February 21–24, 2018
Baltimore, MD, USA

Association for
Computing Machinery

Advancing Computing as a Science & Profession

SIGCSE'18

Proceedings of the 49th ACM Technical Symposium on Computer Science Education

Sponsored by:

ACM SIGCSE

Conference Chairs:

Tiffany Barnes & Dan Garcia

Program Chairs:

Elizabeth Hawthorne & Manuel Pérez-Quiñones

Association for
Computing Machinery

Advancing Computing as a Science & Profession

The Association for Computing Machinery
2 Penn Plaza, Suite 701
New York, New York 10121-0701

ISBN: 978-1-4503-5103-4 (Digital)

ISBN: 978-1-4503-5871-2 (Print)

Additional copies may be ordered prepaid from:

ACM Order Department
PO Box 30777
New York, NY 10087-0777, USA

Phone: 1-800-342-6626 (USA and Canada)
+1-212-626-0500 (Global)
Fax: +1-212-944-1318
E-mail: acmhelp@acm.org
Hours of Operation: 8:30 am – 4:30 pm ET

Welcome from the SIGCSE Chair

Welcome to the 49th SIGCSE Technical Symposium on Computer Science Education (the 2018 Symposium), the premiere technical conference for computer science educators. The 2018 Symposium is sponsored by the ACM Special Interest Group on Computer Science Education (SIGCSE).

SIGCSE is an organization of about 2700 members from more than 70 countries interested and engaged in computer science education. One of the strengths of SIGCSE is the dedication of its members who volunteer to ensure that the activities and events held throughout the year are successful. There are two volunteers in particular who worked very hard to bring the 2018 Symposium to life. Conference co-chairs Tiffany Barnes and Dan Garcia have spent countless hours over the past two years ensuring that the (hopefully around) 1500 attendees at the 2018 Symposium will have a rewarding and inspiring experience. They have led a committee of nearly 100 people in the process of creating an engaging and innovative program, creating opportunities for networking, and handling all the issues big and small that come with a conference of this size. On behalf of the SIGCSE organization and Board, I thank Tiffany and Dan for their hard work and vision that made this conference possible.

This conference also provides us with a chance to honor two people each year for their contributions to computer science education and the SIGCSE community. The annual SIGCSE award for Outstanding Contribution to Computer Science Education will be given to Tom Bell. Bell is best known as the primary author of the CS Unplugged Project, which produced a set of free computer science learning activities that do not use a computer or require programming. His work has influenced many computing educators working to bring computer science to students in schools in many countries around the globe, and it is likely that the impact of his work will be felt for decades to come. The annual SIGCSE award for Lifetime Service will be given to Eric Roberts. Roberts has too many accomplishments to list here, but they include chairing the ACM SIGCSE Java Task Force, serving on the ACM Education Board for nearly 20 years, and continuing to serve on the ACM Education Council. Roberts has earned many awards for his work, including a previous award for Outstanding Contribution to Computer Science Education, making him one of the few people to earn both SIGCSE awards. Please join me and the rest of the SIGCSE Board in congratulating both of them on their well-deserved awards.

The 2018 Symposium will offer you many opportunities to network, whether at sessions, during breaks, at the social events associated with the conference, or simply as you meet people in the halls. I hope that some of the people you will get a chance to talk to will be the members of the SIGCSE Board. Your input and feedback about SIGCSE is important to us, and we want to hear from you. One opportunity to see the Board members will be at the SIGCSE Business meeting on Friday, February 23rd from 5:10 pm to 6 pm in room 308 in the convention center. At this annual meeting we will discuss the overall structure of the SIGCSE organization and share the results of the many SIGCSE projects and events that have been carried out during the past year.

As you attend sessions, meet people, and learn about all the things that SIGCSE members have done, I hope that you will think about what you can bring to the organization. We are always interested in involving new volunteers in SIGCSE, and you can sign up to indicate your interest in volunteering using the online form on the sigcse.org site.

Enjoy the conference!

Amber Settle
SIGCSE Chair, 2016-2019

SIGCSE 2018 Chairs Welcome

We are thrilled to bring the SIGCSE community together from February 21-24, 2018 for the 49th ACM Technical Symposium on Computer Science Education. SIGCSE 2018 is situated in Baltimore, Maryland's Inner Harbor, bustling with live music and arts, harbor tours, restaurants, the Aquarium, and the Science Museum.

The theme for SIGCSE 2018 is *CS for All*, expanding our community and leadership to include everyone, across different groups, educational levels (K-12 to college and beyond), places, and institution types. Inclusion has been threaded throughout our processes. We recruited a larger, more diverse Organizing Committee, with paired junior/senior roles. In 2017, we introduced reviewer discussions and expanded the associate program committee (APC) from 12 to 56 members. In 2018, we established three paper submission tracks, recognizing the differences in scope and review criteria between (1) CS education research and practice, (2) experience reports and tools, and (3) new curricula, programs, degrees, and position papers. These innovations have made our reviewing process more tailored and transparent, and will help us develop new expertise and leadership to foster excellence in computer science education.

We are proud to be co-located with *RESPECT 2018*, the third international conference on Research on Equity and Sustained Participation in Engineering, Computing, and Technology, on Wednesday, February 21st. Other 2018 pre-symposium all-day events include: *New Educators Workshop* (Andrea Danyluk & Zachary Dodds); *Professional Development Workshop for Teaching-Track Faculty* (Mark Sherriff, Susanne Hambrusch, Lori Pollock, & Penny Rheingans); *Jumpstart Teaching Cybersecurity: C5 Instructional Modules Secure Scripting and Cybersecurity and Society* (Melissa Dark, Matt Bishop, Christian Servin, Flo Appel); *POSSE Roundup – Getting Started in an HFOSS Project* (Gregory Hislop, Heidi Ellis, Herman Jackson, Lori Postner, Darci Burdge, Cameron Macdonell); *Integrating Cloud Computing into the Computer Science Curriculum* (Laurie White, Becky Evans); and *CS Education Infrastructure for All: Interoperability for Tools and Data Analytics* (Cliff Shaffer, Peter Brusilovsky, Kenneth Koedinger, Stephen Edwards). Half-day pre-symposium events include: *Computer Science Principles Providers and Teachers Forum* (Lauren Mock, Michael Ball); *Strategies for Integrating the Updated ACM Code of Ethics into the Computing Curriculum* (Karla Carter, Michael Kirkpatrick, Dee Weikle); *RPPforCS for Community Meeting* (Rebecca Zarch, Alan Peterfreund, Leigh Ann Delyser); *Machine Learning in the Classroom* (Tina Ornduff, Sanders Kleinfeld, Phil Wagner); *Microsoft's Mixed Reality 250 Workshop* (Adam Tupler). Joe Chase and Prem Uppuluri will host a *RUSecure Capture The Flag Contest* running throughout the conference.

We have an all-star lineup of speakers who have advanced the concept of *CS for All* in their work. Brenda Wilkerson, President and CEO of the Anita Borg Institute, will give the opening keynote address on Thursday morning, February 22. Eric Roberts, recipient of the 2018 SIGCSE Award for Lifetime Service to the Computer Science Education Community, will speak at the First Timers' lunch. Tim Bell, recipient of the 2018 SIGCSE Award for Outstanding Contributions to Computer Science Education, will give the Friday morning keynote. Finally, Ruthe Farmer, Chief Evangelist of the CSforAll Consortium, will keynote our Saturday lunch.

SIGCSE 2018 will showcase the largest program in its history, with 17 parallel tracks! We have planned a new first-timers' session to help newcomers plan their attendance, expanded the number of submissions we could accept while ensuring high quality, grown from 3 to 4 poster sessions (including one for the ACM Student Research Competition posters), and invited presentations for two new tracks: a *TOCE and Sister conferences* track and an *Inclusion* track. These innovations invite new SIGCSE presenters and broaden the scope of sessions at the conference. To help you manage all these new features, we have also added a new conference app by Whova, where you can build a personalized schedule, message other conference attendees, and vote for people's choice awards.

We hope that our new tracks for Inclusion and Sister journals and conferences will launch a new model of "cross-fertilization" opportunities for the SIGCSE community. At SIGCSE 2017, we piloted a special TOCE track with invited presentations of 8 recent papers from the Transactions on Computing Education (TOCE) journal. This year, we invited 15 TOCE papers, and invited presentations by SIGCAS, SIGGRAPH, SIGHPC, SIGITE, SIGCHI, SIGPLAN, and RESPECT. Our new Inclusion Track seeks to recognize and support groups that are underrepresented in computing and at the conference, including women, people with disabilities, people of color, historically black colleges and universities, Hispanic-serving institutions, community colleges, and more. We have invited community leaders from ACM-W, ACM CCECC, NCWIT, AccessComputing, ECEP, CAHSI, STARS, IAAMCS, CMD-IT, and CRA-W to design sessions to help our community find more ways to be inclusive.

For the first time, "Nifty Assignments" (a SIGCSE favorite, eighteen years running) became its own official track, with veterans Nick Parlante and Julie Zelenski serving as the first co-chairs. We have added a new team to our organizing committee, Puzzles, Social, & Board Games co-chairs Zach Butler and Steven Wolfman will coordinate activities, games and puzzles to help us connect with other participants and have fun together. We will also have a "headshot photo booth" in the exhibit hall to allow our attendees to take a professional headshot for their business cards, web pages and social media accounts.

The SIGCSE Symposium promotes high-quality scholarship and community engagement around computer science education. 1119 volunteers provided each Paper, Panel, Special Session, and Workshop with at least 5 reviews, and each Poster, Birds of a Feather, Demonstration, Lightning Talk, Nifty Assignments, and ACM Student Research Competition submission with at least 3 reviews. These reviewers, along with 56 Associate Program Chairs (APC) and 10 Track Chairs, discussed the papers to come to consensus and make recommendations. The Program Chairs made final selections based on Track Chair and APC recommendations as well as importance to the SIGCSE community, novelty, and timeliness. The table below shows the number of submissions reviewed and accepted in each category.

Proposal Type	Reviewed	Accepted	Acceptance Rate
All Paper Tracks	459	161	35%
CS Education Research	221	82	37%
Experience Reports and Tools	194	57	29%
New Curricula, Programs, Degrees, and Position Papers	44	22	50%
Panel	28	19	68%
Special Session	33	16	48%
Workshop	60	34	57%
Poster	160	90	56%
Birds of a Feather	75	34	45%
Demos	26	10	38%
Lightning Talks	40	26	65%
Nifty Assignments	35	6	17%
ACM Student Research Competition	37	24	65%

Awards recognize outstanding work within SIGCSE and showcase these achievements to ACM and beyond. SIGCSE 2017 awarded three Best Paper awards (for CS Ed Research, Experience Report, and New Programs), and Exemplary Paper awards. 2017 Exemplary Papers were selected by the program chairs from the top ranked of the accepted papers that had no negative reviews, and best papers from each category were selected from among those with best paper nominations and top reviewer rankings. This year, 2018, we awarded 9 Best Papers representing the top three papers in each track. We plan to use our new SIGCSE 2018 conference app and online surveys for people's choice-style awards for various presentations. The Council for Undergraduate Research (CUR) is supporting three new $150 awards for SIGCSE posters authored and presented by undergraduate students. The ACM Student Research Competition (SRC) again invites students from all computing fields to present their research and compete for the chance to enter the national level SRC, and SIGCSE 2018 has four undergraduate submissions and 19 graduate submissions.

This year the Program Chairs selected three best papers, first, second, and third, from each of the paper tracks for their accomplishment of high quality, novelty and broad appeal to reviewers. All best papers received multiple nominations, high ratings, and excellent comments from reviewers.

	CS Education Research -- Best Papers	
1	**The Persistent Effect of Pre-College Computing Experience on College CS Course Grades** Christine Alvarado, Gustavo Umbelino, Mia Minnes, *University of California San Diego*	Sat 8:45 am Room 319
2	**How Near Peer Mentoring Affects Middle School Mentees** Jody Clarke-Midura, Fred Poole, Katarina Pantic, Megan Hamilton, Chongning Sun, Vicki Allan, *Utah State University*	Fri 3:25 pm, Room 321
3	**Enhancing Security Education Through Designing SDN Security Labs in CloudLab** Younghee Park, *San Jose State University;* Hongxin Hu, Hongda Li, *Clemson University;* Xiaohong Yuan, *North Carolina A&T University*	Thu 2:35 pm Room 318
	Experience Reports and Tools -- Best Papers	
1	**Computational Thinking for All - An Experience Report on Scaling up Teaching Computational Thinking to All Students in a Major City in Sweden** Fredrik Heintz, Linda Mannila, *Linköping University*	Thu 1:45 pm Room 317
2	**Reflections of a Diversity, Equity, and Inclusion Working Group based on Data from a National CS Education Program** Nwannediya Ada Ibe, Rebecca Howsmon, Lauren Penney, Nathaniel Granor, *TEALS;* Leigh Ann Delyser, CSNYC; Kevin Wang, *TEALS*	Fri 4:10 pm Room 316
3	**Ethics Education in Context: A Case Study of Novel Ethics Activities for the CS Classroom** Michael Skirpan, Nathan Beard, Srinjita Bhaduri, Casey Fiesler, Tom Yeh, *University of Colorado, Boulder*	Sat 10:45 am Room 321
	New Curricula, Programs, Degrees, and Position Paper -- Best Papers	
1	**Upward Mobility for Underrepresented Students:** **A Model for a Cohort-Based Bachelor's Degree in Computer Science** Sathya Narayanan, *California State University Monterey Bay;* Kathryn Cunningham, *California State University Monterey Bay & Georgia Institute of Technology;* Sonia Arteaga, Hartnell College;William J. Welch, *Hartnell College & Central Texas College*; Leslie Maxwell, Zechariah Chawinga, Bude Su, *California State University Monterey Bay*	Fri 3:45 pm Room 316
2	**A Model for Increasing Gender Diversity in Technology** Penny Rheingans, Erica D'Eramo, *University of Maryland, Baltimore County;* Crystal Diaz-Espinoza, *Baylor University;* Danyelle Ireland, *University of Maryland, Baltimore County*	Fri 11:35 AM Room 316
3	**DIVAS: Outreach to the Natural Sciences through Image Processing** Mark Meysenburg, Tessa Durham Brooks, *Doane University;* Raychelle Burks, *St. Edward's University;* Erin Doyle, Timothy Frey, *Doane University*	Fri 3:45 PM Room 318

Track Chairs and Associate Program Chairs lead our community in discussions to help resolve differences in individual perspectives, and make final recommendations to the program chairs to create a more comprehensive review process. *Track Chairs* are: Workshops: Brett Becker & Michelle Craig, Panels: Christina Gardner-McCune, Special Sessions: Jian Zhang, Birds of a Feather: Lina Battestilli & Jennifer Campbell, Posters: Sarah Heckman, Demos: Peter-Michael Osera, Nifty: Nick Parlante & Julie Zelenski, Lightning Talks: S. Monisha Pulimood, ACM Student Research Competition: Jessica Schmidt & Sarah Heckman. The *Associate Program Committee* includes: Eric Aaron, Joel Adams, Rajeev Agrawal, Meghan Allen, Carl Alphonce, Christine Alvarado, Ruth Anderson, Marie Bienkowski, Aaron Bloomfield, Kristy Elizabeth Boyer, Kevin Buffardi, Tracy Camp, Alistair Campbell, Steve Cooper, Adrienne Decker, Leigh Ann Delyser, Lucia Dettori, John Dougherty, Stephen Edwards, Kathi Fisler, Susan Haller, Sharon Hsiao, Sarah Heckman, Cecily Heiner, Helen Hu, Lisa Kaczmarczyk, Andrew Ko, Deepak Kumar, David

Levine, Gary Lewandowski, Colleen Lewis, Bruce Maxim, Lester McCann, Robert McCartney, Craig S. Miller, Robert Noonan, Jody Paul, Leo Porter, S. Monisha Pulimood, Samuel Rebelsky, Brad Richards, Susan Rodger, Ingrid Russell, Mark Sherriff, Judy Sheard, Simon, Jaime Spacco, Luther Tychonievich, Paul Tymann, Frank Vahid, Jan Vahrenhold, Tammy Vandegrift, Ellen Walker, Henry Walker, Ursula Wolz, and Jian Zhang.

The Program Chairs extend a special debt of gratitude to all the last-minute volunteers who willingly stepped forward to help during the unforeseen natural disasters (hurricanes, earthquakes) that coincided with the reviewing period this year.

Thank you to our SIGCSE 2018 Organizing Committee! We could not do it without you: Scott McElfresh (Treasurer), Cary Laxer, Larry Merkle, and Lynn Degler (Registration), Dave Musicant and Jodi Tims (Supporter / Exhibitor Liaisons), Mark Sherriff (NSF Showcase, Webmaster), Josh Hug (Webmaster), Leen-Kiat Soh (Database), Alison Clear & John Dougherty (Events), Meghan Allen & Dale-Marie Wilson (Kids' Camp), Ruth Anderson (Publications), Adam Blank (Publicity & Social Media), Stacy Branham & Katie Gibson (Local Arrangements), Leigh Ann DeLyser (K12 Liaison, Publicity & Social Media), Ria Galanos (K12 Liaison), Phil East (Evaluations), Zach Butler & Steven Wolfman (Puzzles, Social, & Board Games), and Michael Ball (Photography).

The International Committee, chaired by Elizabeth Patitsas, includes Michelle Craig, Karen Bradshaw, Arto Hellas, Carsten Kleiner, Shitanshu Mishra, Kazushi Ohya, Marco Silva, Claudia Szabo, Gary Wong, and Ming Zhang. The IC ensures that attendees from all over the world find SIGCSE 2018 a welcoming and rewarding experience.

Thanks to our student volunteers who enliven the conference while making sure all goes smoothly. And thanks to Sara Melnick, Darakhshan Mir, and Samuel A. Rebelsky, for organizing them!

Our exhibitors and sponsors enrich the conference by showing off new technologies and tools to support computer science education. We especially thank our platinum sponsors: GitHub, Google, Inc., InfoSys Foundation USA, Intel, and Microsoft; our gold sponsors: Vocareum Inc., Oracle Academy, IBM, Turing's Craft, Inc., ZyBooks, and Codio; and our silver sponsors: ABET, CodeHS, gradescope, and Mimir; and our bronze sponsor: Red Hat Academy. We look forward to visiting their booths, their supporter sessions, and meeting these champions who support CS education and our community.

Amber Settle (President) and Adrienne Decker (SIGCSE conference liaison to the board), and the entire SIGCSE Board have provided support throughout the conference planning. We thank the planners at Executivevents: Roxane Rose, Elizabeth Taggart, Brooke Daley, Shannon Killian, and Cara Candler. Additional thanks go to Bob Beck and Scott Grissom (SIGCSE Symposium Site Coordinators), April Mosqus and Donna Cappo (ACM staff), Lisa Tolles (Sheridan Publishing), Bill Guckert (WRG Design), Paula Hagan (Baltimore Convention Center), and Camille Spilker of Visit Baltimore.

We thank our home institutions (NC State University, UC Berkeley, Union County College, and UNC Charlotte) for their generous support of our service to the SIGCSE community.

We are tremendously grateful for the engagement and support of the SIGCSE community and volunteers. We thank you, and we hope that SIGCSE 2018 will help bring you new ideas, connections, and friends to help us all support CS for All.

Tiffany Barnes
Symposium Co-Chair
NC State University

Dan Garcia
Symposium Co-Chair
UC Berkeley

Elizabeth K. Hawthorne
Program Co-Chair
Union County College

Manuel A.Pérez-Quiñones
Program Co-Chair
UNC Charlotte

Table of Contents

Special Session: Microaggressions

Special Session: Parallel/Distributed Curriculum

First Timer's Lunch Keynote & 2018 SIGCSE Award for Lifetime Service to the Computer Science Education Community

Session Chairs: Dan Garcia *UC Berkeley)* & Tiffany Barnes *(North Carolina State University)*

Paper Session: Computational Thinking #1

Session Chair: Elizabeth Hawthorne *(Union County College)*

Paper Session: Creativity

Session Chair: Dee A. B. Weikle *(James Madison University)*

Paper Session: Cybersecurity #2

Session Chair: Sotirios Kentros *(Salem State University)*

Paper Session: Diverse Topics in CS Ed

Session Chair: Meghan Allen *(The University of British Columbia)*

Paper Session: Pedagogy #2

Session Chair: Brandon Myers *(University of Iowa)*

Paper Session: Science Education

Session Chair: Suzanne Matthews *(United States Military Academy)*

Paper Session: Visualization

Session Chair: Cliff Shaffer *(Virginia Tech)*

Panel Session: Interdisciplinary Capstone

Panel Session: Team-Teaching with Humanities

Special Session: Evaluating CS4All Initiatives

Special Session: Watch them Teach

SRC Session

Session Chair: Jessica Schmidt *(North Carolina State University)*

Panel Session: Team Teaching Computing & Music

Special Session: CS as a Graduation Requirement

Special Session: Introductory CS Courses Using Culturally Responsive Teaching

Morning Keynote & 2018 SIGCSE Award for Outstanding Contributions to Computer Science Education

Session Chairs: Dan Garcia & Tiffany Barnes *(UC Berkeley --- North Carolina State University)*

Paper Session: CS1 #1

Session Chair: Matthew Hertz *(University at Buffalo)*

Paper Session: Curriculum Issues #1

Session Chair: Chris Gregg *(Stanford University)*

Paper Session: Diversity #1

Session Chair: Kinnis Gosha *(Morehouse)*

Paper Session: Curriculum Issues #2

Session Chair: Xuesong Zhang *(Southeast Missouri State University)*

Paper Session: Diversity #2

Session Chair: Andrea Lawrence *(Spelman College)*

Paper Session: Elementary #1

Session Chair: Cecily Heiner *(Southern Utah University)*

Paper Session: Errors

Session Chair: Brian Railing *(Carnegie Mellon University)*

Paper Session: Peer Mentoring

Session Chair: Durga Suresh *(Wentworth Institute of Technology)*

Panel Session: Alternative Paths to Computing Careers to Broaden Participation

Panel Session: Best Practices To Remedy Gender Bias in Tech

Panel Session: Researcher-Practitioner Partnerships in CS4All

Panel Session: Using Real-world Data in Introductory Courses

Special Session: CS4All for Sustainable K-12 CS Implementations

Paper Session: CS1 #3

Session Chair: Brian Harrington *(University of Toronto)*

Paper Session: Diversity #3

Session Chair: Jeff Forbes *(Duke University)*

Panel Session: Maryland Computing Education

Special Session: Filk Circle: Computing in Verse

Special Session: Joint Task Force on Cybersecurity Education

Special Session: Repositories You Shouldn't Be Living Without

Paper Session: Active Learning #2

Session Chair: Chris Mayfield *(James Madison University)*

Paper Session: Ethics

Session Chair: Ruth Anderson *(University of Washington)*

Paper Session: High School #2

Session Chair: Howard Francis *(University of Pikeville)*

Panel Session: CS4NC Summit 2017

Panel Session: Technology We Can't Live Without!, revisited

Special Session: IT2017 Report

Special Session: SIGCSE Committee on Computing Education in the Liberal Arts

Closing Keynote

Session Chairs: Dan Garcia & Tiffany Barnes *(UC Berkeley - North Carolina State University)*

Wednesday Workshops

Friday Workshops

Saturday Workshops

BOF Flock #1

BOF Flock #2

Poster Session #1

Poster Session #2

Poster Session #3

Lightning Talk #1

Session Chair: S. Monisha Pulimood *(The College of New Jersey)*

Lightning Talk #2

Session Chair: S. Monisha Pulimood *(The College of New Jersey)*

Demonstrations

Session Chair: Peter-Michael 2 chairs Osera *(Grinnell College)*

Recipients of the SIGCSE Award for Outstanding Contributions to Computer Science Education

1981 **William F. Atchison**, *University of Maryland*
1982 **Alan Perlis**, *Yale University*
1983 **Karl V . Karlstrom**, *Prentice-Hall*
1985 **Elliot I. Organick**, *University of Utah*
1986 **Donald Knuth**, *Stanford University*
1987 **Niklaus Wirth**, *ETH, Zurich*
1988 **Grace Murray Hopper**, *Rear Admiral, USN, Digital Equipment Corp.*
1989 **Edsger W. Dijkstra**, *The University of Texas at Austin*
1990 **Curriculum '68 Committee**:
William F. Atchison, Samuel D. Conte, John Hamblen, Thomas E. Hull, Thomas A. Keenan, William B. Kehl, Edward J. McClusey, Silvio O. Navarro, Werner Rheinboldt, Earl J. Schweppe, William Viavant, David M. Young, Jr.
1991 **David Gries**, *Cornell University*
1992 **Daniel D. McCracken**, *City College, City University of New York*
1993 **Alan C. Kay**, *Apple Computer*
1994 **Norman E. Gibbs**, *Software Engineering Institute*
1995 **Robert M. Aiken**, *Temple University*
1996 **Nell B. Dale**, *The University of Texas at Austin*
1997 **Andrew Tannenbaum**, *Vrije University*
1998 **William A. Wulf**, *University of Virginia and National Academy of Engineering*
1999 **Peter J. Denning**, *George Mason University*
2000 **Andries Van Dam**, *Brown University*
2001 **Allen B. Tucker**, *Bowdoin College*
2002 **Elliot Soloway**, *University of Michigan*
2003 **Eric Roberts**, *Stanford University*
2004 **Mordechai Ben-Ari**, *Weizmann Institute of Science*
2005 **Kim Bruce**, *Williams College*
2006 **Richard Pattis**, *Carnegie Mellon University*
2007 **Judith Gal-Ezer**, *Open University of Israel* and **John Hughes**, *University of Technology, Sydney*
2008 **Randy Pausch,** *Carnegie Mellon University*
2009 **Elliot B. Koffman**, *Temple University*
2010 **Sally Fincher,** *University of Kent, Canterbury*
2011 **Matthias Felleisen,** *Northeastern University*
2012 **Harold (Hal) Abelson,** *Massachusetts Institute of Technology*
2013 **Michael Kölling**, *University of Kent, Canterbury*
2014 **Robert M. Panoff,** *The Shodor Education Foundation, Inc.*
2015 **Mark Allen Weiss,** *Florida International University*
2016 **Jan Cuny,** *National Science Foundation*
2017 **Gail Chapman,** *Exploring Computer Science*
2018 **Tim Bell**, *University of Canterbury, New Zealand*

Recipients of the SIGCSE Lifetime Service Award

1997 **Richard Austing**, *University of Maryland*
1998 **Della Bonnette**, *University of Southwestern Louisiana*
1999 **Robert Aiken**, *Temple University*
2000 **James E. Miller**, *University of Southern Mississippi*
2001 **Lillian N. (Boots) Cassel**, *Villanova University*
2002 **Joe Turner**, *Clemson University and Zayed University*
2003 **Harriet Taylor**, *National Science Foundation and Louisiana State University*
2004 **Bruce Klein**, *Grand V alley State University*
2005 **Andrew McGettrick**, *University of Strathclyde*
2006 **Joyce Currie Little**, *Towson State University*
2007 **John Impagliazzo**, *Hofstra University*
2008 **Dennis Frailey**, *Raytheon Corporation*
2009 **Michael J. Clancy**, *University of California, Berkeley*
2010 **Peter Denning**, *Naval Postgraduate School*
2011 **Gordon Davies**, *Open University*
2012 **Jane Prey**, *Microsoft Research*
2013 **Henry Walker**, *Grinnell College*
2014 **Andrea Lawrence**, *Spelman College*
2015 **Frank H. Young**, *Rose-Hulman Institute of Technology*
2016 **Barbara Boucher Owens**, *Southwestern University*
2017 **Mats Daniels**, *Uppsala University*
2018 **Eric Roberts**, *Stanford University*

SIGCSE 2018 Technical Symposium Organization

Symposium Co-Chairs:	Tiffany Barnes (North Carolina State University, USA) Daniel Garcia (University of California, Berkeley, USA)
Program Co-Chairs:	Elizabeth K. Hawthorne (Union County College, USA) Manuel A. Pérez-Quiñones (UNC Charlotte, USA)
Program Committee	
Special Sessions Chair:	Jian Zhang (Texas Woman's University, USA)
Panels Chair:	Christina Gardner-McCune (University of Florida, USA)
Workshop Co-Chairs:	Michelle Craig (University of Toronto, Canada) Brett Becker (University College Dublin, Ireland)
Poster Chair:	Sarah Heckman (North Carolina State University, USA)
Birds of a Feather Co-Chairs:	Jennifer Campbell (University of Toronto, Canada) Lina Battestilli (North Carolina State University, USA)
Demos Chair:	Peter-Michael Osera (Grinnell College, USA)
Lightning Talks Chair:	S. Monisha Pulimood (The College of New Jersey, USA)
Student Research Competition Co-Chairs:	Jessica Schmidt (North Carolina State University, USA) Sarah Heckman (North Carolina State University, USA)
Nifty Assignments Co-Chairs:	Nick Parlante (Stanford University, USA) Julie Zelenski (Stanford University, USA)
Organizing Committee	
Pre-Symposium & Affiliated Events:	Alison Clear (Eastern Institute of Technology, NZ) John Dougherty (Haverford College, USA)
Registration:	Lynn Degler (Rose-Hulman Institute of Technology, USA) Cary Laxer (Rose-Hulman Institute of Technology, USA) Larry Merkle (Air Force Institute of Technology, USA)
Publications:	Ruth Anderson (University of Washington, USA)
Database Administrator:	Leen-Kiat Soh (University of Nebraska,Lincoln, USA) Mark Sherriff (University of Virginia, USA)
Webmaster:	Josh Hug (University of California, Berkeley, USA) Mark Sherriff (University of Virginia, USA)
Treasurer:	Scott McElfresh (Longwood University, USA)
Evaluations:	Phil East (University of Northern Iowa, USA)

Supporter/Exhibitor Liaison:	Dave Musicant (Carleton College, USA) Jodi Tims (Baldwin Wallace University, USA)
Student Volunteers & Activities:	Sara Melnick (Independent) Darakhshan Mir (Bucknell University, USA) Samuel A. Rebelsky (Grinnell College, USA)
K-12 Liaison:	Leigh Ann DeLyser (CSNYC, USA) Ria Galanos (Thomas Jefferson High School for Science and Technology, USA)
International Liaison:	Elizabeth Patitsas (University of Toronto, Canada)
Kids' Camp:	Dale-Marie Wilson (UNC Charlotte, USA) Meghan Allen (University of British Columbia)
Puzzles, Social, & Board Games:	Steven Wolfman (University of British Columbia) Zach Butler (Rochester Institute of Technology, USA)
Publicity and Social Media:	Adam Blank (University of Washington, USA) Leigh Ann DeLyser (CSNYC, USA)
Local Arrangements:	Katie Gibson (UMBC, USA) Stacy Branham (UMBC, USA)
International Committee Members:	Michelle Craig (University of Toronto, Canada) Karen Bradshaw (Rhodes University, South Africa) Arto Hellas (University of Helsinki, Finland) Carsten Kleiner (Hochschule Hannover, Germany) Shitanshu Mishra (Indian Institute of Technology Bombay, India) Kazushi Ohya (Tsurumi University, Japan) Elizabeth Patitsas (McGill University, Canada) Marco Silva (Federal University of Technology, Brazil) Claudia Szabo (The University of Adelaide, Australia) Gary Wong (The University of Hong Kong, Hong Kong) Ming Zhang (Peking University, China)
Associate Program Chairs:	Eric Aaron (Vassar College, USA) Joel Adams (Calvin College, USA) Rajeev Agrawal (US Army Engineer Research and Development Center, USA) Meghan Allen (The University of British Columbia, Canada) Carl Alphonce (University at Buffalo, USA) Christine Alvarado (University of California San Diego, USA) Ruth Anderson (University of Washington, USA) Marie Bienkowski (SRI International, USA) Aaron Bloomfield (University of Virginia, USA) Kristy Elizabeth Boyer (University of Florida, USA) Kevin Buffardi (California State University - Chico, USA) Tracy Camp (Colorado School of Mines, USA)

Associate Program Chairs (continued):	Alistair Campbell (Hamilton College, USA) Steve Cooper (University of Nebraska–Lincoln, USA) Adrienne Decker (Rochester Institute of Technology, USA) Leigh Ann DeLyser (NYC Foundation for CS Education, USA) Lucia Dettori (DePaul University, USA) John Dougherty (Haverford College, USA) Stephen Edwards (Virginia Tech, USA) Kathi Fisler (WPI, USA) Susan Haller (SUNY at Potsdam, USA) Sarah Heckman (North Carolina State University, USA) Cecily Heiner (Southern Utah University, USA) Sharon Hsiao (Arizona State University, USA) Helen Hu (Westminster College, USA) Lisa Kaczmarczyk (Independent) Andrew Ko (University of Washington, USA) Deepak Kumar (Bryn Mawr College, USA) David Levine (Saint Bonaventure University, USA) Gary Lewandowski (Xavier University, USA) Colleen Lewis (Harvey Mudd College, USA) Bruce Maxim (University of Michigan, USA) Lester McCann (University of Arizona, USA) Robert McCartney (University of Connecticut, USA) Craig S. Miller (DePaul University, USA) Robert Noonan (William and Mary, USA) Jody Paul (Metropolitan State University of Denver, USA) Leo Porter (University of California San Diego, USA) S. Monisha Pulimood (The College of New Jersey, USA) Samuel Rebelsky (Grinnell College, USA) Brad Richards (Univ. of Puget Sound, USA) Susan Rodger (Duke University, USA) Ingrid Russell (University of Hartford, USA) Judy Sheard (Monash University, USA) Mark Sherriff (University of Virginia, USA) Jaime Spacco (Knox College, USA) Simon (University of Newcastle, Australia) Luther Tychonievich (University of Virginia, USA) Paul Tymann (Rochester Institute of Technology, USA) Frank Vahid (UC Riverside, USA) Jan Vahrenhold (Department of Computer Science) Tammy Vandegrift (University of Portland, USA) Ellen Walker (Hiram College, USA) Henry Walker (Grinnell College, USA) Ursula Wolz (Bennington College, USA) Jian Zhang (Texas Woman's University, USA)

ACM Student Research Competition (SRC) Reviewers

Jonathan Bona (University of Arkansas for Medical Sciences)
Sandra Cleland (UCOL)
Robert Cook (University of Tennessee, Chattanooga)
Amy Csizmar Dalal (Carleton College)
Barb Cutler (Rensselaer Polytechnic Institute)
Lawrence D'Antonio (Ramapo College)
Zhijiang Dong (Middle Tennessee State University)
Felicia Doswell (Norfolk State University)
Ali Ebnenasir (Michigan Technological University)
Paula Evans (California Department of Education)
Hillary Fleenor (Columbus State University)
Eric Fouh (Lehigh University)
S. Jane Fritz (St. Joseph's College)
Rongkai Guo (Kennesaw State University)
Margeret Hall (School of Interdisciplinary Informatics, University of Nebraska Omaha)
William Hendrix (Northwestern University)
Iris Howley (Williams College)
Roberto Hoyle (Oberlin College)
Dugald Hutchings (Elon University)
Jana Jacková (Matej Bel University)
Sarah Judd (Girls Who Code)
Wiliam Kerney (Clovis Community College)
David Levine (St. Bonaventure University)
Jérémie Lumbroso (Princeton University)
Maria Marcelino (University of Coimbra)
Renee McCauley (College of Charleston, Charleston, SC USA)
Charlie Mcdowell (UC Santa Cruz)
James McGuffee (Christian Brothers University)
Chao Mei (University of Texas at San Antonio)
Dagmar Monett (Berlin School of Economics and Law)
Anurag Nagar (The University of Texas at Dallas)
Fabiola Nakamura (Universidade Federal do Amazonas)
Shikha Raturi (University of the South Pacific)
Donna Reese (Mississippi State University)
Durga Suresh (Wentworth Institute of Technology)
Gloria Townsend (DePauw University)
Ellen Walker (Hiram College)
Mark Weiss (Florida International University)

BOF Reviewers

Jennifer Albert (The Citadel)
Michael Ball (Berkeley)
Shankar Banik (The Citadel)
Valerie Barr (Mount Holyoke College)
Nada Basit (University of Virginia)
Aaron Bloomfield (University of Virginia)
Philip Buffum (North Carolina State University)
Yingjun Cao (University of California San Diego)
Lillian Cassel (Villanova University)
Thea Charles (Siegel Family Endowment)
Ankur Chattopadhyay (University of Wisconsin - Green Bay)
Radhouane Chouchane (Columbus State University)
Jonathan Corley (University of West Georgia)
James Davenport (University of Bath)
Nate Derbinsky (Northeastern University)
Paul Dickson (Ithaca College)
John Dougherty (Haverford College)
Jennifer Goodall (University at Albany)
Orit Hazzan (Technion - Israel Institute of Technology)
Sarah Heckman (North Carolina State University)
Cinda Heeren (UBC)
Geoffrey Herman (University of Illinois at Urbana-Champaign)
Justin Hsia (University of Washington)
Siddharth Kaza (Towson University)
Sotirios Kentros (Salem State University)
Richard Kick (Newbury Park High School)
Ed Knorr (The University of British Columbia)
Joan Krone (Denison University)
Clif Kussmaul (Muhlenberg College)
Justin Li (Occidental College)
David Malan (Harvard University)
Andrew McGettrick (University of Strathclyde)
Larry Merkle (Airforce Institute of Technology)
Selvarajah Mohanarajah (UNC-Pembroke)
Christopher Moretti (Princeton University)
Briana Morrison (University of Nebraska at Omaha)
Janice Pearce (Berea College)
Enrico Pontelli (New Mexico State University)
Samuel Rebelsky (Grinnell College)
Ashwin Satyanarayana (City University of New York)

Mark Sherriff (University of Virginia)
Marco Silva (Federal University of Technology - Paraná)
Ken Surendran (Southeast Missouri State University)
Durga Suresh (Wentworth Institute of Technology)
Rajendran Swamidurai (Alabama State University)
Anya Tafliovich (University of Toronto)
Jodi Tims (Baldwin Wallace University)
Cindy Tucker (Bluegrass Community and Technical College)
Luther Tychonievich (University of Virginia)
Gabriela Vilanova
Charles Wallace (Michigan Technological University)
Richard Weiss (The Evergreen State College)
Daniel Zingaro (University of Toronto)

Demonstration reviewers

David Arnow (Brooklyn College (CUNY))
Barb Cutler (Rensselaer Polytechnic Institute)
Yuli Deng (Arizona State University)
Ali Ebnenasir (Michigan Technological University)
Jason Freeman (Georgia Institute of Technology)
Muztaba Fuad (Winston-Salem State University)
Don Goelman (Villanova University)
Rongkai Guo (Kennesaw State University)
Theodore Hays
Dennis Kafura (Virginia Tech)
Saber Khan (Browning School)
Young Lee (none)
Matija Lokar (Faculty of mathematics and physics, University of Ljubljana)
Chao Mei (University of Texas at San Antonio)
Brandon Myers (University of Iowa)
Matthew Peveler (Rensselaer Polytechnic Institute)
Enrico Pontelli (New Mexico State University)
William Turkett (Wake Forest University)
Jeong Yang (Texas A&M University-San Antonio)

Lightning Talk Reviewers

Hisham Al-Mubaid (University of Houston-clear lake)
Ian Barland (Radford University)
Debasis Bhattacharya (University of Hawaii Maui College)
Christopher Bohn (University of Nebraska-Lincoln)
David Bunde (Knox College)
Edward Chapin (University of Maryand Eastern Shore)
Phillip Conrad (UC Santa Barbara)
Marie-Anne Demuynck (Texas Woman's University)
John Dougherty (Haverford College)
Razieh Fathi (University at Buffalo)
Anna Frankfurt (University of Prince Edward Island)
Iris Gaber (mta.ac.il)
Joshua Gross (Blackburn College)
Helen Hu (Westminster College)
Cruz Izu (The University of Adelaide)
Daniel Joyce (Villanova University)
Amardeep Kahlon (Austin Community College)
Zachary Kurmas (Grand Valley State University)
Clifton Kussmaul (Muhlenberg College)
David Largent (Ball State University)
Mary Last (self employed)
Cam Macdonell (MacEwan University)
Luis Macedo (University of Coimbra)
Thomas Marlowe (Seton Hall University)
Suzanne Matthews (United States Military Academy)
Bruce Maxim (University of Michigan)
Amitabh Mishra (University of West Florida)
Anurag Nagar (The University of Texas at Dallas)
Radek Oslejsek (Masaryk University)
Dimitris Papamichail (The College of New Jersey)
Rick Parker (University of Colorado Boulder)
Sravana Reddy (Wellesley College)
Joel Ross (U Washington iSchool)
Vibha Sazawal (University of Maryland)
Bill Siever (Washington University)
Jia Tao (Lafayette College)
Christine Tinner (Colorado Mountain College)
Steve Wolfman (The University of British Columbia)
Fan Yang (University of Toronto)
Sejong Yoon (The College of New Jersey)
Jones Yu (Wentworth Institute of Technology)

Nifty Assignment Reviewers

Beverly Bachmayer (Intel)
Ian Barland (Radford University)
Mike Clancy (University of California, Berkeley)
Phillip Conrad (UC Santa Barbara)

Marie-Anne Demuynck (Texas Woman's University)
Dan Leyzberg (Princeton University)
Thomas Marlowe (Seton Hall University)
Bruce Maxim (University of Michigan)
Dave Reed (Creighton University)
Ellen Spertus (Mills College)
A. Yanushka (Christian Brothers University)

Panel Session Reviewers

Alice Armstrong (Shippensburg University)
Michael Ball (University of California, Berkeley)
Shankar Banik (The Citadel)
Michael Bauer (Leeward Community College)
Leland Beck (San Diego State University)
Celina Berg (The University of British Columbia)
Bradley Beth (The University of Texas at Austin)
Ivona Bezakova (Rochester Institute of Technology)
Jeremiah Blanchard (University of Florida)
Stephen Bloch (Google)
Barry Burd (Drew University)
Randy Connolly (Mount Royal University)
Lucia Dettori (DePaul University)
Ahmed El-Deeb (The American University in Cairo)
Katrina Falkner (The University of Adelaide)
Matthew Forshaw (Newcastle University)
Charles Garrod (Carnegie Mellon University)
Alessio Gaspar (University of South Florida Polytechnic)
Carlos Guerrero (Universitat de les Illes Balears)
Brian Harrington (University of Toronto)
Michael Hewner (Rose Hulman Institute of Techonology)
Aleata Hubbard (WestEd)
Jim Huggins (Kettering University)
Bryn Jeffries (The University of Sydney)
Yerika Jimenez (University of Florida)
David Johnson (University of Oxford)
Colin Johnson (University of Kent)
Yvonne Kao (WestEd)
Edward Kim (Villanova University)
Arthur Lee (Claremont McKenna College)
Chi-Un Lei (Department of Electrical and Electronic Engineering, the University of Hong Kong)
Bruce Maxwell (Colby College)
Jamie Payton (Temple University)
Kelly Rivers (Carnegie Mellon University)
Bill Siever (Washington University)
Melissa Stange (Lord Fairfax Community College)
Roger West (University of Illinois at Springfield)
Howard Whitston (University of South Alabama)
Rina Zviel-Girshin (Ruppin Academic Center)

Paper - CS Education Research Reviewers

Elizabeth Adams (James Madison University)
Shakil Akhtar (Clayton State University)
Ibrahim Albluwi (Princeton University)
Vicki Almstrum (Computing Educators Oral History Project)
Hakam Alomari (Miami University)
Ashish Amresh (Arizona State University)
Sven Anderson (Bard College)
Maurício Aniche (Delft University of Technology)
Gabriella Anton (Northwestern University)
Vaibhav Anu (North Dakota State University)
António Araújo (University of Porto)
Alex Aravind (University of Northern British Columbia)
Gabriela Arevalo (Facultad de Ingenieria - Universidad Austral)
Amadeo Arguelles (Computer Research Centre / National Polytechnic Institute)
Isabel Azevedo (ISEP)
Austin Bart (Virginia Tech)
Ashok Basawapatna (SUNY College At Old Westbury)
Lina Battestilli (North Carolina State University)
Aaron Bauer (University of Washington)
Scott Bell (Northwest Missouri State University)
Jens Bennedsen (Aarhus University)
Marc Berges (Technische Universität München, TUM School of Education)
Gianmario Besana (DePaul University)
Arnab Bhattacharya (Indian Institute of Technology, Kanpur)
Arvind Bhusnurmath (University of Pennsylvania)
William Birmingham (Grove City College, Computer Science Department)
Saul Blanco Rodriguez (Indiana University Bloomington)

Jennifer Blaney (University of California, Los Angeles)
Aaron Bloomfield (University of Virginia)
Cory Boatright (Grove City College)
Steven Bogaerts (DePauw University)
Durell Bouchard (Roanoke College)
Eric Bouwers (Squla)
Erik Brunvand (University of Utah)
Dennis Brylow (Marquette University)
Karan Budhraja (University of Maryland, Baltimore County)
Janet Burge (Colorado College)
Debra Burhans (Canisius College)
Jeffrey Bush (University of Colorado Boulder)
Zack Butler (Rochester Institute of Technology)
Candido Cabo (City University of New York)
Andre Calitz (none)
Johan Calu (khbo)
Jennifer Campbell (University of Toronto)
Sheila Castaneda (Clarke University)
Francisco Enrique Vicente Castro (Worcester Polytechnic Institute)
Albert Chan (Fayetteville State University)
Thea Charles (Siegel Family Endowment)
Joe Chase (Radford University)
Juan Chen (College of Computer, National University of Defense Technology, China)
Wei Kian Chen (Champlain College)
Wai Chong Chia (Sunway University)
Donald Chinn (University of Washington)
Liezel Cilliers (Information Systems Department, University of Fort Hare)
Dawn Cizmar (St. Edwards University)
Peter Clarke (Florida International University)
Eduardo Colmenares-Diaz (Midwestern State University)
Lee Cornell (Minnesota State University, Mankato)
Mary Courtney (Pace University)
Scotty Craig (Arizona State University, Polytechnic)
Tom Crick (Cardiff Metropolitan University)
Edwin P. Curran (University of Ulster)
Lawrence D'Antonio (Ramapo College)
Lucia Dale (Sewanee: The University of the South)
James H. Davenport (University of Bath)
Karen Davis (Miami University)
Don Davis (University of Texas at San Antonio)
Debra Davis (Florida International University)
Josh Dehlinger (Towson University)
Brian Dellinger (Grove City College)
Robert Deloatch (University of Illinois Urbana Champaign)
Leigh Ann Delyser (NYC Foundation for CS Education)
Kamyar Dezhgosha (University of Illinois at Springfield)
Sarah Diesburg (University of Northern Iowa)
Suzanne Dietrich (Arizona State University)
Betsy Disalvo (Georgia Institute of Technology)
Zachary Dodds (Harvey Mudd College)
Marguerite Doman (Winthrop University)
Toby Donaldson (Simon Fraser University)
Yihuan Dong (North Carolina State University)
Mohsen Dorodchi (University of North Carolina, Charlotte)
John Dougherty (Haverford College)
Toby Dragon (Ithaca College)
John Duncan (Indiana University Bloomington)
J. Philip East (University of Northern Iowa)
Joshua Eckroth (Stetson University)
Alex Edgcomb (Sr. Software Engineer at zyBooks. Research Specialist at UC Riverside.)
Jeffrey Edgington (University of Denver)
Jesse Eickholt (Central Michigan University)
Richard Enbody (Michigan State University)
Huseyin Ergin (University of Alabama)
Barbara Ericson (Georgia Institute of Technology)
Paula Evans (California Department of Education)
Nickolas Falkner (The University of Adelaide)
Mohammed Farghally (Virginia Tech)
Russell Feldhausen (Kansas State University)
Ranran Feng (Univ. of Texas at Dallas)
Georgios Fesakis (University of Aegean)
Samantha S. Foley (University of Wisconsin-La Crosse)
Vitaly Ford (Arcadia University)
Eric Fouh (Lehigh University)
Elodie Fourquet (Colgate University)
Diana Franklin (UChicago STEM Education)
Stephen Frezza (Gannon University)
Frank Friedman (Temple University)
Michelle Friend (University of Nebraska Omaha)
Yujian Fu (Alabama A&M University)

Alexandra Funke (Technical University of Munich)
Sat Garcia (University of San Diego)
Christina Gardner-Mccune (University of Florida)
Nasser Giacaman (The University of Auckland)
J Paul Gibson (Mines Telecom)
David Ginat (Tel-Aviv University)
Evan Golub (University of Maryland)
Jean Goulet (Universite de Sherbrooke)
Marco Aurélio Graciotto Silva (Federal University of Technology - Paraná)
Chris Gregg (Stanford University)
Jean Griffin (Temple University)
Andrew Grover (Thiel College)
Joshua T. Guerin (University of Tennessee at Martin)
Nadra Guizani (Gonzaga Univeristy)
Gopal Gupta (The University of Texas at Dallas)
Mandlenkosi Victor Gwetu (UKZN)
Sally Hamouda (Cairo University)
Orit Hazzan (Technion - Israel Institute of Technology)
Bastiaan Heeren (Open University, The Netherlands)
Cecily Heiner (Southern Utah University)
Fredrik Heintz (Linköping University)
James Heliotis (Rochester Institute of Technology)
Arto Hellas (University of Helsinki)
Matthew Hertz (University at Buffalo)
Jalaa Hoblos (Penn State Erie)
William Hochstettler (Antioch University Midwest)
Chad Hogg (King's College)
Cay Horstmann (San Jose State University)
Thomas Horton (Univ. of Virginia, Dept. of Computer Science)
Diane Horton (University of Toronto)
Helen Hu (Westminster College)
Aleata Hubbard (WestEd)
Janet Hughes (The Open University)
Bowen Hui (The University of British Columbia)
Huan Huo (University of Shanghai for Science and Technology)
Petri Ihantola (Tampere University of Technology)
Jana Jackova (Matej Bel University)
Johan Jeuring (Open Universiteit Nederland and Universiteit Utrecht)
Yerika Jimenez (University of Florida)
Karen Jin (University of New Hampshire)
Julie Johnson (Vanderbilt University)
Chris Johnson (University of Wisconsin, Eau Claire)
Dr. Anthony Joseph (Pace University)
Mike Joy (The University of Warwick)
Maria Jump (King's College)
Changyong Jung (Framingham State University)
Dennis Kafura (Virginia Tech)
Pankaj Kamthan (Concordia University)
Amey Karkare (Indian Institute of Technology, Kanpur)
Beth Katz (Millersville Univeristy)
Petros Kefalas (The University of Sheffield)
Hassan Khosravi (The University of Queensland)
Richard Kick (Newbury Park High School)
Michael Kirkpatrick (James Madison University)
Carsten Kleiner (University of Applied Science and Arts Hannover)
Jane Kochanov (Penn State Harrisburg)
Kyu Han Koh (California State University, Stanislaus)
Anna Koufakou (Florida Gulf Coast University)
Stephan Krusche (Technical University of Munich)
Amruth Kumar (Ramapo College of New Jersey)
Deepak Kumar (Bryn Mawr College)
Lisa Lacher (University of Houston - Clear Lake)
Matthew Lang (Google)
Joan Langdon (Bowie State University)
Yedidyah Langsam (City University of New York)
David Largent (Ball State University)
D. Brian Larkins (Rhodes College)
Celine Latulipe (UNC Charlotte)
Bobby Law (Glasgow Caledonian University)
Alina Lazar (Youngstown State University)
Annie Lee (University of Waterloo)
Choong-Soo Lee (St. Lawrence University)
Gilliean Lee (Lander University)
Juho Leinonen (University of Helsinki)
Terry Letsche (Wartburg College)
Chung-Chih Li (Illinois State University)
Huang Libo (National University of Defense Technology)
Panos Linos (Butler University)
Alex Lis-Perlis (Code/Interactive)
Jigang Liu (Metropolitan State University)
Jane Liu (Lamar)
Andrew Luxton-Reilly (The University of Auckland)
Roman Lysecky (University of Arizona)

Mary Maher (University of North Carolina Charlotte)
David Malan (Harvard University)
Jonathan Maletic (Kent State University)
David Martin (Nuance Communications)
Fred Martin (University of Massachusetts Lowell)
Julian Mason (Toyota Research Institute)
Jeffrey Mcconnell (Canisius College)
Frank Mccown (Harding University)
Monica McGill (Knox College)
John Mcmanus (Randolph-Macon College)
Bonnie McVey (St. Norbert College)
Pedro Medeiros (Universidade Nova de Lisboa- Dep. Informática)
Susan Mengel (Texas Tech University)
Rachel Menzies (University of Dundee)
Larry Merkle (Air Force Institute of Technology)
Mia Minnes (University of California San Diego)
Joe Miro (UIB)
Diba Mirza (University of California Santa Barbara)
Sumita Mishra (Rochester Institute of Technology)
Amitabh Mishra (University of West Florida)
Benjamin Mitchell (Villanova University)
Dagmar Monett (Berlin School of Economics and Law)
Nelma Moreira (University of Porto)
Dave Musicant (Carleton College)
Brandon Myers (University of Iowa)
Muhammad Nadeem (Mississippi State University)
Kris Nagel (Georgia Institute of Technology)
Krish Narayanan (Eastern Michigan University)
Thu Nguyen (Rutgers University)
Victor Norman (Calvin College)
Cindy Norris (Appalachian State University)
Suhaib Obeidat (Bloomfield College)
Rainer Oechsle (Trier University of Applied Science)
Peter-Michael Osera (Grinnell College)
Yin Pan (Rochester Institute of Technology)
Rick Parker (University of Colorado Boulder)
David Parker (Salisbury University)
Richard Pattis (UCI)
Arnold Pears (Uppsala University)
Joslenne Pena (The Pennsylvania State University)
Bin Peng (Park University)
Teresa Peterman (GVSU)
Andrew Petersen (University of Toronto)
Zachary Peterson (Cal Poly, San Luis Obispo)
Iasonas Petras (Princeton University)
Raymond Pettit (Abilene Christian University)
Shari Plantz-Masters (Regus University)
Leo Porter (University of California San Diego)
Thomas Price (North Carolina State University)
John Rager (Amherst College)
Brian Railing (Carnegie Mellon University)
Sagar Raina (Mount Saint Mary College)
Saquib Razak (Carnegie Mellon University)
Michael Redmond (La Salle University, Philadelphia, PA, USA)
Dale Reed (University of Illinois Chicago)
Donna Reese (Mississippi State University)
Jan Renz (HPI)
Loren Rhodes (Juniata College)
Kelly Rivers (Carnegie Mellon University)
Michael Robinson (Florida International University)
Guido Roessling (TU Darmstadt)
Audrey Rorrer (UNC Charlotte)
Nicholas Rosasco (Valparaiso University)
Jennifer Rosato (College of St. Scholastica)
John Russo (Landmark College)
Mehran Sahami (Stanford University)
Jeffrey Saltz (Syracuse University)
Ian Sanders (unisa)
Rafi Santo (New York University)
Suzanna Schmeelk (Columbia University)
Karl Schmitt (Valparaiso University)
David Schroeder (Gonzaga University)
Stephanie Schwartz (Millersville University)
Cliff Shaffer (Virginia Tech)
Bonita Sharif (Youngstown State University)
Mohamed Shehab (UNC Charlotte)
Mark Sherman (Massachusetts Institute of Technology)
Swapneel Sheth (University of Pennsylvania)
Beth Simon (University of California San Diego)
Takako Soma (Illinois College)
Jumee Song (CSNYC)
Nathan Sprague (James Madison University)
Bernhard Standl (Vienna University of Technology)
Stuart Steiner (Eastern Washington University)
Tom Stokke (University of North Dakota)

Jeffrey Stone (The Pennsylvania State University)
Kristina Striegnitz (Union College)
David Stucki (Otterbein University)
Kalpathi Subramanian (The University of N Carolina at Charlotte)
Claudia Szabo (The University of Adelaide)
Robert Tairas (Vanderbilt University)
Burcin Tamer (Computing Research Association)
Andrea Tartaro (Furman University)
Rahman Tashakkori (Appalachian State University)
Michael Tashbook (Stony Brook University)
Stephanie Taylor (Colby College)
William Thacker (Winthrop University)
Anastasios Theodoropoulos (University of Peloponnese)
George Thiruvathukal (Loyola University Chicago)
Jakita Thomas (Auburn University)
Andrew Tjang (Rutgers University)
Christian Trefftz (Grand Valley State University)
Deborah Trytten (University of Oklahoma)
Cindy Tucker (Bluegrass Community and Technical College)
Liviana Tudor (Petroleum-Gas University of Ploiesti, Romania)
William Turner (Wabash College)
Hakan Tuzun (Hacettepe University)
Ian Utting (University of Kent)
Frank Vahid (UC Riverside)
David Valentine (Slippery Rock University)
Marko Van Eekelen (Radboud University)
James Vanderhyde (Saint Xavier University)
Jorge Vasconcelos (National Autonomous University of Mexico (UNAM))
Troy Vasiga (University of Waterloo)
Nanette Veilleux (Simmons College)
Giovanni Vincenti (University of Baltimore)
Rebecca Vivian (The University of Adelaide)
Nadine von Frankenberg Und Ludwigsdorff (Technical University of Munich)
David Voorhees (Le Moyne College)
Rosita Wachenchauzer (Universidad Nacional de Tres de Febrero)
Amber Wagner (Kennesaw State University)
Gursimran Walia (North Dakota State University)
Xinli Wang (Michigan Technological University)
Stan Warford (Pepperdine University)
Andrew Watkins (Baldwin Wallace University)
David Webb (University of Colorado Boulder)
Josh Weese (Kansas State University)
Bingyang Wei (Midwestern State University)
David Weintrop (University of Maryland)
Kevin Wendt (University of Minnesota)
Linda Werner (University of CA, Santa Cruz)
Michael Whitney (Winthrop University)
Judith Williams (William Penn University)
Ken Williams (NC A&T State University)
Jim Williams (University of Wisconsin-Madison)
Linda Wilson (Texas Lutheran University)
Zoe Wood (Cal Poly)
Duane Yoder (University of West Georgia)
Evelyn Zayas (One Schoolhouse)
Yuanlin Zhang (Texas Tech University)
Xin Zhang (National University of Defense Technology)
Jian Zhang (Texas Woman's University)
Jian Zhang (Personal)
Jinghua Zhang (Winston-Salem State University)
Ming Zhang (Peking University)
Craig Zilles (University of Illinois at Urbana-Champaign)
Daniel Zingaro (University of Toronto)

Paper - Experience Reports and Tools Reviewers

Joseph Ahor Abandoh-Sam (Valley View University)
Donald Acton (The University of British Columbia)
Elizabeth Adams (James Madison University)
Robert Adams (Grand Valley State University)
Rachel Adler (Northeastern Illinois University)
Irfan Ahmed (University of New Orleans)
Nabeel Alzahrani (University of California, Riverside)
Craig Anslow (Victoria University of Wellington)
Barbara Anthony (Southwestern University)
Luis Gustavo J. Araújo (State University of Feira de Santana)
David Arnow (Brooklyn College (CUNY))

Muhammad Rizwan Asghar (The University of Auckland)
Tugba Ayer (GSU)
Monica Babes-Vroman (Rutgers University)
Doug Baldwin (SUNY Geneseo)
Robert Ball (Weber State University)
David Barnes (University of Kent)
Martin Barrett (East Tennessee State University)
Phillip Barry (University of Minnesota)
Lewis Baumstark (University of West Georgia)
Andrew Berns (University of Northern Iowa)
Kimberly Bertschy (Northwest Arkansas Community College)
Elle Boese (University of Colorado - Boulder)
James Braman (The Community College of Baltimore County)
Stefan Brandle (Taylor University)
Karen Brennan (Harvard University)
Andrej Brodnik (University of Ljubljana)
David Bunde (Knox College)
Barry Burd (Drew University)
Ricardo Caceffo (University of Campinas (Unicamp), Brazil)
Paul Cao (University of California San Diego)
Elizabeth Carter (XL Group, Inc)
Lillian Cassel (Villanova University)
Veronica Catete (North Carolina State University)
Andrew Cencini (Bennington College)
Yongqiang Chen (Tinghua University)
Vanea Chiprianov (University of Pau)
Stefan Christov (Quinnipiac University)
Vincent Cicirello (Stockton University)
John Cigas (Park University)
John Colville (University of Technology, Sydney)
Phillip Conrad (UC Santa Barbara)
Kevin Coogan (Blackburn College)
Jean Coppola (Pace University)
Jose Cordova (University of Louisiana at Monroe)
Amy Csizmar Dalal (Carleton College)
Judy Cushing (The Evergreen State College)
Joan E. Debello (St. John's University)
Sonal S. Dekhane (Georgia Gwinnett College)
G. Barbara Demo (Dipartimento Informatica, Universita Torino)
Anca Doloc-Mihu (Georgia Gwinnett College)
Mohsen Dorodchi (University of North Carolina, Charlotte)
John A. Doucette (University of Waterloo)
Maureen Doyle (Northern Kentucky University)
Wendy Dubow (NCWIT)
Philip East (University of Northern Iowa)
Mary Anne Egan (Siena College)
Roger Eggen (University of North Florida)
Kurt Eiselt (University of California, Davis)
Joseph Ekstrom (Brigham Young University)
Barbara Ericson (Georgia Institute of Technology)
Shannon Ernst (Oregon State University)
Marisa Exter (Purdue University)
K.-Y. Daisy Fan (Cornell University)
Cheri Fancsali (Research Alliance for NYC Schools)
Alan Fekete (The University of Sydney)
Hillary Fleenor (Columbus State University)
Carol Fletcher (UT Austin Center for STEM Ed)
Matthew Forshaw (Newcastle University)
Allan Fowler (Kennesaw State University)
Susan Eileen Fox (Macalester College)
Michelle Friend (University of Nebraska Omaha)
S. Jane Fritz (St. Joseph's College)
Iris Gaber (mta.ac.il)
Ed Gehringer (North Carolina State University)
James Geller (CS Dept., New Jersey Institute of Technology)
Lila Ghemri (Department of Computer Science, Texas Southern University)
Mercedes Gomez-Albarran (Universidad Complutense de Madrid)
Becky Grasser (Lakeland Community College)
Ronald I. Greenberg (Loyola University)
Trina Gregory (University of Southern California)
Yifan Guo (North Carolina State University)
Georgiana Haldeman (Rutgers University)
Tom Halverson (Dakota State University)
Mustafa Hameed (The Islamia University of Bahawalpur)
Nadeem Hamid (Berry College)
Soyeon Han (University of Tasmania)
Meng Han (Kennesaw State University)
Stuart Hansen (UW-Parkside)
Qiang Hao (Computer Science & SMATE, Western Washington University)
Caroline Hardin (University of Wisconsin-Madison)

Brian Harrington (University of Toronto)
Terry Harvey (University of Delaware)
Scott Hawker (Rochester Institute of Technology)
Orit Hazzan (Technion - Israel Institute of Technology)
Phillip Heeler (NWMSU)
Jesse M. Heines (Univ. of Massachusetts Lowell, Dept. of Computer Science)
Fui Chin Hiew (Monash University)
Timothy Highley (La Salle University)
Mark Holliday (Western Carolina University)
Cindy Hood (Illinois Institute of Technology)
Charles Hoot (NW Missouri State University)
Cay Horstmann (San Jose State University)
Brian Howard (DePauw University)
Wen-Jung Hsin (Park University)
Chenglie Hu (Carroll University)
Jim Huggins (Kettering University)
Fran Hunt (Retired)
Deborah Hwang (University of Evansville)
Jorge Eduardo Ibarra-Esquer (Universidad Autónoma de Baja California)
Matt Jadud (Allegheny College)
Hasan Jamil (University of Idaho)
Zhen Jiang (West Chester University)
Mark Johnson (Central College)
Maria Jump (King's College)
Amardeep Kahlon (UT)
Tetsuro Kakeshita (Saga University)
Petros Kefalas (The University of Sheffield)
Thomas Kelliher (Goucher College)
Wiliam Kerney (Clovis Community College)
John Kloosterman (University of Michigan)
Joanna Klukowska (New York University)
Brian J Kokensparger (Creighton University)
James Kolasa (Bluegrass Community and Technical College)
Martha Kosa (Tennessee Technological University)
Joan Krone (Denison University)
Jan Kruger (Unisa SBL)
Zachary Kurmas (Grand Valley State University)
Clifton Kussmaul (Muhlenberg College)
Michael Lachney (Rensselaer Polytechnic Institute)
Richard Ladner (University of Washington)
Mary Last (self employed)
Christopher League (LIU Brooklyn)
Irene Lee (Massachusetts Institute of Technology)
Ben Leong (National University of Singapore)
Scott Leutenegger (University of Denver)
Chun Wai Liew (Lafayette College)
Mark Liffiton (Illinois Wesleyan University)
Qiang Liu (College of Computer, National University of Defense Technology)
Matija Lokar (Faculty of mathematics and physics, University of Ljubljana)
Dastyni Loksa (University of Washington)
Stephanie Ludi (University of North Texas)
Bonnie Mackellar (St John's University)
Joaquim Madeira (University of Aveiro)
Manuel Martins Barata (ISEL - Instituto Superior de Engenharia de Lisboa)
Raina Mason (Southern Cross University)
Suzanne Matthews (United States Military Academy)
Anna Mavroudi (Norwegian University of Science and Technology)
Chris Mayfield (James Madison University)
Chris McDonald (The Univ. of Western Australia)
Steven Mcgee (The Learning Partnership)
Andrew Mcgettrick (University of Strathclyde)
António Mendes (University of Coimbra)
Tyler Menezes (srnd.org)
Larry Merkle (Air Force Institute of Technology)
L. Dee Miller (Apollo Analytics)
Lauren Milne (University of Washington)
Mia Minnes (University of California San Diego)
Shitanshu Mishra (Indian Institute of Technology Bombay)
Idong Mkpong-Ruffin (Faulkner University)
Gabriela Moise (Petroleum-Gas University of Ploiesti)
Alvaro Monge (California State University Long Beach)
Jesús Moreno-León (Programamos.es & Universidad Rey Juan Carlos)
Mirella M. Moro (Univ. Federal de Minas Gerais - UFMG)
Patricia Morreale (Kean University)
Shamsi Moussavi (MassBay Community College)
Paolo Musmarra (Università degli Studi di Salerno)

Dean Nevins (Santa Barbara City College)
Lijun Ni (SUNY, Albany)
Bill Nicholson (University of Cincinnati Clermont College)
Theodore S. Norvell (Memorial University of Newfoundland)
Linda Null (The Pennsylvania State University)
Keith O'Hara (Bard College)
Brian O'Neill (Western New England University)
Edward Okie (Radford University)
Michael Oudshoorn (Northwest Missouri State University)
Youwen Ouyang (Cal State San Marcos)
Younghee Park (San Jose State University)
Rick Parker (University of Colorado Boulder)
David Parker
Allen Parrish (United States Naval Academy)
James Paterson (Glasgow Caledonian University)
Elizabeth Patitsas (University of Toronto)
Raymond Pettit (Abilene Christian University)
Wayne Pollock (Hillsborough Community College)
Irene Polycarpou (UCLan Cyprus)
George Pothering (College of Charleston)
Farzana Rahman (Florida International University)
Rajendra Raj (Rochester Institute of Techinology)
Michael Redmond (La Salle University, Philadelphia, PA, USA)
Suzanne Rivoire (Sonoma State University)
Kevin Robinson (MIT Teaching Systems Lab)
Michael Robinson (Florida International University)
Tobias Rocha (UFRN)
Joel Ross (U Washington iSchool)
Allison Sauppé (University of Wisconsin-La Crosse)
Vibha Sazawal (University of Maryland)
Suzanna Schmeelk (Pace University)
Christian Servin (El Paso Community College)
Ck Shene (Michigan Technological University)
Mark Sherman (Massachusetts Institute of Technology)
Swapneel Sheth (University of Pennsylvania)
Bill Siever (Washington University)
Scott Sigman (Drury University)
Tian Song (Beijing Institute of Technology)
Adalbert Gerald Soosai Raj (University of Wisconsin-Madison)
Ellen Spertus (Mills College)
Stuart Steiner (Eastern Washington University)
Ben Stephenson (University of Calgary)
Jane Stout (Computing Research Association)
Simon Sultana (Fresno Pacific University)
Valdemar Švábenský (Masaryk University)
Paul Talaga (University of Indianapolis)
Cara Tang (Portland Community College)
Fatma Tarlaci (Stanford University)
Rahman Tashakkori (Appalachian State University)
James Teresco (Siena College)
George Thomas (University of Wisconsin Oshkosh)
S. Rebecca Thomas (Bard College)
Megan Thomas (California State University, Stanislaus)
Alfred Thompson (Bishop Guertin High School)
Liviana Tudor (Petroleum-Gas University of Ploiesti, Romania)
William Turkett (Wake Forest University)
Roy Turner (University of Maine)
Robert Van Camp (Marietta College)
Sarah Van Wart (University of California, Berkeley)
Tammy Vandegrift (University of Portland)
J. Ángel Velázquez-Iturbide (Universidad Rey Juan Carlos)
Camilo Vieira (Purdue University)
Gabriela Vilanova (UNPA)
Sally Wahba (NetApp)
Charles Wallace (Michigan Technological University)
Kendra Walther (University of Southern California)
Jayce Warner (The University of Texas at Austin)
David Weintrop (University of Maryland)
Richard Weiss (The Evergreen State College)
Alan Whitehurst (Southern Virginia University)
Eliane Wiese (University of California, Berkeley)
David Williams (National College of Ireland / Pulse College)
Christine T. Wolf (University of California, Irvine)
Jinyue Xia (University Of North Carolina Charlotte)
Benjamin Xie (University of Washington)
Nikhil Yadav (St. John's University)
Fan Yang (University of Toronto)
Sejong Yoon (The College of New Jersey)
Zhen Zeng (Arizona State Univeristy)

Jian Zhang (Personal)
Daniel Zingaro (University of Toronto)

Paper - New curricula, programs, degrees and position papers Reviewers

Paul Addison (Ivy Tech Community College)
Hisham Al-Mubaid (University of Houston-clear lake)
Farha Ali (Lander University)
Steve Andrianoff (St. Bonaventure University)
Owen Astrachan (Duke University)
Donald Bagert (Benedictine College)
Ajay Bandi (Northwest Missouri State University)
Robert Beck (Villanova University)
Brett Becker (University College Dublin)
Michael Bloodgood (The College of New Jersey)
Kevin Buell (Arizona State University)
Lori Carter (Point Loma Nazarene University)
Henry Carter (Villanova University)
Edward Chapin (University of Maryand Eastern Shore)
Robert Chen (Framingham State University (retired))
Sue Inn Chng (Sunway University)
Alison Clear (EIT)
Monica Costa (EST - IPCB)
John Dooley (Knox College)
Peter Drexel (Plymouth State University)
Alan Fekete (The University of Sydney)
Daniel Fokum (The University of the West Indies)
Michael Goldweber (Xavier University)
Ranette Halverson (Midwestern State University)
David Heise (Lincoln University)
William Joel (Graphics Research Group / WCSU)
David Kay (UC Irvine School of Information and Computer Sciences)
Natalia Khuri (Stanford University)
Brian Krupp (Baldwin Wallace)
Anastasia Kurdia (Bucknell University)
Daniela Marghitu (Auburn University)
Thomas Marlowe (Seton Hall University)
Bruce Maxwell (Colby College)
O. William Mcclung (Nebraska Wesleyan University)
James Mcguffee (Christian Brothers University)
Afsaneh Minaie (Utah Valley University)
Mehrgan Mostowfi (University of Northern Colorado)
Michael Murphy (retired)
Lawrence Osborne (Lamar University Faculty)
Young Park (Bradley University)
Janice Pearce (Berea College)
Lambros Piskopos (Wilbur Wright College)
Jari Porras (LUT)
Zhengrui Qin (Northwest Missouri State University)
Beth Quinn (NCWIT)
Detlef Rick (University of Hamburg)
Charles Riedesel (University of Nebraska - Lincoln)
Anthony Ruocco (Roger Williams University)
Anil Shende (Roanoke College)
Jacqueline Smith (University of Toronto)
John Stratton (Whitman College)
Amber Stubbs (Simmons College)
Victor Winter (University of Nebraska at Omaha)
Marty J. Wolf (Bemidji State University)

Poster Reviewers

Joseph Abandoh-Sam (Valley View University)
Reem Ali (University of Minnesota)
Meghan Allen (The University of British Columbia)
Andrew Allen (Georgia Southern University)
Lisa Anthony (University of Florida)
Austin Bart (Virginia Tech)
Lina Battestilli (North Carolina State University)
Lewis Baumstark (University of West Georgia)
Luciana Benotti (Universidad Nacional de Cordoba)
Angela Berardinelli (Mercyhurst University)
Leon Bernard (Towson Univeristy)
Marie Bienkowski (SRI International)
Roberto Bittencourt (UEFS - State University of Feira de Santana)
Kevin Buffardi (California State University - Chico)
Ankur Chattopadhyay (University of Wisconsin - Green Bay)
James Chegwidden (Tarrant County College)
Juan Chen (College of Computer, National University of Defense Technology, China)
John Cigas (Park University)
Barb Cutler (Rensselaer Polytechnic Institute)
Debzani Deb (Winston-salem state university)
Josh Dehlinger (Towson University)
Christo Dichev (WSSU)
Darina Dicheva (Winston-Salem State University)
Gabriella Dodero (ASLERD)

Zhijiang Dong (Middle Tennessee State University)
J.Philip East (University of Northern Iowa)
Ahmed El-Deeb
Heidi Ellis (Western New England University)
Kiran L.N. Eranki (Indian Institute of Technology Bombay)
Yadran Eterovic (Pontificia Universidad Catlica de Chile)
Paula Evans (California Department of Education)
Mohammed Farghally (Virginia Tech)
Monica Gilmore
Cengiz Gunay (Georgia Gwinnett College)
Francisco Gutierrez (Computer Science Department, University of Chile)
Steve Hadfield (US Air Force Academy)
Sally Hamouda (Cairo University)
Brian Harrington (University of Toronto)
Kathy Haynie (Stanford)
Theodore Hays (Clemson University Undergraduate Research Team)
James Heliotis (Rochester Institute of Technology)
José Hilera (Universidad de Alcalá)
Matt Jadud (Allegheny College)
Shan Jiang (The University of Hong Kong)
Xunfei Jiang
Swaroop Joshi (The Ohio State University)
Alark Joshi (University of San Francisco)
Carsten Kleiner (University of Applied Science and Arts Hannover)
John Kloosterman (University of Michigan)
Joanna Klukowska (New York University)
Joe Kmoch (JK Consulting)
Zachary Kurmas (Grand Valley State University)
Lisa Lacher (University of Houston - Clear Lake)
Joan Langdon (Bowie State University)
Qiang Liu (College of Computer, National University of Defense Technology)
Matija Lokar (Faculty of mathematics and physics, University of Ljubljana)
Marcia Lucena (UFRN)
Nicholas Lytle (North Carolina State University)
Lester McCann (University of Arizona)
James McGuffee (Christian Brothers University)
Alexandra Mendes (Teesside University)
Larry Merkle (Air Force Institute of Technology)
Idongesit Mkpong-Ruffin (Faulkner University)
Selvarajah Mohanarajah (UNC-Pembroke)
Gabriela Moise (Petroleum-Gas University of Ploiesti)
Dagmar Monett (Berlin School of Economics and Law)
Frank Moss (Claremont Graduate University)
Alisa Neeman (Muskingum University)
Tom Neutens (Ghent University)
Isabel Nunes (UFRN)
Michael Oudshoorn (Northwest Missouri State University)
Katarina Pantic (Utah State University)
Young Park (Bradley University)
Leo Paschoal (University of São Paulo)
Matthew Peveler (Rensselaer Polytechnic Institute)
Jan Plane (University of Maryland)
Mahmudur Rahman
Brian Railing (Carnegie Mellon University)
Damith Rajapakse (National University of Singapore)
Andrew Rasmussen (Chicago Public Schools)
Samuel Rebelsky (Grinnell College)
Rosario Robinson (FocusGears)
Tobias Rocha (UFRN)
Guido Rößling (TU Darmstadt)
Bianca Santana (Universidade Estadual de Feira de Santana)
Ashwin Satyanarayana (City University of New York)
Madeleine Schep (Columbia College)
Jessica Schmidt (North Carolina State University)
Bruno Sena (University of São Paulo)
Jay Shaffstall (Muskingum University)
Mark Sherriff (University of Virginia)
Amber Solomon (Georgia Institute of Technology)
Cecilia Sotomayor (Universidad de Chile)
Nigamanth Sridhar (Cleveland State University)
Melissa Stange (Lord Fairfax Community College)
Kalpathi Subramanian (The University of N Carolina at Charlotte)
Valerie Summet (Rollins College)
Cynthia Taylor (University of Illinois at Chicago)
Kyle Thayer (Universtiy of Washington)
Anastasios Theodoropoulos (University of Peloponnese)
Charles Thevathayan (RMIT University)

Brian Thoms (California State University Channel Islands)
Armando Toda (University of São Paulo)
Shane Torbert (Fairfax County Public Schools)
William Turkett (Wake Forest University)
Jan Vahrenhold (Department of Computer Science, Westfälische Wilhelms-Universität Münster)
Gabriela Vilanova (UNPA)
Jan Vykopal (Masaryk University)
Xiaojing Weng (The University of Hong Kong)
Linda Werner (University of CA, Santa Cruz)
Chen-Hsiang Yu (Wentworth Institute of Technology)

Special Session Reviewers

Beverly Bachmayer (Intel)
Michael Ball (University of California, Berkeley)
Shankar Banik (The Citadel)
Tiffany Barnes (NC State)
Michael Bauer (Leeward Community College)
Ivona Bezakova (Rochester Institute of Technology)
Jeremiah Blanchard (University of Florida)
Bill Booth (Baylor University)
Veronica Catete (North Carolina State University)
Joan E. Debello (St. John's University)
Lucia Dettori (DePaul University)
Nomusa Dlodlo (Namibia University of Science and Technology)
Yadran Eterovic (Pontificia Universidad Catlica de Chile)
Paul Fodor (Stony Brook University)
Matthew Forshaw (Newcastle University)
Daniel Garcia (UC berkeley)
Joshua Gross (Blackburn College)
Carlos Guerrero
Elizabeth Hawthorne
Sarah Heckman (North Carolina State University)
Curt Hill (Valley City State University)
Hoda Hosny (AUC Egypt)
Bryn Jeffries (The University of Sydney)
David Johnson (University of Oxford)
Yvonne Kao (WestEd)
Salvador López (Universidad Nacional Autónoma de México)
Bruce Maxwell (Colby College)
Larry Merkle (Air Force Institute of Technology)
Manuel Perez-Quinones (University of North Carolina, Charlotte)
Christian Roberson (Florida Southern College)
Jerry Roth (Vanderbilt University)
Christina Schweikert (St John's University)
Bill Siever (Washington University)
Theresa Steinbach (DePaul University)
Steven Vegdahl (University of Portland)
Emily Wenk (The Pennsylvania State University)
Nikhil Yadav (St. John's University)

Workshop Reviewers

Raman Adaikkalavan (Indiana University South Bend)
Ibrahim Albluwi (Princeton University)
Reem Ali (University of Minnesota)
Mark Allison (University of Michigan-Flint)
Cathy Bareiss (Olivet Nazarene University)
Richard Burns (West Chester University)
Bruce Char (Drexel University Department of Computer Science)
Vanea Chiprianov (University of Pau)
Robert Cook (University of Tennessee, Chattanooga)
Jonathan Corley (University of West Georgia)
Michael Cotterell (University of Georgia)
Luigi De Russis (Politecnico di Torino)
G. Barbara Demo (Dipartimento Informatica, Universita Torino)
Mohsen Dorodchi (University of North Carolina, Charlotte)
Kathleen Ericson (University of Tennessee at Martin)
Ronald Finkbine (Indiana University Southeast)
S. Jane Fritz (St. Joseph's College)
Paul Gestwicki (Ball State University)
Mark Gondree (Sonoma State University)
Cengiz Gunay (Georgia Gwinnett College)
Roberto Hoyle (Oberlin College)
Cruz Izu (The University of Adelaide)
Wei Jin (Georgia Gwinnett College)
Deepti Joshi (The Citadel)
Fazel Keshtkar (ST John's University)
Jeff Kinne (Indiana State University)
Daniel Leyzberg (Princeton University)
Justin Li (Occidental College)
Stephanie Ludi (University of North Texas)
Srikanth Mudigonda (Saint Louis University)
Brian O'Neill (Western New England University)
Joonsuk Park (Williams College)
Miranda Parker (Georgia Institute of Technology)

Rebecca Rutherfoord (Kennesaw State University)
Vijayalakshmi Saravanan (University at Buffalo)
Christelle Scharff (Pace University, Seidenberg School of Computer Science and Information Systems)
Michael Scott (Falmouth University)
Ching-Kuang Shene (Michigan Technological University)
Yasuto Shirai (Shizuoka University)
Raja Sooriamurthi (Carnegie Mellon University)
Jonathan Sorenson (Butler University)
Greg Speegle (Baylor University)
Gloria Townsend (DePauw University)
Elizabeth White (George Mason University)
Craig Wills (Worcester Polytechnic Institute)
Greg Wolffe (Grand Valley State University)
Arthur Yanushka (Christian Brothers University)
Timothy Yuen (University of Texas at San Antonio)

The Evolution Before the Revolution

Brenda Darden Wilkerson
President & CEO of AnitaB.org

ABSTRACT

As founder of the original Computer Science for All (CS4All) initiative in the Chicago Public Schools, Brenda Darden Wilkerson set the standard for integrating computer science classes into the curriculum for every student. Now, she's leading the charge to break down barriers for women and members of other underrepresented minorities in the tech industry. She argues that, while many administrators and community leaders see CS4All as merely a key component of a new core curriculum, CS educators are actually sowing the seeds of the next workplace revolution. In this inspirational keynote, Brenda will share the ways that educators on the front lines of this inclusive movement can expect to reap the fruits of their labor — not just professionally, but personally — in surprising ways. And she'll spotlight the historic role of women, and people of color, in technology and computer science, offering examples that will better allow us all to reclaim our rightful seats at the table.

Keywords

Computer Science for All; Computing Education

ACM Reference format:
Brenda Darden Wilkerson. 2018. The Evolution Before the Revolution. In *SIGCSE'18: The 49th ACM Technical Symposium on Computer Science Education, Feb. 21-24, 2018, Baltimore, MD, USA.* ACM, NY, NY, USA, 1 pages. DOI: https://doi.org/10.1145/3159450.3166085

BIOGRAPHY

Brenda Darden Wilkerson is an advocate for access, opportunity, and social justice for underrepresented communities in technology. She currently serves as the President and CEO of AnitaB.org, an organization working to shape public opinion about issues of critical importance to women technologists in academia, industry, and government. She founded the original Computer Science for All program, building computer science classes into the curriculum for every student in the Chicago Public Schools, and serving as the inspiration for the Obama administration's national CS4All initiatives.

SIGCSE '18, February 21–24, 2018, Baltimore, MD, USA

ACM ISBN 978-1-4503-5103-4/18/02.
DOI: https://doi.org/10.1145/3159450.3166085

The Effect of a Web-based Coding Tool with Automatic Feedback on Students' Performance and Perceptions

Luciana Benotti
Universidad Nacional de Cordoba / CONICET
Cordoba, Argentina
benotti@famaf.unc.edu.ar

Federico Aloi
Universidad Nacional de Quilmes
Buenos Aires, Argentina
federico.aloi@unq.edu.ar

Franco Bulgarelli
Mumuki Project
Buenos Aires, Argentina
franco@mumuki.org

Marcos J. Gomez
Universidad Nacional de Cordoba
Cordoba, Argentina
mgomez4@famaf.unc.edu.ar

ABSTRACT

In this paper we do three things. First, we describe a web-based coding tool that is open-source, publicly available and provides formative feedback and assessment. Second, we compare several metrics on student performance in courses that use the tool versus courses that do not use it when learning to program in Haskell. We find that the dropout rates are significantly lower in those courses that use the tool at two different universities. Finally we apply the technology acceptance model to analyse students perceptions.

CCS CONCEPTS

• **Language Classifications → Applicative (functional) languages**; • **Computers and Education → Computer-assisted instruction**;

KEYWORDS

Functional programming; Haskell; Coding tools; Replication; Automatic assessment

ACM Reference format:
Luciana Benotti, Federico Aloi, Franco Bulgarelli, and Marcos J. Gomez. 2018. The Effect of a Web-based Coding Tool with Automatic Feedback on Students' Performance and Perceptions. In *Proceedings of The 49th ACM Technical Symposium on Computer Science Education, Baltimore, MD, USA, February 21–24, 2018 (SIGCSE '18)*, 6 pages.
https://doi.org/10.1145/3159450.3159579

1 INTRODUCTION

While many tools are developed in order to support the teaching and learning of programming, few such tools ever achieve widespread adoption and use. A survey [2] found that one of the most common reasons is the teachers' unwillingness to adopt a new system until its usefulness has been demonstrated.

In general, the evaluations of such tools use ad-hoc metrics and are conducted on a single course (for notable exceptions see [8]). As argued in [8], there is a critical need for replicating studies in different contexts and for evaluating various contributing factors. It is also necessary to use standard metrics in order to better understand the reasons why certain results occur. In this paper we hypothesize that coding tools may have an effect on the high dropout rates observed in introductory programming courses [15].

The main contributions of this paper are:

- We describe a web-based coding tool that is open-source and provides formative feedback and assessment.
- We compare several metrics on student performance in courses that use the tool versus courses that do not use it when learning to program in Haskell.
- We find that the dropout rates are significantly lower in those courses that use the tool at two different universities.
- We apply a standard model, the technology acceptance model (TAM) to analyse students perceptions.

According to a recent review [9], less than 10% of the educational programming tools support functional programming. This paper focuses on the language Haskell, a traditional functional programming language that has gained popularity in recent years.

We begin the paper by reviewing previous work on educational coding tools for functional programming and on previous studies on the effect of such tools on students' performance and perceptions. Then, we describe the online coding tool that we use, called Mumuki, and its rationale. A screenshot can be seen in Figure 1. Moreover, we address the study design followed by our findings. We analyse student passing, failure and dropout rates. Finally, we discuss our findings when applying the technology acceptance model on the courses.

2 PREVIOUS WORK

The topic of online coding tools has received plenty of attention during the last years. Well known examples are Codingbat [13], CodeRunner [12], CodeLab [1] and CloudCoder [14]. These online tools have been shown to be useful helping students' master the syntax of imperative programming languages such as Java and Python [8]. In spite of the attention this topic has received from researchers, the use of online coding tools is not widespread in education [2]. There are studies [8] that use these tools in order to identify students at-risk of dropout. However, longitudinal studies,

ACM ISBN 978-1-4503-5103-4/18/02...$15.00
https://doi.org/10.1145/3159450.3159579

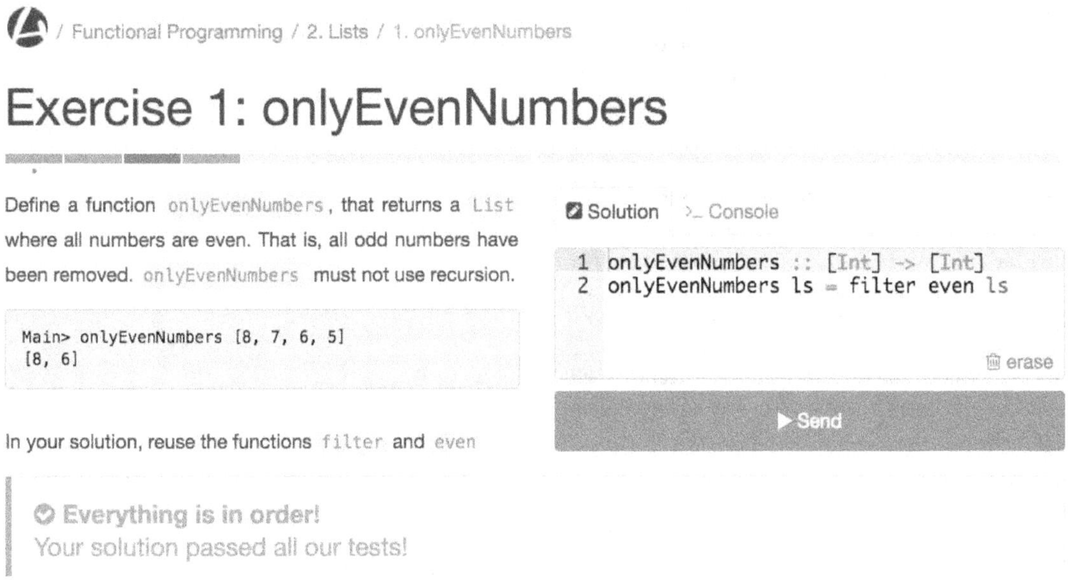

Figure 1: Mumuki screenshot. The left hand panel shows an exercise description. The right hand panel shows the editor where a student wrote a solution. Finally, the bottom of the figure shows the feedback provided when the solution is correct.

where the effect of an intervention would be measured across a number of courses or institutions, are rare.

This paper provides evidence that this kind of systems are useful in introductory programming courses at two different institutions. In particular, we show their usefulness with functional programming languages. In this section we review previous work on educational coding tools for functional programming. As we mentioned in Section 1, almost all educational coding tools focus on imperative languages. To the best of our knowledge, in addition to ours there is only one online coding tool for Haskell that was developed with educational purposes: Ask-Elle.

Ask-Elle [6, 7] is a web-based tutor that shares some features with Mumuki. As well as Mumuki it presents exercises in Haskell and generates automatic feedback to students' programs. Also, similarly to Mumuki, it evaluates the students' solutions using test cases.

Differently from Mumuki, Ask-Elle was conceived as a tutor that provides hints during the intermediate steps of programming a solution to an exercise. Ask-Elle [6] tries to predict which basic steps have to be taken in order to arrive at a solution. They call these steps a "programming strategy" and they derive them automatically from model solutions provided by the teachers. However, in their experiments, they find that it is very difficult to predict the size of the step that students take. Furthermore, often a student's solution cannot be matched to one of the model solutions provided by the teachers by their program transformations. As a result they cannot provide feedback for almost 40% of the student's submissions. The authors note that students usually take steps that are bigger than those expected by the system, frequently submitting complete solutions in one step. Mumuki expects a complete solution whenever it receives a submission. Therefore it is able to provide feedback for all the submissions received.

Another difference between the two tools is that Ask-Elle requires teachers to define model solutions to the exercises while Mumuki does not. Ask-Elle uses QuickCheck [4] which generates random tests cases. QuickCheck developers acknowledge that the major limitation of the software is that there is no measurement of test coverage, since the test cases are generated at random. Mumuki require teachers to manually define test cases so that special attention can be put into border cases and problematic branches. Unlike Ask-Elle, Mumuki also provides a Haskell console for each exercise where students can try their own test cases. Furthermore, in order to verify solution quality, Mumuki allows teachers to define expectations on the submissions. We explain this novel feature in the next section.

Ask-Elle was evaluated at a single university, the Utrecht University, by 40 students. The students used the tool during two laboratory sessions whose duration is not reported. The students attitude towards the tool was also evaluated through a questionnaire as we did. However, the authors do not report following any standard methodology. The students rated the tool an average of 2.82 in the question "The step-size of the tutor corresponded to my intuition" on a Likert scale from 1 to 5. The effect on course dropouts and course pass and failure rates was not reported.

Kumar [10] argues that online coding tools can be used to increase the self-confidence of students in Computer Science. This is particularly useful in the first CS courses when student's self-confidence is lower. Kumar also claims that the impact is stronger on female students. However, they do not report the effect on course performance metrics as we do.

To the best of our knowledge there is only one study [1] where the authors successfully applied a web-based coding tool, CodeLab, across two different institutions. The results and the discussion are encouraging. However, the comparison is purely qualitative, the impact of the tool over quantitative metrics, such as failure and pass rates is not reported. Grades are reported, but only for one of the institutions. The effect on students' performance and perceptions of interactive books [5] and visualisation tools [11] has been better evaluated than the effect of coding tools.

3 MUMUKI: AN ONLINE CODING TOOL

Mumuki is an open-source[1] web-based coding tool that provides automatic formative feedback and assessment, developed in Argentina. This platform provides assistance for teachers and students, in a process conducted by practice where theory arises from the exercises. It supports 17 programming languages, including Haskell, Prolog, Python, JavaScript, C and Ruby. Mumuki is currently used at eight Argentinian universities, five high schools and two coding clubs, with more than 1500 active users per month.

A screenshot can be seen in Figure 1. Practice within the platform is organised across topics with many programming exercises[2] each. The interface includes a progress bar that shows which exercises have been solved (in green), which have been attempted but are incorrect (in red or yellow) and which have not been attempted yet (in grey). The current exercise is marked with a blue dot. The students can solve the exercises in any order they want, but Mumuki suggests an order with the progress bar.

From the student point of view, an exercise includes the description of the problem with at least one example and a list of functions that can or must be reused, as can be seen in the figure in the left hand panel. In the right hand panel it includes a tab with an editor for the solution and another tab with an interactive console where the solution and the reusable functions can be tested. The automatic feedback for the student's solution is shown at the bottom of the screen once she presses the "Send" button . In Figure 1, the solution passed all the tests.

From the teacher point of view, an exercise includes two parts. On the one hand, it includes a description of the problem the student should solve by providing a program, in which generally, no more than a few a few lines of code are required. On the other hand, the exercise designer provides a way to automatically compute feedback for the solution of the exercise at two different levels: correctness and quality. For correctness, a suite of representative unit tests are provided by the teacher and executed against the final program. The final program could include auxiliary functions programmed by the teacher. Although correctness cannot be assured by this technique, it proved to be good enough for the complexity of the existent exercises. Regarding the quality of the student's solution, an analysis of the abstract syntax tree is performed. By using an editor tool, the teacher can pick several predefined patterns, called *expectations* in Mumuki. Expectations are defined so that they must be present or not present in the student's solution. When the student submits a solution, each expectation is evaluated against it.

Student solutions are assessed by Mumuki with three possible values: red, yellow or green. Red indicates that some test result is not correct. Yellow means that all tests are correct but some expectation is not met. An exercise is marked green when all tests are correct

[1]Source code available at https://github.com/mumuki.

[2]The exercises are available at https://mumuki.io (in Spanish)

```
SOLUTION: onlyEvenNumbers [] = []
          onlyEvenNumbers (x:xs)
            | even x    = x:(onlyEvenNumbers xs)
            | otherwise = onlyEvenNumbers xs
```

FEEDBACK:

It worked, but you can do better

Goals that weren't met:

onlyEvenNumbers must not use recursion

Tests results:

onlyEvenNumbers [] is []

onlyEvenNumbers [1, 2, 3] is [2]

onlyEvenNumbers [7, 14, 9, 10] is [14, 10]

Figure 2: Sample solution to an exercise which is assessed as yellow by Mumuki because some expectation is not met.

and all expectations are met. The figure shows an exercise assessed as green. Below we exemplify the other two colors.

The exercise in Figure 1 asks the student to define a function called `onlyEvenNumbers` that returns only the even numbers of a given list. The exercise description is illustrated by the example `onlyEvenNumbers [8,7,6,5] = [8,6]`. The following unit tests are provided by the teacher and not shown to the student until she submits a solution:

- `onlyEvenNumbers [] = []`.
- `onlyEvenNumbers [1,2,3] = [2]`.
- `onlyEvenNumbers [7,14,9,10] = [14,10]`.

The teacher also defines the following expectations. Because the use of `filter` is expected, direct recursion is not allowed. This is specified by the teacher as a pattern that *should not* be found in the student solution. Also, the teacher wants to encourage code reuse, so the solution must use the `even` function provided by Haskell's standard libraries. This is specified by the teacher as a pattern that *should* be found in the student solution.

In Figure 2 the student uses `even` but she uses direct recursion instead of using `filter` in the solution. Mumuki informs the test results are correct but explains that recursion must not be used. Therefore, the exercise is assessed by Mumuki as yellow: tests results are correct but some expectation is not met.

In Figure 3 the student did not use `even` and also made a mistake when programming her version of even. Instead of verifying that the modulus operation is zero, she compares it to one. Both the tests and one of the expectations fail, and this is reported by Mumuki. In this case, the exercise is assessed as red because some test results are incorrect.

Every solution submitted by a student is stored, thus the teacher has access not only to the final solution but also to all the steps that lead to it. The timestamp, the tests and expectations results are also stored, so the full history can be reproduced. It is also used to improve the exercises, to explore common mistakes, etc. The logged data is presented on a web page as shown in Figure 4 and can be accessed only by the teachers. In the web interface, the teachers can monitor students' progress. In the figure, the student has submitted ten different solutions for this exercise. The last one

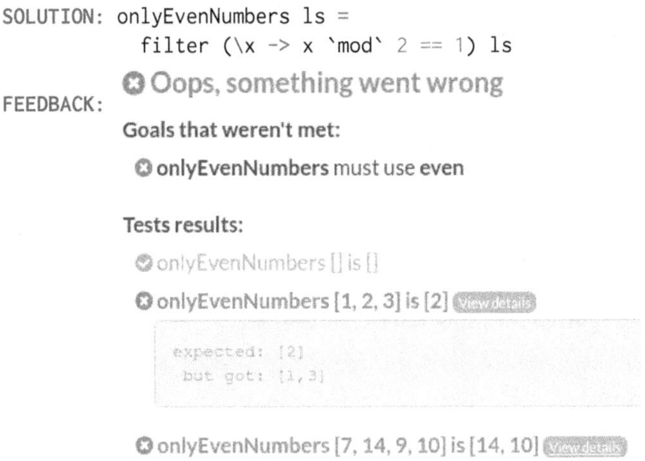

Figure 3: Sample solution to an exercise that is assessed as red by Mumuki because some tests results are incorrect.

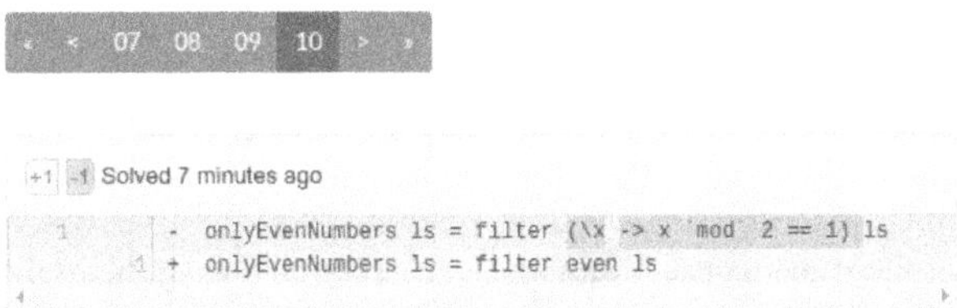

Figure 4: Two solutions for the same exercise and their difference are reported on the teacher's tool, using a diff highlighting tool.

is marked green by Mumuki since it passes all the tests and meets all the expectations.

4 STUDY DESIGN

In this section we describe the contexts where we conducted the observational studies in two different courses at two universities. We pose the following directional hypothesis to be tested at the two courses. H_0 *(null): There is no significant difference between the dropout rate at a course which uses Mumuki and at one that does not.* H_1 *(alt): The dropout rate at a course which uses Mumuki is significantly lower than that of a course that does not.*

4.1 Data Collection and Analysis

We performed interventions in two different public universities. In both of them we taught Haskell using Mumuki.

As we argued in Section 2, most previous work evaluating web-based coding tools are conducted within a single institution and a single course. We selected two institutions that introduce functional programming with Haskell. They have groups of students with different characteristics to replicate our observational study and validate our results. One of the public universities, called UTN, introduces Haskell to CS2 students while the other, called UNC, introduces Haskell to CS1 students. In total, 114 students participated in this observational study. 59 students at CS2 level and 55 students at CS1 level.

Students were asked to solve 82 programming exercises covering introductory functional concepts. Their understanding of the concepts was evaluated with a written test on paper. Neither Mumuki nor other compiler was used for the exam. The exam was manually corrected by the teachers. Students had two opportunities to pass the test; there was at least one month between them.

In order to evaluate their attitude towards Mumuki, we asked the students to complete a questionnaire designed following the Technology Acceptance Model (TAM) methodology [3].

4.2 The CS1 Intervention

UNC is a public university in Argentina where students are full time. Students attend courses approximately 35 hours per week. As a result, there are almost no students that study and work.

From August to October 2016 a university professor, two teaching assistants and one student assistant taught 15 four-hour functional programming lessons to CS1 students at UNC. The course was taught for eight hours a week divided in two days from 9am to 1pm. This is the first programming course of a 5-year degree in Computer Science. The course started with 55 students that enrolled and attended the course at least two days. From the 55 students, only 2 reported previous experience programming imperative languages and none of them reported experience with functional programming. The average age was 21 years old. Each four-hour lecture was divided in two stages of two hours each.

During the first stage, the students used Mumuki in the laboratory programming functions in Haskell. Mumuki provided automated formative feedback but also the professor and the teaching assistants walked around the laboratory answering questions about the exercises.

During the second stage, the students went to a classroom where the professor explained on the blackboard the concepts practiced in the laboratory, presented worked out examples and discussed the most commonly observed errors. No computer was used in the classroom. Students were encouraged to program in Haskell using paper and pencil and to propose test cases in order to manually evaluate their programs.

Summing up, during the course, students used Mumuki during 30 hours. They also used Mumuki outside the course but 85% of their submissions were made during class hours.

4.3 The CS2 Intervention

UTN is a public university in Argentina where students are part time. Students attend courses approximately 20 hours per week. As a result, students can study and work.

From March to May 2016 a university professor, two teaching assistants and six student assistants taught 9 four-hour functional programming lessons to CS2 students at UTN. The course was taught for four hours a week in a single day from 9am to 1pm. Before this course, all the students learn imperative programming in Pascal and C during CS1. The course started with 59 students that attended the course for at least two classes. In the previous semester, Pascal and C languages were used to teach classical control structures and basic data structures such as lists, stacks, and

	2015		2016		t-test	
	n	ratio	n	ratio	p	t
Passed Test	15	.33	22	.37	.62	.49
Passed Re-Test	3	.06	8	.14	.25	1.17
Dropout	13	.28	8*	.14	.05	2.01
Failed	15	.33	21	.35	.75	.32
Total	46	1	59	1	-	-

Table 1: Dropout, passed and failed quantities and ratios in CS2 at UTN in 2015 and 2016. Significant differences between 2015 and 2016 are marked with *, p and t values are reported for unpaired t-test results.

	2014		2015		2016		t-test	
	n	ratio	n	ratio	n	ratio	p	t
Passed Test	21	.32	16	.31	21	.38	.43	.79
Passed Re-Test	3	.05	4	.05	12*	.22	.02	2.3
Dropout	38	.58	34	.59	19*	.35	.01	2.6
Failed	4	.06	4	.05	3	.05	.75	.31
Total	66	1	58	1	55	1	-	-

Table 2: Dropout, passed and failed quantities and ratios in CS1 at UNC in 2014, 2015 and 2016. Significant differences between 2015 and 2016 are marked with *, p and t values are reported for unpaired t-test results.

queues. None of the students reported previous experience with functional programming. The average age was 22 years old.

During the classes, Mumuki was used to introduce new concepts and to practice previously learnt ones. When considered necessary by the professor or the teaching assistant, they stopped the practice and explained some concept in the blackboard or screen projector using Mumuki, discussing errors and sharing different solutions. These explanations lasted 10 minutes in average and never took more than 10% of the total time. Students were not asked to program on paper and they used Mumuki during the whole lecture.

Summing up, during the course, students used Mumuki during 36 hours. They also used Mumuki outside the course, 70% of their submissions were made during class hours.

5 FINDINGS

In this section we describe our findings. We first describe the passed, failed, and dropout ratios, in CS1 and CS2. Then we present our results of applying the Technology Acceptance Model (TAM).

5.1 Dropout, failure and pass metrics

Tables 1 and 2 show performance results for the year 2016, the only year Mumuki was used. Performance results for one or two previous years[3] are also reported. When Mumuki was not used, the students interacted directly with a compiler (Hugs or Ghci) in order to solve the programming exercises. The previous year courses only differ from the 2016 course in the coding tool used. The teaching staff, exercises, types of exam, etc, remained the same. The performance metrics are:

- Passed Test: Number (n) and ratio of students that passed the subject exam the first time they tried.
- Passed Re-Test: Number (n) and ratio of students that passed the subject exam the second time they tried. There is at least one month between the test and the re-test.
- Dropout: Number (n) and ratio of students that enrolled and attended at least two lectures. They either were absent or failed the first test. They were absent during the re-test.
- Failed: Number (n) and ratio of students that failed the test and the re-test.

In both tables, a statistically significant decrease in the dropout can be observed the year Mumuki was used. The statistical analysis used is unpaired t-tests, between the years 2015 and 2016 for all metrics. The values for p and T are reported in the tables. The dropout ratio at UTN in 2016 is .14 while it was .28 in 2015. The dropout ratio at UNC is .35 in 2016 while it was .59 in 2015. These results give evidence for rejecting the null hypothesis H_0(null) in favour of the alternative one H_1(alt): The dropout rate at a course which uses Mumuki is significantly lower than that of a course that does not. This hypothesis was tested in two contexts which are quite different. According to the results, the effect seems to be stronger on our CS1 sample but they are still significant in CS2.

[3]The year 2014 is not reported for UTN because the information was incomplete.

Table 2 shows that the difference between 2015 and 2016 is also significant for the metric Passed re-Test for UNC. We have observed that the students use Mumuki as a tool for preparing themselves for the re-test. During the time between the test and the re-test the course is already over and there are no regular lectures in order to prepare for the re-test. Mumuki gives them a chance to study at their own pace.

The dropout rate in our observational studies is high when comparing it to the one in other countries reported in previous work with an average of 20% [15]. Probable causes could be among the following. Both UNC and UTN are public universities and hence they are completely free. Some students work during their studies and others have weak backgrounds in mathematics.

5.2 Technology acceptance model

Finally we analyse students' perceptions regarding Mumuki's usefulness and ease of use with the Technology Acceptance Model (TAM) [3]. The survey was not mandatory and was completed by 87 students in 2016. We asked the students to indicate their level of agreement with the statements listed in Table 3 using a 7-point Likert scale (from 1 to 7). We also asked students to provide free text comments on the best and the worst features of Mumuki.

In general all students strongly agree with the statements evaluated by the TAM model, predicting that the students would like to continue using Mumuki after the course is over. In particular both groups of students strongly agree with the statements "Mumuki improves my abilities as a Haskell programmer" (6.24 in CS1 and 6.32 in CS2) and "I think that Mumuki is easy to use" (6.44 in CS1 and 6.61 in CS2).

Regarding usefulness, the value that is lower than the others is CS2 students' average value for "Mumuki offers help when I find a task difficult", at 4.53. The students explained that "When I had a syntax error, sometimes I did not understand the explanation given

Statements evaluated (translation from Spanish)	TAM reference	CS1	CS2
1. Mumuki improves my abilities as a Haskell programmer	Improvement	6.24	6.32
2. Mumuki enables me to organise my learning time	Productivity	5.76	5.55
3. Mumuki helps me solve tasks more quickly	Efficiency	5.56	5.74
4. Mumuki offers help when I find a task difficult	Helpfulness	5.52	4.53
5. Mumuki helps me solve tasks correctly	Effectiveness	5.36	5.21
6. Mumuki is useful for learning to program in Haskell	Usefulness	6.16	5.82
7. Learning to use Mumuki was easy for me	Familiarity	6.20	6.74
8. It is easy to get Mumuki do what I want it to	Manageability	4.56	5.24
9. The interaction with Mumuki is clear and understandable	Clarity	5.40	6.08
10. The interaction with Mumuki is flexible	Flexibility	6.28	6.45
11. It was easy for me to become skillful at using Mumuki	Proficiency	6.00	6.37
12. I think that Mumuki is easy to use	Ease of use	6.44	6.61

Table 3: Results of applying the Technology Acceptance Model (TAM) indicators to the CS1 and CS2 courses. The first six statements evaluate usefulness and the other are related to ease of use.

by Mumuki". This is due to the fact that Mumuki report syntax errors by showing the output of the compiler.

Regarding ease of use, the value that is lower than the others is CS2 students' average value for "It was easy to get Mumuki to do what I want it to", at 4.56. The students explained that "It was frustrating to get the same error message again on different submissions". Mumuki does not take into account the history of the interaction when producing feedback. Taking it into account and simplifying the compiler output are topics for future research.

We asked explicitly whether they planned to use Mumuki in order to learn other languages; 95% of them answered affirmatively. Among the many advantages they mention when using Mumuki, the most frequent are the following in their own words: "It tells you when your solution is wrong and you can try many times until you get it right", "The best part is that you get immediate feedback", "You can use it at any time and from anywhere at your own rhythm", "It is particularly useful when you have to miss some lectures".

6 CONCLUSIONS

In this paper we presented a web-based coding tool that is free, open-source and provides formative feedback and assessment. We find that the dropout rates are significantly lower in those courses that use the tool at two different universities.

We applied a standard model, the technology acceptance model (TAM) to analyse students' perceptions which predict, through the strong agreement from the students, that they will continue to use the technology. One of the features better valued by the students is the automated feedback which helps the students correct many errors on their own.

Our results suggest that student dropout rates may diminish significantly when using educational coding tools. Differently from traditional instruction, they allow students to study at their own pace, increasing their chances to pass at re-tests. This paper's goal is to take a further step towards formally showing the effectiveness of such tools in order to motivate their adoption.

ACKNOWLEDGMENTS

This work was partially funded by grants PICT-2014-1833, PDTS-CIN-CONICET-2015-172.

REFERENCES

[1] Valerie Barr and Deborah Trytten. 2016. Using Turing's craft CodeLab to support CS1 students as they learn to program. *Association for Computing Machinery Inroads* 7, 2 (2016), 67–75.

[2] Peter Brusilovsky, Stephen Edwards, Amruth Kumar, Lauri Malmi, Luciana Benotti, Duane Buck, Petri Ihantola, Rikki Prince, Teemu Sirkiä, Sergey Sosnovsky, et al. 2014. Increasing Adoption of Smart Learning Content for Computer Science Education. In *Proceedings of the Conference on Innovation & Technology in Computer Science Education (ITiCSE-WGR)*. ACM, 31–57.

[3] M. Y. Chuttur. 2009. Overview of the Technology Acceptance Model: Origins, Developments and Future Directions. *Sprouts: Working Papers on Information Systems* 9, 37 (2009).

[4] Koen Claessen and John Hughes. 2000. QuickCheck: A Lightweight Tool for Random Testing of Haskell Programs. In *Proceedings of the International Conference on Functional Programming (ICFP)*. 268–279.

[5] Alex Daniel Edgcomb, Frank Vahid, Roman Lysecky, Andre Knoesen, Rajeevan Amirtharajah, and Mary Lou Dorf. 2015. *Student performance improvement using interactive textbooks: A three-university cross-semester analysis*. American Society for Engineering Education.

[6] Alex Gerdes, Bastiaan Heeren, Johan Jeuring, and L Thomas van Binsbergen. 2016. Ask-Elle: an adaptable programming tutor for Haskell giving automated feedback. *International Journal of Artificial Intelligence in Education* (2016), 1–36.

[7] Alex Gerdes, Johan Jeuring, and Bastiaan Heeren. 2012. An interactive functional programming tutor. In *Proceedings of the Conference on Innovation & Technology in Computer Science Education (ITiCSE)*. 250–255.

[8] Petri Ihantola, Arto Vihavainen, Alireza Ahadi, Matthew Butler, Jürgen Börstler, Stephen H. Edwards, Essi Isohanni, et al. 2015. Educational Data Mining and Learning Analytics in Programming. In *Proceedings of Innovation & Technology in Computer Science Education Conference (ITiCSE-WGR)*. ACM, 41–63.

[9] Hieke Keuning, Johan Jeuring, and Bastiaan Heeren. 2016. Towards a Systematic Review of Automated Feedback Generation for Programming Exercises. In *Proceedings of the Conference on Innovation & Technology in Computer Science Education (ITiCSE)*. ACM, 41–46.

[10] Amruth N. Kumar. 2008. The Effect of Using Problem-solving Software Tutors on the Self-confidence of Female Students. *Special Interest Group in Computer Science Education (SIGCSE) Bulletin* 40, 1 (March 2008), 523–527.

[11] Amruth N. Kumar. 2015. The Effectiveness of Visualization for Learning Expression Evaluation. In *Proceedings of the 46th ACM Technical Symposium on Computer Science Education (SIGCSE '15)*. ACM, New York, NY, USA, 362–367.

[12] Richard Lobb and Jenny Harlow. 2016. Coderunner: A Tool for Assessing Computer Programming Skills. *ACM Inroads* 7, 1 (Feb. 2016), 47–51.

[13] Nick Parlante. 2017. CodingBat. http://codingbat.com. (2017). [Online; accessed 17-August-2017].

[14] Jaime Spacco, Paul Denny, Brad Richards, David Babcock, David Hovemeyer, James Moscola, and Robert Duvall. 2015. Analyzing Student Work Patterns Using Programming Exercise Data. In *Proceedings of the 46th ACM Technical Symposium on Computer Science Education (SIGCSE '15)*. ACM, New York, NY, USA, 18–23.

[15] Christopher Watson and Frederick W.B. Li. 2014. Failure Rates in Introductory Programming Revisited. In *Proceedings of the Conference on Innovation & Technology in Computer Science Education (ITiCSE)*. 39–44.

Assessing Bootstrap:Algebra Students on Scaffolded and Unscaffolded Word Problems

Emmanuel Schanzer
Bootstrap/Brown University
schanzer@bootstrapworld.org

Kathi Fisler
Brown University/WPI/Bootstrap
kfisler@cs.brown.edu

Shriram Krishnamurthi
Brown University/Bootstrap
sk@cs.brown.edu

ABSTRACT

Bootstrap:Algebra is a curricular module designed to integrate introductory computing into an algebra class; the module aims to help students improve on various essential learning outcomes from state and national algebra standards. In prior work, we published initial findings about student performance gains on algebra problems after taking Bootstrap. While the results were promising, the dataset was not large, and had students working on algebra problems that had been scaffolded with Bootstrap's pedagogy. This paper reports on a more detailed study with (a) data from more than three times as many students, (b) analysis of performance changes in incorrect answers, (c) some problems in which the Bootstrap scaffolds have been removed, and (d) an IRT analysis across the elements of Bootstrap's program-design pedagogy. Our results confirm that students improve on algebraic word problems after completing the module, even on unscaffolded problems. The nature of incorrect answers to symbolic-form questions also appears to improve after Bootstrap.

ACM Reference Format:
Emmanuel Schanzer, Kathi Fisler, and Shriram Krishnamurthi. 2018. Assessing Bootstrap:Algebra Students on Scaffolded and Unscaffolded Word Problems. In *SIGCSE '18: SIGCSE '18: The 49th ACM Technical Symposium on Computer Science Education, February 21–24, 2018, Baltimore , MD, USA.* ACM, New York, NY, USA, 6 pages. https://doi.org/10.1145/3159450.3159498

1 INTRODUCTION

Integrating CS education with existing disciplines is appealing for both intellectual and logistical reasons (the latter particularly in K-12 contexts). Effective integration helps advance student learning in both computing and the host discipline. However, given the known challenges of transferring skills between disciplines [2, 5], claims that computing curricula foster learning in other disciplines require validation through research.

Bootstrap:Algebra (henceforth BS:A) is a curriculum that has been designed to integrate introductory computing into math classes. Roughly, the curriculum has students build a videogame, where each game feature requires both a new mathematics concept (which already needs to be taught in the (pre)-algebra class) and a corresponding programming construct. Given that math is a high-stakes subject (which is heavily tested in the USA), math teachers are under pressure to use curricula that positively impact students' math scores. Understanding the impact of programs like BS:A on student performance is essential for their long-term adoption.

In 2015, we published a preliminary study showing statistically-significant impacts of BS:A on student performance on function composition and word problems [7]. This paper confirms and extends those results in several ways: we remove some of the problem scaffolds (while retaining performance gains), show that students often make progress even while getting wrong answers, demonstrate performance gains in BS:A skills beyond symbolic form questions, and apply IRT-based analysis to get a richer picture of what is going on across the different elements of the BS:A pedagogy.

2 RELATED WORK

Our work attempts to confirm and extend our initial assessment of student performance gains from BS:A [7]. Our original paper looked at both function-composition and word problems, using paired t-tests to compare performance deltas from pre- to post-tests. The current paper focuses on word problems, adding unscaffolded versions of these questions. Our analyses are now also more nuanced: we explore deltas in students' incorrect answers, compare performance across different parts of the BS:A pedagogy, and include an IRT analysis. Wright, Rich, and Lee [8] studied the impact of BS:A on students' understanding of variables, finding some positive effects. Variables are beyond the scope of this study.

BS:A's curricular design builds on theories about how to achieve transfer of skills from one discipline to another. Both explicit instruction and alignment of problem-solving processes are currently believed to be essential for transfer [2, 5, 6]. BS:A embraces both of these issues, as described in section 3. NCTM (the USA's National Council of Teachers of Mathematics) has raised concerns about casual claims that learning CS enhances learning of math [4]. Our studies leverage questions from state math exams to ground our analysis in performance measures designed for mathematics.

While other projects use computing or software tools to teach algebra concepts, we are not aware of ones that deeply align the *problem-solving process* across math and computing as Bootstrap does (see section 3). Space precludes a review of these other projects.

3 AN OVERVIEW OF BS:A

BS:A is a 20–25 hour curricular module designed to integrate introductory computing and specific learning objective from middle- and high-school algebra [1]. The module is designed to embed into a pre-algebra or algebra 1 class; such courses tend to be offered within the age range 12–15 (in the USA). The module has students design and build a video-game featuring three characters, each of which moves in a single dimension. There is a user-controlled

SIGCSE '18, February 21–24, 2018, Baltimore , MD, USA

ACM ISBN 978-1-4503-5103-4/18/02...$15.00
https://doi.org/10.1145/3159450.3159498

player moving in the y-axis (in response to key-presses), a *target* that the player is trying to catch, and a *danger* that the player is trying to avoid. Both the target and the danger move left-to-right across the screen (in the x-axis, at a fixed y coordinate that changes each time the character wraps around to restart from the left edge of the game). Students customize their games by selecting images for the three characters as well as a background image. This leads to wide variety in the game themes, from chasing credit cards in the mall to avoiding spiders in the desert.

BS:A views animations and games as filmstrips consisting of a sequence of frames. Each frame captures one instant of the animation, just as in the filmstrips used to create movies. For each character in a game, students write a function describing how that character's position changes from one frame to the next. A function such as $f(x) = x + 5$, for example, captures moving a character 5 pixels to the right in each successive frame. Unlike in many popular early programming platforms (such as Scratch or Alice), students do not write loops to generate movement: they focus on the algebraic functions that describe how movement changes between frames. BS:A has students solve a series of word problems, each corresponding to some game feature (moving different characters, wrapping characters around after they leave the screen, responding to key presses, and detecting collisions to compute scores). This alignment in style of problems is a key component underlying the integration of computing and algebra in BS:A.

Why Might BS:A Impact Algebra? Reducing game programming to developing algebraic functions is only one aspect of how BS:A integrates computing and algebra. The algebra connection also lies in a *step-by-step process for solving word problems* that leverages *multiple representations of functions*. Both topics feature in state mathematics standards, the NCTM's (National Council of Teachers of Mathematics) guidelines for math outcomes, and the (USA) Common Core. Algebra standards typically emphasize four representations of functions: symbolic form (like $f(x) = x + 2$), domain and range, input/output tables, and graphs; the standards ask students to relate all four representations across the same conceptual function. BS:A exercises the first three (presently omitting graphs).

Our *Design Recipt Worksheet* (fig. 1) embodies how BS:A connects these representations. Given a word problem, students are taught to first articulate the domain and range of the problem, to write at least two examples of the input/output relationship described in the problem, and only then to write the symbolic form of a function to solve the word problem. The curricular materials explain how to leverage each step when attempting the next step, thus modeling ways in which the different representations depend on one another.

The curriculum teaches a specific way to approach input/output tables, which is designed to help students abstract over examples to derive the symbolic form. Consider the word problem in fig. 1, which asks students to produce a function that computes a new x-coordinate 50 pixels to the right of the input x-coordinate. Students could either write the expected output of examples as the final result of the function or as an *expression that computes the final result.* The difference is illustrated in the table below:

10	60	final result only
5	5 + 50	expression that computes result
8	8 + 50	another expression that computes result

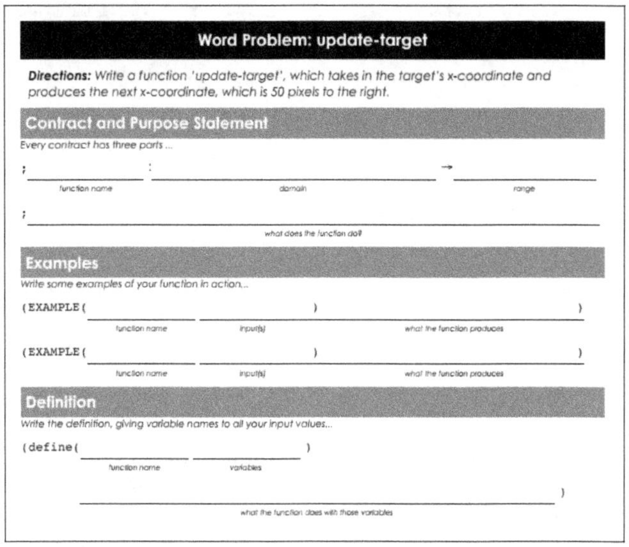

Figure 1: A design-recipe worksheet, showing the process for solving word problems.

The second two examples show the *computation* that would result in the answer. To create a function that solves the word problem, the student needs to abstract over the two expressions, replacing the varying (input) value by a parameter name. The curriculum explicitly teaches this practice: students circle differences between expressions, label the circles with names, then use the names when writing the symbolic form:

$$update\_target(xpos) = xpos + 50$$

This practice of writing output expressions and labeling their differences is not part of conventional mathematics instruction for developing symbolic forms of functions.

The curricular materials provide teachers with several design-recipe worksheets for conventional algebra word problems, in addition to those for the word problems that yield code for creating the videogame. Thus, students are explicitly taught how to transfer the design process from computing to algebra. The transfer literature (section 2) establishes that explicit instruction is generally required before students will transfer skills from one domain to another.

4 STUDY DESIGN

In our original study [7], students solved both function composition and word problems. This new study focuses on word problems alone, with an intent to study them more deeply. (We also lacked a control group; see section 6 for more discussion on this.)

All of the word problems in the original study were scaffolded by the design recipe. This meant that students were asked to explicitly give the domain/range, examples of use, and symbolic form for each word problem. This scaffolding is useful for testing whether students are able to apply the BS:A design steps to algebra problems (rather than game-design problems). It also provides insight into where students might have gone wrong if their symbolic form answer is incorrect. However, typical standardized mathematics

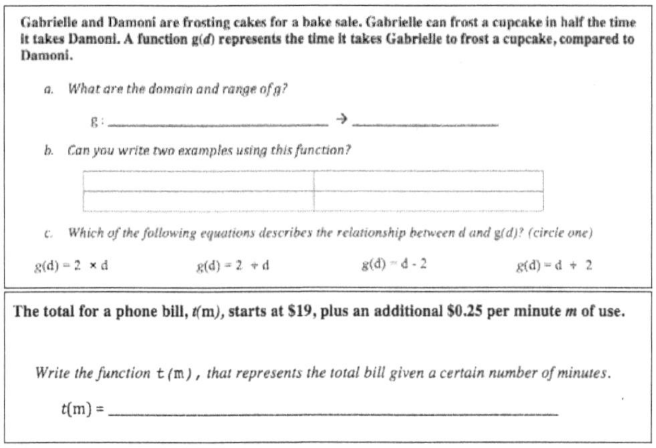
Gabrielle and Damoni are frosting cakes for a bake sale. Gabrielle can frost a cupcake in half the time it takes Damoni. A function g(d) represents the time it takes Gabrielle to frost a cupcake, compared to Damoni.

a. *What are the domain and range of g?*

g: ____________ → ____________

b. *Can you write two examples using this function?*

c. *Which of the following equations describes the relationship between d and g(d)? (circle one)*

g(d) = 2 × d g(d) = 2 + d g(d) = d - 2 g(d) = d + 2

The total for a phone bill, t(m), starts at $19, plus an additional $0.25 per minute m of use.

Write the function t(m), *that represents the total bill given a certain number of minutes.*

t(m) = ____________

Figure 2: Sample questions from our pre and post tests of algebra word problems. The top question includes the BS:A scaffolds, while the bottom question does not. The scaffolded example shown here uses multiple-choice format for the symbolic form; roughly half of our scaffolded questions instead provide a blank link as in the unscaffolded version.

exams (at least in the USA) ask students to provide only the symbolic form. Understanding how BS:A students perform without the scaffolds is therefore critical.

Rather than remove all of the scaffolds, however, we chose to remove the scaffolds on half of the post-test questions (leaving the pre-test fully scaffolded). This design allows us to check whether the same students perform differently on scaffolded vs unscaffolded questions. Naturally, students could be looking at the scaffolded problems for help in solving the unscaffolded ones. This ability adds value to this design: if students perform worse on the unscaffolded problems despite the scaffolding hints being on the same assessment (which was given on paper, so students could see the scaffolded questions alongside the unscaffolded ones), it would suggest that students have not understood the design steps as a process to approaching word problems. Figure 2 gives an example of each of a scaffolded and an unscaffolded question.

Study Logistics. We recruited teachers to participate through a message on the BS:A mailing list. In most cases, we gave teachers PDFs for the pre- and post-tests; the teachers printed the tests, matched the pre- and post-tests by student, and de-identified the tests with unique numbers. This past year, we offered to provide pre-numbered bundles of tests (to save teachers the overhead of matching them). In both cases, teachers mailed the hard/paper copies back to us. We graded all of the tests ourselves to ensure consistency. We asked teachers to allow the students 30 minutes for each test. Teachers gave the pre-test before they started teaching BS:A (or in some cases, within the first week before they got into any of the content on the test); teachers gave the post-test sometime after finishing BS:A (we did not stipulate how close or far the post-test should be given relative to the end of the BS:A unit). Participating teachers received a choice of incentives (Amazon gift cards, BS:A t-shirts for students, or BS:A teaching workbooks for a subsequent school year).

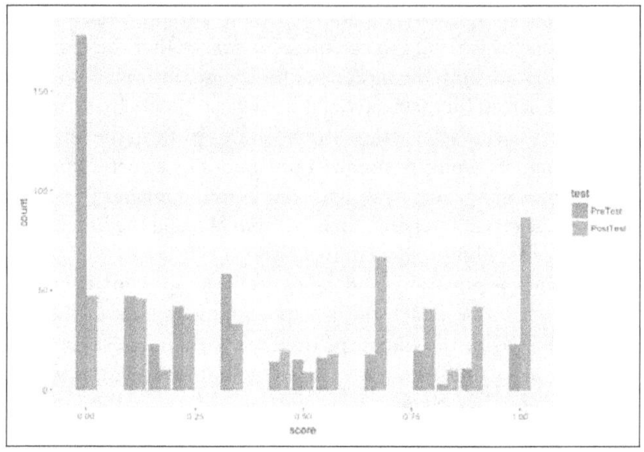

Figure 3: Histogram of Pre and Post Test scores [N=468]. Pre-test scores are the left bar; post-test scores are the right bar.

Participants. Twenty-two distinct teachers provided data. We gathered data between 2014 and 2017. Teachers came from multiple states across the USA and represent several school types and district-level demographics. From across the 22 teachers, we received a total of 468 matched pre- and post-tests. Students who submitted only one of the two tests were dropped (and are not counted in the 468). Most students were in grades 7 through 10 (ages 12 through 15), though at least one teacher provided matched data from eight upper-level high school students (12th grade/age 17). All students (regardless of grade level) did the same problems. Not all teachers provided grade-level data, so we do not include that in our analyses. We did not collect student gender, race, or socio-economic data.

5 ANALYSIS AND RESULTS

In our analyses, we report students' *scores* on each test as the percentage of questions that a student answered correctly. We use percentages rather than question counts because different tests contained different numbers of word problems in different years (sometimes 6, sometimes 9). Questions were weighted equally. We did not give partial credit. Unless noted otherwise, our analyses treat blank answers as incorrect (rather than separate blank answers from incorrect ones).

5.1 Performance on Symbolic Form Questions

Figure 3 shows the distributions of pre and post-test scores on the symbolic form questions across the entire dataset. For scaffolded problems, the symbolic-form questions were part (c) as shown in the top sample in fig. 2; for unscaffolded problems, the symbolic form was the entire question (the blank line in the bottom sample in fig. 2). There is one data point per student (the percentage-based score across all symbolic form questions on the corresponding test).

Using a paired t-test, the differences between pre- and post-test scores are significant ($p < .0001$), with an effect size of .888 (by Cohen's d) and a 95% confidence interval of -0.32 to -0.26. This supports the findings of our original paper [7] showing performance gains on standard algebra assessments.

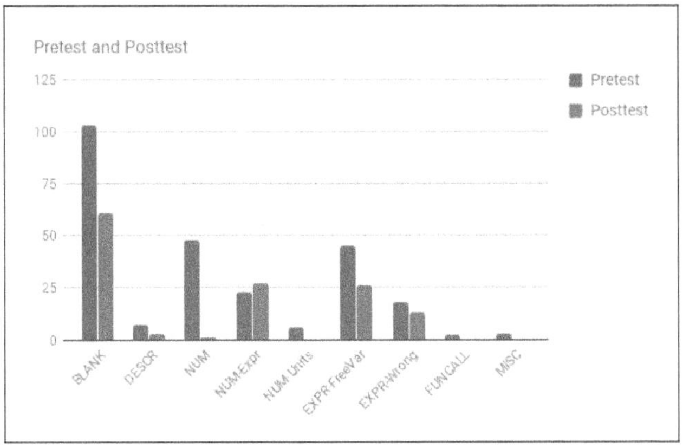

Figure 4: Distribution of types of incorrect free-response answer to symbolic form questions [N=113].

Changes in Incorrect Answers. Even students who answer incorrectly on both the pre- and post-tests could be making progress, depending on the *kinds of wrong answers* that they provide. Figure 4 shows the distribution across categories of wrong answers for questions that asked students to write the symbolic form free-hand (as in the lower problem in fig. 2, though some of these problems were scaffolded with parts (a) and (b) of the upper problem). The categories of mistakes we found were leaving the question BLANK, writing a text DESCRiption of the answer, writing just a constant NUMber, writing a variable-free numeric expression (NUM-Expr, such as "5 + 4"), writing a number and units but not using variables (NUM-Units, such as "3 cans"), writing an expression with a variable other than the given parameter (EXPR-FreeVar), writing an incorrect arithmetic expression over the correct parameter (EXPR-Wrong), writing a call to a function that wasn't named in the problem (FUNCALL, such as "f(10)" for an unknown "f"), and writing unrelated comments (MISC).

Students who used incorrect variables (EXPR-FreeVar) typically fell into two broad camps: those who used the intended function name as a variable, and those who used x or n as a variable (when these were not the given parameter name—these are typical variables used in writing equations and formulas). Typical answers in the EXPR-Wrong category used the wrong operation (+ instead of *), or combined the problem constants and parameter with the wrong operation (such as $5s + 10$ instead of $5 + 10s$).

Figure 4 shows a significant drop in the number of blank answers; the number of students simply entering single numeric answers drops to close to zero. Students make headway on putting only the correct parameter in formulas (EXPR-FreeVar), a discipline which one could expect that writing code would reinforce. The persistence of NUM-Expr errors, in which the symbolic form doesn't reference any variables, points to students who lack a fundamental understanding of functions as a concept. It would be interesting to see whether such students understand this concept in the programming context and haven't transferred it to algebra, or whether they fail to understand the concept in either domain. This is an important topic for future study.

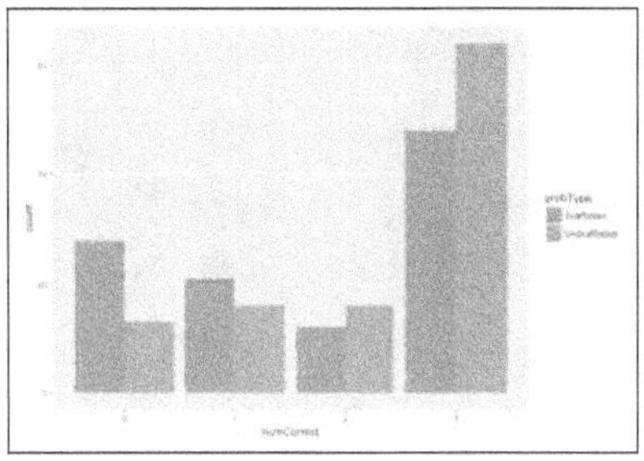

Figure 5: Histogram of scores on scaffolded (left bar) and unscaffolded (right bar) post-test questions [N=109].

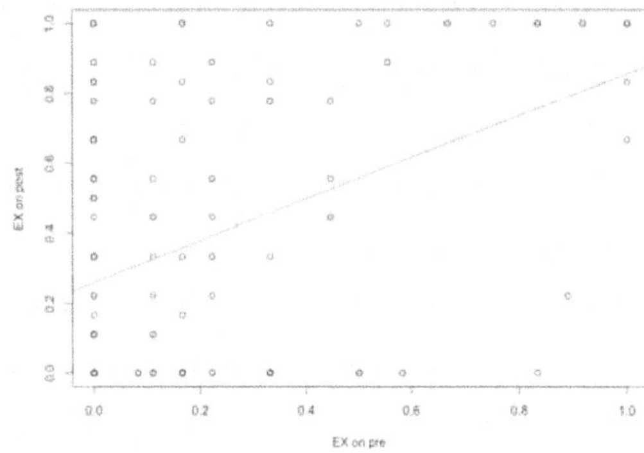

Figure 6: Pre and Post scores on writing examples [N=222].

5.2 Scaffolded Versus Unscaffolded Problems

Figure 5 compares student performance on scaffolded and unscaffolded word problems on the post-test, based on data from 109 students (we only collected data on unscaffolded problems in the last year of our study, after confirming that we were seeing performance gains on the fully scaffolded problems from the first two years). The graph actually shows students having a stronger performance on the *unscaffolded* problems, a result we didn't expect. A paired t-test of scaffolded and unscaffolded problems yields significance of $p < .0001$, but only at an effect size of .39. This result does not appear due to students leaving more scaffolded answers blank: there are 20 instances of a scaffolded symbolic-form question being left blank compared to 35 unscaffolded questions being left blank. It may be related to Heffernan and Koedinger's results that students struggle with expressing word problems in algebraic language more than with figuring out what computation a problem requires [3]. In future work, we need to gather more data and conduct different analysis to confirm and explain these data.

5.3 Performance on Writing of Examples

Writing examples of computations is a key component of the BS:A pedagogy, and aligns with students writing input/output tables in an algebra context. Part (b) of scaffolded word problems asked students to provide two examples for each word problem they were asked to solve (see fig. 2). We are interested in how students evolve

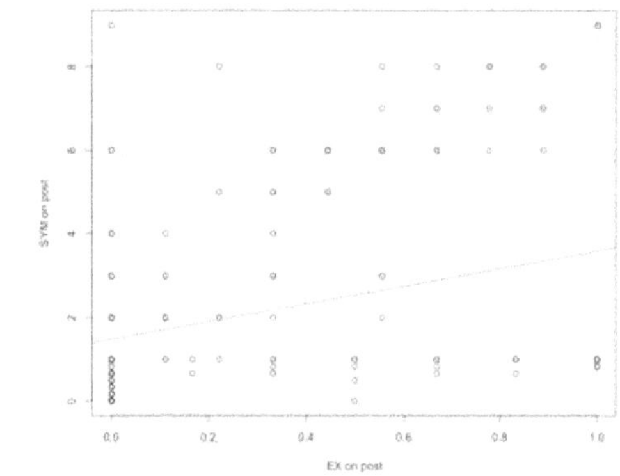

Figure 7: Relationship between examples and symbolic form scores on the post-test [N=222].

in this task, in part because we feel the ability to articulate examples is a valuable skill in both programming and in mathematics.

Figure 6 plots students' scores on writing examples in the pre-test versus the post-test (one data point per student). (We report this data only for students from the last two years of our study (N=222) because we had not tracked data at this detail in the first year of the study.) The graph shows that students are stronger on writing examples in the post-test. A paired t-test shows the differences are significant at $p < .0001$ (with a Cohen's d of .575). These computations, however, do not distinguish wrong answers from examples that are left blank. In 2016-17, we began distinguishing blank and incorrect answers in our grading; for the 140 students in that cohort, the percentage of blank answers does generally decrease from pre to post, but the number of blanks rises for 42 students. No particular variables (such as teacher or grade level) characterize the students in this group; they could have run out of time or not taken the test as seriously. We lack information to unpack this issue further.

Figure 7 plots the relationships between each student's scores on writing examples and answering symbolic form questions on the post test. Spearman's rho shows that writing examples and answering symbolic form are correlated ($p < .0001$, rho = .457). The graph illustrates that some students perform well on each of these two tasks while performing poorly on the other.

5.4 IRT Analysis Across Recipe Elements

For another perspective on how student performance evolves across the different design-recipe elements, we ran an Item Response Theory (IRT) analysis. IRT measures a population's performance on each question as a function of a latent trait θ (e.g., understanding of functions). For each item, IRT provides a measure of the question's difficulty (β) and discrimination (α). A larger α suggests that a particular item was a highly-discriminating measure of θ for that population. A β of 0.25 means that a student who is one quarter of a standard deviation above the mean is expected to have an even chance of generating a correct response, and a higher β implies that a correct answer on a particular item is associated with a higher level of θ (relative to the population).

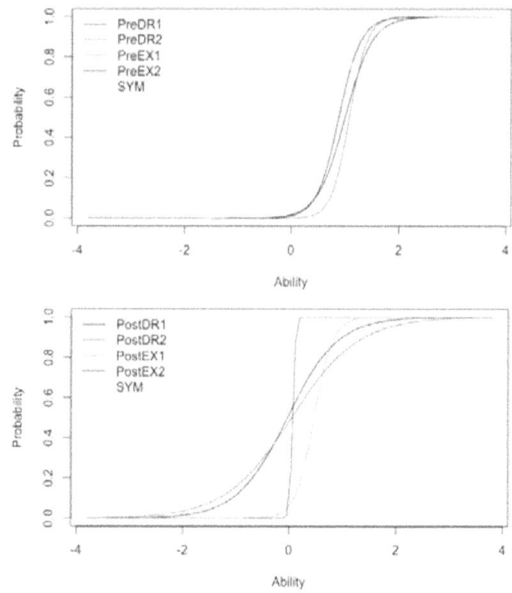

Figure 8: IRT graphs from each step of the design recipe, looking at similar problem from each of the pre- and post-tests. Each IRT plot shows curves for domain, range, two examples, and determining the symbolic form.

For each of the pre- and post-tests, we captured the correctness of students' answers on the domain, range, two examples in the input/output table (each example as a separate score), and the symbolic form of the function. This yields a total of 5 answers for each scaffolded problem and 1 answer for each unscaffolded problem. We ran a separate IRT analysis across all of the answers on each of the pre- and post-test data. Figure 8 shows the characteristic curves for each subpart of one question from each of the pre-test and the post-test (the analysis was done by constructing a latent-trait model using the `ltm` package and function in R). The questions from which these curves arise ask students to produce similar symbolic formulas, but the word problems use different contexts.

The symbolic form curve in the pre-test (SYM, α=2.732, β=0.704) has a gentler slope and is shifted slightly left of the curves for domain (α=3.976, β=1.005), range (α=6.173, β=1.085), and examples (α= 0.891, β=4.938 for both). This suggests that on the pre-test, students were more likely to correctly answer the symbolic form questions than others, regardless of their ability (θ). This is not necessarily surprising: most math classes spend considerable time on this form, but far less (if any) time on the terminology of domain and range, or the practice of writing examples. The higher difficulty and discrimination of these items merely shows that they evaluate specialized knowledge that few students possess during the pre-test.

Given that domain and range play a central role in BS:A's problem-solving strategy, we expect students' understanding to shift from being specialized knowledge (harder, more discriminating) in the pre-test to more general knowledge (easier, less discriminating) in the post-test. Indeed, this expectation in born out in the analysis, as the domain and range curves have a gentler slope and shift left

(β drops from 1.005 and 1.085 to -0.032 and 0.048), indicating that the relative proportion of the students who were able to correctly answer these questions increased from pre to post. α also decreases from pre- to post-test (from 3.976 and 6.173 to 2.139 and 1.619), suggesting that domain and range play a smaller role in discriminating students' level of θ in the post-test than they do in the pre-test.

Interestingly, the α values on the examples curves *increase* relative to the pre-test (from 4.938 on both to 5.85 and 40.690), suggesting that having students provide examples improved as an indicator of their understanding of functions on the post-test. The sharp difference in α between the two post-test example curves may indicate that *asking for a second example* is a more useful measurement of θ than asking for just one, a question worthy of future study.

This effect was even more pronounced for the distribution of correct answers to the symbolic form question. The measure of difficulty dropped from pre (β=0.704) to post (β=0.101), meaning that the likelihood of a correct response required that students be only 0.101 SD above the mean in the post-test, compared to nearly seven times that amount above the mean in the pre-test. The shift in difficulty implies that the portion of students who possessed sufficient θ also increased relative to the pre-test. Meanwhile, the usefulness of this type of question as a discriminator also improved from α=2.732 to α=5.909.

The trends from these particular two problems are similar to what we see across other problems on the pre- and post-tests.

6 THREATS TO VALIDITY

In general, we do not have information on what courses or lessons students were taking in parallel with BS:A. It is possible, for example, that some students were taking another math class in parallel to their BS:A course, and that some of the content tested on our post-test had been covered in the math class. We guard against this in part through having a large number of teachers participating in data collection. In addition, many (though not all) of the teachers who provided data are math teachers who were using BS:A in a math class, so students would not have been taking a math class in parallel. However, teachers use BS:A in different models: some do the curriculum in a concentrated chunk, some spread it over several weeks, and so on. Thus, there are almost certainly variations across the math teachers in how their BS:A curriculum interacted with other aspects of their courses. This paper again relies on a larger teacher population to ameliorate this issue in our analysis.

Unlike in our initial study, we did not have control groups. Our ideal control group would be another section of the same math course taught by a participating BS:A teacher. None of the teachers who provided data were able to provide a control group (for varying reasons). The lack of control groups mainly affects comparisons between pre- and post-test performance. It is not relevant, however, to comparisons of performance on scaffolded versus unscaffolded problems by the same student, or for the IRT analysis. Thus, key parts of our study are not affected by the lack of controls.

7 CONCLUSION AND FUTURE WORK

Our analysis goes beyond our initial paper in several ways. We confirm their findings that students improve significantly on algebra word problems after BS:A, but also go farther: based on the wrong answers to symbolic-form questions, we find students make certain (arguably more serious) errors less often on the post-test. This suggests that the impact of BS:A goes beyond what simply grading indicates, while also pointing to underlying skills that BS:A teachers and curriculum designers should drill more explicitly.

Our study also removes design-recipe scaffolds from half of the post-test questions. Students perform just as well (if not better) on the unscaffolded problems. Since some problems on the post-test were scaffolded, one should wonder whether students were copying scaffolding steps to solve unscaffolded problems. A sample of the actual test papers didn't reveal this behavior, but a future study should contain only unscaffolded problems.

Going forward, we want to explore whether errors that arose on the symbolic form questions manifest similarly in both the programming and mathematical contexts. We want to analyze our error data on domain and range questions (an analysis which did not fit into this paper). Overall, we want to continue to explore finer-grained impacts of the components of the BS:A design recipe, so that we might understand effective ways to integrate math and CS for the benefit of both disciplines.

To this point, our main instructional takeaway is that working with and relating multiple representations of functions—whether in math or computing—seems to positively impact students' abilities to express word problems in code and formulas. Articulating domain/range (types), writing examples (tests), and writing symbolic form (code functions) are important skills for programmers as well as algebra students. While we do not yet know the relative impacts of these skills on understanding and using functions, a multi-representational approach such as the BS:A design recipe seems a useful and lightweight method for developing them.

ACKNOWLEDGMENTS

We thank all the teachers who provided us data. We are deeply grateful to Leigh Ann DeLyser for suggesting and helping us set up the IRT. We are grateful to Peter Hahn for his outstanding work on the data analysis. This work is partially supported by the US NSF.

REFERENCES

[1] Bootstrap:Algebra [n. d.]. The Bootstrap:Algebra Curriculum. http://www.bootstrapworld.org/materials/courses/algebra. ([n. d.]).

[2] J.D. Bransford and D Schwartz. 1999. Rethinking transfer: A simple proposal with multiple implications. In *Review of Research in Education*. Vol. 24. American Educational Research Association, 61–100.

[3] N. T. Heffernan and K. R. Koedinger. 1998. A developmental model for algebra symbolization: The results of a difficulty factors assessment. In *Proceedings of the Twentieth Annual Conference of the Cognitive Science Society*. 484–489.

[4] National Council of Teachers of Mathematics. 2016. Should mathematics course requirements for high school graduation be satisfied by computer science courses? (an NCTM Position Statement). Available online, last accessed Feb 22, 2017 at http://www.nctm.org/Standards-and-Positions/Position-Statements/Computer-Science-and-Mathematics-Education/. (Feb. 2016).

[5] D Perkins. 2009. *Making Learning Whole*. Jossey-Bass, San Francisco.

[6] Peter J. Rich, Keith R. Leatham, and Geoffrey A. Wright. 2013. Convergent cognition. *Instructional Science* 41, 2 (March 2013), 431–453.

[7] E Schanzer, K Fisler, S Krishnamurthi, and M. Felleisen. 2015. Transferring skills at solving word problems from computing to algebra through Bootstrap. In *Symposium on Computer Science Education (SIGCSE)*. 616–621.

[8] Geoff Wright, Peter Rich, and Robert Lee. 2013. The Influence of Teaching Programming on Learning Mathematics. In *Society for Information Technology & Teacher Education International Conference*.

On the Use of Semantic-Based AIG to Automatically Generate Programming Exercises

Laura Zavala
Medgar Evers College | CUNY
Brooklyn, NY 11225
rzgutierrez@mec.cuny.edu

Benito Mendoza
New York City College of Technology | CUNY
Brooklyn, NY 11201
bmendoza@citytech.cuny.edu

ABSTRACT

In introductory programming courses, proficiency is typically achieved through substantial practice in the form of relatively small assignments and quizzes. Unfortunately, creating programming assignments and quizzes is both, time-consuming and error-prone. We use Automatic Item Generation (AIG) in order to address the problem of creating numerous programming exercises that can be used for assignments or quizzes in introductory programming courses. AIG is based on the use of test-item templates with embedded variables and formulas which are resolved by a computer program with actual values to generate test-items. Thus, hundreds or even thousands of test-items can be generated with a single test-item template. We present a semantic-based AIG that uses linked open data (LOD) and automatically generates contextual programming exercises. The approach was incorporated into an existing self-assessment and practice tool for students learning computer programming. The tool has been used in different introductory programming courses to generate a set of practice exercises different for each student, but with the same difficulty and quality.

ACM Reference format:
Laura Zavala and Benito Mendoza. 2018. On the Use of Semantic-Based AIG to Automatically Generate Programming Exercises. In *SIGCSE '18: 49th ACM Technical Symposium on Computer Science Education, Feb. 21–24, 2018, Baltimore, MD, USA.* ACM, NY, NY, USA, 6 pages.
https://doi.org/10.1145/3159450.3159608

1 INTRODUCTION

The literature abounds with research on pedagogies and innovative approaches for introductory computer programming courses (CS1), such as collaborative learning, pair-programming, peer-lead instruction, flipped classrooms, and live coding [1-6]. Many works are motivated by the high failure rates in CS1 courses all over the world. Passing rates are estimated to be around 63%.

Regardless of the approach or the degree to which an approach is used in the classroom, the need for considerable practice in introductory programming courses is indisputable and widely acknowledged. Proficiency in these courses is usually reached through small but frequent assignments. The work in [7] validates the importance of performing multiple exercises with prompt feedback in order for students to gain proficiency on a concept. In [8], evidence is provided that both, practice and reflection, play critical roles in the development of programming proficiency.

Preparing assignments and assessments is a time-consuming task for instructors. Automatic Item Generation (AIG) was used to create a tool that automatically generates programming practice exercises thus relieving the instructor from having to generate them. AIG is an approach for developing test-items or questions for exams, automatically by a program [9]. Existing approaches to AIG are mainly template-based. Instead of creating a question, experts create a template with embedded variables and formulas. By replacing those variables and formulas with different values from a range of values specified by the expert, a high volume of test-items can be generated from a single item template. AIG is critical in applications such as Computer Adaptive Testing (CAT) where a very large bank of items is needed. CAT is a form of computer-based testing that adapts to the examinee's ability level by selecting questions based on what is known about the examinee from answers to previous questions [10]. CAT facilitates precise evaluation at the individual level, which could lead to shorter and faster tests (i.e., the test can stop as soon as an assessment of the student's knowledge has been made).

The type of practice given to students should not be overlooked. Several educational theories emphasize the need for introductory contexts that align with students' interests and goals [11, 12]. Examples in CS1 courses should make sense to students and promote engagement. Recent works [8, 12-21] have explored the use of engaging applications such as robotics, music, games, media, and physical computing in introductory programming courses. Results show that these approaches engage students positively, increase motivation, facilitate understanding, and improve outcomes and retention rates.

Instead of choosing one specific application for a CS1 course, we are concerned with creating numerous practice exercises that are meaningful to a certain degree. It is not easy to create contextual examples for minimal exercises and to manually create plenty of examples that will satisfy a broad variety of learners. We have extended the traditional template-based AIG

SIGCSE '18, February 21–24, 2018, Baltimore, MD, USA

ACM ISBN 978-1-4503-5103-4/18/02...$15.00
https://doi.org/10.1145/3159450.3159608

approach with a semantic-based approach that connects to existing Linked Open Data (LOD)[1] sources to generate different contexts for a practice exercise. To the best of our knowledge, there is no other known work that combines linked open data and automatic item generation to generate contextualized items. We are concerned with introductory programming courses and problem solving as application domain, but our approach is transferable to many other domains.

We have incorporated our semantic-based AIG tool as part of a web-based system that creates and delivers exams online [22][2]. We have used such system in several courses to deliver quizzes. We also used our tool to generate coding problems that we have administered on paper. This paper presents the semantic-based AIG approach used in our tool as well as an initial evaluation based on our experience thus far and the results of a pilot study. Advantages of the semantic-based AIG approach presented here include: a) having a large pool of practice exercises or test items; b) generating different questions for each student and thus making it harder for students to cheat; c) increasing motivation and reducing chances of misunderstanding the question; and d) providing students with plenty of exercises to practice until proficiency is achieved. Although our approach currently has mild contextualization, it can form the basis for a more advanced learning platform with more specialized contextual and CAT and/or intelligent tutoring features.

2 RELATED WORK

Some works have explored the use of AIG in the computer-programming domain. In [23] AIG is used to automatically generate questions in the mathematics, physics and computer programming domains. The late one however, the only variability is in the programming language asked to solve the problem (which assumes students can write in different programming languages). The authors point out that the main point of interest of these exercises is in its automatic grading (through test cases).

In [24-27] the authors present an ontology-based, multiple choice question generation approach. They use ontologies along with some natural language processing to generate factual questions about the domain of the ontology. For example, a geographic ontology is used in [25] to generate questions about geography. No AIG style templates are used. In contrast, we use Linked Open Data and its associated ontologies to insert context into the questions we generate using AIG templates.

The authors in [28] perform an assessment of the usability of Linked Data for the generation of item variables in AIG. Their focus is on the use of LOD as the domain knowledge from which questions can be generated. They raise the issue of data quality and inconsistencies in LOD which can be a problem when LOD is using as source of knowledge. In contrast, we use LOD to contextualize the test items, which do not belong to the same domain as the ontology (the domain is *computer programming*). For example, using a *movies* ontology, [28] would generate quizzes about movies while we instead generate computer programming questions in the context of movies (using movies as part of the problem formulation).

3 SEMANTIC-BASED AIG

3.1 Automated Item Generation

AIG is an approach for developing test-items or questions for exams, automatically by a program. The most common AIG approach is based on the use of test-item templates with embedded variables and formulas. The variables and formulas in the template are resolved by a computer program with actual values to generate test-items. Current approaches to AIG vary by the method used for giving values to the variables: a text [29], mathematical equations [9, 30], or a semantic model [24-28]. The obvious advantage of an AIG system is its ability to produce high volumes of test-items and therefore numerous different tests with the same difficulty and quality.

We use AIG in the computer-programming domain to generate questions of different types, such as open-ended, short answer, multiple choice, and true or false. Figure 1 shows an example of a short answer test-item template and two sample test-items generated from the template. The variables are marked with {{}}. A test-item template is composed of:

- Stem – The stem contains the actual question with embedded variables.
- Options (optional)– For multiple-choice test-items templates, the answer options with embedded variables. The answer options include one correct option and one or more incorrect options or distractors.
- Key – The key is an indicator to the correct answer.
- Script – The script is a computer program that generates values for the embedded variables in the previous elements of the template and generates the key.

3.2 Linked Open Data

Linked Data is a method of publishing data using recognized standards so that it can be interlinked and become more useful through semantic queries. It uses standards and technologies that allow sharing of information in a way that can be read automatically by computers. This enables data from different sources to be connected and queried [31]. Linked Open Data (LOD) is Linked Data that is released under an open license, which does not impede its reuse for free [32].

In LOD, relationships are represented as (*subject, predicate, object*) triples. Resources are represented with URIs (Uniform Resource Identifiers), which can be abbreviated as prefixed names. The *predicate* specifies how the *subject* and *object* are related. A comprehensive introduction to linked open data is out of the scope of this paper. The interested reader can check [31] and [32].

[1] https://www.w3.org/standards/semanticweb/data
[2] http://mz-unbound.com/newipractice/

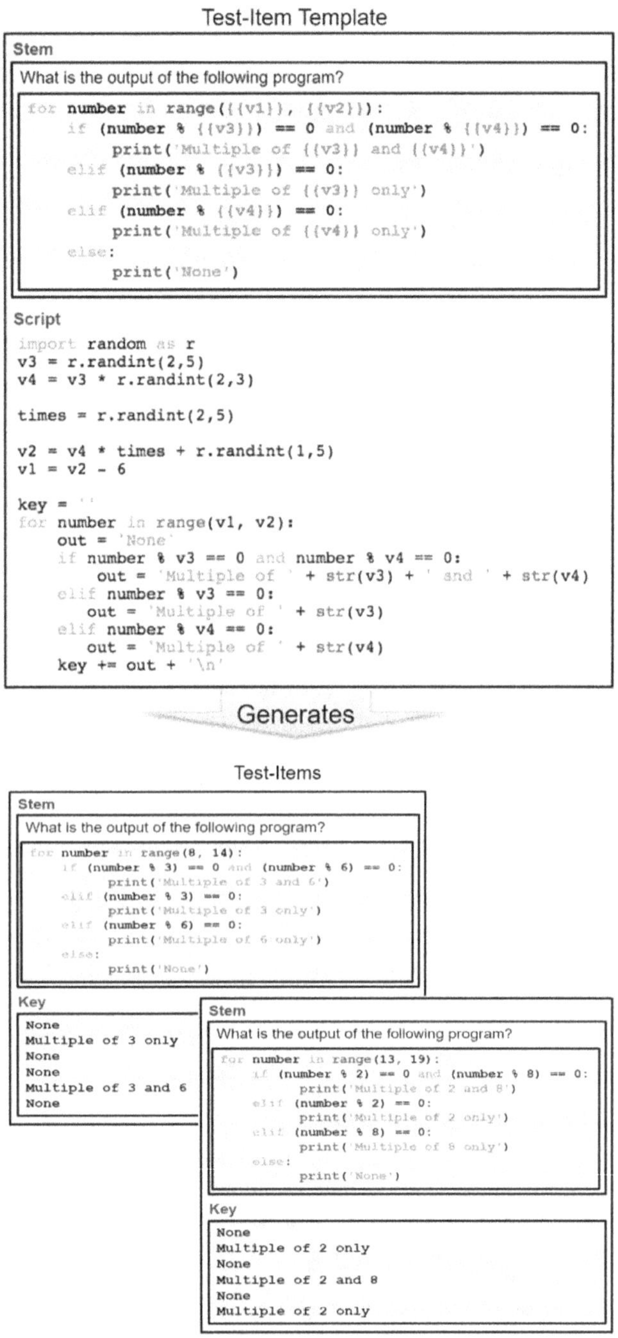

Figure 1: **Example of AIG applied to the computer programming domain: a test-item template, the algorithm to instantiate it, and two of the hundreds of questions that can be generated with the template.**

The DBpedia[3] linked open dataset consists of RDF triples extracted from the *infoboxes* commonly seen on the right-hand side of Wikipedia articles. The following is an excerpt from DBpedia about *The Hunger Games* movie:

```
PREFIX db: <http://dbpedia.org/resource/>
PREFIX dbo: <http://dbpedia.org/ontology/>
PREFIX dbp: <http://dbpedia.org/property/>
PREFIX rdf: <http://www.w3.org/1999/02/22-rdf-syntax-ns#>
db:The_Hunger_Games_(film) rdf:type dbo:Film .
db:The_Hunger_Games_(film) dbo:writer db:Suzanne_Collins.
db:The_Hunger_Games_(film) dbo:starring db:Elizabeth_Banks.
db:The_Hunger_Games_(film) dbo:starring db:Jennifer_Lawrence.
db:The_Hunger_Games_(film) dbo:starring db:Liam_Hemsworth.
db:The_Hunger_Games_(film) dbo:editing db:Juliette_Welfling.
db:The_Hunger_Games_(film) dbo:director db:Gary_Ross.
db:The_Hunger_Games_(film) dbo:producer db:Nina_Jacobson.
db:The_Hunger_Games_(film) dbp:country "United States".
```

Optionally, resources in LOD can be associated with an ontology that specifies the concepts (classes) that a resource can belong to, as well as the types of relations among classes. In the example above, The *Hunger Games* film is specified to belong to the *Film* class. Further, the DBpedia ontology states that a resource of the class *Film* (e.g. *The Hunger Games*) has a *writer* relation to a resource of the class *Person* (e.g. Suzanne Collins). Resources in different LOD datasets can also be interlinked to complement the knowledge about the resources described in the data. For example, the country associated with the *Hunger Games* movie in the previous example is United States:

db:The_Hunger_Games_(film) dbp:country "United States"

Geonames[4], an LOD dataset with knowledge about millions of geographical locations worldwide, could be queried to retrieve further information about the resource *United States.*

LOD is used in our semantic-based AIG approach to populate the variables of the test-item templates in order to generate programming exercises that are associated with real-world concepts and examples. LOD datasets can be queried using the SPARQL query language to query local or remote repositories (e.g. http://dbpedia.org/sparql/). Figure 2 shows an SPARQL query that can be used to get a list of actors from the DBpedia dataset.

We specify ontological elements that can be used to populate the variables in the test-item templates. We use SPARQL to query linked open datasets in order to obtain instances of the ontological elements and use them as values for the variables of a test-item template.

[3] http://wiki.dbpedia.org/

[4] http://www.geonames.org/ontology

```
PREFIX rdf: <http://www.w3.org/1999/02/22-rdf-syntax-ns#>
SELECT DISTINCT ?subject WHERE
{
   ?subject rdf:type <http://dbpedia.org/ontology/Actor> .
}
```

Figure 2: **An SPARQL query to obtain a list of actors from DBpedia.**

Figure 3 provides an example of a short answer, semantic-based test-item template and two sample questions generated from the template. For simplicity purposes, we provide only the algorithm that generates the values for the variables.

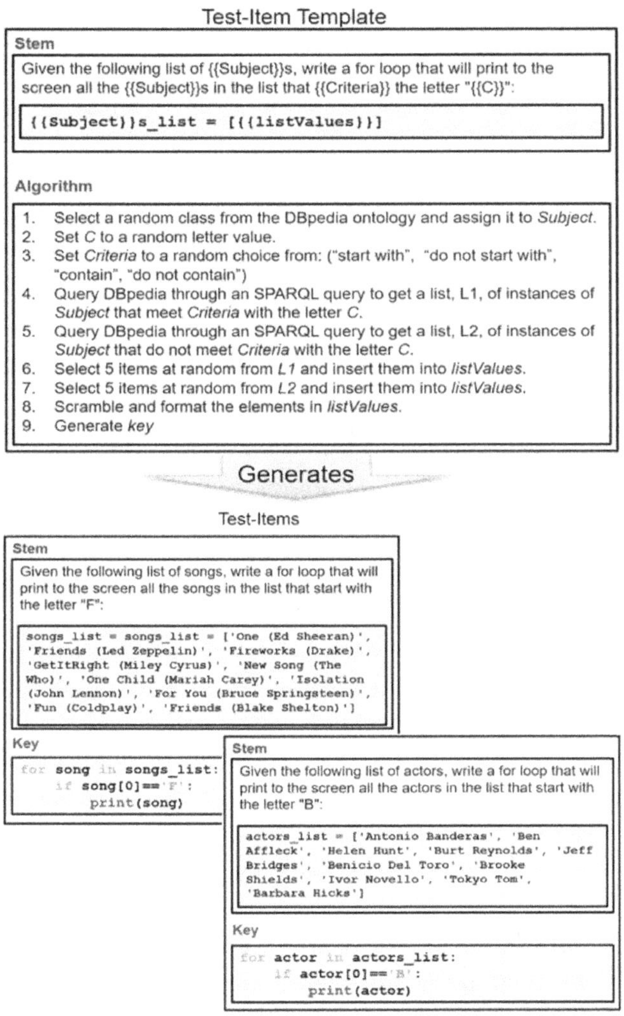

Figure 3: **Example of semantic-based AIG applied to the computer programming domain: a test-item template, the algorithm to instantiate it, and two of the hundreds of questions that can be generated with the template.**

A small number of instances in DBPedia are mapped to the ontology. For example, few actors are declared to be instances of the class *Actor*. However, they are a DBPedia resource and are related to other resources such as films. For example, the *starring* relation associates a film with an actor (even if the actor is not declared as such in the ontology; he might be declared only as a *Person*). Therefore, it can be inferred that the object of the *starring* relation is an *Actor*. Due to this limitation, our approach cannot rely on generic queries like the one in Figure 2. Currently, we have a fixed set of classes/concepts that can be used to instantiate the variables in a template and we have pre-built SPARQL queries for them. The SPARQL queries used in the actors' example of Figure 3 are:

```
PREFIX rdf: <http://www.w3.org/1999/02/22-rdf-syntax-ns#>
SELECT DISTINCT ?actor WHERE
{
  ?movie <http://dbpedia.org/ontology/starring> ?actor.
  FILTER (strStarts(str(?actor), "http://dbpedia.org/resource/B")).
}
PREFIX rdf: <http://www.w3.org/1999/02/22-rdf-syntax-ns#>
SELECT DISTINCT ?actor WHERE
{
   ?movie <http://dbpedia.org/ontology/starring> ?actor.
   FILTER (regex(?actor, "^((?!B).)*$")).
}
```

Queries to LOD can be more complex and detailed than the queries in these examples, allowing for more specific contexts to be defined. For example, in the movies domain, one could query specifically French films, films in a specific genre, or films associated with a particular actor or director.

The content of the LOD cloud is diverse. It comprises data about geographic locations, people, companies, books, music, scientific publications, films, television and radio programs, genes, proteins, online communities, census results, and product reviews. As May 2009, the Web of Data consisted of 4.7 billion triples, which are interlinked by around 142 million RDF links [30]. Currently, we have focused our work on a few LOD datasets (i.e. DBPedia, foaf, and geonames), which are the biggest datasets in the LOD cloud. And as it was mentioned before, we only use a fixed set of concepts from them. Full use of a variety of LOD sources will allow to provide further contextualization.

4 EVALUATION

We have used our semantic-based AIG tool in several courses to generate quizzes with positive outcomes for instructors and students. In this paper, we focus on a pilot study designed to conduct an initial assessment of the impact of explicitly spending extra time on practice exercises generated with our sematic-based AIG tool.

Two sections of an introductory programming course were used for the study. The course is taught at a four-year urban college and uses Python programming language. One section of the course was used to test an intervention strategy implemented with the goal of honing students' programming skills. The other section was used as a control group. Students in both groups were given a test to evaluate their coding skills in the topics learned up to that point. The test was given past mid-semester, when students had already learned some basic programming.

Our semantic-based AIG approach was used to generate a set of practice exercises (four sets of twelve problems) individualized to each student's needs in the intervention group. Students worked on their exercises for a period of two weeks. Some exercises were given to students as in-class lab assignments and others as homework assignments. Nothing else was covered during that period of time in the intervention group while the control group continued with the schedule as planned. A post-assessment was given to students in both groups near the end of the semester to evaluate them on the same skills than in the pre-test. We were interested in observing whether there was any significant difference in the progress made in learning-to-code between the students from the two groups.

Figures 4 to 7 show the results obtained in the pre and post assessments from the control group and the intervention group, respectively. The stacked line charts depict the cumulative students' scores by type of question: 1) code reading (tracing code and indicating the output of a program), 2) code manipulation (modify/extend provided starter code to meet requirements), and 3) code writing (write code from scratch to meet requirements). Students have been anonymized (s1, s2, etc.). The evaluation instrument (quiz) for each skill level had a max score of 100.

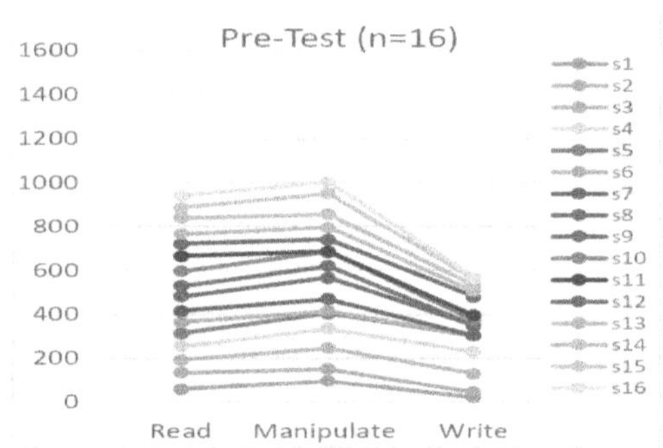

Figure 4: **Pre-test results: Control group cumulative scores by level.**

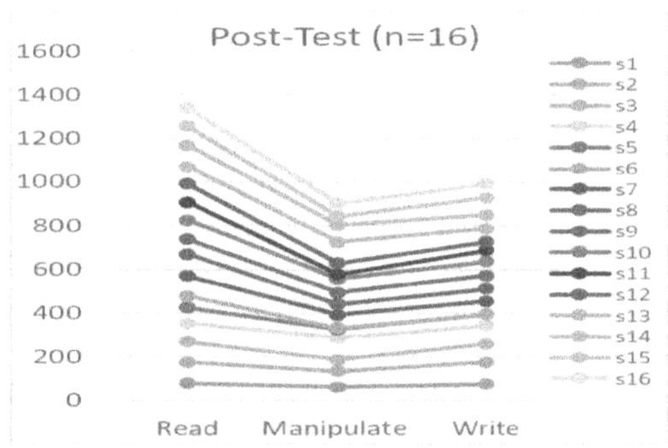

Figure 5: **Post-test results: Control group cumulative scores by level.**

Table 1 shows the average grade of the students on the exams pre- and post-intervention. Both groups exhibited an improvement towards the end of the course. However, students in the intervention group showed a greater improvement than students who did not. All the students in the intervention group finished at a proficient level in code reading questions, while some in the control group did not. A larger improvement was observed in the code writing skills of the students in the intervention group.

Table 1: Average grade obtained by both groups of students, pre- and post-intervention.

	Pre-Test			Post-Test		
Group	**Read**	**Manip.**	**Write**	**Read**	**Manip.**	**Write**
Control	**58.8**	**62.8**	**35.3**	**83.8**	**56.4**	**61.9**
Intervention	**76.3**	**49.4**	**43.8**	**95.0**	**92.3**	**81.5**

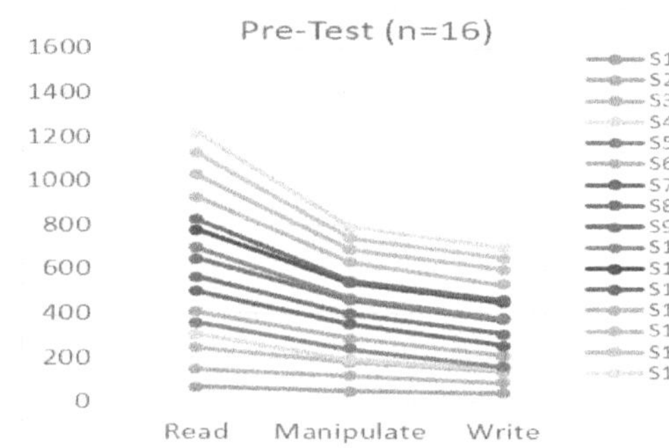

Figure 6: **Pre-test results: Intervention group cumulative scores by level.**

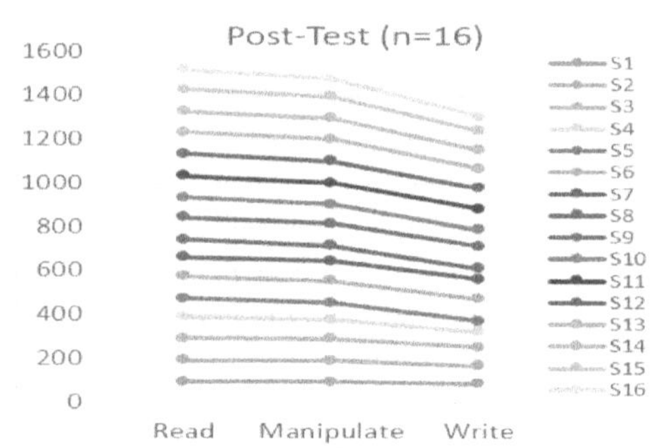

Figure 7: **Post-test results: Intervention group cumulative scores by level.**

6 CONCLUSIONS AND FUTURE WORK

We presented a semantic-based AIG approach to the automatic generation of contextualized programming exercises that can be used for quizzes and homework assignments in introductory programming courses. The approach extends the traditional template-based AIG by connecting to existing Linked Open Data sources to generate different contexts for a programming practice exercise template.

A pilot study assessed the impact of explicitly spending extra time on practice exercises generated with our sematic-based AIG tool. Results obtained from both, an intervention group and a control group, show the benefits of dedicating extra time to practicing. Students that participated in the intervention strategy show a greater improvement in learning-to-code over the students in the control group.

In its current state, our semantic-based AIG approach generates examples with simple contextualization. We will continue our work to devise how LOD and ontologies can be exploited to generate richer and more detailed contexts. We are also interested in evaluating whether it really matters that the students be familiar with the context of the question. Once further contextualization is achieved and preferences of students can be inferred, research must be done to evaluate the impact of this approach on learners' cognition and motivation. In the long term, we are interested in building a suite of CAT and intelligent tutor tools that will offer students the opportunity for plenty of personalized practice that will potentially help them achieve proficiency.

6 ACKNOWLEDGMENTS

We gratefully acknowledge the support of the Research Foundation of CUNY under PSC-CUNY Award 68164-00 46.

REFERENCES

[1] M. McCracken, V. Almstrum, D. Diaz, M. Guzdial, D. Hagen, Y. Kolikant, C. Laxer, L. Thomas, I. Utting, and T. Wilusz. 2001. A Multi-National, Multi-Institutional Study of Assessment of Programming Skills of First- year CS Students. *SIGCSE Bulletin*, 33, no. 4, 125-140.

[2] L. Zavala. 2016. Read, Manipulate, and Write: A study of the role of these cumulative skills in learning computer programming. *Proceedings of the ASEE NE 2016 Conference.* April 28-30, University of Rhode Island, Kingston, RI.

[3] L. Zavala and B. Mendoza. 2017. Precursor skills to writing code. *Journal of Computing Science in Colleges*, 32, 3, 149-156.

[4] J. Sweller, and G. A. Cooper. 1985. The use of worked examples as a substitute for problem-solving in learning algebra. *Cognition and Instruction*, 2, no. 1(1985), 59–89.

[5] M. Guzdial and J. Robertson. 2010. Too much programming too soon? *Communications of the ACM*, 53, no. 3 10-11, ACM, March.

[6] M. Guzdial. 2015. What's the best way to teach computer science to beginners? *Communications of the ACM*, 58, no. 2,12-13, ACM, January.

[7] D. Deb, M. M. Fuad, and M. Kanan. 2017. Creating Engaging Exercises with Mobile Response System (MRS). *Proceedings of the 2017 ACM SIGCSE Technical Symposium on Computer Science Education.* March 08-11, Seattle, Washington.

[8] M. J. Scott, S. Counsell, S. Lauria, S. Swift, A. Tucker, M. Shepperd and G. Ghinea. 2015. Enhancing Practice and Achievement in Introductory Programming with a Robot Olympics. *IEEE Transactions on Education*, vol. 58, no. 4, 249-254.

[9] M. J. Gierl and H. Lai. 2012. The Role of Item Models in Automatic Item Generation. *International Journal of Testing*, 12(3), 273-298.

[10] H. Wainer, N. J. Dorans, D. Eignor, R. Flaugher, B. F. Green, R. J. Mislevy, L. Steinberg, and D. Thissen. 2000. *Computerized adaptive testing: A primer, Second Edition.* Hillsdale, NJ: Lawrence Erlbaum Associates.

[11] J. R. Savery and T. M. Duffy. 1995. Problem based learning: An instructional model and its constructivist framework. *Educational technology*, 35, no. 5, 31-38.

[12] W. W. Cobern. 1993. Contextual constructivism: The impact of culture on the learning and teaching of science. InK. G.Tobin (Ed.),*The practice of constructivism in science education*(pp. 51–69). Hillsdale, NJ: Lawrence Erlbaum Associates.

[13] T. Im, S. Siva, J. Freeman, B. Magerko, G. Hendler, S. Engelman, M. Miller, B. Villa, and T. McKlin. 2017 Incorporating music into an introductory college level programming course for non-majors. *Proceedings of the IEEE Integrated STEM Education Conference (ISEC)*, Princeton, NJ, 2017, pp. 43-48.

[14] J. Stigall and S. Sharma. 2017. Virtual reality instructional modules for introductory programming courses. *Proceedings of the 2017 IEEE Integrated STEM Education Conference (ISEC)*, Princeton, NJ, pp. 34-42.

[15] M. A. Rubio, R. Romero-Zaliz, C. Mañoso and A. P. de Madrid. 2014. Enhancing an introductory programming course with physical computing modules. *Proceedings of the 2014 IEEE Frontiers in Education Conference (FIE)*, Madrid, 2014, pp. 1-8.

[16] F. I. Anfurrutia, A. Álvarez, M. Larrañaga and J. M. López-Gil. 2016. Incorporating educational robots and visual programming environments in introductory programming courses. *Proceedings of the 2016 International Symposium on Computers in Education (SIIE)*, Salamanca, pp. 1-4.

[17] E. Weilemann, P. Brune, and D. Meyer. 2016. Geek Toys for Non-techies? Using Robots in Introductory Programming Courses for Computer Science Non-majors. *Proceedings of the 49th Hawaii International Conference on System Sciences (HICSS)*, Koloa, HI, pp. 31-40.

[18] W. S. Yue and W. L. Wan. 2015. The effectiveness of digital game for introductory programming concepts. *Proceedings of the 10th International Conference for Internet Technology and Secured Transactions (ICITST)*, London, pp. 421-425.

[19] M. Paralič and E. Pietriková. 2014. Learning by game creation in introductory programming course: 5-Year-long study. *Proceedings of the 12th IEEE International Conference on Emerging eLearning Technologies and Applications (ICETA)*, Stary Smokovec, pp. 391-396.

[20] R. Rahul, A. Whitchurch and M. Rao. 2014. An open source graphical robot programming environment in introductory programming curriculum for undergraduates. *Proceedings of the International Conference on MOOC, Innovation and Technology in Education (MITE)*, Patiala, pp. 96-100.

[21] N. Adamo-Villani, T. Haley-Hermiz and R. Cutler. 2013. Using a Serious Game Approach to Teach 'Operator Precedence' to Introductory Programming Students. *Proceedings of the 17th International Conference on Information Visualization*, London, pp. 523-526.

[22] B. Mendoza, J. Reyes-Alamo, H. Wu, A. Carranza, and L. Zavala. 2016. iPractice: A Self-assessment Tool for Students Learning Computer Programming in an Urban Campus. *Journal of Computing Sciences in Colleges*, 31, 3, 93-100..

[23] F. Prados, I. Boada, J. Soler, and J. Poch. 2005. Automatic generation and correction of technical exercices. *Proceedings of the International Conference on Engineering and Computer Education (ICECE 2005)*, Madrid, Spain.

[24] Vinu E.V and P Sreenivasa Kumar. 2015. Improving Large-Scale Assessment Tests by Ontology Based Approach. *Proceedings of the Twenty-Eighth International Florida Artificial Intelligence Research Society Conference.* May 18-20, Hollywood, Florida, USA.

[25] A. Papasalouros, K. Kotis and K. Kanaris. 2008. Automatic generation of multiple-choice questions from domain ontologies. *Proceedings of the IADIS e-Learning 2008 conference*, Amsterdam, Netherlands.

[26] Al-Yahya M. 2014. Ontology-Based Multiple Choice Question Generation. *The Scientific World Journal.* Vol. 2014, Article ID 274949, 9 pages, 2014. doi:10.1155/2014/274949.

[27] M. Cubric and M. Tosic. 2010 Towards automatic generation of eAssessment using semantic web technologies. *In Proceedings of the 2010 International Computer Assisted Assessment Conference*, Jul 2010. University of Southampton.

[28] Foulonneau, M. 2012. Generating Educational Assessment Items from Linked Open Data: the Case of DBpedia. *In: Garcia-Castro, R.e.a. (ed.): Extended Semantic Web Conference Workshops (at the 8th International conference on The Semantic Web)*, Vol. LNCS 7117. Springer, Heraklion, Greece, pp 16-27.

[29] N. Karamanis, L. A. Ha, and R. Mitkov. 2006. Generating multiple-choice test items from medical text: A pilot study. *Paper presented at the Fourth International Conference Natural Language Generation.* Sydney, Australia.

[30] B. Liu, H. Chen, and W. He. 2008. A framework of deriving adaptive feedback from educational ontologies. *Proceedings of the 9th International Conference for Young Computer Scientists*, Zhang Jia Jie Hunan, China.

[31] T. Berners-Lee. 2006. Linked Data. *Design Issues.* W3C. Retrieved 2017-08-18.

[32] C. Bizer, T. Heath, T. Berners-Lee. 2009. Linked Data—The Story So Far. *International Journal on Semantic Web and Information Systems.* 5 (3): 1–22. ISSN 1552-6283.

Mixed Approaches to CS0:

Exploring Topic and Pedagogy Variance After Six Years of CS0

Zoë J. Wood, John Clements, Zachary Peterson, David Janzen, Hugh Smith, Michael Haungs, Julie Workman, John Bellardo, Bruce DeBruhl
Computer Science - California Polytechnic State University
San Luis, Obispo, CA
zwood,clements,znjp,djanzen,husmith,mhaungs,workmen,bellardo,bdebruhl@calpoly.edu

ABSTRACT

Since 2010, the Cal Poly Computer Science Department has required computing majors to select from a variety of CS0 courses to start their academic year. The broad objective of the course is to attract and retain undergraduates that have no prior experience in CS by using authentic problems that demonstrate the relevance and highlight the role of computers in solving "real world" problems. The course is offered in a variety of thematic "flavors" that leverage a student's pre-existing interests (e.g. in music or art), but all share the common goals of introducing students to the basics of programming, teamwork, and college-level study. While there is overlap in overall goals, the courses vary drastically in topic matter (e.g. robotics, gaming, music, computational art, mobile apps, security) and in pedagogical approach (e.g. principles of design, project-based student driven learning, and traditional topic-based programming modules). The introduction of this CS0 course has increased students' commitment to their major and success in follow-on classes. We present these successes and show that student GPAs in a follow-on object oriented programming course do not vary significantly for the differing subtopics and teaching pedagogies employed in the various flavors. Our report includes examining two student subgroups (those experienced with programming and those new to programming). Our evaluations suggest that the existence and goal of the course matter more than the specific content, with all subtopics and pedagogical approaches performing well.

KEYWORDS

Introductory programming, computer science education, CS0, retention

ACM Reference Format:
Zoë J. Wood, John Clements, Zachary Peterson, David Janzen, Hugh Smith, Michael Haungs, Julie Workman, John Bellardo, Bruce DeBruhl . 2018. Mixed Approaches to CS0:: Exploring Topic and Pedagogy Variance After Six Years of CS0. In *Proceedings of SIGCSE '18: The 49th ACM Technical Symposium on Computer Science Education (SIGCSE '18).* ACM, New York, NY, USA, 6 pages. https://doi.org/10.1145/3159450.3159592

SIGCSE '18, February 21–24, 2018, Baltimore , MD, USA

ACM ISBN 978-1-4503-5103-4/18/02...$15.00
https://doi.org/10.1145/3159450.3159592

1 INTRODUCTION

Student success and retention in introductory computer science courses is a nationwide issue [2]. To address first-year retention, since 2010, the Cal Poly Computer Science Department has required students in computing majors to select from a menu of CS0 courses to start their academic year. These CS0 courses, entitled "CPE123: Introduction to Computing," have a shared goal of introducing students to the basics of computing, teamwork, and college-level study through the lens of some pre-existing, personal interest. The courses vary in topic matter or 'flavor' (e.g. robotics, gaming, music, computational art, security, mobile apps) and employ a mix of teaching pedagogies (e.g. How to Design Programs (HtDP), all team work, traditional topic-based programming modules).

Each freshman cohort of computer science (CS), software engineering (SE), and computer engineering (CPE) majors (approximately 250 students each fall) must take our CS0 course. Each section is limited to an enrollment size of approximately 30 students, meaning that eight to ten sections of CS0 are taught, with five to six of the possible topic flavors being offered. Students select their preferred topic within enrollment and scheduling restrictions. Subsequent courses in the computing curriculum introduce students to programming more formally, and use a more consistent course pedagogy (material, style, and development environment) across the numerous sections (again 8-10). Specifically, students follow our CS0 course with three traditional programming classes, our 'CS1' Introduction to Programming, taught in Python, our 'CS2' Introduction to Object Oriented Programming, taught in Java, and our 'CS3' Introduction to Data Structures, taught in Java. [1]

This paper reports on the positive impact that the inclusion of a CS0 course may have had on student graduation rates and students' attitudes towards computer science. We also explore whether the variance in topic and pedagogy affects student success in follow-on courses. Specifically, we report on the variance in students' GPAs for each CS0 flavor in subsequent courses and pass rates in these classes. Our evaluations suggest that the existence and goal of the CS0 course matters more than the specific content, with all subtopics and pedagogical approaches performing well. In addition, we examine the success of two student subgroups (those experienced with programming and those new to programming), with respect to success in follow-on courses and find that once again, even for these two subgroups, each of the flavors of CS0 do equally well in preparing the students for subsequent courses. These explorations include data from six years of these course offerings (2011-2016).

[1] As of this writing, the ordering of this sequence is changing.

2 CS0 GOALS, TOPICS AND PEDAGOGY

In all the CS0 course sections, students engage with core computer science principles through constructivist, open-ended assignments. At a high level, the course aims to: (1) teach core computer science principles and tools, providing a foundation and context for more traditional, introductory CS coursework, (2) explore those core concepts through the lens of some pre-existing interest, contextualizing, and making relevant, often complex topics, and (3) remove barriers commonly attributed to poor CS engagement, including isolation and exclusion, a lack of social relevance, and limitations on creativity. In all sections, no prior programming experience is assumed.

All instructors hold that the following methodologies/ideologies are essential to the course:

- Context based introduction to computing
- Project based learning
- Learn by doing via lab work
- Group work
- Relating CS topics to real-world problem
- Individual creativity in assignments

Outside of these shared goals, each flavor of the CS0 course has been individually created and is taught by a computing faculty member with interest and expertise in that topic. The topic material of the courses varies widely, along with programming environment and pedagogical approach. Over six years, the courses and instructors have varied slightly, but with core topics and teaching methodologies have been fairly consistent. Table 1 highlights some of the teaching methodologies that are valued for each of the flavors. The individual topics and teaching methodologies used in each section are briefly described here, with variance in language and development environment emphasized for quick comparisons, along with instructors individual perceptions of the most distinguishing/unique feature of their flavor of CS0:

2.1 Computational Art

Students in this course explore the relationship of visual aesthetics and computation. Students design and write interactive animated computer programs. By applying computational thinking, mathematics, art and design principles, and principles of animation, students create artistic and expressive computer programs. This course is an introduction to computer graphics and animation in two dimensions, the fun and easy way. *The main development environment is Processing (both Java and javascript, p5.js have been used).*

Course pedagogy: This course employs a topic-based introduction to computing with each topic rooted in the relevance of the associated artistic computational assignment. For example, students are introduced to loops when exploring the artistic principle of texture and the art movement of pointillism and impressionism. Group work and sharing is used regularly throughout the class to help build community along with pair programming for labs and a final project that can be completed individually or as a team (with most students choosing to work in a team). [15]. *One of the most distinguishing features of this flavor is the strong emphasis on creativity and the creative process related to art, design and personal expression.*

2.2 Games

The course on game design explores computing and software development by creating a full-featured computer game. This course includes an overview of the development process of games and an introduction to gaming fundamentals: logic, story and game play. The course focuses on design, teamwork, and using an iterative development process. *Students learn basic programming skills in order to develop a simple 2D game using an object-oriented language, most frequently Java and the Greenfoot game development environment.*

Course pedagogy: The course is rooted in an individual student-driven learning process and project-based learning. Teams are formed early in the class and constructed to provide an educational support system for its members. In the first half of the course, students complete a series of structured programming assignments designed to provide a basic understanding of both Java and the Greenfoot game development environment and, in the second half, further advanced topics (pathfinding, collision detection, animation) are explored based on the requirements of their team's game. Students follow an iterative development process cycling through the following steps: prototyping, playtesting, evaluation and refinement. Both user testing and Agile-based progress updates are key components of the course. The course provides traditional lecture-based learning in teaching game design theory and a flipped-model format for programming instruction. *One of the most distinguishing features of this flavor is the large quarter-long project and 15 page paper requirement.*

2.3 Mobile computing

The course focused on mobile computing started with Android development; due to an instructor change, it switched to iOS in 2013. Students explore computing and software development by creating apps for Android or iOS-based mobile devices. Students work in teams to imagine, design, prototype, build, test, and launch apps for the Android or iOS market. Students gain hands-on experience with the languages and tools needed to build Android/iOS apps, and test their apps on the appropriate device. *For Android, students learned using AppInventor in the first four weeks, then Java in the final six weeks. iOS students use either Objective-C or more recently, Swift.*

Course pedagogy: This course is a mix of traditional topic-based introduction and team project-based learning. Students complete weekly labs in pairs or individually, and complete projects in pairs or larger groups up to five students. *One of the most distinguishing features of this flavor is the fact that students are able to create mobile apps very quickly in first week, then move to professional tools to build an app of their own choosing.*

2.4 Music

In the CS0 course focused on music, students write programs that generate music. Early compositions focus on the elements of western harmony. Later ones allow students to explore timbre and digital sound processing. Students work collaboratively in teams to design, develop, and test their programs and compositions. The course focuses on design, teamwork, and the use of an iterative development process. The course is intended to be an enjoyable introduction to both computer science and elementary composition. *This course*

Table 1: Some of the key methods employed in the various 123 sections other then the universal methods mentioned. A star denotes that this methodology is considered: "Predominantly" important, while a checkmark denotes "Somewhat important".

Pedagogy	Comp. Art	Games	Mobile	Music	Robotics	Security
community building	✓			✓		✓
flipped model		✓			★	
individual creativity	★	★	★	★	✓	✓
individual learning		★	✓		✓	
lecture based learning	★	✓		★		✓
pair programming.			✓			
student feedback (polling)	✓	★		✓		★
student reflections (journal, etc.)	✓	★				★
team projects		★	★	★	★	✓
test 1st design (Htdp)				★	★	
topic based intro to CS	★		✓	✓	★	✓

closely follows the 'How to Design Programs'(HtdP) [6] curriculum and uses Racket as a programming language.

Course pedagogy: The HtdP curriculum is built on several pillars. First, it puts forward a concrete design recipe with six steps to help carry students from problem statement to solution. Second, it focuses on test-first design, and students following the design recipe are required to specify a function's mapping from inputs to outputs with executable test cases. Third, it is algebraic, eschewing state and mutation in order to make functions composable and testable. Fourth, it is data-driven, categorizing problems using the data that they consume, and showing how to use the specifications of each kind of data to construct function templates that guide the students' thinking. Midway through the course students are gathered into teams of three or four, with whom they complete their assignments for the remainder of the quarter including a team final project. Students participate in weekly reflection surveys in order to allow them to consolidate knowledge and identify issues. *One of the most distinguishing features of this flavor is the use of the HdtP design recipe.*

2.5 Robotics

This course is focused on embedded systems and robotics and is structured such that students explore computing, hardware and software development by designing and implementing an embedded system such as a robot or an Internet of Things solution. Students work in teams to imagine, design, prototype, build, and test their own embedded system solution. *The robot used in the curriculum uses an Arduino microcontroller and the students implement their control software using C.*

Course pedagogy: The course includes lectures taught in a flipped format, required labs and a quarter-long design project. The course lecture and lab focus on implementing a wheeled robot. For the flipped lecture format the students are given videos, reading material and quizzes to work on outside of the normal lecture period. Then lecture period is dedicated to individual and group activities that help students master the material which is then used in lab to implement the hardware and software to control their robot. All students also implement a quarter-long design project (for example an embedded system to help the elderly). [14]. *One of the most distinguishing features of this flavor is that the course is taught in a flipped manner, with the quarter long project based on service to others.*

2.6 Security

In the CS0 course focused on security, students learn the fundamentals of computer science through a hands-on exploration of computer security. Specific security topics include: cryptography, authentication, software security, web security, social engineering, digital forensics, and network security. The content is presented in a unique way, using techniques drawn from alternate-reality games (ARGs) [7]. ARGs are designed to encourage players to collaboratively uncover and interpret fragments of a story, distributed across multiple forms of media, using the "real world" as its platform. *Modules are designed to be solved using a variety of approaches, including computer programming (e.g. port scanning for hidden web services), social engineering (e.g. fooling the instructor into entering a flag into a student-designed phishing website), and physical security (e.g. picking a lock, used on a locker containing a cell phone used for two-factor authentication).*

Course pedagogy: The course is organized into modules that explore a different security topic, supported by a set of core CS principles. Students are organized into groups of four, where team members work together throughout the quarter, and prior experience in CS is accounted for, and distributed among the teams. Instruction follows a process-oriented guided inquiry learning (POGIL) approach, where students are encouraged to explore a topic, with only occasional guidance from the instructor. In addition to technical exercises, students are regularly prompted to reflect on their individual experiences. These responses are used for identifying technical misconceptions, social problems within the group, degenerative cases in the challenges, and bugs in the infrastructure.*One of the most distinguishing features of this flavor is the use of an AR game and narrative based assignements in the instruction.*

3 RELATED WORK

The initial development of the CS0 course at Cal Poly is described in an earlier paper [13], with many of the core driving principles of the course founded on related work [1, 5, 12]. For instance, allowing students to start their computing career via different flavors or topics is not unique to our CS0 course [3, 4, 8–10]. Georgia Tech has done excellent work on long term studies of their menu-based introduction to computing [11], examining attitudes towards each track and their varied success.

This work confirms the positive outcomes associated with starting with a context based CS introductory course and suggests a framework for evaluating whether mixed CS0 courses that employ differing topics or pedagogy correlates with the student success in follow-on course. Specifically, we report that there was no statistically significant difference in GPAs in follow-on classes for students in the differing flavored CS0 courses in our setting.

4 EXAMINING STUDENT SUCCESS

Broad success

After six years of teaching our CS0 course, statistics indicate that the course has contributed to positive outcomes in terms of graduation rates, student attitude, and subsequent student grades. All the CS0 course instructors, and indeed the entire CS faculty, believe the course is an important addition to our curriculum.

In terms of the long term success of the CS0 course, graduation rates have increased for all computing majors from those in 2009 (prior to the introduction of the CS0 course). Table 2 shows the increase in graduations rates (4 year and 5 year) for all computing majors. Note that SE graduation rates are more volatile as they are a smaller population with cohort sizes ranging from 31-54 students, versus 79-159 CS majors and 77-124 CPE majors during the relevant graduation time period (2009-2012).

In addition, to increased graduation rates, surveys showed that students' self-efficacy in, and attitudes towards, their major improved. When the students were surveyed after the follow-on data structures course (CS3), of the cohort that did not take our CS0 course (prior to its requirement), only 39% "strongly agreed" that they were excited about computer science, while of those who did take our CS0 course, 47% "strongly agreed" that they were excited about computer science. Similarly, only 76% of those who did not take CS0, but 83% of those who did reported seeing the relevance of CS to their future career.

We also saw an increase in the number of 'A' grades in the follow-on data structures course from 18% for those who did not take our CS0 course to 24% for those who did have the CS0 course. One result that did not show strong improvement was the fact that students still found computer science "harder," "more tedious," "more antisocial," and "less important to society". This hints at the limitation and dangers of selling computer science to be something it is not.

Success in follow-on courses

Given the broad success of the CS0 course, we further examined whether the topic and/or pedagogy of the different flavors reflects any variance in student success in subsequent courses. Our unique setting, with each major cohort of approximately 250 students taking different flavors of CS0, but then all later taking more consistent follow-on programming classes, allows us to examine whether the topic and pedagogy make a difference in student success in subsequent traditional computer science courses.

In our exploration of students' experiences in our early courses, we also considered ways to examine student experience based on their prior programming knowledge. To this end, we have divided the entering freshmen into two subgroups, those who have programming experience and those who do not. These two subgroups are distinguished based on whether the student has any type of AP computer science score (regardless of the score's numeric value) with 443 students of the total 1834 having an AP CS score reported.

Over the course of 2011-2017, 1835 students took our CS0 course. Of these, 1577 students (87%) either passed CS1 in their first attempt or were given credit for it. The number of students passing CS2 in their first attempt or getting credit for it was 1476 (80%). Note that the second set is not a subset of the first, because some students that failed CS1 in their first attempt passed CS2 in their first attempt.

See Figure 1 for an overview of the pass rates per flavor in the follow-on programming courses, over six years. These figures show that all flavors of CS0 courses are performing similarly well in terms of preparing students to pass the subsequent programming courses. These figures are divided into two populations, those students took and passed the CS AP exam in high school and those who did not.

Density of GPAs

Early analysis of our CS0 courses shows that overall student GPAs tend to drop from when the students enter the next more formal programming course. This is not surprising since each CS0 course was intended to be an 'easy and fun' introduction to computing. However, it was noted that there was a variance in the GPA drop experienced by students coming from the various sections. Students transitioning from the music flavor consistently experienced the lowest GPA drop (For example, the average GPA drop for all sections 2011, 2012 and 2013 was -.89%, -.59% and -.91% respectively, while the drop for those in the music section for those same years was -.45%, -.33% and -.27%. This is also reflected in the average retention through our CS2 (OOP) class (i.e. those who received a passing grade), with those in the music section passing CS2 at a rate of 76.4%, while the average pass rate for all sections was 71%. This led to some of the initial work to examine student success in the various CS0 flavors.

In considering whether a specific CS0 section was indeed a better course, we examined the GPA distributions of 1154 students who went on to receive a grade in follow-on programming classes (after two quarters in Object Oriented Programming). We also looked at grade variation for the students after only one quarter (in Introduction to Programming). Note that although we have been teaching the CS0 course since 2010, there have been other changes to the intro series courses (i.e. a switch from C to Python in the Introduction to Programming, etc.), however, we primarily are focused on examining student success in follow on programming courses given starting out in a particular CS0 flavor.

Figure 2 shows the GPA density plot for the different CS0 flavors in the follow-on CS1, for cohorts for the years 2011-2016. All grades are reported for students who did not have an AP CS score (as AP CS students do not take this course). Though there are differences in the GPA densities, ANOVA shows no significant variance (p-value

Table 2: Graduation rates before and after the introduction of CS0

major	4 year Graduation rates prior	2010 cohort	2011 cohort	2012 cohort
computer science	17.1%	27.8%	29.6%	34.6%
computer engineering	21.8%	36.4%	30.6%	25.4%
software engineering	22.6%	19.0%	29.4%	33.3%
majors	5 year Graduation rates prior	2010 cohort	2011 cohort	2012 cohort
computer science	51.7%	62.0%	66.7%	no data
computer engineering	47.8%	61.8%	66.7%	no data
software engineering	66.7%	51.2%	71.4%	no data

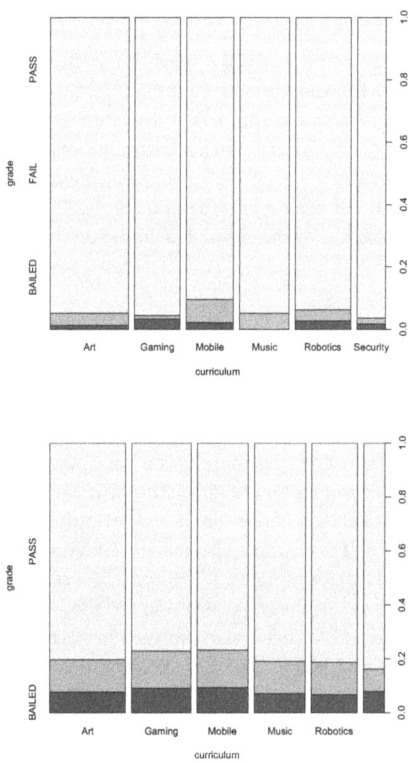

Figure 1: The top figure shows pass/fail rates for the various CS0 courses for the follow-on two programming courses for students with an AP computer science score. The bottom figure shows the same data but for students with no AP CS score. Dark grey shows the population that did not take a follow on course, mid-grey shows those who failed one of the courses and light grey, the majority, shows those who passed. The width of each bar corresponds to the number of students who took each flavor of CS0, for example, 466 students took the computational art flavor versus 136 students took security (a relatively new offering).

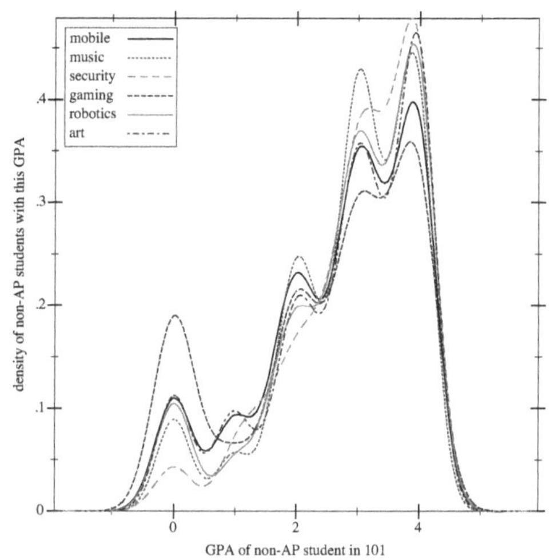

Figure 2: Density plot of GPAs for students from the various flavored CS0 courses in the follow-on 'Introduction to Programming' course for students with no AP CS score. ANOVA shows no significant variance (p-value of .449).

of .449), suggesting that students from the different flavored CS0 courses perform similarly in the follow-on programming course. Figures 3 shows the distribution of the grades in our object oriented programming course (two quarters after our CS0 course) for the two groups of students for the the years 2010-2015. Although there is variance between the grade distributions, ANOVA analysis and Chi-squared analysis showed p-values too large to conclude that any particular section's GPA distribution was significantly different then the others. In all of these graphs, students that elected not to take the course are considered to have earned a GPA of 0.0, except for those that went on to take a later course in the first-year sequence, who are assumed to have bypassed this requirement either through an AP score or by taking the course elsewhere.

5 CONCLUSIONS AND FUTURE WORK

We have presented our explorations of six years of teaching CS0 as a first course for computing majors. Overall, we have experienced that this course is beneficial to our department, contributing to an increase in graduation rates, improvements in students' attitudes towards their major and overall increase in GPAs in follow-on courses. In addition, the unique setting with faculty able to employ various pedagogy and unique material has created a fertile grounds for faculty growth. In a recent survey of the participating faculty (nine in total), 77% said that they had adopted many to a few different

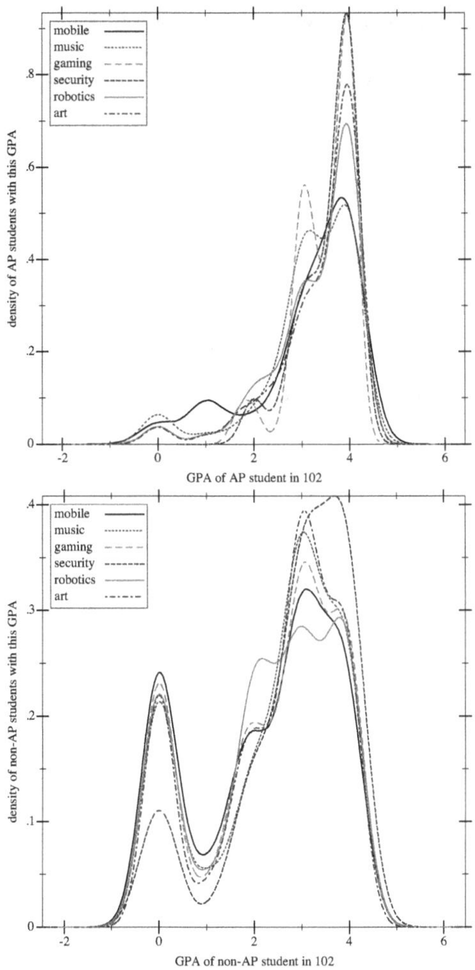

Figure 3: Density plot of GPAs for students from the various CS0 courses in the follow-on 'Object Oriented Programming' course. The top graph shows, all grades for students who entered college with an AP CS score. ANOVA shows no significant variance (p-value: .815). The lower graph shows all grades for students who did not have an AP CS score. ANOVA shows no significant variance (p-value: .581).

teaching strategies based on hearing what other instructors were doing in their sections. One of the most commonly listed practices that was adopted was the weekly reflections/journaling. Some of the faculty comments about the structure include: "It is great to exchange ideas and try to adopt practices that work well in other sections without getting stuck debating the technical minutia." and "I like comparing notes and brainstorming pedagogical approaches; I like that we have a potential to measure and evaluate the efficacy of our varied practices". For a field, renown for language wars, it has been liberating for our faculty to do their 'own' thing and see that all of the students can be prepared via very different approaches.

We examined student success in follow-on courses both in terms of pass and fail rates and GPA distribution and have found that no single flavor of our CS0 course is statistically outperforming the others. This finding in many ways is positive as it demonstrates that no single topic or pedagogy for CS0 of the six variations being used is significantly better. This implies that continuing with all the various flavors and teaching methodologies is appropriate and that any school considering CS0 options could select similar topics and pedagogy to the six presented here.

In the future, we would like to have a more refined subgroup selection process as we acknowledge that many students who do not have an AP score, could have substantial computing experience via summer camps, robotics clubs, etc. In addition, we acknowledge the limitation of drawing conclusions from this exploration. Our graduation rates have increased, but so has the overall popularity of computer science. In addition, this examination gave us an opportunity to think about how we can measure student success and whether any of our teaching pedagogies are perhaps more successful than others (certainly, it is appealing to discover if there is one right way to teach intro CS). We wish to continue to expand our understanding of which factors contribute the most to student success and retention.

REFERENCES

[1] Christine Alvarado and Zachary Dodds. 2010. Women in CS: an evaluation of three promising practices. In *Proceedings of the 41st ACM technical symposium on Computer science education*. ACM, 57–61.

[2] Jens Bennedsen and Michael E. Caspersen. 2007. Failure rates in introductory programming. *SIGCSE Bull. 39* (2007), 32–36.

[3] Elizabeth Bonsignore, Kari Kraus, Amanda Visconti, Derek Hansen, Ann Fraistat, and Allison Druin. 2012. Game design for promoting counterfactual thinking. In *Proceedings of the SIGCHI Conference on Human Factors in Computing Systems.*

[4] Robert Bryant, Richard Weiss, Genevieve Orr, and Kathie Yerion. 2011. Using the Context of Algorithmic Art to Change Attitudes in Introductory Programming. *J. Comput. Sci. Coll.* 27, 1 (Oct. 2011), 112–119. http://dl.acm.org/citation.cfm?id=2037151.2037177

[5] Zachary Dodds, Ran Libeskind-Hadas, Christine Alvarado, and Geoff Kuenning. 2008. Evaluating a breadth-first cs 1 for scientists. In *ACM SIGCSE Bulletin*, Vol. 40. ACM, 266–270.

[6] Matthias Felleisen, Robert Bruce Findler, Matthew Flatt, and Shriram Krishnamurthi. 2001. *How to Design Programs: An Introduction to Programming and Computing.* MIT Press, Cambridge, MA, USA.

[7] M. Gondree and Z.N.J. Peterson. 2015. This is Not a Game: Early Observations on Using Alternate Reality Games for Teaching Security Concepts to First-Year Undergraduates. In *Proceedings of the Workshop on Cyber Security Experimentation and Test (CSET).*

[8] Ira Greenberg, Deepak Kumar, and Dianna Xu. 2012. Creative Coding and Visual Portfolios for CS1. In *Proceedings of the 43rd ACM Technical Symposium on Computer Science Education (SIGCSE '12).* ACM, New York, NY, USA, 247–252. https://doi.org/10.1145/2157136.2157214

[9] Mark Guzdial. 2006. Teaching Computing for Everyone. *J. Comput. Sci. Coll.* 21, 4 (April 2006), 6–6. http://dl.acm.org/citation.cfm?id=1127389.1127390

[10] Mark Guzdial. 2010. Does Contextualized Computing Education Help? *ACM Inroads* 1, 4 (Dec. 2010), 4–6. https://doi.org/10.1145/1869746.1869747

[11] Mark Guzdial. 2013. Exploring Hypotheses About Media Computation. In *Proceedings of the Ninth Annual International ACM Conference on International Computing Education Research (ICER '13).* ACM, New York, NY, USA, 19–26. https://doi.org/10.1145/2493394.2493397

[12] Susanne Hambrusch, Christoph Hoffmann, John T Korb, Mark Haugan, and Antony L Hosking. 2009. A multidisciplinary approach towards computational thinking for science majors. In *Proceedings of the ACM technical symposium on Computer science education.*

[13] Michael Haungs, Christopher Clark, John Clements, and David Janzen. 2012. Improving first-year success and retention through interest-based CS0 courses. In *Proceedings of the ACM Technical Symposium on Computer Science Education.*

[14] H. Smith. 2016. An Embedded System Design Experience for First Year Computing Majors. In *Proceedings of the 8th annual First Year Engineering Experience.*

[15] Z. J. Wood and J. Workman. 2013. Computational art using Processing for CS0. In *Grace Hopper Celebration of Women in Computing.*

Designing an Introductory Programming Course to Improve Non-Majors' Experiences

Jessica Q. Dawson
University of British Columbia
jqdawson@cs.ubc.ca

Meghan Allen
University of British Columbia
meghana@cs.ubc.ca

Alice Campbell
University of British Columbia
alicecam@cs.ubc.ca

Anasazi Valair
University of British Columbia
sazi.valair@ubc.ca

ABSTRACT

Demand for computing courses from students in disciplines outside of Computer Science is growing. This growth has created increasing challenges in offering one-size-fits-all CS1 courses. We found that non-CS majors' experiences and outcomes in our existing CS1 course were worse than those of intended CS majors. In response, we developed an introductory programming course, CS0.5, aimed at meeting the needs of the diverse population of non-CS major students interested in our courses. In this paper, we present the motivation, curriculum design, and evidence of effectiveness for this new course. We describe the specific design decisions we made in response to the experiences of non-CS majors in CS1. We also demonstrate that students' outcomes in CS0.5–measured in terms of students' pass rates, satisfaction, and attitudes–all not only improve compared to non-CS majors in CS1, but also largely match those of CS majors in CS1. Finally, we present student feedback, gathered through surveys and Appreciative Inquiry focus groups, that illustrates how our curriculum design choices better meet our non-major students' needs. The most-valued course design elements, as identified by focus group participants, provide insight for other CS educators who are designing similar courses.

CCS CONCEPTS

• **Social and professional topics → Computer science education;**

KEYWORDS

CS for all; non-majors; curriculum design; CS1; blended-learning; evaluation; appreciative inquiry

ACM Reference Format:
Jessica Q. Dawson, Meghan Allen, Alice Campbell, and Anasazi Valair. 2018. Designing an Introductory Programming Course to Improve Non-Majors' Experiences. In *SIGCSE '18: The 49th ACM Technical Symposium on Computer Science Education, Feb. 21–24, 2018, Baltimore, MD, USA.* ACM, New York, NY, USA, 6 pages. https://doi.org/10.1145/3159450.3159548

SIGCSE '18, Feb. 21–24, 2018, Baltimore, MD, USA

ACM ISBN 978-1-4503-5103-4/18/02...$15.00
https://doi.org/10.1145/3159450.3159548

1 INTRODUCTION

Computer Science departments have seen dramatic increases in enrollments. This growth has been driven by increasing numbers of CS major enrollments, but also by increasing demand for computing courses from non-CS majors who recognize the mounting importance and relevance of computing in their own fields [4, 17]. At our institution, this growth has created new challenges to providing introductory programming courses that fit the needs of all our students. As our student population expands, we want to ensure we offer courses that support diversity in computer science and that students have positive experiences in our courses regardless of their academic area of interest.

Prior to 2016, our university offered only one first-year, introductory programming course (CS1). It is 4-credits, and serves approximately 1500 students per year, including students who intend to be CS majors, students who are required to take the course for their major, and students who are taking the course as an elective. In our CS1 course, which is based on the How to Design Programs curriculum [9], students learn to systematically design readable, well-structured, and well-tested programs using functional teaching languages. While the course has been effective and student feedback has been largely positive, anecdotally, course instructors reported that non-CS majors had worse outcomes, and were more likely to say that they did not enjoy the course, that the pace was too fast, and that the workload was too high.

To serve these students, we proposed a new, first-year, computer science class (CS0.5) about systematic program design for non-major students. Our approach to the CS0.5 curriculum design was driven by the assertion that different disciplines see the world differently [14]. In CS1, we emphasize the core programming and software design skills and concepts that are necessary for computer scientists, but for non-majors we decided that it was more useful to focus on how programming can be used in their own academic discipline. We aimed to shift the emphasis without compromising the integrity of the authentic programming and software design skills that students learn in CS1, particularly as non-majors may only take one computing course.

CS0.5, launched in September 2016, is a 3-credit course that uses a blended-learning approach and is taught in Python. It covers about 40% of the learning outcomes of CS1 over six modules, CS0.5-specific learning outcomes over two modules, and a CS0.5-specific project that is designed so that each student can apply their program design skills to their own area of interest.

In this paper, we report on our experience designing, launching, and evaluating the first two semesters of CS0.5. First, we report on an investigation that examined the differences between CS and non-CS major students' pass rates in and satisfaction with CS1. We also report differences in CS1 students' attitudes towards computing that we gathered using a validated survey tool [7]. In the context of related work, we describe the CS0.5 curriculum and the design decisions we made in response to the experiences of non-CS majors in CS1. We demonstrate that students' outcomes–measured in terms of pass rates, satisfaction, and attitudes–all improve with CS0.5 when compared with non-CS majors in CS1. We present student feedback, gathered through surveys and Appreciative Inquiry [19] focus groups, that illustrates how our curriculum design choices effectively target non-major students' needs. Finally, we discuss student-identified areas of improvement for CS0.5.

2 MAJORS AND NON-MAJORS IN CS1

In 2015/2016, we conducted an evaluation of CS1 to help us better understand the non-CS major population of the course[1]. We wanted to identify similarities and differences between the non-major students' experiences and course outcomes, and those of intended CS majors, in order to guide our development of CS0.5.

2.1 Pass, fail and withdrawal rates

We examined the proportion of students who passed CS1 in 2015/2016 Term 1 and Term 2 (n = 1225; 39% female[2]). We included in the enrollment total all undergraduate students who withdrew within the first two weeks, which is the normal deadline to drop a course without it appearing on their transcript. Overall, 74% of all students passed the course, with 19% failing and 7% withdrawing.

At our institution, most students don't declare their major until after first year, and so we are unable to distinguish intended majors from non-majors using the enrollment data available. As a proxy for comparing CS majors and non-majors, we used the most common faculties that offer majors in CS: Science, Arts, and Commerce[3]. Students from other faculties or schools, such as Forestry or Education or Engineering, also enroll in CS1, but in much smaller numbers.

We found that Science and Commerce students had better pass rates than the overall average, both at 81%. This is 10% higher than for students in Other programs, of whom 71% passed, and 21% higher than for students in Arts, of whom only 60% passed. At our university, the majority of students who major in CS are in the Faculty of Science, although many Science students who take CS1 are also non-CS majors. Roughly two thirds of the Commerce students in CS1 in 2015/2016 were in a combined CS and Business program. A much smaller proportion of CS majors are in the Faculty of Arts. Thus, the lower pass rates for students in Arts and Other programs suggest that non-CS majors were disproportionately more likely to fail or withdraw from CS1.

[1] All evaluations were approved by our institution's Behavioural Ethics Review Board.
[2] Our gender data is from our student information system, which presents gender as binary, and does not accurately represent students with non-binary gender identities.
[3] We also offer a second degree program in computer science for mature students with previous degrees (n=79 in CS1 2015/2016). These students enter as CS majors, and are required to take the existing CS1 course with their cohort. These students are not as useful as a comparison group with non-major students, and have been excluded. We also excluded graduate students, who number only one or two per year.

2.2 Student feedback from surveys

At the end of each term we conducted an online survey to gather information about students' CS1 experiences, which we used to inform the CS0.5 course design. The survey was part of a larger evaluation that extended over the term, and it included a range of questions aimed at course improvement. For this paper we were most interested in exploring the differences between students at the end of the course as opposed to individual shifts from beginning to end. Thus, we present here only results from the end-of-term survey and only questions that relate to the measures of interest in this paper, namely satisfaction and attitudes towards computing.

A total of 626 (55%) of the 1134 students registered at the end of term participated. We asked respondents to specify their intended major(s): those who chose CS as an intended major were classified as CS majors (50%) and all others as non-CS majors (50%). We used unpaired Welch's t-tests to compare the satisfaction and attitudes of CS majors and non-CS majors. See Figures 1 and 2; all questions were optional, so the n varies for each group and question.

Satisfaction: We asked students to rate their satisfaction with various elements of the course. We found that non-CS majors were significantly less satisfied than CS majors with their overall experience, their expected grade, the time and effort that they put into the course, and the skills and knowledge that they learned.

Attitudes towards computing: We asked respondents a subset of questions from the Computing Attitudes Survey (CAS) [7], a validated tool to measure students' expert-like attitudes towards computing. It consists of statements on which there is an empirically-established expert opinion, and which cluster into five empirically-determined subscales measuring different facets of students' attitudes. Respondents rate their agreement with each statement on a 5-point likert scale (strongly agree to strongly disagree).

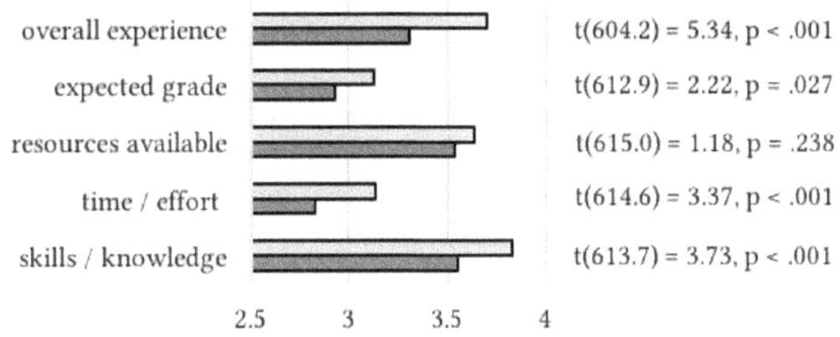

Figure 1: Unpaired t-test of satisfaction in CS1 (2015/2016); 1=very unsatisfied; 5=very satisfied.

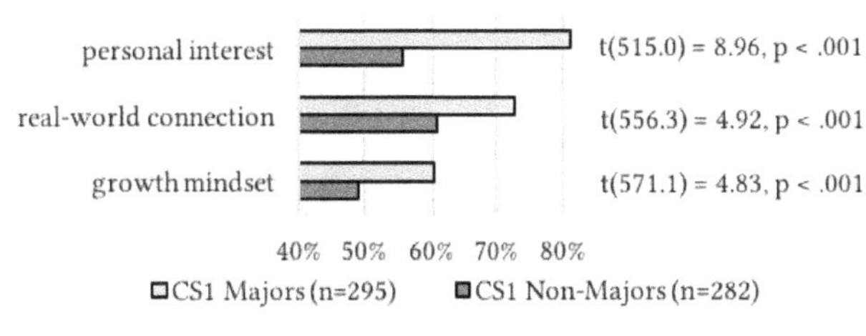

Figure 2: Unpaired t-test of students' agreement with expert opinions on CAS factors in CS1 (2015/2016).

We used a subset of the statements from the three subscales most related to the attitudes we wanted to foster in non-majors. The *real-world connections* subscale (4 statements) focuses on relationships between computing and the real world, e.g. "I think about the Computer Science that I experience in everyday life," where the expert opinion is agreement. The *personal interest* subscale (3 statements) focuses on students' enjoyment and engagement with computing, e.g. "I enjoy solving Computer Science problems," where the expert opinion is agreement. The problem-solving fixed mindset subscale (7 statements), which we call *growth mindset*, focuses on students' confidence and mindset when solving computing problems, e.g. "If I get stuck on a computer science problem, there is no chance I'll figure it out on my own," where the expert opinion is disagreement.

We scored the students' responses to the CAS statements following the standard procedure [7]. We collapsed the responses into a 3-point range (disagree, neutral, agree), and then compared each student's response to the established expert opinion; a student's score on each subscale is calculated as the proportion of statements belonging to that subscale where the student's response matched that of the experts. For each factor, a higher percent agreement suggests more expert-like attitudes, i.e., more personal interest, a stronger appreciation of the relationship between computers and the real world, and more confidence and a more growth-oriented mindset when solving problems. We compared the scores for each group using Welch's t-tests, and found that non-CS majors had significantly less expert agreement than CS-majors on all subscales.

Student comments: To better understand non-CS majors' experiences in CS1 and the reasons for the differences in satisfaction and attitudes towards CS, we open-coded their responses to free-form questions about improvements to CS1, their experiences with the course lectures and labs, and their other comments.

We found that non-CS majors commonly expressed concerns about the difficulty of CS1 (24% of all respondents), the pace of the course (17%), and the high workload required of students (14%). Many of these students found it difficult to balance CS1's workload with their other courses, e.g. "The amount of information is overwhelming for people who had never programmed before. The course load is way [too] much, I personally have 4 other courses and it's taking up way too much time."

10% of all respondents specifically mentioned that they did not feel that CS1 was designed for non-majors or students without prior programming experience. Two of these students explicitly expressed a desire for an introductory programming course better suited to them: "Perhaps if there was a class that taught non-CPSC students how to program in Python and how that would be relevant for any degree [choice], it would be more attractive and get people hooked more"; "I wish there was a course that taught this at a slower and more applicable pace for non-cpsc students."

2.3 Summary

Our evaluations confirmed that students in degree programs with fewer CS majors failed the course at much higher rates. The surveys further confirmed that non-majors were less satisfied than majors with their overall experience in CS1, their expected grade, the workload, and what they learned in CS1. Non-majors also had less expert-like attitudes towards computer science. Not all of these differences are surprising. We would expect, for example, that CS majors might be more interested in computing than non-majors. However, being less interested in computing should not lead to a less satisfactory experience with the introductory course, nor does it mean that these students should be more fixed in their mindsets or be less able to appreciate the connections between computing and their everyday lives.

3 CS0.5 CURRICULUM DESIGN

The findings from the surveys, combined with CS1 instructor reflections and consideration of similar courses elsewhere, led us to a number of goals for CS0.5. We wanted the course to be relevant and engaging to students with various interests, follow the core curricular approach of CS1, have a flexible schedule and slower pace, foster positive attitudes about CS, be scalable to at least 500 students per term, and encourage students to reflect on their learning.

One approach to making CS courses relevant and engaging to non-CS students has been context-based CS1 courses (e.g. [1, 6, 10, 11, 13, 16]). However, rather than make multiple context-specific courses for students in different fields, we wanted to create a single, scalable course that provides flexibility in application topic area. Another common approach has been to use data analysis as a driving problem to introduce computer science concepts, programming, and data visualization (e.g. [2, 3, 18]). We wanted to maintain the focus on systematic program design from our CS1 course, while integrating the ideas of data analysis and visualization into CS0.5. Therefore, our main learning goal for CS0.5 is for students to complete a data analysis and visualization project in which they use computation to systematically solve a problem from a discipline of their choice. We centered the course design around a project because projects have been found to increase student engagement [12]. Every content module of the course focuses on the systematic program design skills and concepts that students will need to use in the project. Each student chooses a topic of interest for their project; we hoped that the ability to personalize the project would improve students' attitudes about computer science, especially students' personal interest in computing and the applications of computing to the real world.

To address concerns about workload and pace we reduced the overall number of learning goals in CS0.5 compared to CS1, and reduced the overall credit count compared to CS1 (3-credits vs. 4-credits). The CS0.5 students learn enough systematic program design to design a readable, well-structured, and well-tested program that uses Python's CSV module to read a .csv file, defines appropriate data types, analyzes the data to answer a specific question, and produces a graph to visualize the results. However, they do not tackle the latter 60% of the CS1 learning outcomes which cover more advanced topics (e.g. trees and generative recursion).

We chose to offer CS0.5 as a blended, reduced-face-time course, as we hoped that increased flexibility would lead to more accessibility for non-majors. Although the workload was the same as it would be for a non-blended course of the same credit count, the students have more control over when and where they complete their coursework. They attend one mandatory 80-minute lecture and one mandatory 50-minute tutorial per week (compared to two 80-minute lectures or three 50-minute lectures and one mandatory

3-hour lab in CS1). In each content module students are assigned pre-class work consisting of reading custom course materials, solving problems using the new concepts, and writing and submitting a brief summary of what they learned and at least one question about the module or how it relates to the rest of the course. In lecture we use Just-In-Time teaching [15] and deliver short mini-lectures to address the questions raised by students in their pre-class work. Students spend the majority of lecture time working in small groups to solve problems on a worksheet package; we usually interject with one or two 5-10 minute mini-lectures and/or wrap-up discussion that focuses on key problems from the worksheets. Completed worksheet packages are collected in the following lecture, graded for completion, and returned electronically. In tutorials, students work in small groups on weekly homework assignments with TA support. They also complete weekly peer review assignments that require them to solve a problem, assess three of their peers' solutions, and complete a self-assessment of their own solution.

We encouraged group work so that the students would have peer support if they started to feel discouraged. We also discussed the growth mindset [8] in class to foster positive attitudes, although we did not teach mindsets explicitly, as done by Cutts et al. [5]. To encourage students to reflect on their own learning, we included reflective questions on each worksheet package. For example, in one package we asked them "Which parts of the course are you finding the most difficult?" and "What is your strategy for mastering the parts of the course that you are finding the most difficult?".

4 CS0.5 YEAR ONE EVALUATION

We offered CS 0.5 for the first time in 2016/2017 Term 1 to 101 students (51% female), and then in Term 2 to 110 students (56% female); CS1 was offered in parallel to 1369 undergraduate students (39% female). We marketed CS1 to students intending to major in CS, as well as non-major students who felt it matched their needs and interests. We marketed CS0.5 as an alternative for non-majors who were interested in an introductory programming course that would allow them to solve problems in the discipline of their choice.

In both terms in 2016/2017 we conducted an evaluation of CS0.5 and CS1 to examine whether CS0.5 was successful in improving outcomes–measured in terms of pass rates, satisfaction, and attitudes–relative to the non-CS majors who remained in CS1. We conducted end-of-term surveys, and in CS0.5 we also ran Appreciative Inquiry focus groups to gain deeper insight into the students' experiences in the course and identify what they most valued about its design.

4.1 Proportions passing CS0.5 and CS1

The pass rates for each degree program are shown in Table 1. Overall, 83% of all students passed CS0.5 (n = 211) and 17% withdrew or failed. This contrasts with CS1 (n=1369), where 75% passed and 25% withdrew or failed. We saw notable increases in CS0.5 pass rates for all degree programs compared to CS1: the proportion was 7% higher for Science students, 15% higher for Arts students, 16% higher for Commerce students, and 12% higher for Other students. The outcomes in CS1 were fairly consistent with the previous year, differing by 5% or less for most groups. This suggests to us that the factors that influence different groups' success in CS1 are fairly steady year over year. A notable exception was the 13% increase

Table 1: Proportion passing in CS0.5 and CS1 in 2016/2017.

	Science	Arts	Commerce	Other
CS0.5	88%	78%	93%	96%
CS1	81%	63%	77%	84%

in the proportion of Other students passing CS1, which may have been caused by more students in Other programs who expected to struggle in CS1 preferentially choosing CS0.5 instead.

4.2 Survey feedback in CS0.5 and CS1

In CS0.5 132 (66%) of the 201 students still registered at the end of term completed the survey, while in CS1, 726 (56%) of the 1307 students still registered completed it. We again asked respondents in the CS1 survey to declare their intended major(s): those students who chose computer science as at least one of their majors were classified as CS majors (52%), while all other respondents were classified as non-CS majors (48%).

We asked students in both courses the same set of satisfaction and CAS [7] questions as in the previous year's CS1 survey. We used one-way between-subjects ANOVAs to examine differences in satisfaction and attitudes between CS0.5 students and CS and non-CS majors in CS1. We performed post-hoc pairwise comparisons using the conservative Bonferroni correction. See Figures 3 and 4; all questions were optional, so the n varies for each group.

Satisfaction: Students' satisfaction varied significantly for overall experience, the expected grade, the amount of time and effort put into the course, and the skills and knowledge learned.

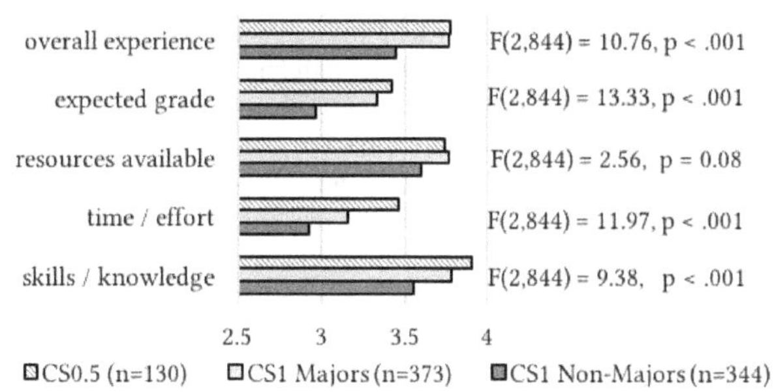

Figure 3: Between subjects ANOVA of satisfaction in 2017/2018; 1=very unsatisfied; 5=very satisfied.

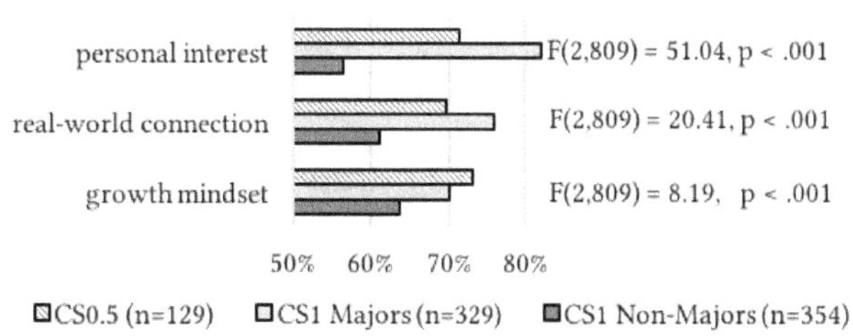

Figure 4: Between subjects ANOVA of students' agreement with expert opinions on CAS in 2017/2018.

Post-hoc comparisons showed that the satisfaction of non-CS majors in CS1 was significantly less than both CS majors in CS1 and CS0.5 students in their overall experience in the course ($p < .001$ and $p < .01$ respectively), their expected grade (both $p < .001$), the amount of time and effort ($p < .05$ and $p < .001$ respectively), and the skills and knowledge ($p < .01$ and $p < .001$ respectively). The satisfaction with the time and effort required was also less for CS majors in CS1 than students in CS0.5; there were no other significant differences between these two groups.

Attitudes towards computing: We found significantly different levels of expert agreement on the personal interest, real world connections and growth mindset subscales.

The post-hoc comparisons showed that non-CS majors in CS1 scored significantly lower than both CS majors in CS1 and CS0.5 students on the personal interest (both $p < .001$), real world connections ($p < .001$ and $p < .05$ respectively), and growth mindset (both $p < .01$) subscales. CS majors scored significantly higher on the personal interest ($p < .01$) measure than CS0.5 students; we found no differences between these groups on the other factors.

CS0.5 student comments: To explore the extent to which the observed outcome improvements could be explained by our curriculum design decisions, we analyzed students' responses to free-form questions about suggestions for improvement, their experiences with the lectures, tutorials, and project, and additional comments.

69% of all respondents remarked on how the project allowed them to apply skills in the course to their personal interests, e.g. "The project made me feel like everything I had learned was put towards a very interesting end-goal. It allowed me to understand the greater contexts within and beyond computer science and how it can be applied in different areas of life".

Students' comments also suggest that the course design supported them in developing a growth mindset in computing, with 33% of all respondents describing growth mindset related concepts or experiences. For example, some describe improving their skills tackling difficult problems: "I improved my ability to systematically work through a problem, looking at each specific aspect instead of immediately trying to go for the big picture, as that can be overwhelming." Others commented on the positive feelings associated with overcoming challenges. For example, one student wrote "the feeling of accomplishment whenever I figured out how to solve a problem is amazing. Anytime I mastered a new skill in general was great." Also related were students' comments on the benefit of having multiple opportunities to interact with course concepts and recognize that they needed help over time, e.g. "I love that ... we had a lot of chances to learn the material and ask for help. [If] we didn't understand it during pre-reading we could understand it during class, and then during the peer review, and then during the tutorial, and then during the practice problems."

4.3 CS0.5 student focus group feedback

In addition to comparing non-CS majors experience in CS0.5 with CS1 through the surveys, we also wanted to deeply explore the students' learning experience in CS0.5, identify the elements of the course design that course participants most valued, and solicit participant-driven ideas for improvements. To answer these questions, we conducted focus groups in CS0.5 using Appreciative Inquiry (AI) [19], an action-driven, participatory research methodology that focuses on what's working well and drives change by enhancing current strengths.

Focus group design: We conducted three 3-hour sessions with a total of 23 students and five teaching assistants. We conducted the first two sessions in the month following the first offering, and the third session the month following the second offering. Two facilitators led each session.

AI uses a four-phase process centered on an affirmative topic, in our case "CS0.5 at its best." In each 3-hour session, a different group of participants completed the first three phases of this process. In the first phase (*Discovery*), the participants conducted storytelling-based interviews in small groups to solicit stories that illustrated CS0.5 at its best. Each storyteller also identified what they valued about themselves or others in their story. The small groups then identified the three to five most salient themes from these stories and wrote them on a large piece of paper to share with the whole group via a gallery walk. Each participant voted on their top priority themes and we carried the most highly-rated themes into the next phase. The participants then formed new small groups, based on the priority theme that they were interested in, and collaboratively generated a drawing and a present-tense, one-sentence description (a provocative proposition) of how they envisioned CS0.5 at its best in relation to their theme (*Dream* phase). Finally, the participants brainstormed course design ideas that could enable this ideal future state (*Design* phase). The final AI phase, *Delivery* on changes, is too large to conduct in a 3-hour focus group; instead, course staff are using the findings to inform future course revisions.

Findings: We found several common themes that participants valued. Many of these aligned with our course design intentions, while some gave us new insight into non-majors' perspectives on their experiences learning CS that we intend to bring forward as we continue to iterate on the course. The project came up frequently, with groups using themes of 'versatility', 'flexibility', 'universal appeal' and 'personal connection' to describe the project and their appreciation of being able to apply new knowledge to their own interests. Envisioning what this could look like, one group wrote the provocative proposition that CS0.5 "enables students to incorporate their own interests and teaches skills that are relevant to their personal goals". Many felt that the project already does this successfully, but the design phase generated several suggestions for further improvement, e.g. collaborating with lab courses to use real observational data, grouping sections into disciplinary clusters, or providing students with more ways to showcase their final projects.

Several themes addressed the 'availability' (two groups), 'accessibility', and 'diversity' of resources, which the respondents appreciated because they could get the type of help they needed when they wanted it. One group's proposition described CS0.5 as "students actively learning how to think systematically by coding whenever they want, wherever they want, whatever they want." Design brainstorming in this area generated many new ideas for resources, such as weekly Q&A live streams, online chats for students who had trouble attending office hours, and dedicated CS0.5 study spaces to work with their peers outside of class time.

The growth mindset arose through several common themes related to the challenges that students encountered with the course concepts and assignments, and how they perceived these challenges:

'perseverance' (three groups) repeatedly came up as a quality that participants valued in themselves at their best in the course, a fourth group raised the related quality of 'self-reliance', and two groups cited the challenge and benefit of 'independent learning.' One group's proposition focused on students being "motivated by success to use resources and pursue solutions to challenging problems." Complementary to this focus on the individual were themes focused on the benefits of interactions with others: 'teamwork', 'support system', 'community' and 'peer review.' Along these lines, one group's proposition described "students asking each other questions, giving feedback, having discussions, and explaining their work," while another described "easily accessible, virtual and in-person resources to facilitate independent and collaborative student learning." These themes prompted many suggestions to enable even more avenues to support students and encourage them when things get tough, such as more opportunities for peer feedback, actively helping students get to know each other better, and new resources like the online chats or dedicated meeting rooms mentioned earlier.

5 DISCUSSION AND CONCLUSIONS

Our evaluation of the first two semesters of CS0.5 confirms that our course design decisions were successful in improving students' outcomes in CS0.5 relative to non-CS major students in CS1. The pass rates of students from all programs improved considerably in CS0.5 over CS1. Not only did students' satisfaction and attitudes improve in CS0.5 when compared with non-CS majors in CS1, we were encouraged to find that these were often in line with those of the CS-majors in CS1.

Survey respondents' reported satisfaction and comments suggest that CS0.5 students found the workload to be much more manageable than non-CS majors in CS1. Compared to non-CS majors in CS1, CS0.5 students were more satisfied not only with the time and effort that they expected to put into the course, but the grade they were able to earn with that effort, and in their overall experience. In addition, CS0.5 students were more satisfied with the skills they learned than non-CS majors in CS1. This suggests that the reduction in the number of learning goals made the course more manageable for non-CS majors, without hurting the course's perceived substance or value. Related to workload, the flexibility of the work-anywhere approach afforded by the blended classroom was identified as particularly valuable by several AI groups.

CS0.5 students' attitudes towards computing also improved on all measures. Compared to non-CS majors in CS1 we saw more expert-like growth mindsets, not only in the CAS scores, but also in the AI and survey comments made by CS0.5 students about overcoming challenges. The CS0.5 students also showed an increased interest in Computer Science and ability to connect computing to real world applications. The AI and survey comments revealed that the personalized project was particularly effective at promoting these attitudes and fostering positive experiences.

One limitation of this work is that the students who participated in evaluations may have been more engaged and thus some measures may be positively overestimated. This is especially likely in CS1, where instructors have noticed that many students who fail the course simply disengage and stop attending. This possibility is further suggested since survey respondents' pass rates are higher than for the courses overall (by 11% in 2015/2016 and 10% in 2016/2017 in CS1; by 8% in C0.5).

Appreciative Inquiry is not yet commonly used in CS education, but we hope our experience will encourage others to try using AI. The students provided rich, actionable feedback and we were impressed with their deep reflections on their learning experiences.

We plan to continue to evaluate the course via surveys and Appreciative Inquiry focus groups, and to respond to student feedback via curricular and pedagogical changes. We are happy to share our course materials; please contact the second author.

ACKNOWLEDGMENTS

We gratefully acknowledge the financial support provided by the UBC Carl Wieman Science Education Initiative and by UBC Vancouver students via the Teaching and Learning Enhancement Fund. We thank Steven A. Wolfman, Albert Xing, Alfred Xing, Giulia Mattia, and Erika Thompson for their contributions to this work.

REFERENCES

[1] Joel C. Adams and Randall J. Pruim. 2012. Computing for STEM Majors: Enhancing Non CS Majors' Computing Skills. In *Proc. SIGCSE '12*. 457–462. doi.org/10.1145/2157136.2157270

[2] Ruth E. Anderson, Michael D. Ernst, Robert Ordóñez, Paul Pham, and Ben Tribelhorn. 2015. A Data Programming CS1 Course. In *Proc. SIGCSE '15*. 150–155. doi.org/10.1145/2676723.2677309

[3] Austin Cory Bart, Ryan Whitcomb, Dennis Kafura, Clifford A. Shaffer, and Eli Tilevich. 2017. Computing with CORGIS: Diverse, Real-world Datasets for Introductory Computing. In *Proc. SIGCSE '17*. 57–62. doi.org/10.1145/3017680.3017708

[4] Tracy Camp, W. Richards Adrion, Betsy Bizot, Susan Davidson, Mary Hall, Susanne Hambrusch, Ellen Walker, and Stuart Zweben. 2017. Generation CS: The Growth of Computer Science. *ACM Inroads* 8, 2 (May 2017), 44–50. doi.org/10.1145/3084362

[5] Quintin Cutts, Emily Cutts, Stephen Draper, Patrick O'Donnell, and Peter Saffrey. 2010. Manipulating Mindset to Positively Influence Introductory Programming Performance. In *Proc. SIGCSE '10*. 431–435. doi.acm.org/10.1145/1734263.1734409

[6] Zachary Dodds, Ran Libeskind-Hadas, and Eliot Bush. 2012. Bio1 As CS1: Evaluating a Crossdisciplinary CS Context. In *Proc. ITiCSE '12*. 268–272. doi.org/10.1145/2325296.2325360

[7] Brian Dorn and Allison Elliott Tew. 2015. Empirical validation and application of the computing attitudes survey. *Computer Science Education* 25, 1 (2015), 1–36. https://doi.org/10.1080/08993408.2015.1014142

[8] Carol S. Dweck. 2006. *Mindset: The New Psychology of Success*. Random House.

[9] Matthias Felleisen, Robert Bruce Findler, Mathhew Flatt, and Shriram Krishnamurthi. 2001. *How to Design Programs*. MIT Press.

[10] Christian T. Jacobs, Gerard J. Gorman, Huw E. Rees, and Lorraine E. Craig. 2016. Experiences with efficient methodologies for teaching computer programming to geoscientists. *J. of Geoscience Ed.* 64, 3 (2016), 183–198. doi.org/10.5408/15-101.1

[11] Cynthia Bailey Lee. 2013. Experience Report: CS1 in MATLAB for Non-majors, with Media Computation and Peer Instruction. In *Proc. SIGCSE '13*. 35–40. doi.org/10.1145/2445196.2445214

[12] Patricia A. Marsh. 2007. What is known about student learning outcomes and how does it relate to the scholarship of teaching and learning. *Int. J. for the Scholarship of Teaching and Learning* 1, 2 (2007), 1–13. doi.org/10.20429/ijsotl.2007.010222

[13] Bruce A. Maxwell and Stephanie R. Taylor. 2017. Comparing Outcomes Across Different Contexts in CS1. In *Proc. SIGCSE '17*. 399–403. doi.org/10.1145/3017680.3017757

[14] Dawn C. Meredith and Edward F. Redish. 2013. Reinventing physics for life-sciences majors. *Physics Today* 66, 7 (2013), 38–43. doi.org/10.1063/PT.3.2046

[15] Gregor M. Novak. 2011. Just-in-time teaching. *New Directions for Teaching and Learning* 2011, 128 (Dec 2011), 63–73. doi.org/10.1002/tl.469

[16] Lauren Rich, Heather Perry, and Mark Guzdial. 2004. A CS1 Course Designed to Address Interests of Women. In *Proc. SIGCSE '04*. 190–194. doi.org/10.1145/971300.971370

[17] Linda J. Sax, Kathleen J. Lehman, and Christina Zavala. 2017. Examining the Enrollment Growth: Non-CS Majors in CS1 Courses. In *Proc. SIGCSE '17*. 513–518. doi.org/10.1145/3017680.3017781

[18] David G. Sullivan. 2013. A Data-Centric Introduction to Computer Science for Non-Majors. In *Proc. SIGCSE '13*. 71–76. doi.org/10.1145/2445196.2445222

[19] Diana Whitney and David Cooperrider. 2011. *Appreciative inquiry: a positive revolution in change*. ReadHowYouWant. com.

Brain-Computer Interface for Novice Programmers

Chris S. Crawford
University of Alabama
Dept. of Computer Science
Tuscaloosa, Alabama
crawford@cs.ua.edu

Christina Gardner-McCune
University of Florida
Dept. of Computer & Information Science & Engineering
Gainesville, Florida
gmccune@ufl.edu

Juan E. Gilbert
University of Florida
Dept. of Computer & Information Science & Engineering
Gainesville, Florida
juan@ufl.edu

ABSTRACT

As CS + X courses become more common, it is important for us to investigate ways to leverage interdisciplinary learning tools to expand the types of experiences available to students. This paper discusses our experiences introducing CS undergraduates to basic Brain-Computer Interface (BCI) concepts using NeuroBlock. Neuroblock is a visual programming environment that allows users to build applications driven by near-real-time neurophysiological (i.e., brainwaves) data. Brainwave data is captured using a commercial-grade BCI device. Students use brainwave data from the BCI device to create interactive hybrid-BCI applications (e.g., games) featuring objects that respond to students' affective states (e.g. engagement, relaxation, and attention) and keyboard events. In this paper, we describe NeuroBlock, three example activities, and results from an exploratory empirical study that suggests exposure to NeuroBlock increased students' confidence in their ability to develop applications that leverage neurophysiological signals. NeuroBlock and the discussed activities have the potential to supplement future CS + X courses by providing students hands on experiences with emerging physiological devices.

CCS CONCEPTS

• **Human-centered computing → Interactive systems and tools**; *Accessibility systems and tools*;

KEYWORDS

Brain-Computer Interface, Block-Based Programming, Neurofeedback

ACM Reference format:
Chris S. Crawford, Christina Gardner-McCune, and Juan E. Gilbert. 2018. Brain-Computer Interface for Novice Programmers. In *Proceedings of The 49th ACM Technical Symposium on Computer Science Education, Baltimore, MD, USA, Feb. 21–24, 2018 (SIGCSE '18),* 6 pages.
https://doi.org/10.1145/3159450.3159603

ACM ISBN 978-1-4503-5103-4/18/02...$15.00
https://doi.org/10.1145/3159450.3159603

1 INTRODUCTION

As computing becomes more prevalent in areas outside of computer science (CS), educators are beginning to apply interdisciplinary approaches in the classroom. This is often accomplished through CS + X courses that integrate CS concepts with a wide range of disciplines. These courses have investigated CS concepts alongside disciplines such as from law [21], robotics [13], music [19], art [10], ecology[6], and biology [6, 8, 9]. The recent emergence of consumer grade Electroencephalography (EEG) Brain-Computer Interface (BCI) devices may support future interdisciplinary approaches that merge introductory CS and neuroscience concepts. BCI devices measure central nervous system (CNS) activity and can be used replace, restore, enhance, supplement, or improve natural CNS output by interpreting brain signals [12].

Although consumer grade BCI devices are relatively new, EEG has existed since the early 1900s [1]. Jacques Vidal coined the term BCI in the early 1970s after creating a computer based system that converted brain signals into commands [25]. Early BCI research mainly focused on clinical/translational applications such as BCI-controlled wheelchairs [3], neuroprosthetics [16], and virtual keyboards [2]. However, non-medical BCI applications such as gaming [4], engagement monitoring [23], and workload estimation [7] are becoming increasingly popular. Thus, the opportunity to introduce students with limited neuroscience backgrounds to non-medical BCI applications through hands-on activities is a promising avenue to spark their interest in areas related to neuroscience. However, many text-based BCI software platforms are designed for experts and may present barriers that hinder novices. NeuroBlock, a block-based programming approach to BCI application development, was designed to address this issue. In this paper, we discuss NeuroBlock and share three example activities that may be used to supplement future introductory neuroscience CS + X courses. Recent work has shown that CS courses designed for specific groups may not enhance students confidence levels [22]. Correspondingly, we present BCI self-efficacy results that suggest NeuroBlock may increase students confidence in their ability to develop applications that leverage neurophysiological data.

2 BCI SOFTWARE TOOLS

Multiple BCI software tools exist that allow users to create BCI applications. However, many of these tools are designed for BCI experts. For example, BCI2000 is a BCI tool that allows users to create BCI applications using a graphical user interface [20]. Nevertheless, sufficient C++ knowledge is needed to create custom feedback applications. BioSig is an alternative BCI tool designed to standardize BCI development and support collaboration. This tool

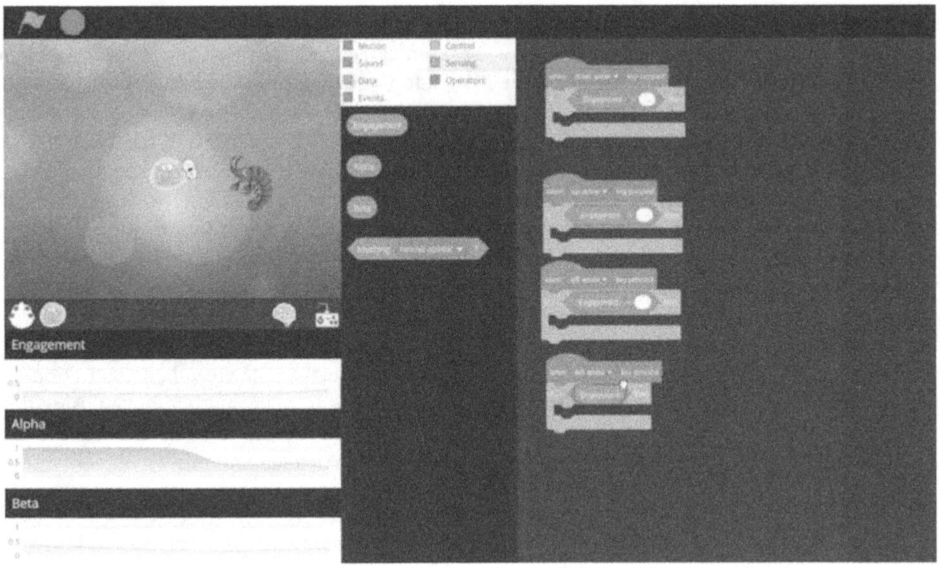

Figure 1: Amoeba application in the NeuroBlock interface.

also requires programming experience for users interested in building custom feedback applications. BCILAB is a MATLAB-based tool that provides various signal processing and classification features for building BCI applications.

Recently, researchers have made efforts to create BCI tools that support users from numerous disciplines. Venthur et al. introduced, Pyff, the first Python-based BCI tool to support growing interest in BCI applications outside of the BCI community [24]. Although this work offers advantages for novices over the C++ based systems, Python programming is still required to meaningfully modify or customize the default applications. OpenVibe attempts to address text-based BCI tools issues by presenting a graphical language for creating BCI applications [18]. The graphical language allows users to modify a BCI application by arranging visual box components. However, this approach may also present issues for novices related to communication between OpenVibe and external feedback applications that require experience with graphics libraries.

In an attempt to address gaps associated with BCI tools for novices, we developed NeuroBlock. NeuroBlock draws inspiration from tools such as Scratch [11] and App Inventor [27] in an effort to reduce barriers to entry for novices to develop BCI applications. Although languages such as Python may also address this goal, block-based programming is often easier to get started and more engaging for learners [26]. We argue that NeuroBlock may provide supplementary hands-on experience for novices investigating topics related to neurophysiology in CS + X courses. To investigate the use of NeuroBlock, we designed three simple neurofeedback exercises for undergraduate students.

In the sections that follow, we present an overview of NeuroBlock and discuss these three exercises. In section 4, we discuss an experiment that features 40 undergraduate students that were tasked with creating neurofeedback applications by completing the three exercises. In Section 6, we discuss results of the experiment related to students BCI self-efficacy followed by a discussion in Section 7. Finally, we present our conclusions in section 8.

3 NEUROBLOCK

NeuroBlock consists of 3 core components: BCI devices (e.g., EEG headset) shown in Fig. 2, EEG data communication, and a web application shown in Fig. 1. The following sections provide details about each of these components.

3.1 BCI Device

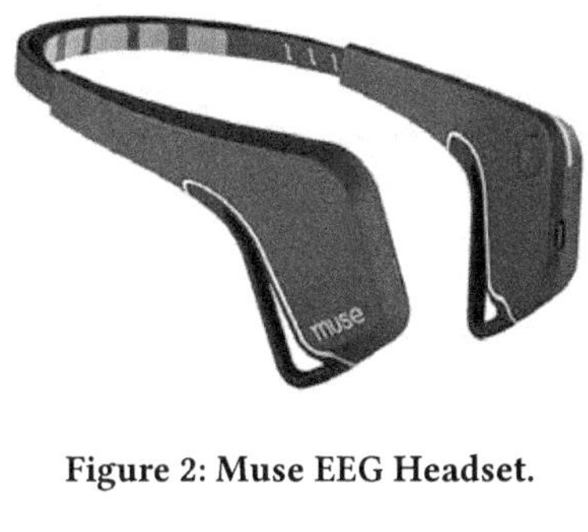

Figure 2: Muse EEG Headset.

A key part of the hands-on experience offered by NeuroBlock is the BCI device. The most recent version of NeuroBlock is compatible with the Muse EEG headset (Fig. 2), a non-invasive wireless Bluetooth device. However, any BCI device capable of communicating with a computer can be made compatible with NeuroBlock. The EEG hardware is responsible for acquiring a user's brain signals. Muse consists of 4 channels (TP9, AF7, AF8, TP10) and 1 reference (FPZ) based on the international 10-20 electrode positioning system. Muse performs at a sampling rate of 220Hz.

Currently, prerecorded data is often investigated in courses covering neurophysiology. When students are restricted to prerecorded data, they may miss the experience of building and testing live closed-loop BCI applications. NeuroBlock addresses this issue by being compatible with a BCI device capable of proving near real-time EEG data.

One drawback of using a tangible device to introduce students to BCI is signal noise. Signal noise is often caused by intense muscle movements. This is especially true for non-invasive consumer-grade devices similar to Muse. However, this can also be a learning lesson for students to assist them with understanding current BCI limitations. Observed issues can also spur discussions on trade-offs between various types of BCI devices. Furthermore, characteristics traditionally viewed as shortcomings could lead to engaging experiences for students new to BCI. For example, BCI devices usually detect intense eye blinks. Although this is not ideal for critical performance-driven medical BCI applications such as neuroprosthetics, witnessing an EEG device detect eye blinks for the first time is often an engaging experience for students new to BCI. Students experiencing mounting the BCI device may also lead to rich discussions on current BCI hardware challenges. Students can be encouraged to discuss interdisciplinary approaches that leverage areas such as fashion and ergonomics to address observed challenges with BCI hardware. These points present a few examples of how hands-on experience with a BCI device may engage students. Future investigations could lead to even more insights on the impact of providing students tangible BCI experiences.

3.2 EEG Data Communication

Once EEG signals are acquired by the EEG headset they are passed to the NeuroBlock web application. Data was captured on a computer using MuseIO, a client application for developers. MuseIO passes alpha, beta, and theta EEG frequency band data to a node.js server which also hosted the web application. EEG frequency bands are related to various affective states such as relaxation (alpha) and alertness (beta). The values were scaled between 0 and 1 prior to being passed to the web application. Abstracting lower level signal processing and communication details may prevent novices from getting discouraged with BCI development early on. Subsequently, NeuroBlock's EEG data communication pipeline only exposes basic yet useful features of the EEG data.

3.3 Web Application

The web application component (Fig. 1) was inspired by block environments such as Scratch and can be organized into 3 features: programming blocks, feedback, and stage.

Programming blocks are essential to creating neurofeedback applications with NeuroBlock. As shown in figure 1, various blocks categories can be used by students at the top center of the interface. Students can use these blocks to move objects (Motion), play sound (Sound), create variables (Data), trigger events (Events), apply logic (Control), detect mouse and affective states (Sensing), and apply mathematical operators (Operator). These blocks can be dragged towards the right to build neurofeedback applications in the workspace area.

Students are provided feedback reflecting data collected by the BCI device in the lower left corner of NeuroBlock's interface. The EEG data discussed in Section 3.2 are presented to students as line graphs. Information about the EEG device's channel quality is presented right above these line graphs as 4 circles superimposed on a top-down graphic of a head. The colors of these circles changes as the quality of a channel vary (green: good, yellow: ok, red: bad, black: none). These forms of feedback often trigger student's curiosity causing them to attempt techniques to alter their cognitive state (i.e., control breathing to relax, mental math to raise alertness). This feedback is also critical to students ability to debug their neurofeedback application. For example, a student attempting to create an application that moves an object based on relaxation levels will monitor Alpha during testing.

Students use the stage component in the top left area of NeuroBlock's interface to view their application. This component holds objects that have been programmed using the workspace. Objects can be added to the stage by clicking the gamepad icon to view object management options.

4 NEUROFEEDBACK EXERCISES

Table 1: Topics featured in neurofeedback exercises.

#	BCI Topics	CS Topics
1	EEG frequency band (Alpha), self-regulation, active-endogenous control	data, conditional logic, loops, mathematical operators, coordinates and directions
2	affective BCI (engagement), hybrid BCI	peripheral input (events), waiting, accumulator, counters, randomness, object collision
3	EEG frequency band (Beta)	concurrency

4.1 Exercise 1

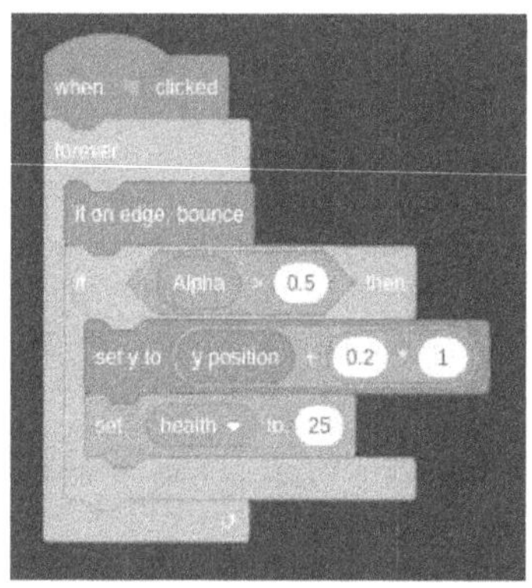

Figure 3: Exercise 1 amoeba object script.

Table 1 presents CS and BCI topics featured in each exercise. During exercise 1, students were tasked with building a neurofeedback application featuring an amoeba object (pink object in Figure 1) that moves upward when a user's relaxation level is high. Figure 3 illustrates an example program completed by a student. To successfully complete the exercise, students were required to apply CS knowledge such as data variables (health block), conditional logics, and loops. Other supplementary skills required were related to mathematical operators, coordinates, and directions.

BCI knowledge was also required to add neurophysiological functionality to the application. This included knowledge of the Alpha EEG frequency band and a general idea of the active-endogenous BCI paradigm. Active-endogenous, involves a user voluntarily inducing specific mental states.

4.2 Exercise 2

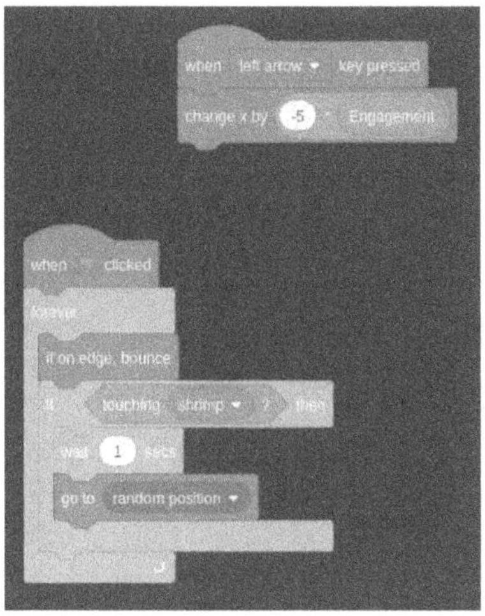

Figure 4: Exercise 2 amoeba object script.

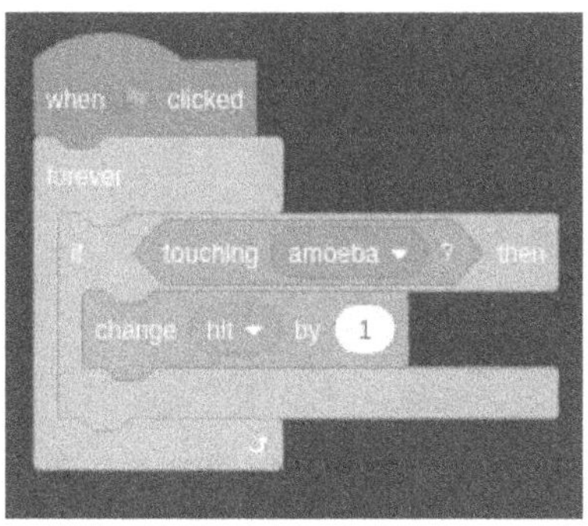

Figure 5: Exercise 2 shrimp object script.

Building off fundamental BCI and CS topics presented during exercise 1, exercise 2 explored students ability to build a slightly more complex neurofeedback application as shown in figure 4 and 5. During this exercise, students created an application that used input from the keyboard and BCI device to control the amoeba object. The amoeba's speed was mapped to engagement levels provided by the BCI device. When the amoeba and shrimp sprites collided the amoeba moved to a random location on the stage. New CS knowledge necessary during exercise 2 included peripheral input ('when key pressed' block), waiting, accumulator ('change by' block), counters, randomness ('go to random position' block) and object collision ('touching shrimp' block). Input from peripheral devices is often used to create hybrid BCI applications. Accordingly, the peripheral input could be useful in future CS + X courses that discuss hybrid BCI systems. The remaining CS topics from exercise 3 provide students experience with designing more interesting control structures that could result in more engaging BCI applications. NeuroBlock features an affective state 'engagement' block. The engagement calculation is based on an EEG frequency band ratio equation [17]. In a classroom setting, this feature could be used to supplement the discussions on the emerging field of affective BCI [14].

4.3 Exercise 3

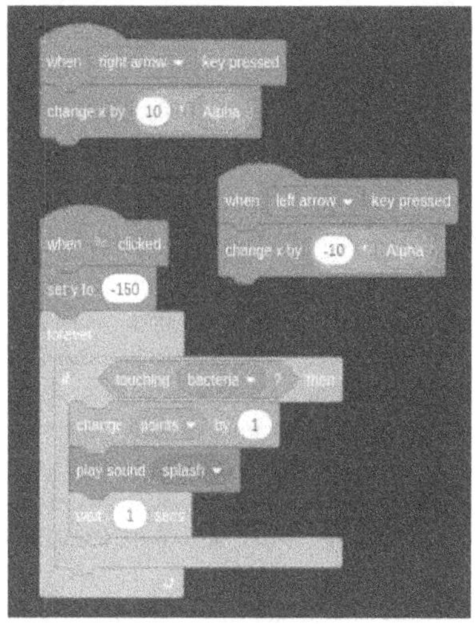

Figure 6: Exercise 3 amoeba object script.

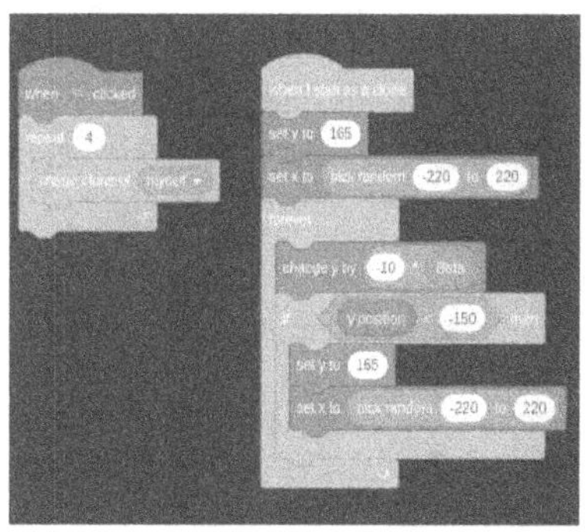

Figure 7: Exercise 3 bacteria object script.

During exercise 3, students leveraged skills they learned during exercise 1 and 2. Students were tasked with creating a neurofeedback application featuring an amoeba and multiple bacteria characters. The resulting application used keyboard and BCI input to control the amoeba. Students were asked to design the application so that the keyboard moved the amoeba left and right while bacteria fell from the top of the stage. To create multiple bacteria the 'create clone of' block had to be used. Students were directed to map the falling speed of the bacteria to attention levels using the 'beta block'. Students were also instructed that the amoeba should move faster as their level of relaxation increased. The instructions directed students to reset the bacteria's position once it fell below the stage view. The goal of the application was to use the keyboard and self-regulation to catch falling bacteria with the amoeba.

Concurrency played an important role in exercise 3 in the form of multiple objects. Students applied concurrent execution of multiple scripts using the 'green flag' block. Although a similar approach was used during exercise 2, students also managed object clones using the 'create clone of' and 'when I start as a clone' blocks in exercise 3. As shown in figure 6 and 7, students paired knowledge gained during exercise 2 of combing EEG frequency band data (Alpha) with peripheral input ('when key pressed'). Students also used skills gained during exercise 1 to leverage the 'beta block' in an active-endogenous manner. Future CS + Neuro courses could investigate additional BCI control paradigms and CS topics with NeuroBlock.

5 EXPERIMENT

Student's completed neurofeedback application development tasks during a study at the University of Florida. A total of 40 students were recruited from an introductory programming course for CS majors. The participants age ranged from 18 to 30. 90% of the participants were between 18-21 years of age. A total of 14 females and 26 males participated in the study. All participants had limited programming experience with Java which was covered in the introductory programming course. Students completed 3 exercises over the span of 5 days with 1-day gaps.

Previous work investigating CS + X approaches observed that some students may feel inadequate or incompetent about computer programming [22]. This lack of self-efficacy may impact a person's ability to perform. To investigate NeuroBlock's impact on students' confidence, a questionnaire assessing students belief in their ability to create applications that utilize brain signals was provided before the exercise. The assessment was a slightly modified version of Compeau and Higgins validated computer self-efficacy scale [5]. The modifications made the survey questions specific to BCI applications.

Afterwards, students watched a tutorial video that explained NeuroBlock's features. Next, the study facilitator covered BCI and CS topics shown in Table 1 with the students. Once the student training was complete, they were provided a list of instructions to reference while building the neurofeedback application. The hybrid-BCI exercises were informed by Bacteria Hunt, a hybrid BCI application presented in previous BCI literature [15]. Students had 20 minutes to complete the exercises. Afterwards, students completed the BCI application development self-efficacy assessment again.

6 RESULTS

To quantify results related to BCI application development self-efficacy, we surveyed students on confidence in their ability to build BCI applications before and after each exercise.

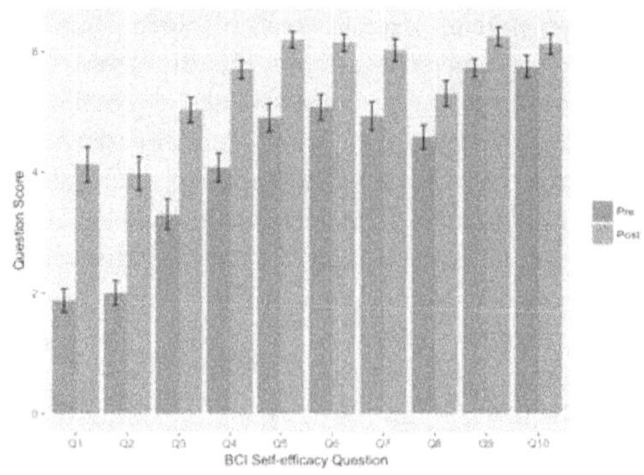

Figure 8: Exercise 1 efficacy scores.

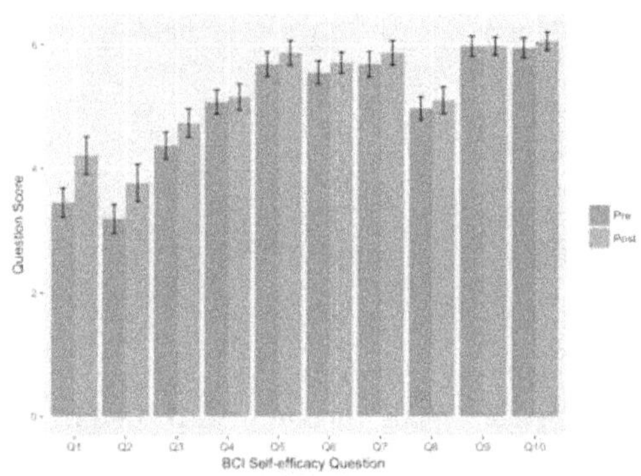

Figure 9: Exercise 2 efficacy scores.

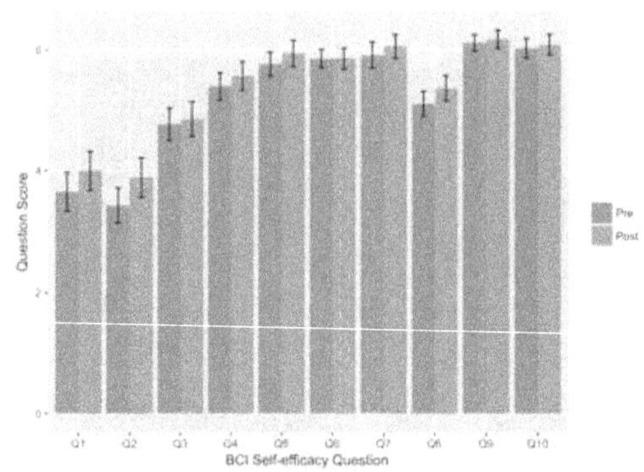

Figure 10: Exercise 3 efficacy scores.

Students reported numerically different scores before and after using NeuroBlock during exercise 1. A Wilcoxon Signed-rank test also showed that there was a significant difference between pre and post BCI self-efficacy score ($Z = -2.4266$, $p < 0.05$). The results to each of these questions are shown in figure 8. These results suggest that NeuroBlock may have positively impacted participants perception of their ability to create neurofeedback applications.

Students also reported different pre and post self-efficacy scores during exercise 2. A Wilcoxon Signed-rank test also showed a signicant difference between these scores ($Z = -3.2932$, $p < 0.001$).

The result for each of the self-efficacy questions are shown in figure 9. Similar to exercise 1, these results suggest that NeuroBlock may have had a positive impact on students BCI application development self-efficacy.

During exercise 3 students' pre and post BCI application development self-efficacy scores differed. A Wilcoxon Signed-rank test showed that there was a significant difference between these two scores ($Z = -2.3178$, $p < 0.05$). The results for each of the BCI self-efficacy questions are shown in figure 10. Similar to what was observed during exercise 1 and 2, these results suggest that further exposure to NeuroBlock positively impacted participants belief in their ability to create neurofeedback applications.

7 DISCUSSION

This work presents our experiences exploring neurofeedback exercises that provide students hands-on BCI development experience. Results from an exploratory empirical study suggest that NeuroBlock had a positive impact on students' confidence in their ability to create neurofeedback applications. This held true for all three exercises. Interestingly, the highest BCI self-efficacy score was observed after exercise 1. This could be due to multiple factors. One potential factor could be the novelty effect of interacting with a BCI device for the first time. Furthermore, the first exercise was the easiest to complete. However, the tasks gradually became more difficult as students moved on to exercise 2 and 3. Much of the novelty effect may have worn off by the time students were working on exercise 3.

Along with demonstrating how NeuroBlock may positively impact students' BCI self-efficacy, this work also provides examples of ways to merge BCI and CS topics. The discussed approach provides basic examples of exercises that could be used to add hands-on interactive activities in CS + X courses related to physiology. One limitation of this work is its focus on a single BCI paradigm (active endogenous). Additional BCI paradigms will be investigated in future work. The presented study features CS students. However, NeuroBlock may be more effective with non-CS students. Additional work is needed to validate this assumption.

8 CONCLUSION

This article presented three neurofeedback exercises for novice programmers. The core purpose of this work is to provide examples of simple neurofeedback application development exercises that may be used in future CS + X courses with NeuroBlock. This approach could allow students to gain experience building neurofeedback applications earlier. Our initial exploratory study suggests that exposure to basic neurofeedback applications development with NeuroBlock may increase students confidence in their ability to build applications that leverage brain signals. We are currently exploring additional exercises that introduce students to alternative BCI paradigms and more complex neurofeedback applications.

REFERENCES

[1] Hans Berger. 1929. ÃIJber das elektrenkephalogramm des menschen. *European archives of psychiatry and clinical neuroscience* 87, 1 (1929), 527–570.

[2] Niels Birbaumer, Nimr Ghanayim, Thilo Hinterberger, Iver Iversen, Boris Kotchoubey, Andrea KÃijbler, Juri Perelmouter, Edward Taub, and Herta Flor. 1999. A spelling device for the paralysed. *Nature* 398, 6725 (1999), 297–298.

[3] P. Brunner, L. Bianchi, C. Guger, F. Cincotti, and G. Schalk. 2011. Current trends in hardware and software for brain-computer interface (BCIs). *Journal of neural engineering* 8, 2 (2011), 025001.

[4] Guillaume Chanel, Cyril Rebetez, Mireille BÃl'trancourt, and Thierry Pun. 2011. Emotion assessment from physiological signals for adaptation of game difficulty. *IEEE Transactions on Systems, Man, and Cybernetics-Part A: Systems and Humans* 41, 6 (2011), 1052–1063.

[5] Deborah R. Compeau and Christopher A. Higgins. 1995. Computer self-efficacy: Development of a measure and initial test. *MIS quarterly* (1995), 189–211.

[6] Judith Bayard Cushing, Richard Weiss, and Yoshiya Moritani. 2007. CS0++ broadening computer science at the entry level: interdisciplinary science and computer science. *Journal of Computing Sciences in Colleges* 23, 2 (2007), 51–57.

[7] Edward Cutrell and Desney Tan. 2008. BCI for passive input in HCI. In *Proceedings of CHI*, Vol. 8. Citeseer, 1–3.

[8] Zachary Dodds, Ran Libeskind-Hadas, and Eliot Bush. 2010. When CS 1 is biology 1: crossdisciplinary collaboration as CS context. In *Proceedings of the fifteenth annual conference on Innovation and technology in computer science education*. ACM, 219–223.

[9] Zachary Dodds, Ran Libeskind-Hadas, and Eliot Bush. 2012. Bio1 as CS1: evaluating a crossdisciplinary CS context. In *Proceedings of the 17th ACM annual conference on Innovation and technology in computer science education*. ACM, 268–272.

[10] Ira Greenberg, Dianna Xu, and Deepak Kumar. 2012. *Processing: Creative Coding and Generative Art in Processing 2*. Apress.

[11] John Maloney, Mitchel Resnick, Natalie Rusk, Brian Silverman, and Evelyn Eastmond. 2010. The scratch programming language and environment. *ACM Transactions on Computing Education (TOCE)* 10, 4 (2010), 16.

[12] Dennis J. McFarland and Jonathan R. Wolpaw. 2011. Brain-computer interfaces for communication and control. *Commun. ACM* 54, 5 (2011), 60–66.

[13] Monica M. McGill. 2012. Learning to program with personal robots: Influences on student motivation. *ACM Transactions on Computing Education (TOCE)* 12, 1 (2012), 4.

[14] Christian MÃijhl, Brendan Allison, Anton Nijholt, and Guillaume Chanel. 2014. A survey of affective brain computer interfaces: principles, state-of-the-art, and challenges. *Brain-Computer Interfaces* 1, 2 (2014), 66–84.

[15] Christian MÃijhl, Hayrettin GÃijrkÃűk, Danny Plass-Oude Bos, Marieke E. Thurlings, Lasse Scherffig, Matthieu Duvinage, Alexandra A. Elbakyan, Sung-Wook Kang, Mannes Poel, and Dirk Heylen. 2010. Bacteria hunt. *Journal on Multimodal User Interfaces* 4, 1 (2010), 11–25.

[16] Gernot R. MÃijller-Putz, Reinhold Scherer, Gert Pfurtscheller, and RÃijdiger Rupp. 2005. EEG-based neuroprosthesis control: a step towards clinical practice. *Neuroscience letters* 382, 1 (2005), 169–174.

[17] Alan T. Pope, Edward H. Bogart, and Debbie S. Bartolome. 1995. Biocybernetic system evaluates indices of operator engagement in automated task. *Biological psychology* 40, 1 (1995), 187–195.

[18] Yann Renard, Fabien Lotte, Guillaume Gibert, Marco Congedo, Emmanuel Maby, Vincent Delannoy, Olivier Bertrand, and Anatole LÃl'cuyer. 2010. Openvibe: An open-source software platform to design, test, and use brainâĂŞcomputer interfaces in real and virtual environments. *Presence: teleoperators and virtual environments* 19, 1 (2010), 35–53.

[19] Alex Ruthmann, Jesse M. Heines, Gena R. Greher, Paul Laidler, and Charles Saulters II. 2010. Teaching computational thinking through musical live coding in scratch. In *Proceedings of the 41st ACM technical symposium on Computer science education*. ACM, 351–355.

[20] Gerwin Schalk, Dennis J. McFarland, Thilo Hinterberger, Niels Birbaumer, and Jonathan R. Wolpaw. 2004. BCI2000: a general-purpose brain-computer interface (BCI) system. *IEEE Transactions on biomedical engineering* 51, 6 (2004), 1034–1043.

[21] Robert H. Sloan, Cynthia Taylor, and Richard Warner. 2017. Initial Experiences with a CS Law Introduction to Computer Science (CS 1). (2017).

[22] Jeffrey A. Stone, Darcy L. Medica, and Leah Ann Fetsko. 2009. Experiences with a CS1 for the health sciences. *ACM SIGCSE Bulletin* 41, 2 (2009), 122–126.

[23] Daniel Szafir and Bilge Mutlu. 2012. Pay attention!: designing adaptive agents that monitor and improve user engagement. In *Proceedings of the SIGCHI Conference on Human Factors in Computing Systems*. ACM, 11–20.

[24] Bastian Venthur, Simon Scholler, John Williamson, Sven DÃďhne, Matthias S. Treder, Maria T. Kramarek, Klaus-Robert MÃijller, and Benjamin Blankertz. 2010. Pyff—A Pythonic Framework for Feedback Applications and Stimulus Presentation in Neuroscience. *Frontiers in neuroscience* 4 (2010), 179.

[25] Jacques J. Vidal. 1973. Toward direct brain-computer communication. *Annual Review of Biophysics and Bioengineering* 2, 1 (1973), 157–180.

[26] David Weintrop and Uri Wilensky. 2015. To block or not to block, that is the question: students' perceptions of blocks-based programming. In *Proceedings of the 14th International Conference on Interaction Design and Children*. ACM, 199–208.

[27] David Wolber, Hal Abelson, Ellen Spertus, and Liz Looney. 2011. *App Inventor*. " O'Reilly Media, Inc.".

CS for All: Catering to Diversity of Master's Students through Assignment Choices

Sohail Alhazmi, Margaret Hamilton, Charles Thevathayan
School of Science, RMIT University, Melbourne, Australia
{sohail.alhazmi, margaret.hamilton, charles.thevathayan}@rmit.edu.au

ABSTRACT

Increasingly, students enrolled into foundational CS courses such as programming fundamentals include those from many non-CS majors including Data Analytics, Business, Science and Social Sciences. Staff teaching foundational programming courses must therefore cater for varying student backgrounds, cognitive abilities and interests while teaching abstract concepts such as encapsulation, inheritance and polymorphism. In the past assignments played a major role in learning such abstract concepts as they allowed students to construct their own meanings experientially. However, a single assignment in a given domain pitched at an average student cannot cater effectively to students with varying cognitive abilities and backgrounds resulting in poor learning outcomes and student satisfaction.

In this paper we report our experience, substantially improving learning outcomes and student satisfaction in a Master's level introductory programming course with weak learning outcomes and poor student satisfaction by offering a choice of assignments. Our novel approach requires designing assignments which take into account the interests of students and their zone of proximal development which determines the extent to which a learner can grasp new concepts. Our pre and post assignment tests and survey feedback clearly show a substantial improvement in learning outcomes and student perception.

CCS CONCEPTS

• **Social and professional topics~ Computer science education**; Student assessment • **Applied computing~** Collaborative learning

KEYWORDS

Assessment Design; Novice Programming

ACM Reference format:

S. Alhazmi, M. Hamilton, and C. Thevathayan. 2018. CS for All: Catering to Diverstiy of Master's Students through Assignment Chooses. In *Proceedings of the* 49th ACM Technical Symposium on Computing Science Education, *Baltimore, MD, USA, February 2018 (SIGCSE'18)*, 6 pages.
DOI: https://doi.org/10.1145/3159450.3194464

1 INTRODUCTION

The ubiquitous nature of computing is attracting diverse cohorts of students into CS majors. Thus staff teaching foundational CS courses such as programming are facing many challenges, as most incoming students have little or no prior experience with problem solving. The object-oriented paradigm covered in the second half of these courses equips non-CS major students with programming skills to store, process and visualize data in various forms. These problems have been exacerbated in recent years with many students from non-CS but related majors (analytics, statistics and business information) enrolling into introductory programming courses [2]. Staff are therefore looking to develop new pedagogies to cater for diversity both in terms of student cognitive abilities and interests.

In the past, pedagogically sound introductory programming languages such as Pascal were focused mainly on control structures and simple algorithms. However, the increasing adoption of the object-oriented paradigm in industry and the need to incorporate prebuilt components has made it necessary to introduce many abstract object-related concepts in introductory programming courses. These problems are exacerbated for our Master's level conversion courses with only three teaching semesters, and where the second semester courses assume a good foundational knowledge of object-oriented concepts. However, a diagnostic test carried out at the beginning of the second semester Advanced Programming course (in 2016) revealed a very poor grasp of these concepts. Some staff suggest teaching object-oriented concepts can be more effective using a constructivist framework with assignments emphasizing high-level design aspects [20]. Others contend that introducing design aspects to novices may lead to cognitive overload [8].

Students are generally believed to perform best when assignments are set near the boundary of their zone of proximal development (ZPD) [1]. The ZPD, however, varies significantly within diverse student cohorts. Above average students who find the assignment tasks trivial may become bored and lose interest in the course while average students given too high a bar often become frustrated and disengaged. Catering to both ends of the students' spectrum therefore requires different formative learning pathways with varying numbers of steps and extent of guidance but leading to the same final outcomes.

Another factor contributing to learning difficulties is setting assignments using unfamiliar problems or in different domains, which have little relevance to the student major context or background. Interest is believed to play a major role in motivating students outside of class where experiential learning takes place. Students become better motivated when they perceive certain skills are useful for their pursuit of an interest

ACM ISBN 978-1-4503-5103-4/18/02...$15.00.
DOI: http://dx.doi.org/10.1145/3159450.3159464

[6]. However, such an approach becomes impractical when dealing with divergent interests of student cohorts.

These problems led to three research questions:

1. How can we design assignments that better match student background, cognitive ability, interest and learning style?
2. Does providing a choice of assignments improve learning outcomes substantially?
3. Does providing a choice of assignments improve student satisfaction?

2 LITERATURE SURVEY OF RELATED WORK

Many researchers have studied the impact of motivation and interest on cognitive processes [9]. Disengaged students were known to become actively involved when assignment tasks are tailored to match their interests [21]. Students interested in computer games have been shown to scale much greater technical depths when game-based assignments were offered even in introductory programming courses [14-15]. A number of researchers have attributed a close link between interest and previous knowledge [18]. Students are known to perform better when assignments build on their prior knowledge [21].

Students relying solely on passive learning often form invalid mental models even with simple programming concepts such as assignments [16]. Constructivism is a learning theory that posits students actively construct their own mental models from sensory data inputs and existing beliefs, instead of passively receiving knowledge [4]. Learners construct their own meanings combining their past knowledge with the information and feedback they receive [12]. Introductory programming students appear to have benefitted when a constructivist approach was combined with incremental visual tasks to introduce control structures and arrays [19]. Novices learning abstract object-oriented concepts also can benefit from a constructivist approach as it allows new knowledge to be constructed on top of prior knowledge [20].

Earlier studies show the use of choices in classroom tasks are able to tap into the intrinsic motivation of students and this can greatly improve their performance in unit tests [17]. Moreover, a phenomenological study of teachers' beliefs showed choice was a popular strategy to motivate students [7]. However, other researchers have cautioned that choices can be effective only when they meet students' need for autonomy and match their competence levels and interests [11]. To the best of our knowledge there has been very little work done analyzing the impact of assignment choices in introductory programming though it is catering to increasingly diverse student cohorts. Moreover, there is a need to compare the effect of guided assignments, assignments with scaffolding and group assignments in reducing the ZPD and improving learning outcomes.

3 OUR CONTEXT AND RESEARCH METHODOLOGY

The Programming Fundamentals (PF) course is a core introductory programming course for those doing a Masters course in CS and IT. The cohort is very diverse, mainly made up of students converting to IT or CS from other disciplines and with over 80% international students. The PF enrollment in 2017 semester 1 was 160, which also included 20% of students from other Masters programs such as Data Analytics, Statistics and Business. The coursework (60%) is made up of three components: the first assignment (20%) covering control structures and algorithms, a series of class tests (15%) and the final assignment covering the main OO concepts (25%). The vast majority of students find the OO concepts in the second part of the course very challenging. The fast pace of PF, the increasing diversity and the steadily increasing enrollment numbers have adversely impacted student learning outcomes and student satisfaction. The University identified the course as being in need of a "minor surgery" at the end of 2016, based on poor student feedback and low teaching scores (GTS).

3.1 Participatory Research for Assignment Choices

The action research methodology we used allowed us to design better assignments to meet student needs by triangulating the data obtained through enrollment data, performance in class tests and student responses in lectures and tutorials. Carr and Kemmis described action researchers as those who see the development of theory or understanding as a by-product of attempts to improve a situation [5]. A participatory action research methodology was used to arrive at suitable assignments. Participatory action research enables teaching staff and co-researchers to step back from familiar duties and power relationships to rethink established practices [3]. Participants included tutors, students and researchers. The data was gathered from student enrollment records, initial assessments and the student feedback on the first assignment. Students were also invited to reflect on existing assignments and give suggestions for new ones as the assignments were released in batches from weeks 6 to 8. Student inputs into assignments included their domains of interest, the structure of assignments (descriptive and incremental or open-ended), level of collaboration (1, 2 or 3 members) and desired feedback mechanisms (face-to-face, written). The analysis was carried out in a semi-structured way during formal and informal tutor meetings with tutors playing an active role in the creation of new assignments. All assignments included a self-reflection component where students were asked to comment on barriers to learning, the effects of the assignment on their own learning, lessons learnt and suggestions for improvement.

3.2 Performance Improvement from Assignment Choices

Pre- and post-tests were designed to measure the performance improvement from assignments. These tests focused on data structures and object-oriented concepts as these were the main learning objectives in the second set of assignments. Statistical techniques were used to measure whether choice of assignments helped to narrow the variation among our diverse student cohort.

3.3 Measuring Student Perception of Assignment Choices.

Student perceptions were measured using three different data gathering exercises:

- The semester-end anonymous survey which included questions using Likert scale and written comments.
- The personal reflection on learning and lessons learnt.
- Students' voluntary feedback related to the assignment through a specially designed survey carried out in week 12.

4 DESIGN OF ASSIGNMENTS

Analysis of diagnostic tests carried out at the commencement of the second programming course revealed that PF had very poor learning outcomes in object-oriented concepts despite half the course being devoted to them. Novice learning difficulties with object concepts such as inheritance, polymorphism and abstract-classes were attributed to poor assignment design [20]. It became increasingly evident that a single assignment pitched at the level of an average student could not cater to the different student backgrounds, interests and cognitive abilities. There were no group PF assignments in the past, despite key ZPD ideas suggesting interacting with more knowledgeable members in well-formed teams can help each individual reach their potential level [10]. The need to structure assignments taking into account cognitive abilities, interests and factors promoting good team dynamics led us to involve the students themselves in assignment setting. Table 1 shows how student preferences and feedback impacted the design of our assignments.

Assignment A1: Timetabling and Enrollment System

Rationale: This assignment involves complex interaction between many different objects, and was intended to highlight the need for good design. Some initial designs and user stories were provided as a guide.

Target: Those who have time and work well in teams of 3.

Bonus marks: Leadership, persistence mechanism, creation of pdf files or GUI for various timetables.

Assignment A2: Monster Chase Player Game

Rationale: This game-based assignment with many extensions was intended to illustrate the need to create extensible and flexible designs through inheritance and polymorphism. Students were provided initial classes for visual objects to motivate\ them.

Target: Those interested in creating games and can learn GUI and Event Handling through self-study in a team of 2.

Bonus marks: Leadership, saving objects and creating dynamic grids at run-time.

Assignment A3: Critical Path and Project Allocation

Rationale: This individual and open-ended assignment was designed to challenge the top students.

Target: Those who love a challenge and are interested in heuristic algorithms and developing tools.

Bonus marks: Automatic allocation of tasks.

Table 1: Gathering Student Feedback and Responding

Stage	Student Preferences/feedback	Response and option
Week (6)	• Choice of group and individual assignments. • Group assignments to make individual contributions clear. • Students to form teams. • Provide regular feedback and face-to-face marking. • Allow challenges such as games but permit changes.	• All assignments to incorporate feedback. • Scaffolding for game based assignments. • Semi-structured assignments for teams of 2 (A2) and 3 (A1). • Challenging assignment for individuals (A3).
Week (7)	• Difficult to form effective teams as most students are working. • Prefer directed assignment with a number of steps. • Make requirements clear.	• An individual assignment (A4) with 6 steps for each new concept. Explicit test cases were created.
Week (8)	• Analytics/statistics students wanted an assignment with data manipulation and visualization.	• Assignment (A5) using sensor data. Additional materials for GUI.

Assignment A4: Car Rental System

Rationale: This assignment was designed to be a structured and guided assignment in 6 increments. For each increment, the expected functionality and test cases were explicitly specified. Test cases for each increment were designed to ensure students reflect on their work and clear any misconceptions before proceeding to the next level.

Target: Individual students with limited problem solving skills who need assistance with each OO concept encapsulation, inheritance, polymorphism, abstract classes, exceptions and persistence.

Assignment A5: Visualization of Pedestrian Data

Rationale: This assignment was designed to meet the interests of those students majoring in Data Analytics. Students are expected to explore GUI and use their analytics knowledge from other courses to develop object-oriented solutions.

Target: Students with interest in Data Analytics and strings and are able to work independently.

Bonus marks: Generic tools able to read data and metadata in different formats.

5 PERFORMANCE IMPROVEMENTS

We noted significant improvement in the understanding of object-oriented concepts from students who undertook each of the above assignment types. The greatest gain in learning outcomes was noticed among the average and below average students who undertook these assignments. We present the feedback in Table 2, which shows the pre and post test results for all students. (The units of the metric for pre-and post-test results were out of 10).

To measure the impact of the choice of assignments on improving learning outcomes, Table 3 shows the impact by comparing the average marks before and after each assignment. The pre-test questions were given to students the week before they selected their assignment. The post-test questions were given the week after the assignment was submitted. The gain column shows the students gained improved understanding of OO concepts, though the percentage gain varied significantly.

Table 2: Gathering Student Feedback and Responding

	Number	Pre Av.	Post Av.	Gain
All	160	6.12	7.74	26.5%
Pre Test>=6.5	79	8.15	8.52	4.54%
Pre Test<6.5	81	4.22	7.07	67%

Table 3: Comparing the Average Marks of Pre and Post Test Results for Each the Assignment.

Assignment	Number	Pre Av.	Post Av.	Gain
A1	16	7.04	7.58	7.6%
A2	6	6.7	8.64	28.9%
A3	3	9.8	9.9	1.02%
A4	127	6.2	7.8	25.8%
A5	8	5.7	7.44	29.8%

The highest improvements in learning outcomes were noted for assignments A5, A2 and A4. The assignments A5 and A2 appear to have motivated students studying or interested in analytics and games respectively, confirming motivation plays a vital role in learning outcomes. Assignment A4 with its well-structured and incremental steps appears to have benefitted the bulk of the students who are transitioning into CS and IT from other disciplines. The improvement for the group assignment A1 was low as some teams were poorly formed being exclusively made up of very weak members. The challenging assignment A3 selected by the topmost students with very high pretest average (9.8) naturally had very little room for improvement (1.02%).

6 STUDENT PERCEPTION AND FEEDBACK

This section summarizes both qualitative and quantitative feedback gathered through three independent means; anonymous assignment feedback survey, students' personal reflection and semester-end mandatory anonymous survey.

6.1 Qualitative Feedback

The assignment feedback survey was specially designed to study the effectiveness of choices and the use of different assignment types from student perspectives. It had 66 responses from a survey population of 160, where students were asked to give the reasons for their assignment choice. Table 4 shows the most common responses students gave for selecting one of the five assignments. The written feedback shows assignment choices were effective as it allowed them to match their own interests and background. Responses to A4 shows students with no programming background preferred the directed and incremental assignment allowing them to learn experientially. Responses to A1 and A2 suggest most enjoyed the teamwork, use of collaboration tools and the ability to learn from one another. A2 appears to have been effective with visual learners interested in game development. A5 shows choosing an assignment relevant to their major such as Data Analytics can be a major motivating factor.

Table 4: Selected Survey Feedback from Students about Assignment

	Reasons student selected the assignment.
A1	*"There is more learning in working as a team."* *"Since it was a group assignment it was a wonderful experience working as a team. I learnt from the other team members and also shared my own knowledge."*
A2	*"I have chosen this assignment because it is a game representation and Visual outputs."* *"I love playing game and I got interested to lean programming to create games in future."*
A3	*"Assignment was open ended. Project allocation assignment was very interesting and was a source of learning therefore I selected that."* *"It was quite challenging and after successfully delivering it, I'm able to write it down in my CV."*
A4	*"Since assignment 2D provided guided instructions as well as practice test cases to ensure that code written is working. In my opinion, this is a perfect assignment for someone who is new to the area of programming."* *"Due to having a background in business not I.T. I felt that an assignment that that was quite structured would make more sense as I could focus on understanding concepts."* *"I am an Accountant by Trade and have no intention of becoming a Programmer and took this unit to learn about programming fundamentals."* *"This assignment is very good to follow what is thought in class. "For students new to programming like myself, this is actionable and relates well the class concepts."*
A5	*"I chose 2E, Data Visualization, I am doing Masters in Data Science, dealing with Data's, CSV files, Python and R coding, so I thought of working with Data in Java."* *"I am doing data science, so like to study how to read dataset and visualize in JAVA."* *"It is related to my major."*

The second source of feedback through personal reflection shows the vast majority gained a better understanding of abstract OO concepts such as polymorphism and inheritance only after completing the assignment tasks. Table 5 shows a cross-section of sample feedback highlighting the sentiments of those in the 5 groups.

In the year-end anonymous-survey question "what are the best aspects of this course?" interesting and challenging assignments were cited as the main reason by 40% of the 68 respondents. Three students, however, commented assignments were too challenging given in the short duration.

6.2 Quantitative Feedback

From a choice of 5 assignments, the majority of the students in the class selected the A4, with 127 out of 160 selecting the directed and incremental assignment (A4). The second most favored assignment was the group assignment A1 with 16 students selecting it, and third was A5 with 8, while the minimum number was 6 for A2 and 3 for the individual advanced assignment A3.

Table 5: **Selected Feedback from Students' Self-Reflection in Each Assignment.**

	Lesson learnt from the assignments
A 1	*"Overall, during the assignment 2, I learnt the logic of design a project, using Arraylist and Hashmap to store datas. This process provided confidence to me on programming."* *"It was the first time that I learnt Java. I thought it was very hard and a little boring. However, I found that it was interesting. I became interested in Java."*
A2	*"Java GUI, searching algorithms, OO principle and design."* *"Leadership, Java OOP, inheritance, polymorphism, constructors."*
A3	*"Objected oriented programming, Javafx."* *"Learned a lot of things about javafx and I appreciate everyone had their own choice of how they would like to work."*
A4	*"This project has very valuable for understanding both O/O concepts and implementation into a working program. Particularly I learnt polymorphism which is difficult to grasp without seeing the effects in front of you."* *"This semester was my first experience with programming, I have thoroughly enjoyed it so far and realise that a keen personal interest and practice in my own time will go a long way in cementing the concepts studied this semester."* *"I very much enjoyed the assignment as there were several areas that made a lot more sense to me putting into a medium size project than trying to learn in a short code segment. I really appreciated the options."* *"I gained a better understanding of almost all the programming taught in class."*
A5	*"I definitely learned a lot about creating graphs in java with Javafx with different graphs such as pie chart, line chart, and so on. I also had a good grasp with handling import values from another class. Also I have a good understanding about reading csv file in java."* *"The purpose of course was delivered accurately. Also the programming assignments including control structures and OOP programming really helped in understanding OOP concepts"*

Quantitative feedback was obtained in the assignment-choice and the year-end surveys through questions designed with 5 Likert scale responses ranging from Strongly Disliked (SD) to Strongly Liked (SL). In the assignment-choice survey, students were asked to rate whether the assignment helped them in learning OO concepts. Fig 2 shows the percentage for each option selected by students in each assignment. Over 75% of the students for assignment categories either *Liked* or *Strongly Liked* suggesting assignment choices have been beneficial to most. During the final face-to-face marking and feedback many team project students displayed excellent learning outcomes with clear evidence of knowledge transfer between members supporting the ZPD. However, 14% and 25% group assignments A1 and A2 respectively, strongly disliked them. There were three main reasons cited in survey responses and informal feedback. The main reason was the inability to find common time, limited time for group assignments and frustration when team members do not contribute. One student commented in self-reflection in A2:

"The assignment was very effective but not easy and requires a lot of time".

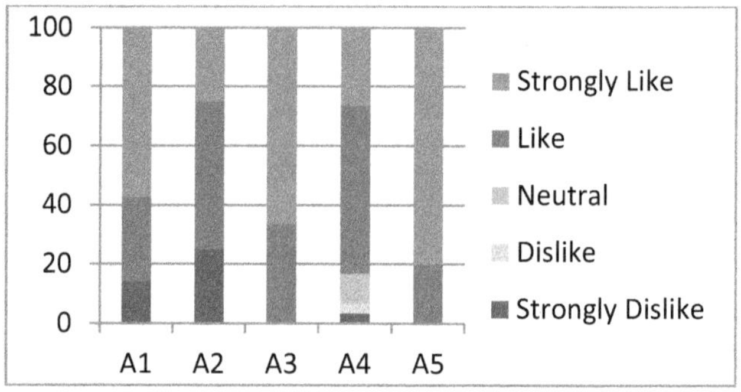

Figure 2: **Student Perception (%) about Assignments**

The semester end survey in 2017 showed over 40% improvement over the previous semester in the Good Teaching Score (GTS). This GTS is calculated from the responses to 5 standardised questions, about feedback, motivation, attention, understanding of problems and lecturer's skill in explaining concepts. For semester 2, 2016, the score had been 62 and at the end of this semester 1, 2017, it had risen to 89 (The highest first semester score at the school for this course). The survey included extra questions to measure student perceptions of their learning using a Likert scale, where SD was Strongly Disagree and SA was Strongly Agree. We present their responses in Table 6 below.

Table 6: **Student Responses to Additional Questions Related to Assignment 2:**

Questions	SD	D	N	A	SA
I found the assessment in this course challenging.	0	3	5	38	48
The course developed my problem-solving skills.	1	0	4	45	44
I enjoy doing this course.	1	4	7	35	44
I enjoy project based learning of this kind.	1	4	5	37	47
My experience with problem based learning in this course will help me work well.	1	4	6	38	45

7 LESSONS LEARNED

Programming assignments play a vital role in imparting abstract object oriented concepts. However, a single common assignment may not appeal to everyone in a diverse group. Encouraging students to participate in the learning and teaching process fosters a less formal relationship with instructors resulting in an atmosphere that aids learning [13]. The proposed approach offers greater choices by involving students in the assignment setting process. Such a process lasting for three weeks helped us to come up with assessment types catering to different target groups. These included incremental and directed, open-ended and challenging, interactive games with the use of scaffolding, data analytics with visualization and a team based one where a partial UML design is given.

Tasks in the directed incremental assignment avoided cognitive overload by creating many small sized increments. The size of increments gradually grew as students became more at ease with object-oriented paradigm. Their success in initial guided iterations spurred them to continue. Over 80% of the students doing the directed assignment successfully completed five of the six increments covering classes, inheritance, polymorphism, abstract classes and use of exceptions. The advanced students with prior knowledge opted to take on the open-ended individual assignment and scaled much greater heights than others. Many of the current approaches catering to student diversity often overlook the need to excite and challenge above average students. In our survey 100% of the students selecting such assignment found the experience rewarding.

Qualitative feedback shows some of the best learning experiences happened in well-functioning teams. Many students noted they only realized the need for OO concepts and design principles after working as a team. The leadership bonus marks helped to improve the extent of collaboration in such teams. Bonus marks, however, made little difference to learning outcomes in poorly formed teams. It is therefore necessary to ensure each assignment group has at least one above average student. Motivation appears to have played the major role for improved learning outcomes in the game and the analytics based assignments. These assignments allowed students to focus on learning the main object oriented concepts by using scaffolding or pre-created objects that handle GUI and event details.

Offering a choice of assignments, however, is likely to increase the workload the first time such an approach is used in a course. Staff must also come up with flexible marking-schemes to ensure students' option for more complex assignments are not unfairly penalized. Catering to diverse students also mandates intermediate progress-check points where staff can provide the necessary give guidance. These challenges, however, are outweighed by the benefits from improvements to retention rates, student satisfaction and preparedness for more advanced courses.

8 CONCLUSIONS

CS courses including introductory programming are increasingly catering to students from many other majors including Data Science, Business, Games and Multimedia. The changing profile of students and the abstract nature of programming and problem solving courses call for innovative teaching techniques founded on cognitive learning theories. A constructivist approach to learning and the crafting of tasks with varying ZPD, have been used effectively to avoid cognitive overload in diverse student cohorts. Therefore our proposed approach provided students a choice of assignments with different group sizes, levels of scaffolding and size of increments. Our techniques have shown significant improvements in learning outcomes especially in the more abstract object-oriented concepts. Catering to a diversity of students coming from different majors, with varying problem solving skills and backgrounds has helped to increase our student satisfaction rates by over 40%. Such an approach can help early computer science courses to cater to increasingly diverse student cohorts.

REFERENCES

[1] Anderson, N and T. Gegg-Harrison. 2013. Learning Computer Science in the "Comfort Zone of Proximal Development". SIGCSE. Denver.

[2] Anderson, R. E., R. Ordonez, and P. P. Tribelhom. 2015. A Data Programming CS1 Course. SIGCSE' 15. Kansa City, ACM.

[3] Bergold, J. and S. Thomas (2012). "Participatory Research Methods: A Methodological Approach in Motion." Qualitative Social Research 30(1).

[4] Ben-Ari, M. (2001). "Constructivism in Computer Science Education." Journal of Computers in Mathematics and Science Teaching 20(1): 45-73.

[5] Carr, W. and S. Kemmis (1986). Becoming critical: education knowledge and action research. Lewes: Falmer Press Lewes, UK, Falmer Press.

[6] Edelson, D. C. and D. M. Joseph, (2004). The Interest-Driven Learning Design Framework: Motivating Learning through Usefulness. 6th international conference on Learning sciences, Santa Monica.

[7] Flowerday, T. and G. Schraw (2000). "Teacher beliefs about instructional choice: A phenomenological study." Journal of Educational Psychology 92: 634-645.

[8] Jenkins, T. (1998). A Participative Approach to Teaching Programming ITiCSE, Dublin.

[9] Jenkins, T. and J. Davy . 2002. *"Diversity and Motivation in Introductory Programming." Innovation in Teaching and Learning in Information and Computer Sciences 1(1): 1-9.*

[10] Kasto, N. (2016). Learning to Program: The development of knowledge in Novice Programmers, Auckland University of Technology.

[11] Katz, I. and A. Assor (2007). "When Choice Motivates and When It Does Not." Educational Psychology Review 19: 429-442.

[12] Koohang, A., L. Riley and T. Smith (2009). "E-Learning and Constructivism: From Theory to Application." Interdisciplinary Journal of E-Learning and Learning Objects 5

[13] Lahtinen, E., K. Ala-Mutka and H.-M. Järvinen (2005). A Study of the Difficulties of Novice Programmers. ITiCSE, Portugal, ACM.

[14] Leutenegger, S. and J. Edgington . 2007. A Games First Approach to Teaching Ontroductory Programming. SIGCSE. Covington, Kentucky, ACM.

[15] Livovsky, J. and J. Poruban . 2014. *"Learning object-oriented paradigm by playing computer games: concepts first approach." Central European Journal of Computer Science 4(3)*

[16] Ma, L.. 2007. Investigating and Improving Novice Programmers' Mental Models of Programming Concepts. PhD, University of Strathclyde.

[17] Patall, E. A., H. Cooper and S. R. Wynn (2010). "The Effectiveness and Relative Importance of Choice in the Classroom." Journal of Educational Psychology 102(4): 896-915.

[18] Renninger, K. A., 1994"The role of interest in learning and development." The American Journal of Psychology 107(2).

[19] Thevathayan, C. and M. Hamilton (2015). Supporting Diverse Novice Programming Cohorts through Flexible and Incremental Visual Constructivist Pathways. ACM Conference on Innovation and Technology in Computer Science Education Lithuania, ACM

[20] Thramboulidis, K. C . 2003. *"A Constructivism-Based Approach to Teach Object-Oriented Programming." Journal of Informatics Education and Research 5(1).*

[21] Tobias, S. 1994. "Interest, Prior Knowledge, and Learning." Review of Educational Research 64(1)

A Landscape Study of Computer Science Education in NYC: Early Findings and Implications for Policy and Practice

Cheri Fancsali
Research Alliance for NYC Schools
285 Mercer Street, 3rd Floor
New York, NY 10003
Telephone number: +1 212-998-5614
Cheri.Fancsali@nyu.edu

Linda Tigani
Research Alliance for NYC Schools
285 Mercer Street, 3rd Floor
New York, NY 10003
Telephone number: +1 212-998-5610
Linda.Tigani@nyu.edu

Paulina Toro Isaza
Research Alliance for NYC Schools
285 Mercer Street, 3rd Floor
New York, NY 10003
Telephone number: +1 212-992-7697
Paulina.ToroIsaza@nyu.edu

Rachel Cole
Research Alliance for NYC Schools
285 Mercer Street, 3rd Floor
New York, NY 10003
Telephone number: +1 212-992-6114
Rachel.Cole@nyu.edu

ABSTRACT

NYC's Computer Science for All (CS4All) is a 10-year, districtwide initiative aimed at providing high-quality computer science (CS) education to all NYC public school students. It aspires to greatly increase the number of students, teachers, and schools exposed to CS in NYC, and to offer meaningful learning experiences that build on prior exposure and skills at every grade level. These plans include providing high-quality professional development (PD) to some 5,000 teachers, designed to help them learn new programs and pedagogies in CS education, as well as strategies for integrating CS into existing courses.

This paper presents findings from an assessment of CS in NYC, conducted in the second year of the CS4All initiative. Using a telephone survey of a representative sample of schools, we describe the current state of CS programming and training in the City. Overall, we found high participation in CS teacher training opportunities (both through and independent of the initiative) and widespread offering of CS courses

Specifically, we estimate just over half of schools districtwide (56%) participated in some type of CS training in the 2015-16 school year, and about two thirds of schools (64%) offered students some kind of CS coursework in the 2016-17 school year (through either stand-alone CS courses or the integration of CS into other subjects). The type of programming and training varied by school level (elementary, middle and high). We also explored the extent to which programming and training are reaching schools and students who are historically underrepresented in CS—including women and girls, students of color, low-income students and students with disabilities. We found that schools offering CS courses and activities served fewer Black and Latino students and more White and Asian Students, compared with schools not offering CS. This work is unique, as it is the only districtwide assessment of CS education conducted anywhere in the country to date, thus adding to an under-researched but important and growing field of study.

ACM 978-1-4503-5103-4/18/02...$15.00.
https://doi.org/10.1145/3159450.3159467

ACM Reference Format:
C. Fancsali, L. Tigani, P. Toro Isaza, and R. Cole. 2017. A Landscape Study of Computer Science Education in NYC:
Early Findings and Implications for Policy and Practice. In *Proceedings of ACM Technical Symposium on Computer Science Education, Baltimore, MD, February 2018 (SIGCSE '18)*, 6 pages.

1. INTRODUCTION

In Fall 2015, the NYC Department of Education launched CS4All through an $81 million, public/private partnership. The initiative's goal is for all 1.1 million NYC public school students to "receive a meaningful, high-quality Computer Science education at each school level: elementary, middle and high school by 2025 [6]."

The City envisions schools implementing this goal in a variety of ways, including semester-long courses and multi-year course sequences, and by integrating CS into other content areas (e.g., science, math, music, and art). To support these efforts, the City plans to provide a range of professional learning opportunities and resources to approximately 5,000 teachers.

In 2015-16, over 400 NYC teachers participated in CS4All PD, ranging from multi-day courses to programs that delivered over 100 hours of PD over three years. These opportunities were offered in three distinct avenues:

Units. PD units offered in partnership with external organizations. Units provide 30+ hours of training and support for teachers across grade levels on incorporating CS into existing curricula.

Courses. CS-focused courses lasting 100+ hours, offered in partnership with external organizations (e.g. Code/ Interactive) to prepare teachers to teach a semester or year-long course in CS (e.g., AP Computer Science Principles course).

Sequences. Teacher training for the Software Engineering Program (SEP) and SEP Jr. Program. SEP is a multi-year, multi-grade, comprehensive, standards-aligned CS and software engineering education program for grades 6-12. SEP Jr. is a one-year, multi-grade computer science experience for grades K-5.

Borough-based CS Education Managers also provide PD, resources and technical assistance to schools and teachers.

As part of an external evaluation, the Research Alliance for NYC Schools and EDC conducted a large-scale telephone survey of NYC public schools during the second year of the initiative, to better understand the current state of CS programming. This data collection effort was guided by the following research questions:

- To what extent have schools participated in CS teacher training?
- To what extent have schools offered CS courses to their students?
- What are the characteristics of schools and teachers participating in CS training and providing CS courses?
- Are there trends or gaps in CS education, particularly for students who have historically been underrepresented?
- What factors promote or hinder implementing CS4All?

This paper presents key findings from the survey. In the next section, we review relevant literature on the state of CS education. In section three, we describe our methodology, including the sample, response rates, measures and data analysis. Section four presents a summary of key findings. Section five provides conclusions and implications for the field. In section six, we note limitations to this research.

2. RELATED WORK

Though there is little research on the state of CS in American K-12 schools, a few key studies provide important information about the extent to which CS is being offered, gaps in access and participation, and barriers to implementation. One recent nationwide study conducted by Google Inc. and Gallup Inc. found that most students, parents and educators support and see the value in CS education [4]. Yet, while there has been a recent uptick in CS opportunities in schools, this same study found that only 60 percent offer at least one CS course to students, and even fewer (40%) offer classes that teach programming and coding. The study documented several barriers to offering CS, including a lack of teachers with necessary skills; lack of funding for computer equipment and software; and limited ability to offer CS because of competing priorities, such as focusing on courses related to state testing requirements.

Further, this and other studies [5,9] have found that students who are historically underrepresented in CS face greater barriers to participation. Specifically, Black and Latino students are less likely than White students to have access to CS learning opportunities in school or access to computers at home. Female students face additional social barriers: They are less likely than male students to report interest in and awareness of CS opportunities, and are less likely to report having ever learned CS.

Previous research, such as the 2010 study by the Association for Computing Machinery (ACM) and the Computer Science Teachers Association (CSTA) [10], echoes these finding. In addition, the ACM and CSTA study found that efforts to support CS policies and practices were impeded by widespread confusion over what should be counted as computer science, with the conflation of terms and concepts, such as technology education, computer science as an academic subject, and computer literacy, for example.

On a more positive note, recent data from Code.org indicate that while large gaps still exist, the percentage of underrepresented students taking the AP CS exam has increased substantially over the last decade [1]. In 2017, 27 percent of test takers nationwide were female, up from 18 percent in 2007. The proportion of underrepresented minority test takers increased from 12 to 20 percent in the same period. This growth has occurred in NYC as well, but it is notable that over 50 percent of AP CS test takers in the City come from just three of approximately 475 high schools [3], illustrating the extent to which access is a continuing challenge.

A review by Code.org of states' efforts to foster growth in CS education also shows a positive trend. The organization reports that 31 states have recently enacted policies to promote CS, such as allowing students to count CS courses toward high school graduation [2]. Nonetheless, there is still much room for more supportive CS policies, for example, requiring secondary schools to offer CS (now in place in only six states), allocating funds for CS PD and course support (in place in 14 states), and establishing rigorous K-12 CS standards (in place in 10 states).

3. METHODOLOGY

In Winter 2016, we conducted a phone survey with schools across New York City's 32 community school districts (CSDs). At each school, we spoke with someone who could answer questions about its CS programming and PD. Most often (47% of the time), we spoke with the principal. We spoke with the assistant principal in 22 percent of the surveys conducted, the technology coordinator or a teacher in 16 percent of surveys, and another teacher or staff member with CS knowledge in 15 percent of surveys.

3.1 Study Sample and Response Rates

We sampled 621 of the City's approximately 1,600 public, non-charter schools. The sample included 234 schools that were identified by the NYC DOE as having participated in the initiative's CS professional development in 2015-16—referred to as "target schools" in this paper. The remaining 387 schools were non-target schools randomly selected from within each CSD and grade configuration. In cases where there were no target schools in a particular CSD/grade configuration category, we over-sampled non-target schools so that each CSD/grade configuration stratum was represented in our sample.[1]

In total, 344 schools responded to the landscape survey, representing an overall response rate of 55 percent. Of the 344 respondents, 153 (44%) were target schools (representing a response rate of 65%), and 191 (56%) were non-target schools (representing a response rate of 49%).

To create an estimate of CS participation for the entire district, we weighted the survey responses to represent all schools districtwide. We weighted the 153 *target* school respondents to represent all 234 target schools in the district, and we weighted the 191 *non-target* school respondents to represent all 1,294 non-target schools in the district.[2] The weighted sample is similar to the district overall with respect to

[1] Target schools are defined as those in which teachers participated in SEP, SEP Jr., Beauty and Joy of Computing, Code Interactive CS AP and Exploring Computer Science, or the STEM Institute in 2015-2016. The NYC DOE identified 246 schools that met this criteria, including 12 schools from Districts 75 (which exclusively serves students with disabilities) and 79 (which serves students who have experienced interruption to their studies), as well as charter schools. We did not include these 12 schools in our sample as they serve a very specific population of students. Schools participating in the TEALS PD were included in the non-target group for this paper, but will be considered a target school in future analyses

[2] In three CSDs by grade configuration sampling strata, no sampled schools responded to our survey. Therefore, these strata are not represented in our weighted sample, and the total number of weighted schools is 1,525 instead of 1,558.

race/ethnicity, economic need, disability and English language learner status, and academic performance. With these data, we are able to estimate how all schools would have responded if we had been able to survey each of them.

Future analyses for our evaluation will include data from other sources, such as the DOE's course characteristic data and a survey of teachers who participated in CS4All PD. These data sources have inherently different strengths and weaknesses in terms of their reliability (e.g., accuracy in respondent recall, consistency in use of CS terms) and completeness (e.g., relying on a sample versus census data). It is important to note that these other sources may yield somewhat different results than the landscape survey alone.

3.2 Data Measures

The survey was comprised of open- and closed-ended items. It included questions about CS courses and activities, such as the grade levels and number of students served, content covered in the courses and activities, and types of technology used. Questions about CS training collected information on the number of teachers participating and the content and length of the PD. We also asked about challenges faced in implementing CS education and the school's motivation for offering CS.

3.3 Data Analysis

We conducted descriptive analyses of the closed- and open-ended survey questions using the weighted sample. Therefore, all percentages presented in this paper are estimates of how all schools in the City would have responded to our survey. Comparison of sample schools that did and did not respond to the survey yielded no observable differences, indicating there was no need to also weight schools to correct for response bias. For closed-ended items, we ran frequencies and cross-tabulations by key subgroups of interest, including school level (elementary, middle, high) and status as a target or non-target school. We also compared responses by school location (community school district and borough). For open-ended items, we conducted a content analysis using an iterative coding process. First, the team inductively developed a set of codes for each open-ended question using the initiative's theory of action and other documents to anticipate possible answers. Then, the team refined and added codes based on respondents' actual answers. Finally, team members discussed the coding scheme and its application to ensure consistent and accurate coding, revising the codes as necessary. Themes that emerged from the open-ended questions were reviewed in conjunction with the close-ended results, providing additional context and detail.

4. FINDINGS

The following section presents findings from our descriptive analyses of the landscape survey data.

4.1 To what extent are schools participating in CS teacher training and offering CS experiences to their students?

Understanding the state of CS education in NYC at this nascent stage of CS4All is crucial for determining the success of the initiative over time. In particular, it is important to know how programming and training opportunities have been distributed, and the extent to which the initiative is serving students historically underrepresented in CS. We were also interested in knowing the extent to which schools outside of the CS4All initiative (i.e., non-target schools) were offering CS programming and training. The landscape survey provides one measure for this early-stage assessment, from which we can monitor the district's progress toward its goals of training 5,000 teachers and ensuring that all students have a meaningful CS experience at each grade level.

4.1.1 CS Trainings

In the first year of CS4All, the NYC DOE reported offering training to over 400 teachers. The initiative prioritized teachers with no previous CS training. Because the DOE is interested in understanding the opportunities to develop teacher capacity to provide CS, we asked schools about participation in initiative-related training as well as CS training that they sought out on their own or through other efforts.

Schools reporting training. Over half of the district's schools (56%) participated in some type of CS training in the 2015-16 school year. Interestingly, among the *target schools*—that is, those identified by the NYC DOE as having participated in CS4All training—just 85 percent reported receiving such training. This may indicate that the survey respondent was mistaken, or that the NYC DOE incorrectly identified some schools. Just over half of the *non-target schools* (51%) also reported receiving training. Thus, a substantial number of schools sought opportunities to participate in CS-related training outside of the initiative, suggesting a sizable demand for such opportunities.

Representation of training across grade bands. There were some differences in training participation by grade configuration. Schools serving grades 6 through 8 (56%) and high schools (56%) were more likely to report participating in CS training than schools serving students in K-2 (39%) and 3-5 (44%).

Type of training received. When asked about training topics and content for the DOE-sponsored PD, we found that 17 percent attended trainings leading to multi-year sequences of CS (e.g., SEP and SEP Jr.), 33 percent attended trainings leading to a year-long course (e.g., AP CSP), and the remaining 50 percent attended trainings leading to integration of a CS unit into existing curricula.

For both DOE and non-DOE PD, schools more frequently reported training focused on coding or programming, compared with topics such as robotics, website development or gaming. While we do not have detailed information on the topics covered, this finding may suggest an emphasis on the theoretical study of computing (e.g., programming), rather than more creative aspects of computing including analysis and prototyping. Future evaluation efforts will attempt to explore this further.

4.1.2 CS Courses

The NYC CS4All initiative's goal is that every student in the district has at least one meaningful CS experience at each school level (elementary, middle, and high school). The DOE defines a meaningful CS experience as one that engages students by:

- A creative application of computing with connections to each student's interests, such as other academic subjects, or real-world scenarios.
- A performance task that assesses students on their ability to think through open-ended tasks.
- Hands-on experience with three CS practices: Analyzing, Prototyping, and Communicating.
- At least three of five key CS concepts: Abstraction, Algorithms, Programming, Data, and Networks [6].

Inherent to the initiative is flexibility for schools to implement CS in ways that best align with their needs and capacity. Our landscape analysis gathered information on the different types of CS programming schools offered. These data provide a picture of how schools choose to enact CS4All, and how it varied in terms of content, format, and whom was served.

Stand-alone CS courses. An estimated 43 percent of schools in the City offered at least one stand-alone CS course (see Figure 1). Among those that did, over half (52%) offered one course, 35 percent offered two, and 13 percent offered three or more. That a majority of schools with CS offered only one course suggests that multi-year sequences are not common. Further, most schools reported that 60 or fewer students took CS courses, suggesting that not all of the students in those buildings had the opportunity to take CS. Future analyses will look at course-level data to examine which students within schools access CS courses.

In terms of content, the most commonly offered subject was Programming, offered by 32 percent of schools, and Introduction to CS, offered by 26 percent of schools. Other commonly reported topics included Technology (21%)[3], and Robotics (15%), Scratch (12%), AP CS Principles (10%), AP CS A (Java) (8%), SEP (8%), Beauty and Joy of Computing (3%), and SEP Jr. (2%).

Figure 1: Schools Offering Stand-Alone Courses and Integrated Courses, 2016-17

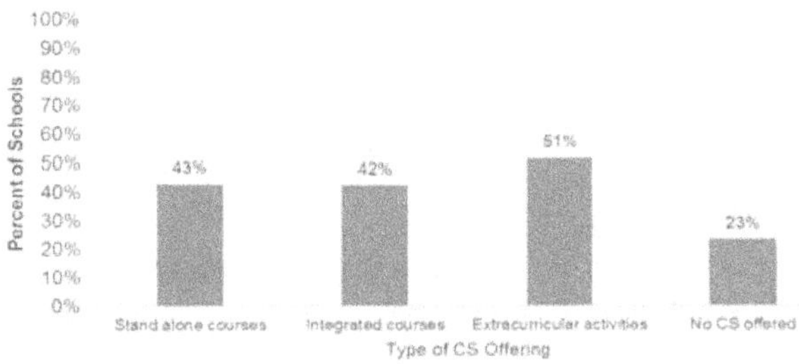

Source: Calculations based on data obtained from the Research Alliance for NYC Schools and EDC CS4All 2017 Landscape Survey. **Note:** n = 344 schools in the survey sample, N = 1,525 schools the weighted sample represents.

Integrated CS courses. Integrating CS into other subject areas is a key strategy to support learning in those areas, as well as to build a foundation in computing and computational thinking. A total of 42 percent of schools districtwide reported integrating CS into other subject-area courses. Among those that did, 44 percent offered one integrated course, 34 percent offered two, and 22 percent offered three or more. CS was most commonly integrated into STEM subjects like science (36%) or math (33%), followed by social studies (24%), English (20%), art or music (21%), and technology (20%). Similar to stand-alone courses, the CS content covered in these integrated courses was most commonly block- and text-based programming.

Differences between target and non-target schools. As with CS PD, we found that schools offering CS courses and programs included both *target* and *non-target schools* (see Figure 2). Among target schools, 87 percent offered CS courses, while 59 percent of non-target schools did so.

Notably, a small proportion of schools that reported participating in CS4All training in 2015-16 (19%) said they did *not* offer any CS courses or activities to their students in 2016-17. This suggests that despite the support of the initiative, some schools faced barriers that prevented them from implementing CS as planned.

Figure 2: Target and Non-Target Schools Offering CS Courses, 2016-17

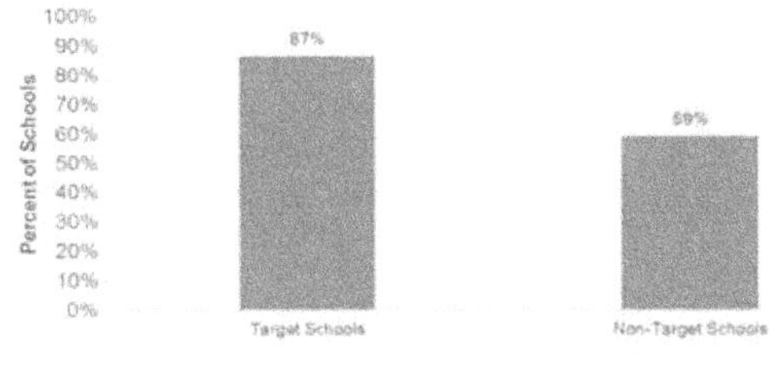

Source: Calculations based on data obtained from the Research Alliance for NYC Schools and EDC CS4All 2017 Landscape survey. **Note:** Non-CS4All Schools n = 191, N = 1,324; CS4All Schools n = 153, N = 234.

Representation across student subgroups. Equitable access is a central goal of CS4All, requiring a focus on students who are typically underrepresented in CS, including girls, students who are Black and Latino, English language learners, and students with special needs. An important contextual factor is that NYC schools serve a large population of students underrepresented in CS: in 2016-17, 67 percent of NYC students were Black or Latino, and 75 percent qualified for free or reduced-price lunch [7].

When we compared the demographic characteristics of schools that offered CS programing with those of schools that did not, we found some notable differences (see Figure 3). Schools offering CS courses and activities served fewer Black and Latino students, and more White and Asian students, than schools that did not offer CS. The schools offering CS also served fewer students in poverty and fewer students receiving special education services, and had higher average academic performance and graduation rates.

The 18 point difference in graduation rates is statistically significant, and the 15 point difference in Black and Latino student enrollment is approaching statistical significance. Other differences are not statistically significant, but suggest a trend of disparities consistent with prior research [4], which warrants continued attention and monitoring.

Figure 3: Comparison of Demographics and Academic Performance of Schools Offering and Not Offering CS Courses

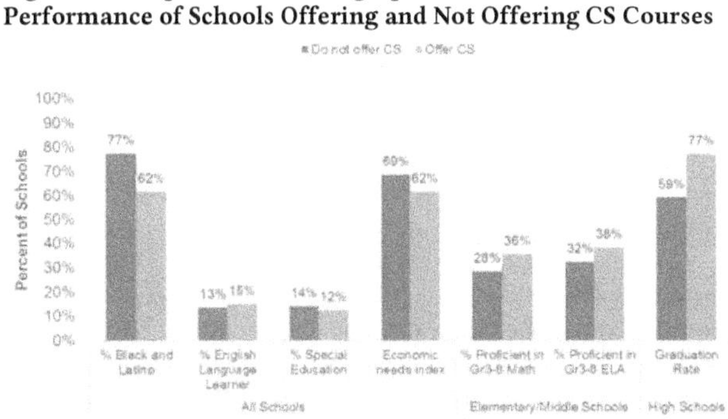

Source: Calculations based on data obtained from the Research Alliance for NYC Schools and EDC CS4All 2017 Landscape survey. **Note:** n = 344, N = 1558.

[3] "Technology" may cover a variety of topics, including courses we would not consider CS, such as keyboarding.

Notably, we did not see demographic differences between schools with teachers who participated in CS PD and those without, indicating equitable access to training that hopefully will translate into equitable access to CS courses.

4.2 What motivated schools to offer CS?

In open-ended questions, we asked schools when they first began offering CS, and their motivation to do so. These responses are useful when thinking about how to get and keep schools engaged in CS efforts.

Number of years offering CS. For most schools in the district, offering CS is a fairly novel experience. A total of 57 percent of schools currently offering CS said this was their first year doing so. Another 14 percent reported becoming involved in CS during the last two years—that is, during the launch and rollout of CS4All. The remaining schools reported having CS in place for longer. The large percentage of schools recently embarking on CS for the first time is likely a result of the City's efforts to promote such adoption.

Who brought in CS and why? Respondents reported several different reasons for bringing CS to their schools: 17 percent reported that CS was part of the school's mission or an explicit career track at the school, while 21 percent described their motivation as wanting to expose students to an important 21st century skill that will be useful in college and careers. In addition, 15 percent attributed their involvement to specific efforts of the NYC DOE, citing training, a grant opportunity, or communication from the DOE, the district, mayor, or superintendent. These findings support the idea that schools are differentially motivated when it comes to CS [8], and suggest that districtwide efforts should consider these diverse motives in developing and communicating to schools about the initiative.

When asked who introduced CS into the school, 52 percent identified a school leader and 52 percent identified a teacher as being responsible for creating CS programming. Examples of the latter included teachers of technology, science, math, Spanish, special education, and media. A few schools reported that it was a parent or PTA that encouraged bringing CS into the school. A substantial number of schools with CS reported that the person who advocated for CS programming had a personal interest or background (e.g., a degree or previous career) in CS. These findings suggest that one strategy to bring CS to schools is to find a "champion" for the work: Someone who has prior experience with CS and believes in its importance for students in K-12 schools.

4.3 What are the barriers to implementing CS4All?

In addition to asking about CS offerings and training, we also wanted to learn more about the barriers to offering CS or implementing it well. Identifying these challenges can surface possible strategies that the NYC DOE and other districts might employ to encourage schools and educators to engage in CS education. When asked about challenges, schools cited a number of issues, ranging from funding for technology to a lack of clarity about what CS is. The challenges cited by schools have also been noted in previous studies of CS education [4, 6].

Funding. The most frequently reported challenge was funding. Schools specifically cited needing additional funding for technology and internet access (50%), implementation (e.g., supporting afterschool programming or student trips, 18%), and training (16%). These findings point to the type of infrastructure needs that likely challenge most districts, and may be difficult to address without additional funding.

Staffing. The second most frequently reported challenge was related to staffing, including limited staff capacity (35%), lack of interest among staff (11%), and an inability to hire the right staff for this work (24%). Principals and teachers expressed concerns that their current staff, even those who had received some training, were not sufficiently well versed in CS (or even basic computing) to offer it in a robust way. This suggests that some teachers may need multiple training opportunities to develop the capacity to provide high-quality CS.

Competing academic priorities. Related to lack of staff interest is the difficulty of implementing CS when schools and teachers already face a heavy load of other responsibilities and expectations (reported by 33% of schools). Respondents said that teachers felt the need to focus on helping students develop stronger basic reading, writing, and math skills; pass high school graduation exams (Regents); and graduate—making it difficult or impossible to take on a new initiative. The issue of competing priorities is particularly salient for lower-achieving schools that may experience even more pressure to focus on improving test scores.

CS confusion. CS confusion (reported by 16% of schools) refers to a lack of clarity about what counts as CS, which curriculum or program a school should use, what companies or organizations to partner with, how to decide on which hardware or software to purchase, and how to integrate CS into existing curriculum. One effort that may help address this confusion is the CS4All "Blueprint," developed by DOE staff and key stakeholders (e.g., educators, researchers, industry representatives), in the NYC CS education community. The Blueprint defines CS and specifies the CS concepts and practices that need to be covered in order for a unit to qualify as high-quality CS education.

5. CONCLUSIONS AND IMPLICATIONS

NYC's CS4All is the largest initiative of its kind to date, set in the largest school district in the country. This paper presents findings from an unprecedented survey effort assessing NYC schools' CS course offerings and participation in CS training, early on in the CS4All initiative. Overall, we were encouraged to find that a high percentage of schools across the City offered students CS instruction (63%), and over half (56%) had teachers who participated in some type of CS training. As expected, most of the NYC DOE-identified target schools offered CS courses to students, but even among non-target schools, over half had participated in CS-related PD, and a similar amount offered CS courses. This finding suggests a substantial appetite for CS across the district. It is also encouraging that efforts to implement CS are not confined to high school advanced placement courses. We see healthy representation of CS participation across schools serving different grade bands, in both stand-alone and integrated coursework.

Most of these schools reported initiating CS within the last two years, which signals that the DOE's efforts to emphasize CS may be taking hold. However, most schools that offered CS reported having only one or two CS courses, suggesting that access to CS instruction within schools is limited. This is an area where we expect to see growth over the next few years, and future analyses will examine the equity of CS participation within schools.

In assessing issues of access and equity, it is important to look at not just the number of schools that send teachers to CS PD and offer CS courses, but the extent to which all students (particularly from underrepresented groups) have access to CS opportunities. This landscape survey suggests possible disparities in who has access to CS that warrant close monitoring in the future. NYC is addressing this issue by targeting schools that serve high proportions of underrepresented students for CS4All training efforts.

Further, the goal of CS4All is to provide *high-quality* CS opportunities. Our landscape survey only measured the presence of CS courses and participation in CS PD. An equally if not more important aspect of measuring the success of this initiative will involve assessing the quality of PD and student learning opportunities, as well as outcomes for teachers (e.g., increased implementation of CS, CS knowledge, comfort level teaching CS) and students (e.g., positive CS attitudes, CS knowledge, computational thinking skills, increased participation in CS coursework). Our evaluation will investigate these issues in future work. A challenge for this study and the larger field is determining how to define and measure quality CS, and identifying expected and reasonable outcomes of these efforts.

The challenges we found are similar to those reported in other studies and may help other districts anticipate and address these barriers. NYC DOE's large investment in CS training and targeted recruitment of schools serving underrepresented populations has clarified that the district sees CS overall and CS equity in particular as priorities. Despite this, many respondents cited competing academic priorities as a challenge to CS implementation, as was found in the Google/Gallup study. This points to the importance of district guidance about where CS instruction fits among other academic priorities—including preparing students for high-stakes tests. Such guidance could help educators feel free to invest the time and effort needed to successfully integrate new material into the curriculum. This is important in part because low-performing schools that feel the most pressure to focus on academic subjects—to the possible exclusion of CS—frequently serve large populations of students under-represented in CS. We see this as a broad challenge for the CS4All movement nationally, as well as in NYC.

Similarly, confusion about what constitutes CS has been cited in other work, and is not surprising given the newness of CS4All in NYC as well as around the country. Efforts to map and articulate a 'Blueprint' for CS education, as seen in NYC, may help guide work here and in other districts. This guidance should include clarity around what is and is not considered CS; what constitutes computational thinking and a 'quality' and 'meaningful' CS unit; and direction about priorities, in terms of the offerings schools should provide and how to allocate funding and resources.

Looking forward, it will be important for CS4All (and other CS initiatives around the country) to consider how needed supports and challenges may differ for schools that adopt CS later on (and who perhaps are less likely to have a 'champion' or strong staff and parent buy-in for the efforts), or that serve students with higher needs and fewer resources (e.g., lower-performing, higher-poverty schools). CS4All initiatives will also need to consider how training and supports can be adjusted to address teacher turnover.

This survey represents a rigorous and unique effort to collect a measure of CS education, early in a districtwide initiative. This provides a crucial assessment of initial progress toward CS4All's goals and feedback that the district can use to inform its efforts and increase the odds of success. Future work will investigate how the landscape has changed over time, as a result of CS4All. We hope that other districts will evaluate the results of their efforts in similarly rigorous ways, contributing to the field's knowledge of how to promote CS for all students.

6. LIMITATIONS OF THE STUDY

As noted earlier, we weighted survey respondents to estimate how all schools would have responded if they had taken the survey. It is possible that the schools that did not respond to our survey were systematically different than the schools that did. This factor introduces some uncertainty into our estimates. The full report on this survey provides the 95% confidence intervals around the point estimates and will be available on our website in early 2018.

REFERENCES

[1] Code.org. 2017. Girls set AP Computer Science record...skyrocketing growth outpaces boys. Retrieved from https://medium.com/@codeorg/girls-set-ap-computer-science-record-skyrocketing-growth-outpaces-boys-41b7c01373a5

[2] Code.org. 2017. K-12 Computer Science Policy and Implementation in States. Retrieved from https://docs.google.com/document/d/1J3TbEQt3SmIWuha7ooBPvlWpiK-pNVIV5uuQEzNzdkE/edit

[3] Leigh Ann DeLyser and Michael Preston. 2015. A public school model of CS education. In *Proceedings of the International Conference on Frontiers in Education: Computer Science and Computer Engineering* (FECS). The Steering Committee of The World Congress in Computer Science, Computer Engineering and Applied Computing (WorldComp), 233-238.

[4] Google Inc. & Gallup Inc. 2016. Trends in the State of Computer Science in U.S. K-12 Schools. Retrieved from http://goo.gl/j291E0

[5] Jane Margolis, et al. 2010. Stuck in the shallow end: Education, race, and computing. MIT Press.

[6] NYC Department of Education. About-CS4All. 2017. Retrieved from http://cs4all.nyc/about/#ee

[7] NYC Department of Education. 2017. Demographic snapshot. Retrieved from http://schools.nyc.gov/NR/rdonlyres/77954FB0-FD24-476B-AB81-3E9BBE8655D9/213559/DemographicSnapshot201213to201617Public_FINAL1.xlsx

[8] S. Vogel, R. Santo, R., & D. Ching. 2017. Visions of Computer Science Education: Unpacking Arguments for and Projected Impacts of CS4All Initiatives. In *Proceedings of the 2017 ACM SIGCSE Technical Symposium on Computer Science Education.* ACM, 609-614.

[9] Jennifer Wang, et al. 2016. Landscape of k-12 computer science education in the US: Perceptions, access, and barriers. *Proceedings of the 47th ACM Technical Symposium on Computing Science Education.* ACM.

[10] C. Wilson, L.A. Sudol, C. Stephenson, & M. Stehlik. 2010. Running on empty. Association for Computing Machinery & Computer Science Teachers Association.

Equal Outcomes 4 All: A Study of Student Learning in ECS

Steven McGee
Randi McGee-Tekula
Jennifer Duck
Catherine McGee
The Learning Partnership
mcgee@lponline.net

Lucia Dettori
DePaul University
lucia@cdm.depaul.edu

Ronald I. Greenberg
Loyola University
rig@cs.luc.edu

Eric Snow
Daisy Rutstein
SRI International
eric.snow@sri.com

Dale Reed
University of Illinois Chicago
reed@uic.edu

Brenda Wilkerson
AnitaB.org
brendadw@anitab.org

Don Yanek
Andrew M. Rasmussen
Chicago Public Schools
DGYanek@cps.edu

Dennis Brylow
Marquette University
brylow@mscs.mu.edu

ABSTRACT
This study investigated patterns in the development of computational thinking practices in the context of the Exploring Computer Science (ECS) program, a high school introductory CS course and professional development program designed to foster deep engagement through equitable inquiry around CS concepts. Past research indicates that the personal relevance of the ECS experience influences students' expectancy-value towards computer science. Expectancy-value is a construct that is predictive of career choices. We extended our research to examine whether expectancy-value influences the development of computational thinking practices. This study took place in the context of two ECS implementation projects across two states. Twenty teachers, who implemented ECS in 2016–17, participated in the research. There were 906 students who completed beginning and end of year surveys and assessments. The surveys included demographic questions, a validated expectancy-value scale, and questions about students' course experiences. The assessments were developed and validated by SRI International as a companion to the ECS course. Overall, student performance statistically increased from pretest to posttest with effect size of 0.74. There were no statistically significant differences in performance by gender or race/ethnicity. These results are consistent with earlier findings that a personally relevant course experience positively influences students' expectancy for success. These results expanded on prior research by indicating that students' expectancy-value for computer science positively influenced student learning.

CCS CONCEPTS
• **Social and professional topics→Computational thinking**; *Model curricula; Student assessment*; *K-12 education*

SIGCSE '18, February 21–24, 2018, Baltimore , MD, USA

ACM ISBN 978-1-4503-5103-4/18/02.
https://doi.org/10.1145/3159450.3159529

KEYWORDS
high school computer science; computer science assessment; computer science attitudes; Exploring Computer Science; Expectancy-Value-Cost; computer science teaching practices

ACM Reference format:
S. McGee, R. McGee-Tekula, J. Duck, C. McGee, L. Dettori, R.I. Greenberg, E. Snow, D. Rutstein, D. Reed, B. Wilkerson, D. Yanek, A.M. Rasmussen, and D. Brylow. 2018. Equal Outcomes 4 All: A Study of Student Learning in ECS. In *SIGCSE '18: 49th ACM Technical Symposium on Computer Science Education, Feb. 21–24, 2018, Baltimore, MD, USA.* ACM, NY, NY, USA, 6 pages. https://doi.org/10.1145/3159450.3159529

1 INTRODUCTION
The Exploring Computer Science (ECS) curriculum and professional development program was developed at the University of California, Los Angeles, with the goal of contributing to broadened participation of women and minorities and increased equity in the field of computer science [18]. Specifically, the ECS curriculum seeks to accomplish this goal of broadening participation by introducing the field of computer science and computational practices in a way that makes the field relevant, engaging, and stimulating for a diverse population of students. The ECS curriculum is composed of activities that are designed to engage students in computer science inquiry around meaningful problems; the ECS professional development program is designed to prepare teachers to implement these inquiry-based activities while also guiding teachers in building a classroom culture that's culturally relevant and inclusive of all students. Prior studies have successfully documented the impact of this professional development on the quality of ECS implementation [13]. Prior studies have also shown that students' perceptions of the relevance of the ECS course experiences influence students' attitudes towards computer science and influence the likelihood that students will pursue further computer science coursework [6,19].

With continued support from the United States National Science Foundation (NSF), a variety of university- and community-based organizations are adopting the ECS program and rapidly expanding its reach to cities across the United States. This study took place during the 2016–17 school year in the context of ECS implementation projects in the state of Wisconsin and in the Chicago Public Schools (CPS). In Wisconsin, there were forty-four teachers who implemented ECS throughout the state. In Chicago, CPS had recently instituted CS as a high school graduation requirement. Over 100 teachers implemented ECS, which fulfills the graduation requirement. In this research, we seek to extend our prior research to investigate the extent to which students' attitudes towards computer science influence the development of computational thinking practices.

2 THE KEY COMPONENTS OF THE ECS CURRICULUM

Key to the design of the ECS curriculum is deep engagement within a community of practice. When computer science is not taught for deep engagement but rather as an abstract academic subject, it privileges access to computer science to mostly Caucasian, male students [16]. To play an integral role in such classrooms, students must master abstract programming for programming's sake. Typically, computer science courses at both high school and college levels have been taught in this abstract way [17]. For non-Caucasian students in low-income neighborhoods, computer instruction has tended to focus on computer applications and has lacked opportunities for engaging in collaborative inquiry [16].

The ECS curriculum is designed to engender deep engagement with important computer science concepts by mimicking important features of communities in which youths participate outside the classroom. General technology use outside of school by youths of all races and genders tends to revolve around making social connections and working on practical problems [15]. Reorienting computer science instruction to be culturally relevant and focused on problem-solving experiences that are meaningful to students has the potential to increase access to computer science content, provide students with integral roles, and create opportunities for students to express themselves [4]. At the college level, computer scientists at Carnegie Mellon made progress at increasing the representation of women in their computer science program by making such changes to the nature of instruction in their introductory courses. Students develop technical fluency through solving problems of interest [17].

At the core of ECS are a set of high-leverage teaching practices [14] that support the three interwoven teaching strands of ECS: equity, inquiry, and CS concepts. The following high-leverage teaching practices enable students to *equitably* participate in student-led *inquiry* around important *CS concepts*: (a) provide a meaningful context for learning; (b) scaffold the development of CS concepts; (c) facilitate peer inquiry and collaboration; and (d) encourage multiple forms of expression [12, pp 7-8]. Inclusiveness is supported by focusing on ideas that are meaningful to students, and activities in the curriculum provide space for teachers to incorporate students' background and culture. In addition, many activities focus on real-life issues in the community—for example, students can make games that communicate messages about healthy eating or about the plight of undocumented students [18]. Resting on equity are inquiry-based activities in which students are "expected and encouraged to help define the initial conditions of problems, utilize their prior knowledge, work collaboratively, make claims using their own words, and develop multiple representations of particular solutions." [18] By engaging students in equitable inquiry through the first two strands, students gain access to the domain content of computer science, the third strand.

3 TRANSLATING THE ECS CURRICULUM INTO CLASSROOM TEACHING

Curriculum materials and activities represent one component of the ECS program. Given the significant shift in the nature of computer science teaching required for successful implementation of ECS, teachers need extended professional development to successfully adapt to the ECS model of teaching [13]. The ECS professional development program is intentionally designed to prepare teachers to implement the inquiry-based activities while also guiding them to build a classroom culture that's inclusive of all students [13]. Professional development begins with a weeklong summer workshop prior to implementing ECS. There are five key components of the ECS professional development model, the first being that teachers engage in the process of collaborative inquiry in small groups in the same way that students will engage in inquiry. The second component is that, throughout the first week, teachers participate in inquiry specifically through a teacher-learner-observer model. Each small group is assigned a lesson in which the group co-plans and teaches the lesson to the rest of the participants, who experience the lesson as learners. After the lesson, all the participants engage in reflective discussion about the experience from the point of view of the three ECS teaching strands (equity, inquiry, and CS content). These first two components of ECS professional development are consistent with what Desimone and Garet [5] call active learning in professional development. Their review of professional development found that active learning was an important component of professional development as it significantly influenced changes in teacher practices.

The third component of ECS professional development is explicit discussion and reflection on equitable practices. During the workshop, the teachers read sections of *Stuck in the Shallow End* [16], which provides rich case study descriptions of the roots of inequity in computer science. The fourth and fifth components of ECS professional development are meant to sustain teacher development over long time spans, which is another key dimension of effective professional development [5]. The fourth component is ongoing professional development during the school year and a second weeklong workshop the summer after their first year of implementation. The fifth component of ECS professional development is the development of a professional learning community. It begins in the summer workshop through the formation of small groups that engage in collaborative inquiry. It's also built up through the trust that teachers develop as they engage in tough, open discussions about equity as well as through open, honest feedback on lesson design and implementation during the workshops.

In prior research, we examined whether teachers were able to translate what they learned in professional development to create meaningful experiences for students. We used a researcher-developed end of course survey, which focused on students' perceptions of the relevance of the course (α=0.67). Almost three-fourths of the students (71%) rated the course as highly relevant. These student ratings of the perceived relevance predicted the students' attitudes towards computer science. In this study, we seek to expand on the initial evidence using instruments that have established convergent validity with measures of teaching practice. The Tripod 7C [11] is a survey of student course experiences that was empirically validated with the Danielson Framework for Teaching as part of the Gates-funded Measurement of Effective Teaching project. Teachers from a variety of subject areas and grade levels were observed and scored using the Danielson Framework. The students of those teachers were surveyed about their course experiences with the teacher using the Tripod 7C survey. The dimensions of the Tripod were correlated with the scores from the dimensions on the Danielson Framework to validate the ways in which students experience the various dimensions of the Danielson Framework. There are seven dimensions of the Tripod 7C: Challenge, Control, Care, Confer, Captivate, Clarify, and Consolidate. These dimensions are well aligned to the three ECS teaching strands.

4 INSPIRING STUDENTS IN COMPUTER SCIENCE

For this research, we seek to build on our prior work by using the expectancy-value-cost model [1] as a mediator for predicting student learning. The expectancy-value-cost model is an extension of the expectancy-value model, which is based on decades of research conducted by Eccles [8,9] on students' choices of majors and careers. These choices are dependent on how much value students put in the field as well as their expectation that they'll be successful. Eccles' research has shown that over time, students' expectations for success are based on successful experiences with relevant school subjects. The value that students place on a particular field is influenced by their enjoyment of experiences in the field, perceptions of whether the field will meet personal goals, and the extent that the field is valued by family, friends, and educators.

Of the corpus of research on the link between expectancy-value and future aspirations, there is one study in particular that is directly related to this research. The study investigates how pedagogical approaches support growth in expectancy-value [23]. The study took place at three middle schools in Greece where students were just finishing their first year of instruction in information technology. The students were surveyed on their expectancy-value as it relates to information technology, as well as the extent to which their teachers used practices that made meaningful connections to the real world through active learning and student collaboration. These practices are similar to the equity and inquiry strands of ECS. The results indicate that exposure to meaningful experiences significantly predicted growth in the value dimension but not the expectancy dimension, providing support for the hypothesis that experiences in ECS could increase the value students place on computer science by engaging them in meaningful tasks.

5 ASSESSMENT OF COMPUTATIONAL THINKING PRACTICES

To measure the development of computational thinking practices, we used assessments that were aligned to the computational thinking practices in ECS [22]. The assessments were developed and field tested by SRI International over two years using Evidence-Centered Design (ECD) [20], an assessment methodology that is especially advantageous when the knowledge and skills to be measured involve complex, multistep performances. The ECD process involved (1) working with various stakeholders to identify the important computer science skills to measure, (2) mapping those skills to a model of evidence that can support inferences about those skills, and (3) developing tasks that elicit that evidence [2]. The assessments were field tested with 941 students over two years [21].

Separate pretest and posttest forms were created. The pretest contains six tasks that measures students' initial understanding of CS concepts and computational thinking practices. For example, in one task students are asked to develop an algorithm to assign students to after school clubs that maximizes students' preferred choice while keeping the enrollment within the limits for each club. There are a series of subtasks that ask students about specific aspects of the problem and the solution. Across the six tasks there are a total of 19 subtasks that are scored independently. The posttest also contained six tasks, two of which were on the pretest and four of which were different. The two common tasks were used to equate the two forms and allow for measurement of growth from pretest to posttest. SRI developed scoring rubrics with student work examples for each of the tasks. Across all of the pretest and posttest tasks, there are a total of 30 question prompts that are each scored individually.

There were three sources of evidence for establishing the validity of the assessments at measuring the computational thinking practices covered in the ECS curriculum [3]. (a) Content validity was established through an expert review of the alignment between the knowledge and skills, the curriculum learning goals, and computational thinking practices. (b) Cognitive think-aloud interviews were conducted with a subset of students participating in the pilot test of the assessments. (c) The reliability of the assessments was moderate to high. The tasks within each assessment are well aligned with each other and with the targeted learning goals. See Snow, Rutstein, Bienkowski, and Xu [21] for additional details on the pilot study and validation results.

6 METHODS

Teachers who had previously participated in the ECS professional development program and were implementing ECS during the 2016–17 school year were invited to participate in the research. There were twenty ECS teachers from Chicago and twenty-seven ECS teachers from Wisconsin who accepted the invitation to participate. We were able to collect pre and post assessments and surveys from the students of eight of those teachers in Chicago and twelve in Wisconsin. The remaining teachers were dropped from the study since they provided only partial data.

There were 906 students who completed the ECS course, agreed to be in the study, completed the surveys and assessments, and whose parents consented for their participation. Table 1 shows the demographic characteristics of these research participants relative to the student demographic characteristics for ECS in CPS and total student population in Wisconsin. Students could select more than one race/ethnicity, so the percentages add to more than 100%. In both Wisconsin

Table 1: Demographic characteristics of ECS research participants

Demographics	CPS Research	CPS ECS	ECS WI	WI
Female	40%	50%	22%	50%
Caucasian	43%	12%	75%	71%
African-American	6%	29%	8%	9%
Hispanic	49%	50%	9%	11%
Asian	10%	7%	7%	4%

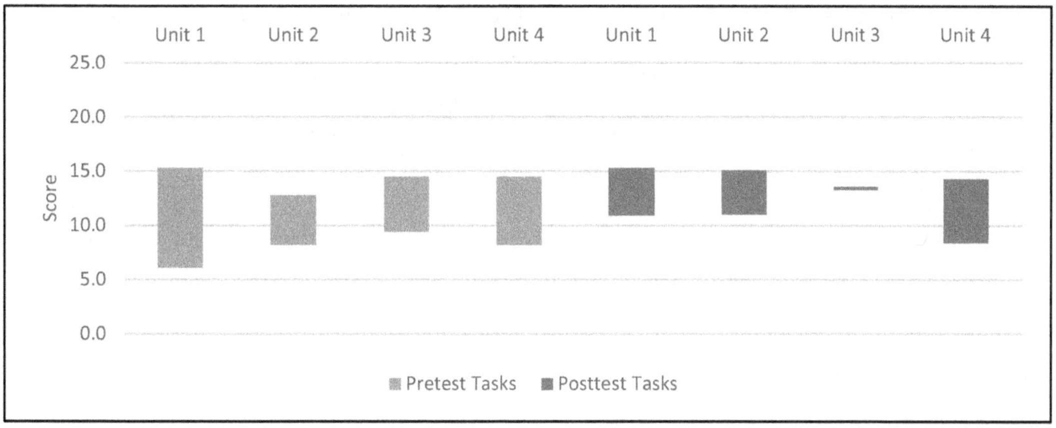

Figure 1: **Range of item difficulties for pretest and posttest performance tasks**

and CPS, there were fewer females than males who were taking an ECS course with the participating research teachers. With the graduation requirement in CPS, thepercentage of female participants is twice as high as for the teachers in Wisconsin.

The racial/ethnic characteristics of the participating students in Wisconsin were reflective of the demographic characteristics of students in the state. In Chicago, the demographic characteristics of the research participants were somewhat skewed relative to the population of students who completed ECS. There were more Caucasian students and fewer African-American students. Given the large sample size, there were sufficient numbers of students in each demographic category to be able to investigate differences in outcomes based on gender and race/ethnicity.

6.1 Assessments

During the 2016–17 school year, teachers administered the SRI-developed ECS pretest at the beginning of the year and the posttest at the end of the year. We hired The Graide Network for scoring the pretests and posttests. The Graide Network recruited and trained 26 undergraduate preservice teachers to score the performances tasks. They were provided training on each of the rubrics prior to scoring. As part of the training, each scorer scored a common set of 80 pretest responses from each question prompt in order to equate the severity of the scorers. For the posttest, we had overlapping subsets of scorers rate the same students. We used the *Facets* software version 3.71.4 to conduct Many-Facet Rasch Measurement analysis (MFRM) [10] to scale the student responses at each administration. *Facets* develops a model based on how well the student performed across the range of question prompts with set difficulties taking into account the severity of the scorer relative to the other scorers. Within MFRM, the goal is not for scorers to arrive at agreement on the scores, but instead to model the variation in how the scorers interpreted the rubrics. As long as the raters are internally consistent in how they apply the rubric, *Facets* can adjust the students' scores based on the severity or leniency of the scores relative to other scorers. We used the pretest tasks as the benchmark for scaling item difficulty. For scaling of the posttest scores, the item difficulties of the two common tasks were fixed based on the pretest scales. The overall model fit of the students, tasks, and scorers at each administration was high. For ease of interpretation, the logit scale produced by *Facets* was converted to a scale ranging from 0 to 25. Figure 1 shows a graphical representation of the range of difficulties for question prompts related to each unit. The bars show the range of difficulties for all of the subtasks related to each of the units. The overall difficulty ranges were similar across units.

6.2 Expectancy-Value-Cost

In this project, we used a validated, shortened version of Expectancy-Value-Cost survey. Barron and Hulleman [1] created separate middle school and high school versions of the survey questions. They conducted an extensive factor analysis to pare the survey length down to the shortest possible length that still provides high levels of reliability and construct invariance. In doing so, they discovered that the best factor structure treats Cost as a separate construct rather than as a negative valence within the Value dimension. The resulting survey instrument takes less than 10 minutes to administer so it can be administered more frequently. The Expectancy-Value-Cost scales were administered on the student survey at the beginning and end of the year. The alpha reliability of the Expectancy, Value, and Cost scales were 0.88, 0.92, and 0.83 respectively. We used the *Facets* software version 3.71.4 to combine the three scales into one EVC index score. The cost scale was reverse coded. We used the combined EVC index score to predict student learning outcomes.

6.3 Teaching Quality

As a proxy for the alignment of teaching practices to the ECS teaching strands, we used a combination of the Tripod 7C [11] and the pedagogical survey used by Vekiri [23]. The combination of scales across these two surveys provide a good approximation of the teaching practices that foster equity, inquiry, and development of computer science concepts. On the Tripod 7C, there are 36 Likert items that correspond to seven dimensions of teaching: *Care* relates to whether the teacher develops supportive relationships with students and is attentive to their feelings. *Challenge* refers to the extent to which the students acknowledge that the teacher places high expectations for rigor and performance. *Captivate* refers to the extent to which the teacher stimulates interest in the lessons. *Control* is related to the degree to which the class is both well-behaved and that the teacher is able to manage the class in such a way that learning can occur. *Confer* refers to the extent to which the

Table 2: **HLM Model results for the student posttest scores by student and teacher characteristics**

Posttest	Coefficient	Standard Error	t-test	p value
Average	**15.07**	**0.55**	**t(16) = 27.22**	**p<0.001**
Student Characteristics				
Pretest	**0.33**	**0.04**	**t(51) = 7.98**	**p<0.001**
Female	0.22	0.14	t(826) = 1.52	p=0.128
Hispanic	-0.03	0.19	t(479) = -0.18	p=0.857
Asian	0.09	0.28	t(826) = 0.34	p=0.734
African-American	0.001	0.31	t(826) = 0.005	p=0.996
Caucasian	0.07	0.18	t(477) = 0.39	p=0.694
Post EVC	**0.36**	**0.09**	**t(195) = 4.00**	**p<0.001**
Teacher Characteristics				
ECS Teaching Experience	**0.56**	**0.26**	**t(16) = 2.18**	**p=0.045**
Teaching Quality Index	-0.33	3.63	t(16) = -0.09	p=0.928

teacher elicits ideas from students and supports student discussion. *Clarify* refers to the extent that students feel that the teacher explains concepts well. *Consolidate* refers to the extent to which the teacher makes the learning experiences coherent for the students, giving feedback, and checking for understanding.

On the Vekiri pedagogy survey, there were 12 Likert items that correspond to three dimensions: *Active learning* relates to whether the teacher encourages exploratory and active learning through design and inquiry-oriented activities. *Collaboration* relates to whether the teacher created opportunities for student interaction and collaboration. *Meaningful learning* relates to whether the teacher highlighted the applications of computer science to the real world and tried to make computer science relevant to students' interests and everyday life.

The students within each class completed overlapping subsets of these scales on the end of course survey. We used *Facets* to develop a scale score for each student and then combined students' scores into a Teaching Quality Index score for each teacher using *WHLM* software version 7.24q.

7 RESULTS

In order to investigate the extent to which students' course experience and their attitudes towards computer science influence the development of computational thinking practices, we developed a series of models to first test the growth of computational thinking practices from pretest to posttest and then test which factors influence the amount of growth, including demographic characteristics, student attitudes, and teaching practices. The average pretest score was 15.2 out of 25 and the average posttest score was 17.0 for a growth of almost two points. We used a paired t-test to determine that this growth was statistically significant ($t(905)=20.3$, $p<0.001$) with a large effect size of 0.74, adjusted for the correlation between the pretest and posttest.

In the next model, we investigated the extent to which students' course experience and their attitudes towards computer science influence the development of computational thinking practices. We used the index of teaching quality and the years of experience teaching ECS as a proxy for students' course experience. In addition, we examined whether there were differences in student performance by students of different gender and racial/ethnic backgrounds. Table 2 shows the results of the analysis. Since students are nested within teachers, we conducted a Hierarchical Linear Model using *WHLM*. Students' demographic characteristics and the Expectancy-Value-Cost (EVC) index were included at student level. At the teacher level, we included the number of years the teacher had taught ECS and the index of teaching quality. After controlling for pretest performance, there were no statistically significant differences in posttest performance by gender or race/ethnicity. There were two statistically significant factors: the end of course EVC index and the number of years of experience teaching ECS. The teaching quality index did not have a direct effect on student posttest performance.

We examined the extent to which student demographic factors, the teaching quality index, and years of ECS teaching

Table 3: **HLM Model results for the student post EVC scores by student and teacher characteristics**

Post EVC	Coefficient	Standard Error	t-test	p value
Average	**2.68**	**0.11**	**t(16) = 23.46**	**p<0.001**
Student Characteristics				
Pre EVC	**0.65**	**0.04**	**t(72) = 15.57**	**p<0.001**
Female	-0.02	0.06	t(28) = -0.39	p=0.703
Hispanic	**-0.18**	**0.07**	**t(242) = -2.67**	**p=0.008**
Asian	0.01	0.11	t(118) = 0.09	p=0.932
African-American	-0.21	0.12	t(98) = -1.77	p=0.080
Caucasian	0.09	0.07	t(182) = 1.35	p=0178
Teacher Characteristics				
ECS Teaching Experience	0.02	0.04	t(16) = 0.46	p=0.649
Teaching Quality Index	**2.53**	**0.61**	**t(16) = 4.14**	**P<0.001**

experience influenced post expectancy. We once again conducted a Hierarchical Linear Model using *WHLM.* Table 3 shows the results of the analysis. There was one statistically significant difference in post EVC by gender or race/ethnicity. Hispanic students had lower levels of EVC after controlling for pre levels. Years of ECS teaching experience did not have a statistically significant effect on post EVC. The teaching quality index did have a statistically significant direct effect on students' levels of post EVC, which in turn influenced student learning outcomes.

8 CONCLUSION

A primary goal of the *Exploring Computer Science* curriculum and professional development program is to contribute to broadened participation of women and minorities and increased equity in the field of computer science. The curriculum is composed of activities that are designed to engage students in computer science inquiry around meaningful problems in the context of a classroom culture that's culturally relevant and inclusive of all students. In this research we examined the outcomes of implementations of ECS in Wisconsin and Chicago. If teachers are successful at implementing ECS in a manner consistent with the curriculum model, we hypothesized that the course experience would have a positive effect on students' expectancy-value and improve student learning outcomes. Overall, students achieved large learning gains from pretest to posttest and those learning gains were spread equitably across gender and race/ethnicity. These learning gains were larger for teachers with more experience teaching ECS, which suggests the extended professional development program provides opportunities for teachers to continue to improve their practices. These results also imply the importance for principals to maintain consistency in ECS teaching assignments from one year to the next.

In this research, we incorporated validated measures of teaching practices that are aligned to the equity, inquiry, and CS concepts teaching strands in ECS. The extent to which students experienced these practices positively influenced their expectancy-value toward computer science, which in turn had a positive impact on student learning. However, after controlling for these teaching practices, Hispanic students had lower levels of expectancy-value. Future research will examine how teachers' implementations of ECS can be better customized to meet the needs of Hispanic students. Despite this ethnic difference in attitude, these results provide evidence that the teachers' emphasis on equity within ECS is contributing to the broadening of participation in computer science. Eccles' prior research on expectancy-value suggests that the overall increased expectancy-value derived from the ECS course experience will lead to increases in the number of students who pursue computer science.

ACKNOWLEDGMENTS

This work was supported by grants CNS-1339392, DRL-1418149, CNS-1543217, CNS-1738515, CNS-1738572, CNS-1738691, and CNS-1738776 from the National Science Foundation (NSF). Any opinions, findings, and conclusions or recommendations expressed in this material are those of the authors and do not necessarily reflect the views of NSF.

REFERENCES

[1] Kenneth E. Barron and Chris Hulleman. 2015. Expectancy-Value-Cost Model of Motivation. In International Encyclopedia of the Social & Behavioral Sciences (2nd ed.), James Wright (Ed.). Elsevier, 503–509.

[2] Marie Bienkowski, Eric Snow, Daisy Rutstein, and Shuchi Grover. 2015. Assessment Design Patterns for Computational Thinking Practices in Secondary Computer Science: A First Look. Technical Report. SRI International, Menlo Park, CA.

[3] Robert L. Brennan (Ed.). 2006. Educational Measurement. Rowman & Littlefield.

[4] Rhonda Christensen, Gerald Knezek, and Theresa Overall. 2005. Transition Points for the Gender Gap in Computer Enjoyment. Journal of Research on Technology in Education 38, 1 (2005), 23–37.

[5] Laura M. Desimone and Michael S. Garet. 2015. Best Practices in Teachers' Professional Development. Psychology, Society, and Education 7, 3 (2015), 252–263.

[6] Lucia Dettori, Ronald I. Greenberg, Steven McGee, and Dale Reed. 2016. The Impact of The Exploring Computer Science Instructional Model in Chicago Public Schools. *Computing in Science & Engineering, 18,* 2 (2016), 10-17.

[7] Oliver Dickhäuser and Joachim Stiensmeier-Pelster. 2003. Gender Differences in the Choice of Computer Courses: Applying an Expectancy-Value Model. Social Psychology of Education 6, 3 (2003), 173–189.

[8] Jacquelynne Eccles. 2009. Who Am I and What Am I Going to Do With My Life? Personal and Collective Identities as Motivators of Action. Educational Psychologist 44, 2 (2009), 78–89.

[9] Jacquelynne S. Eccles. 2005. Studying Gender and Ethnic Differences in Participation in Math, Physical Science, and Information Technology. New Directions for Child and Adolescent Development 110 (Winter 2005), 7–14.

[10] Thomas Eckes. 2011. Introduction to Many-Facet Rasch Measurement. Peter Lang.

[11] Ronald F. Ferguson and Charlotte Danielson. 2014. How Framework for Teaching and Tripod 7Cs Evidence Distinguish Key Components of Effective Teaching. In Designing Teacher Evaluation Systems, Thomas J. Kane, Kerri A. Kerr, and Robert C. Pianta (Eds.). John Wiley, 98–143.

[12] Joanna Goode and Gail Chapman. 2016. Exploring Computer Science (Version 7.0). http://www.exploringcs.org/curriculum (2016).

[13] Joanna Goode, Jane Margolis, and Gail Chapman. 2014. Curriculum is Not Enough: The Educational Theory and Research Foundation of the Exploring Computer Science Professional Development Model. In SIGCSE '14. Association for Computing Machinery, 493–498.

[14] Pam Grossman, Karen Hammerness, and Morva McDonald. 2009. Redefining teaching, re-imagining teacher education. Teachers and Teaching: Theory and Practice 15, 2 (2009), 273–289.

[15] Mizuko Ito, Heather Horst, Matteo Bittanti, danah boyd, Becky Herr-Stephenson, Patricia G. Lange, C. J. Pascoe, and Laura Robinson. 2008. Living and Learning with New Media: Summary of Findings from the Digital Youth Project. John D. and Catherine T. MacArthur Foundation Reports on Digital Media and Learning. (Nov. 2008). http://www.macfound.org/media/article_pdfs/DML_ETHNOG_WHITEPAPER.PDF

[16] Jane Margolis, Rachel Estrella, Joanna Goode, Jennifer Jellison Holme, and Kimberly Nao. 2010. Stuck in the Shallow End: Education, Race, and Computing. MIT Press.

[17] Jane Margolis and Allan Fisher. 2002. Unlocking the Clubhouse: Women in Computing. MIT Press.

[18] Jane Margolis, Jean J. Ryoo, Cueponcaxochitl D. M. Sandoval, Clifford Lee, Joanna Goode, and Gail Chapman. 2012. Beyond Access: Broadening Participation in High School Computer Science. ACM Inroads 3, 4 (Dec. 2012), 72–78. https://doi.org/10.1145/2381083.2381102

[19] Steven McGee, Randi McGee-Tekula, Jennifer Duck, Ronald I. Greenberg, Lucia Dettori, Dale F. Reed, Brenda Wilkerson, Don Yanek, Andrew M. Rasmussen, and Gail Chapman, G. 2017. Does a Taste of Computing Increase Computer Science Enrollment? *Computing in Science & Engineering, 19,* 3 (2017), 8-18.

[20] Robert J. Mislevy and Geneva D. Haertel. 2006. Implications of Evidence-Centered Design for Educational Testing. Educational Measurement: Issues and Practice 25, 4 (2006), 6–20.

[21] Eric Snow, Daisy Rutstein, Marie Bienkowski, and Yuning Xu. 2017. Principled Assessment of Student Learning in High School Computer Science. In ICER '17 Proceedings of the 2017 ACM Conference on International Computing Education Research. 209–216.

[22] Eric Snow, Carol Tate, Daisy Rutstein, and Marie Bienkowski. 2017. Assessment Design Patterns for Computational Thinking Practices in Exploring Computer Science. Technical Report. SRI International.

[23] Ioanna Vekiri. 2013. Information science instruction and changes in girls' and boy's expectancy and value beliefs: In search of gender-equitable pedagogical practices. Computers & Education 64 (May 2013), 104–115.

Challenges Arising from Prerequisite Testing in Cybersecurity Games

Valdemar Švábenský
Masaryk University
Faculty of Informatics
Institute of Computer Science
Brno, Czech Republic
svabensky@ics.muni.cz

Jan Vykopal
Masaryk University
Institute of Computer Science
Brno, Czech Republic
vykopal@ics.muni.cz

ABSTRACT

Cybersecurity games are an attractive and popular method of active learning. However, the majority of current games are created for advanced players, which often leads to frustration in less experienced learners. Therefore, we decided to focus on a diagnostic assessment of participants entering the games. We assume that information about the players' knowledge, skills, and experience enables tutors or learning environments to suitably assist participants with game challenges and maximize learning in their virtual adventure. In this paper, we present a pioneering experiment examining the predictive value of a short quiz and self-assessment for identifying learners' readiness before playing a cybersecurity game. We hypothesized that these predictors would model players' performance. A linear regression analysis showed that the game performance can be accurately predicted by well-designed prerequisite testing, but not by self-assessment. At the same time, we identified major challenges related to the design of pretests for cybersecurity games: calibrating test questions with respect to the skills relevant for the game, minimizing the quiz's length while maximizing its informative value, and embedding the pretest in the game. Our results are relevant for educational researchers and cybersecurity instructors of students at all learning levels.

KEYWORDS

active learning, cybersecurity games, diagnostic assessment, prerequisite testing, self-assessment, linear regression modeling

ACM Reference format:

Valdemar Švábenský and Jan Vykopal. 2018. Challenges Arising from Prerequisite Testing in Cybersecurity Games. In *Proceedings of The 49th ACM Technical Symposium on Computer Science Education, Baltimore, MD, USA, February 21–24, 2018 (SIGCSE '18),* 6 pages.
https://doi.org/10.1145/3159450.3159454

SIGCSE '18, February 21–24, 2018, Baltimore, MD, USA

ACM ISBN 978-1-4503-5103-4/18/02...$15.00
https://doi.org/10.1145/3159450.3159454

1 INTRODUCTION

Cybersecurity games allow participants to test their knowledge and exercise their skills in different areas of computer security. Although carried out in a closed and controlled environment, the games simulate practical, real-world situations. The players can attack and defend computer systems, analyze network traffic, or disassemble binaries without any negative consequences in reality.

Studies confirm multiple benefits of cybersecurity games [16, 17, 21]. They can inspire interest in computer security and motivate participants to explore the field further. Games designed specifically for education enrich the curriculum and test the learners' competence in an authentic setting, enabling them to discover their strengths and weaknesses. Ranking well in competitive games often leads to peer recognition, (monetary) prizes, or job opportunities.

Competitions and games of various difficulty levels and focus are spreading widely, from informal online hacking communities to universities and professional security conferences. The number of participants in cybersecurity games is growing exponentially [17]. At the same time, several authors argue that although high-quality games are available, they offer little educational value to learners [16, 20]. The games often require substantial knowledge of the problem domain, as well as practical expertise, in advance. As a result, the majority of computer science students are unable to participate. Even worse, some students' interest and motivation may diminish after an unsuccessful attempt [16]. Research suggests that games and contests are effective only for already skilled players, whose skills "closely match those required by the competition" [17].

Achieving *game balance* (assigning tasks that are suitable for the player's skill, neither trivial nor impossible to solve [14, 16]) is vital in educational games. One approach to achieving game balance is introducing methods of adaptive learning [4], which change the difficulty of the tasks during the game based on the player's success rate. Another solution is a diagnostic assessment by prerequisite testing, which is the topic of this paper. This approach, suggested in pedagogical theory [9, 13], refers to testing the player before or during a game to determine whether the player's skills are sufficient to finish the tasks, thus providing game balance [16].

This work's main motivation is the demand for timely identification of students who may require help while playing, so that their individual needs can be appropriately addressed. This can be done by providing learners with more precise instructions, hints, or relevant study materials.

To explore the predictive value of both self-assessment and prerequisite tests, we conducted an experiment involving 67 learners and two games. They completed a short questionnaire, played a game, and then reflected on their experience in another survey. Tracking the players' actions during the game allows us to compare the assessment results with the in-game performance. Based on this experiment, we seek to answer two research questions:

(1) Can a prerequisite test accurately model learners' performance in cybersecurity games?
(2) Is self-assessment a reliable indicator of ability in the context of cybersecurity?

2 RELATED WORK

Research into diagnostic assessment of cybersecurity skills is sparse and not yet mature. Therefore, this section also mentions works dealing with assessment and testing in other educational domains.

While Nagarajan et al. [14] stress that measuring skills before and after playing is vital to determine the game's effectiveness, they report that security training programs do not implement this measurement. To the best of our knowledge, we can confirm this observation.

Mirkovic et al. [11, 12] emphasize considering individual skills in team cybersecurity games to balance the teams and give everyone an equal chance to succeed. Before using cybersecurity games in classrooms, Mirkovic and Peterson [11] surveyed the students about their skills to create balanced teams. Unfortunately, the paper does not provide details about the process. In another study [12], the participants reported their knowledge of programming, security, and tools that were to be used later. Again, the survey results were used to balance the teams. However, the authors concluded that this led to inequality among the teams, as the self-assessment was often inaccurate. They recommend "conducting a short quiz-type assessment prior to the event", but do not specify how to do this.

Next, Bolívar-Cruz et al. [3] examined self-assessment of university students in oral communication. Their literature review shows that self-assessment's accuracy is generally low or questionable, but also warns readers about methodological errors in some of the previous studies. Allen and Van Der Velden [1] advocate using self-assessment complemented by independent, objective tests to increase the reliability of results. They argue that people know the level of their skills best but also warn readers of its issues, including misunderstood skill items, an ambiguous rating scale, and the risk of an unreliable answer (either intentional or not).

Finally, Govindasamy [5] suggests applying pretests in e-learning courses to test both minimum requirements and proficiency. Based on the results, the learner can be directed to a simpler or more difficult course, or skip the already familiar areas in the current course. Educational literature [9, 13, 15] advocates the use of prerequisite testing in teaching practice.

3 STRUCTURE OF A CYBERSECURITY GAME

We use instances of a cybersecurity game following a generic format of a hands-on activity, which is performed in a realistic network environment emulated by the KYPO cyber range [19].

Figure 1 shows the scheme of the game, which is structured into successive levels leading to the final objective, such as data theft. Before the start, each player has access to limited network resources and a brief information about the goal. Every level is finished by finding a correct flag (a short string); this accomplishment is awarded a specified number of points contributing to the player's total score. The game ends upon entering the last flag or when a predefined final check of the system's state succeeds.

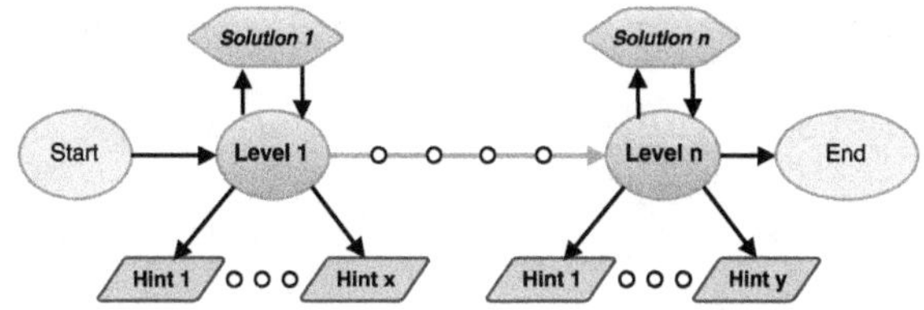

Figure 1: The general structure of the cybersecurity game used in the experiment

Table 1: The design of the experiment with the number of participants and their gender

67 participants				
Session 1 9♂, 1♀	Session 2 4♂, 3♀	Session 3 15♂, 3♀	Session 4 12♂, 0♀	Session 5 19♂, 1♀
Pretest 1 5 items			+ 2 items	Pretest 2 4 items
Self-assessment 3 items				
Game 1 6 levels				Game 2 4 levels
Post-game feedback				

The game provides optional scaffolding by offering hints. If the player struggles with a level, these hints can be used in exchange for penalization by negative points. There is evidence that game elements such as points and levels can improve the overall effectiveness of learning [8]. It is also possible to skip the level, display the recommended solution, and quit the game at any time.

The generic nature of the game format allows us to collect generic game events, regardless of the topic of the particular game and technical infrastructure used. The game events describe the player's interaction with the game interface, namely: starting and ending the game or each level, submitting incorrect flags and their content, using hints, skipping a level, and displaying a solution. Each event contains a timestamp and a unique ID of the player.

4 EXPERIMENT DESIGN

Table 1 summarizes the phases and structure of the experiment. At first, each player completed a prerequisite test and a self-assessment questionnaire. The players then proceeded to a game, where their performance was tracked using the generic game events. Finally, the players filled in a post-game feedback questionnaire. The self-assessment and pretest data were used to create a linear regression model of learners' skill, which is expressed by two metrics: the total game score and number of levels finished.

4.1 Participants

A total of 67 cybersecurity students and professionals of various levels of expertise, background, and nationality participated, covering a broad spectrum of the games' target audience. The players' only motivation was their interest, as they did not receive any incentives

Table 2: Characteristics of the selected games G1 and G2

Level	Score [pts]		Hints		Penalty [pts]	
	G1	G2	G1	G2	G1	G2
1	8	16	2	2	−2, −2	−3, −5
2	12	22	2	2	−2, −3	−7, −5
3	23	27	3	4	−1, −3, −2	−5, −10, −0, −0
4	20	35	2	4	−2, −3	−5, −10, −5, −5
5	22	—	2	—	−3, −4	—
6	15	—	2	—	−5, −2	—
Total	100	100	13	12	−34	−60

for taking part in the study. The participants were informed about the intended use of the acquired data solely for the purpose of this experiment. The data was anonymized during the processing.

The learners were divided into five game sessions, each lasting two hours. The first session included 10 computer science students from St. Pölten University of Applied Sciences, Austria. The second session consisted of 7 employees of the Computer Security Incident Response Team of Pavol Jozef Šafárik University in Košice, Slovakia. The third session included 18 computer science students from Masaryk University, Brno, Czech Republic. The fourth session included 12 finalists of a Czech high school cybersecurity competition. The fifth session included 20 attendees of the AIMS 2017 conference on network security and management, held in Zurich, Switzerland.

4.2 Selected cybersecurity games

We have two games G1 and G2 in this experiment to test various game tasks and prerequisite tests. Table 2 details the maximum score, the number of hints, and scoring penalties for taking the hints in each level of both games.

The topic of the G1 game played in the first four game sessions is information theft from a database server of a fictitious bank. Each player initially controls a single Linux host in an unknown network. The player must gradually gain and maintain access to other hosts that are a part of the bank's network infrastructure, and, finally, steal confidential information. This mission is split into six levels, in which the players exercise penetration testing skills.

To provide comparative data, 20 participants of the fifth game session played another game, G2, with the topic of gaining access to a remote server and destroying stored data. This game is split into four levels with learning objectives similar to the levels of G1.

4.3 Skill measurement before the game

We created quizzes testing prerequisites for each of the two selected games using a model for question design by Beatty et al. [2]. Details about the pretest's design can be found in [22]. In the first three game sessions, the players completed a pretest consisting of five questions. In the fourth session, this pretest was enhanced by two extra questions. In the fifth session, a different but similar pretest consisting of four questions was used. The prerequisite quizzes capture a representative sample of key knowledge and skills exercised in the games. Below is an example of a question for the first level of both games (an asterisk marks the correct answer):

```
What is the effect of the command ping 10.0.0.3?
a)* Tests the reachability of a host with an IP address 10.0.0.3.
b)  Scans open ports of the server with an IP address 10.0.0.3.
c)  Error, the syntax of the command is incorrect.
d)  Measures the number of network hops to a host with an IP address
    10.0.0.3.
```

To evaluate the test, we used a simple *dichotomous* scoring method awarding one point for a fully correct answer, and zero points for a partially or entirely incorrect answer per question. Moreover, after responding to each question, a learner rated the level of certainty in the answer on a five-step scale developed by Hassmén and Hunt [6, 7]. This scoring method, referred to as *confidence assessment*, yielded another test score. In both cases, a sum of the respective scores was considered as an estimate of each learner's total readiness.

Apart from the prerequisite test, each player completed a 3-item self-assessment questionnaire before starting the game. Since there is no standardized methodology for designing the questions, we created them with respect to the content of the particular games. The survey asked the players to self-evaluate their expertise with using three tools needed in the games: for port scanning (Nmap), vulnerability exploiting (Metasploit), and password attacks (John the Ripper). For each tool, the player selected one of four levels of competence on the following ordered scale: zero experience, beginner (basic knowledge), intermediate (some practical experience), and expert (professional working experience). To aggregate the learners' input, we used the median to express the central tendency of each player's self-assessment. Since the self-assessment data are ordinal, we avoided using the arithmetic mean.

4.4 Post-game feedback

After finishing the game, the participants completed a post-game feedback questionnaire. The goal of the survey was to have each player subjectively assess the game's difficulty on a scale from 1 (trivial) to 5 (impossible), and reflect if any learning occurred. This reflection helps to determine if game balance was achieved, and if the player perceived the game as educational. Unfortunately, due to a technical error, we collected the results from only 46 participants.

5 RESULTS

Table 3 reports the examined variables and descriptive statistics of the collected data for G1, which are further detailed in Figure 2. The boxplots show distributions of the game score (T) grouped by the dichotomous quiz score (P_d) and the input from the self-assessment (S). The boxplots showing the distributions of finished levels (L) are almost identical considering patterns of the medians, and thus were omitted. Also, statistically significant ($p \leq 0.02$) Pearson and Spearman correlations (ranging from 0.36 to 0.60) were reported between the score and pretest and between levels completed and pretest (both scoring methods in both cases). Finally, there was strong evidence that all performance predictors and skill descriptors negatively correlate with how difficult the game is perceived ($p \leq 0.02$, coefficients ranging from −0.37 to −0.52).

Next, we modeled the learners' skill (dependent variables T and L) using independent variables P_d, P_c, and S. Three different sets of regression analyses were performed. First, we used the data of the 47 participants playing G1, ignoring the two extra pretest

Table 3: Examined variables and descriptive statistics of the participant data for the four G1 sessions and 5-item pretest

Variable		Possible range	Min	Max	Avg	Med
Self-assessment	S	0 to 3	0	2	0.9	1
Pretest (dich.)	P_d	0 to 5	0	5	3.9	4
Pretest (conf.)	P_c	−300 to 250	−91	240	150.6	155
Game score	T	0 to 100	0	100	49.7	55
Levels finished	L	0 to 6	0	6	3.5	4
Difficulty	D	1 to 5	2	5	3.5	3

Table 4: The overall best linear regression models (see Table 3 for the description of the variables).

Game	Model	R^2	F-statistic	p-value
G1	$T = 8.98 + 10.34 \cdot P_d$	0.17	9.36	0.004
G1	$T = 10.87 + 0.23 \cdot P_c$	0.31	15.66	< 0.001
G1	$L = 1.62 + 0.48 \cdot P_d$	0.14	7.22	0.010
G1	$L = 1.73 + 0.01 \cdot P_c$	0.24	10.99	0.002

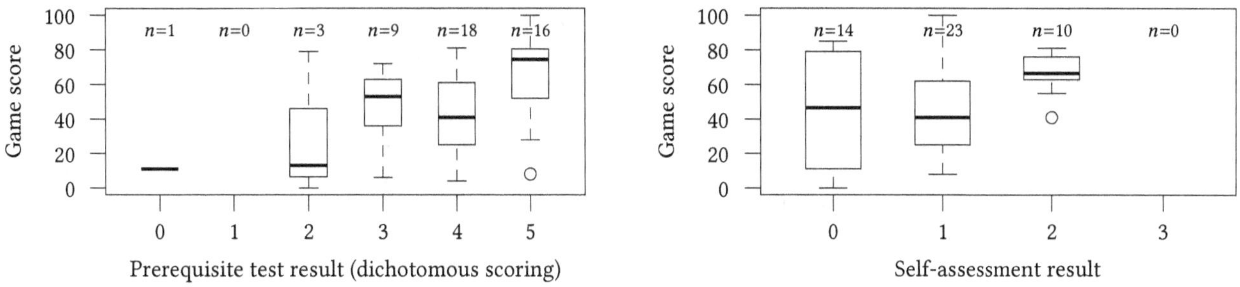

Figure 2: Boxplots depicting relationships between test score, self-assessment, and game score in G1

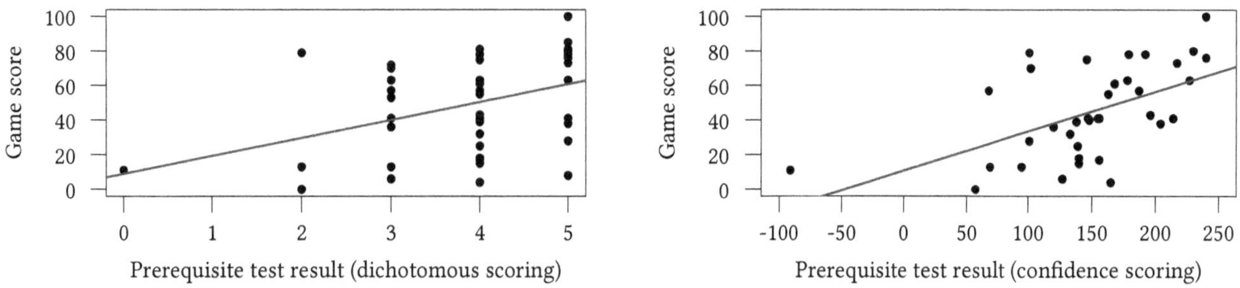

Figure 3: Linear regression models describing game score by pretest for G1

questions given in session 4. Second, we used only the data of the 12 participants playing G1, using the result of the 7-question pretest. Third, we used the data of the 20 participants playing G2.

Table 4 reports the regression models of the first set of analyses. Statistically significant fits were computed for the score or level prediction based on the dichotomously scored pretest ($R^2 = 0.17$ or $R^2 = 0.14, p \leq 0.01$). An even more promising relationship emerged when incorporating confidence testing ($R^2 = 0.31$ or $R^2 = 0.24$, $p \leq 0.004$). The second set of analyses on the subset of players and two extra questions yielded almost identical results to those on the full sample of players from G1. The coefficients in the remaining models did not show statistical significance, and neither did they in other models for G1 nor in any model for G2.

The two best fits for score prediction are graphed in Figure 3. These plots show a certain degree of linearity. The other two plots for predicting completed levels were largely similar and were omitted to conserve space. The regression diagnostic plots (residual plots and Q-Q plots) confirm that the assumptions of homoscedasticity and multivariate normality were met. Based on the leverage plot, the player scoring 0 points in the pretest was identified as an outlier (Cook's distance > 0.5). However, the removal of the data point did not significantly influence the models (the R^2 changed by ± 0.01, and the p-value remained up to 0.01). Thus, we decided to keep the data point in the sample.

6 DISCUSSION

6.1 Quantitative view

Returning to the research questions posed in Section 1, the models accurately predicted the learners' total game score and completed levels when employing prerequisite testing, regardless of the scoring method used, for the game G1. It is interesting that confidence testing revealed guesswork: 8 players randomly guessed at least one correct answer. It also showed misconceptions, since 7 players were quite or absolutely sure about at least one incorrect answer. Most importantly, the confidence testing improved the models, as the value of R^2 almost doubled compared to the dichotomous pretest.

Considering G1, the players from the fourth session exhibited similar results as the whole when using the two extra pretest questions. However, the success was not reproduced in G2. We attribute this to the fact that two of the questions were easy for the players to answer. Moreover, due to unclear formulation of the third question

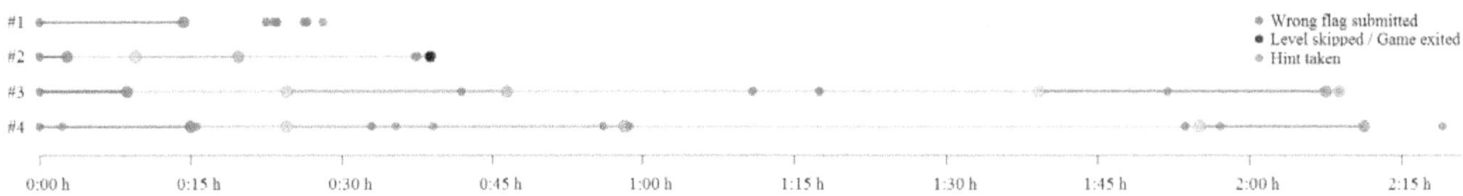

Figure 4: Game events of selected individual players in G1, distributed over time. Each line represents the actions of one player. Finished levels are marked as colored line segments: dark blue displays level 1, light blue level 2, and so on.

we decided to accept even the answers we originally deemed incorrect. As a result, 16 out of 20 players had at least three questions correct, preventing the models from differentiating between them.

To complement the discussion of the regression models, we examined medians in boxplots depicting prerequisite test results (Figure 2). On the one hand, the medians do not show a linear trend, as they are not in ascending order. On the other hand, the players who achieved the highest quiz scores also had the highest medians of the game score and finished levels. Overall, the results confirmed the intuition that players with a high score from the pretest would often perform better in the game compared to the others. The reverse was also true.

However, the regression models employing self-assessment were not statistically significant, and their R^2 values were below 0.07. The models seem unlikely to reach statistical significance even if the sample size increased. The conclusion that the self-assessment is an unreliable skill predictor is consistent with the previous findings by Mirkovic et. al [11], who used a similar self-assessment scale. One possible explanation is that experience with using in-game tools is not a key factor in deciding learners' readiness. Most of the players had worked with a Linux Terminal before the game, thus were able to discover and understand the application of other command-line tools for themselves. Another plausible justification for the poor self-assessment results is that the scale has only four values and three items, which yields data that is too coarse.

6.2 Qualitative view

It can be argued that applying statistical tests and using regression models on a relatively small sample might bias the quantitative results. Therefore, the actions of individual players were further explored from a time perspective (see Figure 4). Several notable anomalies were identified in G1 sessions and are addressed below[1].

Player #1, who we nicknamed "the dropout", reached the full score (5 points) in the dichotomous pretest but got frustrated as early as in level 2. Over the course of less than 6 minutes, he attempted 5 wrong flags, took a hint, and stopped playing. As a result, his game score was only 8 points.

Player #2 ("the achiever") followed the same pattern as "the dropout"; at the beginning, he seemed like a competent learner but got frustrated with the game. "The achiever" scored 4 points in the dichotomous pretest and solved the first three levels quickly. Shortly before the indicative time limit for the fourth level ran out, he took both available hints and then prematurely exited the game. As a result, he scored a, below-average, 43 game points. However, he later reported not knowing that the time limit was only informative and had no impact on the game. Instead, the player thought that if the time runs out, he cannot play anymore, which annoyed him and caused him to quit the game.

We hypothesize that "the achiever" and "the dropout" had possessed the necessary prerequisites for finishing the game. However, they were thwarted by ambiguous game mechanics or design, by insufficient attention paid to the rules, or by some other reason. Due to these unanticipated situations, the dataset includes players scoring well in the pretest but poorly in terms of game score or levels completed. This might have introduced noise in the regression models, as similar misunderstandings could have influenced other players' results.

Another interesting case is player #3 ("the determined one"), who scored 0 in the self-assessment and 2 points in the pretest. Still, he completed 5 levels and scored 79 points in the game: one of the best results in the sample. The player used only 2 hints and attempted only 2 incorrect flags in total, all in the later phases of the game. The time spent in the levels was rather long. This is reflected in the post-game feedback, where he rated the game as hard (4). Although the player did not possess theoretical knowledge from the pretest, his determination allowed him to perform very well.

Finally, the player #4 ("the practitioner") scored 0 in the self-assessment and 3 points in the pretest. However, by taking some hints, using trial and error, and given enough time he was able to complete 5 levels and score 72 game points, which is a good result. This player, like "the determined one", might not have had the theoretical background, but was still able to solve the practical tasks.

These case anomalies show that some unanticipated aspects influence players' performance. An arising challenge is recognizing and deeply understanding all factors that contribute to a successful game. We believe that solving this challenge is essential for designing a useful diagnostic assessment and the whole game.

6.3 Addressing the limitations

Despite using a well-established framework for question-writing [2] and following best practices of assessment design, we were confronted by three main challenges of prerequisite testing. The first is calibrating the test to predict the possession of skills most relevant to the game. While the players often performed well in the quiz, no one finished the last level of G1. It seems that theoretical knowledge might not be enough for succeeding in practical tasks.

The second challenge was the limited time frame for assessing a participant. It is impractical and discouraging to perform a lengthy examination when the learners are eager to play the game. Both the test and self-assessment combined were designed to take 8 minutes at most, yet were perceived by some of the players as

[1] All the players are referred to as males, even if their gender is unknown.

an inconvenience. The third challenge is embedding the pretest in the game. For further experiments, we propose designing and implementing pretests, and, by extension, cybersecurity games differently. Inspired by the results of Lee at al. [10], who report positive effects of assessments in educational games, we propose two main improvements. One is dissolving the assessments into the story of the game. Compared to using questionnaires, which distract the players and shift them into a "testing mode", in-game tests are more engaging [10]. They also allow the use of more assessment questions, which, in turn, brings more validity and reliability to the results. This approach necessitates another improvement in the design of the game itself. Individual levels can be created such that each has only one particular learning outcome. Appropriate prerequisites can be tested before or during that level.

While the experiment proved a link between prerequisite testing and players' performance in the game G1, the generalizability of the results might be questionable, as the model for G2 was not statistically significant. One possible explanation is the dependence on the particular game and its scoring method. Ultimately, successful diagnostic assessment largely depends on the quality of game design. This work attempted to prove the validity of the proposed prerequisite test based, to some extent, on its relationship to the game. However, if the game scoring mechanism or individual levels are poorly designed, this can invalidate the pretest. Therefore, we underline the need for careful consideration of educational game design. Another explanation is that the amount and content of questions in pretest 2 were not sufficient to differentiate the players' skill. Nevertheless, adding more questions in pretest 1 did not seem to bring more validity to the results, as they reflected the results of the analysis performed with the subset of questions.

Finally, the self-assessment had only three items with four distinct values, which was too coarse an input for the linear regression. Introducing questions asking for the frequency of use or applicability to a particular task could increase the reliability of results.

7 CONCLUSIONS

We performed an experimental study investigating the predictive value of prerequisite tests and self-assessment for identifying learners' readiness before playing a cybersecurity educational game. The analysis of game events and information provided by players showed that only a knowledge quiz, and not self-assessment, can model game score and completed levels. The models based on the pretests significantly improved if the quiz contained confidence assessment. However, educators have to pay special attention to the selection and formulation of quiz questions since they fundamentally affect the accuracy of the model.

The major contribution of this pioneering attempt is the new insights provided into hands-on cybersecurity education, which has not been widely researched. This work also motivated the development of an open-source tool for visualizing generic game events over time [18] (see Figure 4). This tool allowed discovering important patterns that would otherwise stay hidden.

In our future work, we will focus on investigating the means of diagnostic assessment into the game story and structure. Since the players rated the games as educational, practical, and interesting, we believe that active learning in cybersecurity is worthy of both security practitioners' and educators' attention. We also encourage fellow researchers to experiment with diagnostic assessment in other domains than cybersecurity.

ACKNOWLEDGMENTS

This research was supported by the Security Research Programme of the Czech Republic 2015-2020 (BV III/1–VS) granted by the Ministry of the Interior of the Czech Republic under No. VI20162019014 – Simulation, detection, and mitigation of cyber threats endangering critical infrastructure. The analysis of the experiment results would not have been possible without a visualization tool developed by Juraj Uhlár. Finally, we thank our colleagues and anonymous reviewers for their helpful comments and suggestions.

REFERENCES

[1] Jim Allen and Rolf Van Der Velden. 2005. The role of self-assessment in measuring skills. In *Transition in Youth Workshop, Valencia, Spain.*

[2] Ian D. Beatty, William J. Gerace, William J. Leonard, and Robert J. Dufresne. 2006. Designing effective questions for classroom response system teaching. *American Journal of Physics* 74, 1 (2006), 31–39.

[3] Alicia Bolívar-Cruz, Domingo Verano-Tacoronte, and Sara M. González-Betancor. 2015. Is University Students' Self-Assessment Accurate? In *Sustainable Learning in Higher Education.* Springer, 21–35.

[4] Mark Gondree, Zachary Peterson, and Portia Pusey. 2016. Talking about talking about cybersecurity games. *USENIX ;login:* 41, 1 (2016), 36–39.

[5] Thavamalar Govindasamy. 2001. Successful implementation of e-learning: Pedagogical considerations. *The internet and higher education* 4, 3 (2001), 287–299.

[6] Peter Hassmén and Darwin P. Hunt. 1994. Human Self-Assessment in Multiple-Choice Testing. *Journal of Educational Measurement* 31, 2 (1994), 149–160.

[7] Darwin P. Hunt. 2003. The concept of knowledge and how to measure it. *Journal of intellectual capital* 4, 1 (2003), 100–113.

[8] Jincheul Jang, Jason J. Y. Park, and Mun Y. Yi. 2015. *Gamification of Online Learning.* Springer International Publishing, 646–649.

[9] Piet Kommers. 2004. *Cognitive support for learning: imagining the unknown.* IOS Press.

[10] Michael J. Lee, Andrew J. Ko, and Irwin Kwan. 2013. In-game Assessments Increase Novice Programmers' Engagement and Level Completion Speed. In *Proceedings of the Ninth Annual International ACM Conference on International Computing Education Research (ICER '13).* ACM, New York, NY, USA, 153–160.

[11] Jelena Mirkovic and Peter A. H. Peterson. 2014. Class Capture-the-Flag Exercises. In *2014 USENIX 3GSE.* San Diego, CA.

[12] Jelena Mirkovic, Aimee Tabor, Simon Woo, and Portia Pusey. 2015. Engaging Novices in Cybersecurity Competitions: A Vision and Lessons Learned at ACM Tapia 2015. In *2015 USENIX 3GSE.* USENIX Association, Washington, D.C.

[13] Gary R. Morrison, Steven M. Ross, Jerrold E. Kemp, and Howard Kalman. 2010. *Designing effective instruction.* John Wiley & Sons.

[14] Ajay Nagarajan, Jan M. Allbeck, Arun Sood, and Terry L. Janssen. 2012. Exploring game design for cybersecurity training. In *IEEE International Conference on Cyber Technology in Automation, Control, and Intelligent Systems (CYBER).* 256–262.

[15] Geoffrey Petty. 2009. *Teaching Today: A Practical Guide.* Nelson Thornes.

[16] Portia Pusey, Sr. David Tobey, and Ralph Soule. 2014. An Argument for Game Balance: Improving Student Engagement by Matching Difficulty Level with Learner Readiness. In *2014 USENIX 3GSE.* USENIX Association, San Diego, CA.

[17] David H. Tobey, Portia Pusey, and Diana L. Burley. 2014. Engaging Learners in Cybersecurity Careers: Lessons from the Launch of the National Cyber League. *ACM Inroads* 5, 1 (2014), 53–56.

[18] Juraj Uhlár. 2017. *Visualization of a run of a security game.* Bachelor's thesis. Masaryk University, Faculty of Informatics, Brno. https://is.muni.cz/th/422160/fi_b/.

[19] Jan Vykopal, Radek Oslejsek, Pavel Celeda, Martin Vizvary, and Daniel Tovarnak. 2017. KYPO Cyber Range: Design and Use Cases. In *Proceedings of the 12th International Conference on Software Technologies - Volume 1: ICSOFT.* INSTICC, SciTePress, 310–321. https://doi.org/10.5220/0006428203100321

[20] Joseph Werther, Michael Zhivich, Tim Leek, and Nickolai Zeldovich. 2011. Experiences in Cyber Security Education: The MIT Lincoln Laboratory Capture-the-flag Exercise. In *Proceedings of the 4th Conference on Cyber Security Experimentation and Test (CSET'11).* USENIX Association, Berkeley, CA, USA, 12–12.

[21] Pieter Wouters, Christof Van Nimwegen, Herre Van Oostendorp, and Erik D. Van Der Spek. 2013. A meta-analysis of the cognitive and motivational effects of serious games. *Journal of Educational Psychology* 105, 2 (2013), 249.

[22] Valdemar Švábenský. 2017. *Prerequisite testing of cybersecurity skills.* Master's thesis. Masaryk University, Faculty of Informatics, Brno. https://is.muni.cz/th/395868/fi_m/.

Assessing the Impact of a National Cybersecurity Competition on Students' Career Interests

Michael H. Dunn
Department of Electrical and Computer Engineering, Air Force Institute of Technology, Wright-Patterson Air Force Base, OH, 45433, USA, michael.dunn.42@us.af.mil

Laurence D. Merkle
Department of Electrical and Computer Engineering, Air Force Institute of Technology, Wright-Patterson Air Force Base, OH, 45433, USA, laurence.merkle@afit.edu

ABSTRACT

It is well documented that there is a sizable shortage of workers in cybersecurity and related careers. Exacerbating this problem are severe imbalances with respect to gender and other underrepresented categories, with one recent study finding only 11% of cybersecurity professionals are women. One approach to addressing these shortages is to attempt to increase interest in cybersecurity careers through extracurricular cybersecurity competitions. CyberPatriot is the largest cybersecurity competition for middle and high school students in North America, with over 14,000 young people participating during the 2016-2017 school year. This paper assesses the impact of this competition on participants' interest in cybersecurity careers. Survey data previously collected by the competition organizers is analyzed with rigorous statistical methods. Results show that participants' interest in cybersecurity increased meaningfully in several dimensions relevant to career selection. Further analysis also finds that despite lower initial interest in cybersecurity careers among female participants, this interest increased by an even greater amount than it did for male participants.

KEYWORDS

Cybersecurity education; K-12 education; underrepresented populations; gender; competitions; CyberPatriot

ACM Reference format:

Michael H. Dunn and Laurence D. Merkle. 2018. Assessing the Impact of a National Cybersecurity Competition on Students' Career Interests. In *SIGCSE '18: 49th ACM Technical Symposium on Computer Science Education, Feb. 21–24, 2018, Baltimore, MD, USA.* ACM, NY, NY, USA, 6 pages. DOI: https://doi.org/10.1145/3159450.3159462

1. INTRODUCTION

Modern society has become dependent on a wide range of networked computer systems, and addressing the many security problems inherent to this dependence is an increasingly difficult challenge.

SIGCSE '18, February 21–24, 2018, Baltimore, MD, USA
ACM ISBN 978-1-4503-5103-4/18/02
https://doi.org/10.1145/3159450.3159462

One of the key components to doing so is employing enough appropriately skilled workers. However, organizations across all sectors of industry are having difficulty filling the existing cybersecurity jobs. Furthermore, the worker shortage is only getting worse as growth in the number of cybersecurity jobs significantly outpaces the number of workers entering the field. A recent study from (ISC)^2 estimated that the cybersecurity worker shortage will grow to 1.8 million by 2022 [13]. Among professionals surveyed in North America, 68% said there were too few cybersecurity workers in their department, and the majority believe that one of the main reasons is difficulty finding qualified people [13]. The U.S. President's Commission on Enhancing National Cybersecurity also identified this challenge, concluding that building the cybersecurity workforce was one of its strategic imperatives for bolstering the nation's cybersecurity posture [8].

Exacerbating this problem is a severe gender imbalance in the cybersecurity workforce. The same (ISC)^2 study found that only 11% of the global cybersecurity workforce are women [14], and multiple studies show that female students have much more negative views of cybersecurity and other computing careers than their male counterparts do [17, 18]. Clearly, addressing the cybersecurity worker shortage must include improving female students' perceptions of cybersecurity as a potential career.

Several approaches to solving this are being pursued by various government, industry, and academic organizations, including scholarships, internships, training camps, new cybersecurity degree programs, and integrating cybersecurity into other related curricula. One approach that is generating growing interest is cybersecurity competitions. Such competitions at the college and professional level have become a well-established and prominent part of the cybersecurity landscape, often in the form of "capture the flag" type challenges [12, 16, 19].

Cybersecurity competitions for secondary school students (i.e. middle and high school) have also been growing in popularity over recent years [15, 21]. With over 14,000 registered participants during the 2016-2017 school year [11], the Air Force Association's CyberPatriot [2] is the largest such program, and the only truly national cybersecurity competition for this age group [16]. Teams of up to six middle or high school students scour a virtual machine for vulnerabilities such as viruses, backdoors, and incorrect security settings, then eliminate those vulnerabilities for points. These teams can come from public or private schools, homeschool groups, Junior ROTC programs, Civil Air Patrol units, or other approved youth organizations serving middle and high school students [2]. The goals of CyberPatriot and similar programs are to increase the number of young people who pursue cybersecurity-related careers and to increase awareness of cybersecurity more broadly. However, it is unclear whether this approach is accomplishing the first goal, and if so, to what extent.

This paper begins to address this question by analyzing results of surveys conducted by the CyberPatriot Program Office and made available to the authors, principally focusing on a survey of participants in the 2016-17 season.

2. RELATED WORK

Recent work suggests academic competitions are effective at stimulating students' interest in specific career fields, particularly in the sciences, and have significant impact on their educational and career choices. In a study of past National Ocean Sciences Bowl participants, 41% said participation influenced their career choice and 39% said it influenced their college major choice [5]. Science fair and science Olympiad participants ranked "fun" and "learning new things" as their leading rewards for participation [1]. External motivators such as pleasing teachers and parents and winning prizes ranked much lower. Students in both competitions said given a choice of future academic competitions, the one in which they just participated would be their top choice.

Academic competitions can also help launch talented students into highly successful careers. A study of past academic Olympiad winners found they significantly outperformed their peers in various measures, including doctorates earned and number of publications. A significant majority of both participants and their parents agreed that the Olympiad programs helped develop their talent and fostered their future accomplishments [6].

However, little is known about the impact of computing and cybersecurity competitions as a means of attracting young people to these fields. One study of past participants in Cybersecurity Awareness Week evaluated personality profiles of competitors, and found that the high levels of "perceived self-efficacy in cybersecurity tasks, rational decision-making style, and investigative interests" correlated with a higher likelihood of participants later choosing a cybersecurity career [4]. A relatively large-scale survey by McGill, Decker, and Settle [18] studies the long-term effects of pre-college outreach activities, especially in relation to students' choice of major (specifically, computing vs. non-computing). These researchers found that there is a strong link between participating in computing educational activities and later choosing to major in a computing field. This correlation is stronger when participation is voluntary than when it is required, and stronger for males than for females [18].

3. METHODOLOGY

The data used for this study came from responses to various surveys conducted by the CyberPatriot Program Office. In 2014, 2015, and 2017 the office conducted "post-season" competitor surveys asking students about their experiences with the program in the preceding school year. Also, in 2014 and 2016 they surveyed all students who had participated in any year of the program ("alumni") and asked them about their current educational and career situations. Summaries of a few of the surveys have been published in reports by the CyberPatriot Program Office ([9, 10]), including basic descriptive statistics; however, this study is the first statistically rigorous analysis of the collected survey data.

The post-season questionnaires, sent to participants from the immediately preceding school years, begin with a series of retrospective questions asking students to "think back to before [they] had ever heard about CyberPatriot" (unfortunately, there were no pre-season surveys to gauge the opinions of students before they participated in the competition). These retrospective questions inquire about students' perceptions of their knowledge of basic cybersecurity principles, their knowledge of and interest in cybersecurity careers, their likelihood of pursuing an education or career in a STEM field, and how "welcoming and accessible" to females they perceived cybersecurity careers to be before they participated. Those questions are then posed again, with the time considered changed to "now" or "currently." Finally, the questionnaires ask participants about how "engaging" and "fun" they thought the competition was after participating.

The alumni questionnaires were sent to CyberPatriot "alumni," i.e. participants of any previous year of the competition, and collect data focusing on the individuals' educational and/or career status and plans. After collecting some basic demographic data, these questionnaires ask respondents if they have graduated from high school yet (i.e. at the time of the survey). High school graduates are then asked if they are enrolled in higher education and if so what field they are studying. Others are asked if they plan on pursuing higher education after high school and in what field. All respondents are then asked if they are employed, and if so, in what sector (public/private/military). They are also asked in what field they are currently employed or hoping to be employed. Finally, respondents are asked to what extent participation in the CyberPatriot program has impacted their education and career goals (none/somewhat/significant).

Three of the five surveys collected personal identifiable information (PII) for use in a survey completion incentive. Prior to our receipt of the data, it was anonymized by replacing each respondent's PII with a unique Hashed Message Authentication Code (HMAC) generated via SHA-256 and a randomly-generated secret key. Thus, the data was de-identified but participants' responses could be linked across surveys by matching their HMACs. This allowed measurement of reliability by comparing an individual's responses to the same question across multiple surveys. It also enabled linking individuals' 2015 post-competition survey responses to those for the 2016 alumni survey.

Due to the significantly larger number of respondents, the 2016 alumni survey and 2017 post-season competitor survey are the primary sources for this study's analysis. The 2015 post-season survey is used primarily to measure reliability.

To measure impact on career interest, responses to the cybersecurity career perception questions are analyzed. The mean value of the responses to each question is calculated, and the means of the "before" and "after" versions compared. A paired t-test is performed for each to determine statistical significance. Effect size is measured by calculating Cohen's d for the difference of means, which is then evaluated against Cohen's conventions for small, medium, and large effect sizes [7].

The impact that participation in CyberPatriot had on female students' perceptions of how accessible a career in cybersecurity is to them is assessed in two ways. First, in the post-season survey, a pair of before and after questions was posed, asking how "welcoming and accessible to females" they thought a career in cybersecurity is. The change in perception from before to after is measured, using a paired t-test, for both male and female students, and the effect size (Cohen's d) calculated for both. Second, the change in the before and after responses to the other career-perception questions is calculated with a paired t-test and Cohen's d specifically for the subgroup of female participants, and compared to the overall group of respondents.

4. RESULTS

The 2017 post-season survey had 2161 respondents – an increase of 274% over the 2015 survey – and the 2016 alumni survey had 2870 respondents – an increase of 1,130% over 2014 (see Table 1).

Table 1: Survey response numbers.

Survey	Total Responses	Male	Female	Decline to Specify
2014 Post-Season	639	516 (80.8%)	115 (18.0%)	8 (1.3%)
2015 Post-Season	790	608 (77.0%)	168 (21.3%)	14 (1.8%)
2017 Post-Season	2161	1553 (71.9%)	576 (26.7%)	32 (1.5%)
2014 Alumni	254	218 (85.8%)	34 (13.4%)	2 (0.8%)
2016 Alumni	2870	2174 (75.7%)	660 (23.0%)	36 (1.3%)

4.1 Demographics

Of the 2161 respondents to the 2017 post-season survey, 187 only answered the first three questions, which were mandatory. These responses were removed, leaving 1974 responses for further analysis (n=1974). Of those respondents, 71.2% were male, 27.3% were female, and 1.5% declined to respond. Ethnicity data was also collected, as summarized in Table 2. The majority (55.0%) were White non-Hispanic, followed by Asian/Pacific Islander (21.2%) and Hispanic (13.1%). The mean age of respondents was 15.8 years; the median age was 16 years, and the mode was 17 years (25.6% of respondents). Grade level was measured by asking respondents what year they will graduate high school. The median grade level of respondents that specified a graduation year was 10th grade (i.e. having two years left in high school), and the mode was 11th grade (23.7% of respondents).

Table 2: Respondents by ethnicity.

Ethnicity	Frequency	Percentage
Am. Indian/Alaskan Native	29	1.5%
Asian/Pacific Islander	419	21.2%
Black (non-Hispanic)	83	4.2%
Hispanic	258	13.1%
White (non-Hispanic)	1086	55.0%
Prefer not to answer	99	5.0%
Total	1974	100.0%

These demographics are similar to those of the sampled population, registered participants in the 2016-2017 CyberPatriot competition season [11]. Females are slightly overrepresented in this survey (27.3% vs 23.0%), as are Asians/Pacific Islanders (21.2% vs 17.8%). Underrepresented demographics include Black non-Hispanic (4.2% vs 6.2%), Hispanic (13.1% vs 17.9%), and 12th-graders (20.8% vs 26.9%).

4.2 Impact on Career Interest

Participants rated their "knowledge of possible cybersecurity careers" at an average of 3.77 on a 1 to 5 scale, somewhere between "some" and "a lot of" knowledge, up from 3.08 before participating in the CyberPatriot program (see Table 3). To gauge the size of the effect from before to after, Cohen's d is calculated. By this measure, the effect size d = 1.06 far exceeds Cohen's threshold of 0.80 for large effect sizes [7].

Table 3: Differences between reported "before" and "after" beliefs in response to questions about (a) knowledge of cybersecurity principles [1-5], (b) likelihood of pursuing an education/career in STEM [1-4], (c) knowledge of cyber-security careers [1-5], (d) how "cool" it would be to work in cybersecurity [1-5], and (e) likelihood of pursuing an education/career in cybersecurity [1-4]. N = 1895, $p \ll 0.001$.

	"Before" $\mu \pm \sigma$	"After" $\mu \pm \sigma$	t	d
a	2.43±0.98	3.76±0.81	57.7	1.33
b	3.16±0.96	3.50±0.73	17.4	0.40
c	2.58±0.99	3.72±0.87	46.1	1.06
d	3.08±1.03	3.77±0.92	28.8	0.66
e	2.24±0.93	3.05±0.83	37.7	0.87

Participants' opinions about how "cool" it would be to work in cybersecurity also increased, from 3.08 to 3.77, again on a 1 to 5 scale. The effect size is not as large (d = 0.66), but still comfortably exceeds the 0.50 threshold for a medium effect size [7].

The most direct question about participants' career interest straightforwardly asked them "how likely [they are] to pursue an education or career in cybersecurity." Here again, there was a marked increase, from a mean of 2.24 before to a mean of 3.05 after, this time on a 1 to 4 scale. The number of participants indicating "somewhat likely" went from 29.6% before to 45.2% after, and the number marking "very likely" rose from 9.4% to

32.3%. The Cohen's d effect size for this question (d = 0.87) comfortably qualifies as a large effect size.

Respondents were asked to rate their cybersecurity knowledge both before and after participating in CyberPatriot. The mean response increased from 2.43 before to 3.76 after, on a 1 to 5 scale. The effect size of d = 1.33 is the largest effect size observed in this question set, and is much larger than Cohen's requirement to qualify as a large effect size.

Participants were also asked about their likelihood to pursue an education or career in the much broader category of Science, Technology, Engineering, and Mathematics (STEM). While this also increased (3.16 before to 3.50 after, on a 1 to 4 scale), the effect is much smaller than the cybersecurity specific questions. Cohen's d = 0.40, which doesn't quite reach the level of a medium effect size. This is primarily due to the fact that the "before" average was already significantly higher than the cybersecurity-specific version of the question (3.16 vs 2.24 on a 1 to 4 scale). This makes sense given that CyberPatriot participants chose to volunteer for an activity that they knew would be somewhat technical.

To gauge the extent to which respondents' self-reported likelihood to enter a cybersecurity field persisted over time, responses to the 2015 post-season survey were linked to responses to the 2016 alumni survey by the same individual. Of the 790 total responses in the 2015 survey, 61 (7.7%) were able to be linked to their responses in the 2016 survey. Of the 17 that had responded in 2015 that they were "very likely" to pursue an education or career in cybersecurity, 13 (76.5%) individuals reported one year later that they were doing so (if they'd graduated) or that they still planned on doing so (if they'd not yet graduated). Two others (11.8%) were pursuing or planning to pursue a degree in a computer science field.

4.3 Female Perceptions of Career Accessibility

Responses to the question of "how welcoming and accessible to females" participants think a career in cybersecurity is rose from a mean of 3.46 before to 3.83 after, on a 1 to 5 scale (see Table 4). Although statistically significant ($t = 19.7$, $p \ll 0.001$), the effect size is not quite medium ($d = 0.45$). When considering just the sub-population of female participants, however, that increases to $d = 0.58$, which constitutes a medium effect size.

Table 4: Perceptions of how "welcoming and accessible" cybersecurity careers are to females.

	"Before"	"After"	Paired t-test ($p \ll 0.001$)		Eff. sz.
	$\mu \pm \sigma$	$\mu \pm \sigma$	t	df	d
All (N=1895)	3.46±1.07	3.83±0.99	19.7	1894	0.45
Female (N=523)	3.02±1.07	3.56±1.04	13.2	522	0.58
Male (N=1343)	3.64±1.01	3.94±0.94	14.5	1342	0.40

Another way to assess how female participants' perceptions of cybersecurity careers changed is to compare their responses on the career perception questions to the responses of male participants. For every single question, although the overall mean response values of the 523 female respondents were lower than those of the 1343 male respondents were, the change in their responses from before to after was greater (see Table 5). The difference in mean change is statistically significant for every question (t between 2.85 and 5.79, $p \le 0.002$), however the effect size is small (two of the questions are close, though just shy of the "small" effect size convention).

Table 5: Mean changes in response, by gender to questions about (a) knowledge of cybersecurity principles [1-5], (b) likelihood of pursuing an education/career in STEM [1-4], (c) knowledge of cybersecurity careers [1-5], (d) how "cool" it would be to work in cybersecurity [1-5], (e) likelihood of pursuing an education/career in cybersecurity [1-4], and (f) how welcoming/accessible cybersecurity is to females [1-5].

	Female	Male	Independent t-test			Eff. sz.
	$\mu \pm \sigma$	$\mu \pm \sigma$	t	df	p	d
a	1.55±1.00	1.26±0.99	5.79	950	0.00	0.30
b	0.52±0.93	0.27±0.82	5.45	855	0.00	0.29
c	1.26±1.11	1.10±1.04	2.85	898	0.002	0.15
d	0.82±1.10	0.65±1.02	3.02	891	0.001	0.16
e	0.99±0.99	0.75±0.89	4.84	871	0.00	0.25
f	0.54±0.92	0.30±0.77	5.11	815	0.00	0.27

4.4 Reliability

To measure reliability for the retrospective questions mentioned above, participants are identified who responded to both the 2015 post-season survey and the 2017 post-season survey. The Pearson r is computed as the reliability coefficient for each question.

Unfortunately, only 16 repeat respondents are identifiable, representing just 2.0% of the respondents to the 2015 survey. Even so, based on one-tailed t tests, all questions but one ("What was your knowledge of possible cybersecurity careers at the time?") are reliable at the $p<0.05$ level of significance.

5. DISCUSSION

5.1 Impact on Career Interest

Responses improved on all five questions related to participant perceptions of cybersecurity and cybersecurity-related careers. These increases are both statistically ($p \ll 0.001$) and practically significant, with effect sizes ranging from medium to very large. The question then, is can these responses really tell us anything about participants' likelihood to enter the cybersecurity workforce? The factors influencing career selection identified by Walters and Bishop [20] can be used as a framework to judge the relevance of the CyberPatriot survey questions and responses. Of the seven factors they identify from the literature and their own study, four are at least partially addressed by the CyberPatriot post-competition survey questions.

Participants' self-reported "knowledge of cybersecurity careers," which increased with a large effect size, is a key dimension of the career selection factors "perception of career tasks" and "interest and awareness" [20]. This is supported by our finding that a self-reported increase in career knowledge is positively correlated with an increase in expressed likelihood to pursue a cybersecurity career ($r = 0.46$). Also contributing to these factors – especially "interest and awareness" – are the students' perceptions of how "cool" a career in cybersecurity would be. These increased by a smaller amount, due in large part to the fact that they started with a higher average (3.08 vs. 2.58). Increases in the response value to this question have the highest correlation with increases in the likelihood to pursue a career ($r = 0.60$), likely because the two questions are the most similar in the sentiment they express. The factor "difficulty of attainment" is partially addressed by the "knowledge of cybersecurity careers" question; 19.8% of respondents answering this question selected "I know a lot about cybersecurity career opportunities, as well as how to pursue them" after participating, up from just 4.2% before. Understanding how to pursue a career in cybersecurity, combined with the increased knowledge of cybersecurity principles, could significantly decrease the perceived difficulty of attaining a career in the field.

Participants' responses to the question of how they would rate their "knowledge of cybersecurity basic principles" is also directly relevant to career selection. One of the factors influencing career selection is "view of self," which is essentially whether the student perceives their abilities, aptitudes, etc. as being sufficient to be successful at a particular career [20]. In fact, in studying past participants of the National Ocean Sciences Bowl, Walters and Bishop found that this self-perception has the strongest influence on students' selection of a career [5, 20]. Perceived competence in a subject has also been found to be a predictor of future achievement [3]. It is noteworthy, therefore, that responses to this question saw the greatest increase of all six career perception questions, with a very large effect size. We did not find it to have the strongest correlation to increased likelihood of pursuing a cybersecurity career, but it is positively correlated ($r = 0.31$).

Summing up the participants' perceptions of cybersecurity as a likely career choice, responses to the question of "how likely [the participant is] to pursue education or career in cybersecurity" increased from 2.24 to 3.05 on a 4-point scale. This increase is statistically significant and has a large effect size. After participating, 32.3% of respondents indicated they were "very likely" to pursue cybersecurity, and 45.1% said they were "somewhat likely" to do so; this is up from 9.4% and 29.5%, respectively, that indicated they were very or somewhat likely to pursue cybersecurity before participating in CyberPatriot. These results are consistent with previous years' surveys [10].

Ultimately, the goal of this program isn't truly fulfilled unless students follow-through with these intentions and actually enter the cybersecurity workforce. Observing participants' responses to multiple surveys over time is the best way to measure if this is really happening. From the limited results found in this study, it appears that the majority of participants do follow-through on their stated intentions. This is also supported by the overall number of CyberPatriot participants who have entered a cybersecurity-related field. The 2016 alumni survey found that 59.2% of those enrolled in higher education were majoring in a cybersecurity or computer science field, and 82.4% of high school grads were employed in or seeking work in a cybersecurity or computer science related field [9].

5.2 Female Perceptions of Career Accessibility

Part of filling the cybersecurity worker shortage has to be increasing the diversity of the talent pool, and one of the most significant diversity challenges is the gender imbalance. Although participation in CyberPatriot suffers from a significant gender imbalance, it is not as severe as the imbalance in the current cybersecurity workforce (23.0% of participants in the 2015-2016 season were female [11] vs. only 11% in the current workforce [14]). Furthermore, it is important to assess how well the program does at influencing those female students that do participate.

According to female participants' survey responses, their perception of how "welcoming and accessible" cybersecurity careers are for females improved in a meaningful way; the improvement in their responses is statistically significant and has a medium effect size. However, perhaps a more meaningful measure is how much female students' opinions changed regarding cybersecurity careers as it relates to *them* specifically. It is possible for a female student to think that a career may be accessible to females generally, but still not think they themselves are "cut out for it." The general trend in the literature that girls tend to perceive themselves as less capable in technical fields than boys do holds for CyberPatriot participants as well. Mean responses to the career perception questions were lower for female respondents than for their male counterparts across the board, both in the "before" questions and in the "after" questions. However, the change in mean response value was higher for female respondents than for males on every question ($p \ll 0.01$). As discussed in the previous section, perceptions improved meaningfully for all students overall, but the improvement was greater for females.

Bolstering the notion that participation in CyberPatriot narrows the gap between male and female students with regard to their interest in cybersecurity careers, female respondents to the alumni survey reported pursuing cybersecurity and computing majors and careers in very similar proportions. Among females enrolled in higher education, 53.6% were majoring in a cybersecurity or computer science field (compared to 59.2% overall), and 80.6% of female high school grads who reported a career field were in cybersecurity or computer science related fields (compared to 82.4% overall [9]).

5.3 Limitations

Due to the retrospective nature of the "before" questions, it is impossible to know with certainty how much a participant's opinions really changed over the course of one or more competition seasons. Reliability is high for all but one question, but the retrospective nature of the questions still introduces error. Additionally, the methods used for linking individual participants across multiple surveys are not as effective as a unique participant identifier, and reduce the number of responses that can be linked. Because the survey questions were originally designed for program evaluation purposes rather than scientific research, they are not as granular or methodical as those used in typical educational research. For instance, although respondents were prompted with multiple-choice selections similar to Likert-type questions, they were not true Likert tests with the formal parameters and procedures that normally entails. Finally, due to the self-selected nature of competition participants and lack of control group, this study cannot make any claims regarding causation. While the results show that participants reported an increase in their positive perceptions toward cybersecurity, it is not known how much these perceptions may have changed on their own, with or without the influence of the CyberPatriot program. Future research should attempt to answer this question by identifying a control group of students with similar interest levels but who do not participate in the competition.

6. CONCLUSIONS

It is evident that the cybersecurity career field is in dire need of more workers. A critical aspect of attaining this objective is recruiting more young people, and a more diverse group of young people, to pursue educations and careers in cybersecurity and related fields. One promising approach to increasing interest in cybersecurity has been student competitions. With over 14,000 participants in the 2016-2017 school year, CyberPatriot is by far the largest such program in the United States for middle and high school students. This paper begins to assess the impact of the CyberPatriot program on the career interests of students by analyzing responses to recent surveys conducted by the competition organizers. The results show that interest in cybersecurity as an educational or career prospect increased meaningfully across multiple dimensions, such as perception of career tasks, interest and awareness, and view of self. The reliability of these self-reported perceptions is bolstered by comparing responses across surveys administered at different times. Our findings indicate that a significant majority of those reporting that they are very likely to choose a cybersecurity field are still planning to do so when asked again one year later.

Our findings also indicate that the CyberPatriot competition is contributing positively to correct the gender imbalance in the cybersecurity workforce. Although a minority of participants in the program are female, it is more than twice the percentage of females in the overall cybersecurity workforce. Furthermore, despite female participants' lower perceptions of cybersecurity careers, they showed a greater increase overall in positive perceptions than their male counterparts, significantly narrowing the gap between male and female responses.

7. FUTURE WORK

Additional work is required to determine what elements of the program contribute most significantly to student impact, and what can be done to attract more students, especially females, to participate. The 2017 survey adds several questions about students' reasons for participating, elements of the competition that were most impactful, how much time they spent training, etc. Analysis of the results of those questions is in progress. Further analysis is also required to quantify impacts on other underrepresented groups, including racial minorities, low-income students, and rural populations. Additionally, a true longitudinal study is needed to measure the long-term impact on participants, including actual career outcomes.

8. ACKOWLDGMENTS

The authors are grateful to Rachel Zimmerman and the staff of the CyberPatriot Program Office for providing the survey data used in this study. This research was sponsored by the Air Force STEM Outreach Office.

9. REFERENCES

[1] Abernathy, T. V. and Vineyard, R.N. 2001. Academic Competitions in Science: What Are the Rewards for Students? The Clearing House: A Journal of Educational Strategies, Issues and Ideas. 74, 5 (May 2001), 269–276.
[2] Air Force Association's CyberPatriot: The National Youth Cyber Education Program: http://uscyberpatriot.org/. Accessed: 2017-07-11.
[3] Akey, T.M. 2006. School Context, Student Attitudes and Behavior, and Academic Achievement: An Exploratory Analysis.
[4] Bashir, M. et al. 2016. Profiling cybersecurity competition participants: Self-efficacy, decision-making and interests predict effectiveness of competitions as a recruitment tool. Computers & Security. 65, (Mar. 2016), 153–165.
[5] Bishop, K. and Walters, H. 2007. The National Ocean Sciences Bowl: Extending the Reach of a High School Academic Competition to College, Careers, and a Lifelong Commitment to Science. American Secondary Education. 35, 3 (2007), 63–76.
[6] Campbell, J.R. and Walberg, H.J. 2010. Olympiad Studies: Competitions Provide Alternatives to Developing Talents That Serve National Interests. Roeper Review. 33, 1 (Dec. 2010), 8–17.
[7] Cohen, J. 1988. Statistical Power Analysis for the Behavioral Sciences. Lawrence Erlbaum Associates.
[8] Commission on Enhancing National Cybersecurity 2016. Report on Securing and Growing the Digital Economy.
[9] CyberPatriot Program Office 2016. CyberPatriot Student Alumni Survey Report: 2016.
[10] CyberPatriot Program Office 2014. CyberPatriot Survey Results: CyberPatriot VI Post-Season Competitor Survey 2013-2014 and CyberPatriot Student Alumni Survey 2014.
[11] CyberPatriot Program Office 2017. National Youth Cyber Defense Competition Registration Report: 2016-2017.
[12] Eagle, C. 2013. Computer security competitions: Expanding educational outcomes. IEEE Security & Privacy.
[13] Frost & Sullivan 2017. 2017 Global Information Security Workforce Study: Benchmarking Workforce Capacity and Response to Cyber Risk.
[14] Frost & Sullivan 2017. The 2017 Global Information Security Workforce Study: Women in Cybersecurity.
[15] Jacobson, D. and Rursch, J.A. 2008. Engaging Millenials with Information Technology: A Case Study Using High School Cyber Defense Competitions. Proceedings of the 12th Colloquium for Information Systems Security Education (CISSE '08), 59–65.
[16] Katzcy Consulting 2016. Cybersecurity Games: Building Tomorrow's Workforce.
[17] McEwan, T. and McConnell, A. 2013. Young people's perceptions of computing careers. 2013 IEEE Frontiers in Education Conference (FIE) (Oct. 2013), 1597–1603.
[18] McGill, M.M. et al. 2016. Undergraduate Students' Perceptions of the Impact of Pre-College Computing Activities on Choices of Major. ACM Transactions on Computing Education (TOCE). 16, 4 (Jun. 2016), Article 15.
[19] Pusey, P. et al. 2016. The Outcomes of Cybersecurity Competitions and Implications for Underrepresented Populations. IEEE Security & Privacy.
[20] Walters, H. and Bishop, K. 2004. Assessing the Impact of the National Ocean Sciences Bowl: A Systems Approach Final Report.
[21] White, G.B. et al. 2010. The CyberPatriot National High School Cyber Defense Competition. IEEE Security & Privacy.

Game based Cybersecurity Training for High School Students

Ge Jin
Purdue University Northwest
2200 169th St, Hammond, IN 46323, USA
ge.jin@pnw.edu

Manghui Tu
Purdue University Northwest
2200 169th St, Hammond, IN 46323, USA
Michael.Tu@pnw.edu

Tao-Hoon Kim
Purdue University Northwest
2200 169th St, Hammond, IN 46323, USA
Taehoon.Kim@pnw.edu

Justin Heffron
Purdue University Northwest
2200 169th St, Hammond, IN 46323, USA
jheffron@pnw.edu

Jonathan White
Purdue University Northwest
2200 169th St, Hammond, IN 46323, USA
white341@pnw.edu

ABSTRACT

Cybersecurity is critical to the national infrastructure, federal and local government, military, industry, and personal privacy. To defend the U.S. against the cyber threats, a significant demand for skilled cybersecurity workforce is predicted in government and industrial sectors. To address this issue, National Security Agency and the National Science Foundation jointly funded GenCyber program to stimulate the K–12 students' interest in the cybersecurity field and raise their awareness of cybersecurity and safe online behavior. Purdue University Northwest has successfully launched four GenCyber summer camps in 2016 and 2017 to 181 high school students, with 51.3% underrepresented minority ratio (Africa American and Hispanics), and about 2:1 male to female ratio. We delivered GenCyber summer camp activities in the format of game based learning and hands-on labs. The use of game-based learning in the camp was an excellent platform to teach concepts of cyber security principles. For example, in Cyber Defense Tower Game, students need to protect their servers from the different types of cyber-attack. They need to select the correct type of defense to stop each wave of cyber-attack. As the students advanced through the game, combinations of the different attacks would come faster, making it more difficult for the students to defend their servers. This game was well received by the students, support staffs, instructors, and site visit team. Learning through these activities provided high school students with an immersive, learner-centered experience, which has been proven very effective on cybersecurity awareness training and practical skill acquisition for learners from diverse backgrounds. Further analysis of survey data revealed that the gamification of cybersecurity education to raise students' interests in computer science and cybersecurity was more effective in male high school students than in female students.

ACM ISBN 978-1-4503-5103-4/18/02...$15.00.
https://doi.org/10.1145/3159450.3159591

CCS CONCEPTS

• Social and professional topics → Computing education → Computing education programs → Computer science education; • Social and professional topics → Computing education → K-12 education; • Applied computing → Computers in other domains → Personal computers and PC applications → Computer games

KEYWORDS

Cybersecurity; Cybersecurity education; Game base learning

ACM Reference format:

G. Jin, M. Tu, T. Kim, J. Heffron, and J. White. 2018. Game based Cybersecurity Training for High School Students. In *SIGCSE '18: 49th ACM Technical Symposium on Computer Science Education, Feb. 21–24, 2018, Baltimore, MD, USA*. ACM, NY, NY, USA, 6 pages. https://doi.org/10.1145/3159450.3159591

1 INTRODUCTION

With the recent high profile cybersecurity incidents targeting Sony Pictures, Target, Anthem and the massive OPM government data breach that followed, cybersecurity has become a top priority for the U.S. government. The U.S. government and major legislative proposals have been passed to enhance U.S. cybersecurity and new government agencies have been proposed to combat cyber threats. Cybersecurity is a shared mission between government and industry, because a large portion of the national cybersecurity infrastructure is in the private sector. Over the past few years, millions of sensitive data records have been compromised and a large number of frauds have been committed, especially in financial and healthcare sectors [1,2]. Such security breaches not only result in substantial financial losses, but also greatly hurt the confidence of customers, business partners and stakeholders [3].

Cybersecurity workforce development is the key to assuring that the nation has adequate security measures to protect and defend information and information systems. However, a global shortage of "1.8 million cybersecurity professionals by the year 2022" has been estimated [4]. According to the U.S. Bureau of Labor Statistics, the growth rate of jobs in information security is projected to be 37% from 2012–2022, and at the same time more than 209,000 cybersecurity jobs in the U.S. will be unfilled every year. The increasing demand for cybersecurity professionals from both government and private sectors makes it a critical mission for higher education institutions to attract and train next generation of cybersecurity workforce and citizenry who are capable of advancing national economic prosperity and security. The U.S. Congress has urged that it is critical to develop high-quality educators to expand cyber education at early age [5]. Expanding cybersecurity education to high schools has been highly advocated, as opinioned by a business leader in The Washington Post, "the key to training more cybersecurity experts is exposing students to STEM education — science, technology, engineering and mathematics — as well as adding some cybersecurity training in high school". To increase K-12 students' interest in cybersecurity and the diversity of cybersecurity workforce, the National Security Agency (NSA) and the National Science Foundation (NSF) have jointly funded more than 300 summer camps to K–12 students and teachers across the nation for the past 3 years [6].

Purdue University Northwest (PNW), a NSA/DHS designated National Center of Academic Excellence in Cyber Defense Education, has successfully launched four GenCyber summer camps for 181 high school students with 51.3% of underrepresented minority (Africa Americans and Hispanics) ratio. PNW GenCyber camp developed innovative game based cybersecurity education modules to provide high school students with hands-on activities in an immersive learning environment. We developed virtual reality (VR) 3D games, robotic programming games, and practical ethical hacking and cyber forensics labs based on simulated cases for cybersecurity training for high school students. The game based cybersecurity education is extremely beneficial to the future cybersecurity workforce by exposing more high school students to the cybersecurity education pathway at a time when they are making decisions regarding higher education. The innovative pedagogical methods and age appropriate game based learning curriculum, has made cybersecurity concepts more accessible to students of varying ability levels. This was supported by the post camp survey conducted for 154 participants.

2 RELATED WORKS

Research indicates that students receiving computer education in high school are 8 times more likely to major in a computer degree, while in the last 20 years; enrollment in computer education courses has seen a dramatic decrease at the high school level [7]. In addition, student participation is unrepresentative of national demographics. These statistics indicate that the key to developing more graduates in the cybersecurity field is establishing a meaningful pathway earlier in the educational process. A primary challenge to achieving this goal is the lack of age-appropriate cybersecurity curricula implemented with pedagogical methods that are most conducive to learning at the high school level [5].

Studies have shown that students learn only 20% of what they hear and read, but can learn 90% of what they have practiced [8]. Traditional teaching uses lectures as the major vehicle to deliver scientific knowledge and technology to learners, which has proven to fall short for learners. Learners at the high school level experience greater cognition if they are given opportunities to actively engage in classroom activities that support the development of critical thinking and problem solving skills. Therefore, there is a critical need for an innovative curriculum and pedagogical methods in the area of cybersecurity education.

The advance of technologies, high-speed connections, and the pervasiveness of mobile devices, have enabled various computer based pedagogical methods. One of the emergent and rapidly mutating forms of computer-based learning is "game based learning." As its name suggests, computer game allows learners to be immersed in an artificial or simulated game environment while experiencing it as real. Game based learning include virtual reality games, web-based games, multi-user virtual environments (MUVEs), massively multiplayer online games, and simulations [9]. Till date, applying game based learning instructional method to cybersecurity education is limited [10].

3 METHODOLOGY

The primary goals of NSA/NSF GenCyber program are: 1) increase interest in cybersecurity, 2) raise general awareness of cybersecurity and help all students understand appropriate and safe online behavior, and 3) increase diversity in the US cybersecurity workforce. As described in the introduction section, PNW GenCyber camp recruited 51.3% of underrepresented minority high school students, and met the goal of increasing diversity of summer camp participants.

To raise general awareness of cybersecurity and safe online behavior of high school students and increase their interest in cyber security, we developed game based cyber security learning modules to meet the GenCyber program goals. The topics of cybersecurity education games were selected in the following areas:

1. Social engineering and information security: Social engineering is the art of manipulating people so they give up confidential information, and social engineering scams such as phishing email have been extremely effective in security attacks. PNW GenCyber camp implemented a 3D VR game to simulate Piggybacking, Tailgating, and Mantrap in a security enhanced office environment to raise general awareness of social engineering scams.

2. Secure online behavior game: Secure online behaviors include identifying phishing emails and appropriately handling them, distinguish between trustworthy web links and insecure links, handling phony phone calls, and protecting personal information. A 3D VR secure online behavior game was developed to simulated high school computer lab and student's bedroom environment. The secure online behavior game allows students to appropriately handle email messages, text messages,

web links and phone calls, using various computing devices such as school computers, mobile phones, laptop computer, and networked game console.

3. Cyber Defense Tower Game: Tower defense game is a subgenre of strategy game to defend a player's territories or possessions by placing defensive structures on or along their path of attack [11]. A Cyber Defense Tower Game was created to allow students to protect their virtual computer server from the different cyber-attacks by applying GenCyber first principles and cybersecurity knowledge. Students need to select the correct types of defense tower to stop each wave of cyber-attacks. As the game progresses, the combinations of the different cyber-attacks would come faster and will make it more difficult for students to defend their servers.

4. 2D GenCyber Card Game: The GenCyber card game is a computerized version of physical GenCyber card game. Physical GenCyber card game requires two players to play the game in face-to-face mode. The computer based GenCyber card game is a single-player version of the GenCyber card game, which allows the students to play the card game by themselves at any convenient time.

3.1 3D Virtual Reality Game Development in Unity3D

Social engineering and secure online behavior game were developed in Unity3D game engine. Both games can be classified as 3D Role-Playing-Game (RPG) genre. The development of 3D RPG cyber security game consists of three major technical components: (1) 3D character and game environment modeling, (2) animation of the 3D game characters, and (3) scripting/programming of the interaction between game characters and dynamic behaviors.

The 3D characters of the game were created from Adobe Fuse software. Instead of modeling a 3D character from scratch, Adobe Fuse allows a user to assemble a 3D character from more than 20 base characters and further customize it into a unique character with different weight, height, skin tones, and texture.

The 3D character from Adobe Fuse was transferred seamlessly into Mixamo software. Mixamo will automatically rig the 3D character and provide hundreds of different motion clips that can be used to animate the character. We selected essential motion clips (such as idle, walk, run, talk, sit, and stand) for each character and export the animated 3D character to Unity3D game engine.

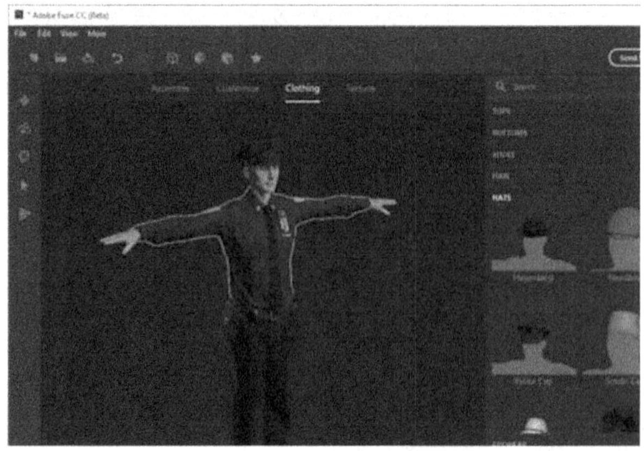

Figure 1: **3D Character Modeling and Customization in Adobe Fuse.**

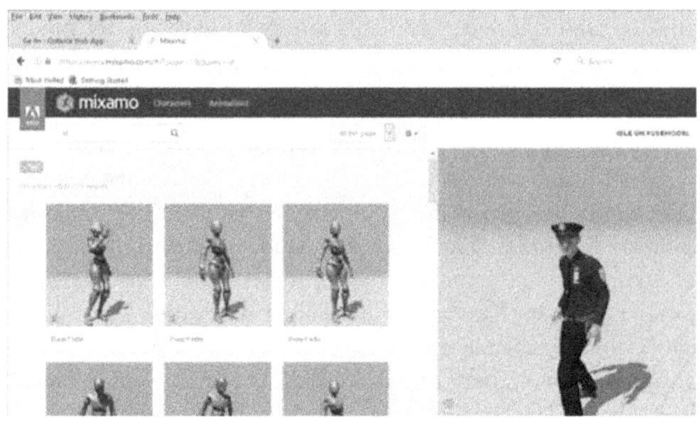

Figure 2: **Character Animation in Mixamo.**

The game environment was modeled mostly using the loyalty-free 3D assets from Unity Marketplace. Several 3D assets that related with social engineering and secure online behavior games were modeling using Autodesk 3D Max and Maya software. The behaviors of the 3D game characters were implemented by programming Unity C# script for each 3D character and dynamic assets in the game environment.

Figure 3: **Programming interactions and dynamic behaviors using Unity C# script.**

The flowing figures were captured from social engineering game and secure online behavior game.

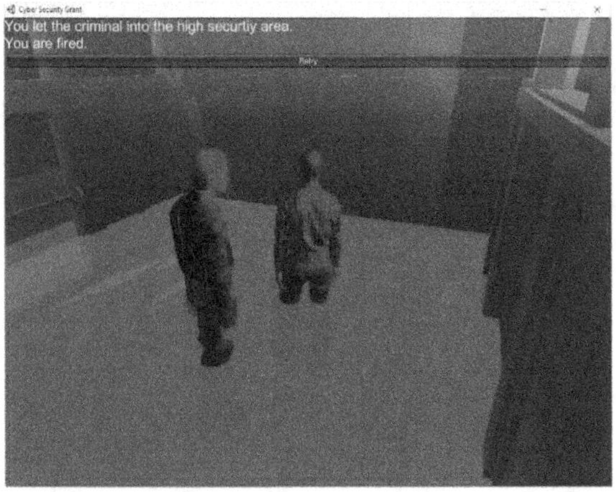

Figure 4: **3D Social Engineering Game.**

Figure 5: **3D Secure Online Behavior Game.**

3.2 Development of Cyber Defense Tower Game in Unity3D

The cyber defense tower game was implemented on top of Tower Defense Toolkit (TDTK) developed by Song Tan [12]. TDTK is a C# coding framework for the easy construction of Tower Defense games. TDTK comes with a bundle of scripts that can be adjusted to fit a variety of Tower Defense gameplay scenarios. The toolkit is designed custom models and art assets, and user can integrate their own art assets to make unique Tower Defense game. We have created 7 unique cyber-attacks (Fig. 6) and 6 cyber defense towers (Fig. 7).

Figure 6: **Cyber-Attacks in Cyber Defense Tower Game.**

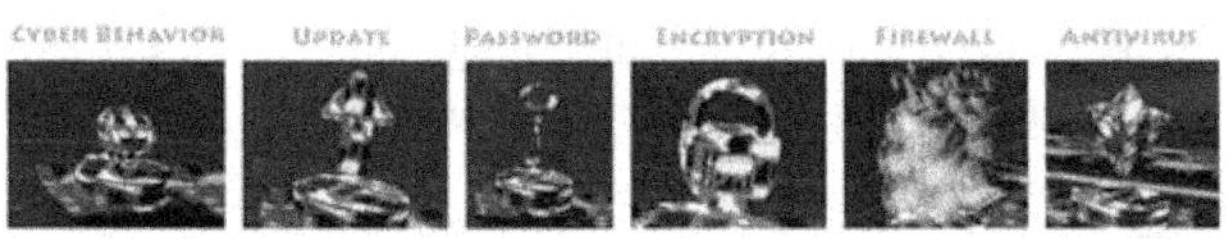

Figure 7: **Defense Towers in Cyber Defense Tower Game.**

One limitation of TDTK is that there are only two types of attacks: ground, air and three types of defense towers: ground, air and hybrid. It's impossible to use the built-in attacks and defense towers to simulate the cyber-attacks and defenses. We have customized the Tower Defense Toolkit to include 7 additional attack types (Virus, Phishing, Trojan, Spyware, Ransomware, DDoS, and Sniffer), and 6 additional defense towers (Antivirus, Password, System Update, Secure Cyber Behavior, Encryption, and Firewall). Some defense towers will defend single type of attack, while other defense towers can defend multiple attack types. For example, the Antivirus tower will defend against Virus, Trojan and Spyware. In addition, certain type of attack can be defended by multiple defense towers. The Sniffer attack can be defended by Password tower and Encryption tower. Cyber Defense Tower Game contains three difficulty levels: tutorial, intermediate and competition level. Fig. 8 is the tutorial level and Fig. 9 is the competition level.

Figure 8: **Tutorial Level in Tower Defense Game.**

Figure 9: **Competition Level in Tower Defense Game.**

3.3 Single-player GenCyber Card Game

The single player version of GenCyber Card game was developed to enhance the students' understanding of 10 Cyber Security First Principles. The original card game was designed and created by Dr. Vincent Nestler at California State University San Bernardino [13]. The computerized GenCyber card game was created by scanning the cards and uploading the images into

Processing programming environment. The site team observed students playing this game during the down time at camp and some students were even creating "cheat sheets" so they could beat their friends' times.

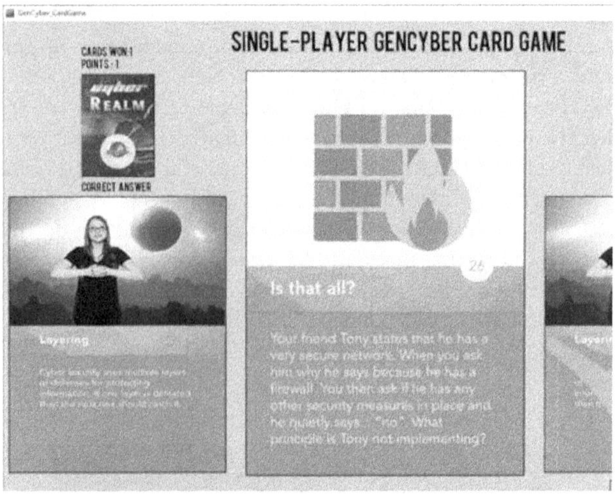

Figure 10: **Single-player GenCyber Card Game.**

4 RESULTS

Purdue University Northwest has successfully launched two 1-week summer camps in June 2016, and another two 1-week summer camps in June 2017. Each GenCyber camp day consists of four 90-minutes sessions; two 15-minutes group discussions, a 60-minute lunch break, and two 15-minutes mini breaks. The day activity will start from 9:00am and ends at 4:30pm. During the 1-week summer camp, each student participated in activities mentored by a team of PNW faculty members and student assistants. The GenCyber team includes 4 faculty members and their roles are listed below: 1) Dr. Ge Jin has 9 years of college teaching and research experience in computer graphics, visualization, animation, with teaching experience in fundamentals of information assurance for CIT program. 2) Dr. Michael Tu has 11 years of college teaching and research in cybersecurity and digital forensics, certified Ethical Hacker, Certified Pen Tester, Certified Hacking and Forensics Investigator, and Certified AccessData Computer Examiner. 3) Dr. Tae-Hoon Kim has 5 years of college teaching and research experience in computer networks, network security and taught computer networks, network security, network design & administration courses at both undergraduate/graduate levels. 4) Dr. Keyuan Jiang has 20 years of college teaching experience in software programming with extensive project management and student advising experiences.

Total of 181 high school students attended the summer camps with 51.3% were underrepresented African American and Hispanic students. The male to female ratio was 2.12 to 1 (Table 1). The students were exposed to cybersecurity first principles and cybersecurity awareness by playing various cyber security computer games during the first two days. About 25 students in one classroom have competed for 3D Secure Online Behavior game, Cyber Defense Tower game and Single-player GenCyber Card game. We picked one winner from each competition and awarded the winner with a small gift on the last day of the summer camp.

Table 1: **Male to Female Ratio of Camp Participants**

Year	Gender	Numer of participants
2016	Male	60
	Female	26
2017	Male	63
	Female	32
Total		181

The post-camp survey was conducted at the last day of the summer camp. A 5-point Likert scale was used to measure the student's satisfactory rate of camp activities and experiences ranging from 5 (strongly agree) to 1 (strongly disagree). The post-camp survey of 154 camp participants indicated that game based learning for cybersecurity has enhanced student's knowledge in cybersecurity, and understanding of the cybersecurity first principles, and educated a digital citizenry with security awareness, and motivated them to pursue higher education and careers in the field of cybersecurity.

Table 2: **Post-camp Survey Questions and Results**

Post-Camp Survey Questions	Rating
I enjoyed learning about computer science	4.36
I would like to learn more about computer science	4.22
I enjoyed learning about cybersecurity	4.27
I would like to learn more about cybersecurity	4.05
The teachers/faculty in this program made me more interested in cybersecurity	4.20
I know what cybersecurity means	4.27
I know more about cybersecurity than I did before this camp	4.36
I know more about computer science than I did before this camp	4.26
I am more comfortable learning cybersecurity concepts now	4.08
I know more about information security than I did before this camp	4.29
I can explain why cybersecurity is important	4.18
Overall this camp was a good experience	4.46
I am glad I attended this camp	4.46
I would like to attend more camps like this	4.17
My opinions and ideas were respected in this camp	4.32
I found the camp activities interesting	4.22
I liked interacting with the teachers at this camp	4.28

The authors further analyzed the survey data to investigate the gender difference in game-based learning. Hypothesis testing for two population means with unequal variance (T-Test) was used to test gender difference for each survey question. The result of hypothesis testing shows that: there are significant differences between male and female students' impression about the camp activities in survey question 1 and survey question 16. It can be interpreted as: the male students thought the game based learning camp activities were more enjoyable and interesting than female students.

5 CONCLUSIONS

In this paper, we introduced an innovative game based learning method for cybersecurity education. Four computer games were developed to educate social engineering and information security concept, secure online behaviors and cybersecurity first principles. The use of game-based learning in the PNW GenCyber camp was an excellent platform to teach concepts of cybersecurity principles and secure online behaviors. This approach is beneficial to the future cybersecurity workforce by exposing more high school students to the cybersecurity education pathway at a time when they are making decisions regarding higher education. The game based learning method was well received by the students, support staff, instructors, and site visit team. This was also supported by the post camp survey conducted for 154 participants with average rating of 4.26 out of 5. To investigate the gender difference of game-based learning, hypothesis testing for two population means with unequal variance (T-Test) was conducted to test gender difference. The hypothesis testing result indicated that the male students thought the game based learning activities were more enjoyable and interesting than female students.

ACKNOWLEDGMENTS

This work was jointly funded by the National Security Agency and National Science Foundation GenCyber grant (NSA Award No. H98230-17-1-0206).

REFERENCES

[1] Eric Johnson and Nicholas Willey. Usability failures and healthcare data hemorrhages. *IEEE Security and Privacy.* 9, 2(2011), 18-25

[2] Manghui Tu and Kimberly Spoa-Harty. Data loss prevention management and control: inside activity monitoring, identification, and tracking in healthcare enterprise environments. *Journal of Digital Forensics, Security, and Law.* 10, 1(2015), 27-44

[3] Lawrence Trautman. Cyberseurity: what about US policy? 2015. [online] https://papers.ssrn.com/sol3/papers.cfm?abstract_id=2548561

[4] A Frost & Sullivan Executive Briefing. Global Information Security Workforce Study. 2017. [online] https://iamcybersafe.org/wp-content/uploads/2017/06/Europe-GISWS-Report.pdf

[5] Jan Cuny and Jim Hamos. NICE cybersecurity in K-12 formal education. 2011 [online] http://csrc.nist.gov/nice/Sept2011-workshop/presentations/Thursday/Thurs_Cuny_NICE_K-12_092211.pdf

[6] Tina Ladabouche and Steve LaFountain. GenCyber: Inspiring the Next Generation of Cyber Stars. *IEEE Security & Privacy.* 14, 5,(2016), 84-86

[7] Stuart Zweben. Computing Degree and Enrollment Trends, from the 2012-2013 CRA Taulbee Survey. 2013. [online] http://www.cra.org/

[8] Michael Findley. The relationship between student learning styles and motivation during educational video game play. *International Journal of Online Pedagogy and Course Design.* 1, 3(2011), 63-73

[9] Abhishek Kumar, Subham Gupta, Animesh Rai, and Sapna Sinha. Social networking sites and their security issues. *International Journal of Scientific and Research Publications.* 3, 4(2013), 1-5

[10] Stephen Tang and Martin Hanneghan. A Model-Driven Framework to Support Development of Serious Games for Game based Learning. *The 3rd International Conference on Developments in e-Systems Engineering.* London, UK. 2010.

[11] Damon Reece. Best Tower Defense Games of All Time. 2015. [online] http://gameranx.com/features/id/13529/article/best-tower-defense-games/

[12] Song Tan. Tower Defense ToolKit (TDTK). 2016. [online] https://www.songgamedev.com/tdtk

[13] Vincent Nestler. Cyber Realm. 2016. [online] http://gencybercards.com/

The Effect of Reporting Known Issues on Students' Work

Iris Gaber Amir Kirsh
The Academic College of Tel-Aviv-Yaffo
Tel-Aviv, ISRAEL

ABSTRACT

Students in Computer Science programming courses often have difficulty with coding, which results in flawed exercises. We asked students working on programming exercises to report known defects in their submission. We distinguish between three types of defects: bugs in the program, missing features, and poorly written code. Results show that students detect and report missing features and bugs quite accurately (59% of the bugs and 61% of the missing features were reported), but they are much less aware of the quality of their code (only 28% of the code issues were reported). After comparing their grades to the grades of the previous year we argue that the request to report defects helps student in submitting exercises with fewer bugs. Finally, the students affirmed that the request to report defects helped them in detecting problems and improved their time management.

CCS CONCEPTS

• **Social and professional topics** → **Software engineering education; Student assessment;** • **Computer science education** → *OOP;*

KEYWORDS

Known Issues, Code Quality, Students Perception, Software Defects

ACM Reference format:
Iris Gaber and Amir Kirsh. 2018. The Effect of Reporting Known Issues on Students' Work . In *SIGCSE '18: The 49th ACM Technical Symposium on Computer Science Education, Feb. 21–24, 2018, Baltimore , MD, USA. ACM, NY, NY, USA,* 6 pages. https://doi.org/10.1145/3159450.3159456

1 INTRODUCTION

The process by which students learn to program is a major topic in computer science educational research. Programming is a fundamental part of the computer science curriculum, and is considered to be challenging. Research shows that students in computer science classes have difficulty with coding and problem solving [5, 9, 10], and as a result the number of students who dropout is high. Reports show that only 44% of the students are retained beyond their freshman year in some of the universities in the U.S. [13]. One of the most fundamental skills the students must acquire is the ability to detect bugs and to correct them. Whether the students end up working as testing engineers or as software developers after graduation, the testing skill will play a major role in their career. Software testing is a critical phase in the Software Development Life Cycle (SDLC). As Bill Gates said: "..we have as many testers as we have developers. And testers spend all their time testing, and developers spend half their time testing" [4]. The major activity performed during software testing is to identify bugs. According to Trivedi et al. [12], more than 40% of the project time is consumed over this activity. Therefore, it is clearly important that programmers report defects they are aware of and save valuable time for the testing team.

Unfortunately, this is one of the major difficulties students encounter. Murphy shows that most students lack the skill of effective debugging. Thus, often when they try to debug their program they end up creating more errors than they fix [11]. Ahmadzadeh et al. [2] show that the students who are good debuggers are also good programmers, while the reverse is usually not true, as many students with a good understanding of programming do not debug their programs effectively. They attribute this to the knowledge of actual program implementation that is gained by debugging. Programming teachers agree that students should spend more time testing their code, and some of them put emphasis on unit testing in their classes. However, many students do not see the use of this. In a discussion at ACM listserv titled: "Value of Unit Testing"[1], many programming professors complain that "it can be difficult to convince folks of the value of unit testing (and test-driven development in general)."

Bryce et al. [6] took interest in the bugs students were aware of and collected the bugs using a tutor lab where students were encouraged to get help from teaching assistants. Their main result is that approximately 22% of the problems are due to problem solving skills, while the remaining problems involve a combination of logic and syntax problems for specific topics. In their paper, they noticed that "Students are not always as descriptive as they should be and sometimes have additional bugs that they do not know about".

The presence of bugs in the exercises students submit, however important, is not the only problem in students' work. In our research we examine programming defects in general. We distinguish between three types of defects: Code, Bug, and Feature. In the 'Code' category we look for 'Code Smell' (see Fowler and Beck [3]), in the 'Bug' category, we check the programming bugs, and in the 'Feature' category we look for features that are not fully implemented.

We asked our students to report known-issues in their exercises, classified under 'Bug', 'Feature' and 'Code'. After checking their exercises, we compared the reports with the actual defects.

SIGCSE '18, February 21–24, 2018, Baltimore , MD, USA

ACM ISBN 978-1-4503-5103-4/18/02...$15.00
https://doi.org/10.1145/3159450.3159456

There can be several objectives to the students' reports. Reports can save time for the exercises' checkers in the same way reporting known issues by developers saves time for the testing team. Also, the reports may help teachers, as they would know what types of problems students are aware of and lack the knowledge of how to fix and what types of problems students are unaware of and need help in detecting.

The first aspect of our research is detecting the defects in the students' exercises, the second aspect is the self detection of defects by the students themselves, and the third aspect of our work is the effect reporting known issues has on the students. We speculate that the need to report the defects helps the students and eventually results in a better exercise. We compare the exercises of two cohorts, where in one cohort, 2017*a*, the students reported defects and in the other, 2016*a*, they did not. Then, we present the opinion of the students about the task of reporting defects.

Summarizing our research questions:

- What are the types of actual defects in students' work?
- What types of issues are the students aware of?
- Does reporting known-issues benefit the students?

The research is based on students in the "Object Oriented Programming and C++ Language" (OOP) course. The students were asked to fill reports regarding their exercises immediately after the exercise submission, specifying problems they were aware of. In addition the students filled questionnaires in which they specified if and how the requirement to report problems helped them or disrupted them in the programming task.

We ask our students to submit their exercises in pairs, as wide research have shown that this benefits the students. Wilson et al. [15] show that collaborative work benefits problem-solving performance required in programming tasks typical of first year university level computing courses. Kirsh and Gaber [8] show that working in pairs on the exercise is a significant factor for predicting success. Some of the pairs may choose to work on one workstation, side by side. This is called 'pair programming'. Williams and Kessler's book [14] discusses its theory, practice and the various studies up to that date. Harsley et al. [7] studied pair programming and showed that while both individual and pair programmers had equivalent learning gains, pair programmers took significantly less time on most problems, consulted fewer examples, coded more efficiently, and showed more signs of engagement. We believe that the pair submission helps our research for two additional reasons: (1) a team member can check his/her partner's code and spot defects that are unnoticed by the coder, and (2) problems which were not reported were actually overlooked by two students, probably indicating more strongly that the students were actually unaware of these flaws.

2 THE RESEARCH

The students that we sampled are students in the "Object Oriented Programming and C++ Language" (OOP) class 2017a in the Academic College of Tel-Aviv-Yaffo. The students are second-year students, who prior to this course have learned the C language over two mandatory courses (including data structures: arrays, linked lists and trees). OOP is the first course in which they learn the object oriented principles. During the semester, the students were given three consecutive exercises. The students did the exercises in pairs. There were 65 teams in the class [1]. Each team reported problems in their submitted exercise. We encouraged the students to report these issues, as a reported known issue would cause a reduced fine in the grade[2]. Also, we recommended the students, who worked in pairs, to divide the work between them such that every team member was responsible of reviewing and testing the code of his/her partner.

We defined three categories of defects: Code, Bug and Feature. We classify the 'Code' issues as: (1) Procedural flaws; (2) Object-Oriented Programming (OOP) flaws; or (3) Design flaws.

Among the types of 'Procedural' flaws there are: (a) long methods; (b) magic numbers - hard coded numbers instead of constants; (c) redundant code; (d) code duplication; and (e) confusing names. The 'OOP' flaws include: (a) missing class; (b) redundant class (lazy class); (c) large class; and (d) inappropriate intimacy between classes. Finally, 'Design' flaws include: (a) flow design problems; and (b) data design problems. The categories and subtypes resemble the 'Code Smell' types introduced by Fowler and Beck [3].

Within the 'Bug' category the students specified the effect of the bug - whether the program crashed or misbehaved. Within the 'Feature' category the students listed the features that were not implemented.

The exercise in discussion required an implementation of a console screen game, where two players compete by solving simple math equations. At each stage one equation is displayed on the screen for both players. Each player on screen is denoted by a character that is controlled by the keyboard. Numbers appear on the screen randomly, and the player that collects the number which solves the current equation wins the stage and a new equation is displayed. A player that collects a wrong number loses the stage.

We checked the exercises before reading the known issues reports. The checking included testing the program and looking into the code, while classifying the issues we detected. Then, we reviewed the reports and compared them with the defects we found. Normally, checking the exercises along with the reports might be helpful, however for the sake of the research we wanted our checking to be independent of the reports.

Finally, we asked the students in two different questionnaires whether having to specify their problems helped them in the programming task. The first questionnaire was filled after the submission the first exercise and the second one at the end of the course.

3 RESULTS

3.1 Distribution of Defects and Reported Issues

We start by analyzing the defects in the exercise as perceived by the students. Table 1 displays the overall number of teams, the number of teams who reported any defects, the total number of reported defects, and the averages of reported defects per team. Table 2 displays the distribution of the three categories: Bug, Code and Feature as classified by the students.

[1] There were 64 teams of two and one team of a single student.

[2] Eventually, in the actual grade, we reduced the penalty for reported defects by 40%, compared to the same defect if not reported. However, for the analysis in this research all defects are graded according to their severity, reported or not.

Table 1: Reported Issues

Total number of teams	65
Number of teams who reported defects	51
Number of reported defects	163
Avg. reported defects per team	3.2

Table 2: Distribution of Reported Issues

	Feature	Code	Bug	Total
Frequency	35	71	57	163
Avg. per team	0.69	1.39	1.12	3.2

After checking the exercises, we went over the reported issues and in several cases we found the classification the students made to be inaccurate. For example, 3 students reported that in some place their code is not well written, however after looking into the code it turned out to be a potential bug. Also, 22 of the reported issues were actually wrongly considered problematic, and are non-issues in our opinion.

Table 3 summarizes our main results. We count the reported defects using our classification and the defects we found but were not reported. For each type we count the number of exercises in which it was found, the number of times the problem was found, and the total number of points reduced due to that type of defect[3]. Table 4 displays the distribution of the reported issues as classified by us, and the distribution of the defects that we found but were not reported. It is noticeable that 61.1% of the 'Feature' defects (22 out of 36) and 58.5% of the 'Bug' defects (62 out of 106) were spotted by the students, however only 27.5% of the 'Code' defects (57 out of 207) were reported. We conclude that students are much more aware of their bugs and missing features than of the quality of their code.

3.2 Examples of Defects

In this section we present a few examples of bugs and code defects found while checking the exercises.

Recall that the exercise is an implementation of a game which takes place on the console. Numbers are placed at different locations and a player collects them according to specific assignments.

We refer to a 'Bug' as any error that was either found during actual runtime or have been noticed in code, regardless whether the bug actually impacts the program behavior. This includes, for example, a memory leak that is clearly a bug but its impact on the program would not be discovered during testing.

Here are a few example of Bugs:

(1) In one math assignment of the game, the player should collect the square of 13. The program mistakenly checked if the square of the collected number is 169, i.e., it expects 13 instead of expecting 169. This is not likely to be a misunderstanding of the requirements as the text presented to the player was correct.
(2) In one math assignment the player should collect a multiple of 7. The program checks if $num/7 == 0$ instead of $num\%7 == 0$.
(3) The program should flush the screen, using cout.flush(), before moving the cursor, otherwise the output is buffered and may be printed later at a wrong location on the screen. In several submissions the call to cout.flush() was wrongly placed.

We refer to a 'Code Defect' as any bad implementation that is not a 'Bug', i.e. would not be considered as an error, but is considered as a bad code practice, i.e 'Code Smell'.

Here are some examples of 'Procedural' code defects:

(1) Massive code duplication: for example, the code in Figure 1 can be written in a much simpler way, by using an array of strings for the mission descriptions.
(2) Redundant code: 'simplify boolean' example as shown in Figure 3 where just returning the expression would be simpler.
(3) Long functions: there were many cases of long functions, most of them reported. Figure 4 demonstrates the problem. We would expect the student to split the different conditions into functions.
(4) Confusing names: some names do not reflect the role of the function or the variable. e.g., a function called "displayInstructions" which only returns a string to be printed.
(5) Bad Overloading: for example, four methods called "isAvailable" in the same class, each with different parameters and each doing different things. See Figure 5.
(6) Inefficient Code: students should check whether some number is prime. Figure 6 shows an inefficient implementation of a loop. The loop does not stop even when it finds a divisor.

Here are some examples of 'OOP' code defects:

(1) Inappropriate intimacy between classes: unrequired intimacy between the classes: 'Point', 'Player', and 'Game'.
(2) Lazy class: having both class 'Point' and class 'Location' which essentially serve the same purpose.
(3) Redundant code: an example is shown in Figure 2. Note that the copy constructor is redundant as the default would be sufficient. Also, the parameter should be passed as const.

Here are some examples of 'Design' code defects:

(1) The students were required to create a menu, with the options of starting a new game, starting a game at a certain level, presenting the players' score table and exiting the program. In the game itself the students were required to allow exiting the game back to the main menu. Some students implemented the return to the main menu as a direct call to a 'menu' function - resulting in a recursion. In order to finally get out of the program these students needed to use the 'exit' function.
(2) Design that does not match the exercise' specifications: some students tend to use code that was presented to them in class, as is, without making the necessary adjustments. It is

[3] Grades are in the scale 0 to 100. Reduced points are in the same scale, according to defect severity, some examples: too long function reduced 1 point, a minor bug - e.g., wrong formula for checking one specific math exercise reduced 1 point, memory leak reduced 5 points.

Table 3: Classification of Reported and Unreported Defects

Classification	Unreported			Reported			Non-issue
	works	freq.	points	works	freq.	points	freq.
Feature							
Req. misunderstanding	1	1	8	4	4	7	1
Fully/ partially missing	10	13	27	9	12	15	9
Did better than req.	0	0	0	6	6	0	0
Code							
Procedural flaw	52	82	70	24	40	36	5
OOP flaw	24	25	63	9	10	23	6
Design flaw	32	43	76	6	7	11	0
Bug							
Memory leak	12	14	75	4	4	23	0
Accessing bad address[a]	0	0	0	3	4	17	0
Potential bug in code[b]	8	8	3	0	0	0	0
Applicative Bugs	11	22	45	28	54	114	1
Total		208	367		141	246	22

[a]The students merely reported a bug which we later detected as accessing bad address
[b]Bugs that we found while looking into the code and not while running the program

Table 4: Classification of Reported and Unreported Defects: Summary of Frequency and Reduced Points

	Frequency			Points		
	Feature	Code	Bug	Feature	Code	Bug
Reported	22	57	62	22	70	154
Unreported	14	150	44	35	209	123
Total	36	207	106	57	279	277
%Reported	61.1%	27.5%	58.5%	38.6%	25.1%	55.6%

like they learned to implement a Zebra and when are asked to implement a Giraffe, they put the entire Zebra code in their program and write code to erase the stripes and pull up its neck. In our case we presented in class an example in which the game board was predefined. Many students pasted the code into their program even though in their exercise the board contained random values, which required a somewhat different approach.

In summary, all the students managed to submit a working program, but many of them did it on the expense of writing low quality code.

3.3 The Effect of Reporting Known Issues

Another research question we addressed was the usefulness of the reporting task. We wanted to check whether reporting defects improves the students' submissions, and whether it causes a different distribution of flaws in the exercise. We conjectured that such reports may benefit the students for the following reasons: (1) It may compel them to think over problems in their work. By doing so they can better manage their time, giving priority to some issues, while writing down others and dealing with them later. (2) It may drive them to test their programs more deeply. (3) They may adopt it as a convenient routine and be more prepared for the industry. (4) Specifying the problems in one exercise may perhaps help them in the subsequent tasks given in the course, which are follow up exercises. (5) Since the exercises were done in pairs, it may encourage them to have each team member review the code of the other and debug it.

Table 5: Exercise Grades Comparison: Without Reporting Known Issues (2016a) and With Reporting (2017a)

	2016a	2017a
Average grade	86.8	90.6
p-value t-test	0.040	
Points Reduced on Average		
Code Defects	4.17	4.29
p-value t-test	0.845	
Bug and Feature Defects[4]	9.05	5.14
p-value t-test	0.018	

In order to check our assumption that the request to report defects aids the students, we looked into the first exercise given last year, 2016*a*, and classified their defects. We then compared the grades the students were given last year with the grades of the exercise in discussion. The results are summarized in Table 5. For the p-value we used a two tailed heteroscedastic t-test. Three findings come up from the comparison. (1) The grades are higher in 2017*a* than in 2016*a*, (2) The points reduced for 'Bug' and 'Feature' defects are significantly lower in 2017*a*, and (3) The points reduced for 'Code' defects are quite similar. The first two results

[4]The comments on the exercises of 2016*a* did not distinguish between 'Bug' and 'Feature' so we combined them. We did distinguish between problems found while running the program and code issues that do not affect the running

```
void Mission::choosMission(int NumMission) {
        switch (NumMission)
        {
          case ONE: //mission one
                gotoxy(20,0);
                cout << "Choose a prime number ";
                cout.flush();
                break;
          case TWO://mission two
                gotoxy(20, 0);
                cout << "Choose a num that Devide By Seven ";
                cout.flush();
                break;
          case THREE://mission three
                gotoxy(20, 0);
                cout << "Choose a number that Devide By Four ";
                cout.flush();
                break;
          case FOUR://mission four
                gotoxy(20, 0);
                cout << "Choose a Square number ";
                cout.flush();
                break;
          case FIVE://mission five
                gotoxy(20, 0);
                cout << "Choose a num that Moddle in 7 give 3";
                cout.flush();
                break;
          case SIX://mission six
                gotoxy(20, 0);
                cout << "Choose the squere of 13 ";
                cout.flush();
                break;
        }
}
```

Figure 1: An example of code duplication

```
Point(Point & p) {              //Point obj ctor
  _row = p.getRow();
  _col = p.getCol();
}
```

Figure 2: Redundant copy constructor

are statistically significant with p-value of 0.04 for the difference in the average grade and p-value of 0.02 for the difference in the reduced points for 'Bug' and 'Feature' defects. We claim that this is unlikely to be attributed to other factors. The exercise given in 2016*a* was of the same format and of the same difficulty level as the exercise given in 2017*a*. Still, it is different enough to prevent students to use the solutions of previous semesters; In both cohorts the students worked in pairs; The teachers were the same teachers, and the pedagogical approach was identical. Furthermore, the students of class 2016*a* are not less skilful than the students of class 2017*a* - the average grade of the final exam in 2016*a* was 73.30 and the average grade of the final exam in 2017*a* was 72.84. The way the exercise was graded in 2016*a* was not more strict. If anything, it was less strict as we put effort in finding all the defects for the sake of the research in 2017*a*, and we used the same score criteria in 2017*a* as we did in 2016*a*.

We conjecture that the request to report issues made the students do more testing and discover more bugs in their submission and fix them. We suspect however, that they are not fully aware of their code quality and do not fully comprehend the principles of good coding.

```
if (num % 7 == 3)
  return true;
else
  return false;
```

Figure 3: Simplify Boolean Returns

```
do {
        y = rand() % 21;
        x = rand() % 79;
   }  while (currentBoard.signInBoard(x, y) == # ||
        currentBoard.signInBoard(x, y) == '@' ||
        currentBoard.signInBoard(x + 1, y) == '#' ||
        currentBoard.signInBoard(x + 1, y) == '@' ||
        currentBoard.signInBoard(x - 1, y) == '#' ||
        currentBoard.signInBoard(x - 1, y) == '@' ||
        currentBoard.signInBoard(x, y - 1) == '#' ||
        currentBoard.signInBoard(x, y - 1) == '@' ||
        currentBoard.signInBoard(x, y + 1) == '#' ||
        currentBoard.signInBoard(x, y + 1) == '@' ||
        x > COLS - 2 || x == 0 || y < 3 || y == 24 ||
        board[y - 1][x] != ' ' || board[y + 1][x] != ' ' ||
        board[y][x + 1] != ' ' || board[y][x + 2] != ' ' ||
        board[y][x + 3] != ' ' || board[y][x - 1] != ' ' ||
        board[y + 1][x] != ' ' || board[y - 1][x] != ' ' ||
        board[y - 2][x] != ' ' || board[y + 2][x] != ' ');
```

Figure 4: Needs to call auxiliary methods

```
void isAvailable(Point& givenPoint, bool& hitSnake, bool& hitNumber,
                                                  Number& eatenNumber);
void isAvailable(Point& givenPoint, bool& hitSnake, bool& hitNumber);
bool isAvailable(Point& givenPoint, Number& eatenNumber);
bool isAvailable(Point& givenPoint);
```

Figure 5: Wrong overloading

```
bool Task::isPrime(int num) {
        bool isPrime = true;
        int n = (int)sqrt(num);
        for (int i = 2; i <= n; i++) {
                if (num%i == 0) isPrime = false;
        }
        return isPrime;
}
```

Figure 6: An example of an inefficient code

3.4 The Students' Opinion about the Requirement to Report Defects

In order to learn about the subjective opinion of the students regarding the requirement to report known issues we passed two questionnaires during the semester. The first was passed after the submission of the exercise, and the second at the end of the course.

The first questionnaire contained multiple choice questions, aiming to find whether the students perceived the task of reporting known issues as helpful, disruptive or neither. For each question we asked them to also elaborate in their own words. We summarize the responses in Figure 7. To the first question: "Did you find reporting the issues to be helpful or disruptive?" 66% of the students marked "Helpful" and only 0.9% (1 student) marked "Disruptive". Looking at the comments, the popular reasons in favor of the reporting task were "It was good to know that the bugs we find will get a reduced fine" , "It made us more responsible", and "It felt like

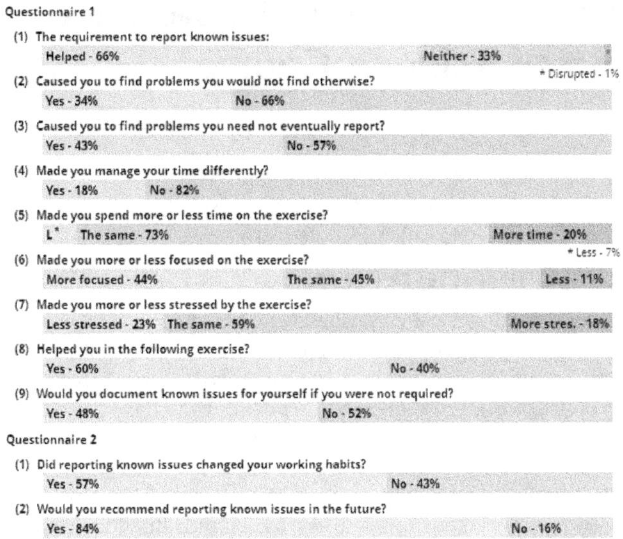

Figure 7: Questionnaires Responses

in the real world". Some students noted that the format of the report sheet was helpful. Another interesting remark was that since the work was done in pairs, sometimes one student wrote down a defect and his partner fixed it.

34% stated that filling the report caused them to find problems they would not have found otherwise. 43% marked "Yes" to the claim that the requirement to report known issues caused them to find problems and fix them, eventually without reporting them.

Another question aimed to check whether the report caused the students to spend more time on the exercise. 20% of the students claimed to have spent more time working on the exercise. However, after reading their comments we learn that only half of those 20% feel the report was a waste of their time and unnecessary, while the other half wrote that the extra time was a time well spent, as it caused them to submit a better exercise. (e.g. "we didn't spend our time on minor problems"). Another thing we checked was the possible negative effects of the report on the students. Less than 18% reported it added to their stress level, where 23% reported it decreased it, and only 11% reported that the task made them less focused, where 44% stated it made them more focused.

The second questionnaire was filled after the submission of all the programming exercises. 57% of the students stated that reporting known issues changed their working habits. 84% would recommend us to continue with the requirement to report known issues also in future semesters. In their remarks, the students who recommended keeping the requirement to report known issues stated the following: "I think filling the report is essential to the design and improvement of every exercise"; "The requirement helps us understand what should be fixed"; "It helped me focus on the important things and reduced my stress level"; "It helps the checker know what problems we are aware of. In addition, it raises our motivation to fix those problems"; "It is kind of a 'TODO list' which helped me. Also, it's nice we can confess on something that is not working and thus show that we are aware of the problem and will probably fix it in the next exercise". Among the students who were against keeping the requirement of reporting known issues, we found the following remarks: "It was more of a burden than a help"; "I think it is not needed because our exercise is not that large".

4 CONCLUSIONS

We asked students to report known issues in their exercise submission. We find that reporting known issues caused students to identify the majority of their bugs and improve their submission. The reporting task was perceived by most of the students as helpful and they recommend us to continue with this requirement. Although students are aware of many of their bugs and missing features, they are not sufficiently aware of the quality of their code. The students are able to solve problems and submit a working exercise at the expense of writing low quality code. Unfortunately most of them do not yet have good programming skills and do not obey the rules of decent procedural code. In order to improve the quality of the students' work we suggest that programming teachers will request their students to report known issues, as it compels them to write down their problems and detect bugs and missing features in their code. We presume presenting in class a catalog of poorly written code snippets and their proposed replacement can increase students' awareness to their code quality. We plan to check in future work if this actually improves the quality of students' code.

REFERENCES

[1] http://listserv.acm.org/scripts/wa-ACMLPX.exe?A2=ind1701A&L=SIGCSE-MEMBERS&D=0&P=5942

[2] Ahmadzadeh M., Elliman D., Higgins C.(2009) An analysis of patterns of debugging among novice computer science students. In Proceedings of the 10th annual SIGCSE conference on Innovation and Technology in Computer Science Education. pp. 84-88.

[3] Fowler M., Beck K. (2000) Bad Smells in Code. in Refactoring: Improving the Design of Existing Code, Addison-Wesley, 2000, pp. 75-88.

[4] Foley J., Murphy C.(2002) , Q&A: Bill Gates On Trustworthy Computing, Information Week, Available on-line: http://www.informationweek.com/qanda-bill-gates-on-trustworthy-computing/d/d-id/1015083?

[5] Guzdial, M. (2011) Education: from Science to Engineering. CACM. 64(2). pp 37-39.

[6] Bryce, R.C., Cooley, A., Hansen, A., Hayrapetyan, N.(2010) A one year empirical study of student programming bugs. In: Frontiers in Education Conference (FIE), 2010 IEEE, pp. 1-7.

[7] Harsley R., Fossati D.,Di Eugenio B., Green N. (2017) Interactions of Individual and Pair Programmers with an Intelligent Tutoring System for Computer Science. Proceedings of the 2017 ACM SIGCSE Technical Symposium on Computer Science Education pp. 285-290.

[8] Kirsh A., Gaber I. (2016) Satisfaction, Time Investment and Success in Students' Programming Exercise. Proceedings of the Programming Experience 2016 (PX/16) Workshop pp. 9-20.

[9] McCartney, R., Boustedt, J., Eckerdal, A., Sanders, K., Zander, C. (2013). Can first-year students program yet?: a study revisited. Proceedings of the Ninth Annual International ACM Conference on International Computing Education Research, pp. 91-98.

[10] McCracken, M.,Almstrum, V., Diaz, D., Guzdial M., Hagan D., Ben-David Kolikant Y., Laxer C., Thomas L., Utting I., Wilusz T. (2001). A multinational, multi-institutional study of assessment of programming skills of first-year CS students. ACM SIGCSE Bulletin 33(4), pp. 125-180.

[11] Murphy C., Kim E., Kaiser G., Cannon A.(2008) Backstop: A tool for debugging runtime errors. ACM SIGCSE Bulletin.40(1) pp. 173-177.

[12] Trivedi, P., Pachori, S.(2010) Modelling and Analysis of Software Defects Prevention Using ODC, International Journal of Advanced Computer Science and Applications (IJACSA), Vol. 1, No. 3, pp 75-77.

[13] Vegso, J. (2010) Freshman interest in cs and degree production trends. Available on-line: www.cra.org/wp/index.php?p=126.

[14] Williams L., Kessler R. (2002) Pair Programming Illuminated.

[15] Wilson J.D., Hoskin N., Nosek J.T. (1993) The benefits of collaboration for student programmers. Proceedings of the twenty-fourth SIGCSE technical symposium on Computer science education. pp. 160-164

Quantifying the Benefits of Prior Programming Experience in an Introductory Computer Science Course

Chris Wilcox
Colorado State University
Fort Collins, Colorado
wilcox@cs.colostate.edu

Albert Lionelle
Colorado State University
Fort Collins, Colorado
lionelle@cs.colostate.edu

ABSTRACT

The superior performance of students with prior exposure to programming has long been evident to faculty that teach introductory courses. In this paper we replicate previous studies that quantify the difference between students with and without previous programming experience, and we provide further focus on gender differences. Our research is based on an initial CS1 course that we divided into a section with students having previous programming experience (P) and two sections for students without (N). Both sections of CS1 were taught with the same curriculum and assessments. We find that the advantages of prior experience are substantial, with P students outscoring N students by more than 6% on exams and 10% on programming quizzes. However, the performance gap between P and N students narrows considerably by the end of the following CS2 course, with no significant difference in overall scores. Analyzing results by gender, our data shows that 22% of N students in CS1 are female versus only 12% of P students. However, the female students with prior exposure outperform their male peers in all areas. Another finding of our research is the confirmation of a significant difference in confidence between female and male students.

CCS CONCEPTS

• **Social and professional topics** → **Computer science education**;

KEYWORDS

CS1; CS2; previous experience, broadening participation

ACM Reference Format:

Chris Wilcox and Albert Lionelle. 2018. Quantifying the Benefits of Prior Programming Experience in an Introductory Computer Science Course. In *Proceedings of The 49th ACM Technical Symposium on Computer Science Education (SIGCSE '18)*. ACM, New York, NY, USA, 6 pages. https://doi.org/10.1145/3159450.3159480

SIGCSE '18, Feb. 21–24, 2018, Baltimore, MD, USA

ACM ISBN 978-1-4503-5103-4/18/02...$15.00
https://doi.org/10.1145/3159450.3159480

1 INTRODUCTION

Several studies have confirmed that students in introductory courses benefit from previous exposure to computer science, see references in Section 2. At our institution we see a disproportionate number of top students that have parents in software engineering or related fields, and we observe that such students perform better because of previous exposure to programming languages or concepts. A study from Google [4] credits early exposure as a key factor in influencing female students towards studying CS, and common sense tells us that students with previous exposure to an activity are more likely to excel at that activity. However, in the United States fewer than 1% of students take the APCS exam, and only 22% of these are female, as reported by the College Board. Thus we find that our incoming students have major differences between genders in level of preparation. This motivates our research to quantify the extent and duration of the advantage that accrues to students with prior programming experience. In addition, we are interested in whether the benefit of prior exposure differs with respect to gender.

At our university we recently revised our introductory CS1 and CS2 courses. The new CS1 covers the traditional set of topics: variables and data types, expressions, methods and parameters, booleans and conditionals, control loops, arrays, and file I/O. We also added several advanced topics to CS1, including interfaces, abstract classes, and recursion. Our new CS2 curriculum covers object-oriented concepts, data structures such as lists, stacks, queues, and graphs, and related algorithms including graph traversal and advanced sorting. A section on parallel programming introduces basic multi-threading and data synchronization.

Following the lead of other institutions, we divided our CS1 course into sections of students with prior programming experience (P) and students without (N). Students self-selected into the appropriate section based on the course catalog description, without testing. We listed the P section as "Java for students with limited programming experience", and the N section as "Java for students without previous programming experience". The course curriculum and schedule were identical, as were all assignments, quizzes, and exams. The first author was responsible for all sections of the initial CS1 course, and taught both sections of the following CS2. Tightly controlling both courses allowed us to observe and measure the differences between students with and without prior exposure to CS concepts.

To summarize our findings, we find that students with prior exposure to programming perform significantly better

	N Grades		P Grades	
	Number	Percent	Number	Percent
Number A's	45	**20%**	38	**37%**
Number B's	59	26%	27	26%
Number C's	45	**20%**	13	**13%**
Number D's	34	**15%**	10	**10%**
Number F's	17	8%	6	6%
Withdrawals	24	11%	10	10%
Total	224	100%	104	100%

Figure 1: Letter Grades for P versus N in CS1.

	N Average	P Average	P - N	Students t-test
Samples	200	94		
Programs	82.00	81.32	-0.68	t = 0.24, p = 0.79
Labs	90.85	89.76	-1.09	t = 1.30, p = 0.45
Peer	84.60	83.93	-0.68	t = 0.35, p = 0.67
Quizzes	72.38	82.89	**10.52**	**t = -3.82, p = 0.01**
Midterm 1	75.39	81.33	**5.94**	**t = -2.44, p = 0.01**
Midterm 2	69.36	74.82	**5.47**	**t = -2.21, p = 0.02**
Final Exam	68.32	74.99	**6.67**	**t = -2.91, p = 0.01**
Total	77.07	80.31	**3.24**	**t = -1.68, p = 0.04**

Figure 2: Average Scores for P versus N in CS1.

in their initial CS1 course. However, their advantage is greatly reduced by the end of a subsequent CS2 course, implying that a lack of experience has been overcome. We also identify topics that we may have introduced too early for many CS1 students, resulting in lower retention rates. In terms of gender differences, we find that inexperienced female and male students perform similarly, but female students with prior experience outperform their male peers. In addition, we confirm the commonly cited differences in confidence between female and male students, and add to the plethora of evidence that shows that incoming females have less prior exposure to programming concepts than males.

2 PREVIOUS WORK

The link between prior programming experience and performance in an introductory CS course has been widely studied [5–7, 10]. Factors that affect retention rates in introductory CS courses have also been investigated [3], as have differences in confidence levels between female and male students [2, 9]. The literature on female participation in CS is too extensive to cite exhaustively, but these references are a starting point [1, 8].

3 METHODOLOGY

We used a variety of data sources to compare P and N student performance. The primary source was our Canvas grade repository, which holds student scores for programming assignments, labs, programming quizzes, peer sessions, reading quizzes, and exams. Canvas computes the average score in each category and the total points based on a weighted average. We also performed an analysis of the final exam in CS1 and CS2 to identify challenging topics.

The second data source was gender identification and academic standing from the registrar, which we processed in a confidential manner. For prior academic performance we used the selection index from the admissions process. This index is a number between 45 and 146, based on ACT or SAT scores and high school GPA. Scores above 130 are considered excellent, 120-129 very good, and 110-119 good. Because the students in CS1 and CS2 are primarily freshman, we consider the selection index to be the best better measure of previous academic performance.

The third data source was a before and after survey administered during the first and last weeks of the semester. The most relevant questions that we asked students related to this research concern prior programming experience, at the beginning of each semester, and confidence in their programming abilities, at the end of each semester.

Our methodology was a straightforward comparison of N and P students, which we further divided by major and by gender. The groups were determined by course section, and confirmed by survey data. As discussed, identification of prior experience was based on self-selection into the P and N sections of CS1. Each section had ample space, so students were able to select a section that matched their preference and experience. We entered all data into an anonymized spreadsheet that allowed us to measure performance differences and run statistical tests.

4 RESULTS

This section provides an analysis of the performance difference between students with prior programming experience and those without. The CS1 data was gathered during Fall 2016, where the combined size of the N sections was 224, and the P section held 104. The subsequent CS2 data was gathered during Spring 2017, and we omitted students in CS2 that did not attend the initial CS1 course.

4.1 P versus N in CS1

Figure 1 shows final letter grades of N and P students in the initial CS1 course. The grades address our basic research question about the extent to which previous programming experience influences academic performance in an introductory CS course. The key result is that only 20% of N students received A grades, compared to 37% of P students. The B grade percentages were almost identical for both groups, but 20% of N students received C grades compared to 13% of P students. Finally, 23% of N students received failing (D or F) grades compared to 16% of P students. Thus the overall performance of students with prior experience was significantly higher. The withdrawal rates of N and P students were similar, but our introductory courses generally exhibit low withdrawal rates for all students.

Figure 2 shows an analysis of the performance difference by category. Throughout this paper we have omitted students that withdrew from the course to avoid biasing the data with low or missing scores. Thus the sample sizes for the average scores are 200 N and 94 P students. Note that assignment and lab scores are almost identical between the sections. We credit our extensive help desk and an unfortunate level of program copying for the uniformity in completing assignments.

	N Average	P Average	P - N	Students t-test
Samples	86	67		
Programs	86.25	84.69	-1.56	t = 0.58, p = 0.56
Labs	92.51	90.14	-2.37	t = 1.05, p = 0.29
Peer	85.19	83.78	-1.41	t = 0.49, p = 0.62
Quizzes	85.97	87.43	1.46	t = -0.53, p = 0.59
Midterm 1	81.21	82.69	1.48	t = -0.79, p = 0.43
Midterm 2	81.43	84.72	3.29	t = 1.59, p = 0.11
Final Exam	84.10	86.07	1.97	t = -0.63, p = 0.52
Total	84.46	85.00	0.54	t = -0.27, p = 0.79

Figure 3: Average Scores for P versus N in CS2.

Plagiarism is outside the scope of this paper, but we have observed that it impacts the performance of many students. Labs are attendance based, so N and P students apparently show up with the same frequency.

The major differences appear on programming quizzes and exam scores, both of which are assessments that require students to work individually. Quizzes force students to demonstrate their programming skills in a controlled lab situation, without help from peers or lab instructors. The difference between N and P is more than 10% on quizzes and close to 6% on exams, suggesting that P students have better programming skills and more understanding of course content. Exams and programming quizzes contribute 60% of the total points in the course, so the exam score disparities account for much of the letter grade difference. Statistically significant differences are shown in bold throughout this paper.

We conclude that prior exposure to programming provides a significant benefit for students in our CS1 course. The self-selection process could also be a factor, but we will show in a separate analysis that N and P students have almost identical academic performance, and the self-selection appears to be very effective, as confirmed both by the performance difference and the survey data presented in 4.7.

4.2 P versus N in CS2

The results in the previous section were not unexpected, but a key goal of our research was to measure the duration of the benefit from prior experience. A follow-on CS2 course was offered as two sections, with a random mixture of N and P students and a small number of new students. Both sections of CS2 used identical materials and the same instructor. Figure 3 shows the average scores from students in CS1 that continued on to CS2, split by membership in the original N and P sections of CS1. The sample size in CS2 is 86 students from the N sections and 67 from the P section, which of course takes into account attrition between CS1 and CS2. Retention rates are analyzed separately in 4.6.

We note that the overall difference in total points for N and P students is less than 1%, and none of the differences are statistically significant. We conclude that the benefit of prior programming experience is considerably diminished in the follow-on CS2 course. The narrowing of the performance gap between N and P was both unexpected and reassuring, implying that students without prior programming can quickly catch up with their more experienced peers. However, we must take into account the high attrition rate from CS1 to CS2 when making this statement.

Content	P + N	N	P	P - N
Java Language	71%	69%	74%	5%
Strings, Math	80%	78%	84%	6%
1D Arrays	81%	79%	85%	6%
File I/O	77%	76%	78%	2%
Array List	89%	89%	89%	0%
Recursion	**65%**	**59%**	**77%**	**19%**
Abstract Classes	**45%**	**41%**	**52%**	**11%**
Sorting	78%	77%	78%	1%
Coding	**75%**	**72%**	**81%**	**8%**

Figure 4: Problem Areas for P versus N in CS1.

Content	P + N	N	P	P - N
Recursion	**54%**	**43%**	**68%**	**25%**
Inheritance, Polymorphism	97%	97%	98%	1%
Lists, Stacks, Queues	**87%**	**90%**	**83%**	**-7%**
Regular Expressions	95%	95%	96%	1%
Expression Trees	70%	71%	69%	-2%
Binary Search Trees	85%	85%	84%	-1%
Hashing, MultiThreading	76%	75%	77%	1%
Graphs: DFS, BFS, MST	**84%**	**82%**	**87%**	**5%**
Graphs: Shortest Path	94%	94%	94%	1%
Coding	**64%**	**62%**	**66%**	**4%**

Figure 5: Problem Areas for P versus N in CS2.

4.3 Problem Areas in CS1 and CS2

Because of the differences in P versus N final exam scores in CS1, we decided it would be worthwhile to perform further analysis to identify problem areas. We analyzed scores from the table of contents of all exams, which corresponded to individual topics. This allowed us to identify topics that were problematic for all students, or that exhibit a large difference between N and P students. Figure 4 shows the CS1 exam scores for both groups by topic.

While the results clearly show the advantage of P students versus N, what we are interested in is the variance by topic. Scores on a handful of topics were almost identical between the two groups, for example sorting, array lists, and file I/O. Other topics had more significant differences, including basic elements of Java such as strings, math, and single dimensional arrays. However, the real differences appear on advanced topics such as recursion and abstract classes. The recursion section of the exam showed a 19% difference between N and P students, and the latter showed a reasonable understanding of the topic. For abstract classes, the difference was 11% but the topic was apparently difficult for both groups, with even the P students scoring only 52%.

We conclude that advanced topics in a CS1 course can be problematic for all students, but may be a disproportionate factor in the failure and attrition rates that we observed for N students. To a lesser extent, the coding section showed a difference of 8%, which is consistent with the general performance difference between N and P students on programming quizzes and other evaluations or programming skills.

Advanced topics from CS1 were revisited in our CS2 course and we made them part of the final exam. This allowed us to

	N Average			P Average		
	Female	Male	Delta	Female	Male	Delta
Samples	46 (23%)	154 (77%)		11 (12%)	83 (88%)	
Programs	83.41	81.58	1.83	91.33	79.99	**11.34**
Labs	92.11	90.48	1.63	96.29	88.89	**7.40**
Peer	83.28	85.00	-1.72	94.18	82.57	**11.62**
Quizzes	68.88	73.43	**-4.55**	86.32	82.44	**3.88**
Midterm 1	72.42	76.26	**-3.85**	82.61	81.16	1.45
Midterm 2	67.33	69.96	-2.64	79.41	74.22	**5.19**
Final Exam	63.18	69.86	**-6.67**	77.00	74.72	2.28
Total	75.51	77.53	-2.02	85.39	79.63	**5.76**

Figure 6: Gender Results for P versus N in CS1.

	N Average			P Average		
	Female	Male	Delta	Female	Male	Delta
Samples	16 (19%)	70 (81%)		10 (15%)	57 (85%)	
Programs	84.36	86.68	-2.32	87.94	84.12	**3.82**
Labs	93.65	92.25	1.40	92.65	89.70	**2.95**
Peer	89.85	84.13	**5.72**	90.12	82.66	**7.45**
Quizzes	84.00	86.41	-2.41	89.10	87.14	1.96
Midterm 1	77.25	82.11	**-4.86**	84.50	82.38	2.12
Midterm 2	81.20	81.49	-0.29	86.17	84.47	1.70
Final Exam	84.78	83.95	0.83	90.53	85.29	**5.23**
Total	84.05	84.56	-0.51	88.22	84.44	**3.79**

Figure 7: Gender Results for P versus N in CS2.

see whether the topics were eventually mastered by both P and N students. Figure 5 shows the CS2 exam scores for both groups by topic. Note that both groups scored approximately equally on a number of advanced topics, including inheritance and polymorphism, which extended the abstract classes topic from CS1. In addition, the overall performance in the course between N an P students was similar.

The exception was recursion, for which the difference actually increased to 25%. Minor differences were also retained in the coding (4%) and graph traversal (5%) topics. The latter may be related to recursion since the algorithms for traversal are recursive. However, on lists, stacks, and queues the N students bested the P students by 7%. Overall the exam scores were higher 12% higher in CS2 at 84%, as compared to CS1 (N) at 68% and CS1 (P) at 73%. We attribute this to culling through failure and attrition between CS1 and CS2, leaving a higher percentage of students that can handle more advanced topics. For the record, we do believe that the majority of students will eventually master topics such as recursion, but doing so in CS2 may be more appropriate.

4.4 Gender Performance in CS1 and CS2

Our next analysis shows student performance by programming experience and gender. Figure 6 shows average scores for male and female students in the N and P sections of CS1. A pervasive but disquieting statistic is the percentage of female students in the N and P categories. Only 12% of P students are female, compared to 23% in the N section. This confirms that female students are exposed to CS at a much lower rate, or are not choosing to pursue CS despite prior exposure. This replicates many previous studies that show that female students are not being given the same opportunities and encouragement as male students.

	N Failures			P Failures		
	Female	Male	Delta	Female	Male	Delta
Samples	51 (23%)	173 (77%)		12 (12%)	92 (88%)	
D's	20%	16%	**4%**	9%	11%	-2%
F's	13%	7%	**6%**	0%	7%	**-7%**
W's	11%	12%	-1%	9%	11%	-2%
Total	43%	36%	**7%**	18%	29%	**-11%**

Figure 8: Failure and Withdrawal Rates in CS1.

A notable result from the gender comparison is that female N students achieve similar performance to male students, but female P students outperform their male counterparts in all categories, with almost a 6% difference in total points. We repeated the gender comparison in CS2, as shown in Figure 7. The gender difference among N students in CS2 remains minimal, but the better performance of female P students persists, with more than 5% higher scores than male P students on the final exam and almost 4% higher on total points. In addition, the N female students appear to have largely overcome their lack of previous exposure to programming. The percentage of females in CS2 remains small, primarily because of their low CS1 participation.

4.5 Failure Rate in CS1

To complete our comparison, we now consider failing and withdrawing students. In this category we include students that received a D or F grade, or that withdrew from CS1 during the semester. Figure 8 shows the number of N versus P students in each of the failure categories, divided by gender. N students failed or withdrew at a 10% higher rate than P students. Female N students had a 7% higher failure rate than males, but female P students had an 11% lower failure rate, which is consistent with their superior academic performance.

The CS1 and CS2 courses described in this paper are designed for CS majors, but still include many non-majors. This is because we currently lack a CS0 course. Compared to previous semesters, our new CS1 curriculum has resulted in a higher level of failure and attrition, as measured by the percentage of students continuing on to CS2. By examining the results previously shown, we see that only 86 of the original 224 students in the N category continued on to CS2, a retention rate of 38%. In the P category, 67 out of 104 students continued on to CS2, for a 64% retention rate.

However, the retention rates cannot be directly compared, because the N sections had a higher percentage of non-majors than the P section to begin with. Such students often take CS1 as a requisite for their majors, but do not continue on. Even so, the high rate of failure for N students is a concern that we discuss in the following section. We have omitted a discussion of the failure rate in CS2 because it was low (6%), which implies that the majority of students surmounting the initial hurdle of CS1 do well in CS2.

4.6 Retention Rate from CS1 to CS2

In 4.5 we stated that comparing the retention rate between N and P students was difficult because the percentage of CS majors varied across sections. This motivated a further

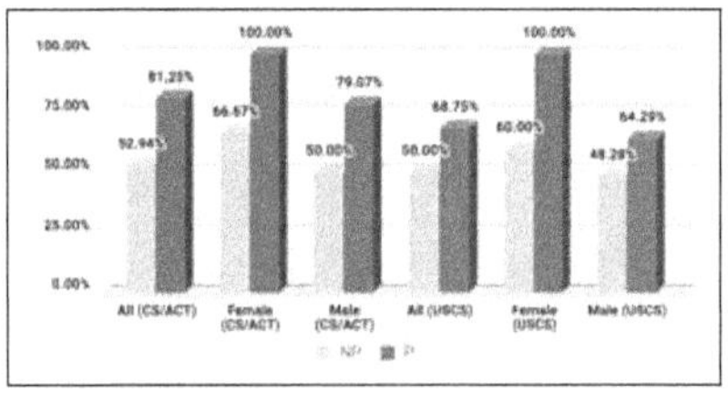

Figure 9: Retention Rate from CS1 to CS2.

investigation of the retention rate in which we identified actual and potential CS majors. Figure 9 shows the result of this study, in which the retention rate from the N and P sections of CS1 into CS2 are shown separately. The leftmost three columns represent students in one of our two computer majors, Computer Science (CS) and Applied Computing Technology (ACT). The rightmost three columns are in the Unspecified Seeking Computer Science (USCS) category. All others have been eliminated from the data, including other science and engineering majors.

Our concern that we may be losing potential majors is clearly shown by the much lower retention among the N students. The problem is particularly noticeable in the case of female students seeking the CS major, where the retention rate was a perfect 100% in the P section and only 60% in the N section. To improve retention and increase female participation we have proposed that our department reintroduce a specialized CS0 course for non-majors that avoids (or defers) some of the advanced topics in our CS1 course.

4.7 Experience and Confidence in CS1

For a number of years we have surveyed students in our CS1 course. The questions that relate directly to the topics in this paper are the type and extent of prior experience, asked in the first week of the course, and the confidence in programming abilities, asked in the last week. Figures 10 and 11 show the wording of both questions. Survey data differs from the objective measures in the previous sections, in that results are reported directly by the students. Assuming students are candid in their responses, our survey data provides a window into how students assess their own experience and skills.

Figures 12 shows the responses from the experience question divided by section and gender. The results clearly confirm the effectiveness of self-selection into N and P sections. Combining genders, 45% of N students had no previous programming, compared to only 3% of P students. Similarly, only 26% of N students had C, C++, or Java experience, compared to 82% of P students. We note that the contrast between female and male students is also stark. For the N section, 60% of female students have no prior experience, compared to 41% for males, and only 6% have previous exposure to Java programming, compared to 17% for males. The P section is equally unbalanced, with 13% of female students having no prior experience compared to 1% for males, and 38% of females with previous exposure to Java programming, compared to 62% for males.

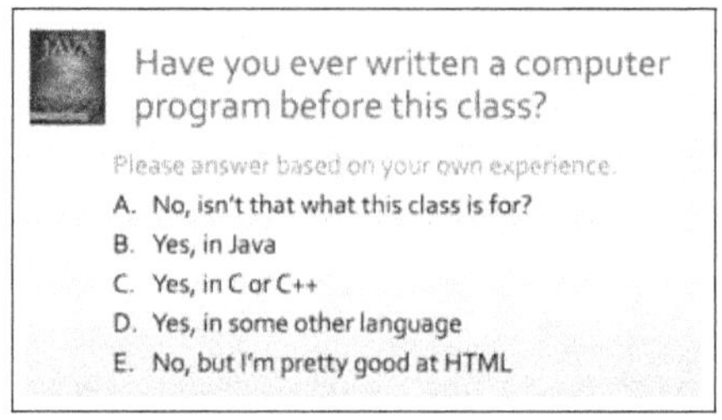

Figure 10: CS1 Programming Experience Question.

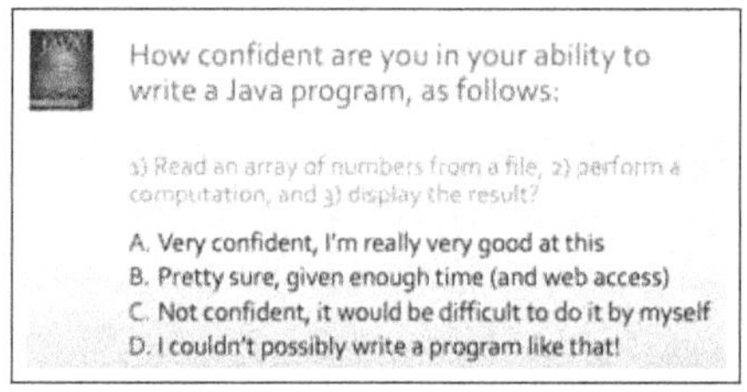

Figure 11: CS1 Programming Confidence Question.

	N Experience			P Experience		
	Female	Male	Delta	Female	Male	Delta
Samples	35	120		8	68	
None	21 (60%)	49 (41%)	19%	1 (13%)	1 (1%)	12%
Java	2 (6%)	20 (17%)	-11%	3 (38%)	42 (62%)	-24%
C or C++	4 (11%)	14 (12%)	1%	2 (25%)	15 (22%)	3%
Other	5 (14%)	30 (25%)	-11%	2 (25%)	9 (13%)	12%
HTML	3 (8%)	7 (6%)	2%	0 (0%)	1 (1%)	-1%

Figure 12: CS1 Programming Experience Results.

	N Confidence			P Confidence		
	Female	Male	Delta	Female	Male	Delta
Samples	37	110		9	59	
Very Confident	14 (38%)	55 (50%)	-12%	6 (67%)	57 (86%)	-19%
Pretty Sure	21 (57%)	45 (41%)	16%	3 (33%)	7 (12%)	21%
Not Confident	2 (5%)	8 (7%)	-2%	0 (0%)	1 (2%)	-2%
Impossible	0 (0%)	2 (2%)	-2%	0 (0%)	0 (0%)	0%

Figure 13: CS1 Programming Confidence Results.

Figures 13 shows the responses from the confidence question, which show a wide disparity between N and P students and between genders. For males, 50% of N students are *Very Confident*, compared to 86% of P students. For females, 36% of N students are *Very Confident*, compared to 67% of P students. The delta between female and male N students that are *Very Confident* is 12% and for P students is even higher at 19%. Thus students without prior programming are less confident than their peers, and female students are less confident than males. This data is especially interesting given that performance for both genders is almost identical in the N section, and the females were dominant in the P section. We note that despite being significantly more confident, males had a much lower rate of retention in both the N and P sections than females.

	N Section		P Section	
	Female	Male	Female	Male
Samples	31	111	9	68
Selection Index	122.84	117.20	117.67	118.97

Figure 14: CS1 Selection Index Averages.

5 THREATS TO VALIDITY

We now address two threats to validity for our study. First, despite our efforts to maintain identical content in the P and N sections, some factors inevitably vary between two sections of a course. In particular, the lecture discussions were often at a higher level in the P section. However, we made every effort to maintain consistency. Lectures and assignments used identical materials, and labs and assessments were given in the same place and time, with a random mixture of N and P students. For this reason, we claim that N versus P experiment has been as tightly controlled as is possible in an academic environment.

Second, there may be other differences besides prior programming experience in the students in the N and P sections. In particular, our method of self-selection introduces the possibility that students will choose a section based on factors other than prior programming experience. Possible factors include the convenience of lecture time or to avoid conflicts with other courses. However, we verified that the P students self-identified as having prior programming experience and N students did not, as shown by our survey.

In addition, we compared the academic performance of both groups. Figure 14 shows the average selection indices of N and P students, differentiated by gender. Note that female N students had a slightly higher selection index (122.84) than female P students (117.67), and male N and P students were almost identical. However, none of the differences were statistically significant, so we conclude that prior programming experience is more relevant than academic stature in predicting performance in our introductory course.

A note on the statistical significance analysis for this paper. Letter grades and gender differences are based on numerical scores. We have therefore included students t-test values on each row of the CS1 and CS2 average scores and problem areas. Statistically significant results are shown in bold font. Gender differentiation is problematic with respect to statistical analysis, because of low female participation. However, we claim that such large disparities in values are relevant despite small sample sizes.

6 CONCLUSIONS

In this paper we have found that the advantages conferred by prior programming experience are statistically significant and biased by gender. The difference in performance is so extensive that it may be difficult to bring N students to the same level as P students in introductory courses. However, our novel result is that disadvantage of not having prior programming experience in CS1 attenuates in the CS2 course that follows. Our research suggests that a less rigorous path into the CS major may be needed in order to attract and retain more diverse students. We derive this conclusion from the higher withdrawal and failure rates of students without prior programming experience, and the disproportionate number of female students in this group, even among declared CS majors. In addition, we confirm that female students have a lower rate of prior exposure to CS than male students, and less confidence.

7 FUTURE RESEARCH

Several topics in this paper motivate future studies. One open question is the extent of programming experience that leads to better performance in an introductory course. Does the programming language, curriculum rigor, and timing of the exposure matter, or is any exposure much better than none? Given the disparities in experience, would introducing a CS0 course decrease the failure rate in CS1, and improve diversity? Also, would moving more advanced topics such as recursion from CS1 to CS2 help our retention rate?

REFERENCES

[1] Christine Alvarado and Zachary Dodds. 2010. Women in CS: An Evaluation of Three Promising Practices. In *Proc. of the 41st ACM Technical Symposium on Computer Science Education (SIGCSE '10)*. ACM, New York, NY, USA, 57–61. https://doi.org/10.1145/1734263.1734281

[2] Sylvia Beyer, Kristina Rynes, Julie Perrault, Kelly Hay, and Susan Haller. 2003. Gender Differences in Computer Science Students. In *Proc. of the 34th SIGCSE Technical Symposium on Computer Science Education (SIGCSE '03)*. ACM, New York, NY, USA, 49–53. https://doi.org/10.1145/611892.611930

[3] Maureen Biggers, Anne Brauer, and Tuba Yilmaz. 2008. Student Perceptions of Computer Science: A Retention Study Comparing Graduating Seniors with Cs Leavers. In *Proc. of the 39th SIGCSE Technical Symposium on Computer Science Education (SIGCSE '08)*. ACM, New York, NY, USA, 402–406. https://doi.org/10.1145/1352135.1352274

[4] Google Corporation. 2014. Women Who Choose Computer Science - What Really Matters. (2014).

[5] Edward Holden and Elissa Weeden. 2004. The Experience Factor in Early Programming Education. In *Proc. of the 5th Conference on Info Technology Education (CITC5 '04)*. ACM, New York, NY, USA, 211–218. https://doi.org/10.1145/1029533.1029585

[6] Charles P. Howerton. 1988. The Impact of Pre College Computer Exposure on Student Achievement in Introductory Computer Programming Courses. *Computer Science Education* 1, 1 (1988), 73–84. https://doi.org/10.1080/0899340880010107

[7] Michael S. Kirkpatrick and Chris Mayfield. 2017. Evaluating an Alternative CS1 for Students with Prior Programming Experience. In *Proc. of the 2017 ACM SIGCSE Technical Symposium on Computer Science Education (SIGCSE '17)*. ACM, New York, NY, USA, 333–338. https://doi.org/10.1145/3017680.3017759

[8] Joan Peckham, Lisa L. Harlow, David A. Stuart, Barbara Silver, Helen Mederer, and Peter D. Stephenson. 2007. Broadening Participation in Computing: Issues and Challenges. In *Proc. of the 12th Annual SIGCSE Conference on Innovation and Technology in Computer Science Education (ITiCSE '07)*. ACM, New York, NY, USA, 9–13. https://doi.org/10.1145/1268784.1268790

[9] Katie Redmond, Sarah Evans, and Mehran Sahami. 2013. A Large-scale Quantitative Study of Women in Computer Science at Stanford University. In *Proc. of the 44th ACM Technical Symposium on Computer Science Education (SIGCSE '13)*. ACM, New York, NY, USA, 439–444. https://doi.org/10.1145/2445196.2445326

[10] Anya Tafliovich, Jennifer Campbell, and Andrew Petersen. 2013. A Student Perspective on Prior Experience in CS1. In *Proc. of the 44th ACM Technical Symposium on Computer Science Education (SIGCSE '13)*. ACM, New York, NY, USA, 239–244. https://doi.org/10.1145/2445196.2445270

Python Versus C++: An Analysis of Student Struggle on Small Coding Exercises in Introductory Programming Courses

Nabeel Alzahrani[1], Frank Vahid[1,3], Alex Edgcomb[1,3], Kevin Nguyen[1] and Roman Lysecky[2,3]
[1] Computer Science and Engineering, University of California, Riverside
[2] Electrical and Computer Engineering, University of Arizona
[3] zyBooks, Los Gatos, California
nalza001@ucr.edu, vahid@cs.ucr.edu, aedgcomb@cs.ucr.edu, knguy092@ucr.edu, rlysecky@ece.arizona.edu

ABSTRACT

Many teachers of CS 1 (introductory programming) have switched to Python rather than C, C++, or Java. One reason is the belief that Python's interpreted nature plus simpler syntax and semantics ease a student's learning, but data supporting that belief is scarce. This paper addresses the question: Do Python learners struggle less than C++ learners? We analyzed student submissions on small coding exercises in CS 1 courses at 20 different universities, 10 courses using Python, and 11 using C++. Each course used either the Python or C++ version of an online textbook from one publisher, each book having 100+ small coding exercises, expected to take 2-5 minutes each. We considered 11 exercises whose Python and C++ versions were nearly identical and that appeared in various chapters. We defined struggle rate for exercises, where struggle means a student spent excessive time or attempts on an exercise. Based on that rate, we found the learning for Python was not eased; in fact, Python students had significantly higher struggle rates than C++ students (26% vs. 13%). Higher rates were seen even when considering only classes with no prerequisites, classes for majors only, or classes for non-majors only. We encourage the community to do further analyses, to help guide teachers when choosing a CS 1 language.

ACM Reference format:
Nabeel Alzahrani, Frank Vahid, Alex Edgcomb, Kevin Nguyen and Roman Lysecky. 2018. Python Versus C++: An Analysis of Student Struggle on Small Coding Exercises in Introductory Programming Courses. In *SIGCSE '18: 49th ACM Technical Symposium on Computer Science Education, Feb. 21–24, 2018, Baltimore, MD, USA.* ACM, NY, NY, USA, 6 pages.DOI: 10.1145/3159450.3160586

1 INTRODUCTION

Python is growing in popularity in introductory programming classes (CS 1). Various factors are stated for switching from languages like C, C++, or Java. One is that Python is interpreted (also known as a scripting language), allowing students to interact immediately by typing print statements or simple calculations, and avoiding some of the complexities of compiling and then running. Another factor is that Python's syntax is simpler, thus preventing students from getting bogged down in syntax errors, and instead allowing students to focus on higher-level programming concepts. A third factor is that Python comes with graphics and other libraries that can make introductory programming courses more engaging for students, who can analyze real data, create graphics-based programs like video games, etc. Other reasons include increasing use of Python in industry, and studies showing fewer lines of code and/or increased productivity among experienced programmers. Key hopes by those who switch is to decrease attrition in CS 1 courses and to attract more people to computing degrees.

But, many teachers disagree, and continue to teach C, C++, or Java in CS 1. Reasons include a belief that new learners should think precisely about details like data types, that learners should not rely so heavily on library functions, that C/C++/Java (or variations) are widely used in industry especially in domains like mobile apps, and that learning Python after C/C++/Java is easier than the other way (strict to less strict being easier than less strict to strict). Some teachers indicate frustration that students who learn Python in CS 1 have trouble in later courses in C/C++/Java, not wanting to be bothered by details. Some engineers state new hires don't understand or respect underlying resources, which can lead to problems on commonly-constrained platforms. Furthermore, cloud-based coding systems for C/C++/Java, where students code in a web window and press "Run", reduce the interpreted/scripting benefit of Python for beginning students.

In previous work, Enbody [1, 2] used Python and C++ for groups in CS 1. They compared the Python-group and C++-group on three outcomes: final exam grade, programming projects scores, and course final grade, and found no significant differences. Using progression analysis, they also found that programming language features had no effect on students' performance in CS 2. For object-oriented programming (OOP), Goldwasser [3] reported that students in CS 1 were overwhelmed by the syntax and semantics of C++ and Java, and found Python provided a simple and consistent model to teach OOP. Prechelt [4] found programmers using a scripting language like Python can solve the same problem with less code and higher productivity vs. a system language such as C++. Zelle [5] found that scripting languages are simpler, safer, and more flexible vs. system

SIGCSE '18, February 21–24, 2018, Baltimore, MD, USA.

ACM ISBN 978-1-4503-5103-4/18/02...$15.00
https://doi.org/10.1145/3159450.3160586

languages like C and C++. Guo [6] stated that Python is the most used CS 1 language in top-ranked U.S. research universities. Such related research suggests how Python can be helpful to teach programming skills. We sought however to determine from the students' experiences whether Python led to less student struggle.

This paper describes our analysis of student struggle rates on identical small coding exercises used in Python and C++ classes across 20 universities. Struggle means spending excessive time or making excessive attempts on such exercises. Some teachers (like ourselves) believe struggle is an important metric because struggle can lead to frustration, and excessive/repeated frustration can lead to students giving up. Struggle is one way (but not the only way) of estimating the learning curve of a language. This paper introduces the small coding exercises, defines a struggle metric, provides data comparing struggle rates for Python and C++ in CS 1 courses showing that struggle rates for Python are not lower (and are actually higher), summarizes a manual investigation into the student submissions to better understand those rates, discusses possible reasons that Python's struggle rates are not lower and are actually higher, and provides conclusions.

2 SMALL CODING EXERCISES

zyBooks [8] is a publisher that creates online textbooks for introductory C, C++, Java, and Python, with those textbooks being very similar but adapted to each language. Over 100 small coding exercises are embedded at the end of sections throughout those books. The exercises are cloud-based, meaning students code directly in a web window and press "Run" to execute their code, so no substantial difference exists between C++'s compile/execute approach and Python's interpreted approach. We abbreviate those exercises in this paper as CA (coding activity). Figure 1 provides some examples.

Each exercise has a coding window with a partial program, and the student is instructed to complete the program to carry out a particular task, like printing numbers by dividing a variable of value 40 until reaching 1 as shown in Figure 1. The instructions usually include a first test case (sample input and output). The student can only edit the relevant portion of the existing program. When the student presses "Run", the program is executed with various test cases that test for proper program output, and the student is shown which test cases passed and which failed (showing the difference in output for failed cases) as shown in Figure 2. Each exercise is worth 2 points: 1 point for passing any test case, and 1 point for passing all test cases. Students can attempt such exercises as many times as desired. Most universities give students some homework points for completing those coding exercises.

The CA in Figure 1, titled "Basic while loop expression", asks the students to print userNum divided by 2 until reaching 1 (given userNum = 40). The shown code is the template. Students change the comment "/* Your solution goes here */" with their code.

Figure 1: Each coding activity (CA) includes instructions, an example, a coding area, and a Run button. For this activity, only lines 8 - 10 are editable.

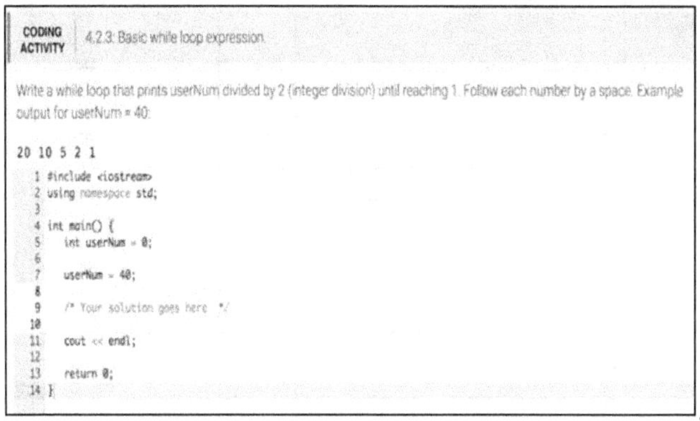

Figure 2: A wrong student solution to the Figure 1 CA. Differences between student and expected output are highlighted.

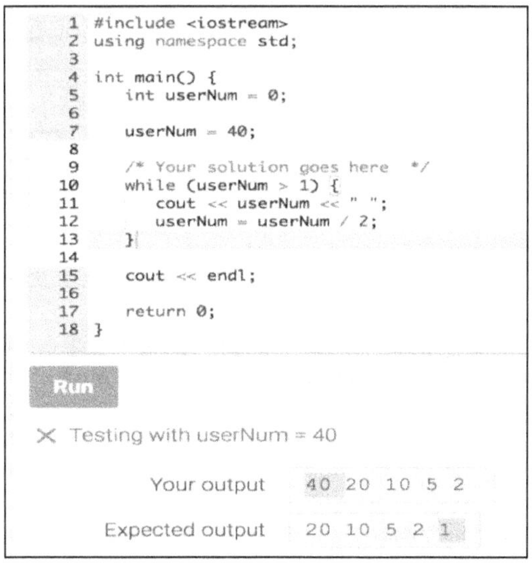

Our institution has taught both Python and C++ in our CS 1, so we wished to compare those languages. We noticed 11 of the CA's were nearly identical in the Python and C++ versions. Those CA's are summarized in Table 1, numbered as CA 1, 2, ..., 11 (which differs from the numbering in the textbooks).

3 STRUGGLE RATE AS A METRIC

To calculate the struggle rate, we first needed to find the number of struggling students for a particular CA. We define struggling students using two parameters: number of attempts (number of submissions), and time spent trying to solve the CA. Students may submit multiple submissions before achieving the correct solution to a CA. We define a struggling student for a particular CA as a student who has spent more than 5 minutes and spent more than double the Baseline time and attempted more than 3 times and attempted more than double the Baseline attempts, or spent more than 15 minutes. The Baseline time is the time spent

Table 1: List of the 11 CA's with their titles and chapters.

CA #	CA title	Ch #	Chapter Title
1	Tree Height	2	Vars / Assgnmt
2	Basic while loop expression	4	Loops
3	Simon says	4	Loops
4	Vector iteration: Sum excess	5	Arrays / Vectors
5	Function call in expression	6	User-Def Fcts
6	Function errors: Copying one function to create another	6	User-Def Fcts
7	Function with loop: Shampoo.	6	User-Def Fcts
8	Constructor overloading	7	Objs & Classes
9	Basic inheritance	10	Inheritance
10	Derived class membr override	10	Inheritance
11	Recursive function: Writing the base case	12	Recursion

by the top 20% students in that class for that CA and the Baseline attempts is the number of attempts by the top 20% students in that class for that CA. We defined a dynamic struggle rate (by referring to top 20% students) rather than a static struggle rate to account for the class (students) background level in programming. A CA's struggle rate is defined as the # of struggling students divided by the # of students in that class. The following formulas summarize a struggling student and the struggle rate.

Struggling student = ((time > 5 min.) AND (time > 2 * Baseline time) AND (# attempts > 3) AND (# attempts > 2 * Baseline attempts)) OR (time > 15 min.)

Struggle rate = # struggling students / # students

Changing the parameters increases or decreases the struggle rate; we based these numbers on teaching experiences. Other struggle rate metrics are possible. For our purposes, the raw % is less important than is the comparison of rates for different languages.

As shown in Table 2, students can make multiple submissions for each CA. Each submission consists of a timestamp, user id #, correctness, and the submitted code. To identify a struggling student for a CA, we do the following: (1) get the student total

Table 2: A snapshot of the student 0xxx submissions for CA2: Basic while loop expression.

Time of submission	User #	Answer correct	Submitted solution

3/10/2017 1:20:44 PM	0xxx	No	while (userNum != 1){
			  cout << userNum << " ";
			  userNum = userNum / 2;
			  }

...	0xxx	No	...

3/10/2017 1:24:51 PM	0xxx	No	while (userNum !=0){
			  while (userNum != 1){
			    cout << userNum << " ";
			    userNum = userNum / 2;
			    }
			  }
			 cout << userNum << " ";

...	0xxx	No	...

3/10/2017 1:30:18 PM	0xxx	Yes	while (userNum >= 1){
			  cout << userNum << " ";
			  userNum = userNum / 2;
			  }

time spent and the student total number of attempts to solve that CA; (2) calculate the top 20% student average time to solve that CA, called "Baseline time", and the top 20% student average number of attempts to solve that CA, called "Baseline attempts"; (3) if the student total time spent is greater than 15 minutes, then the student is a struggling student; or if the student total time spent is greater than 5 minutes and the student total time spent is greater than double the Baseline time and the student total number of attempts is greater than 3 and the student total number of attempts is greater than double the Baseline attempts, then the student is a struggling student. To calculate the struggle rate for a CA, we divide the total number of struggling students for a CA by the total number of students for that CA.

4 RESULTS

We obtained anonymized student submission data for the 11 above-mentioned nearly-identical CAs, for C++ and Python courses at dozens of universities. We chose 11 C++ courses and 10 Python courses at 20 universities to represent a variety of institutions, including 4-year research institutions (none were schools typically ranked in the top 20), non-research 4-year institutions, and 2-year institutions (community colleges). To obtain roughly equal samples from both languages, we generally sought to match each C++ course with a Python course from an institution of the same type and roughly the same numbers of students. Table 3 shows the number of students in the 20 courses per language (C++ and Python). Obviously such matching can't be perfect, but by attempting such matching, coupled with the large numbers of students, we can have more confidence that the two sample populations' statistics can be meaningfully compared.

Table 3: Each row is two similar schools using different languages. A Python-match for row 11 does not exist, but we kept the C++ offering to have data for no-prerequisite and non-majors for C++ CA's.

School	Total # students in C++	Total # students in Python
1 (Research universities)	153	105
2 (Community colleges)	13	33
3 (Teaching universities)	34	23
4 (Research universities)	277	176
5 (Same community college)	21	29
6 (Teaching universities)	48	35
7 (Research universities)	121	92
8 (Community colleges)	14	165
9 (Community colleges)	15	17
10 (Research universities)	167	195
11 (Teaching university)	194	N/A
Total number of students	1057	870

Table 4 shows the struggle rates for the 11 coding exercises, summarized for all 11 C++ courses and all 10 Python courses. For example, the first data row is for CA 1 (Coding Activity 1). 787 C++ students across the 11 C++ courses attempted that CA, while 434 Python students did. Among those students, 5% of the C++ students struggled (39 out of 787), while 9% of the Python students struggled (41 out of 434). Such data is shown for each of the 11 CA's. On average, the C++ struggle rate was 13%, while the Python struggle rate 26%. The average was computed by dividing the total number of students for all the 11 CA's by the total number of struggling students for all the 11 CA's. We did the struggle rate analysis for one community college with similar numbers of students in both C++ (21) and Python (29), and we found nearly identical results with Python students struggling more than C++ students.

Table 4: A comparison of struggle rates on 11 nearly-identical coding exercises for 11 C++ and 10 Python courses.

	C++			Python		
CA	# students	# struggle	struggle %	# students	# struggle	struggle %
1	787	39	5	434	41	9
2	700	131	19	493	159	32
3	489	130	27	362	179	49
4	513	28	5	259	43	17
5	658	51	8	469	46	10
6	630	14	2	420	28	7
7	482	128	27	414	183	44
8	467	19	4	115	30	26
9	193	38	20	77	19	25
10	181	32	18	69	8	12
11	400	103	26	233	118	51
Total	5500	713	13	3345	854	26

Table 5: Struggle rates considering only courses having no computing-related prerequisites, meaning 4 C++ courses and 7 Python courses.

	C++			Python		
CA	# students	# struggle	struggle %	# students	# struggle	struggle %
1	619	33	5	323	33	10
2	602	121	20	388	142	37
3	410	123	30	266	132	50
4	402	25	6	192	34	18
5	564	46	8	365	40	11
6	544	13	2	326	26	8
7	400	115	28	320	153	48
8	247	14	6	32	5	16
9	10	1	10	7	1	14
10	7	0	0	5	1	20
11	220	56	25	165	93	56
Total	4025	547	14	2389	660	28

The data surprised us, so we further sought to see if perhaps the effect was due to differences in the student populations. We did not have access to information about individual students, so we examined the course descriptions. We considered that perhaps the C++ courses were a second course, following a simpler programming course or some other computing-related course. Thus, we excluded any courses that had a computing-related prerequisite, reducing the set to 4 C++ courses and 7 Python courses. Table 5 shows results. The difference in struggle rates continued: 14% for C++, 28% for Python.

We considered that perhaps the C++ courses were taken by majors and Python by non-majors. We thus divided the courses into those intended for majors (per their course descriptions), and those for non-majors. The effect was still seen: 10% vs. 26% struggle for majors (2242 C++ and 383 Python students), and 18% vs. 26% for non-majors (1783 C++ and 1834 Python students).

Because students are anonymized and we have no data on the students themselves, the above analyses should not be considered as perfectly representative of the student populations. For example, the courses intended for non-majors may very well have had some majors. However, the analysis was intended merely to determine if the hypothesis is correct that Python students have a substantially easier learning curve than C++ students. For that purpose, the data seems to suggest that belief is false (and in fact the opposite may be true)

Table 6: % likelihood that any given student would struggle more with Python than with C++

Table	Students population	p-value	Struggle %
Table 4	All students. 11 C++ and 10 Python courses and each course's submissions has 11 CA's.	< 0.0001	12%
Table 5	No prerequisite. with 4 C++ and 7 Python courses.	< 0.0001	12%
Not shown	No prerequisite and CS majors. 2 C++ and 4 Python courses.	< 0.0001	18%
Not shown	No prerequisite and non CS majors. 2 C++ and 3 Python courses.	< 0.0001	6%

5 ANALYSIS

Tables 4 and 5 show Python students struggle more than C++ students. We want to account for the relative number of students per CA because the struggle % is not consistent per CA. For example, in Table 5, CA 8 had 247 C++ students but only 32 Python students. We thus converted the difference of the average C++ and Python Z-scores to a % as follows. For each table, we:

1. Calculated the Z-score per CA: We used the mean and standard deviation of C++ and Python struggle combined per CA.
2. Calculated the p-value for the whole table: We used a Student's t-test to compare the C++ Z-scored struggle to Python Z-scored struggle
3. Calculated the percentage of the average difference: We averaged the C++ Z-scores, and separately averaged the Python Z-scores, then used a Z-score to percentile calculator [7] to convert the difference in average to a percentile.

The final step gives the % likelihood that a given student would struggle more with Python than C++. Table 6 shows that a student is 12% more likely to struggle with Python than C++.

6 MANUAL INVESTIGATION

The analysis above suggests that the Python learning curve, based on the metric of struggle rate on small coding exercises, is not easier than the C++ learning curve. In fact, the analysis suggests (perhaps surprisingly) that the learning curve is actually harder. To better understand, we manually examined student submissions to many of the CA's. Because manual examination is very time consuming, we examined CA's 1, 2, 7, and 10, seeking to spread out the CA's examined.

Table 7 illustrates our findings. For example, for CA 1, which involved converting a math equation into an assignment statement, Python students struggled more with basic assignment concepts, such as missing an = operator, confusing left and right sides, or assigning to an expression rather than a variable. For CA 2, which involved writing a while loop to output a number halved until reaching 0, Python students struggled more on all aspects of the problem, including writing the loop condition, updating the loop counter variable, or placing the output in the correct location.

7 DISCUSSION

Limitations: Other struggle metrics exist, such as measuring struggle on weekly programming assignments, surveying students, measuring performance on exams, etc.

Our analysis involved 1,927 students at courses across 20 universities. While those large numbers and the diversity of populations are strengths of the data and likely minimizes the impact of one particular course's policies or instructor's teaching style, also useful would be a controlled study at one university (which is hard to carry out, since such random assignment is rarely acceptable), or where the university switched from one language to another across semesters (but other factors like teacher and student population may confound results).

The Python/C++ textbooks use a standard approach. Other approaches, such as a media-based approach or objects-first ordering, may yield different results.

The perceived easier learning curve is just one reason some teachers have switched to Python. Other reasons exist, such as built-in libraries. Thus, the above data relates to just one factor among many that influence a CS 1 language decision.

Possible reasons: This study analyzed struggle rate, not the reasons. One possible reason for Python's struggle rate not being lower than for C++ is that learning core programming concepts may overshadow syntax issues. The manual investigation of student submissions seemed to support this reason; few students struggled with syntax in either language. Instead, struggle was due to programming concepts like creating a proper loop to solve a task. The case may be that college students can master the basic syntax of C++ nearly as quickly as they master the slightly-easier syntax of Python. Also, C++ teachers can choose whether or not to dwell on C++ syntax. The textbook in this study avoids potentially-problematic aspects of C++, such as branches/loops without braces (the book always uses braces), assignments in branch/loop expressions (the book avoids those), use of prefix/postfix increment operators (the book avoids except in a for-loop header), etc., instead teaching a common and safer subset of C++.

Python's struggle rate was surprisingly higher. One possible reason relates to programming requiring precision. From the beginning, C++ requires precise thought about variable declarations, variable types, data types resulting from expressions, use of braces, use of = vs. ==, etc. This precision may prime students to think more precisely about language-independent problem-solving as well, like writing loop expressions that iterate exactly as desired. Python's forgivingness might breed a more cavalier attitude that extends beyond syntax/semantics into problem solving as well. This of course is just conjecture; future work may seek to test the idea.

Table 7: CA1, 2, 7, and 10 for all data and the reasons why students struggled, as determined by manual investigation.

CA	C++	Python
	Reasons	Reasons
1	1-Using / instead of * 2-Missing tan() for the angleElevation variable 3-Mistyping variable names	1-Using tan() instead of math.tan() 2-Using / instead of * 3-Missing tan() for the angleElevation variable 3-Mistyping variable names 4-Wrong assignment (using two = symbols, assign to the wrong variable, reverse assignment, etc.)
2	1-Wrong loop condition 2-Wrong/missing loop counter update 3-Missing/wrong location output stmt	1-Wrong loop condition 2-Wrong/missing loop counter update 3-Missing/wrong location output statement 4-Indentation (few: just 5 students)
7	1-Missing for-loop 2-Missing counter inside the for-loop 3-Wrong for-loop counter initial value 4-Wrong for-loop condition 5-Wrong for-loop location 6-Wrong cout() arg inside for-loop	1-Missing for-loop 2-Wrong while-loop update (when using while-loop) 3-Wrong for-loop condition 4-Wrong print() argument inside the for-loop 5-Missing for-loop condition variable inside the for-loop 6-Wrong for-loop location
10	1-Missing ; 2-Wrong cout() argument 3-Not complete cout() arguments 4-Wrong location to call a member function 5-Missing to call a member function 6-Wrong format to call a member function 7-Missing function def	1-Missing function definition 2-Missing call to member function 3-Missing argument to call a member function 4-Extra space when calling print() 5-Wrong call to a member function 6-Wrong print() statement 7-Wrong function argument

We note that cloud-based programming is reducing the difference between languages, eliminating (or postponing) the need to install or even use an IDE.

8 CONCLUSIONS

One factor leading teachers to use Python in CS 1 courses is the belief that Python has an easier learning curve. We analyzed struggle rates for 11 nearly-identical short coding exercises in 11 C++ and 10 Python courses, involving about 1,000 students in each language at 20 universities. We found the Python struggle rate was not lower than C++. One possible reason is that the languages' syntax differences are eclipsed by the difficulty of learning language-independent programming concepts, especially if C++ teachers don't dwell on C++'s complex syntax options.

In fact, our analysis showed Python's struggle rate to be significantly higher than C++. One possible reason is that C++'s focus on precision translates to a more precise approach to programming. As for attrition, at our institution, we have found that a caring talented instructor with good class design, policies, and assignments -- appropriate homework/assignment points ratio, various help resources, encouragement of collaboration, flipped lectures, interesting/relevant assignments -- seem far more important than the language choice. In fact, in our most recent offering of CS 1 in C++, students provided evaluations in the 95'th percentile for all courses in the university of 30,000 students, while performing strongly on programming assignments and exams.

In any case, the analysis might help CS 1 teachers predict whether switching from C++ (or C or Java) to Python might yield the desired benefit of an easier learning curve. We encourage the community to perform more such analyses, so that teachers can be guided by data in making language decisions for CS 1 courses.

REFERENCES

[1] Richard J. Enbody, William F. Punch, and Mark McCullen. 2009. Python CS1 as preparation for C++ CS2. *ACM SIGCSE* Bulletin 41, no. 1 (2009): 116-120.
[2] Richard J. Enbody, and William F. Punch. 2010. Performance of python CS1 students in mid-level non-python CS courses. *In Proceedings of the 41st ACM technical symposium on Computer science education*, pp. 520-523. ACM, 2010.
[3] Michael H. Goldwasser, and David Letscher. 2008. Teaching an object-oriented CS1-: with Python. *ACM SIGCSE* bulletin, vol. 40, no. 3, pp. 42-46. ACM, 2008.
[4] Lutz Prechelt. 2003. Are scripting languages any good? A validation of Perl, Python, Rexx, and Tcl against C, C++, and Java. *Advances in Computers 57* (2003): 205-270.
[5] John M. Zelle. 1999. Python as a first language. *In Proceedings of 13th Annual Midwest Computer Conference*, vol. 2, p. 145. 1999.
[6] Philip Guo. 2014. Python is now the most popular introductory teaching language at top us universities. *BLOG@ CACM*, July (2014): 47.
[7] Measuring U. Z-Score to Percentile Calculator. https://measuringu.com/pcalcz/, accessed Aug, 2017.
[8] zyBooks. https://www.zybooks.com/, accessed Aug, 2017.

Portable Parallel Computing with the Raspberry Pi

Suzanne J. Matthews*
Dept. of Electrical Engineering & Computer Science
suzanne.matthews@usma.edu

Joel C. Adams
Dept. of Computer Science
adams@calvin.edu

Richard A. Brown
Dept. of Mathematics, Statistics, & Computer Science
rab@stolaf.edu

Elizabeth Shoop
Dept. of Mathematics, Statistics, & Computer Science
shoop@macalester.edu

ABSTRACT

With the requirement that parallel & distributed computing (PDC) topics be covered in the core computer science curriculum, educators are exploring new ways to engage students in this area of computing. In this paper, we discuss the use of the Raspberry Pi single-board computer (SBC) to provide students with hands-on multicore learning experiences. We discuss how the authors use the Raspberry Pi to teach parallel computing, and present assessment results that indicate such devices are effective at achieving CS2013 PDC learning outcomes, as well as motivating further study of parallelism. We believe our results are of significant interest to CS educators looking to integrate parallelism in their classrooms, and support the use of other SBCs for teaching parallel computing.

CCS CONCEPTS

• **Computing methodologies → Parallel computing methodologies**; • **Applied computing → Education**;

KEYWORDS

Parallel Computing, Raspberry Pi, Education

ACM Reference Format:

Suzanne J. Matthews, Joel C. Adams, Richard A. Brown, and Elizabeth Shoop. 2018. Portable Parallel Computing with the Raspberry Pi. In *SIGCSE '18: The 49th ACM Technical Symposium on Computer Science Education, Feb. 21–24, 2018, Baltimore, MD, USA.* ACM, New York, NY, USA, 6 pages. https://doi.org/10.1145/3159450.3159558

1 INTRODUCTION

Prior to 2006, parallel & distributed computing (PDC) topics were rarely covered in the computer science (CS) curriculum, let alone at the undergraduate level. The expense of parallel hardware (among other reasons) made PDC challenging to teach. This has largely changed over the last decade, due to the advent of multicore and manycore (GPU) architectures and the emergence of cloud computing. These innovations have greatly decreased the cost and increased the access to parallel architectures.

*Corresponding Author

SIGCSE '18, Feb. 21–24, 2018, Baltimore, MD, USA

ACM ISBN 978-1-4503-5103-4/18/02...$15.00
https://doi.org/10.1145/3159450.3159558

Given the ubiquity of these technologies, the *ACM/IEEE CS 2013 Curriculum Recommendations* [16] moved PDC topics into the core CS curriculum. Unsurprisingly, many of the PDC core curriculum recommendations are focused on topics and concepts specific to shared memory (as opposed to distributed memory) parallel systems. This is due to the fact that all modern phones, tablets, laptops, and desktop systems contain multicore CPUs, making them shared memory parallel multiprocessors. It follows that students who create software need to be educated in the concepts and techniques required to write efficient software for multicore systems. CS 2013 thus requires every CS major to learn about PDC.

This raises many questions, including:

> *What hardware platforms should we use to teach students about parallelism (esp. shared memory)?*

In this paper, we argue that inexpensive single-board computers (SBCs) such as the Raspberry Pi provide a new option for teaching parallel computing. While we focus on the Raspberry Pi in this paper, we believe the same argument applies to other affordable SBCs. The advantages single board computers provide for teaching students about parallel computing include:

Standardization. Pre-configured disk images may be freely downloaded from the Internet (e.g., [7]), ensuring a uniform work environment for each student with the same operating system, compilers, debuggers, integrated development environments (IDEs), and other software development tools. Images can be pre-loaded with pedagogical code examples and instructions.

Ease of setup and maintenance. To start programming, it suffices for students to insert a pre-configured microSD card into their SBC and boot the system. If the disk image gets corrupted, students can simply download a new image and start over. For busy faculty who are new to parallelism and are trying to quickly inject concepts into a course, this ease of setup cannot be overstated.

Affordability. Compared to other parallel platforms, SBCs like the Raspberry Pi are very inexpensive. Some cost less than a typical textbook, potentially allowing each student to purchase her own device. Students can connect their SBCs to university-owned (or previously purchased) peripherals such as monitors, mice and keyboards. To minimimze costs further, students can purchase preloaded microSD cards and boot a university-owned SBC.

Immediacy. On a typical SBC, the CPU, memory unit, storage device, and other components are clearly visible, making them readily available for visual and tactile learners. Since their software is running on actual hardware, students can perform timing and scalability studies without fearing resource contention with other students or performance penalties from virtualization.

2 WHY NOT LAPTOPS, PHONES OR VMS?

Given the ubiquity of multicore CPUs, just about any modern computer has hardware to teach students about parallel computing. However several platforms have drawbacks, including:

Mobile devices (i.e., smartphones and tablets) have small screens, limited ports, and lack IDEs, making them poor platforms for *writing* software.

Student laptops offer larger screens, better ports, and IDEs for writing software, compared to mobile devices. However:

- Students may have different operating systems (e.g., Chrome, Linux, MacOS, Windows) on their laptops. This diversity can make it a challenge for instructors to create instructional materials that work for all students.
- Most laptop operating systems do not come with compilers, debuggers, IDEs, and other software development tools pre-installed. Instead, the student must install and configure these tools, creating a potential barrier to student learning.
- A laptop's expense is often correlated with its number of cores. A course in which students are expected to develop parallel software on their own laptops may thus discriminate against students from disadvantaged backgrounds, who may not be able to afford laptops with four or more cores. This in turn limits the amount of parallelism that can be observed on their system.

Virtual machines (VMs) running on laptops, desktops, or remote servers can be pre-configured in a way that eliminates many of the downsides of student laptops. However in our experience, running parallel software on a VM (especially free ones) incurs a non-trivial performance penalty.

Remote multicore servers can eliminate the preceding drawbacks. However, using remote hardware for parallel computing:

- Requires account management for students in courses, extending instructor or department overhead.
- Requires a mechanism to prevent student programs from interfering with one another. To accomplish this, students may need to use a reservation system, or submit their programs via a batch queuing system.
- Requires students to view the computer as an abstract entity. For students with particular learning styles (e.g., who learn best by seeing and/or by tactile manipulation), a local system they can touch and whose operation they can observe would be preferable.

In short, SBCs eliminate the drawbacks associated with mobile devices, student laptops, virtual machines, and remote servers, making them a viable platform for parallel computing education. They are also fun devices that many students find highly motivating.

3 BACKGROUND AND RELATED WORK

Perhaps the most well-known SBC is the Raspberry Pi, a $35.00 credit-card sized computer. The Raspberry Pi Model 3 features a 1.2 GHz quad-core ARM processor and 1 GB of RAM. Its low cost and small form factor inspires hobbyists to use the Raspberry Pi for various projects, including robots, drones and webservers.

Rasbian, the Raspberry Pi operating system, comes pre-configured with Scratch and Python. A goal of the Raspberry Pi project is to provide an inexpensive, accessible platform that enables children and teachers to learn computing. Notable early efforts include the Glyndŵr/BCS Turing Project [8], and the Bridge21 CPD effort [4]. Both projects aimed to expose high school students and teachers to computing concepts using the Raspberry Pi (the former used the Pi in conjunction with other devices). In both studies, the hands-on approach was well received, with educators in the Bridge21 CPD effort keen to incorporate the Raspberry Pi into their courses [4].

Educators at the Universities of Guelph [19] and Calgary [9, 10] were among the first to use the Raspberry Pi to teach programming topics in a college setting. Guelph students used the Raspberry Pi to learn beginning C programming, while second-year Calgary students used it to learn embedded programming (ARM assembly). At both universities, a dedicated Raspberry Pi lab was created for students to plug in their devices. At Guelph, students bought a custom Raspberry Pi "kit" as part of their standard lab equipment in the course [19]. Calgary students, however, were required to come to the Raspberry Pi lab in order to use their devices. While the Guelph students were markedly enthusiastic for the Pis, the reaction of the Calgary students was more neutral [9] – students were enthusiastic about working with the Pis, but they were frustrated by the "awkwardness" of the lab set up and scarcity of the shared resources [9]. This suggests the "one SBC per student" approach is preferable for CS education. We also note that Raspberry Pis were used to teach assembly at East Tennessee State University [15], though no assessment data was provided.

Early SBCs (including the earlier Raspberry Pis) had one core, so a single SBC did not lend itself well to teaching parallel computing. Instead, researchers and educators started networking SBCs together to form "microclusters", in which communication between the SBC nodes was enabled through the use of the Message Passing Interface (MPI). IridisPi [5] is an early example using Raspberry Pis. Pfalzgraf and Driscoll proposed using single-core Raspberry Pis in conjunction with MPI to teach about HPC concepts [13]. Toth used dual-core Cubie board SBCs to enable each student to have their own 2-node Beowulf cluster [18] in a parallel computing course.

However, modern SBCs have multiple cores and may include access to co-processor or GPU chips. This enables the teaching of shared memory parallelism on SBCs for the first time (see [12] for an example). In this paper, we discuss efforts to use the Raspberry Pi to teach multicore computing. To the best of our knowledge, we are the first to suggest the use of the Raspberry Pi for this purpose. In the sections that follow, we discuss strategies and materials we have used to teach shared memory programming to students at our respective universities and integrate these concepts into our curricula. Motivated by the literature, we present workshop assessment data evaluating the efficacy and enthusiasm SBCs generate when teaching multicore computing concepts.

4 PI TEACHING PLATFORMS & ASSESSMENT

The small form factor of SBCs make them highly portable and amenable for introducing parallel concepts at workshops, without needing to coordinate access to remote architectures. Matthews et al. [7] recently organized a series of workshops (described in Section 4.2) centered on using the Raspberry Pi 3 to learn and teach parallel computing concepts. The workshops were extremely popular, with 15 to 30 people attending each.

In the following subsections, we introduce available teaching materials and present assessment results of using them in the workshop settings. Our goals included observing: (i) how well parallel computing could be taught using an SBC, and (ii) whether or not using an SBC would motivate participants to learn about parallel computing. In the assessments that follow, we focus on the Raspberry Pi 3. However, we stress that almost any SBC offers the same advantages listed in Section 1 – affordability, low power consumption, ease of setup/maintenance, and immediacy. We hypothesize that showing the effectiveness of one SBC for teaching parallelism indicates the effectiveness of others for teaching PDC.

4.1 Available PDC Teaching Modules

We have developed teaching modules, available at *csinparallel.org*, that are designed to be used in a variety of courses in a day or two, enabling instructors to include PDC topics in existing courses. The *csinparallel.org* patternlet modules are especially useful for teaching concepts to students in first and second-year undergraduate courses [2].

Patternlets [1] are small code examples that use established parallel design patterns to demonstrate particular PDC topics. There are currently 17 OpenMP patternlets for teaching shared memory parallel topics, as well as a number of patternlets for POSIX multithreading, MPI, and heterogeneous (MPI+OpenMP) computing.

```
#include <stdio.h>
#include <omp.h>
int main(int argc, char** argv) {
    printf("\nBefore...\n");
//    #pragma omp parallel
    printf("\nDuring...");
    printf("\n\nAfter...\n\n");
    return 0;
}
```

Figure 1: Sample OpenMP fork-join patternlet.

The patternlet examples can be used to achieve several of the CS2013 PD outcomes by enabling students to explore a concept using a simple program (typically one screen of code or less) that, when changed slightly, illustrates the desired learning outcome. Figure 1 shows an OpenMP patternlet that illustrates the fork-join pattern. Students explore this pattern by first running the program shown in Figure 1, observing the results, then uncommenting the pragma and re-running the program to observe changes in output.

The teaching modules accompanying each patternlet use diagrams to further illustrate concepts and provide questions for students to consider while trying out examples [6].

There are additional teaching materials at *csinparallel.org* that can be used in the classroom with the Raspberry Pi. Table 1 depicts the PD Core Tier 1/2 topic areas and learning outcomes from ACM 2013 that can be taught with Raspberry Pi SBCs. Our previous work [3] assessed several of these modules and showed that they met learning objectives similar to those in Table 1 in the Parallel Decomposition, Communication and Coordination, and Parallel Algorithms, Analysis and Programming areas. For example, a module

Table 1: PD Core Topic Areas [16] Teachable on the Pi.

PD Knowledge Area	Outcomes
Parallel Fundamentals	1. Shared resource access 2. Types of synchronization
Parallel Decomposition	1. Explain need for synchronization 2. Identify parallelism opportunities 3. Write correct scalable PD program 4. Use tasked-based decomposition 5. Use data decomposition
Communication & Coordination	1. Use mutual exclusion 2. Give an example of data race 5. Write concurrent task program 6. Use synchronized task queue 7. Explain need for atomicity 8. Write a program that reveals a data race
Parallel Algorithms, Analysis, and Programming	3. Define speedup and scalability 4. Identify independent tasks 5. Describe what can(not) be parallelized 6. Implement parallel divide and conquer
Parallel Architecture	1. Explain shared vs. distributed memory 2. Describe SMP architecture 3. Describe tasks that match SIMD

on multicore programming with OpenMP enables students to use data decomposition, and to observe and fix a race condition on a shared variable.

4.2 Raspberry Pi Workshops

The authors led parallel computing workshops at the 2016 ACM Richard Tapia Conference, the 2017 SIAM Computational Science & Engineering (CSE) Broader Engagement program, and the 2017 ACM SIGCSE Conference. Each workshop lasted about 90 minutes, and used the quad-core Raspberry Pi 3 to introduce the participants to OpenMP programming. Each workshop followed roughly the same format, though were presented to radically different audiences. The workshops at Tapia and CSE were attended primarily by students, while the workshop at SIGCSE was attended by faculty.

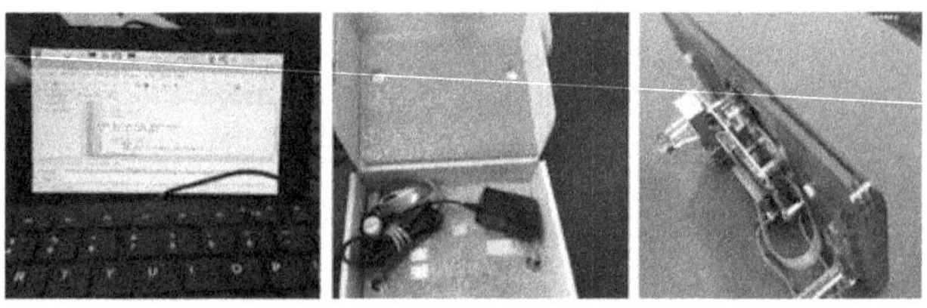

Figure 2: Views of the Pimoroni unit used in workshops.

4.2.1 Workshop Overview. Each pair of participants shared a "Pimoroni" [11] unit: a Raspberry Pi 3 mounted to a Pimoroni 7" display, plus a USB keyboard and mouse (see Figure 2). Each unit cost approximately $150.00. Since the quality of wireless at the workshops was unknown beforehand, paper handouts were prepared for each participant, including a "Raspberry Pi Basics" handout, adapted from the CSinParallel OpenMP patternlets module. We publicly share our workshop materials at this link [7].

Table 2: Results of Pre-Survey and Post-Survey of OpenMP workshops.

	Pre-Survey			Post-Survey			p-values
	T	C	S	T	C	S	
Questions/ Number of Responses	33	16	17	32	16	17	
1. How confident are you that you can describe how to decompose a problem using multiple threads and implement it using a parallel loop?	2.15	2.38	2.88	3.66	4.18	4.06	T: 3.129×10^{-8} C: 1.653×10^{-4} S: 4.556×10^{-3}
2. How confident are you that you could describe the advantages and disadvantages of using parallel programming on shared memory multicore machines to someone familiar with programming?	2.55	3.06	3.17	3.94	4.38	4.18	T: 1.071×10^{-6} C: 6.742×10^{-4} S: 2.753×10^{-2}
3. How confident are you that you can define speedup and describe it to someone familiar with programming?	2.27	2.81	3.12	4.03	4.5	4.23	T: 5.912×10^{-7} C: 1.965×10^{-4} S: 2.081×10^{-2}
4. How confident are you that you can describe what a race condition is and how to avoid it when writing parallel programs that use shared memory?	2.48	2.81	3.12	3.83	4.5	4.17	T: 2.349×10^{-5} C: 6.933×10^{-4} S: 7.663×10^{-3}
5. To what extent did using an inexpensive multicore computer (e.g. the Raspberry Pi) to run parallel programs motivate you to learn more about parallel computing in the future?	n/a	n/a	n/a	4.22	4.13	3.88	n/a

Each workshop began with a short presentation on the Raspberry Pi 3, multicore architectures, and shared memory parallelism. We discussed the differences between processes and threads, and how threads can be executed concurrently or in parallel. The participants spent the next 50 minutes working in pairs, interactively completing the OpenMP exercises in the "Raspberry Pi Basics" handout. In the final 20 minutes of the workshop, the participants used the Pi to run a drug-design CSinParallel module and complete an accompanying worksheet. This module contains three versions of a program simulating the design of pharmaceutical drugs: two using OpenMP (with different thread-scheduling options) and one using C++11 threads. Students ran all three programs, varying the numbers of cores, measured the run times, and calculated speedup. Students were then asked to think about why the three programs ran differently. In the last few minutes of the workshop, we discussed the results, and why the programs behaved differently.

Each workshop had between 15 and 30 participants. While the workshop was designed with computer science undergraduates with no prior exposure to parallelism in mind, we had very diverse audiences. Some attendees were indeed undergraduates who had never been exposed to parallel computing. Others were graduates students with some prior parallel programming experience. Still others were faculty members seeking ideas on how to teach parallelism at their own institutions.

Prior to each workshop, we gave a 4-question pre-survey, asking the participants to rate their confidence on each of four learning objectives, using a scale of 1 to 5 with "1" indicating "not confident at all", "3" indicating "somewhat confident", and "5" indicating "very confident". The survey questions are listed in Table 2.

A post-survey was administered at the conclusion of the workshop that was identical to the pre-survey, except for a fifth question that asked participants to assess (on a scale of 1 to 5) the effect of the Raspberry Pi (or a device like it) in motivating them to learn more about parallel computing. Here, "1" indicated "no increase", "3" indicated "some increase", while "5" indicated "a lot of increase". This question was followed with an invitation to explain their answer further through an open-ended response.

4.2.2 *Results of Assessment.*

Table 2 shows the results of our surveys. The third row reports the number of responses we received on the pre- and post-surveys for the Tapia (T), SIAM CSE (C), and SIGCSE (S) workshops. (For example, 33 Tapia participants completed the pre-survey, while 32 completed the post-survey.) The mean response for each pre- and post-survey question is shown in columns two and three respectively. We conducted a two-sample unpaired t-test using the R statistics package [17] to test the significance of the difference between the mean scores.

For each question, the null hypothesis of the t-test is that the means for the two groups are equivalent, and we reject the null hypothesis when $p < 0.05$. The last column of Table 2 shows the results of our t-test analyses.

There is a significant difference in the means of the pre- and post-surveys for questions 1 through 4 for each of our workshops, despite the fact that each had different mixtures of faculty and students. The Tapia workshop (which had our lowest p-value) had the highest number of novice students; the CSE workshop had more experienced students; and the SIGCSE workshop was made up of almost entirely faculty. Unsurprisingly, more advanced groups had higher p-values than the novice group; however, all measured p-values are below 0.05. This strongly suggests that our approach can be used to cover many of the PDC learning outcomes of Table 1.

The fifth question in Table 2 only appeared on the post-survey. The mean for the fifth question was 4.22 for the Tapia workshop, 4.13 for CSE, and 3.88 for SIGCSE; the more students in a workshop, the greater the positive effect. A histogram depicting the combined set of responses to question 5 is shown in Figure 3.

The overall mean for the fifth question responses was 4.19, and 40 of the 48 total respondents answered either a "4" or "5". This suggests to us that the vast majority of the participants felt the

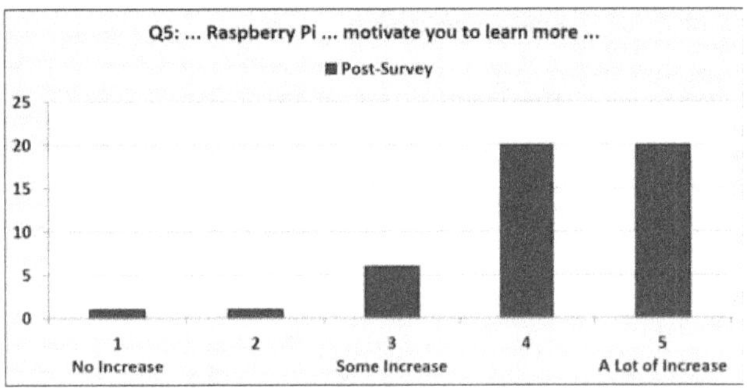

Figure 3: Question 5 histogram of post-workshop survey.

Raspberry Pi 3 SBC was a very positive factor in motivating them to learn more about parallel computing.

More information can be gleaned from the open-ended responses; 40 (83%) of the respondents to the post quiz provided an open-ended response. Their feedback was largely very positive and enthusiastic.

Several participants remarked at the perceived impact of the Raspberry Pi for learning about parallel computing. Said one respondent: *"The impact of it is incredible, would love to learn more."* One of our SIGCSE participants remarked, *"I have experience with parallel processing/programming, but not so much pis. That's why I took the workshop. I love using the pis! Wonderfully motivating! Gets students closer to the hardware and powerful enough to motivate studying parallelism. Great workshop!"*

Still other participants noted how effectively the Raspberry Pi could be used to teach OpenMP. *"Awesome seeing how easy this was to teach"*, said one of our Tapia participants. *"You can get right to the point quickly"*, said another. One of our SIGCSE participants remarked, *"I am impressed with how fast and easy it was to demonstrate this[sic] concepts. This is something I can easily see doing with students. The ease of the examples and the simplicity of the OpenMP inspires me to do this in class!!"*

Perhaps the biggest impact of our workshop was the fact that attendees could explore parallel computing on an inexpensive, personal device. *"Not having to have an expensive computer to try this stuff on is really motivating"*, noted one Tapia participant. *"Accessibility Helps!"* wrote another. *"I'll probably try to get my own Raspberry Pi to practice more and write my own code for it"* remarked one of our CSE attendees. *"Simple system and inexpensive"* stated a SIGCSE participant.

The newness of the Raspberry Pi added an extra dimension of novelty and relevancy to the material for others. *"It's fun to see it work on a small machine and get to play with the tech I keep hearing about (raspberry pi)"*, said a Tapia attendee. *"Amazing parallel processing system with multicore processor!"* remarked a SIGCSE participant. The perceived value was succinctly stated by another Tapia participant: *"Simple, cheap, not too intimidating! Very awesome =)"*.

We acknowledge the concepts taught on the Raspberry Pi can be taught on a workstation or supercomputer node. *"I think it's easier on a workstation"*, grumbled one SIGCSE participant, perhaps due to the Pimoroni's small screen. However, the portability and inexpensiveness of the Raspberry Pi makes it possible to teach parallel computing concepts while maintaining the transferability of knowledge to larger systems. *"It can help run lab experiments that can later be implemented at a larger scale"* observed one attendee. Another noted that *"The somewhat limited resources on the Pi (as compared to KVL or something) really makes you focus on efficiency and proper programming"*.

The true value of the Pi is having a personal machine that is relateable and inexpensive. *"I am already very motivated because I plan to teach the course ..."* said a SIGCSE participant, *"but my expectation is using an inexpensive system will motivate the STUDENTS to do so and I am really interested in how much that is true"*.

4.2.3 Lessons Learned. Teaching OpenMP concepts with the Raspberry Pi in a workshop setting was clearly effective. Furthermore, within a 90-minute period, we were able to touch upon several outcomes listed in the PD knowledge area, including outcomes 1 and 2 under parallel fundamentals; outcomes 1,2, and 4 under parallel decomposition, outcomes 1 and 2 under communication & coordination; outcome 3 under parallel algorithms, analysis, & programming; and outcome 2 under parallel architecture.

The feedback we received from the workshop indicates that people enjoyed using the Raspberry Pi to learn parallel programming. Put differently, our workshop participants found the use of SBCs to be highly motivating, and we believe that students will find the study of PDC using SBCs in the classroom equally motivating.

After the workshops, we held a series of "debriefing" sessions. During these sessions, several of us reflected on how much easier it was (logistically) to conduct this workshop using SBCs, compared to previous workshops in which we used remote HPC systems. In several prior workshops, automated security systems, poor wireless connectivity, electrical storms, misconfigured accounts, and other remote system issues caused problems. Such issues caused a great deal of stress, since we could not fix the systems ourselves. As a result, we always needed to have a "Plan B" system in place for our workshops, just in case something went wrong.

To prepare for our workshop using SBCs, we simply flashed all the devices' disks prior to the workshop, and then re-flashed them with fresh images afterwards. All the units fit into a single pelican case that was mailed to the workshop location prior to the event, and returned afterwards. For the SIGCSE workshop, we were able to check the Pis in their pelican case as a separate piece of luggage.

4.3 Alternative Teaching Platforms

The Pimoroni-based setup for teaching PDC material using Raspberry Pis has proven to be portable and effective, as demonstrated in the workshop experiences described above. This section describes an alternative setup that costs \$50.00 and enables students to interact directly with the Pi's desktop environment via a network connection from a laptop or lab workstation. The system image [7] works as-is on the Pimoroni, or through the configuration described below, and contains the PDC materials used in our workshops.

Each kit (shown in Figure 4) consists of a Raspberry Pi, a Micro-USB card with the system image installed, cables, and a USB-to-Ethernet adapter (for laptops lacking an Ethernet port). The image enables students running Windows, OS X, or Linux to access the Pi desktop environment using open-source virtual network computing (VNC) [14] software. Students connect to the Pi using a direct wired

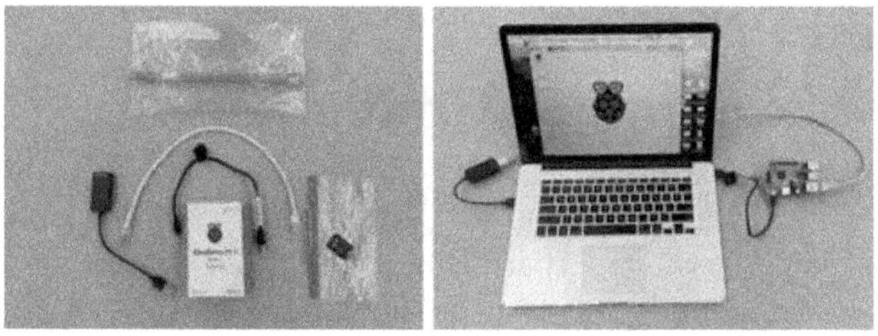

Figure 4: Laptop connection kit.

Ethernet connection between their laptops and the Pi, or through the use of a USB-to-Ethernet adapter.

The right side of Figure 4 depicts a VNC client displaying the Raspberry Pi desktop for user interaction. Users can also interact with their Pi on a command line via SSH (the VNC client requires an underlying SSH session). With printed or video instructions, we found that first-time users can assemble the system and begin computing in 10-15 minutes, even with no prior Raspberry Pi experience (except when hardware issues arise; e.g., a faulty USB socket). After the first time, setup and tear-down time totals about five minutes, making this approach feasible for in-class exercises.

5 CONCLUSIONS AND FUTURE WORK

In this paper, we describe how single board computers like the Raspberry Pi can be effectively used to introduce undergraduate students to parallel computing in a workshop setting. SBCs embody the "hands-on experiential" learning advocated by CS educators, and are a fun way to introduce students to parallel computing.

SBCs can also be networked together to create "microclusters" to introduce students to distributed and heterogeneous computing. For example, our current system image supports building Beowulf clusters through the use of a switch; we plan to extend this image to enable Pis to self-assemble into a cluster.

We have also discussed strategies for teaching parallel computing with the Raspberry Pi. In particular, the Raspberry Pi costs less than many course textbooks. With the availability of free, high-quality teaching materials, Raspberry Pis can be individually purchased by students like a textbook. This makes the Pi useful in a variety of different contexts, including required courses, elective courses, undergraduate research, and outreach experiences.

Our collective experiences strongly suggest that the Raspberry Pi is an inexpensive, accessible, cost-effective, and highly motivating way to introduce undergraduate students to parallel and distributed computing. We hope that our experiences will inspire others to explore the use of the Raspberry Pi and other SBCs to engage their students and help them achieve PDC learning outcomes.

As the price/performance ratios of system on a chip (SoC) architectures continue to improve, we will continue to see SBCs with updated processors. For example, the ODROID XU4 offers an octa-core processor for $59.00. We look forward to future work that explores the use of such systems to increase student engagement through teaching, research, and outreach activities.

ACKNOWLEDGMENTS

We are grateful to the anonymous reviewers for their feedback on this work. Funding for this project was partially provided by the National Science Foundation (NSF) and the DOD High Performance Computing Modernization Program (HPCMP). Adams, Brown, and Shoop are funded under NSF DUE Grants 1225739/1225796/1226172. Matthews is funded under HPCMP MIPRs 61550445/62464243. The opinions expressed in this work are solely of the authors and do not necessarily reflect those of the U.S. Military Academy, the U.S. Army, or the Department of Defense.

REFERENCES

[1] Joel C. Adams. 2014. Injecting Parallel Computing into CS2. In *Proceedings of the 45th ACM Technical Symposium on Computer Science Education (SIGCSE '14)*. ACM, New York, NY, USA, 277–282. https://doi.org/10.1145/2538862.2538883

[2] Joel C. Adams. 2015. Patternlets: A Teaching Tool for Introducing Students to Parallel Design Patterns. In *Proceedings of the 2015 IEEE International Parallel and Distributed Processing Symposium Workshop (IPDPSW '15)*. 752–759. https://doi.org/10.1109/IPDPSW.2015.18

[3] Richard Brown and Elizabeth Shoop. 2011. Modules in community: injecting more parallelism into computer science curricula *(SIGCSE '11)*. ACM, New York, NY, USA, 447–452. https://doi.org/10.1145/1953163.1953293

[4] J. R. Byrne, L. Fisher, and B. Tangney. 2015. Computer science teacher reactions towards raspberry Pi Continuing Professional Development (CPD) workshops using the Bridge21 model. In *2015 10th International Conference on Computer Science Education (ICCSE)*. 267–272. https://doi.org/10.1109/ICCSE.2015.7250254

[5] Simon J. Cox, James T. Cox, Richard P. Boardman, Steven J. Johnston, Mark Scott, and Neil S. O'Brien. 2014. Iridis-pi: a low-cost, compact demonstration cluster. *Cluster Computing* 17, 2 (01 Jun 2014), 349–358. https://doi.org/10.1007/s10586-013-0282-7

[6] CSinParallel. 2013. Patternlets in Parallel Programming. (2013). https://csinparallel.org/csinparallel/modules/patternlets.html

[7] CSinParallel. 2017. Raspberry Pi Workshop Materials. (2017). https://csinparallel.org/csinparallel/raspberry_pi.html

[8] Vic Grout and Nigel Houlden. 2014. Taking Computer Science and Programming into Schools: The Glyndŵr/BCS Turing Project. *Procedia - Social and Behavioral Sciences* 141, Supplement C (2014), 680 – 685. https://doi.org/10.1016/j.sbspro.2014.05.119 4th World Conference on Learning Teaching and Educational Leadership (WCLTA-2013).

[9] Jalal Kawash, Andrew Kuipers, Leonard Manzara, and Robert Collier. 2016. Undergraduate Assembly Language Instruction Sweetened with the Raspberry Pi. In *Proceedings of the 47th ACM Technical Symposium on Computing Science Education (SIGCSE '16)*. ACM, New York, NY, USA, 498–503. https://doi.org/10.1145/2839509.2844552

[10] M Lowey. 2013. Raspberry pi sweetens learning for computer science students. (2013). https://www.ucalgary.ca/utoday/issue/2013-11-13/raspberry-pi-sweetens-learning-computer-science-students

[11] Pimoroni Ltd. 2015. Raspberry Pi 7" Touchscreen Display with Stand. (2015). https://shop.pimoroni.com/

[12] Suzanne J. Matthews. 2016. Teaching with Parallella: A First Look in an Undergraduate Parallel Computing Course. *J. Comput. Sci. Coll.* 31, 3 (Jan. 2016), 18–27. http://dl.acm.org/citation.cfm?id=2835377.2835381

[13] A. M. Pfalzgraf and J. A. Driscoll. 2014. A low-cost computer cluster for high-performance computing education. In *IEEE International Conference on Electro/Information Technology*. 362–366. https://doi.org/10.1109/EIT.2014.6871791

[14] T. Richardson, Q. Stafford-Fraser, K. R. Wood, and A. Hopper. 1998. Virtual network computing. *IEEE Internet Computing* 2, 1 (Jan 1998), 33–38. https://doi.org/10.1109/4236.656066

[15] David Tarnoff. 2015. Integrating the Arm-based Raspberry Pi into an Architecture Course. *J. Comput. Sci. Coll.* 30, 5 (May 2015), 67–73. http://dl.acm.org/citation.cfm?id=2752981.2752998

[16] The ACM/IEEE Joint Task Force on Computing Curricula. 2013. Computer Science Curricula 2013: Curriculum Guidelines for Undergraduate Degree Programs in Computer Science. (December 2013).

[17] The R Foundation. 2009. The R Project for Statistical Computing. Internet Website, last accessed 09-20-16. (2009). https://www.r-project.org/.

[18] D. Toth. 2014. A Portable Cluster for Each Student. In *2014 IEEE International Parallel Distributed Processing Symposium Workshops*. 1130–1134. https://doi.org/10.1109/IPDPSW.2014.126

[19] Michael Wirth and Judi McCuaig. 2014. Making Programs With The Raspberry Pi. In *Proceedings of the Western Canadian Conference on Computing Education (WCCCE '14)*. Article 17, 5 pages. https://doi.org/10.1145/2597959.2597970

A User Space-based Project for Practicing Core Memory Management Concepts

Sam Silvestro
Department of Computer Science
University of Texas at San Antonio
San Antonio, Texas
sam.silvestro@utsa.edu

Timothy T. Yuen
Department of Interdisciplinary Learning and Teaching
University of Texas at San Antonio
San Antonio, Texas
timothy.yuen@utsa.edu

Corey Crosser
Department of Electrical Engineering & Computer Science
United States Military Academy
West Point, New York
corey.crosser@usma.edu

Dakai Zhu
Department of Computer Science
University of Texas at San Antonio
San Antonio, Texas
dakai.zhu@utsa.edu

Turgay Korkmaz
Department of Computer Science
University of Texas at San Antonio
San Antonio, Texas
turgay.korkmaz@utsa.edu

Tongping Liu
Department of Computer Science
University of Texas at San Antonio
San Antonio, Texas
tongping.liu@utsa.edu

ABSTRACT

This paper presents the design and evaluation of a novel project designed to facilitate the learning of memory management concepts and interactions between different components. This project removes the complexity of a full or specific operating system by implementing memory management inside the user space. Evaluation results show that the mean exam scores improved by about 29% to 34%. On average, the total code size is less than 300 lines and time spent working on this project is under 17 hours. Therefore, this project is beneficial in helping students learn memory management while maintaining a reasonable project workload.

ACM Reference Format:
Sam Silvestro, Timothy T. Yuen, Corey Crosser, Dakai Zhu, Turgay Korkmaz, and Tongping Liu. 2018. A User Space-based Project for Practicing Core Memory Management Concepts. In *Proceedings of The 49th ACM Technical Symposium on Computer Science Education (SIGCSE '18).* ACM, New York, NY, USA, 6 pages. https://doi.org/10.1145/3159450.3159581

1 INTRODUCTION

"Operating Systems" is a core course of undergraduate computer science curriculum [1], and memory management is a key component of the OS which determines the efficiency of the entire system, to some extent. Modern operating systems utilize the virtual memory mechanism. Therefore, multiple related concepts (i.e., virtual memory, address space, page tables, address translation, page replacement, page faults, and physical memory management) are required to be covered during lectures as it is important to fully understand the relationship between these concepts. This relationship can be described as follows. In order to support virtual memory, the paging mechanism is typically introduced to overcome the coarse granularity of segments. Physical memory is divided into multiple frames, and the process address space is then divided into virtual pages. The OS is responsible for physical memory management, as well as virtual memory management. Basically, it utilizes per-process page tables to track the relationship between physical frames and virtual pages. An executing program generates a virtual address prior to every memory access, where the page number and page offset can be extracted from this address. The page number of a virtual address is utilized for translation into a physical frame number using the page table, if the page actually exists in main memory. Otherwise, a page fault occurs, and a possible page replacement may be required to find a physical frame. Afterward, a new mapping is created so that the program can access the corresponding page. Each of these concepts themselves are difficult to follow and understand. Further, these concepts should be connected together in order to have a holistic understanding of memory management. So, course projects should be helpful for students to strengthen their understanding of the different concepts and the interactions among them.

ACM ISBN 978-1-4503-5103-4/18/02.
https://doi.org/10.1145/3159450.3159581

2 MEMORY MANAGEMENT PROJECTS

Although there are many existing projects targeting memory management inside the OS [6–10], none can fully serve this purpose. Existing work typically shares two common shortcomings.

First, projects tend to focus on only one aspect of memory management, such as the SLOB memory allocator [7], buddy manager [8], page replacement [10], and page thrashing [6]. Laadan et al. designed several projects to understand internal OS memory usage, such as the working sets and modified sets of a process, and the page uses of each memory region [9], which is still not sufficient to cover all of the concepts described above. Although these projects are helpful for students to understand one particular concept, they cannot present a holistic view of memory management. Many concepts cannot be practiced through these projects, not to mention the interaction between them.

Second, most of these existing projects are too difficult to implement and debug, since students are typically asked to alter an existing OS [2, 7, 9, 10, 13]. For the implementation, students have to understand data structures and the basic architecture of an existing OS, then determine where to insert their implementation, if not given hints. Also, changing an existing OS also increases the complexity of compiling and debugging. Students must recompile the entire OS, then verify whether their specific code has been executed. They also must learn how to debug their code inside the OS itself, which is another well-known challenge, even for experts [5]. Therefore, existing projects significantly increase the complexity of implementation and debugging. Rather than practicing these key memory management concepts, students may end up spending a large amount of time and effort just understanding a particular OS, and learning how to perform debugging within it.

While offering an improvement over a real OS, the issue of complexity holds true for user-level OS's such as Pintos [12]. Additionally, Pintos requires root privileges in order to install the x86 emulator and dependencies needed to run it. The overhead associated with familiarizing oneself with Pintos' installation, configuration, and overall structure would prohibit its use as the basis of a project designed to teach virtual memory concepts. PennOS avoids these issues and does not require special privileges as it is written from scratch in the user space [3]. However, it lacks a memory management component, instead focusing on process management and scheduling, file system and I/O, and shell integration.

3 DESIGN OF A USER SPACE-BASED MEMORY MANAGEMENT PROJECT

This paper presents the novel design of a user space-based project that exercises memory management fully within the user space. This project's design addresses three critical issues for effectively learning memory management: (1) the project should cover most core concepts, as described above, rather than one particular topic; (2) the project's workload should be reasonably low; (3) students should be able to gain a comprehensive understanding of the interaction between the different concepts. A design built in user space provides several benefits: first, it can significantly reduce the complexity of the project. Since it does not rely on an existing OS, students save significant effort spent understanding its implementation. Second, students do not need to recompile the OS upon making changes. Third, the project is significantly easier to debug when problems arise. Students can instead focus on the project itself, rather than interacting with a complicated OS.

Based on these requirements, we adapted **the idea of simulation** [11]. Null et al. designed an interactive tool based on a randomly generated series of memory references. However, their tool is designed to show graphical representations of the memory system and provide step-by-step descriptions of memory management activities inside the OS based on the given memory references. Although this project is also based on a simulated sequence of memory references, students are required to implement the project by themselves starting from scratch. The similarity is limited only to the utilization of a simulated series of memory references.

The overall objective of the project is for students to practice (1) virtual memory management, (2) address translation, (3) page table design, and (4) page replacement algorithms. This project further designs three sub-projects based on a simulated series of memory references.

3.1 Part I: Translation via Page Table

Students implement address translation based on a given one-level page table. They are further provided with basic machine details, such as the page/frame size, the address space of virtual memory, and the size of physical memory. Students write a program that accepts a filename as its only argument. This input file consists of a sequence of 8-byte `unsigned long` values that simulates a sequence of memory accesses, where each value represents a virtual address. For each virtual address, students must refer to a given page table to translate it into a corresponding physical address. The mapping (or page table) between virtual page numbers and physical page numbers is provided by a directed graph, which students are required to translate into a simple array prior to address translation. For simplicity, the given sequence of memory accesses does not include any page faults, where all corresponding addresses are in the range of the given page table. To verify the correctness of their implementation, students should write the sequence of translated physical addresses into an output file in a format similar to the input file. Students can obtain the `md5sum` of this output file [4] and submit the checksum. For a given sequence of memory accesses and a given page table, correct implementations of address translation should always produce the correct and unique checksum.

3.2 Part II: Page Table and Physical Memory Management

Students implement the design of the page table and will manage physical memory. The details of the hardware are provided to the students, such as the page/frame size, the address space of virtual memory and the size of physical memory. From the size of physical memory and the size of a frame, students may compute the total number of physical pages. The difference for the second part is that the page table is not provided. Students must design the page table and manage the physical memory by themselves. To better mimic a real system, it is assumed that the first few pages are reserved for use by the OS, but other pages are initially freed. For simplicity, we assume there is only one application inside the system.

Students are provided with an input file to simulate the memory accesses of the given application. In this part, these memory accesses can cause page faults. For each logical address, students are required to check whether the corresponding physical frame is marked as valid in the page table. If yes, then the student is required to perform the address translation, as in Part I. Otherwise, they must choose a physical frame and update the mapping in the existing page table. Physical frames are assumed to be allocated in sequential order. When there are no available physical frames, students implement the Least-Recently Used (LRU) page replacement policy to evict the LRU frame from the page table, and then reset the page table afterwards. There is no need to swap the page to disk, which is assumed to have been taken care of automatically. Once a frame is selected for replacement, the student must: (1) invalidate the page table entry that is mapped to the current physical frame, and (2) remap the page table entry of the new logical address to the current frame number. The reverse mapping mechanism is introduced in order to identify the corresponding virtual page mapped to the selected physical frame. Upon each reference, the order of accesses for the corresponding physical frames must be updated in order to preserve the LRU policy. Lastly, the students write the sequence of translated physical addresses into an output file and print the total number of page faults that occurred.

To successfully complete this assignment, students must fully understand and integrate different concepts of virtual memory management, including the management of physical pages, LRU page replacement, page-to-frame mapping performed by the OS, and page table management, in addition to the address translation that was exercised in Part I. Part II also helps students understand the details of a physical page table entry, such as the valid bit, and the concept of reverse mapping. With this knowledge, they must simulate the entire process beginning with a memory reference.

3.3 Part III: General Page Table Design

Part III extends the page table for arbitrary system parameters. The student's main program should now accept three additional parameters, which specify a hypothetical machine's page/frame size, virtual memory size, and physical memory size; other conditions remain the same. Students are again required to output the translated physical addresses for the same sequence of memory accesses, as in Part II. This component prompts students to rethink page table design in an abstract situation. Accordingly, students must determine what should be changed to accommodate an arbitrary environment. This part helps students revisit their implementation from the second part in a generalized context, which requires a better understanding of page table design.

4 EVALUATION DESIGN

This section describes the evaluation for this project.

4.1 Sample

This project was implemented in the OS course in the Spring 2017 semester at University of Texas at San Antonio, a large research university in South Texas. There were two sections of this course, taught by the 5th and 6th authors of this paper. There were 64 students in Section 1, and 32 students in Section 2. Of these 96 combined students, 5 were deemed ineligible to include due to not completing the midterm exam, which serves as a test instrument, and were thus eliminated from the sample. For comparison, data from a previous offering of this course in Spring 2016 were included. This section was taught by the 4th author of this paper, and did not include the project, but the same course materials were used for teaching. There were 22 students in this section (Section 0), where no project was assigned.

4.2 Data Sources

4.2.1 Exam Questions. For comparison, we used three identical questions across all sections.

- Question 1 asked students to translate virtual addresses into physical addresses, and show how page tables are stored in memory. Students were provided basic machine parameters such as virtual and physical address spaces, as well as the page/frame size. Students must demonstrate the ability to calculate the number of bits used for each component of both virtual and physical addresses. They must also know how to compute the number of bytes needed for a page table entry, calculate the number of pages required by the entire virtual address space, and produce how many bytes would be needed for the page table of a process on this machine.
- Question 2 tests the students' ability to both perform memory address translation, as well as compute effective access times when given TLB, memory, and disk access times. The students are again provided with basic machine information, such as the page/frame size and virtual/physical address space sizes. Additionally, they are provided with an initial page table and TLB entries. Students must translate four logical addresses into physical addresses, and estimate the access time required by the machine to do so.
- Question 3 tests the students' knowledge of different page replacement algorithms. The question is framed by providing a theoretical maximum number of pages (3 pages) per process. They are then given a sequence of page references from which they must tabulate, by hand, the specific pages currently held in memory after each page reference. Afterward, they must answer with the total number of page faults that occurred for each of the page replacement algorithms in question: FIFO, LRU, and Optimal.

Questions were graded consistently across exams as there was only one correct response for sub-questions in each question. For the sections in which the project was used, this evaluation only includes exam question scores from those students who also completed the project.

4.2.2 Project Results. Student outcomes were also measured through the scores that students received on their projects and completion rates on individual parts of the project. Students were also surveyed on how much time they spent working on the project.

4.2.3 Surveys. Surveys asked students to rate the value of the project, using a 5-point Likert scale, as it related to the topics of address translation, finding the page index inside a virtual address, the concept of frame numbers, physical memory management, LRU, and page offset inside a virtual address. Surveys were used to evaluate students' perception of the project's value as it related to these memory management concepts. The survey also contained open-ended questions asking students to report what they found to be the most difficult part of the project, and why.

5 EVALUATION RESULTS

This section presents the results organized by each evaluation question. A student's data were only included for analysis if s/he had both turned in the project and completed the midterm exam.

5.1 Project Results

Recall the project includes three parts where Part I and Part II are compulsory, and Part III was optional. Table 1 presents the statistics of students' scores for these different parts of the project. In total, 81 out of 91 students submitted the project and took the exam.

The outcomes show that 89% of students were able to complete Part I while about 74% finished Part II across both sections. In terms of scores, there was a very high average score in Part I (around 95.8%), but only around 79% in Part II and Part III. A median score of 100% for Part I indicates that most students were successful in

Section	Submitted	Mean	Stdev	Median
		Part I		
Section 1	89%	97.7%	9.5%	100.0%
Section 2	89%	91.6%	13.6%	100.0%
Combined	89%	95.8%	11.2%	100.0%
		Part II		
Section 1	77%	81.1%	21.0%	90.0%
Section 2	67%	73.8%	22.3%	87.5%
Combined	74%	79.0%	21.5%	87.5%
		Part III		
Section 1	17%	79.1%	8.3%	80.0%
Section 2	15%	77.5%	5.0%	80.0%
Combined	16%	78.7%	7.4%	80.0%
		Parts I & II		
Section 1	89%	77.0%	25.6%	89.2%
Section 2	89%	67.9%	26.8%	70.0%
Combined	89%	74.2%	26.2%	88.3%
		Parts I, II, & III (extra credit)		
Section 1	17%	110.6%	2.2%	111.7%
Section 2	15%	106.7%	3.9%	108.3%
Combined	16%	109.6%	3.0%	110.0%

Table 1: Project results by section and project (both by parts and overall).

	Part I	Part II	Part III	Total
LOC	76.7	220.0	146.7	297.5
Time (h)	5.3	7.4	4.0	16.8

Table 2: Average lines of code for implementation, and average time spent on the project (for each part, and in total).

address translation with a one-level page table. The median score of 87.5% on Part II was lower than Part I, but it still showed that students were moderately successful in managing a page table and physical memory. Note, that grades of zero given to students who did not complete a given project component were not factored into the respective scoring statistics for that part. Furthermore, "completion" is defined as simply having submitted some work product in an attempt to fulfill a given part, without regard to its actual completeness or correctness.

Due to the fact that Part III is provided as extra credit, only 15 students actually submitted this part. The mean score for both sections was 78.7%, which shows that students had average success with address translation on a more general page table design. Note, the percentages given for "Parts I, II, & III" in Table 1 reflect values only for the small subset of students who attempted all three project components. Because this group consists of only 15 students combined, we see significantly higher mean scores than those listed for the other components. The distribution of students' scores is shown further in Figure 1. In total, 64% of students received a score higher than 40 points (or 67%), which also reflects the difficulty of the project.

5.2 Implementation Workload

We wrote a script to obtain the lines-of-code for each part. Note that the total is not the strict sum as these three parts share a large portion of their implementation. A survey was administered to obtain the number of hours spent working on each part.

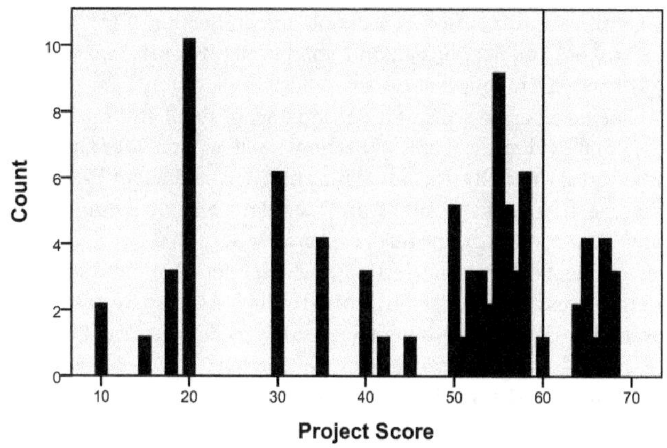

Figure 1: Distribution of student project scores, where the reference line shows maximum combined score for Part I and Part II; Part III is offered as a bonus worth 10 points.

The results are shown in Table 2. Basically, the average LOC for this project was only 297.5, and the average number of hours spent working on this project was only 16.8. As described in Section 1, excluding five outliers, the average hours spent is only 10.8 hours. This indicates that the complexity of this project is totally acceptable, considering the importance of topics covered in an OS course. Also, there is space to extend this project to cover more concepts, if needed, particularly if assigned over a two-week time period.

By manually reviewing the results of 75 surveys, the most commonly reported problems encountered by students were regarding unclear instructions and lack of adequate understanding with respect to the LRU algorithm. As expected, Part II of the project was overwhelmingly cited by students when asked, "What were the most difficult parts of the project, and why?" (with 26 respondents). Specifically, understanding and implementing the LRU algorithm was the most common feedback received (with 10 respondents). Overall, comments that occurred regularly throughout the survey responses were: difficulty in visualizing the concepts; the function and implementation of the LRU algorithm; no means to independently verify correctness of output; understanding what was expected; uneven distribution of work; and too much effort required to complete Part II.

5.3 Exam Results

Table 2 shows the breakdown of scores across both sections, as well as the comparison section (Section 0). Students who did the project (Sections 1 and 2) scored a combined mean of 74% on Question 1, 82.5% on Question 2, and 90.8% on Question 3, which were the exam questions related to memory management. The range of the combined median scores, from 80% to 95% across all three questions, show that most students demonstrated an above average comprehension of memory management. As a comparison, Sections 1 and 2 performed better on the exam questions related to memory management than students in Section 0, who were not assigned the project. An independent samples t-test showed that there was a significant difference in scores between Section 0 (M = 2.08, SD = 0.64) and Sections 1 and 2 combined (M = 2.47, SD = 0.45); $t(101) = -3.335, p = 0.001$.

The mean exam scores for Section 0 were about 15% lower than the combined mean scores of Section 1 and Section 2 for Question 1 on virtual and physical address translation, and about 19% lower than Section 1 and Section 2 on Question 2 on calculating access time. For Question 1, the median score for Section 0 was about 25% lower than Section 1 and Section 2, which infers that more students were successful in translating virtual and physical addresses on the exam. For Question 2, though Section 0's median score of 80% was reasonably good, the median score for Section 0 was 10% lower than Section 1 and 2's median score on calculating access time. There were negligible differences between Section 0 and the other two sections for Question 3, which covered different page replacement algorithms. This result may imply that students do not have much trouble understanding different page replacement algorithms.

	Question 1			
	n	Mean	Stdev	Median
NO PROJECT				
Section 0	22	57.3%	22.7%	55.0%
WITH PROJECT				
Section 1	56	72.5%	26.4%	80.0%
Section 2	25	78.2%	19.6%	85.0%
Combined	81	74.0%	24.6%	80.0%
	Question 2			
	n	Mean	Stdev	Median
NO PROJECT				
Section 0	22	61.4%	38.6%	80.0%
WITH PROJECT				
Section 1	56	82.4%	16.9%	87.5%
Section 2	25	82.8%	21.7%	90.0%
Section	81	82.5%	18.4%	90.0%
	Question 3			
	n	Mean	Stdev	Median
NO PROJECT				
Section 0	22	89.1%	18.5%	100.0%
WITH PROJECT				
Section 1	56	91.6%	13.7%	100.0%
Section 2	25	89.0%	13.3%	95.0%
Combined	81	90.8%	13.6%	95.0%

Table 3: Statistics of examination scores, grouped by project participation status, for each question.

5.4 Perception of Project Value

Seventy-five students, across Sections 1 and 2, responded to the surveys. The survey results, shown in Figure 2, indicate that most students found the project valuable to learning five core memory management concepts. On a scale of 1 (Not valuable at all) to 5 (Extremely Valuable), most students across Sections 1 and 2 found the project to be valuable. Sixty-one percent (61%) of students rated the project experience as 4 or 5 (very to extremely valuable) with respect to understanding address translation, finding the page index inside a virtual address, and the frame number concept. Fifty-three percent (53%) of students rated the project experience as 4 or 5 (very to extremely valuable) with respect to physical memory management and the LRU algorithm.

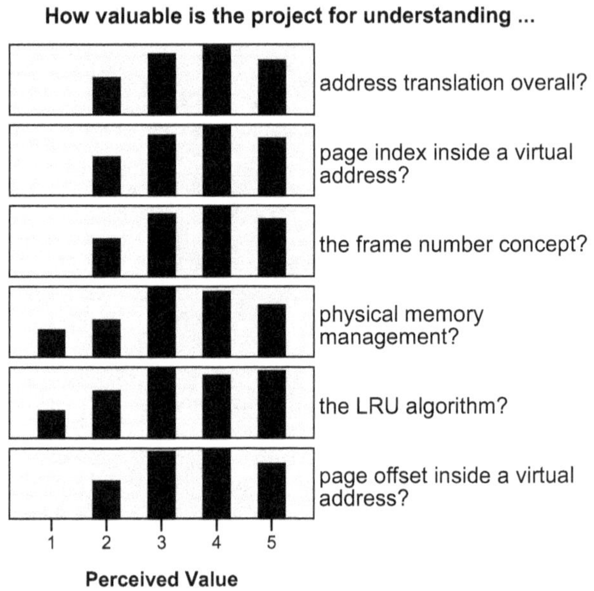

Figure 2: Valuability results on different concepts.

Although most students reported perceiving the project as valuable, they still noted some challenges with it, as well as specific memory management concepts. From the open-ended questions on what students found most difficult in the project, the most commonly reported problems included: unclear instructions and understanding what was expected from them; difficulty in visualizing the concepts; lack of adequate understanding with respect to the LRU algorithm; no means to verify correctness of output, since the answers were not given to students beforehand; uneven distribution of workload between the two required parts; and too much effort required to complete Part II.

6 DISCUSSION

The results showed that this project was beneficial for students in learning about memory management, particularly relating to activities involving address translation and calculating access times. Most students were able to complete the project and received high scores. They also scored higher on exam questions related to memory management as compared to a previous semester, which did not include this project. The only area this project did not necessarily improve upon, when compared to the previous semester, was that of applying different page replacement algorithms, which students appear to have little problem understanding. Student feedback was overwhelming positive in that students found it valuable to learning core memory management concepts. Further, the reported time spent working on the project showed that students spent an appropriate amount of time given the nature of this course. The complexity, as inferred from the grades and time spent on the project, was manageable for the students.

6.1 Potential Project Improvements

The evaluation results, particularly those from student surveys, have been used to improve the project design. One possible revision is to make the overall project a group effort with the hope that collaboration will lead to higher completion rates. Student surveys indicated that Part II took too much effort to complete, which indicates the possibility of dividing that part further. This revision would also make the third part required, which would help students have a more general understanding of page table design. Lastly, this project can teach students the concepts of temporal and spatial locality through utilizing (or constructing an approximation of) real-world memory access patterns for use as project input rather than the random sequences employed in these experiments.

Student surveys suggested that the teaching staff will need to create more resources to help students learn more about the concepts involved before asking to apply them in projects. Also, students recommended more visual resources to help them visualize the concepts. Students also suggested to incorporate inverted page tables, the use of a TLB, and implementing latency calculations for each memory access. The current project could be easily extended to incorporate these concepts. Students regularly expressed their desire to verify the correctness of their programs. Thus, results for a sample set of logical addresses will be provided in order to save students time in verifying the correctness of their programs.

6.2 Novelty

This project differs from other attempts at designing learning environments focusing on memory management. For example, Downey et al. designed a project that allows students to gain experience with paging and thrashing by observing the latency of memory accesses [6]. Hess et al. designed a project for changing the existing SLOB allocator such that the allocator may serve the request in either a best-fit or worst-fit fashion [7]. Laadan et al. designed several projects toward understanding internal OS memory usage, such as the working sets and modified sets of a process, as well as the page uses of each memory region [9]. Singh designed a project that also exercises some key concepts of memory management, such as address translation, updating a two-level page table, and physical memory allocations. However, this project requires the modification of an existing kernel, which may not be easy to control in terms of complexity [13]. These projects presented memory management concepts across several projects whereas our project presented them within the same project to minimize complexity.

Memory management in the user space is not completely new. Nieh and Vaill designed a user-space project for exercising the Buddy algorithm [8]. Arpaci-Dusseau requested students to implement a page fault handler and page replacement policy using LibOS, a library interface to OS services [2]. Null et al. designed their interactive tool based on a randomly generated address reference string [11] by showing students graphical representations of memory activities within the memory system. Thain designed a project that also exercises virtual memory concepts inside the user space [14], which is similar to this project's idea, but their project mainly focused on page replacement policies with page table management functions supplied. Therefore, their project does not provide students with a complete view of how different concepts interact with each other. Further, our project requires students to exercise different memory management concepts by themselves.

7 CONCLUSION

This paper presented a novel project design for an undergraduate Operating Systems course, which focuses on practicing core memory management concepts within the user space. Evaluation results show that this project greatly helps students to understand different concepts related to memory management, with reasonable complexity and effort. The project is now being revised and improved in response to the evaluation results, and will be implemented in subsequent offerings of the OS course. Finally, we have made the project available online at https://github.com/UTSASRG/USMM/.

ACKNOWLEDGMENT

This material is based upon work supported by the National Science Foundation under Award CCF-1566154. The authors would like to thank Shuvra Chakraborty for her help of collecting partial data.

REFERENCES

[1] ACM/IEEE-CS Joint Task Force on Computing Curricula. 2013. *Computer Science Curricula 2013.* Technical Report. ACM Press and IEEE Computer Society Press. https://doi.org/10.1145/2534860

[2] Remzi H. Arpaci-Dusseau. [n. d.]. Project #3: A Real Page Turner. http://pages.cs.wisc.edu/~remzi/Classes/537/Spring2002/p3.html. ([n. d.]).

[3] Adam J Aviv, Vin Mannino, Thanat Owlarn, Seth Shannin, Kevin Xu, and Boon Thau Loo. 2012. Experiences in teaching an educational user-level operating systems implementation project. *ACM SIGOPS Operating Systems Review* 46, 2 (2012), 80–86.

[4] Linux Developers. [n. d.]. md5sum(1) - Linux man page. https://linux.die.net/man/1/md5sum. ([n. d.]).

[5] Jeff Dike. 2000. A user-mode port of the Linux kernel.. In *Annual Linux Showcase & Conference.*

[6] Allen B. Downey. 1999. Teaching Experimental Design in an Operating Systems Class. In *The Proceedings of the Thirtieth SIGCSE Technical Symposium on Computer Science Education (SIGCSE '99).* ACM, New York, NY, USA, 316–320. https://doi.org/10.1145/299649.299796

[7] Rob Hess and Paul Paulson. 2010. Linux Kernel Projects for an Undergraduate Operating Systems Course. In *Proceedings of the 41st ACM Technical Symposium on Computer Science Education (SIGCSE '10).* ACM, New York, NY, USA, 485–489. https://doi.org/10.1145/1734263.1734428

[8] Amit Jain. [n. d.]. Shell Project, part 2 (with Buddy System Memory Manager). http://cs.boisestate.edu/~amit/teaching/552/handouts/p6.pdf. ([n. d.]).

[9] Oren Laadan, Jason Nieh, and Nicolas Viennot. 2011. Structured Linux Kernel Projects for Teaching Operating Systems Concepts. In *Proceedings of the 42Nd ACM Technical Symposium on Computer Science Education (SIGCSE '11).* ACM, New York, NY, USA, 287–292. https://doi.org/10.1145/1953163.1953250

[10] Jason Nieh and Chris Vaill. 2006. Experiences Teaching Operating Systems Using Virtual Platforms and Linux. *SIGOPS Oper. Syst. Rev.* 40, 2 (April 2006), 100–104. https://doi.org/10.1145/1131322.1131323

[11] Linda Null and Karishma Rao. 2005. CAMERA: Introducing Memory Concepts via Visualization. *SIGCSE Bull.* 37, 1 (Feb. 2005), 96–100. https://doi.org/10.1145/1047124.1047389

[12] Ben Pfaff, Anthony Romano, and Godmar Back. 2009. The Pintos Instructional Operating System Kernel. In *Proceedings of the 40th ACM Technical Symposium on Computer Science Education (SIGCSE '09).* ACM, New York, NY, USA, 453–457. https://doi.org/10.1145/1508865.1509023

[13] Jaswinder P. Singh. [n. d.]. Project V: Virtual Memory. http://www.cs.princeton.edu/courses/archive/fall14/cos318/projects/project5/p5.html. ([n. d.]).

[14] Douglas Thain. [n. d.]. Project V: Virtual Memory. http://www3.nd.edu/~dthain/courses/cse30341/spring2009/project5/project5.html. ([n. d.]).

Implementing Malloc: Students and Systems Programming

Brian P. Railing
Carnegie Mellon University
Pittsburgh, PA
bpr@cs.cmu.edu

Randal E. Bryant
Carnegie Mellon University
Pittsburgh, PA
randy.bryant@cs.cmu.edu

ABSTRACT

This work describes our experience in revising one of the major programming assignments for the second-year course Introduction to Computer Systems, in which students implement a version of the malloc memory allocator. The revisions involved fully supporting a 64-bit address space, promoting a more modern programming style, and creating a set of benchmarks and grading standards that provide an appropriate level of challenge.

With this revised assignment, students were able to implement more sophisticated allocators than they had in the past, and they also achieved higher performance on the related questions on the final exam.

KEYWORDS

malloc, programming assignment, systems programming

ACM Reference Format:
Brian P. Railing and Randal E. Bryant. 2018. Implementing Malloc: Students and Systems Programming. In *SIGCSE '18: SIGCSE '18: The 49th ACM Technical Symposium on Computer Science Education, February 21–24, 2018, Baltimore , MD, USA.* ACM, New York, NY, USA, 6 pages. https: //doi.org/10.1145/3159450.3159597

1 INTRODUCTION

Teaching Introduction to Computer Systems, a course developed at Carnegie Mellon University [2] and widely adopted elsewhere, exposes students to the basics of how the architecture, compiler, and operating system work together to support program execution. The course makes use of seven programming assignments, termed labs, that explore different aspects of the computer system. The most challenging lab for the course, distributed as part of the support materials for the Bryant-O'Hallaron textbook [3], requires students to implement a memory allocator based on malloc. Anecdotal reports by students, the instructors of more advanced systems courses, and subsequent employers of the students indicate that this lab provides them an important experience in low-level program implementation, debugging, and tuning.

In reflecting on the existing version of the malloc lab, we noted that high scoring student submissions required identifying particular tricks and knowledge of the testing environment, all the while not exploring the interesting design decisions and implementation work that we would have expected. Furthermore, when faced with the daunting design space during their work, students would often resort to changing and tweaking what they had done so far in hopes of following some random walk to a sufficiently optimized solution that would pass the assignment performance standards.

As a further shortcoming, students were encouraged to follow a programming style with extensive use of macros performing low-level address arithmetic. Many students struggled working with this style of programming—the compiler did not generate meaningful error messages, symbolic debugging tools could only provide a view into the post macro-expanded code, and it was very easy to make mistakes in address computations. A small, but significant number of students failed to write allocators that could even pass all of the correctness tests. The ability of modern compilers to generate efficient code via inline substitution has made most macro-based programming obsolete.

Previously, students would base their malloc on the code in The C Programming Language [6] and Computer Systems: A Programmer's Perspective [3]. From our review of student submissions, we concluded that there were several shortcomings in the assignment and developed four areas for revision to the programming lab. Listed here, these revisions will be discussed in greater detail later in this work:

- *Fully support a 64-bit address space.* This required creating a testing environment that allocated blocks of over 2^{60} bytes, even though no existing system has access to that much memory.
- *Promote a more modern programming style.* Rather than writing macros that performed low-level address calculations, students were required to make best use of the abstractions provided by C, while still achieving high degrees of memory utilization.
- *Use a set of carefully selected benchmark traces.* These benchmarks should challenge students to develop well-engineered designs that achieve an appropriate balance between memory utilization and throughput.
- *Follow a revised time line and grading standards.* We divided the assignment into two phases to help students better manage their time.

The rest of the paper is organized as follows: Section 2 provides the context of the course, Section 3 covers the overview of the malloc assignment, Section 4 explores the changes we made, Section 5 presents our reflections on the results, and Section 6 concludes this paper. Although the focus of this paper is on a specific assignment for a specific purpose, we believe that many of the factors addressed are important considerations for any systems programming assignment and that the approaches we devised have broader applications.

SIGCSE '18, February 21–24, 2018, Baltimore , MD, USA

ACM ISBN 978-1-4503-5103-4/18/02...$15.00
https://doi.org/10.1145/3159450.3159597

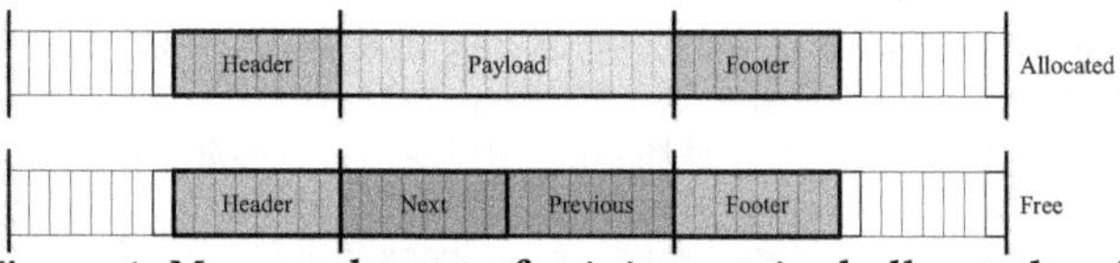

Figure 1: Memory layout of minimum-sized allocated and free blocks for an explicit-list allocator

2 COURSE BACKGROUND

This course is normally taken by Computer Science and Electrical and Computer Engineering majors in their second year, with a significant fraction of non-majors also enrolled, and about equal percentages of each of the three groups. All students are expected to have previous experience with C programming. The course is required for those majors, and the non-majors are usually taking the class to fulfill secondary major or minor requirements. This course also serves as the prerequisite for upper-level systems courses in computer science and engineering, including architecture, compilers, operating systems, and embedded systems. The malloc programming assignment is sixth, and most demanding, of seven assignments.

3 MALLOC PROGRAMMING LAB OVERVIEW

Students are required to implement the functions `malloc`, `realloc`, `calloc`, and `free`, following the API set in the C standard for each function. Their code is then linked into a driver that makes sequences of malloc and free calls. The driver populates allocated blocks with random data and verifies these bytes are preserved until freeing the block. Other correctness checks are also performed.

The lab exposes students to many aspects of systems programming including:

- Implementing library functionality given an API
- Exploring a design space with many choices in data structures and algorithms
- Understanding that heap memory is just an array of bytes that can be partitioned, reused, and redefined as a program executes
- Debugging and tuning code that relies on low-level data structure manipulation to meet targeted requirements
- Exploring possible trade offs between the conflicting goals of high memory utilization and high throughput

The following is a brief discussion of the implementation concerns present when working on this programming assignment. Wilson, et al. [10] has a detailed treatment of the design and evaluation of memory allocators.

Correct malloc implementations are measured with two performance metrics: throughput and utilization. Throughput is the number of operations completed in a measured amount of time. Utilization compares the heap space allocated to the program at the end of execution (the heap never shrinks) compared to the peak data requirement. The excess space required by the implementation is termed *fragmentation*, of which there are two types. Internal fragmentation occurs when the allocated block is larger than the payload, due to extra space required to manage the blocks and to satisfy alignment requirements. And as will be discussed later in Section 4.3, internal fragmentation is greater proportionately with

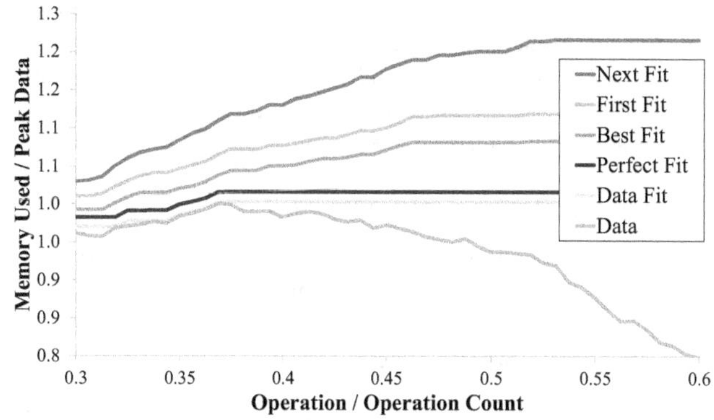

Figure 2: Memory usage for a synthetically generated trace for different free-block selection strategies. Usage is scaled relative to peak data requirement, and operations are scaled relative to the total number of operations

smaller requests. External fragmentation occurs when free blocks are available, but none are large enough to satisfy a request. Each fragmentation type is ameliorated by independent methods. Internal fragmentation is reduced by minimizing the overhead to track the allocated blocks, while external fragmentation is decreased by better selection of which free block to reuse. The fixed nature of pointers in C prevents any form of memory compaction, where allocated blocks are moved into a single region to reduce external fragmentation.

Student implementations start from code using an implicit free list, in which free blocks are located by traversing all allocated and unallocated blocks in memory order. Making the free list explicit with pointers between blocks significantly reduces the time to find whether a unallocated block can be reused. Both implicit and explicit list implementations use boundary tags for coalescing [7], with the layout for a minimum-sized block shown in Figure 1. Students can further improve the throughput of requests by segregating the explicit list based on sizes.

The free lists are searched on subsequent malloc requests to find if there are any blocks that satisfy the request. There are a variety of strategies, including: *next fit* that resumes searching where the previous search finished, *first fit* that selects the first block that could satisfy the request, and *best fit* that checks every block and selects the one closest to the requested size. Other design decisions can include whether to manage the free block list(s) by a FIFO, LIFO, address, or size ordering.

Figure 2 shows the memory usage for different free-block selection strategies focused on the peak, as the peak fragmentation characterizes the memory efficiency of the allocator. In addition to the block-selection strategies, this figure also includes two targets that serve as lower bounds for any allocator: *perfect fit* that assumes there is no external fragmentation, and *data fit* that assumes there is neither internal nor external fragmentation. In the figure, the fit curves continue to increase after the allocation peak, as the different strategies work to handle the churn of allocations and frees. Eventually, a sufficient percentage of memory is free that any new allocation in the trace can be satisfied and there is no further increase in memory usage.

One common optimization is to remove the footer from allocated blocks to allow larger payloads within a block. Other schemes can further improve utilization by special handling of smaller requests, or by reducing the headers for small blocks. Together, these optimizations are focused on reducing the internal fragmentation.

4 ASSIGNMENT REVISIONS

In the following section, we discuss our four revisions to the malloc implementation programming assignment.

4.1 64-bit Address Space

The previous version of the lab was derived from one based on a 32-bit address space. Students found they could exploit limitations of the testing framework. For example, they would deduce that no trace required more than 100MB of memory, and could therefore replace 64-bit pointers with 27-bit offsets and similarly for each block's size field. While these are valuable optimizations in a memory constrained environment, student submissions using this approach do not meet the programming lab objective of developing a general purpose memory allocator.

One possible solution would be to modify the traces to use larger request sizes; however, any such change would always have a known upper bound. Furthermore, students commonly run their code on shared servers, to which significant increases in memory demands could impact the shared platform. Indeed, there are no systems available that have access to the 1.8×10^{19} bytes that a true 64-bit machine could address.

We also felt it was important to provide a testing environment that would truly evaluate the ability of the student programs to handle a 64-bit address space, rather than relying on manual inspection by the students or the grading staff. There are many ways to inadvertently invoke 32-bit arithmetic in C, e.g., by using the expression `1 << n`, rather than `1L << n`, and so explicit testing is important.

To address both of these concerns, we developed an alternative testing infrastructure that would not be limited to the existing memory availability and could then permit testing of request sizes up to the maximum for the `size_t` parameter.

Using the LLVM compiler framework [8], a second, alternative binary `malloc-emulate` was built, where all of the memory operations (loads and stores) were modified to instead call an emulation library. This layer would either emulate the access if it was being made to the heap region or allow direct the access to system memory for other memory regions. The emulator exploits the fact that, even when a very large block is stored on the heap, the allocator need only access the bytes at the very beginning or the very end of the block (assuming no calls to `calloc` or `realloc`.) By emulating a very sparse address space, it can handle allocations of blocks containing 2^{60} or more bytes. With the emulated version, student code can then be tested to support full 64-bit pointers (going beyond current x86 support for 48-bits) and thereby determine if student code was robust against all access sizes or if it had been tuned to the smaller traces.

When running the emulated version, student code has roughly a 9× slowdown versus the native (non-emulated) implementation, and so throughput measurements are run on the native binary. It

```
/* Basic constants and macros */
#define WSIZE 8 /* Word and header/footer size (bytes) */
#define DSIZE 16 /* Double word size (bytes) */
/* Pack a size and allocated bit into a word */
#define PACK(size, alloc) ((size) | (alloc))
/* Read and write a word at address p */
#define GET(p) (*(unsigned long *)(p))
#define PUT(p, val) (*(unsigned long *)(p) = (val))
/* Read the size field from address p. */
#define GET_SIZE(p) (GET(p) & ~0x7L)
/* Given block ptr bp, compute address of
 * its header and footer */
#define HDRP(bp) ((char *)(bp) - WSIZE)
#define FTRP(bp) ((char *)(bp) + GET_SIZE(HDRP(bp))
                                        - DSIZE)
```

Figure 3: Old coding style based on macros (from textbook)

is possible for student code to detect whether it was being run with or without memory emulation, so the emulated tests are made using all of the native traces, and the memory utilization compared against the native execution. This prevents students from using the earlier optimizations during native runs and turning them off in emulation. In addition to rerunning the native traces, additional "giant" traces were prepared that require the emulation support to succeed.

Following the C standard [5], we use the implementation specified alignment for x86-64 [4] and require that student malloc implementations align the allocations to 16-byte boundaries.

4.2 Modern Programming Style

Traditionally, C programming required using macros for common, low-level operations to avoid function call overhead. Also, the emphasis on carefully packing data to minimize memory usage, and the natural reuse of memory blocks in malloc implementations resulted in a significant usage of unstructured pointer arithmetic. This coding style is illustrated in Figure 3, showing excerpts from the allocator code described in the textbook. Many students would struggle when extending this code to support the necessary complexity to pass the assignment.

Modern C standards and compilers provide far greater support for types and performance, such that many of the motivations for macro code are obviated. We rewrote the starter code emphasizing two things: first, insofar as possible, operations should be made using explicit and appropriate type information, and second, inline and optimization decisions should be left to the compiler. Figure 4 is taken from the revised starter code provided to all students. Each internal block in the malloc implementation is now an explicit type; however, the footer cannot be included given that its location is dependent on the size of the payload. By compiling with optimization enabled, the function-based code has the same performance as macro-based code, and it significantly eases their debugging efforts when the optimizations are disabled.

When students make the first change to an explicit free list, they use `union` and `struct` to describe the types and positions of the required pointers. This contrasts with the earlier code where these fields would be known just by their offsets from the header, and

```
/* Basic declarations */
typedef uint64_t word_t;
static const size_t wsize = sizeof(word_t);
typedef struct block {
  /* Header contains size + allocation flag */
  word_t header;
  /* Placeholder for payload */
  char payload[0];
} block_t;
/* Pack size and allocation bit into single word */
static word_t pack(size_t size, bool alloc) {
  return size | alloc;
}
/* Extract size from packed field */
static size_t extract_size(word_t word) {
  return (word & ~(word_t) 0x7);
}
/* Get block size */
static size_t get_size(block_t *block) {
  return extract_size(block->header);
}
/* Set fields in block header */
static void write_header(block_t *block, size_t size,
                         bool alloc) {
  block->header = pack(size, alloc);
}
/* Set fields in block header */
static void write_footer(block_t *block, size_t size,
                         bool alloc) {
  word_t *footerp = (word_t *)((block->payload)
    + get_size(block) - dsize);
  *footerp = pack(size, alloc);
}
/* Locate start of block, given pointer to payload */
static block_t *payload_to_header(void *bp) {
  return (block_t *)(((char *)bp) -
                     offsetof(block_t, payload));
}
```

Figure 4: New coding style based on constants and functions

thereby reduces the chance that the student mixes the meanings of the offsets.

Even in making these changes to the baseline code, we did not do away with all macros. For example, macros are still provided to support assertions, debugging prints, and definitions of constant parameters. All student submissions were screened by a program that detects the use of function-like macros (those having arguments.)

4.3 New Traces

The selection of appropriate traces for the assignment can make a significant difference in establishing appropriate design decisions in the lab. For example, larger request sizes minimize the impact of internal fragmentation on reported utilization but can cause greater external fragmentation. A good allocator must overcome three challenges in achieving high utilization and throughput: (1) it must minimize internal fragmentation by reducing the overhead of the data structures, especially in the fields of the allocated blocks; (2) it must minimize external fragmentation, in which free blocks accumulate due to a poor block placement strategy; and (3) it must maximize throughput by minimizing the time required by each operation. A good set of benchmarks must stress all three of these aspects. No single benchmark can cover all of them, but hopefully a collection of well-chosen and well-designed benchmarks will clearly demonstrate the relative merits of different implementations.

Category	$p:q$	Unit	Maximum
Struct	$70:30$	8	256
String	$60:40$	1	256
Array	$95:05$	4	$\min(2^{18}, 10^9/N)$
Giant array	$60:40$	4	$2^{60}/N$

Figure 5: Power-law parameters for synthetic traces, when generating trace with N allocation operations

We created a new set of benchmark traces that would stress the diversity of program allocation behaviors. We did not conduct a systematic study of real program behaviors, rather we selected several programs with diverse allocation behaviors and also constructed additional synthetic traces to test specific categories of commonly allocated data.

We started with a set of programs and used the compile-time interpositioning method described in [3] to extract the sequence of calls to `malloc` and `free`. We selected sets of input data to these programs to generate a total of 12 traces having between 2,874 and 63,956 allocation requests, with an average of 34,515. Among the largest traces, one requires that the allocator manage up to 44,465 blocks at its peak, while another requires a total of 31.3 MB of payload data at its peak.

In addition, we generated a set of synthetic data that attempted to capture heap-allocated data structures storing structs, strings, and arrays:

Structs: These are used to implement nodes in lists, trees, and graphs. On 64-bit machines, their sizes will typically be multiples of eight to satisfy the alignment of embedded pointers

Strings: These will have no particular pattern of uniformity or size.

Arrays: These will have widely varying sizes, but they will be multiples of 4 or 8.

The block sizes within each of these categories were generated according to a power-law distribution, having a probability density function of the form $p(s) \propto s^{-\alpha}$, for some $\alpha \leq 1$. A power-law distribution can be characterized by a ratio of the form $p : q$, where $0 < p < 100$ and $q = 100 - p$, indicating that percentage p of the generated samples should be less than percentage q of the maximum value. For example, the familiar $80 : 20$ rule states that 80% of the values are less than or equal to 20% of the maximum value. Each class is also characterized by a unit u, defining both the minimum value and a value for which all values must be multiples. Finally, each class has a maximum value M.

Figure 5 specifies the parameters for the different classes. Observe that both strings and structs have maximum sizes of 256 bytes, but strings have $u = 1$, while structs have $u = 8$. This difference has important implications for the internal fragmentation. Arrays have a maximum size of 262,144 (2^{18}) bytes, except when the trace has so many allocations N, that there is a risk that it will require a heap size of more than 100MB. In such cases, the maximum array length is set to $10^9/N$. Normal arrays have an extreme power-law distribution 95 : 5, giving it a very long-tailed distribution. Finally, a class of giant arrays can be generated for traces to test the ability of the allocator to handle 64-bit sizes and pointers. These could have sizes up to $2^{60}/N$ ($2^{60} \approx 1.15 \times 10^{18}$), and with a fairly uniform 60 : 40 distribution. It should be noted that, although these parameters seem reasonable, we made no attempt to systematically evaluate the sizes of heap allocation requests in actual programs.

We generated four benchmark traces, each containing 40,000 allocation requests, for the regular benchmarks: one for each of the three categories, and a fourth containing allocations chosen randomly from the classes struct, string, and array, with probabilities 35%, 30%, and 35%, respectively. We also created a set of five "giant" trace benchmarks, generated allocations that require almost the entire 64-bit address space. The largest allocated block in these has a payload of 8.4×10^{16} (over 2^{56}) bytes.

The difficulty posed by a benchmark trace comes not just from how blocks are allocated, but also how they are freed. For example, a trace that only allocates blocks and never frees them (or frees them at the very end) will have almost no external fragmentation and so the free lists will be very short. These require only reducing internal fragmentation to get good performance. Additionally, block coalescing implies that a trace that frees most of the blocks at some point will end up with a small number of large free blocks. Such a configuration will not pose much challenge for the subsequent utilization or throughput.

We devised a simple scheme for inserting free operations into a trace (both the ones extracted from actual programs, as well as the synthetic traces) that proved successful in stressing both the throughput and the ability to minimize external fragmentation. Consider a trace containing N allocations that are never freed. At each such allocation step i, we generate a *free target* $t = 2i/N$, indicating a target number of free operations to insert after the allocation step. For $t < 1$, we flip a weighted (by t) coin to determine whether or not to insert a free operation. For $t \geq 1$, we repeatedly insert free operations and decrement t until $t < 1$, and then finish with a weighted-coin flip. When inserting a free operation, one of the existing blocks is selected at random to be freed. With this strategy, the program begins by allocating blocks, but freeing them only sporadically. At a midpoint, it approaches an equilibrium, allocating and freeing blocks in roughly equal portions. Then it increases the rate of freeing so that the expected number of allocated blocks at the end should be nearly 0. We also free any allocated blocks at the end to complete the trace.

Figure 2 illustrates the performance of allocators following different block placement policies near the peak for one of the synthetic benchmarks. This is that point where external fragmentation is at its maximum, challenging both utilization and throughput.

We rejected constructing any adversarial traces that might unduly penalize specific design decisions, such as one that would force the allocator's search strategy to fully traverse a FIFO list. The only defense against such traces would be to implement an allocator with strong worst-case performance guarantees, e.g., using balanced tree data structure to implement the free list. Such a requirement was deemed beyond the scope of the course. We also worked to avoid any benchmark trace that would target particular implementation characteristics. Finally, in keeping with the previous lab assignment,

Semester	Version	Assignment Score	Exam Scores
Spring 2016	Old	78.0	78.0
Fall 2016	New	75.1	87.0
Spring 2017	New	75.3	89.0

Figure 6: Malloc Assignment and final exam question scores (both with maximum values of 100), for the old and new versions of the assignments

traces using `realloc` are tested only for correctness and not any performance metrics.

4.4 Grading Standards

Having established a set of benchmarks, existing norms for student submissions no longer apply. Instead we performed an extensive benchmarking process, implementing a number of allocators trying different strategies for reducing internal and external fragmentation. We measured how each performed in terms of throughput and utilization, and then selected cutoff points based on the features we considered achievable by all students versus those of increasing difficulty and complexity. Students implementing segregated free lists, removing footers, and an approximation of best fit would earn a B (around 85%) for the assignment. These features take students a self-reported average of 20–30 hours to complete, which fits with a multiweek assignment. Students completing those features faster generally use additional time to make further improvements to their submissions.

Furthermore, we found that splitting the assignment into two parts by introducing a checkpoint also aided student learning and experience. Given the sequence of features to implement, transitioning the baseline code from implicit free lists to explicit, segregated free lists roughly corresponded to half of student time, as they built up their understanding of the code and the approaches required to debug their implementation. This transition only significantly impacts the throughput of the implementation, which allows students to focus on optimizing for a single constraint. The second part of the assignment requires them to then improve utilization, mostly by reducing internal fragmentation.

5 REFLECTIONS

A major question in any update to course material is whether student learning is improved. As we wrote new traces and grading standards for the assignment, we cannot easily compare before and after the revision on the assignment itself. However, one set of questions on the final exam test students' knowledge of malloc. In Figure 6, we compared the before (Spring 2016) scores with those after revising the lab (Fall 2016 and Spring 2017), as well as including the programming assignment scores for comparison.[1] Using an independent samples t-test, we found no statistically significant difference in the assignment scores, yet a clear difference (p value less than 0.01) in the related exam scores before and after the lab revision. However, the score distribution on the assignment is such that only half of the students in each semester are earning a B.

This assignment gave us considerable exposure to students' efforts to debug their implementations. In particular, corruptions in the internal state of the implementation will not immediately crash

[1]Due to other course changes, we cannot make a broader comparison between semesters.

```
(*(void **)((*(void **)(bp)) + DSIZE)) =
                                (*(void **)(bp + DSIZE));
```

Figure 7: Untyped malloc implementation

```
bp->prev->next = bp->next;
```

Figure 8: Typed malloc implementation

the allocator, but rather instead fail at some later point. Some failures are crashes (segmentation faults or bus errors), but many others are observed as overlapping allocated blocks or corruption of an allocated block's payload. We emphasize the use of gdb, specifically using the two recitations during the assignment to work through debugging techniques using several simple implementations of malloc that have bugs commonly seen by students; however, as observed by others [1] [9], many students will use other debugging approaches. For example, we require students to write a function, the heap checker, that will check appropriate invariants of their implementations. And finally, many students debug their code by manually tracing the state or introducing print statements to observe the state.

Given the design space described in Section 3, this assignment is often one of students' first exposure to a problem with an open design space. Regularly, students attempt to glean specific insights from the instructional staff such as "How many segregated free lists should my implementation use?" or "Now that I have implemented X, what should I do next?". We emphasize the need to test and explore the options available in the potential design space, while providing a basic set of possible features. They both enjoy the ownership that comes from making these decisions, while also expressing frustration with the lack of specific guidance. The guidance is improving as teaching assistants come through the course with the new lab. And for those TAs with experience across both versions of the assignment, they report a greater satisfaction and ease of helping students from this revision.

From the grading and support side, it can be difficult to understand the meaning of purely pointer-based code. Figure 7 provides one extreme example of the minimal level of type information that student code may use. When students ask for assistance debugging similar code, our common response has been to recommend a type-based rewrite, resulting in code similar to Figure 8. And for many, this rewrite is sufficient to find the cause of the bug and fix the original issue.

However, this typed code is not without cost. Those students extending the baseline code with additional pointer casts can violate strict aliasing rules, such as by casting `block_t*` (see Figure 4) directly to `free_block_t*` (or other alternative structure). This cast can have undefined behavior in the C standard, whereas previously all pointers would be `char*` or `void*` and not have this behavior. Identifying undefined behavior that is causing failures is tricky and students can be particularly frustrated that introducing print statements to debug the failing behavior can disrupt the compiler's analysis and optimizations, such that this and other undefined behaviors are no longer failing. Finally, a small percentage of students state a preference for the traditional, macro-based code.

6 CONCLUSION AND FUTURE WORK

This paper has shown our revisions to a demanding systems programming assignment. These changes have helped refocus student effort on the learning objectives for the assignment. And our preliminary analysis of student scores shows a significant improvement, indicating that students are learning the material better than before.

There are several opportunities to continue the assignment rewrite. First, we can revisit the trace generation of Section 4.3 and compare it against a more systematic study of allocation patterns. Second, the throughput measurements can be sensitive to machine configuration and load, so we are investigating how to maintain the time component while minimizing the sources of variation. Finally, we are continuing to update our guidance to students on both how to improve their design and style, as well as exploring how to better prepare students for debugging complex and optimized code.

ACKNOWLEDGMENTS

Matthew Salim, an undergraduate student at CMU, participated in many parts of the lab development. The CMU Eberly Center for Teaching Excellence has provided helpful guidance in how best to assess the effectiveness of the assignment in enhancing student learning, as well as assisting with the collection and analysis of student scores. The National Science Foundation, under grant 1245735, has supported some of our efforts in course material development.

REFERENCES

[1] Basma S. Alqadi and Jonathan I. Maletic. 2017. An Empirical Study of Debugging Patterns Among Novices Programmers. In *Proceedings of the 2017 ACM SIGCSE Technical Symposium on Computer Science Education (SIGCSE '17)*. ACM, New York, NY, USA, 15–20. https://doi.org/10.1145/3017680.3017761

[2] Randal E. Bryant and David R. O'Hallaron. 2001. Introducing Computer Systems from a Programmer's Perspective. In *Proceedings of the Thirty-second SIGCSE Technical Symposium on Computer Science Education (SIGCSE '01)*. ACM, New York, NY, USA, 90–94. https://doi.org/10.1145/364447.364549

[3] Randal E. Bryant and David R. O'Hallaron. 2015. *Computer Systems: A Programmer's Perspective* (3rd ed.). Pearson.

[4] Intel Corporation, Santa Clara, CA 2017. *Intel 64 and IA-32 Architectures Software Developer Manuals.* Intel Corporation, Santa Clara, CA. http://www.intel.com/content/www/us/en/processors/architectures-software-developer-manuals.html.

[5] ISO/IEC 9899:2011 WG14 2011. *Programming Languages - C (C11).* ISO/IEC 9899:2011 WG14. http://www.open-std.org/jtc1/sc22/wg14/www/docs/n1570.pdf

[6] Brian W. Kernighan and Dennis M. Ritchie. 1988. *The C Programming Language.* Prentice Hall Press, Upper Saddle River, NJ, USA.

[7] Donald E Knuth. 1973. *Fundamental algorithms: the art of computer programming.*

[8] Chris Lattner and Vikram Adve. 2004. LLVM: A Compilation Framework for Lifelong Program Analysis & Transformation. In *Proceedings of the International Symposium on Code Generation and Optimization: Feedback-directed and Runtime Optimization (CGO '04)*. IEEE Computer Society, Washington, DC, USA, 75–88. http://dl.acm.org/citation.cfm?id=977395.977673

[9] Laurie Murphy, Gary Lewandowski, Renée McCauley, Beth Simon, Lynda Thomas, and Carol Zander. 2008. Debugging: The Good, the Bad, and the Quirky – a Qualitative Analysis of Novices' Strategies. In *Proceedings of the 39th SIGCSE Technical Symposium on Computer Science Education (SIGCSE '08)*. ACM, New York, NY, USA, 163–167. https://doi.org/10.1145/1352135.1352191

[10] Paul R. Wilson, Mark S. Johnstone, Michael Neely, and David Boles. 1995. Dynamic Storage Allocation: A Survey and Critical Review. In *Proceedings of the International Workshop on Memory Management (IWMM '95)*. Springer-Verlag, London, UK, UK, 1–116. http://dl.acm.org/citation.cfm?id=645647.664690

TMOSS: Using Intermediate Assignment Work to Understand Excessive Collaboration in Large Classes

Lisa Yan
Stanford University
yanlisa@stanford.edu

Nick McKeown
Stanford University
nickm@stanford.edu

Mehran Sahami
Stanford University
sahami@cs.stanford.edu

Chris Piech
Stanford University
piech@cs.stanford.edu

ABSTRACT

As computer science classes grow, instructor workload also increases: teachers must simultaneously teach material, provide assignment feedback, and monitor student progress. At scale, it is hard to know which students need extra help, and as a result some students can resort to excessive collaboration—using online resources or peer code—to complete their work. In this paper, we present TMOSS, a tool that analyzes the intermediate steps a student takes to complete a programming assignment. We find that for three separate course offerings, TMOSS is almost twice as effective as traditional software similarity detectors in identifying the number of students who exhibit excessive collaboration. We also find that such students spend significantly less time on their assignment, use fewer class tutoring resources, and perform worse on exams than their peers. Finally, we provide a theory of the parametric distribution of typical student assignment similarity, which allows for probabilistic interpretation.

CCS CONCEPTS

• **Social and professional topics → Computer science education; CS1; Student assessment**;

KEYWORDS

Programming courses; plagiarism detection; student performance; teaching at scale; undergraduate courses

ACM Reference Format:
Lisa Yan, Nick McKeown, Mehran Sahami, and Chris Piech. 2018. TMOSS: Using Intermediate Assignment Work to Understand Excessive Collaboration in Large Classes. In *Proceedings of The 49th ACM Technical Symposium on Computer Science Education, Baltimore, MD, USA, February 21–24, 2018 (SIGCSE '18)*, 6 pages.
https://doi.org/10.1145/3159450.3159490

1 INTRODUCTION

In the past decade, an increasing number of educators have begun digitizing and transforming the learning experience in order to meet the ever-rising demand for education. This phenomenon is especially apparent in CS education at the undergraduate level, where the nature of the learning material enables efficient use of computing resources. Not only can the content delivery be delivered via online lectures, but also an entire homework assignment can be delivered, submitted, and graded with the aid of autograders.

Due to the size of the CS 1 class at many universities today, it is intractable to monitor every student as they progress through an assignment, even with the use of undergraduate or graduate teaching assistants [5, 19]. Inevitably a large component of the course relies on students performance on assignments, which often must be completed outside of a closed lab setting. Instead of the teacher quickly identifying a student who is struggling, it is often the case that such a student must seek out instructor help through scheduled office hours. At best, teachers can look only at the final homework submission for each student and evaluate whether the student needs additional help based on their final product.

By asking students to take on the responsibility of seeking help, a pressing issue arises. Sometimes, the students who struggle the most will not access the provided learning environments and will instead find their own resources; seeking shortcuts to learning, they can occasionally resort to unpermitted outside resources. This is especially prevalent in large online courses [25].

Two questions arise from the current state of large CS 1 classes: Given that there is a risk of *excessive collaboration* on assignments, where students overly rely on outside resources like peer code or online solutions, how can we identify students who exhibit such behavior? Furthermore, how does excessive collaboration correlate with student assignment work patterns and overall course performance? If we can address these two questions, we can learn more about our students, detect students exhibiting excessive collaboration, and ensure a healthy learning environment.

In this paper we tackle both of these problems by introducing Temporal Measure of Software Similarity (TMOSS), based on the well-known Measure of Software Similarity (MOSS) system [20]. TMOSS is a tool that builds on traditional software *similarity score* measures like MOSS. Instead of looking only at a student's final submission, TMOSS computes similarity on intermediate assignment work. These summaries are then verified by a human to hypothesize which students may have exhibited excessive collaboration. Through this procedure, we demonstrate the effectiveness of the TMOSS algorithm and paint a picture of how excessive collaboration impacts student performance. We further provide a theoretical foundation for interpreting TMOSS and MOSS scores and show that the distribution of similarity scores that do not exhibit excessive collaboration can be modeled with a parametric Gumbel distribution. Such a distribution enables formal analysis and also indicates that the likelihood of false positives in our tool is very low.

Our paper proceeds as follows: After summarizing related work in Section 2, in Section 3 we describe our learning environment and

SIGCSE '18, February 21–24, 2018, Baltimore, MD, USA

ACM ISBN 978-1-4503-5103-4/18/02...$15.00
https://doi.org/10.1145/3159450.3159490

Table 1: Statistics per Breakout repository (1420 students).

	Mean	SE
Start day	-5.22	2.73
# Snapshots	253	199
Hours on task	9.77	4.93
TA hours	4.18	9.09

the process of collecting snapshots of student progress through a programming assignment. Section 4 introduces the TMOSS tool, which uses intermediate student work to compute high similarity scores; these are then used to hypothesize excessive collaboration. Section 5 gives a theoretical framework for the interpretation of similarity scores. Finally, in Section 6 we report our results using TMOSS for three course offerings, and we demonstrate that students that exhibit excessive collaboration and those that do not are meaningfully different in how they interact with the class material—including time on task, use of office hours, and exam performance.

2 RELATED WORK

Many software similarity systems have been developed over the past two decades to detect for software plagiarism [7, 18, 20, 23, 24]. Among these systems, MOSS [20] is commonly used in academic settings to detect student plagiarism in course assignments. People have used biometrics measures like keystroke logging to identify plagiarism [10], which is used in Coursera [11].

Online learning and teaching computer science courses at scale have also prompted new research on modeling and understanding student learning from programming assignment solutions. Spohrer et al. [22] observe and collect student progress based on observation of student programming bugs, whereas Piech et al. [16] use assignment progress repositories to analyze intermediate student work. Social science research in the past has attempted to explain motivations for student plagiarism, citing that plagiarism is most common when there are small penalties and high rewards [3, 13].

Recent work has combined these two areas of research and analyzed how excessive collaboration affects student performance. Pierce et al. [17] developed a tool that correlated plagiarism with negative performance over other assignments in the course, and there has also been anecdotal evidence that over-reliance on outside help can incite negative student experiences in a CS 1 course [15]. Schneider et al. [21] implemented a plagiarism detection tool that analyzes logs of student interaction with course software. To the best of our knowledge, our work is the first to use intermediate student work for identifying cases of excessive collaboration and the first to model the probability of false positives in similarity software detection.

3 DATA

In this study we focus on the first large programming assignment in an undergraduate level CS 1. Breakout, a classic Atari game [14], is a programming assignment used widely in many institutions like Stanford, Cornell, Johns Hopkins, and CodeHS [4, 6, 8, 19]. In the course studied, Breakout is the first large, intensive creative project assignment, and enthusiastic students often extend their work beyond the minimum requirements. At the same time, the assignment unfortunately also creates the first opportunity for excessive collaboration.

In the CS 1 course studied, students complete Java programming assignments individually using the Eclipse Integrated Development Environment (IDE). The IDE has been modified to automatically log snapshots of student code in a local git repository every time a student compiles their assignment project to check program output, which occurs whenever the student tries to run their program. This leads to a series of snapshots with temporal granularity on the order of minutes of programming time. Each snapshot in a student code repository can be indexed by a *snapshot index*, corresponding to a timestamped copy of student code at compile time. When students submit their final code, they also submit the code snapshot repository. A repository can therefore be analyzed for functional information on the student's code development path [16] or for temporal information to quantify student work habits.

We identify broad metrics of student work habits: number of hours worked and which day the student started coding. *Similarity scores*—statistics that will be used for measuring collaboration—are then calculated by analyzing the repository in depth (described more in Section 4). Due to the graphics-based, open-ended nature of the Breakout assignment, we unfortunately did not have unit tests or a functioning autograder and did not have metrics on functionality per snapshot.

We use the Breakout assignment submissions from the CS 1 offerings in Fall 2012 (416 students), Fall 2013 (476 students), and Fall 2014 (528 students). All students from this dataset were taught by the same instructor and had nine days to work on Breakout (with an extra two late days to submit with potential grade penalty). The Breakout assignment is held on week four of a 10-week course. While students work on the assignment individually until the deadline, they can also attend walk-in office hours held Sunday to Thursday evenings to clarify concepts or discuss debugging tips with undergraduate teaching assistants (TAs). In our analysis, we leverage attendance logs of these TA hours—students record their check-in time and their assignment or course issue, and TAs record the students' check-out time and issue resolution. Table 1 provides a summary of how these three sets of students worked through the Breakout assignment. On average, students started the assignment 5.22 (SE=2.73) days before the deadline and spent a mean of 9.77 (SE=4.93) hours on task. TA office hours attended were calculated over the entire course. Hours on task were determined by grouping snapshot times that were within half an hour of each other.

4 METHOD

In this section, we give an overview of the typical process of flagging final student submissions for excessive collaboration with other students or online solutions. We then present TMOSS, a tractable method for identifying excessive collaboration over intermediate versions of student code.

4.1 Traditional software similarity detection

Traditional software similarity detectors compute similarity scores over a student's submitted code; these tools compare the student code to peer submissions and online solutions on various metrics,

ALGORITHM 1: Computing top matches in TMOSS.

```
Input: N students (students)
       n online solutions (online)
Output: N top matches (top_matches). Each student has a
        tuple of (highest similarity score, match code).
top_matches = [];
for i in 1...N do
    compare_set =
        getFinalSubmissions(students - students[i]) + online;
    snapshots = getRepository(students[i]);
    student_matches = [];
    for j in 1...M do
        results = compute_similarity(
            snapshots[j], compare_set);
        student_matches.append(
            argmax_{k=1...N+n-1} results[k].getScore());
    end
    top_matches.append(
        argmax_{j=1...M} student_matches[j].getScore());
end
```

and flag student submissions that deviate from standard statistics [7, 17, 18, 20, 21, 23, 24]. Among these, Measure of Software Similarity (MOSS) is highly regarded as the standard for detecting software plagiarism in the classroom [1, 20]. The software acts as a filtering tool prior to human decision; submissions with high similarity scores are checked manually by course staff, who identify excessive collaboration as plagiarism on a case-by-case basis. These pairwise detectors all scale quadratically with the size of the class, as comparing N student submissions to N peers and $n < N$ known online solutions requires a runtime of $O(N^2)$.

Running these tools on student final submissions can only identify a subset of the students exhibiting excessive collaboration. For example, suppose a student pastes in an online solution momentarily to check the desired output, then removes the online solution and submits his or her own work. While this is a plagiarism case at many academic institutions, existing software similarity detectors cannot flag this student from his or her final submission work.

4.2 TMOSS: Temporal Measure of Software Similarity

TMOSS is a tool designed to extend traditional software similarity detectors by identifying excessive collaboration on any intermediate snapshot of a student's code repository, not just final code submission. While TMOSS (as the name implies) currently implements MOSS-based similarity scores [20], the tool can be easily adapted to different similarity detector backends.[1]

An outline of TMOSS's operation is shown in Algorithm 1. TMOSS produces N top matches—one per student—corresponding to the final peer or online code that returned the highest similarity score over all M snapshots per student repository. The set of peer submissions are from the same course quarter, whereas online

[1]TMOSS is available as an open-source project at https://github.com/yanlisa/tmoss.

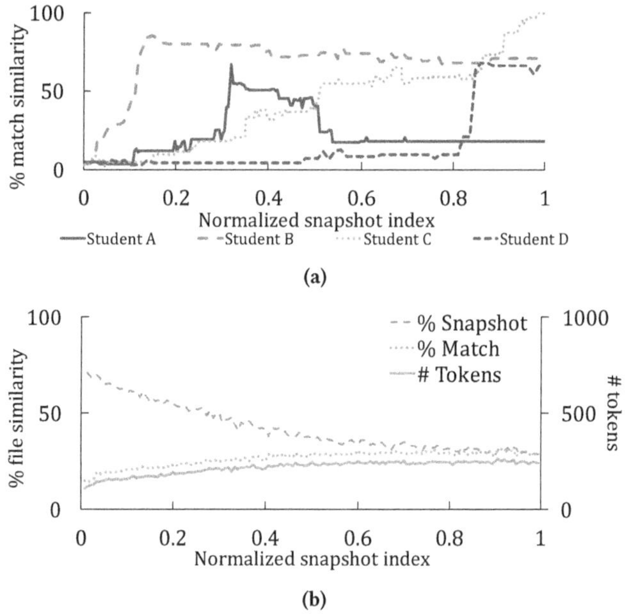

Figure 1: (a) Examples of students in the HEC group; (b) 95th percentiles of different MOSS similarity scores over time.

solutions are those that the teaching staff found via github or coding blogs. The `compute_similarity()` function is our traditional similarity detector backend, which computes similarity scores of a student snapshot to each of the final and online code files. Attempting to run existing pairwise similarity detection algorithms on all M snapshots for each of N students would require $O(N^2M^2)$ runtime, which is impractical. Instead, we avoid pairwise comparison by comparing a snapshot to N final peer submissions and $n < N$ online solutions, thus reducing the runtime per snapshot to $O(N)$ and the overall runtime to $O(N^2M)$. We note that comparing snapshots to final code is often preferable; similarity score algorithms that we surveyed scale much better with larger code files, and comparing two intermediate code files often produces a very low similarity score. Finally, we use human detection as the final step to determine which of these N top matches exhibits excessive collaboration. All students who fall into this category are put into the *hypothesized excessive collaboration* (HEC) group.

Figure 1a shows four students from our dataset who fall into the HEC group, using MOSS as the detector backend for TMOSS. The percent (%) similarity of a match's code to the intermediate code snapshot is plotted over time, here computed as the normalized snapshot index (from their first compiled code at 0.0 to their final submission at 1.0). While all of the students graphed exhibit excessive collaboration, Student A would go undetected by a typical run of MOSS on final submissions.

MOSS similarity scores. While any pairwise software similarity detector that fits the function signature of `compute_similarity()` can be used in TMOSS, we describe MOSS, which is used in our implementation [1, 20]. MOSS returns a triplet of similarity scores for each pair of (snapshot, match), where match refers to a final or online code file: (1) number of tokens—MOSS's internal, tokenized representation of code—shared between the two programs, (2) % snapshot similarity, and (3) % match similarity. The latter two scores are computed as the percentage of shared tokens in the tokenized MOSS representation of the student snapshot code (% snapshot similarity) and the matched peer or online code (% match similarity).

In our implementation of TMOSS, we only consider the first of these metrics—the number of shared tokens—to pick the top match for each student. We ignore the % snapshot similarity score since it varies inversely with the length of the student snapshot, and therefore it will be high when the student starts, and will decrease as the student progresses (Figure 1b). By contrast, the other two metrics do not exhibit this behavior. We further compare the effectiveness of number of tokens and % match similarity as similarity scores in Section 6.

5 THEORY

What is the chance that a student, who did not cheat, is reported as having plagiarized? In this section we provide a theoretical framework for calculating the probability of a false-positive maximum similarity score. The theory presented applies to all similarity measures for plagiarism detection, including MOSS and TMOSS.

Consider a student S who worked independently. When we compute a similarity score X_i between student S and another student i, there is an non-zero probability that the score will be accidentally large. While we suppose that this probability is exceedingly small, the likelihood of a false-positive report for student S increases when we compute a similarity score between them and *every other* student in the history of the course. The score Y that is analyzed for student S is the highest similarity score between the student and all other submissions: $Y = \max_i X_i$, for all other students i. The potential for a large max similarity score arising by chance—in the absence of collaboration—is concerning and worth exploring in detail.

We assume that the probability distribution of X_i is unknown, but that it is exponentially-tailed.[2] We also assume that, as the student did not collaborate with any of their peers, the values X_i should be mutually independent. Finally, it is reasonable to suppose that the X_i scores have the same (though unknown) distribution. The Fisher-Tippett-Gnedenko Theorem, a more obscure cousin of the Central Limit Theorem, tells us that the **max** of exponentially-tailed independent identically distributed (IID) variables can only converge to a *Gumbel* distribution [9]. Since we assumed that Y is the max of exponentially-tailed IID random variables, Y should have a Gumbel distribution; as such,

$$\Pr(Y \geq k) = 1 - e^{-e^{-(k-\mu)/\beta}} \tag{1}$$

holds for all values of k. The parameters of mode (μ) and scale (β) can be estimated using minimal datapoints via the method of probability weighted moments [12]. Once the parameters of Y are known we can answer questions of the form in Equation 1: What is the probability that a student S, who did not work with any other student, has a similarity score Y that is greater than some threshold k used to report plagiarism? The Fisher-Tippett-Gnedenko Theorem should apply for any plagiarism measure—not just MOSS and TMOSS, and not just for programming assignments.

[2] An exponential tail is a reasonable assumption for the token count similarity score X_i. Notably, this assumption has a light impact on the results: If X_i has a sub-exponential tail (for example % similarity has a fixed upper limit and thus has no tail), Y will have a Reverse Weibull Distribution, which along with the Gumbel is a special case of the Generalized Extreme Value Distribution.

Table 2: Results of TMOSS (per snapshot) and MOSS (per final submission) on set of 1420 students.

	MOSS	TMOSS
HEC students	35 (2.5%)	61 (4.3%)
Runtime	0.03 hr	9.77 hr

6 RESULTS

After using TMOSS with human verification, we found 61 students (4.1% of the dataset) in the HEC student group. By contrast, we found only 35 students (2.5% of the dataset) using the traditional MOSS approach with human verification (Table 2). We run both experiments per-quarter by comparing only against peer submissions in the same course offering (in addition to the same set of online solutions across quarters).

We compare the distribution of final submission similarity scores in regular MOSS (Figure 2a) with that of the maximum similarity score over all snapshots in TMOSS (Figure 2b). In both cases, the distribution of similarity scores for the non-HEC student group (1359 students) fit a Gumbel distribution; (TMOSS: $\mu = 153.4, \beta = 37.8$; MOSS: $\mu = 118.8, \beta = 39.2$). However, the distribution of TMOSS scores for the HEC group is easily differentiable from the non-HEC group, where as the MOSS scores for the HEC group are less differentiable, further suggesting that TMOSS is a better metric for detecting students in the HEC group.

We also compare the effectiveness of two different MOSS similarity scores. From Section 3, the number of shared MOSS tokens and % match similarity can both be considered valid scoring backends as they are less dependent on snapshot length. For each similarity score, we filter the TMOSS top matches through various score thresholds k, and we compute the F1 score (a harmonic mean of precision and recall) for each resultant candidate HEC group. We find that the optimal threshold for number of tokens (k = 367 tokens) produces an F1 score of F1 = 0.97, compared to the optimal threshold for % match similarity (k = 46%) at F1=0.58. Moreover, number of tokens performs better as a similarity score at all thresholds.

6.1 Performance analysis

We next consider how excessive collaboration is correlated with assignment work patterns and overall course performance. Table 3 compares various groups of students characterized by their HEC traits. A quick glance at Table 3 shows almost immediately that students in the HEC group compared to those in the non-HEC group tend to start significantly later (an mean of 3.31 days before the deadline, $\delta = 2.0$ days later), have significantly lower midterm and final scores ($\delta = 0.328$, $\delta = 0.351$, respectively), spend 27% less time on task, and often attend fewer TA office hours (51% less over the entire course).

It is important to note that factors other than HEC group membership did not correlate as significantly with student exam performance. A natural one to consider is start date on the Breakout assignment. Figure 2c shows that for non-HEC students, a later

Table 3: Work patterns comparison of different student groups: (a) midterm and (b) final scores; (c) start day as number of days prior to deadline that a student started the assignment; (d) hours on task as computed in Section 3; (e) TA hours attended over the entire course.

	Non-HEC	HEC		Online-Match	Peer-Match		MOSS	TMOSS-only	
# Students	1359	61		55	6		35	26	
	μ (SE)	μ (SE)	$p^\ddagger$	μ (SE)	μ (SE)	$p^\ddagger$	μ (SE)	μ (SE)	$p^\ddagger$
(a) Midterm†	.519 (.282)	.191 (.207)	**<.0001**	.192 (.208)	.183 (.202)	.50	.158 (.161)	.235 (.250)	.08
(b) Final†	.518 (.282)	.167 (.189)	**<.0001**	.169 (.193)	.156 (.148)	.49	.114 (.106)	.246 (.247)	**<.01**
(c) Start day	-5.31 (2.69)	-3.31 (2.92)	**<.0001**	-3.13 (2.95)	-5.00 (1.83)	.07	-2.97 (2.85)	-3.77 (2.94)	.14
(d) Hours on task	9.88 (4.92)	7.23 (4.34)	**<.0001**	6.98 (4.18)	9.54 (5.04)	.09	5.98 (3.65)	8.91 (4.61)	**<.01**
(e) TA hours	4.27 (9.24)	2.10 (4.04)	.02	2.03 (4.18)	2.67 (2.38)	.25	2.38 (4.61)	1.71 (3.08)	.25

† Exam scores are exam ranking per quarter. Students who dropped the class mid-quarter were removed in each group when computing exam statistics.
‡ p-values are computed by bootstrapping for 100,000 iterations on a one-tailed hypothesis test.

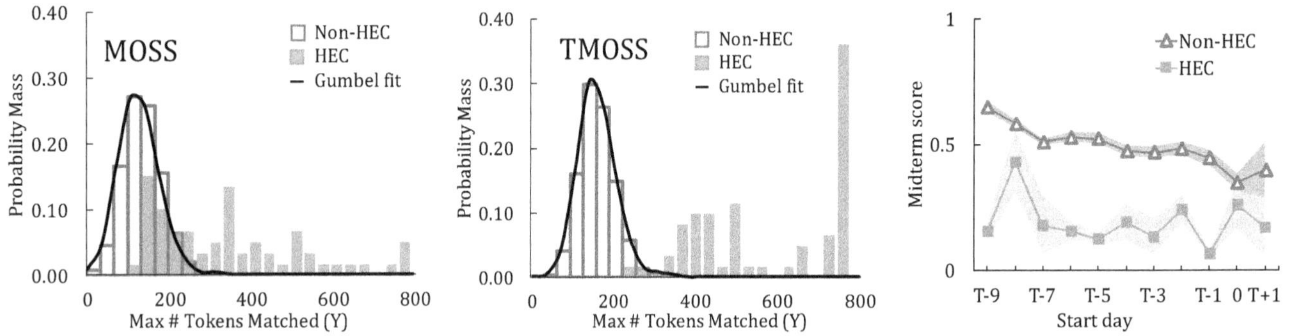

(a) (b) (c)

Figure 2: Distribution of HEC vs Non-HEC scores by (a) MOSS and by (b) TMOSS; (c) Average exam rank with bootstrapped SE.

start on the assignment is correlated with lower performance on the midterm. However, the HEC group performs consistently lower than the non-HEC group regardless of how early or late they start the assignment. The distribution for the final exam scores were consistent with this finding; for clarity they are not shown.

Digging further into the HEC group, we compare students who exhibited excessive similarity with an online solution with those who had high scores with peer final submissions as follows: we construct an undirected connectivity graph of all the top matches of all students, with $N + n$ nodes for all students and all known online submissions, and edges connect student nodes to their top match nodes. We define an *online match* student as one whose top match is connected to an online solution in our graph; all other students are defined as *peer matches.* We find that out of the 61 students in the HEC group, only 6 students were in our peer-match group. We see that students in the online-match HEC group tend to start slightly later than those in the peer-match HEC group; however, the p-values are limited by the small sample size and we are unable to draw any real conclusions.

Finally, we consider the 26 students that were only detectable via TMOSS; these students had high similarity scores over the course of their assignment, but did not exhibit excessive collaboration in their final submission. Again looking at Table 3, we find that the student who were detectable only through TMOSS tend to perform slightly better and work slightly more than those detectable through regular MOSS, but these differences were not as significant.

7 DISCUSSION

Our results show that TMOSS, a temporal analysis of student progress to detect excessive collaboration, is both feasible and more accurate than the final-submission-based detection algorithms used today. Temporal tools are not only effective for detecting unusual patterns of students, but they can also be used to further understand work patterns as correlated with class performance in an effort to provide improved feedback.

We also found that the Gumbel distribution provides us a probabilistic interpretation for scores; this interpretation can be used in a more formal model for separating HEC from non-HEC for a future tool. It also helps absolve students' concerns of a false positive; the likelihood of getting more than 376 tokens (the similarity score threshold determined in our F1 thresholding analysis) is $\Pr(Y \geq 376) < 0.003$. We therefore believe that the likelihood of having a false positive in our results is incredibly low.

We have shown that the students who have a high match with online solutions comprise a large portion of the HEC group, and students who excessively collaborate with peers within their quarter are very low. Work remains to gauge how the HEC group would change when the analysis is expanded to compare against submissions from previous quarters. Moreover, we have yet to understand how the use of TMOSS changes student behavioral patterns. We hope that the use of similarity scores on intermediate work acts as a deterrent and helps engender an academically honest ecosystem. It would even be possible to modify our Eclipse IDE to upload intermediate work periodically, prior to final submission; this would allow us to run TMOSS over the course of the assignment and provide timely interventions for students that help them get back on track.

Finally, we emphasize that TMOSS is not a substitute for human verification; it only helps to provide a more accurate picture of the student landscape. Nor is it intended to impose a negative, pressuring environment on students; instead, we hope that TMOSS is an example of how intermediate student work can be incorporated into the overall feedback system. For instance, TMOSS can be repurposed to evaluate intermediate work on a set of unit tests; an understanding of how a solution functionally evolves over time can guide instructors in giving improved, personalized feedback for each student. We hope that improvements to tools like TMOSS will simultaneously deter plagiarism efforts and facilitate the learning process in future classrooms.

8 CONCLUSION

We have shown that TMOSS can be used to identify students who exhibit excessive collaboration with online or peer solutions and to understand student work patterns over the course of an assignment. The use of MOSS is not critical; any software similarity detector with numerical similarity scores can be used as a backend to TMOSS. TMOSS can thus also be extended to non-programming scenarios; for example, TurnItIn similarity scores [2] can be used instead to check for collaboration in essay grading.

We found that students exhibiting excessive collaboration perform worse on exams and make more limited use of TA office hours. In addition, we have found that a Gumbel distribution fits the distribution of similarity scores in the absence of any excessive collaboration.

TMOSS is just one step in the direction of designing software to better understand students in large classrooms. Such a tool separates typical students from atypical students, and can even be used to indicate at what time a student was experiencing issues. While the use of TMOSS in this work is to detect excessive collaboration, its analysis of intermediate student work can be extended to provide more timely, more accurate feedback. We can therefore identify struggling students in a large classroom, instead of waiting for them to come to us. By reaching out to these students early on, we can give them the right resources to achieve success.

ACKNOWLEDGMENTS

This material is based upon work supported by the National Science Foundation Graduate Research Fellowship under Grant No. DGE-114747.

REFERENCES

[1] A. Aiken. 2014. A System for Detecting Software Plagiarism. Online. (2014). Retrieved October 25, 2016 from https://theory.stanford.edu/~aiken/moss/.
[2] T. Batane. 2010. Turning to Turnitin to Fight Plagiarism among University Students. *Educational Technology & Society* 13, 2 (2010), 1–12.
[3] R. Caldarola and T. MacNeil. 2009. Dishonesty deterrence and detection: How technology can ensure distance learning test security and validity. In *Proceedings of the 8th European Conference on E-Learning*. 108–115.
[4] CodeHS. 2016. Project: Breakout. Online. (2016). Retrieved October 25, 2016 from https://codehs.com/library/course/1/module/469.
[5] J. Forbes, D. J. Malan, H. Pon-Barry, S. Reges, and M. Sahami. 2017. Scaling Introductory Courses Using Undergraduate Teaching Assistants. In *Proceedings of the 2017 ACM SIGCSE Technical Symposium on Computer Science Education (SIGCSE '17)*. ACM, New York, NY, USA, 657–658. https://doi.org/10.1145/3017680.3017694
[6] P. H. Fröhlich. 2016. Department of Computer Science at The Johns Hopkins University: 600.111: Python Scripting. Online. (2016). Retrieved October 25, 2016 from http://gaming.jhu.edu/~phf/2011/fall/cs111/assignment-breakout.shtml.
[7] D. Gitchell and N. Tran. 1999. Sim: A Utility for Detecting Similarity in Computer Programs. In *The Proceedings of the Thirtieth SIGCSE Technical Symposium on Computer Science Education (SIGCSE '99)*. ACM, New York, NY, USA, 266–270. https://doi.org/10.1145/299649.299783
[8] D. Gries, L. Lee, S. Marschner, and W. White. 2016. CS 1110: Introduction to Computing Using Python Fall 2016. Online. (2016). Retrieved October 25, 2016 from http://www.cs.cornell.edu/courses/cs1110/2016fa/.
[9] E. J. Gumbel. 1935. Les valeurs extrêmes des distributions statistiques. *Ann. Inst. Henri Poincaré* 5, 2 (1935), 115–158.
[10] E. Lau, X. Liu, C. Xiao, and X. Yu. 2004. Enhanced user authentication through keystroke biometrics. *Computer and Network Security* 6 (2004).
[11] A. Maas, C. Heather, C. T. Do, R. Brandman, D. Koller, and A. Ng. 2014. Offering Verified Credentials in Massive Open Online Courses: MOOCs and technology to advance learning and learning research (Ubiquity symposium). *Ubiquity* 2014, May (2014), 2.
[12] S. Mahdi and M. Cenac. 2005. Estimating Parameters of Gumbel Distribution using the Methods of Moments, probability weighted Moments and maximum likelihood. *Revista de Matemática: Teoría y Aplicaciones* 12, 1-2 (2005).
[13] D. L. McCabe. 2005. Cheating among college and university students: A North American perspective. *Intl. Journal for Educational Integrity* 1, 1 (2005), 10–11.
[14] N. Parlante, S. A. Wolfman, L. I. McCann, E. Roberts, C. Nevison, J. Motil, J. Cain, and S. Reges. 2006. Nifty Assignments. In *Proceedings of the 37th SIGCSE Technical Symposium on Computer Science Education (SIGCSE '06)*. ACM, New York, NY, USA, 562–563. https://doi.org/10.1145/1121341.1121516
[15] A. Petersen, M. Craig, J. Campbell, and A. Tafliovich. 2016. Revisiting Why Students Drop CS1. In *Proceedings of the 16th Koli Calling International Conference on Computing Education Research (Koli Calling '16)*. ACM, New York, NY, USA, 71–80. https://doi.org/10.1145/2999541.2999552
[16] C. Piech, M. Sahami, D. Koller, S. Cooper, and P. Blikstein. 2012. Modeling How Students Learn to Program. In *Proceedings of the 43rd ACM Technical Symposium on Computer Science Education (SIGCSE '12)*. ACM, New York, NY, USA, 153–160. https://doi.org/10.1145/2157136.2157182
[17] J. Pierce and C. Zilles. 2017. Investigating Student Plagiarism Patterns and Correlations to Grades. In *Proceedings of the 2017 ACM SIGCSE Technical Symposium on Computer Science Education (SIGCSE '17)*. ACM, New York, NY, USA, 471–476. https://doi.org/10.1145/3017680.3017797
[18] L. Prechelt, G. Malpohl, and M. Phlippsen. 2000. *JPlag: Finding plagiarisms among a set of programs.* Technical Report. Universitat Karlsruhe.
[19] E. Roberts, J. Lilly, and B. Rollins. 1995. Using Undergraduates As Teaching Assistants in Introductory Programming Courses: An Update on the Stanford Experience. In *Proceedings of the Twenty-sixth SIGCSE Technical Symposium on Computer Science Education (SIGCSE '95)*. ACM, New York, NY, USA, 48–52. https://doi.org/10.1145/199688.199716
[20] S. Schleimer, D. S. Wilkerson, and A. Aiken. 2003. Winnowing: Local Algorithms for Document Fingerprinting. In *Proceedings of the 2003 ACM SIGMOD International Conference on Management of Data (SIGMOD '03)*. ACM, New York, NY, USA, 76–85. https://doi.org/10.1145/872757.872770
[21] J. Schneider, A. Bernstein, J. vom Brocke, K. Damevski, and D. C. Shepherd. 2016. Detecting Plagiarism based on the Creation Process. *CoRR* abs/1612.09183 (2016). http://arxiv.org/abs/1612.09183
[22] J. G. Spohrer and E. Soloway. 1986. Analyzing the high frequency bugs in novice programs. In *Papers presented at the first workshop on empirical studies of programmers on Empirical studies of programmers.* Ablex Publishing Corp., Norwood, NJ, USA, 230–251. http://portal.acm.org/citation.cfm?id=28897
[23] G. Whale. 1988. Plague: Plagiarism Detection Using Program Structure. In *Tech. Rep. 8805.*
[24] M. J. Wise. 1996. YAP3: Improved Detection Of Similarities In Computer Program And Other Texts. In *SIGCSEB: SIGCSE Bulletin (ACM Special Interest Group on Computer Science Education)*. ACM Press, 130–134.
[25] J. Young. 2012. Dozens of plagiarism incidents are reported in Coursera's free online courses. *The Chronicle of Higher Education* (Aug 2012). http://www.chronicle.com/article/Dozens-of-Plagiarism-Incidents/133697

Social Help-seeking Strategies in a Programming MOOC

Matti Nelimarkka
Aalto University and University of Helsinki
Espoo and Helsinki, Finland
matti.nelimarkka@aalto.fi

Arto Hellas
University of Helsinki
Helsinki, Finland
arto.hellas@helsinki.fi

ABSTRACT

Being able to seek help is a crucial part of any learning process. This includes both collaborative models such as asking for help from others as well as independent models such as using course materials and the vast resources provided by the Web. Currently, MOOC research has addressed social help-seeking within the MOOC course, either using MOOC platform tools (forum, chat) or arranging activities using external platforms (Google Hangout, Facebook groups). However, MOOC learning activities take place in a larger *social ecology*, including friends and teachers, general online communities and alumni communities. Using survey data from a programming MOOC, we show a typology of social learning strategies: non-use of social help-seeking, seeking help from friends and seeking help from alumni and teacher communities. We further show that students using social help-seeking strategies orient themselves more with a surface approach but are also less likely to drop the course. We conclude this work by addressing the various design possibilities identified by this work.

CCS CONCEPTS

• **Applied computing → Education; Collaborative learning; Distance learning; E-learning;**

ACM Reference Format:
Matti Nelimarkka and Arto Hellas. 2018. Social Help-seeking Strategies in a Programming MOOC. In *Proceedings of The 49th ACM Technical Symposium on Computer Science Education, Baltimore, MD, USA, Feb. 21–24, 2018 (SIGCSE '18)*, 6 pages.
https://doi.org/10.1145/3159450.3159495

1 INTRODUCTION

Research into help-seeking in massive open online courses (MOOCs) has mainly focused on quantifying and assisting the help-seeking process. Researchers have, for example, studied students' forum usage [12, 16], ways to deliver information more efficiently [14, 18] and harnessed participants as peer tutors [5, 12, 20, 27]. Most of the work is focused on activities organized within MOOCs and the platform that is used to facilitate the courses.

In this work, we study help-seeking outside the MOOC course and the platform, focusing on social sources of help-seeking such as friends and teachers. Our study is motivated by the recent acknowledgment that much of MOOC activities take place outside the course [31]. For example, students may create online support communities for different language variants on social networking sites [29], and previous participants of a MOOC may independently volunteer to support participants in new course instances [25].

In a broader sense, our work is based on the constructivist paradigm of learning, which suggests that people actively construct knowledge rather than receive and store it [7, 13]. Instead of focusing on MOOC platforms that are used to deliver content and problems, we focus on the larger *social ecology* that the students are a part of an in which they construct their knowledge. The ideas of social constructivism – that is, knowledge "emerges" from social interaction [21, 28] – were dominantly present in early connectivist MOOCs. The recent developments in MOOC research have brought these ideas also into the MOOCs that are primarily extensions of existing university courses.

More specifically, in this work, we study help-seeking strategies in a programming MOOC. We focus on who the participants seek help from, and what factors contribute to the use of specific help-seeking strategies. In addition, we study whether students' course performance can be explained by the help-seeking strategies. Our research questions in this study are as follows:

RQ1 From whom do MOOC participants seek help and how could the behavior be classified into help-seeking strategies?
RQ2 What learning approaches explain the use of particular help-seeking strategies?
RQ3 Do the help-seeking strategies and learning approaches indicate success?

These questions extend the research focused on interaction emerging on MOOC organizers forums and platforms, which have shown peer interaction improves learning outcomes [4, 5]. However, the questions are not specific to a platform, but rather acknowledge that social interaction takes place outside the MOOC platform as well. At the same time, we highlight the importance of the larger *social capital* in MOOC courses as one factor to consider when compared to traditional course instances.

This article is organized as follows. Next, we summarize the related work on social interaction in MOOCs, discuss the pedagogical background for social learning, and outline the RASI questionnaire that is used to study students' learning strategies. We then present the methodology and the context from which the data was collected from. Then we present the results; first by presenting a typology for students' social help-seeking and then by further examining differences observed in this typology. This is followed by a discussion on our insights for MOOC development and limitations of the study. Finally, conclusions and directions for future work are presented.

SIGCSE '18, Feb. 21–24, 2018, Baltimore, MD, USA

ACM ISBN 978-1-4503-5103-4/18/02...$15.00
https://doi.org/10.1145/3159450.3159495

2 BACKGROUND

2.1 Social interaction and MOOCs

MOOCs typically offer a forum for social interaction. Data from these forums have been in the foci of MOOC research on help-seeking and social interaction. A common observation of these studies has been a skewed participation; some of the participants are super-active while the majority is less engaged [12, 16]. Participation can be altered through changing the forum interface and mechanics; one can, for example, use a reputation system [4]. Similarly, researchers have suggested approaches for structuring the discussions differently, for example by using computer-mediated small group discussions in a free-form [3, 20] or in a goal-oriented manner [5, 22].

Students' learning can increase when such social interventions are used [5, 20], and furthermore, social learning tools can improve the MOOC experience [5, 27]. This said, a common challenge with creating social learning activities is their orchestration [5, 20]: the participants are not present all the time, and developing the critical mass needed to ensure the functionality of social interactions can be challenging.

One recently proposed approach is to not only focus on the participants of the current MOOC, but also on all the previous participants [25]. It is possible to create a community of current and alumni members, where the alumni help those currently enrolled. This highlights an important aspect of the social interaction for MOOCs: the target of help-seeking can be outside of the current class. At the same time, the communication mechanisms that are used in the course should integrate with existing communication practices of the alumni for them to continue participation [25].

Furthermore, others have observed social interaction outside a single course environment is valuable for MOOC students. Kasunic et al. [17] discussed how student-led Facebook groups emerged to support the official, platform provided, course forums. Such groups can also support student retention, as they provide an avenue for social engagement and a "real" community. To illustrate, Zheng et al. [29] have found indications that Facebook groups for a course can be more active than the official forums of the course. This novel strand of research shows that social interaction takes place outside a single course iteration [25] and outside the MOOC provided platforms of interaction [17, 29].

2.2 Social knowledge construction

The trend of emphasizing social aspects of learning are visible throughout the history of learning. Therefore, we briefly review the importance learning scholarship has put on the social knowledge construction in a learning activity.

Dewey once wrote that learning is a necessary incident of dealing with real life situations [6]. As – from the perspective of constructivists – knowledge is constructed through interactions with the environment instead of it being simply received and stored [7, 13], utilizing the existing set of tools and social connections for communication and help-seeking is meaningful.

Vygotsky argued that the internal development processes [of a child] operate only when interacting and co-operating with the environment [26]. In the same way, situated cognition theory suggests that individuals learn through shared activities and language that they engage in [2]; knowledge is constructed within and linked to the activity, context, and culture in which it is learned and used. If the activities are constrained to a specific environment, "*students may come to rely, in important but little noticed ways, on features of the classroom context, in which the task is now embedded, that are wholly absent from and alien to authentic activity*" [2].

Lave and Wenger [21, 28] claim that learning to seek for and to ask for help is a part of the learning process. The learner slowly becomes familiar with the community and its practices. This integration can happen through acknowledging newcomers into the community as *legitimate peripheral participants*, where legitimacy means that the newcomers are recognized by members of the community, and peripherality that the newcomers are not expected to fully contribute to the activities of the community – in online courses, this participation can be initiated through forums or other social channels.

2.3 Approaches to Studying

The students' role as an active participant in the learning process has increased in the in higher education. Due to this, the question both in teaching and learning sciences has focused more on what the students do [1].

To understand students' activities, we explore their study strategies [8–10, 15, 23]. The Approaches to Studying Inventory is a survey that measures three distinct strategies that students apply in their studies [8, 10]:

(1) Students with a deep approach focus on comprehension. Their learning focuses on understanding the topic in fully and internalizing at full.
(2) Students with a surface approach focus on gaining a procedural understanding of the material. Here the learning is seen as a tool for an objective and is focused on the teacher set goals (syllabus) and apply memorization.
(3) Students with a strategic approach aim too high achievement in the learning. Students with this approach aim to organize their studies as efficiently as possible and are motivated by grades.

Overall, studies indicate that students with a deep approach tend to achieve higher learning gains and therefore, the goal in higher education is in part to foster the development of deep approaches for teaching [1]. However, the universities have been recently challenged as students with other approaches to studying participate in the classes, as these approaches may require different ways of teaching students [1]. Catering the versatile student body is a problem in traditional in-class education and has been hardly touched in MOOC environments.

3 DATA AND METHODOLOGY

The data for our study comes from a Finnish 14-week introductory programming MOOC that was organized during Spring 2015. The course material is offered as a blended textbook consisting of theory texts, short quizzes, video tutorials and programming assignments, and the content of the course aligns with typical introductory programming courses for computer science majors.

The course offers an embedded social support channel that is facilitated through an Internet Relay Chat (IRC), which is accessible

	(-1)	1	2	3	4	5
Friends (f2f)	75.3	3.5	9.4	5.9	2.0	3.9
Friends (cmc)	80.3	3.9	6.7	5.9	1.6	1.6
Teacher (f2f)	95.7	3.5	0.4	0.4	0	0
Teacher (cmc)	94.9	3.5	1.6	0	0	0
Unknown (cmc)	93.3	3.9	1.2	0.8	0.4	0.4
MOOC IRC	62.0	4.7	12.9	12.2	3.9	4.3

Table 1: Students response distributions (%) on how beneficial particular social sources were for help. Key: (-1) indicates did not use the source, (1) not at all beneficial, and (5) extremely beneficial.

both directly through the course main page and the learning material, as well as through students' own chat applications. Students are also given guidelines on how to access the chat room using their own tools. The channel has previously been studied by Nelimarkka et al. [25], who observed that participants from past courses stay in the channel and volunteer to help newcomers.

To answer the Research Question 1, *From whom do MOOC participants seek help and how could the behavior be classified into help-seeking strategies?* we surveyed the MOOC participants, asking them to grade on a scale from 1 to 5 how relevant different key social sources have been to problems and challenges related to the course. Key social sources included friends, teachers, the MOOC community and strangers on the Internet. We also provided an opportunity to input free-form text to outline additional sources for help. To extend the analysis, and to determine whether there are sub-populations that have different help-seeking strategies, we conducted a k-means clustering on these social sources and self-reported utility of different channels.

To answer the Research Question 2, *What learning approaches explain the use of particular help-seeking strategies?*, we asked the course participants to answer a basic demographic survey and a 30 item questionnaire based on the Revised Approaches to Studying Inventory (RASI) questionnaire [11]. Using the Kruskal-Wallis χ^2-test, we compare the studying approaches from the RASI questionnaire with the sub-populations that have different help-seeking strategies, which were identified as a part of the RQ1.

Finally, to answer the Research Question 3, *Do the help-seeking strategies and learning approaches indicate success?*, we apply a quantitative approach, where we examine the course trajectory of the students in the different sub-populations.

4 RESULTS

The surveys were sent to students who had completed at least one week in the course (n = 982). The survey contained the aforementioned questions on key sources for help, demographic background, and the RASI questionnaire. A total of 263 answers were received, yielding a response rate of 27%, which can be considered acceptable for this study [12, 19]. However, for each question, some responses were discarded due to missing values, and the final analysis was conducted on a subset of 255 users, corresponding to 26% of the whole population and 97% of survey responders.

4.1 Summarizing help-seeking

We asked students to assess how much they benefited from six social sources as they were working on the MOOC assignments: (1) friends through face-to-face (f2f) contact, (2) friends through computer-mediated contact, (3) teachers through face-to-face contact, (4) teachers through computer-mediated contact (CMC), (5) unknown users through the Web and (6) the MOOC supported IRC channel.

	A	B	C	D	E
Friends (f2f)	0.10	−0.77	3.70	0.19	−1.00
Friends (cmc)	2.10	−1.00	1.43	−0.65	−1.00
Teacher (f2f)	−0.40	−0.97	−0.90	−1.00	−1.00
Teacher (cmc)	−0.40	−0.95	−0.90	−1.00	−0.93
From unknown (cmc)	−0.17	−0.95	−0.57	−1.00	−0.90
MOOC IRC	0.83	−1.00	0.20	4.19	2.34
n	30	128	30	26	41
%	11.8	50.2	11.8	10.2	16.0

Table 2: Students clustered based on their help-seeking strategies. The columns indicate the clusters and cell values indicate the mean value of the perceived benefit of each of help sources (rows). The key for the clusters is: (A) CMC Friend, (B) None, (C) Friend, (D) Heavy-MOOC, and (E) MOOC.

We also asked if they sought help from other sources outside the course materials. Students reported e.g. using Google and reading books; a total of 21% of respondents reported the use these non-social forms of help-seeking. Some non-expected social sources were also mentioned, such as family, email and university staff.

As can be seen from Table 1, the majority of the students did not use social help-seeking approaches. The most used venue, the IRC chat room suggested in the MOOC platform, gained attraction from 38% of survey responders. Of them, 88% experienced that they benefited from this help-seeking strategies.

The least used social help-seeking approach related to seeking help from teachers, which was used only by 5% of participants. Friends were used by circa one in four participants, highlighting the aspect that MOOC users extend their help-seeking beyond the MOOC platform. The perceived benefit from this is varied among those who asked their friends to help. Those who received help from friends mostly considered this a little helpful or somewhat helpful (total of 83% of responders), but about 17% felt that they did not receive any support from their friends.

Using the k-means clustering method and the elbow method for determining the optimal number of clusters, we observed that the participants can be summarized using five clusters. We analyzed the descriptive means of each cluster, and classified them as the following learning approaches (see Table 2):

(A) computer-mediated friend-based interaction (CMC-friend)
(B) non-help seekers (none)
(C) friend supported (friend)
(D) heavy MOOC platform benefiters (heavy-MOOC)
(E) MOOC platform benefitters (MOOC)

Approximately one-half of the students did not use social support strategies (51%), and that rest of the students are distributed rather equally among the four different strategies. Overall, we also observe that in each of the clusters, participants considered benefiting from these social help-seeking strategies (i.e. the values are above 2, that is received help "a little").

4.2 Help-seeking and demographics

We then studied participant demographics, including gender, age, level of education, and previous programming experience[1].

We observed that there are gender differences in choosing to use various social help-seeking approaches (Kruskal-Wallis χ^2 = 9.8616, df = 4, p = 0.04283). Overall, men were more likely to not ask for help, while females were, in general, more active as social help-seekers and in using the given support platform. Males, when asking for help, typically used computer-mediated communication.

We observed also a relationship between the age and the social help-seeking approach (Kruskal-Wallis χ^2 = 10.579, df = 4, p = 0.03173). In general, the younger participants belong to those helped by a friend, and older participants use the tools provided by the MOOC platform.

We however did not observe a relationship on the level of education and social help-seeking strategies (Kruskal-Wallis χ^2 = 4.2481, df = 4, p = 0.3735). Thus, education and e.g., social capital gained during higher education did not explain how people seek help.

Similarly, to our surprise, previous programming experience (that is, the subject of the MOOC) was not related to social help-seeking strategies (Kruskal-Wallis χ^2 = 6.7033, df = 4, p = 0.1524). For example, approximately 50% of the most experienced participants who had worked on several group programming projects had sought for help from at least one of the given social help-seeking sources.

4.3 Help-seeking and study approaches

Using the 30 survey items of the Revised Approaches to Studying Inventory (RASI) [11], we studied differences between student clusters and the study approaches. As shown in Table 3, the participants can broadly be described as more deep and strategic learners, and less as surface learners.

We observed that the student clusters that described the help-seeking strategies were not related to deep and strategic approaches. The Kruskal-Wallis χ^2-test demonstrated no relationship, p = 0.769 for deep learning strategy and p = 0.713 for strategic learning approach. However, the surface approach had significant differences between the groups (p = 0.041).

As shown in Table 3, although the differences are modest, the surface approach was highest among the cluster C, the students who relied on their friends for support, and the lowest in the non-help seeking cluster B.

4.4 Help-seeking and course retention

We finally compared the dropout rate of students in each of the different clusters that described students help-seeking strategies. The data included only those students who had completed at least one week of the course. Table 4 shows the proportion of students in different clusters that stayed in the course.

[1]Due to participants not completing both the demographics survey and the RASI survey, the analysis was only conducted with a subpopulation of 102 participants. Their distribution in the cluster groups was even (χ^2= 4.1235, df = 4, p = 0.3896). Gender (male=68%, female=28%, NA=4%), Age (min=18, med=33, max=66), Level of Education (primary/secondary=49%,tertiary=26%,research=25%), Previous programming experience (none=21%,at least some=59%, formal or work experience=20%). Further available from the authors.

	A	B	C	D	E
Deep	37.3	36.8	35.4	36.8	37.8
	(5.8)	(5.7)	(6.4)	(4.9)	(5.5)
Strategic	34.5	33.3	34.4	33.9	35.1
	(6.8)	(5.8)	(5.4)	(6.4)	(6.7)
Surface	26.6	24.3	28.6	26.1	25.5
	(6.3)	(6.0)	(7.0)	(5.2)	(5.9)

Table 3: Mean and standard deviation on the approaches to studying inventory between clusters. A larger value means higher weight on the approach. The key for the clusters is: (A) CMC Friend, (B) None, (C) Friend, (D) Heavy-MOOC, and (E) MOOC. Sub-sample sizes see Table 2.

Weeks	2	4	6	8	10	12	14
A	100%	89%	89%	89%	89%	89%	89%
B	86%	67%	60%	55%	51%	50%	48%
C	85%	78%	68%	62%	59%	52%	52%
D	100%	84%	79%	79%	79%	79%	75%
E	92%	90%	86%	79%	74%	62%	62%

Table 4: Percentage of students in each cluster that were still completing assignments from a given specific course week. The key for the clusters is: (A) CMC Friend, (B) None, (C) Friend, (D) Heavy-MOOC, and (E) MOOC. Sub-sample sizes see Table 2.

Table 4 shows that approximately 50% of those students who did not engage in help-seeking (Cluster B) and those who relied solely on their friends completed (Cluster C) the course. The highest completion rate was among the students who were discussing with friends using computer-mediated communication (Cluster A), and the users who mostly used the tools provided by the MOOC platform fell in between (Clusters D and E).

5 DISCUSSION

Next, we concretize our findings to personas, which can be used to design MOOC courses, followed by further design ideas to improve social help-seeking in MOOC environments.

5.1 Personas

Based on the findings thus far, we idealize five different potential users. These potential users are *personas*, which MOOC system designers and MOOC course teachers can use to help to design their courses. Following standard format of a persona, we give these idealized users a name and provide a short background on them.

Friend over CMC: Ville is around 30 years old. He is keen to understand how programming truly works and is willing to spend time to understand the course exercises. He is connected to some friends who are familiar with programming and who are able to answer his questions in private. He uses Facebook Messenger to stay in touch with his friends but knows them only as they've been bragging about coding in some context in the past. Around 12% of students are like Ville.

None: Matti is around 30 years old. He is keen to understand how programming truly works and is willing to spend time to understand the course exercises. He, however, either do not have friends who know programming or does not want to ask help from them. Instead, he uses Google, StackOverflow, and other online sources when stuck and re-reads the course material. Around 50% of students are like Matti.

Friend: Maija is around 25 years old. She enrolled in the class to learn to program but considers how to most conveniently pass the course. She has some classmates who are also taking the same MOOC course or she happens to be a good friend with someone programming. She asks help for the hard challenges and receives a lot help from them. Around 12% of students are like Maija.

Heavy-MOOC: Anna is around 30 years old. She enrolled in the class to learn to program and wishes to truly understand how programming works. She has found her way to the MOOC support channel and has received a lot of help from them, and occasionally asks also help from some of her friends when they meet. Around 10% of students are like Anna.

MOOC: Leena around 35 years old. She enrolled in the class to learn to program and wishes to understand how programming works. However, she is careful not to spend too much time on the exercises. There is also a life to live! She has found her way to the MOOC support channel and does get help from there, but it is not super critical. Around 16% of students are like Leena.

5.2 MOOC buddy

Our primary finding is that about one in four students seeks help from their friends and that the majority of them also report receiving a little or more support from them. These participants who sought help from their friends did not consider contacts on the MOOC platform beneficial for working with the course assignments. As any MOOC provider can not ensure that each participant has knowledgeable friends, one may question what is the relevance of this finding. However, we see that this finding justifies proposing an intervention which could benefit MOOC students.

A *MOOC buddy* is a person who will help you with your MOOC exercises. Previous research has indicated that MOOC serves also as a platform for social interaction [30]. Furthermore, previous findings have suggested that alumni are willing to engage in supporting new students in MOOCs without extra compensation [25]. Our data can not answer how critical it was that the help-seeking took place from *a friend*, having a social group (and group pressure for studies) or even that there were constantly same persons who could help the MOOC participants. However, the access to participants' social networks via social network sites (e.g., Facebook) could be used to seek both friends and friends-of-friends who a) have relevant knowledge, b) interest on the subject matter or c) have taken the course previously (and are thus alumni), so that they could help existing MOOC participants in a mentor role.

Based on earlier work on social learning, we believe that it is possible to find such participants. Therefore, we argue that through social network mechanics, MOOC buddy system could be scaled to large MOOCs as well. Furthermore, we may be able to reduce the effect of existing friendships (if not found) by providing the opportunity to find some other volunteers if the MOOC participant does not have anyone with a suitable background in their circles.

5.3 Different learners within a MOOC

Our second finding was related to the differences in participants' study approaches. We observed that, overall, course participants were more deeply and strategically orientated and less surface-oriented in their MOOC studies. We, however, observed that especially groups that sought help from their friends were more surface-orientated than other groups. This is not critical, as in all groups the deep learning approach was higher than the surface approach, and no statistically significant differences were observed.

These differences in study approaches can be seen as an indicator of social help-seekers needing more support in the course and may need to be motivated to approach the course using deep study approach. We suggest that, when possible, the social interaction should be constructed so that it supports building a deeper understanding of the course, and not only the strategies needed to solve the course assignments.

If the MOOC buddy program presented above would be initialized, this could take place when mentors enroll. On MOOC platforms, such as IRC in this course, proposing a guideline or etiquette for participants is easily achieved. However, we highlight that this help-seeking takes place also on tools not connected to the MOOC, but on environments that best facilitate the interaction for each specific group.

Therefore, we propose that students would be introduced to a *wireframe for their social help-seeking*, which would introduce questions students should ask when asking for help to ensure they can engage in a deeper course-wise discussion also. Students could use this when engaged to social-help seeking to ask more detailed questions, connecting the exercise and problem to a wider learning context. Furthermore, students could share this material with those helping them to establish an etiquette. Similar practices already exist for solo-work [24].

5.4 Limitations and future work

Our study has several limitations which we address next. First, the course has a specific population. It is related to programming and as such might attract certain types of participants more than others. Furthermore, the course was organized in Finnish, which means that the participants had somewhat similar cultural backgrounds in relation to education and social interaction.

The two points above are also related to the generalizability of our findings. As we used responses from 255 users, which corresponds to 26% of the initial population, it is possible that the results do not generalize to other contexts. The clusters that we presented in this study are a result of the responses that we received, which means that there is also a possibility of participation bias. Similarly, we must highlight that we studied the *benefit* instead of *frequency* of help-seeking, which can also influence the results.

The course under study has also existed several years. It is thus possible that communities have already emerged around the MOOC, which could mean that some of the help-seeking behaviors have been directed at these communities which we do not know of. In the same vein, we do not have more extensive background details on the participants: we do not know if they have deliberately chosen to act in the way they acted in, or if there were other reasons for their behavior.

Finally, any research is as valid as its measurement instruments are. In this research we have used previously validated measurements, translated to the Finnish language by the research team. The translation was performed by two researchers to check the consistency of the terminology and natural presentation. The questions focused on perceived help sources was developed by the research team.

6 CONCLUSIONS

In this work, we studied social help-seeking in a programming MOOC. Based on analysis of our survey, we found five approaches for social help-seeking. First, we observed that the largest group – approximately one-half of the students – did not engage in social help-seeking. They used the existing resources available (e.g., books, search engines) to solve problems they had with their assignments.

Two of the groups primarily sought support from their friends. These groups differed in the type of communication channel they preferred to use. The first group was mostly connected through computer-mediated means, whereas the other used face-to-face communication, supplemented with some computer-mediation. It is important to observe that the interaction in these two groups took place also *outside* the MOOC platforms. The last two groups used the MOOC provided platform (IRC channel) to seek help, but we observed a difference in how helpful they considered the channel.

We also found that women were more likely to engage in social help-seeking, older participants used the MOOC platform more to seek help, and younger participants used more friends as a source of help. Furthermore, while in general the groups corresponded poorly to the RASI learning styles, users who sought help from their friends were marginally more surface oriented. Finally, we observed differences in the drop-out rate between these clusters, which indicates that the clusters provide information on the ways in which students engage in their learning activities.

Based on our findings, we proposed two practices which could assist social help-seeking and improve its overall quality. Our first proposal was a MOOC buddy system, which would ensure access to "friends" who could help on the MOOC. The second practice we proposed related to helping participants to ask the right questions from persons helping them through scaffolded examples.

REFERENCES

[1] John B Biggs. 2011. *Teaching for quality learning at university: What the student does.* McGraw-Hill Education (UK).

[2] John Seely Brown, Allan Collins, and Paul Duguid. 1989. Situated cognition and the culture of learning. *Educational researcher* 18, 1 (1989), 32–42.

[3] Julia Cambre, Chinmay Kulkarni, Michael S Bernstein, and Scott R Klemmer. 2014. Talkabout: Small-group Discussions in Massive Global Classes. In *Proceedings of the first ACM conference on Learning @ Scale conference 2014 - L@S '14.* 161–162. https://doi.org/10.1145/2556325.2567859

[4] Derrick Coetzee, Armando Fox, Marti A. Hearst, and BjÃűrn Hartmann. 2014. Should your MOOC forum use a reputation system?. In *Proceedings of the 17th ACM conference on Computer supported cooperative work & social computing - CSCW '14.* 1176–1187. https://doi.org/10.1145/2531602.2531657

[5] D Coetzee, Seongtaek Lim, Armando Fox, Bjorn Hartmann, and Marti A. Hearst. 2015. Structuring Interactions for Large-Scale Synchronous Peer Learning. In *Proceedings of the 18th ACM Conference on Computer Supported Cooperative Work & Social Computing - CSCW '15.* ACM Press, New York, New York, USA, 1139–1152. https://doi.org/10.1145/2675133.2675251

[6] John Dewey. 1967. *The School and the Society: Rev. Ed.* Univ. of Chicago Press.

[7] Rosalind Driver and Beverley Bell. 1986. Students' thinking and the learning of science: A constructivist view. *School science review* 67, 240 (1986), 443–56.

[8] Angus Duff. 1997. A note on the reliability and validity of a 30-item version of Entwistle & Tait's Revised Approaches to Studying Inventory. *British Journal of Educational Psychology* 67, 4 (1997), 529–539.

[9] Angus Duff. 2004. The Revised Approaches to Studying Inventory (RASI) and its use in management education. *Active learning in higher ed.* 5, 1 (2004), 56–72.

[10] Noel Entwistle, Maureen Hanley, and Dai Hounsell. 1979. Identifying distinctive approaches to studying. *Higher education* 8, 4 (1979), 365–380.

[11] Noel J Entwistle and Hilary Tait. 1994. The revised approaches to studying inventory. *Edinburgh: University of Edinburgh, Centre for Research into Learning and Instruction* (1994).

[12] Nabeel Gillani and Rebecca Eynon. 2014. Communication patterns in massively open online courses. *The Internet and Higher Education* 23 (2014), 18–26. https://doi.org/10.1016/j.iheduc.2014.05.004

[13] Tony Greening. 2000. Emerging Constructivist Forces in Computer Science Education: Shaping a New Future? In *Computer science education in the 21st century.* Springer, 47–80.

[14] Philip J Guo, Juho Kim, and Rob Rubin. 2014. How video production affects student engagement: An empirical study of MOOC videos. In *Proceedings of the first ACM conference on Learning@ scale conference.* ACM, 41–50.

[15] Greg Harper and David Kember. 1989. Interpretation of factor analyses from the approaches to studying inventory. *British J. of Educ. Psych.* 59, 1 (1989), 66–74.

[16] Jonathan Huang, Anirban Dasgupta, Arpita Ghosh, Jane Manning, and Marc Sanders. 2014. Superposter behavior in MOOC forums. *Proceedings of the first ACM conference on Learning @ Scale conference - L@S '14* (2014), 117–126. https://doi.org/10.1145/2556325.2566249

[17] A Kasunic, J Hammer, and R Kraut. 2016. A Preliminary Look at MOOC-associated Facebook Groups: Prevalence, Geographic Representation, and Homophily. *Proceedings of the Third ...* (2016), 205–208. https://doi.org/10.1145/2876034.2893415

[18] Juho Kim, Philip J Guo, Daniel T Seaton, Piotr Mitros, Krzysztof Z Gajos, and Robert C Miller. 2014. Understanding in-video dropouts and interaction peaks inonline lecture videos. In *Proceedings of the first ACM conference on Learning@ scale conference.* ACM, 31–40.

[19] Rene F. Kizilcec, Chris Piech, and Emily Schneider. 2013. Deconstructing Disengagement : Analyzing Learner Subpopulations in Massive Open Online Courses. *Lak '13* (2013), 10. https://doi.org/10.1145/2460296.2460330

[20] Chinmay Kulkarni, Julia Cambre, Yasmine Kotturi, Michael S. Bernstein, and Scott R. Klemmer. 2015. Talkabout: Making Distance Matter with Small Groups in Massive Classes. *Proceedings of the 18th ACM Conference on Computer Supported Cooperative Work & Social Computing - CSCW '15* (2015), 1116–1128. https://doi.org/10.1145/2675133.2675166

[21] Jean Lave and Etienne Wenger. 1991. *Situated learning: Legitimate peripheral participation.* Cambridge univ. press.

[22] Seongtaek Lim, Derrick Coetzee, Bjoern Hartmann, Armando Fox, and Marti A Hearst. 2014. Initial experiences with small group discussions in MOOCs. In *Proceedings of the first ACM conference on Learning @ Scale conference - L@S '14.* 151–152. https://doi.org/10.1145/2556325.2567854

[23] Karen Mattick, Ian Dennis, and John Bligh. 2004. Approaches to learning and studying in medical students: validation of a revised inventory and its relation to student characteristics and performance. *Medical Education* 38, 5 (2004), 535–543.

[24] Robert McCartney, Anna Eckerdal, Jan Erik Mostrom, Kate Sanders, and Carol Zander. 2007. Successful students' strategies for getting unstuck. In *ACM SIGCSE Bulletin*, Vol. 39. ACM, 156–160.

[25] Matti Nelimarkka and Arto Vihavainen. 2015. Alumni & Tenured Participants in MOOCs. In *Proceedings of the Second (2015) ACM Conference on Learning @ Scale - L@S '15.* 85–93. https://doi.org/10.1145/2724660.2724671

[26] Lev Semenovich Vygotsky. 1978. *Mind in society: The development of higher psychological processes.* Harvard university press.

[27] Joe Warren, Scott Rixner, John Greiner, and Stephen Wong. 2014. Facilitating human interaction in an online programming course. *Proceedings of the 45th ACM technical symposium on Computer science education - SIGCSE '14* (2014), 665–670. https://doi.org/10.1145/2538862.2538893

[28] Etienne Wenger. 1999. *Communities of practice: Learning, meaning, and identity.* Cambridge university press.

[29] Saijing Zheng, Kyungsik Han, Mary Beth Rosson, and John M Carroll. 2016. The Role of Social Media in MOOCs: How to Use Social Media to Enhance Student Retention. *Proceedings of the Third ACM Conference on Learning @ Scale* (2016), 419–428. https://doi.org/10.1145/2876034.2876047

[30] Saijing Zheng, Mary Beth Rosson, Patrick C Shih, and John M Carroll. 2015. Understanding Student Motivation, Behaviors and Perceptions in MOOCs. In *Proceedings of the 18th ACM Conference on Computer Supported Cooperative Work & Social Computing - CSCW '15.* ACM Press, New York, New York, USA, 1882–1895. https://doi.org/10.1145/2675133.2675217

[31] Saijing Zheng, Pamela Wisniewski, Mary Beth Rosson, and John M Carroll. 2016. Ask the Instructors: Motivations and Challenges of Teaching Massive Open Online Courses. *Proceedings of the 19th ACM Conference on Computer-Supported Cooperative Work & Social Computing* (2016), 206–221. https://doi.org/10.1145/2818048.2820082

Lightweight Techniques to Support Students in Large Classes

Mia Minnes, Christine Alvarado, and Leo Porter
Computer Science and Engineering
University of California, San Diego
minnes,cjalvarado,leporter@ucsd.edu

ABSTRACT

With surging enrollments in computer science, large classes are becoming standard, even at the upper division. Unfortunately, this new reality can leave students feeling anonymous and unsupported. This work examines the impact of several lightweight interventions on students' sense of connection with instructors and the class. These strategies were employed in a range of large courses at a public research-focused university. The implemented techniques include: opportunities for one-on-one tutoring, seating assignments with consistent teaching staff members seated in class, and assigned small discussion sections, among others. All strategies are lightweight and require only the usual staffing resources afforded to a class. In this report, we evaluate student sense of community and reflect on the benefits and challenges of these techniques.

CCS CONCEPTS

• **Social and professional topics → Computing Education**;

KEYWORDS

Large classes, sense of belonging, educational interventions, classroom community, computing education

ACM Reference Format:
Mia Minnes, Christine Alvarado, and Leo Porter. 2018. Lightweight Techniques to Support Students in Large Classes. In *SIGCSE '18: The 49th ACM Technical Symposium on Computer Science Education, Feb. 21–24, 2018, Baltimore, MD, USA.* ACM, New York, NY, USA, 6 pages. https://doi.org/10.1145/3159450.3159601

1 INTRODUCTION

The reality of large-scale public education is that class sizes will continue to grow. While this growth allows instructors to serve more students (at a lower cost per student), students in large classes can feel anonymous and begin to engage less, which can hurt their learning [10]. This detachment and lack of community may have a stronger negative impact on women and members of underrepresented racial and ethnic groups, who already face barriers to acceptance, particularly in STEM fields [7, 17].

There have been several efforts to improve the student experience in large classes. One approach is to leverage undergraduate and graduate student resources to increase classroom community and student support [11]. Alternatively, technology can be used to allow instructors to better gauge student understanding [12]. Curricular and program efforts to form community-centric learning groups may improve students' sense of belonging, and thereby also (hopefully) improve the overall student experience [3, 6].

New initiatives, though effective, can require significant time and human resources. In our prior work, we reported on a structure called "micro-classes" where students in a 200-person large-format class are organized in groups of 25–30 students, each group led by a designated Teaching Assistant (TA) and a team of undergraduate tutors [1]. We found that the micro-classes structure was successful in increasing students' sense of community compared to a control group. However, the resources required were considerable: three times as many graduate and undergraduate staff were hired, compared to the control course, and significant overhead was needed to train and manage this staff in their larger classroom roles.

Inspired by our prior micro-classes design and its positive results, we explore whether lighter-weight versions of the micro-class strategies and other similar techniques could also produce community gains and other positive effects on students-student and instructor-student interactions, within the time and staffing expectations of a regular course. These strategies include various attendance policies, seating assignments, grouped seating with course staff, course staff being used as personal tutors, and blocked off rows to facilitate course-staff interactions with all students.

We implemented a variety of these strategies in three different classes taught by four different instructors (three of them authors) over the 2016/2017 academic year at a large public research university. We explore the overall utility, benefits, and drawbacks of the various techniques based on our experience teaching these courses as well as on student feedback and measurements of community gains in each course.

2 BACKGROUND

Various techniques have already been shown to increase student engagement, performance and retention, particularly in large (CS) classes. Active learning during class, for example via Peer Instruction (PI), has been shown to improve student pass rates and satisfaction and retention in CS [12, 13]. For labs and out-of-class assignments, Pair Programming has been shown to decrease drop rates while maintaining performance levels in large introductory CS courses [8]. The techniques explored in this experience report are intended to complement (not replace) the existing techniques for supporting student learning.

Course teaching assistants play an important role in shaping students' experiences in large classes. O'Neal et al. found that teaching assistants were particularly important for student retention in science courses [11], while the increased TA interaction with students

SIGCSE '18, Feb. 21–24, 2018, Baltimore, MD, USA

ACM ISBN 978-1-4503-5103-4/18/02...$15.00
https://doi.org/10.1145/3159450.3159601

(along with the decreased student:TA ratio) may be one reason for the community gains in our prior micro-classes structure [1].

However, not all students' interactions with course staff are the same: Smith et al. found that in programming courses at three different universities 5% of students used 50% of tutors' time in the lab [16]. While increasing the number of TAs allocated to a given course might be prohibitively expensive, Smith et al.'s finding suggests that there might be more efficient ways for existing course staff to support students who really need this support. We explore different staff/student interaction models in this report.

One of the main challenges in a large classroom is creating a learning community for all students in the course. Despite some recent work that does not find a connection between stronger sense of classroom community and success in specific computer science courses [1, 4], strong learning communities have long been reported to have many benefits including increased retention in higher-education programs; more engaged, focused, and active learning environments with corresponding gains in learning; and greater student satisfaction [6, 15]. We explore whether classroom policies or actions by the instructor can efficiently help to build this sense of learning community.

3 LIGHTWEIGHT ENGAGEMENT STRATEGIES

We implemented four lightweight engagement strategies designed to complement existing practices for large classes: (1) different types of assigned seating, (2) assignment of undergraduate tutors[1] to support individual students ("personal tutors"), (3) smaller-group, assigned discussion sections, and (4) blocked rows in large classrooms to facilitate instructor and TA/tutor access to students. Each of these additional techniques required few additional staff resources.

3.1 Assigned seating

There is evidence that both lecture seating preference as well as actual lecture seating location correlates with students' grades in large lecture classes [2, 9]. Anecdotally, we have heard from students that assigned seating can help alleviate the social burden for students who do not have close friends in the class, helping them form connections with their peers and feel more comfortable.

On the other hand, assigned seating has its drawbacks. Some students resent not being able to sit in their preferred location. Others may forget their assigned seat and delay the class while looking for it. Seating charts also do require some effort to create and maintain, particularly in the first weeks of the term as enrollments change, but this can be largely automated.

We implemented several different assigned seating strategies to try to find a balance between these benefits and drawbacks. Across these strategies, we varied the degree to which students would be assigned to always sit near the same peers and the same course staff. On one extreme, we randomly assigned students to specific seats and assigned specific TAs and tutors to interact only with students in a particular zone in the classroom, ensuring that students would always interact with the same peers and course staff in class. On the other extreme, we placed no restrictions on where students sat nor assigned staff to regions of the class. Between these extremes, in some classes we used zone-based seating, where students could sit anywhere within given row and seat boundaries, and assigned tutors to cover each particular zone. In this middle option students always interacted with the same course staff and usually, but not always, sat with the same students.

[1] Throughout, "tutor" refers to undergraduate teaching assistants and "TA" refers to graduate teaching assistants; both are hired to work as part of the teaching team.

3.2 Personal tutors

Each class we studied employed both graduate TAs and undergraduate tutors at a student:staff ratio between 40:1 and 55:1, depending mainly on the instructor-selected balance between graduate TAs and undergraduate tutors. TAs carry more responsibility for leading discussion sections and developing assignment-related material (writeups, rubrics, grading scripts) while undergraduate tutors, which typically outnumber TAs, spend more time in student-facing activities (lab or office hours).

Traditionally, tutors and TAs support all students in the class. Despite the availability of these staff resources, some students are still reluctant to reach out for help. To overcome this, in some classes we explicitly assigned each tutor to a particular set of students, so students had a "personally assigned tutor". In addition to standard open office hours offered by instructors and TAs, personal tutors were available for one-on-one meetings with struggling students (by appointment). In some courses, a student's personal tutor also graded all of that student's assignments and so was able to give more detailed, longitudinal feedback. Personal tutors in some classes sent periodic supportive or congratulatory emails to their students. Providing this personal support slightly reduced the number of hours tutors spent in drop-in lab or office hours, since the overall tutor resource level remained the same across all the classes.

3.3 Small group assigned discussion sections

Discussion sections at our university can take several forms but are always scheduled to meet once a week, outside of the lecture session, and are led by TAs. The size of the discussion sections is variable, as is the consistency of the TA leading them, and whether attendance is required. For many classes, discussion sections are not required and students in a class are free to attend any of a set of weekly discussion sections. However, we believed that with a little structure, discussion sections could be an opportunity to help students build community. To try to achieve this goal, discussion sections in some classes were each led by a designated TA, and students were required to attend the section in which they were enrolled. To further enhance the sense of community within the group of students in a discussion, some of the classes coordinated the personal tutors with the discussion sections and with the seating arrangements in the lecture sections.

3.4 Blocked rows in class

Many large classes at our university are taught with the help of various active learning strategies during the lecture period. To facilitate these activities, the instructor and in-class tutors and TAs walk around the room, observing student work, answering questions, and soliciting student feedback. However, the physical layout of the stadium-style seating in most lecture halls makes it challenging to reach students seated far from an aisle.

In some of the classes we studied, we strategically blocked off certain rows in the lecture halls (often relying on the fact that at least 25% of enrolled students don't regularly attend lecture). Instructors and tutors could then walk along these rows to reach students who would otherwise be inaccessible.

4 IMPLEMENTATION AND EXPERIENCE

We implemented several combinations of the lightweight strategies described above during the 2016/2017 academic year at the University of California, San Diego. We selected courses at all levels of the CS program including CS1.5 (a second-quarter introductory programming course designed for students with no pre-college programming experience), CS3 (an Advanced Data Structures course), an upper-division theory of computation course, and an upper-division computer architecture course[2]. Nearly all of the courses we studied had large student enrollments of 150 or more per section; several of these courses had multiple sections. Table 1 summarizes the enrollments and the strategies used in each class.

All of the instructors of these courses were experienced, highly-rated instructors. In all of the courses in this study, instructors used common baseline engagement practices including: frequent formative assessment; peer instruction as well as other active problem solving in class; optional pair programming where appropriate; in-class tutors and TAs who assisted students during in-class exercises and discussions; opportunities for informal feedback by students to the instructional team about conceptual struggles and overall course impressions; and email encouragements and/or feedback to students from the instructor or TA at least once per term.

In all but one case, each course was taught by a different instructor (including three of the authors), while all sections of the same course were taught by the same instructor. However, one of the five sections of CS3 that we examined was taught by a different instructor (not one of the authors), who only taught that one section Also, four of the CS3 sections and the CS1.5 course were taught by the same instructor.

We give the combination of strategies we chose for each course, the motivation for this choice, and our reflections on the results. For those strategies that appeared to promote positive student feedback and sense of community, future work will examine any additional impacts on student performance or retention.

4.1 Introductory Programming (CS1.5)

Context. CS 1.5 at our institution is the second course in a two-term introductory sequence for students with little or no pre-college computing experience. Students in this course learn Java and object oriented programming fundamentals, and complete weekly programming assignments where they may optionally work with a partner engaging in pair programming. In the term included in this report, the course enrolled mostly non computer science majors.

Interventions Employed. In CS1.5 we focused on strategies to provide personal support to students, both in and out of the classroom. Students in this course are still new to Java and debugging, and small errors in their code often cost them hours and leave them feeling discouraged and desperate. To help mitigate this frustration, we provided each student a "personal tutor" as described in section 3.2, to give them extra opportunities for one-on-one help when they struggled and to provide them with personalized grading feedback and email support. In class, we used zone-based assigned seating to help students get to know their peers, and blocked rows so in-class tutors could access all students who came to class.

Reflections. At the end of the quarter, we surveyed students about their experience with the personal tutors. 30% of the 195 respondents to the survey reported working with their personal tutor at least once, and 97% of these students said the interaction with their personal tutor was extremely helpful (54%), somewhat helpful (30%), or a little helpful (13%). Most (63% of) students who did not work with a personal tutor said that they never needed extra help, though 39% (including some who reported not needing extra help) said that they did not work with a private tutor because they failed to contact their tutor to set up a time. Additionally, 7% were unable to schedule a time to meet their tutor and 14% reported being uncomfortable going to their near-peer with their questions.

Despite low attendance (likely due to the 8am class time, the podcast lectures, and a liberal attendance policy), at least some of the students who came to class appreciated the the ability to get to know the tutor in their zone and get help during class. On the end of term evaluation a student reflected, "assigned seating with a students [sic] specific tutor created a welcoming environment that also encouraged taking on challenges... Having a tutor around made it easier to perform these tasks without getting too intimidated."

4.2 Advanced Data Structures (CS3)

Context. CS3 is an advanced data structures course in C++, typically taken by students during their second or third year. It is a challenging course, and serves as the gateway to the upper division for CS and CS-related majors. Students complete bi-weekly programming assignments, optionally with a partner using pair programming. This course is the same course previously studied using micro-classes [1]; several of its sections are included here.

Interventions Employed. In CS3 we focused on exploring how blocked rows in the classroom might improve the ability of the staff to support all students in class. In the fall, we tested the blocked rows seating arrangement in the one (of three) sections where enrollment was substantially below room capacity. In the winter, we implemented it in both sections, but starting a few weeks into the term once attendance had lowered, thus affording enough space in the classroom. We did not use any form of seating assignments in any of the sections; students could sit anywhere they wanted except in the blocked rows. In the winter, we also provided students with personal tutors starting roughly halfway through the term when we realized that this might be a good way to provide struggling with a little extra support, often with cryptic C++ errors.

Reflections. The empty rows were perceived as beneficial by the class staff (including TAs and tutors), but had mixed reviews from students. The staff appreciated being able to walk into the middle of the class during interactive activities to talk with all students, rather than being forced to interact only with the students on the aisles. On the other hand, it was a constant struggle to keep students from sitting in the blocked rows. Each class session required the

[2] The official course numbers for these four courses are CSE 8B, CSE 100, CSE 105 and CSE 141, respectively.

Table 1: Summary of community-building strategies used in each class

Class	Enrollment	Attendance	Assigned Seats	Personal tutors	Assigned Discussions	Extra space
CS1.5 Sp17	215	83	Zone	Yes		Yes
CS3 F16	A:188,B:124,C:132	A:125,B:75,C:85				B only: Yes
CS3 W17	A:227,B:233	A:100,B:170		Yes	Yes	Yes
Theory Sp17	A:193,B:195	A:120,B:129	Individual/Zone	Yes	Yes	
Arch. Sp17	A:187,B:75	A:138,B:43	Individual			

instructors and tutors to make written and oral announcements about the blocked rows and to move individuals who failed to heed the announcements and sat in the blocked rows anyway. Some students reported not seeing the value of the empty rows, while others said it made the class feel too crowded. There were at least a few students who nonetheless commented on the value of the empty rows in the open-ended end-of-course feedback.

4.3 Theory

Context. This theory of computation class is required for both CS majors and a joint Math-CS program at our university. This class is often taken by juniors and seniors and requires students to reason formally, analyze and devise abstract constructions, and write proofs. Most graded student work is weekly written homework (which may be done in groups) and in-class exams.

Interventions Employed. The abstract content of this class is challenging, and students come into the class with different preconceptions about math and formalism. Our interventions in this class focused on reducing students' sense of anonymity and vulnerability and encouraging them to reach out for help when needed. Individual coaching of students by personal tutors was intended to guide students through the process of mathematical discovery at their own pace. At the start of the quarter, randomized lecture seat assignments were announced, and (in one section) were coordinated with the personal tutor assignments and the in-class tutor support. Due to concern from some students with low-vision and students who felt isolated by these assignments, we switched to zone seating for most of the term. In one of the lecture sections, the seating zones corresponded to the discussion sections. Discussion sections were led by the same TA each week, and students were encouraged to attend the section in which they were enrolled.

Reflections. Students valued the opportunities to get help in one-on-one sessions. Only previous assignments or exams could be discussed in these sessions, and students reported being able to correct misconceptions and catch up with difficult concepts.

While somewhat controversial with the students, the zone-based seating assignments were largely seen as positive in the end-of-term student evaluations, with one student writing "Sectioned seating turned out well, since it did not restrict students [but still made] talking with other students ...a little bit better around familiar faces". Reaction to zone-based seating was in marked contrast to the randomized seating that was initially used, and which elicited mid-term feedback like "I really really disliked the seating chart, especially as a woman. Being separated from other women/the guys who [I felt comfortable with] was very isolating." Zone seating appears to strike an important balance between allowing students autonomy to apply learning strategies that have worked for them in the past while still maintaining consistency that can build community.

4.4 Architecture

Context. Computer Architecture is an upper-division required course for the CS major. In this course, students solidify their understanding of hardware systems by connecting combinational and sequential logic with their understanding of assembly programming by learning about processor design fundamentals. Accompanying the course is a separate laboratory course where students complete a term-long project in teams of 2–4 students. Most students take this course and the lab course concurrently.

Interventions Employed. In the larger section, we used seat-based individual assigned seating. A TA or tutor was assigned to each region of the room to build community between staff and students. To allow students some choice in their assigned seat, the seat assignments were determined by the seats students had selected on the second day of the class. Although they were not told in advance that this assignment would be made, on this day students generally were sitting with friends and lab-teams. We also gave students who were unhappy with their specific seat the option to move somewhere in the area of the same TA/Tutor. The smaller section did not have assigned seating as only about 40 students attended daily. Students received support from one TA and the instructor during classroom activities.

Reflections. In the larger section, the method we used for assigning seats mostly struck a good balance between student choice and seating requirements, and the section had a nice rapport with students and staff interacting often in class. Perhaps due to both the seating assignments and the more liberal attendance policy than previous terms, there were many fewer instances of students attending class only to sit in the back, buried in their laptops and refusing to talk to other students. However, there were a few complaints from students who got stuck in the back because they were late on the day seat assignments were determined, who wished they had thought to sit with their lab teams, or, in one case, who got seated next to disruptive students.

Despite its low attendance (or perhaps because of it), the smaller (8am) section had a surprisingly positive classroom environment. Most students who attended were regulars, and roughly half consistently spoke in class.

5 CLASSROOM COMMUNITY

The observations and reflections reported in the previous section shed light on some possible impacts of these techniques. In addition, we collected data on students' perceptions of classroom community.

5.1 Findings on Community

To measure students' sense of community, we administered Rovai's validated Classroom Community Scale (CCS) [14] in each class at the start and end of the term. The CCS measures both sense of learning community and sense of connectedness within a class, with total scores out of 80 points (40 for each sub-scale) and higher scores reflecting a stronger sense of community. At the start of the term, we modified the questions in the survey slightly so that students reported sense of community in all prior CS courses at this university, while at the end of the term we used the survey in its original form, asking them only about the course for which they were taking the survey. The survey was administered online, and linked to a small amount of course credit. Rates of students who responded to both pre- and post- surveys range from 84% and 90% across the five courses, and include both students who did and students who did not regularly attend class.

In Table 2 we report results of the CCS and include the results from both the CS3 micro-class and the CS3 control 1 sections from the micro-classes study for comparison [1]. The control 1 section in [1] includes many of the baseline engagement practices outlined above. We find that community improved in all courses we reported on, with marked increases in Learning Community scores. In fact, many of these CCS gains are statistically significant. Some of the CCS gains approached or even met those seen in our previous CS3 micro-classes section [1]. However, we did not find any significant differences between the CCS gains across the sections of any single class, even when slightly different interventions were used.

5.2 Reflections

The baseline engagement practices, particularly group-based active learning in class, likely play a large part in the increase in community scores in these classes. However, we believe that some of the lightweight practices presented here likely amplify this effect. In particular, seating assignments help stabilize student-student and student-tutor interactions in class, giving students an opportunity to get to know each other and helping students who come into the class not knowing their peers find people to talk to. Personal tutors may also create a sense of community, and this effect is likely strongest when these tutors are assigned early in the term. On the other hand, it does not appear that blocking rows, which allowed tutors to access all students, did much to build community.

High class attendance is not strictly necessary to build community, as seen in the relatively low attendance in CS1.5 and computer architecture (Table 1). Students in these classes who did attend may have got more attention and felt better about the community they built. Students who chose not to attend did not feel forced into being part of an in-class community they did not want to join.

Factors external to the ones discussed here may also have a strong influence on community. For one, the course and the instructor likely play a large role. The CCS score in Computer Architecture likely gets a boost from its companion lab course where students

Table 2: Mean CCS scores before and after each course, including deltas overall and for each subscale (learning and connectedness). * indicates a significant difference between before and after means at the $p < 0.05$ level or lower. For comparison, CS3 MC and Ctrl results use the data from [1].

Course	Before	After	Δ_{Learn}	$\Delta_{Connect}$	Δ_{Tot}
CS1.5	46.7	49.5	**1.7***	**1.0***	**2.8***
CS3 F16	47.0	48.8	**1.5***	**0.5***	**1.8***
CS3 W17	46.7	47.3	**0.8***	-0.2	0.6
Theory	45.7	48.5	**2.3***	0.5	**2.8***
Arch.	45.8	51.7	**3.8***	**2.2***	**5.9***
CS3 (Ctrl)	45.5	47.0	1.3	0.2	1.5
CS3 (MC)	44.4	50.6	**4.1***	**2.1***	**5.2***

work together in teams throughout the quarter. Non-academic factors may also play a significant role. Winter 2017 was a difficult time for many of our students with President Trump's travel ban making many students feel unsafe and unwelcome. These feelings are likely reflected in their overall sense of community in the course.

6 RECOMMENDATIONS

In this section, we collect our lessons learned from these experiences, hoping to provide some insight into the benefits (and pitfalls) of the various techniques for potential adopters.

6.1 Assigned Seats and In-Class Tutor Support

Stability in where students sat in the classroom appears to be beneficial. Seating arrangements that allowed students to work consistently with the same students and in-class staff allowed students to form stronger connections to each other. Moreover, explaining the rationale for the seat assignments gives the instructor another opportunity to motivate active learning and student engagement.

However, seating assignments come with strong cautions. We advise against randomized seat-based assignments, since they may have unintended consequences in isolating members of underrepresented groups from one another. The two alternative seating mechanisms we tried worked reasonably well: (1) allowing students to choose a seat and then declaring that to be their assigned seat, or (2) assigning students to "zones" in the classroom with flexible seating within each zone. In the first option, students always sit next to the same small group of people and may develop closer and deeper peer groups. In the second option, camaraderie within the "zones" of the class is also possible. Asking students to choose names for their seating-zones, or conducting larger group activities within the zones can further enhance this sense of community, as does assigning tutors to consistently support specific zones.

Some instructor support helps ensure smooth in-class interactions between tutors and students. Providing name-tags for in-class staff can help identify them and encourages students to seek the their help. Clear guidelines from the instructor on what tutors are expected to do in-class is also helpful: Where should they sit? When should they circulate among the students? Should they *initiate* interactions with students who appear to need help? Should they approach students who are off-task? With mentoring and guidance, tutors can enrich the course staff and support the students.

6.2 Personal Tutors

We recommend using TAs and tutors to help scale personalization. For example, instead of the instructor sending 200 form e-mails to students, each course staff member can be responsible for a much smaller group, preferably of students with whom they've interacted in class. Staff may, however, need guidance on how to positively and effectively motivate students, taking into account the importance of cultivating growth mindset in students [5].

6.3 Assigned Discussions

We did not observe specific benefits from keeping the TAs for specific discussion section times consistent or from assigning students to particular sections. In our experience, students who choose to attend discussion sections typically attend the same one each week anyway. As such, requiring student to attend the section in which they were enrolled is not necessary for developing a sense of community within those sections. Since attendance at discussion sections is often low, students may not notice when in-class assigned seating is coordinated with the discussion sections.

6.4 Blocked Rows

Staff appreciated being able to move through blocked rows to work with students throughout the class, though some students did not see this value. Blocked rows are most compatible with zone-based seating, where they can be used to give clear boundaries for zones.

6.5 Mitigating factor: Attendance policy

Although not a strategy we explicitly set out to examine, the attendance policy in a class can affect many of the in-class strategies we deployed. A successful attendance policy occupies a middle ground between providing the incentive students need to attend and being overly coercive to the point that students who truly do not wish (or need) to come to class do so begrudgingly. We found that attendance policies that rewarded students for attending class, but that provide alternative ways to earn these rewards, were most successful in creating an engaged classroom community. Policies can also be used to send subtle messages to students: a policy that shifts missed attendance credit to final exam weight can signal that the instructor allows students to demonstrate proficiency at the culmination of the course (without penalty for taking potentially longer to get there); a policy that allows students to earn participation credit weekly, either through attendance or through regular low-stakes quizzes, emphasizes that regular and continual engagement with the course material is important for success. We recognize that there are campuses where the culture around class attendance is more strict. In that context, cultivating a connected and engaged learning community may be even more impactful.

6.6 General Advice

Based on our experiences, and generally accepted wisdom about instructional interventions, we recommend ensuring that whatever policy is adopted is used consistently and communicated clearly to the students. For example, students will be more accepting of seat assignments explained on day one than of a change to assigned seats in the middle of week three. Being upfront with students about why a technique is being used can also help bring students on board. Lastly, being open to feedback when students have concerns can reinforce students' understanding that, at the end of the day, the instructor's focus is on the students' learning experience.

7 CONCLUSION

In this experience report, we reflected on the benefits (and costs) of several lightweight techniques for improving students' experiences in large classes. Across multiple classes in the CS curriculum, we saw consistent gains in students' reported sense of classroom community when we introduced these techniques on top of baseline practices for student engagement. Assigned seating and "personal tutors", both in class and out of class, appear to have particular impact. These techniques are fairly easy to implement and can be achieved without additional staff resources. Future work will study the effects of these strategies on other metrics of student success, including retention and class performance.

8 ACKNOWLEDGEMENTS

We thank the participants in our study and the anonymous reviewers for their valuable feedback. This project was supported in part by the National Science Foundation, grant DUE-1451521.

REFERENCES

[1] C. Alvarado, M. Minnes, and L. Porter. 2017. Micro-Classes: A Structure for Improving Student Experience in Large Classes. In *SIGCSE '17*. 21–26.

[2] M. E. Benedict and J. Hoag. 2004. Seating Location in Large Lectures: Are Seating Preferences or Location Related to Course Performance? *The Journal of Economic Education* 35, 3 (2004), 215–231.

[3] G.M. Besana and L. Dettori. 2004. Together is Better: Strengthening the Confidence of Women in Computer Science via a Learning Community. *J. Comput. Sci. Coll.* 19, 5 (2004), 130–139.

[4] J. Campbell and M. Horton, D.and Craig. 2016. Factors for Success in Online CS1. In *ITiCSE '16*. 320–325.

[5] C.S. Dweck. 2007. The perils and promises of praise. *ASCD* 65, 2 (2007), 34–39.

[6] O.T. Lenning and L.H. Ebbers. 1990. The Powerful Potential of Learning Communities: Improving Education for the Future. *ASHE-ERIC Higher Education Report* 26, 6 (1990).

[7] S. Malcom and M. Feder. 2016. *Barriers and Opportunities for 2-Year and 4-Year STEM Degrees: Systemic Change to Support Students' Diverse Pathways*. National Academies Press, Chapter 5, 59–82.

[8] C. McDowell, L. Werner, H. Bullock, and J. Fernald. 2002. The Effects of Pair-programming on Performance in an Introductory Programming Course. In *SIGCSE '02*. 38–42.

[9] A. McGowan, P. Hanna, D. Greer, and J. Busch. 2017. Learning to Program: Choose Your Lecture Seat Carefully!. In *ITiCSE '17*. 4–9.

[10] C. Mulryan-Kyne. 2010. Teaching large classes at college and university level: challenges and opportunities. *Teaching in Higher Education* 15, 2 (2010), 175–185.

[11] C. O'Neal, M. Wright, C. Cook, T. Perorazio, and J. Purkiss. 2007. The impact of teaching assistants on student retention in the sciences: Lessons for TA training. *J. of College Science Teaching* 36, 5 (2007), 24–29.

[12] L. Porter, D. Bouvier, Q. Cutts, S. Grissom, C.B. Lee, R. McCartney, D. Zingaro, and B. Simon. 2016. A Multi-institutional Study of Peer Instruction in Introductory Computing. In *SIGCSE '16*. 358–363.

[13] L. Porter and B. Simon. 2013. Retaining Nearly One-third More Majors with a Trio of Instructional Best Practices in CS1. In *SIGCSE '13*.

[14] A.P. Rovai. 2002. Development of an instrument to measure classroom community. *The Internet and Higher Education* 5, 3 (2002).

[15] A.P. Rovai. 2002. Sense of community, perceived cognitive learning, and persistence in asynchronous learning networks. *The Internet and Higher Education* 5 (2002).

[16] A.J. Smith, K.E. Boyer, J. Forbes, S. Heckman, and K. Mayer-Patel. 2017. My Digital Hand: A Tool for Scaling Up One-to-One Peer Teaching in Support of Computer Science Learning. In *SIGCSE '17*. 549–554.

[17] G.M. Walton, C. Logel, J.M. Peach, S.J. Spencer, and M.P. Zanna. 2015. Two brief interventions to mitigate a "chilly climate" transform women's experience, relationships, and achievement in engineering. *Journal of Educational Psychology* 107, 2 (2015), 468.

Holistic Approaches to Computer Science

Ali Erkan (Moderator)
Ithaca College
Ithaca, New York
aerkan@ithaca.edu

John Barr
Ithaca College
Ithaca, New York
barr@ithaca.edu

Valerie Barr
Mount Holyoke College
South Hadley, Mass.
vbarr@mtholyoke.edu

Michael Goldweber
Xavier University
Cincinnati, Ohio
goldweber@xavier.edu

Deepak Kumar
Bryn Mawr College
Bryn Mawr, Pennsylvania
dkumar@cs.brynmawr.edu

CCS CONCEPTS

• **Networks → Control path algorithms**; • **Theory of computation → Data structures design and analysis**; • **Applied computing → Education**;

KEYWORDS

Education, Holistic, ACM Guidelines, Operating Systems, Networks, Algorithms

ACM Reference format:
Ali Erkan (Moderator), John Barr, Valerie Barr, Michael Goldweber, and Deepak Kumar. 2018. Holistic Approaches to Computer Science. In *Proceedings of The 49th ACM Technical Symposium on Computer Science Education, Baltimore, MD, USA, Feb. 21–24, 2018 (SIGCSE '18)*, 2 pages.
https://doi.org/10.1145/3159450.3159614

1 SUMMARY

Computer science curricula has been well defined for many years through the publication of the Computer Science Curricula reports developed jointly by the two major professional societies, the Association for Computing Machinery (ACM) and the IEEE Computer Society. These documents define computer science curricula by providing knowledge areas and *course exemplars*. The most recent curriculum report, the Computer Science Curricula 2013 (CSC13 [1]), provides 18 knowledge areas (KAs). Though it stresses that KAs do not necessary represent courses, computer science departments have traditionally created courses around the KAs. Indeed, the *course exemplars* presented in the CSC13 report, for the most part, center around KAs.

This separation of concepts into courses introduces a number of deficiencies in a student's education. In particular, fields within computer science end up appearing to be silo-ed and students lack an understanding of interrelationship between sub-fields. For example, without a comprehension of interrelationships, students may fail to find or modify algorithms to meet efficiency constraints in real-world software.

SIGCSE '18, Feb. 21–24, 2018, Baltimore, MD, USA

ACM ISBN 978-1-4503-5103-4/18/02.
https://doi.org/10.1145/3159450.3159614

We can say that this deficiency is likely to be addressed after years of experience (or graduate school) but, as educators, it is important for us to address it in a more deliberate and timely fashion. A deliberate approach, for example, could be taken in a capstone course or project that requires students to draw upon concepts from several fields. Such a course, however, would come late in a student's development and would therefore be unlikely to fundamentally change a student's understanding of computer science.

This panel will present *holistic* approaches to the cross-disciplinary problem that introduce students to the concept before their final year. Some of the approaches are integrated throughout the curriculum and some involve stand-alone courses, but every approach requires students to draw upon concepts from multiple KAs to solve problems. The panelists are from liberal arts institutions where cross- disciplinarity is prized and a natural part of the culture. Each panelist represents a different curricula approach that she or he will briefly describe before we engage the audience in a discussion of the problems, approaches, and experiences with providing holistic learning to students.

2 DEEPAK KUMAR

At Bryn Mawr College we have been deliberate about the design of our curriculum with the perspective of computer science as a liberal art. Inherently this requires us to take a more holistic approach to the design of courses, course content, and even major/minor requirements. We have identified several design patterns in our curriculum design that go well beyond instantiating a prescription of KAs in curricular recommendations [2]. Some of these include: participation in college-wide interdisciplinary first-year seminars; creating upper-level interdisciplinary courses; humanizing of core computer science courses; breaking down rigid course boundaries; etc. These design patterns have guided us in the development of courses offered in the department. In this panel, I will attempt to summarize these ideas and provide examples of concrete courses.

One of the courses we have created, is titled, *Algorithms: Design & Practice*. This advanced junior/senior-level course is offered in addition to the standard course on *Analysis of Algorithms*. The course focuses on the practice of algorithms: the design, application, implementation, testing, tuning, writing about, talking about, ethics, and presentation of algorithms. Students work on weekly programming assignments and then formally present their results. Assignments are designed to solve real life problems, perform optimizations, measure their performance, make trade-offs, and discuss their work with other students in a formal setting. The course provides an opportunity for students to enhance their knowledge of algorithms, technical writing, presentation, empirical testing, etc. and serves as an opportunity for professional development.

3 VALERIE BARR

As we see increased interest in Data Science, and the role of CS departments in delivering some portion of that curriculum, we will all face the question of how to deliver courses that can appeal to a broad swath of students who have limited CS background. Experience at Union College (my former department) exposes relevant concerns. The Union CS department created a number of courses that follow the CS-1 courses, do not require data structures, and present an alternate pathway for students majoring in another discipline. The primary goal of these courses is to demonstrate the extent to which computing can be applied in ways appropriate for and useful to other disciplines. Example topics included natural language processing, modeling and simulation, data visualization, web programming, bioinformatics, etc.. Because of the minimal prerequisites, these courses have to take a holistic approach with a degree of "just in time" teaching. Various topics normally found in data structures and discrete math courses must be taught so that students are equipped to do assignments and projects.

There are a number of problems with this accessible and holistic approach. First, many of the courses are very attractive to CS majors (CS majors are allowed to count toward the major one course in this group). This frequently leads to tension about course pace and complexity of assignments. Second, in some cases it is difficult to cover the material in a sufficiently rigorous fashion when students have limited background (particularly true in NLP). As a result, the department is now reconsidering the curricular placement of these courses as well as the best ways to address responsibilities to students from outside the CS major.

4 MICHAEL GOLDWEBER

It is precisely because of the observed silo effect of our relatively standard, liberal arts oriented curriculum at Xavier University that I have begun experimenting with a junior-senior level topics course titled "Open-Ended Problem Solving." This course, whose prerequisites are *Algorithms and Data Structures* along with *Software Engineering*, has no required content to be covered or mastered. The primary goal is to practice algorithmic problem solving.

Incorporating the principles from community-engaged learning, the instructor, working with community partners, selects 1-2 open problem to focus on. Students, in hackathon fashion engage in an ideation phase. Once there are n reasonably developed ideas, there is a voting phase to select the two most popular solutions. Finally, students, through preference voting, get sorted into teams.

Teams then self-organize and take most of the balance of the semester to develop a solution to their problem. A key goal is that the problem is such that students need to draw not only upon the concepts they have learned from previous courses (e.g. Algorithms and Data Structures, Databases, Networking), but to also both identify and then self-learn new technologies, algorithms, and concepts that they believe are needed for their solutions. Coping with not knowing what to do next, or even how to start, is a key experience. This past semester, students working in two teams tackled two different aspects of the heroin epidemic that is ravishing Ohio in general and Xavier's local neighborhood in particular.

One difficulty that has been identified is with assessment. The learning outcomes for this course are centered around synthesis (algorithms, data structures, and technologies are tools to be employed when appropriate), and a holistic approach to problem solving. Since these are very difficult to measure, assessment tends toward measuring both the quantity and quality of students' participation.

5 JOHN BARR

Like Bryn Mawr, Ithaca College has been deliberate in our approach to the problem of holistic learning in computer science. Our approach is designed around the reading of technical and research papers in a senior level course called *Algorithms + Organization = Systems*[3]. This course is designed to use research papers as the glue between topics covered in our algorithms course and concepts presented in standard systems oriented courses (such as *Operating Systems, Architecture and Computer Networks*). Students in this course are expected to have taken an algorithms course and a computer organization course, but no other systems courses (such as operating systems or networks). The papers in the course cover algorithms used in one of three areas: operating systems, networks, and architecture.

The overarching purpose of this course is to help students experience the interdependency of two areas of computer science, algorithms and systems, by seeing that algorithms must be implemented in and adapted for a particular systems context. Students are not expected to fully grasp the systems concepts presented in the papers but rather to understand that algorithms can only be successfully implemented when the systems context is considered. In the course, students learn the art of reading and writing technical/research papers and complete several projects that help them understand how algorithms are evaluated in systems contexts.

This course was offered in the fall of 2015 and is again being run in fall 2017. Assessment of the fall 2015 offering of the course indicated that students made gains in their understanding and appreciation of intra-disciplinary connections and also became more adept at designing empirical experiments and reading/writing technical papers.

REFERENCES

[1] ACM and Association for Computing Machinery IEEE Computer Society Joint Task Force on Computing Curricula. 2013. *Computer Science Curricula 2013: Curriculum Guidelines for Undergraduate Degree Programs in Computer Science.* ACM, New York, NY, USA. 999133.

[2] D. Blank and D. Kumar. 2003. Patterns of Curriculum Design. In *Informatics Curricula and Teaching Methods*, L. Cassel and R. A. Reis (Eds.). Kluwer Academic Publishers, 3300 AA Dordrecht, the Netherlands.

[3] Ali Erkan and John Barr. 2016. Algorithms + Organization = Systems. In *Proceedings of the 2016 ACM Conference on Innovation and Technology in Computer Science Education (ITiCSE '16)*. ACM, New York, NY, USA, 65–70. https://doi.org/10.1145/2899415.2899458

Integrating Social Good into CS Education

Douglas H. Fisher
Vanderbilt University
Computer Science
Nashville, TN 37235
douglas.h.fisher
@vanderbilt.edu

Jacqueline Cameron
Atlas Institute
University of Colorado
Boulder, CO 80309
1-412-897-9324
jackiejcameron@gmail.com

Tamara Clegg
University of Maryland
College of Education and
iSchool
College Park, MD 20742
1-301-405-2930
tclegg@umd.edu

Stephanie August
National Science Foundation
EHR/Division of
Undergraduate Education
Alexandria, VA 22314
1-703-292-5128
saugust@nsf.gov

CCS Concepts

• **Computing Education→Collaborative and social computing and tools**

Keywords

computing education; social good; informal education; K-12 education, higher education; sustainability; citizen science; citizenship; social justice; privacy and security

ACM Reference format:

D. Fisher, J. Cameron, T. Clegg, and S. August. 2018. Integrating Social Good into CS Education. In *SIGCSE '18: 49th ACM Technical Symposium on Computer Science Education, Feb. 21–24, 2018, Baltimore, MD, USA.* ACM, NY, NY, USA, 6 pages. https://doi.org/10.1145/3159450.3159622

1. SUMMARY

Computing for social good has become a common topic in computing circles, with professional organizations and conferences sponsoring discussions on the relevance of 'social good' material for computer science research [e.g., 1] and for education [e.g., 12,13,18].

This panel brings together instructors interested in and offering computing courses with exercises and projects on socially important themes, including environmental sustainability, protecting democratic processes, citizen science and science identity among young people, privacy and security, medicine and health, and disaster response. Computing courses with a primary focus on 'social good' applications for computing are also important and relevant.

The presentations cover material that integrates social good into CS education. Additionally, we will summarize past recommendations for infusing societal good applications by other authors into CS curricula [e.g., 7, 9, 10, 11, 12, 13, 18]. Audience participation is an important aspect of this special session, because we don't imagine that our coverage will be complete.

In addition to talking about subject matter ideas for assignments and courses, we address issues relating to "difficult conversations" [e.g., 8] regarding applications of social good in CS classes, because there are opportunities for disagreements between instructors, students, and parents (in the case of K-12).

ACM ISBN 978-1-4503-5103-4/18/02.
https://doi.org/10.1145/3159450.3159622

Finally, one panelist (August) addresses funding possibilities, particularly from NSF, for the infusion of social good into CS curricula. Social Good engages a cross-cutting, interdisciplinary audience, has implications for broadening participation, and prepares today's students for tomorrow's workforce, as we learn to develop and encourage practices that increase computing's bang for the buck relative to societal concerns.

2. IMPACT OF SOCIAL GOOD IN CS

Social good can be used to contextualize CS methods and concepts, which has positive implications for CS education.

- Students are often interested in making an impact, and that can be harnessed as a way to more deeply engage them. Many students are motivated by social relevance, and so inclusion of social good material can attract students, including underrepresented groups, into computer science [9, 13, 14].
- Social good contextualization increases opportunities for exercising communication skills and for considering the implications of computing, both of which are ABET-dictated outcomes for CS students:
  - "(h) An ability to communicate effectively with a range of audiences" [5]
  - "(g) An ability to analyze the local and global impact of computing on individuals, organizations, and society" [5]
- Our students will have opportunities to contribute to society, and we have a duty as instructors to prepare them for real-world scenarios.

3. AREAS AND TYPES OF INTEGRATION

The panel addresses several areas of 'social good' coverage explicitly, including environmental sustainability, protecting democratic processes, citizen science and science identity among young people, privacy and security, medicine and health, and disaster response, suggested both by panelist experience and prior proposals [e.g., 13].

Social good can be infused into formal CS curricula at multiple levels [10, 11], including fine-grained component-level integration of exercises, projects, and other assessments. For example, one panelist (Fisher) describes a database project that reverse-engineers the database necessary to support the Oberlin Dorm Energy monitoring project [17], which introduces students to issues of energy and environment, as well as exercising core competencies in database, and communication skills. Platforms for curating social good exercises in CS can include Wikibooks [11] and Nifty Assignments [15], as but two examples.

Course-level integration introduces whole courses that are focused on social good topics for computer science. These can be special topics courses and independent study courses. One panelist (Cameron) describes a theater production on data ethics as an independent study for CS students, which integrated both accessibility and sustainability lessons into an HCI curriculum. Courses in computing and sustainability have been offered at a fair number of institutions [10], and CS courses with still broader treatments of social good have been offered as well [6].

In addition to infusion of social good applications into computing curricula, computing can be integrated into courses in other disciplines, such as integrating computational thinking into a social justice course (Cameron). This can also extend to informal learning activities, such as learning experiences and programs to support children's scientific inquiry engagement in everyday life contexts, to include topics at the nexus of computing and the social good [3, 4]. One panelist (Clegg) addresses how interactive computing is being used as a vehicle for informal education in the NatureNet project to promote conservation among college undergraduates [2]. One panelist (August) will describe projects recently funded by NSF that integrate social good into both formal and informal computer science education and suggest how convergence plays a role in these efforts and elsewhere.

4. CONCLUDING REMARKS

In sum, the special session spotlights specific opportunities for incorporation of social good topics into computing education, as well as the potential for incorporation of computing into education in other disciplines. The session discusses some of the difficulties of including social good material in a classroom setting when disagreements are present, and we explore potential funding opportunities as well.

5. ACKNOWLEDGEMENTS

Fisher was supported by NSF 1521672 Collaborative Research: CompSustNet: Expanding the Horizons of Computational Sustainability. NatureNet (Cameron, Clegg) was funded by NSF 1423207 to U Maryland, 1221513 and 1423212 to the UNC Charlotte, and 1423338 to the U Colorado at Boulder. Cameron was also supported by John S. and James L. Knight Foundation.

6. REFERENCES

[1] Artificial Intelligence for Social Good, CRA/CCC, http://cra.org/ccc/events/ai-social-good/

[2] Boston, C., Clegg, T., Pauw, D., Preece, J., Warrick, E., Abdellahi, S., Christian, T., Grace, K., Maher, M. L., Cameron, J., and Yeh, T. (2017). Supporting Environmental Stewards' Needs with Technology. In Companion of the 2017 ACM Conference on Computer Supported Cooperative Work and Social Computing (CSCW '17 Companion). ACM, New York, NY, USA, 151-154.

[3] Clegg, T. (2013). Keynote: The Potential of Technology for Enhancing Scientific Disposition Development. Presented at the 2nd Annual Learning Science Workshop: Research and Innovation for Enhancing Achievement and Equity. Carnegie Mellon University, Pittsburgh, PA.

[4] Clegg, T., Preece, J., Pauw, D., Warrick, E., and Boston, C. (2016). Environmental Learning through the Lens of Affinity Spaces: Transforming Community Members into a Community Force. International Conference of the Learning Sciences Proceedings, 2016, pp. 851-854.

[5] Criteria for Accrediting Computing Programs, 2017-2018, IEEE ABET, http://www.abet.org/accreditation/accreditation-criteria/criteria-for-accrediting-computing-programs-2017-2018/

[6] CS + Social Good, Stanford University http://125.stanford.edu/cssocial-good/

[7] Cui, Y. (2010) Integrating Sustainability into Undergraduate Computing Education, In SIGCSE-10, ACM, Retrieved from http://dl.acm.org/citation.cfm?id=1734439.

[8] Difficult Dialogues, Center for Teaching, Vanderbilt University https://cft.vanderbilt.edu/guides-sub-pages/difficult-dialogues/

[9] Fisher, D. (2008). AI and Developing Socially-Engaged Computational Thinkers, AAAI Spring Symposium http://www.vuse.vanderbilt.edu/~fisherdh/socially-engaged-computational-thinkers/SS08FisherD.pdf

[10] Fisher, D., Bian, Z., Chen, S. (2016) Incorporating Sustainability into Computing Education, IEEE Intelligent Systems, Vol. 31, Issue 5. 93-96. And follow-up https://s3.amazonaws.com/vu-my/wp-content/uploads/sites/484/2017/06/02093224/CompSustNetTechReport.pdf

[11] Fisher, D., Dilkina, B., Eaton, E., Gomes, C. (2012).Incorporating Computational Sustainability into AI Education through a Freely-Available, Collectively-Composed Supplementary Lab Text. In Proceedings of the Third AAAI Symposium on Educational Advances in Artificial Intelligence https://www.seas.upenn.edu/~eeaton/papers/Fisher2012IncorporatingEAAI.pdf

[12] Goldweber, M., Barr, J., Patitsas, E. (2013) Computer Science Education for Social Good, Proceedings of SIGCSE'13 The 44th ACM Symposium on Computer Science Education (pp. 15-16) https://dl.acm.org/citation.cfm?id=2445208

[13] Goldweber, M., Barr, J., Clear, T., Davoli, R., Mann, S., Patitsas, E., Portnoff, S. (2012). A Framework for Enhancing the Social Good in Computing Education: A Values Approach. In ITiCSE-WGR '12 Proceedings of the final reports on Innovation and technology in computer science education 2012 working groups, pp. 16-38 https://dl.acm.org/citation.cfm?id=2426639

[14] Margolis, J., Fisher, A. (2002). Unlocking the Clubhouse. The MIT Press, Cambridge, MA.

[15] Parlante, N. (ongoing) Nifty Assignments Retrieved from http://nifty.stanford.edu.

[16] Nature Net (ongoing) http://research.nature-net.org/

[17] Petersen, J., Shunturov, V., Janda,K., Platt, G., Weinberger, K. (2011). "Dormitory residents reduce electricity consumption when exposed to real-time visual feedback and incentives", International Journal of Sustainability in Higher Education, Vol. 8, No. 1 http://www.emeraldinsight.com/doi/pdfplus/10.1108/14676370710717562

[18] SIGCAS Symposium on Computing for the Social Good: http://www.sigcas.org/sigcas-symposium-on-computing-for-the-social-good-educational-practice

What Would You Say if... Responding to Microaggressions, Bias, and Other Nonsense

Colleen M. Lewis
Harvey Mudd College
301 Platt Blvd
Claremont, CA 91711
lewis@cs.hmc.edu

Catherine Ashcraft
NCWIT
University of Colorado, Boulder
Boulder, CO 80309
catherine.ashcraft@ colorado.edu

Kyla McMullen
University of Florida
432 Newell Dr.
Gainesville, FL 32611
drkyla@ufl.edu

Keywords
Microaggressions; bias; inclusive teaching

ACM Reference format:
Colleen M. Lewis, Catherine Ashcraft, and Kyla McMullen. 2018. What Would You Say if ... Responding to Microaggressions, Bias, and Other Nonsense. In *SIGCSE '18: 49th ACM Technical Symposium on Computer Science Education, Feb. 21–24, 2018, Baltimore, MD, USA*. ACM, NY, NY, USA, 6 pages. https://doi.org/10.1145/3159450.3159458

1. SUMMARY
Many SIGCSE attendees are committed to inclusive teaching practices and creating an inclusive culture within their classrooms; yet, advocating for and sustaining these initiatives may require having difficult conversations with our colleagues and students. Understandably, many faculty are unsure about how to talk about sensitive topics such as race and gender with their colleagues and students. Research suggests that practicing some of these difficult conversations is essential to achieve the goals of inclusive teaching and culture. Most SIGCSE attendees probably use active learning throughout their teaching, but we rarely see active learning at SIGCSE - let's try it! In this interactive session, attendees will learn strategies for responding to bias in academic settings. Attendees will then practice those strategies in small groups. This will be facilitated by playing two rounds of a research-based game learning approach developed by the NSF project CSTeachingTips.org (#1339404), which has been tested in group of 200 teaching assistants. This is the fifth iteration of the game-learning approach and all attendees will receive a printed copy of the game and a link to download and print more copies.

2. OBJECTIVE
The special session seeks to help attendees broaden participation and create more inclusive environment by building their capacity to address and respond to bias in their academic environments. Most importantly, attendees can replicate this session at their institution because all materials will be provided online.

3. OUTLINE OF ACTIVITIES
3.1 Group Formation
As attendees arrive, they will be asked to create groups of three to six people. Before the session starts, the presenters will circulate to encourage attendees to be proactive in forming and splitting groups as needed. This will be familiar to most attendees' likely experience in organizing students into groups. This group formation will also encourage faculty to form connections before the session begins.

ACM ISBN 978-1-4503-5103-4/18/02.
DOI: https://doi.org/10.1145/3159450.3159634

3.2 Presentation of Session Goals (5 minutes)
The session will begin with a brief introduction by the presenters to the structure and goals of the session.

Session Goals:

- Develop and practice strategies for responding to bias or problematic statements in the classroom.
- Practice explaining the benefits of inclusive teaching strategies to faculty and students who may be skeptical.
- Create connections among SIGCSE attendees committed to inclusive teaching practices.

After reviewing the goals for the session, the presenters will explain the first interactive portion of the special session. Groups will be provided a printed copy of the instructions and these instructions will be displayed on the screen for easy reference.

3.3 Interactive Portion 1 (15 minutes)
Groups will be asked to do a quick round of introductions before beginning the first interactive portion of the game.

In addition to the instructions, each group will have a set of eight cards. Each card addresses a common teaching challenge such as "What would you do if one student seems to dominate class discussion?" One member of the group, the judge, draws a card and reads the question aloud. Each of the other group members are asked how they would respond. After each of the group members have responded or passed, the person who read the card picks their favorite answer. Each card also has a brief paragraph to read aloud before moving on to the next card. This paragraph describes one possible strategy for responding and a bit of background about how this relates to creating and sustaining an inclusive classroom climate. The role of the judge rotates between each card.

Cards will have the following questions, which all begin "What would you do if..."

- students never ask questions during class?
- a student is always late and seems disengaged in class?
- one student shouts out answers to your questions?
- during class a student with a lot of prior CS experience asks questions about advanced topics outside of the scope of the class content?

- some students did very poorly on a recent exam?
- barely any students are asking for help outside of class?
- a student says that they don't know how to get started when approaching a problem?
- students have varied prior CS experience in your class?

Groups will vary in the speed that they progress through each of the cards and we expect few groups to get through more than three or four cards. With funding provided by Harvey Mudd College, we will bring enough sets of cards for each attendee to have a copy. This will allow everyone who wants a set to have one and some attendees to be able to take multiple sets home.

The attendees may all have experience with these scenarios, and they can learn from each other to better be able to promote an inclusive classroom community.

3.4 Introduction to Strategies for Responding to Bias (15 minutes)

The presenters will first summarize strategies for responding to the scenarios above and will emphasize the two themes:

- **Empathize:** Assume that there is a reason for students' behavior when they seem unengaged or are pursuing ineffective learning strategies.
- **Promote belonging:** Respond to behavior that may unintentionally signal to students that they don't belong in CS. This may be particularly important for students with less experience or who do not identify with the stereotypes of computer scientists.

The presenters will then introduce the following themes that are helpful in responding to bias:

- **Challenge stereotypes:** Stereotypes can have negative consequences for students. Even seemingly positive stereotypes, like "Asians are good at math," are still problematic because they ignore individual variation, create unfair expectations, and may implicitly insult another group of people.
- **Change structures:** Sometimes initiatives to promote inclusions in CS focus on strategies for how students can respond to bias that they face. While these may be helpful strategies, they may unintentionally send the message that the student is as fault. Instead, we should focus on changing the structures that lead to bias or other forms of marginalization.

3.5 Interactive Portion 2 (15 minutes)

Attendees will remain in the same groups for the second interactive portion. The flow of the game will be identical and the only difference will be the content of the cards. This round will more directly address bias and issues of inclusivity with the following prompts that begin "What would you say if your colleague said..."

- We want diversity, but we don't want to water down the content.
- Students should just tell me if I say something that offends them.
- The faculty candidate didn't seem like they'd be a good fit for the department culture.
- Women just aren't interested in CS.
- There are so few Black and Latinx students in CS, it is a lot easier for them to get CS jobs.
- Programs for certain groups are divisive and unfair to others.
- I would think women would like to have classes with lots of men. Lots of dating options!
- Brenda just needs to learn to be more confident.
- Rochelle just needs to be more professional.

3.6 Q&A (25 minutes)

In the last twenty_five minutes, the presenters will answer questions from attendees. The presenters will also highlight how their responses might vary based upon their identities, the power dynamics, and context of any given statement.

4. PRESENTERS

Colleen Lewis is an assistant professor of CS at Harvey Mudd College where typically 40% to 50% of the CS majors identify as women. Colleen Lewis researches how people learn CS and how people feel about learning CS. Her research seeks to identify effective teaching practices for creating equitable learning spaces where all students have the opportunity to learn. Lewis is the PI for CSTeachingTips.org, a NSF-sponsored project (#1339404) for disseminating effective CS teaching practices.

Catherine Ashcraft is Director of Research and a Senior Research Scientist with the National Center for Women & Information Technology (NCWIT) at the University of Colorado Boulder. Her research focuses on issues related to gender, diversity, and technology; organizational change and curriculum reform; and popular culture, media representations, and youth identity (especially as it relates to race-ethnicity, gender, class, sexuality). She also has taught, presented at national and international venues on these topics, and led bias-busting sessions for a variety of audiences for the past 15 years. She also has worked with a variety of government entities, advocating for CS/IT/ICT education and workplace policy.

Kyla McMullen is an Assistant Professor of Computer and Information Science and Engineering at the University of Florida. Dr. McMullen is the leader of the SoundPAD Laboratory at the University of Florida, which focuses on the Perception, Application, and Development of 3D audio in various contexts. Dr. McMullen also researches programming self-efficacy as an effect of IDE design, paired-programming, and active learning methodologies.

5. SUITABILITY FOR A SPECIAL SESSION

This innovative and interactive format would only be possible as a special session. This special session could be particularly helpful for new attendees so that they can meet other attendees. The session provides the important opportunity for attendees to become better prepared to address microaggressions, bias, and other nonsense at their institution.

6. ACKNOWLEDGEMENTS

The development of CSTeachingTips.org and the special session content were funded by NSF grant #1339404.

NSF/IEEE-TCPP Curriculum Initiative on Parallel and Distributed Computing – Status Report

Sushil K. Prasad
Georgia State University
25 Park Place, Suite 717
Atlanta, GA 30303-2904 USA
+1 678-793-3953
sprasad@gsu.edu

Charles C. Weems
University of Massachusetts
Amherst, MA 01003-4610
+1 413-545-3163
weems@cs.umass.edu

John P. Dougherty
Haverford College
370 Lancaster Avenue
Haverford, PA 19041 USA
+1 610-896-4204
jd@cs.haverford.edu

Debzani Deb
Winston-Salem State University
601 S. Martin Luther King Jr. Drive
Winston-Salem, NC 27110 USA
+1 336-750-2496
debd@wssu.edu

Keywords
Parallel and distributed computing; education; curriculum guidelines; status report

ACM Reference format:
Sushil K. Prasad, Charles C. Weems, John P. Dougherty, and Debzani Deb. 2018. NSF/IEEE-TCPP Curriculum Initiative on Parallel and Distributed Computing – Status Report. In *SIGCSE '18: 49th ACM Technical Symposium on Computer Science Education, Feb. 21–24, 2018, Baltimore, MD, USA.* ACM, NY, NY, USA, 6 pages.
https://doi.org/10.1145/3159450.3159632

1. SUMMARY

A working group proposed a curriculum in 2010 for computer science and engineering undergraduates on parallel and distributed computing (PDC), with the goal that every undergraduate in computing and engineering related fields should be exposed to courses and experiences in PDC-related topics. This group produced an edited book of contributed chapters on teaching PDC topics in the undergraduate curriculum in computing and engineering [1], and also provided updates to the SIGCSE community in 2011 [2] and again in 2014 [3]. In 2017, an expanded working group, including some early adopters, has undertaken a revision of this curriculum, especially considering the emerging aspects of Big Data, power, and distributed computing and identifying a set of cross-cutting topics, as well as formulating concrete exemplars for various PDC topics, modules, and courses.

The proposed session will provide an opportunity for the computing education community to interact with the working group on parallel and distributed computing education. Specifically, this session is intended to (i) brief the community on the proposed PDC curriculum updates toward its second version, (ii) obtain feedback from the community on the updated curriculum draft, (iii) engage the community for future early adoption activities (with seed grants) and for contributions to the Center for Parallel and Distributed Computing Curriculum Development and Educational Resources (CDER) courseware site and in authoring and reviewing book series contributions, and (iv) to further develop the community of interest.

ACM ISBN 978-1-4503-5103-4/18/02.
https://doi.org/10.1145/3159450.3159632

2. OBJECTIVE

Background: CDER is an NSF supported project to develop curricular guidance and supporting materials to facilitate preparation of computer science and computer engineering undergraduates with the knowledge of PDC. The CDER working group is composed of researchers from academia, government and industry. This preparation is presently considered an essential part of a bachelor's degree in computing, and is expected to grow in importance and in number of applications in the future. Thus, CDER provides instructor resources such as a sample curriculum and an edited textbook, as well as reports from about one hundred early adopter institutions from around the world. The guideline influenced and was referenced by the ACM 2013 Computer Science Curriculum [4] and the working group is now working closely with the CC2020 ACM/IEEE Computer Science Curriculum Joint Task Force. The current guideline emphasizes on four sub areas such as architecture, programming, algorithms, and cross-cutting topics and various PDC topics and subtopics are organized around this categorization along with their level of coverage (*i.e.,* Bloom Classification). The guideline further identifies where in current core courses these topics could be introduced, and has provided examples of how they might be taught.

During a series of recent workshops in 2017, an expanded working group recognized the need for reorganization and prioritization within areas. This special session will focus on the rationale for the proposed reorganization involving three major areas (namely, architecture, programming, and algorithm) and several emerging aspects within each area, such as Big Data, power and distributed computing as well as cross-cutting topics and exemplars within each area. The working group recognized that distributed computing was not as well covered as parallel in the original curriculum, and that we should strengthen it in this current revision by considering it as a separate aspect within each three major areas. The group also realized that parallel and distributed computing is a matter of paramount importance for mitigating scaling and efficiency challenges for the Big Data applications and therefore emphasizes must be placed in the revised curriculum to tackle related issues. Considering the importance of power and energy efficiency in the advancement of future exascale systems, the group agreed to cover these aspects in all three primary areas under the revised curriculum. The working group further intends to solicit important feedback from the SIGCSE community to guide and improve this revision.

Why is the proposed session important? The proposed session, which would be our third appearance at SIGCSE, should help us to promote our vision of experts from various agencies and disciplines coming together periodically to find effective (and perhaps novel) ways to inject PDC into the computing curriculum. Given the diversity of institutions preparing students in computing, CDER is working to provide flexible yet practical resources that can be applied throughout these institutions. The feedback received will help us to see which approaches and methods have worked up to this point, and that will direct how we will proceed in the future.

3. OUTLINE

The following outline is proposed for this special session

1. Introduction to the Curriculum Initiative and Revision – 5 minutes
2. Updated Curriculum and Rationale for updates in Architecture, Programming and Algorithms Topics – 10 minutes
3. Rationale for Emerging Aspects – 10 minutes
   a. Big Data
   b. Power
   c. Distributed Computing
4. Rationale for Cross-cutting Topics and Exemplars – 10 minutes
5. Discussion and Q&A – 30 minutes
6. Feedback Collection – 10 minutes

4. EXPECTATIONS

The intended audience consists (i) early adopters and/or authors of the book project and (ii) a wider group of computing and engineering educators (and perhaps students) who are interested in PDC, or who teach related courses (in particular, CS0, CS1 and CS2), or are interested in adopting some of the PDC topics. There has already been interest from industry, including from chipmakers and parallel software and tool creators (*e.g.*, Intel, NVidia, RedHat and IBM); therefore, some attendees from industry are expected as well. A similar status report session 2014 [3] drew approximately 50 attendees in addition to the part of the working group itself; we anticipate a similar amount of interest for the session proposed here.

We plan to promote this session (and increase attendance) via the SIGCSE listserv. We will have summary materials of the curricula with links to more complete online resources at CDER. Finally, we plan to solicit feedback via questionnaire during the session. This feedback will be important and timely to the group.

5. SUITABILITY FOR A SPECIAL SESSION

In this session, multiple committee members will cover the current curriculum, its yearlong activities, our proposed revision, and the current and future roadmap. The session also intends to discuss and collect direct feedback (via questionnaire) from the community, which will influence our subsequent round of revisions. The format and organization of the proposed session such as presentations followed by questions and discussions, and finally the collection of completed questionnaires is not appropriate for a conventional symposium session. A special session that spans for 75 minutes will properly accommodate the amount of material we plan to cover and discuss, as well as obtain critical feedback from the community.

6. ACKNOWLEDGEMENTS

This initiative is partially supported by IEEE TCPP, Intel, nVIDIA and IBM.

7. REFERENCES

[1] Prasad, S.K., Gupta, A., Rosenberg, A.L., Sussman, A. and Weems, C.C. eds., 2015. *Topics in Parallel and Distributed Computing: Introducing Concurrency in Undergraduate Courses.* Morgan Kaufmann.

[2] Prasad, S.K., Chtchelkanova, A.Y., Das, S.K., Dehne, F., Gouda, M.G., Gupta, A., Jaja, J., Kant, K., La Salle, A., LeBlanc, R. and Lumsdaine, M., 2011, March. NSF/IEEE-TCPP curriculum initiative on parallel and distributed computing: core topics for undergraduates. In SIGCSE (Vol. 11, pp. 617-618).

[3] Prasad, S.K., Chtchelkanova, A., Gupta, A., Rosenberg, A., and Sussman, A. 2014. NSF/IEEE-TCPP curriculum initiative on parallel and distributed computing: core topics for undergraduates (abstract only). In *Proceedings of the 45th ACM technical symposium on Computer science education* (SIGCSE '14). ACM, New York, NY, USA, 735-735. DOI: http://dx.doi.org/10.1145/2538862.2544255

[4] Joint Task Force on Computing Curricula, Association for Computing Machinery (ACM) and IEEE Computer Society. 2013. *Computer Science Curricula 2013: Curriculum Guidelines for Undergraduate Degree Programs in Computer Science.* ACM, New York, NY, USA.

Teaching Computer Science in a Time of Opportunities and Challenges

Eric Roberts
Department of Computer Science
Stanford University
Stanford, CA, USA
eroberts@cs.stanford.edu

ABSTRACT

Academic computer science is at a critical juncture that offers both challenges and opportunities. More students than ever before are choosing to major in computer science and an even larger number of students are taking computer science courses in recognition of the fact that knowledge of computing is essential in the modern world. That interest, of course, is exciting. At the same time, most computer science departments are overwhelmed by the growing demand from students. In this talk, I draw on my own experience as a young faculty member in the similarly challenging 1980s to offer advice on how to make the most of the opportunities that are intrinsic to teaching in such a vibrant field.

Author Keywords

Computer Science Education

ACM Reference format:
Eric Roberts. 2018. Teaching Computer Science in a Time of Opportunities and Challenges. In *SIGCSE '18: 49th ACM Technical Symposium on Computer Science Education, Feb. 21–24, 2018, Baltimore, MD, USA.* ACM, NY, NY, USA, 1 page
https://doi.org/10.1145/3159450.3166086

BIOGRAPHY

After receiving his Ph.D. in Applied Mathematics from Harvard University in 1980, Eric Roberts taught at Wellesley College from 1980-85, where he organized and chaired the Computer Science Department. From 1985-90, he was a member of the research staff at Digital Equipment Corporation's Systems Research Center in Palo Alto, California, focusing on programming tools for multiprocessor architectures. In September 1990, Roberts joined the Stanford faculty, where he remained until he retired from teaching in 2017. He is now the Charles Simonyi Professor of Computer Science, emeritus, and a Bass University Fellow in Undergraduate Education.

From 1990 to 2002, Professor Roberts was Associate Chair and Director of Undergraduate Studies for Computer Science. In that capacity, he was the principal architect of Stanford's introductory programming sequence. He has written seven computer science textbooks that are used at many colleges and universities throughout the world. From 1998 to 2005, Roberts directed the Bermuda Project, which developed the computer science curriculum for Bermuda's public secondary schools.

Professor Roberts has been active in professional organizations dedicated to computer science education. He is a Fellow of both the Association of Computing Machinery (ACM) and the American Association for the Advancement of Science (AAAS). From 1998 to 2001, Roberts served as co-chair and principal editor for the ACM/IEEE-CS Joint Task Force on Computing Curricula 2001, which published a detailed set of curriculum guidelines in December 2001. He also chaired the ACM Java Task Force from 2003 to 2007.

In 2003, Roberts received the annual Award for Outstanding Contribution to Computer Science Education from the ACM's Special Interest Group in Computer Science Education (SIGCSE). In 2012, Roberts received both the Karl V. Karlstrom Outstanding Educator Award from the ACM and the Taylor Booth Education Award from the Institute for Electrical and Electronic Engineers Computer Society (IEEE-CS).

ACM ISBN 978-1-4503-5103-4/18/02.
https://doi.org/10.1145/3159450.3166086

Computational Thinking for All – An Experience Report on Scaling up Teaching Computational Thinking to All Students in a Major City in Sweden

Fredrik Heintz
Linköping University, Sweden
fredrik.heintz@liu.se

Linda Mannila
Linköping University, Sweden
linda.mannila@liu.se

CCS CONCEPTS

• **Social and professional topics → Computing education; K-12 education; Computational thinking;**

KEYWORDS

K-9 education, teacher professional development, digital competence, programming, computational thinking

ACM Reference Format:
Fredrik Heintz and Linda Mannila. 2018. Computational Thinking for All – An Experience Report on Scaling up Teaching Computational Thinking to All Students in a Major City in Sweden. In *SIGCSE '18: SIGCSE '18: The 49th ACM Technical Symposium on Computer Science Education, February 21–24, 2018, Baltimore , MD, USA.* ACM, New York, NY, USA, 6 pages. https://doi.org/10.1145/3159450.3159586

1 INTRODUCTION

The increased exposure to technology raises a need for understanding how the digital world works, in the same manner as we get to know the physical world. Consequently, during recent years, we have witnessed an active discussion surrounding the role of programming and computer science (CS) for everyone (see e.g. [6, 9, 13]). As a result, an increasing number of countries have introduced or are in the process of introducing CS in their school curriculum. For instance in Europe, the majority of countries (17 out of 21) taking part in a survey conducted by the European Schoolnet in 2015 reported doing so [1]. The way in which this is accomplished varies. Some countries focus on K-12 as a whole, whereas others primarily address either K-9 or grades 10-12. Some countries have introduced CS as a subject of its own (e.g. Computing in England [3]) while others have decided to integrate it with other subjects, by for instance making programming an interdisciplinary element throughout the curriculum (e.g. Finland [5]). The role of CS and information technology in school curricula has – in general – varied over the years, placing focus on different areas, ranging from using technology as a tool to learning how the computer works and how to use it to create programs. This has also been the case in Sweden.

SIGCSE '18, February 21–24, 2018, Baltimore , MD, USA

ACM ISBN 978-1-4503-5103-4/18/02...$15.00
https://doi.org/10.1145/3159450.3159586

Introducing new content in curricula affects many teachers. When the content is new, such as programming and digital competence, most of the teachers affected have no prior experience in teaching the content. Consequently there is a large need for professional development and training initiatives. In this paper we present our experience from a three year long project, aiming at training Swedish teachers (grades 1-9) in teaching programming and computational thinking.

Although the Swedish government decided on including programming in the curriculum as late as in March 2017, the discussion on this had already been vivid since around 2014. To those involved it was more a question of when this would happen, rather than if. As a result, many projects focusing on programming and digital competence at primary and lower secondary school, were initiated already several years ago. For instance, Sweden's innovation agency Vinnova funded several such projects already in 2014. One of these projects was "A model for computational thinking in Swedish primary school", which received renewed funding under the new project name "Computational thinking for all" in 2016. Both are lead by the authors of this paper.

The first project aimed at introducing programming and computational thinking to a small group of teachers, who then were to implement the ideas and plans created in their own classroom. The later project, built on the previous one, now involving a larger group of teachers, who were not only to implement the ideas in their own classroom, but also to spread it to other teachers at their schools.

Both projects took place in Sweden's fifth largest city, Linköping, as a collaborative effort between the Computer Science Department at Linköping University and Linköping Municipality. The university was responsible for the project and all the project activities, while the municipality took care of the administration at the city level and the contact with the teachers.

The rest of the paper is structured as follows. We start in Section 2 with a background on digital competence, programming and computational thinking in Swedish education. In Section 3, we present the first part of our project, the pilot study. In Section 4, the second and larger part of the project is presented. In Section 5, we discuss the lessons learned from the projects and in Section 6, we draw conclusions and give some recommendations for the future.

2 DIGITAL COMPETENCE IN SWEDISH K-9 EDUCATION

The role of computer science and IT in Swedish schools has varied throughout the years [10]. In fall 2015, the Swedish government gave the National Agency for Education (Skolverket) the task of preparing a proposal for K-12 education on how to better address the competences required in a digitalized society. In June 2016, Skolverket submitted a proposal putting a much stronger emphasis on digital competence and introducing both digital competence and programming as interdisciplinary traits. It also provides explicit formulations in subjects such as mathematics (programming, algorithmic thinking, and problem solving), technology (controlling physical artifacts) and social sciences (fostering aware and critical citizens in a digital society). In March 2017, the government accepted the proposal, which has to be implemented by fall 2018 at the latest. In October 2017, the government also decided on a National IT Strategy which was significantly weaker than the one Skolverket proposed in June 2016.

The Swedish school debate has in recent years circled around poor PISA results, difficulties in providing all children and youth with equal opportunities, and about modernizing the curriculum in order to meet future job market requirements. As "programmer" is the most common job in the capital Stockholm, and the need for software professionals is estimated to increase heavily both in Sweden and internationally, some have argued that the education system should teach programming in order to prepare young people for these jobs. Others, the authors of this paper included, believe that school should offer all students general preparation for any kind of work, and have therefore argued for digital competence as part of all-round-learning, including computational thinking as a set of general problem solving skill useful for all in the spirit of Jeannette Wing [14].

In 2012, the Swedish government established the Digitalization Committee (Digitaliseringskommissionen) with the task of providing guidelines for the future of work related to digitalization in Sweden. One of the committee's reports [4] highlights the need for the school system to put larger focus on digital competence. The report explicitly points out the need for including programming in the curriculum as part of existing subjects. As a result of the discussion around schools, programming and CS as part of all-round learning, persons representing school, universities and industry engaged in voluntary initiatives to help overcome the lack of CS in Swedish basic education. Teacherhack (http://teacherhack.com) is a non-profit organization aiming at inspiring "teachers to hack the current curriculum (Lgr 11) to include the essential skills that students need in a digital world". The Teacherhack website provides reviews of all subjects in Lgr 11 with practical advice on how the current texts can be interpreted in order to allow for a more active inclusion of content and practices related to CS, programming and the Internet, as well as security and integrity issues.

Extracurricular activities such as CoderDojos, code camps, after-school clubs and makerspace activities are organized to give children and youth access to informal learning opportunities. Teachers throughout the country are experimenting and sharing experiences from introducing programming in different subjects, ranging from languages to handicraft and music. Heintz et. al. [8] present an overview of ongoing activities related to CS and computational thinking in Sweden, highlighting several projects that show how one can introduce CS already within the current curriculum.

In September 2015, the Swedish government gave the National Agency for Education (Skolverket) the task of presenting a national IT strategy for the Swedish school system. As one part of this work, Skolverket was to update the curricula for primary (K-9) and upper secondary education (grades 10-12). The government explicitly stated that the curriculum should 1) strengthen students' digital competence and 2) introduce programming at K-9 level.

In March 2017, the Swedish government accepted Skolverket's proposal. The revised curriculum will be mandatory starting in fall 2018, but schools have the option to introduce it already in fall 2017.

The revision introduces a new general section on digital competence. Skolverket acknowledges that the meaning of digital competence changes over time due to changes in society, technology and available services [11]. Skolverket's definition is based on the set of key competences developed by the European commission [12] and the work by the Digitalization Committee [4]. In the Swedish curriculum, digital competence includes four aspects: 1) understanding how digitalization affects individuals and society, 2) understanding and knowing how to use digital tools and media, 3) critical and responsible usage of digital tools and resources, and 4) being able to solve problems and implement ideas in practice. In a supplemental material [11], Skolverket stresses that helping students develop their digital competence is a cross-curricular responsibility and aspects of digital competence should hence be covered in all subjects. Programming is considered part of this definition. The supplemental material clarifies that focus is not on coding skills, but on programming as a pedagogical tool and a problem solving process including many phases. Programming should also be seen in a wider context, including "creation, controlling and regulating, simulations and democratic dimensions" [11, p.10, freely translated]. Skolverket emphasizes the importance of seeing programming in this wider perspective both as a basis for teaching and as part of all four aspects of digital competence.

For a more detailed overview see [7].

3 THE PILOT STUDY

The first project was a pilot study in the spring of 2015. It involved 10 teachers in different subjects and from different schools, who had been selected by the municipality. Their background varied, from those that had been working with Bebras (http://bebras.org) and Hour of Code (http://code.org) to those that had absolutely no previous experience. The study took place during one semester and included three 3 hour workshops. The goal was for each teacher to carry out at least three activities with their students. In the end more than 300 students from more than 14 classes from grade 1 to grade 9 participated in computational thinking activities as part of the pilot study.

The first workshop was a lecture style introduction to computational thinking, which gave a motivation to why it is important, an introduction to what it is, concrete examples of computational thinking in different subjects, both with and without computers, and an introduction to programming using ScratchJr/Pyonkee. To introduce computational thinking, tasks from the international Bebras challenge were used. To introduce programming without a computer, material from CS Unplugged [2] was used. To introduce programming we used Hour of Code and ScratchJr/Pyonkee. The fact that these resources were easily available simplified our work notably.

The second workshop was a workshop style discussion around how to introduce computational thinking in the participating teachers' particular subjects. The teachers were divided into groups based on their subject. There were three groups: Swedish/language teachers, math teachers, and science/technology teachers. Each group was given the explicit task to come up with at least two activities related to computational thinking that they could carry out in their classes in the coming month: one unplugged activity and one involving a tablet or a computer. After the group discussions, the whole group discussed the suggested activities together. The workshop ended with each teacher having to commit to doing one unplugged activity, one Hour of Code session, and one programming activity using a digital device (tablets were more common than computers) before the third and final workshop.

At the third workshop the teachers presented what they had done in their classes and we discussed their experience and lessons learned. The teachers also filled out an evaluation form for each activity they had completed. In total we received information about 17 activities. One example of an activity that a teacher developed introduced a treasure hunt covering angles and fractions in mathematics. The students were given a grid map of the school yard and a sequence of instructions on the form "walk 1 3/4 squares forward", "turn 270 degrees to the right", etc. They then had to calculate where the treasure was hidden before actually executing the program to see if they could find the treasure. This is a good example of combining developing computational thinking skills with outdoor activities.

The final review of the pilot study revealed four major lessons learned:

(1) The teachers were in general positive and felt that the training made it possible for them to adapt the material provided and run an activity as part of their own teaching. Nevertheless, they only did this once and as far as we know the teachers did not continue to develop more activities after the pilot study was over.
(2) The teachers reported that other students than the usual suspects did best on the activities. Students that were usually quiet and low key were more excited and engaged in the activities than normally.
(3) According to teacher's experience, Scratch and ScratchJr worked well at lower grade levels, while students in grade 7-9 were not motivated by the cute graphics and cartoons. One teacher used Code Combat (http://codecombat.com/) instead together with grade 9 students, which he reported worked well.
(4) The students were in general positive towards the activities and engaged in them.

The conclusions from the pilot study are that it was definitely possible to get teachers to introduce computational thinking in their teaching with a limited amount of professional development, as long as it was directly connected to their subject. However, it did not seem to get a lasting effect. This seems to be a general observation, it is relatively easy to do one or a few activities, but it is much harder to make it part of the standard practice and integrate it into everyday teaching.

4 CT FOR ALL

As the conclusions from the pilot study were positive, while it was clear that this only affected a small number of students, the continuation project focused on addressing the question on scaling up. The basic question is: Now that we know how to get individual teachers to start including computational thinking in their classes, how can we scale this up in both the number of teachers/students and also in the regularity/longevity of the activities. The general plan for the project was to provide professional competence development to at least one teacher at each school and to build up a central support function within the municipal administration to support the teachers. The goal of the project was that 80% of all students in the municipality should have at least one activity per month related to computational thinking.

4.1 Organization

The municipality has 50 schools and about 14000 students in comprehensive education (grade 1-9) organized in 5 school districts. Due to the hierarchical organization, the communication from the central municipal administration is always through the school district, which can decide whether to forward information to the principals, or not. Each principal decides whether information should be forwarded to the teachers and, if so, whom to inform. All communication from the project to the teachers were taken care of by the project's municipality representative, who is also a teacher.

The original plan was to build an organization with one teacher from each school and a support group within the central administration consisting of one representative from each of the school districts and one representative from the central education development office (who would also be responsible for the whole project). We as the university representatives were outside the organization as our role was to bootstrap the change. Our responsibility was to provide teacher training, expert advice and to study the introduction of computational thinking in the schools.

Even though the central municipal administration has been very supportive and positive we have not managed to form a central support group and the representative from the municipality has been replaced three times during the project period of three years. Based on this experience, the school organization appears to be rather volatile with people constantly changing positions, but it could also be a coincidence that the municipality was in a shift of staff.

Luckily, we have managed to get representatives from more than 40 out of the 50 schools, which means that we actually reach at least 80% of the schools. Initially we got about 30 teachers in the spring of 2016, which was increased to about 70 teachers from the fall of 2016 after the head of education had sent out a request to all the schools. The group was mostly unchanged during fall 2016 and spring 2017, but the engagement and activity of these teachers varied substantially. Normally about 40 of the teachers showed up to the workshops. Finding suitable workshop times and getting teachers to commit is both hard and important.

4.2 Workshops and Activities

The workshops have been the backbone of the project. We have arranged three half-day workshops per semester at the university, resulting in total 12 workshops during 2016 and 2017. Each workshop has had a theme and a program including both information or new material from us and discussions to activate the teachers. We have also given the teachers assignments to do between the workshops.

In addition to the workshops we have also encouraged participation in events such as Bebras and Hour of Code. We have also developed a handbook with computational thinking activities and an introductory material for teaching computational thinking. This material is freely available in Swedish as it is designed for Swedish teachers.

Workshop Program.

(1) Introduction to computational thinking, overview of the proposed new curriculum, introduction to Bebras, Hour of Code, and Scratch Jr. *Discussion:* What support do you need to implement the new curriculum?
(2) Assessment of computational thinking skills. *Discussion:* How to assess digital competence and programming in the new curriculum?
(3) Introduction to our handbook on computational thinking. *Discussion:* Now that you have learned the basics, how should you proceed? This was the first workshop with the full group, so we had a parallel session for the new teachers, where we summarized the content of the first two workshops to bring them up to speed.
(4) Bebras and models for introducing programming and computational thinking in K-9. Hands on programming exercises for those that were new to programming and a seminar on the computer science behind Scratch for the more experienced.
(5) The results from Bebras and introduction to Hour of Code. Programming in Python for those with programming experience and a hands on introduction to Hour of Code for those that were new to programming.
(6) Presentation of the introductory material for computational thinking. *Discussion:* Experiences from trying out Bebras and Hour of Code, how can these resources be used in teaching?
(7) Presentation of how others have worked with the new curriculum. Workshop on Micro:bit (http://microbit.org) and Swift Playgrounds (http://apple.com/swift/playground). *Discussion:* What do you think of the introductory material to computational thinking and how does it work in your class?
(8) From block programming to textual programming and programming and algorithms in mathematics. *Discussion:* How will you introduce programming in your teaching this fall?
(9) Progression and more on algorithms in mathematics. *Discussion:* What should students know after grade 3, grade 6 and grade 9? (The Swedish curriculum lacks details, so it is up to teachers to interpret the curriculum.)
(10) Spreading to other teachers at the same school. *Discussion:* How to spread the workshop contents and lessons learned to other teachers, get all teachers involved in order to have continuity at school level (instead of the level of digital competence teaching at a given school being dependent on a single teacher personally driving the change)?
(11) Lessons learned and moving forward. *Discussion:* How will you continue the work now that you have to work more independently?

4.3 Intro to Computational Thinking Package

To provide the teachers with a joint basic material on how to introduce computational thinking, we put together a small resource package. The material defines the main computational thinking concepts, provides examples of concrete activities and exercises that the teacher can use in his or her classroom, and presents a model for how to assess the attitude and maturity of the computational thinking of the students.

The material covers five concepts:

(1) step by step instructions (or how the computer works);
(2) detecting and finding patterns;
(3) breaking down a problem into smaller parts;
(4) abstraction and representation; and
(5) algorithms and programming.

The progression basically follows these concepts, so teachers start with the first and work through them one by one.

The material also considers seven attitudes:

(1) dealing with complexity;
(2) dealing with ambiguity and open problems;
(3) adapting solutions to new situations;
(4) evaluating own and others solutions;
(5) experimenting and troubleshooting;
(6) grit; and
(7) communication and collaboration.

The learning objectives of the material, when used in teaching, is for students to:

- know that a computer does things step-by-step;
- have experience working with different types of problems where he/she has benefited from or has developed concepts and attitudes related to computational thinking;
- recognize computational thinking as a problem solving process together with computers that are based on a set of concepts and attitudes; and
- be able to assess his/her own level of computational thinking.

The material consists of a set of slides presenting the concepts and attitudes, in addition to two matrices. The first matrix defines the concepts. In addition, concrete activities and examples related to math, technology and other subjects are provided for each concept. The activities are either Bebras tasks or activities from our handbook on computational thinking activities. Most activities can be carried out without a computer. The second matrix provides an assessment tool where each attitude progresses through three stages based on work by Phil Bagge, Mark Dorling, and Thomas Stephens (http://code-it.co.uk/attitudes). Each step is in the form of a concrete question for the student to answer.

4.4 Impact

Measuring the number of students that have participated in the project is challenging. The most specific figure we have is the number of students that participated in the Bebras contest. In the 2016 contest 3756 students from 47 different schools in Linköping participated. This corresponds to close to 30% of the students in grades 2-9, which is three times as many as the year before when the corresponding number was 1277 students. The Linköping students represented more than 40% of all students that participated in Bebras in grade 2-9 at a national level in Sweden. This shows that the project has had a large impact. Unexpectedly, the number of students that participated in Bebras in 2017 fell to 2209 students from 30 different schools. The comments we got indicates that the Bebras tasks are very popular but that the schools do not like to participate in the contest itself. In addition to Bebras, many students participated in the Hour of Code, but for that activity we lack concrete statistics.

The informal impact is very high as almost all schools in Linköping participate in the project and we have been invited to present the work to all school leaders in the municipality. It is very likely that this effort will be the main effort by the municipality to introduce the new curriculum.

5 LESSONS LEARNED

The project has provided many lessons learned.

As mentioned above, the project was organized around a municipality representative taking care of all direct contact with the teachers. This was challenging from two perspectives. First, teachers changing jobs or tasks at their work place led to the municipality representative changing several times throughout the project. This makes it difficult to have continuity in the project even if the representatives have all been very good and active. Second, having one person in charge of all teacher contacts complicated our communication with the teachers, as everything had to go through the middleman. One important lesson learned is hence to have an active coordinator at the municipality level, both for teachers who need somebody they can easily contact and for us as the university. Another, but closely related, observation is that it can be rather difficult to get communication across in large organizations.

Another lesson learned is related to teacher activity and the role played by school leadership. Regardless of the current and highly relevant topic of digitalization in schools, teachers were not able to prioritize the project. There is a need for a clear vision at the leadership level and resources that make it possible for teachers to not only take part in a limited number of workshops, but also to learn more and experiment on their own and together with colleagues. It is quite surprising to us that even if the new curriculum is decided and our program is available for free for the teachers the interest from school leaders is quite low (this could be a consequence of the difficulty of communication as we have no direct contact with school leaders either).

While introducing the basics of programming and algorithms can be considered rather easy, moving beyond unplugged programming, apps, Hour of Code and simple block based programming is not as straightforward. Questions such as what to use after Scratch or how to integrate programming in mathematics and other subjects in grades 7-9, are not as easy to answer. The suggestions made by us often were seemed as too advanced and hard. One lesson learned is hence that progression is important in many respects and that there is a need for teacher centric research in order to learn more about suitable ways to integrate programming at different grade levels. In Sweden, comprehensive school is organized in three main stages: K-3, grades 4-6 and grades 7-9, and it is between these stages that students shift schools and teachers. It is therefore crucial to have a joint progression, to make it easier for teachers at different levels both in order to know what to expect from students when they transition to their stage and to know what minimal level they have to reach before moving on to the following stage.

The question "what to do now that we know Scratch" is also not a straightforward one. Does it imply that the person knows how to use the tool Scratch or actually how to program in Scratch? For most teachers, the question seems to imply the former. They have used the tool quite extensively and feel that they know how to use it, therefore they believe they know how to program. This claim is based on our experience with assuming that the teachers actually had learned to program. For those teachers, who felt that they needed to learn more advanced topics, we tried to introduce text-based programming in a more university style manner. The first attempt was to take Scratch as the starting point, go through the different blocks and constructs and explain the computer science behind them. This turned out to be too complex. The second attempt was to take a subset of the introductory lecture in our university Python course, explaining the basics of programming in Python, and then do a hands on exercise writing a function which computes the maximum of two numbers. This went much better than the first attempt, but it was still clear that the step from block programming to text-based programming is quite big. The step was made even bigger by the fact that many schools in the region have opted for tablets, and teachers had to do all the programming on an iPad. From this we draw two conclusions. First, going from block-based programing to text-based programming is hard. Second, teachers who express that they are ready to move from Scratch probably do not need another tool or programming language, but rather more experience in developing interesting tasks and problems, where students can use Scratch, or some other block-based environment, as a tool solve the task or implement an idea.

The teachers participating in our projects had quite heterogeneous backgrounds, as some did not have any prior experience in programming, while others had already done quite a lot, both on their own and together with their students. This did not cause any problems during the workshops, as the participants were divided into groups with different program based on their background. However, making all activities suitable to everyone, regardless of subject taught and prior background, requires significant resources.

Most teachers in the project have done activities with their class and many have done activities with other classes at their school, but it is much harder to spread it to other teachers at their school. Some of the reasons expressed by the teachers are:

- lack of time;
- lack of mandate, they only have the mandate to participate in these activities not to take their own initiatives at their schools;
- lack of school leadership, in some cases they didn't even have a principal as a new was under recruitment; and
- lack of a clear idea on how to introduce programming and digital competence in a sustainable manner.

6 CONCLUSION

In this paper we have described our experience from introducing programming and computational thinking at a large-scale in a Swedish city. The goal was to reach at least 80% of all the schools and at least 80% of all the students. The plan was to provide professional training to the participating teachers the first semester, support them in carrying out a series of activities during the second semester and then support them to spread their knowledge to their colleagues during the third semester. The goal turned out to be too optimistic. First, it took longer to recruit teachers to the project so we had to restart the professional training the second semester. Second, getting the teachers to activate their colleagues requires both the mandate and the support from their local school leaders, which was outside of our control. Third, large organizations are constantly changing both in terms of directives and in terms of people, so finding a stable backbone is quite hard.

The main conclusions of the project are:

- it is possible to provide good teacher training with relatively modest efforts;
- it is possible to get these teachers to carry out activities in their own classrooms and usually also in other classes;
- the teachers are usually good at adapting the material we present and turn it into their own lessons; and
- it is much harder to get the teachers to do their own local teacher training and to get more local teachers at their schools to adopt the new material as it requires an explicit mandate from the local school leaders.

An observation that might be important is that it seems that the teachers who learn Scratch (or other similar languages), learn it as a tool not as a realization of common programming concepts. When they have learned the tool, they feel that they know programming, but when you start discussing the programming concepts or show how to do the same thing in another language, such as Python, they do not really follow. Scratch in all its greatness also seems to lure people into believing that they know more than they do, which is something we have to be aware of and try to mitigate.

If we were to carry out the project again, the most important thing we would do differently would be to explicitly get the commitment of the principals and the school leaders at the highest level. Having their explicit support would greatly empower the teachers to get more done at their schools and feel that they have a clear mandate and resources needed to inspire to change.

Overall we are satisfied with the project as we have gained valuable and important insights, and we know for a fact that we have reached more than 80% of the schools and at least 30% of all the students in city, probably significantly more.

REFERENCES

[1] Anja Balanskat and Katja Engelhardt. 2015. Computing our future. Computer programming and coding. Priorities, school curricula and initiatives across Europe. (2015).

[2] Tim Bell, Ian H. Witten, and Mike Fellows. 2015. *CS Unplugged – An enrichment and extension programme for primary-aged students.*

[3] Department for Education. 2013. National Curriculum in England: Computing programmes of study. (2013). https://www.gov.uk/government/publications/national-curriculum-in-england-computing-programmes-of-study.

[4] Digitaliseringskommissionen. 2014. *En digital agenda i människans tjänst : en ljusnande framtid kan bli vår : delbetänkande.* Technical Report SOU 2014:13.

[5] Finnish National Board of Education. 2014. Perusopetuksen opetussuunnitelman perusteet 2014. (2014).

[6] Fredrik Heintz, Linda Mannila, and Tommy Färnqvist. 2016. A Review of Models for Introducing Computational Thinking, Computer Science and Computing in K-12 Education. In *Proc. IEEE Frontiers in Education Conference (FIE).*

[7] Fredrik Heintz, Linda Mannila, Lars-Åke Nordén, Peter Parnes, and Björn Regnell. 2017. Introducing Programming and Digital Competence in Swedish KâĂŞ9 Education. In *Proc. ISSEP.*

[8] Fredrik Heintz, Linda Mannila, Karin Nygårds, Peter Parnes, and Björn Regnell. 2015. Computing at School in Sweden – Experiences from Introducing Computer Science within Existing Subjects. In *Proc. ISSEP.*

[9] Informatics Europe and ACM Europe. 2015. Informatics in Education: Europe Cannot Afford to Miss the Boat. (2015). Report of the joint Informatics Europe and ACM Europe Working Group on Informatics Education.

[10] Lennart Rolandsson and Inga-Britt Skogh. 2014. Programming in school: Look back to move forward. *Trans. Comput. Educ.* 2, 14 (2014), 12:1–12:25.

[11] Skolverket. 2017. Få syn på digitaliseringen på grundskolnivå. (June 2017).

[12] Stephanie Carretero Gomez and Riina Vuorikari and Yves Punie. 2017. DigComp 2.1: The Digital Competence Framework for Citizens with eight proficiency levels and examples of use. (2017).

[13] White House. 2016. Computer Science for All. (2016). https://www.whitehouse.gov/blog/2016/01/30/computer-science-all.

[14] Jeanette Wing. 2006. Computational thinking. *Commun. ACM* 49, 3 (2006), 33–35.

Analysis of Collaborative Learning in a Computational Thinking Class

Bushra Chowdhury
Department of Engineering Education
Virginia Tech
bushrac@vt.edu

Austin Cory Bart
Department of Computer Science
Virginia Tech
acbart@vt.edu

Dennis Kafura
Department of Computer Science
Virginia Tech
kafura@vt.edu

ABSTRACT

Collaborative learning can help reduce the anxiety level of learners, improve understanding and thus create a positive atmosphere for learning. This study analyzes students' collaborative learning experiences within small interdisciplinary "cohorts" while learning computational thinking in a university-level class. The cohort allows students from different disciplines to contribute diverse perspectives, socially interact with each other and in turn create situations where two or more students learn together. This study uses both qualitative and quantitative means to explore students' collaborative learning experiences. Ethnographically-informed qualitative data using Stahl's collaborative framework is analyzed. The analysis revealed that most students found the cohort model to be valuable in learning computational thinking by allowing them to ask about and explain problems, especially with students from different disciplines who perceive and explain a problem differently. Quantitative data from a multi-term survey complements and confirms the findings from the qualitative data. Our study helps to inform those teaching foundational computing concepts to a diverse audience of learners.

CCS CONCEPTS

• **Human-centered computing**→ Collaborative and social computing→ Collaborative and social computing design and evaluation methods→ Ethnographic studies.

KEYWORDS

Computational thinking, collaborative learning, cohort, interdisciplinary groups

ACM Reference format:

Bushra Chowdhury, Austin Cory Bart, Dennis Kafura, 2018. Analysis of Collaborative Learning in a Computational Thinking Class. In *Proceedings of the ACM SIGCSE conference, Baltimore, Maryland, USA. February 2018 (SIGCSE'18)*, 6 pages.

1 INTRODUCTION

Computational Thinking (CT) has caught the attention of a broad academic community [1, p.38]. Wing defined "computational thinking" as "a universally applicable attitude and skill set everyone, not just computer scientists, would be eager to learn and use" [2, p.33]. Being able to think computational has been identified as a major skill "21st Century" [3] in part because nearly three out of four jobs will require significant CS skills and knowledge [5. As the availability of big data and integration of computing in different disciplines increases, the necessity of people in diverse disciplines with the ability to think computationally has also increased. Thus different initiatives for integrating CT within existing curricula at various academic levels have started to gain footing.

Educators in the field of computer science are grappling with the challenge of teaching their discipline to an audience more diverse in their backgrounds and goals than has been traditional. This is even more the case for teaching CT to undergraduates who are unlikely to pursue a career in computer science and may not have a strong analytical background. Thus, it is important to assess the pedagogical approach of teaching CT to non-CS majors.

Collaborative learning has emerged as a technique that researchers have found to be generally applicable and effective for teaching Computer Science concepts [6, 7]. Collaboration can help reduce the anxiety level of learners, improve understanding and thus create a positive atmosphere to learn CT [8]. In collaborative learning particular forms of interaction are expected to occur which would trigger learning [9, p.5]. During collaboratively learning, individuals negotiate and share meanings relevant to the problem-solving task at hand [10, p. 70]. Collaborative interactions between students majoring in different disciplines can thus promote not only a disciplinary notion of CT but also an interdisciplinary notion of CT that fosters transfer of computational concepts across disciplines [11].

This study, focusing on experiences of non-computer science majors enrolled in a general education CT course, makes two contributions:

- presents a multi-disciplinary collaborative learning "cohort model" appropriate for CT, and
- shows the value of this model by analyzing the experience of students using ethnographic and survey methods.

This paper gives lengthier treatment to the ethnographic study in order to convey more vividly the cohort learning experience.

The cohort model has five features:

Multi-disciplinary: Each cohort had students from multiple majors. The cohorts were assigned by the instructor. A strong attempt was also made to achieve gender balance with no cohort having fewer than two female students.

SIGCSE'18, February 21-24, 2018, Baltimore, MD, USA.

ACM ISBN 978-1-4503-5103-4/18/02...$15.00.
DOI: http://doi.org/10/1145/3159450.3159470

Persistent: Students were assigned to a cohort in the second week of the semester and the cohort lasted throughout the remaining 14 weeks of the semester. The longevity of the cohort allows students to develop a degree of social acceptance that lowers the barriers to collaboration.
Active peer learning: Each class day students sit together as a cohort at a table and perform all class room activities within their cohort. Students were strongly encouraged and guided in how to interact with their cohort members. A cohort "contract" was developed and signed by each cohort at the beginning of the semester. This contract outlined their responsibilities to the cohort and to each other. Students could also collaborate virtually using the course book, a custom-built, interactive web-based platform with embedded coding activities and real-time, shared text writing.
Individual evaluation: The class room activities, as well as virtually all other course work, was done individually but freely provided and received clarification, explanation, and encouragement to others in their cohort.
No cohort evaluation: Believing that a cohort assessment would interfere with its social dynamics, no assessment or self-assessment of the cohort members' level or quality of participation was done. This allows students to participate at whatever level they are comfortable with. It is possible for a student to engage minimally or not at all and still receive as high a grade as someone who more fully interacted in their cohort.

The collaborative learning that occurred within the cohort model is analyzed as follows. The qualitative methods (Section 2) use Stahl's major influences of collaborative learning as a lens to study the student's experiences [12]. The results are presented (Section 3) and discussed (Section 4). The quantitative survey and its results are given in Section 5. The survey analysis complements the ethnographic findings but is independent, having been conducted over a different and larger student population in a different semester. Conclusions are given in Section 6.

2 Theoretical Framework and Research Design

Studies focusing on collaborative learning usually consider group of learners collaboratively solving a task together. In this study, the "cohort" approach of collaboratively learning was slightly different because students in a cohort were solving the same problem individually at the same time. The cohort was designed to act as a supportive sub community within the classroom setting, taking more of naturalistic peer learning model. Thus, the study required a research framework that was flexible enough to incorporate such variations of collaborative learning. According to Stahl, the framework is not intended to be a model of objects and processes but rather illustrates how members of small groups can engage in a cognitive activity. Hence the framework seemed suitable for this particular study which allowed the researcher to focus on students' experiences of learning in general as well as the collaborative features emerging from their experiences.

2.1 Stahl's major influences of Collaborative Learning

Various factors of a setting and the participant's personal attributes influence collaborative learning. Group members'

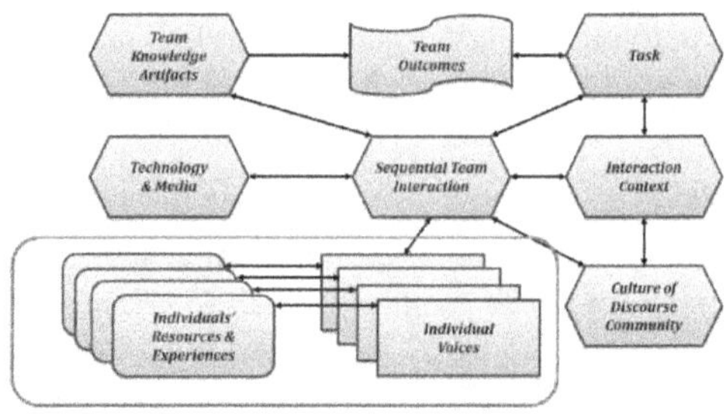

Figure 1 Major influences of collaborative learning [12]

prior knowledge, perspective, abilities, understanding of the task to be completed, the technology and media used, the context of interactions and, finally, the culture of the community, all play vital roles in the collaborative process. **Error! Reference source not found.** illustrates the major influences of collaborative learning as described by Stahl [12].

According to Stahl's framework, all the major influences in a collaborative learning environment interact with the sequential team interaction goal. In the context of learning CT in a classroom setting, interactions between learners, learners and the instructors, and learners and the course materials can be considered as collaborative interactions. These interactions weave all the other influences to each other. Among other influences, a student's background, prior knowledge and perspective specifically impact how s/he interacts in a collaborative environment. This study focuses on these major influences on student learning CT collaboratively, particularly on "individual' resources and experiences". According to Stahl, "much of the power of collaborative learning can come from the pooling of different knowledge and alternative perspectives distributed within the group" (page 257).

Thus, in order to better understand the role disciplinary background and how it shapes a student's experience in learning CT collaboratively, ten undergraduate students (majoring in different non-computer science) who had enrolled in a CT course were interviewed.

2.2 Research Design

The goal of this study was to investigate how students in a CT course experience collaboration. The study used ethnographically-informed data collection methods (observations, interviews and surveys). Interviews as a data collection method allows a researcher to gain better understanding of people's experiences and perceptions. Researchers focusing on social interactions have interviewed participants to know how the participants felt doing an activity, and to reflect on their experiences [14]. This study thus mainly focuses on qualitative data coming from semi-structured interviews in order to gain better understanding on student's perceptions of peer interactions in the general education CT class. The study also collected quantitative survey data.

The study was conducted in a state university in the Southeast U.S. As part of the strategic plan the university has been offering a general education course titled "Introduction to CT" to students from all disciplines. In spring 2015, when the ethnographic study was conducted the class enrolled approximately 45 students and met twice a week for 75 minutes sessions. Each class began with a 10-15 minute review of the days topic followed by active class work. A short (5-10 minutes) discussion period concluded the class.

In order to better understand major influences experienced by students while learning collaboratively, members of three of the eight cohorts (**Error! Reference source not found.**) were individually interviewed in the last two weeks of the semester. A total of 10 students were interviewed. The semi structured interviews typically lasted 15 to 40 minutes were audio recorded and transcribed. The interview protocols were informed by Stahl's collaborative learning framework, primarily focusing on students' background, goals, interests, and experiences while learning CT. The interview participants were voluntary. The researcher obtained Human Subjects Research Approval through the Institutional Review Board (IRB) of the corresponding University before initiating the interview for the study. Consent of the participants was obtained prior to the initiation of data collection. The full interview protocol can be accessed at https://think.cs.vt.edu/resources/ct-protocol.

Table 1: **Profile of students interviewed**

Cohort	No. of students interviewed	Total no. of students in the cohort	Major
Cohort Alpha	3 (senior:2 freshman:1)	5	History, Political Science, Architecture, Chemistry, Public Relations, Housing, Theater Arts, Journalism
Cohort Beta	4(senior:3, sophomore:1)	6	
Cohort Gamma	3(sophomore:2, freshman:1)	6	

All transcribed audio recording of individual student interviews were coded using a prior code informed by Stahl's collaborative learning framework. Two independent researchers coded separately for the purpose of cross-checking coding and emerging themes. Discrepancies with codes were discussed and resolved. To protect the anonymity, pseudonyms were assigned to each of the interview participant.

3 RESULTS

A brief summary of the findings are given and then explained in detail. First, for most of the non-science majors, learning to code was learning something conceptually different than they were used to. These students struggled to write code, finding it difficult to comprehend how precise one had to be. Nevertheless, most of the students could comprehend the value of learning CT and its applicability to their own discipline. Second, most of them found the long term cohort model to be valuable resources in learning CT. Asking and explaining problems to cohort members were not only useful to advance through a problem but also valuable to one's own learning process. Discussing problems with students coming from different disciplines allowed them to see how differently students perceive and explain a problem. Students coming with a science background could recognize the struggle non-science majors faced while learning to code. Third, providing ample time for students to actively learn CT during class time, acknowledging that students will make mistakes, allowing students to casually communicate with each other, and the overall structure of the course were few salient features of the CT course that students brought up during their interviews.

The following sections summarize student's personal CT learning experiences according to the major influences highlighted in Stahl's framework.

3.1 Individual's Resources and Experiences. All students of this study were taking the CT course to fulfill a general education requirement in quantitative reasoning. A course in calculus was the most common class taken by student to satisfy this Area 5 requirement prior to the offering of this CT course. Most of the participants found math difficult and the option of taking something different encouraged them to take the CT class.

Students majoring in different disciplines were able to relate the use of CT to their fields. For some students, the final project of the CT class helped them to make this connection. For example, a student in journalism was able to describe how big data is being used to analyze and predict crime-related behaviors. A student in Public Relations understood that s/he might need to apply his/her computation skill while developing websites. The student majoring in chemistry explained how computational analytics help chemists to discover new drugs. The following excerpts are taken from the conversation between the journalism, architecture and chemistry majors respectively:

"It's sort of on the cusp of journalism is now, they're going through very large things of data. Most recently, the Chicago red light thing that was going on with red light cameras in Chicago. Somebody had to go through all 4 million instances of red light tickets. And you could go through them manually, or you can have a programmer go through all of it. If you can do that as a journalist it's getting more and more to where you kind of need to have a niche position. Almost as if the job has never been there before, like Washington Post or something like that. Somebody's going through all that data to create the graphs that end up on the news." [Journalism Major]

"I'll probably be able to use it ... The coding, the different rules for coding. I'm actually working on a website in another of my classes so it's helpful to know how coding works. Then also just how we're working on the visualizations for the final project right now, I think that's going to be pretty helpful in the future to be able to analyze data in my PR I'll probably be able to use that." [Architecture Major]

However, some students still had a very rudimentary perception on CT and were not able elaborate on the applicability of CT in their own field. For example, in the following quote, a History major gives a very brief definition of CT:

"I would just say using computers to analyze data." [History Major]

The profiles of the interviewed participants revealed that students who were more advanced in the study of their discipline were able to elaborate on the connection of CT to their own discipline while freshman and sophomore were not clear in making the connection. This difference could be explained by the fact that the freshman and sophomore students were new to their own disciplines and their disciplinary perspectives were not fully formed.

3.2 Individual voices (Role of a student). Students can take on various roles in a collaborative environment [13]. In this study the roles students assumed were oriented towards peer learning in a cohort where each student was solving the same problems individually but could voluntarily ask help from their cohort members.

The main roles students conveyed in their interviews were asking a question, responding to a question and taking the role of a mentor. Most of the students interviewed explained their role in the cohort as both giving and receiving help. Students would work on the problems by themselves and if they got stuck, they would ask help from a cohort member.

"During the class we would work on our own and if we had questions we would ask each other sometimes I would ask, sometimes someone else would ask me" [Architecture Major]

One particular student, Joe (not his real name), assumed more of a mentor role. Joe had prior programming experience and was willing to help others. As a result he was seen helping out most of the other students in his cohort. His cohort members also found his presence to be assuring. In the following quote, a Liberal Arts major describes Joe's role:

"I really liked our group. We would just work on our stuff and mostly ask questions, we'd go to Joe because he's the only one who has any CS background. So he knows everything compared to us. We would ask him a lot of questions. He's a super helpful guy and super talkative...I had lots of learning opportunities, from Joe especially and then from other people much less so. I think also another reason that everybody was here all the time is because we had Joe. He had that kind of background experience. Even if nobody else was getting it, Jonathan gets it. I think we always felt safe to come to class" [Liberal Arts Major]

Joe describes his first couple of weeks of CT mentoring experience as follows:

"I wasn't really prepared to take on this role, so I wasn't thinking I need to be a leader. It was sort of like oh, I know about this stuff and you guys don't really know all that much about this stuff, I guess I should help you out, and it was sort of a last minute thing. It kind of shook me for the first couple of weeks. I was like these people really need my help." [Science Major]

3.3 Culture of discourse community. The students believed the cohort model to be beneficial to learning. The students appreciated the in-class time allowed to learn CT with cohort members.

"I think it's because we were provided ample time every single class to work as a group... I think that was probably the biggest facilitator of the group interaction was just being in the same place at the same time at a time that was convenient for everyone, because we were planning on being there for class." [English Major]

The Journalism Major appreciated the cohort as a natural conversational mode with cohort members.

"I guess I was really fond of the way we could just casually bring up the conversation instead of formally raising your hand, and the class would stop ... I just felt like it was more natural conversation." [Journalism Major]

One of the main reasons why students found the cohort model to be helpful is to have someone at the same level of learning explain a problem.

"Mostly because we're all kind of on similar levels of understanding, my cohort members and I, so when they explain it in their own words, it's just easier for me to understand" [History Major]

According to the History major it is helpful when a learner with the same level of understanding explains a problem in their own words.

"And for me, I personally would rather hear a student's point of view on a problem because I probably relate to them more than an instructor. Usually the student will give some sort of example to coincide with the problem. So, I guess it's not as hard to grasp. While the instructor will use more of the technical terms which I probably don't know so, it's harder for me to grasp the concept."[Political Science Major]

A Political Science major preferred an explanation from a peer student rather than the instructor. This particular student found the use of technical terms by the instructor to be difficult to interpret. In the excerpt bellow a student majoring in Theater Arts describes that at times when he was burdened thinking over a problem another cohort member would explain the problem in more basic terms which was helpful.

"Like if I was more confused, if I was overthinking a problem in something, my cohort members would boiled it down to more bare basics. That was helpful." [Theater Arts Major]

In the two excerpts below a student majoring in English and another majoring Architecture describe that explaining a problem to another cohort member can be helpful for one's own understanding.

"A lot of times we would just say the things we were doing, especially in [the block-base language], as we were doing them. I've definitely learned, not just in this class but overall as a psychology thing, being able to explain back something that you've been told is a really good way of gauging understanding. It's always funny when you ask a question to our group because you'll get some really interesting answers. Part of them will be funny and part of them will be legitimate, but we all shared the struggle I guess." [English Major]

"Others helping me helps me learn it through, like on a one-to-one scale with a person my age. It's kind of relatable. So you're learning with someone who's learning with you, and if they know something, it's like oh, I can learn it too. And if I know something they don't, they can learn it too, and we're just helping each other grow. Of course, if I help him with something, and I can verbally communicate it with him that means that I'm understanding it more, and that's definitely a learning skill." [Architecture Major]

The Architecture major in the above excerpt elaborates on the aspect of enhancing self-confidence. Seeing someone with similar experience in learning CT able to solve a problem helped him to believe that he could also solve the problem.

Liberal Arts students found learning CT to be a different type of learning then they were used to. For example:

"I don't get this. I'm not used to having to be so precise and so logical about everything." [Political Science Major]

When the student was asked to elaborate on what he meant by "being precise and logical" the Political Science Major elaborated, *"There is more than one way to write the same thing. Even if your sentence is not fully formed others can figure out what you want to say. But with computers, it has to be picture perfect, or else it doesn't work."*

"I'm not really good with ... My brain's more of the English and history side versus science and math" [English Major]

Students appreciated the exchange of ideas with cohort members and having students coming from different disciplines in their cohort.

"Students coming from different discipline had a different take on how they explained a problem or solution of a problem and that was nice". [Political Science Major]

3.4 Interaction context. The students mentioned that it was important not only to talk about and solve problems in a cohort but to get to know each other, attend class regularly, tell a joke and laugh about things happening in each other's lives. These non-academic conversations made them feel comfortable to ask questions to each other and probably also kept the cohort functional.

"Building that sense of community, just friendship and working relationships with the people in my cohort was such a huge part I think for us of how we got along so well, just little things here and there. We weren't just coming to do the group work, we were all getting to know each other and I think that really helped." [English Major]

Students appreciate the long lasting cohort model for the community aspect it provided for the students:

"Since we're able to all talk about it, like we're comfortable sharing our problems or our complications with each other, it was easy to learn like that, because it was just like you weren't afraid to ask for help, and sometimes, your cohort members would explain something a different way, and then it would help you understand it." [History Major]

3.5 Technology and media. Students in the CT class did not only communicate with their cohort members within class but also on Facebook. They had a Facebook group where they communicated, shared their experiences, problems they were having with home works and help one another outside the class room.

"We have a Facebook message for if we're doing homework or something and we need help that we're all linked into so we all see it. We can then message, "Oh, well I see your code. You really need to put a parenthesis here. You're not counting this right," or something like that. We can all help each other, not while we're even just in the classroom. We can meet outside the classroom." [Science Major]

4 DISCUSSION

In studying small group cognition, Stahl suggested focusing on the role, interactions and discourse between group members [15]. In this study, students' experiences while learning CT were also influenced by other factors that contribute to small group cognition. Students' role and the discourse within the CT class were shaped by the resources that were available, and the interactions student had with their peers, the instructor and the TAs. Fig. 3 maps Stahl's collaborative framework to factors influencing the experiences of students.

The findings reveal that most students taking this CT class

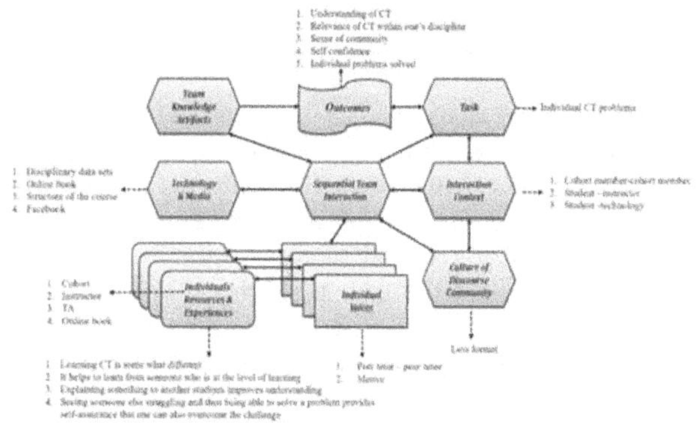

Figure 3: **Factors influencing non-computer science majors' experiences in learning CT within small groups**

did not have prior experience in learning computational concepts and were enrolled in non-STEM majors. Only a few students had some prior programming experience. Most of the students were taking this course as alternative to a math course (calculus). Thus, student's discipline and prior experience in computing were considered as the background of the participants. The discourse in the small groups as well in the class was less formal. Students could casually start talking to one another.

In terms of available resources, students found having a semester long small groups (cohort model) helpful to learning CT. Students characterized their role in the small groups as a tutee (mostly asking questions) or as a tutor (providing explanations). Some students also characterized their role as mentors. Students found it beneficial to explain and be able to see how others solved a problem. The students found it comforting that they were able to work on a data set from their own discipline. The disciplinary data sets allowed the students to bring in their own disciplinary knowledge and combine what they had learned from the CT class.

In terms of experiences, students described learning CT to be different than typical type of learning they were commonly used to. Breaking down problems to its very basic level so that a computer can understand seemed difficult for them to comprehend. For some students learning to code was like learning another language. However, for a student majoring in science, learning CT was not that much different.

In terms of outcome, students referred to being able to comprehend what CT is, the applicability of CT within one's own discipline, the ability to write a computer program and having a sense of community within the class.

4.1 Implications for practice. Students with a non-science background can find learning CT difficult. On the other hand, the process of learning CT is more intuitive and comes naturally to the students coming from a science background with prior programing experience. Using discipline specific datasets can be helpful to keep students interested and motivated to learn CT. Forming semester long groups/cohorts can be beneficial for novice learners. These small groups provide students a sense of belonging, a place to share thoughts and anxieties. Students find it is easier to naturally ask questions to group member than help from instructors. An explanation coming from a peer who is at the same learning level is easier to understand and relate to. Educators should also keep in mind that some students may struggle and need extensive support.

4.2 Limitations and future directions Students who participated in this study were self-selected. For this reason, it is likely that most of them had a positive attitude towards the CT class. Also, most of the students interviewed in this study were taking this particular CT course to avoid taking a course in 'math'. This could have influenced the findings of this study. There were disciplines from which students were enrolled in the course but were not interviewed. Interviewing students from a larger number disciplines could have allowed the researcher to gain a broader perspective. A future direction of this work could be to investigate the similarities and dissimilarities within student's disciplinary backgrounds that support or hinder learning of CT for undergraduate students.

5 QUANTITATIVE ANALYSIS

Complementing the ethnographic analysis a survey was conducted over two semesters (Fall 2016 and Spring 2017). The survey was voluntary, had no weight in the course grade, and was done under an IRB approved protocol. A total of 176 out of 191 students (a 91% response rate) gave consent to participate in the study. Approximately 60% of the students were female. There was a distribution over academic years (freshmen and sophomores were each 30% of the class while juniors and seniors were each 20%).

The survey asked six questions which are identified in Figure 4 as: Giving (I felt comfortable giving help to others in my cohort.), Interaction (I felt the others in my cohort often interacted with me and the others.), Learning (I felt my cohort helped my learning.), Seeking (I felt comfortable getting help from others in my cohort.), Useful (I believe that the course material is useful.), and External/Useful (I felt the others in my cohort believed that the course material is useful). Each question was answered on a 7 point Likert scale as shown in the figure.

The survey shows an overall strong and positive response to the cohort experience. Students felt extremely comfortable in giving assistance and only slightly less comfortable in seeking assistance. A small minority was less than comfortable seeking assistance though none were uncomfortable giving assistance. The frequency of interaction was rated slightly higher than the contribution to learning though the positive view of each was extremely strong. It is interesting to note that individuals believed more strongly that the material was useful then they perceived this to be the case of others in their cohort.

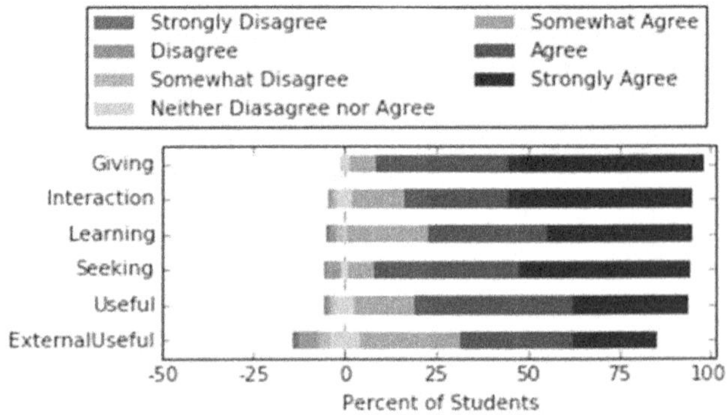

Figure 4 Results of Survey Data

6 CONCLUSIONS

Findings of this study suggest that novice CT learners from different disciplines had varied experiences in learning CT. The students valued the cohort model of learning CT collaboratively. Disciplinary data sets allowed students to combine their disciplinary knowledge with computational skills learned from the CT class. The students also valued having a learning environment where they could learn from peers who they have come to know and trust. Taken together, these results suggest the benefits of collaborative learning and the need for further mixed-methods analyses of how students work together to learn about computational thinking

REFERENCES

[1] Grover, S. and R. Pea, *Computational Thinking in K–12 A Review of the State of the Field.* Educational Researcher, 2013. **42**(1): p. 38-43.

[2] Wing, J., *Computational thinking.* Communications of the ACM, 2006. **49**(3): p. 33-35.

[3] National Research Council, *A framework for K-12 science education: Practices, crosscutting concepts, and core ideas.* 2012: National Academies Press.

[4] *Education for Life and Work: Developing Transferable Knowledge and Skills in the 21st Century*, ed. W.P. James and L.H. Margaret. 2012: The National Academies Press.

[5] Bureau of Labor Statistics, U.S. Department of Labor. *Occupational Outlook Handbook, 2016-17.* Computer and Information Research Scientists; Available from: https://www.bls.gov/ooh/computer-and-information-technology/computer-and-information-research-scientists.htm (visited June 03, 2017).

[6] McDowell, C., et al. *The effects of pair-programming on performance in an introductory programming course.* in *ACM SIGCSE Bulletin.* 2002. ACM.

[7] Kavitha, R. and M.I. Ahmed, *Knowledge sharing through pair programming in learning environments: An empirical study.* Education and Information Technologies, 2015. **20**(2): p. 319-333.

[8] Hmelo-Silver, C.E., *The international handbook of collaborative learning.* 2013: Routledge.

[9] Dillenbourg, P., *What do you mean by collaborative learning?* Collaborative-learning: Cognitive and Computational Approaches., 1999: p. 1-19.

[10] Roschelle, J. and S.D. Teasley. *The construction of shared knowledge in collaborative problem solving.* in *Computer supported collaborative learning.* 1995. Springer.

[11] Lattuca, L.R., L.J. Voigt, and K.Q. Fath, *Does interdisciplinarity promote learning? Theoretical support and researchable questions.* The Review of Higher Education, 2004. **28**(1): p. 23-48.

[12] Stahl, G., *Guiding group cognition in CSCL.* International Journal of Computer-Supported Collaborative Learning, 2010. **5**(3): p. 255-258.

[13] Wasserman, S. and K. Faust, *Social network analysis: Methods and applications.* Vol. 8. 1999: Cambridge university press.

[14] Belbin, M., *Belbin team roles.* Book Belbin Team Roles, 2004.

[15] Stahl, G., *Theories of Cognition in Collaborative Learning*, in *International Handbook of Collaborative Learning*, C. Chinn, et al., Editors. 2013. p. 74-92.

The Computational Algorithmic Thinking (CAT) Capability Flow: An Approach to Articulating CAT Capabilities over Time in African-American Middle-school Girls

Jakita O. Thomas
Auburn University
1301 Shelby Center
Auburn, AL 36849
jnt0020@auburn.edu

ABSTRACT

Computational algorithmic thinking (CAT) is the ability to design, implement, and assess the implementation of algorithms to solve a range of problems. It involves identifying and understanding a problem, articulating an algorithm or set of algorithms in the form of a solution to the problem, implementing that solution in such a way that the solution solves the problem, and evaluating the solution based on some set of criteria. Supporting Computational Algorithmic Thinking (SCAT) is both a longitudinal between-subjects exploratory research project and a free enrichment program supporting and guiding African-American middle school girls over three years as they iteratively design a set of games for social change. This paper explores the CAT Capability Flow, which begins to describe the processes and sub-skills and capabilities involve in CAT. To do this, we engage in an approach which results in an initial flowchart that depicts the processes students are engaging in as an iteratively-refined articulation of the steps involved in computational algorithmic thinking.

KEYWORDS

Computational algorithmic thinking, CAT capability flow, African-American, middle school, girls

ACM Reference format:

Jakita O. Thomas. 2018. The Computational Algorithmic Thinking (CAT) Capability Flow: An Approach to Articulating CAT Capabilities over time in African-American Middle-school Girls. In *SIGCSE '18: 49th ACM Technical Symposium on Computer Science Education, Feb. 21–24, 2018, Baltimore, MD, USA.* ACM, NY, NY, USA, 6 pages.
https://doi.org/10.1145/3159450.3159473

1 INTRODUCTION

Our research makes explicit a critical aspect of computational thinking through its focus: the design, development, and implementation of algorithms to solve problems [34, 35,36].

SIGCSE '18, February 21–24, 2018, Baltimore, MD, USA

ACM 978-1-4503-5103-4/18/02...$15.00
https://doi.org/10.1145/3159450.3159473

Computational algorithmic thinking (CAT) is the ability to design, implement, and assess the implementation of algorithms to solve a range of problems. It involves identifying and understanding a problem, articulating an algorithm or set of algorithms in the form of a solution to the problem, implementing that solution in such a way that it solves the problem, and evaluating the solution based on some set of criteria. CAT is focused on the algorithms designed, adapted, implemented, and discarded by the human (as computing agent) on the journey toward choosing the "right" abstractions. [35, 28]. CAT is an important scaffolded on-ramp as students develop more advanced computational thinking capabilities and apply computational thinking to solve problems that are more constrained and require greater expertise. CAT has roots in Mathematics [22], through problem solving and algorithmic thinking [26, 10, 15], and it lies at the heart of Computer Science, which is defined as the study of algorithms [27].

While there is a great deal of research that examines how to engage students in computational thinking and learning in CS, there is a scarcity of research that focuses on understanding and describing how the development of CAT happens over time as a complex cognitive capability. This paper begins to address the research question: How do individual and small-group computational algorithmic thinking capabilities of African-American middle school girls develop over time? We address this question by describing our early findings in articulating CAT based on data that was collected over 3.5 years and is still being fully analyzed. This research is significant because CAT has previously not been articulated or described. This articulation serves as a first critical step in describing and identifying changes in the development of CAT capabilities over time. To describe CAT, we create a visual representation of the process(es) Scholars engage in as they enact CAT in the context of game design for social change.

2 THEORETICAL FRAMEWORK

The National Research Council [18] outlines eight practices as being "essential elements of the K-12 science and engineering curriculum": defining problems, developing and using models, planning and carrying out investigations, analyzing and interpreting data, using mathematics, information and computer technology, computational thinking, designing solutions, engaging in argument from evidence, and obtaining, evaluating, and communicating information. While the major competencies that students should have by the 12th grade and sketches regarding how that competence should progress are described, the NRC states "there is very little research evidence as yet on the developmental trajectory of each of these practices" (p. 3-6).

The acquisition and development of skills and practices involves the changing of declarative knowledge, or independent pieces of factual knowledge, to procedural knowledge, or connected knowledge that forms a process for carrying out a skill [2, 1]. Applied in context and/or among a community, a process evolves into a practice [19, 16]. While skills, or abilities refer to what one can do in the present, capabilities refer to what one can learn to do with instruction and scaffolding [3, 4, 31, 8]. However, moving learners from capability to ability requires several things [8, 19, 30]. First, learners need opportunities to make connections between their experiences and the knowledge/skills they are learning. Second, learners need enough time to learn and develop skills and capabilities so that they can use them flexibly in appropriate situations. Third, learners should be supported as they attempt to represent problems at higher levels of abstraction. Finally, learners should be both encouraged to monitor their learning and supported as they learn metacognitive strategies.

As a domain, engaging in game design aligns with the eight practices outlined by the NRC [18]. The iterative game design lifecycle involves several phases as shown in Fig. 1, which are iterative themselves [12]. During brainstorming, game designers generate many game ideas, narrow them down to a small subset, and choose the idea to pursue. Next, a solid storyboard or gameplay treatment is created, which is then playtested. Playtesting involves bringing actual players from the target user group in and observing them as they play the game in real time, getting feedback about the game experience to inform the design of the game [12, 11]. Game designers then create a playable physical prototype, which is developed using craft materials and is also playtested. Next, designers create a set of rough software prototypes, which each model some aspect(s) of core gameplay followed by more playtesting. Next comes creating the design document, a dynamic document that outlines every aspect of the game, including how it will look, feel, function, and behave. This is followed by implementing the game with playtesting throughout. Finally, if the game is produced, quality assurance testing is done with continued playtesting.

Game design has also been shown to be an effective approach to broadening participation by groups who are normally under-represented in Computer Science (i.e., women and minorities) and in improving computing capabilities, interest in Computer Science, and retention [24, 11, 5, 6, 33, 32, 17]. Rooted in Constructionism and project-based learning, young people can construct, or design, their own games and "create new relationships with knowledge in the process" both in formal and informal settings [13, 14, 7, 21, 25]. The literature reveals that engaging in game design has been shown to improve participants' programming skills, technology fluency, algorithmic thinking capabilities, retention and interest in Computer Science, modeling capabilities, and abstraction capabilities at many different levels (K – 14). In other words, they have impacted students' computational thinking capabilities. Our research seeks to go one level deeper into understanding how African-American middle-school girls develop CAT capability over time.

3 SUPPORTING COMPUTATIONAL ALGORITHMIC THINKING (SCAT)

SCAT is a longitudinal between-groups research project that explores how African-American middle-school girls develop CAT capabilities over time (i.e., three years) in the context of game design for social change. SCAT is also a free enrichment program designed to expose middle school girls to game design. Spanning three years, participants developed CAT capabilities as they design more and more complex games that address issues or problems identified by the Scholars themselves. SCAT Scholars began the program the summer prior to their 6th grade year and continued through their 8th grade year (i.e., June 2013 – May 2016). Each year, Scholars engaged in 3 types of activities: 1) a two-week intensive game design summer experience; 2) twelve technical workshops where Scholars implemented the games they designed using visual and programming languages in preparation for submission to national game design competitions; and 3) field trips where Scholars learned about applications of CAT in different industries and careers. Scholars also had several scaffolds in the learning environment to support them in the ways cognitive apprenticeship suggests including the facilitator, four undergraduate assistants, the Design Notebook as well as other scholars [9, 23, 28, 29].

As mentioned previously, game design is all about algorithms, and computational algorithmic thinking is enacted in a number of places throughout the game design cycle [29]. The game design cycle itself is an algorithm consisting of seven phases as described in Section 2. As Scholars move through the phases of the game design cycle, they engage in computational algorithmic thinking. For example, during the Storyboarding phase, Scholars engage in computational algorithmic thinking as they draw stills that depict the gameplay for the player from beginning to end as well as the non-visual elements of the game. In fact, the storyboard is the first enactment of CAT as it visually describes many of the game's algorithms. During the Physical Prototyping phase, Scholars articulate the rules and procedures of the gameplay, which are the primary algorithms that govern gameplay and how players engage with the game. The implementation phase involves Scholars not only articulating algorithms in SCRATCH to implement gameplay functionality and behavior, but also adapting and implementing SCRATCH algorithms (e.g., creating a scrolling screen, keeping score, enacting a timer, detecting and responding to a collision between objects, etc.). As Scholars move through the phases of the game design cycle, they articulate the algorithms in their games more and more specifically as they move toward a more fully functional game.

4 CONSTRUCTUING THE CAT CAPABILITY FLOW – METHODS AND TECHNIQUES

The CAT Capability Flow should not be thought of as an absolute or complete description of CAT, but rather as a way to begin describing a process that has not been described in detail before, informing possible developmental changes that may occur in Scholars' ability to design, implement, and assess algorithms over time. In addition, the CAT Capability Flow serves as a starting point in the development of a coding scheme that will be used to analyze Scholar artifacts to detect shifts in aspects of CAT capability over time, the full description of which is outside the scope of this paper. The CAT Capability Flow will inform the dimensions (categories) that should be included in the coding scheme [20, 30]. This paper describes the first step of this process: constructing the CAT Capability Flow.
spatial profiles.

4.1 The Pilot Study

From January-March 2013, we piloted the SCAT Workshops and Game Design Competition activity. One major purpose of this 8-week pilot study was to begin identifying and describing the sub-processes that exist for each phase of CAT through the CAT Capability Flow. During this study, twenty African-American 6th grade girls worked in dyads to design and implement a game for social change. It is important to note that data collection for the full implementation of the SCAT project took place from July 2013 – May 2016, with full data analysis beginning in June 2016 and continuing to date. As such, the volume of data collected and the careful analysis of that data (especially video observations) has taken a great deal of time. To describe capability development over time appropriately, it is important to start from the beginning: the pilot study.

4.2 Setting and Participants

The pilot study took place at Spelman College in Atlanta, GA, a private, liberal arts, Historically Black College for women. Spelman College has been a leader in training minorities and women in Science, Technology, Engineering Mathematics, and Computer Science (STEM+CS) areas. We worked with 20 African-American 6th grade girls from across the metro-Atlanta area. They met 8 Saturdays for 6-7 hours each time to design games for social change (2 Saturdays) and to implement those game (6 Saturdays).

4.3 Data Sources

We gathered various data during the pilot study including completed Design Notebook pages, physical prototypes, implementations of games (using SCRATCH), design documents, video observations (both whole class and small group/dyad), pictures, and written direct observations. However, to inform the creation of the CAT Capability Flow, we focused mainly on the whole class video observations, direct observations, and pictures, which captured how the game design cycle was enacted during the pilot study.

4.4 Data Analysis

Using our video observations, direct observation notes, and pictures taken each day of the summer game design experience as well as the twelve workshops, six members of the research team began our analysis by describing the enactment of these activities. To do this, we watched the whole class video observations of the 8-week enactment, which represented over 64 hours of video data. For each phase in the game design cycle, two research team members were responsible for individually documenting and describing the enactment based on video observations for their assigned phase(s) and those descriptions were discussed. Using these descriptions, we mapped each phase of the game design cycle to our high-level definition of CAT described in Section 1. Next, we prioritized the activities conducted during each phase of the game design cycle captured during video observations and described in the observation notes of the research team, with a focus on the order in which activities occurred within a phase as well as activities that may have occurred simultaneously.

5 CREATING THE CAT CAPABILITY FLOW

5.1 Mapping the Game Design Cycle onto CAT

Figure 2 shows the mapping of the game design cycle onto our high-level definition of CAT described in Section 1. During the brainstorming phase, Scholars described game ideas at a very high level, articulating only the formal and dramatic elements of the game. During the storyboarding phase, Scholars visualized the formal and dramatic elements of the game, describing visually how the characters looked and moved, what the context of the game, or game world, looked like, how objects within the game world moved, where resources were situated within the game, the perspective of the player (e.g., first person, third person, etc.), how the player moved, and any non-visual elements that the player might experience as they played (e.g., music). During the physical prototyping phase, Scholars represented gameplay and the core gameplay mechanic in the physical realm using craft materials. They had to define even further how characters, resources, objects, the game world, etc. looked as well as how player actions informed object interactions within the game. They also had to clearly define how player progress was measured as well as how progress toward the goal was rewarded and progress away from the goal was determined and penalized.

As Scholars implemented their games in SCRATCH, they had to translate their designs to represent the game world, sprites and the look of their game in SCRATCH as well as the functionality of their games by creating blocks that described how player actions changed the behavior of sprites within the game world. As Scholars reviewed and discussed the feedback they received during playtesting sessions (where they played each other's games and gave feedback), they were able to better understand how to convey the problem in their games to players in such a way that they were motivated to play the game to learn more about the issues addressed in the game and to achieve the game's objective(s).

Figure 2 allowed us to understand which phases of the game design cycle addressed various aspects of CAT. For example, during the physical prototyping phase, dyads understood the problem they were trying to address through their games better because building the physical prototype forced them to be more specific about their idea as they represented each aspect of the game using physical media. Dyads also designed algorithms to solve the problem in the form of rules and procedures, implemented those algorithms by creating a physical representation of the game world and providing written instructions for how to play the game, and assessed those

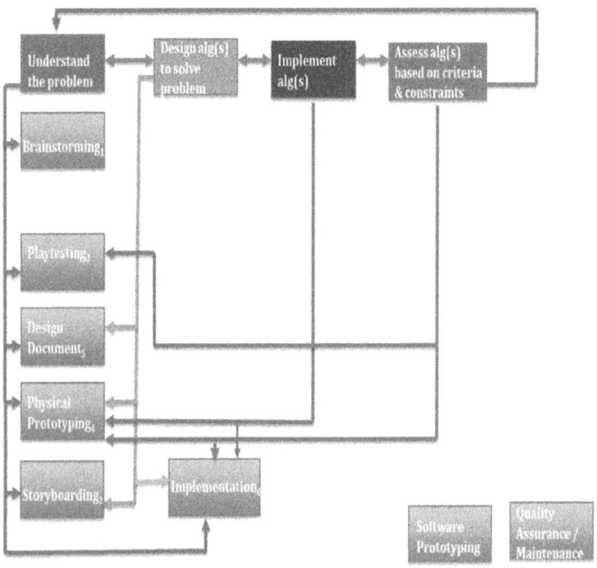

Figure 2. CAT Capability Flow Iteration 1: Mapping CAT definition to the Game Design Cycle

algorithms by having their peers playtest their games and give feedback on the physical representation as well as the gameplay. During these sessions, dyads also gave feedback on other dyad's games. In addition, dyads also collaboratively assessed that feedback to inform design decisions for and changes to their games. The Software Prototyping and Quality Assurance/Maintenance phases are not connected to the rest of the flow because these phases were not included in the pilot study enactment due to time constraints. It should be noted that each phase has a subscript: Brainstorming (1), Playtesting (2) Storyboarding (3), Physical Prototyping (4), Design Document (5), and Implementation (6). These subscripts will be used later as the enactment for each phase is described.

5.2 Specifying Each Phase of the Game Design Cycle

As described earlier, after we mapped the game design cycle onto our definition of computational algorithmic thinking, we then prioritized the activities conducted during each phase of the game design cycle. To do this, we analyzed the data captured during video observations as well as pictures and described in the observation notes of the research team, with a focus on the order in which activities occurred within a phase as well as activities that may have occurred simultaneously or in any order. We prioritized the activities for each phase to provide a chronological description of the enactment of each phase. An example of how that was carried out is described in detail below for the first two phases, Brainstorming and Storyboarding and the current first iteration of the CAT Capability Flow is presented.

5.2.1 Brainstorming Phase

Based on our review of the whole group video observations, direct observation notes, and pictures taken during SCAT pilot study sessions, the prioritized set of activities that Scholars engaged in during the Brainstorming phase included: 1 &2) generated ideas and/or adapted known games, 3) narrowed their ideas down to at least three, 4, 5 & 6) described the characters, formal elements, and dramatic elements in their ideas (which they could do in any order), and 7) created power point presentations for their top 3 ideas, which they 8) presented to the larger group. Fig. 3 shows this prioritized enactment of the Brainstorming$_1$ phase substituted for the Brainstorming block depicted in Fig. 2.

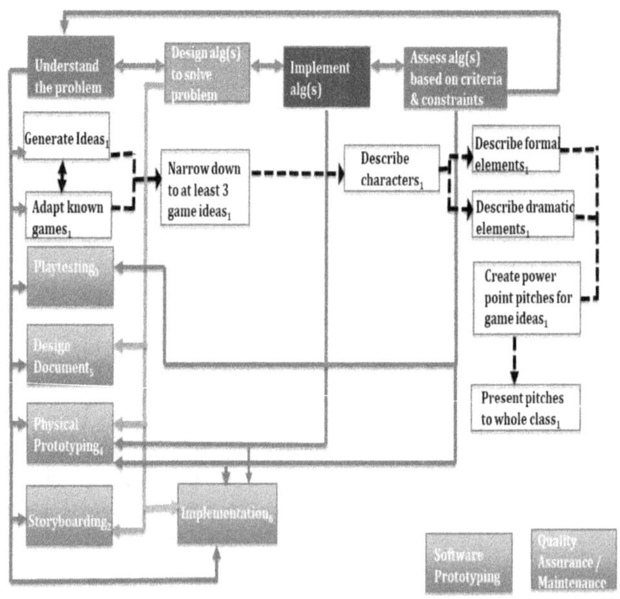

Figure 3. CAT Capability Flow with Fleshed Out Brainstorming Phase

5.2.1 Storyboarding Phase

During the Storyboarding phase, dyads used the My Storyboard Design Notebook page. This scaffold helped dyads align the visual and non-visual elements of their game idea, and helps them to visually specify the formal and dramatic elements of the game as well as begin articulating the core gameplay mechanic, game functionality, user interface, and interaction model. Dyads use multiple My Storyboard Design Notebook pages to represent their game idea from the opening screen to the concluding screen of gameplay. For this phase, dyads either 1) drew stills for each action within their game as well as each level within the game, or, for each action that was represented by a button click (for example, next, play, back, etc.), they 2) mapped that button to a still that depicted what the player would see upon clicking the button. Finally, they 3) described the non-visual elements. Figure 4 depicts the flow with the Brainstorming$_1$ and Storyboarding$_3$ phases fleshed out including playtesting$_2$.

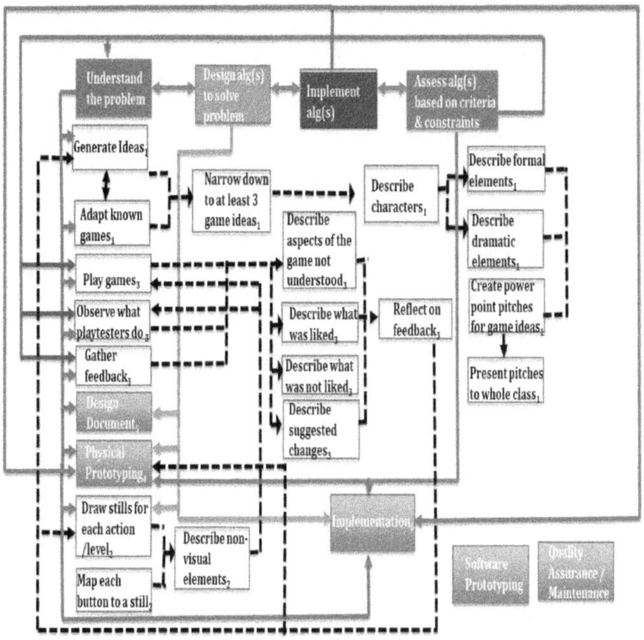

Figure 4. CAT Capability Flow with Fleshed out Brainstorming and Storyboarding Phases (including Playtesting)

Due to space limitations, we will describe the prioritized set of activities that Scholar dyads engaged in during the Physical Prototyping, Design Document, and Implementation phases in the presentation of this paper.

5 DISCUSSION

Our analysis of the CAT Capability Flow to date reveals some compelling insights. First, enacting CAT in the context of game design is a non-trivial endeavor. Recall that the game design cycle is an iterative cycle of phases which are themselves iterative. The CAT Capability Flow represents both the serial, parallel, and iterative nature of the enactment of CAT in the context of game design. Second, our analysis reveals that different aspects of CAT show up in different places of the game design cycle for this population (i.e., African-American middle-school girls). For example, while *'Understand the problem'* maps to every phase of the game design cycle, *'Implement algorithm(s)'* (described as *'Implement alg(s)'*) maps to the Physical Prototyping and Implementation phases. Prior research reveals that subsequent phases of the game design cycle require the game designers (i.e., Scholars working in dyads) to describe their game in more and more specific ways [29]. This increased specification over subsequent phases could result in a deeper understanding not only of the game, but also potentially of the problem or social issue itself. Analysis of the dyad video observations will reveal whether dyads discussed or conducted further research on their social issue as they moved through subsequent phases of the game design cycle.

Finally, our analysis revealed two phases where all aspects of CAT were mapped onto, namely, the Physical Prototyping$_4$ and Implementation$_6$ phases. While analysis of dyad video observations and dyad artifacts will uncover fully what this suggests about CAT capability development in African-American middle-school girls, previous research [29] suggests that the Physical Prototyping and Implementation phases were two phases where dyads reported experiencing the most difficulties as they were designing their games. As such, our analysis suggests that phases with multiple arrows coming into them may be phases where additional scaffolds are required to support Scholars as they move through those phases. Our continued analysis of dyad video observations will provide more insight into what kinds of additional scaffolds may be needed.

6 FUTURE WORK

This submission described early findings describing CAT. We used an approach which resulted in the continued iterative refinement of the CAT Capability Flow. This iteration of the CAT Capability Flow is a first step in describing a capability that, to date, has not been described before. As steps are iteratively refined, the connection between the enactment and the underlying cognitive processes will become more salient.

ACKNOWLEDGMENTS

We are grateful for the generous support of the National Science Foundation (DRK-12 1150098).

REFERENCES

[1] Anderson, J. R. (2000). *Cognitive Psychology and Its Implications: Fifth Edition.* New York: Worth Publishing.

[2] Anderson, J. R., Greeno, J. G., Kline, P.J. & Neves, D.M. (1981). Acquisition of problem-solving skills. In J. R. Anderson(Ed.), *Cognitive skills and their acquisition.* Hillsdale, NJ: Lawrence Erlbaum Associates.

[3] Bandura, A. (1994). Self-efficacy. In R. J. Corsini (Ed.), Encyclopedia of psychology (2nd ed., Vol. 3, pp. 368-369). New York: Wiley.

[4] Bandura blog entry. Ability and Capability. Downloaded from Bandura's blog, http://des.emory.edu/mfp/AbilityCapability.html.

[5] Barnes, T., Richter, H., Chaffin, A., Godwin, A., Powell, E. (2007). Game2Learn: Building CS1 Learning Games for Retention. Accepted by ITiCSE2007, Dundee, Scotland, June 2007.

[6] Barnes, T., Richter, H., Chaffin, A., Godwin, A., Powell, E., Ralph, T., Matthews, P. & Jordan, H. (2007). Game2Learn: A study of games as tools for learning introductory programming. In Proceedings of SIGCSE 2007.

[7] Barron, B., Schwartz, D.L., Vye, N.J., Moore, A., Petrosino, A., Zech, L., Bransford, J. D. & The Cognition and Technology Group at

Vanderbilt (1998). Doing with understanding: Lessons from research on problem- and project-based learning. *Journal of the Learning Sciences*, 7(3&4), 271-311.

[8] Bransford, J. D., Brown, A.L., & Cocking, R. R. (1999). *How people learn: Brain, mind, experience, and school.* Washington, DC: National Academy Press.

[9] Collins, A., Brown, J.S., & Newman, S.E. (1989). Cognitive apprenticeship: Teaching the crafts of reading, writing, and mathematics. In L.B. Resnick (Ed.), *Knowing, learning, and instruction: essays in honor of Robert Glaser*, 453-494. Hillsdale, NJ: Lawrence Erlbaum Associates.

[10] Crawford, C. (2010) *How to Think: Algorithmic Thinking*, In the *Journal of Computer Game Design* v.7.

[11] DiSalvo, B. J., Guzdial, M., Mcklin, T., Meadows, C., Perry, K., Steward, C. & Bruckman, A. (2009). Glitch Game Testers: African American Men Breaking Open the Console. In Proceedings of DiGRA 2009.

[12] Fullerton, T., Swain, C., and Hoffman, S. (2004). Game Design Workshop: designing, prototyping and playtesting games. San Francisco, CA: CMP Books.

[13] Kafai, Y. B. (2006). Playing and Making Games for Learning: Instructionist and Constructionist Perspectives for Game Studies. In *Games and Culture*, 1(1), pp. 36-39.

[14] Koschmann, T. (1996). Paradigm shifts and instructional technology: An introduction. In T. Koschmann (Ed.), *CSCL: Theory and practice of an emerging paradigm*, 1-23. Mahwah, NJ: Erlbaum.

[15] Kramer, Kramer, D. (2002). *Algorithms Should Mind Your Business*, downloaded from http://www.outsourcing-russia.com/docs/?doc=680.

[16] Lave, J., & Wenger, E. (1991). Situated learning: Legitimate peripheral participation. Cambridge, UK: Cambridge University Press.

[17] Maloney, J., Burd, L., Kafai, Y., Rusk, N., Silverman, B., and Resnick, M. (2004). Scratch: A Sneak Preview. Second International Conference on Creating, Connecting, and Collaborating through Computing. Kyoto, Japan, pp. 104-109.

[18] National Research Council (2011). *A Framework for K-12 Science Education: Practices, Crosscutting Concepts, and Core Ideas.* Washington, DC: The National Academies Press.

[19] Nersessian, N.J. (2008) *Creating Scientific Concepts.* Cambridge, MA: MIT Press.

[20] Owensby, J.N. (2006). *Exploring the Development and Transfer of Case Use Skills in Middle-School Project-Based Inquiry Classrooms.* Completed Dissertation, Georgia Institute of Technology. Proquest (1115125971).

[21] Papert, S. (1993). *The children's machine: Rethinking school in the age of the computer.* New York: Basic Books.

[22] Polya, G. (1973). *How to Solve It: A New Aspect of Mathematical Method, 2nd Edition.* Princeton, NJ: Princeton University Press.

[23] Rankin, Y., Thomas, J.O., Irish, I., and Hawkins, S. (2014). From Consumers to Producers: African American Middle School Students as Game Designers. In Proceedings of Foundations of Digital Games (FDG) 2014, Liberty if the Seas, Caribbean, April 2014.

[24] Repenning, A. and Ioannidou, *Broadening Participation through Scalable Game Design*, ACM Special Interest Group on Computer Science Education Conference, (SIGCSE 2008), (Portland, Oregon USA), ACM Press.

[25] Repenning, A., Webb, D., & Ioannidou, A. (2010). *Scalable Game Design and the Development of a Checklist for Getting Computational Thinking into Public Schools.* In the proceedings of the 2010 ACM Special Interest Group on Computer Science Education (SIGCSE) Conference, Milwaukee, WI.

[26] Schoenfeld, A. H. (2010). *How we think: A theory of goal-oriented decision making and its educational applications.* New York: Routledge.

[27] Schneider, G. M. & Gersting, J. L. (2010). *Invitation to Computer Science, 5th Edition.* Boston, MA: Course Technology, Cengage Learning, 4-16.

[28] Thomas, J. O; Minor, R.; and Odemiwingie, O. C. (2016). Exploring African-American Middle School Girls' Perceptions of Computational Algorithmic Thinking and of Themselves as Game Designers. In C. Looi, J. Polman U. Cress and P. Reimann (eds): *ICLS '16: Proceeding of the 12th International Conference of the Learning Sciences Volume 1., Singapore, 20 June – 24 June 2016.* Singapore: International Society of the Learning Sciences, pp. 960 – 962.

[29] Thomas, J.O., Rankin, Y., Minor, R. & Sun, L. (2017). Exploring the Difficulties African-American Middle School Girls Face Enacting Computational Algorithmic Thinking over three Years while Designing Games for Social Change. In *Journal of Computer Supported Cooperative Work* (2017) 26: 389.

[30] Thomas, J.O. (2008). *Scaffolding Complex Cognitive Skill Development: Exploring the Development and Transfer of Case Use Skills in Middle-School Project-Based Inquiry Classrooms.* VDM Publishing.

[31] Vygotsky, L. S. (1978) *Mind and society: The development of higher mental processes.* Cambridge, MA: Harvard University Press.

[32] Werner, L., Campe, S., & Denner, J. (2005, October). Middle school Girls + games programming = Information technology fluency. *ACM special interest group in information technology education (SIGITE).* Newark, NJ.

[33] Werner, L., Denner, J., Bliesner, M., and Rex, P. (2009, April). Can middle-schoolers use Storytelling Alice to make games? Results of a pilot study. *Fourth International Conference on the Foundations of Digital Games.* Orlando, FL.

[34] Wing, J.M. (2006). *Computational Thinking.* In CACM Viewpoint, March 2006, pp. 33-35.

[35] Wing, Jeannette M. (2008). Computational thinking and thinking about computing. *Philosophical Transactions of the Royal Society A: Mathematical, Physical and Engineering Sciences*, vol. 366, no. 1881, April 2008, pp. 3717-3725.

[36] Wing, J.M. (2010). "Computational Thinking". Presented at the Centre for Computational Systems and Biology, Trento, Italy, December 2010.

Examining the Impact of Computational Creativity Exercises on College Computer Science Students' Learning, Achievement, Self-Efficacy, and Creativity

Markeya S. Peteranetz
Dept. of Educational Psychology
University of Nebraska-Lincoln
114 Teachers College Hall
Lincoln, NE 68588-0345
markeya.dubbs@huskers.unl.edu

Shiyuan Wang
Dept. of Geriatrics and Gerontology
Rowan University School of Osteopathic Medicine
One Medical Center Drive, Suite 246
Stratford, NJ 08084
wangs1@rowan.edu

Duane F. Shell
Dept. of Educational Psychology
University of Nebraska-Lincoln
114 Teachers College Hall
Lincoln, NE 68588-0345
dshell2@unl.edu

Abraham E. Flanigan
Dept. of Educational Psychology
University of Nebraska-Lincoln
114 Teachers College Hall
Lincoln, NE 68588-0345
abrahamflanigan@gmail.com

Leen-Kiat Soh
Dept. of Computer Science and Engineering
University of Nebraska-Lincoln
256 Avery Hall
Lincoln, NE 68588-0115
lksoh@cse.unl.edu

ABSTRACT

The purpose of the present study was to investigate how the inclusion of computational creativity exercises (CCEs) merging computational and creative thinking in undergraduate computer science (CS) courses affected students' course grades, learning of core CS knowledge, self-efficacy, and creative competency. CCEs were done in lower- and upper-division CS courses at a single university. Students in CCE implementation courses were compared to students in the same courses in different semesters. *Propensity score matching* was used to create comparable groups (control and implementation) based on students' GPA, motivation, and engagement. Results showed that implementing CCEs in undergraduate CS courses enhanced grades, learning of core CS knowledge, and self-efficacy for creatively applying CS knowledge. However, CCEs did not impact creative competency. The effect of the CCEs was consistent across upper- and lower-division courses for all outcomes. Unlike previous studies that only established the *support* for CCEs, such as positive dosage effects, the results of this study indicate that CCEs have a *causal* effect on students' achievement, learning, and self-efficacy, and this effect is independent of general academic achievement, motivation, and engagement. These findings establish the CCEs as a validated, evidence-based instructional method.

CCS CONCEPTS

• **Social and professional topics~Computational thinking** • *Social and professional topics~Model curricula* • *Social and professional topics~Computer science education*

KEYWORDS

Computational creativity; computational thinking, computer science education

SIGCSE'18, February 21-24, 2018, Baltimore, MD USA

ACM ISBN 978-1-4503-5103-4/18/02...$15.00
https://doi.org/10.1145/3159450.3159459

ACM Reference format:
M. S. Peteranetz, S. Wang, D. F. Shell, A. E. Flanigan, L-K. Soh. 2017. Examining the Impact of Computational Creativity Exercises on College Computer Science Students' Learning, Achievement, Self-Efficacy, and Creativity. In *Proceedings of* 49th ACM Technical Symposium on Computing Science Education, *Baltimore, MD, USA, February 21—24, 2018 (SIGCSE'18)*, 6 pages. https://doi.org/10.1145/3159450.3159459

1 INTRODUCTION

A primary goal of computer science (CS) education is to produce students who are capable of practicing computational thinking and applying it effectively to problem solving situations in their chosen field [1, 8]. Meanwhile, as is true of many STEM and non-STEM disciplines, effectively solving complex problems in CS fields requires more than knowledge of basic principles or the application of algorithmic processes. It involves integrating knowledge and skills and adapting them in a way that is compatible with the novelty of a given problem. In order to solve complex problems in CS, one must think systematically, yet flexibly, computationally, yet creatively. This approach to thinking and problem solving has been called computational creativity [27]. Computational creativity is one possible route to enhancing students' learning of computational thinking skills and CS principles while also fostering creative problem solving skills. In the computational creativity framework, computational thinking and creative thinking are viewed as separate but compatible cognitive tools that individually expand the ways knowledge and skills can be applied to problem solving.

Computational thinking is a systematic approach to solving problems, building systems, and understanding human behavior that draws on the power and limits of computing [28]. It involves skills such as conceptualizing at multiple levels of abstraction and generalization, recognizing patterns, designing and executing algorithms, decomposing a problem, and evaluating the correctness and effectiveness of problem solutions.

Epstein's Generativity Theory [4, 5, 6] identifies four core competencies of creative thinking. First, capturing novelty refers to the capacity to recognize and note unique ideas as they occur. Second, challenging established thinking and behavior patterns refers to the capacity to generate new approaches to problems. Third, broadening one's knowledge beyond one's discipline allows for the novel integration of ideas. Fourth, surrounding oneself with new social and environmental stimuli can lead to new experiences and ideas. Importantly, Epstein notes that these competencies are skills that can be practiced and developed by anyone in any context [4, 5].

This integration of computational and creative thinking is motivated by the complementary benefits that each affords the other. Computational thinking can lend structure to the creative process, improving the process's efficiency, whereas creative thinking facilitates novelty and ingenuity in solving computational problems, improving a solution's effectiveness. For example, challenging leads to computational tools being used in novel ways leading to the development of new computational approaches to old and new problems, and capturing forces consideration of new ways to represent and save data and solution procedures. Through computational creativity, students can leverage creative thinking skills to "unlock" their understanding of computational thinking while their growing computational thinking skills enhance the tools available for creatively solving challenging problems [27].

Prior research has shown that exercises designed to integrate computational and creative thinking can support students' learning, achievement, and self-efficacy [11, 12, 15, 20, 21], independent of individual differences such as motivation and gender [12]. However, to date, research on Computational Creativity Exercises (CCEs) has not employed research designs that allow for strong causal interpretations of effects. Extending prior research, the present study uses one such design, propensity score matching, that makes it possible to draw conclusions about causality. Results indicate CCEs have a positive causal impact on students learning, achievement, and self-efficacy. These findings establish the CCEs as a validated, evidence-based instructional method.

2 COMPUTATIONAL CREATIVITY EXERCISES (CCEs)

Previous research has produced a set of CCEs where group activities are designed to train students in both creative competencies and computational thinking skills [12, 27]. As discussed in [12, 27], the principles underlying the design of the CCEs are (1) balancing of attributes between computational and creative thinking and (2) mapping between computational and creative concepts and skills as they manifest in different disciplines. Here we provide a summary of these CCEs and refer readers to [11, 26, 27] for details.

Each exercise has four basic components: (1) Objectives, (2) Tasks, (3) CS Light Bulbs, and (4) Questions. Each exercise is supported using an online collaborative wiki platform [2]. The objectives include a set of creative objectives, computational objectives, and collaborative problem solving objectives. Creative objectives are based on Epstein's four competencies: capturing, challenging, broadening, and surrounding. Computational objectives include two aspects: CS concepts, such as sorting and logical conditionals, and computational thinking skills, such as problem decomposition, pattern recognition, abstraction, generalization, algorithmic design, and evaluation. The collaborative nature of the CCEs facilitates creative thinking by bringing together students from diverse backgrounds. These objectives help students contextualize the purpose of the exercises by showing how an exercise lacking any programming code is related to CS concepts and indicate how students can use relevant creative thinking skills to complete the exercises.

The Task component lists all the tasks the group must complete during the two weeks of the exercise. Tasks require collaboration among the students and some require individual contributions. They are designed to engage group members with different backgrounds, encourage creative approaches, and promote open-ended discussions as the group produces specific artifacts.

The CS Light Bulbs are text snippets embedded within the exercise handout that explicitly connect the task activities and CS topics specific to each participating course. These snippets help students relate what they do for the exercise to real-world issues and practices that utilize computational thinking and CS concepts.

The Questions component presents open-ended questions that require students to reflect on their solutions and analyze potential issues with their solutions, encouraging them to evaluate the results of their original tasks using computational thinking and imagine further improvements using creative thinking.

3 RELATED RESEARCH FINDINGS

Previous studies have collectively found that the CCEs are associated with better student learning and achievement in computer science courses. Studies of CCEs in introductory CS1 courses [11, 12, 15, 20] have found a linear increase in learning outcomes (i.e., grades and computational thinking test scores) with each additional CCE completed. This "dosage" effect was generally consistent for CS majors and non-majors, first-year students and upper-classmen, and men and women [12]. This dosage effect was again found in [26] where lower- and upper-division courses were studied. This indicated that even though the basic computational thinking principles at the core of the CCEs would be covered in CS1 courses, with minimal adaptations, the CCEs appear to be effective in courses at all undergraduate levels and across an array of CS topics. A separate quasi-experimental study was conducted examining the CCEs in a foundational CS1 course for engineering majors [21]. Again, including CCEs in the course led to higher computational thinking test scores and self-efficacy for applying CS knowledge in a future career field. These findings suggested that CCEs are a viable instructional tool for enhancing student learning in CS1 classes for CS majors and non-CS majors.

In all of these studies, the "dosage effect" and implementation–control group differences were distinct from general student achievement as students' overall GPA was controlled. Also, the effects in CS1 classes have been shown to be distinct from students' motivation and strategic self-regulated engagement in the course [15]. *This suggests that the CCEs have an independent instructional effect that is not an artifact of student general academic ability or motivation.*

Even though the evidence supporting the above reviewed finding—that the CCEs are effective in increasing student course achievement and learning across multiple replications—is compelling, with the exception of [21], the *evidence comes from correlational research designs rather than from experimental or quasi-experimental designs with a control group that would allow for more causal interpretation.* Only the findings from [21] were based on a quasi-experimental treatment-control group design that would support a causal interpretation. But, [21] was confined to *a single CS1 course for engineering students.* Other CS courses like those in which the dosage effect was found have *not* been examined with a similar treatment-control group experimental design. Also, although [15] found that the dosage effect was consistent across different profiles of student motivated strategic engagement, students with different levels of motivation did complete *different* numbers of exercises. As a result, motivation cannot be completely ruled out as a factor.

4 STUDY PURPOSE, DESIGN, AND RESEARCH QUESTIONS

The purpose of this study was to address the limitations identified in the previous research on CCEs. While the most desirable research design for determining effectiveness would be a randomized trial, the use of actual courses generally precludes any type of random assignment of courses to treatment and control conditions, especially in upper division courses with smaller enrollments where only one section is offered in a semester. Furthermore, we wanted to examine whether effects for the CCEs could be found when these were done as an integral part of the course as a regular course assignment. Randomly assigning some students to do the CCEs and others to a no-CCEs control group within the same course would negate the examination of their effects when implemented as an integral part of the course.

The most powerful alternative research design to randomized trials for determining causal effects is Propensity Score Matching (PSM) [7]. In randomized trials, the randomization process results in treatment/intervention and control groups that are expected to be equivalent in terms of all potentially confounding variables. When participants cannot be randomly assigned—which is often the case in actual classroom settings either because only a single section of a class is offered or because administratively students cannot be barred from a section when it is offered at the only time that does not conflict with other courses–PSM can be used to equate intervention and control groups by matching each student in the intervention group with a control group student, perhaps from another semester of the same course, who has similar characteristics. Propensity scores are derived through logistic regression, with matching variables that are related to outcome variables.

This study sought to use PSM to examine the effectiveness of CCEs for increasing student achievement and learning, self-efficacy, and creative competencies when implemented in regular CS classrooms from the freshmen to senior level. We had two guiding research questions.

Research Question 1: What was the effect of completion of CCEs on students' class grades, learning CS knowledge, self-efficacy for applying CS, and creative competency? We hypothesized that students in the CCE implementation group would have higher grades, knowledge retention, self-efficacy, and creative competency, than matched students in the control group.

Research Question 2: Did the effect of CCEs differ by course level (lower division [freshmen and sophomore] vs. upper division [junior and senior])? We hypothesized that any differences would be more salient in lower division courses.

5 METHOD

5.1 Classes and Participants

The study was approved by the university IRB and students participated voluntarily in data collection. The CCEs were implemented during the Fall 2015 semester (implementation group semester) with 376 students in four undergraduate and one combined undergraduate/graduate CS courses. For PSM, control group data were collected from 439 students in these same five courses (control group semesters) during the Fall 2014 and/or Spring 2015 semesters. The instructors were the same for each course during control and intervention semesters. The courses examined were (1) 100 level: CS1: Engineering and Science Focus (3 CCEs), (2) 200 level: Computer Organization (4 CCEs), (3) 300 level: Data Structures and Algorithms (3 CCEs), (4) 300 level: Programing Language Concepts (3 CCEs), and (5) 400 level: Automata (2 CCEs). CCEs were deployed using the Written Agora system [2], a wiki system designed to facilitate online collaboration between groups of students.

5.2 Propensity Score Matching

Prior studies [11, 12, 20, 26] found that improvements in learning, achievement, and self-efficacy only occurred when students completed most of the CCEs assigned. Because different numbers of CCEs were implemented in the different classes based on how instructors aligned the CCEs with course topics, the CCE intervention group was created from those students in each class who completed the minimum number of CCEs required to have an effect based on prior dosage effect findings. The CCE completion criteria were: for courses with two CCEs, students had to complete both; for courses with three CCEs, two or more; for courses with four CCEs, three or more.

To build a comparable propensity score matched control group from the students in the control semester classes, a one-to-one matching procedure was used. Each student in the implementation group was matched with one student from the same course in the control group semester [7].

For the PSM for testing course grade, matching measures were from a pre-survey motivation questionnaire done during the first week of the semester, student enrolled course, and student cumulative Grade Point Average (GPA). Because most students in the classes completed the pre-survey, this allowed for the maximum number of students available for matching regardless of whether students completed other survey or outcome measures.

For the PSM for testing the knowledge test, creative competencies, and self-efficacy, matching measures were from a more comprehensive post-survey questionnaire of motivation, strategic self-regulation, studying, and affect done during the last week of the semester; student enrolled course, and student cumulative GPA. These comprehensive surveys allowed for more variables in the PSM, which should increase matching accuracy. However, fewer students completed these post-surveys than the pre-survey. This did not affect the sample for testing the knowledge test, creative competencies, and self-efficacy outcomes as these were done at the same time as the post-survey. But, using the post-survey for grades would have reduced the available sample relative to the pre-survey, which is why different criterion variables were used for our PSM-matching testing different outcomes.

After PSM-matching, 277 students were included in the course grade comparison (128 in control group, 149 in CCE implementation group; 227 male, 48 female; 180 in lower-division courses, 97 in upper-division), and 224 students were included in the knowledge test, creative competency, and self-efficacy comparisons (88 in control group, 136 in CCE implementation group; 179 male, 43 female; 160 lower-division courses, 64 in upper-division). One senior course was excluded from the examination of knowledge scores, self-efficacy, and creative competency because of too few participants (N = 13) at post-survey, but it was retained for grades. Sample sizes differ because of student attrition between the pre- and post-survey.

5.3 Propensity Score Matching Variables

Students' overall GPA was obtained from university records. Students' motivation was assessed with an instrument battery used and validated in prior studies. These measured (1) students' goal orientation for the class [3, 13, 17, 22, 24]; (2) students' ratings for the connectedness between academic coursework and a STEM career ad perceived instrumentality of specific course work for attaining STEM academic and career goals [9, 10, 13, 22, 24]; and (3) students' emotional or affective course reactions [e.g., 14].

Strategic self-regulation was assessed with the Student Perceptions of Classroom Knowledge Building instrument (SPOCK) [13, 22, 23, 24]. The SPOCK assesses four aspects of student self-regulated engagement: (1) general metacognitive self-regulation and strategy use; (2) knowledge building/deep learning strategies; (3) engagement evidenced through active question asking; and (4) lack of engagement evidenced through reports of study and learning difficulties. Engagement was further measured by self-reported study time and perceived study effort [13, 22, 24].

5.4 Outcome Variables

Course grades were obtained from university records and were *z*-score standardized within each course. Students' computational thinking knowledge and skills from the course were measured with a computational thinking/CS knowledge test (13 conceptual and problem-solving items) developed by CS and engineering department faculty at the university where the study was conducted [13, 24]. The Cronbach's alpha was .77.

Creative competencies were measured with a researcher-developed instrument adapted from the Epstein Creative Competencies Inventory (ECCI) [6]. The score was the mean of the items (Cronbach's alpha = .79).

Self-efficacy was measured by asking students to rate their confidence in their knowledge of 12 computational thinking and CS topics with emphasis on application in their chosen field and enhancing creativity in their field ("Your ability to use computational algorithms to solve problems in your field;") [25]. Ratings were done on a scale from 0 (Completely Unconfident) to 100 (Completely Confident). The self-efficacy score was the mean of the items (Cronbach's alpha = .98).

6 RESULTS

6.1 Research Question 1

To test Research Question 1, independent samples *t*-test was conducted (means and standard deviations shown in Table 1). Consistent with our hypothesis, the implementation group with CCEs had higher course grades ($t = -3.78$, $p < .01$). This indicates that students who completed most or all of the CCEs in a course achieved higher grades relative to their classmates than did their PSM-matched controls. The effect size (Cohen's $d = .77$) was large. And, the course grades for the control semester PSM-matched students was essentially identical to the overall z-score standardized mean for the courses, which was zero. This means that the control group students did not differ as a group from others in their course who were not matched with implementation group students. The implementation group students who completed most or all CCEs, however, averaged .42 standard deviations higher than the course z-score standardized mean of 0.0.

Results for the CS/computational thinking knowledge test were not as dramatic (t = -2.34, p = .02, Cohen's d = 0.35), but students in the implementation group averaged about 1.2 more questions correct than control group students. There were similar results for student self-efficacy for using their CS knowledge in their field (t = -2.65, p = .01, Cohen's d = .39). In both of these tests, the effect sizes would be considered medium.

There was not a significant difference in creative competencies (t = .28, p = .78, Cohen's d = -0.05) (as shown in Table 1). Scores on the creative competencies test were essentially the same for the two groups. It is possible that an effect was not found because the test used is not sensitive enough to detect change in a time frame as short as one semester.

Table 1: Achievement, Creative Competency, and Self-Efficacy

	Control		*Implementation*	
	M	SD	M	SD
Course Grade	.01	1.03	.42	.64
Knowledge Test	6.68	3.12	7.84	3.36
Creative Competency	2.51	.69	2.47	.84
Self-efficacy	63.11	21.81	70.88	18.41

6.2 Research Question 2

To test Research Question 2, a 2 (course level) x 2 (implementation/control) ANOVA was conducted. Means and standard deviations are shown in Table 2. The germane test for determining whether there were differences in the effects of CCE completion is the interaction. If the results for the implementation group and control group are different for upper and lower division courses, the interaction effect will be significant. For course grades ($F = .22$, $p = .64$, partial $\eta^2 = .001$), CS/computational thinking knowledge test scores ($F = .48$, $p = .49$, partial $\eta^2 = .003$), self-efficacy ($F = .09$, $p = .76$, partial $\eta^2 = .001$), and creativity competency ($F = 2.74$, $p = .10$, partial $\eta^2 = .02$) there was no significant interactions. Thus, the patterns of difference were the same for upper- and lower-division courses. Consistent with the findings for the entire sample, students in the implementation semester had higher grades, knowledge test scores, and self-efficacy but there was no difference in creative competency scores in both lower and upper division courses.

Although the pattern of higher knowledge test scores for the implementation group relative to the control group was the same for both upper- and lower-division classes, upper-division courses had significantly higher knowledge test scores ($F = 4.12$, $p = .04$, partial $\eta 2 = .02$). For creativity competency, although there was no difference between implementation group and control group students, students in upper-division courses scored significantly higher ($F = 5.25$, $p = .02$, partial $\eta 2 = .04$), suggesting that creative competencies do improve as students move through their post-secondary education.

Table 2: Achievement, Creative Competency, and Self-Efficacy in Lower- and Upper-Division Courses

	Lower-Division		Upper-Division	
	Control	Implementation	Control	Implementation
	M (SD)	M (SD)	M (SD)	M (SD)
Course Grade	.02	.41	-.04	.46
	(1.06)	(.70)	(.96)	(.49)
Knowledge Test	6.24	7.63	7.71	8.36
	(2.97)	(3.29)	(3.29)	(3.56)
Creative Competency	2.47	2.30	2.56	2.88
	(.63)	(.81)	(.77)	(.79)
Self-efficacy	61.37	69.61	67.73	73.98
	(21.05)	(18.04)	(23.56)	(19.26)

7 DISCUSSION

This study used propensity score matching (PSM) to examine the causal effect (if any) of implementing CCEs in undergraduate CS courses. The CCE implementation group used CCEs while the control group did not. Students in the CCE implementation group, in two lower-division and three upper-division courses, were paired with a control group student who had similar GPA, motivation, and engagement, who was taking the same course, from the same instructor.

Generally, the findings supported our hypotheses. First, students in the CCE implementation group earned higher grades, scored higher on the knowledge test, and had higher self-efficacy for using their CS knowledge in their field than students in the control group who did not do CCEs. These results were the same for both upper (junior and senior) and lower (freshmen and sophomore) division courses.

PSM is considered a strong design for inferring causal effects, equivalent to a randomized trial design [7]. The findings should, therefore, be interpreted as indicating a causal effect of the CCEs on student grades, learning, and self-efficacy. This extends beyond the previous "dosage effect" found in prior studies [11, 12, 15, 26] and prior quasi-experimental findings [21].

CCEs, however, did not impact creative competencies. Prior studies [11] using student focus group and post-survey responses indicated that, for the most part, students do not see the CCEs as being useful or connected to course content. This was also true in the current study. The learning that occurs in the CCEs does not need to be conscious [18]. The creative competencies, however, were assessed with a survey instrument. This type of survey requires that students be aware of the changes being rated. While the CCEs did provide them with broadened experiences, challenging tasks, surrounding with new collaborative partners, and opportunities to capture their finding and thoughts, these may not have been obvious. Students might have better creative competency skills but not recognized them. Some evidence for this can be found in the self-efficacy increases. The self-efficacy measure assesses creative application of CS knowledge to the students' field. That this significantly increased suggests that students may actually feel more creative, but not necessarily in terms of the specific creative competencies. This issue requires additional study.

8 CONCLUSIONS AND FUTURE WORK

The findings support the idea that the incorporation of the CCEs into classes can improve learning of CS content and computational thinking in CS courses from freshmen to senior level. Consistent with the Unified Learning Model [18], completing CCEs provides additional retrieval and repetition of course content beyond the other class assignments, which strengthens knowledge connections, leading to better understanding of course content and more potential for creative application of computational thinking and CS.

The findings from this and other previous studies reported in this area [11, 12, 15, 21, 26] confirm that the merger of computational and creative thinking can be realized in exercises that can be implemented in CS courses across the entire curriculum from freshmen to senior level, and these exercises can help students improve their course achievement and learning of CS and computational thinking. In previous studies, the "dosage effect" was distinct from general student achievement as students' overall GPA was controlled, and distinct from students' motivation and strategic self-regulated engagement [15]. In this study, the effect was found by matching students on these same potential confounding factors. The PSM allows us to infer a true causal impact of the CCEs that was not possible in prior studies which indicates that CCEs are exerting an independent instructional effect. If students complete the CCEs, they learn more and achieve higher grades.

These findings support recommending CCEs as an addition to CS courses, as suggested by [27]. Acting on the recommendations by [15, 26], in this study there was a significant attempt to help instructors integrate CCEs into courses. This work showed that CCEs can be modified to fit curriculum in courses from the freshmen to senior level with adaptations to tasks and lightbulbs. But, as in prior studies [11], student focus group and post-survey responses indicated that, for the most part, students are not self-aware of either the usefulness of the CCEs or the connection of the CCEs to the course. In courses where CCEs were more fully integrated into the class, focus group responses indicated that students enjoyed them and appreciated the rationales behind them. But, as reported previously, it appears that if CCEs are not required, then students will differ in how many they complete voluntarily [11, 12, 15, 26]. To achieve maximum benefits, CCEs need to be a required part of the course. To effectively integrate the CCEs, instructors need to overtly connect the CCEs to the course by (1) discussing exercises in class and going through the exercise assignments with students, (2) explicitly mapping activities in CCEs to class topics, and (3) relating computational and creative objectives to real-world problems.

In recognition of the importance of collaboration as one of the essential skills for effective problem solving in the 21st century [1, 8], CCEs have been refined by the addition of collaborative objectives based experience working in teams and coordinating student group work. There is a stand-alone computational creativity course that has been developed and delivered, with an on-line deliverable version. These courses are currently being evaluated.

ACKNOWLEDGMENTS

This work was partially supported by the National Science Foundation (Grants No. 0829647, 1431874, and 1122956).

REFERENCES

[1] ACM/IEEE-CS Joint Task Force on Computing Curricula. (2013, Dec.). Computer Science Curricula 2013. [Online]. Available: http://dx.doi.org/10.1145/2534860

[2] A. Eck, L-K., Soh, and C. Brassil. 2013. Supporting active wiki-based collaboration. In *Proc. CSCL'2013* (Madison, WI), 176-183.

[3] A. J. Elliot, K/ Murayama, and R. Pekrun. 2011. A 3 X 2 achievement goal model. *J. of Educ. Psychol.*, 103, 632-648.

[4] R. Epstein. 1996. Cognition, creativity, and behavior: Selected essays. Praeger, Westport, CT.

[5] R. Epstein. 2005. Generativity theory and creativity. Theories of creativity. In *Theories of Creativity,* M.A. Runco and R.S. Albert, Eds. Hampton Press, Cresskill, NJ.

[6] R. Epstein, S. M. Schmidt, and R. Warfel. 2008. Measuring and training creative competencies: Validation of a new test. *Creativity Res. J.*, 20, 7-12.

[7] S. Guo, and M. W. Fraser. 2015. *Propensity score analysis: statistical methods and applications.* Sage Publications, Thousand Oaks, CA.

[8] M. Guzdial. 2008. Paving the Way for Computational Thinking. *Commun. ACM,* 51, 25-27.

[9] J. Husman, and J. Hilpert. 2007. The intersection of students' perceptions of instrumentality, self-efficacy, and goal orientations in an online mathematics course. *Zeitschrift für Pädagogische Psychologie/ German J. of Educ. Psychol.*, 21, 229-239.

[10] J. Husman and D. F. Shell. 2008. Beliefs and perceptions about the future: A measurement of future time perspective. *Learning and Individual Differences,* 18, 166-175.

[11] L. D. Miller, L.-K. Soh, V. Chiriacescu, E. Ingraham, D. F. Shell, and M. P. Hazley. 2013. Improving learning of computational thinking using creative thinking exercises in cs-1 computer science courses. In *Proc. FIE'2013* (Oklahoma City, OK), 1426-1432.

[12] L. D. Miller, L.-K. Soh, V. Chiriacescu, E. Ingraham, D. F. Shell, and M. P. Hazley 2014. Integrating computational and creative thinking to improve learning and performance in CS1. In *Proc. SIGCSE'2014 (SIGCSE'2014),* (Atlanta, GA), 475-480).

[13] K. G. Nelson, D. F. Shell, J. Husman, E. J. Fishman, and L.-K. Soh. 2015. Motivational and self-regulated learning profiles of students taking a foundational engineering course. *J. Eng. Educ.*, 104, 74-100. DOI= 10.1002/jee.20066

[14] R. Pekrun, A. Frenzel, T. Goetz, and R. P. Perry. 2007. The control value theory of achievement emotions: An integrative approach to emotions in education. In *Emotion in Education*, P.A. Schutz and R. Pekrun, Eds. Academic Press, San Diego, CA.

[15] M. S. Peteranetz, A. E. Flanigan, D. F. Shell, and L.-K. Soh. 2017. Computational creativity exercises: An avenue for promoting learning in computer science. *IEEE Trans. on Ed.*, 99, 1-9. DOI: 10.1109/TE.2017.2705152

[16] P. R. Pintrich. 2003. A motivational science perspective on the role of student motivation in learning and teaching contexts. *J. of Educ. Psychol.*, 95, 667-686.

[17] C. Senko, C. S. Hulleman. and J. M. Harackiewicz. 2011. Achievement goal theory at the crossroads: Old controversies, current challenges, and new directions. *Educ. Psychologist,* 46, 26-47.

[18] D. F. Shell, D. W. Brooks, G. Trainin, K. Wilson, D. F. Kauffman, and L. Herr. 2010. The Unified Learning Model: How Motivational, Cognitive, And Neurobiological Sciences Inform Best Teaching Practices. Springer, the Netherlands.

[19] D. F. Shell, M. P. Hazley, L.-K. Soh, E. Ingraham, and S. Ramsay. 2013. Associations of students' creativity, motivation, and self-regulation with learning and achievement in college computer science courses. In *Proc. FIE'2013* (Oklahoma City, OK), 1637-1643.

[20] D. F. Shell, M. P. Hazley, L.-K. Soh, E. Ingraham, and S. Ramsay. 2014. *Impact of creative competency exercises in college computer science courses on students' creativity and learning.* Presented at the Annual Meeting of the Amer. Educational Res. Assoc., (Philadelphia, PA), Apr. 3-7.

[21] D. F. Shell, M. P. Hazley, L.-K. Soh, L. D. Miller, V. Chiriacescu, and E. Ingraham. 2014. Improving learning of computational thinking using computational creativity exercises in a college CS1 computer science course for engineers. In *Proceedings of the 44th Annual Frontiers in Education (FIE) Conference,* (Madrid, Spain), 3029-3035.

[22] D. F. Shell, and J. Husman. 2008. Control, motivation, affect, and strategic self-regulation in the college classroom: a multidimensional phenomenon. *J. of Educ. Psychol.*, 100, 443-459.

[23] D. F. Shell, J. Husman, J. E. Turner, D. M. Cliffel, I. Nath, and N. Sweany. 2005. The impact of computer supported collaborative learning communities on high school students' knowledge building, strategic learning, and perceptions of the classroom. *J. of Educ. Comput. Res.*, 33, 327-349.

[24] D. F. Shell and L.-K. Soh. 2013. Profiles of motivated self-regulation in college computer science courses: Differences in major versus required non-major courses. *J. of Sci. Educ. and Tech.*, 22, 899-913.

[25] D. F. Shell, L.-K. Soh, A. E. Flanigan, and M. S. Peteranetz., 2016. Students' initial course motivation and their achievement and retention in college CS1 courses. In *Proc. SIGCSE'2016* (Memphis, TN), 639-644.

[26] D. F. Shell, L.-K. Soh, A. E. Flanigan, M. S. Peteranetz, and E. Ingraham. 2017. Improving Students' Learning and Achievement in CS Classrooms through Computational Creativity Exercises that Integrate Computational and Creative Thinking. In *Proc. SIGCSE'2017* (Seattle, WA), 543-548

[27] L.-K. Soh, D. F. Shell, E. Ingraham, S. Ramsay, and B. Moore. 2015. Learning through computational creativity. *Commun. ACM,* 58, 8, 33-35.

[28] J. Wing, 2010. Computational Thinking: What and Why. Link Magazine.

Creativity, Customization, and Ownership: Game Design in Bootstrap:Algebra

Emmanuel Schanzer
Bootstrap/Brown University
Providence, RI, USA
schanzer@bootstrapworld.org

Shriram Krishnamurthi
Brown University/Bootstrap
Providence, RI, USA
sk@cs.brown.edu

Kathi Fisler
Brown University/WPI/Bootstrap
Providence, RI, USA
kfisler@cs.brown.edu

ABSTRACT

Game programming projects are concrete and motivational for students, especially when used to teach more abstract concepts such as algebra. These projects must have open-ended elements to allow for creativity, but too much freedom makes it hard to reach specific learning outcomes. How many degrees of freedom do students need to make a game feel like one they genuinely designed? What kinds of personalization do they undertake of their games? And how do these factors correlate with their prior game-playing experience or with their identified gender?

This paper studies these questions in the concrete setting of the Bootstrap:Algebra curriculum. In this curriculum, students are only given four parameters they can customize and only a few minutes in which to do so. Our study shows that despite this very limited personalization, students still feel a strong sense of ownership, originality, and pride in their creations. We also find that females find videogame creation just as satisfying as males, which contradicts some prior research but may also reflect the nature of games created in this curriculum and the opportunities it offers for self-expression.

ACM Reference Format:
Emmanuel Schanzer, Shriram Krishnamurthi, and Kathi Fisler. 2018. Creativity, Customization, and Ownership: Game Design in Bootstrap:Algebra. In *SIGCSE '18: SIGCSE '18: The 49th ACM Technical Symposium on Computer Science Education, February 21–24, 2018, Baltimore , MD, USA.* ACM, New York, NY, USA, 6 pages. https://doi.org/10.1145/3159450.3159471

1 INTRODUCTION

Many authors [3, 7, 11] emphasize the creative benefits of computing. A game or physics simulation author can design novel characters or means of input, experiment (or do away) with gravity, and so on. Many are attracted to computing precisely because of this creative power, and constructionism [8] embraces this kind of power as a central part of its pedagogy.

When discussing K-12 CS curricula, "creativity" is often used colloquially (as opposed to formally, as in psychology [15]), referring to a combination of student engagement, motivation, or flexibility for students to choose their learning tasks. In a traditional curricular setting, too much flexibility can be problematic. If a course has concrete topics to cover—especially in the context of an externally administered exam—then teachers may not have the flexibility to engage in free-form exploration. Here, we do not go into the question of whether this is a reasonable attitude or not. We take it as a given and important constraint of many teachers and schools, and note that curriculum designers that want to succeed in a large number of schools—thereby bringing computing to *all*—must take into account such constraints.

Three factors amplify these costs:

- Some attempts at bringing computing to all take it to non-computing subjects. Their instructors may be ill-equipped to aid students in unstructured explorations.
- These problems as exacerbated when computing is embedded into topics like algebra, which are subjected to high-stakes testing. These tests often push teachers to stick to a regimen likely to meet their testing goals, and create anxiety about too much deviation. Thus, a curriculum that wishes to embed itself into such a topic must minimize variance.
- Finally, not all students themselves necessarily appreciate a lack of fetters. As research has shown [6], too much choice can negatively impact motivation and engagement.

In this paper, we examine these issues in the context of a specific curriculum, Bootstrap:Algebra[1] (henceforth BS:A). In BS:A, students build a videogame that is purportedly "of their own design", but in actuality is highly constrained. The benefit of this curriculum for math transfer has been studied before [14], but does it come at a cost of hurting computing satisfaction? Indeed, many CS teachers balk at how little "creative control" students are given over their games, especially in relationship to free-form curricula that build on tools like Scratch [12]. In response to those teachers, we investigate the impact of the small amount of customization BS:A provides. Is this enough for students to feel a sense of satisfaction or ownership over their product? Do they view this as an authentic game-building experience? Along the way, we also consider the impact of identified gender, providing new data on how female students relate to game design.

2 CREATIVE EXPRESSION IN BOOTSTRAP:ALGEBRA

BS:A is a 20–25 hour module embedded into math classes in US grades 7–10, and is designed to teach students the essence of functions. To motivate learning, students approach this topic by creating

[1]Bootstrap is the umbrella name for a family of four curricula. The Algebra curriculum is the oldest of these, and referred to simply as "Bootstrap" in older publications.

ACM ISBN 978-1-4503-5103-4/18/02...$15.00
https://doi.org/10.1145/3159450.3159471

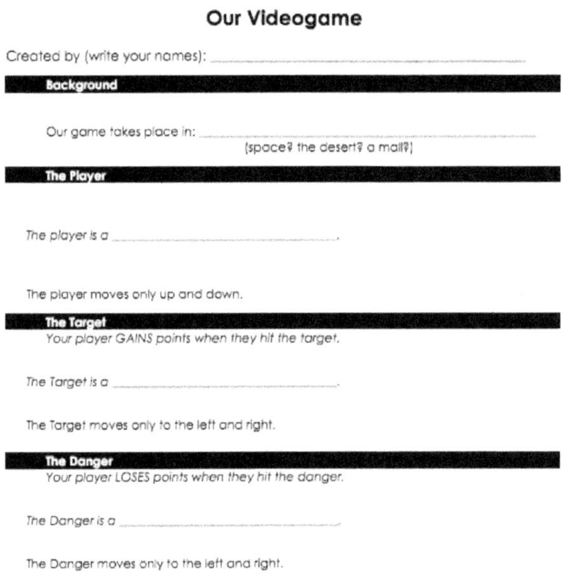

Our Videogame

Created by (write your names): ____________________

Background

Our game takes place in: ____________________
(space? the desert? a mall?)

The Player

The player is a ____________________.

The player moves only up and down.

The Target

Your player GAINS points when they hit the target.

The Target is a ____________________.

The Target moves only to the left and right.

The Danger

Your player LOSES points when they hit the danger.

The Danger is a ____________________.

The Danger moves only to the left and right.

Figure 1: Game Design Worksheet

a videogame. Concretely, students write several functions to define the behavior of various game elements: the movement of characters, the detection of walls (to implement "side-scrolling"), the calculation of distances (to check for collisions), and the production of game visuals. To meet its math curricular needs, the game design obeys a careful progression to motivate every next needed mathematics topic, in close alignment with math standards, and with significant scaffolds [13] to stage the math/game progression.

To motivate students, teachers tell them that they will *create their own videogame*. This is followed by a discussion about the importance of teamwork and pair-programming[2], and setting student expectations.

Students are then shown a simple game with four components:

- *background* (static image over which the game takes place)
- *player* (avatar, moves along y-axis via keypresses)
- *danger* (moves along x-axis; player wishes to avoid)
- *target* (moves along x-axis; player wishes to catch)

The game score increases when the player collides with the target, and decreases when it collides with the danger.

At this point, students are given time to design their game. In fact, the only "design" they can perform is to customize these four elements. Furthermore, they are then given merely *five minutes* to (in pairs) come up with the design elements. Their design is written down on the worksheet shown in fig. 1. Having come up with this design, they are given a few minutes on Google Images [images.google.com] to find images corresponding to these choices.[3]

In principle, there is still ample room for creative expression. One team might use an underwater background, a diver for a player, a treasure chest for the target, and a shark for the danger. Another might use a mall as the setting, a teenager as the player, jewelry as the target, and a mall cop as the danger. Some games borrow from existing narratives (a *Twilight*-themed game, for example, might use characters from the well-known franchise), while others have a social mission (a student avoids drugs and gangs while collecting As and Bs that fly across the screen). Two sample screenshots are shown in fig. 2.[4] On the left, the heart tries to catch the cap and avoid the monster. On the right, the net tries to catch space junk while avoiding asteroids. The BS:A infrastructure maintains the score (initial value of 100, +20 for catching the target, -50 for colliding with the danger) and automatically overlays it atop the game.

Because there is an enormous gap between the popular commercial games they have named and what they are being allowed to design for themselves, students may not find this an authentic experience. Furthermore, the movement of characters is also fairly scripted (they can only move in certain dimensions; thus, the only flexibility they have is in how far they move, which is usually a function of the sizes of images). To a mathematically-minded viewer, then, the games might seem essentially isomorphic. Do students also view them that way?

Note that working in pairs further affects these issues. When grouped, student are forced to come to an agreement. While this may lead to more creative options, it also requires a degree of compromise, which may further reduce the sense of personalization and hence ownership. Nevertheless, studying the effect of working in pairs is a broad topic outside the scope of this paper, so we leave this question for future study.

Concretely, in this paper we ask the following questions:

- Do the students play videogames themselves? Their frequency of play may impact how they perceive the (lack of) flexibility they are given.
- Do students feel excitement about building a game? If they felt overly constrained or scripted, that is likely to reflect in a lack of excitement.
- Do students feel pride in the game they built? The closer they associate with the game, the more pride they are likely to feel; the small degrees of freedom they are given may result in a lack of pride in the result.
- Do students feel their game is "real"? It is quite possible that choosing four parameters with limited motion greatly impacts their sense of realism, especially when compared to the blockbuster games they have played.
- Do students feel their games are different from each others'? Given the high degree of behavioral similarity between the games, is the small amount of customization they perform sufficient for them to feel like their games are distinctive?

We also study the impact of gender on these questions.

3 STUDENT SURVEY

We conducted a survey across students who had just completed BS:A. We had a choice of a small-scale, in-depth study or a large-scale one with fewer details. While the former would and will be instructive, we wanted results with sufficient numbers to arrive at statistically significant conclusions. Therefore, we opted for a

[2]Though the BS:A curriculum strongly recommends that teachers have students work in pairs, some teachers permit some or all students to work individually.

[3]Teachers are instructed about Google Images filters to enable students to search for images with suitable usage rights [support.google.com/websearch/answer/29508].

[4]These images were obtained from programs voluntarily provided by students.

Figure 2: Sample Student Game Screenshots

lighter-weight study to encourage participation and completion. Our goal was to examine whether there was even preliminary evidence in favor of personalization and ownership before conducting a richer study. In this paper, we use $\Longrightarrow$ to indicate some of the issues we either explicitly left out of our study (to keep it short) or that have arisen as a result of seeing the data we obtained.

In response to our request on the primary BS:A mailing list, we received responses from 21 schools. These spanned both middle- and high-schools. All but one were public middle and high schools in the USA, with one international school in Nigeria. The survey was administered using a Google Form, which teachers forwarded to their classes; no personally-identifying information was collected.

A total of 225 students responded, evenly distributed across the schools. Of the respondents,[5] 94 identified as female, 104 as male, and 11 marked Other or preferred to not answer. (The ratio of about 43% female is consistent with the overall BS:A student demographic.) While it is impossible to check that students were taking the study seriously, we felt any lack of seriousness would be manifest in the free-form textual answers. As we did not find instances of this, we used all survey responses in our analysis.

4 STUDENT BACKGROUND

We now analyze student responses to answer the questions raised in section 2. We begin by exploring the student population.

Game Playing. We first determine to what extent students themselves play videogames.

How often do you play videogames?

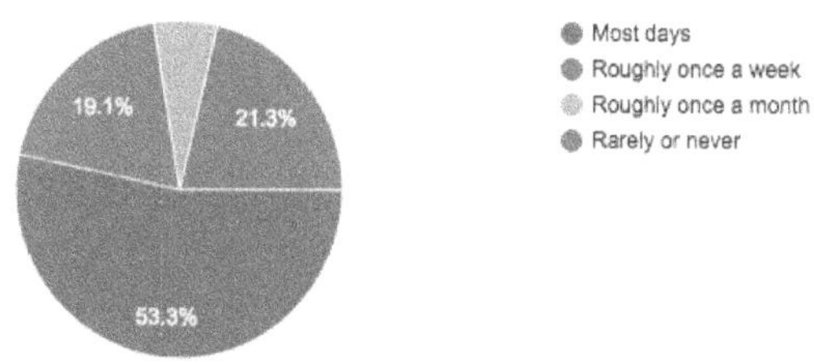

As we can see, roughly half are avid game players. We did not ask them for specific styles of games, allowing their self-definition of games to suffice for this purpose. $\Longrightarrow$This is an example of a question a richer study could include, e.g., as a free-form textual box where students could name the games they play, and the research team or outside experts could classify these by styles of games.

[5]Due to a form error, this question was missing from the survey that the first few students saw. Therefore, these data alone are for 209, not 225, respondents.

Game Creation Confidence. We also asked students whether, before they started, they felt confident they could create a game. Note that this question was posed at the end of the class, so their recall may not be perfect. Nevertheless, student confidence in completing the task was high. This could be attributed to having had some prior experience with tools like Scratch [2]; $\Longrightarrow$additional research is needed to understand why students have this confidence.

Before I started this project, I was confident I could make a game

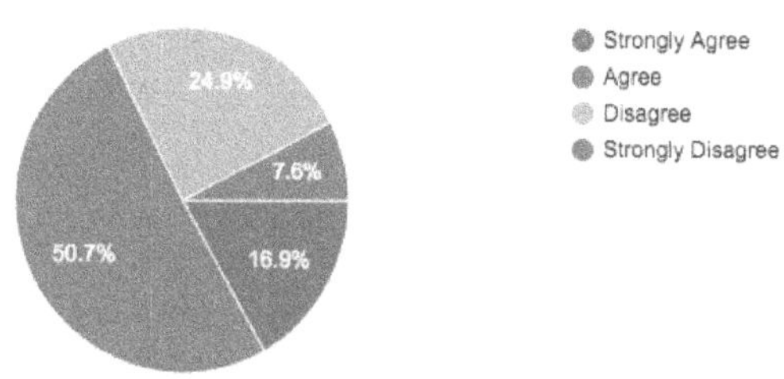

5 AUTHENTICITY AND OWNERSHIP

Now we focus on student responses that help us understand their perception of the games they created.

Excitement. In light of the previous data, it is conceivable that many students, being confident about their ability to create a game and being game habituants, did not feel much excitement from their accomplishment. However, we find that that is not true:

I am excited that I made a game

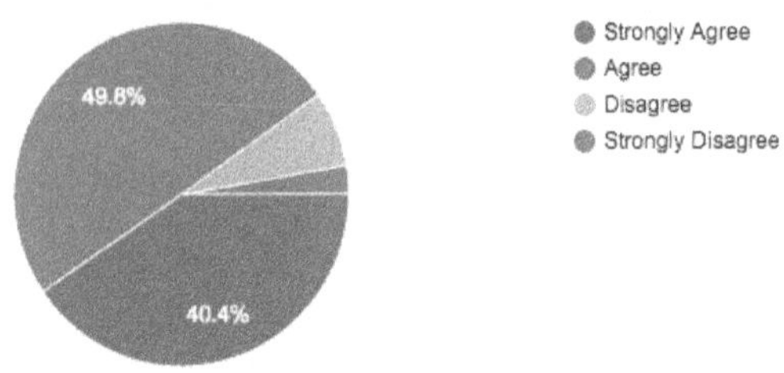

In particular, only six students are in the strong disagreement group.

Pride. Beyond excitement, we were interested in a more subtle emotion: pride in their product. It is conceivable that students were excited by the activity but did not feel a deeper sense of pride, which would result in a more lasting positive impact [5].

I am proud of the game I made

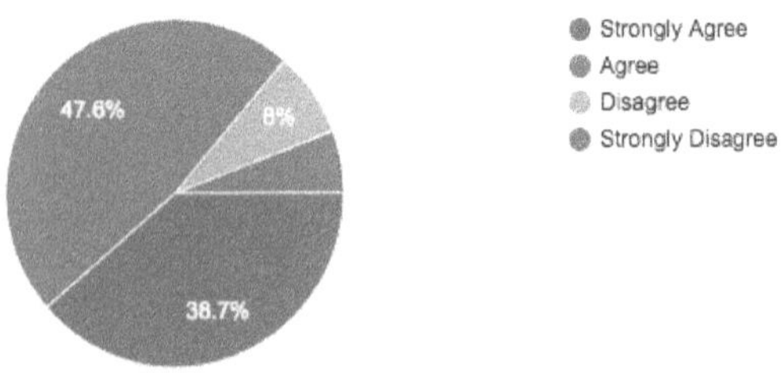

We note that students feel pride to essentially the same extent as they feel excitement. (Indeed, student ratings for the two questions are essentially identical.) ⟹It is possible students interpreted the two questions in essentially the same way; in-depth studies would be needed to determine their perceptions.

Having established a baseline sense of accomplishment, now we get to the two most important questions relevant to this paper: does the small degree of customization they were able to perform (a) result in authentic-feeling games and (b) help differentiate their games from those of others?

Realism. First, we asked students how *real* they felt their game was. It is easy to see that a simple game with just three entities and highly constrained movement might not feel real. In that case, students might view their activity as no more than a disguised math task and might not feel they have done any computer programming. However, the data (shown in the next chart) do not bear this out.

It is noteworthy that about a quarter of students slightly or strongly disagreed with the realism of their games. Indeed, we would have been surprised, and been suspicious about the attention students were paying to the questions, had this not been so: given the very artificial nature of the games, a significant number of students should have felt this way. In light of that, we find it interesting that nearly three-quarters (71.1%) somewhat or strongly felt their game was realistic. In section 6 we analyze these data further,

I feel like I made a real game

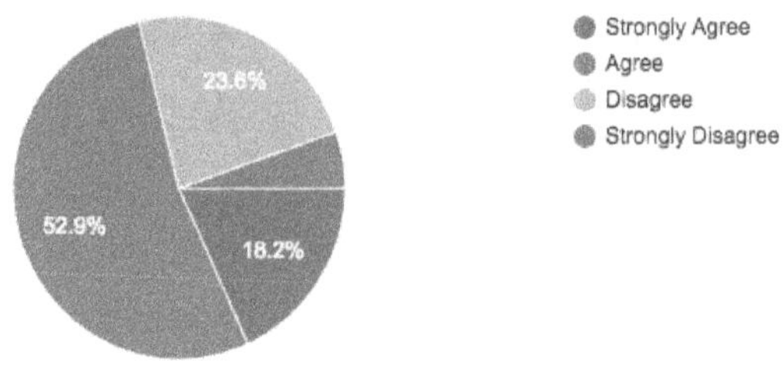

in particular comparing the perception of realism with students' gaming activity and with gender.

⟹A natural follow-up is to determine what factors of the games felt realistic. For instance, if scoring were removed, would that impact realism? Did students want more freedom in choosing components? Was the restriction to one-dimensional motion for each moving object to blame? (This is a restriction that many students want to remove; the Bootstrap:Reactive [www.bootstrapworld.org/materials/spring2017/courses/reactive] curriculum was created as a follow-up to Bootstrap:Algebra precisely to provide this power.)

My game is different from the ones other students made

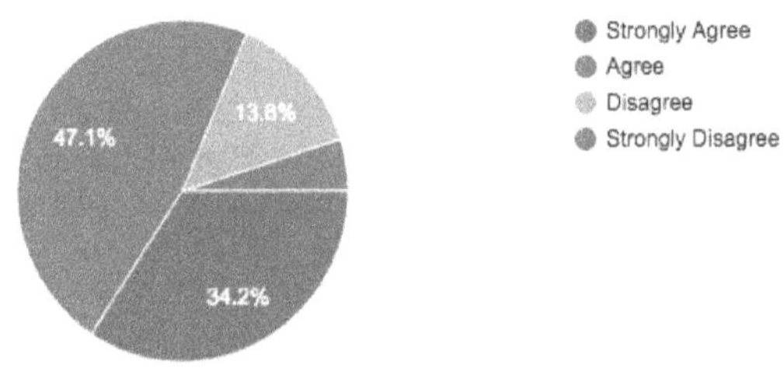

Difference. Another important question is whether the similarities that are clear from a mathematical perspective are evident to the students, or at least whether they *matter.* We asked students this directly. A total of 18.7% feel that their game is *not* different from those of others, with only 4.9% feeling *strongly* this way. What this indicates is that even the small amounts of customization permitted by BS:A are sufficient to get students to view their games as different from those of others; indeed, over a third feel *strongly* that their games are different, nearly double the disagreement groups put together.

⟹It would be useful to understand the students who do *not* perceive differences. We conjecture several hypotheses. Some might be procedural:

- All games started by customizing the same worksheet.
- All games were produced in lock-step in a class setting.

More intriguingly, however, students might have perceived the underlying mathematical similarity between the games, and might thus have looked past the visual and narrative differences.

Equally interesting is why students *did* view the games as different: did they understand the underlying mathematical similarity and consciously choose to overlook it, or did the visual and narrative differences occlude that similarity?

Visibility. One other measure is how students feel about sharing these games with people outside their class. Here we find that 64% would like others to see their game.

I want people from outside my class to see my game

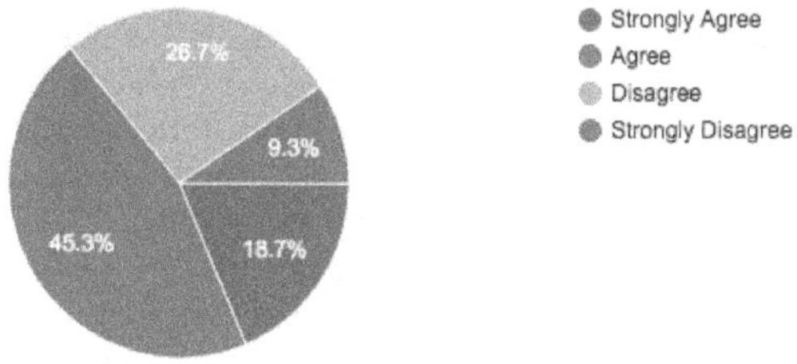

⟹Of course, there are many reasons why a student might *not* want others to see their game. They may not feel sufficient pride in their product; they may be nervous about criticism or even just calling attention to themselves; they may be embarrassed about how their parents might distribute their work. In addition, we have to also consider social factors, such as students not wanting to be seen by their friends and peers as overly academic [4]. These factors demand significantly more study.

Design Inspiration. Finally, we ask students for the inspirations for their game designs: both how they chose the characters in their game, and whether they got interesting ideas from seeing or playing other students' games. Students cited numerous influences on the former: a quarter chose "They remind me of a book, movie or TV show that I like"; another 14% chose "They remind me of something I like to do"; 7.6% chose it because of their partner. 20% had no particular reason for their choice.

Because we permitted free-form answers, we received many that evinced personalization in one of the above categories. Some chose to write in specific TV shows (e.g., The Simpsons) or bands (e.g., Migos). Several mentioned either specific videogames that inspired their design (e.g., Minecraft, Clash Royale), genres ("who doesn't like a good zombie game!"), or a generic desire to mimic a videogame. We also received some other categories of responses, such as [all quotes are verbatim, including typos]:

- "They represented something I was extremely passionate about; the enviorement and environmental protection."
- "we thought it was funny and we like dogs"
- "it has a good meaning: to always pick up trash"
- "Sloths are cute. Zombie marshmallows are a necessity of life."
- "i chose batman as my them because my sister oves batman and she kind of wonted me to make the about that so i chose to make her happy"
- "To raise animal endangerment"
- "it's a true story. Me and my partner just changed it a little bit though."

Some of these responses represent recurrent themes: animals they like or animal rights in general, social goals (such as reducing littering or protecting the environment), or humor.

We also see some conflict. Two students commented that they were forced to change their choices by their teacher. Both students, one male and one female, who may have been partners (both were taught by the same teacher), strongly disagreed on most of the questions above (e.g., on excitement and pride). The teacher's comment on this intervention was: "After some experience with poor decisions made by my 8th grade students, I had to restrict any racial stereotypes and political figures. I had a couple of groups over the years make some games that were very offensive to the parents and staff that the students were presenting to." These issues are not widely reported by BS:A teachers, but are nevertheless something to consider when students have freedom to choose from the unlimited palette of the Web, as opposed to highly restricted characters provided by some systems.

We also see evidence of inspiration from one another:

I got some interesting ideas from seeing or playing other students' games

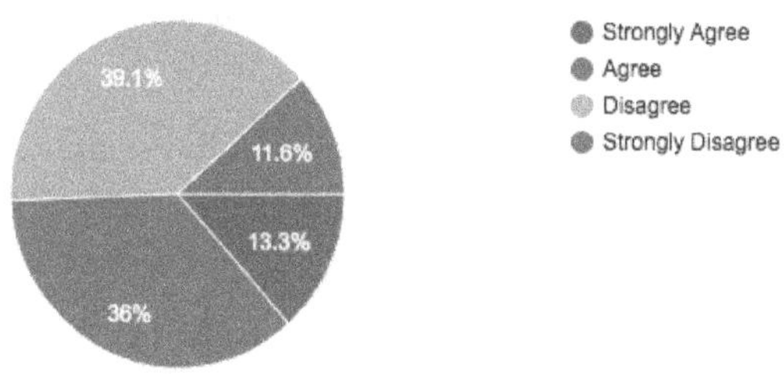

Observe that over 40% of students claimed to get interesting ideas. Surely this could not happen if they all considered their games to be the same, so this is further evidence that students did not do so, even to the point of getting new ideas from each other.

6 ANALYSIS

Finally, we examine some correlations of interest.[6] We abbreviate question names and give responses ordinal values (Strong Agree = 4 down to Strong Disagree = 1) to summarize responses.

- *Does the frequency with which a student plays games impact how they feel about their games?*
  PlayFrequency has a positive, weak relationship with OutsiderSee (0.16), but the relationship is somewhat significant ($p = 0.01645$). No other factor shows significance.
- *Does students' confidence going into Bootstrap impact how they feel about their games?*
  Yes! PreConfidence has a positive, weak relationship (0.17–0.26) with PostPride, PostExcitement, OutsiderSee, and PostAuthentic ($p < 0.001$ to 0.11).
- *Does the frequency with which a student plays games impact their amount of confidence about being able to make one?*
  PlayFrequency has a positive, weak relationship with PreConfidence (0.26), and the relationship is significant ($p < 0.001$). This is noteworthy given the previous two.

We also performed an ordered logistic regression [1] to identify which effects might have been significant in arriving at our key outcomes. When factoring in *frequency of playing videogames*, *confidence in being able to make a game*, and *gender*, the only effect to

[6]We use correlations rather than ANOVA as the variables are not independent.

show true significance (t = 2.223) is that identifying male leads to a feeling the videogame is not real. No other factors are significant.

The Impact of Gender

The following table summarizes the responses by gender for the 198 students who self-identified as one of male or female (section 3).

Measure	*Males*	*Females*	$p < \cdots$	*Significant?*
PlayFrequency	3.56	2.41	**0.001**	yes
PreConfidence	2.87	2.56	*0.011*	somewhat
PostPride	3.16	3.26	0.2248	**no**
PostExcitement	3.23	3.19	0.39	**no**
PostAuthentic	2.72	2.89	0.11	**no**
PostUnique	3.09	3.18	0.4033	**no**
OutsiderSee	2.75	2.65	0.4049	**no**
GotIdeasFromOthers	2.5	2.54	0.7322	**no**

The data show that there *is* a difference between the extent to which males and females play games, *but* these do not translate into other measurable differences. Females seem to get every bit as much excitement, pride, and sense of authenticity out of this educational experience. These results are consistent with prior research on gender and games that distinguish game *play* from game *design*. Lucas and Sherry [10] found that male adolescents were more likely to play games, to play them for longer, and to enjoy different qualities of gameplay, but Kafai [9] reports on multiple studies (some from other researchers) showing that gender differences are much smaller when looking at game design. In Kafai's design studies, gender differences manifest in the *nature* of games (i.e., themes and characters) that students choose. Examining whether similar differences arise in Bootstrap games would be an interesting question for future work.

7 DISCUSSION AND CONCLUSION

Our study offers several important lessons. First, it questions how much creativity is really needed for students to feel proud and have a sense of ownership of their work, showing that very small amounts can have large impact, even when the subsequent programming is largely identical. Second, it fails to find any significant outcome differences between male and female students, indicating that a videogame programming curriculum can be just as effective with female students. Finally, it demonstrates that BS:A students feel a sense of accomplishment over their computing artifact, which is independent of any math learning outcomes achieved.

A few details are worth noting. Once students have designed their scenario, they are allowed to get images from the Web. This means they have access to the "entire world" of images. It is possible that students' sense of realism comes from this array of choices, in contrast to the curated selection found in tools from Code.org, Scratch, and Alice.

Is more room for creative expression better? Perhaps not! A previous version of BS:A had one more opportunity for customization: a projectile. When this was given to students, most games ended up looking like "shooter" or "shoot 'em up" games. Concerned about the negative connotations of a projectile, the BS:A team removed this option from the standard curriculum in 2009. Yet this effectively liberated students, as a result of which the games now produced are much harder to classify. We believe this shows that there is a great deal more study needed to understand what constitutes creativity and freedom in computing.

How lasting is the impact of our findings? Will students' sense of pride dissipate quickly? Would they feel less pride if they were to see a friend's game written in a more free-form setting? These issues may not be relevant for the original purpose—of invigorating their math learning—but would matter in a broader CS setting.

Finally, we note that some of the games have very strong social and personal components. Their student designers are essentially using games for self-expression. To what extent does this happen in other game-based programming curricula, and what are the curricular design factors that enable or inhibit it? And how can we draw on these experiences to create a more socially meaningful form of computing?

ACKNOWLEDGMENTS

Emma Youndtsmith, Rosanna Sobota, Ed Campos, and dozens of other BS:A members helped refine the curriculum. We thank Matthias Felleisen for inspiration. We appreciate the detailed reviews, some of whose good ideas we could not execute due to space limitations. Preston Tunnell Wilson helped with the data analysis. This work is partially funded by the US National Science Foundation.

REFERENCES

[1] A. Agresti and M. Kateri. 2003. Categorical Data Analysis. 482 (2003).
[2] M Armoni, O Meerbaum-Salant, and M Ben-Ari. 2015. From Scratch to "real" programming. *ACM Transactions on Computing Education* 14, 4 (2015), 25.
[3] D. Clements. 1991. Enhancement of creativity in computer environments. *American Educational Research Journal* 28, 1 (1991), 173–187.
[4] B DiSalvo. 2012. *Glitch game testers: the design and study of a learning environment for computational production with young African American males.* Ph.D. Dissertation. Georgia Institute of Technology.
[5] C. Ingleton and K. O'Regan. 2002. Recounting mathematical experiences: Emotions in mathematical learning. *Literacy and Numeracy Journal* 11, 2 (2002), 95–107.
[6] S.S. Iyengar and M.R. Lepper. 2000. When choice is demotivating: Can one desire too much of a good thing? *Journal of Personality and Social Psychology* 79, 6 (2000), 995.
[7] Y. Kafai and K. Peppler. 2011. Youth, Technology, and DIY: Developing Participatory Competencies in Creative Media Production. *Review of Research in Education* 34 (2011), 89–119.
[8] Y. B Kafai, K. A Peppler, , and R. N. Chapman. 2009. *The Computer Clubhouse: Constructionism and Creativity in Youth Communities.* Teachers College Press.
[9] Yasmin V. Kafai. 1998. Video game designs by girls and boys: variability and consistency of gender differences. In *From Barbie to Mortal Kombat: gender and computer games.* MIT Press, 90–114.
[10] Kristen Lucas and John L. Sherry. 2004. Sex Differences in Video Game Play: A Communication-Based Explanation. *Papers in Communication Studies* 20 (2004).
[11] A. Repenning, D.C. Webb, C. Brand, F Gluck, R Grover, S Miller, H. Nickerson, and M. Song. 2014. Beyond Minecraft: Facilitating computational thinking through modeling and programming in 3d. *IEEE Computer Graphics and Applications* 34, 3 (2014), 68–71.
[12] M. Resnick, J. Maloney, A. Monroy-Hernández, N. Rusk, E. Eastmond, K. Brennan, A. Millner, E. Rosenbaum, J. Silver, B. Silverman, and Y. Kafai. 2009. Scratch: programming for all. *Commun. ACM* 52, 11 (2009), 60–67.
[13] E Schanzer, K. Fisler, and S. Krishnamurthi. 2013. Bootstrap: Going beyond programming in after-school computer science. In *SPLASH Education Symposium.*
[14] E Schanzer, K Fisler, S Krishnamurthi, and M. Felleisen. 2015. Transferring skills at solving word problems from computing to algebra through Bootstrap. In *Symposium on Computer Science Education.* 616–621.
[15] Robert J. Sternberg. 2006. The Nature of Creativity. *Creativity Research Journal* 1 (2006), 87–98.

Updating Introductory Computer Science with Creative Computation

Dianna Xu
Bryn Mawr College
Bryn Mawr, PA, USA
dxu@brynmawr.edu

Ursula Wolz
Bennington College
North Bennington, VT, USA
ursulawolz@bennington.edu

Deepak Kumar
Bryn Mawr College
Bryn Mawr, PA, USA
dkumar@brynmawr.edu

Ira Greenberg
Southern Methodist university
Dallas, TX, USA
igreenberg@smu.edu

ABSTRACT

This paper reports on the results of a multi-year project in which we identified essential pedagogy and curriculum for teaching introductory computing courses focused on Creative Computation using Processing. The curriculum aligns with a traditional 'CS1' approach as well as 'AP CS A', and goes well beyond 'CS Principles' standards to teach foundations of computer science and programming. We addressed the bridge between high school and entry-level college curriculum in computer science (American freshman high school to freshman college) and demonstrated how algorithmic art provides a powerful vehicle for diverse student populations within a broad range of pedagogical frameworks ranging from traditional structured classrooms to inquiry-based student-driven project labs. A secondary result is that instructors require long-term engagement with mentors to extend their own knowledge of computing, visual arts and appropriate pedagogy.

CCS CONCEPTS

• Social and professional topics • Professional topcs→Computing Education

KEYWORDS

CS AP; K-12 Computing; CS0; CS1; creative computation; Processing

ACM Reference format:
D. Xu, U. Wolz, D. Kumar, and I. Greenberg. 2018. Updating Introductory Science with Creative ComputationIn SIGCSE '18: 49th ACM Technical Symposium on Computer Science Education, Feb. 21–24, 2018, Baltimore, MD, USA. ACM, NY, NY, USA, 6 pages.
https://doi.org/10.1145/3159450.3159539

1 INTRODUCTION

Creative Computation via Processing[1] [4,5] is a curriculum and pedagogy that provides contextualized computing through which a diverse student population can be introduced to foundational principles of computer science and develop novice expertise as programmers. Creative Computation is an emergingdiscipline that combines theory and methodology from computer science and engineering with aesthetic principles, creative practice and pedagogical approaches from the fine and graphic arts. As a highly interdisciplinary approach [3], it is an example of contextualized computing that can serve to attract a diverse student population to computer science. It draws from prior work in media computation [6], robots [8,10], games/animation [11,13], and music [2].

Our goal was to strengthen formative/introductory CS education in high school and college by catalyzing excitement, creativity, and innovation. The digital representation of data, access to authentic sources of big data, and creative visualization techniques are revolutionizing intellectual inquiry in many disciplines, including the arts, social sciences, and humanities. We assert that CS1 should be updated with contemporary, diverse examples of computing in a modern context. This paper reports on the success of adapting a curriculum and pedagogy, namely a traditional CS1 scope and sequence, with an art studio pedagogy in which students engage in highly individual artistic design. This paper summarizes the qualitative evidence to date that Creative Computation can be successfully integrated into a variety of high school and undergraduate introductory courses.

Contextualized computing is increasingly being introduced into American grades 6-11, articulating with the Common Core Standards in Language Art. With few exceptions such as [12], the primary emphasis is on computing principles applied to a sampling of disciplines rather than immersion in an interdisciplinary domain. Using a qualitative research approach we studied the degree to which an established introductory curriculum could be disseminated to high school and diverse undergraduate institutions with a broad range of pedagogical perspectives.

Through short-duration workshops and mini-grants, several school instructors have adapted our Creative Computation curriculum to courses including High School Pre-AP Computer Science, AP CS Principles, AP CS A, High School Post-AP, Community College Computer Science, Community College Media Studies, Computer Science 0 (CS0), and Computer Science 1 (CS1). The institutions ranged from small private elite high schools and colleges, to large urban public high schools and universities, with course structure including teacher-centric instruction and inquiry-based labs. The curriculum was

[1] Processing.org

SIGCSE'18, February 21-24, 2018, Baltimore, MD, USA.

ACM ISBN 978-1-4503-5103-4/18/02...$15.00.
DOI: http://dx.doi.org/10.1145/3159450.3159539

successfully adapted as modules in semester or yearlong courses, as full courses that ranged from quarter, to tri, to semester and full year duration, and one instance adapted the curriculum for an online course for both high school students and undergraduates.

Reports from participant instructors in the workshops and mini-grant program suggest that Creative Computation was universally successful. This can be attributed to the objective to create a flexible curriculum and pedagogy that can be adapted by instructors, rather than requiring adoption of a highly structured scope and sequence. This would seem obvious with the objective of promoting contextualization. The remainder of this paper documents how a traditional CS1 over-arching structure, that emphasizes individual student creativity in the arts, can meet the needs of a diverse constituency and provide meaningful contextualization.

A secondary outcome was to provide further evidence that the current popular model of short duration workshops with online resources is insufficient for developing instructor expertise. Contextualized computing in general and creative computation in particular require interdisciplinary expertise. Providing sufficient resources for such interdisciplinary professional development remains an open question. The workshop and mini-grant participants all requested more extended engagement in both in-person and internet-based venues. We propose recommendations for next-steps in adequately supporting professional development specifically in Creative Computation in CS1, and for contextualized computing in general.

2 CREATIVE COMPUTATION FOR CS1

Creative Computation showcases the theory of visual arts rendered through computer code. In addition to a firm grounding in programming principles, students learn essential graphics operations such as transformations, iteration and randomization, algorithmic drawing, animations, basic physics-based simulations, and interactivity. Domains of inquiry go well beyond commercial level media graphics (e.g. what you might see on a web-page or mobile device) and include creative use of image processing and emergent systems. As a true blending of science and art, Creative Computation requires understanding of and practice in the intersection of analysis and aesthetics. For example, pixel-based image manipulations require mastery of efficient algorithms for data structures such as two and higher-dimensional arrays; text and data visualization require a fusion of artistic design and application of sophisticated data structures and algorithms; rendering L-systems requires deep understanding of recursion and recursive structures.

Creative Computation [4,5] requires students to engage in artistic creative acts to practice and master essential concepts, not only in media arts, but in computational thinking, algorithm design and programming. Used as a vehicle for teaching introductory computer science, our approach required blending opportunities for individual artistic expression with a traditional Java-based CS1 scope and sequence. The curriculum follows a standard CS1 course, but instead of solving for roots of polynomials, simulating gas station/cash registers, or implementing well-known algorithms and techniques, our labs provide avenues for highly individual creative expressions to produce artwork, interactive multimedia, data visualizations, and games.

2.1 Scope and Sequence

The CS1 scope and sequence shown in Table 1 is a variation of an *Objects Gently* approach to teaching programming with Java [7]. Object-oriented concepts are introduced neither at the beginning or the end of the semester.

Programming Concepts	Creative Computation Technique
What is programming	Built-in drawing functions; primitive shapes, coordinate systems, creative coding principles
Variables, data types, expression	Drawing in scale, proportional distance and size to a vanishing horizon specified by a y-variable
Mouse/keyboard interactions	Shapes drawn via mouse clicks
Control structures: loops and conditionals	Use of simple iterations to draw many shapes Use of conditionals in simple simulations: ball drop, bouncing ball
Writing functions with control structures, randomization	Parameterized shape drawing: location, size, color etc.; Randomize display
Simple objects, super and subclasses, object instantiation vs class definition	Shapes modeled as objects: data fields store parameters, methods implement rendering and animation, dynamic instances generated by mouse click
One dimensional arrays	Complex scene with many shapes(objects) stored in arrays
Math applications: polar coordinates, trigonometry, rotational geometry	Mandala art, complex abstract/geometric design, composition of polygons, stars and line strings, creative aesthetics
OOP principles, inheritance, abstract classes and interfaces	Collaborative project with generic object types, instructor provides interface, students contribute sub classes
Manipulating two dimensional arrays	Image processing, Game of Life, tiling and tessellation
Recursion, recursive functions	Procedural art (e.g. fractals), L-systems
Data sets, data mining, data visualization, strings and files	Visually manipulate string Visualization techniques

Table 1: Creative Computation Scope and Sequence

Exercises consist of a sequence of programming projects in which students individually or collaboratively construct a work of art, ranging from still graphics as shown in Figure 1, to data visualizations and interactive games. For example, to teach object inheritance, each student is asked to create a subclass of a sea-creature interface/abstract class. The hierarchy is combined into a single project instantiating the contributed subclasses in a creature aquarium. Every exercise has a well-defined basic part and offers students the opportunities to explore open-ended creative projects. Students take ownership of their work. As a consequence, no two submitted projects are the same, and plagiarism is visually obvious.

2.2 Creative Computation in Processing

Our approach follows in the footsteps of John Maeda, who is both a formally trained artist and computer scientist. Inventor of the programming environment Design by Numbers [9], a precursor to Processing, he pioneered an approach to "creative coding" that radically *re-contextualized* computer code–from an applied math notation to a creative medium, on par with charcoal, paint, clay, etc. Creative coding is an exploratory and aesthetically driven approach, where students build visual designs and artworks iteratively as they expand their projects.

Our curriculum assumes use of the Processing IDE. It should be stressed that this is not a curriculum to learn Processing, but rather a traditional CS1 – introduction to programming, problem solving and foundations of computer science utilizing the rich and friendly graphics library of Processing. It can be taught in any programming language with a mature graphics API.

Processing is built on top of Java with a simplified syntax and an API that focuses on graphics/media programming. It is a robust and full-featured language that has use both in the classroom and beyond; it is used widely in industry and growing quickly in popularity. It supports code writing in Java, Python and JavaScript. A Processing project is developed in Java or Python in a simple IDE that dispenses with the complexity of creating a complex object structure in Java or mastering library imports in Python. Within the last two years P5.js [2] provides a JavaScript web-supporting framework in which to write Processing functions using JavaScript syntax. Our CS1 curriculum is implemented entirely in the Java version to align with the AP CS A and traditional Java based curricula. Sample code in our repository is entirely in Java, however lab assignments can be adapted to either JavaScript or Python to accomplish the learning goals stated in the materials. We also have a successful adaption of our curriculum in C++ with openFrameworks[3].

3 CURRICULUM ADAPTION

The efficacy of the Creative Computation approach comes from a series of opportunities to experiment with how the curriculum as a whole, and in part, could be adapted by a range of institutions. Through initial deployment in two undergraduate institutions and two high schools, a series of short-duration workshops introduced educators to the curriculum and pedagogy. Through mini-grants, nine institutions adapted the curriculum and provided qualitative analysis of results to an external evaluator and are summarized here.

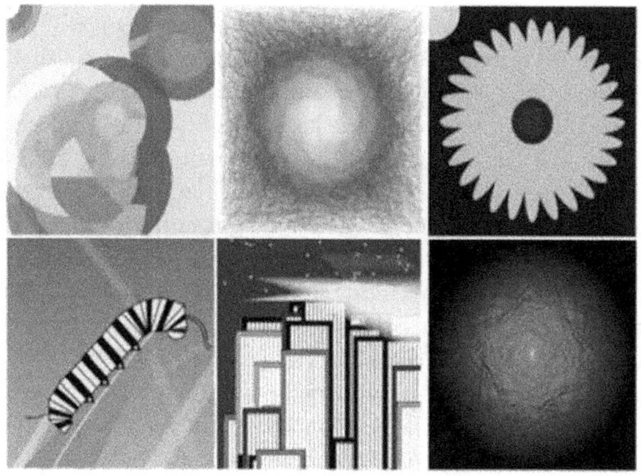

Figure 1: Student artwork

3.1 Initial Undergraduate Implementation

The curriculum outlined above has been in place within undergraduate introductory courses at Bryn Mawr College, Bryn Mawr, PA and Southern Methodist University, Dallas, TX for the past eight years.

Bryn Mawr Collge (BMC) is a small, all-women's liberal arts college in the suburbs of Philadelphia that enrolls 1,300 undergraduates. BMC teaches and values critical, creative and independent habits of thought and expression in an undergraduate liberal arts curriculum for women. The Computer Science Department offers a B.A. in Computer Science as well as a minor in Computer Science and in Computational Methods.

Southern Methodist University (SMU) is a private university of 11,000 students (6,000 undergraduates) near the vibrant heart of Dallas, TX. SMU offers nationally competitive undergraduate and graduate CS and Engineering programs to a larger and more conventional student body. The Creative Computation Program is supported through both the School of the Arts and the Department of Computer Science and Engineering housed in the School of Engineering and offers degrees in both Computer Science and Computer Engineering.

In both institutions Creative Computation was developed and adapted to fit the local intellectual culture. Over a dozen different instructors not associated with the grant have successfully offered our curriculum more than twenty times. See www.cs.brynmawr.edu/visual for more information.

3.2 Initial High School Implementation

As a curriculum intended to support the bridge from high school to college, a natural consequence was to investigate how it could be adapted to the cultures of high school. Two

[2] P5js.org P5js.org
[3] openframeworks.cc/

high schools were initially selected [14]. The courses were taught in these two schools that are at the extreme end of the spectrum of high school cultures, using pedagogy that is similar in the emphasis on project work, but markedly different in use of materials and presentation style. Sidwell Friends School (SFS) is a private coeducational PK-12 Quaker school in Washington, DC, in which computer science is taught entirely through a project-based lab with heavy emphasis on student-centered inquiry. James Martin High School (MHS) is a large urban public school in Texas that enrolls over 3300 students in grades 9-12, where computer science instruction models traditional high school mathematics instruction. As a large public high school that accommodates a diverse population with a full range of socio-economic needs, expectations for achievement require significant reinforcement via extensive use of highly structured materials. The computer science program at MHS is targeted toward Advanced Placement and formal lecture is reinforced through worksheets and exercises that lay the groundwork for structured project assignments. The participant teachers in both schools successfully adapted the college-level creative computation model to the following courses: as in [14]:

- An introduction to computer science course that starts with 4 weeks of Python following by Creative Computation with Processing. The course covers materials traditionally associated with CS1 with an introduction to classes but without inheritance.
- An introduction to computer science course that uses Creative Computation with Processing exclusively and covers material traditionally associated with CS0.
- An advanced computer science course that parallel expectations for a traditional CS1/CS2 experience exclusively taught with Creative Computation in Processing.
- An AP CS course that requires students to sit for the AP exam. Creative Computation projects are used intermittently because the test is not contextualized to the arts, but uses draws from a broad spectrum of applications.
- An Artificial Intelligence and Game Design course that has evolved into a significant example of Creative Computation that goes beyond the fine arts.
- An advanced computer science class that covers material traditionally found in CS2 as well as providing opportunities for kinesthetic game design.

3.3 Summer Workshops

In 2014, a four-day summer workshop was held at Bryn Mawr College[4]. There were fifteen participants: seven high school teachers and eight college faculty. Five public and two private high schools were represented including a leading K-12 school for students with learning disabilities. The college faculty included a large research university, two small private liberal arts colleges, as well as a public university and two community colleges. Feedback from participants was overwhelmingly positive. Five contributed projects to our repository, and all but one indicated plans to adapt the curriculum into their programs.

In 2015, we held a second four-day summer workshop at Soutern Methodist University. Despite a budget limited to twenty participants, thirty-three people were accepted into the workshop; twenty-eight attended. Of those twenty-eight, twenty-one were faculty members: twelve high school teachers and nine professors from colleges and universities around the country. Among the teachers, nine were from public schools, and three from private schools. The college faculty members ranged from a well-known research university, a small private liberal arts college, three public universities, and an Ivy League university. There were also non-faculty participants: tech industry and non-profit organizations that run extracurricular and youth summer camps for computing. All of the participants either indicated intention to adopt the Creative Computation approach, or were already teaching with Processing in some form and intended to adapt our curricular materials and approaches.

3.4 Mini-grant Institutions

Between 2014 and 2017 instructors from ten different institutions were awarded mini-grants to adapt and implement the Creative Computing curriculum in their own classrooms. Nine of these filed final reports summarizing successful implementation, one initial grantee withdrew before implementation, due to local institutional staffing and course scheduling difficulties. Additionally, an external evaluator carried out pre-post interviews and student surveys on all these courses.

The curriculum was implemented at four high schools (2 public, 2 private), a public 2-year community college, a private 4-year liberal arts college and three 4-year universities (2 public, one private). One college course was offered online for both high school and college students. The four major regions, as defined by the US Census, were represented: one each in the Northeast and South (both high school), three in the West (two high school, one undergraduate) and four in the Midwest (four undergraduate, one on-line allowing high school student to register).

The courses that were offered spanned a full range of traditional levels in computer science and in introductory media arts. Introductory computer science is comparatively new and lacks a consensus on foundation.[5] As a metric for evaluating the efficacy of Creative Computation we use the following generally

[4] http://cs.brynmawr.edu/visual/bmcworkshop.html.

[5] See http://www.acm.org/education/curricula-recommendations for CS0 and CS1, http://www.exploringcs.org/ for Pre-AP HS – e.g Exploring Computer Science, https://apcentral.collegeboard.org/courses for AP CS A and AP CS Principles. We have not found a professional society standard for Media Arts programming.

accepted curricular foci to categorize the courses taught in the mini-grant program.

- Pre-AP High School: As exemplified by the nationally recognized *Exploring Computer Science.*
- AP CS principles/CS0: CS0 is considered a foundations course for non-majors or entering college CS majors with no background in computer science. The AP CS Principles course is intended to articulate with that college level offering.
- AP CS A/CS1: The traditional computer science course for entering CS majors.
- Media Arts Coding: A course offered in Digital Arts programs that introduces programming.

The high school courses were titled: AP CS A, AP CS principles, Introduction to Programming (Pre-AP), Pre-AP CS A (three instances).

The undergraduate level courses were titled: Applied Logic (A prerequisite for CS1, not a CS0), Beyond Photoshop (A CS0 course), Critical Games (A media arts course), CS1.

Implementation ranged from modules (in the AP CS A courses) to full semester adaption of the creative arts projects curriculum outlined in section 2 for courses at the pre-AP and AP Principles High School level, and for all of the undergraduate courses as pre-CS1 (e.g. Logic and CS0), CS1, and for Media Arts.

Our initial efforts at both the college and especially the high school level identified a broad spectrum of pedagogical styles from highly structured to intensively inquiry-based. The mini-grant offerings, not surprisingly fell in the middle without clear metrics for distinguishing between them. They all did however include the following:

- Short lecture and resource materials to introduce programming (e.g. variables, control structures) and creative arts concepts.
- Practice via short-guided assignments that allowed for individual creativity.
- Opportunities for large project work with a focus chosen by the student.

The remaining sections summarize outcomes and recommend changes for curricular and teacher professional development.

4 OUTCOMES

The major expected outcome of this work was that Creative Computation as an adapted curriculum can successfully meet a broad range of curricular goals at the bridge between high school and introductory college computer science. A key element is the emphasis on project work in which students can express artistic creativity and create an individual agenda for project goals. This project also demonstrated that the traditional CS1/CS AP A curriculum structure is viable as a vehicle for introductory computing, provided there is contextualization, in this case media arts. Quotes from mini-grant participants provide insight:

> *We have been teaching [CS 0] for 5 years. This was by far the most engaged group of students we have worked with; the combination of technical rigor, criticality, and contemporary themes/materials/topics seems to have inspired and encouraged an unusually open and responsive group dynamic.*

> *These creative tasks allowed for both computational and "artistic" success. Students could produce something that was simplistic in terms of code, but successful in terms of humor or emotional appeal. This allowed for a wonderful classroom climate in which students of all levels felt capable of producing work they would be proud to share with classmates.*

A hoped for, but not necessarily expected outcome, was that the short-duration workshop that exposed participants to a studio art experience would support adaptation of our pedagogy to their own needs. Evidence to that effect is that all of the mini-grant participants reported that they successfully completed their course and were going to continue using Creative Computation. Consider this example:

> *Their projects and the process was a success, and one that I intend to replicate after the AP test. The entire class became more collaborative and kids were motivated not from a grade, but from seeing something on the screen that they wanted to replicate. In addition, it has been rare for students who do not know each other to enter into a discussion. With this project, many were looking and asking how to take their own projects to the next level. Many kids who were checked out for most of the year, basically came back to write more code than they did the entire year, and they were doing it based on their own purpose-driven initiatives. I could hardly keep them out of the computer lab. ⊠I would like to use this more next year in all my classes, but in particular, AP Computer science just because many kids find the current grind a bit more than they care to take.* ⊠

Unexpected outcomes did, of course, occur. The commitment to NSF was to produce a workshop model and repository of material resources. This proved inadequate. Each mini-grant participant expressed a need for more mentorship with experts to expand their computing and artistic skills, to brainstorm pedagogy, and to identify curricular connections. An attempt to create an online community of our own during the mini-grant course execution period did not generate sufficient traffic to engage the group. However, all participants did articulate goals to pursue Creative Computation further through existing resources.

We address the question of what merits claiming success. In this paper we do not list statistics of diversity, nor increased enrollments, nor attitudinal outcomes. Seven years ago when this project started, increasing enrollment was seen as a bell-weather of success. But interest in computer science has exploded with enrollments stretching teaching resources in both high school and undergraduate programs. Consequently, there is no statistically valid correlation between Creative Computation and increased enrollment, nor, we suggest, can any contextualized approach make that claim. Similarly statistics on who enrolls in introductory computer science classes is not correlated with successful curriculum. Schools on both sides of the bridge now require computer science, often because of state mandates. In institutions without an explicit requirement, due to lack of teaching resources, students cannot enroll or are placed in over-crowded classrooms. A companion paper will present a methodology and conclusions on student affect. Consequently, we report here on how the curriculum was successfully used by the simple standard that teachers self-evaluated their success, critiqued their short comings and articulated what they would improve in the next round. Throughout, the reporting has been consistently positive.

5 RECOMMENDATIONS

The AP CS Principles curriculum was intentionally developed to address the shortcoming of the AP CS A – that it was inaccessible to many students, with too much emphasis on the Java programming language and not enough emphasis on core computer science principles. The Creative Computation curriculum illustrates that the depth of code development, problem solving, and principles of software design explicit in the CS1, AP CS A curricula can be taught in a manner that engages students. Programming is essential to learning computer science, but the coding must be purposeful. In the curriculum presented here, that purposefulness comes from the emphasis on creative arts. This speaks to a need for reconsideration of *how* foundations of programming are introduced rather than *depth of knowledge* of those foundations. While we promote creative art as a vehicle for the *how,* this is certainly not the only framework, but we do assert that the *depth of knowledge* should not be minimized. Programming, problem solving, and software design are skills that, like any other skill, need to be practiced and mentored. Consequently, our recommendation on both sides of the bridge is to keep the depth of knowledge, but to identify how standard curricula can be *adapted* to the local goals, objectives and projected outcomes.

Simple adoption of curriculum requires teacher professional development. Adapting curriculum to local goals requires expertise in both the subject area and the pedagogy. This project illustrated that minimal training via short duration workshop and static online materials was sufficient to bootstrap adaption. But a significant outcome of the mini-grant program was the hunger among all the participants for more – of everything. A compelling question for the computer science community is how to provide those resources in a way that engages a community – that provides the kind of art studio approach we promoted to the very hard task of teacher professional development.

ACKNOWLEDGMENTS

This project is supported in part by grants from The National Science Foundation (DUE-0942626, DUE-0942628, DUE-1323463, DUE-1323305, CCF-0939370, and CCF-1140489).

REFERENCES

[1] Jessica D. Bayless and Sean Strout. Games as a "Flavor" of CS1. In *proceedings of SIGCSE 2006.* ACM Press 2006.

[2] Robert E. Beck, Jennifer Burg, Jesse M. Heines, and Bill Manaris. Computing and Music: A Spectrum of Sound. *Special Session, SIGCSE 2011.* Dallas, TX, March 2011.

[3] Cassel, L. and Wolz, U Interdisciplinary Computing, Successes and Challenges. In *Proceedings of SIGCSE 2013.* ACM Press 2013.

[4] Ira Greenberg, Deepak Kumar and Dianna Xu. Creative Coding and Visual Portfolio for CS1. In *Proceedings of SIGCSE 2012.* ACM Press 2012.

[5] Ira Greenberg, Dianna Xu, and Deepak Kumar. *Creative Coding and Generative Art in Processing 2.0.* friends Of ed/Apress 2013.

[6] Mark Guzdial. Introduction to computing and programming with Python: A Multimedia Approach.

[7] Prentice-Hall, 2004.

[8] Elliot Koffman, E. and Ursula Wolz, CS1 using Java language features gently. In *Proceedings of SIGCSE/ITiCSE 1999.* ACM Press 1999.

[9] Deepak Kumar, Doug Blank, Tucker Balch, Keith O'Hara, Mark Guzdial, Stewart Tansley, Engaging Computing Students with AI and Robotics. *Symposium on Using AI to Motivate Greater Participation in Computer Science,* 2008.

[10] John Maeda *Design by Numbers,* MIT Press 2001.

[11] Jay Summet, Deepak Kumar, Keith O'Hara, Daniel Walker, Lijun Ni, Doug Blank, and Tucker Balch. Personalizing CS1 with Robots. In *Proceedings of ACM SIGCSE 2009.* ACM Press 2009.

[12] Ursula Wolz, Christopher Ault and Teresa Nakra, "Teaching Game Design through Cross-Disciplinary Content and Individualized Student Deliverables", *The Journal of Game Development,* adapted based on invitation from presentation at the 2nd Annual Microsoft Academic Days Conference on Game Development , February 22 - 25, 2007

[13] Ursula Wolz, Kim Pearson, S.Monisha Pulimood, Meredith Stone, Mary Switzer. Computational Thinking and Expository Writing in the Middle School: A novel approach to broadening participation in computing, *Transactions on Computing Education,* 2011, Volume 2, article 9.

[14] Dianna Xu, Douglas Blank, and Deepak Kumar. Games, Robots and Robot Games: Complementary Contexts for Introductory Computing Education. In *Proceedings of Third International Conference on Game Development in Computer Science Education* (GDCSE'08), 2008.

[15] Dianna Xu, Aaron Cadle, Darby Thompson, Ursula Wolz, Ira Greenberg, and Deepak Kumar. 2016. Creative Computation in High School. In Proceedings of the 47th ACM Technical Symposium on Computing Science Education (SIGCSE '16). ACM, New York, NY, USA, 273-278. DOI: https://doi.org/10.1145/2839509.2844611

Timely Feedback in Unstructured Cybersecurity Exercises

Jan Vykopal
Masaryk University, Institute of Computer Science
Brno, Czech Republic
vykopal@ics.muni.cz

Radek Ošlejšek
Masaryk University, Faculty of Informatics
Brno, Czech Republic
oslejsek@fi.muni.cz

Karolína Burská
Masaryk University, Faculty of Informatics
Brno, Czech Republic
burska@mail.muni.cz

Kristína Zákopčanová
Masaryk University, Faculty of Informatics
Brno, Czech Republic
zakopcanova@mail.muni.cz

ABSTRACT

Cyber defence exercises are intensive, hands-on learning events for teams of professionals who gain or develop their skills to successfully prevent and respond to cyber attacks. The exercises mimic the real-life, routine operation of an organization which is being attacked by an unknown offender. Teams of learners receive very limited immediate feedback from the instructors during the exercise; they can usually see only a scoreboard showing the aggregated gain or loss of points for particular tasks. An in-depth analysis of learners' actions requires considerable human effort, which results in days or weeks of delay. The intensive experience is thus not followed by proper feedback facilitating actual learning, and this diminishes the effect of the exercise.

In this initial work, we investigate how to provide valuable feedback to learners right after the exercise without any unnecessary delay. Based on the scoring system of a cyber defence exercise, we have developed a new feedback tool that presents an interactive, personalized timeline of exercise events. We deployed this tool during an international exercise, where we monitored participants' interactions and gathered their reflections. The results show that learners did use the new tool and rated it positively. Since this new feature is not bound to a particular defence exercise, it can be applied to all exercises that employ scoring based on the evaluation of individual exercise objectives. As a result, it enables the learner to immediately reflect on the experience gained.

ACM Reference format:
Jan Vykopal, Radek Ošlejšek, Karolína Burská, and Kristína Zákopčanová. 2018. Timely Feedback in Unstructured Cybersecurity Exercises. In *Proceedings of The 49th ACM Technical Symposium on Computer Science Education, Baltimore, MD, USA, Feb. 21–24, 2018 (SIGCSE '18)*, 6 pages.
https://doi.org/10.1145/3159450.3159561

SIGCSE '18, Feb. 21–24, 2018, Baltimore, MD, USA

ACM ISBN 978-1-4503-5103-4/18/02...$15.00
https://doi.org/10.1145/3159450.3159561

1 INTRODUCTION

Cyber attacks threatening ICT infrastructure have become routine. Their intensity and complexity are growing with the increasing number of interconnected devices exposed to attackers and the influx of new vulnerabilities being revealed each year. Unfortunately, there is a significant global shortage of cybersecurity workers equipped with the skills necessary for preventing or responding to the attacks [6].

Cyber defence exercises (CDX) [1] represent a popular type of training that aims to fill this skill gap. They enable participants to experience cyber attacks first-hand with real-life limitations, including a lack of information and resources, the need for communication and making decisions under stress.

CDX are usually intensive, short-term events lasting several days. Tens to hundreds of professional learners participate and are grouped in teams. The target groups are administrators of ICT systems, incident responders, and security managers. The exercises deliver rich immediate experience of ongoing attacks and the opportunity to practice crisis procedures and techniques.

In contrast to structured, step-by-step hands-on training guided by an instructor, teams of learners have to figure out all the issues on their own, in the order they agree on, within the team. These settings simulate real operation but prevent any direct feedback from instructors (exercise organizers). Learners can only presume what they did was correct, what worked and what did not. The only feedback they are given during the exercise is often through an exercise score with no further details about score breakdown. Some exercise organizers provide technical reports after the exercise, which reveal some details highlighting important moments from the perspective of a particular team of learners. The after-action report is sometimes also complemented by a short workshop, which provides an opportunity to discuss the content of the exercise with the instructors in person. Nevertheless, all these methods of feedback are delivered with a significant delay after the actual exercise because they require preparation from the instructors that cannot begin before the end of the exercise.

In this paper, we study whether learners benefit from simple, but individualized feedback provided just after the end of a two-day intensive exercise. In our study, each team was provided with an interactive timeline of its score development during the exercise, with important events emphasized. The timeline was generated automatically from data stored by an existing scoring system. All interactions of exercise participants (mouse clicks and movements) were logged with the scoring timeline. After that, participants were asked to fill out short evaluation questionnaire. The data and answers we obtained show that learners valued the feedback, even though they still lack more details about particular events.

2 STATE OF THE ART

Research on providing feedback in complex and unstructured cybersecurity exercises is very scarce. The following overview is therefore based not only on a review of academic literature but also on technical reports published by organizers and the experience of authors who participated in several CDXs.

One of the world's largest exercise is Locked Shields [8], which is organized annually by the NATO Cooperative Cyber Defence Centre of Excellence in Tallinn, Estonia. Immediate brief feedback to learners is provided at a so-called "hot wash-up" session right after the exercise since any time lag will diminish the learning impact [7]. Educators provide a summary of the exercise's progression and comment on key moments that drove it. More comprehensive and detailed feedback is available only at a workshop which is held a month later, and furthermore, not all learners come to this event.

Another international exercise organized by NATO is Cyber Coalition. Very brief feedback is provided a day later in-person at a hot wash-up session. More specific information is available only in the form of an after-action report at a workshop, which takes place a month later [9]. A very similar type of feedback, with an even longer delay is provided in Cyber Europe, another international exercise organized by ENISA. [2]

Granåsen and Andersson [4] focused on measuring team effectiveness in CDXs. They thoroughly analysed system logs, observer reports, and surveys collected during Baltic cyber shield 2010, a multi-national civil-military CDX. They concluded that these multiple data sources provided valuable insight into the exercise's run. However, they did not mention how to use these data for providing feedback. The only feedback provided to learners was during a virtual after-action review the day after the exercise, where only the leaders of learners' and organizers' teams summarized and discussed their experience.

Henshel et al. [5] also focused on the assessment model and metrics for team proficiency in CDXs. They analysed learners' and observers' input from surveys and intrusion detection logs from the Cyber Shield 2015 exercise. Similarly to the Baltic cyber shield exercise, the feedback provided to learners was not based on an analysis of acquired data since the analysis was done manually and required significant human effort.

Since existing CDXs do not provide any timely and personalized feedback to the learners, we also mention a feedback-related study in learning, which does not concern CDXs. Gibbs and Taylor [3] focused on the theory that personalized feedback does not hold such importance or a value compared to its time-consumption for the instructor.

3 EXPERIMENT SETUP

In this experiment, we studied the behaviour and interactions of participants at a complex cyber defence exercise held on May 23–24, 2017 at Masaryk University, Brno, Czech Republic. The exercise is focused on defending critical information infrastructure (particularly railway infrastructure administration) against skilled and coordinated attackers.

Table 1: Phases of the exercise with time allocation

Order	Phase	Duration	Day
1	Exercise familirization	3 hrs	1
2	Actual exercise	6 hrs	2
3	Post-exercise survey	5 mins	2
4	Break	25 mins	2
5	Scoring timeline interaction	10 mins	2
6	Scoring timeline survey	5 mins	2
7	Quick exercise debriefing	15 mins	2

First, the learners got access to the exercise infrastructure to become familiar with virtual hosts in their network. Then, they took part in an intensive exercise where they faced challenges posed by simulated attackers and legitimate users. Right after the end of the exercise, the learners were asked to express their immediate impressions about the exercise in a short post-exercise survey. After a short break, a timeline depicting the score of each team was presented in the exercise portal. Finally, the learners were asked to evaluate the timeline via a very short questionnaire. Time allocated for each phase of the experiment is shown in Table 1.

3.1 Exercise participants

The experiment involved a Red vs. Blue exercise with 40 participants working in an emulated ICT infrastructure. The structure of the exercise is inspired by the Locked Shield exercise [8, 10]. The participants were divided into four groups according to their role and tasks in the exercise. Their interactions are depicted in Figure 1.

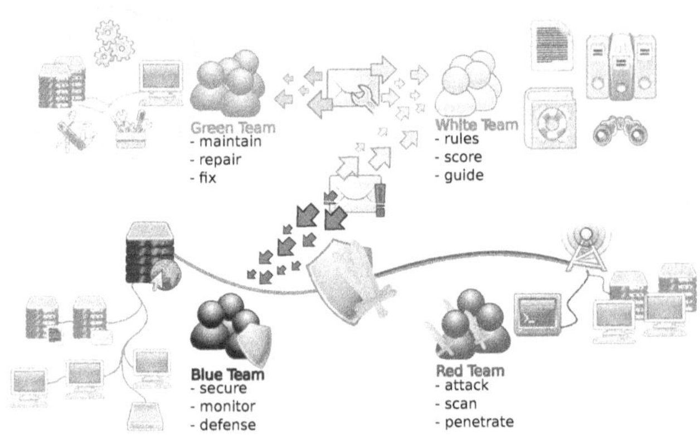

Figure 1: Exercise participants, their interactions and tasks.

Twenty professional learners formed five *Blue teams* (T1–T5) which were put into the role of emergency security teams sent into five organizations to recover compromised networks. Each team of 4 learners was responsible for securing the compromised networks, dealing with the attacks, collaborating with other emergency teams, and collaborating with the coordinator of the operation and media representatives. They had to follow the exercise's rules and local cybersecurity law. Each team represented one real cybersecurity response team from one country in Central Europe.

All attacks against infrastructure defended by Blue teams were conducted by *Red team*. This team consisted of cyber security professionals who carefully followed a predefined attack scenario to equally load the Blue teams. This means they should not use any other arbitrary means of attack against the Blue teams. Based on the success of attacks, the Red team assigns penalty points to the Blue teams since the amount of points is based on non-trivial factors that need expert review.

Exercise managers, referees, organizers, and instructors worked in *White team*. During the exercise, this team assigns tasks (called injects) to the Blue teams and thus simulates the requests of many entities, such as legitimate users of the defended organization, the operation coordinator which needs situational reports, media inquiries, and law enforcement agencies. Then the White team assesses the promptness and quality of a Blue teams's reactions to these tasks and assigns penalties and points.

Finally, the *Green team* is a group of operators and system administrators responsible for the exercise infrastructure. They have full access to the exercise network so they can provide assistance to Blue teams in trouble in an exchange for penalty points.

3.2 Exercise phases

Before the actual exercise (Phase 1 in Table 1), learners are provided with a background story to introduce them to the situation before they enter the compromised networks. Then they access their part of the emulated network for 3 hours to get familiar with the exercise infrastructure. This is very important since the exercise is not set in a known environment and learners have no previous knowledge about who is who in the fictitious scenario (e. g., users in their organization, a popular news portal, superordinate security team).

The exercise (Phase 2) is driven by a detailed scenario which includes the actions of attackers (Red team) and assignments for the defenders prepared by the organizers (White team). Attackers exploit specific vulnerabilities left in the compromised network in a fixed order. This follows a common attack life cycle in a critical information infrastructure. On top of that, learners should also answer media inquires and requests from users doing their routine job in the defended network. The performance of each Blue team is scored based on successful attacks or their mitigation, the availability of specified critical services and the quality of reporting and communication. The score is either computed automatically from events, processed by the logging infrastructure (e. g., a penalty for inaccessible services) or entered manually (e. g., attacks completed by the Red team). An aggregated score is shown to participants in real-time. Table 2 shows the structure of the scoreboard and the values of aggregated score.

Immediately after the end of the exercise, we asked the learners to evaluate the exercise and their experience by rating several statements using the Likert scale (Phase 3).

3.3 Scoring timeline application

After a break (Phase 4), the score acquired by each team during the exercise was presented to the Blue teams in the form of an interactive application, as shown in Figure 2 (Phase 5). It provided automatically generated personalized feedback. Members of each team could only see their own scoring timeline with individual exercise events.

Table 2: The scoreboard presented to the learners during the exercise.

Team	Services	Attacks	Injects	Users	Access	Total
T1	91,843	-8,500	9,000	-1,100	0	91,243
T5	92,230	-5,000	3,600	-400	0	90,430
T2	81,280	-10,750	6,425	-4,000	0	72,955
T4	74,518	-11,000	6,650	0	-4,000	66,168
T3	85,756	-12,000	2,475	-1,700	-9,500	65,031

Note: Teams are sorted according to their final score.
"Injects" is an abbreviation for communication injects of the White team.

The initial score of each team is 100 000 points. In the graph, the main, predominantly descending line represents the development of a team's total score over time. The score is computed from penalties and awarded points that were either recorded automatically for the inaccessibility of required network services or assigned manually by the Red or White team. The colourful dots are interactive and they are related just to the manual rating. The red dots represent Red team penalties, white dots represent the rating of communication injects by the White team, yellow dots indicate the rating of user simulated injects by the White team, and grey dots indicate requests for assistance from the Green team (to grant temporary remote access to a machine or revert to the initial state). Each dot contains textual information that specifies the reason for the rating. This information is shown in each dot's tooltip.

Learners were able to provide us with their reflection on their penalty and awarded points very easily by clicking on the coloured dots and choosing one of predefined options (Phase 5; see right-hand side of Figure 2), e. g., whether they recognized the attack or not, or why they did not respond to the inject of the White team. Moreover, all scoring timeline interactions, including mouse clicks, mouse movements, and selected options were logged. This data, together with answers from a short survey on the scoring timeline (Phase 6) were used to evaluate the usefulness of the timely feedback.

Finally, representatives of the Red and White team provided a short debrief of the exercise ("hot wash-up", Phase 7) from their perspective. They highlighted important breaking points of exercise and pointed out exemplary or interesting decisions and actions took by Blue teams. This part is mentioned here only for completeness, no input from learners was required for the experiment.

4 RESULTS

4.1 Post-exercise survey

The post-exercise survey was focused on general qualitative aspects of the exercise. Relevant statements to this study are listed in Table 3 and marked as E1–E4 for further reference. The statistical distribution of individual answers across all teams is depicted in Figure 3.

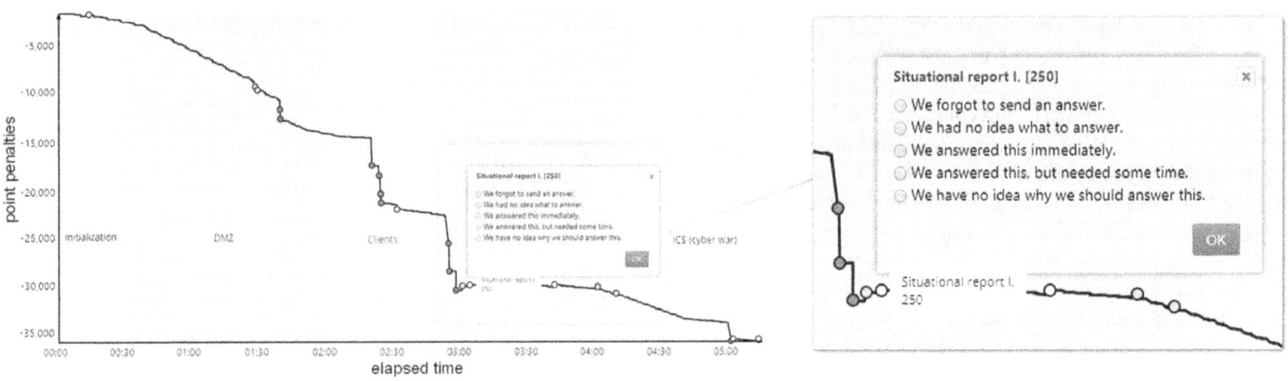

Figure 2: A screenshot of a scoring timeline providing personalized feedback for each team right after the exercise.

Table 3: Team statistics for the post-exercise and scoring timeline surveys

	Statement	Team 2	Team 1	Team 5	Team 4	Team 3	Average
E1:	My knowledge and skills were sufficient.	3.75	3	2.6	2.5	2	3.05
E2:	I found exercise difficult for me.	3.33	3	4	4.25	5	3.8
E3:	Exercise was well organized and structured.	2.66	3.25	3.3	4	5	3.75
E4:	Exercise was beneficial and useful to me.	2.66	3.5	4	4.5	5	3.85
F1:	The scoring timeline of my team displayed after the end of the exercise provided useful feedback.	3.25	2.5	-	4.25	3.66	3.53
F2:	Do you have any comments on the scoring timeline?	D	M	-	M	M	

1 = strongly disagree, 5 = completely agree, D = there was a delay in inserting points by a Red and White team, M = add more details about the depicted events

We collected answers from all 20 participants. However, four of them did not provide their identification and so their answers were omitted from the team statistics. Team values were computed as the average from a five-point Likert scale answers (1 = strongly disagree, 5 = completely agree). The *Average* column represents the average value across all answers regardless of teams.

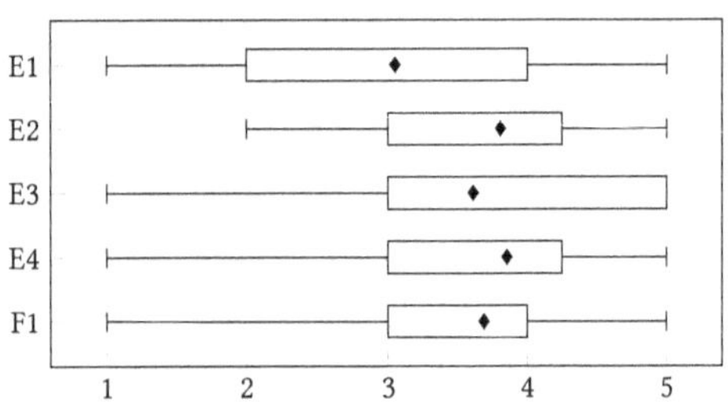

Figure 3: Distribution of all answers to E1 – E4 and F1.

The aim of E1 and E2 was to reveal the level of expertise of individual teams and the difficulty of the exercise. Individual answers to E1 significantly varied, which indicates that learners had significantly different expertise. However, the average values calculated for each team reveal that the exercise was well balanced with no extremely weak or strong team. The answers to E2 indicate that the overall difficulty of the exercise was considered as rather high.

Two statements in the questionnaire, E3 and E4, were focused on satisfaction with the organizational aspects and usefulness of the exercise. Both statements brought very similar answers. Teams that were more satisfied with the organization also considered the exercise more beneficial. Even though the opinion differed across the teams, learners considered the exercise rather beneficial and well organized in general.

4.2 Scoring timeline interaction

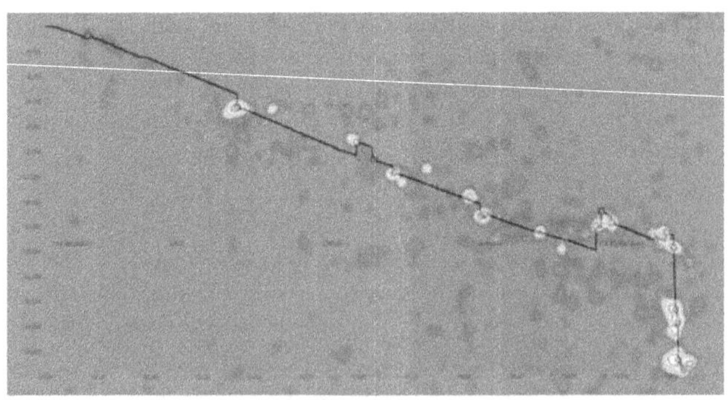

Figure 4: An example of a heatmap of mouse movements and clicks on a screen of a scoring timeline.

In order to evaluate the scoring timeline, we were actively recording learners' interactions with a tool. We obtained data from 18 learners, 2 learners were missing due to technical issues. The data consisted of 2,994 individual low-level events (mouse clicks, mouse hovers, etc.). Moreover, we recorded heatmaps of mouse positions on the screen (see an example in Figure 4). Putting this data together, we were able to estimate the focus of the learners during their exploration of the scoring timeline. A deeper analysis did not reveal any preference patterns in the sense that learners would be more interested in some kind of objectives, such as Red team attacks, White team injects, or penalties from later critical phases of the exercise. On the contrary, it seems that the learners were interested in all the penalties and awards roughly the same.

Analyses of timestamps revealed that the time spent by individual learners with the scoring timeline ranged between 1m 22s and 8m 27s It is worth noting that there was no significant difference between teams. They spent approximately 3 to 5 minutes with the feedback application on average. We also did not find any relation between the time spent with the timeline and the willingness to provide their reflection on particular penalties or awards. Many learners just spent a long time with only a passive exploration of the timeline.

Seven learners from four teams also gave us an active reflection to penalties in addition to passively exploring the scoring timeline. The values in Table 4 represent the numbers of collected answers per team and objective type. Blue team 1 is omitted from the table because we got no data from them. These results are discussed in Section 5.

Table 4: Numbers of responses of each team to objectives.

	Teams				
Objectives	T2	T3	T4	T5	$\sum$
Red team attacks	7	13	5	1	26
Users injects	5	7	0	1	13
Communication injects	0	5	0	2	7
Green team assistance	0	4	2	0	6

4.3 Scoring timeline survey

The usefulness of the feedback provided via the scoring timeline was evaluated with a short survey. We got answers from 13 learners (out of 20) because Blue team 5 did not respond at all. The statements and their team statistics are shown in Table 3 under the labels F1 and F2.

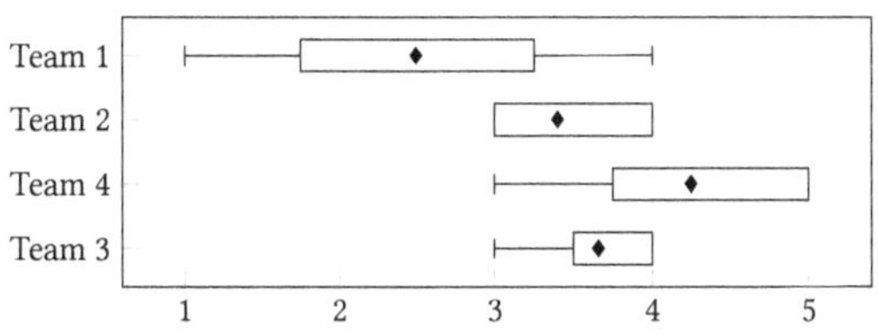

Figure 5: Distribution of answers to F1. Teams are sorted according to the final score (the best on the top).

The data shows that the usefulness of the feedback can be considered to be "rather useful" (the average value across all the teams is 3.53). A detailed distribution of answers depicted in Figure 5 reveals that the most successful team considered the feedback less useful than other teams.

Answers to the open question F2 provided four comments on possible improvements. Three teams requested more details about penalties. They would appreciate knowing "how it happened" in addition to "what happened" (marked as M in Table 3). One comment objected that "some attacks were happening way sooner in reality than on the timeline" (marked as D in Table 3). This is true because attack penalties were inserted by the Red team manually with some delay.

5 DISCUSSION

The validity of the timely feedback evaluation would be affected by dissatisfaction with the exercise so the learners would not be interested in the feedback at all or they would provide distorted data. Dissatisfaction can be caused by poor organization, unfulfilled expectations, or by a disparity between the difficulty of the exercise and the knowledge of learners. In general, this exercise was considered slightly difficult and was also assessed positively (see Section 4.1). Although the exercise was attended by skilled teams whose members had previous experience with similar exercises, they still considered it rather difficult, challenging and useful. Therefore, we believe that conclusions drawn from the analysis based on this particular exercise and its participants are plausible. In the following part, we put together the results of the post-exercise survey, the scoring timeline survey, and the exploration of the timeline and analyse their mutual relationships.

Teams sought out feedback. A deeper analysis of learners' interactions with the scoring timeline shows that all teams were using it intensively, regardless of what reflection they provided in the scoring timeline survey. All teams explored all the penalties depicted in their timeline. They also gave us an evaluation of the majority of displayed objectives. The only exception was Team 4, probably due to technical issues. Team 5, which did not respond to the scoring timeline survey at all, still explored their timeline actively. Team 1 rated the scoring timeline as less useful than other teams. It was the most successful team according to the final score and, therefore, the feedback may not have been so interesting for them because they might have already known about their failures. However, even this team was interested in the timely feedback because they explored the scoring timeline for the longest.

A need for more detail. Answers to the open question F2 confirmed our assumption that more precise and more detailed information provided by the timely feedback makes the feedback even more attractive to learners. Nevertheless, the need for more detail can also be indirectly inferred. For example, a further analysis of the White team's injects (users and communication injects) indicates that teams often underestimated time-dependant response to this type of "soft" request. Teams could either consider these requests "annoying" and not so important in comparison with attacks or they could just be too busy with the attacks, for instance. A deeper understanding of their behaviour also requires collecting more detailed and better structured data from the timely feedback.

Benefits for instructors. Although the scoring feedback was intended primarily for learners, the previous discussion shows that it is very valuable also for organizers and educators who can learn about the exercise and then fine tune its parameters, e. g., by better scheduling of the White team's injects with respect to the attacks. Since learners are not usually aware of this value, they do not make more effort than necessary into providing quality and valuable information for instructors. However, if providing reflections is intuitive and quick for them, they are motivated to use it. Furthermore, since the feedback is generated automatically, organizers can get valuable data without any additional effort.

Limitations of the study. This study is limited in two respects. First, data were obtained from a single exercise with a relatively small group of participants. The reason is that the organization of such a complex exercise is expensive and time-consuming and it is organized rarely for only a narrow group of experts. Nevertheless, we consider the sample to be representative because the learners were highly qualified experts, often with experience in similar exercises and the exercise received a positive rating from them. Second, the timeline evaluation questionnaire was simple and freely structured. However, this was intentional since the survey took place at the end of an exhausting two-day exercise and thus a more sophisticated questionnaire might not have guaranteed more precise results.

6 CONCLUSIONS AND FUTURE WORK

To best of our knowledge, this paper is the first attempt to study the means of providing feedback to learners participating in cyber defence exercises. The literature review and our own experience showed that feedback provided in state-of-the-art exercises is very limited or delayed. The most often used method is an exercise scoreboard displayed to the learners throughout the exercise. Another method is a short verbal evaluation by exercise observers or organizers right after the end the exercise or its phases. The last commonly used method is after-action reports highlighting key conclusions from a laborious manual analysis of heterogeneous data acquired during the exercise (survey, written communication, scoring and monitoring logs, and checks).

The lack of timely feedback results in the learners having limited opportunity to learn from their experience. They undergo numerous real-life situations during the exercise, but they are not supplied with an explanation why such situations occur. We therefore complemented these means by a novel approach which provides feedback to learners right after the end of the exercise with no additional effort required from educators. Learners can explore a scoring timeline depicting increases and decreases in their team's score and display details about individual events (name and type of the exercise objective, and the number of awarded points or penalty points). Also, they have an opportunity to provide their reflections to educators and indicate their awareness about a particular objective and its solution. The exploration and interaction with the scoring timeline enables learners to reflect on their experience and thus strengthen the learning impact of the exercise.

In order to evaluate this approach, we ran an experiment involving a two-day, complex cyber defence exercise with 24 objectives, and 20 professional learners from five security teams. The results, based on an analysis of user surveys and interactions with the new tool, suggest that learners welcomed the new feature even though the feedback was mined automatically and thus provided a very limited level of detail about particular events.

The experiment also outlined directions for future work. First, learners would appreciate more detail about a particular event in the timeline. This can be easily done by adding a detailed description of the objective related to the event. Another option is to extend the scoring application so that instructors can not only assign points, but also provide a comment on each exercise objective. Second, the timeline could be enriched with a display of the relationship between all exercise objectives. This would highlight that an event that the team may not have been aware of was caused by several previous events they encountered. The context can be then built not only from a time perspective, but also from the topology of the exercise network. Providing information on which host or service was affected by the particular event may help learners to recall the particular situation and understand it better. Finally, the ultimate goal is to provide a "replay function", which would show how attackers proceeded and what could have been done better to prevent or mitigate attacks.

ACKNOWLEDGMENTS

This research was supported by the Security Research Programme of the Czech Republic 2015-2020 (BV III/1–VS) granted by the Ministry of the Interior of the Czech Republic under No. VI20162019014 – Simulation, detection, and mitigation of cyber threats endangering critical infrastructure.

REFERENCES

[1] Elena García Díez, Daniel Fírvida Pereira, Marco A. Lozano Merino, Héctor R. Suárez, and Darío Beneitez Juan. 2015. *Cyber Exercises Taxonomy.* Technical Report. INCIBE. https://www.incibe.es/extfrontinteco/img/File/intecocert/EstudiosInformes/incibe_cyberexercises_taxonomy.pdf

[2] European Union Agency for Network and Information Security. 2016. *Cyber Europe 2016 – After action report : findings from a cyber crisis exercise in Europe.* Technical Report. ENISA. https://doi.org/10.2824/218244

[3] Jennifer C Gibbs and Jim D Taylor. 2016. Comparing student self-assessment to individualized instructor feedback. *Active Learning in Higher Education* 17, 2 (2016), 111–123. https://doi.org/10.1177/1469787416637466

[4] Magdalena Granåsen and Dennis Andersson. 2016. Measuring team effectiveness in cyber-defense exercises: a cross-disciplinary case study. *Cognition, Technology & Work* 18, 1 (01 Feb 2016), 121–143. https://doi.org/10.1007/s10111-015-0350-2

[5] D. S. Henshel, G. M. Deckard, B. Lufkin, N. Buchler, B. Hoffman, P. Rajivan, and S. Collman. 2016. Predicting proficiency in cyber defense team exercises. In *MILCOM 2016 - 2016 IEEE Military Communications Conference.* 776–781. https://doi.org/10.1109/MILCOM.2016.7795423

[6] (ISC)2. 2015. The 2015 (ISC)2 Global Information Security Workforce Study. (2015). https://iamcybersafe.org/wp-content/uploads/2017/01/FrostSullivan-ISC%C2%B2-Global-Information-Security-Workforce-Study-2015.pdf

[7] Kaie Maennel. 2017. *Improving and Measuring Learning Effectiveness at Cyber Defence Exercises.* Master's thesis. University of Tartu, Institute of Computer Science. https://pdfs.semanticscholar.org/777d/3e2e5e8994dc9cb2bb7268881a3d13535f63.pdf

[8] NATO Cooperative Cyber Defence Centre of Excellence. 2017. Cyber Defence Exercises. (2017). http://ccdcoe.org/event/cyber-defence-exercises.html

[9] NATO Supreme Headquarters Allied Powers Europe. 2016. Cyber Coalition 16: NATOs largest cyber defence exercise. (2016). https://www.shape.nato.int/2016/cyber-coalition-16-ends-natos-largest-cyber-defence-exercise

[10] Jan Vykopal, Martin Vizváry, Radek Ošlejšek, Pavel Čeleda, and Daniel Tovarňák. 2017. Lessons Learned From Complex Hands-on Defence Exercises in a Cyber Range. In *2017 IEEE Frontiers in Education Conference.* IEEE, Indianapolis, IN, USA.

Teaching Cyber Security Using Competitive Software Obfuscation and Reverse Engineering Activities

Muhammad Rizwan Asghar
The University of Auckland
New Zealand
r.asghar@auckland.ac.nz

Andrew Luxton-Reilly
The University of Auckland
New Zealand
a.luxton-reilly@auckland.ac.nz

ABSTRACT

Teaching cyber security techniques can be challenging due to the complexity associated with building secure systems. The major issue is these systems could easily be broken if proper protection techniques are not employed. This requires students to understand the offensive approaches that can be used to breach security in order to better understand how to properly defend against cyber attacks. We present a novel approach to teaching cyber security in a graduate course using an innovative assessment task that engages students in both software obfuscation and reverse engineering of obfuscated code. Students involved in the activities gain an appreciation of the challenges in defending against attacks. Our results demonstrate a positive change in the students' perception during the learning process.

CCS CONCEPTS

• **Security and privacy → Software reverse engineering**;

KEYWORDS

Cyber Security, Competition, Obfuscation, Reverse Engineering, Contributing Student Pedagogy, Peer Learning, Active Learning

ACM Reference Format:
Muhammad Rizwan Asghar and Andrew Luxton-Reilly. 2018. Teaching Cyber Security Using Competitive Software Obfuscation and Reverse Engineering Activities. In *SIGCSE '18: The 49th ACM Technical Symposium on Computer Science Education, February 21–24, 2018, Baltimore , MD, USA.* ACM, New York, NY, USA, 6 pages. https://doi.org/10.1145/3159450.3159489

1 INTRODUCTION

As software becomes ubiquitous in our lives, the security of that software becomes of critical importance. ACM/IEEE Computer Science Curricula 2013 [12] recognised the growth in importance of security since CS2008 [3], and introduced the knowledge area IAS (Information Assurance and Security), while noting that security is embedded throughout other knowledge areas in the curriculum.

Engaging students in activities in which they attempt to develop and break security systems provides practical experiences that demonstrate the difficulties of software security. To write secure code, students need to think about vulnerabilities and to anticipate possible attacks when writing defensively. Asking students to attack code by exploiting vulnerabilities is a valuable exercise that may improve students ability to write more secure code and defend against malicious attacks [11, 15].

Software obfuscation is a promising technique to protect sensitive information in application code when applications are run by untrusted users. Software obfuscation makes it difficult for attackers to extract sensitive information from the code consisting of private data (*e.g.*, password matching) and program control flow (*i.e.*, business logic). The basic idea is to transform code in such a manner that it can function but it becomes hard to interpret for a human. To address this issue, researchers and industry have developed sophisticated reverse engineering mechanisms and tools that aim at analysing the code in a fully or semi-automated fashion. In other words, one can easily understand the code by using reverse engineering tools. For designing obfuscation methods, it is necessary to test them against available reverse engineering tools.

Techniques for teaching reverse engineering have rarely been discussed in the literature, and until relatively recently, it was not obvious that it was an important part of the curriculum [1]. Mahoney and Gandhi present their experience of teaching reverse engineering and observe that it appears to be more of an art than a science, and that some students "get it" while others do not[13].

Although there are several examples of cooperative and competitive activities involving security, there are no reported activities that engage students in competitive obfuscation and reverse engineering of software. In this paper, we describe a case study illustrating how software obfuscation and reverse engineering activities have been used as part of a competitive assignment in a graduate cyber security course.

2 RELATED PEDAGOGIES

Constructivism is based on the idea that individuals learn by building their own knowledge through processes of assimilation, in which students incorporate new knowledge into an existing schematic framework, and accommodation, in which students adjust their framework to fit new experiences into their view of the world [2]. Vygotsky extended the view of constructivism to acknowledge the role that social interaction plays in learning, advancing the sociocultural theory of development in which learning occurs when it is supported by an instructor, or by peers [21].

The approach described in this paper is informed by previous work on Contributing Student Pedagogies. A Contributing Student Pedagogy (CSP) is an approach that encourages students to contribute to the learning of others and to value the contributions of others [9]. Characteristically, these pedagogies include a focus

SIGCSE '18, February 21–24, 2018, Baltimore , MD, USA

ACM ISBN 978-1-4503-5103-4/18/02...$15.00
https://doi.org/10.1145/3159450.3159489

on the contribution of content used for peer learning, the assessment of the quality of contributions, the development of learning communities, and the use of technology as a facilitator.

Although it can be challenging for students to work in groups, particularly in competitive environments [19], the benefits of peer assisted [18], and cooperative [17] learning are well established, and are particular value to CS students [16] who are likely to work in teams in their professional lives.

Teaching Using Competitive Activities. Several researchers have used authentic competitive activities in teaching practice. Any domain can use competition as a motivator, simply by publicly ranking student achievement. However, in the software domain, there are some natural contexts, such as software testing and cyber security, in which competition is authentic.

Live security competitions, or "Capture the Flag" competitions are a popular way to engage students in security education. Although they have been adopted by both academia and industry [4, 5, 22] they are difficult to design, implement and run effectively [20].

Goldwasser presented a case study of a more structured activity, in which students submitted both an implementation of a program and a set of tests. The implementation was tested by running the tests submitted by other students, and in turn, the test set submitted by a given student was used to test other students' implementations. Although Goldwasser recommends this approach, the administration was time-consuming and automated tools were advised for large classes [8]. Similar approaches have been reported at several other universities [6, 7, 10, 11, 14] with positive responses reported from both students and teachers.

Hooshangi *et al.* [11], described a competitive activity that was divided into two parts. In the first part, students were asked to develop a defence monitoring program that stopped a user from reading data, writing over existing data, or writing new data to the end of a file if the user did not have the appropriate permissions. In the second part, students were given the defensive programs submitted by their peers and asked to write attack programs that would bypass as many defence programs as possible. The authors conclude that student attack programs had a high degree of uniqueness, and there is a relationship between good attack programs and good defensive programs.

3 PROPOSED TEACHING METHOD

The Computer Science Department at the University of Auckland is a large department with graduate classes typically consisting of 30–100 students. *Security for Smart-Devices (COMPSCI 702)* is a 12-week long graduate course, focusing on security architectures of smart devices (covering both Android and iOS). Students in this course are expected to demonstrate a critical understanding of research literature, and to develop novel problem solving and research-informed ideas. The course assessment consists of three components: 15% individual seminar, 25% group project, and 60% final exam.

The group project was conducted in the same way in 2016 and 2017. We describe here the 2017 version, which was formally evaluated. There were 70 students divided into 13 groups.

Students were permitted to self-organise into groups for the group project. Each group consisted of 5–6 members and operated as a startup, delivering several project artefacts including an obfuscated app, an obfuscation tool, a research report, and a project presentation (optionally including a demonstration of their app and/or tool). To monitor group progress throughout the course, we adopted a scrum methodology and managed each group through Basecamp[1], a project management and team communication tool.

There were two phases to the project: a development phase and a challenge phase.

3.1 Development Phase

In the development phase, each group was asked to develop an Android app using Java, and to produce an obfuscation tool in a programming language of their choice.

3.1.1 App Development. We set some broad guidelines for the development of the app, but allowed students the freedom to design and develop an app on any topic desired. The guidelines stated that the app should consist of 400-1000 lines of code, and should have a clear separation between UI and business logic.

To provide context, we mention three Android apps that students developed in 2017. The first one is a Bus Tracker app, shown in Figure 1. This app enables users to search for specific or nearby bus stops. Furthermore, a user can add a bus stop to their favourite list.

Figure 1: Bus Tracker app.

Two other groups developed two health-related apps, including a Calories Calculator app, and a Drink Up app, shown in Figures 2 and 3, respectively.

Figure 2: Calories Calculator app.

[1]https://basecamp.com

Figure 3: Drink Up app.

The former app calculates calories burnt while taking into account user inputs including weight, type, and length of exercise. Moreover, it gives calorie information about user's input for a particular food. The latter app tracks water consumption. Users can set their goal by specifying the number of glasses per day. They receive reminders if notifications are set up.

3.1.2 Development Phase — Obfuscation Tool. The obfuscation tool was used to automate the obfuscation process used by the group. We allowed students to build an obfuscation tool from scratch, or to extend an existing tool.

Code obfuscation aims at hardening the process of reverse engineering by protecting intellectual property in the program. Students were given an introductory lecture to describe the various forms of code obfuscation. In the context of the group project, we expected students to focus on data obfuscation and control obfuscation. The former technique aims at preventing adversaries from extracting information from the data used in the program, while the latter approach is used to obscure the control flow information of the program. Students were encouraged to read the literature and develop their own obfuscation strategy.

The length of the development phase was approximately 9 weeks and the main outcome was an obfuscated app, which was obfuscated using the obfuscation tool developed by the group.

3.2 Challenge Phase

The second phase was the challenge phase, which started immediately after the end of development phase.

The obfuscated apps developed in the first phase were distributed to other groups. Since there were 13 groups in total, each group received 12 obfuscated apps and was expected to reverse engineer each of the apps by identifying the obfuscation techniques used. To help students, we shared a set of obfuscation and reverse engineering tools with students in the beginning of the course.

The challenge phase lasted for 2 weeks, after which each group submitted a research report explaining their proposed idea, providing a literature review, reporting an evaluation, and covering some discussion. In the proposed idea, they were asked to explain their obfuscation technique. For the literature review, students were expected to highlight how their technique was novel, by justifying how their technique was different from existing approaches and tools. In the evaluation part, students were required to discuss the strength of their obfuscated app, performance overhead, and storage overhead. Students were also expected to report on reverse engineering of the obfuscated apps developed by other groups. The last part of the report was a discussion for covering limitations, possible extensions, and how obfuscated apps could be debugged and updated.

3.3 Other coursework

Following the challenge phase, students were expected to deliver a presentation based on the research reports they submitted. The project presentation provided an opportunity for the whole group to give a joint presentation to share obfuscation technique and the process of reverse engineering as well as to demonstrate the app and obfuscation tool. There was a QA session (of 10 minutes) at the end of each group presentation (up to 20 minutes).

Students were encouraged to use Piazza[2] (which was set up with the anonymous feature enabled) to engage in discussion between groups.

4 EVALUATION

The first time we used this approach to teach obfuscation and reverse engineering (in 2016), students responded very positively, and appeared to be engaged and enthusiastic. Subsequently, we decided to collect evidence to support the anecdotal findings.

4.1 Methodology

To evaluate the effectiveness of the competitive project, we conducted two anonymous online questionnaires: one after the development phase (the *pre-challenge questionnaire*), and the other after the challenge phase and project presentations (the *post-challenge questionnaire*). The questionnaire response rate was 30% for the pre-challenge questionnaire (21 students) and 40% for the post-challenge questionnaire (28 students).

Table 1: Questions asked in the both the pre-challenge and post-challenge questionnaires.

Q1	Difficulty of coming up with a novel idea for obfuscation
Q2	Difficulty of reverse engineering app created by others
Q3	Difficulty that other groups will encounter reverse engineering your app

4.2 Questionnaires

A small number of questions were asked in both the pre-challenge questionnaire and the post-challenge questionnaire, to analyse changes in attitude that occur during and after the challenge phase. These questions are listed in Table 1. A larger set of questions administered in the post-challenge phase asked students to reflect on aspects of the entire course. All of these questions were answered on a categorical scale. Additionally, students were provided with open-text fields and asked what they liked most and what they liked least. Finally, students were invited to make any further comments they thought were relevant.

[2]https://piazza.com

Figure 4 illustrates the perception of students after the development and challenge phases. In the development phase, students found the obfuscation task quite challenging as we can see in Figure 4(a). Although some students (more than 14%) thought the obfuscation task was going to be easy, they found it challenging when they started working on it.

Responses to the question asking students what they liked most indicated that students enjoyed developing the app and working on the obfuscation technique/tool, making comments such as:

- *"Creating the app".*
- *"The research was interesting, I enjoyed learning about different available techniques".*
- *"Writing our obfuscation tool was both challenging and rewarding".*

In 2016, we observed (anecdotally) that students anticipated that it would be very difficult to reverse engineer obfuscated code, and perceived that the challenge phase would be difficult. However, after completing the challenge phase, students discovered that reverse engineering code obfuscated by their peers was easier than expected. The questionnaire results from the 2017 course we capture this change in perception before and after the completion of challenge phase.

To determine if the changes in perception were statistically significant, we used the two-tailed Mann-Whitney U test, where alpha was .05. We found that the p-value was .05486. Although our results are not statistically significant at the .05 level the p-value was borderline and indicative that a real change in perception is likely to have occurred.

Students also perceived that it would be more difficult for other groups to reverse engineer their obfuscated app. However, after the challenge phase, they realised that their code was not as difficult to reverse engineer as they originally thought (see Figure 4(c)). A two-tailed Mann-Whitney U test indicated a statically significant change (Z-Score -2.41426 and p-value .01596) in the perception of how difficult it is for other groups to reverse engineering the obfuscated code.

To reflect what students managed to reverse engineer, we illustrate the performance of groups in the reverse engineering phase in Figure 5. In both years, we noticed that all the groups managed to reverse engineer almost all the obfuscated apps, although some of them did not manage to completely reverse engineer some parts of few apps.

Note that there was a very strict policy that we enforced for grading the reverse engineering component. Basically, we looked for whether the groups identified the right technique, and if so, we expected them to provide an example or two of reverse engineered code (*i.e.,* code snippets). Groups that identified the correct technique, but did not provide an example were awarded partial marks.

Figure 6 illustrates students' responses when we asked them about improving their obfuscation technique. Surprisingly, all the students indicated that they would like to improve their obfuscation technique. This reflects an active student learning from their peers, where they realised themselves that there are some flaws in their techniques. It does not mean that their technique was totally useless; as we can see in Figure 6, none of them chose *'entirely a new technique'.* This self-reflection suggests that all students considered that they had partial success, but had further room for improvement.

Figure 7 shows student responses in regards to usefulness in enhancing their skill to be a good team player such that they can prepare themselves for serving in teams in industry. The majority of the students found the project quite helpful.

Figure 8 illustrates different aspects for personal learning of students. Overall, students found it quite helpful to work on different things including app development, obfuscation technique and tool, and reverse engineering. It was extremely helpful for students to work on app development and reverse engineering. As expected, group presentation was helpful only for a few students. To monitor the progress of projects, we are using Basecamp since 2015. Although Basecamp enables communication within each team, the results show that students did not find it very helpful.

In few cases, we noticed in both 2016 and 2017 that students performed better in group presentations as compared to individual presentations. In the group presentation, almost all the students participated. We believe that the group presentation in such a project appeared to be more enjoyable rather than a stressful activity. During QA sessions held at the end of group presentations, we observed some students asking questions, though they never asked any question during class lectures and courses. One possible reason of this positive change in behaviour could be the peer review nature of this new innovative method involving development and challenge phases, which resulted in active learning.

Figure 9 highlights three aspects of the project including stimulation of student interest in the learning process, motivating and interesting nature of the method, and recommending it for other courses. As we can notice, this teaching approach is perceived positively by the students.

5 DISCUSSION

In this section, we discuss various aspects of this method. We stress that this method might not be effective in all situations and there are some limitations. There are following aspects to be aware of when one is going to follow such a teaching method.

It might be possible for the teacher to provide an app, and reduce the time spent by students developing their own app, and therefore allow students to spend more time on the obfuscation and reverse engineering phases. However, this may be time-consuming for teachers if there are large numbers of groups.

Although students were asked to use obfuscation tool for automating obfuscation process, we also allowed students to do manual obfuscation in case they could not fully automate their obfuscation technique. This flexibility was desired for this course project due to its time limit, which was 10 weeks. Since most groups manually obfuscated some parts of their app, it was beneficial for students to have the detailed understanding of code that comes from writing the code themselves.

Additionally, students reported that they enjoyed developing apps as discussed in Section 4.2. They also enjoyed breaking obfuscated apps developed by their colleagues, as mentioned by one student in the post-challenge questionnaire:

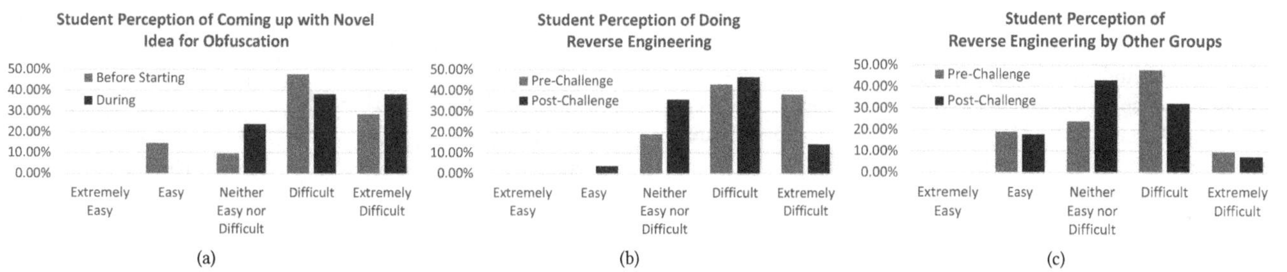

Figure 4: Student perception of (a) coming up with novel idea for obfuscation, (b) doing reverse engineering, and (c) their obfuscated app being reverse engineered by other groups.

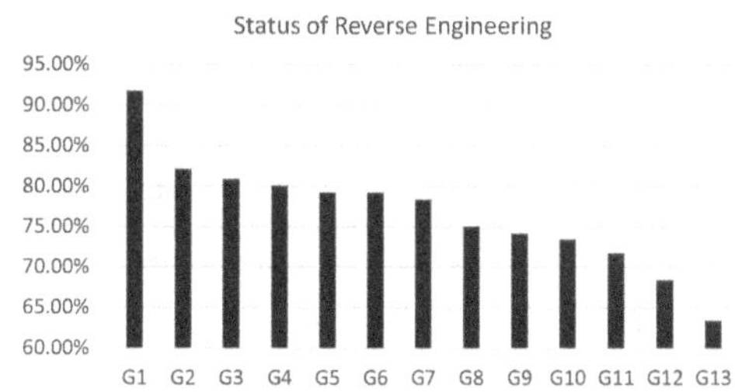

Figure 5: Performance of groups in the reverse engineering part.

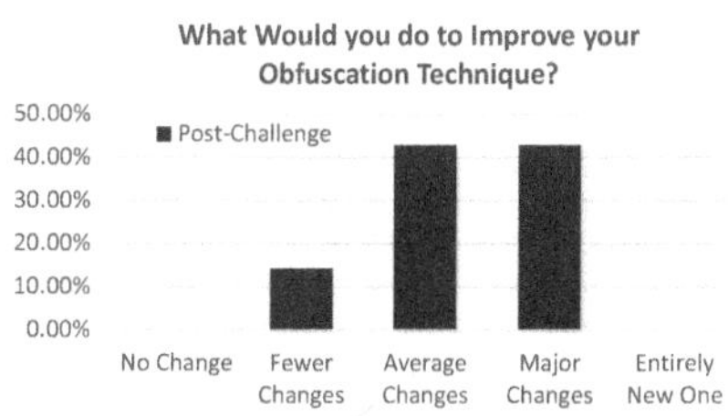

Figure 6: Students' responses to the question on improving their obfuscation technique.

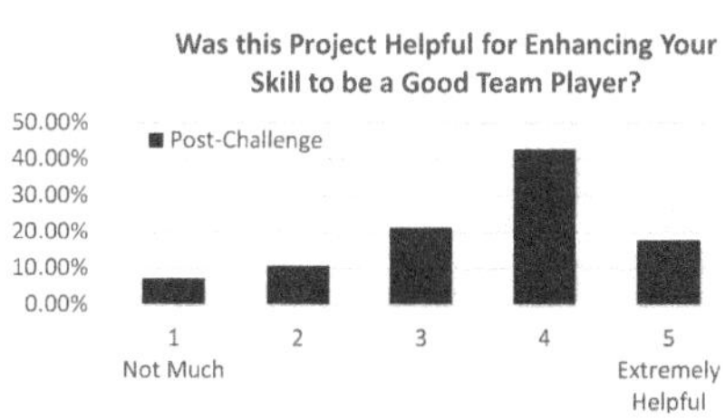

Figure 7: Helpfulness of the project in enhancing skill to be a good team player.

- *"Live the challenge phase because it encourages everyone to do their best obfuscating and it's just fun to crack other teams' app".*

We have to stress that a care must be taken when using this teaching method. That is, this method worked well with a class of 40 students in 2016. However, we observed a comparatively lower

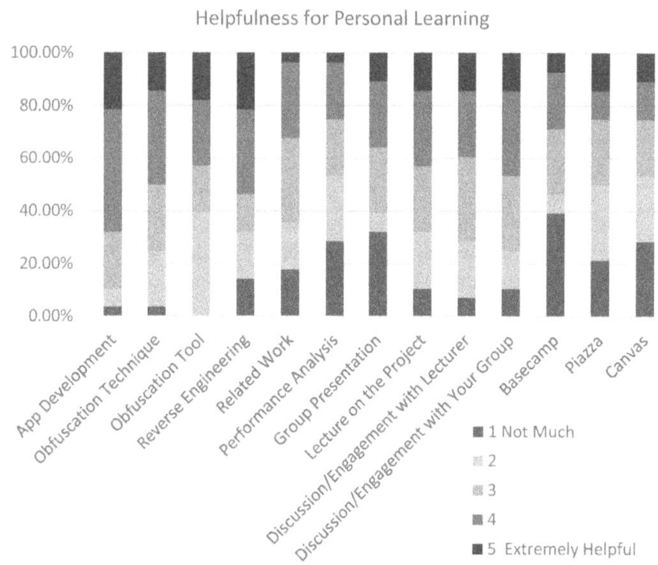

Figure 8: Usefulness of different aspects for personal learning.

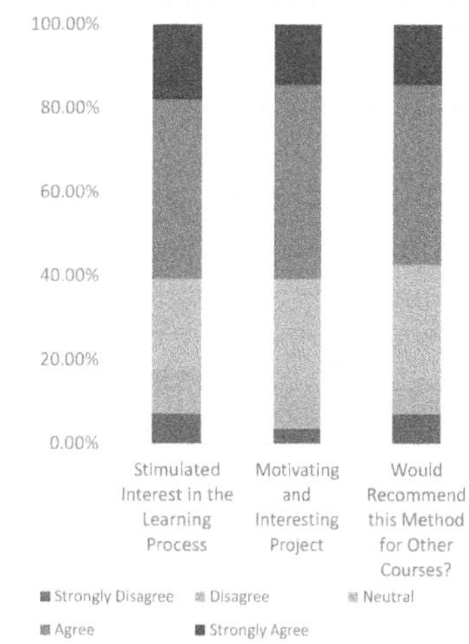

Figure 9: Interesting project and recommendation of this innovative teaching method for other courses.

score in course evaluations when the class increased to 70 students in 2017.

We required students to reverse engineer the apps produced by **all** the groups, so as the number of students increased (between 2016 and 2017), the workload for students increase commensurately. In 2016, we had 7 groups with 4 or 5 members each. In 2017, we had 12 groups with 5 or 6 members. In total, this resulted in approximately 70% extra workload with only 20% additional resources (*i.e.,* students) in each group. We strongly recommend placing a limit on the number of apps that students are expected to reverse engineer.

Below is what we noted in the open comments in 2017:

- *"The amount of effort needed for the project seemed very heavy for the number of marks it was worth."*

Even if we have more balanced workload for a large class, there is still a very important factor when it comes to the group work, namely, how to balance groups. It is quite a challenging task to make balanced groups, particularly in classes that have students from different backgrounds. One way to ensure balanced groups is by making it compulsory to have at least one student from each discipline, *e.g.,* one from computer science, one from information system, one from engineering, and so on. In 2017, we received verbal and written complaints about this issue. Here is what one student wrote in the post-challenge questionnaire:

- *"Having to deal with less than ideal teammates."*

From the comments, we noted a number of students enjoyed this course and the course project appeared to be a pleasant experience for them. Below are some comments we found in the post-challenge questionnaire:

- *"enjoyed course"*
- *"Great experience."*
- *"Overall, the course has been helpful."*
- *"Great course, highly recommend. I wish I had taken this last year due to how interesting it is. A student who does the work will learn app development, obfuscation technique development, reverse engineering, giving technical presentation, writing technical paper and about the security in smart devices which is a major issue in the work today (and will be more so in the future)."*

6 CONCLUSIONS AND FUTURE DIRECTIONS

In this paper, we have described a novel approach to teaching software obfuscation and reverse engineering that uses competitive group projects. One on hand, we can see a positive change in student perception and learning activities, and students appear to have more realistic expectations about the difficulty of effectively preventing code from being reverse engineered.

On the other hand, there is more administrative work for a course instructor to follow this teaching method in managing multiple projects. More students mean more meetings with them, more emails to reply, more questions to answer on Piazza, and more workload for grading projects. In short, there is a trade-off between what one can get out of this innovative teaching method and the amount of effort needed to run the projects. However, on balance, we believe that this has been a positive experience for both students and teaching staff, and we plan to continue to both use and evaluate this approach in future.

ACKNOWLEDGMENTS

This project was approved by the University of Auckland Human Participants Ethics Committee — Reference Number 019274.

REFERENCES

[1] M. R. Ali. Why teach reverse engineering? *SIGSOFT Softw. Eng. Notes*, 30(4):1–4, July 2005.
[2] M. Ben-Ari. Constructivism in computer science education. *Journal of Computers in Mathematics and Science Teaching*, 20(1):45–73, 2001.
[3] L. Cassel, A. Clements, G. Davies, M. Guzdial, R. McCauley, A. McGettrick, B. Sloan, L. Snyder, P. Tymann, and B. W. Weide. Computer science curriculum 2008: An interim revision of cs 2001. Technical report, New York, NY, USA, 2008.
[4] A. Conklin. The use of a collegiate cyber defense competition in information security education. In *Proceedings of the 2Nd Annual Conference on Information Security Curriculum Development*, InfoSecCD '05, pages 16–18, New York, NY, USA, 2005. ACM.
[5] G. Conti, T. Babbitt, and J. Nelson. Hacking competitions and their untapped potential for security education. *IEEE Security and Privacy*, 9(3):56–59, May 2011.
[6] S. H. Edwards, Z. Shams, M. Cogswell, and R. C. Senkbeil. Running students' software tests against each others' code: New life for an old "gimmick". In *Proceedings of the 43rd ACM Technical Symposium on Computer Science Education*, SIGCSE '12, pages 221–226, New York, NY, USA, 2012. ACM.
[7] A. Gaspar, S. Langevin, N. Boyer, and R. Tindell. A preliminary review of undergraduate programming students' perspectives on writing tests, working with others, & using peer testing. In *Proceedings of the 14th Annual ACM SIGITE Conference on Information Technology Education*, SIGITE '13, pages 109–114, New York, NY, USA, 2013. ACM.
[8] M. H. Goldwasser. A gimmick to integrate software testing throughout the curriculum. In *Proceedings of the 33rd SIGCSE Technical Symposium on Computer Science Education*, SIGCSE '02, pages 271–275, New York, NY, USA, 2002. ACM.
[9] J. Hamer, Q. Cutts, J. Jackova, A. Luxton-Reilly, R. McCartney, H. Purchase, C. Riedesel, M. Saeli, K. Sanders, and J. Sheard. Contributing student pedagogy. *SIGCSE Bull.*, 40(4):194–212, Nov. 2008.
[10] M. Hauswirth, D. Zaparanuks, A. Malekpour, and M. Keikha. The javafest: A collaborative learning technique for java programming courses. In *Proceedings of the 6th International Symposium on Principles and Practice of Programming in Java*, PPPJ '08, pages 3–12, New York, NY, USA, 2008. ACM.
[11] S. Hooshangi, R. Weiss, and J. Cappos. Can the security mindset make students better testers? In *Proceedings of the 46th ACM Technical Symposium on Computer Science Education*, SIGCSE '15, pages 404–409, New York, NY, USA, 2015. ACM.
[12] A. f. C. M. A. Joint Task Force on Computing Curricula and I. C. Society. *Computer Science Curricula 2013: Curriculum Guidelines for Undergraduate Degree Programs in Computer Science.* ACM, New York, NY, USA, 2013. 999133.
[13] W. Mahoney and R. A. Gandhi. Reverse engineering: Is it art? *ACM Inroads*, 3(1):56–61, Mar. 2012.
[14] W. Marrero and A. Settle. Testing first: Emphasizing testing in early programming courses. In *Proceedings of the 10th Annual SIGCSE Conference on Innovation and Technology in Computer Science Education*, ITiCSE '05, pages 4–8, New York, NY, USA, 2005. ACM.
[15] M. Mink and F. C. Freiling. Is attack better than defense?: Teaching information security the right way. In *Proceedings of the 3rd Annual Conference on Information Security Curriculum Development*, InfoSecCD '06, pages 44–48, New York, NY, USA, 2006. ACM.
[16] B. Plimmer and R. Amor. Peer teaching extends hci learning. In *Proceedings of the 11th Annual SIGCSE Conference on Innovation and Technology in Computer Science Education*, ITICSE '06, pages 53–57, New York, NY, USA, 2006. ACM.
[17] R. E. Slavin. Cooperative learning. *Review of Educational Research*, 50(2):315–342, 1980.
[18] K. Topping. Peer assessment between students in colleges and universities. *Review of Educational Research*, 68(3):249–276, 1998.
[19] K. J. Topping. Trends in peer learning. *Educational Psychology*, 25(6):631–645, 2005.
[20] G. Vigna, K. Borgolte, J. Corbetta, A. Doupé, Y. Fratantonio, L. Invernizzi, D. Kirat, and Y. Shoshitaishvili. Ten years of ictf: The good, the bad, and the ugly. In *2014 USENIX Summit on Gaming, Games, and Gamification in Security Education (3GSE 14)*, San Diego, CA, 2014. USENIX Association.
[21] L. S. Vygotsky. *Mind in Society.* Harvard University Press, Cambridge, MA, 1978.
[22] M. E. Whitman and H. J. Mattord. The southeast collegiate cyber defense competition. In *Proceedings of the 5th Annual Conference on Information Security Curriculum Development*, InfoSecCD '08, pages 1–4, New York, NY, USA, 2008. ACM.

Enhancing Security Education Through Designing SDN Security Labs in CloudLab

Younghee Park
San Jose State University
younghee.park@sjsu.edu

Hongxin Hu
Clemson University
hongxih@clemson.edu

Xiaohong Yuan
North Carolina A&T State University
xhyuan@ncat.edu

Hongda Li
Clemson University
hongdal@clemson.edu

ABSTRACT

Software-Defined Networking (SDN) represents a major shift from ossified hardware-based networks to programmable software-based networks. It introduces significant granularity, visibility, and flexibility into networking, but at the same time brings new security challenges. Although the research community is making progress in addressing both the opportunities in SDN and the accompanying security challenges, very few educational materials have been designed to incorporate the latest research results and engage students in learning about SDN security. In this paper, we presents our newly designed SDN security education materials, which can be used to meet the ever-increasing demand for high quality cybersecurity professionals with expertise in SDN security. The designed security education materials incorporate the latest research results in SDN security and are integrated into CloudLab, an open cloud platform, for effective hands-on learning. Through a user study, we demonstrate that students have a better understanding of SDN security after participating in these well-designed CloudLab-based security labs, and they also acquired strong research interests in SDN security.

KEYWORDS

Software-Defined Networking, Security, CloudLab

ACM Reference Format:

Younghee Park, Hongxin Hu, Xiaohong Yuan, and Hongda Li. 2018. Enhancing Security Education Through Designing SDN Security Labs in CloudLab. In *Proceedings of The 49th ACM Technical Symposium on Computer Science Education (SIGCSE '18).* ACM, New York, NY, USA, 6 pages. https://doi.org/10.1145/3159450.3159514

1 INTRODUCTION

Software-Defined Networking (SDN) has progressed from a purely theoretical concept [10, 11, 13, 18] to an increasingly popular new paradigm that numerous networking vendors are not only embracing, but also are pursuing as their model for future enterprise network management. According to a recent report from Google, SDN-based network management helped Google run wide-area networks at close to 100% utilization compared to other state-of-the-art network environments that yielded only 30% to 40% network utilization [16].

Along with the rapid growth of SDN, there are many new security issues in SDN that are different from traditional network security problems [7, 9, 12, 14, 15, 17, 19, 26, 27]. It is imperative that research results on SDN should be brought into cybersecurity education with effective delivery approaches to prepare our students, as the future workforce and pillars of the nation, with security awareness and readiness sufficient to protect the emerging SDN-based network infrastructure. However, there are few hands-on lab materials to address SDN security issues. A traditional lab setting with multiple interconnected physical computers for cybersecurity training presents problems both in terms of associated overhead costs and in terms of setup, configuration, installation, and scheduling and management of equipment [22]. Usually, the SDN learning environment is also limited to simulation-based exercises. Furthermore, commercial cloud platforms like Amazon Web Service (AWS) are unflexible and expensive to use, and have restrictions on conducting some security labs [22]. In addition, no existing *commercial* cloud platforms can directly provide SDN features that are critical for implementing SDN security labs.

This paper presents our initial progress to develop Cloud-based SDN security labs. We develop an open laboratory for SDN security education, leveraging unique features provided by CloudLab [1], an open cloud platform. CloudLab is specially built for research and education purposes and hence it is completely *free* to use. In addition, CloudLab supports OpenFlow [18] and other software-defined networking technologies that are particularly important for building SDN security labs. It engages students in SDN security education through hands-on lab development. Our designed labs cover various security issues, such as denial-of-service (DoS) attacks and application attacks, from the data plane to the control plane in SDN. We also introduce pilot labs related to two main security problems in SDN and students participate in survey after finishing the labs. Our survey results show that the designed labs provide students with a positive learning experience in SDN security.

The rest of this paper is organized as follows. Section 2 introduces CloudLab. Section 3 presents various SDN security labs, and also gives example lab modules. Section 4 discusses student experiences in the proposed SDN security labs in CloudLab. Section 5 reviews related work and lastly Section 6 concludes this paper.

SIGCSE '18, Feb. 21–24, 2018, Baltimore, MD, USA

ACM ISBN 978-1-4503-5103-4/18/02...$15.00
https://doi.org/10.1145/3159450.3159514

2 CLOUDLAB FOR SDN SECURITY EDUCATION

SDN as an new emerging network technology has raised a lot of new research problems, especially in security areas. Even though SDN has rapidly adopted in both industry and academia with significant research outcomes, there are very few education materials from the latest research results in order to effectively teach students in SDN security. Therefore, we aim to build a cloud-based open laboratory for hands-on labs in SDN security.

Several studies [22, 29, 31] have demonstrated the use of cloud computing as an effective delivery approach for cybersecurity education; unfortunately their emphasis involves leveraging *commercial* cloud platforms, such as Amazon Web Services (AWS), which are expensive to use and have restrictions on conducting some security labs [22]. More importantly, no existing commercial cloud platforms can directly provide SDN features that are critical for conducting our hands-on labs on SDN security.

CloudLab is an NSF-sponsored project that enables the academic research community to develop and experiment with novel cloud architectures and to develop new cloud computing applications. CloudLab provides the substrate on which instructors can build their own flexible cloud environment that will give them both control and visibility all the way down to the hardware.

CloudLab has some specific advantages for building an open laboratory for SDN security education. First, unlike the creation of security exercises using the commercial cloud, which is quite costly, CloudLab was designed for educational purposes, which means that it is *free* of charge. Second, CloudLab supports OpenFlow (an open SDN standard through which instructors may run experimental protocols on campus networks) and other SDN technologies. This is significant requirements for SDN security education. In the case of exclusive-access bare metal switches, users will get direct and complete OpenFlow access to switches to many SDN security experiments. Third, CloudLab uses a profile to encapsulate everything needed to run an experiment. The profile consists of two main parts: a description of hardware, storage, and network resources needed to run the experiment, and software artifacts that run on those resources. A profile can be created and published by an instructor. Students use the profile to provision an entire cloud inside of CloudLab within minutes, which greatly reduces the set-up time for experiments, making it easier to repeat them and compare results. Last, existing research [22] has confirmed that unlike CloudLab, the Amazon AWS cloud or other commercial cloud alternatives may be unsuitable for many cybersecurity labs, such network security exercises involving eavesdropping and Man-In-The-Middle (MITM) attacks.

We leverage the unique benefits provided by CloudLab to build an *open* laboratory specifically for the SDN security education purpose. Using the CloudLab-based open laboratory, an instructor designs and publishes an experiment simply by creating a profile and distributing it to the students. There are two ways to create a profile: 1) cloning an existing profile, which is useful if the instructor wants to design an experiment using a previous record, and 2) writing a new profile in RSpec format [2]. CloudLab provides two methods [3] to easily generate valid profiles in RSpec format. The graphical user interface (GUI) method is straightforward, based on Jacks, an embeddable RSpec editor. The programming language binding method is useful when the user wants to create large, complicated profiles in the RSpec format by writing programs in an existing, popular language (like Python). Geni-lib [4] is being evaluated for this purpose.

3 DESIGN OF SDN SECURITY LABS

3.1 Lab Module Overview

The SDN security labs designed with the support of CloudLab consist of five lab modules to learn five important security problems in SDN. Each module has a problem definition to address a specific security issue in SDN, a learning objective and outcome to evaluate student achievement, and research challenging questions to encourage students to participate in research in the specific SDN security issues.

3.1.1 Lab 1: *Data-to-control Plane Saturation Attacks to the SDN Controller*

. Problem Definition: Data-to-control plane saturation attacks present the biggest security threat to the SDN controller because the controller is a logically centralized framework [24, 33, 34]. The lack of scalability can cause control plane saturation attacks by inundating communication between the controller and the switch. When a table-miss flow entry occurs in an OpenFlow switch, the packet is forwarded to the OpenFlow controller. The controller responds with one or more flow rules for packet processing actions. Such design in SDN becomes a scaling bottleneck since anomalous burst traffic, such as flash crowds, denial-of-service attacks, and even botnets, quickly saturate the control plane with new flow requests. An adversary could exploit the feature by mounting a control plane saturation attack that disrupts network operations in SDN.

Learning Objectives: Students will learn the communication logic between the controller and the data plane as to connection establishment and flow rule installation.

Learning Outcomes: Students will be able to understand fundamental security issues in the controller. They can generate TCP-based flood attacks on the controller, and analyze flow rules and response delays under attack.

Challenging Questions: Students will brainstorm how to increase scalability and resilience in the controller. Students will discuss pros and cons of using multiple controllers to prevent or defeat saturation attacks [33].

3.1.2 Lab 2: *Flooding Attacks to the SDN Data Plane*

. Problem Definition: An attacker can produce a large amount of table-miss flow entries in messages to consume resources in the data plane [28, 34]. The impact of this data-to-control plane saturation attack differs for various target applications. For example, a load balancing application is more vulnerable than a hub application since it requires high programming complexity to handle complicated computations for load balancing. The controller installs flow rules in the switch flow table. The flow rules can be installed proactively or retroactively. Since the switch has a limited number of flow tables, the data plane is vulnerable to saturation attacks.

Learning Objectives: Students will learn different attack techniques to saturate data plane resources and understand the different characteristics of SDN applications that can affect flow rules proactively or reactively. Students will be able to understand the internal architecture of the data plane.

Learning Outcomes: Students understand the packet processing policies for different types of SDN applications. They can generate UDP or ICMP based flood attacks to launch saturation attacks in the data plane [28]. They can identify table-miss cases.

Challenging Questions: Students will brainstorm ways to keep the major functionalities of the SDN infrastructure working under a saturation attack in the data plane.

3.1.3 **Lab 3**: *API Misuse Attacks to the SDN Controller*

. Problem Definition: Networking functionalities can be implemented in software as applications on top of the control plane in SDN. Each application has its own distinct functional requirements for accessing the controller. Fallacious network applications that misuse APIs in the controller can cause serious security threats to network resources, services, and functions through the control plane due to lack of authentication and authorization for applications and lack of standard open APIs [20]. Students will explore how these unprivileged applications can crash the controller and launch memory leakage attacks [25].

Learning Objectives: Students will learn the internal structure of the controller and understand how applications can misuse APIs to cause attacks.

Learning Outcomes: Students can implement SDN applications and understand the architecture for interaction between applications and controller APIs. Students will be able to identify additional software vulnerabilities by investigating the internal code space.

Challenging Questions: Students will brainstorm security requirements for SDN applications. Different applications must have different privileges to access network information and resources. For example, a load balancing application needs network statistics while Intrusion Detection Systems (IDS) need to scrutinize packet header fields.

3.1.4 **Lab 4**: *Man-in-the-middle Attacks in the SDN Data Plane*

. Problem Definition: OpenFlow vulnerability is caused by insecure network management protocols where the adoption of transport layer security has lagged. Even though OpenFlow specifications support the use of Transport Layer Security (TLS), many vendors of both switches and controllers have failed to fully implement the specifications due to the complexity of TLS configuration, such as switch certificates, signing of certificates with a site-wide private key, and installing correct keys and certificates on all devices. The lack of adequate TLS implementation enables adversaries to infiltrate OpenFlow networks through a man-in-the-middle attack [6, 8]. Attackers place a device on a communication path between the switch and the controller, or simply copy the flow to his/her machine. As a result, attackers can fully control any down-stream switches and execute stealthy eavesdropping attacks in-band (i.e., links carry both data and OpenFlow traffic).

Learning Objectives: By using security protocols in the transport layer, student will learn how to establish a secure communication between the controller and switch. Students will understand OpenFlow protocol vulnerability.

Learning Outcomes: Students will be able to launch the man-in-the-middle attack in SDN and understand how attackers can steal information. They will learn security protocols like TLS, IPSec, and SSH and their usage between the controller and the switches. They will learn authentication methods needed for all devices connected to the controller or switches to ensure secure communication.

Challenging Questions: Students will brainstorm efficient authentication methods based on existing SDN features to reduce communication costs.

3.1.5 **Lab 5**: *Topology Poisoning Attacks to the SDN Controller*

. Problem Definition: The controller has a vast amount of important data, such as topological information, device information, and link information, all of which can be compromised by attackers. To accomplish this, attackers exploit the host tracking service in the controller. They can tamper with host location information to break through the controller and impersonate the target host. In that case, all traffic on the target host will be routed to the attacker's host. TopoGuard [14] was the first to demonstrate network poisoning attacks designed to compromise the network topology information based on the LLDP (Link Layer Discovery Protocol) protocol. It is but one example of many possible network poisoning attacks in SDN.

Learning Objectives: Students will learn link discovery methods to discover network topology. They will be able to identify important data structures in the controller, such as the topology. They can understand new attacks that compromise the controller database.

Learning Outcomes: Students will be able to generate a host location hijacking attacks by using the LLDP protocol. They can understand the procedure for maintaining network topology information in SDN. They can develop other exploits to poison other information in SDN.

Challenging Questions: Students will brainstorm a method to verify switch port properties by using model checking or symbolic execution to defend against the topology poisoning attack.

Table 1 summarizes the five security labs in SDN. The prerequisite for these labs is basic knowledge related to traditional networks and security. Without the prerequisite, it may be difficult to understand the difference between traditional network security problems and new SDN security problems. The table identifies learning outcomes, the concrete results that students will be able to accomplish after finishing each lab. After finishing all of the labs, students will understand new security issues with overall SDN knowledge.

Table 1: Five Lab Modules for SDN Security in CloudLab

Lab Num.	Pre-requisite Knowledge	Learning outcomes in a new SDN Security
Lab 1	Flooding attacks	Communication logic in the controller Connection establishment Flow rule installation
Lab 2	Flooding attacks	Flow table management in the data plane
Lab 3	Malicious applications Software vulnerability	Core APIs in the controller System architecture for SDN controller
Lab 4	MITM attack Security protocols like SSH	OpenFlow protocol vulnerability Authentication in SDN
Lab 5	LLDP	Link discovery in SDN

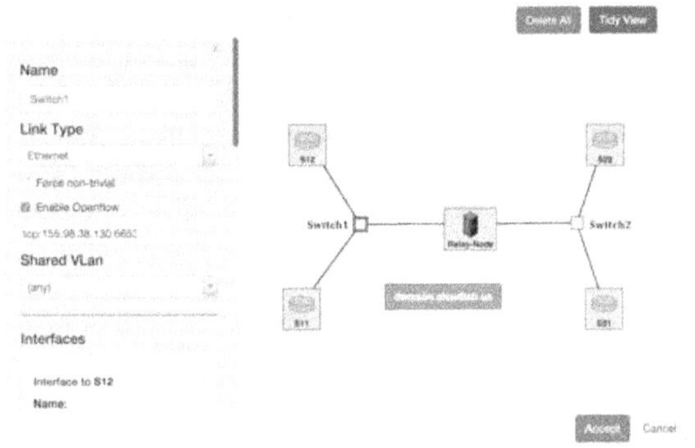

Figure 1: Network Topology Generated in CloudLab-based Laboratory

Figure 2: A Screenshot after DoS Attacks in the SDN Data Plane

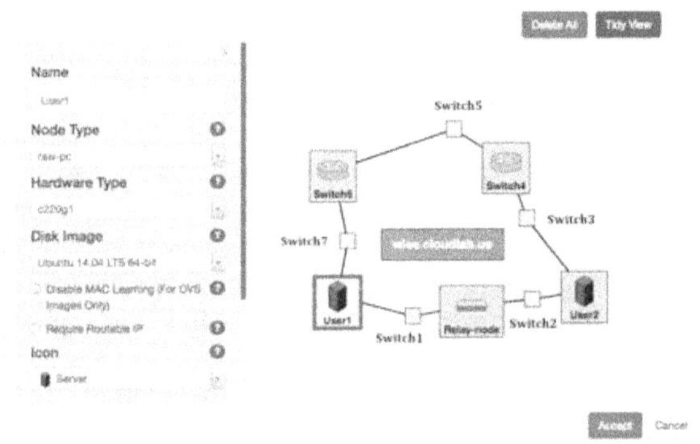

Figure 3: Network Topology Generated in CloudLab-based Laboratory for MITM Attack Lab.

3.2 Example Lab Modules

In this section, we demonstrates two pilot lab modules for teaching students in SDN security by using CloudLab. Each lab consists of three steps: a brief introduction to CloudLab; a detailed explanation of each security problem; and the steps to launch an attack in CloudLab. The introduction to CloudLab is shared by all labs to ensure that students are familiar with the CloudLab environment. However, each lab will have different problem statements and steps to execute corresponding attack.

We next illustrate how to set up our CloudLab-based open laboratory. First, the instructor creates a profile describing the resources required for the experiment. Each experiment requires at least two OpenFlow switches and one other node (Relay-Node). The network topology is shown in Figure 1. On the left, the properties of the selected entity are listed, in this case the switch, Switch1. The instructor can check the Enable Open-flow option and assign a valid OpenFlow controller (tcp:155.98.38.130:6653, not shown in this topology), which will convert Switch1 to an OpenFlow switch. On the right, the GUI visualizes the current network topology, which is helpful to the instructor when the network topology becomes quite complicated. Once the design is accepted, a profile will automatically be generated. The instructor can then distribute this profile by providing the students with a link to it. The shared link is always to the latest version of this profile, so the instructor need not republish every time a profile is updated. Note that each profile for each lab will be somewhat different depending on attack scenarios. Students can easily copy and paste the shared link into a web browser address bar to instantiate an experiment. The procedure of instantiation is as simple as clicking the "next" button, prompting CloudLab to automatically perform the set up. Once the experiment is successfully set up, the instructor is able to see an entry for this experiment under the instructor's account. The instructor can then log in to any of the assets with root privileges if she/he wants to troubleshoot, monitor the experiment's procedure, or assess the experiment.

The SDN security problem for each lab was discussed in the previous section. Based on that information, students can understand the scope of each lab problem. Next, we use the Lab 2 and the Lab 4 as examples to articulate the detail of our lab design.

The Lab 2 addresses flooding attacks to the SDN data plane. This lab aims to design a new type of DoS attack in the SDN data plane. As mentioned before, the lab includes major components: an introduction to CloudLab; a detailed explanation of flooding attacks in the data plane; and launching a flooding attack in CloudLab. In this lab, students first create nodes shown in Figure 1 with predefined profiles for CloudLab. Second, students generate a number of Ping packets moving from one node to the other nodes and check the flow entries in the flow tables in the data plane. Flow rules are installed up to the maximum number of available flow entries. The large number of Ping packets results in the maximum being reached very quickly so that new flow rules overflow the flow entries in the data plane. Therefore, they cannot be installed and are dropped. Figure 2 shows the result of DoS attacks in the data plane. When the flow table on a switch is full, upon receiving an instruction to install a flow rule, the switch detects that there is no more space in the flow table. As the switch cannot install this rule, it sends an OFPT_ERROR message to the controller with the error code OFPFMFC_TABLE_FULL. It then drops this packet. The switch cannot forward buffered packets until there is space in the flow table to install new flow rules.

In the Lab 4, a man-in-the-middle (MITM) attack in the SDN data plane is addressed. Students are able to launch an MITM attack in an SDN network and understand how attackers can steal information by using TLS, IPSec, and SSH protocols. The topology of the lab design has two hosts and seven switches, as shown in Figure 3. Due to space limitations, we will not explain the profile used to create the topology, but it will be shared with students in the lab. Students will set up the routing path from Host 1 to Host 2, for example with Switch 3, Switch 4, Switch 5, Switch 6, and Switch

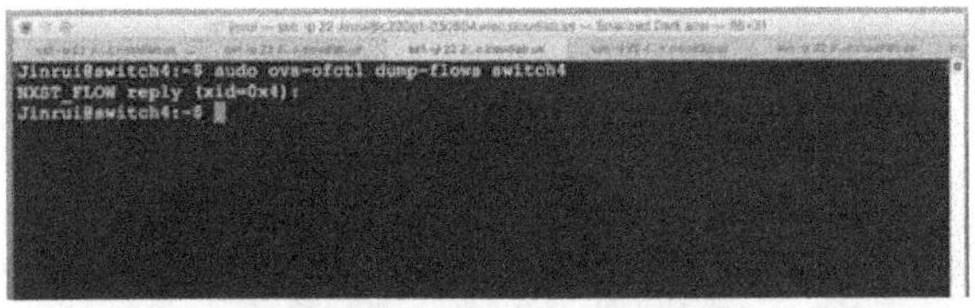

(a) No Traffic on Switch 4

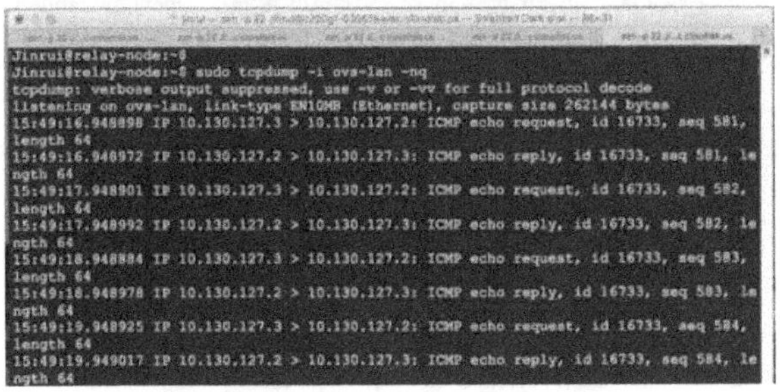

(b) Sniffed Traffic on Relay Node

Figure 4: Screenshots after MITM Attack

7 by installing flow rules in these OpenFlow-enabled switches, as shown in Figure 3. By using TCPdump, students can easily check the traffic passing through the designated path from Host 1 to Host 2. An attacker can cause the relay node shown in Figure 3 between Switch 1 and Switch 2 to forge a virtual link in the relay node by using the following commands:

- ovs-vsctl add-br ovs-lan
- ovs-vsctl add-port ovs-lan eth0
- ovs-vsctl add-port ovs-lan eth1
- ifconfig eth0 0
- ifconfig eth1 0
- ifconfig ovs-lan 10.130.127.1 netmask 255.255.255.0 up
- ovs-vsctl set-controller ovs-lan tcp:128.104.222.42:6653

An SDN-enabled virtual switch is created in the relay node machine and it is connected to the SDN controller. Because the SDN controller does not authenticate the SDN virtual switch, the switch can easily be registered in the SDN controller with the relay-node MAC address. Finally, the attacker captures all of the traffic between Host 1 and Host 2 through the relay node even though the hosts are able to ping each other. As shown in Figure 4, the traffic does not pass through the original path from Switch 3 to Switch 7. The traffic can only be captured between Switch 1 and Switch 2 through the relay node.

4 USER STUDY FOR SDN SECURITY LABS IN CLOUDLAB

We performed a user study with the sample labs described in Section 3.2. We recruited 35 students who have taken an SDN security course, which is an elective course to cover the fundamental techniques related to SDN. Thus, the 35 students are familiar with the SDN technique. In addition, the 35 students understood basic security concepts and general attacks, such as DoS attack and MITM attack, in networks. However, it was their first time to use CloudLab to study SDN security. The students conducted the sample lab modules and participated in a survey to evaluate the effectiveness

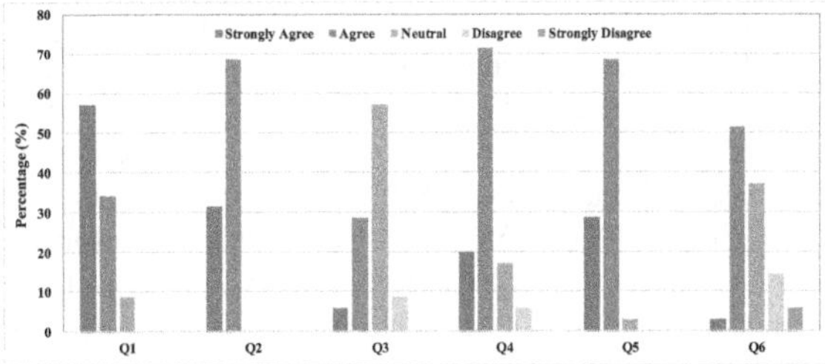

Figure 5: Survey Results. X-axis represents each question. Y-axis indicates the percentage for each answer.

of the designed labs. The survey asks students the following six questions:

- Q1: The lab helps students understand SDN security issues.
- Q2: The lab provides good hands-on skills to understand SDN security issues.
- Q3: The lab material is well-designed and easy to practice.
- Q4: The lab encourages students to be interested in SDN security issues.
- Q5: CloudLab helps students to understand a practical SDN environment.
- Q6: The lab makes student understand the difference between traditional network security issues and SDN specific security issues.

Figure 5 shows the results of this survey. More than 90% of students gave positive feedback on all evaluation questions except for the survey statements Q3 and Q6. Around 90% of students can understand SDN security issues even though none of the participating students has prior experience in SDN security issues. Therefore, around 90% of the students agreed that the designed lab in CloudLab would be an effective platform to understand real SDN security issues through hands-on experience. Furthermore, around 92% of the students showed research interests in SDN security after finishing the sample labs.

Even though they enjoyed the labs, some students gave negative feedback about the lab set-up and procedure. For the third survey statement (Q3), only around 35% of students can easily follow the instructions to finish the two labs. The rest of them showed a little difficulty to perform attacks in the CloudLab-based SDN environment. The reason is that it is the first time for all of them to use CloudLab and study the specific SDN security problems. They suggested putting video clips for demos since they lacked the security background to clearly understand the lab materials in SDN security. For this reason, around 57% of students gave a neutral response to the third survey statement (Q3). However, the survey showed that CloudLab is an effective platform to learn security issues. All students could finish one lab in less than five hours.

To summarize, our SDN security labs designed based on CloudLab results in positive feedback from students. The labs can provide a strong motivation for students to learn SDN security knowledge. The labs can also improve student learning skills based on CloudLab.

5 RELATED WORK

Many recent efforts have been devoted to addressing various security challenges in SDN, such as scanning attack prevention [15, 19],

DDoS attack detection [9], and topology poisoning attack prevention [12, 14]. Cloud-based education has become a promising trend for teaching cybersecurity [5, 21, 23, 30, 32]. Previous work has proposed hands-on cybersecurity assignments based on cloud services for cybersecurity education [5, 21, 23]. In [32], the authors focused on using the EDURange framework, a cloud-based resource for hosting on-demand interactive cybersecurity scenarios. In [32], the researchers introduced an assessment of student performance after they performed a network reconnaissance exercise. They explored the use of command line history and visualization to simplify the assessment of student performance [30]. However, none of the previous work on Cloud-based security have designed SDN security labs, despite the prevalence of SDN in networks today. This work is the first to structure hands-on security labs for SDN security education with the open cloud platform, CloudLab.

6 CONCLUSION

Cybersecurity education is critical for the development of future cybersecurity professionals, and for protecting IT assets. The advent of new network technology, SDN, has resulted in a high degree of flexibility in network infrastructure, but at the same time brought new security challenges. We have designed CloudLab-based SDN security labs to help students understand specific security issues in SDN and to encourage them in doing SDN security research. Our user study shows that students were satisfied with our designed SDN security labs in terms of high usability, effective cost, and hands-on experience.

ACKNOWLEDGMENT

This work was partially supported by grants from National Science Foundation (NSF-DGE-1723663, NSF-DGE-1723804, and NSF-DGE-1723725). Dr. Younghee Park is a corresponding author.

REFERENCES

[1] 2014. CloudLab. (2014). https://www.cloudlab.us/.

[2] 2014. RSpec. (2014). http://groups.geni.net/geni/wiki/GENIExperimenter/RSpecs.

[3] 2014. Two methods to generate a profile in RSpec in CloudLab. (2014). http://docs.cloudlab.us/index.html.

[4] 2017. geni-lib. (2017). https://bitbucket.org/barnstorm/geni-lib.

[5] Mhd Wael Bazzaza and Khaled Salah. 2015. Using the Cloud to Teach Computer Networks. In *Utility and Cloud Computing (UCC), 2015 IEEE/ACM 8th International Conference on*. IEEE, 310–314.

[6] Kevin Benton, L. Jean Camp, and Chris Small. 2013. OpenFlow Vulnerability Assessment. In *Proceedings of the Second ACM SIGCOMM Workshop on Hot Topics in Software Defined Networking (HotSDN '13)*. ACM.

[7] Kevin Benton, L Jean Camp, and Chris Small. 2013. Openflow vulnerability assessment (Poster). In *Proceedings of ACM SIGCOMM workshop on Hot topics in software defined networking (HotSDN'13)*. ACM, 151–152.

[8] Kevin Benton, L. Jean Camp, and Chris Small. 2015. Secure communication Between OpenFlow Switch and Controllers. In *Proceedings of the Seventh International Conference on Advances in Future Internet*. AFIN.

[9] Braga Braga, Mota Mota, and Passito Passito. 2010. Lightweight DDoS flooding attack detection using NOX/OpenFlow. In *Proceedings of the 2010 IEEE 35th Conference on Local Computer Networks (LCN'10)*. IEEE, 408–415.

[10] Martin Casado, Michael J Freedman, Justin Pettit, Jianying Luo, Nick McKeown, and Scott Shenker. 2007. Ethane: Taking control of the enterprise. In *Proceedings of the ACM SIGCOMM 2007 conference*. ACM.

[11] Martin Casado, Tal Garfinkel, Aditya Akella, Michael J Freedman, Dan Boneh, Nick McKeown, and Scott Shenker. 2006. SANE: a protection architecture for enterprise networks. In *Proceedings of the 15th conference on USENIX Security Symposium*. USENIX Association.

[12] Mohan Dhawan, Rishabh Poddar, Kshiteej Mahajan, and Vijay Mann. 2015. SPHINX: Detecting Security Attacks in Software-Defined Networks. In *Proceedings of the 22nd Annual Network and Distributed System Security Symposium (NDSS'15)*.

[13] Albert Greenberg, Gisli Hjalmtysson, David A Maltz, Andy Myers, Jennifer Rexford, Geoffrey Xie, Hong Yan, Jibin Zhan, and Hui Zhang. 2005. A clean slate 4D approach to network control and management. *ACM SIGCOMM Computer Communication Review* 35, 5 (2005), 41–54.

[14] Sungmin Hong, Lei Xu, Haopei Wang, and Guofei Gu. 2015. Poisoning Network Visibility in Software-Defined Networks: New Attacks and Countermeasures. In *Proceedings of the 22nd Annual Network and Distributed System Security Symposium (NDSS'15)*.

[15] Jafar Haadi Jafarian, Ehab Al-Shaer, and Qi Duan. 2012. Openflow random host mutation: transparent moving target defense using software defined networking. In *Proceedings of ACM SIGCOMM Workshop on Hot Topics in Software Defined Networking (HotSDN'12)*. ACM, 127–132.

[16] Sushant Jain, Alok Kumar, Subhasree Mandal, Joon Ong, Leon Poutievski, Arjun Singh, Subbaiah Venkata, Jim Wanderer, Junlan Zhou, and Min Zhu. 2013. B4: Experience with a globally-deployed software defined WAN. In *ACM SIGCOMM Computer Communication Review*, Vol. 43. ACM, 3–14.

[17] Diego Kreutz, Fernando Ramos, and Paulo Verissimo. 2013. Towards secure and dependable software-defined networks. In *Proceedings of ACM SIGCOMM workshop on Hot topics in software defined networking (HotSDN'13)*. ACM, 55–60.

[18] Nick McKeown, Tom Anderson, Hari Balakrishnan, Guru Parulkar, Larry Peterson, Jennifer Rexford, Scott Shenker, and Jonathan Turner. 2008. OpenFlow: enabling innovation in campus networks. *ACM SIGCOMM Computer Communication Review* 38, 2 (2008), 69–74.

[19] Syed Akbar Mehdi, Junaid Khalid, and Syed Ali Khayam. 2011. Revisiting traffic anomaly detection using software defined networking. In *Proceedings of the 14th international conference on Recent Advances in Intrusion Detection (RAID'11)*. Springer-Verlag, 161–180.

[20] T. Nadeau. 2011. Software driven networks problem statement by Network Working Group. (2011). https://tools.ietf.org/html/draft-nadeau-sdn-problem-statement-00.

[21] Khaled Salah. 2014. Harnessing the cloud for teaching cybersecurity. In *Proceedings of the 45th ACM technical symposium on Computer science education*. ACM, 529–534.

[22] Khaled Salah, Mohammad Hammoud, and Sherali Zeadally. 2015. Teaching Cybersecurity using the Cloud. *IEEE Transactions on Learning Technologies* (2015).

[23] Khaled Salah, Mohammad Hammoud, and Sherali Zeadally. 2015. Teaching Cybersecurity Using the Cloud. *IEEE Transactions on Learning Technologies* 8, 4 (2015), 383–392.

[24] Seungwon Shin and Guofei Gu. 2013. Attacking Software-defined Networks: A First Feasibility Study. In *Proceedings of the Second ACM SIGCOMM Workshop on Hot Topics in Software Defined Networking (HotSDN '13)*. ACM.

[25] Seungwon Shin, Yongjoo Song, Taekyung Lee, Sangho Lee, Jaewoong Chung, Phillip Porras, Vinod Yegneswaran, Jiseong Noh, and Brent Byunghoon Kang. 2014. Rosemary: A robust, secure, and high-performance network operating system. In *Proceedings of the 2014 ACM SIGSAC Conference on Computer and Communications Security*. ACM, 78–89.

[26] Seungwon Shin, Vinod Yegneswaran, Phillip Porras, and Guofei Gu. 2013. AVANT-GUARD: scalable and vigilant switch flow management in software-defined networks. In *Proceedings of the 20th ACM conference on Computer and communications security (CCS'13)*. ACM, 413–424.

[27] Haopei Wang, Lei Xu, and Guofei Gu. 2015. FloodGuard: A DoS Attack Prevention Extension in Software-Defined Networks. In *Dependable Systems and Networks (DSN), 2015 45th Annual IEEE/IFIP International Conference on*. IEEE, 239–250.

[28] Haopei Wang, Lei Xu, and Guofei Gu. 2015. FloodGuard: A DoS Attack Prevention Extension in Software-Defined Networks. In *Proceedings of the 45th Annual IEEE/IFIP International Conference on Dependable Systems and Networks (DSN'15)*.

[29] Richard Weiss, Michael Locasto, Jens Mache, and Vincent Nestler. 2013. Teaching cybersecurity through games: a cloud-based approach. *Journal of Computing Sciences in Colleges* 29, 1 (2013), 113–115.

[30] Richard Weiss, Michael E Locasto, and Jens Mache. 2016. A reflective approach to assessing student performance in cybersecurity exercises. In *Proceedings of the 47th ACM Technical Symposium on Computing Science Education*. ACM, 597–602.

[31] Richard Weiss, Jens Mache, and Michael Locasto. 2014. EDURange: hands-on cybersecurity exercises in the cloud. *Journal of Computing Sciences in Colleges* 30, 1 (2014), 178–180.

[32] Richard S Weiss, Stefan Boesen, James F Sullivan, Michael E Locasto, Jens Mache, and Erik Nilsen. 2015. Teaching cybersecurity analysis skills in the cloud. In *Proceedings of the 46th ACM Technical Symposium on Computer Science Education*. ACM, 332–337.

[33] Guang Yao, Jun Bi, and Luyi Guo. 2013. On the cascading failures of multi-controllers in Software Defined Networks. In *Network Protocols (ICNP), 2013 21st IEEE International Conference on*.

[34] Ying Zhang, N. Beheshti, and M. Tatipamula. 2011. On Resilience of Split-Architecture Networks. In *Global Telecommunications Conference (GLOBECOM 2011), 2011 IEEE*.

Understanding Professional Identities and Goals of Computer Science Undergraduate Students

Amanpreet Kapoor
Computer & Info. Science & Engineering
University of Florida
Gainesville, FL, USA 32611
kapooramanpreet@ufl.edu

Christina Gardner-McCune
Computer & Info. Science & Engineering
University of Florida
Gainesville, FL, USA 32611
gmccune@ufl.edu

ABSTRACT

Understanding professional goals and identities of undergraduate Computer Science (CS) students is critical for curriculum decisions, workforce development, and retention programs. This paper aims to explore the ways in which undergraduate CS students describe their professional goals and identities, and gauge how these goals and identities vary across gender and academic standing. This paper is part of a larger study aimed at understanding how students form their professional goals and identities. In the study presented in this paper, we surveyed 109 CS undergraduate students and interviewed 14 CS undergraduate students across gender and academic standing. The data were qualitatively analyzed using inductive coding and thematic analysis. Our findings indicate that most students identify themselves professionally as software development professionals, various specialized CS professionals, and by their majors. We also found that both male and female students were interested in becoming entrepreneurs, and females were more likely to have professional goals to move into management. This paper contributes to the fields' growing knowledge of undergraduate students' professional goals and professional identities. This knowledge can help CS departments to better align their degree programs, curriculum, and specialization tracks with student goals. Such an alignment has the potential to increase retention in the major as well as prepare students to be competitive in the workforce.

ACM Reference format:

Amanpreet Kapoor and Christina Gardner-McCune. 2018. Understanding Professional Identities and Goals of Computer Science Undergraduate Students. In *SIGCSE '18: 49th ACM Technical Symposium on Computer Science Education, Feb. 21–24, 2018, Baltimore, MD, USA.* ACM, NY, NY, USA, 6 pages. DOI: https://doi.org/10.1145/3159450.3159474

SIGCSE '18, February 21–24, 2018, Baltimore, MD, USA

ACM ISBN 978-1-4503-5103-4/18/02...$15.00
https://doi.org/10.1145/3159450.3159474

1 INTRODUCTION

Computing professionals are diverse and form intersecting communities of practice. While there are official pathways to earning credentials to become part of most professional communities of practice, participation in the community is essential for membership within the community [13]. Lave & Wenger's theory of Legitimate Peripheral participation [6] suggests that most people start off on the periphery of communities of practice. In the context of undergraduate degree programs, courses, projects, internships, research, and full-time employment offers a student an initial opportunity to participate in computing communities of practice. As academic institutions, our role is to create pathways for career preparation through our degree programs to help students gain entry into various computing communities of practice. Thus, we play a role in the initial development of students' professional identities.

Professional identity enables a person to be technically competent, self-confident, and experience a sense of belongingness to the profession [9]. We know from prior research that students are more likely to persist in CS1 when they are able to make connections between computing concepts and their goals and life experiences [7]. We also know that we experience attrition during the first two years of our degree programs as students re-evaluate their interest and fit [1]. While research has linked persistence among women and underrepresented minorities to belongingness [12], there is also research that suggests that students of both genders often leave because of their perceptions of computing, the computing community, and its alignment with students' lifestyle goals [2].

Therefore, we argue in this paper, that it is necessary to understand the development of students' professional identities, career goals, and degree expectations over the span of their 4+ years in our undergraduate CS programs as it shifts and changes. The research presented in this paper is part of a larger study aimed at understanding students' computing professional identity and goals through the development of their technical competency and confidence gained through their degree experiences, professional experiences, independent skill development, and social supports. For this paper, we focus on identifying students' professional goals and identities.

2 BACKGROUND

Identity theory research describes identity and identity development as multiple dimensional. The operational definition of identity put forth in the Handbook of Identity Development by Schwartz, Luyckx, and Vignoles [10] states *"viewed through the lens of an individual person, identity consists of the confluence of the person's self-chosen or ascribed commitments, personal characteristics, and beliefs about herself; roles and positions in relation to significant others; and her membership in social groups and categories (including both her status within the group and the group's status within the larger context)"* [10].

Theories of personal identity tend to focus especially on individual-level processes and often emphasize the agentic role of the individual in creating or discovering his or her own identity [5]. Marcia's identity status theory suggests that professional identity is just one facet of an individual's identity that also includes an individual's social, personal, and cultural identity. Marcia suggests that professional identity is formed usually between the ages of 17-23, traditional college age [5]. Marcia's theory proposes that a well-developed professional identity gives a sense of one's strengths, weaknesses, and individual uniqueness [5]. Marcia's Identity Status theory also suggests that identity changes over time based on a person's active or passive exploration and commitment to their chosen profession [8]. We believe this theory offers insight into how and why undergraduate students' awareness and development of their professional identity and goals changes during their 4+ years in our degree programs.

We define *Computing Professional Identity* as the transformation of one's interest in computing into seeing one's self as a person who does computing and self-identifies with one or more computing sub-disciplines and career paths. Evidence of computing professional identity development is demonstrated by a commitment to develop technical competencies and skills and to engage in continued professional development within one or more computing fields, or an interest in using technical skills and knowledge to solve problems and/or generate new knowledge with computing approaches, techniques, and tools.

3 METHODS

3.1 Study Design

The study presented in this paper focuses on identifying the professional identities and goals of CS undergraduate students and investigates the variation of CS professional identity and goals across gender and academic standing. The study was approved by our university Institutional Review Board. We surveyed and interviewed students enrolled in an undergraduate CS degree program at the University of Florida, Gainesville in the United States. The university has a population of 1700 undergraduate CS majors. The degree program does not offer a specialized track in any subdomains of CS. The average age of the participants was 18 to 23 based on our enrolled population. Our study explored the following research questions:

RQ1. What are CS students' professional identities?

RQ2. What are CS students' five-year professional goals?

RQ3. How do CS students' professional identities and goals vary across gender and academic standing?

3.2 Participants

Surveyed Participants

Students were recruited from our university's CS1, data structures, software engineering, AI for Computer Games, and senior design courses, as well as several HCI and CS technical electives. The survey participants were given extra credit for participating in this study - not more than 1% towards their final grade based on pre-approval by the respective course instructors. The second author was one of the instructors who offered extra credit in the software engineering course, but the data was collected by the first author and not shown to the second author until after grades were submitted for the course. 148 students responded to our survey: 115 students completed the survey, 32 completed less than 18% of the survey, and 1 participant did not consent to research. Out of the 115 students, 6 students did not major or minor in CS or Computer Engineering (CE). We chose CE students to include in our sample population as both CS and CE degree programs are offered through the CS department at our university. Thus, we were left with 109 survey participants who completed the survey and were CS or CE majors/minors. These 109 survey participants were undergraduate students who majored in CS (61.5% n=67), CE (33.0%, n=36) or double majored in CS and another subject (3.7%, n=4), or minored in CS (1.8%, n=2). 84 males, 24 females, and one student who did not specify gender participated in the survey. Other demographic details are shown in Table 1.

Table 1: **Demographics of Study Participants**

	Academic Standing (By Year)					Gender	
	Year 1	Year 2	Year 3	Year 4	Year 5-6th	Male	Female
Survey (N=109)	18.3% n=20	14.7% n=16	30.3% n=33	32.1% n=35	4.6% n=5	77.1% n=84	22.0% n=24
Interview (N=14)	21.4% n=3	21.4% n=3	21.4% n=3	35.7% n=5	-	57.1% n=8	42.9% n=6

Interviewed Participants

The interviewed participants were recruited by email, flyers, and a separate question at the end of our survey which asked them if they were willing to participate in an interview. A pool of 14 participants was chosen from 56 students, ensuring that we had a representation of gender, academic standing, and degree program. The interview participants were given a $10 gift card for their participation in a 45-minute interview. The 14 interviewed participants were CS majors (50.0%, n=7), CE majors (42.9%, n=6) or CS minors (7.1%, n=1). Other demographics of interview participants are shown in Table 1.

3.3 Data Collection

We used Qualtrics to administer the survey and gain consent for the study participation. Before the survey and the interviews, participants completed a consent form, followed by a demographic questionnaire. The surveys were completed on average within 24 minutes and each interview session lasted around 35-45 minutes. For the larger study, the survey participants were asked 12 qualitative questions along with 39 multiple answer questions, and the interview participants were asked 27 open-ended questions, regarding their sense of professional identity, degree experience, professional experience, and social supports. For this paper, we focused our analysis on 2 qualitative questions from the interviews, as well as 1 qualitative and 1 quantitative question from the survey which are relevant to answer our research questions. We interviewed the participants to get a richer data set of students' goals, experiences, and expectations to complement our larger survey data set, and to ensure we were capturing students career interests accurately in the survey. The semi-structured interviews were conducted in person by the first author. The interviews were audio recorded, then transcribed by a commercial transcription service, and reviewed for accuracy by the first author.

3.4 Data Analysis

For this paper, we analyzed student responses to the following two questions asked in the interviews as well as the survey:

Q1. How do you identify yourself professionally?

Q2. Where do you see your career going three to five years after you graduate?

On the survey, Q1 was presented as a multiple select question with a textbox that allowed students to select multiple professional interests (e.g., software engineer, web developer, data analyst, networks engineer, etc.) or add unlisted options to the textbox, and Q2 was an open-ended question. The options on the survey for Q1 were selected using the knowledge areas specified in the ACM 2013 CS Curricula report [14]. 109 participants answered Q1 in the survey, while 107 participants answered Q2 (2 responses were random words). In the semi-structured interviews, these questions were open-ended.

Student responses to Q1 were used as evidence to explore professional identities (RQ1). Likewise, Q2 was used to explore professional goals (RQ2). Further, Q1 and Q2 were used as evidence to explore the variation of students' professional identities and goals across gender and academic standing (RQ3).

We analyzed our data using inductive content analysis and thematic analysis in Microsoft Excel 2016. We were following a grounded theory process of inductive coding [11]. We started with the raw data and created codes inductively using words from participants responses. The first author created primary codes and the second author reviewed the codes and data until a consensus was reached about the code accuracy and reliability. The primary codes were then clustered to form categories, and these categories formed the basis of our codebook. From survey/interview questions Q1 and Q2, we identified 23 categories for each question from our data. From these categories, 5 themes were identified for Q1 and 10 themes for Q2. Table 2 highlights an example of our inductive content and thematic analysis [11].

We then combined categories into themes. This was followed by a frequency analysis of responses within each theme. We counted unique participants when computing these frequencies, to avoid counting multiple responses from the same participant within any theme. The frequency analysis was done separately for the survey and the interview data. In presenting our findings we include the percentage of both survey and interview participant responses to highlight the representative nature of our interview quotes to the larger participant pool of our survey participants.

Table 2: **Inductive Content and Thematic Analysis example**

Where do you see your career going three or five years once you graduate?			
Raw Data	I've always wanted to have my *own company*, just because like I never really liked the idea of like working under someone.	What I want to do is get some experience, and really like hone my skills and then try to *make my own business*.	I'm starting out by doing something stupid and going into independent game development. If everything goes well, I would be *self- employed making games*.
Primary Code	Entrepreneur /Startup	Work at a company - prior to business	Self-employed - making games
Categories	Entrepreneurship		Self Employed
Themes	Entrepreneurship/Self-Employed		

4 FINDINGS

We identified 5 themes for professional identities and 10 themes for professional goals across our survey and interview data. Table 3 represents the themes found in our study. Given the space constraints of this paper, we will highlight prominent trends within each theme in the narrative text and use Table 4, 5, 6 and 7 to summarize our frequency analysis across gender and academic standing for both the survey and the interviews.

Table 3: **Themes for Professional Identities and Goals**

Identities
Software Development
Specialized CS/CE
Identification by major
Indecisive/ Unknown
Non-CS

Goals	
Getting a job/ Working in industry	Area: Software
Graduate school/ Research	Area: Specialized CS/CE
Other goals: location, success, etc.	Area: Management
Entrepreneur/ Self-employment	Area: Non-CS
Indecisive/Unknown	Area: Technical

4.1 Professional Identities

In both the survey and the interviews, the participants described their professional identities as software development professionals, specialized CS/CE professionals, and by their majors. However, there were a small number of participants who were indecisive about their professional identity, or identified themselves as non-CS professionals. In the following sections we will present the findings for each of the identity themes.

Software Development

"I would wanna be a software engineer at this point. That's like where I would go towards. I'm not really a hardware person. Like I like the idea that, sort of, like actually making the systems and stuff. I really like the coding and programming aspect."

- Student A, female, freshman

Like Student A, 50.0% of the 14 interviewed participants (n=7) identified themselves as software professionals, in particular, they identified themselves as software engineers, software developers, or software programmers. Likewise, 81.7% of the 109 survey participants (n=89) described a similar identity. We found that the majority of both male and female participants in the survey identified themselves as software professionals: 79.2% females (n=19) and 82.1% males (n=69) identified themselves as software professionals. Similarly, across academic standing over 77% of participants in the survey identified themselves as software professionals (Table 5).

Specialized CS/CE Professional

"I think the coolest thing is augmented reality, and just augmenting people, in general. So that's my goal, probably."

- Student B, male, sophomore

We also found a dominant theme around students describing themselves professionally as specialized CS/CE professionals. 42.9% of the 14 participants (n=6) in the interviews and 58.7% of the 109 participants (n=64) in the survey were interested in pursuing careers in specialized CS or CE. Subfields in CS/CE or cross-disciplinary fields, including cybersecurity, data science, web development, and product management were included in the specialized CS/CE theme. Out of 64 students in the survey who identified themselves as specialized CS/CE professionals, Web Development (62.5%, n=40), Computer Security (20.3%, n=13), and UX Design (18.8%, n=12) were the most prominent professional interests. Further, most females (54.2%, n=13) and males (60.7%, n=51) in our survey identified themselves as specialized CS/CE professionals. Results from our surveys show a growing interest in CS/CE specializations from 45.0% during freshman year to 71.4% during the senior year.

Identification by major

"I feel like a computer scientist, not a software engineer."

- Student C, male, senior

Some students like Student C explicitly described their professional identity by their degree major. The categories that were included as a part of this theme included identification as CS/CE Engineer, well-rounded professional in CS and Electrical Engineer (EE), and Computer Scientists. 42.9% of the 14 interview participants (n=6) and 17.4% of the 109 survey participants (n=19) described their identity by their major. We also observed in the interviews that more males (50.0%, n=8) were prone to designate themselves by their majors when compared to females (33.3%, n=2). In addition, juniors (100%, n=3), and seniors (60%, n=3) were more likely to define their professional identities by their majors when compared to freshmen (0%, n=0) and sophomores (0%, n=0). These findings were consistent with the survey (Table 5).

Table 4: **Themes for Professional Identities in Interviews**

Themes	N=14	Academic Standing				Gender	
		Year 1 n=3	Year 2 n=3	Year 3 n=3	Year 4 n=5	Male n=8	Female n=6
Software	50.0%	100.0%	33.3%	33.3%	40.0%	37.5%	66.7%
Specialize CS/CE	42.9%	66.7%	66.7%	0.0%	40.0%	37.5%	50.0%
Major	42.9%	0.0%	0.0%	100.0%	60.0%	50.0%	33.3%
Indecisive	14.3%	0.0%	33.3%	0.0%	20.0%	0.0%	33.3%
Non-CS	0.0%	0.0%	0.0%	0.0%	0.0%	0.0%	0.0%

Table 5: **Themes for Professional Identities in the Survey**

Themes	N=109	Academic Standing				Gender	
		Year 1 n=20	Year 2 n=16	Year 3 n=33	Year 4 n=35	Male n=84	Female n=24
Software	81.7%	90.0%	81.3%	81.8%	77.1%	82.1%	79.2%
Specialize CS/CE	58.7%	45.0%	50.0%	54.5%	71.4%	60.7%	54.2%
Major	17.4%	10.0%	12.5%	21.2%	20.0%	19.0%	8.3%
Indecisive	5.5%	5.0%	12.5%	9.1%	0.0%	3.6%	12.5%
Non-CS	1.8%	5.0%	0.0%	0.0%	0.0%	2.4%	0.0%

Indecisive/Unknown

"That's a question I've just been asking myself recently as I near graduation and as of right now, I find it kind of hard to decide."

- Student D, female, senior

Similar to Student D, 14.3% of the 14 interview participants (n=2) and 5.5% of the 109 survey participants (n=6) were not sure about their professional identity. They either reported that they were trying to explore and figure out their identity, or perceived that they were too inexperienced in CS to decide their professional identity. 8 participants: 33.3% of 6 females (n=2), 0% of the 8 males (n=80) in the interviews, 12.5% of 24 females (n=3) and 3.6% of 84 males (n=3) in the survey, reported that they were indecisive about their professional identities.

Non-CS Professionals

"History, law" *- Student E, male, freshman*

Two male students like Student E, 1.8% of the 109 students in the survey (n=2) described their professional identities as Non-CS professionals including occupations like a lawyer, and a historian. 1 of these participants was a freshman double major in CS and history, while the other was a 5th year CS major.

4.2 Professional Goals

In both the survey and the interviews, the participants were asked to describe their 3-5-year career goals. We identified 10 themes shown in Table 3. These themes were divided into two aspects: their career goals and the areas of interest in their workplaces. Most of the career goal areas aligned with their professional identities. A frequency analysis of these themes for the interviews and the survey is shown in Table 6 and Table 7 respectively. Two male students, a freshman, and a junior responded random words as their professional goals in the survey and were excluded from the frequency analysis leaving the total survey participants to 107 for professional goals.

Getting a Job/Working in Industry

"Straight into industry. Maybe will have worked at two different companies 5 years after graduation."

– Student A, male, junior

Like Student A, 85.7% of the 14 students (n=12) in the interview expected to work in the industry after they graduate. Similarly, in the survey, 64.5% of 107 participants (n=69) preferred to work in the industry. Out of these 69 survey participants, 55.0% participants (n=38) aspired to work in any type of company, 27.5% had career goals to work for an established corporation (n=19), 13.0% wished to work for a start-up (n=9), 4.3% for a small company (n=3) and 1.4% for a nonprofit (n=1). The ranking of the type of workplaces was consistent across the interviews. Over 63% of the males and females expected to get a job. Across academic standing, more than 71% seniors expected to work in the industry.

Table 6: **Themes for Professional Goals in Interviews**

Themes	N=14	Academic Standing				Gender	
		Year 1 n=3	Year 2 n=3	Year 3 n=3	Year 4 n=5	Male n=8	Female n=6
Industry/Job	85.7%	66.7%	100.0%	66.7%	100.0%	87.5%	83.3%
Grad School	14.3%	0.0%	0.0%	66.7%	0.0%	12.5%	16.7%
Other	21.4%	0.0%	0.0%	0.0%	60.0%	25.0%	16.7%
Indecisive	14.3%	33.3%	0.0%	33.3%	0.0%	12.5%	16.7%
Entrepreneur	28.6%	66.7%	0.0%	0.0%	40.0%	37.5%	16.7%
Areas							
Software	50.0%	33.3%	33.3%	33.3%	80.0%	50.0%	50.0%
Specialize CS/CE	64.3%	66.7%	66.7%	66.7%	60.0%	50.0%	83.3%
Management	57.1%	66.7%	66.7%	33.3%	60.0%	25.0%	100.0%
Non-CS	7.1%	0.0%	0.0%	33.3%	0.0%	12.5%	0.0%
Technical	21.4%	33.3%	0.0%	33.3%	20.0%	25.0%	16.7%

Table 7: **Themes for Professional Goals in the Survey**

Themes	N= 107	Academic Standing				Gender	
		Year 1 n=19	Year 2 n=16	Year 3 n=32	Year 4 n=35	Male n=82	Female n=24
Industry/Job	64.5%	63.2%	75.0%	56.3%	71.4%	63.4%	66.7%
Grad School	24.3%	10.5%	31.3%	28.1%	22.9%	18.3%	41.7%
Other	17.8%	21.1%	18.8%	12.5%	17.1%	18.3%	16.7%
Indecisive	15.0%	21.1%	6.3%	15.6%	17.1%	12.2%	25.0%
Entrepreneur	12.1%	15.8%	12.5%	9.4%	14.3%	12.2%	12.5%
Areas							
Software	21.5%	15.8%	18.8%	28.1%	22.9%	22.0%	20.8%
Specialize CS/CE	18.7%	5.3%	18.8%	15.6%	31.4%	19.5%	16.7%
Management	6.5%	5.3%	12.5%	12.5%	0.0%	6.1%	8.3%
Non-CS	6.5%	15.8%	0.0%	3.1%	5.7%	7.3%	4.2%
Technical	0.9%	0.0%	0.0%	0.0%	2.9%	0.0%	4.2%

Graduate School/Research

"I plan on going to grad school and getting an MBA in Information Systems. I would like to be a Database Administrator"

- Student B, female, junior

We found that 14.3% of 14 students (n=2) in the interviews, and 24.3% of 107 students (n=26) in the survey, described their career goals as pursuing graduate school. Out of these 26 students who wanted to pursue graduate school, 61.5% wished to pursue a master's degree (n=16), 26.9% Ph.D. (n=7) and 11.5% MBA (n=3). Further, female students were inclined to pursuing graduate school as compared to males: 41.7% females (n=10) and 18.3% males (n=15) in the survey and 16.7% females (n=1) and 12.5% males (n=1) in the interviews.

Other Professional goals: location, success, creating an impact, major, working on projects, etc.

"Hopefully somewhere I can get a job in the southeastern US."

- Student C, male, junior

We also found a dominant theme around students who defined their career goals in terms of their motivations: working at a specific regional location, being successful, or working on impactful projects: 21.4% of 14 students (n=3) in the interviews, and 17.8% of 107 students (n=19) in the surveys.

Indecisive/Unknown

"As I am only a sophomore, I feel that I am not close enough to determine my career path within the scope of CS just yet since I have yet to take the more specialized courses within my major."

- Student D, male, sophomore

Some students like Student D were not sure about their professional goals. They mentioned that they were not sure or were exploring options. These included 14.3% of the 14 interview participants (n=2) and 15.0% of the 107 survey participants (n=16). Altogether, 11 males and 7 females were indecisive about their career goals. Out of these 18 students, 6 students were seniors, 6 juniors, 1 sophomore and 5 were freshmen.

Entrepreneurship/Self Employment

"I want to own my own tech company where I invent different products ranging from software and devices for cybersecurity to devices for miscellaneous activities."

- Student E, female, freshman

We also found that some students were interested in becoming entrepreneurs, starting their own business, or working for themselves. 28.6% of the 14 interview participants (n=4): 1 female, 3 males; and 12.1% of the 107 survey participants (n=13): 3 females and 10 males. We observed from the survey data that the percentage of male and female students who wanted to become entrepreneurs was almost equal, respective to their population (Table 7). In addition to this, we found that freshmen and seniors were more likely to define their professional goals as entrepreneurship when compared to sophomores and juniors. This was consistent across both the survey and the interviews.

Areas to Work in – Software, Specialized CS/CS, Management, Technical, Non-CS

"I plan to work at a large tech company and earn my MBA, for experience to earn a managerial position."

- Student F, female, sophomore

We also found that some students described their career goals to work in specific areas in their career. In the interviews, students preferred to work in the following areas: 64.3% specialized CS/CE (n=9), 57.1% management (n=8), 50% software (n=7), 21.4% technical (n=3), and 7.1% non-CS (n=1). We also found that females preferred moving into management when compared with males (Table 6, 7).

5 DISCUSSION AND IMPLICATIONS

Overall, we found that CS undergraduate students have various professional goals including pursuing careers in industry, entrepreneurship, graduate school, creating an impact, and as being indecisive about their professional goals. They want to work in areas defined by their professional identities such as software, specialized CS/CE fields, management, technical and non-CS. These goals were consistent with a similar study in Europe [4] in which the authors' observed students' affinity towards software professions, management, and entrepreneurship. Undergraduate CS students are also interested in specialty CS professional occupations. There is a need to prepare our students for these specialty occupations like Web Development, Information Security, Database Administration, etc. due to their self-interests and the demand in industry for these jobs which are projected to grow annually at 27%, 18%, and 11% respectively from 2014-2024 [3]. In addition, these results are consistent with McCartney et al.'s [9] findings that students relate their professional identities with jobs in the industry. Hence, there is a need to map our current curriculum of our degree programs to help our students accomplish their career goals by including specializations or cross-disciplinary tracks specifically tailored towards software development or subdomains in CS/CE.

Findings from our study also show that a substantial number of females preferred moving into management when compared with males, and freshmen and seniors were more likely to define their career goals as entrepreneurship when compared with sophomores and juniors. The former results are consistent with research that shows that women are interested in having socially impactful careers [12]. We believe participants' interest in management and entrepreneurship may be related to our universities' initiatives to promote these skills through cross-university programs and business incubators. Given students' interest and growth in these areas, universities may need to create incubation centers for startups to provide support for students to pursue entrepreneurial and leadership endeavors. We believe that these results can be leveraged to address retention rates of CS students especially females by incorporating aspects of technical management, leadership, and entrepreneurship into preliminary years of a CS degree programs.

Findings from our study also indicated that students in our study were interested in pursuing graduate school. Results from our study indicated that females were twice as likely to pursue graduate school when compared to males. We believe this may be due to our university's curricular requirement to participate in at least one semester of research. However, we still need to analyze whether these students have genuine interests to pursue a master's degree or Ph.D., or if it is due to a lack of confidence to get a job after completing their undergraduate degree. In the former case, this suggests that CS degree programs may need to ensure that their curriculum is preparing students to get into the best graduate schools in areas they want to work or conduct research in. In the latter case, the degree program, as well as the faculty, need to ensure that students participate in career support programs within the university to encourage student involvement in the communities of practice.

6 LIMITATIONS

The findings presented in this paper represent a snapshot of the current professional goals and identities of a sample of CS student population at the research university where the study was performed. A possible limitation of this study is that reported professional identities may be overstated because survey participants did not have distinct "Not known" or "Unsure" professional identity options available to them. Thus, both students who responded as unsure and unknown used the other's option and specified it qualitatively. Given that this study gave students extra credit at the end of the semester, the study participants could have either been high performing students that wanted to take every opportunity to secure a good grade in their course or low performing students that wanted an extra grade boost. Overrepresentation of any of these groups may skew the generalizability of these results. In the future, additional data on students' GPA, family background, and ethnic diversity might help to better characterize the population.

REFERENCES

[1] Bank, B.J., Delamont, S. and Marshall, C. 2007. *Gender and Education: An Encyclopedia.* Westport, Conn : Praeger Publishers.

[2] Biggers, M., Brauer, A. and Yilmaz, T. 2008. Student Perceptions of Computer Science : A Retention Study Comparing Graduating Seniors with CS Leavers. *ACM SIGCSE Bulletin.* 40, 1 (March 2008), 402–406. DOI:https://doi.org/10.1145/1352322.1352274.

[3] Employment Projections: https://data.bls.gov/projections/occupationProj. Accessed: 2017-10-13.

[4] Kinnunen, P., Butler, M., Morgan, M., Nylen, A., Peters, A.-K., Sinclair, J., Kalvala, S. and Pesonen, E. 2016. Understanding initial undergraduate expectations and identity in computing studies. *European Journal of Engineering Education.* (Feb. 2016), 1–18. DOI:https://doi.org/10.1080/03043797.2016.1146233.

[5] Kroger, J. and Green, K.E. 1996. Events associated with identity status change. *Journal of Adolescence.* 19, 5, (1996), 359–380. DOI:https://doi.org/10.1006/jado.1996.0045.

[6] Lave, J. and Wenger, E. 1991. Situated learning: Legitimate peripheral participation. *Learning in doing.* 95, (1991), 138. DOI:https://doi.org/10.2307/2804509.

[7] make it matter | EngageCSEdu: https://www.engage-csedu.org/engagement/make-it-matter. Accessed: 2017-09-02.

[8] Marcia, J.E. 1966. Development and validation of ego-identity status. *Journal of Personality and Social Psychology.* 3, 5 (1966), 551–558. DOI:https://doi.org/10.1037/h0023281.

[9] McCartney, R. and Sanders, K. 2015. School/Work: Development of Computing Students' Professional Identity at University. Proceedings of the eleventh annual International Conference on International Computing Education Research - ICER '15 (New York, New York, USA, 2015), 151–159.

[10] Schwartz, S., Luyckx, K. and Vignoles, V. 2011. *Handbook of Identity Theory and Research.* Springer Science & Business Media.

[11] Corbin, J., & Strauss, A. 2008. *Basics of qualitative research: Techniques and procedures for developing grounded theory.* Thousand Oaks.

[12] Tamer, B. and Jane, S. 2016. Recruitment and Retention of Undergraduate Students in Computing: Patterns by Gender and Race/Ethnicity. Available from: http://cra.org/cerp/research-findings/

[13] Wenger, E. 1998. *Communities of Practice: Learning, Meaning, and Identity.* Cambridge university press.

[14] Joint Task Force on Computing Curricula, Association for Computing Machinery (ACM) and IEEE Computer Society. 2013. *Computer Science Curricula 2013: Curriculum Guidelines for Undergraduate Degree Programs in Computer Science.* ACM, New York, NY, USA.

Who Teaches Accessibility? A Survey of U.S. Computing Faculty

Kristen Shinohara
Golisano College of Computing and Information Sciences
Rochester Institute of Technology
Rochester, NY
kristen.shinohara@rit.edu

Saba Kawas*, Andrew J. Ko*, Richard E. Ladner†
*The Information School,
†Paul G. Allen School of Computer Science & Engineering
DUB Group, University of Washington
Seattle, WA
*{skawas, ajko}@uw.edu, †ladner@cs.washington.edu

ABSTRACT

Industry demand for software developers with knowledge of accessibility has increased substantially in recent years. However, there is little knowledge about the prevalence of higher education teaching about accessibility or faculty's perceived barriers to teaching accessibility. To address this gap, we surveyed 14,176 computing and information science faculty in the United States. We received a representative sample of at least one response from 318 of the 352 institutions we surveyed, totaling 1,857 responses. We found that 175 institutions (50%) had at least one instructor teaching accessibility and that no fewer than 2.5% of faculty overall teach accessibility. Faculty that teach accessibility are twice as likely to be female, to have expertise in HCI and software engineering, and to know people with disabilities. The most critical barriers to teaching accessibility that faculty reported were the absence of clear and discipline-specific accessibility learning objectives and the lack of faculty knowledge about accessibility. Faculty desired resources that were specific to the areas of computing in which they teach rather than general accessibility resources and guidelines.

KEYWORDS

Computing education, accessibility, curriculum change

ACM Reference format:

Kristen Shinohara, Saba Kawas, Andrew J. Ko, Richard E. Ladner. 2018. Who Teaches Accessibility? A Survey of U.S. Computing Faculty. In Proceedings of the 2018 ACM SIGCSE Technical Symposium on Computer Science Education (SIGCSE '18). ACM, New York, NY, USA. DOI: https://doi.org/10.1145/3159450.3159484

1 INTRODUCTION

People with disabilities rely on a range of access technologies to interface with the digital world, including screen readers, text-to-speech, speech-to-text, and alt-tags for images on the web. However, software has to be designed to work these technologies. Because of this, many companies view accessibility as not only an essential component of software design, but also an essential component of their engineers' expertise. Consortia like TeachAccess (teachaccess.org), led by Yahoo!, Facebook, Microsoft, Google, and Adobe, represent this increased demand for accessibility knowledge, and are leading efforts to increase the number of computer and information science faculty teaching accessibility. In parallel, professional societies such as ABET have recently added accessibility into engineering design accreditation requirements.

Incorporating instruction on accessibility at scale requires two major elements: (1) methods for how to teach accessibility in computer science (CS) and related fields, and (2) large scale adoption and implementation of these methods by faculty. Most prior work has focused on the first element. For example, some have incorporated accessibility in software engineering courses [5,9,15], as part of introducing web development [8,12], or in HCI and design courses as a central component of design process [13,14]. Others have discovered that teaching accessibility also requires teaching empathy[2,10]. In the most comprehensive study to date, Putnam et al., summarized the practices of 18 faculty across 15 universities [11], documenting a range of pedagogies for teaching accessibility, including engaging with multiple diverse perspectives, and incorporating project-learning and creative approaches, such as field trips, guest speakers and videos. Others still aimed for more ambitious curricular change, developing four-year integrated curricula that span multiple courses [16] and investigated the importance of student and administration interest in sustaining accessibility infused programs in information and technology curriculum [3].

Although these pedagogical and curricular innovations are necessary, little work has investigated the second element to curricular change: faculty adoption. In fact, we know little about how much computer and information science faculty are teaching accessibility, and what barriers exist to more faculty doing so. Research on curricular change provides us some predictions. For example, theories of curricular change argue that change only comes through social and instructional discourse among faculty organically contributing to, and constructing, instructors' knowledge [1,7]. Additionally, Kezar and Eckel, in an examination of several institutions, determined that institutional culture could enhance or stymie curriculum changes [6]. These works suggest that large scale curricular change is not a matter of top-down decree, but one of fostering local change agents who are

SIGCSE '18, February 21–24, 2018, Baltimore, MD, USA

ACM ISBN 978-1-4503-5103-4/18/02...$15.00
https://doi.org/10.1145/3159450.3159484

intimately aware of the culture of specific institutions and who can devise and implement strategies to work within them.

If these theories of curricular change are true, then a next step in increasing the prevalence of accessibility instruction is to discover:

- RQ1. Who is teaching accessibility?
- RQ2. What barriers do faculty see to teaching accessibility?
- RQ3. What factors predict who is teaching accessibility?

To answer these questions, we designed and disseminated a survey to nearly all computing and information science faculty in the U.S. In the rest of this paper we discuss our findings and offer recommendations for teaching accessibility at scale.

2 METHOD

In this section, we cover our inclusion criteria, sampling, survey instrument, and data collection and cleaning.

2.1 Defining and Recruiting Participants

We defined our population as faculty in computer science, information science and other interdisciplinary computing departments at 4-year universities and colleges. We chose this demographic because they are traditionally tasked with teaching many of the students who pursue careers in technology-based fields (we scoped studies of community colleges and coding bootcamps for future work). Because the survey was sponsored by AccessComputing [8] and supported by TeachAccess, and both organizations focus on technology access in the U.S., we targeted instructors and professors in the U.S. We obtained a full list of institutions by merging accredited computer science and engineering programs from Wikipedia and departments members of Computing Research Association. For Information Science programs we merged the Wikipedia list with the iSchool Caucus charter list updated in 2014.

We used Mechanical Turk to crowdsource contact information from publicly facing university websites. We gathered the site links for the faculty directory for each of department and college on the list above. We set up the Mechanical Turk task for two different workers to collect the contact information from the same website. For sites that listed more than 30 faculty names we split the list into two or three different tasks. We then matched the responses from the different workers and flagged the instances where there was a mismatch. In those cases, we checked the responses manually and compared it to the contact information on the website. This resulted in email addresses for 14,176 faculty.

2.2 Survey Instrument

Our survey began by asking "Do you teach courses that incorporate topics about accessibility?" We asked respondents about barriers they faced "incorporating accessibility topics in your teaching," and to indicate their agreement with the statement "Accessibility should be taught as part of computer science." We next asked their gender, years of teaching experience, and if the respondent had "colleagues, acquaintances, friends, or family with disabilities."

If the respondent indicated that they teach accessibility, we also asked "What accessibility learning objectives does your course cover?", "What readings are made available to students?", and "what pedagogies do you use to teach about accessibility?", providing a list of responses for each and an option for a free response. We also asked "In your course, how often do students interact with people with disabilities?", "How many years experience do you have teaching accessibility related topics?", and "How would you rate your knowledge of accessibility?" Finally, we asked whether the respondent identified as having a disability, and if so, which ones. Due to a design oversight, we did not ask all respondents this last question, only those that indicated they teach accessibility.

We did several pilot tests with faculty in our home institution to gauge the clarity of the questions and the length of the survey overall. To encourage a high response rate, we aimed for a survey that did not take more than 5 minutes to complete. We used SurveyGizmo to create and distribute our survey, conducting several piloting rounds with SurveyGizmo to verify distribution and presentation ensured completion.

We emailed surveys to 14,176 instructors in three separate waves due to limits on how many emails the tool would send at once. We sent emails on Mondays, and a reminder email one week later to those who had not completed the survey, prompting them to start or complete the survey.

Table 1. Survey emails, responses, and response rates

First Launch	9,736	1,302	13.4%
Second Launch	4,207	547	13.0%
Third Launch	233	22	9.4%
Total	14,176	1,857	13.1%

2.3 Data Collection and Cleaning

We received 1,857 full responses, for a response rate of 13%. We did not include partial responses because incomplete surveys did not have enough data for analysis of our research questions. Table 1 shows the distribution of surveys sent per launch, the number of full responses received, and corresponding response rates.

We downloaded all the survey responses and filtered out partial responses. Then, we merged the response with the respondent's institution name and its geographic location. Some faculty (45) responded "Yes" to "Do you teach courses that incorporate topics about accessibility?" but later responded "I do not teach courses that incorporate topics about accessibility." We counted these faculty as not incorporating accessibility topics in their courses.

3 RESULTS

3.1 RQ1: Who is teaching accessibility?

In this section, we describe who responded to the survey and then compare those who did and did not report teaching accessibility. We then discuss what faculty reported teaching.

The faculty who responded to the survey reflected CS departments broadly. Respondents had a range of experience, with 7.4% reporting less than a year of experience, 23.3% more than 25 years, and within this range, a mode of 10 years. Of all respondents, 72.6% identified as male, 23.2% identified as female, and 4.3% preferred not to indicate their gender (this proportion reflects the gender distribution reported in the 2016 Taulbee Survey: 79.4% men, 20.6% women). The geographic distribution of respondents included faculty from 48 states in the U.S., Washington DC and Puerto Rico, with a concentration of respondents in California (188), New York (187), Pennsylvania (126), and Michigan (101), which are four of the ten most populous states in the U.S. In total, we received at least one response from 318 out of the 352 institutions who received the survey.

Table 2. Gender identity and who teaches accessibility

	Female	Male	Non-Binary	Prefer not to say
All Respondents	23.2%	72.6%	0.3%	4.0%
Who Teach	37.6%	59.5%	0.3%	2.7%
Who Do Not	19.6%	75.9%	0.3%	4.3%

Table 3. Proportion of faculty who do and do not teach accessibility and who know someone with a disability

Relationship?	All	Teaches	Doesn't
No	27.1%	19.2%	29.1%
Yes, close family	23.9%	31.7%	21.9%
Yes, close friends	13.4%	21.6%	11.3%
Yes, personal acquaintances	30.5%	39.7%	28.2%
Yes, professional acquaintances	35.1%	50.9%	31.0%

Overall, 20% of faculty (375) responded "Yes" to the prompt "Do you teach courses that incorporate topics about accessibility?" These faculty represented 175 unique colleges and universities, and were dominated by University of Washington (21), Kent State University (12), Indiana University at Bloomington (11), Rochester Institute of Technology (11), University of Michigan (11), Carnegie Mellon University (10), University of Maryland, Baltimore County (9), University of Maryland, College Park (9), and University of Missouri (8), with 75 universities having at least 2 faculty teaching accessibility. Thus, with the caveat of not knowing the prevalence of faculty who did not respond to the survey, an estimate of the floor of the total number of computing and information science faculty in the U.S. teaching accessibility is at least 375 out of 14,176 of the faculty surveyed, about 2.6%, and at least 175 institutions out of 352 institutions, or 50%.

There were several notable differences between respondents who do and do not teach accessibility. For instance, Table 2 shows a greater proportion of those who reported not teaching accessibility also identified as male (75.9%), compared with those who identified as female (19.5%). The data show how those who teach accessibility identified (not how male and female declared they teach accessibility), thus, in looking at the proportions of those who reported teaching accessibility and identified as female or male, a significant proportion identified as female ($\chi^2(df = 1, N = 1856) = 54.597, p < 0.0001$), specifically, 37.6% compared with 19.6% who do not teach accessibility.

Across all faculty, nearly 73% knew someone with a disability. However, as shown in Table 3, those who taught accessibility were significantly more likely to report knowing someone with a disability ($\chi^2(df= 1, N = 1857) = 15.0, p < 0.0001$).

For respondents who reported teaching accessibility, we asked detailed questions about their experience with disability, what content they taught about accessibility, and what teaching methods they used to do so. Of those who reported teaching accessibility, 17% reported having a disability themselves, including 5.3% identifying as an older adult, 4.8% as having hearing impairments, 4.3% as having a physical or mobility disability, 2.9% as having vision impairments, 2.4% with a cognitive or learning disability, 2.4% reported having "other" disabilities, 1.9% as neurodiverse, and 0.5% as having motor impairments. Based on 2013 statistics from the U.S. Center for Disease Control and Prevention [4], these are lower rates of disability than in the U.S. population.

Of the 1,857 responses, 424 respondents included a description of their area of expertise. We counted each mention of a distinct specialization, as many faculty mentioned multiple areas of expertise. We categorized these according to the 2013 ACM Curriculum Guidelines "Knowledge Areas," ignoring case and minor differences in terminology. Based on this categorization, the top 5 areas of expertise across all respondents were algorithms and theory, machine learning, robotics, human-computer interaction, software engineering, and networking and communication. Of the 280 that reported teaching accessibility and described their expertise, the most common expertise was HCI (28%), with a long tail of software engineering, information assurance and cybersecurity, library and information science, computer science education and other applied areas of computing. Among the 984 that reported not teaching accessibility, the most common expertise was algorithms, theory, artificial intelligence, machine learning, and programming languages. Only 1.8% of those reporting HCI expertise reported not teaching accessibility. This suggests that those teaching about accessibility are faculty with expertise on human and social factors in computing.

Of those who taught accessibility, we asked what they taught and how they taught it. The majority of faculty taught a course with accessibility content once a year (55.5%), while 18.4% reported teaching once a semester or quarter, 13.1% reported teaching every other year and 10.1% taught accessibility less than every other year. Only 2.9% reported teaching more than one course per semester or quarter. Within a given course, respondents included accessibility as part of a lecture (31.7%), in a few classes (22.9%), or in at least one class (20.5%), whereas 16% included accessibility as an occasional informal class mention, and 8.8% included accessibility course-wide. Of those that taught accessibility, we asked respondents to judge their knowledge of accessibility; 10.7% reported "Not knowledgeable," 66.1% reported "Some knowledge," 18.7% reported "Knowledgeable," and 4.5% reported "Expert." Note that there were only 17 self-identified faculty experts in accessibility, and only three institutions had more than one (Rochester Institute of Technology, University of Maryland at College Park, and University of Missouri). The most common disabilities that faculty mentioned teaching about were vision (77.9%) and hearing impairments (46.1%). Next were physical/mobility (40.5%), older adults (40.5%), and motor impairments (35.7%). Fewer respondents reported teaching accessibility related to cognitive or (29.3%) learning disabilities (27.2%), or neurodiversity (13.5%). Only 1.8% reported "none of the above," which we interpreted as teaching about general accessibility related topics, such as web accessibility guidelines or heuristics, rather than focusing on specific disabilities.

Finally, drawing on reported objectives and pedagogies from related work [11], we asked respondents to indicate which objectives they focus on in their teaching. Table 4 shows that the majority of respondents focused on barriers to using technology design paradigms such as universal design and inclusive design. Table 5 shows that most faculty taught these learning objectives via lectures, in-class activities, and homework, with few using service learning or disability simulation exercises.

3.2 RQ2: What barriers exist?

Our second research question focused on barriers instructors encountered to teaching accessibility, regardless of whether they taught accessibility or not.

Table 4. Learning objective faculty reported teaching

Understand technology barriers faced by people with disabilities	66.1%
Understand design concepts: universal design, ability- based design, inclusive design, participatory design, etc.	65.9%
Engage with individuals from diverse populations appropriately	40.0%
Be able to evaluate web pages by accessibility standards and heuristics (e.g., W3C, WCAG)	36.5%
Be able to develop accessible web technologies (e.g., use of alt-tags, captioning videos, and describing images)	36.0%
Be able to employ design techniques: personas, paper prototyping, high-fidelity prototyping	35.2%
Understand legal accessibility regulations (e.g., Section 508, Americans with Disabilities Act, etc.)	31.5%
Understand the different models of disability (e.g., social, medical or legal models)	15.2%
Be able to develop with accessibility focused technical languages and tools (Apple's UI Accessibility Programming Interface, Android's Accessibility Events, Universal Windows Platform)	6.1%
Other	4.8%
None of the above	3.2%

Table 5. Methods faculty used to teach accessibility

Lectures and class meetings	95.9%
In-class activities	39.2%
Homework assignments	32.0%
Team projects	29.9%
Individual projects	17.9%
Simulation exercises	9.6%
Service learning, going to/seeking out organizations to work with	8.5%
None of the above	1.6%

3.2.1. Barriers. We asked faculty about a set of challenges identified in prior work [11] to incorporating accessibility in computing curriculum. As Table 6 shows, across all respondents, most reported the two main challenges were that accessibility was not a core part of their curriculum and that they did not know enough to teach it. Of those that already teach accessibility, expertise was not reported as a challenge as often, but curricular integration was still a central issue, as were the lack of resources such as textbooks and pedagogies for engaging students. Notably, few faculty (only 8.2%), whether they taught accessibility or not, believed a lack of demand in industry discouraged teaching accessibility. We performed a chi-square test comparing selection of each of the barriers between those who do and do not teach accessibility (see Table 6), finding that the two groups had largely different perspectives about all barriers except student and administrator awareness. The largest differences in perspectives was between having sufficient knowledge, textbook availability, and challenges engaging students: twice as many faculty who did not teach accessibility viewed these as significant barriers as those who did.

3.2.2. Accessibility as part of computing. To understand social and cultural factors that may influence whether respondents teach

Table 6. Barriers to teaching accessibility

	All	Teaches	Doesn't	χ^2
Not a core part of curriculum	52.3%	45.6%	54.0%	8.4**
Don't know enough to teach it	49.1%	26.1%	54.9%	99.3**
Lack of appropriate textbook	14.9%	24.8%	12.4%	32.6**
Lack of students and administrator awareness	14.1%	17.1%	13.4%	3.3
None of the above	13.5%	17.3%	12.6%	5.6*
Other	13.1%	12.0%	13.4%	
Lack of support for topics addressing real challenges for people with disabilities	13.1%	21.3%	11.0%	25.3**
Difficult engaging students	10.2%	19.2%	7.9%	36.3**
Lack of demand in industry	8.2%	11.5%	7.4%	6.7**
Difficult to recruit people with disabilities	7.2%	12.8%	5.8%	19.1**
All of the above	6%	2.7%	6.0%	11.2*

*$p < .05$, **$p < .01$

Table 7. Accessibility should be taught in CS

	All	Teaches	Doesn't
Strongly Agree	4.1%	42.2%	12.5%
Agree	42.6%	45.1%	42.0%
Neither Agree nor Disagree	29.9%	5.6%	36.0%
Disagree	4.8%	1.3%	5.7%
Strongly Disagree	4.1%	5.6%	3.7%

accessibility, we asked instructors to indicate their level of agreement with the statement "Accessibility should be taught as part of computer science." Table 7 summarizes the responses, showing that overall, there was either neutral or positive support for the topic, and that the only difference between those who do and do not teach accessibility was how strongly they believe it should be part of computing (Mann-Whitney U=159094, $p < .0001$).

3.2.3. What faculty need. To determine resources faculty perceived they needed, we asked them "If you wanted to incorporate accessibility into your curriculum, what resources would be helpful?" Because responses were open-ended, we inductively coded the responses, then developed axial codes to categorize themes. High-level codes that emerged were: connecting with or bringing people with disabilities into the classroom; having useful resources, like specific tools, technologies, guidelines, and problem examples; having access to curriculum building and curricular samples to use in specific courses; and faculty training and expertise.

Some did not see accessibility as relevant to their field, and desired arguments for relevance, as one respondent conveyed:

Appropriate lesson plans for different classes (algorithms, theory, intro programming). This should be taught across the CS curriculum, not just in a specialty topics course. But, I feel that students and faculty feel that "it is not directly related to the curriculum" and so they don't incorporate it.

Faculty mentioned many specific gaps. Some desired teaching modules that could be picked up and easily integrated into specific courses without too much modification or customization per discipline. Others wanted textbooks that adequately address accessibility in computing, or sample material for lectures, assignments and projects, or guidance on how instructors can include accessibility related topics for specific sub-disciplines within CS (like algorithms or data structures). For example, this instructor desired materials that were customized to sub-topics they were teaching, not just overarching and general material:

I teach operating systems to an undergraduate audience. I am unsure if there are relevant accessibility topics at this layer of systems. If I am wrong, resources discussing accessibility in lower layers of the system would be very helpful!

The dearth of resources corroborates findings from Putnam et al. [11], but our findings offer more detail: responses reflected a lack of reliable examples or curricular modules that could be used to teach practical skills or within specific knowledge areas, including knowing which research papers (or finding any relevant to their area of expertise), or having relevant training or access to updated guidelines or best practices. Finally, some faculty suggested that the survey was asking the wrong questions because accessibility was not a relevant topic for typical courses in computing, except when teaching students with disabilities. For example, in the quote below, the respondent balked at the notion that the survey had the "presumption" that accessibility could fit within certain sub-disciplines of CS:

I'm unclear how the issue would be relevant for the courses I teach. Not everything has an accessibility dimension. This survey seems to start from a presumption that accessibility would be a sensible unit even in a course on databases, or theoretical systems. Well, I just don't see that as being the case, or as making a lot of sense, frankly.

Despite the outlook that accessibility is "not in my area" of CS, others acknowledged that this perception was a pervasive cultural view within CS. To that view, the idea was that things could change, if the discipline as a whole took on the "challenge" to change. One respondent identified barriers as bias:

Materials to motivate why a culture change in computing is needed to both broaden participation and address sources of implicit bias. The largest hurdle is the mindsets that currently pervades computing that is oriented towards financial bottomlines and achievable but incremental pursuits. Accessibility must be seen as a grand challenge for computing.

Finally, we note that some respondents thought the question was asking how to make courses accessible to students with disabilities, not how to include accessibility as part of course topics. To the former, it is unclear if respondents wanted training to know how to teach accessibly, or to know how to include accessibility in content. In either case, however, confusion indicates that respondents were unfamiliar with how CS-focused pedagogy ought to incorporate accessibility. Clarifying the distinction between the two appears to be another barrier to teaching about accessibility.

Table 8. Logistic regression predicting teaching accessibility, showing coefficients (B), standard errors (SE), chi-squared statistics (Wald), and odds ratios (OR) for each factor

Factor	B	SE	Wald	OR
Female	0.70	0.14	26.5	2.0
Accessibility is part of CS	0.76	0.08	94.1	2.1
Sufficient expertise	1.25	0.13	86.8	3.5
Knows someone w/ disability	0.39	0.15	6.5	1.5

3.3 RQ3: What predicts teaching accessibility?

Modeling which factors predict who teaches accessibility may reveal additional insights about what factors may be necessary for overcoming these barriers. In particular, our hypothesis was that the dominating predictive factors would be knowing someone who had a disability, knowing enough to teach it, believing it should be taught, and, based on our results to RQ1, that a faculty member was female. To test this hypothesis, we built a binomial logistic regression, predicting who reported teaching accessibility from each of the above binary and ordinal variables.

The model, shown in Table 8, was statistically significant ($\chi^2(4) = 277.6$, $p < 0.00001$), as were all of the factors ($p < 0.01$). The model explained 21.9% (Nagelkerke R^2) of the variance in reporting teaching accessibility topics and correctly classified 81.7% of the cases. Interpreting the odds ratios (OR) in the table, those who taught accessibility were 1.5 times as likely to know someone with a disability, 2.0 times as likely to be female-identified, 2.1 times as likely to agree that accessibility is part of computing, 3.5 times as likely to report having sufficient knowledge to teach accessibility.

While the factors included in the model have predictive power, they only explained a fraction of the variance, suggesting that other factors dominate whether faculty teach accessibility.

4 DISCUSSION

Our discoveries are as follows:

- About 20% of faculty reported teaching accessibility, representing 2.5% of all faculty surveyed.
- About 50% of responding institutions reported teaching accessibility in at least one elective course, and 75 institutions had at least two faculty teaching accessibility.
- There were only 17 self-described faculty accessibility experts in our sample, spread across 14 institutions.
- Of faculty who responded, those who teach accessibility are twice as likely to be female, to know someone who has a disability, to have expertise in accessibility, and to strongly believe that accessibility should be part of CS curricula.
- Nearly all HCI experts teach accessibility.
- Most faculty who teach accessibility teach it once a year, cover it in a class or two, and focus on barriers that people with vision, hearing, and mobility impairments face, and design paradigms for preventing these barriers.
- Most respondents believe accessibility should be taught in CS degrees, but see the lack of expertise and sub-area specific materials as key barriers.

These results paint a picture of knowledge of accessibility as scarce, teaching of accessibility as prevalent but shallow, but support for teaching accessibility among U.S. faculty as broad.

These discoveries are consistent with prior work on curricular change [1,7]: change ultimately comes from local change agents, and many of the 375 faculty who teach accessibility now are likely already acting as those agents, teaching about accessibility despite the lack of curricular and resource support. However, there were also hundreds of faculty in the sample who do not yet teach accessibility, but believe it should be part of computing curricula. Some of those faculty hold a latent capacity for curricular change that appears to be held back only by a lack of knowledge and resources. There is some evidence in our data that some faculty cultures may be ambivalent to accessibility, with sentiments that "Not everything has an accessibility dimension." This may explain the absence of accessibility learning objectives in computing standards, and therefore its absence in concrete computing curricula. This also illustrates, in the words of Kirk and MacDonald, that "instructional discourse is embedded in regulative discourse, suggesting an organic relationship that involves inextricable connection, constant change and mutual–although not necessarily even–adaptation" [7]. In other words, what computing faculty teach and what faculty believe they should teach co-evolve.

What will trigger this co-evolution? Our findings suggest that knowledge of accessibility, plus materials that integrate accessibility into specific sub-areas of CS, as key. The 375 faculty who teach it now likely acquired their expertise in classes, or in their research, but the hundreds of others who support teaching accessibility may not have a context in which to learn this knowledge. Our data show that the training and teaching materials should not be on general accessibility knowledge, but on specific sub-areas of computing and information science. Based on these findings, we recommend: (1) investigating how accessibility is relevant to theory, algorithms, architecture, artificial intelligence, graphics, networking, software engineering, robotics, data science, and other areas, for future computing education research and (2) creating materials and modules that incorporate accessibility in these specific sub-areas; (3) finally, devising ways to teach faculty how to incorporate modules to include accessibility in their teaching, empowering them as change agents in their institutions.

Our survey has several limitations. We sent surveys on the same day of the week (Mondays), but our inability to send all emails at the same time impacted who received solicitations first. Faculty who teach accessibility who recognized the survey authors may have been more likely to respond, leading to response bias. And, some individuals indicated they suspected the solicitations were inauthentic, which may have limited responses systematically.

Despite these limitations, next steps are clear: if current champions of accessibility want to increase the number of students who know about accessibility, the focus must be on how accessibility fits within computing curriculum and on promoting faculty learning about accessibility. Some concrete recommendations include:

- For institutions with no HCI researchers, hire HCI faculty who are almost certain to teach accessibility.
- Develop and disseminate materials at the course- and class-level that are discipline-specific.
- Devise scalable ways to teach faculty key accessibility concepts.

With a few strategic investments in these efforts, academia appears ready to teach accessibility. AccessComputing [8] is beginning to gather and implement some of these resources, but it will take a whole community to succeed at scale.

4 ACKNOWLEDGMENTS

This work is supported by National Science Foundation Grants 1539179, 1314399, 1240786, 1153625, and Microsoft, Google, Adobe.

5 REFERENCES

1. Ronald Barnett, Gareth Parry, and Kelly Coate. 2001. Conceptualising Curriculum Change. *Teaching in Higher Education* 6, 4: 435–449.
2. Kimberly E. Bigelow. 2012. Designing for Success: Developing Engineers Who Consider Universal Design Principles. *Journal of Postsecondary Education and Disability* 25, 3: 211–225.
3. Paul Bohman. 2012. Teaching accessibility and design-for-all in the information and communication technology curriculum: Three case studies of universities in the United States, England, and Austria. Utah State University, Logan, UT.
4. Elizabeth A Courtney-Long, Dianna D Carroll, Qing C Zhang, Alissa C Stevens, Shannon Griffin-Blake, Brian S Armour, and Vincent A Campbell. 2015. Prevalence of disability and disability type among adults - United States, 2013. *Morbidity and Mortality Weekly Report Centers for Disease Control and Prevention* 64, 29: 777–783.
5. Israel Martin-Escalona, Francisco Barcelo-Arroyo, and Enrica Zola. 2013. The introduction of a topic on accessibility in several engineering degrees. In *2013 IEEE Global Engineering Education Conference (EDUCON)*, 656–663. https://doi.org/10.1109/EduCon.2013.6530177
6. Adrianna J Kezar and Peter D Eckel. 2002. The Effect of Institutional Culture on Change Strategies in Higher Education: Universal Principles or Culturally Responsive Concepts? *The Journal of Higher Education* 73, 4: 435–460. https://doi.org/10.1353/jhe.2002.0038
7. David Kirk and Doune MacDonald. 2001. Teacher voice and ownership of curriculum change. *Journal of Curriculum Studies* 33, 5: 551–567. https://doi.org/10.1080/00220270010016874
8. Andrew J. Ko and Richard E. Ladner. 2016. AccessComputing Promotes Teaching Accessibility. *ACM Inroads* 7, 4: 65–68.
9. Stephanie Ludi. 2007. Introducing Accessibility Requirements through External Stakeholder Utilization in an Undergraduate Requirements Engineering Course. In *Proc Software Engineering '07*, 736–743.
10. Cynthia Putnam, Maria Dahman, Emma Rose, Jinghui Cheng, and Glenn Bradford. 2015. Teaching Accessibility, Learning Empathy. In *Proc ASSETS 2015*, 333–334.
11. Cynthia Putnam, Maria Dahman, Emma Rose, Jinghui Cheng, and Glenn Bradford. 2016. Best Practices for Teaching Accessibility in University Classrooms: Cultivating Awareness, Understanding, and Appreciation for Diverse Users. *ACM TACCESS* 8, 4: 1–26.
12. Brian J. Rosmaita. 2006. Accessibility first!: a new approach to web design. In *Proc SIGCSE 2006*, 270–274.
13. Kristen Shinohara, Cynthia L. Bennett, and Jacob O. Wobbrock. 2016. How Designing for People With and Without Disabilities Shapes Student Design Thinking. In *Proc. ASSETS '16.*, 229–237.
14. Kristen Shinohara, Cynthia Bennett, Jacob Wobbrock, and Wanda Pratt. 2017. Teaching Accessibility in a Technology Design Course.
15. Stephanie Ludi. 2002. Access for everyone: introducing accessibility issues to students in Internet programming courses. In *32nd Annual Frontiers in Education*, S1C–7. https://doi.org/10.1109/FIE.2002.1158617
16. Annalu Waller, Vicki L. Hanson, and David Sloan. 2009. Including accessibility within and beyond undergraduate computing courses. In *Proc. ASSETS '09*, 155–162.

A Survey of Instructors' Experiences Supporting Student Learning using HFOSS Projects

Lori Postner
Nassau Community College
Garden City, NY, USA
lori.postner@ncc.edu

Heidi J. C. Ellis
Western New England University
Springfield, MA, USA
ellis@wne.edu

Gregory W. Hislop
Drexel University
Philadelphia, PA, USA
hislop@drexel.edu

ABSTRACT

Studies have shown that Humanitarian Free and Open Source Software (HFOSS) projects provide a rich learning environment for students, allowing them to gain a range of both technical and professional skills. Although there have been a number of studies on student attitudes toward learning within HFOSS projects, little has been documented about instructors' experiences supporting their students in the classroom. This paper examines survey results from 26 faculty members who participated in an NSF-funded Professors' Open Source Software Experience workshop with the goal of incorporating HFOSS into their curriculum. The survey was designed to identify barriers to using HFOSS in the classroom, to understand the type of classes where instructors incorporated HFOSS, the successes attained and challenges faced by instructors, and to understand instructors' future plans. The data gathered was used to enhance semi-structured interviews that are currently being analyzed. This paper focuses on the hurdles reported by faculty members, the cross-section of uses of HFOSS in the classroom as well as factors that may influence one's ability to integrate HFOSS into the curriculum. The results of the survey demonstrate that faculty have successfully incorporated HFOSS into a wide range of courses across all four years of the curriculum with both large and small classes. The major hurdles are time to prepare materials for one's course as well as finding time within an existing course to integrate HFOSS material.

CCS CONCEPTS

• **Social and professional topics** → **Computer science education**; • **Software and its engineering** → *Open source model*;

KEYWORDS

Open source software, HFOSS, computing education

ACM Reference format:
Lori Postner, Heidi J. C. Ellis, and Gregory W. Hislop. 2018. A Survey of Instructors' Experiences Supporting Student Learning using HFOSS Projects. In *Proceedings of The 49th ACM Technical Symposium on Computing Science Education, Baltimore, MD, USA, February 21–24, 2018 (SIGCSE'18)*, 6 pages.
DOI: 10.1145/3159450.3159524

978-1-4503-5103-4/18/02...$15.00
DOI: 10.1145/3159450.3159524

1 BACKGROUND

The characteristics of Free and Open Source Software (FOSS) projects including transparency, meritocracy, community development, accessible artifacts, distributed and global development, and openness to contributions, provide a rich learning environment for students [7, 20, 26]. Students gain exposure to a sizable real-world project that is accompanied by a professional development community. Students can learn technical skills such as development tools, design, maintenance, software life-cycle, etc. [13, 17] as well as professional skills including communication, collaboration, and problem solving [27].

Humanitarian FOSS (HFOSS), is FOSS that improves the human condition in some manner. Examples include electronic medical records, disaster management software, micro-finance applications and more. The Humanitarian FOSS effort was founded in 2006 [22] in the hope of revitalizing computer science enrollments which were in a slump at the time [11, 21, 23]. In 2009, more formal studies of student opinion of motivation and learning that results from participation in an HFOSS project began [15]. Since that time, research results indicate that HFOSS can motivate students and aid in learning [6, 8, 16]. Student involvement in HFOSS has a significant positive impact on:

- Student attitude towards computing
- Perceived learning of software engineering
- Technical and professional knowledge
- Understanding how to plan, develop and maintain such a project, and female students demonstrate significantly greater understanding

In addition to gaining understanding about student learning, the authors gained experience in providing guidance to instructors on how to support student involvement in HFOSS [4, 5, 9, 10]. Results of this foundation include:

- Identification of an approach for selecting appropriate HFOSS projects for student involvement
- Identification of approaches for structuring computing learning within HFOSS participation
- Understanding of how to support development of an HFOSS project using integrated teams across levels and institutions
- Development of materials to help faculty get started with student involvement in HFOSS
- Founding a community of instructors who are involving students in HFOSS

Even with guidance provided to instructors when supporting student participation in HFOSS, the benefits from HFOSS come at a cost. HFOSS projects present learning curves for both faculty members and students related to project domain, tools, culture and more. HFOSS projects typically have less structure than an academic classroom which may present difficulties to student learning within this dynamic environment. Communication with the HFOSS community, identifying potential student contributions, fit to course schedule, FERPA, and institutional requirements may also create challenges for faculty trying to utilize HFOSS within the classroom [12].

In 2009, Red Hat started to address the need for faculty members to understand open source culture by creating the Professors' Open Source Summer Experience (POSSE) workshop [14]. The workshop, held in summer, helped faculty members understand how open source software communities worked by immersing them in open source culture. However this version of POSSE did not address the inclusion of open source in the classroom. In addition, faculty were not provided lodging or travel support so participation was typically limited to only faculty local to the POSSE location or having other sources of travel support. In 2013, an NSF grant awarded to the authors allowed the POSSE content to be revised to address curriculum and pedagogy and the name was updated to Professors' Open Source **Software** Experience since the workshops are not confined to summer [9]. The grant also funded participant faculty member travel and lodging. As of 2017, about 200 faculty members from over 100 academic institutions have attended a POSSE workshop.

The success of the POSSE workshops is demonstrated by the reports of alumni describing various aspects of student involvement in HFOSS. MacDonell [18] reports on incorporating Ushahidi, open source crisis mapping software, into his senior software engineering course. Rebelsky [25] incorporated Ushahidi into a data structures course. Four POSSE alumni [24] presented a panel that reported on their individual experiences involving students in HFOSS. One panel member worked with an interdisciplinary team of students and faculty to create an open source application that tracks the spread of Wavyleaf Basketgrass, an invasive grass first found in Maryland in 1997. Walden [28] developed an introductory workshop to guide faculty members through the key aspects of an HFOSS project. Buffardi [2, 3] describes an approach used to help manage open source project unpredictability by forming a local open source organization with students, professors, and professionals making up the community.

While this success is encouraging, there is still much to learn about the factors that either lead to the success of student involvement in HFOSS or perhaps inhibit such involvement in the classroom. This paper reports on results of a survey to elicit information on positive and inhibiting factors for faculty members supporting student involvement in HFOSS.

2 METHODS

In order to obtain a better understanding of the contexts in which instructors are supporting student involvement in HFOSS as well as the successes achieved and challenges faced by instructors, a two-phase plan was implemented. The first phase, reported here, was a survey of instructors to identify the hurdles encountered by instructors, the cross-section of uses of HFOSS in the classroom, and factors that may influence instructors' ability to integrate HFOSS into the curriculum. The second phase, based on the surveys, was semi-structured interviews to obtain more detailed information on instructor observations. Analysis of these interviews is currently ongoing.

2.1 Subjects

Subjects were selected from the 77 faculty members teaching at U.S. institutions who completed one of the five POSSE workshops held between June 2013 and June 2016. The authors identified a subgroup of workshop participants who, during the POSSE workshop, were actively engaged and highly enthusiastic about incorporating HFOSS into their curriculum as potential participants. Each faculty member was then categorized by the amount of student participation in HFOSS (high, medium, low, none). This categorization was based on information that the authors had learned about faculty member activity from various post-workshop interactions. To avoid similar responses and to diversify the academic institutions, the subject pool was limited to one faculty member per institution. 39 faculty members were identified as prospective participants and contacted via email inviting them to complete an on-line survey about their use of HFOSS in their classes. They were told that the authors were interested in those who had been unable to incorporate HFOSS as well as those who had been successful adopters. A second follow-up email was sent to prospective participants who had not completed the survey by the deadline date. The data described in this paper consists of 26 faculty members (66% response rate), 10 women and 16 men.

Survey participants answered a variety of demographic questions about their rank at their current academic institution, years in computer science education, years of industry experience and years of open source experience. Table 1 below shows the demographics of the survey participants. The preponderance of respondents were Associate or Full Professors. This makes sense as Assistant Professors are typically pre-tenure and less likely to risk any classroom intervention that could negatively impact their tenure case. Similarly, the majority of participants had more than 10 years of education experience. Perhaps more interesting was the number of faculty who had industry experience. Only seven participants had no prior industry experience and five had over 10 years. It was also interesting to observe that many participants had more than a year of open source experience.

Of the 26 faculty who responded, 20 had incorporated HFOSS into their courses in some form, six reported being unable to incorporate any HFOSS.

2.2 Survey

The purpose of the survey was two-fold: the first purpose was to gather demographic information and document instructors' experiences using HFOSS in the classroom, the second purpose was to serve as background information for follow-up semi-structured interviews with the survey participants. This paper focuses on the survey data. The instructor interviews are in the preliminary stages of analysis. The survey was conducted on-line and contained 18 questions. It was IRB approved and contained a consent form which stated the purpose as "This study involves an investigation of instructor support for student learning in open source software

Academic Rank		
Assistant Professor	6	23%
Associate Professor	13	50%
Professor	6	23%
Other Academic Rank	1	4%
Years CS Education Experience		
2-5 years	4	15%
6-10 years	5	19%
> 10 years	17	65%
Years Industry Experience		
0 years	7	27%
1-4 years	10	39%
5-10 years	4	15%
> 10 years	5	19%
Years Open Source Experience		
0 years	5	19%
1-4 years	13	50%
5-10 years	5	19%
> 10 years	3	12%

Table 1: Survey Participant Demographics

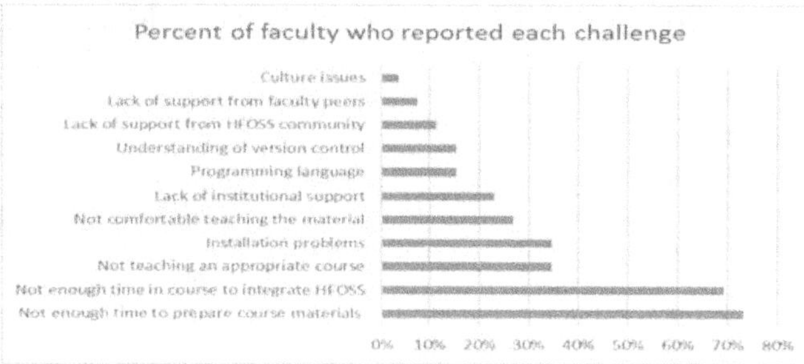

Figure 1: Barriers to Instructor Support of Student Involvement in HFOSS.

CS Ed Exp.	HFOSS Use	No HFOSS Use	Pct HFOSS Use
0-1 Years	0	0	NA
2-5 Years	4	0	100%
6-10 Years	3	2	60%
> 10	13	4	76.5%

Table 2: CS Education Experience and HFOSS Inclusion

projects. Specifically, the focus of the project is to expand student learning in the computing disciplines via involvement in Humanitarian Free and Open Source Software (HFOSS) projects." In order to fulfill the two purposes, the survey questions included demographic information about the participant as well as specific questions regarding barriers to incorporating HFOSS into the classroom, courses and projects where HFOSS was used and use of on-line activities from the POSSE workshop organizers. The goal of survey questions was to help answer the following research questions:

- Research Question 1 (R1): What are the biggest hurdles to incorporating HFOSS into the curriculum?
- Research Question 2 (R2): Does the number of years the faculty member has been involved in CS Education, Industry or Open Source influence his/her ability to incorporate HFOSS into the curriculum?
- Research Question 3 (R3): For which courses were faculty successful in incorporating HFOSS?

The on-line survey can be viewed at: URL HERE

3 RESULTS

3.1 R1: What are the biggest hurdles to incorporating HFOSS into the curriculum?

The survey asked instructors to identify all the barriers that they encountered related to involving students in HFOSS (select all that apply). Figure 1 shows the factors that instructors identified as barriers. It was not surprising that faculty members cited lack of time as the primary hurdle to incorporating HFOSS into the curriculum. 73% of the participants cited lack of time to prepare course materials as a major hurdle to incorporating HFOSS into their courses and 69% said that they didn't have enough time in their courses to integrate HFOSS. The next most frequent answers were that instructors did not have an appropriate course to teach (35%), getting the HFOSS project installed was difficult (35%) and the instructor did not feel comfortable with the HFOSS material (27%). It was surprising that only 15% cited version control as an issue since that is a popular topic of the POSSE workshops, and that most people felt that their institution was supportive of their effort to include HFOSS in their courses (only 23% cited institutional support as a hurdle). Since this was a check list, other hurdles may be identified from the interview data.

3.2 R2: Does the number of years the faculty member has been involved in CS Education, Industry or Open Source influence his/her ability to incorporate HFOSS into the curriculum?

Although only 6 of the respondents cited being unable to incorporate HFOSS, it was interesting to see that neither the faculty's rank, nor the number of years involved with CS education, nor the number of years of industry experience appeared to have any influence on the ability to incorporate HFOSS into the curriculum. An examination of these factors indicates that experience in CS education and experience in industry does not appear to impact the success of faculty members incorporating HFOSS into the classroom. There does seem to be a weak correlation between previous open source experience and success in incorporating HFOSS in the classroom, however the number of respondents was too small for statistical significance. Tables 2 and 3 demonstrate that faculty with all types of experience have successfully incorporated HFOSS into their classrooms.

Years Industry Experience and HFOSS Inclusion			
	HFOSS Use	No HFOSS Use	Pct HFOSS Use
0 Years	6	1	85.7%
1-4 Years	8	2	80%
5-10 Years	3	1	75%
> 10	3	2	60%
Years Open Source Experience and HFOSS Inclusion			
	HFOSS Use	No HFOSS Use	Pct HFOSS Use
0 Years	2	3	40%
1-4 Years	10	2	83.3%
5-10 Years	4	1	80%
> 10	4	0	100%

Table 3: Industry/Open Source Experience and HFOSS Inclusion

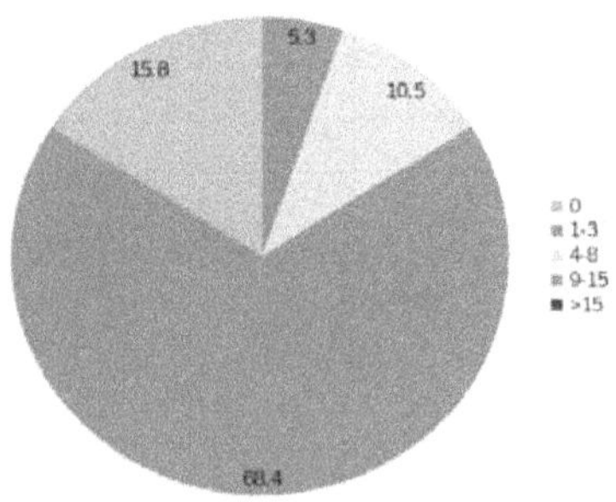

Figure 2: Percentage HFOSS Activities Used.

3.3 R3: For which courses were faculty successful in incorporating HFOSS?

Survey results indicated that faculty members had involved students in HFOSS in 18 different courses for a total of 37 different sections. The courses included expected courses such as Software Design and Software Engineering, but also included Data Structures, Parallel Computing, Secure Computing, Mobile Development, Object Oriented Design and Data Mining. Faculty cited using HFOSS in courses for both majors and non-majors across all four years of the curriculum. Class size did not appear to influence faculty's choice to use HFOSS as it was used in large lecture classes of 100-150 as well as in small classes (10 or fewer students) and independent studies (with 1-2 students). This provides evidence that HFOSS can be incorporated into a wide range of courses.

In order to help the authors understand if POSSE alum had used any of the materials provided during the workshop, the survey asked faculty how many HFOSS learning activities they had used. Figure 2 shows the distribution of the number of HFOSS learning activities that were used by faculty members. It is interesting to note that the majority of faculty members used only 1-3 activities from the over 100 available within their class. The hurdles identified in the previous section may be hindering greater usage.

3.4 HFOSS Projects

In addition to asking information about courses, the survey also asked information about the project used in the classroom. Figure 3 shows the projects used in classes and their frequency. It should be noted that some instructors included HFOSS in multiple classes and therefore utilized more than one HFOSS project. Based on Figure 3, OpenMRS was clearly the most widely used project. This is interesting as OpenMRS is also the largest and most complex project in the set of projects listed. One reason why it was used so widely could be due to OpenMRS having a relatively large community that is accustomed to working with student contributors. 47.4% of instructors either agreed or strongly agreed that they would use the project again in the future and 42.1% were neutral about using the same project.

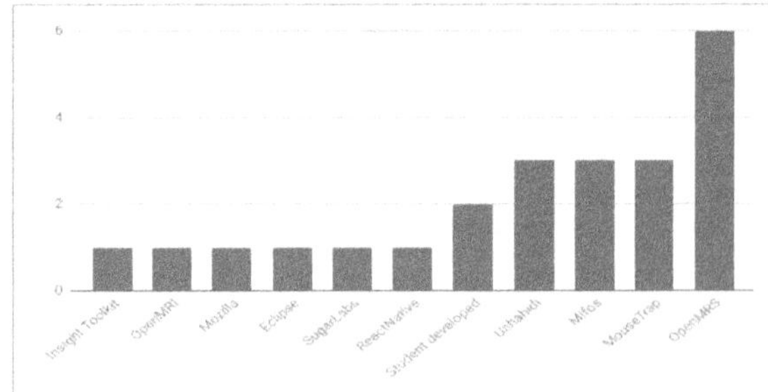

Figure 3: HFOSS Projects Used.

When asked about their role in the HFOSS project, the majority of instructors (84.2%) reported that they were lurkers within projects. Some 10.5% reported serving as contributors and 15.8% served as mentors (faculty members served more than one role across projects). This provides strong evidence that faculty members do not need to be core contributors to a project in order to support student participation in HFOSS.

60% of instructors either agreed or strongly agreed that their contact person within the community was helpful. This provides some evidence that one success factor for student involvement in HFOSS in the classroom is having a contact person within the HFOSS project community to whom to ask questions.

3.5 Future Use of HFOSS

In order to assess if faculty would begin or continue using HFOSS in their future classes, the survey asked them their future plans. Three of the six faculty who had not incorporated HFOSS at the time of the survey said they hoped to incorporate it into a course with the next year or two depending upon the courses they were teaching.

Of the 20 faculty who had incorporated some HFOSS into their courses, four indicated that they would not continue in the future. The reasons for this included not teaching an appropriate course and change in job status. The remaining 16 faculty members planned to continue to use HOSS in their courses. Two faculty members mentioned expanding HFOSS into Independent Studies and one proposed introducing a workshop series. Several faculty members mentioned expanding the use of HFOSS into Testing or SQA courses. Several also mentioned expanding into senior capstone courses including the senior seminar. Interestingly, two instructors mentioned developing new courses (Open Source Tools, Open Source Software) in which HFOSS would be utilized. One faculty member mentioned hosting an Open Source Day and several faculty members mentioned developing additional materials for use in their classes. This mention of expanding use of HFOSS and development of materials is encouraging evidence that faculty members find student participation in HFOSS provides a positive learning experience.

4 DISCUSSION

The survey data provided insight into how faculty use HFOSS in their classrooms and what they found to hinder their efforts. One of the goals of the survey was to provide the authors with information to help refine the POSSE workshop and to provide additional support for faculty who want to incorporate HFOSS into the classroom.

4.1 R1: Hurdles to Incorporation of HFOSS

Two major hurdles identified by survey participants had to do with lack of time, both time to prepare for a course using HFOSS and time to implement HFOSS within an existing course. There are several possible ways to surmount the time issues. First, the NSF-funded foss2serve project (foss2serve.org) has a collection of over 100 teaching activities that have been developed by instructors. These activities range from introductory activities appropriate for non-majors to advanced activities appropriate for software engineering or capstone courses. All activities focus on HFOSS but may be easily generalized to FOSS. In the authors' experience, incorporating 1-2 HFOSS teaching activities into an existing course is an excellent way to start supporting student involvement in HFOSS. Survey results indicate that faculty use few of the existing materials (on average 1-3 activities). The authors need to investigate barriers to broader adoption of HFOSS activities as well as how to help make existing materials easier to find and use.

Second, the Teaching Open Source community (teachingopensource.org) is another resource for teaching materials. While there is some overlap in materials between the foss2serve and Teaching Open Source sites, teachingopensource.org also contains links to existing courses that utilize FOSS or HFOSS to provide examples of ways to incorporate HFOSS into a course. There are also multiple examples of courses taught using HFOSS and FOSS [1, 3, 18–20, 24] that can provide instructors with insights on a variety of ways to utilize HFOSS within a course.

Third, the authors have started to map the teaching activities on the foss2serve site to the ACM Curricular Guidelines, specifically the Computer Science and Software Engineering guidelines. With such a mapping in place, faculty could easily search for materials to meet specific course outcomes. The team is also running additional post-POSSE meetings which allow faculty members to meet in groups to collaborate on course materials.

Lastly, communities of faculty members are starting to form around specific projects. For example, instructors from Dickenson College and University Complutense Madrid have students who are collaborating on the Sahana project. Instructors from Berea College, Western New England University, and Nassau Community College are collaborating on the Accessibility aspects of Mozilla Dev Tools. These communities are jointly creating materials that support student involvement in HFOSS.

Another hurdle that came up in the survey that has also come up during the POSSE workshop is difficulty finding an HFOSS project whose development environment can be easily downloaded and installed. To address this hurdle, the authors are designing a workshop to bring together faculty who have already completed POSSE so that they can spend a full day working with other faculty and with a faculty mentor on a specific HFOSS project. They will install the development environment, identify a bug, attempt to fix and submit a solution to the bug. The goal of this is not only to provide faculty with the time needed to focus on a project and the support necessary to get started, but also to provide a support group moving forward. This effort will help to develop faculty communities around HFOSS projects.

4.2 R2: Prior Experience

The finding that the number of years faculty members have taught or worked in industry did not seem to influence their ability to incorporate HFOSS is encouraging as it shows that time and motivation on the part of the faculty is most important. It was not surprising that faculty with prior Open Source experience would be likely to incorporate HFOSS into their classrooms, but it was also clear that this was not a requirement.

4.3 R3: Environments Using HFOSS

The survey results demonstrated that the most common classes where faculty are using HFOSS are software engineering and senior capstone courses. However, the results also show that these are not the only classes where faculty have incorporated HFOSS in some form. Class size is often in the 8-20 student range, however large classes as well as small independent studies have been used. The breadth of classes indicates that there are lots of opportunities where faculty can utilize the rich learning environment of HFOSS.

4.4 Future Plans

A few faculty mentioned using HFOSS in new courses they would be teaching. It is exciting that schools are creating new courses focusing on Open Source software and tools. In addition, independent studies were mentioned as well as expanded use in projects courses based upon student interest. Many faculty stated that they would use HFOSS if they were assigned courses where they felt it would be appropriate. The fact that faculty were actively finding ways to introduce students to HFOSS is encouraging and demonstrates that although there are a number of hurdles involved that faculty believe the approach is worth the effort.

4.5 Generality

The faculty who have attended POSSE are a self-selected group who have applied to the workshop and participated in a 6-8 week on-line training prior to the face-to-face workshop. Since this study selected a subset of this group, the faculty involved are not likely to be representative of Computer Science faculty in general. However, the sample represented in this paper does provide a glimpse into the struggles and successes that motivated, enthusiastic faculty have when trying to incorporate HFOSS into the curriculum. The small number of respondents made it difficult to perform much statistical analysis on the data set, particularly with regard to the subset of the sample who were not able to incorporate any HFOSS into the classroom.

5 CONCLUSIONS AND FUTURE WORK

This study of instructor experiences using HFOSS supports the belief that, although there are significant hurdles, faculty with a wide variety of backgrounds, from multiple institutions have been successful in incorporating HFOSS into many different environments. One future direction is to look at faculty success rate based upon HFOSS project they have chosen to use. In this study faculty used a variety of established projects with varying degrees of success. The authors hope that the interview data will help provide additional information about how individual projects may influence a faculty member's success and interest in using this approach in the future.

ACKNOWLEDGMENTS

This material is based on work supported by the National Science Foundation under Grant Nos. DUE-1525039, DUE-1524877, and DUE-1524898. Any opinions, findings and conclusions or recommendations expressed in this material are those of the author(s) and do not necessarily reflect the views of the National Science Foundation (NSF).

REFERENCES

[1] Grant Braught, John MacCormic, James F. Bowring, Quinn Burke, Barbara Cutler, David Goldschmidt, Mukkai Krishnamoorthy, Wesley Turner, Steven Huss-Lederman, Bonnie MacKellar, and Allen Tucker. 2018. A Multi-Institutional Perspective on H/FOSS Projects in the Computing Curriculum. *Trans. Comput. Educ.* forthcoming (2018).

[2] Kevin Buffardi. 2015. Localized Open Source Collaboration in Software Engineering Education. In *Proceedings of the 2015 IEEE Frontiers in Education Conference (FIE) (FIE '15)*. IEEE Computer Society, Washington, DC, USA, 1–5. DOI: http://dx.doi.org/10.1109/FIE.2015.7344142

[3] Kevin Buffardi. 2017. Comparing Remote and Co-located Interaction in Free and Open Source Software Engineering Projects. In *Proceedings of the 2017 ACM Conference on Innovation and Technology in Computer Science Education (ITiCSE '17)*. ACM, New York, NY, USA, 22–27. DOI: http://dx.doi.org/10.1145/3059009.3059019

[4] Darci Burdge, Lori Postner, Heidi J. C. Ellis, and Gregory W. Hislop. 2014. Preparing for Student Participation in HFOSS Projects: FOSS Tools and Techniques. *J. Comput. Sci. Coll.* 29, 3 (Jan. 2014), 74–75. http://dl.acm.org/citation.cfm?id=2544322.2544338

[5] Darci Burdge, Lori Postner, Becka Morgan, Heidi J.C. Ellis, Stoney Jackson, Gregory W. Hislop, and Michelle Purcell. 2014. Teaching with HFOSS to Provide Students with Real World Experience: An Introduction (Abstract Only). In *Proceedings of the 45th ACM Technical Symposium on Computer Science Education (SIGCSE '14)*. ACM, New York, NY, USA, 744–745. DOI: http://dx.doi.org/10.1145/2538862.2539017

[6] Heidi J.C. Ellis, Gregory W. Hislop, Josephine Rodriguez, and Ralph A. Morelli. 2012. Student Software Engineering Learning via Participation in Humanitarian FOSS Projects. *119th Annual ASEE Conference and Exhibition* (2012).

[7] Heidi J. C. Ellis, Gregory W. Hislop, Mel Chua, and Sebastian Dziallas. 2011. How to Involve Students in FOSS Projects. In *Proceedings of the 2011 Frontiers in Education Conference (FIE '11)*. IEEE Computer Society, Washington, DC, USA, T1H-1-1–T1H-6. DOI: http://dx.doi.org/10.1109/FIE.2011.6142994

[8] Heidi J. C. Ellis, Gregory W. Hislop, Stoney Jackson, and Lori Postner. 2015. Team Project Experiences in Humanitarian Free and Open Source Software (HFOSS). *Trans. Comput. Educ.* 15, 4, Article 18 (Dec. 2015), 23 pages. DOI: http://dx.doi.org/10.1145/2684812

[9] Heidi J. C. Ellis, Gregory W. Hislop, Michelle Purcell, Mel Chua, and Sebastian Dziallas. 2013. Towards a Model of Faculty Development for FOSS in Education. In *26th International Conference on Software Engineering Education and Training (CSEE&T) (CSEET '13)*. IEEE Computer Society, Washington, DC, USA, 269 – 273. DOI: http://dx.doi.org/10.1109/CSEET.2013.6595259

[10] Heidi J. C. Ellis, Gregory W. Hislop, Michelle Purcell, and Lori Postner. 2013. Project Selection for Student Participation in Humanitarian FOSS. *J. Comput. Sci. Coll.* 28, 6 (June 2013), 16–18. http://dl.acm.org/citation.cfm?id=2460156.2460162

[11] Heidi J. C. Ellis, Ralph A. Morelli, Trishan R. de Lanerolle, Jonathan Damon, and Jonathan Raye. 2007. Can Humanitarian Open-source Software Development Draw New Students to CS? *SIGCSE Bull.* 39, 1 (March 2007), 551–555. DOI: http://dx.doi.org/10.1145/1227504.1227495

[12] Heidi J. C. Ellis, Ralph A. Morelli, and Gregory W. Hislop. 2008. WIP: Challenges to Educating Students within the Community of Open Source Software for Humanity. In *Proceedings of the 2008 Frontiers in Education Conference (FIE '08)*. IEEE Computer Society, Washington, DC, USA. DOI: http://dx.doi.org/10.1109/FIE.2008.4720515

[13] Swapna Gokhale, Thérèse Smith, and Robert McCartney. 2013. Teaching Software Engineering from a Maintenance-centric View Using Open-source Software. *J. Comput. Sci. Coll.* 28, 6 (June 2013), 189–191. http://dl.acm.org/citation.cfm?id=2460156.2460191

[14] Red Hat. 2017. Open Source in Education. (2017). https://www.redhat.com/en/about/open-source-education/educators

[15] Gregory W. Hislop, Heidi J.C. Ellis, and Ralph A. Morelli. 2009. Evaluating Student Experiences in Developing Software for Humanity. In *Proceedings of the 14th Annual ACM SIGCSE Conference on Innovation and Technology in Computer Science Education (ITiCSE '09)*. ACM, New York, NY, USA, 263–267. DOI: http://dx.doi.org/10.1145/1562877.1562959

[16] Gregory W. Hislop, Heidi J.C. Ellis, S. Monisha Pulimood, Becka Morgan, Suzanne Mello-Stark, Ben Coleman, and Cam Macdonell. 2015. A Multi-Institutional Study of Learning via Student Involvement in Humanitarian Free and Open Source Software Projects. In *Proceedings of the Eleventh Annual International Conference on International Computing Education Research (ICER '15)*. ACM, New York, NY, USA, 199–206. DOI: http://dx.doi.org/10.1145/2787622.2787726

[17] Clif Kussmaul, Heidi J.C. Ellis, and Gregory W. Hislop. 2012. 50 Ways to Be a FOSSer: Simple Ways to Involve Students & Faculty (Abstract Only). In *Proceedings of the 43rd ACM Technical Symposium on Computer Science Education (SIGCSE '12)*. ACM, New York, NY, USA, 671–671. DOI: http://dx.doi.org/10.1145/2157136.2157393

[18] Cam Macdonell. 2015. Ushahidi: A Crisis Mapping System. *SIGCAS Comput. Soc.* 45, 2 (July 2015), 38–38. DOI: http://dx.doi.org/10.1145/2809957.2809969

[19] Bonnie K. MacKellar, Mihaela Sabin, and Allen Tucker. 2013. Scaling a Framework for Client-driven Open Source Software Projects: A Report from Three Schools. *J. Comput. Sci. Coll.* 28, 6 (June 2013), 140–147. http://dl.acm.org/citation.cfm?id=2460156.2460184

[20] Robert Marmorstein. 2011. Open Source Contribution As an Effective Software Engineering Class Project. In *Proceedings of the 16th Annual Joint Conference on Innovation and Technology in Computer Science Education (ITiCSE '11)*. ACM, New York, NY, USA, 268–272. DOI: http://dx.doi.org/10.1145/1999747.1999823

[21] Ralph Morelli, Trishan de Lanerolle, and Janardhan Lyengar. 2008. Teaching and Building Humanitarian Open Source Software. *J. Comput. Sci. Coll.* 23, 5 (May 2008), 5–6. http://dl.acm.org/citation.cfm?id=1352627.1352628

[22] Ralph Morelli, Trishan de Lanerolle, and Allen Tucker. 2012. *The Humanitarian Free and Open-Source Software Project: Engaging Students in Service-Learning through Building Software.* John Wiley & Sons, Inc., 117–136. DOI: http://dx.doi.org/10.1002/9781118319130.ch5

[23] Ralph Morelli, Allen Tucker, Norman Danner, Trishan R. De Lanerolle, Heidi J. C. Ellis, Ozgur Izmirli, Danny Krizanc, and Gary Parker. 2009. Revitalizing Computing Education Through Free and Open Source Software for Humanity. *Commun. ACM* 52, 8 (Aug. 2009), 67–75. DOI: http://dx.doi.org/10.1145/1536616.1536635

[24] Christian Murphy, Kevin Buffardi, Josh Dehlinger, Lynn Lambert, and Nanette Veilleux. 2017. Community Engagement with Free and Open Source Software. In *Proceedings of the 2017 ACM SIGCSE Technical Symposium on Computer Science Education (SIGCSE '17)*. ACM, New York, NY, USA, 669–670. DOI: http://dx.doi.org/10.1145/3017680.3017682

[25] Samuel A. Rebelsky. 2015. HFOSS-Lite in CS2: Incorporating the Ushahidi Crowdmapping Program in a Data Structures and Algorithms Course (Abstract Only). In *Proceedings of the 46th ACM Technical Symposium on Computer Science Education (SIGCSE '15)*. ACM, New York, NY, USA, 514–514. DOI: http://dx.doi.org/10.1145/2676723.2691885

[26] Therese Mary Smith, Robert McCartney, Swapna S. Gokhale, and Lisa C. Kaczmarczyk. 2014. Selecting Open Source Software Projects to Teach Software Engineering. In *Proceedings of the 45th ACM Technical Symposium on Computer Science Education (SIGCSE '14)*. ACM, New York, NY, USA, 397–402. DOI: http://dx.doi.org/10.1145/2538862.2538932

[27] Eleni Stroulia, Ken Bauer, Michelle Craig, Karen Reid, and Greg Wilson. 2011. Teaching Distributed Software Engineering with UCOSP: The Undergraduate Capstone Open-source Project. In *Proceedings of the 2011 Community Building Workshop on Collaborative Teaching of Globally Distributed Software Development (CTGDSD '11)*. ACM, New York, NY, USA, 20–25. DOI: http://dx.doi.org/10.1145/1984665.1984670

[28] James Walden. 2014. Teaching with Humanitarian Free/Open Source Software. *J. Comput. Sci. Coll.* 30, 1 (Oct. 2014), 103–104. http://dl.acm.org/citation.cfm?id=2667369.2667388

Supporting Differentiated Instruction in Programming Courses through Permanent Progress Monitoring

Nuno Gil Fonseca
College of Technology and Management of Oliveira do Hospital, Polytechnic Institute of Coimbra
Oliveira do Hospital, Portugal
nuno.fonseca@estgoh.ipc.pt

Luís Macedo
Center for Informatics and Systems of the University of Coimbra, Dep. of Informatics Eng., University of Coimbra, Coimbra, Portugal
macedo@dei.uc.pt

António José Mendes
Center for Informatics and Systems of the University of Coimbra, Dep. of Informatics Eng., University of Coimbra, Coimbra, Portugal
toze@dei.uc.pt

ABSTRACT

Several studies showed that teacher's support is essential to the students learning process. Often it is difficult for teachers to follow all their student's evolution and make timely interventions when needed. Often, in the same class, there are students with substantially different performance levels, and many times a teacher intervention is crucial to help lower performing students. To help the teacher identify these students, we propose the use of *CodeInsights*, a tool able to capture autonomously and unobtrusively real-time information about the students' performance based on snapshots of their code. The information available can be used by the teachers to support the adoption of the necessary measures to address each student needs or difficulties in a more grounded manner. We present the system and some results of a field test involving students from an introductory course on PHP programming.

ACM Reference format:

Nuno Gil Fonseca, Luís Macedo, and António José Mendes. 2018. Supporting Differentiated Instruction in Programming Courses through Permanent Progress Monitoring In *SIGCSE '18: 49th ACM Technical Symposium on Computer Science Education*, Feb. 21–24, 2018, Baltimore, MD, USA. ACM, NY, NY, USA, 6 pages. https://doi.org/10.1145/3159450.3159578

1 INTRODUCTION

Numerous authors have focused their research on learning and teaching programming, in particular, concerning introductory courses (generally designated as CS1) [1].

Studies have shown that learning programming is not a simple or trivial task and that many students experience a series of difficulties along the way [2]. In particular, the first steps are crucial to determine their future success in introductory programming courses, and in computing degrees in general.

Regardless of all the advances from the last decades, there are still several challenges that the programming teachers have to deal with on a daily basis [3]. Among those challenges, we may find the diversity of students, which generally translates into completely different results (grades). Some authors argue that this diversity in the final results is mainly influenced by the student's prior knowledge [4], while other authors explain this behavior with concepts like *Learning Edge Momentum* [5] or the questionable existence of a "Geek Gene" that some gifted students may have, which makes them more able to learn to program than other [6]. One thing is certain: there are indeed students learning/working at considerably different paces, in a normal classroom.

According to Raabe et al. [7], the students' performance is highly coupled with the capacity that the teachers have to detect their difficulties and react within useful time. However, due to the high number of students per class and/or the inhibition of the students to expose their weaknesses, students may be facing difficulties that are unnoticed by their teachers.

Particular attention should be given to those students that, although may not be facing difficulties, are consistently working at a slower pace, as well as those students that have a learning pace much faster than the rest of the class [8]. Since all these situations can prevent the student's progress or make them lose interest in the classes, it is crucial to identify them and provide the proper attention and motivation as quickly as possible.

In this paper, we describe the use of *CodeInsights*,, a monitoring tool able of autonomously capture information based on the code snapshots produced by the students while they are solving their assignments. This information about the students' performance is then available to the teacher in real-time, allowing him/her to identify situations that justify some intervention.

In the next section, we present some relevant related work. We proceed by presenting details of our approach, the main results of a field test and, finally, we make some conclusions and provide some suggestions for future improvements.

SIGCSE '18, February 21–24, 2018, Baltimore, MD, USA

ACM ISBN 978-1-4503-5103-4/18/02...$15.00
https://doi.org/10.1145/3159450.3159578

2 RELATED WORK

In recent years, several authors developed systems that collect and analyze snapshots from the source code developed by the students to characterize them and their behavior. An example of such systems is *Retina* [9], which consists of a Java tool that enables teachers to browse through the student's source code and have access to some statistics about their performance. Another interesting system is *TestMyCode* [10], which is mainly an automatic assessment tool, but also collects the snapshots and allows teachers to browse through them and provide feedback to the students (if they request it). *SnapViz* [11] was designed as a straightforward tool that can be used to visualize some aspects of collections of snapshots. *CodeBrowser* [12] is another tool that can be used to browse through student's code snapshots. Aimed especially to visualize data collected from the *BlueJ IDE*, *ClockIt* [13] is another example of a tool that can be used to show aggregate statistics of the student's programming session. Other tools such as *SCORE* [14] or *CSQuiz* [15] rely on low-grained data about the student's behavior while solving a specific assignment.

Authors like Jadud [16, 17], Watson et al. [18], Vihavainen et al. [19], Blikstein et al. [20], Ahadi [21–23] or Bumbacher et al. [24] have proposed metrics and algorithms, not necessarily integrated into a specific tool to characterize the students' performance, progress or behavior. These metrics and algorithms can then be used to identify problematic situations, predict the risk of dropping out or predict the overall performance of the students based on the analysis of code snapshots, or low-grained data. An exhaustive study on the use of data mining and learning analytics techniques, for the purpose of assisting programming students/teachers, was conducted by Ihantola et al. [25].

In general, these tools/approaches require the teacher to browse through the snapshots and try to find patterns himself. Some are highly coupled to a specific set of assignments, other are not much flexible concerning the students' solutions or require much work from the teachers to prepare the assignments (e.g., *TestMyCode* relies on the use of pre-prepared Eclipse projects with the code skeleton and unit tests already provided to the students).

In some of these systems, the data is collected locally in the student's computers and has to be uploaded later to a central repository, meaning that the data is not available in real time, and consequently it may not be possible to intervein in useful time, which in our opinion is a significant limitation.

3 OUR APPROACH

Most teachers provide worksheets with training assignments aimed to prepare the students for more complex assignments. Students that have difficulties solving the simpler assignments will most likely also have problems with the more complex ones. Unfortunately, frequently the students don't submit their solutions to these assignments. Therefore, an important source of information about their performance is discarded, and valuable opportunities to give feedback to the students are lost.

While some students will only work on the assignments during the classes, others will also work at different times and some of them may miss several classes, but still keep solving the assignments. If it is already difficult to track the work done during the classes, without the use of a proper tool it is almost impossible to be aware of what happens outside them.

If no measures are taken, there is a high probability that some students will lose interest in the classes or stay well behind the rest of the colleagues, which may result in drop out or failure.

With this in mind, *CodeInsights* allows teachers to obtain real-time information about their student's performance while solving the assignments, no matter when or where they are. Then, the teachers can identify problematic situations and act proactively to address them. To use *CodeInsights*, the students only need to add one plug-in to the IDE used in the course (e.g., Eclipse or Atom). It is very important to highlight that the students that use this plug-in will not have any disadvantage compared to atudents not using it. The IDE will behave equally for all students.

CodeInsights takes as input snapshots of the source code that the students are writing to solve a particular assignment. These snapshots are automatically sent to a server each time the students run their programs (in most IDEs, running a program implies it is automatically compiled before running it). When the snapshots arrive at the server, the code is compiled and tested locally using a "black-box" automatic assessment technique, and a series of information is collected. The teacher has immediate access to the collected information in the form of a series of visualizations and pre-processed data. Fig. 1 shows a partial view of *CodeInsights'* main dashboard where the teacher has access to a variety of aggregated data about the performance of his/her students.

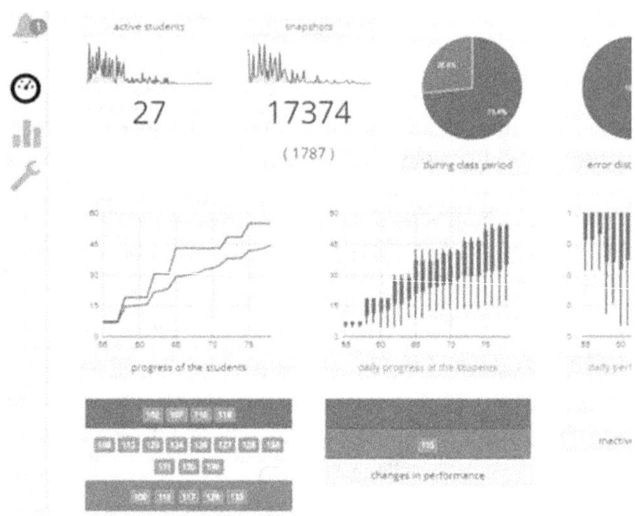

Figure 1: **Partial view of *CodeInsights'* main dashboard**

Unfortunately, the teachers most likely don't have time to be constantly looking at the charts or browsing through the data and snapshots, particularly outside the classes period. So, to call their attention, we have developed an automatic notification system that will notify the teacher about situations that eventually can lead to problems. These include an unusual number of lines of code, compilation errors, number of attempts per assignment, assignments not even attempted, or number of "unfinished" assignments. In reality, *CodeInsights* can generate notifications about virtually any aspect that can be observed from the data.

Let's consider a scenario where the teacher has presented a worksheet with ten "one-function" training assignments. Ideally, the students should keep a similar working pace while solving them. It would be easier for the teacher to decide when to explain the purpose of the next assignment or present some concept needed to address a particular assignment. Unfortunately, this hardly happens, and while faster-paced students may already be solving assignment 9, others may be stuck on assignments 2 or 3.

In order to identify these situations, the system periodically checks if some students are working considerably faster or slower than the colleagues. The process starts by measuring each student's performance at a given moment *t*, SP_t. In general terms, the performance is defined as the percentage of assignments that each student solved correctly for a period of time (since the worksheet is published till the deadline).

$$SPt = \frac{WD}{G} \qquad (1)$$

The value for SP_t is obtained using Equation 1, where *WD* represents the work done in that period by the student (i.e., the assignments solved correctly). Since not all assignments have the same difficulty level, a *wi* weight is used to reinforce the difficulty of each assignment (easy → *wi* = 1; medium → *wi* = 1,5; difficult → *wi* = 2). The value for *WD* is then is obtained by summing all the *wi* values for the assignments that the student could solve correctly. In (1), *G* represents the goals for that period and it is the sum of the *wi* values for all the assignments that were supposed to be solved in that period.

For instance, let's consider a worksheet with 5 assignments (2 easy, 2 medium and 1 difficult) published on day *t1* with *t4* as the deadline. If at moment *t2*, student "A" could solve all the assignments, the value of SP_{t2} is 1 (7 / 7). For this student, the value of SP_t at *t3* and *t4* will also be 1, which means that s/he was able to solve the proposed tasks very fast. If in the same scenario, student "B" could solve only one easy assignment at *t2*, SP_{t2} = 0.14 (1/7). If at *t3* s/he was able to solve an additional assignment of medium difficulty, SP_{t3} = 0.36 (2.5/7). Finally, if at *t4* s/he could solve all easy and medium assignments, SP_{t4} = 0.71 (5/7).

We are mainly interested in identifying outliers (i.e., students with a performance that is substantially different from the average). So, after determining the value of SP_t for each student, the system will determine the mean (λ) and mean absolute deviation around the mean (*MAD*) for these values. Finally, for each student, the system will compare SP_t with $\lambda \pm MAD$.

If $SPt > (\lambda + MAD)$, we consider that the student is currently performing at a fast pace (faster than most of the colleagues). On the other side, if $SPt < (\lambda - MAD)$, we will consider that the student is performing at a slow pace (slower than most of the colleagues). The remaining students will be regarded as working at an average pace. Fig. 2 illustrates this process where each dot represents the SP_t value for a particular student.

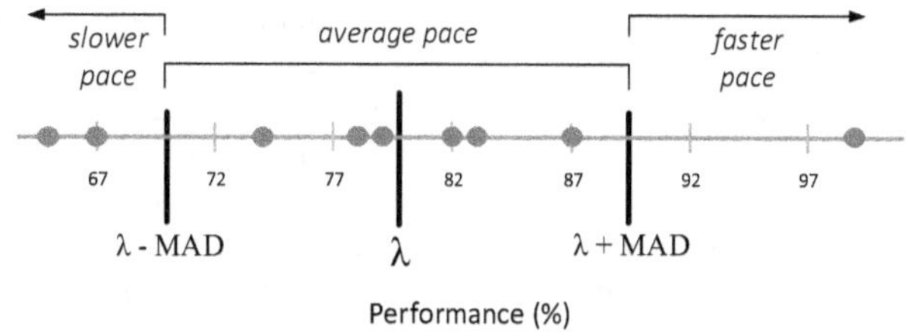

Figure 2: **Illustration of the approach used to determine which students are considered slow or fast paced**

When the system identifies some students working at a slower or faster pace than most of their colleagues, a notification to the teacher is generated (Fig. 3).

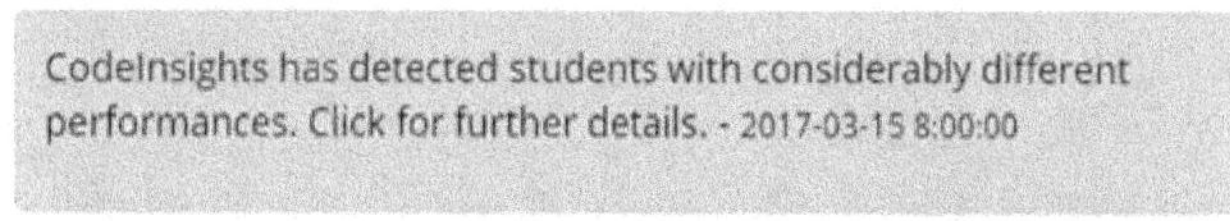

Figure 3: **Example of one notification about the existence of students working with considerably different paces**

If, in the period under consideration, a student was not active, that information is also stored as it may be useful in the future. After characterizing each student's performance, the system will also look for considerable changes (e.g., a student was previously considered "slow paced" and currently is "average paced").

The occurrence of changes can be an indication that a student may be facing difficulties, losing interest in the classes or on the contrary, may indicate a sudden increase in the interest and thereby on the performance of a particular student. Either way, we believe that it is important that the teacher is aware of these changes and therefore the system will also notify the teacher (Fig.4). In both cases presented previously, an email with the content of the notifications will also be sent to the teachers.

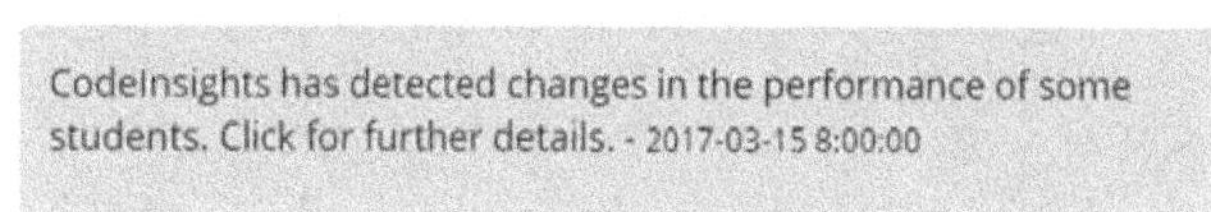

Figure 4: **Example of one notification about the existence of changes in the student's performance**

When the teacher sees the notifications or the emails, s/he can explore further details, such as the list of students that were inactive or that are performing faster and slower than the rest of the class. For each student, the teacher has access to information about the evolution and consistency of the performance through time in comparison with the class; the list of assignments that the student attempted to solve (and the final result); and the list of programming concepts related to the assignments that the s/he is having difficulties to solve correctly.

Fig. 5 shows details about the performance of a student that was performing consistently as an "average" student, but suddenly had a significant drop in his performance and a halt in the overall progress (blue lines in both cases).

The teacher has access to all the attempts the students made for an assignment. S/he can browse through the source code, view a series of metrics (e.g., number of lines of code, execution time, number of errors), check the compilation or run-time errors, or how the code behaved with the test cases. The teacher can also temporarily edit the source code and test it. (Fig. 6).

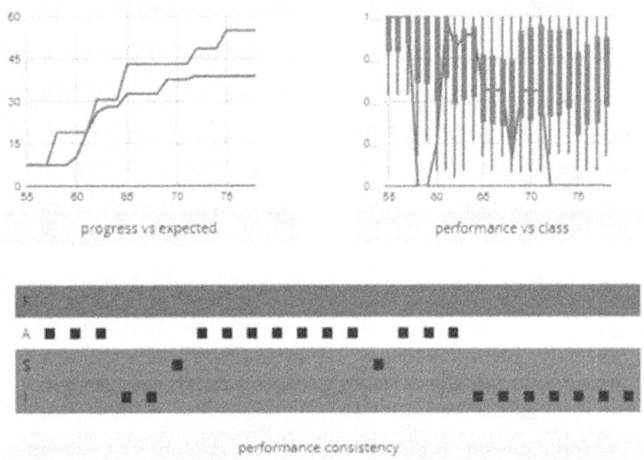

Figure 5: **Partial view of the details about the progress/ performance of a student**

Figure 6: **Partial view of the details of a particular snapshot**

Supported by all the information available, the teacher can provide differentiated assistance to each student, according to his/her individual needs/difficulties. For instance, if a student has difficulties with nested loops, the teacher can provide him/her with additional examples. To keep the students that are working at a faster pace motivated, the teachers could, for instance, provide some more advanced assignments.

In any case, if needed, the teacher can give feedback to the student about a specific snapshot directly on the system. In this case, an email with the source code and the feedback provided by the teacher will be sent to the student.

One significant aspect involving the use of *CodeInsights* concerns the ethical and privacy issues of collecting and using this type of data. It is important to highlight that the data collected is only used for the purpose strictly related to assisting the teacher's to improve their student's performance.

4 FIELD TEST

CodeInsights was evaluated during the first weeks of an Introduction to Server-side Web Development with PHP course in a higher education school. Although PHP might not be the most obvious option to test the system, the results obtained in this experiment are consistent with the results previously obtained while using Java or Python.

The student's involvement in the experiment was voluntary, and there were no consequences for those not participating. Though, before the start of the experiment, the teacher explained in detail which data would be collected and for what purposes.

During the period of the experiment, the students were expected to solve 51 "one-function" assignments with different difficulty levels. The system received approximately 13.500 valid snapshots, from 27 different students (17 were enrolled in the course, and 10 were repeating it due to a previous failure).

Approximately 61% of the snapshots were received outside the classes period. Interestingly, the students with a faster pace worked essentially during the classes period and within minutes immediately after the classes (even while attending a different class). Students working with a slower pace needed more time outside the class to keep progressing.

The system checked for the existence of differences in the student's performance, on a daily basis at 8h00.

Through the experiment, the teacher made approximately 100 direct interventions outside the classes period using *CodeInsights* (the students received feedback via email) and approximately 60 direct interventions during the classes (the students received feedback from the teacher in person). Some of these interventions were made in response to notifications, while others took place because the teacher was browsing through the data and visualizations and found situations that needed to be addressed. As an example, at some point, several students were making the same mistake while building an if clause with two conditions. Instead of `if($a>10 && $a<20)` they were doing `if(10 < $a < 20)`, which obviously resulted in error.

In most cases, after receiving the feedback, the students accepted the recommendations and took the adequate measures to correct their code. In a small number of situations, the teacher provided feedback to the student about a specific assignment more than once. There were also situations where the student took the initiative to request help from the teacher.

The teacher also made several general interventions using the whiteboard to give additional examples to all the students (as he was able to see in *CodeInsights* that several of them were having similar difficulties). Finally, the teacher provided several additional assignments to students working at a faster pace, since they were able to complete the proposed assignments very quickly, and there was the need to keep them motivated.

Fig. 7 shows the distribution of the SP_t values for all the days of the experiment (each column represents one day). The lower value for each column represents the student(s) with the lowest value for SP_t while the upper value represents the student(s) with the highest value of SP_t for that day. The rectangle on top of each line corresponds to the interval ranging value from $\sigma - MAD$ to $\sigma + MAD$ (average zone). The figure also contains information about the start of each period (WS1-WS5).

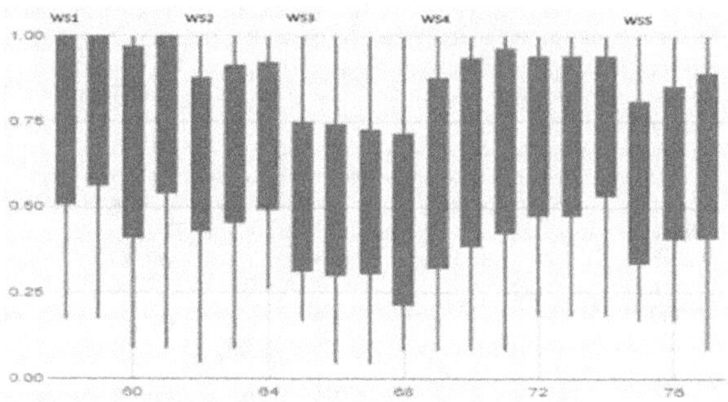

Figure 7: **Evolution of the value for *SP***

It is possible to observe that in the first day of all periods (worksheet) there were some students able to complete all proposed assignments for the period. On the other hand, some students were not even able to complete 25% of the assignments at the end of the same period. It is also possible to see that the value for *MAD* was very consistent through the experiment, which means that there was always a high dispersion in the student's performance (even after the teacher interventions). Obviously, the ideal scenario would be that all students have a similar performance, but that is not common, and it didn't also happen in our experiment.

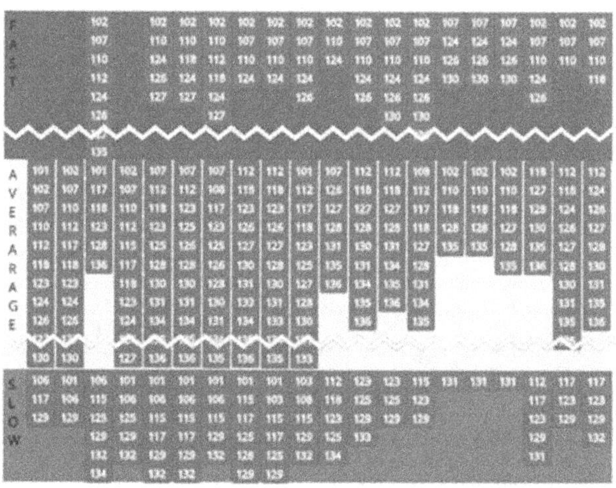

Figure 8: **Distribution of the students by working pace**

The teacher has access to another visualization containing information about the students that are classified in each group. In Fig. 8, each column represents a different day of the experiment, and each small rectangle contains the id of a student. When the teacher hovers a specific rectangle, a tooltip with the name of the student will be shown, and if the teacher clicks on it, the system will display a page similar to Fig. 5, allowing him/her to access detailed information about that student.

Observing Fig. 8, it is possible to see that the performance of some students was not consistent as they were moving from one "group" to the other, in particular between "average" and "fast".

When analyzing the profile of the students that were frequently classified as working at a slower pace, we find mainly students that had already been enrolled in this course in the past, and most of them revealed a severe lack of reasoning and programming skills. In part, this explains why they were not able to move forward even after the teacher gave them feedback. Most of these students ended up dropping out, and only one of them was able to pass with the lowest possible grade (10 in a 0-20 scale).

On the opposite side, in the "fast-paced" group, we find mostly students that were enrolling the course for the first time, in most cases, they had an excellent performance in previous programming courses using C and Java.

In the end, only one of the students classified at least once as working at a "fast pace" was not able to pass. All the other students were approved with excellent grades (16-19 in a 0-20 scale). Most of the students more consistently present in the "average" group were also able to pass with good grades, while, unfortunately, some other failed.

If we don't take into account the "ghost" students (students that didn't participate in any activity), this year's approval rate was approximately 62% which highly contrasts with the previous year's approval rate of 38% (also not considering the "ghost" students). Obviously, we cannot argue that these results are a direct result of the use of *CodeInsights*. However, we are absolutely confident that it had a significant contribution, as it allowed the teacher to use a different approach with the students.

Unfortunately, not all students took good advantage of the teacher feedback. Still, some of them mentioned that they felt more secure while programming since they knew that the teacher was monitoring them, and could support them whenever needed.

It is worth highlighting that *CodeInsights* will not take any autonomous action or automatically provide feedback to the student. The purpose of the system is only to collect, process and make the data available to the teacher. It is entirely up to the teacher to decide if and what should be done to overcome the problems that the students may be facing. Although the experiment occurred only in the first weeks of the course, it was able to provide valuable insights into what was to come.

5 CONCLUSIONS

With this work, we have presented *CodeInsights*, a tool that can be used by teachers to monitor, in real time, the performance of the students and identify those that are working at a pace considerably faster or slower than their colleagues. With the information available, the teachers can make the adequate pedagogical interventions (e.g., different assignments, additional instructional materials) to keep the students motivated and help those that might be facing difficulties.

It is important to notice that the use of the system per se will not have any direct impact on the students' performance. *CodeInsights* provides data, visualizations, and notifications to the teachers, but if they do not check the system regularly and if they don't act based on the information provided then the impact of the system will be close to null.

The duration of the experiment and the number of students involved may limit the validity of our study. However, we believe that the results allowed us to show that the system can, in fact, provide the teacher a real insight into the student's performance and assist him/her in taking appropriate measures.

All the visualizations included in this paper were taken directly from *CodeInsights* without any editing, and these visualizations were immediately (and automatically) available to the teacher as soon as the snapshots were processed.

Currently, the system is deciding if the notifications should or not be displayed to the teachers based on a simple approach. We have already implemented an artificial selective attention mechanism based on cognitive and affective feelings (namely, surprise) more adequate to the human being's cognitive processes [26], which is currently being tested.

Other aspects that will deserve our attention in the near future concern the eventual integration of aditional metrics to measure the student's performance and progress as well as investigate which measures taken by the teachers while using *CodeInsights* were more effective.

Although *CodeInsights* was created to be used in the context of programming classes using code snapshots as input, with minor adjustments it could be used in other courses and with other inputs such as data coming from clickers used in the classes [27].

ACKNOWLEDGMENTS

The authors would like to thank the teacher and all the students that participated in the experiment.

REFERENCES

[1] Arnold Pears, Stephen Seidman, Lauri Malmi, Linda Mannila, Elizabeth Adams, Jens Bennedsen, Marie Devlin, and James Paterson. 2007. A Survey of Literature on the Teaching of Introductory Programming. *Working Group Reports on ITiCSE on Innovation and Technology in Computer Science Education* (New York, NY, USA, 2007), 204–223.

[2] Anabela Gomes and António J. Mendes. 2007. Learning to program - difficulties and solutions. *International Conference on Engineering Education* (Sep. 2007).

[3] Janet Carter. 2010. The problems of teaching programming: Do they change with time? *In 11th Annual HEA-ICS conference* (Durham, Aug. 2010), 182–196.

[4] Malcolm Morrison and Timothy S. Newman. 2001. A Study of the Impact of Student Background and Preparedness on Outcomes in CS I. *Proceedings of the Thirty-second SIGCSE Technical Symposium on Computer Science Education* (New York, NY, USA, 2001), 179–183.

[5] Anthony Robins. 2010. Learning edge momentum: A new account of outcomes in CS1. *Computer Science Education.* 20, 1 (2010), 37–71.

[6] Raymond Lister. 2011. COMPUTING EDUCATION RESEARCH: Geek Genes and Bimodal Grades. *ACM Inroads.* 1, 3 (Sep. 2011), 16–17.

[7] André Raabe and Júlia Silva. 2004. Um Ambiente para Atendimento as Dificuldades de Aprendizagem de Algoritmos. *Anais do XXV Congresso da Sociedade Brasileira de Computação* (2004).

[8] Janet Carter, Su White, Karen Fraser, Stanislav Kurkovsky, Colette McCreesh, and Malcolm Wieck. 2010. ITiCSE 2010 Working Group Report Motivating Our Top Students. *Proceedings of the 2010 ITiCSE Working Group Reports* (New York, NY, USA, 2010), 29–47.

[9] Christian Murphy, Gail Kaiser, Kristin Loveland, and Sahar Hasan. 2009. Retina: Helping Students and Instructors Based on Observed Programming Activities. *Proceedings of the 40th ACM Technical Symposium on Computer Science Education* (New York, NY, USA, 2009), 178–182.

[10] Arto Vihavainen, Thomas Vikberg, Matti Luukkainen, and Martin Pärtel. 2013. Scaffolding Students' Learning Using Test My Code. *Proceedings of the 18th ACM Conference on Innovation and Technology in Computer Science Education* (New York, NY, USA, 2013), 117–122.

[11] Evan Balzuweit and Jaime Spacco. 2013. SnapViz: Visualizing Programming Assignment Snapshots. *Proceedings of the 18th ACM Conference on Innovation and Technology in Computer Science Education* (New York, NY, USA, 2013), 350–350.

[12] Kenny Heinonen, Kasper Hirvikoski, Matti Luukkainen, and Arto Vihavainen. 2014. Using CodeBrowser to Seek Differences Between Novice Programmers. *Proceedings of the 45th ACM Technical Symposium on Computer Science Education* (New York, NY, USA, 2014), 229–234.

[13] Cindy Norris, Frank Barry, James B. Fenwick Jr., Kathryn Reid, and Josh Rountree. 2008. ClockIt: Collecting Quantitative Data on How Beginning Software Developers Really Work. *Proceedings of the 13th Annual Conference on Innovation and Technology in Computer Science Education* (New York, NY, USA, 2008), 37–41.

[14] Maximilian Wittmann, Matt Bower, and Manolya Kavakli. 2011. Using the SCORE software package to analyse novice computer graphics programming. *Proceedings of the 16th annual joint conference on Innovation and technology in computer science education.* (Darmstadt, Germany, Jun. 2011).

[15] Daniel Toll. 2016. *Measuring Programming Assignment Effort.* Linnaeus University.

[16] Matthew C. Jadud. 2006. Methods and Tools for Exploring Novice Compilation Behaviour. *Proceedings of the Second International Workshop on Computing Education Research* (New York, NY, USA, 2006), 73–84.

[17] Matthew C. Jadud and Brian Dorn. 2015. Aggregate Compilation Behavior: Findings and Implications from 27,698 Users. *Proceedings of the Eleventh Annual International Conference on International Computing Education Research* (New York, NY, USA, 2015), 131–139.

[18] Christopher Watson, Frederick W. B. Li, and Jamie L. Godwin. 2013. Predicting Performance in an Introductory Programming Course by Logging and Analyzing Student Programming Behavior. *Proceedings of the 2013 IEEE 13th International Conference on Advanced Learning Technologies* (Washington, DC, USA, 2013), 319–323.

[19] Arto Vihavainen, Matti Luukkainen, and Jaakko Kurhila. 2013. Using Students' Programming Behavior to Predict Success in an Introductory Mathematics Course. *Proceedings of the 6th International Conference on Educational Data Mining* (Memphis, Tennessee, United States, 2013).

[20] Paulo Blikstein, Marcelo Worsley, Chris Piech, Mehran Sahami, Steven Cooper, and Daphne Koller. 2014. Programming Pluralism: Using Learning Analytics to Detect Patterns in the Learning of Computer Programming. *Journal of the Learning Sciences.* 23, 4 (Oct. 2014), 561–599.

[21] Alireza Ahadi. 2016. Early Identification of Novice Programmers' Challenges in Coding Using Machine Learning Techniques. *Proceedings of the 2016 ACM Conference on International Computing Education Research* (New York, NY, USA, 2016), 263–264.

[22] Alireza Ahadi, Raymond Lister, and Arto Vihavainen. 2016. On the Number of Attempts Students Made on Some Online Programming Exercises During Semester and Their Subsequent Performance on Final Exam Questions. *Proceedings of the 2016 ACM Conference on Innovation and Technology in Computer Science Education* (New York, NY, USA, 2016), 218–223.

[23] Alireza Ahadi, Raymond Lister, Shahil Lal, Juho Leinonen, and Arto Hellas. 2017. Performance and Consistency in Learning to Program. *Proceedings of the Nineteenth Australasian Computing Education Conference* (New York, NY, USA, 2017), 11–16.

[24] Engin Bumbacher, Alfredo Sandes, Amit Deutsch, and Paulo Blikstein. 2013. Student Coding Styles as Predictors of Help-Seeking Behavior. *Artificial Intelligence in Education* (Jul. 2013), 856–859.

[25] Petri Ihantola et al. 2015. Educational Data Mining and Learning Analytics in Programming: Literature Review and Case Studies. *Proceedings of the 2015 ITiCSE on Working Group Reports* (New York, NY, USA, 2015), 41–63.

[26] Nuno Gil Fonseca, Luís Macedo. and António José Mendes. 2017. Monitoring the Progress of Programming Students Supported by a Digital Teaching Assistant. *Progress in Artificial Intelligence. EPIA 2017. Lecture Notes in Computer Science.* vol 10423. Springer, Cham 2017 .

[27] Leo Porter, Daniel Zingaro, and Raymond Lister. 2014. Predicting Student Success Using Fine Grain Clicker Data. *Proceedings of the Tenth Annual Conference on International Computing Education Research* (New York, NY, USA, 2014), 51–58.

Reflections on 17 Years of ICT Capstone Project Coordination: Effective Strategies for Managing Clients, Teams and Assessment

Nicole Herbert
University of Tasmania
Australia
Nicole.Herbert@utas.edu.au

ABSTRACT

Many undergraduate ICT degrees culminate with students completing a team-based capstone project under academic supervision. Capstone projects provided by external clients facilitate authentic experiential learning, but sourcing external projects can be difficult, and there can be issues managing industry clients within an academic setting. Capstone projects also provide an opportunity for professional skill development to increase student employability, though to fully assess generic learning outcomes requires evaluating more than the final product created for the client. Teamwork can have a positive impact on student learning, however it is challenging to determine a process of assessment that enables formative and summative assessment that does not require an academic to immerse themselves within a team to evaluate an individual's contribution. Team members are often the best source of meaningful information, and self and peer assessment is commonly used as part of an assessment scheme, but to ensure the objectivity and integrity of the final grade it is necessary to correlate data from a variety of sources. This experience report reflects on a team-based capstone project approach that has been offered for 17 years and proposes some effective strategies for coordinating the more challenging aspects of capstone projects.

ACM Reference format:

Nicole Herbert. 2018. Reflections on 17 years of ICT capstone project coordination: effective strategies for managing clients, teams and assessment. In *Proceedings of The 49th ACM Technical Symposium on Computer Science Education, Baltimore, MD USA, February 2018 (SIGCSE'18)*, 6 pages. DOI: https://doi.org/10.1145/3159450.3159584

1. INTRODUCTION

Capstone projects allow students to apply the knowledge and technical and non-technical skills they have acquired throughout their degree to a substantial real world project, while developing professional skills such as teamwork and project management. Capstone projects have become commonplace in Information and Communication Technology (ICT) bachelor's degrees and there are many resources available for coordinators [2,3,4]. Capstone projects involving real experiences (such as creating software that will be used) are a form of authentic learning and enable students to bridge theory and practice by actively engaging in the work of their professional community, and they better prepare students for their post-graduate career than a typical assignment [5]. Research has shown that authentic learning experiences allow students to turn information into application of knowledge [6].

This report proposes some effective combinations of strategies for managing the more challenging aspects of coordinating capstone projects: sourcing projects and client management, team formation and management, assessing student learning against generic learning outcomes, and ensuring individual accountability.

SIGCSE '18, February 21–24, 2018, Baltimore, MD, USA

ACM 978-1-4503-5103-4/18/02...$15.00
https://doi.org/10.1145/3159450.3159584

2. OUR CONTEXT

The University of Tasmania is responsible for developing work-ready graduates for a broad local ICT industry. A renewed ICT curriculum was implemented in 2014 [1], which focuses on professional and technical ICT skills. The long-standing capstone project continued largely in its current form due to its overwhelming success as indicated by: the number of industry awards received for student software; the extremely low failure rate; the feedback from clients on the final products; success of the graduates in finding employment; and the number of awards received by staff for the design and delivery of the experience.

ICT Project is our compulsory capstone experience for final year students in our three-year Bachelor of Information and Communication Technology degree offered on two campuses. All students have the same core background knowledge in the areas of project management, programming in a number of languages, databases, web development, software design, and some students have knowledge in game design and development. ICT Project is a 26-week experience divided into two 13-week units; the students get two grades. Students normally work in teams of six or seven students on their own team project. The student's final grade is based on a team mark and an individual mark for their contribution.

3. SOURCING REAL PROJECTS

Our projects involve developing a significant piece of software for real clients who will use the software and fall under a broad range of domains: PC applications, web applications, game or virtual reality systems, online content systems, mobile applications, systems administration software, internet system software, or data management systems. Obtaining a broad range of projects for the students to choose from, particularly for a regional university, can be difficult especially as there should be more projects available than teams to give students choices to match career goals [4].

***Look beyond the ICT industry for real clients*:** Students perform better on capstone projects when their projects engage with real clients and the end product will be used [7]. 17 years ago it was difficult for us to source projects with real clients but it became easier each year as students demonstrated what they were capable of and as our alumni transitioned into the industry and were able to nominate projects either for their own entrepreneurial business or persuade their employers of the benefits for them (e.g. free software, preview future employees). An effective strategy to source projects is to look beyond the ICT industry for "real clients" to provide the variety of projects to meet the future career paths of students. Meaningful projects can be undertaken for local ICT businesses either for their clients or as an in-house software system, government departments that lack human resources for non-critical software projects, non-ICT businesses that require IT-related solutions, researchers in scientific organisations that require a software tool for data gathering or analysis. Table 1 illustrates the spread of projects undertaken in ICT Project.

***In-house projects can broaden the local ICT industry*:** ICT academic staff can provide meaningful projects related to their research or their teaching that have the potential to broaden the local industry impacted by a regional university e.g. our games research group offer projects with a view to growing our local games industry. In-house projects though do not provide the experience of dealing with an external client. One effective strategy is to have the staff member involve some external people in the project that the students will have to deal with e.g. an external research organisation or staff from a different discipline.

Table 1. ICT Project Client-Type Data

Year	ICT	Government	Non-ICT	Research	In-house
2014	3	1	2	2	
2015	3	1	5	1	2
2016	3	1	4	1	1
2017	4		4	1	3

4. MANAGING CLIENTS IN ACADEMIA

Academia presents a number of issues that don't normally exist when managing a project: zero budget, inflexible timeframes, inexperienced developers, and academic assessment. The three major client-related problems that impact on students the most are: absentee clients at a critical time; lack of client supplied content/data to fully demonstrate the software; and excessive scope creep particularly in the final stages when clients are more aware of the quantity and quality that the students can achieve. Preparing students is critical; these are real world problems (and ones that most lead to project failure in industry).

***Ensure students interact often with client*:** Students need to be aware of the seriousness of these issues. To reduce the risk and minimise the impact they need to keep the client involved, request information early and consistently at each meeting with the client. The appointment of a client liaison (discussed next section) can help mitigate the problems, as communication is paramount. An effective strategy for scope creep and lack of content is to allow many opportunities for clients to provide input and feedback early into the project process enabling them to see the necessity for the content and also make suggestions for additional features early.

***Ensure clients understand the academic constraints*:** An effective strategy for managing clients is to provide them with documentation that outlines their obligations and for the coordinator to remind clients and students at critical intervals of key behaviours that can lead to project failure. "Client issues" should be a regular topic at meetings with the coordinator to allow students to seek suggestions on how to manage their client. The coordinator also needs to establish a cut-off date with all clients for the supply of content and after that allow the use of temporary content that will demonstrate that the software works, that can be removed before handover. An effective strategy for scope creep is to prevent the inclusion of features that could lead to non-completion once a certain point is reached (for us that is week 18). Our students produce a reference manual that includes instructions on how to modify the software with a focus on new features that have been requested but can't be included within our timeframe.

5. TEAM FORMATION

For some students there is a lot of anxiety associated with forming a team and getting the project they really want, particularly for something that is such a critical part of their degree. In ICT Project all teams are formed and projects allocated on day one during a 5-hour workshop held on each campus to reduce the longevity of this anxiety. Prior to the workshop students are expected to have read an extensive manual that explains all key elements of the capstone experience and a brief (one-page each) description of all available projects for that year.

***Ensure students explore the range of projects*:** Students will tend to choose projects with someone they know. They also tend to choose projects on the basis of relevance to future career goals [7], i.e. web project or game project, and as there are a number of projects for each type they need more information to differentiate the intricacies of each project. "Speed-dating" is an effective strategy to combat these problems. All the potential clients attend the initial workshop and talk for two minutes about their project to the entire class and then the students interview (in random groups) 5-7 potential clients for 10 minutes each. This results in more external clients being selected as they learn more about the projects and begin to form a relationship with the client.

Use project preference to form teams: During the workshop each student submits their top five project preferences allowing them to match their project with their future career aspirations and they also have the opportunity to submit names of four people they would like to work with. Once in employment students will have little influence over whom they work with, so while they can submit team member preferences this is not the key-determining factor in forming the teams. Every attempt is made to give students their first preference as this can have an impact on commitment [7] and we are successful 60% of the time. This is sometimes not possible as too few students express interest in a project to form a team (on average < 12% of class) and sometimes too many students want to do the same project. One effective strategy to manage this problem is to give students the opportunity to write a case for a particular project, this is similar to applying for employment (on average < 15% of class take this opportunity). The coordinator can then consider a student's case for a particular project and allocate accordingly. The other information about preferred team members and lower ranked project preferences are then used to form teams of the appropriate size for the project.

6. TEAM MANAGEMENT

It takes time and experience to develop the skills to be an effective team member. Placing students in teams and expecting them to be ideal team members and successfully manage their first real project is unrealistic. It is necessary to provide sufficient guidance and consistent supervision to individuals and teams.

Ensure consistent supervision of teams: Our most effective strategy for team management is having the one coordinator supervise all the teams on both campuses, 200 km apart, for 17 years. Having just one supervisor for all teams means there is no time spent managing and training supervisors to ensure that all teams receive equivalent supervision. All the coordinator time can be spent on the teams. Our coordinator had industry experience having worked in the industry for 10 years, but was relatively inexperienced with academia. Over time the coordinator has developed a knowledge bank of potential problems and solutions for capstone projects, and acts as a valuable mentor to all teams. While the coordinator travels regularly to the remote campus, communication with all teams is largely via email, apart from scheduled meetings with each team. This approach might raise concerns with workload. We operate a workload model based on hours taken to complete the associated tasks for a unit (a unit is one of eight subjects that a student completes each year). The total time for ICT Project (two units) was approximately 626 hours in 2017 (based on 75 students and 12 teams); this includes all classes, team meetings, material preparation, student consultation, travel time, and assessment. For comparison, another typical unit represents 462 hours of work (not taken by just one person).

Provide oversight without intrusion: To effectively manage the teams it is necessary to meet regularly with each team. These meetings are important for developing an understanding of the inner workings of a team and the information can be used to determine an individual grade for each student. In ICT Project face-to-face communication between the coordinator and each team is largely conducted at management meetings which are held initially fortnightly for the first six weeks and then every 3 weeks for the rest of the project. Each meeting lasts for 20-30 minutes and the main purpose is to provide formative feedback on work products and discuss any issues related to the current phase, team or client. These meetings can be kept this short because before the meetings are held there is a 2-hour lecture where all current tasks and associated assessment can be explained and general questions answered, and thus the meetings can be restricted to discussing just the project specific details. These meetings (and other accumulated data that is discussed later) mean that the coordinator doesn't need to intrude into the day-to-day workings of the team and thus influence the way teams work [8].

Allow self-management of teams: An effective strategy for team management is to allow self-management by giving the students' roles and clear duty statements (which they should be encouraged to further develop themselves). These are administrative roles, not authoritative roles, and the students should rotate roles (we rotate each semester) as they provide significant learning experiences. Our key roles are:

Client liaison: provides easy access for the client to the team, coordinates the communication with the client, organises client meetings, keeps the client informed of progress and requests relevant content/data.

Project manager: coordinates the team, runs the team meetings. Their main role is managing task allocation across all aspects of the project; the different leads (below) supply the tasks and the project manager ensures all tasks are allocated (task allocation should be as fair and democratic as possible).

Lead Programmer: locates useful tools and software for the project, implements prototypes and the starting codebase, manages configuration and integration, and identifies implementation tasks to be allocated to team members.

Lead Designer: one of the main visionaries of the overall software. They coordinate the analysis and design documentation, and identify tasks related to particular documents to be allocated.

Lead Artist/Interfacer: oversees the art/interface prototyping, manages the asset library, and maintains the artistic vision and visual consistency of the artwork/interfaces throughout the software. They identify artwork/interfaces tasks to be allocated.

It is important to note that these roles are identifying a leader, but all team members work on the programming, design and interfaces. These are substantial development projects and each team member can spend more than 200 hours programming.

Identify team issues early: Another effective strategy for managing teams is early identification of team related issues and providing them with strategies to deal with them. A later section will discuss self and peer assessment which is one of the main forms for identifying issues, but problems can also be indicated by poor process products submitted for assessment, emails by concerned students to the coordinator, and the students themselves raising the issues in the management meetings. For these mechanisms to work the students must have confidence in the coordinator to maintain their confidentiality and for the students to be assured that the identification of an issue is not going to cause loss of marks. This is important: the impact of an issue can lead to loss of marks as it results in poor work being submitted. Having issues and learning how to deal with them is a key aspect of the entire learning experience.

7. ASSESSMENT OF STUDENT LEARNING

Providing an authentic experience typically has students work in teams on different projects. Performing a consistent and accurate assessment of individual student contributions to the work produced by a team as well as assessing teamwork itself presents numerous challenges; particularly when the projects themselves are significantly different [4]. Capstone projects should assess more than the final software product as there is much more learning than just software development. Clear [9] spoke about the three p's in capstone project assessment: product, process and progression in learning. Capstone projects can also be extremely valuable in verbal and written communication and teamwork skill development so assessment of professionalism is also warranted.

***Assess the four P's*:** An effective strategy for assessment of capstone projects is to include evaluation of the product, process, professionalism and progression in learning [9]. To do this the capstone project should include a number of assessment activities. In ICT Project in the first semester teams progress through a number of phases each requiring process work products: concept, analysis, and design, and implementation of release one of their software. In second semester the phases are: design review, implementation of release 2 including testing, marketing and manuals. Basing capstone project results solely on the software product does not recognize the difference between individual students' contributions during the different phases of the software development lifecycle. Initially over assessment was an issue, but the assessment strategy has been refined by ending first semester with the implementation of release one and reducing the elements required in the design review, testing and marketing phases in second semester to allow them to focus on the implementation. Table 2 shows the break down of our assessment activities.

In our assessment the final product is only worth approximately a third of the final grade for each semester. In semester one there is a focus on process and the documentation that is produced during the early phases of a project. In each semester there are marks for professionalism, which is not easy to measure but we evaluate timesheets as a record of individual contribution, interaction with the client via a survey, and teamwork via self and peer assessment. In semester 2 the teams develop their verbal communication via a final presentation in front of the client and external assessors and production of a team movie. It is important to note, and this will be discussed in the next section, that team members receive individual grades for all the components based on their level of contribution.

Table 2. Assessment Tasks for ICT Project

Semester 1		Semester 2	
Concept Report	10%	Design Review	10%
Analysis Report	15%	Testing Reports	7%
Design Report	20%	Manuals	15%
Release 1	30%	Release 2	35%
Teamwork	5%	Teamwork	5%
Client Interaction	5%	Client Interaction	3%
Timesheets	5%	Timesheets	5%
		Presentation/Movie	15%
Reflection Report	10%	Reflection Report	5%

Key: Product | Process | Professionalism | Progression

***Use reflection to improve outcomes*:** A self-reflection report can help students improve the way they work [8,9]. In 2014 we introduced an individual reflection report at the end of both semesters to assess "progression in learning" and provide formative feedback to help students learn from semester one heading into semester two. This report asks students to reflect on their contribution during each phase and their role but also focus on their impact on the project as a whole and their individual growth in learning. They reflect on why things went well/not-so-well for their team, their biggest lesson learnt, and the impact of the project on their confidence. The reflection report is a significant self and team evaluation tool. An effective strategy to maximise the benefits from the reports is for the coordinator to summarise the key and common elements that each student reports on within a team at the end of semester one and use them as elements for discussion at the first management meeting in semester two as guidance for areas of improvement both in process and teamwork.

***Provide formative assessment to increase learning*:** Capstone projects provide significant learning experiences throughout the entire process and with the aid of formative feedback the learning can be increased. If there is too much focus on just summative assessments, students focus on obtaining good grades rather than effective learning [8]. An effective strategy for increasing the formative feedback is to allow students to request feedback on incomplete work products, particularly in first semester to get their project off to a solid start by using the expertise of the coordinator built over many years. The onus to seek formative feedback should be on the students, and we do not allowed them to seek it the day of or the day before something is due to encourage them to complete tasks early. The final mark should not be affected by whether they sought formative feedback, the teams will realise that the feedback can significantly increase the quality of final products and thus the final mark.

Another effective strategy to increase the formative feedback is to turn summative feedback into formative feedback. In the real world if a mistake or improvement was identified in an early work product it would be acted upon. In ICT Project we allow resubmission for assessment of key work products after the summative feedback to encourage students to make these improvements to lead to better outcomes for students and clients.

Include external assessors for moderation: When there is one supervisor for all teams it ensures that the assessment is consistent across projects. It is good practice though to get some external validation to ensure that no bias has developed over the duration of the project. An effective strategy is to have other assessors evaluate some of the final work products. In ICT Project the client and two other academic assessors along with the coordinator evaluate release two and the presentation.

8. INDIVIDUAL ACCOUNTABILITY

Teamwork can have a positive impact on student learning, however it is challenging to determine a process of assessment that does not require an academic to immerse themselves within a team to evaluate an individual's contribution. Too much weight given to a team result can allow individuals to be carried, and likewise a focus on individual assessment could result in individuals not working towards common goals [8]. In ICT Project each student gets an individual mark for each assessed work product e.g. an individual mark for the concept report. Each student's result is based partly on the evaluation of the work product and partly on how they contributed to that work product. Overall each student's final grade consists of an individual component that is marked out of 45 and a team component that is marked out of 55 – this near even split ensures that individuals work towards team goals but also ensures individuals do their share to pass. To pass a student must achieve at least 50% overall with at least 45% for both components.

Ensure integrity of individual grade: Gates, Delgado, Mondragon [10] identified the importance of structuring individual accountability to ensure that all members of a team contribute to the project concluding that team members are often the best source of meaningful data. Self and peer assessment is used throughout ICT Project allowing for early identification of under (and over) performing students. The most effective strategy to ensure the integrity of the final grade is to correlate data from a variety of sources [11]. A range of tools are used in ICT Project to allow students to indicate their own contribution and that of team members, the evolution of each tool is described in detail in [12]:

- Timesheets – weekly online timesheets for students to enter the time spent on each project related task that week.
- Self/Peer Evaluation Surveys (SPES) – students rate each team member (including self) on a list of behavioural characteristics of good teamwork.
- Individual Contribution Reports (ICR) – a personal report detailing their contribution to a work product. Each student also has to indicate agreement or disagreement with the reports written by each of their team members and a write a comment evaluating the performance of the team member (covering quality, quantity, timeliness of work completed and any aspects that they rated lowly in the SPES).
- Work Product Pay Packet (WPPP) – each team member gives a quantitative opinion of how much each team member contributed to a work product, they also have to include an explanation for why they have distributed the pay that way. It is useful to have an understanding of the "formula" each individual has used to quantitatively assess each person.

Provide timely individual feedback: While timely, individual feedback is central to facilitating learning, providing detailed, quality feedback to a large number of students is an extremely time-consuming task. An effective strategy is to use an online system [12] that enables the regular collection of a large amount of information on quantity and quality of individual contributions to the team's work and the individual's performance as a team member so that timely feedback can be provided to large and diverse student cohorts in a manageable way. In ICT Project timesheets are completed weekly, the other tools are used four times each semester at the end of each phase. Students can view team member's timesheets as well as a summary of how much each team member contributed to a particular task. With our tools students can see aggregated feedback from their team members, while maintaining the anonymity of the author. Once the due date has passed students can view feedback from the SPES and the WPPP and compare where they have rated themselves against the aggregated results of their team members.

Discuss team issues to increase learning: Our tools have now been used for many years and some refinements have been made to increase learning. Initially in the SPES each individual made recommendations for improvement to each of their team members. We discovered that forcing the students to give suggestions for improvement made them mention things that weren't important and trivial issues were taken totally out of perspective and actually created team issues. Students are now required to add comments evaluating an individual's performance in the ICR and an explanation justifying the quantification in the WPPP; only the coordinator can view these comments. Having students write private comments allows the coordinator to amalgamate the information to identify any real team issues.

Discussing team issues at a meeting is an effective strategy to improve teamwork. In ICT Project once the work product has been assessed a meeting is held with the coordinator to receive feedback on the work product and discuss the peer assessment and any teamwork issues identified. While these discussions can be quite confronting for an individual, in many cases the issues are related to how the team is working together and the discussions can prove very valuable learning experiences for everyone.

Establish clear criteria for the different grades: The nature of teamwork can lead to students getting higher grades than they earn due to other team members doing more than their share. It is important to set the standards and criteria for the different grades so that the high achievers know what they need to do, and the other team members can appreciate that while the mark for a work product is high, their contribution to the process and professionalism was not at the required standard. In ICT Project the criteria for each grade, shown in Table 3, are presented in the first and mid-semester lecture each semester and used when determining an individual's final grade.

Table 3. Grade Criteria for ICT Project

Pass:
Product: Contributed adequately to the work product. The team must have produced at least a semi-functional work product. *Process*: Demonstrated ability to follow the process prescribed by the coordinator. *Professionalism*: Acceptable level of attendance and engagement with respect to both internal (team) and external (client) related activities during the phase.
Credit in addition to Pass expectations:
Product: Contributed strongly and consistently to the work product over the duration of the phase. The team must have produced a solid functional work product using good design standards and practices. *Process*: Demonstrated ability to accurately follow the process documented by the coordinator and the team. *Professionalism*: An active level of engagement (internal and external), including organisation and leadership responsibilities for an element of the phase.
Distinction in addition to Credit expectations:
Product: Contributed significantly, consistently and to a high standard, to the work product over the entire phase. *Process*: Demonstrated contribution to the definition and ongoing improvement of good process used by the team. *Professionalism*: An active level of contribution across multiple areas or responsibilities during the phase, including significant input to important decisions.
High Distinction in addition to Distinction expectations:
Professionalism: Active leadership/ownership of key responsibilities resulting in high quality outcomes for the work product. As indicated by providing support and leadership to members of the team for at least one key area of the phase. Leadership in this context may refer to knowledge, technical, or managerial responsibilities; it is not confined to a role.

9. CONCLUSION

This experience report reflected on a team-based capstone project unit utilizing external clients that has been offered for over 17 years. In that time there has only been one team failure (failed to deliver a useable product) out of more than 200 teams, the client feedback on the final software has consistently averaged above 80% (a rating that indicates the client will use it with trivial modifications) and many products are in use by clients, and some have even won industry standard awards. The client feedback on the professionalism of the students has averaged around 90% and most of our graduates find employment within months of graduating, many gain employment before graduation.

Throughout this paper effective strategies were proposed for the more challenging aspects of coordinating capstone projects:

- sourcing projects and client management – use real clients and ensure clients understand the academic constraints;
- team formation and management – project preferences are paramount, consistent supervision is essential and self-management is a valuable learning opportunity;
- assessing student learning against generic learning outcomes – evaluate product, process, professionalism and progression in learning [9], use reflection and provide formative feedback to increase learning; and
- ensuring individual accountability – use a variety of tools and sources for peer assessment and establish clear criteria to ensure the integrity of individual grades and discuss teamwork issues to increase learning.

While some of the individual strategies are novel (consistent supervision, team self-management, individual accountability tools and criteria), when the strategies are combined (particularly assessment of learning and individual accountability) it can lead to an increase in student learning and a better software product for the client. The strategies proposed should be adaptable to any teamwork capstone project experience involving the development of a significant software product.

Our next challenge is to adopt a more agile approach in the second semester to more align with current industry practice and adapt the assessment to work for capstone projects that do not involve the development of a software product but are focused on a different area of the ICT industry, e.g. cyber-security system to align with current industry demands for graduates in this area.

REFERENCES

[1] Nicole Herbert, Kristy de Salas, Ian Lewis, Julian Dermoudy, and Leonie Ellis. 2014. "ICT curriculum and course structure: the great balancing act." In *Proceedings of the Sixteenth Australasian Computing Education Conference-Volume 148*, pp. 21-30. Australian Computer Society, Inc.

[2] Sally Fincher, Marian Petre, Martyn Clark. 2001. Computer science project work: principles and pragmatics, Springer-Verlag, London, UK

[3] Tony Clear, Michael Goldweber, Frank H. Young, Paul M. Leidig, Kirk Scott. 2001. Resources for instructors of capstone courses in computing, ACM SIGCSE Bulletin, v.33 n.4

[4] Nicole Clark. 2005. "Evaluating student teams developing unique industry projects." *Proceedings of the 7th Australasian conference on Computing education-Volume 42.* Australian Computer Society, Inc.

[5] Andres Neyem, Jose I. Benedetto, Andres F. Chacon. 2014 Improving software engineering education through an empirical approach: lessons learned from capstone teaching experiences, Proceedings of the 45th ACM technical symposium on Computer science education, Atlanta, Georgia, USA

[6] Jan Herrington, and Ron Oliver. 2000. "An instructional design framework for authentic learning environments." *Educational technology research and development* 48.3: 23-48.

[7] Jacqueline Whalley, Michael Goldweber, and Harley Ogier. 2017. "Student values and interests in capstone project selection." *Proceedings of the Nineteenth Australasian Computing Education Conference.* ACM.

[8] Maria Vasilevskaya, David Broman, Kristian Sandahl. 2014. An assessment model for large project courses, Proceedings of the 45th ACM technical symposium on Computer science education, Atlanta, Georgia, USA

[9] Tony Clear. 2009. Thinking ISsues: the three p's of capstone project performance, ACM SIGCSE Bulletin, v.41 n.2.

[10] Ann Q. Gates, Nelly Delgado, and Oscar Mondragón. 2000. "A structured approach for managing a practical software engineering course." *Frontiers in Education Conference, 2000. FIE 2000. 30th Annual.* Vol. 1. IEEE.

[11] Nicole Herbert. 2007. Quantitative peer assessment: can students be objective?, Proceedings of the ninth Australasian conference on Computing education, p.63-71, Ballarat, Victoria, Australia

[12] Nicole Clark, Pamela Davies, Rebecca Skeers. 2005. Self and peer assessment in software engineering projects, Proceedings of the 7th Australasian conference on Computing education, p.91-100, Newcastle, New South Wales, Australia

Design and Evaluation of an Undergraduate Course on Software Development Practices

Paul Gestwicki
Ball State University
Computer Science Department
Muncie, IN, USA
pvgestwicki@bsu.edu

ABSTRACT

This paper describes the design, evolution, and evaluation of a second-year undergraduate course on professional software development practices. The course design arose from two properties of a curriculum revision: the removal of redundancy across Discrete Mathematics, Data Structures, and Algorithms coursework and the identification of desired skills for students entering the upper-division courses. A research-informed design for the course incorporates code quality, version control, teamwork, user-centered design, risk management, design thinking, and reflective practice, presented in keeping with the values of agile software development. We describe the evolution of the course over its six years of implementation, including a transition from a Java-specific textbook to a more generic book about code quality and the transition from a six-week to a nine-week project. The course has become a linchpin for mid-major assessment of students' software development skills, and we discuss the strengths, weaknesses, and results of our assessment strategy. We provide a reflection of the role this course has had within our program and advice for those who might wish to adopt or adapt this design.

ACM Reference Format:
Paul Gestwicki. 2018. Design and Evaluation of an Undergraduate Course on Software Development Practices. In *Proceedings of SIGCSE'18, February 21–24, 2018, Baltimore, MD, USA*, , 6 pages.
https://doi.org/http://dx.doi.org/10.1145/3159450.3159542

1 INTRODUCTION

One of the most important creative tasks of university faculty is the design and evaluation of curricula and their courses. These designs define our students' experiences as well as the day-to-day work of ourselves and our colleagues. Accrediting bodies have long emphasized the importance of effective assessment strategies, and we have seen an increasing interest in course, program, and institutional assessment in recent years. Perhaps the most common form of such assessment is the feedback loop, where assessment data from one iteration is used as input to curricular changes for the next. Such approaches ideally combine with research-informed pedagogy and scholarship of teaching as described by Boyer [5] and Glassick et al. [8]. Framing the creation of courses and curricula as a design problem highlights the many stakeholders and their sometimes-conflicting desires and constraints.

This paper describes the creation of *Advanced Programming*, a required course for sophomore Computer Science majors and minors. It was designed to solve local problems and leverage local opportunities. The course was created from whole cloth, being based on neither curriculum recommendations nor extant courses in other institutions. The course was formally introduced in 2010, and it has undergone a series of changes based on formal and informal assessments. We hope that by sharing the context, design, evaluation, and impact of this course, we make a contribution to the wider community of practice, so that others may build upon this design and to enable future research on curriculum design and assessment processes.

2 CONTEXT

This work took place in the Computer Science Department at Ball State University, a public university in the American Midwest of approximately 22,000 students, with high undergraduate enrollment. The university is ranked as Higher Research Activity according to the Carnegie classifications, with a distinction for community engagement. The Computer Science Department is home to approximately 375 undergraduate majors and two masters degree programs enrolling approximately 25 students. The department undertook a significant evaluation of the undergraduate curriculum during the 2009-10 academic year, inspired in part by the *Computer Science Curriculum 2008* report [1] with careful attention paid to the "foundations" courses—courses that students take during their first two years in the major. Figure 1 provides an overview of the foundations curriculum at the time. The first two programming-oriented courses—*Computer Science 1* and *Computer Science 2*—were four credit-hour courses with mandatory lab meetings, while the others were three. Courses were available during the conventional 15-week semester or during five-week summer sessions, and all were in face-to-face rather than online or hybrid formats. The courses follow the conventional topics one might expect based on their names, their topic lists generally being related to chapters in standard textbooks.

The focus of our attention here is on *Data Structures*, a course that would be taken by a Computer Science major or minor in their third semester. All upper division courses at the time used this course as a prerequisite, which made it a bottleneck in the curriculum. Students who struggled with this course could not

SIGCSE'18, , February 21–24, 2018, Baltimore, MD, USA

ACM ISBN ISBN 978-1-4503-5103-4/18/02...$15.00
https://doi.org/http://dx.doi.org/10.1145/3159450.3159542

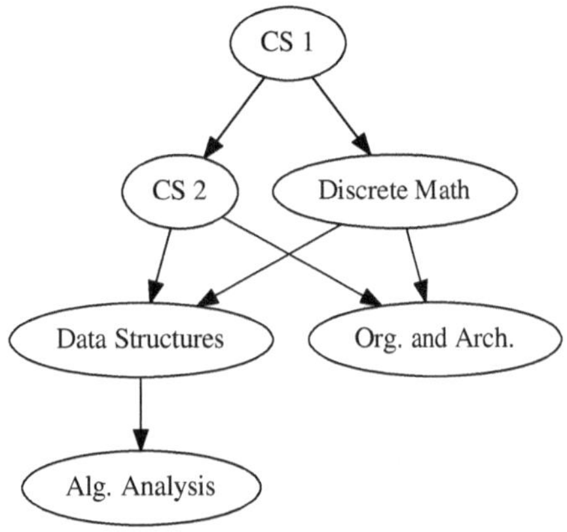

Figure 1: Foundations Curriculum Prerequisites, 2009-10

proceed in the major at all, leading to extra semesters at the university or, frequently, dropping the major. Our analysis revealed significant topic redundancy across *Computer Science 2, Data Structures*, and *Algorithm Analysis*. There was particular overlap between the first two of these courses: both of which were taught in Java and included significant programming work, although the latter emphasized mathematical abstraction over software development. Framing the course content in terms of the ACM/IEEE curriculum recommendations [1] clarified the redundancy, as we were able to see the the same topics from PF/DataStructures and the Algorithms and Complexity knowledge area across these three courses. Counting the recommended core hours for each knowledge unit, we realized it would be possible to rearrange the content into two three-credit courses.

The department was also starting a shift toward defining courses by learning outcomes rather than topic lists. This forced us to carefully consider why *Data Structures* was a bottleneck. Almost none of the upper-division courses actually drew upon specific data structures knowledge, even though they all listed this course as a prerequisite, directly or transitively. Informal survey of the faculty teaching these courses revealed that the course was, in fact, a proxy for something else—something ambiguous often referenced as "programming maturity." We note that this echoes the concept of "mathematical maturity" that arises in mathematics education, and it suffers from the same lack of rigor and specificity: it seems to be a thing that is desired but that no one can accurately define, measure, or predict. The honest scientist then must consider it to be folklore or myth rather than pedagogic principle. However, identifying this phenomenon was invaluable for our purposes, since it helped us realize that faculty did want their students to have more programming experience prior to taking upper-division courses, but that the content of that experience did not necessarily matter to them. Furthermore, we recognized that the content *did* matter to the students, and so we were able to capitalize on pedagogy designed to foster student motivation and knowledge transfer.

It is important to consider, for this contextualization, the department's decades-long tradition of a full-year senior capstone. The capstone consists of a two-course sequence of Software Engineering courses taken in the Fall and Spring semester. The sequence combines traditional content of Software Engineering (following various versions of Pressman [18], for example) along with a service-learning project. Students form teams and work with a community partner to develop an original software system. Years of implementation and conversations with alumni informed us that students gained significant and noteworthy experience through the capstone, such as working on a team, dealing with ambiguity and changing requirements, and the technical skills used in contemporary software development. Indeed, alumni have consistently cited this experience as fundamental to their success in the job market. Many faculty, however, wanted students to learn these particular skills much sooner in the curriculum, and for highly pragmatic reasons: it would enable more challenging and authentic projects in upper-division courses, and it would mean better-prepared undergraduate research assistants.

The Computer Science department articulated the following goals for our curricular revision: to remove the bottleneck in the curriculum; to remove unnecessary redundancy, particularly around data structures and algorithms material; and to prepare students with contemporary software development skills that can be leveraged in upper-division courses and research experiences. These goals would be addressed in the development of a new, required, sophomore-level course on professional software development—our focus for the remainder of this paper.

3 NEW COURSE DESIGN

The most dramatic change in response to the analysis above was the introduction of a new required course. The new course was titled "Advanced Programming" in order to emphasize its pragmatic focus; although some of the content was extracted from the Software Engineering capstone sequence, the department felt that it was prudent to give it a distinctive name. The initial design for the course emphasized coverage of these topics: advanced features of a programming language; interactive debugging; testing; build configurations; and one or more projects of significant size. The course plan allowed an instructor to choose any language, platform, and toolchain that was within their expertise, so that students would have the best practical experience. The course also included the minimum eight core hours from CS2008's Human-Computer Interaction area [1], which were previously only available to those students who enrolled in the elective, upper-division Human-Computer Interaction course. The original syllabus also mandates that at least half of the student's grade be determined from their work on programming projects.

The inaugural offering of the course established a structure wherein the first six weeks were spent covering material from the topic list in a fairly conventional approach: in-class demonstrations and mini-lectures combined with active-learning activities such as small-group discussions and programming challenges. Required readings were taken from *Effective Java* [4], with assignments given in each of the two weekly class meetings. The following two weeks were spent on a small-scale project, to be completed by pairs of students. The project, which varied from semester to semester, was designed with two outcomes in mind: first, that students put into practice what they had read and done in assignments; second, that students be given the opportunity to reflect on what it meant to work together. The latter manifested in post-project reflective writing assignments. The rest of the semester was spent on a major project that was completed by teams of four in two three-week iterations. Teams pitched their own projects and worked with the instructor to refine their requirements to be within scope. Collaborative projects reap the benefits of being a High-Impact Educational Practice [12], and students' being able to define their own projects raises student motivation. We leverage the epistemic value of writing to inculcate reflective practice [20], with students completing reflections at the end of each major project iteration.

As for the rest of the curriculum, *Advanced Programming* allowed for a balancing of prerequisites to minimize the bottleneck. This course replaced the previous *Data Structures* course as prerequisite to all the programming-intensive upper-division courses such as *Database Design*, *Game Programming*, and the capstone. The algorithms course, as well as some less-intensive programming electives such as *Web Programming*, could build directly off of *Computer Science 2*. This provided students with more flexibility in scheduling, particularly helping those students who needed to repeat a foundations course.

The course design has evolved since its initial offering. The *Advanced Programming* syllabus was revised in keeping with the department's continued emphasis on learning outcomes over topic lists. It stated specifically that a student who satisfactorily completes the course should be able to:

(1) Explain, justify, and follow heuristics of code quality, including: coding standards and style documents; refactoring as a technique for improving code quality; clear naming and language-specific naming conventions; using abstraction and decomposition to eliminate redundancy; prudent use of comments and version control commit messages
(2) Demonstrate and justify software development practices that incorporate the compiler, debugger, version control, and testing features of a modern integrated development environment
(3) Apply code review techniques to identify design and implementation defects; create and analyze software following conventions of object-orientation, including the Single Responsibility Principle and model-view separation
(4) Apply user-centered philosophy to design simple graphical user interfaces, justify usability considerations, and implement the user-interface in a high-level programming language.
(5) Plan, manage, present, and evaluate multi-week programming projects created by small teams using an incremental and iterative approach
(6) Demonstrate reflective practice for professional improvement

There have been two other major revisions to the course, the first being a revision to the course schedule. Instructors observed that practically every team struggled with the first iteration of the six-week project, and then most did better in the second iteration. However, a troubling proportion of teams still performed poorly. By the the end of the second iteration, teams seemed to become aware of their problems and begin to show evidence of improvement, but too late in the semester to capitalize on it. The course shifted to spending nine weeks on this project, now consisting of three three-week iterations. This led to much higher rates of project success despite having to cut the introductory portion of the course almost in half. The current conventional course structure is to have three weeks of reading and exercises, two weeks on a small project, and nine weeks on the major project. Additionally, the three iterations of the major project are graded to reflect the formative nature of early iterations: most instructors weight each iteration by the square of its number.

The other major revision was a transition away from the Java-centric examples in Joshua Bloch's *Effective Java* [4] to the more general code quality heuristics and explicitly Agile values presented in Robert C. Martin's *Clean Code* [14]. This coincided with the introduction of Test-Driven Development as a required element of the course, with required excerpts from Kent Beck's *Test-Driven Development By Example* [3]. Although the *Computer Science 2* prerequisite is ostensibly object-oriented, we identified that many students harbored serious misconceptions about OO design philosophy. It is worth noting that Martin [14] spends an entire chapter defending a semantic distinction between "data structures" and "objects" as they manifest in object-oriented programming languages; from this perspective, it seems that trying to teach both data structures and object-orientation simultaneously may be doomed to conflating them.

Advanced Programming has come to place particular attention to issues of object-oriented programming, particularly model-view separation via domain modeling [7] and the Single Responsibility Principle [13]. Students complete a required reading from the first chapter of *Holub on Patterns* [10], which contains an excellent and accessible overview of object-oriented design philosophy. A vast majority of students' reflective responses claim this reading is perspective-altering, particularly the section unabashedly entitled "Getters and Setters are Evil."

Some instructors have used *essential questions* [15] as a way to frame their course plans. Essential questions are a fundamental element of the Understanding by Design framework [22]. They encourage framing a course around a small number of open-ended questions, such that working through the course brings one to a deeper understanding of the questions. For *Advanced Programming*, we have used the following:

- What is *software craftsmanship*?
- How do you know when a feature is done?
- How do small teams of developers coordinate activity?
- How does a software developer use ubiquitous and chaotic information to be a lifetime learner?

Many of the reflective writing assignments in the course require a student to relate their experiences back to one of the essential questions. For example, students' end-of-iteration essays must explicitly draw from their experience to address one of the course's essential questions. We have found that essential questions provide a synergy with the content of the course, given that we are studying a field that is always changing and where there is often not one right approach—where every decision is a design decision with concomitant trade-offs.

4 EVALUATION OF STUDENT WORK

The syllabus for the course does not mandate a student evaluation policy besides at least half the grade being related to programming projects. However, convention has been that students are evaluated in three categories: performance on assignments from the first three weeks of the course; performance on the two-week and nine-week projects; and the earning of achievements. We will investigate each of these in turn below. Some faculty additionally evaluate students based on attendance and participation, although this is not shared across all sections.

One or two assignments are given each week preceding the two-week project. Many assignments involve reading an assigned text and then acting upon its content. Sometimes this action is a simple reflective essay, but one of the most successful assignment structures requires students to read their own previously-written programs and analyze them in light of the rules of *Clean Code* [14]. Most of the students have never reconsidered the programs they wrote in *Computer Science 1* or *2*; when they look back on their previous work and realize that they cannot make sense out of it, the students are convinced of the value of good naming practices and structuring principles.

The two-week project uses instructor-specified functional requirements, while the nine-week project requirements are written and iteratively revised by the students. In both cases, these projects are evaluated along two dimensions: structural rules, which include naming, commenting, and formatting conventions; and procedural rules, which include Test-Driven Development, proper use of version control, and compliance with acceptance testing specifications. Faculty do not directly evaluate functional correctness to no perceivable ill effect. We hypothesize that students' motivation to complete the project drives them to complete the functionality without additional incentives.

During the first few years teaching the course, we observed that many high-achieving students would voluntarily undertake extra challenges in their nine-week projects. However, their grades did not necessarily reflect their excellent work, and in fact, they would sometimes earn lower grades than less-ambitious peers. In 2013, *achievements* were added as a student assessment category. This timing coincides with the popularity of educational gamification, as described by Kapp [11]. The achievement system was designed based on recommendations from the evaluation of the MacArthur Foundation Digital Badges for Lifetime Learning project (see Hickey et al. [9], for example). Achievements were designed that would recognize, encourage, and reward students for taking on challenges that were relevant to, but separable from, the core course content; for example, achievements could be earned by using new platforms, participating in departmental colloquia, engaging with alumni, and giving in-class presentations.

All of these evaluations of student work are customarily evaluated using triage grading [19] or a variation of it. Briefly, this grading philosophy involves grading each item on a four-point scale. An item may be essentially correct (3 points), partially correct (2 points), or essentially incorrect (1 point), with zero points reserved for work not submitted. These map to the letter grades A (3 points), C (2 points), D (1 point), and F (0 points); B and +/- grades emerge through linear interpolation. Experience has shown this to be a powerfully expressive system for evaluating source code quality in particular. *Clean Code* [14] presents a rich set of heuristics for determining the quality of code, many of which permit multiple interpretations. For example, Martin exhorts developers to minimize a method's number of parameters ideally to zero or one, while acknowledging that while it is always possible, it is not always prudent. Students can be taught the mechanics of such a refactoring, but understanding when *not* to do this requires experience and wisdom. Hence, a program containing high-arity methods can either be essentially correct or only partially correct. The instructor's role here is to evaluate the context and communicate to students whether such decisions were justifiable. Once students overcome their unfamiliarity with triage grading, they find it clear and fair: the textual feedback accompanying the grade justifies it and points them toward improvement. From a faculty perspective, it reduces grading effort and eliminates "grade grubbing." It may be worth noting that triage grading bears much in common with Specifications Grading [16] and meets most—if not all—of the design criteria expressed therein; however, a detailed comparison and critique of these two grading methods is beyond the scope of this paper.

5 PROGRAMMATIC ASSESSMENT

Just before *Advanced Programming* was first offered, the Computer Science Department articulated a revised set of five departmental learning outcomes along with a new assessment strategy. The learning outcomes were strongly inspired by ABET's student outcomes. The following departmental learning outcome is relevant to our discussion:

> Design and development skills: Given an appropriate set of software requirements, the student will be able to formulate a specification from which to design, implement and evaluate a computer-based system, process, component or program that satisfies the requirements. At a minimum, this must include the ability to design, implement and evaluate a software system using a high-level programming language, following the conventions for that language, and using good practices in software design to satisfy the given requirements.

This outcome was to be measured at two points using embedded assessments: at the mid-major point while taking *Advanced Programming* and at the end of the major while taking the capstone. *Advanced Programming* has served as an advantageous position from which to assess this particular outcome since it involves both rigorous programming work and explicit reflection on past programming-oriented coursework. The corresponding assessment data has been useful as we transitioned our *Computer Science 1* course to use media computing, peer instruction, and pair programming in order to reap the benefits described by Porter and Simon [17]; our data showed no loss in programming ability at the mid-major point by switching from traditional Java to media-oriented Python.

It is less clear whether the course has had significant impact upon the student outcomes at the end of the major. Seniors' performance on the relevant sections of the ETS Major Field Test has not changed, yet we recognize that the skills developed by this new course are not what is being measured by that exam. Holes in the assessment procedures for the capstone have left the department without adequate data about relative performance before and after the introduction of the course. However, for faculty teaching upper-division, programming-intensive courses, the change has been dramatic. Faculty know that they can insist upon high-quality code and industrial-strength practices such as version control, Test-Driven Development, and effective collaboration. We have seen this improvement in both conventional courses as well as undergraduate research opportunities and independent studies.

More recently, the department has begun to evaluate all of its foundations course plans in light of the syllabus review approaches reported by Stanny et al. [21]. Their instruments explicitly address research-supported best practices for teaching, and *Advanced Programming* routinely rates highest among the foundations courses. This has inspired curriculum committees to investigate how additional improvements can be made to more traditional existing courses.

6 DISCUSSION

Based on observation, student evaluations, and personal communication, the course is transformative for many students. Students are given relatively little freedom in the introductory programming courses, where exercises are designed to assess specific, discrete knowledge. *Advanced Programming* instead gives them the opportunity to pursue their own interests, and so we have seen projects ranging from internationalized media players to role-playing game character generators to Instagram friend-finders, and every team has to learn something new in order to meet their collective goals. Students recognize that the reflective practice modeled in this course is clearly applicable to their interests and appropriate to the careers they anticipate. We will note briefly that—as one might expect—many students want to create video games. We have adopted a policy of strongly warning against this but not actively prohibiting it. Game prototyping involves significant experimental gameplay programming, which is a context that is not ideal for also practicing Test-Driven Development, and so we advise students toward problems that will more readily demonstrate the learning objectives.

The course was explicitly designed to allow faculty to bring their preferred toolchain to the classroom, specifically considering Java and Microsoft .NET platforms. However, in practice, the course has always been taught using Java. The reason for this appears to be that the first instructor was most comfortable with Java, and contract faculty in subsequent years built their courses upon the specific plans laid out by this instructor. This brings us to one of the most significant challenges we have faced in implementing *Advanced Programming*, which is that, by and large, faculty are inadequately prepared to teach it. Practical software development skills have often fallen outside the traditional realm of Computer Science education; certainly, none of our faculty have had coursework on these topics. It appears to be that the most prepared faculty to teach the course are those who have faced the problems that arise from the absence of Clean Code, version control, design thinking, and iteration planning; these faculty have tacit understanding of why the course is important and can bring enthusiasm and expertise.

While *Clean Code* [14] is an excellent resource that is highly respected in industry, it seems nearly invisible in higher education. It is not a "textbook," and so faculty must invest the time to create their own teaching materials. The closest to a conventional textbook we have discovered for these topics is by Crookshanks [6], whose book describes itself as "an overview of tools and techniques used in enterprise software development, many of which are not taught in academic programs." However, none of our instructors has actually implemented a course using this book. Note that many *Advanced Programming* course plans are publicly available online, and interested readers are welcome to investigate and adapt them; see https://www.cs.bsu.edu/~pvg/courses/cs222Fa17 for a recent example.

One of the explicit goals for the course was to prepare students for upper-division project work, and we find that faculty who draw upon these skills are pleased with the students' preparation. While one semester is not enough time to master agile software craftsmanship, having this course means that students can draw upon its concepts when required by future instructors or employers. However, we have observed an unfortunate counterpoint, that many students do not use what they learned in *Advanced Programming* if they are not required to. For example, we see very few students holding themselves to the standards of *Clean Code* in upper-division courses where it is not explicitly required. When an upper-division operating systems or networking textbook flagrantly violates structural and naming conventions of Clean Code, such as with single-letter variable names or very long methods, we see students following suit rather than critically reflecting upon it. This suggests that although the course is preparing students with skills, it is not adequately preparing them in terms of judgment. Although students have successfully evaluated, analyzed, and synthesized knowledge in the course—from the perspective of Bloom's taxonomy of the cognitive domain [2]—many neither transfer this knowledge nor incorporate it into their own professional practice.

The curricular bottleneck was lessened by the introduction of *Advanced Programming*, as upper-division courses without significant programming components could rely on other prerequisites instead; the bottleneck has not been completely eliminated, however, since many upper-division courses that relied on sound programming skills simply swapped the *Data Structures* prerequisite with *Advanced Programming*. Eliminating the redundant *Data Structures* course has not had any observable impact on student performance in other courses or in assessments. The inclusion of *Advanced Programming* course has given some benefits as mentioned above, and it appears to still meet the desires of courses for which it is a prerequisite. This course has also become a "mini-capstone" for Computer Science minors: previously, their curriculum involved only conventional coursework, but with this new project-oriented course, they could potentially develop a project worthy of including in a portfolio or job application.

The programmatic assessment scheme described in Section 5 has proven useful for foundations courses. Unfortunately, overall program assessment has been hindered by incomplete participation in assessment reporting activities. While perhaps only tangential to the issues of this paper, it speaks to the importance of faculty commitment to the culture of assessment. The departmental committee that oversees the foundations courses has been able to perform evidence-driven revisions, while other potential improvements have languished due to lack of assessment data.

This report has not addressed individual or aggregate student behavior since we did not have the requisite human-subjects protocols in place during the period in question. However, the design, implementation, and iterative refinement of this course has led us to identify several avenues for potential future research. We noted how students who show evidence of learning within *Advanced Programming* rarely transfer these skills spontaneously into other programming experiences, yet this kind of transfer is the goal in practically all of higher education. A study of how programming skills and design philosophies are integrated by students could contribute significantly to the body of scholarship on knowledge transfer. We have collected several years of data around students' use of the achievements grading system, and although it is based on established theories of motivation and learning, we have not yet conducted the analysis to see how this system compares to others, in part because the specifics continue to evolve. Finally, we notice—and hear rumors about—students choosing which section to take depending on whether it is taught by a regular faculty versus contract faculty, with high-achieving students opting for the former and effort-avoiding students seeking the latter. However, we have little scientific understanding of how students make these decisions beyond advising sessions. A qualitative inquiry into how students choose such courses could help us improve our advising.

REFERENCES

[1] ACM/IEEE Interim Review Task Force. 2008. Computer Science Curriculum 2008: An Interim Revision of CS2001. (2008).
[2] Lorin W. Anderson and David R. Krathwohl. 2001. *A taxonomy for learning, teaching, and assessing: a revision of Bloom's taxonomy of educational objectives.* Longman, New York.
[3] Kent Beck. 2002. *Test-Driven Development: By Example.* Addison-Wesley, Boston.
[4] Joshua Bloch. 2008. *Effective Java* (second ed.). Addison-Wesley, Boston.
[5] Ernest Boyer. 1990. *Scholarship Reconsidered.* Jossey-Bass, San Francisco.
[6] Edward Crookshanks. 2014. *Practical Software Development Techniques.* Apress, New York.
[7] Martin Fowler. 2002. *Patterns of Enterprise Application Architecture.* Addison-Wesley, Boston.
[8] Charles E. Glassick, Mary Taylor Huber, and Gene I. Maeroff. 1997. *Scholarship Assessed.* Jossey-Bass, San Francisco.
[9] Daniel T. Hickey, Note Otto, Rebecca Itow, Katerina Schenke, Cathy Tran, and Christine Chow. 2014. Badges Design Principles Documentation Project: Interim Report. Center for Research on Learning & Technology, Indiana University. (Jan. 2014).
[10] Allen Holub. 2004. *Holub on Patterns: Learning Design Patterns by Looking at Code.* APress, New York.
[11] Karl M. Kapp. 2012. *The Gamification of Learning and Instruction: Game-Based Methods and Strategies for Training and Education.* Pfeiffer, Hoboken, NJ.
[12] George D. Kuh. 2008. *Excerpt from high-impact educational practices: What they are, who has access to them, and why they matter.* Association of American Colleges and Universities, Washington, DC.
[13] Robert C. Martin. 2003. *Agile Software Development, Principles, Patterns, and Practices.* Prentice Hall, Upper Saddle River, NJ.
[14] Robert C. Martin. 2008. *Clean Code: A Handbook of Agile Software Craftsmanship.* Prentice Hall, Upper Saddle River, NJ.
[15] Jay McTighe and Grant Wiggins. 2013. *Essential Questions: Opening Doors to Student Understanding.* Pearson Education, Upper Saddle River, NJ.
[16] Linda B. Nilson. 2014. *Specifications Grading: Restoring Rigor, Motivating Students, and Saving Faculty Time.* Stylus, Sterling, VA.
[17] Leo Porter and Beth Simon. 2013. Retaining Nearly One-third More Majors with a Trio of Instructional Best Practices in CS1. In *Proceeding of the 44th ACM Technical Symposium on Computer Science Education (SIGCSE '13).* ACM, New York, NY, USA, 165–170.
[18] Roger S. Pressman. 2014. *Software Engineering: A Practitioner's Approach* (8th ed.). McGraw-Hill Education, New York.
[19] William J. Rapaport. 2011. A Triage Theory of Grading: The Good, the Bad, and the Middling. *Teaching Philosophy* 34, 4 (Dec. 2011), 347–372.
[20] Donald A. Schon. 1984. *The Reflective Practitioner: How Professionals Think in Action.* Basic Books, New York.
[21] Claudia Stanny, Melissa Gonzalez, and Britt McGowan. 2015. Assessing the culture of teaching and learning through a syllabus review. *Assessment & Evaluation in Higher Education* 40, 7 (2015), 898–913.
[22] Grant Wiggins and Jay McTighe. 2006. *Understanding by Design* (expanded 2nd ed.). Pearson Education, Upper Saddle River, NJ.

Low-Cost Programmable Air Quality Sensor Kits in Science Education

Bjørn Fjukstad
Department of Computer Science
UiT The Arctic University of Norway

Nina Angelvik
Department of Computer Science
UiT The Arctic University of Norway

Maria Wulff Hauglann
Department of Computer Science
UiT The Arctic University of Norway

Joachim Sveia Knutsen
Kongsbakken Videregående Skole

Morten Grønnesby
Department of Molecular Biology
UiT The Arctic University of Norway

Hedinn Gunhildrud
Science Centre of Northern Norway

Lars Ailo Bongo
Department of Computer Science
UiT The Arctic University of Norway

ABSTRACT

We describe our citizen science approach and technologies designed to introduce students in upper secondary schools to computational thinking and engineering. Using an Arduino microcontroller and low-cost sensors we have developed the *air:bit*, a programmable sensor kit that students build and program to collect air quality data. In our course, students develop their own research questions regarding air quality before using their own air quality sensor kit to answer their respective questions. This project combines electronics and coding with natural sciences providing a truly interdisciplinary course.

We have open-sourced the teaching materials including the building and coding instructions. In addition, students can contribute to our web-based platform for storing, visualizing, and exploring the collected air quality data. It also provides an open API for anyone to download air quality data collected by the students. Through the website, available at airbit.uit.no, students are motivated to contribute air quality data open to the public.

We describe lessons learned from our pilot project in a Norwegian upper secondary school and how we are deploying it in 10 schools across Northern Norway. In the pilot, students successfully built and coded the air:bits, and after two months of data collection they could correctly describe local patterns in the air quality. We believe that by combining electronics and coding with the natural sciences we motivate students to engage in all scientific disciplines.

ACM Reference Format:

Bjørn Fjukstad, Nina Angelvik, Maria Wulff Hauglann, Joachim Sveia Knutsen, Morten Grønnesby, Hedinn Gunhildrud, and Lars Ailo Bongo. 2018. Low-Cost Programmable Air Quality Sensor Kits in Science Education. In *SIGCSE '18: The 49th ACM Technical Symposium on Computer Science Education, Feb. 21–24, 2018, Baltimore, MD, USA.* ACM, New York, NY, USA, 6 pages. https://doi.org/10.1145/3159450.3159569

SIGCSE '18, Feb. 21–24, 2018, Baltimore, MD, USA

ACM ISBN 978-1-4503-5103-4/18/02...$15.00
https://doi.org/10.1145/3159450.3159569

INTRODUCTION

From a recently published Norwegian Official Report on the future of education in Norway, the authors argue that technology affects all subjects in the Norwegian school system and that digital skills should be expressed in these.[1] While countries such as the UK, Finland, and Estonia have already, or are now, introducing programming and computational thinking in school curricula from primary school and upwards[2], Norway is falling behind. This is both due to the lack of mandatory courses, teaching materials, tools, and courses for teachers without any programming background.

We have developed a course that aims to introduce computer programming and engineering to Norwegian upper secondary schools. Our course combines engineering and computer programming with natural sciences. We developed a maker-inspired citizen science approach focused on air pollution data collection monitoring. We believe this engages both male and female students that are not primarily interested in programming and engineering. It also teaches scientific thinking since students themselves have to collect and verify data. As part of the course we developed an air pollution sensor kit that we have named *air:bit* to collect data. We provide teaching materials including the design, assembly instructions, example source code for the sensors, and a cloud based service for students to upload and explore their collected datasets.

The air:bit shown in Figure 1 measures air quality using low-cost sensors and the Arduino UNO microcontroller.[1] It measures i) dust particles, ii) temperature, iii) air humidity, iv) location, v) time and date, and log these to a memory card in an open format. The total cost of each kit is $40 USD. The cloud service provides data storage and visualization that can be used by students and the public to view current and previous trends in air quality. The cloud service also facilitates download of the air quality datasets through an open API.

The rest of this paper gives an introduction to air quality and related projects that aim to create awareness and engagement; describe our course and how it is structured; gives an overview of

[1] arduino.cc

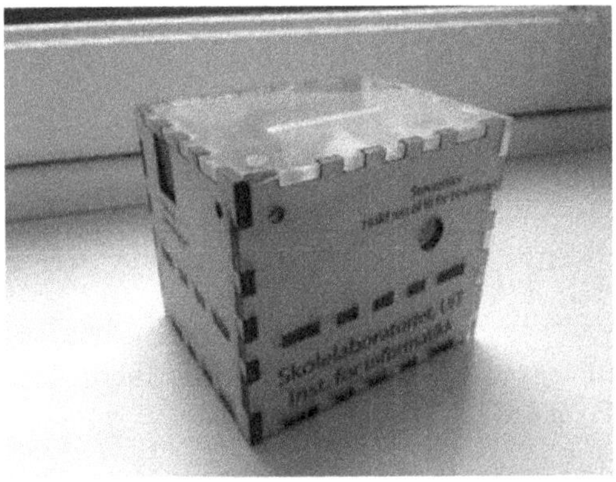

Figure 1: The air:bit.

the air:bit and the computational resources; discuss our experiences from a pilot project; and lastly we provide future directions for the project.

BACKGROUND

We provide a background in air quality and describe related projects that aim to create public awareness and information on air quality.

Air pollution

Air pollution is a global issue since it reduces quality of life in polluted areas and causes diseases. The WHO has termed air pollution as the largest single environmental health risk[3], and has both health, environmental and climate effects.[4] Both short and long term exposure to poor air quality as a result of air pollution is contributing to respiratory disease, cardiovascular disease, and certain cancers.[4–8] In Norway, both European and Norwegian legislation ensure that the air quality is monitored and that air quality forecasts are available to the public. Air pollution originate from a range of different sources. From chemical emissions in factories, chemicals used as a fertilizer in agriculture, exhaust from combustion engines burning fossil fuel, to micro-particles from cars driving on snow-free roads with studded tires[4, 9]. This wide range of sources generate different pollutants, e.g. nitrogen oxides (NO_x), Ozone (O_3), Particulate Matter (PM), and Carbon Monoxide (CO).

In Northern Norway the air quality is rapidly changing in the winter months, especially while the seasons are changing from winter to spring, and fall to winter mainly due to the use of spiked tires on dry roads that generate dust particles in the air, and the emissions from diesel powered cars. Reducing the use of cars will improve air quality in these months, and by creating awareness on the local conditions and their impact on health we believe that it is possible to reduce car usage without enforcing it. However, the monitoring is typically done using stationary equipment that provides high-quality data, but due to their high cost are not affordable to locate throughout all populated areas. Therefore citizens may not find available data on the air quality in their city or neighborhood and it's not possible to increase awareness around poor air quality and simple measures to improve it.

Recent initiatives to use low-cost, easy-to-use micro-sensors for air quality monitoring[10–13] to replace the expensive instruments currently to gather high-quality air quality data. These projects are often targeted towards crowd sourcing air quality data, and must therefore provide an easy-to-use platform that anyone can use. In our project we focus on building the sensor kits to give the students a deeper understanding on how the technology works and not just how to use it. We have focused on measuring PM since it is the major cause of poor air quality in Tromsø, and there are simple and reasonably priced sensors available to measure dust densities in the air.

Air Pollution Engagement Projects

There are many recent projects that aim to engage the public to collect air quality data using a citizen science approach using various air quality kits.

Friskby Bergen is a Norwegian project with a similar aim as our project to develop a project for school classes to build air quality monitoring base stations and collect air quality data. Their technology is based on the Raspberry Pi computer and use low-cost sensors to measure air quality. Their monitoring stations are stationary and log data directly to their open web services over wifi. While the Friskby sensor kits provide live monitoring of air quality by directly uploading air quality measurement over wifi, our air:bit is equipped with a memory card to store measurements before being uploaded by the students afterwards. This simplifies both the software and makes it possible to use the kits without any wifi coverage.

The aim of the hackAIR project is to develop a simple DIY kits that enable citizens and organizations to engage in air quality data generation and sharing.[14] We share the same technical platform as the hackAIR project, and we have initiated a collaboration to share both data and experiences between the two projects.

The CITI-SENSE project has developed 'citizens observatories' for citizens to contribute to and participate in environmental governance[11]. Citizens use the Little Environmental Observatory (LEO) sensor packs to measure NO, NO_2, O_3, temperature and relative humidity. Data is uploaded to a online service for users to view and explore, similar to our approach.

Another project that share our technological platform is the Luftdaten project which aims to promote air quality awareness in Germany.[15] Through the luftdaten.info site they provide instructions on how to build and code the air quality sensor, in addition to interactive maps with live data. The Luftdaten project also host frequent meetups for citizens who need help with the air quality kits or want to learn more about the project. We share the approach with the Luftdaten project, but we target high-school students as the main audience.

Computer Science Education

There is a wealth of platforms and software tools to introduce programming and technology. One such approach is to combine electronics and coding through the cheap Arduino microcontroller architecture and electronic components such as LEDs, buttons or other sensors.[16, 17] An example of one such approach was to create or hack existing toys or build new ones to make "noise"[18].

Figure 2: Students soldering different components of the air quality sensor kits to the custom PCB Arduino Shield.

Another is to use Arduinos in Physics experiments in the areas of Optics, Thermodynamics, and Waves.[19]

COURSE CONTENTS

Our course has been given once in spring 2017 at UiT The Arctic University of Norway to science students at a local High School, and is planned again in spring 2018 across 10 upper secondary schools across Northern Norway. We host the course at the university both to recruit new students but also as a part of the outreach program at the university.

To make the course fit into different subjects in the upper secondary school in Norway, we have surveyed the relevant subjects and their specific learning goals and requirements. By creating a project where students build, code and use a sensor kit to investigate air pollution we cover learning outcomes from the subjects Technology and Research Learning (Teknologi og Forskningslære), Physics (Fysikk), Chemistry (Kjemi), Information Technology (Informasjonsteknologi), and Mathematics (Matematikk for realfag).

The course is run over the duration of a semester and given in four segments; first an introduction to air quality and research on the topic; a hands-on introduction to electronics and coding, as well as assembling and coding the air:bit; air quality data collection; and finally an evaluation where students summarize their work in a written report and/or a presentation. We followed the students' presentations both to get an overview of their learning outcome and get feedback on the project.

Figure 3: Students browsing their collected air quality data on the web site.

The course is designed for students in Norwegian upper secondary school, typically around 17-18 years old. Students may have some experience with basic circuits and electronics through science classes, but since there are no mandatory courses on computer programming so we do not expect any prior experience with coding. We can expect them to have basic computer skills and access to individual laptops.

As for the teaching staff at the individual institutions we cannot expect them to have more knowledge on air quality, microcontrollers, or extensive coding experience. Prior to the project we therefore invite teachers for an intensive two-day workshop that take the teachers through the four segments of the course. We host this two-day workshop at our department.

Following the two-day workshop teachers will return to their schools with parts and instructions to complete the course at their respective institutions. We provide an online forum for questions and answers, both from students and teachers, if they encounter any difficulties with assembling, coding or collecting data. The project is typically run in the spring months to capture the changing air quality from winter to spring.

In the course, teachers can themselves choose if they want to provide research questions to the students or if they want students to develop these themself. The imporant point is that the students all contribute to a large database with air quality measurements, but each student group each decide on what aspect of air pollution they want to investigate. For example, one student group investigated the relationship between snow coverage of roads and dust particles in the air.

SENSOR KIT AND CLOUD COMPUTE INFRASTRUCTURE

In this section we describe our air quality measurement kit, its relevant documentation, the backend storage system, and the frontend visualization platform. The students collect air quality data and upload it to the backend storage system. To view and download data, users access a frontend web application. This application interfaces with both student-collected data in our local backend storage system, as well as open air quality data from the Norwegian

Table 1: A list of the different components in the air:bit along with their cost (as of August 2017).

Component	Cost (USD)
Arduino Uno microcontroller	\$3.14
NEO6MV2 GPS module	\$8.19
Sharp GP2Y1010AUOF optical dust sensor	\$5.99
DHT11 temperature and humidity sensor	\$1.00
SD Card reader and 16GB memory card	\$4.74
Portable power bank	\$15.00
Two indicator leds and resistors	\$1.00
Custom PCB circuit board	\$2.00
Total:	\$41.06

Institute of Air Research (NILU) and the Norwegian Meteorological Institute (MET).

air:bit

We have designed the air quality sensor kit as a small microcontroller based data logger that collects measurements of dust particles, air temperature, air humidity, location, and time and date. The kit is enclosed in a laser cut box, equipped with an external power source that makes the kit portable and withstanding of different weather conditions. Figure 1 shows the first prototype. The kit was built as simple as possible to facilitate use in an educational setting. Table 1 lists the different components and their respective cost.

To simplify the assembly and soldering of the components to the microcontroller we have designed a custom PCB circuit board. The circuit board has pre-defined pins for each sensor, and fits on top of the popular Arduino UNO board. Figure 4a shows the underlying circuit and Figure 4b shows the custom designed PCB circuit board.

Students assemble the kit soldering the components to the custom PCB circuit board. The sensors and circuit board is then mounted on top of an Arduino UNO before enclosed in the pre-cut box.

To program the air:bit we use the standard Arduino IDE together with additional libraries to interface with the different sensors. Through the Arduino IDE students code and upload programs to the Arduino. Arduino programs are written in C++ and by the end of the project students will end up with a working solution at about 150 lines of code. While this is the final version, we expect students to write at least 500 lines of code during the project to test sensors and experiment with different solutions. The Arduino IDE features a console for monitoring communication from the Arduino, allowing students to read data in real time from the different sensors before taking it outside.

Since the kits are programmed in upper secondary school classes where both teachers and students have little or no coding experience, we aim to keep the code as simple as possible. In the project we distribute example code to interface and collect data from the individual sensors[2]. These are small ĩ00 lines of code examples that typically take 20 minutes each to implement. The students must write their own program that collects data from all sensors simultaneously and write them to a memory card. We do not put any restrictions on how their code should look like, the only restriction is on the format of the output data written to the memory card.

We designed a simple data exchange format for the air:bit based on the simple CSV file format. Sensor kits create a single log file and append to it as it collects new measurements. A line (row) in the output file is an observation and consist of measurements for all available sensors. Listing 2 shows an example data file. Using simple Arduino libraries students write the data files to memory cards and they can view them using standard applications, such as Excel, on their laptops.

Listing 1: A simplified code example to collect and print temperature and humidity data from a DHT sensor every second.

```
void setup() {
  Serial.begin(9600);  // Start Serial communication to
  dht.begin();         // receive messages from the Arduino
}                      // and initialize the DHT sensor.

void loop() {
    // Collect data and print them.
    float humidity = dht.readHumidity();
    float temperature = dht.readTemperature();
    Serial.print(temperature);
    Serial.print(", ");
    Serial.print(humidity);
    Serial.print("\n");
    delay(1000);
}
```

Listing 2: Example data file. Every line in the file is a measurement.

```
Time and date, Latitude, Longitude, Dust, Temperature, Humidity
26/10/2016 18:48:41, 69.682121, 18.978985, 88.98, 21.00, 20.00
26/10/2016 18:48:46, 69.682114, 18.978952, 95.70, 22.00, 17.00
26/10/2016 18:48:51, 69.682114, 18.978891, 99.06, 22.00, 17.00
26/10/2016 18:48:55, 69.682106, 18.978865, 98.22, 22.00, 17.00
...
```

Backend data storage

We built a backend cloud based data storage system to handle the large quantities of student data. Students upload data directly from their memory cards to the backed system. The backend also serves queries for air quality data within given time intervals. Since we want to support a query-like interface to the collected air quality data, we used a relational database to build the backend storage system. Student access a lightweight web interface to upload data files from the air:bits, which are parsed and inserted into the database represented by a record for each measurement. Records are indexed using a combination of the time and date, and location. Invalid records are rejected and users will receive an error message to indicate any invalid data or formatting. The backend data storage system exposes a small REST API to allow the frontend (and other applications) to retrieve air quality data. The API will accept queries to retrieve all data within a given time interval. There is no limitation on the length of the time interval, and the API will return a single file with all measurements within the time period.

Frontend visualization

To simplify the process of accessing the collected air quality data, we built a web application. Students and the public can explore air quality data from the last 24 hours, or view and download data from any time period. The web application is built around a

[2]Available online at airbit.uit.no

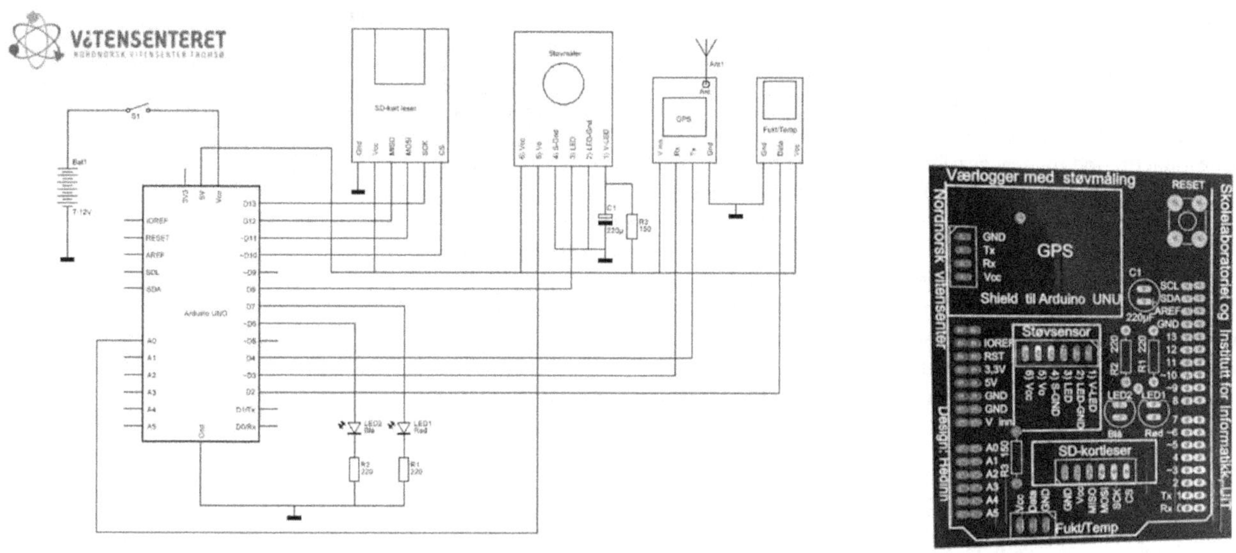

(a) The Air Quality Sensor Kit circuit diagram.

(b) The custom PCB Arduino shield.

Figure 4: air:bit circuit diagram and custom PCB.

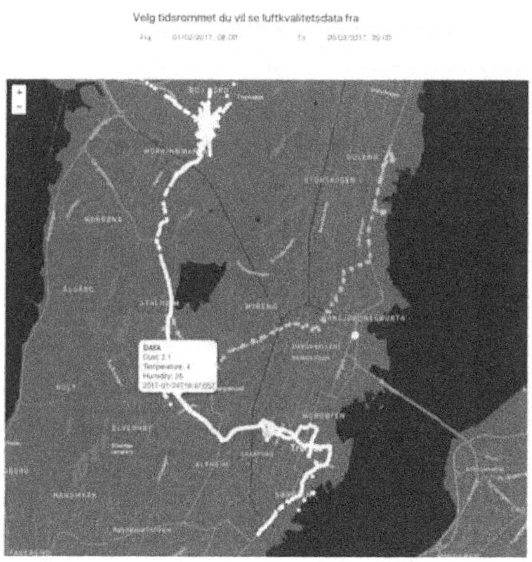

Figure 5: Screenshot from the web application for exploring collected air quality measurements.

paneled visualization consisting of a map with measurement points plotted at their geographical location, in addition to other line plots visualizing the different measurements over time. Figure 5 shows a screenshot from an early version the web application with measurements from two different air:bits carried around in Tromsø, Norway.

EXPERIENCES

Our course has been delivered once in spring 2017 at the University of Tromsø to science students at a local High School (Kongsbakken Videregående Skole). The class consisted of 26 students divided into groups of 3-4 students. The teacher formed groups consisting of students at the same level of experience. The students had varying previous experience with soldering, and no one except one student had coding experience.

The assembly of the kit went almost without any issues. The groups had to present their soldering to one in the staff before moving on to the coding. This allowed us to verify their soldering. We observed that students took turns soldering, and offered each other help. It was clear that some students had done more prior soldering than others.

Coding the kit was a more challenging task. Since most students had little experience writing software, it was oftentimes not clear that they understood the structure of a program and where to start debugging it. The Arduino IDE helped a bit, but most groups had difficulties completing the coding without any help from the instructors. We believe that this is related to the minimal code examples and instructions we provided the students. An interesting point made by one of the students was that it would be helpful with some tool (test suite) that could verify that their implementation was correct.

The students collected data over a 2 month period, each group deciding on when and where to bring their kits on their own. This resulted in measurements from different areas over different time periods. We believe that this stems from our instructions not being clear enough that they should focus on collecting data at the same locations and time of day to make the interpretation simpler. One group ended up with mounting the kit outside their house to simplify data collection. Another group also photographed the road while they were collecting dust data to quantify the amount of snow and ice later.

Due to the scattered data points, the students experienced some difficulties interpreting the data. Because of this, groups with 'good' and complete datasets shared their data with other groups to help them answer their respective research questions. However due to the very simple dust sensor, groups had difficulties with comparing their data with official PM measurements.

After the project was complete we collected oral feedback from both the students and the teacher. Students enjoyed the interdiciplinary nature of the project, especially in groups where students could assign tasks evenly according to interest. The coding was by far the most difficult part of the project for the students as well as the teacher. Because the data interpretation was difficult because of the sensors and scattered data, students had to reflect on the study design and quality of the data before making any conclusions. While we are going to improve the data quality by using improved sensors, the teacher enjoyed the student's reflection on study design and data collection.

FUTURE WORK

While we successfully deployed the air:bit project in a upper secondary school class of 26 students, we have identified areas for improvement and some future directions for the project.

We will improve data quality from the air:bit by using an air quality sensor that can measure both PM2.5 and PM10 concentrations in the air. The current Sharp GP2Y1010AU0F optical dust sensor measures only the total amount of dust particles and cannot be directly compared with the air quality stations from the NILU. We will use the Nova SDS011[3] that both measures PM2.5 and PM10. We will also replace the DHT11 temperature and humidity sensor with the DHT22 temperature and humidity sensor since its readings more accurate and can read temperatures below 0 °C. With these new sensors we are aiming to perform a formal evaluation of their accuracy by sampling air quality data at one of the air quality measurement stations of NILU. We estimate that the new sensors will increase the total cost of each kit by USD $15.

We are also re-writing both the interface for students to explore their collected data, as well as redesigning both the backend storage solution, and the frontend to facilitate users from different parts of Norway. The current backend does not provide the low latencies required by the frontend visualization interface.

To make it possible to scale the project to 10 new schools we are improving the teaching materials that we distribute to the classes. Since we cannot host every class ourselves, we provide video lectures on the background material such as air quality and climate, as well as instructional videos on assembly of the kit and soldering. We are also re-writing the example code that we distribute to the students with better documentation and clearer code. We believe this will simplify and make the coding-part of the projects more pedagogical.

CONCLUSIONS

We have shown how we designed the air:bit, a simple programmable sensor kit for measuring air quality, and how we built a upper secondary school course for students to build and program the kit. We believe that by introducing students to electronics and coding in a citizen science project we motivate students to engage in both technology and the environment.

[3] aqicn.org/sensor/sds011

ACKNOWLEDGEMENTS

We would like to thank MET for providing open weather observations through data.met.no and yr.no. We would like to thank NILU for providing air quality measurements through their luftkvalitet.nilu.no portal. We would also like to thank Thomas Olsen, Torkjel Sandanger, and Juan Carlos Aviles Solis for their presentations and input on the projects.

REFERENCES

[1] "NOU 2015: 8 - fremtidens skole." https://www.regjeringen.no/no/dokumenter/nou-2015-8/id2417001.

[2] European Schoolnet, "Computing our future. computer programming and coding - priorities, school curricula and initiatives across europe." http://www.eun.org/c/document_library/get_file?uuid=521cb928-6ec4-4a86-b522-9d8fd5cf60ce&groupId=43887, 2014.

[3] W. H. Organization, "World health assembly closes, passing resolutions on air pollution and epilepsy." http://www.who.int/mediacentre/news/releases/2015/wha-26-may-2015/en, 2015. [Online; Accesssed: 02.06.2017].

[4] C. Guerreiro, "Air quality in europe: 2013 report," 2013.

[5] R. Beelen, O. Raaschou-Nielsen, M. Stafoggia, Z. J. Andersen, G. Weinmayr, B. Hoffmann, K. Wolf, E. Samoli, P. Fischer, M. Nieuwenhuijsen, *et al.*, "Effects of long-term exposure to air pollution on natural-cause mortality: an analysis of 22 european cohorts within the multicentre escape project," *The Lancet*, vol. 383, no. 9919, pp. 785–795, 2014.

[6] R. D. Brook, S. Rajagopalan, C. A. Pope, J. R. Brook, A. Bhatnagar, A. V. Diez-Roux, F. Holguin, Y. Hong, R. V. Luepker, M. A. Mittleman, *et al.*, "Particulate matter air pollution and cardiovascular disease," *Circulation*, vol. 121, no. 21, pp. 2331–2378, 2010.

[7] O. Raaschou-Nielsen, Z. J. Andersen, R. Beelen, E. Samoli, M. Stafoggia, G. Weinmayr, B. Hoffmann, P. Fischer, M. J. Nieuwenhuijsen, B. Brunekreef, *et al.*, "Air pollution and lung cancer incidence in 17 european cohorts: prospective analyses from the european study of cohorts for air pollution effects (escape)," *The lancet oncology*, vol. 14, no. 9, pp. 813–822, 2013.

[8] M. Pascal, M. Corso, O. Chanel, C. Declercq, C. Badaloni, G. Cesaroni, S. Henschel, K. Meister, D. Haluza, P. Martin-Olmedo, *et al.*, "Assessing the public health impacts of urban air pollution in 25 european cities: results of the aphekom project," *Science of the Total Environment*, vol. 449, pp. 390–400, 2013.

[9] J. A. Hagen, P. Nafstad, A. Skrondal, S. Bjørkly, and P. Magnus, "Associations between outdoor air pollutants and hospitalization for respiratory diseases," *Epidemiology*, vol. 11, no. 2, pp. 136–140, 2000.

[10] J. Dutta, C. Chowdhury, S. Roy, A. I. Middya, and F. Gazi, "Towards smart city: Sensing air quality in city based on opportunistic crowd-sensing," in *Proceedings of the 18th International Conference on Distributed Computing and Networking*, p. 42, ACM, 2017.

[11] N. Castell, M. Kobernus, H.-Y. Liu, P. Schneider, W. Lahoz, A. J. Berre, and J. Noll, "Mobile technologies and services for environmental monitoring: The citi-sense-mob approach," *Urban climate*, vol. 14, pp. 370–382, 2015.

[12] A. Antonić, V. Bilas, M. Marjanović, M. Matijašević, D. Oletić, M. Pavelić, I. P. Žarko, K. Pripužić, and L. Skorin-Kapov, "Urban crowd sensing demonstrator: Sense the zagreb air," in *Software, Telecommunications and Computer Networks (SoftCOM), 2014 22nd International Conference on*, pp. 423–424, IEEE, 2014.

[13] D. Oletic and V. Bilas, "Design of sensor node for air quality crowdsensing," in *Sensors Applications Symposium (SAS), 2015 IEEE*, pp. 1–5, IEEE, 2015.

[14] hackAIR, "The hackair project." http://www.hackair.eu/pages/about-hackair, 2017. [Online; Accesssed: 16.08.2017].

[15] Luftdaten, "luftdaten.info – feinstaub selber messen." http://luftdaten.info, 2017. [Online; Accesssed: 16.08.2017].

[16] J. D. Brock, R. F. Bruce, and S. L. Reiser, "Using arduino for introductory programming courses," *Journal of Computing Sciences in Colleges*, vol. 25, no. 2, pp. 129–130, 2009.

[17] L. Buechley, M. Eisenberg, J. Catchen, and A. Crockett, "The lilypad arduino: using computational textiles to investigate engagement, aesthetics, and diversity in computer science education," in *Proceedings of the SIGCHI conference on Human factors in computing systems*, pp. 423–432, ACM, 2008.

[18] E. Brunvand and N. McCurdy, "Making noise: Using sound-art to explore technological fluency," in *Proceedings of the 2017 ACM SIGCSE Technical Symposium on Computer Science Education*, pp. 87–92, ACM, 2017.

[19] C. A. Petry, F. S. Pacheco, D. Lohmann, G. A. Correa, and P. Moura, "Project teaching beyond physics: Integrating arduino to the laboratory," in *Technologies Applied to Electronics Teaching (TAEE), 2016*, pp. 1–6, IEEE, 2016.

A Biology-themed Introductory CS Course at a Large, Diverse Public University

Tanya Berger-Wolf, Boris Igic, Cynthia Taylor, Robert Sloan, Rachel Poretsky
University of Illinois at Chicago
Chicago, IL
{tanyabw,boris,cynthiat,sloan,microbe}@uic.edu

ABSTRACT

We present the curriculum and evaluation of a pilot Biology-themed CS1 course offering at a large public university. Inspired by Harvey Mudd's CS 5 Green, we adapt CS1 + Bio to fit the needs of our student body, which is much more typical for those US institutions that produce the bulk of the nation's CS undergraduate degrees. This course was team-taught by a computer science professor and a biology professor, and combined typical CS1 topics with relevant biology content. Our initial offering attracted students who would not otherwise have taken CS1, and was the only one of our three CS1 courses where more students reported planning to major in CS after the course than before it.

CCS CONCEPTS

• **Social and professional topics** → *Computer science education*;

KEYWORDS

CS1, CS + X, Contextualized CS, CS1 + Biology

ACM Reference format:
Tanya Berger-Wolf, Boris Igic, Cynthia Taylor, Robert Sloan, Rachel Poretsky. 2018. A Biology-themed Introductory CS Course at a Large, Diverse Public University. In *Proceedings of SIGCSE '18: The 49th ACM Technical Symposium on Computer Science Education, Baltimore , MD, USA, February 21–24, 2018 (SIGCSE '18),* 6 pages.
https://doi.org/10.1145/3159450.3159538

1 INTRODUCTION

This work looks at an introductory Computer Science course with a biology theme developed by adapting Harvey Mudd College's "CS 5 Green" introductory course [1, 8, 9] for use at the University of Illinois at Chicago (UIC), a large, public, diverse research university. Our goals include enabling biology majors and minors to use the power of computing and computational thinking, and attracting more women into computer science.

Alvarado et al. [1] showed CS 5 Green to be highly effective in drawing women into Computer Science *in the context of Harvey Mudd*, a small, private, highly selective, and STEM-focused college. According to its Common Data Set [10], it has a total of 804 students across all years and fields, and three-quarters of its entering students have either an ACT score of at least 33, or an SAT Math score of at least 740. According to *US News and World Report*, Harvey Mudd's acceptance rate was 13 percent in 2015 [17]. Anecdotally, Harvey Mudd has very few biology majors.

Elite STEM schools are outstanding places to start STEM education experiments. However, if we really want to change biology education, we must go to schools that have large numbers of biology majors. UIC has between 1500 and 2000 biology majors, and just over 1000 CS majors, each number being more than the entire enrollment of Harvey Mudd College. To change CS education at the national level, and especially to make major progress on the dismal nationwide statistics on the percentage of women in CS, we must eventually make changes at the schools that produce the most bachelor's degree graduates. The most recent Taulbee Report tells us that public, Ph.D.-granting universities now average nearly 900 Computer Science majors per department, split between about 725 "majors" and 150 "pre-majors" [23]. That is, the average public Ph.D.-granting institution has more CS majors than Harvey Mudd has total students.

CS 5 Green requires substantial reworking to be really useful for such schools. In its original form, the course is aimed at very strong students who are ready, starting with absolutely no CS background, to cover in a single semester, among other things: recursion, recursion on trees, memoization, and computability theory. For many students at our broad set of target schools, this topic list is somewhat ambitious, given that we must simultaneously teach Python programming, as well as a fair amount of biology to a diverse student population with disparate levels of experience.

The Harvey Mudd College context is different from most other schools in two more ways, as well. First, Harvey Mudd is a school targeting the STEM disciplines, and the overwhelming majority of all Mudd students major in a STEM field. Second, every student at Harvey Mudd is required to take an introductory CS course, regardless of major. Most institutions do not require such a course of every undergraduate—ours certainly does not. While today we and many, many other CS programs are feeling overwhelmed by the overall demand for our courses, we nevertheless want to have an introductory CS course, or an array of introductory CS courses, that appeals to a broad range of students. While we may have difficulties meeting the demand for courses, it is crystal clear that it is an advantage to our institution's students if *all* of them take at least one CS course. We expect that a CS+Bio intro course aimed only modestly more broadly than Harvey Mudd's course ought to attract students who would otherwise never take such a course at

SIGCSE '18, February 21–24, 2018, Baltimore , MD, USA

ACM ISBN 978-1-4503-5103-4/18/02...$15.00
https://doi.org/10.1145/3159450.3159538

other institutions with a wide mix of students and no campus-wide CS requirement.

2 WHY BIOLOGY?

According to *Vision and Change in Undergraduate Biology Education: A Call to Action* [2], the study of modern biology requires more emphasis on modeling, computation, and data analysis tools than ever before. Undergraduate biology students are expected to acquire knowledge of related disciplines, specifically including computer science. Biology has long been on a path to becoming quantitatively and computationally intensive, yet undergraduate biology curricula have not kept up with this new reality [3, 14].

Many graduates with degrees in biology lack the training in analytical and information-processing skills needed to tackle growing and increasingly complex datasets. These skills often constitute basic requirements for jobs in industry or academic careers. As a result, the inclusion of computer programming in biology coursework is a developing national trend for undergraduate education, endorsed by the NSF and AAAS [2], and used in biology programs nationwide.

There is considerable demand among some of our Biology department undergraduates for greater exposure to computer science and, unlike the situation at Harvey Mudd College, many of our entering students are unaware of the relevance of computational biology and bioinformatics. Providing our Biology department undergraduates with basic programming skills will make them more competitive and prepared for the workforce.

3 COURSE

In this section, we describe the course content and instructional methods.

3.1 Course Content

To ensure the fit of this course for our students, we built on the syllabi of the existing introductory courses at our institution in Biology and Computer Science, ensuring that no prior knowledge in either subject is required. As a starting point, we also used material from the Harvey Mudd CS 5 Green, and the Rosalind [20] platform for learning bioinformatics.

The combined syllabi of our two-course introductory Biology sequence include: processes of cellular and organismic function, cell structure, respiration photosynthesis, molecular genetics and development, structure, and physiology of plants & animals in Bio 1; and in Bio 2: species richness, population biology, community ecology, biogeography, biogeochemical cycles, conservation biology, speciation, and extinction.

Our CS+Bio course includes more biology background and concepts than the Harvey Mudd CS 5 Green course. We begin the semester by defining life and discussing the structure and function of DNA, RNA, and proteins. The reasons for this include the fact that many of our CS students enter the course with little to no knowledge about biology, as well as our hope that this course will at least partially fulfill some of the learning goals of our introductory biology sequence, or reinforce them. To aid this goal, we provide lectures and readings in biology, in addition to the computer science text.

Our standard CS1 course syllabus includes topics in encoding of data, variables, data types, basic statements and operators, simple input and output, while loops and relational operators, method calls and parameters, `for` loops, `if` statements, Boolean operators, return values from methods, and usage of basic data structures (e.g., lists).

Assignments and labs closely intertwined this biology curriculum with the standard CS1 topics (Table 1). Biologically meaningful datasets, including real and simulated nucleotide gene sequences, genotypes, and genomes, provided the source data for a variety of exercises packaged into weekly labs and three larger projects, following the CS curriculum in a manner otherwise nearly identical to our standard CS1. As an instructive example, we spent one biology lecture on the theory of molecular clock and a historical overview, and then used the same hemoglobin sequences (α-globin & β-globin) as Zuckerandl, Jones, and Pauling [22] for CS material on file I/O and a variety of basic string manipulations, as well as molecular distance calculations.

Our CS+Bio syllabus is shown in Table 1. Details on the current or most recent offering of the course are available at: https://www.cs.uic.edu/CS111Green/, and on the Fall 2016 offering, described in this paper at: https://www.cs.uic.edu/CS111GreenFA16/. Interested readers are encouraged to contact the authors for access to full course assignments and more information. The course syllabus followed our standard CS1 course very closely, with the selection from the standard biology syllabus that best matched the CS material, while creating a coherent and self-contained educational unit.

3.2 Adaptation and Differences from CS 5 Green

As mentioned in the introduction, the main goals of our course, and the motivation behind modifying the course design of Harvey Mudd's CS 5 Green, were to serve a student population which is typical for a public Research 1 university, without extremely selective admission, with many students entering with very little or no CS background, and no requirement of a CS intro course for the biology major. Thus, our course aimed to closely follow the existing intro curricula in CS and Bio, which are tuned for our students and would appeal as an elective alternative for biologists (and other majors).

Harvey Mudd's CS 5 Green is listed as covering: "data, lists, and functions", "recursion and functional programming", "combination circuits", "memory, registers and machine language", "the imperative paradigm: loops and accumulators", "maintaining modularity!", "algorithm design: the use-it-or-lose-it idiom", "2d data, memoization and algorithm efficiency", and "algorithm complexity and uncomputability" [8]. Of these topics, the CS1 course at our institution covers "data, lists and functions", "the imperative paradigm: loops and accumulators", and perhaps, if we are being generous, some algorithm design. As a result, the Harvey Mudd assignments and lesson plans were well out of scope for our CS1 course, after the initial introductory material.

We used only Parts 0 and I of the textbook created for the Harvey Mudd CS 5 Green course [12], which is about a third of the material covered by that book. This represented about half of the material

Biology	CS	Example Assignments
Intro to Bio	Intro to CS	
DNA	Variables and statements, Python syntax	(1) Write a program that sets the number of bases of each type (A, C, T, G) into a string (DNA molecule), and then computes and prints its length. You should have variables for the number of each nucleotide, and your program should print the total number. (2) Create a string variable of any length that contains the letters A, C, T, and G. Print a string that is a tandem duplicate of the original string.
Genes, Cells, Central Dogma of Molecular Biology	Sequences, lists, indices, and slicing	Find the first three base pairs of a given gene. Use the codon translation table to find the amino acid for which it codes. Print the first nucleotide in *each* codon of the gene, as a single string.
GenBank	File I/O and manipulation	Access *GenBank* [5]. Find the nucleotide sequences for the human α-globin (HBA1) and β-globin (HBB). Create a file that contains these two DNA sequences, each in a separate line. Add lines that contain each of these two gene sequences, but in reverse.
GC percentage of DNA, transcription, strand orientation, ORF	Functions	Write a simple gene finder with a function that calls other functions, and then use it to find reading frames in a *Salmonella* sequence (obtained from GenBank).
Pathogenicity	Control flow, `if/else`, loops	Write a function that takes four file names (provided), reads the sequence contained in each, then compares sequences at each position, and reports the overall pairwise percentage differences.
Heredity, population genetics	Random numbers	Write a simple population simulation which illustrates Mendelian genetic inheritance and its properties. Create a founder population, randomly mate them with other individuals to produce offspring with a genetic makeup that follows Mendel's laws, thus creating the next generation. Do this for many (N) generations, and calculate the frequencies of different genotypes in the population, following how those change with every generation.
Models of sequence evolution, phylogenetic trees	Dictionaries and arrays, plotting	Write a simple simulation of DNA genome evolution for a group of virtual species. Begin by simulating the first virtual organismal genome of arbitrary length with arbitrary probabilities. Next, implement an algorithm that allows your species to give birth, become extinct, or neither, and undergo mutation in each time step. Finally, implement a procedure to calculate differences between your evolved species' genomes.

Table 1: The CS+Bio Syllabus, listing the topic correspondence between the two disciplines, as well as example assignments.

covered in our class. However, we spent significantly more time covering biological material in class, and covered the computer science content more slowly. In addition, basic operations of File I/O are not explicitly covered by Harvey Mudd course, and the subject of random numbers, necessary for population biology and evolution (or any biology, really) is covered only minimally. Overall, even for the parts of the course which overlapped with the Harvey Mudd course material, we significantly modified the lecture notes and examples to reflect the biological content.

We matched the coverage of introductory biology, but generally provided more detail, and diverged from the Mudd CS 5 Green to follow our standard biology curriculum more closely. Specifically, we progressed along the biological hierarchy, from sequences to genes, to populations, and species (and groups of species). The major changes in our course included coverage of genome structure, molecular evolution (molecular clocks, DNA sequence models, etc.), and expanded population genetics.

3.3 Team Teaching and Peer Instruction

Our course was team-taught by two instructors, one each from the Biology and Computer Science departments. After initial experiments with the timing and combining the biology and computer science lecture material, and after receiving feedback from the students, we settled on lectures alternately devoted to either computer science or biology material. Students explicitly preferred this and noted that switching in the middle of the lecture from one field to another was jarring and disruptive. For practical reasons, we continued to use the split lecture arrangement for the first week of class, for the purpose of introduction and initial material exposure.

Both instructors were present for all lectures (unless precluded by travel or illness).

Peer-instruction-based materials were developed for the course. Peer instruction is a pedagogical technique, which has been emphasized in physics for over 20 years, and is well documented as increasing the students' conceptual understanding of topics [6]. It is increasingly used in computer science [7, 13, 15, 16, 18, 21]. Under peer instruction, throughout the lecture, students are given a multiple-choice question, with one correct answer and two to four distractor answers. They first vote individually on an answer, typically by using an electronic clicker device [4]. They then discuss the question in small, assigned groups, and after a brief discussion, the group votes on a single answer. Peer instruction is effective in developing cross-disciplinary communication skills in an interdisciplinary setting [11], one of the goals of the course.

3.4 Student Recruitment

Students were recruited from three sources: (1) incoming engineering (including CS) majors could take this course instead of our regular CS1, (2) incoming biology majors were able to take the course as an elective, and (3) all Honors College students were able to take the course as an honors elective. The course was open to every student at our institution as a free elective. Undergraduate advisors in three colleges (Engineering, Liberal Arts & Sciences, Honors) received information about the course.

4 EVALUATION

During Fall 2016, we offered three sections of our CS 1 course: The biology-focused section, a new law-focused section [19], and a section using media computation that previously had been our only offering of CS1. The biology section of CS1 had 27 students in this initial offering, in comparison with 45 students in our law section, and 158 students in our media computation section.

All sections were offered in the standard CS1 format for our institution: two lecture sections of an hour and fifteen minutes each a week lead by the course instructors, as well as an additional weekly hour long lab section lead by a TA. All instructors and TAs had office hours available to the students, and additional general CS tutoring hours were available for all the students.

We surveyed students in all three courses before and after the course, and had five identical common short questions across all three final exams, and one similar longer coding question across all three final exams. We also had access to the regular end-of-term course evaluations for our biology-focused section, and demographic information for all three courses.

4.1 Student Learning

We asked five identical multiple-choice questions on all three sections' final exams: three on control structures, and two on function calls and parameters. The students in the CS + Bio section performed comparable to the other two sections, with 61%±15 average overall answering questions correctly, compared to 62%±23 for the general section and 77%±6 for the law section.

We also asked one broadly similar coding question on all the sections' final exams. It asked students to produce a weighted sum of two sequences, with some sort of limiting rule of the form, "If the weighted sum is greater than x in absolute value, use x with the appropriate sign as the value." For the biology section, this was posed as following: Write a function combineProb, which takes two dictionaries of DNA probabilities as inputs and returns one dictionary of DNA probabilities which is the average of the input dictionaries. That is, for all the dictionaries the keys are the nucleotide letters and the values are the probabilities of that nucleotide. For this question, students in the biology section (earning on average 71%) performed similar to the general section (71%) but better than the law (61%).

A tentative conclusion would be that the CS + Bio section was at least as effective as the other sections in teaching Computer Science concepts.

Table 2: Ethnicity, gender, and CS major data in percentages, compared to two other Fall 2016 sections of CS1, and the Fall 2015 single CS1 (media computation) section.

	Bio	Media	Law	Fall 15
Asian	29	30	31	39
Black	11	6	4	6
Hispanic	30	22	20	15
International	11	5	2	6
Multiracial	4	2	7	2
White (non-Hispanic)	15	34	33	30
Female	22	22	18	25
Male	78	78	82	75
CS Majors	74	87	53	NA

4.2 Student Comments

Students generally found the instructional approach worthwhile and particularly enjoyed the active learning approach. Here is a selection of comments in response to "Please comment on specific characteristics of the course that were most beneficial to you" in our institution's regular post- course course evaluation:

- "Ideal learning environment and ideal instruction for introduction to Python/programming."
- "Excellent overall instruction, much greater than anticipated. Instructor catalyzed new found interest in bioinformatics. Optimal integration of biological and computer sciences."
- "Detailed slides with perfect amount of information."
- "Being able to discuss solutions with my table and then learn if it is correct."
- "We would go through some programs as groups and regroup as an entire class."
- "The pace that [instructor] taught the biology portion of the class was at a good pace."

4.3 Course Demographics

We obtained complete demographic information for the students from our institution. As shown in Table 2, the biology section had more black and Hispanic students, and fewer white students. While the population differences between the courses were not statistically

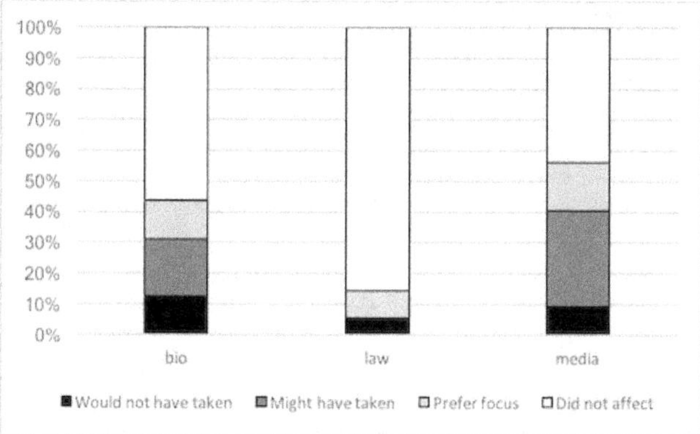

Figure 1: Answers to the question "How important was the Law/Media Computation/Biology focus in you deciding to take this course? A. Would not have taken an introductory computer science course with a different focus B. Might have taken a different introductory computer science course, but focus was the deciding factor C. Would have taken a different introductory computer science course, but prefer one with this focus D. Did not factor into decision to take an introductory computer science course."

significant, this is a promising sign towards using biology as a target domain to attract diverse students.

Unfortunately, this section did not succeed in recruiting any more women than any of our other CS1 offerings. This may be partially due to the fact that the course was developed relatively late, and we were not able to advertise it to Biology students before the end of Spring semester. We hope future offerings with more targeted recruiting will be able to attract more women. However, it is possible that without being a requirement, this course will not be able to recruit more women to the CS major.

4.4 Survey Data

We now examine results from a pre- and post-course survey given to students in all three of the CS1 sections. This survey consisted of a series of five-point Likert scale questions aimed at assessing student's feelings about the importance of computer science, and their computer science related self-efficacy. Survey data was evaluated using the Kruskal-Wallis test to determine if there was a statistically significant difference between the three groups, followed by pair-wise Mann-Whitney tests, if a difference was found.

4.4.1 Importance of Biology Focus. The biology focus was relatively important to students in choosing to take this course, as shown in Figure 1. Fifty-six percent of CS 1 + Bio students said the biology focus did not factor into their decision to take the course, compared to 85% of law students and 44% of media computation students. The biology section also had the highest percentage of students who would not have taken a CS course without the focus at 13%, compared to 6% in the law section and 9% in the media section. There was a statistically significant difference between biology and law courses (p-value=0.00038), although not between biology and media computation.

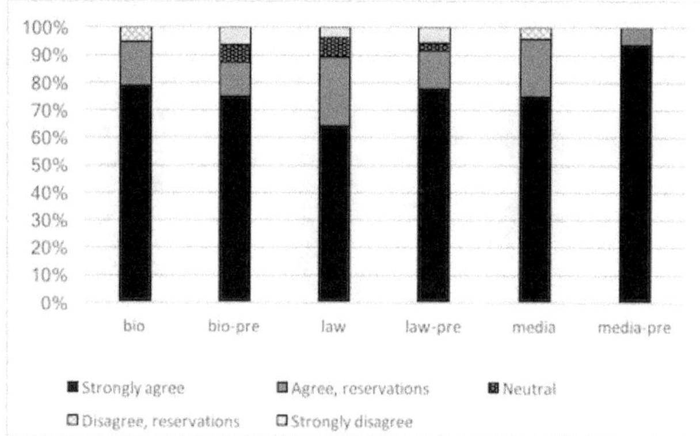

Figure 2: Responses to the statement "I plan to major in Computer Science", before and after taking the course. "-Pre" indicates responses from the pre-course survey.

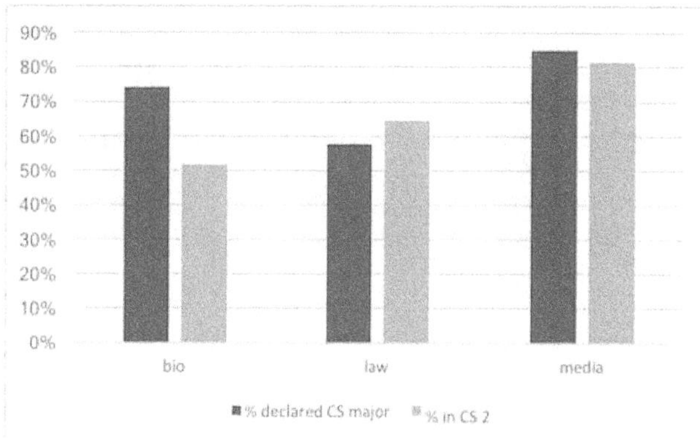

Figure 3: Percentage of each class to major, and to take CS 2.

4.4.2 Likelihood to Major. Student agreement with the statement "I plan to major in Computer Science" is shown in Figure 2. While there was no statistically significant difference between the distributions, the biology focused course stands out as the only course where students were more likely to agree with the statement **after** rather than before taking the course. (On a 5 point Likert Scale where "Strongly Agree" was coded as 1, Biology had a mean of 1.5 pre-course and 1.32 post course, compared to Law with 1.42 and 1.54, and Media Computation with 1.06 and 1.33.)

As shown in Figure 3, as of a semester after the course was offered, 74% of the biology section has declared a CS major, and 52% took CS 2 in the next semester, as compared to 58% and 64% from the law section, and 85% and 82% in the media section. It is worth noting that quite a few students at our school always choose to defer CS 2 from the spring to the summer session.

4.4.3 Student Self-Efficacy. Students in the biology section were more likely to agree with statements like "I like writing computer programs" (shown in figure 4, mean of 1.63 versus 2.29 in law and 2.083 in media computation), "I think I could handle more difficult programming problems" (mean of 1.74 versus 2.04 in law and 2.00 in media computation), and "I am sure that I can learn programming" (mean of 1.26 versus 1.39 in law and 1.42 in media computation.)

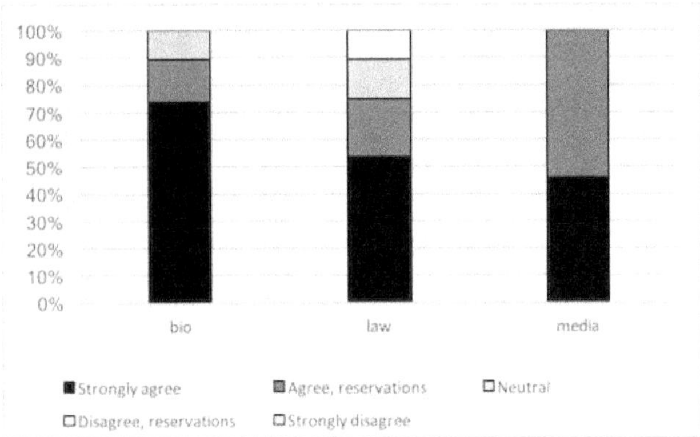

Figure 4: Responses to the statement "I like writing computer programs".

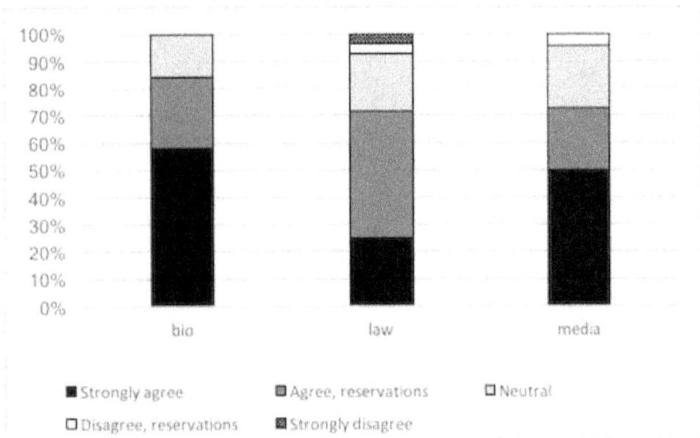

Figure 5: Responses to the statement "I would recommend this course to a friend".

While these results were not statistically significant, we take them as a promising sign of student self-efficacy.

4.4.4 Student Enjoyment of the Course. Students in the biology section were more likely to agree with the statement "I would recommend this course to a friend", as shown in Figure 5, with a mean of 1.74 on a five point Likert scale, versus 2.5 and 2.14 in the other two sections. Although that difference was not statistically significant, this is a promising sign that students enjoyed the course.

5 CONCLUSION

A CS + Biology approach to CS1 can be beneficial for both computer science and biology students. In this paper, we described the results of our initial offering of a Biology-themed CS1 course, created by very heavily modifying Harvey Mudd's CS 5 Green, to meet the needs of students at a large public university. We attracted a diverse set of students, including some that would not otherwise have taken a CS1 course. Students did just as well as traditional CS1 students on comparable questions on the final exam, indicating similar knowledge of CS content. Students who took the course report enjoyment of the course, and computer science in general.

6 ACKNOWLEDGEMENTS

This material is based upon work supported by the National Science Foundation under Grant No. DUE-1612113.

REFERENCES

[1] Christine Alvarado, Zachary Dodds, and Ran Libeskind-Hadas. 2012. Increasing Women's Participation in Computing at Harvey Mudd College. *Inroads* 3, 4 (2012), 55–64.

[2] American Association for the Advancement of Science. 2011. Vision and Change in Undergraduate Biology Education: A Call to Action. (2011). http://visionandchange.org/finalreport/

[3] William Bialek and David Botstein. 2004. Introductory science and mathematics education for 21st-century biologists. *Science* 303, 5659 (2004), 788–790.

[4] Jane E. Caldwell. 2007. Clickers in the Large Classroom: Current Research and Best-Practice Tips. *CBE Life Sciences Education* 6, 1 (March 2007), 9–20.

[5] K. Clark, I. Karsch-Mizrachi, D. J. Lipman, J. Ostell, and E. W. Sayers. 2016. GenBank. *Nucleic Acids Res.* 44, D1 (Jan 2016), 67–72.

[6] Catherine H. Crouch and Eric Mazur. 2001. Peer Instruction: Ten Years of Experience and Results. *American Journal of Physics* 69, 9 (2001), 970–77.

[7] Quintin Cutts, Angela Carbone, and Kelsey van Haaster. 2004. Using an Electronic Voting System to Promote Active Reflection on Coursework Feedback. In *Proceedings of ICCE 2004*. APSCE.

[8] Zachary Dodds, Ran Libeskind-Hadas, and Eliot Bush. 2010. When CS 1 is Biology 1: Crossdisciplinary Collaboration as CS Context. In *Proceedings of the 15th Annual Conference on Innovation and Technology in Computer Science Education (ITiCSE)*. 219–223. https://doi.org/10.1145/1822090.1822152

[9] Zachary Dodds, Ran Libeskind-Hadas, and Eliot Bush. 2012. Bio1 as CS1: Evaluating a Crossdisciplinary CS Context. In *Proceedings of the 17th Annual conference on Innovation and Technology in Computer Science Education (ITiCSE)*. ACM, 268–272. https://doi.org/10.1145/2325296.2325360

[10] Harvey Mudd College. 2015. Common Data Set. Online at https://www.hmc.edu/institutional-research/institutional-statistics/common-data-set/. (2015).

[11] Sharon K Lanning, Sonya L Ranson, and Rita M Willett. 2008. Communication skills instruction utilizing interdisciplinary peer teachers: program development and student perceptions. *J Dent Educ* 72, 2 (Feb 2008), 172–182.

[12] Ran Libeskind-Hadas and Eliot Bush. 2014. *Computing for biologists: Python programming and principles*. Cambridge University Press.

[13] Roy P. Pargas and Dhaval M. Shah. 2006. Things are Clicking in Computer Science Courses. In *Proceedings of the 37th ACM Technical Symposium on Computer Science Education (SIGCSE)*. ACM, 474–78. https://doi.org/10.1145/1124706.1121489

[14] Pavel Pevzner and Ron Shamir. 2009. Computing Has Changed Biology—Biology Education Must Catch Up. *Science* 325, 5940 (2009), 541–542.

[15] Leo Porter, Cynthia Bailey Lee, Beth Simon, Quintin Cutts, and Daniel Zingaro. 2011. Experience Report: A Multi-classroom Report on the Value of Peer Instruction. In *Proceedings of the 16th Annual Confernece on Innovation and Technology in Computer Science Education (ITiCSE)*. ACM, 138–142. https://doi.org/10.1145/1999747.1999788

[16] Leo Porter, Cynthia Bailey Lee, Beth Simon, and Daniel Zingaro. 2011. Peer Instruction: Do Students Really Learn from Peer Discussion in Computing?. In *Proceedings of the Annual ACM International Computing Education Research (ICER)*, Michael E. Caspersen, Alison Clear, and Kathryn Sanders (Eds.). ACM, 45–52. Online at http://dl.acm.org/citation.cfm?id=2016911.2016923.

[17] U.S. News & World Reports. [n. d.]. Top 100 - Lowest Acceptance Rates. ([n. d.]). Retrieved August 31, 2017 from https://www.usnews.com/best-colleges/rankings/lowest-acceptance-rate Fall 2015 Acceptance Rate when last accessed.

[18] Beth Simon, Michael Kohanfars, Jeff Lee, Karen Tamayo, and Quintin Cutts. 2010. Experience Report: Peer Instruction in Introductory Computing. In *Proceedings of the ACM Technical Symposium on Computer Science Education (SIGCSE)*. 341–45. http://dl.acm.org/citation.cfm?id=1734263.1734381

[19] Robert H. Sloan, Cynthia Taylor, and Richard Warner. 2017. Initial Experiences with a CS + Law Introduction to Computer Science (CS 1). In *Proceedings of the 2017 ACM Conference on Innovation and Technology in Computer Science Education (ITiCSE '17)*. 40–45. https://doi.org/10.1145/3059009.3059029

[20] University of California at San Diego, Saint Petersburg Academic University, and the Russian Academy of Sciences. [n. d.]. Rosalind, a platform for learning bioinformatics through problem solving. http://rosalind.info. ([n. d.]). http://rosalind.info/

[21] Daniel Zingaro. 2010. Experience Report: Peer Instruction in Remedial Computer Science. In *Proceedings of World Conference on Educational Multimedia, Hypermedia & Telecommunications(Ed-Media)*, Jan Herrinton and Bill Hunger (Eds.). AACE, 5030–35. Online at http://editlib.org/p/36184/.

[22] Emile Zuckerkandl, Richard T Jones, and Linus Pauling. 1960. A comparison of animal hemoglobins by tryptic peptide pattern analysis. *Proceedings of the National Academy of Sciences* 46, 10 (1960), 1349–1360.

[23] Stuart Zweben and Betsy Bizot. 2017. 2016 Taulbee Survey. *Computing Research News* 29, 5 (2017). http://cra.org/crn/wp-content/uploads/sites/7/2017/05/2016-Taulbee-Survey.pdf

Programming the Central Dogma: An Integrated Unit on Computer Science and Molecular Biology Concepts

Anna Ritz
Reed College
Biology Department
3203 SE Woodstock Boulevard
Portland, Oregon 97202-8199
aritz@reed.edu

ABSTRACT

Much of modern biology requires quantitative and computational skills for the proper analysis of large-scale datasets, and there is a recognized need for computational training in undergraduate biology programs. This experience report describes a four-week unit designed to introduce fundamental computer science concepts and molecular biology concepts in an integrated fashion. The unit serves as the first four weeks of an introductory course taught within the Biology Department at an undergraduate institution, and is designed to introduce computational thinking to non-computational science majors. Survey results reveal that the course has attracted students from all years (first years through seniors), the majority of students have been women, and students have large self-perceived learning gains in computer science concepts. The unit shows promise for engaging non-computational students through applications in introductory molecular biology. Materials are available at http://www.reed.edu/biology/courses/bio131/resources.html.

CCS CONCEPTS

• **Social and professional topics → Computational thinking; Computer science education;** • **Applied computing →** *Bioinformatics*;

KEYWORDS

Computational biology; introductory programming; undergraduate education; computational thinking

ACM Reference format:
Anna Ritz. 2018. Programming the Central Dogma: An Integrated Unit on Computer Science and Molecular Biology Concepts. In SIGCSE'18: *The 49th ACM Technical Symposium on Computer Science Education, Baltimore, MD, USA, February 21–24, 2018.* ACM, NY, NY, USA. 6 pages. https://doi.org/http://dx.doi.org/10.1145/3159450.3159590

1 INTRODUCTION

Biology has seen an explosion of enormous, complex datasets that require computational methods to process, store, and analyze them. The number of publications that involve *bioinformatics*, loosely defined as research at the intersection of biology and computer science, is expected to grow by as much as 93% by 2025 [15]. A current challenge in biology education is to introduce quantitative skills into the curriculum that engages students who may otherwise be unprepared for quantitative and computational reasoning [24]. There is a recognized need for computational biology courses as part of scientific training, and recent efforts have established communities of educators focused on bioinformatics within biology [8] and computer science [2]. However, many existing computational biology courses are typically intended for graduate or upper-level undergraduate students [17].

This experience report aims to introduce computational concepts to biology majors early in their undergraduate education. The overall goal of the four-week unit is to provide a crash course on introductory programming that is intertwined with biology concepts. The computational problems posed in the three main assignments are critical in computational biology, and capture much of the programming concepts necessary for first-year programmers. While this is not a rigorous computer science course, the immediate application to real data aims to engage non-computational students.

1.1 Related Work

Computational biology education has been a focus for over twenty years [1, 17], and there is a growing amount of training materials for biologists [10, 21, 23]. Workshops developed by Software Carpentry [28] and Data Carpentry [25] have helped train current practitioners as well as students entering the field. Pavel Pevzner and Phillip Compeau have developed a six-course Coursera series on Bioinformatics Algorithms, which uses a textbook combined with Rosalind, a web-based platform for learning about computational biology by problem solving [6].

In addition to online resources, computational biology training has appeared at the undergraduate level across many institutions. Computational biology is a common elective course in computer science programs, where it is typically presented as an upper-level algorithms course on biological sequence analysis. These courses draw on textbooks that describe algorithms on strings and their applications [5, 12, 14]. The Coursera series on bioinformatics algorithms grew out of Pavel Pevzner's introductory courses at University of California, San Diego [5, 6, 14], which has been a leading example of undergraduate training in computational biology.

Within undergraduate biology programs, computational biology courses have a notably different flavor. Computational topics in biology courses aim to teach students how to use well-established

SIGCSE'18, February 21–24, 2018, Baltimore, MD, USA

ACM ISBN ISBN 978-1-4503-5103-4/18/02.
https://doi.org/http://dx.doi.org/10.1145/3159450.3159590

tools such as BLAST for local sequence alignment and Clustal for multiple sequence alignment [17]. Recent textbooks written by biologists [13] or co-authored by biologists and computer scientists [4] are promising resources for including more programming concepts into undergraduate biology courses.

Many computational biology topics covered in tool-based and algorithmic-focused classes are similar – they include sequence alignment, motif finding, genome assembly, and phylogenetic reconstruction – but the courses are usually intended for intermediate to advanced undergraduate students [17]. There are notable exceptions, however, and a well-known example is Harvey Mudd's introductory BioCS1 course, which has successfully placed equal emphasis on biology and computer science topics at an introductory level [9, 16]. The course is team taught with computer science and biology faculty, which is the ideal scenario if there is enough faculty support at the institution, and materials have been adapted by other institutions. This report offers suggestions for a smaller unit that introduces computational thinking within an introductory biology curriculum.

1.2 Audience and Academic Environment

This four-week unit is the first component of an *Introduction to Computational Biology* course taught in the Biology Department at Reed College, a primarily undergraduate institution in Portland, Oregon. This course is separate from the recently-established Computer Science program at Reed, yet it is grounded in computer science concepts and taught by a computer scientist affiliated with the Biology Department. *Introduction to Computational Biology* was developed based on initial lectures from a Computational Thinking course from Brown University's Department of Computer Science [20], and uses the Compeau and Pevzner textbook [5] along with the companion Rosalind website [22].

Introduction to Computational Biology requires no programming or computer science experience, but students are expected to have completed first-semester introductory biology or equivalent. In addition to three hours of lecture, there is a two hour computational laboratory with structured labs that lead into the relevant assignment. The professor and an undergraduate TA are available during the lab sections. To-date, 49 students have completed the course over three semesters. Students range from first years to seniors and include both biology and non-biology majors (Figure 7). There are typically a few students who are familiar with programming and computer science concepts (e.g. they have complete CS1 or equivalent). More details about the introductory course are presented in Section 3.

1.3 The Central Dogma

The Central Dogma is a concept coined by Francis Crick that, at its most fundamental level, describes the transfer of information within a cell [7]. The genome is comprised of a double-stranded molecule called DNA, carefully organized and packed into chromosomes. Our DNA is nearly identical in every one of our trillions of cells, yet cells perform dramatically different functions. The information from our genome is selectively transferred into the synthesis of proteins, molecules that carry out complex biochemical reactions that result in a cellular response (such as grow and divide, recycle components, or move). This transfer of information typically requires a single-stranded molecule called RNA. The phrase "DNA makes RNA makes protein," while over-simplified, summarizes the transfer of information that has been collectively defined as the Central Dogma of molecular biology (Figure 1).

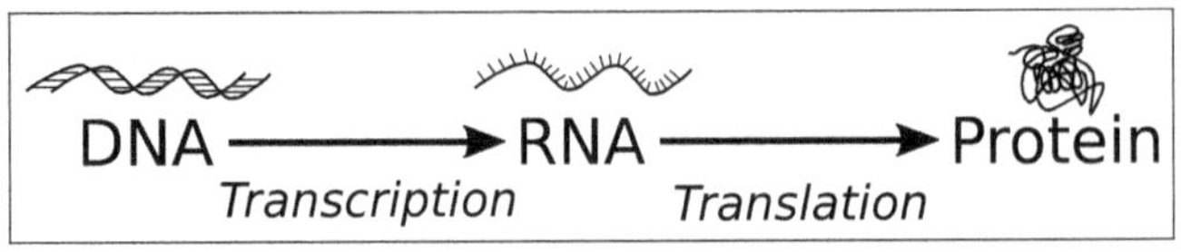

Figure 1: Simplified View of the Central Dogma.

2 CONTENT

The transfer of information summarized by the Central Dogma can be formalized as straightforward computational problems that introduce fundamental programming concepts. The unit is centered around eight computational problems that are directly related to sequence analysis (Table 1), which are described in further detail in the following subsections.

2.1 Week 1: Introduction to Functions

The first week of the unit does not begin with Python programming – it begins with Excel. Nearly every student has worked with spreadsheets; the point of the first few lectures is to reveal that they already know what a function is. The first assignment cements the following concepts within a spreadsheet environment: (a) variables and assignments, by referencing values by their cell location (e.g., A1), (b) types, by formatting cells as numeric or strings, and (c) using built-in functions such as LEN and SUM, and learning how to look up functions in an API. In addition to basic calculations, the first assignment aims to convey the difficulty of working with strings in Excel. Questions that involve standard Excel functions include calculating the length of a string, concatenating strings, removing characters from a string, and counting the number of occurrences of a character in a string. The last question in the assignment poses the first computational problem:

Problem 1 (HAM). Count the number of character differences between two strings s_1 and s_2 of equal length.

This problem is commonly known as computing the Hamming Distance [5], and appears at multiple points throughout the course. Students complete functions in the blue cells in Figure 2, and are assessed based on whether the function is correct and updates when different characters are entered into the green cells. Extensions of this problem include shifting the strings by prepending spaces to one of s_1 or s_2 (Figure 2 bottom), providing the optimization formulation of Problem 1:

Problem 2 (HAM-SHIFT). Find a shifted alignment by prepending spaces that minimizes the number of character differences between two strings s_1 and s_2.

Problem 2 describes a variant of a sequence alignment problem, namely global ungapped alignment. Sequence alignment is covered in the middle of the semester; when gaps are allowed within the

Problem	Programming Concepts	Rosalind
In Excel	Variables & Assignments	
1 HAM	Variable Types	
2 HAM-SHIFT	Built-in Functions	
	String Manipulation	
In Python	Strings, Ints, and Floats	
3 COUNT	Iteration	*DNA*
1 HAM	Conditionals	*HAMM*
4 REVCOMP	User-Defined Functions	*REVC*
5 TRANSCRIBE	Lists	*RNA*
6 SPLICE	Slicing	*SPLC*
7 TRANSLATE	Program Organization	*TRANSLATE*
8 DOGMA	Dictionaries (advanced)	

Table 1: List of Computational Problems. Last column denotes most similar problem from Rosalind's Bioinformatics Stronghold Track [22].

strings, this problem becomes a classic motivation for dynamic programming. The goal of the first assignment is to convey that, while Excel is powerful for numeric data, it is a pain for text manipulation.

2.2 Week 2: String manipulation

Lectures from the end of Week 1 begin teaching basic Python programming concepts, starting with using the interpreter as a calculator. The second assignment includes a Python skeleton script where students "fill in holes" by working through directions in the comments. This includes standard programming assignments that introduce expressions and assignments, types (ints, floats, and strings), lists and indexing into strings and lists, and iteration.

During lectures, students begin manipulating toy DNA sequences. They learn about the double-stranded DNA molecule, which is comprised of four nucleotides (for simplicity, we will keep them as A/C/G/T). They first implement a customized LENGTH code snippet that uses a counter to compute the length of the string. They then learn about conditionals, which allows students to count the frequency of nucleotides in a string of DNA:

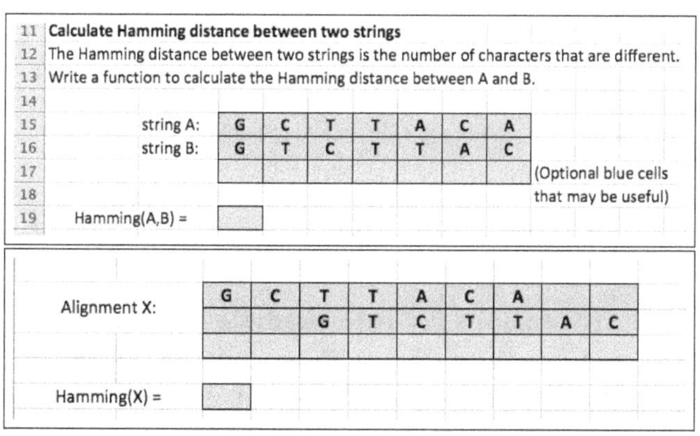

Figure 2: Hamming Distance Problem in Excel.

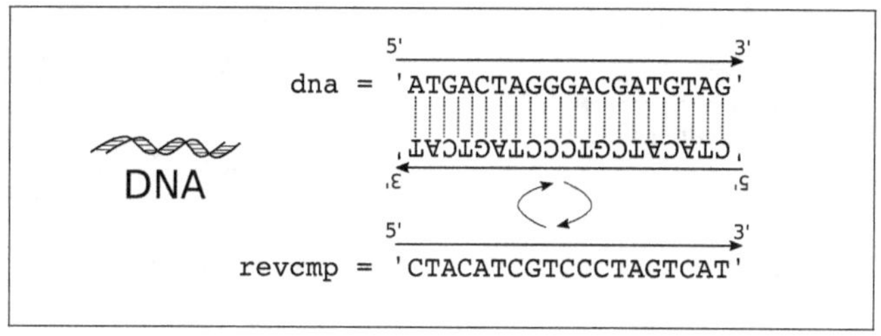

Figure 3: DNA Reverse Complement Problem.

Problem 3 (COUNT). Given a string $s \in \{A, C, G, T\}^*$, count the number of A's, C's, G',s and T's.

The final problem in this assignment is related to the fact that DNA is double-stranded and nucleotides have an affinity for A/T pairs and C/G pairs. Further, there is a notion of directness for a strand of DNA, typically referred to as the 5' and 3' ends (and always read in the 5'-to-3' direction). Thus, given a string s of DNA in the 5'-to-3' direction, students write code to compute the reverse complement of s, which will also be in the 5'-to-3' direction (Figure 3):

Problem 4 (REVCOMP). Given a string $s \in \{A, C, G, T\}^*$ (assuming the 5'-to-3' direction), return the reverse complement of s (in the 5'-to-3' direction).

The solution to this problem can be solved in two pieces: (a) creating a string comprised of the complement of each letter (e.g., A matched with T, C matched with G), and (b) reversing the contents of the string. This provides an opportunity to introduce functions, and establish a modular solution to the problem. By this point, students will gain familiarity with simple Boolean operations for string equality. As demonstration of their one-week progress, students can re-solve Problem 1 for any two strings of equal length.

2.3 Week 3: Transcription

The second half of the unit is designed to reinforce concepts learned in the first two weeks through small programming problems, while introducing more details about the Central Dogma. As shown in Figure 1, there are two main steps involved in the transmission of information from DNA to proteins. The first step converts the contents stored in DNA into RNA, a single-stranded nucleic acid that serves as an intermediary between DNA and proteins. DNA and RNA are structurally similar molecules, with notable differences in the type of ribose used as the "backbone" of the nucleic acid (deoxyribose in DNA vs ribose in RNA), and the fact that RNA is comprised of A/C/G/U rather than A/C/G/T. Pieces of DNA are discretized into regions called *genes*, which may be hundreds to thousands of nucleotides long. Genes are transcribed into RNA molecules by proteins that form a complex machinery, which will not be described here. While students learn about this process (especially the directionality of the process), the computational problem for transcribing a segment of DNA to RNA is straightforward (Figure 4):

Problem 5 (TRANSCRIBE). Given a string $s \in \{A, C, G, T\}^*$, return the transcribed RNA.

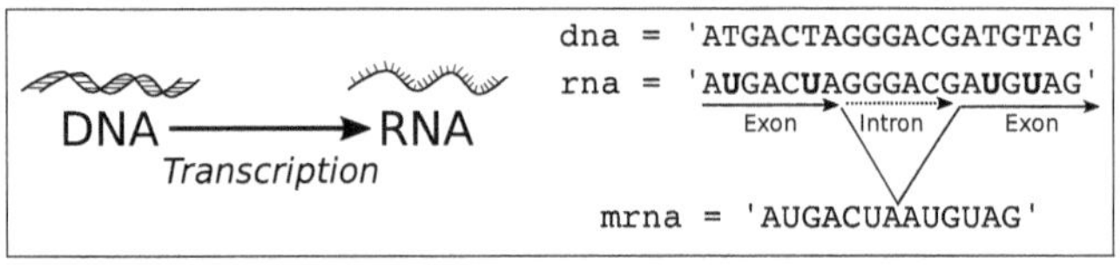

Figure 4: Transcription and RNA Processing Problem.

While RNA is commonly thought as the intermediary for producing proteins, recent work has revealed a diverse set of functions for RNA. The RNA molecules that code for proteins must be further processed into messenger RNA (mRNA) before they can move on to the next step of the Central Dogma. Genes that are encoded in DNA have small segments that describe parts of the proteins, called *exons*, separated by much larger segments that contain irrelevant sequence to the protein, called *introns*. Machinery must splice out the intronic regions of the transcribed RNA (Figure 4). While students learn about RNA processing (including other components of the messenger RNA), they can solve the following problem:

Problem 6 (SPLICE). Given a string $s \in \{A, C, G, U\}^*$ and a list of exon and intron starts, return the mRNA comprising only the exons.

This problem can be complicated by the structure of the inputs. The current form of the assignment provides two lists of equal length: one list denotes exon start indices and the other list denotes intron start indices. As a warm-up, students are given a hypothetical gene `'eeeeeeiiiiiiiieeeee'` with coordinates that should splice out (remove) the `i` characters in the string. Students can also calculate basic statistics about each gene that includes the number of exons, the average exon length, and the average intron length.

2.4 Week 4: Translation

In the final week of the unit, the focus shifts to the underlying molecular biology as we discuss the second step of the Central Dogma, which converts mRNA into protein, which are comprised of amino acids. During translation, mRNA is partitioned into non-overlapping substrings of length three called *codons*, where each codon maps to one of 20 possible amino acids (Figure 5). Amino acids are attached to a growing protein by "reading" the mRNA sequence in groups of three letters.

The first computational question we discuss is *why are codons three nucleotides long?* This is a classic information theory question: with an alphabet of four nucleotides, a single-letter code would only describe four items, a two-letter code would describe $4^2 = 16$ items, and a three-letter code would describe $4^3 = 64$ items. There are 20 amino acids (plus a signal for "stop"), so one needs the three-letter code to distinguish them. As a result, multiple codons map to the same amino acid. This redundancy has a pattern of variance in the third nucleotide due to the physical structure of the translation mechanism.

The computational problem of translating an mRNA to protein is formulated as follows:

Problem 7 (TRANSLATE). Given a string $s \in \{A, C, G, U\}^*$ (where mod(length(s),3)=0) and a codon table, return the protein described by the codons.

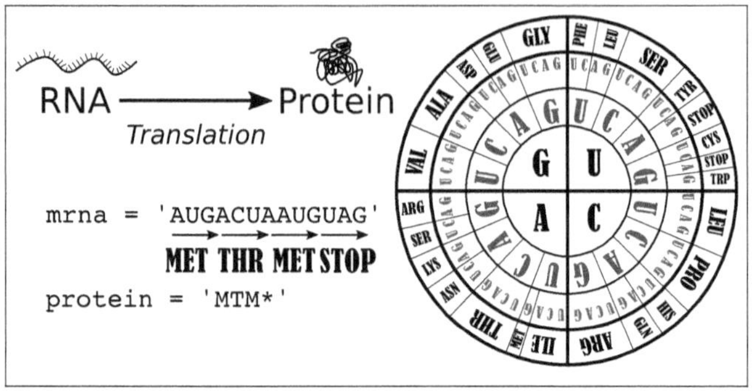

Figure 5: Translation Problem. Circular codon table adapted from [18].

The assignment includes a `codon_to_aa()` function that maps each 3-letter codon to the appropriate amino acid. The last task of the assignment is to put the entire pipeline together:

Problem 8 (DOGMA). Given a string $s \in \{A, C, G, T\}^*$ in the 5'-to-3' direction with a list of exon and intron starts, return the protein.

2.5 Case Study: Cancer Genes

Public repositories contain the sequences that comprise the human genome, and have been extensively revised since the sequenced genome was announced in the early 2000s. The UCSC Genome Browser is one of the most popular repositories, offering a searchable database that annotates genetic segments and a programmatic API [26]. Students are able to compute the solutions for Problems 3–8 on real gene sequences, meaning that the students begin working with real data at about the same time that they learn their first python programming concepts. As a case study, the last problem is framed as one that transcribes and translate cancer genes.

Cancer is a disease characterized by mutations at the DNA (gene) level, and many genes that are related to cancer have been studied for decades [27]. SRC (pronounced "sark") is one such gene whose overexpression (in terms of RNA abundance) is associated with colon, breast, ovarian, and lung cancers, among many others [11]. This gene is over 22,000 nucleotides long, containing 13 exons that create a 1,611 nucleotide long mRNA sequence. This sequence is transcribed into a protein with 546 amino acids and one "stop" codon. The UCSC Genome Browser contains information about the DNA sequence, the mRNA sequence, and the protein sequence, as well as the exon and intron starts. Students are given all these pieces of information, and require their code to contain tests that evaluate whether the computed mRNA matches the real mRNA sequence and whether the computed protein matches the real protein sequence. Students are also provided with hypothetical genes for testing on a smaller scale, and require outputs to be printed to screen (Figure 6).

2.6 Extensions for Intermediate Programmers

This unit can be understandably slow-paced for students who are familiar with some programming. However, there are points that can be extended for more challenging problems. First, students are encouraged to write user-defined functions for standard built-in functions such as `len()` and `reverse()` for practice; students

```
Dataset: testPos
DNA: CCCATGGTCGGGGGGGGGGAGTCCATAACCC
Num exons: 2
strand: +
RNA (from file): AUGGUCAGUCCAUAA
peptide (from file): MVSP*

Computed mRNA: AUGGUCAGUCCAUAA
mRNA matches!

Computed Peptide: MVSP*
Peptide matches!
```

Figure 6: Output from Problem 8 for a test gene.

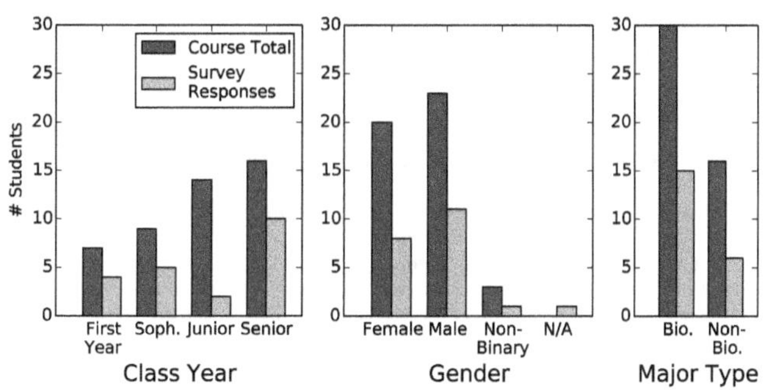

Figure 7: Number of students by year, gender, and type of major.

end up adopting more built-in functions in the later part of the course. Second, students can write their own codon_to_aa() function using dictionaries. Finally, an advanced assignment is to extend Problem 8 for handing genes on the *negative strand* of a DNA molecule. The UCSC Genome Browser has standardized the format of storing gene sequences, returning the negative strand (in the 5'-to-3' direction) but always reporting exon boundaries according to the *forward* strand of the DNA. Students can handle the negative strand by re-mapping the exon boundaries (and reversing the order of the exons) before solving Problem 8, but it requires careful thought. This subtlety introduces students to both the complexity of standardization and file processing skills.

3 CONTEXT WITHIN A COURSE

The remaining components of this course use elements of the widely-used bioinformatics algorithms textbook by Compeau and Pevzner [5]. The units in the class are framed by the biological motivations within each chapter, but are adapted for an introductory audience (rather than an intermediate or upper-level undergraduate audience). They include:

- **Identifying the origin of DNA replication** by searching for frequently-occurring strings of length k (k-mers).
- **Finding DNA-binding protein motifs** with a greedy algorithm.
- **DNA assembly** by constructing a de Bruijn graph and identifying Eulerian cycles.
- **Sequence alignment** by implementing dynamic programming.

Each of the topics above has an associated programming assignment, where students implement basic aspects of the content. The last two weeks of the course are structured around final projects. Projects are wide-ranging, but many have involved extensions of the Central Dogma unit. For example, single-stranded RNA molecules tend to fold in on itself due to the A/U and C/G pairing; and intermediate programmers have successfully implemented the Nussinov dynamic program to compute the optimal number of nucleotide pair matchings given a string [19].

4 STUDENT RESPONSES

Student response from the *Introduction to Computational Biology* course evaluations has been positive overall. However, as one of the few introductory science courses with a small number of students (typically 15-20), these responses may be inflated due to the structure of the course and the individualize attention, rather than the effectiveness of the course itself. Further, the student evaluations were about the entire course, rather than this four-week unit. Thus, all 49 students who have completed the course to-date were anonymously surveyed to gather responses related to learning gains and preparation for the remainder of the course.[1] While there are established issues with surveys that assess undergraduate self-reported gains [3], the goal here was to identify changes in *self-perceived* learning gains, which are associated with a confidence in the subject.

Twenty-one students completed the survey, reflecting the diversity by year and gender (Figure 7). Before the start of the course, the majority of students were comfortable with molecular biology concepts, and the majority of students were unfamiliar with computational skills (Figure 8). Self-perceived learning gains in biology were not large, which is expected since students believed they had background in the subject before taking the course. This is also reasonable given the large proportion of juniors and seniors in the course (Figure 7). Strikingly, self-perceived gains in computational concepts are very large, especially when aggregated across all concepts (Figure 9).

Students were also asked about the usefulness of the assignments in preparation for the rest of the course. The assignments were listed as HW1 (Excel), HW2 (Python Practice) and HW3 (Central Dogma), which was further subdivided into transcription and translation. While the Excel homework was not as useful to students as the subsequent homework assignments, only one individual found HW1 to be not helpful and confusing (Figure 9). Written comments revealed that some students were unfamiliar with Excel, making the first assignment more difficult than intended. The usefulness of the transcription and the translation components of HW3 were listed as equally useful, and are not shown here.

[1] This survey, disseminated as a Google Form, was deemed to be exempt by the Institutional Review Board.

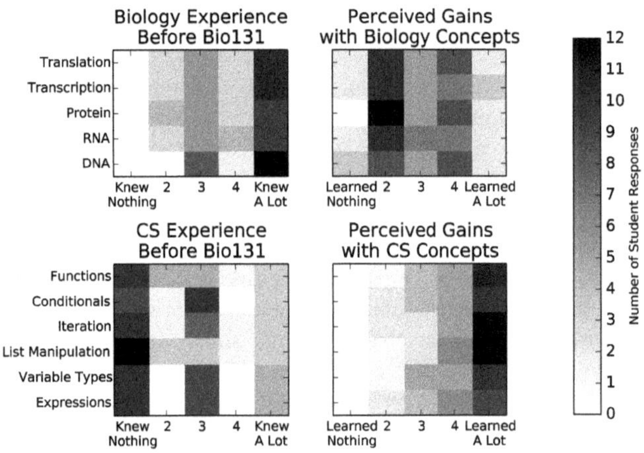

Figure 8: Student responses about biology and CS concepts on a 5-point scale.

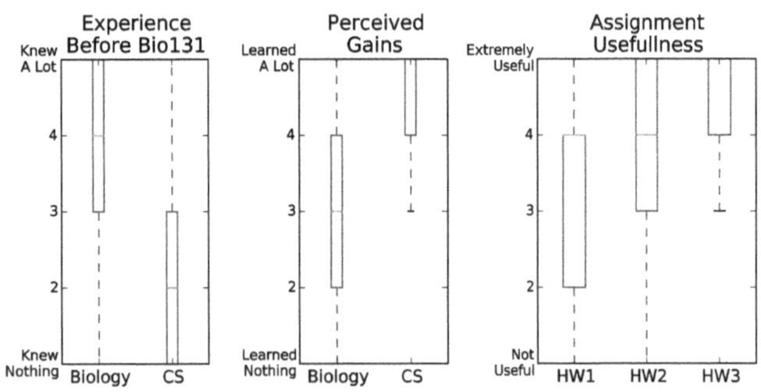

Figure 9: Self-perceived experience, learning gains, and assignment usefulness. First two plots summarize the data in Figure 8.

5 CONCLUSION

New biological technologies are producing enormous datasets, requiring significant training in computational and quantitative skills. While computational biology courses exist at institutions, they are usually offered within computer science as upper-level electives. Thus, there is a need to introduce biology majors to computational reasoning early in their undergraduate education. This introductory-level unit integrates computational problems with molecular biology concepts, providing biology students an immediate connection and meaning for programming. The unit may also be useful in cross-disciplinary courses, where it is important to get everyone on the same page as quickly as possible. Student responses indicate that the unit helped cement computer science concepts, and the assignments were useful preparation for the remainder of the course. Future work includes developing a tool to automatically pull down and process *any* UCSC gene for the unit, providing full flexibility for students to pursue genes related to diseases of interest. This will help produce more robust faculty development materials for others to easily adapt the four-week unit in their courses.

REFERENCES

[1] Russ B. Altman. 1998. A curriculum for bioinformatics: the time is ripe. *Bioinformatics* 14, 7 (1998), 549–550.

[2] Teresa K Atwood, Erik Bongcam-Rudloff, Michelle E Brazas, Manuel Corpas, Pascale Gaudet, Fran Lewitter, Nicola Mulder, Patricia M Palagi, Maria Victoria Schneider, Celia WG van Gelder, et al. 2015. GOBLET: the global organisation for bioinformatics learning, education and training. *PLoS computational biology* 11, 4 (2015), e1004143.

[3] Nicholas A Bowman and Patrick L Hill. 2011. Measuring how college affects students: Social desirability and other potential biases in college student self-reported gains. *New Directions for Institutional Research* 2011, 150 (2011), 73–85.

[4] Caroline St Clair and Jonathan E Visick. 2013. *Exploring Bioinformatics.* Jones & Bartlett Publishers.

[5] Phillip Compeau and Pavel Pevzner. 2015. *Bioinformatics algorithms: an active learning approach.* Active Learning Publishers.

[6] Phillip Compeau and Pavel A Pevzner. 2015. Life After MOOCs. *Commun. ACM* 58, 10 (2015), 41–44.

[7] Francis Crick. 1970. Central dogma of molecular biology. *Nature* 227, 5258 (1970), 561–563.

[8] Elizabeth Dinsdale, Sarah CR Elgin, Neal Grandgenett, William Morgan, Anne Rosenwald, William Tapprich, Eric W Triplett, and Mark A Pauley. 2015. NIBLSE: A network for integrating bioinformatics into life sciences education. *CBE-Life Sciences Education* 14, 4 (2015), le3.

[9] Zachary Dodds, Ran Libeskind-Hadas, and Eliot Bush. 2010. When CS 1 is biology 1: crossdisciplinary collaboration as CS context. In *Proceedings of the fifteenth annual conference on Innovation and technology in computer science education.* ACM, 219–223.

[10] Berk Ekmekci, Charles E McAnany, and Cameron Mura. 2016. An introduction to programming for bioscientists: A python-based primer. *PLoS computational biology* 12, 6 (2016), e1004867.

[11] Margaret C Frame. 2002. Src in cancer: deregulation and consequences for cell behaviour. *Biochimica et Biophysica Acta (BBA)-Reviews on Cancer* 1602, 2 (2002), 114–130.

[12] Dan Gusfield. 1997. *Algorithms on strings, trees and sequences: computer science and computational biology.* Cambridge university press.

[13] Steven Harold David Haddock and Casey W Dunn. 2011. *Practical computing for biologists.* Sinauer Associates Sunderland, MA.

[14] Neil C Jones and Pavel Pevzner. 2004. *An introduction to bioinformatics algorithms.* MIT press.

[15] Jonghoon Kang, Seyeon Park, Aarya Venkat, and Adarsh Gopinath. 2015. Quantitative analysis of the trends exhibited by the three interdisciplinary biological sciences: biophysics, bioinformatics, and systems biology. *Journal of microbiology & biology education* 16, 2 (2015), 198.

[16] Ran Libeskind-Hadas and Eliot Bush. 2013. A first course in computing with applications to biology. *Briefings in bioinformatics* 14, 5 (2013), 610–617.

[17] Alejandra J Magana, Manaz Taleyarkhan, Daniela Rivera Alvarado, Michael Kane, John Springer, and Kari Clase. 2014. A survey of scholarly literature describing the field of bioinformatics education and bioinformatics educational research. *CBE-Life Sciences Education* 13, 4 (2014), 607–623.

[18] Kenneth R Miller and Joseph S Levine. 2006. Prentice hall biology. *Boston, MA: Pearson Prentice Hall. Retrieved on February* 4 (2006), 2014.

[19] Ruth Nussinov and Ann B Jacobson. 1980. Fast algorithm for predicting the secondary structure of single-stranded RNA. *Proceedings of the National Academy of Sciences* 77, 11 (1980), 6309–6313.

[20] Laura Pappano. 2017. Learning to Think Like a Computer. *The New York Times: Education Life* (2017).

[21] Jeffrey M Perkel. 2015. Pick Up Python. *Nature* 518, 7537 (2015), 125.

[22] Pavel Pevzner. 2012. Rosalind. (2012).

[23] Ashley Shade and Tracy K Teal. 2015. Computing workflows for biologists: a roadmap. *PLoS biology* 13, 11 (2015), e1002303.

[24] Susan Singer and Karl A Smith. 2013. Discipline-Based Education Research: Understanding and Improving Learning in Undergraduate Science and Engineering. *Journal of Engineering Education* 102, 4 (2013), 468–471.

[25] Tracy K Teal, Karen A Cranston, Hilmar Lapp, Ethan White, Greg Wilson, Karthik Ram, and Aleksandra Pawlik. 2015. Data carpentry: workshops to increase data literacy for researchers. *International Journal of Digital Curation* 10, 1 (2015), 135–143.

[26] Cath Tyner, Galt P Barber, Jonathan Casper, Hiram Clawson, Mark Diekhans, Christopher Eisenhart, Clayton M Fischer, David Gibson, Jairo Navarro Gonzalez, Luvina Guruvadoo, et al. 2016. The UCSC Genome Browser database: 2017 update. *Nucleic acids research* 45, D1 (2016), D626–D634.

[27] Bert Vogelstein and Kenneth W Kinzler. 2004. Cancer genes and the pathways they control. *Nature medicine* 10, 8 (2004), 789.

[28] Greg Wilson. 2006. Software Carpentry: Getting Scientists to Write Better Code by Making Them More Productive. *Computing in Science & Engineering* (2006).

PVC: Visualizing C Programs on Web Browsers for Novices*

Ryosuke Ishizue
Department of Computer Science and Engineering
Waseda University
Tokyo, Japan
ishizue@ruri.waseda.jp

Kazunori Sakamoto
National Institute of Informatics
Tokyo, Japan
exkazuu@nii.ac.jp

Hironori Washizaki
Department of Computer Science and Engineering
Waseda University
Tokyo, Japan
washizaki@waseda.jp

Yoshiaki Fukazawa
Department of Computer Science and Engineering
Waseda University
Tokyo, Japan
fukazawa@waseda.jp

ABSTRACT

Many researchers have proposed program visualization tools for memory management because this is a challenging concept for novice programmers. For example, SeeC and PythonTutor (PT) are state-of-the-art tools for C languages. However, three problems hinder the use of these and other tools: capability (P1), installability (P2), and usability (P3). (P1) Tools do not fully support dynamic memory allocation or File Input / Output (I/O) and Standard Input. (P2) Novice programmers often have difficulty installing SeeC due to its dependence on Clang and setting up an offline environment that uses PT. (P3) Revisualization of the modified source code in SeeC requires several steps. To alleviate these issues, we propose a new visualization tool called PlayVisualizerC (PVC). PVC, which is designed for novice C language programmers to provide solutions (S1–3) for P1–3. S1 offers complete support for dynamic memory allocation, standard I/O, and file I/O. S2 involves installation in a user web browser and its server program is initiated by executing a jar file. S3 reduces the steps required for revisualization. To evaluate PVC, we conducted an experiment and questionnaire involving 30 students. Students using PVC solved a set of four programming tasks on average 1.7 times faster and with 19% more correct answers than those using a current state-of-the-art visualization tool.

CCS CONCEPTS

• **Human-centered computing** → *Visualization systems and tools*; • **Social and professional topics** → *Computer science education*;

KEYWORDS

C language, visualization, web application

*This paper is an extended version of a poster "An Interactive Web Application Visualizing Memory Space For Novice C Programmers"[11] presented at the 48th ACM Technical Symposium on Computer Science Education (SIGCSE 2017).

SIGCSE '18, Feb. 21–24, 2018, Baltimore, MD, USA

ACM ISBN 978-1-4503-5103-4/18/02.
https://doi.org/10.1145/3159450.3159566

ACM Reference Format:
Ryosuke Ishizue, Kazunori Sakamoto, Hironori Washizaki, and Yoshiaki Fukazawa. 2018. PVC: Visualizing C Programs on Web Browsers for Novices. In *SIGCSE '18: The 49th ACM Technical Symposium on Computer Science Education, Feb. 21–24, 2018, Baltimore, MD, USA.* ACM, New York, NY, USA, 6 pages. https://doi.org/10.1145/3159450.3159566

1 INTRODUCTION

Various visualization techniques have been proposed to aid programmers in understanding the program execution status [1, 3, 7, 18, 21]. Most existing debuggers and integrated development environments such as GDB and Eclipse provide limited features to visualize the program execution status. Typically, these applications display simple text outputs, but do not visualize the relationships between variables, pointers, and memory. Learning how to use these tools is often difficult for novice programmers (hereafter referred to as novices) [1]. Instead of enhancing the understanding of programming languages, these tools often hinder novices.

C programming language (C language) is popular and is typically one of the first languages learned by novices. However, mastery of C language requires that users learn a basic but difficult-to-grasp concept of memory management, including pointers and dynamic memory allocation. This can be extremely challenging for novices [2, 14, 17].

To assist novices, previous studies have proposed tools to visualize the program execution status [6, 12, 13, 20]. For example, SeeC and Python Tutor (PT) are state-of-the-art tools that effectively visualize C programs. However, three problems affect these and other tools: **capability (P1), installability (P2), and usability (P3). (P1)** SeeC does not fully support dynamic memory allocation. It displays the size of the allocated memory in bytes, but omits more detailed memory values. PT does not support file Input / Output (I/O) and standard Input. **(P2)** It is difficult for novices to install SeeC due to its dependency on Clang, a compiler. Moreover, students struggle to use PT in an offline environment, and teachers must setup PT for C language on their computer. **(P3)** SeeC is a desktop application consisting of a compiler and a visualizer. Users cannot modify the source code during SeeC's visualization. Thus, SeeC requires many steps to modify and revisualize C programs. PT

[1]A **novice** is defined as a person learning C language who is currently trying to understand the concept of memory management, including pointers and dynamic memory allocation.

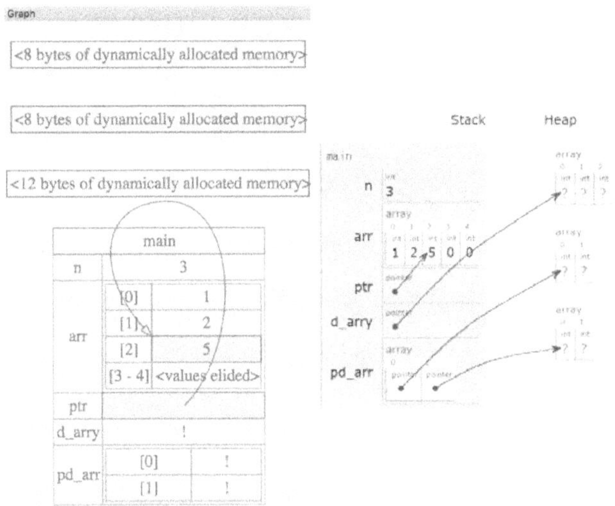

Figure 1: Screenshots of SeeC (left) and PT (right).

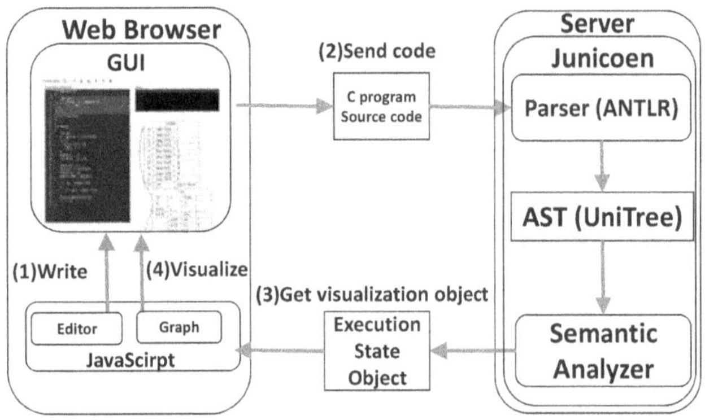

Figure 2: Overview of the PVC architecture

does not have this problem because it is a web application running on a browser window.

To solve **P1–3**, we propose PlayVisualizerC (PVC), which is an interpreter of C language with features to visualize the program execution status. PVC provides three solutions **(S1–3)** to the problems outlined above. **(S1)** PVC can fully visualize variables, pointers, arrays, dynamically allocated memory, and their relationships. It supports standard I/O and file I/O. **(S2)** PVC is implemented as a web application. Because installation requires only a browser, executing a jar file can start the server program. **(S3)** PVC allows users to revisualize a program after source code modifications using a single button click.

The novel contributions of this paper are as follows:

(1) PVC can aid novices in understanding the program execution status and behaviors.
(2) PVC is published as a web application at `http://play-visualizer-c.herokuapp.com`, and as a standalone version at `https://github.com/RYOSKATE/PlayVisualizerC/releases`.
(3) We conducted an experiment and a questionnaire to verify that PVC addresses **P1–3**.

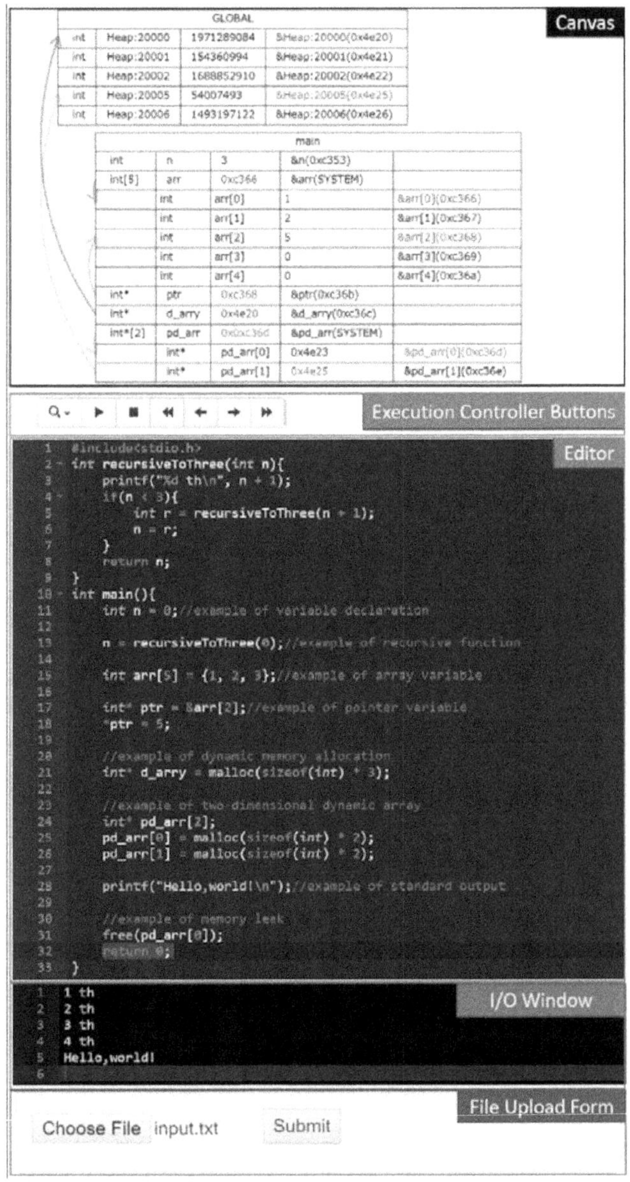

Figure 3: Screenshot of the PVC interface

2 RELATED WORKS

Previous studies have indicated that the concepts of memory and pointer are extremely challenging for novices. For example, Lahtinen et al. investigated the difficulties faced by novices in learning programming languages [14] and found that more than 500 students indicated that finding bugs in a program is the most difficult part of learning to program. Moreover, pointers and references are identified as two of the hardest programming concepts.

Milne and Petersen also investigated challenges surrounding learning and teaching of object-oriented programming (OOP) [17]. Their questionnaire showed that learning copy constructor and virtual function is difficult, primarily due to the fact that memory and pointer are hard concepts to grasp. These studies reveal that

Table 1: Comparison of PVC, SeeC, and PT functionality

Comparison items	PVC	SeeC	PT
Summary			
Capability (P1)	OK	(NG) It does not support malloc.	(NG) It does not support I/O.
Installability for client (P2)	(OK) Only a browser	(NG) Difficult to setup	(OK) Only a browser
Installability for server (P2)	(OK) Launch the playvisualizerc.jar file.	(NG) Not supported (Desktop application)	(NG) Very difficult to setup
Usability (P3)	(OK) Open in a browser, write the code, and press execute button.	(NG) Compiling is necessary beforehand. Visualizer cannot edit the code.	(OK) Open in a browser, write the code, and press execute button.
Language feature support			
malloc	Y	N	Y
I/O	Y	Y	N
Visualization expression			
Variables grouped by stack	Y	Y	
Pointer references represented by arrows	Y	Y	Y
Addresses of variables shown	Y	N	N
Display values of uninitialized variables	Random number	! or ? mark	An emoji
Visualization method	Run and create trace data using a proprietary execution environment (Junicoen).	Create execution trace data using LLVM (Clang).	Create execution trace data using GCC and a hacked Valgrind.

understanding memory and pointer are important steps towards progressing in programming ability.

Many studies have proposed visualization techniques and tools, which can effectively aid novices' understanding of these programming concepts. Some research has focused on visualizing the memory state of C language. Koike and Go proposed SuZMe, which visualizes the memory state by byte unit with a horizontal straight line [13]. SuZMe also checks the values of variables and memory allocation in detail. Milne et al. proposed a program visualization tool named OGRE [18]. OGRE generates planes to represent memory space such as Global, Heap, main(), and function(). An object is represented as a figure within three-dimensional space and cylinders connecting figures represent references. Egan and McDonald proposed SeeC, which visualizes the running state of a C program [6]. Moreno et al. proposed Eliot, which is an interactive animation environment to visualize algorithms written in the C programming language [15].

Other tools such as Jeliot [19] and OOP-anime [7] support OOP languages such as Java. These tools show the relationship between class, instance, and variable with figures such as lines and boxes.

Similar to our efforts for PVC, previous studies have developed these tools as web applications to improve accessibility. One example is Python Tutor (PT), which is a program visualization tool proposed by Guo that specializes in supporting Python and the embeddability in web-pages [9, 10]. Currently, PT supports visualization of other languages, including C language. Our literature investigation revealed that SeeC and PT are currently the most useful and widely available state-of-the-art tools for novices to learn about memory management in C language.

3 PROBLEMS WITH STATE-OF-THE-ART TOOLS

Figure 1 (left) and 1 (right) show the visualization results of SeeC and PT, respectively. The effectiveness of these two visualization expressions are similar. They have three common problems: **capability (P1), installability (P2), and usability (P3).** Table 1 summarizes these programs and compares the features of PVC, SeeC, and PT.

Capability (P1): SeeC does not support dynamic memory allocation (e.g., malloc) completely. Instead it shows the byte size of dynamically allocated memory in text. Figure 1 (left) illustrates an example of a visualization result from SeeC, which includes only the line < *n bytes of dynamically allocated memory* >. As this example shows, SeeC users cannot see the content of the memory allocated by programs such as *malloc*. On the other hand, PT does not allow file I/O and standard Input due to security issues. It is inconvenient that these functions cannot be used.

Installability (P2): The dependency of SeeC on Clang makes installation somewhat difficult. Many novice-oriented visualization tools proposed in previous studies require users to setup an execution environment. This is the main obstacle preventing users from installing these kinds of tools, regardless of a tool's usefulness [5]. Moreover, these tools are usually restricted to specific operating systems.

Another problem with PT is installability on a server computer. Even if students or teachers try to use PT, setting up a server program for C language on their own computer can be burdensome.[2] The other problem is the stability of the connection with the server. Users may not be able to visualize with PT due to the internet connection environment. For example, one study found that PT could not send back the visualization result when the client was connected to the Internet via *eduroam*, a famous academic Internet service.[3]

For these reasons, SeeC and PT are insufficient for novices to write and visualize their programs in class.

Usability (P3): Users cannot modify source code during SeeC's visualization because the source code is shown in a read-only text area. To revisualize a program, SeeC requires users to execute the following four steps each time the source code is modified:

[2] Github of PT says "it can be hard to run your own visualizer locally for non-Python languages, since there are complex setups in v4-cokapi/ that I haven't yet cleanly packaged up."

[3] Eduroam is an academic wireless LAN roaming infrastructure developed in GEANT (formerly TERENA) in Europe. It is the de facto standard of campus wireless LAN in 80 countries and regions in the world [8]. It has some limitations such as port restrictions.

(1) Modify the source code file with an external editing application.
(2) Recompile to generate an executable file with SeeC on a terminal or command prompt.
(3) Open the executable file to generate a recording file for program behavior and execution status visualization.
(4) Open the recording file in SeeC's viewer.

PT does not have such a problem.

4 OVERVIEW OF PVC

We implemented PVC with HTML5, JavaScript, C parser, and a semantic analyzer to overcome **P1–3**. The C parser and the semantic analyzer work on the server side. Figure 2 systematically overviews the program, while Fig. 3 shows a screenshot of PVC. To implement our design, we used *ANTLR*, which parses the source code, and *Junicoen*, which creates and executes the abstract syntax tree (AST), *UniTree*, in C language on the server [16]. PVC is a web application that simply requires users to input the URL into a web browser. Additionally, we provide a standalone version that launches a server-side system running on Java on a local computer. The standalone version does not require an internet connection. Therefore, PVC provides a solution **(S2)** to **installability (P2)**.

4.1 Tool Usage

Figure 3 shows an execution example in PVC. PVC has five GUI components: (1) editor, (2) execution controller buttons, (3) I/O window, (4) canvas for visualization, and (5) file upload form. Users can write source code in the editor. Clicking on the execution control buttons initiates the step execution. The I/O window shows the content of the standard output written by the program (e.g., *printf*) and accepts standard input (e.g., *scanf*). Canvas shows the program's execution status using tables and figures. PVC adaptively changes its layout to correspond with the size of the browser window.

The top of the GUI in Fig. 3 shows the program's execution controller. The controller includes the following six buttons: (i) change editor font size, (ii) initiate program execution, (iii) stop program execution, (iv) go backward for all step, (v) go backward one step, (vi) go forward one step, and (vii) go forward all steps. A statement unit executes each step.

Users also can upload files to a temporary space on the server side created for each browser session from the user files form. They can use these files via programs such as *fgets, fputc.*

PVC requires three steps:

(1) Input the URL of PVC into a web browser.
(2) Insert the source code into the editor to visualize it.
(3) Press the button to execute the program.

Simply changing the code and pressing the execution button during visualization allows the users to change the program. Thus, PVC provides a solution **(S3)** to **usability (P3)**.

4.2 Visualization Features

PVC, SeeC, and PT use a similar approach for visualization. The programs show values, names, and types of variables using arrows and boxes to represent pointer and stack references. For example, colored arrows and variable addresses help users understand that references differ. Movable figures make it easier to see the visualized results, while the display depth of the recursive functions informs users of how many times it has been called.

Table 2: Examination questions (T1–4) and questions in the questionnaire about usefulness (Q1–4)

T1	What are the final values of variables a, b, c, d, e?
T2	What are the values of variables n, r, (*pn) when the function f is returned for a third time?
T3	What are the final values of heap memory, which has not been freed, and of the pointer variable, which refers to the memory when the main function return?
T4	When are the values of n=1, a='B', b='A', c='C'?
Q1	Do you think this visualization tool helps solve the problems in the experiment?
Q2	Do you think this visualization tool is useful for C language novices?
Q3	Do you think this visualization tool is more accessible than other visualization or debugging tools (e.g., Eclipse, Visual Studio, GDB) that you have used?
Q4	In which areas of C language is this visualization program a useful learning tool? (multiple answers allowed) (A. variable, B. pointer, C. array, D. function, E. dynamic memory allocation, F. structure, G. data structures and algorithms, H. other)

Only PVC supports the following important features:

- Dynamically allocated memory visualized[4)]
- Memory addresses value displayed in hexadecimal
- File and standard I/O

Figure 3 presents an example of visualization with PVC. There are two boxes on the canvas: *main* and *GLOBAL*. *main* represents a stack of the main function, while *GLOBAL* contains dynamic variables for heap memory allocated by *malloc*. The table columns in the box show (1) type, (2) name, (3) value, and (4) address of each variable. For example, the first line of *main* refers to a variable of *n*, which is a type *int* and has a value of 3. Moreover, some variables, such as *ptr* and *d_arr*, refer to other variables. The pointer reference is represented as an arrow with the same color as the reference address (e.g., the green arrow from the row containing *ptr* to the row containing *arr*[2]).

Figures 1 (left) and 3 visualize the same code. Although SeeC stops its visualization, PVC visualizes the allocated heap memory referred to by the pointer variable d_array, which is not free. Therefore, PVC can be useful for debugging a program with memory leak action calls. Consequently, PVC provides a solution **(S1)** to **capability (P1)**. Thus, PVC can visualize pointer and dynamic memory allocation (Fig. 3). These solutions are summarized in Table 1.

5 EXPERIMENT

We investigated the following research questions (RQ):

- RQ1 Is PVC useful for informing users of the status of running programs?

4)Dynamically allocated memory can be visualized if *sizeof(type)* is used in arguments of *malloc*

Table 3: Comparison of PVC, SeeC, and no tool in terms of median, mean, and statistical test

		Number of correct answers	Time to answer [s]
Median (Mean)	no tool	3 (2.5)	1002.5 (1148.4)
	SeeC	2 (2.1)	1030 (1045.5)
	PVC	3 (3.1)	620.5 (623.3)
Steel-Dwass test (p-value)	PVC / no tool	<0.1	<0.01
	PVC / SeeC	<0.05	<0.05
	no tool / SeeC	n.s.	n.s.

- RQ2 Is PVC useful for novices who are learning C programming language concepts?
- RQ3 Is PVC as useful as similar tools for visualizing running program status, and is it more accessible as an application?

We conducted an experiment and a survey to evaluate PVC with respect to RQ1–3.

5.1 Experimental Setting

The participants were 30 undergraduate or graduate students majoring in computer science and engineering. Ten performed the tasks using PVC, 10 using SeeC [5)], and remaining 10 did not use a visualization tool (viewed the code only and used a pen and paper). After completing the tasks, all participants used PVC and answered the questionnaire.

The experiment involved four tasks. The source code used in this experiment was the same as the code shown on our demo site[6)]. Table 2 shows the examination questions (T1–4) for each task and the questions (Q1–4) in the questionnaire. The participants completed the questionnaire upon finishing the tasks using PVC. Prior to the experiment, we explained PVC and provided a tutorial on how to use it. (The explanation was almost identical to that in Fig. 3.). During the experiment, we measured the time taken to answer each question and checked the answers. Q1 to Q3 were evaluated on a scale from 1 to 5, where 5 is the most positive.

5.2 Experimental Results

Figure 4 shows a box plot of the time taken to answer each task, while Fig. 5 shows a bar graph of the percentage of correct answers for the tasks. Figures 6 and 7 show the questionnaire responses. Figure 6 shows the participants' answers to Q1–3, which evaluate the usefulness and accessibility of a tool, whereas Fig. 7 shows the answers to Q4, which assesses the utility of PVC. In other words, Fig. 6 represents a measure of the usefulness and accessibility of the PVC program (Q1–3), while Fig. 7 relates the appropriateness of the tool to the application (Q4).

RQ1: Figures 4 and 5 clearly indicate that the group using PVC generally answered the questions more accurately and faster than the other groups. Table 3, which compares the mean values of these results, shows that the group using PVC answered the questions on average 1.8 times faster and gave 24% more correct responses than the group working without a tool (no tool). Compared to the group working with SeeC, those working with PVC responded 1.7 times faster and provided 19% more correct answers, demonstrating that PVC is well suited to the tasks.

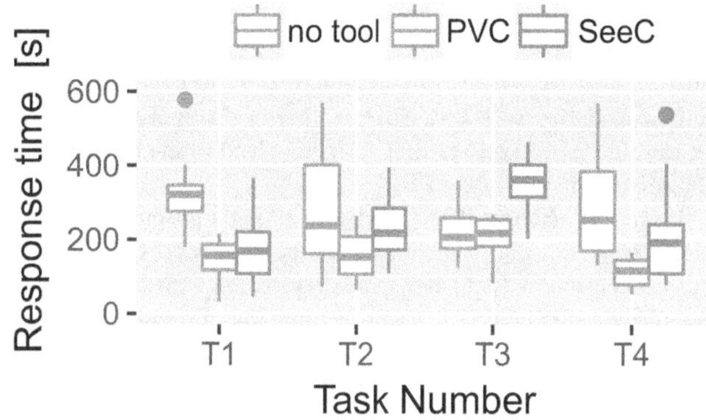

Figure 4: Box plot of the time required to complete each task

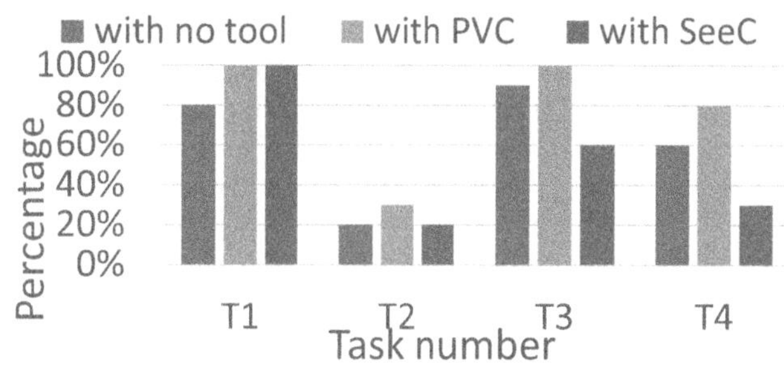

Figure 5: Percentage of correct answers for T1–T4 (for RQ1)

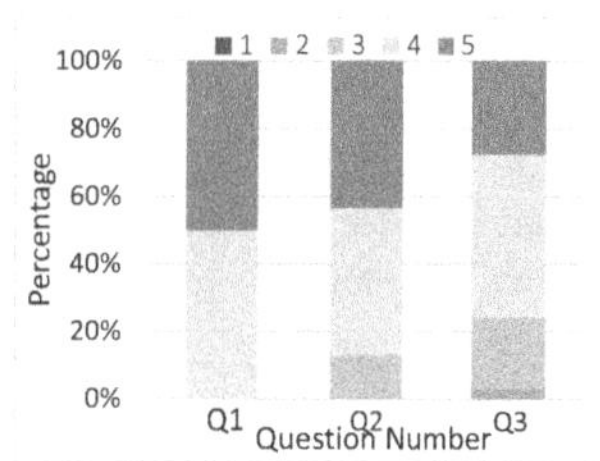

Figure 6: Results of Q1-3 (for RQ2 and RQ3)

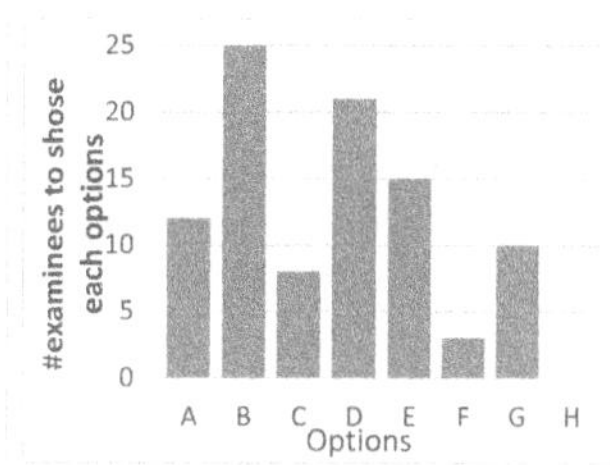

Figure 7: Result of Q4 (for RQ3)

Figure 4 shows the results as a box plot. Table 3 also shows the p-values between the groups and evaluates them using the Steel-Dwass test [4] [7)]. A significant difference exists between the groups, except for the relationship between the SeeC and the no tool groups.

Focusing on the results of T3 and T4 of the SeeC group, the correct answer rates are worse than the no tool group, which was unexpected. Moreover, for T3, the SeeC group took more time on average to answer than the no tool group. We speculate that the

[5)]For the above reason, we judged that there is no visualization difference between PT and SeeC. Hence, the experiment only employed SeeC. If PT was selected, T3 would change to a File I/O problem.

[6)]http://play-visualizer-c.herokuapp.com

[7)]We selected the Steel-Dwass test, which is a non-parametric test, because it is difficult to determine whether the scores and times of the tasks follow a normal distribution that strictly avoids multiple test.

reasons for these are as follows: T3 — SeeC does not fully support dynamic memory allocation. Thus, participants become confused or have to switch to working with pen and paper, which is more time-consuming. T4 — PVC can visualize the depth of recursive call as a number, but SeeC cannot. This may lead to the difference in the correct answer rate.

Moreover, the result of Q1 (shown in Fig. 6) indicates that all participants felt that PVC is very useful for solving the problems in the experiment. (All participants responded with 4 or 5.) These results indicate that PVC can convey the status of running programs to programmers in general.

RQ2: About 90% of the participants feel that PVC is useful for novices learning some concepts of C programming language (Fig 6, Q2). As expected, most users felt that PVC is a useful aid for learning pointer and dynamic memory allocation (Fig. 7, Q4). Additionally, participants felt that the program is also useful for functions. Based on these results, we speculate that PVC is useful for checking the answer to T2, which is challenging as it involves a recursive function. Given that task T2 yielded the lowest percentage of correct answers, it is inferred that it is the most challenging part of the experiment.

RQ3: About 80% of the participants felt that PVC is more accessible than other existing visualization or debugging tools (Fig. 6, Q3).

Hence, the experiment confirms that PVC mostly satisfies RQ 1–3 proposed at the beginning of the study

5.3 Threats to Validity

All the participants in this study had basic knowledge of the C language and we provided a tutorial of PVC. However, the degree of proficiency varied within the groups. Some participants used PVC very well, while others struggled in the experiment. These attributes may affect the results of the experiment and pose a threat to internal validity.

Most participants are students of Waseda University. If we repeated this experiment with people belonging to another group or organization, the results may vary. The results may depend on demographic (e.g., age), programming skill level, and experience in the field, posing a threat to the experiment's external validity.

5.4 Limitations

Currently, PVC does not support minor language features, built-in functions, and compiler features. For example, it does not support *union* and external libraries. However, PVC is designed for novices. Consequently, we believe that these oversights are acceptable because these concepts are difficult for novices to comprehend. Moreover, PVC does not display compiler error messages because PVC is a visualization tool and not a compiler. In addition, PVC cannot hide or fold up figures, which may be confusing to users if there are numerous variables.

6 CONCLUSIONS AND FUTURE WORK

We proposed new visualization technique for C languages called PVC. It is a browser-based web application inspired by previous studies. The application is open-access and free to try at the listed address (see Section I). The experiment reveals that PVC is useful not only for novices, but also programmers in general.

In the future, we plan to investigate whether PVC can help students learn programming by evaluating users' programming skills after using PVC. Moreover, we will continue to develop and improve PVC. For example, our visualize application currently supports only C language. It does not support the full range of C language syntax and standard library functions.

ACKNOWLEDGMENTS

This work was partially supported by JST Presto Grant Number JPMJPR14D4.

REFERENCES

[1] Herbert Baerten and Frank Van Reeth. 1998. Using VRML and JAVA to visualize 3D algorithms in computer graphics education. *Computer networks and ISDN systems* (1998).

[2] Michelle Craig and Andrew Petersen. 2016. Student difficulties with pointer concepts in C. In *Proceedings of the Australasian Computer Science Week Multi-conference*. ACM.

[3] Wim De Pauw, Erik Jensen, Nick Mitchell, Gary Sevitsky, John Vlissides, and Jeaha Yang. 2002. Visualizing the execution of Java programs. In *Software Visualization*. Springer.

[4] MM Desu and Damaraju Raghavarao. 2003. *Nonparametric statistical methods for complete and censored data*. CRC Press.

[5] Stephen H Edwards, Daniel S Tilden, and Anthony Allevato. 2014. Pythy: improving the introductory python programming experience. In *Proceedings of the 45th ACM technical symposium on Computer science education*. ACM.

[6] Matthew Heinsen Egan and Chris McDonald. 2014. Program visualization and explanation for novice C programmers. In *Proceedings of the Sixteenth Australasian Computing Education Conference-Volume 148*. ACS.

[7] Micaela Esteves and AJ Mendes. 2003. OOP-Anim, a system to support learning of basic object oriented programming concepts. In *Proceedings of the CompSysTech*.

[8] Licia Florio and Klaas Wierenga. 2005. Eduroam, providing mobility for roaming users. In *Proceedings of the EUNIS 2005 Conference, Manchester*.

[9] Philip J Guo. 2013. Online python tutor: embeddable web-based program visualization for cs education. In *Proceeding of the 44th ACM technical symposium on Computer science education*. ACM, 579–584.

[10] Philip J. Guo, Jeffery White, and Renan Zanelatto. 2015. Codechella: Multi-user program visualizations for real-time tutoring and collaborative learning. In *Proceedings of the IEEE Symposium on Visual Languages and Human-Centric Computing (VL/HCC) (VL/HCC '15)*. 79–87. https://doi.org/10.1109/VLHCC.2015.7357201

[11] Ryosuke Ishizue, Kazunori Sakamoto, Hironori Washizaki, and Yoshiaki Fukazawa. 2017. An interactive Web Application Visualizing Memory Space for Novice C Programmers. In *Proceedings of the ACM SIGCSE*. ACM, 710–710.

[12] Richardo Jiménez-Peris, Cristóbal Pareja-Flores, Marta Patiño-Martínez, and J Ángel Velázquez-Iturbide. 1997. The locker metaphor to teach dynamic memory. In *ACM SIGCSE Bulletin*. ACM.

[13] Nobuya Koike and Kentaro Go. 2012. A Proposal of Interaction on Visualization Using Address Space Representation in Runtime Program. *Interaction* (2012).

[14] Essi Lahtinen, Kirsti Ala-Mutka, and Hannu-Matti Järvinen. 2005. A study of the difficulties of novice programmers. In *ACM SIGCSE Bulletin*. ACM.

[15] S-P Lahtinen, Erkki Sutinen, and Jorma Tarhio. 1998. Automated animation of algorithms with Eliot. *Journal of Visual Languages & Computing* 9, 3 (1998), 337–349.

[16] Yoshiaki Matsuzawa, Kazunori Sakamoto, Takashi Ohata, and Katsuhiko Kakehi. 2015. A Programming Language Translation System for Programming Education. In *SIGCE*. IPSJ.

[17] Iain Milne and Glenn Rowe. 2002. Difficulties in learning and teaching programming-views of students and tutors. *Education and Information technologies* (2002).

[18] Iain Milne and Glenn Rowe. 2004. Ogre: Three-dimensional program visualization for novice programmers. *Education and Information Technologies* (2004).

[19] Andrés Moreno, Niko Myller, Erkki Sutinen, and Mordechai Ben-Ari. 2004. Visualizing programs with Jeliot 3. In *Proceedings of the working conference on Advanced visual interfaces*. ACM, 373–376.

[20] Linda Null and Karishma Rao. 2005. CAMERA: Introducing memory concepts via visualization. In *ACM SIGCSE Bulletin*. ACM.

[21] Jaishankar Sundararaman and Godmar Back. 2008. HDPV: interactive, faithful, in-vivo runtime state visualization for C/C++ and Java. In *Proceedings of the 4th ACM symposium on Software visualization*. ACM.

Instructor Perspectives on Comparative Heatmap Visualizations of Student Engagement with Lecture Video

Jinyue Xia
University of North Carolina at Charlotte
Charlotte, NC
jxia3@uncc.edu

David C. Wilson
University of North Carolina at Charlotte
Charlotte, NC
davils@uncc.edu

ABSTRACT

The use of online video in learning environments is prevalent – serving in a variety of roles, such as multimedia textbook, video lecture, or medium for documenting student coursework. For instructors who employ video as a learning material, it is becoming increasingly important to gain a deeper understanding of the fit of video content across student cohorts, as well as the impact on student engagement, learning, and success. In order to better understand instructor interests and needs in this regard, we developed a learning analytics visualization tool that links data on student viewing and video interactions with student demographics and performance measures. Instructors can use the tool to generate and compare correlated heatmap visualizations representing student engagement across segments of the video. This paper describes an initial user study conducted with instructors in an HCI course context to understand how this kind of feedback can inform their use of video in the classroom. Results show that instructors find such feedback very useful across a variety of use cases.

CCS CONCEPTS

• **Applied computing** → **Learning management systems**; • **Human-centered computing** → *Visual analytics*;

KEYWORDS

Video; Learning Analytics; Visualization

ACM Reference format:
Jinyue Xia and David C. Wilson. 2018. Instructor Perspectives on Comparative Heatmap Visualizations of Student Engagement with Lecture Video. In *Proceedings of The 49th ACM Technical Symposium on Computer Science Education, Baltimore , MD, USA, February 21–24, 2018 (SIGCSE '18),* 6 pages. https://doi.org/10.1145/3159450.3159487

1 INTRODUCTION

Video has become a useful and pervasive learning tool [6, 10, 12, 13, 19]. The 2017 Horizon Report for Higher Education[1] notes that video is a key enabling technology for learning spaces and blended learning. And research has shown that integrating video material can help to improve the active learning experience [3, 7, 8, 17] across domains such as population health [20], management [1], and chemistry [9]. Online video can be employed as part of different strategies for flipped classroom learning [21, 22], such as integrating critique / selection of videos as part of the learning experience [16].

For instructors who employ video as a learning material, it is becoming increasingly important to gain a deeper understanding of the fit of video content across student cohorts, as well as the impact on student engagement, learning, and success. Modeling student engagement through interaction measures has been shown to help improve outcomes for using video materials. For example, displaying user engagement can potentially change the user's watching behavior [18], and it can help to make video more engaging from the perspective of video production [11]. Modeling user engagement can help to support task-based video navigation. For example, a one-minute long segment in a video with a higher number of views may warrant more attention because it might mean the segment is interesting, important or confusing [11, 12]. Studies have also investigated different behavioral patterns of high- and low-achieving students through user engagement with MOOC videos [2]. And duration has been studied as a lecture video design parameter for user engagement. For example, one study suggested a limit of 6 minutes for MOOCs [11], but others suggest this may be different in more traditional course context [14].

Previous research, however, has typically focused on holistic visualization of engagement models. In this research, we examine the potential for comparative visualizations of video engagement. In order to better understand instructor interests and needs in this regard, we developed a learning analytics visualization tool that links data on student viewing and video interactions with student demographics and performance measures. Instructors can use the tool to generate and compare correlated heatmap visualizations representing student engagement across segments of the video.

A class instructor, for example, may want to find out how the user engagement evolves as the time goes. She might be interested in how the watching behavior changes from a week to a semester. Or a lecture video producer may want to improve the video and to find if an unclear part is causing a problem for lower performing students. Then she may want to know whether a different behavior implies different performance levels by comparing the user engagement of students with better performance and poorer performance.

This paper describes an initial user study conducted with instructors to understand how this kind of feedback can inform their use of video in the classroom. The study examines the following research questions in the context of a foundational computing course on Human-Computer Interaction.

[1] https://www.nmc.org/publication-type/horizon-report/

SIGCSE '18, February 21–24, 2018, Baltimore , MD, USA

ACM ISBN 978-1-4503-5103-4/18/02...$15.00
https://doi.org/10.1145/3159450.3159487

- **RQ1** By exploring the interface of multiple heatmaps, how do the class instructors or video owners interpret the heatmaps of user engagement with online videos?
- **RQ2** How does the heatmap of user engagement influence the class instructor in self critiquing the teaching method?

2 VISUALIZING VIDEO ENGAGEMENT

As part of an ongoing research effort in video analytics for learning, we developed a data collection and analysis toolkit that aggregates student viewing and interaction behavior with a given video. We refer to the toolkit as VIVA – Video Interaction Visual Analytics. For analysis, the video is divided into half-second segments. As a given video is watched over time, the analytics tool tracks (1) segments of the video watched and re-watched; (2) click data such as play, pause, and skip; and (3) metadata such as playback speed for segments watched. We recognize that there are many perspectives on what is meant by "engagement." Here, we presume that engagement correlates and can be modeled by interaction cues. Thus VIVA employs a visual analytics model to create a heatmap visualization of the interaction data to represent engagement, which we refer to in general as VIVA-HM. Details of the model are beyond the scope of this paper, as the focus here is on how instructors could use such models to explore and engage with video interaction data. An example VIVA-HM for a lecture video is shown in Figure 1. The heatmap corresponds directly to the video timeline, displaying a color that represents the overall degree of engagement at that point in the video. In this research, a green to red color scheme mapping was selected for heatmap display, where green colors represent lower levels of engagement than red colors and lighter versions of each color represent lower levels of engagement than darker. By showing a heatmap in direct parallel to the video timeline, the overall interaction of a given student cohort with that video can be seen at a glance. The VIVA-HM component also acts as a navigation tool, clicking at a point in the heatmap skips the video playback to the corresponding time.

Figure 1: Example VIVA-HM heatmap integrated with a lecture video.

2.1 Comparative Heatmap Tool

VIVA collects data at the level of individual interactions, so it is possible to create a set of related VIVA-HM visualizations by filtering the underlying data. Filters can be set using dimensions of the audience (e.g., graduate vs. undergraduate, course grade, etc.) or dimensions of the video watching context (e.g., time of day, semester(s), etc.). This provides a great deal of flexibility to explore student video interactions in context. Moreover, multiple VIVA-HM visualizations that have different filters applied can be aligned together to allow flexible visual comparisons across multiple contexts. We refer to such coordinated VIVA-HM sets as VIVA-HMX visualizations.

For this research, we developed a comparative heatmap tool that enabled instructors to build their own customized VIVA-HMX visualizations to explore and compare student video engagement using a baseline set of filter options. Figure 2 shows the interface setup, which employs the same color scheme as described for VIVA-HM. On the left is the video player and controls with an integrated VIVA-HMX visualization containing two heatmaps for the video shown. On the right is a set of controls for specifying a new filter and adding an additional heatmap for comparison. No limit was placed on the number of filtered-heatmaps that could be added. To help manage multiple heatmaps, each individual VIVA-HM visualization component includes functionality to delete and reorder within the overall VIVA-HMX component, as well as to show tooltip information on the underlying filter conditions. An overall "Clear Criteria" allows for clearing all added heatmaps. The filter interface incorporated demographic and academic data options: course grade, GPA in the semester when they registered the class, gender and citizenship. It also incorporated options for cohort (level, semester) and timeframe.

The example in Figure 2 illustrates a comparison based on video watching context. The upper heatmap shows watching behavior at the time the video was first assigned in the first semester (1 week of interaction data from initial assignment), while the lower heatmap shows watching patterns for the entire two-semester period. Note that many of the lighter colors in the upper heatmap (initial viewing) are darker in the lower heatmap (with additional viewing throughout the semesters). This could be used, for example, to understand how students engage with the video material during initial learning in comparison to review throughout a semester – or at quiz / exam times.

3 USER STUDY

For this study, we randomly selected a lecture video from a set that had been employed over several semesters in a course on Human-Computer Interaction. The selected video was a lecture video on analyzing user study data, close to 20 minutes in length. The collected user interaction data for this video included 141 watching sessions from a pool of 101 students (both undergraduate and graduate) across two semesters. We obtained the demographic and academic data for the students represented in the interaction data. This included program level (e.g. graduate and undergraduate), grade, GPA, gender and citizenship – summarized as domestic or international.

The study selection criteria required that participants were class instructors or teaching assistants who had experience with flipped

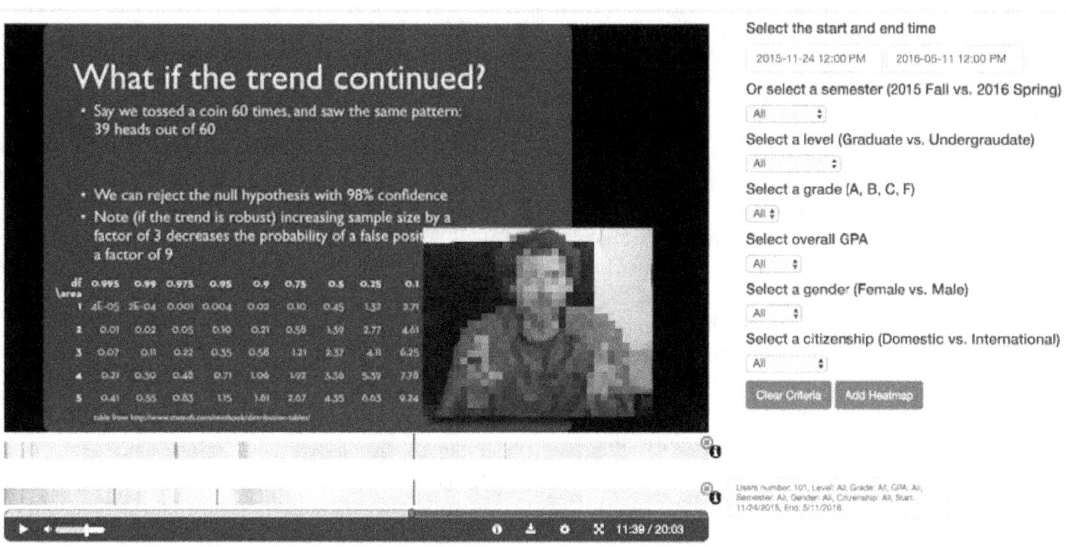

Figure 2: VIVA-HMX comparative heatmap visualization tool.

classroom or using video materials for course material. Ten participants signed up for the study and each one received a $25 Starbucks gift card as compensation. The ten participants consist of seven class professors / lecturers and three PhD student TAs experienced with the video material. Four out of the seven professors had directly taught the class and had used the selected video as course material. The remaining professors had substantial experience using online videos as course material. The average study duration was 30 minutes.

3.1 Procedures

We adopted a "Think Aloud" approach [5] for the user study. The computer's screen and the participant's voice were recorded for later coding and analysis. Prior to showing the interface, participants were asked what they would hope to discover if they were able to track and compare the different patterns from the student audience.

The study employed a semi-structured session [4], where the participants interacted freely with the interface and the experimenter asked pre-determined questions, with follow-up on topics of interest pointed out by the participants. By using the comparative heatmap interface (as shown in Figure 2), participants were able to discover, explore and compare any combination of the following criteria: temporal data across two semesters, program level, course grade, GPA, gender and international status. During the think aloud process, the facilitator consistently prompted for:"Why did you make this choice?", "What did you find from the comparison?", and "Did the outcome look as what expected?". Depending on the context, the facilitator sometimes also prompted for: "why did you do X? why not Y?".

Once the participant finished exploration, a brief post-study interview was conducted. Following [15], the interview questions included:

(1) Did you meet troubles when you used the interface? If yes, what are they?
(2) What comparison did you find most interesting? Why are they interesting? How may you use the comparisons?
(3) What additional information do you want to know why the pattern is like it is? What are they?
(4) Do you think you can use this tool to develop your future lectures / teaching preparations?
    - *Follow-up:* If the videos are from a third party, how would you revise your lectures. If you were able to make your own videos, what would you like to use the tool to help you do?
    - *Follow-up:* If the tool is not helpful at all, can you tell us why and what other tools you want to use?
(5) Do you have other comments or suggestions?

4 ANALYSIS AND RESULTS

A qualitative coding analysis was conducted to analyze the data [4]. Two coders (one of whom was the interviewer) iteratively coded the data for emerging concepts expressed by the participants, with joint review after each iteration. The resulting concepts are organized into three general themes:

Theme 1 *Perceptions of Comparative Heatmaps.* Instructors shared some common general perceptions about heatmap visualizations of student engagement with video material.

Theme 2 *Applications of Comparative Heatmaps.* All participants mentioned their potential applications for multiple heatmap comparisons. Two main use cases emerged: (2.1) Making teaching better (particularly for using third-party videos) and (2.2) Making video better (particularly when using self-created videos).

Theme 3 *Why Comparisons are Interesting.* All participants explained to some degree why their selected comparisons of watching patterns were interesting.

A number of concepts emerged in each theme during the coding process. The concepts were found from at least 5 participants. In the following discussion, anonymized participants are referred to with a numerical designation, *P1, P2, etc.*.

4.1 Prior Expectations

In order to help calibrate responses, before being introduced to the comparative heatmap tool participants were asked what they hoped they would be able to do, if they were able to track different video watching patterns from students. *All* participants indicated that if there were such a tool they would like to compare the patterns and interpret the segments that significantly differentiate others. For example, *P10* mentioned "...The second thing would be to look at the hot spots, em..., to see either what was the most engaging but also maybe it was confusing. Then I have to what to interpret...". Three participants wanted to have a tool that could help them find correlations between the patterns and the video content. Interestingly, four responders wanted a tool which could help them simply identify whether the students had watched the video or not. Some participants were interested in very specific functions that would be possible, but were not implemented in the interface for the study. For example, a few participants were looking for the number of loops, pauses or plays on a segment. For instance, *P3* stated "...numbers of times they stopped or looped, or went back or that kind of thing and then number of times that they re-watched the whole video, when they watched the video, that kind of thing,...". Overall, the functionality of the comparative heatmap tool for the study was a reasonable fit to address the majority of participants' expected use cases and avenues for exploration.

4.2 Theme 1: General Perceptions

Overall, we observed that participants had a very positive experience with the multiple heatmap comparison. "Interesting" (any words with stemming from "interest") is the term most often mentioned (120 occurrences) across all participants' interaction with different heatmaps. Other positive indicators include "fascinating" (11 times) and "fantastic" (9 times).

During exploration, all participants tried to correlate heatmap patterns with the selected filter criteria based on their previous teaching experience. For example, five participants compared the difference in watching patterns between domestic and international students. They linked this to previous teaching experience and tried to analyze why language understanding might present a challenge in this video. For example, *P3* mentioned "Maybe for international students, English is their second language. A word they don't know, they can go pause or something then generate a different pattern."

Three main concepts emerged during coding for this theme. Table 1 summarizes the overall number of participants referencing the concept and the overall number of references in the study.

Concepts	Sources	References
Matching teaching experience	5	8
Surprised by the heatmap(s)	3	5
Uncertainty	2	3

Table 1: Theme 1 General Perceptions

4.2.1 Matching teaching experience. Five participants confirmed that some watching patterns definitely matched their impressions about the filtered groups of students. For example, *P3* (comparing graduate & undergraduate watching) "I think the outcome makes sense. It looks like graduate students worked more consistently versus the undergraduate students maybe just click in the areas and watch." *P4* (comparing domestic & international watching) explained "it confirms my suspicions that international students are watching the videos a lot more, ..., because of the language." Moreover, the majority of the participants expressed interesting or exciting motion when they recognized such patterns.

4.2.2 Surprised by the heatmap(s). Three instructors expressed surprise when a selected heatmap filter did not match their experience. One participant said "That surprises me. I was absolutely thinking the females are more attentive, that actually dispelled some notions I have about male and females students. Look, the males stay quite engaged with it almost all the way where the women sort of stopped earlier."

4.2.3 Uncertainty. In some cases, participants expressed uncertainty about what they had found from the heatmaps. For example, *P5* mentioned "we want to know why, it could be caused by whether or not the students are mature enough. You know, the young guys are losing ..., or it is because the content is designed badly suited for the graduate students, but I don't know." When some parts of the video showed an unusual pattern, participants sought evidence for why the pattern happened, and expressed an interest in getting access to more detailed interaction data to do so.

4.3 Theme 2.1 Making Teaching Better

Three concepts were identified during coding as falling within this theme. Table 2 summarizes the overall number of participants referencing the concept and the overall number of references in the study.

Concepts	Sources	References
Make explanations	7	11
Make quiz	6	6
Show heatmaps to students	3	3

Table 2: Theme 2.1 Change teaching

4.3.1 Explaining material. A majority of participants (7) mentioned that comparative analysis would impact classroom coverage of material or concepts covered in the video. Both the "hot" and "cold" spots gained attention. Three of the seven noted that hot spots could indicate difficulty in students' understanding of the material, and would warrant additional review in class. On the other hand, four were concerned about cold spots that contain particularly important concepts. This could indicate that many students had missed or neglected critical points, which would also warrant additional review in class. *P10* said "I would probably just start with that as a baseline data and look at where the low spots were. First of all look at the overall patterns, so if I do this before class, I look at historical data and look at the overall patterns and then look at where do I have concerns, ... , I would find out what I am not happy with, with these patterns, what can I do is trying to combine them."

4.3.2 Quizzing. Six participants noted that they would use less-watched segments as a reference for creating quizzes. And all of the participants who indicated they would use a quiz to reinforce concepts noted that they would link quiz content to the spare spots. *P2* explained: "So when I am in the class, ... , for the clicker quiz I could put more focus on the second part, they could get the chance to learn what they missed." The "second part" refers to the heatmap where contains lots of green areas.

4.3.3 Showing heatmaps to students. Another common theme was to show the heatmaps to students directly as a motivation / learning aid. When *P4* noticed different watching patterns across student performance levels, *P4* became excited and commented: "I would actually like to show students this, I would show students, look, these are the students who are getting the A, these are the students who are getting C, ..., so I would use that as a way to inform the students about how they can do better.". Participant *P9* would use the heatmaps to guide discussion, noting: "so when I'm in the class I could talk to the students about the part that was red. And enquire with them whether they thought that was something that was hard to understand."

4.4 Theme 2.2 Making Video Better

Using heatmaps to refine video content, was pointed out both by participants who created their own videos for class and those who did not. Two main concepts emerged within this theme. Table 3 summarizes the overall number of participants referencing the concept and the overall number of references in the study.

Concepts	Sources	References
Refine the video	6	8
Shorten video / less content	4	5

Table 3: Theme 2.2: making a better video

4.4.1 Refine the video. Five participants discussed video content modifications based on the results of comparative analysis. Six participants suggested remaking videos to address video content issues that cause lower than expected engagement in segments with important content. For example, one participant *P4* commented "so if I was making a lecture video and I use it in one semester, and I saw that it seems to have a lot of problems in confused students through the interface, then that would give me an opportunity to not just remake the video but to remake video knowing exactly what's wrong with it...". Other instructors (*P7, P8, P10*) suggested refinement is to change the video content to motive the students. Three instructors indicated that they could incentivize students to pay attention and focus on the video by revising video content to address identified issues. For example, *P10* said " I'm not going to penalize them for not watching it but everyone needs incentives and motivation." Another approach to motivate the students on less-engaged segments is to embed evaluation content. *P5* noted "... So I try to somehow make them like several important segments, okay. I also want to embed like quiz or like questions in the videos."

4.4.2 Shorten video / less content. At close to 20 minutes, the lecture video for the study can be considered relatively long. Four participants observed a watching pattern that may indicate many students lose attention about halfway through the video. Moreover, their previous teaching experience matched the observation from the heatmap. Thus, the concept of shortening the video or placing less content in a video stood out.

Four participants stated that making a shorter video could help students focus more on the video content. For instance, after *P6* realized students may drop off in middle of the video, *P6* stated "Basically it shows me that it is very very easy to see that this point some where people dropped off the video. Really it tells me that not to create a video more than 10 minutes long. Because a lot of people seems to drop off."

While two of the four instructors saw value in making shorter videos, they also noted a common problem existing for online education. Unlike the traditional classroom environment, they lack the instant audience feedback from the classroom. *P6* commented "One worry I have, for the online-course, is that I do not have their feedback. I do not know whether or not I'm running too fast or too slow, which concept students do not understand. This is a very bad thing, this is very, very bad thing from their educational side, ..., On the network, we usually ran faster because there is no feedback. I don't repeat." Simply shortening video length has the potential to result in too much content density. *P6* noted that heatmaps could help calibrate the length-density, saying " I will try to, you know, to make the video so even if I make a 12 minutes video, I probably will talk about a few things."

4.5 Theme 3: Why Comparisons are Interesting

On average, each participant used three to four heatmaps together for a given comparison, with as many as six together. Comparisons included a wide variety of filter combinations. As part of the interview, participants described the most interesting comparisons and the reason why those comparisons were interesting. Participant feedback was varied, even for similar threads of comparison. For example, three participants mentioned comparing heatmaps based on gender was interesting, but some compared in the context of a single semester while some ones focused on all semesters. Overall, there was no clear comparison that stood out as most interesting across all participants in the study. However, we did observe an emergent theme about the reasons why they were interested in the comparisons. Three main concepts were noted for this theme based on the participants' descriptions. Table 4 summarizes the overall number of participants referencing the concept and the overall number of references in the study.

Concepts	Sources	References
Interesting results	4	4
Confirmed / disconfirmed experience	3	3
Help improve teaching	3	3

Table 4: Theme 3 Reasons for interesting comparisons

Participants commented on the reasons why they were interested in a particular comparison from two perspectives: (1) the visual results from multiple heatmaps and (2) the functionalities of the multiple heatmaps. The first two concepts were captured from the participants who were interested in the results of comparing multiple heatmaps, whereas the last concept is more about how the interesting comparison could possibly help future teaching.

4.5.1 Interesting results. Four participants were either excited or interested in the heatmaps when the generated heatmaps showed a huge and obvious difference. For example, three instructors compared heatmaps for students grouped by course grade: A, B, C, and F. Students with a grade of A or B seemed to watch the same video very differently from students with a grade of C or F. One participant commented that "the comparisons when there was a big difference with the most interests. Not necessarily, it was most interesting because of what I could select but most interesting because of the difference." Another participant (*P5*) indicated this could be a way to help lower-performing students. *P5* noted "I want to look at the grade,..., basically I want to see, what cause the problem, in other words, how can we help the C students.".

4.5.2 Confirmed / disconfirmed experience. This concept emerged as part of user perceptions. During the coding process of the second interview question, this pattern was confirmed again because of the watching patterns that were displayed by the heatmaps. Three participants described patterns as most interesting because it confirmed their teaching experience, while one participant noted that the most interesting pattern was a surprising one, because it did not match their teaching impression for selected group of students. For example, *P6* (confirming experience) commented "... because it confirmed my theory of what I've observed in my class and it's good to know that I'm right, that is really what's happening".

4.5.3 Help improve teaching. Three participants answered the question in a way that considered the functionalities of comparing watching patterns with heatmaps. They pointed out the comparison is most interesting because it is a kind of useful tool to develop and improve their teaching. Most participants considered the grade based comparison to be the most interesting, because the different patterns could help them discover potential problems in different student groups. For example, *P2* stated that "I want to know how a good student work compared with not really good ones, that could help me plan accordingly, ...I mean we don't want to watch students for fun, we want to know what is the problem so we can make it better."

5 CONCLUSION

In this paper, we presented an initial user study on instructor exploration of students' engagement with video lecture material using a comparative heatmap visualization tool. Results for **RQ1** (instructor interpretation) indicate that instructors explore based on how the engagement visualizations fit their expectations from previous teaching experience (confirmation, surprise, uncertainty), as can be seen in Theme 1 and Theme 3 concepts. Results for **RQ2** (self critiquing) indicate that instructors respond to issues highlighted by the engagement visualizations by in-class explanation and quizzing linked to concepts in the identified video segments, or by refining the video in those areas, as can be seen in Theme 2 and Theme 3 concepts. Overall, instructors were very positive about using this kind of data-driven visual analytics feedback to help understand the fit of video lecture content to student engagement and learning outcomes. In future research, we plan to explore other filter parameterizations and visualizations with VIVA in larger scale deployments and user studies.

ACKNOWLEDGMENTS

This material is based upon work supported by the National Science Foundation under Grant No. (1500195).

REFERENCES

[1] Michael Albert and Brian J Beatty. 2014. Flipping the classroom applications to curriculum redesign for an introduction to management course: Impact on grades. *Journal of Education for Business* 89, 8 (2014), 419–424.
[2] Ashton Anderson, Daniel Huttenlocher, Jon Kleinberg, and Jure Leskovec. 2014. Engaging with massive online courses. In *Proceedings of the 23rd international conference on World wide web*. ACM, 687–698.
[3] Athula Balachandran, Vyas Sekar, Aditya Akella, Srinivasan Seshan, Ion Stoica, and Hui Zhang. 2012. A quest for an internet video quality-of-experience metric. In *Proceedings of the 11th ACM Workshop on Hot Topics in Networks*. ACM, 97–102.
[4] AE Blandford. 2013. Semi-structured qualitative studies. Interaction Design Foundation.
[5] T. Boren and J. Ramey. 2000. Thinking aloud: reconciling theory and practice. *IEEE Transactions on Professional Communication* 43, 3 (Sep 2000), 261–278.
[6] Derrick Coetzee, Armando Fox, Marti A Hearst, and Björn Hartmann. 2014. Should your MOOC forum use a reputation system?. In *Proceedings of the ACM conference on Computer supported cooperative work & social computing*.
[7] Florin Dobrian, Vyas Sekar, Asad Awan, Ion Stoica, Dilip Joseph, Aditya Ganjam, Jibin Zhan, and Hui Zhang. 2011. Understanding the impact of video quality on user engagement. *SIGCOMM Comput. Commun. Rev.* 41, 4 (2011).
[8] Jacob Enfield. 2013. Looking at the impact of the flipped classroom model of instruction on undergraduate multimedia students at CSUN. *TechTrends* 57, 6 (2013).
[9] Alison B Flynn. 2015. Structure and evaluation of flipped chemistry courses: organic & spectroscopy, large and small, first to third year, English and French. *Chemistry Education Research and Practice* 16, 2 (2015), 198–211.
[10] Dan B Goldman, Chris Gonterman, Brian Curless, David Salesin, and Steven M Seitz. 2008. Video object annotation, navigation, and composition. In *Proceedings of the 21st annual ACM Symposium on User Interface Software and Technology*.
[11] Philip J Guo, Juho Kim, and Rob Rubin. 2014. How video production affects student engagement: An empirical study of mooc videos. In *Proceedings of the first ACM conference on Learning@ scale conference*. ACM, 41–50.
[12] Juho Kim, Philip J Guo, Carrie J Cai, Shang-Wen Daniel Li, Krzysztof Z Gajos, and Robert C Miller. 2014. Data-driven interaction techniques for improving navigation of educational videos. In *Proceedings of the 27th annual ACM symposium on User interface software and technology*. ACM, 563–572.
[13] Juho Kim, Philip J Guo, Daniel T Seaton, Piotr Mitros, Krzysztof Z Gajos, and Robert C Miller. 2014. Understanding in-video dropouts and interaction peaks inonline lecture videos. In *Proceedings of the first ACM conference on Learning@ scale conference*. ACM, 31–40.
[14] Larry Lagerstrom, Petr Johanes, and Umnouy Ponsukcharoen. 2015. The Myth of the Six-Minute Rule: Student Engagement with Online Videos. In *Proceedings of the ASEE Annual Conference & Exposition*.
[15] Jonathan Lazar, Jinjuan Heidi Feng, and Harry Hochheiser. 2010. *Research methods in human-computer interaction*. John Wiley & Sons.
[16] Mary Lou Maher, Celine Latulipe, Heather Lipford, and Audrey Rorrer. 2015. Flipped classroom strategies for CS education. In *Proceedings of the 46th ACM Technical Symposium on Computer Science Education*. ACM, 218–223.
[17] Roger C Schank. 1994. Active learning through multimedia. *IEEE multimedia* 1, 1 (1994), 69–78.
[18] Klaus Schoeffmann, Frank Hopfgartner, Oge Marques, Laszlo Boeszoermenyi, and Joemon M Jose. 2010. Video browsing interfaces and applications: a review. *Journal of Photonics for Energy* (2010).
[19] Daniel Seaton, Isaach Chuang, Piotr Mitros, David Pritchard, et al. 2013. Who Does What in a Massive Open Online Course? *EducationXPress* 2013, 9 (2013).
[20] Vicki Simpson and Elizabeth Richards. 2015. Flipping the classroom to teach population health: Increasing the relevance. *Nurse Education in Practice* 15, 3 (2015), 162–167.
[21] Vikash Singh, Sarah Abdellahi, Mary Lou Maher, and Celine Latulipe. 2016. The Video Collaboratory As a Learning Environment. In *Proceedings of the 47th ACM Technical Symposium on Computing Science Education (SIGCSE '16)*.
[22] Vikash Singh, Celine Latulipe, Erin Carroll, and Danielle Lottridge. 2011. The choreographer's notebook: a video annotation system for dancers and choreographers. In *Proc. of the 8th ACM Conference on Creativity and Cognition*.

Supporting Self-Regulated Learning with Visualizations in Online Learning Environments

Kalle Ilves, Juho Leinonen, Arto Hellas
University of Helsinki
Helsinki, Finland
{firstname.lastname}@helsinki.fi

ABSTRACT

In this article, we study how visualizations could be used to support students' self-regulation in online learning. We conducted a randomized controlled trial with three groups: one control group without visualization, one treatment group with textual visualization, and one treatment with graphical visualization with information on peers' average achievement. We studied how different visualizations affect students' academic performance and behavior. We focused on four factors; starting, scheduling, earliness and exercise points, where the first three are related to time management and self-regulation. The last factor measures course performance in terms of completed exercises. Our results suggest that the lowest performing students can benefit from a visualization, whereas the highest performing students are not affected by the presence or absence of a visualization. We also found that visualizations that do not provide the means to compare your own performance with others may even be harmful to performance oriented students.

CCS CONCEPTS

•**Human-centered computing → Visualization; Visualization systems and tools;** •**Applied computing → Education;** *Interactive learning environments; E-learning;*

ACM Reference format:
Kalle Ilves, Juho Leinonen, Arto Hellas. 2018. Supporting Self-Regulated Learning with Visualizations in Online Learning Environments. In *Proceedings of The 49th ACM Technical Symposium on Computer Science Education, Baltimore , MD, USA, February 21–24, 2018 (SIGCSE '18),* 6 pages.
DOI: 10.1145/3159450.3159509

1 INTRODUCTION

Students have been found to have different motivations for trying to achieve learning goals [10]; in broad terms, students can be categorized as mastery oriented learners who seek to understand and develop their competence, and as performance oriented learners who seek to perform well and contrast their performance to others. Our study focuses both on visualizations for supporting self-regulated learning as well as on students' motivations.

SIGCSE '18, February 21–24, 2018, *Baltimore , MD, USA*

978-1-4503-5103-4/18/02...$15.00
DOI: 10.1145/3159450.3159509

We examine how different visualizations affect students' academic performance and behavior in an online learning environment. For the purposes of this study, we developed two different visualizations: a textual and a radar visualization. These visualizations show the students their exercise points and time management when completing the problems on a course. The textual visualization gave the students a score on each measured factor and provided textual feedback on how to improve their score, while the radar visualization also provided the means to compare the performance to others in the class. The two visualizations were developed with students' different motivations in mind: by comparing the visualizations' impact on performance of differently motivated students we could potentially find a way to support differently motivated students with different kinds of visualizations.

Academic performance was measured through the number of exercise points, which was a convenient measure for our course and an often used measure in previous studies. We also measured whether the visualizations can be used to influence how early and on how many days the students solve exercises before the deadline to see whether a visualization encourages behavior which has been shown to lead to better academic performance. These behavioral measures on top of the number of exercise points were the key visualized aspects in the visualizations we developed. As a summary, our overarching research question for this study is *"How do visualizations that support self-regulated learning affect students' academic performance and behavior?"*.

Achievement goals and visualizations have been previously studied by, e.g., Auvinen [3], who suggested that students' performance is only slightly influenced by visualizations. Achievement goals have been also studied by Zingaro and Porter [17, 18], who suggested that both performance and mastery orientation can influence students grades and exam scores. Similarly, students' behavior has been studied by e.g. [12], who sought for interventions that reduce procrastination.

This work is organized as follows. Section 2 covers the background information related to scheduling and completing programming exercises, goal orientation in self-regulated learning, and visualizations developed for supporting self-regulated learning. Section 3 addresses the methodology of our study, describing the course in which this study was conducted and its learning environment, the visualizations that were used, and other key aspects of the study. In Section 4 we present and discuss the results of our study. Finally, Section 5 concludes this work by summarizing our findings and outlining the future work that we are planning to conduct.

2 BACKGROUND

2.1 Scheduling and completing exercises

Students' academic performance on a course has been measured using for example factors like the amount and quality of completed exercises, exam scores, the final grade, and drop-out-rate [5, 11, 13, 16]. Studies have revealed that the total number of exercises the student has completed, the number of days that the student has been working on the exercises and how early the student starts working on the exercises correlate with students' performance.

Spacco et al. [16] studied the relationship between the amount of completed exercises and students' exam scores. In the study, students completed a set of programming exercises which were similar to the programming questions asked in the exam. The study revealed that the amount of exercises attempted and answered had a positive correlation with exam scores.

Spacing out learning over time has been shown to be a more effective way of learning compared to learning the same material in a single session [5]. Leppänen et al. [11] studied how students space out their work in a programming course. Students participating in the study attended school work on average three times a week. The study revealed that students with higher exam scores averaged less working days per week, while the study conducted by Cepeda et al. [4] indicates that spacing out work over time is beneficial for students' performance.

Martin et al. [13] studied how starting school work early or starting it late affected the quality of finished work. The study was conducted on a course which involved four separate programming projects, with students being given approximately one month for each assignment. The study revealed that individual students underestimated the effort required to complete the assignments 72% of the time.

2.2 Goal orientation in self-regulated learning

Goal orientations can be defined as purposes for achievement behavior [10]. Rather than focusing on *what* people try to achieve, goal orientation characterizes the individual's *motivation* for achieving various objectives. Adopting different orientations is associated with different quality of engagement in school work as well as with different emotional experiences in school.

Perception of the number and the definition of orientations that people may adopt in achievement situations vary among researchers. Nevertheless, goal orientation research focuses mostly on two main orientations: *mastery* and *performance* goals. Mastery orientation refers to the purpose of developing competence. Mastery-oriented students focus on learning, understanding, developing skills, and mastering information. Performance orientation on the other hand refers to the purpose of demonstrating competence. Performance-oriented students strive to perform well relative to others and seek to appear competent.

Mastery and performance orientation can be divided into *approach* and *avoidance* [6]. When pursuing performance-approach goals, the student is oriented towards demonstrating high ability. In contrast, a student pursuing performance-avoidance goals is seeking to avoid showing low competence. Similarly, students with a mastery-approach seek to master the task, while the mastery-avoidance students seek to avoid failing in the task.

Mastery-oriented students have been suggested to also have higher self-efficacy, persistence, preference for challenge, self-regulated learning and positive affect and well-being [10]. Performance-oriented students, on the other hand, have been found to be associated with positive outcomes such as persistence and positive affect as well as negative outcomes such as anxiety, disruptive behavior and low retention of knowledge [10].

It is common to assess the existence of mastery and performance goal orientations with questionnaires constructed with inventories using Likert type scales [10]. In this study, we use the questionnaire by Elliot and McGregor [7].

2.3 Visualizations for supporting self-regulated learning

Multitude of systems supporting students' monitoring and reflection of their own behavior have been developed. The impact of such systems to students' performance is typically evaluated both empirically and using feedback surveys or usability studies. The following systems share similarities with our study in that they also visualize students' performance with different variables such as exercise points and time spent in the learning materials, and also provided a way to compare own performance to peers' performance.

iTree [14] is a mobile based system, which allows students to interact, exchange information, engage in discussion, and collaborate on projects. It visualizes the activity of each individual student as a tree that changes its form depending on the student's number of posts, number of times posts are read, number of replies to posts and the ratio of total forum posts to replies. Students who used the system spent more time reading posts and created more posts on the discussion forum than the students who did not use it.

Student Activity Meter (SAM) [8] aims to assist both teachers and learners with self-reflection and awareness of what and how students are doing. It visualizes, e.g., work periods on a time line, number of accessed resources and the time spent with them, forum activities and comparison to peers. The system also recommends resources based on the resources accessed by the student.

StepUp! [15] empowers students to reflect on their own activity, and that of their peers, in open learning environments. The system tracks the time students spend in different activities on websites and the Eclipse development environment. It visualizes social interaction, time spent, artifacts produced, resource use, and allows comparison to other students. Feedback received from students suggested that the system helps students to assess how they are doing on the course and allows them to better compare themselves with their peers. Many students considered the feeling of being observed as a negative aspect.

Course Signals [1] allows teachers to send personalized emails to students that contain information about their current performance in a given course, encourage students to visit various help resources on campus or office hours and employs learning analytics to predict students' performance. The performance is measured using past academic history and the amount of interaction with the learning environment. At-risk students are sent emails that visualize their risk level as a traffic light and include pointers to various help resources on the campus. A study revealed that courses that implement Course Signals had a strong increase in satisfactory grades, and a decrease in unsatisfactory grades and withdrawals.

Finally, Auvinen et al. [3] developed a set of eight different visualizations visualizing students' average number of attempts per exercise, average points of the first attempts to each exercise, average time interval between consecutive attempts to the same exercise and average distance of the submissions to the deadline. Six of the visualizations are heat maps where color represents past students' final exercise points based on their behavior. Two of the visualizations are line charts with a thick line representing final exercise points and a gray area lower and upper quartiles. All the visualizations have a "You are here" label plotting student's own behavior, allowing students' to compare themselves to peers. The majority of students found visualizations reasonably easy to interpret but claimed that visualizations did not affect how exercise were done and submitted. There was also no significant change observed in the earned exercise points from the group who used the visualizations.

3 METHODOLOGY

3.1 Context and Data

The data for this study comes from an eight and a half-week online introductory programming course that was organized during the Spring 2017 at University of Helsinki, a European research first University. The course uses a blended online textbook with videos, instructional materials and embedded programming assignments that were automatically assessed. The course had a total of seven exercise sets that were released weekly; at the beginning of the course, the participants had a 20-day window to the first deadline. There was no limit or penalty for submitting incorrect answers, and the students could resubmit the assignments as many times as they wished.

The course had a total of 753 students, from whom 442 were included in this study. The 311 students were excluded for reasons including not wanting to participate in the study, not answering the provided questionnaires, or not attending more than a single week of the course.

The 442 students were divided randomly into three groups. The control group consisted of 168 students, the treatment group A consisted of 141 students, and the treatment group B consisted of 133 students. For analysis, the three groups were then divided further into four groups based on their goal orientation determined by the survey by Elliot and McGregor [7]. In both treatment groups and the control group, the vast majority of the students were classified as mastery approach students. A small smoothing for orientations with less students was applied to distribute students with weaker mastery approach orientation to the second strongest orientation. The final group sizes used for the analysis in this study are shown in Table 1.

In this study, we focus on the overall populations in the different conditions as well as on the influence of the treatments to performance and mastery approach oriented students.

3.2 Treatment and Visualizations

We attempted to influence students' working habits using visualizations embedded into the course materials. The specific metrics that we chose to visualize were chosen based on earlier work indicating that they influence students' academic performance [5, 11, 13, 16].

Table 1: Sizes of the control group and the treatment groups which are divided into goal orientations.

	Control	Grp A/Radar	Grp B/Text
mastery approach	55	45	48
performance approach	49	49	42
mastery avoidance	35	27	25
performance avoidance	29	20	18
total	187	141	133

Figure 1: The textual visualization of a problem set. The students could see the Scheduling metric by scrolling down.

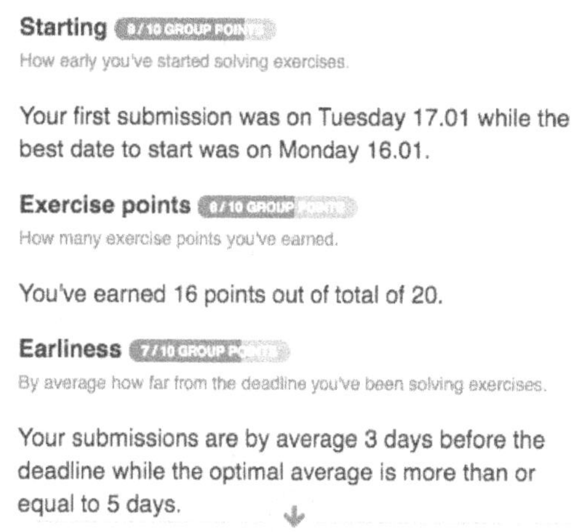

The four metrics that were used to describe students' behavior are as follows: *starting*, *scheduling*, *earliness* and *exercise points*. *Starting* measured how soon after the release of an exercise set the student started to work on the exercises; *Scheduling* measured the number of days that the student worked on an exercise set; *Earliness* measured the average distance from the deadline of a specific exercise set; and *Exercise points* measured how many points the student had received from the exercises of a certain exercise set. Each metric was normalized to a range from 0 to 10, where 0 indicated poorest performance and 10 indicated the best performance. The visualizations showed data for each separate week in the course, which corresponded to separate pages in the course material.

Two types of visualizations were used: the *textual* and the *radar* visualization. The textual visualization showed the variables as a list of values. Each variable had the name of the metric, a short description of it, the value of the metric as a progress bar with a numerical label and a description of where the points came from and how to maximize the value of the metric (see Figure 1). For example, for the scheduling metric, the student could see a guiding text "You've been solving exercises on 2 days while the optimal number of days is at least 3".

The radar visualization showed the metrics using a radar chart. The radar chart consisted of a sequence of spokes where each spoke represented one of the four metrics. The length of each spoke was defined by the value of the metric the spoke was representing. The

Figure 2: The radar visualization of a problem set.

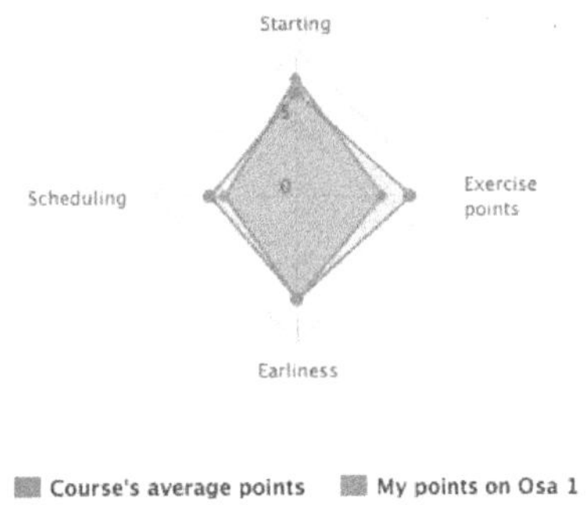

same textual suggestions than in the textual visualization were available when hovering on the values using a mouse. The radar chart was layered so that the student's performance was displayed using a blue layer and the average performance of all students in the course was displayed as a gray layer (see Figure 2).

The differences in the visualizations were motivated by performance oriented students striving to perform well relative to others whereas mastery oriented students strive to develop competence [10]. In the radar visualization, students had an opportunity to compare their points to their peers' points which should motivate performance oriented students. The textual visualization on the other hand was more focused in visualizing the student's own behavior and provided suggestions on how to improve it. We hypothesized that this would motivate mastery oriented students.

Group A was assigned the radar visualization, and Group B was assigned the textual visualization.

4 RESULTS AND DISCUSSION

Table 2 lists the means (denoted by μ) and standard deviations (denoted by σ) of the variable values for control and treatment groups and for goal orientations within the groups. The size of each group is denoted by n.

4.1 Visualizations and exercise completion

When comparing the average exercise points from the control group ($\approx$ 160.35) to the treatment groups ($\approx$ 170.23 for radar and $\approx$ 147.67 for textual), no statistically significant difference was found. This applies to comparing the treatment groups as a whole to the control group as well as comparing both treatment groups individually to the control group.

When comparing the treatment groups, Wilcoxon test revealed a statistically significant difference between the treatment groups ($p \approx 0.014$). Students in the radar visualization group earned on average 170.23 exercise points, whereas students in the textual visualization group earned on average 147.67 exercise points. The difference between the treatment groups is approximately 22.56 exercise points. In other words, students in the radar group completed approximately 15% more exercises than the students in the textual group.

When we examine the control group and treatment groups further by dividing them into tertiles based on the number of exercise

Table 2: Mean and standard deviation values for exercise points and behavioral variables for the different groups in the study.

Control	exercise points	starting	earliness	scheduling
total $n = 187$	$\mu \approx 160.35$ $\sigma \approx 68.94$	$\mu \approx 8.19$ $\sigma \approx 6.92$	$\mu \approx 12.99$ $\sigma \approx 7.38$	$\mu \approx 2.89$ $\sigma \approx 1.43$
mast. app. $n = 55$	$\mu \approx 164.98$ $\sigma \approx 68.82$	$\mu \approx 9.1$ $\sigma \approx 7.11$	$\mu \approx 12.51$ $\sigma \approx 7.69$	$\mu \approx 2.88$ $\sigma \approx 1.53$
perf. app. $n = 49$	$\mu \approx 173.59$ $\sigma \approx 65.9$	$\mu \approx 8.3$ $\sigma \approx 6.7$	$\mu \approx 13.86$ $\sigma \approx 7.48$	$\mu \approx 3.05$ $\sigma \approx 1.42$
mast. avoid. $n = 35$	$\mu \approx 121.77$ $\sigma \approx 72.3$	$\mu \approx 4.38$ $\sigma \approx 3.99$	$\mu \approx 12.84$ $\sigma \approx 7.12$	$\mu \approx 2.62$ $\sigma \approx 1.45$
perf. avoid. $n = 29$	$\mu \approx 145.66$ $\sigma \approx 76.72$	$\mu \approx 9.15$ $\sigma \approx 8.32$	$\mu \approx 10.48$ $\sigma \approx 7.21$	$\mu \approx 2.46$ $\sigma \approx 1.41$
Radar	exercise points	starting	earliness	scheduling
total $n = 141$	$\mu \approx 170.23$ $\sigma \approx 61.42$	$\mu \approx 8.64$ $\sigma \approx 6.55$	$\mu \approx 13.45$ $\sigma \approx 7.18$	$\mu \approx 3.12$ $\sigma \approx 1.55$
mast. app. $n = 45$	$\mu \approx 176.27$ $\sigma \approx 59.43$	$\mu \approx 8.52$ $\sigma \approx 6.2$	$\mu \approx 14$ $\sigma \approx 7.1$	$\mu \approx 3.5$ $\sigma \approx 1.72$
perf. app. $n = 49$	$\mu \approx 185.06$ $\sigma \approx 58.7$	$\mu \approx 9.92$ $\sigma \approx 6.63$	$\mu \approx 13.5$ $\sigma \approx 7.33$	$\mu \approx 2.84$ $\sigma \approx 1.47$
mast. avoid. $n = 27$	$\mu \approx 127.48$ $\sigma \approx 72.14$	$\mu \approx 6.29$ $\sigma \approx 7.19$	$\mu \approx 11.5$ $\sigma \approx 8.01$	$\mu \approx 2.77$ $\sigma \approx 1.54$
perf. avoid. $n = 20$	$\mu \approx 138.15$ $\sigma \approx 70.1$	$\mu \approx 7.8$ $\sigma \approx 6.98$	$\mu \approx 10.98$ $\sigma \approx 7.11$	$\mu \approx 2.6$ $\sigma \approx 1.6$
Textual	exercise points	starting	earliness	scheduling
total $n = 133$	$\mu \approx 147.67$ $\sigma \approx 71.13$	$\mu \approx 8.76$ $\sigma \approx 6.55$	$\mu \approx 11.17$ $\sigma \approx 6.46$	$\mu \approx 2.70$ $\sigma \approx 1.62$
mast. app. $n = 48$	$\mu \approx 158.54$ $\sigma \approx 65.26$	$\mu \approx 8.99$ $\sigma \approx 6.94$	$\mu \approx 11.94$ $\sigma \approx 6.83$	$\mu \approx 3.08$ $\sigma \approx 1.7$
perf. app. $n = 42$	$\mu \approx 155.12$ $\sigma \approx 71.49$	$\mu \approx 10.31$ $\sigma \approx 6.41$	$\mu \approx 10.6$ $\sigma \approx 5.86$	$\mu \approx 2.46$ $\sigma \approx 1.38$
mast. avoid. $n = 25$	$\mu \approx 105.4$ $\sigma \approx 71.05$	$\mu \approx 5.05$ $\sigma \approx 4.63$	$\mu \approx 10.23$ $\sigma \approx 6.45$	$\mu \approx 2.23$ $\sigma \approx 1.4$
perf. avoid. $n = 18$	$\mu \approx 151.78$ $\sigma \approx 69.26$	$\mu \approx 9.22$ $\sigma \approx 6.09$	$\mu \approx 11.13$ $\sigma \approx 6.67$	$\mu \approx 2.79$ $\sigma \approx 1.92$

points earned, we notice that the exercise points vary in the lowest two thirds. Table 3 displays the mean exercise points (denoted by μ) and the standard deviations (denoted by σ) of the lowest, middle and highest thirds of the treatment groups and the control group. The size of each group is denoted by n.

The highest performing students earned on average almost all of the available points in the course (the maximum was 216 exercise points) with a standard deviation of less than two in each of the treatment groups and in the control group. This indicates that the highest performing students, regardless of the visualization, earned

Table 3: Exercise points of the lowest, middle and highest tertiles.

	lowest third	middle third	highest third
control $n = 164$	$\mu \approx 65.02$ $\sigma \approx 25.83$ $n = 54$	$\mu \approx 194.20$ $\sigma \approx 24.89$ $n = 55$	$\mu \approx 215.89$ $\sigma \approx 0.31$ $n = 55$
radar $n = 137$	$\mu \approx 86.31$ $\sigma \approx 36.42$ $n = 45$	$\mu \approx 204.15$ $\sigma \approx 14.15$ $n = 46$	$\mu \approx 215.87$ $\sigma \approx 0.34$ $n = 46$
textual $n = 132$	$\mu \approx 55.98$ $\sigma \approx 22.18$ $n = 44$	$\mu \approx 171.12$ $\sigma \approx 32.56$ $n = 43$	$\mu \approx 214.91$ $\sigma \approx 1.70$ $n = 45$

the maximum points in the course without nearly any variance. A hypothesis for the reasons behind these results is that the students who have strong task related or self-regulatory skills do not benefit from the external feedback provided by the visualizations as much as the students with weaker skills.

The lowest two thirds reveal a difference between the groups. Students in the middle third are akin except when using the textual visualization, which seems to be harmful. Students in the lowest third of the radar visualization group earned on average 86.31 exercise points, whereas students in the lowest third of the textual visualization group earned on average 55.98 exercise points. Additionally, the lowest third in the control group earned on average 65.02 exercise points. The differences between the radar visualization group and the other groups were statistically significant (Wilcoxon, $p \approx 0.0029$ for control, $p < 0.001$ for textual), while the difference between the textual visualization and the control group was not statistically significant. This finding emphasizes that even if the positive impact of a visualization might not be that large on the whole group of students, positive impacts can be observed within student subpopulations.

4.2 Visualizations and goal orientation

Exercise points earned by the performance approach oriented students differed significantly in the treatment groups (Wilcoxon, $p \approx 0.01$). Performance approach oriented students in the radar visualization group complete more exercises than the performance approach oriented students in the textual visualization group: students in the radar visualization group earned on average nearly 30 more exercise points than the ones in the textual visualization group. This difference is also in line with goal orientation theory, which suggests that performance approach oriented students draw motivation from outperforming others – something that is supported by the radar visualization. However, at the same time, the mastery oriented students also performed better in the radar group than the students in the textual group.

Performance approach oriented students in the control group earned approximately on average 173.59 exercise points, while they earned on average 155.12 points in the textual visualization group. This difference was confirmed significant by a Wilcoxon test ($p \approx 0.027$). That is, the performance approach oriented students who had no visualization performed better than the performance approach oriented students with the textual visualization. This indicates that a visualization may even be harmful to performance approach oriented students if the visualization does not provide a comparison to other students.

This observation suggests that performance and mastery approach oriented students may benefit from different types of visualizations – or from the lack of a visualization. To our knowledge, previous work has not reported negative effects of visualizations on students. One reason for the lack of observed negative effects could be that most studies only measure the effects of the visualizations on the whole population of students without diving students by their goal orientation and measuring their differences. However, Auvinen et al. [2] divided the student population by their goal orientation but did not find any negative effects in any student groups. Another possible reason for lack of research on negative effects could be that reporting positive results is far more common than reporting negative results [9].

4.3 Visualizations and time management

The length of the delay in days students submit their first exercise after an exercise set is published (*starting*) does not vary between groups with a significant difference. However, the mean difference in days between all the student's exercise submissions during an exercise set and the deadline of the exercise set (*earliness*) differed significantly between the groups. Students in the radar visualization group submit exercises on average 13.45 days before the deadline whereas students in the textual visualization group submit exercises on average 11.17 days before the deadline. A Wilcoxon test suggests that the difference can be statistically significant ($p \approx 0.04$).

Exercise submission earliness of the performance approach oriented students varied in the treatment groups. In the radar visualization group performance approach oriented students submitted exercises approximately on average 13.5 days before the deadline whereas performance approach oriented students in the textual visualization group 10.6 days before the deadline. A Wilcoxon test again confirmed that the groups differed significantly ($p \approx 0.047$). Similar difference in exercise submission earliness was observable between the performance approach oriented students in the control group and the textual visualization group. Performance approach oriented students in the control group submitted exercises 3.26 days earlier than the performance approach oriented students in the textual visualization group. A Wilcoxon test confirmed a significant difference between the groups ($p \approx 0.038$).

When considering scheduling, i.e. dividing the work across multiple days, we observe that the visualizations did not increase the number of days during which the students worked on the assignments. On the contrary, performance approach oriented students in the textual visualization group submitted exercises on average on 2.46 days whereas performance approach oriented students in the control group submitted exercises on average on 3.05 days. The difference between the groups was statistically significant ($p \approx 0.031$). It is possible that the visualized metrics influence each other; the performance approach oriented may have striven to gain all the exercise points as fast as possible, ignoring the feedback related to spacing out their effort.

4.4 Limitations of the study

Next, we address both internal and external validity concerns related to our study. While our visualizations were evaluated using a randomized between-subject experiment which provides a good confidence that the differences between the treatment and control groups are due to the intervention, there is a possibility of random variations in the pre-test performances of the groups. It is also possible that some of the students learned of the experiment from their peers, which could have affected the study outcomes.

It is also possible that there is a self-selection bias in the goal orientation and in the final survey feedback. This might have resulted in some goal orientation or opinions to have a stronger presence than others. For example, avoidance-oriented students might skip some of the survey to minimize effort, or to avoid checking or noticing if they perform poorly when compared to others.

The results could be dependent on the arrangements of the course, the participants of the course, and the culture. Our course was a university level course and the participants provide a very biased sample. In a more competitive culture, the effects related to the performance approach oriented students might also manifest in a stronger fashion. Also, in some cultures students may be more dependent on external support, which can affect how they behave in self-regulated learning activities.

Finally, any research is as valid as the used measurements are. In this study, we used the questionnaire by Elliot and McGregor [7], which may not be optimal for assessing mastery and performance orientation – similarly, the link between different goal orientations and course performance needs to be studied further in different contexts.

5 CONCLUSIONS

In this work, we studied whether different types of visualizations embedded to the course materials can influence students' performance on the visualized variables. We conducted a randomized controlled trial, where the student population of an online programming course was divided into three groups, where one group had no visualizations, one group had a textual visualization, and one group had a radar visualization that also compared their progress to the progress of others in the course. Furthermore, we studied whether students' goal orientation influences their behavior.

Our study suggests that visualizations can have both negative and positive effects on students. Based on our results, the lowest performing students can benefit from a visualization the most, whereas highest performing students completed on average all the exercises on the course regardless of their visualization. Our results also indicate that a visualization that does not provide the means to compare your own performance to the performance of others can even be harmful to performance approach oriented students. The students with the radar visualization had overall better performance than the textual visualization group, and in some cases, the students with the textual visualization actually performed worse than the students in the control group with no visualization.

There was no clear indication that the visualizations would have a positive effect in behavior which is considered to lead into better academic performance. On the contrary, performance approach oriented students in the textual visualization group submitted exercises closer to deadline than those in the control group who did not receive any visualization. On the other hand, the students in the radar visualization group submitted exercises earlier than students in the textual visualization group. This difference was most significant within the performance approach oriented students.

Our results can be used as a guideline when designing course material visualizations; there is no clear consensus on the best visualization, but it is clear that students' goal orientations should also be taken into account. As a part of our future work, we are conducting a similar controlled experiment that studies only the radar visualization. In the study reported here, the students with the radar visualization performed on average better than the students in the other conditions. We hypothesize that the reason for the improved performance was that the students could compare their behavior to others, but as we did not explicitly study two versions of the radar visualization, this has to be confirmed.

REFERENCES

[1] Kimberly E Arnold and Matthew D Pistilli. 2012. Course signals at Purdue: using learning analytics to increase student success. In *Proc. of the 2nd international conference on learning analytics and knowledge*. ACM, 267–270.

[2] Tapio Auvinen et al. 2015. Educational Technologies for Supporting Self-Regulated Learning in Online Learning Environments. (2015).

[3] Tapio Auvinen, Lasse Hakulinen, and Lauri Malmi. 2015. Increasing students' awareness of their behavior in online learning environments with visualizations and achievement badges. *IEEE TLT* 8, 3 (2015), 261–273.

[4] Nicholas J Cepeda, Harold Pashler, Edward Vul, John T Wixted, and Doug Rohrer. 2006. Distributed practice in verbal recall tasks: A review and quantitative synthesis. *Psychological bulletin* 132, 3 (2006), 354.

[5] Frank N Dempster. 1988. The spacing effect: A case study in the failure to apply the results of psychological research. *American Psychologist* 43, 8 (1988), 627.

[6] Andrew J Elliot and Marcy A Church. 1997. A hierarchical model of approach and avoidance achievement motivation. *Journal of personality and social psychology* 72, 1 (1997), 218.

[7] Andrew J Elliot and Holly A McGregor. 2001. A 2× 2 achievement goal framework. *Journal of personality and social psychology* 80, 3 (2001), 501.

[8] Sten Govaerts, Katrien Verbert, Erik Duval, and Abelardo Pardo. 2012. The student activity meter for awareness and self-reflection. In *CHI'12 Extended Abstracts on Human Factors in Computing Systems*. ACM, 869–884.

[9] John PA Ioannidis. 2005. Why most published research findings are false. *PLos med* 2, 8 (2005), e124.

[10] Avi Kaplan and Martin L Maehr. 2007. The contributions and prospects of goal orientation theory. *Educational Psychology Review* 19, 2 (2007), 141–184.

[11] Leo Leppänen, Juho Leinonen, and Arto Hellas. 2016. Pauses and spacing in learning to program. In *Proc. of the 16th Koli Calling International Conference on Computing Education Research*. ACM, 41–50.

[12] Joshua Martin, Stephen H. Edwards, and Clfford A. Shaffer. 2015. The Effects of Procrastination Interventions on Programming Project Success. In *Proc. of the Eleventh Annual International Conference on International Computing Education Research (ICER '15)*. ACM, New York, NY, USA, 3–11. https://doi.org/10.1145/2787622.2787730

[13] Joshua Martin, Stephen H Edwards, and Clfford A Shaffer. 2015. The Effects of Procrastination Interventions on Programming Project Success. In *Proc. of the eleventh annual International Conference on International Computing Education Research*. ACM, 3–11.

[14] Jun Nakahara, Shinichi Hisamatsu, Kazaru Yaegashi, and Yuhei Yamauchi. 2005. iTree: Does the mobile phone encourage learners to be more involved in collaborative learning?. In *Proc. of th 2005 conference on Computer support for collaborative learning: learning 2005: the next 10 years!* International Society of the Learning Sciences, 470–478.

[15] Jose Luis Santos, Katrien Verbert, Sten Govaerts, and Erik Duval. 2013. Addressing learner issues with StepUp!: an evaluation. In *Proc. of the Third International Conference on Learning Analytics and Knowledge*. ACM, 14–22.

[16] Jaime Spacco, Paul Denny, Brad Richards, David Babcock, David Hovemeyer, James Moscola, and Robert Duvall. 2015. Analyzing student work patterns using programming exercise data. In *Proc. of the 46th ACM Technical Symposium on Computer Science Education*. ACM, 18–23.

[17] Daniel Zingaro. 2015. Examining interest and grades in computer science 1: A study of pedagogy and achievement goals. *ACM Transactions on Computing Education (TOCE)* 15, 3 (2015), 14.

[18] Daniel Zingaro and Leo Porter. 2016. Impact of student achievement goals on CS1 outcomes. In *Proc. of the 47th ACM Technical Symposium on Computing Science Education*. ACM, 279–296.

Fostering Meaningful Collaboration in an Interdisciplinary Capstone Course

Liz Hutter
(Moderator)
Valparaiso University
Department of English
1400 Chapel Drive
Valparaiso, IN 46383
(612) 964-0995
liz.hutter@valpo.edu

Halcyon M. Lawrence
Georgia Institute of Technology
Writing and Communication
215 Bobby Dodd Way
Atlanta, GA 30318
(773) 240-2884
hlawrence7@gatech.edu

Melinda McDaniel
Georgia Institute of Technology
College of Computing
801 Atlantic Drive
Atlanta, GA 30318
(770) 378-3090
mcdaniel@cc.gatech.edu

Marguerite Murrell
Georgia Institute of Technology
College of Computing
801 Atlantic Drive
Atlanta, GA 30318
(404) 610-2908
mmurrell6@gatech.edu

CCS Concepts

- **Social and professional topics → Computing education** → Computing education programs

Keywords:
Agile Collaboration; Capstone; Interdisciplinary; Pedagogy

ACM Reference format:

Liz Hutter, Halcyon M. Lawrence, Melinda McDaniel and Marguerite Murrell. 2018. Fostering Meaningful Collaboration in an Interdisciplinary Capstone Course. In *SIGCSE '18: 49th ACM Technical Symposium on Computer Science Education, Feb. 21–24, 2018, Baltimore, MD, USA. ACM, NY, NY, USA,* 2 pages. http://dx.doi.org/10.1145/3159450.3159625

1. SUMMARY

The benefits of interdisciplinary collaboration are not new to the field of computer science [1], [2]. At Georgia Tech, the College of Computing and the Writing and Communication Program currently offer a unique interdisciplinary, year-long computer science capstone course which is integrated with a technical communication course. Every semester, the integrated capstone enrolls 600 students, requires a dozen teaching faculty, and works with approximately 50 clients. The capstone's administrative infrastructure (i.e., syllabus, course policies, and course deliverables) is distinct in that it presents a single, unified technical communication and computer science experience for students. Our panel recognizes that collaboration must be inclusive and happen at different levels (i.e., course planning, design, and implementation) if students are to engage successfully with the software development life cycle. In this presentation, each panelist addresses a different experience of interdisciplinary collaboration, reflecting on issues that arise from administrative, pedagogical, teacher, and student-learner contexts.

For example, course administrators have had to understand how learning outcomes from two fields are aligned; instructors from different disciplines have had to build common ground around their individual disciplinary expertise; and students have had to learn to work on a team with other students who bring specialization in different sub-disciplines. The breadth of collaborative experiences this panel examines can guide administrators and instructors wishing to integrate more collaborative opportunities in computer science curricula at their respective institutions. While our panel presents both theoretical and individual perspectives, each panelist addresses the following questions:

1. How have we tried to make our individual expertise (e.g. programmer or technical communicator) relevant and useful to the other discipline?
2. How do we make the experience of collaboration one of integration rather than something piecemeal, where one part is added on to the other?
3. How do we resolve the challenges we experience as we try to collaborate within or across disciplines?

While these questions are designed to reflect on our own experiences in the capstone, the panel will provide an opportunity for the audience to raise questions and provide perspectives from their own institutional experiences.

ACM ISBN 978-1-4503-5103-4/18/02.
DOI: http://dx.doi.org/10.1145/3159450.3159625

2. RESOLVING ADMINISTRATIVE CHALLENGES THROUGH COLLABORATION (LAWRENCE)

One of the more pressing needs of a growing program such as ours is streamlined administrative practices. All courses incur some administrative load that needs to be managed; however, courses taught across disciplinary units have an added challenge of disciplinary differences that need to be understood and negotiated for the successful administration of the course. As noted by Bohen and Stiles [3 pp. 41], "existing administrative structures are not oriented toward promoting or supporting collaborative work, particularly that which crosses disciplinary, department or school boundaries." Beyond some of the more obvious resource-related issues [4] of funding, staffing, and training, our disciplinary differences require us to put at the forefront of our planning: (1) the need for strong vertical and lateral channels of communication within and across disciplines; (2) the need to develop long-term sustainable administrative practices; and (3) the need for clear allocation of responsibilities and a plan of accountability. I discuss each of these needs and highlight how integral collaboration is to the administrative success of the course. For example, since the integration of the two courses, co-administrators have successfully written and communicated policies and procedures for the course, provided initial onboarding for new faculty, along with regular semester check-ins, and worked with college advisors to streamline registration procedures.

3. RESOLVING PEDAGOGICAL DIFFERENCES THROUGH COLLABORATION (HUTTER)

Understanding how knowledge is created in a discipline is important when designing syllabi and assignments in an integrated course. This understanding is especially useful as computer science students come to the course already possessing the skills that would allow them to complete writing tasks. However, students do not easily make the connection between the two disciplines and often see writing and coding as distinctly different forms of knowledge creation [5]. While the field of technical communication recognizes that concepts such as audience/user, syntax, and revision/iteration, are common to both disciplines [6], these commonalities are not conspicuous to computer science students. Therefore, there is a need to teach computer science students how to use what they already know about coding to compose effective technical communication artifacts (e.g. specifications, detailed system design, or feasibility reports). To accomplish this pedagogical goal, an instructor needs to understand the disciplinary culture of computer science. She needs to observe, listen, and experience how the students learn a new coding concept and how they apply that concept to the code they write. This presentation examines how collaborative dialogue in an interdisciplinary computer science classroom might address the challenge of making explicit to students how the process of coding is analogous to writing.

4. COLLABORATION IN ACTION: TEACHER/TEACHER EXPERIENCE (MCDANIEL)

I came into the capstone course excited about the prospect of applying Agile methodologies to a course at Georgia Tech. I felt that my role would be to cover software design and implementation issues while allowing my co-instructor to teach rhetoric and writing. As the course progressed, my opinion of the importance of writing to the Agile methodology expanded, and I grew to appreciate my colleague's ability to synthesize what the students were trying to express into clear, precise specifications. This type of expressive communication is very similar to what a programmer needs to do when developing software. She must keep in mind who will be using the software just like a writer must keep in mind the rhetorical context. A programmer must develop software that works for all cases and has been fully tested, just as good writing must make sure that there are no ambiguities and that all ideas are clearly expressed. I developed an appreciation for collaboration with a colleague possessing very different skills than myself. The students saw that when skills are equally valued, the environment becomes inclusive, and each student's skills are strengthened.

5. COLLABORATION IN ACTION: STUDENT /TEAM EXPERIENCE (MURRELL)

As a computer science student at Georgia Tech, I have worked in many interdisciplinary settings. From programmer to project manager to teaching assistant, my varying roles in projects have given me a unique perspective on interdisciplinary collaboration and its necessity for success in creating a valuable end product. Through my experiences creating software and facilitating projects with my peers in different STEM fields, I have discovered certain methodologies of collaboration that are integral to success and others which proved more challenging. For example, within this capstone course for which I'm a teaching assistant, I've noticed that students will often take one of two routes when creating their software or their writing assignments. Students will either divvy the work week by week, passing the baton at the end of an iteration to the next teammate, or teammates will collaborate on *every* aspect of a project during an iteration. The first of these tactics leaves students in one field to work within the confines of what they know, contributing to the project in areas they are strong in, but nothing more, and ultimately never inhabiting the other field. The end project is merely the sum of all the disciplinary parts. The latter method is preferable, because it allows teammates the opportunity to understand a project from the inside out, resulting in the exchange of differing opinions and varying backgrounds of work and style and a smoother end product. This aggregation of results from true interdisciplinary collaboration is the key to success in this capstone course.

6. REFERENCES

[1] R. F. Dugan, "A survey of computer science capstone course literature," *Computer Science Education*, vol. 21, no. 3, pp. 201–267, 2011.

[2] S. Kurkovsky, "Mobile game development: improving student engagement and motivation in introductory computing courses," *Computer Science Education*, vol. 23, no. 2, pp. 138–157, 2013.

[3] S. J. Bohen and J. Stiles, "Experimenting with models of faculty collaboration: Factors that promote their success," *New Directions for Institutional Research*, vol. 1998, no. 100, pp. 39–55, 1998.

[4] M. Hukill and D. Lassner, "Interdisciplinary studies in communication and information sciences: Promises and problems," *Proceedings of the Twenty-Second Annual Hawaii International Conference on System Sciences*. Vol. IV: Emerging Technologies and Applications Track, 1989.

[5] J. Ford, "Knowledge transfer across disciplines: Tracking rhetorical strategies from a technical communication classroom to an engineering classroom," *IEEE Transactions on Professional Communication*, vol. 47, no. 4, pp. 301–315, 2004.

[6] R. E. Cummings, "Coding with power: Toward a rhetoric of computer coding and composition," *Computers and Composition*, vol. 23, no. 4, pp. 430–443, 2006.

Team-Teaching with Colleagues in the Arts and Humanities

Panel

Keith J. O'Hara
Bard College
Annandale-on-Hudson, NY, USA
kohara@bard.edu

Sven Anderson
Bard College
Annandale-on-Hudson, NY, USA
sanderso@bard.edu

David Musicant
Carleton College
Northfield, MN, USA
dmusicant@carleton.edu

Amber Stubbs
Simmons College
Boston, MA, USA
stubbs@simmons.edu

Thomas Way
Villanova University
Villanova, PA, USA
thomas.way@villanova.edu

KEYWORDS

Team-Teaching; Interdisciplinary Courses; Computing for All; Humanities Computing; Arts

ACM Reference Format:
Keith J. O'Hara, Sven Anderson, David Musicant, Amber Stubbs, and Thomas Way. 2018. Team-Teaching with Colleagues in the Arts and Humanities: Panel. In *SIGCSE '18: SIGCSE '18: The 49th ACM Technical Symposium on Computing Science Education, February 21–24, 2018, Baltimore , MD, USA.* ACM, New York, NY, USA, 2 pages. https://doi.org/10.1145/3159450.3159617

1 SUMMARY

This panel will include experience reports from five computer science faculty members who have team-taught courses with professors from outside the sciences. Specifically, we will discuss lessons learned and best practices with collaborating with faculty from the arts and humanities. Courses that look outward have the potential to broaden participation and promote computing's role in the broader world beyond software engineering concerns. The panelists will highlight how to: find a topic, find a collaborator(s), design the course, maintain rigor in both disciplines, target the right audience, assess how well it worked, and do it more than once.

2 SVEN ANDERSON

I collaborated with a professor of literature, Collin Jennings, to develop and co-teach a course entitled "Technologies of Reading: Human and Machine Approached to Literature." This course assumed no background in computing and was attended primarily by students in literature. We sought to highlight the history of scholarly activity that included both humanist and computational approaches to literary analyses, particularly ideas associated with close reading. The course was organized historically, and used computation to re-create and then extend analyses performed in the papers on literary analyses we read, combining basic elements of computation with more powerful algorithms adopted from the Natural Language Toolkit, including parsing, sentence generation, language modeling, and creation of high-dimensional semantic spaces. I will focus on how we determined the arc of the course topics, how we balanced the pull of literary studies versus basic programming. The long-term prospects of the course and its effect on later teaching by both professors will be discussed.

ACM ISBN 978-1-4503-5103-4/18/02...$15.00
https://doi.org/10.1145/3159450.3159617

3 DAVID MUSICANT

Stephen Mohring (Professor of Art, Carleton College), and I have offered a course three times called "Art, Interactivity, and Robotics." In this hands-on studio centered course, we explore and create interactive three-dimensional art. Using basic construction techniques, microprocessors, and programming, this class brings together the fundamentals of computer science, sculpture, engineering, and aesthetic design. Students engage the nuts-and-bolts of fabrication, learn to program computers, and study how robots think. The class culminates in a campus-wide exhibition. I will describe my experience from having taught the course three times, specifically regarding lessons learned in marketing an interdisciplinary course such as this one, as well as how we faced challenges in producing assignments in a course that introduces dramatically different sorts of skills from multiple disciplines.

4 AMBER STUBBS

Kris Erickson (Communications Department, Simmons College) and I will offer a "learning community" course titled "Choose Your Own Adventure: Coding and Digital Storytelling." Learning Communities are part of Simmons College's effort to incorporate multidisciplinary learning into every student's curriculum by bringing together different fields of study. In our Learning Community, students will learn programming fundamentals (variables, if/else, loops, arrays, functions, etc, using JavaScript) and simple HTML and CSS, along with basic photography, photo manipulation, and video processing to create immersive, interactive, and responsive stories through. Finding a balance between integrating and maintaining rigor in both disciplines can be difficult, but there are ways to use each discipline to motivate the other. I will discuss how Professor Erickson and I developed our current version of the course, which uses individual and team-taught classes to provide instruction, as well as related work using the Twine platform (twinery.org) to teach programming with the Boston chapter of Science Club for Girls.

5 KEITH O'HARA

With Ben Coonley (Film & Electronic Arts Department, Bard College), I offered an 8-credit course called "Games at Work: Participation, Procedure and Play." The course was part of a campus-wide initiative to create "big ideas" courses that connects programs in different divisions of the college. These courses targeted first and second-year students, and therefore, did not require any prior coursework in the involved disciplines. This single course satisfied two college-wide general education distribution requirements: Mathematics & Computing and Practicing Arts. Students created a variety of digital and non-digital games: remixing classics like Candyland and Fluxus Event Scores; programming with Twine, P5/JavaScript and Unity. I will describe my experience with an intimate (15 students; 2 faculty members), intensive (6 hours/week) course including challenges (e.g., time management, scalability, sustainability) and successes (e.g, student engagement, improved pedagogical practice, incubating continued collaboration). Moreover, I will compare this model of intensive team-teaching with other interdisciplinary models like linked/conjoined classes[1] and module-based approaches, both of which I have employed at Bard with humanities and art collaborators.

6 TOM WAY

Two French professors in my university's Department of Romance Languages & Literature, Seth Whidden and later Francois Massonnat, and I collaborated for the past six years on a parallel, conjoined approach to team-teaching[2].

We taught courses for our majors and minors on the same days and times in adjoining classrooms, meeting together about 10 times a semester to explore shared topics of interest and work together on projects. French students were in their Writing and Stylistics in French course while Computer Science students studied in my Machine Translation course. Motivated by a university initiative to foster interdisciplinary teaching, we designed our approach because we wanted to find a fun and fulfilling collaboration while maintaining rigor within our respective disciplines. I will report on how we pleased our chairs and dean by overcoming the "who gets credit for how much teaching" hurdle and on the successful student and faculty collaboration that resulted. Presented will be some of the interesting language analysis projects devised by cross-disciplinary teams of students using NLTK, along with the many positives and few negatives we gleaned through three iterations and our plans for the next offering in Fall 2018.

REFERENCES

[1] Keith J. O'Hara. 2012. Pedagogical Explorations in Computational Perception for Performance. In *Proceedings of the Twenty-Sixth AAAI Conference on Artificial Intelligence (AAAI'12)*. AAAI Press, 2375–2376. http://dl.acm.org/citation.cfm?id=2900929.2901069

[2] Thomas Way and Seth Whidden. 2016. A Parallel, Conjoined Approach to Interdisciplinary Computer Science Education. In *Proceedings of the 2016 ACM Conference on Innovation and Technology in Computer Science Education (ITiCSE '16)*. ACM, New York, NY, USA, 363–363. https://doi.org/10.1145/2899415.2925486

SIGCSE Special Session
Evaluating CS4All Initiatives—Challenges and Opportunities

Cheri Fancsali
Research Alliance for New York City Schools
285 Mercer Street, 3rd Floor
New York, NY 10003
Telephone number: +1 212-998-5614
Cheri.Fancsali@nyu.edu

Linda Tigani
Research Alliance for New York City Schools
285 Mercer Street, 3rd Floor
New York, NY 10003
Telephone number: +1 212-998-5610
Linda.Tigani@nyu.edu

Paulina Toro Isaza
Research Alliance for New York City Schools
285 Mercer Street, 3rd Floor
New York, NY 10003
Telephone number: + 1 212-998-5546
Paulina.ToroIsaza@nyu.edu

Rachel Cole
Research Alliance for New York City Schools
285 Mercer Street, 3rd Floor
New York, NY 10003
Telephone number: +1 212-992-6114
Rachel.Cole@nyu.edu

Wendy Martin
Education Development Center
96 Morton Street, 7th Floor
New York, NY 10014
Telephone number: +1 212-807-4200
wmartin@edc.org

CCS Concepts

• Social and professional topics ~ Computing education programs ~ K-12 education

Keywords

Evaluation Design; CS Education Research; K-12 CS Education; Computer Science for All

ACM Reference format:
Cheri Fancsali, Linda Tigani, Paulina Toro Isaza, Rachel Cole, and Wendy Martin. 2018. SIGCSE Special Session: Evaluating CS4All Initiatives—Challenges and Opportunities. In *SIGCSE '18: 49th ACM Technical Symposium on Computer Science Education, Feb. 21–24, 2018, Baltimore, MD, USA*. ACM, NY, NY, USA, 6 pages.
https://doi.org/10.1145/3159450.3159458

1. SUMMARY

The last 10 years have been marked by an explosion of computing across almost every industry and a dramatic increase in STEM jobs that require computational thinking skills. In response, there has been a growing call for CS4ALL initiatives—at the district, state, and national levels [1]. The thrust of these initiatives is for all students to have opportunities to become proficient computational thinkers and be exposed to computer science curricula and courses throughout their educational careers. According to a review conducted by Code.org, major computer science initiatives currently exist in 31 states across the United States, with an additional seven states implementing policies that allow for computer science courses to count as math or science credit toward graduation [2].

One of the largest and most ambitious efforts is the NYC CS4All initiative. CS4All is a 10-year, districtwide public/private venture to bring high-quality CS education to all students in the nation's largest school district. It aspires to greatly increase the number of students, teachers, and schools exposed to CS in NYC, and to provide meaningful learning experiences that build upon prior exposure and skills at every grade level.

These plans include providing high-quality professional development (PD) to some 5,000 teachers, aimed at helping them learn new programs and pedagogies in CS education, as well as strategies for integrating CS into existing courses.

With the national proliferation of CS initiatives like NYC's CS4ALL comes a clear need for rigorous, thoughtful evaluation. Such evaluations can help guide the development and improvement of CS efforts, highlight whether and how these initiatives are accomplishing their intended goals, and determine the impact of these efforts on students, teachers, schools, and districts.

The purpose of this special session will be to engage members of the CS research community in sharing best practices, tools and resources for evaluating CS efforts. We will present the NYC CS4All evaluation as a case study of a multi-faceted, mixed-method evaluation of a complex and large-scale CS4ALL initiative, from which other efforts may find guidance. We believe there is much to be learned from the experience of the NYC CS4ALL initiative and evaluation, given its scope, depth and complexity.

2. OBJECTIVES

Given the relative newness of the CS4All movement, little research has been conducted on these efforts to date. Researchers working in this space have few resources to draw on in terms of standard practices for identifying and measuring appropriate outcomes, or well-tested instruments. Further, CS initiatives face inherent challenges associated with evaluating multi-faceted, large-scale, and complex enterprises.

As the external evaluators of NYC's CS4All initiative, the Research Alliance for New York City Schools and Education

ACM ISBN 978-1-4503-5103-4/18/02.
DOI: https://doi.org/10.1145/3159450.3159638

Development Center (EDC) are employing a mixed-method, longitudinal study that will document the launch and development of this ambitious system-wide effort. The nine-year evaluation is examining implementation across CS4All's many activities, tracking the growth and evolution of the initiative over time, and assessing the impact of CS education on a variety of district, school, teacher, and student outcomes. The study has a strong focus on issues of equity and access for all, and will pay particular attention to the experiences and outcomes of students who have traditionally been underrepresented in CS.

The objective of this session is to increase evaluator capacity to study CS education initiatives and to share knowledge and resources with the CS education research community. We plan to use the session to share our own experience as evaluators of the NYC CS4All initiative, and to brainstorm effective strategies and approaches to address the challenges inherent in evaluating such efforts. In the session, we will pay particular attention to identifying and developing reliable and valid measures of teacher, student and district outcomes.

Working in small groups, session participants will have an opportunity to share their own evaluation designs and instruments and get feedback from other researchers. After the session, the organizers will compile key themes and ideas discussed in small groups, as well as instruments and evaluation design documents. These will be disseminated to the participants through a shared platform (such as a shared folder on Google Drive, a Dropbox or by collaborating with an existing group like the CS Consortium to post resources online).

Specific objectives of the proposed session will be to:

1. Briefly review the NYC CS4All initiative goals and describe the external evaluation design and methods.
2. Surface and discuss challenges and opportunities associated with evaluations of CS initiatives.
3. Discuss and identify appropriate outcomes and measures for CS4ALL initiatives.
4. Share CS research instruments, data collection methods, and best practices.

3. OUTLINE

- **Introduction** (2 mins) – The organizers will introduce the agenda and objectives of the session.
- **Present NYC CS4All research design** (15 mins) – The research team will provide an overview of the NYC CS4All initiative goals and evaluation design, with a focus on the key outcomes and measures used to determine the initiative's success.
- **Small group work** (45 mins) – Attendees will be invited to work in small groups on focused topics of discussion. Topics will include school outcomes, teacher outcomes, student outcomes, district outcomes, and implementation measures. Each small group will be facilitated by a member of the CS4All research team and a volunteer from the audience. Participants are encouraged to bring and share their own research designs and instruments.

  Questions motivating the small group discussion will be tailored to the topics. The session organizers will prepare a handout with guidelines on how to facilitate the discussion, including protocols for ensuring all voices are heard and suggesting key questions to address. Example questions include:

  - What are the key outcomes of interest for (teachers, students, schools, districts)?
  - How should districts operationalize and measure equity and access in CS?
  - Who are the key mediators and moderators of the outcomes?
  - What are the most appropriate ways to measure the outcomes of interest? How might that be different for different grade levels?
  - What are the key contextual factors that must be taken into consideration in studying CS initiatives?
- **Group share out** (13 mins) – Participants will share out key ideas and themes from their small group. The discussion will be documented by members of the research team and made available to attendees following the conference through a shared platform.

4. EXPECTATIONS

The intended audience for this session includes CS researchers who are currently working on or are interested in evaluations of CS initiatives. It may also be of interest to other CS initiative stakeholders (e.g., developers, administrators, leadership) who are establishing outcomes and objectives for their initiative and working with external evaluators. The session will provide an opportunity for CS education researchers and relevant stakeholders to work together, share resources and learn from one another. Participants will be able to discuss and debate the most appropriate goals and measures for CS4All initiatives as well as identify what necessary measurement tools are missing and in need of development. These discussions will fill a critical gap and help advance the field of CS education research, with the potential of improving the quality and usefulness of such work.

5. SUITABILITY FOR A SPECIAL SESSION

This proposed session is well suited for a special session as it will allow participants to engage in meaningful discussions and collaborate in small groups around common interests in a way that is not possible in a paper session or panel.

6. REFERENCES

[1] Smith. M. 2016. Computer science for all. White House Blog. https://www.whitehouse.gov/blog/2016/01/30/computer-science-all).

[2] Code.org. 2017. K-12 Computer Science Policy and Implementation in States. https://docs.google.com/document/d/1J3TbEQt3SmIWuha7ooBPvlWpiK-pNVIV5uuQEzNzdkE/edit .

Five Slides About: Abstraction, Arrays, Uncomputability, Networks, Digital Portfolios, and the CS Principles Explore Performance Task

Colleen M. Lewis
(moderator)
Harvey Mudd College
Claremont, CA 91711
lewis@cs.hmc.edu

Leslie Aaronson
NCWIT
1111 Engineering Drive
Boulder, CO 80309
leslie.aaronson@ncwit.org

Eric Allatta
Academy for Software Engineering
New York, NY 10003
eallatta@afsenyc.org

Zachary Dodds
Harvey Mudd College
Dept. of Computer Science
Claremont, CA 91711
dodds@cs.hmc.edu

Jeffrey Forbes
Duke University
Dept. of Computer Science
Durham, NC 27708
forbes@cs.duke.edu

Kyla McMullen
University of Florida
Comp. & Info. Sci. & Eng.
Gainesville, FL 32611
drkyla@ufl.edu

Mehran Sahami
Stanford University
Computer Science Dept.
Stanford, CA 94305
sahami@cs.stanford.edu

ACM Reference format:
C.M. Lewis, L. Aaronson, E. Allatta, Z. Dodds, J. Forbes, K. McMullen, and M. Sahami. 2018. Five Slides About: Abstraction, Arrays, Uncomputability, Networks, Digital Portfolios, and the CS Principles Explore Performance Task. In *SIGCSE '18: 49th ACM Technical Symposium on Computer Science Education, Feb. 21–24, 2018, Baltimore, MD, USA*. ACM, NY, NY, USA, 6 pages.
https://doi.org/10.1145/3159450.3159645

Keywords
Teaching demonstrations; pedagogy; innovative teaching.

1. SUMMARY
SIGCSE is packed with teaching insights and inspiration. However, we get these insights and inspiration from hearing our colleagues *talk* about their teaching. Why not just watch them teach? This session does exactly that.

Each of six exceptional educators will be given ten minutes to teach the audience something. After this, the moderator will draw the attention of the audience to particular pedagogical moves that the instruction included. Attendees can see a new approach to introducing a topic or a new pedagogical move. No matter what, we expect attendees will be taking ideas from this session directly back to their teaching!

The format is based upon a practice in chemistry of sharing "Five Slides About," which introduce a topic in a novel or concise way (https://www.ionicviper.org/types/five_slides_about). Resources from each of the presenters will be shared on the website CSTeachingTips.org.

2. OBJECTIVE
The goal of the session is to inspire SIGCSE attendees by highlighting innovative instruction by exceptional educators. The specific content of the innovative instruction may be applicable for some attendees, and the discussion of the underlying pedagogical move within each innovation can be applied across the attendees' teaching.

ACM ISBN 978-1-4503-5103-4/18/02.
DOI: https://doi.org/10.1145/3159450.3159645

3. STRUCTURE
Six exceptional educators will present their favorite piece of innovative lecture content just as they would their students. The moderator, Colleen Lewis, will describe the central pedagogical move within the innovation and how this connects to education research. We believe this is an innovative session that will be well received by the SIGCSE community.

4. PRESENTERS

4.1 Abstraction - Mehran Sahami
Abstraction is a critical topic in teaching introductory CS, especially programming. Many students, however, find the concept of abstraction as well as the attendant notion of information hiding to be (with a slight pun intended) too abstract. To help students better understand this concept, we teach it using real-world examples of abstraction, often including real-world physical objects, such as kitchen appliances or digital media players. Such examples help students more concretely understand what abstraction is, how it can be useful, and how it is a powerful concept that is applicable in a variety of situations. We then draw parallels from these real-world examples to the case of abstraction in programming, leveraging what students understand about the concrete examples to help them better appreciate abstraction in programming.

Mehran Sahami is a Professor and Associate Chair for Education in the CS Department at Stanford University. He is also the Robert and Ruth Halperin University Fellow in Undergraduate Education at Stanford.

4.2 Arrays - Kyla McMullen
Due to the amount of interactivity, active learning is oftentimes a challenge in large lecture contexts. To help facilitate active learning in large settings of hundreds of students, I use a combination of think-pair-share and cloud computing technologies to seamlessly allow students to discuss and apply the concepts they have learned in lecture while receiving real-time feedback on their solutions. After I teach about arrays I give the students a piece of code that's missing a line and they pair with a neighbor to write the missing line of code. Students then

submit their code using a live-updated Google Form. I grab a few correct and incorrect answers and run them. Students come up with incorrect solutions I wouldn't have thought of and I can explain the nuances that arise in each.

Kyla McMullen is an Assistant Professor of Computer and Information Science and Engineering at the University of Florida. Dr. McMullen is the leader of the SoundPAD Laboratory at the University of Florida, which focuses on the Perception, Application, and Development of 3D audio in various contexts. Dr. McMullen also researches programming self-efficacy as an effect of IDE design, paired-programming, and active learning methodologies.

4.3 Uncomputability - Zachary Dodds

Uncomputability is a beautiful CS topic, widely considered spider-man central to the field's intellectual core. Independent of its historical and theoretical importance, I believe uncomputability can also invite a clarifying, big-picture perspective on the frustrations and triumphs of students' intro-computing experience. We invert the traditional "for some functions, it's impossible to create programs that compute them" with a more sympathetic equivalent: "some functions simply *cannot* be debugged." Students wholeheartedly agree with this latter sentiment, *especially* at the end of their first CS course! From there, it's only a small step to see just how correct -- and deep -- their intuition already is.

Zachary Dodds is a Professor in Harvey Mudd College's CS department. He enjoys teaching CS1, a course that, at HMC, precedes students' choice of major/other academic paths.

4.4 Networks - Jeff Forbes

The science of networks examines how entities are interconnected and how that connectivity impacts collective behavior. In CS1, I introduce topics, tools, and methods from the modeling and analysis of social networks as a way of motivating CS and other fields. Networks help motivate graph structures and algorithms. I ask students how to choose the vertices and edges to model a particular problem. We model the Hollywood universe by considering how actors are connected by co-starring in movies. Students consider the difference between different centrality measures as proxies for popularity. The study of networks also leads to a discussion of the power of online social networks and the data that they generate.

Jeffrey Forbes is an Associate Professor of the Practice of CS at Duke University. From 2011-2014, he served as a Program Director for the Education & Workforce program in the United States' National Science Foundation's Directorate for Computer & Information Science & Engineering.

4.5 Digital Portfolios - Leslie Aaronson

There are organic opportunities in CS education for students to document and reflect on their learning by creating a digital artifact through digital portfolios. This process makes the content matter and builds confidence. With the portfolios students are able to articulate their learning by embedding their CS projects and writing reflections about their work and learning for an audience outside the classroom, plus they will write and update resumes that include their new CS skills. In five slides, I introduce students to the technology they will use to make a digital portfolio and why it will be important.

Leslie Aaronson is the Strategic Director of K12 Initiatives for NCWIT (National Center for Women & Information Technology) and the Teacher in Residence at LA Promise Fund where she manages Girls Build LA. Leslie was awarded Teacher of the Year by LAUSD for her work as the Lead Teacher and Coordinator of Foshay Learning Center's Technology Academy where she taught CS to 10-12th graders for thirteen years.

4.6 CS Principles Explore Performance Task - Eric Allatta

In the AP CS Principles Explore Performance Task, students are required to research a "computing innovation," which must "consume, produce, and/or transform data." Students must develop a lens for looking at the world and seeing the data behind the innovation. Functional programming languages can facilitate this programming/impact connection. Functional languages allow for a data first pedagogy rooted in examining the world in terms of data. Students learn to apply functions by learning their contracts: the name, domain, and range of the function. When students are developing their proposals for the Explore Performance Task, they must identify the data an innovation consumes, transforms, and produces, which parallels the identification of the domain and range of a function. Students write contracts for the innovations they research, and use them to guide their performance task.

Eric Allatta is a CS teacher at the Academy for Software Engineering, an unscreened NYC public school with a core CS sequence required of all students. Eric leads the school's effort to design and implement a four-year layered curriculum sequence, aligned with the school's broader mastery-based learning goals. Each CS course has identified vertically aligned skills, and described criteria for assessing those skills at four levels of mastery.

5. Moderator

Colleen Lewis is a professor of CS at Harvey Mudd College who specializes in CS education. Lewis researches how people learn CS and how people feel about learning CS. Her research seeks to identify effective teaching practices for creating equitable learning spaces where all students have the opportunity to learn. Lewis curates CSTeachingTips.org, a NSF-sponsored project for disseminating effective CS teaching practices.

SRC: Student Research Competition

A Four Point Student-Led Strategy for Attracting Diverse Small College Commuter Campus Students to Computer Science

Gabrielle I. Zahuantitla, *SUNY Old Westbury*
Aryanna Holder, *SUNY Old Westbury*
Contact: gzahuant@oldwestbury.edu

Currently, there is a push for integrating computer science education and computational thinking into the classroom. For example, major local and national organizations such as CS4ALL: NYC and Code.org aim to expose all students, including typically underrepresented groups, to computer science education nurturing students' intrinsic motivation. Furthermore, current research indicates that first-exposure to computer science is an important deciding factor as to whether students are open to computer science in future endeavors. Being one of the most diverse campuses in the nation, and a commuter campus, The State University of New York (SUNY) Old Westbury provides a unique opportunity to pilot how one might go about creating a motivating first exposure to computer science. Through a four point student-led strategy, we explore student pre-conceived attitudes towards computer science and programming to better understand what strategies might increase CS engagement. In order to do this, we host workshops revolving around creative computer science activities such as 3D game design and multimedia art projects. During these workshops, we collect pre and post questionnaires and use their data to gain insight into the Old Westbury student body's notions of computer science. Initial analyzed pre-survey data shows that 70% of students thought Computer Science was difficult. However, post-survey data shows that, after the experience, approximately 90% of students want to take additional workshops involving Computer Science.

Keywords: Computer Science Education; Undergraduate Exposure; Game design; Workshops; Computational Thinking

DOI: https://doi.org/10.1145/3159450.3162331

A Mental Approach to Software Testing

Pedro Valdivia, *California State University, Chico*
Contact: pvaldivia1@mail.csuchico.edu

Many software engineering students make the transition from an academic setting to professional software development careers. Due to its popularity in the software industry, it is important for students to learn software testing skills and adhere to professional practices to prepare them for their transition and be successful. Software testing is an important skill for students but there are many different approaches that enables students to gain this skill. We created a unique approach that enables students to learn software testing with a unique mentality and developed a tool to make educational assessments and feedback quick and scalable. Our approach is implemented within an undergraduate classroom where students are separated into two groups. Each group develops software tests through Test-Driven Development (TDD) with a different mentality. With this approach, we hope to see an improvement in the quality of software that students produce.

ACM ISBN 978-1-4503-5103-4/18/02.

Keywords: test driven development (TDD); software development; software testing; unit testing

DOI: https://doi.org/10.1145/3159450.3162332

Software Engineering Education

William Zamora, *California State University, Chico*
Contact: wzamora@mail.csuchico.edu

Software Engineering courses are essential for undergraduates to achieve a smooth transition from higher education to a career. However, many of these courses encounter complications that forbid them from meeting their goals such as: Real products and customers, project duration, software sophistication and more. At Chico State, we have implemented the Tech Startup Model in which the Software Engineering students partner with entrepreneurship students to allow for more collaboration and the creation of a customer-employee relation to address some of these issues. This model utilizes both Lean Startup as well as Agile Development to continuously test a student's ability to adapt to the customer's needs. The data accumulated from the past couple of semesters allowed us to analyze student behavior when exposed to the Tech Startup Model as opposed to other methods tested from previous semesters.

Keywords: FOSS; Engineering; Lean Startup; Agile Development; Software; Education

DOI: https://doi.org/10.1145/3159450.3162333

Air Pollution Data Analysis Platform for Computer Science Education Projects

Nina Angelvik, *UiT The Arctic University of Norway*
Contact: nan016@post.uit.no

We have developed an applied computer science project to introduce students in upper secondary schools to computer science and engineering. In the project, students build and code their own air quality sensor kits before investigating a research question by analyzing their collected data. An important part of the analysis is to investigate the air quality data in context of other data sources, such as data from other sensor kits or climate data. The task of curating such datasets are too complex for such an introductory project and it therefore requires a specialized service. In this poster we present the design and implementation of an air pollution data analysis platform that stores air quality measurements collected by students, combines it with open environmental data, and provides students with an open interface to analyze their data. During spring 2018, ten school classes from Northern Norway are going to use the platform, online at airbit.uit.no, to study air quality patterns across Northern Norway. We also provide the source code for the platform at the same address.

Keywords: Air quality; Microcontrollers; Computational thinking; Cloud; Open source

DOI: https://doi.org/10.1145/3159450.3162334

Developing a Blocked Based Language for the Adafruit Circuit Playground

Blayde Dill, *University of Alabama*
Contact: badill@crimson.ua.edu

With the integrated use of technology in daily activities, the need for more end-users who can program solutions in their domain of expertise is increasing. There is also growing interest to introduce children to coding activities that are engaging and appropriate for their experience level. Additional resources are needed that initiate and teach computer science in a way that incorporates hardware components to children and first-learners. This poster introduces a new block-based programming environment (called CodePlayground) built from Google's Blockly Developer Tools. The Blockly library injects an editor into an HTML file that represents coding concepts as interlocking blocks, and then outputs the blocks as syntactically correct code. CodePlayground was designed to be compatible with the Adafruit Circuit Playground, which was released as an all-in-one low cost device that can be used for education. CodePlayground allows teachers to utilize the Circuit Playground as an educational device that includes both hardware and software elements. The Circuit Playground uses the firmata provided by Adafruit to communicate with Python code generated by CodePlayground. Blockly Developer Tools was used to create the frame for the language and Atom was used to insert the specialized JavaScript for code generation. After the language was complete, 90 sample programs were created and evaluated to demonstrate the ability of CodePlayground to serve as a programming environment for first learners.

Keywords: computer science education; block-based languages; Adafruit Circuit Playground

DOI: https://doi.org/10.1145/3159450.3162335

Weather Radar Algorithm Development using Google Blockly

Eric Tilley, *University of Alabama*
Contact: evtilley@crimson.ua.edu

NADER (NEXRAD Algorithm Development Environment) is a desktop-based programming environment that allows users to build algorithms for the analysis of NEXRAD level-II Doppler weather radar data. NEXRAD level-II data provides a high-resolution 3D mapping of precipitation intensity and wind speeds around a radar site. These datasets are available from NCEI (National Centers for Environmental Information, a division of the National Oceanic and Atmospheric Administration) both from archives and in real-time, providing nearly endless opportunities for automated algorithmic analysis of weather features. The language provided by NADER is block-based and is built on the powerful Google Blockly platform. In addition to blocks for logic, math, and control flow functions, NADER also presents the user with a succinct set of blocks providing abstractions for common radar data structures. NADER also includes a visualization tool for level-II data, allowing users to clearly see exactly what data is passed into their algorithms and exactly what data is output. With NADER, users can develop a huge variety of algorithms— for example, an algorithm for hail detection, an algorithm for tracking snowfall, or even an algorithm for estimating tornado damage.
NADER strives to accomplish two main objectives. One objective is to provide beginning programmers with a straightforward programming environment with an intriguing, real-life application. The other objective is to provide meteorology experts with a rapid-feedback prototyping environment for developing new algorithms.

Keywords: Block-based programming; Computer Science Education; Meteorology

DOI: https://doi.org/10.1145/3159450.3162336

Toward Continuous Assessment of the Programming Process

Ayaan M. Kazerouni, *Virginia Tech*
Contact: ayaan@vt.edu

Assessment of software tends to focus on postmortem evaluation of metrics like correctness, mergeability, and code coverage. This is evidenced in the current practices of continuous integration and de- ployment that focus on software's ability to pass unit tests before it can be merged into a deployment pipeline. However, little attention or tooling is given to the assessment of the software development process itself. Good process becomes both more challenging and more critical as software complexity increases. Real-time evalu- ation and feedback about a software developer's skills, such as incremental development, testing, and time management, could greatly increase productivity and improve the ability to write tested and correct code. My work focuses on the collection and analysis of ne-grained programming process data to help quantitatively model the programming process in terms of these metrics. I report on my research problem, presenting past work involving the col- lection and analysis of IDE event data from junior level students working on large and complex projects. The goal is to quantify the programming process in terms of incremental development and procrastination. I also present a long-term vision for my research and present work planned in the short term as a step toward that vision.

Keywords: Programming process; educational data mining; testing behavior; repository mining

DOI: https://doi.org/10.1145/3159450.3162337

ACM ISBN 978-1-4503-5103-4/18/02.

Quantum Artificial Intelligence for Natural Language Processing Applications

Ramin Ayanzadeh, *University of Maryland, Baltimore County*
Contact: aramin1@umbc.edu

Natural Language Processing and Semantic Web include several NP complete/hard problems that are intractable for classical computing machines. Even though distributed computing has provided remarkable advances (more precisely in dealing with big data), non-decomposable NP problems are still intractable in many real-world applications. And, from quantum computing perspective, solving complex problems with universal quantum gates requires developing of quantum algorithms. Considering commercializing quantum annealing machines by D-Wave, achieving global optimum for discrete optimization problems has been realized. In this study, a novel approach has been introduced to convert symbolic AI problems into quadratic unconstrained binary optimization (QUBO) form. More narrowly, this method represents classification of text documents (fragments) as optimizing a QUBO function. After embedding the train corpus into a QUBO function, D-Wave quantum annealer is used to classify new observations with finding the minimum energy level of the system.

Keywords: Quantum Artificial Intelligence; Natural Language Processing; Semantic Web; Text-Mining; Machine Learning

DOI: https://doi.org/10.1145/3159450.3162338

Modelling Correct Operation of Webcams for Security Purposes

Blaine Billings, *College of Charleston*
Xenia Mountrouidou, *College of Charleston*
Contact: billingsbt@g.cofc.edu

In October of 2016, we saw a Denial of Service (DoS) attack, the Mirai botnet, which made use of machines on a global scale, primarily targeting often-unprotected devices like webcams and routers. Due to the widespread use of the Internet of Things (IoT), and, specifically, webcams, the attack surface available to malicious actors has increased dramatically. Whereas some researchers tackle this problem by measuring and increasing the efficiency of existing Intrusion Detection Systems (IDSs) or by creating models for the purpose of characterizing cyber-attacks, such solutions do not investigate the problem of identifying when a system itself is behaving under incorrect operation. Through our research, we established a set of stochastic models that are able to accurately and efficiently model the correct operation and behavior of webcams. In order to verify the efficacy and validity of such models, we ran a multitude of normal-operation scenarios and cyber-attacks against webcams using an isolated network. Using the data from these emulated experiments, we correlated network traffic data and audit logs to verify the correctness and accuracy of our models.

ACM ISBN 978-1-4503-5103-4/18/02.

Keywords: Network Security; Denial of Service Attack; Systems Security; Webcam; Behavior Model

DOI: https://doi.org/10.1145/3159450.3162339

Study Genie: An Intelligent and Collaborative Web-based Study Platform

Jiaqi Wu, *Arizona State University*
Terry Wen, *Arizona State University*
Contact: jiaqiwu@asu.edu

Research has shown that the cheat sheet preparation process helps students with performance in exams. However, results have been inconclusive in determining the most effective guiding principles in creating and using cheat sheets. The traditional method of collecting and annotating cheat sheets is time consuming and exhaustive, and fails to capture students' preparation process. This work examines the development and impacts of a new web-based study preparation tool, Study Genie, supporting collaborative note creation, editing, sharing, and cheat sheet organization. This new educational technology enables big-data learning analytics, permitting quantitative data modeling on connecting formal and informal digital learning footprints. Study Genie also systematically automates cheat-sheet quality evaluation, which traditionally could only have been done qualitatively. A classroom study was conducted to measure the technology and learning effects in an introductory computer science programming course. Results suggest that actions associated with editing and organizing cheat sheets are positively correlated with exam performance, and that there is a significant difference between the activity of high-performing and low-performing students. Through these results, Study Genie presents itself as an opportunity for mass data collection, providing insight into the assembly process rather than just the finished product in cheat sheet creation.

Keywords: Study Genie; Cheat Sheet; Computer Science; Web Application; Learning Analytics; Educational Technology

DOI: https://doi.org/10.1145/3159450.3162340

Automation for Instruction Enhancing Feedback

Luke Gusukuma, *Virginia Tech*
Contact: lukesg08@vt.edu

Automated feedback needs instructor input to be most effective. The increasing demand in computing education necessitates automated feedback systems for teaching programming. However, most current automated feedback tools do not incorporate instructor input. Great strides are being made with identification and code edit steps for automated student feedback, but tools for instructor crafted feedback are lacking in the field of computing. My research, currently targeted at novice programmers aims to close that gap with a hybrid approach of a teacher in the loop feedback system I facilitate writing instructor feedback delivered to students in an automated fashion to give meaningful, instruction enhancing feedback. I also evaluate these mechanisms in classrooms by measuring learning gains, student perception, and other metrics.

Keywords: Knowledge Components; CS1; CS Education; Assessment; Instructional Design; Automated Feedback

DOI: https://doi.org/10.1145/3159450.3162341

Social Motivators and Inhibitors for Women Entering Software Engineering through Coding Bootcamps vs. Computer Science Bachelor's Degrees

Sherry Seibel, *Simmons College*
sherry.seibel@gmail.com

The gender disparity in technology related fields is well known and well documented. Only 18% of computer science undergraduates and 26% of computer science professionals are women. Despite numerous interventions in the past decade, there is still not gender parity in the undergraduate pipeline. However, 43% of post-baccalaureate "coding bootcamp" participants were women in 2016, indicating that this population may have different characteristics, attitudes, and mindsets than younger women and girls. In this project, the authors have investigated these changes in gender role perceptions that create barriers for girls but are seemingly resolved for some adult women. We hypothesize that older women come to view their own abilities as well as the impact of failure differently than girls and younger women. By recruiting a subject pool of women who have entered the computer science profession through traditional baccalaureate as well as non-traditional bootcamp pathways and posing reflective as well as current questions in semi-structured interviews we assess the changes in attitudes regarding the subjects' self-efficacy and mindset with respect to technical work. From these findings, we hope to identify triggers and possible interventions.

Keywords: Coding Bootcamps; Gender Disparities; Women in Technology

DOI: https://doi.org/10.1145/3159450.3162342

Intelligent Group Suggestions Based on Students' Conceptual Understanding

Elisabeth Kimmich Mitchell , *Ithaca College*
Toby Dragon, *Ithaca College*
Contact: ekimmichmitchell@ithaca.edu

Collaborative learning can be beneficial for students, but its success is highly dependent on the characteristics of the students grouped together. Structuring group interactions enhances the effectiveness of collaborative learning [1] and therefore the structuring must be done appropriately. Creating successful groups is challenging for instructors, who generally do not have the ability to hand-select groups. We have created a system to dynamically recommend student groups for short-term collaboration. Instructors can request group suggestions based on various criteria related to students' performance on assessment materials. This system creates groups based on different pedagogical theories we find to be salient to group learning.

Keywords: Computer Supported Collaborative Learning (CSCL); group formation; concept maps; Intelligent Tutoring Systems (ITS)

DOI: https://doi.org/10.1145/3159450.3162343

ACM ISBN 978-1-4503-5103-4/18/02.

Below C Level: A Simulator for Visualizing x86-64

Caitlin Fanning, *University of San Diego*
Contact: caitlinfanning@sandiego.edu

Students often encounter assembly language during the course of their education as part of learning about the low-level operation of computer systems. While there are many assembly languages ranging from simple to complex, x86-64 is widely used in introductory level computer systems courses. Unfortunately, students often have difficulty visualizing the execution of an x86-64 program. Interactions between instructions, relevant registers, and the effect that instructions have on memory are all concepts that students struggle to understand. While students can use GDB or other debuggers to help them step through the execution of a program, there are currently no x86-64 simulators aimed at introductory computing students.
Below C Level (BCL) is an x86-64 simulator aimed at helping novices overcome the barriers to learning this challenging language. BCL visualizes program state, specifically the program stack and register file in order to assist novice x86-64 programmers in tracing the execution of their programs.
One of the primary motives for the creation of BCL was the desire for a simulator with a simple and intuitive interface that enables the user to spend more time focusing on the task at hand rather than attempting to understand a complex program. BCL provides this simple interface, which allows users to view firsthand the effects their code has upon the program stack and registers.

Keywords: assembly language; simulator; x86-64; visualization

DOI: https://doi.org/10.1145/3159450.3162344

Summit Selection: Designing a Feature Selection Technique to Support Mixed Data Analysis

Duc Manh Doan, *University of the District of Columbia*
Clayton Gordon, *University of the District of Columbia*
Dong H. Jeong, *University of the District of Columbia*
Contact: duc.doan@udc.edu

Since data size is continuously increasing, analyzing large-scale data is considered as one of the major research challenges in computational data analysis. Although researchers have proposed numerous approaches, most of them still suffer from analyzing the data efficiently. To overcome the limitation, identifying the optimal number of features is critical for analyzing the data. In this paper, we introduce a newly designed feature selection technique, called Summit Selection, which boosts model performances by determining optimal features in noisy mixed data. First, testing all features is conducted to determine an initial base feature that satisfies a pre-defined criterion for maintaining the highest performance score. Then, a continuous evaluation is managed to build a model by successively adding or removing features based solely on the performance score tested with chosen computational models. To show the effectiveness of our proposed technique, a performance evaluation study was conducted to determine fraudulent activities in the UCSD Data Mining Contest 2009 Dataset. We compared our proposed technique with different feature extraction techniques such as PCA, ANOVA test, and Mutual Information (MI). Specifically, multiple machine learning techniques such as Decision Tree, Random Forest, and k-Nearest Neighbor (KNN) are tested with the feature extraction techniques to determine performance differences. As results, we found that our proposed technique showed about 8.78% performance improvement in detecting fraudulent activities. Since our technique can be extended to a cloud computing environment, we also performed a scalability testing with a known distributed cloud computing model (i.e., Apache Spark).

Keywords: Feature Selection; Data Analysis; Cloud Computing

DOI: https://doi.org/10.1145/3159450.3162345

Creating a Classroom Programming Lab Using Android and Blockly

Don Kerrigan, University of West Florida
Contact: donkerrigan@gmail.com

Current tools required for teaching computer science at any level of education are expensive and require a dedicated lab. With an increasing desire for early computer science education, pairing with the expensive costs for computers, there is an increasing need for a solution. In this paper, I will investigate a mobile-based solution to more effectively, both educationally and financially, solve this problem. I will describe the system and how it could be used as an effective solution.

Keywords: Google Blockly; Visual Programming; K-12 Education; Android; Web Application; Mobile

DOI: https://doi.org/10.1145/3159450.3162346

Change Impact using Dynamic History Analysis

Sydney Pugh, *Loyola University Maryland*
David Binkley, *Loyola University Maryland*
Contact: sfpugh@loyola.edu

As the complexity of software systems grows, it becomes increasingly difficult for developers to be aware of all the dependencies that exist between a system's artifacts (e.g., its files or methods). Change impact analysis has been proposed as a technique to overcome this problem, as it suggests to a developer relevant source-code artifacts related to his/her changes. Association rule mining has shown promise for determining change impact by uncovering relevant patterns in a system's change history.

State-of-the-art change impact mining typically makes use of a history of tens of thousands of transactions. This makes a priori generation of all possible rules costly and thus led to the introduction of targeted association rule mining, which only generates rules for transactions relevant to a particular query. Because the set of relevant transactions is much smaller than the complete history, these algorithms are more efficient. However, they still require processing the history's complete set of relevant transactions.

Our work considers the dynamic selection of relevant transactions. It can be viewed as a further constrained version of targeted association rule mining, in which as few as a single relevant transaction might be considered when determining change impact. This initial look at dynamic algorithms empirically studies seven algorithm families. These are referred to as families because some are parameterized and thus give rise to multiple algorithms. Using over 20,000 queries from 19 systems, we empirically show that dynamic algorithms are viable, can be just as applicable as start-of-the-art algorithms, and even outperform them for certain queries.

Keywords: Software Change Impact Analysis; Evolutionary Coupling; Historical Co-change; Targeted Association Rule Mining; Change Recommendation; Algorithms; History

DOI: http://dx.doi.org/10.1145/3159450.3162347

WebBCI: An Electroencephalography Toolkit Built on Modern Web Technologies

Pierce Stegman, *University of Alabama*
Contact: pwstegman@crimson.ua.edu

In recent years, advances in electroencephalography (EEG) brain-computer interfaces (BCIs) have led to the development of applications that allow users to control prosthetic arms, fly drones, and play video games using only their thoughts. However, these use cases are occasionally restricted to laboratory environments. As BCI software is often designed to work with research-grade equipment, it can be inaccessible to the average consumer. This research poster describes why JavaScript-based BCIs would be more accessible to developers and students. We also discuss the current issues with JavaScript-based BCIs and introduce a new library, WebBCI, which is designed to take the initial step towards addressing these issues. Example BCI systems that can be created with WebBCI are described in this poster, along with the outputs of these systems given sample EEG data.

Keywords: Brain-computer interface (BCI); Electroencephalography (EEG); JavaScript

DOI: https://doi.org/10.1145/3159450.3162324

Reported Development of Computational Thinking, Through Computer Science and Programming, and its Benefits for Primary School Students

Caitlin Duncan, *University of Canterbury*
Contact: caitlin.duncan@pg.canterbury.ac.nz

Across the world there has been a paradigm shift in school education, as many countries are incorporating Computer Science (CS), programming, and Computational Thinking (CT), into their K-12 curriculums for the first time. In 2018 these subjects will be introduced to the New Zealand (NZ) Digital Technologies curriculum under the subject of "Computational Thinking". Like the majority of countries who have introduced these topics, NZ faces challenges in preparing teachers, and in successfully implementing a curriculum which achieves its educational goals. To support this curriculum, we have been conducting studies in primary schools across NZ, trialing resources with teachers and students.

Building on a 2014 exploratory study on CS and programming in intermediate school, this project investigates the existing assumptions around CT education in K-12. It aims to address the specific questions: How do we teach CT concepts and approaches to primary aged students? If they learn CT, does it have the

ACM ISBN 978-1-4503-5103-4/18/02.

expected positive impacts on students learning? And, what other positive and negative impacts does this have?
Throughout 2015 and 2016 a study was conducted with 18 primary school teachers from across NZ, who used CS Unplugged and educational programming languages in their classrooms. Teachers submitted feedback on these classes through an online form, and participated in semi-structured interviews. The feedback responses and interview transcripts were analysed using a thematic approach, which revealed many positive impacts on students general learning, minimal negative impacts, and observations of CT development.

Keywords: Computational Thinking; Problem Solving; Primary School; Programming Education

DOI: https://doi.org/10.1145/3159450.3162325

Developing Software Engineers: A Study of Professionalization in a CS Senior Capstone

Rick Parker, *University of Colorado*
Contact: rick.parker@colorado.edu

My research investigates the role of practical experience on professionalization and confidence in students of software engineering during their university-to-work transition. Practical experience comes in many forms, including internships, capstone projects, and "year-in-industry" experiences. These hands-on opportunities place the learner into an authentic role using professional methods and tools to accomplish legitimate work. Improved understanding of the positive and negative influences of practical experience during the university-to-work transition may support ongoing discussions of the potential for integrating such experiences earlier in the learning pipeline. I apply a mixed-methods approach to studying the implementation of a computer science software engineering capstone course at an R1 research institution. My work integrates a case study of the artifacts produced during the capstone, qualitative interviews of student reflections about their experiences in the capstone, and a pilot run of a quantitative survey on professional identity and behaviors. Taken together, the three methods shed light on different roles that professional experience plays during the university-to-work transition.

Keywords: Practical Experience; Senior Capstone; Community of Practice; Qualitative Interviews; Educational Artifacts; University to Work Transition

DOI: http://dx.doi.org/10.1145/3159450.3162326

BeginToReason: An Introduction to Symbolic Reasoning

Megan Fowler, *Clemson University*
Tim Schwab, *Clemson University*
Contact: mefowle@g.clemson.edu

ACM ISBN 978-1-4503-5103-4/18/02.

Computer science (CS) students often evaluate the behavior of the code they write by running it on specific inputs, studying the outputs, and then inductively reasoning to a more general understanding of the code. This is a good starting point in the student's career, but successful graduates must be able to reason deductively about the code they create and encounter. They must be able to reason about the code on all inputs, without running the code. This paper describes an online system named "BeginToReason" that is designed to introduce symbolic reasoning, and the results of its use. One hundred and fourteen students were asked to use BeginToReason after receiving no prior instructions on formal reasoning. Several weeks later, a question on their final exam tested their ability to utilize formal reasoning. Across all question variations presented to the students, they completed an average of at least 80% correctly indicating that the online tool is a useful tool for teaching formal reasoning. Subsequent analysis of the results indicates that student responses may have been influenced by the phrasing of the questions as well as their use of concrete numerical examples to solve the problem.

Keywords: Symbolic reasoning; reasoning tool; online system; verification engine

DOI: https://doi.org/10.1145/3159450.3162328

Improve Feedback Mechanism in Programming Assessment Systems with Progress Indicators and Reward to Foster Students' Growth Mindset

Zhiyi Li, *Virginia Tech*
Contact: zli04@vt.edu

When students learn programming, the assignment feedback information from current automatic programming assessment systems, such as Web-CAT [1] is often negative, objective, and unfriendly. These feedback information can easily frustrate students to lose interest in programming related activities. The negative feedback information can have possible serious consequences to students. We work to improve current feedback mechanism in mindset perspective: encourage students by positive feedback with a group of fifteen progress indicators and possible reward. The fifteen progress indicators were designed and implemented based on students' sequential programming submissions. These fifteen indicators include seven general purpose indicators about various aspects when students construct solutions for assignments; eight other software testing indicators concentrate on students' progress when students self-checking their code [3]. We did statistical analysis for these fifteen indicators' suitability to a collection of programming assignments data set including 257 students. In order to validate fifteen progress indicators' effectiveness, we also apply a student performance model: Recent-Performance Finite Analysis model (R-PFA) [4] to the same programming assignment data set we used before. We calculate R-PFA model's prediction accuracy and apply learning curves analysis. In learning curve analysis, eight software test indicators demonstrate students gradually learn positively when they work on their assignment submissions. Based on progress indicators information, we plan to give students possible reward when they make progress. We will research on reward mechanism, reward format, and timing, etc. In this way, moves students to growth mindset [2] - belief that hard work and practices can improve their skills and capabilities.

Keywords: indicator; feedback; growth mindset; fixed mindset; automatic grading; R-PFA model; reward

DOI: https://doi.org/10.1145/3159450.3162329

Teaching Programming Style in CS 1 with Erroneous Examples

Adam Koehler, *University of California, Riverside*
Contact: akoeh001@cs.ucr.edu

Students in introductory computer science courses (CS 1) typically receive little formal instruction in proper programming style. They may gain limited understanding of proper style by reading code samples, observing an instructor write code with proper style, or by receiving feedback on homework submissions. In our research, we evaluate the effectiveness of an alternative pedagogical approach in which students are provided brief instruction on proper style and are then asked to critique examples of improper style. This research answers three questions: First, when a student knows style will be graded, is proper style utilized? Second, does the student's ability to use proper style correlate with academic performance? Third, do our exercises increase the student's ability to employ proper style? We investigated the first two of these questions using data from three CS 1 courses with distinct forms of style assessment: 1) no style grading and no feedback; 2) automated style grading with feedback; and 3) hand-graded style with feedback. We investigated the third research question, by augmenting the first two course forms with our pedagogical approach. In all courses, a CS 1 style guide was distributed at the beginning of the term and similar lecture examples were used. We found that grading of style is necessary to motivate students, and that our approach shows some promise in increasing ability to use proper style.

Keywords: computer science education; CS 1; erroneous examples; programming style

DOI: https://doi.org/10.1145/3159450.3162330

ACM ISBN 978-1-4503-5103-4/18/02.

Providing Meaningful Feedback for Autograding of Programming Assignments

Georgiana Haldeman
Rutgers University
mgh80@cs.rutgers.edu

Andrew Tjang
Rutgers University
atjang@cs.rutgers.edu

Monica Babeş-Vroman
Rutgers University
babes@cs.rutgers.com

Stephen Bartos
Rutgers University
scb167@scarletmail.rutgers.edu

Jay Shah
Rutgers University
js2279@scarletmail.rutgers.edu

Danielle Yucht
Rutgers University
dry11@scarletmail.rutgers.edu

Thu D. Nguyen
Rutgers University
tdnguyen@cs.rutgers.edu

ABSTRACT

Autograding systems are increasingly being deployed to meet the challenge of teaching programming at scale. We propose a methodology for extending autograders to provide meaningful feedback for incorrect programs. Our methodology starts with the instructor identifying the concepts and skills important to each programming assignment, designing the assignment, and designing a comprehensive test suite. Tests are then applied to code submissions to learn classes of common errors and produce classifiers to automatically categorize errors in future submissions. The instructor maps the errors to concepts and skills and writes hints to help students find their misconceptions and mistakes. We have applied the methodology to two assignments from our Introduction to Computer Science course. We used submissions from one semester of the class to build classifiers and write hints for observed common errors. We manually validated the automatic error categorization and potential usefulness of the hints using submissions from a second semester. We found that the hints given for erroneous submissions should be helpful for 96% or more of the cases. Based on these promising results, we have deployed our hints and are currently collecting submissions and feedback from students and instructors.

KEYWORDS

Autograding, concepts/skills-based hints, error categorization

ACM Reference format:
Georgiana Haldeman, Andrew Tjang, Monica Babeş-Vroman, Stephen Bartos, Jay Shah, Danielle Yucht, and Thu D. Nguyen. 2018. Providing Meaningful Feedback for Autograding of Programming Assignments. In *Proceedings of SIGCSE '18: The 49th ACM Technical Symposium on Computing Science Education, Baltimore , MD, USA, February 21–24, 2018 (SIGCSE '18),* 6 pages. https://doi.org/10.1145/3159450.3159502

SIGCSE '18, February 21–24, 2018, Baltimore , MD, USA

ACM ISBN 978-1-4503-5103-4/18/02...$15.00
https://doi.org/10.1145/3159450.3159502

1 INTRODUCTION

The current demand for computing professionals is unprecedented, with a short supply in the US, and the gap between demand and supply is predicted to increase even more in the next few years [13]. Correspondingly, universities are seeing tremendous enrollment growths in computing classes and are faced with the challenge of teaching programming at scale [4].

According to Ambrose et al., *"goal-directed practice coupled with targeted feedback are critical to learning"* [1]. Programming assignments are the tools of choice for providing students with hands-on practice in many computing classes. However, as autograding systems are deployed to scale the grading of programming assignments in increasingly large classes, providing meaningful feedback remains an open problem. Many deployed autograding systems do not provide feedback. Even when feedback is available, the feedback provided does not assist students in correcting errors [10] and does not address underlying misconceptions. A recent work seeks to address these issues using a hybrid approach that combines program synthesis and instructor code review and feedback generation [7].

In this paper, we propose a methodology that is similar in spirit to the approach in [7], but focuses on linking errors to concepts and skills central to a programming assignment and does not depend on compilation tools. Rather, our approach depends on collecting and analyzing assignment submissions to generate hints that can be used in future semesters.[1] More specifically, when designing an assignment, we propose that the instructor explicitly define the set of concepts and skills, called the *knowledge map*, that students need to master to complete the assignment. After the assignment has been written, a comprehensive test suite should be developed with the goal of teasing out misunderstandings of the knowledge map along with correctness testing for grading.

Next, the assignment is released and student submissions are collected. The instructor runs the test suite against the submissions and manually inspects sets of submissions with the same outcome patterns (called signatures) to identify errors, refining the test suite as needed or desired. Finally, the instructor maps the errors to specific items in the knowledge map and generates hints to guide

[1] Supporting the evolution of assignments while still making use of collected data is an important extension that we intend to explore in the near future.

the students toward reviewing and improving their understanding and mastery of the applicable concepts and skills. The observed signatures can be used to produce a classifier that automatically categorize future erroneous submissions, allowing the autograding system to provide the corresponding hints as meaningful feedback.

The above methodology encapsulates two key ideas: (1) the inspection of a set of submissions with the same signatures for a comprehensive, well designed suite of tests can help the instructor identify high-level logical errors, and (2) the mapping of errors to concepts and skills in the knowledge map can aid in the generation of hints that direct students to conceptually reconsider their code, rather than making local, code specific suggestions that can lead to highly convoluted solutions (e.g., many unnecessary nested conditional statements). Understanding common errors in light of the knowledge map can also aid the instructor in adjusting classroom teaching in the current and future offerings of the course.

We applied our proposed methodology to two assignments in our Introduction to Computer Science course. We collected large numbers of submissions for the two assignments across two semesters, Spring 2016 and Spring 2017. We designed test suites for the assignments and used submissions from Spring 2016 to learn classes of common errors, produce classifiers for automatic error categorization of future submissions, and write hints. We then used the classifiers to attach hints to erroneous submissions from Spring 2017. Four of the authors manually reviewed the results of this experiment, and found that over 91% and over 87% of the hints for the two assignments, respectively, fully captured the errors in the corresponding submissions. These percentages rise to over 96% when we count hints that partially captured the errors. Based on these promising results, we have deployed the error categorization and corresponding hints for the two assignments in the Fall 2017 semester, and are currently collecting submissions and feedback from students and instructors.

2 RELATED WORK

Our work explores the extension of autograding systems to provide feedback to students. Web-CAT [5] and Autolab [12] are two autograding tools that we have used in our Introduction to Computer Science course. Web-CAT includes a library that allows a hint to be attached to each test case. When a submission fails a test, the associated hint is returned as feedback. In our experience, it is difficult to balance between writing hints that are overly specific and overly vague based on the result of one test case. Thus, our approach uses the results from an entire test suite for identifying common errors and providing hints.

One research effort for automated grading has focused on defining a problem-independent grammar of features, and by using a supervised learning algorithm trained on teacher graded examples to assign grades to new student submissions [18]. This work is related but focuses on grading rather than providing feedback.

Commonly, the generation of feedback is a two step process: first, the code is assessed to identify mistakes or bad practices; then, appropriate feedback is generated based on the assessment from the first step. Methods for assessing students' code are unit testing, stylistic checking [10], property-based testing [2], execution traces [14], and program synthesis [19]. Automated generation of feedback often relies on the assumption that students in large classes share common errors [6]. Student submissions are clustered based on failed test cases, compiler errors or runtime exceptions [6], stylistic checking [17], AST tree edit distance [9], probabilistic semantic equivalence [15] or program synthesis [3]. Our categorization approach is based on testing and manual review of submitted code.

Providing personalized feedback in Intelligent Tutoring Systems (ITS) is done by using rule-based and constraint-based methods [8]. However, this approach does not scale well for assignments that have multiple solutions (classes 2 and 3 in [11]). Data-driven procedures improve existing methods. One approach [16], for example, uses the AST distance to guide students from an erroneous submission to a correct solution. Their work is complementary to our work. Another recent effort focuses on designing a system that propagates the feedback of the teacher on one submission to the rest of the submissions that need the same code fixes by using program synthesis [7]. We already discussed how our system is different in Section 1.

3 CONCEPT AND SKILLS BASED FEEDBACK GENERATION FRAMEWORK (CSF^2)

We propose the Concepts and Skills based Feedback Generation Framework (CSF^2) for designing programming assignments based on the concepts and skills that students are required to master, and analyzing submissions with respect to these concepts and skills to generate hints for assisting students in correcting their errors. The approach is described as a sequence of steps, but the ordering can be modified as discussed in Section 6. The proposed steps are as follows.

- Step 1 Carefully consider the knowledge map (concepts and skills) that students need to master to complete the assignment.
- Step 2 Write the assignment with the knowledge map in mind.
- Step 3 Design a test suite to assess student submissions. Full path coverage of a reference solution is typically a good start (but will need expansion). Each test should output a code representing the outcome when it is run against a submission.
- Step 4 Release the assignment and collect student submissions.
- Step 5 Automatically run the test suite against the collected submissions and group submissions into buckets based on the outcome signatures, where a signature is the concatenation of the codes output by all the tests in the test suite. Each signature may indicate one or more logical errors. Our hypothesis is that submissions with the same signatures are likely to have similar logical errors.
- Step 6 Manually inspect each bucket of submissions to see whether subsets of submissions have different logical errors. If yes, then refine the test suite to separate these subsets into different buckets. The knowledge map may also need to be refined (for example, to include a concept that has to be mastered for the assignment but was accidentally omitted in Step 1).
- Step 7 Repeat Step 5 and Step 6 as needed.
- Step 8 Map the errors identified for each bucket to concepts and skills in the knowledge map. Then, manually inspect and combine buckets of submissions with the same errors or

knowledge deficiencies. Our hypothesis is that mapping errors to the knowledge map will help instructors reduce the number of hints that need to be written, as well as write hints that provide conceptual guidance rather than very specific coding changes.

Step 9 Write a hint for each bucket. The outcome of Step 8 and Step 9 is a classifier, manually trained on past student submissions, that maps the outcome signature of a well designed test suite to meaningful hints.

Step 10 When the assignment is run again, the autograding system can use the classifier to automatically categorize errors and provide hints for submissions that fail one or more tests.

While the work in this paper is focused on generating meaningful autograding feedback, the above process is also useful in gaining a better understanding of students' errors and misconceptions. The instructor can use this information to improve the quality of classroom teaching, for example, in identifying concepts and skills that should be reinforced, as well as adjusting the teaching of the concepts and skills in the future.

As described above, CSF^2 is most useful when an assignment is reused over multiple offerings of a class, with previous submissions being used to generate and improve hints for subsequent uses of the assignment. Currently, CSF^2 does not directly support the evolution of an assignment (for example, changes to the assignment to circumvent cheating or to improve the assignment) across time (although we have successfully experimented with changing *TwoSmallest* to an isomorphic assignment while still making use of analysis results from previous submissions; see Section 6). This is an important challenge that we plan to address in the future.

Finally, while the manual inspection of assignments is labor intensive, it is possible to get help from advanced undergraduate students when CSF^2 is applied to early computing classes. We have successfully done this with our case studies: three of the authors are undergraduate students who helped with exactly this task.

4 CASE STUDIES

In this section, we describe the application of CSF^2 to two programming assignments in the Introduction to Computer Science course at Rutgers University. Even though CSF^2 proposes that an instructor starts with a knowledge map when designing an assignment, our case studies work with existing assignments because we already collected a large number of student submissions across several semesters. In essence, we reversed the ordering of Steps 1 and 2 in CSF^2, and extracted the knowledge maps from the existing assignments.

Steps 1 and 2: Extracting the Knowledge Maps

We studied two assignments, *PayFriend*, a class 2 assignment according to [11], which means that it has one solution strategy with multiple possible implementations, and *TwoSmallest*, a class 3 assignment, which means that it has multiple solution strategies. *PayFriend* asks the students to compute the fee associated with making an e-payment when given a tiered fee structure, with different fees for four payment ranges, requiring a good understanding of conditional statements. *TwoSmallest* asks the students to read a sequence of floating point values that starts and ends with a sentinel value and output the two smallest values in the sequence, requiring algorithmic thinking and understanding of initialization and loops (in addition to conditional statements).

Table 1: Number of students and assignment submissions.

	Spring 2016	Spring 2017
Number of students	511	437
***PayFriend* Submissions**	1152	723
***TwoSmallest* Submissions**	1339	870

Each assignment requires the solution to be implemented inside a method with a prescribed method signature. Students are also asked to submit code in a specific format, including predefined file and class names and to omit all `package` and `import` statements. Failure to follow all instructions results in compilation errors and zero credit.

When we started this research, *PayFriend* and *TwoSmallest* had already been designed and used several times. We worked with the lead instructor to determine the knowledge maps he had in mind when designing them. Some of the concepts and skills in the knowledge maps are shown in the right column of Table 2 below.

Step 3: Designing the Test Suites

We developed a reference solution for each assignment and designed 13 test cases for *PayFriend* and 20 for *TwoSmallest* that led to a full path coverage of the reference solutions. Next, we considered more challenging inputs, especially for novice programmers. For example, it is well known that many programming bugs involve the handling of boundary cases. Thus, for *PayFriend*, we designed test cases with input values close to the tier boundaries, as well as values from the middle of the tiers. This test design process was iterative (as discussed in Steps 5–7 of CSF^2). After all refinements were made, *PayFriend*'s test suite contained 20 test cases and *TwoSmallest*'s contained 30. In previous offerings of the assignments, *PayFriend* and *TwoSmallest* were graded using 10 and 7 test cases, respectively.

Step 4: Collecting Student Submissions

We collected student submissions for the two assignments during the Spring 2016 semester using Web-CAT [5] and during the Spring 2017 semester using Autolab [12]. Table 1 shows the number of students and submissions collected for each assignment during the two semesters. Each submission included anonymized student information, a time stamp, and code. In this study, we only looked at the submitted code; all submissions were anonymized by removing all information, including comments, other than the actual code. The submissions from Spring 2016 were used for Steps 5–8 of CSF^2. The submissions from Spring 2017 were used to evaluate our ability to correctly identify the most important errors associated with incorrect submissions, with the ultimate goal of providing meaningful hints. This was a partial evaluation of the effectiveness of Step 10.

Steps 5–7: Refining Tests and Partitioning Submissions

We generated a test outcome signature for each submission by running the test suite developed in Step 3 against the submitted code. Then, submissions with the same signature were grouped in

Table 2: Mapping of common errors to concepts and skills in the knowledge map.

Code	Error	Concept / Skill
	Both assignments	
COMP	compilation errors	writing compilable code
INS	errors regarding the required format, e.g., incorrect filename	following instructions
IO	IO errors, e.g., wrong numbers or types of inputs/outputs	data representation / following instructions
INF	used infinite loops	control flow
	PayFriend	
CF	output only in some branches	control flow
COND	used incorrect conditional statements	translating word problems into conditional statements
FORM	used incorrect calculation inside a range	translating word problems into formulas
	TwoSmallest	
SEQ	read and processed incorrectly a sequence of values	data representation / following instructions
INIT	wrongly initialized min values	algorithmic thinking
UPDT	wrongly updated min values	algorithmic thinking

the same bucket. Each signature could indicate one or more logical problems. A bucket could be mapped to two or more independent errors with their own associated hints, but all the submissions in the same bucket needed to have the same errors so that a meaningful corresponding hint could be generated. If, for a given bucket, some of the submissions had one error while others had a different error, we refined the test suite to obtain a better partitioning.

We manually inspected the students' code in each bucket to identify the main reason for the code failing one or more tests. For buckets containing submissions with *different* knowledge deficiencies, we refined or extended our test suite to further partition the buckets. We iterated through Steps 5–7 once for *PayFriend* and several times, making small refinements each time, for *TwoSmallest.* We found that iterations with small refinements were easier to think about. By the end of the process, we added 7 additional test cases for *PayFriend* and 10 for *TwoSmallest.* The final test suites led to 109 non-empty buckets for *PayFriend* (using 20 tests) and 137 non-empty buckets for *TwoSmallest* (using 30 tests).

Steps 8 and 9: Combining Buckets and Generating Hints

Next, we manually mapped the main reason for code failure in each bucket to a deficiency in a concept or skill as shown in Table 2. As already mentioned, we found that many of the buckets were different manifestations of similar knowledge deficiencies. Thus, we grouped many of the buckets together, leading to 8 "super-buckets" for *PayFriend* and 7 for *TwoSmallest* (Table 3). Clustering student submissions for assignments in class 2 and 3 is a particularly challenging task because the solution space can be large. Since unit testing mostly focuses on the functionality of the code rather than the style, we were able to cluster stylistically different student submissions with the same logical error.

Finally, we wrote a hint for each bucket, and the hints have been deployed in Autolab for the Fall 2017 semester. We are still in the process of collecting data, including student feedback, to assess the impact of our hints on student learning.

5 RESULTS

In this section, we present the most relevant findings from our case studies. We first assess the accuracy of the automatic error categorization of submissions and whether the hints capture these errors. Then, we show examples of common errors and corresponding hints. We discuss how the outputs of the test suites help identify logical errors and how the knowledge maps help produce hints on a more conceptual level. We have improved some of the hints (over the ones deployed for Fall 2017) in the process of writing this paper, although we did not fundamentally change any of the hints.

5.1 Accuracy of Error Categorization and Hints

As described in Section 4, we used our test suites and submissions from Spring 2016 to manually generate an error classifier for each of *PayFriend* and *TwoSmallest.* We also wrote hints to be given as feedback from the autograder. We then used the same test suites, classifiers, and hints to identify, categorize, and attach a hint to each erroneous submission from Spring 2017.

Three of the authors manually reviewed the Spring 2017 submissions to assess the accuracy of the classifier and potential efficacy of the corresponding hints. These authors are currently enrolled in the undergraduate Computer Science program at Rutgers, and have previously taken the Introduction to Computer Science course. We believe that having done the assignments themselves while taking the course gave them a good perspective in this evaluation. Their task was to label each (erroneous submission, hint) pair as *Correct, Partially Correct,* or *Incorrect. Correct* meant that the automatic diagnosis and corresponding hint fully captured the logical errors in the submission, and so would potentially provide useful guidance to the student. Note that we say "potentially" since the labeling was done by people other than the owners of the submissions. *Possibly Correct* meant that the diagnosis and hint only partially captured the errors in the submission. *Incorrect* meant that the errors were misdiagnosed and so the hint was misleading. Each submission was inspected and evaluated by at least two authors. The results were analyzed by a fourth author to resolve conflicts.

Table 3 presents the results. Examination of *Incorrect* cases for both assignments revealed errors that would be difficult to detect with black box testing. Thus, improving accuracy would likely require the use of additional complementary or more powerful methods for assessment (for example, compiler analysis techniques).

We conclude that the automatic error categorization and corresponding hints are appropriate for the vast majority of the erroneous submissions, and so we have deployed them in the Fall 2017 semester.

5.2 Examples of Common Errors and Hints

Example 1. For *PayFriend,* common errors include incorrect conditional expressions leading to incorrect answers for boundary values,

Table 3: Accuracy of error categorization and hints for Spring 2017 submissions. Each row presents statistics for a bucket of submissions with the same errors.

Error Codes	Automatic Categorization	*Correct*		*Partially Correct*	
	PayFriend				
COMP	34	34	100%	0	0%
INS	111	111	100%	0	0%
IO	119	114	95.8%	3	2.5%
INF	7	4	57.1%	3	42.9%
CF	38	26	68.4%	4	10.5%
COND	44	39	88.6%	4	9.1%
COND, FORM	91	82	90.1%	9	9.9%
FORM	83	72	86.7%	4	4.8%
Total	**527**	**482**	**91.5%**	**27**	**5.1%**
	TwoSmallest				
COMP	39	39	100%	0	0%
INS	105	104	99%	1	1%
SEQ	51	47	92.2%	4	7.8%
INIT	67	56	91.8%	5	8.2%
UPDT	158	129	87.2%	19	12.8%
SEQ, INIT	157	137	91.9%	12	8.1%
SEQ, UPDT	176	145	85.8%	24	14.2%
Total	**767**	**671**	**87.5%**	**65**	**8.5%**

and incorrect formulas for one or more fee tiers leading to incorrect answers for entire tiers. It is useful to differentiate between the two errors when giving students hints. We were able to make this distinction using the combined outputs of multiple tests.

More specifically, if a submission fails test cases with input values inside one tier, *I*, but passes test cases with input values in other tiers, it is likely that the code does not correctly calculate the fee for tier *I*. This signature leads to the following hint for tier ($100 to $1000): *"It seems that you are not correctly calculating the fee for payments in the range (100, 1000). Review the assignment instructions, check that your formula for computing the fee is correct, then follow the steps used in the calculation of the fee in your code and make sure that they implement the correct formula."*

On the other hand, if the submission passes test cases with input values inside *I*, but fails test cases with inputs near the upper or lower boundaries of *I*, it is likely that the code uses incorrect conditional expressions. This may arise from misunderstandings of conditional statements and expressions, and/or misunderstandings of the assignment write-up, hence the mapping to the skill *translating word problems into conditional statements.* For example, discriminating between ≥ and > in a conditional expression requires understanding of boundary values and how they differ among data types. For integers, $x < 100$ is equivalent to $x \leq 99$, but this is not true for real values. We thus wrote the following hint: *"It seems that you did not split the input intervals correctly, where some values at the boundary between intervals may have been included under the wrong formula/rule; that is, your conditional expressions may be incorrect, for example you may have ≥ 101 instead of > 100 which are not equivalent expressions for double values."*

Example 2. For *TwoSmallest,* given the material that has been taught in class, most students develop algorithms that have two major steps: (1) initialize two variables used to hold the two smallest values, and (2) read the input sequence and update the variables. Many students make the algorithmic error of not considering what the initial values of the variables should be, and often initialize them to inappropriate values such as 0. Comparing the results of several test cases with input values that are positive, negative, and mixed can tell us whether or not a submission has this error. Also, the mapping of this error to *algorithmic thinking* in the knowledge map reminds us to view the error in light of the student's algorithmic design effort. This leads to the hint: *"It seems that you did not initialize the variables used to hold the minimum and secondMinimum to reasonable values. Think about how the starting values would affect your algorithm for finding the two smallest values. In particular, what would happen if the input values in the sequence were greater, equal or less than the starting values for your minimum and secondMinimum."*

Updating the two variables in *TwoSmallest* requires algorithmic thinking, and can be a challenge for students new to programming. Many students tend to think about the update process in fragmented, poorly coordinated pieces. To assess if the update of the variables is done correctly, we test input sequences that are permutations of two and three numbers. If the submitted code passes all the test cases with a valid input of size two but fails the test cases where the third value is less than the minimum value, then it is highly likely that the student is not updating the minimum value correctly. The mapping of the error to "algorithmic thinking" again leads us to write a hint designed to steer students toward developing this skill: *"It seems that you did not update the variables holding the minimum and/or secondMinimum values correctly. Think carefully about the algorithm that you are developing to update your variables. It may help to think about what would happen if the sequence had the same number appearing multiple times; for example, all possible permutations of 3 numbers with repetition."*

6 DISCUSSION

CSF^2 is designed to be flexible enough to serve the needs of many programming courses that use autograding. It can assist instructors in various tasks from creating assignments, to reviewing course material, to encouraging interactions between students through discussion of the hints. In this section, we discuss possible modifications to CSF^2 and the use of the knowledge map.

6.1 Modifications to the Framework

The process described in Section 3 is meant to be a guideline for best practices. As written, it describes a top-down approach to the design of assignments using knowledge maps. The advantage of this approach is that assignments are carefully and systematically written to target specific course material. However, in practice and as we see in our case studies, instructors have their assignments already written and have already used them over the course of a few semesters. In these situations, a "bottom-up" approach can be used with a few advantages: previously collected submissions can be used to guide the extraction of the knowledge map, design or improve the test suite, and generate the error classifiers and hints.

Much of the manual work done for this research is labor intensive. While we have manually reviewed all 527 and 767 erroneous submissions for *PayFriend* and *TwoSmallest* in this work, it may be that reviewing only a sample of submissions would be sufficient. We are currently exploring the use of random subsets of various sizes to gauge the sensitivity of the error categorization and hint generation on sample size.

6.2 Using the Knowledge Map

One advantage of using a knowledge map and a classifier is the ability to query which concepts and skills students are struggling with, similar to the results shown in Tables 2 and 3. With this knowledge, instructors can devise specific interventions targeting knowledge deficiencies that can be deployed prior to the administration of the assignment. Some of these proposed interventions may include additional exercises, textbook references, and/or video lessons.

Instructors can also take advantage of the knowledge map when assigning partial credit to autograded assignments. Traditionally, grading rules have been very rigid, following the boundaries of unit testing and leading to a linearly scaled grade based on the percentage of passed test cases. Relying on test cases alone to grade submissions resulted in some unexpected behaviors. Instructors at our university reported that students at either end of the scoring spectrum (that is, those who received no credit and those who earned nearly full credit despite still having important misconceptions and mistakes), gave up working on and completing their programming assignments. With our proposed knowledge map, instructors can assign scores based on the importance they allot to each concept or skill. For example, for *PayFriend* we weighted all the tested concepts starting with compilation and ending with conditional statements. Students who understood the assignment but previously would have received low grades due to failed test cases, were more fairly assigned scores that reflected their understanding of the problem and its solution using the knowledge map. Conversely, we found submissions that previously would have received near perfect scores since they only failed a few tests. The weighted knowledge map scoring lowered their scores because these test failures showed misunderstandings of core concepts, serving as a motivation for the students to improve their solutions.

Finally, the knowledge map and buckets of common errors can aid in the generation of isomorphic assignments while reusing the error classifier and hints. For example, in Fall 2017, we modified *TwoSmallest* into *TwoLargest*, where the students were asked to output the two largest values in a sequence. In this instance, we were able to reuse the test suite, classifier, and hints with only small changes. This can be a starting point for extending CSF^2 to support the evolution of assignments over time (for example, to circumvent cheating) while reusing classifiers and hints.

7 CONCLUSIONS

In this paper, we presented a methodology which bridges the gap between autograding and the knowledge assessment of programming assignments to provide meaningful feedback to students. Our methodology asks the instructor to systematically analyze programming assignments with respect to knowledge maps to ensure course cohesion between the specific challenges posed to students by the programming assignments and the material taught in class. The methodology also outlines an approach for finding common errors in a set of submissions for an assignment, and generating an error classifier and hints that can be used by an autograder to give feedback for future submissions. This process can also give instructors insight on how to adjust class material to address observed knowledge deficiencies. We have applied our methodology to two assignments in our introductory course, and found that the hints should provide useful feedback for the vast majority of incorrect submissions.

Acknowledgement. This work was partially supported by a Google Computer Science Capacity Award.

REFERENCES

[1] S. A. Ambrose, M. W. Bridges, M. DiPietro, M. C. Lovett, and M. K. Norman. *How Learning Works: Seven Research-based Principles for Smart Teaching*. Jossey-Bass, 2010.

[2] C. Benac Earle, L. A. Fredlund, and J. Hughes. Automatic Grading of Programming Exercises Using Property-Based Testing. In *Proceedings of the 2016 ITiCSE Conference*, 2016.

[3] S. Bhatia and R. Singh. Automated Correction for Syntax Errors in Programming Assignments using Recurrent Neural Networks. *CoRR*, 2016.

[4] Computing Research Association. Generation CS: Computer Science Undergraduate Enrollments Surge Since 2006. https://cra.org/data/Generation-CS/.

[5] S. H. Edwards and M. A. Perez-Quinones. Web-CAT: Automatically Grading Programming Assignments. In *ACM SIGCSE Bulletin*, volume 40, 2008.

[6] E. L. Glassman, A. Lin, C. J. Cai, and R. C. Miller. Learnersourcing Personalized Hints. In *Proceedings of the 2016 CSCW Conference*, 2016.

[7] A. Head, E. Glassman, G. Soares, R. Suzuki, L. Figueredo, L. D'Antoni, and B. Hartmann. Writing Reusable Code Feedback at Scale with Mixed-Initiative Program Synthesis. In *Proceedings of the 2017 Conference on Learning @ Scale*. ACM, 2017.

[8] J. Holland, A. Mitrovic, and B. Martin. J-LATTE: a Constraint-based Tutor for Java. In *The 2009 International Conference on Computers in Education*, 2009.

[9] J. Huang, C. Piech, A. Nguyen, and L. Guibas. Syntactic and Functional Variability of a Million Code Submissions in a Machine Learning MOOC. In *Proceedings of the 2013 Workshop on Massive Open Online Courses at the 16th Annual Conference on Artificial Intelligence in Education*, 2013.

[10] H. Keuning, J. Jeuring, and B. Heeren. Towards a Systematic Review of Automated Feedback Generation for Programming Exercises. In *Proceedings of the 2016 Conference on Innovation and Technology in Computer Science Education*, 2016.

[11] N.-T. Le and N. Pinkwart. Towards a Classification for Programming Exercises. In *Proceedings of the 2nd Workshop on AI-supported Education for Computer Science*, 2014.

[12] D. Milojicic. Autograding in the Cloud: Interview with David O'Hallaron. *IEEE Internet Computing*, 2011.

[13] National Center for Women & Information Technology. Projected Computing Jobs and CIS Degrees Earned. http://www.ncwit.org/sites/default/files/file_type/usnatgraphic2022projections_10132014.pdf.

[14] B. Paaßen, J. Jensen, and B. Hammer. Execution Traces as a Powerful Data Representation for Intelligent Tutoring Systems for Programming. In *Proceedings of the 2016 International Conference on Educational Data Mining*. International Educational Datamining Society, 2016.

[15] C. Piech, J. Huang, A. Nguyen, M. Phulsuksombati, M. Sahami, and L. J. Guibas. Learning Program Embeddings to Propagate Feedback on Student Code. *CoRR*, 2015.

[16] K. Rivers and K. R. Koedinger. Data-Driven Hint Generation in Vast Solution Spaces: A Self-Improving Python Programming Tutor. *International Journal of Artificial Intelligence in Education*, 27, 2017.

[17] S. Rogers, D. Garcia, J. F. Canny, S. Tang, and D. Kang. ACES: Automatic Evaluation of Coding Style. Master's thesis, EECS Department, University of California, Berkeley, May 2014.

[18] G. Singh, S. Srikant, and V. Aggarwal. Question Independent Grading Using Machine Learning: The Case of Computer Program Grading. In *Proceedings of the 2016 SIGKDD International Conference on Knowledge Discovery and Data Mining*, 2016.

[19] R. Singh, S. Gulwani, and A. Solar-Lezama. Automated feedback generation for introductory programming assignments. *SIGPLAN Not.*, 48(6), 2013.

ArTEMiS - An Automatic Assessment Management System for Interactive Learning

Stephan Krusche
Technische Universität München
Munich, Germany
krusche@in.tum.de

Andreas Seitz
Technische Universität München
Munich, Germany
seitz@in.tum.de

ABSTRACT

The increasing number of students in computer science courses leads to high efforts in manual assessment of exercises. Existing assessment systems are not designed for exercises with immediate feedback in large classes. In this paper, we present an **A**u**T**omated ass**E**ssment **M**anagement **S**ystem for interactive learning.

ArTEMiS assesses solutions to programming exercises automatically and provides instant feedback so that students can iteratively solve the exercise. It is open source and highly scalable based on version control, regression testing and continuous integration. ArTEMiS offers an online code editor with interactive exercise instructions, is programming language independent and applicable to a variety of computer science courses. By using it, students gain experiences in version control, dependency management and continuous integration.

We used ArTEMiS in 3 university and 1 online courses and report about our experiences. We figured out that ArTEMiS is suitable for beginners, helps students to realize their progress and to gradually improve their solutions. It reduces the effort of instructors and enhances the learning experience of students.

CCS CONCEPTS

• **Social and professional topics** → **Software engineering education**; *Computer science education*; • **Applied computing** → **Interactive learning environments**; **Learning management systems**;

KEYWORDS

Automated Assessment, Programming Exercises, Continuous Integration, Version Control, Instant Feedback, Online Editor, Interactive Exercise Instructions, Online Courses, In-class Exercises.

ACM Reference Format:
Stephan Krusche and Andreas Seitz. 2018. ArTEMiS - An Automatic Assessment Management System for Interactive Learning. In *SIGCSE '18: SIGCSE '18: The 49th ACM Technical Symposium on Computing Science Education, February 21–24, 2018, Baltimore, MD, USA.* ACM, New York, NY, USA, 6 pages. https://doi.org/10.1145/3159450.3159602

SIGCSE '18, February 21–24, 2018, Baltimore, MD, USA

ACM ISBN 978-1-4503-5103-4/18/02...$15.00
https://doi.org/10.1145/3159450.3159602

1 INTRODUCTION

The amount of students in university classes and online courses is increasing. The number of freshmen at our computer science department increased by 67 % between 2013 (1110) and 2016 (1840). In addition, the number of enrollments in online courses such as MOOCs is increasing as well. Class Central recently reported 35 million students which have signed up for at least one MOOC. With such large numbers of students, manual assessment of programming exercises in computer science and software engineering courses is no longer feasible. Yet, programming exercises are essential in computer science education [17].

While automatic assessment is an established concept, large courses raise new challenges for instructors and tools. Automated assessment must be scalable to handle a large number of students and provide immediate feedback. The effort for an instructor conducting an programming exercise has to be independent of the number of participating students. Instant feedback to students is required to allow resubmissions and learning from failures. This is particularly important in courses based on active learning [3], where the programming exercises happen in-class in specific time frames. During the exercise, instructors need to be able to get an overview of submitted solutions and typical problems to react and guide the students.

There are many existing tools for automatic assessment and grading but most of them are custom tailored solutions for specific programming languages and requirements (compare Section 5). This makes it particularly hard to integrate them into existing infrastructure and use them in large scale courses.

Continuous integration (CI) is an approach allowing to detect defects and failures in programs [7]. This idea can be used for programming exercises to validate the correctness and completeness of source code with test cases. Students upload their solution to a version control system (VCS) and receive instant feedback about the result of their submissions from the CI server. While doing the exercise, they get used to VC and CI, which are important skills in software development.

In this paper, we describe our experiences with ArTEMiS, an open source **A**u**T**omated ass**E**ssment **M**anagement **S**ystem for interactive learning. In Section 2, we cover the basic background behind the methodology and tools for our approach. Section 3 presents the approach behind and the use of ArTEMiS in more detail. We describe its scalability and show the applicability of the system within large university courses and an online course in a multi case study in Section 4. We analyze the participation of students in the case study and provide insights. Section 5 relates and differentiates ArTEMiS to other automated assessment tools. In Section 6, we conclude the paper and provide directions for future work.

2 FOUNDATIONS

ArTEMiS uses version control (VC) and continuous integration (CI) to automatically assess programming exercises in interactive learning environments. This sections describes its foundations.

2.1 Interactive Learning

Interactive learning combines lectures and exercises into interactive classes with multiple iterations of theory, example, exercise, solution and reflection [12]. Educators teach and exercise small chunks of knowledge in short cycles. They focus on immediate feedback to exercises to improve the learning experience in large classes so that students reflect and increase their knowledge incrementally.

Hands-on activities in class increase students' motivation and engagement and allow continuous assessment over the course [13]. This approach expects active participation of learners and the use of computers (laptops, tablets, smartphones) in the classroom. Instructors provide guidance during the learning process to prevent misconceptions and to facilitate the learning process.

2.2 Continuous Integration

CI was first described by Grady Booch as concept to avoid risky late integrations [4]. Martin Fowler defines CI as follows: "Continuous Integration is a software development practice where members of a team integrate their work frequently, usually each person integrates at least daily – leading to multiple integrations per day" [7].

Each developer works on a local copy of a shared code base. After implementing source code, the developer integrates the changes into the shared code base. An automated build (including test cases) verifies each integration to detect compile, test, and integration errors as soon as possible [7]. The build is triggered on the developer's machine or on a central CI server. While CI does not require special tools, developers use dedicated servers to perform it.

Figure 1 illustrates a common CI workflow. (1) The process starts with a developer committing code changes to a VCS. (2) The CI server regularly checks the VCS for code changes and (3) automatically triggers the build and test process on every commit. Tests can range from small unit tests over larger integration tests to complete system tests. (4) After the build has either succeeded or failed, the developer is notified about the build result. Every commit triggers a build, so the developer responsible for the failure is notified immediately to fix the problem.

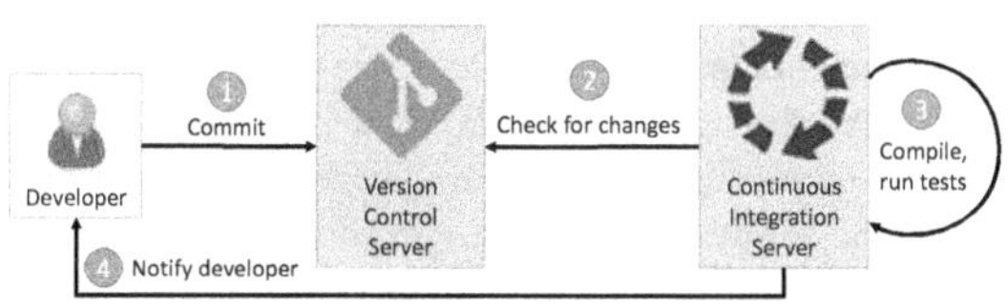

Figure 1: Typical continuous integration workflow

2.3 Automatic Assessment

"The [manual] assessment of [programming] assignments places significant demands on the instructor's time and other resources" [5]. To solve this problem and due to the logical character of programming, the task of assessing programming exercises can be automated. A first example was a grading program for punch card programs by Hollingsworth [9]. Since then, many automatic assessment tools (e.g. [6], [11], [15]) have been developed, together with guidelines on how programming exercises should be assessed.

Automatic assessment systems provide feedback on students' solutions for programming exercises [19]. Compared to manual assessment, they are able to provide consistent feedback for every student without bias while significantly reducing the effort for instructors and TAs. Ala-Mutka describes different types of assessments [1]. The historically most common type is dynamic assessment. Its main aspects are to assess functionality, efficiency, and testing skills by executing a program with test input data and checking the output for correctness. Another type is static analysis, which provides feedback on style, programming errors or software metrics by analyzing the code without executing it.

Students using automatic assessment tools achieve important learning goals: they develop a clean and reusable code style, reflect critically on errors and establish a testing culture. These goals are achieved by multiple methods, e.g. varying the amount of feedback provided or allowing to work incrementally on a solution. They can be effectively implemented using different assessment techniques such as black-box testing, white-box testing or peer reviews.

3 APPROACH

We identified the following goals for ArTEMiS by analyzing the applicability of existing tools for large interactive courses:

Independence of programming language: different programming languages are taught in university courses [17]. The system should work independently of a specific programming language.

Scalability: the system should be scalable usable in university classes and online courses. It should work with hundreds of participating students at the same time, e.g. during an interactive class. The workload for preparing and grading exercises must be independent of the number of participating students.

Instant feedback: the system should provide instant feedback for submitted solutions and describe why the particular solution is correct or wrong so that students can improve it.

Learning from failures: students can learn, reflect and iteratively submit new solutions even if they fail initially. Students should have the chance to resubmit their solutions as often as they want (potentially limited to a specific time frame).

Different exercise types: the system allows programming exercises in different areas of the software engineering process including programming basics, system design, object design, testing and build and release management.

Different assessment ways: the system should allow different ways to assess submissions. For programming exercises the system has to support different test types (e.g. structural, behavioral, runtime, performance or functional tests).

Traceability: the system must ensure traceability for instructors and for students. With regards to team exercises, the contribution of each team member should be accountable. Traceability enables early detection of difficulties for the students in the assignment and lets the instructor react accordingly.

Immediate evaluation: solutions and results are easily accessible and evaluable for instructors enabling them to remove ambiguity, answer open questions, or extend the given working time.

Interactive exercise instructions: dynamic tasks and UML diagrams visualize the current progress of students. They update their color from red (incomplete) to green (complete) when students submit their solution and when associated test cases pass.

Easy to use online editor: to simplify the participation and improve the learnability, programming beginners can work on programming exercises in an interactive and lightweight online editor. They can submit their solutions with just one button click.

ArTEMiS fulfills these goals by using the concepts of VC and CI. Each student works with a given template code in his own repository and has a build plan which executes test cases after each commit. Students can solve the programming exercise in an online editor, on the local computer using an IDE or with a mix of both. When using the online editor, they don't need to setup a VC client and an IDE. If they work on their own computer, they need to apply version control and install an IDE (e.g. Eclipse) and have more functionalities in the code editor (e.g. auto completion, error highlighting, etc.). Conducting a programming exercise consists of 7 steps distributed among instructor, ArTEMiS and students:

1. **Instructor prepares exercise:** set up a base repository containing the exercise code and test cases. Set up a base build plan on the CI server, and create the exercise on ArTEMiS.
2. **Student starts exercise:** click on *Start Exercise* on ArTEMiS. This automatically generates a copy (fork) of the base repository with the exercise code and a copy of the base build plan. ArTEMiS sets the permissions so that students can only see their personal repository.
3. **Student clones repository:** optionally clone the personalized repository from the remote VCS to the local machine.
4. **Student solves exercise:** Solve the exercise with an IDE of choice on the local computer **or** in the online editor.
5. **Student submits solution:** upload source code changes to the VCS by committing and pushing them to the remote server **or** by clicking *Commit & Run Tests* in the online editor.
6. **CI server verifies solution:** verify the student's submission by executing the test cases (see step 1) and provide feedback which parts are correct or wrong.

7a. **Instructor reviews course results:** review overall results of all students, and react to common errors and problems.

7b. **Student reviews personal result:** review build result and feedback using ArTEMiS. In case of a failed build, reattempt to solve the exercise (step 4.).

Figure 2 shows this approach as UML activity diagram. CI server, VCS, and ArTEMiS are combined in the *System* actor. The approach consists of 2 phases, exercise preparation and exercise execution.

Exercise preparation: an instructor sets up a VC repository containing the exercise code (template) handed out to students and test cases to verify students' submissions (*base repository*). This repository typically includes a small sample project including some predefined classes, dependencies to external libraries, e.g. a testing framework, and test cases. A combination of behavioral (black-box) and structural (white-box) tests allows to check for both functionality and implementation details of the submitted code. In addition, the instructor stores the tests separately in a test repository, which is not accessible to students, to prevent that they adapt the test cases. It can make sense to completely hide the tests from the students to prevent reverse engineering the solution.

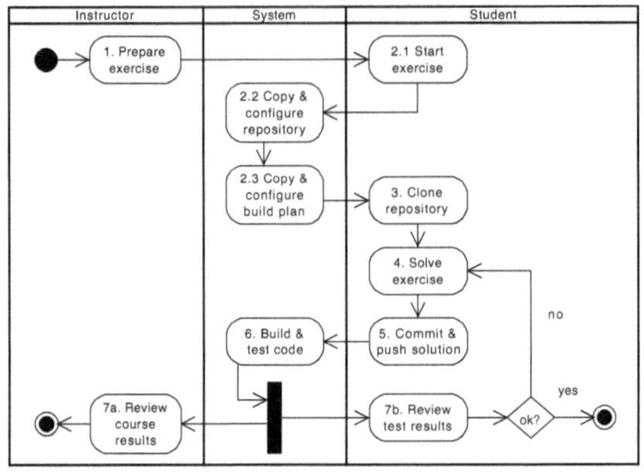

Figure 2: Process for automated assessment in ArTEMiS

After setting up the base and test repositories, the instructor configures the build plan on the CI server which compiles and tests the exercise code using the previously defined test cases (*base build plan*). This build plan includes a task to pull the source code from the base repository and the test repository whenever changes occur, and to combine them so that the tests can be executed in the second step. A final task, which is also executed when compilation or test execution fails, notifies ArTEMiS about the new result. The instructor finally creates an exercise on ArTEMiS by selecting the preconfigured base repository of the VCS and the preconfigured base build plan of the CI server.

Exercise execution: a student starts an exercise with a single click, triggering the setup process: ArTEMiS creates a personal copy of the base repository, the *student repository*, and provides access only to this student. It creates a personal copy of the base build plan, the *student build plan*, and configures it to be triggered when the particular student uploads changes to this personal student repository. The student can usually not access the build plan to hide its complexity. Personalized means that each student gets one repository and one build plan. When 200 students participate in an exercise, ArTEMiS creates 200 student repositories and 200 student build plans. Students only have access to their personal repository, they cannot access other student repositories. This prevents cheating, because students cannot access code of each other.

After the setup is complete, ArTEMiS displays the clone URL and/or allows the student to open the exercise in the online editor. The student clones the repository to the local computer and starts working on the exercise. When the students uploads a new solution to the personalized repository, the personalized build plan of the student assesses the solution. Students upload solutions by committing and pushing changes in their source code to their personal repository or by submitting their changes in the online editor (which triggers a commit and a push operation in the background). The new commit on the personal repository triggers the personal build plan to assess the solution on a build agent. The build agent pulls the submitted code from the personal repository and the tests from the test repository, and combines them in a working directory. It compiles the code, executes the tests and uploads the results to ArTEMiS in a few seconds, so that the student can immediately review the feedback and iteratively improve their solution.

In case of an incorrect solution, the feedback includes how many tests failed and the corresponding failure message for each failed

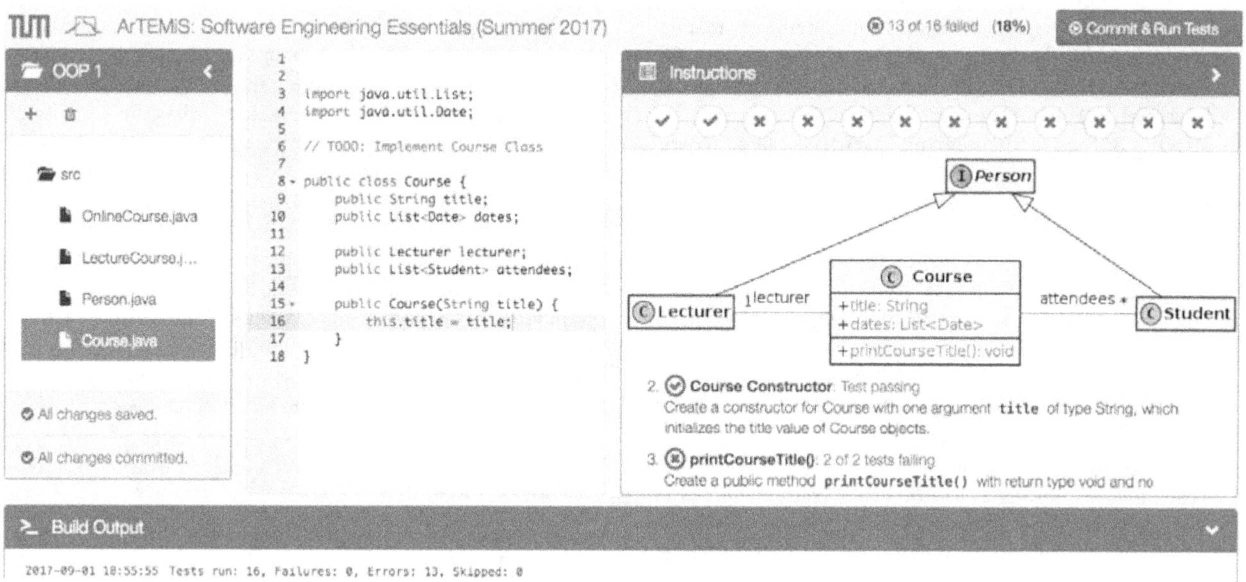

Figure 3: Screenshot of the ArTEMiS online editor with interactive exercise instructions on the right

test. The student can now reattempt to solve the exercise and submit a new solution. The instructor can review the results, gain insights on the exercise progress and react immediately to errors and problems during the exercise. ArTEMiS acts as facade to the CI process and hides complex details, which enables less experienced students to participate in the exercise. Every student has a personalized build plan, so the approach can be used to teach the concepts of CI. Then, students get access to their build plan and have to configure it on their own. Students can only see, edit and adjust their personalized build plan. They cannot inspect build plans of their fellow students.

ArTEMiS includes an online editor that allows unexperienced students to participate in exercises without dealing with the complex setup of VC and IDEs. Figure 3 shows the online editor with interactive and dynamic exercise instructions on the right side. Interactive instructions change their color depending on the progress of students. Already completed tasks are marked with a green tick, incomplete tasks are marked with a red cross. This helps students to identify which parts of the exercise they have already solved correctly. When they submit their current solution with the *Commit & Run Tests* button in the upper right corner, the interactive instructions dynamically update. The exercise tasks and the UML diagram elements are referenced by the predefined test cases. They change their color from red to green when all test cases associated with the task or diagram element pass. This allows the students to immediately recognize which tasks are already fulfilled and is particularly helpful for beginners.

Figure 4 shows the system architecture of ArTEMiS. A student uses the *ArTEMiS Application Client* (a browser) and a *VC Client* of his choice to obtain the exercise code and to submit solutions. *VC Server, CI Server, Local Build Agents,* and the *ArTEMiS Application Server* run on the university's infrastructure. The *CI Server* delegates the builds to local and/or remote agents, e.g. on Amazon Web Services, depending on how much capacity is required for the number of participating students. This makes it easy to scale the approach by adding additional build agents. ArTEMiS uses the university's *User Management System.* The components *VC Server* and *CI Server* are exchangeable, resulting in a flexible system which can be adapted to the specific requirements of instructors.

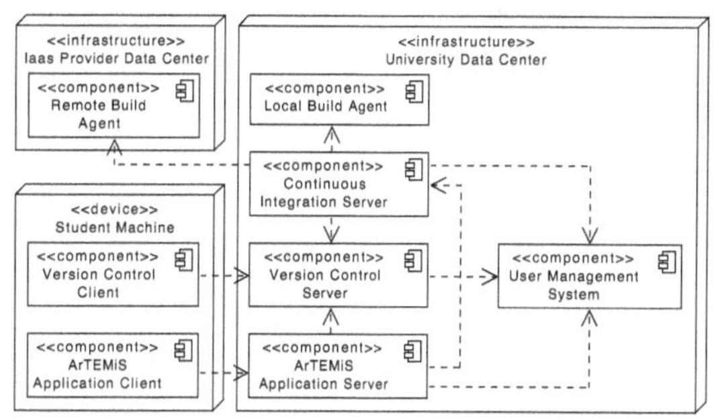

Figure 4: System Architecture of ArTEMiS

The use of CI leads to several benefits: the programming language for programming exercises is freely configurable. Compilation and testing of student solutions is not a matter of ArTEMiS, it only depends on the configuration of the build system. Students learn the concepts and workflows of VC, CI and testing, all important skills in software development. The system is scalable and can react to the number of assessments to be handled with a corresponding number of build agents. Adding more build agents allows more students to submit their solution at the same time and still receiving instant feedback. This is crucial for interactive learning based exercises that are integrated into a class.

4 CASE STUDY

We use ArTEMiS in 3 large university course (UC) and in a MOOC:

(1) **UC - Introduction to Software Engineering**: mandatory subject, 1400 bachelor students (2nd semester), 6 exercises, 814 students participated
(2) **UC - Patterns in Software Engineering**: elective subject, 400 master students, 34 exercises, 334 students participated

(3) **UC - Project Organization and Management**: mandatory subject for business informatics, elective subject for computer science, about 300 bachelor and master students, 1 exercise, 224 students participated
(4) **MOOC - Software Engineering Essentials**: 300 active students, 10 exercises, 257 students participated

In the beginning of these courses, we go through a short interactive tutorial together with the students to show them how to use ArTEMiS. In all these courses, we recommend to use Eclipse as IDE and SourceTree as VC client (git). Students could individually decide which VC client to use to retrieve the assignment, and hand in their solution. We describe 4 typical exercises from our courses:

(1) **Programming:** write source code for a problem statement or UML model. Typical examples are the implementation of the quick sort algorithm or the strategy pattern. Test cases assess the correctness of the solution.
(2) **Testing:** write test cases for the given program code and mock parts of the program. The instructor creates test cases that assess the test cases of the students with the given correct program code and by injecting wrong program code to review if the tests of the students are correct.
(3) **Merge conflict:** experience a merge conflict in git and have to resolve it.
(4) **Release management:** learn how commits trigger the CI server, which produces new build artifacts. Students get direct access to their personalized build plan to be able to view its configuration in detail.

By automizing all setup steps, we decreased the effort for students and instructors. The instructor can dynamically adapt the working time for different assignments based on the students' progress in class. This allowed students to actively think about the exercises instead of just following along with the solution.

4.1 Results

In simulations with 800 students and 2000 submissions over a period of 10 minutes, ArTEMiS assessed solutions in an average of 10 seconds. In our courses, we measure the average assessment time. This allows us to constantly evaluate whether ArTEMiS fulfills its scalability goals under real classroom conditions. In a quantitative analysis, we found the following results:

(1) Scalability: ArTEMiS can handle 200 submissions per minute.
(2) Feedback: ArTEMiS provides feedback within 10 seconds.
(3) Usability: Programming beginners are able to use ArTEMiS.

Table 1 displays an overview of the number of students and submissions for each exercise together with the average assessment time. The number of submissions per student varies from 1.6 to 4.3 on average. In one exercise, where students could only use the online editor, this number was higher: 7.2. If students participate in the exercise and submit solutions, most of them also successfully solve the exercise. The assessment time, i.e. the time for students to wait from the moment they submit their solution until they see the test results and the feedback, varies from 5.1 to 10.3 seconds on average depending on the complexity of the exercise, the number of tests and the number of external dependencies. In exercises with more complex tests, e.g. asynchronous client-server tests with timeouts, this number can increase. In such cases, it makes sense to distribute tests to students so that they can also execute them on their computer. ArTEMiS uses a separate test repository so that students who try to cheat and change tests locally, e.g. to let all tests pass immediately without solving the exercise, can be detected.

We asked the students for feedback regarding the use of ArTEMiS. Most students had less experience in the areas of distributed VC and CI, nonetheless they had no issues working with ArTEMiS. They stated, that the test results and the feedback was helpful to solve the exercises, they enjoyed working with it and preferred the usage of ArTEMiS over the previous process where there was no automatic and instant feedback. In an online questionnaire, we found that more than 90 % of the students consider the interactive exercise instructions helpful in solving the exercise. They are particularly valuable in online courses, where students are distributed and instructors cannot guide them directly in case of problems.

	(1) Programming	(2) Testing	(3) Merge conflict	(4) Release management
Participating students	317	167	224	248
Submitting students	209 (66 %)	109 (65 %)	211 (94 %)	149 (60 %)
Successful students	200 (96 %)	108 (99 %)	183 (87 %)	135 (91 %)
Overall submissions	340	340	904	285
Correct submissions	236	236	291	198
Test cases	12	12	2	0
Assessment time*	10.3 s	8.3 s	5.1 s	9.6 s
Submissions per student*	1.6	3.1	4.3	1.9

Table 1: Numbers in typical exercises (* on average)

4.2 Discussion

ArTEMiS provides flexibility in how instructors conduct exercises. It allows them to distribute assessment tests to students so that they can find their own errors during debugging easier. However, this might facilitate that students only work on getting the tests passed and do not take the time to understand the actual problem and solve it on their own. In such cases, instructors can hide the tests and only show the test results on ArTEMiS.

Another choice is the use of the online editor vs. the use of an IDE on the local computer. While the online editor lowers the entrance barrier, it has limited features. In a comparison, we found that students prefer the local IDE if they are already familiar with it, as it offers more features such as syntax and error highlighting, auto completion and debugging. In an experiment, we forced them to use the online editor, however some students copied the code file by file into their local IDE, solved the exercise there, and copied the code back. An open question at this point is whether providing features such as auto completion is beneficial to the learning experience. Novice programmers often heavily depend on such features [18]. This may make students reliant on them and may prevent learning the correct syntax of the programming language. It could be a viable strategy to provide only minimal features in a code editor.

ArTEMiS supports in-class exercises with hundreds of students and can additionally be used for homework exercises. We use it in online courses where students are distributed and rely on the exercise instructions and in university classes where instructors can guide the students in addition. The costs of providing the system are not negligible. We could use already existing, self-hosted CI and VC systems. These are hosted at our institution, but we have to take care of the maintenance. Alternatively, cloud-based solutions such as GitHub Education, GitLab or Bitbucket Cloud can be used. These usually offer attractive opportunities for educational institutions.

5 RELATED WORK

A variety of systems for automatic assessment exists. Multiple surveys have been published, summarizing and categorizing these systems. The first extensive surveys on this topic were done by Ala-Mutka [1] and Douce et al. [5]. They describe multiple auto assessment tools and categorize them into dynamic and static assessment and differentiate between local and web based systems.

The survey by Ihantola et al. focuses on identifying key features of automatic assessment tools, such as supporting different programming languages, allowing resubmissions, or providing a sandbox environment to handle malicious submissions [10]. The authors state most systems are not open source or available otherwise, even if a publication describes the development of a prototype. A survey by Queiros states interoperability and compatibility to other services is a key factor for automatic assessment systems [14]. He concludes that this factor is not considered for many existing assessment tools and that future solutions have to improve this. Our approach fulfills many of the stated features by connecting to university user management or providing interfaces to VCS.

From those surveys, we identified multiple publications related to our system. WebCAT was first created in 2003 and is arguably one of the most complete automatic assessment tools [6]. It has been developed as open-source software and allows extensibility by plugins. In terms of assessment, it supports student written tests, test coverage, static code analysis and a combination of both automatic and manual grading. Our approach covers most of the features of WebCAT, while removing the dependence on a single software product. Instead, our approach consists of multiple independent software systems that are connected using common interfaces. This leads to a higher flexibility as individual parts of the architecture can be replaced, for example in favor of lower costs, superior support, larger communities or general management decisions.

Marmoset focuses on information collection during the development process of students [16]. The system takes regular snapshots of the students' progress. It allows the instructor to study the development process of the students and to identify common bug patterns. By using VCS and teaching its application, we achieve the same outcome. Students commit multiple iterations of their solution, resulting in a commit history that can be evaluated. This allows to identify common mistakes and study problem solving behavior. Amelung et al. propose a system thats splits e-learning and e-assessment platforms into separate systems, allowing independent deployment and easier adoption [2]. Our approach targets the same idea, but our goal is not to implement another closed source assessment system. Instead, we reuse workflows provided by existing CI tools to achieve similar results.

Gruenewald et al. focus on the challenge of conducting programming lectures as MOOCs [8] integrating active experimentation and relating to concrete experience. Those aspects are considered in ArTEMiS as well. In recent years, commercial products have become available for automatic grading, including Vocareum, Turing Craft, etc. An open source and free alternative is Codeboard, developed by ETH Zurich. These online tools are cloud based and use regression testing, a technique used for quality control in software development. They allow students to edit and submit source code in the browser to simplify the participation.

6 CONCLUSION

ArTEMiS combines VC and CI with automated assessment of programming exercises and immediate feedback. This enables high flexibility and scalability in large classes. Our experiences in 3 university courses and 1 online course show that programming beginners are able to use the system, improve their solutions iteratively with immediate feedback and increase their learning experience.

Dynamic and interactive exercise instructions are particularly helpful for beginners to immediately recognize which tasks are resolved. The effort for instructors and TAs is reduced. They can evaluate student results immediately during the exercise to help students when problems occur. ArTEMiS is free and open source on https://github.com/ls1intum/ArTEMiS, so that other instructors can use it in their courses. We will support additional interactive exercises in the future, in particular quizzes and modeling.

ACKNOWLEDGMENTS

We want to thank Dominik Münch, Andreas Greimel and Josias Montag who participated in the development of ArTEMiS.

REFERENCES

[1] K. Ala-Mutka. 2005. A Survey of Automated Assessment Approaches for Programming Assignments. *Computer Science Education* (2005), 83–102.
[2] M Amelung, P. Forbrig, and D. Rösner. 2008. Towards Generic and Flexible Web Services for E-Assessment. *SIGCSE Bulletin* (June 2008), 219–224.
[3] C. Bonwell and J. Eison. 1991. *Active Learning: Creating Excitement in the Classroom.* ASHE-ERIC Higher Education Reports.
[4] G. Booch. 1991. *Object Oriented Design with Applications.* Benjamin-Cummings Publishing Co., Inc., Redwood City, CA, USA.
[5] C. Douce, D. Livingstone, and J. Orwell. 2005. Automatic Test-Based Assessment of Programming: A Review. *Journal on Educ. Resources in Computing* (2005).
[6] S. Edwards. 2003. Improving student performance by evaluating how well Students test their own programs. *Journal on Educ. Resources in Computing* (2003).
[7] M. Fowler. 2006. Continuous Integration. http://www.martinfowler.com/articles/continuousIntegration.html. (2006).
[8] F. Grünewald, C. Meinel, M. Totschnig, and C. Willems. 2013. Designing MOOCs for the Support of Multiple Learning Styles. In *European Conference on Technology Enhanced Learning.* Springer, 371–382.
[9] J. Hollingsworth. 1960. Automatic Graders for Programming Classes. *Commun. ACM* (1960), 528–529.
[10] P. Ihantola, T. Ahoniemi, V. Karavirta, and O. Seppälä. 2010. Review of Recent Systems for Automatic Assessment of Programming Assignments. In *Koli Calling Conference on Computing Education Research.* ACM, 86–93.
[11] M. Joy, N. Griffiths, and R. Boyatt. 2005. The BOSS Online Submission and Assessment System. *Journal on Educational Resources in Computing* (2005).
[12] S. Krusche, A. Seitz, J. Börstler, and B. Bruegge. 2017. Interactive Learning: Increasing Student Participation through Shorter Exercise Cycles. In *Proceedings of the 19th Australasian Computing Education Conference.* ACM, 17–26.
[13] S. Krusche, N. von Frankenberg, and S. Afifi. 2017. Experiences of a Software Engineering Course based on Interactive Learning. In *Proceedings of the 19th Workshop on Software Engineering Education in Universities.* 32–40.
[14] R. Queirós and J. Leal. 2012. Programming Exercises Evaluation Systems – An Interoperability Survey. In *Conference on Computer Supported Education.* 83–90.
[15] R. Singh, S. Gulwani, and A. Solar-Lezama. 2013. Automated feedback generation for introductory programming assignments. *SIGPLAN Notices* (2013), 15–26.
[16] J. Spacco, D. Hovemeyer, W. Pugh, F. Emad, . Hollingsworth, and N. Padua-Perez. 2006. Experiences with Marmoset: Designing and Using an Advanced Submission and Testing System for Programming Courses. *SIGCSE Bulletin* (2006), 13–17.
[17] T. Staubitz et al. 2015. Towards Practical Programming Exercises and Automated Assessment in Massive Open Online Courses. In *International Conference on Teaching, Assessment, and Learning for Engineering.* 23–30.
[18] A. Vihavainen, J. Helminen, and P. Ihantola. 2014. How novices tackle their first lines of code in an IDE: Analysis of programming session traces. In *Koli Calling Conference on Computing Education Research.* ACM, 109–116.
[19] M. Vujošević-Janičić, M. Nikolić, D. Tošić, and V. Kuncak. 2013. Software Verification and Graph Similarity for Automated Evaluation of Students' Assignments. *Inf. Softw. Technol.* 55, 6 (2013), 1004–1016.

MRS: Automated Assessment of Interactive Classroom Exercises

Debzani Deb
Dept. of Computer Science
Winston-Salem State University, NC, USA
debd@wssu.edu

Muztaba Fuad
Dept. of Computer Science
Winston-Salem State University, NC, USA
fuadmo@wssu.edu

James Etim
Dept. of Education
Winston-Salem State University, NC, USA
etimj@wssu.edu

Clay Gloster
Dept. of Computer Systems
NC A&T State University, NC, USA
cgloster@ncat.edu

ABSTRACT

Classroom formative assessment augmented with timely and frequent feedback has become one of the most prominent teaching practices in education research. On the context of Computer Science (CS) courses that expose students to the functionality and dynamic aspects of various algorithms, traditionally, students are evaluated by exploring in-class paper-based exercises. In these exercises, they simulate the steps of an algorithm by drawing several instances of a diagram. This traditional approach is time consuming, is inherently difficult for students to express the dynamics of an algorithm, does not allow timely feedback, and restricts the number of exercises that students can practice and receive feedback on. Mobile Response System (MRS) is a software environment that facilitates in-class exercises and their real-time assessment using mobile devices and therefore focuses on addressing many of the above-mentioned problems. In this paper, we present results of eight semester-long studies using MRS in two of the required CS courses at Winston-Salem State University (WSSU). Our experimental evaluation shows the educational benefits of the proposed approach in terms of enhanced student retention of covered concepts, reduced failing rate, and increased student engagement and satisfaction.

ACM Reference format:
Debzani Deb, Muztaba Fuad, James Etim, and Clay Closter. 2018. MRS: Automated Assessment of Interactive Classroom Exercises. In *SIGCSE '18: 49th ACM Technical Symposium on Computer Science Education, Feb. 21–24, 2018, Baltimore, MD, USA.* ACM, NY, NY, USA, 6 pages. https://doi.org/10.1145/3159450.3159607

1. INTRODUCTION

Since the pivotal work of Black and William [1], classroom formative assessment has become one of the most important teaching practices in education research. Bell & Cowie [2] defined it as the repeated use of assessment-based information to recognize and respond to students' needs to enhance learning. Many studies [3, 4] found the classroom formative assessment extremely effective when it is augmented with timely feedback. According to them, a timely and frequent feedback informs students about their current comprehensions and competencies, their progression toward learning, and assist and encourages students to take the next learning step [4].

In CS education, understanding the functionality and dynamic aspects of an algorithm is a crucial skill that every student should be proficient at. Traditionally, these concepts are hard for many students to comprehend as they are abstract and mathematical in nature. Therefore, careful consideration must be given to the methods that are used to assess the student understandings of these concepts in the classrooms. Usually, instructor evaluates the student comprehension of the algorithmic process by offering them paper-based exercises to solve, where they demonstrate their proficiency by drawing several instances of a diagram to simulate operations of an algorithm. While drawing these static images can aid students to mentally conceptualize the abstract phenomena described by an algorithm, it is very hard to simulate and comprehend dynamically evolving algorithms in terms of few diagrams. Moreover, it is time consuming and difficult to draw separate instance of a diagram to reflect each and every step of an algorithm, therefore often student tends to combine several operations of an algorithm (in many occasions by erasing the result of the previous stage with the result of the current stage) in a single instance of a diagram. This shortcut process often generates mistakes and confusions and impedes students' learning process. Time consuming nature of many of these practice exercises also implies that the manual grading can take several weeks for students to receive feedback on their works. As the class sizes grow, this in-class assessment model quickly becomes unsustainable and fails to offer any benefit. Even for a small class size and/or with substantial amount of grading resources (e.g. TAs), only a finite set of exercises can be made available to the students where they can receive feedback. Limited number of graded exercises also prohibits students from evaluating their understanding on a broad range of challenging tasks with various orders of difficulties. However, this exposure is very important in order to stimulate students' cognitive conflicts and engage them in higher-level thinking process.

The MRS [5, 6] project emphasizes on addressing the above-mentioned shortcomings of the in-class assessment model that traditionally instructors employ while teaching algorithms to the CS students. In particular, MRS framework facilitates in-class proficiency exercises and their real-time assessments using mobile devices. We argue that as mobile devices are becoming more pervasive and are being used profusely by students, it will be intuitive for them to perform visual and interactive exercises in their preferred devices. MRS is therefore designed as client server software that allows the instructor to dynamically intervene the students with carefully designed exercise Apps, synchronized with the lecture material, in their mobile devices.

SIGCSE '18, February 21–24, 2018, Baltimore, MD, USA

ACM ISBN 978-1-4503-5103-4/18/02...$15.00
https://doi.org/10.1145/3159450.3159607

Students are able to actively interact with the graphical representation of the exercise while recognizing the effect of their dynamic interactions visually at different stages of the algorithm and send their solutions back to the server computer. MRS then facilitates grading of the exercise automatically by comparing the student made sequence of interactions with the model sequence of interactions. Since MRS software automatically administers the delivery, time keeping and grading of these exercise Apps, instructor could use them more frequently in the classroom and learners could actively participate in more exercises where they can receive feedback. The overall aim of this mobile-based, visual, and interactive exercise is to activate students cognitively in understanding these harder concepts by making the learning processes more explicit and responsive to them. MRS accomplishes this aim in a novel way, by providing App-based visualization exercises, whereas other such systems provide web-based exercises.

Our previous works [5, 6] focused on exploring the design, development and deployment of MRS software environment and exercise Apps and evaluated its effectiveness within a single CS course where students' short-term knowledge acquisition and satisfaction were measured immediately after the MRS-enabled classroom interventions. We found significant evidence that MRS is effective in increasing student understanding of difficult concepts [5] and with MRS it is possible for the instructor to offer more hands-on-activities with increasing order of difficulties to the students during the class time [6]. We then extended MRS intervention to two of the required CS courses (one sophomore and one junior level course) at WSSU and studied MRS's effectiveness in students' long-time knowledge retention, perception of learning and perception of engagement for eight semesters. This paper summarizes the student-generated evidence of the strong and weak points of our interventions and also discusses some of the appealing and challenging aspects from an instructor's perspective.

2. MRS SYSTEM FEATURES

In MRS, the server component hosts questions, manages users, and maintains communication and synchronization, and the client component executes in learner's mobile devices and allows them to login to the system and facilitates interactive exercises. In current MRS implementation, the server has been developed in Java and the client has been developed in Android. MRS allows the instructor to import the interactive exercises (IE) within MRS and to broadcast them to students' mobile devices. When the MRS client receives a new exercise from the server, the corresponding App that renders the given exercise is executed, which allows student interaction with the App. The App then captures learner interaction at every stage (screen) and sends it back to the server for grading. When the server receives all answers back, it uses the corresponding server-side grading component in order to grade learner submissions and creates grading and other statistics.

In each of the IE Apps, students are required to work on a visual representation of a problem and to develop the answer following a set of steps guided by a particular algorithm or process. In each step, students make key choices (for example clicking the table or array indices for selection or swap, selecting from a drop-down menu, selecting a tree node or an edge of a graph etc.) that impact their next step of interaction. Table 1 lists the IE Apps that are utilized in this study along with their visualization and course information.

Table 1. Interactive Exercise (IE) Apps Details

App	Visual Representation	Which Course?
Interactive matching	Clickable 2-D array	Sophomore
Analytical answering	Free writing & word cloud	Sophomore
Truth Table formation	Clickable 2-D array	Sophomore
K-map simplification	Clickable 2-D array	Sophomore
Bubble Sorting	Clickable 1-D array	Junior
Selection Sorting	Clickable 1-D array	Junior
Prim's minimum spanning tree	Clickable logical graph and dynamic table	Junior
Dijkstra's single source shortest path	Clickable logical graph and dynamic table	Junior

The design and development of the MRS system and IEs are out of scope of this paper and interested readers are advised to explore MRS website [7] for downloadable modules and publications [5, 6] to learn more. However, following is a brief description of the important features of MRS, so that readers can gain a good idea about the intervention.

1. MRS supports immediate and automated grading of the interactive exercises. Once all answers are submitted, the server grades them and each student receives an email containing their grade for that exercise, the visual representation of the correct answer, and a visual representation of their submitted answer. The email is preferred as delivery method as screen captures can be attached and the information can be secured for future references. Immediate grading allows the students to obtain faster and frequent feedbacks that reinforce their learning and help them to identify misconceptions and problem areas.
2. MRS provides anonymous and summative grading statistics of the class which is calculated and projected instantly for the instructor to share with the students after each grading session. This instant visualization of class grade distribution allows the instructor to have real-time evidence of students' comprehension of covered lecture materials on a particular class and also helps instructor to identify the concepts that need to be repeated or reinforced. Students are also able to assess their progress toward learning the concept and to compare it with their peers in the class. Along with the grading statistics, MRS also analyzes a wealth of students' mobile device usage and interactions data (i.e. button clicks, time spent, navigation behavior etc.), anonymizes and summarizes them, and makes them available for immediate visualization. This summarized information allows instructor to better understand and interpret student mental model and attitudes during problem solving.
3. MRS also supports in-class anonymous communication, where students can send anonymous question/feedback to the instructor and additionally can vote on existing pool of questions (submitted by other students) that instructor may choose to review and answer at the end of the class.
4. MRS supports multi-step interactive exercises that typically spans into many screens, where students can transition between screens by utilizing "Next" and "Back" button. Pressing "Next" button will lead to a screen where students can see the results of their interactions in the previous screen reflected on the graphical representation of the problem, on the other hand, pressing "Back" button will undo all previous interactions. It is therefore possible to start the exercise from a clean slate by utilizing "Back" button multiple times.
5. In order to support unlimited practice and graded exercises, the interactive exercise Apps are designed to accept inputs as parameters, where parameters can be populated with either

randomly generated values or instructor generated values to create many different variations of a problem. An exercise definition is stored as an XML file and contains exercise parameters such as problem components, time to answer, special instructions etc., which are used to render the corresponding App in the client device. The file additionally contains different rubric and grading parameters such as correct answers, grading weights, etc. to support server-side automated grading. Therefore, creating a new exercise instance (with input data and grading rubrics) does not involve changing any programming code. More importantly, one single exercise definition file can contain many problem instances and importing that file into MRS server allows the instructor to prompt the students with as many practice and graded exercises as the class time permits.

6. MRS uses step-wise grading and students can receive partial credit for partially correct answer. Checkpoints are utilized in the client devices to monitor students' interaction throughout the exercise. The system then formulates a sequence of interactions as student submission and compares them with the model sequence at the server to determine how much of the exercise was answered correctly. This grading methodology obligates students to correctly follow all intermediate algorithmic steps rather than guessing the final answer.

3. EXPERIMENTAL EVALUATION

We postulate that students' increased engagement with the mobile-friendly, interactive and instant-feedback nature of MRS, as well as visually seeing the consequence of their interactions in different stages of a multi-step problem, while going back and forth, will allow the students to comprehend and retain the subject material better. We are also interested to explore MRS's impact on various levels of students, students' open-ended feedbacks and instructors' perspective regarding the strengths and limitations of using MRS. Our Research Questions (RQs) are as follows:

1. RQ1 - Are the students using MRS become more engaged, retain concepts better, and enjoy enhanced learning than the non-intervened students?
2. RQ2 - Is there any notable difference between how the intervention impact CS sophomore vs. junior students?
3. RQ3 - What feedback do students from the intervened group provide regarding their experience?
4. RQ4 - What do the instructors, willing to deploy MRS in their classroom, need to consider?

3.1 The Study Setting

The MRS software and associated IE Apps were deployed in two courses during the period of Spring 2015 (S15) to Spring 2017 (S17) semesters with a total of 97 students being intervened. One course, entitled as, "Intro. to Computer Hardware Organization" (CSC 2320, offered with MRS during S15-S17 semesters) is a sophomore level course and the other is a junior level course, "Analysis of Algorithms" (CSC 3331, offered with MRS at S15, S16 and S17 semesters). Both courses focus on concepts involving functional dynamics whereas the junior (algorithm) course emphasizes on a large number of such topics.

Before MRS, both courses were taught with lectures, paper-based in-class assessment exercises, take-home assignments, midterm and final exams. During the intervened semesters, the paper-based in-class assessment was replaced with MRS-based IEs where students had a chance to practice some IEs before participating in multiple graded exercises while progressively being exposed to higher-order problems. For comparison, student performance data gathered during the F13 (N:11) and S14 (N:17) offerings of the sophomore course and the S13 (N:19) and S14 (N:11) offerings of the junior course were utilized as baseline data. The same instructor taught all offerings of a particular course and the course setting and teaching practices have been consistently maintained both before and during the MRS interventions. Table 2 shows some course and participant related information. In an effort to diminish the impact of confounding variables such as size, display and appearance of mobile devices, each student was provided with an identical Samsung tablet in the classrooms while performing IE Apps.

Table 2: Course-wise MRS Intervention Information

	Junior			Sophomore				
	S15	S16	S17	S15	F15	S16	F16	S17
#Students	18	19	14	14	8	8	5	11
#IE Apps	2	3	3	2	3	4	4	3
#Graded IE	4	10	7	3	8	10	13	10

3.2 Study Design

In a typical intervened class of 75 minutes, the instructor spent the first 30 minutes to convey a lecture covering a specific concept and problem-solving exercises related to that concept by utilizing slides and whiteboards. In the next 15 minutes, students applied their understanding of the concept by practicing some IEs, followed by completing the first graded IE (same paper-based exercise was offered to the control group), which is similar to the already lectured examples in terms of the degree of difficulty. As all students received instant email with their answers and correct answer after completing the first graded IE, instructor then spent the next 5 minutes pointing out the mistakes and clarifying the concepts more. The next 10 minutes were spent by the students solving a second graded IE, which is of higher order of difficulty than the examples and exercises covered previously. The following 5 minutes were spent by the instructor to reinforce the topic and correct student misconceptions (if any). Students spent the last 10 minutes of the class performing a difficult graded IE that required critical thinking and involved unfolding scenarios that were not explicitly taught before. It should be noted that this is a tentative outline of activities and there is room for flexibility (e.g. having two or four graded exercises instead of three) depending on the difficulty of the lectured concept, student comprehension level and amount of questions that they have, and other class logistics.

3.3 Metrics

In order to measure students' retention of knowledge in the long term, we utilized the final course grade as evaluation metric. The graded MRS-based class exercises contribute toward 10%-15% of the total course grade. However, student's long-term knowledge acquisition is further tested on the same topics during the midterm and final exam and each of these exams contributed 15% to 20% toward the total course grade. In addition to that, course failing rates are also considered as a measure of knowledge retention.

To assess student engagement and perception of the MRS environment and its overall effectiveness, an anonymous experience survey (Table 3) was offered to the learners only after they completed all MRS related in-class activities. The students gave their opinion about eight statements using a Likert scale of four values (Strongly Agree, Agree, Disagree and Strongly

Disagree), with an agreement scale ranging from strongly agree (4) to strongly disagree (1). The survey questions were then grouped into thematic categories of *perception of learning* and *perception of engagement.* In order to ensure that students are actually looking at the content of the survey, not just "clicking through", the survey was designed to contain both positive and negative questions. Additionally, the survey includes following two open-ended questions.

1. Tell us about the MRS features that you found to be most useful.
2. What would you suggest in order to improve MRS environment or your experience?

Table 3. Thematic Categories of Student Survey Questions

Questions about Students' Perception of Learning
Q1. MRS is helpful in understanding concepts such as A, B & C.
Q2. MRS helps in visualizing the steps in A, B & C.
Q3. Using MRS did not improve my understanding of A, B & C.
Questions about Students' Perception of Engagement
Q4. I am enjoying this experience.
Q5. I feel competent & confident to solve problems in MRS than in a pen- and paper-based setting.
Q6. The A, B & C Apps are intuitive and easy to use.
Q7. Seeing my grades immediately after taking the exercises is really helpful.
Q8. Learning to use MRS software & related Apps is additional work beyond normal course work.

3.4 Results & Discussions

Final Course Grade: Table 4 shows the descriptive statistics for final course grade (out of 100) attained by the intervened and non-intervened group of students in the junior and the sophomore classes. The results indicate that the average grades attained by the treated groups in both classes are significantly higher than the average scores attained by the non-treated groups. The treated group also performed more uniformly than the control group, which is reflected in its much lower standard deviation value. A two-tailed independent samples t-test assuming unequal sample variances, with 5% significance level, was performed on the final course scores and shows significant differences between groups for both courses. The results also show that the sophomore students were benefitted marginally more than the junior students due to the use of MRS. These results affirmatively answer RQ1 and verify that the students, who are intervened with MRS, learned contents better and had better retention of topics covered over the entire course than the non-intervened group of students. The results further confirm that the MRS impacts different levels of students slightly differently and positively answer RQ2.

Course Failing Rate: Fig. 1 shows the comparison of overall course grade distributions for the junior class during the intervened (S15, S16, S17) and the non-intervened (S13, S14) semesters. On average, 28% of the non-treated group of students received a course failing (D/F) or withdrawal (W) grade, on the other hand, only 9% of treated group of students received the D/F/W grades. Interestingly, although the average percentage of students receiving A or B grades remain the same (59%) in both treated and non-treated semesters, the percentage of students receiving A grade enhanced from 19% to 34% in intervened semesters. This observation indicates that along with reducing course failing and withdrawal rate, MRS intervention was also helpful for average or above average students, who otherwise would receive grade B, however with MRS intervention they were able to enhance their understanding and achieved higher grades.

Table 4: Descriptive Statistics of Final Course Grade

	Junior Control (N: 30)	Junior Treated (N:51)	Sophomore Control MRS(N:28)	Sophomore Treated (N:46)
Average	71.2	81.30	73	84
Std. Deviation	26.2	15.27	19.1	12.1
F-Test	F = 2.91, p = 0.0004		F = 2.45, p= 0.002	
T-Test	**t = -2.19, p = 0.031**		**t = -2.97, p = 0.004**	

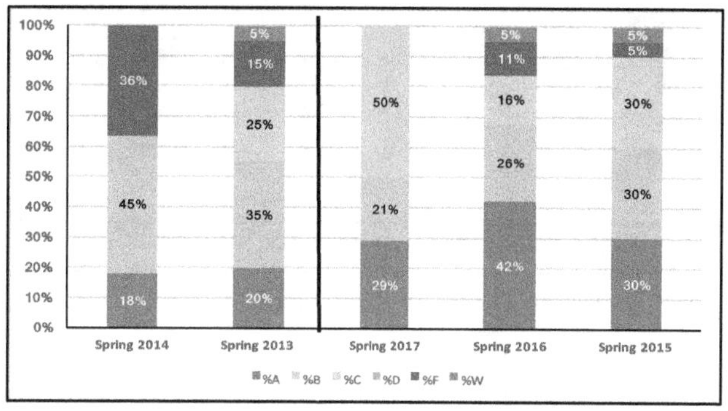

Figure 1: Grade Distributions for the Junior Class

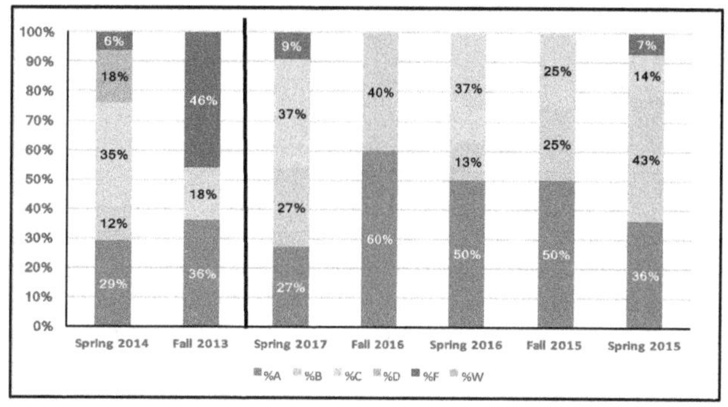

Figure 2: Grade Distributions for the Sophomore Class

Fig. 2 details the grade distributions for the sophomore class during the intervened (S17, F16, S16, F15, S15) and the non-intervened (S14, F13) semesters. Similar to the junior class, MRS intervention helped in reducing D/F/W rates from 35% to 3%. Unlike the junior class, the percentage of student receiving A or B grade enjoyed a substantial enhancement from 39% in non-intervened semesters to 74% in intervened semesters. Similar to the junior class, on average, more students received an A grade in treated semesters (45%) than the non-treated semesters (33%). These results, again, positively confirm both RQ1 and RQ2.

Student Survey: Table 5 shows the descriptive statistics for the student survey results gathered during all intervened semesters and thematically organized into two categories such as *perception of learning* and *perception of engagement.* These results represent a strong student approval of the proposed approach and positively attest RQ1. While considering positive questions (only) for all intervened semesters, students on average reported very high levels agreement on perceived learning and perceived engagement for both classes (Table 5). In order to investigate whether there is any statistically significant difference between the perceptions of students from the junior class and sophomore class, we compared the survey responses by using the

Table 5: Descriptive Statistics of Student Survey Results.

	Perception of Learning	Perception of Engagement
Junior Class (N: 47)	Mean = 3.76 Stdev = 0.02	Mean = 3.6 Stdev = 0.02
Sophomore class (N: 42)	Mean = 3.71 Stdev = 0.19	Mean = 3.62 Stdev = 0.20

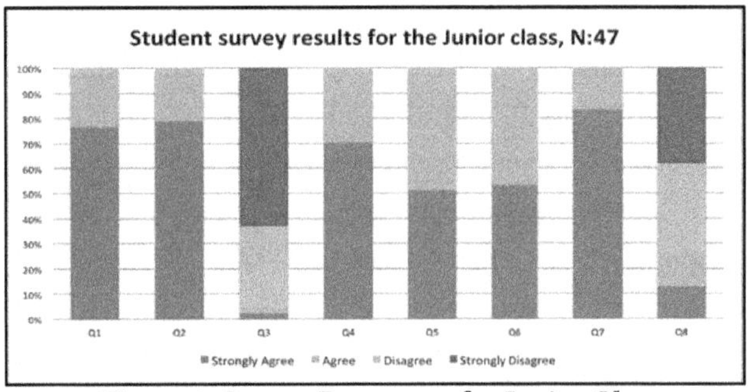

Figure 3: Survey Responses for Junior Class

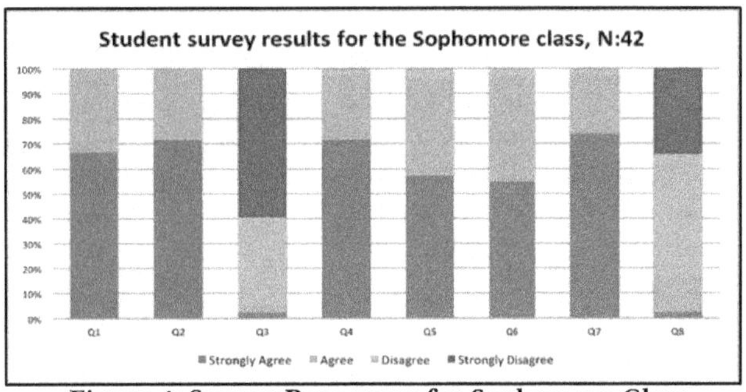

Figure 4: Survey Responses for Sophomore Class

Mann-Whitney U Test and the result came out as insignificant. However closer look at the question-wise responses for the junior class (Fig. 3) and the sophomore class (Fig. 4) reveal some interesting phenomenon. It is evident that, all students of the both groups equivocally appreciated the enhanced understanding (Q1) and visualization (Q2), while about 10% more junior students strongly approved them than the sophomore students. In both classes, a small percentage of the students (2% to 5%) did not find MRS to be enjoyable (Q4), preferable over paper-based exercises (Q5), or intuitive and easy to use (Q6). Similar percentage of students (~4%) in both classes also attested that they did not experience enhanced learning after using MRS (Q3). Interestingly, a substantial group of students complained about the additional workload that is involved with MRS (Q8). About 26% of the junior students confirmed that learning to maneuver the exercise Apps are additional work, whereas only 18% of the sophomore students found it to be difficult. As the junior course covers harder concepts and algorithms than the sophomore course, it is possible that a considerable number of students recognized the extra effort.

Students' Comments: The survey also contained two open-ended questions and 95% of the junior students taking the survey generously expressed their perspective in the comments section, where 70% of the sophomore students provided comments. The students' comments for both questions are categorized according to the themes that we observed and their distributions are shown in Table 6 and Table 7. Table 6 reflects that, students' positive attitude toward the visual way of learning and immediate feedback and their appreciation regards to the improved understanding of the difficult concepts arise frequently in their answers. However, junior students admired visual and interactive exercises considerably more than the sophomore students. On the other hand, sophomore students appreciated the detailed email feedback much more than the junior students. The students of the junior class found hands-on-learning and the use of back button more useful than the sophomore students; on the contrary, sophomore students really valued the repeated practice and the support for anonymous question.

Table 6: Response Distribution (%) for Question: "Tell us about the MRS features that you found to be most useful."

Themes	Junior class	Sophomore class
Immediate and automated grading	24%	24%
Visual and interactive exercises	22%	15%
Instant email feedback with correct and submitted answer	10%	18%
Improved understanding	15%	13%
Hands-on-learning	7%	0%
Use of back button	8%	2%
Immediately projected model sequence of interactions after completing the exercise	1%	4%
Immediately projected class-wise grade distribution	1%	6%
Repeated Practice	4%	8%
Better Exam Preparation	4%	2%
Instructors' in-class re-explanation	3%	0%
Anonymous Question	1%	8%

Table 7 reflects the distribution of student-suggested improvements of MRS and is extremely helpful for us to identify the current limitations of MRS and future enhancements. It should be noted that, many of these suggestions are already implemented in the later versions of MRS since their first appearance as comments. For example, currently MRS provides email feedback with correct and submitted answers, which was suggested by a group of students during earlier deployments. There were many App specific suggestions and bug reports and later versions of MRS addressed many of those suggestions successfully. A considerable number of students (especially junior) expressed the desire to receive the grade instantly as part of the App along with the detailed email feedback. Many students of the junior class wanted more algorithmic concepts to be supported my MRS, on the other hand, sophomore students wanted more frequent use of it in the classrooms. Both group of students expressed the desire to see MRS being adopted in the mid-term and final exams and in the other CS/IT classes, which clearly indicates their positive attitude towards it. Many students emphasized on downloading MRS and accessing the practice problems not only in the classrooms, but anytime and anywhere as they wish. Majority of the students suggested that a better, simpler and more appealing interface would benefit them more. A large group of junior students suggested having a "Reset" button in order to start from a clean slate, which would be much easier than pressing back buttons multiple times. The students' comments and suggestions provide a detailed insight for RQ3 and indicate that the students took the time to explore MRS, found it to be useful and wanted more and better use of it in future. The frequency distributions of respective themes (Table 6 & 7) also suggest that the junior and the sophomore students found different aspects of MRS appealing and their suggestions also vary significantly (RQ2).

Table 7: Response Distribution (%) for Question: "What would you suggest in order to improve MRS environment or your experience?"

	Junior	Sophomore
Add more concepts to MRS	16%	3%
Use more often in the classroom	6%	14%
Support for downloading the Apps in students' devices and for practicing the Apps anytime, anywhere.	3%	14%
App specific suggestions.	9%	13%
Show correct answer instantly and send it via email for future reference.	0%	3%
Add helpful "tips" in the Apps to steer student toward correct answer.	0%	3%
Port MRS to iOS/Apple device.	0%	6%
Better, simpler and more appealing interface.	17%	13%
Add Stylus to improve interaction.	3%	6%
Use MRS in other CS/IT classes.	3%	6%
Add virtual discussion board to participate in discussion outside of classroom.	0%	6%
Show grade instantly in App after completing the exercise.	15%	3%
Offer MRS-based midterm and final exam.	3%	3%
Fix bugs in the Apps.	3%	6%
Send grade by text message as opening and reading emails takes time.	0%	1%
Have a "Reset" button that will start the App from the beginning.	22%	0%

Instructors' comments: Both instructors appreciated the immediate grading, instant visualization of class grade distribution and App tracking data, anonymous questions, and the support for offering more practice problems to the students. By exploiting MRS, instructors could receive an instant snapshot of her classroom comprehension and could change the pace of the class dynamically such as broadcasting more challenging problems to the students instantly if the students comprehend concepts quicker. However, MRS-based classes need a considerable amount of organization and preparation in terms of updating the tablets with necessary Apps, creating the exercise definition (XML) file etc. At certain times during the junior class, the instructor found out that some students took too long to complete their exercises because of using the back button too many times since they did not understand the concept well enough to make a concrete decision. In those cases, the whole class had to wait for the slower students to complete before receiving their grades. However, the problem only occurs during the first few practices of an exercise and at certain times, instructor had to reduce the amount of allowed time to make the wait shorter for the rest of the class. The real-time "Back Button Usage" statistics provided by MRS also becomes helpful to detect such situations. These comments provide important insight regarding RQ4.

4. RELATED WORKS

TRAKLA2 [8] is the pioneering learning environment that supports algorithm simulation exercises, automatic assessment and visual feedback. JHAVÉ [9] is a java application that renders algorithm visualizations and allows learner explorations by pop-up questions. VisuAlgo [10] is an online collection of visualizations that generates questions for the learners to answer based on the content. OpenDSA [11] and related JSAV [12] supports algorithm visualization and proficiency exercises. However, all of them support content delivery via web browser and therefore utilized technologies such as HTML, Java, JavaScript etc. and none to our knowledge do so via native mobile App like MRS.

5. CONCLUSIONS

This paper presents the results of eight semester-long studies using MRS in two required CS courses at WSSU. More specifically, we studied the student-generated evidence of the strong and weak points of the MRS interventions and explored various research questions around those evidences. Our comparative study based on students' final course grade and course failing rate showed that the intervened group of students had better retention of the topics covered over the entire course and performed significantly better than the non-intervened group. Analysis of survey responses showed very high levels of agreement on perceived learning and perceived engagement. Answers to the open-ended questions revealed the mostly appreciated features of MRS and considerable differences were noticed between junior and sophomore responses. Instructor comments' identified few challenging aspects of deploying MRS in the classrooms Overall, students enjoyed MRS, explored it enough to suggest important improvements and expressed the desire to experience more of it beyond the two intervened courses. In future, the focus will be on making the App interface and IEs simpler and more appealing. We will also work toward extending MRS to support out-of-class practices and activities.

ACKNOWLEDGMENTS

This research was supported by National Science Foundation grant #1332531.

REFERENCES

[1] P. Black, & D. Wiliam, "Assessment and classroom learning" Assessment in Education: Principles, Policy & Practice, v.5, n.1, p.7–74, 1998.

[2] B. Bell, & B. Cowie, "The characteristics of formative assessment in science education", Science Education, v.85, n.5, p. 536–553, 2001.

[3] J. Hattie, "Visible learning: A synthesis of over 800 meta-analyses relating to achievement", New York, NY: Routledge, 2009.

[4] J. Hattie, & H. S. Timperley, "The power of feedback" Review of Educational Research, v.77, n.1, p.81–112, 2007.

[5] M. M. Fuad, D. Deb, J. Etim & C. Gloster, "Using Interactive Exercise in Mobile Devices to Support Evidence-based Teaching and Learning", 21st ACM Conference on Innovation and Technology in CS Education (ITiCSE), July, 2016.

[6] D. Deb, M. M. Fuad, M. Kanan, "Creating Engaging Exercises with Mobile Response Systems (MRS)", 48th ACM technical symposium on Computer science education (SIGCSE'17), March, 2017.

[7] Mobile Response System, mrs.altl.org, 2017.

[8] L. Malmi. et. al., "Visual algorithm simulation exercise system with automatic assessment: TRAKLA2", Informatics in Education, v.3 n.2 p.267–288, 2004.

[9] T. L. Naps, "Jhavé: Supporting algorithm visualization", Computer Graphics and Applications, IEEE, v.25 n.5 p.49- 55, 2005.

[10] S. Halim, et. al., "Learning algorithms with unified and +interactive web-based visualization," Olympiads in Informatics, v.6, p.53–68, 2012.

[11] E. Fouh, et. al., "Exploring students learning behavior with an interactive eTextbook in Computer Science Courses", Computers in Human Behavior n. 41, p. 478-485, 2014.

[12] V. Karavirta, C. A. Shaffer, "Creating Engaging Online Learning Material with the JSAV JavaScript Algorithm Visualization Library," in Learning Technologies, IEEE Transactions on, no.99, p.1-1, 2015.

Incorporating Computational Thinking in the Classrooms of Puerto Rico: How a MOOC Served as an Outreach and Recruitment Tool for Computer Science Education

Patricia Ordóñez Franco
University of Puerto Rico Río Piedras
San Juan, Puerto Rico
patricia.ordonez@upr.edu

Joseph Carroll-Miranda
University of Puerto Rico Río Piedras
San Juan, Puerto Rico
joseph.carroll@upr.edu

María López Delgado
University of Puerto Rico Río Piedras
San Juan, Puerto Rico
maria.lopez13@upr.edu

Eliud Gerena López
University of Puerto Rico Río Piedras
San Juan, Puerto Rico
eliud.genera@upr.edu

Grace Rodríguez Gómez
University of Puerto Rico Río Piedras
San Juan, Puerto Rico
grace.rodriguez6@upr.edu

ABSTRACT

This paper intends to share both the experience of teachers and document the research of the design, implementation, and evaluation of a massive open online course (MOOC). The primary purpose of the MOOC was to do outreach and build community to interest teachers from any discipline in Puerto Rico to incorporate Computational Thinking (CT) into their curriculum and peak their interest in Computer Science Education (CSE). Additional objectives were to use CT as a way to build self-efficacy in high school teachers as integrators of this newly gained knowledge while investigators learned the state of CSE and technology integration in schools of Puerto Rico. The MOOC titled Integrating Computational Thinking into the Curriculum was the first free online Professional Development offered to educators in Puerto Rico and has served as the launching board for the Computer Science Teachers' Association (CSTA) in Puerto Rico. This paper will describe the course's development, content and pertinent activities as they relate to the established goals of the project. Finally, it will share some vignettes of the educators' experiences as well as the results of a survey that was administered to 164 participants of the MOOC in its second rendition and had a 32% response rate.

CCS CONCEPTS

• **Applied computing** → **Distance learning**; • **Social and professional topics** → *Computational thinking*; *Informal education*; *Adult education*; K-12 education;

KEYWORDS

MOOC, Computational Thinking, K-12 Professional Development, Cultural Relevance

ACM ISBN 978-1-4503-5103-4/18/02...$15.00
https://doi.org/10.1145/3159450.3159544

ACM Reference Format:
Patricia Ordóñez Franco, Joseph Carroll-Miranda, María López Delgado, Eliud Gerena López, and Grace Rodríguez Gómez. 2018. Incorporating Computational Thinking in the Classrooms of Puerto Rico: How a MOOC Served as an Outreach and Recruitment Tool for Computer Science Education. In *Proceedings of The 49th ACM Technical Symposium on Computer Science Education (SIGCSE '18).* ACM, New York, NY, USA, 6 pages. https://doi.org/10.1145/3159450.3159544

1 INTRODUCTION

Much has been said about MOOCs. Some celebrate them as a revolutionary transformation of education, while other are more cautious to affirm such claims [13, 20]. Leaning more towards the side of caution, MOOCs need to be treated separately for they lack consistency in terms of design, mission, purpose and strategies [1]. Half a decade later, MOOC powerhouses like Coursera, have shifted to a common course management system that is currently exploring ways to improve their online education services [13, 20]. Issues such as language, instructional design, technical support and student mindset have generated more questions than answers as to what constitute a good MOOC experience.

Although it is not the focus of this paper, much has been published about MOOCs academic rigor, credentials, quality of education and economic viability [1]. Guzdial [12] raises salient points as he problematizes cookie cutter approaches to education such as: 1.Overelying on lectures; 2. Teachers are experts in their domain due to their pedagogical content knowledge; 3. Educators should be motivators instead of filters. Consistent with Guzdial, Bali [1] found that the generic approach of lecture-quiz-forum and low teacher participation undermines the MOOCs potential as a good educational experience.

There is much in the literature that argues both about the pros and cons of MOOCs. It all depends on the established objectives of the provider and the expectations of the user [15]. The bulk of the findings as to the effectiveness and impact of MOOCs are centered on the scenario of Higher Education.

In an attempt to identify patterns, tendencies, and communalities about MOOCs research and literature, Liyanagunawardena et al. [15] conducted a systematic study of MOOC literature from 2008-2012. A total of 45 peer reviewed papers about MOOCs were part of their study. In their analysis they identified 8 categories. These are: 1. introductory, explaining basic aspects of MOOCs; 2. concept, threats and opportunities of MOOCs in higher education; 3. MOOCs case studies; 4. educational theory; 5. technology, software and hardware used in MOOCs; 6. participant focus, perspective of the user; 7. provider focused, perspective of the creators, designers, and host organization; and 8. other for two papers that didn't fall into any other category. Nevertheless, in our research we have not encountered a research paper that concentrates on how a MOOC may be used as both outreach and motivation for CSE amongst educators in the K-12 scenario.

While in terms of participants, this course many not be considered a MOOC, it was designed as a MOOC for Puerto Rico with the intention of reaching the high school teachers of the entire country, but should be considered a hybrid MOOC pilot. It reached approximately 550 teachers across the island which is considerable given the technological and financial limitations of our project. Our experience with the *Integrating Computational Thinking into the Curriculum* MOOC offers a different perspective as to how MOOCS may be used beyond their predominant use in higher education. We expect that our experiences with this MOOC will contribute to the ongoing debate as to what are the different type of practices and what constitutes an effective MOOC experience. The design of this MOOC is a positive step for both creating good informal training experiences for working adults online and for motivating K-12 educators to integrate CS in their classrooms.

2 THE NEED FOR OUTREACH TO TEACHERS IN PUERTO RICO

The state of CSE in Puerto Rico is sparse. The island has a centralized educational system such that all courses and curriculums in the public schools must be approved by the Puerto Rico Department of Education (PRDE). Currently, the PRDE does not: a) have any CS curriculum in schools, b) offer any CS courses in schools, c) have any CS teacher certification or credentials, d) offer any Professional Development in CSE, and e) there is no teacher preparation program that prepares educators in CSE [19].

Prior to 2014, aside from a series of isolated summer camps and informal teacher training sessions, very little has been done to establish a statewide/national strategy to offer CSE in the schools of Puerto Rico[19]. Nonetheless, in spring of 2014, the College of Education and the Department of Computer Science of the University of Puerto Rico Río Piedras forged an alliance to advocate for the need to offer CSE in the schools of Puerto Rico. In fall of 2014, this alliance created an online professional development MOOC to integrate CT into the curriculum, an initiative financed by Google's CS4HS project. This MOOC had over 550 registered educators interested in CSE and served as both as an outreach and recruitment tool that promotes CSE in Puerto Rico. The CS4HS Puerto Rico project played an instrumental role in the process of facilitating the first constituency meeting for a CSTA chapter in PR in February 2016 [11]. The CSTA chapter of Puerto Rico was officially established in May 2016. All of its founding members were participants of our MOOC.

3 OBJECTIVES

The MOOC, named *Integrating Computational Thinking into the High School Curriculum in Puerto Rico*, was sponsored by Google's CS4HS initiative and was originally targeted for high school teachers. However, it soon became clear to us that the principles could apply to any teacher in K-12. The first edition was offered in the spring of 2015. We had little registration until the Tuesday before the MOOC began. That day an advertisement was posted in a local paper and in one night, 74 teachers signed up for the course. By Saturday, February 7, 2015 (the course start date) and first face-to-face meeting, we had 184 teachers registered and 35 appear in person. By February 28, 2015 when we closed the registration, we had 228 teachers signed up. We had requests from 12 more teachers from all over the island until the end of the MOOC on May 7, 2015.

The second edition of the MOOC in the spring of 2016, 390 teachers signed up by the first face-to-face meeting on Saturday, February 28, 2016. By the time we closed registration on March 20, 2016 we had 459 teachers registered for the course. Out of those only 347 registered on Piazza and only 181 activated their accounts.

In both cases, the number of people that actually registered for the course is higher than the ones which participated. Although a high drop out rate in MOOCs is very common, we suspect that requiring registration on two learning management systems, Piazza and Moodle, may have been a factor. Piazza was selected as the means for communication, and Moodle as the content keeper and manager of submissions and grades.Thus, the interest by teachers in the integrating computing into their non-CS classrooms is strong in Puerto Rico, whereas resources are not. Most programs in Puerto Rico for computing focus on students and entrepreneurs. The creation of the course sparked the creation of other initiatives such as C3Tec [4] and CodeTrotters [5] which focus on educator professional development. This MOOC laid the ground work for current initiatives and efforts to incorporate CS into the curriculum of all K-12 schools on the island.

The primary objective of the MOOC was to do outreach to create a community of non-CS educators who would be interested in incorporating CT in their curriculum. By introducing them to an interdisciplinary way of incorporating CT into their courses, we expected to be able to identify the educators with the most potential in becoming future CS curriculum builders. We also used this online course as the basis to conduct a survey on the state of CSE in Puerto Rico by tying participation in the course to a needs assessment survey of the school. The participants were asked to measure the state of Technology Infrastructure and Use of Technology, and to find Potential Content Knowledge Experts for curriculum development in the future at each school.

Other objectives included creating a course that was culturally relevant to Puerto Rican educators across the island. We wanted it to align with teachers' schedules and be accessible to everyone. By creating a MOOC, teachers from all parts of Puerto Rico and even in other Spanish-speaking countries were able to register and view a course in Spanish that taught them what CT was in their native language and explained to them the importance of incorporating it in all disciplines. The concept was that the course would be taught by Puerto Rican Professors and Developers for Puerto Ricans. In the process of design, we asked the professors to add Puerto Rican slang and references so that participants could relate with the material. The intent was to motivate the teachers as they saw professors from one of the top universities on the island that spoke like them.

For futher motivation, the Center for Excellence in Academia (CEA) [17] of the University of Puerto Rico Río Piedras, also, offered each module of the course as part of its online curriculum. The College of Graduate Education and the Department of Computer Science of the UPRRP provided certificates for every module that was completed to emphasize that each module was an accomplishment and the CEA provided certificates for anyone who completed the MOOC to give a greater incentive for the teachers to complete the course.

Originally, the primary objectives of the hybrid online course were to:

(1) Create a community of high school educators who are interested in integrating CT into their curriculum,
(2) Identify potential CS curriculum developers around the island,
(3) Conduct research on the state of technological infrastructures and use of technology in Puerto Rico' high schools,
(4) Generate awareness of both the pervasiveness and interdisciplinary nature of CS in the world today,
(5) Use CT as a way to build self-efficacy in high school teachers as integrators of computational thinking into their curriculum and as potential future developers of a CS curriculum in their respective schools, and
(6) Design an online course in CT that is offered in Spanish for Puerto Ricans and was developed by Puerto Ricans.

While the objectives for the MOOC were designed for High School teachers, many teachers of other levels were eager to take the class and we allowed them to do so. The participants were required to turn in their projects in a particular format, so that the MOOC became a course that generated content for a future website which would host the developed activities. The collaboration between the College of Education and the PR Department of Education allowed for the creation of content that would adhere to the upcoming standards in Computational Thinking from the Computer Science Teachers Association (CSTA) and the standards of each subject as set by the PRDE.

To create a community, we had three face-to-face meetings in San Juan, PR. The first two face-to-face meetings were designed to create community among the participants and have those participants serve as leaders in the online community. In the first meeting, we focused on explaining the problem with the lack of diversity in the field of computing and explained what CT was and why it was important for them to incorporate it into their courses. Then participants shared why they had come. Many stated that they realized the importance of doing so because otherwise their students were going to fall behind or that they felt they personally were falling behind in their own lives in terms of technology and welcomed the opportunity to improve their personal experience with technology at no cost. One teacher even drove over two hours across the island to attend the meeting. We did an activity that emphasized the importance of creating community and becoming leaders in the online community so that teachers would not feel alone.

The second face-to-face meeting was designed to build the educators' self-efficacy in completing the course by having them learn to program in Python, whether or not they would be using it in their classroom. The class basically consisted of following one of the two videos offered in the course, the intermediate or beginner video, but having experienced mentors helping participants through the course by doing the video step-by-step with the class. To our surprise, no one registered for the intermediate video. When we completed the day, everyone who attended (except for one teacher who arrived several hours late) had written their first program and the excitement was in the air as can be seen in the following documentary about the day [9]. Many of these teachers became leaders online for the course in both sessions.

The third face-to-face meeting was the graduation ceremony where we handed out certificates and a gift to participants. We had a keynote speaker for the first edition of the MOOC with the Chief Information Officer of Puerto Rico at the time, Giancarlo González, who is continues to be one of the most vocal advocates of CSE on the island. The first year we gave t-shirts with the logos and the second year USBs sticks with the logo of the university. Everyone received a certificate the first year, but in the second year we only gave paper certificates to those that completed the entire course and emailed electronic certificates to everyone else in the hope that it would inspire more people to complete the course. In the second year that the course was offered, the community had grown to the point that we were able to create a CSTA Puerto Rico with participants from both cohorts, founded in May 2016, instead of having a keynote speaker.

4 COURSE DEVELOPMENT

The development of the MOOC on a low cost budget required over 30 volunteers of whom 10 were faculty of the University of Puerto Rico Río Piedras (UPRRP), 10 students of the UPRRP, 15 videographers from the community, and required the teaching of the videotaping software to all professors and students involved. A professional videographer was hired to help create videos to promote the MOOC. An administrative assistant was hired to help with the paperwork of the project. Two students were hired as Teaching Assistants for the course every semester. Everyone else was a volunteer. The MOOC was a six week course spread over February to May. We also created a promotional video to recruit educators for the MOOC filmed and editted by a professional videographer in Puerto Rico, Javier Colón [6].

4.1 Technology Used

For the building of the course, we used the same technology that Sal Khan of Kahn Academy did - Camtasia Studio 8 for video recording and editing, the Wacom Bamboo Wireless Touchpad with digital stylus, which allowed you to draw on Microsoft Power Point Presentations, and a laptop. Because we wanted complete autonomy, we bought a domain name on Namecheap and created the online platform with a WordPress Template for the webpage to recruit teachers [11]. The Moodle Learning Management System was incorporated through the Namecheap website. We used Google Forms for registration to stay within the $15K budget.

4.2 First academic year (2014-2015)

The first year we focused on creating the course and had difficulty recruiting a programmer for the project, and thus, one of the investigators became the web develper for the project. Therefore, in the first semester, the investigators and one student assistant worked to recruit the best professors to teach the course and the students for the promotional video. As a result, the investigators had to create the course as it was taking place. The investigators taught two more student assistants how to create a video in the first month and the students learned to edit the videos to make them more interactive. From then on, each student and investigator had a computer and taught one of the professors how to create a video. We purchased five laptops to have everyone creating and editing courses in parallel.

In the second semester, the two student assistants were hired as Teaching Assistants. The Teaching Assistants took responsibility for editing the videos and doing technical support. The investigators worked with the professors on creating the videos. Once the course began, the four ran the MOOC where teaching assistants managed Piazza and the investigators focused on organizing the in-person events and creating the course in Moodle. All professors worked for the promotional video session and in creating their own video.

4.3 Challenges

Given the limited budget, we had several challenges to overcome to make the course run. Most of the budget went to the purchasing of the hardware and software, and the payment of teaching assistants, food for face-to-face activities, and video production. The recruitment of professors and students was also a challenge due to the novelty of the course and the volunteer time required to learn the technology and create the course. Other significant challenges were 1) finding a location for in-person meetings for the courses, 2) paying contractors on time, 3) marketing in the first year, 4) relying on an online server for the course, and 5) battling the skeptical reactions of participants when creating the MOOC.

5 COURSE DESCRIPTION

The MOOC was based on the definition of Computational Thinking of the ISTE and the CSTA [14] which is described as a problem-solving process that includes the following characteristics:

- Formulate problems in a way that enables us to use a computer
- Logically organize and analyze data
- Representing data through abstractions such as models and simulations
- Automate solutions through algorithmic thinking (a series of ordered steps)
- Identify, analyze, and implement possible solutions with the goal of achieving the most efficient and effective combination of steps and resources
- Generalize and transfer this problem solving process to a wide variety of problems

Thus, the developers of the course aimed to reinforce the learning of CT by having volunteer professors of the UPRRP apply the above techniques to the creation of an activity that educators can integrate into one of their courses in their respective disiciplines. The professors were recruited as volunteers and were selected for their reputation for being excellent teachers. We also aimed to recruit Puerto Rican professors with the belief that they would serve as greater motivation for Puerto Rican educators and create more culturally relevant curriculum. The only exception was one of the authors of the paper who is of Colombian descent, but was selected because of her expertise in equity in CSE.

5.1 Design

In designing the MOOC, we wanted to consider the demanding life style of a high school teacher and provide the necessary flexibility to allow for educators to successfully complete the course. Thus, we started the course early in the semester in February, and spread out the six modules of the course over several months and completed it in early May. We did not assign work over spring break, and we allowed teachers to turn in their homework two weeks late and even more if necessary. We also decided to make the course a hybrid course in that the first lecture was given in person to whomever could attend so that we could create community of teachers to lead the online course through a tool called Piazza.

5.2 Content

The course consisted of six online modules with the option of the third module in person at the university with mentors.

5.2.1 *Module 1: Introduction to Computational Thinking and Computer Science.*

Instructors: *Joseph Carroll Miranda & Patricia Ordóñez.* ***Description:*** The objective of the first week was to instill in the teachers the urgency for completing the course by highlighting the importance of equity for the women and Latinos in the computing and technology world. This module presented the theoretical and pedagogical concepts that define Computational Thinking particularly those pedagogical models that support and sustain the integration of CT into the curriculum. The introduction to Computer Science was embedded in a discussion of the research Stuck in the Shallow End by Jane Margolis, Joanna Goode and others to emphasize the importance of equity in Computer Science Education [16]. ***Objective:*** To motivate participants to complete the course and to build self-efficacy so that they are able to integrate CT into their curriculum. To emphasize the importance of offering Computer Science Education for all.

5.2.2 *Module 2: Computational Thinking without Computers.*

Instructors: *Luis López & María López.* ***Description:*** Given the lack of consistent access to internet and technology in schools, this module introduces a series of activities that demonstrate how you can integrate computational thinking into the curriculum without the use of computers. ***Objective:*** To share games and pedagogical activities based on many exercises derived from CS Unplugged [3] that can foment the development of computational thinking for the solving of problems and to build self-efficacy.

5.2.3 *Module 3: Introduction to Programming in Python.*

Instructors: *Sasha Méndez & Rafael Arce Nazario.* ***Description:*** This module provided an introduction to programming using Python at the command line or Trinket [18], which is a visual web-based interface for Python designed for novice programmers. Participants only needed to complete one of the two tracks but were encouraged to try both. A "Codeathon" was held on a Saturday morning in the Department of Computer Science at the UPRRP where the primary intructors and the teaching assistants of the course provided step-by-step support as each participant completed the module. Afterwards, participants enjoyed lunch to celebrate their achievements and create community. ***Objective:*** To provide a positive first coding experience for teachers with caring and patient mentors and help build the self-efficacy of the participants for programming.

5.2.4 Module 4: Ethics, Intellectual Property, Netiquette and Cyberbullying.

Instructors: *José Alejandro Medina Cruz, Ramphis Castro, Margarita Delgado.* ***Description:*** This module was designed to expose participants to the concepts of Cybersecurity and Intellectual Property through a discussion amongst experts in the field. It was also designed to serve as a change of pace and to allow participants to catch up with the material in the course. It aims to introduce the participants to the importance of teaching students about Netiquette and the dangers of the cyberbullying and the internet. ***Objective:*** To explain concepts of intellectual property and emphasize the importance of addressing netiquette (etiquette for the Internet), cyberbullying, and cybersecurity with their students.

5.2.5 Module 5: Integrating Computational Thinking into Your Curriculum.

Instructors: *Kariluz Dávila, Carmen Pacheco, Luis López, Mayra Lebrón.* ***Description:*** This module provides concrete examples of how professors from the University of Puerto Río Piedras have integrated Computational Thinking into their curriculum. There are examples in Chemistry, Learning Technology, Mathematics and Physics. ***Objective:*** To share a series of activities that integrate computational thinking into the curriculum. Examples from a range of disciplines were provided as mentioned in the Description. In the future, we aim to add an example for non-STEM disciplines such as English, Spanish and History on using logical operators for Google search.

5.2.6 Module 6: Integrating a Computational Thinking Activity into your Course.

Instructor:*Joseph Carroll Miranda.* ***Description:*** This module was designed to motivate the participants to develop pedagogical activities that integrate Computational Thinking into the curriculum that they teach. ***Objective:*** To motivate and offer direct support in the process of designing and developing a diverse set of pedagogical activities that integrate computational thinking into the curriculum of the participant.

6 CONCLUSIONS

The primary purpose of the MOOC was to do outreach and build community to interest teachers from any discipline in Puerto Rico to incorporate Computational Thinking into their curriculum and peak their interest in CSE. Additional objectives were to use CT as a way to build self-efficacy in high school teachers as integrators of this newly gained knowledge while learning the state of computing education and technology integration in schools of Puerto Rico. In order to assess the effectiveness of the MOOC, we conducted an online survey with 164 participants for which we received Institutional Review Board approval. Out of those 164 participants a total of 51 answered the survey (31%). Approximately 32% of the MOOC were participants from January-May of 2016. Through their answers, we evaluated our effectiveness with the following objectives:

(1) Create a community of educators who are interested in integrating Computational Thinking into their curriculum,
(2) Identify potential Computer Science curriculum educators around the island,
(3) Generate awareness of both the pervasiveness and interdisciplinary nature of Computer Science,
(4) Use Computational Thinking as a way to build self-efficacy as they integrate CT into their classrooms, and
(5) Conduct research on the state of technological infrastructures and use of technology in Puerto Rico's schools.

6.1 Self-Efficacy

Self-efficacy is one's self-belief in one's ability to succeed at or complete a task [2]. Confidence in the understanding of the concepts essential for success in the course is one of the strongest experiences that this MOOC provided to educators. The concepts used to document self-efficacy on a 5 point Likert scale were: 1. Computational Thinking; 2. Breaking down the problem; 3. Abstraction; and 4. Algorithms. With the concept of computational thinking, 60% strongly agreed and 37.5% agreed they had a better understanding of this concepts thanks to their experience with the MOOC. In addition, 45% participants strongly agreed, while 45% of participants agreed with the statement of being more comfortable with the concept of computational thinking. Considering the concept of breaking down problem, 32.5% strongly agreed and 55% agreed they felt more comfortable with this concept. With the concept of abstraction, 57.5% agreed and 15.5% strongly agreed that they felt more comfortable. In addition, with the concept of algorithms, 30% strongly agreed and 57.5% agreed that they felt confident with this concept. In terms of self- efficacy, 62.5% strongly agreed and 32.5% agreed that computational thinking will help them integrate technology into their classroom, while 50% strongly agreed and 32.5% agreed that they feel more comfortable integrating technology into their classrooms thanks to their experience with the MOOC.

6.2 Generating Awareness

Findings from the survey attest that this MOOC helped to generate awareness around Computer Science. As a result of this MOOC, 55% of our participants strongly agreed while 37.5% agreed with the statement: "This course changed the vision I had of Computer Science." Furthermore, the research helps document that one of the ways our participants' vision of Computer Science changed was by 42.5% of our participants strongly agrees and 55% agreed with the following statement: "I am conscious of the ubiquity and interdisciplinary nature of Computer Science." Finally 43.6% of our participants strongly agree and 51.3% agree with the statement:

"This course changed my perception of the Computer Science professional."

6.3 Motivation

Our research documented how MOOC participants were motivated by their experience with the course. 55% of participants both strongly agreed and 42.5% agreed that they were motivated to learn how to code. 42.5% of participants both strongly agreed and 40% agreed that they were motivated to teach their students how to code. Participants after the MOOC were motivated to incorporate Computational Thinking into their classroom by indicating that 50% strongly agreed and 40% agreed to do so. Probably the biggest impact in terms of motivation, we found that 62.4% strongly agreed and 30% agreed expressed interest in being certified as a Computer Science educator.

6.4 Building CSE Advocacy

As a result with their experiences with MOOC, we found that 64% strongly agreed and 32.5% agreed with the statement : "The integration of Computational Thinking into curricula is important." In addition our participants indicated that 60% strongly agreed and 37.5% believe that Computational Thinking should be incorporated in the curriculum of all schools in Puerto Rico. Moreover, 61.5% of the participants strongly agreed and 33.3% agreed that Computer Science should be taught in all schools of the island.

6.5 Tech Infrastructure and Use

This research documented a disparity in the ratio of technology infrastructure versus technology use. An overwhelming 95% of participants indicated that their schools had Internet access. While 97% of participants had personal access to the Internet in their schools, an interesting fact worth mentioning is that an overwhelming 95% indicated that they provided their own technology in their classroom. This contrasted with 72% that indicated that the school provides technology to be used in the classroom.

When asked what type of technology they used in the classroom, 78% indicated they had a laptop or PC in the classroom, 80% said they had a projector in their classroom, while 25% indicated they had a smartboard in their classroom. Furthermore, the research documented that 75% of students have access to Internet in the school, 65% of students have Internet access in their classroom, 90% had access to a public space pc or laptop. Nevertheless, it is interesting to note that although there is a high penetration rate in terms of access to Internet and equipment, the actual use of such in the classroom is not as common. This research documented that 43% have access to computers in the classroom, 48% of students bring their own device, and 48% have access to mobile devices in the classroom. In terms of technology courses offered in the schools, only 48% of the participants indicated they had some course relating to technology in the school. Many of them expressed that the technological courses in the schools deal with MS Office literacy. This is fairly consistent with the findings of the research conducted by Margolis [16].

7 ACKNOWLEDGEMENTS

Our thanks to Google for Education's CS4HS Program [10] for funding this effort and then to the many, many volunteers who committed their time or charged much lower for their time in order to create the course and be able to offer it for two years. This course would not have been possible without the cooperation of Xiomara Figueroa Fontanez and Roxana González Burgos, undergraduate students majoring in Computer Science at the time and co-founders of Include Girls [8], who helped in the writing of the proposal and provided much creativity to the concept of how to recruit teachers for the course. Many thanks to Javier Colón, the founder of Spanglish Films [6], who brought a large crew to help create the high quality promotional videos that will motivate teachers and students for many years to come. Thanks also to thirty plus faculty and student volunteers who participated in the creation of the course and promotional videos and are noted in the credits of the videos [7].

REFERENCES

[1] Maha Bali. 2014. MOOC pedagogy: Gleaning good practice from existing MOOCs. *MERLOT Journal of Online Learning and Teaching* 10 (03/2014 2014), 44–56. http://jolt.merlot.org/vol10no1/bali_0314.pdf
[2] Albert Bandura. 1977. Self-efficacy: Toward a unifying theory of behavioral change. *Psychological Review* 84, 2 (March 1977), 191–215.
[3] Tim Bell, Ian Witten, and Michael Fellows. 2017. CS Unplugged: Computer Science without a Computer. (2017). Retrieved December 7, 2017 from http://csunplugged.org
[4] C3TEC. 2017. Centro Criollo de Ciencia y Tecnologia del Caribe. (2017). Retrieved December 7, 2017 from http://c3tec.org/inicio
[5] Codetrotters. 2017. Rock star coding onsight or online. (2017). Retrieved December 7, 2017 from http://www.codetrotters.com/
[6] Javier Colon. 2017. Spanglish Films. (2017). Retrieved December 8, 2017 from http://www.spanglishfilms.com/
[7] Javier Colon and Patricia Ordonez. 2015. Why CS should be in High Schools: Voices from CS students. (2015). Retrieved September 1, 2017 from https://youtu.be/AQVhGUioUyI
[8] Xiomara Figueroa, Cassandra Schaening, and Roxana Gonzalez. 2016. Include Girls. (2016). Retrieved December 8, 2017 from https://www.facebook.com/includeGirls/
[9] Spanglish Films. 2016. CS4HS Puerto Rico Hackathon 2015. (2016). Retrieved September 1, 2017 from https://vimeo.com/128060748
[10] Google for Education. 2017. Educator Grants Application Process. (2017). https://edu.google.com/computer-science/educator-grants/process.html.
[11] Roxana Gonzalez and Patricia Ordonez. 2016. Google CS for HS Puerto Rico. (2016). Retrieved September 1, 2017 from http://cs4hspuertorico.org/
[12] Mark Guzdial. 2013. MOOCs are a fundamental misperception of how teaching works. (2013). https://computinged.wordpress.com/2013/01/04/moocs-are-a-fundamental-misperception-of-how-learning-works/
[13] Phil Hill. 2016. MOOCs are Dead. Long live online higher education. (Sept. 2016). Retrieved September 1, 2017 from http://www.chronicle.com/article/MOOCs-Are-Dead-Long-Live/237569
[14] ISTE and CSTA. 2017. Operational Definition of Computational Thinking for K-12 Education. (2017). Retrieved September 1, 2017 from http://www.iste.org/docs/ct-documents/computational-thinking-operational-definition-flyer.pdf
[15] Tharindu Liyanagunawardena, Andrew Adams, and Shirley Williams. 2013. MOOCs: A systematic study of the published literature 2008-2012. *The International Review of Research in Open and Distributed Learning* 14, 3 (2013), 202–227. http://www.irrodl.org/index.php/irrodl/article/view/1455
[16] Jane Margolis. 2008. *Stuck in the Shallow End: Education, Race, and Computing.* The MIT Press, Cambridge, MA.
[17] University of Puerto Rico Rio Piedras. 2017. Centro para la Excelencia Academica. (2017). Retrieved September 1, 2017 from http://cea.uprrp.edu/
[18] Trinket. 2017. Code is Your Canvas. (2017).
[19] Kiara Sofia Vega-Bellido. 2016. Why Puerto Rican Students need to take computer science education into their own hands. (2016). Retrieved September 1, 2017 from https://www.cienciapr.org/en/blogs/uprm-science-communication-initiative/why-puerto-rican-students-need-take-computer-science
[20] Jeffrey R. Young. 2016. Are MOOCs forever? (Sept. 2016). Retrieved September 1, 2017 from http://www.chronicle.com/article/Are-MOOCs-Forever-/237130

Increasing Student Self-Efficacy in Computational Thinking via STEM Outreach Programs

Russell Feldhausen
Kansas State University
Manhattan, Kansas
russfeld@ksu.edu

Joshua Levi Weese
Kansas State University
Manhattan, Kansas
weeser@ksu.edu

Nathan H. Bean
Kansas State University
Manhattan, Kansas
nhbean@ksu.edu

ABSTRACT

This paper describes our experiences developing and teaching two different interventions focused on computational thinking and computer science at a yearly STEM outreach program hosted by a local school district. We describe the creation of our lesson plans, how we worked with experienced and pre-service teachers alike to deliver the lessons, and how we assessed the effectiveness of each intervention. We will discuss our successes and failures, and provide information on our future plans to incorporate more formalized education theory, pedagogy, and research methodology in future years to further this project.

Based on our assessment results, we observed statistically significant gains in student self-efficacy with creating computer programs that perform a variety of operations. In addition, students reported a significantly higher understanding of how computer programming can be used in daily life. Our survey also highlighted differences in student self-efficacy between the two interventions, and we discuss possible sources for that result. We discuss observed results based on student groups with various backgrounds, previous STEM experiences, and socioeconomic status.

CCS CONCEPTS

• **Social and professional topics → K-12 education**; *Computational thinking*; *Student assessment*;

KEYWORDS

pedagogy; self-efficacy; stem; outreach; k-12; middle school

ACM Reference Format:

Russell Feldhausen, Joshua Levi Weese, and Nathan H. Bean. 2018. Increasing Student Self-Efficacy in Computational Thinking via STEM Outreach Programs. In *SIGCSE '18: The 49th ACM Technical Symposium on Computer Science Education, February 21–24, 2018, Baltimore , MD, USA.* ACM, New York, NY, USA, 6 pages. https://doi.org/10.1145/3159450.3159593

1 INTRODUCTION

As the world becomes more reliant on technology, it is vital for students to learn relevant skills for navigating an increasingly computerized society. By introducing computational thinking (CT) to students in middle school, educators hope to have a positive impact on students' interest in computer science (CS) as well as their comfort level working with technology. Unfortunately, many K-12 curriculum standards do not include these skills. [6, 27] STEM (science, technology, engineering, mathematics) outreach programs are one effective way to introduce students to CS and CT. They provide freedom for educators to teach skills and subjects outside the normal curriculum standards, and create a fun and positive atmosphere for students to learn about possible future college majors and careers. [39]

A local school district invited us to assist with bringing CS to an ongoing STEM outreach program. We developed two intervention lesson plans to teach CT concepts to middle school students through this partnership. We collaborated with experienced educators and pre-service teachers to present the lessons to several cohorts of students, and collected assessment data on how the interventions impacted student self-efficacy with CT concepts.

2 RELATED WORK

In her seminal Viewpoint article, Wing described CT as a "fundamental skill for everyone." [40] She further expanded her definition in 2011, describing it as "the thought processes involved in formulating problems and their solutions so that the solutions are represented in a form that can be effectively carried out by an information-processing agent." [41] This clearly implies that, while learning programming definitely teaches CT, there is a much broader realm of knowledge that fits this definition. Indeed, the Royal Society provided another take on CT, stating that it "is the process of recognising aspects of computation in the world that surrounds us, and applying tools and techniques from Computer Science to understand and reason about both natural and artificial systems and processes." [33] Using that definition, it is clear that CT can be applied to and taught within a variety of STEM fields.

Brennan and Resnick provided a more concrete definition for CT in terms of computational concepts, practices, and perspectives through their study of the Scratch [23] programming environment. [8] Similarly, Google also uses a list of concepts and skills to further define CT. [19] Weese and Feldhausen created a list of CT concepts and related CS principles based on those works, adapted below in Table 1, which informed the curriculum design in this work. [37]

Efforts to include CT in existing K-12 curricula are ongoing, but the progress is slow. Many states within the United States have voluntarily adopted the Common Core State Standards [26] and Next Generation Science Standards [35] within their K-12 schools. Reviews by Pokorny [27] and Bienkowski [6] individually state that while each set of standards include applicable mathematical

SIGCSE '18, February 21–24, 2018, Baltimore , MD, USA

ACM ISBN 978-1-4503-5103-4/18/02...$15.00
https://doi.org/10.1145/3159450.3159593

Table 1: CT Concepts and Related Computer Science Principles [37]

Abbr.	Description
ALG	**Algorithmic thinking** - sequence of steps that complete a task. Operators and expressions are also included
ABS	**Abstraction** - generalized representation of a complex problem, ignoring extraneous information
DEC	**Problem decomposition** - breaking a problem into smaller, more manageable parts that can be solved independently of each other
DAT	**Data** - collection, representation, and analysis of data [19]
PAR	**Parllelization** - simultaneous processing of a task [19]
CON	**Control flow** - directs an algorithm's steps when to complete
IAI	**Incremental and iterative** - building small parts of the program at each step instead of the whole program at once
TAD	**Testing and debugging** - performing intermediate testing and fixing problems while developing
QUE	**Questioning** - working to understand each part of the code instead of using code that is not understood well
USE	**Reuse and Remix** - making use of other people's work and resources to solve a problem

or CT skills, they fall short of deeply integrated CT. The Computer Science Teachers Association (CSTA) has also published a set of broad curricular standards for K-12 education, [3] based on the K-12 Computer Science Framework, [21] but our state has not adopted those standards. Wiebe et al. shared results of a statewide survey of student attitudes toward STEM fields, showing the importance of increased awareness and frequent exposure to STEM in encouraging students to consider future STEM careers. Since students may not be getting that exposure in the classroom due to limited support for CT and CS in K-12 standards, we must look to after-school outreach programs to fill the gap and connect students to STEM fields and practicing professionals. [39]

Research by Tai et al. published in the journal *Science* shows that, among students graduating with a 4-year college degree who were previously asked in 8th grade to list their possible future careers at age 30, those who expected to have a science-based career were "1.9 times more likely to earn a life science baccalaureate degree," and "3.4 times more likely to earn physical science and engineering degrees than students without similar expectations." [36] Similarly, that research showed that students with high mathematics scores were also much more likely to graduate with physical science and engineering degrees. This clearly demonstrates that early interest in science and mathematics, two major parts of STEM, has a large impact in future career choices.

In 2014, a group of CS education researchers concluded that "[t]he greatest need in providing computing education in schools is to provide more teachers." [13] Bean et al. described a program training pre-service teachers in CT, with the goal of encouraging them to integrate more CT and programming into their future classrooms. [5] The STEM program described below similarly involves pre-service teachers to achieve the same goal.

There are many methods to assess CT in students. One possibility is to use evidence-centered design to create assessments and quantitatively measure student learning outcomes. [32] However, due to the informal and fun nature of STEM outreach programs, this approach was deemed unreasonable.

Another approach is to measure student self-efficacy, described by Bandura as "how people judge their capabilities" and the effect that judgement has on their own "motivation and behavior." [4] Ramalingam et al. studied the self-efficacy of students before and after a programming class, and compared that to the measured mental models of the participants. They found that not only do most students experience significant gains in self-efficacy, but student self-efficacy itself was a significant predictor of student performance, along with the student's own mental model. [29] Lishinski et al. furthered this work by studying how self-efficacy and "self-regulated learning" aspects relate to course performance over time. They confirmed that self-efficacy is the strongest predictor of student performance in classes when compared to other predictors such as student goals and metacognitive strategies. [24]

3 INTERVENTION DESIGN

We developed two different interventions for this STEM outreach program, each for a different age group and with a different theme. Each intervention included four 3-hour sessions each week, and was presented to four different groups of 12 to 18 students each summer. Below we discuss the design of each intervention, focusing on our own intentions and thoughts when developing the interventions. More details on the interventions can be found in Weese and Feldhausen [37] and online. [18]

3.1 Saving the Martian

Saving the Martian is an intervention for 5th and 6th grade students that focuses on introducing CT through unplugged activities and scaffolded examples using the Scratch programming environment. We found inspiration in the book *The Martian*, by Andy Weir, [38] by looking for scenarios that could be generalized into activities for the class, such as the protagonist's struggle to grow food and communicate. We could then use the book to provide additional framing for the activities along with the field of space travel, hoping to engage students with an interesting theme. The class focused on four primary areas: programming, algorithms, data, and artificial intelligence. Each area included unplugged activities, scaffolded programming exercises, and discussion of how each related to CS and other topics.

As we introduced programming via the Scratch environment, we related programming terms to the familiar concept of a school play. We also used activities to create simple programs, clearly describing the thought processes a programmer would use to complete the task, while giving students ample time to experiment and build their own knowledge. This process follows the paradigms of educational constructivism and constructionism popularized by Piaget and Papert. [2] To introduce algorithms, we used sorting algorithms in both unplugged and programming activities, coupled with a discussion of simple algorithmic analysis to compare different algorithms for the same task. We also created simple computer simulations to manipulate data variables, showing how chemical reactions would take place in order to grow food on Mars. When dealing with data, students learned both binary and hexadecimal number systems, as well as ASCII, all to build a program to translate communicated data. We also included some ambiguous messages in our activity, prompting a discussion of reliable communication methods. Finally, our activities for artificial intelligence included a discussion of the Turing test, an unplugged activity introducing artificial neural networks, and programming projects to create perceptron-based AIs for video games and navigation.

Throughout the week, we focused on blending both unplugged and programming activities to show how CT and CS work in different fields. We also provided outside information and expansive framing whenever possible to link our activities and CS in general to the broader world. By showing how CS can have an impact in everyone's daily lives, we hope to encourage students to consider CS as a future career.

3.2 Mighty Micro Controllers

Mighty Micro Controllers (MMC) is an intervention for 7th through 9th grade students, focused on teaching CT through programming Arduino Uno micro controllers using Scratch, the Arduino IDE, and a text-based language. Our goal for MMC was to use physical computing as a means to engage students with CS and CT, which has been shown to be successful. [25, 28] The format of this class included guided examples creating simple circuits and programs, followed by problem-driven exploration to build programming, electrical, and CT skills. We also used pair programming extensively to further aid student success. [7]

We taught students the basic principles of electricity, circuits, and signals. As these concepts are new to many students, it can be overwhelming at first, so we drew upon unplugged examples to manage the challenge. For example, we adopted Kuphalt's physical illustration of electricity using marbles flowing in a hula-hoop. [22] Similarly, students were challenged to rank resistors from weakest to strongest through a hands-on experiment by plugging the resistors into a blinking LED circuit, discovering that the weaker resistors let the LED shine bright, while the strongest let nearly no light out at all.

Each successive activity had an increasing focus on CT. These were scaffolded to emphasize the CT and software side of micro controllers, rather than the physical implementation. Students were given detailed circuit diagrams for each activity, and guided through the steps to enable the required pins on the Arduino. This left students to program their own ideas into each activity. With most of the circuits done with LEDs, groups were encouraged to show originality in patterns and light shows. However, we found that the physical devices can be distracting. When given time to explore after finishing a guided activity, students often spent time focusing on getting the hardware to work instead of the code. This issue arose in debugging as well. When an LED would not light up, students often focused on the circuit, though the cause was typically a misplaced block of code.

Students were also introduced to sensors. One final guided activity used ultrasonic sensors within the Arduino IDE, since Scratch was not able to accurately work with these sensors. We introduced students to a text-based programming language, showing how it directly mirrored the structure of a Scratch program. This gave context for students to connect how the blocks they had been using corresponded to a real-world application. Students were then given ample time to complete a final group project for the class. Some students truly innovated in creating their own projects by going beyond the examples given in class, while others simply continued projects done throughout the week. This is one of the fundamental principles of CT; however, we saw many groups that relied too heavily on reusing their old material and programs without sufficient changes and innovation, an area we would like to improve in future implementations.

4 STEM SUMMER INSTITUTE

The *STEM Summer Institute,* [1] hosted by the Manhattan-Ogden USD 383 school district and funded by a grant though the United States Department of Defense, "is designed to raise student achievement levels and increase enrollments in science, technology, engineering and math, or STEM, careers" [31] for students in 5th grade through 9th grade. Teachers from the school district, pre-service teachers from the Kansas State University College of Education, and subject-matter experts are grouped together to develop and teach each class during the camp.

We filled the role of subject-matter experts, and were paired with teachers from the school district interested in our field. We worked collaboratively with the teachers to develop each intervention plan in the spring. Typically, we developed the lessons, and the teachers helped us make sure they were appropriate for the younger students. They also provided feedback on how to link our lessons with the school's curricula. At the start of each summer camp, we were joined by one to three pre-service teachers for each intervention. They were primarily there to gain in-class teaching experience while also getting exposure to STEM disciplines to be used in future classrooms. Pre-service teachers were required to teach at least one lesson during the last week to demonstrate their capability working with the material.

During the first two weeks, we would lead the class through most of the activities, with the teachers observing and assisting as needed. The teachers would also frequently add more information or clarify something if needed, helping us to refine our lesson plans to fit the students. For the last two weeks, the teachers would progressively lead more and more of the class, with us offering advice or corrections as needed.

5 ASSESSMENT

As discussed in the related work, we were unable to perform direct knowledge assessments since it would not be appropriate for the program. Instead, we focused on measuring student self-efficacy in problem solving and computer programming. In doing so, we hope to show that our interventions increase student interest in CS and comfort level with CT concepts, thereby making them more likely

Table 2: Self-Efficacy Survey Questions and Related CT Skill [37]

	When solving a problem I...	
1	create a list of steps to solve it	ALG - Algorithms
2	use math	ALG - Algorithms
3	try to simplify the problem by ignoring details that are not needed [41]	ABS - Abstraction
4	look for patterns in the problem	ABS - Abstraction
5	break the problem into smaller parts	DEC - Problem Decomposition
6	work with others to solve different parts of the problem at the same time	PAR - Parallelization
7	look how information can be collected, stored, and analyzed to help solve the problem	DAT - Data
8	create a solution where steps can be repeated [30]	CON - Control Flow
9	create a solution where some steps are done only in certain situations [32]	CON - Control Flow
	I can write a computer program which...	
10	runs a step-by-step sequence of commands	ALG - Algorithms
11	does math operations like addition and subtraction	ALG - Algorithms
12	uses loops to repeat commands	CON - Control Flow
13	responds to events like pressing a key on the keyboard	CON - Control Flow
14	only runs specific commands when a specific condition is met	CON - Control Flow
15	does more than one thing at the same time	PAR - Parallelization
16	uses messages to talk with different parts of the program	PAR - Parallelization
17	can store, update, and retrieve values	DAT - Data
18	uses custom blocks	ABS - Abstraction
	When creating a computer program I...	
19	make improvements one step at a time and work new ideas in as I have them	IAI - Incremental and Iterative
20	run my program frequently to make sure it does what I want and fix any problems I find	TAD - Testing and Debugging
21	share my programs with others and look at others' programs for ideas	USE - Reuse and Remix
22	break my program into multiple parts to carry out different actions	DEC - Problem Decomposition
	Impact	
23	I understand how computer programming can be used in my daily life	QUE - Questioning

to choose a STEM major or career in the future. The assessments used for this program are detailed in Weese and Feldhausen, [37] and related survey questions are included in Table 2.

In addition, we asked students about their previous experiences with various programming environments, other STEM programs, and simple questions measuring a student's socioeconomic status. [14, 17, 20] Those questions help us further categorize our students to observe any relevant differences between groups.

6 RESULTS

During 2016 and 2017, we taught each intervention to a total of 214 students across 16 groups. Of those, we collected valid pre- and post-surveys from 184 students. Students were excluded from the survey for failing to complete either a pre- or post-survey, or by opting-out of the research. We failed to administer the post-survey to one Saving the Martian intervention due to time constraints, accounting for a majority of students excluded from the results. We did not observe significant differences between each year's data, and therefore combined them. Our combined results for Cohen's *d* effect size [10] for both years are detailed in Table 3. Effect sizes are marked as small, medium, or large effect following Cohen's recommended reference points, [10] with significant results shaded based on the associated *p*-values. The results are divided into the following groupings:

- **Mars** - Saving The Martian
- **MMC** - Mighty Micro Controllers
- **Male** - Male-identifying students
- **Female** - Female-identifying students
- **NoS** - Haven't previously attended a STEM event
- **STEM** - Have previously attended a STEM event
- **SB** - Have previously attended STARBASE
- **>$10** - More than $10 in weekly spending money
- **≤$10** - $10 or less in weekly spending money
- **Cell** - Have a cell phone of their own
- **NoC** - No cell phone of their own
- **MS** - At least one parent has MS degree or higher
- **NoMS** - No parent has MS degree or higher

Our data shows that we clearly achieved gains in student self-efficacy related to CT skills when framed as writing computer programs, but not when those skills were framed within problem solving. This supports the claim that learning CT is not the same as learning problem solving, and that simply teaching a student about programming will not necessarily make them better problem solvers. We found significant gains in student self-efficacy in a

Table 3: Effect Size (*post* − *pre/stdev*) [10] for Problem Solving (PS) and CT Concepts. Italicized values indicate a small (≥.2) effect, bold values indicate a medium (≥.5) effect, and bold italicized values indicate a large (≥.8) effect. Shaded values indicate a *p*-value ≤.01. Columns marked with an asterisk include data from 2017 only

Skill	All	Mars	MMC	Male	Female	NoS	STEM	SB	>$10*	≤$10*	Cell*	NoC*	MS*	NoMS*
PS - ALG	0.15	*0.28*	0.05	0.12	*0.25*	0.19	0.15	*0.21*	0.14	0.16	0.13	*0.22*	0.15	-0.04
PS - ABS	0.01	0.09	-0.07	0.01	0.00	0.02	0.00	0.10	0.02	-0.08	-0.02	-0.15	-0.02	-0.08
PS - DEC	0.12	*0.23*	0.01	0.08	0.17	0.00	0.15	0.18	*0.36*	-0.11	0.03	-0.09	0.00	0.13
PS - PAR	0.05	0.16	-0.05	0.04	0.10	0.00	0.07	0.11	-0.05	-0.02	0.13	-0.44	-0.33	*0.24*
PS - DAT	0.11	0.04	0.17	0.04	*0.21*	-0.02	0.15	*0.32*	0.15	-0.03	0.03	-0.04	-0.09	0.00
PS - CON	0.15	*0.21*	0.10	0.12	*0.22*	0.13	0.16	*0.26*	0.05	0.04	0.07	-0.05	-0.11	0.04
CT - ALG	*0.41*	**0.56**	*0.28*	*0.45*	*0.33*	*0.47*	*0.39*	**0.58**	*0.39*	*0.39*	*0.39*	*0.40*	*0.42*	**0.65**
CT - ABS	**0.66**	*0.48*	***0.84***	**0.71**	**0.61**	*0.48*	**0.71**	***0.80***	***0.89***	**0.77**	**0.76**	***0.93***	**0.66**	***1.52***
CT - DEC	*0.39*	*0.48*	*0.29*	*0.30*	**0.55**	*0.41*	*0.38*	**0.55**	*0.40*	*0.40*	*0.44*	*0.30*	*0.40*	**0.70**
CT - PAR	*0.42*	*0.48*	*0.37*	*0.45*	*0.36*	*0.44*	*0.42*	**0.57**	*0.47*	*0.44*	*0.48*	*0.35*	*0.37*	**0.56**
CT - DAT	**0.66**	**0.74**	**0.58**	**0.69**	**0.61**	**0.57**	**0.69**	***0.86***	*0.50*	**0.76**	**0.65**	**0.82**	*0.45*	**0.57**
CT - CON	*0.29*	*0.33*	*0.26*	*0.28*	*0.34*	*0.27*	*0.30*	*0.42*	*0.38*	*0.35*	*0.37*	*0.34*	*0.47*	*0.33*
CT - IAI	*0.29*	0.19	*0.39*	*0.28*	*0.27*	*0.34*	*0.28*	*0.36*	**0.60**	*0.28*	*0.30*	**0.51**	*0.34*	**0.60**
CT - TAD	*0.26*	*0.27*	*0.26*	*0.26*	*0.27*	*0.30*	*0.25*	*0.34*	*0.23*	*0.47*	*0.38*	*0.49*	*0.25*	**0.61**
CT - USE	0.19	0.18	*0.20*	*0.26*	0.05	*0.33*	0.15	0.15	-0.23	*0.28*	0.12	*0.22*	*0.28*	-0.12
CT - QUE	*0.41*	**0.54**	*0.30*	**0.51**	*0.26*	**0.54**	*0.37*	**0.61**	*0.39*	*0.50*	*0.44*	**0.59**	*0.39*	**0.61**
# Students	184	90	94	121	61	42	142	51	21	58	58	21	41	9
Pre Mean	3.68	3.76	3.61	3.70	3.64	3.65	3.69	3.73	3.72	3.64	3.68	3.59	3.70	3.69
Post Mean	4.03	4.17	3.89	4.05	3.99	4.01	4.03	4.21	4.06	3.98	4.04	3.89	4.01	4.08

variety of CT skills, with each skill except reuse and remix (USE) showing at least a small effect size, with appropriately significant *p*-values. Our largest effect sizes were observed in the areas of abstraction (ABS), data (DAT) and questioning (QUE). Students in the Mars group showed higher gains in algorithms (ALG) than any other group, primarily due to that class's focus on algorithms. We observed lower effect sizes for students in MMC, which we attribute to the increased cognitive load of learning circuits along with programming. Males and females were largely similar, though female students had a larger effect size in the area of problem decomposition (DEC) while males were higher in the overall questioning and impact (QUE) area.

Students in the STEM group had larger effect sizes than students in the NoS group in most areas, which we attribute to repeated positive exposure to STEM; students who have already gained some experience in STEM may be more likely to engage with the material. Similarly, we observed medium and high effect sizes in students who have previously attended STARBASE, a structured STEM program for 5th graders in the area. [34] We did not observe significant differences between student groups based on self-reported socioeconomic information. While the data indicates that students with a lower socioeconomic status tend to experience larger effect sizes in some areas, the small population size makes it difficult to draw any definitive conclusions. We hope to continue this research in future years to get additional data in this area.

Based on experiences throughout the camp, we observed a significant increase in the ability of partnered teachers to engage with CT concepts and instruct students in a variety of technical activities. In most cases, we were able to completely allow them to lead the entire class for the last week each summer, only adding a few comments when students had questions. We found this to be a very valuable way to bring CT to educators outside CS. In addition, working with experienced teachers allowed us to improve our own skills working with younger students. We learned techniques for maintaining student attention, encouraging students to discuss among themselves, and how to link our own activities back to things they have already covered in their classrooms. They also provided valuable comments and suggestions for our intervention designs, allowing us to refine them each week based on their feedback. We found this to be a very positive experience for everyone involved, and believe it is an effective method to improve our own teaching and outreach efforts.

7 CONCLUSIONS AND FUTURE WORK

We developed two STEM interventions targeted at 5th through 9th grade students, and partnered with teachers from a local school district as well as pre-service teachers from our university to teach these interventions during a summer STEM camp in 2016 and 2017. We observed significant gains in student self-efficacy with many CT skills framed within computer programming. We did not observe similar gains in CT skills framed within problem solving. Additionally, we found that working with practicing and pre-service teachers was a positive experience for everyone involved, and we feel that it greatly improved our intervention design and teaching skills. Finally, we gained valuable experience creating STEM intervention curricula and performing basic research, informing our future efforts to formalize our curriculum design and research methods.

We plan to continue this project using more formalized research methods. First, we would like to revisit each intervention's design and add techniques from educational theory and pedagogy, particularly cognitive apprenticeship [9, 11, 12] and expansive framing, [15, 16] both of which could have positive impacts on student learning and closely match our existing design. We also plan to continue to refine our self-efficacy assessment by combining it with knowledge-based assessments to confirm that students are indeed learning the material while also becoming more confident in the field. While we cannot directly assess student learning through exams, we hope to make use of student trivia games with evidence-based questions to drive that research. Finally, we plan on expanding the scope of our research by using activities from each intervention during other outreach events while collecting data from participants. This will help expand our pool of research and give us insight into how other student populations and events affect our results.

REFERENCES

[1] Manhattan-Ogden USD 383. 2017. STEM Summer Institute. (2017). Retrieved July 13, 2017 from http://www.usd383.org/manhattan-ogden/district-office-/teaching-and-learning/stem/stem-summer-institute
[2] Edith Ackermann. 2001. Piaget's Constructivism, Papert's Constructionism: What's the Difference. In *Constructivism: Uses and Perspectives in Education*. 85–94.
[3] Computer Science Teachers Association. 2017. CSTA K-12 Computer Science Standards, Revised 2017. (2017). Retrieved July 31, 2017 from http://www.csteachers.org/standards
[4] Albert Bandura. 1982. Self-efficacy Mechanism in Human Agency. *American Psychologist* 37, 2 (02 1982), 122–147.
[5] Nathan Bean, Joshua Weese, Russell Feldhausen, and Richard Scott Bell. 2015. Starting from Scratch: Developing a Pre-service Teacher Training Program in Computational Thinking. In *2015 IEEE Frontiers in Education Conference (FIE)*. 1–8. https://doi.org/10.1109/FIE.2015.7344237
[6] Marie Bienkowski. 2016. Deepening Learning in High School Computer Science Through Practices in the NGSS. In *Proceedings of the 47th ACM Technical Symposium on Computing Science Education (SIGCSE '16)*. ACM, New York, NY, USA, 694–694. https://doi.org/10.1145/2839509.2850557
[7] Grant Braught, Tim Wahls, and L. Marlin Eby. 2011. The Case for Pair Programming in the Computer Science Classroom. *Trans. Comput. Educ.* 11, 1, Article 2 (Feb. 2011), 21 pages. https://doi.org/10.1145/1921607.1921609
[8] Karen Brennan and Mitchel Resnick. 2012. New frameworks for studying and assessing the development of computational thinking. In *Proceedings of the 2012 Annual Meeting of the American Educational Research Association*.
[9] John Seely Brown, Allan Collins, and Paul Duguid. 1989. Situated Cognition and the Culture of Learning. *Educational Researcher* 18, 1 (1989), 32–42. https://doi.org/10.3102/0013189X018001032
[10] Jacob Cohen. 1988. *Statistical Power Analysis for the Behavioral Sciences - Second Edition*. Lawrence Erlbaum Associates.
[11] Allan Collins. 1988. Cognitive Apprenticeship and Instructional Technology. Technical Report. *BBN Systems and Technologies Corporation* (1988).
[12] Allan Collins, John Seely Brown, and Ann Holum. 1991. Cognitive Apprenticeship: Making Thinking Visible. *American Educator* 15, 3 (1991), 6 – 11, 38–46.
[13] Stephen Cooper, Linda Bookey, and Peter GruenBaum. 2014. *Future Directions in Computing Education Summit Part One: Important Computing Education Research Questions* . Technical Report CS-TR-14-0108-SC. Stanford University. http://ilpubs.stanford.edu:8090/1117/
[14] Candace E. Currie, Rob A. Elton, Joanna Todd, and Stephen Platt. 1997. Indicators of socioeconomic status for adolescents: the WHO Health Behaviour in School-aged Children Survey. *Health Education Research* 12, 3 (1997), 385–397. https://doi.org/10.1093/her/12.3.385
[15] Randi A. Engle, Diane P. Lam, Xenia S. Meyer, and Sarah E. Nix. 2012. How Does Expansive Framing Promote Transfer? Several Proposed Explanations and a Research Agenda for Investigating Them. *Educational Psychologist* 47, 3 (2012), 215–231. https://doi.org/10.1080/00461520.2012.695678
[16] Randi A. Engle, Phi D. Nguyen, and Adam Mendelson. 2011. The Influence of Framing on Transfer: Initial Evidence from a Tutoring Experiment. *Instructional Science* 39, 5 (01 Sep 2011), 603–628. https://doi.org/10.1007/s11251-010-9145-2
[17] Doris R. Entwisle and Nan Marie Astone. 1994. Some Practical Guidelines for Measuring Youth's Race/Ethnicity and Socioeconomic Status. *Child Development* 65, 6 (1994), 1521–1540. http://www.jstor.org/stable/1131278
[18] Russell Feldhausen. 2017. Curriculum Resources. (2017). Retrieved August 31, 2017 from http://people.cs.ksu.edu/~russfeld/curriculum/
[19] Google. 2017. Computational Thinking Concepts Guide. (2017). Retrieved August 24, 2017 from https://docs.google.com/document/d/1i0wg-BMG3TdwsShAyH_0Z1xpFnpVcMvpYJceHGWex_c/edit
[20] Robert M. Hauser. 1994. Measuring Socioeconomic Status in Studies of Child Development. *Child Development* 65, 6 (1994), 1541–1545. http://www.jstor.org/stable/1131279
[21] K-12 Computer Science Framework. 2016. K-12 Computer Science Framework. (2016). http://www.k12cs.org
[22] Tony R. Kuphaldt. 2014. Lessons in Electric Circuits. (2014). Retrieved August 29, 2017 from https://www.allaboutcircuits.com/textbook/
[23] MIT Media Lab. 2017. Scratch - Imagine, Program, Share. (2017). Retrieved July 21, 2017 from https://scratch.mit.edu/
[24] Alex Lishinski, Aman Yadav, Jon Good, and Richard Enbody. 2016. Learning to Program: Gender Differences and Interactive Effects of Students' Motivation, Goals, and Self-Efficacy on Performance. In *Proceedings of the 2016 ACM Conference on International Computing Education Research (ICER '16)*. ACM, New York, NY, USA, 211–220. https://doi.org/10.1145/2960310.2960329
[25] Raina Mason and Graham Cooper. 2013. Mindstorms robots and the application of cognitive load theory in introductory programming. *Computer Science Education* 23, 4 (2013), 296–314. https://doi.org/10.1080/08993408.2013.847152
[26] Council of Chief State School Officers National Governors Association Center for Best Practices. 2010. Common Core State Standards. (2010). Retrieved August 14, 2017 from http://www.corestandards.org/
[27] Kian L. Pokorny. 2013. What Will They Know? Standards in the High School Computer Science Curriculum. *J. Comput. Sci. Coll.* 28, 5 (May 2013), 218–225. http://dl.acm.org/citation.cfm?id=2458569.2458616
[28] Mareen Przybylla and Ralf Romeike. 2014. Physical computing and its scope-towards a constructionist computer science curriculum with physical computing. *Informatics in Education* 13, 2 (2014), 225.
[29] Vennila Ramalingam, Deborah LaBelle, and Susan Wiedenbeck. 2004. Self-efficacy and Mental Models in Learning to Program. *SIGCSE Bull.* 36, 3 (June 2004), 171–175. https://doi.org/10.1145/1026487.1008042
[30] Mitchel Resnick, John Maloney, Andrés Monroy-Hernández, Natalie Rusk, Evelyn Eastmond, Karen Brennan, Amon Millner, Eric Rosenbaum, Jay Silver, Brian Silverman, and Yasmin Kafai. 2009. Scratch: Programming for All. *Commun. ACM* 52, 11 (Nov. 2009), 60–67. https://doi.org/10.1145/1592761.1592779
[31] Patrice Scott. 2012. Summer STEM Institute is an academic adventure. (Jun 2012). Retrieved July 12, 2017 from https://www.k-state.edu/today/announcement.php?id=4050
[32] Eric Snow, Geneva Haertel, Dennis Fulkerson, M Feng, and P Nichols. 2010. Leveraging evidence-centered assessment design in large-scale and formative assessment practices. In *Proceedings of the 2010 Annual Meeting of the National Council on Measurement in Education (NCME)*.
[33] The Royal Society. 2012. Shut down or restart? The way forward for computing in UK schools. (2012). Retrieved August 23, 2017 from https://royalsociety.org/~/media/education/computing-in-schools/2012-01-12-computing-in-schools.pdf
[34] Kansas STARBASE. 2017. Kansas STARBASE. (2017). Retrieved August 31, 2017 from http://www.kansasstarbase.org/
[35] NGSS Lead States. 2013. Next Generation Science Standards. (2013). Retrieved August 14, 2017 from https://www.nextgenscience.org/
[36] Robert H. Tai, Christine Qi Liu, Adam V. Maltese, and Xitao Fan. 2006. Planning Early for Careers in Science. *Science* 312, 5777 (2006), 1143–1144. https://doi.org/10.1126/science.1128690
[37] Joshua Levi Weese and Russell Feldhausen. 2017. STEM Outreach: Assessing Computational Thinking and Problem Solving. In *2017 ASEE Annual Conference & Exposition*. ASEE Conferences, Columbus, Ohio. https://peer.asee.org/28845
[38] Andy Weir. 2014. *The Martian*. Crown.
[39] Eric N. Wiebe, Malinda Faber, Jeni Corn, Tracey Louise Collins, Alana Unfried, and LaTricia Townsend. 2013. A Large-scale Survey of K-12 Students about STEM: Implications for Engineering Curriculum Development and Outreach Efforts (Research to Practice) . In *2013 ASEE Annual Conference & Exposition*. ASEE Conferences, Atlanta, Georgia. https://peer.asee.org/19073
[40] Jeannette M. Wing. 2006. Computational Thinking. *Commun. ACM* 49, 3 (March 2006), 33–35. https://doi.org/10.1145/1118178.1118215
[41] Jeannette M. Wing. 2011. Research notebook: Computational thinking - What and why? (2011). Retrieved July 21, 2017 from http://www.cs.cmu.edu/link/research-notebook-computational-thinking-what-and-why

Introducing Computational Thinking through Non-Programming Science Activities

Youwen Ouyang
California State University San Marcos
San Marcos, CA 92096, USA
ouyang@csusm.edu

Katherine L. Hayden
California State University San Marcos
San Marcos, CA 92096, USA
khayden@csusm.edu

Julie Remold
SRI International
Menlo Park, CA 94025, USA
julie.remold@sri.com

ABSTRACT[1]

Many programs offer informal experiences in programming for select students who may qualify or whose parents pay fees for attending. Integrating computational thinking (CT) in the formal classroom setting provides equal opportunities to develop valuable problem-solving skills for all students. However, such integration poses challenges since teachers may have limited experiences in computing and may be pressured by time constraints due to the need to cover Common Core and Next Generation Science Standards (NGSS) as well as district specific initiatives. A 2-year intervention has been designed to target upper elementary level self-contained classrooms to increase teachers' knowledge and ability for integrating CT into science lessons. Twenty teachers from four school districts in Southern California participated in the first year of the project's professional development activities. These schools have varying levels of diversity and socioeconomic status of student populations. Instead of using popular drag-and-drop programming tools such as Scratch or Tynker, the first year of the project focused on key CT concepts and helped teachers connect these concepts with skills important for student success in science activities. This paper reports on the study of the project's impact on student learning of key CT concepts among students from project classrooms. The main elements of the professional development are also described.

ACM Reference format:

Youwen Ouyang, Katherine L. Hayden, and Julie Remold. 2018. Introducing Computational Thinking through Non-Programming Science Activities. In *SIGCSE '18: 49th ACM Technical Symposium on Computer Science Education, Feb. 21–24, 2018, Baltimore, MD, USA.* ACM, NY, NY, USA, 6 pages. https://doi.org/10.1145/3159450.3159520

SIGCSE '18, February 21-24, 2018, Baltimore, MD, USA

ACM 978-1-4503-5103-4/18/02... $15.00
https://doi.org/10.1145/3159450.3159520

1 INTRODUCTION

Recent initiatives demonstrate the interest in, and demand for, computing education resources among the nation's teachers. The Hour of Code has been the largest campaign in recent years to promote computing at a young age, attracting tens of millions in more than 180 countries. According to Code.org, over one hundred thousand teachers signed up to introduce various online "Hour of Code" tutorials to their students. However, teachers' involvement in students' coding and problem-solving processes during the hour of code vary greatly. Currently, formal school-based interventions on computing education have mostly focused on high school and middle school levels. The visionary CS10K initiative [1] aims to offer quality CS education, including Explore Computer Science (ECS) and AP Computer Science Principles, in 10,000 high schools, providing equitable access for students of diverse backgrounds. oDREAMS is a project aimed to provide professional development for 200 teachers in nine states to embed Scalable Game Design in existing computing and STEM courses [8]. The Middle Years Computer Science (MyCS) project has designed and piloted CS curriculum in the Pomona, CA and Kaua'i, HI school districts and is now turning the curriculum into a Massive Open Online Course (MOOC) to reach a broader audience [9].

At the elementary level, digital storytelling and animations through tools such as Scratch and Alice have attracted teachers to explore programming activities with their students. However, like Hour of Code, teacher involvement with Scratch is typically self-selected and the focus of their integration is often on student creativity and engagement. In addition, it is not uncommon to hear teachers comment about how students can be much more advanced in coding than teachers. More teachers shy away from integrating computational thinking (CT) into their subject area content due to their own lack of programming experience. The *Quality Understanding and Engagement for Students and Teachers on Computational Thinking* (QUEST CT) project is an exploratory research project conducted at the 5th and 6th grade levels in eight schools that reflect varying levels of diversity and socioeconomic status (see Table 1 for student demographics). The schools are part of the following four school districts: Cardiff, Encinitas Union, Escondido Union Elementary, and

Santee. Names of schools are not included in Table 1 to provide anonymity to project participants.

Table 1: **Student Demographics in Participation Schools**

School	Enrollment	% Hispanic	% Free Lunch
1	554	46.8	35.6
2	381	17.9	13.9
3	982	27.3	31.1
4	854	17.8	27.6
5	506	24.3	50.4
6	748	94.3	92.2
7	784	92.1	93.6
8	773	93.7	93.1

The project targets 5th and 6th grade levels for two reasons: (1) self-contained classrooms provide maximum contact time between teachers and their students, affording more flexibility in schedule and potential for sustained impact, and (2) these grades are critical times for students to build interest and foundations in STEM while many teachers in these classrooms have limited STEM and computing background. The specific goals of the project are to:

- Increase teachers' knowledge and ability to integrate CT to create engaging science lessons and activities;
- Increase students' understanding and knowledge of CT concepts through contextually rich STEM-based formal and informal learning activities; and
- Broaden the participation of diverse student communities by providing multiple opportunities for engagement with STEM+C experiences.

This paper reports what we have learned from the project's first year where we helped project teachers use non-programming science activities to introduce CT concepts and improve student CT skills. Currently, there exist several variations for defining CT in K-12 classrooms. Our project adopts the operational definition of computational thinking and nine vocabulary terms [6] taken from the 2010 collaboration between the Computer Science Teacher Association (CSTA) and the International Society of Technology in Education (ISTE). While the activities don't involve programming, we ask teachers to explicitly highlight how their students are thinking like computer scientists when appropriate. The next section of the paper describes key elements of the professional development for the first year of the project. Section 3 presents a study of the project impact on students from participating teacher classrooms. Concluding discussions and remarks are provided in Section 4.

2 PROFESSIONAL DEVELOPMENT

The following diagram reflects the iterative nature of the project's professional development model that allows teachers to continuously design CT-integrated science lessons, field-test and refine pedagogical strategies in introducing CT to students. The key conceptual frameworks that guide the design include principles for how people learn [4], the Biological Sciences Curriculum Study (BSCS) 5E Instructional Model [2] and a professional learning community structure for teacher collaboration. It follows promising "best practices" [10]: intensive, sustained, job-embedded professional development focused on the content of the subject that teachers teach and is more likely to improve teacher knowledge, classroom instruction, and student achievement.

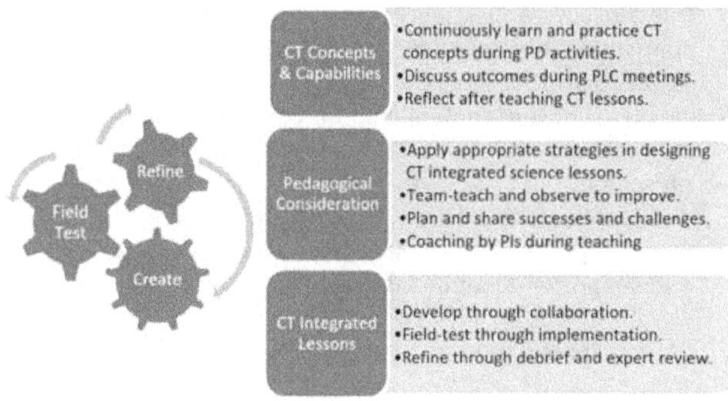

Figure 1: **Iterative process of professional development**

2.1 Intensive Summer Academy

Teachers participated in an intensive *Teacher Summer Academy* in July 2016 to not only jumpstart their understanding and knowledge of CT, but also to design science lessons that emphasized CT skills. The academy began with bonding activities to build community and understanding of CT definitions and vocabulary. The newly released ISTE student standards provided a foundation for how CT aligns with K-12 technology standards [7]. Teachers were asked to make connections by identifying how their prior lessons may already have alignment with the nine CT terms: data collection, data analysis, data representation, algorithms and procedures, problem decomposition, abstraction, simulation, parallelization, and automation. They reflected on how their current lessons provided many opportunities to integrate CT to increase student problem-solving skills. After gaining a foundation in CT and becoming part of a safe community of peers, teachers were led through development of CT-integrated lessons working in grade level teams. Teachers also had opportunities to connect with scientists who shared how computing supports their research and teachers collaborated in teams on lesson ideas to incorporate CT. These lessons were then team-taught and refined by the participating teachers during a *Student Summer Camp* to allow them to build confidence as they observed students engage in CT activities. Teachers were led through reflection activities based on student outcomes to provide insight and strategies in teaching CT. These activities established entry points for their fall CT integrated curriculum. The structure of the academy was based on the **5E Instructional Model** [2] that has demonstrated significant impact on science education.

- ***Engagement:*** Example CT resources and activities were presented in the context of science to help teachers make connections to past experiences and expose potential misconceptions about CT concepts and processes.

- ***Exploration:*** Teachers explored different CT concepts and processes in order to solve science problems. These activities were carried out on the same technology platform their students use. This exploration allowed teachers to ask questions about CT, gain confidence in using the technology, and recognize the opportunities to align CT with NGSS.
- ***Explanation:*** Teachers designed lessons that introduced CT concepts and science activities to engage students in sharpening and applying CT skills.
- ***Elaboration:*** Teachers identified how CT could be applied to other lesson content and/or considered additional CT concepts that could be incorporated in the lessons presented.
- ***Evaluation:*** Teachers worked in groups to assess effectiveness of the lesson and discussed how to measure and support student outcomes.

2.2 Coached Lesson Study

The QUEST CT *Coached Lesson Study (CLS)* promotes understanding of how students respond and understand content, which lead to the development of effective teaching practices [5]. By clarifying and incorporating teachers' individual beliefs, values, and priorities during the planning phase, *CLS* circumvents a common roadblock toward improvement, providing time to discuss teacher perceptions. The *coaching* component, led by the PIs, is critical for supporting the development of CT skills for teachers during their implementation of lesson study rotations. According to Cornett and Knight [3], when teachers are given only a description of new instructional skills, only 10% used the skill in the classroom. However, when coaching was added to staff development approximately, 95% of teachers implemented the new skills in their classrooms. In addition, Cornett and Knight found that when coaching was added to professional development follow-up sessions, the rate of implementation increased from 15% to 75% and the skills were more likely to be sustained.

The CLS cycle includes four components. ***Lesson Planning:*** teachers collaboratively plan CT integrated lessons on a Saturday working in grade level team with the help of a facilitator. Each team identifies a day, host site, schedule and roles for implementation of the lesson. ***Coached Team Teach:*** Teachers team-teach the lesson they have planned collaboratively during an identified day at a team member's school. Team members team teach, reflect, discuss and refine through two or more cycles using different student groups. ***Individual Teach:*** Following the Coached Team Teach day, teachers implement the refined lessons in their own classrooms. Some teachers may expand or further modify the lesson after the Coached Team Teach day to accommodate their student population needs. ***Debrief & Refine:*** The culmination for each CLS cycle is for teachers to debrief together and polish lessons based on implementation and analysis of student work.

The first iteration of *CLS* occurred in July 2016 when teachers planned CT-integrated science activities during the *Teacher Summer Academy* and team taught, debriefed, and refined the lessons during *Student Summer Camp* the following week. In addition, each teacher participated in two *CLS* iterations during the school year, one in Oct. 2016 and another in Feb. 2017.

2.3 Ongoing Support

Ongoing ***mentoring and support*** from project leadership allowed teachers to continue expanding their CT skills after the *summer academy,* and supported them in development of additional CT integrated lessons. PI visits to project classrooms during September 2016 and April 2017 provided personalized coaching during a CT lesson taught by each teacher and feedback through a virtual follow-up meeting when teachers discussed the outcomes as they engaged in discussion with other teachers and leadership in small groups. In addition, quarterly afterschool workshops provided time for teacher reflection on outcomes and strategies for teaching CT within science, and sharing of lessons taught successfully. Guest speakers were invited to present during afterschool workshops on topics selected based on teacher needs. Experts presented resources, tools and/or content related to the learning of CT and science. Throughout the year, project leaders connected with teachers to ensure early identification and resolution for any issues that arose.

2.4 Classroom Implementation

To prepare students for use of a shared language throughout the school year, a 45-minute to 1-hour lesson was designed collaboratively by teachers during the summer academy to introduce the ISTE/CSTA CT vocabulary through images that help children connect with their prior experiences. The lesson was tested and refined by project teachers during the *student summer camp* in July that followed the academy. At the beginning of the school year, each teacher took the lesson back to their own class, adding their own modifications. Many expanded the lesson into multiple sessions each covering a subset of the terms.

During the three CLS iterations (summer, fall, and spring) teachers worked collaboratively in grade-level teams with support from the PIs as facilitators, to design, field-test, and refine science activities that would support students thinking like computer scientists. While each lesson might provide multiple opportunities for integration of CT concepts, teachers were asked to select a primary and possibly a secondary CT focus for each lesson in order to provide enough time to engage students in a deeper understanding and application of the concept. For example, one 5th grade team developed a lesson on the water cycle that engaged students in creating digital models that could be used by computer scientists to create a simulation for kids to learn the stages of the water cycle. Through this lesson, students learned about different ways of representing data in a model, with the end goal that the model could be simulated by a program. The secondary CT focus for the lesson was abstraction, asking students to think about how their model stemmed from observations of water cycle events. The afternoon of the CLS debrief days and afterschool workshops provided additional opportunities for teachers to collaborate with other teachers to design and/or share additional CT-integrated lessons.

Five times throughout the year, teachers were asked to describe an example of a recent CT-integrated lesson they had designed and taught in their classroom by completing a survey that shared, a) the goals of the lesson, b) the primary CT focus, and c) other lesson information such as plans for reusing and modifying the lesson. The survey also allowed a secondary CT focus to be associated with each lesson. Teachers were specifically instructed not to submit lessons from CLS as their survey responses in order to collect lessons designed individually by teachers. Figure 2 summarizes the number of times each of the CT terms was associated with an example lesson submitted by teachers in the data collected from the five surveys. .

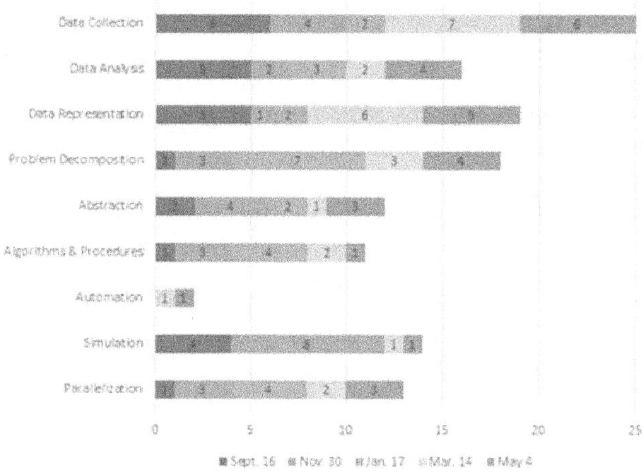

Figure 2: **Teacher Self-reported CT Integration**

It is important to note, however, that these data do not reflect all CT-integrated lessons implemented by teachers. The timing of the surveys coincided with project supported professional development activities to ensure high completion rate. Teachers might choose a particular lesson to submit based on how much detail they remembered about the lesson. It is no surprise that very few teachers focused on "automation" in their lessons due to their limited experience in the use of programming to automate. The responses also reflect science teachers' priority in engaging students in data collection, analyses, and representation. Through interviews and informal discussions with teachers, we often heard that CT had changed how they approached science activities. Instead of setting up data tables and worksheets for students to record measurements in appropriate slots, they now involved students in an iterative process of decision making to determine what data to collect, how data are relevant, what patterns exist, and how to best illustrate findings. Another commonly covered CT term was "Problem Decomposition" as teachers found it to be the critical gear in problem solving activities, often driving the success of the other terms.

3 ASSESSING STUDENT LEARNING

3.1 The Assessment Instrument

The student assessment used to measure student learning of CT, contains two parts. The first part focuses on how one applies CT skills in problem solving. The first five questions are multiple choice items with one correct answer. Each question is scored at one point. The last question has five possible options and asks students to select all that apply. For this last item, each option correctly identified as true or not true was worth 0.5 points for a total possible score of 2.5 points. Together the maximum score on all of the part one items was 7.5 points.

The second part of the assessment has six questions, each one evaluating student understanding of one of the CT terms of the ISTE standards[2]. These items are scenario based. Each question asks students to choose the right CT term from three options based on a described activity. To minimize reading required of student participants, three questions were developed for each of two scenarios. The questions were weighed equally for a total possible score of 6 points.

3.2 Data Collection

The two-part assessment was administered to students in project classrooms via SurveyMonkey at two time points during the year[3]. The pre-assessment data was collected in September 2016 and completed by 425 students. The post-assessment was administered in May 2017 and completed by 453 students. Data were cleaned to resolve duplicate student ID entries (26 and 25 in the pre- and post-test) and then data from pre and post assessment were matched by student ID. When more than one survey or assessment was submitted with the same student ID, we selected the most complete or the earliest when completion levels were equal. 327 matched pairs of pre- and post-assessments were identified. Some students were absent during either the pre or post survey and there was some turnover of students during the school year. In addition, it is possible some students did not enter their ID consistently between the two assessments. Therefore, the number of matched pairs is smaller than the total number of students who took the assessment. Table 2 provides an overview of the number of matched pairs of assessment data that were provided from students at each grade level.

[2] The six terms included in the assessment were Data Collection, Data Analysis, Data Representation, Problem Decomposition, Parallelization, and Algorithms and procedures. The remaining three terms from the ISTE standards could not be readily incorporated into scenario-based word problems at the appropriate reading level.

[3] We used a pre-post design for the evaluation. An experimental design with comparison group was outside the scope of the evaluation research.

Approximately half of the students in project classrooms from which we collected assessment data were girls. Teachers reported that about 34% of students in project classrooms were English Language Learners (ELL) and about 34% were significantly behind grade level in reading. The ELL status and percent behind grade level varied greatly across the participating schools. In one school, teachers reported no ELL students while another school reported 89% of students in project classrooms were ELL students. Similarly, the percent of students behind grade level ranged from 6% in one school to 67% in another.

Table 2: **Students from which matched pairs of pre- and post-tests were submitted**

Grade Level	Number of Students
4th	16 (5%)
5th	196 (60%)
6th	98 (30%)
Missing grade level data	17 (5%)
Total	**327**

3.3 Analyses and Findings

Several analyses were performed to help determine the project's impact on student learning of CT by calculating gains in student scores from pre- to post-assessment. Paired t-tests were performed to determine if the mean differences between pre- and post-test are statistically significant for both the assessment as a whole and the sub-scores. We also tested for significance of test score gains among different subsets of the student population such as English language learners (ELL) versus non-ELL and girls versus boys. For items with binary outcomes (0 or 1), such as when we analyzed gains for individual assessment items, McNemar's tests were also used to determine whether student gain is statistically significant on each of the items.

The histograms in Figure 3 show the distributions of the test scores at the two time points (pre-test at left, post-test at right). The histograms show the total scores distributed across the full range of the possible scores, indicating that the test was effective in differentiating students at different levels. Both distributions are unimodal and slightly skewed with more students at the higher end. Distribution of the post test is more left skewed than the distribution of the pre-test, indicating the improvement of student performance on average.

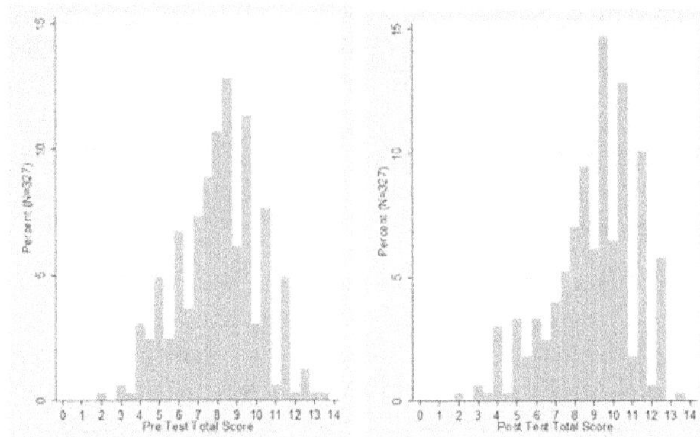

Figure 3: **Distributions of individual scores (pre-test on left, post-test at right)**

Table 4 provides an overview of student gains on the assessment and each of the sub-scores for the entire population of students. We found statistically significant gains in test scores for both the overall assessment score (all questions) and for each of the two assessment sub-scores: 1) student capacity to apply CT skills in problem solving and 2) student capacity to correctly identify CT terms. This resulted in student-level gains data for all students who completed the assessments. The larger growth in part 2 of the assessment, concerning CT terms, may be due to the fact that students scored lower on these items in the pre-test leaving more room for growth.

Table 4: **Mean percentage of correctness for all students**

	Pre-test	**Post-test**	**Gain**	**Cohen's d**
Overall: All items	59.6%	66.5%	6.9%***	.42
Part 1. CT Application	71.9%	77.5%	5.6%***	.30
Part 2. CT Terms	45.2%	53.5%	8.3%***	.20

*p < .05, **p < .01, ***p < .001

Table 5 further investigates student performance on the six vocabulary items by showing the percentage of students who responded correctly for each item. McNemar's tests were performed to determine whether the gain is statistically significant on each of the items. The one term with the largest gains, parallelization, was a topic we learned had been incorporated in many recent lessons, even those not specifically focused on this term. Other terms with significant and large gains included, *algorithms and procedures* for which pre-test scores were especially low, and *data collection,* the term teachers reported integrating in their instruction most often.

Table 5: **Mean performance on each of the six vocabulary items.**

	Pre-test	Post-test	Gain
Data Collection	67%	74%	7%*
Data Analysis	48%	53%	5%
Data Representation	67%	73%	6%
Problem Decomposition	28%	29%	1%
Parallelization	31%	57%	26%***
Algorithms and procedures	27%	35%	8%*

*p < .05, **p < .01, ***p < .001

Some student demographic data was available to allow comparison of assessment scores across different subsets of the student population. As shown in Table 6, statistically significant gains were found for all student groups analyzed. However, boys showed slightly higher scores at both pre- and post-test time points as well as larger gains between the time points. In addition, the gap in terms of both pre- and post-test scores and assessment gains was larger when comparing students who spoke English at home with those who do not.

Table 6: **Changes between pre- and post-assessment items percent correct for matched pairs of students in matched pairs of student assessments.**

	Pre-test[4]	Post-test	Gain	Cohen's d
Girls	59.7%	65.3%	5.6%***	.34
Boys	60.5%	67.4	6.9%***	.43
English spoken at home (n=244)	61.2%	70.2%	9%***	.39
English not spoken at home (n=66)	56.2%	61.9%	5.7%**	.35

*p < .05, **p < .01, ***p < .001

[4] Pre-test scores reported here for both girls and boys are higher than the average scores reported in table 5 for the entire population. This is because there are 17 low-scoring students who declined to provide gender data.

4 CONCLUSIONS

The QUEST CT project successfully provided professional development for 20 upper elementary classroom teachers, which led to their development and implementation of CT integrated lessons providing CT experiences for their students. Presenting the parallel between CT concepts and the Next Generation Science Standards (NGSS) science and engineering practices makes it easier for teachers to recognize opportunities to deepen student understanding of CT concepts and improve related CT skills as they engage students in science activities throughout the school year. The data from the student assessment shows a significant increase with all scores going up, and statistically significant gains for girls and ELL students, even though their overall scores were lower. The gap shown in the data for students underrepresented in STEM (girls and minority populations) is being addressed by the project by providing additional CT opportunities for students from these populations. Project leadership is also working with teachers to identify strategies to support student sub-groups with lower scores overall, and we hope that the next year will show improvement in this area.

ACKNOWLEDGMENTS

The QUEST CT project is supported by the National Science Foundation under Grant # 1543258. Any opinions, findings, and conclusions or recommendations expressed in this material are those of the authors and do not necessarily reflect the views of the National Science Foundation.

REFERENCES

[1] Briggs, A., & Snyder, L. (2012). Computer science principles and CS 10K initiative. ACM Inroads, 3(2), 29-31.
[2] Bybee, R. (1997). Achieving Scientific Literacy, Portsmouth, NH: Heinemann.
[3] Cornett, J., & Knight, J. (2008). Research on coaching. In J. Knight (Ed.), Coaching: Approaches and perspectives (pp.192-216). Thousand Oaks, CA: Corwin Press.
[4] Donovan, M.S., & Bransford, J.D. (2005). How students learn: Science in the Classroom. Washington, DC: National Academy Press.
[5] Hayden, K., Ouyang, Y., Scinski, L., Olszewsk, B., and Bielefeldt, T. (2011). Increasing Student Interest and Attitude in STEM: Professional Development and Activities to Engage Learners. Contemporary Issues in Technology and Teacher Education, Vol. 11, No. 1, pp 47 – 69
[6] ISTE/CSTA (2011) Computational Thinking Teacher Resources, 2nd ed. Retrieved from http://iste.org/computational-thinking/
[7] ISTE, (2016). ISTE Standards for Students. Retrieved from http://www.iste.org/standards/standards /for-students-2016
[8] Repenning, A., Webb, D. C., Brand, C., Gluck, F., Grover, R. et. al. (2014). Beyond Minecraft: Facilitating computational thinking through modeling and programming in 3D. Computer Graphics and Applications, 34(3), 68-71.
[9] Schofield, E., Erlinger, M., & Dodds, Z. (2014). MyCS: a CS curriculum for middle-years students. Journal of Computing Sciences in Colleges, 29(4), 145-155.
[10] Wayne, A. J., Kwang, S. Y., Zhu, P., Cronen, S., & Garet, M. S. (2008) "Experimenting with Teacher Professional Development: Motives and Methods", Educational Research, 37(8): 469 – 479.

Teaching NoSQL Databases to Undergraduate Students - A Novel Approach

Sriram Mohan
Rose-Hulman Institute of Technology
Terre Haute, Indiana
mohan@rose-hulman.edu

ABSTRACT

An increase in data tracking by organizations has created a need for systems that can handle a variety of data models at scale. NoSQL databases and Polyglot persistence - the industry's preferred solution to modern data problems is not covered in sufficient detail, if covered at all in the undergraduate curriculum. The paper reports on our experience of introducing NoSQL paradigms using a four-tiered learning model to undergraduate students over the last two years. We believe that our methodology exposes these new ideas in an approachable manner and would provide a great starting point for other programs interested in teaching modern database paradigms and distributed data modeling and processing.

CCS CONCEPTS

• **Information systems** → **Information storage technologies**; • **Social and professional topics** → **Information science education**; • **Software and its engineering**;

KEYWORDS

NoSQL, Polyglot persistence, Databases, Education, Curriculum, Undergraduates

ACM Reference Format:
Sriram Mohan. 2018. Teaching NoSQL Databases to Undergraduate Students - A Novel Approach. In *SIGCSE '18: The 49th ACM Technical Symposium on Computer Science Education, Feb. 21–24, 2018, Baltimore, MD, USA*. ACM, New York, NY, USA, 6 pages. https://doi.org/10.1145/3159450.3159554

1 INTRODUCTION

Relational database systems have long been the dominant database model of choice and the widely used storage medium that powers industry. Most academic programs including Rose-Hulman provide sufficient coverage of this concept. However, relational databases suffer from several drawbacks including:

(1) Representation mismatch - the type of data that needs to be stored does not naturally fit the relational model [5]. For instance, the data that needs to be stored might be a graph of relationships, that better fits a graph database than a relational database.
(2) Transactional Model - Relational databases offer a very strict model of transaction control(Atomicity, Strongly Consistent, Isolation, Durability - commonly called ACID) that is not needed for many types of applications. A strict transactional model can reduce the performance of many systems [16].
(3) Scalability - Scaling relational databases can be challenging and requires constant tuning for efficiency [4].
(4) Fixed Schema - Most relational databases expect the data in a particular table to follow a fixed schema. This can create problems when some rows do not have the need for certain attributes or in the future could gain extra attributes. While there are solutions around this problem, it is inelegant and can create performance issues.
(5) Data Modeling - relational data modeling places an emphasis on normalized data. Application developers tend to prioritize performant data structures that prioritize aggregation over normalization, leading to mismatch issues [3].

In response to these issues, numerous NoSQL databases have been developed in industry. Unlike the standardized relational model, each NoSQL database has been developed in response to a specific problem and brings along with it, its own underlying concepts and language for interaction. These NoSQL databases have become the technology of choice in startups, and fortune 500 companies are beginning the transition to these systems.

1.1 What is NoSQL?

NoSQL as a term has been used to refer to different types of databases. Originally, it stood for databases that did not use SQL to query and was also used as a term that covered all non-relational databases. Increasingly, the word NoSQL is used to mean "Not Only SQL" and is used to refer to databases that do not use the row/column tabular approach that forms the basis of relational databases. NoSQL databases are characterized by the following:

(1) Data models other than tabular models (graph, tree, key value, document etc.)
(2) Typically, a lack of rigidity in schema definition
(3) Implicit support for horizontal scaling
(4) Eventual consistency [17] as opposed to strong consistency

The rise of these NoSQL systems has also been characterized by the popularity of another idea - "Polyglot Persistence". [14]. Similar in concept to Polyglot Programming[1], Polyglot Persistence refers to the notion that it is best to use multiple data stores to meet the needs

[1]Applications must use a variety of programming languages to leverage the suitability of different languages for different needs

SIGCSE '18, Feb. 21–24, 2018, Baltimore, MD, USA

ACM ISBN 978-1-4503-5103-4/18/02...$15.00
https://doi.org/10.1145/3159450.3159554

of an information system. Given the plethora of database choices, each with its unique strengths and weaknesses, and ability to store different type of data models, Polyglot persistence encourages the use of the right database for the right feature. It must be pointed out that with polyglot persistence, the application developer has to consider techniques for keeping the various databases in use consistent.

Lastly, another important notion in NoSQL is the CAP theorem[2]. It provides some constraints on properties that are vital to modern distributed systems namely: 1) Consistency, 2)Availability &, 3) Partition Tolerance. The CAP theorem states that a distributed system can utmost satisfy only 2 of these properties at any given time.

1.2 NoSQL in Industry

Data driven decision making is increasingly common in organizations. A survey by Gartner [7] reveals that a striking 75% of organizations in a variety of sectors are investing in Big Data projects. Big data with its emphasis on data from a variety of sources/formats, along with IoT devices has created a need to store and process both structured and unstructured data at scale. This is also confirmed in a recent survey by Forrester [19]. It reveals that 29% of the surveyed organizations have already implemented a NoSQL solution with a further 20% planning to implement in the next year. Anecdotal evidence from our career fairs confirms a sharp increase in demand for students with exposure to NoSQL.

1.3 NoSQL in Academia

An analysis of current undergraduate curriculum reveals the following themes:

(1) A significant minority of programs do not require a course in database systems. Among programs that require databases as a part of graduation requirements, the focus is purely on relational databases. This was confirmed during a Birds of the Feather discussion organized at SIGCSE [9] .
(2) A dearth of papers describing techniques to cover these rapid changes in the world of databases. [8]

Computer Science as a discipline places an emphasis on problem based learning. Realistic usecases and experiences are vital to enhance learning in Computer Science [18]. Several studies have confirmed the value addition offered by learning through doing [6, 15]. The value of "learning by doing" to databases was specifically confirmed by Ramakrishna [13]. The rest of this paper describes our experience with a new approach to teaching NoSQL databases. This course utilizes a tiered model of learning and emphasizes hands-on experience with a variety of NoSQL databases. The course provides students with the opportunity to learn and practice with several NoSQL paradigms.

2 EDUCATIONAL CONTEXT

We currently offer undergraduate programs in Software Engineering, Computer Science and International Computer Science. Students graduating with a degree in our programs are required to take a course on the fundamentals of database systems. This course has traditionally focused on the theoretical and practical aspects of the design and development of an information system. The department also requires students to take four electives within the discipline and students who favor a career in the world of data typically take a follow on courses in one of the following areas:

- Modern Database Paradigms
- Introduction to the Hadoop Ecosystem
- Independent Research

As a four year school, that places an emphasis on undergraduate education and teaching, our programs place a strong emphasis on active learning inside the classroom and problem based learning outside the classroom. To meet this principle, our courses are typically taught in the studio format with a lot of labs and in-class activities that require students to apply concepts in scenarios similar to the one's they may face in industry. All classes also require a team (3-4 students) project that serves as a way to assess student mastery of the concepts covered in class. As a part of these programs, graduating students are required to complete a year long senior capstone experience [12]. This experience requires students to work on teams of about four students on a project for a real client to understand the need for, design, and develop a system that meets the identified needs. We have seen a remarkable increase in the use of NoSQL databases in these projects.

This course on Modern Database Paradigms has to function in this setup. As such the course had to support several labs/activities similar to those seen in industry with a team project that provided realistic exposure to the use of NoSQL in industry.

3 OUR COURSE ON NOSQL

A quick glance at the state of art on databases, reveals that there are several NoSQL databases, each with its own unique features. This raises a natural question - how does one begin to identify the concepts and the databases that should be covered in a class on NoSQL? It is conceivable that one could choose to offer a class on each of these NoSQL databases, similar to techniques use to teach SQL and relational databases. Unlike the standardized relational model, each NoSQL database has been developed in response to a specific problem and brings along with it, its own underlying concepts and language for interaction. A successful database developer needs to be curious about the state of the world of NoSQL databases, keep up to date in this rapidly changing industry and see connections and patterns between concepts they are familiar with and techniques being introduced in new systems. Further, a developer needs the ability to recommend the right set of database technologies to be deployed in a project to drive maximum value for the client. As such, we realized that this called for a course that would introduce students to several flavors of NoSQL databases. Our courses run for 10 weeks and gave us ample time to introduce 4-5 flavors of NoSQL systems. We chose a representative & popular tool from each of the following flavors:

(1) Document Oriented - MongoDB
(2) Graph - Neo4J
(3) Search - SOLR
(4) Memory Based / Key Value - REDIS
(5) Columnar - Cassandra [2]

For each of these systems, we covered data modeling, querying, scaling and building a small information system to demonstrate the

[2]We did not have enough time to cover this in some offerings.

utility of the system. This course was targeted at Juniors/Seniors and had the following objectives.

Students who complete this course[11] will be able to

(1) Explain basic storage structures and access techniques for relational and post-relational systems.
(2) Develop information systems in a variety of database paradigms (such as graph databases, document databases, memory based, & key value stores) using the features unique to those paradigms.
(3) Identify the semantic similarities and differences between a new database and previously known databases.
(4) Differentiate between commonly used consistency models.
(5) Decide the NoSQL/SQL databases to deploy based on the data to be stored and desired availability, scalability and consistency requirements.
(6) Develop information systems that employ polyglot persistence using NoSQL databases.

To meet the above outcomes, we covered the following topics:

- The downside of relational databases
  - Evaluation of relational operators
  - Limitations of join algorithms in a distributed environment
  - Transaction management
  - Deadlock handling
  - Recovery
- Scaling Databases
  - Why Scale?
  - Eventual Consistency
  - Distributed data models
  - Paxos
- Key Value & Memory Stores
  - Introduction to REDIS
  - Commands/Querying in REDIS
  - Data Modeling in REDIS
  - REDIS Persistence
  - Replication
  - Application Development
- Document Store
  - MongoDB Data Modeling
  - Commands in MongoDB
  - MapReduce in MongoDB
  - MongoDB Replication
  - MongoDB Sharding
  - Application Development
- Graph Database
  - Why Graphs?
  - Modeling in Graphs
  - Cypher Queries & Neo4J
  - Indexing, Constraints, & Transactions in Neo4J
  - Application Development
- Search
  - What is SOLR?
  - Key Concepts in Search
  - Indexing
  - Text Analysis
- Columnar Store[3]
  - Data Modeling in Cassandra
  - Consistency & Replication
  - Application Development

[3]We did not have enough time to cover this in some offerings.

We have refined the list of topics mentioned above over the last two years, based on feedback we have received from students, alumni and in consultation with data engineers in industry.

3.1 Textbooks

NoSQL databases that were covered in this class changed on a regular basis. We reviewed several books that offered detailed insight into each of these tools that were published within the last year. Most of these books were obsolete at the last offering of the class. The class relied mostly on the official documentation published by these NoSQL databases. These pages provided a good overview of data model, query language, scaling features and included common use cases and problems encountered. A complete list of useful web pages is available on the class website[11]. The official documentation was supplemented by notes written by the instructor. We will note that that "In Action" series of books published by Manning [10] publishers to be mostly up-to-date and were assigned as reference books.

3.2 Infrastructure

Each student in the class was provided with a virtual machine with the latest version of Ubuntu installed on it. Each machine had about 16 GB of RAM, 500 GB of storage and 4 i5 cores. These machines were provided from our department's existing infrastructure. It is also possible to receive discount codes from Google Cloud Platform to host these virtual machines for no cost. The students used these machines to install the NoSQL databases in question (instructions were provided) and follow along with the concepts covered in class. These machines were also used by students to finish homework assignments and were later used by student teams for projects as a part of 3-4 node cluster. The cluster was needed for students to scale the NoSQL databases used in the project.

4 LEARNING MODEL

Continuous learning is important to stay relevant as the world of NoSQL continues to reinvent itself. This requires the ability for our students to be able to explore connections and patterns between their existing knowledge base and new paradigms they encounter. The course[4] was designed with this philosophy in mind. Throughout the course, we made constant connections between the NoSQL databases that were discussed in class and students were required to reflect about their experiences with these databases. Reflection when coupled with hands on learning, allows students to master the final details of the database, compare paradigms, pick up new patterns and learn a new database quickly. Further, we wanted students to be able to choose the right set of NoSQL databases for a given application and it supporting usecases. There is no magic formula that can be applied to determine the right NoSQL system to choose for the right usecase. The tool of choice will depend a lot on a) the type of data, b) the type of queries ,and c) the frequency of queries. It is imperative that students have a project experience

[4]Complete details of all the activities mentioned in this section are available in the class website [11].

that simulates this to give them hand on experience with selecting a NoSQL system to use. With these goals in mind, we decided to utilize a four-tier learning model to provide numerous opportunities for our students to practice and develop a mastery of these vital skills. The tiers include:

(1) Tier 1 - In-class Concepts & Practice
(2) Tier 2 - Labs
(3) Tier 3 - Research
(4) Tier 4 - Project

4.1 Tier 1 - In Class Concepts & Practice

Active learning has proven to be very effective in communicating concepts in computer science [6, 15], specifically databases [13]. Every session was designed with this in mind and several in-class activities were designed for the various concepts, techniques and databases that were covered in class.

- Data Modeling Exercises: Students in this class were comfortable with Entity Relationship diagrams, Normalization and modeling relational databases. NoSQL data modeling tends to emphasize a) Data Aggregation to reduce joins,b) Denormalized data, c)Data access patterns - types & frequency, d) Data structure support, and e) Anticipated number of reads & writes. In our experience, data modeling tends to be an optimization problem across these constraints and students require extensive practice. Each database covered in class spent an extensive amount of time on data modeling. Students were first instructed using an interactive live modeling session. Following the session, students were divided into ad-hoc teams and asked to work on a sample data modeling activity. The teams had to come up with a data model and provide a rationale for their design based on the criterion mentioned before. Teams were assigned 30 minutes for the activity. At the end of the activity, the teams reported their work to the class and the session concluded with an instructor led analysis on the designs produced by the ad-hoc teams.
- Live Programming: Live programming was used to cover the querying capabilities of each NoSQL system. Following the live programming, students had the ability to practice queries on similar problem sets. Depending on the concept being covered, students had as few as one query or as many as 10 queries to write and execute during class. These activities were made available to the student as a worksheet after the class.
- Scalability: Scaling in the NoSQL world typically falls under the umbrella of horizontal scaling. Most databases implement scaling using replication, sharding or a combination of the two. A successful deployment of a NoSQL database requires that students have comprehension of the supported scaling techniques. To help achieve this, our sessions on scaling were divided into two distinct activities - a) One session on the mechanism used by the database to implement scaling. This session went into details on processes and workflow used by the NoSQL database under discussion. b) A live instructor led demonstration on scaling the database during class. This session provided students with a worksheet they could use to follow along as the instructor went through the steps. The session was further supplemented with information about common bugs encountered and system tuning to improve performance.
- Quizzes: Quizzes were inspired by the principle of "Test First Teaching" [1] and involved the use of select queries and analysis that students completed while listening to concepts in class. These quizzes are part of the culture at Rose-Hulman and serve the following needs:
  - Gauge comprehension of the topics covered on a daily basis. Based on the number of students who were able to solve a particular problem on the quiz, we gained immediate feedback on the class and could adjust the schedule and reengage the students on certain concepts as needed.
  - Student often use the quiz to take notes and as a way to learn material before an exam.

Care was taken to compare and contrast the various databases throughout the class. Time was provided for student led reflection on advantages/disadvantages of utilizing one of these databases as a part of a set of systems to bring about polyglot persistence.

4.2 Tier 2 - Labs

Every NoSQL database that was covered in class was accompanied by a lab. The labs were designed to give students experience with building an application using the NoSQL database in question. All labs required students to build the exact same application - a library information system with support for a rudimentary interface(Command Line, or Web based). The feature set for the information system was carefully curated to include features that would be very simple to implement on some systems (direct support) and complicated on others. The hidden theme behind these labs was to help students organically understand the need for polyglot persistence. A sampler of the feature set is provided below. The full feature set is available on the class website [11].

(1) CRUD[5] operations on Books
(2) CRUD operations on Borrowers
(3) Search
(4) Support for multiple authors
(5) Checkout & Check-in Books
(6) Recommendation Engine

Students were required to demonstrate their finished lab to the instructor in person. During the demonstration, students had to justify their data model & design choices.

The final lab in the class was a design activity and was scheduled for the last week of classes. Students were asked to redesign the Library Information System with polyglot persistence in mind. The lab required the students to think about:

(1) Would it make sense to use just one database? If more than one database is used, how should the features be distributed across the databases?
(2) How do you keep the information consistent across the databases that were chosen?
(3) Identify strengths and weaknesses of their proposed design.

[5]Create,Retrieve,Update,Delete

4.3 Tier 3 - Research

In the modern database world, the features drive the database of choice, and it is relatively common for a data warehouse to have several database tools in the production pipeline. A NoSQL developer needs the ability to identify the right database, learn it quickly and leverage the database to fit the requirements for a project.

The purpose of this research was to provide a realistic experience of the learning they might encounter in industry. Students were required to identify a unique NoSQL database and research it as a team. Teams may not be allowed to research the same tool if numerous teams within the section have opted for the same database. Some potential NoSQL databases that have been studied using the model include:

- ArangoDB - A NoSQL database with a graph data model and support for other models as well
- RIAK - a distributed Key-Value Store
- CouchBase - a distributed multi-model documented oriented system
- CRUD operations with Apache HBase - a distributed multi-dimensional sorted map

Each team was required to research and produce a lab on their database. The teams were graded both on the content of the lab as well as the quality of the lab. The lab's produced by teams had to address the following components:

(1) Introduction to the NoSQL database
(2) Introduction to the underlying data model with examples
(3) Installation of the NoSQL database
(4) Configuration of the NoSQL database
(5) Simple activities to introduce query model & other relevant ideas and concepts
(6) A mini-project that demonstrates common use of the NoSQL database
(7) A follow on project that interested students completing the lab can work on to demonstrate their mastery of the NoSQL database
(8) Description of scalability options with instructions for setting up replication/sharding/or the option supported by the NoSQL database
(9) Lists of issues and unique things to keep an eye on while using this NoSQL database
(10) Links to relevant documentation about the NoSQL database

Student teams started their research around the half-way point of the class. Work produced by teams were monitored using an Agile methodology with several milestones similar to those mentioned for the project in the next section. At the end of the class, the labs were distributed to the class to serve as a reference for future work.

4.4 Tier 4 - Project

The final project provides student teams with the opportunity to develop an information system (no. of features is twice as much as that of the labs) using a NoSQL system. Students had complete freedom in determining the requirements as long as the minimum complexity was met. One of the goals for the project was that students learn and use a NoSQL system that wasn't covered in class. Students had to choose a NoSQL system that could work well with their feature set.

The second goal of the final project was polyglot persistence. This required the teams to use at least two other NoSQL systems. For this category, teams could choose a NoSQL system that was covered in class as long as the features were a good match. Polyglot persistence also required the teams to keep the data consistent across all 3 NoSQL systems. Student teams had to come up with a design that could keep the data eventually consistent across all 3 systems. For instance, if a team chose REDIS, MongoDB and ArangoDB for their project, as long as one of the databases is up and running, the system is considered available and should continue to accept user input and interact with users. When the other two systems are brought online, they should be able to catchup to the actions that happened during their downtime. The class had guest lectures from industry that provided students with designs that utilized a publish-subscribe system like Kafka or the use of a log to meet this goal.

The third goal for the project was scalability. The teams should identify a scaling strategy for at least 2 of their NoSQL systems and implement it successfully. To help the students meet these goals, we divided the work into the following milestones:

(1) Milestone 1 - Problem Statement with feature listing(at least 7 features), Identify NoSQL databases and map databases to features.
(2) Milestone 2 - Stand-up a 3-4 node cluster, install, configure and deploy all NoSQL databases identified in previous milestone. Demonstrate tool readiness using sample programs.
(3) Milestone 3 - Identify strategy for scaling for at least 2 NoSQL databases. Provide plan for implementing the strategy.
(4) Intermediate Status Reports - Weekly sprints as teams start implementing the final project. We had a total of 5 sprints. The teams had to focus 2 of the sprints on polyglot persistence and 1 of the sprints on scaling the system.
(5) Final Report & Reflection - Captures the state of the system on delivery and includes instructions for deploying the system and a report on its strengths and weaknesses with recommendations for future work.

Teams had the freedom to modify the features associated with the project during sprints, as long as learning objectives were met.

5 EVALUATION AND DISCUSSION

We used regular anonymous surveys during the class to obtain feedback from the students on the course. Students were instructed to focus their feedback on the day-to-day running of the class, concepts covered and changes that could be made to concept delivery. The class also used anonymous feedback associated with every student artifact and a general purpose anonymous feedback form to gauge student sentiment. We responded regularly to student concerns and structured course delivery and materials (if appropriate) in response to student feedback. This gave students a sense of ownership to the class and was conducive to enhanced student learning.

In addition to the regular feedback, students were surveyed at the end of the term. The end of term summative assessment is comprised of the following questions:

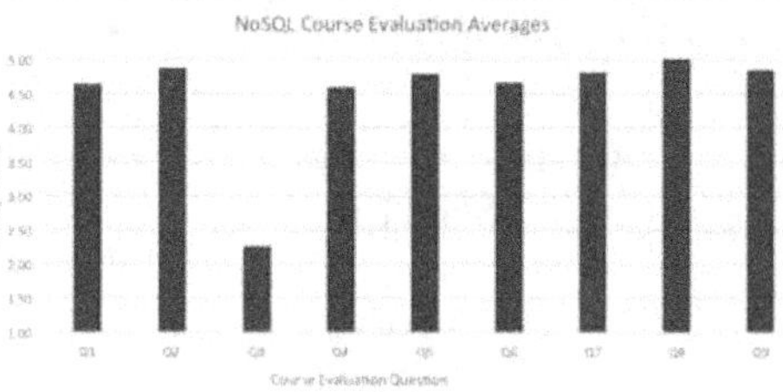

Figure 1: NOSQL Course Evaluation Averages over the last 2 years (n = 50)

(1) Please rate the quality of your learning in the class
(2) The laboratory assignments and the course material reinforced one another
(3) The work load for this course in relation to other courses
(4) Overall, how would you rate this class
(5) The professor was well prepared for this class
(6) The professor used teaching techniques that helped me learn
(7) The professor was available for help outside of class
(8) The professor was genuinely interested in teaching the class
(9) Please rate the professor's overall performance in the class.

Q1, Q2, Q4, Q5, Q6, Q7, Q8, Q9 were evaluated using a 5 point Likert scale with the following options: a) strongly agree - 5, b) agree - 4, C) neither agree nor disagree - 3 , d) disagree - 2, and e) strongly disagree - 1. The results from the student survey are provided to the instructor in the form of a mean and standard deviation and are reported in Figure 1. Student responses to these surveys over the last two years (n=50) have demonstrated the quality as well as the quantity of learning that students gained in the course. Students also appreciate the range of experiences and the realistic nature of the work that was done during the class.

Q3 is a measure of workload and is evaluated using a 5 point Likert scale with the following options: a) much lighter - 5 , b) lighter - 4, c) about the same - 3, d) heavier - 2 and e) much heavier - 1. Lower the rating, heavier the workload in that class and as shown in Figure 1 student attribute this class to be heavier than most classes offered at the school.

The author continue to have regular conversations with our alumni in industry and engineers in the NoSQL world about the class. The feedback we receive from these constituents is positive and provides another good data point about the direction of this class. In addition to these questions, students also had the option to provide free form responses to the following questions:

(1) Explain why your learning was at this level
(2) Describe one or more strengths of this course
(3) Describe one or more ways this course can be improved
(4) Explain why you gave the instructor this rating

More details are not provided due to space restrictions, but we will be happy to share the full results. We include the following comment to summarize student sentiments: *"The content was interesting to learn. The labs were great for reinforcing our knowledge of the subject matter. Learning how to ensure polyglot persistence and horizontally scale databases will prove useful in my future. I felt very accomplished when I finally figured out how to keep data between all three of our databases consistent."*

6 CONCLUSION

NoSQL databases are increasingly used to drive web applications in industry and have seen rapid adoption in a variety of organizations. Current undergraduate curriculum computer science is focused mainly on relational systems and pays scant attention to NoSQL paradigms. We believe, that exposure and experience with a variety of NoSQL paradigms and data models is a critical part of the student skill set and will help them make a successful transition to industry. We also believe that students need to be exposed to multiple NoSQL paradigms and be provided with the opportunity to practice and reflect on their work as outlined in our learning model. Student assessment and reports from companies that hire our students have consistently pointed out the value & efficacy of our approach.

REFERENCES

[1] Mark A. Ardis and Cheryl A. Dugas. 2004. Test-First Teaching: Extreme Programming Meets Instructional Design in Software Engineering Courses.
[2] Eric A. Brewer. 2000. Towards Robust Distributed Systems (Abstract). In *Proceedings of the Nineteenth Annual ACM Symposium on Principles of Distributed Computing (PODC '00)*. ACM, New York, NY, USA, 7–.
[3] Eric Evans. 2002. Domain Driven Design: Tackling Complexity in the Heart of Business Software. (2002).
[4] Sean Hull. 2013. 20 Obstacles to Scalability. *Queue* 11, 7, Article 20 (July 2013), 7 pages. https://doi.org/10.1145/2508834.2512489
[5] Christopher Ireland and David Bowers. 2015. Exposing the myth: object-relational impedance mismatch is a wicked problem. In *DBKDA 2015, The Seventh International Conference on Advances in Databases, Knowledge, and Data Applications.* IARIA XPS Press, 21–26.
[6] Karl Kapp. 2005. Review of "Learning by Doing: A Comprehensive Guide to Simulations, Computer Games and Pedagogy in E-learning and Other Educational Experiences by Clark Aldrich". *eLearn* 2005, 9 (Sept. 2005).
[7] Lisa Kart and Nicholas Heudecker. 2015. Survey analysis: Practical challenges mount as Big Data moves to mainStream. *Gartner Group* (September 2015).
[8] Carsten Kleiner. 2014. No News in Database Education by All Accounts: Seriously? (Abstract Only). In *Proceedings of the 45th ACM Technical Symposium on Computer Science Education (SIGCSE '14)*. ACM, New York, NY, USA, 728–729.
[9] Carsten Kleiner. 2015. New Concepts in Database System Education: Experiences and Ideas (Abstract Only). In *Proceedings of the 46th ACM Technical Symposium on Computer Science Education (SIGCSE '15)*. ACM, New York, NY, USA, 698–698.
[10] Manning. 2017. Publications. (2017). https://www.manning.com/
[11] Sriram Mohan. 2017. Modern Database Paradigms - Course Website. (2017). https://sites.google.com/site/rhitadb/ accessed:July 21st 2017.
[12] Sriram Mohan, Stephen Chenoweth, and Shawn Bohner. 2012. Towards a Better Capstone Experience. In *Proceedings of the 43rd ACM Technical Symposium on Computer Science Education (SIGCSE '12)*. ACM, New York, NY, USA, 111–116.
[13] M. V. Ramakrishna. 2000. A Learning by Doing Model for Teaching Advanced Databases. In *Proceedings of the Australasian Conference on Computing Education (ACSE '00)*. ACM, New York, NY, USA, 203–207.
[14] Pramod J. Sadalage and Martin Fowler. 2012. *NoSQL Distilled: A Brief Guide to the Emerging World of Polyglot Persistence* (1st ed.). Addison-Wesley Professional.
[15] Michael Skirpan and Tom Yeh. 2015. Beyond the Flipped Classroom: Learning by Doing Through Challenges and Hack-a-thons. In *Proceedings of the 46th ACM Technical Symposium on Computer Science Education (SIGCSE '15)*. ACM, New York, NY, USA, 212–217. https://doi.org/10.1145/2676723.2677224
[16] Michael Stonebraker. 2010. SQL Databases V. NoSQL Databases. *Commun. ACM* 53, 4 (April 2010), 10–11. https://doi.org/10.1145/1721654.1721659
[17] Werner Vogels. 2009. Eventually Consistent. *Commun. ACM* 52, 1 (Jan. 2009), 40–44. https://doi.org/10.1145/1435417.1435432
[18] Ellen L. Walker and Oberta A. Slotterbeck. 2002. Incorporating Realistic Teamwork into a Small College Software Engineering Curriculum. *J. Comput. Sci. Coll.* 17, 6 (May 2002), 115–123.
[19] Noel Yuhanna. 2016. The Forrester Wave: Big Data NoSQL, Q3 2016 Scalability, Multimodal, Flexibility, And Lower Cost Drive Enterprise Adoption Of NoSQL. *Forrester Group* (August 2016).

A Visual Introduction to Conceptual Database Design for All

Don Goelman
Villanova University
Villanova, PA
don.goelman@villanova.edu

Suzanne W. Dietrich
Arizona State University
Phoenix, AZ
dietrich@asu.edu

ABSTRACT

The goal of the presented pedagogical tool is to engage all disciplines in learning how to understand their data and the relationships among the data, and subsequently representing those data in a relational database. The tool provides a visual introduction to important concepts in database design using Entity Relationship Diagrams as the primary visual design model, relating these same concepts to other models, such as UML diagrams and the crow's feet notation used in MySQL Workbench. Once the conceptual design is realized, the tool visually presents a methodology for mapping the various data concepts to a collection of relations. Relational databases are ubiquitous and conceptually simple for all majors to understand based on the analogy of a spreadsheet with named columns. A unique feature of this tool is a built-in formative self-assessment feature, called a checkpoint, to engage learners in reflecting on what they have learned. The checkpoint provides 20 questions, multiple-choice and true/false, over a given conceptual design to test the student's understanding of the design features and mapping to relations. Another novel capability of this tool is its ability for instructors to customize the example to their discipline, supporting the introduction of database topics within the context of the domain to which it is being applied. There are already customizations of the tool available in several disciplines, broadening the accessibility of data design to many majors. Experience has shown that the tool supports visual learners in all majors, including computer science.

CCS CONCEPTS

• **Information systems → Entity relationship models**; *Relational database model*;

KEYWORDS

courseware; visualizations; computer science for all

ACM Reference Format:
Don Goelman and Suzanne W. Dietrich. 2018. A Visual Introduction to Conceptual Database Design for All. In *SIGCSE '18: SIGCSE '18: The 49th ACM Technical Symposium on Computer Science Education, February 21–24, 2018, Baltimore , MD, USA.* ACM, New York, NY, USA, 6 pages. https://doi.org/10.1145/3159450.3159555

SIGCSE '18, February 21–24, 2018, Baltimore , MD, USA

ACM ISBN 978-1-4503-5103-4/18/02...$15.00
https://doi.org/10.1145/3159450.3159555

1 INTRODUCTION

"Databases for All" is a notable subtheme within the context of how computer science can reach out to all interests and all majors. Data and Information is one of the seven "big ideas" for the Computer Science Principles project [1]. The importance of databases in this conversation was incorporated early on, e.g., in the first edition of the Snyder and Henry book [23] in 2002, and the challenges of designing a database course for non-majors were discussed in Goelman's paper [13]. The pedagogical tool and experience described in this paper relates specifically to this subtheme.

This research is a component of an NSF sponsored project [7], whose goal is to introduce the fundamental concepts of database technology to students of many majors. One of the objectives of the project is to use visualization to engage students in the learning process. Two animations had been developed before the work described in this paper. The first one, referred to as "IntroDB," introduces students to relational databases and their similarities to/differences from/advantages over familiar spreadsheets. The second one, "QueryDB," provides more depth on queries by introducing students to important operators (e.g., sets, filtering, and joins) for getting information from a database and, ultimately, to SQL, the industry standard query language. The animations were used in various courses and supported by cooperative learning exercises. Evaluation of the animations [10] indicates that the animations support student learning.

The experience described in this paper deals with a newly developed third visualization in the sequence, Conceptual Database Design, or "DesignDB." IntroDB and QueryDB help students interpret the data when given a relational database over which they can ask questions or queries. The goal of DesignDB is to empower students with the knowledge to design their own relational database. As noted by Chilton,"the concept of designing a relational database can be a difficult one for beginning students to assimilate" [5]. DesignDB was developed to assist beginners of conceptual database modeling by visually illustrating the methodology to model the data with its relationships as an Entity Relationship (ER) Diagram and to map the design to a relational database schema.

The database visualizations are novel in several aspects. First, the tools have a built-in formative self-assessment feature, called a checkpoint, so that students can reflect on what they have learned. These checkpoints consist of 20 questions, multiple-choice ("mcq's" in our discussion below) and true/false, that quiz the student comprehensively over the learning outcomes of the visualization. Second, the visualizations are customizable, allowing instructors of all disciplines to change the default example to a contextual example for introducing database concepts within their class. All three visualizations, and supporting curricula, are freely available on the project's Web site [7], including customizations to various disciplines, such as astronomy, computational molecular biology, environmental science/ecology, forensics, geographic information systems, and statistics.

This paper describes in depth the structure of DesignDB and reports on the initial experiences with using DesignDB in a course for non-majors. Related work on visualizations and formative assessment are briefly presented in Section 2, contextualizing some of the decisions in the design and use of the visualizations. Section 3 describes the content of the DesignDB visualization for enhancing student learning of conceptual modelling and the design of its formative self-assessment feature for students to reflect on their learning. Section 4 describes the experience of using DesignDB in a non-majors database course, and the paper concludes with a discussion of plans and recommendations for going forward.

2 RELATED WORK

The pedagogical benefits of visualizations have been noted in the research literature in general [26], in STEM disciplines [16], and, most specifically, in computer science [3]. The ADbC project [18] provides a Web-based interface for walking computer science majors through database concepts, but it is not a visualization per se.

Probably the seminal paper on the topic of the pedagogy of visualization was the product of an ITiCSE Working Group [19], which was a major factor in informing the development of this project's products. In that paper the authors warn that the success of visualization is strongly dependent on how it is presented in (and out of) class. Therefore, cooperative exercises were designed to accompany the current database visualizations for in-class use. The research supports positive learning effects by the addition of discrete steps that provide the meaning of the structure of the animation as well as points that can be selected within the animation for replay [24]. Visual cues and focus during a visualization has also been shown to enhance learning [24, 25]. Both discrete steps and visual cueing have been incorporated into the database visualizations.

Another area of research that has influenced the current project is that of formative self-assessment. The initial implementations of the IntroDB and QueryDB visualizations did not include this feature, which we call a checkpoint, based on the database metaphor. Although the evaluation shown in [10] indicated that the animations support student learning, anecdotal reports supported student overconfidence in understanding the concepts, which is not uncommon with visualizations [25]. Therefore, checkpoints were added after an extensive review of the existing literature, showing formative self-assessment as an important ingredient in pedagogy. A typical definition is given by McMillan and Hearn [17] as "self-monitoring, self-evaluation, and identification and implementation of instructional correctness," while formative self-assessment adds to this the dimension of feedback during learning. Researchers recommend that student participation be required, not optional ([22] and [6]). Other influences on the design of our checkpoints included articles by Nicol [20], who recommends seven feedback principles; and, again, by Ross [22], who cautions against the reliability of some self-reported accomplishments on the checkpoints.

A unique aspect of the checkpoints in the visualizations is that the questions can also be customized to the discipline-specific example. The design and implementation of the checkpoints in IntroDB and QueryDB have been discussed by the authors [8]. This paper will elaborate on the design of the DesignDB checkpoint with respect to learning outcomes as part of the next section, which describes the visualization in depth.

3 CONCEPTUAL DESIGN

The pedagogical tool of DesignDB uses dynamic presentation and visual cues to present the fundamental concepts on database design. Table 1 shows an overview of the structure of the tool with its themes that are on the left-hand side navigation bar, along with its corresponding tool tip, and the names of the discrete steps within that theme. The themes and steps within each theme represent points in the animation that a student can restart or replay. This inherent structure provides the students with cues on the meaning of the animation, which leads to positive learning effects [24]. The Home theme provides the information about the pedagogical tool and project information along with a button to "Run Tutorial in Demonstration Mode". This mode is useful for presenting in class but students will choose each theme or topic to run the tutorial interactively. The Design theme motivates the process that the tool is capturing, by gathering the concepts to be represented in an ER diagram, which is then mapped to a relational database. The remainder of the themes are further described below.

3.1 Entities and Relationships

The themes overviewing entities and relationships introduce the notations for describing both concepts along with attributes that describe their properties. An important component of relationships are the cardinality and participation constraints of the associations between the entities. The "how many" question is introduced instead of the more formal "cardinality" term. How many times does the entity participate in the relationship - one time or multiple times? This question is answered in the context of M:N (ManyToMany), 1:N (OneToMany), and 1:1 (OneToOne), with illustrative examples over the sample enterprise. The "participation" question is posed, asking whether an entity is required to participate in the relationship or not. Again, examples are used to illustrate the concepts. Once the conceptual design of the enterprise is captured in an ER diagram, the diagram must be mapped for implementation. Based on the simplicity and popularity of the relational data model, the following mapping theme presents the methodology for mapping an ER diagram to a collection of relations.

3.2 Mapping

The mapping of an ER diagram to a relational database uses the canonical mapping approach discussed in many database texts [12]. The novelty provided by the pedagogical tool is its use of visual cues to enhance the presentation of the mapping. Each component is highlighted in the ER diagram and subsequently highlighted in its mapping within its corresponding relation. The mapping of relationships is shown in general as the inclusion of the primary key of each entity involved in the relationship as a foreign key in the resulting relation, and includes any descriptive attributes of the relationship itself. The primary key of the mapped relation is based on the cardinality of the relationship. This mapping approach is reiterated for each cardinality ratio. Also, the alternative mapping

Table 1: Visualization Structure

Theme: *Tool Tip*	Steps in Theme
Home: *Introduction to Designing Databases*	
Design: *What is Conceptual Design?*	Design
ERDiagram: *Overview of Entity Relationship Diagrams*	Intro Sample
Entities: *What concepts are to be stored in the database?*	Intro Composite Identify Summary
Relationships: *How are the concepts related?*	Intro Attributes HowMany ManyToMany OneToMany OneToOne Participation
Mapping: *How are ER diagrams mapped to tables?*	Intro Entities Relationships ManyToMany OneToMany OneToOne More1toN More1to1 Review
MoreDiagrams: *What concepts are to be stored in the database?*	Intro UML MySQL
Checkpoints: *Quiz yourself on another example - click the Show Checkpoint ERD button to see the ER diagram*	20 Questions T/F and mcq

approaches for 1:N and 1:1 relationships are presented, visually showing the combination of the two tables from the canonical approach having the same primary keys. At the end of the mapping theme, the Review step shows an ER diagram and the resulting visual relational schema. A unique aspect of this review is the ability to click a component on the ER diagram, which will be highlighted on both the ER diagram and its mapping in the visual schema. For example, Figure 1 illustrates how the AdvisedBy 1:N relationship is mapped using the alternative approach, including the key (FID) representing the student's one adviser in the Students table.

Figure 1 also illustrates the ability to show a textual abstraction of the relational schema, which is captured in Figure 2. Instead of using database jargon, the term "Summary Syntax" was introduced to represent a summary of the table and attribute names, with the primary key attributes of the table being underlined, and foreign keys represented in these simple examples by the naming convention of attributes. This textual syntax is commonly used

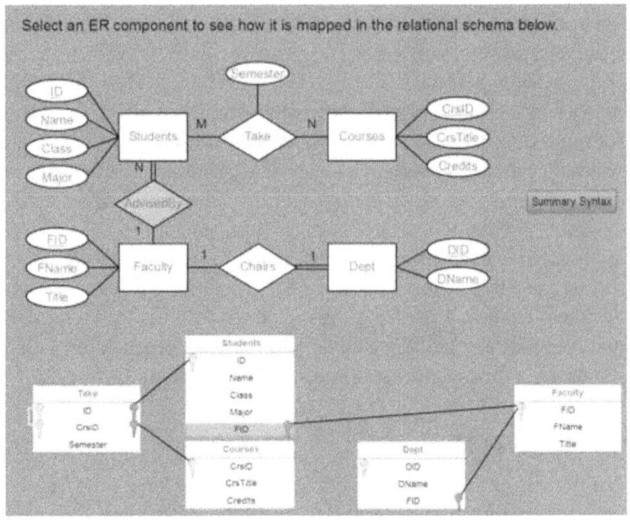

Figure 1: Visual Mapping Review.

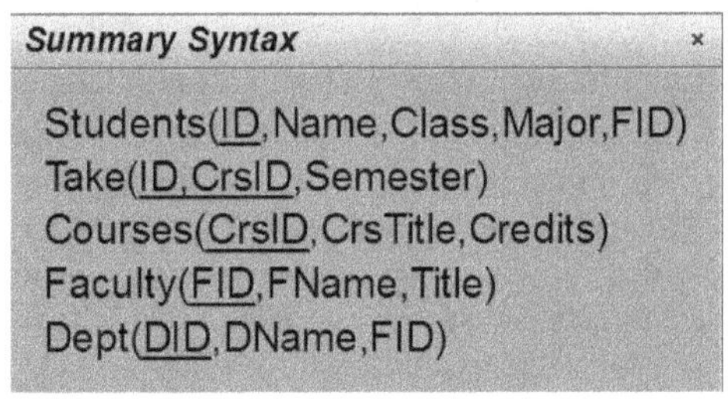

Figure 2: Summary Syntax.

in the abstraction of a schema. The visualization illustrates this summary syntax throughout the mapping process, after presenting the visual schema, and utilizes this abstraction in the presentation of the checkpoint.

3.3 Alternative Designs

There are several alternative diagrams that are also commonly used to represent the conceptual design of databases, including UML class diagrams [11] and the crow's foot notation used by a popular open-source database, MySQL, in its Workbench client software [21]. The visualization briefly explores both of these notations, illustrating that the different diagrams represent similar information: important concepts and their descriptive properties, associations or relationships between these concepts, and a depiction of the participation of each concept in the relationship. The UML and MySQL diagrams for the example enterprise appear in the visualization.

3.4 Checkpoints

The DesignDB checkpoint builds on the foundation of the formative self-assessment introduced in IntroDB and QueryDB with the use of customizable multiple-choice and true/false questions that assist students on reflecting on the state of their learning. The DesignDB checkpoint presents a generic example shown in Figure 3: items

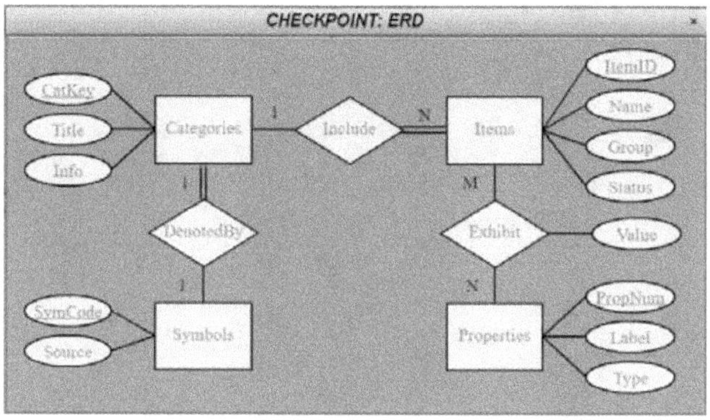

Figure 3: Checkpoint Entity Relationship Diagram.

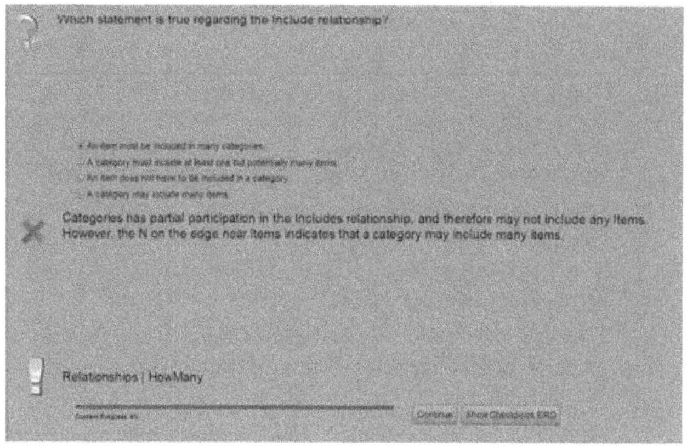

Figure 4: Sample Checkpoint Question with Feedback.

exhibiting properties, items classified into categories, and categories denoted by a symbol. The goal of this generic example is to ease the burden of instructors having to customize the 20 checkpoint questions to be domain specific.

Again in DesignDB, the checkpoint presents questions randomly to the student and randomizes the answer choices for multiple-choice questions as well. Figure 4 shows a sample multiple-choice question that has been answered incorrectly, as indicated by the red X. A green checkmark is used for a correct answer. In either case, the feedback explaining the underlying concepts is presented to the students, which is a recommended practice [6]. (Note that the extra space on the screen is to allow for longer questions and feedback in the customization process.) The yellow exclamation mark alerts the student to the concept being tested in the animation, which is the HowMany step of the Relationships theme for the question shown. Students can explore that concept by clicking on the words and later return to the checkpoint to complete the questions. There is a Continue button for students to proceed to the next question. The Show Checkpoint ERD button pops up a window with the ER diagram over which the checkpoint questions are being asked (Figure 3).

The checkpoint questions are designed to be comprehensive in covering the various learning outcomes of the visualization. Table 2 indicates the Question number, its type (T/F or Multiple-Choice["mcq"]), and its associated learning outcomes. Note that the question numbers are not shown to students during the formative self-assessment but are shown to instructors who wish to customize the checkpoint.

Table 2: Checkpoint Question Learning Outcomes

#	Type	Learning Outcome
1–3, 20	mcq	identify components (entity, relationship, attribute, composite attribute) in an ER diagram
4	mcq	identify primary keys in an ER diagram
5–7	T/F	interpret the participation and cardinality constraints indicated on the ER diagram to answer statements regarding the enterprise being modelled
8–10	mcq	interpret the cardinality ratios for relationships on an ER diagram to identify statements describing the enterprise being modeled
11,17–19	mcq	map an entity to its representation as a table, indicating its primary key
12–16	mcq	map a relationship (M:N, 1:N, 1:1) to its representation as a table, including alternative mapping techniques based on cardinality ratios (1:N, 1:1), and correctly identifying its primary key based on the cardinality ratio of the relationship

4 EXPERIENCE

The experience presented here relates to the use of DesignDB in the non-majors database class. The students first learned about the relational model, because of its simple tabular structure, before they saw the ER model [15]. They did cooperative exercises related to DesignDB, and the instructor screened it briefly in class; most reviewed it at least once on their own. They also had the opportunity to earn a point towards the relevant examination in return for exhibiting a screen shot of achieving at least 70% on DesignDB's Checkpoint segment. Finally, the instructor asked students for some feedback on their perceptions of the visualization.

4.1 Evaluation

Table 3 provides the assessment questions asked of the student regarding DesignDB, including the range of the Likert scores, together with the resulting mean of the results. On average, students viewed the DesignDB animation 2.7 times. The student responses indicated that they found DesignDB moderately helpful in understanding ERD's and their mapping to RDB's. In general, more students agreed than disagreed that the checkpoints in the visualization are an important component of the animation.

In addition, the students were asked the following open-ended question: Please provide feedback on the visualization and the checkpoint. A quantitative content analysis was performed by two researchers, coding the 16 responses received using an inductive data-driven approach. The two major categories that resulted from

Table 3: Assessment Questions and Results

#	Question	Mean (N = 18)
Q1	About how many times did you screen the visualization DesignDB?	2.7
Q2	On a scale of 0 (not at all) to 3 (very much so), how helpful was DesignDB in understanding ERD's and mapping them to RDB's)?	2.2
Q3	Take the statement "The checkpoints in the visualization are an important learning component of the animation." Classify your opinion as (1) Strongly agree; (2) Agree; (3) Neither agree nor disagree; (4) Disagree; (5) Strongly disagree. Breakdown: (1)#3, (2)#6 (3)#7(4)#1(5)#1	2.5

the coding are Helpful and Caveats. Subcategories of Helpful were introduced to capture how the visualization was helpful: Checkpoints, Visual Learner, Studying, Different Mode, and Generic (helpful or effective with no specific reason stated). Sample student comments follow:

- The visualizations were extremely helpful to me as I was preparing for exams and allowed me to see things unfold in a different way than in the traditional PowerPoint slides or through examples done in class. The checkpoints were important as they allowed me a gauge for how well I truly understood what I had just watched.
- I loved the checkpoints! Kind of tricky questions at first, but once I kept re-watching the visualizations, the checkpoints were very helpful. When I knew I could do the checkpoints, I knew I had a firm understanding of the material. Also, the extra point on the exams didn't hurt!
- The visualizations and checkpoints were extremely helpful in my opinion because I have never seen a database before. So, as a new learner of databases visualizing what to do/click/create is important to understanding not only how to create databases, but understanding what you are doing so you can replicate the process.
- I'm more of a visual learner so these kinds of things really help out and solidify what it is I need to work on and keep track of.

The intent of the Caveat category is to capture the responses that included a limitation. Here are some examples of these responses:

- Time consuming but effective.
- I thought they did an okay job at helping understand the concepts, but they were a bit clunky in their operation.
- I thought that some of the visualizations and checkpoints were helpful when preparing and reviewing for the exam, but if there was a concept that I didn't quite understand, I didn't feel that I could learn it from the visualizations.
- I thought that the visualizations and checkpoints themselves are an amazing addition to the course material as a whole. Although I did not utilize them that much personally, I could see how they could be extremely useful to someone who is more of a visual learner. I tend to do my best when I read a conceptual explanation of something and then am forced to work on a problem or example in front of me, but that is just my personal learning process.

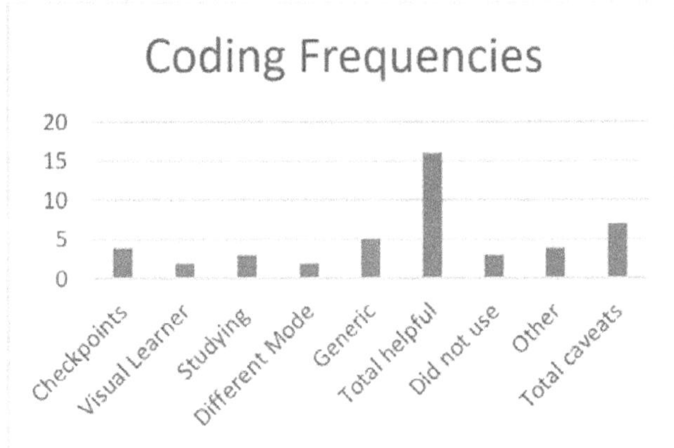

Figure 5: Quantitative Content Analysis of Responses.

Figure 5 shows a quantitative content analysis of the student responses. The Caveat subcategories are Did Not Use and Other, where the Other coded comments are included in the student responses provided above. Note that one comment could contribute to multiple coding subcategories. For example, the "Time consuming but effective" contributed to counts in Helpful: Generic and Caveats: Other.

4.2 Reflection

The student feedback was quite encouraging. Almost all students commented that the visualizations helped them learn. DesignDB was also made available as an optional supplement for a database class for computer science majors. Anecdotal feedback from majors also indicated the helpfulness of the visualization, especially for studying for exams. These results are also consistent with the evaluation of the IntroDB and QueryDB checkpoints [8], where student perceptions supported the helpfulness and importance of the visualizations and associated checkpoints.

5 DISCUSSION

The goal of engaging the broader community with the fundamental concepts of databases is an ongoing process. The visualizations provide an engaging presentation that introduces the novice to various concepts: the importance of a relational database versus a spreadsheet (IntroDB), how to query a relational database using SQL (QueryDB) and how to design a relational database (DesignDB). The checkpoints form an integral part of the learning in the animations by providing the learner with formative self-assessment. The customizations of the visualizations by instructors to various domains broaden the impact of the project [2, 4, 14]. Our domain partners are enthusiastic about engaging their respective communities with the power of databases and are working on building domain-specific cooperative exercises with snapshots of real-life data from their field.

The authors see the impact of the visualizations in their own field of computer science. There are a majority of students who say that they are visual learners and welcome the animations as a useful tool in acquiring and reviewing knowledge in their database classes. In fact, the visual schema presented in the animations is now typically included as part of the specification on all assignments, as it more clearly illustrates the connections between the tables through the use of foreign keys, which tend to be hidden in a textual schema representation.

The project is ongoing. In the near term, there is a visual tool that is being tested to aid instructors with the customization process [9], generating the files needed as a basis to customize each animation to their example. The domain partners will endeavor to provide custom cooperative database exercises for their respective fields. All visualizations, including customizations, are available on the project's Web site [7] along with supporting curricula. The source code for the visualizations will be released as open source at the project's completion. We look forward to additional recruits in computer science and other fields in spreading the appreciation of databases' relevance to all.

ACKNOWLEDGMENTS

This material is based upon work supported by the National Science Foundation under Grant No. DUE-1431848, Grant No. DUE-141431661, Grant No. DUE-0941584, and Grant No. DUE-0941401. Any opinions, findings, and conclusions or recommendations expressed in this material are those of the author and do not necessarily reflect the views of the National Science Foundation.

REFERENCES

[1] Owen Astrachan and Amy Briggs. 2012. The CS Principles Project. *ACM Inroads* 3, 2 (June 2012), 38–42. https://doi.org/10.1145/2189835.2189849

[2] Becky Ball, Suzanne W. Dietrich, and Don Goelman. 2017. An Interactive Learning Module for Teaching Ecology Students (and Professors) about Databases for Managing and Querying Large Datasets. (2017). Poster. In Ecological Society of America Annual Meeting, Portland, OR, August 2017.

[3] Mordechai Ben-Ari, Roman Bednarik, Ronit Ben-Bassat Levy, Gil Ebel, Andrés Moreno, Niko Myller, and Erkki Sutinen. 2011. A decade of research and development on program animation: The Jeliot experience. *Journal of Visual Languages & Computing* 22, 5 (2011), 375 – 384. https://doi.org/10.1016/j.jvlc.2011.04.004

[4] Jennifer Broatch. 2017. Databases! A Web-Based Introduction to the Data Science Techniques of Database Querying and Design. (2017). Poster. In USCOTS (United States Conference on Teaching Statistics) 2017, State College, PA, May 2017.

[5] Michael A. Chilton. 2006. Data Modeling Using Entity Relationship Diagrams: A Step-Wise Method. *Journal of Information Systems Education* 17, 4 (2006), 385-394.

[6] Concetta A. DePaolo and Kelly Wilkinson. 2014. Recurrent Online Quizzes: Ubiquitous Tools for Promoting Student Presence, Participation and Performance. *Interdisciplinary Journal of E-Learning and Learning Objects* 10 (2014), 75–91. http://www.ijello.org/Volume10/IJELLOv10p075-091DePaolo0900.pdf

[7] Suzanne W. Dietrich and Don Goelman. 2017. Databases for Many Majors. (2017). Retrieved November 27, 2017 from https://databasesmanymajors.faculty.asu.edu

[8] Suzanne W. Dietrich and Don Goelman. 2017. Formative Self-Assessment for Customizable Database Visualizations: Checkpoints for Learning. In *2017 ASEE Annual Conference & Exposition*. ASEE Conferences, Columbus, Ohio. https://peer.asee.org/27853

[9] Suzanne W. Dietrich and Don Goelman. 2017. A New Tool for Guiding Faculty in Customizing Database Visualizations for Learners of Many Majors. (2017). NSF Showcase, SIGCSE 2017, Seattle, WA.

[10] Suzanne W. Dietrich, Don Goelman, Connie M. Borror, and Sharon M. Crook. 2015. An Animated Introduction to Relational Databases for Many Majors. *IEEE Transactions on Education* 58, 2 (May 2015), 81–89. https://doi.org/10.1109/TE.2014.2326834

[11] Suzanne W. Dietrich and Susan D. Urban. 2010. *Fundamentals of Object Databases: Object-Oriented and Object-Relational Design.* Morgan Claypool, San Rafael, CA, USA. https://doi.org/10.2200/S00315ED1V01Y201012DTM012

[12] Ramez Elmasri and Shamkant B. Navathe. 2015. *Fundamentals of Database Systems* (7th ed.). Pearson.

[13] Don Goelman. 2008. Databases, Non-majors and Collaborative Learning: A Ternary Relationships. *SIGCSE Bull.* 40, 3 (June 2008), 27–31. https://doi.org/10.1145/1597849.1384281

[14] Kimberly Kobojek. 2017. Visualizations for Introducing Database Concepts in Forensic Science. (2017). Poster. In AAFS (American Academy of Forensic Sciences) 2017, New Orleans, LA, February 2017.

[15] David M. Kroenke and David J. Auer. 2015. *Database Concepts.* Pearson Education Limited.

[16] Michael B. McGrath and Judith R. Brown. 2005. Visual learning for science and engineering. *IEEE Computer Graphics and Applications* 25, 5 (Sept 2005), 56–63. https://doi.org/10.1109/MCG.2005.117

[17] James H. McMillan and Jessica Hearn. 2008. Student Self-Assessment: The Key to Stronger Student Motivation and Higher Achievement. *Educational Horizons* 87, 1 (2008), 40–49. http://www.jstor.org/stable/42923742

[18] Meg Murray and Mario Guimaraes. 2008. Recent Upgrades to an Animated Database Courseware (ADbC). In *Proceedings of the 46th Annual Southeast Regional Conference on XX (ACM-SE 46).* ACM, New York, NY, USA, 515–516. https://doi.org/10.1145/1593105.1593242

[19] Thomas L. Naps, Guido Rößling, Vicki Almstrum, Wanda Dann, Rudolf Fleischer, Chris Hundhausen, Ari Korhonen, Lauri Malmi, Myles McNally, Susan Rodger, and J. Ángel Velázquez-Iturbide. 2002. Exploring the Role of Visualization and Engagement in Computer Science Education. *SIGCSE Bull.* 35, 2 (June 2002), 131–152. https://doi.org/10.1145/782941.782998

[20] David Nicol. 2007. E-assessment by design: using multiple-choice tests to good effect. *Journal of Further and Higher Education* 31, 1 (2007), 53–64. https://doi.org/10.1080/03098770601167922

[21] Oracle. 2017. MySQL Workbench. (2017). Retrieved November 27, 2017 from https://www.mysql.com/products/workbench/

[22] John A. Ross. 2006. The reliability, validity, and utility of self-assessment. *Practical Assessment, Research & Evaluation* 11, 10 (Nov 2006). http://pareonline.net/pdf/v11n10.pdf

[23] Lawrence Snyder and Ray Henry. 2017. *Fluency with Information Technology: Skills, Concepts, & Capabilities.* Pearson Education, Limited.

[24] Ingrid A.E. Spanjers, Tamara van Gog, Pieter Wouters, and Jeroen J.G. van Merriënboer. 2012. Explaining the segmentation effect in learning from animations: The role of pausing and temporal cueing. *Computers & Education* 59, 2 (2012), 274 – 280. https://doi.org/10.1016/j.compedu.2011.12.024

[25] Herre Van Oostendorp, Michiel J. Beijersbergen, and Sam Solaimani. 2008. Conditions for Learning from Animations. In *Proceedings of the 8th International Conference for the Learning Sciences - Volume 2 (ICLS'08).* International Society of the Learning Sciences, 438–445.

[26] C. Douglas Wetzel, Paul H. Radtke, and Hervey W. Stern. 1994. *Instructional effectiveness of video media.* Lawrence Erlbaum Associates, Hillsdale, NJ, USA.

Improving Classroom Preparedness Using Guided Practice

Saturnino Garcia
University of San Diego
San Diego, California
sat@sandiego.edu

ABSTRACT

Numerous studies have demonstrated the effectiveness of flipped classrooms (e.g. peer instruction) in computer science courses. Flipped classrooms rely on students having obtained first exposure to concepts through pre-class activities such as viewing videos or reading a textbook. Having engaged with the material before class, class time can be spent on more challenging activities with feedback from the instructor and classmates. These pre-class activities can be a challenge for students, who often do not have the skills necessary to critically engage with the assigned reading/viewing. As a result students often come to class under-prepared despite completing the pre-class activities.

This paper presents the author's experience with adding *guided practice* worksheets to improve student preparedness in two courses: a CS1 course and a lower-division "Introduction to Computer Systems" course. These pre-class worksheets provided a structured set of learning objectives for students to focus on in their reading as well as exercises to test those objectives. Limited results indicate a high worksheet completion rate and a strong positive correlation between individual completion rates and final course grade. This paper also presents recommendations for those instructors wishing to adopt guided practice in their class.

ACM Reference Format:
Saturnino Garcia. 2018. Improving Classroom Preparedness Using Guided Practice. In *SIGCSE '18: The 49th ACM Technical Symposium on Computer Science Education, Feb. 21–24, 2018, Baltimore, MD, USA.* ACM, New York, NY, USA, 6 pages. https://doi.org/10.1145/3159450.3159571

1 INTRODUCTION

Active learning has been widely studied as an alternative to standard lecture-based teaching. While there are a number of educational activities that fall under the umbrella of active learning (e.g. think, pair, share exercises and flipped classrooms), *peer instruction* in particular has been shown to be an extremely effective at improving student learning outcomes [2]. While peer instruction was originally developed for teaching physics, recent studies have demonstrated its effectiveness in a wide range of computer science classes, from the introductory level [6] on up to upper-division classes [5].

SIGCSE '18, Feb. 21–24, 2018, Baltimore, MD, USA

ACM ISBN 978-1-4503-5103-4/18/02...$15.00
https://doi.org/10.1145/3159450.3159571

Peer instruction is a type of flipped classroom pedagogy, where students get their initial exposure to course concepts through pre-class reading or video lectures. With this initial exposure out of the way, students spend the class period working on deepening their understanding of these concepts. During class, students are presented with a number of challenging, conceptual multiple-choice problems that they have to solve on their own before working together with a small group of students to solve. Students submit their answers to these multiple choice questions twice: first after they work on their own, then again after they discuss with their group. Instructors use various techniques (e.g. clicker devices or apps) to gather student answers then hold a classwide discussion after each question to address any lingering misconceptions.

Like other flipped classroom pedagogies, peer instruction relies on students having engaged in the course material in a meaningful way before attending class. Without this initial exposure, students are not prepared to engage in meaningful conversations with their peers. When a small percentage of students come unprepared it is mostly them who suffer, but when significant portions of students come unprepared it can reduce class time discussions to those of basic terminology rather than deep conceptual understanding. Instructors who use peer instruction therefore generally use some mechanism to ensure that most students have spent time on the material before class.

The most widely used technique for ensuring students engage in pre-class activities is to assign a short "reading quiz" on the assigned material. This reading quiz can either be administered online through a learning management system (e.g. Blackboard) or at the beginning of class via multiple-choice voting. While reading quizzes force students to look at material before class, they suffer from a number of drawbacks.

First, these quizzes are generally multiple-choice and focus on basic definitions with which a student must be familiar. Students can easily circumvent meaningful engagement in the reading by simply skimming for definitions. Second, these quizzes do not provide adequate guidance on the full scope of learning objectives that students are expected to master both before class and then during/after class. This often leads students–especially younger, less experienced students–to underestimate what is required from them before, during, and after class; in essence it makes it easier to miss the forest for the trees. While reading quizzes are still a valuable tool in assessing students' pre-class knowledge–and taking advantage of the well-known *testing effect* [7]–they alone are not necessarily adequate in preparing students for class.

One way to address the shortcomings of reading quizzes, is to supplement them with what is known as *guided practice* [8]. Guided practice revolves around the use of worksheets with two main components: a set of learning objectives that the students are expected to master, and a set of exercises that allow students to practice the skills necessary to master some or all of the listed objectives. To further aid students in their preparation, the learning objectives can be split up into those that students are expected to be proficient in before class (i.e. basic objectives) and those that will be worked on during class and that will further need to be practiced after class (i.e. advanced objectives).

Guided practice works nicely as a precursor to a reading quiz. The worksheets make explicit the objectives that students will be expected to master, which addresses the second drawback of reading quizzes. They also also provide an opportunity for students to practice skills that may be difficult to exercise in a reading quiz, thus addressing the first downside of reading quizzes.

To the author's knowledge there have been no formal studies into the effectiveness of guided practice. This paper details one instructor's experiences with introducing guided practice into courses that use peer instruction. In particular, guided practice worksheets were added into two courses. The first was a CS1 course that the instructor had taught many times in the past. The second was a lower-division, "Introduction to Computer Science" course that the instructor had taught on one previous occasion. Based on these experiences, this paper provides some general recommendations for introducing guided practice into courses. While the focus of this paper is on peer instruction-based courses, it is likely to apply equally well to any course that uses a flipped classroom format where students first gain exposure to material before coming to class.

The rest of this paper is organized as follows. Section 2 explains the details of how guided practice was implemented in the two courses in which it was used, including example learning objectives and exercises. Section 3 looks at results of guided practice worksheets, including completion rates and their correlation to overall course grades. Section 4 discusses the instructor's experiences, including some limitations, potential improvements, and general recommendations for potential adopters. Finally, Sections 5 concludes this paper.

2 IMPLEMENTATION

In this section we will examine how guided practice was implemented in the classroom. This will include not only the basic integration mechanisms, but also examples from specific guided practice worksheets. While used in two separate courses, a CS1 course and a lower-division Intro to Computer Systems (ICS) course–the implementation in both courses was nearly identical.

2.1 Course Integration

Because peer instruction is a type of flipped classroom pedagogy, students were assigned reading that was to be completed before class. This reading was nearly always from the required course textbook and roughly half of all class meetings had assigned readings. Each reading assignment was accompanied with two pre-class activities: a guided practice worksheet and a reading quiz. The reading quizzes were available on the course's LMS (Blackboard) and were due an hour before class, while the exercises on the guided practice worksheet were due–in paper format–at the beginning of class. While the syllabus hinted at the preferred ordering–first guided practice exercises *then* the reading quizzes–it was not explicitly stated in writing, so students were free to complete these activities in whatever order they preferred.

These pre-class activities were given a weight of 7% of the student's final grade, but individual weights associated with guided practice and reading quizzes were left undefined to the students. The guided practice exercises were graded on a two point scale that was based on effort rather than correctness: 2 points for a reasonable attempt at *all* problems, 1 point for attempting only *some*, and 0 for attempting *none* of the problems. This grading scale was chosen because the exercises were meant to be a type of *formative* assessment rather than a *summative* assessment. Conversely, reading quizzes were graded for correctness, as they were a type of summative assessment for their understanding entering each class. Students were given permission to work with one other student on the guided practice exercises, but with the caveat that their solutions must be their own work and not simply a copy of their partner's work. Conversely, students were required to work alone on reading quizzes.

One notable difference between the implementation in the CS1 course and the ICS course was in the distribution of solutions to the guided practice exercises. In the former, answers were never released. Instead, students were encouraged to discuss the answers with their classmates or to attend office hours to discuss the questions. In the latter, answers were distributed on Blackboard; generally this occurred before a quiz or an exam where the answers could be used as a study guide.

2.2 Guided Practice Worksheet Overview

Each guided practice worksheet consisted of the five following sections.

(1) A short introduction providing a high-level overview of the reading.
(2) The required reading associated with the worksheet–or, on the rare occasion a link to a video.
(3) A set of "Basic" Learning objectives. These objectives were prefaced with a statement that students were responsible for being proficient in these objectives **before** class and that they would be tested on the reading quiz.
(4) A set of "Advanced" Learning objectives. Again these were prefaced with a statement, but this time indicating that they were skills that would be mastered both during class and after class (e.g. through homework assignments).
(5) A set of problems aimed at gaining experience with the basic learning objectives. There were a few occasions (less than 10%) where worksheets did not have this section.

The first step in developing each worksheet was to review the assigned reading and develop a list of learning objectives. This also happened to be the most time-consuming step. While the set of "big picture" objectives for a given reading might have been small, the instructor also needed to consider smaller-scale objectives that students should actively work on in order to build up to these bigger objectives.

After developing a complete list of learning objectives, each objective needed to be classified as either basic or advanced. Differentiating between basic and advanced learning objectives played a key role in the development of the worksheets. The basic objectives needed to be complete enough to provide the necessary background for meaningful in-class discussion but not so complex that students could not reasonably complete them on their own. It was also important that these basic objectives were not simply focused on remembering key terms from the reading, as the reading quizzes that were already being used were adequate in that regard.

To aid in the classification of learning objectives, the instructor made use of Bloom's revised taxonomy [4]. Each objective was placed in one of the following categories: remembering, understanding, applying, analyzing, evaluating, and creating. As a general rule-of-thumb, objectives at the bottom of the revised Bloom's hierarchy (remembering, understanding, and applying) were placed into the "Basic" objectives category while those at the top of the hierarchy (evaluating, creating) were placed in the "Advanced" objectives category. Objectives that were classified as *analyzing* were sometimes placed in the Basic category–often when they involved comparing and contrasting in a way that mirrored the book's discussion–while other times they were placed in the Advanced category.

After finalizing the set of basic objectives, a small number of exercises were either developed by the instructor or curated from the textbook. The goal was to test as many of the basic objectives as possible, either through worksheet exercises, reading quiz questions, or a combination of both.

2.3 CS1 Worksheet Example

The CS1 course examined here was an introduction to computer programming taught using the context of media computation. Students were not expected to have any experience with programming prior to entering the course. It was taught at a liberal arts college with small classes (enrollment was capped at 25 students per section).

The course was required for computer science majors and minors, mathematics majors, and was one of two options for all engineering majors; otherwise, it attracted students who were simply interested in computer science and/or programming. Students in the class were overwhelmingly freshmen and sophomores–with the former group being the largest. These levels of students are often still developing effective learning habits; aiding in the development of strong study skills was in fact one of the major motivations for introducing guided practice.

Throughout the semester the instructor developed 128 learning objectives, split across 20 guided practice worksheets. Of the 128 objectives, 90 were classified as basic objectives and the reminder (38) were advanced objectives. Space limitations prohibit presenting all of the objectives here, they–along with the guided practice worksheets–are available at https://home.sandiego.edu/~sat/gp.

Below we will present five learning objectives from each of the two categories. These objectives are taken from five separate guided practice worksheets that spanned the semester. To draw some parallels, the corresponding number in each category corresponds to the same guided practice worksheet. For example, Basic and Advanced Objectives 1 both came from the first worksheet of the semester.

2.3.1 Example Basic Learning Objectives. Below is the sample list of basic learning objectives for the CS1 course.

(1) Declare and assign values to primitive variables and String variables, using proper variable naming.
(2) Describe the roles of the *initialization area, continuation test,* and *change area* in a `for` loop.
(3) Write a Java statement that prints out a message only when a specific condition is met.
(4) Compare and contrast the method headers of accessors (getters) and modifiers (setters).
(5) Use the `put` method to add an entry into a given `HashMap` object.

In terms of Bloom's revised taxonomy, objective 2 can be classified as *understanding*; objectives 1, 3, and 5 can be classified as *applying*; and objective 4 can be classified as *analyzing*.

The instructor deliberately avoided objectives for the *remembering* category for several reasons. First, the instructor wanted to emphasize that the goal wasn't to memorize key terms. Second, the key terms were integrated into higher level objectives (e.g. in objective 2 above) so it is clear to students that they need to know these terms. Third, a number of explicit objectives for defining terms or producing lists would have further increased an already significant number of learning objectives. This could have a negative impact on students who are already unsure about their abilities, as a long list of objectives could be overwhelming to the student.

Without the guided practice worksheets, these basic objectives would likely be implicitly embedded within other course objectives rather than explicitly stated. By making them explicit, students have a fuller understanding of the many smaller steps it takes to build up to the more advanced/abstract objectives, and their reading can take on new meaning.

2.3.2 Example Advanced Learning Objectives. Below is the sample list of advanced learning objectives for the CS1 course.

(1) Trace the execution of a series of Java statements using a *memory map.*
(2) Find and fix array index out-of-bounds exceptions in a `for` loop.
(3) Modify a method to make it more "flexible" by replacing constants with parameters.
(4) Identify the commonalities between all getters and setters.
(5) Identify cases when you would use a `HashMap` to solve a problem.

In terms of Bloom's revised taxonomy, objective 1 can be classified as *applying*; objectives 2 and 4 can be classified as *analyzing*; objective 5 can be classified as *evaluating*; and objective 3 can be classified as *creating*.

Note that objective 1 is an example of *applying* being part of an advanced objective. While it was generally true that objectives classified as *applying* were considered Basic objectives, some algorithms or concepts are more difficult to apply so were bundled under the Advanced objectives. For this particular example students must do some small-scale analysis in order to determine whether a value is a primitive (e.g. `int`) or an object (e.g. `String`).

2.3.3 Example Practice Exercises. As previously discussed, most worksheets had associated example exercises meant to help students become proficient in the basic learning objectives. Below are a couple examples of these practice questions.

- Complete the following Pixel method so that it prints "Woah, that's seriously red!" if the red component of the calling object is greater than 200.

```
public void printIfVeryRed()
{
  // Fill in the code that goes here.
  // Remember that this is a Pixel method
  // so "this" refers to a Pixel object.
}
```

- Write Java code to create three new Picture objects and add them to the 'gallery' map, using whatever titles you want.

The first and second question exercise basic learning objective 3 and 5, respectively.

2.4 ICS Worksheet Example

The course described here was an introductory course on computer systems (ICS). This course is generally the third computer science course taken by computer science majors, with the pre-requisite being a CS2 course that covers basic data structures and algorithms.

The course aimed to introduce students to the fundamental concepts of computer systems, with a focus on the *instruction set architecture* and *operating system* levels of abstractions. Students were tasked with learning to program in C–for most, their first exposure to a second language–as well as the x86-64 assembly language. They would also explore the concept of the memory hierarchy (with a focus on caching) and operating systems concepts such as processes, virtual memory, and concurrency.

The course textbook [1] is widely used but is quite dense and previous student feedback indicated they had a difficult time learning from it. Part of the goal of introducing guided practice into this course was to help them develop better skills in reading comprehension for technical material, specifically developing a goal-oriented mindset rather than a memorization mindset.

The instructor developed 172 learning objectives, split across 22 guided practice worksheets. Of the 172 objectives, 118 were classified as basic objectives and the reminder (54) were advanced objectives. Again, a full list of these objectives and their accompanying worksheets are available at https://home.sandiego.edu/~sat/gp.

Below we will present three learning objectives from each of the two categories. These objectives are taken from three separate guided practice worksheets that spanned the semester.

2.4.1 *Example Basic Objectives.*

(1) Describe the role of each of the *condition code registers.*
(2) Contrast the line matching process in direct-mapped caches with that in a set associative cache.
(3) Given the size of a page and the virtual address size, calculate the number of *page table entries* (PTEs).

In terms of Bloom's revised taxonomy, objectives 1 and 2 can be classified as *understanding* while objective 3 can be classified as *applying*.

Again the instructor purposely avoided objectives targeted at the *remembering* level of the taxonomy, partly to deemphasize memorization and partly to limit the number of learning objectives presented to students.

	2 points	1 point	0 points
Mean	14.642	1.821	2.536
Std. Dev.	3.456	1.338	3.029
Median	15	1.5	2

Table 1: CS1 Worksheet Grades. (N = 28 students) The median number of submissions (out of 19) that received full credit was 15.

2.4.2 *Example Advanced Objectives.*

(1) Convert between C code that contains if-else statements and the equivalent x86-64 assembly code.
(2) Simulate the operation of a set (or fully) associative cache with an LRU replacement policy on a stream of memory accesses.
(3) Given a page table entry, determine whether the virtual page is on the disk, in physical memory, or has not yet been allocated.

In terms of Bloom's revised taxonomy, each of these objectives can be classified as *applying*. Developing learning objectives targeting the highest-levels of Bloom's taxonomy (evaluating and creating) was especially challenging for this course. This was largely a result of two factors: the complex nature of modern computer system design and the goals of the course. An advanced course on computer system design (e.g. a principles of operating systems course) would be a better fit for objectives that involve designing and evaluating complex systems.

3 RESULTS

The guided practice worksheets were meant to increase student preparedness in a flipped classroom environment. In this section we will present some limited results to help characterize guided practice's potential effectiveness. Specifically, we will look at the rate at which students completed the worksheet exercises and the correlation between the number of completed worksheets and the final course grade for each student.

Please note that this work is intended as an experience report and therefore presents only limited results. Future work could include more detailed statistical analysis with larger sample sizes.

3.1 CS1 Data

As described in Section 2.1, worksheet exercises were graded on a two point scale based on completion rather than correctness. Table 1 shows the mean, median, and standard deviation values for the number of submissions receiving each grade (2, 1, or 0 points) in the CS1 course. There were 19 total guided practice problem sets that were graded for each of the N = 28 students in the course (split across two sections).

The table shows that most students fully completed (i.e. received 2 points) roughly 75% of the worksheets (Median: 15/19). This table also shows that it was relatively rare for a student to submit solutions that did not reasonably attempt all problems in the worksheet; more common–although still relatively rare–was for students to simply not submit anything (Median: 2/19).

This completion data indicates that students were largely motivated to complete the worksheet exercises. We viewed this as an

	2 pts	1 pt	0 pts
Mean	10.643	1.714	5.643
Std. Dev.	5.576	1.332	5.665
Median	12	2	4

Table 2: ICS Worksheet Grades. (N = 14 students) The median number of submissions (out of 18) that received full credit was 12.

encouraging sign as getting buy-in for these additional exercises is key to ensuring they have maximum effect. Combined with the relatively low weighting of these exercises on the overall grade (see: Section 2), it appears as though students thought the exercises were worthwhile on their own. Future work could include attitudinal surveys so as to better understand the students' motivations in completing the exercises.

Being prepared for class means that students are ready to learn the covered topics, and are therefore more likely to perform well on homework, quizzes, and exams. If the guided practice worksheets improve preparedness, we would expect there to be a positive correlation between the percentage of worksheets in which a student received a 2 (variable X) and their final course letter grade (variable Y).

Our null hypothesis (H_0) was that the Pearson correlation coefficient (r) between X and Y is 0, indicating no correlation between worksheet completion rates and final letter grades. The alternative hypothesis (H_1) is that $r \neq 0$, i.e. there is a correlation between the two variables. We calculated r to be 0.433, which for $N = 28$ results in a $p - value$ of 0.011. Because $p - value < 0.05$ we can reject the H_0 and accept H_1.

3.2 Intro to Computer Systems (ICS) Data

Table 2 shows the mean, median, and standard deviation for the ICS course. In this course there were 18 total guided practice problem sets and a total of $N = 14$ students.

The results once again indicate that most students submitted reasonable answers to all the questions on a strong majority of worksheets (Median: 12/18). While the number of students submitting only partially completed problem sets was similar to the CS1 course (Median 2/18), the number of non-submissions was twice as high (Median: 4/18) as the other course. The exact reason for the larger number of non-submissions is unclear; future work could survey students as a way to better understand the difference.

We once again tested our null hypothesis (H_0) that there is no correlation between worksheet completion rate and final letter grade. For this course, the we calculated r to be 0.875, which for $N = 14$ results in $p - value$ of 0.000021. We were once again able to reject the null hypothesis and conclude there is a correlation.

4 DISCUSSION

The goal of introducing guided practice worksheets was to increase student preparedness in a flipped classroom environment like peer instruction. In this section we will discuss some limitations of our implementation of guided practice and some possible future improvements. We also provide recommendations for possible adopters.

4.1 Limitations

One of the key components of the guided practice sheets was the list of learning objectives. These learning objectives can encourage active engagement with the reading, as students are aware of the ultimate goals of the reading beyond simple memorization of key terms. The obvious downside is that the instructor needs to build this list of learning objectives.

While some textbooks provide learning objectives–e.g. the CS1 textbook [3] contained a list of learning objectives at the beginning of each chapter–many do not–e.g. the textbook in the Intro to Computer Systems [1]. Even for those textbooks that do provide learning objectives, the quality or scope of the objectives may not be appropriate for the guided practice worksheets. For example, one of the learning objectives from an early chapter in [3] reads, "To write methods (functions)." While this is a well-written objective that fits into the *creating* category of Bloom's revised taxonomy, introductory students often need more guidance in the form of objectives at a lower level of Bloom's taxonomy. For example, the instructor developed several lower-level objectives for this chapter in the textbook, including the following objectives: "Identify each component of a *method declaration*" and "Describe what it means for a method to have a *return type* of `void`."

Developing these learning objectives can be time-consuming. However, instructors looking to adopt guided practice for their CS1 or Intro to Computer Systems courses can take advantage of those developed by the instructor that are freely available at https://home.sandiego.edu/~sat/gp. Guided practice worksheets for other classes will also be available.

Another limitation of guided practice is the increased amount of grading required by instructors, teaching assistants, and/or course graders. While this limitation is ameliorated by having problem sets graded based on completion, each submission still needs to viewed by a grader who must make a judgment about the quality of the student's effort.

This extra grading overhead could possibly be reduced by an auto-grading system but that could limit the types of questions that could be asked (e.g. multi-choice, matching, or fill-in-the-blank). These limited types of questions may not be as useful in assessing students at this very early stage of learning. This is especially true for learning objectives based on *applying*, where the steps taken to get the answer are likely just as important as getting the final, correct answer.

Finally, another limitation is the additional class prep-time required by each student. Many students are often stretched thin from other classes, extracurricular activities, and personal obligations. If not explained correctly, it can seem like the worksheets are just forcing extra work on the students. It is therefore important to explain–in class, the syllabus, or both–to students that the worksheets are there to help them structure their learning and develop the skills necessary to get the most out of their study time.

4.2 Future Improvements

While we consider the introduction of guided practice in these two courses to be a success, we identified several possible improvements for future implementations.

The first suggested improvement is to do electronic submission of the guided practice exercises and provide immediate feedback to the students. While solutions were provided in the Intro to Computer Systems course, there was sometimes a lengthy delay between the due date and the release of the reference solutions. Students need this feedback to help identify misconceptions; delaying this feedback is likely detrimental to their learning.

This is a fairly simple improvement to make. In a more recent teaching of the course, the instructor utilized their school's course management system (CMS) to allow students to submit their work online. After submission, the reference solutions automatically became available to the students.

A second suggested improvement would be to introduce a new "Post-class Exercises" section to the worksheets. While the "Pre-class Exercises" were aimed at testing the basic learning objectives from the worksheet, the only means of exercising these advanced objectives outside of class were the course programming projects. Students would likely benefit from additional, lower-overhead means of practicing these advanced objectives in preparation for quizzes and exams. A set of post-class exercises would be very similar to typical homework problem sets; instructors who have previously given homework problems could easily merge those into the guided practice worksheet. The instructor would need to decide whether these post-class problems would be part of the grade or only suggested problems for more practice.

One final improvement might be to introduce a new type of learning objective into the guided practice worksheet, a learning objective that crosses the boundaries of assigned readings and therefore might not be appropriately encapsulated in a single worksheet. For example, the aforementioned "To write methods (functions)" is a simple example of one of these cross-cutting objectives. Another example for a CS1 course might include "Utilize existing classes to solve a new problem."

These type of objectives are the high-level objectives that often show up on a course syllabus. By adding these objectives to the guided practice worksheet, they explicitly tie individualized readings to the larger goals of the course and can help reinforce the "big picture" goals that may be obscured when students are learning complex new topics.

4.3 Recommendations for Adopters

Those wishing to adopt guided practice for their courses should keep the following recommendations in mind:

- When developing your own learning objectives, backwards design can be of great use. Start with a question you asked on a recent exam and then list all of the steps requires to solve that problem. For each of these steps, develop a learning objective and identify the spot in the reading where this objective is first introduced.
- Make the guided practice exercises due at least an hour before class. While it may not be possible to grade them before class, looking at a sample of the submissions can help identify the basic learning objectives that students are still struggling with. Similarly, the instructor could ask students to optionally submit any questions they have about the basic objectives and could spend a few minutes at the beginning of class addressing the common questions.
- The list of advanced learning objectives can make an effective study guide for quizzes and exams. Encourage students to develop new questions aimed at these objectives and share them with the class; you may also want to offer incentives (e.g. extra credit) for doing so.
- One important goal of teaching is to create *self-regulated learners*, those who understand how they learn most effectively and can tailor their study accordingly. Guided practice worksheets can be part of scaffolding this process, specifically when it comes to reading new material. At the beginning of the semester, guided practice worksheets can contain complete lists of objectives. As the semester progresses, the exercise questions can remain but students can be tasked with developing the learning objectives themselves. Ultimately, students should be able to create a complete guided practice worksheet on their own, demonstrating not only their mastery of the content but also the process of learning the content.

5 CONCLUSION

This paper examined the use of guided practice worksheets in two separate lower-division computer science classes. These worksheets are meant to provide additional support for instructors using a flipped classroom course structure such as peer instruction. By adding explicit learning objectives and exercises to be completed before students come to class, these worksheets can improve student preparedness, allowing for class-time to focus more on advanced learning objectives.

A strong completion rate as well as a positive correlation between completion rate and final course grade provide some evidence of the level of student buy-in as well as the utility of the guided practice worksheets. For those interested in adopting guided practice in their courses, a complete set of worksheets for both a CS1 and an Intro to Computer Systems course are freely available at https://home.sandiego.edu/~sat/gp.

REFERENCES

[1] Randal E. Bryant and David R. O'Hallaron. 2016. *Computer Systems: A Programmer's Perspective* (third ed.). Pearson.
[2] Catherine Crouch and Eric Mazur. 2001. Peer Instruction: Ten years of experience and results. *American Journal of Physics* 69, 9 (2001), 970–977. https://doi.org/10.1119/1.1374249
[3] Mark Guzdial and Barbara Ericson. 2007. *Introduction to Computing & Programming with Java: A Multimedia Approach.* Pearson.
[4] David R. Krathwohl. 2002. A Revision of Bloom's Taxonomy: An Overview. *Theory Into Practice* 41, 4 (2002). https://doi.org/10.1207/s15430421tip4104_2
[5] Cynthia Bailey Lee, Saturnino Garcia, and Leo Porter. 2013. Can Peer Instruction Be Effective in Upper-division Computer Science Courses? *Transactions on Computing Education* 13, 3, Article 12 (Aug. 2013), 22 pages. https://doi.org/10.1145/2499947.2499949
[6] Leo Porter, Dennis Bouvier, Quintin Cutts, Scott Grissom, Cynthia Lee, Robert McCartney, Daniel Zingaro, and Beth Simon. 2016. A Multi-institutional Study of Peer Instruction in Introductory Computing. *ACM Inroads* 7, 2 (May 2016), 76–81. https://doi.org/10.1145/2938142
[7] Henry L. Roediger III and Andrew C. Butler. 2011. The critical role of retrieval practice in long-term retention. *Trends in Cognitive Sciences* 15, 1 (2011), 20–27. https://doi.org/10.1016/j.tics.2010.09.003
[8] Robert Talbert. 2013. Inside the inverted proofs class: Guided Practice holds it together. http://www.chronicle.com/blognetwork/castingoutnines/2013/03/13/inside-the-inverted-proofs-class-guided-practice-holds-it-together/. (2013).

Unencapsulated Collection—A Teachable Design Smell

Giuseppe De Ruvo
Dep. of Electrical and Computer Engineering, The University of Auckland, Auckland, New Zealand
g.deruvo@auckland.ac.nz

Ewan Tempero
Andrew Luxton-Reilly
Dep. of Computer Science, The University of Auckland, Auckland, New Zealand
e.tempero@auckland.ac.nz
a.luxton-reilly@auckland.ac.nz

Nasser Giacaman
Dep. of Electrical and Computer Engineering, The University of Auckland, Auckland, New Zealand
n.giacaman@auckland.ac.nz

ABSTRACT

Design smells are design structures that indicate poor design quality. Many identified smells are difficult to teach as they require a degree of experience and judgement that novices, by definition, do not have. We have identified a design smell, which we call "unencapsulated collection", that is common in novice designs. It is simple to describe, allowing it to be objectively detected, and the refactoring steps needed to remove the smell are usually simple to illustrate. We give a description of the smell and present the results of an empirical study showing its prevalence. We outline the general steps for refactoring the smell, and illustrate it with a case study. The simplicity of this smell makes it a good candidate for teaching good design principles to novices.

KEYWORDS

Software Engineering, Design smells, Abstraction, Collections

ACM Reference Format:
Giuseppe De Ruvo, Ewan Tempero, Andrew Luxton-Reilly, and Nasser Giacaman. 2018. Unencapsulated Collection—A Teachable Design Smell. In *SIGCSE '18: SIGCSE '18: The 49th ACM Technical Symposium on Computing Science Education, February 21–24, 2018, Baltimore , MD, USA.* ACM, New York, NY, USA, 6 pages. https://doi.org/10.1145/3159450.3159469

1 INTRODUCTION

Teaching design is hard. It's hard because there are few objective criteria for identifying good or bad designs, or rules that can be blindly followed that lead to designs that would be generally recognised as being good. We know good design when we see it—but only if we have had sufficient experience. We often cannot convey our understanding of what makes a good design to novices because they—by definition—do not have the experience to appreciate what we see. In order to be able to teach design, we need such objective criteria. It does not have to be many, just something to bootstrap a students' design experience. We offer "unencapsulated collection" as a good candidate.

SIGCSE '18, February 21–24, 2018, Baltimore , MD, USA

ACM ISBN 978-1-4503-5103-4/18/02...$15.00
https://doi.org/10.1145/3159450.3159469

The importance of teaching what makes good design is well understood. The ACM/IEEE Curriculum Guidelines for Undergraduate Programs in Computer Science (CS2013) includes the following topics in the Core-Tier1 SDF/Algorithms and Design unit:

- Abstraction
- Program decomposition
- Encapsulation and information hiding
- Separation of behavior and implementation

The Curriculum Guidelines for Undergraduate Degree Programs in Software Engineering (SE2014) has Software Design as a Knowledge Area in its own right.

However, teaching good design principles to novice programmers is difficult [10, 18]. Even for students in advanced programming courses to be more reflective about their design, explicit guidance and requirements is still necessary [11]. Yet, it is appreciated that students should be exposed to software design to develop their modeling skills as early as possible [7].

The question we want to address is how to teach novice programmers the beginnings of good design. While design advice such as design patterns [14], design smells [13], anti-patterns [21], and the like are accepted as leading to good design, they are not suitable to teach to novices due to the need for experience to use these ideas successfully—they are not "teachable" to novices.

To effectively teach design at an introductory level we need good candidates of design advice that:

(i) is accessible to novices, so that they can appreciate their value, and the wider value of design in general,
(ii) has objective criteria for determining whether or not the principle can be applied, or has been applied correctly, so that students can gain experience applying design criteria and may be integrated into development environments for timely feedback and assessment [18], and
(iii) has clear advice to follow if it is determined the principle has not been applied correctly, so that students can appreciate the consequences of improving design through refactoring.

The overall goal of our research is to improve our ability to teach good design. Our experience is that novices prefer rules to follow or objective criteria to apply, so we would like to identify such rules or criteria. We have identified the "unencapsulated collection" design smell as a possibility.

In this paper we argue that it is a design smell that is accessible to novices, and is one that novices would benefit from knowing about. Specifically:

RQ1: Does unencapsulated collection have the desired properties?

RQ2: To what degree does the unencapsulated collection design smell occur in student work?

For RQ1 we need to demonstrate that the design smell can be detected through the application of objective criteria (and in fact, can be detected automatically), and that the advice for removing it is sufficiently mechanical that it would be accessible to novices. This is Section 3.

For RQ2 we need to demonstrate that novices do create designs with the unencapsulated collection smell often enough that teaching it will be of benefit. This is Section 4.

A good object-oriented design will have classes representing abstractions that made sense to the purpose of the program. While many interesting programs will use one or more collections, in most cases the collections themselves are not abstractions associated with the program's purpose. Instead they are part of a relevant abstraction.

For example, consider a program to read in a data file containing a list of numbers with the purpose of providing statistics (sum, mean, median, etc) of the numbers on demand. A reasonable design would be to have a method that reads the numbers from the file and then supplies the result to other methods (which we will call *clients*). A reasonable multi-class design would have the method reading the file in a separate class from the client method that (for example) outputs the mean value for the data to read.

Suppose the method reading the file returns a "naked" or *unencapsulated* collection (e.g., in Java a `java.util.List`). In this design, the collection is not obviously related to the purpose of the program. A list of numbers could be used for many purposes other than statistics. Furthermore, any client would then have to do the necessary processing related to its responsibility. For example, the method for outputting the mean would have to both compute the mean as well as send it the result to the appropriate output location. Another method, possibly in a different class, with the responsibility of outputting the sum would do something very similar (but not identical).

An alternative design would be to create a class (e.g. "DataSet") that encapsulates the collection. The collection would be a field in this class, and the class' public interface would provide methods providing an abstraction relevant to the purpose of the program (e.g. `sum`, `mean`, possibly also `loadFromFile` that reads the data from the file). This choice would more obviously convey how the class contributes to the overall purpose. It would also gather together all the code that processes the collection into one place, rather than having it scattered over several other classes.

The remainder of this paper is organized as follows. Section 2 deals with related work on design. The unencapsulated collection design smell is defined in Section 3 and its prevalence in student code is discussed in Section 4. Section 5 examines a case study. In Section 6 we explain the genesis of the unencapsulated collection design smell. Finally, in Section 7 we present the conclusion and future directions.

2 RELATED WORK

Designing good software is as much of an art as it is a science. In a special issue of IEEE Software, Baker et al. observe that

> ... we don't have a sufficient understanding of what effective professional software designers do when they design, nor much well-founded guidance about how to match method to context [5, p. 28]

The substantial variability in the practice of design in the software industry, and the lack of codified design strategies, apart than a few design patterns, makes it difficult to teach software design in the university environment [15]. The difficulty in teaching design perhaps explains why graduating students still have significant difficulties with design tasks [20]. Although students' software design strategies have not been extensively studied, Stuurman et al. [22] conducted a small qualitative study investigating the way that graduate students approached a software *redesign* task that required them to refactor their code. They observed that graduate students lacked the ability to design using top-down breadth-first strategies used by experts, but rather used local and concrete approaches more typical of novices. They conclude that students need more specific, and more concrete guidelines.

Object-oriented programming requires students to make decisions about how classes are designed. Whether to teach objects early or late has been the subject of some debate [4, 6, 19], but regardless of when object-oriented programming is taught, there is widespread agreement that the design of OO programs involves notions of abstraction, encapsulation and information hiding.

Armstrong identified a set of 88 sources that specified concepts that were central to object-oriented programming. Encapsulation was the fourth most common concept, after Inheritance, Object and Class. Armstrong defines encapsulation as:

> a technique for designing classes and objects that restricts access to the data and behavior by defining a limited set of messages that an object of that class can receive.[2, p. 125]

Encapsulation is often taught in CS1, particularly in courses that take an objects-first approach [23]. However, students frequently struggle to understand how to design classes that use the principles of encapsulation effectively. Wick et al. [24] claim that students with poor understanding of encapsulation frequently use accessor methods to access member data inappropriately. They advocate teaching students to adhere to four simple design rules for accessor methods. For example, the first design rule suggests that whenever a client attempts to access private member data, identify why the client requires the data and write a method for achieving the behaviour rather than providing a getter/setter pair [24, p. 101].

At the design level, the *names* of member data and methods that operate on the data are in the forefront. There has been a recent and growing interest in 'naming' by software engineering researchers [8, 17]. In fact, poor names make software difficult to understand and hinder the maintainability of a code base, particularly when "70% of source code of a software consists of identifiers" [12].

Laurie et al. [16] state that good identifiers come from existing words in dictionaries, well-known abbreviations and stopwords. They made this conclusion by splitting identifiers into separate words, e.g. *ServerVendorMngr* is split into *Server*, *Vendor* and *Mngr*. Butler et al. [8] investigated the role of Java identifier names, their conventions, and how they affect not only code comprehension but even research and tools that rely on names [9]. Arnaoudova et al. [3] analysed the inconsistency among naming, documentation, and implementation regarding methods and attributes. They abstracted such inconsistencies into 17 recurring antipatterns called "Lingusitic antipatterns (LAs)". An important aspect we have to take into account is that students make a variety of mistakes [1] because most of the time they focus on the algorithm and problem itself and not on how they are writing the code, e.g. naming variables and functions/methods.

3 UNENCAPSULATED COLLECTION

We define the design smell Unencapsulated Collection as follows:

Unencapsulated Collection. *A method returns a collection and clients of the method perform operations on what the method returns.*

In this definition, "collection" means anything that represents a group of elements and provides an interface that treats the group as a whole or the individual elements. This includes arrays, lists, maps, sets, queues, stacks, and so on.

Should such a design smell be identified, then the refactoring advice is to encapsulate the collection, that is:

(1) Identify operations performed by clients of the method
(2) Use the operations identified to determine what abstraction is intended
(3) Create a class for the abstraction, with the collection as a field
(4) Move the code for the operations performed on the result of the method into the new class (this may include the original method, perhaps as a constructor)
(5) Refactor the clients to use the new class.

Encapsulating a collection means hiding it behind an interface that presents an abstraction consistent with the purpose of the program. While parts of the interface may still reflect the collection nature of the abstraction (e.g. "size"), there will also be aspects of it that are domain-specific.

In principle it is possible to encapsulate any collection. For example, a stack can be implemented by encapsulating a list. Whether it is appropriate depends on the impact to the overall design. For example, if the implementation of all methods in the interface is to just invoke a method on the collection (e.g. `size()`) then there is likely to be little change to the overall design. If however, some implementations involve non-trivial manipulation of the underlying collection (e.g. iterating over the list to sum its contents), then the abstraction being provided is more appropriate for the program's purpose.

This is not to say the decision will always be clear. The implementation of methods for a stack that encapsulates a list will be very simple, yet we find value in distinguishing the stack and list abstractions. Similarly, if we want to use a collection that we only ever add elements to or iterate over, then encapsulating the collection with a simple interface restricting to just those operations would more clearly convey its purpose.

While this decision may not be always obvious, it does provide a good example of what it means to make design decisions. The value of examining this decision is that it is objective enough that novices can identify for themselves cases that need such a decision, and simple enough that they can understand the possibilities and their consequences.

However, if the Unencapsulated Collection design smell does not occur very often in novice programmer designs, then the value in discussing it will be limited. We next discuss the degree to which this smell is likely to occur. In fact, we have implemented a prototype tool that parses the Java Abstract Syntax Tree in order to find all the methods returning collections and their uses. Results are displayed in a user friendly web interface thus we were able to analyse and validate them. The results list every instance of Unencapsulated Collection found with references to the location in the original source. In other words, it is possible to navigate directly to the interested clients using those methods with highlighting on the method's calls.

4 PREVALENCE OF UNENCAPSULATED COLLECTION

We have argued Unencapsulated Collection is teachable. However this is only of value if students create designs with this smell. To determine whether this happened we examined two datasets, each containing submissions to an assignment for two courses at the University of Auckland. One, which we call "KalahGrad", contains 42 implementations of the Kalah game [25]. These have been tested by an automatic framework created by the instructor to assess correctness. A stated requirement for this assignment was that the submissions should have a "good" design, as determined by the student. The other dataset, which we call "SpellcheckerUnderg", contains 77 implementations of a system to provide a spelling quiz and record the results. The only requirement for this assignment was that it provided correct functionality.

We analysed the two datasets to identify methods that returned collections, and then manually analysed the results to determine which, if any, represented instances of Unencapsulated Collection. Table 1 shows the results. In it, "Projects" is the number of projects in each dataset, "RC methods" is the number of methods that returned collections, and "RC projects" is the number of projects that had at least one method that returns a collection. "UC Projects" is the number of projects that had at least one occurrence of the design smell.

We discovered that a number of methods that returned collections were `private` ("RC private"), and thus could be considered implementation details. It could be argued that creating classes to encapsulate the returned collections is of little value, although there were instances where doing so would have improved the design. Nevertheless we decided to exclude such cases for this analysis.

Despite our claims that the criteria for detecting the smell are clear, we nevertheless found instances where the decision was not that easy. We have already mentioned the fact that some of the methods were private. The other main difficulty was in assessing whether the operations performed by the clients were sufficiently non-trivial to be considered a smell. In some we saw cases where the collection was returned, and the only operation performed on it (for all calls of the method) was something simple such as `size()`. In such cases, it was unclear why the method could not have just performed the operation directly rather than return the list. As this suggested confusion on the part of the student as to what the

```
class Player {
  ...
  public ArrayList<House> getHouses(){
    return this.houses;
  }
  ...
}
```

Figure 1: Instance of the Unencapsulated Collection design smell

```
// method getScore in Player
public int getScore() {
  int score=0;
  for(int seed=0; seed < this.getHouses().size(); seed++){
    score = score+this.getHouses().get(seed).getSeeds();
  }
    score = score + this.getStore().getSeeds();
    return score;
}
```

Figure 2: A client of `getHouses()`

abstraction was, we concluded such cases should be recorded as having the design smell.

Our conclusion is that about half of the projects in each dataset had instances of the Unencapsulated Collection design smell. To illustrate how we might use the identification of a design smell to provide feedback on a student's design, we now give a case study based on one of these projects.

5 CASE STUDY

In this section we present a complete example of Unencapsulated Collection and we explain all the steps performed to do the refactoring – according to definition 3.

Fig. 1 shows an example the Unencapsulated Collection smell in a project of the KalahGrad dataset, implementing the Kalah game [25]. While this appears to be a standard "getter", to appreciate the impact of this choice, we need to consider the whole design.

We begin by identifying the clients of the method performing operations on what the method returns. Method **getHouses()** belongs to the class **Player**. It used by itself (Fig. 2) and the classes **Printer** and **Kalah** (Fig. 3).

All three uses of `getHouses()` involve iterating over the list and determining some property of it. The properties relate to the elements in the list, rather than the list itself, so we propose creating an abstraction that captures the use of those elements. Since the list contains instances of `House`, we create a class `HouseGroup`. Based on the client operations, we give it the interface summarised in Fig. 4.

Table 1: Data for prevalence of UC design smell

	KalahGrad	SpellcheckerUnderg
Projects	42	77
Min SLOC	126	303
Max SLOC	671	1167
Min Classes	1	1
Max Classes	36	20
Min Methods	8	4
Max Methods	74	106
RC Projects	24 (57%)	42 (32%)
RC methods	47	126
RC Private	7	19
UC Projects	22	35

Having created `HouseGroup` we can now refactor the original clients of `getHouses()` as shown in Figs. 5, 6, and 7. The code implementing the operations those classes performed on the original list is now moved into `HouseGroup`. As a result, each of those classes is now smaller (which in itself makes them easier to understand), but more importantly are more cohesive, since code not directly related to their respective responsibilities has been removed. The `HouseGroup` class provides an abstraction that is more meaningful in the context of Kalah than the original `ArrayList<House>`, meaning it is easier to understand its role in the design.

6 DISCUSSION

Part of our contribution with this work is how we got to what we present here. We did not set out to identify a new design smell, teachable or otherwise. We were interested in how we might more easily assess student designs, and were exploring whether choices of names might help. While there has been interest in evaluating names against coding conventions (See Section 2), as far as we are aware there has been little work using choice of names as indicators of possible design problems.

We explored using the Linguistic Antipatterns (LAs) of Arnaoudova et al. [3] to determine whether they gave us any insight regarding the design. One LA in particular "A4 – Expecting but not getting a single instance" provided us interesting results. This LA is defined as: "The name of a method indicates that a single object is returned but the return type is a collection." An example of this LA would be a method called `getHouseGroup()`, suggesting a single thing is being returned, but returning a `List` of `House`—that is, a collection.

In reviewing the results for the A4 LA, we noticed that often the name of the method signalled an abstraction that was relevant to the purpose of the program, however the collection returned did not exactly match the abstraction. This suggested that the student had a reasonable idea of what the design should look like, but failed to capture it fully in the design. Our early speculation that the A4 LA would allow us to identify such design problems was quickly refuted when we realised that the underlying problem—not providing the right abstraction—was more widespread than just what the A4 LA indicated, and led us to identifying what we now call the Unencapsulated Collection design smell.

Our initial idea that choice of names may help identify design issues turned out to be right, but not in the way we expected. We now believe choice of names will *in some cases* indicate examples

```
// in Printer
private void printPlayer(Player player) {
    StringBuffer line = new StringBuffer();
    boolean countUp = true;
// other code not included
 [...]
for(int x=0; x< player.getHouses().size(); x++){
    if(countUp){
        House house = player.getHouses().get(x);
        line.append("|" + (house.getId())+ "[" + house.getSeedsString() + "]");
   }else{
        House house = player.getHouses().get(player.getHouses().size()−x−1);
        line.append("|" + (house.getId())+ "[" + house.getSeedsString() + "]");
}
}
// other code not included
[...]
}
// in Kalah
private Player currentlyPlaying;
private boolean didGameFinish() {
    boolean fullHouse = false;
    for(int house=0;
        house<currentlyPlaying.getHouses().size();
        house++){
    if(currentlyPlaying.getHouses().get(house).getSeeds()>0){
        fullHouse = true;
        break;
}
}
    return !fullHouse;
}
```

Figure 3: Other clients of `getHouses()`

```
public class HouseGroup {
private ArrayList<House> houses =
                    new ArrayList<House>();
public void add(House house){...}
public House get(int houseid){...}
public int getSeeds(){...}
public void setOrderOfPlay(Player player,
                         boolean clockwise){...}
public void asString(StringBuffer line,
                     boolean clockwise){...}
}
```

Figure 4: HouseGroup, encapsulating a collection of `House`

of a more general design issue. We suggest there is considerable scope in exploring this idea.

We have only formally examined two datasets. This raises the question as to whether what we have seen in them generalises to other student groups. There is nothing in our student groups that

```
private HouseGroup houses= new HouseGroup();
public HouseGroup getHouses(){
    return this.houses;
}
```

Figure 5: Refactoring of getHouses() in Player

```
private void printPlayer(Player player) {
    StringBuffer line = new StringBuffer();
    boolean countUp = true;
    // other code not included
    [...]
    player.getHouses().asString(line, countUp);
    // other code not included
    [...]
}
```

Figure 6: Refactoring of printPlayer() in Printer

```
// refactored portion
private Player currentlyPlaying;
private boolean didGameFinish() {
    return currentlyPlaying.getHouses().getSeeds() == 0;
}
```

Figure 7: Refactoring of Kalah

would suggest they are particularly prone to this (or any) design smell. One consisted of undergraduate students, while the other was graduate students. The graduate group is of particular interest as it included not only students from the undergraduate programme at university, but also a significant number of international students. The results are similar enough to suggest no particular bias.

Another reason the graduate dataset is of interest is the nature of their task. They were asked to produce a "good" design. While no specific criteria were given regarding what this might mean (explaining this was part of the assignment), there was an incentive to avoid "obvious" design problems. This suggests our results not only confirm the difficulties graduating students have with design (c.f. Section 2), but the prevalence of the Unencapsulated Collection design smell.

7 CONCLUSION AND FUTURE WORK

We have proposed the Unencapsulated Collection, a design smell that we believe will be useful for teaching design to novices. The greatest value of examining a student's design for occurrences of Unencapsulated collections is that it would provide a very accessible way to discuss the design, a way that is not dependent on intuition or experience, but instead can be explained in concrete objective terms. We have demonstrated that the proposed design smell represents such objective criteria and it is also easy to detect automatically in order to provide fast feedback to students.

What we have proposed is in contrast with other design smells. Many have a subjective element that requires expert judgement in order to appreciate the benefits. For example, the "God Class" anti-pattern is described as "a class knows too much or does too much"—characterising at what point a class is doing "too much" is quite challenging. Novices by definition do not have the necessary expertise to make this determination and so such smells are difficult to explain to them.

About 50% of the 119 student submissions we examined exhibited the Unencapsulated Collection. This suggests it is common enough that using it as the basis for discussing good design will help many students. Because it is accessible to novices, we expect that it will also help them appreciate the goals of good design. We suggest there is value in identifying other teachable design smells.

REFERENCES

[1] Amjad Altadmri and Neil C.C. Brown. 2015. 37 Million Compilations: Investigating Novice Programming Mistakes in Large-Scale Student Data. In *Proceedings of the 46th ACM Technical Symposium on Computer Science Education (SIGCSE '15)*. ACM, New York, NY, USA, 522–527. https://doi.org/10.1145/2676723.2677258

[2] Deborah J. Armstrong. 2006. The Quarks of Object-oriented Development. *Commun. ACM* 49, 2 (Feb. 2006), 123–128.

[3] Venera Arnaoudova, Massimiliano Di Penta, and Giuliano Antoniol. 2016. Linguistic antipatterns: What they are and how developers perceive them. *Empirical Software Engineering* 21, 1 (2016), 104–158.

[4] Owen Astrachan, Kim Bruce, Elliot Koffman, Michael Kölling, and Stuart Reges. 2005. Resolved: Objects Early Has Failed. In *Proceedings of the 36th SIGCSE Technical Symposium on Computer Science Education (SIGCSE '05)*. ACM, 451–452.

[5] Alex Baker, Alex van der Hoek, Harold Ossher, and Marian Petre. 2012. Guest Editors' Introduction: Studying Professional Software Design. *IEEE Softw.* 29, 1 (Jan. 2012), 28–33.

[6] Anders Berglund and Raymond Lister. 2007. Debating the OO Debate: Where is the Problem?. In *Proceedings of the Seventh Baltic Sea Conference on Computing Education Research - Volume 88 (Koli Calling '07)*. 171–174.

[7] Jean Bezivin, Robert B France, Martin Gogolla, Øystein Haugen, Gabriele Taentzer, and Daniel Varro. 2009. Teaching modeling: why, when, what?. In *MoDELS Workshops*, Vol. 6002. Springer, 55–62.

[8] Simon Butler, Michel Wermelinger, and Yijun Yu. 2015. Investigating naming convention adherence in Java references. *2015 IEEE International Conference on Software Maintenance and Evolution (ICSME)* 00 (2015), 41–50.

[9] Simon Butler, Michel Wermelinger, and Yijun Yu. 2015. A Survey of the Forms of Java Reference Names. In *Proceedings of the 2015 IEEE 23rd International Conference on Program Comprehension (ICPC '15)*. IEEE Press, 196–206.

[10] David Carrington and S-K Kim. 2003. Teaching software design with open source software. In *Frontiers in Education, 2003. FIE 2003 33rd Annual*, Vol. 3. IEEE, S1C–9.

[11] John W Coffey. 2017. A Study of the Use of a Reflective Activity to Improve Students' Software Design Capabilities. In *Proceedings of the 2017 ACM SIGCSE Technical Symposium on Computer Science Education*. ACM, 129–134.

[12] Florian Deissenboeck and Markus Pizka. 2006. Concise and consistent naming. *Software Quality Journal* 14, 3 (2006), 261–282.

[13] Martin Fowler. 1999. *Refactoring: improving the design of existing code*. Addison-Wesley, Boston, MA, USA.

[14] Erich Gamma, Richard Helm, Ralph E. Johnson, and John Vlissides. 1994. *Design Patterns*. Addison-Wesley.

[15] Chenglie Hu. 2016. Can Students Design Software?: The Answer Is More Complex Than You Think. In *Proceedings of the 47th ACM Technical Symposium on Computing Science Education (SIGCSE '16)*. 199–204.

[16] Dawn Lawrie, Henry Feild, and David Binkley. 2007. Quantifying identifier quality: an analysis of trends. *Empirical Software Engineering* 12, 4 (2007), 359–388.

[17] B Lin, S Scalabrino, A Mocci, R Oliveto, G Bavota, and M Lanza. 2017. Investigating the Use of Code Analysis and NLP to Promote a Consistent Usage of Identifiers. In *17th IEEE International Working Conference on Source Code Analysis and Manipulation.*

[18] Stephen Paul Linder, David Abbott, and Michael J Fromberger. 2006. An instructional scaffolding approach to teaching software design. *Journal of Computing Sciences in Colleges* 21, 6 (2006), 238–250.

[19] Raymond Lister, Anders Berglund, Tony Clear, Joe Bergin, Kathy Garvin-Doxas, Brian Hanks, Lew Hitchner, Andrew Luxton-Reilly, Kate Sanders, Carsten Schulte, and Jacqueline L. Whalley. 2006. Research Perspectives on the Objects-early Debate. In *Working Group Reports on ITiCSE on Innovation and Technology in Computer Science Education (ITiCSE-WGR '06)*. ACM, 146–165.

[20] Chris Loftus, Lynda Thomas, and Carol Zander. 2011. Can Graduating Students Design: Revisited. In *Proceedings of the 42Nd ACM Technical Symposium on Computer Science Education (SIGCSE '11)*. 105–110.

[21] James E. McDonough. 2017. *Design Anti-Patterns*. Apress, Berkeley, CA, 347–348.

[22] Sylvia Stuurman, Harrie Passier, and Erik Barendsen. 2016. Analyzing Students' Software Redesign Strategies. In *Proceedings of the 16th Koli Calling International Conference on Computing Education Research (Koli Calling '16)*. 110–119.

[23] Allison Elliott Tew and Mark Guzdial. 2010. Developing a Validated Assessment of Fundamental CS1 Concepts. In *Proceedings of the 41st ACM Technical Symposium on Computer Science Education (SIGCSE '10)*. 97–101.

[24] Michael R. Wick, Daniel E. Stevenson, and Andrew T. Phillips. 2004. Seven Design Rules for Teaching Students Sound Encapsulation and Abstraction of Object Properties and Member Data. In *Proceedings of the 35th SIGCSE Technical Symposium on Computer Science Education (SIGCSE '04)*. 100–104.

[25] Wikia. 2017. Kalah Game. http://mancala.wikia.com/wiki/Kalah. (2017). [Online; accessed August 2017].

Instructional Design + Knowledge Components: A Systematic Method for Refining Instruction

Luke Gusukuma
Department of Computer Science
Virginia Tech
Blacksburg, Virginia
lukesg08@vt.edu

Austin Cory Bart
Department of Computer Science
Virginia Tech
Blacksburg, Virginia
acbart@vt.edu

Dennis Kafura
Department of Computer Science
Virginia Tech
Blacksburg, Virginia
kafura@cs.vt.edu

Jeremy Ernst
School of Education
Virginia Tech
Blacksburg, Virginia
jvernst@vt.edu

Katherine Cennamo
School of Education
Virginia Tech
Blacksburg, Virginia
cennamo@vt.edu

ABSTRACT

This paper reports on a systematic method used to improve an existing unit of instruction. The method is distinctive in combining steps of instructional design with "knowledge components" from a cognitively-based framework of learning. Instructional design is used to develop assessment instruments that incorporate information about student misconceptions. The method uses the assessment instruments to evaluate student performance and learning gains, while statistical analysis evaluates the quality of the instruments themselves using measures of difficulty and discrimination. Fine-grain insight into possible improvements is enabled by the knowledge components implicated by the assessment. The method is illustrated and evaluated by applying it to a unit of instruction on collection-based iteration in a computational thinking class. Data gathered during this evaluation highlights a number of opportunities within the unit to refine the instruction.

CCS CONCEPTS

• **Applied computing → Education**; Learning management systems;

KEYWORDS

Knowledge Components, CS1, CS Education, Assessment, Instructional Design

ACM Reference format:

Luke Gusukuma, Austin Cory Bart, Dennis Kafura, Jeremy Ernst, and Katherine Cennamo. 2018. Instructional Design + Knowledge Components: A Systematic Method for Refining Instruction. In *Proceedings of SIGCSE '18: The 49th ACM Technical Symposium on Computing Science Education, Baltimore , MD, USA, February 21–24, 2018 (SIGCSE '18),* 6 pages.
https://doi.org/10.1145/3159450.3159478

ACM ISBN 978-1-4503-5103-4/18/02...$15.00
https://doi.org/10.1145/3159450.3159478

1 INTRODUCTION

Revision is a crucial component of course design. Frequently, however, the original instruction and accompanying assessments have not been developed using any kind of formal process, but instead were developed from informed experience while using informal means. In other cases, the instruction was "inherited", often with overlapping contributions and viewpoints from various instructors. Of course, experienced instructors often have valuable insight into the misconceptions held by students. When instructors have the opportunity to refine a curriculum, or even rebuild it from the ground up, the process can benefit from this prior knowledge. Still, using ad-hoc processes can limit the effectiveness of a revision opportunity in the same way that large software projects suffer without guidance from formal design methodologies.

Course revision can benefit from formal methods of Instructional Design (ID) even when these methods were not used in the original development. There are a variety of ID models and frameworks that systematize the design of learning experiences [2, 4, 7]. Elements of ID have been used for Needs Assessments [9] and comparing instructional strategies [3]. Some works even note the parallels of Software Engineering and ID [5, 6], However, there are few guides for targeted ways to incorporate ID into curriculum redesign [1], suggesting a need for a well-described model suitable for computing education practitioners.

In this paper, we describe our activities in the practical improvement of a targeted unit of existing instruction. This paper makes two contributions:

- The development of a method for improving a targeted unit of instruction that combines steps of instructional design with elements of a cognitively-based framework of learning and is particularly suited for the design of computing instruction, and
- The illustration and evaluation of the method as applied it to a unit of instruction on collection-based iteration in a introductory computing class.

The audience for this paper are instructors seeking an approachable and effort-conscious way of improving a specific part of their course. We believe the method is approachable; while it does require some reading and preparation, it does not require extraordinary training or overly-sophisticated statistical analysis. The method is effort-conscious, requiring a modest time investment. We estimate that creating the assessment instruments (the first step of the method) involved three of the co-authors working intermittently over several weeks, so conservatively two person-weeks of effort. The analysis step took four of the co-authors less than a week to conduct. Finally, the method is (at least in our view and use) focused on a "unit" of instruction (i.e., a single topic) which in our case was a unit lasting four class days on the topic of collection-based iteration. While the method can be used to incrementally improve an entire course, one unit at a time, we realize that in practice not all units in a course may require improvement. Rather, especially critical or under-performing units can be targeted. This work also makes a partial contribution toward the development of a concept inventory [10, 11], specifically for the topic of iteration.

We give an outline of our method and use this outline as a guide to the organization of the paper. The method has four steps:

(1) Design assessment
  - identify instructional goals (Sec 2.1)
  - identify misconceptions (Sec 2.2)
  - conduct instructional analysis (Sec 2.3)
  - create assessment instruments (Sec 2.4)

(2) Collect assessment data
  - administer assessment instruments (Sec 3.1)
  - tabulate student performance and learning gains (Sec 3.2 and Table 1 and Figure 2)
  - tabulate item analysis to identify item difficulty and discrimination (Sec 3.2 and Table 2)

(3) Analyze student learning and assessment instruments
  - identify items with weak learning gains and valid assessments (Sec 4.1 and 4.2)
  - identify implicated knowledge components (Sec 4.2)

(4) Improvement (Sec 4.1 and 4.2)
  - correct suspect items in assessment instruments
  - improve instruction (presentation, problems, feedback)

Roughly, the steps in the design assessment step are a subset of the Dick and Carey instructional design process [4], though specialized. For example, in our method, the Dick and Carey step of identifying instructional goals is limited to identifying the goal of the unit of instruction selected for improvement. The instructional analysis and assessment instrument steps are the same. We do not claim that the method is unique in conception, but a selection and integration of existing techniques.

A deficiency in many ID processes is a lack of a model of the learners' understanding.To overcome this, the ID model that we describe leverages the cognitive modeling aspects of the Knowledge Learning Instruction Framework (KLI) [8] within a sub-set of a formalized ID process [4], Operationally, a Knowledge Component (KC) is "an acquired unit of cognitive function or structure that can be inferred from performance on a set of related tasks" [8]. Examples of such cognitive functions/structures include, but are not limited to, concepts, skills, misconceptions, and facts [8]. KCs can be generated by an iterative process using insights from: (1) misconceptions: mistakes reveal by analysis of prior student work (Sec. 2.2), (2) content: the tasks and performance objectives defined by instructional analysis (Sec. 2.3), and (3) assessment: the correct and distractor alternatives used to measure student learning (Sec. 2.4).

The steps to analyze student learning and the assessment instruments use standard statistical techniques. Through this analysis, specific KCs are implicated by assessment items with reasonable difficulty and discrimination and with less than desired student performance or learning gains. Comparison across different assessment items refine the list of implicated KCs.

2 DESIGN ASSESSMENT

Assessment-driven improvement of instruction relies on assessment instruments that are directly relatable to the instruction. Some systematic instructional design process must be used to achieve this linkage. In our case, a subset of the Dick and Cary model [4] was used where some steps were narrowed or refined for the task.

2.1 Identifying Instructional Goals

We targeted one of the most difficult and important parts of our curriculum, collection-based iteration. Not only is collection-based iteration difficult for our learners, it is also central to our curriculum, which revolves around data science. Specifically, students must be able to use iteration to compute simple quantitative measures of list-oriented data (e.g., averages) and generate visualizations (e.g. histograms). Two instructional goals emerged: "Construct an algorithm that outputs a quantitative measure of the values in a given list" and "Construct an algorithm that produces a visualization based on the values in a given list". Each goal expresses an observable skill that we expect our students to learn from the instruction. For brevity, only the first is considered in this paper.

2.2 Identify Misconceptions

An initial list of student misconceptions about collection-based iteration was developed through personal observation and semi-automated analysis. Personal observations in the classroom were done informally. In our course format, instructors walk around the classroom and help students who are engaged in active learning exercises with other students. The interaction with students helped build our intuition regarding misconceptions and student knowledge. Semi-automated inspection of previous student code supported our personal observations. The tools used in the inspection allowed the replay of the students' steps in writing their code, comparison of their code to a model answer, and k-means clustering of similar student programs. For brevity, we do not discuss these tools. The misconceptions played a role both in identifying KCs (a misconception suggests one or more partially understood or misunderstood KCs) and in developing distractors on the multiple choice assessment questions. While we developed tools for the semi-automated analysis of student code, this is not a requirement of using the method. Any information regarding student misconceptions, from formal or informal data sources, is useful.

2.3 Instructional Analysis

The next step is to perform Instructional Analysis whose major purpose is "...to identify the skills and knowledge that should be

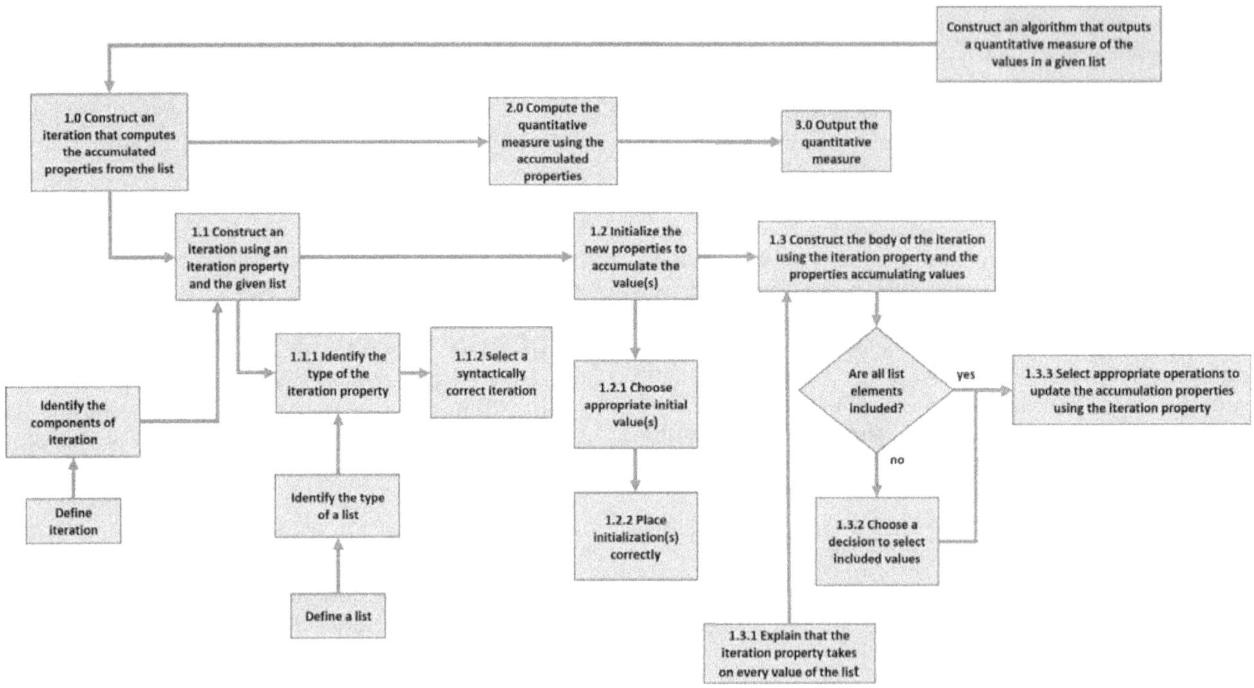

Figure 1: Final iteration of Instructional Design Diagram

included in our instruction ..." [4, page 41] that leads students to achieve the identified instructional goal. This process involves identifying the major components of instruction, subordinate skills, and their relationships. For our instructional goal we determined the baseline knowledge we expected students to have at the beginning of the iteration unit. The units prior to iteration provide instruction on basic initialization, Boolean logic, if-else constructs, as well as a knowledge of the basic data types (string, integer, and float). Determining the baseline knowledge of the students is important to having well defined boundaries about what was, and was not, in the scope of our instructional analysis.

Using our instructional goal, Bloom's taxonomy, our list of misconceptions, the baseline knowledge, and previous course material as guides, we created a rough task analysis diagram [4] of skills we wanted our students to be able to perform. To break the instructional goal down into subtasks and steps, we went through the process of discerning what skills were being exercised and used to produce our instructional goal. We used Bloom's taxonomy as a guide to make sure we included items from lower cognitive levels to higher cognitive levels. The list of misconceptions helped us identify items in the diagram. For example, we included "Identify a subtype of list" as a task because our observations showed that students would occasionally use strings instead of numbers when constructing a list. After establishing a hierarchy of tasks, we formalized our task analysis into an instructional design diagram. The diagram shown in Figure 1 is a final iteration of the diagram.

We also generated performance objectives for each task in the diagram. A performance objective identifies for a given task what the student will be able to accomplish and with what accuracy. For example, for Task 1.1.1 "Construct an interation property", two performance objectives are:

(1) Given a list explain what type of value the iteration property will have.
(2) Given a list select the type of the iteration property from among several choices.

Many other performance objectives are possible for this task. The value of stating these performance objectives is that they lead directly to assessment questions. They are the linkage between the assessment data gathered later and the instructional steps.

2.4 Assessment Instruments

Our assessment instruments (the pretest and post-tests) were multiple choice that assessed the individual subtasks in the instructional analysis diagram. To generate the multiple choice questions, we drew upon the performance objectives defined earlier, using those that could be cast into a multiple choice form. The misconceptions that we found in our earlier analysis (semi-automated inspection and observation) and refined in our instructional analysis drove the creation of the distractors we used for the test.

After creating the test, we used the answer choices to refine the list of KCs as the student's selection of an answer choice represents knowledge we can infer the student to have (or not have). These KCs were developed for our student population and using our instructional design. While other instructors may formulate the KCs differently due to differences in instructional design and student population, a large number of these KCs are likely transferable to other situations, or may serve as a starting point for other instructors. A full list of KCs is available at https://think.cs.vt.edu/resources/ct-kcs.

3 COLLECT AND TABULATE DATA

The data was collected using parallel pre- and post-tests administered before, during, and after the unit of instruction. The tabulated data allows both an analysis of student learning and an evaluation of the instruments used to measure that learning (i.e., the pre- and post- tests). Both analyses are needed because gains or deficiencies in student learning should not be ascribed on the basis of a suspect instrument.

3.1 Administer Assessment

The primary unit of instruction on iteration that we sought to improve took place over three consecutive class days. During this time, the students used a block-based programming language. Following this unit, the students transitioned to using a text language (Python) where they learned a more complex data structure (lists of dictionaries) and used iteration to process such data. We were interested in assessing the students learning within the block-based portion and also the transfer of this learning to the text-based portion. Therefore, multiple tests were constructed to assess student learning at different stages.

Each test has nine multiple choice questions. The questions concern the initialization (number or list) prior to the iteration (Q3 and Q7), the relationnship between the selected element on each iteration the list (Q1 and Q5), the "syntax" and body of a "for" statement (Q2 and Q4), and selecting a correct algorithms (Q6, Q8, and Q9). The ordering and content of the multiple choice questions remained the same, but the details of the questions (e.g. summing distances vs. summing prices) and the ordering of the answer choices changed between tests. The tests were administered in an online format via a learning management system where each question was presented one at a time, with students not being able to go back to a previous question. This format was used because later questions in the test can give away answers to previous questions in the test (e.g., the code in a later question could give the answer to an earlier recall question).

The assessment consisted of one pretest and three post-tests. A pretest was given at the end of the class prior to the onset of unit instruction. The pretest established each student's baseline knowledge on the material being taught. The first post-test, sometimes called an embedded post-test, was given at the beginning of the third day of instruction. The second post-test was given two class days after the first post-test. The first two post-tests assessed the student learning within the block-based language portion and used a block-based representation of code for the questions and answer choices. The third post-test, sometimes called a far transfer test, was given eight class days after the second post-test. This post-test was administered after the students had completed the Python coding portion of the class and was administered using the text representation for questions and answer choices. This post-test assessed the transfer of the student learning from the earlier instruction in a block-based form to a text-based form. The authors will provide the assessment questions upon request.

The tests were administered over two sections of the class that each met twice a week. The number of consenting participants were 67 for the pretest, 75 for post-test 1, 72 for post-test 2, and 69 for post-test 3 with 55 students participating in all three tests.

All tests were planned to be administered in class. However, an issue with the learning management system for one section necessitated the pretest for that section to be administered as a take home test. To insure that the difference in pretest administration did not invalidate the outcome measure we conducted an independent 2-group Mann-Whitney U test between the two sections. The p-value of 0.8157 suggests that there were no significant differences caused by taking the test at home instead of in the classroom.

3.2 Tabulate Data

Table 1 presents the data on student learning showing the percent of student answering each question correctly on each test. Learning gains were calculated as $\frac{post-pre}{1-pre}$ where pre and post represent the percentage of students who correctly answered each assessment question. The percent correct is an absolute measure of student performance while the learning gains is a measure relative to the students' starting (pretest) point. The learning gains are presented graphically in Figure 2.

Table 2 presents the data for the assessment of the three post-test instruments on an item (i.e., question) by item basis. The item difficulty is a proportion of collective correct responses. The discrimination ability of post-test items is characterized through summary correlation between a continuous and binary variable (overall outcome in relation to item-level association).

The assessment data can be described as follows. Based on response items of the post-test, question 1 showed a proportional decline in post-test 1 and post-test 3 with a slight proportional increase in post-test 2 in relation to the pretest. Questions 2-9 have notable increases in learning outcome while there was no detectable learning gain for question 1 across the 3 tests. Based on item difficulty, questions 2 and 5 had the highest proportional outcome on the post-test, reflected in the student learning gains on post-test 1, post-test 2 and post-test3. Questions 3 and 6 had very little change in learning gains (average change of less than 0.03), and were identified by the portion of correct responses as items of lower difficulty, but with stronger discriminative power. Question 4 has a comparatively higher level of post-test difficulty in relation to questions 2, 3, 5, 6, and 9 and has moderate discriminative power (summary correlation of 0.599). Question 7 shows reasonably high learning gains on post-tests 2 and 3 (0.834 and 0.914 respectively), but shows much smaller progressions of learning gains in the first post-test. The resulting difference in learning gains is highlighted in the discussion section. Questions 8 and 9 had strikingly similar behaviors in their learning gains curves (see Figure 2) as well as their interesting learning gain drops on post-test 3 and are also highlighted.

4 ANALYZE DATA

The tabulated assessment item data is analyzed in two steps. First, areas of possible improvement are identified. Assessment instrument improvements are indicated by low quality questions (i.e., those with problematic difficulty or discrimination). Improving these questions leads to a better assessment instrument. Instructional improvements are indicated by high quality questions where materially better student performance is possible. Second, for instructional improvements the related KCs are identified.

Table 1: Learning Outcomes

	Percent of students correct				Learning Gains		
Question	pre	post1	post2	post 3	post1	post2	post 3
q1	0.646	0.547	0.708	0.594	-0.279	0.177	-0.145
q2	0.633	0.947	1.000	1.000	0.855	1.000	1.000
q3	0.329	0.947	0.931	0.942	0.921	0.896	0.914
q4	0.241	0.693	0.708	0.797	0.596	0.616	0.733
q5	0.709	1.000	1.000	1.000	1.000	1.000	1.000
q6	0.519	0.907	0.875	0.899	0.806	0.740	0.789
q7	0.329	0.467	0.889	0.942	0.205	0.834	0.914
q8	0.367	0.507	0.819	0.725	0.221	0.715	0.565
q9	0.443	0.773	0.931	0.812	0.593	0.875	0.662

Table 2: Item Analysis

	Average		Standard Deviation	
	Proportion Correct	Discrimination	Proportion Correct	Discrimination
Q1	0.616	0.588	0.068	0.040
Q2	0.982	-0	0.025	-0
Q3	0.940	0.222	0.007	0.066
Q4	0.733	0.599	0.046	0.105
Q5	1	-0	0	-0
Q6	0.893	0.546	0.013	0.111
Q7	0.766	0.398	0.213	0.127
Q8	0.684	0.659	0.131	0.114
Q9	0.838	0.356	0.067	0.044

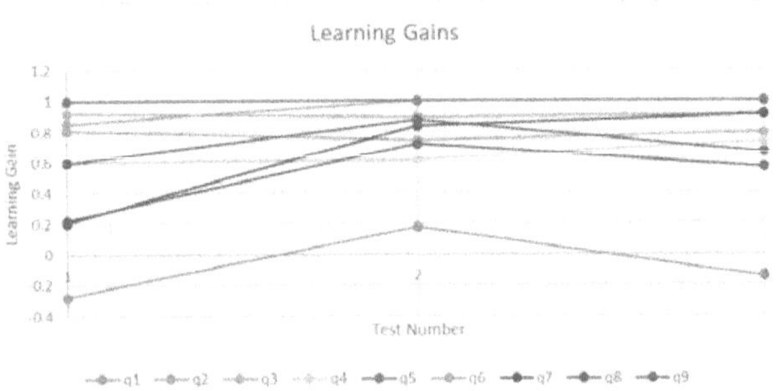

Figure 2: Learning Gains by Question

4.1 Identify Possible Improvements

Question 1 has an inconsistent and low level of correct responses and the learning gains are very poor (Table 1). The overall level of performance is the lowest of all items (Table 2). Three possible causes of this poor performance are: (1)there is some ordering effect that distorted the learning outcomes; (2) the item was compromised because the content for this question was based on identifying data types which limited developing parallel questions on each test; or (3) our instruction on types was insufficient. Further testing is needed to know whether improvement are needed in the assessment item or in the instruction.

Question 1 appears to be of low quality. The level of correct responses is inconsistent and low and the learning gains are very poor (Table 1). The overall level of performance is the lowest of all items (Table 2). We are not sure if there is some ordering effect that affected this question and distorted the learning outcomes. Additionally, the content for this question was based on identifying data types which limited developing parallel questions on each test as the only suitable types for the distractors were float, integer, and string. It is also possible that our instruction on types was insufficient. Analysis of this question highlights a need for item revision.

Questions 2, 3, and 5 (all with learning gains consistently above 0.855 and never dropping) leave little room for improvement. Question 6 has acceptable learning gains by post-test 3 (0.789). Questions 7 through 9 have low learning gains on the first post-test because the material for those questions was not yet taught. Question 7 shows good learning gains on post-tests 2 and 3 (0.834 and 0.914). Questions 8 and 9 have significant drops in learning gains between post-tests 2 and 3 (0.715 to 0.565 and 0.875 to 0.662, respectively). One hypothesis is that the introduction of dictionaries between post-tests 2 and 3 resulted in confusion on those questions. This suggests that material involving dictionaries should be a focus for future improvement.

Question 4 is a high quality question that shows improvement in student performance. The students showed lower learning gains than we would have liked (0.596, 0.616, and 0.733 across the three post-tests, respectively). The low learning gains flags this question as containing concepts that our students are not sufficiently mastering. The fact that 73% of students get this question correct, and the fact that it's discrimination is 0.599, we can tell that the content of the question itself, and not the clarity of it, is something we need to address.

In summary, we have identified an assessment item that may need improvement (Question 1), a topic for the future application of our method (dictionaries as indicated by Questions 8 and 9), and a current topic to study further (Question 4).

4.2 Identify Knowledge Components

Exploring the KCs of a question, like Question 4, that points to possible instructional improvements allows for a fine-grain understanding of precisely what in the instruction needs to be improved. For brevity, we'll focus on answer choice "a" for Question 4 (see Figure 3) that was one of the two most commonly selected distractors. We want to know what KCs led students to select this distractor. From answer choice "a", we can infer that the students have the following KCs (see Table 3): 6, parts of 18, and to some confidence, 23. The missing pieces of knowledge are other subparts of KC 18 as well as KCs 12 and 22.

By identifying the KCs, we have a list of specific ideas against which we can review our instruction. For instance, we know the student has at least some partial competency with regards to KC 18. So an instructional improvement from the syntactic perspective is to clarify the basic accumulation pattern for summing a list using iteration. However, another approach, using KC 12, is to make

```
When using the iteration shown below to compute the sum of the
numbers in the distance_list, which of the following is the
correct statement to be in the body of the iteration?

distance_sum = 0
for distance in distance_list:
    pass

a: distance_sum = distance_list + distance
b: distance = distance_sum + distance
c: distance_sum = distance_sum + distance_list
d: distance_sum = distance_sum + distance
e: distance_list = distance
f: distance_sum = distance_sum + 1
g: distance_sum = distance_list
```

Figure 3: Question 4 template

Table 3: Knowledge Components for Question 4

KC Number	Description
KC006	The iteration property takes on each value of the list
KC012	The sum and the list are two different items
KC018	Update for sum is sum = sum + iteration_ property (has 6 different sub parts)
KC020	You can't add the list to a number
KC022	The list is not used in accumulation
KC023	The list is not used as an accumulator

clearer how a list is distinctly different from a sum, or a way of summarizing a list. A third approach would be to use direct instruction: "don't use the list in for loop". A fourth approach is to include in our programming environment tests for this misconception and provide immediate feedback linked to "just-in-time" instruction.

In summary, we have identified four different approaches to address the misconceptions revealed by the KCs in Question 4. Other guidance could be gained by examining other associated KCs in this question and studying how these same KCs appear in other questions. For example, Question 3 also contains KC 12 but performance on Question 3 question is on the upper end (learning gains averaging .9). Does this mean that students generally have KC 12 and the problem is elsewhere? Or does it mean that KC 12 in the context of accumulation is problematic? Further analysis can reveal the answer.

5 CONCLUSION

In this paper we have presented a pragmatic method for improving instruction by combining KCs from a cognitively-based framework with selected steps from a commonly referenced model of instructional design.

This four-step method begins by developing an assessment of the instruction targeted for improvement. In this step, a limited number of formal and informal methods are combined to define the high-level goal of the instruction, break-down the instruction into a set of related steps (visualized in an instructional diagram), identify student's misconceptions using whatever means are at hand - including experienced observation, and use all of this information in a deliberate way to create assessments that can be directly related to the instruction. We have reported our own experience on using this method to develop an assessment for a unit of instruction on collection-based iteration.

The second step applies the assessment during the teaching of the material and tabulating this data to derive measures of performance, learning gain, difficulty and discrimination. Calculating these measures is straightforward and does not require statistical sophistication. We have reported our experience explaining how we structured our assessment test to gain measures during the primary class days when the material was presented in a block-based language and also a later test to gauge the transfer of this learning to a text-based language. We encountered the usual situation where the administration of one of the tests did not go as planned and we discussed how we recovered from this problem.

The third step analyzes the assessment data to identify weakness in the instruction and specific "knowledge components" that students have not sufficiently mastered. We reported our efforts to relate the assessment to improving the questions on the assessment itself and how one question pointed us to an area where we could improve our instruction. We are now in the process of performing the fourth step - improving the instruction and the assessment.

We have shown how we have applied this method to our instruction of collection based iteration in a computational thinking course. We hope that this work better informs the community about the possibility of using principled methods to assess and revise critical topics with reasonable level of effort.

ACKNOWLEDGMENTS

This work is supported in part by National Science Foundation grants DUE 1624320, DUE 1444094, and DGE 0822220.

REFERENCES

[1] Austin Cory Bart and Clifford A. Shaffer. 2016. Instructional Design is to Teaching As Software Engineering is to Programming *(SIGCSE '16)*. 240–241.

[2] Robert K Branson, Gail T Rayner, J Lamarr Cox, John P Furman, and FJ King. 1975. *Interservice procedures for instructional systems development. executive summary and model.* Technical Report. DTIC Document.

[3] Michael E. Caspersen and Jens Bennedsen. 2007. Instructional Design of a Programming Course: A Learning Theoretic Approach *(ICER '07)*. 111–122.

[4] Walter Dick, Lou Carey, James O Carey, and others. 2001. *The systematic design of instruction.* Vol. 5. Longman New York.

[5] Ian Douglas. 2006. Issues in software engineering of relevance to instructional design. *TechTrends* 50, 5 (2006), 28–35.

[6] J. Philip East. 2004. Applying Software Design Methodology to Instructional Design. *Computer Science Education* 14, 4 (2004), 257–276.

[7] Peter J Esseff and Mary Sullivan Esseff. 1998. Instructional Development Learning System (IDLS). (1998).

[8] Kenneth Koedinger, Albert T Corbett, and Charles Perfetti. 2012. The Knowledge-Learning-Instruction Framework: Bridging the Science-Practice Chasm to Enhance Robust Student Learning. *Cognitive science* 36.5, Article 5 (2012), 757-798 pages.

[9] Nasir I. Mohd, Azilah N. Nor, and Naufal U. Irfan. 2010. Instructional Strategy in the Teaching of Computer Programming: A Need Assessment Analyses. *TOJET: The Turkish Online Journal of Educational Technology* 9, 2 (2010).

[10] Cynthia. Taylor, Daniel Zingaro, Leo Porter, Kevin C. Webb, Cynthia Bailey Lee, and M. Clancy. 2014. Computer science concept inventories: past and future. *Computer Science Education* 24, 4 (2014), 253-276.

[11] Allison Elliott Tew and Mark Guzdial. 2011. The FCS1: a language independent assessment of CS1 knowledge. In *Proceedings of the 42th ACM Technical Symposium on Computer Science Education.* ACM, 111–116.

An Explicit Strategy to Scaffold Novice Program Tracing

Benjamin Xie
University of Washington
The Information School, DUB Group
bxie@uw.edu

Greg L. Nelson
University of Washington
The Allen School, DUB Group
glnelson@uw.edu

Andrew J. Ko
University of Washington
The Information School, DUB Group
ajko@uw.edu

ABSTRACT

We propose and evaluate a lightweight strategy for tracing code that can be efficiently taught to novice programmers, building off of recent findings on "sketching" when tracing. This strategy helps novices apply the syntactic and semantic knowledge they are learning by encouraging line-by-line tracing and providing an external representation of memory for them to update. To evaluate the effect of teaching this strategy, we conducted a block-randomized experiment with 24 novices enrolled in a university-level CS1 course. We spent only 5-10 minutes introducing the strategy to the experimental condition. We then asked both conditions to think-aloud as they predicted the output of short programs. Students using this strategy scored on average 15% higher than students in the control group for the tracing problems used the study (p<0.05). Qualitative analysis of think-aloud and interview data showed that tracing systematically (line-by-line and "sketching" intermediate values) led to better performance and that the strategy scaffolded and encouraged systematic tracing. Students who learned the strategy also scored on average 7% higher on the course midterm. These findings suggest that in <1 hour and without computer-based tools, we can improve CS1 students' tracing abilities by explicitly teaching a strategy.

KEYWORDS

Program tracing, instructional intervention, sketching, think-aloud.

ACM Reference format:
Benjamin Xie, Greg L. Nelson, and Andrew J. Ko. 2018. An Explicit Strategy to Scaffold Novice Program Tracing. In *Proceedings of The 49th ACM Technical Symposium on Computing Science Education, Baltimore, MD, USA, February 21–24, 2018 (SIGCSE '18),* 6 pages.
https://doi.org/10.1145/3159450.3159527

1 INTRODUCTION

Program tracing, the process of emulating how a computer executes a program [6], is a necessary precursor to the ability to write [12, 13, 22], debug [17], and maintain code [28]. However, there is substantial evidence that novice programmers, such as those in introductory computer science (*CS1*) courses, struggle with tracing.

Prior work suggests this is from fragile understanding of program semantics and weak strategies for tracing [11, 14, 17]. For example, novices struggle with tracing variable values as they update because they often try to remember these values [29]; this extraneous load on working memory [1, 26] increases as programs become longer and more complex. Students also struggle to produce external representations of program state, perhaps because of an incomplete understanding of the function of code elements [27] or an inability to put the "pieces" of a program together [25].

Computer-based tools to support tracing are not easily integrated into CS1 curricula, which often require students to trace code on paper. Tools enable students to see a visualization of the program state [8, 15], but they often lack active engagement, having students passively step through code execution [23]. Virtual Program Simulation could improve engagement [24], but this work has yet to be evaluated and focuses on computer-based tools. Low-level tracing without the aid of tools is necessary for expert code comprehension [28], so novices must learn to trace without tools.

As an alternative to tools, researchers have investigated *sketching*, writing visualizations of program state or other computing processes, as a pedagogical tool [3]. Previous work has investigated using sketching to assess object-oriented programming knowledge [10] and integrating sketching into pedagogy [9], with other work proposing standardization of sketched memory diagrams [4]. Cunningham et al. framed sketching as a technique for managing cognitive load and found that complete tracing sketches correlated with improved performance [3]. These findings suggest a correlation between sketching an external representation of memory and improved tracing performance, but fall short of evaluating whether teaching sketching is the cause of this improvement.

We explore these causal effects of sketching. We theorize that sketching is a form of scaffolding [21] that lessens the load on students' working memory and makes changing program state more visible. We predict that explicitly teaching a lightweight sketching strategy will offer two benefits: 1) by encouraging students to trace line-by-line "like a computer does" [15], it will reduce their temptation to create their own strategies or shortcuts which may lead to errors [18]; 2) by having students make updates to an external representation of variable values as the code executes, it will reduce the extraneous working memory load of remembering values, lowering working memory retrieval errors [1]. We hypothesize that explicitly teaching a tracing strategy will take a short amount of time and improve students' performance for tracing code on paper.

To test this hypothesis, we ask the following questions: **1) Does explicitly teaching a tracing strategy improve novice programmers' performance? 2) How do novices trace code and how does an explicit strategy change their behavior?**

2 THE STRATEGY: LINE-BY-LINE + SKETCH

The goal of our strategy was to help novices *embody the computer.* Our strategy achieved this by providing 1) step-by-step instructions

SIGCSE '18, February 21–24, 2018, Baltimore, MD, USA

ACM ISBN ISBN 978-1-4503-5103-4/18/02...$15.00
https://doi.org/10.1145/3159450.3159527

on how to apply the syntactic and semantic knowledge novices have been learning to tracing questions and 2) a visual representation to explicitly track variables which we refer to as *memory tables*. The strategy instructions consisted of three steps:

(1) Read question: Understand what you are being asked to do. At the end of the problem instructions, write a check mark.
(2) Find where the program begins executing. At the start of that line, draw an arrow.
(3) Execute each line according to the rules of Java.
  (a) From the syntax, determine the rule for each part of the line.
  (b) Follow the rules.
  (c) Update memory table(s).
  (d) Find the code for the next part.
  (e) Repeat until the program terminates.

When tracing through the code, a participant creates a *memory table* with each method call, as shown in Figure 1. This memory table keeps track of parameters passed into and variables instantiated in a given method, similar to sketches from previous work [3, 4]. These were the instructions for using a memory table :

(1) Create a new Memory Table every time a method is called.
(2) Write the method name in the box at the top of table.
(3) When a variable is created, add it as a row in the table (variable name in the "name" column; value in "value" column.
(4) When a variable is updated, find the variable by name, cross out the previous value and write in the new one.
(5) After the method finishes running, write the value for the return and cross out the entire table.

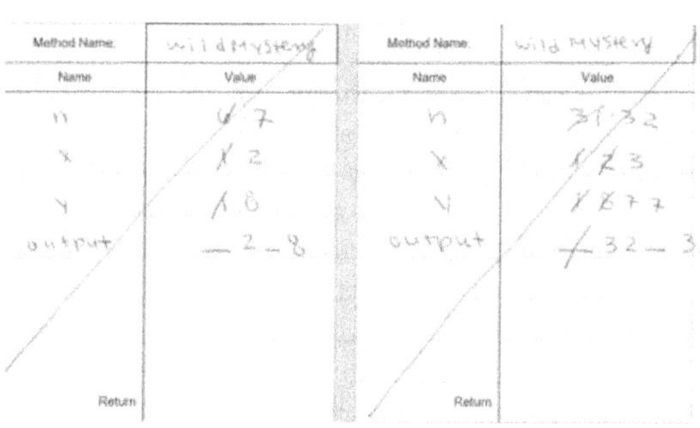

Figure 1: Two memory tables for 2 calls to the same method (Prob. 3). The participant wrote the method name at the top, variable names in the *Name* column, and variable values on the *Value* column. When variables updated, they crossed out the previous value and wrote in the new value. After each method finished executing, they crossed out the table.

In designing the strategy, our intentions were to enable instructors to teach the strategy without major changes to their pedagogy and to enable novices to easily understand and apply the strategy to any tracing problem. From our pilot testing, we found the instructions were easy to recall and discouraged participants from deviating from line-by-line tracing. We designed the memory tables so participants could easily sketch their own tables. We emphasized the separation of variable names and values to ensure variable names were differentiated from Strings and to ensure variable names from different scopes were not passed in as parameters. We emphasized using a new table for each method call to enforce scope.

3 EXPERIMENT: TRACING + THINK-ALOUD

We designed an experiment in which students enrolled in the same CS1 course worked through problems that required them to predict the output of 6 Java programs while verbalizing their thoughts. The control group used their own strategies, while the strategy group was encouraged to use the strategy from Section 2.

Our target population was novices who were just beginning to learn programming. This ensured some exposure to the syntax and semantics of a programming language, but little experience with tracing code. We advertised the study as preparation for an upcoming midterm, with participants receiving tutoring after the problem solving session. We recruited students who had taken 0 or 1 CS courses prior to the course they were enrolled in.

Ultimately, 24 students participated in the study. Eleven identified as males and 13 as females. Nineteen were enrolled in their first CS course, 1 was retaking the course, 1 had previously taken a CS1 course at local community college, 1 had taken AP Computer Science, and the 2 others specified they had previously completed an unspecified CS course. Most participants were in their first year of college (16), with 7 others in years 2-4, and 1 having a Master's degree and taking the course to change careers. Most were *not* CS majors. Only 3 were majoring in CS, with others majoring in another engineering discipline (8), Informatics (4), a non-engineering major (3), were undecided (5), or were not pursuing a major (1).

3.1 Study design: Think-aloud while tracing

The study sessions occurred 3-6 days prior to the course midterm and participants worked through 6 tracing problems that covered potential midterm concepts. Participants met individually at self-selected times with a researcher and completed a pre-survey (demographics, prior knowledge, self-efficacy [19]) prior to arriving. We attempted to block randomize participants by self-reported number of previous CS courses completed and hours spent programming or learning to program. Because of cancellations, there were 11 in the control group and 13 in the strategy group.

After introducing the study and asking a few questions (# of practice midterm problems attempted, describe tracing strategy), we spent 5-10 minutes introducing think-aloud (protocol from [5]). We then asked participants to work through 6 tracing problems in a fixed order while verbalizing their thought process. After each question, they were asked to recall what they remembered thinking. Following the completion of all problems (≈40 min on average, although they could work for as long as they wanted), we asked them to describe their strategy, how they learned it, what strategies their CS1 course taught, and had them complete a post-survey (mindset, study feedback). We then tutored them for ≈ 30 minutes, reviewing study problems, the midterm format and the cheat sheet.

For the strategy group, we spent ≈5 minutes after practicing think-aloud to teach the tracing strategy. We provided the instructions on a sheet of paper and 4 example memory tables on another sheet of paper and walked through the instructions with the participant. We provided help applying the strategy to the 1st problem, with the help typically involving us reiterating some of the written instructions. Our intention was to help the participant learn the strategy without providing hints which may unfairly support their knowledge of syntax and semantics.

#1 (created)

```
public class StrategyPractice {
    public static void main(String[]
        args) {
        int x = 1;
        int y = 2;

        int z = x;
        x = y;
        y = z;

        printSum(x, y);
        printSum(z, y);

        int val = getSum(x, y+z);
        System.out.println(val);
        System.out.println("Bye!");
    }

    public static void printSum(
        int a, int b) {
        System.out.println(a + b);
    }

    public static int getSum(int a, int b) {
        return a + b;
    }
}
```

#2 (midterm)

```
public class Farmer {
    public static void main(String[] args) {
        String farm = "here";
        String old = "macdonald";
        String macdonald = "there";
        String everywhere = "farm";
        String here = "everywhere";
        String there = "old";
        String quack = "duck";

        mystery(old, macdonald, farm);
        mystery("quack", here, "there");
        mystery(quack, "here", "farm");
        mystery(old, everywhere, there);
    }

    public static void mystery(String
        macdonald, String farm, String old) {
        String end = ".";
        if (macdonald.length() >
        farm.length()) {
            end = "!";
        }
        System.out.println(old + " " +
         macdonald + " had a " + farm + end);
    }
}
```

#3 (midterm)

```
public static void wildMystery(int n) {
    int x = 1;
    int y = 1;
    String output = "";
    while (y < n) {
        x++;
        if (x % 2 == 0) {
            n++;
        } else {
            output = n + " ";
        }
        y = 10 * y - x;
    }
    output = output + x + " " + y;
    System.out.println(output);
}
```

```
wildMystery(0);  ___
wildMystery(6);  ___
wildMystery(31); ___
```

#4 (SCS1)

```
public class Conditionals {
    public static void
    main(String[] args){
        int x = 3;
        int y = 9;
        int z = 5;
        manipulate(x, y, z);
        manipulate(y, z, z);
    }

    public static void manipulate
    (int x, int y, int z) {
        if (y % x == 0) {
            if (y >= z) {
                x = x * x;
            } else {
                z = z * z;
            }
        } else {
            if (z >= x) {
                if (y >= z) {
                    y = y * y;
                }
            } else {
                z = z * z;
            }
        }
        if (y % x == 0) {
            x = x + 3;
        } else {
            y = y * 2;
        }
        System.out.println(
          "x = " + x);
        System.out.println(
          "y = " + y);
        System.out.println(
          "z = " + z);
    }
```

#5 (SCS1)

```
public class Greeting {
    public static void main(String[] args) {
        String banner = "Good Night";
        System.out.println("banner");

        greet("Alice", "night");
        System.out.println(banner);

        greet("Bob", "night");
        System.out.println(banner);
    }

    public static String greet(String name, String
    time) {
        String greeting = "Good " + time + " " +
        name;
        if (name.equals("Alice")) {
            return greeting;
        }
        greeting = greeting + "!";
        System.out.println(greeting);
        return greeting;
```

#6 (created)

```
public class OddMystery {
    public static void main(String[] args) {
        int x = 2;
        int y = 3;

        System.out.println(x + y + "!");

        compute(y, x);

        double val = compute(x, y + 1);

        System.out.println(val);
    }

    public static double compute(int
    x, int y) {
        int z = y;
        y = x;
        x = z;

        System.out.println("x" + y + z);

        return Math.pow(x, y);
    }
}
```

Figure 2: The 6 problems for the study, each asking for the program's output. Bold denotes changes to adapted items.

3.2 Problems: Fixed-code tracing questions

The study had 6 *fixed-code* problems which covered early CS1 concepts and required participants to trace provided code and determine the output. In contrast, the midterm assessed tracing (≈50% of midterm), code construction (≈40%), and invariants (≈10%).

Figure 2 shows the 6 problems. Problem 1 helped participants practice using memory tables with variable updates, repeated method calls with parameters passed in, and calls to different methods. Problems 2 and 3 were from practice midterms and Problems 4 and 5 from the SCS1 [16]. Problem 6 assessed midterm concepts not covered in other problems. We used notes from the think-aloud sessions to develop a scoring rubric for the problems completed during the study. The rubric attempted to differentiate scores based on what participants found difficult about each problem. We did not look at participant responses until after the rubric was created.

After the midterm, we sent an online survey to participants to solicit their midterm grades and experiences (perceived problem difficulty, how they prepared for the midterm, how the study may have helped). We also asked the participants in the strategy group to describe the strategy we taught them (to ensure they remembered it) and whether they used the strategy. Of the 24 participants, 17 responded (8 control, 9 strategy, with 1 not sharing their grade).

4 RESULTS

Our data included background information, participants' sketches and responses, researcher notes, audio recordings of participants thinking aloud, and self-reported midterm grades.

4.1 The explicit strategy improved correctness

We answer our first research question by comparing the performance of the two groups on the study problems and midterm. We found a strong linear correlation ($r = 0.91$, Pearson) between the scores on the study problems and the midterm grades, suggesting both measure similar concepts. Because the distributions of scores for each problem in the study deviated from normality ($p < 0.05$, Shapiro-Wilk [20]), we conducted a one-tail non-parametric t-test (Mann-Whitney U test [20]) to determine significance without making assumptions on the distribution shape. Participants' total scores and midterm scores did *not* deviate from normality, so we used a one-tail parametric t-test (Welch t-test [20]) to compare total scores and midterm scores between conditions. We calculated a *Common Language* (CL) effect size from Cohen's d [7, 20] for the parametric test and by dividing the test statistic U by the product of the sample sizes for the non-parametric test [7].

Although we designed the 6 problems to be harder than midterm problems, a large portion of students got many problems correct. Because of this skew, we use the median as the average and the interquartile range (IQR, 3rd quartile/75% - 1st quartile/25%) to measure dispersion for scores on individual problems. For all problems, the median for the strategy group was greater than or equal to the control group's and the IQR was lesser, as shown in Figure 3. The strategy group tended to perform better and with less variability.

Strategy group participants performed significantly better on Problem 4 (p=0.021), which required them to keep track of multiple variables through nested if/else statements. Figure 3 shows that 11 of 13 participants in the strategy group scored perfectly on this problem and above the median score of the control. The U statistic is 101.5, which we interpret as a CL effect size to say that there is a 71% chance that a randomly selected participant from the strategy group scores better than one from the control group on Problem 4.

For the total score across all problems, we found that the strategy group performed on average 15% better and with 46% less variability. We could model the distributions of total problem scores as

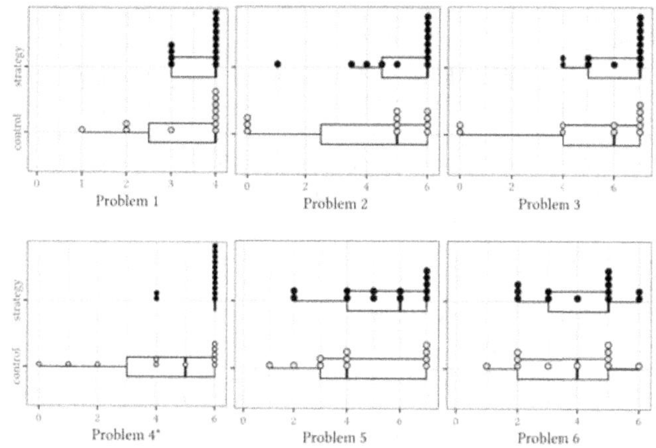

Figure 3: Scores for the 6 study problems by condition. Each dot denotes a participant score. Each boxplot shows the interquartile range. * denotes $p < 0.05$.

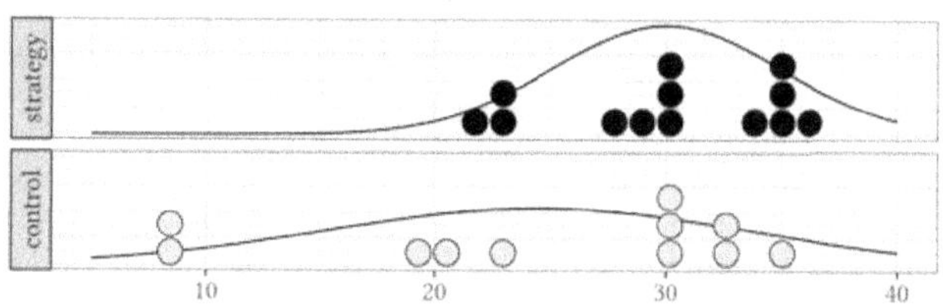

Figure 4: Total scores for study problems by condition (max 36). A dot is a participant score and a curve is a fitted normal curve. ($\bar{x}_s$=30.00, σ_s=4.91). ($\bar{x}_c$=24.55, σ_c=9.16). p=0.049.

approximately normal, so we used mean and the standard deviation to measure dispersion. Figure 4 shows the distributions, where the strategy group performed significantly better (p = 0.049). Ten of the 13 students who learned the strategy performed better than the mean of the control group. We interpret the Cohen's d of 0.7243 as a CL effect size and say that there is a 70% chance that a randomly selected participant from the strategy group scores better than one from the control group on the study problems.

Seven of the 8 strategy group participants who provided midterm grades said they used the strategy on the midterm. These 8 scored on average 7% better than the control group and had 42% less variability. Figure 5 shows the distributions of midterm scores and fitted normal curves. The class average of 80.4 was within 0.5 standard deviations of the control group mean of 84.5 (Z=-0.36, σ_c=9.16) but was over 1.5 standard deviations below the strategy group mean of 91.5 (Z=-1.66, σ_s=4.91). We expected both groups to perform above the class average because of the tutoring. We found a trend towards significance (p=0.083) that the strategy group performed better than the control group on the midterm. The tracing questions on the midterm were easier, so the difference in performance came largely from the code writing questions which were more challenging.

Considering these performance scores together, our data show that explicitly teaching a strategy can improve tracing performance, even on a midterm which assesses more than just tracing ability.

4.2 An explicit strategy reduced errors

In this section, we qualitatively investigate the reasons for the performance increases in the previous section. To perform this analysis,

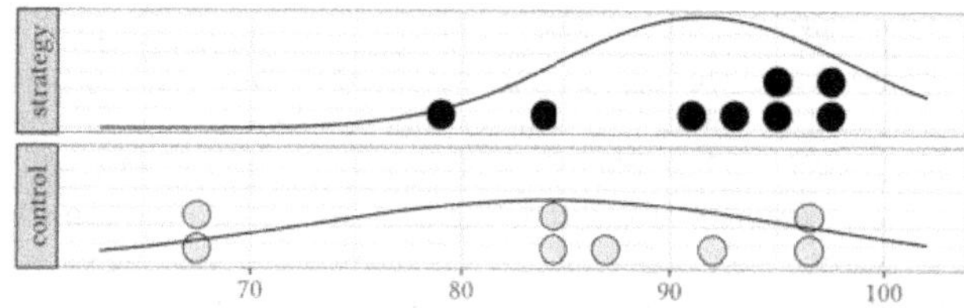

Figure 5: Midterm scores by conditions (max 100). A dot is a participant's score and a curve is a fitted normal curve. ($\bar{x}_s$=91.5, σ_s=6.68). ($\bar{x}_c$=84.5, σ_c=11.5). p=0.083.

we triangulated across think-aloud recordings, sketches, solutions, and researcher notes to characterize the tracing strategy that each participant used. We compare and contrast the strategies that we observed through this process by describing high and low performers in each condition, describing similarities within each subgroup and go into detail on one member of each group (called C_{max}, C_{min}, S_{max}, S_{min} for control/strategy participant with max/min score).

4.2.1 Control group's low performers. The two lowest performing members of the control group demonstrated incomplete knowledge of semantics and often deviated from line-by-line tracing. They deviated because they skipped past an unfamiliar concept (e.g. x++) or they made incorrect assumptions about the control flow (e.g. choosing to skip a method call in Problem 4 because they felt the method would not output anything). They often focused on trying to determine if a problem was similar to one they had previously practiced. Both participants quit partway through several problems, either because of a lack of semantic knowledge overwhelming them or inadequate strategy leaving them unsure what to do next.

C_{min}: One of the lowest scoring members of the control group scored 9/36. He had attempted 5 practice midterm questions prior to the study. His strategy involved trying to comprehend the code's overall purpose and translating the code to English. This strategy and an incomplete understanding of Java semantics overwhelmed him, resulting in him giving up and not answering half of the problems. He tried to look at the code holistically before tracing, but either found the code "really weird" for unfamiliar problems or recognized the problem as similar to one he had previously seen, but failed to recall how to solve it ("I swear I've done a problem like this. I just forgot how to do it."). He had trouble applying concepts he learned in class. He often focused on translating code into natural language but was usually unable to do this for the entire problem. In Problems 4 and 6, he considered writing down intermediate values ("Maybe if I write down the variables?"), but did not do it. He also inappropriately drew upon knowledge from other domains, such as seeing a number followed by an exclamation point in a string ("5!", Prob. 6) and thinking it referred to a factorial. Longer code segments (Prob. 4) were more overwhelming, with the participant "thinking that this is crazy, I don't know where to start."

4.2.2 Control group's high performers. The six highest performers in the control group scored 30-35 of 36. They were able to trace code line-by-line and also update a sketch of intermediate values, although they did not consistently create sketches. Some looked at code holistically before tracing line-by-line, often looking for print/output statements and return statements, but did not do this for longer code segments (Prob. 4) or for later, more complex problems (Prob. 5, 6). Others immediately began tracing line-by-line.

High performing participants in the control group tended to intermittently sketch a tabular external representation to keep track of intermediate values. They often began sketching as a response to specific "cues," such as when the code instantiated multiple variables or when a variable began updating ("I needed to make a table to keep track of the variables because there are a lot of moving parts"). Their tracing of intermediate values also appeared to vary by data type, often sketching numeric variables in tables, but ignoring String variables. This may be because Strings take longer to write, something noted by many members of the strategy group.

C_{max}: The highest scoring participant from the control group scored 35/36 and used both inline (next to code) and tabular (separate from code) annotations to track intermediate values. She completed 4 practice midterm questions prior to the study and reported the highest programming self-efficacy [19] of all participants. She self-described her tracing strategy as "writing out the values that were given and keeping track of the series of manipulations as they went through." Like most of the control group, she recognized Problem 2 and applied a problem-specific strategy learned in class. For other problems, she immediately began tracing the code line-by-line. She wrote intermediate values inline when they were numeric and did not update. She created a separate table when values were Strings or when they updated. The only error she made was when she used the + operator incorrectly (Prob. 6).

4.2.3 Strategy group's low performers. The 3 lowest strategy group participants did not use the strategy appropriately, scoring 22-23.5 of 36. Despite being taught the strategy, they still deviated from line-by-line tracing, sometimes unintentionally (not checking an if/else conditional because they believe it is always true, Prob. 3), and sometimes intentionally (see S_{min}). One participant did not create memory tables for the last 3 problems she did. These participants found sketching the memory tables time-consuming and often unnecessary. In sharp contrast to the control group, these low performers never became overwhelmed or gave up.

S_{min}: The lowest scoring participant in the strategy group scored 22/36, still within 3 points of the mean score of the control group. He reported having done 0 practice problems prior to the study. Prior to being taught the strategy, he tried to interpret what the code was doing and translate it to pseudocode, while also trying to remember variable values. When applying the strategy, he still deviated from line-by-line tracing intentionally, such as in Problem 5 when he correctly traced through the first call to a method and realized it resulted in no printed output or stored return, then skipped the second call to the method which had different parameters passed in and would have printed an output. He justified his decision by thinking that "since [the method] doesn't do anything with the return value, I just ignore it. I don't need to write another memory table. It doesn't affect the output in any way. At least, I don't think it does." He also unintentionally deviated from line-by-line tracing, such as in Problem 4 when he correctly interpreted an if condition as false, but skipped past the else statement. S_{min} found the strategy familiar and reliable, "having a very structured set of rules to follow that would generally work for any code".

4.2.4 Strategy group's high performers. The four highest performing participants scored 34-36 of 36, using the strategy as intended to complement their Java semantics knowledge. Participants had strong understanding of Java, even on more advanced concepts which often confused most other participants (e.g. scope, return). They used the strategy as intended, tracing line-by-line and creating and updating memory tables as they traced. One participant felt the strategy "forces you to think through what you're doing...forces you not to skip around." Another noted that he "didn't have to keep thinking about values because they were on paper," suggesting that the strategy does offload values from working memory. Some participants actively kept track of where they were in the code either by pointing at the line they were executing or by crossing out previously executed lines. The most common error among this group was returning an integer instead of a double in Problem 6.

S_{max}: The highest scoring participant from the strategy group was the only one to score perfectly on all 6 problems. S_{max} self-reported having attention deficit hyperactivity disorder (ADHD) and completing around 100 practice problems prior to the study, which is much greater than the average participant who had completed less than 10 practice problems. She was also the only one who was not an undergraduate, already having a Master's degree in an unrelated field. She immediately began tracing the code line-by-line while also filling in the memory tables completely. She also wrote check marks after lines in the main method were executed, perhaps misinterpreting the 2nd step of the strategy. While other participants in both conditions deviated from line-by-line tracing, she never deviated from line-by-line tracing. This enabled her to avoid strategic errors other participants made when skipping line by line tracing. S_{max} found the strategy useful "for keeping track of what a value is," especially when variables were updating or when there were multiple methods (multiple scopes). She recognized that the strategy required time and paper to write down the memory tables, but she felt "like you have to write this stuff down" to solve the problem. With this method, S_{max} felt "you can focus on the calculations without wondering what [a variable] equals."

4.3 Limitations

Because we conducted this study days before course midterms, we were mindful of participants' time constraints. We relied on proxy measures of prior knowledge (est. hours programming, # of CS courses). Our performance measurements are not validated, although we found a strong correlation between the study and midterm scores. Students self-selected to participate in the study, so selection bias may exist. Some students dropped out of the study, resulting in our block-randomization on prior experience slightly favoring the strategy group. Participants took the midterm only 3-6 days after the study, so longer term retention is unclear. Think-aloud and recall may have influenced their thinking, although we followed best practices on protocol analysis [5]. We observed some carryover effect between problems even though we did not provide feedback. Our statistical analysis assumes applying the strategy has the same effect for all participants. A mixed model may more appropriately represent the effect and generalize better [20].

5 DISCUSSION

Our results show that explicitly teaching a tracing strategy that emphasizes line-by-line tracing and an external representation for tracking state may improve tracing performance. We also found that novices who performed well tended to be more able to apply knowledge of semantics, trace line-by-line systematically, and write down intermediate values rather than try to remember them. This was true regardless of whether a student used our strategy, but when a student did, they tended to perform even better. These findings support prior work that identified poor problem solving as a cause of novice programmers' poor tracing [14] and found correlations between sketching and tracing performance [3, 10].

There are many ways to interpret our results. First, confounds such as differences in prior knowledge, self-efficacy, motivation, fatigue, and amount studied could have influenced participants' performance. We did not find significant differences between groups relating to fatigue before the study (# hrs slept) or the amount of practice prior to the study or midterm (# of practice problems attempted). There was a significant difference in average programming self-efficacy [19] favoring the control group ($p<0.01$, 2-sided Welch t-test). Our sample size was also small and limited to students from a single course, so course instruction (instructor demonstrated tracing with tables, students used jGRASP debugger [2]) could have influenced how participants traced. Replication is necessary to increase confidence in the effects of teaching a strategy.

One interpretation is that the strategy helped lower performers make progress and not give up. Those in the control group (e.g. C_{min}) tended to become overwhelmed and gave up on problems in part because their strategies (e.g. translating code to English, looking at code holistically) were inappropriate for their current abilities. In contrast, those in the strategy group (e.g. S_{min}) used the strategy to make incremental progress, never becoming overwhelmed.

Another interpretation is that strategy did indeed help, but that it did not compensate for a lack of syntactic or semantic knowledge. This was reinforced by our qualitative results, which showed that lower performing participants in both groups tended to make mistakes reflecting incomplete semantic knowledge.

The implications for teaching are simple: help students practice an explicit strategy. That said, our strategy was not necessarily optimal. Our participants had to do additional work to keep track of their place in the code (pointing, crossing lines out). We found the memory tables to be effective for primitive data types and Strings, but this may not hold true for data structures (e.g. arrays) or objects. Integrating this strategy with more advanced representations [4] and determining long-term benefits (e.g. transfer to code writing ability) may be promising future work.

6 ACKNOWLEDGEMENTS

We have archived the study materials at https://github.com/bxie/archive/tree/master/sigcse2018. This material is based upon work supported by the National Science Foundation under Grants No. 1314399, 1735123, 1703304 and the NSF GRFP under Grant No. 12566082. Any opinions, findings, and conclusions or recommendations expressed in this material are those of the authors and do not necessarily reflect the views of the National Science Foundation.

REFERENCES

[1] Alan D. Baddeley and Graham Hitch. 1974. Working Memory. *Psychology of Learning and Motivation* 8 (Jan 1974), 47–89.

[2] J. H. Cross, D. Hendrix, and D. A. Umphress. 2004. JGRASP: an integrated development environment with visualizations for teaching java in CS1, CS2, and beyond. In *34th Annual Frontiers in Education, 2004. FIE 2004.* 1466–1467.

[3] Kathryn Cunningham, Sarah Blanchard, Barbara Ericson, and Mark Guzdial. 2017. Using Tracing and Sketching to Solve Programming Problems: Replicating and Extending an Analysis of What Students Draw. In *2017 ACM Int'l Computing Education Research Conf. (ICER '17)*. ACM, 164–172.

[4] Toby Dragon and Paul E. Dickson. 2016. Memory Diagrams: A Consistant Approach Across Concepts and Languages. In *47th ACM Technical Symp. on Computing Science Education (SIGCSE '16)*. ACM, 546–551.

[5] Karl Anders Ericsson and Herbert Alexander Simon. 1993. *Protocol Analysis: Verbal Reports as Data Revised Edition.* The MIT Press.

[6] Sue Fitzgerald, Beth Simon, and Lynda Thomas. 2005. Strategies That Students Use to Trace Code: An Analysis Based in Grounded Theory. In *First Int'l Workshop on Computing Education Research (ICER 2005)*. ACM, 69–80.

[7] Robert J. Grissom and John J. Kim. 2012. *Effect Sizes for Research: Univariate and Multivariate Applications, Second Edition.* Routledge.

[8] Philip J. Guo. 2013. Online Python Tutor: Embeddable Web-based Program Visualization for Cs Education. In *Technical Symp. on Computer Science Education (SIGCSE '13)*. ACM, 579–584.

[9] Matthew Hertz and Maria Jump. 2013. Trace-based Teaching in Early Programming Courses. In *Technical Symp. on Computer Science Education (SIGCSE '13)*. ACM, 561–566.

[10] Mark A. Holliday and David Luginbuhl. 2004. CS1 Assessment Using Memory Diagrams. In *Technical Symp. on Computer Science Education (SIGCSE '04)*. ACM, 200–204.

[11] Raymond Lister, Elizabeth S. Adams, Sue Fitzgerald, William Fone, John Hamer, Morten Lindholm, Robert McCartney, Jan Erik Moström, Kate Sanders, Otto Seppälä, and et al. 2004. A Multi-national Study of Reading and Tracing Skills in Novice Programmers. In *Working Group Reports from ITiCSE on Innovation and Technology in Computer Science Education (ITiCSE-WGR '04)*. ACM, 119–150.

[12] Raymond Lister, Colin Fidge, and Donna Teague. 2009. Further Evidence of a Relationship Between Explaining, Tracing and Writing Skills in Introductory Programming. In *14th Annual ACM SIGCSE Conf. on Innovation and Technology in Computer Science Education (ITiCSE '09)*. ACM, 161–165.

[13] Mike Lopez, Jacqueline Whalley, Phil Robbins, and Raymond Lister. 2008. Relationships Between Reading, Tracing and Writing Skills in Introductory Programming. In *4th Int'l Computing Education Research Workshop (ICER '08)*. ACM, 101–112.

[14] Michael McCracken, Vicki Almstrum, Danny Diaz, Mark Guzdial, Dianne Hagan, Yifat Ben-David Kolikant, Cary Laxer, Lynda Thomas, Ian Utting, and Tadeusz Wilusz. 2001. A Multi-national, Multi-institutional Study of Assessment of Programming Skills of First-year CS Students. *SIGCSE Bull.* 33, 4 (Dec 2001), 125–180.

[15] Greg L. Nelson, Benjamin Xie, and Andrew J. Ko. 2017. Comprehension First: Evaluating a Novel Pedagogy and Tutoring System for Program Tracing in CS1. In *2017 ACM Int'l Computing Education Research Conf. (ICER '17)*. ACM, 2–11.

[16] Miranda C. Parker, Mark Guzdial, and Shelly Engleman. 2016. Replication, Validation, and Use of a Language Independent CS1 Knowledge Assessment. In *2016 ACM Int'l Computing Education Research Conf. (ICER '16)*. ACM, 93–101.

[17] David Perkins and Fay Martin. 1985. *Fragile Knowledge and Neglected Strategies in Novice Programmers.*

[18] D. N. Perkins, Chris Hancock, Renee Hobbs, Fay Martin, and Rebecca Simmons. 1986. Conditions of Learning in Novice Programmers. *J. of Educational Computing Research* 2, 1 (Feb 1986), 37–55.

[19] Vennila Ramalingam and Susan Wiedenbeck. 1998. Development and Validation of Scores on a Computer Programming Self-Efficacy Scale and Group Analyses of Novice Programmer Self-Efficacy. *J. of Educational Computing Research* 19, 4 (Dec 1998), 367–381.

[20] J. Robertson and M. Kaptein (Eds.). 2016. *Modern Statistical Methods for HCI.* Springer.

[21] B. Rosenshine and C. Meister. 1992. The use of scaffolds for teaching higher-level cognitive strategies. *Educational Leadership* 49, 7 (Apr 1992), 26.

[22] Elliot Soloway. 1986. Learning to Program = Learning to Construct Mechanisms and Explanations. *Commun. ACM* 29, 9 (Sep 1986), 850–858.

[23] Juha Sorva, Ville Karavirta, and Lauri Malmi. 2013. A Review of Generic Program Visualization Systems for Introductory Programming Education. *Trans. Comput. Educ.* 13, 4 (Nov 2013), 15:1–15:64.

[24] Juha Sorva, Jan Lönnberg, and Lauri Malmi. 2013. Students' ways of experiencing visual program simulation. *Computer Science Education* 23, 3 (Sep 2013), 207–238.

[25] James C. Spohrer and Elliot Soloway. 1986. Novice Mistakes: Are the Folk Wisdoms Correct? *Commun. ACM* 29, 7 (Jul 1986), 624–632.

[26] John Sweller. 1994. Cognitive load theory, learning difficulty, and instructional design. *Learning and Instruction* 4, 4 (Jan 1994), 295–312.

[27] Lynda Thomas, Mark Ratcliffe, and Benjy Thomasson. 2004. Scaffolding with Object Diagrams in First Year Programming Classes: Some Unexpected Results. In *Technical Symp. on Computer Science Education (SIGCSE '04)*. ACM, 250–254.

[28] Rebecca Tiarks. 2011. What maintenance programmers really do: An observational study. In *Workshop on Software Reengineering*. 36–37.

[29] Vesa Vainio and Jorma Sajaniemi. 2007. Factors in Novice Programmers' Poor Tracing Skills. In *12th Annual SIGCSE Conf. on Innovation and Technology in Computer Science Education (ITiCSE '07)*. ACM, 236–240.

Future-Oriented Motivation and Retention in Computer Science

Markeya S. Peteranetz
Dept. of Educational Psychology
University of Nebraska-Lincoln
114 Teachers College Hall
Lincoln, NE 68588-0345
markeya.dubbs@huskers.unl.edu

Abraham E. Flanigan
Dept. of Educational Psychology
University of Nebraska-Lincoln
114 Teachers College Hall
Lincoln, NE 68588-0345
abrahamfl nigan@gmail.com

Duane F. Shell
Dept. of Educational Psychology
University of Nebraska-Lincoln
114 Teachers College Hall
Lincoln, NE 68588-0345
dshell2@unl.edu

Leen-Kiat Soh
Dept. of Computer Science and Engineering
University of Nebraska-Lincoln
256 Avery Hall
Lincoln, NE 68588-0115
lksoh@cse.unl.edu

ABSTRACT

Retaining students in computer science (CS) courses and majors is a concern for many undergraduate CS programs in the United States. A large proportion of students who initially declare a major in CS do not complete a CS degree. The impact of future-oriented motivational constructs such as career aspirations and future connectedness on retention has received relatively little research attention, but these are potential contributors to students' retention in CS courses. The purpose of this study was to investigate how future-oriented motivation related to CS students' retention in CS courses over three consecutive semesters. Students enrolled in CS courses (four 100-level courses, one 200-level course, three 300-level courses, and five 400-level courses) completed survey measures of future-oriented motivation, and course enrollment data were collected for the three semesters. Logistic regression was used to determine whether motivation variables could distinguish between students who were enrolled in at least one CS course during a given semester and students who were not enrolled in any CS courses. Results indicate that, across all three semesters, career aspirations and knowledge of CS career paths were associated with a greater likelihood of continuing to take CS courses, and stronger future connectedness was associated with a lower likelihood of continuing to take CS courses. Implications for CS educators are discussed.

CCS CONCEPTS

• Social and professional topics~Computer science

KEYWORDS

Computer science education; retention; future-oriented motivation; future time perspective

ACM Reference format:
M. S. Peteranetz, A. E. Flanigan, D. F. Shell, L-K. Soh. 2018. Future-oriented motivation and retention in computer science. In SIGCSE '18: 49th ACM Technical Symposium on Computing Science Education, Feb. 21–24, 2018, Baltimore, MD, USA. ACM, NY, NY, USA, 6 pages. https://doi.org/10.1145/3159450.3159513

1 INTRODUCTION

Undergraduate achievement and retention in STEM majors is of interest to many stakeholders in the United States because STEM jobs have been steadily growing in number and importance for several decades [12]. However, research indicates that many students who adopt a STEM major later switch to a non-STEM major [19, 24]. Within STEM, CS historically has seen large proportions of students not completing the CS degree they initially pursue [4]. In order for the United States to meet future workforce demands for STEM and CS professionals [11], the number of students who complete STEM and CS courses must increase.

Low retention and degree completion rates in CS have prompted research into factors that contribute to retention. For example, researchers have considered prior exposure to CS and programming [10], personality characteristics [2], the learning environment [4], and achievement in introductory CS courses [10] as factors that might predict students' retention in CS. In the broader realm of education research, many popular motivation constructs are present-oriented, that is, they center on students' immediate experiences (e.g., belongingness), states (e.g., interest, flow), or pursuit of proximal outcomes (e.g., achievement goals). Future-oriented motivation constructs are studied less but are particularly relevant when studying outcomes that extend further into the future than a chapter test or course grade, as is the case with retention.

The purpose of this study was to examine the relationship between students' future-oriented motivation and continued enrollment in CS courses for three semesters by using official enroll-

ACM ISBN 978-1-4503-5103-4/18/02..$15.00
https://doi.org/10.1145/3159450.3159513

ment data. Much of the research on retention in CS has relied on students' self-reported intentions to study or continue studying CS [2, 4, 18]. While self-reported intentions can provide useful insights into students' plans for their education, objective records of students' continued course enrollment provide information about what students actually do. The research question guiding this study was as follows: Is retention in CS courses related to students' future-oriented motivation? We hypothesized that all future-oriented motivation variables would be positively associated with retention in CS courses. Logistic regression analyses were conducted on retention data in order to answer this question.

In this paper, we report on the findings of what we believe to be the first investigation into how future-oriented motivation relates to retention in CS. The method described in this paper, including the data collection procedure and the survey instruments used to gauge students' future-oriented motivation, serves to inform the CS education community on viable processes for collecting more such data. The discussions and implications for CS educators can potentially help increase student retention in CS through better informing students on career choices as well as nurturing students' future time perspective.

For the rest of this paper, we first review future-oriented motivation in Section 2. Then, we detail our design method, including the participants and courses from which we collected the data, our data collection procedure, and survey instruments used in Section 3. Section 4 presents the results. We discuss the results in Section 5 and offer implications for CS educators in Section 6, before concluding and outlining future directions in Section 7.

2 FUTURE-ORIENTED MOTIVATION

Future Time Perspective (FTP) is a set of psychological constructs that together explain some of the differences we see in students' tendency to plan for the future, delay gratification, and make responsible life choices [25]. FTP is conceptualized as a multi-faceted, hierarchical construct [6, 8, 23]. At the highest level, FTP deals with the ability to conceptualize a personal future. Individuals envision possible future selves [13] based on the future outcomes they have knowledge of and perceive as being attainable. From these possible future selves, one derives more specific career aspirations [14]. Career aspirations serve as a type of long-term goal that generally guides one's behavior toward the desired possible future self [20]. The link between these career aspirations and the future enacts through connectedness. FTP connectedness [9] refers to how much people see their present behavior as contingently linked to the attainment of future outcomes and goals. Connectedness itself has been shown to be multifaceted and hierarchical with general feelings of connectedness influencing and being influenced by specific connectedness, such as connectedness for a career [6, 7, 8]. In academic settings, FTP constructs have been associated with student academic achievement [14, 21], student self-regulation and engagement [6], and student course withdrawal [22].

Another relevant construct that does not fall under the umbrella of FTP is information on careers, that is, the degree to which one is aware of possible career paths and the steps involved in pursuing a given career. Whereas FTP has to do with "seeing" and planning a specific potential future, information on careers has to do with whether one presently knows how to make that specific future a reality. The concept of information on careers is part of the questionnaire portion of the Programme for International Student Assessment (PISA), an international survey of education systems and students that has been conducted every three years since 2000 [16]. In the PISA survey, students respond to items about their knowledge of careers in a domain such as science [15]. Research using PISA data has shown that students' knowledge of science careers is related to their interest in pursuing science-related careers [1].

3 METHOD

3.1 Participants and Courses

The study was approved by the university IRB and students participated voluntarily in data collection. Students enrolled in undergraduate CS courses at a large, public, Midwestern university participated in this study (N = 753; 629 males, 124 females). Participants represented all academic levels (316 freshmen, 203 sophomores, 138 juniors, 96 seniors) and were recruited from five 100-level courses (lower-division; n = 534), one 200-level course (lower-division; n = 63), three 300-level courses (upper-division; n = 87), and five 400-level courses (upper-division; n = 69). Students who did not enroll in any classes for a given term were not included in the analyses for that term because of the variety of reasons students might not enroll in classes (e.g., graduation, transferring to a different institution, dropping out of school). As a result, each regression has a different sample size.

3.2 Procedure

Data collection took place as part of a larger NSF-funded study aimed at improving undergraduate CS education. No interventions were conducted during the semesters from which these data were collected. All participants provided informed consent before participating, and they separately provided consent for the researchers to access their ongoing enrollment data. Primary data collection took place in CS courses during the fall 2014 and spring 2015 semesters. During the first week of the semester, participants completed a web-based survey that included a battery of motivation, self-regulation, and affect scales. Only the instruments used in the present study are reported here. For three subsequent semesters, enrollment data were collected from the university. Enrollment data listed all courses for which each participant was registered. Data were recoded into a binary variable indicating whether a participant was enrolled in at least one CS course for the given semester. Below, the three subsequent semesters—during which we measured retention—are referred to as Semesters 1, 2, and 3.

3.3 Instruments

3.3.1. Career Aspirations. Career aspirations were measured with a scale that was adapted from the career aspirations scale used in the PISA assessment [14, 15]. The scale used in the PISA assessed high school students' career aspirations for the future in general subject matter domains such as science. For this study, questions were reworded to ask about students' aspirations toward careers involving CS (e.g., "In whatever career I choose, I would like to work in a job that uses computer science applications, programming, or computational thinking"). Participants responded to three items using a 5-point scale ranging from 1 (strongly disagree) to 5 (strongly agree). The mean of item responses was computed and used as a scale score in the analyses. The coefficient alpha reliability estimate for the scale was .94.

3.3.2. Information on Careers. The Information on Careers scale was based on the scale used in the PISA assessment [14, 15]. The scale used in the PISA assessed high school students' awareness of careers in general domains such as science. The adapted scale used in this study assessed participants' perceived knowledge of CS careers and the steps involved with finding a CS job (e.g., "How much do you know about careers and jobs that involve computer science applications, programming, or computational thinking?"). The scale consisted of four items that were presented with a 4-point scale ranging from 1 (very little) to (a lot). The mean of item responses was computed and used as a scale score in the analyses. The coefficient alpha reliability estimate for the scale was .85.

3.3.3. Future Connectedness. An adapted version of the Connectedness subscale from the Future Time Perspective Scale [9] was used to measure future connectedness. Eleven items from the full 16-item subscale were revised so that items referred to the connectedness between the present and one's future career (e.g., "I have been thinking a lot about what I am going to do in the future in my career"). Items were presented with a 5-point scale ranging from 1 (strongly disagree) to 5 (strongly agree). The mean of item responses was computed and used as a scale score in the analyses. The coefficient alpha reliability estimate for the scale was .88.

3.4 Logistic Regression Models

We used logistic regression to examine the relationship between future-oriented motivation and retention. Logistic regression is conceptually parallel to linear regression, but is used with discrete outcome variables such as category membership or binary outcomes. In logistic regression, independent variables are used to estimate the likelihood of belonging to one of the groups. Because estimations are of probability, the primary effect size of interest is the odds ratio. An odds ratio indicates the expected increase (or decrease) in probability of the outcome based on a one-unit changes in the independent variable. For example, if the relationship between a test score and passing a class has an odds ratio of 2, one-unit change in the test score makes it twice as likely one will pass the class. Other effect sizes of interest are the Cox & Snell R^2 and the Nagelkerke R^2. These two measures of effect size are analogous to R^2 as it is used in linear regression and are interpreted similarly. That is, both the Cox & Snell R^2 and the Nagelkerke R^2 reflect how well the entire model accounts for variability in the outcome variable.

Other statistics reported below include B coefficients, standard error, Wald test statistics, and classification percentages. The B coefficient and standard error in logistic regression are analogous to the same statistics as used in linear regression, but do not have the same direct unit-to-unit-change interpretation. The Wald test statistic is similar to the t-test statistic used in linear regression, and it is used to determine the statistical significance of individual variables in the model. Finally, the classification percentage indicates the percentage of cases in the data set that were correctly classified by the model. With a binary outcome variable, a classification percentage of 50% would reflect chance levels and suggest that the independent variables do not contribute to one's ability to classify cases.

4 RESULTS

Career aspirations, information on careers, and future connectedness were mean-centered (i.e., rescaled so the mean of all scores was zero) prior to analysis so that interactions between variables could be included in the regression models. Mean-centering can reduce multicollinearity and aid in interpreting interaction effects in regression [5]. In order to test the research question posed in Section 1, a series of three two-step logistic regressions was conducted (one for each of the three semesters). The mean-centered career aspirations, information on careers, and future connectedness variables were included in the models at step 1, and the three two-way interactions between the three centered variables were included in the model at step 2.

During Semester 1, there were 624 students enrolled in classes, of which 303 were enrolled in at least one CS course. At step 1, the regression model was significant ($\chi2(3) = 228.67, p < .001$), indicating that the set of predictors reliably distinguished between those who were enrolled in at least one CS course and those who were not. The Cox & Snell estimated $R^2 = .31$, the Nagelkerke estimated $R^2 = .41$, and 79.0% of students were classified correctly. Adding the three two-way interaction terms at step 2 made a significant contribution to the model ($\chi2(3) = 16.40, p = .001$), and slightly increased the Cox & Snell estimated R^2 and the Nagelkerke estimated R^2 to .33 and .43, respectively. The full model correctly classified 79.2% of students. Statistics for individual predictors for both steps are shown in the top section of Table 1. Career aspirations and information on careers were positively associated with retention, and future connectedness was negatively associated with retention.

During Semester 2, there were 544 students enrolled in classes, of which 240 were enrolled in at least one CS course. At step 1, the regression model was significant ($\chi2(3) = 156.41, p < .001$), indicating that the set of predictors reliably distinguished between those who were enrolled in at least one CS course and those who were not. The Cox & Snell estimated $R^2 = .25$, the Nagelkerke estimated $R^2 = .34$, and 76.1% of students were classified correctly. Adding the interaction terms at step 2 did not make a significant contribution to the model ($\chi2(3) = 4.79, p = .188$). The full model correctly classified 77.2% of students. Statistics for individual predictors for both steps are shown in the middle section of Table 1.

During Semester 3, there were 494 students enrolled in classes, of which 213 were enrolled in at least one CS course. At step 1, the regression model was significant ($\chi2(3) = 170.88, p < .001$), indicating that the set of predictors reliably distinguished between those who were enrolled in at least one CS course and those who were not. The Cox & Snell estimated $R^2 = .29$, the Nagelkerke estimated $R^2 = .39$, and 78.7% of students were classified correctly. Adding the interaction terms at step 2 did not make a significant contribution to the model ($\chi2(3) = 5.70, p = .127$), but it did slightly increase the Cox & Snell estimated R^2 and the Nagelkerke estimated R^2 to .30 and .40, respectively. The full model correctly classified 79.6% of students. Statistics for individual predictors for both steps are shown in the bottom section of Table 1.

5 DISCUSSION

Results from this study indicate students' future-oriented motivation is associated with later retention in CS courses. Across all three retention semesters, career aspirations, information on careers, and future connectedness were significant predictors of retention in CS courses. Stronger CS-related career aspirations and greater information on CS careers was associated with an increased likelihood of continuing to take CS courses, and stronger future connectedness was associated with a decreased likelihood of continuing to take CS courses.

These direct relationships held across all three retention semesters. It is not surprising that of the three variables, career aspirations had the strongest direct effect on retention: Students who aspire to CS-related careers are expected to take more CS courses than students who do not aspire to CS-related careers.

Table 1: Logistic Regression Statistics for All Predictors and Models

	B	S.E.	Wald	p	Odds ratio
Semester 1; N = 624					
Step 1					
Career aspirations	1.40	0.14	104.60	<.001	4.05
Information on careers	0.53	0.17	9.62	.002	1.70
Future connectedness	-0.47	0.18	7.06	.008	0.63
Step 2					
Career aspirations	1.58	0.16	103.05	<.001	4.84
Information on careers	0.79	0.21	14.72	<.001	2.20
Future connectedness	-0.57	0.18	9.66	.002	0.57
Career aspirations*Information on careers	-0.78	0.24	10.58	.001	0.46
Career aspirations*Future connectedness	0.48	0.20	5.61	.018	1.62
Information on careers *Future connectedness	0.00	0.27	0.00	.990	1.00
Semester 2; N = 544					
Step 1					
Career aspirations	1.18	0.14	77.09	<.001	3.26
Information on careers	0.43	0.18	5.79	.016	1.53
Future connectedness	-0.57	0.19	9.29	.002	0.57
Step 2					
Career aspirations	1.23	0.14	76.89	<.001	3.42
Information on careers	0.60	0.20	8.83	.003	1.82
Future connectedness	-0.60	0.19	9.68	.002	0.55
Career aspirations* Information on careers	-0.44	0.22	4.12	.042	0.64
Career aspirations* Future connectedness	0.05	0.22	0.04	.837	1.05
Information on careers *Future connectedness	0.28	0.31	0.86	.354	1.33
Semester 3; N = 494					
Step 1					
Career aspirations	1.36	0.15	79.82	<.001	3.88
Information on careers	0.55	0.20	7.80	.005	1.74
Future connectedness	-0.43	0.20	4.64	.031	0.65
Step 2					
Career aspirations	1.41	0.16	80.21	<.001	4.08
Information on careers	0.71	0.22	9.90	.002	2.03
Future connectedness	-0.53	0.21	6.40	.011	0.59
Career aspirations* Information on careers	-0.38	0.25	2.34	.126	0.69
Career aspirations* Future connectedness	0.24	0.24	1.07	.300	1.28
Information on careers *Future connectedness	0.48	0.33	2.02	.155	1.61

Note. B = regression coefficients, S.E. = standard error.

The negative effect of future connectedness indicates that, for a given level of aspirations and information, students who perceive a stronger connection between the present and the future were more likely to stop taking CS courses. Considering the majority of participants were initially enrolled in lower-division CS courses, it is possible that these students did not initially take CS because they intended to continue in the CS major, but that the skills and knowledge gained in their lower-division CS course was helping them progress in other domains, such as engineering. Additionally, it is possible that for students early in their academic careers, a weaker connection to the future might be more conducive to the slow, step-by-step progression through a major course sequence.

As for the interactions, the negative coefficient for the interaction between career aspirations and information on CS careers indicates that the relationship between aspirations and retention was stronger when information was low than when information was high (the interaction in Semester 1 is shown Figure 1). The effect of this interaction was rather pronounced during the first retention semester (odds ratio = 0.46), and was present but less pronounced during the second retention semester (odds ratio = 0.64). The interaction between career aspirations and future connectedness was also significant during the first retention semester (odds ratio = 1.62). The positive coefficient for this interaction indicates that the relationship between aspirations and retention was stronger when future connectedness was high than when future connectedness was low. This is consistent with FTP theory [6, 8, 23] that proposes that future outcomes like career aspirations are more salient motivationally for students with a stronger connection to the future.

Interactions, however, diminish in significance as the semesters become more distal. By the third semester only the main effects of career aspirations, information on careers remained significant. This suggests that conditional effects lessen as time goes by and only the students' individual levels of aspirations, information, and connectedness matter.

6 IMPLICATIONS FOR EDUCATORS

The finding that information on CS careers is related to increased retention suggests that teaching students about CS careers and the steps involved in obtaining a CS career could encourage them to continue taking CS courses. While many CS programs have seminar courses that provide information about career paths, that information only reaches students who are already engaged enough to sign up for the seminar course. CS educators might need to look for other ways to provide career information to students who come to CS courses from other programs, such as engineering. Furthermore, we also infer from our findings that informing students on CS careers can impact students beyond just job search or career placement. That is, informing students on CS careers can improve retention, instead of informing students for the sake of recruiting them into the computing discipline and for the sake of preparing them for graduation towards the end of their undergraduate studies. In a way, informing students on CS careers exposes students to the varied purposes of studying in CS. Ways to inform students on CS careers in introductory courses include, for example, having guest speakers or panels from industry and academia from not just traditionally CS fields but also emerging interdisciplinary areas. These efforts can complement well proven practices to improve retention in the major, such as media computation, pair programming, and peer instruction, reported by [17].

Figure 1. The Interaction between Career Aspirations and Information on Careers during Semester 1.

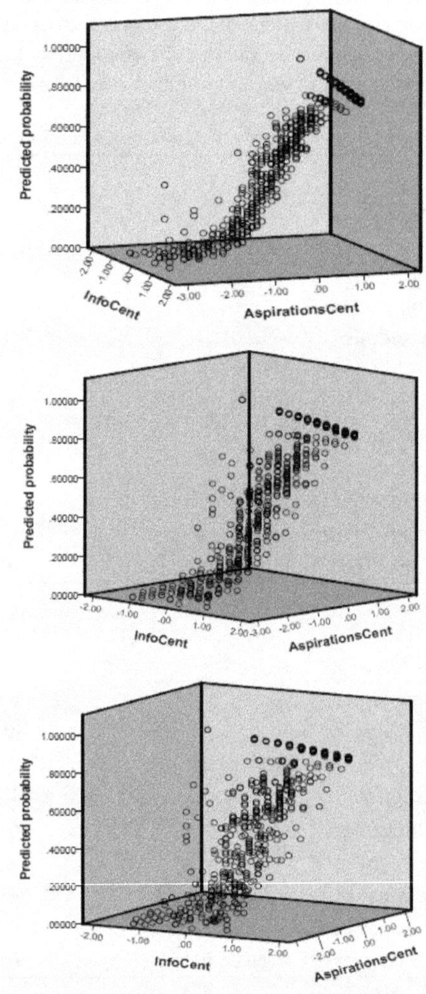

Note. InfoCent = mean-centered information variable; AspirationsCent = mean-centered information variable. Figure shows the same data rotated around the y-axis.

Additionally, fostering students' CS-related career aspirations might also encourage retention in CS courses and programs. Teaching practices such as drawing connections between skills learned in class and specific workplace tasks is one possible way to help students connect CS courses to existing career goals. Furthermore, as more STEM and non-STEM disciplines encourage or require their students to take CS courses such as CS1, it is likewise increasingly important to connect CS-related tasks or roles to their discipline-specific career aspirations. Again, activities such as inviting industry or academic professionals in those disciplines to discuss specific examples of CS- and computing-related solutions in their problem solving or their daily responsibilities can help retain non-CS-majors. Facilitating mentor-mentee programs between industry and classroom can also potentially foster students' CS-related career aspirations.

Finally, these findings support the importance of having role models in computer science or computing for women and under-represented groups. When informing students of career choices, providing examples of or access to successful professionals that are members of under-represented groups might make information on careers even more impactful and also foster career aspirations. As one example, it is important to have panels that are inclusive and diverse. Likewise, including mentors of diverse backgrounds from the industry or conducting an industry fair could help encourage participation in computing [3], and in turn, improve retention in CS courses.

7 CONCLUSIONS AND FUTURE WORK

In this study, future-oriented motivation was associated with retention in CS courses for three semesters after future-oriented motivation was measured. Students' future-oriented motivation shows promise as an entry point for educators to impact retention in CS courses. For example, educators could tell students how specific skills learned in class are used by professionals in specific careers. In contrast to inherent, unchangeable student attributes (e.g., prior exposure to CS, demographic variables), career aspirations and increase knowledge of CS careers have the potential to be changed. Research is needed to determine whether interventions targeting future-oriented motivation can have a positive impact on retention. Additionally, future research on subgroups of students (e.g., men and women, introductory and advanced students) should investigate potential group differences in the relationships between future-oriented motivation and retention.

ACKNOWLEDGMENTS

This work was partially supported by the National Science Foundation (Grants No. 0829647, 1431874,and 1122956).

REFERENCES

[1] J. Basl. 2011. Effect of school on interest in natural sciences: A comparison of the Czech Republic, Germany, Finland and Norway based on PISA 2006. Internat. J. of Sci. Educ., 33, 145-157.

[2] S. Beyer. 2014. Why are women underrepresented in Computer Science? Gender differences in stereotypes, self-efficacy, values, and interests and predictors of future CS course-taking and grades. Compu. Sci. Education, 24(2-3), 153-192.

[3] W. M. Dubow, B. A. Quinn, G. Childress Townsend, R. Robinson, and V. Barr. 2016. Efforts to make computer science more inclusive of women. ACM Inroads, 7(4), 74-80.

[4] M. N. Giannakos, I. O. Pappas, L. Jaccheri, and D. G. Sampson. 2016. Understanding student retention in computer science education: The role of environment, gains, barriers and usefulness. Education and Information Technologies, 1-18.

[5] A. F. Hayes and J. Matthes. Computational procedures for probing interactions in OLS and logistic regression: SPSS and SAS implementations. Behavior Research Methods, 41, 924-936.

[6] J. C. Hilpert, J. Husman, G. S. Stump, W. Kim, W. Chung, and M. A. Duggan. 2012. Examing students' future time perspective: Pathways to knowledge building. Japanese Psychological Research, 54, 229-240.

[7] J. Husman, S. K. Brem, S. Banegas, D. W. Duchrow, and S. Haque. 2015. Learning and future time perspective: The promise of the future–rewarding in the present. In M. Stolarski, N. Fieulaine, & W. van Beek (Eds.), Time perspective theory; Review, research and application: Essays in honor of Philip G. Zimbardo (pp. 131-141), Springer International Publishing.

[8] J. Husman, J. Hilpert, and S. Brem. 2016. Future time perspective connectedness to a career: The contextual effects of classroom knowledge building. Psychologica Belgica, 56, 210-225.

[9] J. Husman and D. F. Shell. 2008. Beliefs and perceptions about the future: A measurement of future time perspective. Learning and Individual Differences, 18, 166-175.

[10] S. Katz, D. Allbritton, J. Aronis, C. Wilson, M. J. and Soffa. 2006, fall. Gender, achievement, and persistence in an undergraduate computer science program. The DATA Base for Advances in Information Systems, 37(4), 42-57.

[11] D. Langdon, G. McKittrick, D. Beede, B. Khan, and M. Doms. 2011, July. STEM: Good jobs now and for the future (Issue Brief #03-11). Washington, DC: U.S. Department of Commerce, Economics and Statistics Administration.

[12] L. S. Liben and E. F. Coyle. 2014. Developmental interventions to address the STEM gender gap: Exploring intended and unintended consequences. In L. S. Liben & R. S. Bigler (Vol. Eds.) The Role of Gender in Educational Contexts and Outcomes. In J. B. Benson (Series Ed.), Advances in Child Development and Behavior: Vol. 47 (pp. 77–116). London: Elsevier.

[13] H. Markus and P. Nurius. 1986. Possible selves. American Psychologist, 41, 954-969.

[14] B. Nagengast and H. W. Marsh. 2012. Big fish in little ponds aspire more: Mediation and cross-cultural generalizability of school-average ability effects on self-concept and career aspirations in science. J. of Educational Psychol., 104, 1033-1054.

[15] Organisation (sic) for Economic Co-operation and Development. 2009. PISA 2006 technical report. Paris, France.

[16] Organisation (sic) for Economic Co-operation and Development. Programme for International Student Assessment: About PISA. Retrieved from http://www.oecd.org/pisa/aboutpisa/.

[17] L. Porter and B. Simon. 2013. Retaining nearly one-third more majors with a trio of instructional best practices in CS1, SIGCSE'2013, 165-170.

[18] L. J. Sax, K. J. Lehman, J. A. Jacobs, M. A. Kanny, G. Lim, L. Monje-Paulson, and H. B. Zimmerman. 2017. Anatomy of an enduring gender gap: The evolution of women's participation in computer science. The J. of Higher Education, 88(2), 258-293.

[19] E. Seymour and N. M. Hewitt. 1997. Talking about leaving: Why undergraduates leave the sciences. Westview Press, Boulder, CO.

[20] D. F. Shell, D. W. Brooks, G. Trainin, K. Wilson, D. F. Kauffman, and L. Herr. 2010. The Unified Learning Model: How Motivational, Cognitive, And Neurobiological Sciences Inform Best Teaching Practices. Springer, the Netherlands.

[21] D. Shell and J. Husman. 2001. The multivariate dimensionality of personal control and future time perspective in achievement and studying. Contemporary Educational Psychol., 26, 481–506.

[22] D. F. Shell, L.-K. Soh, A. E. Flanigan, and M. S. Peteranetz., 2016. Students' initial course motivation and their achievement and retention in college CS1 courses. In Proc. SIGCSE'2016 (Memphis, TN), 639-644.

[23] J. Simons, M. Vansteenkiste, W. Lens, and M. Lacante. 2004. Placing motivation and future time perspective theory in a temporal perspective. Educational Psychol. Review, 16, 121-139.

[24] J. Watkins and E. Mazur. 2013. Retaining students in science, technology, engineering, and mathematics (STEM) majors. J. of College Sci. Teaching, 42(5), 36–41.

[25] P. G. Zimbardo and J. N. Boyd. 2009. The time paradox: The new psychology of time that will change your life. Simon and Schuster, New York, NY.

Helping Underrepresented Students Succeed in AP CSA and Beyond

Barbara Ericson
Georgia Institute of Technology
801 Atlantic Drive
Atlanta, GA, 30332
ericson@cc.gatech.edu

Tom McKlin
The Findings Group
2646 Woodridge Dr.
Decatur, GA 30033
tom@thefindingsgroup.org

ABSTRACT

Rise Up 4 CS was created at Georgia Tech in the spring of 2013 to help African American students succeed in their Advanced Placement (AP) Computer Science A (CSA) high school course and on the exam. The AP CSA course is intended to be equivalent to a college level CS1 course. In the fall of 2014, Sisters Rise Up 4 CS was also created to help female students succeed. Rise Up (RU) and Sisters Rise Up (SRU) both offer remote and in-person help sessions led by undergraduate students, who serve as near-peer role models. The long-term goal of these projects is to attract more underrepresented students to computing careers by increasing their self-efficacy. Self-efficacy is the belief that one can succeed in a particular task or field. Thanks to generous support from Google, RU and SRU have been offered at several other colleges and universities as well. This paper summarizes the results from spring 2013 to summer 2016, reports on an alumni survey answered by 68 (32%) of the 211 alumni, and includes excerpts from five semi-structured interviews. The majority (63%) of the alumni survey respondents, who are in college, are majoring in computing. A similar percentage of the alumni who are still in high school intend to major in computing (62%). When asked about the programs' impact on their career choices and interest in computing, 61% of respondents indicated that the program increased their interest in computer science and 24% indicated that it changed their career plans to computing.

KEYWORDS

Advanced Placement (AP); African Americans, Females; Self-Efficacy; Identity; Outreach; Hispanics; URM

ACM Reference format:

Barbara Ericson and Tom McKlin. 2018. Helping Underrepresented Students Succeed in AP CSA and Beyond, In *SIGCSE '18: 49th ACM Technical Symposium on Computer Science Education, Feb. 21–24, 2018, Baltimore, MD, USA.* ACM, NY, NY, USA, 6 pages. https://doi.org/10.1145/3159450.3159517

ACM ISBN 978-1-4503-5103-4/18/02...$15.00
https://doi.org/10.1145/3159450.3159517

1 INTRODUCTION

The average number of computer science majors at doctoral granting institutions has more than doubled since 2011 [11]. However, women, and Underrepresented Minorities (URM) are still not well represented in computing. URM includes African Americans, Hispanics, Native Americans, and Pacific Islanders. Women earned only 16% of computer science bachelor degrees awarded at doctoral-granting institutions in 2015, though they are roughly half the population [4; 10]. In 2015, URM students earned 13% of computer science bachelor degrees at doctoral granting institutions, though they are roughly 30% of the population [4; 10].

Interest in computing is also increasing at the high school level. The number of AP CSA exams taken nationwide over the last five years has more than doubled from 2012 (24,782) to 2016 (54,379) [2]. However, women, African Americans, and Hispanics are still not well represented as shown in Table 1. Females were less than a quarter of all AP CSA exam takers in 2016 and had a lower pass rate on average than males. African Americans, who are approximately 13% of the U.S. population, were only 3.7% of exam takers in 2016 and their average pass rate was nearly half that of Caucasian students [10].

Table 1: **National Data for AP CSA Exam Takers for 2016**

Gender	Number	Percent	Pass Rate
Females	12,642	23.2%	60.7%
Males	41,737	76.8%	64.7%
Ethnicity			
African American	2,027	3.7%	33.2%
Hispanic	6,256	11.5%	41.5%
Asian	15,913	29.3%	72.7%
Caucasian	26, 698	49.1%	65.7%

Failing the AP CSA exam could decrease underrepresented students' confidence in their ability to succeed in a computing career. Research has shown that believing that you can succeed is a key factor in choosing a career [17]. Women and URM are already at risk for low self-efficacy in computing because the prevailing stereotype of a computer scientist is a White or Asian male [23; 34]. High achieving high school girls often turn away from STEM subjects, such as math in high school, because they tend to believe that if they are finding a subject difficult then they do not have the ability to do well in the subject [16; 36].

Nearly half (46%) of the students who dropped an introductory course in computing in college felt that it was too challenging and 75% of those who dropped were female [24]. Prior research has shown that females are more likely to succeed in college-level computer science courses if they had prior experience, such as an AP CSA course in high school [5]. Helping more underrepresented students succeed in AP CSA could increase the diversity of the field.

Ericson at Georgia Tech created RU and SRU to help African American and female students in Georgia succeed in their AP CSA course and on the exam [19; 22; 20]. This paper summarizes the results from spring 2013 to summer 2016, presents the findings from an alumni survey, and contains excerpts from alumni semi-structured interviews. Our research questions were: 1) To what extent did the alumni persist or intend to persist in post-secondary computing? 2) What role did RU and SRU play in developing their interest and enabling them to persist in computing?

2 RELATED RESEARCH

Harvey Mudd [3] and Carnegie Mellon University [25] have greatly increased their percentage of females in undergraduate computer science, but the majority of institutions have not [4]. Ways to attract underrepresented students to computing and to help them succeed in computing include computing summer programs [1; 14; 21; 30; 39], bridge programs [38], and revising the first course in computing at the college level [12]. While results from many of these projects have been encouraging, the long-term effects are not known. Given the limitations of space, this section will only cover efforts that targeted high school students and prepared them to pass an AP course and exam. This section also describes other research, in self-efficacy and how people learn, which informed the design of RU and SRU.

2.1 Glitch

The three-year Glitch project successfully increased African American male high school students' interest in computing careers by paying them to be game testers and by teaching them computing concepts [13]. When the project started only 20% of the participants were interested in a career in computing. One year after the project ended, 65% of the participants who were attending college (*n*=25) had pursued some form of post-secondary computing. Project features included exposure to a college campus, a community of practice, competitions, and undergraduate students as near-peer role models who led the instruction in computing concepts.

2.2 Advanced Placement Incentive Program

The Advanced Placement Incentive Program (APIP), run by AP Strategies, increases the number of students who take and pass Advanced Placement exams by offering extra help sessions, teacher professional development, and financial incentives for both teachers and students [29]. The financial incentives range from \$100 to \$500 for each passing score (three or higher). More females and underrepresented minorities are taking AP courses at APIP participating schools and more are passing the exams. However, these programs are costly. The National Math and Science Initiative (NMSI) has replicated this program [40], and has had similar results.

2.3 Research on Self-Efficacy

Self-efficacy is one's belief in one's ability to succeed at a particular task or subject [6]. Self-efficacy is very important in career selection [17]. People quickly remove career fields from consideration if they do not think they can succeed in them [6]. There is a significant correlation between self-efficacy and interest in a field [33]. High self-efficacy results in more persistence in technical or scientific majors than low self-efficacy [32]. Females have a lower self-efficacy in computing than males [26; 35], which may be an important factor in their underrepresentation in computing. Self-efficacy in a field can be improved by success [15], exposure to similar role models in the field [7], and social encouragement [6]. Research has shown that encouragement and positive feedback from instructors raises self-efficacy for minority students for scientific fields [28].

2.4 Research from the Learning Sciences

One of the challenges for RU and SRU was how to help underrepresented students succeed in their AP CSA course and on the exam. The exam consists of 40 multiple-choice questions and four free response questions with multiple parts that require the students to write Java code on paper. We incorporated spaced practice, worked examples plus practice, and a community of practice to provide social support and encouragement.

Practice is very important in developing expertise [9] and spaced practice (i.e. practice over a length of time) is better than massed practice, (cramming for an exam) for long-term retention [8]. One of the ways to improve the efficiency of learning is through worked examples, especially with interleaved practice problems [42; 43]. A worked example is an expert's detailed solution to a problem. A community of practice is a group of people interacting regularly that share a common interest or goal [44]. Communities of practice have been shown to improve learning and the formation of identity in a field [31].

3 SUMMARY OF RESULTS - 2013 TO 2016

RU and SRU incorporated undergraduate student near peer role models who lead the help sessions, exposure to a college campus, and a community of practice from Glitch [13]. The undergraduate students were paid an hourly rate. We hired three undergraduate students per project. Most of the undergraduate student leaders were underrepresented in computing (African American, Hispanic, or female), but not all.

RU and SRU originally replicated the student incentives from APIP [29], but reduced the cost by offering smaller incentives (\$100) and by offering remote and in-person help sessions. RU and SRU tried to improve the participants' self-efficacy in computing by helping the students succeed in the AP CSA course, through exposure to near peer role models, and through social support in a community of practice. The project provided spaced practice through one-hour weekly remote and three-hour monthly in-person help sessions and through the use of an interactive ebook, which was developed for the project, with worked examples and interleaved practice problems [18].

RU has been offered at Georgia Tech every year since January 2013 [19; 22]. Based on feedback from the first cohort we started in the fall rather than the spring after the first year. SRU started in the fall of 2014 and has been offered at Georgia Tech every year since then [20]. Table 2 shows the percentage of participants who completed the project by attending at least four help sessions, which has varied from 35% to 76%. The pass rate for completers has varied from a low of 31% to a high of 64%, but is usually higher than the pass rate for that same group in Georgia as shown in Table 2. For the first three years we paid participants who attended a required number of help sessions and passed the exam with a score of three or higher $100. In years two and three we also paid participants an additional $100 for attending the required number of help sessions (4). Only a few of the participants mentioned the payments as a reason for joining or completing the project, and some who qualified for the payment never filled out the paperwork to receive it. To test the need for these monetary payments, we did not include them in SRU. As seen in Table 2, SRU had similar completion and pass rates to RU. We stopped offering monetary incentives after the 2014-2015 academic year, which reduced the cost of the project.

Table 2: **Rise Up and Sisters Rise Up in Georgia**

Georgia RU and SRU	N	Number Comp.	# Comp. Passed	GA % Passed
RU Spr 13	27	14 (52%)	9 (64%)	21.7% AA
RU 13-14	33	18 (55%)	7 (39%)	22.6% AA
RU 14-15	21	16 (76%)	5 (31%)	31.6% AA
RU 15-16	19	11 (58%)	7 (64%)	34.5% AA
SRU 14-15	21	12 (57%)	6 (50%)	48.3% F
SRU 15-16	20	7 (35%)	3 (43%)	51.3% F

Thanks to support from Google, we have been able to offer RU and SRU at other locations as shown in Table 3. Bowie State University offered RU in Maryland (MA) in the spring of 2014 and again during 2014-2015 [22]. However, due to administrative problems, they did not collect all the scores for the participants from 2014-2015. Florida International University offered RU in the spring of 2015 for African Americans, however not many African American enrolled. During the 2015-2016 academic year they allowed any underrepresented student to enroll and had mostly Hispanic students. Westminster College in Utah ran SRU in the spring of 2016. However, not many female students enrolled as seen in Table 3. These replication projects had high pass rates for completers, especially when compared to the pass rates for the targeted underrepresented group in the that state.

Table 3: **Rise Up and Sisters Rise Up in Other States**

Location and Year	N	# Comp.	# Comp. Passed	% Passed in State
MA RU Spr 14	22	9 (41%)	6 (67%)	30.2% AA
MA RU 14-15	19	6 (31.6%)	1 score rec.	37.9% AA
FL RU Spr 15	6	3 (50%)	3 (100%)	25.7% AA
FL RU 15-16	14	8 (57%)	7 (88%)	41.3% H
UT SRU Spr 16	8	2 (25%)	2 (100%)	68.8% F

Participants have shown statistically significant attitude changes from pre to post and have reported an increase in interest in a career in computing [19; 22; 20]. Several participants have credited RU or SRU with helping them succeed in their AP CSA courses and on the exam. Even students who did not pass the exam have credited RU and SRU with sustaining or increasing their interest in a computing career.

One of the participants from Florida International University's Rise Up 4 CS in 2015-2016 was a 9th grade Hispanic male. He chose AP CS A because he thought the course "*sounded cool.*" However, he found the first few assignments uninteresting, felt that he was "*just taking down notes,*" and became lost when object-oriented programming was introduced. He got further behind when he went on vacation with his family and lost his flash drive with his assignments. By the end of the first quarter his grade had dropped to a D. His teacher recommended joining RU. He participated in the twice-weekly webinars and a tutor offered individualized support. He passed the exam with a 5, the highest possible score. This demonstrates how easy it is for a student to get behind in AP CSA and how valuable extra help can be.

4 LONG TERM IMPACT IN GEORGIA

One way to measure the long-term impact of RU is examine the AP CSA data for Georgia. Table 4 shows the number of African American exam takers in Georgia from 2012 to 2016, the number who passed the exam, the pass rate in Georgia, and the pass rate nationally. Notice that the number of African American students passing the exam has more than doubled since 2013 and the pass rate has increased each year since we started RU in the spring of 2013. We can not claim that this increase is due to RU, but we have had participants who say that they would not have passed the exam without the project. The pass rate for African Americans in Georgia was below the national average when we started in 2012, but exceeded the national average for African Americans in 2016.

Table 4: **African American data from 2012 to 2016**

Year	GA # AA	GA # AA Passed	GA AA Pass Rate	National AA Pass Rate
2012	137	22	16.1%	27.3%
2013	129	28	21.7%	35.6%
2014	155	35	22.6%	33.4%
2015	174	55	31.6%	37.7%
2016	174	60	34.5%	33.2%

More females in Georgia have been taking the AP CSA exam and passing it since we started SRU in the fall of 2014 as shown in Table 5. Note that the number of females passing the exam in Georgia has doubled from 2014 to 2016. The percentage of females that pass the exam in Georgia is still less than the national average, but it has increased each year since we started SRU.

Table 5: **Female data from 2014 to 2016 in Georgia**

Year	GA # Fem.	GA # Fem. Passed	GA Fem. Pass Rate	National Fem. Pass Rate
2014	285	119	41.8%	57.1%
2015	315	152	48.3%	60.6%
2016	464	238	51.3%	60.7%

We can not claim that this increase in females taking and passing the AP CSA exam is due to SRU, since the number of females passing the exam is far higher than the number of participants in SRU. However, we send out letters to underrepresented students in Georgia who do well on the PSAT to encourage them to take AP CSA and to let them know about RU and SRU. Some of our female participants have told us that the letter convinced them to try AP CSA, since they knew they could get help from SRU. Participants have credited SRU with increasing their interest in computing and their ability to succeed in their course and on the exam [20]. We also hope that these projects have a ripple effect by showing that underrepresented students can succeed in computing.

5 ALUMNI SURVEY

In February of 2017, the 211 alumni of RU and SRU were emailed a request to complete an online survey. Those who completed the survey were entered into a drawing for a prize worth $150. Responses were received from 68 program alumni, for a 32.2% response rate. This rate is slightly higher than the typical response rate (25-30%) for emailed surveys [45]. Fig. 1 shows the percentage of survey respondents by their year of participation and location.

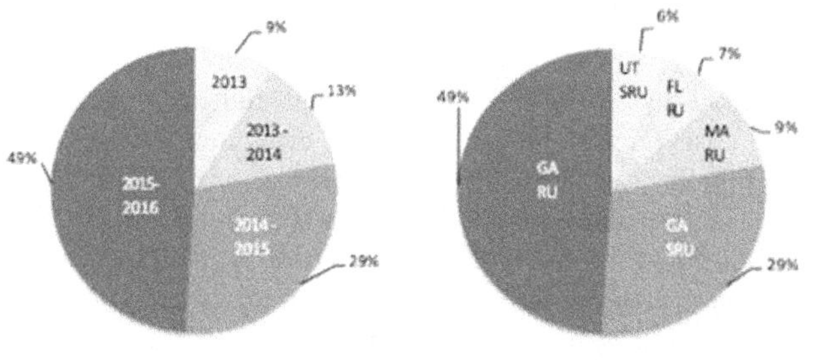

Figure 1: **Percentage of survey respondents by year and location**

Of those responding to the survey, 42 (62%) were high school graduates while the remaining 26 (38%) were still enrolled in high school. Of those who had graduated from high school 41 (98%) were currently attending college. The remaining student was not enrolled in college for health reasons. Table 6 provides the number and percentage of survey respondents for each ethnicity and gender as well as the percentage of alumni in each category.

Table 6: **Survey Respondents by Race and Gender**

Ethnicity	# Resp.	% Resp.	% Alumni
African American	42	62%	74%
Asian	14	21%	11%
Caucasian	5	7%	8%
Hispanic	5	7%	6%
Two or More Races	2	3%	1%
Gender			
Female	37	55%	46%
Male	31	45%	54%

The majority of the survey respondents, who were enrolled in college, were majoring in computing (63%, n=26). One student was minoring in computing. Of the students who were enrolled in college and not majoring or minoring in computing, 6 had taken a computing course in college, and 7 had used programming in their major. Of the students who were still in high school (n=26), 62% report that they intend to major in computing.

The majority of survey respondents (61%, n=38) indicated that the program increased their interest in computer science. Several of the open-ended comments showed how the participants felt that the project improved their self-efficacy in computing. *"It made it easier and more interesting, I felt better when doing it and my confidence in my abilities grew my interest in CS."* A female alumnus wrote, *"I thought CS was too hard or not for me before joining SRU."* Another alumnus wrote, *"It showed me that I can do well in this field, it just takes hard work and determination."*

Alumni were asked if RU or SRU changed their career plans. The majority of them (n=45, 73%) reported that it had not changed their career plans, however 27% (n=17) reported that it did. Two of these students said that it helped them realize that they did not want to major in computing. One of these students said, "*the complexities of coding scared me away*". This student went on to write, *"I would like to pick up coding again because I think it's a very effective skill in the work force."* The remaining 24% (n=15) of the alumni reported that it changed their career plans to include computing. One alumni wrote, "*I was planning to go into prosthetic research with Biomedical Engineering, but I realized that Computer Science is much more fitting for me.*" Another wrote, *"This program encouraged me to go into the computing field; it was a huge component of my decision."*

6 INTERVIEWS WITH ALUMNI

In order to gain a deeper understanding of the ways that RU and SRU impacted our alumni, we held semi-structured interviews with five of them. Three were female and two were male. Three were African American, one was Asian, and one was Caucasian.

We interviewed one student from spring 2013, one from 2013-2014, one from 2014-2015, and two from 2015-2016.

Students told us that they were able to improve their understanding of computing concepts with the help of RU and SRU, even if their teachers were not knowledgeable. *"She didn't know the material herself. So, everyone in the class was confused. By then, like I was getting 100s on free responses and stuff and everyone was getting 30s. They're like, 'How do you know this stuff?'"* Another alumnus said, *"I had a teacher who didn't take computer science and really didn't know anything about it. So, he did the best he could with it. But at the end of the day, thankfully to Rise Up, I was able to kind of go back and look and try to cram so much stuff in just to kind of get a better understanding of everything."*

Even students who were already interested in computing were discouraged by the difficulty of the AP CSA course [37]. *"So, I was like, 'I'm going to love the AP class. I'm going to animate. I'm going to make awesome scenes every day.' We had been working with just Alice (2). In AP, we were working in Alice 3...We actually did a lot of just plain coding, and it was very difficult. So, I definitely needed Project Rise Up... With Rise Up, I liked the one-on-one. I love that there were online sessions so I could join at home, and watch, and type my questions, as well as going in in person and meeting like-minded individuals who either excelled in the program and wanted to see the other ways they could solve equations or were just like me and needed as much help as they could get."* This quote shows that this student valued the community of practice.

Alumni said that the undergraduates could relate to their difficulties and help them understand concepts, even more than knowledgeable teachers. *"They knew the struggle of trying to understand... That's the problem that my teacher couldn't do, because he knew it, but he didn't know how to teach other people how to know it."* The undergraduate students also helped attract students to computing by serving as role models. As one alumni said, *"...they exuded enthusiasm for computer science. I mean, meeting people that really love what they're doing really makes you think, 'Oh, maybe I want to be as happy as they are with what they're doing.' And they all seemed to have really cool internships and job opportunities. They just really have cool things going on."* One of the proven ways to improve self-efficacy is to see others like yourself succeed [6].

One of the interviews with a female student in SRU was originally feeling a lack of self-efficacy in computing. She was one of only four women taking the course online compared to about 70 males. *"I thought computer science was taught more for guys. Like I had one friend that went to a different school taking it, and he seemed to get it easily and had other guys to work with. I was like, 'You know, maybe there's a reason only guys are majoring in this, or mostly guys.'"* After working with SRU she started understanding more and improved. The reaction of her male friend shows how hard it can be for women to overcome the prevalent stereotypes. *"So, he knew I was significantly worse at computer science than him at the beginning. Then at one point, I got a better grade than him on an assignment and he's like, 'Oh, did you cheat?' Like he just didn't see that I can figure stuff out and had been learning, which was what I got out of the program."* She was understandably annoyed at being accused of cheating. Though this student did not pass the AP CSA exam, she is majoring in computing at Georgia Tech and is one of the undergraduate leaders of SRU.

7 DISCUSSION

Prior research had shown that Rise Up and Sisters Rise Up had increased the participants' intent to pursue post-secondary computing studies [19; 22; 20]. However, underrepresented students face stereotypes that can discourage them from pursuing particular careers [41], so it was possible that they might not feel that way a year or more later. Our first research question was to what extent did the alumni persist or intend to persist in post-secondary computing? Over 60% of the alumni survey respondents are majoring in computing or plan to when they reach college. In addition, 79% of the respondents who are in college have taken more computing courses.

Our second research question was what role did RU and SRU play in developing their interest and enabling them to persist in computing? The majority (61%) of the survey respondents credit RU and SRU with increasing their interest in computing and 24% say that it changed their major to computing. The interviews provide evidence that the projects improved understanding, provided social encouragement through a community of practice, and increased interest through undergraduate role models.

A limitation of this study is that the survey response rate was 32.2%. While higher than we might expect for an email survey, the respondents may not represent the majority of the alumni. Also, nearly half of the respondents were from the 2015-2016 academic year, so while they intend to continue in computing, that could change. More follow-up studies should be done to verify these results over time.

8 CONCLUSIONS

Underrepresented students are especially at risk of failure in introductory computing due to less prior experience and a lack of encouragement [24; 27]. With the enrollment surge at the college level, which has increased class sizes, less help is available for novice students [4]. This means that it is more important than ever for underrepresented students to have prior experience before taking college-level computing courses. This paper provides evidence for the long-term effects of RU and SRU, which help underrepresented students succeed in the AP CSA course and on the exam. It provides evidence that these projects attracted underrepresented students to computing and encouraged them to persist in computing in their post-secondary education by improving their self-efficacy in computing. By helping more underrepresented students succeed in AP CSA we may be able to improve the gender balance in computing and the representation of underrepresented minorities.

ACKNOWLEDGMENTS

The funding for RU and SRU came from the National Science Foundation grant CNS-1228352 as well as RISE awards TFR14-00363 and TFR14-03256 from Google. We thank the undergraduate students who led RU or SRU in Florida, Georgia, Maryland, and Utah. We also thank the reviewers for their comments, which improved the clarity of the paper.

REFERENCES

[1] Adams, Joel C., 2007. Alice, middle schoolers & the imaginary worlds camps. In *Proceedings of the 38th SIGCSE technical symposium on Computer science education* (Covington, Kentucky, USA, 2007), ACM, 1227418, 307-311.

[2] Advanced Placement Data From 2016, https://research.collegeboard.org/programs/ap/data/participation/ap-2016, Accessed 2016, May 20

[3] Alvarado, Christine and Dodds, Zachary, 2010. Women in CS: an evaluation of three promising practices. In *Proceedings of the 41st ACM technical symposium on Computer science education* (Milwaukee, Wisconsin, USA, 2010), ACM, 1734281, 57-61.

[4] Association, Computing Research, 2017. Generation CS: Computer Science Undergradute Enrollments Surge Since 2006.

[5] Babes-Vroman, Monica, Juniewicz, Isabel, Lucarelli, Bruno, Fox, Nicole, Nguyen, Thu, Tjang, Andrew, Haldeman, Georgiana, Mehta, Ashni, and Chokshi, Risham, 2017. Exploring Gender Diversity in CS at a Large Public R1 Research University. In *Proceedings of the 2017 ACM SIGCSE Technical Symposium on Computer Science Education* (Seattle, Washington, USA, 2017), ACM, 3017773, 51-56.

[6] Bandura, Albert, 1997. *Self-efficacy: The exercise of control.* Macmillan.

[7] Barnir, Anat, Watson, Warren E, and Hutchins, Holly M, 2011. Mediation and moderated mediation in the relationship among role models, selfâ efficacy, entrepreneurial career intention, and gender. *Journal of Applied Social Psychology 41*, 2, 270-297.

[8] Bjork, Robert A., Dunlosky, John, and Kornell, Nate, 2013. Self-Regulated Learning: Beliefs, Techniques, and Illusions. *Annual Review of Psychology 64*, 417-444.

[9] Bransford, John D., Brown, Ann L., and Cocking, Rodney R., 2000. How People Learn NATIONAL ACADEMY PRESS, Washington D.C.

[10] Bureau, United States Census, Quick Facts, https://www.census.gov/quickfacts/fact/table/US/PST045216, Accessed 2017, August 27, 2017

[11] Camp, Tracy, Adrion, W. Richards, Bizot, Betsy, Davidson, Susan, Hall, Mary, Hambrusch, Susanne, Walker, Ellen, and Zweben, Stuart, 2017. Generation CS: the growth of computer science. *ACM Inroads 8*, 2, 44-50.

[12] Cohoon, James P and Tychonievich, Luther A, 2011. Analysis of a CS1 approach for attracting diverse and inexperienced students to computing majors. In *Proceedings of the 42nd ACM technical symposium on Computer science education* ACM, 165-170.

[13] Disalvo, Betsy, Guzdial, Mark, Meadows, Charles, Perry, Ken, Mcklin, Tom, and Bruckman, Amy, 2013. Workifying games: successfully engaging African American gamers with computer science. In *44th ACM technical symposium on Computer science education (SIGCSE)* (Denver, Colorado, USA, 2013), ACM, 317-322.

[14] Doerschuk, Peggy, Liu, Jiangjiang, and Mann, Judith, 2007. Pilot summer camps in computing for middle school girls: from organization through assessment. In *Proceedings of the 12th annual SIGCSE conference on Innovation and technology in computer science education* (Dundee, Scotland, 2007), ACM, 1268789, 4-8.

[15] Doyle, Eileen, Stamouli, Ioanna, and Huggard, Meriel, 2005. Computer anxiety, self-efficacy, computer experience: An investigation throughout a computer science degree. In *Frontiers in Education, 2005. FIE'05. Proceedings 35th Annual Conference* IEEE, S2H-3.

[16] Dweck, Carol, 1986. Motivational Processes Affecting Learning. *American Psychologist 41*, 10, 1040-1048.

[17] Eccles, Jacquelynne, 2009. Who am I and what am I going to do with my life? Personal and collective identities as motivators of action. *Educational Psychologist 44*, 2, 78-89.

[18] Ericson, Barbara, Java Review Book for the AP CS A exam https://runestone.academy/runestone/static/JavaReview/index.html, Accessed 2016, April 25

[19] Ericson, Barbara, Engelman, Shelly, Mcklin, Tom, and Taylor, Ja'quan, 2014. Project rise up 4 CS: increasing the number of black students who pass advanced placement CS A. In *Proceedings of the 45th ACM technical symposium on Computer science education* (Atlanta, Georgia, USA, 2014), ACM, 2538937, 439-444.

[20] Ericson, Barbara J., Parker, Miranda C., and Engelman, Shelly, 2016. Sisters Rise Up 4 CS: Helping Female Students Pass the Advanced Placement Computer Science A Exam. In *Proceedings of the 47th ACM Technical Symposium on Computing Science Education* (Memphis, Tennessee, USA, 2016), ACM, 2844623, 309-314.

[21] Ericson, Barbara and Mcklin, Tom, 2012. Effective and sustainable computing summer camps. In *Proceedings of the 43rd ACM technical symposium on Computer Science Education* (Raleigh, North Carolina, USA, 2012), ACM, New York, NY, 289-294.

[22] Ericson, Barbara and Mcklin, Tom, 2015. Helping African American Students Pass Advanced Placement Computer Science: A Tale of Two States. In *Research on Equity and Sustained Participation in Engineering, Computing, and Technology (RESPECT)* (Charlotte, NC, USA, 2015), IEEE.

[23] Fisher, Allan and Margolis, Jane, 2002. Unlocking the clubhouse: the Carnegie Mellon experience. *SIGCSE Bull. 34*, 2, 79-83.

[24] Fisher, Lawrence M., 2016. Booming enrollments. *Commun. ACM 59*, 7, 17-18.

[25] Frieze, Carol and Quesenberry, Jeria, 2015. Kicking Butt in Computer Science: Women in Computing at Carnegie Mellon University. Dog Ear Publishing.

[26] Google and Gallup, 2016. Diversity Gaps in Computer Science: Exploring the Underrepresentation of Girls, Blacks and Hispanics.

[27] Google and Gallup, 2015. Searching for Computer Science: Access and Barriers in U.S. K-12 Education.

[28] Hackett, Gail, Betz, Nancy E, Casas, J Manuel, and Rocha-Singh, Indra A, 1992. Gender, ethnicity, and social cognitive factors predicting the academic achievement of students in engineering. *Journal of counseling Psychology 39*, 4, 527.

[29] Jackson, C. K., 2010. A little now for a lot later: A look at a Texas Advanced Placement incentive program. *Journal of Human Resources 45*, 591-639.

[30] Lau, Winnie W.Y., Ngai, Grace, Chan, Stephen C.F., and Cheung, Joey C.Y., 2009. Learning programming through fashion and design: a pilot summer course in wearable computing for middle school students. In *Proceedings of the 40th ACM technical symposium on Computer science education* (Chattanooga, TN, USA, 2009), ACM, 1509041, 504-508.

[31] Lave, Jean and Wenger, Etienne, 1998. Communities of practice. *Retrieved June 9*, 2008.

[32] Lent, Robert W, Brown, Steven D, and Larkin, Kevin C, 1984. Relation of self-efficacy expectations to academic achievement and persistence. *Journal of counseling Psychology 31*, 3, 356.

[33] Lent, Robert W, Larkin, Kevin C, and Brown, Steven D, 1989. Relation of self-efficacy to inventoried vocational interests. *Journal of vocational behavior 34*, 3, 279-288.

[34] Margolis, Jane, Estrella, Rachel, Goode, Joanna, and Holme, Jennifer Jellison, 2008. *Stuck in the Shallow End: Education, Race, and Computing.* The MIT Press Cambridge, MA.

[35] Miura, Irene T, 1987. The relationship of computer self-efficacy expectations to computer interest and course enrollment in college. *Sex Roles 16*, 5, 303-311.

[36] Muenks, Katherine and Miele, David B, 2016. Students' ™ thinking about effort and ability: The role of developmental, contextual, and individual difference factors. *Review of Educational Research*, 0034654316689328.

[37] Pausch, Randy, 2008. Alice: a dying man's passion. In *Proceedings of the 39th SIGCSE technical symposium on Computer science education* (Portland, OR, USA, 2008), ACM, 1352137, 1-1.

[38] Roberts, Eric S, Kassianidou, Marina, and Irani, Lilly, 2002. Encouraging women in computer science. *ACM SIGCSE Bulletin 34*, 2, 84-88.

[39] Scott, Allison, Martin, Alexis, Mcalear, Frieda, and Koshy, Sonia, 2017. Broadening Participation in Computing: Examining Experiences of Girls of Color. In *Proceedings of the 2017 ACM Conference on Innovation and Technology in Computer Science Education* (Bologna, Italy, 2017), ACM, 3059054, 252-256.

[40] Sherman, Dan, Darwin, Marlene J., Song, Mengli, Li, Yibing, and Statchel, Suzanne, 2016. Evaluation Findings for the College Readiness Program on Student Outcomes. In *American Educational Research Association*, Washington, D.C.

[41] Steele, Claude M, 1997. A threat in the air: How stereotypes shape intellectual identity and performance. *American Psychologist 52*, 6, 613.

[42] Sweller, John and Cooper, Graham, 1985. The Use of Worked Examples as a Substitute for Problem Solving in Learning Algebra. *Cognition and Instruction 2*, 1, 59-89.

[43] Trafton, John Gregory and Reiser, Brian J., 1993. The contributions of studying examples and solving problems to skill acquisition. In *15th Annual Conference of the Cognitive Science Society* (Hillsdale, NJ, 1993), Lawrence Erlbaum Associates, Inc., 1017–1022.

[44] Wenger, Etienne, 1998. *Communities of practice: Learning, meaning, and identity.* Cambridge university press.

[45] Yun, Gi Woong and Trumbo, Craig W., 2000. Comparative Response to a Survey Executed by Post, E-mail, & Web Form. *Journal of Computer-Mediated Communication 6*, 1.

The Components of a Successful S-STEM Program: What Works at Appalachian State University

Rahman Tashakkori, Cindy Norris
Department of Computer Science
Appalachian State University
Boone, NC
tashakkorir,norrisca@appstate.edu

Mary E. Searcy
Department of Mathematical Sciences
Appalachian State University
Boone, NC
searcyme@appstate.edu

ABSTRACT

In 1999, the National Science Foundation created the "Computer Science, Engineering, and Mathematics Scholarships" (CSEMS) program to provide funding for institutions to supply scholarships for academically talented and financially needy students to complete an associate, baccalaureate, or graduate degree in computer science, computer technology, engineering, engineering technology, or mathematics. In 2004, the program was renamed to "Scholarships for Science, Technology, Engineering, and Mathematics" (S-STEM) and modified to include students from physical and life sciences. Appalachian State University (ASU) has been the recipient of four CSEMS/S-STEM awards since 2001 and the scholarships have funded 161 students. Nearly all of these students have high levels of financial need and the majority are first generation college students. Overall, the program has retained 87 percent of these students; 12 percent of the scholars completed a bachelor's and then continued on to complete a master's degree or are in the process of doing so. The retention rate has increased as our program has improved. The retention rate of the current cohort of S-STEM students is 92.3 percent; 31 percent of the students in the current program completed a bachelor's degree and are pursuing or have completed a master's degree. These retention numbers are significantly higher than the 31 percent national average reported by the U.S. Department of Education. In addition, these retention numbers are higher than those found at our own institution for all Computer Science and Mathematics majors. This paper discusses the components of our successful program.

CCS CONCEPTS

• **Social and professional topics → Computing education**; **Model curricula**; **Computer science education**;

KEYWORDS

Computer Science, S-STEM, student retention

SIGCSE '18, February 21–24, 2018, Baltimore , MD, USA

ACM ISBN 978-1-4503-5103-4/18/02...$15.00
https://doi.org/10.1145/3159450.3159600

ACM Reference Format:
Rahman Tashakkori, Cindy Norris and Mary E. Searcy. 2018. The Components of a Successful S-STEM Program: What Works at Appalachian State University. In *SIGCSE '18: The 49th ACM Technical Symposium on Computing Science Education, February 21–24, 2018, Baltimore , MD, USA.* ACM, New York, NY, USA, 6 pages. https://doi.org/10.1145/3159450.3159600

1 INTRODUCTION

According to the U.S. Bureau of Labor and Statistics, the number of computer and information technology jobs will grow 12 percent from 2014 to 2024 [1]. In particular, 488,500 new jobs are expected to be added during that time period. However, the demand for people with expertise in computing far exceeds the availability. At present, code.org reports more than 500,000 open computing jobs in the United States. Although the number of students graduating with degrees in Computer Science is increasing, the number of graduates remains far less than the demand [12]. Giffi et al. predict that the shortage of candidates with technology skills within the manufacturing sector alone could reach two million over the next decade [13]. In addition to the negative impact on industry, non-STEM college graduates are missing out on lucrative salaries since starting salaries for STEM graduates tend to be higher than those of their non-STEM peers [11].

However, simply recruiting into the STEM majors is insufficient for increasing the STEM workforce as many students that pursue a STEM major either change majors or drop out altogether. A U.S. Department of Education study of the 2004/09 Beginning Postsecondary Students Longitudinal data found that 48 percent of bachelor's degree students and 69 percent of associate's degree students who entered a STEM program between 2003 and 2009 left those programs by 2009 [7]. 28 percent of those students switched majors. 20 percent left without earning a degree. Attrition rates varied by discipline. Among bachelor's degree seeking students, the U.S. Department of Education study found that the STEM attrition rate for computer/information sciences major was 59 percent, the highest among the STEM disciplines.

The study also found that STEM dropout rates are particularly high for female students and under-represented minority students [7]. A larger percentage of females than male students changed from a STEM major to a non-STEM major (32 percent versus 26 percent). However, a larger percentage of male students in STEM dropped out of college altogether (24 percent versus 14 percent). Among ethnic groups, African-American students are the most likely to leave the STEM major by either switching to a non-STEM major (36 percent) or dropping out of college (36 percent).

Chen also determined that STEM attrition correlated with a range of factors including family income, level of family education, academic preparation for college, and performance in the first year [7]. In particular, the intensity and the type of courses in the first year and the success in those STEM courses was strongly associated with whether a student remained in the major. Students that took less intense STEM courses and performed poorly in those courses were more likely to change majors. Poor performance in college as indicated by the GPA and a large number of dropped or failed STEM courses was associated with an increased probability of dropping out altogether.

There are equally high attrition rates at our institution. The four year retention rate for the 571 students entering Appalachian State between Fall 2006 and Fall 2014 intending upon majoring in Computer Science was only 30.6 percent. 32.7 percent of the students in that group changed majors and 36.6 percent of the students left the institution altogether. The four-year retention rates for the 420 Mathematics majors during the same time period was slightly higher. 37.9 percent of students remained Mathematics majors, 37.9 percent of students changed majors, and 24.3 percent left the institution. These percentages also include any S-STEM students (with much higher retention) that were in the S-STEM program during that time period because of the difficulty of removing the S-STEM students from the data set.

Researchers have investigated a variety of reasons for students leaving or remaining in STEM majors. Cheryan et al. noted that changing the objects in the computer science classroom to those not typically associated with the geek culture (i.e. replacing Star Trek posters by nature posters) can increase the level of interest of female undergraduates [8]. Unwelcoming classroom environments can make it difficult for minority students to succeed [6]. Su et al. found significant differences in vocational interest among males and females, which may contribute to the low number of females in Computer Science [22]. However, some schools have improved diversity in Computer Science by changing the Computer Science I course to include assignments with broad appeal and separating students into classes based upon their previous experience [2, 9, 18]. Other research has focused on self-efficacy and a sense of belongingness. Marra et al. found that poor teaching and advising, curriculum difficulty, and a lack of belonging were the most significant three factors in causing a student to exit an engineering program [17]. Of the three factors, evidence indicated a sense of belonging was the greatest influence on whether a student decided to stay in the engineering major.

Appalachian State University has been the recipient of four CSEMS/S-STEM awards since 2001 and the scholarships have funded 161 students. The program has retained 87 percent of these students. Our current S-STEM program, which started in Spring 2014 and is ending in Fall 2017, has funded 39 students and has a retention rate of 92.3 percent. Table 1 compares the retention rates of our four CSEMS/S-STEM programs. In addition, it displays the percentage of students in each program who completed bachelor's degrees and decided to stay in the program to complete a master's degree.

This paper discusses the components of our successful S-STEM program, what we have done to improve the program over time, and further improvements that can be made.

Program	BS and MS	Retention Rate
CSEMS	13.2%	87%
S-STEM 1	0%	75%
S-STEM 2	0%	90%
Current S-STEM	31%	92.3%

Table 1: ASU CSEMS/S-STEM Programs

2 ASU HIGH-ACHIEVERS SCHOLARSHIP PROGRAM IN COMPUTER SCIENCE AND MATHEMATICS

Appalachian State University is a public, comprehensive university that enrolls about 18,000, primarily undergraduate, students. The current S-STEM program is a joint program between the departments of Mathematical Sciences and Computer Science. The Mathematical Sciences Department offers BS, MA, and BA degrees in Mathematics and a BS in Actuarial Sciences. The Mathematical Sciences Department enrolls about 250 undergraduate students and 20 graduate students. The Computer Science Department offers BS and MS degrees in Computer Science and enrolls about 490 undergraduate students and 20 graduate students.

The current S-STEM program has a 1:3 Math to CS ratio for the number of majors in the program. The goals of the program are to increase the high technology workforce and the number of CS and Math students pursuing graduate degrees by providing opportunities for talented, economically disadvantaged students. Out of the 39 participants in the current S-STEM program, 38 demonstrated high financial need and one had moderate need as determined by the expected family contribution reported by FASFA. Students coming from families in which the expected family contribution is less than $5,234 (a value based upon the cost of attending our institution) are categorized as having high need. Our program has retained all but three of the scholars (92.3 percent). One of the three students who resigned from the program joined the military after his first semester and two students switched from CS to Computer Information Systems.

Our S-STEM program also encourages students to continue their education and 13 of the 39 students have completed, or are in the process of completing, graduate degrees at our university. Considering that 96 percent of our university's population is Caucasian, we have had some success in diversifying our S-STEM program where 15 percent are non-white. In addition, 23 percent of our S-STEM population is female and more than 68 percent of our S-STEM scholars are first generation college students.

Although our CSEMS/S-STEM programs have evolved since our initial CSEMS program in 2001, all four of the programs have emphasized research and collaboration. At present, the significant components of the program include: leadership building, collaboration, research, and academic support. Of these four components, participants rank research as the component that is the most important to them and their career goals.

The activities of the ASU S-STEM program, entitled the High-Achievers Scholarship Program in Computer Science and Mathematics, center around a weekly STEM seminar. Participants, whom we call scholars, are required to attend this one credit hour, graded seminar. Undergraduate students can earn a maximum of three

	1	2	3	4	Score
Research Experiences	38.10%	38.10%	4.76%	19.05%	2.05
Collaborative Experiences	23.81%	38.10%	38.10%	0%	2.14
Leadership Building Experiences	19.05%	14.29%	23.81%	42.86%	2.91
Academic Support Experiences	19.05%	9.52%	33.33%	38.10%	2.90

Table 2: Scholar's Ranking of Program Components

hours for attending the seminar; none of the hours count toward the graduate degree. During the seminar, students have the opportunity to listen to guest speakers, engage in leadership building activities, and present their own research. Outside of the STEM seminar, scholars are required to collaborate on a research project and attend study halls. Other activities are also promoted to encourage the development of an S-STEM community, including intramural sports, movie nights, hiking, etc. A small number of students from two other scholarship programs participate in the S-STEM program activities, including the STEM seminar; the retention rate of these students, although also high, is not included in this paper.

In an S-STEM program survey during the 2016-2017 academic year, the 21 scholars in the program at that time were asked to rank the S-STEM program components, with 1 given the highest ranking. Table 2 contains the ranking. The score column provides the ranking as a weighted average. As can be seen, scholars rank Research Experiences as the most important component to them and their career goals. The remainder of this section discusses each of these components.

2.1 Research

ASU S-STEM scholars are organized into research clusters where students work together in teams of three or four to solve CS, Math, or interdisciplinary problems. For example, research clusters worked on the following problems during the 2016-2017 academic year:

- Converting Piano Input to Sheet Music
- Creating a Kinect Pong Game
- Chemistry Calculator and Converter
- Manga Reader - Manga is a style of cartooning that originated from the historical art traditions of Japan. MangaReader developed in Android Studio provides streaming Manga content for Android 5.1 and above.
- NEAT - Collecting renewal energy device data in a uniform database
- Rhythmos - An Angular-based system that utilizes IndexDB, WebGL, NPM, and Typescript and allows multiple tightly-coupled database system upgrades independently
- Stereotype Threat and Perceptions of Mathematics Experiences
- Slackurity System - A Secure Raspberry Pi-based Surveillance System

Beyond that, during the 2016-2017 academic year about 95 percent of the scholars worked on an undergraduate research project under the direction of a faculty mentor. About 70 percent of the scholars presented their work at our university's Undergraduate Research Day. About 23 percent of the scholars presented their work at a regional or national conference.

A number of the conference presentations have pertained to honey bees, which is an active interdisciplinary area of research within the Computer Science department. An ongoing project is BeeMon, a honey bee monitoring system which was created six years ago by two of the S-STEM scholars. Since its inception the BeeMon project has involved more than twelve students who have consistently improved the hardware and software of the system. In addition, the BeeMon system has created a large number of video and audio recordings that are being used by faculty and students at our university to understand bee behavior. As a result of the BeeMon project, three S-STEM scholars have completed Master's theses and more than 10 papers have been presented at various conferences including the National Conference of Undergraduate Research [3–5, 10, 14–16, 19–21, 23, 24].

We believe that the opportunity to participate in research significantly contributes to the retention of these students. Indeed, our students indicate research as the most important component of the program. Approximately 85 percent of the surveyed scholars indicated they applied to the program because of its research emphasis. The survey respondents were asked to explain their rankings of various components of the S-STEM program. A number of students commented on the importance of the research component:

- *The research aspect of SSTEM has introduced me to a great number of fields and technologies that I would not otherwise have been made aware of during my coursework. The act of participating as a team member and trying to work in the areas that need to be filled as well as pulling information from others has been very eye-opening.*
- *Several of the people who have come in to give us talks from industry have said that projects and working in teams are vital to finding a job in computer science.*
- *The research opportunities were a very strong reason behind me being accepted into an extremely awesome internship.*

2.2 Collaboration

Overall, scholars rank collaboration as the second most significant component to them and their careers. In addition, 100 percent agreed or strongly agreed that the S-STEM program activities prepared them to work in collaborative environments when they graduate. Some of the scholars specifically noted collaboration in their explanations of the benefits of the S-STEM program:

- *Working with other people on a project of our choosing.*
- *Being involved in research projects and collaborating with other students in my field. Developing skills and friends.*
- *Leadership training and connections with other people*
- *Collaboration with fellow students, study halls, weekly presentations on varied topics from varied departments.*

2.3 Academic Support

One of the goals of the project is to improve the student support infrastructure available to all CS and Math students. The program offers study halls, mentoring and tutoring services to all Computer Science and Mathematics students. The survey results indicated the scholars were engaged in academic support activities in the following ways:

- all respondents participated in study halls (2 hours weekly are mandatory for all students)
- approximately 85 percent participated in group study sessions.
- approximately 76 percent made a connection with a former S-STEM program participant through our S-STEM alumni mentorship program
- approximately 71 percent were mentored by an S-STEM-related faculty member
- approximately 71 percent were mentored by another S-STEM student
- approximately 62 percent mentored another S-STEM student.

When asked to evaluate their level of satisfaction with the academic support, 85 percent indicated that the academic support helped them succeed in their classes. In addition, 76 percent indicated that they were able to use the information learned in the S-STEM program in other classes. Here are some comments that the students made about the importance of academic support:

- *Without members who help me academically, I would struggle to do well in my CS courses.*
- *The research projects and study halls focus on collaboration and academic support which makes up most of S-STEM.*
- *I have found that through the academic support of S-STEM I can accomplish stuff in that it forces me to study hard.*

Because the program has been active off and on since 2001, we have a rich pool of CSEMS/S-STEM alumni that are helpful in making the current program successful. The alumni return to campus to give presentations in the STEM seminar about industry and technology. In addition, the alumni serve as mentors to current scholars. As noted earlier, 76 percent of the current scholars have connected with an alumni mentor. The scholars received advice about courses to take, technologies to learn, research, the job search, and surviving school. Here are comments that students provided about working with an alumni mentor:

- *I asked a former student after a presentation what he would do for a summer position (research or internship) and he gave me some pretty great advice from his perspective.*
- *I had correspondence with a former S-STEM student. I learned how to make a good impression with employers outside of college.*
- *I was offered a potential career path by my alumni mentor.*

Since its inception, a handful of scholars have earned GPAs that are lower than the required GPA to remain in the S-STEM program, which is a minimum 2.8. In the first semester after the GPA drop, these students can continue to participate in S-STEM program activities and receive 1/2 of the scholarship. After that, if their GPAs remain below the minimum, the students receive no scholarship but can remain in the program. Often students will elect to remain with no scholarship. We have had some students remain in the program when their financial status has changed and they no longer qualify as financially needy. This is evidence, albeit anecdotal, that students recognize the importance of the program to their academic and career success.

2.4 Leadership Building

Several times during the past two years, ASU professor Dr. Jim Street of the Office of Student Leadership Development attended the S-STEM seminar to conduct leadership workshops. These workshops provided students the opportunity to learn about themselves, learn how to collaborate with others and work in teams, and develop their capacity to lead. These skills are important preparation for the workforce. Some of the workshop topics are:

- Notions of Leadership - Students have the opportunity to develop and refine their mental model of leadership.
- Keeping Commitments - Identifying and keeping commitments is critical to the leadership process. Identifying the obstacles to keeping commitments is equally valuable.
- Balance - The balanced student is the effective student. Students have the opportunity to identify areas in their life that need attention.
- Team Building - Most of the STEM students will be working in teams in their careers. Understanding how teams work most effectively is a valuable skill to master.
- Risk Taking and Failure - Each failure brings a group closer to the answer. Students will come to value the power of taking risks and learning from failure.

3 HOW WE HAVE IMPROVED

The retention rate of our CSEMS/S-STEM programs has increased as we have improved the program. In particular, we have increased our scholars' sense of connection to the program and increased the value of the program to them. We have accomplished this via the following:

Connecting with the real-world experts: An early challenge involved connecting scholars of the program to external experts. We were able to recruit industry experts to give talks in the STEM seminar about exciting research and technologies, but our scholars were not able to form lasting connections with these speakers. Now that our fourth CSEMS/S-STEM program is in progress, we have a substantial pool of CSEMS/S-STEM alumni from which we can recruit speakers for presentations and more significantly, for alumni mentoring. As noted in section 2.3, a relationship with an alumni mentor is very important to our scholars. In addition, the alumni mentoring program keeps the S-STEM alumni connected to us. Both the current S-STEM program and the S-STEM alumni have developed a sense of belonging to a program that is meaningful and lasting.

Instilling a sense of ownership: In our initial CSEMS program, some scholars thought a few of the program activities were unnecessary chores. In particular, some students did not see the value of attending study halls. Students also did not want to participate in community building activities such as movie nights, hiking, and intramural sports. In recent programs, we have done a better job of convincing students of the importance of these activities. More importantly, we have instilled in the students a sense of ownership by regularly reminding the scholars that this is their program: their success and the success of their peers is up to them. Having a large set of alumni also helps since the alumni are good mentors to our scholars, which in turn inspires scholars to mentor one another.

Creating a culture of engagement: Success breeds success. Successful scholars and alumni have inspired the new scholars to embrace the activities of the program. Our current group of scholars are active in healthy living activities such as sports and hiking, social activities, and clubs. In addition, the new scholars see the academic success of the older scholars and alumni and they too have become interested in performing research and giving presentations.

Increasing the quality of research and innovation: Research projects in the early programs were completed within a semester or two. The current research projects are more advanced, often interdisciplinary, and typically require a year or more to complete. We have become better at helping students define projects that are both significant and tractable. In addition, the research performed by scholars in the earlier program has laid the foundation for some of the research that is currently being performed. For example, the initial bee project laid the foundation for a number of related projects. The quality of the research has improved and consequently, students view the opportunity to perform research to be extremely valuable as can be seen by comments in section 2.1.

4 RETENTION

Scholars have been surveyed regularly since the program's conception for evaluation purposes. In these surveys, scholars rank research experiences as the component of the program that is most significant to them. Thus, we theorize that the opportunity to perform research motivates students and inspires them to stay STEM majors. A more recent survey of both current and former scholars specifically asked participants to "Indicate the one or two most significant components of the scholarship program that you believe contributed to you remaining a STEM student." 36 scholars (15 current, 21 former) completed the survey. An analysis of the results found that almost all responses referred to either the opportunity to perform research, community and friendship, and/or the financial support. We coded responses that contained phrases such as *research project, group project,* and *new possibilities in research* as one that indicates research opportunities contributed to their retention. Phrases that caused a response to be coded as one that indicates community included: *group of people, mentoring component, study group support network, peer interaction.* Several response are given below. The first response indicates community; the second response indicates both community and research; the last response indicates financial support.

- *Being around and having a close relationship with those who are further ahead in the major. Having a group of people who have my back and I can depend on to help me whenever I am struggling or just need motivation.*
- *Working with like-minded students on research projects related to my major.*
- *Helps me financially so I can continue to study.*

Although current scholars largely name research as the component that is most significant to them, when asked which component contributes to them staying in the STEM major, when grouped together the current and former scholars indicate community and friendship. Specifically, 50 percent of all survey participants named research and 63.8 percent indicated community (note: survey participants can indicate both). In addition, the perception that community was the most influential factor upon their retention is much stronger among alumni scholars. 80.9 percent of the former scholars indicated community as an influential factor, while only 40 percent of the current scholars indicated that aspect. In contrast, 52.4 percent of former scholars and 46.7 of current scholars indicated research. One possibility for this difference is that the quality of the research has improved and thus current scholars view it to be more significant than previous scholars. Another possibility is that the friendships developed among S-STEM scholars can continue past graduation, while the research performed does not. Thus, S-STEM alumni will continue to value the friendships past graduation. Figure 1 display the distribution of factors indicated by all, current, and former scholars.

Most scholars did not name the financial award as the most significant component to their retention. Specifically, 27.8 percent of all scholars, 26.7 percent of current scholars, and 28.6 percent of former scholars indicated money as very significant. This could indicate that a program such as ours which provides components that allow students to perform research in teams and build strong relationships with their peers could engender retention even without the financial incentive. However, it is unclear whether students would be willing to participate in the program, given the level of commitment required, without financial gain.

5 WHERE WE CAN IMPROVE

100 percent of the surveyed scholars agreed (85 percent strongly agreed) that they would recommend the S-STEM program to other students. Nevertheless, students also offered ideas for improvement. Several of the suggestions pertained to study halls:

- *I would have the study halls be more potent and meaningful in some way. Replacing them with something student-skill development related would be abundantly helpful. Such as assigning a member of SSTEM to present on a practice, principle, or tool they use during that weeks study hall in an INTERACTIVE manner.*
- *Add something that allows with help for specific courses. The study halls are great, and I think that any changes need to be student led, but it would be nice to have study hall options explicitly for specific courses.*
- *I feel study halls are not utilized well. Maybe replace them with an extra class.*

Scholars are required to attend study halls for 2 hours a week. This provides a structure that can help students with less than stellar study habits to succeed. However, a few students do not perceive study halls to be useful to them. One way we could improve this component is to develop a more flexible organization of study halls that is arranged around courses and deadlines, such as lab deadlines.

Another set of suggestions refer to the research clusters:

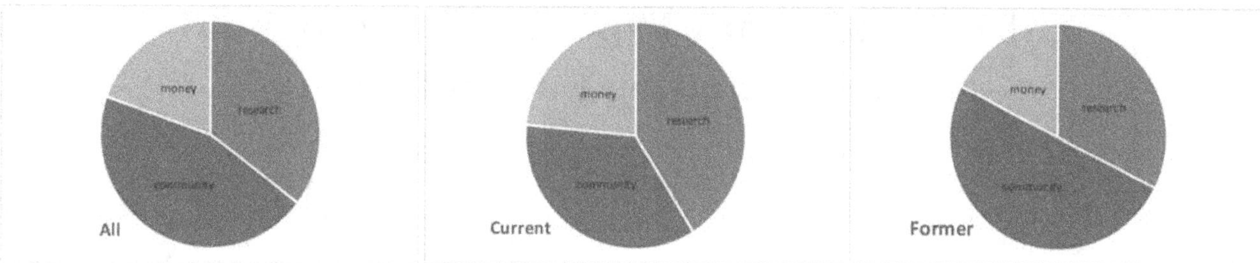

Figure 1: Factors indicated by scholars to engender retention

- *Having a teacher or someone with knowledge available to help groups who are having issues functioning well together.*
- *Group higher level students together, keep groups closer in terms of skill, so they can be on the same page for the project hand.*
- *I think there should be more leader check-ins for the research project throughout the semester to ensure quality control and good team direction.*

Each research cluster consists of an upper undergraduate or graduate student and beginning students. This can make it harder to choose a project to which all members can contribute. As the comments note, this can be frustrating to the students. However, this organization enables a mentoring relationship between the upper level and lower level students, which is more significant than the drawbacks. Although students might not recognize the relationship as one of mentoring, their comments make clear that they value the relationships they have formed with other scholars:

- *Relationships with people who are willing to help me with my studies. I can't tell you how many times I've needed help on a program in a course I'm taking and someone from STEM has been willing to help.*
- *I made lots of friends, and I have a large network of people I know I can rely on.*

Although it is not in the best interest of scholars to change how research clusters are organized, we can address the concerns expressed by students that refer to helping teams work better together and defining and meeting regular deadlines.

6 CONCLUSIONS

A U.S. Department of Education study found that the STEM attrition rate for computer/information sciences major was 59 percent, the highest among the STEM disciplines [7]. Our current S-STEM program, which has a 1:3 Math to CS student ratio, has an attrition rate of just 7.7 percent. We attribute the success of that program to activities that establish a strong sense of community among participants and allow students to work on a research project.

We thank the National Science Foundation for the support of our CSEMS [0122168, 0324002] and S-STEM [0630984, 0806814, 1259496] programs. In addition, we thank the Szulik Family Foundation and ECRS Software Corporation for the support of our McKinney and ECRS scholars who also participate in the S-STEM program activities.

REFERENCES

[1] 2015. Occupational Outlook Handbook. U.S. Bureau of Labor and Statistics, Postal Square Building, 2 Massachusetts Avenue, NE Washington, DC 20212-0001.
[2] Christine Alvarado, Zachary Dodds, and Ran Libeskind-Hadas. 2012. Increasing Women's Participation in Computing at Harvey Mudd College. *ACM Inroads* 3, 4 (Dec. 2012), 55–64.
[3] Jonathan Brotherton. 2017. Estimating Daily Beehive Activities using Image Processing. In *National Conference on Undergraduate Research.*
[4] Gurney Buchanan. 2016. Determining the Net Traffic at the Entrance of a Honeybee Hive. In *State of North Carolina Undergraduate Research Symposium (NCUR2016).*
[5] Gurney Buchanan and Edward Shuffler. 2017. Determining the Net Traffic at the Entrance of a Honeybee Hive. In *National Conference on Undergraduate Research (NCUR2017).*
[6] M. J. Chang, M. K. Eagan, M. H. Lin, and S. Hurtado. 2011. Considering the Impact of Racial Stigmas and Science Identity: Persistance Among Biomedical and Behavorial Science Aspirants. (2011).
[7] X. Chen. 2013. STEM Attrition: College Students' Paths Into and Out of and Out of STEM Fields (NCES 2014-001). (2013).
[8] S. Cheryan, V. C. Plaut, P. G. Davies, and C. M. Steele. 2009. Ambient belonging: How stereotypical cues impact gender participation in computer science. (2009), 1045-1060 pages.
[9] James P. Cohoon. 2007. An Introductory Course Format for Promoting Diversity and Retention. *SIGCSE Bull.* 39, 1 (March 2007), 395–399.
[10] Michael Crawford. 2017. *Automated Collection of Honey Bee Hive Data Using the Raspberry Pi.* Master's thesis. Appalachian State University, Boone, NC.
[11] Arne Duncan. 2017. Educational equality and excellence will drive a stronger economy. (Mar 2017).
[12] National Center for Education Statistics. 2017. The Condition of Education. (Apr 2017). https://nces.ed.gov/programs/coe/
[13] C. Giffi, B. Dollar, M. Drew, J. McNelly, G. Carrick, and B. Gangula. 2015. The skills cap in U.S. Manufacturing. (2015).
[14] Nathaniel Hernandez, Michael Crawford, and Alexander Ratzloff. 2014. Remote Beehive Surveying. In *State of North Carolina Undergraduate Research and Creativity Symposium.*
[15] David Kale. 2017. *Automated Beehive Surveillance using Computer Vision.* Master's thesis. Appalachian State University, Boone, NC.
[16] David Kale and Rahman Tashakkori. 2015. Automated Beehive Surveillance Using Computer Vision. In *IEEE SoutheastCon 2015.*
[17] Rose M. Marra, Kelly A. Rodgers, Demei Shen, and Barbara Bogue. 2012. Leaving Engineering: A Multi-Year Single Institution Study. *Journal of Engineering Education* 101, 1 (2012), 6–27. https://doi.org/10.1002/j.2168-9830.2012.tb00039.x
[18] Rita Manco Powell. 2008. Improving the Persistence of First-year Undergraduate Women in Computer Science. In *Proceedings of the 39th SIGCSE Technical Symposium on Computer Science Education (SIGCSE '08).* 518–522.
[19] Scott Shuffler and Ahmar Gordan. 2015. Automated Beehive Surveillance Using Raspberry Pi. In *State of North Carolina Undergraduate Research and Creativity Symposium.*
[20] Scott Shuffler and Ahmar Gordan. 2016. Automated Beehive Surveillance Using Raspberry Pis. In *National Conference on Undergraduate Research (NCUR2016).*
[21] Chris Smith. 2015. Analysis of Frequencies in Beehive Audio Recordings. In *State of North Carolina Undergraduate Research and Creativity Symposium.*
[22] Rong Su, James Rounds, and Patrick Ian Armstrong. 2009. Men and things, women and people: A meta-analysis of sex differences in interests. *Psychological Bulletin* 135, 6 (2009), 859–884. https://doi.org/10.1037/a0017364
[23] Rahman Tashakkori, Nathan Hernandez, Michael Crawford, Alek Ratzloff, and Ahmad Ghadiri. 2017. A Honeybee Hive Monitoring System: From Surveillance Cameras to Raspberry Pis. In *IEEE SoutheastCon 2017.*
[24] Preston Wilson and Chris Smith. 2017. Bee Audio Frequency Analysis. In *National Conference on Undergraduate Research (NCUR2017).*

Enhancing Robotic Experiences throughout the Computing Curriculum

Michael V. Doran
University of South Alabama
Department of Computer Science
Mobile, Alabama
mdoran@southalabama.edu

George W. Clark
University of South Alabama
Department of Computer Science
Mobile, Alabama
georgewclark@southalabama.edu

ABSTRACT

The study of robotics is often an excellent recruitment motivation for students entering a computing curriculum. It is also often cited that Artificial Intelligence (AI) and related robotics is a critical area of future innovation in computing. However, there are a number of challenges to implementing a robotic curriculum at the university level. A few of those challenges include, lack of a uniform hardware platform, incongruity in the software used, and the missing significant deliverable artifacts by students at the end of a term to encourage learning and further interest. Educational robotic activities are often treated as advanced research topics with high associated costs that prohibit widespread integration into the curriculum. In this paper, we present the deployment of a multi-stage robotic platform that attempts to address these challenges and overcome the obstacles. We detail the evolution of the hardware from using a readily available LEGO Mindstorm base platform to next include the addition of an Arduino and Raspberry Pi. Likewise, we detail the transition from the basic LEGO Mindstorm software to the use of leJOS and PYTHON. At each stage, additional sensors and software libraries can likewise be added. Finally, we present an achievable academic goal for students to use the hardware and software platforms to develop a model autonomous vehicle with aspects of intelligent control, learning and adaptive behaviour. All levels of projects can be undertaken at the appropriate level of maturity for the students in the computing curriculum.

ACM Reference format:

Michael V. Doran, and George W. Clark. 2018. U Enhancing Robotic Experiences throughout the Computing Curriculum. In *SIGCSE '18: 49th ACM Technical Symposium on Computer Science Education, Feb. 21–24, 2018, Baltimore, MD, USA.* ACM, NY, NY, USA, 4 pages. https://doi.org/10.1145/3159450.3159580

SIGCSE '18, February 21–24, 2018, Baltimore, MD, USA

ACM ISBN 978-1-4503-5103-4/18/02...$15.00
https://doi.org/10.1145/3159450.3159580

1 INTRODUCTION

Robotics has always been a strong source of motivation for the recruitment of CS students. Prior papers have reported how robotics is also an excellent vehicle to teach many core CS topics and concepts [1, 2, 3]. Even as early as CS1 the initial concepts have been taught using robots [4]. Advanced courses such as AI often utilize robotic activities. The role of AI is often cited as tying together all CS concepts into a capstone experience [5]. The use of robots in AI is a very clear and visible way to explore and demonstrate these concepts [6, 7]. Robotics can even serve to give students an enriched interdisciplinary learning experience [8]. This certainly will lead to the necessary advances in robotics and CS for the future including potential social robots that work alongside and in partnership with humans [9]

Our Computer Science Department has utilized robotic laboratories for over 20 years. Initial and sustaining funding was secured from NSF, local industry and by internal university grants. These labs have included a wide variety of hardware platforms ranging from LEGOs to industry grade hardware acquired from i-Robot, Joker Robotics and Lynxmotion. In some cases even custom hardware was fabricated for specific projects or curricular activities. This is probably the case for many other similar institutions wishing to engage in a meaningful robotic experience for their students.

As a medium sized urban institution, with a diverse student population, it is often difficult to sustain a critical mass of students participating in these activities. Expertise gained by the small group of students can quickly be lost if others do not follow immediately. It is also the case that due to the limited size of our faculty, with heavy teaching and service expectations, sufficient time to spend in lab with students is likewise a problem.

Our experience using robots has also influenced our K-12 outreach. On a regular basis for almost 20 years, summer robotic camps and academic year workshops have focused on giving a wide range of K-12 students a meaningful set of activities using robotic equipment. These camps typically used LEGO robotic platforms. Visiting campers learn how to program these robots quickly and by the end of camp can perform a variety of tasks and conquer various challenges.

When recruiting CS majors these camps and outreach experiences draw many K-12 students to attend and become involved with robotics. Also, many students who enter CS are well aware of the potential opportunities associated with working with robots. However, when only provided the limited capabilities of the LEGOs they feel that meaningful work is not possible. If they start using LEGOs they feel that the transition is abrupt and disjoint to a more sophisticated platform. The concepts might be similar but the artifacts from the LEGOs are useless in other environments. An added obstacle is that the associated cost of the more sophisticated platforms limits that availability to ultimately only a few students. Recently, we have found a cost-effective alternative that has not only opened up more complex challenges to a greater number of students but has also given new ways to consider and prototype actual research projects.

2 INITIAL ROBOT ACTIVITIES

Our journey of using robots throughout the curriculum has been a long one. It is now best described as a multi-stage approach. This has evolved over the past 4 years as the result of what we were doing at that time in several courses. The use in any course was ad hoc and there was not an apparent linkage or coordination between the activities. Some limited undergraduate research took place from time to time but serious research was restricted to a few students using more sophisticated platforms. The following section describes that status of isolated robot deployment.

In CS1, as others have pointed out, an early use of robots can be beneficial [4]. We have also done this in a variety of ways over the years. One of the main advantages found has been the almost immediate transition to the use of leJOS as an operating and programming environment. Students in CS1 use Java as their primary programming language. By using the Java based leJOS, students quickly realize how their programs can do real things and not just provide solutions to artificial abstract "toy" problems. Likewise in AI and Real-Time systems, as others [6, 7] have pointed out the use of robots in the initial AI course was a common activity. Students would often identify a challenge that a robot could be used to demonstrate intelligent behavior. A course in Real-Time systems likewise would often utilize robots to demonstrate core concepts of that course. In most cases, the course was restricted to using the readily available LEGOs. Many students were happy to have a physical system to interact with but also expressed the view that the simple platform did not provide the richness of programming to fully explore the concepts of the courses.

Our university has grown an extensive support system for undergraduate research and many CS majors have participated in these efforts. Some students, especially those who were part of the Honors Program, would start projects as early as their freshmen year following the above mentioned CS1 activities. Work often started where the CS1 ended and led to long term projects that in some cases served as senior capstone projects or theses. An added benefit of this undergraduate research activity was to recruit these talented students into our MS degree and often continue using more advanced robotic platforms as part of an MS thesis.

3 UNIFIED APPROACH

The above-mentioned approach is common in similar academic institutions and suffers from the problems faced by those wishing for a unified and more challenging research agenda. Over the past several years we have undertaken to overcome this and provide a more advanced research agenda while still using a readily available and cost effective robotic platform. The platform remained the basic LEGO hardware. However, the usual LEGO NXT programmable brick is replaced by either a Raspberry Pi or Arduino board. Both boards provide a more advanced programming platform and the ability to use languages and libraries in C, Java and Python. The following section describes the multi-stage approach taken to introduce this environment and the role it has played in a more advanced research agenda.

A graduate student who had taken the AI course in the fall and the Real-Time system course in the spring which had used the basic LEGO robot kit agreed to participate in a summer directed study course. In the recent Real-Time course he and a partner had created a very accurate table tilter board maze game. This was done with an unmodified LEGO NXT robot kit. They were able to incorporate a small camera to track the ball movements. They were advanced graduate students with extensive hardware and software experience which they used to overcome the platform limitations. This motivated one of the students to consider how the use of more sophisticated components would lead to more efficient and effective implementations to more complex problems. The goal of his follow-up directed study project course was to explore how the course projects in AI and Real-Time could be enhanced and promote the creation of more challenging projects. The student modified the basic platform by adding an Arduino board and the necessary interface board. This allowed the addition of wireless XBee communication and RFID readers. This initial reconfiguration allowed for at first a more challenging project of a predator/prey task. The task required the sensors to obtain a larger amount of data rapidly. However, this data could not be processed in real-time and on board and therefore required the wireless communication device was needed to transmit the data to a PC. Once the data was processed, the PC would transmit instructions back to the robot where the Arduino board would perform limited computations and low level control of actions. A major contribution of this project was the inclusion of new more advanced sensors and devices. Also, the library routines could now be a more significant artifact that future projects could draw upon and build on.

Concurrently, two recent freshmen were finishing a project using the basic LEGO platform to control and schedule an HO scale model train [10]. Using the ultrasonic sensors found in the basic LEGO NXT robot kit, they created an environment where the train would arrive at designated locations (stations) by a specific deadline. The speed of the train was controlled by a simple robotic "hand" that could grip the control knob on the voltage regulator. As an added challenge, a turnout track was added to vary the distance the train might travel on a cycle from one station to another. The basic NXT programmable brick was used for processing and control commands while a second NXT brick was used to gather sensory data from the ultrasonic sensors. The NXT bricks were physically connected to exchange data. An exhaustive set of experiments were conducted to evaluate performance of various scheduling strategies. However, this project did not include additional sensors besides those found in the basic robot kit and was limited to processing and communication provided by the NXT bricks. Figure 1 shows the layout of the train environment.

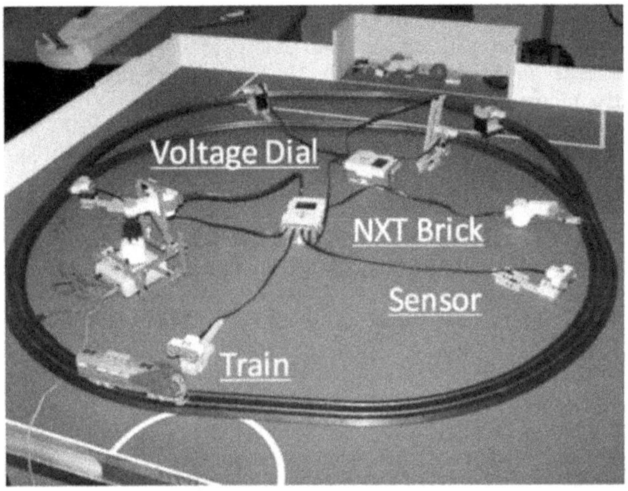

Figure 1: LEGO NXT train environment

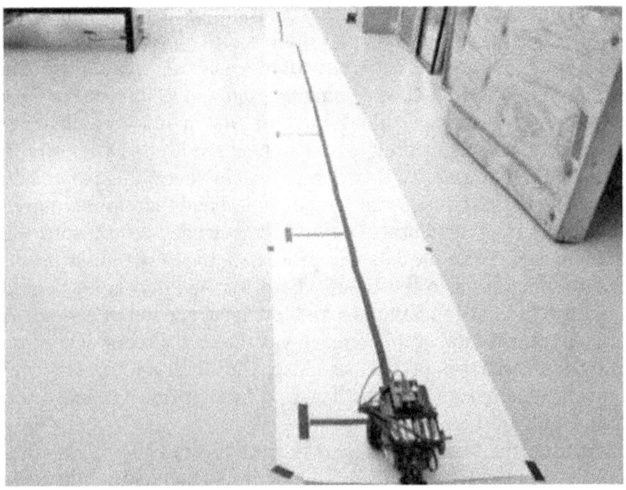
Figure 2: Scale model layout of factory

Upon completion of the train project, the two students were able to quickly transition to use the new enhanced platform and libraries created by the graduate student's recently completed directed study effort. The focus of the new enhanced platform was a factory simulation project [11]. Meeting with a local manufacturing business, the students devised a model of their factory operations and after an in-depth simulation of the operations, a scale model of the factory was created. The LEGOs, now modified to include a Raspberry Pi, were added to the Arduino to perform the tasks of the simulated environment and provide reasonable empirical data of performance. Figure 2 shows the scale model layout of the factory floor.

Following that effort, a modified version of the earlier predator/prey task was reattempted using the Arduino. This led to an Honors senior thesis on a limited Machine Learning (ML) project [12]. Figure 3 shows the RFID grid system and 2 robots used in the ML thesis project. Both this and the factory project had to transmit sensor data to a remote PC for processing of the intelligent control and learning of the AI algorithms.

Figure 3: RFID grid layout for ML thesis

Finally, a serious research effort involving ML has been undertaken building on the enhanced platforms to investigate the possible attack methods on a physical system's ML model. To accomplish this it was necessary to design and build a robot to emulate the operation of an autonomous vehicle. This section details the design of the Jaguar Autonomous Vehicle (JAV).

The design and construction of JAV's body was accomplished by using the LEGO Mindstorms NXT education robotics kit. To emulate the functionality of an autonomous vehicle, several sensors were needed to handle lane detection, collision avoidance, and location awareness. An actual autonomous vehicle might accomplish these functions using cameras for lane detection, LiDAR for collision avoidance, and a GPS navigation system for location awareness. To achieve lane detection functionality, JAV used the two LEGO NXT light sensors included in the education kit. These sensors were mounted side by side on the front of JAV. Using the light sensors, JAV detected a deviation on either side of a two-inch piece of black tape which is used to represent a street lane. For collision avoidance JAV made use of a single LEGO NXT Ultrasonic sensor included in the education kit. This sensor was mounted on the front of the vehicle and can detect an obstruction up to twenty centimeters in front of the path of JAV.

Location awareness for JAV was accomplished by using two additional sensors not included in the LEGO NXT education kit. For directional awareness, a LEGO NXT compatible digital compass manufactured by HiTechnic was used. The compass was mounted at the front of the vehicle and provides a bearing range of 0 – 179 degrees where North is at 0 degrees, East is at 45 degrees, South is at 90 degrees and West is at 135 degrees.

To detect the specific location, a Radio Frequency Identification Device (RFID) reader module was used in conjunction with RFID coin tags. The RFID reader module is the model EM4100 manufactured by Asiawill. The RFID module consists of an antenna for detecting the RFID coin tags and an interface board for power and communicating with the controller via the serial port. The interface board was mounted underneath JAV towards the rear and wires were routed from the board to the controller. The antenna portion of the sensor was mounted underneath JAV. The range of the antenna is approximately 5 cm and allows for the reading of 125 KHz RFID coin tags on the surface of JAV's operating environment. This provides JAV with a pseudo navigation system with respect to its operating environment.

The controller unit used for JAV is the Raspberry Pi 3 (RPi3). The RPi3 is a small inexpensive development board commonly used for educational purposes that is also popular among hobbyists. It contains a 1.2 GHz quad-core ARM CPU, a 400 MHz Broadcom GPU, 1 GB of SDRAM, 4 USB ports, a 10/100 MBPS Ethernet port, and built in 802.11n wireless LAN. The RPi3 was chosen for its low cost, availability of open source code, and its processing power.

An interface board was needed for the RPi3 to communicate with the LEGO NXT sensors and motors used on JAV. The BrickPi3 produced by Dexter industries was chosen for this purpose. It can be stacked on top of the RPi3 and interfaces via the General-Purpose Input Output (GPIO) port of the RPi3. The BrickPi3 provides four ports for attaching LEGO NXT motors and an additional four ports for attaching LEGO NXT compatible sensors. Additionally, it provides a 12-volt power input for powering the LEGO NXT motors and sensors along with the RPi3. The BrickPi3 base kit includes a case for holding and mounting the combined RPi3 and BrickPi3. The case with boards were mounted towards the rear of JAV. The BrickPi3 base kit also included a battery case for holding 8 AA batteries used to power JAV. The batteries were mounted towards the center of JAV as they had the most weight.

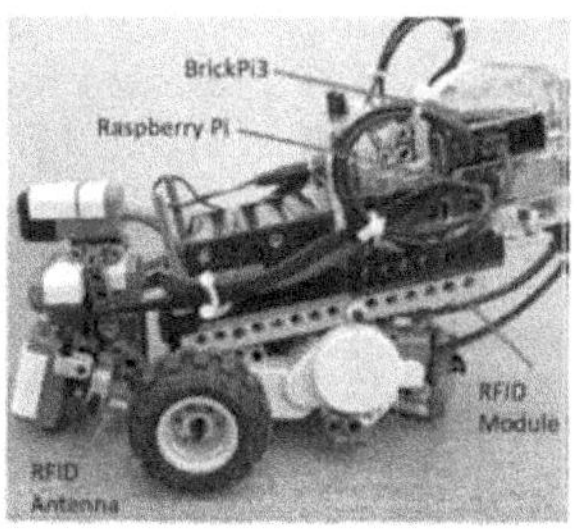

Figure 4a: Front view of JAV. Figure 4b: Side view of JAV.

The completed JAV is shown in figure 4a with labels for each of the sensors, motors, RPi3 and BrickPi3 boards and power supply. Figure 4b shows a side view of JAV and the mounting locations for the RFID antenna and interface board. Numerous web sites provide a simple wiring diagram for connecting the RFID interface board to the RPi3.

Once JAV was assembled, the Dexter Industries Raspian for Robots Linux distribution needed to be installed on the RPi3. The OS was installed on the RPi3's 16 GB micro SD card. In addition to the Linux OS functionality, the Raspian for robots customized Linux distro provides all the necessary tools for interfacing the BrickPi3 to the RPi3, including software libraries (written in C, Python, Scratch) for communicating with the LEGO NXT sensors and motors.

To simulate an autonomous vehicle's ability to receive over the air updates, the RPi3's wireless network connection was enabled and connected to the wireless network in the lab. All software and firmware updates were carried out over the wireless connection.

The software for JAV was developed using the Python language. This language was chosen mainly because it was one of the three supported by the BrickPi3 libraries. However, it was also chosen due to the abundance of RPi3 open source code available over the Internet from hobbyists and developers. Additionally, there are several free Python ML libraries available such as Keras, Tensorflow, and Theanos which provide more options for the development of JAV's ML model.The code for JAV was developed using a free multi-platform IDE by Microsoft called Visual Studio Code (MVSC). This IDE provided full support for the Python language as well as support for remote debugging.

4 CONCLUSION

A multi-stage robotic development environment is now available to CS majors throughout the curriculum. The basic platform remains the LEGO NXT which can be introduced as early as CS1 but as the students advance through the curriculum appropriate modules and languages can be included. These additions provide a more realistic experience. But more importantly they provide continuity and meaningful artifacts to carry forward between projects. The final platform presented allows for an independent computational platform for AI related tasks (learning, planning, security sensor fusion, etc). Previous projects had to rely on remote processing of the intelligent tasks by a PC. Finally, with the appropriate experience and expertise, a true research agenda can be considered without the need for specialized or expensive equipment.

ACKNOWLEDGMENTS

The authors wish to acknowledge W. Brad Glisson who contributed to the review of this document.

REFERENCES

[1] R. D. Beer, H. J. Chiel and R. F.Drusbel, Using autonomous robotics to teach science and engineering, Communications of the ACM, 42(6), 1999.

[2] E. Sklar, S. Parsons and M. Q. Azhar, Robotics across the curriculum. In Proceedings of the 2007AAAI Spring Symposium on Robots and Robot Venues: Resources for AI Education, 2007.

[3] S. Magnenat, J. Shin, F. Riedo, R. Siegwart and M. Ben-Ari, Teaching a Core CS Concept through Robotics, ITiCSE'14, Proceedings of the 2014 Conference on Innovations and Technology in Computer Science Education, Uppsala, Sweden, June 2014.

[4] J. Summet, D. Kumar, K. O'Hara, D. Walker, L. Ni, D. Blank and T. Balch, Personalizing CS1 with Robots, SIGCSE'09, Proceedings of the 40th ACM Technical Symposium on Computer Science Education, Chattanooga, TN, March 2009.

[5] R. Aiken, The new hurrah: creating a fundamental role for artificial intelligence in the computing science curriculum, Education & Computing vol 7 1991.

[6] A. Goel, AI Education for the World, AI Magazine, Vol. 38 #2, Summer 2017.

[7] M. Wollowski, T. Neller, J. Boerkoel, Artificial Intelligence Education, AI Magazine, Vol. 38 #2, Summer 2017.

[8] E. Eaton, Teaching Integrated AI Through Interdisciplinary Project-Driven Courses, AI Magazine, Vol. 38 #2, Summer 2017.

[9] M. Ferguson, N. Webb and T. Strzalkowski, Nelson: A Low-Cost Social Robot for Research and Education, SIGCSE'11, Proceedings of the 42nd ACM Technical Symposium on Computer Science Education, Dallas, TX, March 2011.

[10] A. Henderson, J. Maynard and M. Doran, Scheduling a Real-Time Railroad System Using Lego MindStorm Hardware, International Conference on Computers and Information Science and Technology (CIST'15), Otawa, Canada, May 2015.

[11] J. Maynard and A. Henderson, Intelligent Management of Autonomous Vehicle in a Factory Setting: Simulation and Scale Model, Fall Conference Proceedings Mid-Southeast Chapter of the ACM, Gatlinburg, TN, November 2015

[12] A. Henderson, Independent Competitive Algorithms in a Multi-Robot System, University of South Alabama, Honors Program Senior Thesis, School of Computing, Department of Computer Science, Mobile, Alabama, May 2017.

Enhanced Robotics! Improving Building and Programming Learning Experiences for Students with Visual Impairments

Stephanie Ludi
Computer Science & Engineering Dept.
University of North Texas
USA
Stephanie.ludi@unt.edu

Debra Bernstein
TERC
USA
debra_bernstein@terc.edu

Karen Mutch-Jones
TERC
USA
karen_mutch-jones@terc.edu

ABSTRACT

Making technology and computer science learning experiences accessible to students with disabilities is an important step in preparing them to enter the workforce of the future—one in which many jobs will require skills to solve problems with technology. This paper presents the tool and curricular enhancements developed to make the *Exploring Computer Science* Robotics unit accessible to students with visual impairments (VI). It describes the evolution of enhancements, based on formative evaluation studies, to increase support as VI students engaged in building and programming LEGO Mindstorms robots. Results describe the ways in which enhancements were iteratively designed in response to student engagement and confidence, as well as their emerging understanding of top-down and bottom-up processes in robotics design and programming.

ACM Reference Format

Stephanie Ludi, Debra Bernstein, & Karen Mutch-Jones. 2018. Enhanced Robotics! Improving Building and Programming Learning Experiences for Students with Visual Impairments. In *SIGCSE '18: 49th ACM Technical Symposium on Computing Science Education, Feb. 21–24, 2018, Baltimore, MD, USA*. ACM, NY, NY, USA, 6 pages. https://doi.org/10.1145/3159450.3159501

1 INTRODUCTION

Recent trends in STEM education emphasize technology, recognizing the educational benefits and career opportunities computing offers for all students [11]. Creating access and supporting students with disabilities is essential, particularly given their lower achievement levels in STEM [29] and lack of representation in STEM fields, particularly in computer science. [2, 21]

While students with visual impairments reflect their sighted peers in terms of cognitive ability [14], their participation in STEM can be limited by insufficient resources and instruction, and a lack of teacher preparation in computing and non-visual teaching methods [12, 13]. Ultimately this closes down access to the 'STEM pipeline' of courses and activities in high school, college, and (eventually) the workplace [3]. STEM participation can impact students' attitudes towards STEM fields [19], which are highly correlated with later STEM achievement [17, 28].

Participation in enhanced STEM programming can make a big difference in students' attitudes towards the STEM fields and potential careers [19]. Specifically, programs that make STEM 'active' by using hands-on materials and engaging students in design-based tasks, have been shown to increase students' interest in STEM [17, 25].

Participation in robotics activities, in particular, can: promote students' computational thinking, critical thinking, and problem solving skills [8, 27]; and increase understanding of complex systems [1]. Robotics provides opportunities to practice teamwork and collaboration [6, 22], which can influence student self-efficacy [9, 23]. Enabling teamwork is especially important for students with VI, who tend to be more socially isolated than their sighted peers [30].

Moreover, robotics is a well-used vehicle for teaching computer science concepts and skills [5, 7], and engaging students in engineering design tasks [6].

LEGO Mindstorms robots, which are used in the Robotics Unit of the Exploring Computer Science (ECS) curriculum [10] have been used to teach computer science concepts such as variables, control flow, constants, procedures and problem decomposition, expressions, and arrays [5]. Having students create their own robots encourages them to use their knowledge and understanding in creative ways [24], while engaging them in a design process that itself promotes critical thinking and problem solving [4]. Thus, designing robots introduces and allows students to iteratively practice computer science and engineering skills.

This paper presents our work in creating an accessible ECS Robotics Unit for 3 cohorts of students with visual impairments, which included designing hardware and software accommodations. Both aspects evolved over the course of the project, and this paper will show the evolution to demonstrate the challenges and rewards of the effort, both technically and in terms of student engagement.

SIGCSE '18, February 21–24, 2018, Baltimore , MD, USA

ACM ISBN 978-1-4503-5103-4/18/02...$15.00
https://doi.org/10.1145/3159450.3159501

2 EXPLORING COMPUTER SCIENCE: ROBOTICS UNIT

ECS is a high school curriculum comprised of 6 units: Robotics, the focus of this paper, as well as Human-Computer Interaction, Problem Solving, Web Development, Programming, and Data Analysis [10]. Several tools, activities, and resources used in the ECS curriculum are not accessible to students with visual impairments. As a result IECS, where the 'I' stands for Inclusive, was designed [20]. The Robotics Unit is expected to be taught in about 7 weeks. The instructional breakdown of the Robotics Unit can be found within the ECS Teacher Guide [10]. This paper will focus on building (Hardware) and programming (Software) accommodations.

3 HARDWARE & SOFTWARE ACCOMODATIONS

The ECS Robotics Unit requires students to build and program a robot, however there are many barriers that impede VI students' ability to do such work. The LEGO Mindstorms building instructions and the block-based programming software that come with the kits are not accessible to students with visual impairments due to the graphical nature of each. In order to make the ECS Robotics Unit accessible both the hardware and software aspects required significant accommodations.

3.1 Hardware

LEGO building instructions, as shown in Figure 1, are provided but are not accessible to students with visual impairments. One challenge involved identifying and differentiating LEGO Mindstorms pieces, so we created a prototype tray where parts were organized and easily accessible.

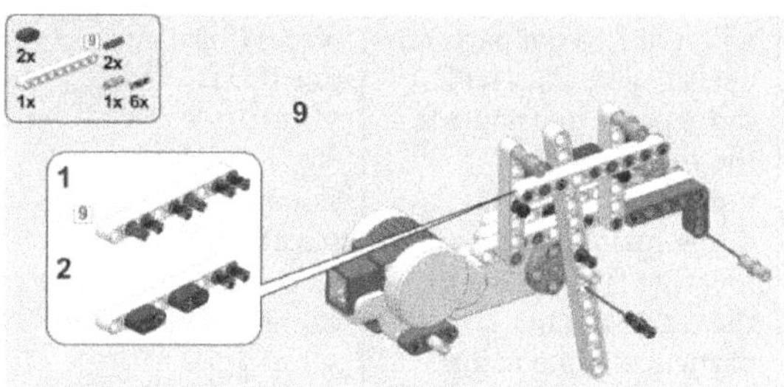

Figure 1. Sample of visual LEGO building instructions [26]

Each section had a flap with parts glued to it, so students could quickly feel the type of part within a section. Having sample pieces enabled students to visually or tactily browse for pieces without disrupting the contents of the tray. In addition, similar parts were in nearby sections (e.g., inner wheels of various sizes), so that students could evaluate their choices (e.g., a tiny, small, medium, or large wheel) and select the part needed.

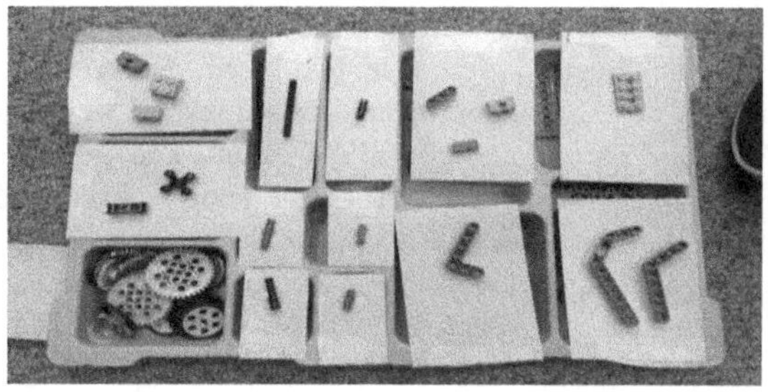

Figure 2. A tray prototype with exemplar pieces on flaps

The next challenge was for students to learn how pieces fit together generally, and then how to use them to create robots. Unstructured tactile exploration is inadequate and lacks efficiency. To support the development of building skills, the team conducted an activity with the third cohort that provided a guided exploration that transitioned into explorative small building (sans the LEGO Brick itself). Figure 3 shows group work as a whole alongside a close-up of students doing some exploratory building. In the activity, students learned about the pieces by type: Structural Elements, Connectors, Wheels and Treads, Motors. Our approach required students to form highly collaborative teams that could compare and contrast individual parts for identification; and use a visual and tactile guide to map parts to their proper names, based on their degree of vision. Via self-created mini-builds, they also explored how different types of pieces impact robot design.

Figure 3. a) An overview of the group tactile activity and b) a close-up of students exploring pieces

This exploration scaffolds engineering design decisions that students will make later in the process. Through this activity, students were able to practice how to attach connectors to different supports and to appreciate their different functions. This activity was successful with a small group, but in order to scale up, we would need to restructure the process so that larger numbers of students could move through stations that are organized by type of materials (e.g., all parts related to wheels).

The third challenge was providing accessible building instructions for an initial robot to be used with the programming tutorial. The ECS curriculum includes a set of initial building instructions that are pictorial. As an alternative, one of the authors developed instructions describing the pieces, how to orient them, and how to navigate to where they must be placed on the model. This approach is based on work by a blind high school student [18]. Our text-based version of the instructions for the same robot model used in ECS was tested with the third cohort of students. The Results and Discussion section will talk about the feedback in more detail. While promising, the pilot revealed that students had trouble orienting the model, attaching sub-models to the main robot, and using LEGO terminology. Therefore, revisions to the building instructions and tray design will be conducted based on student feedback.

3.2 Software

JBrick is the software used to program LEGO Mindstorms robots. The language is NXC (Not eXactly C), thus JBrick serves as an accessible, programming tool that both sighted and visually impaired students can use when completing the ECS Robotics Unit. In contrast to many block-based tools that introduce novice programmers to robotics, JBrick requires students to program in a text-based language. Prior work has outlined the evolution of JBrick with students with visual impairments [15, 16]. Accessibility features include:

- Screen reader compatibility (Mac and PC)
- Compatibility with refreshable Braille displays
- Customization of text size, background and text colors
- Audible line numbers
- Audio feedback for compilation and program download
- Keyboard shortcuts for tasks (e.g. compile, save)
- Highlight of the current line for easier navigation
- The ability to jump the cursor to the line with the compiler error

In addition to JBrick itself, a set of tutorials provides students with the means to get started with programming, using JBrick, and working with the LEGO Mindstorms robots.

4 EVALUATION

The evaluation was designed to offer formative findings to the development team, enabling them to revise and strengthen the enhancements to better meet the learning and accessibility needs of VI students.

Data were collected via evaluator observations of students as they designed, built, and programmed robots, as well as through surveys and interviews with students, and interviews with undergraduate mentors. These instruments were designed to: 1) assess the usability of hardware and software enhancements, identifying which students were best supported by the enhancement (e.g., those with particular kinds of prior computer science experience, those who were blind vs. those with low vision); 2) gauge the influence of enhancements on student interest and engagement in computer science; and 3) identify components of the enhanced robotics unit where barriers remained.

Three cohorts of students—17 male and 2 female in total—participated in the CS Academy's robotics unit during the summers of 2013, 2015, and 2016. Participants were recruited from across the US. Eleven students (58% of participants) had limited vision, and the rest were blind. Students were entering grades 8 to 12, and were homeschooled, attending public schools, or schools for the blind. Most had little to no experience with robotics design or programming.

5 RESULTS AND DISCUSSION

Evaluation findings over three years suggest that in order to fully address accessibility needs for robotics learning, both top-down and bottom-up supports are required for VI students. For instance, enhancements can be designed to scaffold students' high-level thinking about design and problem-solving processes and to help students learn specific skills like appropriate use of programming syntax. These supports are provided by enhancing (or, when needed, re-designing) the software, hardware, and curriculum activities.

5.1 Accessibility Support for Designing and Building (Hardware)

Designing and building robots requires understanding both top-down and bottom-up processes. For example, students need to understand both how to assemble individual components of the robot and how those components can come together to create a functional piece of hardware (see table 1). Merging these two types of knowledge was essential for students with VI to successfully complete the robot design and building task.

Table 1. Top-Down and Bottom-Up Design/Build understanding that was supported by enhancements.

	Top-Down	Bottom-Up
Designing/Building	Engineering the robot's form and function – What will it do? What parts are needed, and what will those parts contribute to the robot's overall function? How will different components fit together (e.g., where is the right spot for particular components, like the robot's 3rd motor). Coordinating hardware and software	Familiarity with individual/groups of Lego pieces (form and function) Steps and details of assembling Lego structures (e.g., what pieces go together, or connect other pieces?) Using groups of Lego pieces to make larger components (e.g., assembling pieces into a support arm for a sensor)

Enhancements to support top-down understanding. In the first year of the project, evaluators noted that some students gravitated toward building robots and others toward programming with JBrick. The students were quite aware of their preferences, saying things like "I'm really not a big Lego guy" or "I'm not good at coding." Often the two activities were divorced, most observably when two boys worked together with one building a robot and the other programming, and neither checking in with the other about design until much later in the process. As a result, the physical design of the robot didn't match the movements that were programmed, creating a fair amount of frustration for this pair. Even after extensive troubleshooting which left them without a satisfying conclusion (their robot never really fulfilled the requirements of the Challenge), it was hard to tell whether they understood that it was essential to collaborate on both building and programming.

It became clear that the project needed to provide more support to overtly help students link hardware and software design processes, which necessitated engaging all students in hardware exploration. During the second project year, all students broke into groups to build a complete robot (with assistance from a mentor). The process was collaborative, making the workload more manageable for those with limited building experience. Three blind students in this cohort developed shared verbal descriptions of Lego pieces to facilitate sorting and building (e.g., 'I'm putting all the round pieces in here'), and took turns retrieving pieces and assembling the robot while the mentor read out loud from the construction manual.

Observing the robot building process, mentors noted the importance of students (particularly blind students) being able to feel the entire robot and well as the sections and individual parts, in order to create a 'schematic' of the final product in their heads. But this observed benefit came with a challenge. Keeping the big picture in mind, while at the same time remembering the shape and size of parts, the types of connectors required to create robot sections, and the ways in which these sections fit together to create the full robot, increased memory load beyond some students' capacity. As a result, additional memory supports were developed and offered to the final cohort (as described in Section 3.1).

Students in the final year of the program responded well to these changes, and were able to form a full understanding of robot design, including which components of a design could be flexible. As one student from this cohort noted, "[what] was easy was that you could change things [on the robot]. Like anything could be kind of changed to your liking. The hard part was like knowing what you could change and what you couldn't. So... you can change the body of the robot. You can change how it's formed and stuff, but you can't really change that like some wheels just won't turn, and some structures just won't move too fast or too slow."

Enhancements to support bottom-up understanding. In the early years of the program, many students (especially those who were blind) struggled with identifying Lego pieces, discerning how/where to connect them while building, and remembering the shape of the robot/robot sections they were trying to build to meet the design challenge. Thus, to enable all students to develop basic building skills, three enhancements were designed to guide bottom up learning: the trays and scaffolded exploration as described in Section 3.1, and building cloths that provided a clean surface and a tactile edge (so students could tell where to stop looking for pieces).

Data collected from students suggest that these basic enhancements were helpful. When surveyed, the majority of students (6 out of 10) agreed that it was 'easy to locate parts' and physically assemble the Lego pieces. One student commented, "it was confusing, but got easier over time. Had to get used to it at first, I'm not used to playing with those kinds of Legos."

While one student with low vision said he preferred to search for parts that were in their original bags, all of the other student felt the trays were "way better". Some recalled challenges they faced while working with Legos when younger. For instance, one blind student said, "I was in a robotics class back in elementary school. It was really bad...where everything was just thrown into a huge [bin]. Then we had to go in there and just look and look and look." These students particularly liked having the Lego piece taped to a flap on top of each section so they could slide their hands across the tray's surface and locate the section/pieces rapidly. One student suggested adding a Braille description next to the actual part (e.g., a connector with two holes). Several students thought making the flaps sturdier (a plastic piece or a stronger cardboard) would help them to lift and manipulate pieces with greater ease.

Taking time to explore parts as a group also seemed valuable. Quick activities, like passing around parts by type, engaged student and got them thinking about building robots. For instance, after feeling several key pieces, the instructor asked students to figure out how one piece could be connected with another or how two parts might work together. This led to some limited building in small groups, and the excitement during this time was visible and audible. As they reflected on this portion of the enhancement, all students said that the exploration activities were valuable. In fact, several of them wanted more. These students wanted to feel every part within a category to more fully identify differences, and to spend more time understanding sensors and motors before using them in their robots.

With a set of tested enhancements in place for our Y3 cohort, we found that addressing top-down and bottom-up needs in an integrated fashion led to improved confidence while building robots (see Figure 4).

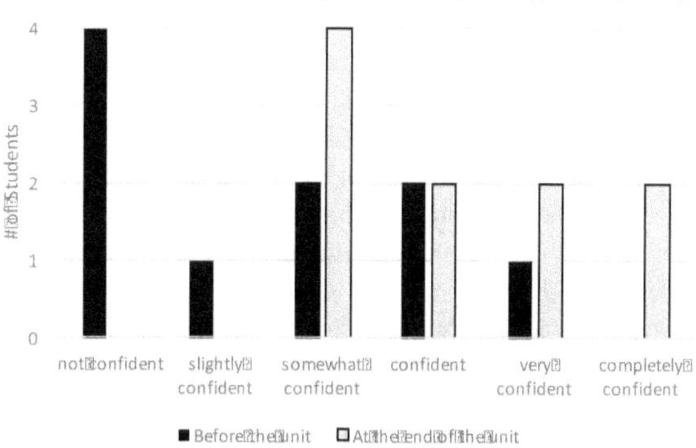

Figure 4. Students' confidence ratings about building robots; Year 3 cohort (n=10).

5.2 Accessibility Support for Programming (Software)

Programming robots requires students to engage in top-down planning (e.g., deciding what the program will accomplish, including sections in the correct order) while understanding how to use the syntax and commands of a particular language (see Table 2). IECS enhancements sought to support students in mastering top-down and bottom-up elements of programming.

Table 2. Top-Down and Bottom-Up Programming understanding that was supported by enhancements.

	Top-Down	Bottom-Up
Programming	What the whole program is designed to accomplish Coordinating hardware and software Flow of the program (i.e., order of components)	Syntax of programming What individual programming commands do and how to use them Steps of programming, debugging Programming sequences/parts of programs that need to go together (e.g., specify which motor port + speed + direction of motor)

Enhancements to support top-down understanding. Many of the IECS participants felt that learning how to program was challenging and required persistence, but in the end felt highly satisfied with their accomplishments. One student from the Y1 cohort noted that programming was, "like [learning] a language; as you practice it gets easier." Another student, from the final cohort, expressed enthusiasm about the way a program could control different components of his robot: "motors are the things that really fascinated me. And that's just going back to coding. It really fascinated me how I could write some code, plug a brick Lego in, and then download it, and then make it so the Lego would spin, rotate, move a certain amount of time, wait a certain amount of time. You know? It would just kind of fascinate me."

The relationship between the written program and the robot's actions was reinforced through the use of JBrick tutorials. The tutorials introduced students to different concepts and commands available in JBrick (e.g., moving forwards, backwards, using sensors, if statements) and provided an opportunity to for students to immediately test out short programs on their robots. For example, one section of the tutorial deals with motors and encourages students to see how different motor speeds and wait times look on their robot. Blind students would often run the programs with one hand on the robot to gauge its speed. These exercises helped prepare students to create their own programs later on by showing them how to break the programming challenge into smaller parts, and drill down further to design and program. When needed the undergraduate mentors stepped in to help students break down a challenge into a set of smaller goals, or to help with programming.

Enhancements to support bottom-up understanding. Unlike Mindstorms, a drag and drop software application that requires vision to manipulate the programming blocks, JBrick requires that students write code to program robots. The evaluators noted that while accommodations for students with disabilities often make the work easier, in this case JBrick makes the work harder, even though it increases *visual* access.

Some students found the syntax-heavy programming language to be a challenge. One student noted, "I found it hard to actually type in the code...it's cap sensitive, and you have to put a semi-colon at the end of every line." Another student noted there were "so many weird punctuation marks; I get a lot of compilation errors." However, other students found that because JBrick offered clear robotics command about each function, they were easy to remember. One student explained: "So if you're in the code, you'd see clear motors and then off motors, for example. So you'd understand it means turn off the motors [or]...if you see task main in the line of code, you know that that's where it's going to start...It's pretty easy to understand the actual code."

To help mitigate syntax challenges, the tutorials provided segments of sample code that students could paste into JBrick and then edit to create their own code. This allowed students to achieve their programming goals without first having to master all of the syntax. It also served as a memory cue for the different commands. Many students did cut and paste program segments as they were beginning to program, but then moved on to writing independent code when they wanted their robots to perform actions not described in the tutorials.

JBrick also offers other supports including auditory prompts and tools to help alleviate memory load (such as line numbering that helped students locate their place in a program). Again, with tested final enhancements in place, we asked Y3 students to rank how useful those features were in helping them program their robot. A great majority of the cohort indicated that having a *screen reader* to read their code and *audio feedback,* which indicated that their program was downloaded, was very or extremely helpful. And 75% of the group rated the clarity of menus as moderately to very helpful in finding commands.

Students with low vision were able to access the line numbering option, but they had mixed reviews about its helpfulness, in part because this sub-group still needed to hear which line they were on. Unfortunately, the NVDA screen reader did not read the line numbers, so this feature wasn't used fully. A couple of students also used a feature that allowed them to change the size and color of their code, but most students relied on the screen reader.

Overall findings from our Y3 cohort suggest that the final version of JBrick and the supportive curriculum structure led to improved student confidence about programming robots.

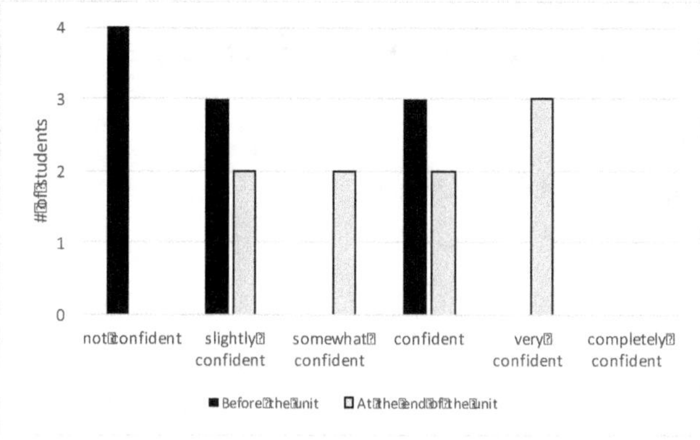

Figure 5. Students' confidence ratings about programming robots; Year 3 cohort (n=10).

5 SUMMARY & FUTURE WORK

Evaluation findings illustrate the ways in which hardware and software accommodations for the ECS Robotics Unit reduce tool and curricular barriers, and increase access for students with VI. Evaluating the tools and activities for such a complex (Robotics) unit, can help teachers provide new resources to maximize access to all students. As a result of our accessibility evaluation, we now have a complete set of tested and revised enhancements, enabling us to measure longitudinal change in student engagement and learning.

In terms of development, our future work will include written and video materials for teachers and students, to illustrate the tactile exploration activities. In addition, next steps for the development team are to include the LEGO Mindstorms EV3 platform, and simplify code reuse to help students use blocks of code more easily. A more ambitious project underway is our accessible block-based tool that also supports LEGO Mindstorms programming, but JBrick will continue to evolve.

ACKNOWLEDGMENTS

This work is supported by the National Science Foundation awards CNS-1240856 and CNS-1240809. We also thank our mentors, participants and their parents.

REFERENCES

[1] Barab, S. (2014) Design-Based Research: A methodological toolkit for engineering change, in The Cambridge Handbook of the Learning Sciences, edited by Sawyer, R.K., 151-170. New York: Cambridge University Press.

[2] Burgstahler, S., & Ladner, R.E. (2007). Increasing the participation of people with disabilities in computing fields. Computer. 40(5), 94-97.

[3] Burgstahler, S. & Chang, C. (2009). Promising interventions for promoting STEM fields to students who have disabilities. Review of Disability Studies: An International Journal, 5, 29-47.

[4] Cross, N. (1982). Designerly ways of knowing. Design Studies, 3(4), 221-227.

[5] Fagin, B. S., Merkle, L. D., & Eggers, T. W. (2001, September). Teaching computer science with robotics using Ada/Mindstorms 2.0. In ACM SIGAda Ada Letters (Vol. 21, No. 4, pp. 73-78). ACM.

[6] Gomez, K., Bernstein, D., Zywica, J., & Hamner, E. (2012). Building technical knowledge and engagement in robotics: An examination of two out-of-school programs. In B.Barker, G. Nugent, N. Grandgenett, &V.I. Adamchuk (Eds.), Robotics in K-12 Education: A New Technology for Learning (pp. 222-244).

[7] Grabowski, L. M., & Brazier, P. (2011, October). Robots, recruitment, and retention: Broadening participation through CS0. In 2011 Frontiers in Education Conference (FIE) (pp. F4H-1). IEEE.

[8] Grover, S. & Pea, R. (2013). Computational thinking in K-12: A review of the state of the field. Educational Researcher, 42(1), 38-43.

[9] Hutchinson, M.A., Follman, D.K., Sumpter, M., & Bodner, G.M. (2006). Factors influencing the self-efficacy beliefs of first-year engineering students. Journal of Engineering Education, 95(1), 39-47.

[10] Into the Loop (2011). Retrieved at: http://www.exploringcs.org/

[11] Israel, M., Pearson, J.N., Tapia, T., Wherfel, Q.M., & Reese, G. (2015a). Supporting all learners in school-wide computational thinking: A cross-case qualitative analysis. Computers & Education, 82, 263-279.

[12] Israel, M., Wherfel, Q.M., Pearson, J. Shehab, S. & Tapia, T. (2015b). Empowering K-12 student with disabilities to learn computational thinking and computer programming. Teaching Exceptional Children, 48(1), 45-53

[13] King, H. (2011). Supporting STEM teaching and learning of visually impaired students: An ISE research brief discussing in Rule et al. Impact of adaptive materials on teachers and their students with visual impairments in secondary science and mathematics classes. Retrieved from http://www.relatingresearchtopractice.org/article/250

[14] Kumar, D., Ramasamy, R., & Stefanich, G. (2001). Science for students with visual impairments. Electronic Journal of Science Education, 5. Retrieved from http://ejse.southwestern.edu/article/view/7658/5425 30 April 2013.

[15] Ludi, S., & Reichlmayr, T. (2011). The Use of Robotics to Promote Computing to Pre-College Students with Visual Impairments. ACM Transactions on Computing Education. ACM New York, NY, Volume 11 Issue 3, October 2011. doi>10.1145/2037276.2037284

[16] Ludi, S. (2014) Robotics Programming Tools for Blind Students. Journal on Technology and Persons with Disabilities. CSUN Center on Disabilities, http://scholarworks.csun.edu/handle/10211.3/125008, pp. 81-91.

[17] Maltese, A.V., & Tai, R.H. (2011). Pipeline persistence: Examining the association of educational experiences with earned degrees in STEM among U.S. students. Science Education, 95, 877-907.

[18] McDonald, C. (2016). A New System Lets Blind Kids Build Lego Sets. Popular Science. Retrieved at: http://www.popsci.com/blind-high-school-student-helps-make-legos-accessible

[19] Moore, J.L. (2006). A qualitative investigation of African American males' career trajectory in engineering: Implications for teachers, school counselors, and parents. Teachers College Record, 108(2), 246-266.

[20] Mutch-Jones, K., Bernstein, D., Ludi, S. (2016). Creating access to computer science: Enhancing engagement and learning for students with visual impairments. Visual Impairment and Deafblind Education Quarterly, 61(4), 38-51.

[21] National Science Foundation (2015). Division of Science Resources Statistics. Women, minorities, and persons with disabilities in science and engineering. Arlington, VA: NSF 15-311.

[22] Nourbakhsh, I., Crowley, K., Bhave, A., Hamner, E., Hsiu, T., Perez-Bergquist, A., et al., (2005). The Robot Autonomy Mobile Robotics Course: Robot Design, Curriculum Design and Educational Assessment. Autonomous Robotics Journal 18(1).

[23] Nugent, G., Barker, B.S., Grandgenett, N., & Adamchuk, V.I. (2010). Impact of robotics and geospatial technology interventions on youth STEM learning and attitudes. Teacher Education Faculty Publications. Paper 33. Available at http://digitalcommons.unomaha.edu/tedfacpub/33

[24] Resnick, M., Berg, R., & Eisenberg, M. (2000). Beyond black boxes: Bringing transparently and aesthetics back to scientific investigation. Journal of the Learning Sciences, 9(1), 7-30.

[25] Reynolds, B., Mehalik, M.M., Lovell, M.R., & Schunn, C.D. (2009). Increased student awareness of and interest in engineering as a career option through design-based learning. International Journal of Engineering Education, 25(4), 788-798.

[26] Robot Building Instructions. Retrieved from: http://robotsquare.com/2012/02/27/tutorial-manty/

[27] Sullivan, F., (2008). Robotics and science literacy: Thinking skills, science process skills and systems understanding. Journal of Research in Science Teaching, 45(3), 373-394.

[28] Tai, R.H., Liu, C.Q., Maltese, A.V., & Fan, X. (2006). Planning early for careers in science. Science, 312, 1143-1144.

[29] US Department of Education. (2011). The Nation's Report Card: Science 2011. Retrieved from http://nationsreportcard.gov/science 2011/g8_nat.aspx?subtab_id=Tab _6&tab_id=tab3#chart

[30] Wolffe, K., & Sacks, S. Z. (1997). "The Lifestyles of Blind, Low Vision, and Sighted Youths: A Quantitative Comparison", Journal of Visual Impairment and Blindness, May-June, 91, (3), pp. 245-257

Experiences in Teaching the Internet of Things Courses

Farha N. Ali
Department of Mathematics and Computing, Lander University
Greenwood, SC, USA
fali@lander.edu

ABSTRACT

With the increasing impact of the Internet of Things (IoT) in our everyday lives, it is imperative that a work force would be needed not only to develop the new IoT solutions but also to maintain the established IoT systems. In this paper, we discuss our experiences in curriculum development for three courses on the topic of IoT. This paper's main focus is course development for the latest offering (Spring 2017), and a discussion about what we changed from the previous two offerings. We discuss our weekly lecture plans for IoT topics' coverage along with programming assignments and other assessment activities. We also discuss our observation of students' interest levels, and how we used an incremental project development approach to keep students engaged and motivated. We conclude with our observations of what did and didn't worked for us. We also discuss what we missed because of time constraints but would try to include in our next offering.

CCS CONCEPTS

• **Computer systems organization** → **Embedded systems**; *Redundancy*; Robotics; • **Networks** → Network reliability;

KEYWORDS

The Internet of Things, networks, protocols, algorithms, sensor networks, distributed systems

ACM Reference Format:

Farha N. Ali. 2018. Experiences in Teaching the Internet of Things Courses. In *SIGCSE '18: SIGCSE '18: The 49th ACM Technical Symposium on Computer Science Education, February 21–24, 2018, Baltimore , MD, USA.* ACM, New York, NY, USA, 6 pages. https://doi.org/10.1145/3159450.3159549

1 INTRODUCTION

The last few years have witnessed the exponential growth of the Internet of Things (IoT) field [9, 19]. With IoT technology woven in many aspects of our daily life [7, 8] in the near future, we can envision a need for professionals trained for designing, developing, monitoring, and maintaining IoT applications. Hence, It is evident that there is a need to include IoT application development in computer-related disciplines in colleges. Fortunately, IoT applications are built using multiple concepts that are already core components of most computer related undergraduate programs. Below we summarize the components of an IoT application.

To develop an IoT application one must be able to understand the following concepts: i) hardware architecture of microprocessors used in embedded devices and use of sensors and actuators etc. ii) programming principles for programming the microcontroller-based embedded devices to sense and collect data, iii) analog and digital data communication, iv) technologies like Bluetooth BLE [1] and Zigbee [27] used for building local area networks of embedded devices, v) client server programming for data communication among devices, vi) Internet communication protocols, and vii) distributed computing. It can be observed that the knowledge needed to develop a complete IoT application is covered in various core courses of a computer science program. The main objective of a course on IoT is then to tie-in all these concepts to develop an IoT application. Consideration of these requirements can help us decide an appropriate background/prerequisite requirement for an IoT course, and can help an instructor decide the topics that must be covered in the course.

We assume that junior level standing is an appropriate time for students to take an IoT course . By this time the students have usually taken the core courses in programming, computer architecture, computer networking, and information sciences. Students can then learn basic concepts of embedded programming and required data communication and distributed computing concepts very quickly.

This paper is organized as follows. Section 2 dicusses the efforts of our peers in teaching IoT related courses. Section 3 covers the course structure of our course. Section 4 covers the changes that we made in this offering from the feedback we received from previous two offerings of the same course. Section 5 discusses our observations of students' interest level and their evaluation of the course. Section 6 concludes this paper with a brief summary.

2 RELATED WORK

This section discusses some efforts regarding the teaching of the Internet of Things (IoT) concepts. While searching for efforts similar to ours we look for two resources: i) syllabi of courses on the topic of IoT concepts and ii) the published literature where educators have discussed their experiences and courses' layouts. In our observations, we see that most courses focus deeply on one aspect among the many aspects of IoT technology i.e. some courses focus on the networking aspect of the IoT, some focus on the hardware and programming aspect of the IoT, whereas some focus on the web

SIGCSE '18, February 21–24, 2018, Baltimore , MD, USA

ACM ISBN 978-1-4503-5103-4/18/02...$15.00
https://doi.org/10.1145/3159450.3159549

application aspect of the IoT. Our focus was to develop a course that covers the breadth of concepts needed to develop an IoT application rather than focusing on some aspects of IoT development.

We start our discussion with a syllabus [18] for a course about the Internet of Things concepts. The main focus of the course is discussion of network protocols for various layers of TCP/IP suite. A very small percentage of course covers IoT definitions and case studies, and that only in the last few lectures. The course objectives expected the following outcomes from the course: understanding the limitations, performance, and opportunities available to wireless networks. In our opinion, this course is better suited as a networking course rather than an IoT course. Our course expects the students to possess the basic networking knowledge and focus more on concepts needed to develop an IoT application.

Next we discuss course syllabus [10] which covers IoT application development more closely. Topics covered in the course include discussion of evolution of IoT from M2M to full scale IoT applications. The objectives of the course include introducing students to evolution of IoT, IoT in marketplace, hardware involved in developing an IoT application, and design constraints in IoT application development. The syllabus does not mention coverage of distributed computing which is an important part of a full-scale IoT application. In our course we covered distributed computing along with concepts regarding wired and wireless communication and data storage and retrieval using a web-based application.

Forster et al., [13] discuss an experience in teaching a course on IoT. The course covers several topics regarding IoT including hardware architecture of an IoT device, the software pattern for IoT programs, technologies to develop wireless communication protocols among devices. The course also covers the Bluetooth BLE and Zigbee protocols but only in lectures. There was a poster activity to assess students' understanding of the concepts, but we do not see any hands-on activity where students actually used Bluetooth BLE or Zigbee technologies. The students also did not develop their own servers. But this could be attributed to the fact that some of the students were not computer science majors. In our course we not only covered Bluetooth BLE and Zigbee protocols in lectures,we also required students to complete two graded programming assignments using these technologies. We also provided students with a web application where they were required to learn to interact with a storage and data visualization provider and store their data on the server using the HTTP protocol.

Lastly, we discuss our previous experiences of teaching [2] two offerings of IoT course, and how they differ from each other. We incorporated feedback from students and our own observations from previous offerings in our third offering. We also added hands-on Bluetooth BLE and Zigbee exercises.

3 COURSE DESIGN

This paper discusses the third offering of a course on IoT concepts offered by us. We made several changes in the approach from our previous offerings [2]. In previous offerings, we focused mainly on concepts regarding embedded programming and communication among the embedded devices via the Internet using the TCP/IP protocols. In the most recent offering, we added Bluetooth and Zigbee communications as local area network protocols. We divided the course in five sections, each focusing on a portion of IoT application development. The sections were taught such that each section helps students to understand one or more concepts. The hands-on activities and programming assignments were designed such that each section's work is used as a component in the next sections' assignments. Students' grade for the class included the following activities: written quizzes, programming assignments, a presentation on an IoT-related topic, and a final project requiring the design, implementation, and presentation of an IoT application.

We provided students with the hardware needed for the course. The hardware included the SimpleLink WiFi CC3200 devices [22] (we will refer to these devices as CC3200 in rest of the paper), NRF24L01 radios [17], Bluetooth BLE HC-05 devices [26], some colored LEDs, photo resistors, breadboards, and jumper wires. Students were allowed to keep the hardware for whole semester. The CC3200 devices were provided to us from Texas Instruments as a grant, and we arranged for the other pieces of hardware. In the following discussion, we present concepts covered in each section along with assessments, programming assignments, and hands-on in-class activities.

3.1 Course Sections

Following is a discussion of how we divided our course into multiple sections and what each section covered. we also discuss the programming assignments and written assessments.

3.1.1 Course Section 1. The first three weeks of the course were dedicated to introduce students to the idea of embedded systems programming. Students were familiar with the programming concepts after having completed the three programming courses as the core major requirement. Some were also familiar with the Arduino [4] and raspberry pi [20] programming. The first three weeks were used to level the field and for making sure that all students understand the basic concepts of embedded programming. The lectures for this section covered fundamental building blocks that form the Internet of Things. Topics included overview of the following: definition of IoT, basic hardware units used in development of the IoT, the role of software in controlling the hardware used in the IoT, different local area network and Internet level protocols used to facilitate the communication among the devices involved in an IoT application, digital and analog data communication, and an overview of different applications using IoT in various fields of life. The hands-on activity part of this section involves downloading and installing Energia IDE [12]. Students learned about downloading custom libraries and placing them in right locations on their computer to make sure they work with Energia IDE. We used the CC3200 as our embedded device. We discussed basic components of the CC3200 board, introducing students to the board pins and their functions and on-board sensors. The assessment for this section involves a written quiz and developing a simple embedded programming application. The quiz evaluated students' knowledge on the topics covered and the programming lab required students to represent the amount of light sensed by a photo resistor as a binary code between 0 and 7 using three LEDs. Students also learned about the difference between analog and digital input and outputs and why one should be careful in choosing the right type of pin for any specific type of data.

3.1.2 Course Section 2. The second section of the course was taught over the next two weeks. The focus of this section was to introduce students to client server programming, and how it is used to facilitate data communication between devices of different computational capability. Students were familiar with the Java programming language and object-oriented programming concepts. Although all students have taken the core programming course sequence, some have not taken a database course. Keeping this in mind, we started our lectures with the discussion about client server programming. Students were introduced to basic pattern of a client server program and developed a Java client and server application during an in-class activity. Then we introduced the basic pattern of a database program. The CC3200 library provides support for client server programming. Students use that to develop a client server program where the client was a CC3200 device and the server was a Java application running on their computer. The application worked as follows: The device reads the light and temperature values from the sensors, and then send them to the server using a pre-agreed protocol. The server then extracts the information, stored it in a database, and also displayed it on the computer screen. The written assessment involved short answer type questions about the client server and database applications' design and implementation.

3.1.3 Course Section 3. The third section of the course involves teaching students how to send data to a web server application. The job of the web server was to receive and store data and display it upon users' requests. The focus was on learning the HTTP protocol and using it in the client server program from the previous section. The basics of HTTP protocol were covered in the lectures. We discussed HTTP's GET and POST requests. A revision of basic HTML and CSS concepts is also conducted. During the in-class activities students sent data to a web application which saved it to a database. The Web application also displayed the data on a web page. The purpose of this exercise was for the students to be able to use several available data collection websites [15, 16, 21] where sensor data can be stored and viewed. We have noticed that most of these websites require an understanding of HTTP protocol. We also discussed the importance of making sure that data is strictly associated with the device sending it. Students were asked to determine a way of generating a unique ID for each device. The assessment for this section required students to send data to a test website [3] and then view it on website's portal, making sure they were successfully able to send data to an application developed by a third party. For that purpose we developed a website which can register devices, receive data from devices, and then display it. Students were asked to follow instruction given on the website and then display sensor data collected by their device on the website. Written assessment involved questions about HTTP protocols and HTML.

3.1.4 Course Section 4. This was the longest section of our course. This section focused on teaching the concepts regarding the development of local area networks for IoT devices. There are several embedded boards available with the on-board WiFi capability, but to be able to work in a commercial production environment students must know different choices available for developing their own local area networks using serial and radio transmissions. We started the discussion by introducing the concept of serial communication. We discussed the similarities and differences of different protocols used for serial communication. We covered I2C [14], SPI [24], and UART [23] protocols. Students were asked to develop a simple protocol to send a text string from one device to another by using serial communication between the two CC3200 devices. Students learned to pack data in data frames, making sure that start of packet is visible and clear to the receiving device. We then introduced the idea of sending data using radio communication. We started the discussion by first introducing the concept of sending data bit by bit from the device to the hardware module responsible for sending the data over the air. We discuss the conceptual hardware architecture of the radio module. We then provide the students with a Bluetooth communication hardware module and an NRF2401L module. The Bluetooth modules cost about $8 each whereas the NRF2401L modules cost around $1 each. The first programming assignment was a group assignment. Students were asked to develop a Bluetooth communication protocol. Each team was supposed to use two devices. One device acted as a Bluetooth slave and the second device acted as a Bluetooth Master. The Master device was responsible for collecting data from sensors on the slave devices and its own sensors, and then pass the data to a server, which in turn forwarded it to the database. Another Java program was also developed to display the data from the database. In order to enable Bluetooth communication among the devices, the students have to first configure their Bluetooth modules. Using the AT commands [26] students set up one-to-one communication among modules of their team. The second programming assignment was also similar as the one discussed except that the students were asked to replace the Bluetooth hardware with the NRF2401L radio modules. The Bluetooth module was connected to the device using the UART interface whereas the NRF2401L used the SPI connections. Students were responsible for finding the correct pins to connect their devices. Both of these projects were received with great interest, and students participated enthusiastically in the class discussions during the time when these projects were being developed.

3.1.5 Course Section 5. This was the last section of the course. We introduced students to the topic of hardware interrupts. Students have already taken the core programming classes and were familiar with the idea of event listeners and call back functions. We used those concepts as the basis of introducing the hardware interrupts and interrupt handlers. The assessment for this part of the course consisted of converting a 3 bit binary number into a decimal value. The binary numbers were entered by the push of a button. Each push generates an interrupt and the duration between subsequent pushes determined the value 0 or 1 of the entered bit. Students were responsible for writing the logic for interrupt handler. The last topic of our course was discussion of middleware. Students were introduced to the importance of middleware in IoT application. Because of the time constraint, students developed a program in class to connect to the eclipse [11] IoT server.

3.2 Class Presentations

Students were asked to choose a topic of their choice related to Internet of Things application and give a short presentation about the topic. The grade was determined by the quality of research and presentation skills. Students chose some very interesting topics including: smart cities, smart parking, smart baby monitor, smart basketball, use of IoT in preservation of endangered wildlife, and a project regarding an electronically controlled dragonfly.

3.3 Final Project

One part of students' final grade required them to develop an IoT-based project. Students were required to present an idea, prove that the idea represents a feasible project, develop the hardware needed, and design and implement the software components of the project. After successfully completing the project, students were required to collect data using their IoT project, and prove that their project has some merit. Students were also required to present a poster of their projects in a class poster showcase. We meet with each team and discuss their project with them. There were four teams of students. Following is a discussion of each individual project. The first project involved developing a system to detect emergency alarm tones and sending the information to a computer. Students used the CC3200 devices to form a local area network using Bluetooth connections. Among all the devices in the network, one device was responsible for connecting to WiFi and collecting data sent from the individual CC3200 devices. The collected data is then forwarded to the main server. The main server then can choose to spread the warning as suitable. The project was able to differentiate among various alarm tones for different types of threats, and turned on a different colored LED for the received threat. Students used the Java programming language to develop the main server to collect warnings. The system was tested for different tones and a working demo was presented during the class showcase. A poster for this project is shown in Figure 1.

Figure 1: Severe Weather Warning System

The second project involved developing an IoT application for determining the moisture level in a plant pot. The system sent an email to the user if the moisture level went below a given threshold. A moisture sensor was used to determine the level of humidity in the pot. Students collected data for one full day and determined the best place to place their plant where it can receive appropriate sunlight and still be able to keep the moisture level satisfactory. The Java programming language is used to develop the a server to collect data sent from the CC3200 device. A poster for this project is shown in Figure 2.

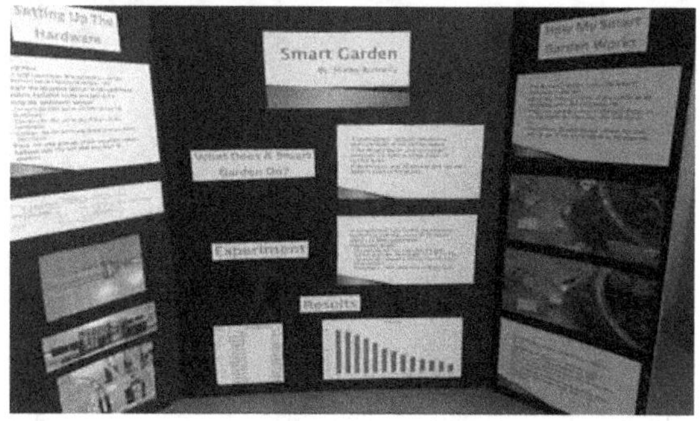

Figure 2: Smart Garden

The third project was developed to help the waiting staff in a restaurant. Students developed a special coaster that can sense the weight of the beverage glass or cup, and if the weight is below a certain level, an information message is sent to a central server. The central server can then display the table number on a screen, thus providing the waiting staff with a visual of all beverage levels on all tables. The Java programming language is used for developing the main server and students used NRF2401L radios for facilitating the local area communications. A poster for this project is shown in Figure 3.

Figure 3: Akatsuki Cup Holder

The last project involved developing an IoT application for determining the path of a moving device. Students made use of NRF2401L radios in this project. One device was designated as a roaming node and other three devices were placed inside three locations. Depending the number of packets received form each of the stationary nodes, students develop an algorithm to determine the distance. The Java programming language is used to develop a server that collected information from all the CC3200 devices and stored it in a database. Using the developed algorithm students recreated the path of the roaming device. A poster for this project is shown Figure 4.

We want to add here that these projects do not have a high research merit as that was not our objective. These projects required

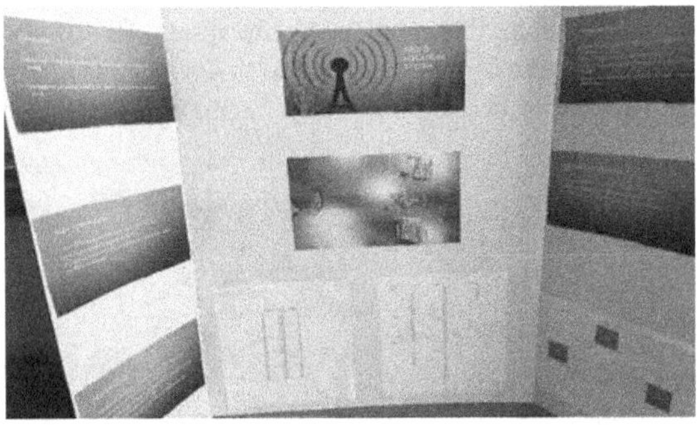

Figure 4: Radio Location System

students to use knowledge gained during the course and apply it to develop a project with some merit. We found that students were highly motivated and went above and beyond our expectations.

4 INCORPORATING FEEDBACK

We offered the same course in the Springs of 2013 and 2015. The most recent offering was in Spring 2017. When we taught the course for the first time in Sprng 2013, we used both ATMega168 [6] chips and Netduino Plus [25]. We programmed the ATMega168 chips using a programmer device and used Atmel Studio [5] for developing and downloading the program on the chips. Netduino plus devices are programmed using the C# language. We realized that students' background was not enough for them to be able to program at the low level that Atmel Studio required. Students were not able to complete many assignments. Programming at that level required them to set register values and pin directions at bit and byte levels, and they soon lost interest. When we introduced Netduino plus devices in the second half of course, students liked programming with C#. Students' projects also showed lack of interest level. From student feedback and our own observations, we decided to use the Energia IDE in our next offering.

In our second offering in Spring 2015, we used the CC3200 devices from Texas Instruments. These devices can communicate using WiFi and can be programmed very easily using the Energia IDE. The language used is C, but several libraries make it easy to make function calls. We also were able to incorporate many distributed programming concepts in this offering. The Java programming language was used to teach client server programming to reinforce those concepts. Students like the programming part. We also required students to make 50 minutes presentations in class for a topic of their choice. This was not received very well. We observed that students did not have appropriate background and knowledge to prepare a 50 minute presentation, and both the presenter and the audience seem dissatisfied during the presentations. In course evaluations students did mention that they would have preferred more programming exercises and shorter presentations.

In our recent offering (Spring 2017) we incorporated the students' feedback from previous courses. Student evaluations for this offering were positive. We also observed that students stayed engaged and motivated during the course.

5 EVALAUTION

In this section we discuss our reflections after teaching the course. We will also discuss students feedback through out the course during each section of the course.

During the first section we found students a bit confused about how to choose the appropriate pins for analog or digital data. We think that dedicating a whole class for hands-on activities was very beneficial. During that class we did not give a lecture, students' just worked on some simple embedded programs with our help. At the end of that section students were able to write simple embedded systems program correctly. We found that slowing down the pace in this activity helped students built confidence in embedded programming and raised their interest in the class. The grades for the written quiz assessment were also satisfactory.

The second section of course was little different. In this section we covered client server programming concepts. We observed that the students were interested and participated actively during the lecture discussions. A relatively minor problem that we noticed was in the development of application level protocol. We felt the same in our previous offerings of this class. We resolved this by involving students in multiple hands-on activities focusing on protocol development. By the end of this section students showed satisfactory level of understanding of the concepts covered, and were able to develop custom client server programs. We had issues with WiFi connection availability for the CC3200 devices. These devices were running a very lightweight library of HTTP protocol and could not authenticate themselves to communicate on university network. We were granted a special permission for the devices. Students performed well on the written and programming assignments.

The third section involved discussion of web programming and HTTP protocol. This section did not go as smoothly as the previous two sections. Students have problems understanding the basic web programming concepts. We used PHP programming language to retrieve data from the GET requests sent from the students' CC3220 devices. Students had problems generating correct GET requests from their CC3200 devices. We revisited several discussion in this section. The quiz assessment showed a lack of understanding of these concepts. Based on the result of written assessment, we discussed the weak points in students' understanding and give them some extra time to finish the programming assignment. We realized that we must reserve a longer time duration for this section in the future. The time dedicated for this section was not enough to grasp the basic concepts of web programming and HTTP protocol.

Fourth section of course was dedicated for coverage of technologies used to built local area networks of embedded devices. To our surprise this section was received with enthusiasm. Student showed great interest in learning different ways of transmitting the data. Building their own communication protocols to make sure data reached to the other node correctly kept them interested and motivated, and this is the point where we noticed students started discussing ideas about their final projects. By the time we reached this section students had a fairly good grip on what is involved in development of on IoT application, and they seem excited for their final projects. The written assessment of this section showed satisfactory results. Students were able to successfully complete the assigned programming projects for this section.

During the fifth and last section of the course students were busy building their projects and we covered topics of programming Interrupts in embedded devices and its importance along with the concept of middleware. An in-class programming activity was assigned for a quiz grade and and written quiz assessment was also used. Students performed satisfactorily for both activities.

For class presentation we see students putting a lot of effort in developing presentation about their chosen topic. We also see that all students showed great interest in presentations and asked many questions.

Students put a lot of effort in their final project and completed their projects with minimal help from us.

During this course we noticed that observing students' perception and understanding of the topics covered during any particular section helped us in maintaining the pace of the course. The incremental development approach where concepts covered in one section were used in explaining the topics in the next section was also helpful.

During final project demonstrations students commented that they liked the freedom of choosing their own project and that way they feel a responsibility of finishing the project.

6 CONCLUSIONS

With the rapid adoption of the Internet of Things (IoT) paradigm in our everyday lives, we see a future need for professionals trained in developing and manipulating the IoT solutions. Although the technologies and concepts used to build the IoT solutions are taught in core CS courses, not many courses are available that integrate all these concepts for developing IoT application. In this paper, we presented our efforts in developing a course for IoT applications for the third time. we discussed what we learned from our previous offerings, and how we used that knowledge to improve our most recent offering. We included our lecture plans, programming assignments,and assessment activities. We hope that our experience may help other educators in developing their own courses for teaching IoT concepts.

ACKNOWLEDGMENTS

We would like to acknowledge the support from Texas Instruments in developing this course. Texas Instruments provided us with a grant for CC3200 Simplelink Wi-Fi devices which we used in the course.

REFERENCES

[1] Adafruit. Adafruit. https://learn.adafruit.com/, 2017.
[2] F. Ali. Teaching the internet of things concepts. In *Proceedings of the WESE'15: Workshop on Embedded and Cyber-Physical Systems Education*, WESE'15, pages 10:1–10:6, New York, NY, USA, 2015. ACM.
[3] F. Ali. Smart app web. http://www.smartappweb.com, 2017.
[4] Arduino. Arduino. https://www.arduino.cc/, 2017.
[5] Atmel. Avr studio 4. http://www.atmel.com/dyn/products, 2011.
[6] Atmel Corporation. ATmega168 datasheet. http://www.atmel.com/Images/doc2545.pdf/.
[7] M. Brereton, A. Soro, K. Vaisutis, and P. Roe. The messaging kettle: Prototyping connection over a distance between adult children and older parents. In *Proceedings of the 33rd Annual ACM Conference on Human Factors in Computing Systems*, CHI '15, pages 713–716, New York, NY, USA, 2015. ACM.
[8] Q. Chen, X. Wang, and F. Liang. Intelligent control and information management system for plant growth cabinet based on internet of things. In *Proceedings of the 2017 ICMSS*, ICMSS '17, pages 246–249, New York, NY, USA, 2017. ACM.
[9] Denise Lund, Carrie MacGillivray,Vernon Turner, Mario Morale. Worldwide and Regional Internet of Things (IoT) 2014âĂŞ2020 Forecast: A Virtuous Circle of Proven Value and Demand. https://https://pdfs.semanticscholar.org/2af9 /2e352bd1b5c497515d2a191a661638751bf8.pdf/, 2017.
[10] Dr. Gowrishankar. Internet of Things (IoT) Syllabus. http://gowrishankarnath.com/468-2/, 2016.
[11] Eclipse. Open Source for IoT . https://iot.eclipse.org/, 2017.
[12] Energia. Energia. http://energia.nu/, 2017.
[13] A. Förster, J. Dede, A. Könsgen, A. Udugama, and I. Zaman. Teaching the internet of things. *GetMobile: Mobile Comp. and Comm.*, 20(3):24–28, Jan. 2017.
[14] I2C Bus. Traciixl 2.0 i2c bus what's that. http://www.i2c-bus.org, 2012.
[15] IBM. BlueMix and Internet of Things. https://www.ibm.com/cloud-computing/bluemix/internet-of-things, 2017.
[16] IBM. Xively. http://www.sense-iot.com/get-started/, 2017.
[17] Nordic Semiconductors. nRF24L01 Ultra low power 2.4GHz RF. http://www.nordicsemi.com/eng/Products/2.4GHz-RF/nRF24L01, 2017.
[18] F. B. of Science and Technology . Syllabus for Internet of Things. http://www.uu.se/en/admissions/master/selma/kursplan /?kKod=1DT094, 2017.
[19] V. P. P. Suresh, J. V. Daniel and R. H. Aswathy. A state of the art review on the internet of things (iot) history, technology and fields of deployment. In *2014 International Conference on Science Engineering and Management Research (ICSEMR)*, pages pp. 1–8., Chennai, India. IEEE.
[20] Raspberry Pi. Raspberry Pi. https://www.raspberrypi.org/, 2017.
[21] sensoiot. senseiot. http://www.sense-iot.com/get-started/, 2017.
[22] Texas Instruments. CC3200 SImplelink Wi-Fi, Internet of Things Solution. http://www.ti.com/lit/ds/symlink/cc3200.pdf, 2017.
[23] Wikipedia. Basics of UART Communication. http://www.circuitbasics.com/basics-uart-communication, 2017.
[24] Wikipedia. Serial peripheral Interface Bus. https://en.wikipedia.org/wiki/Serial_Peripheral _Interface_Bus, 2017.
[25] Wilderness Labs. Power Connected Things With Netduino. https://www.wildernesslabs.co/, 2017.
[26] www.electronica60norte.com. Datasheet for hc05. http://www.electronica60norte.com/mwfls/pdf /newBluetooth.pdf, 2017.
[27] Zigbee Alliance. Zigbee. http://www.zigbee.org/, 2017.

Enhancing Interest in Cybersecurity Careers: A Peer Mentoring Perspective

Vandana P. Janeja, Abu Zaher Md Faridee, Aryya Gangopadhyay, Carolyn Seaman, Amy Everhart
Department of Information Systems, University of Maryland, Baltimore County
{vjaneja,faridee1,gangopad,cseaman,everhart}@umbc.edu

ABSTRACT

The focus of this paper is an evaluation of our peer mentoring framework designed to encourage more students to seek cybersecurity career pathways through providing peer interactions. We present and compare results from two years (Spring 2016 and 2017) of interaction between students in an introductory Information Systems class *(IS 300: Management of Information Systems)* and an upper-level elective Cybersecurity course *(IS 471: Data Analytics for Cybersecurity)*. Our results show a continuation of the general trend observed in the 2016 study. The students who receive peer mentoring show more interest in cybersecurity issues and careers and gain more overall knowledge throughout the semester, than those who don't. This is reflected by the results of an anonymous survey and overall grade improvements. These students show more variations regarding their choice of cybersecurity as a career compared to students who did not receive any mentoring, demonstrating that they are able to make more informed decisions. Female students exhibit more pronounced responses to peer mentoring in contrast to their male counterparts.

KEYWORDS

Cybersecurity; Workforce Development; Peer Mentoring; Information Systems

ACM Reference Format:
Vandana P. Janeja, Abu Zaher Md Faridee, Aryya Gangopadhyay, Carolyn Seaman, Amy Everhart. 2018. Enhancing Interest in Cybersecurity Careers: A Peer Mentoring Perspective. In *SIGCSE '18: The 49th ACM Technical Symposium on Computer Science Education, Feb. 21–24, 2018, Baltimore, MD, USA.* ACM, New York, NY, USA, 6 pages. https://doi.org/10.1145/3159450.3159563

1 INTRODUCTION

Cybersecurity career pathways and roles are an ever increasing need of the workforce as the world becomes more connected and more emerging threats are identified in multiple and newfangled areas of our lives ranging from traditional networks, mobile devices to Internet of Things [22]. Workforce development in this area is inadequate as cybersecurity certificates and programs are few and limited in their scope. Moreover, there is a lack of awareness of the myriad of career options in the cybersecurity field. Our work is motivated to fill this gap. Academic programs are uniquely placed to address this need by encouraging students with a deeper understanding of the cybersecurity career spectrum. We have created a unique undergraduate certificate program in the Information Systems Department that targets the student curriculum at the intersection of Data analytics and cybersecurity. In addition to the new curriculum, we have also instituted a peer mentoring program where students in an introductory technology course are able to interact with students in the upper level cybersecurity elective class.

Peer mentoring refers to the matching of more experienced students with less experienced students who are typically in the early stages of their programs. Peer mentoring has been well accepted and known to be effective [1–11, 13–20, 23–28] in inculcating (a) better academic performance after the first year and reduction of student attrition over all four years in the student mentees and (b) an increase in critical thinking, leadership skills, and abilities for the student mentor. Our framework is based on the evidence from these prior studies indicating that peer mentoring works well in a structured curriculum and shows increased retention with students in the experimental groups earning higher grades and developing critical thinking skills. In this paper we outline the structure of the peer mentoring exercise for undergraduate students, established between the advanced cybersecurity course, *IS 471: Data Analytics for Cybersecurity*, with *IS 300: Management of Information Systems*, a gateway course and the first IS-specific course that IS majors take. Courses before IS 300 build specific foundational skills in programming, economics, and math. This is also the place where students are beginning to explore career pathways. Moreover, this gateway course offers an opportunity to increase participation in advanced technology courses as the gender and under represented groups are still at a slightly higher percentage than in some of our advanced electives. On an average UMBC has about 46% female and 22% underrepresented groups, while the IS department as a whole has roughly 19% female and 22% underrepresented groups. In some of our upper level electives such as Data Mining (2017 Fall) we have 23% female and 33% underrepresented minorities. In IS 300 we have seen over 27% females and 27% minorities (2017 Spring). Thus, we hope to encourage some of these students into advanced technology careers through peer mentoring and increase participation in this important area of STEM education and cybersecurity careers.

In this paper our aim is threefold,

- We evaluate the peer mentoring model and compare findings across two semesters of this study to evaluate whether we have been able to encourage students to pursue cybersecurity careers. We also investigate if, beyond the peer mentoring

SIGCSE '18, Feb. 21–24, 2018, Baltimore, MD, USA

ACM ISBN 978-1-4503-5103-4/18/02...$15.00
https://doi.org/10.1145/3159450.3159563

exercise, more and more students (particularly with diversity) are enrolling in the advanced cybersecurity electives across the two years.
- We evaluate the impact of cybersecurity exercises as part of regular lectures (in a Control section of IS 300) as compared to peer mentoring (Experimental section of IS 300) to see if the impact is significant especially for the underrepresented groups.
- We also discuss qualitative results by evaluating student assignments in the IS 300 courses to see the depth of knowledge gained by the experimental vs the control group. Both these courses are offered by the same instructor who provided additional qualitative insights.

The rest of the paper is organized as follows: we begin with a brief outline of the intervention study design. In section 3 we evaluate, compare and analyze the trend from the two year data. Finally, we discuss the future directions of the project in section 4.

2 METHODOLOGY

The methodology of the peer mentoring approach is based on earlier work [12], discussing peer mentoring results from a one semester offering of this intervention. Figure 1 summarizes the study methodology across the two sections (experiment IS 300E and control IS 300C) of IS 300 and the interactions with peers from IS 471.

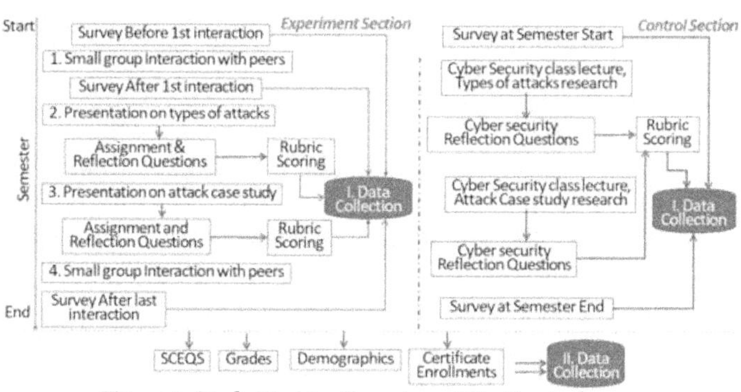

Figure 1: Study Design: Experiment Vs. Control

2.1 Peer Mentoring Approach

Once every month, students in IS 300E interacted with the IS 471 students in a classroom setting through small-group conversations and presentations from the advanced class of students. The two courses were scheduled in the same time slots to facilitate coordination. Both IS 300C&E were taught by the same instructor. IS 471 students provided advanced insights, knowledge, and skills to IS 300E students to enhance relevant assignments in cybersecurity. As peer-mentors the IS 471 students also provided information and insights into cybersecurity careers to potentially raise the IS 300 students' awareness of and interest in course work and career paths in cybersecurity. IS 300 students wrote short reflection statements, discussing insights gained and lessons learned through the cybersecurity presentations as well as their interactions with IS 471 students as part of two assignments. IS 471 students responded to reflection questions and surveys to reflect on the benefits they gained through these interactions. The interactions between IS 300E and IS 471 included two short interactions (at the beginning and end of the semester) where small groups (with a mix of IS300E and IS471 students) interacted with each other through unstructured discussions, guided by some leading questions regarding cybersecurity careers. Throughout the semester IS 300E students attended presentations on types of attacks and attack case studies done by the IS 471 students. These were quick, short presentations that were highly animated and interactive with lots of Q&A. Following these presentations students completed short essay type questions on these topics by selecting a type of attack and a case study to research for their assignment. In IS 300C these presentations from peers were replaced by classroom lectures and research done by the students individually.

There were two surveys conducted before and after the interventions in the IS 300E and 471 classes. There were also two surveys conducted in the control section of IS 300 to evaluate the efficacy of classroom instruction about cybersecurity and self-guided assignments. The pre-survey done before the first interaction in IS 300 included questions such as: *"Do you know what cybersecurity is?", "Are you interested in learning more about cybersecurity?", "Do you know of careers in cybersecurity?", "How likely is it that you will pursue a career in cybersecurity?"*

The post-survey after the fourth intervention repeated these questions and included additional questions on how they evaluated their interactions with IS 471 students. Some of the survey questions for IS 471 included: *"How helpful to you was having a conversation with the IS 300 students, particularly in thinking through reasons for your interest in cybersecurity as an area of study?", "Did this interaction help you gain confidence in talking about your understanding of cybersecurity?"*

2.2 Differences across 2016 and 2017

We wanted to introduce redundancy to better understand the interactions between students and reasons for their answers through their responses to additional position statements over time. Therefore, we asked students to choose one of five position statements in all of the surveys (before and after) for both IS 300 groups and IS 471: *"Learning Cybersecurity is interesting", "Cybersecurity topics do not change over time", "I think cybersecurity is hard", "I believe I can master Cybersecurity knowledge and skills", "Understanding Cybersecurity will help solve important problems such as data leaks, national security etc."*. All of these questions had five possible responses: *Strongly agree, Agree, Neither agree or disagree, Disagree, Strongly disagree.* These additional questions proved much more valuable during our analysis when we found a few contradictory results (discussed in section 3).

We next discuss results obtained by evaluating the surveys.

3 RESULTS

The results compare the data collected through the surveys to evaluate (a) perceptions before and after the interactions, (b) results across the control and experiment sections and (c) results across two years.

The gender and ethnicity distribution of the sections across the years 2016 and 2017 are detailed in table 1 and 2 respectively. The total number of students in each group is denoted by **'N'** in the table headers. The percentage of female students almost doubled from 2016 to 2017. Anecdotally we also saw some students from

Gender	Spring 2017 IS300E (N=39)	Spring 2017 IS300C (N=40)	Spring 2017 IS471 (N=22)	Spring 2016 IS300E (N=38)	Spring 2016 IS300C (N=33)	Spring 2016 IS471 (N=22)
Male	59%	75%	67%	82%	91%	82%
Female	38%	20%	33%	15%	6%	18%
Unspecified	3%	5%	0%	3%	3%	0%

Table 1: Gender Distribution (in percentage)

Ethnicity	Spring 2017 IS300E (N=39)	Spring 2017 IS300C (N=40)	Spring 2017 IS471 (N=22)	Spring 2016 IS300E (N=38)	Spring 2016 IS300C (N=33)	Spring 2016 IS471 (N=22)
Unspecified	8%	5%	6%	3%	24%	13%
White	28%	35%	32%	42%	18%	31%
African-American	15%	17%	16%	16%	15%	15%
Asian	46%	32%	39%	26%	33%	30%
Multiple races	0%	5%	3%	13%	6%	10%
Other	3%	5%	4%	0%	3%	1%

Table 2: Ethnicity Distribution (in percentage)

the peer mentoring interactions in 2016 enrolling for IS 471. So in general these exercises are generating more interest across the department as a majority of the students are passing through either of the IS 300C or IS 300E courses. This is indeed an encouraging finding.

3.1 Comparison across 2016 and 2017 in IS 300E and IS 471

In 2016 we observed that a majority of the students in IS 300E and IS 471 found these interactions helpful. That trend continues to improve in 2017. In 2016 the percentage of students in IS 300 who found these interactions *very* or *moderately helpful* were 82%, in 2017 we found 92% of the students responding with similar positivity to these questions (figure 2).

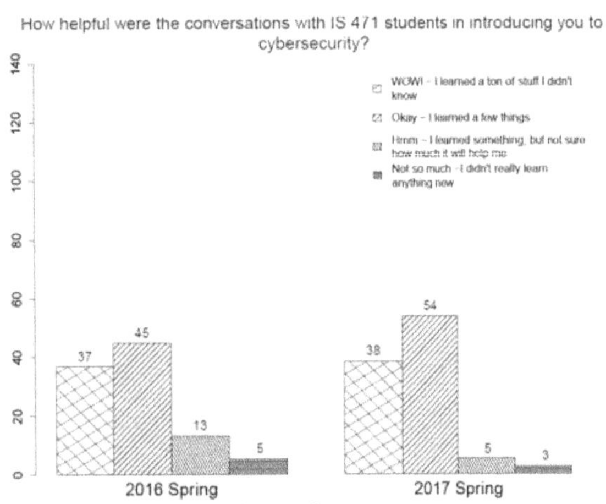

Figure 2: Helpfulness of conversations: IS 300E

Figure 3 shows IS 471 students' response to the question regarding the *helpfulness* of the interactions. Compared to 2016, in 2017 the IS 471 students found these interactions much more helpful. After final interaction, in 2016 54% found these interactions to be between *moderately* to *extremely helpful*, 2017 saw that percentage rise to a complete 100% and there were no students who had any negative response to these interactions. Another interesting observation is that during the 2016 study, the IS 471 students found these interactions a little *less helpful* (14%) towards the end of the semester, whereas in 2017 the IS 471 students felt that these interactions are getting much *more helpful* (25%) as they approach the end of the semester. This indicates the level of confidence gained by the IS 471 students in talking about cybersecurity, which was also observed by the faculty teaching IS 471 through classroom discussions about the peer mentoring exercises. This is possibly also a result of managing the interactions better across the years. There is some level of noise in these descriptive statistics, given the size of the dataset. In our future work we plan to perform statistical tests of significance across three years of this study to conclude with significant findings.

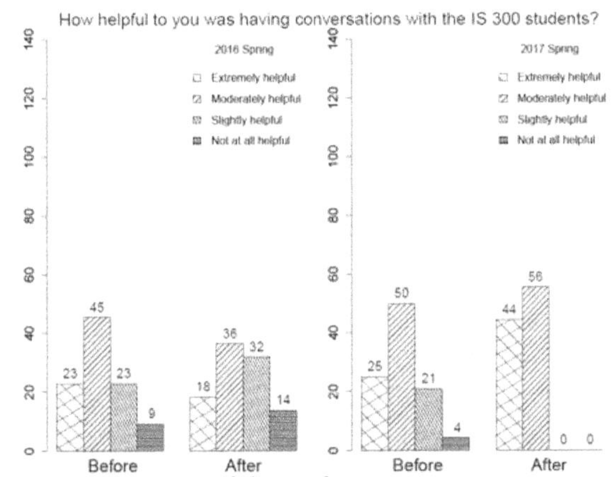

Figure 3: Helpfulness of conversations: IS 471

In 2016, more than two thirds (68%) of the students in IS 300 reported an increased interest in cybersecurity as a result of the interactions. 2017 saw the number raise to 79% (net 11% increase) with zero reporting on any decreased interests (Figure 4)

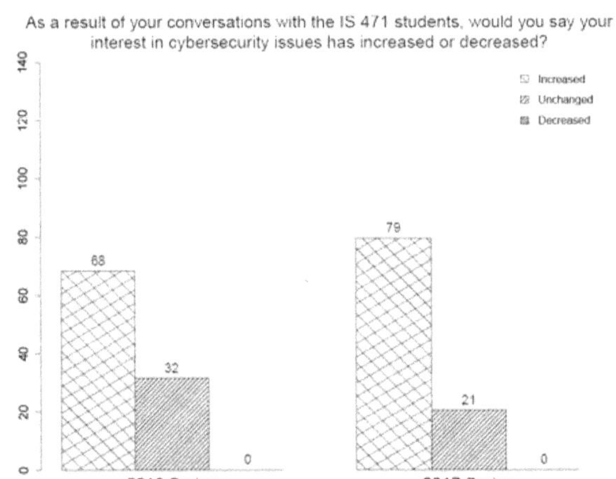

Figure 4: Increased Interest in Cybersecurity: IS 300E

2016 saw a general improvement in response to the question about likelihood of IS 300 students pursuing cybersecurity careers both in the control and experiment section. IS 300 students who had interactions with IS 471 students were around 4% more likely to pursue cybersecurity careers than the students who did not have the interactions by the end of the semester. The results are slightly different in 2017; while the difference for *highly likely* is the same (12% more), it appears that students from the experiment group are at least 8% *less likely* to choose a career in cybersecurity (Figure 5). However, we do see some interesting findings in gender based comparisons discussed later.

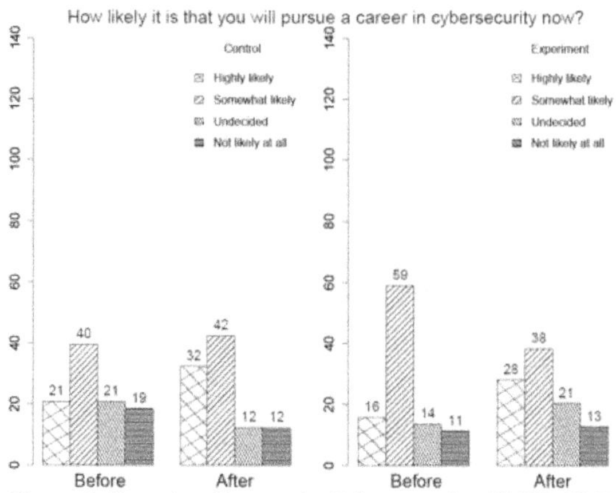

Figure 5: Pursuing Careers in Cybersecurity, IS 300, 2017

A possible explanation for this result could be that as the students in the experiment section have access to IS 471 students' interaction and case study presentations sessions and are able to better judge the depth of their knowledge, interests and career options, they can become more opinionated compared to the students from the control section. This hypothesis can be tested by analyzing the position statements from 2017. The summary of the results are shown in table 3 (due to space constraint, we are only showing the significant differences). The experiment section does not find cybersecurity as interesting as the control section and they find cybersecurity a bit harder than their control counterparts, but at the same time more of them think they can master cybersecurity knowledge and skills and more of them think that cybersecurity is important for national security. These observations show that the experiment section makes more informed decisions later on as they have more interactions. They become more confident about their abilities with cybersecurity topics but this does not necessarily translate to their responses to choosing cybersecurity careers in general. This needs to be further evaluated in the third year of our study as these position statements have only been introduced in 2017 so there is no comparison across 2016. It is also possible that these interests will be evident later on in their careers as we saw in the case of some students going through the peer mentoring exercise in 2016, who enrolled in the IS 471 class in 2017.

3.2 Gender Specific Differences in Responses

In both years of the study, we have observed an encouraging and consistent trend that female students exhibit more positive responses to the questions compared to their male counterparts. The female students generally find these interactions more helpful and interesting and their self-assessment of knowledge gain is also higher than the male students. When asked about choosing cybersecurity as a career their responses are still not as positive as their male counterparts, but they show increased interest (for example from not interested to undecided) and variations in their responses

	Control	Experiment	Observation
Learning Cybersecurity is interesting	26% increase in strongly agree (rest decreasing)	11% increase in agree (rest decreasing)	Control section shows stronger agreement to the statement
Cybersecurity topics do not change over time	18% increase in strongly disagree (rest decreasing)	5% increase in agree & 10% increase in disagree (rest decreasing)	Control section shows stronger disagreement to the statement
I think cybersecurity is hard	6% combined increase in disagreement (rest decreasing)	6% decrease in undecided, almost even increase in agree & disagree percentage	Control section shows more disagreement to the statement
I believe I can master Cybersecurity knowledge & skills	4.1% increase in undecided (rest decreasing)	4% increase in strongly agree & 11% increase in undecided (rest decreasing)	Experiment section shows more agreement to the statement
Understanding cybersecurity will help solve important problems such as data leaks, national security	9% increase in strongly agree & 2% increase in strongly disagree (rest decreasing)	13% increase in strongly agree, 3% increase in neither & 5% increase in strongly disagree (rest decreasing)	Experiment section shows more agreement to the statement

Table 3: IS 300 Spring 2017 Position Statement Results

as compared to the male students. For example, in 2016 all of the female students (100%) in the experiment section found the interaction with IS 471 students *extremely helpful* compared to a 77% male positive response (Figure 6). The next year (2017), we also saw a 100% response in the helpful side compared to a 87% male positive response. (Figure 7)

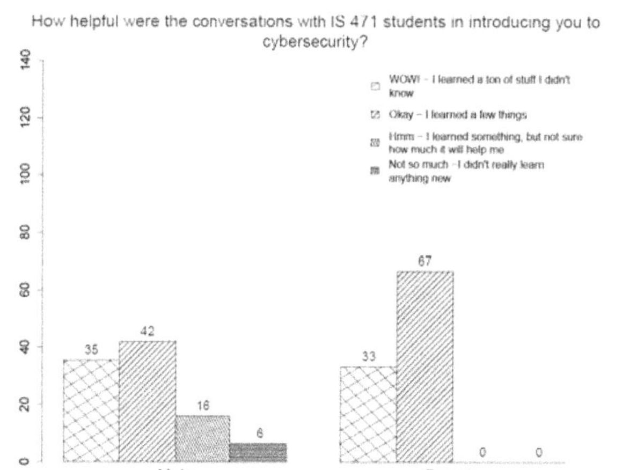

Figure 6: Helpfulness of Interactions 2016, IS 300E Females Vs. Males

Female students in the experiment section also show equal or higher increased interest in cybersecurity issues as a result of their conversation with IS 471 students as compared to the male students of the same section. When comparing the responses to their female counterparts from the control section, we also observed the evidence of positive effect of peer mentoring. In response to the question *"Do you know what is cybersecurity"*, the female students from the experiment section show 60% knowledge gain compared to 29% knowledge gain by the male students (in 2017, figure 8). Without the peer mentoring intervention, the knowledge gain increases are 23% and 37% for female and male students respectively

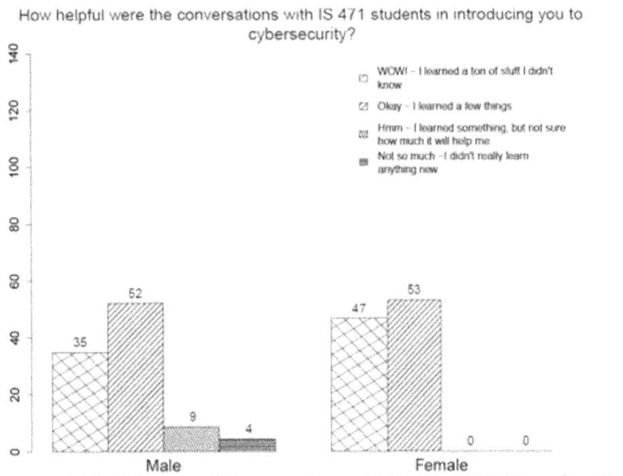

Figure 7: Helpfulness of Interactions 2017, IS 300E Females Vs. Males

(figure 9). The increased knowledge gains appear to greatly influence the responses regarding the interests in cybersecurity learning and career choice for female students. The responses to the question *"Are you interested in learning more about cybersecurity?"* is much more varied in the female students in the experiment section compared to males in contrast to the same comparison on control section (Figure 10 and 11).

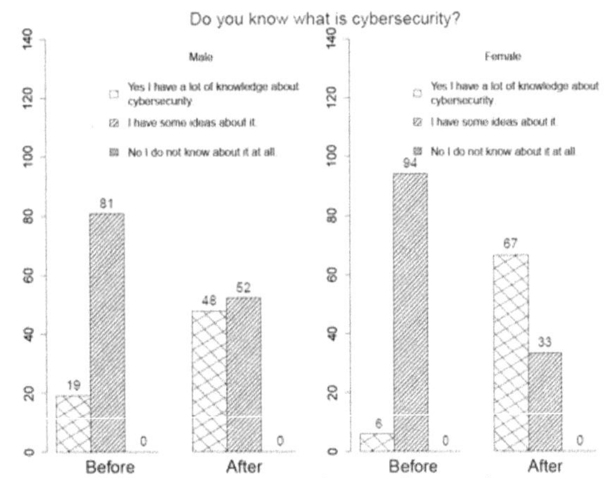

Figure 8: 2017, IS300E: Do you know what is cybersecurity?

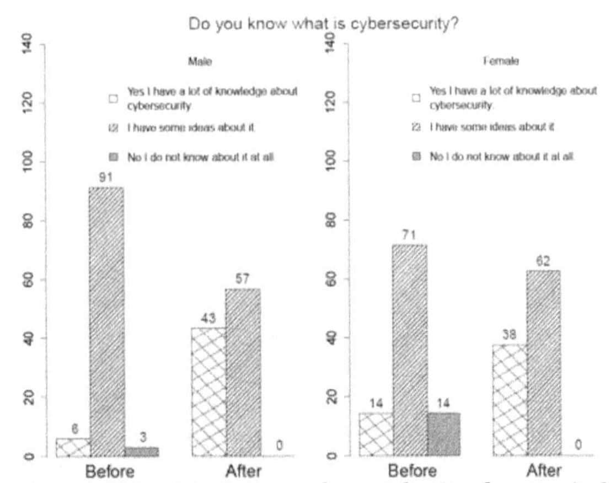

Figure 9: 2017 IS300C: Do you know what is cybersecurity?

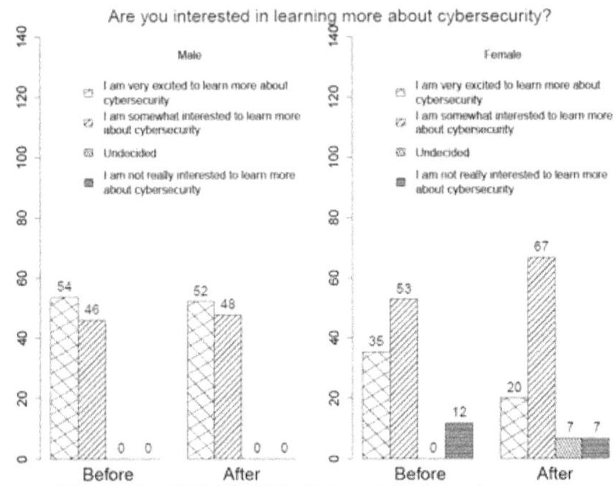

Figure 10: 2017 IS300E: Interest in learning more

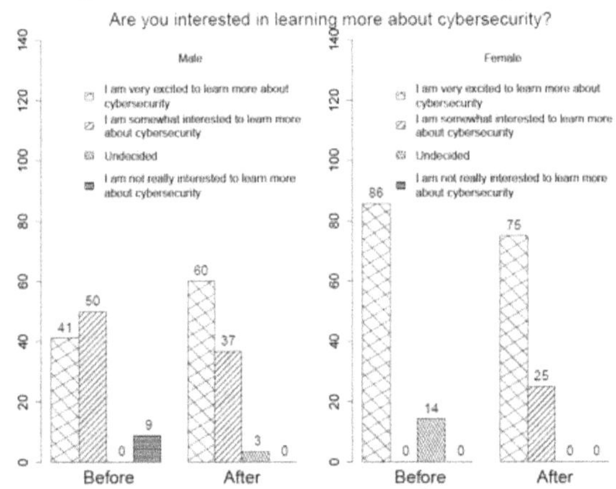

Figure 11: 2017 IS300C: Interest in learning more

These show that female students are much more receptive to the peer mentoring interventions and they are more likely to make more rigorous informed decisions on further cybersecurity study and careers compared to their male counterparts.

3.3 Grade Analysis of the Cybersecurity Assignment

IS 300 students from both control and experiment sections were given two assignments on cybersecurity throughout the semester. The first assignment was on *types of cyber attacks*, where the students were asked to write an essay on a specific type of cyber attack from a predefined list. They were asked to provide a description of the attack, example incidents, commonly affected businesses and preventive measures against the attack. The second assignment was a *cyber attack case study* where the students were asked to write an essay on a recent cyber attack incident. They were asked to provide the background, estimated damage, targeted audience, resolution and lessons learned from this case study. The difference between the experiment and control section was that the IS 300E students attended presentations made by IS 471 students on multiple *types of cyber attacks* and *case studies* prior to these two assignments. The assignments were graded by the same instructor who taught both the control and the experiment section during that same semester.

On the first *types of cyber-attack* assignment, the IS 300 students from the control section have slightly higher class average and lower standard deviation than the experiment section, but at the later part of the semester when they are given the *case study* assignment, they fall behind compared to the students from the experiment section. For the *types of attack* assignment, the control section students may be able to find adequate information over the traditional Internet resources, but the *attack case study* assignment is much more complex in nature; the IS 300E students are possibly able to gain more knowledge here, as they attend the presentations and accompanying Q/A sessions from the IS 471 students. They are able to better understand these complex issues in contrast to the students from the control section who can only use self guided research as the primary resource. This pattern is observable in both 2016 and 2017, experiment section's average score increases in the second assignment and variance goes down, the control section exhibits the the opposite trend in both years.

4 CONCLUSION & FUTURE WORKS

In this paper we outlined results of two years of a peer mentoring study. An earlier study was introduced in [12]. The compilation of two years of data helped to validate the results from the 2016 study; that the students receiving peer mentoring gain more overall knowledge about cybersecurity issues and careers and are able to make more informed decisions about their career choices. Having more overall positive responses from female students under peer mentoring is also a very promising result, given the general lower percentage of females in cybersecurity and in general STEM careers [21]. The works presented here are just a small portion of the full analysis being done on the two years of data collected. We did not discuss the text analysis comparisons (readability, expressiveness and sentiment analysis) of the essays written by the students of both the experiment and control groups. In the upcoming spring 2018, we plan to use improved questionnaires to better understand the difference in the self-reported change in interest vs the derived change in interest in cybersecurity of the IS 300 students. We also plan to investigate a measure of knowledge gain between the groups to avoid potential false positives and incorporate robust statistical analysis. The increased interest in cybersecurity could be further examined to determine if the interest resulted in an increase in enrollment or majors. It would also be interesting to conduct exit surveys over years to find how many students actually sought and got cybersecurity jobs.

5 ACKNOWLEDGMENTS

This work is funded by the National Science Foundation Grant #1515358 titled *'Integrating Cybersecurity with Undergraduate IT Programs'*

REFERENCES

[1] Alexander W. Astin. 1997. *What Matters in College: Four Critical Years Revisited.* Jossey-Bass. http://www.amazon.com/exec/obidos/redirect?tag=citeulike07-20&path=ASIN/078790838X

[2] Alexander W. Astin and Helen Astin. 1993. *Undergraduate science education: The impact of different college environments on the educational pipeline in the sciences.* Technical Report. University of California, Graduate School of Education, Higher Education Research Institute.

[3] Albert Bandura. 1995. *Self-Efficacy in Changing Societies.* Cambridge University Press, New York.

[4] Laura L. Bierema and Sharan B. Merriam. 2002. E-mentoring: Using Computer Mediated Communication to Enhance the Mentoring Process. *Innovative Higher Education* 26 (2002), 211–227. Issue 3. http://dx.doi.org/10.1023/A:1017921023103 10.1023/A:1017921023103.

[5] Toni A. Campbell and David E. Campbell. 1997. Faculty/Student Mentor Program: Effects on Academic Performance and Retention. *Research in Higher Education* 38 (1997), 727–742. Issue 6. http://dx.doi.org/10.1023/A:1024911904627 10.1023/A:1024911904627.

[6] Toni A. Campbell and David E. Campbell. 2007. Outcomes of mentoring at risk college students: gender and ethnic matching effects. *Mentoring & Tutoring: Partnership in Learning* 15, 2 (2007), 135–148. https://doi.org/10.1080/13611260601086287 arXiv:http://www.tandfonline.com/doi/pdf/10.1080/13611260601086287

[7] Janet W. Colvin and Marinda Ashman. 2010. Roles, Risks, and Benefits of Peer Mentoring Relationships in Higher Education. *Mentoring & Tutoring: Partnership in Learning* 18, 2 (2010), 121–134. https://doi.org/10.1080/13611261003678879 arXiv:http://www.tandfonline.com/doi/pdf/10.1080/13611261003678879

[8] Stephen Cooper, Wanda Dann, and Randy Pausch. 2003. Teaching objects-first in introductory computer science. In *Proceedings of the 34th SIGCSE technical symposium on Computer science education (SIGCSE '03).* ACM, New York, NY, USA, 191–195. https://doi.org/10.1145/611892.611966

[9] John P. Dugan and Susan R. Komives. 2007. *Developing leadership capacity in college students: Findings from a national study.* Technical Report. National Clearinghouse of Leadership Programs.

[10] Kassie Freeman. 1999. No services needed? The case for mentoring high-achieving african-american students. *Peabody Journal of Education* 74, 2 (1999), 15–26.

[11] Maryann Jacobi. 1991. Mentoring and Undergraduate Academic Success: A Literature Review. *Review Of Educational Research* 61, 4 (Jan. 1991), 505–532.

[12] Vandana P Janeja, Carolyn Seaman, Kerrie Kephart, Aryya Gangopadhyay, and Amy Everhart. 2016. Cybersecurity workforce development: A peer mentoring approach. In *Intelligence and Security Informatics (ISI), 2016 IEEE Conference on.* IEEE, 267–272.

[13] A. Kahveci, S.A. Southerland, and P.J. Gilmer. 2006. Retaining undergraduate women in science, mathematics, and engineering. *Journal of College Science Teaching* 36, 3 (2006), 34–38.

[14] Ross Kirkham and Damian. Ringelstein. [n. d.]. Student Peer Assisted Mentoring (SPAM): A Conceptual Frameworke-Journal of Business Education & Scholarship of Teaching. *E-Journal of Business Education & Scholarship of Teaching* 2, 2 ([n. d.]), 39–49.

[15] Susan R. Komives, Felicia C. Mainella, Susan D. Longerbeam, Laura Osteen, and Julie E. Owen. 2006. A leadership identity development model: Applications from a grounded theory. *Journal of College Student Development* 47 (2006), 401–418.

[16] George D. Kuh, Jillian Kinzie, John H. Schuh, Elizabeth J. Whitt, and And Associates. 2005. *Student Success in College: Creating Conditions That Matter* (1 ed.). Jossey-Bass. http://www.amazon.com/exec/obidos/redirect?tag=citeulike07-20&path=ASIN/0787979147

[17] William D. Mangold, LuAnn G. Bean, Douglas J. Adams, William A. Schwab, and Scott M. Lynch. 2003. Who Goes Who Stays: An Assessment of the Effect of a Freshman Mentoring and Unit Registration Program on College Persistence. *Journal of College Student Retention* 4, 2 (2003), 95–122.

[18] Barbara Moskal, Deborah Lurie, and Stephen Cooper. 2004. Evaluating the effectiveness of a new instructional approach. *SIGCSE Bulletin* 36, 1 (March 2004), 75–79. https://doi.org/10.1145/1028174.971328

[19] Ralph Pagan and Runae Edwards-Wilson. 2003. A Mentoring Program for Remedial Students. *Journal of College Student Retention* 4, 3 (2003), 207–225.

[20] Ernest T. Pascarella and Patrick T. Terenzini. 2005. *How College Affects Students : A Third Decade of Research.* Jossey-Bass. http://www.amazon.com/exec/obidos/redirect?tag=citeulike07-20&path=ASIN/0787910449

[21] Donna Peacock and Alastair Irons. 2017. Gender Inequality in Cybersecurity: Exploring the Gender Gap in Opportunities and Progression. *International Journal of Gender, Science and Technology* 9, 1 (2017), 25–44.

[22] Rodrigo Roman, Jianying Zhou, and Javier Lopez. 2013. On the features and challenges of security and privacy in distributed internet of things. *Computer Networks* 57, 10 (2013), 2266–2279.

[23] Elaine Ross-Thomas and Charles E. Bryant. 1994. Mentoring in higher education: A descriptive case study. *Education* 115, 1 (1994), 70–76.

[24] Geri Salinitri. 2005. The effects of formal mentoring on the retention rates for first-year, low-achieving students. *Canadian Journal of Education* 28, 4 (2005), 853–873.

[25] F. Sana, M. V. Pachai, and J.A. Kim. 2011. Training Undergraduate Teaching Assistants in a Peer Mentor Course. *Transformative Dialogues: Teaching & Learning Journal* 4, 3 (2011).

[26] M. Sorrentino, Diane. 2007. The SEEK mentoring program: An application of the goal-setting theory. *Journal of College Student Retention* 8, 2 (2007), 241–250.

[27] Patrick T. Terenzini, Alberto F. Cabrera, Carol L. Colbeck, John M. Parente, and Stefani A. Bjorklund. 2001. Collaborative Learning vs. Lecture/Discussion: Students' Reported Learning Gains. *Journal of Engineering Education* (2001), 123–130.

[28] Abel R. Wallace, D. and Becky R. Ropers-Huilman. 2000. Clearing a path for success: Deconstructing borders through undergraduate mentoring. *The Review of Higher Education* 24, 1 (2000), 87–102.

Evaluating Two Methods for Integrating Secure Programming Education

Madiha Tabassum, Stacey Watson, Bill Chu and Heather Richter Lipford
University of North Carolina at Charlotte
Charlotte, North Carolina
[mtabassu,swatso50,billchu,Heather.Lipford]@uncc.edu

ABSTRACT

Security vulnerabilities are still prevalent in today's software, yet many can be prevented with standard secure programming techniques. Thus, educators of future developers need to teach students not just how to program, but how to program securely. Many researchers advocate integrating secure programming knowledge and skills across the computer science curriculum. In this paper, we report the results of a study comparing two such methods: our own tool ESIDE, which provides students with security warnings on assignment code, and a security-clinic approach, a one-on-one session with a teaching assistant. Both methods suffered from challenges in incentivizing students to incorporate secure programming techniques into their code. We discuss the relative strengths and weaknesses of these methods, and the challenges of timing and motivation of secure programming education.

KEYWORDS

Secure Programming; CS Education; Motivation and Timing

ACM Reference Format:
Madiha Tabassum, Stacey Watson, Bill Chu and Heather Richter Lipford. 2018. Evaluating Two Methods for Integrating Secure Programming Education. In *SIGCSE '18: SIGCSE '18: The 49th ACM Technical Symposium on Computing Science Education, February 21–24, 2018, Baltimore , MD, USA.* ACM, New York, NY, USA, 6 pages. https://doi.org/10.1145/3159450.3159511

1 INTRODUCTION

Software security vulnerabilities are a critical problem that put both an organization and its users at the risk of security attacks and data breaches. Software developers who produce the applications are primarily responsible for preventing such vulnerabilities by employing secure coding techniques. Yet, secure programming knowledge and skills are not regularly taught in computing curricula. Security education researchers have recognized the importance of integrating security concepts throughout the computing curriculum to train future developers [6–8]. We have been investigating one approach towards achieving that goal - a tool to provide vulnerability warnings and education in the IDE while students are working on programming assignments [9, 10]. ESIDE, Educational Security in the IDE, is a Java plug-in for Eclipse which is designed to help students address potential security vulnerabilities while they write code. Through our previous evaluations, we have demonstrated that ESIDE increases student awareness and knowledge of secure programming. We have also learned the importance of incentivizing learning about secure programming, and carefully timing the introduction of such concepts and skills through our tool [9].

In this paper, we report on our most recent study to compare ESIDE against a similar approach utilizing person-to-person feedback on security for student assignments, referred to as a security clinic [2, 4]. Our goal is to understand the strengths and weaknesses of our tool-based approach, and inform design ideas to improve student engagement and interaction with our tool based on similar personalized feedback. We conducted our study in an advanced computing course during two different semesters, Fall 2016 and Summer 2017. Our results provide evidence of the relative strengths and weaknesses of these two different methods. At the same time, our study also further demonstrates how challenging it is to introduce secure programming concepts such that students have enough time and motivation to learn them while still fulfilling the primary goal of learning and practicing the course content.

2 BACKGROUND

As future software developers, students need to have sufficient knowledge of how to prevent common security vulnerabilities in order to develop secure software. "The ability to write secure code should be as fundamental to a university computer science undergraduate as basic literacy" [3], yet secure programming is often taught too little and too late in a computing program. As such, a number of researchers are investigating various methods for integrating secure coding practices into the computer science curriculum [1], through techniques such as security modules, hand-on-activities, and assignments [6–8]. However, there will likely be only a limited amount of time within any particular programming course to explicitly cover secure programming. As such, other techniques, including ours, focus on developing these skills alongside course content and programming assignments.

Bishop et al. proposed the use of security clinics to reinforce secure programming habits within assignments [2, 4]. Security clinics are similar to writing clinics. Students send their code to the clinic, the clinic members review the code and then have one-to-one discussions with students about the security implications of their code. This approach provides a rich interaction between students and clinic members, and, in their studies, they found that almost all of the participants who attended the clinic fixed the problems pointed out by the clinician. In other words, the security clinic was

SIGCSE '18, February 21–24, 2018, Baltimore , MD, USA

ACM ISBN 978-1-4503-5103-4/18/02...$15.00
https://doi.org/10.1145/3159450.3159511

found to increase awareness and understanding of the potential problems in students' code [2, 4]. Though this approach has been shown to be effective in improving student's secure programming behavior, it can also be time-consuming and resource intensive. Skilled clinicians, such as teaching assistants, need to take the time to first review each student's code and then attend a session with each student. This approach would require universities to have a sufficient number of skilled clinicians to support the program.

We have proposed a tool-based approach, where students are provided with immediate security-related instructional feedback in their IDE as they develop their assignments. In this way, secure programming knowledge can be introduced early and reinforced throughout a students' education. We provide an overview of the tool below. We have previously evaluated ESIDE in a 3-hour laboratory study[10] and two field studies: one for 14 days and another for an entire semester with students in an advanced web development course[9]. We observed a significant increase in students' secure programming awareness and knowledge with ESIDE. Students also reported an appreciation of the tool. However, we also noticed that interaction with ESIDE was very brief, and that almost no students actually modified their code to mitigate the detected vulnerabilities [9]. Not surprisingly, students were most concerned with completing functionality and did not want to impact that functionality with additional security-oriented code. Thus, we are still investigating how to best engage students with learning about and actually performing secure coding behaviors. We decided to compare our approach with the security clinic which has similar goals, yet with human interaction would presumably be more personalized and engaging to students. Thus, in this paper, we provide the results of comparing students' interactions with ESIDE versus their interactions with a teaching assistant (TA) similar to a security clinic to inform design ideas for enhancing our tool.

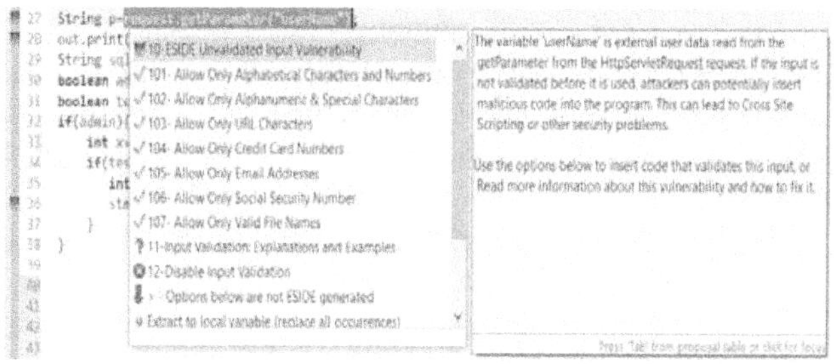

Figure 1: ESIDE provides a list of quick fixes that can be applied to address the selected warning.

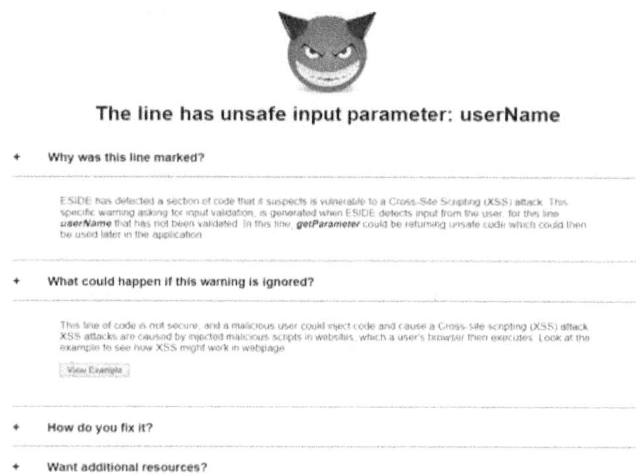

Figure 2: Portion of input validation explanation and example page.

3 ESIDE

ESIDE is a proof-of-concept Eclipse plug-in for Java, which integrates secure programming support and education into the IDE. ESIDE works in the background and provides instructional intervention the moment students write insecure code. In this way, ESIDE enhances the students' learning experience as they can directly apply the secure programming lessons they learned in the classroom to their coding practices.

ESIDE works by scanning a selected project for code patterns that match predefined heuristic rules of security vulnerabilities. Though there are many code related vulnerabilities in Java, currently ESIDE includes only a few of the most common, namely: vulnerabilities caused by the lack of input validation, output encoding, access control checks and dynamic SQL statements. If left unresolved, these code patterns can lead to real and common security vulnerabilities such as cross-site scripting (XSS) and SQL Injection.

Once ESIDE discovers a potential vulnerability, it places an icon in the left margin of the code editor beside the vulnerable line of code. Hovering over the marker reveals a short message about the type of vulnerability and a single click reveals a list of options for learning more and possibly adding code to resolve the vulnerability. Each item on the list is accompanied by an explanatory pop-up, as shown in Figure 1. For a more in-depth explanation about that vulnerability, students can go to the explanation and example page where they can read more detailed information about what the vulnerability is, what could happen if it is left unresolved, and examples of how to fix that vulnerability as shown in Figure 2.

ESIDE also auto-generates remediation code for vulnerabilities caused by lack of input validation and output encoding. Students can choose any of the remediation options as quick fixes from the pop-up list by double clicking on that option. ESIDE will then insert the corresponding input validation and output encoding routine in the code available from ESAPI, an open source secure application development library [5]. For dynamic SQL statements, ESIDE does not provide any quick fixes to generate code, and instead provides a detailed explanation about how to write prepared SQL statements [9]. ESIDE's messages have been iteratively developed over the course of multiple evaluations with students to communicate clear, simple, and concrete information about vulnerabilities and their mitigations.

4 USER STUDY METHODOLOGY

Our study aimed to examine the strengths and weaknesses of tool and in-person approaches to teaching secure programming techniques to students in a programming course. We compared ESIDE against a similar idea of a security clinic using a teaching assistant to examine the potential of both of the approaches to influence the student's secure coding practices and security awareness, with the goal of improving the design of our tool to be more engaging and effective.

The study goals are to examine the following questions:

- How do students interact with ESIDE versus the TA to learn about security implications of their code?
- How does ESIDE help students advance their secure programming knowledge versus what they learn from the TA?
- What are the questions frequently asked by the students? Can ESIDE provide the answers to those questions?
- How do students incorporate what they learned from ESIDE versus a TA into their assignments?

Student participants were recruited from our university's Network Based Application Development (NBAD) course in Fall 2016 and Summer 2017. The course was offered to both graduate and undergraduate students. In this course, students incrementally develop a Java-based web application using Java Servlet technology. While students may have taken an introduction to security course, that course does not cover secure programming.

Based on the time they signed up for, participants were assigned to use either ESIDE or meet with a TA, for a one time, 30-minute session. Students were not informed before arriving for the study whether their session would be with ESIDE or with the TA. We had two TAs for the Fall'16 semester: one was a male undergraduate student who is a former TA of our "Software Security Penetration Testing" course, and the other was a male Ph.D. student who does research in software security and had previously taught the NBAD course. For the Summer'17 study, only the Ph.D. student served as the TA. The students and the TAs signed a consent form before participating. All methods were approved by our university IRB.

4.1 First Study: Fall 2016

We recruited 23 students from the Fall 2016 NBAD course, which was an online course that semester. The course instructor assigned students to read a brief web-based tutorial, developed by us, where they were introduced to basic secure programming techniques (i.e., prepared statements, input validation and output encoding). The students received no additional secure programming training in the course. The instructor also agreed to add security requirements to the project to help incentivize students to utilize that training. However, the instructor chose to only require the use of prepared SQL statements, with no mention of input validation or other security requirements as we had requested.

The students were offered a $10 Amazon gift card for participating in the study in the initial recruitment email. Unfortunately, students did not respond to that email. A follow-up email by the instructor offered extra credit points instead of the gift card, which did prompt a number of students to volunteer for the study. However, we discovered that they did so only after their projects were completed and were about to be or already turned in. As a result of this timing, students were not at all motivated to modify their code after the study session. Thus, we decided to improve the timing of the study and run it again.

4.2 Second Study: Summer 2017

13 students from the NBAD course participated in the study in the first and second summer sessions of 2017. Both sessions had the same instructor (different from Fall 2016), who covered the same course material in a condensed 7 weeks. The students were briefly introduced to basic secure programming techniques such as prepared statements, input validation, output encoding, and access control in the course. Though there were no additional security-related requirements in the project, students were offered bonus points for both participating in the study and adding security into their code. While students did participate in the study session before turning in their project, this was still only 1 or 2 days prior to submission because of the tight summer schedule.

4.3 Study Setup

The ESIDE session took 15-20 minutes of code investigation with ESIDE and 5 minutes of a post-test and survey. Each participant was first given a brief tutorial on how ESIDE works by being shown an example vulnerability and how to fix it in a sample project. Because students did not use the Eclipse IDE for the course (Netbeans was used), we preloaded their assignment code into the Eclipse IDE with the ESIDE plug-in on our study machine prior to the session. The participants were then asked to go through their code, investigate ESIDE's warnings and explanations, and were invited to fix the vulnerabilities in their code. Interactions with the tool were captured by screen recordings and the session was audio recorded. We exported from Eclipse and emailed the projects back to the students if they made any changes and wanted the updated code.

The TA session took 15-20 minutes for discussion of the vulnerabilities in students' code and 5 minutes for a post-test and survey. The TA reviewed the student's code prior to the session for a few minutes to find vulnerabilities. We chose not to have the TA utilize ESIDE for discovering vulnerabilities as we did not want to complicate the session or have the TA overly influenced by our tool. During the session, the TA went over the code with the student, discussed the findings, and answered questions regarding how to fix the vulnerabilities and addressed any other security concerns students had. This conversation was audio recorded, and interactions with the code were captured in screen recordings. Students in both conditions were asked to share the code of their project after it was completed and submitted so we could analyze whether and how they performed any secure programming.

4.4 Post-Test and Survey

Participants from both studies were asked to take a post-test and survey at the end of their session. The post-test questions were the same for both conditions and consisted of three questions asking to identify whether a code segment is vulnerable to SQL injection or required input validation or output encoding and why, as well as three more general questions about SQL injection, input validation, and output encoding. For each question, we asked participants to mark the level of confidence in their answer using a Likert scale. The following is an example of two test questions:

(1) What is the purpose of output encoding?
(2) Why might the following declared variable require subsequent validation? String title= request.getParameter("Title");

In addition to secure coding test questions, we also asked participants for subjective impressions and recommendations about either ESIDE or the TA session.

5 RESULTS

In total, there were 36 (23|13) participants: 18 male(13|5) and 18 female(10|8) in the two studies. 28(23|5) were masters students, and 8(0|8) were undergraduates. Out of 36 students 19(12|7) were scheduled to have a TA session and the rest used ESIDE(11|5).

5.1 Summary of ESIDE Sessions

Table 1 summarizes the interactions students had with both input validation and output encoding warnings. ESIDE showed output encoding warnings for debugging print statements in the Fall'16 study, which could be considered a false positive. Thus we have decided to keep the field under "Output Encoding" for "Correct" blank for the Fall study. Overall, students saw and interacted with a large number of warnings. The number of warnings is smaller for the summer sessions, both because student projects were less complex and because we stopped showing output encoding warnings for debugging print statements. In general, students went through warnings in order and clicked on most of them. Students did not modify any code manually, instead choosing the quick fix options. However, they often chose the first option (87% for Fall'16 and 66% for Summer'17), which was a generic option to only allow letters and numbers. However, this was not always the correct option. For example, password inputs would need to also allow special characters to function properly. Students in the summer semester were more accurate in their choices, possibly because they were not as overwhelmed by the volume of warnings.

	Input validation			
	Seen (Avg.)	Clicked	Fixed	Correct
Fall'16	34.91 (SD:21.87)	74.47%	67.44%	69.11%
Summer'17	13.67 (SD:2.58)	93.90%	90.24%	80.52%
	Output Encoding			
	Seen (Avg.)	Clicked	Fixed	Correct
Fall'16	6.36 (SD:3.13)	47.14%	15.71%	
Summer'17	1.83 (SD:0.75)	100%	100%	45.45%

Table 1: Summary of input validation and output encoding warnings

We also examined student interactions with explanatory popups shown alongside the warning menu and via the "explanation and example page." In the Fall'16 study participants investigated 25.52% of the input validation warnings that were clicked and in the Summer'17 study, only 22.07% such warnings were investigated. Most of the time participants examined the labels of the quick fixes to decide which validation code to insert rather than reading any accompanying explanations. Only 4 of the participants clicked on the "explanation and example" option for an input validation warning. One did not read anything and immediately closed the page. The other 3 read the page for an average of 93.33 seconds.

Students already utilized prepared SQL statements in their code, and thus only 3 students saw warnings related to having dynamic SQL statements. Two did visit the explanation page for more than 2 minutes, and 1 student attempted to change to a prepared statement afterwards as a result. Finally, in the Summer'17 sessions students also received access control warnings. Six students saw around 4 warnings each. However, students did not seem to understand access control vulnerabilities and were mostly confused by the warnings. As a result, they ignored them and did not explore further. No students kept the changes they made with ESIDE in their final code that they turned in.

To summarize, students tended to go through all of their warnings and fixed them using the quick fixes options. However, participants did very little reading and exploring the information available with the warning. Thus, we suspect that although ESIDE is giving the students awareness about the number of vulnerabilities of their code, they are not learning enough about these vulnerabilities and how to correctly fix them.

5.2 Summary of TA Sessions

We used the screen and audio recordings to examine participants' interaction behavior with the TAs. We provided TAs with participant's code 5-10 minutes before the session. During the session, the TAs went over the code with students and discussed the identified vulnerabilities with them. They also explained vulnerabilities to students by providing both explanations of how they can be exploited by attackers in general and how specific vulnerabilities that resided in students' code affect the security of their applications. The TAs also then explained how to prevent those attacks. The TAs covered on average 3.32 specific lines of vulnerable code per participant.

In response, students asked TAs for clarification when they were confused about the explanation. In Fall'16, students ask on average 1.33 clarifying questions per session whereas in Summer'17 they asked 2.28 questions per session. The following is an example conversation between a TA and a participant:

TA: In the place where you are using a variable someone else typed in, not something that is created by the program itself. You should always use COUT or some other sort of encoding thing to prevent XSS.

Participant: Ok.

TA: Something like this. This is generated by one of your functions; you wouldn't ....

Participant: This would go in the COUT thing?

TA: You wouldn't have to put COUT into it because you are generating it by yourself. So, it's safe.

Participant: So, if something generated by something else we need to use COUT?

TA: Yes, user input. Like if you make an account with username and you wanted to say hello username. You would wanna use COUT that in case someone has put a script there or something.

Students asked questions about both security attacks and other security issues an average of 1.67 times per session, particularly about passwords, salting, and hashing. The TAs responded to students' questions by explaining with relevant examples. For example,

Student: One thing which I wanted to know is we type the password into the database. You store it somewhere right... like when a new user want to register at the website, so he needs to give his passwords, we have to encrypt it right... How would you do that?

The TA then proceeded to explain hashing and salting. Despite these examples of TA-student interaction, much of the session and conversation was driven by the TA.

The TAs discussed different types of security concepts, vulnerabilities and attacks such as cross-site scripting (XSS), SQL injection, man-in-the-middle, access control and denial of service. Information provided to the students differed a great deal between the TAs. TA1, the undergraduate who was a TA for a security class, spent most of the session seeking out vulnerable spots in the student's code by looking at the code and asking participants how the application works (on average 6 times per participant). Only a small portion of time was spent on explaining the vulnerabilities. But the time that was spent, was spent on specific vulnerable lines of code and how to fix them. In contrast, TA2, a Ph.D. student who had previously taught the course, talked about input validation, output encoding, and SQL injection in detail even if he did not find specific examples of such vulnerabilities in the student's code. In contrast with TA1, he did not spend much time learning about how the code works. Instead, TA2 spoke significantly more, and covered concepts more generally. Thus, he treated his sessions more like general education sessions, while TA1 used his sessions more to find and fix specific issues in the code. This experience emphasized how different a session could be based upon the clinician, and how and what they were trained to provide students. Again though, the effectiveness of the session was greatly reduced by the lack of incentives for students to remember and utilize what they learned. In the Summer'17 study, only the second TA conducted the session, and we instructed him to be more code specific and to describe the security problems by pointing out the exploitable lines of code.

As with the ESIDE sessions, we found no evidence that any students modified their code based on their TA session.

5.3 Survey Results

The survey asked students what they liked and disliked about their sessions. Students in both conditions were quite positive. ESIDE participants commented on the instant warnings and quick fixes:

"It takes and checks all the lines of the code and gives users good suggestions to improve their code. That's pretty good."

Similarly TA session participants reported that they like the suggestions given and the opportunity to ask questions:

"Information was clearly delivered. Had the opportunity to ask questions to the tutor and get instant answers."

However, a number of the participants (n=8) thought the TA session was not long enough, and the explanations provided were not detailed enough to clearly understand the idea. One stated:

"It did feel just a little rushed, fifteen minutes is hardly enough to look for every security flaw that was present."

Most students performed poorly on the knowledge questions, answering only about 50% correctly, with no real difference between sessions. This demonstrates that students did not learn much about secure programming within their class materials, and not surprisingly, did not learn much in such a short study session.

6 DISCUSSION

As with our previous evaluations[9, 10], students responded positively to their interaction with ESIDE. They were equally positive regarding their interactions with a TA. However, we already knew that at least modest incentives are required to motivate students to learn about and perform secure programming in their assignments [9]. The problems we ran into with the Fall'16 study setup and timing only reiterated this. Thus, despite our efforts, students were still not very motivated to learn and apply any secure programming skills. This limits the effectiveness of either of these methods, and what we could learn in our study. Still, we have some evidence of the relative strengths and weaknesses of each method and we learned additional lessons regarding the incentives and timing of secure programming education.

6.1 Awareness, Knowledge, and Behaviors

The most significant difference we found between the ESIDE and TA sessions were the number of vulnerabilities covered. ESIDE marked on average 33.88 vulnerable lines of code, whereas TAs pointed out only 3.32 lines of code per session. Students visited most of the ESIDE warnings and fixed many by quick fixes, giving them insight about the volume of security flaws in their code and also how to fix them. In contrast, the TAs pointed out only a few lines of vulnerable code and described vulnerabilities and remediation techniques more generally, leaving students to write the fixes by themselves if they desired.

Yet, students talking with the TA heard more information about vulnerabilities and could ask clarifying questions. ESIDE students rarely read any of the additional explanations or examples. Thus, using ESIDE may provide greater awareness of the number of vulnerabilities, and help students quickly implement fixes. Yet, students talking with a TA seem to have a greater chance of actually understanding vulnerabilities and their potential remediation. In addition, students had the chance to ask the TAs any security related questions, including concepts not related to secure programming. This further helps students implement security in their code. For example:

"Will there be any kind of attack if my website is linking to some external websites? Can something happen over there?"

Overall, students asked 32 questions to the TAs, and ESIDE could potentially answer only 14 of them. We could modify ESIDE to answer more of those questions and to restructure the information provided by ESIDE to answer questions rather than just provide explanations of menu options. However, students still have to notice ESIDE's content and be willing to spend time reading it.

Because of the lack of sufficient incentives, no students actually modified the code they turned in to include secure programming. Thus, both methods suffer from the same issues of how to go beyond awareness to actually impact student behavior.

6.2 Incentivizing Students

The first challenge we faced is how to incentivize and influence students to learn and use secure programming techniques where the primary need is to learn and practice the course content. Despite our efforts to incentivize students to use that knowledge, we struggled to actually achieve this. Both of the instructors we worked with were more willing to give extra credit as incentives instead of making security a requirement for the assignment. In the Fall'16 study, it was not possible for us to determine whether students would have added input validation or output encoding functions in their final project because of the timing of the study. However, we suspect that they would not have because there was no incentive for them to do so. Despite the bonus points offered in the summer sessions, none of the students who participated in the study incorporated secure programming changes in their final assignments. Thus, extra credit points did motivate students to participate in our study, yet were not sufficient to actually influence them to do secure programming. Some students reported that they already had good enough grades on the project, and did not need the bonus points. Others reported a fear of breaking the functionality if they tried to change the code to improve the security of their project.

Bonus points tend to be useful only if students complete the basic requirements first and, as with our participants, will be ignored if not needed. Thus, only a small group of students with sufficient functionality may be motivated to work towards bonus points to improve their grade. Additionally, using bonus points only reinforces the notion that security-related concepts are an add-on and not integral to the course content.

In future studies, we would like to convince course instructors to make security a requirement in some way, and not simply use bonus points. However, security-related concepts will only ever be a small percentage of the learning objectives in a programming course. Thus, secure programming requirements will also only be worth a small amount of credit towards the final grade. We will do additional research to understand the incentives and rewards that can influence students of all levels to practice secure programming.

6.3 Timing

In both semesters, instructors provided some in class instructions about secure programming. Though that motivated students to participate in the study, they did not employ the secure programming techniques they learned in their assignment code. Beyond incentives, we believe another reason was that students participated in the study at the end of the semester. Students did not have enough time to work on the lessons they learned from the study and were not confident enough to add the security fixes without breaking the functionality of their project. On the other hand, we found from our previous studies[9], students tend to ignore secure coding if introduced earlier in the semester before they sufficiently understand how to construct the program. We are still investigating the sweet spot for introducing secure programming concepts when they make the most sense, and then reinforcing them within assignments.

If we can sufficiently incentivize students, we believe ESIDE has the potential to consistently reinforce secure programming knowledge, as students can work incrementally on fixing vulnerabilities as they work on their assignments. Yet, they may merely learn to rely on a tool instead of learning the concepts more deeply. We have yet to determine how this will compare with sessions with a security clinician. A TA could meet students at their level of understanding and engage students at the moment they think they are ready. However, students would then be responsible for utilizing that knowledge on their own. We plan to further investigate how timing and different incentives effect student behavior with these two approaches to be able to provide guidance for faculty and course designers on how to best integrate secure programming instructions into their courses.

7 ADDITIONAL LIMITATIONS

Our study was conducted in a laboratory and has several limitations. First, the sample size is still small although on par with other similar studies. Moreover, most of the participants were graduate students from the same course. Student interactions might be different with a larger balanced sample of both novice and advanced students. We also think that students might exhibit more interaction and knowledge about secure programming if the duration of the sessions were longer. Students were also voluntarily participating in the study, rather than using the techniques as a natural part of their course, which may have changed their interaction with the tool or TA.

8 CONCLUSION

The risk of security attacks can be reduced by following secure programming guidelines during software development. Developers need to be experienced and knowledgeable enough to apply these guidelines in their work. Hence, educating current and future developers about secure coding guidelines is a necessary yet challenging task. Both ESIDE and security clinics have the potential to train students as they learn to program, without adding to their existing course load. Though we believe ESIDE raises awareness about security vulnerabilities, students do not yet engage much with the tool due to the challenges of effectively timing and incentivizing secure programming training. We will continue to study these issues and approaches in future courses to provide better guidance as to how to effectively teach students to program securely.

ACKNOWLEDGMENTS

We would like to thank all the participants, TAs and instructors for their time. This work is funded partially by NSF-DGE #1523041 and NSF-CNS #1318854.

REFERENCES

[1] S. Azadegan, M. Lavine, M. O'Leary, A. Wijesinha, and M. Zimand. 2003. *A Dedicated Undergraduate Track in Computer Security Education.* Springer US, Boston, MA, 319–331.

[2] M. Bishop. 2010. A Clinic for "Secure" Programming. *IEEE Security Privacy* 8, 2 (March 2010), 54–56.

[3] M. Bishop and D. A. Frincke. 2005. Teaching secure programming. *IEEE Security Privacy* 3, 5 (Sept 2005), 54–56.

[4] M. Bishop and BJ Orvis. 2006. A clinic to teach good programming practices. In *Proceedings of the 10th Colloquium for Information Systems Security Education.* 168–174.

[5] OWASP Foundation. 2016. OWASP enterprise security api. https://www.owasp.org/index.php/Category:OWASP_ Enterprise_Security_API. (2016).

[6] K. Nance. 2009. Teach Them When They Aren't Looking: Introducing Security in CS1. *IEEE Security Privacy* 7, 5 (Sept 2009), 53–55.

[7] Blair Taylor and Shiva Azadegan. 2006. Threading Secure Coding Principles and Risk Analysis into the Undergraduate Computer Science and Information Systems Curriculum. In *Proceedings of the 3rd Annual Conference on Information Security Curriculum Development (InfoSecCD '06).* ACM, New York, NY, USA, 24–29.

[8] Michael Weeks, Yi Pan, and Yanqing Zhang. 2016. Increasing Security Awareness in Undergraduate Courses with Labware. In *Proceedings of the 47th ACM Technical Symposium on Computing Science Education (SIGCSE '16).* ACM, New York, NY, USA, 687–687.

[9] Michael Whitney, Heather Lipford-Richter, Bill Chu, and Jun Zhu. 2015. Embedding Secure Coding Instruction into the IDE: A Field Study in an Advanced CS Course. In *Proceedings of the 46th ACM Technical Symposium on Computer Science Education (SIGCSE '15).* ACM, New York, NY, USA, 60–65.

[10] Jun Zhu, Heather Richter Lipford, and Bill Chu. 2013. Interactive Support for Secure Programming Education. In *Proceeding of the 44th ACM Technical Symposium on Computer Science Education (SIGCSE '13).* ACM, New York, NY, USA, 687–692.

Using Virtual Machine Introspection for Operating Systems Security Education

Manish Bhatt
University of New Orleans
mbhatt@uno.edu

Irfan Ahmed
University of New Orleans
irfan@cs.uno.edu

Zhiqiang Lin
The Ohio State University
lin.3021@osu.edu

ABSTRACT

Historically, hands-on cybersecurity exercises helped reinforce the basic cybersecurity concepts. However, most of them focused on the user level attacks and defenses and did not provide a convenient way of studying the kernel level security. Since OS kernels provide foundations for applications, any compromise to OS kernels will lead to a computer that cannot be trusted. Moreover, there has been a great interest in using virtualization to profile, characterize, and observe kernel events including security incidents. Virtual Machine Introspection (VMI) is a technique that has been deeply investigated in intrusion detection, malware analysis, and memory forensics. Inspired by the great success of VMI, we used it to develop hands-on labs for teaching kernel level security. In this work, we present three VMI-based labs on (1) stack-based buffer overflow, (2) direct kernel object manipulation (DKOM), and (3) kernel integrity checker which have been made available online. Then, we analyze the differences in approaches taken by VMI-based labs and traditional labs and conclude that VMI-based labs are better as opposed to traditional labs from a teaching standpoint because they provide more visibility than the traditional labs and superior ability to manipulate kernel memory which provides more insight into kernel security concepts.

ACM Reference format:
Manish Bhatt, Irfan Ahmed, and Zhiqiang Lin. 2018. Using Virtual Machine Introspection for Operating Systems Security Education. In *Proceedings of SIGCSE'18, February 21–24, 2018, Baltimore, MD, USA, SIGCSE '18: The 49th ACM Technical Symposium on Computing Science Education,* 6 pages. DOI: https://doi.org/10.1145/3159450.3159606

1 INTRODUCTION

The hands-on cybersecurity exercises have always helped students reinforce the core concepts of cyberattacks and defenses. They typically involve running malware, exploits, and/or security tools on machines to generate or thwart local/remote cyberattacks. Unfortunately, the traditional hands-on exercises fail to provide a deep understanding of cyberattacks, and are mostly limited to teach the execution steps of the attacks. For instance, the Zeus bot injects an executable in `svchost.exe` in MS Windows. When students perform the hands-on exercise that requires them to infect a benign machine with Zeus bot executable, the changes in the memory (made by the bot) are mostly not transparent to students. These changes are essential to understanding the underlying concept of the Zeus bot infection.

To address this problem, we propose to adopt and utilize virtual machine introspection (VMI) [14] (currently offered by many popular hypervisors such as Xen, and KVM) for developing more effective hands-on exercises (than traditional approaches). In a virtualized environment, VMI with the help of a hypervisor allows a privileged host to examine and directly modify the physical memory and hard disk content of a guest virtual machine (VM) from outside the VM.

Our approach uses VMI to eliminate unnecessary abstraction in the hands-on exercises by letting students make the changes (such as mentioned in the Zeus bot example) directly to the memory of a VM via read/write memory operations, and more importantly, observe their effect within or outside the VM. In particular, VMI is useful to develop the challenging hands-on exercises on operating-system (OS) kernel-level attacks. For instance, an exercise may involve loading a malicious kernel module and then, observe its impact on the infected computer system. VMI allows students to experience sufficient low-level details of the target malicious functionality of the module including the exploitation of the internals of an OS kernel.

In this work, we develop three VMI-based hands-on exercises and make them available on gitlab [3]. The two exercises focus on the techniques employed for a kernel attack (i.e., DKOM or direct kernel object manipulation) and defense (i.e., kernel patch protection, a.k.a. PatchGuard). The third exercise is on buffer overflow. We present significant implementation details of these exercises and compare them with their respective traditional hands-on exercises using four characteristics, i.e., completeness, flexibility, portability, and creativity (previously identified by Joyce *et al.* [18] for evaluating hands-on exercises). The analysis results show that VMI-based labs are better as opposed to traditional labs from a teaching standpoint because they provide more visibility and superior access to low-level details (such as the operating system internals) than the traditional labs.

The rest of the paper is organized as follows: Section 2 discusses the related work. Section 3 presents a general framework for developing VMI-based hands-on exercises followed by the implementation of three VMI-based security labs in section 4. Section 5 presents a comparative analysis between VMI and traditional hands-on exercises. Section 6 concludes the paper.

2 BACKGROUND/RELATED WORK

Hypervisor or Virtual Machine Monitor (VMM) is the foundation of the virtualization technology for system developers to achieve unprecedented levels of security, reliability, and manageability mainly because of their ability to package software in a contained environment, and also to shift the state of a VM to outside VMM to isolate the in-VM and the out-of-VM programs. In recent years,

SIGCSE'18, February 21–24, 2018, Baltimore, MD, USA
© 2018 ACM. ISBN 978-1-4503-5103-4/18/02...$15.00
DOI: https://doi.org/10.1145/3159450.3159606

VMMs have been widely adopted for intrusion detection, malware analysis, memory forensics, and also for cybersecurity education-particularly in virtualized computer labs.

2.1 Virtual Machine Introspection

Hypervisors were first introduced in the 1960s [23]. While this computing model was originally designed to logically divide the resources for time sharing of different applications in mainframes, it now underpins today's cloud computing and data centers. In addition to pushing computer paradigm for multi-tasking to multi-OS, hypervisors also pushed system monitoring from traditional in-VM monitoring to out-of-VM monitoring [2]. Because guest OSs run on virtual resources [1] provided by the VMM, system designers gain new opportunities for flexibility and control since VMM is essentially a software layer and software is easy to monitor, migrate and modify. Through extracting and reconstructing the guest OS states in the host, the out-of-VM instrumentation of the OS known as VMI becomes possible which empowers the monitoring system to control, isolate, interpose, inspect, secure and manage a VM from the outside [6]. VMI based monitors, as opposed to traditional in-VM monitors, have been widely adopted because they run at higher privilege level and are isolated from attacks in the guest OSs they monitor and can trap all the guest OS events as they are one layer below the guest OS. VMI has been widely used in security applications ranging from read-only introspection [11, 14] to writable reconfiguration, repair and management [12, 13, 19], passive intrusion detection [17] to active prevention [22] etc.

2.2 Virtualization in Education

Because of the efficient support for scalability and diversity in a lab infrastructure at a much lower cost, universities prefer virtual computing labs to physical computing labs. For instance, Cavanagah *et. al.* [5] used VMware ESXi to create a virtualized information security laboratory mainly for the purpose of organizing Maine Cyber Defence Competition using a Dell PowerEdge R610 machine with Dual Xenon E5620 2.4 GHz processors, each with 12MB cache, 24GB RAM, and a 146GB RAID-configured storage system of 6 disks, and a quad-port Gigabit NIC which as opposed to creating a Physical Lab. Nance *et. al.* [20] described virtual labs established in Carnegie Mellon University(CMU) and the University of Alaska Fairbanks using VMware server for packaging hands-on training materials available on demand. Burd *et. al.*[4] described the virtual lab in the University of New Mexico using VMware ESX and VMware Lab Manager where the lab manager created and managed configurations with required virtual machines to support specific courses or lab exercises. Moreover, some universities such as the United States Military Academy(USMA) and the University of New Mexico(UNM) have converted their physical Windows XP labs to virtual labs [4]. Hay *et. al.*[16] developed ASSERT using the university's surplus computers stored in a warehouse. Du *et. al.* developed SEED (SEcurity EDucation) project [8, 9] for cybersecurity education. This project resulted in the development of over 30 SEED labs to cover topics like vulnerabilities, attacks, software security, system security, network security, web security, authentication, cryptography, etc.

In summary, the primary use of virtualization has been to package labs. To the best of our knowledge, VMI has never been explored for cybersecurity education. This paper is the first effort to use the capabilities provided by VMI for improving the pedagogical efforts and instruction in cybersecurity education.

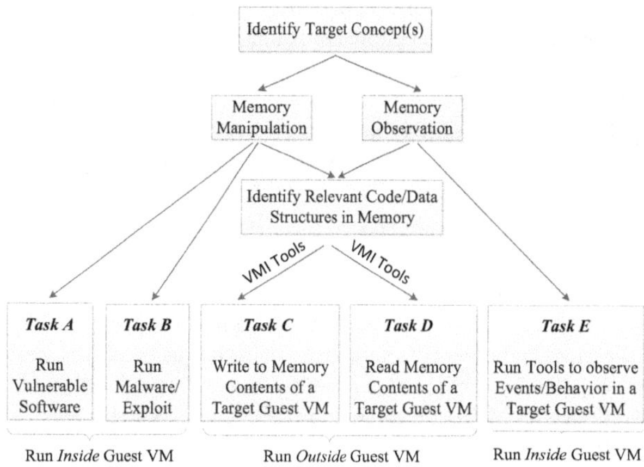

Figure 1: Framework for developing a VMI-based cybersecurity lab exercise. A task is run either inside or outside a target guest VM. Outside tasks are executed via VMI. Only relevant tasks are included in a lab exercise and can be executed in any defined order.

3 FRAMEWORK FOR DEVELOPING VMI LABS

In figure 1, we present a generalized framework for developing a VMI-based security lab. It consists of two main components: memory manipulation, and memory observation. *Memory manipulation* refers to the tools and techniques that change the contents of the memory actively when they are run, while *memory observation* monitors memory contents passively.

To develop a VMI lab exercise, a target concept is identified and further elaborated and broken down into tasks to comprehend a complete kernel security concept. Each task primarily must be either for memory manipulation or memory observation and can be implemented as one of the five task categories described at the lowest level of the framework. Tasks C and D implement tools that use VMI to write to and read from the memory from outside a target guest VM. The tools need to locate the pertinent memory locations containing target code and data structures for a lab exercise. We address this problem in two ways: first by using a debugger in a target guest VM; second by using the tools provided with a VMI library.

Tasks A, B, and E do not use VMI, execute directly inside a guest VM, and are included in the framework to provide flexibility of incorporating standard tools and techniques in a hands-on exercise. Tasks A and B run benign (potentially vulnerable) software, and malware in a guest VM respectively. They are placed under memory manipulation component and are useful to directly involve a target software in an exercise. For instance, a Zeus bot executable is run in a benign VM, and its changes (infection) are observed using a VMI tool (in Task D) from outside the VM.

On the contrary, Task E runs tools (such as debugger and OS utilities) in a guest VM to observe its events and behavior. For instance, a VMI tool (in Task C) mimics a rootkit functionality and alters the memory contents of a guest VM accordingly. The impact of the changes is observed inside the target guest VM using the standard monitoring tools in Task E.

It is worth mentioning that since our focus is to leverage VMI capabilities, it is essential that a hands-on exercise must include at least one of the Tasks C and D containing VMI tools. Otherwise, the hands-on exercise would be closer to traditional hands-on approach.

4 VMI-BASED HANDS-ON EXERCISES

We developed three VMI-based cybersecurity lab exercises; one is on buffer overflow (a user-land attack), and the other two are on 1) direct kernel object manipulation (a kernel-land attack), and 2) Kernel patch protection a.k.a., PatchGuard (a kernel-land defence), introduced by Microsoft in Windows OS to check the integrity of kernel code and critical data structures. The exercises are publicly available at gitlab [3]; each includes a comprehensive tutorial.

Lab Setup. The exercises are developed and tested on a desktop computer running a Ubuntu 16.04 facilitated XEN-hypervisor 4.6.5. A target VM running 64-bit MS Windows 7 is instantiated. For VMI support, LibVMI [21] library is installed at the host OS, Ubuntu. The VMI tools created for the exercises run on the host OS and use LibVMI to access the RAM content of the target VM from outside.

This section presents both traditional and VMI-based approaches for the exercises and further describes their shortcomings and advantages.

4.1 Stack-based Buffer Overflow Lab

The *objective* of the lab is to make students acquainted with a popular user-mode attack known as stack-based buffer overflow. The main *target concept* for the exercise is that the attack modifies the return instruction pointer in a stack-frame to redirect the system control flow to an unexpected (potentially malicious) code.

4.1.1 Traditional Buffer Overflow Labs. In a normal program execution, when a function is called, the pointer to the next instruction (a.k.a return instruction pointer) is stored in a stack frame along with any arguments. A local buffer that stores user input is also located in the frame. If a program has buffer overflow vulnerability, it accepts more user input than the buffer size. An attacker exploits the vulnerability to overwrite the pointer to make the program jump to the attacker's intended location in the memory. Figure2 shows the state of the stack before and after the buffer overflow exploitation.

For a typical lab exercise, students are provided with a vulnerable program and a well-crafted input string that exploits the vulnerability to redirect the system control flow to some other function in the program. To perform the exercise, the students provide the input string to the program and observe the output generated from the redirected function.

The exercise is sufficient to demonstrate that a buffer overflow vulnerability can be exploited. However, the students do not directly experience the modification of the pointer.

4.1.2 VMI-based Buffer Overflow Lab. In our VMI-based exercise, students observe the current value of the return address in the stack and can directly modify it to another function pointer and then, observe the change in the vulnerable program behavior.

The whole exercise comprises of the following tasks; each is derived from the framework (refer to Section 3).

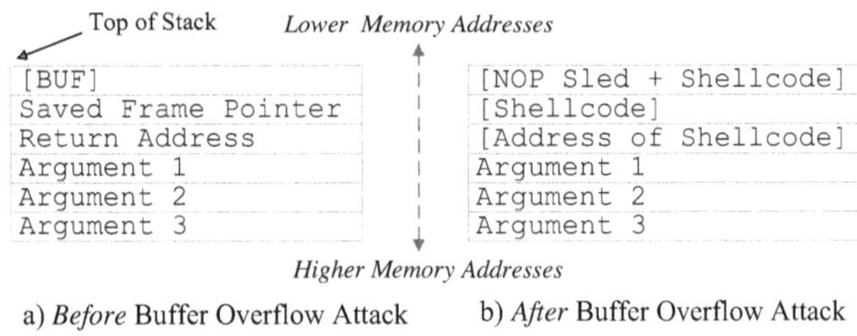

Figure 2: Program stack, *before* and *after* buffer overflow attack

(Task A). This task consists of a vulnerable C program consisting of three functions, viz. `main()`, `vulnerable_function()`, and `not_called()`. The `vulnerable_function` is using `strcpy` function that has a buffer overflow vulnerability. The `not_called` function is using a system call to execute *calc.exe* to spawn a calculator.
(Task D). This task consists of a VMI program that reads the process memory in the target VM, fetches the relevant stack frame contents and displays them to the terminal. The program enables the students to observe the current value of the return address pointer when needed.
(Task C). This task consist of a VMI program that accesses the location of the return address pointer and replaces it with the address of the `not_called` function. It causes the execution of the program to be redirected to the `not_called` function and pops open a calculator.

The program has to identify the address of the `not_called` function, and the location of the return address on the stack. Since the program runs outside the VM, it suffers from the *semantic gap* problem, which is the problem of extracting high-level semantic information from low-level data sources like the OS memory[7]. To resolve this issue, we use `GDB` debugger and MinGW C compiler running inside the target VM to leak the required information to the VMI program.

Execution of the Tasks. Students begin with Task A and run the vulnerable C program inside the target VM, followed by the Task D to obtain the current value of the return address pointer. Then, the students pause the vulnerable program and run Task C that provides the address of the `not_called` function that they are asked to note down. Now, the students resume the vulnerable program until the second pause to update the return address location on the stack with the not_called function address. Students, then, rerun Task D to verify the modification of the return address and then execute the vulnerable program to completion. As opposed to what the program was supposed to be doing, the students see that the vulnerable program now spawns the calculator.

The VMI exercise eliminates unnecessary abstractions by directly focusing on the memory content, and provides better ability to manipulate the stack-space and memory as opposed to the traditional buffer overflow exercise.

4.2 Direct Kernel Object Manipulation Lab

The *objective* of the lab is to make students acquainted with the Direct Kernel Object Manipulation (DKOM) attack. The main *target*

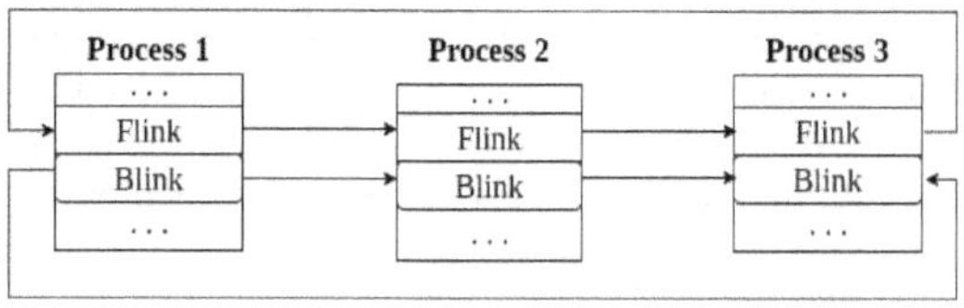

(a) **Active Process List entries in a normal state.**

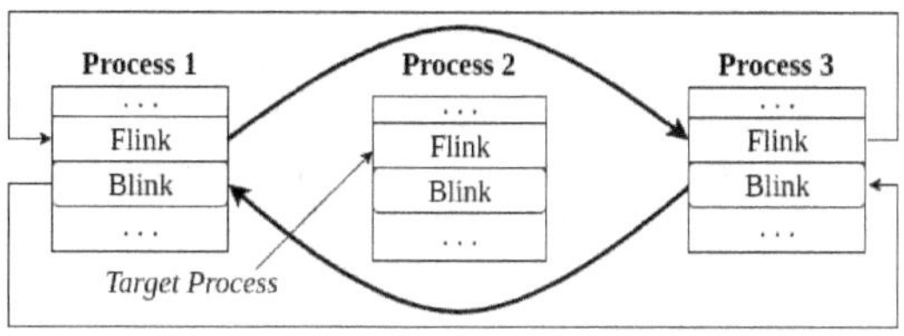

(b) **Process 2 has been unhooked from the List.**

Figure 3: Illustration of DKOM.

Data: receivedPid
Result: process with receivedPid absent or unhooked
initialization;
while *receivedPid not equals PidFromList* **do**
  Keep going to the next process;
  if *nextPid = receivedPid* **then**
    a = previousProcess;
    b = nextProcess;
    a.flink = currentprocess.flink;
    b.blink = currentprocess.blink;
    return unhooked;
  else
    go back to the beginning of current section;
  end
  return absent;
end
Algorithm 1: Algorithm to replicate DKOM functionality

concept for the exercise is that the attack manipulates the doubly-linked list of the processes (maintained by OS kernel) to hide a target process from the list.

4.2.1 Traditional DKOM Lab. A typical hands-on exercise (in MS Windows environment) involve spawning a notepad application, for instance, using Windows Task Manager to verify that the notepad process is present, and then running the FU rootkit to hide the process and further observe that the notepad process becomes hidden in Windows Task Manager. FU rootkit is a kernel module that makes changes in the doubly-linked list to hide the target process. Each node of the list is represented by the EPROCESS data structure.

The exercise is useful to demonstrate that the rootkits can hide OS processes. However, students do not directly experience or observe the state changes in the process list, which is key to understanding the DKOM.

4.2.2 VMI-based DKOM Lab. In our VMI-based exercise, students traverse the doubly-linked list of processes, observe the forward and backward pointers in each node, and then perform DKOM by directly manipulating these pointers to hide the target process.

We derive the following tasks from the framework described in Section 3. The whole exercise comprises of these tasks.
(Task A). This task runs a notepad or a similar benign program.
(Task D). MS Windows maintains the active process list in a doubly-linked circular linked-list. Each process in the list has a link to the next process, called forward link(`Flink`) and also a link to the previous process, referred to as `Blink`. This task consists of a VMI program that traverses the list and displays the name of each process, and its corresponding pointer values of `Flink` and `Blink`.
(Task C). The task consists of a VMI program that takes in the process id of the process the student wants to hide. Then, it iterates through the active process list and finds the process. Now, the program creates references to the previous process and the following process, and maps the `Flink` of the previous process to the address in `Flink` of the current process and the `Blink` of the previous process to the `Blink` of the current process as shown in the Figure 3 and Algorithm 1.
(Task B). This task runs FU rootkit inside a target VM running MS Windows OS.
(Task E). This task observes the list of processes inside the VM using monitoring tools such as the Windows Task Manager and tasklist.

Execution of the Tasks. Students begin with Task A to instantiate the OS process of a benign program followed by Task D to go through the process list and identify a target process and observe the `Flink` and `Blink` pointers of the target process and its adjust nodes. At this stage, students perform DKOM either via Task C or Task B. Task C allows students to modify the pointer values in the list via VMI directly. Task B runs FU rootkit and is useful to provide experience with real malware. In either case, students perform Task D to verify the intended modifications in the list. Task E can be used to corroborate further that the target process is invisible to the user applications in the target VM such as Windows Task Manager or tasklist utilities.

4.3 Kernel Modules Integrity Checker Lab

The *objective* of the lab is to make students acquainted with the functionality of Kernel Patch Protection in MS Windows, also known as PatchGuard.

The main *target concept* for the exercise is that the kernel code and critical data structures do not change once setup in the memory; at this stage, any changes in their memory content indicate unwarranted and unsupported patching or hooking.

The rationale behind PatchGuard is that some 32-bit device drivers used to modify the behavior of Windows in unsupported ways. For instance, they patch the system call table to intercept system calls or patch the kernel image in memory to add functionality to specific internal functions. To prevent these kinds of changes, MS Windows introduced PatchGuard. Its job is to attempt to deter common techniques for patching or hooking a system. The components that are protected by PatchGuard [25] include ntoskrnl.exe, global descriptor table (GDT), interrupt descriptor table (IDT), and system service descriptor table (SSDT) or syscall table.

```
Data: moduleName
Result: Is module compromised?
initialization;
dump all modules in ./original/ folder;
store names of all modules in module-list;
check initial integrity status of modules and store it in a file;
pick a non-essential kernel module like srv2.sys;
modify n-bytes in memory for srv2.sys;
check integrity status again;
if status has changed then
    use xen-hvmcrash utility to crash VM;
    return module crashed;
else
    return module not compromised;
end
```

Algorithm 2: Algorithm for Kernel Module Integrity Checker

The PatchGuard computes and compares hashes of the kernel code and data structures periodically. If any changes are detected, it crashes the system with `0x109-CRITICAL-STRUCTURE-CORRUPTION`.

4.3.1 Traditional PatchGuard Lab. Traditionally, PatchGuard functionality was demonstrated to the students via writing a kernel driver to make changes in SSDT/IDT on windows supporting PatchGuard. After computing the hash value, PatchGuard would detect those changes and would crash the system with `CRITICAL-STRUCTURE-CORRUPTION` exception, which is famously known as the blue screen of death (BSoD). This approach is useful to demonstrate that the PatchGuard is functioning. However, it provides no insight into its mechanism. Moreover, correctly executing the lab required the knowledge of driver compilation and initialization which strays away from the point.

4.3.2 VMI-based PatchGuard Lab. In our VMI-based exercise, students replicate the PatchGuard functionality using VMI and observe that the kernel code and the data structures being monitored do not change and that any attempts to change them cause BSoD. The algorithm 2 shows the logic of the VMI program that replicates PatchGuard.

We divide the whole exercise into tasks derived from the framework described in Section 3.

(Task D). This task consists of a VMI program that reads the whole memory of a Kernel module, computes its hash value, dumps it in a file on disk.

(Task C). This task comprises of a VMI program that alters the memory content of a Kernel module.

Execution of the Tasks. Students begin with Task D. They pick a non-essential kernel module, create its memory dumps across a period of time, followed by Task C to make changes in the module in memory. The hash value will change after Task C. The students can also compute the `md5sum` of the memory dumps to verify that the memory dump after Task C has different hash value and thereby, indicating a kernel compromise. At this stage, the students intentionally crash the VM using a Xen utility, *xen-hvmcrash*.

This lab demonstrated that students can play with the kernel modules directly in the memory and view the effects of the changes more effectively using VMI. Moreover, it excluded the need of the student to learn about kernel drivers to understand the concept of PatchGuard. Additionally, had the student made changes to an essential kernel module such as hal.dll being monitored by PatchGuard, the environment would have crashed. However, since the damage is encapsulated inside a VM, the environment can be reset to a previous setting quite easily.

5 ANALYSIS OF THE EXERCISES

We use four characteristics of an effective cybersecurity to make the comparison between traditional and VMI based lab exercises. The characteristics are completeness, flexibility, portability, and creativity identified by Joyce *et al.* [18]. In this section, we define what those features signify regarding hands-on security exercises and use them to gauge VMI based kernel security labs against their traditional counterparts.

5.1 Completeness

A hands on kernel security lab is complete if:

(1) It provides a complete picture of the mechanism of the attack/defense.
(2) The changes made in the kernel because of the attack/defense is directly visible.
(3) the effect of the changes made in the kernel is visible.

Buffer Overflow Lab. Both the traditional and VMI buffer overflow labs provide a complete picture of the mechanism of attack, provide the means to see the effect of those changes(by use of a debugger and VMI program respectively) and provide means to look at the effects of said changes.

DKOM Lab. Traditional DKOM lab, as opposed to VMI lab, is limited because it does not provide a complete picture of the attack-/defense and the changes made in the kernel aren't directly visible. The student does not get to see what pointers are changed or what the data structures look like.

PatchGuard Lab. Traditional PatchGuard lab performed in windows 7 64 bit VM is performed by the Windows kernel itself, and the traditional version does not provide any transparency at all.

5.2 Flexibility

Kernel security labs are flexible when *the student can play with the code without causing lasting damage to the environment.* Traditionally, all kernel security labs are executed and performed inside a VM. Since they may manipulate the OS kernel of the VM, thus, can crash. In this case, the students may loose their work or have to reset the VM to start all over. It restricts student's ability to play with the code to observe the effects. VMI labs, on the other hand, isolate any possible damage inside the encapsulated VM and the VMI tools run outside the VM. Hence, VMI kernel security labs are more flexible than traditional kernel security labs.

5.3 Portability

The following criterion describes when kernel security labs are portable: *The students can use the same set of programs in different computers with same or similar operating systems and similar environments without recompilation.* Both traditional labs and VMI labs are C based and are not independent of the machines. Both of them would need recompilation. Hence, neither traditional nor VMI labs are portable.

Characteristics	Traditional vs. VMI Labs	Buffer Overflow Lab	DKOM lab	PatchGuard Lab
Completeness	Traditional Lab	✓	×	×
	VMI Lab	✓	✓	✓
Flexibility	Traditional Lab	×	×	×
	VMI Lab	✓	✓	✓
Portability	Traditional Lab	×	×	×
	VMI Lab	×	×	×
Creativity	Traditional Lab	✓	✓	✓
	VMI Lab	✓	✓	✓

Table 1: Comparison between Traditional and VMI Cybersecurity labs using four characteristics i.e. completeness, flexibility, portability, and creativity

5.4 Creativity

Traditionally, kernel security labs have always stimulated creativity, which refers to: *the ability of the student/instructor to use same/similar frameworks to come up with exercises or labs about other attacks and/or defenses.*

Buffer Overflow Lab. Techniques used in buffer overflow can also be used in heap overflow exploit and in advanced exploits such as ROP[24].

DKOM Lab. The techniques used in DKOM are used in advanced exploits such as evolutionary DKOM[15].

PatchGuard Lab. The techniques used in Patchguard for computing hashes can be used in the labs such as digital signatures[10]. Hence, in general, both traditional and VMI labs stimulate creativity.

Table 1 presents the result of comparison of VMI based labs against traditional labs. Here, we see that leveraging VMI in kernel security labs has advantages on two fronts, i.e improvement of completeness and flexibility of kernel security exercises. It provides better visibility and ability to manipulate the guest OS memory space, which decreases the abstraction warranted by traditional exercises by a great deal.

6 CONCLUSION AND FUTURE PLANS

We demonstrated the use of VMI for developing labs successfully by creating three kernel-security labs and making them available online[3]. We then compared VMI-based approach against traditional approach for creating these three labs and found that VMI provided more visibility to the kernel's memory and allowed modification of the guest kernel with lot fewer restrictions than the traditional approach. Hence, leveraging VMI to develop kernel security exercises is a superior approach to designing kernel security labs from a teaching standpoint. We believe that educators and students will benefit from this approach. However, we see much scope for future work and improvement.

Until now, we have developed three labs. We would like to extend the idea of using VMI to more cybersecurity concepts such as *return oriented programming* and *in-memory fuzzing*. We would also like to solve the semantic gap problem by introducing some way to make the labs OS agnostic. We would also like to conduct quantitative studies after all labs have been completed to establish statistically supported the efficacy of VMI in kernel security education.

ACKNOWLEDGMENTS

This work was supported by the NSF grant #1623276 and #1623325.

REFERENCES

[1] Paul Barham, Boris Dragovic, Keir Fraser, Steven Hand, Tim Harris, Alex Ho, Rolf Neugebauer, Ian Pratt, and Andrew Warfield. 2003. Xen and the art of virtualization. In *ACM SIGOPS operating systems review*, Vol. 37. ACM, 164–177.

[2] Erick Bauman, Gbadebo Ayoade, and Zhiqiang Lin. 2015. A Survey on Hypervisor Based Monitoring: Approaches, Applications, and Evolutions. *Comput. Surveys* 48, 1, Article 10 (Aug. 2015), 33 pages.

[3] Manish Bhatt. 2017 (accessed August 18, 2017). *VMI Exercises*. https://gitlab.com/mbhatt1/VMITool

[4] Stephen D Burd, Xin Luo, and Alessandro F Seazzu. 2013. Cloud-based virtual computing laboratories. In *System Sciences (HICSS), 2013 46th Hawaii International Conference on*. IEEE, 5079–5088.

[5] C Cavanagh and R Albert. 2011. Goals, Models, and Progress towards Establishing a Virtual Information Security Laboratory in Maine. In *Proceedings of the SAM '11 Conference*. 496–500.

[6] Peter M Chen and Brian D Noble. 2001. When virtual is better than real [operating system relocation to virtual machines]. In *Hot Topics in Operating Systems, 2001. Proceedings of the Eighth Workshop on*. IEEE, 133–138.

[7] Brendan Dolan-Gavitt, Tim Leek, Michael Zhivich, Jonathon Giffin, and Wenke Lee. 2011. Virtuoso: Narrowing the semantic gap in virtual machine introspection. In *Security and Privacy (SP), 2011 IEEE Symposium on*. IEEE, 297–312.

[8] Wenliang Du. 2011. SEED: hands-on lab exercises for computer security education. *IEEE Security & Privacy* 9, 5 (2011), 70–73.

[9] Wenliang Du and Ronghua Wang. 2008. SEED: A suite of instructional laboratories for computer security education. *Journal on Educational Resources in Computing (JERIC)* 8, 1 (2008), 3.

[10] Shimon Even, Oded Goldreich, and Silvio Micali. 1989. On-line/off-line digital signatures. In *Conference on the Theory and Application of Cryptology*. Springer, 263–275.

[11] Yangchun Fu and Zhiqiang Lin. 2012. Space Traveling across VM: Automatically Bridging the Semantic-Gap in Virtual Machine Introspection via Online Kernel Data Redirection. In *Proceedings of the 2012 IEEE Symposium on Security and Privacy*. San Francisco, CA.

[12] Yangchun Fu and Zhiqiang Lin. 2013. Exterior: Using a dual-vm based external shell for guest-os introspection, configuration, and recovery. *ACM SIGPLAN Notices* 48, 7 (2013), 97–110.

[13] Yangchun Fu, Junyuan Zeng, and Zhiqiang Lin. 2014. HYPERSHELL: A Practical Hypervisor Layer Guest OS Shell for Automated In-VM Management.. In *USENIX Annual Technical Conference*. 85–96.

[14] Tal Garfinkel, Mendel Rosenblum, and others. 2003. A Virtual Machine Introspection Based Architecture for Intrusion Detection.. In *Ndss*, Vol. 3. 191–206.

[15] Mariano Graziano, Lorenzo Flore, Andrea Lanzi, and Davide Balzarotti. 2016. Subverting Operating System Properties Through Evolutionary DKOM Attacks. In *Detection of Intrusions and Malware, and Vulnerability Assessment*. Springer, 3–24.

[16] Brian Hay, Kara Nance, and C Hecker. 2006. Evolution of the ASSERT computer security lab. In *Proceedings of the 10th Colloquium for Information Systems Security Education. Adelphi, MD*.

[17] Ashlesha Joshi, Samuel T King, George W Dunlap, and Peter M Chen. 2005. Detecting past and present intrusions through vulnerability-specific predicates. In *ACM SIGOPS Operating Systems Review*, Vol. 39. ACM, 91–104.

[18] Daniel Joyce, Deborah Knox, Jill Gerhardt-Powals, Elliot Koffman, Wolfgang Kreuzer, Cary Laxer, Kenneth Loose, Erkki Sutinen, and R Alan Whitehurst. 1997. Developing laboratories for the SIGCSE computing laboratory repository: guidelines, recommendations, and sample labs (report of the ITiCSE'97 working group on designing laboratory materials for computing courses). In *The supplemental proceedings of the conference on Integrating technology into computer science education: working group reports and supplemental proceedings*. ACM, 1–12.

[19] Zhiqiang Lin. 2013. Toward guest OS writable virtual machine introspection. *VMware Technical Journal* 2, 2 (2013), 9–14.

[20] Kara Nance, Brian Hay, Ronald Dodge, James Wrubel, Steve Burd, and Alex Seazzu. 2009. Replicating and sharing computer security laboratory environments. In *System Sciences, 2009. HICSS'09. 42nd Hawaii International Conference on*. IEEE, 1–10.

[21] Bryan D Payne. 2011. *LibVMI*. Technical Report. Sandia National Laboratories.

[22] Bryan D Payne, Martim Carbone, Monirul Sharif, and Wenke Lee. 2008. Lares: An architecture for secure active monitoring using virtualization. In *Security and Privacy, 2008. SP 2008. IEEE Symposium on*. IEEE, 233–247.

[23] Gerald J Popek and Robert P Goldberg. 1974. Formal requirements for virtualizable third generation architectures. *Commun. ACM* 17, 7 (1974), 412–421.

[24] Marco Prandini and Marco Ramilli. 2012. Return-oriented programming. *IEEE Security & Privacy* 10, 6 (2012), 84–87.

[25] Mark E Russinovich, David A Solomon, and Alex Ionescu. 2012. *Windows internals*. Pearson Education.

Writing in CS: Why and How?

Mia Minnes (Moderator)
Computer Science and Engineering
University of California, San Diego
minnes@ucsd.edu

Bruce Maxwell
Computer Science
Colby College
bmaxwell@colby.edu

Stephanie R Taylor
Computer Science
Colby College
srtaylor@colby.edu

Phillip Barry
Computer Science and Engineering
University of Minnesota
barry@cs.umn.edu

KEYWORDS

Writing, professional development, communication, curriculum design, assessment.

ACM Reference Format:
Mia Minnes (Moderator), Bruce Maxwell, Stephanie R Taylor, and Phillip Barry. 2018. Writing in CS: Why and How?. In *SIGCSE '18: The 49th ACM Technical Symposium on Computer Science Education, February 21–24, 2018, Baltimore , MD, USA.* ACM, New York, NY, USA, 2 pages. https://doi.org/10.1145/3159450.3159620

1 SUMMARY

The importance of written communication and critical thinking in Computer Science is widely acknowledged. It was called out specifically in the curriculum guidelines ACM CS2013 [6] and has been the topic of a number of previous SIGCSE papers, for example [1–4]. Moreover, writing as a pedagogical practice can help make CS more accessible for a broader population. However, special challenges may arise for students who are English-language learners or have writing-specific learning differences.

In this panel, we share our experiences teaching Writing in CS and, in particular, leveraging resources from writing experts to address these opportunities and challenges. The panelists come from both a private liberal arts college and two large public research-intensive universities. We will share how we have engaged in writing in different ways: large-scale curricular development designed to incorporate "writing to learn" in an entire undergraduate program vs. a specific writing-intensive non-technical class where students explore professional development. A common theme of our experiences is that connecting with colleagues across campus, specifically experts in writing pedagogy, can give computer scientists both the confidence and the language with which to meaningfully teach writing in our own context.

During the panel, we'll share our motivations for bringing writing into the classroom, outline the nuts and bolts of how to do so without massively increasing the load on teachers and students, and give strategies for assessing the results. We will solicit contributions from participants about where and how writing is incorporated in their courses, and field questions.

ACM ISBN 978-1-4503-5103-4/18/02.
https://doi.org/10.1145/3159450.3159620

2 MIA MINNES

Myths about CS and engineering sometimes obscure the essential role of writing and communication in CS. In light of this, how do we motivate our students to devote time and energy to developing effective communication and writing skills? In my professional development course at UC San Diego, students write informally on a weekly basis while they are working full-time at summer internships. They write about technical accomplishments, about interpersonal struggles and successes, and about how they see themselves progressing on their professional journey. The weekly reflections are shared with peers working at other CS internships.

In this course, writing serves both as a vehicle for learning and as one of its key subjects. The course takes place while students are off-campus, spread across many states (and countries). The online written discussion forum is an essential component of the communal learning space. Moreover, many of the topics discussed in the course focus on professional communication itself: why it's important, what are common pitfalls, and what are strategies for improving it. By teaching these concepts in an authentic and immediately relevant setting (while students need to work with managers and co-workers), it becomes easier to get student buy-in. Students are developing their written communication while seeing why this is useful.

A complementary goal for this course, in addition to improving students' writing proficiency, is to help students recognize and appreciate the connections between their on-campus coursework and real-world applications in which they are engaging during their internships. Analyzing samples of student writing from the beginning and the end of the summer revealed that, indeed, students' writing demonstrated greater depth of integrative learning [5]. In collaboration with the UC San Diego Writing + Critical Expression Hub, I've been able to sharpen the focus of writing assignments and identify key lessons for the students.

3 BRUCE MAXWELL

Communication and writing is an important skill for computer scientists in both academia and industry. The CS Department at Colby College has integrated writing into weekly projects for the past decade, primarily by requiring brief written reports for all of our weekly assignments in our core sequence. The sequence includes

Introductory Computer Science, Data Structures and Algorithms, Data Analysis and Visualization, and Programming Languages. In addition, all faculty have required some form of presentation and writing in our 400-level capstone experience courses. However, despite believing the writing to be an important part of the assignment, we had only a rough idea of what we wanted from student writing, and it was difficult to help students improve.

After discussions with our own Writing Center, we partnered with the University of Minnesota to implement their Writing Enriched Curriculum (WEC) concept. The overall process had us examine and identify the types of writing we wanted our students to undertake, clearly state what constituted good writing, and identify a coherent progression within our curriculum so that students went through beginner, intermediate, and advanced writing tasks. Having to describe to a non computer scientist the types of writing we felt were important was a challenging, but worthwhile exercise. It helped us to understand and focus our attention on the skills we believed were the most important.

The outcome of this process was a set of clear and unambiguous statements of both the types of writing, and what constituted good writing for each type. For example, we identified five types of writing–persuasive, descriptive, explanatory, analytic, and code–along with specific qualities of good writing in each category. These descriptions helped us to build a comprehensive plan for integrating writing throughout the curriculum.

4 STEPHANIE TAYLOR

I worked closely with the Writing Center and others in the department to develop a plan for students to develop the writing skills we identifed earlier in the WEC process. We started by identifying where in the curriculum they should work on each skill, and at what level. One goal was to ensure that students experienced beginner and intermediate level writing expectations and exercises before being expected to undertake more advanced writing. Another goal was to develop a teaching plan and other materials based on our writing types and rubrics to enable us to teach the relevant skills and clearly communicate to students our expectations.

Our implementation is based on short writing lessons to supplement the writing accompanying every coding project. Briefly, each programming assignment involves a blog-style report that summarizes the project's coding and non-coding goals. For example, if a project has students use the Python turtle to draw a picture, the written report involves a description of the elements in the picture along with the coding approaches used to create those elements, such as for loops. The students also reflect on what they learned.

The short writing lessons focus on specific aspects of the reports, such as the summary, or how well they integrate text and pictures or text and code. These lessons are strategically placed in the semester so students can reflect on their prior report and see improvement on their next report. The lessons also recur, with increasing sophistication, as students move through the progression of core courses. Students see each topic twice, in different courses, to emphasize and strengthen prior experience.

A key factor in the success of the writing lessons is giving feedback that is timely, relevant to the skill being learned, and avoids correcting grammar and fine details. In addition, we have to be able to train student graders to provide feedback on writing. Designing clear rubrics that we can communicate to students, graders, and faculty has been critical, and we are seeing clear evidence of improvement in student writing in the context of project reports.

5 PHILLIP BARRY

Many of the challenges of teaching writing in CS involve assessment. How effective is students' writing in a given class? How good are students' written communication skills once they complete their degree? How proficiently do we teach writing in a given class? How proficiently do we teach it in our entire curriculum?

The Department of Computer Science and Engineering at the University of Minnesorta has been a participant in the university's WEC (Writing Enriched Curriculum) program for over five years. Our WEC activities involving assessment include the following:

- Faculty discussions of where writing occurs in our curriculum. In particular, this helped us identify "writing gaps" and the need to emphasize writing more in our introductory classes.
- Faculty discussions of rating criteria for student writing in general. These criteria are used in writing instruction, in grading rubrics, and in programmatic evaluations of writing.
- Experimenting with different practices that give students feedback for revision.
- Development of grading rubrics for certain writing assignments.
- Training material for teaching assistants in large, writing-heavy classes. Because of of our large class sizes, teaching assistants play an important role in assessing writing, and therefore need special training.
- Assessment and revision of various key writing assignments.
- Formal ratings of student writing samples. Every three years the WEC program has a formal rating of student work that provides a variety of feedback to the department.

Most of these are ongoing activities in the sense that we have made some progress, are analyzing their effectiveness, and are working to improve them. In particular, three keys themes in our WEC activities are (1) the use of assessment data in improving writing instruction and activities; (2) the variety of different types of assessment and assessment-related activities; and (3) writing assessment as a fertile area for discussion within our department, with other departments and centers — such as the Center for Writing — at the University of Minnesota, and with colleagues at other institutions.

REFERENCES

[1] Alan Garvey. 2010. Writing in an Upper-level CS Course. In *SIGCSE '10.*
[2] Mark E. Hoffman, Timothy Dansdill, and David S. Herscovici. 2006. Bridging Writing to Learn and Writing in the Discipline in Computer Science Education. In *SIGCSE '06.*
[3] Lisa C. Kaczmarczyk. 2003. A Technical Writing Class for Computer Science Majors: Measuring Student Perceptions of Learning. In *SIGCSE '03.*
[4] David G. Kay. 1998. Computer Scientists Can Teach Writing: An Upper Division Course for Computer Science Majors. In *SIGCSE '98.*
[5] Mia Minnes, John Mayberry, Melissa Soto, and Jace Hargis. in press. Practice Makes Deeper? Regular Reflective Writing During Engineering Internships. *Journal of Transformative Learning* (in press).
[6] ACM-IEEE Joint Task Force on Computing Curricula. 2013. Computer Science Curricula 2013: Curriculum Guidelines for Undergraduate Degree Programs in Computer Science.

Perfect Harmony: Team Teaching Computing & Music

Richard Weiss
Computer Science & Mathematics
The Evergreen State College
weissr@evergreen.edu

James Caristi
Dept. of Computing & Info. Sciences
Valparaiso University
james.caristi@valpo.edu

Jesse M. Heines
Dept. of Computer Science
Univ. of Massachusetts Lowell
jesse_heines@uml.edu

Aaron Koehl
Mason School of Business
College of William & Mary
aaron.koehl@mason.wm.edu

Kelly Rossum
Dept. of Music
Christopher Newport University
kelly.rossum@cnu.edu

ABSTRACT

One of the ways to attract a more diverse group of students to computer science is by offering courses that are interdisciplinary. Some of the first examples of this combined multimedia with programming. There are many more possibilities, but as computer scientists, we often do not have the domain knowledge to teach these courses alone. Team teaching offers a solution to this dilemma. The goal of this panel is to present some of the problems we have encountered and to discuss some of the solutions.

CCS CONCEPTS

• **Applied Computing → Arts and Humanities →** Sound and Music Computing
• **Applied Computing → Education →** Collaborative Learning

KEYWORDS

Team Teaching; Computing and Music; Interdisciplinary

ACM Reference format:

R. Weiss, J. Caristi, J. Heines, A. Koehl, and K. Rossum. 2018. SIG Computer Science Education. In *SIGCSE '18: 49th ACM Technical Symposium on Computer Science Education, Feb. 21–24, 2018, Baltimore, MD, USA.* ACM, NY, NY, USA, 2 pages.
https://doi.org/10.1145/3159450.3159619

ACM ISBN 978-1-4503-5103-4/18/02.
https://doi.org/10.1145/3159450.3159619

1 POSITION STATEMENTS (in alphabetical order)

1.1 James Caristi

I have twice team taught a course on Computing and Music with the chair of the Music Department at Valparaiso University, and we have plans to make this a regular offering in the General Education Program. There are, in fact, two courses involved: one with a MUS number and one with a CS number. They meet at the same time and place with both of us. Each course has its own set of learning objectives, but students learn both sets, even though they only get either Fine Arts credit (if they took MUS) or Quantitative Literacy credit (if they took CS). Students use Scratch to produce musical sounds and develop a project that is displayed to passersby during our Hour of Code day. The course is evolving toward more algorithmic composition and machine learning. Although our course is immensely popular and extremely highly rated, our detailed assessment shows that a negligible number of non-CS students intend to take another CS course after this experience. But this course does make them feel much more comfortable and knowledgeable about computing.

1.2 Jesse Heines

I team taught an interdisciplinary course called "Sound Thinking" once per year for eight years with three different colleagues in my university's Dept. of Music. (Please see jesseheines.com/~heines/91.212/91.212-2015-16s/ for the most recent course website, and compthinkinsound.org for the book by Music Prof. Gena Greher and myself on our experience team teaching this course.) Our experience with the students was consistently fantastic, and course enrollment tripled over the eight years. The interpersonal relations between faculty were always respectful, of course, but small clashes sometimes arose when the different demands of our different departments caused us to have different priorities. None of these small clashes was egregious, but it was important to keep in mind and account for the differences in our departments. Despite such small setbacks, I can say without reservation that the team teaching experience was as enriching for the participating professors as it was for the students.

1.3 Aaron Koehl

Our University was looking to explore interdisciplinary, co-taught courses. What two disciplines could be more orthogonal? Computer science changes rapidly with new advancements in technology, while music (academically) is considered new after 1850, so we took the challenge to integrate the two! I teamed up with our director of jazz studies and we attended an NSF workshop on computing and music to explore the idea. During the workshop, we sketched a design for what ultimately became Computing and Electronic Dance Music (EDM), a cross-listed major elective for both computer science and music. The offering was our most successful interdisciplinary course to date. We consciously avoided a course divided in half by discipline. Instead, both instructors were present and contributed at each class session, which required coordination and frequent meetings. After an exploration of the EDM genre, a viewing of a documentary on the Roland 808 drum machine, and sessions on music theory, students were introduced to technology in a well-equipped music lab. A discussion of sound waves led to sound synthesis of high hats, kick, and snare in PureData. This provided adequate foundation for students to develop their own sounds and sequenced music using Logic Pro, a professional digital audio workstation (DAW). Special class sessions were dedicated to rhythm, bass, software plugins, and the "Drop," a hallmark of the EDM genre. The course concluded with software-based lighting control and discussions of the Digital Multiplex (DMX) protocol. Students exhibited their final projects publicly during a "rave night" held in our studio theatre, with professional lighting and sound equipment.

1.4 Kelly Rossum

I served as the co-instructor (with Aaron Koehl) of the "EDM - Computing and Electronic Dance Music" course at our university. This class served as a special topics experiment to expand traditional music pedagogy into the realm of computer science and electronic dance genres. In addition to university level computational fundamentals, basic music theory, notation, and compositional approaches were delivered to a mixed class of physicists, information systems, and computer science majors, with the inclusion of a handful of interested musicians. As an indirect result of this course, the department has hired an electronic/new music specialist to lead a "Creative Studies" program that would include a music technology degree track. The overwhelming success of the EDM class has created a buzz within the student body, and we will probably be developing this course full-time in the near future.

1.5 Richard Weiss

I have taught Music, Math and Cybernetics with composer and music faculty Arun Chandra. This was a 16-credit program, in which students learned the basics of programming, 16-channel sound synthesis, and the principles of cybernetics as applied to social and musical systems. Evergreen does not have departments, so we did not have external constraints on the content of this class. This kind of team teaching is the norm. The students came from a range of backgrounds and about half of the students continued in computer science. It allowed them to combine their interests in music and computing. For the coherence of the class, it was important for Arun and me to talk frequently about the learning goals and scheduling events such as attending concerts. We had planned to create a piece together, but we did not allow enough time to do that.

2 PLAN FOR AUDIENCE PARTICIPATION

Each panelist will introduce his experience in no more than 8 minutes. With 75 minutes allocated for the panel, this will leave about 30 minutes for audience discussion. We will encourage audience members to raise issues with and obstacles to team teaching that we can all address collectively. Such issues might include difficulties in finding a compatible partner, in getting classes approved by governing parties, in synchronizing disparate schedules, and reconciling different department expectations. We expect a lively discussion from many perspectives, as the panelists themselves are from vastly different types of institutions. A summary of the obstacles and solutions presented will be prepared dynamically during the session and made available to all participants on a publicized website.

CS as a Graduation Requirement: Catalyst for Systemic Change

Lucia Dettori
DePaul University
Chicago, Illinois
lucia@cdm.depaul.edu

Ronald I. Greenberg
Loyola University Chicago
Chicago, Illinois
rig@cs.luc.edu

Steven McGee
The Learning Partnership
Western Springs, Illinois
mcgee@lponline.net

Dale Reed
University of Illinois at Chicago
Chicago, Illinois
reed@uic.edu

Brenda Wilkerson
Anita Borg Institute
Palo Alto, California
brendadw@AnitaB.org

Don Yanek
Chicago Public Schools
Chicago, Illinois
dgyanek@cps.edu

CCS CONCEPTS

• **Social and professional topics → K-12 education**; *Computational thinking*; *Model curricula*; *Student assessment*;

KEYWORDS

high school; graduation requirement; instructional coaching; systemic change; CSforAll; Exploring Computer Science; teacher professional development; Chicago Public Schools

ACM Reference Format:

Lucia Dettori, Ronald I. Greenberg, Steven McGee, Dale Reed, Brenda Wilkerson, and Don Yanek. 2018. CS as a Graduation Requirement: Catalyst for Systemic Change. In *SIGCSE '18: The 49th ACM Technical Symposium on Computer Science Education, February 21–24, 2018, Baltimore , MD, USA.* ACM, New York, NY, USA, 2 pages. https://doi.org/10.1145/3159450.3159646

1 SUMMARY

Since President Obama's announcement of the Computer Science for All Initiative in 2016, there has been a surge in the number of districts that are planning for or newly implementing computer science (CS) offerings at their schools. Chicago Public Schools (CPS) is the first large school district to have adopted Computer Science as a high school graduation requirement, taking this significant step along the path towards systemic change. The foundation was laid eight years ago when an informal alliance was formed between a CPS high school CS teacher, a CPS administrator, and three university computer scientists. With the addition of an education researcher, the alliance later formalized as a researcher-practitioner partnership: the Chicago Alliance for Equity in Computer Science, known as CAFÉCS. With CE21 funding from NSF (CNS-1138417), the alliance initiated work on the Taste of Computing project with a pilot cohort of 11 teachers. Through multiple public (CNS-1543217, CNS-1542971, DRL-1640215, CNS-1738691, CNS-1738776) and private grants since then, the alliance has developed 15 CPS peer facilitators who have provided professional development to over 200 CPS teachers. In the alliance's first 5 years, ECS has been taught in 40 CPS high schools to over 13,000 students. Of these students, 47% have been Hispanic, and 38% have been African American, both of which match the overall CPS demographics; 44% of the students have been female. Currently, ECS is being taught in 63 schools to over 11,000 students by over 150 teachers. The alliance has also contributed to the literature on the impact of the ECS course on students' attitudes towards computer science [3], students' choices about future CS coursework [4], and students' development of computational thinking practices [5]. Lessons learned in Chicago over the last eight years can inform this process in other school districts.

The panel will present discussion questions revolving around key factors for constructing a successful CS initiative. Following the ethos of ECS, participants will have the opportunity to share and to discuss their own district's progress with peers in small groups. These discussions will lead to a larger groups discussion focusing on best practices and lessons learned.

SIGCSE '18, February 21–24, 2018, Baltimore , MD, USA

ACM ISBN 978-1-4503-5103-4/18/02.
https://doi.org/10.1145/3159450.3159646

2 OBJECTIVE

The history of achieving the computer science graduation requirement contains important lessons for other school districts large and small. Beginning eight years ago with a small group of like-minded Chicago high school teachers, administrators, and university professors, our effort has evolved into a grassroots movement resulting in endorsement and support from the Chicago city government, expansion of CS into elementary as well as high schools, collaborations with industry partners, and connections to nationwide systemic change with Exploring Computer Science, Code.org and NSF-funded CSforAll.

The successful creation of a high school computer science requirement requires more than just inspiration and a group of willing teachers. Our evolution began in the classroom with students and teachers, and has expanded to include the larger academic and political community in Chicago. Along the way successes and failures have taught us lessons from which others can benefit. Key ingredients in our recipe for success have been:

(1) Growing at the pace of relational trust. It takes time to cultivate a geographical community of partners. It takes time to establish common vision among stakeholders, to find appropriate equity-based curriculum, for teachers to change their pedagogy, for principals to embrace the change, and for a school system to adopt a new course requirement.
(2) Implementing best-practices professional development for long-term growth, implementing an inquiry approach not only for the curriculum but for the PD experience itself.

(3) Transitioning ownership into the school system, and building institutional structure to sustain the effort: examples are CPS' adoption of ECS as the flagship high school CS curriculum, CPS' hire of a full-time ECS coach, and the expansion of the computer science-related district administrative staff toward levels enjoyed by traditional core subjects, building out the CS deptartments.
(4) Handling the failures that come with success. For instance once CS was required in CPS, it became more common at professional development sessions to have teachers attend only because they were required to be there rather than because they were otherwise personally invested in it.

The objective of the session is to share Chicago successes and failures with participants and provide an interactive forum for participants to brainstorm how to adapt elements of Chicago's success to their own local contexts.

3 OUTLINE

An initial brief history of CAFÉCS and the Chicago story will give overall context to the discussion (10 minutes). Special session question leaders and team members will include Brenda Wilkerson (CPS CSforAll champion), Don Yanek (CPS teacher, CSTA president, ECS coach), University partners (Lucia Dettori of DePaul, Ron Greenberg of Loyola, Dale Reed of UIC), Steven McGee (external evaluator and researcher), along with additional CPS staff and teachers (Andy Rasmussen, Troy Williams, Faythe Brannon).

Each of the implementation areas are given below, along with emphasis areas for each one. Session leaders will first summarize each question (1 min.) as a lead-in to brief small group discussion. Groups will be asked to consider how various solutions apply to their own local contexts (4 min.), and will take turns reporting out as part of the larger group discussion (5 min.). This process will be repeated for each question.

(1) **What are steps to building a good researcher/practitioner partnership involving teachers, university partners, and district leaders?** *Emphasis:* It is important to have a champion within the system, which in our case was Brenda Wilkerson.
(2) **How can a good pilot be leveraged for systemic change?** *Emphasis:* Initial seed funding and commitments from a highly motivated core group can provide a proof-of-concept pilot to be used to sway leadership.
(3) **For building institutional capacity what is the relative importance of curriculum, PD, coaching, and systemic endorsement? Which should come first?** *Emphasis:* While all these are important, start with the right curriculum, then adopt an effective PD model.
(4) **From teachers' perspectives, what are the most pressing needs in implementing CS across a school system?** *Emphasis:* Teachers need community support to get started, and coaching support to continue.
(5) **How would a CS graduation requirement fit into the existing curriculum?** *Emphasis:* Find the path of least resistance, with the requirement drafted in such a way that it works politically with the existing curriculum structure.
(6) **What are primary concerns from the school district administrator point of view?** *Emphasis:* Funding and political support go hand-in-hand.
(7) **What are the problems you might expect once the graduation requirement has been adopted?** *Emphasis:* It is not one-and-done. Real work continues after the graduation requirement. There are many schools that are not ready, more teachers will be needed to meet the demand, and frequent leadership turnover means we need to continue to convince administrators of the importance of CS.

4 EXPECTATIONS

Intended Audience: K–12 teachers and administrators, university professors, policy makers.

The session will cover the evolution of creating a high school graduation requirement. The audience will learn a pathway and strategies to investigate as well as critical people to engage in the mission. They will become aware of possible pitfalls and issues.

5 SUITABILITY FOR A SPECIAL SESSION

With the announcement of the CSforAll initiative, many states and municipalities are allocating budgets around the investigation of how to implement Computer Science education in K–12. The Chicago CAFÉCS is a mature implementation of CSforAll, having worked as a cohesive team on this unified vision for the last eight years, leading to Computer Science being adopted as a graduation requirement for all CPS high school students a year ago.

The session goal is to enable participants to consider what elements of Chicago's success can be replicated within their own local context. For this reason the session is designed to be interactive, capturing participant dialogue. We have learned from both our successes and failures and presenting these in this session coupled with small group discussions will help participants to consider what elements of the Chicago story might be appropriate to help bring about systemic change in their own contexts.

REFERENCES

[1] J. Century, M. Lach, H. King, S. Rand, C. Heppner, B. Franke, and J. Westrick. 2013. Chicago: District Partnership In Stories from the Field. In *Building an Operating System for Computer Science Education*. CEMSE, University of Chicago with UEI. http://outlier.uchicago.edu/computerscience/OS4CS. Includes narratives by Taste of Computing project personnel.
[2] Chicago Public Schools. 2016. New CPS Computer Science Graduation Requirement to Prepare Students for Jobs of the Future. Press release http://cps.edu/News/Press_releases/Pages/PR2_02_24_2016.aspx. (Feb. 2016).
[3] Lucia Dettori, Ronald I. Greenberg, Steven McGee, and Dale Reed. 2016. The Impact of The Exploring Computer Science Instructional Model in Chicago Public Schools. *Computing in Science & Engineering (Special Issue: Best of RESPECT 2015)* 18, 2 (March/April 2016), 10–17. http://doi.org/10.1109/MCSE.2016.39
[4] Steven McGee, Randi McGee-Tekula, Jennifer Duck, Ronald I. Greenberg, Lucia Dettori, Dale F. Reed, Brenda Wilkerson, Don Yanek, Andrew M. Rasmussen, and Gail Chapman. 2017. Does a Taste of Computing Increase Computer Science Enrollment? *Computing in Science & Engineering (Special Issue: Best of RESPECT 2016)* 19, 3 (April 2017), 8–18. http://doi.org/10.1109/MCSE.2017.50
[5] Steven McGee, Randi McGee-Tekula, Jennifer Duck, Catherine McGee, Lucia Dettori, Ronald I. Greenberg, Eric Snow, Daisy Rutstein, Dale Reed, Brenda Wilkerson, Don Yanek, Andrew Rasmussen, and Dennis Brylow. 2018. Equal Outcomes 4 All: A Study of Student Learning in ECS. In *SIGCSE '18*.
[6] Dale Reed, Brenda Wilkerson, Don Yanek, Lucia Dettori, and Jeff Solin. 2015. How Exploring Computer Science (ECS) Came to Chicago. *ACM Inroads* 6, 3 (Sept. 2015), 75–77. http://doi.org/10.1145/2807703

Striving for Excellence in Introductory Computer Science Courses Using Culturally Responsive Teaching (CRT)

Alla Webb
Department of Engineering, Physical and Computer Sciences
Montgomery College
51 Mannakee Street
Rockville, MD 20850
240-567-7934
alla.webb@montgomerycollege.edu

Ray Gonzales
Department of English Language for Academic Purposes and Linguistics
Montgomery College
51 Mannakee Street,
Rockville, MD 20850
240-567-7439
ray.gonzales@montgomerycollege.edu

CCS Concepts
• Computing education→ Computing education programs→ Computer science education

Keywords
Culturally responsive teaching (CRT); introduction to computer science; effective teaching practices.

ACM Reference format:
Alla Webb and Ray Gonzales. 2018. Striving for Excellence in Introductory Computer Science Courses Using Culturally Responsive Teaching (CRT). In *SIGCSE '18: 49th ACM Technical Symposium on Computer Science Education, Feb. 21–24, 2018, Baltimore, MD, USA.* ACM, NY, NY, USA, 6 pages. https://doi.org/10.1145/3159450.3159631

1. SUMMARY
This special session will focus on a multi-year project based on an AAC&U Teaching to Increase Diversity and Equity in STEM (TIDES) grant focused on integrating Culturally Responsive Teaching (CRT) in Computer Science courses at Montgomery College, a highly diverse urban-suburban community college in Maryland. The presenters will discuss the project's development of a CRT model based on a "Discover-Adjust-Assess" process that took into account the realities of the college's faculty and student contexts. Attendees will participate in awareness-raising activities, analyze case studies involving common teaching-learning challenges using CRT-based concepts and tools, and be presented with sample data in the form of student/faculty survey results and interview responses. Several CRT resources created as part of the project will also be presented.

2. OBJECTIVE
As college and university student populations become increasingly diverse, the role of Culturally Responsive Teaching, or CRT [1], in guiding them to success has become a critical topic in higher education. This is especially true for diverse students in Computer Science (CS), a discipline with its own culture that can seem quite "foreign" to these students. CRT can be defined as utilizing information about our students' backgrounds and learning to tailor instruction in ways that increase their opportunities for success. As such, CRT aims to make learning in CS and other disciplines more relevant to students and their lives.

CRT and its sister approaches including Culturally Relevant Teaching [2] are quite broad and often misunderstood topics. This session will first help attendees understand the most important components of CRT, including the meaning of culture within this approach and the importance of being aware of one's implicit biases and assumptions about teaching and learning.

Faculty are also naturally concerned with how they can practically apply CRT in their courses, especially given their limitations on time inside and outside of the classroom. As such, the second part of this session will take attendees on an interactive tour of the "Discover, Adjust, and Assess" CRT process developed as part of the TIDES grant project and implemented in introductory and other Computer Science courses over several semesters. How faculty can "discover" their students, especially those "cultural factors" affecting their learning in the course, and then use that knowledge to "adjust" instruction accordingly will be one focus of this part of the presentation. By following this process, students are more likely to perceive a greater sense of caring on the part of their instructors, a critical component in student success and retention. Another intended result of CRT is to increase students' sense of self-efficacy. Sample student survey results indicating increases in these areas during the project will be presented. In addition, the critical role of continuous "assessment" as part of this process will be discussed. In this part of the session, attendees will also analyze and discuss several case studies of actual classroom challenges encountered by computer science faculty utilizing CRT principles and concepts.

Finally, to facilitate implementation of CRT, available resources in the form of effective teaching practices are critical. The final part of the session will focus on various resources, including an online "Teaching Toolkit", and explain the process of how they were developed by involving the college's faculty and professional development division.

This session will be a "hybrid" in terms of organization: presentation, brainstorming, case-study analysis and discussion, especially of attendees' relevant experiences.

ACM ISBN 978-1-4503-5103-4/18/02
https://doi.org/10.1145/3159450.3159631

3. EXPECTATIONS

This session will provide a brief overview of Culturally Responsive Teaching (CRT), followed by a focus on how CRT can be practically implemented in the classroom, case study analyses using CRT concepts, and a presentation of CRT resources developed primarily by faculty at Montgomery College. The primary intended audience is Computer Science faculty. However, the CR concepts and model that will be presented are applicable to all disciplines and players involved in students' overall college experience (e.g. advisors, instructional designers, administrators).

The audience will come away from this session with a clear understanding of CRT's main components, experience analyzing classroom challenges using CRT principles, and models of applying CRT in the classroom and involving faculty in the development of CRT resources. Feedback from the audience will be central to this session and will be elicited through individual and group reporting of brainstorming and reflections, writing of responses on poster paper, and brief written responses.

4. REFERENCES

[1] Gay, G. 2000. *Culturally Responsive Teaching: Theory, Research, & Practice.* Teachers College Press. New York.

[2] Ladson-Billings, G. 1995.*Toward a Theory of Culturally Relevant Pedagogy.* American Educational Research Journal, 32, 3, (Fall 1995), 465-491.

What's the Big Idea with CS Education in K-12?

Tim Bell
Department of Computer Science and Software Engineering
University of Canterbury
New Zealand
Tim.Bell@canterbury.ac.nz

ABSTRACT

Computer Science is seen in many different ways in society; some may consider it to be an esoteric collection of jargon-laden skills, while others view it as an essential topic of study for all citizens. Many of us are very passionate about sharing our enthusiasm for the subject with others, and we are at a time in history where much of the hard work to get the public to understand that it is something special is starting to bear fruit, as we see Computer Science and Computational thinking appearing in K-12 curricula around the world. But what is it about Computer Science that makes it so important and exciting? Is it a subject in its own right that deserves space in the curriculum? We will explore the reasons that young students should become engaged with the subject, illustrated using an Unplugged perspective.

CCS Concepts

• Social and professional topics~K-12 education • *Social and professional topics~Computing education* • *Social and professional topics~Computational thinking* • Applied computing • Applied computing~Education

Keywords

Computer Science Unplugged; K-12; Computing Education

ACM Reference format:
Tim Bell. 2018. What's the Big Idea with CS Education in K-12??. In *SIGCSE '18: 49th ACM Technical Symposium on Computer Science Education, Feb. 21–24, 2018, Baltimore, MD, USA.* ACM, NY, NY, USA, 6 pages. https://doi.org/10.1145/3159450.316087

BIOGRAPHY

Tim Bell is a professor in the Department of Computer Science and Software Engineering at the University of Canterbury. His "Computer Science Unplugged" project is being widely used internationally with the supporting materials (books and videos) having been translated into over 20 languages. Tim's awards for his work in computing education including the ETH (Zurich) ABZ International Honorary Medal for Fundamental Contributions in Computer Science Education (in 2013) and the IITP President's Award for Contribution to the IT Profession in 2014. Since 2008 he has been actively involved in the design and deployment of teaching Computer Science and Computational Thinking in New Zealand schools.

ACM ISBN 978-1-4503-5103-4/18/02.
https://doi.org/10.1145/3159450.3166087

Longitudinal Data on Flipped Class Effects on Performance in CS1 and Retention after CS1

Celine Latulipe, Audrey Rorrer, Bruce Long
University of North Carolina at Charlotte
Charlotte, NC
{clatulip,arorrer,nblong}@uncc.edu

ABSTRACT

We present results of a college wide undergraduate retention study tracking student retention in computing, comparing students who experience a flipped, active learning version of CS1 against those who experience a traditional lecture and lab version of CS1. We examine demographic subgroups to understand retention differences between sexes and racial/ethnic groups. Specifically, we examine which students exit computing majors in the semester immediately after taking CS1, and those who leave following one academic year. This allows us to focus on how the immediate experience of the CS1 teaching approach impacts desire to continue in computer science during the critical first year in CS. Our dataset includes 698 CS majors who took CS1 in either the flipped or traditional style, between Fall 2013 and Fall 2016, at a large, comprehensive, urban research university in the US. Our results show that women were less likely to switch majors after taking the flipped version than after taking the traditional version. Conversely, male students were more likely to be retained following the traditional course, and less likely to be retained following the flipped course. Performance of CS majors in CS1, as measured by DFW rates, is statistically higher in the flipped classes than performance in the traditional classes. One-year retention in the major for under-represented groups (women and racial minorities) was higher in the flipped classes for new freshmen taking CS1, but not for transfer students.

KEYWORDS

flipped classes, lightweight teams, retention, sex, gender, race, CS1

ACM Reference Format:
Celine Latulipe, Audrey Rorrer, Bruce Long. 2018. Longitudinal Data on Flipped Class Effects on Performance in CS1 and Retention after CS1. In *SIGCSE '18: The 49th ACM Technical Symposium on Computer Science Education, Feb. 21–24, 2018, Baltimore, MD, USA.* ACM, New York, NY, USA, 6 pages. https://doi.org/https://doi.org/10.1145/3159450.3159518

1 INTRODUCTION

There is a growing trend towards fully or partially flipping introductory computer science courses and employing active learning techniques during class time [6, 11, 16, 17, 23]. In fully flipped classes, students absorb the informational content outside of the classroom through short videos, readings, interactive textbooks, etc., and then apply that learning in the classroom through active learning activities, often in collaboration with peers. Students in flipped classes get to try applying their knowledge in a classroom setting, surrounded by peers, teaching assistants (TAs) and instructors, which means that they have help when they get stuck. Getting stuck in CS1 can take on many forms: students may not know the right syntax, may not understand how a programming feature applies to a given problem, or may not understand how to interpret a compiler error, or how to logically construct a solution. While help may be available online for some problems, that help is out of context. By facing these problems in the classroom with others working through the same activity, peers can learn from each other and receive contextually-sensitive help. This can reduce the high levels of frustration that can occur while working in isolation.

The peer interaction that is often part of flipped class structures, beyond being useful for helping students get 'unstuck', can provide many other benefits. Students get practice with social interaction and teamwork, and also communication practice within their discipline. In earlier work, we presented the 'Lightweight Teams' structure for flipped classes, which specifies that students are put into teams with a fixed seating arrangement for the entire semester [14]. The teams are lightweight, meaning that there is no significant assignment or project that the teams have to do together. They only work on low-stakes active learning activities while in class. This takes away the grade stress that often plagues class project teams, and results in teams that are positively engaged in social learning, rather than coordination headaches and blame games. This model can improve student engagement and learning outcomes in subsequent classes. We argued that by telling students where to sit and who to sit with, we removed significant levels of freshman anxiety associated with entering a large lecture hall. In addition, we showed that students reported making many new friends as a result of the Lightweight Teams structure [14]. We had also hypothesized that such a structure, because of the many new friends, would result in students being retained in the major, as they would have developed a strong support network of peers that they could rely on in later computing classes when they faced challenges. However, as we were only able to report early results, we were unable at that time to test the retention hypothesis.

1.1 Local Context

The University of North Carolina at Charlotte is a large, urban campus with more than 29,000 undergraduates, which serves the local state population, drawing mostly from the greater metropolitan area. We are a minority-serving institution[1], with more than 25%

[1]Characteristics of Minority-Serving Institutions and Minority Undergraduates Enrolled in These Institutions, U.S. Department of Education, NCES 2008-156

SIGCSE '18, Feb. 21–24, 2018, Baltimore, MD, USA

ACM ISBN 978-1-4503-5103-4/18/02.
https://doi.org/https://doi.org/10.1145/3159450.3159518

Table 1: Flipped vs. Traditional CS1 Class at our institution

	Traditional Class	Flipped Class
Homework	Assigned Readings	Videos, Readings, Prepwork Quiz
Class Activities	Lecture	Active Learning Peer Instruction Quizzes and Activities
Class Sizes	60-200	80-126
Teams	None	Lightweight Teams for whole semester
Seating	Arbitrary	Assigned
Setting*	Lecture Halls and Classrooms	Classrooms and Active Learning Classrooms
Labs	individual or paired programming	Gender-paired programming
Lab Sizes	20-24	35-45
Language	Java (C++ before 2015)	Java

of freshman students identifying as African American or Hispanic. The average age of our undergraduate student population is 25; half our new students are transfers, a population that is likely to have adult obligations and time constraints.

Our computing college has experienced a 62% increase in undergraduate enrollment over the last five years, from 995 to 1616 in 2016. The introductory courses offered in our college enroll approximately 200 students each semester, most of whom are first year students, i.e. freshmen and transfer students. Many students arrive unprepared to learn programming for a myriad of reasons, e.g. lack of pre-course exposure to programming, and college readiness in general. As a result, it is not surprising that the percentage of students receiving D, F, and W grades is high, at an average of 40% for CS1. Many students have to repeat these gateway courses, and low performers are ill-prepared for higher level course work.

Retention among the CS freshmen and transfer student populations has tended to fluctuate, rather than show a steady rise. One-year new freshmen retention bounced from 71% in 2012, to a high of 82% in 2014, and down to 73% in 2015. Two-year freshmen retention rates are at 60%. For female students, since 2012, we have lost 29-37% of new freshmen and transfers after one year. For minority students, we lose over half after their first year: 64% of new freshmen and new transfers did not return to the major one year later in 2015. In an effort to address these issues, we have created a set of flipped introductory CS courses in our college. To set the stage for the analysis presented in this paper, Table 1 presents the similarities and differences between the flipped class and traditional versions of CS1, which is our focus.

In this work, we present data collected over four years that compares one-semester and one-year retention in the major rates for both freshmen and transfer students who took either a flipped CS1 or a traditional CS1. Our data is broken down by sex and race so we can report retention rates across those demographics. We do not report graduation rates at this point, as at our institution very few students graduate within four years, with most graduating in the fifth or sixth year. We also report on class performance (DFW rates) across flipped vs. traditional classes, for all CS1 students.

2 RELATED WORK

2.1 Retention Issues in CS

Failure rates in introductory programming courses are generally between 30-50% worldwide [2], though most data on failure rates tends to be anecdotal rather than systematic [26]. Some have argued that traditional introductory computer programming education fails because it is antisocial, boring, tedious, irrelevant and competitive instead of presented as socially relevant and cooperative [21]. As a result, the number of alternative teaching methods being explored in CS education is increasing, with many promising approaches. Active learning, online learning, hybrid learning, social learning are just a few of the popular methods being discussed, tried, and adapted for teaching CS. Yet the effect of these new teaching methods, along with a deeper understanding of the impact of interventions on specific student populations remains unclear.

Luxton-Reilly argues that the retention problem in early college computing courses relates to unrealistic expectations that students can learn how to program in a single semester[15]. This is too much too soon, especially for students without a CS course background from high school. In our state, CS courses are not required for a high school diploma or applicable for STEM credit, and many of our students arrive to CS1 with no prior computing experience. In a recent survey of students taking our sophomore-level data structures course, none of the female students and only a minority of the male students had taken a high school computing course.

Climate issues also appear to be a major factor contributing to women and under-represented minorities leaving CS. Women in CS and STEM tend to feel more isolated [24]. Research has shown that ambient cues in the environment of a computer science lab can negatively impact women's feelings of belonging [4].

2.2 Active Learning and Flipped Classes

Active learning is not a clear or narrowly defined concept [23], but is a term that encompasses a variety of pedagogical practices that are different from traditional lecturing. Active learning is generally seen as a positive teaching strategy that increases student engagement and gets students more involved in the process of learning [20, 25]. Pair programming, an active learning strategy with a long history in computing, is shown to improve retention in CS1 [17]. One of the most common active learning techniques is peer instruction activities in which students engage together in answering multiple-choice questions posed by the instructor. Peer instruction has been shown to increase student self-efficacy in CS1 classes [27]. Peer instruction is considered a 'best practice' for CS1 classes [22].

Research on flipped classes in computing has increased, and most report positive results [3, 11, 12, 14]. Flipping the classroom provides a structure in which the majority of in-class time can be devoted to active learning strategies [16]. Research suggests that creating a structured learning environment with active learning, as exemplified in most flipped classrooms, provides better results across all demographic groups, but is especially helpful to under-represented groups and first-generation college students [8]. Some research from the life sciences has shown that the effectiveness of flipped classroom structures are due to the better pre-class preparation that the structure enforces [10]. Research has also shown that the flipped classroom structure, with significant peer interaction, improves students' perceptions of their creative fluency [1].

2.3 Team-based Learning

Team-based learning has been shown to have positive pedagogical results across a variety of domains [18, 19]. The benefits of team-based learning include communication practice, exposure to multiple perspectives, and the ability to attack larger problems. Much of the previous work on team-based learning concerns project teams in which students in a class are assigned to groups so that they can work together on an assignment or large project, that may last a few weeks up to an entire semester. This type of project team is typically not useful in CS1 courses where students haven't yet acquired basic programming skills. The lightweight teams approach we introduced [14] allows CS1 students to benefit from peer instruction and social interaction, but the teams do not have any assignments or projects that they have to complete together. The teams are lightweight because the grade weights related to team activities are extremely low. The teams sit together throughout the semester and work on in class active learning activities together.

The Lightweight Teams approach echoes the socio-academic integrative moments theory advanced by Deil-Amen [7]. This theory was developed to capture the experience of two-year community college students for whom the social aspects of the college experience are limited, and for whom the community that they belong to is their home community, not the college community. These students, who typically commute to college between work and other commitments, do not tend to get involved in student organizations on campus. Thus, the ability for them to become socially integrated into the college community is greatly diminished and the only opportunity they may have to develop a campus community is through interaction with students and faculty during class times. Flipped, active learning classes are more likely to provide this type of socio-academic integrative moment than lecture classes.

3 RESEARCH QUESTIONS

The research questions we address are how the flipped vs. traditional class approach differs in terms of student performance, and how these two approaches impact retention in the major. In this paper we investigate retention rates based on students' first university exposure to a CS class. We investigate student retention for two groups of CS1 students: those who took a flipped, lightweight teams version vs. those who took a traditional lecture version.

4 METHODS

We requested anonymized data from the Institutional Research Office at our institution. In our analysis, the independent variable is the instructional dimension: whether students took their initial CS1 course as a flipped class with lightweight teams or a traditional lecture and lab. The dependent variable is the percentage of students who switched out of their CS major. This dependent variable can be broken down across various dimensions:

- Enrollment Dimension: New Freshman vs. Transfer Students. Students entering CS majors are classified as new freshmen (first time university students, entering directly from high school) or transfer students (from other colleges or universities who have declared a CS major). Roughly half the incoming students each year are new freshman.
- Sex Dimension: Male vs. Female. Our university allows two sex classifications at enrollment, male or female, and does not capture chosen gender identity.
- Racial/Ethnic Dimension: Underrepresented Minority Groups. Underrepresented minority groups in this study are defined as African American, Hispanic/Latino, Native American, Multi-ethnic, and Pacific Islander. Caucasian and Asian students define the majority group. International students and the unknown classifications are omitted from this study because the numbers are extremely small.

For the academic performance analysis, all students who enrolled in CS1 during fall and spring terms between 2013 and 2017 were included. There were 166 students in the flipped version, and 1573 in the traditional version. Grade performance was analyzed by pass (A,B,C) or fail (D,F,W).

5 RESULTS

In this section we present both descriptive results on retention in CS across the dimensions of freshmen vs. transfer students, males vs. females, racial/ethnic background, and interactions across these. Our independent variable is retention in the major immediately after taking either the flipped or traditional CS1 class. For all the statistics below, the number of students in each category is the number of students who **completed** the CS1 course, except where we specifically discuss DFW rates.

5.1 Descriptive Results

In these descriptive statistics, we show results for students who changed out of the major, but these do not include students who dropped out of university entirely. The raw data in Table 2 shows that no females changed major out of CS after CS1 flipped, but 7% of males did. For CS freshmen that took the traditional CS1 class, 3% of females changed major and 3% of males changed major.

If we look at the impact on racial/ethnic minorities, no minorities changed majors out of CS after taking the flipped CS1, while 5.3% of asian and white students changed major out of CS after taking the flipped CS1. In contrast, 5% of minority CS majors changed major after taking the traditional CS1, while only 2% of asian and white CS majors changed out of the major after taking traditional CS1. Note that this data represents only students taking our CS1 class who had already selected a CS major. Our CS1 classes often have many students from other majors.

Table 2: Count of CS freshmen (not transfer) students completing CS1 and count of students changing major out of CS next term, from Spring 2013-Spring 2016, by sex, majority vs minority group and instructional method

		All CS Freshmen		Afr-Amer & Hisp		Asian & White	
Type	Sex	# Completed	# Changed Major	# Completed	# Changed Major	# Completed	# Changed Major
Flipped	Female	29	0	6	0	22	0
	Male	70	5	11	0	53	4
	Total	99	5	17	0	75	4
Traditional	Female	69	2	15	1	41	1
	Male	530	14	82	4	404	10
	Total	599	16	97	5	445	11

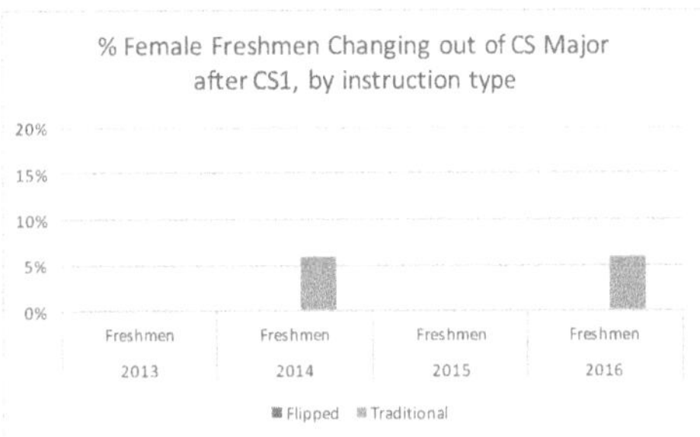

Figure 1: The % of freshman female CS majors who change major immediately after CS1, by instructional method.

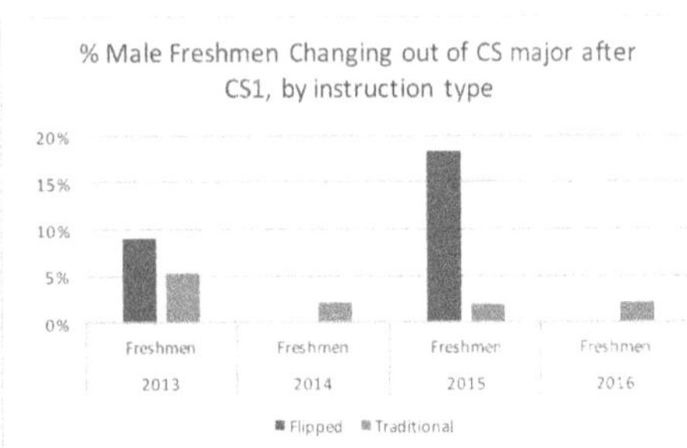

Figure 2: The % of freshman male CS majors changing out of the major immediately after CS1, by instructional method.

5.2 Statistical Analysis

To analyze retention by course type, a series of non-parametric analyses were conducted. First, students were grouped by admission type (freshmen/transfer), by sex (male/female), and by underrepresented minority group, and then by retention status. Retention is defined as continuing in the major; not-retained is defined as changing out of CS or leaving the university. Due to small numbers in some cases, statistical analyses were not possible, so a second series of non-parametric analyses were performed, that combined female students into the underrepresented minority group. Underrepresented Minority Group students are indicated by URM, and include non-white and non-asian students. Underrepresented Student Group (URS) includes all URM students and white and asian

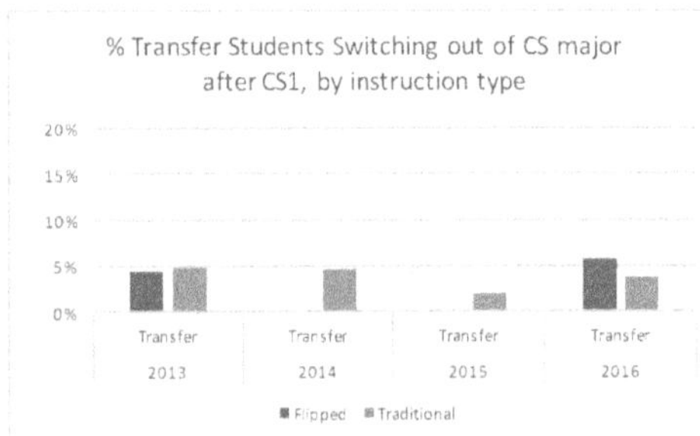

Figure 3: The % of transfer CS students changing out of the major immediately after CS1, by instructional method.

women. Each analysis was conducted for retention after one year in the major, and repeated for retention in the term following taking CS1. Figure 4 displays the analyses that were performed and bolds those with statistically significant findings.

5.2.1 Academic Performance. For all CS majors who enrolled in CS1 during fall and spring terms between 2013 and 2017 (freshmen and transfers), there were 166 students in the flipped version, and 1573 in the traditional version. Grade performance was analyzed by pass (A,B,C) or fail (D,F,W), and chi square revealed statistically significant differences in performance outcomes among the courses, $x(1) = 6.369, p = .012$. More students passed flipped CS1 than expected, and fewer passed traditional CS1 than expected.

5.2.2 One Year Retention. Underrepresented minority students in computing (women, African American, Hispanic, Native American, Pacific Islander and Multi-racial) were compared to majority students (white and asian males) in one year retention in the computing major having taken the flipped course or the traditional course. Statistically significant differences were observed for transfer students, $x(1) = 4.153, p = .042$; fewer transfer underrepresented minority students were retained in the flipped course than expected while more were retained in the traditional course than expected. New freshmen underrepresented minority students were retained significantly higher than expected in the flipped course than the traditional course, $x(1) = 16.202, p = .000$.

When the student groups were further separated by sex and then by underrepresented minority ethnicity (African American, Hispanic, Native American, Pacific Islander, Multi-ethnic vs Majority),

Non-parametric Analyses Performed by Population			
R1. Are 1-year retention rates in CS different based upon taking Flipped vs Traditional CS 1 Course?			
Overall	Freshmen Retained/Not-Retained Transfer Retained/Not-Retained		
Gender	~Freshmen Females Retained/Not-Retained Transfer Females Retained/Not-Retained ***Freshmen Females/Males, Retained/Not-Retained*** Transfer Females/Males, Retained/Not-Retained	URM	~Freshmen URM Retained/Not-Retained ***Transfer URM Retained/Not-Retained*** Freshmen URM/Majority, Retained/Not-Retained ~Transfer URM/Majority, Retained/Not-Retained
Females + URM = Underrepresented Students			~Freshmen URS Retained/Not-Retained **Transfer URS Retained/Not-Retained** ***Freshmen URS/Majority, Retained/Not-Retained*** Transfer URS/Majority, Retained/Not-Retained
R2. Are Next-Term retention rates in CS different based upon taking Flipped vs Traditional CS 1 Course?			
Overall	Freshmen Retained/Not-Retained Transfer Retained/Not-Retained		
Gender	~Freshmen Females Retained/Not-Retained Transfer Females Retained/Not-Retained ***Freshmen Females/Males, Retained/Not-Retained*** ***Transfer Females/Males, Retained/Not-Retained***	URM	~Freshmen URM Retained/Not-Retained ~Transfer URM Retained/Not-Retained Freshmen URM/Majority, Retained/Not-Retained ~Transfer URM/Majority, Retained/Not-Retained
Females + URM = Underrepresented Students			~Freshmen URS Retained/Not-Retained Transfer URS Retained/Not-Retained ***Freshmen URS/Majority, Retained/Not-Retained*** Transfer URS/Majority, Retained/Not-Retained

Figure 4: Summary of Non-parametric analysis by population. Items in bold represent statistically significant relationships, while items marked ~represents populations with too few students in flipped cells for analysis.

statistically significant differences were again observed. Female students were retained at a higher rate than expected when taking the flipped course and less than expected when taking traditional course, $x(1) = 22.347, p = .000$, while male students were retained at a higher rate in the traditional course than in the flipped course. For minority ethnicity transfer students, fewer were retained than expected in the flipped course and more than expected in the traditional course, $x(1) =, 3.859, p = .049$.

5.2.3 Next Term Retention. When next term retention of all new freshmen was compared by sex and course, a statistically significant difference was obtained, $x(1) = 20.992, p = .000$. Female students were retained at a higher rate than expected when taking the flipped course and less than expected when taking the traditional course, whereas male students were retained more than expected in the traditional course. When transfer students were compared by sex and course, female students were retained more than expected in the flipped course with less retained in the traditional course; the opposite was found for males, who were retained at a higher rate than expected in the traditional course, $x(1) = 10.339, p = .001$.

Underrepresented minority students in computing (women, African American, Hispanic, Native American, Pacific Islander and Multi-racial) were compared to majority students who haven taken the flipped course or the traditional course. Statistically significant differences were observed for freshmen students, $x(1) = 7.892, p = .005$; more underrepresented students were retained in the flipped course than expected, and fewer in the traditional, with fewer majority students retained in both the flipped course and traditional course than expected. Fewer transfer underrepresented minority students were retained in the flipped course than expected while more were retained in the traditional course than expected.

6 DISCUSSION

Our findings suggest that female and underrepresented minority group students are retained at higher rates when taking a flipped CS1 course when entering as freshmen, and no female students left the major after taking a flipped introductory course. This is unsurprising given that we know female and minority students have been shown to have higher retention in computing when they can develop a sense of community [5]. What is surprising is that majority male students were retained better in traditional CS1 courses, because researchers have suggested that what works well for underrepresented students will work equally as well for majority students [9, 13]. We interpret these findings as strong indications that one size does not fit all students, and that further study is needed to parse out impact of instructor, student prior computing exposure, and other possible confounding variables on retention. Faculty advisors should inform students about their choice of course style so that they can make the most appropriate decision for their own personal preference. The findings that minority transfer students did not reap the retention benefits from flipped courses may be because their identity as transfer student trumps their minority identity. Transfer students are typically older than freshmen, indicative that these students are more mature, and may face pressures of adulthood beyond those of a typical freshman.

The flipped class approach with required prepwork forces students to spend more time learning to program, which may account for some of the success, inline with earlier research [10]. An increase in the time spent on preparation supports the idea that 'programming is easy' but takes time [15]. This is likely especially helpful for students who come in without programming experience.

The social aspects of lightweight teams in our flipped classes means that students see that others also struggle with the new concepts. As they see their peers overcome, it gives them confidence and self-efficacy that they also can persevere. This means they are less likely to think they don't fit the CS mold. Because they have made friends, they have people they can call on when they get stuck on something, and study with for tests.

7 LIMITATIONS

Our analysis has certain limitations. As with most post-hoc analysis in higher education, there is almost no ability to control for between subjects population confounds, as students tend to select course section based on what suits their schedules. In addition, the institutional data we acquired that is used to understand one-semester and one-year retention effects is based on students who *passed* the CS1 class, ignoring the students who may have failed these classes and left (though this is captured in the DFW analysis). Institutional enrollment numbers hide non-gender binary students, requiring them to select a binary sex category.

As with all educational research, there are contextual confounds. Our introductory CS courses have been in flux, with a move to make all CS1 classes taught in Java, though some of the courses represented in our data were taught with C++. Additionally, we did not control for instructors as variables, and many of the traditional courses have begun to be redesigned to incorporate some degree of active learning activities. As enrollments increase over time, we anticipate being able to control for instructor variables, such as experience with and usage level of active learning techniques.

8 CONCLUSIONS

We have presented a longitudinal analysis based on four years of data that examines how flipped vs. traditional CS1 classes impact student retention in the following year. We showed that female students and underrepresented racial minority students are less likely to switch out of the CS major after taking a flipped version of CS1, while the opposite is true for male students and transfer students. We also showed that female students and under-represented minority students were less likely to fail a flipped version of CS1.

9 ACKNOWLEDGMENTS

This work is supported by the National Science Foundation, IUSE/Professional Formation of Engineers: Revolutionizing engineering and computer science Departments (RED), Award 1519160.

REFERENCES

[1] A. M. Al-Zahrani. From passive to active: The impact of the flipped classroom through social learning platforms on higher education students' creative thinking. *British Journal of Educational Technology*, 46(6):1133–1148, 2015.

[2] J. Bennedsen and M. E. Caspersen. Failure rates in introductory programming. *SIGCSE Bull.*, 39(2):32–36, June 2007.

[3] J. Bergmann and A. Sams. *Flip your classroom: Reach every student in every class every day.* International Society for Technology in Education, 2012.

[4] S. Cheryan, V. C. Plaut, P. G. Davies, and C. M. Steele. Ambient belonging: how stereotypical cues impact gender participation in computer science. *Journal of personality and social psychology*, 97(6):1045, 2009.

[5] T. Dahlberg, T. Barnes, K. Buch, and A. Rorrer. The stars alliance: Viable strategies for broadening participation in computing. *ACM Transactions on Computing Education (TOCE)*, 11(3):18, 2011.

[6] S. L. Dazo, N. R. Stepanek, R. Fulkerson, and B. Dorn. An empirical analysis of video viewing behaviors in flipped cs1 courses. In *Proceedings of the 2016 ACM Conference on Innovation and Technology in Computer Science Education*, ITiCSE '16, pages 106–111, New York, NY, USA, 2016. ACM.

[7] R. Deil-Amen. Socio-academic integrative moments: Rethinking academic and social integration among two-year college students in career-related programs. *The Journal of Higher Education*, 82(1):54–91, 2011.

[8] S. L. Eddy and K. A. Hogan. Getting under the hood: how and for whom does increasing course structure work? *CBE-Life Sciences Education*, 13(3):453–468, 2014.

[9] J. Goode and J. Margolis. Exploring computer science: A case study of school reform. *ACM Transactions on Computing Education (TOCE)*, 11(2):12, 2011.

[10] D. Gross, E. S. Pietri, G. Anderson, K. Moyano-Camihort, and M. J. Graham. Increased preclass preparation underlies student outcome improvement in the flipped classroom. *CBE-Life Sciences Education*, 14(4):ar36, 2015.

[11] N. A. Hamid. A functional flipped CS1. *J. Comput. Sci. Coll.*, 32(2):120–126, Dec. 2016.

[12] D. Horton, M. Craig, J. Campbell, P. Gries, and D. Zingaro. Comparing outcomes in inverted and traditional CS1. In *Proceedings of the 2014 Conference on Innovation & Technology in Computer Science Education*, ITiCSE '14, pages 261–266, New York, NY, USA, 2014. ACM.

[13] G. Ladson-Billings. Culturally relevant pedagogy 2.0: aka the remix. *Harvard Educational Review*, 84(1):74–84, 2014.

[14] C. Latulipe, N. B. Long, and C. E. Seminario. Structuring flipped classes with lightweight teams and gamification. In *Proceedings of the 46th ACM Technical Symposium on Computer Science Education*, SIGCSE '15, pages 392–397, New York, NY, USA, 2015. ACM.

[15] A. Luxton-Reilly. Learning to program is easy. In *Proceedings of the 2016 ACM Conference on Innovation and Technology in Computer Science Education*, ITiCSE '16, pages 284–289, New York, NY, USA, 2016. ACM.

[16] M. L. Maher, C. Latulipe, H. Lipford, and A. Rorrer. Flipped classroom strategies for CS education. In *Proceedings of the 46th ACM Technical Symposium on Computer Science Education*, SIGCSE '15, pages 218–223, New York, NY, USA, 2015. ACM.

[17] C. McDowell, L. Werner, H. E. Bullock, and J. Fernald. Pair programming improves student retention, confidence, and program quality. *Commun. ACM*, 49(8):90–95, Aug. 2006.

[18] L. K. Michaelsen, A. B. Knight, and L. D. Fink. *Team-based learning: A transformative use of small groups.* Greenwood Publishing Group, 2002.

[19] L. K. Michaelsen and M. Sweet. Fundamental principles and practices of team-based learning. *Team-based learning for health professions education: A guide to using small groups for improving learning. Sterling (VA): Stylus Publishing*, pages 9–31, 2008.

[20] J. Pirker, M. Riffnaller-Schiefer, and C. Gütl. Motivational active learning: Engaging university students in computer science education. In *Proceedings of the 2014 Conference on Innovation & Technology in Computer Science Education*, ITiCSE '14, pages 297–302, New York, NY, USA, 2014. ACM.

[21] L. Porter, M. Guzdial, C. McDowell, and B. Simon. Success in introductory programming: What works? *Commun. ACM*, 56(8):34–36, Aug. 2013.

[22] L. Porter and B. Simon. Retaining nearly one-third more majors with a trio of instructional best practices in CS1. In *Proceeding of the 44th ACM Technical Symposium on Computer Science Education*, SIGCSE '13, pages 165–170, New York, NY, USA, 2013. ACM.

[23] K. Sanders, J. Boustedt, A. Eckerdal, R. McCartney, and C. Zander. Folk pedagogy: Nobody doesn't like active learning. In *Proceedings of the 2017 ACM Conference on International Computing Education Research*, ICER '17, pages 145–154, New York, NY, USA, 2017. ACM.

[24] P. Sankar, J. Gilmartin, and M. Sobel. An examination of belongingness and confidence among female computer science students. *SIGCAS Comput. Soc.*, 45(2):7–10, July 2015.

[25] A. Vihavainen, J. Airaksinen, and C. Watson. A systematic review of approaches for teaching introductory programming and their influence on success. In *Proceedings of the Tenth Annual Conference on International Computing Education Research*, ICER '14, pages 19–26, New York, NY, USA, 2014. ACM.

[26] C. Watson and F. W. Li. Failure rates in introductory programming revisited. In *Proceedings of the 2014 Conference on Innovation & Technology in Computer Science Education*, ITiCSE '14, pages 39–44, New York, NY, USA, 2014. ACM.

[27] D. Zingaro. Peer instruction contributes to self-efficacy in cs1. In *Proceedings of the 45th ACM Technical Symposium on Computer Science Education*, SIGCSE '14, pages 373–378, New York, NY, USA, 2014. ACM.

Does Native Language Play a Role in Learning a Programming Language?

Adalbert Gerald Soosai Raj
Department of Computer Sciences and Education
University of Wisconsin-Madison
gerald@cs.wisc.edu

Kasama Ketsuriyonk
Department of Computer Sciences
University of Wisconsin-Madison
ketsuriyonk@cs.wisc.edu

Jignesh M. Patel
Department of Computer Sciences
University of Wisconsin-Madison
jignesh@cs.wisc.edu

Richard Halverson
Department of Educational Leadership and Policy Analysis
University of Wisconsin-Madison
rich.halverson@wisc.edu

ABSTRACT

Computer Science (CS) is taught in India, using English as the medium of instruction, to students whose native language is not English. This places a high cognitive load on students who learn programming for the first time and who are not very proficient in English. The problems these students face become even harder since learning to program can be an incredibly difficult task. Our study aims to find out if a student's native language has any effect on the student's ability to learn programming. We taught linked list, a basic concept in CS, to two groups of undergraduate students for a week in Tamil Nadu, India. We used *English* to teach one group of students and *English and Tamil* (the native language in Tamil Nadu) to teach the other group. Our intervention consisted of three lectures and one live-coding session. We collected quantitative and qualitative data using technical tests and open-ended feedback respectively. We found that although teaching programming using both English and Tamil is no different when compared to using only English with respect to student learning, students have expressed positive opinions about teaching and learning CS using two languages.

CCS CONCEPTS

•Social and professional topics → Computer science education;

KEYWORDS

CS Education; Native Language; Bilingual Education

ACM Reference format:

Adalbert Gerald Soosai Raj, Kasama Ketsuriyonk, Jignesh M. Patel, and Richard Halverson. 2018. Does Native Language Play a Role in Learning a Programming Language?. In *Proceedings of The 49th ACM Tech-nical Symposium on Computer Science Education, Baltimore, MD, USA, February 21–24, 2018 (SIGCSE'18),* 6 pages.
DOI: http://dx.doi.org/10.1145/3159450.3159531

DOI: http://dx.doi.org/10.1145/3159450.3159531

1 INTRODUCTION

Students in India learn their subjects during their K-12 (kindergarten (K) through twelfth grade (12)) either in English or their *native/first language* (i.e., the language that a person has spoken from earliest childhood). This choice of language depends on whether the student studies in an English-medium school or a native-language-medium school during their K-12. Although there are two mediums of instruction during K-12, almost all the STEM (Science, Technology, Engineering and Mathematics) subjects in undergraduate education are taught mostly in English [1, 12]. Computer Science, one of the STEM subjects, is also taught in Indian colleges in English. The main reason for teaching CS in English is because software companies in India use English as their language of communication as most of them are affiliated with U.S. based companies [3]. Therefore, students who aren't very comfortable in English (e.g., students who studied in a Tamil-medium school during their K-12 and students who aren't proficient with English even though they may have studied in an English medium school) find it difficult to understand programming concepts since the subject is already new to them and they are also forced to learn it in a language that they are not comfortable with [18, 22]. As a result, these students end up failing their programming courses, and eventually develop inferiority complexes about their programming abilities [17].

Our research started with the following question: Can we reduce the difficulties faced by these students by teaching them CS using both English and their native language? To answer this question and to better understand the impact of the medium of instruction to teach CS, we conducted an experiment where we taught programming using both *Tamil and English* to a group of students (experimental group) whose native language was Tamil. We also taught programming to another set of students (control group) *only in English* even though their native language was also Tamil. We used *English along with Tamil* to teach the experimental group since we believe that even though Tamil may help students to better understand programming concepts, English is needed for them to communicate with other programmers around the world. Moreover since the documentation of the programming languages (e.g., K&R C [13]) and the online programming forums (e.g., Stack Overflow) are in English, it is very important for these students to learn English along with programming.

To teach CS using two languages, we use techniques like *code-switching* [8] and *translanguaging* [9, 16] while communicating with the students. *Code-switching* is a technique of alternating between two or more languages in the same conversation. Code-switching, especially from the secondary to the primary/native language helps the students to focus, clarify and reinforce lesson materials that leads to better understanding of the subject [8]. *Translanguaging* is a pedagogical practice where certain aspects of the pedagogy (e.g., classroom discussion) are done in the primary language and other aspects (e.g., writing, exams, etc.) are done in the secondary language. This helps the students to gain a deeper understanding of the subject matter and to improve their proficiency with the secondary language [2].

The reason why bilingualism will be beneficial in CS is because it is one of the subjects where students will be greatly benefited if they understand the meaning of keywords. Many of the concepts in programming languages would be easy to remember and recall if students understood the meaning of those words in English. Examples of such concepts/keywords are static, abstract, virtual, inheritance, polymorphism, encapsulation, etc. The number of non-native speakers of the English language (as of 2003) around the whole world outnumbered the native speakers by a ratio of 3 : 1 [6]. We consider our study to be a small first step towards broadening the impact of computing education not just to predominantly English-speaking regions but to the entire world.

2 RELATED WORK

Pal and Iyer analyzed the effects of medium of instruction on acquiring programming abilities among students in North India whose native language is mostly Hindi [19–21]. Programming was taught to two groups of first-year undergraduate students from Hindi-medium background (i.e., students who studied in Hindi-medium schools during their K-12) using English-only, and Hindi-only medium of instruction. The programming abilities of the two groups of students were tested and compared, and it was found that the students from Hindi-medium background learnt programming better when they were taught in Hindi when compared to when they were taught in English. Our work differs from this work in various aspects. First of all, the native language that we used in our study was Tamil (a South-Indian language, spoken by people in Tamil Nadu) which is a completely different language than Hindi (spoken by people in many parts of India but not in Tamil Nadu). We don't use Tamil-only to teach programming but instead we use a combination of Tamil and English to teach programming since we recognize the benefits of using both languages. We don't target students who are from a Tamil-medium background but instead we target all students whose native language is Tamil, even though they may have studied in an English-medium school during their K-12. We compared the effectiveness of our approach by using the gain and the post-test score while Pal et.al. used only the post-test score to compare the effectiveness of their approach even though they had conducted a pre-test in their study.

Lau and Yuen studied the impact of medium of instruction on teaching and learning computer programming [14]. They conducted their study among two groups of K-12 students from Chinese-medium and English-medium schools in Hong Kong. They taught bubble sort using either C or Pascal to these students, and reported that Chinese-medium students appear to understand programming concepts better than their English-medium counterparts. In our study, the students were not separated into two groups based on their medium of instruction during K-12 since CS is taught using English as the medium of instruction in undergraduate colleges in India, irrespective of the students' prior medium of instruction.

Boulet studied the role of language in teaching and learning of Mathematics [4]. The author addresses some specific issues pertaining to languages that students use to define mathematical terms to read and interpret mathematical notations, and to describe mathematical processes. The teacher's role to foster productive mathematical discourse in the classroom using their language as a tool is also highlighted. In our study too, we used all the technical terms in CS as it is in English. For example, the terms like *linked lists, arrays, pointers, structures*, etc, were used as they are used in English. Tamil was used only to explain the programming concepts.

Probyn interviewed some teachers in South Africa who use English along with Xhosa, an official South African language, to teach Science [22, 23]. The study shows that the language of learning and teaching frequently creates a barrier to learning when it is not the native language of the learners. The benefits of code-switching between the two languages for increased comprehension among students is also highlighted. We consider our study as an extension to this study where we try to find if the vernacular has any effect on learning programming, mainly by measuring student learning using pre-and-post technical tests.

Fennema-Bloom studied the value of naturally occuring code-switching during bilingual content instruction in Mandarin/English among non-traditional immigrant high school students [8]. The author found that code-switching is a valuable pedagogic tool used by bilingual teachers to make content more comprehensible. Our work targets on finding the value of code-switching for CS Education.

3 RESEARCH QUESTIONS

Our research aims at addressing the following questions:

(1) Does using the native language (Tamil) along with English for teaching programming have any effect on student learning when compared to teaching only in English?

(2) What are the students' opinions about using their native language along with English for teaching programming within the classroom?

Our *hypothesis* is that using the native language (Tamil) along with English for teaching programming will have a positive impact on student learning when compared to using only English, for first year undergraduate students whose native language is Tamil.

4 METHODOLOGY

In this section, we explain the methodology that we used to conduct the experiment and to collect the data.

4.1 Participants

The experiment was conducted in a well reputed Engineering college in Tamil Nadu. Two groups of first-year students, enrolled in two different sections of a data structures course were selected for the study. One group was treated as the control group and the other group was treated as the experimental group. The total number of students in the control and experimental group were 52 and 51 respectively. All these students have previously taken a programming course in C [13] and data structures was their second programming course. There was only one student in the experimental group who was from a Tamil-medium background during K-12 and there were two such students in the control group.

4.2 Experimental Design

The experiment was conducted using a *nonrandomized control group pre-test post-test design* [7]. In this design, the participants were not randomly assigned to groups but remained in their pre-assigned groups. This increases the external validity of the design by reducing the reactive effects of the experimental procedure [7]. We acknowledge that the problem with this approach is that even if there are any post-test differences between the groups, they may be attributed to characteristic difference between the groups rather than to the intervention. We take this issue into consideration in our result analysis by choosing our statistical models for pre-test post-test comparison very carefully (see Section 5 for more details).

The reason behind using this experimental design is that we didn't want the students to know that they were part of an experiment comparing the effects of teaching programming using their native language along with English versus using only English. We felt that if students knew these details about our experiment before our intervention then the results may be unreliable since some students may try to bias their test results based on their preferred method for learning programming.

We coordinated with the two teachers who were teaching data structures for these two groups so that we can teach linked lists at the appropriate time during the course. The teachers introduced the researcher (and the observer) as guest lecturers to the students. The researcher taught the students and the observer took field notes during the intervention. After our intervention was over, we informed the students that they were part of a teaching intervention and gave them the option to withdraw their test and feedback data, if they didn't want them to be included in our study. No student withdrew from our experiment.

4.3 Experimental Procedure

The following activities were performed with both the control group and the experimental group as a part of our intervention. There was a pre-test, three in-class lectures, a live-coding session, and a post-test. The programming (coding) was done in C [13] (a high-level programming language) and the questions in the pre-test and the post-test were in English for both groups. We collected an open-ended feedback from the students in both groups to understand what they felt about our intervention.

4.3.1 Pre-test. A pre-test was conducted to determine the students' understanding of key programming concepts like *pointers*, *structures*, and concepts about *stack and heap memory* in C programming. There were a total of 10 questions in the pre-test. There were 4 questions on pointers, 2 questions on structures, 2 questions on stack and heap memory, and 2 questions on some basic concepts in C. The pre-test was conducted for a total of 10 points, one point for each question. The pre-test (and post-test) questions were chosen from a set of frequently asked programming interview questions [11].

These topics were tested in the pre-test as they are the prerequisites for learning linked lists in C. We also wanted a way to determine how much the students learnt during the one week session, so the pre-test scores were used as a baseline for each student. The complete pre-test can be found at this link: http://bit.do/pretest_questions.

4.3.2 Three lectures on linked lists. Three classroom-based lectures, each of 50 minutes duration, were taught for both groups. The basics of linked lists were taught in those three lectures. Topics discussed were: declaring a node structure for the linked list, adding a node at the beginning of the linked list, deleting a node from a linked list, calculating the length of a given linked list, printing a linked list, etc. The same topics were taught to both the groups.

The main differences between the lectures for the two groups were the following: The lectures were taught *only in English* for the students in the control group. Also, the students in the control group were required to communicate with the instructor and their classmates during the lecture only in English.

On the other hand, the lectures were taught using both *English and Tamil* in the experimental group, and the students were free to communicate in any of those two languages, whichever they felt more comfortable with. The instructor used both English and Tamil nearly equally (i.e., 50% time in English - 50% time in Tamil) while teaching the experimental group. Based on the observer's field notes, we found that more than 90% of the questions that were asked by the students in the experimental group during the lecture were in Tamil. The instructor answered the questions during the lecture using the same language (either English or Tamil) in which they were asked.

The instructor used *code-switching* between Tamil and English in the following way. He used English to introduce a topic, to explain the syntax, and to explain some technical terms (e.g., self-referential structures). He switched to Tamil whenever he felt that a particular topic needed detailed explanation in order to help the students understand the idea in a better way (e.g., How to change the head of a linked list when we add an element at the beginning?). The instructor used *translanguaging* as follows. He used Tamil only for oral explanations, discussion, and answering students' questions. He wrote all the content (e.g., code snippets, definitions, etc.) on the chalk-board during the lectures only in English.

4.3.3 Live coding session. Following the three classroom-based lectures on linked lists, a live-coding session [25] was conducted for about 90 minutes. The instructor projected his laptop on a screen, and wrote C code for the following linked list functions from scratch: adding a node at the beginning of the linked list, printing all the elements in the linked list, deleting all the nodes from the linked list.

The instructor was thinking aloud throughout the live-coding session. He showed the students how he would go about writing the code for these three functions. He also showed them some common sources of errors while writing code for linked lists. The content taught during the live-coding session was the same for both the control group and the experimental group.

4.3.4 Post-test. The post-test consisted of 15 questions on linked lists from the following three categories:

(1) Syntax of linked lists (5 questions - 1 point each)
(2) Conceptual understanding (5 questions - 2 points each)
(3) Predict the output (5 questions - 3 points each)

All the questions on the post-test were based on the material taught during the classroom-based lectures and the live-coding session. The post-test was conducted for a total of 30 points. The complete post-test can be found at this link: http://bit.do/posttest_questions.

4.3.5 Open-ended feedback. We collected open-ended feedback from the students about our bilingual teaching methodology. All the students in both groups wrote their feedback in English, although the choice of language for the feedback was left to the students. Sample feedback from students is shown in Section 5.3.

5 RESULTS

The mean of the pre-test scores and the post-test scores for the two group are shown in Table 1 and Table 2 respectively.

Table 1: Mean of pre-test scores for the two groups

Group	N	Mean	Std. Dev.	Std. Error of Mean
Control	52	33.9	15.2	2.1
Experimental	51	25.3	14.5	2.0

Table 2: Mean of post-test scores for the two groups

Group	N	Mean	Std. Dev.	Std. Error of Mean
Control	52	76.7	17.3	2.4
Experimental	51	65.4	17.4	2.4

The mean of the pre-test score for the control group is higher than the mean of the pre-test score for the experimental group (see Table 1). This indicates that the control group and the experimental group were at different levels with respect to the prior knowledge in programming before our intervention. We were aware that this issue may occur in our results since we used a *nonrandomized control group pre-test post-test design*. In order to account for these initial differences between the two groups, we did the following to measure student learning:

(1) Compared the *gain scores* using *Independent Samples t-test*
(2) Compared the *post-test scores* using *ANCOVA (ANalysis of COVAriance)* with the pre-test score as a covariate.

According to the literature on measuring change using a pre-test and post-test, both the gain scores [26] and the post-test scores [15] are considered to be good indicators of student learning [5]. Hence, we compared both these metrics using appropriate tests of significance to find out if there was any statistically significant difference between the two groups due to our intervention. We used an alpha level of .05 for all statistical tests.

5.1 Comparison of Gain Scores

The mean of the gain scores for the two groups are shown in Table 3. The mean gain for the control group is higher than that of the experimental group. We performed Independent Samples t-test [10] to compare the gain scores between the control group and the experimental group and found *no significant difference* in gain scores (t(103) = .702, df = 101, p = .485).

Table 3: Mean of gain scores for the two groups

Group	N	Mean	Std. Dev.	Std. Error of Mean
Control	52	42.8	18.8	2.6
Experimental	51	40.1	20.1	2.8

5.2 Comparison of Post-Test Scores

The pre-test scores of the students in both the groups varied significantly before our intervention. We performed Independent Samples t-test to compare the pre-test scores between the control group and the experimental group and found *a significant difference* in pre-test scores (t(103) = 2.92, df = 101, p = .004). Therefore, we cannot directly compare the post-test scores between the two groups using Independent Samples t-test as we did for the gain scores [7]. Instead we use a statistical model to analyze and find if there was a significant effect on the post-test score of a student (response variable) because of the student's group (categorical variable) while controlling for the pre-test score of the student (predictor variable). Hence, we performed ANalysis of COVAriance (ANCOVA) [10] on post-test scores of the two groups as described below.

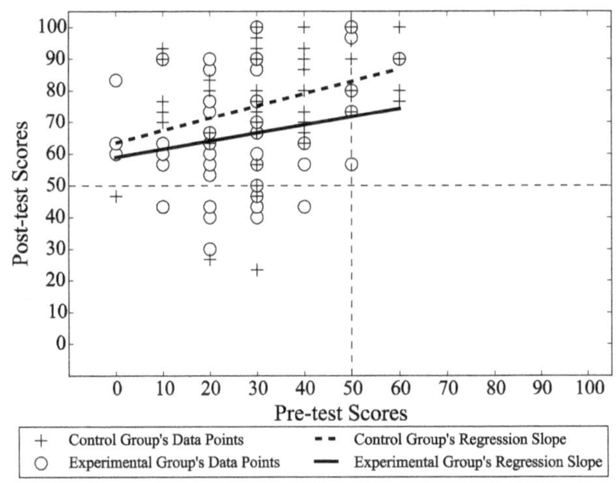

Figure 1: A scatter plot showing each student's pre-test score plotted on the x-axis and the post-test score plotted on the y-axis. The regression lines are also plotted for each group which shows the relationship between the pre-test and post-test score.

We plot a scatter plot in Figure 1 using the pre-test and the post-test scores of the students in both the groups. In this scatter plot the x-axis represents the pre-test scores of the students and the y-axis represents the post-test scores of the students. The two lines shown in this scatter plot are the regression lines for a particular group that summarizes the relationship between the post-test score and the pre-test score for that group. The regression lines for both the groups have nearly equal *positive slopes* (0.26 for the experimental group and 0.39 for the control group) which means that our intervention had a similar positive effect on both the groups. The y-intercept of the control group's regression line (63.51) is slightly higher than the y-intercept of the experimental group's regression line (58.98) which means that for a given pre-test score, a student in the control group had a better post-test score when compared to a student in the experimental group. The homogeneity of the regression slopes tells us that it is valid to create an ANCOVA regression model for finding out if there was any significant difference between the two groups due to the native language.

The results from our analysis of covariance are shown in Table 4. The p-values shown in this table are for the interaction of each variable with the response variable (i.e., post-test score).

Table 4: ANCOVA Results

Variable	p-value
Pre-test score	0.000324
Group	0.016056
Interaction between the pre-test score and the group	0.554225

The *pre-test score of a student* had a *significant effect on the post-test score* of the student after controlling for the effect of the student's group (p-value = 0.000324). This means that irrespective of the group that a student belongs to, generally, if a student did well on the pre-test then that student also did well on the post-test.

The *group of a student* had a *significant effect on the post-test score* of the student after controlling for the effect of the student's pre-test score (p-value = 0.016056). This is due to the fact that even before our intervention, the control group was better than the experimental group with respect to the knowledge of programming.

The interaction between the *pre-test score and the group of a student* has *no significant effect on the post-test score* of that student. In other words, the post-test scores of two students with the same pre-test score were not statistically significant based on the student's group. This means that the post-test scores of the two groups are not statistically significant due to our intervention.

5.3 Sample Students' Feedback

Tamil was used to explain difficult concepts in the experimental group. All the students' comments about the usage of Tamil to explain programming were very positive. Selected comments include: *"Your class made me more attentive in the class."; "The lecture was really very useful and it was easy to understand since the mixture of English and Tamil language helps us to learn better."; "The usage of both the languages Tamil and English actually kept us engaging."*

Some students in the experimental group also mentioned that they *felt more comfortable within the classroom* during our intervention. We believe that the usage of the native language within the classroom may be one of the main reasons for these students to have felt this way. Some sample students' comments: *"It is very helpful for us to understand the concept. I really felt comfortable in learning this topic that taught us in both the languages. "; "This class was just rocking, we feel comfortable when we are taught in both the language. As far from my part linked list is the toughest portion in C programming, but you made us understand easily. There was full freedom throughout the class (with respect to using the language of our choice)."; "Really the lectures are awesome. It is very useful for us. The method is really good. I feel very comfortable and it is little easy to understand when compared to normal teaching (using only English)."; "The lecture was simply awesome. True to my heart it was excellent. It was very comfortable for me to learn programming in this way."*

The feedback from the control group was also positive about our intervention. A detailed analysis of the comparison of students' sentiments between the two groups can be found in this study [24].

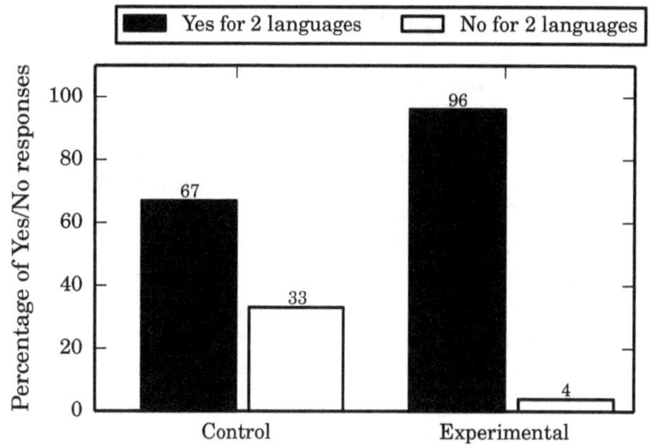

Figure 2: The student responses to the survey question "If given an option would you learn programming in a classroom where the teacher would use both English and Tamil to teach the concepts in programming?"

We also asked the following question in the feedback that we collected from the students at the end of our intervention: *If given an option would you learn programming in a classroom where the teacher would use both English and Tamil to teach the concepts in programming?*

This question was asked to students in both the groups, even though we didn't use Tamil in the control group. We wanted to get a sense of what might be the difference in students' opinions about learning using two languages between the two groups, one of them exposed to such an intervention while the other wasn't.

The student responses for this question are shown in Figure 2. The percentage of students favouring the use of both the languages was higher in both the groups.

6 DISCUSSION

Our study tried to find if using the native language (Tamil) along with English for teaching programming had any effect on students' learning of programming when compared to using only English. We measured the student learning in terms of gain scores and post-test scores.

The difference between the two groups with respect to the gain score is not statistically significant (see Section 5.1). This shows that there is no difference between teaching programming using only English and teaching programming using the native language (Tamil) along with English.

Also, the difference between the two groups with respect to the post-test score (with the pre-test score as a covariate) is not statistically significant (see Table 4). Therefore, based on these ANCOVA results we understand that since our intervention had similar positive effects on both the groups, we need more quantitative experiments in this area to better understand the impact of the native language on students' understanding of programming.

This further confirms that there is no difference between the two teaching methodologies on student learning.

Our finding that using the native language (Tamil) along with English is no different from using only English for teaching programming is different from the findings of Pal and Iyer [19–21] which suggests that the native language (Hindi) had a significant positive effect on students who did their schooling in a Hindi-medium school. The main reason for this difference is that in our study even though the native language of all students was Tamil, the majority of students (100 out of 103 students) studied in an English-medium school during their K-12. On the other hand, 50% of students in Pal and Iyer's study were from a Hindi-medium background. Also, while their study compared the difference between using Hindi-only and English-only medium of instruction, our study compared the difference between using two languages (English and Tamil) with English-only medium of instruction.

The feedback received from the students about using their native language (Tamil) along with English for teaching programming were completely positive. No student had any issues or concerns with using their native language for teaching programming within the classroom although they were only used to an English-only medium of instruction within the classroom until now. Also, many students in the experimental group have expressed that they felt very comfortable during our lectures since we used both the languages for instruction within the classroom. The students in the experimental group have expressed more positive opinions about learning using two languages when compared to those in the control group. We believe that the reason for this increased interest among the experimental group may be due to the fact that they were exposed to the teaching methodology of using two languages while the control group wasn't. Therefore, our other finding is that almost all the students exposed to our bilingual teaching methodology have preferred it over the current practice of teaching only in English.

One limitation with our study is that since we used the *non-randomized control group pre-test post-test design*, the two groups varied significantly with respect to their programming knowledge before the start of our intervention. Although we have taken this pre-test difference into consideration in our analysis of results, we acknowledge that the results would have been more reliable if these initial differences didn't exist among these groups. To minimize the effects due to the initial differences among the two groups, as a part of our future work, we plan to conduct more controlled experiments with a *randomized control group pre-test post-test design* [7] to better understand the effects of the native language for learning programming. Another limitation with our study is that we did not control for the students' English proficiency which we plan to do in our future experiments by conducting tests for English proficiency.

7 CONCLUSIONS

Our study didn't find any significant impact of using Tamil along with English on student learning of linked lists. We conclude that we need more studies in this area to verify if there is any significant difference in student learning between teaching programming using only English and using two languages (English and Tamil). We also conclude that, even though the effectiveness of using Tamil and English for teaching programming with respect to student learning is still unknown, students have expressed positive opinions about learning programming using the two languages. We believe that our work has potential implications in making CS education accessible to everyone around the world irrespective of their native language.

ACKNOWLEDGMENTS

We thank Prof. Saswati Mukerjee and Prof. Annie Bennet for helping us conduct experiments in India. Our sincere thanks to Prof. Michael Swift, Devin Wixon, Harshad Deshmukh, Ayebuke Turker, and Kaviya Lakshmipathy for their valuable feedback on our work. We also thank the anonymous reviewers for their comments on the earlier versions of this paper.

REFERENCES

[1] E Annamalai, JW Tollefson, and ABM Tsui. 2004. Medium of power: The question of English in education in India. *Medium of Instruction Policies–Which Agenda? Whose Agenda?* (2004).

[2] Colin Baker. 2003. Biliteracy and transliteracy in Wales: Language planning and the Welsh national curriculum. *Bilingual education and bilingualism* (2003).

[3] Peri Bhaskararao. 2002. English in contemporary India. *ABD* (2002).

[4] Genevieve Boulet. 2007. How does language impact the learning of mathematics? Let me count the ways. *Journal of Teaching and Learning* (2007).

[5] Edward Roland Cimler. 1973. *Gain vs. posttest scores as predictors of future performance.* Master's thesis. Citeseer.

[6] David Crystal. 2012. *English as a global language.* Cambridge university press.

[7] Dimiter M Dimitrov and Phillip D Rumrill Jr. 2003. Pretest-posttest designs and measurement of change. *Work* (2003).

[8] Jennifer R Fennema-Bloom. 2009. Code-scaffolding: A pedagogic code-switching technique for bilingual content instruction. *Journal of Education* (2009).

[9] Ofelia Garcia and Claire E Sylvan. 2011. Pedagogies and practices in multilingual classrooms: Singularities in pluralities. *The Modern Language Journal* (2011).

[10] Gene V Glass and Kenneth D Hopkins. 1970. *Statistical methods in education and psychology.* Prentice-Hall Englewood Cliffs, NJ.

[11] Sandeep Jain. 2017. GeeksforGeeks: A computer science portal for geeks. http://www.geeksforgeeks.org/. (2017). http://www.geeksforgeeks.org/

[12] N Jayaram. 1993. The language question in higher education: trends and issues. *Higher Education* (1993).

[13] Brian W Kernighan and Dennis M Ritchie. 2006. The C Programming Language. (2006).

[14] Wilfred WF Lau and Allan HK Yuen. 2011. The impact of the medium of instruction: The case of teaching and learning of computer programming. *Education and Information Technologies* (2011).

[15] Frederic M Lord. 1956. The measurement of growth. *ETS Research Report* (1956).

[16] Catherine M Mazak and Claudia Herbas-Donoso. 2015. Translanguaging practices at a bilingual university: A case study of a science classroom. *Bilingual education and bilingualism* (2015).

[17] T Murugavel. 2011. The Problems of Non-English Medium Engineering Students and Possible Solutions. (2011). http://worldlitonline.net/the-problems-of-non-english.pdf

[18] Yogendra Pal. 2016. *A Framework for Scaffolding to Teach Programming to Vernacular Medium Learners.* Ph.D. Dissertation. IIT, Bombay.

[19] Yogendra Pal and Sridhar Iyer. 2012. Comparison of English versus Hindi Medium Students for Programming Abilities Acquired through Video-Based Instruction. In *T4E*. IEEE.

[20] Yogendra Pal and Sridhar Iyer. 2015. Classroom Versus Screencast for Native Language Learners: Effect of Medium of Instruction on Knowledge of Programming. In *ITiCSE*. ACM.

[21] Yogendra Pal and Sridhar Iyer. 2015. Effect of medium of instruction on programming ability acquired through screencast. In *LaTiCE*. IEEE.

[22] Margaret Probyn. 2001. Teachers voices: Teachers reflections on learning and teaching through the medium of English as an additional language in South Africa. *Bilingual Education and Bilingualism* (2001).

[23] Margaret Probyn. 2005. Learning science through two languages in South Africa. In *The 4th International Symposium on Bilingualism, Somerville, MA.*

[24] Adalbert Gerald Soosai Raj, Kasama Ketsuriyonk, Jignesh M Patel, and Richard Halverson. 2017. What Do Students Feel about Learning Programming Using Both English and Their Native Language?. In *LaTICE 2017*. IEEE.

[25] Marc J Rubin. 2013. The effectiveness of live-coding to teach introductory programming. In *SIGCSE*. ACM.

[26] Donald W Zimmerman and Richard H Williams. 1982. Gain scores in research can be highly reliable. *Journal of Educational Measurement* (1982).

Tracing vs. Writing Code: Beyond the Learning Hierarchy

Brian Harrington
Dept. of Computer and Mathematical Sciences
University of Toronto Scarborough
brian.harrington@utsc.utoronto.ca

Nick Cheng
Dept. of Computer and Mathematical Sciences
University of Toronto Scarborough
nick@utsc.utoronto.ca

ABSTRACT

Much work has been done on the achievement gap between code tracing and code writing in CS1 students. The generally accepted explanation for this gap is that tracing and writing form separate steps in a learning scaffolding; students must first learn to trace code before they can be expected to write code. The expectation is that once students have mastered these skills, future grades will be driven by their ability to understand the deeper learning concepts, and so the gap between tracing and writing should disappear.

In this paper, we detail and evaluate a study on 384 CS2 students to evaluate whether a tracing-writing gap still exists, and assess whether anything can be deduced about students who continue to exhibit such a gap. We find that not only does the gap seem to have closed by CS2, students are equally likely to show a reverse gap in the writing-tracing direction. However, further analysis shows a strong correlation between students who do continue to have a gap (in either direction) and poor overall performance in the course.

CCS CONCEPTS

• **Social and professional topics → Computing education**; **Computer science education**; **CS1**;

KEYWORDS

Assessment, CS1, Computer Science Education, Code Tracing, Code Writing, Exam Questions

ACM Reference Format:

Brian Harrington and Nick Cheng. 2018. Tracing vs. Writing Code: Beyond the Learning Hierarchy. In *SIGCSE '18: The 49th ACM Technical Symposium on Computer Science Education, Feb. 21–24, 2018, Baltimore, MD, USA.* ACM, New York, NY, USA, 6 pages. https://doi.org/10.1145/3159450.3159530

1 INTRODUCTION

Modern CS1 and CS2 examinations are often broken into two modalities of questions: tracing and writing. In tracing questions students are given some completed code and asked to analyse the code in some way. Typically students are asked to reproduce the output of the code, but other variations may include reproducing the memory model at a certain point, or providing the order/number of times a certain line is executed. For writing questions students are expected to generate code in order to fulfil certain requirements. The most basic version of this is to simply ask students to write code to meet given specifications, but many variations on this also exist.

It is not uncommon for CS1 students to be able to competently complete tracing questions, but be unable to handle writing questions. And the prevailing theory is that students learn programming concepts in a hierarchical manner, with tracing being a basic level upon which writing rests. Thus it is understandable that students who had not mastered tracing would be unlikely to perform well on the writing sections of an exam.

If this theory is correct, then we should see that once students have moved beyond the basic stages of tracing and writing in their learning hierarchy, then performance on examinations should be relatively independent of the modality of the question. Thus one should expect that in a CS2 course, it would not matter whether we ask students to trace or write code, the results should be approximately the same. However, if a gap does still exist, this may indicate that the hierarchical learning paradigm is either flawed, or overly simplistic (perhaps there is some sort of cyclical hierarchy with students needing to re-learn the lower levels for each new concept visited).

In this study, we develop an experiment to evaluate whether a gap exists in students ability to trace or write code in a CS2 course. Unlike previous studies where students were all asked the same questions, and analysis was largely done on relative scores, our study performs an A-B comparison of questions. Two questions were generated for the final exam of our course that were deemed to be equally difficult, and could be answered in either a tracing or writing modality. Students were then randomly assigned to trace one question and write the other such that each question was traced by approximately half the students and written by the other half. This allows us to directly compare the same questions being asked in different ways, and to analyze students tracing vs writing skills on questions where we can be sure that the difficulty level and complexity is normalized.

In our results, we found that, as the hierarchy theory predicts, the gap between tracing and writing abilities had disappeared. In fact, there was no statistically significant difference in performance across either question in either modality. In particular, while some students did still have an achievement gap between the tracing and writing questions, the gap was as likely to be due to higher achievement on the writing question as on the tracing.

Further analysis shows that some students did still have a gap between their tracing and writing skills. A strong inverse correlation was found between the size of the gap and performance in the course. Interestingly, this effect is actually stronger when the direction of the gap is not taken into account. This indicates that the issue is not that students have not properly moved up the learning hierarchy, but perhaps these students have compartmentalized

SIGCSE '18, Feb. 21–24, 2018, Baltimore, MD, USA

ACM ISBN 978-1-4503-5103-4/18/02...$15.00
https://doi.org/10.1145/3159450.3159530

tracing and writing as separate skills, and appear to be struggling with the surface aspects of the questions rather than focusing on deeper understanding of the concepts.

2 BACKGROUND

Several studies have evaluated and attempted to explain the gap in CS1 student performance between tracing and writing questions on exams. Lopez, Whalley, Robbins, and Lister [5] found a correlation between students performance on tracing, writing and "explain in plain English" tasks on a CS1 exam, and used stepwise regression to suggest the existence of a learning hierarchy of tasks, with tracing being a necessary step before moving on to writing and explanation. Similar findings by Lister, Fidge, and Teague [4] indicated that these findings held across multiple cohorts, institutions and programming languages, and attempted to further delineate the learning hierarchy, placing explanation above tracing, but below writing. Venables, Tan, and Lister [8] showed that the relationship between explanation and coding was less reliable and at least partially dependent on the way in which the question was asked, but provided further evidence for the hierarchy between tracing and writing.

Most of the existing studies use Parson's Problems [6] for their writing questions. Parson's Problems (alternatively: Parson's Puzzles) ask a student to take a series of statements provided in a random order, and input these statements (or the line number given to these statements) into a given structure. Studies have shown that student performance in Parson's Problems correlates highly with performance in 'traditional' writing questions [3]. Our study uses Code Mangler style questions [2], which are similar to Parson's Problems, but generally do not provide a scaffolded structure in which to place the code, and allow for more flexibility and variety of problems. Performance on Code Mangler questions has also been shown to have a strong correlation with performance on writing questions [2].

3 METHODOLOGY

The study for this paper was performed during the Winter Term of 2017. CSCA48: Introduction to Computer Science II is a CS2 course intended for majors and specialists in the computer science program, and enrolment in the course requires a passing grade in our institution's CS1 course. Students are generally discouraged from taking CSCA48 unless they feel completely comfortable with the CS1 material (an unofficial suggestion is that students receiving less than 65% in the CS1 course meet with the course instructor to discuss whether this course is a viable option for them). The course had an enrolment of 450 students, of which 384 wrote the final examination, and is split into 3 lectures sections, all taught by the same instructor.

CSCA48 uses Python as its language of instruction and covers standard CS2 material including OOP, Principles of Software Engineering and Design, Linked Data Structures (including linked lists and trees), Recursion and Complexity Analysis. Both the CS1 and CS2 courses have 2 term tests and a final examination, each of which had at least one tracing question and one Code Mangler style writing question. 70% of the marks for both courses came from these examinations, with the remaining 30% coming from weekly exercises and larger programming assignments.

The final exam for the course consisted of 6 questions written over a 3 hour period. All questions are answered with pen & paper, and no aids are allowed. All students had question 4 as a tracing question and question 5 as a writing question, so the order of presentation remained constant.

The two questions used in this study both directly related to the final course assignment (a 'formula game' assignment where students had to take various formulae, represented as either strings or trees, and attempt to provide truth assignments for variables in order to either make the formula evaluate to true or false), which had been completed by all students. This was done to ensure a uniform familiarity with the background. One question involved writing a function that would take an n-ary tree structure and simplifying it by collapsing hierarchies of repeated node types. We will call this question `simplify`. A second question asked students to write a function that would take a formula tree, and produce the string representation of the formula. We will call this question `tree`.

The tracing questions provided the students with completed code with commenting removed and the function name replaced by an unhelpful word. Students were then asked to trace the output of the function on a simple tree, and then a more complex one. Finally students were asked to provide a sensible name for the function and provide a docstring that clearly explained what the function does. 2 marks were awarded for tracing the simple tree, 2 marks for the complicated tree, and 4 marks for the docstring. An example of the complicated tree question can be seen in Figure 1.

What does `voodoo(root)` return if `root` is the root of the following tree?

```
              -
              |
              -
              |
   -----------*-----------
  /     -----/|\-----     \
 /     /      |      \     \
a     -       +       -     h
      |    __/|\__    |
      b   c   d   *   g
                 / \
                e   f
```

Figure 1: An example of a complicated tree upon which students were asked to trace the code.

For the writing questions, a docstring was given for the function, and students were told that the code had been 'mangled' by the code mangler. All internal documentation and spacing was removed, and the lines of code were scrambled. The students were then asked to re-construct the original code. 4 marks were given for internal comments, and 4 marks were given for the code itself, with 1 mark being deducted for each line that was improperly placed or indented. An excerpt from a writing question showing the code that the students were required to 'un-mangle' can be seen in Figure 2.

```
def simplify_tree(root: 'FormulaTree') -> None:
    """
    Modify the FormulaTree rooted at root so that no
    AND node is the child of an AND node, and no
    OR node is the child of an OR node.

    (Do this by combining grandchildren with children,
    resulting in nodes with >2 children as needed.)
    """

elif root.symbol in "*+":
else:
for c in root.children:
if c.symbol == root.symbol:
if root.symbol == '-':
newchildren = []
newchildren.append(c)
newchildren = newchildren + c.children
root.children = newchildren
simplify_tree(c)
simplify_tree(root.children[0])
```

Figure 2: An example of mangled code which students were required to correct.

Two versions of the final exam were created. Version A asking the students to trace simplify and write tree, and version B asking the students to trace tree and write simplify. The exams were otherwise identical except for a small, nondescript A or B on the front cover. The exam was written in a large lecture hall, and exams were placed in alternating order at each available seat. Students were allowed to choose any seat they wished. In total 195 Version A and 189 Version B exams were written, the minor discrepancy in numbers due to exam no-shows and seats not being filled.

4 RESULTS

In this section we will explain the way in which our data was analyzed and provide the resulting statistics. We will attempt to narrate our thought process in choosing our statistical tools, but deeper analysis of the results will be left to a later section.

4.1 Verifying the Setup

The first order of business in analyzing our data was to ensure that our experimental design was viable. In order for the data to be meaningful, it is important to establish that the two questions, and two modalities of those questions were of equal difficulty, and the performance of students was based on the type of the question, and not its intrinsic relative difficulty. The averages of the two questions with both modalities were within a range of 1.5%, indicating that the relative difficulties were even and no global adjustments needed to be made. The means of all question-modality pairs can be found in Table 1.

Having similar average performance doesn't necessarily imply that the questions were equally difficult. For this reason, we compared relative student performance on each question pairing along

Table 1: Mean Score (out of 8) by Question and Modality

question-modality	mean
simplify-tracing	6.48
simplify-writing	6.46
tree-tracing	6.48
tree-writing	6.58

with a control question (a technical question about arranging pointers on linked lists). We computed a Kendal tau-b (τb) rank correlation coefficient (tau-b was used because our data contained ties) and found that each question had a moderate and statistically significant pairwise performance correlation. Each question pair produced a p value of less than 0.001. Scatter plots can be found in Figure 3, and Kendal Tau coefficients are given in Table 2.

Table 2: Kendal tau-b rank correlation scores: Question pairing

Question pairing	τb	p
simplify-tracing vs tree-writing	0.4869	< 0.0005
tree-tracing vs simplicity-writing	0.4674	< 0.0008
tracing (combined) vs control	0.4013	< 0.0001
writing (combined) vs control	0.4131	< 0.0001

A Spearman Rank Correlation test showed a moderate but statistically significant rank correlation between performance on the tracing and writing questions for all students ($r_s = 0.4397, p < 0.000001$).

4.2 Searching For Gaps

Having established that the methodology is relatively sound, and the questions were not inherently biased; we could begin to look at the gaps in student performance between tracing and writing. As shown in Figure 4, approximately 56% of students had a gap of 1 or fewer marks (out of 8) between their tracing and writing scores. This is positive evidence for a diminished achievement gap among CS2 students, but the data becomes even clearer when looking at a directed rather than an absolute gap. While Figure 4 shows the absolute value difference between the tracing and writing score for each student, Figure 5 shows the distribution of 'scaffolded differences': tracing scores minus writing scores. If the remaining gaps in the CS2 class were attributable to the same scaffolding model as proposed by Lopez et al [5], then we would expect to see most or all of the gaps be in the positive direction (tracing scores higher than writing scores). However, in our data, students were actually slightly more likely to have a negative scaffolded difference (i.e., more students had a higher writing score than a higher tracing score).

4.3 Analyzing Student Gaps

In order to analyze the relationship between student performance and tracing-writing ability gap, student exam grades (as calculated on the final exam excluding the two questions used in this study)

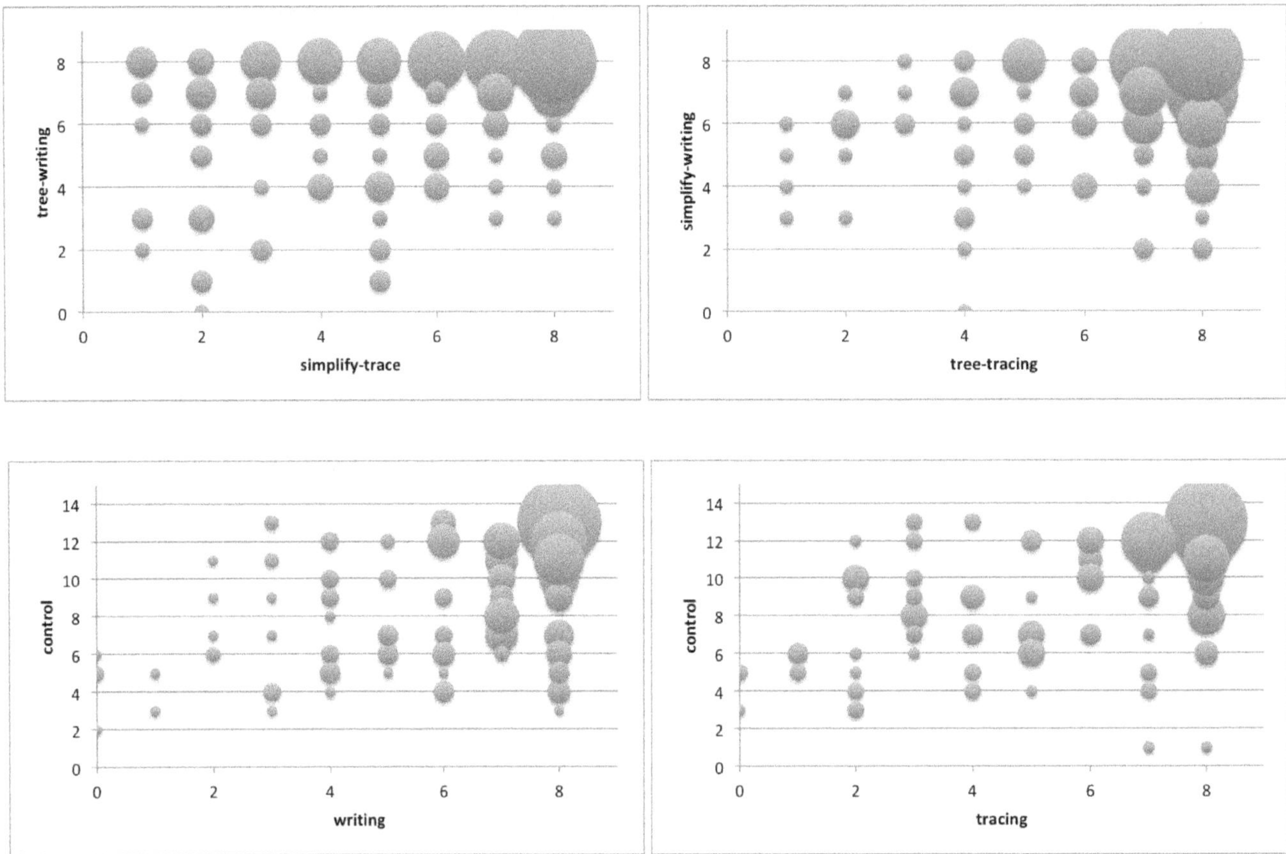

Figure 3: Plots of question score correlations. The width of the dot represents the number of students at that data point.

were correlated with both absolute and scaffolded gaps. Kendal's Tau-b showed a weak statistically insignificant relationship between scaffolded gaps and exam grades, and a moderate, statistically significant relationship between absolute gaps and exam grades. Correlations were also done between both types of gaps and final course grades (it should be noted that the questions directly studied in this paper are included in those course grades, but count for less than 10% of the total grade). Kendal's Tau-b showed a weak, statistically significant relationship between scaffolded gaps and course grades, and a moderate, statistically significant relationship between absolute gaps and course grades. Scatter plots can be found in Figure 6, and Kendal Tau coefficients are given in Table 3. In both cases (exam grades and course grades) scaffolded relationships were positive and absolute relationships were negative.

Table 3: Kendal tau-b rank correlation scores: Gap size vs grade

Relationship	τb	p
scaffolded gap vs exam grade	0.0541	0.1449
absolute gap vs exam grade	-0.2153	< 0.00001
scaffolded gap vs course grade	0.1177	0.0012
absolute gap vs exam grade	-0.3314	< 0.00001

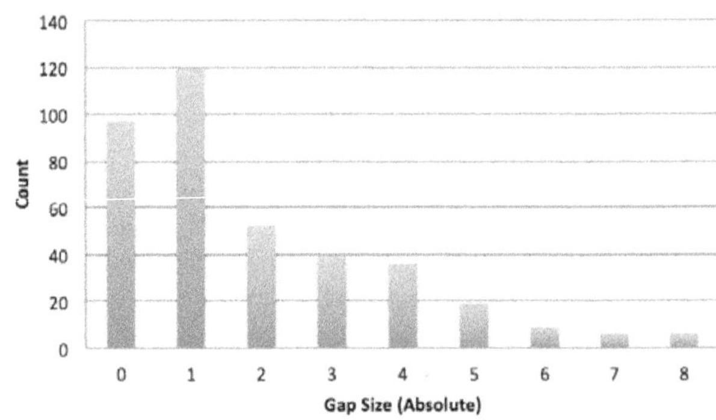

Figure 4: Count of examinations with absolute difference between tracing and writing scores.

5 ANALYSIS

Our novel method for evaluating tracing-writing gaps does not rely on assumptions about relative question difficulty. Our A-B approach appears to have resulted in fairly balanced and directly comparable questions of different modalities, and has removed any discrepancies that may be due to the questions themselves and their

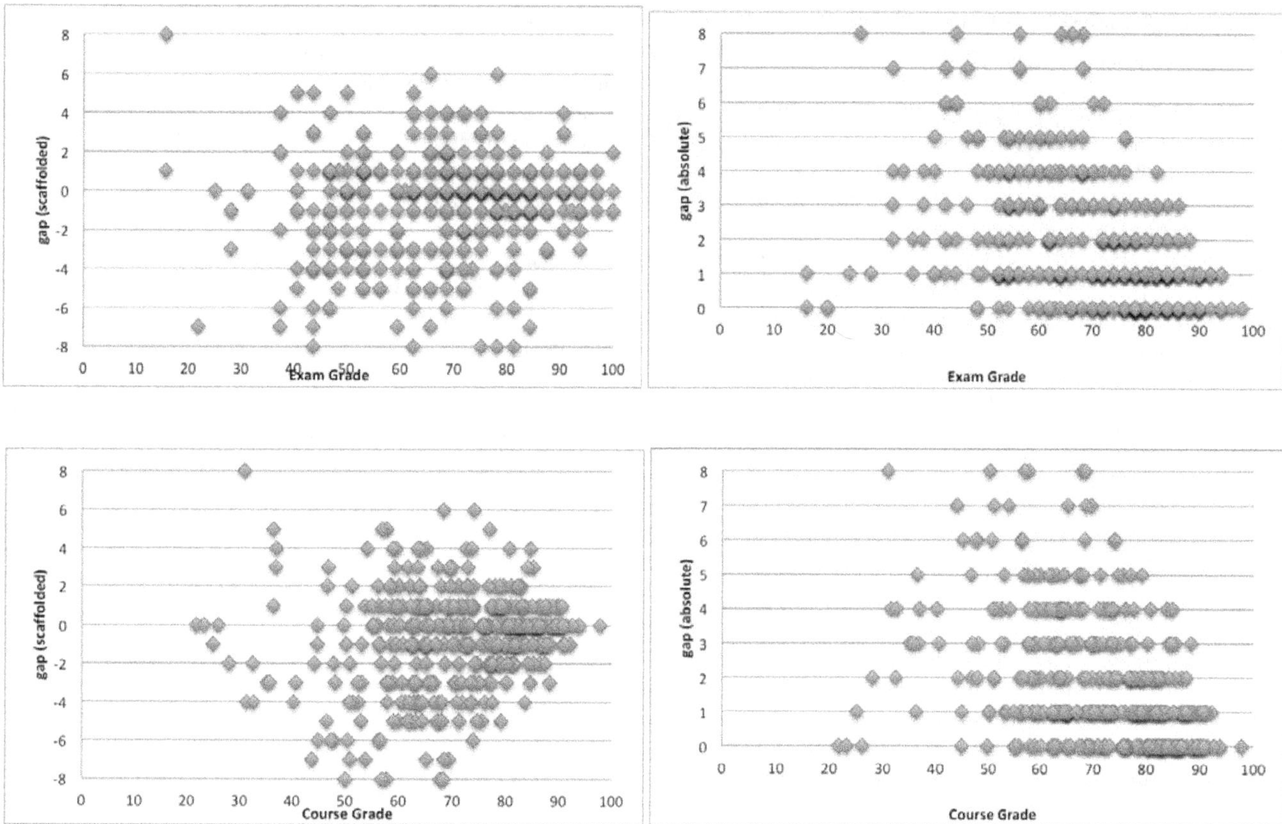

Figure 6: Plots of gap-outcome correlations.

Figure 5: Count of examinations with scaffolded difference between tracing and writing scores (calculated as *tracing* − *writing*).

relative difficulties. Our personal experience in developing questions combined with good luck meant that our questions naturally balanced and had good rank correlation. However, had that not been the case, we could have made post-hoc adjustments to either our marking scheme, or directly to our mark allocation in order to ensure fairly comparable questions. This was something that is not possible with other methodologies.

Our data show that, as the scaffolding theory suggests, the directed gap between competency in tracing and writing of code has essentially disappeared by the end of our CS2 course. While there are still gaps present (44% of students still had a gap of 2 or more), the directed gap distribution indicates that students are equally likely to have the higher scoring question be writing as tracing. This indicates that any remaining systematic gaps are not explainable by the scaffolding theory and therefore require an alternate explanation.

Analyzing the correlation between gaps and student performance, it appears that there is a statistically significant correlation between scaffolded gap and student achievement (on the overall course grade). However, the strength of this correlation is quite weak. This is not surprising, as Kendal's Tau assumes a directed relationship, and as we have already established, the gaps appear to be equally distributed in either direction. The correlation between absolute gap size and student achievement is statistically significant, and moderately strong. This indicates that the size of the gap and not its direction is a good indicator of student success. Regardless of whether it is the tracing or the writing that is performing better, a student who has a significant difference between their performance on the two types of questions is likely to be struggling with the course overall.

6 DISCUSSION & FUTURE WORK

The primary contributions of this work are as follows:

(1) We developed and tested a new method for analyzing tracing-writing gaps that allows for post-hoc control of question difficulty and does not rely on relative analysis.
(2) We provided evidence that directional gaps between tracing and writing competencies, while commonplace in CS1 courses do not appear to be present in our CS2 course.
(3) We showed that continued existence of tracing-writing gaps correlates significantly with decreased performance in both the examination and the course overall.

With respect to our experimental design, we believe that while this methodology does require some more setup (printing of multiple exams, staggering layout, etc), it provides a more concrete and easily manipulable experimental design for future work. We intend to use this design to replicate the study in our CS1 course to further verify its validity and usefulness. However, this methodology can also be used for a variety of other purposes. We have already used this technique to analyze our work [2], and hope to find more uses for it in future.

The lack of a systematic directed gap between tracing and writing skills in CS2 does not come as a surprise. The scaffolding theory predicts that such gaps would disappear once the fundamental skills are mastered in CS1. We have merely provided evidence to support that claim. However, the implications of this are quite interesting. The modality in which a question is asked can greatly affect multiple factors of an exam, including writing time, marking time, focus (number of core concepts required to answer the question) and student satsifaction [7]. It is clear that in CS1 we must ask questions in a variety of modalities in order to ensure adequate coverage of concepts and to assess multiple levels of the learning hierarchy. However, if these findings seem to indicate that this is not necessary for CS2 exam, and perhaps instructors can use their time and energy more wisely by designing questions that are easier to create and mark, and that focus more directly on the concepts they wish to evaluate, rather than worrying about ensuring that every exam has fair weighting between tracing and writing questions. We hope to study this idea further by developing a wider variety of CS2 examination questions and analyzing in greater detail which modalities are easiest to create, mark, evaluate and focus. We will also perform additional experiments to further assess whether it is necessary to include all modalities of question on an examination, or whether it is viable to simply choose the modality/modalities that work best for the course instructor at the time.

A gap between tracing and writing skills in CS1 indicates that a student has not progressed along the concept hierarchy. We have shown that a gap (in either direction) in CS2 correlates negatively with course outcomes. But why should that be? Beyond the obvious: that a gap means that they student is performing poorly in at least one exam question, why should a gap between tracing and writing skills indicate that a student is likely to be struggling in other areas of the course? We propose here that this correlation is a sign that the student is focusing on surface manipulation of the code rather than gaining a deeper understanding of the core concepts being tested.

It is entirely possible that a student could pass CS1, and continue on to CS2 by spending time practicing tracing and writing as independent skills. Focusing on getting good at manipulating the code, or developing a simplistic model of code tracing that would allow them to answer these questions without having to resort to a deeper understanding of core CS concepts such as memory management and data manipulation. This essentially means a student who is stuck at a lower level of Bloom's Taxonomy [1] than their peers, but continues to succeed in their courses through aptitude at surface manipulation. Such a student would be likely to have gaps in their tracing-writing performance (they could simply be unable to perform the surface manipulation on a particular question, or their simplified memory model would fail them); their gaps would be equally likely to occur in either direction (as their methodologies for answering the questions do not rely on a scaffolded approach); and their lack of deep understanding would be likely to manifest itself in poor performance in other areas of the course.

We would like to develop a series of experiments to gain a clearer picture of how depth of understanding vs ability to perform directed tasks impacts grades in CS1 and CS2, and possibly develop an early warning system based on ability gaps that could indicate that a student is focusing their time and energy on surface abilities rather than deeper understanding of the core concepts being taught.

REFERENCES

[1] Lorin W Anderson, David R Krathwohl, P Airasian, K Cruikshank, R Mayer, P Pintrich, J Raths, and M Wittrock. 2001. A taxonomy for learning, teaching and assessing: A revision of Bloom's taxonomy. *New York. Longman Publishing. Artz, AF, & Armour-Thomas, E.(1992). Development of a cognitive-metacognitive framework for protocol analysis of mathematical problem solving in small groups. Cognition and Instruction* 9, 2 (2001), 137–175.

[2] Nick Cheng and Brian Harrington. 2017. The Code Mangler: Evaluating Coding Ability Without Writing any Code. In *Proceedings of the 2017 ACM SIGCSE Technical Symposium on Computer Science Education*. ACM, 123–128.

[3] Paul Denny, Andrew Luxton-Reilly, and Beth Simon. 2008. Evaluating a new exam question: Parsons problems. In *Proceedings of the fourth international workshop on computing education research*. ACM, 113–124.

[4] Raymond Lister, Colin Fidge, and Donna Teague. 2009. Further Evidence of a Relationship Between Explaining, Tracing and Writing Skills in Introductory Programming. In *Proceedings of the 14th Annual ACM SIGCSE Conference on Innovation and Technology in Computer Science Education (ITiCSE '09)*. ACM, New York, NY, USA, 161–165. https://doi.org/10.1145/1562877.1562930

[5] Mike Lopez, Jacqueline Whalley, Phil Robbins, and Raymond Lister. 2008. Relationships Between Reading, Tracing and Writing Skills in Introductory Programming. In *Proceedings of the Fourth International Workshop on Computing Education Research (ICER '08)*. ACM, New York, NY, USA, 101–112. https://doi.org/10.1145/1404520.1404531

[6] Dale Parsons and Patricia Haden. 2006. Parson's programming puzzles: a fun and effective learning tool for first programming courses. In *Proceedings of the 8th Australasian Conference on Computing Education-Volume 52*. Australian Computer Society, Inc., 157–163.

[7] Andrew Petersen, Michelle Craig, and Daniel Zingaro. 2011. Reviewing CS1 Exam Question Content. In *Proceedings of the 42Nd ACM Technical Symposium on Computer Science Education (SIGCSE '11)*. ACM, New York, NY, USA, 631–636. https://doi.org/10.1145/1953163.1953340

[8] Anne Venables, Grace Tan, and Raymond Lister. 2009. A Closer Look at Tracing, Explaining and Code Writing Skills in the Novice Programmer. In *Proceedings of the Fifth International Workshop on Computing Education Research Workshop (ICER '09)*. ACM, New York, NY, USA, 117–128. https://doi.org/10.1145/1584322.1584336

Understanding the New ABET Computer Science Criteria

Michael J. Oudshoorn
Northwest Missouri State University
Maryville, Missouri
oudshoorn@nwmissouri.edu

Stan Thomas
Wake Forest University
Winston-Salem, North Carolina
sjt@wfu.edu

Rajendra K. Raj
Rochester institute of Technology
Rochester, New York
rajendra.k.raj@rit.edu

Allen Parrish
United States Naval Academy
Annapolis, Maryland
aparrish@usna.edu

ABSTRACT

The Computing Accreditation Commission of ABET accredits over 300 Computer Science programs worldwide under the Computer Science program criteria. In the past few years, the Commission has engaged the computing community to modify and update these criteria, and has now signed off on an updated set of program criteria that take into account factors such as the CS2013 curricular guidelines, impact on currently accredited programs, structural changes to clarify the criteria, and the reduction of the assessment burden. These recent changes to the Computer Science program criteria primarily impact student outcomes (what program graduates are expected to know and be able to do by graduation) and curriculum. Those changes will impact computer science programs in a variety of ways and degrees—some programs will be impacted significantly while others will be affected in a relatively minor way. This paper examines the changes that will take effect starting in the 2019-20 accreditation cycle, covering the rationale for those changes and exploring the likely impact on computer science programs that are currently accredited or seeking accreditation in the near future.

CCS CONCEPTS

• **Social and professional topics → Accreditation**; **Computer science education**;

KEYWORDS

Computer science degree programs; computing programs; program accreditation

ACM Reference Format:
Michael J. Oudshoorn, Stan Thomas, Rajendra K. Raj, and Allen Parrish. 2018. Understanding the New ABET Computer Science Criteria. In *Proceedings of SIGCSE '18: The 49th ACM Technical Symposium on Computer Science Education, Baltimore, MD, USA, February 21–24, 2018 (SIGCSE '18)*, 6 pages. https://doi.org/10.1145/3159450.3159534

SIGCSE '18, February 21–24, 2018, Baltimore, MD, USA

ACM ISBN 978-1-4503-5103-4/18/02...$15.00
https://doi.org/10.1145/3159450.3159534

1 INTRODUCTION

The Council for Higher Education Accreditation (CHEA) describes higher education accreditation as "... a collegial process based on self and peer assessment for public accountability and improvement of academic quality" and states "Accreditation involves judgments of quality and effectiveness of an institution/program against a set of expectations (standards, criteria)" [5]. With respect to the accreditation of computing programs by ABET, the expectations of programs are documented in the ABET Criteria for Accrediting Computing Programs (Criteria) [2, 3].

Accreditation of Computer Science programs has been ongoing since visits were conducted by the Computer Sciences Accreditation Board (CSAB) in the 1985-86 academic year. CSAB continues to play a role in computing accreditation as one of thirty-three cooperating member societies of ABET [6]. The integration of CSAB into ABET occurred in 2001 with the formation of a new ABET commission to focus on computing accreditation, the Computing Accreditation Commission (CAC). CSAB continues to play a key role in the formulation of accreditation criteria for computer science, information systems, information technology and software engineering programs, and recruits and trains program evaluators. The CAC of ABET conducts program reviews against the relevant criteria and makes accreditation decisions. Presently, CAC accredits 461 programs at 354 institutions around the globe, including 338 undergraduate computer science programs, 58 information systems programs, and 50 information technology programs [1].

1.1 The Computer Science Criteria

The CAC Criteria for Accrediting Computing Programs [2, 3] are composed of the General Criteria that apply to all computing programs, and Program Criteria specific to computer science, information systems, or information technology, as determined by the program name. This paper focuses on the recently approved revisions to those portions of the CAC Criteria that apply to computer science programs, which we refer to as the computer science criteria. We refer to the revised criteria as the 2019 criteria, as they will required in the 2019-20 cycle, and the current criteria as the 2017 criteria.

We review the rationale for the 2019 criteria revisions and the potential impact on computer science programs that are currently accredited or seeking accreditation in the near future.

2 FACTORS GUIDING CRITERIA REVISIONS

The last major change to the accreditation criteria for computer science occurred around 2006 when CAC adopted a version of Engineering Criteria 2000 (EC 2000) [8], and transitioned from a standards-based approach to an outcomes-based approach. This significant change helped to shift the foundation of accreditation from *what is taught* by a program to *what is learned* by students by the time they graduate from the program. Since then, although computing infrastructure and technologies have evolved significantly, there have not been significant changes in the CAC accreditation criteria, thus creating a groundswell for criteria revisions.

2.1 CS 2013

The Computer Science Curricula 2013 report (CS2013) [4], published by ACM and the IEEE-Computer Society in December 2013, is likely to impact computer science curricula for many years. The report, developed over a four year period with broad community input, represents a comprehensive revision of previous curriculum recommendations and includes a redefined body of knowledge, desirable characteristics of graduates, and many exemplars of courses and programs from a variety of institutional contexts. Consideration of revisions to the CAC computer science criteria was informed by the body of knowledge and characteristics of graduates identified in CS2013.

2.2 Student Outcomes

Criterion 3 (Student Outcomes) of the 2017 computing criteria allows programs to identify their own student outcomes based on the objectives of the program and the expectations of external constituencies. Criterion 3 also defines eleven program characteristics, which are shown in Table 1. Often referred to simply as (a)–(k), these characteristics must be enabled but—unlike student outcomes—not necessarily assessed and integrated with the program's continuous improvement process. This distinction between characteristics and outcomes has been confusing to both programs and evaluators over the years.

The 2019 criteria resolve this structural ambiguity, but more importantly, they institute a philosophical change by specifying required outcomes. Rather than allowing programs to select outcomes based on goals and expectations of external constituencies, the criteria now specify required outcomes for *all* computer science programs. At the same time, a program is still permitted to articulate additional outcomes.

2.3 Assessment

As described previously, computer science programs which are accredited under the 2017 criteria can currently elect to adopt characteristics (a)–(k) as the program's student outcomes. If they do so, then the program must assess at least eleven outcomes. There was a desire to reduce this assessment burden to focus the assessment process toward more meaningful continuous improvement. In addition, the use of common outcomes is intended for programs to be able to build common and consistent approaches and tools for assessment, thus leading to the sharing of assessment artifacts, helping to reduce assessment cost.

Table 1: 2017 Criteria: Student Characteristics [2]

The program must enable students to attain, by the time of graduation:

a. An ability to apply knowledge of computing and mathematics appropriate to the program's student outcomes and to the discipline.
b. An ability to analyze a problem, and identify and define the computing requirements appropriate to its solution.
c. An ability to design, implement, and evaluate a computer-based system, process, component, or program to meet desired needs.
d. An ability to function effectively on teams to accomplish a common goal.
e. An understanding of professional, ethical, legal, security and social issues and responsibilities.
f. An ability to communicate effectively with a range of audiences.
g. An ability to analyze the local and global impact of computing on individuals, organizations, and society.
h. Recognition of the need for and an ability to engage in continuing professional development
i. An ability to use current techniques, skills, and tools necessary for computing practice.
j. An ability to apply mathematical foundations, algorithmic principles, and computer science theory in the modeling and design of computer-based systems in a way that demonstrates comprehension of the tradeoffs involved in design choices.
k. An ability to apply design and development principles in the construction of software systems of varying complexity.

2.4 Other Factors

While a primary goal was to reflect the evolving discipline of computer science, the 2019 revisions to the criteria attempted to maintain backward compatibility with existing criteria, to increase consistency with pertinent engineering criteria, to allow for flexibility in program design, and not to unduly increase requirements without providing trade-offs. An increased degree of consistency between the computer science criteria and the engineering criteria is desirable as many computer science programs are housed within a College of Engineering, and increased consistency helps reduces confusion and workload as each program within the college prepares its self-study report.

3 CHANGE PROCESS

3.1 Committee formation

The change process was managed by a Criteria Committee made up of ABET CAC members and CSAB-appointed volunteers. The committee worked at two levels: (a) an Executive Committee that provided overall management and leadership of the process; and (b) individual subcommittees for each of the disciplinary areas, including computer science, information systems and information technology—as well as a subcommittee for cybersecurity, which was simultaneously developing its own initial draft program criteria for cybersecurity [7].

Revisions were debated within the subcommittees and then submitted to the Executive Committee for further consideration and synthesis across all disciplines. The proposal from the Criteria Committee was approved by the Computing Accreditation Commission in July 2017 and subsequently obtained final ABET approval in

Table 2: 2019 Criteria: Student Outcomes [3]

Graduates of the program will have an ability to:

1. Analyze a complex computing problem and to apply principles of computing and other relevant disciplines to identify solutions. *General Criteria*
2. Design, implement, and evaluate a computing-based solution to meet a given set of computing requirements in the context of the program's discipline. *General Criteria*
3. Communicate effectively in a variety of professional contexts. *General Criteria*
4. Recognize professional responsibilities and make informed judgments in computing practice based on legal and ethical principles. *General Criteria*
5. Function effectively as a member or leader of a team engaged in activities appropriate to the program's discipline. *General Criteria*
6. Apply computer science theory and software development fundamentals to produce computing-based solutions. *Computer Science Program Criteria*

October 2017 for use in evaluations scheduled for the 2019-20 accreditation cycle. Programs may also opt to use the 2019 criteria in the 2018-19 accreditation cycle.

3.2 Feedback regularly sought

The changes leading to the 2019 criteria were developed over a five-year period. This period culminated with a one-year review-and-comment period. During this review-and-comment period, the criteria were posted on the ABET Website and feedback was obtained from the community, both via a web survey and via in-person comments obtained during presentations at conferences such as ACM SIGCSE, ACM SIGITE, IEEE Frontiers in Education, as well as the annual ABET Symposium. A large number of useful comments were obtained during this process. Each comment was analyzed by the appropriate subcommittee and resulted in a recommendation for disposition of that comment, which involved either changing the criteria or leaving the criteria unchanged. Each disposition was documented for internal process traceability.

4 IMPACT OF CRITERIA CHANGES ON COMPUTER SCIENCE PROGRAMS

Of the eight criteria used by ABET to accredit all programs, the CAC criteria changes were limited to only two of them: Student Outcomes and Curriculum. These two, however, are the ones most closely tied to each discipline representing what the students learn and what curricular areas are taught by each accredited program.[1]

Under the Student Outcomes of the 2019 criteria, computer science programs will be required to satisfy six outcomes (five from the General Criteria, and one from the Computer Science Program Criteria) [3]. These outcomes have been consolidated and are shown in Table 2.

The 2019 changes to the Curriculum criterion have been made in both the General Criteria and in the Program Criteria. For ease

Table 3: 2019 Criteria: Curriculum [3]

General Criteria—Curriculum:
The program's requirements must be consistent with its program educational objectives and designed in such a way that each of the student outcomes can be attained. The curriculum must combine technical, professional, and general education components to prepare students for a career, further study, and lifelong professional development in the computing discipline associated with the program.

The curriculum requirements specify topics, but do not prescribe specific courses. The program must include mathematics appropriate to the discipline and at least 30 semester credit hours (or equivalent) of up-to-date coverage of fundamental and advanced computing topics that provide both breadth and depth.

The computing topics must include:

1. Techniques, skills, and tools necessary for computing practice.
2. Principles and practices for secure computing.
3. Local and global impacts of computing solutions on individuals, organizations, and society.

Computer Science Program Criteria—Curriculum:
The curriculum requirements specify topics, but do not prescribe specific courses. These requirements are:

a. Computer science: At least 40 semester credit hours (or equivalent) that must include:
   1. Substantial coverage of algorithms and complexity, computer science theory, concepts of programming languages, and software development.
   2. Substantial coverage of at least one general-purpose programming language.
   3. Exposure to computer architecture and organization, information management, networking and communication, operating systems, and parallel and distributed computing.
   4. The study of computing-based systems at varying levels of abstraction.
   5. A major project that requires integration and application of knowledge and skills acquired in earlier course work.

b. Mathematics: At least 15 semester credit hours (or equivalent) that include discrete mathematics and must have mathematical rigor at least equivalent to introductory calculus. The additional mathematics might include course work in areas such as calculus, linear algebra, numerical methods, probability, statistics, or number theory.

c. Science: At least six semester credit hours (or equivalent) in natural science course work intended for science and engineering majors. This course work must develop an understanding of the scientific method and must include laboratory work.

of understanding, the revised Curriculum section under General Criteria and the Computer Science Program Criteria have been consolidated in Table 3.

Most computer science programs will be impacted in some way by the criteria revisions. Changes to Criterion 3, Student Outcomes, will have a more profound impact on some programs than others, depending on the program's current student outcomes. Changes to

[1] It should be noted that although the CAC criteria obviously are applicable to other computing disciplines, this paper focuses on the criteria as applicable to computer science programs.

Criterion 5, Curriculum impact all programs equally. These issues are examined in the remainder of this section.

4.1 Student Outcomes

The 2019 criteria specify six required Student Outcomes (five in the General Criteria for all programs, and one additional outcome for Computer Science), as shown in Table 2. In contrast, the 2017 criteria did not require any outcomes, but instead specified a collection of characteristics, (a)–(k), to be enabled by all programs; these characteristics are shown in Table 1.

Showing that a characteristic is enabled is a weaker standard than showing to what extent a student outcome is being met. Specifically, data collection and evaluation, and documentation of the consideration of that information to enact program improvements is necessary for student outcomes, whereas enabling a characteristic can be demonstrated by showing that students have an exposure or opportunity to gain that skill. That is, these characteristics represent topics that need to be covered in the curriculum, not outcomes that need to be assessed.

However, under the 2017 criteria, programs had the flexibility to create their own student outcomes and assess the level to which these outcomes were being realized. Programs chose one of two approaches to devise their student outcomes:

(1) Adopt the eleven characteristics, (a)–(k), as their own student outcomes, or
(2) Create their own student outcomes different from the (a)–(k).

Programs that took the first approach, i.e., elected to adopt the eleven student characteristics (a)–(k) as their outcomes, will be minimally impacted by the new six required outcomes, since the previous eleven characteristics served as the basis for creating the six outcomes in the 2019 criteria. While the wording of the outcomes differs from the previous eleven characteristics, the content is substantially similar in terms of assessment and evaluation. Programs treating the characteristics as outcomes should already be collecting relevant assessment data. The only change that will be required is potentially converting from eleven to six substantially similar outcomes. For example, 2019 Criteria student outcomes 2, 3, 4 and 5 correspond fairly well to 2017 Criteria student characteristics c, f, e, and d respectively, while outcome 1 covers both characteristics a and b, and outcome 6 more or less covers characteristics j and k.

Programs that took the second approach—elected to identify student outcomes different from the eleven characteristics—often did so to clearly identify differentiating aspects of their programs as compared to their competitors. These programs are not being asked to abandon their outcomes and the assessment data that they have gathered in the past. However, under the 2019 criteria, these programs will need to support the assessment of the six newly required outcomes, in addition to any other outcomes that they want to retain to support continuous improvement. Note that the 2019 criteria permit additional outcomes beyond the required six.

As an example, Table 4 illustrates student outcomes that a program might have selected under the 2017 Criteria [2]. In this example, mapping to the 2019 criteria's student outcomes will require careful consideration. Assessment data currently collected for this program's student outcomes A, B and C would need to be re-factored to allow for a correspondence with the 2019 criteria's student outcomes 1, 2 and 3. However, assessment data previously collected relating to outcomes D, E and F would likely be applicable to the 2019 criteria's student outcomes 5, 3 and 4 respectively.

Table 4: An Example of Program-defined Student Outcomes under the 2017 Criteria [2]

	By the time of graduation, students will have the ability to:
A.	Apply the theory and principles of computer science.
B.	Demonstrate fluency in several programming languages, environments, and tools.
C.	Demonstrate knowledge of computer organization, operating systems, and networks.
D.	Apply computing skills and work effectively in teams in industry or research.
E.	Prepare technical documents and make effective oral presentations.
F.	Analyze and apply legal and ethical issues involving computing in society.

4.2 Computing Curriculum

CS2013 [4] de-emphasizes some aspects of computing such as computer architecture and places grater emphasis on other areas such as information management. It also introduces a number of topics that were not covered in previous curriculum recommendations. These include computer security and information assurance, which is now pervasive throughout the CS2013 recommended curriculum. The 2019 criteria does not increase the minimum amount of computer science (40 credits or $1\frac{1}{3}$ years) that a student is exposed to, but does allow for more computing content to be added if a program desires, through reduction of the mathematics and science credits that a student must complete.

In line with the changes in CS2013, the General Criteria requires exposure to principles and practices of secure computing, as appropriate for the computer science discipline the Computer Science Program Criteria requires exposure to computer architecture and organization, information management, networking and communications, operating systems, and parallel and distributed computing. Several of these are new topics that were not previously specified or required. Care has been taken to explicitly point out that these are not necessarily courses that should be introduced into programs, but rather these are topics that ought to be covered somewhere in the program requirements. For example, some topics may be covered in a relatively small number of lectures embedded within an existing course.

The 2017 criteria require coverage of the fundamentals of algorithms, data structures, software design, concepts of programming languages and computer organization and architecture. In comparison, the 2019 criteria requires substantial coverage of several core computer science topics including algorithms and complexity, computer science theory, concepts of programming languages, and software development. These are regarded as fundamental areas of computer science and a knowledge set that differentiates a computer science graduate from a graduate of an information systems, information technology, or cybersecurity program.

The 2019 criteria states that there must be "Substantial coverage of at least one general-purpose programming language". This is a change from "in-depth" coverage of a "high-level language". Most programs are unlikely to be affected by this change which is intended to ensure all students gain proficiency in at least one general-purpose language. The aim is to prevent programs from claiming that they meet this criteria by only requiring a specialized language such as a markup language or an application specific language.

Under the 2019 criteria, students are expected to "study computing-based systems at varying levels of abstraction". Many programs will be unaffected by this change as they already examine computing systems in this way. This can be satisfied in many ways and could include overage of the OSI 7-layer network model, design patterns, ER-models, etc. The goal is for students to be able to abstract away details in order to talk about high-level concepts or to be able to drill down to the appropriate level to identify and solve problems in multi-level systems.

Finally, students must complete a major project that requires integration and application of knowledge and skills acquired in earlier coursework. This is not necessarily intended to be a capstone experience, although it could be one way of meeting the requirement. The intent is that students assimilate and synthesize the knowledge they have gained in their studies and deliver a project that is substantive in nature. This would not typically be a weekly assignment, or maybe even one that a student completes over a 3-week period. Apart from the need for the project to integrate and apply knowledge, nothing is said about the nature of the project to provide programs with flexibility. As this is a significant change, several accredited programs will be impacted unless each develops an approach to meeting this requirement in an appropriate manner.

4.3 Mathematics and Science

The 2017 criteria stated that each "program must include mathematics appropriate to the discipline beyond the pre-calculus level". In addition, the Computer Science Program Criteria stated that there had to be a minimum of one year of mathematics and science of which at least half a year must be mathematics. The mathematics requirement was further elaborated such that it must include discrete mathematics and might consist of other courses such as calculus, linear algebra, and others. The science requirement stated that the courses had to develop an understanding of the scientific method, include exposure to laboratory work, and be classes suitable form science and engineering majors.

There was confusion as to what "beyond pre-calculus" meant and many institutions believed that it was necessary to include pre-calculus as a pre-requisite for all mathematics courses. The list of exemplar courses was also taken somewhat literally by some institutions who clung to other criteria which required calculus courses. There was also confusion as to what a year of mathematics and science meant, with some new programs inquiring if it merely meant two semesters which included a mathematics and science course.

CS2013 does not specify mathematics and science requirements but focuses on the computer science content of programs. Mathematics and science requirements were the topic of significant debate within the criteria committee and at various venues and forums where feedback was sought. Significant feedback suggested that the mathematics and science requirement be reduced or even eliminated. However, the majority still believed that half a year of mathematics was not only appropriate, but necessary, to properly prepare students. A vocal majority also believed that merely one science course, permitted in the previous criteria, was inadequate. Feedback from industry participants strongly supported the need for mathematics and science in many jobs and the belief that students would be poorly served by reducing these requirements.

To address the concerns and confusion, the revised criteria discusses curriculum needs in terms of semester credit hours. The mathematics requirements still require discrete mathematics but indicate that other mathematics courses must have mathematical rigor at least equivalent to introductory calculus. The intent is to signal to programs that calculus is not necessarily required if it does not support the program's objectives as well as other mathematics courses. The list of exemplar courses still remains because many felt that it was necessary to provide some advice to programs, but it is intended to be a list of topics, not names of courses, that might suitably support many currently accredited programs.

The science requirement now explicitly states that there must be at least six credits of natural science course work, which must include laboratory work, and be intended for science and engineering majors. The explicit mention of natural science was to make it clear that course in areas such as the social sciences would not satisfy the criteria.

The impact on programs is that the minimum amount of mathematics and science necessary has decreased from 30 to 21 credits, but the minimum number of science credits is specified as six. Previously, a program with three credits of science and 27 credits of mathematics beyond pre-calculus would have satisfied the criteria. Hence, a potential impact is that some programs may need to increase their science requirement in the degree. There is no reduction in the minimum mathematics requirement, but it is hoped that programs see it as an opportunity to include mathematics courses that best support the program rather than simply requiring traditional courses such as calculus.

5 CONCLUSIONS

The development of accreditation criteria is a challenging process seeking the consensus of a large community with a diversity of opinions. The 2019 ABET computer science criteria ensure that several topics newly identified in CS2013 are now factored into the accreditation process. These criteria also provide a common set of student outcomes as opposed to forcing programs to design their own. These generic student outcomes provide a basis for building a comprehensive continuous improvement process, without being too prescriptive and without forcing programs to go through a potentially elaborate process of reinventing the wheel when developing their own outcomes.

The computer science criteria will continue to evolve in the future, as the discipline matures and comes to closure on what it means to be a BS Computer Science graduate. For example, more work is needed to better capture the role of mathematics in computer science education, an area where additional consideration is needed in the community *writ large*. In addition, having a single set of Student Outcomes for all programs, several of which are based on non-technical capabilities related to team and communication skills, calls for further analysis and consideration.

ACKNOWLEDGMENTS

The following people served on the ABET Computer Science criteria subcommittee in 2016/17: Michael Oudshoorn (co-chair), Stan Thomas (co-chair), Maria Altebarmakian, David Bover, Deepak Garg, Cary Laxer, George Pothering, Gerald Thomas, and Joe Turner. The following people served on the ABET Criteria Executive Committee in 2016/17: Allen Parrish (co-chair), Rajendra Raj (co-chair), Jean Blair, Andrew Borchers, David Cordes, Joseph J. Ekstrom, Scott Murray, Michael Oudshoorn, Srini Ramaswamy, Mark Sebern, Ed Sobiesk, Judy Solano, Stan Thomas, and Heikki Topi. In addition, thanks are expressed to all those who provided input and feedback into the criteria proposal as it evolved over the past three years.

REFERENCES

[1] ABET, Inc. 2017. ABET Webpage. (2017). http://abet.org Accessed: November 14, 2017.

[2] ABET, Inc. 2017. Criteria for Accrediting Computing Programs. Effective for Review During the 2017-18 Accreditation Cycle. (2017). http://www.abet.org/wp-content/uploads/2016/12/C001-17-18-CAC-Criteria-10-29-16-1.pdf Accessed: November 14, 2017.

[3] ABET, Inc. 2017. Criteria for Accrediting Computing Programs, Effective for Review During the 2019-20 Accreditation Cycle. (2017). http://www.abet.org/wp-content/uploads/2017/11/CAC-Criteria-Version-2.0-2018-19.pdf Accessed: November 14, 2017.

[4] ACM/IEEE-CS Joint Task Force on Computing Curricula. 2013. *Computer Science Curricula 2013*. Technical Report. ACM Press and IEEE Computer Society Press. https://doi.org/10.1145/2534860 Accessed: November 14, 2017.

[5] Council for Higher Education Accreditation. 2017. What Is Accreditation? (2017). http://www.chea.org/4DCGI/cms/print.html?Action=CMS_Document&DocID=308&MenuKey=main Accessed: November 14, 2017.

[6] CSAB, Inc. 2017. CSAB Webpage. (2017). http://csab.org Accessed: November 14, 2017.

[7] Joseph J. Ekstrom, Barry M. Lunt, Allen Parrish, Rajendra K. Raj, and Edward Sobiesk. 2017. Information Technology as a Cyber Science. In *Proceedings of the 37th SIGITE technical symposium on Information Technology education (SIGITE '17)*. ACM, New York, 84–89.

[8] Lisa R. Lattuca, Patrick T. Terenzini, and J. Fredricks Volkwein. 2015. Engineering Change: A Study of the Impact of EC2000. (2015). http://www.abet.org/wp-content/uploads/2015/04/EngineeringChange-executive-summary.pdf Accessed: November 14, 2017.

Computer Science Curricular Guidance for Associate-Degree Transfer Programs

Cara Tang
Portland Community College
12000 SW 49th Ave
Portland, OR, U.S.A.
cara.tang@pcc.edu

Cindy Tucker
Bluegrass Community and Technical College
500 Newtown Pike
Lexington, KY, U.S.A.
cindy.tucker@kctcs.edu

Christian Servin
El Paso Community College
919 Hunter Dr.
El Paso, TX, U.S.A.
cservin1@epcc.edu

Markus Geissler
Cosumnes River College
8401 Center Parkway
Sacramento, CA, U.S.A.
markus.geissler@crc.losrios.edu

ABSTRACT

After two years of intense curriculum development effort, the ACM CCECC (Committee for Computing Education in Community Colleges) published Computer Science Curricular Guidance for Associate-Degree Transfer Programs with Infused Cybersecurity, known as CSTransfer2017. Based on Computer Science Curricula 2013 (CS2013), this guidance was specially designed to aid in the smooth transfer from associate degrees to baccalaureate degrees. The curriculum contains 17 of CS2013's 18 knowledge areas, and a variety of knowledge units appropriate in the first two years of a computer science degree. The guidance comprises over 200 learning outcomes, 64 of which are infused with cybersecurity, along with a three-tiered assessment rubric using measurable verbs from Bloom's Revised Taxonomy. In addition to the CSTransfer2017 task group consisting of 20 community college educators, input from both two- and four-year educators was collected via surveys administered to a global audience, as well as two rounds of public review and comment on drafts of the guidance. Examples of degree and certificate programs that align with CSTransfer2017 are part of a growing repository hosted on the CCECC website, ccecc.acm.org. These program examples demonstrate the adaptability of this competency-based curriculum approach to a variety of computing programs. The CCECC invites institutions to highlight their computer science degree program by submitting a program example at ccecc.acm.org/correlations.

SIGCSE '18, February 21–24, 2018, Baltimore , MD, USA.

ACM ISBN 978-1-4503-5103-4/18/02...$15.00.
https://doi.org/10.1145/3159450.3159536

CCS CONCEPTS

• Social and professional topics → Model curricula • Social and professional topics → Computer science education

KEYWORDS

Curriculum Guidelines; CSTransfer2017; CS2013; Community College; Two-Year College; Transfer Programs; Computer Science Education.

ACM Reference format:

C. Tang, C. Tucker, C. Servin, and M. Geissler. 2018. Commputer Science Curriculum Guidance for Associate-Degree Transfer Programs. In *SIGCSE '18: 49th ACM Technical Symposium on Computer Science Education, Feb. 21–24, 2018, Baltimore, MD, USA*. ACM, NY, NY, USA, 6 pages. https://doi.org/10.1145/3159450.3159536

1 INTRODUCTION

In 2015, under the auspices of the ACM Education Board the ACM CCECC (Committee for Computing Education in Community Colleges) began updating the ACM *Computing Curricula 2009: Guidelines for Associate-Degree Transfer Curriculum in Computer Science* [3]. Several driving factors motivated the update: 1) the dated 2009 guidance; 2) the release of ACM *Computer Science Curricula 2013* (CS2013) [1]; 3) tremendous need expressed by community college educators during a SIGCSE 2015 BoF session [11]; and 4) a top U.S. priority to build a highly capable cybersecurity workforce including computer science professionals [7].

To this end, the CCECC established a task force of community college educators to review CS2013 and identify foundational material in CS2013 that is appropriate for the first two years of a computer science baccalaureate degree. To further inform the guidance, the CCECC administered surveys to a global audience of computer science educators, both 2- and 4-year, to solicit input related to CS2013 knowledge areas (KAs), knowledge units (KUs), and cybersecurity topics which are appropriate for associate-degree computer science transfer programs, reflecting the growing importance of cybersecurity in all aspects of computing. The CCECC and the task force hosted community engagement workshops at SIGCSE 2016 [10] and SIGCSE 2017 [5, 8], and collected input via a poster session as ITiCSE 2016 [9]. The guidance has been through two rounds of public review and comment on draft versions. In early 2017, the guidance, called CSTransfer2017, was endorsed by the ACM Education Board, and published in June as *Computer Science Curricular Guidance for Associate-Degree Transfer Programs with Infused Cybersecurity* [2].

2 OVERVIEW OF THE GUIDELINES

2.1 Structure and Differences from CS2013

CSTransfer2017 is aligned with CS2013 to facilitate smooth transfer with 4-year university partners. The guidance maintains the knowledge area (KA) and knowledge unit (KU) structure of CS2013, with learning outcomes for each knowledge unit. To facilitate integration into competency-based curriculum typical at many two-year schools, learning outcomes are expressed using Bloom's Revised Taxonomy [4] rather than the custom system used in CS2013. In addition, all learning outcomes are accompanied by a three-tiered assessment rubric providing meaningful evaluation metrics. The lists of topics from CS2013 are absent, reflecting the emphasis on what students can do over what students know.

Included in the associate-degree guidance are 17 of CS2013's 18 knowledge areas. Table 1 shows the 17 KAs and the percentage of the guidance each KA makes up, based on the number of learning outcomes in the KA. The only knowledge area not included is intelligent systems, which consists of upper division content judged not appropriate in the first two years. Two KAs, software development fundamentals (SDF) and discrete structures (DS), are included in their entirety. For the remaining KAs, those knowledge units and learning outcomes determined appropriate for the first two years of a computer science program are included. The information assurance and security (IAS) knowledge area has been renamed Cybersecurity (CYB) to reflect the terminology used in the community, as well as the forthcoming ACM undergraduate curriculum guidelines for cybersecurity education [6]. As in CS2013, the Platform-based Development KA does not have any learning outcomes associated with it, but represents the reality that the design and development of software applications resides on specific software platforms in which platform-specific constraints may apply.

A detailed mapping of CSTransfer2017 learning outcomes to CS2013 can be found on the CCECC website at ccecc.acm.org/guidance/computer-science-2017/classification-mappings. Mappings of CSTransfer2017 to other curricular guidelines, such as Advanced Placement - Computer Science A (AP-CS A), are also included.

The guidance presented in CSTransfer2017 is intended for use by both 2-year and 4-year computer science programs, and should be especially helpful in articulation discussions.

2.2 Learning Outcomes

The guidance consists of a total of 214 learning outcomes (LOs), 64 with infused cybersecurity as applied to computer science. The LOs in the guidance fall across the upper five levels of Bloom's taxonomy: *understanding*, *applying*, *analyzing*, *evaluating*, and *creating*. There are no LOs at the lowest level of Bloom's Revised Taxonomy, *remembering*. Figure 1 shows the distribution of Bloom's levels in the 200+ learning outcomes. The emphasis is on student performance, with half of the learning outcomes at the *applying* level, 22% at the *analyzing* level, and 7% at the *evaluating* and *creating* levels. Only 21% of LOs are at the comprehension level of *understanding*.

Table 1: Knowledge Areas in CSTransfer2017

Knowledge Area	Percentage
Algorithms and Complexity (AL)	7.7%
Architecture and Organization (AR)	5.2%
Computational Science (CN)	0.5%
Cybersecurity (CYB)	10.3%
Discrete Structures (DS)	20.6%
Graphics and Visualization (GV)	1.0%
Human-Computer Interaction (HCI)	2.6%
Information Management (IM)	3.1%
Networking and Communications (NC)	2.6%
Operating Systems (OS)	5.2%
Parallel and Distributed Computing (PD)	1.5%
Platform-based Development	0%
Programming Languages (PL)	7.7%
Software Development Fundamentals (SDF)	15.5%
Software Engineering (SE)	7.7%
Systems Fundamentals (SF)	2.6%
Social Issues and Professional Practice (SP)	6.2%

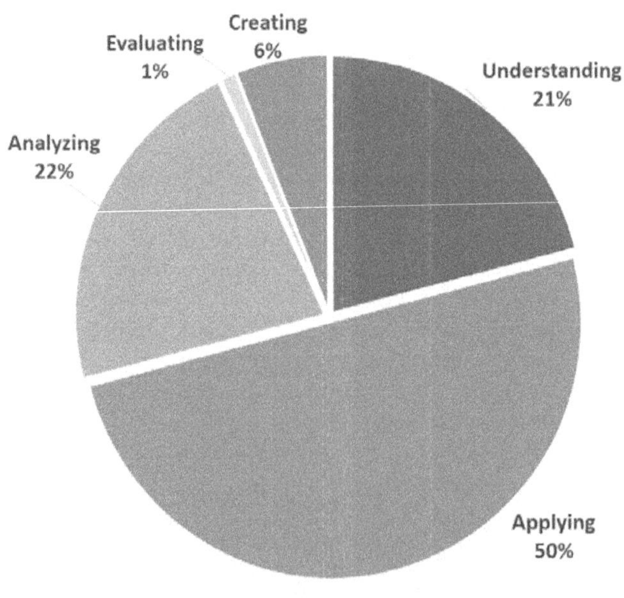

Figure 1: Distribution of learning outcomes in CSTransfer2017 across levels of Bloom's Revised Taxonomy.

Table 2 shows a sampling of the learning outcomes in the guidance, with cyber-infused LOs bolded. Bloom's levels are indicated after each learning outcome. The table of verbs used for the learning outcomes, categorizing the verbs according to Bloom's level, can be found at ccecc.acm.org/assessment/blooms.

Table 2: **Selected Learning Outcomes from CSTransfer2017**

KA-#. Learning Outcome [*Bloom's level*]
AL-01. Analyze best, average, and worst-case behaviors of an algorithm. [*Analyzing*]
AL-06. Investigate the use of random/pseudo random number generation in cybersecurity applications. [*Applying*]
AR-01. Diagram the digital components of computing architecture. [*Applying*]
CN-01. Illustrate the concepts of modeling and abstraction with respect to problem solving. [*Applying*]
CYB-15. Construct input validation and data sanitization in applications, considering adversarial control of the input channel. [*Creating*]
DS-11. Apply each of the proof techniques (direct proof, proof by contradiction, and induction) correctly in the construction of a sound argument. [*Applying*]
GV-05. Perform information hiding through steganography in images, messages, videos, or other media files. [*Applying*]
HCI-06. Analyze the interaction between a security mechanism and its usability. [*Analyzing*]
IM-05. Describe approaches to scale up information systems. [*Understanding*]
NC-01. Diagram the basic structure of the Internet. [*Applying*]
OS-09. Illustrate the concepts of virtual memory, including paging, thrashing, and partitioning. [*Applying*]
OS-10. Investigate the features and limitations of an operating system used to provide protection and security. [*Applying*]
PD-01. Analyze the goals of parallelism and concurrency. [*Analyzing*]
PL-01. Design a simple class hierarchy using superclasses, subclasses, and abstract classes. [*Creating*]
PL-03. Use access and visibility modifiers to secure class data and methods. [*Applying*]
SDF-04. Create simple programs that use abstract data types (ADTs). [*Creating*]
SDF-19. Carry out a code review on a program component using a provided security checklist. [*Applying*]
SE-03. Diagram the phases of the secure software development lifecycle (SecSDLC). [*Applying*]
SE-10. Describe the cost and tradeoffs associated with designing security into software. [*Understanding*]
SF-01. Illustrate the basic building blocks of computers and their role in the historical development of computer architecture. [*Applying*]
SP-08. Support the ethical responsibility of ensuring software correctness, reliability, and safety. [*Evaluating*]
SP-16. Use effective oral, written, electronic, and visual communication techniques with stakeholders. [*Applying*]

Of the 64 cybersecurity-infused learning outcomes, 25 are in the Cybersecurity (CYB) knowledge area. The rest are distributed throughout the other knowledge areas, as shown in Figure 2. The majority of the cybersecurity-related LOs appearing in other knowledge areas demonstrates the importance of security being integrated into the computer science curricula, rather than (only) a separate topic.

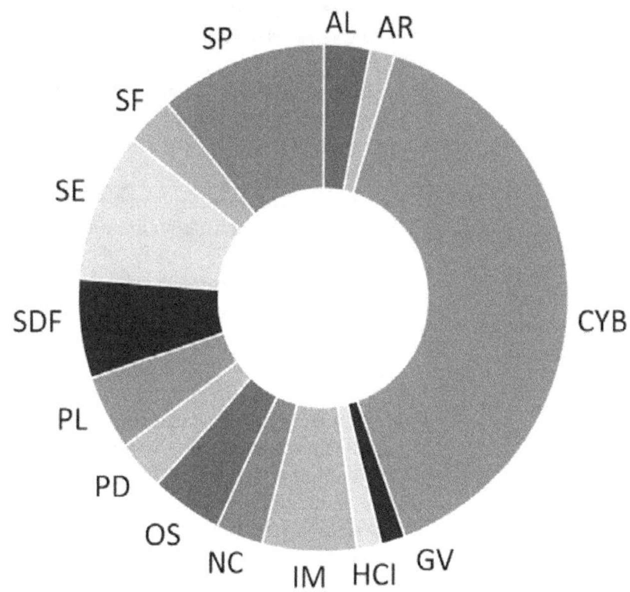

Figure 2: **Cybersecurity-infused learning outcomes across the knowledge areas of CSTransfer2017.**

Table 3 shows a small number of learning outcomes with their full three-tiered assessment rubric. The lowest level in the rubric, Emerging Standard, represents students who are still emerging in their competency and have not yet achieved the indicated outcome. The Developed Standard represents students who have developed the competency, and the Highly Developed Standard represents those students who have gone above and beyond the given outcome.

Table 3: **Selected Learning Outcomes with Assessment Rubric**

Learning Outcome	Assessment Rubric
AR-03. Illustrate how fixed-length number representations could affect accuracy and precision, causing vulnerabilities. [*Applying*]	**Emerging Standard:** Explain how fixed-length number representations could affect accuracy and precision, causing vulnerabilities. [*Understanding*] **Developed Standard:** Illustrate how fixed-length number representations could affect accuracy and precision, causing vulnerabilities. [*Applying*] **Highly Developed Standard:** Examine how fixed-length number

	representations could affect accuracy and precision, causing vulnerabilities. [*Analyzing*]
CYB-11. Use the principles of secure design. [*Applying*]	**Emerging Standard:** Demonstrate some of the principles of secure design as related to cybersecurity. [*Understanding*] **Developed Standard:** Use the principles of secure design, such as least privilege, isolation, fail-safe, and deny-by-default. [*Applying*] **Highly Developed Standard:** Choose appropriate secure design principles for a given cybersecurity scenario. [*Evaluating*]
SDF-06. Create programs which use defensive programming techniques, including input validation, type checking, and protection against buffer overflow. [*Creating*]	**Emerging Standard:** Investigate defensive programming techniques. [*Applying*] **Developed Standard:** Create programs which use defensive programming techniques, including input validation, type checking, and protection against buffer overflow. [*Creating*] **Highly Developed Standard:** Create complex programs which use defensive programming techniques, including input validation, type checking, and protection against buffer overflow. [*Creating*]
SDF-11. Compare the efficiency of basic operations across various data structures. [*Analyzing*]	**Emerging Standard:** Investigate the efficiency of basic operations across various data structures. [*Applying*] **Developed Standard:** Compare the efficiency of basic operations, such as insertion and deletion, across various data structures. [*Analyzing*] **Highly Developed Standard:** Critique the efficiency of basic operations across various data structures. [*Evaluating*]

The full list of learning outcomes and assessment rubrics can be found in the published guidance [2] or explored interactively at the ACM CCECC computer science curricular guidance website: ccecc.acm.org/guidance/computer-science-2017.

3 PROGRAM EXAMPLES

Examples of degree and certificate programs that align with CSTransfer2017 are part of a growing repository hosted on the CCECC website. These program examples demonstrate the adaptability of this competency-based curriculum approach to a variety of computing programs. Three program examples are described here, with a summary of how each program correlates to the guidance depicted in Table 4. The table shows what percentage of CSTransfer2017 learning outcomes from each knowledge area are included in the given school's program.

3.1 El Paso Community College (EPCC)

The two-year Computer Science Field of Study at El Paso Community College prepares students to transfer directly into a Bachelor's Degree Program in Computer Science at a four-year institution. The Computer Science Field of Study provides a balanced program which gives students a strong concentration in computer programming. In this program, it is highly recommended that students complete the Math and Physics sequence at the same institution. The Computer Science Field of Study consists of the following four courses:

- **COSC 1436: Programming Fundamentals I.** Introduces the fundamental concepts of structured and object-oriented programming, and provides a comprehensive introduction to programming for computer science and technology majors. Includes topics on software development methodology, data types, control structures, functions, arrays, and the mechanics of running, testing, and debugging. This course assumes computer literacy.
- **COSC 1437: Programming Fundamentals II.** Focuses on the object-oriented programming paradigm, emphasizing the definition and use of classes along with fundamentals of object-oriented design. Includes basic analysis of algorithms, searching and sorting techniques, and an introduction to software engineering processes. Students will apply techniques for testing and debugging software.
- **COSC 2336: Programming Fundamentals III.** Provides further applications of programming techniques, introducing the fundamental concepts of data structures and algorithms. Includes topics on recursion and fundamental data structures, including stacks, queues, linked lists, hash tables, trees, and graphs.
- **COSC 2425 Computer Organization and Machine Language.** Introduces the organization of computer systems using assembly language. Includes topics on basic concepts of computer architecture and organization, memory hierarchy, data types, computer arithmetic, control structures, interrupt handling, instruction sets, performance metrics, and the mechanics of testing and debugging computer systems. Introduces systems and device interfacing

3.2 Bluegrass Community and Technical College (BCTC)

The A.S. Transfer degree in Informatics at Bluegrass Community and Technical College focuses on software development and databases. In addition to general education requirements, the degree includes the following five courses:

- **INF 120: Elementary Programming.** An elementary introduction to programming for those with no previous programming experience. Emphasis on understanding of algorithm development, procedural and object-oriented software development, secure coding, testing, and execution of program. This is a CS1-level course, which includes secure software development techniques.
- **INF 260: Object-Oriented Programming.** Elementary object-oriented programming concepts and practice: types, decisions, loops, methods, arrays, classes; design and

problem solving. An intensive introduction intended for students with programming experience. This is a CS2-level course, which includes secure software development techniques.

- **INF 282: Introduction to Databases.** Core concepts for the design, creation, and manipulation of relational databases. Analysis of data requirements, conceptual modeling, definition of the relational model, relational database design and normalization, and database implementation; manipulation of relational databases using relational algebra with SQL.
- **CIT 120: Computational Thinking.** Promotes understanding of computer programming and logic by teaching students to "think like a computer". Covers skills needed to develop and design language-independent solutions to solve computer-related problems. Covers development and design basics including use of variables, control and data structures, and principles of command-line and object-oriented languages.
- **CIT 111: Computer Hardware and Software.** Presents a practical view of computer hardware and client operating systems. Covers computer hardware components; troubleshooting, repair, and maintenance; operating system interfaces and management tools; networking components; computer security; and operational procedures.

3.3 Folsom Lake College (FLC)

Folsom Lake College's Associate Degree in Computer Science provides a comprehensive exposure to computer science in preparation for upper-division computer science courses. The program also prepares students for entry level employment in the computer and related industries. Students must complete either CISP 400 or CISP 401, and either CISP 310 or ENGR 303: Introduction to Logic Design (not analyzed here). The Computer Science Associate of Science (AS) Degree may be obtained by completion of the required program, plus general education requirements, and sufficient electives to meet a 60-unit total.

- **CISC 310: Introduction to Computer Information Science.** This course is an examination of information systems and their role in business. The focus is on information systems, database management systems, networking, e-commerce, ethics and security, computer systems hardware and software components. Students will develop experience applying these concepts and methods through hands-on projects creating computer-based solutions to business problems.
- **CISP 300: Algorithm Design/Problem Solving.** This course introduces the Computer Science major to methods for solving classical computer problems through algorithm design. Topics covered include introduction to structured design, control structures, arrays, object oriented programming, and file processing. Students will learn how to assess and analyze computer problems in a top-down, divide-and-conquer approach that leads to a programming solution. It also includes creating programming plans and detailed design documents from which source code versions of programs will be created.
- **CISP 310: Assembly Language Programming for Microcomputers.** This course is an introduction to computer architecture using assembly language programs. Topics include binary representation of data and instructions, memory addressing modes, subroutines and macros, operating system interrupts, processor architecture, and interfacing with high level languages.
- **CISP 360: Introduction to Structured Programming.** This course is an introduction to structured programming. The topics covered include: top-down design, input/output considerations, control structures and flow control, variables, constants, the use of libraries, simple to intermediate data structures, functions, and arguments. An introduction into objects will be included.
- **CISP 400: Object Oriented Programming with C++.** This course is an introduction to object-oriented programming using the C++ programming language. This course is designed to enhance students' abilities to implement object-oriented programs and to further develop programing proficiency. Detailed topics include classes, storage class and scope, encapsulation, polymorphism, inheritance, function overloading and overriding, virtual functions, operator overloading, templates, exception handling, stream I/O, file processing, and the Standard Template Library. Also covered are introductions to Graphical User Interface (GUI) development using class libraries, and object-oriented design methodology.
- **CISP 401: Object Oriented Programming with Java.** This course is an introduction to Object Oriented Programming using the Java language. Topics include: objects, classes, UML, function overloading, inheritance, static and dynamic class relationships, polymorphism, components, graphical user interfaces, event driven programming, class associations, interfaces, error handling, threads, file I/O, testing and debugging. This provides the student with a well-rounded background in Java and is good preparation for advanced topics.
- **CISP 430: Data Structures.** This is a course in data structures for Computer Science. Topics include time complexity analysis and big-O notation, recursion, searching and sorting, linked lists, stacks, queues, priority queues, binary trees, B-trees, graphs, hashing, and basic encryption algorithms.
- **CISP 440: Discrete Structures for Computer Science.** This course is an introduction to the essential discrete structures used in Computer Science, with emphasis on their applications. Topics to be covered include: binary number representation and arithmetic, sets, relations, functions, formal propositional logic and proofs, digital logic and combinational circuits, finite state machines, regular expressions and formal grammars. Students will implement programs to illustrate principles of discrete structures.

Table 4: **Program Examples**

Knowledge Area	EPCC Computer Science Transfer	BCTC Informatics Transfer	FLC Computer Science Transfer
AL	88.2%	76.5%	94.1%
AR	100%	63.6%	81.8%
CN	33.3%	0%	66.7%
CYB	72%	72%	88%
DS	48.4%	0%	85.3%
GV	60%	60%	60%
HCI	100%	50%	83.3%
IM	46.1%	84.6%	92.3%
NC	33.3%	75%	75%
OS	83.3%	61.5%	84.6%
PD	20%	20%	20%
PL	100%	80%	100%
SDF	94.7%	100%	89.5%
SE	57.1%	64.3%	14.2%
SF	66.6%	33.3%	33.3%
SP	86.3%	45.5%	40.1%

4 DISCUSSION

The three program examples included here show three diverse ways that a program can align with the CSTransfer2017 guidelines. As seen in Table 4, none of the programs aligns 100% with every knowledge area, but nearly all knowledge areas are included in each program to some extent. The knowledge areas do not represent courses; a typical course is composed of content from multiple knowledge areas. For example, a CS1 course may include content from the KAs Algorithms and Complexity, Cybersecurity, Human-Computer Interaction, Programming Languages, Software Development Fundamentals, Software Engineering, Social Issues and Professional Practice, and others. The learning outcomes in the guidance can be mixed and matched into courses in a variety of ways to meet the needs of a given program and its local situation and transfer partner(s).

The ACM CCECC invites institutions to highlight their computer science degree program by submitting a program example at ccecc.acm.org/correlations. A spreadsheet can be downloaded for easy offline preparation of the program example, which can then be entered in to the online form at the website.

ACKNOWLEDGMENTS

The CCECC thanks the many reviewers and those who provided input and feedback on CSTransfer2017, especially the task group leaders Teresa Moore (Volunteer State Community College, TN), Lambros Piskopos (Wilbur Wright College, IL), and Christian Servin (El Paso Community College, TX). Thanks also to Caleb Fowler (Folsom Lake College, CA) for providing the FLC program example.

REFERENCES

[1] ACM and IEEE Computer Society. 2013. *Computer Science Curricula 2013.* ACM, New York, NY. DOI: http://dx.doi.org/10.1145/2534860.

[2] ACM Committee for Computing Education in Community Colleges. 2017. *Computer Science Curricular Guidance for Associate-Degree Transfer Programs with Infused Cybersecurity.* ACM, New York, NY. DOI: http://dx.doi.org/10.1145/3108241.

[3] ACM Two-Year College Education Committee. 2009. *Computing Curricula 2009: Guidelines for Associate-Degree Transfer Curriculum in Computer Science.* Available at http://ccecc.acm.org/files/publications/2009ComputerScienceTransferGuidelines.pdf. Accessed 30 August 2017.

[4] Anderson, L.W. and Kratwohl, D.R. eds. 2001. *A Taxonomy for Learning, Teaching and Assessing: A Revision of Bloom's Taxonomy of Educational Objectives.* New York, Longman.

[5] Elizabeth Hawthorne, Cara Tang, Cindy Tucker, and Christian Servin. 2017. Computer Science Curricular Guidelines for Associate-Degree Transfer Programs (Abstract Only). In *Proceedings of the 2017 ACM SIGCSE Technical Symposium on Computer Science Education* (SIGCSE '17). ACM, New York, NY, USA, 725-725. DOI: https://doi.org/10.1145/3017680.3022348.

[6] Joint Task Force on Cybersecurity Education. Cybersecurity Curricula 2017 (CSEC 2017) Website. http://www.csec2017.org/. Accessed 30 August 2017.

[7] National Initiative for Cybersecurity Education (NICE). 2017. *NICE Cybersecurity Workforce Framework.* NIST Special Publication 800-181. DOI: https://doi.org/10.6028/NIST.SP.800-181.

[8] Cara Tang, Cindy Tucker, Elizabeth Hawthorne, Christian Servin, and Teresa Moore. 2017. Curricular Guidance for Associate-Degree Transfer Programs in Computer Science with Contemporary Cybersecurity Concepts (Abstract Only). In *Proceedings of the 2017 ACM SIGCSE Technical Symposium on Computer Science Education* (SIGCSE '17). ACM, New York, NY, 717-717. DOI: https://doi.org/10.1145/3017680.3022398.

[9] Cara Tang, Elizabeth Hawthorne, Cindy Tucker. 2016. ACM Undergraduate Curricular Guidance in Computer Science: The First Two Years. In *Proceedings of the 2016 ACM Conference on Innovation and Technology in Computer Science Education* (ITiCSE '16, Arequipa, Peru). ACM, New York, NY. 357-357. DOI: https://doi.org/10.1145/2899415.2925480.

[10] Cara Tang, Cindy Tucker, Elizabeth Hawthorne. 2016. Updating Curricular Guidelines for Associate-Degree Computer Science Programs. In *Proceedings of the 47th ACM Technical Symposium on Computing Science Education* (SIGCSE '16). ACM, New York, NY, 490-491. DOI: http://doi.org/10.1145/2839509.2844671.

[11] Cindy Tucker, Cara Tang, Elizabeth Hawthorne. 2015. Perspectives on How Computer Science Curricula 2013 Influences Two-Year College Programs (Abstract Only). In Proceedings of the 46th ACM Technical Symposium on Computer Science Education (SIGCSE '15). ACM, New York, NY, 698-698. DOI: 10.1145/2676723.2691833.

A Systematic Review of the Use of Bloom's Taxonomy in Computer Science Education

Susana Masapanta-Carrión
Pontificia Universidad Católica del Ecuador
Quito, 17012184, Ecuador
smmasapanta@puce.edu.ec

J. Ángel Velázquez-Iturbide
Universidad Rey Juan Carlos
28933 Móstoles, Madrid, Spain
angel.velazquez@urjc.es

ABSTRACT

Bloom's taxonomy is a model that allows characterizing students' learning achievements. It is frequently used in computer science education (CSE), but its use is not straightforward. We present a systematic review conducted to know actual use of the taxonomy in CSE. We found that it was mostly used in programming education and to assess students' performance. A more relevant contribution is a classification of authors' difficulties. In particular, the most often reported difficulty is determining the level of the taxonomy where an assessment task can be classified. In addition, we present authors' hypotheses about possible causes of the difficulties and the solutions they adopted.

CCS CONCEPTS

• Social and professional topics~Computer science education

KEYWORDS

Computer science education; Bloom's taxonomy; difficulties.

ACM Reference format:

S. Masapanta-Carrión, and J. Á. Velázquez-Iturbide. 2018. A systematic review of the use of Bloom's taxonomy in computer science education. In *Proceedings 49th ACM Technical Symposium on Computing Science Education, Baltimore, MD, USA, February 2018 (SIGCSE '18)*, 6 pages.
https://doi.org/10.1145/3159450.3159491

1. INTRODUCTION

Bloom's taxonomy is a model that allows characterizing students' learning achievements. According to Bloom *et al.* [3], learning objectives are "explicit formulations of the ways in which students are expected to be changed by the educative process". The original taxonomy [3] establishes hierarchy of six levels of learning. The revised taxonomy [1] does not establish a strict hierarchical relation between levels and it differentiates two dimensions. The cognitive process dimension is similar to the original taxonomy, whereas the knowledge dimension classifies the knowledge the student is expected to achieve.

Bloom's taxonomy is probably the most widely used taxonomy to state learning goals in computing studies. Even curricular recommendations by ACM/IEEE specify learning goals by means of the revised version of Bloom's taxonomy (more faithfully in the 2008 edition [4] and in a simplified way in the 2013 edition [6]).

However, some authors reported that the use of the taxonomy was problematic. For instance, different instructors may classify a given exercise at different levels of the taxonomy. Actually, the second author used Bloom's taxonomy in the past but, in spite of the taxonomy appeal, he found difficulties of use [10]. A few years later, a working group was created at the ITiCSE 2007 conference. In its final report [6], the group includes a comprehensive review of academic literature on different learning taxonomies, their use in computer science education (CSE) and their associated problems. The working group also proposed a new taxonomy that could be used in programming courses. However, the review of problems reported on the use of the taxonomy was not exhaustive.

Britto and Usman made a systematic review of the use of Bloom's taxonomy in software engineering education [4]. However, their analysis is descriptive and does not deepen, at least, in difficulties of use of the taxonomy.

The goal of this work is to expand knowledge of difficulties reported by authors using Bloom's taxonomy for CSE. The structure of the paper is as follows. In Section II, the methodology used for the systematic review is described. Section III presents answers to research questions, according to the review. Finally, Section IV contains a brief discussion of our findings and Section V summarizes our conclusions.

2. METHODOLOGY

In this section, we describe in detail the process followed for the systematic review. We followed the guidelines proposed by Barbara Kitchenham [12].

2.1 Research Questions

The following research questions were formulated:

RQ1. What version of Bloom's taxonomy was used?
RQ2. Is any other learning taxonomy used?
RQ3. In what subject matters is Bloom's taxonomy used?
RQ4. What is the purpose of using Bloom's taxonomy?
RQ5. Did the authors report any difficulty of use of Bloom's taxonomy? In the affirmative case, what difficulties?

SIGCSE '18, February 21–24, 2018, Baltimore, MD, USA

ACM ISBN 978-1-4503-5103-4/18/02...$15.00
https://doi.org/10.1145/3159450.3159491

2.2 Documentation Sources

The search was focused on the most relevant journals and conferences on CSE. At the risk of excluding some valuable publications, we expected that the results would be representative of the use of Bloom's taxonomy in CSE. We selected prestigious journals and conferences sponsored by SIGCSE, plus the journal Computer Science Education:

- Transactions on Computing Education (TOCE).
- ACM Conference on International Computing Education Research (ICER).
- ACM Technical Symposium on Computer Science Education (SIGCSE).
- ACM Conference on Innovation and Technology in Computer Science Education (ITiCSE).
- Australasian Computing Education Conference (ACE).
- Koli Calling International Conference on Computing Education Research.

2.3 Search Terms

Search terms were selected by taking into account the use of Bloom's taxonomy in computer science and in programming, as well as the possibility of other ways of indirectly referring to the taxonomy. The search string used was:

("Bloom's taxonomy" OR "Bloom taxonomy" OR
"cognitive taxonomy")
AND
(programming OR "computer science")

The search for the journal Computer Science Education was conducted in the on-line version of Taylor & Francis and, for the rest of sources, in the ACM Digital Library.

2.4 Selection Criteria

The search of the above-specified string yielded a result of 314 publications, not all of them useful. Therefore, we applied exclusion and inclusion criteria to determine relevant articles. The selection process was conducted in three stages:

- Duplicated publications were discarded, as well as results corresponding to conference proceeding volumes (without the papers). As a result, 306 publications were selected.
- We applied the following inclusion criteria: (a) the abstract referred to the use of Bloom's taxonomy, or (b) the string "Bloom" was present in the list of key words. The number of publications was reduced to 45.
- A second exclusion process was conducted given that, on analyzing these 45 publications, we noticed that some works reported the same research effort, usually presented differently (e.g. one was an extended version of another one). We decided to keep the publication containing more details related to our research. The resulting number of publications was 40.

Table 1 summarizes the process described above, with the figures resulting after each step. The list of the 40 publications finally selected can be found in a technical report [13].

2.5 Methodology of Analysis

Research questions 1 and 2 only admitted a restricted number of answers, therefore they were counted and handled statistically. Questions 3-5 were open, therefore they were analyzed qualitatively. We elaborated a matrix where the authors' comments about difficulties of use of the taxonomy were recorded. On analyzing a publication, we only considered the comments of its authors, not citations or quotations of other authors.

Table 1. Results of applying selection criteria

Document source	Found	Discarding duplicates	Satisfying inclusion criteria	Discarding similar works
CSE	7	7	7	6
TOCE	17	17	1	1
ICER	42	39	5	5
SIGCSE	119	117	13	11
ITiCSE	86	85	11	10
ACE	30	29	7	6
Koli Calling	13	12	1	1
Total	**314**	**306**	**45**	**40**

The qualitative analysis was conducted without predefined categories, as *grounded theory* advocates [7], and proceeded through numerous iterations. The iterations may be grouped into two stages:

1. Difficulties were classified into internal difficulties (i.e. inherent to the taxonomy) and external difficulties (i.e. related to the use of the taxonomy). However, this analysis criterion did not provide a clear classification instrument, being common the uncertainty about the subcategory where each difficulty best fitted. Finally, we discarded this classification scheme.
2. We analyzed whether each commentary reported on a difficulty of use, a cause of the difficulty hypothesized by the authors, or a solution adopted by them. This classification provided greater precision, thus we adopted it.

Each stage comprised a high, undetermined number of iterations, with frequent analysis forward and backward of the 40 publications. Most analysis iterations were conducted by the first author, but the second author also was involved in the analysis. The analysis ended when both authors achieved a consensus.

3. RESULTS

We first present the results of closed questions and then we present the results of open questions.

3.1 Results of Closed Questions

RQ1 inquired the version of Bloom's taxonomy actually used by the authors. The original taxonomy was used in 30 publications (75%), while the remaining 10 (25%) used the revised version.

RQ2 was intended to know whether other taxonomies also were used. Most publications exclusively used Bloom's taxonomy (34 publications, 85%). Other publications used the SOLO taxonomy [2], either after discarding Bloom's taxonomy (4, 10%) or jointly with Bloom's (2, 5%).

3.2 Results of Open Questions

In order to interpret correctly the results of research questions 3 to 5, note that some publications do not provide answers to some questions. For instance, the authors of an article report on one or more plausible causes of their difficulties of use of Bloom's taxonomy, but they do not report on any adopted solution. Consequently, the total number of answers to each question is not equal to the number of publications selected (40).

3.2.1 Matters where Bloom's Taxonomy Was Used

In general, the publications reported the use of the taxonomy in just one course. However, three publications reported its use in either two or three courses. In total, the number of courses reported is 45. The results, classified into subject matters, are shown in Table 2.

Table 2. Subject matters where Bloom's taxonomy was used

Subject matter	Number	Percentage
CS1	23	51%
Data structures or algorithms	4	9%
Other programming courses	3	7%
Software engineering	6	13%
Other computing topics	5	11%
High school course	4	9%
Total	**45**	**100%**

The two first subject matters are self-explanatory. "Other programming courses" comprises courses on programming languages or functional programming. "Software engineering" gathers five publications reporting general courses on software engineering and one publication reporting a specialized course on requirements engineering. In "Other computing courses" we include courses on data bases, networking, security, human-computer interaction, and computing professionalism. The category "High school course" refers to courses at the high school level and the *AP Computer Science* exam.

3.2.2 Uses of Bloom's Taxonomy

We analyzed the use that authors made of Bloom's taxonomy. One of the publications reports two uses, thus we computed 41 uses in total (see Table 3).

Nearly half the publications (46%) used Bloom's taxonomy in relation to assessment. Note also that a substantial number of publications (37%) mention that they have used or have based on Bloom's taxonomy, but they do not make clear how.

In the following, categories and subcategories are explained:

- Assess students (19 publications). The taxonomy is used to measure students' knowledge. This category groups three subcategories:
  - Develop questions or problems aimed at given cognitive levels.
  - Classify questions or problems previously developed into cognitive levels.
  - Classify students' performance into cognitive levels.
- Schedule instruction (2 publications). Bloom's taxonomy is used to schedule instructional activities in a course in order to enhance students' learning.
- Specify the learning goals of a course (2 publications).
- Others (3 publications):
  - Create a new taxonomy. Bloom's taxonomy is modified to obtain a new taxonomy, supposedly more adequate for CSE.
  - Develop educational software. The taxonomy is used as a basis to develop a tutorial on how to use Bloom's taxonomy itself.

Table 3. Uses of Bloom's taxonomy

Category	Subcategory	Num.	Total in category	%
Assess students	Develop questions	10	19	46%
	Classify questions	7		
	Classify students' learning	2		
Schedule instruction	–	2	2	5%
Specify learning goals	–	2	2	5%
Others	Create a new taxonomy	2	3	7%
	Develop educational software	1		
Undetermined	–	15	15	37%
TOTAL		**41**	**41**	**100%**

- Undetermined (15 publications). They mention the use of Bloom's taxonomy without additional details.

3.2.3 Difficulties of Use of Bloom's Taxonomy

Only 15 publications (38%) report that their authors had any difficulty using the taxonomy. Let us analyze in detail the difficulties reported by their authors.

We successively present the difficulties identified, their plausible causes, and the solutions adopted to overcome them. In order to enhance the understanding of our findings, we include some quotations. Unfortunately, given the lack of space, we are unable to include a quotation for every category.

3.2.3.1 Difficulties

Three of the fifteen publications reporting difficulties cite two difficulties, therefore the total amount of reported difficulties reaches 18. We may distinguish four classes of difficulties (see Table 4), being the difficulty in classifying learning goals or assessment tasks into the taxonomy levels the most frequent (77%). In the following, the categories are described.

- Difficulty in classifying learning goals or assessment activities. It is common to consider several promising candidate taxonomy level that fit the best. Whalley *et al.* [18] comment: "... categorising programming MCQ's by cognitive complexity applying Bloom's taxonomy, has proven challenging even to an experienced group of programming educators".
- Difficulty in precisely specifying the knowledge associated to each learning goal or assessment task. The problem emerges when the instructor switches without intention between related, but not equal, concepts. For instance, Starr *et al.* [16] draw our attention about switching between "iteration" and "*for* loop"; notice that the former is a more general concept than the latter.

- Difficulty in measuring student's progress. It is difficult to know whether a student's cognitive process to solve a given problem progresses, for example, moving to upper levels in the taxonomy. Meerbaum-Salant *et al.* [14] claim: "We wanted to work with a strictly hierarchal taxonomy, enabling us to monitor students' progress, but one that matched the context of the study and its objectives."

Table 4. Classes of difficulties on using Bloom's taxonomy

Difficulty of use	Num.	%
Classifying learning goals or assessment tasks	14	77%
Specifying precisely the knowledge associated to each learning goal or assessment task	2	11%
Measuring student's progress	1	6%
Understanding the taxonomy	1	6%
TOTAL	**18**	**100%**

- Difficulty in understanding the taxonomy. The difficulty comes from having doubts about how to interpret some of the taxonomy concepts in a computing context. Thompson *et al.* [17] comment the difficulty in understanding the meaning of "applying a process" or "creating a process" in the revised taxonomy, referred to a programming context.

3.2.3.2 Causes

Authors of the publications often guess plausible causes for the difficulties they found on using Bloom's taxonomy. We classify them into five categories (see Table 5). Here, we did not find one major cause, but four main causes: need to know the educational context, limitations of the taxonomy, deficient understanding of the taxonomy, and terminology of the taxonomy. Remember that we do not express our opinions, but we reproduce opinions by the authors of the reviewed publications. A description of categories and subcategories follows:

- Need to know the educational context. The authors point out that ignorance of the way contents were instructed makes difficult to classify into a specific level of the taxonomy. Gluga *et al.* [9] remark "The example highlights the tight dependence on knowledge of the teaching context to correctly classify exam questions using Bloom.". This category of causes comprises two subcategories:
  - Different students may make different cognitive efforts to solve the same problem, since they may apply different ways of reasoning, corresponding to different levels of the taxonomy.
  - Instructors may address a particular approach to problem solving, which must therefore be known in order to properly classify the assessment into the corresponding level of the taxonomy.
- Limitations of the taxonomy. This category gathers those causes that are inherent to the taxonomy, such as its definition or its structure. It includes three subcategories:
  - Incomplete or inadequate set of levels for programming tasks. Authors think that the taxonomy levels hardly fit the concepts and tasks involved in programming [14].
  - Overlapped set of levels. The levels are not well differentiated, therefore a question or concept may be categorized at different levels by different persons.
  - Conceived to assess and not to specify goals.
- Deficient understanding of the terminology. The difficulties may be due to instructors' misunderstandings of the meaning of each level. Some subcategories are:
  - Shallow knowledge. Instructors often have beliefs and misunderstandings about the meaning of the levels of the taxonomy. Gugla *et al.* [8] say "... the use of Bloom's Taxonomy in a computer science context has generally been inconsistent. A possible reason for this is that the computer science educators performing the Bloom's classifications did not have a strong understanding and/or a common understanding of the theory".
  - Different understanding, depending on the instructors' experience. The interpretation of each level of the taxonomy, as well as the cognitive effort, are different in experienced and in novice instructors. Difficulties come when instructors with varying experience meet in the same assessment group.
  - The use of the taxonomy demands a notable memorization effort. Note that, according to the revised Bloom's taxonomy [1], there are 4 levels and 11 sublevels in the knowledge dimension, and 6 levels and 19 sublevels in the cognitive process dimension.
- Terminology used to define the taxonomy. Actually, we may consider this category a particular case of the previous one but we keep it separate, given its specific relation to language use. We differentiate two subcategories:

Table 5. Causes of the difficulties of use of Bloom's taxonomy

Category	Subcategory	Num.	Total	%
Need to know the educational context	Varying students' cognitive effort	4	8	31%
	Need to know how the contents is instructed	4		
Limitations of the taxonomy	Incomplete or inadequate set of categories	5	7	27%
	Overlapped set of categories	1		
	Conceived to assess and not to specify goals	1		
Deficient understanding of the taxonomy	Shallow understanding	3	5	19%
	Different understanding, depending on experience	1		
	Demand of a notable memorization effort	1		
Terminology	Lack of illustrative examples	3	5	19%
	Peculiar terminology	2		
Complexity of computer science	–	1	1	4%
TOTAL		**26**	**26**	**100%**

- Lack of examples of computing that illustrate the levels and sublevels in the taxonomy. Whalley *et al.* [18] comment: "The examples given by the taxonomy's authors are not easy to translate into the programming domain. In many cases the categories within the knowledge domain, did not readily fit with concepts and tasks required in computer programming".
- Peculiar terminology of the taxonomy. The terminology used in computing, in particular in programming, has different connotations than the terminology used in Bloom's taxonomy. For instance, the task of analyzing the complexity of an algorithm typically does not correspond to the analysis level of Bloom's taxonomy but to the application level, i.e. application of a procedure.

- Complexity of computer science. The intended cognitive level not only depends on the topics under study but also on the tool. Although different tools may have the same purpose, their complexity may vary, resulting in classifications at different levels of the taxonomy. For instance, "...in the systems modeling field, comparing the number and nature of symbols in Data Flow Diagrams (DFDs) to those in the formal specification language Z makes evident the considerable disparity between them. Whereas DFDs have only a few graphical symbols, Z has a complex mathematical notation. These differences superimpose a degree of difficulty at all levels of the taxonomy, leading to a paradigm shift between these two examples" [15].

3.2.3.3 Solutions

We gathered the solutions that some authors adopted to solve their difficulties and grouped them into categories (see Table 6). We found 4 publications that did not report any solution, 3 publications reporting 2 solutions and 1 publication reporting 3 solutions. The most frequent solution was to adopt a criterion and to apply it consistently (38%).

The categories for solutions adopted follow:

- Give guidelines of use. These authors gave two kinds of guidelines: to make decisions on the level corresponding to a given class of programming exercise, or to interpret the terms of the taxonomy and indicate how to use them in computer science. For example, Thompson *et al.* [17] redefine each level of the taxonomy based on specific examples of programming.
- Training instructors in the use of the taxonomy. For instance, Gluga *et al.* [8] conclude, after a review of the literature, that the use of Bloom's taxonomy is not straightforward; consequently, academics willing to use Bloom's taxonomy must be trained.
- Extend the taxonomy. Three kinds of solutions were grouped into this category: to extend the taxonomy with other dimensions (in particular, complexity and difficulty), extend it with an additional "higher application" level, and use it jointly with the SOLO taxonomy. For instance, the latter solution was adopted by Meerbaum-Salant *et al.* [14], who created a new taxonomy that combines some categories of Bloom's and SOLO taxonomies. Based on the specifics of their student population, they only used the understanding, applying and creating levels from Bloom's taxonomy and the unistructural, multistructural and relational levels from SOLO. The authors use such a combined taxonomy to design assessment questions and to analyze the answers.
- Change the terminology. They recommend using terms related to computing for each level of the taxonomy.
- Know the context of assessment questions within a course.
- Determine the cognitive level that students will use. They propose guessing the cognitive level that most students will achieve.

Table 6. Solutions adopted to overcome difficulties

Solutions	Num.	%
Give guidelines	6	38%
Training	3	19%
Extend the taxonomy	3	19%
Change the terminology of the taxonomy	2	12%
Know the educational context	1	6%
Determine the cognitive level that students will apply	1	6%
TOTAL	**18**	**100%**

4. THREATS TO VALIDITY

The main validity threat to this work is the coverage of relevant literature. It was the result of adopting a trade-off between wider coverage and capacity to handle a (foreseeable) very high number of publications, at least in the first stages of selection. However, we consider that the decision of limiting ourselves to most of the publications organized or sponsored by ACM SIGCSE, as well as the Computer Science Education journal, was correct. Other forums could have contributed with additional publications, especially those organized or sponsored by IEEE. However, according to preliminary search results, many of them refer to engineering education. Engineering and computing often overlap, especially in the topic of computer programming. However, we wanted to focus on computer science education.

Another threat may be the specific string search used. As an additional check of the search results, we tested whether a number of publications about the topic we were aware of had been selected. The result was affirmative in all the cases.

Another threat is the classification of difficulties, causes and solutions. To mitigate this threat, both authors were involved in the classification process. Actually, the first author did a bigger effort, but consensus was necessary to validate the classification. Consensus was not simple and, as reported in Section 2.5, we successively used two categorization schemes. The first scheme distinguished between internal and external difficulties, inspired by other classification techniques used in computing (such as pattern languages). However, we often disagreed, thus we found confusing this criterion. When we distinguished among difficulties, causes and solutions, it was much simpler to come to a consensus.

5. DISCUSSION

Some results of the systematic review match the results of our previous paper [10], as well as those of the working group led by Ursula Fuller [6], but the final overview is more comprehensive. According to the selected papers, we might be tempted to conclude that Bloom's taxonomy is the most often used educational taxonomy in computing. However, this claim cannot be supported by our study because the search string, as well as inclusion and exclusion criteria, were biased in behalf of Bloom's taxonomy. We do may claim that Bloom's taxonomy has been mostly used in programming courses and with the goal of assessing students' performance.

About one third of the reviewed publications acknowledge having used Bloom's taxonomy, but they do not even sketch for what purpose or how. Furthermore, over half the publications analyzed do not refer any difficulty of use. However, the rest of publications report severe difficulties, often suffered by experienced researchers. Both facts raise the issue of whether the use of the taxonomy often is very shallow.

The main difficulty found by authors was the classification of a learning goal, course contents or an assessment test in a cognitive level of the taxonomy. There is more disparity in the causes hypothesized about such difficulties, with four causes being the most frequently guessed: need to know the educational context, deficiencies of the taxonomy, deficient understanding of the taxonomy, and terminology of the taxonomy. Finally, we also find diversity of solutions proposed to overcome these difficulties, being guidelines of use the most frequently adopted solution.

6. CONCLUSIONS

We have presented in detail a systematic review of the use of Bloom's taxonomy in computer science education. The resulting landscape is perplexing. On the one hand, the high frequency of use of the taxonomy allows considering it a valuable educational tool, especially to assess students. On the other hand, common report of difficulties, as well as the variety of causes hypothesized and solutions adopted makes difficult to find clear lines of action to let instructors use the taxonomy with confidence. Currently, we are studying in depth the results of the systematic review to suggest plausible solutions that may (ideally) provide aids to instructors willing to use Bloom's taxonomy.

ACKNOWLEDGMENTS

This work was supported by research grants TIN2015-66731-C2-1-R of the Ministry of Economy and Competitiveness, and S2013/ICE-2715 of the Regional Government of Madrid.

REFERENCES

[1] L.W. Anderson, D.R. Krathwohl, P.W. Airasian, K.A. Cruikshank, R.E. Mayer, P.R. Pintrich, R. Raths, and M.C. Wittrock. 2001. *A Taxonomy for Learning, Teaching and Assessing. A Revision of Bloom's Taxonomy of Educational Objectives*, Addison-Wesley Longman.

[2] J.B. Biggs, and K.F. Collis. 1982. *Evaluating the Quality of Learning: The SOLO Taxonomy (Structure of the Observed Learning Outcome)*, Academic Press.

[3] B.S. Bloom, M.D. Engelhart, E.J. Furst, W.H. Hill, and D.R. Krathwohl. 1956. *Taxonomy of Educational Objectives: Handbook I: Cognitive Domain*, Longmans Group.

[4] R. Brito, and M. Usman. 2015. Bloom's taxonomy in software engineering education: A systematic mapping study. In *Proceedings of the Frontiers in Education Conference (FIE 2015)*, IEEE Xplore. DOI= 10.1109/FIE.2015.7344084.

[5] CS2008 Review Taskforce, 2008. Computer Science Curriculum 2008: An Interim Revision of CS 2001, ACM & IEEE Computer Society. Retrieved 24th April 2017 at http://www.acm.org/education/curricula/ComputerScience2008.pdf.

[6] U. Fuller, C.G. Johnson, T. Ahoniemi, D. Cukierman, I. Hernán-Losada, J. Jackova, E. Lahtinen, T.L. Lewis, D.M.Thompson, C. Riedesel, and E. Thompson. 2007. Developing a computer science-specific learning taxonomy. In *ITiCSE-WGR '07 Working Group Reports*, 2007, ACM DL, 152-170. DOI= 10.1145/1345443.1345438.

[7] B.G. Glaser, and A.L. Strauss. 2009. *The Discovery of Grounded Theory: Strategies for Qualitative Research*, Transaction Publishers.

[8] R. Gluga, J. Kay, R. Lister, and S. Kleitman. 2013. Mastering cognitive development theory in computer science education. *Computer Science Education*, 23(1), 24-57, DOI= 10.1080/08993408.2013.768830.

[9] R. Gluga, J. Kay, R. Lister, S. Kleitman, and T. Lever. 2012. Over-confidence and confusion in using Bloom for programming fundamentals assessment. In *Proceedings of the 43rd ACM Technical Symposium on Computer Science Education*, 2012, 147-152. DOI= 10.1145/2157136.21571.

[10] I. Hernán-Losada, C.A. Lázaro-Carrascosa, and J.Á. Velázquez-Iturbide. 2004. On the use of Bloom's taxonomy as a basis to design educational software on programming. In *Engineering Education in the Changing Society*, C. da Rocha Brito y M.M. Ciampi (eds.), COPEC, 2004, 351-355. Retrieved 24th April 2017 at http://copec.eu/congresses/wcete2004/

[11] The Joint Task Force on Computing Curricula,. 2013. Computer Science Curricula 2013 – Curriculum Guidelines for Undergraduate Degree Programs in Computer Science, ACM & IEEE Computer Society. Retrieved 24th April 2017 at http://www.acm.org/education/CS2013-final-report.pdf.

[12] B. Kitchenham. 2004. Procedures for performing systematic reviews. Technical Report TR/SE-0401. Keele University. Retrieved 24th April 2017 at http://www.inf.ufsc.br/~aldo.vw/kitchenham.pdf.

[13] S. Masapanta-Carrión, and J.Á. Velázquez-Iturbide, 2017. Una revisión sistemática del uso de la taxonomía de Bloom en la enseñanza de la informática. Technical Report DLSI1-URJC 2017-02, Universidad Rey Juan Carlos. Retrieved 24th April at http://www.lite.etsii.urjc.es/technical-reports/.

[14] O. Meerbaum-Salant, M. Armoni, and M. Ben-Ari, 2010. Learning computer science concepts with Scratch. In *Proceedings of the Sixth International Workshop on Computing Education Research (ICER'10)*, 69-76. DOI= 10.1145/1839594.1839607.

[15] D. Oliver, T. Dobele, M. Greber, and T. Roberts. 2004. Comparing course assessments: When lower is higher and higher, lower. *Computer Science Education*, 14(4), 321-341, DOI= 10.1080/0899340042000303465.

[16] C.W. Starr, B. Manaris, and R.H. Stalvey. 2008. Bloom's taxonomy revisited: specifying assessable learning objectives in computer science. In *Proceedings of the 39th SIGCSE Technical Symposium on Computer Science Education*, 261-265, DOI= 10.1145/1352135.1352227.

[17] E. Thompson, A. Luxton-Reilly, J.L. Whalley, M. Hu, and P. Robbins. 2008. Bloom's taxonomy for CS assessment. In *Proceedings of the Tenth Conference on Australasian Computing Education*, 155-161.

[18] J.L. Whalley, R. Lister, E. Thompson, T. Clear, P. Robbins, P.K. Kumar, and C. Prasad. 2006. An Australasian study of reading and comprehension skills in novice programmers, using the Bloom and SOLO taxonomies. In *Proceedings of the 8th Australasian Conference on Computing Education*, 243-252.

Culturally-Centric Outreach and Engagement for Underserved Groups in STEM

Danielle Cummings
US Air Force Academy
danielle.cummings@usafa.edu

Loretta Cheeks
StrongTIES
loretta.cheeks@gmail.com

Rosario Robinson
Anita Borg Institute
rosario.robinson@gmail.com

ABSTRACT

The intersection between Science, Technology and the Arts is providing an insightful and rich playground for engaging historically underrepresented and underserved youth. This paper discusses an innovative and effective approach for learning Science, Technology, Engineering, the Arts and Mathematics (STEAM) with an emphasis on using expressive arts as a culturally-centered engagement tool. Our framework incorporates a multimodal model that considers unconventional learning styles that appeal to underrepresented and underserved students, the power of cultural cues and the presence of minority STEM professionals to shape students learning experiences. In addition to demonstrating the importance of culturally-centered learning approaches, we've identified methods of engaging students' families and communities as a means of strengthening the pipeline to continued education in STEM.

ACM Reference Format:
Danielle Cummings, Loretta Cheeks, and Rosario Robinson. 2018. Culturally-Centric Outreach and Engagement for Underserved Groups in STEM. In *SIGCSE '18: The 49th ACM Technical Symposium on Computer Science Education, Feb. 21–24, 2018, Baltimore, MD, USA.* ACM, New York, NY, USA, 6 pages. https://doi.org/10.1145/3159450.3159565

1 INTRODUCTION

The tradition of music-making and performance, although pervasive throughout African American culture, is often segmented in the educational system. This is especially true when considered in conjunction with the sciences. This segmentation is surprising given the number of non-western cultures that embrace a strong tradition of music and performance which often presents itself in situations that may be atypical by western standards (e.g. greeting visitors, settling disputes, preserving history, etc.) [34]. Many West African cultures embrace music and ritual performance as, not only an avenue of self-expression, but also an integral part of fellowship, play, sport, education, work, and all mannerisms of daily life [12]. Despite heavy criticism and suppression in the New World (17th century) the tradition of music and performance remains an integral part of the African American experience [12, 21].

The use of music and performance arts in youth education is not a novel concept. However, technology has revolutionized the way today's youth interacts with music, going beyond the role of listener to active music-makers and social influencers. Unfortunately, the education system continues to fall short in keeping pace with the way music and performance intertwines with youth culture [14]. The use of these art forms in curriculums, classrooms, and in informal learning environments with respect to STEM is lacking and presents a missed opportunity. Studies have shown that the integration of culture within the context of STEM learning experiences has demonstrated value for increasing the number of students who enter these disciplines [19].

In addition, underrepresented students benefit from seeing cultural representation when exposed to unfamiliar and challenging content. Young people interpret their confidence and abilities through various lenses of identity as gained through observational modeling of who they want to become [5, 8, 31]. Therefore, having a connection with relevant representatives who understand the African, Latino, or Indigenous American experience presents an archetype of success and creates a learning environment wherein perceived intellectual, social and economical shortcomings may be overcome [11].

When attempting to address complexities that exist in the learning experiences of underrepresented youth, a single approach is inadequate. An effective approach requires an integration of multiple modes, hence our goal to link STEM education with cultural representation, music and performance. In this paper we present teaching methods that are firmly grounded in these culturally-relevant mediums as a means of introducing and engaging underrepresented youth in Computer Science. We hope this approach may lead to the development of a unique pedagogy in STEM education.

2 RELATED WORK

The authors' careful selection of music and performance as tools for introducing and engaging disadvantaged youth is an acknowledgement of music's association with emotional reactions, motivation, positive moods, expression and problem-solving [7, 22, 23]. Motivation often precedes engagement, which is essential for learning [15]. Scholarly research suggests linkages between short-term engagement that is predictive of improved grades, conduct and academic achievement in the long-term [18, 24, 25]. Furthermore, scholars underscore the importance of motivation that leads to engagement (i.e. a change in behavior) as a necessary factor for youth learning achievements, particularly resulting from the integration of cultural relevance in education [27, 32].

Despite these promising findings, recent reports state that due to unknowns about the long-term effectiveness of short-term STEM programming, it is unclear if this approach is predictive of an overall positive learning achievement. These reports suggest that the

SIGCSE '18, Feb. 21–24, 2018, Baltimore, MD, USA

ACM ISBN 978-1-4503-5103-4/18/02...$15.00
https://doi.org/10.1145/3159450.3159565

unknowns are attributed to the limitations of existing formalized instruments and measures (given the time spent in short-term STEM programs and available collective measures for data). In spite of these limitations and mixed perspectives, the authors relied on longstanding evidence of the benefits of out-of-school programming in the design and implementation of their STEAM program [13].

Existing research notes there is significant value of learning in informal learning environments (i.e. out-of-school time) as this setting has been found to be effective in reducing achievement gaps [2, 9]. These findings align with reports that support informal STEM learning in libraries, museums, science centers, or other community gathering locations such as recreation centers and after school clubs [3, 4, 20]. There is a shared view by educators that learning is life-long and opportunities for learning STEM may occur outside formal institutions, particularly, during the summer months [1, 10].

The resulting teaching methodology builds on models that a) address the complexities and unique needs of African, Latino, and Indigenous American youth, b) integrate music and performance arts with relevant cultural representation as a means of reinforcing both an educational and social connection and c) capitalize on standing research that supports the value of out-of-school informal learning for stimulating interest and engagement in STEAM disciplines [16].

3 CONCEPTUAL FRAMEWORK

In 2013, members of Black Women in Computing (BWiC), a Systers affinity group sponsored by the Anita Borg Institute, established a mission that supports efforts aimed at increasing the number of black women and other underrepresented and underserved groups in computing-related fields. One of these efforts included the implementation of a series of workshops and parent panels, called Pathways to STEM. The Pathways to STEM program focuses on introducing and engaging underrepresented and underserved youth (e.g. low income, African American, Latino/a (Hispanic), Native American, Pacific Islander, and girls) to the power of computing and careers in STEM.

The purpose of these workshops is to:

- Creatively engage students to increase their interest in computer science and programming
- Promote education and careers in science, technology, engineering and mathematics (STEM)
- Support historically underrepresented and underserved students with limited opportunities or access to critical resources in these areas
- Present a diverse group of tech professionals (serving as teaching assistants, tutors and role models) that mirrors the target student population
- Provide guidance and resources via a parent's panel focused on keeping children engaged in STEM education following the workshop

Many of the workshops have occurred, by design, in conjunction with the Grace Hopper Celebration for Women in Computing Conference and the ACM Tapia Celebration of Diversity in Computing. Aligning the workshops with these conferences has offered multiple advantages. African Americans, Latinos and Native Americans combined represent less than 3% of graduates with advanced degrees in Computer Science [35]. Conferences that target these underrepresented populations in computing offer prime opportunities for engaging computing professionals as well as students who converge in one area at the same time. Volunteers from these populations are recruited strategically to represent the various stages of the STEM pipeline ranging from college freshman majoring in Computer Science to senior executives. As a result, our volunteers have a wide range of academic and industry expertise and experience. As stated earlier, the presence of these underrepresented STEM professionals is essential for developing a rapport with the students, and also for presenting culturally-similar role models, to which students may not have daily access.

In addition, s.w.a.g donations from companies that attend and sponsor these conferences help to demonstrate the various career opportunities, potential financial security and demand for professionals in computing fields. Not only do the students delight in the "goodie bags", but they are often surprised to find that they could potentially work for TIME magazine, HBO, the US Government, and various other companies in addition to Microsoft and Google. Companies that donate these items for the workshops are happy to contribute to efforts that support the local community, raise awareness about opportunities at their company with potential future STEM professionals, and decrease extensive costs to ship unused materials back to a home office. In turn, partnerships with potential sponsors are developed for future workshops, which ends up being advantageous for everyone involved.

Another highlight of the program is a showcase of various careers in computing that pertain to students' interests. For example, students that are interested in art enjoy the discussion about Joseph Teran, mathematics professor at UCLA, and how his work contributed to the realistic look of snow in the movie Frozen; for those that love video games, the story of Gerald Lawson, the African American inventor of the video game console, peaks their interest.

The workshops' strengths also manifest through collaboration with community-building partners who use this program as a framework for scaling nationwide. For instance, Strong TIES, a STEAM education organization based in the Phoenix metropolitan area, used this program for impacting over 120 students collectively in recent years through its annual city-wide event titled Turn Up for STEAM. Partnerships with national leaders and innovators in game design, app design, visual design, and music education have been vital for ensuring the program implementation is inclusive and rigorous. The program team also seeks partnerships with local community organizations that pursue shared goals or program offerings, as well as educators from local colleges and universities. They are encouraged to contribute through information sharing and an exchange of ideas during the parent panels. This allows for parents to receive resources for starting their child on the path to STEM education or continuing their own educational journey in STEM.

Students selected to participate in these workshops are residents of the conferences' host cities. On average, each workshops serves thirty (30) students, ranging in age from 10-18, with a 60:40 male to female enrollment ratio (figure 1). Grade makeup is 8th (43.5%), 9th (15.2%), 10th (21.7%), 11th (8.7%) and 12th (10.9%). The student

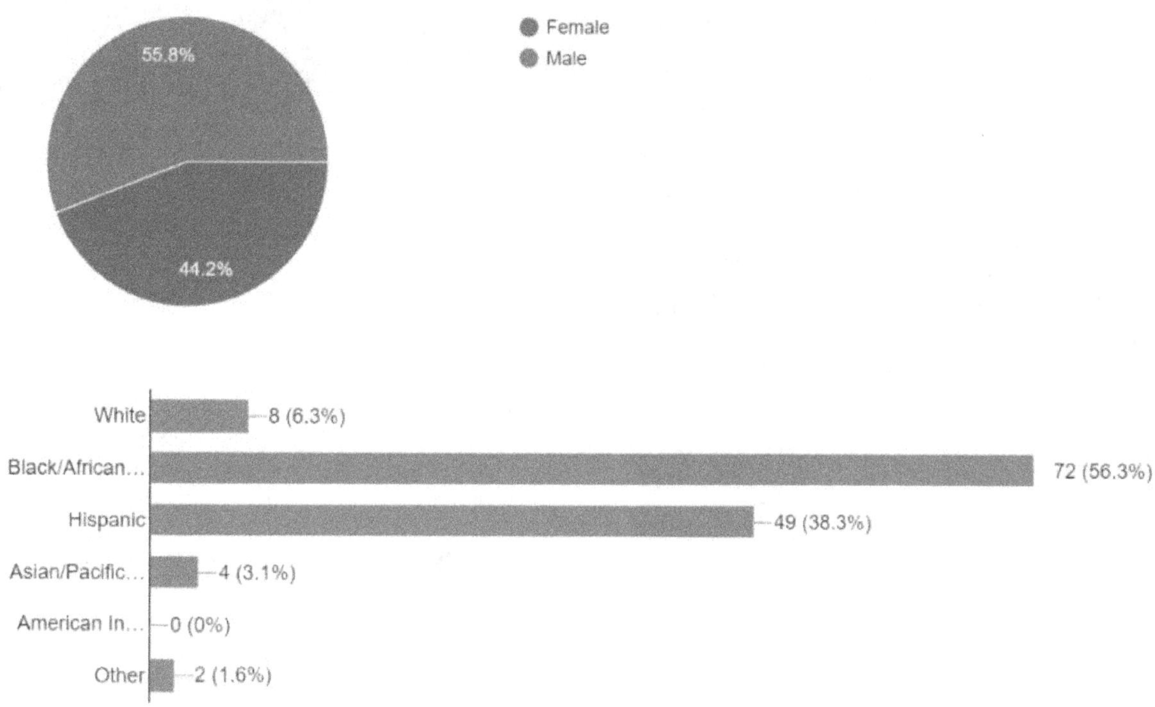

Figure 1: Demographics for workshop students in 2016

to mentor ratio is 4:1 and approximately 50% of the students receive free or discounted lunches. The workshop has undergone six iterations of design and implementation in the following US cities: Portland OR, Phoenix AZ, Houston TX (twice), Austin TX, and Atlanta GA. In each iteration, the planning and development teams focused on 1) creating a safe and supportive environment for youth to engage in a new (and perhaps intimidating) subject matter 2) showcasing various career paths in computing and successful tech professionals whose ethnic and socio-economic background is similar to that of the student audience and 3) incorporating culturally-centered and expressive art forms as a means to break down learning barriers.

4 CONTEXT CASES

Recent implementations of the Pathways to STEM workshop incorporated hip-hop to create a learning bridge between game development and mathematical concepts (e.g. linear algebra, transforms, and geometry). Improvisation and performance exercises were also used to allowed students to practice and improve their presentation skills. The overall goal was to transform students from player to game creator/entrepreneur through activities that emphasized creativity, problem-solving, collaboration and experiential learning.

As students and parents entered the workshop, they were immediately greeted by workshop mentors, teaching assistants and volunteers. After a short welcome presentation, the parents were directed to a parent/guardian information session which is discussed in detail in a later section. The workshop began with an ice breaker activity to wake the students up and allow them to become more comfortable with their surroundings, the volunteers and each other. After the ice breaker, the students were given a presentation about Computer Science and its many applications (including the discussion of various minority professionals and their contributions to the field).

The curriculum was built to employ tools such as Scratch, EarSketch and Beta the Game because they allow students to apply basic programming concepts and quickly see the results of their actions [17, 26, 30]. Volunteers were paired with students to help reinforce a brief lesson on what a program is and how variables, values and decision and flow structures can be used to perform various tasks in a program. Students were walked through simple tasks with the help of their volunteers such as using a variable to change the value of an equation and output the result, getting input from the user and responding, etc.

This development session was followed by lunch during which students got to learn about the volunteers' various computing careers. Students were encouraged to ask questions and talk with the volunteers about their own interests and get advice on how to pursue them. Not only did this time serve as another informal ice breaker for the students, but it allowed the students to learn more about the volunteers and bond over common interests and/or experiences. The lunch session was followed by the music and performance portion of the workshop.

Figure 2: Using music to learn cartesian coordinate system

4.1 Music and Math

Part of the game development tasks focused on the creation of a simple interactive video game such as Paddle Ball (the target game varied depending on the curriculum and tools being used). In order for the students to understand the mechanics of the interaction between the ball and paddle (or any two objects in the Scratch environment) they had to first understand the cartesian plane and how coordinates and angles are represented in the game development environment. The Music Notes team was recruited to help the students accomplish this task.

Music Notes is a group of mathematics educators and the creators of a music education portfolio for engaging students in understanding math principles. However, the presentation of this learning method goes far beyond the traditional approach to singing a song as a means to promote memorization in the classroom. The Music Notes performance is an edutainment experience complete with music, lights, speakers and the energy of a live hip-hop concert. During the performance, Music Notes often engaged students in a call-and-response style of rapping/singing in which the students would echo or respond to the lyrics which served to help illustrate math concepts displayed on a large screen (figure 2). While the students were energized, each song was followed by an interactive, yet anonymous, audience-polling quiz (using Kahoot!, an eLearning platform) and/or additional explanation from the performers to help reinforce the concepts presented [29]. The integration of music, singing and dance paired with anonymous group evaluation transformed the classroom into a safe environment where both students and volunteers were able to actively enjoy learning and embracing their culture through "a collective connection to hip-hop" [11].

Figure 3: Using movement, dance and improv to teach presentation skills

4.2 Improvisation and Performance

A key part of the workshop was a final presentation by the students in which they showcased their game for a panel of fictitious CEOs from gaming companies (represented by the senior-level volunteers) for prizes. This activity encouraged entrepreneurship and taught students that in addition to being creators of technology, they could also potentially build and run their own tech companies. The main learning objective for this task was to practice and demonstrate effective presentation skills with an emphasis on how to best sell their game design concept to the audience. The students were informed that they were not being evaluated on their final product. Instead, the goal was to teach students that the presentation, like most situations in life, is a performance and when performance seems scary or challenging, the best approach is to "fake it until you make it" (i.e. to master the ability to seem confident even though they may feel otherwise). Improvisation techniques and role playing exercises were used to help the students practice this art of performance and learn how to exhibit confident behavior in stressful and frightening situations. For example, in one of the workshops held in Texas, a mentor who was a trained actress and performance artist, lead the students in an activity where they danced throughout the workspace to calm their nerves and mitigate their fears of "looking foolish in front of a crowd" (figure 3). She then taught them how to project their voice to an audience by imagining they were shouting at someone in order to avert a catastrophic event. Volunteers participated alongside the students and shared their own methods for overcoming performance anxiety and self-doubt.

This lack of confidence in underrepresented students can sometimes be the result of feeling over-challenged, misunderstood or even discriminated against in traditional organized educational activities [6, 33]. However, this occurrence is not unique to students; many underrepresented professionals in STEM report feeling added social and psychological pressures related to feelings of inadequacy known as impostor syndrome or impostor phenomenon [28]. These feelings are often reinforced by an environment that is not inclusive or culturally responsive. Many of the volunteers share these experiences and therefore are equipped to provide supportive advice on

Figure 4: Panel session for parents and guardians

how to manage these situations with the students and with each other.

4.3 Fostering Support at Home

Parents play an important part in motivating students to select STEM careers. Providing information on local STEM education opportunities to parents allows them to steer their children toward activities and opportunities that may lead them to a career in STEM. Therefore a parent/guardian panel focused on informing and empowering parents in their efforts to actively support their children's STEM education was added to the workshop (figure 4).

The panel session included STEM professionals who gave practical advice and community partners who provided resources (information on local youth programs, scholarships, internships, career information, etc.) related to STEM. Panelists were recruited from academia, industry and community organizations to answer parents' questions and provide suggestions on ways to keep their child motivated to continue their STEM education after the workshop ended.

In consideration of the low socio-economic status of many of the workshop participants, the authors recognize that many of these potential future first generation professionals may be committed to financially supporting parents, siblings and other family members. Therefore, panelists, mentors, teachers and all volunteers were instructed not to shy away from telling students and parents just how lucrative a career in technology can be. The probability that a career in STEM will result in the advancement of, not only the student, but multiple members of an underserved community by association, warrants close consideration and intentional focus. While appreciation for the intrinsic value of a STEM career is admirable, it is important to consider that a more effective motivation for underrepresented students may be socioeconomic gains for self and family.

5 LEARNING OUTCOMES

In the Pathways to STEM workshops, both informal and online questionnaires were administered to evaluate any changes in students' thoughts and attitudes towards computer science and STEM in general. This data was used to track the level of immediate impact and improve the workshop from city to city. Over the course of four workshops, the following change in responses obtained before and after the workshop were observed:

- 17.5% increase in students that strongly agree that "Scientists make a meaningful difference in the world"
- 8.3% increase in students that strongly agree that "they could be successful at Computer Science"
- 11.5% increase in students that strongly agree that "they would like a career in Science, Technology, Engineering or Math"

In addition to quatitave data, qualitative observations have revealed a noticeable difference in the level of engagement from both students and volunteers that participate. Students often arrived at the workshop reserved and withdrawn, and asked few questions. However, once the activities and interaction with volunteers began, students became more responsive. There were also notable increases in the level of experimentation attempted during the workshop; students were more likely to try new things, make mistakes and learn from them without extensive guidance from the volunteers compared to previous workshops that didn't employ music and performance. In addition, when asked what they liked most about their experience in the workshop, many students rated the concert and programming with the volunteers as the most enjoyable activities. However, the most significant observations came from the parents. Parents were invited to view the students' final presentations and many expressed surprise in seeing their children speak in front of an audience.

Because the workshop is offered in a different US city each year, recruitment from the target populations often presents a challenge. Therefore, it's critial to contact and collaborate with entities that specifically serve minority communities (e.g. churches, youth outreach organizations, school districts, fraternities/sororities, minority civic organizations, academic institutions, etc.) as early as possible. Doing so helps to capitalize on existing relationships between these local establishments and the parents and students in their communities, and it also serves to reinforce the STEM pipeline once the workshop is over. By employing this method, each workshop has successfully recruited a student body that represents a majority of the target underrepresented groups as well as an acceptable gender mix.

Critical to this relationship-building process is the growth of a volunteer network for engaging the community as a whole and ensuring the retention of underrepresented professionals already in STEM. These professionals often don't have time to participate in volunteer activities in their hometown, and one Saturday a year (served in conjunction with attendance at a computing conference) is, for many, a manageable commitment. Following each workshop, volunteers often stated that serving as mentors for the students left them with feelings of pride and fulfillment. Many also reported feeling a sense of community resulting from sharing their story and engaging with other professionals who experience similar challenges related to being underrepresented in a science field.

6 CONCLUSION

Throughout the development of these workshops, the ACM Richard Tapia Celebration for Diversity in Computing and the Grace Hopper Celebration for Women in Computing conferences have been an ideal venue for conversations centered on discovering unique methods of engaging minority youth and supporting existing underrepresented professionals through culturally-centered learning activities in STEM education. With the launch of programs like CSforAll and efforts to standardize a computer science curriculum in K-12 schools, it is important that students of color are engaged to the same extent as their classmates whenever possible. However, attempting to incorporate music, improvisation and other methods from an ethnocentric view of the instructor can be counterproductive. When introducing new, challenging and often intimidating subject matter to underrepresented students in the classroom, it is important that instructors capitalize on the benefits of incorporating culturally-relevant mediums in their teaching methodology. This approach to introducing and teaching CS concepts will create a supportive learning environment and hopefully will empower underrepresented students to positively view computer science as something they can learn and perhaps master. Regardless of their chosen career path, this confidence is vital for underrepresented students to be able to thrive in a constantly advancing digital world.

ACKNOWLEDGMENTS

The authors would like to thank all corporate and community sponsors whose contributions make the Pathways to STEM efforts possible. The BWiC workshops have been supported in part by GoDaddy, Prairie View A&M University, Microsoft, the Arizona Community Foundation and many others. The past two workshops have been supported by grants from the Motorola Solutions Foundation, with assistance from the Center for Minorities and People with Disabilities in IT (CMD-IT).

The authors would also like to thank members of Black Women in Computing and our community partners including Hidden Level Games, Music Notes, Strong TIES, the Anita Borg Institute and numerous volunteers for their generous donations, support and committment to the education of our youth.

REFERENCES

[1] Karl L. Alexander, Doris R. Entwisle, and Linda Steffel Olson. 2007. Lasting Consequences of the Summer Learning Gap. *American Sociological Review* 72, 2 (2007), 167–180. https://doi.org/10.1177/000312240707200202 arXiv:https://doi.org/10.1177/000312240707200202

[2] Afterschool Alliance. 2015. *Full STEM Ahead: Afterschool Programs Step Up as Key Partners in STEM Education.* Technical Report.

[3] H Anderton. 2012. STEM, Teens, and Public Libraries: It's Easier Than You Think! *Young Adult Library Services* 10, 2 (2012).

[4] Linda Braun. 2011. The Lowdown on STEM: A formula for luring teens toward science and math. *American Libraries* (2011). https://americanlibrariesmagazine.org/2011/09/20/the-lowdown-on-stem/

[5] Marilynn B. Brewer and Wendi Gardner. 1996. Who Is This "We"? Levels of Collective Identity and Self Representations. *Journal of Personality and Social Psychology* 71, 1 (7 1996), 83–93.

[6] Ronald J Burke and Mary C Mattis. 2007. *Women and minorities in science, technology, engineering, and mathematics: Upping the numbers.* Edward Elgar Publishing.

[7] Ron Butzlaff. 2000. Can Music Be Used to Teach Reading? *Journal of Aesthetic Education* 34, 3/4 (2000), 167–178. http://www.jstor.org/stable/3333642

[8] Clark D. Campbell. 2008. *Best Practices for StudentâĂŞFaculty Mentoring Programs.* Blackwell Publishing Ltd. 325–343 pages. https://doi.org/10.1111/b.9781405133739.2007.00020.x

[9] National Research Council. 2015. *Identifying and Supporting Productive STEM Programs in Out-of-School Settings.* The National Academies Press, Washington, DC. https://doi.org/10.17226/21740

[10] Douglas B. Downey, Paul T. von Hippel, and Beckett A. Broh. 2004. Are schools the great equalizer? Cognitive inequality during the summer months and the school year. *American Sociological Review* 69, 5 (10 2004), 613–635.

[11] Christopher Emdin. 2010. *Urban Science Education for the Hip-hop Generation: Cultural perspectives in science education.* Sense Publishers.

[12] Samuel A Floyd. 1995. *The power of Black music: interpreting its history from Africa to the United States.* Oxford University Press.

[13] STEM Education Coalition Policy Forum. 2016. *The Case for Investing in Out-of-School Learning as a Core Strategy in Improving Science, Technology, Engineering, and Mathematics (STEM) Education.* Technical Report. Washington, D.C.

[14] Gena R. Greher. 2011. Music Technology Partnerships: A Context for Music Teacher Preparation. *Arts Education Policy Review* 112, 3 (2011), 130–136. https://www.learntechlib.org/p/109192

[15] Philip J. Guo, Juho Kim, and Rob Rubin. 2014. How Video Production Affects Student Engagement: An Empirical Study of MOOC Videos. In *Proceedings of the First ACM Conference on Learning @ Scale Conference (L@S '14).* ACM, New York, NY, USA, 41–50. https://doi.org/10.1145/2556325.2566239

[16] Khe Hew. 2015. Promoting engagement in online courses: What strategies can we learn from three highly rated MOOCS: Engagement: lessons from MOOCs. 47 (01 2015).

[17] Hidden Level Games. [n. d.]. Beta the Game. ([n. d.]). http://betathegame.com/

[18] Laura Griner Hill and Nicole E. Werner. 2006. Affiliative motivation, school attachment, and aggression in school. *Psychology in the Schools* 43, 2 (2006), 231–246. https://doi.org/10.1002/pits.20140

[19] Schellenberg E.G. Hunter P.G. 2010. Music and Emotion. In *Music Perception*, Mari Riess Jones, Richard R. Fay, and Arthur N. Popper (Eds.). Springer-Verlag New York, New York, Chapter 4, 129–164.

[20] ilms.gov. 2014. *Talking Points: Museums, Libraries and Makerspaces.* Technical Report. Washington, D.C.

[21] Irene V Jackson. 1985. *More Than Dancing: Essays on Afro-American Music and Musicians.* Greenwood Press.

[22] Patrik N. Juslin, Simon LiljeströÄűm, Petri Laukka, Daniel VÄďstfjÄďll, and Lars-Olov Lundqvist. 2011. Emotional reactions to music in a nationally representative sample of Swedish adults. *Musicae Scientiae* 15, 2 (2011), 174–207. https://doi.org/10.1177/1029864911401169 arXiv:https://doi.org/10.1177/1029864911401169

[23] Suvi Laiho. 2004. The Psychological Functions of Music in Adolescence. *Nordic Journal of Music Therapy* 13, 1 (2004), 47–63. https://doi.org/10.1080/08098130409478097 arXiv:http://dx.doi.org/10.1080/08098130409478097

[24] Shui-fong Lam, Bernard P. H. Wong, Hongfei Yang, and Yi Liu. 2012. Understanding Student Engagement with a Contextual Model. In *Handbook of Research on Student Engagement.* 403–419.

[25] S.J. Maddox and R.J. Prinz. 2003. School Bonding in Children and Adolescents: Conceptualization, Assessment, and Associated Variables. *Clinical Child and Family Psychology Review* 6, 1 (2003), 31–49. https://doi.org/10.1023/A:1022214022478

[26] Brian Magerko, Jason Freeman, Tom Mcklin, Mike Reilly, Elise Livingston, Scott Mccoid, and Andrea Crews-Brown. 2016. EarSketch: A STEAM-Based Approach for Underrepresented Populations in High School Computer Science Education. *Trans. Comput. Educ.* 16, 4, Article 14 (Sept. 2016), 25 pages. https://doi.org/10.1145/2886418

[27] Richard H Milner. 2010. *Start Where You Are, but Don't Stay There: Understanding Diversity, Opportunity Gaps, and Teaching in Today's Classrooms.* Harvard Education Press, Cambridge, MA.

[28] Bridgette J. Peteet, LaTrice Montgomery, and Jerren C. Weekes. 2015. Predictors of Imposter Phenomenon among Talented Ethnic Minority Undergraduate Students. *The Journal of Negro Education* 84, 2 (2015), 11.

[29] Carolyn M. Plump and Julia LaRosa. 2017. Using Kahoot! in the Classroom to Create Engagement and Active Learning: A Game-Based Technology Solution for eLearning Novices. *Management Teaching Review* 2, 2 (2017), 151–158. https://doi.org/10.1177/2379298116689783 arXiv:https://doi.org/10.1177/2379298116689783

[30] Mitchel Resnick, John Maloney, Andrés Monroy-Hernández, Natalie Rusk, Evelyn Eastmond, Karen Brennan, Amon Millner, Eric Rosenbaum, Jay Silver, Brian Silverman, and Yasmin Kafai. 2009. Scratch: Programming for All. *Commun. ACM* 52, 11 (Nov. 2009), 60–67. https://doi.org/10.1145/1592761.1592779

[31] Belle Rose Ragins Roosevelt Eleanor, Day O'Connor Justice Sandra and Kathy E. Kram. 2008. The Roots and Meaning of Mentoring. In *The Handbook of Mentoring at Work: Theory, Research, and Practice*, Belle Rose Ragins and Kathy E. Kram (Eds.). SAGE Publications, Inc., Thousand Oaks, California, Chapter 1.

[32] Kimberly A. Scott, Kevin Clark, Elisabeth Hayes, Cynthia Mruczek, and Kimberly Sheridan. 2010. Culturally Relevant Computing Programs: Two examples to Inform Teacher Professional Development. In *Proceedings of Society for Information Technology & Teacher Education International Conference 2010*, David Gibson and Bernie Dodge (Eds.). Association for the Advancement of Computing in Education (AACE), San Diego, CA, USA, 1269–1277. https://www.learntechlib.org/p/33532

[33] Sandra D. Simpkins, Nathaniel R. Riggs, Bic Ngo, Andrea Vest Ettekal, and Dina Okamoto. 2016. Designing Culturally Responsive Organized After-School Activities. *Journal of Adolescent Research* 32, 1 (2016), 25.

[34] Christopher Small. 1987. *Music of the Common Tongue: Survival and Celebration in African American Music.* J. Calder, Indiana University.

[35] Stuart Zweben and Betsy Bizot. 2016. 2016 Taulbee Survey. *Computing Research News* 29, 5 (May 2016).

Looking Beyond Representation: How Women Develop Their Leadership Perceptions During the Introductory Computing Course

Jennifer M. Blaney
University of California, Los Angeles
Moore Hall, 457 Portola Plaza
Los Angeles, CA 90095
jmblaney@ucla.edu

ABSTRACT

While the gender gap in undergraduate computing is often discussed in reference to the representation of women in the computing major, less is known about leadership and other affective outcomes for women and men in computing. This study examines how gender shapes (a) introductory computing students' perceptions of their leadership, including measures of both general self-rated leadership ability and perceived capacity for leadership in computing, (b) how these perceptions change during the introductory computing course, and (c) the experiences that are related to change in leadership outcomes. Findings reveal gender differences in how incoming introductory course students report both their general leadership abilities and their perceived capacity for leadership in computing. Additionally, both women and men experience a decline in their perceived capacity for leadership in computing during the introductory course. These and other findings are discussed, with attention given to the implications for both researchers and instructors seeking to broaden women's participation in computing.

ACM Reference Format

Jennifer M. Blaney. 2018. Looking Beyond Representation: How Women Develop Their Leadership Perceptions During the Introductory Computing Course. In *SIGCSE '18: 49th ACM Technical Symposium on Computing Science Education, Feb. 21–24, 2018, Baltimore, MD, USA.* ACM, NY, NY, USA, 6 pages. https://doi.org/10.1145/3159450.3159458

1 INTRODUCTION

Despite women's advancements in higher education, women remain sorely underrepresented in computing majors [7], tech careers [7, 9], and leadership roles in the field of computing and technology [1]. In light of these stark gender inequities, women's representation in computing has become a national focus of research. However, much of this work focuses on undergraduate women's recruitment, retention, and graduation rates, and little attention has been given to aspects of women's affective development in computing majors. It is important to address this gap in the literature so that researchers and practitioners can better understand women's experiences in computing, particularly those that may shape their career trajectories in the field.

This study considers one aspect of undergraduate women's development in computing: their perceptions of leadership. Over the last few decades, there has been a wealth of research surrounding undergraduate leadership across disciplines [3], some of which considers undergraduate women's leadership [5, 7, 10]. This research has revealed that undergraduate men tend to more favorably rate their leadership abilities compared to their female counterparts [8]. Prior research also suggests that gender inequities in leadership are particularly prevalent in male-dominated fields [3].

In the field of computing and technology, women's underrepresentation in leadership has gained national attention [1]. However, little is known about how women's leadership develops during undergraduate computing. This study seeks to fill this gap in the literature by focusing on gender and leadership perceptions among introductory computing students. Specifically, this study examines gender differences in how women and men report their leadership at the beginning of the introductory course, how those perceptions of leadership change during the course, and the experiences that predict those changes in leadership perceptions.

2 Methods

2.1 Research Questions

The following three questions frame this inquiry:

1. How do incoming introductory computing students report their leadership, both in general and in computing, and how do those leadership perceptions vary by gender?

SIGCSE '18, February 21–24, 2018, Baltimore, MD, USA

ACM ISBN 978-1-4503-5103-4/18/02...$15.00
https://doi.org/10.1145/3159450.3159458

2. How do perceptions of leadership change during the introductory course? How might this vary by gender?
3. What factors predict change in leadership perceptions? How does this vary by gender?

2.2 Sample

This study utilized a longitudinal sample of students who were surveyed at the beginning and end of their introductory computing course. Specifically, a pre-test survey was administered to students enrolled in introductory courses at 15 participating institutions across the United States during the 2015-2016 academic year. The pre-test was administered during the first two weeks of the course and received 3,945 responses (a response rate of 33%). Of the students who took the pre-test survey, 34% also responded to a post-test that was administered during the last week of their introductory course, yielding a matched sample of 1,355 responses. Women represented approximately 42% of the sample, and a quarter of respondents were students from underrepresented minority groups.

2.3 Measures

Leadership perceptions. This study focuses on two primary outcomes of interest: general self-rated leadership and self-rated leadership capacity in computing. To measure perceptions of general leadership ability, students were asked to rate their leadership ability on a five-point scale compared to the average person their age (*1=Lowest 10%; 2=Below Average; 3=Average; 4=Above Average; 5=Highest 10%).* To capture self-rated leadership confidence in computing, students were asked to indicate their agreement with the following statement on a five-point scale (*1=Strongly Disagree; 2=Disagree; 3=Neither Agree Nor Disagree; 4=Agree; 5=Strongly Agree*): *I am confident that I can become a leader in the field of computing.* Both survey items were included on the post-test survey and were also directly pre-tested (i.e., the items also appeared on the pre-test survey).

Major. Because this study examined students enrolled in introductory computing courses, the sample included a mix of computing and non-computing majors. Importantly, men in the introductory course were more frequently computing majors. For this reason, the regression included a control measure for whether or not the student was a computing major when they entered the course. Computing was broadly conceptualized, and students were counted as a computing major if they selected at least one of the following: Computer Science; Computer Information Systems or Informatics; Bioinformatics; Computing and Business; Information Technology; Computer Engineering; Other Computing. Major was then coded dichotomously (*0=non-computing major; 1=computing major*).

Gender and underrepresented minority (URM) status. Students were also asked to indicate their gender by selecting one of the following: woman; man; non-binary or something else. Due to small numbers of non-binary students, I used a dichotomous measure of gender (0=man; 1=woman). Students also indicated their race/ethnicity, and their responses were aggregated into the following categories: URM (including Black; Latinx; Native American; Native Hawaiian or Pacific Islander; Arab, Middle Eastern, or Persian) and majority (including White and Asian). Students who selected more than one race/ethnicity were counted as URM if they selected at least one URM group. Both gender and URM status were measured on the pre-test survey.

Independent Variables. Komives et al.'s model of Leadership Identity Development [LID] [6] was used to frame the independent variables included in the regression analysis. Specifically, the LID model identifies adult interactions (in the case of this study, family support and mentorship), peer interactions, and involvement as three important factors shaping leadership development [6]. All of these variables were measured on the post-test survey. Descriptives for these variables are shown below in Table 1.

Family support. Family support was measured using a composite measure that included the following four items: *My family encourages me to pursue a computing degree*; *My family questions why I would pursue a computing degree* (reverse-coded); *My family wonders why I invest so much time and effort into studying computing* (reverse-coded); *My family emphasizes the value of earning a computing degree.* Participants responded on a five-point scale ranging from *strongly disagree (1)* to *strongly agree (5)*. These items were added together to create a measure that ranged from 1 (low family support) to 20 (high family support).

Mentorship. Mentorship was measured using a composite variable ranging from 1 (low mentorship) to 20 (high mentorship). This measure was made up of items asking students to report how frequently their mentor(s) do any of the following: *Helps you improve your computing skills*; *Shows compassion for any concerns and feelings you discussed with them*; *Shares personal experiences as an alternative perspective to your problems*; *Explores career options with you.* For each item, students responded on a five-point scale: *1=Not at all; 2=A little; 3= Somewhat; 4= Quite a bit; 5=Very much.*

Peer support. Peer support was also measured using a composite variable and included four items asking students the extent to which the following types of support are available from other computing students: *Someone to hang out with; Someone to confide in or talk about your problems*; *Someone to get class assignments for you if you were sick*; *Someone to help you understand difficult homework problems.* These items were measured using the same five-point scale as the family mentorship items (*1=Not at all*; *5=Very much)* and also had a range of 1 (low peer support) to 20 (high peer support).

Involvement. This study focused on one aspect of involvement: participating in computing-related student groups. This was measured using a single item where students were asked to indicate the number of hours they spend each week in student groups by selecting one of the following: *1=None; 2=Less than 1 hour; 3=1-2 hours; 4=3-5 hours; 5=6-10 hours; 6=11-15 hours; 7=16-20 hours; 8=Over 20 hours.*

Table 1. Descriptive Statistics for Independent Variables

	N	Mean	SD
Family support	1146	11.702	3.086
Mentorship	1242	11.117	5.026
Peer support	1251	12.379	4.596
Hours per week (HPW) in computing student groups	1244	2.350	1.598

2.4 Data Analysis and Hypotheses

The first two research questions required descriptive analyses (i.e., frequency distributions and t-tests) to examine leadership ratings among introductory students. Based on prior literature, I hypothesized that men would report their leadership abilities more favorably than women. I also hypothesized that leadership ratings would remain relatively stable during the introductory course. To examine the final research question, which asked about the predictors of leadership perceptions at the end of the term, I used multiple regression analysis. All independent variables included in the table above were standardized prior to the regression analyses. Based on Komives et al.'s LID model [6] as well as other prior literature, I hypothesized that family support, mentorship, peer support, and involvement in student groups would be positive predictors of leadership perceptions at the end of the course.

3 FINDINGS

3.1 Research Question One

Research question one asked about introductory students' incoming perceptions of leadership, focusing on how those perceptions vary by gender. To explore research question one, I first examined frequency distributions for the incoming leadership variables. I found that when students were asked about their general incoming leadership ability, 10% of intro students reported that they were either "below average" or in the "lowest 10%", nearly one-third (31%) indicated that they were "average", and the remaining 59% indicated that they were either "above average" or in the "highest 10%". However, when students were asked if they believed that they had the ability to become a leader in the field of computing, their reports were less positive. A third disagreed or strongly disagreed, 29% neither agreed nor disagreed, and 37% either agreed or agreed strongly that they could become a leader in the field of computing. Put more simply, while the majority of students believed that their leadership abilities were at least above average, only 37% believed that they had the capacity to become a leader in the field of computing. Thus, students who report high leadership abilities may still have low confidence in their leadership efficacy in computing.

The second half of research question one asked about gender differences in students' incoming leadership perceptions. To examine this, I ran t-tests to determine mean differences by gender on the two measures of incoming leadership. T-tests revealed that women's general self-rated leadership (M=3.53; SD=0.907) was significantly lower than men's (M=3.74; SD=0.955), $t(1271)=3.935$, p=.000. The same pattern held true for self-reported leadership capacity in computing. That is, men's average perceived leadership capacity (M=3.26; SD=1.207) was significantly higher than the mean for women (M=2.74; SD=1.299), $t(1205)=7.184$, p=.000.

3.2 Research Question Two

Research question two asked about how leadership perceptions change during the introductory computing course. To examine this, I first used two separate paired-sample t-tests to compare pre- and post-test scores on both leadership variables. The paired t-tests revealed that general self-rated leadership did not change during the introductory computing course. However, students' perceptions of their capacity to become a leader in computing declined during the introductory course. Means, standard deviations, and results of the paired-sample t-tests are summarized in Table 2.

Additional analyses were used to examine whether *changes* in leadership perceptions might vary by gender, revealing no significant gender differences. In other words, while women and men enter the introductory course with differences in how they report their leadership perceptions, they experience similar rates of change during the course.

Table 2. Mean Leadership Perceptions Over the Course of Introductory Computing

	Measure				
	Pre-test (SD)	Post-test (SD)	t	Sig.	df
General Leadership	3.649 (0.948)	3.642 (0.914)	-0.146		1244
Computing Leadership	3.023 (1.279)	2.891 (1.228)	4.205	***	1183

Note. *p<.05; **p< .01; ***p<.001. Standard deviations are shown in parentheses. df=degrees of freedom.

3.3 Research Question Three

The third and final research question asked about the experiences that predict leadership perceptions at the end of the introductory course. Given that general leadership perceptions did not significantly change during the introductory course, I focused these analyses on the predictors of self-reported capacity for leadership in computing. To examine this question, I used linear regression, controlling for the pre-test of computing leadership capacity at the beginning of the course, major, gender, and URM status. Komives et al.'s [6] leadership identity development (LID) model was used to frame the additional independent variables included in the regression.

The regression model is shown in Table 3. Unsurprisingly, the strongest predictor of perceived leadership capacity in computing at the end of the term was the pre-test measure of perceived leadership capacity at the beginning of the term. Also as one might expect, students who entered the course with a computing major reported greater capacity for leadership in computing. Controlling for all other variables, being a woman was a negative predictor of the outcome, while URM status was not significant in the final model.

After controlling for the pre-test of computing leadership, major, gender, and URM status, all of the independent variables of interest were positive predictors of the outcome. More specifically, family support, followed by mentorship, hours per week spent in computing-related student groups, and peer support each positively predicted perceptions of leadership capacity in computing at the end of the course.

The final model explained 47% of the variance in the outcome (R^2=0.47), though it is important to note that 39% of the variance was explained by the pre-test alone. However, the additional variables did significantly contribute to the model. In other words, while the majority of the explained variance in the dependent variable was due to incoming differences in perceived leadership capacity in computing, this study identifies several variables that predict the outcome, above and beyond the impact of the pre-test measure.

Table 3. Regression Predicting Perceived Leadership in Computing

	Beta	b	Std. Error	Sig.
Leadership pre-test	0.477	0.576	0.034	***
Major	0.104	0.249	0.064	***
Gender (W)	-0.103	-0.249	0.060	***
URM	0.029	0.081	0.068	
Family support	0.141	0.174	0.032	***
Mentorship	0.072	0.087	0.031	**
Peer support	0.062	0.075	0.031	*
HPW in computing student groups	0.064	0.078	0.031	*

Note. **p*<.05; ** *p*<.01; ****p*<.001. This table shows only the main effects of the regression model (i.e., coefficients before interaction terms entered the model).

Finally, I also wanted to examine whether the predictors of self-rated leadership in computing might vary by gender (i.e., interaction effects). To examine this, I computed four interaction terms by multiplying gender by each of the following variables: family support, mentorship, peer support, and hours per week in computing-related student groups. Next, the four interaction terms were entered into the model one at a time to test for conditional effects. These analyses revealed one significant interaction effect: *gender and peer support*, *Beta*=0.073, *t*(957)=2.281, *p*<.05. A further investigation of this interaction effect revealed that, while the main effect of peer support was significant (see Table 3), peer support was actually only a significant predictor for women. That is, feeling more supported by peers was a significant and positive predictor of the outcome for women, but was a non-significant positive predictor for men. In other words, men's perceptions of their capacity to become a leader in computing were not dependent on the extent to which they felt supported by their peers. At the same time, women's perceptions of their leadership in computing were, in part, a product of how supported they felt by their computing classmates. This relationship is shown below in Figure 1.

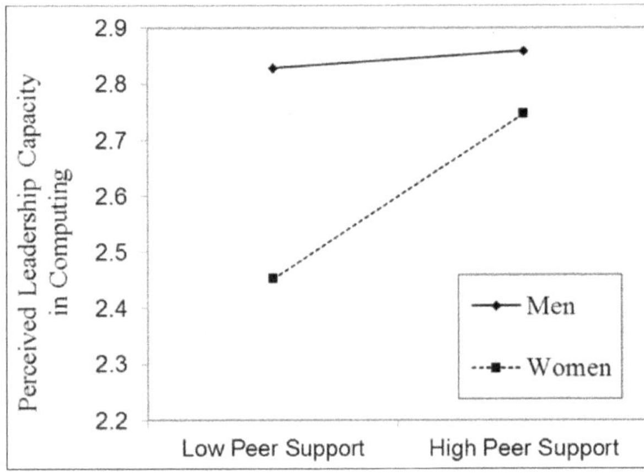

Figure 1. Conditional Peer Support

4 LIMITATIONS

It is important to consider some key limitations when interpreting findings from this study. Because of the nature of this study, we cannot infer causation between the independent variables and the outcome. For example, it could be the case that students with higher ratings of their leadership capacity also report more positive interactions with their peers (rather than peer support leading to enhanced leadership perceptions). To mitigate this limitation as much as possible, I controlled for the pre-test of perceived leadership capacity in computing in the regression analysis.

This study also relied on self-reports of leadership perceptions, which makes it impossible to discern whether gender differences in how students perceive leadership are actually present. It may be the case that gender differences are due to differences in how women and men *report* their perceptions on surveys. More qualitative inquiry is needed in order to determine how women and men are conceptualizing their leadership abilities.

5 DISCUSSION

This study contributes to existing literature in several key ways. Consistent with prior research, findings from this study reveal gender differences in how undergraduates perceive their leadership abilities. This study also adds to the literature by examining leadership perceptions specifically in the context of computing, revealing that the gender gap was present among computing students, regardless of whether or not they were responding about their general leadership or their leadership in computing. Further, this study provides insight into how students report their leadership when primed to think about a male-dominated field (in this case, computing). More research is needed to better understand how findings from this study might be applicable to other contexts both in and out of computing.

This study also contributes to our understanding of student development in introductory computing. While I hypothesized that there would be minimal change in leadership perceptions during the introductory course, this was only partially the case. As expected, perceived leadership abilities remained largely the same during the course. However, perceptions of leadership capacity in computing declined. That is, students left the introductory course feeling less confident about their capacity for computing leadership, relative to their perceptions when they started the course. While both women and men experienced similar declines, it is important to be particularly mindful of this for women, given that women enter the course with lower reported perceptions of their capacity for computing leadership.

In addition to revealing inequities in perceived leadership among computing students, this study also reveals several factors that predict leadership outcomes at the end of the introductory course. These findings point to several action items that may be employed in computing classrooms, which will be discussed in the implications section below. As I hypothesized, family support, mentorship, peer support, and time spent in student groups were all positively associated with perceived leadership capacity in computing.

Further, findings revealed a conditional effect, such that the relationship between having supportive classmates and perceiving that one has the capacity to become a leader in computing was stronger for women than it was for men. Another way of interpreting this interaction effect is that, controlling for all other variables, the gender gap in perceived leadership capacity in computing was smaller when students felt that they were supported by their classmates. This underscores previous literature on the importance of peer interactions.

Interestingly, even after controlling for the pre-test and all other variables in the regression analysis, being a woman was still a negative predictor of perceived leadership capacity in computing. In other words, controlling for the gender gap in incoming leadership perceptions and holding other variables in the model constant, women still have more negative perceptions of their leadership capacity in computing; this suggests that some important aspects of the environment may not be captured in this study. Future research should examine other college experiences that might contribute to this gender inequity.

6 IMPLICATIONS

6.1 Implications for Research and Theory

This study reveals gender inequities in how undergraduate computing students perceive their leadership abilities and capacity, highlighting the importance of considering leadership development and other affective outcomes among undergraduates in computing. Future research should examine the extent to which the predictors of leadership and other affective outcomes differ from the predictors of more traditionally studied behavioral outcomes (e.g., retention and graduation in computing). Further, while this study sheds light on the factors that predict leadership perceptions among computing students, more research is needed to better understand *how* undergraduate women in computing develop their perceptions of leadership.

These findings contribute to what is known about college student leadership development. Specifically, this study confirms parts of the Leadership Identity Development model by highlighting the important role of family, mentorship, peers, and student involvement (time spent in computing student groups), showing the model's applicability to computing students. Further, given the important role of peer support for women's leadership perceptions (i.e., the interaction effect), this study suggests that some factors may take on heightened importance in different contexts, particularly in settings where individuals are marginalized (e.g., women in computing). Future research should explore this more closely.

6.2 Implications for Practice

Findings from this study point to several implications for practitioners seeking to reduce gender inequities in their computing classrooms.

Demystifying leadership and tech careers. For many students, the introductory computing course may be their first significant exposure to computer science. Thus, it is telling that students leave the intro computing course, on average, with lower perceptions of their leadership capacity in the field, despite the fact that their perceptions of their general leadership abilities remain relatively stable. One reason for this decline in perceived computing leadership might be that as students learn more about the field during their first computing course, they may be intimidated or unable to visualize themselves in a computing career, let alone a leadership position. To mitigate this, introductory course instructors can share information about tech careers, examples of their own experiences navigating the field, and encouragement to students as they consider different career options in computing. Such interventions may go a long way in developing introductory computing students' efficacy for computing leadership. At a minimum, these interventions might help students to maintain the leadership efficacy that they bring with them to the introductory course.

Teaching collaboration and support. The findings reviewed above reveal that women who feel more supported by their peers in computing tend to have more positive perceptions of their leadership capacity in the field. This suggests that instructors should work to teach students to be supportive and helpful to their peers by sharing notes, providing homework help, and offering other types of support and encouragement. One way to create this type of collaboration in class might be to assign homework groups or partners so that students have designated people who they can reach out to if they need extra help. However, interactions with peers must be supportive in order for them to be beneficial. As such, efforts to increase peer interactions must also be accompanied by activities that teach students how to be supportive of their classmates. Given that the gender gap was smaller when students reported high peer support (see Figure 1), fostering supportive classroom environments may be one way that instructors can reduce the gender gap in leadership perceptions.

Engaging families. After incoming leadership perceptions, family support was the strongest predictor of perceived leadership capacity in computing. Thus, helping students to feel supported by their families may be key to developing their leadership efficacy. Perhaps one way to do this is to provide opportunities for families to attend events that showcase students' work and demonstrate the important contributions of computing. Such events might go a long way in challenging stereotypical beliefs about computing and helping families to see the importance of computer science. Instructors may also provide students with tips for communicating the value of computing to family members who may or may not be familiar with the field.

7 SUMMARY AND CONCLUSION

Women and men enter introductory computing with differences in how they report their leadership. Compared to their male counterparts, women report slightly lower confidence in their general leadership abilities and perceived capacity for computing leadership. However, it is important to note that self-reported leadership ability should not be used as a proxy for actual abilities. In fact, there is a wealth of literature that firmly concludes that women and men equitably exemplify effective leadership skills [4]. At the same time, inequities in how individuals *perceive* their leadership abilities should be considered, as these perceptions may shape motivation to lead and aspirations for leadership [2], thus contributing to gender inequities in society. Future research should further examine this topic at the K-12 level to better understand the social structures that contribute to gender inequities among incoming college students.

Further, this study revealed that both women and men experience declines in how they perceive their capacity for leadership in computing. These declines may be particularly detrimental for women, given the gender gap in incoming leadership perceptions. Fortunately, findings from this study also point to several factors that are associated with enhanced perceptions of leadership in computing at the end of the course. In light of those findings, this paper highlights implications for practice, including suggestions for demystifying leadership in the field, teaching students to collaborate and support each other, and connecting with students' families to help students build a support system for their computing aspirations. These suggestions may enhance leadership perceptions for all students, regardless of gender. However, some practices, particularly those related to peer support, may be especially important for women in computing. Thus, fostering supportive peer environments within computing classrooms may be a way to reduce the gender gap in how undergraduates perceive their leadership.

Together, these findings shed light on gender inequities in undergraduate computing students' perceptions of leadership, as well as experiences that may lead to enhanced leadership perceptions for women. It is important to understand these gender inequities because, in order to address the larger gender gap in undergraduate computing, we must also consider leadership and other affective components of student development. Women will only reach parity in undergraduate computing programs when they are not only equitably represented, but also have access to equitable opportunities to develop themselves, including their perceptions of leadership. This paper highlights the important role that educators can play in reducing the gender gap in computing by considering leadership development.

ACKNOWLEDGMENTS

This study utilizes data from the larger Building, Recruiting, and Inclusion for Diversity (BRAID) Research Study and is funded by the National Science Foundation (#152573), AnitaB.org, the Computing Research Association, Facebook, Google, Microsoft, and Intel.

REFERENCES

[1] Anita Borg Institute [ABI]. 2016. Top companies for women technologists: Measure what matters. Accessed via: http://anitaborg.org/awards-grants/top-companies-for-women-technologists/2016-top-companies/
[2] K. Y. Chan, and F. Drasgow. 2001. Toward a theory of individual differences and leadership: Understanding the motivation to lead. Journal of Applied Psychology, 86(3), 481.
[3] A. H. Eagly, and L. L. Carli. 2007. Through the labyrinth: The truth about how women become leaders. Harvard Business Press. Chicago, IL.
[4] A. H. Eagly, S. Karau, and M. Makhijani. 1995. Gender and the effectiveness of leaders: A meta-analysis. Psychological Bulletin, 117, 125–145.
[5] A. Kezar, and D. Moriarty. 2000. Expanding our understanding of student leadership development: A study exploring gender and ethnic identity. Journal of College Student Development, 41(1), 55–69.
[6] S. Komives, S. Longerbeam, J. Owen, F. Mainella, and L. Osteen. 2006. A leadership identity development model: Applications from a grounded theory. Journal of College Student Development, 47(4).
[7] National Center for Education Statistics. (2016). Bachelor's degrees conferred by degree-granting institutions, by gender and field of study.
[8] L. Sax. 2008. The gender gap in college: Maximizing the developmental potential of women and men. San Francisco, CA: Jossey-Bass.
[9] J. Teague. 2002. Women in computing: What brings them to it, what keeps them in it? SIGCSE Bulletin, 34(2), 147–158.
[10] E. Whitt. 1993. I can be anything! Student leadership in three women's colleges. Journal of College Student Development, 35, 198–207.

A Model for Increasing Gender Diversity in Technology

Penny Rheingans
UMBC
Baltimore, MD
rheingan@cs.umbc.edu

Erica D'Eramo
UMBC
Baltimore, MD
deramo@umbc.edu

Crystal Diaz-Espinoza
Baylor University
Waco, TX
Crystal_Diaz-Espinoza@baylor.edu

Danyelle Ireland
UMBC
Baltimore, MD
direland@umbc.edu

ABSTRACT

At our university, women are a minority in all computing and engineering majors. This situation is mirrored at other universities nationwide, as well as in technical industries. Stereotype threat, the risk of confirming a negative stereotype about one's social group, can result in women not performing as well as their male counterparts in computing, mathematics, and engineering courses. The aftermath of these experiences cause women to fear they do not belong or are not "smart enough", resulting in women switching to a different major. Even high-performing women can be subject to these pressures. We present a Scholar model for increasing gender diversity in technology fields and an evaluation of its impact on the retention and success of women in computing and engineering majors. We compare the performance of Scholars to that of non-Scholars with similar demographic and academic backgrounds who entered into the College of Engineering and Information Technology at the University of Maryland, Baltimore County.

CCS CONCEPTS

• **Social and professional topics → Model curricula**; **Gender**; *Race and ethnicity*;

KEYWORDS

Diversity, Gender, Community, Scholar Programs

ACM Reference Format:
Penny Rheingans, Erica D'Eramo, Crystal Diaz-Espinoza, and Danyelle Ireland . 2018. A Model for Increasing Gender Diversity in Technology . In *Proceedings of ACM SIGCSE conference, Baltimore, MD USA, March 2018 (SIGCSE '18)*, 6 pages.
https://doi.org/10.1145/3159450.3159533

SIGCSE '18, March 2018, Baltimore, MD USA

ACM ISBN 978-1-4503-5103-4/18/02...$15.00
https://doi.org/10.1145/3159450.3159533

1 INTRODUCTION

Engineering and computing are important fields at the forefront of solving the world's problems and maintaining American competitiveness. Employment opportunities in these fields remain strong, with the Bureau of Labor Statistics predicting that demand in these fields will outstrip supply in the coming years [3]. Drawing broadly from the available talent base of students with strong math and science backgrounds is essential to meeting this growing demand. Additionally, a diverse talent pool will help ensure better quality solutions to complex problems, as technologists with different life experiences bring those experiences to bear on crafting solutions. Simply put, a diverse pool of students in computing is critical in terms of both quantity and quality of graduates.

Nationally, women account for a relatively small fraction of computing and engineering students. In 2016, the percentage of women among those receiving Bachelor's degrees was 17.9% in computer science, 12.6% in computer engineering and 22.9% in informatics [11]. The percentage of computing degrees earned by women is much lower than it was in the 1980s, but has been creeping up in recent years. In most engineering disciplines, the situation is similar. In 2015, women received 32.4% of Bachelor's degrees in chemical engineering and 13.2% of degrees in mechanical engineering, with other engineering disciplines falling between. In both of these engineering disciplines, the national trend for women has been climbing slowly [10].

Potential theories abound for the persistence of extremely low percentages of women in computing fields. Proposed causes include problems with the public image of computing, a belief that computing careers preclude a family life, and stereotype threat. Stereotype threat describes the situation in which concern about being judged negatively according to a stereotype about one's group results in reduced performance or other negative effects [6]. Research on stereotypes indicates that academic performance is undermined by the extra pressure created by stereotype threat. Additionally, limited real-world relevancy of computing curricula, poor teaching and inaccessible advising in some computing departments, confidence issues in computing students, and more attractive options in other fields can encourage women to leave computing. These issues are not unique to the women in these fields, but underrepresented populations tend to suffer greater effects from adverse conditions.

The Center for Women in Technology (CWIT) Scholars program has proven to be effective at increasing persistence and graduation of women in computing and engineering at the University of Maryland, Baltimore County (UMBC). This model involves a strong community of women and allies who work together to create a welcoming environment for women in technology. The very intentional, research-based elements of this program include multiple mentoring programs, a first-year experience course, academic and professional programming, staff support and advising, a living learning community (LLC), and community-building social events.

2 BACKGROUND

Women have remained underrepresented in computing with computer science being the only science, technology, engineering and mathematics (STEM) major experiencing a decline in the representation of women at the undergraduate level [1]. The academic experience for women in STEM can be characterized by isolation, a lack of mentors, and a shortage of role models [2]. Attrition typically happens after the first year in college and may be caused by a lack of a sense of belonging and a lack of self-confidence during the first year [9]. Additionally, there is evidence that suggests stereotypes about computer science (often negative) are powerful influences for women considering careers in the field [1].

Research also emphasizes the effect of peers on women in STEM. While female peer interactions can have a positive impact on women within STEM majors or when deciding to enter STEM majors, negative social interactions with male peers within study groups or social circles can negatively influence a woman's decision to persist in STEM [5]. Additionally, peer-to-peer interactions have been shown to positively affect the development and retention of college students [8]. Academic and social support are key to increasing the persistence and advancement of women and underrepresented minorities in STEM [4]. The development of women's self-concept is greatly improved when receiving encouragement from role models at school [7]. The CWIT Scholars Program is designed to offer women in computing an environment that counteracts many of these negative influences through an engaging and supportive community of peers, allies, and role models.

3 INSTITUTIONAL CONTEXT AND GOALS

Situated between Baltimore and Washington, DC, UMBC is a mid-sized, public research university of approximately 14,000 students, about 11,000 of them undergraduates. UMBC is among the top three research universities in information technology degrees awarded nationally. UMBC's College of Engineering and Information Technology (COEIT) offers six undergraduate degrees: a BS in Information Systems (IS), a BA in Business Technology Administration (BTA), a BS in Computer Science (CMSC), a BS in Computer Engineering (CMPE), a BS in Mechanical Engineering (ME) and a BS in Chemical, Biochemical, and Environmental Engineering (CBEE). COEIT accounts for a significant percentage of UMBC undergraduates, with 3487 students in the Fall 2016. This group is fairly computing heavy, with a total of 2424 in the four computing majors. In all COEIT undergraduate programs, women are a minority of students, ranging from 16% in computer science to 37% in chemical, biochemical and environmental engineering in the 2016-2017 academic year. In most programs, the percentage of women has increased slowly over the last several years.

CWIT was founded in 1998 as an online resource for research and resources about women and technology, including a focus on global issues in technology access for women. The CWIT Scholars Program was introduced in 2001. The first few cohorts were limited to students in computing majors, with engineering majors added in 2006. In 2008, the CWIT mission was revised to focus more firmly on improving the success of women in technology at UMBC. An Affiliates program for other COEIT students interested in the CWIT mission was launched in 2009 to increase the reach of CWIT on campus beyond Scholars, while global and business programs were phased out. The current mission of CWIT is to increase the diversity of those who will create technology through initiatives on campus and in our community.

We have identified four goals key to this aspiration: 1) sustain and strengthen vital Scholar programs for undergraduates committed to increasing the representation of women in computing and engineering fields, 2) work with allies to foster a supportive community for all women in computing and engineering at UMBC 3) improve climate for diversity in COEIT, and 4) broaden the pipeline of talented women interested in computing with K-12 outreach programs. This paper will concentrate on the Scholars Programs, more specifically on the CWIT Scholars Program.

4 PROGRAM MODEL

The Scholars programs within CWIT are at the core of all CWIT initiatives, with Scholars acting as peer-leaders for other program elements. Scholars participate in a series of academic and extracurricular activities designed to foster a supportive community for women and underrepresented minorities within computing and engineering. Our goal is to support Scholars academically and socially, by creating an environment that aids them in their technical pursuits. CWIT prepares Scholars to be leaders and advocates in their academic and professional fields, either by pursuing industry leadership as entrepreneurs, technical leads, or technical management, or by advancing to doctoral programs and an academic career. Both paths require strong academic performance and mastery of professional and leadership skills.

4.1 Scholar Selection

The CWIT Scholars Program is open to high-achieving students who enter COEIT majors as freshmen. Potential Scholars apply to the program in January of their senior year of high school. Scholar Selection is made on four equally weighted categories: 1) strong interest in computing and/or engineering field, 2) academic ability to succeed in the major, 3) drive to contribute through leadership within CWIT and UMBC communities, and 4) passion for increasing diversity in computing and engineering fields. The most promising applicants are invited to campus for an interview with faculty, current Scholars, CWIT alumni, and other industry professionals.

In addition to transcripts for course selection and grades, the selection committee also reviews essays, recommendation letters, and interview answers to glean clearer insight into a student's unique academic, cultural, and leadership background. While most of those selected to be Scholars have exceptionally strong academic backgrounds, the committee also selects some Scholars with strong potential but less clearly strong academic backgrounds.

4.2 Scholar Program Elements

CWIT Scholar Program elements have been intentionally introduced and refined over the years. Each program element has specific learning objectives and regular assessment. According to NCWIT [7], successful strategies for reforming undergraduate computing include implementing a recruiting plan for creating a pipeline of diverse students with appropriate competencies, helping students understand how their classes and internship or research experiences support their future identities as computing professionals, aligning assignments and coursework with students' goals and interests, and fostering a positive student-to-student and student-to-faculty environment with meaningful interactions contributing to their sense of belonging.

4.2.1 Community-building Events. The creation of a strong and supportive community is perhaps the most important element of the CWIT Scholars model. Community-building activities help build connections on all levels within the community, strengthening Scholars' ability to overcome possible academic challenges and creating an atmosphere where Scholars support one another. Additionally, a strong sense of belonging to a community of successful women can help protect against the vulnerability that can result from stereotype threat [6]. Specific community-building activities include a summer retreat to jump-start connections and skills, monthly program or cohort meetings, receptions to celebrate major events, and periodic social events.

The New Scholar Retreat is a three-day on-campus residential retreat for all incoming first-year Scholars. The Retreat includes sessions about transitioning to college, gender issues in technology, diversity, networking, campus resources, team-building, and opportunities to meet College faculty. A planning committee of returning Scholars designs and presents several of the sessions and attends the Retreat as resident peer mentors. There are three concrete benefits to having peer planners and presenters compared with staff presented sessions: a closer alignment with the interests and concerns of incoming Scholars, the greater persuasive power of peers, and the opportunity for leadership experience.

Cohort meetings provide opportunities for students with similar issues to receive targeted advice and share experiences and strategies. Stage-based cohorts give students at the same academic stage an opportunity to discuss academic challenges and transitions, job searching, or decision points. Major-based cohorts give students in the same major the chance to share discipline-specific strategies. The Allies in CWIT cohort gives men, gender non-conforming, and other CWIT allies in the community an opportunity to discuss strategies for becoming effective allies and advocates for diversity.

4.2.2 Living- Learning Community. The CWIT Living-Learning Community (LLC) complements other elements of the Scholar program by strengthening community ties, providing proximity for effective peer-mentoring opportunities, enabling easy access to students in the same classes, and providing an opportunity for residential leadership. All CWIT Scholars are required to live in the CWIT LLC during their first year and can apply to return for their sophomore year. After their sophomore year, Scholars tend to move to university-owned apartments, often with others from the LLC. The LLC is typically one third first-year Scholars, one third returning sophomores and one third CWIT Affiliates. Men supportive of the CWIT mission are welcome on the LLC, but women constitute a strong majority of floor residents. Students wishing to return to the CWIT LLC as sophomores must participate in one of three Engagement Teams: 1) Academic Team, focused on programming for academic success, 2) Social Team, focused on programming for community building 3) Retriever Connection, focused on connecting students to the larger UMBC community. The presence of sophomores on the floor provides convenient role models for first-year students and the structure of the Engagement Teams provides leadership opportunities for sophomores.

4.2.3 Academic Support. Academic support concentrates on the development of specific academic skills and coaching in academic strategies. A major academic initiative is a one-credit first-year course in fall of the freshman year. This course includes sessions led by upperclass Scholars on topics ranging from academic strategies and time management to networking and oral presentation skills. Other specific academic activities include mandatory study groups for STEM courses for underclassmen, workshops for selecting classes, and programming to strengthen academic skills such as test-taking, technical reading, communicating with professors, and time management. Scholars are encouraged to give back academically by serving as a resource for study groups, providing tutoring, serving as undergraduate teaching assistants, and working in departmental help centers.

Another major component of the CWIT Scholar experience is monthly one-on-one meetings with the CWIT staff. At the beginning of each semester, Scholars set goals for themselves, which are revisited every month to track progress. Overall goals for the meetings are that students will self-reflect on their academic past and present academic performance, communicate academic challenges or barriers hindering their success at maintaining the required GPA, understand the importance of seeking help when needed, better understand CWIT and UMBC resources, and display a willingness to effectively utilize suggested strategies for improvement. These meetings allow Scholars to develop a meaningful relationship with a staff member who can serve as a support system and an early alert system for academic struggles.

4.2.4 Mentoring Programs. Mentoring activities include a peer-mentoring program in which first-year Scholars are paired with an older Scholar in their academic major, a pairing with a faculty mentor during their first year, an industry mentoring practicum and match with an industry mentor during their junior year, and informal meetings with distinguished visitors to campus. The industry mentoring practicum includes face-to-face connections with industry mentors as well as sessions dedicated to helping the Scholars develop their professional identities and understand the career or graduate school process. Scholars are encouraged to meet monthly with their industry mentor for personalized discussions. Small groups of industry mentors join each class session, giving Scholars a chance to get to know the mentors of other Scholars and mentors to get to know one another. These multiple forms of interaction help build deeper bonds and a richer mentoring experience for all involved. CWIT also encourages research experiences for

Scholars by partnering with campus initiatives supporting undergraduate research.

4.2.5 Leadership Development. Leadership training addresses the need for soft skills to complement academic performance. Important complementary skills include public speaking, networking, project planning and execution, working with a team, advocacy, and workforce preparation. This programming draws on the expertise of CWIT alumni, the UMBC Career and Shriver Centers, and partners in local companies. A foundation for leadership is laid with a leadership practicum in the spring of the sophomore year. Scholars are encouraged to practice leadership skills by speaking on panels, becoming active in technical and professional organizations, serving as student representatives on department committees, and participating in student government and activism. In order to provide additional leadership practice, large-scale CWIT networking and outreach events are typically organized by a student planning team working in conjunction with CWIT staff.

5 EFFECTIVENESS OF THE MODEL

Since 2002, the CWIT Scholars program has served 174 students; 86% of CWIT Scholars identified as women and 12% were from underrepresented racial-ethnic minority backgrounds. Historically, CWIT Scholars have a 91.7% retention rate in computing and engineering majors, an overall 87.6% graduation rate, and an average time to degree of 4.2 years. Our primary goal is to increase the academic performance, retention, and graduation of CWIT Scholars relative to the overall COEIT undergraduate population; thus, we evaluate the performance of the CWIT Scholars in comparison to their peers with similar incoming profiles.

5.1 Methodology

Using anonymized institutional data from UMBC cohorts entering COEIT from Fall 2002 to Fall 2012 (N=6,681), we employed a case-control matching procedure in SPSS Statistics software (version 24) to draw a matched sample and assess differences in academic outcomes between CWIT Scholars and non-CWIT Scholars. A sample of CWIT Scholar cases was matched to non-CWIT Scholar cases on gender (male/female), race-ethnicity (underrepresented minority / non-underrepresented minority), UMBC cohort, incoming COEIT major, math SAT score, and high school GPA. Match tolerance levels were set at .3 for high school GPA and 50 for math SAT score. These parameters yielded a sample of 134 cases; 67 matches representing 56% of the 120 CWIT Scholars who entered as freshman between Fall 2002 and Fall 2012).

Descriptive statistics and histograms of the total 134 cases were run to examine the distribution and normalcy of the data. Independent samples t-tests and Mann Whitney U tests were run to confirm that the CWIT Scholar cases and non-CWIT Scholar cases did not differ significantly on the matching variables (pre-UMBC characteristics) and to examine any significant differences on academic outcomes. The outcome variables assessed were average cumulative GPA, average years to degree, graduation from UMBC, graduation within four years, graduation within five years, graduation within six years, and retention in a computing or engineering major.

Table 1: CWIT Scholars compared the non-CWIT Scholars entering UMBC Fall 2002 to Fall 2012. Bold rows show statistically significant differences.

Academic Outcomes	CWIT Scholars	Non-CWIT Scholars
Average years to degree	4.26	4.33
Last reported cum. GPA	3.30	3.11
Overall graduation rate	82.1%	71.6%
Four-year graduation rate	**61.2%**	**41.8%**
Five-year graduation rate	79.1%	64.2%
Six-year graduation rate	79.1%	70.2%
Retention rate in COEIT	**86.6%**	**71.6%**

5.2 Results

Comparisons of academic outcomes among CWIT Scholars and non-CWIT Scholars indicate that the CWIT Scholar program model is meeting its intended goals. Compared to matched peers with similar profiles, CWIT Scholars have higher cumulative GPAs and UMBC graduation rates, and shorter time to degree. Additionally, Mann Whitney U tests indicated that there was a statistically significant difference in the number of CWIT Scholars graduating within four years (41) compared to the number of non-CWIT Scholars graduating within four years (28); $z = -2.239$, $p = .025$. There was also a statistically significant difference in the number of CWIT Scholars retained in a COEIT major (58) compared to the number of non-CWIT Scholars retained in a COEIT major (48); $z = -2.117$, $p = .034$. Additional differences on academic outcomes were observed, though not statistically significant at the .05 level. A summary of the group differences between sampled CWIT Scholars and non-CWIT Scholar peers is presented in Table 1.

6 ADAPTING THE MODEL

The CWIT Scholars model includes elements that have been successfully adapted to serve other student populations. The following are two examples of how the CWIT Scholars model was adapted to create 1) a transfer Scholar program (T-SITE) and 2) a CWIT Affiliates program. We also provide tips for implementing aspects of the CWIT Scholars program at other institutions and describe some of the challenges organizers might face during the planning and implementation process.

6.1 T-SITE Scholar Program

The T-SITE (Transfer Scholars in Information Technology and Engineering) program applies the structure and community focus of the CWIT Scholar model to high-achieving transfer students with financial need to increase their success in computing and engineering majors. As with CWIT Scholars, we provide T-SITE Scholars with academic and professional development opportunities, including connections to internships and research experiences.

Since its inception in 2012, the T-SITE program has served 32 transfer students with diverse backgrounds from Maryland community colleges who are majoring in engineering or computing and have demonstrated financial need. Forty-seven percent of these scholars identify as women, and 50% identify as an underrepresented racial-ethnic minority. Scholars in the first five cohorts entered UMBC with an average transfer GPA of 3.55 and 65 credits completed. The average time to graduation for T-SITE Scholars is three years after transferring to UMBC. One hundred percent of all students in the first five T-SITE cohorts have been retained in engineering or computing majors.

Demographically, T-SITE Scholars have different characteristics than incoming freshman. They tend to be older, with different responsibilities and motivations than first-time freshmen. Most have worked full-time while attending community college and may have spouses and/or children. Although transfer students have completed many courses at community college, they may not have strategically planned courses that will lead to completion of a four-year degree. The psychological and emotional aspects of transferring from a community college to a four-year institution pose challenges not generally experienced by typical incoming freshmen. The CWIT model of support safeguards the transition process and nurtures the development of T-SITE Scholars as successful UMBC students and future professionals in engineering and computing.

6.2 Affiliates Program

We have adapted elements of the CWIT Scholar experience to increase our reach within the College. The CWIT Affiliates program was created to offer a strong sense of community and connection among the approximately 600 women in COEIT. It includes a peer mentoring program, the first-year experience course, networking events, social events, and workshops focused on topics ranging from academic success strategies to career skills and issues for women in technology. Additionally, incoming freshmen can apply to the CWIT LLC. The Affiliates program is designed to leverage the CWIT infrastructure and community to offer connections and resources to students without the need for individualized attention from staff.

Affiliates who live in the CWIT LLC are provided with additional academic advising from the CWIT staff to place both Scholars and Affiliates in the same course sections. This allows for increased peer support and easy development of study groups throughout the semester. Not only are Affiliates active participants in programs provided by CWIT staff but they are also leaders within the community by serving as CWIT peer mentors, CWIT Student Council members, CWIT office student assistants, and coordinators of CWIT Affiliate retreats and workshops.

The CWIT Affiliates Workshop series leverages the expertise of faculty and staff who work within COEIT, Residential Life, and Academic Affairs Offices. The bi-weekly workshop topics include diversity issues in technology, imposter syndrome exercises, decreasing test anxiety, leadership styles in computing fields, applying to graduate school, the STEM pipeline and ways to give back, microaggression in the classroom, and digital image curation.

The primary challenge of the Affiliates program is keeping students engaged in the face of many competing demands for their time. We conduct end-of-year surveys of Affiliates and solicit advice from an Affiliates advisory board to ensure that our programming continues to be relevant and valuable to busy students. In 2016-2017, approximately 190 students were identified as Affiliates.

6.3 Adapting for Other Institutions

The CWIT Scholars Program is a model with elements that can easily be adapted by universities seeking to support women in engineering and computing. While the CWIT Scholars Program does offer scholarship support, this is not necessary to replicate many of the initiatives. The following are best practices, resources, and potential challenges for implementation.

Peer Mentoring. The peer mentoring program can be offered to first-year students (freshmen and transfer) as a way of connecting them to a more experienced student in their major. This can be done through both formal and informal gatherings. Time and effort in executing this program mostly occurs at the beginning of the year. Once in place, monthly emails about ways to continue the relationship don't require extensive time. The challenges to consider are creating an application that provides enough information for the organizer to make a positive match for mentor and protégé. With additional financial and time resources, a peer mentor program can include more events and giveaways that foster a close relationship.

Faculty Mentoring. Pairing incoming students with a passionate and engaged faculty mentor is a great way to establish university norms, academic goals, and create positive faculty and student relationships. A large challenge to this program for many institutions is the time commitment faced by many faculty members, but by using a similar process as the Peer Mentoring program, matches can be made within students' intended majors.

Industry Mentor Program. The industry mentoring program can be offered with either in person mentors or by leveraging an online mentoring program (such as mentornet.org or another). Whether students are meeting with their mentors in person or virtually, they can come together regularly to share what they've learned from their experiences with industry mentors. The benefit of this is twofold, 1) students are able to connect with one another and 2) students are able to hear multiple perspectives from industry professionals. Organizers can build upon the existing relationships that the Career Center and Alumni Relations have with individuals in the computing and engineering fields. The challenges that this program faces are 1) lack of pre existing industry relationships, 2) time and commitment ability for mentors, and 3) providing consistent experiences for all mentors and protégés.

First-Year Experience Course. The first-year experience course can also be adapted to become individual workshops or be offered as a full one-credit course as it is within CWIT. Potential topics for a first-year experience course are limitless and can be easily adapted to fit any university. Several institutions have a version of a first-year experience course where a few sections could be tailored for women in computing and engineering majors to provide the instructor with the opportunity to focus general topics on specific ways women can succeed in these majors. Additionally, students can collaborate with one another in selecting future courses, allowing for increased female representation in specific sections and creating study groups together. Alternatively, for universities without a first-year experience course, these could become topical workshops advertised to students in ITE majors and conducted on a bi-weekly or monthly basis. Key challenges to adding anything to an already packed curriculum is the impact of an additional one-credit course, deciding whether it is mandatory for students, and finding the financial support to pay instructors and program expenses.

Living-Learning Communities (LLC). Women who are interested in computing and engineering majors and living on campus can greatly benefit from being placed together on a floor with programming related to success in their major. Not only does this increase the ability for students to study similar subjects together, but they are surrounded by other women who are passionate about these fields. Challenges for implementing an LLC for women in technology include space limitations within residential life, having the ability to train a student resident assistant in issues related to women in technology, and monetary resources.

Summer Community Retreat. A one to three day community retreat for interested new students can review topics such as diversity in technology, team building, identity development, brave space guidelines, networking and professional development, what to expect when moving to campus, allies in action, and academic resources. Each topic area is covered with the goal of increasing knowledge and success in computing and engineering majors. The challenge with providing retreats are financial resources and limitations of the time to deeply discuss several topics. If possible, a three-day on campus retreat provides students with additional social experiences and community building experiences that gives them a jumpstart to the academic year and knowing more people. This will decrease anxiety as they start their first semester.

Affiliates Workshop Series. This program is a great way to utilize the experts at individual institutions. After identifying a consistent day of the week, time, and location, organizers can contact faculty and staff regarding topics related to increasing the success of women in computing and engineering. The challenges in running a successful workshop series is having consistent attendance, reaching your target market through advertising, and cultivating the relationships with the experts at the specific institution.

7 LIMITATIONS

There are external and internal limitations to the successful increase of women in computing and engineering fields. The dominant culture and lack of representation of women in computing and engineering fields in the media impact the K-12 pipeline to higher education and advanced degrees. The ability to provide extended programs to the hundreds of women currently studying COEIT majors is constrained by resources, both availability of funds and limited staff. The Scholar model described here requires substantial resources for a lean public university, with limited staff resources being harder to overcome than limited program support funds. Scholarships increase interest in programs and give staff leverage to mandate participation in activities. Without the scholarship component (as in the Affiliates model described here), staff must work much harder to convince busy students to participate.

A possible critique of the CWIT Scholars program is that most Scholars are academically high achieving and would succeed without the interventions of the program. While high achieving women may complete these majors with or without interventions, challenges such as microaggressions, imposter syndrome, lack of confidence, and others are inevitably part of their experience. We show better outcomes for Scholars, even among these high-performing women. When we only focus on graduation numbers as the outcome, we neglect to consider that women who complete these majors may have had a negative experience that may have lasting impact as they enter the workforce or graduate school. The CWIT Scholars program works to minimize and educate students about these intangible barriers and support them so they have a more positive experience throughout their undergraduate years thus more likely to continue pursuing their professional and academic goals.

8 CONCLUSIONS

The CWIT Scholar program model is an effective model for increasing the retention and success of women in undergraduate computing and engineering majors. The core of this model is the development of a strong, welcoming, and multi-faceted community that can provide academic and professional resources to help women feel connected to others in their discipline, and support women through times of doubt or difficulty. Scholars have overcome stereotype threat by building community among women in computing and engineering fields at UMBC. This model has been successfully adapted to other Scholar programs at UMBC and has elements that could be adopted at other universities.

9 ACKNOWLEDGMENTS

The other members of the CWIT staff have been instrumental in the success of the CWIT Scholars Program model. Susan Martin took the lead on adapting the model to become the T-SITE Scholars Program, while Cindy Greenwood has been instrumental in the success of the Affiliates Program. The T-SITE Scholars Program is supported by NSF through S-STEM grants 1154300 and 1458343.

REFERENCES

[1] S. Beyer. 2014. Why are Women Underrepresented in Computer Science? *Computer Science Education* 24, 2-3 (2014), 153–192.

[2] S. Brainard and L. Carlin. 1998. A six-year longitudinal study of undergraduate women in engineering and science. *Journal of Engineering Education* 87, 4 (1998), 369–75.

[3] Bureau of Labor Statistics. 2017. *Occupational Outlook Handbook.* Available online at https://www.bls.gov/ooh/.

[4] Cinda-Sue Davis, Edward St John, Darryl Koch, Guy Meadows, and Derrick Scott. 2011. Making academic progress: The University of Michigan STEM academy. *Women in Engineering ProActive Network* (2011).

[5] Casey A Shapiro and Linda J Sax. 2011. Major selection and persistence for women in STEM. *New Directions for Institutional Research* 2011, 152 (2011), 5–18.

[6] Steven J Spencer, Christine Logel, and Paul G Davies. 2016. Stereotype threat. *Annual review of psychology* 67 (2016), 415–437.

[7] Leisa D Thompson, Lecia J Barker, Rita Manco Powell, Catherine E Brawner, and Tom McKlin. 2012. Initiatives to support systemic change for women in undergraduate computing. In *Proceedings of the 43rd ACM technical symposium on Computer Science Education.* ACM, 163–164.

[8] UMBC Office of Institutional Research, Analysis, and Decision Support. 2017. Databook. http://www.oir.edu/databook/student-term-headcount-enrollment/undergraduate-enrollments. (2017).

[9] M Lee Upcraft, John N Gardner, and Betsy O Barefoot. 2005. Introduction: The first year of college revisited. *Challenging and supporting the first-year student: A handbook for improving the first year of college* (2005), 1–12.

[10] Brian L Yoder. 2016. Engineering by the Numbers. In *American Society for Engineering Education.*

[11] Stuart Zweben and Betsy Bizot. 2017. 2016 Taulbee Survey. *Computing Research News* 29, 5 (2017). Available online at http://cra.org/crn/wp-content/uploads/sites/7/2017/05/2016-taulbee-survey.pdf.

The Impact of AP Computer Science Principles – Are You Ready to Change Your Undergraduate Courses?

Paul T. Tymann
Rochester Institute of Technology
Rochester, NY 14623
+1 585-475-7908
paul.tymann@rit.edu

Dale Reed
University of Illinois at Chicago
Chicago, IL 60607
+1 312-413-9478
reed@uic.edu

Chinma Uche
Academy of Aerospace and Engineering
Windsor, CT 06095
+1 860-243-0857
cuche@crec.org

Carol S. Yarbrough
Alabama School of Fine Arts
Birmingham, AL 35203
+1 205-252-9241
cyarbrough@asfa.k12.al.us

ACM Reference format:

Paul T. Tyman, Dale Reed, Chinma Uche, and Carol S. Yarbrough. 2018. The Impact of AP Computer Science Principles – Are You Ready to Change Your Undergraduate Courses? In *SIGCSE '18: 49th ACM Technical Symposium on Computer Science Education, Feb. 21–24, 2018, Baltimore, MD, USA*. ACM, NY, NY, USA, 6 pages. https://doi.org/10.1145/3159450.3159612

1.SUMMARY

In the last few years, there has been a groundswell of programs to support more and better computer science (CS) education in K-12. A large number of organizations and institutions including ACM, Code.org, CSTA and the National Science Foundation (NSF) have worked to make CS more available and engaging and in this way increase the CS into post-secondary CS programs. NSF's CS10K initiative, for example, aimed to "have rigorous, academic curricula incorporated into computing courses in 10,000 high schools, taught by 10,000 well-trained teachers" [3]. These initiatives have energized the education world and have resulted in sweeping changes in the way that computing is being taught at in K-12. Examples include the College Board's CS Principles Course [1], the Beauty and Joy of Computing [2,4], UTeach CS Principles [5, 41], and Mobile CSP [6, 7].

These courses are attracting a broad and diverse collection of students to computing and teaching them basic computational thinking skills. To date almost all efforts to broaden computing education have focused on students at the K-12 level. As these more computationally literate students enter college they will expect the same relevant and meaningful educational experiences that they have had during their K-12 educational career. This new generation of students, who have a deeper understanding of computing, will require introductory courses that engage, excite, and retain them.

SIGCSE '18, February 21–24, 2018, Baltimore, MD, USA

ACM ISBN 978-1-4503-5103-4/18/02.
https://doi.org/10.1145/3159450.3159612

The higher education community has a rare opportunity to change the content of introductory courses and the pedagogy used in these courses. The design of introductory course experiences can now leverage the high level of computational sophistication of incoming students and integrate computation, appropriate to the discipline, from the very start of a student's educational career. While computing departments will be impacted the most, it is a mistake to think that only computing departments will be affected. All higher education programs, both STEM and non-STEM, need to rethink and redesign their core curricula to accommodate these students and develop new content and pedagogical approaches that leverage the knowledge set brought in by these students. Unless higher education rethinks and retools the way in which students are taught in the first year of their college experience, the potential gains in diversity and depth of coverage that has been fueled by these initiatives will not be realized.

This panel will explore post-secondary CS education in a post-AP CS Principles world. It will examine the impact recent K-12 CS developments have had on student knowledge, skills, and expectations, focusing specifically on ways in which incoming students are likely to change as CS becomes a staple in pre-college education. It will introduce participants to pedagogy being used in K-12 classrooms to teach the course and introduce strategies that higher education institutions are undertaking prepare for the students who have taken these courses. The session will conclude with a discussion session that will focus on strategies that participants can use to adopt similar models at their institutions.

2. PAUL TYMANN

Paul Tymann is currently serving as the Chief Reader for the AP CS Principles exam and has developed and is teaching a CS Principles course at the Rochester Institute of Technology (RIT). He is currently working with faculty across RIT to integrate computing into their respective disciplinary-based programs. Tymann will serve as the moderator of the panel.

3. DALE REED

Dale Reed is a Clinical Professor and teaches a CS Principles course at the University of Illinois at Chicago (UIC). He is part of the Chicago team that got Computer Science to be a high school graduation requirement in Chicago Public Schools. He was a College Board CSP Development Committee member for 3.5 years and has been a professional development facilitator for Exploring Computer Science for the past six years. He has a passion for making CS compelling and relevant for every student.

Widespread adoption of the AP CSP course is increasing the number of students who have some CS background when they arrive at the university. This is increasingly true across the K-12 spectrum, where earlier and earlier students are experiencing meaningful computational thinking experiences through curriculum such as that provided by Code.org, Project Lead the Way (PLTW), and Exploring Computer Science (ECS). Over the next five years I anticipate this will cause a shift in which curricular topics are covered at which levels. In spite of computing tools such as Scratch and App Inventor becoming increasing powerful and accessible to novices, the level of abstraction of some topics makes them more appropriate for older students. For instance, while sorting is covered in kindergarten using wooden blocks, at the other end of the spectrum the efficiency of various sorting algorithms is of great interest to university researchers. Over the next five years as computer scientists interested in educational research we will need to parse which concepts at what level of abstraction are most appropriately covered at which grade levels. This will lead to changes in our university introductory CS courses.

4. CHINMA UCHE

Chinma Uche is a Math and Computer Science (CS) teacher at the Academy of Aerospace and Engineering (AAE) and the Greater Hartford Academy of Math and Science (GHAMAS). She is the 2015 CREC Teacher of the Year. She has been at GHAMAS since 2002 and has taught Algebra I, Algebra II, PreCalculus, Advanced Math, AP Calculus AB. As a CS teacher, she has taught AP CS A and the defunct AP CS AB. She has been a pilot instructor for the new AP CS Principles course the College Board is developing. She participated in Pilot II, Pilot III and is currently involved in the Phase II pilot of CS Principles course. Chinma is a graduate of the University of Nigeria, Nsukka and holds a Ph.D from Imperial College of Science, Technology and Medicine, London. In her spare time, Chinma advocates for CS education for all K-12 students. She is currently the President of the Connecticut Chapter of the Computer Science Teachers Association. She is a co-PI to a CE21 project, "Using Mobile Learning to Teach CS Principles in Connecticut Schools". Chinma is also a member of Computer Science Advocacy Leadership Team (CSALT). She enters teams into the Moody Mega Math Challenge, the Technovation Challenge and supervises the CS Programming team which participates in programming contests within and outside the state of Connecticut. Chinma has been an AP CS A reader since 2006.

5. CAROL YARBROUGH

Carol Yarbrough is the Computer Science Instructor at the Alabama School of Fine Arts, a public magnet school for the arts in Birmingham, Alabama. Carol began teaching high school computer science after a 20+ year career as a software developer in industry. She is actively involved in training teachers from multiple disciplines, across the state of Alabama, to teach computer science. She believes that all students should have an understanding of computer science and how it can enhance their future career path. Her work often focuses around helping students realize that computing is a new medium for artistic expression. Carol enjoys teaching AP Computer Science Principles to both Arts and Math/Science majors.

6. REFERENCES

[1] Astrachan, O., and Briggs, A., (2012) "The CS Principles project." ACM Inroads, 3(2), pp. 38-42.

[2] The Beauty and Joy of Computing. http://bjc.berkeley.edu/index.html, accessed:

[3] Forbes, J., (2014) "Building a talent pool: the CS 10K project." Journal of Computing Sciences in Colleges, 29(4), pp. 112-113.

[4] Garcia, D. Barnes, T., Ball, M., Biga, E., Paley, J., Hill, M., Rose, J., Mattix, N., Safa, P., Morris, S., Kenner, S., (2016) "AP CS Principles and The Beauty and Joy of Computing Curriculum," Proceedings of the 47th ACM technical symposium on Computer Science.

[5] Mickel, J., Bradley B., (2016) "K-12 Teacher Support for Computer Science Principles: An Introduction to the UTeach Course, Thriving in Our Digital World," Proceedings of the 47th ACM technical symposium on Computer Science Education, Memphis, TN.

[6] The Mobile CSP Project. http://mobile-csp.org, accessed: November 28, 2016.

[7] Morelli, R., Uche, C., Lake, P., Baldwin, L., (2015) "Analyzing Year One of a CS Principles PD Project," Proceedings of the 46th ACM technical symposium on Computer Science Education, Kansas City, MO.

[8] UTeach CS Principles. https://cs.uteach.utexas.edu, accessed: November 28, 2016.

A Summer Program to Attract Potential Computer Science Majors

Scott Vandenberg, Sharon G. Small, Meg Fryling, Robin Flatland, MaryAnne Egan
Computer Science Department
Siena College
vandenberg, ssmall, mfryling, flatland, maegan@siena.edu

ABSTRACT

Computer Science (CS) is not taught in enough high schools thus many students arrive at college or university knowing little about it and often do not consider taking a CS course during their first year. At the same time, we encounter many college or university juniors and seniors who, while taking their first CS course, discover an aptitude and interest, at which point it is too late. We describe an innovative one-week residential summer program designed to educate non-computer science majors, before their second year of college or university, about the field's many areas and long-term prospects. The program has succeeded at encouraging undecided students to major or minor in CS and thus somewhat ameliorates the lack of CS in K-12 education and furthers the conference goal of "CS For All".

KEYWORDS

CS Summer Program, Recruitment, Retention, CS Education, Outreach, Computer Science Majors, Non-majors, STEM

ACM Reference format:

S. Vandenberg, S. G. Small, M. Fryling, R. Flatland, M. Egan. 2018. A Summer Program to Attract Potential Computer Science Majors. In *Proceedings of SIGCSE '18: The 49th ACM Technical Symposium on Computer Science Education, Baltimore, MD, USA, Feb 21-24, 2018 (SIGCSE'18)*, 6 pages. https://doi.org/10.1145/3159450.3159562

1 INTRODUCTION

Many college and university-level Computer Science (CS) faculty worldwide have encountered the following situation: A high-performing 3rd- or 4th-year student in an introductory CS course approaches you after class one day and says, "*I'm really enjoying this class and I'm doing very well in it. I wish it wasn't too late to change my major. Why didn't somebody tell us about this field earlier?*" In many cases they are also out of time to complete a minor, but they still want to take as many CS courses as they can. We encountered this often enough at Siena College, a four-year post-secondary liberal arts college, that we decided to try to do something about it. A program similar to ours could be implemented at any college or university offering a typical four-year CS degree, and references to "college" should generally be interpreted as "college or university".

It is well known that a large percentage of secondary schools in the United States and other countries offer little in the way of real CS education [3]. In addition, very few colleges and universities explicitly require CS, though some (including Siena) do allow certain CS courses to count as courses in a required area such as quantitative reasoning or analysis. Thus, while a large percentage of college or university freshmen will be taking a mathematics course (a worthwhile thing, to be sure), relatively few of them will be taking a CS course.

In order to help a certain cohort of students understand the nature and possibilities of the field, we hypothesized that exposing them to the field prior to their sophomore year might help them end up "in the right place" by allowing them to make an informed decision about a major or minor with enough time left for them to do something about it. Having them take a course would be ideal, but we needed something to get them into that first course, at which point we have an opportunity to give them a more complete picture of CS. Our program exclusively targets students who have not declared CS as a major, that is we do not invite CS majors to apply to the program.

We have run this program three times (summers 2015-2017) and will be running it at least two more times. More complete results will be reported in several more years, when we know graduation and retention rates, but we believe these early results are very encouraging and warrant dissemination so that others may be able to run similar programs: waiting any longer may result in more students missing out on their true calling. The program is being run in the setting of a 4-year liberal arts college with approximately 3000 total full-time undergraduate students. We have a relatively healthy CS major for a liberal arts college, with about 150 majors total and 13 tenure-track faculty. Siena College also has a successful School of Business, unusual for a liberal arts college. Our department teaches, in addition to a typical CS curriculum, a number of Information Systems (IS) courses. We also offer an IS minor and certificate.

ACM 978-1-4503-5103-4/18/02...$15.00
https://doi.org/10.1145/3159450.3159562

The next section of this paper reports on related work, followed by a section describing the summer program itself, with enough detail to be replicable. Section 4 describes our outcomes based on the first two years of the program, Section 5 describes our next steps, and the final section contains conclusions and lessons learned.

2 SUMMER PROGRAMS – RELATED WORK

There appears to currently be very little work in summer recruitment efforts for students entering their first and second year of college. There are instances of programs that do reach out and educate students while still in high school and there are bridge programs to improve college readiness. There are also programs that focus on retention by offering research opportunities early in the student's college career: freshman and sophomore years to students who are CS majors [9]. Since the program is so unique in its combination of content and cohort served, our goal here is to present it and demonstrate that it works, not to say that it works better or worse than other programs designed for very different cohorts.

A program most similar to ours is the IMPACT program [2] run annually at Siena College in the Fall semester of each year. High school juniors who are strong in mathematics, and their teachers are recruited to attend the day-long event. Students spend the day learning about CS topics through interactive sessions. This program is similar in goal to our work. The distinctions are that IMPACT is for high school juniors while our summer program is for incoming college freshmen and sophomores, and ours is a 1-week residential program.

Programs offered over the summer tend to be bridge programs, focusing on improving a student's college readiness. The National Center for Postsecondary Research evaluated [1] eight of these types of programs in Texas. These programs all included accelerated instruction in math, which should improve course performance in typical required math courses for the CS major potentially improving retention for students that participated in these types of programs.

Research programs are also being offered to students earlier in the CS program, freshman and sophomore years, in an effort to improve student retention. One such program funded by the National Science Foundation at Appalachian State University [9] has shown some promising results. In their latest reported year 79% of the students indicated that their participation in the research program was either *Very Helpful* (61%) or *Helpful* (17%) with only 22% indicating that it was *Little Helpful*.

Markowitz [7] describes a general summer science program with positive results, and [4] describe positive long-term results of a summer science program, but these are designed specifically for high school students, not for rising sophomores and freshmen within the college as ours is, and are not specific to CS.

These other efforts gave us encouragement that a summer program could be successful, but finding no evidence that others had tried what we were planning, we had no real model to go by, so we devised the program described in the next section.

3 OUR SUMMER PROGRAM

We first describe how we select students for the program, followed by a description of the week's activities and some important logistical details. Data we gathered[2] from our college before starting this program indicated that 65% of undecided science majors ended up not obtaining a degree in a STEM field (either because they did not graduate or they changed to a non-STEM major). Of incoming science students with a declared major, 47% did not obtain a STEM degree. Furthermore, a large portion of both of these groups had not been previously exposed to CS. At the same time, other data from our college indicated that significant numbers of undecided students from non-science fields might have the aptitude to succeed in CS, based on their Math SAT scores being higher than the average Math SAT score of CS majors. Obviously this is only one limited metric, but it encouraged us enough to hope that there were enough undecided students in the college as a whole who had the quantitative, analytical, and symbolic reasoning proficiency, and possibly the interest, to succeed in CS.

3.1 Student Selection

The program is designed for about 18-24 students per year. We start by identifying undecided (students who have not declared a major yet) rising sophomores near the end of the freshman year (typically in March). The motivation here is that undecided students are more likely to consider something new, and we want to get them before it's too late for them to complete the major. We target students from all areas of the college (science, liberal arts, and business). Most of the seats in the program are filled in this way. Each year, however, we have had room for a number (5-7) of incoming freshmen to attend the program. All invited students are full-time students at Siena College.

We obtain academic records and contact information for current undecided freshmen (rising sophomores) from our institutional research office. Specifically, we request cumulative GPA and test scores, if available, for the SAT math test and/or the ACT math test. We then invite the subset of students from that list who have a GPA of at least 2.8 and a math SAT score of at least 540 (ACT equivalent about 21). These criteria are used for one main reason: there is an academic threshold that demonstrates a student's ability to be successful in CS and it would be a disservice to recruit a student into CS who is unlikely to succeed. We are also able, if we think it necessary, to examine the students' complete academic records online to help us decide whether to extend an invitation to apply. These invitations go out in mid-to-late April, and we give them several weeks to respond. The invitations to rising sophomores are sent in three ways: via email to the student's college account, via paper to their campus post office box (if they live on campus), and via US mail to their home address (whether they live on campus or not).

[2] Data cited are for graduation years 2014-2017

The application process for the students is online and brief (contact information, housing preferences for the program, brief response about why they are interested, and any other students they may know who may have a similar interest – just in case we missed someone good in our process). After the deadline, we send out acceptance notifications. During the first three years of the program, we have accepted 100% of the sophomores who applied (this is unsurprising, because we would not have invited them to apply if we didn't think they would benefit from the program). The acceptance notification requires the students to confirm (or reject) their attendance at the program; we also threaten to penalize their college financial account by $75 if they confirm attendance but then don't show up. This is to ensure that we don't end up with empty seats that could have been filled by someone else interested in the program. (In practice we have not had to enforce this; our only no-show so far was a student who never bothered to show up for college at all.)

	Year 1	Year 2	Year 3
Sophomore Pool	180	179	394 (65 Biology +159 Undecided +170 Business)
Sophomore Invites	83	85	155 (35 Biology +72 Undecided +48 Business)
Sophomore Attended	15	13	18 (8 + 5 + 5)
Freshman Undecided	225	207	124
Freshman Invites	85	96	68
Freshman Attended	5	7	5
Total Invites	168 (82 female)	181 (98 female)	223 (113 female)
Total Attended	19	20	23
% Females Attended	53	55	52

Table 1: Program Invite, Application, Participation Data, Years 1-3

We have had room, at least the first 3 years, for all the interested rising sophomores, with some space left over for incoming freshmen, who are invited separately (and after the rising sophomores, since we normally don't know until after May 1st who will be attending in the fall). In year 3 (Spring 2017), we expanded the list of invited rising sophomores to include selected biology majors and business majors who may be looking for a second major or a new major, or a minor. In part this was done because this is where we find students at Siena College who later discover they are "in the wrong major". We also expanded in this direction because the number of undecided sophomores and freshmen were both decreasing (Table 1). This expansion was done with the enthusiastic support of the relevant academic administrators (department chairs and deans): while the program certainly is a recruitment tool, and everyone knows that, we have been careful to structure it in such a way as to educate and raise awareness, and we are always careful to emphasize that our purpose is to help the students make an informed decision, not to indoctrinate them. Our biology department, for example, is highly selective, and thus has a relatively low retention rate, with over 24% of students not graduating from the college, and another 44% not graduating in a STEM field. This is one potential area for finding students who may find a home in CS and, if we find them early enough, many still graduate in four years.

The undecided incoming freshmen are again identified for us by our institutional research department, with some help from admissions, in early-to-mid May. In the case of these freshmen, we do not send out paper invitations to apply. Instead, we send two emails, one to their college account and one to the contact email address listed on their college application. We narrow down this list similarly to how we limit the rising sophomores list, but instead of cumulative college GPA we use their high school grade average, and require it to be at least a B or 3.0. Freshmen are invited to apply in late May or early June, and are again given a few weeks to respond.

Table 1 contains some invitation/application/attendance numbers for the first three years of the program. One interesting trend is the diminishing number of undecided students, which was one reason we expanded the recruitment of rising sophomores to include students from selected majors. We are also encouraged by the percentage of women (over 50%) participating in the program: this is a historically underrepresented group in CS.

3.2 Program Structure

The main goal of the program is to expose the students, via specific, targeted activities, to the thinking and problem-solving that goes into CS. The schedule of activities for the program in Year 2 (2016) is shown in Figure 1. The schedules for Years 1 and 3 are similar. We have omitted faculty names and replaced them with numbers. As you can see from the figure, this is not a "programming boot camp", nor is it just a compressed version of an Introduction to CS (CS0 or CS1) course. It is a combination of computer-based and non-computer-based activities, as well as panel discussions, that together give a fairly complete picture of the kinds of thinking and problem-solving involved in CS. This does include some programming, but it also includes web page design, game design, work with finite automata, simulations of sorting algorithms, visualizations of data compression, etc.

All sessions involve all participants and are hands-on/interactive. Each session is led by 1 or 2 tenure-track CS faculty: notice from Figure 1 that 9 different faculty participated in this way. This program can and should not be a "one-person show". It is too much for one person to do, and it is beneficial for the students to see a variety of faculty, thus a variety of ways of thinking about problems and thinking computationally. Of course, we could have done it with fewer faculty, but we are fortunate to have a very participatory group!

The morning sessions are all "unplugged" in the sense that the students do not use computers for anything. Students sit at round 4-6 person tables (no computers at the tables) and typically work in groups on activities that illustrate the kind of thinking and problem-solving involved in CS. Some of these activities were drawn from existing literature such as CS Unplugged[3], and others are "home-grown".

	Mon 29 Aug	Tue 30 Aug	Wed 31 Aug	Thu 1 Sep	Fri 2 Sep
9AM – noon	Welcome Introductions Making it Fit: Data Compression (Faciulty 1,2)	*Software Engineering and Tinkertoys (Faculty 2)*	*Computing Without Computers: Models of Computation (Faculty 5)*	*Mind Your Own Business: Privacy, Secrecy, and Encryption (Faculty 6)*	Discuss Movie (Faulty 1); Who's Next? Putting Things in Order (Faculty 9)
12pm – 1	Lunch				
1PM – 4PM	*Time to Make Stuff: 3D Printing (Faculty 3)*	*Put Yourself Out There: Making a Mobile Web Page (Faculty 4)*	*Time to Play: Game Development using GameMaker (Faculty 3)*	*Robotics (Faculty 7, 8)*	*Joyful Noise: Making Music with Python (Faculty 1)*
4-6:30	Free time/dinner				
6:30PM-8:30PM	Alumni Panel: Life after College	Intern & Research Panel: Life at College Beyond the Classroom	Faculty Panel: Life at College in and out of Classroom, Career Opportunities, etc.	Movie Night: TBA	Have a great weekend!

Figure 1: Summer Program Schedule, Year 2 (2016)

The afternoon sessions have the students on computers (using various lab rooms in our CS facilities). On the first day, for example, they use 3D printing software to design an object, which is printed out for them and given to them at the end of the week; the context of 3D printing can be used to learn about process and abstraction [5]. The GameMaker software package is used on the third day (game design can be used to teach computational thinking [8]).

The Robotics session on Thursday involves programming our department's robots (used also in our upper-level robotics course). The amount of actual programming done is minimal early in the week: they learn concepts, possibilities, and strategies the first 3 afternoons. Though some would consider much of what they do to be programming, they are not writing code in a general-purpose programming language until Day 4 – and what they do there is mainly "fill in some blanks". On the last day, the afternoon activity involves simple programming by creating music in Python [6].

[3] http://csunplugged.org

The evening sessions are panel discussions. The first one is comprised of 4-6 CS alumni from Siena College who give brief introductions of what they have been doing after college, then answer questions from the participants. The second night's panel is structured similarly, but involves panelists who are current CS majors and have done some sort of internship or research activity. The faculty panel on the third night gives the faculty an opportunity to describe the CS curriculum briefly, advise students on what courses to take for a major/minor/etc., and to talk to them more about career and internship opportunities from a faculty perspective. Thursday's evening activity is a movie with some sort of CS theme, and there is no Friday evening activity.

In each of the years of the program so far, we have been fortunate to have been able to have two student assistants (CS majors) to help us out during the daytime sessions. They work with the participants to help them with concepts or problem-solving or (in the afternoon sessions) software and syntax issues. We believe it is good for the participants to see not just the faculty, but also their fellow students who are CS majors and can give them different perspectives on the field.

3.3 Logistics

At this point the reader may wonder how we convinced about 20 students each year to give up a week of their summer to do this. Of course, we hope it is because they have seen a sample program from a previous year and are intellectually stimulated enough to want to learn more. And that is genuinely the case with most of them. But we have added inducements. First, we hold the program the week before classes: students can simply return to campus and move in one week early (or commute if they live locally). College is a very fun place when you have no homework, and the students appreciate being able to move in early. We also offer them the option to stay in the dorms for the week even if they typically live off-campus: the intent is that this is a residential program.

We also do not want this program to cost the students anything, so their food and lodging are paid throughout the program, from Sunday dinner through Friday lunch (the students arrive Sunday to check in so we can get a full week of the program in). In addition, each student completing the program is given a $100 stipend upon completion (full attendance required, though we have been a little flexible with genuine conflicts such as required freshman orientation activities). Practically, we have to be a little flexible for highly active students who may have legitimate conflicts with 1 or 2 sessions but will still gain value from participating. Currently the program is funded by the National Science Foundation; we address sustainability issues in Section 5.

At the end of Friday's activities, students can meet with a faculty advisor if they want to make any last-minute changes to their fall schedule, such as enroll in our Introduction to CS course (we reserve at least 8-10 seats for students from this program, spread among 4-5 sections, before "opening it up" again to everyone else). They may also speak with an advisor in more general terms, or they may plan a sequence of courses in CS that begins in the spring instead of the fall semester.

4 OUTCOMES

The results of the program, by several measures, demonstrate a great deal of success. Of course we realize these results are preliminary, since the program is only in its third year right now and the students who took it as rising sophomores in Year 1 will be seniors in Fall 2017. But the outcomes to date are very positive and have encouraged us to disseminate the ideas so that others can take advantage of them.

We have completed 2 years of the program, which means the participants from Year 1 have completed 4 semesters (2 years) since they experienced the program, and none have graduated. We have some interesting results based on course registrations post-program; major and minor declarations post-program; student survey feedback (a survey is administered at the end of the program); and grade data. We should note also that the program has a 100% completion rate through the first two years (no student dropped the program and only one student had attendance issues).

A basic outcome, of course, is that 20 students per year learn about CS earlier than they would have. But we would also like to know that they have decided, after the program, to continue on with more CS education. Table 2 shows the numbers of course registrations, minors declared, and majors declared for participants from Years 1 and 2 of the program (the number of courses is courses completed as of the end of spring semester 2017). From Table 2, we see that in each year, about 75% of the students took at least one additional CS course (and some of those declared a major or minor).

	YEAR ONE (n=19)	YEAR TWO (n=20)
# taking no more CS courses	5	6
# taking 1 CS course	3	7
# taking 2 CS courses	2	5
# taking 3 CS courses	2	0
# taking 4+ CS courses	7	2
# declared minors	1	1
# declared majors	7	5

Table 2: Participants Enrolling, Minoring, and Majoring in CS After the Program

As can be seen in Figure 2, overall, 31% of the participants have declared a major in CS after their participation in the program. From Year 1, 37% of the participants declared a CS major and from Year 2, 25% (so far) have declared a CS major. All of these students were previously undeclared majors. The percentage of undeclared students who did not participate in the program but still declared a CS major is 2.3%, so our program participants are much more likely (31% vs. 2.3%) to declare a CS major. The numbers for declared CS minors from these same cohorts are also quite favorable: 5.13% of the participants declared a minor in CS versus only 1.64% of non-participating undeclared students.

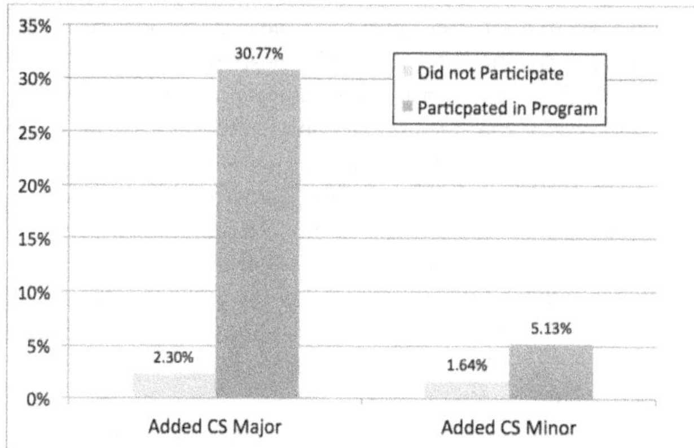

Figure 2: Major & Minor Effects from Summer Program

Of course, one would hope that students accepting our invitation to the program would enroll in the major or minor at a higher rate than the group of all undecided students. But, as can be seen in Figure 3, we also compared the numbers of undecided students that added the CS major and minor in the four semesters after our program began to the four semesters before our program began. Both comparisons, which measure the proportion of students who were undecided at some point during those four semesters and then switched to CS during those four semesters, show a significant improvement in the percentages of undecided students who declared new CS majors and new CS minors after we began our Summer Program.

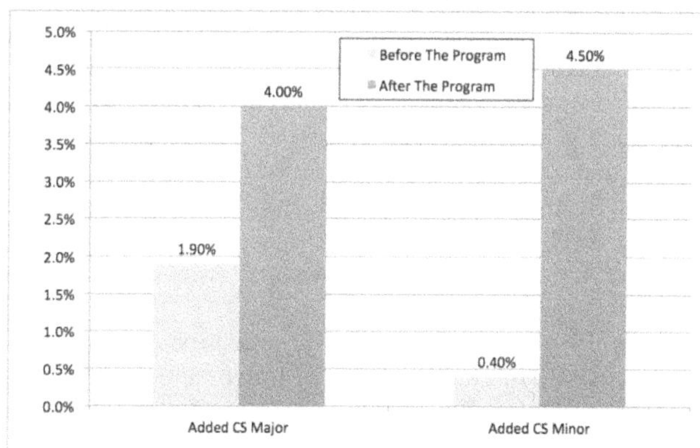

Figure 3: Major & Minor Effects: % of Undecided Students Adding CS Major/Minor for the Four Semesters Before and After the Summer Program was First Offered

In addition to the very positive enrollment results, we have some very valuable and favorable feedback from surveys. We administered online surveys, both pre-program and post-program, in Years 1 and 2. The basic results from these surveys indicate the students enjoy the program and find it worthwhile and helpful in career exploration.

More specifically, participants indicated that they enroll in the program to learn more about CS, move in early, help decide on a major, and to have fun. The post-surveys indicate the students had a very positive and educational experience, that they appreciated the breadth of topics offered, they liked the faculty, and they found the panels very worthwhile. Half of the participants, at the end of program, "agree" or "strongly agree" that they are considering majoring in CS (measured on a 5-point Likert scale from "strongly agree" to "strongly disagree"). In addition, about two-thirds are considering a minor. Nearly all participants found the program interesting and would recommend it to others, thought it encouraged critical thinking, and increased their interest in CS.

Finally, in examining grades, we wanted to see how these participants have fared academically. We compared the average overall GPA of students completing the program who switched to the CS major (3.11) with the average GPA of students who switched to the CS major without participating in the program (3.07). These numbers assure us that one potentially negative outcome of the program has not occurred: We have not enticed students into the major who are not capable of doing the work. They aren't just riding a temporary wave of excitement from the summer program and then flaming out.

5 NEXT STEPS

Through National Science Foundation funding, the program will be run five times, each summer through 2019. More complete results will be reported in several more years, when we know graduation and retention rates. Following that, we hope to sustain the program via institutional funds or other sources (talks are already under way with the administration, with positive indications so far: the program helps retain students, and administrators like that). Of course, the program is not free, but neither is it prohibitively expensive. The annual budget for the program is about $7500. About $2000 of that is for the stipends for the participants, with the bulk of the remainder covering food and lodging for the participants as well as payments for the two student assistants. The faculty donate their time.

We will continue to monitor the numbers of undeclared students, and if they do not rise, we will continue with our expanded invitation list (including selected biology and business majors) in subsequent years.

6 CONCLUSIONS & LESSONS LEARNED

The program has been a great success, based on our "rate of return" on new majors, new minors, and students simply taking another CS course. The program is fun for the students and for the faculty; hopefully word will spread via the students not just about the program but about the possibilities of CS. In addition, it can help show the participants, who may not have encountered many computer scientists up to this point in their education, that we (faculty and students in CS) are people too and maybe this can help break down some of the popular misconceptions of our field, making it easier to achieve "CS For All".

We have presented a 1-week summer residential program, held just before classes begin, that introduces undeclared rising sophomores (and a few incoming freshmen) to the wonders of CS. The program includes interactive, faculty-led sessions both with and without a computer as well as panels of alumni, students, and faculty. The goal of the program is to expose more students, especially those with relevant aptitudes, to the field of CS as a whole. The results have been very positive and gratifying, with over 30% of participants declaring a CS major, 5.13% minoring in CS, and most of the rest taking at least one more course in the field. We hope to continue the program indefinitely, as long as it continues to work, and we encourage other institutions to try similar programs.

ACKNOWLEDGMENTS

This work was supported by NSF grant 1432198. We would also like to thank the anonymous referees for their comments.

REFERENCES

[1] R. H. Bork, A. K. Mayer, J. Pretlow, H. D. Wathington, M. J. Weiss. 2012. Bridging the gap: An impact study of eight developmental summer bridge programs in Texas. New York: National Center for Postsecondary Research.

[2] MaryAnne L. Egan and Timoth Lederman. 2011. The impact of IMPACT: assessing students' perceptions after a day of computer exploration. In Proceedings of the 16th annual joint conference on Innovation and technology in computer science education (ITiCSE '11). ACM, New York, NY, USA, 318-322.

[3] Gallup Poll. 2016. Trends in the State of Computer Science in U.S. K-12 Schools.

[4] E.G. Helm, J.E. Parker, M.C. Russell. Education and career paths of LSU's summer science program students from 1985 to 1997. Academic Medicine: April 1999. Journal Article: PDF Only.

[5] Chris Johnson. 2017. Toward Computational Making with Madeup. In In Proceedings of the 2017 ACM SIGCSE Technical Symposium on Computer Science Education (SIGCSE '17). ACM, pp. 297-302.

[6] Bill Manaris, Andrew R. Brown. 2014. Making Music with Computers: Creative Programming in Python, CRC Press.

[7] Dina G. Markowitz. Journal of Science Education and Technology September 2004, Volume 13, Issue 3, pp 395–407. Evaluation of the Long-Term Impact of a University High School Summer Science Program on Students' Interest and Perceived Abilities in Science.

[8] Alexander Repenning, David Webb, Andri Ioannidou. 2010. Scalable Game Design and the Development of a Checklist for Getting Computational Thinking into Public Schools. In Proceedings of the 41st ACM technical symposium on Computer Science Education (SIGCSE '10). ACM, pp. 265-269.

[9] Rahman Tashakkori , Barry L. Kurtz , Dolores A. Parks , James B. Fenwick, Jr., Alice A. McRae, Early participation of CS students in research, Proceedings of the 42nd ACM technical symposium on Computer science education, March 09-12, 2011, Dallas, TX, USA [doi>10.1145/1953163.1953185]

Docendo Discimus: Students Learn by Teaching Peers Through Video

Pablo Frank-Bolton
The George Washington University
Washington, DC
pfrank@gwu.edu

Rahul Simha
The George Washington University
Washington, DC
simha@gwu.edu

ABSTRACT

This study presents and evaluates a scalable approach for improving learning outcomes by having students "teach" peers in the same course via video. The approach was tested in a standard upper-level undergraduate computer algorithms course with material commonly considered challenging to teach: combinatorial optimization and NP-complete problems. An important design goal was to incentivize students to learn deeply in crafting their instructional videos while minimizing the added burden on instructors to review their products, allowing for scalability. A learning assessment administered to two successive cohorts (N=89) showed statistically significant improvement ($P < 0.0001$) in learning for students who make the videos compared to those who merely study the materials or view the videos. Students not only enjoyed applying their creativity in making videos but, in the process, also strengthened their conceptual learning. While much of the existing research on student-created videos has shown its effectiveness in motivating students, few studies exist that directly isolate learning gains in those who *craft* instructional videos.

KEYWORDS

Active learning; Student-centered learning; Student-created videos; Improved conceptual learning; Scalable Instructional resources; ACM proceedings; SIGCSE

ACM Reference Format:

Pablo Frank-Bolton and Rahul Simha. 2018. Docendo Discimus: Students Learn by Teaching Peers Through Video. In *Proceedings of The 49th ACM Technical Symposium on Computer Science Education, Baltimore, MD, USA, Feb. 21–24, 2018 (SIGCSE '18)*, 6 pages.
https://doi.org/10.1145/3159450.3159466

1 INTRODUCTION

The notion of learning by teaching can be traced back to the Latin phrase *docendo discimus* ("by teaching, we learn") attributed to the Roman philosopher Seneca the Younger (4BC – 65AD). Instructors know all too well the experience of acquiring insight while preparing to teach: "the best way to learn something is to teach it." At the same time, getting students to learn by teaching others is fraught with risk: Will they reinforce wrong concepts by teaching them? Will they take the task seriously enough to go deep into the subject matter? Who has the time to evaluate their teaching "products"?

The ubiquity of smartphones and of free and simple editing software makes the cost of crafting video extremely low. This offers an opportunity for a scalable approach in which students make videos that "teach" a topic, which can then be peer-studied in a manner similar to peer-graded writing. The trick is to design a protocol that has the right incentives to address the risks mentioned above. The goal of our project was to design and evaluate such a protocol, which has now been refined over two semesters. A learning assessment (a quiz) showed statistically significant gains in learning when applied to a module of an upper-level undergraduate algorithms course. The video assignment was one of many assignments in the course but the only one to focus on the topic of combinatorial optimization and NP-complete problems.

The protocol can be summarized as follows (details are given in Section 3). Students are placed in teams; each team is assigned a topic and tasked with crafting a video that explains the topic along with a number of required contextual aspects. Each student, independent of the video production team to which they are assigned, is also given a second topic to *study*. The "studiers" are given links to text material and required to watch the video produced by the team assigned their second (study) topic. Students under the production and study treatments are incentivized to learn the material to do well on a quiz, but if the docendo discimus theory holds, producers should do better. Furthermore, we expect producers to do better on the conceptually harder questions in the quiz.

The contributions of this paper are:

- The design and evaluation of a scalable protocol for engaging students to learn by teaching.
- Addressing incentives for students so that they put sufficient effort into their assignment both as producers and as studiers.
- A small learning study (N=89) that provides evidence supporting the approach.

Prior studies that examine the effectiveness of video in learning have focused on instructor-created videos [2, 3]. While some have examined student-generated videos, these tend to focus on either motivation or overall learning in the course, making it difficult to tease out the "I learned something deeply because I had to teach it" effect. Our study focused narrowly on this effect with statistically significant evidence in support of the approach.

Students received and carried out the project enthusiastically. This too aligns with studies [10, 11, 17, 21] that show greater student engagement with video and media, as well as studies that show

SIGCSE '18, Feb. 21–24, 2018, Baltimore, MD, USA

ACM ISBN 978-1-4503-5103-4/18/02...$15.00
https://doi.org/10.1145/3159450.3159466

increased engagement when students are given autonomy and opportunities to be creative [5, 27, 31].

2 RELATED WORK

Student-produced objects, and videos in particular, have been the subject of increased focus in pedagogical research. This is due in large part to the rise of active learning techniques and the growing accessibility of cheap recording and editing methods.

2.1 Student engagement

Kearney and Schuck [13] focused primarily on student and teacher perception of the potential of student-generated video to enhance the learning experience, particularly in the area of *authentic learning*, which they define as "learning in ways that fit with real world contexts". They found that the video projects helped motivate students, particularly if they knew that their classmates would be the target audience. In two follow-up studies [14, 27], they found clear evidence that student-generated video projects strongly enhanced their motivation and autonomy, and that allowing them to present in their own style, and the feeling of ownership this produced, were key factors in enhancing the learning process. They highlight the need for a well-designed project and the importance of the instructor's guidance when discussing the contents of the student presentations.

Several other studies found clear support for the benefits of student-produced videos on motivation, self-confidence, and engagement, and that they promoted the acquisition of technical and communication skills [5, 10, 11, 21]. Chi et al. [4] present empirical evidence of increased learning across four modes of learning activities and engagement behaviors:*interactive, constructive, active, or passive*, Under this framework, a team activity aimed at video production would appear to fall under the highest learning level.

While these studies demonstrate an overall improvement of student experience and the indirect learning benefits that come from student-produced videos, a key finding in some of these studies was a low level of conceptual development [27]. In the same vein, Pirhonen et al. [21] report a lack of evidence for improved learning.

2.2 Assessment

Another area of focus has been the use of the video-project as an assessment mechanism. This was mentioned in the work by Kearney and Schuck [27] as a key part of assessment strategies. An in-depth study by Murray et al. [18] determined, through the use of surveys, that the majority of students preferred video assessment over traditional methods like exams or reports. They underline the importance of having the instructor moderate any type of peer assessment to prevent any anxiety that might arise because of the prospect of judgment from their classmates. Walters et al. [29] implemented an assessment protocol using student videos, where they determined that it was an acceptable and even "pleasing" assessment method. They concluded that the effectiveness of learning environment can be enhanced by multimedia technology when using a learner-generated approach.

2.3 Improving conceptual learning

Studies disagree on whether or not student-produced videos promote an actual improvement in conceptual development. Little or no evidence was found in [21, 27]. Another study where this is supported is in the work by Draus et al. [6] where, despite there being an increase in perceived value from learned content, no measurable difference in student outcome was detected. On perceived value, Ryan et al. [26] report that students were uncertain about the effectiveness of the video projects on their learning.

On the other hand, in the work of Box et al. [1], they found small-to-large effects on the number of correct responses for laboratory quizzes. Willmott et al. [31] found statistically significant increase in scores of self-evaluation surveys measuring perceived improvements on learning. In the work by Brecht [2], it was determined that videos were used as tutorials, and that their application in classrooms improve initial learning, reduces dropout rates, and has a positive impact on course grades. Walters et al. [29] found that, when using video projects as an assessment tool, there was a substantial increase in passing grades as compared to written examinations. Greene et al. [11] found, through the use of surveys, that creating videos helps students reinforce concepts they have been exposed to in class. Roscoe et al. [23, 24] argue that two key activities to take advantage of knowledge-building opportunities are *self-explanation* and *peer-questioning*. A properly constructed team-based video-creation protocol would promote both of these key activities and contribute to conceptual learning.

2.4 Areas of application

The technique of having students create tutorial videos has been successfully applied in several areas, like history, science, language, media studies, marketing, distance learning, and more [6, 16, 27]. While some areas and classes lend themselves naturally to video presentation, others, like computer science and mathematics might appear to focus on subject matter inimical to this medium. This is not so, as evidenced by the work of [1, 15, 17, 18] which show clear positive effects of student-created projects in the areas of mathematics, aerospace engineering, information technology, and organic chemistry, respectively. In the work by Nordstrom and Korpelainen [19], it was pointed out that non-conventional tools like video can promote deep learning of scientific facts. For an in-depth report of active learning as a positive influence in science, engineering, and mathematics, see [8].

Student-produced videos may constitute a reusable peer learning resource [22, 26, 27]. While some content might not age well, the concepts taught in STEM courses are less likely to change over time due to the largely consistent nature of the material they present, which makes a large stock of conceptual videos a very useful long-term resource.

There is research supporting the use of active learning in computer science [8], and even the use of video-lectures as a valid resource [20], but there seems to be little work devoted to the effect on conceptual learning of student-produced video presentations in computer science. One of the few studies that looks into the use of videos in CS is the work by Gehringer and Miller [9], where they found an increase in student attentiveness, rather than increased conceptual learning.

3 METHODS AND EXPERIMENTAL DESIGN

3.1 The course

The video project was implemented in two successive offerings (2015, 2016) of an upper-level semester-long undergraduate algorithms course that featured both theory and programming. The course topics are fairly standard: searching, sorting, advanced data structures, graph algorithms, dynamic programming, combinatorial optimization, NP-complete problems, along with a few advanced topics. The course pedagogy included lectures interspersed with active-learning exercises, followed up with reinforcement through weekly homeworks and assignments. It is one of these assignments, focused on the topic of combinatorial optimization problems, that we reformulated for the video project.

3.2 Specific goals for the study

We designed this study with several specific goals in mind. First, we sought a scalable approach to allow its application to large classes, requiring modest additional effort on the part of the instructional team. Second, we wanted to devise a quiz that would measure whether students that produced a video demonstrated a significant improvement in the understanding of complex concepts. Third, we were also interested in finding a suitable way to exploit the potential of teamwork, especially in the crafting of videos.

3.3 The video-assignment protocol

At a high level, the following steps describe our approach.

- Students are divided into teams of three. In our case, we typically had 30-50 students per class.
- The instructor selects subtopics and assigns one subtopic to each team. We assigned a different NP-complete problem of similar structure and subject matter to each team.
- The instructor designs one assessment per subtopic, ideally with at least one challenging question to tease out whether the video-producing team really dug into the topic. This part is the most time-consuming for the instructor, but only needs to be done once and can be reused for future offerings.
- Each team is then given their subtopic and asked to produce an explanatory video that satisfies a list of criteria (which we describe below).
- Separate from the teams, each individual student is given one of the subtopics to *study*, ensuring that no student is given the same topic for both production and study. Thus, each subtopic has a producer and some "studiers." For any given subtopic, we provide links to reading materials for both producers and studiers. Conveniently, in our case, Wikipedia has a page on each NP-complete problem.
- Students are given a week to produce their videos. We also told students that they had to describe their sources (in an accompanying document), and to explain how each team member contributed. We informed them that, should it prove necessary, we would reserve the right to question any team member on any aspect of the video.
- After the videos are crafted, they are made available to the studiers. Everyone is asked to study both from the materials and the video for their assigned "study" subtopic.
- Finally, each student takes two quizzes: the first quiz is on the subtopic of their *production* while the second is on the subtopic of their *study*.
- Team points are assigned for the quality of video production, while individual points are given for performance on the quiz. This creates an incentive to spend enough time on crafting the video because the producing students realize that they can optimize by digging deep into their subtopic both for production points and study points. They also have an incentive to study for their assigned study subtopic.

All but two of the steps above scale with class size. The exceptions are the one-time effort needed for devising the quizzes, and the time needed for grading the videos. In the former case, several different teams in a large class can be assigned the same subtopic, perhaps with care taken to avoid publicizing which team is assigned which subtopic. For the latter, if instructional resources are not sufficient for video review, one could opt for peer-review of videos (each student is assigned some videos to review with a criteria-satisfying rubric), or use undergraduate learning assistants from students who have taken the course before.

In developing criteria for video production, we sought to achieve a balance between encouraging self-expression and originality, on the one hand, and avoiding confusion and wasted effort on irrelevant video effects. Prior work has highlighted the importance of this balance [21, 22, 27]. In particular, we wanted to avoid making the video project about learning new media skills. We therefore opted to let the students choose the method in which they recorded and presented the videos, as long as the following basic criteria were met:

- The video must contain a technical description of the problem as well as an explanation in plain English.
- A concrete example must be completely explained and solved.
- In addition to the formal technical explanation, the video should explain the application.
- The audio, video, and effects must be clearly understandable.
- The video must be no more than 10 to 15 minutes in length.

A duration of 10 to 15 minutes constitutes a reasonable compromise that allows for content completeness without risking a decrease in engagement and attention [12]. It also facilitates evaluation, since the videos have clear sections and a reasonable duration. In sum, this protocol is in alignment with principles on student-produced videos described in the literature [5, 13, 21, 27].

3.4 Design of study

The study was carried out in the 2015 and 2016 Fall semesters, with 39 and 50 students respectively, for a combined N=89 students. The NP-complete problems selected as subtopics were chosen to have a similar degree of complexity and so that each had an understandable application. Thus, problems like traveling salesman make sense whereas something in timed petri-nets would be too theoretical and require significant background.

Before being distributed to the studiers, the videos were reviewed for satisfying the criteria. A simple checklist was used for this purpose. In our study, all but a few submissions passed this step. For those that did not, students were given specific notes on any issues and how to address them before resubmitting. We did this so that there would be a level playing field for all the studiers.

Students were given the same number of days to study their assigned "study" subtopic as they were given to make a video for the "production" subtopic. Once available, students were given two days to study the video for their "study" subtopic (which was produced by another team). In accordance with the protocol, each student took two quizzes, the first on the subtopic assigned for production and the second on the subtopic assigned for study. Note that every subtopic was assigned as a production subtopic for one team, and assigned as a study subtopic for a different set of 2 or 3 students.

Each quiz consisted of four questions designed to gauge the level of understanding of the specifics of the problem and the context in which it was studied. It is very important to mention that all quizzes were designed to ask about the technical and high level concepts in the same way for all different subtopics, thus ensuring that no particular topic was more challenging than another.

Question one in each quiz was especially designed to assess deeper technical understanding. An example of one of the quizzes can be seen in Figure 1, in which the first question is the hardest one. Note that all the choices for this question contain language and terminology used in the correct definition of the problem, but only one does so correctly, and some of the others are deliberately misleading. The nature of the description is somewhat technical, so that only someone who understands the problem well enough can see the equivalence between the technical description in the choices and their assigned subtopic.

The second question relates the problem to the general area of combinatorial optimization. This requires the generalization of the elements of the problem as well as integration with the previous lectures on problem complexity and related categories of algorithms and problems. This is a free-form question in which three specific requirements need to be clearly stated for the answer to be complete. Partial credit was awarded.

Question 3 requires that the student understand the particulars of the problem scenario, as well as its possible application to an actual problem. This is a free-form question in which students may relate any examples presented in the video that explained it, or create a new problem instance from what they have learned. Partial credit was awarded.

Question 4 is another free-form question where the student is asked to pose a possible real-world application of the concepts surrounding the problem.

Questions 3 and 4 require the least amount of detailed technical knowledge, but both require the student to contextualize the concepts, reinforcing what Kearney and Schuck call *authentic learning* [13].

Data analysis consisted of gathering the per-question grades from each of the (N = 89) students in the *produced quiz* (taken by those who produced for that subtopic) and the *studied quiz* (taken by those who studied for that subtopic). These constituted a collection of paired samples of four questions per student.

In all but the first question, the Wilcoxon signed paired test [7] was used to statistically analyze the paired samples of the final grades. To implement the test, we used the *stats* package in R [28].

(1) Which of the descriptions below comes closest to describing the problem you were assigned?
   (a) Suppose U is a set of points $(x_1, y_1), \ldots, (x_n, y_n)$ in the plane. For each pair of points in the set, define the midpoint as the point exactly halfway in between. Any midpoint that's at most distance W from its end points is called a center, where W is a given bound in the problem. The goal is to compute the centers.
   (b) Suppose U is a set of points $(x_1, y_1), \ldots, (x_n, y_n)$ in the plane, and V is another set of points $(a_1, b_1), \ldots, (a_m, b_m)$. For each point x_i, y_i in U and a_j, b_j in V, let $d(i, j)$ denote the distance between the two points. For each such pair, let p, q denote the point halfway in between (the midpoint). We'll call this the center. The goal of the problem is to compute the centers.
   (c) Suppose U is a set of points $(x_1, y_1), \ldots, (x_n, y_n)$ in the plane, and V is another set of points $(a_1, b_1), \ldots, (a_m, b_m)$. A point p in the set V is called a center, if the distance from every point in U to the center is less than some given number W. The goal is to identify which of the points in V are centers.
   (d) Suppose U is a set of points $(x_1, y_1), \ldots, (x_n, y_n)$ in the plane, and V is another set of points $(a_1, b_1), \ldots, (a_m, b_m)$. For any point $p = (x_i, y_i)$ in U, let $f(p)$ denote the closest point in V to p, and $d(p)$ be the distance between p and $f(p)$. Define $D = \max_p f(p)$. The goal of the problem is, given a set U with n, find a set of m points V to minimize D.
(2) Explain how your problem is a combinatorial optimization problem. That is, explain why it satisfies the three requirements.
(3) Create an instance (example) of your problem, with a drawing or illustration where needed. Show a couple of candidate solutions where one solution is better.
(4) Write down a potential application for your problem.

Figure 1: Example quiz (Euclidean p-center problem)

To measure effect size, we use the standard z-score approximation [25] to Cohen's d measure: $d \approx r = \frac{z}{\sqrt{N}}$

Because Question 1 is scored either right or wrong, we use the McNemar test with Yate's continuity correction for binary paired data. This is performed using the *gmodels* package in R [7, 28, 30]. For the McNemar test, the conditional odds ratio $OR = \frac{c}{b}$ is used in place of an effect size, where b and c are the number of discordant pairs i.e., those where a negative or positive change occurred between treatments, respectively.

4 RESULTS

For the overall grades, as well as for questions 1−3 seen individually, there was a statistically significant improvement (those marked with a $*$) when going from the study to the production treatment. A summary of results can be seen in Table 1. Because Question 1 is binary, its results are analyzed separately. Given that these are paired tests between the video-production and the study treatments, the data can be arranged by the change from one treatment to another. The paired results can be seen in table 2.

Table 1: Summary of results

Question	Test	Statistic	P	effect size
1	McNemar	6.283	0.0061*	0.44
2	Wilcoxon	978	0.001*	-0.35
3	Wilcoxon	677	0.03337*	-0.23
4	Wilcoxon	22	0.57	NA
Full	Wilcoxon	705	<0.0001*	-0.43

Table 2: Q1 Contingency Table (numbers represent pairs)

		Produced		
		Correct	Incorrect	Total
Studied	Correct	a=26	**b=14**	40
	Incorrect	**c=32**	d=17	49
	Total	58	31	89

For the first question, the ratio of correct responses went from $40/89 \approx 45\%$ to $58/89 \approx 65\%$, with an odds ratio of $OR = 0.438$. A student that prepares for Question 1 by producing a video has his or her odds of getting a correct answer increased by 44%. For Question 2, we found a statistically significant improvement ($P = 0.001$) from the study treatment (median of 90%, mean of 78.5% with a $SD = 25.9\%$) to the video production treatment (median of 90%, mean of 85.5% with a $SD = 21.9\%$) and an effect size of $r = -0.349$, which is considered to be a small-to-medium effect size. In Question 3, we found a statistically significant improvement ($P = 0.03337$) from the study treatment (median of 100%, mean of 83.4% with a $SD = 27.2\%$) to the video production treatment (median of 100%, mean of 88.7% with a $SD = 22.4\%$) with an effect size of $r = -0.225$, which is considered to be a small effect size. In Question 4, we found that there was no statistically significant improvement between treatments.

When looking at the overall grades, we found a statistically significant improvement ($P < 0.0001$) from the study treatment (mean of 75.5% with a $SD = 20.9\%$) to the video production treatment (mean of 84.1% with a $SD = 16.3\%$) with an effect size of $r = -0.429$, which is considered to be a small-to-medium effect size. The Box plots for questions 2, 3 and the full quiz can be seen in Figure 2. A boxplot for Question 1 is not included because the data is binary.

The type of question plays a role in the magnitude of the improvement that was obtained. Figure 3 shows the improvement obtained per question.

5 DISCUSSION

By design, Question 1 required the deepest knowledge of the problem. The distractors (wrong choices) were very similarly worded so that choosing the wrong option was likely if students were hazy on the details of the problem and the interplay of its parts. The fact that it was graded as all-or-nothing meant that the effect this question had on the overall quiz grade was large. It is important to consider this possibility of confusion when considering the results of Table 2. Many of the possible errors might come from simply misreading the options. Even when considering these type of errors, the increase in the ratio of correct answers, as well as the fact that we are considering paired samples, allows us to conclude that there

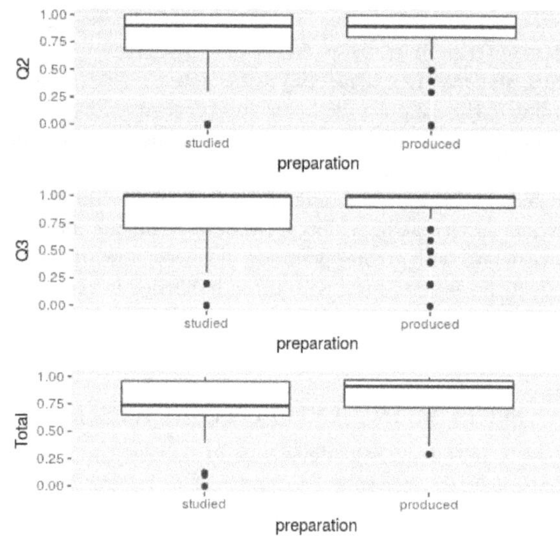

Figure 2: Box plot for Questions 2, 3 and the overall grade

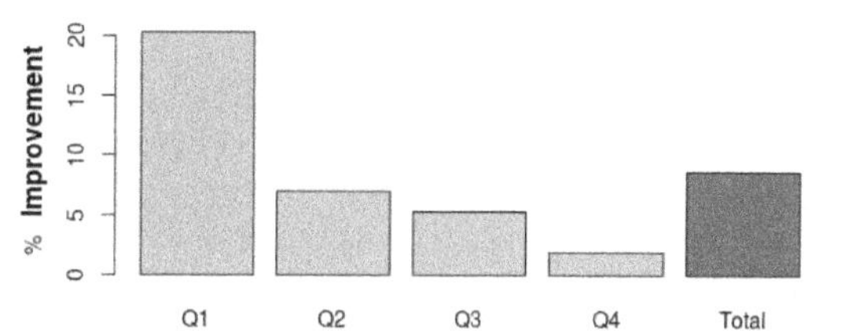

Figure 3: Grade improvement per question

is a clear improvement in the student performance while under the video production treatment.

The remaining questions were considered to be easier because it was possible to get a fair amount of partial credit by being able to contextualize the problem and relate it to real-world scenarios. Questions 2, 3, and 4 move away from the details and into high level understanding of the problem in its context. Students had a much easier time doing those, which is evidenced by the high medians obtained in these questions (100% in both studied and produced treatments). In all but the most general question (Question 4), a clear advantage was noticed for those students that produced a video. It is worth noting, that for questions 2, 3 and for the full quiz grade, the quantiles are tighter for produced-video treatment. This points to more consistent results for producers than for the study treatment. We believe that group work plays a part in this reduced grade variance. One explanation for this effect is that, along with the positive effects on individual performance, collaboration provides an environment in which to compare and corroborate ideas, which reduces the possibility of maintaining misconceptions and hazy notions. A higher and closer grade range also opens the possibility of using the group average as a grade for all students, which could potentially motivate a fair division of work, and allow for the application of this protocol to larger teams.

We think that the reason that Question 4 showed no improvement between treatments is due to the fact that it was the most general question and it allowed for basic/general knowledge of the problem to result in a greater chance of a high grade.

Thus, *students do considerably better when producing a video*, according to the data. We think that this is because the production of the instructional video requires the grounding of a multitude of concepts as well as their integration into a wider theoretical context, which aids in the understanding of the particulars with respect to the whole as well as providing a framework for the memory to retrieve details with greater precision. It is worth mentioning that the effect size is consistent with those published in earlier meta-analyses in the area of active learning for sciences, engineering and mathematics [8].

6 CONCLUSIONS AND FUTURE WORK

This study found statistical evidence to support the claim that student-produced videos provide significant improvements in terms of learning retention, contextualizing, and applying of theoretical concepts in the field of computer science. We also noted that there was less variability in response qualities for both specific and context-related questions.

A careful description of the project, as well as continued guidance is important to maintain video-content correctness and quality. We found that allowing students to express themselves through various modes of presentation and styles did not hinder the effort, and in fact, might have made the whole experience more memorable. This has the added benefit that a large amount of tailor-made stock footage of good quality can be accessed by future classes. The protocol described here can be replicated with very little overhead because most of the required knowledge and equipment is provided by the students themselves. This allows for a scalable procedure that can improve student engagement and attitudes, and has a considerably positive effect on the quality of the initial knowledge retention and its relation to the theoretical context.

Since this protocol is group-based by design, in the future, we would like to differentiate the production of videos from the precise effects of team collaboration on improvement. Additionally, we would like to refine the protocol to further tighten intra-team variation. Lastly, we would also like to explore the long-term benefits of this approach by surveying previous generations.

REFERENCES

[1] Melinda C. Box, Cathi L. Dunnagan, Lauren A.S. Hirsh, Clinton R. Cherry, Kayla A. Christianson, Radiance J. Gibson, Michael I. Wolfe, and Maria T. Gallardo-Williams. 2017. Qualitative and Quantitative Evaluation of Three Types of Student-Generated Videos as Instructional Support in Organic Chemistry Laboratories. *Journal of Chemical Education* 94, 2 (2017), 164–170. https://doi.org/10.1021/acs.jchemed.6b00451

[2] H David Brecht. 2012. Learning from Online Video Lectures. *Journal of Information Technology Education* 11 (2012), 227–250.

[3] MC Carlisle. 2010. Using YouTube to enhance student class preparation in an introductory Java course. In *Proceedings of the 41st ACM technical symposium on Computer science education.* 1–5. https://doi.org/10.1145/1734263.1734419

[4] Michelene T.H. Chi and Ruth Wylie. 2014. The ICAP Framework: Linking Cognitive Engagement to Active Learning Outcomes. *Educational Psychologist* 49, 4 (2014), 219–243. https://doi.org/10.1080/00461520.2014.965823

[5] Jo Clemmons and Ray Posey. 2016. Creating Dynamic Learning through Student-Created Video Projects. *Currents in Teaching & Learning* 8, 2 (2016).

[6] Peter J Draus, Michael J Curran, and Melinda S Trempus. 2014. The Influence of Instructor-Generated Video Content on Student Satisfaction with and Engagement in Asynchronous Online Classes. 10, 2 (2014), 240–255.

[7] Andy Field, Jeremy Miles, and Zoe Field. 2012. *Discovering statistics using R.*

[8] Scott Freeman, Sarah L Eddy, Miles McDonough, Michelle K Smith, Nnadozie Okoroafor, Hannah Jordt, and Mary Pat Wenderoth. 2014. Active learning increases student performance in science, engineering, and mathematics. *Proceedings of the National Academy of Sciences of the United States of America* 111, 23 (2014), 8410–5. https://doi.org/10.1073/pnas.1319030111 arXiv:arXiv:1408.1149

[9] Edward F Gehringer and Carolyn S Miller. 2009. Student-generated active-learning exercises. In *ACM SIGCSE Bulletin*, Vol. 41. ACM, 81–85.

[10] Caroline Rosenthal Gelman and Carol Tosone. 2006. Making it real: Enhancing curriculum delivery through the use of student-generated training videos. *Journal of Technology in Human Services* 24, 1 (2006), 37–52.

[11] Henry Greene and Cheryl Crespi. 2012. The value of student created videos in the college classroom - an exploratory study in marketing and accounting. *International Journal of Arts and Sciences* 5, 1 (2012), 273–283.

[12] Philip J Guo, Juho Kim, and Rob Rubin. 2014. How Video Production Affects Student Engagement: An Empirical Study of MOOC Videos. (2014). https://doi.org/10.1145/2556325.2566239

[13] Matthew Kearney and Sandy Schuck. 2004. Authentic learning through the use of digital video. In *Proceedings of the Australian Computers in Education Conference.* 1–7.

[14] Matthew Kearney and Sandy Schuck. 2005. Students in the director's seat: Teaching and learning with student-generated video. In *EdMedia: World Conference on Educational Media and Technology.* Association for the Advancement of Computing in Education (AACE), 2864–2871.

[15] Adeel Khalid. 2014. Use of Student Generated Videos to Enhance Teaching Quality in Aerospace Engineering Classes. In *ASEE Southeast Section Conference American Society for Engineering Education.*

[16] Wolfram Laaser and Eduardo A Toloza. 2017. The Changing Role of the Educational Video in Higher Distance Education. *International Review of Research in Open and Distributed Learning* 18, 2 (2017).

[17] Jill Lazarus and Geoffrey Roulet. 2013. Creating a YouTube-Like Collaborative Environment in Mathematics: Integrating Animated Geogebra Constructions and Student-Generated Screencast Videos. *European Journal of Contemporary Education* 4, 2 (2013), 117–128.

[18] David E Murray, Tanya J McGill, Danny Toohey, and Nik Thompson. 2017. Can Learners Become Teachers? Evaluating the Merits of Student Generated Content and Peer Assessment. *Issues in Informing Science and Information Technology* 14 (2017), 021–033.

[19] Katrina Nordstrom and Päivi Korpelainen. 2011. Creativity and inspiration for problem solving in engineering education. *Teaching in Higher Education* 16, 4 (2011), 439–450.

[20] Chaohua Ou. 2016. Designing Videos with Pedagogical Strategies : Online Students ' Perceptions of Their Effectiveness. *Proceedings of the Third ACM Conference on Learning @ Scale* (2016), 141–144. https://doi.org/10.1145/2876034.2893391

[21] Juhani Pirhonen and Päivi Rasi. 2017. Student-generated instructional videos facilitate learning through positive emotions. *Journal of Biological Education* 9266, August (2017), 1–13. https://doi.org/10.1080/00219266.2016.1200647

[22] Annie Prud'homme-Genereux. 2014. Student-Produced Videos for the Flipped Classroom. *Journal of College Science Teaching* 45, 3 (2014), 58–62.

[23] Rod D Roscoe. 2014. Self-monitoring and knowledge-building in learning by teaching. *Instructional Science* 42, 3 (2014), 327–351. https://doi.org/10.1007/s11251-013-9283-4

[24] Rod D Roscoe and Michelene T H Chi. 2007. Understanding Tutor Learning: Knowledge-Building and Knowledge-Telling in Peer Tutors' Explanations and Questions. *Review of Educational Research* 77, 4 (2007), 534–574. https://doi.org/10.3102/0034654307309920

[25] Robert Rosenthal. 1991. *Meta-analytic procedures for social research.* Vol. 6. Sage.

[26] Barry J. Ryan. 2013. A Walk Down the Red Carpet : Students as Producers of Digital Video-Based Knowledge . *International Journal of Technology Enhanced Learning* 5 (2013), 24–41. https://doi.org/10.1504/IJTEL.2013.055950

[27] Sandy Schuck and Matthew Kearney. 2006. Capturing learning through student-generated digital video. *Australian Educational Computing* 21, 1 (2006), 15–20.

[28] R Core Team. 2017. *R: A Language and Environment for Statistical Computing.* R Foundation for Statistical Computing, Vienna, Austria. https://www.R-project.org/

[29] Simon R Walters, Julia Hallas, Sean Phelps, and Erika Ikeda. 2015. Enhancing the Ability of Students to Engage With Theoretical Concepts Through the Creation of Learner-Generated Video Assessment. (2015), 102–112.

[30] Gregory R. Warnes, Ben Bolker, Thomas Lumley, Randall C Johnson. Contributions from Randall C. Johnson are Copyright SAIC-Frederick, Inc. Funded by the Intramural Research Program, of the NIH, National Cancer Institute, and Center for Cancer Research under NCI Contract NO1-CO-12400. 2015. gmodels: Various R Programming Tools for Model Fitting. (2015). https://CRAN.R-project.org/package=gmodels R package version 2.16.2.

[31] Christopher J R Willmott. 2015. Teaching bioethics via the production of student-generated videos. *Journal of Biological Education* 49, 2 (2015), 127–138. https://doi.org/10.1080/00219266.2014.897640

Two-Stage Programming Projects: Individual Work Followed by Peer Collaboration

Lina Battestilli
North Carolina State University
lbattestilli@ncsu.edu

Apeksha Awasthi
North Carolina State University
aawasth@ncsu.edu

Yingjun Cao
University of California, San Diego
yic242@eng.ucsd.edu

ABSTRACT

Programming projects are widely used in CS1 classes to develop students' coding skills. To improve the learning impact of these projects, we propose and study a special project format named two-stage project in an introductory computer science course. For the first stage, students submit their programming projects individually followed by a second stage where they are paired to work on the same project in order to create an improved solution. Through peer collaboration, students review each other's work from the first stage, and write correctly-styled, well-documented, and more thoroughly tested code during the second stage. We used isomorphic assessments before and after the second stage of a project to measure students' understanding of the course material. Results indicate that two-stage projects tend to improve student understanding of course learning objectives. We also studied students' perceptions and experiences with two-stage projects, and their confidence toward computing. Students liked working on two-stage projects because they saw new ways to approach the same problem, and they liked discussions with their peers.

CCS CONCEPTS

• **Applied computing → Collaborative learning**; • **Social and professional topics → Computing education**; **CS1**;

KEYWORDS

CS1; Two-Stage Project; Collaborative Project; Peer Collaboration

ACM Reference Format:
Lina Battestilli, Apeksha Awasthi, and Yingjun Cao. 2018. Two-Stage Programming Projects: Individual Work Followed by Peer Collaboration. In *SIGCSE '18: SIGCSE '18: The 49th ACM Technical Symposium on Computer Science Education, February 21–24, 2018, Baltimore , MD, USA.* ACM, New York, NY, USA, 6 pages. https://doi.org/10.1145/3159450.3159486

1 INTRODUCTION

Providing constructive and detailed feedback on assignments is an essential part of student learning across different areas [2, 10]. Feedback in introductory computer science courses, however, tends to be automated due to the surging enrollment [6, 12]. Typically, students are provided a grade and some feedback but don't have a chance to remedy any issues with their work before moving on to the next assignment. In other words, students do not submit a corrected second version of the assignment thus limiting the impact of assignments on their learning. This is an important problem because learning how to program is often difficult for students and leads to high attrition rates in the first-year computer science courses [26].

One approach to remedy this problem is to use individual two-stage submissions where students turn in the assignment and receive instructor's feedback instead of a grade, then students address the feedback, and resubmit the assignment for a final grade [25]. Another approach is to allow students to first work alone and then in groups [3, 23].

For this study, we adopt the collaboration approach of two-stage submissions of programming projects. For the first stage, students work alone on the project and are given an individual grade and feedback. For the second stage, students address the feedback with an individual reflection, then peer review each other's code and re-submit a pair-coded version of the project. The second-stage group submissions are graded again and this new grade potentially could increase students' final grade for the project.

Often, when students are paired together, they tend to copy from each other instead of discussing the material and together coming up with a solution [19]. To address this issue, we paired students who received similar individual grades on the first stage of the project so that they had to work together to improve the code of their projects. This technique worked well because students like when the instructor creates the pairs rather than self-selection [13]. To assess whether students made learning gains after the two-stage pair-coding, we administered pre and post assessments using isomorphic questions as described in [14].

In summary, we explore the effects of two-stage programming projects in an introductory CS1 course. We focus on the following two research questions:

- **RQ1.** What are the impacts of two-stage programming projects on students' learning of the course material?
- **RQ2.** What are the students' experiences with and attitudes toward two-stage projects?

2 BACKGROUND

Introductory programming courses can be difficult for students because many students come with the preconception that learning how to program can be very hard. Students also fear poor performance in the course due to lack of prior experience. In recent years, however, the interest in computer science has significantly increased the number of students enrolling in CS1 courses. Unfortunately, this leads to large size classes where an instructor's individual feedback is often limited [25]. **Pair programming** and

SIGCSE '18, February 21–24, 2018, Baltimore , MD, USA

ACM ISBN 978-1-4503-5103-4/18/02...$15.00
https://doi.org/10.1145/3159450.3159486

peer code review can be used to provide students with extra feedback from their peers on programming assignments. Studies have shown that the learning outcomes are greater when they have the opportunity to review other students' assignments [15, 20]. Students who pair program are more likely to choose Computer Science as their major [28] and show higher rates of retention and a higher promise of succeeding in future courses in which they would have to work alone [16]. When working in groups, students become more confident in their work and find it more enjoyable. They benefit from communication with their peers and might even make new friends.

Metacognition is another way to help students benefit from grading feedback via individual reflections after each assignment. Metacognition is the process of analyzing whether a goal has been met or what a person could do to meet it. Students that develop their metacognitive skills tend to have more academic success [5]. Exam wrappers have been used in multiple studies to encourage metacognition by asking students to reflect on their study habits and what topics they still need to master [7, 24] though its impact is questionable. Often, students get their grades for assignments but don't even look at the feedback to evaluate what they might have done wrong or what they could do to improve [1]. Metacognition can help students develop **Growth Mindset**, the thinking that one's intelligence level and ability to learn is not fixed [9, 11] but rather it is possible to improve it. Students with Growth Mindset are more likely to succeed than those with Fixed Mindset.

In our study we use two-stage submissions of projects. The two-stage idea is also used in **Peer Instruction (PI)**, which is a student-centric pedagogy where students move from the role of passive listeners to active participants. Recently, there has been significant research regarding the value of PI in computer science [17, 18, 21]. In PI, students answer each question individually in the first stage. In the second stage, students discuss with their peers in a small group and come up with a group answer. Typically, PI is used during lectures with clicker questions to engage students in the two-stages.

Another application of the two-stage idea is **Two-Stage Exams** where the students take some parts of a test individually and other parts in small groups. The group portion of the test improved students' knowledge on the topic in the short term [3]. The benefits of two-stage exams have also been explored across other fields as well such as physiology [4], physics [22], etc.

Our study builds upon **PI**, **two-stage exams**, **pair programming**, **code review** and **reflections**. We extend the two-stage concept of working individually and then collaboratively on programming projects in an introductory computer science course. To the best of our knowledge, this is a first study of two-stage projects in CS1.

3 METHOD

Three sections of a CS1 class in Java at a large public university participated in this study during spring 2017. This course is the first programming course that students take in the computer science major, and it is also taken by other majors. The course learning objectives include basic programming (variables, data types, loops, conditionals, methods) and introductory object-oriented concepts. One section was the experimental section, and there were two control sections. Students in the experimental section were given the opportunity to participate in two-stage projects while students in the control sections were not. Each section had 29 students with a total enrollment of 87. However, 2 students from the experimental section and 15 students from the control sections did not consent to this research. One of the authors of this paper is the instructor of the experimental section while the control sections were taught by a different instructor.

The course has six programming projects, two tests, a final exam, and other low-weight formative assignments. In this study, we focus on the programming projects which were the same across all three sections and were written by a third instructor who is the overall course coordinator. The grading rubric and guidelines for the projects were identical across all sections of the course.

In the experimental section, 33.3% of students were females while 66.7% were male students; 40% were freshman, 40% were sophomores, and 20% were seniors; 33.3% were computer science majors, 33.3% being other STEM majors, and 33.3% were undecided.

3.1 Experimental Design

Students in this CS1 course normally work on programming projects and submit them individually. To implement the second stage for projects and to evaluate its impact on student learning, we added the components shown in Figure 1.

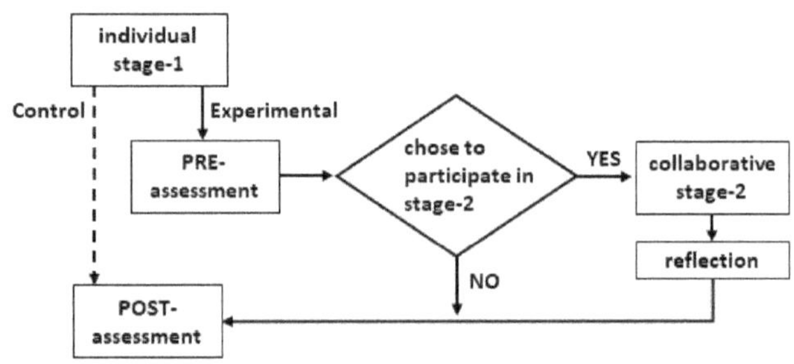

Figure 1: Flowchart for the experiment.

Stage-1(S1) Individually-coded Project: In the first stage, students were to complete and submit the project individually. The first stage submissions were graded, and the students were given feedback.

Stage-2(S2) Pair-coded Project: The second stage of the project was completed by students in pairs. This stage was optional in the experimental section. Students chose to do it or not after they had completed the first stage of a project. When students signed up to do the second stage, they did not know their grades for the first stage. Students had to submit a form where they agreed to be a contributing partner for the second stage. Second stage participants were told that if they were not a helpful partner then they would not be given the opportunity to participate in the second stage on future projects. Partners were assigned by the instructor based on students' grades in the first stage of the project. Students with similar grades were paired together. This was done so they can work together to improve their grades. However, if a student got a failing grade, then they were paired with someone who got a high grade. The purpose for this is that the student with the failing grade can see a good solution for the project. The two partners were to work on the project together and submit an improved pair-coded version of the project together.

Pre-Assessment (PRE_A) and Post-Assessment ($POST_A$): These assessments were short isomorphic quizzes that each student had to take individually. The pre-assessment was given before the second stage and measured students' baseline knowledge level at the end of the first stage. The pre-assessment was taken only by the students in the experimental section. The post-assessment was taken by all the students in the experimental and the two control sections. For the 2-stage participants, the results from the pre and post-assessments allowed us to measure their learning after pair-coding and discussion with a partner. The post-assessment results allowed us to compare the learning of the students that did participate in the second stage and those that didn't. The assessments had one or two questions based on the learning objectives of the project. The pre-assessment was given the day after the first stage was submitted and the post-assessment was generally given the day after the second stage was submitted.

Isomorphic Questions in Pre/Post Assessments were used to measure any potential learning changes for both control and experimental groups [14, 19]. The isomorphic property of the questions was independently validated by another experienced instructor from another institution. One sample question in the second project's pre-assessment is included in Figure 2. The content assessed is Java Graphics object and user input via console window.

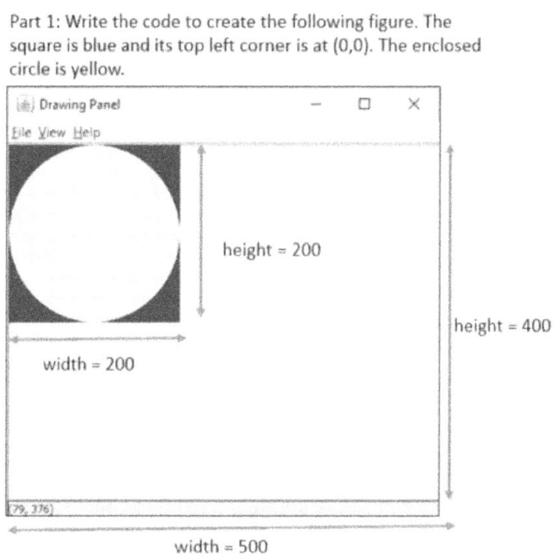

Figure 2: Sample Pre-Assessment Question

Reflections(RE): Students who signed up for the second stage were also encouraged to complete an individual reflection about their experience. They were asked to reflect on where they had lost points, how they had managed the individual completion, and about their experience of working with a partner during the second stage. Most of the reflections consisted of open ended questions, except the project management part which consisted of 5-point Likert-scale statements. Students were asked if they attended office hours, posted on the course's forum, planned to start the next project earlier, etc. In other words, students reflected on their strategy of completing the first stage of the project and were given some ideas on how they can perform better for the next project.

Grade Calculation: In the experimental section, for students who participated in the second stage, a new grade was calculated which replaced their stage one project grade only if it increased their grade. The final project grade was calculated using the following formula:

$$FinalGrade = S1 + (S2 - S1) * 0.3 + RE * 0.01$$
$$(PRE_A + POST_A)/2 * 0.02$$

This formula gives students 30% of the point difference between stage-one and stage-two. Also, a very small percentage was given for completing the assessments and the reflections. The reason for this is that we did not want the project grades to be too inflated based on the additional work, but we wanted to give these components some weight as an incentive for students to complete them well.

3.2 Projects

The learning topics of the six programming projects are shown in Table 1.

Table 1: Descriptions of the six projects in the course.

Project	Topics Addressed
1	For loops and Java classes for text-based output to the Console Window
2	Loops and Java classes for text-based inputs/outputs; selection logic with if/else statements; static methods; graphics/basic animation
3	While loops; using Java classes for text based input/output; methods with multiple parameters and return; unit tests.
4	Reading/writing to files; loops; writing methods and using Java classes
5	Construct and use one and two dimensional arrays; arrays of objects
6	Object-Oriented Design; Writing Classes that drive a GUI

For each project, students typically submitted source files, structure diagrams, black box and unit tests. The project grading rubric took into account implementation, Javadoc documentation, correctness of structure diagram and teaching staff tests. Projects were graded and feedback was provided to students as to why they lost points if they did. The due dates for these projects were spaced about every two weeks. This created a tight timeline for this study where students were generally given about three days to work on stage-two before they had to start working individually on the next project. We were able to implement the two-stage setup only for the first five projects since the sixth project's due date was at the end of the semester.

3.3 End-of-Semester Survey and Focus Group

At the end of the semester students were given a survey inquiring about their experiences with two-stage projects. The survey also asked questions about confidence and attitude toward computing which were pulled from existing surveying instruments [8, 27]. Students who had participated in the second stage of projects were asked what they did or didn't like about the second stage. Otherwise, students were asked why they had not chosen to participate in any of the second stages of the projects.

For richer qualitative results, we also held a 30-minute focus group with students from the experimental section. This was done at the end of the semester after final course grades were submitted. The focus group was facilitated by an undergraduate research assistant. Students were asked about how two-stage projects might have affected their attitude and confidence towards the course material and what they did and didn't like.

4 RESULTS

4.1 Learning The Course Material (RQ1)

Figure 3 shows the pre/post assessment scores of the two-stage project participants in the experimental section. There is an improvement from the pre-assessment to the post-assessment on all the projects except for Project 4. Two-sample U-test was used, and no statistical significance was observed.

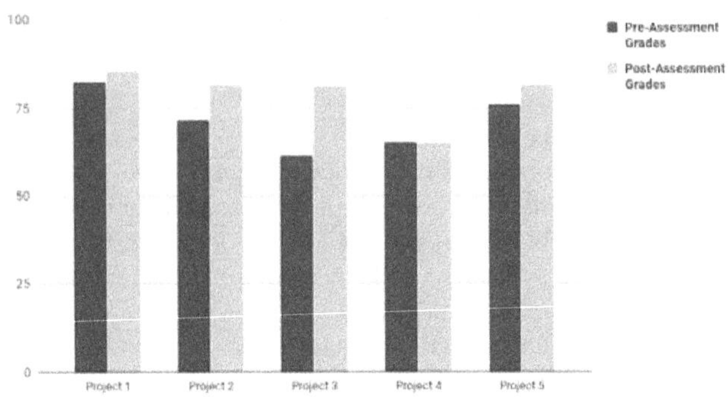

Figure 3: Average pre/post-assessment grades of the stage-two participants from the experimental section. Project 1: n=13; Project 2: n=13; Project 3: n=13; Project 4: n=14; Project 5: n=9

The post-assessment scores for the students that participated in the second stage from the experimental section and those that did NOT participate from both the experimental and two control sections are compared in Figure 4. Students that did not participate in the second stage scored lower on every project. Two-sample U-tests were used, and Project 1 showed a significant difference between the second stage participants (μ_{post}=91.80%, N=13) and the non-participants (μ_{post} = 67.56%, N=75) with p=.003 and a large effect size as .97. No other projects showed statistical significance. Data was not collected for Project 3 from the control sections due to scheduling issues.

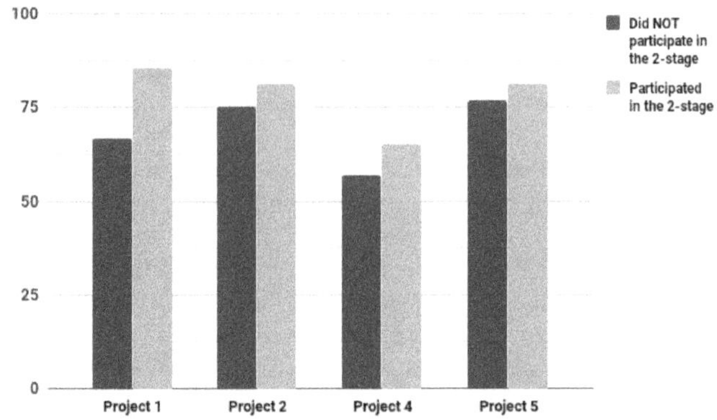

Figure 4: Average post-assessment grades for students that did and did not participate in the second stage. Project 1: n_{exp} =13; n_{ctrl} = 75;Project 2: n_{exp} = 13, n_{ctrl}=74, Project 4: n_{exp} = 14, n_{ctrl} = 68, Project 5: n_{exp} = 9, n_{ctrl} = 56

4.2 Students Experiences (RQ2)

End-Of-Semester Survey Results: Data from the survey (see Section 3.3) provided an insight on how students felt about the two-stage projects. There was 100% response rate as the survey was administered during class time. 77% of the students in the experimental section participated in at least one two-stage projects. The result from the open ended survey question about students' experience is shown in Table 2.

Table 2: Stage-two participants on what they did or didn't like about the two-stage projects

Answer	Number Students
Showed me a different perspective	6
Helped me understand my errors	3
Helped me understand difficult material	3
Time was very limited	3
Didn't help me	2
Helped the other person, but not me	2
My code didn't need any improvement	2
Partner wanted points, but didn't want to talk about concepts	2
Did not provide an answer	2
Didn't like being randomly paired	1

Table 2 was coded using an open coding approach. One coder went through the data and came up with the initial themes and then a second coder confirmed and refined them. Many students showed Growth Mindset and felt that working with a partner in stage-two helped them learn. However, there were students who simply focused on grades rather than learning. Also, some students that chose to participate in stage-two already had good grades on stage-one and thus chose not to submit new code for stage-two.

Students who did not participate in any stage-two of the projects were also surveyed on the reasons why. These students mainly chose not to participate in stage-two because of the limited time allotted to work with a partner or they felt they had done well-enough on stage-one. In this particular experiment, the tight schedule was necessary because projects were due approximately every two weeks. There were eight sections of this CS1 course taught at the institution, and all sections had to complete the same projects so that all students develop the same practical skills before moving to CS2.

Reflections Results: The data from individual student reflections revealed that as projects became harder, the time the students spent on stage-one increased from less than 3 hours to 8 or more hours, while the time that students spent on stage-two stayed around 1-2 hours. 83.7% of students felt that working with a partner in stage-two was a good experience, they received help, saw a different perspective and reviewed someone else's code. The rest of students reported that stage-two didn't help them because their grade was already good enough, their partner didn't respond or they were tight on time.

We also asked two-stage participants of each project to reflect on their performance in stage-one, and the results are shown in Table 3. For Project 2 and 4, all of the two-stage participants submitted a reflection and most lost points due to style and wrong functionality. As the projects got more complex, points were also lost due to incorrect or incomplete black box and unit testing.

Table 3: Stage-two participants on why they lost points or what they did not understand in Stage-one of each project.

Answer	P1	P2	P3	P4	P5
Did not loose points	2	2	3	1	0
Style/Javadoc	5	6	1	5	6
Wrong functionality/Output	0	7	0	9	6
Wrong structure diagram	0	2	0	1	1
Testing	0	2	0	5	1
Num of Completed Reflections	7	14	4	12	5
Num of two-stage Participants	13	14	14	12	7

Focus Group Results: As described in Section 3.3, we held a focus group and asked questions pertaining to students experiences and attitudes towards two-stage projects. The audio recorded from the focus group was transcribed via a third party and then open theme coded. Students' answers reinforced some of the findings from the survey. Students expressed that the two-stage projects helped them see new ways to approach a problem. One student said two-stages projects helped them see more efficient ways to solve the same problem. Students also enjoyed the two-stage projects because it opened communication with their peers. The time-constraint was their biggest challenge with stage two. Students also did not like the automated and limited feedback from stage-one. If paired students for stage-two had failed the same exact teaching staff test case in stage-one, then they did not know what the problem was and how to fix it before stage-two.

In the focus group, we found that students felt that their attitudes didn't change very much throughout the semester. They had started the semester with an open and conscientious attitude towards programming, and two-stage projects played no role in their attitudes. Students expressed that their confidence in the course material had significantly improved because they either had no experience before the course or felt that the course improved their understanding of the material. Students agreed that two-stage projects overall helped them have more confidence in explaining their own code.

5 DISCUSSION

This study is an attempt to scaffold Peer Instruction, Pair Programming, and Peer Code review to produce a meaningful impact on student learning. Figure 3 shows that students in general performed better after the second stage of the project. Due to the small sample sizes, no statistical significance was observed. However, the general trend of higher post assessment scores in four out of five projects tends to indicate a positive impact of this project format on its participants.

Figure 4 indicates that second stage participants tend to outperform the non-participants in all four projects. Though only one statistical significance was observed, the overall trend again shows a promising impact of the collaborative second stage.

We also examined which students chose to participate in the second stage of projects based on their average test grades (Figure 5). A

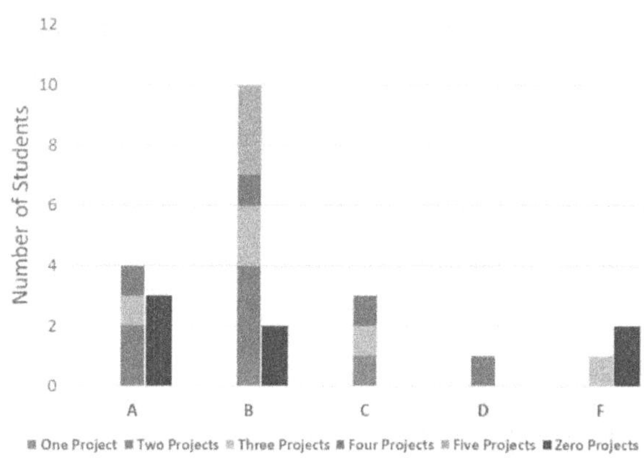

Figure 5: The distribution of number of two-stage projects students completed against the their average test grade

weak positive correlation ($r = 0.173$) was observed between these two factors. There were two tests and a final exam taken individually by students. Thus those grades weren't affected by external factors like extra credit and were a good indicator of the students' understanding of the course material. From the 12 students that got Bs, only 2 did not participate in the second-stage of a project, and 3 of them participated in all five second-stages. This might indicate that these students were determined to get a better mastery of the subject. Interestingly, 4 students with As chose not to participate in any of the second-stage. Most likely, that is because these students were probably confident in their skills and did not think the collaborative discussion of the second stage will have a benefit for them. The Cs and Ds chose to participate in at least some of the second stage. We conjecture that this group benefits the most from reviewing and discussing code with their partner in the second stage of one project before moving to the first stage of the next project. Therefore, it might be better to make the second-stage of the projects mandatory rather than optional. This could improve the learning of lower grade students. It is also important to highlight to the A students the benefits for participating in the second stage. One better retains knowledge when they teach or explain it to another person. The reason we made stage-two optional during our experiment is because we wanted the assigned partners to be both willing and eager to work together and create a better pair-coded project solution.

5.1 Threats to Validity

The experimental group and control group were taught by two different instructors, which could affect the results of the assessments. However, the learning gains before/after stage-two for the control section alone indicate the advantage of this intervention. Another threat to this study is the lack of statistical significance, and we hypothesize that it is most likely due to the small sample size. The overall pattern is promising. Finally, the opt-in to participate in the second stage might also impact the results. If all students were asked to participate in the second stage, that would add more confidence in the reported learning gains.

6 CONCLUSION

This study examined the effects of two-stage programming projects on students' understanding of the course material and their attitude and confidence towards programming and computer science. Students showed improvement in their learning and enjoyed working with a partner on the second stage. Two-stage projects, however, had little effect on students' attitudes or confidences toward computing. Further studies are needed to determine the effects of longer timeline for the students to complete stage-two and determine how to provide more detailed feedback to the students for stage-one. We recommend the stage-two projects be made mandatory rather than optional to encourage students to adapt to a Growth Mindset, review others' code, and practice working with partners. We plan to extend this work by also comparing 2-stage submission of projects individually rather than in pairs. This will help answer the question whether the learning benefits are due to the multiple submission stages or the peer work.

ACKNOWLEDGMENTS

The authors would like to thank Dr. Jessica Schmidt, for running the experiment in the control sections and providing the data.

REFERENCES

[1] Randy Elliot Bennett. 2011. Formative assessment: a critical review. *Assessment in Education: Principles, Policy & Practice* 18, 1 (2011), 5–25.
[2] Paul Black. 1998. Formative assessment: raising standards inside the classroom. *School Science Review* 80, 291 (1998), 39–46.
[3] Yingjun Cao and Leo Porter. 2017. Evaluating Student Learning from Collaborative Group Tests in Introductory Computing. In *SIGCSE 2017*. 99–104.
[4] R. N. Cortright, H. L. Collins, D. W. Rodenbaugh, and S. E. Dicarlo. 2003. Student Retention Of Course Content Is Improved By Collaborative-Group Testing. *AJP: Advances in Physiology Education* 27, 3 (2003), 102–108.
[5] Savia Coutinho. 2007. The relationship between goals, metacognition, and academic success. *Educate* 7, 1 (2007).
[6] CRA. [n. d.]. Computing Research Association, The Taulbee Survey. ([n. d.]). http://cra.org/crn/wp-content/uploads/sites/7/2017/05/2016-Taulbee-Survey.pdf. Accessed August 11, 2017.
[7] Michelle Craig, Diane Horton, Daniel Zingaro, and Danny Heap. 2016. Introducing and Evaluating Exam Wrappers in CS2. In *SIGCSE 2016*. 285–290.
[8] B Dorn and A. E. Tew. 2015. Empirical Validation and Application of the Computing Attitudes Survey. *Computer Science Education* 25, 1 (2015), 1–36.
[9] Carol S. Dweck. 2008. *Mindset :the new psychology of success*. Ballantine Books.
[10] Barry J Fraser, Herbert J Walberg, Wayne W Welch, and John A Hattie. 1987. Syntheses of educational productivity research. *International Journal of Educational Research* 11, 2 (1987), 187–212.
[11] Aaron Hochanadel and Dora Finamore. 2015. Fixed And Growth Mindset In Education And How Grit Helps Students Persist In The Face Of Adversity. 11 (01 2015), 47.
[12] Petri Ihantola, Tuukka Ahoniemi, Ville Karavirta, and Otto Seppälä. 2010. Review of recent systems for automatic assessment of programming assignments. In *Koli Calling*. 86–93.
[13] Michael S. Kirkpatrick. 2017. Student Perspectives of Team-Based Learning in a CS Course: Summary of Qualitative Findings. In *SIGCSE 2017*. 327–332.
[14] Eric Kjolsing and Lelli Van Den Einde. 2016. Peer Instruction: Using Isomorphic Questions to Document Learning Gains in a Small Statics Class. *Professional Issues in Engineering Education and Practice* 142, 4 (2016).
[15] Xiaosong Li. 2006. Using Peer Review to Assess Coding Standards - A Case Study.. In *Frontiers in Education*.
[16] Charlie McDowell, Linda Werner, Heather E. Bullock, and Julian Fernald. 2006. Pair Programming Improves Student Retention, Confidence, and Program Quality. *Commun. ACM* 49, 8 (Aug. 2006), 90–95.
[17] Leo Porter, Cynthia Bailey Lee, and Beth Simon. 2013. Halving Fail Rates Using Peer Instruction: A Study of Four Computer Science Courses. In *SIGCSE 2013*. 177–182.
[18] Leo Porter, Cynthia Bailey Lee, Beth Simon, Quintin Cutts, and Daniel Zingaro. 2011. Experience Report: A Multi-classroom Report on the Value of Peer Instruction. In *ITiCSE 2011*. 138–142.
[19] Leo Porter, Cynthia Bailey Lee, Beth Simon, and Daniel Zingaro. 2011. Peer Instruction: Do Students Really Learn from Peer Discussion in Computing?. In *ICER 2011*. 45–52.
[20] Ken Reily, Pam Ludford Finnerty, and Loren Terveen. 2009. Two Peers Are Better Than One: Aggregating Peer Reviews for Computing Assignments is Surprisingly Accurate. In *GROUP 2009*. 115–124.
[21] Beth Simon, Michael Kohanfars, Jeff Lee, Karen Tamayo, and Quintin Cutts. 2010. Experience Report: Peer Instruction in Introductory Computing. In *SIGCSE 2010*. 341–345.
[22] Chandralekha Singh. 2005. Impact of Peer Interaction on Conceptual Test Performance. *American Journal of Physics* 73, 5 (2005), 446–451.
[23] Michelle K Smith, William B Wood, Wendy K Adams, Carl Wieman, Jennifer K Knight, Nancy Guild, and Tin Tin Su. 2009. Why peer discussion improves student performance on in-class concept questions. *Science* 323, 5910 (2009), 122–124.
[24] Ben Stephenson, Michelle Craig, Daniel Zingaro, Diane Horton, Danny Heap, and Elaine Huynh. 2017. Exam Wrappers: Not a Silver Bullet. In *SIGCSE 2017*. 573–578.
[25] Claudia Szabo and Nickolas Falkner. 2017. Silence, Words, or Grades: The Effects of Lecturer Feedback in Multi-Revision Assignments. In *ITiCSE 2017*. 293–298.
[26] Christopher Watson and Frederick W.B. Li. 2014. Failure Rates in Introductory Programming Revisited. In *ITiCSE 2014*. 39–44.
[27] E.N. Wiebe, L. Williams, K. Yang, and C. Miller. 2003. *Computer Science Attitude Survey*. Technical Report. North Carolina State University Technical Report.
[28] Laurie Williams, Charlie McDowell, Nachiappan Nagappan, Julian Fernald, and Linda Werner. 2003. Building Pair Programming Knowledge Through a Family of Experiments. In *ISESE 2003*.

A Computer Science Study Abroad with Service Learning: Design and Reflections

Lori Pollock, James Atlas
University of Delaware
Computer and Information Sciences
{pollock,jatlas}@udel.edu

Tim Bell, Tracy Henderson
University of Canterbury
Computer Science and Software Engineering
{tim.bell,tracy.henderson}@canterbury.ac.nz

ABSTRACT

Study abroad offers students the opportunity to experience other cultures, languages, and environments while obtaining credits toward their degree. Students are also taught to appreciate the diversity of people and culture, such that they may dismiss stereotypes and learn to communicate and collaborate cross-culturally in a global economy. Unfortunately, few universities offer study abroad programs directed specifically to computer science and particularly in combining student technical learning with service learning for broadening participation in computing throughout the world.

In this paper, we describe a service-learning-based model for computer science students and other university students with minimal prior computer science experience to engage and inspire themselves and the next generation of computational thinkers through learning, teaching and creating web-based learning games along with local children and teachers in a foreign country. We describe the model focusing on learning objectives, curriculum, field component, planning, and partnership building. We describe the products that undergraduates were able to create in four weeks and their CS education service learning field experiences. Finally, we investigate the impact of the study abroad model on undergraduates' content knowledge, and their career and personal development.

ACM Reference format:
Lori Pollock, James Atlas and Tim Bell, Tracy Henderson . 2018. A Computer Science Study Abroad with Service Learning: Design and Reflections. In *Proceedings of The 49th ACM Technical Symposium on Computer Science Education, Baltimore, MD, USA, Feb. 21–24, 2018 (SIGCSE '18)*, 6 pages.
https://doi.org/10.1145/3159450.3159589

1 INTRODUCTION

The Forum on Education Abroad defines a *study abroad program* as education that occurs outside the participants' home country and results in progress toward an academic degree at a student's home institution[7]. A *service learning program* is a specially designed experience combining reflection with structured participation in a community-based project to achieve specified learning outcomes[7]. Studies of students' participation in study abroad and service learning experiences have indicated that participants obtain significant gains in cultural, academic, and linguistic knowledge, are more likely to examine their values and strengths, develop a stronger sense of self, and gain maturity and confidence, and demonstrate significant increases in their empathy toward others as a result of interactions with diverse individuals [2]. Despite the benefits and global nature of computer science, few universities offer study abroad programs specifically for computer science, particularly by combining student technical learning with service learning for broadening participation in computing throughout the world.

This paper describes the design of a study abroad program focused on computer science education, offering undergraduates an experience to use agile development to create learning games for teaching computer science concepts to beginners/non-CS students and deploy the games in local community centers as well as to plan and help facilitate several workshops for K-12 students and teachers in the host country. The program integrates technical computer science learning with the benefits of service learning and study abroad, while providing the opportunity for undergraduates with less technical background to participate through offering an alternative of computer ethics combined with the service learning experience abroad. The program was highlighted by a unique culturally-centered workshop with the local indigenous community, where the community leaders led authentic cultural protocols, traditions, and history-focused activities for the local indigenous children and undergraduate study abroad students together, which was followed by undergraduates helping the children as they created culturally-focused Scratch games to reinforce what they had learned about the important aspects of their culture.

This paper demonstrates how a study abroad program can be designed to include technical computer science learning and team-based projects culminating in a software product, deployment, and feedback in a short time period, service learning based on outreach to teachers and students with the goal of broadening participation in computer science, reciprocating this learning with a significant integration of host country cultural experience with the computer science learning and outreach goals.

2 RELATED WORK

In 2005, ITiCSE formed a working group to investigate ways to improve computer science students' learning and understanading of the global nature of computing[4]. They described why an international experience is important to a computer science student's education, given its inherently international nature. In addition to student and faculty exchanges and joint collaborative projects, the working group recommended study abroad programs. In 2015, Goldweber organized a SIGCSE birds-of-a-feather session for computer

SIGCSE '18, Feb. 21–24, 2018, Baltimore, MD, USA

ACM ISBN 978-1-4503-5103-4/18/02...$15.00
https://doi.org/10.1145/3159450.3159589

science educators interested in creating successful study abroad experiences for computer science students[5].

Despite the interest and recommendations, we could find only a few descriptions of study abroad programs targeting computer science students. Doyle et al. developed a study away program for computer science students at Northern Kentucky University (NKU) to explore the concept and controversy of agile software development by spending a spring break week in San Francisco visiting companies and cultural sites[1]. Fry at Baylor University described a 41-day summer study abroad program for Baylor computer science and engineering students to take technical and professional writing and digital networks in the Netherlands[3].

3 CS STUDY ABROAD COURSE MODEL

The CS study abroad trip was 29 days in the host country during our university's winter January 2017 session with three days of travel to/from the U.S.[1] The study abroad group was based at a single host university campus with field experiences in teacher workshops and K-12 student camps in computer science hosted at the university computer science labs, at local community centers, and at another university campus in another city, which provided an opportunity to travel to a new location for four days as part of the official itinerary. In addition to the field experience days, official excursions were planned to learn about the indigenous peoples' culture, history, and natural environment. Students were given one 4-day weekend, one 3-day weekend, and two 2-day breaks to travel and explore on their own. Two faculty directors, both computer science faculty at the U.S. university, organized and led the trip, with one graduate teaching assistant, who helped with grading.

3.1 General Learning Objectives

In addition to the standard objectives of study abroad and service learning objectives, at the end of this program, the students should:

- in learning game development, be able to design an educational game with good design and play strategy and implement a prototype using agile process
- in software engineering, use user-centered research and iterative design process
- in communication, develop skills for presenting, analytic thinking, teaching, collaborating in a team, and mentoring
- in teaching, adapt lesson plans and facilitate CS learning using engaging pedagogy
- in computing ethics, assess potential benefits and harmful uses of a technology, defend positions with rational arguments, and be aware of social and ethical issues of computing

Students contribute directly to the national effort to train elementary and middle school teachers in computer science and teach middle school students computational principles. Service learning is tracked through reflection journals, lesson plans, and computational artifacts produced during the field experience.

3.2 Curriculum

While this program primarily targeted computer science majors, we took a multi-pronged approach to make sure we were able to recruit enough students. The audience for this experience was all university students who have taken at least one computer science course. We offered three courses, of which a given student must register for two courses. We chose the courses from existing on-campus courses such that students with varied backgrounds would be able to use all 6 credits towards their graduation requirements. Thus, we offered : Learning Game Development, Field Experiences in Teaching Computer Science, and Computer Ethics.

Specific curricular requirements are met through all 3 course offerings. Computer Ethics is a degree requirement for all CS majors. Learning Game Development satisfies either a technical or concentration elective requirement (students need 4 courses of each total). The field experiences course satisfies a concentration elective (students need 4 total). This program secondarily targeted computer science minors. The field experiences and learning game development both satisfy minor elective courses. Finally, this program targeted all university majors who need a breadth requirement and have taken at least one computer science course. Computer ethics counts towards breadth for several colleges and counts towards the Creative Arts & Humanities university breadth requirement.

We describe the courses' content, format, and requirements here.

Learning Game Development. This course lets students experience the software engineering process through creating educational games for youth; open-ended, project-oriented team learning while assisting regional teachers in integrating computing and computational thinking into the classroom; interact with teachers as clients, hone communication skills and experience design-studio-based critiques of their ideas. The course is project based with studio-based learning for in-class sessions.

The course met regularly either as a class or team meetings in the classroom, team meetings with the instructor, or participating in field experiences teaching game development to children. Student teams were provided big time slots to design and build their learning games. There was no textbook for this course, similar to on campus. Instead, much of the learning material for this course is tutorials that the students did independently to learn HTML5 and Phaser, or Unreal Engine technology, from which they implemented their games. The course was designed following the agile software development model so students created initial prototypes in a short time, got feedback through demos to everyone, revised for their alpha, beta, and final games. The games were demoed to the public for feedback at two local malls and the community playground in the country being visited, all arranged through a local non-profit.

Field Experience In Teaching Computing. This course is an introduction to computer science teaching methodology which is immediately put into practice in local schools. Lectures hone teaching and classroom skills while examining the state of CS education. Students produce written lesson plans, journals, and collaborative projects. The course started with a few orientation sessions the first week by and then all the students' hours of field experiences were distributed across the various events: 3-day Ages 10-13 Coding Camp, 2-day game development camp, 1-day 12-hour game hackathon, 2-day Teacher Professional Development workshop, 3-day summer camp on Arduinos and robots, E-textiles, and CS

[1]For anonymity during the review, we do not identify the specific country or locations of the excursions and field experiences in the submission.

Unplugged, and the 2-day teen programming camp with the indigenous children after a 1-day cultural learning day in an authentic setting. The students were also required to write reflective journals on their field experiences.

Computers, Ethics, and Society. This course explores relationships among information technology, society and ethics by examining issues raised by increasingly widespread use of computers. Topics include ethics for computer professionals, computer impact on factory work, office work, personal privacy and social power distribution. This course met regularly once a day for about 1 1/4 hours, 16 days. The format was very interactive both in class and online. Other class time (1 hour each team) was by meeting with student teams separately to guide them in preparing for their class facilitation and final oral argument, and online through a student online discussion forum where students were required to identify, post, and start a discussion on a current events article involving computer ethics and then comment on others' discussion threads once a week (5 times total for about 10 hours total). Each student's final activity was to identify, read, summarize, and lead a discussion on a news event in the host country that involved computer ethics.

3.3 Field Component

The field component of the study abroad offered significant opportunity to interact with many children and adults (teachers) in the host country beyond daily living in the host country. All students, despite the courses they chose, participated in some amount of field experience in teaching computer science (through the field experiences course) or demoing their learning games (learning game development course). Any student who wanted to participate beyond their required participation was encouraged to get involved.

The field component consisted of five multi-day coding camps for children, each focusing on different technologies, including Scratch, Unreal Engine, Arduinos and robots, and e-textiles. All included CS Unplugged activities. Most camps were arranged by university personnel while two were arranged in collaboration with non-profit organizations. Students also assisted with a multi-day teacher workshop in Scratch and python programming. Lastly, one of the student camps was followed by a whole day 12-hour hackathon of game development in Scratch or Unreal Engine, with undergraduates matched as mentors for each team.

3.4 Student Assessments

Given the shortened time (29 days), student assessments needed to be modified from standard semester versions of the courses. The learning game development course assessment consisted of assessments for the project design challenge, user-centered research, concept generation and selection, prototype, testing and revision, the final game deliverable and demo, peer review, and reflective journal. The field experience course assessment focused on participation in field work, class activity participation, reflective journal entries and final essay. The computer ethics course assessment consisted of in-class exercise participation, online discussion entries, a group debate facilitation, and final essay and oral argument.

4 PLANNING, RECRUITING, & LOGISTICS

Planning started a year in advance of departure with a proposal due to the study abroad office. The two faculty directors identified the existing on-campus courses that would achieve the objectives in offering a study abroad targeted at computer science, but also attracting broader participation with diverse backgrounds. We contacted potential partners in the host university and host city organizations to organize field experiences in teaching computer science as well as cultural excursions related to the study abroad and culture, history, and environment of the host country. These partnerships and course planning culminated in a month-long schedule of activities. We modified the course requirements and assessments in the on-campus versions of each course to fit the study abroad context.

To recruit for the trip, we held information sessions in spring 2016. We advertised through the university study abroad web site, posters, the main CS building, emails sent to all CS majors and minors, and personal invitations and announcements in CS courses. We interviewed 54 applying students for 15 minutes each with a consistent set of interview questions, and selected 35 students with a wait list. Of the 35 students, 12 were female, 23 male, which is a much higher percentage of women in CS than our regular majors and classes, where it is approximately 15%. There were mostly CS majors, but also CS minors, with majors in electrical engineering, chemical engineering, math, visual communications, and MISY. Of the 35 students, there were 19 in the Computer Ethics course, 30 in the Learning Game Development course, and 21 in the Field Experience in Teaching CS course. We held three orientation meetings in fall 2016 for the participants, each focusing on different aspects of the trip preparation.

The 35 participants were grouped into eight teams by using criteria for diversity, computer science background, and course selection. Each team chose a name based on local native animals, was assigned time slots in the field based on their course enrollment, and teams enrolled in the learning game development course collaborated on the development of a learning game.

5 METHODOLOGY

5.1 Research Questions

In this paper, we focus on answering the following research questions with regard to the CS study abroad program model:

(1) What kinds of CS learning games can undergraduates design and implement in a 4-week study abroad program?
(2) What kinds of CS service learning activities can undergraduates design and facilitate in a foreign country during a 4-week program?
(3) What is the impact of the study abroad on undergraduate student participants regarding their content knowledge, soft skills, and personal and career development?
(4) What is the impact of involving undergraduate students in CS education service learning in another country?

Specifically for this paper, we examined what worked well during the planning and implementation of the study abroad experience, and what, if anything, should be changed to increase impacts of the program on undergraduates and the partnering organizations and their constituents.

Table 1: Undergrad and Event Participants

Event	Undergrads	Attendees
Scratch Coding Camp	35	40
Game Dev Workshop	30	40
Game Dev Hackathon	35	50
Arduino, E-textiles Camp	9	120
Cultural Exchange Workshop	35	40
Demos@Community Centers	35	150
Teacher Workshop	21	50
Total Participants	35	490

5.2 Data Collection and Analysis

To answer our research questions, we collected data using several sources. First, a key component of the program was reflective journals written by undergraduates, which were collected and examined. A minimum of 5 journal entries per student were written during the program period. Although the length of each reflective entry varies from week to week and from participant to participant, the average length of each entry was 343 words. Second, all undergraduate participants responded to an evaluation survey, which asked questions about each course as the academic component, their exposure to the culture of the host country, excursions, and overall positive and negative aspects of the program, and any life-changing or important impacts. Third, artifacts created by the students, including learning games, lesson plans, demos, and essays were also collected and analyzed. Fourth, students completed a 500 word final reflective essay and a 15 minute exit interview with the instructors. Lastly, the instructors and teaching assistant made observations of the students during the workshops, camps, and demos.

To answer our research questions, we analyzed the data qualitatively. We read the reflection entries, essays, and evaluation survey answers. We compared data across participants to identify similarities and emerging themes[6].

5.3 Participants

Table 1 shows the counts of participants in the field experiences, separated by undergraduates and attendees at each outreach event. In total, the undergraduates reached 490 children and teachers through their field work during 29 days on study abroad.

6 FINDINGS

6.1 Undergraduate-made Learning Games

Table 2 describes the computer science concepts or topics, descriptions and technologies used to develop each learning game that was developed by the study abroad undergraduate teams.

For each learning game project, the teams produced an initial concept document describing their learning objective, aesthetic, mechanics, and dynamics. 1-week agile development sprints were used to produce alpha, beta, and final versions complete with write-ups, posters, and demos to their client, other teams, children at a workshop, and three community center events. Students worked in groups of 4-6 and estimated that each project represented 40-80 hours of work per member over the 4-week study abroad.

Their client was the local computer science education research group who plans to use the prototypes as a base for their online interactive computer science activities for K-12 teachers and students. The final prototypes after 4 weeks of intense development were similar in quality to final prototypes of non-study-abroad regular 15 week semester projects. Two of the projects met their learning objectives and stability criteria so well that the client has dedicated resources to immediately develop them into production releases. All of the projects impressed our client and will help development of their future computer science education online interactives.

6.2 CS Service Learning Activities Abroad

During the study abroad, students took on multiple roles in service to the local community - lesson planner, learning facilitator, teacher, teaching assistant, team mentor, and game demonstrator. Some workshops were organized by the host university, and the undergraduates served as teaching assistants in helping young students learn and develop projects in Scratch and python. In other workshops, the students created Arduino wheeled robot lessons, Raspberry PI sensor programming lessons, and e-textiles lessons and projects, and co-led the workshop in their team. During the 12-hour game development hackathon,undergraduate pairs were teamed with participant teams of 2-4 and served as their mentor for the day. In one workshop, students helped the local children to incorporate their history and culture into their coding through character sprites, stories, and animation. Students in the learning game course set up tables in local community centers (i.e., two malls and a large playground) and introduced and observed children in playing their games, gathering user feedback from the intended users. Following good practice for service learning, the students were required to write a journal entry reflecting on their service learning experiences after each event.

6.3 CS Study Abroad Impacts on Undergrads

In final reflective essays and reflective journals, undergraduates indicated that they learned how to explain computer science concepts to non-technical people, and became more confident in communicating about computer science with technically-knowledgeable peers and young students just learning to code. One student writes "I think one of the biggest benefits I got out of this class was the practice in communicating about computer science at a student's level. After working with students for 30+ hours, I was able to understand what jargon they were familiar with and other ways to describe technical terms."

Another student writes "The field experience definitely built up some confidence in my teaching abilities. Before the first teaching experience, I doubted in my capability to teach young students how to develop a game from Scratch. Nearly a week later I was confidently helping to run a seven hour event teaching Unreal Engine." Yet another student writes "My favorite part of the course was the chance to lead a lesson plan about a topic in computer science. The power of being able to guide discussion and learning made me feel like I was impacting the lives and learning of others. Seeing all of the kids in the room jumping to answer a question about what might happen next was very empowering and instilled a great feeling of satisfaction."

Table 2: Learning Game Artifacts Developed by Undergrads

CS Concept	Game Description	Technology
Computer image representations with RGB colors	A first-person shooter paintball game with RGB bit selection guns to shoot matching enemies	Unreal Engine
Bit parity	Player escapes rooms of a pirate adventure by looking for and solving parity puzzles	Unreal Engine
Network transmission protocols	Player navigates spaceship carrying packets through maze choosing powerups to keep data intact through error barriers	Unreal Engine
Neural network AI	Player tries to pick up final stick from a pile, while playing against a learning AI with fully transparent neural net training algorithm	Phaser, javascript
Image processing with filters	Solve a mystery involving missing turtles inside Professor Pixel's mansion by matching turtle images that have filters applied	Phaser, javascript
Facial recognition	Using webcam, take your picture, locate facial points, and find out which rugby player matches you closest	Phaser, javascript
Intuitive GUI design	Make a bird fly around obstacles to collect coins while your GUI functionality changes	Phaser, javascript

Students also repeatedly mentioned having to gauge their audience before deciding how to communicate an idea. For example, one student writes "I definitely had to alter my communication style, and I found that some of the most effective techniques were to get on the child's level physically (sit next to them rather than stand over them), and to ask them to explain what they were working on to you, so that you could gauge their communication style and choose your response fittingly."

Students recognized the importance of improving their communication skills. One student writes "Communication is such a major part of computer science. Employers love seeing that a candidate has the ability to communicate and collaborate. This experience has undeniably made me better at both. I've learned how to communicate what I'm thinking in a clear and concise manner. I've also learned to be patient as no matter what your age or background there are always things that need to be learned. "Another student writes "As a future consultant when talking to layman about computing I may have to answer general questions about how computers work. Learning these styles of teaching will help me give better explanations in these situations." Another writes that "keeping explanations simple and understanding the technical aptitude of my target audience will be very beneficial in my career."

Along the same vein, undergraduates in the learning game course became more aware of the important role of the end user as they watched the young students playing their games in the community centers. One student summarized it as "My views of computing have changed in that my experiences have reinforced that keeping in mind who the programs and games are being made for is the most important. That being a computer scientist is not just about programming, but more about understanding others and that we are making our programs for someone else." They also increased their awareness of the importance of collaboration. One student writes ". I think being involved in the collaborative process of thinking of ideas for what the young students could create and the discussion after the workshop was beneficial in emphasizing for me how collaboration and working together is essential to accomplishing more and better things."

Findings indicate that undergraduates became more aware of the importance of universal access to computing, and that it does not necessarily mean losing tradition. One student states "It had never occurred to me how important computing and computer science could be to groups that had not been previously involved in the subject. When we were at the (anonymous location), I learned that the average (anonymous population) lives in a fairly low income bracket. By getting kids interested in computer science, we can get them into a subject that could potentially double their family income." Another student notes "It mainly taught me that you don't have to sacrifice tradition for advancement. In other words, I thought it was really cool that we spent one day with the kids learning about their culture with the traditional greeting, the songs, language and norms. And the next day we spent coding in a computer lab. A field like computer science that might be the most new and innovative field out there, doesn't have to exclude anyone. You can still be part of a developing community and world while at the same time preserving your culture and traditions."

Undergraduates recognized and gained pride in the role they can play as computer scientists in broadening participation of computing with even very young children. Many students wrote reflections similar to this one - "My favorite part of this course is definitely seeing what the students make by the end of the day. Almost always I am amazed at what the kids have created, and they always seem to want to continue to expand on their projects or create something new. This, along with the big smiles, leaves me feeling like I have made a positive impact in their learning, and that is what I find important and worthwhile."

Students also repeatedly commented on how much harder teaching is than they imagined, how much preparation goes into planning and preparing for lessons behind the scenes, challenges of dealing with a mixed audience of student background, how surprised they were at how young you can teach computer sciende,and how it is all about engaging the students, not giving out information. Many commented on the joy and satisfaction of working one-on-one with the children and bringing in the culture with creating projects.

6.4 CS Study Abroard Impacts on Community

Having the opportunity to collaborate internationally with study abroad students impacted positively on all groups who learned from them during their field work. A key observation was that both local students and teachers were able to make the connection that computer science and computational thinking is an international subject, and that the hosting university's computer science department is not alone in its passionate about teaching K-12 students. The fact that their tutors came from overseas, and it was a unique experience for local students meant that local students looked up to their visiting tutors.

Another key observation was the length of time young students were engaged in their programming activities and how much their learning accelerated. When asked during the reflection sessions, students mentioned that it was because they had their "own experts" who were able to take the time to explain carefully what they had to think about, rather than either quickly showing them or giving hints that didn't always make sense. This can be attributed to the small ratio of one tutor to three local students. There are local students who now are considering studying computer science to be able to join study abroad groups.

Teachers who attended the two day workshops commented positively on having an international connection and appeared more confident in their programming ability, when comparing confidence observed between the January workshops to followup July workshops, where the ratio was 1:6 tutors. One teacher commented "thanks to students, got lots of help". Overall, the teachers were impressed with the study abroad group's knowledge and willingness to patiently explain what they were programming.

The impact on the indigenous students and their leaders was the most substantial of all the groups mentored by the study abroad students. There were three students who said that their next step was to attend similar workshops at the study abroad's home university. The indigenous students learned alongside their study abroad tutors to create a meaningful program about their culture. The combination of having subject matter experts (students studying indigenous culture, language and traditions), technical experts (the study abroad students), and the local students who were interpreting what they had learned meant that collaboratively these teams were able to create quality programs in a short period of time.

One indigenous student, age 11, had very complex ideas, and having a study abroad student to help work through them meant that this student not only created the desired program, but was able to learn the computational thinking and computer science needed to make this work. Since attending these workshops, this indigenous student now leads computer science projects at school, where they speak and learn in their native language. Both the study abroad student and this indigenous student expressed their excitement and there was definitely a connection between the two of respect as to what each could achieve.

There is a wider impact of hosting the indigenous workshops. There were two other visiting lecturers who also attended these workshops. They were motivated and moved by what they observed and they in turn are exploring opportunities to combine a study abroad program with indigenous peoples to expand their students' acceptance and understanding of different cultures and how they can meaningfully contribute to the indigenous cultures' preservation and revitalization.

Locally, the impact of these workshops has led to other organizations within the indigenous network to contact the host university team to open discussions on how this model could be adopted both locally and internationally, with all parties involved exploring how it could be developed further into an ongoing and sustainable model. One of the ideas is to travel with indigenous students to the University of Delaware to reciprocate the experience of travelling abroad and learning about other indigenous cultures, while celebrating their own and learning computer science.

7 DISCUSSION AND CONCLUSIONS

In this paper, we described the design, implementation and impacts of a computer science study abroad with both technical and service learning components. Findings indicate that the experience has positive impacts on undergraduate participants in terms of communication skills, confidence in communication skills, awareness of the importance of broadening access and participation in computing, and recognition of the important role they can play with their technical and communication skills. Findings also indicate significant positive and broadly reaching impacts on local participants in engagement, accelerated learning, increased interest in pursuing computer science careers, indigenous cultures preservation, and open discussions of sustainable models for computer science collaborations with indigenous peoples.

In terms of future directions, findings from our work revealed several components that were key to the success of the study abroad model but presented room for improvement. We think it would be useful to only offer 2 courses so that all students had equal requirements for time spent on their courses, alleviating some concerns as the game development course required more time from students than the other two courses. We also would ensure only one field experience happens at a time; our flexibility with community partners meant that on our busiest day, we had three overlapping events and had to manage the logistics of our undergraduates being seperated into three groups at three different locations.

REFERENCES

[1] Maureen Doyle, Candace Gibson, Michelle Melish, and Rees Storm. 2016. Agile Software Development Study Away. In *47th ACM Technical Symposium on Computing Science Education (SIGCSE '16)*.

[2] M. E. Engberg. 2013. The Influence of Study Away Experiences on Global Perspective-Taking. *Journal of College Student Development* 54, 5 (2013).

[3] Cynthia C. Fry. 2004. The development of a summer study abroad program for engineering and computer science students at Baylor University. In *Proceedings of the 34th ASEE/IEEE Annual Frontiers in Education*.

[4] Ursula Fuller, June Amillo, Cary Laxer, W. Michael McCracken, and Joseph Mertz. 2005. Facilitating Student Learning Through Study Abroad and International Projects. *SIGCSE Bull.* 37, 4 (Dec. 2005), 139–151.

[5] Michael Goldweber. 2015. Study Abroad Experiences in Computer Science (Abstract Only). In *Proceedings of the 46th ACM Technical Symposium on Computer Science Education (SIGCSE '15)*. 699–699.

[6] M. B. Miles and A. M. Huberman. 1994. Qualitative data analysis: An expanded sourcebook. Sage.

[7] The Forum on Education Abroad. 2015. Standards on Good Practice. https://forumea.org/resources/standards-of-good-practice/.

Combining Agile Software Development and Service-learning: A Case Study in Experiential IS Education

Spencer Robinson, Margeret Hall
University of Nebraska Omaha
School of Interdisciplinary Informatics
Omaha, USA
spencerrobinson@unomaha.edu; mahalll@unomaha.edu

ABSTRACT

Experiential learning is ever-more popular with educators, industry, and with students themselves. Finding and delivering appropriate applied use cases can be challenging though, as on one hand industry partners may not willing to give insights to non-employees into their systems for creating truly meaningful case studies, and on the other hand the appropriate balance between instruction and application is ill-defined. Service learning projects are one solution for filling in the applied project gap. This case study takes place in the nexus between blended classrooms, applied software development, and service learning. Junior and senior level students partnered with a community actor to develop deployable software applying the Agile methodology. The service-learning project enabled students to engage in a full-cycle development project, from requirements gathering to hypercare. However, significant trade-offs in structure and classroom management must be made when the focus of the class is a full implementation. Blended technologies and course delivery were found to aid delivery and project management in a seamless manner. Drawing on feedback from stakeholders and students, this experience report makes a series of recommendations for implementing applied software development. Our contribution is the introduction and assessment of a method to marry (online) information systems education with service learning.

KEYWORDS

Information systems education; undergraduate instruction; agile software development; service learning; experiential learning.

ACM Reference format:
Spencer Robinson, and Margeret Hall. 2018. Combining Agile Software Development and Service-learning: A Case Study in Experiential IS Education. In *SIGCSE '18: 49th ACM Technical Symposium on Computer Science Education, Feb. 21–24, 2018, Baltimore, MD, USA.* ACM, NY, NY, USA, 6 pages. https://doi.org/10.1145/3159450.3159564

SIGCSE '18, February 21–24, 2018, Baltimore, MD, USA

ACM ISBN 978-1-4503-5103-4/18/02...$15.00
https://doi.org/10.1145/3159450.3159564

1 INTRODUCTION

One under-addressed experiential learning approach is found in service learning [7]. In contrast to industry-directed projects, service learning is based in community needs and wants. In service learning students work directly with community partners/community to develop and implement a solution. Service learning projects contain several elements interesting for experiential learning. In particular, the content is highly applied and requires the creation of a (minimally viable) solution for and by the completion of the course(semester). Community partners engaged in service learning often (though not always) have less-strict cooperation requirements, meaning students can take advantage of a full development cycle [7]. Service learning intersects with Agile development methods naturally in its necessity to have strong feedback loops with the community partner/community partner/client [1].

Implementing experiential learning in the classroom poses specific pedagogical challenges. In order to achieve a successful implementation, some portion of lecture time must be allocated to group activities, community partner/client-facing time or requirements discovery. This necessarily takes away from traditional lecturing. In order to convey the needed information to meet learning objectives, a compromise solution must be delivered. This is well-addressed in a blended classroom [11, 13], a time-effective course delivery mechanism which re-focusses in-class time to active learning and homework to learning the materials previously covered in lectures.

This article describes an experiential learning scenario employing blended classrooms technology and service-learning elements. The class worked in conjunction with a community partner specializing in ex-patriate elder care. Students were tasked with creating a study aid for seniors to study for the US Citizenship Exam. First the course and team structure are introduced (Sections 2 and 3). As in all group work scenarios, pedagogical methods to support student learning and avoid free-riding [6] were required (Sections 3 and 4). The core of the contribution is found in the Validation (Section 4) and Discussion (Section 5). Section 6 closes with an overview of Limitations and Future Work.

CASE STUDY: APPLIED SERVICE-LEARNING IN IS EDUCATION

Course Format and Curriculum

'Agile Development Methods' is a required 3-credit course for the Bachelor of Science in IT Innovation programme focussing on third and fourth year students. This is a once-yearly Spring semester course with regular course meetings twice a week for 1 hr 15 per session. Additional in-person and online meetings are scheduled in-group. The course was taught in English, along with all assignments, evaluations, and course communications. The course was managed as a hybrid blended classroom [13], where assignment and course materials were hosted in the course management system (CMS) and student applied the week's content in-classroom. In addition to a CMS, the open source platforms Slack and Trello were implemented to assist in project management.

Course Content and Intended Learning Outcomes

The aim of Agile Development Methods is providing a course-based environment to learn (i) rapid prototyping (ii) project management and (iii) teamwork skills (see [5, 12] for detailed information on Agile classroom outcomes). Agile courses are applied courses and must mimic an actual Agile scenario closely, lest the students gain incorrect exposure. The blended environment supported this aim particularly well, allowed course time to be allocated to hands-on activities and group planning [11]. The course is the final requirement in the course module before students undertake their final capstone or thesis work in preparation for graduation from the program.

In the first part of the course students learn the theories and techniques of Agile Development and SCRUM. They are introduced to the organization's stakeholders, begin needs gathering, and meet with various research and practical topic experts. Students had nine scheduled in-classroom or on-site visits and three subject matter expert discussions in-class. The expert visits were in gerontology, learning science, and a recent successful US Civics exam test-taker.

The students then break into functional teams, write software requirements, finally implementing minimally viable software in four, 2-week sprints. The course objectives were written as such:

At the end of this course students:

- Have knowledge of the processes, methods, and tools that are used in agile IT application development approaches.
- Are able to apply agile methods and processes to small and middle-sized projects software development.
- Have learned how to determine system requirements and how to create a logical incremental design for an IT application.
- Are familiar with UML modelling techniques.
- Are able to utilize SCRUM methods and techniques to support agile project management.
- Are able to prepare and run project meetings.
- Are able to actively participate in the team-based analysis and design of an innovative IT application.
- Have honed teamwork, critical thinking, and communication skills, through active involvement in project teams and cooperative learning groups.
- Demonstrate the ability to make professional presentations and reports by applying learned knowledge and skills.
- Demonstrate professionalism, respect for others (both oral and written), and high ethical conduct.

The blended classroom enabled spending class time in experiential sessions and was employed throughout the semester. Classroom time was spent clarifying, discussing the methodology and processes, and in group-based work. Groupmates were guaranteed to have a minimum of two meetings per week. Project management tools like Slack and Trello were employed to enable transparency and real-time updating between and across teams, and with the professor.

Within the broad specifications of the project, students were granted significant autonomy in selection of the implemented study aid mechanism, programming language, and individual role in the project. The goal of the class was to simulate an Agile software development cycle as closely as possible, requiring a higher level of autonomy than a traditional lecture-based course.

Student Composition and Competency Profiles

18 students (two females) registered for and completed this course. Registered students are third or fourth year students in the IT Innovation programme. To register for the class all students must have passed or shown equivalency in Java programming (two semesters), C programming (one semester), and Management of Databases (one semester). Approximately half of the class had previous experience with Agile Development through other courses or internships.

Of the 18 students in the course during the term under observation, two had migration backgrounds. Both students with migration backgrounds reported assisting family members with studying for the US Citizenship Exam. The exam was unfamiliar to the rest of the course participants.

Three functional teams convened (Table 1): Backend, Admin, and Quiz. Each team had one SCRUM Master, a tester and a combination of developers and User Experience roles. The structure is resultant of the project in place. One Proxy Product Owner (PPO) was also in place to centralize communication between the student groups, the community partner/client, and the professor. This was a double role with the SCRUM Master of the Backend team.

Students self-selected into roles via ballot submitted to the professor. Fig. 1. displays the employed ballot and potential roles. In all but one case, students were placed into their top or second most preferred role.

Scale: 1 - 10

1 = absolutely not!

10 = Would make my YEAR

___ SCRUM Master

___ Product Owner

___ Developer, Browser

___ Developer, IOS or Android - (circle one)

___ Developer Architecture

___ Tester

___ UI Designer

___ Database Developer

___ Other - please name

Figure 1. SCRUM role ballot

Teams submitted a team contract including an agreed-upon definition of "done," an internal accountability process and conflict management plan, and a communication strategy.

Table 1. Team Structure

Team 1: Admin	Team 2: Backend	Team 3: Quiz
SCRUM	SCRUM/PPO	SCRUM
Development/ Architecture/ Database DDA	DDA	DDA
DDA	DDA	DDA
User eXperience	UX	DDA
UX	T/QA	UX
Tester/Quality Assurance T/QA	-	UX
-	-	T/QA

10-minute standing meetings were a feature of the course. Groups were in near-daily communication, with deadlines and graded materials set to coincide with the end of the week.

TRADE-OFFS AND TENSIONS IN TEAM MANAGEMENT

A chief difference in Agile methodologies compared to historical software development methods is its tolerance of and for ambiguity. While this is an attribute in fast-changing development environments, it poses specific pedagogical challenges [14]. In addition, group assignments invite free-riding problems [6]. In this course it resulted in two major trade-off scenarios: Individual vs SCRUM Master Responsibility and Big Picture vs Skill-based Thinking. These two ambiguous aspects caused the first sprint to fail, meaning that no instantiation was produced.

SCRUM Master Responsibility ↔ Personal Responsibility

Agile software development classroom environments are unique because of participants' unfamiliarity with the agile methodology combined with unenforceable management structures along with external distractions. These combined factors can lead to failed sprints and setbacks that stack up and eliminate the possibility for an agile process because of the finite semester schedule.

Students initially struggled with breaking down their own project section into smaller tasks, and task structuring as delivered by the team's SCRUM Master. This is partially due to the structure of traditional classrooms: tasks and outcomes are mandated by the lecturer rather than self-organized or tasked by a peer. With many distributed responsibilities, it can be difficult for students to prioritize (as well as guide groupmates) effectively. Students were bottlenecked by their expectation of hierarchical accountabilities.

This problem caused the greatest detriment to group morale and seemed to be contagious. Agile is theoretically a modular process [12] but undergraduate students inevitably prioritise competing (academic and non-academic) demands [9]. When there is an uneven understanding of the development environment or task prioritisation, teams can be limited by low output. In consultation with the students, two linked processes to counter the effect were put in place. As the fundamental challenge was one of experience and not capability [4], students were encouraged to employ self-management and refer to the team contract in cases of conflict or differing performance expectations. In order to ensure mutual accountability and continuous evaluation [10], 30% of the students' participation grade was reallocated to reflect self- and time management.

Big Picture ↔ Individual Skills

A foundational principle of Agile development is community partner/client interaction [1]. Particularly the concept of epics and user stories (informal descriptions of software requirements from the perspective of the end user) drives all development in an agile system.

Students understandably concentrated on applying their existing skill sets to the project [14]. However, a mismatch between student skills and project requirements occurred on the Quiz Team. The developers on the Quiz Team focussed on implementing the game with the Unity development platform rather than in a standard programming language (i.e., Java), with which they were less competent. The implementation delivered a smooth, game-like experience, which was a community partner/client requirement. However, another community partner/client requirement was deprioritised by this implementation, namely that the implementation be highly functional with low latency. The Unity implementation could not directly interact with the developed Cake PHP database, causing the developers to create a complicated, intensive workaround solution. In addition, the implementation was not functional on several of the work stations in use at the community centre due to the age of the machines.

The challenge represented here is less of a pedagogical issue and more of a project management challenge. It however prompted a change in future class projects; students in future courses will receive a briefing on interoperability of technologies before the sprints.

VALIDATION

We were particularly interested in the nexus between student and community partner/client feedback to find evidence for the effectiveness or limitations of this course. The coming section is broadly based on qualitative written and focus-group feedback received as a part of the course.

As part of the university's policy, all courses are subject to a standardized evaluation scheme that students have to complete after or during the last lecture. Due to the scheduled timing of the standardized evaluation form, extensive formal feedback is left for a future extension of the paper. In the following sections we give a short overview of feedback received from the student teams, community partners/clients and the students.

Sprint Reviews and Retrospectives

Sprints were two week iterations. At the end of each sprint students presented then submitted a team-based sprint review and an individual sprint retrospective. The review established the progress and challenges compared to the sprint plan. This was scored for deviation from the submitted sprint plan and actions taken to remedy any deviations.

The retrospectives allowed each student to evaluate their group as a whole, their groupmates individually, as well as their own contribution. In addition, two sprints had an in-class conversation based retrospective covering the sprints' overarching themes, accomplishments, and challenges.

Table 2 reflects the scoring of students in roles by all other students. Students awarded 'points' to each person on their team from 0-100. Self-assessments are extracted from this matrix. Note that with one SCRUM master and one tester per team there is no cross-scoring possible unless self-assessments are included. SCRUM masters were generally well-regarded across the three teams. Students generally rated their own performance well, with a high of 100 and a low of 75 across 18 students in four, two-week sprints.

Table 3. Ratings of performance by role averaged and rounded across sprints and teams

	SCRUM Master	Developer	UX	Tester
SCRUM Master	-	87	90	92
Developer	95	97	91	89
UX	91	83	94	75
Tester	97	72	79	-

In-class retrospectives were a vehicle to discuss highs and lows as well as recalibrate classroom and/or project management strategies in a public forum. Several positive outcomes came from these discussions, including the redirected 30% of the participation score, a swarming approach to aid the Quiz Team developers in connecting the game and the database, a change in time for the standing meeting from the beginning of class to the end of class, and a unified deadline for all weekly assignments at the end of the week to better facilitate development and CMS work.

Stakeholder Feedback

Nine scheduled visits and along with several ad-hoc client visits happened throughout the semester. Two main and two secondary contacts from the senior centre staff were in contact with the student teams. The meetings were held at the senior centre (4x) and in-class (5x). Students were encouraged to use these sessions for requirements gathering, proof of concept validation, and user acceptance. The community partners/clients were likewise encouraged to push back on implementations, question features, and guide future development cycles.

Whereas the student groups had significant autonomy in implementing the game section of the artefact, the administrative section received considerable feedback and was re-developed over several iterations. This is due to strict requirements for reporting that are in place from various granting agencies funding the work of the community centre. From a simple interface listing individual students and last scores, the administrator's page gained group analytics, ability to alter questions and answers, a leader board, player progress scoring by quartile by week and month, as well as individual player progress tracking.

The three quotes (from emails between the main contacts at the senior centre and the instructor) below illustrate the relationship between the student groups and the clients:

"[...] it is a privilege to be part of such wonderful class, your students are amazing. We are very excited about this project and I am sure the outcomes will be remarkable once everything is done." (emailed, 2/20/2017)

"[We] were both impressed with the progress the students had made and their thoughtful questions to us." (emailed, 3/20/2017)

"We are so lucky to have you all your students working in this project. I do believe we are the ones who have to be more thankful because you have help us to provide to our seniors an easier way to practice their knowledge to become citizens." (emailed, 5/19/2017)

The strongest positive feedback came from an ad-hoc visit by a group of developers and UX students performing user acceptance testing at the senior centre. Working directly with the senior citizens, students took feedback on the design and performance of the game. Seniors reported:

> "[...] *feeling heard and empowered because the students wanted to listen to their opinions. They were so happy to have participated in the development process.*" (phone call, 3/27/2017)

A secondary positive result is that one student was offered a part-time IT administrator position for the senior centre.

Student Feedback

Students submitted a final reflection after project handoff. No student feedback on the blended course delivery mechanism was received. This indicates that such delivery is acceptable, if not commonplace. Overall student satisfaction with the course was high. Many students (40%) also wrote (at length) about the importance of good group work and being a good teammate in a group development scenario.

> *"I learned it is hard to work in a big team, it takes a lot of management to diffuse confusion and remedy apathy because of that confusion. I learned that I am not a manager type, I did not envy the scrum masters during the project duration. That being said I feel like I did gain confidence in my communication skills by being force to do it to finish the project."* (Q1)

Students overwhelmingly preferred the hands-on aspect of the course (Q2).

> *"I liked the pressure this project brought. Having actual clients, and an actual quiz that needs to be delivered provided a different viewpoint than other classes. It gave more real world experience than simply learning through lectures and papers. I was able to adapt quickly throughout this project, being a tester was the foundation of development, and constantly being prepared to run changes in the game was important."*

> *"I like that we were able to work on a real life problem and that there are people that need this product and they will be using it. I also like that we did not waist (*sic*) our time developing a product that will never see the light or no-one will use it."*

It must however be noted that several students wished that there had not been an actual client as it added undue pressure (Q2). This could be a reflection of the added vulnerability of the user population at hand.

> *"I think we should participate in activities without the stress of creating a product for someone who actually needs it."*

While most enjoyed the team environment (Q6):

> *"I liked that I could work with a group. This is something that I could put on my resume or tell a potential employer about when I apply for a job. I could communicate effectively and ask for help when needed. I completed some tasks within a day and helped speed up development."*

fissures were also apparent (Q7).

> *"Sometimes my team would not communicate with me, so I did not know what needed it to be tested, and sometimes when I tested something and it was working, so I would record my results but the developer would make some changes without telling me what changes they made so I could test it one more time, so I had to figure out myself what need it to be test it."*

Though perfect harmony should not be expected in a (student) group project, so some amount of discord along with the learning process was expected. Issues such as above are more likely indicative of individual dynamics than a broad course-based issue.

DISCUSSION AND RECOMMENDATIONS

Reiterating, the goals of this class are (i) rapid prototyping (ii), developing project management as well as (iii) teamwork skills. To this extent several pedagogical tools were employed. Concentrated group work and development time was enabled by the application of blended classrooms. Additional tools and approaches to support a successful outcome included expert guidance, community partner/client visits, and online project management tools. A series of recommendations and proposed and discussed below.

Implement Sprint 0

A significant amount of stumbling blocks can be avoided by implementing a preparation Sprint (Sprint 0). Sprint 0 contains standard preparation aspects like finalizing requirements and preparing the burn chart, but also gets students 'used to' the agile process. Sprint 0 can contain sections like effective standing meeting management, conflict role-play, tech crash courses, communication planning, or best practices like interoperability in software design. Though students may come to class with some knowledge of the Agile process, students reasonably need a standard starting point [2]. The value of a leadership and a communications plan cannot be overstated [3].

Spread the Accountability

With interlocked artefacts, if single items fail, the entire software fails. Even in graded situations [6, 14] established that students are still likely to rely on a small group of dedicated students to implement the project even in the best of systems. An interesting approach from behavioural economics was proposed in the 1970's [15] to situate the class as a social choice function experiment, but few follow-up works exist to validate the results in a modern classroom.

Trust but Validate

It has been shown that trust must be present in agile processes [8]. To support trust development students and lecturers should embrace more frequent iteration validation than the standard sprint review process allows for. The classroom-based exercise necessitates more frequent showing of progress (homework-style submissions) due to its more infrequent meetings times. This level of oversight seems contrary to Agile methods as it requires committed software much more frequently than the sprint allocates. However, this is both fairer for students in the grading process as well as easier for the staff in case of implementation issues. Each timeboxed item should be submitted to the lecturer for evaluation. This need not be graded exercises; but will assist in transparent feedback with individuals and groups [16].

Best Not Easiest

While students understandably want to develop and implement in their most familiar programming languages, full autonomy is not optimal inside of a semester-based course. Students may lack the foresight of interoperability challenges (see **Sprint 0**), have a limited time scope for implementation, and in contrast to employees in a similar situation, cannot be available at the end of the project (semester). In this case, a client-focussed 'best' standard is critical for project success. Even in cases of an individual being able to implement something "better" another way, a spike considering the delta between global best and individual better must be carefully analysed.

LIMITATIONS AND FUTURE WORK

Classroom environments have the greatest chance for students to learn an approach as well as the technology being used to develop. Via service-learning projects, student developers will have already worked in similar environments and have years of experience building systems. This is particularly valuable for future corporate or entrepreneurial endeavours: while the students in this course had passed several programming classes, no classes had undefined goals. In this instance, ambiguity led to hesitation, which quickly led to a failed sprint, putting the entire project behind. In addition, students enjoy working with and for their communities (see **Student Feedback**).

For students to truly process the experience of performing agile roles, students are necessarily in the roles of SCRUM master and product owner. These members manage the backlog, assign tasks, and resolve productivity issues. However, students are unable to hold fellow students accountable. If a student SCRUM master finds someone continuously slowing development, their best option for reprimanding the offender is reporting the issue to the instructor so that they receive a lesser grade; This is not ideal as it still puts the accountability and management responsibility into the professor's hands rather than the SCRUM master's or product owner's.

To fix agile implementation in a classroom environment, a team must be able to first develop a network of trust [8]. Sprint planning and backlog prioritization is addressed as a result of stakeholder meetings, but implementing them requires the full cooperation of all team members. This requires common accountability standards to enforce performance requirements. The most effective way to do this in a classroom environment is to implement the tools necessary to make SCRUM masters the primary reporter to the lecturers. In this way, an inexperienced SCRUM master is not deciding the academic fate of an inexperienced developer, but they are the ones providing insight. With well-enforced deadlines, developers will feel more obligated to finish on time and get through sprints in a timelier manner.

Future work has several directions. Minor changes in content delivery must be made to more fully support the development process. It is worth considering employing a Teaching Assistant to fill the role of Product Owner in order to maintain student autonomy while keeping a strong validation process in place.

This course is an ongoing, required course and observed and qualitative classroom data exists in full for +3 years. This will be analysed in full. In future iterations of the course, the data collected will be moved from qualitative to quantitative (which is a current limitation of the approach in place). This will allow for statistical analysis of student outcomes.

REFERENCES

[1] Beck, K. et al. 2001. The Agile Manifesto.

[2] Boehm, B. et al. 2002. Balancing Plan-Driven and Agile Methods in Software Engineering Project Courses. Computer Science Education. 12, 3 (2002), 187–195.

[3] Cervone, H.F. 2014. Improving Strategic Planning by Adapting Agile Methods to the Planning Process. Journal of Library Administration. 54, 2 (2014), 155–168.

[4] Chen, C.S. 2002. Self - regulated Learning Strategies and Achievement in an Introduction to Information Systems Course. Information Technology, Learning, and Performance Journal. 20, 1 (2002), 11–23.

[5] Devedzic, V. and Milenkovic, S.R. 2011. Teaching Agile Software Development: A Case Study. IEEE Transactions on Education. 54, 2 (2011), 273–278.

[6] Hall, D. and Buzwell, S. 2013. The problem of free-riding in group projects: Looking beyond social loafing as reason for non-contribution. Active Learning in Higher Education. 14, 1 (2013), 37–49.

[7] Hoxmeier, J. and Lenk, M.M. 1999. Service-Learning in Information Systems Courses: Community Projects that Make a Difference. Journal of Information Systems Education. 14, 1 (1999), 91–100.

[8] McHugh 2012. Agile Practices: The Impact on Trust in Software Project Teams. IEEE Software. 29, 3, 71.

[9] Mehl, M.R. and Pennebaker, J. 2003. The sounds of social life: a psychometric analysis of students' daily social environments and natural conversations. Journal of personality and social psychology. 84, 4 (2003), 857–870.

[10] Moskal, P. et al. 2013. Blended learning: A dangerous idea? Internet and Higher Education. 18, (2013), 15–23.

[11] Napier, N.P. et al. 2011. Transitioning to blended learning: Understanding student and faculty perceptions. Journal of Asynchronous Learning Network. 15, 1 (2011), 20–32.

[12] Read, A. et al. 2014. Developing entrepreneurial skills in IT courses: The role of agile software development practices in producing successful student initiated products. Proceedings of the Annual Hawaii International Conference on System Sciences. (2014), 201–209.

[13] Rutherfoord, R.H. and Rutherfoord, J.K. 2013. Flipping the classroom: is it for you? Proceedings of the 14th annual ACM SIGITE conference on Information technology education (2013), 19–22.

[14] Umphress, D.A. et al. 2002. Software process in the classroom: The capstone project experience. IEEE Software. 19, 5 (2002), 78–85.

[15] Walker, H.M. et al. 1976. Deviant classroom behavior as a function of combinations of social and token reinforcement and cost contingency. Behavioral Therapy. 7, 1 (1976), 76–88.

[16] Wormeli, R. 2006. Accountability: Teaching Through Assessment and Feedback, Not Grading. American Secondary Education. 34, 3 (2006), 14–27.

Social Software Design to Facilitate Service-learning in Interdisciplinary Computer Science Courses

Brian Thoms
California State University, Channel Islands
Brian.Thoms@csuci.edu

Evren Eryilmaz
California State University Sacramento
Evren.Eryilmaz@csus.edu

ABSTRACT

Service-learning continues to play an increasing role in higher education as instructors look to incorporate high impact practices that challenge students through active and experiential learning. Yet limitations in learning management systems (LMS) can be barriers to service-learning project success. In this paper, we present an experience report on the design and implementation of an interdisciplinary service-learning course for computer science. We also present on the design and implementation of specialized social networking software as a mechanism to support service-learning across interdisciplinary computer science courses. More specifically, this research introduces customized social software, consisting of blogging, wiki and discussion software as tools for facilitating the specialized needs of these courses. These needs range from the ability for project management and milestone tracking, which are supported through wiki technology and messaging, self-reflection, which is supported through blogging and information exchange and knowledge sharing, which are supported through online discussion boards, social bookmarking and file-sharing. Results were largely positive, with a majority of students indicating that the course learning environment supported learning, collaboration and course community.

ACM Reference format:
Brian Thoms, and Evren Eryilmaz. 2018. Social Software Design to Facilitate Service-learning in Interdisciplinary Computer Science Courses. In *SIGCSE '18: 49th ACM Technical Symposium on Computer Science Education, Feb. 21–24, 2018, Baltimore, MD, USA*. ACM, NY, NY, USA, 6 pages. https://doi.org/10.1145/3159450.3159572

1 INTRODUCTION

According to Pew Research [1], Generation Y, commonly referred to as Millennials, overtook Baby Boomers as the largest demographic group in the United States and is comprised of over 75 million individuals. As this generation matured, higher education struggled to keep pace with their prowess for technology and penchant for collaboration. As traditional millennial-aged college students continued on into the workplace, higher education is seeing an influx of new digital natives with even greater technical prowess and emersion. Referred to as Generation Z, Post-Millennials also embrace active learning, collaboration and meaningful learning experiences [2].

A pedagogical approach grounded in active learning and one that aims to provide students with meaningful learning experiences is service-learning. As explored in [3], service-learning is a high-impact educational practice that provides students direct experiences with discipline specific concepts and with ongoing efforts to analyze and solve problems within the broader community. Pedagogically, service-learning begins with the assumption that experience is the foundation for learning and considers community service as an experiential basis for such learning [4]. For Post-Millennials, the method of pedagogical delivery of courses is also important. And within higher education the predominant mechanism for course delivery is through a learning management system (LMS). However, LMS systems may not be best suited for service-learning course delivery and, more importantly, may not be the best way to deliver content to digital natives. Experian Research estimates that 98% of adults between the ages of 18 and 24, which includes subsets of Millennials and Post-Millennials, engage in some form of online social networking [5]. Yet, as identified in [6], LMS systems are limiting in terms of their social networking capabilities such as profile building, peer-to-peer interaction and friending.

In this study, we explore the design and implementation of online social networking (OSN) software as a mechanism to support participants in service-learning courses. More specifically, we implement customized OSN software as a tool for supporting the unique needs of service-learning courses in interdisciplinary teams. These needs range from the ability for project management and milestone tracking, which is supported through wiki technology, self-reflection, which is supported through blogging technologies and information exchange and knowledge sharing, which is supported through online discussion boards. We present on both the implementation of this interdisciplinary service-learning course as well as the implementation of the OSN.

2 BACKGROUND

2.1 Course Design

The computer science course, COMP342 - Internet Based Social Networking, explores the ongoing evolution of internet-based social networks using an interdisciplinary approach. The course incorporates research from sociology, computer science, media studies, and philosophy to understand Internet based social networks, cultural and structural conditions of online

SIGCSE '18, February 21–24, 2018, Baltimore, MD, USA

ACM ISBN 978-1-4503-5103-4/18/02...$15.00
https://doi.org/10.1145/3159450.3159572

communication, virtual identity construction, management of digital media, and the impact online social networks have on various institutions of society. As an interdisciplinary course, COMP342 is cross-listed with computer science, communication and sociology and looks to synthesize broad perspectives, skills, interconnections, and epistemology surrounding internet-based social networks. The cross-listed course is available to any student with junior standing or better and fulfills the university's general education technical requirement. Cross-listed computing courses offer unique opportunities for computing programs and introduce more reluctant students to areas of computer science through the integration of theories and concepts of other disciplines [7].

In spring 2016, COMP342 was redesigned as a service-learning course and implemented in spring 2017. The overarching goal of the redesign focused on establishing a course-based project that could meet the general education requirements, while also supporting the needs of select community partners. The course redesign aimed to showcase the important role multiple disciplines play within technical projects. As a testament to this, the course project would center on the development of a single social media strategy for each of our community partners and students would work in cross-disciplinary teams and with their service-learning partners to achieve these goals.

2.2 OSN Design

2.2.1 OSN. In computer science education, and higher education in general, instructors are faced with numerous options when deciding on a collaborative learning environment. While constructivist research offers instructors important lessons on how individuals learn and places the individual at the center of a learning environment, modes of delivery and how they can support individual learning play increasingly important roles. Some environments leverage popular OSN software like Facebook or Bebo, while others leverage social components integrated within institutional LMS systems. In [8], researchers implement LMS software to facilitate service-learning, which provided basic communication and interpersonal exchange as well as archiving learning objects. However, in [9], researchers identified OSN software to be more effective at supporting project teams in capstone courses compared against a traditional LMS, which resulted in high levels of course learning, software satisfaction and course satisfaction. For the scope of this study, we categorize service-learning courses as niche subsets of project-based courses, where students work with external organizations towards the completion of project milestones. In COMP342, the final project was to develop a social media strategy, which could be shared with course participants and community partners.

2.2.2 Elgg OSN. The underlying OSN implemented in this study was Elgg. Out of the box, Elgg provides a basic set of social technologies and is customizable to match the look and feel of any organization. The user interface is simple, clean and is geared towards ease-of-use. A default installation provides an online discussion board, blog, file gallery, profile building and the ability to establish connections. Advanced features allow for the creation of sub-communities, a critical feature, which allows organizations to implement sub-groups within a single installation. Sub-groups allow instructors to create multiple courses, while allowing students to interact with peers outside their respective course community as well. Additionally, Elgg allows restrictions across multiple levels, including individual-level, community-level and logged-in-user-level restrictions, making it a choice system for project-based communities, who may wish to share project information with community partners.

Illustrated in Figure 1 is the course landing page for the COMP342 Elgg group. Within this environment, members are able to add customizable modules and RSS feeds to present them with real-time community activity. By default, users are presented with active content from across the site, including discussion activity, blog posts, file uploads and wiki updates. Notifications can also be toggled on, which provide site or email alerts when content is added or modified. Advanced features used during COMP342 were blogging and wiki documenting.

Figure 1: **COMP342 Landing Page**

2.2.3 Elgg Wiki. Wiki software affords groups of users the ability to create, read, update and delete content in collaborative fashion. Wikis typically maintain a running history of contributions, which are timestamped and available for rollback when necessary. Not only are wikis an effective mechanism for obtaining information and knowledge, such as with Wikipedia, the world's largest encyclopedia, they are also an effective technology for facilitating asynchronous virtual collaboration. Wikis also provide a shared dialogue and centralize information among group project collaborators. Additionally, as reported in [10], wikis allow members to engage in group learning and share in knowledge construction within a virtual community. Related specifically to project-based computer science courses, Xu [11] found wikis to be effective in centralizing and capturing project activities when documents were maintained by both the instructor and students. Within COMP342, the wiki played a significant role and helped coordinate all service-learning milestones, detailed further in Section 3. These notions are paramount for project teams working collaboratively towards shared goals and shared understandings. Additionally, a wiki can provide project teams with a level of coordination and synchronization not afforded by other means, which offers a final artifact that can be shared between students and community partners; one that may be revisited after the course and in later projects.

2.2.4 Elgg Blog. Blog, short for weblog, is a technology that fosters user-centric content creation. Blogs can be standalone websites, such as wordpress.com or embedded within a larger online environment, for example, Elgg. Blogs differ greatly from wikis, and are typically single-authored. Academic blogging has been widely studied and helps to promote reflection, which can lead to intellectual identity [12]. As part-service, part-learning, the blogging component supports service-learning reflection by students on relevant course topics.

2.2.5 Elgg Asynchronous Online Discussion. Illustrated in Figure 2, asynchronous online discussions (AOD) facilitate back and forth discourse among participants, which are usually grounded in a central topic. Typically, AODs are multi-threaded for easier navigation and information digestion. AODs play an integral component within learning environments and help bind individual learning experiences to greater course community. AODs are best conceptualized by their ability to facilitate cognitive, on-topic, on-task, and sustained discussion among students [13]. While the wiki offered team-based collaboration and the blog provided self-reflection, the AOD allowed all COMP342 students to interact across relevant course concepts.

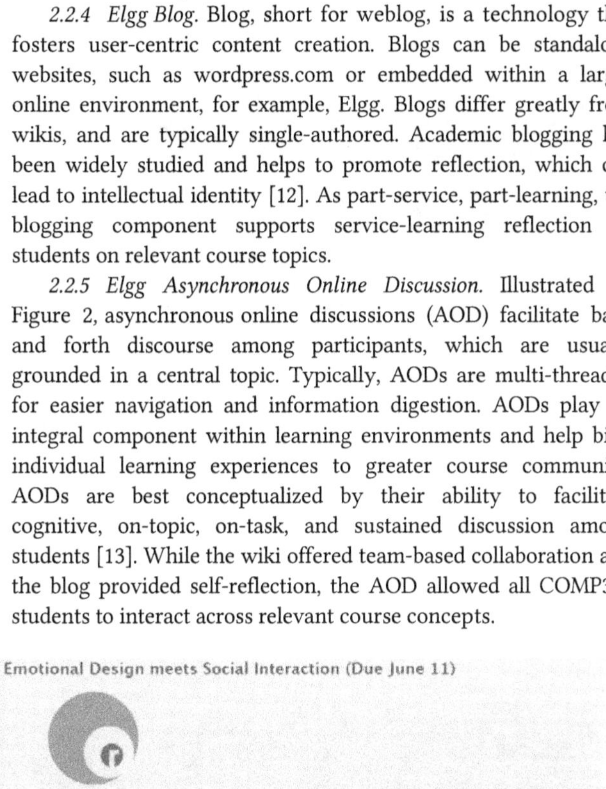

Figure 2: **Elgg AOD– Course Discussions.**

3 INTERVENTION

3.1 Community Partner Selection

Prior to the start of COMP342, the instructor met with key university stakeholders from the Center for Community Engagement (CCE). During these initial meetings, best practices in service-learning were reviewed and preliminary course objectives were identified. During the weeks that followed, the instructor solidified the course syllabus using criteria established in [14]. While components such as service-learning objectives, project measurement, assignments and reflection could be predetermined, other service-learning criteria required coordination with community partners such as community needs, community placement and required time commitments.

Working with the CCE, a subset of ten community partners were selected from a potential list of more than 70 available community partners. Initial meetings with partners helped to collect more background on the scope and specific needs of these organizations. Also during these meetings, the instructor shared the work-in-progress syllabus, including high-level service-learning goals that aligned with course learning objectives. Break-out discussions and question-answer sessions helped narrow the scope of potential projects and better align service-learning goals with the needs of the community partners. Prior to the start of the semester, a more manageable subset of six partners were selected for inclusion in COMP342. At this stage, the instructor met with each partner individually to clearly document the basic needs of the organization. This information was updated into the COMP342 OSN and made available to students from the onset.

3.2 Student Population

The number of course participants was 23, not including the instructor and course stakeholders. All participants were traditional college-aged students with ages ranging from 20-25. The demographic composition of the class was 52% female and 48% male. Student majors consisted of computer science majors (20%), communication majors (20%), sociology and psychology majors (20%), non-profit management majors (20%) and liberal arts majors (20%). All project teams were comprised of students from multiple disciplines and formal team roles were not defined.

An anonymous survey captured students' experience with OSN technologies. All students completed the survey and results identified that the majority of students were experienced or very experienced (92%) with social networking technologies, while no participants indicated having little or no experience. Students were also presented with a specialized Elgg tutorial, which detailed all technologies. Expectations for netiquette and digital citizenship were also provided and reviewed in class.

3.3 Service-learning Phases

3.3.1 Phase 1, Project Initiation. During Phase 1, Project Initiation, students were introduced to the six community partners. Organizational information and links to external resources were made available through the course wiki prior to an initial meet-and-greet. During the first week of classes, community partners presented students with the mission and scope of their organization. This also provided students with the chance to meet one-on-one with community partners during break-out sessions. In total, six service-learning projects were identified consisting of teams of 2 or more.

Phase 1 also required students to select a partner and investigate the organization's mission and scope and present the information back to the classroom using the course project wiki. A sample wiki document is illustrated in Figure 3. The wiki document structure can be observed to the right of the document and was preformatted for each phase, yet students could create, update and delete pages at their discretion.

Figure 3: **Wiki documenting as a mechanism for information management.**

3.3.2 Phase 2: Requirements Gathering. During Phase 2, students performed a more detailed analysis of existing OSN technologies in order to better understand which types of social technologies support various individuals and groups. During this phase, students were required to work closely with community partners to identify OSN strategies that could support the organizational needs identified during Phase 1. Phase 2 also required students to discover more about their respective organizations, target audience and service needs. This task was realized through the construction of user-personas (1 per student). Illustrated in Figure 4, a user persona is a software design technique and an effective method for understanding and characterizing individual users of a system. Illustrated in Figure 5, students were also required to align specific internet-based social networking technologies within the social media design framework (SMDF) to understand what aspects of the technology could be useful for their partner organizations.

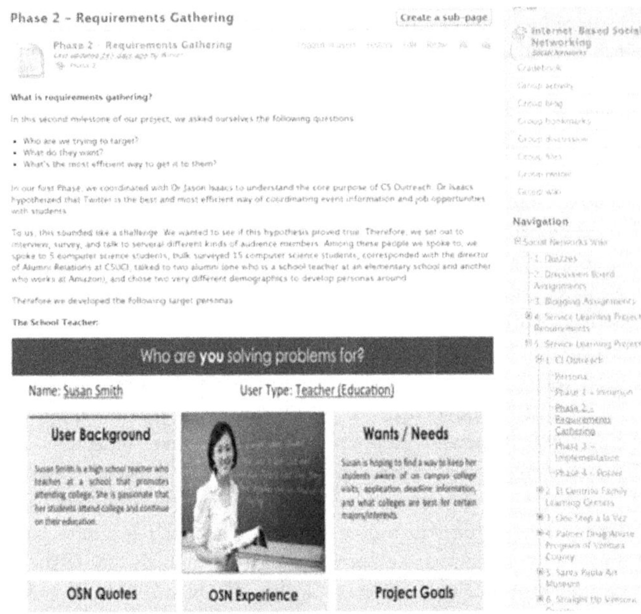

Figure 4: **Wiki documenting as a mechanism for project management and requirements gathering.**

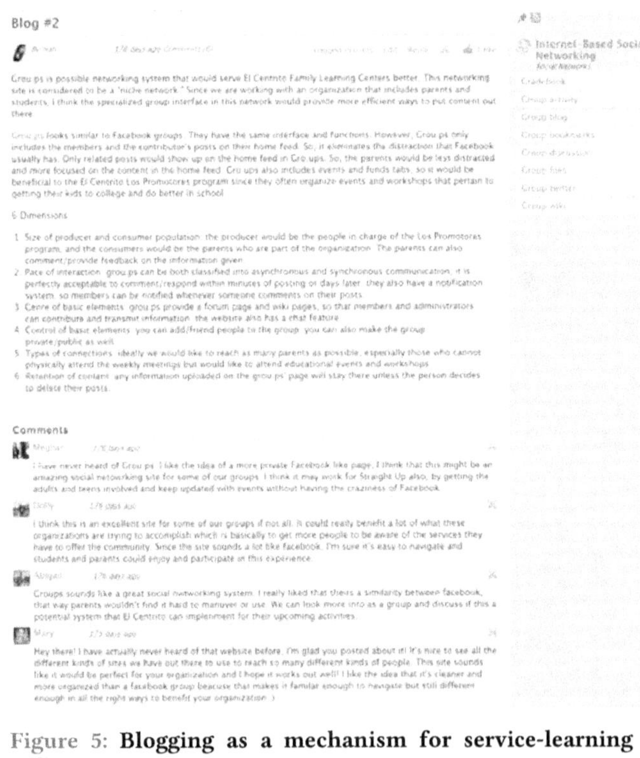

Figure 5: **Blogging as a mechanism for service-learning reflection.**

3.3.3 Phase 3: Implementation. In Phase 3, students were required to finalize their working framework or design documents and provide details on how organizations could achieve the objectives set forth in Phase 1 and Phase 2. These documents consisted of guidelines, best practices and tutorials for how partner organizations might integrate various social networking technologies and social media. Students utilized the course wiki to manage Phase 3 documentation. Wiki documents also served as the primary artifact for knowledge transfer with organizations and the instructor. The benefits of the wiki come from its ability to assign public read-only access, allowing teams to share their work with community partners at the conclusion of the course.

3.3.4 Phase 4: Presentation. In Phase 4, project teams were required to construct comprehensive posters highlighting their project work and achievements. Invitations were sent to community partners to attend the Celebration of Service held by the CCE. The event allowed students to share their work publicly with all CCE community partners. Additionally, posters were uploaded to the OSN discussion and classmates had the opportunity to reflect on their service-learning projects and respond to their classmates' work.

4 OUTCOMES

4.1 Service-learning Results

As part of the requirements for a service-learning course, students provided a personal reflection and summary of the work they performed, summarized and presented below.

4.1.1 SL Group 1. Group 1's partner organization was a community youth organization. The organization utilizes improvisational techniques for engaging and creating drug awareness and prevention. Service-learning goals centered on establishing a social media campaign to solicit funding, create brand awareness, extend outreach and promote events. Group 1 goals centered on using Instagram as a promotional tool to promote events through interactive giveaways in order to increase their number of followers, likes and facilitate overall exposure of the program. Additionally, the group helped to identify clear guidelines for posting to social media accounts, including how much content to post and the types of images to include. Challenges this group faced involved time management, communication and limited technical knowledge.

4.1.2 SL Group 2. Group 2's partner organization was a non-profit museum, which provides educational programs and rotating art exhibitions. While the museum had an existing social media presence on Facebook and Instagram, it was receiving limited engagement from its base audience. Group 2 was tasked with identifying a social media strategy that could promote greater awareness to the organization's programs. Their project involved constructing an online survey, which the organization could use to better understand their base demographic. This team also created a social media campaign that would best operationalize the results of this survey. Challenges Group 2 faced included time management issues, intra- and inter-team communication and logistical problems surrounding the location of the museum.

4.1.3 SL Group 3. Group 3's partner organization was a substance abuse program for adolescents. As our smallest partner organization with only a handful of coordinators, this organization was struggling to reach out to potential donors and was having a difficult time creating awareness of its programs. Group 3 looked to ameliorate these issues through a simplified, yet strategic social media campaign. The service-learning team searched for low-hanging fruit and implemented easy-to-use technologies such as LinkedIn and Facebook to more effectively publicize the organization's mission. The challenges facing this team involved generational issues, as the management team for this organization was a much older demographic and contributed to issues in communication and technology transfer.

4.1.4 SL Group 4. Group 4's partner organization was educational outreach. The goal for this partnership was to help better engage the organization with the surrounding community and facilitate connection-making with potential partners and donors. To facilitate this, Group 4 established a Twitter account and identified an entire social media campaign based on a survey that the team constructed. Challenges this group faced included intra-team communication and general project focus.

4.1.5 SL Group 5. Group 5's partner organization provides bi-lingual educational services for children. For this organization, parent engagement is instrumental, since parents are the target demographic that the organization provides services for. Group 5 was tasked with creating a Facebook campaign that would better engage the organizations 60+ Facebook followers. Some of the potential solutions this group identified involved sharing Facebook posts across other social media sites including Twitter and Instagram, establishing an email listserv to keep parents updated on programs, and establishing consistent guidelines for posting to social media. A significant barrier for this group was the organization's mission to provide English and Spanish-language material.

4.1.6 SL Group 6. Group 6's service-learning partner was a community youth organization, which looks to engage adolescents in after-school activities and programs. The role of service-learning was to use social media to help create awareness about programs and expand the organizational mission through the use of social networking and social media. The final artifacts included a set of best practices for social media, a strategy for rebranding the organizational website and a campaign to create awareness on environmental justice, which the partner deemed as an important mission pillar. The primary challenge facing this team was logistical in nature, as the organization was located further than any other partner organization.

4.2 System Usage

The OSN played an instrumental role throughout the semester. The total number of pageviews generated across the OSN by active, logged-in users was 20,136. Wiki pages, which captured required project documentation, received the most pageviews and constituted 25% of all site activity. This was followed by the homepage and activity page which received 23% of all page views. Blogs, which supported student reflection, received 13% of pageviews and course discussion boards received 10%. Bookmarks, which linked to course-related documents, received 12% of pageviews. All other pages, including file uploads, profiles and messaging received the remaining 17% of pageviews.

4.3 System Feedback

While challenges and limitations to the system design exist, anonymous survey instruments captured aspects of the system related to learning, interaction if course community. Of 20 respondents completing the survey, 85% agreed that the OSN increased interaction, with 10% neither agreeing nor disagreeing and 5% strongly disagreeing. Of the same set of responses, 90% indicated that the software supported learning, with 5% neither agreeing nor disagreeing and 5% strongly disagreeing. Regarding course community, 95% indicated that the software supported community, with 5% neither agreeing nor disagreeing. Lastly, 95% of respondents agreed or strongly agreed that the OSN was important for the course with 5% strongly disagreeing.

5 CONCLUSIONS

5.1 Interdisciplinary Service-Learning Courses

One of the mission pillars of the university, centers on community engagement. Service-learning courses facilitate this engagement and can help strengthen the bond between the college and partner organizations, providing substantial benefits for both.

5.1.1 Student Benefits of Service-learning. While often above and beyond the demands of traditional classes, students are challenged with real-world problems and needs and are required to collaborate with classmates and partner organizations. These partnerships often result in rich relationships with community organizations. In reflective essays at the end of the semester, students indicated a strong bond with partners. One student wrote, "I fully intend to volunteer with this non-profit after graduation," while another stated, "I will be continuing to volunteer through the summer". Other students reflected on the experiences they had working collaboratively. One student stated, "I'm really glad I got to work with my group, we all got along great and always seemed to be on the same page" and another remarked, "Our group rocked the challenge of social media together!" Regarding the overall service-learning experience students made such comments as, "The satisfactions of SL was making connections, going out of my comfort zone, and exploring more of the area that I probably wouldn't be aware of had it not been for this class" and "Regardless of the miscommunication and potential struggles within the service learning project, it was very interesting to explore the cultural and needs of the organization."

5.1.2 Partner Benefits of Service-learning. For community partners, service-learning offered a new lens for viewing how social networking technologies might be leveraged. In addition to possible technical improvements, service-learning also helped partner organizations enhance awareness of their organization since students presented their work in a public forum at the end of the semester. Furthermore, the use of an OSN provided community partners with a permanent final artifact that persisted even after the course concluded.

5.1.3 Computer Science Benefits of Service-learning. From the perspective of the computing field, interdisciplinary, service-learning courses present students with a perspective to organizational problem solving that they would rarely, if ever, experience in other courses. More so, many students did not realize the scope of the computing field and how it requires thinking and strategies from numerous disciplines to help solve real-world organizational problems. For example, it was encouraging to see teams with diverse compositions assigning tasks relevant to their field such as survey instrument creation (psychology), technical design (computer science) and coordination and planning (communication and non-profit management).

5.2 OSN Integration

Overall, OSN software provided a viable and beneficial environment for supporting interdisciplinary service-learning courses. The strengths in OSN software come from its focus on social interaction through collaborative writing, connection-making, discussion boards and blogs. As an interdisciplinary service-learning course, students were required to work in teams to coordinate on service-learning project milestones, which were supported through the project wiki. System usage and user feedback provided valuable insight into the potential for using social networking software as a mechanism for supporting future service-learning courses.

6 REFERENCES

[1] Fry, R. (2016). "Millennials overtake Baby Boomers as America's largest generation," Retrieved on Aug. 1, 2017 from http://www.pewresearch.org/fact-tank/2016/04/25/millennials-overtake-baby-boomers.

[2] Rickes, PC. (2016). "Generations in Flux: How Gen Z Will Continue to Transform Higher Education Space," *Planning for Higher Education*; Ann Arbor 44(4).

[3] Kuh, GD. (2008). High-impact educational practices: What they are, who has access to them, and why they matter. Washington, DC: Association of American Colleges and Universities.

[4] Morton, K., Troppe, M. (1996). "From the Margin to the mainstream: Campus compact's project on integrating service with academic study," *Journal of Business Ethics*, 15(1).

[5] Experian Marketing Service (2011). "The 2011 Social Media Consumer Trend and Benchmark Report," Retrieved Aug. 15, 2017, from http://www.experian.com/assets/simmons-research/brochures/2011-social-media-consumer-report.pdf.

[6] Thoms, B., Eryilmaz, E. (2014). "How Media Choice Affects Learner Interactions in Distance Learning Classes," *Computers & Education*, v75.

[7] Carter, L. (2014). "Interdisciplinary computing classes: worth the effort," In *Proceedings of the 45th ACM technical symposium on Computer science education* (SIGCSE '14). ACM, New York, NY, USA.

[8] Kathy L., Guthrie, Holly McCracken. (2010). "Making a difference online: Facilitating service-learning through distance education," *The Internet and Higher Education*, 13(3).

[9] Thoms, B., Eryilmaz, E. (2015). "Online Learning Community Software to Support Success in Project Teams," *The Fifth International Conference on Advanced Collaborative Networks, Systems and Applications*, Oct. 2015.

[10] Boulos, M., Maramba, I., Wheeler, S. (2006). "Wikis, blogs and podcasts: a new generation of web-based tools for virtual collaborative clinical practice and education," *BMC Medical Education*, 6(41).

[11] Xu, L. (2007). "Project the wiki way: using wiki for computer science course project management," *Journal of Computing Sciences in Colleges*, 22(6).

[12] Kirkup, G. (2010). "Academic blogging: academic practice and academic identity," *London Review of Education*, *8*(1).

[13] Pituch, K., Lee, Y. (2006). "The influence of system characteristics on e-learning use," *Computers & Education*, 47(2).

[14] Ballard, SM, Elmore, B. (2009). "A labor of love: Constructing a service-learning syllabus," *The Journal of Effective Teaching*, 9(3).

Understanding the Software Development Industry's Perspective on Coding Boot Camps versus Traditional 4-year Colleges

Quinn Burke
College of Charleston
burkeqq@cofc.edu

Cinamon Bailey
College of Charleston
kerrcs@g.cofc.edu

Louise Ann Lyon
ETR Associates
louann.lyon@etr.org

Emily Green
ETR Associates
emily.green@etr.org

ABSTRACT

This study reports on the perceived capacity of coding boot camps versus computer science (CS) undergraduate programs to instill a range of software development skills from an industry perspective. We present findings from a series of national focus groups and individual interviews with representatives from the software development industry, who spoke about their hiring procedures and preferences as well as how they perceived coding boot camp applicants in comparison to graduates from four-year CS degree programs. We also present findings on how the boot camp and university participants viewed their role in developing necessary skills for employability. Results indicate that hiring managers filling positions, generally have a favorable perspective of coding boot camp hires in relation to their demonstration of "soft" skills, such as teamwork, passion, and persistence; With regards to four-year university hires, several industry representatives indicated that a four-year degree is mandatory for hire, while also listing a solid understanding of CS principles and substantial exposure to mathematics. The Discussion section focuses on the future potential of coding boot camps as an alternative training ground for the software development industry.

KEYWORDS

Coding boot camps; industry needs; experiential learning

ACM Reference Format

Q. Burke, C. Bailey, L. A. Lyon, and E. Green. 2018. Understanding the Software Development Industry's Perspective on Coding Boot Camps versus Traditional 4-year Colleges. In *SIGCSE '18: 49th ACM Technical Symposium on Computer Science Education, Feb. 21–24, 2018, Baltimore, MD, USA.* ACM, NY, NY, USA, 6 pages. https://doi.org/10.1145/3159450.3159485

ACM ISBN 978-1-4503-5103-4/18/02...$15.00
https://doi.org/10.1145/3159450.3159485

1. INTRODUCTION

One of the most prominent challenges facing U.S. higher education in the STEM fields is meeting the ever-growing computing needs of the U.S. workforce. The U.S. Bureau of Labor Statistics [1] projects the United States will have over one-million unfulfilled software engineering jobs by 2020, with the non-profit Code.org [2] listing the current openings in the U.S. at over 600,000. While post-secondary computer science enrollments have steadily risen since 2006 [3], the country is still drastically under-producing the computing literate workforce that an ever-growing number of industries demand.

Into this gap, a new educational player has emerged. Multi-week coding schools, such as CoderFoundry (http://www.coderfoundry.com) and Coding Dojo (http://www.codingdojo.com), offer students intensive introductions to coding, with the goal that their graduates can land entry-level software development positions after a relatively brief, yet intensive, introductory course (10-12 weeks on average according to Course Report [4]). The price tag for such education represents a steep upfront cost at $12,147 on average [4]. The average cost of a 4-year degree currently at $98,440 [5].

Most information we have about these camps comes from popular media articles detailing "rags to riches" success stories [6, 7] or cautionary tales about hopeful students, who are cheated by bad operators in the field [8]. Our exploratory research intends to move beyond the rather casual sketches of coding boot camps offered by popular media and further delve into the role of coding boot camps in the growing post-secondary STEM education market by examining the software development industry's perspective of these programs and how they compare and fit in with traditional 4-year degree programs in CS. This paper examines what particular skill sets industry representatives expect of their entry level software developers, and to what degree coding boot camps and 4-year degree programs are meeting such needs. After a review of the relevant literature around the requisite mix of "hard" and "soft" skills characteristic of effective software developers, this paper reports on the findings of a series of national focus groups and interviews with software development representatives, boot camp representatives, and university representatives. We also discuss potential limitations of the current research as well as detail our next steps, particularly with the addition of boot camp and college student perspectives to offer a counter perspective to industry's professed outlook.

2. BACKGROUND

In order to pinpoint skills that are necessary for employability and career success, it is critical to have clear definitions of these skills. In their paper "What Makes a Great Software Engineer?" Li, Ko, and Zhu [9] arrived at a total of 53 distinct attributes that mark exceptional software engineers and noted that across these attributes, effective software engineering is clearly not just about content productivity but likewise about the manner with which such content is produced (i.e., the "how" is stressed much more often by interviewees than the "what").

Within industry, this distinction between "how" and "what" often translates into the distinction between "soft" and "hard" skill sets. "Soft" skills refer to those skills that relate to a person's personality and ability to work with others (communication, critical thinking, empathy, conflict resolution, flexibility, adaptability, and creativity among others). Yet despite the poplar moniker of "soft", such skills are increasingly being identified as the crucial attributes for success in the current marketplace, with prominent institutions [10], Meanwhile, "hard" skills refer to specific knowledge and cognitive capabilities required for a job (computer programming, mathematics, data analysis, etc.). With regards to "hard" skills, an individual may possess procedural knowledge (how something works in a certain way) and/or conceptual knowledge (why something works the way it does) [11].

Hatano and Inagaki [12] offered a more nuanced split between skills, differentiating between "routine" and "adaptive" expertise. Individuals, who have learned a set of routines that they master and continue to become more efficient in applying, are said to have routine expertise. They will continue to learn throughout their lifetime but will often only apply their new knowledge in a manner that makes the existing procedures/routines more efficient. On the other hand, an individual with adaptive expertise will utilize the knowledge they obtain and apply it to new, innovative procedures or solutions to problems.

The question for our study is the degree to which software development companies value/search out these respective skills sets, and to what extent they report 4-year CS programs and coding boot camps have the capacity to inculcate these crucial elements.

3.1 Participants

Fifteen industry representatives/hiring managers (8 females, 7 males) from twelve different software development companies voluntarily participated in this study. Three of these companies were classified as small sized (<50 employees), four were classified as medium sized (51-250 employees), and five were classified as large sized (>250 employees). Additionally, eleven national boot camp volunteer representatives (4 females, 7 males) from eleven different boot camps participated. The third group of participants consisted of nine university professors (3 females, 6 males) from nine different undergraduate computer science programs.

Participants were recruited through online postings via the National Center for Women in IT (NCWIT), the Special Interest Group in Computer Science listserv (SIGCSE), "cold" emailing Boot Camps directly through the contacts made available through CourseReport [4], as well as "cold" emailing to prospective industry representatives, and through connections via the grant's advisory panel.

3.2 Data Collection & Analysis

From August 2016 through December 2016, the research team conducted a total of three industry focus groups and four one-on-one interviews with industry managers/ directors about their hiring needs and procedures for entry-level software developers. Questions focused on (1) student/ employee recruitment and retention; (2) skills, knowledge, and competencies expected by graduates of each training ground, and (3) what companies expected of code camps and universities alike. All focus groups were semi-structured and intended to provoke free responses and wider discussion. The boot camp and university participants (instructors or faculty who determine their department's CS curriculum) were likewise interviewed with questions focused on (1) curriculum design/ implementation (2) recruitment, admission, and assessment procedures (3) student profiles and (4) skills emphasized within program.

All focus groups and interviews were subsequently transcribed and qualitatively analyzed using both NVivo and Dedoose software. The research team constructed a preliminary coding schema [13], consisting of a series of primary overarching coded categories and two levels of subcategories (i.e. "secondary" and "tertiary" codes).

With their coding, the research team had a threefold purpose. First, to what extent was the drafted coding schema effective as a tool to consistently capture and classify relevant participant responses? Second, to what degree was there inter-coder reliability with regards to the utterances selected to be coded? Campbell [14] refers to this selection of coded utterances as "unitization". Third, to what degree would their codes match on the overarching primary, secondary, and tertiary levels? Reliability was calculated based on three sample coding comparisons between two coders. Across these three, there was 100% agreement on the 4 primary codes, 94% agreement on the secondary codes, and 87% agreement on the tertiary codes. As expected, primary codes saw the highest percentage of agreement, while the increasingly nuanced secondary and tertiary sub-categories saw inter-rater agreement slightly decrease incrementally. Such a decline is expected as the increased nuance and specificity of the sub-categories can result in a wider fluctuation in interpretation [15]. Table #1 offers the project's overall research questions and coding schema.

Primary code	Secondary (and Tertiary Codes)
RQ: What kinds of learners are attracted to different learning opportunities and why?	
Recruitment and Admission	Program for Recruitment & Admission; Recruitment of a Diverse Student Body; and Student Reason or Motivation
Learner Profile	Demographics; Cognitive Characteristics; Interpersonal Characteristics; and Intrapersonal Characteristics
RQ: What kinds of s/w development learning opportunities are offered by undergrad programs? Boot camps?	
Learning Opportunities	Training Environment (Professor Designed, Student Experience, Underrepresentation, and Institutional Realities); Programmatic Outcome (Anticipated or Stated, and Actual or Experienced); Practice; and Skills and Knowledge (Developing Cognitive Skills, Developing Interpersonal Skills, and Developing Intrapersonal Skills)
RQ: How well do the settings align with regional s/w development industry's needs?	
Industry Needs	Hiring Practices/Standards and Expectations for Hiring; Industry Partnerships; Skills and Knowledge (Cognitive Skills, Interpersonal Skills, and Intrapersonal Skills); and Working Environment (Employee Experienced, Underrepresentation, and Workplace Expectations/Realities)

TABLE #1: Research Questions and Coding Schema

4. RESULTS

4.1 Soft Skills & Hard Skills as Hiring Indicators

Over the course of the hour-long focus groups with industry representatives, "soft" skills were uniformly the most prevalent topic of discussion. 100% of industry participants noted the importance of soft skills in hiring and as the table below indicates, soft skills were twice as likely to come up than "hard" skills in the focus groups discussions.

	Utterances About Soft Skills	Utterances About Hard Skills	Total Utterances
Small sized companies	67	20	87
Medium sized companies	35	14	49
Large sized companies	83	62	145
Total	185	96	281

TABLE #2: Mention of "Soft" Versus "Hard" Skills Based on Company Size

Multiple industry participants pointed to how extensive their interview process is, as this is where "soft" skills are assessed. The graph below represents those requisite "soft" skills that came up most often among focus group participants, with teamwork and communication (36.8%) as the leading expectation of new hires and with the ability/ desire to continue learning as the second leading expectation (29.2%).

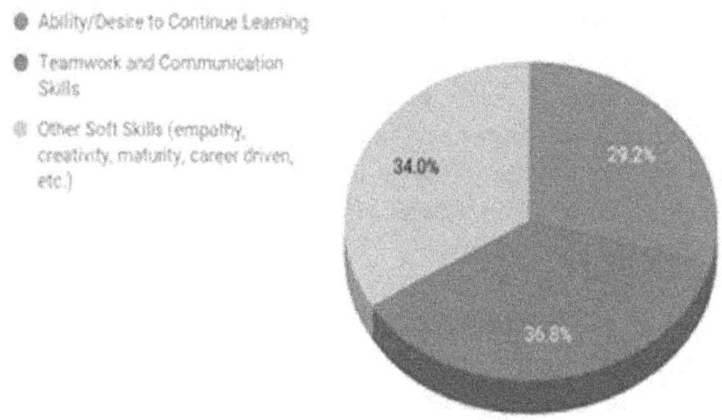

GRAPH #1: Breakdown of Soft Skills desired by Industry Representatives

90% of these industry participants also indicated that routine skill sets, such as the capacity to program, were a necessary initial indicator for hiring. A director of a Southeast big data engineering company noted that "you have to have the technical baseline understanding and aptitude. You wouldn't pass that first screening if you didn't have that." Several of the participants also noted that these requirements often change rapidly within this industry; whereas, the desire to hire individuals, who demonstrate "soft" skills, such as teamwork and the ability/desire to continue to learn, remains consistent with time. In fact, as one hiring manager stated, "if it's someone that they don't think they could get along with, they simply will turn the person down, even if that individual has very strong skills in terms of the technical know-how."

4.2 Employer Preference: Coding Boot Camp or 4-year degrees?

Several companies listed a 4-year degree (or higher) as essential for hire. Many of these companies did not list a specific preference for CS university degrees. In fact, some indicated that hires with alternative degrees, such as music, physics, or education degrees were successful due to similar problem solving traits as CS graduates as well as "the breadth of education that you would get from a 4-year degree, just from baseline knowledge, and experience perspective, versus people that have come through maybe a boot camp situation." A hiring manager from a small data analytics company listed a preference for candidates with a 4-year degree or higher because "some of the practice areas, especially in a data science area, require a pretty heavy mathematical background, so they need an education in statistical math that's deeper than you would get through a boot camp." Three companies recognized university graduates for having more theoretical knowledge and knowing "the best algorithm to make something work". Some companies do not even bother to interview boot camp graduates due to either having enough college candidates to choose from or not "view[ing] it as much of an asset" to the company.

On the other hand, several companies (including companies focused on consulting, software development and support, automobile technology, and digital marketing for education and healthcare) stated that in certain cases, they actually prefer their boot camp hires. These participants praised their coding boot camp hires based on the fact that they were often older and had more experience with hands-on projects as well as more efficient problem-solving skills based on their work and educational experiences. Furthermore, software development companies prefer candidates with up-to-date knowledge. Four of the managers interviewed noted that a boot camp hire tends to have more current knowledge; whereas, the undergraduate hire may not have been exposed to newer software programs/hardware. Participants also indicated boot camp hire strengths in the areas of communication, code development, more experience pairing, better reactions to critical feedback, and passion and perseverance in work projects. For example, a large online travel and entertainment company states "when you have this input algorithm that works, and then you have someone that's basically just putting it into code, the code you end up with is much more readable and much more logical, and just much more common sense coming out of a boot camp graduate than from a computer science graduate". A large automobile technology company stated that CS graduates are "generally not so much taught to code. They don't come out as the best developers, and they may be able to analyze a problem very well... They can think about the theory really well and explain the theory of things really well, but then when they actually sit down to code, their habits aren't great. Their naming conventions aren't great. They generally are unfamiliar with just basic development tools."

It was also notable that more often than not, code camp hires actually also had a college degree, albeit not in CS. In the focus groups with code camp administrators, we learned that most of their students already had at least a four-year degree (66% on the low end to 80%, on the high end), typically in a liberal arts major/ concentration.

4.3 Perspectives from Coding Boot Camp & Undergraduate CS Programs

As the data in the above sections indicate, positive hire attributes include a mix of both soft and hard skills. Prior work experience counts considerably as does the desire for continuous learning, the capacity to work in teams and ability to receive critical feedback. In terms of hard skills, industry representatives regularly cited the need to know CS principles (data analysis, algorithms) and have a solid background in rigorous mathematics. Industry also pointed toward the need for efficient coding practices and some stressed up to date knowledge of current software development platforms.

So where are these skills inculcated within undergraduate CS programs and coding boot camps? Of the nine CS undergraduate faculty members who participated in this study, all indicated that the development of hard skills is built into their respective curricula. Mandatory classes are offered in data structures, design patterns, software architectures, as well as classes that focus on understanding how computer science is used on the job. Undergraduates instructors were less agreed upon where their students learned soft skills in the classroom, such as teamwork and clear communication. Participants reported that often these skills were not explicitly taught in their classrooms but were tacitly encouraged through the nature of assignments. As one professor points out, simply exposing undergraduates to multiple languages helps them "get over fear of, 'Oh, here's another language I have to learn.'" She added this this exposure to multiple languages also had the side benefit of making her students "more willing to go and explore other languages and take on opportunities." Sometimes instruction was more explicit. Multiple undergraduate instructors reported that they would directly tell students about the importance of continuous learning; some engaged in role playing with senior capstone work, while others had students work in pairs and in teams on select assignments. Six of the nine college/ university participants mentioned inviting in guest industry speakers as a way to ground students' learning in actual application. However, undergraduate CS faculty also reported on the challenges associated with inculcating so-called "soft" skills, such as large class sizes, their own inability to change departmental curricula in a timely manner to meet industry needs, and the challenge of teaching from textbooks in which the solutions to the problems have already been posted on the web. Some professors stated outright that they do not believe that teaching the latest languages and platforms was the role of the university. One professor stated that "the university is about education and not training."

The eleven coding boot camp instructors and administrators, who participated had no such problem categorizing their programs as training. The majority classified their programs as a form of experiential learning and spoke to the daily projects and assignments, which often mimicked real life projects and workplace conditions. As one boot camp representative stated, "the best way to learn is to actually teach. The second-best way to learn is by actually by doing it yourself. Experiential learning...That's a large part of what they do here and that's a large part of what their employer will expect to do as a professional." Other methods used to develop student skills include job prep courses, internships, options to repeat modules following feedback, alumni mentorship programs, seat assignments, project-based learning, portfolio development, development of continuing learning groups for alumni, lectures, group projects, and forming industry partnerships and collaborations. With regards to class size, one boot camp participant noted "Sometimes we have 25 students in the class, sometimes we have more like 15." Finally, coding boot camps reported to be necessarily more responsive to current industry needs. As one administrator stated, code camps are in "a unique position to pivot really quickly, and address those needs." They are able to change curriculum in between student cohorts in order to" fix things that are not working, get the feedback, improve it and so on."

5. DISCUSSION

Our national focus group discussions with software development managers support the same conclusion that Li, Ko, and Zhu [9] posit in "What Makes a Great Software Engineer?": software development is very much a *socio*technical undertaking, not just a technical one. But based on our data, for industry, this "socio" element takes considerable more effort in terms of recruiting and retaining new talent.

While the research presented here is still in early stages, it does not appear from these focus groups that code camps are a threat to four-year programs. Data in this study in fact suggests that most boot camp hires also have an undergraduate degree. Also, it appears that there are human resource requirements mandating hiring candidates with at least a college degree. However, this data also suggests that companies, which prefer college degrees do not necessarily prefer a CS degree. Furthermore, while our preliminary research with industry managers and directors is hardly a representative sample, it does indicate that some companies are quite willing to interview and hire boot camp graduates—a finding supported by Course Report's [4] annual job placement statistics for boot camp graduates. It is likewise quite clear from our research that the hard (routine) skill of programming is increasingly not enough to land a job. At this point, coding boot camps seem to be fulfilling the role of continuing educational facilities to assist with career growth, career change, and add additional skill sets for resume building. While this may not affect undergraduate CS programs, it could impact future graduate school admissions as candidates may opt for the less expensive route for further education.

What is less clear from our research at this time is to what degree undergraduate programs and coding boot camps inculcate the leading soft and hard skills we have detailed here. Are teamwork and perseverance, in fact, skills that can be developed in these educational programs? Are they even skills, or are they attributes that the individual student enters a program with?

In the next phase of our data collection—individual interviews with CS undergraduates and code camp students—we begin to investigate these questions more directly. What technical proficiencies have these students gained over their respective post-secondary educational environments? What soft skills have they learned (or further developed)? Or do they feel these skills are ones they already had prior to admission? Among those first-year graduates who have already landed a position at a software development company, to what extent did their respective training prepare them for year one of the job? This next step offers a corollary and balance to the industry perspectives we have reported here.

ACKNOWLEDGEMENT

The writing of this paper was supported by through a pair of National Science Foundation (NSF) Core Research and Development Grants to the first and third author. The views expressed in this paper are their own and not necessarily those of the NSF nor their respective institutions.

REFERENCES

[1] The U.S. Bureau of Labor Statistics. 2017. Retrieved from https://www.bls.gov.

[2] Code.org. 2017. Computer science education stats. Retrieved from https://code.org/promote.

[3] Computing Research Association. 2017. Generation CS: CS undergraduate enrollments surge. Retrieved from http://cra.org/data/Generation-CS.

[4] Course Report. 2017. Retrieved from https://www.coursereport.com/.

[5] College Data. 2017. What's the price tag for a college education?" Retrieved from http://www.collegedata.com/cs/content/content_payarticle_tmpl.jhtml?articleId=%2010064

[6] Margo Greenman. 2016. Intensive training helps coding newcomers land technology jobs. (September 2016). Retrieved from http://425business.com/ intensive-training-helps-coders-land-technology-jobs/.

[7] Steve Lohr. 2017. A new kind of tech job emphasizes skills, not a college degree. (June 2017). *The New York Times.* Retrieved from https://www.newyorktimes.com/2017/06/28/technology/tech-jobs-skills-college-degree,html?mcubz=2.

[8] Sarah McBride. 2016. Want a job in Silicon Valley? Keep away from coding schools. (December 2016). *Bloomberg Technology.* Retrieved from https:// www.bloomberg.com/news/features/2016-12-06/want-a-job-in-silicon-valley-keep-away-from-coding-schools.

[9] Paul Luo Li, Andrew J. Ko, & Jiamin Zhu, J. 2016. What makes a great software engineer?" n *Proceedings of the 37th International Conference on Software Engineering - Volume 1* (ICSE '15), Vol. 1. IEEE Press, Piscataway, NJ, USA, 700-710.

[10] James Pellegrino. 2016. What is the evidence on teaching & learning 21st Century skills? *Presentation at the National Research Council on 21st Century Skills.* Retrieved https://www.youtube.com/watch?v=RctULp9Gugo.

[11] James Hiebert & P. Lefevre. 1986. Conceptual and procedural knowledge in mathematics. *Science and Education* (pp. 1-27). Hillsdale, NJ: Erlbaum.

[12] Giyoo Hatano & Kayoko Inagati. 1986. Two courses of expertise. In H. Stevenson, H. Azuma, & K.

[13] Matthew Lombard, Jennifer Snyder-Duch & Cheryl Campanella Bracken. 2010. Practical resources for assessing and reporting intercoder reliability.. Retrieved from http://matthewlombard.com/reliability/.

[14] John L. Campbell. 2013. Coding in-depth semi structured interviews: Problems of unitization and intercoder reliability and agreement. *Sociological Methods & Research ,42 (3),* 294-320.

An Experience Report on a Boot-Camp Style Programming Course

Yu-Cheng Tu
Department of Computer Science
The University of Auckland
yu-cheng.tu@auckland.ac.nz

Gillian Dobbie
Department of Computer Science
The University of Auckland
g.dobbie@auckland.ac.nz

Ian Warren
Department of Computer Science
The University of Auckland
i.warren@auckland.ac.nz

Andrew Meads
Department of Computer Science
The University of Auckland
andrew.meads@auckland.ac.nz

Cameron Grout
Department of Computer Science
The University of Waikato
cameron.grout@waikato.ac.nz

ABSTRACT

Recently, there has been a strong demand for talented ICT (Information and Communication Technology) graduates in the software industry in New Zealand. To meet this demand, in 2015, the government of New Zealand provided funding for three new ICT Graduate Schools. The challenge for the schools was twofold: to provide a qualification for students transitioning into ICT and to prepare those with an ICT education for the workforce. Each of the Schools offer different programmes. We offer two postgraduate programmes for growing talent and knowledge to support the New Zealand's ICT sector. In this paper, we describe our experience with delivering one of the postgraduate programmes, the Postgraduate Certificate in Information Technology. The programme consists of two courses, Programming for Industry and Programming with Web Technologies. The courses focus on providing industry-focused education to students with non-ICT backgrounds for a career in IT. The programme has been running for 2 years and runs over one semester (12 weeks) in a "boot-camp" style, which has proved to be successful. In this paper, we provide an overview of the features of the programme, which incorporates industry-focused activities for building students' knowledge relevant to the software industry. Finally, we discuss key challenges and identify directions for improvement.

KEYWORDS

bootcamps; learning by doing; programming education

ACM Reference format:
Yu-Cheng Tu, Gillian Dobbie, Ian Warren, Andrew Meads, and Cameron Grout. 2018. An Experience Report on a Boot-Camp Style Programming Course. In *Proceedings of SIGCSE '18: The 49th ACM Technical Symposium on Computer Science Education, Baltimore , MD, USA, February 21-24, 2018 (SIGCSE '18),* 6 pages.
DOI: https://doi.org/10.1145/3159450.3159541

SIGCSE '18, February 21-24, 2018, *Baltimore , MD, USA*

DOI: https://doi.org/10.1145/3159450.3159541

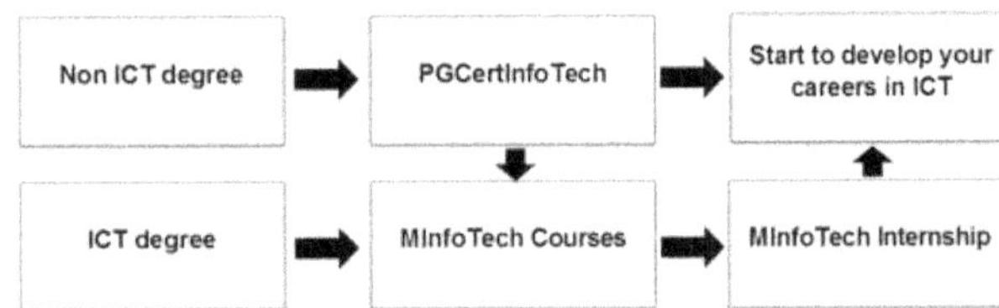

Figure 1: Pathways of our programmes.

1 INTRODUCTION

The software industry in New Zealand has a strong demand for talented and skilled ICT (Information and Communication Technology) graduates. To meet the demand, the New Zealand government provided funding for three new ICT Graduate Schools in 2015. Each school offers different programmes to meet the Government's goals of delivering industry-focused education as well as producing graduates with work-relevant and business-focused skills [3]. The challenge in meeting the goals is twofold:

- To provide a qualification for students transitioning into ICT, and
- To prepare those with an ICT education for the workforce.

Our school is a joint collaboration between two universities in New Zealand. We offer two postgraduate programmes to grow talent and knowledge in supporting the ICT sector. The two programmes are the Postgraduate Certificate in Information Technology and the Master of Information Technology. Both programmes aim to provide industry-relevant education and to connect students with ICT businesses. Figure 1 illustrates the pathways of the two programmes.

The Master of Information Technology (MInfoTech) enables students with relevant ICT degrees to progress further in ICT education and applied research. The MInfoTech allows students to specialise in ICT areas such as mobile security, networking, and data management. The MInfoTech also develops students' industry-relevant soft skills, such as communication and project management, through business-focused courses and workshops. Moreover, each MInfoTech student undertakes a 10-week internship in the software industry. By the end of the Masters programme, students are able to meet industry needs with the technical and complementary skills developed from their studies, workshops, and internship components. Students are also be able to demonstrate critical thinking and communication skills gained from the programme to prospective employers.

The Postgraduate Certificate in Information Technology (PGCertInfoTech) provides the opportunity for anyone with a non-ICT background to upskill and to pursue a career in IT. The PGCertInfoTech has run over one semester (12 weeks) in a "boot-camp" style since 2015. The programme consists of two courses that focus on principles of programming and web development. The programme is aimed at students who already have a Bachelors degree in a non-ICT area and who want to gain essential ICT skills. We have taught a wide range of students with different academic backgrounds and experience. For example, we have taught students who just graduated from University majoring in Biomedical Science, Engineering, Finance, Law, Psychology and the Arts. In addition, we have taught students working full-time in areas such as banking, human resources, and law enforcement.

There are universities that offer similar summer or "boot-camp" style programmes for high school students [5] and undergraduate students [8]. There is also a university that offers a week-long summer programming boot camp for retaining female students majoring in IT [4]. Furthermore, there are short on-line courses and coding camps offered by private organsiations. Example coding camps include Coding Dojo and Dev Bootcamp. Similarly, there are coding camps in New Zealand such as Dev Academy for web development training [1]. According to Thayer and Ko [15], these coding bootcamps provide opportunities for people, especially women, to enter the software industry.

Like the coding camps and programmes offered by other organisations, the PGCertInfoTech programme is intensive. However, unlike the camps and other programmes, the PGCertInfoTech is taught across semesters and includes the application of theoretical concepts. The coursework of the programme involves daily lab exercises, weekly tests, and a final group project. The programme also focuses on industry-relevant attributes that help to build students' professionalism. One of the major strengths of the programme is that the faculty staff running the programme have both an academic background and relevant software industry experience, providing the programme with a good balance between academia and industry. Students coming to the PGCertInfoTech programme have developed critical thinking and communication skills from their previous tertiary studies. They also already have the proven ability to learn which is an important attribute for the software industry [14]. Once students have successfully completed the PGCertInfoTech, they can progress further with the MInfoTech. Alternatively, students can seek entry-level developer positions in the software industry.

In this paper, we present our experience developing and running the PGCertInfoTech programme. In the following section, we give an overview of the key features of the programme. We further describe the industry-focused activities as well as the challenges of developing and teaching such a programme and identify directions for improvement.

2 PROGRAMME STRUCTURE

The PGCertInfoTech programme consists of two courses, which are equivalent to one semester (12 weeks) of full-time study. The courses are:

- Programming for Industry
- Programming with Web Technologies

Programming for Industry examines object-oriented programming and design using Java as the primary language. The course aims to foster students' ability to solve problems relating to software development. The topics covered in the course range from introductory programming concepts such as program structure and boolean operators to more advanced concepts such as concurrency and design patterns. The course covers the key principles of object-oriented programming including inheritance and polymorphism. The course also covers good practices of programming and testing that are important in the software industry.

The second course, Programming with Web Technologies, focuses on building web-based applications. The course exposes students to different technologies for web development and provides the essential knowledge for students to develop modern web applications. The course covers front-end web development using HTML, CSS, and JavaScript. It also introduces popular frameworks such as Bootstrap. Additionally, the course exposes students to server-side development with the use of a relational database, Java Servlets, and a servlet container. The components covered in the course include source and version control systems with Git, web deployment, and remote database servers.

We took a holistic approach when developing the programme. There are two main elements of the programme, those that are academic-focused and others that have an industry focus, as shown in Figure 2. The academic-focused elements include coursework and academic seminars. They provide students with essential ICT education and an overview of different Computer Science topics. On the other hand, the industry-focused elements provide students with an overview of software applications in the real world and opportunities to practise their programming knowledge with activities that originated from the software industry. We have an industry advisory group that provided feedback while the programme was being developed. Additionally, the programme is reviewed after each offering and improved based on feedback from both the faculty and students.

By successfully completing the programme, students have developed transferable knowledge and skills for entering into the ICT sector. In the next section, we present how the topics are supported through the academic-focused and industry-focused elements.

3 ACADEMIC-FOCUSED ELEMENTS

The main goal of the programme is to transition students into ICT and to prepare them for the workforce. To achieve this goal, the programme provides intensive training, where students attend lectures and labs from 9am - 4pm Monday to Thursday for the first 10 weeks. Tests are held every Friday with alternate academic and industry seminars in the afternoon. The academic and industry seminars are a part of broadening students' knowledge in the ICT area as the programme is designed for students who have little or no prior experience with Computer Science or Information Technology.

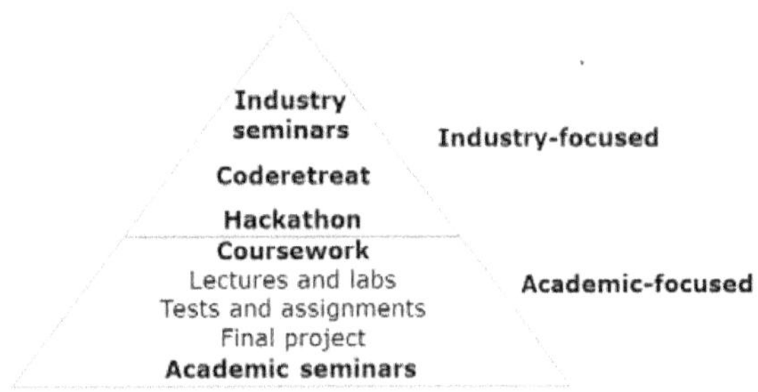

Figure 2: Elements of the PGCertInfoTech programme.

It is mandatory for students to attend the seminars. In the last two weeks of the programme, students work in groups on a final project.

3.1 Lectures and Labs

In the first 10 weeks of the programme, we hold lectures every morning, Monday to Thursday, from 9am. The lecture duration is usually 1 - 1.5 hours. We use a mix of traditional lecturing and active learning strategies [10] to deliver academic content to the class. The lecturer presents the new concepts of the day and regularly engages students with open questions and problem-based tasks during the lecture. We utilise the idea of the "think-pair-share" strategy to encourage students to work together to answer questions about particular programming concepts. For example, in the lecture on inheritance, we first present theory to students and distribute different sets of cartoon stickers that contain farm animals, dinosaurs, or sea creatures. We divide students into groups of three or four and ask each student to think about the attributes and possible behaviours of the creatures in the given set of stickers. Students then share their thoughts within their group and come up with a design that would represent each creature as well as the supertype. Afterwards, students come together to discuss the design they produced.

After the morning lectures, we have supervised lab time until 4pm for students. Students can also use this time to revise material and to look at further recommended readings. We promote a "learning by doing" environment for our students through a series of lab exercises that are related to the new concepts of the day. Students are encouraged to complete the lab exercises as they are worth 20% of their final mark. During the lab sessions, tutors are available to students to answer questions as well as provide guidance on lab exercises. Tutors also provide feedback to students on their approaches and solutions to problems. We typically use the last hour of the day as a reflection, where the class discusses the new concepts learned for the day. The lecturer also demonstrates how to approach complex problems and explains the underlying theory. This style of teaching in the lab is similar to the extreme apprenticeship method proposed by Vihavainen et al. [16]. The extreme apprenticeship method, which extends from the cognitive apprenticeship model, emphasises the importance of learning by doing with guided programming exercises. The method involves practices such as giving clean guidelines on solving exercises, encouraging students to look for information, and providing help and continuous feedback in labs. The extreme apprenticeship method helps students to acquire and to master the necessary skills for software development [16].

3.2 Tests and Assignments

In the first 10 weeks of the programme, students are assessed every Friday morning with alternating tests for the two courses. Each test covers two weeks of material and is open book. In Programming for Industry, we assess students' understanding of programming concepts using a short written test. Furthermore, we assess how well students have understood such concepts using a two-hour practical test. The practical test also assesses students' ability to apply the material and to solve programming problems.

For Programming with Web Technologies, we currently give students a one-hour written test and a bi-weekly practical assignment. We give students assignments instead of practical tests for the web development course, because the two-hour practical tests that we initially had were ineffective in assessing students' actual ability in building web pages and simple web applications. Students were unable to finish the practical tests on time, and were mostly relying on search engines to find the right answers. Consequently, we replaced the practical tests with assignments. However, with this change, it becomes more difficult to distinguish the top students.

3.3 Final Project

In the last two weeks of the programme, students work in assigned groups of three or four on the final project. The final project is a joint project for the two courses, which is worth 30% of the final mark. Students are required to build a blogging system, which has the following main features:

- login / logout
- register / delete users
- add / delete articles and comments

Students are also required to build other features such as enhancing security of the system to avoid SQL injection, enabling multimedia in their blogging systems, and providing a simple GUI application to manipulate data.

Prior to the commencement of the project, we ask students to adopt agile project management where they break down the required features into stories and estimate the effort in completing each story using the planning poker process. The planning poker process is an estimating and planning technique that is used in agile software development. The process involves developers discussing and estimating the work involved in implementing each story. At the end of the process, everyone in the team should come to a consensus on the work to be done [7]. We also ask students to use a Kanban board to manage their tasks for each week. The Kanban board is a simple visualisation tool that helps everyone see all the tasks that need to be done, the tasks that are currently been undertaken, and the completed tasks [13]. During the two project weeks, the lecturer acts as a scrum master and has daily stand-up meetings with each group to ensure students are following their plans and updating their Kanban boards. In the daily stand-up meeting, we ask three simple questions:

(1) What did you do yesterday?
(2) What are you doing today?
(3) Is there anything impeding your progress?

At the end of the project, each group of students is asked to present their blogging systems based on a specific scenario. The kinds of specific scenarios we have set for the presentations are:

- the groups are meeting with potential buyers that have technical knowledge, and
- a product launch for a general audience.

Students are also asked to submit individual reports reflecting on their contributions as well as their experience working in teams and applying course material.

3.4 Academic Seminars

We invite academics to give an one-hour overview covering different topics in computer science, that we are unable to cover in the course due to time constraints. The topics include binary representation, graphics and data encoding, searching, sorting, security, and networking. The academic seminars provide students with the opportunity to view very important areas of computer science and to encourage students to study further in the areas of their interest.

4 INDUSTRY-FOCUSED ELEMENTS

The industry-focused elements consist of industry seminars, a coderetreat, and a hackathon. The main goal of these elements is to broaden students' knowledge about the software industry and to enable them to apply the concepts learned from the programme in industry-relevant activities.

4.1 Industry Seminars

We invite guest speakers from the ICT industry to present to students. The goal of the seminars is to introduce students to the breadth of software applications in the real world. The seminars also inform students of the type of careers they can pursue in IT as well as providing an understanding of the kinds of graduate attributes software companies require. Moreover, the industry seminars provide the opportunity for students to network with software company representatives. Guest speakers are drawn from a variety of domains, not limited to crime-fighting, data analytics, and healthcare. We also bring in people from professional bodies, such as New Zealand's IITP (Institute of Information Technology Professionals), to discuss with students issues such as ethics and civic responsibility in the context of the software industry.

4.2 Coderetreat

The PGCertInfoTech programme is an intensive programme with "boot-camp" style education developing industry-focused programming skills. Before the commencement of the final project, we run a one-day class activity to help students revise all the concepts learned throughout the semester. The one-day class activity is known as the code retreat. Code retreats have been hosted by the software industry, where software developers come together to hone their software craftsmanship. Such events in industry enable software developers to practise fundamental software development skills and to learn various software implementation techniques free from interruptions and pressures. Software developers can make mistakes safely, and learn how to improve by attempting the same set of problems multiple times with different approaches. Moreover, feedback from a code retreat survey [12] suggests that the events provide great platforms for software developers to improve their software craftsmanship. Software developers can take away what they have learned, and apply their learnings at work, which in turn results in improvement of their code quality in the workplace [12]. Therefore, the code retreat has been promoted as an effective means of improving and enhancing the knowledge and skills of software developers [6, 11, 12].

We use the format of a legacy code retreat, where students are given an existing codebase. We primarily focus on refactoring and testing during the event as these are two of the most important concepts in the software industry. In the event, students work in different pairs to solve problems. Throughout the event, the lecturer and tutors act as facilitators to give guidance and feedback to students. At the end of the day, we reflect on the programming problems and the approaches used to solve such problems. The event has been successful as it enables students to practice what they have learned in the past 10 weeks in an environment without the pressure of being assessed. Moreover, it provides another opportunity for students to interact closely with fellow students. The event also enables the faculty to engage with students in a different way and to see how well students have applied the concepts in practice.

4.3 Hackathon

"Hackathons" are events in which software developers (and often those from other disciplines) collaborate intensively over a short time-frame on problems to be solved by software. They are becoming increasingly common in industry and software development circles [2]. We run a two-day game development hackathon for our full-time students at the half-way point in the course. In the hackathon, students form teams of between three and five people to develop a simple game of their own design. Food is provided and tutors are available to work with the students, but the direction of each team's project is entirely up to them. The primary objective is to give our students the opportunity to cement their new-found object-oriented programming knowledge. The open-ended scenario additionally encourages creativity and problem-solving skills, while the environment fosters a cohort feel amongst the students.

5 VARIATIONS OF THE PROGRAMME

After the first full-time cohort, we received many expression of interests for part-time classes. To accommodate such requests, we started running the part-time version of the programme in July 2016. The part-time programme is suitable for people who are already working full-time, and wish to upskill their IT knowledge or to switch careers into IT. The part-time programme runs in the evenings over two semesters. The classes are from 5:30pm - 8:30pm, Tuesdays and Thursdays.

This programme is also intensive, but students only study one course at a time. The two courses run independently allowing students to start either with Programming for Industry or Programming with Web Technologies. The academic content for the two courses are the same as the full-time programme, but the delivery has had to be altered due to scheduling and time constraints. In order to run the courses independently, we need to decouple the use of Java from Programming with Web Technologies. Therefore, the second half of Programming with Web Technologies has changed, where Node.js is taught as the server-side technology. The coursework for the part-time programme is similar to the full-time version with the following differences:

- **Lectures and labs.** Similarly to the full-time programme, we utilise active learning strategies to deliver academic content to the class. We encourage part-time students to read the lecture slides and recommended readings before each class. We also have supervised lab times for students to work on exercises. The labs are not assessed as students often do not have enough time to complete the exercises in class. However, we encourage students to practise as much as they can as well as encourage them to use Piazza, an on-line Q&A platform, to ask questions.
- **Assessments.** For the part-time programme, we use online quizzes and assignments instead of the lab exercises. We also have short written tests and two-hour practical tests for both courses.
- **Final projects.** For each course, students are assigned a final project in the last two weeks. In Programming for Industry, students work individually on completing a GUI application that involves Java concurrent processing. They also write a report reflecting on their learning experience. In Programming with Web Technologies, students work in groups of three or four, creating a blogging system. The final project for the Programming with Web Technologies has similar requirements to the full-time final project.
- **Academic and industry seminars.** Because of the time constraints, we could not have the same series of academic and industry seminars as the full-time programme. We have only industry seminars for the part-time students as these benefit students if they were planning to change their careers. To inform students about different computer science topics, we provide relevant textbooks and resources for those who are interested.

6 RESULTS

The PGCertInfoTech programme has been running successfully with positive feedback from students. Students have responded positively on the programme organisation, the clearness of the aims, the resources provided in the programme, and the quality of small-group teaching. Students have also expressed that the hands-on practice with supervision in labs have been effective for their learning. For example, a student from the recent cohort commented on labs and small-group teaching:

> The daily labs were very helpful for my learning. The small class size and the number of tutors to students for these labs were crucial to achieving this.

Over the past two years, more than 40 students have completed the programme (including 6 part-time students). The proportion of women in the programme is slightly higher than the proportion of women studying in the Computer Science department at one of our institutes. Of the students enrolled in the full-time or part-time programme, 35% are female, whereas 23.5% of the students studying computer science at the same institute are female [9]. Currently, more than 80% of the full-time students continue to the Master of Information Technology programme. We have had one part-time student continue to the Master programme.

With the experience of delivering the programme, we have identified and addressed the following issues:

- **Student workload.** The programme is intensive – which leaves little time for students to take any breaks from study. Students are in class everyday to complete lab exercises, assignments, and to study for the tests. The intensive programme helps students to concentrate on software development, but we did have a few students who felt they could not cope with the pace and who decided to withdraw after 2 weeks of study. This is similar in the part-time programme where students are required to study 20 hours a week on top of their full-time employment. Therefore, at the start of the programme we set clear expectations to both full-time and part-time students that the programme is fast-paced and involves many hours of hands-on practice.
- **Teaching and learning activities.** One of the challenges with the programme is that students come from various academic backgrounds and might be used to different styles of teaching and learning from their disciplines. Students with engineering backgrounds often prefer lectures with concrete step-by-step examples, whereas students with arts and law backgrounds tend to prefer readings and group discussions. Over the past two years, we find "learning by doing" with hands-on help has been the most effective way for students to master programming. We also face the challenge of delivering the same academic contents to students in the part-time programme. We could not use the same teaching and learning activities for the part-time students as the time for the part-timers with faculty and tutors is shorter. Therefore, we have revised the coursework for the part-timers as discussed previously.

We have also identified the ongoing challenges and areas for improvement for the programme:

- **Faculty workload.** The "boot-camp" style class requires much greater student contact time than traditional lectures. A lecturer typically spends 3 hours each day with students. In addition, we have a ratio of one tutor per five students and each tutor works five hours a day. As a result, the cost of running the programme is considerably higher than traditional programmes. In the future, we are looking at revising the staff-student ratio as the enrollment number increases. We are looking at how we can reduce the staff-student ratio while maintaining the quality of effective lab supervision.
- **Student engagement with industry.** The opportunities for students to engage with industry are currently only during the industry seminars on Friday afternoons. However, due to the intensiveness of the programme, students often become fatigued and less engaged with the industry representatives on Fridays.
- **Destinations for students.** Currently, many students continue to the Masters programme. However, we have

not carried out any formal surveys of where other students go after finishing the programme. We know a few students found full-time employment straight after completing the programme, but little is known as to how much they learned from the programme is being applied in their jobs or how useful the programme was to them when they entered the software industry.

- **Student space.** Due to the increased number of students at one of our institutes, we are facing issues of finding a computer lab or a study space that is available from 9am - 4pm every day. It is important for the students to have their own study space to develop a collaborative learning environment for students with different academic backgrounds to work together. In the past, our part-time students have created their own private study group using the available study space. The private study group not only helped students' learning, but it has also created a cohort feeling for that particular part-time class.
- **Continuous course improvement.** As the technologies and software tools nowadays are evolving fast, they can quickly become obsolete. To ensure we are not just teaching the technologies of the day, we regularly review the course material and attempt to make the lecture slides as well as lab exercises independent of the tools used. For example, we separate the instructions on using IDEs such as Eclipse and IntelliJ from the lab exercises. An advantage of this approach is that we retain the academic content and focus on the key principles. At the same time, we can easily provide up to date information to students on relevant technologies and tools used in the software industry.
- **Coordination and collaboration between universities.** The School is a joint collaboration between two universities in two different cities in New Zealand. Students can study the same programme at either university. To maintain the quality and standard of the programme, we work on being consistent across the two institutes in terms of course delivery and grading. We have had joint industry seminars with the use of video conferencing, attempting to create a sense of cohort between the two universities. However, it has not been easy due to practical factors such as different semester start dates and different environments. Moreover, it has been difficult to build a sense of cohort between the universities as students could not easily interact with one another effectively via video conferencing. The distance between the two universities also makes it difficult for students from one university to travel to the other.

7 CONCLUSIONS

The "boot-camp" style PGCertInfoTech programme has been successful at our institutes. The programme enables people with non-ICT backgrounds to gain a postgraduate qualification relating to ICT. The two courses, Programming for Industry and Programming with Web Technologies, provide firm foundations of programming concepts and relevant web development technologies. Significantly, the programme offers a holistic approach for students migrating to ICT; in addition to its sound academic underpinning, the programmes includes several industry-focused elements that are key to preparing students for industry practice.

Once students have successfully completed the programme, they are able to continue and develop more specialist skills in ICT through the associated MInfoTech programme. Alternatively, PGCertInfoTech graduates can opt to enter the software industry as junior developers. Throughout the programme, students enhance their knowledge and skills with hands-on practice as well as regular feedback from faculty. Moreover, the academic seminars and industry seminars broaden students' knowledge in the ICT area and the industry.

In this paper we have reported on our two-year experience of developing and delivering the programme. We have identified and addressed issues relating to the workload of students, and teaching and learning activities for students with diverse academic experience. We also identified ongoing challenges for the programme. In the future, we plan to run a formal evaluation regarding what our graduates do after completing the PGCertInfoTech. In particular, we would like to determine the extent to which our programme has helped students to obtain skilled positions in the IT industry, and the value of their studies in preparing them for their new careers.

REFERENCES

[1] Dev Academy. 2017. Web Development Bootcamp. (2017). Retrieved August 21, 2017 from https://devacademy.co.nz/course-details/

[2] Gerard Briscoe and Catherine Mulligan. 2014. Digital innovation: The hackathon phenomenon. (2014).

[3] Tertiary Education Commission. 2016. ICT graduate schools. (Nov. 2016). Retrieved August 25, 2017 from http://www.tec.govt.nz/funding/funding-and-performance/funding/fund-finder/ict-graduate-schools/

[4] Sonal Dekhane, Kristine Nagel, and Nannette Napier. 2015. Summer Programming Boot Camp: A Strategy For Retaining Women In IT. In *Proceedings of the 46th ACM Technical Symposium on Computer Science Education*. ACM, 678–678.

[5] Barbara Ericson and Tom McKlin. 2012. Effective and sustainable computing summer camps. In *Proceedings of the 43rd ACM Technical Symposium on Computer Science Education*. ACM, 289–294.

[6] Corey Haines. 2016. Coderetreat. (2016). Retrieved October 24, 2016 from http://coderetreat.org/

[7] Nils Christian Haugen. 2006. An empirical study of using planning poker for user story estimation. In *Agile Conference, 2006*. IEEE, 9–pp.

[8] Timothy J Hickey and Pito Salas. 2013. The entrepreneur's bootcamp: a new model for teaching web/mobile development and software entrepreneurship. In *Proceeding of the 44th ACM Technical Symposium on Computer Science Education*. ACM, 549–554.

[9] The University of Auckland. 2016. University of Auckland Equity Profile 2015. (2016). Retrieved August 30, 2017 from https://cdn.auckland.ac.nz/assets/auckland/about-us/equity-at-the-university/plans-reports-reviews/university-of-auckland-equity-profile-2015.pdf

[10] The University of Minnesota. 2015. Basic Active Learning Strategies. (2015). Retrieved May 23, 2017 from https://cei.umn.edu/support-services/tutorials/what-active-learning/basic-active-learning-strategies

[11] David Parsons, Anuradha Mathrani, Teo Susnjak, and Arno Leist. 2014. Coderetreats: Reflective practice and the game of life. *IEEE Software* 31, 4 (2014), 58–64.

[12] David Parsons, Teo Susnjak, and Anuradha Mathrani. 2016. Design from detail: Analyzing data from a global day of coderetreat. *Information and Software Technology* 75 (2016), 39–55.

[13] Mary Poppendieck and Michael A Cusumano. 2012. Lean software development: A tutorial. *IEEE software* 29, 5 (2012), 26–32.

[14] Sarah Putt. 2013. Developer bootcamps - good or bad? (May 2013). Retrieved August 21, 2017 from https://www.computerworld.co.nz/article/488039/developer_bootcamps_-_good_bad_/

[15] Kyle Thayer and Andrew J. Ko. 2017. Barriers Faced by Coding Bootcamp Students. In *Proceedings of the 2017 ACM Conference on International Computing Education Research (ICER '17)*. ACM, New York, NY, USA, 245–253. https://doi.org/10.1145/3105726.3106176

[16] Arto Vihavainen, Matti Paksula, and Matti Luukkainen. 2011. Extreme apprenticeship method in teaching programming for beginners. In *Proceedings of the 42nd ACM Technical Symposium on Computer Science Education*. ACM, 93–98.

A Collaborative Course for Learning How to Teach Summer Java Coding Camps

Kelvin Sung Karen Gourd Ann McMahon Kulsoom Mansoor Riley Gaggero
Computing and Software Systems School of Education Studies Office of Research
University of Washington Bothell

ABSTRACT

Summer coding or programming camps are popular. With sufficient organization, offering these camps at higher education institutions can facilitate outreach objectives including engaging underrepresented groups. However, the challenges involved in organizing and offering a camp are many, including: recruitment of instructors and campers, camp management, finances, and curriculum development. We addressed these challenges by engaging a non-profit summer camp provider, Pacific Science Center (PSC), to handle camp logistics; and offered a new course for students with backgrounds in computer science (CS) or education (ED) to learn to teach Java programming and develop a curriculum appropriate for middle school aged campers. The university students then worked as paid summer camp instructors. Three professors, one each from CS, ED, and the Office of Research, co-planned and co-facilitated the course. Reflecting a hands-on and collaborative learning philosophy of PSC camps, the course grouped students into multidisciplinary teams and challenged the teams to learn by collaboratively developing and practice teaching the content. By the end of the course, we had classroom-ready instructors with technical knowledge in both programming and learning theories and a customized curriculum ready for use. This paper details our project, including results from the summer camps. With all developed materials freely available. Interested institutions can either adapt the curriculum or offer a similar course.

ACM Reference format:

K. Sung, K. Gourd, A. McMahon, K. Mansoor, and R. Gaggero. 2018. A Collaborative Course for Learning How to Teach Summer Java Coding Camps. In *SIGCSE'18: 49th ACM Technical Symposium on Computer Science Education, Feb. 21–24, 2018, Baltimore, MD, USA.* ACM, NY, NY, USA, 6 pages. https://doi.org/10.1145/3159450.3159610

1. INTRODUCTION

During the summer of 2016, the University of Washington Bothell (UWB) and Pacific Science Center (PSC) experimented with a collaboration in offering two week-long Java coding camps for students in grades six-eight. UWB's goals were to further understand the multi-faceted working relationship with community partners and to explore an outreach infrastructure for building pipelines of students for its competitive Computer Science degree programs. PSC was interested in expanding its summer camp offerings beyond the metropolitan Seattle area as well as integrating academic rigor into its programming.

SIGCSE '18, February 21–24, 2018, Baltimore, MD, USA

ACM ISBN 978-1-4503-5103-4/18/02...$15.00
https://doi.org/10.1145/3159450.3159610

Both of the week-long camps were fully enrolled with maximum wait-lists. Based on results from the Game-Themed Computer Science (GTCS) project and using curriculum materials designed for college introductory courses [1]–[3], two Computer Science (CS) students, each with prior experience from a community outreach class that teaches young kids programming concepts,[1] were recruited as camp instructors (CIs).[2] With minimum refinements of the curriculum and no additional training, the CIs showed up on the first day of camp and dynamically adapted to the campers' needs. While the first day of the first camp began with challenges, by the end of the first week, campers and their parents were both engaged and enthusiastic with the results. The second week was an all-girls camp and concluded with high praises.

Encouraged by the results, plans to offer seven similar camps in the summer of 2017 began early in Autumn of 2016 with the intent to develop an infrastructure needed for consistency and sustainability. A course was established to involve computer science (CS), educational studies (ED), and a specialist in broader impacts from the Office of Research. The course was designed and offered in spring quarter 2017 to 12 CS students and four ED students. These students collaborated and produced a customized summer camp curriculum, including detailed lesson plans with accompanying hands-on, game-themed exercises. Eight of the CS and three of the ED students went on and led the seven summer Java camps.

Our experiences with the cross-disciplinary course and the detailed summer curriculum and materials provide options for continued collaboration between UWB and PSC for offering Java camps. The course can be offered again to generate further refined materials. Alternatively, CS and ED students can be recruited as CIs and trained to work with the existing materials prior to the camps. In these ways, this course can provide a cross-disciplinary learning experience, recruit and train competent CIs, and serve as a reliable pathway for the production of high-quality lesson plans. As all materials described in this paper are freely available,[3] similar results may be achieved by other institutions.

This paper contextualizes our work among existing efforts in summer coding camps and identifies the distinctive features of our approach—beginning with a university course to engage college students as CIs, and produce Java-based curriculum for middle school aged campers. The paper then details the design and implementation of the course; presents results related to university student learning outcomes and examples of games created by the summer camps; and concludes with a discussion of limitations of the project and potential future work.

[1] http://courses.washington.edu/css295/

[2] *CIs* are college students, *campers* are the middle school students.

[3] Materials freely available at https://depts.washington.edu/cmmr/GTCS/.

2. BACKGROUND

Summer coding (or programming) camps are popular and there are many varieties. For example, DeWitt et al. surveyed the CS education literature and the Internet to identify 480 camps [4]. Besides serving as fun and engaging summer activities for youth, many of the camps are designed with additional explicit goals including: outreach to underrepresented groups in gender (e.g., [5]) or race (e.g.,[6]); and to create pipelines for students for CS/STEM majors (e.g., [7]). Almost all of these camps operate in one-week formats.

The programming languages of choice for middle school summer camps are based mostly on the drag-and-drop paradigm, including: Alice (e.g., [8]), Scratch (e.g., [9]), or App Inventor (e.g., [10]). Traditional text-based programming languages like Java are typically reserved for the more advanced students (e.g., grades 9 to 12 [11]). As a result of the recent high profile and successful efforts in early integration of languages like Alice [12] or Scratch [13] into K-12 classrooms, many middle school students already have had first-hand experience working with these systems. Summer camps based on these languages may run the risk of being perceived as routine and thus boring and unchallenging [14].

Building *interactive graphical systems*, or videogame-like applications is a common *theme* for many of the camps (e.g., [7]). Other camps are designed around additional potentially engaging themes, including Artificial Intelligence [5], 3D Worlds [15], storytelling [16], or real-world needs in the community [10]. These camps engage young learners [17] by involving topics that interest the campers [18].

While well-organized information and guides on approaches [19] are available, the operational logistics of summer camps—including marketing; equipment and equipment configurations; registration, meals, safety and insurance issues; parental communication; emergency contacts; and finance—can still be logistically challenging for higher education institutions.

3. THE PROJECT

In addition to community outreach and building a pipeline of future students for our CS degree programs, at UWB, organizing summer coding camps, is a way to fulfill our core mission of serving and engaging our community in learning.

3.1 Decisions and Rationale

Middle school students are targeted because this is a critical time period for youth to make decisions about the extent to which they identify with careers in STEM fields [20].

Java, the choice of language for our camp, is based on the experience of teaching foundational programming concepts by building casual video games in Java [21], [22]. Together with PSC's interest in academic rigor, we approached the design of the Java coding camps by referencing popular college-level introductory programming textbooks in Java (e.g., [23]).

While the interactive graphical application or videogame-theme is similar to many camps based on Alice and Scratch, because of the language of choice, our campers were able to experience the entire spectrum of frustration and joy of coding—from dealing with syntax issues to the freedom and power of working with actual programming instructions.

Logistical aspects of camp preparations and operations were turned over to PSC, while UWB provided the curriculum and recruited college CS and ED students as CIs. The net revenues from the camps are shared equitably.

3.2 Challenges

These ideas were first implemented in Summer 2016 with two fully subscribed and highly praised PSC Java coding camps for middle school kids. Though the camps were successful, several important lessons were learned.

- **Curriculum and lesson plans**: Adapting materials developed for college introductory courses during the actual camps is not a sustainable approach. A custom curriculum with detailed lesson plans, including non-technical activities, should be developed.
- **The art of teaching and classroom management**: Being technical experts does not mean CS students can teach or manage a dynamic learning environment. Training and additional expertise in how to teach are needed.
- **Communication with PSC**: Even with the clear separation of responsibilities, there are unforeseen issues, and it is often difficult to get in contact after such issues arise. The communication should be planned, extensive, and frequent.
- **Sustainability**: Build on the success from 2016, an infrastructure can and must be organized to institutionalize the efforts. Long-term planning could include curriculum updates, annual offering of camps, and potential expansions to different age groups.

None of the major challenges encountered were related to the technical content of the camps. It was clear that a collaborative team effort would be required.

3.3 The Solution

In the autumn of 2016, a cross-disciplinary team was formed—one faculty member from CS, one from ED, and one from the Office of Research in the area of strategies for broad impact—to focus on the scope and requirements of the project including: expanding intentional and regular collaboration and communication with PSC, designing a curriculum with detailed lesson plans and instructional materials, and recruiting and training students to learn how to engage youth in learning to code.

A new collaborative course would be designed to address the challenges from the previous summer. Students with knowledge in teaching or backgrounds in programming who are interested in summer camp instruction would be recruited and prepared to be camp instructors through an iterative process of identifying content, designing teaching materials, practice teaching, and applying peer and instructor feedback to revise content, materials, and instructional activities. The resulting materials could then be used for subsequent years of Java coding camps.

3.4 Evaluation Criteria

Three outcomes define the success of the current project: (1) the new course, (2) the summer camps, and (3) continuing collaborations between UWB and PSC.

The UWB collaborative course. The purpose of the course was to ensure that a Java curriculum would be available to camp instructors (CIs). Where the CIs would be prepared with knowledge and confidence in content and pedagogy to enable them to adapt the curriculum to the needs and interests of campers by using instructional strategies supported by learning theory and well-aligned with the content of the curriculum. Descriptions of the intended course outcomes follow.

- **Curriculum**: Targeted for the middle-school age group, customized for typical week-long summer camps, appropriate for learning introductory programming concepts based on Java, and fun and engaging for youth.

- **Student learning outcomes**: For students with CS knowledge (e.g., background in CS2 if not majoring in CS), success would mean that they are ready and capable of meeting daily challenges and lead the teaching of the summer camps. For typical ED students, success would mean that they can teach basic CS1 concepts including: Java syntax, variables, conditionals, loops, and functions.

The Java coding camps. As in all summer activities with hidden academic agendas, success would mean a pleasant experience with demonstrated competency by the campers at the conclusion.

The collaboration with PSC. By the conclusion of all seven Java coding camps, both UWB and PSC would be enthusiastic about offering similar camps the following year.

4. THE COURSE

The design of the course followed a targeted summer camp experience: collaborative and hands-on in learning while building engaging computer games. The course required students to integrate learning theories, instructional strategies, and programming concepts as they constructed a curriculum and associated lesson plans and materials to demonstrate competency.

4.1 The Overall Course Design

To foster collaboration and adapt to practical constraints, the class was grouped into four teams each with one ED student. The group membership changed regularly. To ensure a hands-on learning experience for all, the first half of the course was dedicated to bringing learning theory to CS students and programming concepts to ED students. The progress was divided into four main stages: (1) Introduction; (2) Learning; (3) Contextualization; and (4) Demonstration. The next section provides details of each stage.

4.2 The Implementation

The course met for two hours, twice weekly according to a 10-week academic quarter. The four stages of the class design were implemented as follows.

Stage 1: Introduction (Weeks 1 and 2). The goals of this stage were for students to trust each other, experience the GTCS technology, learn foundations of relevant learning theory, and gain insights about teaching summer camps. During this stage, class time was spent discussing the concept of "*listening to students as your most important instructional strategy*" [14], [24], [25]. As take home assignments, each team designed and built a game to showcase the GTCS technology. In this endeavor, the ED students led the design while the CS students learned the tool (GTCS API) and used the tool to build the games. At the end of the second week, in the presence of the PSC camp manager, the teams presented their games in class. The visitor also provided relevant details of the camps (e.g., typical camper backgrounds and abilities, daily camp schedule).

Stage 2: Learning (Weeks 3 to 5). The goals of this stage were for students to gain knowledge useful to designing and building the curriculum. Students were assigned readings on videogames and CS education [26] and how people learn [27] and were asked to reference the relevant chapters in a CS1 Java textbook [23]. Instructors stressed that the main purpose of the camps would be to teach programming fundamentals and not videogames and that people learn in different ways. The teams selected materials to develop from the following topics: development environment, conditionals, loops, functions, and functions with parameters. During the first hour of class periods, the ED student on each team taught the rest of the class the topic of their choice based on custom-built GTCS demonstration examples. The second hour of class time was used to provide verbal feedback to each team, discuss the readings, and plan strategies for applications.

Stage 3: Contextualization (Week 6). With a strong foundation established, this stage aimed to guide students in articulating and structuring their knowledge for specific purposes. The main goal of this stage was to produce the camp curriculum and schedule. New teams were formed, and based on their CS subject matter knowledge, understanding of how learners learn, and a template schedule provided by the PSC camp manager, the teams proposed different solutions, presented their work to the class, evaluated each other, and voted to adopt the best approach.

Stage 4: Demonstrations (Weeks 7 to 10). The goals of this stage were for the teams to select topic areas, to customize and build materials to present their topic according to the adopted curriculum schedule, to align to topic materials with the content to precede and follow theirs, to finalize detailed lesson plans, and to experience presenting their materials to the class. With different team memberships, a process similar to Stage 2 was repeated whereby teams selected topic areas, built GTCS examples, developed detailed lesson plans, and presented the materials in the class. The main difference was that all members were expected to take turns instructing. Again, the second hour of each class focused on peers and instructors providing feedback to be applied to revisions of lesson plans.

During the last stage, when time allowed, various engaging activities[4] and theatre games [28] were introduced and practiced, so they could be used as ice breakers and tools to engage campers' interests beyond coding. The PSC camp manager came to a session to view and provide feedback on planned lessons and to share additional information for CIs (e.g., CI hiring and training process, coordinating planned breaks, keeping track of campers).

Throughout the course, feedback sessions were accompanied by the students posting written versions of the feedback on the class discussion board. This feedback was in turn reviewed and commented on by course instructors. After the final class session, the curriculum was compiled by using the final version of each teams' materials.

4.3 Discussion

This course was a passionate overload for all three collaborators, and all three attended nearly all class meetings. In hindsight, the implementation stages seem rather clear and purposeful. However, in practice, initially each week began at the brink of collapsing and chaos for the collaborators.

The entire Stage 1 and early parts of Stage 2 succeeded based mainly on the prior related independent experiences of the collaborators. The collaborators began focused weekly meetings in week 4. These meetings helped the course progress in a more purposeful and seemingly controlled manner. These meetings should have begun before week 1.

It was amazing that with little to zero programming experience, all of the ED students were able to quickly pick up

[4] http://csunplugged.org/

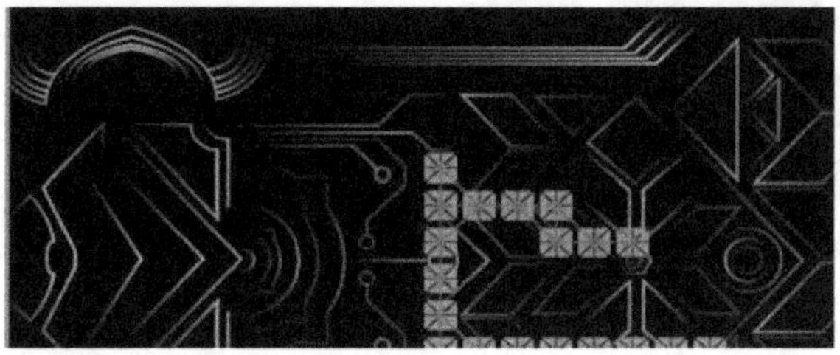

```
import Currupted_ProceduralAPI.*;       // Work with GTCS API
public class Lab6 extends CorruptedProceduralAPI {
  int x = 15, y = 5;                    // init tile position
  // init the game, called once by the API
  public void buildGame() {
     drawTile(x, y); }                  //draw at (x,y) with default color
  //update is called continuously >40 times per second
  public void updateGame() {
     if (pressingLeft()) {              //left-arrow pressed
        x = x - 1;                         //move position left
        drawTile(x,y);  }                  //draw a new tile
     if (pressinDown()) {               //down-arrow pressed
```

Figure 1: GTCS Example for Teaching Conditionals

BlueJ IDE and learn to code. This observation reinforces the idea that anyone can learn to code.[5] Perhaps the two most important lessons for all involved was (1) the appreciation for the complexity of some concepts that are perceived to be *simple* and (2) the need to teach the concepts by connecting them to learners' existing knowledge.

5. RESULTS

Encouragingly, as the 2017 PSC Summer camps came to a conclusion, the parties involved—UWB faculty members, PSC camp manager, and the CIs—are all enthusiastic about the continuation of this collaboration and planning meetings for 2018 camps are already underway. Though not equivalent to being "*sustainable,*" continued collaboration is assured. In the next sections, results of the course and summer camps are detailed.

5.1 Results: The UWB Course

The two important outcomes are: the curriculum and students' ability in teaching introductory programming concepts.

5.1.1 The Curriculum

A 53-page document based on a PSC-supplied, week-long template camp schedule was developed by CS and ED students for use by CIs. Coding concepts accompanied by GTCS examples along with suggested physically engaging activities are organized into three-and-a-half days of hands-on challenges that are clustered into 1.5-hour blocks. In this way, the first day of the camp introduces GTCS and coding fundamentals, variables, and simple conditionals; day two teaches functions, Boolean operators, and coordinate systems; day three covers for-loops; and the first half of day four is designed to be a *buffer,* where more advanced topics in functions (e.g., return types, and parameters) can be taught if time allows. A detailed guide for campers to design and build their own final game completes the curriculum.

Figure 1 shows a screenshot and the corresponding source code for one of the GTCS examples designed for teaching conditionals. Note the simple and intuitive interface of the GTCS procedural API where the *buildGame()* function is called once at the beginning for building the game, and *updateGame()* function is called at a real-time rate of around 40-times a second. In this example, campers only need to know about the *drawTile()* and the *pressingKey()* functions. This example is designed to be used toward the end of the first day. Campers must examine the source code and use conditionals to complete the support for the tile right- and up-ward movements (the screenshot was taken from running a completed exercise). Figure 2 shows two additional examples for teaching functions (mid-day 2), and for-loops (day 3). The two star-shaped tiles on the right of the function example (top of Figure 2) represents goal posts that the player must move the blue tile through. This example allowed campers to practice working with Boolean operators, variables, and function calls. The loop example (bottom of Figure 2) consists of separate loops that draw tiles of specific colors.

Figure 2: GTCS Examples for Functions (top) and Loops (Bottom).

The GTCS examples are really simple graphical applications designed to highlight and support interactive examination of specific programming concepts. As illustrated in the case of Figure 1, these examples often present a partial solution to the campers, challenge them to understand the given code, and then require them to practice the concept by completing the tasks. GTCS API functions are introduced only when they are required as part of the teaching materials. Except day-1's introduction session, no dedicated time was spent on teaching the API.

5.1.2 Student Learning Outcomes

With the ultimate goal of students teaching CS1 concepts to middle school campers, the actual outcomes included: (1) decomposing concepts for explaining, (2) constructing materials for teaching, (3) creating a presence and holding an audience's attention for communicating ideas, and ultimately, (4) dynamically adjusting materials based on learners' needs.

The first two outcomes, in the context of CS1 concepts, can be verified based on the quality and scope of the produced curriculum. Outcome (3) was continuously assessed, commented on, and improved during the many class presentations. By Stage-4 teaching demonstrations, it appeared that the quietest CS students were comfortable in leading discussions, and all of the ED students were able to teach their team's technical content. Ideally, the best assessment for outcomes (3) and (4) should be based on CIs' teaching the summer camps. These will be detailed in Section 5.2.

[5] http//www.pbs.org/newshour/making-sense/how-anyone-can-learn-to-code/

Figure 3: Sample Summer Camp Final Projects: **Left**: Week 1; **Middle**: Week 7; **Right**: Week 7.

5.1.3 Class Survey Results

After the course, a survey was conducted to assess students' self-perceived learning, to check if the course had met students' expectations, and to receive general feedback. Of the 16 students (12 CS and 4 ED), 13 (10 CS and 3 ED) responded to the survey.

CS and ED students responded that, with teammates from *another* discipline, they learned different ways of thinking and approaches to collaborate. CS students remarked that they had not realized how complex the act of teaching is, and they appreciated learning how people learn. Most students of both disciplines remarked that the course challenged them both cognitively and socially—appreciation for problem solving approaches and friendships of students from another discipline. Many expressed that they would have liked more opportunities to practice teaching the lessons they created.

On a five-level Likert scale, 11 of the respondents rated the course as *Excellent* (scale-5) or *Very Good* (scale-4) with 2 students rating the class as *Good (scale-3).* Eight of the respondents said that they would recommend the course to their peers, with two stated that due to the experimental nature of the course, they would actively discourage their peers from taking this course. The high faculty to student ratio and the small number of students suggest that these data be interpreted more anecdotally than statistically.

5.1.4 Discussion

The ED students were comfortable acknowledging their limited skills in programming and raised questions that helped identify the need for detail and clarity. Their status as beginners provided a lab for the CS students to practice sharing familiar concepts with people who do not share their knowledge or background. As the course progressed, the students developed awareness and began to significantly rely on each other's expertise, they became more confident in what they knew and less concerned about what they did not know. The cross-disciplinary nature of the course was indeed invaluable.

In the long run, scalability in number of students may be a potential limitation. It is essential that students must have adequate opportunities to present, provide and receive feedback in class. The experience seems to suggest 15-20 students to be an ideal size. Considering that the class should be collaboratively offered by faculty members from CS and ED, the institutional budget may be a concern. Fortunately, the revenue from the camps allowed for potential creative solutions.

5.2 Results: The Summer Camps

Eight of the CS and three of the ED students were able to commit their summer schedules and form interdisciplinary instructional teams of two CS and one ED CIs for leading all but one camp. The teams were formed based on CIs' schedules and varied each week. Some CIs ended up teaching more than others.

Most of the campers were from well-to-do families attending private schools, and with minimal to no coding experience where prior exposures were mainly from school elective or math courses, or popular on-line resources.[6] In all cases, the exposures were limited to Scratch-like drag-and-drop paradigms. Though the campers were motivated and eager to "*type code in Java,*" most were in the camps as a result of their parents' choice. The campers were more excited about *"building videogames*" and not "*learning more about coding.*"

These camps must be assessed from two perspectives: results from the camps and learnings of the CIs.

5.2.1 Results from the Camps

Figure 3 shows selected screenshots of games built by three of the campers from Weeks 1 (left) and 7 (middle and right). These are games that the campers designed and built during the last two days of the camp.

The game on the left challenges a player to navigate the maze to reach the green *win* tiles on the right where hidden untouchable *death* tiles must be avoided along the way. The game in the middle races against time where the yellow robot must touch and save the two red robots before the continuously closing-in green wall swallows them all. The game on the right consists of a hero fish, two bombs, six moving sharks, five shells, one treasure, and seaweed. The hero fish must avoid the bombs and the sharks, collect all the shells to uncover the treasure in the seaweed, and pick up the treasure to win the game.

The games in Figure 3 were among the most interesting visually, there were other creative and sophisticated ones with simpler displays. For example, one game requires the player to press the space bar at precise moments to rotate a horizontal set of tiles by 45-degrees in order to touch well-hidden winning tiles; or advancing a hero tile while avoid collisions with advancing walls.

These final games represented the campers synthesizing coding concepts and skills acquired over the week. The quality of these results are, though indirect, indications that the CIs likely communicated technical concepts with the campers, thereby supporting the learning outcome (3) as listed in Section 5.1.2.

5.2.2 Learning of The CI's

A thumb drive containing a *master curriculum* was updated and maintained by CIs of the Java camps. Additionally, during each camp, the CIs shared their insights and reflections via a group email list. From this communication, it was evident that the CIs deviated, sometimes significantly, from the developed materials.

For example, "[we] *decided that we would not teach them functions ... because the kids don't need to use them to make their games and that it would add more complexity than necessary ...*" In this case, the campers were interested in creating multiple versions of simpler games instead of one larger and more complex final game.

[6] Examples: https://hourofcode.com/ or https://code.org/

In another example when dealing with diverse student background and alignments of expectations, "*a lot of students in this class had coding experience and therefore [we] could give them challenges to try out which amplified the awesomeness of their games. ... We teach material and give challenges but recognize that the kids would rather not learn about why a code works but rather what to code to get their game to do certain things. We try to find a happy medium with this dynamic because ultimately it is important for them to understand the code too.*"

Finally, the games presented in Figure 3 from Weeks 1 and 7 were taught by the same CIs. Perhaps because the CIs gained experience and learned from others' reflections, Week 7 projects contained significantly more complexities. For example, only the player-controlled hero can be in motion in the Week 1 game, whereas all tiles can be in motion in the Week 7 games. Additionally, both of the Week 7 games consisted of customized tile images.

This evidence suggests adaptation to learners' needs and skill levels in support of learning outcome (4) as listed in Section 5.1.2.

5.2.3 Discussion

After the camps a survey was conducted to assess CIs experience, and usefulness of the UWB course and the curriculum they had developed. Of the 11 CIs, six responded. All responses were positive, attributed their preparedness to the curriculum development process, and yet clearly referred to the actual document as a reference. All stated emphatically that knowing what they know now they would again take the spring course and be a CI for the summer camps.

As the collaboration with PSC continues, pre- and post-camp evaluations should be developed and administered to the campers. A more challenging task would be attempts to assess knowledge retention and the camps' effect on middle school students' choices of academic pursuit.

6. CONCLUSION

While the camps have been successful, the campers from the well-to-do families are not the ideal ultimate audience for the developed curriculum. Pathways are being investigated on bringing these materials to typical public school audiences (e.g., as afterschool enrichment programs). However, this project does demonstrate that collaboration across disciplinary boundaries supports students' learning. Additionally, collaborations between universities and community organizations can lead to impactful outcomes otherwise challenging to achieve. This experience has produced a template that can be used to create summer camps and other broad-impact efforts in other disciplines.

The presented findings can be applied at two levels: others can conduct their own course based on our template or download and use the developed summer camp curriculum.

The next steps for this project should include a rigorous data collection and detailed analysis [29], and formulation of approach to support longitudinal studies (e.g., [30]) for assessing actual impacts.

ACKNOWLEDGMENTS

A heartfelt thank you to the students in our experimental class for their willingness to tolerate and accompany us in this exploration. Thanks to Carolyn Brennan and the UWB Office of Research for supporting our work. Thanks to Leilani Nussman from PSC who helped with our class and ensured the sanity of everyone. Ahnya Redman, Dana Bigham, and Ann Bush helped recruited students and ensured we have a classroom.

REFERENCES

[1] K. Sung, M. Panitz, C. Hillyard, R. Angotti, D. Goldstein, and J. Nordlinger, "Game-Themed Programming Assignment Modules: A Pathway for Gradual Integration of Gaming Context into Existing Introductory Programming Courses," *IEEE Transactions on Education*, vol. 54, no. 3, pp. 416–427, Aug. 2011.

[2] B. Chau, R. Nash, K. Sung, and J. Pace, "Building Casual Games and APIs for Teaching Introductory Programming Concepts Game-themed instructional modules: a video case study," in *FDG 2015*.

[3] K. Sung, R. Nash, and J. Pace, "Building Casual Game SDKS for Teaching CS1/2: A Case Study," *J. Comput. Sci. Coll.*, vol. 32, no. 1, pp. 129–143, Oct. 2016.

[4] A. DeWitt *et al.*, "What We Say vs. What They Do: A Comparison of Middle-School Coding Camps in the CS Education Literature and Mainstream Coding Camps (Abstract Only)," in *SIGCSE 2017*, pp. 707–707.

[5] M. E. Vachovsky, G. Wu, S. Chaturapruek, O. Russakovsky, R. Sommer, and L. Fei-Fei, "Toward More Gender Diversity in CS Through an Artificial Intelligence Summer Program for High School Girls," in SICSE 2016, pp. 303–308.

[6] K. Nagel, S. Dekhane, and N. Napier, "Can Programming Boot Camp Help Under-represented College Students Succeed in Computing Degrees? (Abstract Only)," in *SIGCSE 2015*, pp. 702–702.

[7] M. Guzdial and B. Ericson, "Georgia Computes!: An Alliance to Broaden Participation Across the State of Georgia," *ACM Inroads*, vol. 3, no. 4, pp. 86–89, Dec. 2012.

[8] R. Van Camp, "Alice Summer Camps: Evaluating Multiple Formats," in *Proceedings of Alice Symposium on Alice Symposium*, New York, NY, USA, 2013, p. 16:1–16:1.

[9] J. C. Adams, "Scratching Middle Schoolers' Creative Itch," in *SIGCSE 2010*, pp. 356–360.

[10] L. Ni, M. Sherman, D. Schilder, and F. Martin, "Computing with a Community Focus: An App Inventor Summer Camp for Middle School Students (Abstract Only)," in *SIGCSE 2016*, pp. 690–690.

[11] A. Wagner, J. Gray, J. Corley, and D. Wolber, "Using app inventor in a K-12 summer camp," in *SIGCSE 2013*, pp. 621–626.

[12] S. Cooper, S. H. Rodger, M. Schep, R. H. Stalvey, and W. Dann, "Growing a K-12 Community of Practice," in *SIGCSE 2015*, pp. 290–295.

[13] K.-T. Foerster, "Integrating Programming into the Mathematics Curriculum: Combining Scratch and Geometry in Grades 6 and 7," in *SIGCSE 2016*, pp. 91–96.

[14] K. Cushman and What Kids Can Do (Organization), *Fires in the bathroom: advice for teachers from high school students*. New York; York: New Press; Signature Books Services [distributor, 2005.

[15] C. Hulsey, T. B. Pence, and L. F. Hodges, "Camp CyberGirls: Using a Virtual World to Introduce Computing Concepts to Middle School Girls," in *SIGCSE 2014*, pp. 331–336.

[16] B. Ericson and T. McKlin, "Effective and Sustainable Computing Summer Camps," in *SIGCSE 2012*, pp. 289–294.

[17] M. Guzdial and E. Soloway, "Teaching the Nintendo generation to program," *Commun. ACM*, vol. 45, no. 4, pp. 17–21, 2002.

[18] M. Guzdial, "Contextulized Computing Education," in *Invited Presentation, Microsoft Research Faculty Summit, http://home.cc.gatech.edu/guzdial/169*, 2008.

[19] K. Roy, K. Nagel, and S. T. Dunton, "How to Plan and Run Computing Summer Camps: Logistics (Abstract Only)," in *SIGCSE 2017*, pp. 742–742.

[20] R. Tai, C. Qi Liu, A. Maltese, and X. Fan, "Planning early for careers in science," *Science*, vol. 312, pp. 1143–1144, 2006.

[21] K. Sung, R. Nash, and J. Pace, "Learn CS1/2 by Playing and Building Commercial Grade Casual Games: No Background Required," in *FDG 2015*.

[22] K. Sung, R. Nash, and J. Pace, "Learn CS1/2 by Playing and Building Commercial Grade Casual Games (Abstract Only)," in *SIGCSE 2016*, pp. 716–716.

[23] W. Savitch, *Absolute Java*, 6th ed. Pearson, 2016.

[24] H. Mills, T. O'Keefe, and L. B. Jennings, *Looking closely and listening carefully: learning literacy through inquiry*. Urbana, Ill: National Council of Teachers of English, 2004.

[25] R. Ritchhart, *Creating cultures of thinking: the 8 forces we must master to truly transform our schools*. San Francisco: Jossey-Bass & Pfeiffer Imprints, Wiley, 2015.

[26] K. Sung, "Computer Games and Traditional Computer Science Courses," *Communications of the ACM*, vol. 52, no. 12, pp. 74–78, Dec. 2009.

[27] Bransford, National Research Council (U.S.), and National Research Council (U.S.), Eds., *How people learn: brain, mind, experience, and school*, Expanded ed. Washington, D.C: National Academy Press, 2000.

[28] A. Boal, *Games for actors and non-actors*, 2nd ed. New York: Routledge, 2002.

[29] A. Decker, M. M. McGill, and A. Settle, "Towards a Common Framework for Evaluating Computing Outreach Activities," in *SIGCSE 2016*, pp. 627–632.

[30] C. N. Outlay, A. J. Platt, and K. Conroy, "Getting IT Together: A Longitudinal Look at Linking Girls' Interest in IT Careers to Lessons Taught in Middle School Camps," *ACM Trans. Comput. Educ.*, vol. 17, no. 4, p. 20:1–20:17, Aug. 2017.

Strategies for Basing the CS Theory Course on Non-decision Problems

John MacCormick*
Dickinson College
jmac@dickinson.edu

ABSTRACT

Computational and complexity theory are core components of the computer science curriculum, and in the vast majority of cases are taught using *decision problems* as the main paradigm. For experienced practitioners, decision problems are the best tool. But for undergraduates encountering the material for the first time, we present evidence that *non-decision problems* (such as optimization problems and search problems) are preferable. In addition, we describe technical definitions and pedagogical strategies that have been used successfully for teaching the theory course using non-decision problems as the central concept.

CCS CONCEPTS

• **Theory of computation** → **Complexity classes**; **Problems, reductions and completeness**; • **Applied computing** → **Education**;

KEYWORDS

theory course; decision problems; computability theory; complexity theory

ACM Reference Format:
John MacCormick. 2018. Strategies for Basing the CS Theory Course on Non-decision Problems. In *SIGCSE '18: The 49th ACM Technical Symposium on Computer Science Education, Feb. 21–24, 2018, Baltimore, MD, USA.* ACM, New York, NY, USA, 6 pages. https://doi.org/10.1145/3159450.3159557

1 INTRODUCTION

Many undergraduate computer science curricula include a "theory" course, covering some aspects of automata theory, computability, and complexity. Central questions addressed by a theory course include: (a) Given a computational problem C, can we solve C using a computer program? (b) If so, can we do so in polynomial time? A strong majority of popular theory textbooks focus on computational problems that are in fact *decision problems*—problems that have a yes/no answer. An alternative approach, advocated by this paper, is to consider *general* computational problems—including non-decision problems such as *optimization problems* and *search problems*—while narrowing in on decision problems when appropriate.

There are two principal objectives of this paper. First, we explain why non-decision problems are pedagogically advantageous for introductory theory courses, supporting the explanation with empirical evidence based on a survey of computer science majors. Second, we describe technical details and pedagogical strategies for using non-decision problems as the central concept in the CS theory course, based on experience with four years of course offerings and a recent textbook [16]. The use of non-decision problems is the single most important idea for the suggested approach, but additional strategies for making the CS theory course accessible are also described. This includes the use of real computer programs processing ASCII strings, instead of the more common model of Turing machines processing symbols from an arbitrary alphabet.

The nature of the audience is crucial to our considerations. In this paper, the primary target is undergraduate students who are seeing computability and complexity theory for the first, and quite possibly the last, time. We will refer to such students as the *novice audience.* We focus only on the novice audience in this paper, ignoring other theory course scenarios such as graduate courses or hybrid courses taught to a mixture of graduate students and advanced undergraduates. We also ignore the possibility of theory courses that focus mostly on automata theory, assuming instead that computability and complexity theory comprise at least a majority of the course.

For this audience, the key advantage of non-decision problems is that they are more realistic: they match the previous programming and algorithms experience of undergraduates more closely. As a concrete example (details are given later), a decision problem may ask the yes/no question, "Does this graph have a Hamilton cycle?" The corresponding non-decision problem is, "Please give me a Hamilton cycle of this graph if it has one." A program that solves the non-decision version produces a useful result that could conceivably be used in a real-world application, whereas a program solving the decision version yields only a single bit: it tells us whether or not a Hamilton cycle exists, but gives no additional information. For the novice audience, focusing on these single-bit decision problems potentially positions the course as abstruse and irrelevant. Focusing on non-decision problems with meaningful solutions, on the other hand, provides more direct connections to earlier courses. In section 4, we provide a combination of educational theory and empirical evidence to support these claims.

However, it is important to note at the outset that we do not suggest decision problems should be jettisoned from the theory course. On the contrary, there are some compelling reasons to incorporate decision problems into any theory course, including: (i) some theorems and proofs are more concise and elegant when phrased in terms of decision problems; (ii) the vast majority of

*Also affiliated with School of Computing Sciences, University of East Anglia, 2017–19

SIGCSE '18, Feb. 21–24, 2018, Baltimore, MD, USA

ACM ISBN 978-1-4503-5103-4/18/02...$15.00
https://doi.org/10.1145/3159450.3159557

existing CS theory literature considers only decision problems, so it is essential that any student planning to take a subsequent graduate-level theory course has been exposed to the decision problem framework. Therefore, in this paper we advocate a hybrid approach, whereby the earlier topics in the theory course are taught with a focus on non-decision problems. When NP-completeness is introduced—typically sometime in the second half of a one-semester course—we suggest transitioning to the classical approach and focusing only on decision problems (with some minor exceptions described later). This hybrid approach allows the novice audience to establish an initial appreciation of the relevance and importance of CS theory via non-decision problems, while still being well-versed in the classical approach by the end of the course.

As a basis for comparing and contrasting various approaches to the theory course, we will refer to a selection of ten textbooks covering the relevant material [2, 5, 10–13, 18, 19, 21, 24]; please see the technical report [15] for details about the selection of comparison textbooks.

2 RELATED WORK

There are several strands of related work aiming to make CS theory courses more practical, accessible, or meaningful. We might classify these strands as: (i) interactive automata software tools such as JFLAP and DEM [3, 22, 23]; (ii) lab assignments and visualizations for NP-completeness, an approach sometimes described as "NP-completeness for all" [4, 6, 14]; (iii) recasting the theoretical ideas themselves, for example by emphasizing non-decision problems and including holistic discussions about the implications of NP-completeness and P-versus-NP [8–10, 17, 20]. The present paper falls firmly in category (iii). The ideas described here are orthogonal to categories (i) and (ii). Indeed, the ideas of this paper have been employed over a four-year period in a course that also uses JFLAP and practical programming assignments, thus benefiting from all three strands of literature on the CS theory course.

To the best of our knowledge, Goldreich's position paper [9] and subsequent textbook [10] comprise the previous work most similar to the present paper. Goldreich makes several important, insightful, and useful suggestions for improving the theory course, including strong advocacy for the use of non-decision problems. The novel contribution of the present paper is to recast the use of non-decision problems in a manner that is more accessible to the novice audience, thus enabling instructors to focus on non-decision problems and deliver the consequent educational benefits to students.

3 A PRACTICAL DEFINITION OF COMPUTATIONAL PROBLEMS

Before the advantages of non-decision problems can be explained, we review some elementary background material to establish notation and give a formal definition of a "computational problem," which can of course be either a decision problem or a non-decision problem. The background review in this section also includes several ancillary recommendations for how to present this material to a novice audience.

Computational theory is often developed in terms of an arbitrary *alphabet* (i.e. a finite set of symbols) denoted Σ. The set of all possible *strings* (i.e. finite sequences of symbols) on Σ is denoted Σ^*. Experienced practitioners understand that the choice of alphabet is irrelevant for most purposes. But for students being introduced to complexity theory for the first time, it may be preferable to employ a more familiar and obviously relevant alphabet—one that is used by programmers to describe the inputs and outputs of computer programs in practice. This motivates us here to take the ASCII alphabet as our primary example of Σ.

For similar reasons, we use real computer programs as our main computational model, rather than the Turing machines which are more common in the theory literature. A program P receives a single ASCII string w as input and the output is either undefined (e.g. if P crashes or enters an infinite loop) or is an ASCII string denoted $P(w)$. When $P(w)$ is defined, we say P *rejects* w if $P(w) =$ "no" and P *accepts* w if $P(w) \neq$ "no".

A central concept in complexity theory is a *language* (sometimes called a *formal language*), defined as a subset of Σ^*. The intuitive notion of "solving a problem" is usually formalized as "deciding a language." Thus, a central concept in many treatments is that a program P *decides* a language L if P accepts all strings $s \in L$ and rejects all $s \notin L$.

What is the connection between "deciding a language" and "solving a problem"? For so-called *decision problems*, there is a direct and simple connection. Informally, decision problems are computational questions that have a yes/no answer, such as "Given an integer $m > 0$, is m prime?" or "Given a graph G, does G contain a Hamilton cycle?". Formally, one could define a decision problem as a function from Σ^* to {"yes", "no"}. When taking Σ as the ASCII alphabet, we first agree an encoding of the relevant mathematical objects into ASCII. For example: the integer $m = 43552$ might be encoded as the ASCII string "43552"; a graph that is a three-cycle with three vertices labeled a, b, c might be encoded as the ASCII string "a,b b,c c,a".

For a given decision problem D, strings for which the answer is "yes" are called *positive instances* of D and all other strings are *negative instances*. This leads to a simple and obvious mapping between languages and decision problems. Any language L corresponds to a decision problem D_L defined as follows: for $s \in \Sigma^*$, $D_L(s) =$ "yes" if and only if $s \in L$. The reverse mapping is also simple and obvious: a decision problem D corresponds to a language L_D with the property that $s \in L$ if and only if $D_L(s) =$ "yes".

As a result of the exact correspondence between decision problems and languages, the theory of computability and complexity is usually described in terms of languages. As already mentioned in the introduction, the advantages of doing so include simple notation and compact statements of certain theorems, but disadvantages for the novice audience include a high level of abstraction and the restriction to decision problems, which may appear unfamiliar and irrelevant.

To illustrate the distinction between decision and non-decision problems, we will use two running examples throughout the paper:

- FACTOR: The input is a string representing a positive integer m in decimal notation (e.g. "35"), and a solution is any factor of the input other than 1 and m (e.g. "5" or "7" for $m = 35$), or "no" if no such factor exists. FACTORD is the corresponding decision problem, with solution "yes" if m has a non-trivial factor and "no" otherwise.

- HamCycle: The input is a string representing a graph G (e.g. "a,b b,c c,a"), and a solution is any Hamilton cycle of G (e.g. "a,b,c" for the given example of G), or "no" if no such cycle exists. HamCycleD is the corresponding decision problem, with solution "yes" if G has a Hamilton cycle and "no" otherwise.

We also assume the reader is familiar with Sat (which asks for a satisfying assignment to a Boolean formula) and SatD (the decision variant, which asks whether a satisfying assignment exists).

Several important differences between the decision and non-decision variants should be immediately obvious from the Factor and HamCycle examples:

- Non-decision problems can have multiple solutions (e.g. an integer m can have multiple non-trivial factors; a graph G can have multiple distinct Hamilton cycles), whereas decision problems always have a unique solution ("yes" or "no").
- It is possible for decision and non-decision variants of the same problem to have apparently different complexity properties. Factor is a classic example here, since FactorD can be solved in polynomial time by the AKS algorithm [1], whereas Factor has no known polynomial-time method of solution.[1]
- Non-decision variants appear to be more "natural." For example, it is hard for the novice audience to imagine an application where it is useful to determine the mere existence of a Hamilton cycle, rather than determining the sequence of vertices in the cycle.[2]

A significant fraction of theory textbooks give no formal definition of a non-decision problem. In our sample of ten books, seven give no formal definition [2, 5, 11–13, 18, 24]. One [21] gives a brief definition; Papadimitriou [19] and Goldreich [10] give detailed definitions and analysis. These last two define non-decision problems in terms of binary relations with certain technical properties: they are *polynomially decidable* and *polynomially bounded* (or *balanced*). This approach is correct and concise, but perhaps more abstract than necessary for a novice undergraduate audience. Instead, the following concrete definition is recommended for the novice audience:

> A *computational problem* (which may or may not be a decision problem) is a function F, mapping ASCII strings to sets of ASCII strings. If $F(x) = \{s_1, s_2, \ldots\}$, we call $\{s_1, s_2, \ldots\}$ the *solution set* for x, and each s_i is a *solution* for x. If $F(x) = \{\text{"no"}\}$, then x is a *negative instance* of F; otherwise x is a *positive instance*. If F has unique solutions, F is a *function problem*. For function problems, we can drop the set notation, for example writing $F(x) = y$ instead of $F(x) = \{y\}$.

For example: "35" is a positive instance of Factor, and we have Factor("35") = {"5", "7"}; "29" is a negative instance, and we have Factor("29") = {"no"}. Note that neither Factor nor HamCycle is a function problem, since both problems can have multiple solutions. The definition of computational problem can obviously be adapted to non-ASCII alphabets, but we omit those details here.

[1] For NP-complete problems like HamCycleD, however, this never happens: given a non-decision problem C whose decision variant is an NP-complete problem C', it is known that C always has a polynomial time reduction to C'. This property is sometimes known as *self-reducibility* [10].

[2] In contrast, expert practitioners know that sometimes the single-bit decision *is* useful. For example, determining whether an integer is prime or composite is important in cryptographic applications.

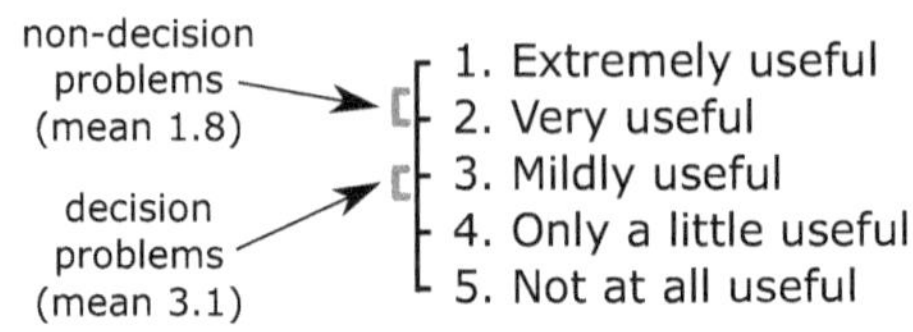

Figure 1: Students perceive programs solving non-decision problems as considerably more useful than programs solving decision problems. The red bars represent 99% confidence intervals for the mean.

The above definition has an intuitive connection to computer programs that produce meaningful output (as opposed to a single accept/reject bit). Formally, we say a computer program P *solves* the computational problem F if $P(x) \in F(x)$ for all x. That is, the program always terminates and outputs a correct solution.

4 EMPIRICAL EVIDENCE FOR PEDAGOGICAL BENEFIT OF NON-DECISION PROBLEMS

The core motivation for our approach is the well-established pedagogical principle that students learn new concepts more effectively when those concepts are placed in a familiar context. The effectiveness of learning is further enhanced if the new concept is perceived as *useful* or *applicable* [7]. Non-decision problems conform to these two criteria—familiarity and applicability—much more closely than decision problems. The familiarity criterion is indisputable, since almost every computer program written by students, beginning with the first programming course and continuing throughout their careers, computes meaningful answers to general problems rather than producing a single-bit accept/reject decision. The second criterion of perceived usefulness or applicability also seems plausible, but requires supporting evidence. To investigate this, a sample of 41 computer science majors were given descriptions of four computer programs which solved decision and non-decision variants of two different problems. Participants rated the usefulness of each program on a Likert scale from 1 (extremely useful) to 5 (not at all useful). The order of presentation (decision versus non-decision variants) was varied to eliminate ordering effects. We control for the intrinsic perceived usefulness of any given problem by presenting decision and non-decision variants of the *same* problems. A total of $n = 81$ paired (i.e. decision versus non-decision) responses were received from the 41 participants. Further details of the survey design, demographics, and results are available in an accompanying technical report [15].

The results show that programs solving non-decision problems are perceived as significantly more useful than programs solving decision problems (mean 1.8 vs 3.1 on the Likert scale, with standard deviations of about 0.7 and 0.8 respectively, leading to standard errors of less than 0.1 in both cases). A 99% confidence interval for the population mean, formed from plus-or-minus three standard errors, is shown on figure 1; the intervals suggest a large and significant difference. Two more rigorous tests confirm this: (i) a Wilcoxon signed-rank test for asymmetry of the paired differences has a negligible p-value ($p < 10^{-11}$); (ii) the same test run on shifted data, with the non-decision responses shifted away from "useful" by an entire Likert gradation, also has a negligible p-value ($p < 10^{-6}$). We conclude that the difference in student perceptions of usefulness is rather large—certainly more than one Likert gradation and hence exceeding the distinction between "very useful" and "mildly useful," as shown on figure 1.

It is worth emphasizing here that this difference in perceived usefulness exists in a *novice audience* (as defined in section 1), and this underpins the key pedagogical point of the paper. Experienced practitioners know that decision programs can often be converted to equivalent non-decision programs with only a logarithmic increase in running time. But because the novice audience does not share this intuition, we should exploit the novices' perception that non-decision programs are useful. We conclude that elementary concepts in an introductory computer science theory course should be taught using non-decision problems whenever possible.

5 COMPUTABILITY FOR NON-DECISION PROBLEMS

The previous section established the key pedagogical advantages of non-decision problems: familiarity and applicability. The remainder of the paper describes technical details of how to teach the standard material of a CS theory course using non-decision problems. This brief section tackles *computability theory*, and the following section tackles *complexity theory*.

We say a computational problem is *computable* if there exists a program that solves it. Note that computability is a generalization of decidability, which applies only to decision problems. Most undergraduate theory treatments use *undecidability* as the central concept to convey the profound idea that "there are some problems that computers can't solve." In the approach advocated by this paper, the notion of *uncomputability* replaces undecidability as the central concept. We can still use classical decision problems as examples of uncomputable problems (e.g. the halting problem, or the question of whether a given program computes a given function). But in addition, we can discuss other interesting uncomputable problems that are not decision problems (see [15, 16]). In all cases, we retain the pedagogical advantage of working in a framework that is perceived by the novice audience as familiar and applicable.

6 ELEMENTARY COMPLEXITY THEORY FOR NON-DECISION PROBLEMS

We now move from computability theory to complexity theory. Here, the use of non-decision problems as the central focus requires some new notation and terminology, compared to the traditional approach. The most fundamental classical complexity classes (P, NP, Exp) contain only decision problems, so we need new notation for analogous classes that contain both decision and non-decision problems. Here, we will denote these new classes by Poly, NPoly, and Expo respectively. Formally, then, Poly is the set of computational problems for which there exists a program (or Turing machine) that solves the problem in polynomial time. NPoly is the same but we allow nondeterministic programs[3]; and Expo is the same but we allow exponential time.

The literature already has classes FP and FNP, which are similar in spirit to Poly and NPoly respectively—so we need good justification for introducing new terminology into such well-trodden territory. One reason is that FP is sometimes defined in terms of function problems only (which excludes problems with multiple solutions such as FACTOR and HAMCYCLE). And even when FP is defined in terms of general problems, it is usually done via the polynomially bounded relations mentioned above, which is unnecessarily complicated for the novice audience. Therefore, we prefer to introduce the new classes Poly, NPoly, and Expo.

A comparison with our ten sample books is interesting here: five do not mention FP, FNP, or any analogous complexity class [5, 11–13, 24]; three briefly cover one or both of FP and FNP [2, 18, 21]; and two give more thorough analyses of FP and FNP or analogous classes (Papadimitriou [19], Goldreich [10]). Papadimitriou's definitions of FP and FNP are closest to the Poly and NPoly defined here. However, they are not equivalent, because of the restriction to polynomially balanced relations mentioned above. Goldreich is the only one of the ten sample books to adopt non-decision problems as a central concept. Goldreich defines the interesting non-decision complexity classes PF (for "polynomial time find") and PC (for "polynomial time checkable"), but they are again not equivalent to Poly and NPoly. Moreover, PF is not a subset of PC (in contrast to the intuitive relationships P⊆NP, Poly⊆NPoly, FP⊆FNP), making PF and PC less than ideal for the novice audience. The overall conclusion from analyzing the selection of textbooks is twofold: (i) few textbooks discuss non-decision problems in any detail, even via the well-established complexity classes FP and FNP; and (ii) for technical reasons, the various non-decision classes FP, FNP, PF, and PC are unsuitable for the novice audience and we instead recommend Poly, NPoly, and Expo as defined above.

Introducing novice audiences to complexity theory via the non-decision classes Poly, NPoly, and Expo has a striking advantage that is worth discussing further: the concrete impact of polynomial time algorithms on cryptography is more obvious. To see this, note that one way to crack the popular RSA cryptosystem is to factor a large integer. So, if it turned out to be true that FACTOR∈Poly, the extraordinary consequences (namely, that RSA would be vulnerable to attack) are immediately obvious to the novice audience. In contrast, the consequences are unclear when the same concepts are taught in terms of decision problems: we already know that FACTORD∈P, but that doesn't help to crack RSA since we get only the existence and not the value of the factors. There are ways of rephrasing factorization in terms of decision problems,[4] but the extra technical complexity of rephrasing the problem obscures the key point for novice audiences.

What about more abstract problems such as HAMCYCLE or SAT? In these cases, the pedagogical advantages of familiarity and applicability are compelling. To see why, first note that both HAMCYCLE and SAT can be reduced fairly easily to their decision variants.

[3]The details of defining the outputs of nondeterministic programs that can produce more than a yes/no solution are interesting and important, but are omitted here for space reasons. See [16] for details.

[4]Specifically, we can ask if there exists a factor within a given range. The search problem of finding a factor reduces to this decision problem, via binary search.

Therefore, to an experienced practitioner, it makes absolutely no difference whether we discuss algorithms for HAMCYCLE or HAMCYCLED (and similarly for SAT vs SATD). But to the novice audience, the act of finding a Hamilton cycle or satisfying assignment is much more compelling than determining their existence. This distinction becomes especially important when discussing nondeterminism, since nondeterministic programs can easily and efficiently compute factors, Hamilton cycles, and satisfying assignments. In fact, a beneficial and enlightening homework assignment is for students to write multithreaded programs that compute solutions to these problems in nondeterministic polynomial time. As emphasized in section 4, the fact that the outputs of such programs are perceived as "useful" is an important factor in achieving positive learning outcomes.

7 THE VERIFIER-BASED DEFINITION OF NPOLY

It is well-known that NP has two equivalent definitions: (i) decision problems that can be decided by a polynomial time nondeterministic program; and (ii) decision problems whose positive instances can be verified in polynomial time by a deterministic program, when provided with a suitable *certificate* (also known as a *witness*, or *hint*). Most modern textbooks cover both definitions, usually introducing (ii) first and later proving the equivalence to (i). Can we generalize these definitions to non-decision problems in a way that appeals to the novice audience? Yes we can, but with some caveats.

Definition (i), based on nondeterminism, was discussed in the previous section. Here we focus on definition (ii), based on verification. According to this definition, NPoly is the class of computational problems which have polynomial time verifiers. And NP is defined in a precisely analogous way: it is the class of *decision* problems which have polynomial time verifiers. When we move to defining *verifier*, however, there are key differences in the decision (NP) and non-decision (NPoly) scenarios. Details of these differences can be found in the accompanying technical report [15]. Here, we mention just one key aspect. Recall that every positive instance of an NP problem must be verifiable in polynomial time when provided with some certificate c. Typically, the certificate c encodes a solution to the underlying non-decision problem. For example, a HAMCYCLED instance can be verified by providing a legitimate Hamilton cycle as the certificate. But unfortunately, it turns out that certificates for NP problems can also work in less intuitive ways. For example, it is possible to define a HAMCYCLED verifier that uses only partial Hamilton cycles as certificates. This discrepancy between certificates and underlying solutions is a source of confusion for the novice audience.

It turns out that if we work with non-decision problems, this potentially confusing "looseness" in the definition of certificates is eliminated. In essence (and please see the technical report [15] or textbook [16] for additional details), the certificate c is replaced by two separate strings: a solution s and hint h. Both strings are given as input to the verifier. For successful verifications of positive instances, the solution s really is a solution for the given instance; the hint h provides any additional information needed for verification. The explicit roles of s and h provide additional clarity to the novice audience.

To the best of our knowledge, no textbook other than [16] employs this formulation, which ensures that verified solutions are meaningful while still permitting hints for problems that need them. This is one key difference between the approach of this paper and that of Goldreich [10].

8 REDUCTIONS AND NP-COMPLETENESS

We noted in the introduction that some of the theorems and proofs in computational complexity theory are more elegant when expressed in terms of decision problems, and the vast majority of literature takes this approach. Therefore, even if we choose for pedagogical reasons to introduce elementary concepts in terms of non-decision problems, it makes sense to eventually transition to the decision problem viewpoint. Over a four-year period, we experimented with making this transition at various points in the course. For reasons discussed below, we found the best choice is to make the transition when students first encounter polynomial time reductions, and hence also before introducing NP-completeness.

For the novice audience it seems preferable to focus on the simplest type of reduction, which is variously known as a *Karp reduction, polynomial time mapping reduction,* or *many-one reduction.* In focusing on Karp reductions, we are now in line with eight of our ten sample textbooks (with the same two outliers [10, 19] as previously). However, we still break slightly from the eight standard treatments, because instead of defining reductions between *decision* problems, we define reductions from decision computational problems to *general* problems (i.e. *to*, but not *from*, general problems). This difference again calls for new terminology, and we use the term "polyreduction" for this.

Formally, a *polyreduction* from the decision problem D to the general computational problem G is a map $r : \Sigma^* \to \Sigma^*$, such that $r(w)$ is a positive instance of G if and only if w is a positive instance of D. We also require that r is computable in polynomial time. With this definition, students can first examine trivial polyreductions such as HAMCYCLED→HAMCYCLE, then move on to more interesting ones such as DIRECTEDHAMCYCLED→UNDIRECTEDHAMCYCLED.

With a little more effort, we can define polyreductions between general problems F and G. To do so, we need polynomial time maps in both directions. First, $r : \Sigma^* \to \Sigma^*$ maps instances of F to instances of G. Then $r' : \Sigma^* \to \Sigma^*$ maps solutions of G back to solutions of F. The correctness condition is that, given any program G that solves the problem G, we must have $r'(\mathsf{G}(r(w))) \in F(w)$ for all w. (In words, the solution of G for $r(w)$ must map back to a solution of F for w.) We have experimented with teaching this concept to novice audiences and met with a certain amount of success. Goldreich also recommends this approach [9]. However, as already stated, on balance we recommend avoiding this extra level of generality, instead restricting polyreductions to be maps from decision problems to general problems via the simpler definition in the previous paragraph.

In the same spirit, we might attempt to teach "NPoly-completeness" for general computational problems. But in this case, our experience has been that the benefits of using non-decision problems are clearly outweighed by the disadvantages of dealing with arbitrary solutions when stating and proving theorems about NPoly-completeness. Therefore, it seems preferable to stay solidly in the traditional realm of decision problems when teaching NP-completeness. As a small bonus, the fact that our definition of polyreduction allows decision problems to be reduced to *general* problems leads to an elegant definition of NP-hardness: a problem G is NP-hard if some NP-complete problem D polyreduces to G. Holistic discussions of P versus NP (although defined formally in terms of decision problems) also take on a more practical tone when the majority of concepts earlier in the course have been taught in terms of non-decision problems.

9 CONCLUSION

The paper advocated the use of non-decision problems in CS theory courses. The paper consisted of two separate strands: (i) an explanation of *why* non-decision problems are preferable, based on a combination of empirical survey results and educational theory; and (ii) an explanation of *how* to use non-decision problems in the theory course, using reformulations of classical concepts. In the first strand (section 4), we demonstrated via an empirical survey of CS majors that programs solving non-decision problems are perceived as much more useful and applicable than programs solving decision problems. Invoking the well-known educational principle that learning outcomes are likely to be better for a course that uses materials perceived as "useful," we concluded that non-decision problems should be used if possible. In the second strand (sections 3 and 5–8), we suggested new definitions, terminology, and notation that are designed to employ non-decision problems and to maximize the accessibility of CS theory concepts for the novice undergraduate audience. The approach has been tested and refined over four years of teaching, culminating in a recent textbook [16]. Looking to the future, we hope this approach will not only improve learning outcomes for undergraduates receiving their first taste of computer science theory, but will also lead to theory courses that are taught earlier in the curriculum, to a wider range of undergraduates, at a wider range of institutions.

REFERENCES

[1] Manindra Agrawal, Neeraj Kayal, and Nitin Saxena. 2004. PRIMES is in P. *Annals of Mathematics* 160, 2 (2004), 781–793.
[2] S. Arora and B. Barak. 2009. *Computational Complexity: A Modern Approach.* Cambridge University Press. https://books.google.com/books?id=8Wjqvsoo48MC
[3] Carlos I. Chesñevar, María L. Cobo, and William Yurcik. 2003. Using Theoretical Computer Simulators for Formal Languages and Automata Theory. *SIGCSE Bulletin* 35, 2 (June 2003), 33–37. https://doi.org/10.1145/782941.782975
[4] Pierluigi Crescenzi, Emma Enström, and Viggo Kann. 2013. From Theory to Practice: NP-completeness for Every CS Student. In *Proc. ITiCSE.* 16–21. https://doi.org/10.1145/2462476.2465582
[5] Martin Davis, Ron Sigal, and Elaine J Weyuker. 1994. *Computability, Complexity, and Languages: Fundamentals of Theoretical Computer Science* (2nd ed.). Morgan Kaufmann.
[6] Emma Enström and Viggo Kann. 2010. Computer lab work on theory. In *Proc. ITiCSE.* 93–97.
[7] L Dee Fink. 2013. *Creating significant learning experiences: An integrated approach to designing college courses* (2nd ed.). John Wiley & Sons.
[8] Lance Fortnow. 2013. *The golden ticket: P, NP, and the search for the impossible.* Princeton University Press.
[9] Oded Goldreich. 2006. *On Teaching the Basics of Complexity Theory.* Springer, 348–374. https://doi.org/10.1007/11685654_15 In *Theoretical Computer Science: Essays in Memory of Shimon Even*, ed. Goldreich, Rosenberg, Selman.
[10] Oded Goldreich. 2010. *P, NP, and NP-Completeness: The Basics of Computational Complexity.* Cambridge University Press.
[11] John E. Hopcroft, Rajeev Motwani, and Jeffrey D. Ullman. 2006. *Introduction to Automata Theory, Languages, and Computation* (3rd ed.). Pearson.
[12] Harry R Lewis and Christos H Papadimitriou. 1997. *Elements of the Theory of Computation* (2nd ed.). Prentice Hall.
[13] Peter Linz. 2011. *An Introduction to Formal Languages and Automata* (5th ed.). Jones & Bartlett.
[14] Andrea F. Lobo and Ganesh R. Baliga. 2006. NP-completeness for All Computer Science Undergraduates: A Novel Project-based Curriculum. *J. Comput. Sci. Coll.* 21, 6 (June 2006), 53–63. http://dl.acm.org/citation.cfm?id=1127442.1127450
[15] John MacCormick. 2017. *Strategies for basing the CS theory course on non-decision problems.* Technical Report. Dickinson College.
[16] John MacCormick. 2018. *What Can Be Computed?: A Practical Guide to the Theory of Computation.* Princeton University Press.
[17] Dino Mandrioli. 1982. On teaching theoretical foundations of Computer Science. *ACM SIGACT News* 14, 3 (1982), 36–53. Part 2 appears in 14(4):58–69.
[18] Cristopher Moore and Stephan Mertens. 2011. *The Nature of Computation.* Oxford University Press.
[19] Christos H. Papadimitriou. 1994. *Computational Complexity.* Addison Wesley, Massachussetts.
[20] Christos H Papadimitriou. 1997. NP-completeness: A retrospective. In *International Colloquium on Automata, Languages, and Programming.* Springer, 2–6.
[21] Elaine Rich. 2007. *Automata, Computability and Complexity: Theory and Applications.* Pearson.
[22] Susan H Rodger and Thomas W Finley. 2006. *JFLAP: an interactive formal languages and automata package.* Jones & Bartlett Learning.
[23] Susan H Rodger, Eric Wiebe, Kyung Min Lee, Chris Morgan, Kareem Omar, and Jonathan Su. 2009. Increasing engagement in automata theory with JFLAP. In *ACM SIGCSE Bulletin*, Vol. 41. ACM, 403–407.
[24] Michael Sipser. 2013. *Introduction to the Theory of Computation* (3rd ed.). Cengage.

Epplets: A Tool for Solving Parsons Puzzles

Amruth N. Kumar
Ramapo College of New Jersey
Mahwah, NJ 07430
USA
amruth@ramapo.edu

ABSTRACT

Performance on Parsons puzzles has been found to correlate with that on code-writing exercises. Parsons puzzles are preferred by students over alternative programming tasks. In order to make Parsons puzzles widely available to students in the introductory programming course, we developed a tool that administers the puzzles in C++, Java and C#, called epplets. Our design of the tool improves upon the work done by earlier researchers in several ways: students rearrange lines of code rather than program fragments; they get credit based on the number of actions they take to reassemble the code; they get feedback that helps them fix their incorrect answer; and the tool adapts to the needs of the student. The tool runs as a Java Web application. We describe our experience using the tool for two years: how it benefited the students; the revisions made to address the feedback provided by the users; and our plans for future work. We found that practicing with the tool helped reduce the time and actions with which students solved successive puzzles.

ACM Reference format:

Amruth N. Kumar. 2018. Epplets: A Tool for Solving Parsons Puzzles. In *SIGCSE '18: 49th ACM Technical Symposium on Computer Science Education, Feb. 21–24, 2018, Baltimore, MD, USA*. ACM, NY, NY, USA, 6 pages. https://doi.org/10.1145/3159450.3159576

1 INTRODUCTION

In a Parsons puzzle [13], the student is presented with a problem statement, and the program written for it. The statements in the program are provided scrambled, along with distracters that are incorrect syntactic or semantic variants of existing lines of code. The student is asked to reassemble the statements in their correct order and delete any distracters. Parsons puzzles were designed to be an engaging way to learn programming [13].[1]

Parsons puzzles have since been proposed for use in exams [3], since they are easier to grade than code-writing exercises, and yet, scores on Parsons puzzles correlate with scores on code-writing exercises. Researchers have found solving Parsons puzzles to be part of a hierarchy of programming skills alongside code-tracing [11]. In electronic books, students have been found to prefer solving Parsons puzzles more than other low-cognitive-load activities such as answering multiple choice questions and high-cognitive-load activities such as writing code [4]. Solving Parsons puzzles was found to take significantly less time than fixing errors in code or writing equivalent code, but resulted in the same learning performance and retention [5]. So, Parsons puzzles have been gaining popularity among educators of introductory programming.

Software to administer Parsons puzzles have been developed for Turbo Pascal [13] and Python (e.g., [1,7]). We wanted to make the puzzles more widely available to students in introductory programming courses. Therefore, we developed a Parsons puzzle tool for C++, Java and C#, three of the most widely used languages in introductory programming courses today. Our tool differs from prior Parsons puzzle solvers in several respects, including design, delivery, puzzle generation, and grading. To date, we have developed six modules: one on sequence, two on selection statements and three on loops. The tool is called epplets (short for extended Parsons puzzle problets) and is accessible online for free for educational use. Additional information about epplets can be found at epplets.org.

2 PARSONS PUZZLE TOOL DESCRIPTION

We will first describe the user interface of the tool, followed by description of its unique features vis-à-vis design, delivery, problem generation and grading.

2.1 User Interface

A snapshot of our tool is shown in Figure 1 at the end of this paper. The problem statement is displayed in instruction panel (I). The code written for this problem is presented in problem panel (P), both scrambled and unindented. The student has the following **action**s available for solving the puzzle:

- Drag a line of code from Problem panel (P) to solution panel (S);
- Drag a line of code from Problem panel (P) to Trash panel (T) to delete it – this is applicable to distracters in the puzzle;
- Reorder a line of code in Solution panel (S) by moving it up or down;
- Indent/outdent a line of code in Solution panel (S) to improve readability;

- Return a line from either the Solution panel (S) or Trash panel (T) back to the Problem panel (P), whereupon the line is placed back in its original scrambled order in the Problem panel (P);
- Move a line from the Solution panel (S) to the Trash panel (T) or vice versa.

Feedback is provided to the student in the feedback panel (F). When the student is solving the puzzle, every action taken by the student is listed in the Feedback panel (F).

The student can attempt to submit the solution by clicking on "Submit Answer" button (shown at the bottom right). The student's solution is not considered to be complete until the student has moved all the lines of code from the Problem panel (P) to either the Solution panel (S) or Trash panel (T). Until the student's solution is complete, whenever the student clicks on "Submit Answer" button, the feedback displayed in the Feedback panel (F) simply asks the student to complete the solution first. Once the solution is complete, it is checked for correctness when the student clicks on the "Submit Answer" button:

- If the solution is correct, a summary of the actions taken by the student is listed in the Feedback panel (F). "Next Problem" button (shown at the bottom right) becomes enabled and the student can click on it to advance to the next puzzle.
- If the solution is incorrect, the first line in the Solution panel (S) that is not in its correct location is highlighted. Feedback is presented in the Feedback panel (F) asking the student to move the line to its correct location later in the code. If the first incorrect line in the Solution panel (S) is a distracter, the feedback also lists why the line of code is incorrect (e.g., "The operator between `principal` and `rate` should be multiplication, not division.") So, the student is given the opportunity to fix the solution one line at a time.

  The student can take as many actions as necessary to correct the solution. Once the solution is correct, the student is provided a summary of the actions in the Feedback panel (F) and "Next Problem" button is enabled as described earlier.

  If the solution remains incorrect, once the student has executed twice as many actions as the number of lines in the code, "Quit" button becomes enabled (shown at the bottom right), and the student can abandon solving the puzzle by clicking on it. If the student does so, the correct solution to the puzzle is displayed in the Feedback panel (F) and the problem is marked as not having been completed by the student.

  So, the only way a student can advance to the next puzzle is by solving it completely and correctly (after zero or more corrections) or by quitting the puzzle.

Help menu is always available – if the student clicks on it, drag-and-drop instructions for solving the puzzle are displayed in a separate window.

The tool allows students to indent/outdent lines of code to improve its readability. But, true to the nature of C++/Java/C# programs, indentation is ignored during grading. If the tool were to be extended to cover Python, the grading scheme would have to be extended to also consider indentation, as is done in 2-D Parsons puzzles (e.g., [8]).

2.2 Unique design: One line at a time

In all prior Parsons puzzle solvers, the student reassembled the code one fragment at a time, a fragment consisting of one or more lines of code. E.g., the following is a fragment in Pascal [13]:

```
writeln( "You win" );
end;
```

Another fragment in the same puzzle is [13]:

```
writeln( "You lose" );
end;
```

Combining multiple lines into a fragment provides two benefits: It eliminates interchangeability when the same line appears multiple times in a program (e.g., `end` statement in the above two fragments, else clause, open and close braces, etc.): each instance of the repeated line can be incorporated into a unique, non-interchangeable fragment, as shown above. It also addresses the issue that the order of some of the lines in a program is often partial rather than total, e.g., variables could be declared in any order without affecting the semantics of the program. In such cases, lines can be incorporated into fragments so that the order among the fragments is total rather than partial, e.g., all the variable declarations could be encapsulated into one program fragment. So, using fragments considerably simplifies grading in Parsons puzzle solvers.

In our design, the student re-assembles the code *one line at a time*. This approach has two benefits: it makes the puzzles harder to solve since the number of lines in a program is greater than or equal to the number of fragments. More importantly, since students write code one line at a time, solving a puzzle one line at a time makes the puzzle more epistemic [2]. It forces students to think about the solution in terms of lines which are canonical units of code rather than code fragments which are often contrived aggregations of contiguous lines of code.

If code fragments encapsulate abstract steps in a program, Parsons puzzles with code fragments can be said to promote puzzle-solving at a more abstract level. But, in reality, fragments were not proposed as encapsulations of abstract steps: the two examples of code fragments listed earlier [13] are neither a single step nor an abstract step, but rather, a sequence of lines aggregated to eliminate the ambiguity of placing multiple `end` statements in the code. One can place such contrived code fragments in their correct location often based merely on their unique composition, and without considering their algorithmic role in the overall program. So, using contrived code fragments reduces the pedagogic benefits of Parsons puzzles.

Having students solve the puzzle one line at a time instead of one code fragment at a time meant that we had to handle two issues: the interchangeability of a line of code (e.g., brace) when it appears in multiple locations in a program; and that the order among some lines of code (e.g., declaration statements) is not strict, but rather flexible. We solved these issues in a manner intrinsic to the nature of programming. When a line appears multiple times in a program, our tool awards correct credit for placing any instance of the line in any of its correct locations in the code.

We introduced comments in the code to enforce strict order among the lines of code that could otherwise be listed in any order, e.g., in a program to calculate interest on a loan, the loan amount, duration of the loan and interest rate may be input in any order. We introduced comments into the code that could not be reordered, and that enforced a strict order among these three inputs as follows:

```
// Input the loan amount
...
// Input the rate of interest
...
// Input the duration of loan
...
```

This approach of using comments reinforces the good programming practice that code should follow comments. It requires students to associate lines of code with the purpose for which they were written, as expressed in the comments. Finally, comments serve as sub-goal labels, and research shows that sub-goal labels help students solve puzzles statistically better [12].

2.3 Tool Delivery

In prior approaches, the Parsons puzzle solver was built to administer and grade puzzles. We built our tool to also be *adaptive*, i.e., cater to the puzzle-solving needs of the student.

In our tool, each puzzle is associated with a learning objective. The student's current knowledge is modeled in terms of these learning objectives. The tool first administers a puzzle on each learning objective, to determine whether the student can solve it completely, correctly and with the fewest actions. Thereafter, for each learning objective on which the student could either not solve the puzzle correctly or took redundant actions to solve it correctly, the tool presents additional puzzles until the student demonstrates mastery, i.e., solves puzzles with no more than a pre-determined number of actions [9].

The adaptive nature of our tool ensures that students do not solve unnecessary puzzles; they solve additional puzzles on only the learning objectives they have not yet met; and their progress in solving puzzles on each learning objective can be documented. Adaptation personalizes the practice provided by the tool, and leverages the benefits of using technology for learning.

2.4 Generation of puzzles

Our tool generates puzzles as randomized instances of parameterized puzzle templates. A puzzle template is written in BNF notation. For example, the template for a variable declaration and initialization statement is:

```
<T1><V1> = <R1>;
```

<T1> is a BNF non-terminal that represents a data type, <V1> represents the name of a variable and <R1> represents a random value of data type <T1>. The template may also contain constraints, as in:

```
<T1#real#> <V1#rate,percent,interest #> = <R1#3<=R1<=12>;
```

In this template, the data type is constrained to be a real type (e.g., `float` or `double`). The possible names for the variable are `rate`, `percent` and `interest`. The value of R1 is constrained to be within the range 3 through 12. So, the line of code generated from this template could be any of the following:

```
float percent = 5.0;
double rate = 9.0;
float interest = 7.0;
```

The template of a puzzle is the template of an entire program in the correct order. When generating a puzzle from its template, the tool first replaces all the BNF non-terminals in the template with randomly chosen terminals that obey applicable constraints and are appropriate for the programming language being used (C++, Java or C#). The result is a complete and correct program. The tool next scrambles the lines of code in the program. Finally, the tool adds distracters to the scrambled code.

Distracters are syntactically / semantically buggy versions of the correct code e.g., `5 = count;` instead of `count = 5;`. We used a library of bug specifications to implement distracters. A bug specification contains a regular expression pattern which is used to match each line of code; a code transformation that is used to generate the distracter; a statement that is presented as feedback if the student fails to delete the distracter; and the programming languages and topics to which the bug applies.

For example, consider the following bug specification:
Pattern: ^(.*)\+=(.*)$
Transformation: $1+ =$2
Feedback: Space is not allowed within assignment operator +=
Languages: C++, Java, C#
The line of code `count += 5;` matches the pattern. As a result, the distracter `count + = 5;` is generated. If the student fails to discard the distracter, "Space is not allowed within assignment operator +=" is presented as feedback.

The tool contains 100 bug specifications. It generates at most one distracter per line in the code. It can be configured to specify the total number of distracters per puzzle. It can also be configured to place the distracter either at a random location in the code or right before/after the line for which it was generated – the latter placement is known to reduce cognitive load [3].

Initially, the tool generates all possible distracters for each line in the program. Next, it randomly picks a line and randomly picks a distracter for the line. If it is configured to generate n distracters per puzzle, it repeats this process n times, while also making sure that no two distracters are exactly the same.

Since our tool generates puzzles as randomized instances of parameterized templates and adds distracters that are randomly selected from among the available distracters, no two puzzles will be exactly the same even when they have been generated from the same puzzle template. This ensures that no two students will see the same puzzle, and no student will see the same puzzle twice. In addition, each of the 6 modules of the tool contains 15-20 puzzle templates. Therefore, students can practice solving puzzles with the tool as long and as often as they wish.

The tool can be configured to present puzzles in one of two modes:

- Shell-unscrambled mode: The shell of the program is provided to the student in its correct order in the Solution panel (S) at the start of the puzzle-solving session. The student cannot reorder any of its lines. The student is expected to drag and drop only the lines of code contained within the program. Figure 1 shows an example of this mode at the start of a puzzle-solving session.

- None-unscrambled mode: No lines of code are provided unscrambled – the student must reassemble all the lines of code including the shell of the program.

In both the modes, comments in the program are always provided unscrambled in the Solution panel (S) and cannot be reordered. The benefit of shell-unscrambled mode is that students can focus on reconstructing the program and ignore the minimum syntactic baggage needed to make the program compilable, such as `import` statements in Java. This is the mode in which we have been using the tool.

2.5 Grading of student solution

As mentioned earlier, wherever the order of lines of code is not strict, comments are used to disambiguate their order and impose a strict order. So, each puzzle has only one correct solution. The student is required to solve the puzzle completely and correctly before moving on to the next puzzle. The student can execute any number of actions to solve a puzzle. The number of actions is used as the measure of the student's ability to solve the puzzle.

In order to solve a puzzle containing n lines of code, a student needs n and no more actions: one action per line to drag and drop the lines of code into their correct location in the Solution panel (S) and one action per line to drag and drop distracters into the Trash panel (T). In order to allow for unintentional drag-and-drop mistakes, the tool was configured to allow a leeway of 10% more actions without penalty. So, anyone who solved the puzzle within 1.1 * n actions was given full credit by the tool. Thereafter, partial credit was awarded inversely proportional to the number of unnecessary actions taken by the student.

Recall that once the student has cleared the Problem panel (P), whenever the student attempts to submit the answer, feedback is provided describing which line is not in its correct location and how it can be fixed. However, students cannot game the system by repeatedly trying to submit an incorrect solution and fixing the solution using the feedback provided to them, because actions over 1.1* n are negatively graded. This is also why once the student has executed 2*n actions, the tool determines that the student is thrashing and enables Quit button that the student can click to abandon the solution.

3 EXPERIENCE REPORT

The tool is deployed as a Java Web application. It was used by multiple schools each semester in 2015-2017 in their introductory programming course. Students typically used the tool for after-class assignments. They could use each module as often as necessary.

In order to determine whether the ability of the students to solve Parsons puzzles improved with practice, we analyzed the data collected by the module on selection statements over two years. This module presented puzzles on two learning objectives:

1. Programs that used a single `if-else` statement
2. Programs that used nested `if-else` statements.

None of the puzzles administered by the module on selection statements used any control construct other than `if-else` statements. On each learning objective, the module was configured to present 6 different puzzles in a row, as needed by the student: the first puzzle to determine whether the student needed additional practice and subsequent ones to help the student practice solving puzzles. If students got better at solving Parsons puzzles with practice, we expected to see that with each successive (and different) puzzle, we would find a reduction in:

1. the time spent solving the puzzle;
2. the number of actions taken to solve the puzzle.

The number of lines of code varied with the puzzles – some puzzles had more lines of code than others. In order to facilitate comparison of these metrics across different puzzles, we analyzed the time spent per line of the puzzle and number of actions taken per line of the puzzle instead.

The module on selection was used by the students of 24 instructors over the two years data was collected. For our analysis, we used data from the students who had given permission for their data to be used for research purposes. We eliminated those who had solved only one puzzle on a learning objective. For the students who had used the module multiple times, we considered data from only their first complete session.

3.1 Puzzles with a single selection statement

The 6 puzzles administered by selection module on this learning objective, in order, were on the following problems:

1. Read two numbers and print the smaller value among them
2. Read a number and print whether it is odd or even
3. Read sound in decibels and print whether it is loud or not
4. Read body temperature in Celsius, print whether the person has fever
5. Read the price and earnings of a stock and recommend buying/selling the stock based on price to earnings ratio
6. Read two numbers and print the absolute difference between them

Although these puzzles were very different both syntactically and semantically, especially in the eyes of a novice programmer, they all shared the same underlying algorithm.

Table 1 lists the mean of the time in seconds spent by the students per line of code on successive puzzles. The last column lists the statistical significance at 95% confidence level of conducting paired t-test on the times spent on problems n-1 and n for the values of n from 2 to 6. Each successive puzzle was solved by fewer students because of the adaptive nature of the tool. The mean time spent per line of code dropped significantly on each successive puzzle from the first puzzle to the fourth. Subsequent changes in the mean times were not statistically significant.

Table 1: Time spent and actions executed per line of code of each puzzle with a single selection statement

		Time spent (sec)		Actions executed	
Puzzle	N	Mean	p	Mean	p
1	194	21.803		1.695	
2	194	16.130	0.005	1.242	$p < 0.001$
3	179	11.642	0.021	1.159	0.012
4	57	8.294	0.005	1.088	0.016
5	51	10.743	0.078	1.108	0.281
6	15	9.133	0.186	1.163	0.188

Table 1 also lists the mean number of actions carried out per line of code on successive puzzles. On the first puzzle, students executed an average of 69% more actions than needed to solve the puzzle. This mean dropped significantly from the first puzzle through the fourth. Subsequent changes were not statistically significant.

So, on this learning objective, students improved significantly with practice, both in terms of the time spent and the actions executed per line of code through the first four puzzles. There are a few plausible explanations for why this trend did not continue to the fifth and sixth puzzles:

- The sample size N is too small, especially on the sixth puzzle;
- Students who continued to solve puzzles past the fourth puzzle without demonstrating mastery were either less prepared, not engaged or did not stand to benefit from solving puzzles;
- Puzzles on this learning objective take about 8-10 seconds to solve per line of code and about 8-16% more actions than necessary, and no significant further improvements in either metric should be expected.

We plan to test these hypotheses with additional data in the future.

3.2 Puzzles with nested selection statements

The 6 puzzles administered by selection module on this learning objective, in order, were on the following problems:

1. Read numerical grade, print the corresponding letter grade A/B/C/D/F (5)
2. Read the month, print the corresponding season (4)
3. Read angle in degrees, print the corresponding quadrant (4)
4. Read altitude in miles, print the name of the corresponding atmospheric layer (5)
5. Read the wavelength of light, print the corresponding color (6)
6. Read wind speed, print the corresponding enhanced Fujita hurricane scale (6)

Listed in parentheses against each problem above is the number of options handled by the code in the puzzle. In each puzzle, the problem statement clarified the ranges needed to correctly solve the puzzle, e.g., red is 620-750 nm, and 158-206 mph is F3 hurricane. Once again, these puzzles were very different both syntactically and semantically, but, they all shared the same algorithm.

Table 2 lists the mean of the time in seconds spent by the students per line of code on successive puzzles. Although the mean time appeared to drop through the fourth puzzle, only the drop from second to third puzzle was marginally significant. The other drops were not statistically significant.

Table 2: Time spent and actions executed per line of code of each puzzle with nested selection statements

		Time spent (sec)		Actions executed	
Puzzle	N	Mean	p	Mean	p
1	176	18.152		1.561	
2	176	19.404	0.427	1.200	p < 0.001
3	145	9.636	0.075	1.120	0.002
4	72	8.903	0.132	1.156	0.131
5	57	11.663	0.173	1.165	0.424
6	23	9.941	0.286	1.292	0.047

Table 2 also lists the mean number of actions carried out per line of code on successive puzzles. The mean dropped significantly from the first puzzle through the third. Subsequent changes in the mean were not statistically significant except the last one.

The puzzles on this learning objective were conceptually harder than those on the previous learning objective. We still found a significant drop from 56% to 20% redundant actions per line of code from the first to the third puzzle. It could very well be that students need at least 10 seconds per line and at least 20% more actions than necessary to solve puzzles on this leaning objective. More data is needed to test this hypothesis.

4 DISCUSSION

One of the items of feedback provided by the students who used the tool in the first year was that they would have liked to get a better sense of progress as they went about solving each puzzle. So, we updated the tool to list the number of lines in the puzzle (e.g., 36 in Figure 1) and the number of actions with which it could be solved (e.g., 39 in Figure 1). In addition, the tool enumerates the actions taken by the student so that the student knows how many more actions are available before negative grading kicks in. However, these changes did not seem to positively benefit students [10]. In the future, we also plan to display the edit distance of the student's solution from the correct solution on a visible scorecard to further motivate students during the puzzle-solving process – when the edit distance reduces to zero, the solution is complete and correct.

The current scheme of grading rewards students who have a clear idea of the purpose of each line of code. It penalizes exploration, wherein a student might try several alternative locations for each line before placing it for the final time. In the future, we plan to implement an alternative grading scheme which will penalize only the actions needed to correct the solution after the student submits a complete solution for the first time. In this scheme, all the exploratory actions taken by the student until the first submission are forgiven. Until then, the only feedback provided by the tool is to direct the student to complete the solution by clearing all the lines of code from the Problem Panel. Currently, the leeway of extra actions allowed by the tool for full credit is 10%. In the future, we plan to investigate whether it is beneficial to adaptively set the leeway based on the collected data (e.g., 15% for the first learning objective in selection and 20% for the second one) and physical needs of the learner.

Our tool helped students solve Parsons puzzles in less time and with fewer missteps. Whether this results in better ability to write code is an interesting hypothesis for future exploration. Another interesting line of enquiry is to mine the collected data to extract patterns of how students solve the puzzles, as has been attempted by other researchers [6]. Finally, we plan to extend the tool to additional topics including functions, arrays and classes. We also plan to extend it to Python.

ACKNOWLEDGMENTS

Partial support for this work was provided by the National Science Foundation under grants DUE-1502564 and DUE-1432190.

REFERENCES

[1] Nick Cheng and Brian Harrington. 2017. The Code Mangler: Evaluating Coding Ability Without Writing any Code. In *Proceedings of the 2017 ACM SIGCSE Technical Symposium on Computer Science Education* (SIGCSE '17). ACM, New York, NY, USA, 123-128.

[2] Collins, A. and Ferguson, W. Epistemic forms and epistemic games: Structures and strategies to guide inquiry. *Educational Psychologist.* 28 (1), 1993, 25-42.

[4] Ericson, B.J., Guzdial, M.J., and Morrison, B.B. 2015. Analysis of Interactive Features Designed to Enhance Learning in an Ebook. In *Proc.11th annual International Conference on International Computing Education Research* (ICER '15). ACM, New York, NY, USA, 169-178

[5] Barbara J. Ericson, Lauren E. Margulieux, and Jochen Rick. 2017. Solving parsons problems versus fixing and writing code. In *Proceedings of the 17th Koli Calling Conference on Computing Education Research* (Koli Calling '17). ACM, New York, NY, USA, 20-29.

[6] Juha Helminen, Petri Ihantola, Ville Karavirta, and Lauri Malmi. 2012. How do students solve parsons programming problems?: an analysis of interaction traces. In *Proceedings of the ninth annual international conference on International computing education research* (ICER '12). ACM, New York, NY, USA, 119-126.

[7] Ihantola, P. and Karavirta, V. 2010. Open source widget for parson's puzzles. In *Proc. Fifteenth annual conference on Innovation and technology in computer science education* (ITiCSE '10). ACM, New York, NY, USA, 302-302

[8] Ihantola, P. and Karavirta, V.Two-Dimensional Parson's Puzzles: The Conceot, Tools, and First Observations. *Journal of Information Technology Education: Innovations in Practice.* Vol 10. 2011. 119-132.

[9] Kumar, A.N. A Scalable Solution for Adaptive Problem Sequencing and its Evaluation. *In Proc.* Fourth International Conference on Adaptive Hypermedia and Adaptive Web-Based Systems (AH 06), Dublin, Ireland, 2006, 161-171.

[10] Kumar, A.N. The Effect of Providing Motivational Support in Parsons Puzzle Tutors. *In Proc.* AI-ED 2017, Wuhan, China, June 2017, 528-531.

[11] Lopez, N., Whalley, J., Robbins, P. and Lister,, R. 2008. Relationships between reading, tracing and writing skills in introductory programming. In *Proc. 4th international Workshop on Computing Education Research* (ICER '08). ACM, New York, NY, USA, 101-112.

[12] Morrison, B., Margulieux, L., Ericson, B. and Guzdial, M. 2016. Subgoals Help Students Solve Parsons Problems. In *Proc. 47th ACM Technical Symposium on Computing Science Education* (SIGCSE '16). ACM, New York, NY, USA, 42-47.

[13] Parsons, D and Haden, P. 2006. Parson's programming puzzles: a fun and effective learning tool for first programming courses. In *Proc. 8th Australasian Conference on Computing Education - Volume 52* (ACE '06), Vol. 52. Australian Computer Society, Inc., Australia, 157-163.

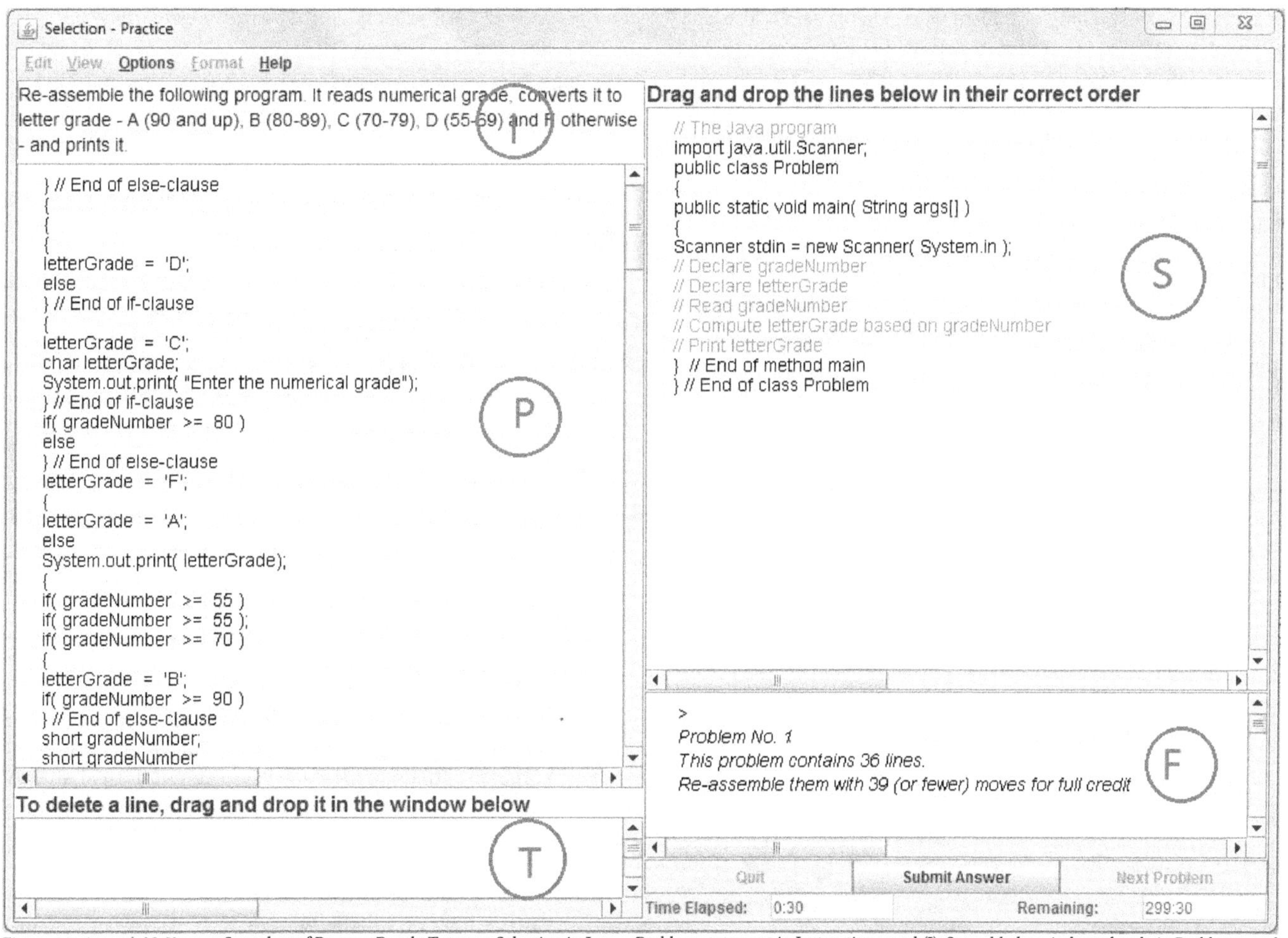

Figure 1 © Amruth N. Kumar: Snapshot of Parsons Puzzle Tutor on Selection in Java – Problem statement in Instruction panel (I); Scrambled un-indented code in Problem panel (P); Student solution in Solution panel (S); Deleted lines in Trash panel (T); Feedback in Feedback panel (F). A problem on conversion from numerical grade to letter grade is in progress.

Connect the Dots to Prove It

A Novel Way to Learn Proof Construction

Mark McCartin-Lim
University of Massachusetts Amherst
Amherst, Massachusetts
markml@cs.umass.edu

Beverly Woolf
University of Massachusetts Amherst
Amherst, Massachusetts
bev@cs.umass.edu

Andrew McGregor
University of Massachusetts Amherst
Amherst, Massachusetts
mcgregor@cs.umass.edu

ABSTRACT

This paper describes a new method for helping students improve their ability to develop proofs, a skill necessary for comprehending and appreciating the foundational topics of computer science. Our method transforms ordinary pen-and-paper homework problems into a puzzle-like game, where students connect dots to justify assertions, in a quest to reach a desired goal. We have implemented a software tutoring system using this method, for students to use at home as an optional study aid. Potentially, our system could one day become a full replacement for traditional hand-written homework, which has the additional benefit for course instructors of automating the grading of student work. Our system is also easy to adapt to any class that requires students to write proofs, and it is easy for instructors to create new problems to use with this system. This stands in contrast to many other educational tools for teaching proofs, which are limited to specific topic domains. We have demonstrated the versatility of our system by testing it in two computer science classes at a large public university. One was a Sophomore-level discrete mathematics course where the students were learning first-order prepositional logic, and the other was a Junior-level algorithms course where students were being first exposed to the concept of NP-completeness. Students from our experiments reported that they would like our system to be used in more of their classes.

CCS CONCEPTS

• **Social and professional topics** → **Computer science education**; *Student assessment*; • **Theory of computation** → *Logic*; • **Applied computing** → **Computer-assisted instruction**; *Interactive learning environments*; E-learning; • **Mathematics of computing** → *Discrete mathematics*;

KEYWORDS

proofs, intelligent tutoring systems, automated grading, theoretical computer science, discrete math, logic, complexity theory, algorithms, active learning, e-learning

SIGCSE '18, February 21–24, 2018, Baltimore, MD, USA

ACM ISBN 978-1-4503-5103-4/18/02...$15.00
https://doi.org/10.1145/3159450.3159609

ACM Reference format:
Mark McCartin-Lim, Beverly Woolf, and Andrew McGregor. 2018. Connect the Dots to Prove It. In *Proceedings of The 49th ACM Technical Symposium on Computing Science Education, Baltimore, MD, USA, February 21–24, 2018 (SIGCSE '18),* 6 pages.
https://doi.org/10.1145/3159450.3159609

1 INTRODUCTION

In 2014, when Maryam Mirzakhani became the first female mathematician to win the prestigious Fields Medal, she explained how she first developed a passion for mathematical proofs [4]:

> *"It is fun — it's like solving a puzzle or connecting the dots in a detective case."*

Our goal is to inspire all students with that same passion, and we aim to accomplish that goal by introducing a puzzle-based platform for proof construction, where the pedagogical method is to have students construct proofs by literally *connecting the dots.*

As computer science researchers, we specifically developed this platform as part of a tutoring system for helping computer science students in their theoretical courses [12].

Computer science educators have lamented the difficulty of teaching students how to write rigorous proofs in discrete mathematics courses [8, 10]. From our own experience grading student papers, we have found that many students also struggle to write rigorous proofs in more advanced theoretical computer science courses as well, such as those covering algorithms and the theory of computation.

Our proof construction platform provides the following benefits:

- **The puzzle-like game structure should increase engagement.** Puzzles have a rich history of being used to teach mathematics [15], and more recently Puzzle-Based Learning has been adopted in computer science and engineering pedagogy [6]. Digital game-based learning has also been shown to affectively motivate learners in numerous fields [18].
- **Students are encouraged to be precise and meticulous.** Our platform constrains students to only construct rigorous proofs. That way, students are guided away from the common pitfalls that frequently plague informal student proofs such as semantic ambiguity, insufficient detail, gaps in justification, and logical inconsistency.
- **Immediate feedback is provided to the student.** Traditional homework practice is non-ideal because it does not provide timely feedback for students to rectify learning deficiencies. It may be weeks before students get their corrected homework back, and some students may find themselves pushed to the next topic in the course before they have mastered the previous topic.

- **Homework can be graded automatically.** When our platform is used to replace some or all of the traditional written homework, it reduces the amount of resources needed for manually grading student work. This could be a major benefit for teaching very large courses such as MOOCs.
- **It is easy to adopt the platform in a wide variety of contexts.** Instructors can easily adapt it to any topic that involves proof instruction. The simplicity of the interface makes it equally suitable for introducing logic problems to K-12 students or teaching highly abstract mathematics to college students.

In this paper, we describe the platform in detail and we report our findings from a pilot study where we used the platform to provide supplemental aid to students in a discrete mathematics course and to students in an algorithms course.

2 BACKGROUND

2.1 Existing Proof Tools and Their Limitations

There are many Computer Assisted Instruction (CAI) systems designed to help students construct proofs in formal logic courses, including Wilfried Sieg's AProS [20], Peter Andrew's ETPS [1], and the EPGY theorem proving environment [13]. An overview of these and many more can be found in [19]. Many have a lengthy history – for instance, Wilfried Sieg has been developing AProS for decades. These tools automatically verify the correctness of each step of a student's proof. Some have been bundled with popular textbooks [2, 21], while others are Intelligent Tutoring System [7, 11, 16] and provide students with additional hints and feedback.

These tools have not been adapted much for use in computer science courses other than to familiarize students with formal logic. The one exception we are aware of is the equational logic system that Gries and Schneider used to teach a whole course in discrete mathematics [8].

There are technical challenges that make it difficult to adapt most logic-based proof tools to new domains. These tools require proofs to be constructed from a small set of primitive inference rules and axioms. The tedious steps involved in using these rules to construct even the most elementary of proofs taught in undergraduate math and computer science classes is vaguely reminiscent of developing a large software package in assembler code. Therefore, these tools cannot be pedagogically useful outside of teaching pure logic, unless they permit students to skip steps while still supporting the correct verification of the student's proof. This can be accomplished with automated theorem proving as demonstrated in [13] but there is still the problem of determining how many steps to let the student skip. Marvin Schiller's PhD Dissertation [19] looked at resolving this problem, and he has made some progress, as demonstrated in ActiveMath [14].

However, even when those challenges can be resolved, none of these tools permit students to construct proofs in natural language. Outside of formal logic courses, most instructors and textbooks use natural language to describe proofs and expect their students to do the same. Furthermore, a student's ability to construct proofs with a tool that only uses symbolic logic may not directly transfer to their ability to reason correctly using natural language, without explicitly training them to use the same kind of reasoning for natural language. The "Mental Models" theory of cognitive science predicts that humans make systematic logical errors when reasoning, because our natural method of reasoning is inconsistent with formal logic [9].

2.2 The Difference in Our Approach

Our proof construction platform allows students to construct proofs in natural language as well as symbolic logic and is agnostic to the many different flavors of formal systems. Informal proofs explained by an instructor in class can easily be adapted to our platform.

The reason this is possible is because our platform gives the student all the written assertions they need to construct a valid proof of whatever problem they are working on. In other words, they are given all the puzzle pieces they need to construct a proof (as well as some pieces not needed) and are left with the task of figuring out how those pieces connect together.

This is analogous to Parson's Problems [17], a similar kind of puzzle used to teach programming. With Parson's Problems, students are given blocks of code that they need to rearrange to create a program with a desired functionality. A study found a strong correlation between the ability to solve Parson's Problems and the ability to correctly write code from scratch, and concluded that these tasks likely require the same skills [5]. Similarly, constructing proofs with our platform may require much of the same deductive skills needed to construct proofs without the platform.

3 HOW THE PROOF CONSTRUCTION PLATFORM WORKS

We will illustrate how our platform works with the following logic problem: "Emily and Catherine each have their own pizza. Using the given assumptions, prove that Emily is not lactose intolerant." Figure 1 is a screenshot of the completed proof construction using our platform. We are given three assumptions:

(1) "Either Catherine's pizza or Emily's pizza, or both, has pepperoni, but Catherine's pizza does not have cheese."
(2) "Any pizza that has pepperoni also has cheese."
(3) "If someone is lactose intolerant, then their pizza does not have cheese."

Assumptions and assertions are used to complete the proof. An assumption is a statement considered valid without need of substantiation, such as an axiom. An assertion is a statement that needs substantiation before it is considered valid. Assertions may be validated by connecting them with assumptions and other assertions.

3.1 Placing the Dots

To solve the problem, a student will select assumptions and assertions from prescribed lists on the screen. The student will drag assertions and assumptions from the lists into a proof space shown on the screen. When an assumption or assertion is moved into the proof space, a specific dot will appear with written text stating the assumption or assertion. The student will click individual dots to select them and connect them to other dots with arrows in the proof space.

Our platform allows a student to start the proof construction with any assumption or assertion and complete the proof in a roundabout

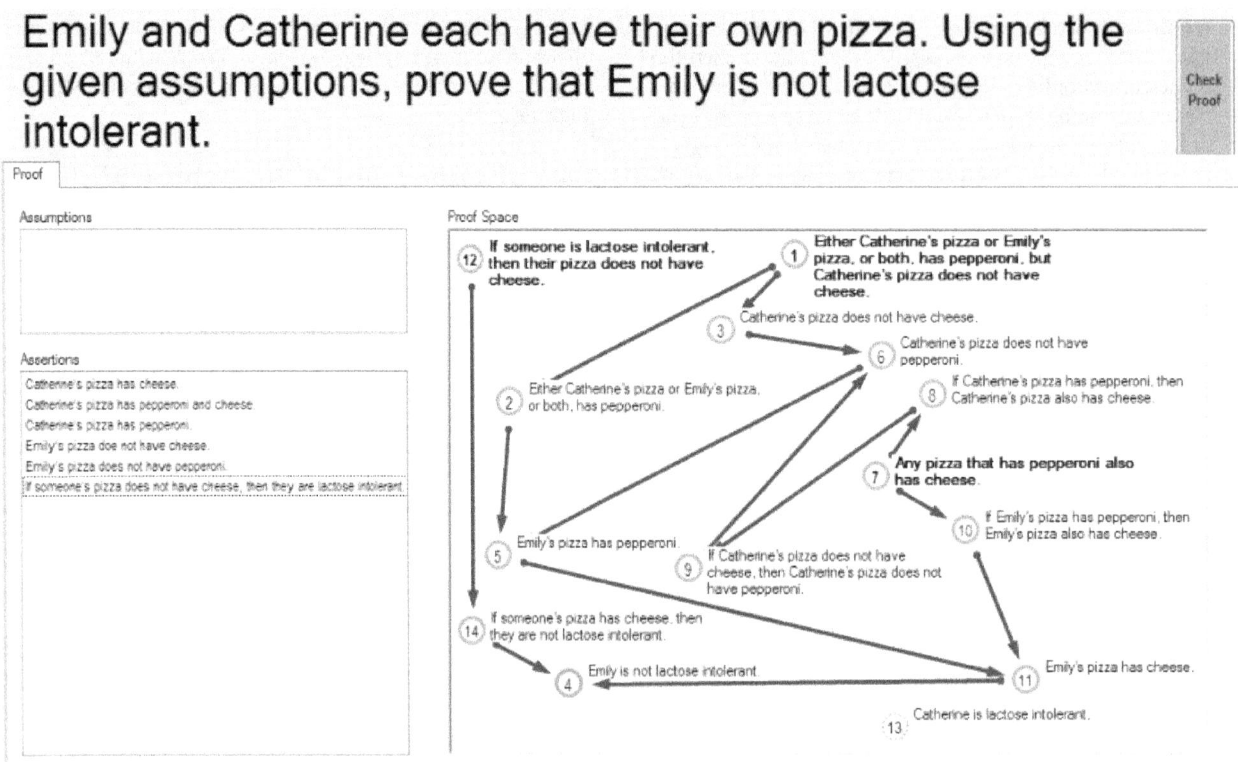

Figure 1: Screenshot of completed Pizza Proof Problem with text toggled on, assumption text is in bold print.

manner, like approaching the proof backward or using a mixture of going forward and backward to solve the proof problem.

After studying the three assumptions and the assertions on the prescribed lists adjacent to the proof space, in Figure 2, suppose the student decides to drag the assumption "Either Catherine's pizza or Emily's pizza, or both, has pepperoni, but Catherine's pizza does not have cheese." into the proof space. Notice that when this assumption is moved into the proof space, the text of the assumption appears with a dot "1" adjacent to the text. Also notice the text of the assumption is displayed in bold print to distinguish it from assertions which are displayed in regular print.

The student then determines what should follow this assumption. The student peruses the list of assertions, in Figure 2, decides the assertions "Either Catherine's pizza or Emily's pizza, or both, has pepperoni." and "Catherine's pizza does not have cheese." could follow the assumption in the proof space, and drags these two assertions into the proof space. The text of the two assertions appear with partial dots "2" and "3". A partial dot means the associated assertion needs substantiation to be validated. When an assertion is validated, its partial dot will change to a complete dot.

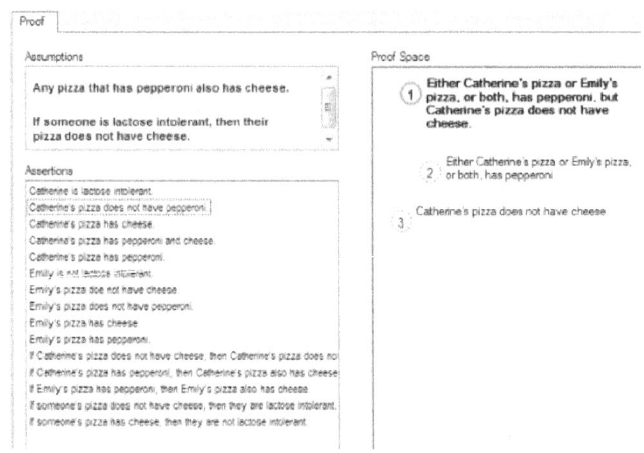

Figure 2: Moving assumptions and assertions into proof space, assumptions are complete dots and assertions are partial dots.

3.2 Connecting the Dots

To see if the decision that the two assertions follow the assumption was correct, the student left clicks dot "1" (assumption) followed by a left click of partial dot "2" (assertion). An arrow will appear to connect the dots with the arrow pointing at dot "2" as shown in Figure 3. Also notice that the partial dot "2" has changed to a complete dot "2" indicating the assertion was validated by the connection with the assumption dot "1". The student repeats this process to connect dots "1" and "3". As shown in Figure 3, an arrow connects the two dots and the partial dot "3" is changed to a complete dot indicating the assertion associated with dot "3" was substantiated and validated by the connection.

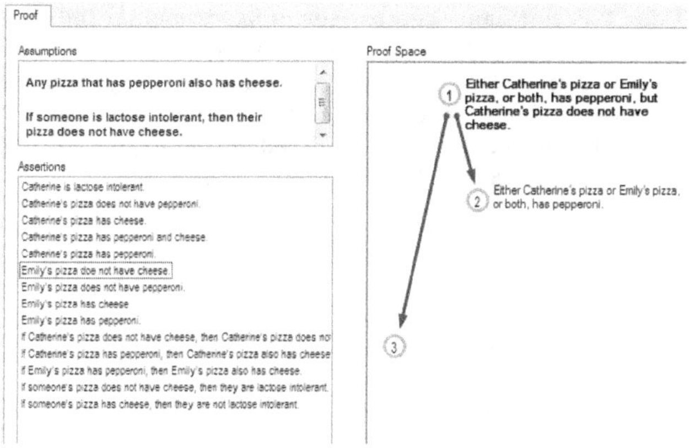

Figure 3: Connecting the dots, validated assertions become complete dots, toggling text and relocating dots.

Notice in Figure 3 that dots "2" and "3" have moved from their original locations shown in Figure 2. Our platform permits the student to drag the dots to different locations in the proof space to arrange the proof spatially in the way that makes the most sense to them.

Also notice the text associated with dot "3" is not shown in Figure 3. The platform allows the student to make the text associated with a dot disappear and reappear by double clicking the dot. This feature allows the student to hide the text of dots they are not considering at the moment. This can reduce cognitive load and promote better focus and efficiency for the student to solve the part of the problem they are currently working on [3]. Additionally, when students hover their mouse pointer over any dot, it will intermittently display the associated assertion, if it has been hidden.

3.3 Completing the Proof

The student continues selecting assertions and assumptions from the lists, moving them into the proof space, and connecting them until the proof is completed. The proof is completed when the goal assertion is validated (its partial dot has been converted into a complete dot) and all assertions leading to the goal assertion have also been validated. Notice that Figure 1 shows the goal assertion dot "4" and all of the other connected dots are complete dots. The tutoring system will also display a message on the computer screen that the proof has been successfully completed.

Notice the remaining assertions in the list even after the proof is completed in Figure 1. These assertions are *distractors*, unnecessary to complete the proof. Some of the distractors are valid assertions that can actually be justified in the proof space, but will lead down paths that do not connect with the goal. Others are "bugs" that get denoted with hashed dots when dragged into the proof space.

3.4 Authoring New Problems

New problems can be authored for this platform using the Python scripting language. The following is example code for the syllogism, *"All men are mortal. Socrates is a man. Therefore, Socrates is mortal."*

```
ProblemDescription.Text = "Prove Socrates is mortal."
ax1 = ProofItem("All men are mortal.")
ax1.isAssumption = True
ax1.show()
ax2 = ProofItem("Socrates is a man.")
ax2.isAssumption = True
ax2.show()
goal = ProofItem("Socrates is mortal.")
goal.Requirements.Add(ax1)
goal.Requirements.Add(ax2)
goal.show()
```

In the future, we are considering creating a graphical tool for constructing new problems.

4 EVALUATION

Over the course of two semesters, we did a study to evaluate students using our proof construction platform to solve problems in two different Computer Science courses at an R1 public university. Overall, there were 59 students who got to test the platform and their feedback is reported here.

We started with a pilot experiment in the Fall 2016 semester in a Junior-level algorithms course. The experiment commenced near the end of the semester, and we gave participants a problem related to the topic of NP-Completeness. This was one of the last topics covered in the course, and students had virtually no practice with or assessment on this topic before they participated in the study. A total of 26 students used the platform in this experiment, and an additional 22 students were part of a control group.

In Spring 2017, we continued with an experiment in a Sophomore-level discrete math course. This experiment also occurred near the end of the semester. We gave participants three pure logic problems. Two were written in plain English, and a third used a mixture of English and symbolic formulas. These problems were similar to many practice problems that the students had already completed in their homework. They had also been given a similar problem on their midterm exam. A total of 33 students used the platform in this experiment, and additional 36 students were part of a control group.

4.1 Methodology

Students received a small amount of extra credit on their final exam for participating in the study, but were not required to participate and could drop out at any time without penalty. We followed the same general protocol for both Fall 2016 and Spring 2017 experiments.

We announced our study at the beginning of a lecture. We told the students general details about the study, but to avoid biasing the distribution of volunteers, we did not tell students what kind of problems they would be given or even the nature of the software they would be using, besides indicating that it was designed to help them in the course.

Volunteers were assigned to one of two groups, experimental or control. We asked the instructor to ensure that both groups were equal in size and were randomly selected in a way to ensure that both groups had the same grade distributions based on their performance from a midterm exam. After the groups were selected, some students dropped out, resulting in the groups being slightly unequal in size but this did not change the distribution much. We believe that slightly more students may have dropped from the experimental groups because they could not run the software if they did not have Windows.

The experimental group solved problems with the proof construction platform. They were instructed to download the software with the selected problems, watch a short instructional tutorial[1] on the software, and attempt to solve the problems. While they were using the platform, we automatically video recorded their screen interactions and asked them to upload the videos to us. After uploading their data, they were asked to do an online survey.

The control group worked the same problems, but without the platform, either writing or typing their solutions as they would a normal homework assignment. They uploaded PDF copies of their written work to us, and we returned feedback similar to what they would receive on a homework assignment in the course.

Both groups were graded on how well they performed on the problems in the experiment. The control group was graded using the same standards normally used for homework problems in the course. The experimental group was graded based on what we observed in the videos, with variable scores assigned for incomplete proofs based on how many connections were missing.

We took extreme care to ensure that all participants in the study were anonymous to us. They generated random identifiers that tracked them anonymously throughout the study. We setup an anonymous file drop service for them to upload their data to us, which was either videos files for the experimental group or PDF files for the control group. The feedback given to the control group was also delivered via anonymous email drops. Most importantly, the survey responses were also anonymous and only linked to the anonymous identifiers.

4.2 Description of Problems

The following problem was given for the experiment in the algorithms course: "*Let PATH* = $\{\langle G, s, t\rangle \mid G$ *is a graph with a path from s to t}. We know PATH is in P. Prove that if* $P = NP$*, PATH is NP-Complete.*"

We had three logic problems used in the discrete math course, which we refer to as the "Pizza Problem", the "Muddy Dog Problem" and the "Murder Mystery Problem". The "Pizza Problem" is described in Section 3, and we omit the full descriptions of the others to save space. "Muddy Dog" is moderately difficult, requiring 42 dot connections for successful completion. The "Murder Mystery Problem" required 55 dot connections for successful completion, and was challenging because it mixed symbolic formulas with English descriptions. The others were written completely in English.

4.3 Results and Discussion

The video recordings submitted by the experimental students were analyzed to determine if the students encountered difficulties in using the software or user interface, and if they were able to solve the proof problems with the tutoring system. No significant difficulties were observed in the students using the software. Table 1 gives statistics for how the control and experimental groups performed on

[1] https://youtu.be/3jQM_T1qZvY

Table 1: Performance comparison of Experimental and Control Groups. N = NP-Completeness Problem, P = Pizza Problem, D = Muddy Dog Problem, M = Murder Mystery Problem. For each problem, scores ranged from 0-100. The "Perfect" row indicates the percentage of students who got a perfect score amongst those who attempted the problem.

	N		P		D		M	
	Experimental	Control	Experimental	Control	Experimental	Control	Experimental	Control
Mean	94	59	95	96	79	82	49	46
Median	100	55	100	100	95	100	50	50
Perfect	88	27	90	92	55	60	44	31

the problems. For most of the problems, the statistics are very similar for both groups, with the exception of the "NP-Completeness Problem". Students in the control group had significant conceptual difficulties with that problem, and often conflated the concepts of NP and NP-Complete in their proofs. Many tried to argue that PATH was NP-Complete because it can be verified in polynomial time, which indicates that PATH is in NP but not that it is NP-Complete. We think that the guided help that the platform gives the experimental group kept them from getting lost, and helped them solve what is an easy problem for students who have no conceptual difficulties with the material.

However, for the other problems given to the students in the discrete math course, we do not believe that many of the students in either group had conceptual difficulties. The differences in performance seem to be more indicative of the innate challenge provided to students in figuring out the proof, not difficulty understanding the material. Given that the statistics are so similar for both groups, we theorize that our puzzle-based method of discovering proofs is just as challenging and rewarding as the normal pen and paper method.

The data from the surveys were analyzed and the results that mainly pertain to the usefulness of the platform are shown in Figure 4. Student comments from the surveys are italicized below.

One attraction of the proof construction platform is it could be amusing and entertaining to the students using it. One student stated that it was a *"fun way to learn"* and another said, *"It is way more interesting than traditional homework."* But the main benefit of the proof construction platform is exemplified by this survey comment: *"I think if I had more practice using this application, it would be beneficial to my proof construction skills."*

Other students elaborated on what they found helpful:

"It's very helpful in visualizing the proofs."

"Having the pieces already helps to understand what parts are required whereas with a pen and paper you are on your own."

"One thing that is useful is being able to do the forward backward proof method. It was very straightforward to do backward proofs. Another thing that I thought was useful was being able to solve the problem in chunks. E.g. I could solve two different parts of a problem then use the 'backward' proof method to link the two parts together."

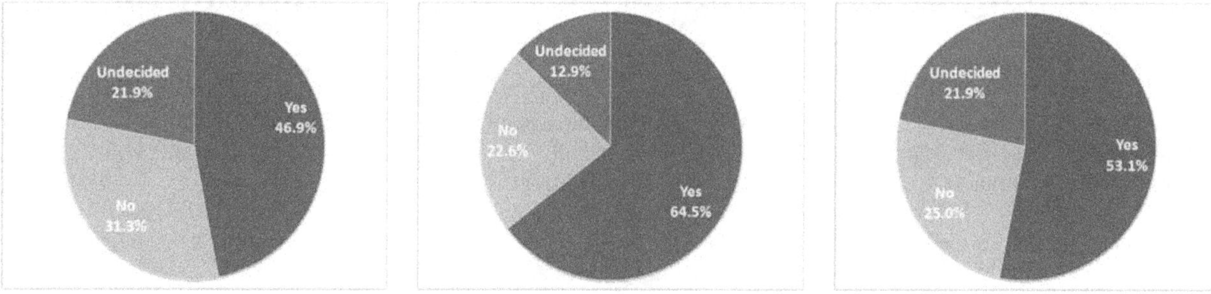

(a) Did you find the tutoring system helpful in your learning proof construction?

(b) Do you want the tutoring system to be available in other courses with proof construction?

(c) Would you recommend the tutoring system to others learning proof construction?

Figure 4: Responses from Questionnaires

Many of the surveys comment on how the platform forced them to be meticulous: *"It was good at making me remember the smaller steps. You aren't allowed to jump, you really have justify everything."*, and *"It takes much more time than do it by hand."* With pen and paper, many students skip lots of steps. In the future, a feature may be developed for the platform to assess a student's ability to solve specific types of proofs by looking at past performance. When a student has mastered a particular proof type, we can reduce the granularity of proof steps to allow abbreviated proofs for those types of proofs.

There were many comments requesting the provision of hints when using the proof construction platform; e.g., *"If there is a hint while I am stuck in a problem, it will be great. Otherwise I will just give up after many tries."* This is also a feature we plan to introduce in the future.

The results of the experiments show the proof construction platform is indeed helpful to students learning proof construction.

5 CONCLUSION AND FUTURE WORK

In this paper, we have presented and evaluated a new tool for helping students learn the process of constructing proofs from assertions in two different computer science theory classes. Overall feedback from students who used the tool was positive, and our empirical results indicate that students who use our software were able to overcome conceptual difficulties that the control group struggled with, as illustrated with the NP-completeness problem. In the future, we plan to look at how the use of the software affects exam performance as an indicator of retention of critical proof construction skills. We also plan to add a hint feature to guide students in the construction process, and a search feature that will allow students to find specific assertions more rapidly. We aim for our tool to become an indispensable asset to students of computer science.

Acknowledgements: We thank Dave Barrington for providing assistance to facilitate the experiments.

REFERENCES

[1] Peter B Andrews, Chad E Brown, Frank Pfenning, Matthew Bishop, Sunil Issar, and Hongwei Xi. 2004. ETPS: A system to help students write formal proofs. *Journal of Automated Reasoning* 32, 1 (2004), 75–92.

[2] David Barker-Plummer, Jon Barwise, and John Etchemendy. 2011. *Language, Proof, and Logic: Second Edition* (2nd ed.). Center for the Study of Language and Information/SRI.

[3] Roland Brünken, Roxana Moreno, and Jan L Plass. 2010. *Cognitive Load Theory*. Cambridge University Press.

[4] Bjorn Carey. 2014. Stanford's Maryam Mirzakhani wins Fields Medal. (12 Aug. 2014). Retrieved August 31, 2017 from http://news.stanford.edu/news/2014/august/fields-medal-mirzakhani-081214.html

[5] Paul Denny, Andrew Luxton-Reilly, and Beth Simon. 2008. Evaluating a new exam question: Parsons problems. In *Proceedings of the fourth international workshop on computing education research*. ACM, 113–124.

[6] Nickolas Falkner, Raja Sooriamurthi, and Zbigniew Michalewicz. 2010. Puzzle-based learning for engineering and computer science. *Computer* 43, 4 (2010), 20–28.

[7] João Carlos Gluz, Fabiane Penteado, Marcel Mossmann, Lucas Gomes, and Rosa Vicari. 2014. A student model for teaching natural deduction based on a prover that mimics student reasoning. In *International Conference on Intelligent Tutoring Systems*. Springer, 482–489.

[8] David Gries and Fred B Schneider. 1994. *A new approach to teaching mathematics*. Technical Report TR94-1411. Department of Computer Science, Cornell University.

[9] Philip N Johnson-Laird. 2010. Mental models and human reasoning. *Proceedings of the National Academy of Sciences* 107, 43 (2010), 18243–18250.

[10] Richard Jay Lipton. 2015. Why Is Discrete Math Hard To Teach? (27 Dec. 2015). Retrieved August 31, 2017 from https://rjlipton.wordpress.com/2015/12/27/why-is-discrete-math-hard-to-teach/

[11] Josje Lodder, Bastiaan Heeren, and Johan Jeuring. 2017. Generating hints and feedback for Hilbert-style axiomatic proofs. In *Proceedings of the 2017 ACM SIGCSE Technical Symposium on Computer Science Education*. ACM, 387–392.

[12] Mark McCartin-Lim. 2016. Complexity Tutor: Developing an Interactive Tutoring System for Computational Complexity (Abstract Only). In *Proceedings of the 47th ACM Technical Symposium on Computing Science Education (SIGCSE '16)*. ACM, New York, NY, USA, 494–494. https://doi.org/10.1145/2839509.2850524

[13] David McMath, Marianna Rozenfeld, and Richard Sommer. 2001. A computer environment for writing ordinary mathematical proofs. In *Logic for Programming, Artificial Intelligence, and Reasoning*. Springer, 507–516.

[14] Erica Melis and Jörg Siekmann. 2005. e-Learning Logic and Mathematics: What We Have and What We Still Need. *Essays in Honor of Dov Gabbay* (2005).

[15] Zbigniew Michalewicz and Matthew Michalewicz. 2007. Puzzle-based learning. In *Proceedings of the 2007 AaeE Conference*. 1–8.

[16] Behrooz Mostafavi and Tiffany Barnes. 2017. Evolution of an intelligent deductive logic tutor using data-driven elements. *International Journal of Artificial Intelligence in Education* 27, 1 (2017), 5–36.

[17] Dale Parsons and Patricia Haden. 2006. Parson's programming puzzles: a fun and effective learning tool for first programming courses. In *Proceedings of the 8th Australasian Conference on Computing Education-Volume 52*. Australian Computer Society, Inc., 157–163.

[18] Marc Prensky. 2001. *Digital Game-based Learning*. McGraw-Hill.

[19] Marvin R. G. Schiller. 2010. *Granularity Analysis for Tutoring Mathematical Proofs*. Ph.D. Dissertation. Saarland University, Saarbrücken, Germany. Advisor(s) Siekmann, Jörg.

[20] Wilfried Sieg. 2007. The AProS project: Strategic thinking & computational logic. *Logic Journal of IGPL* 15, 4 (2007), 359–368.

[21] Daniel J. Velleman. 1994. *How to Prove It: A Structured Approach*. Cambridge University Press.

Rising CS Enrollments: Meeting the Challenges

Eric Roberts (moderator)
Stanford University
Department of Computer Science
Stanford, CA 94305-9015
USA
eroberts@cs.stanford.edu

Tracy Camp
Colorado School of Mines
Brown 280E
1500 Illinois Street
Golden, CO 80401
USA
tcamp@mines.edu

David Culler
University of California, Berkeley
465 Soda Hall
Berkeley, CA 94720
USA
culler@berkeley.edu

Charles Isbell
Georgia Institute of Technology
801 Atlantic Drive
Atlanta, GA 30332
USA
isbell@cc.gatech.edu

Jodi Tims
Baldwin Wallace University
275 Eastland Road
Berea, OH 44017
USA
jtims@bw.edu

CCS CONCEPTS

• Social and Professional Topics → Professional Topics → Computing Education

KEYWORDS

CS education, enrollment growth, National Academies

ACM Reference format:

Eric Roberts, Tracy Camp, David Culler, Charles Isbell, and Jodi Tims. 2018. Rising CS Enrollments: Meeting the Challenges. In *SIGCSE '18: 49th ACM Technical Symposium on Computer Science Education, Feb. 21–24, 2018, Baltimore, MD, USA.* ACM, NY, NY, USA, 6 pages. https://doi.org/10.1145/3159450.3159628

1 SUMMARY

In recent years, computing enrollments have increased rapidly throughout the United States, creating serious challenges for many institutions. The participants on this panel have been members of the National Academies Committee on the Growth of Computer Science Undergraduate Enrollments and will share the findings and conclusions of the committee's report.

2 BACKGROUND

Over the past decade, the number of computer science majors has skyrocketed. Faculty numbers have not kept pace. Figure 1 shows the growth rates for undergraduate majors compared with the growth in tenure- and teaching-line faculty. [1]

In many ways, the growth in student numbers—which arises not only from a rapid rise in the number of majors but also from increased interest by non-majors in computer science courses—is not surprising. Computing is a rapidly growing sector of the economy and offers an array of well-paying jobs. To meet the level of student demand, institutions need to expand the resources available to computer science.

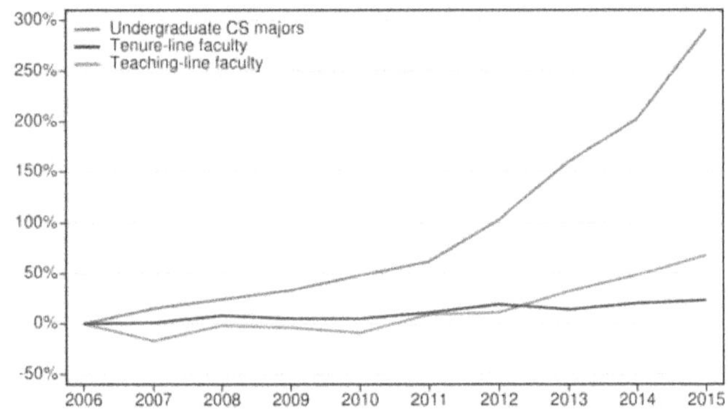

Figure 1: Relative growth rates for majors and faculty.

Academic institutions, however, face a range of challenges hiring new computer science faculty. For public institutions in particular, reduced funding makes it difficult to hire in any field, even when student demand is undeniable. Worse still, even computer science departments that get permission to hire often cannot attract enough candidates to fill the advertised positions. The shortage of computer science faculty reflects two unusual characteristics of the discipline: (1) computer science produces a smaller fraction of Ph.D.s than other similar disciplines, and (2) most new Ph.D.s take positions in industry rather than in academia.

Faced with seemingly relentless growth in student demand and a shortage of available faculty, institutions are increasingly taking steps to limit the number of computer science majors and to restrict enrollment in computer science courses. Although this approach can relieve immediate pressures, it has a significant cost. First, students are prevented from pursuing their chosen major and from enrolling in courses they need to succeed in

ACM ISBN 978-1-4503-5103-4/18/02.
https://doi.org/10.1145/3159450.3159628

their careers. Second, the economy already needs more CS graduates that the nation's educational institutions produce; reducing the supply of graduates further would make that situation worse. Third, the imposition of similar limits in the past has been associated with declines in student diversity, particularly for women.

Although the challenges associated with student growth have been anticipated for some time [2, 3], the problems have reached a level that has attracted significant national attention, both from the professional societies and from agencies at both the federal and state level. In March 2017, the Computing Research Association released a report entitled *Generation CS: Computer Science Undergraduate Enrollments Surge Since 2006* [1]. In 2016, the National Academies convened a Committee on the Growth of Computer Science Undergraduate Enrollments, which released its final report in prepublication form in October 2017 [4]. The panelists were all members of this committee and will report on its findings and lead a discussion with the audience about solution strategies.

3 TRACY CAMP

Tracy Camp is Department Head of Computer Science at Colorado School of Mines and led the CRA Enrollments Committee that collected data on the enrollment growth across North America. Tracy will provide the latest information available on the enrollment growth in computer science, including data concerning non-majors. Interest by non-majors in computer science courses across the nation is increasing at all levels (intro-level, mid-level, and upper-level). Any analysis of the enrollment growth that does not consider non-majors is underrepresenting the increased demands that computer science is facing.

4 DAVID CULLER

David Culler is Professor of Electrical Engineering and Computer Science at the University of California, Berkeley, where he now serves as Dean of the newly established Division of Data Sciences. David will share several of the most important results of the committee's investigations, some of which came as a surprise even to members of the committee. For example, contrary to the common assumption that past enrollment declines resulted from industry downturns, the evidence collected by the committee shows that institutional actions to restrict enrollment have been the primary factor affecting degree production. David will also share information about how the pressures of rising enrollments affects different institutions in different ways and summarize the findings about how the low rate of Ph.D. production and the tendency of those Ph.D.s to seek industry employment create serious challenges for faculty hiring.

5 JODI TIMS

Jodi Tims is Professor of Computer Science at Baldwin Wallace University in Berea, OH, where she currently serves as Chair of the Department of Mathematics and Computer Science, and chair of ACM-W, which supports, celebrates, and advocates internationally for the full engagement of women in all aspects of the computing field. Jodi will discuss the committee's findings on how enrollment increases affect student diversity. Enrollment increases in computing programs can have a positive effect on the participation of women and underrepresented minorities in the discipline. The enrollment surges of the mid-1980s and early 2000s both saw increased interest in pursuing computing majors among females. Currently, there is evidence that diversity has increased in recent years and that the percentage of women and underrepresented minorities, in aggregate, is improving [1]. However, as previous enrollment surges waned, interest in computing by females dropped more significantly than for males and has never recovered to previous levels.

While it is not possible to prove that institutional policies to address enrollment pressures directly *caused* reduced levels of diversity in computing, it is clear such actions have the *potential* to reduce diversity, and universities must therefore take diversity into account when deciding how to address the challenges of the current enrollment boom. Enrollment-management strategies must mitigate the bias inherent in policies that emphasize prior exposure to or achievement in computer science as such policies favor those groups that currently comprise the majority of computer science majors. In addition, high-engagement pedagogical practices that have been shown to be effective in attracting and retaining women and underrepresented minorities to computer science programs must be continued even in the face of large class sizes and increased faculty workload.

6 CHARLES ISBELL

Charles Isbell is Professor and Executive Associate Dean for the College of Computing at the Georgia Institute of Technology and co-chairs the Computing Research Association's Subcommittee on Education. Charles will move the discussion from an analysis of the problem to the search for solutions by looking at how institutions are responding to the challenges. The discussion will explore the options available to individual institutions but will also consider ways that those institutions, together with support from the professional societies, industry, and government can address the critical shortage of computer science faculty.

REFERENCES

[1] CRA Enrollment Committee. 2017. Generation CS: Computer Science Undergraduate Enrollments Surge Since 2006. Computing Research Association. http://cra.org/data/generation-cs/

[2] Eric Roberts. 2011. Meeting the challenges of rising enrollments. *ACM Inroads* 2, 3 (August 2011), 4–6. DOI=http://dx.doi.org/10.1145/2003616.2003617

[3] Ed Lazowska, Eric Roberts, and Jim Kurose. 2014. Tsunami or sea change? Responding to the explosion of student interest in computer science. Presentation at the CRA Conference at Snowbird, July 2014. http://lazowska.cs.washington.edu/NCWIT.pdf

[4] National Academies. 2017. *Assessing and Responding to the Growth of Computer Science Undergraduate Enrollments.* Prepublication version. https://www.nap.edu/catalog/24926/

2018 Panel of Computing Students with Disabilities

Richard E. Ladner
Moderator
Paul G. Allen School of Computer Science and Engineering
University of Washington
Seattle, WA 98195-2350
ladner@cs.washington.edu

Ramin Ayanzadah
University of Maryland, Baltimore County
Baltimore, MD 21250

Kavita Krishnaswami
University of Maryland, Baltimore County
Baltimore, MD 21250

Samsara N. Counts
George Washington University
Washington DC 20052

Kevin Wolfe
Gallaudet University
Washington DC 20002

CCS Concepts
Social and professional topics → Computing education

Keywords
Education; Disability; Accessibility

ACM Reference format:
Richard E. Ladner, Ramin Ayanzadah, Kavita Krishnaswami, Samsara N. Counts, and Kevin Wolfe. 2018. 2018 Panel of Computing Students with Disabilities. In *SIGCSE '18: 49th ACM Technical Symposium on Computer Science Education, Feb. 21–24, 2018, Baltimore, MD, USA.* ACM, NY, NY, USA, 2 pages. https://doi.org/10.1145/3159450.3159615.

1. SUMMARY
A panel of students with disabilities who are pursuing computing degrees will describe their experiences both in and out of the classroom. The goal of the panel is to provide the audience with an opportunity to hear first-hand how their educational needs were met as non-traditional computing students. In addition to the panelists' short presentations, the moderator will facilitate a dialog between the members of the audience and the panelists.

2. INTRODUCTION
Because of the Individuals with Disabilities Education Act (IDEA) originally passed in 1975, the Rehabilitation Act of 1973, Section 504, and the Americans with Disabilities Act of 1990 more and more students with disabilities are pursuing college and advanced degrees in computing fields. As a result we educators of computer science are more likely now than in the past to have a blind, low-vision deaf, hard of hearing, mobility disabled, or cognitively disabled students in our classrooms and research labs. The purpose of this panel is for educators in computing fields to learn first-hand from students about their educational needs and how they can be met. No doubt there will be members of the audience at the panel who have experiences with students with disabilities which will enliven the discussion.

ACM ISBN 978-1-4503-5103-4/18/02.
https://doi.org/10.1145/3159450.3159615

3. ACCESSCOMPUTING
AccessComputing (The Alliance for Access to Computing Careers), founded in 2006, is a NSF-funded Broadening Participation Alliance with the goal of increasing the number and success of students with disabilities in computing fields. This panel is part of our effort to foster institutional change that will help make computing departments and organizations more welcoming and accessible to students with disabilities. In the past eleven years we have held many capacity building workshops for educators and administrators to help empower them to improve the accessibility and welcoming atmosphere of their departments and organizations. We have found that one of the most effective ways to get the attention the workshop attendees is by having a panel of students with disabilities. Hearing the compelling stories from the students first-hand has had a huge impact on the attendees of these workshops.

In addition to institutional change the AccessComputing is involved in interventions that directly impact students with disabilities in building their capacity to succeed in the field. This is achieved through a large network of collaborators and partners at more than 50 institutions and organizations. We have had more than 750 students with disabilities participate in the AccessComputing Team. The team forms a peer mentoring group that we are in close contact with on a regular basis. The four panelists from our AccessComputing Team live reasonably close to Baltimore, MD, the site of SIGCSE 2018. AccessComputing will pay their registration so they can participate in the full conference. We held a similar student panel at SIGCSE 2014 in Atlanta, GA, that was highly successful [1].

4. PANEL STRUCTURE
The panel will consist of four mature and thoughtful students with disabilities moderated by Richard Ladner. The students will have a variety of disabilities in order to address the kinds of needs that will arise. All the students will be in some computing field. The students will be asked to make short 10 minute presentations that include the following:

- Demographic information: name, academic background, current school, year, disability.
- Description of accessibility needs in their computing classes and other academic activities, such as office hours, group projects, and research group meetings.
- Description of how those needs were met at the university level, department level, and instructor level.

- Description of any physical or attitudinal barriers that needed to be overcome.
- Description of future goals.

After these introductory remarks the moderator will solicit questions from the audience and encourage a dialog between the students and members of the audience. Those attending the panel will be provided informational packets including:

- Equal Access: Universal Design of Computing Departments
- Equal Access: Universal Design of Your Project
- Equal Access: Universal Design of Computer Labs
- Equal Access: Universal Design of Instruction

5. PANELISTS

Ramin Ayanzadah is a PhD student of computer science at University of Maryland, Baltimore County (UMBC). He is mainly interested in quantum artificial intelligence through whitch, he is working with Prof. Tim Finin to extend usage of quantum machines for NLP and semantic web applications. He is also working with Prof. Milton Halem to explore applications of D-Wave quantum annealer for NASA science missions.

Samsara N. Counts is a junior at George Washington University double-majoring in Computer Science and Mathematics with a Creative Writing minor. Her research uses Artificial Intelligence to promote fairness and diversity in the hiring process, advised by Dr. John P. Dickerson at the University of Maryland College Park. In 2017 she was awarded a HackHarassment grant from Intel to research online harassment and host a hackathon, Hackital, to create technological solutions to combat it. She is continuing this work with Dr. Robert Pless, using deep learning to detect harmful content online. As Academic Affairs Chair of GW's ACM chapter, she frequently leads workshops and events for the computing community. In her free time, she reads incessantly and writes poetry.

Kavita Krishnaswami is a Ph.D. candidate in Computer Science at the University of Maryland, Baltimore County (UMBC) working with Dr. Tim Oates. She is a Microsoft Research Fellow and Google Lime Scholar. She was both a Ford Foundation Predoctoral and National Science Foundation Graduate Research Fellow. She has also worked at the Quality of Life Technology Center (QoLT) in Carnegie Mellon and University of Pittsburgh and IBM Business consulting services. As a professional researcher with a physical disability, Kavita is motivated by a powerful, innate force: autonomy is the soul of independent daily living that is achieved with the advancement of technology. Her research involves the development of robotic systems to provide assistance and increase independence for people with disabilities. She is developing several prototype robotic systems that will support transferring, repositioning, and personal care, with a focus on accessible user interfaces for control that are feasible for persons with severe disabilities.

Kevin Wolfe graduated from Gallaudet University and received Bachelor of Science in Information Technology, Concentration: Network/Database/Web. His interest is in working with researchers to improve the classroom experience for Deaf and Hard of Hearing using technology. He is currently pursuing a career in Web programming, network administration, Cybersecurity, and Information Technology Specialist.

Richard E. Ladner, **moderator**, is a professor emeritus in the Paul G. Allen School of Computer Science and Engineering at the University of Washington. He is the Principal Investigator for AccessComputing. He has taught students with disabilities for the past 25 years in various enrichment programs. He has mentored numerous students with disabilities from high school through graduate school levels. He has an active research program in accessible technology.

6. DISCUSSION

Panels at SIGCSE are quite varied, covering topics such as curriculum, diversity, policy, and opportunities. It is seldom that we get to hear our students' points of view. Educators hearing from other educators only provides a second-hand view of their needs and how they were met. A more powerful approach is to hear directly from the students. Attendees will expect to learn something new and personal, not just boiler-plate from their university's office of disability services for students.

7. ACKNOWLEDGMENT

AccessComputing is funded by the National Science Foundation (CISE BPCA awards #CNS-0540615, CNS-0837508, CNS-1042260 and CNS-1539179.) Any questions, findings, and conclusions or recommendations expressed in this material are those of the author and do not necessarily reflect the views of the federal government.

8. REFERENCES

[1] Richard E. Ladner, Jillian Hall, Samir Jain, CeAhna Lathon, and Vincent Martin. 2014. Panel of computing students with disabilities. In Proceedings of the 45th ACM technical symposium on Computer science education (SIGCSE '14). ACM, New York, NY, USA, 271-272.

How am I Going to Grade All These Assignments? Thinking About Rubrics in the Large

John Cigas
Park University
Parkville, MO, USA
cigas@acm.org

Adrienne Decker
Rochester Institute of Technology
Rochester, NY, USA
adrienne.decker@rit.edu

Crystal Furman
The College Board
Atlanta, GA, USA
cfurman@collegeboard.org

Timothy Gallagher
Winter Springs High School
Winter Springs, FL, USA
timothy_gallagher@scps.k12.fl.us

SUMMARY

With the record growth in computing classes, it has been challenging for faculty to keep up with the logistics of the classroom, particularly in assessment. Automatic grading software and unit tests have been employed successfully in many settings to help ensure proper scoring of programming assignments. However, assignments that are not necessarily complete programs (in-class short quizzes, homework problems or worksheets, exams) present different challenges for scoring. In this session, we propose some tips and techniques for scoring such assessment items quickly and consistently, with the added benefit that grading criteria are clearer to the students.

CCS CONCEPTS

• **General and reference~Evaluation** • **Social and professional topics~Computer science education** • *Social and professional topics~Student assessment*

KEYWORDS

Rubrics; assessing student work; training team of graders

ACM Reference format:

J. Cigas, A. Decker, T. Gallagher, C. Furman. 2018. How am I Going to Grade All These Assignments? Thinking About Rubrics in the Large. In *SIGCSE '18: 49th SIGCSE Technical Symposium on Computer Science Education, Feb. 21–24, 2018, Baltimore, MD, USA*. ACM, NY, NY, USA, 2 pages. https://doi.org/10.1145/3159450.3159641

ACM ISBN 978-1-4503-5103-4/18/02.
DOI: http://dx.doi.org/10.1145/3159450.3159641

1 OBJECTIVE

The format of this special session is a tutorial. During the session, we will engage the participants by showcasing a set of strategies for grading large numbers of assignments quickly and consistently. The method described is based on the way the rubrics and training are conducted for the annual Advanced Placement Computer Science A (AP CSA) exam.

When discussing the grading of student assignments, there are numerous things that have been written about the process and sessions and workshops devoted to the topic, [1, 2, 4, 5, 7] but perhaps the most succinct list comes from Henry Walker [12, p. 14] when he states that grading should:

- be fair and consistent,
- reinforce high-level course goals and themes,
- provide students with feedback, and
- be reasonably fast for the instructor.

Many assignments in computing classrooms are programs and faculty have turned to various means to grade these programs consistently and quickly. One approach is to utilize a system that provides practice problems and gives feedback to the students (Problets [9], CodingBat [3], Practice-It [8]). There are also automatic grading and submission systems available that provide feedback to the students upon submission (Web-CAT [11], Gradescope [6], zyLabs [13]). Many of these auto-graders are built on the idea of unit testing the submitted code. Some faculty simply make students write their own unit tests to demonstrate that the assignment works as specified. All of these approaches are reasonable for grading digital program artifacts, but fail to be helpful on paper and pencil exercises, homework problems, or exams.

Further, unit testing and other testing frameworks focus on functionality of a computer program (implementation), not necessarily on higher-level concepts. The purpose of this session is to showcase the methodology used in creating rubrics for the AP CSA exam as well as the training that is given to those applying the rubrics so that consistency can be maintained.

2 OUTLINE

The following section describes the content of this special session and gives an outline of the topics that will be discussed.

2.1 Overview of Goals for CSA Assessment

Every AP assessment is designed to measure both content knowledge and reasoning processes. The AP program has identified a set of disciplinary practices that require students to demonstrate their understanding through the application of both content knowledge and reasoning processes. In this part of the session, the presenters will describe disciplinary practices assessed on the free response portion of the AP CSA exam and provide examples of past free response questions that illustrate these practices.

Audience members will be tasked to think about their courses and the types of skills and knowledge that their course assesses as the first step in thinking of how to create useful rubrics.

2.2 Creating a Rubric

For purposes of illustration, the presenters will show the process of creating a rubric using a released AP CSA question. The rubric for a question is developed concurrently when the question is written based on the topics and skills intended to be assessed. Through a series of iterations, the rubric is refined. Key aspects of what makes a good rubric will be presented, including clarity of the wording, possible exceptions that can be encountered, and clear separation of points. Discussion will also include the weighting of points, elements of holistic grading, and some other alternative grading techniques [10].

2.3 Training to apply a Rubric

Grading a large number of assignments consistently, even for a single grader, can be a challenge. Having a rubric helps a single grader maintain a consistent view of the scoring criteria. However, when multiple graders are scoring the same assessment, such as TAs in different lab or recitation sections, it is essential that everyone have the same interpretation of the rubric and apply it in the same way. In this part of the session, we offer training tips and techniques based on our experience guiding 40-80 people to apply a rubric consistently over the course of a week. While most teaching staffs are not as large, the same techniques can be used with some modification to ensure consistency when grading with a smaller staff.

2.4 Discussion and Q&A

After the initial presentations, we will have time for discussion and questions from the audience (approximately 30 minutes). We would like to solicit experiences with using and implementing rubrics and questions they may have about the process we have just presented.

3 EXPECTATIONS

The intended audience for this special session are those computing educators who are grading assignments and looking for ways to improve that process, either from the creation or implementation standpoint. Participants should leave with concrete ideas of how to create rubrics and how to implement grading using those rubrics in their classrooms.

REFERENCES

[1] Don Blaheta and Adrienne Decker. 2016. Rubricking Like a Boss: Writing and Using Rubrics For Faster, Fairer Grading of Student Assignments (Abstract Only). In *Proceedings of the 47th ACM Technical Symposium on Computing Science Education* (SIGCSE '16). ACM, New York, NY, USA, 715-716. DOI: https://doi.org/10.1145/2839509.2844704

[2] Veronica Cateté, Erin Snider, and Tiffany Barnes. 2016. Developing a Rubric for a Creative CS Principles Lab. In *Proceedings of the 2016 ACM Conference on Innovation and Technology in Computer Science Education* (ITiCSE '16). ACM, New York, NY, USA, 290-295. DOI: https://doi.org/10.1145/2899415.2899449

[3] CodingBat. 2017. CodingBat code practice. Retrieved August 29, 2017 from http://codingbat.com/java

[4] Karen Donathan and Paul Tymann. 2010. The development and use of scoring rubrics: (or how to grade thousands of exams without losing your mind). In *Proceedings of the 41st ACM technical symposium on Computer science education* (SIGCSE '10). ACM, New York, NY, USA, 477-477. DOI: http://dx.doi.org/10.1145/1734263.1734423

[5] Sue Fitzgerald, Brian Hanks, Raymond Lister, Renee McCauley, and Laurie Murphy. 2013. What are we thinking when we grade programs?. In *Proceeding of the 44th ACM technical symposium on Computer science education* (SIGCSE '13). ACM, New York, NY, USA, 471-476. DOI: http://dx.doi.org/10.1145/2445196.2445339

[6] Gradescope. 2017. Retrieved August 29, 2017 from https://gradescope.com/

[7] Sam Kavanagh and Andrew Luxton-Reilly. 2016. Rubrics used in peer assessment. In *Proceedings of the Australasian Computer Science Week Multiconference* (ACSW '16). ACM, New York, NY, USA, , Article 10 , 6 pages. DOI=http://dx.doi.org/10.1145/2843043.2843347

[8] Practice-It. 2017. Retrieved August 29, 2017 from https://practiceit.cs.washington.edu/

[9] Problets. 2017. Problets - The Home Page. Retrieved August 29, 2017 from http://problets.org/

[10] Rapaport, William J. 2011. "A Triage Theory of Grading: The Good, the Bad, and the Middling", *Teaching Philosophy* 34(4): 347–372.

[11] Web-CAT. 2017. Web-CAT: Automatic Grading Using Student-written Tests. Retrieved August 29, 2017 from https://web-cat.cs.vt.edu/

[12] Henry M. Walker. 2010. Classroom issues: Grading and the allocation of points. SIGCSE Bull. 41, 4 (January 2010), 14-16. DOI=http://dx.doi.org/10.1145/1709424.1709431

[13] zyLabs. 2017. zyLabs: Programming. Retrieved August 29, 2017 from https://www.zybooks.com/catalog/zylabs-programming/

SIGCSE Filk Circle: CS Parody Songs for Learning, Engagement, and Fun

Patrick Virtue
EECS, Univ. of California Berkeley
253 Cory Hall
Berkeley, CA USA
virtue@eecs.berkeley.edu

Steven A. Wolfman
CS Dept, Univ. of British Columbia
201-2366 Main Mall
Vancouver, BC, Canada
wolf@cs.ubc.ca

John P. Dougherty
Haverford College
370 Lancaster Avenue
Haverford, PA USA
jd@cs.haverford.edu

Categories and Subject Descriptors

• **Applied computing → Education**

Keywords

Filks; music; singing; parodies.

ACM Reference format:

Patrick Virtue, Steven A. Wolfman, and John P. Dougherty. 2018. SIGCSE Filk Circle: CS Parody Songs for Learning, Engagement, and Fun. In *SIGCSE '18: 49th ACM Technical Symposium on Computer Science Education, Feb. 21–24, 2018, Baltimore, MD, USA*. ACM, NY, NY, USA, 2 pages. https://doi.org/10.1145/3159450.3159640

1. SUMMARY

In a session with live music and collaborative parody, we celebrate the long tradition of computing parody songs ("filks") and their potential to contribute to education and a fun environment in CS courses. We perform several new and classic CS filks, such as "Like it Called on Me (QuickSort)" [1], interspersing discussion of how and why these parodies were written. We also propose a song for the audience to parody and walk them through a structured small-group activity to help them brainstorm topics and lyrical phrases and fit them to the existing lyrics and music. Attendees should expect to laugh (and possibly cry) with the singing and to leave inspired to incorporate filks and other creative activities into their computing education practice: playing, performing, or writing songs themselves, and encouraging their students to do so as well.

2. OBJECTIVE

The session intersperses live performance of high-quality CS filks with discussion of how and why the songs were created, how these songs can be used in classrooms, and hands-on activities designing new parody lyrics. The immediate goals are to have fun and spur attendees to continue the fun within their own learning communities. However, both filks and music more generally also have long traditions in computing education and may offer powerful, alternative approaches to learning in the field. [2, 3]

The computing filk tradition extends back at least to Guy Steele's "The Telnet Song", published in 1984 under his pseudonym "The Great Quux" [4]. These songs are fun, but also address and explore genuinely challenging computing concepts such as information hiding in software engineering [5] and NP-completeness [6]. Songs like "Code Monkey" [7] also explore cultural issues in computing. Knowing good filks helps instructors identify hooks they can use to enliven their courses.

ACM ISBN 978-1-4503-5103-4/18/02.
https://doi.org/10.1145/3159450.3159640

3. OUTLINE

The session follows the timeline:

- Introduction (15 minutes) [JD]
  - Opening computing parody song, "Stuck in an Infinite Loop" (by John Dougherty, to the tune of "Stuck in the Middle with You" by Stealers Wheel) [8]
  - Introduction of session leaders
  - Outline of the session
  - Discussion of how and why the first parody song was created, with emphasis on research and themes
- Scansion, Rhyme, and Range (15 minutes) [Pat]
  - Second computing parody song, "The Red-Black Tree Song" (by Sean Sandys, to the tune of "Paint It Black" by The Rolling Stones) [9]
  - Discussion of how to pick a target song and matching scansion and rhyme
  - Discussion of the history and research on songs in education
- Designing a filk exercise (35 mins) [all leaders]
  - Attendees breaks into small groups to brainstorm and select a promising topic and target for a filk; leaders distribute lyrics of the target songs to parody, annotated with scansion and rhyme patterns
  - Play choruses of well-known songs that are good parody targets (Adele's "Hello", Billy Joel's "We Didn't Start the Fire", Meghan Trainor's "N∅", Pharrell Williams's "Happy")
  - Small groups choose a familiar song and brainstorm words and phrases, rhymes, and good scansion matches in the song

  - Small groups share their favorite phrases and verses with the whole group
- Conclusion (10 minutes) [Steve]
  - Quick rundown of resources and references for filks and parody song creation
  - Closing parody song (with a sing-along chorus): "Like It Called on Me (QuickSort)" (by Steve Wolfman et al. to the tune of "Like a Wavin' Flag" by K'naan)

4. EXPECTATIONS

Audience members need not meet any prerequisites except a willingness to enjoy live, amateur performances and try their hands (vocal chords optional) at brainstorming elements of a new parody song. Audience members will leave with a catalog of good parody songs, the skeleton of a new parody in an area of interest to them, an idea of how to flesh that out into a full song, and connections to others interested in the same song.

5. SUITABILITY FOR A SPECIAL SESSION

This session combines performance with hands-on activities in a way that can only work as a special session. Session leaders bring an openness to public embarrassment and varied experience in what some would call music—including authorship of 15 computing related filks, many more live performances survived, and instrument mastery ranging from guitar to shaker all the way to YouTube karaoke tracks.

6. REFERENCES

[1] S. Wolfman, S. Bradley, R. Pottinger, N. Wolfman and C. S. 320 2016W2 TA Staff, "Like It Called on Me (QuickSort)," 5 April 2017. [Online]. Available: http://www.cs.ubc.ca/~wolf/songs/like_it_called_on_me_quicksort.html. [Accessed 31 August 2017].

[2] B. Schreiber and J. P. Dougherty, "Assessment of introducing algorithms with video lectures and pseudocode rhymed to a melody," in *48th Annual Special Interest Group on Computer Science Education (SIGCSE) Technical Symposium*, Seattle, WA, USA, 2017.

[3] E. V. Siegel, "Why Do Fools Fall Into Infinite Loops: Singing To Your Computer Science Class," in *4th Annual Conference on Innovation and Technology in Computer Science Education*, Cracow, 1999.

[4] J. G. L. Steele, "THE TELNET SONG: ("Control-Uparrow Q.")," *Commun. ACM,* vol. 27, no. 4, pp. 347-348, 1984.

[5] V. Sazawal, K. Yasuhara and N. Spring, "Educational Materials to Assist in Instruction of Information Hiding Basics," 10 May 2002. [Online]. Available: https://www.cs.umd.edu/~nspring/papers/ease-of-change.ps. [Accessed 31 August 2017].

[6] D. J. Barrett, "Find the Longest Path," 14 January 2010. [Online]. Available: https://www.youtube.com/watch?v=a3ww0gwEszo. [Accessed 31 August 2017].

[7] J. Coulton, *Code Monkey,* 2006.

[8] J. P. Dougherty, "Computational Singing." [Online]. Available: https://goo.gl/CpphJd. [Accessed 31 August 2017].

[9] S. D. Sandys, "The Red-Black Tree Song," 1995. [Online]. Available: http://webhome.csc.uvic.ca/~ruskey/classes/326/TreeSong.html. [Accessed 1 September 2017].

Quick-Sort: A Pet Peeve

Arthur Nunes-Harwitt
Rochester Institute of Technology
Rochester, New York
anh@cs.rit.edu

Matt Gambogi
Rochester Institute of Technology
Rochester, New York
matt.gambogi@csh.rit.edu

Travis Whitaker
Alphasheets, Inc.
San Francisco, California
travis@programmable.computer

ABSTRACT

The traditional functional formulation of quick-sort is simple and elegant. But is it fast? Through a dialog, we observe that this traditional formulation does not retain certain crucial properties of the imperative version. We include a known derivation of a higher performing functional implementation together with a graph that illustrates the differences. Our pet peeve is that the faster quick-sort is frequently left out of texts on functional programming.

CCS CONCEPTS

• **Applied computing → Education**; • **Theory of computation → *Divide and conquer***;

KEYWORDS

Algorithms, Quick-Sort, Functional Programming, Performance, Education

ACM Reference Format:
Arthur Nunes-Harwitt, Matt Gambogi, and Travis Whitaker. 2018. Quick-Sort: A Pet Peeve. In *Proceedings of SIGCSE '18: The 49th ACM Technical Symposium on Computer Science Education, Baltimore , MD, USA, February 21–24, 2018 (SIGCSE '18)*, 3 pages.
https://doi.org/10.1145/3159450.3159535

1 INTRODUCTION

We sat in the classroom waiting. The professor came in and stopped suddenly. He was staring at the board with a scowl. We looked too and noticed the following code [9, 13].

$$
\begin{aligned}
&quicksort :: Ord\ \alpha \Rightarrow [\alpha] \rightarrow [\alpha]\\
&quicksort\ [\,] \qquad = [\,]\\
&quicksort\ (p : xs) = quicksort[y \mid y \in xs, y \leq p]\ +\!\!+\\
&\qquad\qquad\qquad [p]\ +\!\!+\\
&\qquad\qquad\qquad quicksort[y \mid y \in xs, y > p]
\end{aligned}
$$

"If I see quick-sort in Haskell one more time, I'm going to be sick!" he declared.

"What's wrong?" we asked. "Doesn't that implementation beautifully express the essence of the quick-sort algorithm?"

SIGCSE '18, February 21–24, 2018, Baltimore , MD, USA

ACM ISBN 978-1-4503-5103-4/18/02...$15.00
https://doi.org/10.1145/3159450.3159535

"Yes and no," replied the professor. "It certainly gets at how the sorting happens, but it doesn't shed light on the 'quick' aspect. Consider the following imperative formulation [5, 8]."

def SORT(A) :
  SORT3(A, 0, $len(A) - 1$)

def SORT3(A, p, r) :
  if $p < r$:
    $q \leftarrow$ PARTITION(A, p, r)
    SORT3($A, p, q - 1$)
    SORT3($A, q + 1, r$)

"Notice that partitioning happens in a single pass, that there is no work involved in combining the subsequences, and that the second recursive call is in tail position[1]. That's why the imperative version is fast. It's not even clear that the Haskell formulation is faster than merge-sort."

2 COMPARISON TO MERGE-SORT

"We've already written merge-sort in Haskell:"

$$
\begin{aligned}
&mergesort :: Ord\ \alpha \Rightarrow [\alpha] \rightarrow [\alpha]\\
&mergesort\ [\,]\ = [\,]\\
&mergesort\ [x] = [x]\\
&mergesort\ xs\ =\\
&\quad let\ (half1, half2) = split\ xs\\
&\quad in\ merge\ (mergesort\ half1)\ (mergesort\ half2)
\end{aligned}
$$

$$
\begin{aligned}
&split :: [\alpha] \rightarrow ([\alpha], [\alpha])\\
&split\ xs = splita\ xs\ [\,]\ [\,]
\end{aligned}
$$

$$
\begin{aligned}
&splita :: [\alpha] \rightarrow [\alpha] \rightarrow [\alpha] \rightarrow ([\alpha], [\alpha])\\
&splita\ [\,] \qquad e\ o = (e, o)\\
&splita\ (x : xs)\ e\ o = splita\ xs\ o\ (x : e)
\end{aligned}
$$

$$
\begin{aligned}
&merge :: Ord\ \alpha \Rightarrow [\alpha] \rightarrow [\alpha] \rightarrow [\alpha]\\
&merge\ [\,] \qquad ys \qquad = ys\\
&merge\ xs \qquad [\,] \qquad = xs\\
&merge\ (x : xs)\ (y : ys)\\
&\quad \mid x < y \qquad\qquad = x : (merge\ xs\ (y : ys))\\
&\quad \mid x > y \qquad\qquad = y : (merge\ (x : xs)\ ys)\\
&\quad \mid otherwise \qquad = x : y : (merge\ xs\ ys)
\end{aligned}
$$

"We used GHC version 8.0.1 with packages from Stackage resolver lts-7.3. A 2-core i386 Ubuntu 16.04 VM with 4 GB of memory was used as the underlying machine. The criterion benchmarking

[1] Of course, tail-recursion does not necessarily imply a speed improvement; it only entails a space improvement.

suite was used to capture all result data. We found that the quick-sort implementation is about 1.45 times faster than the merge-sort implementation." (In the comparison, we call the original version of quick-sort *quicksort1*. See Figure 1.)

"OK," replied the professor. "But it's not that much faster. Quick-sort should be faster than that."

3 IMPROVING PARTITION

"Improving the partition phase by reducing the number of passes is not hard. We've written the following one-pass function."

```
partition :: Ord α ⇒ α → [α] → ([α], [α])
partition pivot lst =
    let part []       leq gt            = (leq, gt)
        part (x : xs) leq gt | x > pivot = part xs leq (x : gt)
        part (x : xs) leq gt            = part xs (x : leq) gt
    in part lst [] []
```

"Using it instead of the list comprehensions yields a performance increase. The new version is about 1.67 times faster than the original version, and it is about 2.44 times faster than merge-sort." (We call this version of quick-sort *quicksort2*. See Figure 1.)

"Fine," commented the professor. "But it will be impossible for you to eliminate all the work involved when combining the results."

4 IMPROVING COMBINING

"We can completely eliminate the linear-time list append operations (++)," we replied.

"The very nature of functional programming requires that you assemble the results returned. If you are not using append, then surely you are using some other similar operation."

"It's true that we cannot eliminate all work. We use a single constant-time cons (:) operation."

"Is that all?" The professor was surprised. "That's a big improvement. How can you get away with only that?"

"We make use of an accumulation parameter [6] that implicitly appends. Here is the equation for the invariant."

$$qsAccum\ \ell\ a = (quicksort\ \ell) +\!\!+\ a$$

"The base case is then simple calculation [3]."

$$qsAccum\ []\ a = (quicksort\ []) +\!\!+\ a = a$$

"The recursive case is not too bad either."

$$\begin{aligned}
&qsAccum\ (p : xs)\ a && =\\
&(quicksort\ (p : xs)) +\!\!+\ a && =\\
&(quicksort\ leq) +\!\!+\ ([p] +\!\!+\ ((quicksort\ gt) +\!\!+\ a)) && =\\
&(quicksort\ leq) +\!\!+\ (p : (qsAccum\ gt\ a)) && =\\
&qsAccum\ leq\ (p : (qsAccum\ gt\ a))
\end{aligned}$$

where $(leq, gt) = partition\ p\ xs$

"Putting it all together, we get the following alternative functional quick-sort formulation [2, 4, 11, 12]."

```
quicksort3 :: Ord α ⇒ [α] → [α]
quicksort3 lst =
    let qsAccum []       a = a
        qsAccum (p : xs) a =
            let (leq, gt) = partition p xs
            in qsAccum leq (p : (qsAccum gt a))
    in qsAccum lst []
```

"Further, this version does, in fact, perform significantly better. It is about 1.64 times faster than the previous version, it is about 2.75 times faster than the original version, and it is about 4.01 times faster than merge-sort." (See Figure 1.)

5 CONCLUSION

"I like it," commented the professor.

"It's still purely functional, but the final version does partitioning in a single pass, the work for combining the subsequences involves only a small constant, and one of the recursive calls is in tail position. Further, the graph clearly shows how much faster it is than merge-sort.

"Now that I see the derivation, it is obvious. But I had assumed that it wasn't possible since I've seen so many texts [1, 6, 7, 9, 10, 13] that have only the initial formulation of quick-sort. Perhaps the authors of those texts consider it a small leap, but why not publicize the good news?! I hope that in the future authors will include both formulations."

6 ACKNOWLEDGEMENTS

We would like to thank Tim Fossum and Jim Heliotis for carefully reading previous drafts of this paper.

REFERENCES

[1] Umut A. Acar and Guy E. Blelloch. 2017. *Algorithm Design: Parallel and Sequential.* http://www.parallel-algorithms-book.com/.
[2] Richard Bird. 1998. *Introduction to Functional Programming using Haskell.* Prentice Hall.
[3] Rod M. Burstall and John Darlington. 1977. A Transformation System for Developing Recursive Programs. *Journal of the ACM (JACM)* 24, 1 (1977), 44–67.
[4] William Clocksin and Christopher S. Mellish. 1987. *Programming in PROLOG.* Springer.
[5] Thomas H. Cormen, Charles Eric Leiserson, Ronald L. Rivest, and Clifford Stein. 2009. *Introduction to Algorithms.* MIT press.
[6] Matthias Felleisen, Robert Bruce Findler, Matthew Flatt, and Shriram Krishnamurthi. 2001. *How to Design Programs: An Introduction to Programming and Computing.* MIT Press.
[7] Brian Harvey. 1997. *Computer Science Logo Style: Beyond Programming.* Vol. 3. MIT press.
[8] Charles A. R. Hoare. 1962. Quicksort. *Comput. J.* 5, 1 (1962), 10–16.
[9] Miran Lipovača. 2011. *Learn You a Haskell for Great Good! A Beginner's Guide.* no starch press.
[10] V.S. Manis and J.J. Little. 1995. *The Schematics of Computation.* Prentice Hall. https://books.google.com/books?id=jIyIQgAACAAJ
[11] Lawrence C. Paulson. 1996. *ML for the Working Programmer.* Cambridge University Press.
[12] Fethi Rabhi and Guy Lapalme. 1999. *Algorithms: A Functional Programming Approach.* Addison-Wesley Longman Publishing Co., Inc.
[13] Simon Thompson. 2011. *Haskell: The Craft of Functional Programming.* Addison-Wesley Publishing Company.

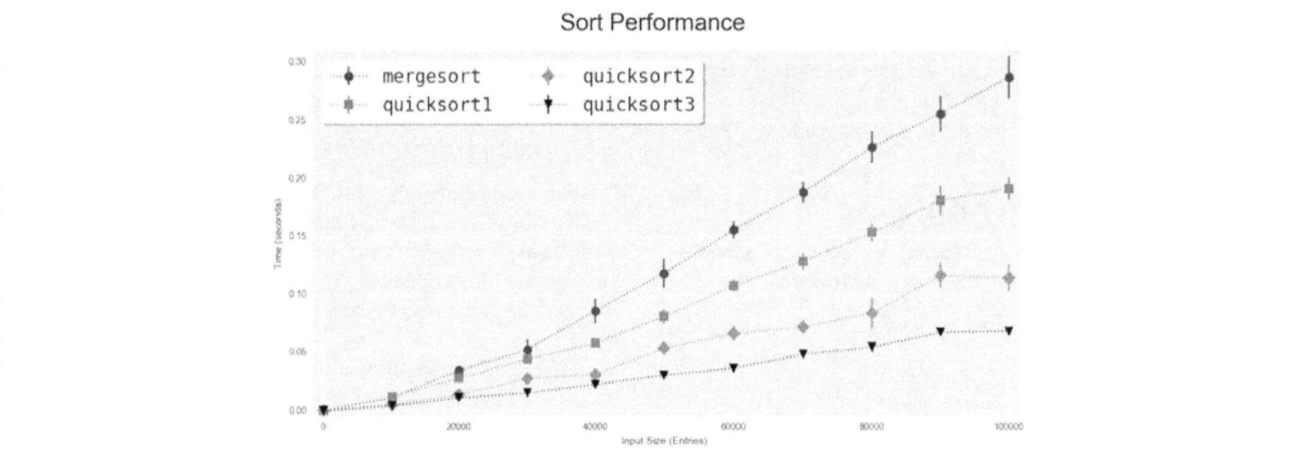

Figure 1: Sorting performance graph

Map-based Algorithm Visualization with METAL Highway Data

James D. Teresco
Siena College
Loudonville, New York
jteresco@siena.edu

Razieh Fathi
University at Buffalo
Buffalo, New York
raziehfa@buffalo.edu

Lukasz Ziarek
University at Buffalo
Buffalo, New York
lziarek@buffalo.edu

MariaRose Bamundo
Siena College
Loudonville, New York
mr26bamu@siena.edu

Arjol Pengu
Siena College
Loudonville, New York
a30peng@siena.edu

Clarice F. Tarbay
Siena College
Loudonville, New York
cf13tarb@siena.edu

ABSTRACT

We present the algorithm visualization capabilities of the METAL project. Using METAL's graph data which represents highway systems, a selection of interactive algorithm visualizations are performed. Progress of the algorithm is shown by changing the colors of the graph's vertices and/or edges overlaid on Google Maps and in color-coded tabular form, including contents of important data structures. Advantages include the real-world data set and the variety of data sizes available, enhancing student engagement. While many visualizations and visualization tools exist for graph and related algorithms, most focus on small, synthetic graphs. We describe our algorithm visualization capabilities, which include implementations of sequential search, graph traversals, Dijkstra's algorithm, and convex hulls. These can be executed on graphs ranging in size from a few vertices and edges to hundreds. We also present results of a survey of students who have used METAL's algorithm visualizations.

CCS CONCEPTS

• **Applied computing → Education**; **Interactive learning environments**; • **Theory of computation** → *Graph algorithms analysis*;

KEYWORDS

Pedagogical tools, Graph algorithms, Algorithm visualization.

ACM Reference Format:
James D. Teresco, Razieh Fathi, Lukasz Ziarek, MariaRose Bamundo, Arjol Pengu, and Clarice F. Tarbay. 2018. Map-based Algorithm Visualization with METAL Highway Data. In *Proceedings of SIGCSE '18: The 49th ACM Technical Symposium on Computer Science Education (SIGCSE '18).* ACM, New York, NY, USA, 6 pages. https://doi.org/10.1145/3159450.3159583

ACM ISBN 978-1-4503-5103-4/18/02...$15.00
https://doi.org/10.1145/3159450.3159583

1 INTRODUCTION

The Map-based Educational Tools for Algorithm Learning (METAL) project provides real-world graph data sets representing systems of highways and the ability to visualize the data and results of computations on that data [13–15]. In this paper we introduce METAL's newest capability: a map-based, dynamic, interactive algorithm visualization (AV) system. The implementation leverages Google Maps to handle graphs ranging from a few vertices and edges to thousands. Color-coded visual cues, in both map and tabular form, show the data being processed at each step of an algorithm's execution, along with the contents of underlying data structures used to implement the algorithm. METAL's AVs can use small graphs to illustrate the low-level details of an algorithm, then seamlessly "scale-up" for a view of how the algorithms perform on larger data sets. Users can pan and zoom for a closer view of interesting parts of the visualization as well as control the speed of the visualization.

The ability to see the algorithms in action at a wide range of speeds and scales is very exciting. After watching the visualization on a small graph, likely at a slow simulation speed, a student can then load a larger graph and watch the simulation at high speed. Watching graph traversals, for example, on a graph with hundreds of vertices clearly shows how the breadth-first traversal moves out in "waves" from the source vertex, and depth-first proceeds to a dead end and then backtracks, demonstrating the essential differences between the two.

The paper is organized as follows. The data provided by METAL is described briefly in Section 2. METAL's AV capabilities are described in detail in Section 3. Pedagogical usage and the results of a student survey are presented in Section 4. We relate METAL's AVs to other efforts in Section 5. Section 6 offers some concluding remarks and discussion of future directions.

2 HIGHWAY GRAPH DATA

Before describing METAL's AV system, we first present its data. METAL's graph data is one of the major features of the project [15]. This data set has several important and desirable features.

- The graph vertices represent actual places, and edges represent the roads that connect them.
- Hundreds of graph data files are provided, ranging in size from fewer than a dozen vertices and edges to hundreds of thousands of vertices and edges.

- The data can be used as examples for a variety of algorithms, either as a simple collection of points (i.e. vertex coordinates only) or as a graph.
- The data itself can be visualized in map form.

METAL's graph data is derived from highway data created by the Travel Mapping (TM) project[1], as described in [15]. TM is a travel enthusiast project that allows its users to track their cumulative travels and see maps and statistics of those travels. Project volunteers continuously expand and improve the highways represented in TM. As of this writing, 30,626 routes have been plotted for 987,274 miles. 456,587 unique locations have been plotted as starting, ending, intersecting, or other interesting waypoints along these routes. Data is derived only from permissible, open sources[2], most often from maps in the OpenStreetMap project [7] or open government satellite or topographic imagery.

TM's daily update process converts its route-based highway data to a graph format for METAL. Each graph represents a subset of the world's highway systems. These have been used successfully for class examples and assignments for several years [13–15]. TM data and source code is available in public repositories[3]. Details of graph construction and examples of the data's use in classes are given in [15].

3 ALGORITHM VISUALIZATION IN METAL

METAL's AVs are implemented within its freely-available *Highway Data Examiner (HDX)*[4] HDX was originally created to visualize the graph data itself and the (static) results of computations performed over the data. We focus here on METAL's new support for interactive visualization for a set of algorithms.

Figures and descriptions in this section give a sense of the HDX UI, but the reader is encouraged to try it live, or view videos of these AVs in action[5].

3.1 Design and Implementation Discussion

A complete description of METAL's AV framework implementation is well beyond the scope of this paper. Instead, we give an overview and mention a few interesting issues.

The map[6] is the primary user interface (UI) feature, with other information overlaid on the map. JavaScript lacks direct multithreading support, so the simulation is event-driven. An AV proceeds by performing a single step (typically one iteration of a loop) of the algorithm, then scheduling a timer event that will be responsible for the next iteration. This yields control to the browser, so it can update the screen and respond to UI events until the timer event is triggered. Each AV is implemented as functions that set up, begin execution, continue execution, and clean up, and are called by UI and/or timer event handlers. Our experience indicates that algorithms can be fairly easily implemented in an event driven form.

3.2 User Interface Features

Before detailing specific AVs, we first intorduce the overall UI. The design is driven by some underlying principles that we mention in this section, as well as feedback from students, including survey responses (Section 4.1).

When HDX is loaded, options to load data are presented in the Algorithm Visualization Control Panel (AVCP). Typical AV users will obtain a list of graphs from which one can be selected for loading. No downloading or uploading is needed; the graph is loaded directly.

On successful loading, the graph is displayed on the map and its waypoints (graph vertices) and connections (graph edges) are shown in tabular forms. The underlying Google Maps UI supports pan and zoom, and all waypoints and connections are clickable to bring up additional information. The AVCP and waypoints/connections tables can be moved, resized, or hidden, as desired.

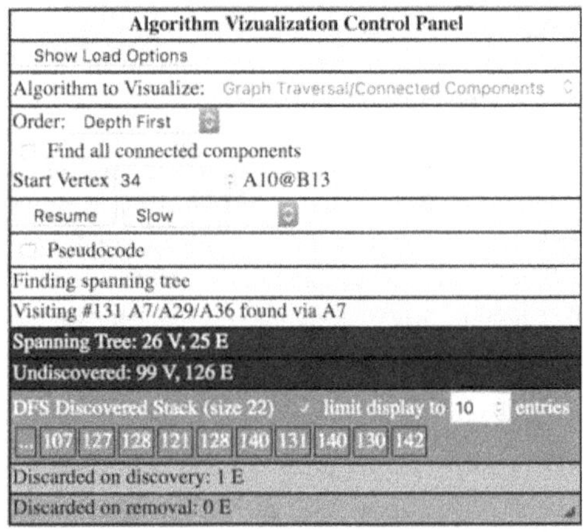

Figure 1: A closer view of the contents of the HDX AVCP for the depth-first traversal shown in progress in Figure 2.

When an algorithm is selected from the "Algorithm to Visualize" dropdown, controls to select any additional simulation parameters are presented. The top half of the AVCP in Figure 1 shows the algorithm-specific controls for the "Graph Traversal/Connected Components" AV: (*i*) traversal order, (*ii*) whether to find all connected components, and (*iii*) the start vertex. The start vertex can be selected by number, or by clicking on that box, then on any vertex/waypoint on the map or in the waypoints table. Common to all algorithms is the "Start"/"Pause"/"Resume" button (label and functionality changes as appropriate), the simulation speed control, and a checkbox to show pseudocode for the selected algorithm.

An AV in execution, as shown in the figures in Section 3.3, displays information about the variables and data structures in the AVCP (whose labels also act as a color legend), and consistently colors vertices and/or edges on the map, and in the waypoint and connection tables. We also strive to keep colors consistent across AVs where it makes sense (e.g., dark gray usually denotes "unvisited" entities and yellow denotes an entity currently being visited).

Figure 1 shows a closer view of the information shown in the AVCP during execution of the depth-first graph traversal in Figure 2. The color-coded entries here show key variables and statistics for

[1] See http://tm.teresco.org/
[2] See http://tm.teresco.org/credits.php
[3] https://github.com/TravelMapping.
[4] http://courses.teresco.org/metal/hdx/, runs in any standards-compliant browser.
[5] http://courses.teresco.org/metal/cse18/
[6] The map uses the Google Maps JavaScript API, https://developers.google.com/maps/.

the AV. The stack is the interesting structure in this example. To save display space, the default limits the view to only a subset (the top 10 elements) of the stack. This behavior can be disabled, or the limit modified during the AV by the user. When limiting, the entries nearest the top of the stack are shown, as these are the ones most recently added and those that will come out soonest. Other AVs use queues, generic lists/arrays, and priority queues. The displays are similar, but, for example, with queues, the middle of the queue is collapsed from view when the display is limited, since it is most interesting to see the items that are about to come out and the items that were most recently added.

We continue to expand and improve the UI for ease of use, better control over the AV, and to highlight the most important and instructive information for the user. Sedig and Parsons [9] bring together the work of many researchers on what makes an effective visualization, and most importantly for us, what makes an effective visual pedagogical tool. For example, Bertin [2] outlined eight visual variables for information visualization: size, value, texture, color, orientation, shape, and the two planar dimensions. METAL's AVs take advantage of nearly all of these. We will continue to be informed by this extensive body of research as we transform our AVs into complete teaching modules to help students understand the algorithms more quickly and at a deeper level. More information and more options in an AV are not always better, in terms of the cognitive load on the users [16]. This is particularly important to consider as we look to make AVs accessible to students at a wide variety of levels.

3.3 Available AVs

Of course, graph data can be used as input for graph algorithms, but taking the vertices as a field of points opens up a variety of other possibilities. As of this writing, four major algorithms and groups of related algorithms are supported: (*i*) a sequential search of the vertex or graph data for extreme values (e.g., the northernmost vertex, or the longest edge), (*ii*) graph traversals, including breadth-first, depth-first, random-first, with options to find a single spanning tree or all connected components of the graph, (*iii*) Dijkstra's algorithm for single-source shortest paths, and (*iv*) a brute-force algorithm for finding the convex hull of the vertices. Additional algorithms are in progress or planned.

3.3.1 Sequential Search. Our vertex-based sequential search visualization traverses the graph's vertices to locate the extreme points (i.e., the northern-, southern-, eastern-, and western-most) and the points with the longest and shortest labels. Sequential search is a fundamental algorithm that can be understood by non-programmers, but the details can be confusing to beginning programmers. The essential points here are that we track the *leader* for each search criterion, and as each candidate (in this case, vertex) is visited, we check to see if it is the new leader. If it is, we remember it. Our system shows this in action in both tabular and map form.

Edge-based sequential searches work similarly. In that variant, the edges with the longest and shortest lengths and the longest and shortest labels are located.

3.3.2 Graph Traversals. To illustrate graph traversals, we present the breadth-first (BFT) and depth-first (DFT) algorithms. An example of each in progress using HDX on a small graph, the highways on the Isle of Man, is shown in Figure 2.

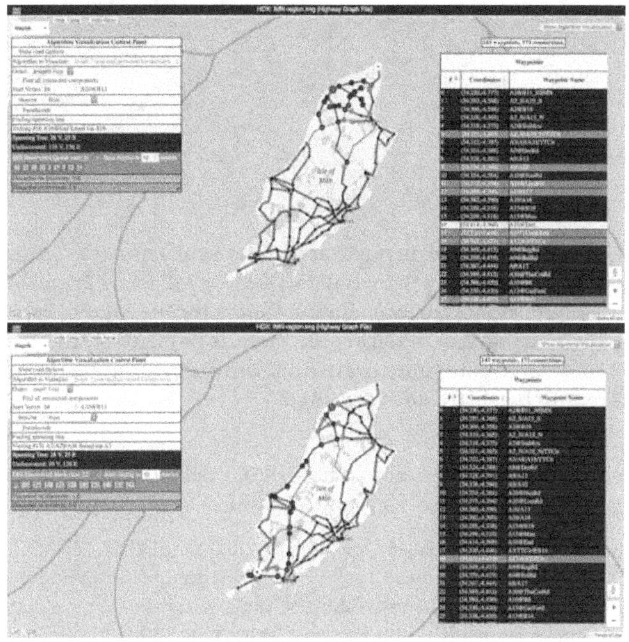

Figure 2: BFT (top) and DFT (bottom) in progress in HDX using METAL's graph of the highways on the Isle of Man when the algorithm has added the 26th vertex to the spanning tree. Vertices and edges are colored on the map and in the table to show their status in the simulation. The starting vertex is shown in magenta. Other colors match the AVCP entries more easily visible in Figure 1.

As those familiar with these algorithms would be aware, the algorithms are identical, save the data structure used to maintain a list of *discovered* vertices (LDV), i.e., those connected (by edges) to the part of the graph visited so far. However, they result in radically different traversal orders. BFT uses a queue, and DFT uses a stack[7]. By running each ordering on the same graph, the difference between them becomes quickly apparent by watching the portion of the graph in the LDV and growth of the spanning tree.

This AV was used with good success in the course for which the student survey (Section 4.1) was conducted.

Graph traversals also have the option of finding all connected components of the graph. When this option is selected, each time the LDV becomes empty, the spanning tree just computed is repainted with a unique color, and an unvisited vertex is selected to begin the next traversal to find the next connected component. An example of this in progress on the graph of the TM-plotted routes in the West Indies is shown in Figure 3. This graph is much larger (3848 vertices, 4964 edges), so individual vertices and edges are

[7] HDX includes a third option, not illustrated here, called *random-first* traversal, where the next vertex is chosen randomly from the LDV.

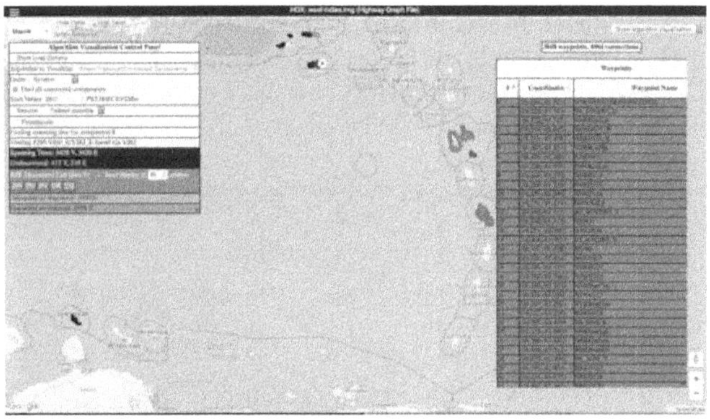

Figure 3: A random-first traversal finding all connected components shown in progress in HDX using METAL's graph of the highways on the West Indies. Colors for the current component being discovered are the same as in Figure 2, and the 7 completed components are each shown in a unique color. Areas in black are not yet visited.

not easily seen. It does demonstrate HDX's ability to handle larger graphs. An interactive user can also pan and zoom to see detail.

3.3.3 Dijkstra's Algorithm. The original motivation for METAL's predecessor project was to come up with a better Dijkstra's algorithm for single-source shortest paths assignment for a data structures course [13]. It is also an excellent algorithm to visualize on a map using highway data. Figure 4 shows Dijkstra's algorithm in progress and at completion on METAL's graph of the U.S. state of Delaware. The start vertex is `DE1A@RehAve_E`, which is the corner of Rehoboth and Bayard in Rehoboth Beach, and the destination vertex is `DE1@104`, interchange 104 on Delaware Route 1 in Dover.

The Dijkstra's algorithm AV was not implemented until after the course for which student surveys (Section 4.1) were conducted. However, it was the most-requested new AV in those surveys.

3.3.4 Brute-Force Convex Hull. Convex hull algorithms can be challenging for students. The idea is simple enough, but the details are less obvious. METAL's brute-force convex hull AV is shown in Figure 5. In the brute-force algorithm, each pair of vertices is considered as a candidate to be added to the convex hull. The innermost loop checks whether all other points lie on the same side of that line. If they do, the points are added to the hull. As soon as a vertex is found that lies on the opposite side, that pair is rejected.

Brute-force convex hull was chosen for implementation as a METAL AV to demonstrate a non-trivial algorithm that operates on vertex data only.

4 PEDAGOGICAL USAGE

METAL's AV capabilities present multiple new opportunities for classroom use beyond what was previously reported [15]. Actual course usage of the AV capabilities so far has been in Teresco's Analysis of Algorithms course at Siena College, where it was used in conjunction with other assignments using METAL data. Two AVs were used: sequential search and graph traversals. The sequential search AVs were part of a lab exercise which was reviewing search algorithms, while introducing the students to METAL's data

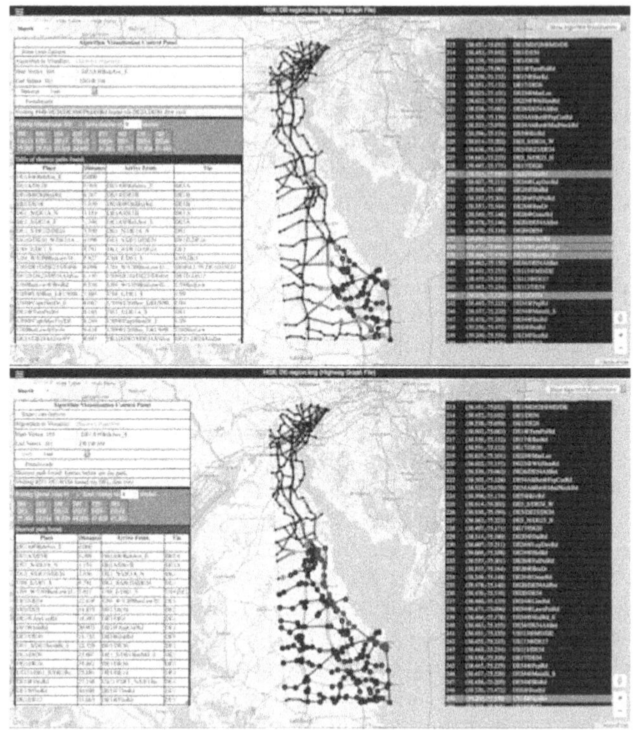

Figure 4: An instance of Dijkstra's algorithm shown in progress (top) and completed (bottom) in HDX using METAL's graph of the highways in Delaware. In purple are the start (dark) and destination (light) vertices. Blue vertices and edges are those to which a shortest path has been found and the edges used to get to them, each of which has an entry in the table of shortest paths found. Green vertices and edges are those currently in the priority queue. In the bottom figure, the computed shortest path is shown in dark red, and only those entries remain in the table of shortest paths.

and to HDX. Students were asked to watch a vertex search before writing their own program to do the same (in Java) on METAL vertex data. This allowed the students to compare the results of the AV with their own implementations on the same input graphs. The graph traversal AVs supplemented more traditional whiteboard and pencil-and-paper examples. The AVs were used to emphasize the differences between breadth-first and depth-first traversals. These were especially successful, and were mentioned by several students in the post-course survey described later in this section. The number of AVs has grown and is expected to grow further before the next offering, when these new AVs will be used in additional class examples and lab exercises. Students can interact with the AV and try out different graphs and algorithm parameters.

The real value here is in watching the simulation live. A user can very quickly see the difference in traversal order, how vertices are selected to be added to the data structure, and how they are removed to be visited. Our sample video list[8] includes examples of several AVs. We believe that seeing these algorithms on different

[8] http://courses.teresco.org/metal/cse18/

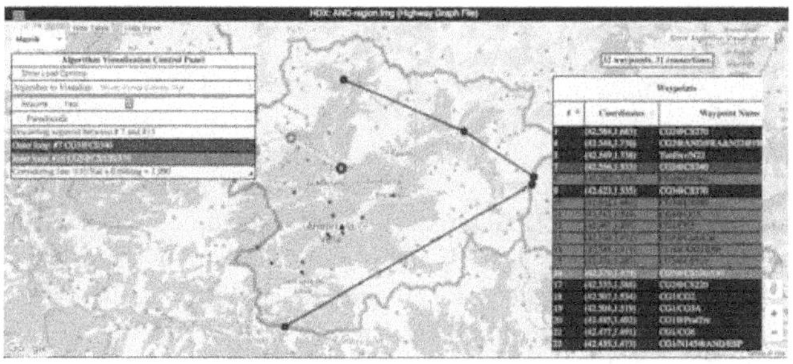

Figure 5: An instance of the brute-force convex hull algorithm shown in progress in HDX using METAL's graph of the highways in Andorra. Blue vertices and line segments (not graph edges!) have been found to be part of the convex hull. The red vertex and the maroon vertex and the yellow line segment between them are the ones being considered as a candidate for inclusion in the hull. Light gray vertices no longer need to be considered at all, green vertices are ones that still need to be considered in the inner loop, and dark gray vertices are those that still need to be considered by the outer loop.

size graphs representing a real-world data set in this manner has two benefits. First, the overall behavior, such as the differences between the orderings for the traversal types, is more apparent on a larger graph. Second, students can see the utility of the algorithms as they apply to map data.

There is little if any barrier to adoption for an instructor interested in using an AV. HDX is web-based, so there is nothing to download or install[9]. After just a few minutes experimenting to become familiar, an instructor could easily use a METAL AV in class examples or help students begin to use it.

4.1 Student Evaluation

METAL's data and visualization capabilities have enabled class examples and assignments that students have found engaging and challenging. Students in the most recent course to work with METAL, and the first to work with the AV capabilities, in the Spring 2017 Analysis of Algorithms course at Siena College, were administered a short survey about their experience (IRB #04-17-049). 34 students responded and the results were very encouraging.

Students worked with two of METAL's interactive AVs: the sequential searches (both vertex-based and edge-based data), and graph traversals. They were asked to "indicate their level of agreement with each of the following statements about METAL's interactive algorithm visualization system" using a Likert scale ranging from 1 (strongly disagree) to 7 (strongly agree). Results are shown in Figure 6. The responses to all were very positive, with at least 70% of students responding "Strongly agree" or "Agree" on each.

Further, in free-form responses to a question "Was there a usage of METAL this semester that you found especially helpful or interesting?", the most common response was that the visualization helped students to understand the differences between breadth-first

[9]Unless an instructor wishes to have his or her own instance of HDX.

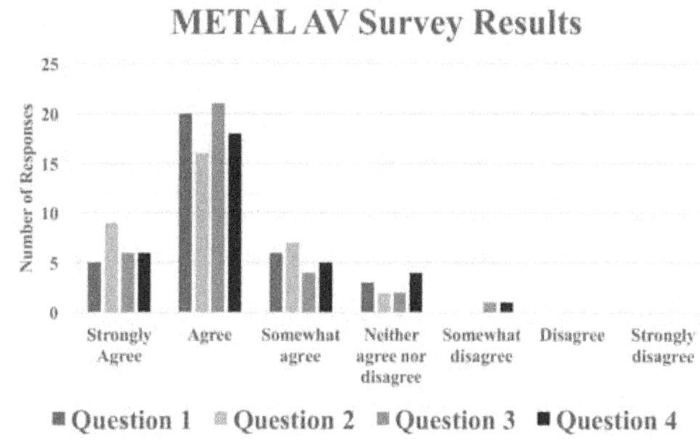

Figure 6: Survey results summary. Question 1: The visualization of sequential search helps me understand the nature of that algorithm. Question 2: The visualization of breath-first and depth-first traversal helps me understand those algorithms and the differences between them. Question 3: Running algorithm visualizations using small graphs helps me see the fine-level details of an algorithm. Question 4: Running algorithm visualizations using larger graphs helps me see the "big picture" overview of an algorithm's progress.

and depth-first graph traversals. Others mentioned two of the original motivations for the project: that the real-world data was more engaging and that seeing the data on the map was helpful.

We acknowledge that this survey was not a formal study of the effectiveness of METAL. The survey was conducted to gain a more complete understanding of the student perspective and to guide our future use and development of the project. Much of the feedback on the tool itself helped guide the priorities for the project that enhanced and expanded AV capabilities during Summer 2017. We intend to conduct more formal studies in future courses.

5 COMPARISONS WITH OTHER AV SYSTEMS

A comprehensive survey of AV systems (e.g., [10]) is well beyond our scope, so we will discuss some of what distinguishes METAL's AVs from some other projects with similar goals.

We begin by acknowledging the limitations of METAL's AVs. We focus strictly on graph data representing highways, and only on algorithms that can take advantage of the spatial and/or connectivity information of our data. However, we believe these also lead to METAL's greatest strengths: the real-world data that can be visualized in map form on a wide variety of sizes and other characteristics make it an engaging tool for students to use. Naps, et al. [6] concluded that visualization has no value in improving learning until it can become a tool for engagement. Even outside of AV, engagement is shown to be important for student learning [1, 3].

BRIDGES [12] is a powerful and flexible system that focuses on bringing a variety of real-world data such as that from social networks into data structure visualizations. Their focus is more on having students visualize the operation of data structures rather than algorithms built on those structures.

To our knowledge, METAL provides the only AVs that operate both on a variety of scales and on a large collection of real-world data. AV tools such as DisViz [11], Galle's "Data Structure Visualizations"[10], VisualGraph [5], Visualgo[11], and Algomation[12] provide a wide variety of AVs but on smaller or synthetic data. GraphExploiter [4] operates on synthetic graphs but at larger scales.

METAL also brings a narrative texture to its AVs, which can enhance engagement. For example Rowe, et al. [8] found that a narrative environment enhanced the ability of high-achieving students, and motivates curiosity about the subject among lower achievers.

6 CONCLUSIONS AND ONGOING WORK

We believe our approach offers some distinct advantages. The data has a real-world connection that students can relate to immediately, we can visualize in map form, and the data includes graphs at a wide variety of scales. After watching the visualization on a small graph, likely at a slow simulation speed, a student can then load a larger graph and watch the simulation at high speed. Watching the progress of the graph traversals, for example, on a graph with hundreds of vertices (or more) is fascinating and, we believe, instructive and engaging.

While highly useful in its current form, we see the work presented here as a foundation on which we can build much more. Of course, we will expand the selection of AVs. Building on our dynamic display of the contents of key data structures, we would like to highlight additional variables and lines of code in execution during the simulations. We can change the speed of and pause and restart AVs, but it is potentially helpful to be able to step through or even reverse the simulation.

Efficiency is essential to the study of algorithms. While it is tempting to use a visualization to compare algorithm efficiency, we argue that this can be misleading. In our implementation, the constant factors from map and UI updates would make timings difficult to interpret. Operation counts are being added to our framework, which will allow some meaningful algorithm efficiency studies by running the algorithms on a variety of data sizes.

To date, our focus has been on data and infrastructure development, allowing our first several AVs to be implemented. Earlier versions of METAL have been used in classes, but the only somewhat formal feedback of the utility of its AVs that has been gathered to date is that presented in Section 4.1. As development progresses on this and other METAL tools, we plan to study the effectiveness of these tools more formally.

Since METAL's AV capabilities are new, they have not yet been well integrated into the examples and assignments that have used METAL data and static visualization capabilities successfully. More complete modules are planned for the next Analysis of Algorithms offering that will integrate METAL AVs with other class examples and assignments. Ideally, a topic like graph traversals or Dijkstra's algorithm would be largely moved out of lecture and learned by the students with guided examples and exercises centered around current and future METAL AVs. We hope these modules will not only be useful in data structures and algorithms courses, but possibly in courses like networking or machine learning where similar algorithms arise, and students might need some extra resources to understand them better.

[10]https://www.cs.usfca.edu/~galles/visualization

[11]http://visualgo.net

[12]http://www.algomation.com/

ACKNOWLEDGMENTS

This work was supported in part by the Summer Scholars 2017 Program, Center for Undergraduate Research and Creative Activity (CURCA), at Siena College. Thank you to the contributors of Travel Mapping and its predecessor project, Reichard's Clinched Highway Mapping, for providing the raw data from which the METAL data is created. Early versions of HDX were based on programs written by Reichard. Students whose work provided the basis upon which HDX's AV capabilities were developed include students in the Spring 2015 and Spring 2016 Software Engineering courses at The College of Saint Rose. Finally, thank you to all students in courses that have used METAL and its predecessor projects for their patience and feedback.

REFERENCES

[1] Austin Cory Bart, Eli Tilevich, Simin Hall, Tony Allevato, and Clifford A Shaffer. 2014. Transforming introductory computer science projects via real-time web data. In *Proceedings of the 45th ACM technical symposium on Computer science education*. ACM, 289–294.

[2] Jacques Bertin. 1983. Semiology of graphics: diagrams, networks, maps. (1983).

[3] Michael Buckley, John Nordlinger, and Devika Subramanian. 2008. Socially relevant computing. *ACM SIGCSE Bulletin* 40, 1 (2008), 347–351.

[4] Victor Lequay, Alexis Ringot, Mohammed Haddad, Brice Effantin, and Hamamache Kheddouci. 2015. GraphExploiter: Creation, Visualization and Algorithms on Graphs. In *Proceedings of the 2015 IEEE/ACM International Conference on Advances in Social Networks Analysis and Mining 2015 (ASONAM '15)*. ACM, New York, NY, USA, 765–767. https://doi.org/10.1145/2808797.2808803

[5] Jeff Lucas, Thomas L. Naps, and Guido Rößling. 2003. VisualGraph: A Graph Class Designed for Both Undergraduate Students and Educators. *SIGCSE Bull.* 35, 1 (January 2003), 167–171. https://doi.org/10.1145/792548.611960

[6] Thomas L. Naps, James R. Eagan, and Laura L. Norton. 2000. JHAVÉ – an Environment to Actively Engage Students in Web-based Algorithm Visualizations. *SIGCSE Bull.* 32, 1 (March 2000), 109–113. https://doi.org/10.1145/331795.331829

[7] OpenStreetMap contributors. 2016. OpenStreetMap. http://www.openstreetmap.org/. (2016).

[8] Jonathan P Rowe, Lucy R Shores, Bradford W Mott, and James C Lester. 2010. Individual differences in gameplay and learning: a narrative-centered learning perspective. In *Proceedings of the Fifth International Conference on the Foundations of Digital Games*. ACM, 171–178.

[9] Kamran Sedig and Paul Parsons. 2016. Design of Visualizations for Human-Information Interaction: A Pattern-Based Framework. *Synthesis Lectures on Visualization* 4, 1 (2016), 1–185.

[10] Clifford A. Shaffer, Matthew L. Cooper, Alexander Joel D. Alon, Monika Akbar, Michael Stewart, Sean Ponce, and Stephen H. Edwards. 2010. Algorithm Visualization: The State of the Field. *Trans. Comput. Educ.* 10, Article 9 (August 2010), 22 pages. Issue 3. https://doi.org/10.1145/1821996.1821997

[11] Alexander A. Sherstov. 2003. Distributed Visualization of Graph Algorithms. In *Proceedings of the 34th SIGCSE Technical Symposium on Computer Science Education (SIGCSE '03)*. ACM, New York, NY, USA, 376–380. https://doi.org/10.1145/611892.612011

[12] Kalpathi Subramanian, Jamie Payton, David Burlinson, and Mihai Mehedint. 2016. Bringing Real-World Data And Visualizations Into Data Structures Courses Using BRIDGES. In *Proceedings of the 47th ACM Technical Symposium on Computing Science Education*. ACM, 590–590.

[13] James D. Teresco. 2010. A Dijkstra's algorithm shortest path assignment using the Google Maps API: poster session. *J. Comput. Small Coll.* 25, 6 (2010), 253–255.

[14] James D. Teresco. 2012. Highway data and map visualizations for educational use. In *Proceedings of the 43rd ACM technical symposium on Computer Science Education (SIGCSE '12)*. ACM, New York, NY, USA, 553–558. https://doi.org/10.1145/2157136.2157295

[15] James D. Teresco. 2017. Improved Highway Data and Map Visualizations for Teaching Data Structures and Algorithms. In *2017 Proc. EDSIG Conference*, Li-Jen Lester, Neelima Bhatnagar, Jeffrey Cummings, and Jason Sharp (Eds.), Vol. 3. ISCAP (Information Systems & Computing Academic Professionals), http://iscap.info, Austin. ISSN 2473-3857, http://proc.iscap.info/2017/pdf/4325.pdf.

[16] M Eduard Tudoreanu and Eileen Kraemer. 2008. Balanced cognitive load significantly improves the effectiveness of algorithm animation as a problem-solving tool. *Journal of Visual Languages & Computing* 19, 5 (2008), 598–616.

Student Misconceptions of Dynamic Programming

Shamama Zehra
University of Toronto Mississauga

Aishwarya Ramanathan
University of Toronto Mississauga

Larry Yueli Zhang
University of Toronto Mississauga

Daniel Zingaro
University of Toronto Mississauga

ABSTRACT

Dynamic Programming (DP) is considered to be one of the most difficult topics for students to understand in theoretical CS. Prior work suggests that misconceptions arise even when students have completed a course in which there is considerable focus on learning how to solve DP problems. We conducted think-aloud interviews with students who have completed the DP portion of the Algorithms course at a top North American research university. We report on three themes and their misconceptions discovered through this process. The first theme delves into students' struggles defining the notion of a subproblem and identifying particular subproblems. The second theme focuses on the understanding and usage of DP solution techniques compared to other algorithmic approaches. The third theme is composed of misconceptions related to defining and using recurrences. Analysis of each misconception provides insight into student thinking and offers ideas for improving the education of DP to university students.

CCS CONCEPTS

• **Social and professional topics** → **Computing education**; • **Theory of computation** → *Dynamic programming*;

KEYWORDS

Algorithms, Dynamic Programming, Misconceptions

ACM Reference Format:
Shamama Zehra, Aishwarya Ramanathan, Larry Yueli Zhang, and Daniel Zingaro. 2018. Student Misconceptions of Dynamic Programming. In *SIGCSE '18: The 49th ACM Technical Symposium on Computer Science Education, February 21–24, 2018, Baltimore , MD, USA.* ACM, New York, NY, USA, 6 pages. https://doi.org/10.1145/3159450.3159528

1 INTRODUCTION

The CS education research community has studied in depth the difficulties and misconceptions of students in CS1 [12]. And for good reason: elevated failure rates in CS1 persist even with the latest pedagogical research [14], and students demonstrate misconceptions of even the most rudimentary concepts [7]. Save for isolated instances (e.g., Digital Logic [6]), courses beyond the introductory levels have been given considerably less attention. For two reasons, it is important for research to focus on more advanced courses, even while the community continues to solve pressing issues at the introductory level. First, for students who do continue to advanced courses, we want to avail ourselves of teaching that is based on knowledge of student misconceptions. Second, misconceptions at this level are likely to be largely disjoint from CS1 misconceptions, so work at different levels of the CS curriculum can be conducted in parallel.

In this paper, we offer a think-aloud study of students as they solve Dynamic Programming (DP) problems. This topic was chosen based on difficulties reported in recent research on student algorithmic misconceptions [4]. We interviewed juniors at a top North American research institution, and sought students at a wide range of algorithmic facility. We document considerable difficulties with the DP problems, some of which replicate prior research, but others that, to our knowledge, are reported for the first time.

2 LITERATURE REVIEW

There is a recent research push to study student misconceptions of advanced CS material. For example, one study reports on student misconceptions of binary search trees and hash tables [8]. Another reports on student experiences with the Build-Heap algorithm [13]. There is considerably less research on algorithm design techniques such as Dynamic Programming and Divide-and-Conquer.

Dynamic Programming (DP) is a powerful algorithmic problem-solving technique and a core part of the Algorithms and Complexity knowledge unit of Computing Curricula 2013 [1]. DP is typically taught in a second- or third-year Algorithms course, but see [9] for a call to integrate DP across the curriculum. Recursion itself is challenging for students [10], and recursion is but one step in the generation of a DP solution. In particular, it is thought that students struggle to find recurrences based on the optimal substructure of solutions [4].

Enström and Kann [4] report on multi-year action research of their Algorithms, Data Structures and Complexity course. The research consisted of cycles of determining topics of difficulty, improving teaching on those topics, and evaluating the results. A core focus of the research was improving student understanding of DP. The authors introduced concrete assignments, used visualizations, and were careful to provide examples that demonstrate each aspect of DP solutions that can vary (e.g., number of dimensions in the recurrence, array-filling order). Finally, the authors separately taught different phases of the DP process to reduce cognitive load: recognizing the problem structure and producing a recurrence relation were taught separately from finding a correct array-filling order. In general, students responded positively to these changes, suggesting that DP misconceptions are within the purview of educators

SIGCSE '18, February 21–24, 2018, Baltimore , MD, USA

ACM ISBN 978-1-4503-5103-4/18/02...$15.00
https://doi.org/10.1145/3159450.3159528

to address. Unfortunately, specific misconceptions and challenges with DP were not provided.

Another study [11] used lightweight methods (e.g., multiple-choice or fill-in-the-blank questions) to detect student misconceptions of algorithm design and object-oriented concepts. In terms of DP, students were asked two multiple-choice questions: one on the coin-changing problem (given particular coin denominations, what is the minimum number of coins required to make n cents) and one on the knapsack problem. In each problem, students were asked to fill-in the **copy** (when the new item under consideration does not help) or **update** (when the new item does help) code required to extend a subsolution to a larger solution. The authors found that the coin-changing problem is more challenging than the knapsack problem; and that, within the same problem, **copy** correctness and **update** correctness were significantly associated.

We know of only one DP study that includes specific student misconceptions supported by data [3]. That study used multiple-choice questions and student interviews as the data-collection instruments. Misconceptions included writing a naive recursive solution instead of a DP solution, reasoning incorrectly about bottom-up solutions, and conflating DP with Divide-and-Conquer algorithms. Only 2 of 23 students were able to fill-in missing code for a solution to the coin-changing problem. Compared to that study, our study uses what we consider to be conceptually-simpler problems, and we ask students to conduct each step of the DP problem-solving approach rather than fill-in missing pieces of skeleton code.

3 METHOD

We conducted in-person interviews that targeted students who were taking the third-year Algorithm Design and Analysis course at a research-intensive North American university. DP was taught from Week 3 to Week 5 of the 12-week course, and our interviews were conducted in Week 11. Student interviewees were recruited through announcements made on our behalf by the course instructor. In particular, the announcements gave no hint that our focus was DP, instead generally noting that we sought interviewees to inform our research on student conceptions of algorithms. Participation was voluntary and was compensated with a gift card. Students were selected for interview participation based on a pre-screening survey, where we asked for their academic year and self-reported expected grade in the Algorithms course. Fourteen interviews were conducted over four days, each of which lasted approximately one hour.

Algorithm design problems were prepared and used as the interview questions. We sought questions that demonstrate the types of variation possible in DP problems [4]. Specifically, we sought 1D- and 2D-array problems, as well as concrete and more abstract problems. We also chose problems that were unlikely to have been covered in the course or studied online by students. We used three DP problems in our interviews, the first two of which are the focus of this paper:

- **Q1: Coin Row**: There is a row of n coins whose values are positive integers $c_1, c_2, \ldots, c_n$. The goal is to pick up the maximum-value coins such that no two coins adjacent in the initial row can be picked up. (This problem can be solved by DP using a 1D array. Letting subproblem $D[i]$ represent the maximum-value solution using the first i coins, $D[i]$ is the maximum of $c_i + D[i-2]$ (when c_i is picked up) and $D[i-1]$ (when c_i is not picked up). This problem is concrete in the sense that the row of coins is provided as input to the algorithm and can be visualized.)
- **Q2: Consecutive 1's**: Describe an algorithm to find the number of binary strings of length N that do not contain any two consecutive 1's. (This problem can be solved by DP; interestingly, it uses structurally the same subproblem recurrence as that of the Coin Row problem. This problem is less concrete than the Coin Row problem as there is no input array provided.)
- **Q3: Maximum Pixel Sum**: Given a 2D image where each pixel can be represented by a value between 0 and 1, find a connected path of pixels that results in the smallest sum of pixel values. The path must begin somewhere in the first row of the image and end somewhere in the last row of the image. (This problem can be solved with a 2D DP strategy; the problem is quite concrete as the input is a grid of pixels.)

For each of the three problems, we presented the following questions to the students:

- What is the most appropriate algorithm design technique for solving this problem? Note that we did **not** ask students to use DP right away; this let us explore variation in how students' navigate the algorithm design space. We did direct them to a DP solution after several minutes had they not settled on DP on their own by then.
- What are the sub-problems of this problem and what is the recurrence that relates the sub-problems?
- Write the pseudocode of a bottom-up Dynamic Programming solution to this problem.

These steps mirrored the "DP recipe" that was taught to these students in their Algorithms course.

We felt that our DP problems were considerably easier than those used in prior research [3]. Still, given the degree of student struggle in that prior research, we worried about students not being able to make any progress at all. With that in mind, we produced two additional problems that could be solved without using DP:

- **Q4: Stock Market**: Given a sequence of historical daily prices for a stock on consecutive days, find the days on which someone should have bought the stock and then sold the stock so as to maximize earnings. (A Divide-and-Conquer solution can be used to solve this problem in $O(n \log n)$ time; a linear-time scan through the array is also possible.)
- **Q5: Peak-Finding**: Given an array of numbers that we know ascends up to some maximum value and then descends until the end of the array, find the maximum element of the array. (This problem can be solved in $O(\log n)$ time using an approach based on binary search.)

These simpler problems served as "morale boosters" in case the DP problems were not going well for a student. A small number of our students did become agitated or lost confidence when unable to solve a DP problem. We were cautious of demoralizing students in that way and then letting them leave the interview; the non-DP problems were used to mitigate this possibility. Note that these problems were used only when we felt it extremely unlikely that a

T#	M#	Misconception	# of Students
T1	M1	Student struggles to write iterative code to solve the problem.	7/14
T1	M2	Student struggles to compose subproblems or define what is meant by "subproblem".	8/14
T2	M3	Student uses sets for the DP problem.	5/14
T2	M4	Student uses Divide-and-Conquer for the DP problem.	4/14
T2	M5	Student uses a Greedy approach for the DP problem.	8/14
T3	M6	Student struggles to write a recurrence.	4/14
T3	M7	Student fails to use previous experience with a recurrence to solve an analogous problem.	4/10

Table 1: Prevalent Student Themes (T) and Misconceptions (M)

student would progress on the DP problems (e.g., long stretches of no progress, giving up). Finally, for such students, these non-DP problems were also used as calibration for evaluating overall level of knowledge in algorithm design.

A think-aloud protocol [5] was used in conducting the interviews. This technique involves asking students to verbalize their thoughts as they solve problems. Note that we did not ask students to explain **why** they think in the ways that they do; asking **why** is known to change the problem-solving process [5]. Two researchers jointly conducted each interview, with one researcher notetaking and prompting the student to verbalize their thoughts when required, and the other focusing exclusively on notetaking. We made students aware that we would not be able to provide hints or answer their questions while they worked on a problem, as doing so would influence their thinking and impede our ability to study what they can do on their own. That said, when it became clear that students were not making progress, we did provide hints to inform our understanding of what students can do with help. Once hints were given, however, further data was analyzed in the context of that hint, with pre-hint and post-hint progress distinguished in our analysis.

Each student was first given the Coin Row problem. The second problem was selected based on the student's approach and progress on the first problem. If the student made at least minimal progress on Coin Row, or understood the general idea of DP and tried to apply it, then Consecutive 1's or Maximum Pixel Sum was selected as the second problem. If the student failed to make any progress or gave up on Coin Row, then we chose one of the non-DP problems as the second problem and used Consecutive 1's for the third problem. All of the interviewees were presented at least two of the DP problems.

For each interview, a digital smart pen device was used to record both the audio of the interview and the student's written work on scrap paper. After the interview, all recordings, written work, and interviewer notes were analyzed independently by two researchers. Each researcher segmented each interview and tagged the transcripts with codes representing misconceptions. Misconceptions were then clustered into themes. Finally, the researchers met to discuss the themes and codes that were generated as part of their individual analyses. Themes and misconceptions are included below only when both researchers agreed on the coding decisions. Researchers also jointly coded student progress on each question on a scale of 0 to 1. A score of 0 indicated no understanding of the question; a score of 1 indicated achieving at least a partially-correct solution which, with minor refinement, could become a fully-correct solution; intermediate scores were assigned when warranted. This progress-scoring was negotiated by the researchers and each score was agreed-upon before proceeding with additional scoring.

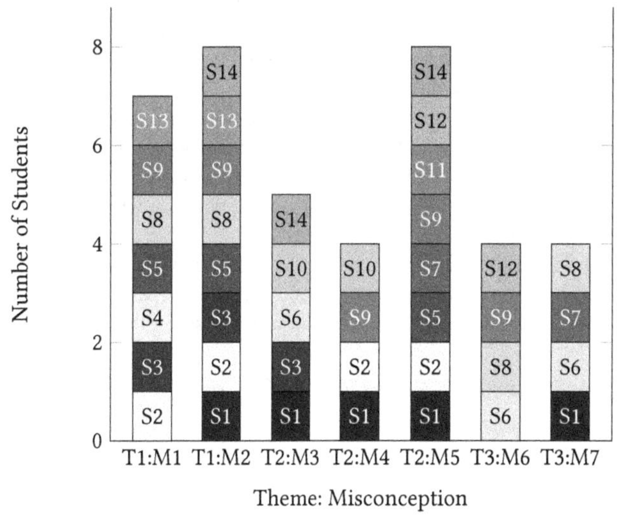

Figure 1: Overview of Student Misconceptions. This stacked bar graph represents the misconceptions that were observed across students (S1-S14).

4 RESULTS

Our quantitative and qualitative data reveal many student misconceptions related to DP. In this section, we report on three broad themes that were evident from patterns in student misconceptions, as shown in Table 1 and Figure 1. Each student in Figure 1 is represented by a colour and label on the graph, and it is evident that certain misconceptions co-occur. As an example of interpreting this figure, consider the student labelled S14. We can see that this student did not understand how to use subproblems or what is meant by "subproblems" (M2), used sets to state a solution on a DP Problem (M3), and also chose to use a Greedy technique on a DP problem (M5). Each DP question highlighted unique misconceptions. However, for the purposes of understanding student thinking across contexts, the most valuable misconceptions are those seen across questions and students.

4.1 Theme 1: Subproblem Identification

The first theme was that students were unable to identify or define subproblems (T1). That is, students were unable to state an optimal substructure property of the problem. As this is often the first step in developing a DP solution [2], difficulties here are particularly problematic.

One of the key misconceptions from this theme occurred when students used the notations `D[i]` or `OPT[i]`, but without stating the subproblem solutions represented by `D` or `OPT`. This disconnect between using notation and defining subproblems is further evident for the 6 students who were unable to justify their array's dimensions. Follow-up discussion suggested that these students had seen or remembered 2D DP examples from lecture, and so reasoned that 2D arrays would similarly work on Q1. Of these 6 students, 2 proposed while solving the question that a 2D array might not be a promising approach. After struggling and being provided hints, another 2 students realized that their thinking was incorrect. Students with this 2D misconception, and who were asked Q3 after Q1, generally made good progress on Q3, where a 2D solution was in fact viable.

In general, students identified in this theme were quite eager to "solve the problem", and simply skipped the steps of thoroughly understanding the problem and identifying subproblems.

4.2 Theme 2: Solution Technique

The second key theme observed was that students used other algorithmic problem-solving techniques to solve DP problems (T2).

This theme emerged when the student had an unclear understanding of the problem or of DP problem-solving techniques. There were 5 students who struggled to remember the steps to solve DP problems, causing them to resort to other solution techniques. We suspect that other students had the same trouble, but did not explicitly articulate it as these 5 did.

Students relied on a small set of non-DP techniques, reflecting those that were learned in their Algorithms course or in their prior CS programming courses. One such solution approach, used by 4 students, was that of Divide-and-Conquer (D&C), a fundamental technique that one is typically taught prior to learning DP. This heavy reliance on D&C suggests that these students had learned the rudiments on which DP is based: recursion, breaking a problem into subproblems, and using subproblem solutions to solve larger problems. Yet, students were not able to advance past the ill-fated D&C attempts, even when prompted to try DP solutions.

Another incorrect approach on which students relied was characterized by use of set terminology in expressing their solution. Interestingly, there were also 2 students who attempted to use finite state machines (deterministic finite automata) to solve the DP problems. This was particularly evident when solving Q2, where these students interpreted "not contain any two consecutive 1's" as two separate states where a 1 is or is not allowed, respectively. Some students did understand that these techniques would not solve the problem, but still chose to attempt these incorrect strategies until asked to use DP.

The most worrisome result here is that interviewers observed 4 students who were unable to think of any approach to the DP problems, even after struggling and being given several hints.

4.3 Theme 3: Defining a Recurrence

The final theme that emerged from the misconceptions was that students were unable to clearly define a recursive solution to the problem (T3). In contrast to Enström and Kann's findings [4], some students had difficulty observing recursive relationships in Q1, Q2, and Q3.

Discovering misconceptions in this theme was most straightforward when we interviewed students who could identify subproblems but could not compose the subproblems to solve the original problem. For 5 students who were not making progress, we offered a hint and asked them to think about how a solution to problem size $n-1$ could be used in a solution of size n; that is, we gave them a hint about the optimal substructure and asked them to compile that knowledge into a recurrence. After such hints, students were generally able to recite and recognize the steps of DP. However, most of these students were not able to correctly identify the step that they were to solve next, or incorrectly explained one or more steps when asked to summarize their progress to this point. Many were aware of the necessity of having the recursive solution before attempting to write a bottom-up solution, but failed to define a recurrence and so could not proceed to the bottom-up code. It seems that the given hints did not help students who lacked the ability to define the recurrence on their own.

We end this subsection with a preliminary hypothesis on the fragility of understanding recurrences. Q1 and Q2 can be solved using recurrences that are structurally very similar. Only 1 student explicitly identified similarities between the two problems when attempting a solution to Q2. Moreover, many students that were able to solve both problems did not note or use any similarity between the two recurrences.

5 ADDITIONAL OBSERVATIONS

5.1 Concrete vs. Abstract Problems

In our study, two of the problems that were presented (Q1 and Q2) had very similar recursive decompositions. As the "cover stories" for these two questions were of different forms, we wondered to what extent student facility with identifying and composing subproblems holds across contexts. We present such an analysis in Figure 2. 4 out of the 10 students who were presented both problems were able to progress through more of Q1 (the seemingly easier problem) as compared to Q2. However, there were 4 students who progressed much further in Q2 than Q1; in fact, they were not able to form any solution, despite repeated hints, for Q1. The other 2 students performed equally well in both problems.

For the 4 students that performed well on Q1 but failed to find a solution to Q2, it is possible that they were able to make connections in Q1 with concrete concepts. Q1 presents the problem in terms of objects with which students are familiar (coins), rather than an abstract concept that they may have only learned relatively recently (binary strings). We also note that the similarity in recurrence between Q1 and Q2 is highly nonobvious: one problem has to do with picking up coins, the other with enumerating binary strings of a given property. But inasmuch as the recurrence is "simple", based only on a single parameter, we hypothesize that the concreteness of Q1 facilitated its discovery compared to Q2 that did not. Based on previous research presented by Enström and Kann [4], we concur

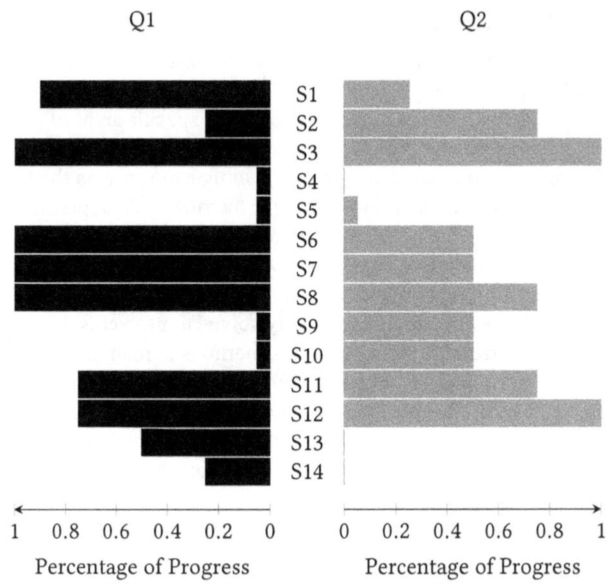

Figure 2: Preliminary Analysis for M7. This graph indicates how students (S1-S14) progressed on Q1 versus Q2, on a scale of 0-1 for each question.

that one of "the most difficult tasks... [is] related to seeing the structure of subproblems and their solutions...". It may therefore be very difficult for students to reach a point in Q2 where the analogous solutions for the two problems are evident. That is, while students **may** be able to transfer knowledge from Q1 to Q2, the challenging cover story of Q2 prevents students from identifying the features of Q1 that are relevant for Q2.

An interesting pattern emerged for those who were able to solve Q2 but not Q1. There were 4 students who failed to make progress on Q1 to whom we gave the Stock Market problem (Q4) after Q1 and prior to Q2. 3 of these 4 students performed much better on Q2 than Q1; at present, it is not clear why these students were able to do so. Did the Stock Market question somehow "clear their minds" in preparation for a fresh attempt at Q2? Would these students have made progress on Q2 had we presented it immediately after Q1? Our data does not admit answers to these questions.

5.2 Expectations and Confidence

Though not a primary focus of our interviews, we report preliminary results on interactions between student performance on the one hand and expectations and confidence on the other.

First, our data showed that students who predicted themselves to be in the highest (A) grade range progressed almost to completion on most problems during the interview. Similarly, students who predicted themselves to be in the lower (C) grade range had poor progress in solving the interview problems. Patterns among students in the middle (B) grade range were inconclusive; students who determined themselves to be in this range had a variety of performance levels in the interviews. The student who projected themselves at the lowest grade level (D) was also an anomaly, as they progressed beyond 7 others in the DP programming problems.

Second, we report a preliminary observation of student confidence levels throughout the problem-solving process. Interviewers periodically asked students their level of confidence in their solution, especially when a hint had been given for the question. Some students indicated high confidence in incorrect solutions, which was often followed by a desire to stop solving the problem and continue on to the next one. Another set of students self-expressed discontentment with correct answers, and then further reflection led them astray to other, incorrect solutions. However, most students were able to self-identify when they achieved a correct solution. Since DP questions may have multiple correct recurrences, it is important that students be able to not only define but also identify a correct recurrence.

6 DISCUSSION

In our analysis of student misconceptions, we discovered findings in line with previous research as well as novel results. In general, we found that students have difficulty across every step in the DP design process. Students specifically struggle with determining whether and how DP applies and, when it does, designing both top-down and bottom-up solutions.

6.1 Theme 1: Subproblem Identification

Students were unable to identify the subproblems, or the connections between subproblems, to form the solution to the larger problem (M1 and M2). This demonstrated that students were not able to grasp the core concept of DP: that the solution to subproblems can be stored and used to solve a bigger problem [2]. M1 and M2 are related, as difficulty with iterative code suggests a struggle with "bottom-up" array solutions, and solutions to subproblems are precisely what the array stores. Interestingly, most students who were able to identify the subproblem space were able to write iterative code. One can imagine a disconnect between defining subproblems and writing the bottom-up code, but as seen in Figure 1, only 1 student (S4) who was able to define "subproblem" and compose subproblems struggled with writing iterative code. This is an encouraging result, as it suggests that writing bottom-up code is not itself inherently challenging for students who understand the subproblem space.

Still, these common misconceptions are problematic because progress of any kind is unlikely without having identified the subproblems. Anecdotally, in books and lectures, we observe that subproblems and optimal substructure are often simply stated, with little insight into the process that led to the identification of subproblems and their relationships. It seems prudent to focus on this crucial design stage in order to help students past this initial hurdle.

6.2 Theme 2: Solution Technique

Another finding is that students conflate D&C and Greedy Algorithms with DP problems (M4 and M5). This finding is in line with previous research showing student difficulty distinguishing D&C and DP solutions [3]. In addition, we observed some students trying to apply automata and sets, two approaches not commonly-associated with problems of the type that we presented. If the student was not comfortable solving problems using DP, perhaps these were simply attempts to invoke well-understood, practiced knowledge from prior courses. However, it is not clear why so many of the students thought that these techniques were promising, even when these techniques did not lead to progress.

When students used incorrect strategies and made no progress, they were often quite confident in their answers. This suggests that further time could be spent attuning students to the features of problems that may suggest one algorithmic technique over another, or revisiting previously-learned techniques to compare and contrast them with more advanced techniques.

6.3 Theme 3: Defining a Recurrence

Many students proposed using a recurrence by beginning to name it with `D[i]` or `OPT[i]`, but were not able to decide how a recursive relationship could be expressed, even when they had decided on the subproblems. Furthermore, they were not able to recognize how the recursive relationship between the elements in the array would lead to a DP solution. This suggests that students have difficulty with recurrences and building an array from the recurrence, or deciding on how the array would be used. Hints given to students about how to form the array or connect subproblems generally did not help students progress.

How is it that students can sometimes identify subproblems but not be able to use them? We suspect that this has to do with students reciting information learned in lecture or tutorial, without understanding the relationship between the various steps of DP. This suggests that core notions of DP itself are not understood by the student. In accordance with results of Enström and Kann [4], students tend to find the idea of evaluating subproblems in the correct order to be a difficult concept to grasp.

7 FUTURE WORK

A single think-aloud study is insufficient for validating student misconceptions. We offer three areas here for future work.

First, recall that students who struggled on Q1 were next given Q4, and then often did well on Q2. Future work involves replacing Q4 with another, simpler DP problem (perhaps generating the nth Fibonacci number). Are the Q1-Q2 patterns sustained in this case? What would result from the interviewer intervening with explicit instruction on students who struggle on Q1? And are students able to apply this guidance to Q2?

Second, our interview protocol was not designed to assess prior knowledge that is likely to be prerequisite for solving DP problems. For example, we did not explicitly seek to identify student thinking on D&C problems, Recursion, Greedy Algorithms, or Algorithm Design in general. In particular, we suspect that some of the difficulty in T3 can be traced to student misconceptions of recursion and recursive structure, rather than some "new" misconceptions specific to DP.

Third, it is necessary to offer other DP questions to students, in order to generalize or refute misconceptions presented in this paper. What are the features of DP problems that lead to considerable difficulty? Are students able to progress easily on more introductory DP examples?

8 CONCLUSION

We have presented three themes that emerge from 7 misconceptions held by upper-level CS Students solving Dynamic Programming (DP) problems. The misconceptions explore specific areas of problematic thinking across all steps of the DP problem-solving process. We hope that this work may serve a similar purpose as the CS1 misconceptions literature: fostering for instructors an appreciation of the ways in which students can misapply core CS material.

We offer a tentative conclusion based on the students that we interviewed: typical DP instruction is insufficient if our goal is for students to be able to independently solve DP problems. Improving such instruction likely requires methods similar to those of Enström and Kann [4]. Based on our results, it seems prudent to intervene at the beginning of the DP design process, improving instruction on how students can identify subproblems and how and why composing those subproblems is important to a correct DP solution.

REFERENCES

[1] ACM/IEEE-CS Joint Task Force on Computing Curricula. Computer science curricula 2013. Technical report, ACM Press and IEEE Computer Society Press, 2013.

[2] T. H. Cormen, C. E. Leiserson, R. L. Rivest, and C. Stein. *Introduction to Algorithms, Third Edition.* The MIT Press, 2009.

[3] H. Danielsiek, W. Paul, and J. Vahrenhold. Detecting and understanding students' misconceptions related to algorithms and data structures. In *Proceedings of the 43rd ACM Technical Symposium on Computer Science Education*, pages 21–26, 2012.

[4] E. Enström and V. Kann. Iteratively intervening with the "most difficult" topics of an algorithms and complexity course. *Transactions on Computing Education*, 17(1):4:1–4:38, 2017.

[5] K. A. Ericsson and H. A. Simon. *Protocol Analysis: Verbal Reports as Data.* MIT Press, 1993.

[6] G. L. Herman, M. C. Loui, and C. Zilles. Creating the digital logic concept inventory. In *Proceedings of the 41st ACM Technical Symposium on Computer Science Education*, pages 102–106, 2010.

[7] L. C. Kaczmarczyk, E. R. Petrick, J. P. East, and G. L. Herman. Identifying student misconceptions of programming. In *Proceedings of the 41st ACM Technical Symposium on Computer Science Education*, pages 107–111, 2010.

[8] K. Karpierz and S. A. Wolfman. Misconceptions and concept inventory questions for binary search trees and hash tables. In *Proceedings of the 45th ACM Technical Symposium on Computer Science Education*, pages 109–114, 2014.

[9] Y. Kortsarts and V. Kolchenko. Dynamic programming across the CS curriculum (abstract only). In *Proceedings of the 43rd ACM Technical Symposium on Computer Science Education*, pages 671–671, 2012.

[10] R. McCauley, S. Grissom, S. Fitzgerald, and L. Murphy. Teaching and learning recursive programming: a review of the research literature. *Computer Science Education*, 25(1):37–66, 2015.

[11] W. Paul and J. Vahrenhold. Hunting high and low: Instruments to detect misconceptions related to algorithms and data structures. In *Proceedings of the 44th ACM Technical Symposium on Computer Science Education*, pages 29–34, 2013.

[12] A. Robins, J. Rountree, and N. Rountree. Learning and teaching programming: A review and discussion. *Computer Science Education*, 13(2):137–172, 2003.

[13] O. Seppälä, L. Malmi, and A. Korhonen. Observations on student misconceptions—a case study of the Build-Heap Algorithm. *Computer Science Education*, 16(3):241–255, 2006.

[14] C. Watson and F. W. Li. Failure rates in introductory programming revisited. In *Proceedings of the 19th ACM Conference on Innovation and Technology in Computer Science Education*, pages 39–44, 2014.

BlueBook: A Computerized Replacement for Paper Tests in Computer Science

Chris Piech
Stanford University
Stanford, CA
cpiech@stanford.edu

Chris Gregg
Stanford University
Stanford, CA
cgregg@stanford.edu

ABSTRACT

This paper presents *BlueBook*, a lightweight, cross-platform, computer-based, open source examination environment that overcomes traditional hurdles with computerized testing for computer science courses. As opposed to paper exam testing, *BlueBook* allows students to type coding problems on their laptops in an environment similar to their normal programming routine (e.g., with syntax highlighting), but purposefully does not provide them the ability to compile and/or run their code. We seamlessly transitioned from paper exams to *BlueBook* and found that students appreciated the ability to type their responses. Additionally, we are just beginning to harness the benefits to grading by having student answers in digital form. In the paper, we discuss the pedagogical benefits and trade-offs to using a computerized exam format, and we argue that both the students and the graders benefit from it.

KEYWORDS

Computerized Exam; Assessment; Pedagogy

ACM Reference Format:
Chris Piech and Chris Gregg. 2018. BlueBook: A Computerized Replacement for Paper Tests in Computer Science. In *SIGCSE '18: SIGCSE '18: The 49th ACM Technical Symposium on Computer Science Education, February 21–24, 2018, Baltimore, MD, USA.* ACM, New York, NY, USA, 6 pages. https: //doi.org/10.1145/3159450.3159587

1 INTRODUCTION

Although it is not universal, most university introductory computer science courses give traditional paper exams, asking students to hand-write code for the problems that test programming ability. Pedagogically, there are legitimate reasons for having students hand-write code. However, hand-written code does have its downsides, including the tedious nature of undoing (hand-erasing) incorrect work, messy handwriting (leading to longer grading times), and space limitations on paper. More importantly, students who are used to typing code for their assignments are forced to write code in a completely different manner when taking paper-based exams, and this can be stressful and does not necessarily assess the students accurately. Additionally, grading handwritten exams cannot benefit from automatic grading tools, which can be tremendously helpful as course enrollments escalate. In this paper, we present *BlueBook*, a lightweight, cross-platform, computer-based, open source examination environment that students can run on their laptops. There is nothing particularly fancy about *BlueBook* (see Section 3), though it does include public-key password-protection (so the students can download exams), encrypted local backups, and the ability to automatically submit exams to a server with a historical log of student work during the exam. *BlueBook* also provides syntax highlighting for code writing, but we purposely decided not to include any ability for students to compile and/or test their code (see Section 5).

With BlueBook, we believe that we have finally reached a point in our courses where computerized testing is a better assessment tool than paper-based testing. Our computer science department experimented with a computerized testing framework roughly a decade ago and at that time we were disappointed with the results. This was primarily due to two reasons: scaling the testing to large classes was difficult, and allowing the students to compile and test their code inhibited students' ability to finish the exams.

The scaling issue was almost purely technology-limited. At that time, not all students had laptops, and battery-technology was also at a point where most laptops could not hold a charge for an entire 3-hour final exam. Therefore, the tests were administered in a computer lab on campus, and this presented logistical problems for large classes. Now, 100% of our students have laptops, and while there are still some battery issues, we have found that in a class of 300 students, approximately 10% needed access to mains power, which was easy to provide through the use of power strips and extension cords.

The other main reason we ended the original computerized testing experiment was because we found that students who were able to compile and test their code spent too much time on getting the code to work. They were not finishing the exam problems and were frustrated when they could not produce fully-working solutions. Although we would still like to explore a modified compile-and/or-test framework, for *BlueBook* we decided to only allow students rudimentary syntax highlighting, and we found that students were able to complete the exams on time. See Section 5 for a discussion on allowing students to compile their code.

In this paper, we demonstrate how *BlueBook* can be both beneficial to students and graders, and we present pedagogical arguments for the use of a computerized testing environment. We also present evidence of our successful transition away from paper-based exams, as well as some of the remaining challenges that can be expected from using this type of test-taking system.

2 RELATED WORK

Computer-based testing (especially in computer science) has a long history of research and experimentation. The main focus of much of the research has been regarding student performance: is there a

SIGCSE '18, February 21–24, 2018, Baltimore , MD, USA

ACM ISBN 978-1-4503-5103-4/18/02...$15.00
https://doi.org/10.1145/3159450.3159587

quantitative difference in student performance between paper exams and computerized exams? Although this paper does not focus on that aspect particularly, we did not want to embark on our project without understanding the potential ramifications of student performance if we transitioned to computerized exams. Most of the research indicates that student performance is comparable between paper and computerized exams, and in many cases assessment was improved with the use of novel computerized tests. For example, in the early 1990s, Syang and Dale describe "Intelligent Tutoring Systems" that uses an adaptive test to assess performance[21], and adaptive testing is used on some prominent standardized tests, such as the SAT and the GRE[17, 24] We wanted *BlueBook* to model a paper-based exam as much as possible, though in Section 8 we discuss modifications that will diverge from this idea. There are also many reports on web-based testing[20, 26] and tablet-based testing[4, 23]. Because of the limited security available with web browsers, and because of the necessity for Internet access for web-based tests, we did not pursue a web-based model. We also wanted a test that was accessible by all of our students, and 100% of our students have laptop computers, so we decided to make it a Java-based program that could run on typical laptop computers.

Grissom et al.[8], and Lappalainen et al.[13] both reported that computer-based alternatives to paper tests gave students a better chance to fix errors, although in both experiments students were allowed to compile and test their code. As we discuss in Section 5, we purposefully did not allow students to compile or test their code, but this is a possible extension of the project.

Most of the research we have read indicates that there are no significant differences in performance between paper and computerized tests, particularly in early programming classes[3, 9, 12, 16, 19, 22, 23]. There are further studies that show distinct benefits to computer-based testing[11, 14, 25], and others that claim computerized testing has gender-equalization benefits[3, 25]. However, there are some reports that computerized testing can be detrimental, particularly when general access to computers (based on socioeconomic and cultural factors) was taken into account[15]. Because our students already use laptops on a daily basis, access is not an issue, but we think more research could be done to investigate this concern.

Another concern of ours was the student perception of a computerized test versus a paper-based test. Students are used to taking paper exams for many of their classes, but they have also taken many computerized standardized tests in their academic path, as well. We were also concerned about their anxiety regarding computerized exams. There have been a number of studies to address student perception and anxiety, and they predominantly show that students prefer computer-based exams[6, 7]. Some studies show mixed results, potentially based on gender and familiarity with computers in general[10], but others claim that there are benefits to taking a computerized exam for low-achieving students[18].

3 BLUEBOOK DETAILS

BlueBook is a Java program for administering exams. The program runs in full-screen mode (to inhibit students from attempting to use other programs, or the Internet), as can be seen in Figure 1. Students choose from among the problems listed at the top of the screen, and the question appears on the left side of the screen with a basic editor for answers on the right side of the screen. The questions can include both formatted text and graphics, and answers are typed into the editor. Code answers can be syntax-highlighted based on programming language. There is a count-down timer at the top of the screen, and this can be modified for different groups of students taking the exam (e.g., students who are allowed extra time can get an exam with a longer timer). *BlueBook* can be set up to either stop the test at the end of the timer, or it can simply act as a reminder.

Creating a *BlueBook* exam is straightforward, with problems written in basic HTML and answer starter code in plain text. Instructors run a separate Java program that creates the exam data with a given password, time limit, and other constants (e.g., a server address and directory location for results), and the exam data is then packaged with the *BlueBook* exam program. Students can download the exam data and *BlueBook* program prior to the exam. The exam data is encrypted with a public/private key encryption that would make it materially impossible for students to determine the questions before the exam time. Students do not need Internet access during the exam itself, though they submit the exams at the end via the Internet (or they can copy it to a flash drive for submission, if necessary).

When the exam is administered, students are given a password to begin the exam. *BlueBook* backs up student responses at an instructor-defined time interval (we have found that every 30 seconds provides adequate granularity), and the entire history of student answers is uploaded to the server (see Section 8, which discusses using this historical data). The backup is also encrypted with public key encryption.

During the exam, *BlueBook* keeps the computer screen maximized and does not allow students to exit out of the program without closing it. We have also disabled switching to other programs, and *BlueBook* is the only program that can run during the exam. That said, there are potential ways for students to break the system (e.g., with a Virtual Machine), but we have done what we can to mitigate the potential for cheating.

When students finish the exam, they can submit the exam to a server automatically, which utilizes the `scp` protocol. Students do need Internet access for this step, but in a class of 400+ students, we did not find any issues with submissions. If students can't submit online, they can email the solutions, or provide them to us on a flash drive. Students receive an email receipt for their submission and the encrypted history is also kept on their laptops in the event that the submission did not get properly saved on the server.

If *BlueBook* crashes while a student is taking the exam, there is also a *Crash Recovery* program that can be used to retrieve the encryped answers and return the student to the exam. This requires an additional password that instructors or TAs type in (so the student cannot recover the data on his or her own).

Once the answers are received on the server, instructors can extract the data to either `json` or plain text format for grading. We have created an additional utility that produces PDF files for uploading into a grading program (e.g., Gradescope[1]).

As *BlueBook* is open source, features can be added or modified as necessary, and we hope that other developers add interesting features as the program matures. Please email the authors for access to the current source code.

4 PRACTICAL CONSIDERATIONS

In this section we discuss the practical reasons we have decided to transition to *BlueBook* from a paper-based exam system. The initial inspiration for *BlueBook* arose from the simple desire to reduce the

Figure 1: *BlueBook* Screenshot. The program runs in full screen mode, and prohibits students from switching between programs. Problems are stated on the left, and students answer on the right. Answers can be syntax-highlighted based on programming language.

amount of paper being used, and to minimize the logistical issues that using paper entails. Upon consideration of the ramifications of a digital exam, we quickly realized that there were numerous areas where we could benefit from the idea.

Our paper-based workflow included time consuming printing and scanning (we use an online grading system that accepts scanned PDF exams), and it seemed feasible to cut out the analog steps on both ends: if producing the exams is digital, and grading the exams is digital, we reasoned that it would be ideal to keep the exam experience digital, as well. For a 400 student class (which is about the average size of the introductory courses at Stanford), a 10-page, double-sided exam produces 2000 pages (four reams!) of paper. To physically produce an exam takes a significant amount of time, even if the printing and copying technology works perfectly. Once the exam is over, the scanning process involves removing staples (and keeping track of the loose pages of the exams), and running the exams through a scanner. Our department has an excellent scanner, but for large classes this process can take many hours, and getting the scanner to produce readable scans reliably often requires fine-tuning the scanner settings and some good luck.

The exam-taking process itself can also benefit from a computer-based exam. *BlueBook* is secure enough to allow students to download the encrypted questions ahead of time, so students can come into the exam, sit down, and start the exam immediately upon receiving the password. There is no need to hand out the exam, although we do allow students to use scratch paper, which is freely available around the exam room. Students do need to use their own laptops to take the exam, but we found that less than 10% of students needed access to power-points for their computers, and we were able to accommodate that even for very large classes. The timing of the exam is easier to manage, as well: students who show up a few minutes late will have their own timer on the exam and (if allowed) can simply take the extra minutes at the end of class to finish. This completely fixed the issue of trying to pry the exams from students at the end of the exam. Additionally, students who receive extra time on an exam can have their own data files that give them a timer appropriate for their accommodations. Because the exams are submitted wirelessly (and this is the only time students need Internet access), there is no need to physically collect anything at the end of the exam.

Because exam delivery is digital, we also found significant benefit for students who needed to take the exam remotely. Some of our classes have offsite students who take the exam with a local proctor, and *BlueBook* significantly improved the test-taking process for these students. The proctor simply needs to know the exam password to give to the students at the start of the exam. Other students who needed to take the exam remotely (e.g., traveling athletes) benefited similarly.

By and large, the students were happy with the practical benefits they received by using *BlueBook*. We heard many comments that the experience was better than taking a paper exam, and that it was more like their normal programming practice. See Section 6 for details on student experience.

Graders for *BlueBook* exams were unanimous in their support for using the program. Issues related to reading handwriting disappear with *BlueBook*, and grading typed text is altogether easier than grading scanned, handwritten answers. An additional benefit derived from our ability to have students graded anonymously. In our pre-*BlueBook* grading, graders could use handwriting and a students name to infer either the individual or demographic details of the student they are grading. When grading digital exams we can avoid these unmeasured and undesirable problems.

We implemented an auto-grading system that allows graders to run student code during grading. This saved considerable time in grading students who had correctly or almost-correctly working code, and the only downside we noted was that virtually all student code starts with at least some syntax errors, and correcting those can take some time during grading. See Section 8 about ideas we are working on to mitigate this aspect of the auto-grading, and see Section 5 about why we don't allow students to compile and test their code during exams.

Practically, transitioning to a computer-based exam saves time and physical resources (e.g., paper and toner), students like it better than paper exams, and it opens up new grading avenues that are not available when the exams are analog.

5 PEDAGOGY

When we created *BlueBook*, we were understandably concerned about whether the idea was pedagogically sound. There is a long history of students handwriting code (both on exams and in general), and there are good arguments to suggest that students should demonstrate these skills while in a CS1 or CS2 course. Some of the arguments in favor of paper-based testing are listed below:

(1) By forcing students to write out their code, they will need to plan it out (whether in pseudocode or another form), and that planning is critical to being a good programmer.
(2) Many coding interviews require applicants to hand-write code (on paper or a white board, for instance), and handwriting code for exams gives students practice in these skills.
(3) When students take computer-based exams, they write too much code and by limiting the space on paper, they are forced to think through their code to create concise responses.

We do not necessarily find fault in the points listed above, but our opinion is that they are minor concerns that can be mitigated elsewhere in the computer science curriculum (or even in CS1 and CS2 courses in different assessments). Additionally, except in programming interviews, programmers rarely write code out by hand. We do think that it can actually be detrimental to students to have to hand-write programs when they are used to typing them, and during an exam we would rather students focus on solving the problem than potentially being distracted by a new way of writing their programs down.

When we brought up the idea to try a computerized test in our department, we learned that it had been tried before, with poor results. In the previous experiment, students were expected to write their answers and also had the ability to compile their code, and (most importantly) to run the code through a suite of tests. This proved disastrous, as students spent too much time trying to get their code to pass the tests, and many students did poorly on the overall exam because they were not willing to move to other problems if their code was failing tests. Partially because of this data, and particularly because we wanted *BlueBook* to mimic a paper testing environment as much as possible, we made the decision to disallow any compiling or running of code during the exam. Although occasionally students requested those features, the majority of students did not concern themselves with it, and seemed more pleased with the syntax highlighting and with the simple ability to type their answers. From a pedagogical standpoint, disallowing compiling or running of code does force students to think through their answers fully, and students can not simply try different solutions until they land on one that works (as is, unfortunately, what some students do on coding assignments).

Argument (3) discusses the limiting effect of a paper exam, to encourage students to write concise code that fits on the paper. We did not limit code size in *BlueBook*, and we did find that some students wrote more code than was required to answer some problems. We were initially concerned that this would be a bigger issue than it was, and it would be easy to modify *BlueBook* to limit student answer length. We also sometimes add in the problem description a length suggestion (e.g., "the reference solution is ten lines of code"), and this influences students to produce a similar length for their answers. Additionally, when limiting paper answer space, students with larger (or messier) handwriting are unfairly penalized, and this bias is eliminated with typewritten answers.

6 STUDENT EXPERIENCES AND FEEDBACK

When we first introduced *BlueBook* to one CS2 class, we gave the students a practice exam using *BlueBook* a few days before a normally scheduled midterm, which was to be available with both *BlueBook* and on paper (student's choice). We had roughly one hundred students take the practice exam, and we "exit polled" them after the exam to get their feedback and to provide *beta* test bug reports for the software. The feedback was predominantly positive, with over 95% of the students polled indicating that they would elect to take the exam using *BlueBook* for the actual midterm. The following represents a (paraphrased) sample of the specific responses to our questions:

- I liked the ability to type answers and to edit my responses.
- I didn't feel as constrained with space as on a paper exam.
- The countdown timer was helpful so I could pace myself.
- I was able to answer questions faster and better because I type faster than I write.
- My hand doesn't feel cramped like it does after paper exams.
- I liked having the question and answer on the same page, so I didn't have to flip back and forth.
- The syntax highlighting was helpful.
- We're saving the trees!

During the practice exam the program crashed for three students, but they were able to quickly get back to the exam with the help of a TA with the crash recovery password. No data was lost.

For the midterm and final exam for the initial CS2 class, roughly two-thirds of the students elected to take the exam using *BlueBook*. We allowed students the use of as much scratch paper as they wanted to use, and we provided power strips for those worried about battery life. The following is a sample of reasons students elected to take the paper-based exam:

- My laptop can't last for the entire exam [*note*: despite available power strips].
- I'm used to paper and it feels more normal.
- The font is too small on my computer [we have fixed that issue]

After the midterm exam, we polled the class about whether they wanted us to administer the final exam using *BlueBook*. There was an overwhelming desire from the students to allow them to use it, to the point that the course staff admitted that there would be a great number of upset students if we didn't have a *BlueBook* option.

One concern we have about the student experience is that laptops, by the nature of their vertical screens, are easily viewable by nearby students. We don't know if there was more cheating during *BlueBook* exams, but this is a downside to the format.

We have successfully used *BlueBook* during a subsequent CS2 offering, and we only allowed paper exams on a case-by-case basis. We gave students practice *BlueBook* exams (to take on their own), and we reminded them about having a full battery multiple times before the exams. Less than five percent of the students ended up taking the exam on paper (for similar reasons as above). We did not receive any direct complaints about using *BlueBook*, and students readily accepted the exams in that format.

7 GRADING BENEFITS

Although we did not initially anticipate it, we found that having digital answers was a boon for exam grading. As discussed in Section 4, we saved a considerable amount of time post-exam with no need to shuffle vast amounts of paper for scanning into the online grading program. For the final exam in the most recent course to use *BlueBook*, we scheduled the grading for three hours after the exam, and we could have cut that time down if necessary. We do have to post-process the exams for the auto-grader and for uploading to the online grading program, but we have scripted this to streamline it.

Graders were happy that they did not have to struggle to read handwritten code, and we also realized that we likely reduced grading bias that might happen with neat-vs-messy handwriting.

We wrote an online auto-grader for student code that is still in its preliminary stages but that shows great promise (see Section 8 for our anticipated future work). All code problems from *BlueBook* get uploaded to an online database that is available to graders, and a web-based front-end allows graders to compile and run student code in a testing framework. As with any auto-grading, the specific code tests do have to be prepared separately, and this is not necessarily trivial. However, we found that creating the grading tests before the exam provided a nice forcing function to ensure that the exam questions were reasonable and that the rubric solutions worked correctly.

Interestingly, very few student responses compile straightaway, but the graders quickly get used to fixing syntax errors to get the code to compile. The workflow for most graders was as follows:

(1) Scan the student response in the grading software.
(2) Switch to the auto-grader and attempt to fix syntax errors and test.
(3) If the testing showed correct results, immediately mark the answer as correct.
(4) If the testing showed incorrect results, revert to the grading rubric, fixing the code to test as needed.

Graders reported that having the auto-grader was normally helpful, and if it did not always save time, it gave the them additional peace-of-mind that they were grading the problems better. We frequently found graders helping each other debug student code to enhance grading.

8 FUTURE WORK

We have a number of enhancements planned for *BlueBook* itself, for improving the grading after the exam has been processed, and also for research purposes. As we mentioned before, we also hope that by making *BlueBook* open source it can improve even faster.

8.1 BlueBook Enhancements

Compiling/Running Code Despite the past discouraging results of allowing students to compile and test their code, we would like *BlueBook* to have the option for one or both of those features. We think there is a the potential to allow students to at least compile (or perform *lint*-like behavior) so they can fix some of their own syntax errors (so graders do not have to do it). We are considering allowing students to compile only at the end of the exam for a certain amount of time, or only to compile a fixed number of times. As discussed in Section 5, allowing testing of code during an exam is riskier, but having the option would allow for interesting research about how students run code in a timed testing environment.

Live Exam Updating As every instructor knows, exams are rarely perfect, and in-class announcements about problems are sometimes necessary. In its current state, *BlueBook* does not require Internet access during examinations, but we would like to introduce an update functionality to allow for tests to be updated mid-exam for typos and clarifications. This could cut down on announcements, although there is a concern about how the news is delivered to the students (e.g., as a pop-up message?)

Increased Security We are confident that the current security for *BlueBook* is adequate, but there is a potential for cheating if students aren't taking the exam at the exact same time (e.g., for remote students). We plan on adding a feature that logs students when they first start the exam (which will require temporary Internet access), so that we can track when the exam was accessed.

Per-problem Timer Although students reported that the timer was beneficial to their pacing of the exam, we are considering adding more granularity in the form of an individual timer per problem that shows students how much time they have spent on a particular problem. This could be further expanded by providing students an "optimum response time," as described by Delen[5].

Graphics and Math Answers At the moment, *BlueBook* works well for plain-text and coding questions, but it is not appropriate for courses where students need to answer with drawings, or with mathematical symbols. Both of these features could be added. Mixing text with drawing provides a challenge for auto-grading, but that problem is not insurmountable. If we were to add a math/equations editor, students would necessarily need practice using it before it would make practical sense to use for an exam.

8.2 Better Grading

Auto-Syntax Correction Because we now have digital exam answers, we can use the information to better inform our grading. We would like to enhance the auto-grader in a couple of particular ways. The first is to attempt some basic automatic syntax error correction. Automatic syntax error correction is a decades-old problem (see [2], for instance), but during grading we see regular syntax errors that we don't penalize students for (unless they are egregious), and we would like to investigate fixing them automatically. Very few student code answers compile immediately, but most can be fixed with a small number of easy-to-see corrections.

Nearest Correct Code Another area we have started implementing is to provide a "nearest correct code" window alongside code that needs to be graded. Any code that has been graded as correct will be flagged in the database, and as graders are looking at an ungraded problem, the closest correct solution will be shown in an adjoining window. We are working on a neural network that determines which of the correct solutions is the closest. We expect that such a feature will have the dual benefit of speeding up grading and also helping to normalize grades for similar solutions.

8.3 Research Opportunities

Because *BlueBook* captures student work at an instructor-defined frequency (we have set ours to collect responses every 30 seconds), there is a tremendous amount of data that can be mined regarding how students take examinations. For example, how long do students spend on individual problems, and do they spend more or less time on earlier problems? Do students routinely go back and make significant changes to early problems? Do students write code all at once, or do they make frequent pauses?

As mentioned above, there are potential research questions regarding allowing students to compile and/or run their code during examinations, and once we implement these features into *BlueBook*, we will be able to investigate them.

Finally, we would like to collect data on how graders are assessing students when they have the ability to run and test student code. With some of the grading updates mentioned above, we can start research in that direction.

9 SUMMARY

Our implementation and use of the *BlueBook* computerized exam software has had multiple and significant benefits to our CS2 course. It has helped streamline and improve our exam logistics both before, during, and after the exams. Students have embraced the software and have had provided predominantly positive feedback. Indeed, some students would have been disappointed if they were not allowed to use *BlueBook* on exams. Graders were happy to improve their experience with the ability to compile and test student responses. We likely minimized bias and saved time due to handwriting issues. We are excited about the research avenues we are planning based on *BlueBook*'s data gathering and reporting, and by future enhancements to the software.

ACKNOWLEDGMENTS

The authors would like to thank Stanford undergraduates Ali Malik and Brahm Capoor, who have spent countless hours helping with the coding and roll-out of BlueBook.

REFERENCES

[1] [n. d.]. Gradescope. https://gradescope.com. ([n. d.]). Accessed: 2017-08-24.
[2] Alfred V Aho and Thomas G Peterson. 1972. A minimum distance error-correcting parser for context-free languages. *SIAM J. Comput.* 1, 4 (1972), 305–312.
[3] Eren Can AYBEK and R Nükhet DEMİRTAŞLI. 2014. A Comparison of Psychometric Properties of a General Ability Test Which Administered In Paper-Pencil and Computer Based Form. *Elementary Education Online* 13, 4 (2014), 1400–1413.
[4] Matthew J Cheesman, Prasad Chunduri, Mary-Louise Manchadi, Kay Colthorpe, and Ben Matthews. 2015. Student Interaction with a Computer Tablet Exam Application Replicating the Traditional Paper Exam. *Mobile Computing* 4 (2015), 10–21.
[5] Erhan Delen. 2015. Enhancing a Computer-Based Testing Environment with Optimum Item Response Time. *EURASIA Journal of Mathematics, Science and Technology Education* 11, 6 (2015), 1457–1472.
[6] Robert Deloatch, Brian P. Bailey, and Alex Kirlik. 2016. Measuring Effects of Modality on Perceived Test Anxiety for Computer Programming Exams. In *Proceedings of the 47th ACM Technical Symposium on Computing Science Education (SIGCSE '16)*. ACM, New York, NY, USA, 291–296. https://doi.org/10.1145/2839509.2844604
[7] Victor Faniran and Nurudeen Ajayi. 2016. Students' perceptions of computer-based assessments: A case of UKZN. In *IST-Africa Week Conference, 2016*. IEEE, 1–9.
[8] Scott Grissom, Laurie Murphy, Renée McCauley, and Sue Fitzgerald. 2016. Paper vs. Computer-based Exams: A Study of Errors in Recursive Binary Tree Algorithms. In *Proceedings of the 47th ACM Technical Symposium on Computing Science Education (SIGCSE '16)*. ACM, New York, NY, USA, 6–11. https://doi.org/10.1145/2839509.2844587
[9] D. Gürsoy. 2016. Assessing novice programmers' performance in programming exams via computer-based test. (June 2016). http://essay.utwente.nl/70114/
[10] Pari Delir Haghighi, Judy Sheard, Chee-Kit Looi, David Jonassen, and Mitsuru Ikeda. 2005. Summative Computer Programming Assessment Using Both Paper and Computer.. In *ICCE*. 67–75.
[11] Monirosadat Hosseini and Seyyed Morteza Hashemi Toroujeni. [n. d.]. Replacing Paper-Based Testing with an Alternative for the Assessment of Iranian Undergraduate Students: Administration Mode Effect on Testing Performance. ([n. d.]).
[12] Hanho Jeong. 2014. A comparative study of scores on computer-based tests and paper-based tests. *Behaviour & Information Technology* 33, 4 (2014), 410–422.
[13] Vesa Lappalainen, Antti-Jussi Lakanen, and Harri Högmander. 2016. Paper-based vs Computer-based Exams in CS1. In *Proceedings of the 16th Koli Calling International Conference on Computing Education Research (Koli Calling '16)*. ACM, New York, NY, USA, 172–173. https://doi.org/10.1145/2999541.2999565
[14] Karen A Maguire, Daniel A Smith, Sara A Brallier, and Linda J Palm. 2010. Computer-based testing: A comparison of computer-based and paper-and-pencil assessment. *Academy of Educational Leadership Journal* 14, 4 (2010), 117.
[15] Óscar Marcenaro-Gutiérrez and Luis Alejandro López-Agudo. 2016. MIND THE GAP: ANALYSING THE FACTORS BEHIND THE GAP IN STUDENTSâĂŹPERFORMANCE BETWEEN PENCIL AND COMPUTER BASED ASSESSMENT METHODS. *Revista de Economía Aplicada* 24, 71 (2016).
[16] Alan D Mead and Fritz Drasgow. 1993. Equivalence of computerized and paper-and-pencil cognitive ability tests: A meta-analysis. *Psychological Bulletin* 114, 3 (1993), 449.
[17] Craig N Mills and Manfred Steffen. 2000. The GRE computer adaptive test: Operational issues. In *Computerized adaptive testing: Theory and practice*. Springer, 75–99.
[18] Stavros A Nikou and Anastasios A Economides. 2016. The impact of paper-based, computer-based and mobile-based self-assessment on students' science motivation and achievement. *Computers in Human Behavior* 55 (2016), 1241–1248.
[19] Jan M Noyes and Kate J Garland. 2008. Computer-vs. paper-based tasks: Are they equivalent? *Ergonomics* 51, 9 (2008), 1352–1375.
[20] Sanjay Kumar Singh and Arvind Kumar Tiwari. 2016. Design and Implementation of Secure Computer Based Examination System Based On B/S Structure. *International Journal of Applied Engineering Research* 11, 1 (2016), 312–318.
[21] Angel Syang and Nell B. Dale. 1993. Computerized Adaptive Testing in Computer Science: Assessing Student Programming Abilities. *SIGCSE Bull.* 25, 1 (March 1993), 53–56. https://doi.org/10.1145/169073.169109
[22] Krisztina Tóth. 2015. *THE COMPARATIVE ANALYSIS OF PAPER-AND-PENCIL AND COMPUTER-BASED INDUCTIVE REASONING, PROBLEM SOLVING AND READING COMPREHENSION TEST RESULTS OF UPPER ELEMENTARY SCHOOL STUDENTS.* Ph.D. Dissertation. szte.
[23] Andrew Valentine, Iouri Belski, and Margaret Hamilton. 2017. Developing creativity and problem-solving skills of engineering students: a comparison of web-and pen-and-paper-based approaches. *European Journal of Engineering Education* (2017), 1–21.
[24] Howard Wainer, Eric T Bradlow, and Zuru Du. 2000. Testlet response theory: An analog for the 3PL model useful in testlet-based adaptive testing. In *Computerized adaptive testing: Theory and practice*. Springer, 245–269.
[25] Patricia Wallace and Roy B Clariana. 2005. Gender differences in computer-administered versus paper-based tests. *International Journal of Instructional Media* 32, 2 (2005), 171.
[26] Yuan Zhenming, Zhang Liang, and Zhan Guohua. 2003. A novel web-based online examination system for computer science education. In *33rd ASEE/IEEE Frontiers in Education Conference*. 5–8.

Using a Computer-based Testing Facility to Improve Student Learning in a Programming Languages and Compilers Course

Terence Nip*
University of Illinois at Urbana-Champaign
Urbana, Illinois
nip2@illinois.edu

Elsa L. Gunter
University of Illinois at Urbana-Champaign
Urbana, Illinois
egunter@illinois.edu

Geoffrey L. Herman
University of Illinois at Urbana-Champaign
Urbana, Illinois
glherman@illinois.edu

Jason W. Morphew
University of Illinois at Urbana-Champaign
Urbana, Illinois
jmorphe2@illinois.edu

Matthew West
University of Illinois at Urbana-Champaign
Urbana, Illinois
mwest@illinois.edu

ABSTRACT

While most efforts to improve students' learning in computer science education have focused on designing new pedagogies or tools, comparatively little research has focused on redesigning examinations to improve students' learning. Cognitive science research, however, has robustly demonstrated that getting students to practice using their knowledge in testing environments can significantly improve learning through a phenomenon known as the testing effect. The testing effect has been shown to improve learning more than rehearsal strategies such as re-reading a textbook or re-watching lectures. In this paper, we present a quasi-experimental study to examine the effect of using frequent, automated examinations in an advanced computer science course, "Programming Languages and Compilers" (CS 421). In Fall 2014, students were given traditional paper-based exams, but in Fall 2015 a computer-based testing facility enabled the course to offer more frequent examinations while other aspects of the course were held constant. A comparison of 292 student scores across the two semesters revealed a significant change in the distribution of students' grades with fewer students failing the final examination, and proportionately more students now earning grades of B and C instead. This data suggests that focusing on redesigning the nature of examinations may indeed be a relatively untapped opportunity to improve students' learning.

*Now at Google.

SIGCSE '18, February 21–24, 2018, Baltimore, MD, USA

ACM ISBN 978-1-4503-5103-4/18/02...$15.00
https://doi.org/10.1145/3159450.3159500

CCS CONCEPTS

• **Social and professional topics → Computing education; Student assessment;** • **Software and its engineering → General programming languages; Compilers;**

KEYWORDS

Programming languages, compilers, testing effect, computer-based testing

ACM Reference format:
Terence Nip, Elsa L. Gunter, Geoffrey L. Herman, Jason W. Morphew, and Matthew West. 2018. Using a Computer-based Testing Facility to Improve Student Learning in a Programming Languages and Compilers Course. In *Proceedings of SIGCSE '18: The 49th ACM Technical Symposium on Computing Science Education, Baltimore, MD, USA, February 21–24, 2018 (SIGCSE '18),* 6 pages.
https://doi.org/10.1145/3159450.3159500

1 INTRODUCTION

While most efforts to improve students' learning in computer science education have focused on designing new pedagogies (e.g., pair programming [32] and CS unplugged [30]) or new pedagogical tools (e.g., block languages [36] and informative compiler error messages [28]), comparatively little research has focused on redesigning traditional models of assessment. The lack of research and development on efforts to change the way that we test students may mean that we are leaving valuable and viable options for improving students' learning untapped. One of the most robust findings in cognitive science, the testing effect, suggests that we can improve students by engaging them in more test-taking behaviors and discouraging them for from engaging only in rehearsal strategies such as rereading the textbook or rewatching a video lecture [3, 11, 15]. Unfortunately, weaker students are the ones most likely to persist in these less effective learning strategies [15].

Class sizes continue to grow at the University of Illinois at Urbana-Champaign, increasing the difficulty of assessing students in a fair and timely manner. In response to these difficulties, we recently created a engineering college-wide Computer-Based Testing Facility (CBTF) with the goal of reducing the overhead of administering examinations and thus enabling faculty to give more frequent and smaller exams to their students. The CBTF provides a central testing facility with continual proctoring [39]. Rather than schedule a single hour for an exam with 100 or more students (and afterwards accommodate any students who cannot attend that hour due to time conflicts), each student selects an hour that is convenient for them during an exam window to take a proctored exam [37]. These exams have randomized content to discourage cheating and enable this asynchronous testing environment [7]. In Spring 2017, the CBTF ran 37,000 exams for 4,500 students in 18 courses from 5 engineering departments.

During Fall 2015, the enrollment of "Programming Languages and Compilers" nearly doubled from 104 students to 188 students. As enrollments had been increasing, the instructors were increasingly concerned that learning outcomes were declining and that failure rates were rising. From the instructors' perspective, students seemed to be relying too much on their peers or other resources when completing their machine problems (i.e., intensive coding problem sets) and were not actively engaging on their own. Consequently, the instructors, like many other instructors using the CBTF, increased the number of times that students were tested in a semester. In addition to the standard two midterms and a final examination, students were also tested four times on their understanding of their code for week-long machine problems. For the remainder of this paper, we treat this change in the course as a quasi-experimental study investigating the effect of using examinations as a learning tool. Most aspects of the course remained the same between semesters, having the same instructor and approximately the same assignments. The only major changes made were the shift from paper-based examinations to computer-based examinations, and the switch to using short examinations to assess students' efforts on and understanding of their machine problems. We evaluate the impact of these changes on students' learning by comparing students' performance on the final examination from both semesters. We explore the following research question, did switching to exam-based assessments for machine problems improve students' learning in programming languages and compilers?

2 BACKGROUND

Left to their own devices, students typically select study strategies that tend to be passive and focus on encoding processes such as rereading a textbook, reviewing notes, or rewatching lectures [15]. Students, especially those who are lowest performing, tend to select inefficient study strategies. Retrieval practice, often in the form of test taking, has been shown to produce better long-term retention in both clinical studies [9, 31] as well as secondary and university classrooms [1, 22, 25, 27], compared with restudying materials. For example, McDermott et al. [27] utilized a within-subjects design with middle school students where the course material was randomly assigned to be either tested, restudied, or not tested or restudied. Students recalled facts at a higher rate for course material that was tested than for course material that was either restudied or not tested. Similar results were found for factual recall with undergraduate students in an online Psychology course [1].

The benefits of retrieval practice, also known as the testing effect or test-enhanced learning, are likely due to the ways in which testing facilitates the representation and retrieval of information stored in memory. Successful retrieval is thought to change the information's representation in memory such that it becomes easier to retrieve in the future [2]. However, the beneficial effects of testing are also found for items that were answered unsuccessfully during initial testing, suggesting that merely engaging in retrieval attempts may potentiate future learning of material [29]. Kornell, Hays, and Bjork [16] suggest that retrieval attempts during testing facilitate deep processing of the material, strengthen pathways for correctly recalled information, and weaken pathways for information which was incorrectly recalled.

Although most research concerning the testing effect has used either identical questions or very similar questions as those used in the retrieval practice, a few studies have demonstrated improvements for rephrased questions [22]. Other studies have shown improved performance on new inferential questions covering previously tested material [4]. In addition, some studies have found that retrieval attempts enhances performance on related but untested material [6, 8, 19]. However, other studies have found no testing effect for related, but untested material [20, 38].

In the laboratory, much of the research concerning the testing effect has focused on memory tasks, while research in the classroom has utilized content focused on declarative memory, such as word pairs in second language learning [13], factual recall in psychology [24, 26], short answer questions in medical education [17], recalling facts from a lecture [5], and multiple choice questions involving recalling or applying definitions in a middle school science course [21]. The benefit of testing on problem-solving tasks, such as those found in computer science courses, is less clear. Some researchers have asserted that testing effects are lessened as the complexity of the information increases [10, 35]. However, other researchers have documented testing effects for more complex tasks such as reading comprehension and inference tasks, learning spatial relationships, and constructing concept maps [12, 14]. For example, McDaniel, Howard, and Einstein (2009) had undergraduate students read two passages explaining how pumps and brakes operate [23]. After either studying or engaging in retrieval practice, students completed a free-recall task, multiple-choice factual recall, and a short-answer inference task that asked them to apply their knowledge about brakes and pumps in novel ways. Students engaged in retrieval outperformed students who reread the material on all three measures. However, retrieval was not more effective than note taking for the inference task.

To our knowledge, only three studies have examined the benefits of testing in mathematical problem-solving contexts. Leahy, Hanham, and Sweller [18] engaged elementary students in solving problems involving reading a bus schedule. Students who engaged in repeated studying of worked examples outperformed those who studied an example and then completed practice problems on immediate post-test and performed the same as those who completed practice problems on a delayed post-test. Van Gog and Kester engaged novices in learning to solve problems involving electrical circuits by either studying four worked examples or studying two worked examples followed by attempting to solve two isomorphic problems [33]. Participants in the study-only condition scored the same as those in the testing condition on the immediate post-test and higher on the delayed post-test one week later. Van Gog et al. compared retrieval versus restudy in students engaged in learning problem solving from worked examples across four experiments and found no advantage for testing over repeated studying for problem-solving tasks involving electrical circuits or probability distributions [34]. However, these findings may be the result of samples with low prior knowledge and motivation to learn from the worked examples. In these studies, the participants had very little experience with the topic, indicated by their low pre-study conceptual scores. In addition, the authors do not indicate whether the participants received feedback from their retrieval attempts.

3 METHODS

CS 421, "Programming Languages and Compilers", is a large enrollment (100-200 students per semester) upper division course. Students learn about language design principles, abstract data types, functional programming, and type systems. Students also learn about the basics of lexing, parsing, syntax-directed translation, semantic analysis, and code generation.

In Fall 2014, 104 students took CS 421. The course administered 11 written homework assignments, 11 machine problems, 2 paper-based midterm examinations, and a paper-based final examination. Examinations were composed of short programming problems, a few computation problems, and a few multiple true-false questions. In Fall 2015, 188 students took CS 421. That semester, the course migrated to the CBTF while most other aspects of the course remained unchanged (e.g., students were still given 11 homework assignments). The content coverage and question structure of the midterm and final examinations were kept similar (e.g., true/false questions were kept the same, but students used graphical tools to draw parse trees rather than create them by hand). However, the course changed the way that four of the machine problems were submitted. Rather than turn in code at the end of a week of work on the problem, students were given a test in the CBTF that required the students to code one fifth of the machine problem. Which fifth the students completed was randomly selected by the testing environment in the CBTF.

As a quasi-experimental study, we argue that most aspects between the course were held constant. The instructor was the same both semesters. Students taking the course in Fall 2014 and Fall 2015 had taken similar prior coursework and had spent a similar number of semesters in the degree program. The number of assignments was held constant. Only the modality of the midterm and final examinations and the modality of assessment of four machine problems were changed. As we describe in the next following subsection, the instructors strove to maintain parity between semesters in how students were assessed on midterm and final examinations. Consequently, we believe that the switch to using the CBTF to test students' understanding of the machine problems constituted the primary treatment for students' learning.

This sequential study design has the added benefit of avoiding ethical dilemmas arising from randomly withholding the treatment from students and the logistical challenges of requiring a single instructor to run two different versions of the course in parallel. Although we could not use random assignment for the treatments, thus limiting the causal claims that we can make, the ecological validity, large sample size, and similarity of the students provide a sufficiently controlled and well-powered study to conclude that the findings from the study may be considered to be robust.

3.1 Details of the computer-based examinations

The testing environment for the CBTF relies on a web-based homework system called PrairieLearn. PrairieLearn is an open-source platform that provides native support for standard question types such as multiple-choice, short-answer, and multiple true-false. It also allows students to upload files such as text files or PDFs. Beyond these basic functions, the system also allows instructors to supply their own client- and server-side code to generate new question types.

When migrating the paper-based midterm and final examinations to the CBTF, the CS 421 instructors used many of the standard features in an attempt to mirror the content from the paper-based exams, asking students to complete multiple true-false questions, provide answers to computation problems in short-answer boxes, and had students upload text files to be graded manually by the course staff. The instructors also developed additional tools such as creating an in-browser code editor that enabled students to write their code within the PrairieLearn environment rather than write code in a separate program and upload it.

Further, the instructors developed two libraries using HTML and JavaScript: one to display proof trees (and have students be able to identify errors in the proofs) (Figure 1), and another to allow students to construct proof trees from scratch (Figure 2). Similarly, the instructors created a library that allowed students to "draw" parse trees in the browser so that students could demonstrate their mastery of grammars - in particular, recognizing when a grammar is ambiguous and how strings can be parsed given an unambiguous grammar. The instructors created the libraries so that students could perform similar tasks to what they performed on the paper-based examinations, maintaining as much parity as possible with examinations across semesters.

3.2 Analysis

To compare student performance across semesters, we compared student performance on the final examinations. The final examination is a stronger measure of student learning than course grades as there are fewer sources of variation in student grades in a single examination than over the course of semester (i.e., a student may get sick and fail to submit an assignment, dramatically reducing their grade even if the student learned the content). We perform an independent samples t-test to compare overall student performance on the final examination. We perform χ^2 tests to compare the distribution of students' grades on the final examination.

The statistical analysis reported in this paper was conducted by a educational psychology graduate student who is not affiliated with either CS 421 or the CBTF, minimizing bias in the reporting and interpretation of findings.

4 RESULTS

The mean final exam score was 4% higher in Fall 2015 (mean = 76.8%, sd = 15.6%) than in Fall 2014 (mean = 72.5%, sd = 18.6%). To determine whether altering the assessment schedule led to greater

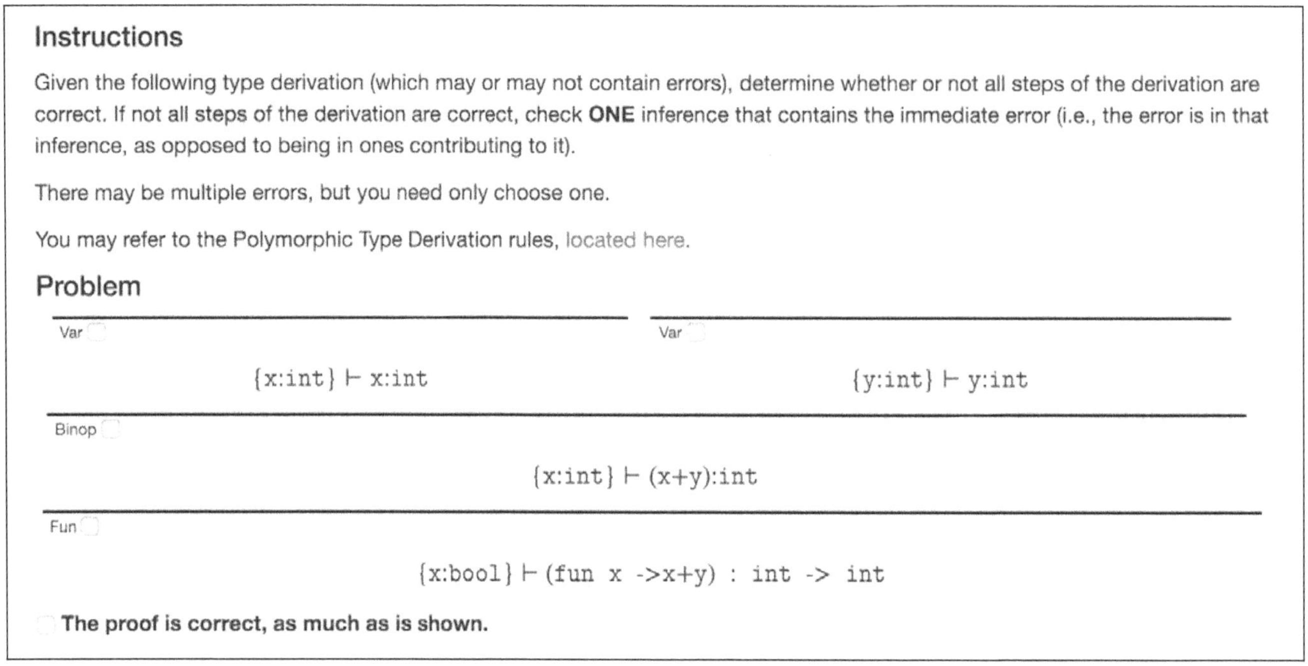

Figure 1: A proof tree with checkboxes for identifying mistakes.

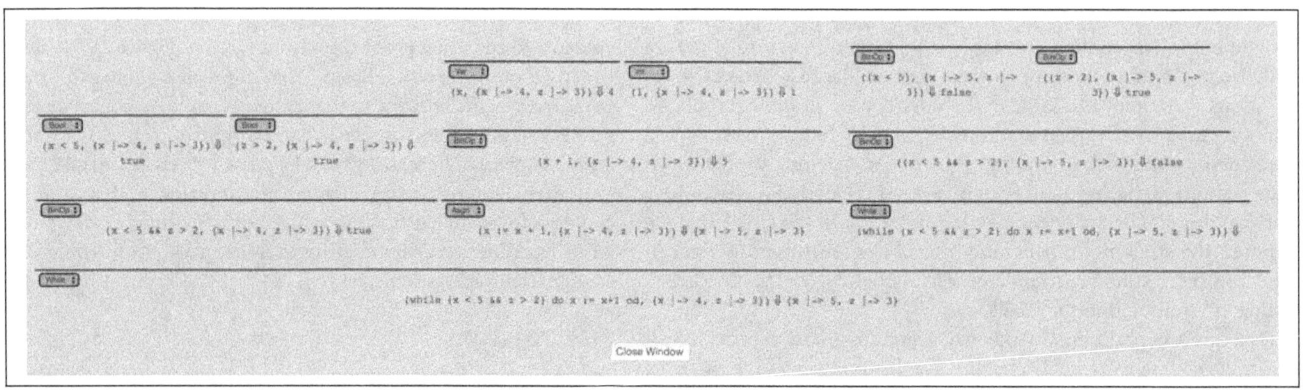

Figure 2: An example complete proof tree derivation.

performance on the final exam, we conducted an independent samples t-test. The assumption of equal variances was tested with the folded F-test. The variance was different between the two semesters ($F' = 1.43$, $p = .04$), therefore a Satterthwaite correction was used. Shapiro-Wilk's tests of normality indicated that the distribution of exam grades deviated from normality for both semesters. The central limit theorem suggests that independent samples t-tests are robust to deviations from normality with large sample sizes. Since this study employed large samples and the distributions were similarly negatively skewed, this test is appropriate for the data. The results indicate that students completing the final exam in Fall 2015 scored higher on the final exam than did students completing the final exam in Fall 2014 ($t(183.1) = 2.01$, $p = .046$) with a small effect size (d = .25) roughly equivalent to four-tenths of a letter grade (See Table 1).

Table 1: Comparison of mean scores on the final examination of Programming Languages and Compilers between Fall 2014 and Fall 2015

Fall 2014 mean (sd)	Fall 2015 mean (sd)	t-test	Effect Size Cohen's d
72.5% (18.6%)	76.8% (15.6%)	$p = .046$	d = .25

Because the instructors were deeply concerned about increasing failure rates and students failing to achieve core learning objectives, we further examined the effect of the new testing regime on pass/fail rates in the course. The letter grade on the final exam for

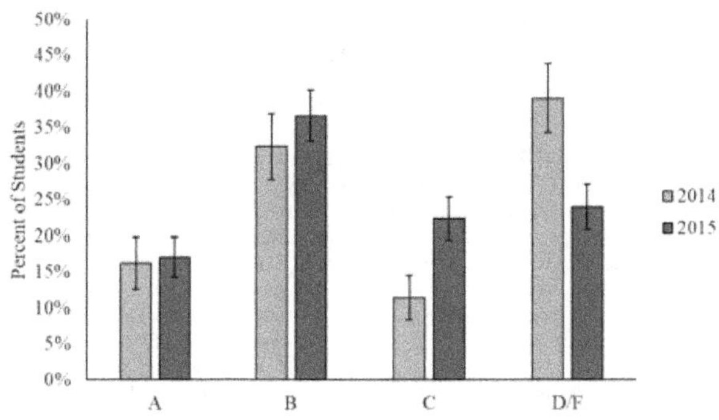

Figure 3: Final exam score distribution by letter grade.

each student was calculated and the grade distributions for the two semesters are shown in Figure 3. The grade distributions between the two semesters were statistically significantly different as measured by a chi-Square test of independence [$\chi^2(3) = 10.00$, $p = .02$]. The percentage decrease in the number of D/Fs (failing grades) is proportional to the increase in the number of B/Cs (passing grades).

5 DISCUSSION

This study primarily examined the effect of testing students on their machine problems rather than simply letting them submit their code after a week's worth of work. We found that this increased use of testing coincided with improved student performance on the final examination, indicating improved learning. In particular, we found that the distribution of grades was significantly different between semesters. After the increased use of testing, the percentage of failing grades (D/Fs) decreased proportionally with the increase in the percentage of low passing grades (B/Cs). These findings suggest that the use of increased testing primarily helped weaker students who may have otherwise failed the final examination. The stronger students appeared to be relatively unaffected, as the percentage of students earning A grades was not substantially different between semesters.

Alternate explanations of the findings include more lenient grading, an easier final examination, or an improved test-taking environment for students. Because the change to the CBTF was concurrent with the change in assessment philosophy for the machine problems, it is impossible to tease apart whether the improvement was environmental or due to the change in assessment strategy. We, however, argue that these explanations are weaker interpretations of the data. As mentioned in the methods sections, when making the switch to the CBTF, the instructors created their tools and examinations in an effort to maintain parity across semesters. The instructors actively sought to maintain the rigor of the examinations and went to great lengths to maintain similar modalities of testing in the CBTF. Additionally, a secondary motivation for the instructors to switch to the CBTF was to cope with the increasing scale of the course and to combat some of the ethical challenges that come with increasing class size (i.e., over-reliance of students on either their peers or external resources), in turn hopefully both stopping the decline in grades and motivating students to garner a greater understanding of the course material. The improvement in students' grades was rather much a surprise to the instructors, rather than a specifically sought after outcome biasing the study.

In contrast, the addition of an individualized test of understanding for the machine problems likely provided additional motivation for students to develop their own understanding of their code rather than overly rely on peers. Because students often rely on rehearsal strategies, such as reading someone else's code, they easily mistake familiarity with a solution for understanding of that solution. Requiring students to demonstrate their understanding in a test environment likely required students to develop their own understanding. This explanation is also compelling because we see that improvements in learning were primarily seen among weaker students (those earning failing grades). While the strong students (those earning As) likely were already learning the course content well before the change, the weaker students were now placed in a situation that aided their learning.

6 CONCLUSIONS AND FUTURE WORK

This study provides evidence that switching the assessment of students' understanding of an extended coding problem from simply turning in the code to testing their understanding of a portion of their code in an exam environment may improve students' learning. Critically, this switch significantly lowered the failure rate for students on the final examination. This finding is particularly exciting as the community continues to grapple with ways to improve retention rates and reduce failure in all core CS courses. Future studies will need to tease apart what effect a computer-based testing environment has relative to traditional paper-based examinations. Critically, these findings suggest that we should increasingly look to using the testing effect to improve students' learning in addition to our efforts to improve pedagogy and content.

ACKNOWLEDGMENTS

This research was supported in part by the National Science Foundation under Grants DUE 1347722 and CMMI 1150490. Any opinions, findings, and conclusions expressed in this material are those of the authors and do not necessarily reflect the views of the National Science Foundation.

REFERENCES

[1] R. L. Bangert-Downs, J. A. Kulik, and C. Kulik. 1991. Effects of frequent classroom testing. *The Journal of Educational Research* 85 (1991), 89–99.
[2] R. A. Bjork. 1975. . Erlbaum, Hillsdale, NJ, Chapter Retrieval as a memory modifier: An interpretation of negative recency and related phenomena, pp. 123–144.
[3] P. C. Brown, H. L. Roediger, III, and M. A. McDaniel. 2014. *Make It Stick: The Science of Successful Learning.* Belknap Press.
[4] A. C. Butler. 2010. Repeated testing produced superior transfer of learning relative to repeated studying. *Journal of Experimental Psychology: Learning, Memory, and Cognition* 36 (2010), 1118–1133. https://doi.org/10.1037/a0019902
[5] A. C. Butler and H. L. III. Roediger. 2007. Testing improves retention in a simulated classroom. *European Journal of Cognitive Psychology* 19 (2007), 514–527. https://doi.org/10.1080/09541440701326097
[6] J. C. K. Chan. 2010. Long-term effects of testing on the recall of nontested materials. *Memory* 18 (2010), 49–57. https://doi.org/10.1080/09658210903405737
[7] B. Chen, M. West, and C. Zilles. 2017. Do Performance Trends Suggest Widespread Collaborative Cheating on Asynchronous Exams?. In *Proceedings of the Fourth (2017) ACM Conference on Learning at Scale.* https://doi.org/10.1145/3051457.3051465
[8] M. T. H. Chi, P. J. Feltovich, and Glaser R. 2012. Using spacing to enhance diverse forms of learning: Review of recent research and implications for instruction. *Educational Psychology Review* 24 (2012), 369–378. https://doi.org/10.1007/s10648-012-9205-z

[9] C. F. Darley and B. B. Murdock. 1971. Effects of prior free recall testing on final recall and recognition. *Journal of Experimental Psychology* 91 (1971), 66–73. https://doi.org/10.1037/h0031836

[10] J. Hanham, W. Leahy, and J. Sweller. 2017. Cognitive load theory, element interactivity, and the testing and reverse testing effects. *Applied Cognitive Psychology* 31 (2017), 265–280. https://doi.org/10.1002/acp.3324

[11] M. K. Hartwig and J. Dunlosky. 2012. Study strategies of college students: Are self-testing and scheduling related to achievement? *Psychonomic Bulletin and Review* 19 (2012), 126–134. https://doi.org/10.3758/s13423-011-0181-y

[12] C. I. Johnson and R. E. Mayer. 2009. A testing effect with multimedia learning. *Journal of Educational Psychology* 101 (2009), 621–629. https://doi.org/10.1037/a0015183

[13] S. H. K. Kang, T. H. Gollan, and H. Pashler. 2013. DonâĂŹt just repeat after me: Retrieval practice is better than imitation for foreign vocabulary learning. *Psychonomic Bulletin & Review* 20 (2013), 1259–1265. https://doi.org/10.3758/s13423-013-0450-z

[14] J. D. Karpicke and W. R. Aue. 2015. The testing effect is alive and well with complex materials. *Educational Psychology Review* 27 (2015), 317–326. https://doi.org/10.1007/s10648-015-9309-3

[15] J. D. Karpicke, A. C. Butler, and H. L. Roediger. 2009. Metacognitive strategies in student learning: Do students practice retrieval when they study on their own? *Memory* 17 (2009), 471–479. https://doi.org/10.1080/09658210802647009

[16] N. Kornell, M. J. Hays, and R. Bjork. 2009. Unsuccessful Retrieval Attempts Enhance Subsequent Learning. *Journal of Experimental Psychology: Learning, Memory, and Cognition* 35 (2009), 989–998. https://doi.org/10.1037/a0015729

[17] D. P. Larsen, A. C. Butler, and H. L. III. Roediger. 2009. Repeated testing improves long term retention relative to repeated study: A randomised controlled study. *Medical Education* 43 (2009), 1174–1181. https://doi.org/10.1111/j.1365-2923.2009.03518.x

[18] W. Leahy, J. Hanham, and J. Sweller. 2015. High element interactivity information during problem solving may lead to failure to obtain the testing effect. *Educational Psychology Review* 27 (2015), 291–304. https://doi.org/10.1007/s10648-015-9296-4

[19] J. L. Little, E. L. Bjork, R. A. Bjork, and G. Angello. 2012. Multiple-choice tests exonerated, at least of some charges: Fostering test-induced learning and avoiding test-induced forgetting. *Psychological Science* 23 (2012), 1337–1344. https://doi.org/10.1177/0956797612443370

[20] J. L. Little, B. C. Storm, and E. L. Bjork. 2011. The costs and benefits of testing text materials. *Memory* 19 (2011), 346–359. https://doi.org/10.1080/09658211.2011.569725

[21] M. A. McDaniel, P. K. Agarwal, B. J. Huesler, K. B. McDermott, and H. L. III. Roediger. 2011. Test-enhanced learning in a middle school science classroom: The effects of quiz frequency and placement. *Journal of Educational Psychology* 103 (2011), 399–414. https://doi.org/10.1037/a0021782

[22] M. A. McDaniel, J. L. Anderson, M. H. Derbish, and N. Morrisette. 2007. Testing the testing effect in the classroom. *European Journal of Cognitive Psychology* 19 (2007), 494–513. https://doi.org/10.1080/09541440701326154

[23] M. A. McDaniel, D. C. Howard, and G. O. Einstein. 2009. The read-recite-review study strategy: Effective and portable. *Psychological Science* 20 (2009), 516–522. https://doi.org/10.1111/j.1467-9280.2009.02325.x

[24] M. A. McDaniel, H. L. III. Roediger, and K. B. McDermott. 2007. Generalizing test-enhanced learning from the laboratory to the classroom. *Psychonomic Bulletin & Review* 14 (2007), 200–206. https://doi.org/10.3758/BF03194052

[25] M. A. McDaniel, R. C. Thomas, P. K. Agarwal, K. B. McDermott, and H. L. Roediger. 2013. Quizzing in middle school science: Successful transfer performance on classroom exams. *Applied Cognitive Psychology* 27 (2013), 360–372. https://doi.org/10.1002/acp.2914

[26] M. A. McDaniel, K. M. Wildman, and J. L. Anderson. 2012. Using quizzes to enhance summative-assessment performance in a web-based class: An experimental study. *Applied Research in Memory and Cognition* 1 (2012), 18–26. https://doi.org/10.1016/j.jarmac.2011.10.001

[27] K. B. McDermott, P. K. Agarwal, L. DâĂŽAntonio, H. L. III. Roediger, and M. A. McDaniel. 2014. Both multiple-choice and short-answer quizzes enhance later exam performance in middle and high school classes. *Journal of Experimental Psychology, Applied* 20 (2014), 3–21. https://doi.org/10.1037/xap0000004

[28] Raymond S. Pettit, John Homer, and Roger Gee. 2017. Do Enhanced Compiler Error Messages Help Students?: Results Inconclusive.. In *Proceedings of the 2017 ACM SIGCSE Technical Symposium on Computer Science Education (SIGCSE '17)*. ACM, New York, NY, USA, 465–470. https://doi.org/10.1145/3017680.3017768

[29] L. E. Richland, L. S. Kao, and N. Kornell. 2013. Can unsuccessful tests enhance learning. *Educational Psychology Review* 25 (2013), 523–548. https://doi.org/10.1007/s10648-013-9240-4

[30] Brandon Rodriguez, Stephen Kennicutt, Cyndi Rader, and Tracy Camp. 2017. Assessing Computational Thinking in CS Unplugged Activities. In *Proceedings of the 2017 ACM SIGCSE Technical Symposium on Computer Science Education (SIGCSE '17)*. ACM, New York, NY, USA, 501–506. https://doi.org/10.1145/3017680.3017779

[31] H. L. III. Roediger and J. Karpicke. 2006. Test-enhanced learning: Taking memory tests improves long-term retention. *Psychological Science* 17 (2006), 249–255. https://doi.org/10.1111/j.1467-9280.2006.01693.x

[32] Karthikeyan Umapathy and Albert D. Ritzhaupt. 2017. A Meta-Analysis of Pair-Programming in Computer Programming Courses: Implications for Educational Practice. *Trans. Comput. Educ.* 17, 4, Article 16 (Aug. 2017), 13 pages. https://doi.org/10.1145/2996201

[33] T. van Gog and L. Kester. 2012. A test of the testing effect: Acquiring problem-solving skills from worked examples. *Cognitive Science* 36 (2012), 1532–1541. https://doi.org/10.1111/cogs.12002

[34] T. van Gog, L. Kester, K. Dirkx, V. Hoogerheide, J. Boerboom, and P. P. J. L. Verkoeijen. 2015. Testing after worked example study does not enhance delayed problem-solving performance compared to restudy. *Educational Psychology Review* 27 (2015), 265–289. https://doi.org/10.1007/s10648-015-9297-3

[35] T. van Gog and J. Sweller. 2015. Not new, but nearly forgotten: The testing effect decreases or even disappears as the complexity of learning materials increases. *Educational Psychology Review* 27 (2015), 247–264. https://doi.org/10.1007/s10648-015-9310-x

[36] David Weintrop and Uri Wilensky. 2015. To Block or Not to Block, That is the Question: Students' Perceptions of Blocks-based Programming. In *Proceedings of the 14th International Conference on Interaction Design and Children (IDC '15)*. ACM, New York, NY, USA, 199–208. https://doi.org/10.1145/2771839.2771860

[37] M. West and C. Zilles. 2016. Modeling student scheduling preferences in a computer-based testing facility. In *Proceedings of the Third ACM Conference on Learning at Scale*. 309–312. https://doi.org/10.1145/2876034.2893441

[38] C. L. Wooldrige, J. M. Bugg, M. A. McDaniel, and Y. Liu. 2014. The testing effect with authentic educational materials: A cautionary note. *Journal of Applied Research in Memory and Cognition* 3 (2014), 214–221. https://doi.org/10.1016/j.jarmac.2014.07.001

[39] C. Zilles, R. T. Deloatch, J. Bailey, B. B. Khattar, W. Fagen, C. Heeren, D. Mussulman, and M. West. 2015. Computerized Testing: A Vision and Initial Experiences. In *Proceedings of the American Society for Engineering Education (ASEE) 2015 Annual Conference*. https://doi.org/10.18260/p.23726

Including Coding Questions in Video Quizzes for a Flipped CS1

Lisa L. Lacher
University of Houston - Clear Lake
Houston, Texas
lacher@uhcl.edu

Albert Jiang
Trinity University
San Antonio, Texas
xjiang@trinity.edu

Yu Zhang
Trinity University
San Antonio, Texas
yzhang@trinity.edu

Mark C. Lewis
Trinity University
San Antonio, Texas
mlewis@trinity.edu

ABSTRACT

In an effort to improve student performance in a flipped classroom environment, this paper explores the impact of including auto-graded coding questions in gate check quizzes associated with videos for a flipped CS1 course. Previous work showed that having students complete multiple choice questions that were intended to verify that they had done the preparation work did not have a statistically significant impact on outcomes as measured through written quizzes and exams. In an attempt to engage higher-level processing of learned information, this work builds on top of that by adding questions that require students to write short segments of code for most of the quizzes in addition to doing some multiple choice questions. We found that students who were given these coding video quizzes performed better on written assessments, especially for the final exam.

CCS CONCEPTS

• **Social and professional topics → Computer science education**; **CS1**;

KEYWORDS

flipped classroom; inverted classroom; flipped learning; CS1; assessments; novice programming; video quizzes; active learning; blended learning; programming

ACM Reference Format:

Lisa L. Lacher, Albert Jiang, Yu Zhang, and Mark C. Lewis. 2018. Including Coding Questions in Video Quizzes for a Flipped CS1. In *SIGCSE '18: The 49th ACM Technical Symposium on Computer Science Education, February 21–24, 2018, Baltimore, MD, USA.* ACM, New York, NY, USA, 6 pages. https://doi.org/10.1145/3159450.3159504

1 INTRODUCTION

The flipped or inverted classroom is considered by some to be one of the most valuable educational technologies in current use [5]. The basic idea behind flipped learning is that it reverses the learning process from the traditional classroom. In a flipped class, students review new content, often by watching videos which contain normal lecture material, prior to class, and then use class time to work on problem solving exercises, projects, and homework assignments in order to promote higher-order learning. Continuing advances in technology make it easier than ever to create and post content for students to view and interact with on many platforms and in many locations, which led to an increase in the use of flipped classrooms. New learning communities, such as SOPHIA and the Flipped Learning Network, have been established to help interested educators implement the flipped model by providing them with knowledge and resources. One indication of the growing interest in flipped learning can be seen by membership surveys in these communities. A survey conducted by both communities indicated a ten-fold increase in membership. It also found that the number of educators that flipped at least one lesson has almost doubled between 2012 and 2014, and that 96% of educators who have flipped a lesson would recommend the method to others [18].

The flipped classroom has certainly been gaining momentum within higher education; especially within Computer Science, as it allows students to spend more of the valuable class time doing hands-on activities instead of passively listening to a lecture[7]. This increased adoption is not surprising as research suggests that millennial students prefer the interactive learning that the flipped model provides [17]. Student engagement is just one of the benefits touted by many flipped classroom researchers[15]. Many studies show other promising benefits of the flipped model beyond student engagement. Some of these benefits include students in the flipped classrooms outperforming students in lecture based classrooms[2, 8], more positive attitudes, better learning habits, development of critical thinking skills [9], and the ability to cover more course material [15].

However, there are still many challenges with the flipped model. Not all studies actually show improved student performance [3]. Another challenge is that the flipped model requires students to be more responsible for their own learning and not all students are comfortable with or prepared for that responsibility [20]. University freshman, in particular, need much more motivation from instructors to take responsibility [7]. Yet other issues are a lack of student accountability to complete the instruction that happens outside of class and the inability to monitor how well the students have understood the pre-class instructional materials [6]. Thus, we

SIGCSE '18, February 21–24, 2018, Baltimore , MD, USA

ACM ISBN 978-1-4503-5103-4/18/02...$15.00
https://doi.org/10.1145/3159450.3159504

can see that the flipped classroom method provides much promise, but there are still many pitfalls that mainly center around student preparedness. The effectiveness of the flipped method depends on how well prepared the students show up to class. If a sufficient number of students do not adequately prepare, then the instructor has few other options than to revert back to the traditional lecture format. For this reason, instructors who use the flipped method would benefit by having a mechanism that increases the likelihood that students will show up to class having completed the recommended preparation work. It is necessary that they will have gained enough prior knowledge so that they will have more time to conduct higher level cognitive activities during class time.

This work builds on [10, 12], which explored the value of simple gate-check quizzes using multiple choice questions in a CS1 flipped classroom to help the students be more accountable and prepared for class. Both studies found that the multiple choice question style of gate-check quizzes was not effective in helping students adequately prepare. In this paper, we discuss a study that used coding questions, in addition to multiple choice questions, for the gate-check quizzes. Our goal was to see if questions that required the student to invoke higher forms of thinking and *apply* knowledge that they should have gained by watching videos would be more beneficial than simply *memorizing* or *looking up* answers.

2 BACKGROUND

Bloom's taxonomy differentiates between cognitive skill levels. It calls attention to learning objectives that require higher levels of cognitive skills that lead to deeper learning, and transfer of both knowledge and skills to a greater variety of tasks and contexts [1]. The fundamental idea of the flipped learning model is to have students do the lower levels of cognitive work, such as gaining knowledge by remembering and understanding, outside of class. Then instructors can attempt to more positively impact the students' higher level cognitive work during class time by using more active learning activities where students apply, analyze and create, whilst getting immediate assistance and feedback from the instructor or their peers. However, in order to achieve the potential of the higher cognitive levels students must take the initiative outside of class to prepare and achieve a sufficient level of understanding of the material. Because most CS1 courses are composed of freshmen, and they often have lower levels of learning readiness [7, 20], educators must use a mechanism to assist in their motivation.

Some researchers have used gate-check quizzes in flipped classrooms to motivate students to prepare [6], but little is known about the actual makeup of the quizzes. A gate-check quiz is administered after the student has consumed the materials to give the student feedback about their level of understanding before they would enter the classroom – to let them know if they are ready to go through the gate. Thus the feedback from this quiz should be immediate. There is a lack of research about the *type* of questions that could be used in gate-check quizzes to improved learning outcomes in a flipped classroom. Zhang et al.[21] suggest that interactive quizzes (multiple-choice style) within videos can be used to improve learning effectiveness. However, Horton [8] found that "Students who passively watch the videos and click through the in-video quizzes without much thought may get a false sense of mastery over the material". Also, not all instructors have the technology available to create interactive video quizzes or insert them into preexisting videos. Stanger-Hall [19] found that using constructive response questions in addition to multiple choice questions significantly improved students' performance. Constructive response requires more thought and according to [1], students who engage in tasks that require higher levels of cognitive skills engage in deeper learning which aids in their understanding of the material.

We preformed a previous study about the effectiveness of gate-check quizzes in a CS1 class that used online multiple choice questions. Although it was found that the multiple choice question style of gate-check quiz was not effective in helping students adequately prepare to learn (measured by grade performance on written quizzes and exams) in a flipped classroom; there was some evidence that it might have helped raise the grades of students who have a propensity toward surface learning [10, 12].

We believe that the limited nature of multiple choice quiz questions did not adequately test the students' understanding and provide the necessary feedback to them so that they knew what they did and did not understand. It also did not stimulate the students' motivation to learn and understand the course material. In other words, multiple choice questions did not promote deep learning. The multiple choice quiz style was a surface learning tool, not something that prompted students to think more deeply, make connections, or question their assumptions. Based upon what we learned in that study, we conceived the idea of adding questions with more cognitive complexity. We felt that including coding questions, which necessitate some application or simple analysis of ideas or concepts introduced during the videos, would engage a higher level of cognitive thinking that would produce deeper learning and understanding. Because writing program code is one of the primary ways CS1 students communicate their understanding of material, we wanted questions that required students to write programming code solutions to simple problems. Students need to apply some programming concepts in order for students to fully understand these concepts [4].

3 STUDY DESIGN

This study looks at five sections of CS1 taught by two instructors in the fall semester of 2015. All sections used a flipped approach where students watched videos outside of class, and then spent class time applying the knowledge they should have acquired from the videos. We designed the study to answer the question of whether the use of coding gate-check quizzes was helpful in improving the students' learning as measured by the in-class quiz and exam scores. We administered pre-tests in order to assess each student's computer programming aptitude. The study compares the performance of students that were required to complete pre-class coding quizzes that provided immediate feedback to students that were not required to take such quizzes.

3.1 Hypotheses

For this study we had two hypotheses related to requiring the coding style gate-check video quizzes as a means of assisting students learning preparation before coming to class.

- Hypothesis 1: Students taking the coding gate-check video quizzes have higher grades on the assessments than students who do not have to take the coding quizzes.
- Hypothesis 2: Students with lower programming aptitudes benefit more from coding gate-check quizzes than students who have medium or high programming aptitudes.

The rationale behind the first hypothesis is that making the students *apply* knowledge learned from the videos would stimulate deeper thinking to help them really understand programming concepts. Successfully completing a coding question should help better prepare the student to engage in the active learning activities that occur in the classroom so that they get more out of that learning experience and earn better grades. As coding ability is important to learning the fundamental concepts in CS1, this type of question can better inform the instructor about the students' abilities. This type of knowledge can help the instructor design a better learning experience for the classroom to assist in student learning. You cannot get that type of feedback from multiple choice questions.

We based the second hypothesis on the belief that students with high programming aptitudes would generally do well regardless of pre-class preparation and, as such, would not benefit much from the coding quizzes. On the other hand, forcing the lower aptitude students to work harder at their preparation by writing small pieces of code that force them to focus on details of both syntax and semantics would help them be more successful in the class.

3.2 Participating Subjects

There were eighty-five undergraduate students enrolled in five sections of CS1 at Trinity University. Trinity University is a small, selective liberal arts college with 2500 undergraduate students, during the fall semester of 2015. The courses used [14] and the associated videos that are available on the author's YouTube channel [13]. Prior to the beginning of classes, the instructors randomly choose which class sections would use video quizzes and which class sections would not use video quizzes. Sixty-nine of the students participated in the study and completed quizzes and tests: forty-one participants took the video quizzes and twenty-eight did not take video quizzes. Instructors urged every section of students to watch the videos and/or read the textbook before attending class. Instructor A taught two video quiz sections and one non-video quiz section. Instructor B taught one video quiz section and one non-video quiz section. We would have liked to do a statistical analysis of the impact for each instructor separately, but the sample size would have been too small.

3.3 Artifacts

The classes used identical in-class quizzes for the quizzes that were included in the study. There were minor differences in the material presented late in the semester between the instructors. As a result, Instructor A offered a sixth quiz, which was not included in the study. Each student took a midterm and a final at the same point in the semester. Students had advanced knowledge of the dates of all quizzes and exams. Two of the sections taught by Instructor B, one with the video quizzes and one without, had three 50 minute periods each week. The other sections, taught by Instructor A, each had two 75 minute periods each week. To compensate for this, the midterm tests were identical for the first seven questions and the 75 minute sections had an extra three questions. Although the majority of the final test questions were identical between all sections, there was one question that was different due to the pace of the classes. Instructor B's classes ended up one week behind Instructor A's classes. Again, there was always a balance between courses with the video quizzes and courses without the video quizzes using different versions. The fact that both courses with and without the video quizzes had identical exams balances out the overall statistics for this work.

We created one rubric for each quiz to aid with consistency in grading. One teaching assistant, using the rubric as a guide, graded all the quizzes. Instructors graded the tests, with each instructor being responsible for a certain set of questions. This ensured consistency in grading across all tests. Each day in class, the students worked on writing code solutions for a variety of problems posed by the instructor. There was consistency in the problems posed between sections.

The students also completed four homework assignments. However, those homework assignments were not included in the study because students who put forth time and effort basically received full or nearly full credit. Because we did not track time and effort spent on homework assignments, those assignment grades do not provide a useful way to analyze the impact that the coding gate-check quizzes would have had on them.

3.4 Experimental Procedure

To evaluate the hypotheses posed, the study contained a control group and an experiment group. We give the details of the experiment steps below.

3.4.1 Course Assessments. Three of the sections had ten percent of the grade determined by short quizzes that students completed after watching the videos and before their scheduled class meeting times. We give details of these quizzes, including the nature of the coding questions, below. It was felt that ten percent of a grade was sufficient incentive to ensure that students took the gate-check quizzes seriously. To determine a composite grade for this study, in-class quiz scores contributed twenty-five percent, and the midterm and final contributed equally to the remaining seventy-five percent of the grade. Actual course grades used a different formula to include assignments and other coding activities not directly factored into this work.

3.4.2 Pre-Test. Students were asked at the beginning of the semester to complete a computer programming aptitude test created by the University of Kent [16]. It consists of twenty-six questions composed of numerical problem solving, logical reasoning, attention to detail, pattern recognition, and the ability to follow complex procedures. As it does not require students to have any programming knowledge, it is appropriate for CS1 students. Numerical problem solving is similar to the logical thinking and trouble shooting skills required in programming. Pattern recognition is necessary in understanding the representations of symbols and procedures. The ability to follow complex procedures is necessary to trace code. Students had forty minutes to complete this test. The University of Kent breaks scores into three groups. Scores >= 19 are considered

Table 1: Grade Results: Quiz n=41, NoQuiz n=28.

	Q1	Q2	Q3	Q4	Q5	Midterm	Final	Combined Grade
QuizAvg	8.09	5.94	3.56	6.91	6.03	49.54	59.39	66.4
QuizMedian	8.5	6	3	7	6	65	75	68.5
NoQuizAvg	7.17	5.07	2.89	5.37	5.32	48.0	49.22	57.0
NoquizMedian	7	5	2	4.5	5.25	63	60	53
p	0.075	0.142	0.364	**0.039**	0.427	0.350	**0.030**	**0.00072**

high-aptitude; scores 13-18 are considered average aptitude, and scores 12 or below are considered low aptitude.

3.4.3 Gate-check Quizzes. The "video quizzes" included questions that required the students to write simple expressions or small functions as well as multiple choice questions when suitable coding questions could not be written for a topic. The sections took between twenty and twenty-two of these video quizzes. The quizzes were generally available at least two days before they were due.[1]

For the twenty-two video quizzes there were eighteen coding questions and thirty-three multiple choice questions. The majority of the coding questions were before the midterm when students were learning basic coding concepts like conditionals, functions, and loops. There were more multiple choice questions in the second half of the semester for topics like GUIs, graphics, and sorting. Students could only answer each multiple choice question once, but the coding questions allowed for unlimited submissions. There were more multiple choice questions than coding questions because if a topic lent itself to coding questions, there would generally only be one or possibly two coding questions on the quiz, while a quiz with only multiple choice questions would have three or four such questions for the same amount of material.

In addition to allowing unlimited submissions for the coding questions, students could ask for assistance from the professor[2] or work with other students on the coding question. Allowing unlimited attempts and using the professor and/or other students as resources helps minimize anxiety. Practicing programming involves trial and error and allowing multiple submissions permits trial and error. Allowing students to talk to the professors provides students another source of feedback to help with their learning and this is particularly advantageous if the students do not understand what is wrong with their submissions. The motivation for allowing communications with other students is to potentially enable collaborative learning, but our experience is that students do not often collaborate on the quizzes. Once again, the purpose of the pre-class video quiz questions is to make sure the students put in the necessary preparation so that they can get the most out of the active learning exercises they will be doing in class.

Here are four sample coding questions used in the video quizzes in the first half of the semester.

- In math you would write 0<x<5 to indicate that x is between 0 and 5. What would you write in Scala to express this same restriction? Write the proper expression and assume x is a Double.
- Write an expression that assumes there is a List[Int] called nums which calculates the sum of the even values in the List.
- Write a function called sumOdds that takes n:Int and returns the sum of all the odd numbers between 1 and n inclusive. So if you call sumOdds(8) it should return 16 because 1+3+5+7=16.
- Write a function that takes a List[Int] and returns the index of the first number divisible by 5. If there is no such number, return -1.

The coding questions were auto-graded by executing student code on a suite of randomized inputs and checking their results against a correct solution. If students submitted incorrect answers for a coding question, they were only told that their response was incorrect, with no details on the nature of the error. Students were strongly encouraged to test their code on their own before submitting. Multiple submissions were common. A section with sixteen students generally had 50+ submissions and some problems had closer to 100 attempts for a given problem. Once a student got the problem correct, going back to the quiz showed them the code from their correct submission as un-editable text.

3.4.4 In-class Quizzes and Tests. The questions on the in-class quizzes and tests used for assessment were very different from the questions on the video quizzes. There were three types of questions: short answer, coding, and tracing. We used an equal amount of each type. There were no multiple choice questions, and the coding questions were typically larger in scope than the coding questions on the video quizzes. The medium used for the in-class quizzes and tests was paper.

4 ANALYSIS AND RESULTS

We carried out statistical analyses on the data collected during the study and tested the described hypotheses to determine the usefulness of the coding gate-check quizzes in improving student understanding as proven out by grades. Independent samples t-tests were performed to determine if differences were statistically significant. We selected an alpha value of 0.05 for judging the significance of the results.

4.1 Hypothesis 1

The students taking the coding gate-check video quizzes have higher grades on the assessments than students who do not have to take the coding quizzes.

Table 1 shows the numeric values for means and medians of all of the grades collected for both the video quiz and non-video quiz

[1]They were available for a longer period of time if there was a weekend between classes.

[2]Professors in the Trinity CS department have open-door office hours, and are highly available through email, so all students had the ability to ask questions, regardless of whether or not they were in the video quiz group.

sections. It also shows the p value for a t-test to see if the differences in the means are statistically significant. While the difference for individual grades are only significant for quiz four and the final exam, the group that took the video quizzes had a higher mean and median for all of the grades, so the combined grade shows a advantage for the group that was taking the video quizzes.

Note that this is in direct contrast to the results of [10, 12] where the gate-check video quizzes only included multiple choice questions. The results here support the hypothesis, indicating that the addition of coding questions to the video quizzes was the primary factor in improving the effectiveness of the video quizzes as measured by student grades.

The final showed a much larger difference than the midterm. We believe that this is not just an anomaly due to the small number of students, but a real effect that indicates that the true benefit of adding coding questions to the video quizzes was fully manifest in the second half of the semester, even though many of the video quizzes in the second half of the semester often lacked coding questions. This is because the material in CS1 is very implicitly cumulative. Each topic has a tendency to build on the ones before it. The CS1 curricula used in this study also tends to get more challenging for many students after the midterm. Students who have an inferior mastery of the material from the first half of the semester get lost and struggle more in the second half of the semester. So while students who had not fully mastered the material might have been able to sufficiently study enough to get by the midterm, the second half of the semester made their lack of mastery more obvious which, most likely, caused them to fall further behind in the second half of the semester. We believe that the coding questions on the video quizzes helped students achieve mastery, which paid off by the end of the course. It definitely presented a good opportunity to make students code more which should have had a positive impact on their learning.

Given the small sample size, we cannot do statistical analysis on groups broken out by instructor, but there were no significant effects due to a difference in instructors. To illustrate this, Figure 1 shows the mean grades for each of the written evaluations in the order students completed them during the semester, broken out by groups for instructor and whether or not they took the coding video quizzes. In this plot, there are 14 pairs of vid/no-vid groupings, seven for each instructor. It is worth noting that of those 14 pairs, there are only three cases where students who did not take the video quizzes scored higher than students who did take the quizzes for the same instructor. Those cases are quizzes #2 and #3 for Instructor B and quiz #4 for Instructor A. In all three cases, the margin was small. This plot shows that while there were differences between the instructors on the various written assessments, the overall impact of the coding video quizzes is not generally instructor dependent.

4.2 Hypothesis 2

Students with lower programming aptitudes benefit more from coding gate-check quizzes than students who have medium or high programming aptitudes.

Figure 2 shows the course grades of students in the two groups plotted against aptitude along with trend lines. Our hypothesis was

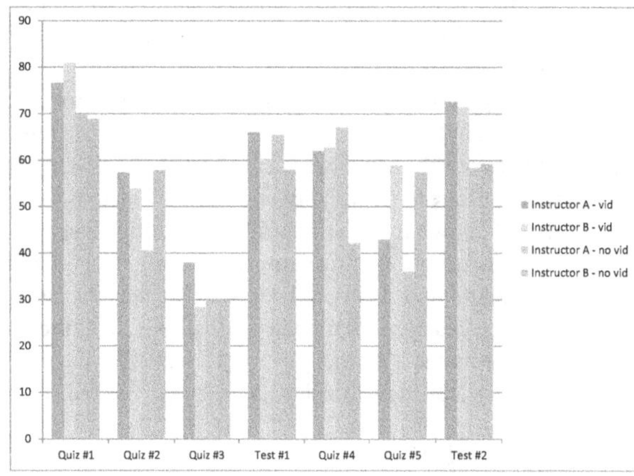

Figure 1: This figure shows the median grades for each quiz and test broken out by instructor and whether or not the section used the video quizzes. The sample sizes for each group are as follows: Instructor A vid - 28, Instructor A no-vid - 14, Instructor B vid - 13, Instructor B no-vid - 14.

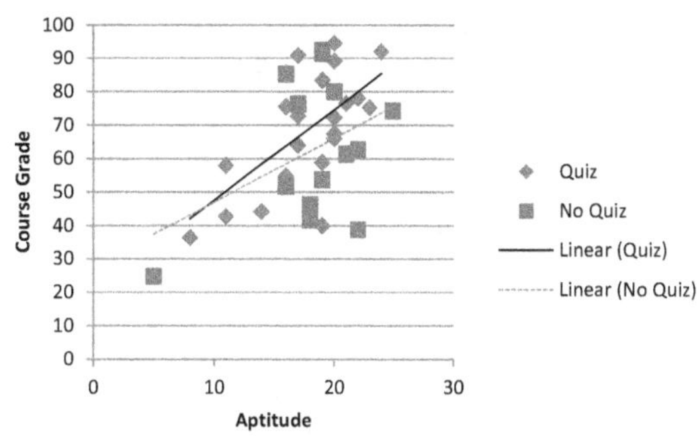

Figure 2: Cumulative student grades plotted against aptitudes. The fit for the video quiz group is $y = 2.7027x + 20.449$ with $R^2 = 0.39$. The fit for non-video quiz group is $y = 1.9053x + 27.94$ with $R^2 = 0.1724$. In both groups there is a positive correlation between aptitude and grades.

that being forced to do regular coding on the video quizzes would provide the most benefit to the low aptitude students. Though it is hard to draw strong conclusions here given the general dearth of low aptitude students, the trend lines indicate that this hypothesis was incorrect. Instead, it appears that the low aptitude students performed at roughly the same level between the two groups, and it was the higher aptitude students who received the most benefit.

Figure 2 is significant for other reasons as well. First, both groups show a clear positive slope.[3] This would be expected for a valid aptitude test as high aptitude students should be more likely to do

[3]The slope of the non-video quiz group is effectively determined by the one low aptitude outlier. Removing that point causes the trend line to have a slightly negative slope over the small range of aptitudes in the sample.

well on standard assessments. This result basically shows further support for the University of Kent aptitude test being a valid metric of student aptitude that is independent of any programming background.

In addition, given the smaller number of students involved in this study, it would have been possible for students to be unevenly distributed between the two groups based on aptitude. That would have been a challenge to the validity of all the conclusions presented here. This plot shows that the aptitude distribution between the two groups was roughly equivalent. If anything, the quiz group had more students with lower aptitude, so the fact that they had higher overall scores appears to indicate that the use of the coding video quizzes provided a benefit, even if it does not appear to have benefited the low aptitude students as we had predicted.

5 CONCLUSIONS

This work found that student grade outcomes benefited in a flipped classroom when using gate-check quizzes that force the students to write code related to the topic of the new material. This is in contrast to previous work where the gate-check video quizzes aimed at simply verifying that students watched the videos, not whether they had learned enough from them to apply that knowledge, included only multiple choice questions.

This benefit was not uniform for all students. Students with higher aptitudes for CS seemed to accrue most of the benefits, contrary to our hopes and expectations. Still, we feel that these results provide a strong motivation for including these techniques in any type of inverted classroom because we did see positive results. Unfortunately, it does not seem to provide significant benefits to the population of students who probably need it the most. More work needs to be done to see how lower aptitued students can be helped. Analysis of this study data related to how to deal with low aptitude students in introductory computer science courses is discussed presented in [11].

There were several limitations with this study. The study was performed at a small, private liberal arts university and the class sizes are constrained to rooms that seat 21. We call on others with larger student populations to continue this work. We also realize that we required the experimental group to take video quizzes and that there was no equivalent effort or work required for the control group. We took this approach because we wanted to create circumstances as similar as possible to previous work so that we could more accurately measure this new gate-check quiz approach. This is why we brought in comparisons from previous work. Previous work found the same confounding variable - the study required the experimental group to take video quizzes and there was no equivalent work required for the control group. Yet, the evidence suggests that the addition of coding questions to the gate-check quizzes had a more positive impact on students than just using multiple choice questions. Another threat includes the fact that we had two different instructors and instructors may have different teaching styles. However, to achieve as much balance as possible, each instructor had students who took the video quizzes and students who did not take the video quizzes. Plus, all instructors used the flipped classroom approach and all student watch the same video lectures.

REFERENCES

[1] N. E. Adams. Blooms taxonomy of learning objectives. *Journal of the Medical Library Association*, pages 152–153, Jul 2015.

[2] A. Amresh, A. R. Carberry, and J. Femiani. Evaluating the effectiveness of flipped classrooms for teaching cs1. In *2013 IEEE Frontiers in Education Conference (FIE)*, pages 733–735, Oct 2013.

[3] W. G. Bowen, M. M. Chingos, K. A. Lack, and T. I. Nygren. Interactive learning online at public universities: evidence from a six-campus randomized trial. *Journal of Policy Analysis and Management*, 33(1):94–111, 2014.

[4] S. Cummins, A. R. Beresford, and A. Rice. Investigating engagement with in-video quiz questions in a programming course. *IEEE Transactions on Learning Technologies*, 9(1):57–66, 2016.

[5] T. Economides. The state of the art in educational technology. In *Global Humanitarian Technology Conference (GHTC), 2013 IEEE*, pages 285–287, Oct 2013.

[6] J. Enfield. Looking at the impact of the flipped classroom model of instruction on undergraduate multimedia students at csun. *TechTrends*, 57(6):14–27, 2013.

[7] Y. Hao. Exploring undergraduates' perspectives and flipped learning readiness in their flipped classrooms. *Computers in Human Behavior*, 59:82–92, 2016.

[8] D. Horton and M. Craig. Drop, fail, pass, continue: Persistence in cs1 and beyond in traditional and inverted delivery. In *Proceedings of the 46th ACM Technical Symposium on Computer Science Education*, SIGCSE '15, pages 235–240, New York, NY, USA, 2015. ACM.

[9] S. C. Kong. Developing information literacy and critical thinking skills through domain knowledge learning in digital classrooms: An experience of practicing flipped classroom strategy. *Computers & Education*, 78:160–173, 2014.

[10] L. Lacher and M. C. Lewis. The value of video quizzes in a computer science flipped classroom: An empirical study. In *The 2014 International Conference on Frontiers in Education: Computer Science & Computer Engineering*, pages 94–100. CSREA Press, 2014.

[11] L. L. Lacher, A. Jiang, Y. Zhang, and M. C. Lewis. Aptitude and previous experience in cs1 classes. In *Int'l Conf. Frontiers in Education: CS and CE | FECS'17*, pages 87–95, 2017.

[12] L. L. Lacher and M. C. Lewis. The effectiveness of video quizzes in a flipped class. In *Proceedings of the 46th ACM Technical Symposium on Computer Science Education*, pages 224–228. ACM, 2015.

[13] M. C. Lewis. Instructional youtube videos. https://www.youtube.com/channel/UCEvjiWkK2BoIH819T-buioQ.

[14] M. C. Lewis. Introduction to the art of programming using scala, 2012.

[15] G. S. Mason, T. R. Shuman, and K. E. Cook. Comparing the effectiveness of an inverted classroom to a traditional classroom in an upper-division engineering course. *IEEE Transactions on Education*, 56(4):430–435, 2013.

[16] U. of Kent. University of kent. https://www.kent.ac.uk/careers/tests/computer-test.htm.

[17] C. R. Phillips and J. E. Trainor. Millennial students and the flipped classroom. *Journal of Business and Educational Leadership*, 5(1):102, 2014.

[18] Sophia.org. Growth in flipped learning. https://www.sophia.org/flipped-classroom-survey, 2014. [Online; accessed 22-August-2016].

[19] K. F. Stanger-Hall. Multiple-choice exams: An obstacle for higher-level thinking in introductory science classes. In *CBE life sciences education*, 2012.

[20] J. F. Strayer. How learning in an inverted classroom influences cooperation, innovation and task orientation. *Learning Environments Research*, 15(2):171–193, 2012.

[21] D. Zhang, L. Zhou, R. Briggs, and J. Nunamaker. Instructional video in e-learning: Assessing the impact of interactive video on learning effectiveness. *Information and Management*, 43(1):15–27, 1 2006.

Understanding Computing in a Hybrid World

On the Undergraduate Curriculum Front-End Development

Laura Benvenuti
Hogeschool van Amsterdam
Amsterdam, the Netherlands
l.benvenuti@hva.nl

Erik Barendsen
Radboud Universiteit,
Open Universiteit
Nijmegen, the Netherlands
e.barendsen@cs.ru.nl

Gerrit C. van der Veer
Dalian Maritime University
Dalian, China
gerrit@acm.org

Johan Versendaal
Open Universiteit
Heerlen, the Netherlands
johan.versendaal@ou.nl

ABSTRACT

Computing is an interdisciplinary field that can be approached from different points of view. Each point of view has its goals, aims and fundamental assumptions. This makes computing a complex discipline. Moreover, new computing disciplines appear regularly. With the trend that ICT-professionals should have non-ICT competences as well, and non-ICT-professionals should have ICT-competences, new computing curricula are often *hybrid* in nature. As a hybrid computing curriculum cannot cover the full range of computing, it is interesting to investigate the 'computing part' of such curricula.

Our analysis framework consists of three elements: the curricular components 'goals and objectives' and 'instructional strategies', and the underlying epistemological view on the discipline ('cultural styles'). Taking a historical perspective, we describe the origins of the ACM/IEEE Curriculum Recommendation series. We discuss the three main cultural styles of computing: theoretical, scientific and engineering.

Observing that in a curriculum the above elements should be aligned, we present three trade-offs for the case of hybrid computing curricula. We apply our results to two concrete examples, *Liberal Arts and Computer Science* and *Front End Development.* Based on our investigation, we formulate recommendations for designers of hybrid computing curricula. We recommend, for example, discussing disciplinary boundaries and resulting trade-offs explicitly while designing and documenting curricula.

SIGCSE'18, February 21-24, 2018, Baltimore, MD, USA.

ACM ISBN 978-1-4503-5103-4/18/02...$15.00.
https://doi.org/10.1145/3159450.3159532

CCS Concepts

• Social and professional topics ~ Computing education programs
• Social and professional topics ~ History of computing

Keywords

Interdisciplinary programs (CS+X); Hybrid undergraduate curricula; Cultural styles in computing; Front End Development

ACM Reference format:

Laura Benvenuti, Erik Barendsen, Gerrit van der Veer and Johan Versendaal. 2018. Understanding computing in a hybrid world. In *Proceedings of SIGCSE'18, February 21–24, 2018, Baltimore, MD, USA.* 6 pages. https://doi.org/10.1145/3159450.3159532

1 INTRODUCTION

New computing curricula often are hybrid in nature. Since the introduction of the World Wide Web, new areas, commonly referred to as Creative Technologies, have gained importance. Educational programs appear, meant to foster these developments by stimulating crossovers between computing and non-technological sectors as fashion, health etc. The corresponding curricula only partially concern computing, since a considerable part is devoted to sector specific topics. Designing curricula for hybrid contexts poses interesting questions. Which part of computing is relevant for hybrid programs, in how far should we consider graduates of these curricula as computing professionals? The answer to these questions is controversial.

Recent research on the Dutch labor market [7] observes that boundaries between Information and Communication Technology (ICT) and other sectors are fading away. It refers to the European e-Competence Framework (eCF) [8] that divides specific ICT competences in primary ICT skills, as software development, and secondary ICT skills supporting primary skills, like information security strategy development of user support. Specific ICT competences are increasingly requested in other professions than the computing professions listed in eCF. If professional profiles were classified by the required ICT competences, argues the Dutch report, the computing professions would double. The report predicts a shortage of professionals having primary ICT skills in the immediate future, in particular a shortage of software developers. It also warns against the growth of hybrid undergraduate computing curricula, where 'hybrid' is defined as: "programs that primarily concern other areas than computing". According to the Dutch researchers, hybrid curricula focus too much on secondary ICT skills to comply with the industry's demand.

We question the researchers' conclusions about the education of software developers. But we do acknowledge that designing computing content for hybrid setting is a challenge. This paper strives at understanding computing, to scaffold choices, necessary to design hybrid curricula. Which part of computing is relevant in hybrid contexts, and why?

In our pedagogical analysis we consider two central curricular themes (cf. [1]), namely *Goals and objectives of computing curricula* and *Instructional strategies specific for teaching computing*. The underlying cultural or epistemological view on the discipline [19] is a third theme, which we refer to as *Cultural styles*. In a balanced curriculum, the above three themes are *aligned*, that is, goals and instructional strategies fit together and are consistent with an underlying cultural style.

We will conduct our investigation from a historical perspective. In Section 2 we will sketch the preamble for the joint ACM/IEEE series of curriculum guidelines, to better understand the international guidelines for the undergraduate computing curricula, in particular with respect to goals and objectives of computing curricula.

In Section 3, we will further examine the interdisciplinarity of computing. Besides a comparison of the different cultural styles in computing, we will discuss the implications for computing education, especially concerning instructional strategies.

We explore the challenges for hybrid curricula in terms of trade-offs between the three themes in Section 4. In Section 5 we apply our analysis to two particular hybrid curricula, *Liberal Arts and Computer Science* and *Front End Development*. We conclude with a summary and recommendations in Section 6.

2 COMPUTING CURRICULUM GUIDELINES

North America has a tradition of dialogue between professionals covering different roles in the computing community: scholars, professionals, engineers, and theoreticians. This is remarkable; in the Netherlands, the computing community was shaped by debates and is still divided today [4]. In this section, we will explore the preamble to the Joint Task Forces on Curriculum Recommendation, that were initiated in North America but operate worldwide today.

The usage of programmable computing machines for practical purposes took off with the Second World War in the United States, Germany and Great Britain. But the European computers did not survive the war. The German Z3 was destroyed in an allied bombardment of Berlin in 1943; the British Colossi were considered highly classified and were dismantled for that reason. Things went differently in the U.S.A. The ENIAC was announced to the press in 1946. In the summer of that year, the Pentagon organized lectures about the construction of digital electronic computers, and invited computing professionals from the United States and Great Britain [12]. The dissemination of the ideas underlying computing construction starts here.

Societies for computing professionals were quickly established: one of the precursors of IEEE (the Subcommittee on Large-Scale Computing of the American Institute of Electrical Engineers) in 1946, followed by ACM in 1947. American organizations of computing professionals have collaborated since the early days [9] by sponsoring joint conferences.

Tedre [20] draws a detailed picture of the debates that have shaped the discipline in the second half of the 20th Century. Until the 1960s, mathematicians collaborated with engineers to realize computing machines and languages to program them. These activities resulted in artifacts that have an impact on the world, an impact that sometimes is measurable, but not always. Should computing be considered an art or a science? Should practical topics as programming be taught in academy; is computing an academic discipline at all?

2.1 A theoretical approach

The first edition of the ACM curriculum recommendations, published in 1968, took a stance in this debate. Computer Science (CS) had to be considered an academic discipline studying information structures and processes [20]. Its core issue was handling abstraction. Mathematics provided for theoretical foundation of the discipline. In these days, computer scientists were accommodated in Departments of Mathematics or in Departments of Electronic Engineering. Training for the positions of programmers could be supplied by technology programs, vocational education or junior colleges.

2.2 The software crisis

The theoretical approach appeared not to be able to solve all the problems of the booming discipline. In the late 1960s, software complexity increasingly had become problematic. Complexity did not only arise from the parts of a system – object of study in the Computer Science (CS) departments - but from the connections between these parts [20]. This software crisis uncovered a lack of methodology for understanding and controlling software systems that were too big for single programmers. Software Engineering (SE) emerged, a discipline that considers software development as the effort of a team whose members might have contrasting intentions.

The update of the ACM Curriculum in 1978 brought programming back in the academic curriculum. With the software crisis, the focus of computing had shifted from a discipline studying information structures into an application-centered discipline [20]. Computing had gained independence from mathematics and engineering, but a clear definition of the discipline had been lost.

Curriculum '78 has been criticized for too strongly identifying computing with programming. In their objection to that view, Ralston and Shaw [14] stated that mathematics lays a foundation under both science and engineering, and that understanding of any of these disciplines is impossible without understanding mathematics. Also, the mathematic foundations of computing are stable, where specific skills rapidly become obsolete. Giving students a background in mathematics would protect them from this obsolescence, pleaded Ralston and Shaw.

2.3 The Snowbird conferences in the 1980s

Starting with 1972, the Heads of CS Departments offering PhD in the USA and Canada held biennial meetings in Snowbird, Utah. Members of government and representatives from the computer industry attended these meetings, which evolved towards meetings of the North American computing community.
The 1980 Snowbird Report [5], "A discipline in crisis", depicts a worrisome situation of Computer Science Departments. The computing field was growing explosively. Universities were overburdened by the growth of undergraduate enrollments. There was no time for supervision of graduate students. The best students were hired by industry, which caused a shortage of PhDs. The situation threatened the ability to conduct basic research in Computer Science.

As an answer to the problems described in "A discipline in crisis", dialogues were improved between academia, the industry, government agencies and professional organizations [22]. The 1984 report (Future Issues in Computer Science) [17] addresses the question of the lack of agreement about the accreditation of undergraduate programs. ACM and IEEE had started investigating the desirability of cooperating in the accreditation process at the 1982 Snowbird conference [22]. By 1984, the professional organizations had created a Computer Science Accreditation Board (CSAB); the volunteers necessary to administrate the CSAB were provided by academy.

One of the aims of CSAB was: providing a more common view of a core description, at least for the undergraduate curriculum. ACM and IEEE formed a joint task force to describe the intellectual substance of the computing field in 1985[6]. A joint task force for the definition of the undergraduate curricula was formed in 1988 [15].

2.4 The ACM/IEEE curriculum reports

The Task Force, chaired by P. Denning, presented its final report "Computing as a Discipline" in 1989. The Task Force uses the phrase *discipline of computing* as an umbrella term for scientific and engineering aspects of computing. It starts with stating having extended its task to both Computer Science and Computer Engineering because it had concluded that *no fundamental differences exist between the two fields in the core material.* [6] The report distinguishes three major paradigms, or cultural styles, for the computing discipline: theory (rooted in mathematics), abstraction (rooted in the experimental scientific method), and design (rooted in engineering). The three cultural styles are fundamental for the discipline, which is described as a blend of interaction among theory, abstraction and design.

"Computing as a discipline" addresses the question, in which area of computing majors should be competent. The answer is cautious: discipline-oriented thinking should be the primary goal of every curriculum for computing majors, based on solid mathematical foundations. Teaching paradigms emphasizing inquiry and orientation in the computing literature are recommended, instead of lectures presenting answers.

"Computing as a discipline" pleads against a strong identification of computing with programming. It also states that every computing major should be competent in programming. The Task Force remarks, that the distinctions between the computing disciplines are embodied in the differences between programming languages, and recommends programming languages to be treated as a vehicle to access these distinctions.

Since 1989, the ACM/IEEE has jointly formed Task Forces that have published and iterated overview reports with recommendations for computing curricula. They appeared in 1991 and 2005. These reports have a triple ambition. They aim at (1) training the professionals requested by industry, (2) training the students' intellectual skills necessary to find employment, enter the Master level and keep up with future developments, and (3) granting the development of the discipline of computing.

Over the years, the amount of sub disciplines has narrowed to 5 [2]: Computer Science, Computer Engineering, Information Systems, Information Technology, and Software Engineering. Undergraduate curriculum recommendations for each of these areas were published in 2005. Specific committees of ACM and IEEE representatives worldwide have updated them since then. CS2013 applies to Computer Science, one of the sub-disciplines of computing. It falls outside the scope of this investigation.

2.5 Hybrid computing curricula

Until the 1970s, computers were used in professional setting in the industry, in academia and in big governmental institutions. The first computer users were programmers, but the user base changed as the costs of hardware lowered [20]. New interdisciplinary fields of study emerged, as Management Information Systems, combining computing topics with topics from other disciplines.

Today, all computing curricula are "hybrid" to a certain extent. Non-computing topics as Risk Management or Interpersonal Communication are taught in most undergraduate computing programs. But there also is a "core of computing", common to all these programs. The last ACM/IEEE Overview Report, CC2005 [2], provides 10 knowledge areas and 40 topics every Computing Curriculum should cover. The weight of these topics in single curricula can differ, and some topics might not be covered at all, but the clear intention of the Report is to describe a core, common to the five sub disciplines of computing.

Today, there also are undergraduate curricula covering a significant part of the core of computing, but omitting another significant part. Some examples are: Medical Information Systems [7], Business Analytics [7], Liberal Arts and Computer Science [10]. We will adopt the Dutch researchers' definition and will indicate as "hybrid" these curricula dedicating less than half of their program to topics belonging to the core of computing.

3 CULTURAL STYLES IN COMPUTING

The Task Force's view on three cultural styles of computing [6] was not new. In 1969, Peter Wegner had held a lecture at the annual meeting of the American Association for the Advancement of Science. Its title was: Three computer traditions [21]. Wegner objected to a single view of computing. CS, argued Wegener, is *in part a scientific discipline concerned with the empirical study of a class of phenomena, in part a mathematical discipline concerned with the formal properties of certain classes of abstract structures, and in part a technological discipline concerned with the cost-effective design and construction of commercially and socially valuable products.*

In a recent article [19], Tedre and Apiola discuss the different cultural styles of computing, or (in their terminology) three traditions of computing. According to the authors, these three traditions fulfill different roles in the development of the discipline of computing. The scientific tradition copes with the fundamental problem: does an abstract model fit the world? The engineering tradition copes with the question, how to translate abstract models into working artifacts. The theoretical tradition aims at building a coherent abstract framework supporting understanding of notions as algorithms, complexity, data structures. All authors agree upon the importance of intertwining the traditions in the computing practice.

Despite the statement in the 1989 report, that "no fundamental difference exists between the [...] fields in the core material", founding the discipline on three traditions is a challenge. Tedre and Apiola [19] analyze the differences between the three cultural styles, and the implications of these differences implications for basic (K-12) computing education. They state that, however intertwined and overlapping, the three cultural styles are fundamentally different in their aims, in the status of the knowledge they pursue and in their methodological views.

The aim of the theoretical tradition is to produce coherent structures, in order to describe algorithms and cope with complexity. The scientific tradition aims at understanding the world by modeling phenomena (such as the weather, the mind) and testing the accuracy of the models. The engineering tradition aims at changing the world, by producing artifacts that fulfill social needs or desires.

In the theoretical tradition, knowledge is considered independent of what people may think. It is considered universal and is validated in its theoretical context. Also the scientific tradition claims to aim at value-free knowledge, which should be descriptive. This is opposed to the engineering tradition, in which knowledge is partially value-free (where it concerns physical constraints) and partially value-laden (where it concerns social needs and desires). The Body of Knowledge in the engineering tradition is partially descriptive and partially normative (know-how).

The theoretical tradition analyzes ideas. Propositions should be proven. The scientific tradition observes the world. Claims should be sustained by empirical results. The engineering tradition acts. It evaluates tangible products. Engineers must be able to act, even without having sufficient information to fully sustain the design of the artifact.

Tedre and Apiola's paper concerns K-12 computing education. The authors plead for aligning learning objectives with the corresponding computing traditions (expressed in pedagogic approaches and educational resources), because a mix would not result in effective educational interventions. If the learning objectives of the school concern construction processes, assessment tasks should not be propositional (quizzes), but procedural (assessment of design artifacts), because they better fit in the related tradition, which in this case is engineering. The authors stress that educators should understand all the traditions of computing. They warn for bias induced by hidden ethos elevating one of the traditions above the others, both inside schools as in university departments educating teachers.

Tedre and Apiola reflect on the role of computing traditions in educational design. The authors recommend matching the tradition with the learning objectives of educational units. In the end, it is an argument about the efficacy of educational interventions. It does not concern the learning objectives themselves, nor the goals and objectives of computing curricula.

4 DISCUSSION: CURRICULAR TRADE-OFFS

In this section we will reflect on hybrid computing education using the three pedagogical themes described earlier. Alignment of the three themes in combination with the limited space for computing in a hybrid curriculum gives rise to challenges. Below we will discuss three of these challenges: representing all cultures (cultural styles), fostering of discipline oriented thinking (goals and objectives) and the role of mathematics (goals and objectives, again). In our opinion, the trade-offs involved with curricular choices ought to be made explicit by authors of hybrid curricula. In Section 5 we will discuss two cases in more detail.

4.1 Incorporation of the three cultural styles

In 1989, the Task Force on the Core of Computer Science described a common core of the discipline of computing. Content from each cultural style should be treated by all undergraduate computing curriculums. To prepare students for the future –which was uncertain– the 1989 recommendations included *inquiry-based* learning activities and orientation in the computing literature, instead of lectures presenting answers.

According to Tedre and Apiola, the three cultural styles not only entail different approaches to the discipline, but also respect different epistemological values. Should value-laden knowledge be accepted (as it is in the engineering culture) or should knowledge always be value-free? Should ideas be analyzed (theoretical culture) or evaluated empirically (scientific culture)?

An inquiry-based curriculum appears not to be neutral from this perspective. There is a risk that Institutions (schools, academies, departments) prefer one culture, one approach to research above others. Even an inquiry-based educational approach can canalize students' understanding of the discipline, towards values, consistent with the method of inquiry.

A possible direction for a solution is given by "Computing as a discipline" in stating that "*most of the distinctions in computing are embodied in programming notations*". It suggests using differences between programming languages as a vehicle to discuss differences between approaches to computing. We will return to this in Section 5.2.

4.2 Fostering discipline oriented thinking

The ACM/IEEE curricula are written from a triple ambition: to serve the students, serve the industry and grant the development of a (unified) discipline. In the light of Tedre's and Apiola's findings, we are not optimistic about the possibility of fulfilling all the ACM/IEEE curricular ambitions by any of the undergraduate computing curricula. Especially the aims concerning overview of the discipline and employability appear to be scarcely compatible with each other. Mixing content from cultural styles will not automatically grant overview of the discipline, since knowledge is also rooted in the understanding of research methods. Nor will an investigative approach to education necessarily support discipline oriented thinking.

Employability and capability to keep up with future developments often suppose up-to-date knowledge in one of the sub disciplines and related research skills. Once acquainted with one of the cultural styles, the graduate is likely to pursue a career path compatible with it, reinforcing the chosen orientation.

If granting overview of the discipline is challenging for hybrid curricula, explicating boundaries becomes necessary.

4.3 The role of mathematics

Both the 1989 Task Force and the authors of "Computing as a discipline" recognized the importance of a solid mathematical foundation to foster discipline oriented thinking.

We partially agree on the overall importance of mathematical thinking for computing professionals. Yes, the theoretical cultural style does support discipline oriented thinking, because it provides a common language to discuss computing constructs. It certainly does support formal reasoning. But Mathematics too is a vast discipline. Different branches of computing rely different branches of Mathematics. A course on continuous mathematics supports skills that are relevant to computer engineers, not necessarily to information scientists. The existence of one form of mathematical training, apt to foster overall understanding of computing, is debatable.

5 HYBRID CURRICULA: TWO CASES

In this section we will apply our findings to two existing hybrid programs: Liberal Arts and Computer Science and Front End Development, respectively. For each of these we will examine our pedagogical themes and the appearance of trade-offs.

5.1 Liberal Arts and Computer Science

The Liberal Arts and Computer Science (LACS) curriculum (USA) [10], has its origin in a reaction to ACM's Curriculum '78, a strongly engineering oriented curriculum [3][20]. Liberal Arts undergraduate programs traditionally emphasize intellectual growth of students, rather than preparing them for a specific career. In 1984, a consortium of small Liberal Arts colleges offering computing degrees, was formed to discuss the problems these colleges had with the implementation of Curriculum '78. The meetings resulted in the first Model Curriculum for a Liberal Arts Degree in Computer Science (LACS), which appeared in 1986.

LACS offers a Bachelor of Arts degree. Roughly 40% of the curriculum is dedicated to Computer Science, 5-10% to other science courses and the remaining 50-55% to humanities and social sciences [10]. LACS is a hybrid computing curriculum.

It is interesting to see, what the LACS curriculum guidelines states about the role of mathematics. Mathematical education is considered part of the Computer Science curriculum, for several reasons. Computing relies on mathematical objects (as sets, relations) and mathematical reasoning (logic, algorithms, correctness proofs); mathematical tools as probability and statistics allow analysis of software [10].

5.1.1 Cultural styles LACS chooses a generalist approach and de-emphasizes specific technical details. It acknowledges the importance of mathematics in this - hybrid - curriculum. In terms of Tedre's and Apiola's work, the theoretical and the scientific view are combined in the LACS curriculum, but the engineering viewpoint is somehow overshadowed.

5.1.2 Goals and objectives LACS strives to train generalists. The curriculum de-emphasizes specific technical details; its ambition is to develop student's intellectual skills. The objective of the curriculum is to support durable intellectual growth, combined with (generalist, discipline oriented) helicopter view.

5.1.3 Trade offs The LACS curriculum explicitly makes concessions to its ambitions towards software development.

5.2 Front End Development

We will refer to the discipline, specialized in the development of multimodal user interfaces as Front End Development (FED) and the corresponding professional figures, Front End Developers (FEDs):.

"A front-end developer specializes in building the front end, or client-side, of a web application, which encompasses everything that a client, or user, sees and interacts with. Front-end development is all about what's *visible* to the user." [16] .

There is not yet consensus about an undergraduate curriculum for FED. In Amsterdam, FED is a major of the undergraduate curriculum Communication and Multimedia Design, in the domain Creative Technologies. FEDs are professional users of client-side technology. They work in interdisciplinary teams in developing projects. FEDs produce software that interacts with APIs, services and other ready-to-use software components, written by other computing professionals.

5.2.1 Cultural styles FED is teamwork and aims to produce maintainable software products. For these reasons, we tend to include FED among the disciplines emphasizing primary ICT skills as described in section 1. Still, not all of computing is relevant for FEDs. Most of the Front End Developer's work is visible to the user and can be tested directly. There is no need for correctness proofs in FED. FEDs need Mathematics to interpret quantitative research data. Acquaintance with basic abstract structures as sets and enumerations is needed, since every Front End communicates with other computer systems through abstract interfaces. In how far modeling skills are necessary for FEDs is subject to discussion. In terms of Tedre's and Apiola's work, the engineering and the scientific aspects of computing are emphasized by this program, at the expenses of theoretical aspects.

5.2.2 Goals and objectives FED is characterized by focus on craftsmanship, in the context of interdisciplinary developing teams and rapid technologic evolution. It strives at training competent manpower for the discipline of FED, who will be able to to comply with future developments in FED.

5.2.3 Instructional strategies Front-end developing languages are introduced stressing their aims and their boundaries, conform the Task Force's remark on programming languages: "Software, written with HTML, performs behavior that is visible. It is not necessary to express intended outcomes in formal statements; the software can be tested. To support interaction with abstract agents, professional HTML code should respect conventional semantics. These are defined by a political process". This supports future FEDs' understanding of the scope of their craftsmanship, helps them to follow the evolution of their discipline, and to participate in that process.

5.2.4 Trade offs. The choice for an engineering-based FED curriculum, at the expense of the theoretical content, has consequences. Graduates are not all-round software developers. Their sphere of activity is limited to the user interface. FEDs are trained in making Front-End artifacts, not in developing Front-End technology. They use and research the possibilities of existing technology. The question, whether FEDs should develop simple APIs is still open.

FED graduates are granted access to the Master's level in hybrid computing disciplines as Digital Communication and Media, not to Master's programs in Software Engineering.

6 CONCLUSIONS

We investigated the possibility to type hybrid computing curricula. Our conclusion is: refer to the complex epistemological background of computing to type hybrid curricula. It is inevitable for designers of hybrid curricula to make choices. This approach gives insight in the related trade-offs; it is relevant for both educational institutions and accreditation boards.

We do think that some of the hybrid computing curricula can train developers, although bound to specific contexts, like FEDs. Though, it is fundamental to describe and stress the boundaries of such programs, and of the corresponding professions. Defining and tuning undergraduate computing curricula is not only a matter of training manpower requested by industry. We saw that the field of computing was shaped by a joint effort of industry, academy and governmental institutions, and urge designers of hybrid curricula, to take responsibility for the definition of new disciplines. Trade-offs, involved by curricular choices, should explicitly be discussed in broad communities including: related computing disciplines in academy, the industry and the public authorities.

Following Tedre's and Apiola's observations, we also recommend that all educators of computing topics understand the complex nature of computing. This applies in particular to those lecturing in hybrid curricula, a condition that is not always met. We address educators, to warn them against a sloppy approach to computing: (1) lecturing the outcomes without the method would not result in durable knowledge; (2) lecturing technology without mentioning its trade-offs would not allow students to position themselves as professionals in the dynamic field of computing; (3) lecturing the method without the philosophical motivations would mean not taking students seriously enough to invite them to join the conversation about their own professional future.

REFERENCES

[1] Van den Akker, J. (2003). Curriculum perspectives: An introduction. In: Van den Akker, J., Kuiper, W., Hameyer, U. (eds.) *Curriculum landscapes and trends* (pp. 1-10). Springer Netherlands.

[2] ACM/IEEE. (2005). Computing Curricula 2005. The Overview report, Retrieved from https://www.acm.org/education/curricula-recommendations, 10.6.2016

[3] Bruce, K. B., Cupper, R. D., & Drysdale, R. L. S. (2010). A history of the liberal arts computer science consortium and its model curricula. ACM Transactions on Computing Education (TOCE), 10(1), 3.

[4] Dael, R. L. H. V. (2001). 'Iets met computers': over beroepsvorming van de informaticus. Delft: Eburon.

[5] Denning, P. J., Feigenbaum, E. A., Gilmore, P., Hearn, A. C., Ritchie, R. W., & Traub, J. F. (1981). A discipline in crisis. Communications of the ACM,24(6), 370-374.

[6] Denning, PJ, DE Comer, D. Gries, MC Mulder, A. Tucker, AJ Turner, and PR Young (1988). "Computing as a discipline." Communications of the ACM 32, no. 1 (1989): 9-23.

[7] Dialogic & Matchcare (2016). Digitaal vakmanschap, van de ICT arbeidsmarkt naar de arbeidsmarkt voor ICT'ers, retrieved from https://www.nederlandict.nl/news/tekort-aan-developers-neemt-toe/2.11.2016

[8] eCF, European e –Competence Framework 3.0, retrieved from http://www.ecompetences.eu, 02.6.2016

[9] Joint Computer Conferences, retrieved from https://en.wikipedia.org/wiki/Joint_Computer_Conference , 18.3.2016

[10] Liberal Arts Computer Science Consortium. (2007). A 2007 model curriculum for a liberal arts degree in computer science. Journal on Educational Resources in Computing (JERIC), 7(2), 2.

[12] Moore School Lectures, retrieved from https://en.wikipedia.org/wiki/Moore_School_Lectures, 12.01.2016

[13] Ralston, A. (1981). Computer science, mathematics, and the undergraduate curricula in both. The American Mathematical Monthly, 88(7), 472-485.

[14] Ralston, A., & Shaw, M. (1980). Curriculum'78 - is computer science really that unmathematical?. Communications of the ACM, 23(2), 67-70.

[15] Reilly, E. D. (2004). Concise encyclopedia of computer science, 4th edition (p.291). John Wiley & Sons.

[16] http://www.skilledup.com/articles/web-developer-job-descriptions-skills-they-require retrieved 25-5-2016

[17] Tartar, J., Arden, B., Booth, T., Denning, P., Miller, R., & Van Dam, A. (1985). 1984 Snowbird Report: Future Issues in Computer Science. Computer, 18(5), 101-105.

[19] Tedre, M., & Apiola, M. (2013). Three computing traditions in school computing education. In: Kadijevich, D. M., Angeli, C., & Schulte, C. (eds.). Improving computer science education. Routledge, 2013, CH. 7.

[20] Tedre, M.: lecture Notes on the Philosophy of Computer Science, retrieved September, 3rd 2015 from http://cs.joensuu.fi/~mmeri/teaching/2007/philcs/

[21] Wegner, P.(1970) Three computer traditions: Computer technology, computer mathematics, and computer science. Advances in computers, 10, 7-78.

[22] Yau, S. S., Ritchie, R. W., Semon, W., Traub, J., Van Dam, A., & Winkler, S. (1983). Meeting the Crisis in Computer Science. Communications of the ACM, 26(12), 1046-10

Curriculum-Aligned Work-Integrated Learning: A New Kind of Industry-Academic Degree Partnership

Gail Carmichael
Shopify
Ottawa, Ontario
gail.carmichael@shopify.com

Christine Jordan
Shopify
Ottawa, Ontario
christine.jordan@shopify.com

Andrea Ross
Shopify
Ottawa, Ontario
andrea.ross@shopify.com

Alison Evans Adnani
Shopify
Ottawa, Ontario
alison.evansadnani@shopify.com

ABSTRACT

Work-integrated learning is a common approach to add practical, real-world work experience to academic settings. Traditional co-op programs in colleges and universities alternate courses with semesters spent as an intern at a relevant workplace. We have designed an academic-industry partnership that takes work-integrated learning further by deliberately aligning workplace experience to the academic curriculum. Our students earn a Bachelor of Computer Science from the university, and are paid employees of the industry partner throughout their degree. While advanced courses and electives are taken on campus as usual, some core computer science classes and practicum courses are delivered with the industry partner so as to integrate them with placements on site. Assessment remains the responsibility of the university. In this report, we describe the partnership from the perspective of the industry partner. We describe our goals, partnership design, and first two iterations of the implementation. We discuss the challenges we have faced with our first cohort, and share suggestions for others looking to create similar programs.

ACM Reference Format:
Gail Carmichael, Christine Jordan, Andrea Ross, and Alison Evans Adnani. 2018. Curriculum-Aligned Work-Integrated Learning: A New Kind of Industry-Academic Degree Partnership. In *Proceedings of The 49th ACM Technical Symposium on Computer Science Education, Baltimore, MD, USA, Feb. 21–24, 2018 (SIGCSE '18)*, 6 pages.
https://doi.org/10.1145/3159450.3159543

1 INTRODUCTION

The educational needs of the twenty-first century's workforce are constantly in flux as scientific breakthroughs and new technologies redefine the nature of work. Educational institutions are not structured to be immediately responsive to changing skills demands, and require time to redesign and rejuvenate their curricula. Not enough students are graduating with the skills necessary to meet the technology industry's workforce needs [6]. The gap between skills provided by higher educational institutions and those that are needed in the workforce is especially apparent in computer science education, where programming languages, tools, and best practices are constantly evolving. The challenges facing computer science education relating to its rapid evolution along with the employability of graduates has been a topic of discussion and debate for many years [2, 5].

Several work-integrated learning models have been implemented in post-secondary educational institutions, such as industry-focused capstone projects and cooperative education projects. One way that work has been integrated with student learning is by having students perform capstone projects working with industry. A capstone project typically happens in the last year of a student's degree, as a culminating project that builds upon the knowledge the student has gained throughout the course of their degree program. An example of this is the Undergraduate Capstone Open Source Projects (UCOSP) [1] program that allows Canadian undergraduate computer science students to work on open source software projects for academic credit. With capstone projects happening at the end of a degree, it may be several years until students are able encounter the real-world applications of the theory they are learning. A disadvantage of this approach is that students do not get the motivational benefit of problem-based learning when a concept is introduced.

Cooperative education has been a popular model of work-integrated learning, but has remained mostly unchanged since its initial inception in 1957 [4]. It provides students with alternating learning terms at an academic institution and work terms in the workplace. Depending on the program, students may complete all their working terms at the same employer, or acquire a variety of work experiences by changing employers each term. It benefits students by allowing them to connect with their community of practice and work on real-world applications. However, there are several short-comings of the cooperative education model; in particular, the work performed in work terms is not guaranteed to reinforce the concepts that students have been learning or align with students' coursework. With learning and work terms being performed consecutively, students must wait months before being able to see the applications of the theory they have learned in class.

SIGCSE '18, Feb. 21–24, 2018, Baltimore, MD, USA

ACM ISBN 978-1-4503-5103-4/18/02...$15.00.
https://doi.org/10.1145/3159450.3159543

Shopify and Carleton University have partnered to deliver Carleton's Bachelor of Computer Science degree in a whole new way. Instead of separating coursework and work placements, students in the program are immersed in the work environment and have the opportunity to connect the two deliberately and deeply. We call our approach curriculum-aligned work-integrated learning (CAWIL). In this report, we describe our partnership from the perspective of the industry partner. We introduce details of CAWIL in Section 2, including goals and the high level design of the partnership. In Section 3, we discuss the first and second iterations of implementing the partnership. We conclude in Section 4 with some suggestions for those considering their own CAWIL programs based on lessons we have learned so far.

2 CURRICULUM-ALIGNED WORK-INTEGRATED LEARNING

2.1 Partnership Goals

It is our philosophy that excellent software developers come from many types of backgrounds, and that a background incorporating both theory and practice is particularly valuable. We decided to partner with a local university to try a new approach to delivering a Bachelor of Computer Science degree. The university covers the theoretical aspects of the program as usual, while we not only provide relevant work experience, but deliberately align workplace competencies with the material learned on campus. We call our model **curriculum-aligned work-integrated learning** (CAWIL).

Our goal is to create a model that is different from other computing education initiatives. We are not trying to replicate the idea of a bootcamp, where the focus is much more heavily on specific industry technologies. We are also not offering an apprenticeship in the traditional sense, though there are aspects of apprenticeship in our team placements. We are closest to the idea of co-op. However, we are not alternating team placements with semesters on campus and hoping that students see how theory from courses can be applied on the job. Instead, students work and study at the same time, and we explicitly connect the two.

We consider a successful curriculum-aligned work-integrated learning experience to have the following characteristics:

- student coursework is deliberately and intentionally connected to team placements
- students have opportunities to master academic learning outcomes through their team placements and our in-house supporting curriculum
- whenever possible, students experience a concept in a practical setting through their team placements before they see the associated theory
- the time that passes between experiencing a concept and learning the theory is minimized
- students are given formal opportunities to reflect on connections between theory and practice

Shopify is a software company providing a commerce platform to entrepreneurs. Shopify's priorities naturally focus on its business. Broadly, our business goals are:

- increase the pipeline of **talented, qualified computer science graduates** to our company and more generally in Canada, all with a favorable opinion of Shopify as an employer
- improve Shopify's ability to **onboard and accelerate the impact of junior employees**, thus widening the pool of talent we can recruit
- achieve these goals in a way that delivers the **highest possible return on investment** (for example, by having our students contribute to the company in a meaningful way by the end of their degree)

To reach our business goals, we strive to support our students in becoming:

- **competent computer scientists** – Our students should build strong theoretical knowledge and deep experiential wisdom, and see meaningful connections between the two.
- **co-creators of an exceptional learning experience** – Students and educators should co-create a learning environment that is active, learner-centered, and problem-based.
- **resilient and in control** – Students should understand what is expected of them throughout their degree. They should not feel overwhelmed by the program's difficulty, and be able to maintain a reasonable work/life balance. They should feel well supported, for example through on-site coaching.
- **cultural role models** – Students should be able to fit well into the company's culture and be committed to its mission.
- **empowered and valued employees** – Students should see that they are contributing to the company through their work, and not feel indebted when they finish school.
- **connected collaborators** – Students should build camaraderie among their cohort, and become well connected both within and outside of the company.

In the following, the design of our partnership, and our experience implementing it over the past year, should be read in the context of these goals.

2.2 Partnership Design

Both Carleton University and Shopify contributed to the design of our partnership. On the university side, changes were required to accommodate the team placements in a way that supports CAWIL. Fortunately, we did not require the creation of a new degree program. Instead, we were able to add a special option to the existing Bachelor of Computer Science Honours program. It is very important to note that Carleton is still granting the degree, not Shopify. Carleton fully owns the assessment of students and assignment of grades. The same standards apply to all students, whether part of our partnership or not.

Students participating in the partnership are paid Shopify employees throughout their degree, both through a salary and tuition grant. There is no need to take on a part time job during school, and students can graduate debt free. After some time focused on learning fundamental computing skills, students join development teams and contribute to our products while learning competencies in a practical setting. After joining teams, students spend time both studying and working, ideally integrating practice and theory as per the goals of CAWIL. They are able to finish their degree in four years, and graduate with at least as many hours of work experience as a typical co-op program that usually takes five years to complete.

Most credit requirements in the degree remain the same, except that eight free electives become practicum credits. Practicums are pass/fail courses that capture the industrial skills students are learning at the company, both through their team placements and through educational material developed at Shopify. Practicums are also used to give credit for the acquisition of soft skills and exploration of other CS topics of interest. Two practicums are covered each year, and each year has a theme.

The degree includes eight core computer science courses that all students take, including CS1, CS2, and web development fundamentals. It is through the core courses that we want to tie theory and practice together especially tightly. We aim to have the competencies from these courses mastered on site at Shopify through active learning workshops, self-directed learning, and work on team placements.

Math courses, advanced computer science electives, and breadth electives are taken on campus as usual. We encourage students to take breadth electives later in their degree than is typical, pushing CS content earlier. We do this to ensure students are ready to join teams as soon as possible, and to help students find electives later on that can connect to their computing skills and interests.

Students interested in participating in our partnership for their degree must apply for one of a limited number of places. Students apply first to the university, and if they are accepted to the Bachelor of Computer Science Honours program, they submit an application portfolio to Shopify. We screen students based on their applications, then interview them in a process quite similar to other Shopify interns. We look for students who have a demonstrated passion for wanting to solve real-world problems with computing, along with a strong academic background and/or at least some prior experience with computing. We believe strongly in the value of diversity, and work hard to encourage underrepresented groups in tech to apply.

Accepted students can expect to receive extra support from Shopify staff. Our team provides coaching before students join teams and instructional support for material delivered on site. We help them get used to what is quite a new way of learning for most of them, and help them navigate a career as a software developer – this will be the first job many of our students have had. Placement teams provide mentors and coaching after students start working.

3 PARTNERSHIP IMPLEMENTATION

Shopify welcomed our first cohort of students in September 2016. They experienced the first implementation of the partnership design described above, and encountered our first set of challenges. Both are discussed below as the alpha version of the implementation. We took what we learned from our first cohort and designed the beta version of the partnership, which will partially be implemented for the first cohort and fully implemented for the second cohort that joined us in September 2017.

3.1 Alpha Implementation

Our first cohort of students joined us in September 2016 for the alpha implementation of our program. We had eleven students total (six female, five male). Four were mature students, returning to school having completed another degree some time in the past. We tested the alpha implementation design for two semesters before transitioning to the beta design.

Figure 1 summarizes the structure of the alpha implementation. Students took up to three courses and a practicum each semester, including over the summer (on-campus students typically take five courses each in the fall and winter semesters). Team placements began in the second semester, when material for the core computer science courses was learned through placements as well as workshops and self-paced learning delivered on site. Students would be working on teams every semester after that except for two, when they would attend courses on campus full time.

One of our most important goals is to increase the number of talented software developers primarily at Shopify, as well as in the greater community in Canada. As such, we designed an unconventional path through Carleton's Bachelor of Computer Science. Students typically take CS1 and CS2 in their first and second semesters respectively, which then opens up a number of core courses that can be taken in second year; math courses and breadth electives fill out most of the first year. We wanted to accelerate when our students acquired fundamental computing skills so they could meaningfully contribute to the company as soon as possible. Delivering both CS1 and CS2 back to back in the first semester helped meet this goal, as did getting students onto placement teams as fast as possible.

Not shown in Figure 1 is a Ruby on Rails bootcamp given to students at the beginning of the second semester. After the two week long intensive introduction to the technology used on web-centric teams at Shopify, students started their first placements. In the second semester, web development and data structures competencies were meant to be mastered through work on teams, self study, and active-learning workshops delivered on site. Students participated in the assessments given on campus. The plan was for students to rotate their team placements every two semesters with the goal of performing work closely related to the competencies of the core courses delivered in that timeframe.

Mentoring was structured such that each student received one-on-one time with a mentor from the education team. During biweekly meetings (and additionally as needed), the mentor and student discussed academic progress and personal development. The student was also encouraged to provide feedback about the partnership. Mentors also met with each other biweekly to discuss the topics to cover in the next sessions and to raise any issues that need to be addressed by the team.

3.2 Alpha Challenges

As is to be expected with an undertaking this large, we ran into several challenges with the alpha implementation of our partnership. Some of these were due to time and staffing constraints on the company side, and others indicated where we could improve our design. We collected data from our mentorship and instructional sessions, interactions with education staff, and formal anonymous surveys sent regularly to students to measure against the goals of Section 2.1.

Our first semester with CS1 and CS2 was largely successful. Students performed well in the online, self-paced courses and generally maintained a reasonable balance with their on-campus course, their

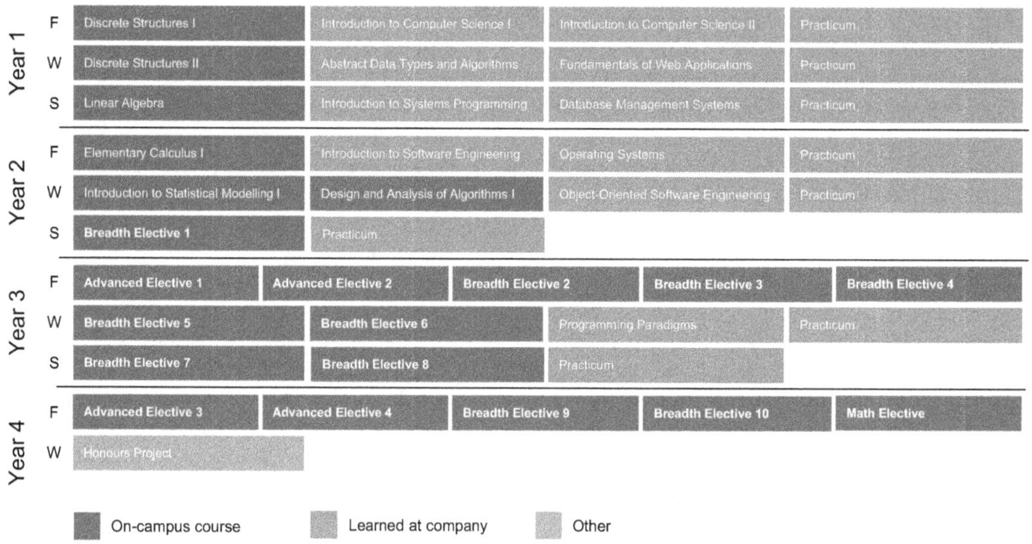

Figure 1: Course sequence for alpha implementation.

practicum, and getting settled into life at Shopify. We had originally planned to deliver our Ruby on Rails bootcamp for three to four weeks at the end of the semester, but were unable to dedicate time to its development. Instead, we held a two week bootcamp created by another Shopify employee at the beginning of the second semester.

Students joined teams immediately after the bootcamp, but were not sufficiently prepared. The bootcamp was too short, and could have been better designed pedagogically. Further, students were not proficient enough in GitHub, which we intended for them to use for their practicum projects and which was covered again only superficially during the bootcamp. In some cases, students had not developed strong enough programming skills for the particular teams they were joining.

Teams were not sufficiently prepared to accept our students, either. It took us an unexpectedly long time to find teams willing and able to take on our relatively junior students when they were used to interns further on in their education. As a result we ran out of time to prepare the teams that did agree. We did not set proper expectations of what level our students would be at and what kind of work they should do. Developing scaffolds to be used in the future would benefit not only our own students, but the ability of all teams across the company to take on more junior employees.

Delivery of our two second semester courses – web development and data structures – failed to meet our goals of CAWIL. Students had the option of participating in just the final exam for each course, but did not want their entire mark based on one test. They opted to take the midterm as well as submit assignments, the latter to help prepare for the former. Unfortunately, by participating in all the assessments, we were very tightly tied to the cadence of the on-campus course, yet we did not get information from instructors any sooner than the students. In the case of the web development course, we also found ourselves tied to the technologies used on campus, which did not match what we used in house. Students struggled with the self-directed learning we assigned them and yearned for more structure. Because of these challenges, placement work did not contribute directly to learning the core CS courses and we were unable to spend time in workshops making connections to it.

The difficulties of the second semester negatively affected our students' well being. Joining teams too early caused them a large amount of stress and anxiety. We discovered that their trust in the education team diminished. With team members acting as mentors as well as instructors, students were not forthright and often did not bring forward their actual concerns, or tell us if they were in crisis. Additionally, most students coming from high school were experiencing their first professional job experience. Not all knew how to behave in some situations without additional coaching, sometimes escalating situations further.

One interesting issue that arose that may have contributed to some of the other problems is that of student perception. After team placements began, we found that some students felt that they were getting "a raw deal" with this program. They compared themselves with full time engineering staff and felt badly that they were the lowest paid, with the least vacation and the most work on their plate. A group coaching session helped these students shift their perspective to that of their peers, who felt very lucky to be part of a program with many perks compared to other students taking the traditional path through the degree.

Finally, we found that our model for mentoring needed adjustment. As mentioned above, having our staff play the role of mentor, instructor, and program developer led to not receiving accurate information and feedback from students. The model would also not be scalable as we welcome new cohorts each year and expand with new partnerships.

3.3 Beta Implementation

After two semesters of the alpha implementation, we began working on the beta implementation design (simply referred to as beta

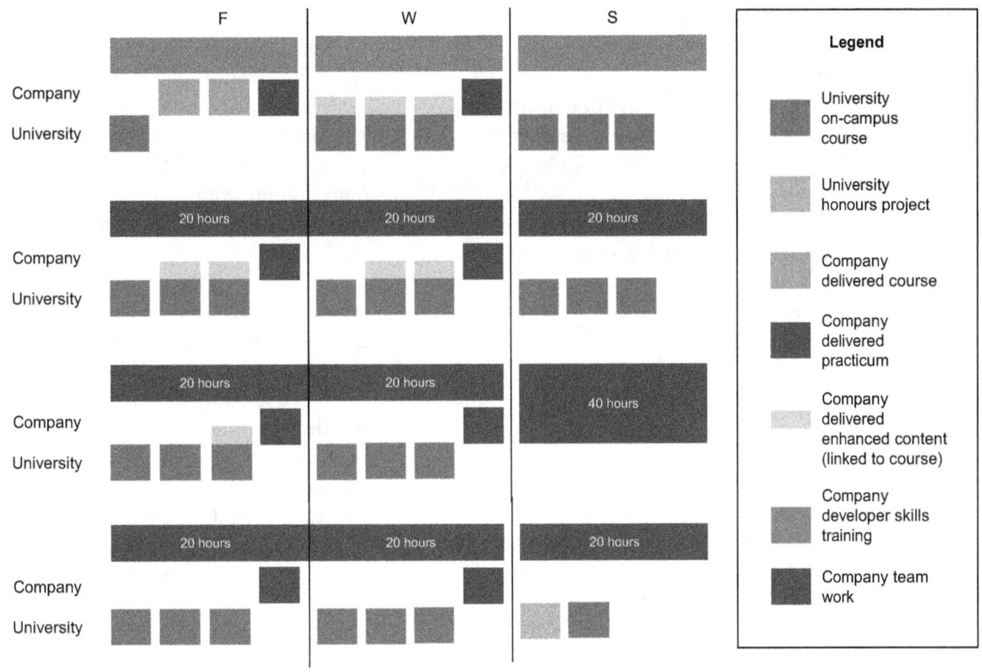

Figure 2: Course structure for beta implementation.

from here on) to address some of the challenges outlined above. Our second cohort of students began in September 2017 and will experience beta fully. Our first cohort of students will experience a modified version of beta that fits with what they have completed in alpha so far. The key areas of improvement for beta are centered around curriculum, placements, and student wellbeing.

With respect to curriculum, the most important changes bring us closer to meeting our CAWIL goals. The structure of beta is summarized in Figure 2. In beta, we focus our time on our greatest strengths: industry-specific knowledge and how it fits with theory. Rather than find ourselves watching what instructors are doing on campus and trying to replicate it, we will add a new layer between academic courses and work at Shopify. Starting second semester, students will take most core computer science classes on campus, and then engage with additional material and workshops at Shopify that link the theory they learn to industry practice. Practicums in beta capture this enhanced content layer as well as team placements.

CS1 and CS2 will remain as online courses run back to back first semester. However, the first practicum in beta works differently than in alpha. Instead of group projects of the students' choosing, students participate in developer skills training courses in topics such as command-line interfaces, and GitHub. Developer skills training continues in the second and third semesters, sometimes tied directly to on-campus course and sometimes as standalone topics.

Students will now begin their first team placements at the beginning of their second year. By pushing back when students join teams, we are better able to prepare them in terms of technical and professional skills. In turn, development teams will benefit from more productive students, and place higher trust in the value of the partnership. Students should also feel significantly less pressure to perform at too high a level early. Another benefit of later placements is the ability to better match students to the *right* team in terms of skills, personality, need for mentoring, and so on.

Perhaps most importantly, we have put a much greater focus on student wellbeing for beta. We saw first hand in alpha how important a positive student experience is, and that performance in both academics and work placement is significantly affected if student wellbeing degrades. As a result, we have created a dedicated role in our education team to facilitate a positive student experience. We have also designed a *Life at Shopify* program that matches students with mentors outside of the education team. The lead of the education team is additionally available to students, as is the lead of their work placements when those begin.

3.4 Data Collection

We currently have several mechanisms for collecting data about our program. In the future, we hope to conduct a more in-depth analysis of our data. At present, our data informs us on how students are performing and what changes we can make on an ongoing, realtime basis.

Student weekly reports: Students submit a weekly report on Fridays using a stoplight rating for wellbeing, academics, and work placement. Green signifies no significant issues, yellow signifies some issues but nothing serious, and red signifies serious issues. Students reflect on their work from the past week and share plans for the next week, what they need help with, and any other general comments.

Mentor bi-weekly reports: Each placement mentor submits a performance evaluation report every second Friday, again using a stoplight rating for wellbeing, academics, and work placement results. Mentors also numerically rate students on various dimensions ranging from dependability to impact.

Practicum term reports: Students submit summative practicum reports that tie academic learning objectives to work placements in the fall and winter terms and allow for reflection on work placements and the program as a whole.

Student life one-on-ones: About once a month, students have an informal meeting with one of our staff. Additional meetings may also occur if there are discrepancies in the above reports.

Check-in surveys: Quarterly surveys measure student well being and other characteristics that can be compared to other Shopify employees.

3.5 Future Directions

To fully realize our goals of CAWIL, we would like to fully take on delivery of the core computer science courses at Shopify. By doing so, time already spent on developer skills training and in work placements could go toward mastering the competencies of a particular course, and we would be able to use specific technology to illustrate the theoretical competencies. With a more flexible schedule, theory could be mastered at just the right time – ideally after gaining some practical experience to motivate the theory – through independent learning or workshops that could be developed in collaboration with the university.

Developing competencies is one way to achieve full adoption of courses while ensuring assessment remains with the university. We define a competency as skills or knowledge in a topic that through various learning experiences help a student achieve a defined learning outcome. Upon achieving the learning outcome, the student can claim a new level of mastery such as those inspired by ACM and IEEE's Computer Science Curricula [3]: familiarity, usage, and assessment. For each course to be delivered at Shopify, both partners would work together to list the competencies that all students should be mastering. When these are agreed upon, exams can be designed to test to these outcomes in a technology agnostic way. Then, how a student comes to master the competencies – whether on campus or at Shopify – no longer matters, so long as they can succeed on the exam.

As we develop the enhanced content layer for core courses, we hope to also start building a proposed set of competencies. Eventually, we hope to be able to move toward fully delivering the core courses on site.

4 CONCLUSION

We have described a new kind of partnership between academia and industry following what we call curriculum-aligned work-integrated learning (CAWIL). This special option to the Carleton's Bachelor of Computer Science program is delivered jointly on campus and at Shopify. Students are paid, have their tuition covered, and graduate with many hours of practical work experience that is tied to the theory learned in class.

After iterating on the program's design, we have several lessons learned that may help others considering a similar endeavor. Our suggestions are listed below, organized loosely by topic.

- General:
  - Consider experimenting with CAWIL for a semester with select core courses before trying an entire degree program.
  - Expect to hire a substantial number of skilled staff for your education team, and expect this not to be easy.
  - Recognize there are three pillars for a program like this (curriculum, work placements, and wellbeing). Pay close attention to wellbeing because if it degrades, the other two will follow.
- Curriculum:
  - Allow sufficient time to develop quality curriculum.
  - Look for ways to allow core computer science courses to overlap as much as possible with work placements (in the best case, meeting course learning objectives by delivering the learning experience completely at the industry partner).
- Work placements:
  - Carefully consider each development team's capacity for working with students and their availability for providing support through mentorship, supervision, checking of work, and so on.
  - Carefully consider the minimum set of skills and experiences required to join development teams and be successful. These will vary from team to team.
  - Formally and prominently link performance evaluation and prestige of those working with students to the successful development of the student. In other words, ensure student mentors get recognized.
- Student experience:
  - Students will tend toward self-reporting results that are more positive than reality. Mentors often struggle with giving complete and candid feedback. Students often struggle with receiving constructive feedback, causing a vicious cycle.
  - Consider proactively giving both mentors and students workshops on crucial skills such as giving and receiving feedback, forthright discussion, and other related communication skills.
  - Ensure students have mentors outside of the education staff and ensure they can speak freely through appropriate venues.

REFERENCES

[1] Undergraduate Capstone Open Source Projects. http://ucosp.ca/ [accessed August 2017].

[2] L Harris. No end to ICT skills crunch. *ITWeb Brainstorm Magazine*, pages 78–83, 2011.

[3] Association for Computing Machinery (ACM) Joint Task Force on Computing Curricula and IEEE Computer Society. *Computer Science Curricula 2013: Curriculum Guidelines for Undergraduate Degree Programs in Computer Science*. ACM, New York, NY, USA, 2013. 999133.

[4] Bruce A McCallum and James C Wilson. They said it wouldn't work: A history of cooperative education in Canada. *Journal of Cooperative Education*, 24(2-3):61–67, 1988.

[5] Yma Pinto. A strategy, implementation and results of a flexible competency based curriculum. *ACM Inroads*, 1(2):54–61, 2010.

[6] Alex Radermacher and Gursimran Walia. Gaps between industry expectations and the abilities of graduates. In *Proceeding of the 44th ACM technical symposium on Computer science education*, pages 525–530. ACM, 2013.

Integrating A Career Preparedness Module into CS2 Curricula Through The Teaching C++ and Java Side-by-Side

Ryan Rybarczyk
Indiana University-Purdue University Indianapolis
723 W. Michigan St. , Indianapolis IN 46202
rrybarcz@cs.iupui.edu

Lingma Acheson
Indiana University-Purdue University Indianapolis
723 W. Michigan St. , Indianapolis IN 46202
linglu@cs.iupui.edu

ABSTRACT

A key learning objective of the CS2 curriculum is for a student to obtain the necessary computer science skills to be proficient in the understanding and usage of software objects in an object-oriented programming language. In typical CS programs there are two prevalent object-oriented languages that are used to fulfill this requirement: Java and C++. In most instances, one language is selected as the primarily tool in which to teach these concepts. In other instances, both languages may be used, but not in a side-by-side fashion which can often leave the students confused or with an incomplete understanding of both languages. Each language has its documented trade-offs (benefits and drawbacks) when it comes to adequately preparing students. An aspect that is often overlooked as part of this traditional course structure is the ability to leverage a teaching component that allows the students to analyze trade-offs between languages and the Why/When/How to select a given language based upon their analysis. We provide an outline for how these two languages can be successfully taught in a side-by-side, or simultaneous, fashion that will still satisfy all of the existing expectations and requirements of a course. We describe how this component can be integrated into a career preparation module that will further augment the students' overall learning experience and their academic preparation. Results of this trial demonstrate that student satisfaction, understanding, learning of concepts, and educational preparation can be improved while maintaining the necessary standards set forth as part of the CS2 curriculum.

ACM Reference Format

R. Rybarczyk and L. Acheson. 2018. Integrating A Career Preparedness Module into CS2 Curricula Through The Teaching C++ and Java Side-by-Side. In *SIGCSE '18: 49th ACM Technical Symposium on Computer Science Education, Feb. 21–24, 2018, Baltimore, MD, USA.* ACM, NY, NY, USA, 6 pages. https://doi.org/10.1145/3159450.3159552

CCS CONCEPTS

• **Computing education → Computer and Information Science Education**; *computer science education, curriculum*;

ACM ISBN 978-1-4503-5103-4/18/02...$15.00
https://doi.org/10.1145/3159450.3159552

KEYWORDS

CS2, Curriculum, Java, C++, Career Preparation

1 INTRODUCTION

The Computer Science I (CS1) and Computer Science II (CS2) curriculum, as designed, provide a set of guidelines for the first two primary computer science (CS) courses that a typical major will take during their degree pursuit at United States colleges and universities. The goal of the CS1 curriculum is to introduce students to programming in a higher level language and explore concepts like variables and looping. A CS2 course takes this initial step and builds upon CS1's introduction by exploring the object-oriented (OO) programming paradigm and discussing topics like abstract data types and structures. Python has become a popular choice for use in the CS1 curriculum [1] due to its lack of basic complexity (e.g., syntax, memory management, data structures). Meanwhile for CS2 courses common languages in use are: C, C++, and Java [2]. Each of these languages have inherent consequences (both positive and negative) [3] when it comes to use in the CS2 curriculum. Typically, the course instructor makes a selection for which language(s) will be taught. Often this process is completed without providing justification to the students for why that selection has taken place.

In this paper, we are proposing a technique for teaching two programming languages (C++ and Java) at the same time, side-by-side, in accordance with the CS2 specified curriculum. We have created a teaching component that will allow the students to weigh in on the Why/When/How a language should be selected and then include this decision making process as part of a career preparation module in the course. We demonstrate that through this teaching model it is possible to provide students with hands-on experience with common problems that arise in industry and allow them to learn by "doing." This approach allows the students to weigh the tradeoffs between languages first hand by allowing them a choice of language to use on at-least one assignment during the semester.

2 CS2 LANGUAGE SELECTION

Language selection is an important part of constructing a well-rounded programming course. Various factors weigh-in on the How and the Why a given language is selected for inclusion in a course. From the complexity (e.g., difficulty learning/understanding the languages' syntax) of the language to style of the language (e.g., compiled or interpreted); these criteria are used in the decision making process by a course creator. In addition to the language specific factors, a second aspect that works its' way into the decision making process for language selection in a CS2 course is that of the expected student population. A CS2 course makeup may consist of primarily major students or can be a mixture of major students and students that are taking the course to satisfy a Mathematics requirement, or are non-traditional (or non-major) students that may have come from a very different and diverse academic background in CS.

In most CS programs in the United States, the traditional CS2 course is taught using one of the following three languages: C++, Java, or Python [4-6]. Each of these languages, and a host of other candidate languages, provide the necessary structure to meet the needs and requirements of the CS2 curriculum. In addition to meeting the needs of the CS2 curriculum, these languages are also extremely relevant for career preparation due to their popularity in industry. An August 2017 report indicates that the Top 5 programming languages used in software today are: Java, C, C++, C#, and Python [7].

Outside of the popularity, and relevance, of a given language, another step that is also taken by course creators is a survey of materials and resources that are available for a given language. If the course has previously been taught in your department there is a tendency to use that language again as the wealth of materials and best practices learned can be leveraged for the course. Experience with a language and related course content (e.g., course textbook, resources, assignments/projects, etc.) may also heavily influence a decision of language. The monetary cost for using a given language may also be a factor in deciding which programming language to select for the course. Some instructors may want to use a specific language that requires a license to obtain the necessary software on which the students will be required to do their programming assignments with.

In many instances multiple languages may be selected for use in a course and taught. Typically, these are not taught side-by-side and often this teaching of the languages is done in a segmented fashion and can lead to confusion for the students. In this scenario the students also do not gain an appreciation for how the languages were selected for the task of teaching the CS2 concepts and principles and therefore an important teaching moment is missed. In this paper, we are arguing for an adapted approach in which two languages may be taught side-by-side to provide a more well-rounded experience for the students and provide them with a career guidance and preparation learning module to better prepare the students for life beyond academic study.

3 CAREER GUIDANCE & DEVELOPMENT

Typically, career guidance is conducted through a dedicated office at the school or university level. This office provides professional assistance in resume writing, interview preparation, and job hunting, among other advising activities. While these are all essential to a student's career development, students in the CS discipline have additional needs that are not part of this general guidance. In addition, students normally seek guidance when they start to look for internships or jobs, which typically happens in their third or fourth year of academic study. An alternative to this existing approach is to integrate career guidance into their curriculum, however, traditional CS curriculum, specifically the CS2 curriculum, focuses on hard skills, which are core knowledge required in mastering the discipline. The rigor of these courses often prevents instructors from spending valuable classroom time on non-course related topics (e.g., career guidance). Even in the case the career guidance can be included it is often fragmented and its availability highly varies from course to course and semester to semester. In some universities, such as [8] and [9], a group counselling approach is used, but only for first-year students. Thus a gap exists for students after their initial semester of study.

Our department uses a four-step strategy that is seamlessly integrated into a student's four year CS curriculum, which includes the students' CS1 and CS2 courses. As part of this idea, a required first year seminar course is provided to help introduce core concepts in each of the concentration areas found in the CS degree. In the student's sophomore year, a career planning module named "You and Your Options" will be embedded into various classes to help further expose the students to their career possibilities. This particular module is the focus of our CS2 course discussion and will be adapted as part of the course content. During their junior year, students are provided the opportunity to be engaged in service-learning projects where their soft skills such as time management, conflict resolution, problems solving, communication and global citizenship can be developed. Finally, in their senior year, a capstone or internship course is required for every student in which they will complete a project that combines knowledge and skills from at least three areas in CS.

This close integration with the existing curriculum provides students with hands-on and personalized attention, yet does not require much additional classroom time and instructor efforts. Because the planning is done at the department level, involvement with other offices on campus such as Office of Career Development, Office of Gateway to Graduation, Office of Curriculum Internationalization are more systematic and strategic, resulting in much effective approaches.

The aspect of career development and preparation can also be integrated into the existing course structure as part of this module. In many instances the career guidance that is provided, in terms of opportunities, is presented separately from the course content or not directly related back to the material being covered. While all courses are leading towards providing students with career development, here we suggest that additional opportunities are being missed as part of the traditional CS2 curriculum to better educate the students' on the finer points of programming language selection. Instead, we argue, that this career development (e.g., language selection) should be included as part of this career guidance module in CS2 courses to better aid the students in understanding what a specific career will look like from a technical point of view. This will provide the students with additional preparation for their future careers.

4 CS2 COURSE OVERVIEW

In this section we will introduce our proposed changes to an existing CS2 course. While we will use specific examples that are relevant for our particular course setup and structure the goal is to provide a generalized framework or template for providing such an implementation in any CS2 course.

The first programming language that students are introduced to as part of our curriculum path is Python, in the CS1 course. This language was selected for use in CS1 due to its ease of understanding as an introductory programming language. However, not all students in the course have this experience. Students may transfer course credit from another program or have received high school AP credit. This may or may not have adequately prepared them for the CS2 course. Therefore we must begin with a basic review of the core content that is covered in CS1. This ensures that all students have the same level of understanding. This understanding does not however mean that the students will have the same experience level or background in programming. This is ok as we are prepared to introduce the concepts at a level and in a format such that all students have an equal chance to not only complete the course but succeed in mastering the course content. By starting with Python in CS1, the students are able to familiarize themselves with a programming language without concerning themselves with the syntax related errors commonly found in C++ or Java.

In previous offerings of this CS2 course the two primary programming languages utilized for teaching were C++ followed by Java. The existing approach to integrating these languages into the CS2-based curriculum was to present them as two separate modules for discussion. In each module, specific highlights of the respective language were stressed and exercises were done to help familiarize the students with the language. This type of approach is widely used by CS departments in the United States as a means for introducing advanced topics in CS2 courses to students. To stay consistent with other departmental offers we decided to maintain the course structure of teaching both C++ and Java at the CS2 level.

In the redesign of our CS2 course, the first step was to chart out all of the key requirements and concepts on a white board that needed to be included and covered as part of the CS2 curriculum. The items identified became our learning objectives for the course and teaching modules created, as shown in Table 1. An example of one such module, Topic #2, includes a discussion of the concept and use of recursion and how it can be used to solve problems in CS. Based upon a class survey, 20% of the students in the course responded that they had at-least a basic or general understanding of recursion and its role in CS. A few of these students responded that they had "some" experience in writing code or being exposed to code that could leverage this important concept. As a tangible artifact of this learning module an assignment was given to test the students' ability to master this concept.

Special consideration was given to the fact that the proposed lectures would be introducing key concepts and demonstrating and discussing these concepts using two different languages in a side-by-side fashion. The question arose: would this approach lead to potential confusion and lower level of confidence for those

Table 1: **CS2 Course Topics**

Topic	Description
1	Course & Tools Introduction
2	Programing Language Introduction: C & Recursion
3	Memory Management: Stack vs. Heap
4	Object-Oriented Introduction: C++ & Java
5	Class Structure
6	Abstract Data Types
7	Composition - Inheritance
8	Composition - Aggregation
9	Polymorphism
10	Algorithm Analysis
11	Software Design Discussion

students struggling to learn a key concept – specifically, would proposed change to our offering of the CS2 curriculum is are we overloading the students with too much complex syntax information when they should be concentrating on learning the core concepts? Lessons were learned from how natural languages are taught to students and these best practices were evaluated in our course formation.

To address this question, we have attempted to distinguish the two languages as clearly as possible during any lectures, examples, exercises, and lab sessions. The key to success of this collaboration between languages is to be very clear to the students as to which language you are currently working in. If this care is not taken in the presentation the students will leave confused and often intermix language constructs when attempting to solve problems. The method that we have selected to use in our course is to color coordinate the use of the languages in your lecture slides and examples. For instance, every usage of C++ code is indicated by a Red font color while every usage of Java is indicated by a Blue font color. This information is disseminated to the students at the start of the semester and periodic reminders are provided to the students during the course of the semester so they know what to expect when viewing the content. The use of color coded examples also allow for ease of viewing when direct side-by-side comparisons.

An example of such side-by-side comparison takes place in an early introductory lecture in which we discuss and then demonstrate the semantics of a FOR-loop, a concept that they should have mastered as part of CS1, and then show what a FOR-loop looks like, in terms of syntax, in both languages. In this comparison we can highlight the differences and similarities between the syntax of the two languages while stressing that the semantics of the overall structure stay the same. This is helpful for students to see this direct comparison and gain a better understanding how the same problem is solved in two different programming languages. This differs from the existing approach in which one language is introduced early in the semester and then later in the semester the other language is introduced.

In the transition from introductory exercises to more advanced topics (e.g., data structures and the OO paradigm), it is important to clearly outline the strengths and weaknesses of each language and how to identify these and weigh this tradeoff. This is discussion takes place in most courses but the hands-on feel of using two languages adds to the belief and the importance of this task. This is an excellent place in the course to introduce the first component of the career guidance and development module. This component involves allowing the students to experience a real-world problem of language selection for a given problem and outlines careers that CS graduates have. We can highlight the need for problem solvers and how learning such concepts can help them successfully interview for a job or internship. In the module, "You and Your Options," the students are given a task of determining which language to use for the problem at hand and are given a set of constraints; similar to what would be found as a job or internship interview question. A side effect of this module is that the student completes it feeling more comfortable and confident when facing a new programming language. Instead of focusing on the syntax of a given language – the process has forced the students to focus more on the semantics of problem solving.

Two questions arose when examining the existing course and how improvements could be made to improve overall learning outcomes. Firstly, why modify the existing CS2 course? Secondly, why teach two languages side-by-side? The first question is driven by a need to better prepare the students and adjust to the experience level of the students entering the CS program. With the increase in CS education at the K-12 level [10], more and more students are entering university study with experience and exposure to at-least one programming language. Many students may have even taken a CS or Programming course as part of their high school curriculum. The second question can be answered as an extension of the first question. In a voluntary survey of first year undergraduate major students in our program, it was discovered that 75% students who responded had some exposure to at-least one programming language at some point in their academic study up until that point. Through their exposure to multiple languages we felt it was an excellent opportunity to teach them about programming language selection and use.

5 COURSE STRUCTURE

The structure of the course is as follows: a review of principles and concepts covered as part of the CS1 curriculum; an introduction to the C programming language. This allows the students a first look at a programming in which there is a strong reliance on the syntax; an introduction to the object-oriented paradigm; at this point in the semester we begin our treatment of the introduction of C++ and Java. We make the transition from C to these languages by explaining how the syntax and structure is related. The individual learning modules that are covered during the semester are shown in Table 1. We now describe the specific alterations to the course in more detail.

During the transition into the discussion about C, there is a learning component that highlights various problem solving strategies and discusses the terms syntax and semantics with respect to programming languages. Introducing C requires that the students learn a new language and a new set of syntax rules. This introduction is often one of the hardest components of the course as students are familiar with the more relaxed syntax rules of Python and the first time they are introduced to more strict rules of syntax they become very unsure and often disheartened. A brief discussion about the process of compilation is included and then the students write their first C program. This program is of the traditional "Hello World" form and allows the students to begin the process of grasping preprocessors, functions, types, variables in the language along with the specific syntax found with C.

In breakout sessions in the lab these concepts are reinforced and the students are walked through a tutorial of how to compile and run the code on a departmental server. The lab sessions are structured to follow a peer-led team learning (PLTL) approach. This approach specifies that a peer, or recitation, leader is assigned to a small group of students (e.g., $\leq$ 15 students per group) and is then responsible for helping facilitate communication and discussion between the students to solve a given task. In each lab session the students are given a lab handout in which they are to work through the given set of tasks or exercises. These tasks include the traditional tasks (e.g., doing sample exercises and compiling them) as well as non-traditional tasks (e.g., discussing the consequences of pass-by-reference in programming languages). Here the focus is to foster an environment of collaboration and an exchange of ideas with their peers. The peer leader's role in this scenario is to ensure that the students remain on task and make progress on the exercises or tasks. The peer leaders may also interject their own experiences into the discussion. This helps to augment the students' overall experience in lab and makes for less formal discussions of course material. By adding their experiences the students may learn more about job opportunities and internships that may be available at later stages in their academic career. This component can be described as an informal career preparation and development module in which the students are provided a discussion, informal Q/A, on possible career options.

The first formal assignment, as shown in Table 2, in the course is provided in order to demonstrate the power of recursion written in C. Skeleton code is provided to the students and they are expected to complete the code and ensure that it compiles and runs correctly. The students submit their assignments in a private GitHub repository in which the instructor and any teaching assistants are expected to be added as collaborators. In addition to submitting the source code for the assignment the students are also required to write an "algorithm" for how they plan to solve the problem. This algorithm contains the following components: goal, problem, input, output, and step-by-step details for how they plan to solve the given problem. It is expected that each student complete this task prior to writing any code. This is a challenge for some students as they are used to just jumping right in and pounding out code on their keyboard. This is an excellent opportunity to introduce a career guidance and development module by discussing the different roles that a Computer Scientist or Software Engineer may play out in industry.

At the completion of a CS2 course we expect students to be able to write and understand OO code and basic data structures – however at this point in their academic study the students' have not had any exposure to Software Engineering or software design concepts. In most instances these will come later in their academic

Table 2: **CS2 Course Assignments**

Assignment	Language	Title
1	C	Not Your First C Program
2	C++	Pointers For The Win!
3	C++/Java	Class Madness
4	C++/Java	Stacks Upon Stacks
5	C++/Java	A Healthy Dose of Inheritance
6	C++/Java	Polymorphism, Sorting, Big-O My!

study – however a brief introduction is often necessary to reinforce "good practices." When students are given a programming assignment often missing is a discussion of how the requirements and specifications for the assignment were identified. By integrating a career guidance and development module here in the course structure we can discuss with the students how these two components were identified and why they are important in the overall development process. Here we can leverage practical examples from industry in which a programmer may very well just be handed a design specification – and allow the students to see how this design specification looks and what sort of expectations and desired outcomes are to come from the production of the necessary software component.

After an introduction to C, we next transition into our discussion and teaching of C++ and Java side-by-side. The students should now feel comfortable with the C syntax and the look and feel of a compiled language. In our discussion of C we have deferred our in-depth discussion of memory management techniques until later in the course. We begin by discussing how memory is managed, or how the students think or expect memory to be managed by our programming languages. We revisit concepts we introduced in our C lesson and now begin to build the bridge between C and C++. This initial transition provides the students with some comfort as the general structure and overall syntax is now familiar to them. Using the color coordinate source code in the lecture helps to assist the students in visually seeing the side-by-side difference between the two languages but prompts allow them to better understand how the languages provide the same behavior through different constructs.

Once we have bridged this transition between C and C++ we are now able to introduce Java as a derivative of C++. We remind the students that at the beginning of the semester we examined the overview and hierarchy of common programming languages. We explain how concepts and ideas are inherited from languages in much the same way we as humans inherit given traits from our parents. We demonstrate how to construct a "Hello World" program in both C++ and Java – side-by-side as an in-class exercise. We demonstrate to the students that while the syntax is vastly different between the two programs the underlying meaning, or semantics, remains the same. The students are given introductory tutorials in the subsequent lab sessions that they are expected to complete to help reinforce these concepts.

During this period of the course the students are introduced to the notion of the OO paradigm as this is an essential component of grasping the Java programming language. In the initial stages less attention is paid to the concept of objects in languages. Once a basic understanding of the core syntax and structure of the languages is achieved we next turn to a discussion about objects, and what the OO paradigm means for us in programming terms. When introducing objects we also must provide a thorough treatment of dynamic memory and how each language manages memory. A discussion of the Heap and the Stack are provided during a learning module here. The students are then given the task of identifying, in snippets of code, what is stored on the Heap and what is stored on the Stack. This is done for each language – and we make sure that the differences or similarities between the two languages are clearly identified and discussed.

After providing a treatment on dynamic memory management we are off to discussing the finer points of abstract data types (ADT) and provide an introduction to one such type through both in-lecture tutorials as well as an assignment. Here for an exercise we build a Stack data structure that can handle String data types as part of our in-lecture discussion. The students guide the instructor on how and why to include the different features (e.g., Push and Pop). Once this construct has been built the students are now required to modify it to select any data type. This becomes another programming assignment for the students and they are expected to choose one of the languages to submit this assignment in. A discussion regarding the behavior of an ADT is included as part of lecture and then through a lab session the students are able to gain a better understanding for how it can be represented in both C++ and Java using objects.

After a discussion regarding ADT's we transition into our final learning module, that of system composition. Again, this module is not meant to be a full treatment on the subject, but instead is to be an introduction into Software Engineering concepts as part of their understanding of programming. In this component we primarily discuss the different types of composition and explore Inheritance in detail. With this discuss we provide an understanding of the concept of Polymorphism and this is worked into their final assignment for the system which allows them to construct a robust software application.

The semester ends with a comprehensive final examination. The exam is structured such that it is a mixture of True/False, multiple choice, and short answer. The short answer questions are made up of scenarios (often practical-based) in which the students' are required to decide which language would be the most beneficial and then provide snippets of code to satisfy the problem at hand. While this type of question would appear to be the most challenging, students' have reported that this style of question is also the most rewarding and beneficial as they are able to directly apply the knowledge that they have been given over the course of the semester to a given problem.

6 RESULTS

During the semester in which this pilot study was integrated into the CS2 course content anonymous surveys were conducted and progress tracked as part of the existing course structure. These surveys were voluntary in nature with the hope that this would entice students to provide honest feedback regarding the course. The course consisted of 146 students in this initial pilot study. The lab recitation leaders were also surveyed as they had taken previous iterations of the course. The purpose of the surveys was to gauge how the learning was progressing through each learning module. The responses initially surprised us as the first set of surveys early in the semester described an environment in which the students were excited about the new approach and learning two languages at once. The opinion shifted slightly once the module on C was conducted. In this instance the students cited that learning the new syntax was often challenging and that they feared learning two languages side-by-side may be overwhelming. Overall, student feedback and satisfaction were overwhelmingly positive, 90% reported satisfaction with regards to the format of the course and how the material was presented in a side-by-side fashion.

A real benefit to this approach was noted however not from the surveys but from the instructor as well as the lab recitation leaders. The students that were coming to office hours or asking for help in the lab sessions were asking questions not necessarily about the syntax but asking deeper questions about the core concepts. The questions turned from simply being about how to do something, to rather why something works/behaves in a given way? This was an extremely pivotal moment for us in this process of trying this new approach as it demonstrated that the students were beginning to think about these concepts in a much deeper fashion and were not getting bogged down by the syntax of the language.

One of the challenges when examining the empirical data collected as part of the course is the fact that there will always be students that struggle with learning a new language or concept. The hope is to minimize the number of students that experience this struggle and instead find ways to best help them find success in a course. When applying this pilot study we found that the Fail rate of the students dropped 4%, as shown in Fig. 1, compared to the previous semester(s). We also found that through exit surveys students felt better prepared for facing a new language based upon their experiences in the course. Future studies are needed to validate the performance of students in intermediate and high level courses to see if this indeed does hold true.

7 CONCLUSIONS

In summary, we have provided the template for teaching two languages side-by-side in a CS2 course. We have enhanced the overall course content with career preparation and guidance modules that help to reinforce the principles and concepts that we cover in lecture. We have demonstrated that through this pilot study we have seen an increase in the overall satisfaction of the students and an improvement in their ability to understand a given programming language. Empirically, we have found that the Fail rate has decreased in the CS2 course while at the same time increasing the enrollment. These results demonstrate that it is indeed possible to teach two programming languages side-by-side and have success in doing so.

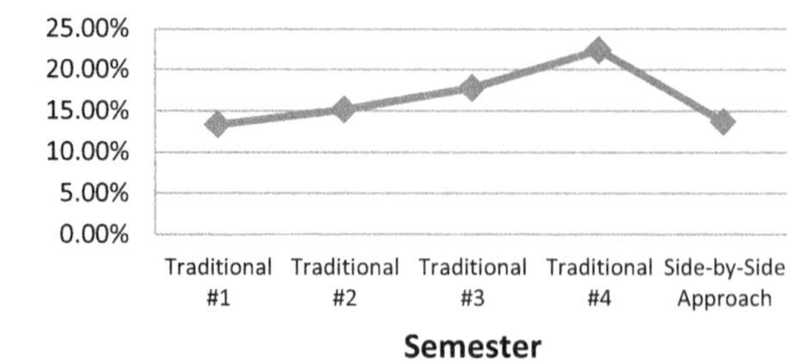

Figure 1: **CS2 Failure Rate**

Future work includes continuing this study for multiple semesters and tracking the progress of the individuals that have completed this course as they progress through the rest of their academic careers in the department. Other work includes forming industrial partnerships to aid in the sample problems that can be given to help reinforce the different concepts that we teach as part of the CS2 curriculum. Finally, ongoing work in the area of study around the PLTL approach applied to CS is being carried out to better understand how the model, when applied to CS, can bring about improved student success.

REFERENCES

[1] R. J. Enbody, W. F. Punch, and M. McCullen, "Python CS1 as preparation for C++ CS2," *ACM SIGCSE Bulletin*, vol. 41, pp. 116-120, 2009.

[2] L. Ficocelli and D. Gregg, "Coping with Java as the core CS educational language: an evolutionary experience," in *Proceedings of the 16th Western Canadian Conference on Computing Education*, 2011, pp. 38-42.

[3] J. Bergin, A. Agarwal, and K. Agarwal, "Some deficiencies of C++ in teaching CS1 and CS2," *ACM SIGPlan Notices*, vol. 38, pp. 9-13, 2003.

[4] A. M. Berman, R. Decker, D. X. Nguyen, R. J. Reid, and E. Wallingford, "Using C++ in CS 1/CS 2," *ACM SIGCSE Bulletin*, vol. 26, pp. 383-384, 1994.

[5] S. Reges, "Back to basics in CS1 and CS2," in *ACM SIGCSE Bulletin*, 2006, pp. 293-297.

[6] K. K. Agarwal and A. Agarwal, "Python for CS1, CS2 and beyond," *Journal of Computing Sciences in Colleges*, vol. 20, pp. 262-270, 2005.

[7] TIOBE. (2017). *TIOBE Index for August 2017.* Available: https://www.tiobe.com/tiobe-index/

[8] L. Penttinen and M. Vesisenaho, "Career repertoires of IT students: A group counselling case study in higher education," *International Journal for Educational and Vocational Guidance*, vol. 13, pp. 203-215, 2013.

[9] M. Vesisenaho, H. Puhakka, J. Silvonen, E. Sutinen, M. Vanhalakka-Ruoho, P. Voutilainen, *et al.*, "Need for study and career counselling in computer science," in *Frontiers in Education Conference, 2009. FIE'09. 39th IEEE*, 2009, pp. 1-6.

[10] Google. (2016, August 2016). Trends in the State of Computer Science in U.S. K-12 Schools. Available: http://services.google.com/fh/files/misc/trends-in-the-state-of-computer-science-report.pdf

Informal Mentoring of Adolescents about Computing: Relationships, Roles, Qualities, and Impact

Andrew J. Ko, Leanne Hwa, Katie Davis, and Jason C. Yip
The Information School
University of Washington
Seattle, WA
{ajko,lkhwa,kdavis78,jcyip}@uw.edu

ABSTRACT

Influencing adolescent interest in computing is key to engaging diverse teens in computer science learning. Prior work suggests that informal mentorship may be a powerful way to trigger and maintain interest in computing, but we still know little about how mentoring relationships form, how mentors trigger and maintain interest, or what qualities adolescents value in informal mentors. In a 3-week career exploration class with 18 teens from underrepresented groups, we had students write extensively about their informal computing mentors. In analyzing their writing, we found that most teens had informal computing mentors, that mentors were typically teachers, friends, and older siblings (and not parents or school counselors), and that what teens desired most were informal mentors that were patient, helpful, inspiring, and knowledgeable. These findings suggest that computing mentors can come in many forms, that they must be patient, helpful, and inspiring, but that they also require content knowledge about computing to be meaningful. Future work might explore what knowledge of computing is sufficient to empower teachers, parents, peers, and family to be effective computing mentors.

KEYWORDS

Informal mentorship; interest development; adolescence.

ACM Reference Format:
Andrew J. Ko, Leanne Hwa, Katie Davis, and Jason C. Yip. 2018. Informal Mentoring of Adolescents about Computing: Relationships, Roles, Qualities, and Impact. In *Proceedings of SIGCSE '18: The 49th ACM Technical Symposium on Computer Science Education (SIGCSE '18)*. ACM, New York, NY, USA, 6 pages. https://doi.org/http://dx.doi.org/10.1145/3159450.3159475

1 INTRODUCTION

Computing has become an integral part of society, increasing the importance of future generations learning about computing. In most places in the world, whether an adolescent engages in computing education is a decision based partly on their *interest* in computing as a subject [25, 26]. As a psychological and motivational construct, interest can be viewed as a predisposition to reengage with certain ideas over time, shaped by the interaction between a learner and their environment over time, and evolving from something that is external and situational to something personal and individual [14].

Unfortunately, prior work has shown that many adolescents are either not interested, or actively disinterested in learning computing, viewing it as boring, antisocial, irrelevant, male, and competitive (e.g., [6, 24, 25]). Changing these adolescents' interests is hard. Theoretically, interest must be both triggered and maintained *situationally* before it becomes internalized enough to drive further learning [14]. Both triggering and maintenance require ongoing effort by both the adolescent and also by people in an adolescent's life. For example, adolescents might become interested because someone fosters pleasure in learning about a subject, concern about a problem related to the subject, identity around knowledge of the subject, or curiosity about the subject [4, 11]. Interest can also be fostered through social means, such as becoming part of a social group, or meeting some social obligation [11]. The maintenance of deeply engaged interest development is rarely about a particular domain of interest, but rather a constellation of concerns, domains, values, goals, practices, and communities that make practice of an interest meaningful along different time scales [2]. In the context of computing, this general literature on interest development suggests that an Hour of Code experience might *trigger* an interest in computing, but adolescents will need a strong social and "multitopical" component over time to develop an individual interest [2].

One way to facilitate this exploration is through *mentoring* relationships [20]. Mentors can be "intimate strangers," in that the student may not know a mentor as a person, but the mentor nevertheless offers sustained help in accomplishing an authentic task that youth have chosen to work on [13]. Mentors can be people like teachers, community members volunteering at a coding summer camp, or even classmates, siblings or parents [3]. The educational paradigm of connected learning views these mentoring relationships as not just helpful to developing interest, but central to embedding youth in social networks and communities of interest that they can call on for support and encouragement [18, 19]. A recent national survey of interest in computing reinforces this view, finding strong correlations between interest and the confidence and encouragement that mentors can provide [38].

Most research on mentoring has focused on *formal* mentoring programs, in settings such as the workplace [16, 17] or in educational contexts (e.g., [28, 33, 35, 39]), in which mentors are assigned or matched as part of a structured program. This focus on formal mentoring is also true of research on computing mentoring. This work has found that strong communication skills and an appropriate personality are key [29, 31, 32, 37], mirroring general research

SIGCSE '18, February 21–24, 2018, Baltimore , MD, USA

ACM ISBN 978-1-4503-5103-4/18/02...$15.00
https://doi.org/http://dx.doi.org/10.1145/3159450.3159475

on formal mentoring [12, 20, 33]. By following these practices, CS faculty can influence enrollment decisions [36], increase retention [7], and produce more effective learning [10]. Formal *peer* mentoring, in contrast, poses challenges that may do more harm than good [15], but can improve learners' sense of community [9].

While there has been substantial prior work on formal mentoring relationships both inside and out of computer science education, we still know little about the *informal* mentoring relationships that develop organically, particularly among adolescents [20]. Recent efforts to define mentorship primarily focus on formally designed mentoring interventions, decomposing models along dimensions such as relative seniority, tie strength, mentee selection, training, monitoring, and policy [8]. Informal mentoring relationships have some of these features, but lack any intentionality in their qualities. A recent definition (and the one we use in this paper) defines informal mentoring relationships as determined not by the setting a learner is in, but rather as relationships that developed as extensions to existing social support structures, developing gradually over time [1, 21]. By this definition, prior work shows that many adolescents have informal mentors in their lives: one national survey of U.S. teens found that more than 4 out of 5 adolescents identified informal mentors that they obtained through their social networks [27]. Another study of Los Angeles teens showed that more than half of adolescents had informal mentors, viewing key mentor attributes as showing respect, offering someone to talk to, and supporting social and learning activities [5].

Only recently have researchers begun to investigate informal mentoring of adolescents about *computing*. This work has found that many students mention the importance of mentors in deepening their interest in computing [22], that interest is associated with having and gaining an informal mentor [23] and that informal mentors included friends, siblings, parents, neighbors, cousins, and teachers. What makes informal computing mentorship notable is just how strongly predictive it is of interest: in a recent study [23], having an informal mentor predicted more than 25% of the variation in self-reported interest in learning computing, an order of magnitude more than gender or socioeconomic status.

While this work shows the importance of mentorship, it leaves open several questions about mentoring relationships:

- What kinds of informal mentoring relationships form?
- What do mentors do to trigger and maintain interest?
- What qualities do youth value in their mentors?
- What impact do youth believe their mentors have?

Our approach to answering these questions was to teach a small group of 18 low-income, racially diverse teens from the city of Seattle, Washington, USA, and have them write about their interests and informal mentoring relationships. We hoped a longitudinal encounter with a trusted teacher and among trusted peers would be more revealing than brief interviews or surveys, while also acknowledging teens' active and evolving sense of identity and interest.

2 METHOD

Our method engaged students both retrospectively and prospectively, relying partly on their memories of current and recent mentoring relationships, but also their active engagement in developing academic interests. We devised a 10-hour class to elicit these perspectives, split across ten days of 1-hour sessions over three weeks. We offered the class as part of our university's Upward Bound program. The class sought to introduce students to careers in web design by engaging them with the experiences that led to their interests and by helping them to develop these interests.

Upward Bound (UB) is a U.S. federally-funded college preparation program that helps high school students who are low-income and/or have no parent or guardian with a bachelor's degree. There are currently 826 programs in the U.S., many of which have existed since the 1964 Economic Opportunity Act that founded them. The program we worked with serves three urban south Seattle public high schools and reaches about 125 students per year. The program is free; students receive lunch money and a stipend to attend. In 2017, 79% were both low-income and first-generation immigrants, 50% identified as female, 35% as South Asian, 19% as African, 16% as Asian, 14% as Hispanic/Latino, 10% as Black, 4% as two or more races, and 2% as White. The program's high school graduation rate is 98% and its college graduation rate is consistently above 60%.

The UB program offers a 6-week summer curriculum. We offered a three-week course titled "Web Design" as part of a six-week "Career Exploration" course, the other half of which introduced students to careers in architecture. Our course description was:

> *Love the Internet? Want to learn more about how to create content and experiences for it? In this course, you'll learn these things and more, learning modern technologies for web design and the big ideas in computing that make the Internet work. You'll create real websites that people in your life can visit and work together with your classmates to make them great. We'll also spend time helping you develop plans for further learning, discussing classes, degrees, and careers related to computing and the web.*

Program administrators solicited student preferences and then randomly assigned students to their 1st and 2nd choices, ensuring a balance along racial and gender lines; however, administrators also encouraged students to focus on classes that would satisfy graduation requirements, which biased enrollment against our course.

We aimed to provide a course that was genuinely helpful in teaching students about computing education and careers, while doing so in a way that generated data useful for answering our research questions. The premise of the course, as conveyed to students, was that "computing is everywhere," and that computing had some connection to their interests. To help them find these connections, we asked students, over the course of the three weeks, to create a site using the Google Sites platform, spanning five pages:

- An "About" landing page that gave context to who the student was and what their interests were.
- An "Interests" page, which provided a narrative about the student's general academic interests and their thoughts on computing, including details about the people in their life that contributed to those interests and disinterests.
- A "Mentor" page, which elaborated on one of the people in their narrative, giving detail about how they came to be mentored by the person and how that person contributed to their interests (computing or otherwise).
- A "Goals" page, in which students expressed the activities they wanted to engage in to further their interests.
- A "Who Can Help" page, which described qualities of their ideal mentor and listed people who could match their ideal.

Students created these five pages across the ten days, with the guidance and help of the first and second authors. To help students understand the genre of content and the level of detail we were seeking, the second author, an undergraduate student studying information science, created a site of her own, as an exemplar. Additionally, each evening after class, the second author also read each page, embedding clarifying questions, both to help students reflect on their past and future, but also to ensure sufficient detail in the content for our research goals.

Additionally, at the beginning of the course, we administered a brief survey of age, racial identity, gender identity, grade level, language fluency, and reasons for enrolling in the class. We also coarsely measured prior knowledge by having students self-report what technology classes they had taken at their school and what programming languages they had used at least once. We measured interest in computing education by adapting an existing validated scale for STEM education [30].

At the end of the course, students presented their sites at an end of summer ceremony to their parents, siblings, and other teachers. After their final edits, we archived their pages for analysis.

Because students in Upward Bound engage in both their third and fourth years of high school, the class did have 4 students whom the first author had taught the year prior to this study. Therefore, there was some potential that those students would write about the first author as an informal mentor. The first author explicitly raised this as a possibility and encouraged students to focus broadly on everyone who had impacted their interests, and that they should be honest about the limited impact that the first author might have had on their interests, so he could improve his efforts in future years. Of course, these students may have censored some of their more negative thoughts about the first author's mentorship, since he held power over their grades in the summer course.

The first two authors, as the instructors of the course, also engaged in mentoring best practices, writing individual feedback to each student's homework assignments and web pages that guided their lives outside of school, providing encouragement and guidance in class, and offering mentorship after the class was over.

2.1 Participants

The class ultimately enrolled 18 students, 8 female-identified, between the ages of 16 and 18 years. Students lived in a dozen distinct neighborhoods of south Seattle, and all were entering their junior or senior year of high school. Only 7 students spoke English at home, with the rest of the students speaking a range of languages, including Spanish, Vietnamese, Chinese, Amharic, Oromo, Kiswahili, and Somali at home. Nine students identified as Asian (of these, six as Vietnamese), 4 as Hispanic, 4 as Black, and 1 as Native Pacific Islander. Only one student had a parent who had finished more than some college; this student's father had recently finished college and started a job as a software engineer. The majority of the remaining students had parents or guardians who had finished no more than some high school. The students' reported parent occupations including nurse, janitor, barber, construction manager, gardener, and waitstaff, or listed unemployed or retired.

We asked students for their reasons for enrolling. Eight reported being explicitly interested in learning about programming and web design, five mentioned being interested in the architecture portion of the career exploration elective, 3 reported being forced to take it because they either did not want to take the other electives or their preferred elective was full, and 2 mentioned taking it because they enjoyed taking the first author's class in the previous year. All but one student was aware of a computing course at their high school or community college, but only 8 mentioned having taken it or an Upward Bound computing course. Six students reported not having ever used a programming language, and the others reported languages such as Java, JavaScript, Scratch, and Excel. On an aggregate scale measuring interest in learning about computing, interest was positive for 10 of the students, and neutral or negative for the other 8. On their websites, students explicitly described academic interests in health, medicine, math, law, business, art, science, music, sports, environment science, biomedical engineering, and aerospace engineering. None mentioned interests related to computing, despite the class's explicit focus on computing.

2.2 Analysis

Our unit of analysis was an *informal mentoring relationship*. To analyze relationships, we systematically read each student's homework submissions and web pages, extracting all sentences referring to an informal mentor. We extracted and categorized four types of information: the *relationship* the student had to the mentor, *actions* the mentor performed in their role as a mentor, *qualities* the student described their mentor having, and *perceived impact* from the mentoring relationship. Our process for coding mentor statements began with open coding of the set of statements that concerned a mentor to generate categories consistent with the content of the sentences. Then, we performed axial coding of the entire set of sentences for each mentor, systematically assigning categories from open coding to each mentoring relationship. Given the small, non-representative sample, we did not seek to quantify the frequency of categories. Our results are therefore the categories themselves, inferred from students' writing.

3 RESULTS

Throughout, we quote students anonymously. All spelling and grammar issues in quotes are students' own, and are due to many of them recently learning English.

3.1 What kinds of informal mentoring occur?

The 18 students we taught mentioned 47 informal mentoring relationships that influenced their interest in learning computing. Students mentioned anywhere from 1 to 7 relationships, with a median of 2. All relationships emerged from social contexts not originally intended to produce mentorship. Many of the students mentioned the first two authors who taught the course as mentors, and so we include students' perspectives on us as well.

Students wrote in widely varying detail about their mentors, but there was sufficient information to classify each according to well-defined social role. By far the most common role was *teacher*, which was 25 (50%) of the relationships mentioned. By "teacher," however, students were not referring to the role of managing a classroom, providing instruction, and administering tests, but rather the mentoring role of providing guidance and encouragement to them individually and often outside of class, beyond the boundaries of what students viewed as teachers normally providing. We will therefore call these teachers *teacher-mentors*.

There were two types of teacher-mentors. The most common was Upward Bound teachers, which 9 students mentioned. These mentors included six distinct people, including the first two authors of the paper, and other past instructors of computing courses, two of whom were doctoral students. All of these teacher-mentors developed relationships with each individual student and viewed their role as guiding students to and through college.

Nine students also mentioned teacher-mentors from their public schools who individually encouraged interest in computing:

> *One of my mentors that shaped my interest in computing was my 8th grade tech teacher, [-]. He is also the school's Spanish teacher and librarian. Our previous librarian had retired and it was [-]'s first year at the school. We became acquainted since I usually visit the library often during recess. I was surprised to hear that he was going to teach the brand new tech course. (F, African, 17)*

Students described these teachers as interacting directly with them and providing them meaningful attention outside of class.

Nine students mentioned a *sibling* or *cousin*. For example:

> *...my older sister by 21 months. She is the smartest person I know, or at least one of the smartest. When I was little and before I met a lot of people, she is the person that I would say is the smartest besides my dad... I live with her so I can just barge into her room whenever I need help. But she's going to college so she'll probably not have time for me. (M, Asian, 16)*

Not all sibling relationships were constructive. One older brother encouraged a student to take AP CS, but offered little support:

> *Sometimes, he would yell at me for my troubling grade in the class but he could not able to listen to me looking out for support... Also, he do not spent much time with me to be able to understand my problem in the class or unable to help me on it... Throughout, the AP class I would cried myself to sleep in silent without letting my older brother know my struggle in class... (M, Asian, 17)*

Six students described *friends* as informal mentors. In all but one case, these were friends in the students' schools with whom they interacted regularly. The nature of these relationships was quite diverse. Some were acquaintances that students met through classes, clubs, or their community and shared their knowledge. Others were best friends who had some computing knowledge:

> *Later on my best friend [-], who was a year younger, introduced me to the concept of coding and web design after she took a class at school sophomore year. (F, Hispanic, 17)*

One student mentioned an online friendship that emerged from starting a Minecraft server. A high school student in Canada that was one year older decided to help him set it up, teaching him over the course of a year how to run and configure a server, learning how to write Java in the process. The Canadian student spent multiple hours on Skype, helping the student solve programming problems and providing him guidance on how to run the online community.

Only three students described *parents* as informal mentors (two mothers and two fathers) and one mentioned an employer. Students provided almost no detail about these relationships with adults, mentioning only superficial guidance.

3.2 What do informal computing mentors do?

Next we discuss what actions these mentors took that triggered students' interests. Students shared three types of actions.

First was simply *teaching a skill*. Whether the mentor was a teacher-mentor, a sibling, a friend, or a parent, teaching a skill was by far the most common form of mentorship, mentioned as a critical role in 37 of the 47 relationships. The skills mentors taught ranged from basic computer skills such as how to use the internet, to programming and debugging in various platforms. For example, one student described how her friend shared the knowledge she was learning in class:

> *One day, she told me how her friend was making a game for her AP Computer Science class and that she was asked to design the characters and the visuals. During the rest of the school year would kept on show me the progress that she made and would even work on it during homeroom. (F, Asian, 17)*

In describing their teacher-mentor's efforts, students highlighted the importance of their teachers helping with problems they encountered in school and out of class activities, and providing feedback and guidance on learning these skills.

Six students also described the impact of mentors sharing *new perspectives*. For example, writing about the first author, one student wrote:

> *During one of his brief lectures one day, [-] explained to the entire class how computing happens everywhere, not just with people who major in computer science. He then showed us a list of careers that utilize computing. Aerospace engineering, a career I am interested in was on that list! That moment changed my views of computer science because it plays a large role in the field of engineering. After this day I became more open minded with computing as the class was very enjoyable. (M, Asian, 16)*

Only three students mentioned their mentors offering *encouragement*. A few mentioned parents playing this role superficially:

> *Dad really wanted me to have a career in computing becasue it's 'easy' and has a good pay. Good Impact. (M, Asian, 17)*

> *My mom has always expressed some of her desire for me to pursue computer science as a career because she heard that it is a very popular field in this day and age. She would always try to persuade me to take computers classes in school which I had no desire to take... This slight pressure actually had the opposite affect and made me not want to go into this field. (F, Asian, 17)*

In both of these cases, students perceived the encouragement to be unrelated to the student's interests.

Aside from skills, perspectives, and encouragement, students did not mention other elements of mentoring described in prior studies, including goal setting or psychological support.

3.3 What qualities do adolescents value?

In creating their "Mentor" page, we explicitly prompted students to describe what they valued about their mentors, and in our effort to help them develop goals and plans, also asked them to characterize the qualities of an "ideal" mentor. We analyzed these statements and found a range of mentor qualities.

A small number of adjectives and phrases dominated youths' descriptions. Table 1 shows the most frequent qualities described more than once, including *patient*, *helpful*, *inspiring*, and *supportive*.

These manifested in similar ways across each role. For example, students characterized teachers as focused on helping students build confidence, identity, and skills:

> *Ms. [-] was caring person and very inspirational. Due to the fact that she was an African American woman into computer engineering, she really inspired me that anything thing can be done and that if you gain enough interest into computing you can use that skills to build skills that will make you successful. She did not want me to discourage myself and assume I was not good with computer. She was caring enough to work with me alone to help me build my skills with computer so that I don't become left out from the class. (F, African American, 17)*

Table 1: Frequency of qualities students used to describe their informal mentors (left) and their ideal mentors (right).

patient	||||||||	patient	|||||||||||
helpful	||||||||	expert	||||||||||
inspiring	|||||	older	|||||||
supportive	||||	similar age	||||
fun	|||	easy to talk to	||||
interactive	|||	understanding	||||
kind	||	comfortable	|||
caring	||	kind	|||
clear	||	positive	|||
encouraging	||	encouraging	|||
humble	||	fun	||
African American	||	open-minded	||

Students described their friends and siblings in similar terms, emphasizing how comfortable and supported they felt:

[-] is easy to work with because he is very humble and laid back as well as supportive and patient. He also has a good sense of humor and is only a year older than me so it is easy for us to talk and relate. (M, Asian, 17)

What's most important about my sister is that she even until this very day she puts me first in everything. I was lucky to have a sister who is humble and caring. (F, Hispanic, 17)

In their "Who can help" page, students described their ideal mentors, and people in their lives who might fit those ideals. The qualities they described (also shown in Table 1) mirrored those of their past and current informal mentors:

The most important quality I would value in a mentor is motivation. I think as a mentor it is very important to encourage your mentee to do better at anything in there life, and especially to be able to bring them up and empower them when something happens that brings them down. (F, African American, 17)

My ideal mentor would be someone who I'm comfortable around. This is probably the most important trait. I have this fear of messing up in front of other people and it causes me to just malfunction. When I'm alone, I can just laugh over my mistake and move on but in front of others I just can't. (F, Hispanic, 17)

Patient. So they can put up with my shit. (M, Asian, 17)

While students mentioned a desire to be close to their mentors, they also mentioned the importance of mentors having wisdom and genuine expertise in computing:

Someone who has a lot of experience in my interests. They will be able to tell me what kind of experience I need, what classes to take, and so forth. I could go to this person for advice and ask for help. (F, Pacific Islander, 16)

I would like my mentor to be an expert because I want to be able to learn a lot and achieve my goal... I prefer mentors who interactive, fun, outgoing, easy to talk to, and flexible. My mentor's age doesn't matter much to me because friends can be mentors too... (M, Asian, 17)

In reflecting on who in their life might fit these ideals, most students wrote about existing mentors already in their life, with whom they were already comfortable speaking. Several, however, described people they already knew who might be able to support them, including teachers they admired but never talked to, siblings with whom they had never shared their interests, and friends who knew about computing but had never shared their knowledge:

A person who would fit my ideal mentor would be my sister [-]. She is very understanding and patient. Though she does not know a lot about any of my interest, she will be able to teach some of it. (F, Pacific Islander, 16)

Few students mentioned their parents, lamenting that they did not have the knowledge to guide them in their academic interests.

3.4 What impact do youth perceive?

In describing their mentors' contributions to their lives, many students described how their *identity* shifted:

9th grade summer's Web Design class left me unsure in my coding capabilities and disappointed in myself. On the other hand, 10th grade summer's Web Design class helped me understand the role of coding in life, as well as reaffirm my self-confidence... Thanks in large part to [-]'s teachings, I once again believed that even someone like me can excel at coding with enough practice. (M, Asian, 17)

Going to [-]'s class everyday for the past few weeks has been very eye opening for me. It has made me wondered why I was so disinterested with computing to begin with. Not only has [-] allowed me to learn about the field of computer science, but I have also learned more about myself and what I want to do in the future. (M, Asian, 17)

Others focused on how mentors shifted their *interests*:

He greatly advised me to follow my ambitions in what ever career that caught my attention and never be lured by the income I would be earning. I could tell by just looking at his lifestyle of what kind of ambitions he was advising me about... We have become great friends despite the wide age gap between us. (M, African, 18)

In other cases, mentors shaped students' *perspectives on the world* and their role in it:

All my teachers had a positive impact on me and showed me that code isn't just used for building websites, but showed me that coding is used for almost everything we interact with. (M, Hispanic, 17)

All three of these types of perceived impact centered on helping to *develop* an adolescent by giving them knowledge about computing. This focus on knowledge, and its impact on interest, is consistent with the mutually reinforcing roles of identity, values, and goals in developing interest over time [2].

4 DISCUSSION

Prior work shows that most adolescents have informal mentors from their social network that offer respect, support, and encouragement of their social and learning activities [5, 27]. Our work builds upon these findings in many ways.

First, the types and distribution of informal mentoring relationships we observed reinforce prior work showing that informal mentoring relationships emerge naturally from existing social relationships [1, 21]. Our work extends this to computing, showing that even among students with lower socioeconomic status and without parents who have earned college degrees, attending school that offers computing can indirectly produce informal mentorship about computing.

Our results also show that teachers in *any* subject area can play an instrumental mentorship role in not only teaching computing skills, but offering guidance, encouragement, and perspective on computing. When asked to select a mentor to describe, most chose a teacher, partly because that was the only informal computing mentor they had, but also because of the pivotal role that teachers played in offering individual guidance on the subject.

Unlike prior work showing the role that parents can play in triggering computing interest [3], the adolescents we taught relied more on teachers, siblings, and friends. This might be explained by demographic differences: none of our youth had parents with college degrees, and none of their parents had knowledge of computing. In contrast, Barron et al. studied youth with parents working in Silicon Valley. Another explanation is age: adolescents can be more interested in developing identity with peers and other adults than with their parents [34].

Finally, students' characterization of qualities of an ideal mentor were strikingly consistent: they sought mentors who would not judge them for their failures, who would inspire them to learn, and who had the expertise to guide them. Students reported that their mentors having sufficient expertise was just as important as having a comfortable relationship with them. These qualities, while often found in great teachers, can also apparently be found in great friends, great older siblings, and even online friends.

These results have many implications. First, these findings point to the need for a deeper understanding of what aspects of adolescents' relationships give them the capacity for informal mentorship. Are there ways of providing peers, parents, and teachers with enough content knowledge about computing to thrive as mentors? Could we teach potential informal mentors this content at scale? What explicit steps might schools take to foster these informal mentoring relationships organically? If we can answer these questions, we may be able to not only trigger more interest in computing, but maintain and develop it over time among more diverse groups.

ACKNOWLEDGMENTS

We thank the 18 students who participated in class and shared their perspectives on mentorship. This material is based upon work supported by the National Science Foundation under Grants 1240786, 1314399, and 1441523.

REFERENCES

[1] Tammy D. Allen and Lillian T. Eby. 2011. *The Blackwell handbook of mentoring: A multiple perspectives approach.* John Wiley & Sons, USA.

[2] Flávio S Azevedo. 2013. The tailored practice of hobbies and its implication for the design of interest-driven learning environments. *J. of the Learning Sciences* 22, 3 (2013), 462–510.

[3] Brigid Barron, Caitlin K. Martin, Lori Takeuchi, and Rachel Fithian. 2009. Parents as learning partners in the development of technological fluency. *Int'l J. of Learning and Media* 1, 2 (2009), 55–77.

[4] Sreyashi Jhumki Basu and Angela Calabrese Barton. 2007. Developing a sustained interest in science among urban minority youth. *J. of Research in Science Teaching* 44, 3 (2007), 466–489.

[5] Margaret R Beam, Chuansheng Chen, and Ellen Greenberger. 2002. The nature of adolescents' relationships with their "very important" non-parental adults. *American J. of Community Psychology* 30, 2 (2002), 305–325.

[6] Sapna Cheryan, Benjamin J Drury, and Marissa Vichayapai. 2013. Enduring influence of stereotypical computer science role models on women's academic aspirations. *Psychology of Women Quarterly* 37, 1 (2013), 72–79.

[7] Gloria Crisp and Irene Cruz. 2009. Mentoring college students: A critical review of the literature between 1990 and 2007. *Research in Higher Education* 50, 6 (2009), 525–545.

[8] Phillip Dawson. 2014. Beyond a definition: Toward a framework for designing and specifying mentoring models. *Educational Researcher* 43, 3 (2014), 137–145.

[9] Peggy Doerschuk. 2004. A research and mentoring program for undergraduate women in computer science. In *Frontiers in Education.* IEEE, IEEE, New York, NY, S2H-7-12.

[10] Daryl D'Souza, Margaret Hamilton, James Harland, Peter Muir, Charles Thevathayan, and Cecily Walker. 2008. Transforming learning of programming: a mentoring project. In *Conf. on Australasian Computing Education.* Australian Computer Society, Inc., Australian Computer Society, Inc., Australia, 75–84.

[11] Daniel C. Edelson and Diana M. Joseph. 2004. The interest-driven learning design framework: motivating learning through usefulness. In *Int'l Conf. on Learning Sciences.* Int'l Society of the Learning Sciences, ICLS, ICLS, 166–173.

[12] John C. Hall. 2003. *Mentoring and Young People: A Literature Review.* ERIC, New York.

[13] Shirley Brice Heath. 2012. Seeing our way into learning science in informal environments. In *Research on schools, neighborhoods, and communities: Toward civic responsibility,* William F. Tate (Ed.). American Educational Research Association, New York, Chapter 13, 249–267.

[14] Suzanne Hidi and K Ann Renninger. 2006. The four-phase model of interest development. *Educational psychologist* 41, 2 (2006), 111–127.

[15] Mark A Holliday and David R Luginbuhl. 2004. Peer-centered service learning. In *Frontiers in Education.* IEEE, IEEE, New York, F3E-1-6.

[16] Beth K Humberd and Elizabeth D Rouse. 2016. Seeing you in me and me in you: Personal identification in the phases of mentoring relationships. *Academy of Management Review* 41, 3 (2016), 435–455.

[17] David M. Hunt and Carol Michael. 1983. Mentorship: A career training and development tool. *Academy of management Review* 8, 3 (1983), 475–485.

[18] Mizuko Ito, Sonja Baumer, Matteo Bittanti, Rachel Cody, Becky Herr Stephenson, Heather A Horst, Patricia G Lange, Dilan Mahendran, Katynka Z Martínez, CJ Pascoe, et al. 2009. *Hanging out, messing around, and geeking out: Kids living and learning with new media.* MIT press, Cambridge, MA.

[19] Mizuko Ito, Kris Gutiérrez, Sonia Livingstone, Bill Penuel, Jean Rhodes, Katie Salen, Juliet Schor, Julian Sefton-Green, and S Craig Watkins. 2013. *Connected learning: An agenda for research and design.* BookBaby, Pennsauken, NJ.

[20] Thomas E. Keller. 2005. The stages and development of mentoring relationships. *Handbook of youth mentoring* 1 (2005), 82–99.

[21] Rhodes Jean E. Klaw, Elena L. and Louise F. Fitzgerald. 2003. Natural mentors in the lives of African American adolescent mothers: Tracking relationships over time. *J. of Youth and Adolescence* 32, 3 (2003), 223–232.

[22] Andrew J Ko. 2009. Attitudes and self-efficacy in young adults' computing autobiographies. In *IEEE Symposium on Visual Languages and Human-Centric Computing.* IEEE, IEEE, New Jersey, 67–74.

[23] Andrew J. Ko and Katie Davis. 2017. Computing mentorship in a software boomtown: Relationships to adolescent interest and beliefs. In *ACM Int'l Computing Education Research Conf.* ACM, ACM, New York, 236–244.

[24] Colleen M Lewis, Ruth E Anderson, and Ken Yasuhara. 2016. I don't code all day: Fitting in computer science when the stereotypes don't fit. In *ACM Int'l Computing Education Research Conf.* ACM, ACM, New York, 23–32.

[25] Jane Margolis, Rachel Estrella, Joanna Goode, Jennifer Jellison Holme, and Kim Nao. 2010. *Stuck in the shallow end: Education, race, and computing.* MIT Press, Cambridge, MA.

[26] Jane Margolis and Allan Fisher. 2003. *Unlocking the clubhouse: Women in computing.* MIT press, Cambridge, MA.

[27] Kathryn T McLearn, Diane Colasanto, Cathy Schoen, and Michele Y Shapiro. 1999. Mentoring matters: A national survey of adults mentoring young people. In *Contemporary Issues in Mentoring,* J. B. Grossman (Ed.). Public/Private Ventures, Philadelphia, 66–83.

[28] Barnes J.C. Miller Holly V. Miller, J.M. and Layla McKinnon. 2013. Exploring the link between mentoring program structure & success rates: Results from a national survey. *American J. of Criminal Justice* 38, 3 (2013), 439–456.

[29] Emma Norling. 1995. Encouraging networking through informal mentoring: a look at a newly-established mentor scheme. In *Second Australasian Women in Engineering Forum.* RMIT, RMIT, Australia.

[30] Youn Joo Oh, Yueming Jia, Mhora Lorentson, and Frank LaBanca. 2013. Development of the educational and career interest scale in science, technology, and mathematics for high school students. *J. of Science Education and Technology* 22, 5 (2013), 780–790.

[31] Kate Philip and Leo B Hendry. 2000. Making sense of mentoring or mentoring making sense? Reflections on the mentoring process by adult mentors with young people. *J. of Community & Applied Social Psychology* 10, 3 (2000), 211–223.

[32] SS Pisimisi and MG Ioannides. 2005. Developing mentoring relationships to support the careers of women in electrical engineering and computer technologies. An analysis on mentors' competencies. *European J. of Engineering Education* 30, 4 (2005), 477–486.

[33] Jean E Rhodes. 2009. *Stand by me: The risks and rewards of mentoring today's youth.* Harvard University Press, Cambridge, MA.

[34] Wendy M Rote and Judith G Smetana. 2015. Parenting, adolescent-parent relationships, and social domain theory: Implications for Identity development. In *The Oxford handbook of identity development.* Oxford University Press, Chapter 27, 437–453.

[35] DĂI'ana Aeolani Scipio. 2015. *Developing mentors: Adult participation, practices, and learning in an out-of- school time STEM program.* Ph.D. Dissertation. University of Washington, Seattle.

[36] Amber Settle, Sarah Pieczynski, Liz Friedman, and Nathan Kizior. 2013. Evaluating a prospective student mentoring program. In *Frontiers in Education.* IEEE, IEEE, New York, 1.

[37] Rahman Tashakkori, James T Wilkes, and Edward G Pekarek. 2005. A systemic mentoring model in computer science. In *ACM Southeast Regional Conf.* ACM, ACM, New York, NY, 371–375.

[38] Jennifer Wang, Sepehr Hejazi Moghadam, and Juliet Tiffany-Morales. 2017. Social perceptions in computer science and implications for diverse students. In *ACM Int'l Computing Education Research Conf. (ICER '17).* ACM, New York, NY, 47–55.

[39] Sarah Wood and Evan Mayo-Wilson. 2012. School-based mentoring for adolescents: A systematic review and meta-analysis. *Research on Social Work Practice* 22, 3 (2012), 257–269.

A National Study of Undergraduate Research Experiences in Computing: Implications for Culturally Relevant Pedagogy

Audrey Smith Rorrer
University of North Carolina Charlotte
9201 University City Blvd.
Charlotte, NC 28223
audrey.rorrer@uncc.edu

Joseph Allen
University of North Carolina Charlotte
9201 University City Blvd.
Charlotte, NC 28223
jallen17@uncc.edu

Huifang Zuo
University of Chicago
1467 E. 60th St.
Chicago, IL 60637
hzuo@uchicago.edu

ABSTRACT

In this paper, we describe a large-scale, long-term study of a National Science Foundation undergraduate research program via the Computer and Information Science and Engineering (CISE) Research Experiences for Undergraduates (REU) Evaluation Toolkit project. The overarching research questions are: what attitudinal shifts occur for undergraduate research experience student participants, and do experience perceptions differ based upon student demographics? Results across two cohort years showed statistically significant gains for several key program level outcomes. However, intent to go to graduate school decreased in both cohorts. Gender and ethnicity differences were observed. Women and underrepresented minority group students had significantly higher scores for several factors. These findings are discussed in context of culturally relevant pedagogy for undergraduate research programs. This study is unique in its scale and scope, providing a depiction of student outcomes across multiple cohorts of a national sample including over 58 computing research sites and more than 900 undergraduate students.

CCS CONCEPTS

• **Applied Computing Education. Special and professional topics** → **Computing education**; *Computing education programs*

KEYWORDS

Undergraduate research experiences; computing education; gender; underrepresented minority; culturally relevant pedagogy

ACM Reference format:
A. Rorrer, J. Allen, and H. Zuo, 2018. A National Study of Undergraduate Research Experiences in Computing: Implications for Culturally Relevant Pedagogy. In *Proceedings of SIGCSE'18: The 49th ACM Technical Symposium in Computer Science Education, Baltimore, MD, USA, Feb. 21–24, 2018, Baltimore, MD, USA. ACM, NY, NY, USA, 6 pages.*
https://doi.org/10.1145/3159450.3159510

ACM ISBN 978-1-4503-5103-4/18/02...$15.00
https://doi.org/10.1145/3159450.3159510

1 INTRODUCTION

The National Science Foundation (NSF) has formally supported undergraduate research programs to enhance student education since 1953 and began the Research Experiences for Undergraduates (REU) program in 1986 [16]. The NSF sponsors approximately 700 REU programs for undergraduate research project sites with 7,000 college student participants in scientific disciplines at US universities each year, and 60-80 site within the CISE domain (800 students). Many of these programs seek to increase student retention and to encourage students to pursue graduate education [1, 22, 28]. In a study of computer science faculty regarding undergraduate research experiences, Matzen and Alrifai [24] found that REU programs share similar objectives of developing student research skills, preparation for graduate school and professional development. While REU sites share common goals, each site has unique research project objectives. A clear challenge in evaluating program outcomes in the computing domain is balancing the need for individual site context with the need for broader, generalizable program impact [13,26] that is not conflated with other scientific domains [4].

Literature shows that research experiences are effective teaching and training tools in the sciences [20, 21, 32]. Undergraduate research experiences have been demonstrated as effective recruiting and retention tools in computing disciplines [10, 22, 28]. While there are many case studies and descriptive accounts presented [16, 26], there are limited systematic studies across specific REU directorates of the impact of undergraduate research programs [22, 32]. Measuring undergraduate research outcomes is a noted issue within the computing community [6].

Among the few larger studies about the value of undergraduate research, participation benefits have been shown among a liberal arts student population [17], across a wider array of scientific disciplines and institutions [17, 22, 32, 36, 37], and among women in research programs [4, 8]. This study is part of a larger project that seeks to strengthen the research knowledge base about federally funded undergraduate research programs in computing, and to provide the CISE REU directorate with tools tailored to the discipline. There is a recognized need to broaden participation in computing generally, and more specifically on increasing the diversity within the research pipeline [9, 35], because it has been widely recognized that creativity within the discipline is enhanced through broadening participation [28].

Given that women and underrepresented minority groups value different components from educational experiences [12], and that these students are culturally situated within multiple perspectives, not within privileges middle-class majority students [11, 27, 31], understanding computing REU program outcomes from a diversity inclusion perspective is imperative. Undergraduate research programs have demonstrated their co-curricular value to student development and education [17, 22, 32]. Recent studies have shown that underrepresented minority students (URM) experience greater benefit from REUs [30, 35], or little to no differential outcomes at all [21, 22, 32]. Weinman, et al [37] report that computer science students report lesser gains than do students in other STEM fields.

This study focuses on computing undergraduate research program participants to address the need to measure aggregate program outcomes within computing and to examine what distinctions may exist for underrepresented students in computing. A national sample of computing REU participants across two cohort years within the CISE domain has been examined to measure overall program outcomes, and to discern distinctive outcomes among underrepresented student populations. A brief description of the CISE REU Evaluation Toolkit is provided along with a description of the study rationale and approach. Results are presented and discussed in terms of culturally relevant computing pedagogy.

2 BACKGROUND

2.1 CISE REU Evaluation Toolkit

The CISE REU Evaluation Toolkit project, hereafter referred to as the Toolkit [https://reu.uncc.edu/cise-reu-toolkit], began as a grassroots initiative among the community of faculty Principal Investigators (PIs) who sought to identify common indicators across the program sites that could be collectively examined. The project goal is to conduct research beyond the typical case study methodology, to provide comprehensive descriptions of project outcomes. In so doing, an aggregate picture of program wide outcomes can inform the community about holistic successes and lessons learned directly applicable to computing.

The overarching goals for the Toolkit project are to facilitate REU site project assessment and to provide overall evaluation of the national program. The Toolkit contains: evaluation instructional materials, an inventory of assessment tools and techniques employed within the community, a standardized program applicant management tool called the Common Application, and an instrument to measure student outcomes known as the A la Carte Survey. The Toolkit provides benefits to the REU community by providing cost-effective, sustainable assessment tools, a community forum for localized project assessment, and a national program evaluation to assess overall program outcomes [29]. Since its development in 2010, the Toolkit has provided direct evaluation services through its Common Application and survey to 110 CISE REU sites, and been adapted within Engineering and Chemistry programs.

2.2 Study Approach

Primary research questions were developed collaboratively by the community of PIs at large. The overarching research questions guiding the study of student outcomes are: what attitudinal shifts occur for undergraduate research experience participants, and do demographic factors such as gender and underrepresented ethnicity influence participant perspectives? More specific research questions include: a) to what degree do students attitudes change over the course of their summer research experience; b) do attitudes vary by gender, ethnicity and/or academic level; and c) how do students feel about their research experiences and the mentoring that occurred? The hypothesis is that positive gains would be found for student attitudinal shifts, and that perspectives would vary by demographic variables (gender, underrepresented minority group), and academic level. In order to be able to address the primary research questions of the project site assessments and the collective program evaluation, a survey instrument was developed to measure a set of expected outcomes for undergraduate students participating in summer CISE REU programs; these are identified as common indicators for the program. The develop of the survey, survey methodology, and results are described in the following sections.

3 A la CARTE SURVEY

3.1 Origin of Common Indicators

A review of computing undergraduate research programs was conducted at the onset of the Toolkit project, to identify central goals and desired student outcomes for the CISE domain. The commonly held goals are to provide quality undergraduate research experiences that recruit, retain, and prepare students for graduate study and/or careers in computing. Attention toward reducing the disparity of women and underrepresented minority groups is also a primary focus. Essentially, faculty seek to engage students in undergraduate research to entice and prepare them for graduate school, and in particular, seek to attract students who are not well represented in computing-women and minority ethnic groups. The indicators found to be central across sites were developed into the following survey construct variables: self-efficacy, intent to attend graduate school, attitudes towards computing disciplines, academic help-seeking/coping skills, research skills, scientific leadership skills, scientific identity, and mentoring satisfactions. These common indicators are grouped as student perceptions of the research experience (self-efficacy, attitudes towards computing, mentoring), skill development (help-seeking/coping, research), and career identity (intent to pursue graduate school, scientific leadership and identity).

Self-efficacy, attitudes toward computing, and academic help-seeking/coping have been shown to correlate with academic retention in computing disciplines [9]. Because actual graduate school enrollment is unable to be tracked in the direct project lifecycle, a proxy measure is necessary. Research has shown that behavioral intentions are predictive of actual behaviors [2], and therefore the intention to attend graduate school construct was developed. The computing self-efficacy construct was developed on the basis of Bandura's [3] theory and from items on the LAESE instrument [23]. The intention to attend graduate school construct was developed from Ajzen's theory of planned behavior [2]. The computing attitudes and academic help-seeking/coping constructs were modifications of existing subscales with reported reliability demonstrating strong psychometric properties [14, 34]. Research skill items were adapted from the Survey of Undergraduate Research Experiences developed by the Howard Hughes Medical Institute [14]. The scientific leadership and identity constructs were adapted from the work designed to address underrepresented minority students in scientific disciplines [7]. The mentoring items were adapted from work in the medical community [5].

The A la Carte Survey includes a total of 111 items measuring eight constructs. An additional set of 13 demographic items identify gender, ethnicity, level in school, and current college major, with 9 items about overall program satisfaction in the post-survey. For a detailed discussion of these variables, refer to the Toolkit website and [29].

3.2 Survey Deployment

The study design was a quasi-experimental repeated measures assessment. An online survey was administered to REU site participants during the first week of the REU experience (pre-survey). The same survey was administered during the final week of the REU experience, with additional program evaluation items. All CISE REU PIs were invited to participate in the study via direct email. The primary researcher sent the pre-survey web link to the participating PIs along with informed consent and an email invitation to be distributed to their site participants during the first week of the REU. PIs also provided the start and end dates of their site programs and total number of student participants to ensure the appropriate timing of the pre and post administration for each site and allow for response rate calculations. The survey included informed consent to participate in the study and a request for student permanent email addresses, enabling the researchers to administer the post-survey directly to REU participants at the conclusion of the REU site experiences. Human subjects research compliance was obtained from the researcher's institution prior to the start of the study.

Following survey data collection, each site participating in the survey receives their site's response data in anonymous form for individual site program analysis. The student data package includes syntax codes for establishing the common indicator construct variables, and a code sheet of the items and response keys. This procedure facilitates PI ability to evaluate their individual site. Aggregate response data are maintained at the researcher's institution for collective evaluation of the program. Twenty-eight sites deployed the survey in 2015, and 30 sites deployed it in 2016, representing 41% of the sites for both year's CISE REU programs.

4 METHODS

4.1 Participants

Total participation in the study included 924 undergraduate students. Participants included in the analysis were 349 undergraduate students in the summer 2015 program, and 575 undergraduate students in 2016. In the 2015 cohort, 180 students completed the pre-survey and 169 students completed the post-survey. In the 2016 cohort, 305 students completed the pre-survey and 270 completed the post-survey. Because the researcher only had access to student emails from the pre-survey responses, all post-survey participants were also pre-survey participants. Students had the option to participate anonymously; because of all faculty reported their total number of students, response rates are estimated based upon a site number of 10 students, the NSF average, and calculated by the post-survey responses. Estimated response rates are 60% for 2015 and 90% for 2016. Additional follow up reminders were conducted in 2016 to increase response rates. Participant demographics were similar across both cohorts with 36% and 42% female and 30% and 34% URM student participants in 2015 and 2016 respectively. Ethnic majority groups included Asian and Caucasian, and URM included African American, Hispanic/Latino, Pacific Islander, Native American, and Multi-ethnic groups.

4.2 Survey Analysis

The construct variables computing self-efficacy, intent toward graduate school, computing attitudes, academic help-seeking/coping skills, research skills, leadership skills, scientific identity, and mentoring were analyzed. All items were rated on a 5-point Likert-type scale, ranging from 1 (strongly disagree) to 5 (strongly agree). The construct variables were treated as dependent variables. Independent variables included time effect (pre- and post-surveys), gender (female and male), ethnicity (majority and underrepresented minority groups).

Multivariate analysis of variance (MANOVA) was used to examine how these independent variables affected the dependent variables. In particular, time, gender, and ethnic membership, main effects were observed therefore pairwise comparisons were used to investigate gender and ethnicity differences.

5 RESULTS

5.1 Overall CISE REU Program Outcomes

Gains were observed across construct variables with respect to time (pre- and post-surveys). In the 2015 cohort, statistically significant gains were observed for computing self-efficacy (F=43.063, p<.001), research skills (F=68.669, p<.001), and scientific leadership skills (F=6.567, p<.001). In the 2016 cohort, statistically significant gains were observed for computing self-efficacy (F=116.385, p<.001), research skills (F=209.524, p<.001), scientific leadership (F=5.308, p=.022), and scientific identity (F=10.185, p=.001). A significant decrease was obtained in 2016 for intent to attend graduate school (F=3.881, p=.049) and for attitudes about computing (F=23.370, p<.001). Table 1 shows the means, standard deviations, and significance at pre- and post-surveys for each of the construct variables for both cohorts. Mentoring relationship satisfaction was only measured at post-survey.

Table 1. Survey Construct Means, Standard Deviations, and Significance by Time

Construct	2015 Cohort Means (*SD*)		2016 Cohort Means (*SD*)	
	Pre-Survey	Post-Survey	Pre-Survey	Post-Survey
Self-efficacy	3.87 (.64)	***4.34** (.59)	3.67 (.61)	***4.21** (.53)
Graduate School	3.86 (.76)	3.78 (.89)	3.83 (.75)	***3.70** (.88)
Attitudes	4.33 (.55)	4.23 (.66)	4.33 (.51)	***4.09** (.74)
Help-Seeking/ Coping	3.99 (.49)	4.01 (.51)	4.27 (.61)	4.35 (.64)
Research Skills	3.37 (.69)	***4.04** (.61)	3.15 (.66)	***3.92** (.59)
Scientific Leadership	4.24 (.57)	***4.37** (.56)	4.18 (.60)	***4.30** (.65)
Scientific Identity	3.62 (.88)	3.81 (1.06)	3.42 (.91)	***3.68** (1.0)
Mentoring	NA	4.47 (.74)	NA	4.38 (.84)

*p<.05, indicating post-survey was significantly different from pre-survey

Mentoring relationship satisfaction was observed at the end of the summer research experience. Overall satisfaction level means were as follows: 4.47 (*SD*=.74) in 2015 and 4.38 (*SD*=.84) in 2016. This is indicative that students found the mentors to be supportive and approachable. Having a matched gender mentor had no significant impact on student mentor satisfaction in either cohort.

5.2 Outcomes by Demographics

Based on significance of the overall MANOVA for time, interaction effects were examined next with none found between time, gender, and URM group students. In the 2015 cohort, gender showed a significant difference on scientific identity (F=4.83, p=.029, partial eta squared=.15) with a higher mean (3.91) than males (3.65), meaning female participants reported a higher degree of professional identity as a scientist. Statistically significant differences for ethnicity were observed for computing self-efficacy (F=4.885; p=.028, partial eta squared=.015), academic help-seeking/coping (F=10.127, p=.002, partial eta squared=.031), research skills (F=5.103, p=.025, partial eta squared=.016) and scientific leadership (F=5.412, p=.021, partial eta squared=.017). In the 2016 cohort, gender showed a significant difference on scientific leadership (F=7.572, p=.006, partial eta squared=.031) with a higher mean (4.49) than males (4.25), meaning females reported a higher degree of scientific leadership skills. Statistically significant differences were observed for URM groups for computing self-efficacy (F=4.138, p=.043, partial eta squared=.017). Significant results of pairwise comparisons for gender and URM groups are presented in Tables 2 and 3.

Table 2. Significant Construct Mean Differences by Gender

Cohort	Construct	Female Mean	Male Mean	*p* Value
2015	Scientific Identity	3.91 (.09)	3.65 (.08)	.029
2016	Scientific Leadership	4.49 (.07)	4.25 (.06)	.006

Table 3. Significant Construct Mean Differences by Ethnic Group

Cohort	Construct	URM Mean	Majority Mean	*p* Value
2015	Self-efficacy	4.23 (.06)	4.06 (.05)	.028
2015	Academic Help-seeking/Copin g	4.14 (.05)	3.95 (.03)	.002
2015	Research Skills	3.85 (.07)	3.67 (.05)	.025
2015	Leadership Skills	4.42 (.06)	4.26 (.04)	.021
2016	Self-efficacy	4.32 (.52)	4.17 (.52)	.043

5.3 Limitations

The interpretation of findings from this study are made with caution. Self-responses are susceptible to response bias. Causal links between REUs and participant attitudes cannot be made due to the quasi-experimental design, and the inability in this study to match participants between pre- to post-survey. Additionally, effect sizes are small, not uncommon in education research. These research challenges are prominent in education in general, and pervasive in the study of undergraduate research programs [20]. However, Lopatto [21] argues that student reports of individual attitudes and personal gains are indeed best obtained by asking students directly. Since this sample contains the same respondents within the pre- and post-survey participants, albeit un-paired, results represent a description of CISE REU program outcomes and general differences of female and URM students.

6 DISCUSSION

6.1 Overall Student Outcomes

The key findings from this study corroborate similar studies in other STEM disciplines. Gains in self-efficacy and research skills have been supported [20, 21, 22, 30]. It is anticipated that students gain in research ability as REU programs explicitly educate in these areas. With acquisition of new skills comes increased belief in one's own abilities, i.e. self-efficacy. Additionally, this study shows new support for the development of student leadership skills and professional identity formation as scientists. Leadership and identity may be as critical to continuing into graduate research as are attitudes and intentions. Professional identity gains were expected, as undergraduate research has been deemed a 'critical incident' to developing professional identity [25].

Mixed results with intentions to attend graduate school have been reported [22, 28, 32, 36], yet factors related to graduate school interest are not understood. The decrease in graduate school interest among the 2016 cohort, alongside declining means scores in attitudes towards research (albeit not statistically significant), suggest that CISE REU programs may not be demonstrating the relevance of research as much as necessary to appeal to students [36], and that individual identity may be paramount to developing student interest in research.

6.2 Gender

The gender difference in scientific leadership and identity are somewhat surprising given the literature surrounding STEM [11, 15, 27, 31] that describes the particular challenges for women being lagging exposure, gender identity contexts such as stereotype threat, etc. However, this study corroborates recent studies showing higher gains for underrepresented students in computing [36]. The intersectionality between gender and minority status creates a multilayered perspective worth examining [27], such as the possibility that female and URM group students may face differential selection criteria for participating in research. Being cognizant of the gender complexity with mentoring relationships, and that encouragement matters [12] can go a long way in addressing the layers of complexity surrounding the intersection of gender and research culture, particularly in light of literature surrounding academic mentoring as 'cloning' and that women scientists report fewer opportunities to be mentored [35].

6.3 Underrepresented Minority Groups

URM groups reported higher levels of self-efficacy, academic help-seeking/coping, research skills, and leadership skills. These findings support other research demonstrating enhanced benefit to minority group students [30, 36]. In light of the noted challenges for URM students in computing, e.g. lack of privilege [11, 31], lack of mentorship [35], less exposure [12], stereotype threat [33], these finding suggest that REU programs are providing engagement opportunity for underrepresented students in computing and that these students may also be facing selection bias when applying to REUs. These findings were observed among overall declining interest in graduate education and attitudes about research. While it is fitting that students leverage REU programs to explore the possibility of graduate education, and also fitting that some students discern graduate work is not desirable, it is troubling that an increased interest in graduate school was not found, despite gains in self-efficacy, academic help-seeking/coping, research skills, and professional skills (leadership, scientific identity). A plausible explanation is related to the timing of the post-survey collection, which falls during the final, and likely stressful, week of research projects. Other possible explanations, such as cultural relevance of the research experience, need to be further investigated.

7. IMPLICATIONS

What we know about undergraduate research programs specifically within computing is largely case based, localized examples. Among the larger studies specific to computer research outcomes, mixed results have been exhibited regarding interest in graduate school, with noted distinctions of perceptions for female and URM group students [36]. The summation of these findings points to the complexity of cultural context within educational programs, and bring attention to the known challenges associated with achieving gender and ethnic parity in computing. This begs the questions: with improving research skills, and self-efficacy, why aren't students indicating a resounding interest in graduate education?; with higher overall means in some variables for women and underrepresented minority students, why aren't they interested in graduate school and research?; is there a selection bias for recruiting women and underrepresented minority students? We suggest the answer lies within the cultural contexts within each REU site, as do Tamer and Stout [36]. There is noted variability among site administration and research topics [4, 36]. Key factors that propel women and underrepresented minority group students into research careers include collaboration and social relevance [9, 10, 36], and mentoring [9, 10].

What this study implies can be described as culturally relevant pedagogy [18]. In describing successful educational practice that are embedded within students' cultural views, Ladson-Billings [19] proposes that these strategies promote success among all students. The key to culturally relevant pedagogy is linking learning with culture, by focusing on meaningful academic achievement that is situated within a socio-political consciousness that has meaning for the student [19]. In the context of CISE REUs, this means connecting the research to personal meaning, offering collaborative environments that mentor students where they are, and being open and intentional about program learning outcomes. For example, students would shape their research experiences to fit themselves, not just adapt into a current research paradigm. The culturally relevant research approach would facilitate the students' consideration of research topics into meaningful research within their cultural identity.

8. CONCLUSION

REU program evaluation has been a localized endeavor, often led by faculty who find themselves ill equipped to plan and conduct rigorous project evaluations. The contribution of this study is in the Toolkit itself and in corroboration of general STEM findings to computing REUs. The Toolkit aligns measurement, forming a central language for measuring CISE REU sites both individually and holistically. Results from the two cohorts of student outcomes support findings that students benefit from REUs, but increasing interest in graduate school may not be a program outcome. These findings suggest that CISE REU sites be cognizant of factors that have been shown to engage students in research and lead them into research careers, i.e. collaboration and meaningful research. Simply stated, these factors are explicit features of culturally relevant pedagogy, and we suggest REU programs adopt this pedagogical design. Additionally, this study is pertinent to the ongoing conversation surrounding collective efforts to broaden the research computing pipeline by being aware of and attentive to the cultural subtexts within computing education. Future recommendations for REU research should include rigorous study of the recruitment and selection process, and the complexity of student identities among lab cultures.

ACKNOWLEDGMENTS

This work was partially supported by the National Science Foundation under grant numbers 1645846 and 1346847. The authors wish to also acknowledge the support of the Toolkit by the CISE REU PI Assessment Work Group of 2009-10, especially Teresa Dahlberg, Guy-Alain Amassou, Chris Aberson.

REFERENCES

[1] Aspray, W., and Bernat, A. (2000). Recruitment and retention of underrepresented minority graduate students in computer science: Report of a workshop, March 4-5, 2000. Washington, DC: Computing Research Association.

[2] Ajzen, I. (2001). Nature and operation of attitudes. Annual Review of Psychology, 52, 27-58.

[3] Bandura, A. (1997). Self-efficacy: The Exercise of Control. New York: W. H. Freeman and Company.

[4] Barker, L. (2009). Student and faculty perceptions of undergraduate research experiences in computing. ACM Trans. Comput. Educ. 9, 1, Article 5 (March 2009), 28 pages.

[5] Berk, R. A., Berg, J., Mortimer, R., Walton-Moss, B., & Yeo, T. P. (2005).Measuring the effectiveness of faculty mentoring relationships. Academy of Medicine, 80(1), 66-71.

[6] Bischof, H., Furst, J.D., Raicu, D.S., and Urban, S. (2011). Top Issues in Providing Successful Undergraduate Research Experiences. SIGCSE '11, March 9-12, 2011, Dallas, TX.

[7] Chemers, Zurbriggen, Syed, Goza, and Bearman (2011). The role of efficacy and identity in science career commitment among underrepresented minority students. Journal of Social Issues, 67(3), 469-491, September 2001.

[8] Cohoon, M.J., Wu, Z., and Luo, L. (2008). Will they stay or will they go? In Proceedings of the ACM Special Interest Group on Computer Science Education, SIGCSE 2008: 397-401.

[9] Dahlberg, T., Barnes, T., Buch, K. & Rorrer, A. (2011). The STARS Alliance: Viable strategies for broadening participation in computing. Transactions on Computer Education, Special Issue on Broadening Participation, 11 (3),18.

[10] Gates, A. Q., Teller, P. J., Bernat, A., and Delgado, N. (1998). Meeting the challenge of expanding participation in the undergraduate research experience. In Proceedings of the Frontiers in Education Conference, 1998.

[11] Goode, J., and Margolis, J. (2011). Exploring Computer Science: A Case Study of School Reform. July 2011 ACM Transactions on Computing Education (TOCE): Volume 11 Issue 2, July 2011.

[12] Guzdial, M., Ericson, B., & McKlin, T. (2012). A statewide survey on computing education pathways and influences: factors in broadening participation in computing. ICER 2012, September ICER'12, September 9–11, 2012, Auckland, New Zealand.

[13] Hardré, P. L., Slater, J. & Nanny, M. (2010). Redesigning and Aligning Assessment and Evaluation for a Federally-funded Math and Science Teacher Education Program. Evaluation and Program Planning, 33, 498-510.

[14] Hoegh, A., & Moskal, B. M. (October, 2009). Examining science and engineering students' attitudes toward computer science. Paper presented at 39th Frontiers in Education Conference, San Antonio, Texas.

[15] Irani, L. (2004). Understanding gender and confidence in CS culture. IGCSE'04, March 3–7, 2004, Norfolk, Virginia, USA.

[16] Kinkead, J. What's in a Name? A brief history of undergraduate research. Council on Undergraduate Research, Fall 2012, Volume 33, No. 1. https://www.cur.org/assets/1/7/331Fall12KinkeadWeb.pdf.

[17] Kuh, G.D. (2008). High-Impact Educational Practices: What They Are, Who Has Access to Them, and Why They Matter. Washington, D.C.:AAC&U.

[18] Ladson-Billings, G. (1995). Toward a Theory of Culturally Relevant Pedagogy. American Educational Research Journal, Vol. 32, No. 3. (Autumn, 1995), pp. 465-491.

[19] Ladson-Billings, G. (2014). Culturally Relevant Pedagogy 2.0: a.k.a. the Remix. Harvard Educational Review: April 2014, Vol. 84, No. 1, pp. 74-84.

[20] Lopatto, D. (2004). Survey of Undergraduate Research Experiences (SURE): First Findings. Cell Biology Education, 3, 270-277. Available: http://www.grinnell.edu/academics/areas/psychology/assessnebts/sure-iii-survey

[21] Lopatto, D. (2007). Undergraduate research experiences support science career decisions and active learning. CBE - Life Sciences Education, 6, 297-306.

[22] Laursen, S., Hunter, A., Seymour, E., Thiry, H., & Melton, G. (2010). Undergraduate Research in the Sciences: Engaging Student in Real-Science. San Francisco, CA: Jossey-Bass.

[23] LAESE Survey, AWE Assessment Project, Survey, V3.1, Available: https://www.engr.psu.edu/awe/default.aspx

[24] Matzen, R., and Alrifai, R. (2012). Defining undergraduate research in computer science: A survey of computer science faculty, Journal of Computing Sciences in Colleges, 27, 31-37.

[25] McCartney, R., & Sanders, K. (2015). School/Work: Development of computing students' professional identity at university. CER'15, August 9–13, 2015, Omaha, NB, ACM ISBN DOI: http://dx.doi.org/10.1145/2787622.2787732.

[26] McDavid, J. C., & Hawthorn, L. R. L. (2006). Program evaluation and performance measurement: An introduction to practice. Thousand Oaks, CA: Sage.

[27] Ong, M., Espinosa, L. L., and G. Orfield, G. (2011). Inside the double bind: A synthesis of empirical research on undergraduate and graduate women of color in science, technology, engineering, and mathematics. Harvard Educational Review, 81(2), 172-208.

[28] Peckham, J.L., Stephenson, P., Herve, J., Hutt, R., and Encarnacao, M. (2007). Increasing student retention in computer science through research programs for undergraduates. In Proceedings of the ACM Special Interest Group on Computer Science Education, SIGCSE 2007: 124-128.

[29] Rorrer, A. (2015). Evaluation and Program Planning, 55, 103-111, April 2016. https://doi.org/10.1016/j.evalprogplan.2015.12.006.

[30] Russell, S. H., Hancock, M. P., and McCullough, J. (2007). Benefits of undergraduate research experiences. Science 316, 548–549.

[31] Scott, A., Martin, A., McAlear, F., and Koshy, S. (2017). Broadening Participation in Computing: Examining Experiences of Girls of Color. June 2017 ITiCSE '17: Proceedings of the 2017 ACM Conference on Innovation and Technology in Computer Science Education. July 3-5, 2017, Bologna, Italy.

[32] Seymour, E., Hunter, A.B., Laursen, S. L., and Deantoni, T. (2004). Establishing the benefits of research experiences for undergraduates in the sciences: First findings from a three-year study. Science Education, 88, 493-534. DOI 10.1002/sce.10131.

[33] Steele, C. M. (1997). A Threat in the Air: How Stereotypes Shape Intellectual Identity and Performance. American Psychologist, 52 (6), 613-629.

[34] Struthers, C. W., Perry, R. P., & Menec, V. H. (2000). An examination of the relationship among academic stress, coping, motivation, and performance in college. Research in Higher Education, 41, 581-593.

[35] Sullivan, P., Simmons, M., Moore, K., Meloncon, L., and Potts, L. Intentionally recursive: A participatory model for mentoring. ACM SIGDOC 2015, July 16-17, 2015, Limerick, Ireland. http://dx.doi.org/10.1145/2775441.2814672.

[36] Tamer, B. and Stout, J. (2016). Understanding How Research Experiences for Undergraduate Students May Foster Diversity in the Professorate. SIGCSE'16. March 2-5, Memphis, TN.

[37] Weinman, J., Jensen, D., and Lopatto, D. (2015). Teaching Computing as Science in a Research Experience. SIGCSE 2016, March SIGCSE'15, March 4-7, 2015, Kansas City, MO.

Diversity Across a Decade: A Case Study on Undergraduate Computing Culture at the University of Illinois

Heather E. Metcalf
Association for Women in Science
Washington, DC
metcalf@awis.org

Tanya L. Crenshaw
New Relic
Portland, OR
tcrenshaw@newrelic.com

Erin Wolf Chambers
Saint Louis University
Saint Louis, MO
erin.chambers@slu.edu

Cinda Heeren
University of British Columbia
Vancouver, BC, Canada
cheeren@cs.ubc.ca

ABSTRACT

While we celebrate the dramatic increase in women's undergraduate enrollment at computer science programs around the country, to see this surge translate into career-long outcomes, we cannot ignore ongoing gendered and racialized disparities in computing, particularly as they relate to a student's sense of belonging. Even in times of high enrollment, fostering a sense of belonging cannot occur just through ad-hoc methods, the goodwill of a few faculty, or a standalone mentoring program. Policies and structures must be put into place and enacted holistically.

We report on a multi-phase, 10-year case study of undergraduate student experiences at the University of Illinois (2007, n=61; 2017, n=339). Our 2017 study explores the policies and structures enacted over a decade and their impact on departmental culture. We report on three areas: i) Inclusive classroom experiences; ii) Quality of mentorship opportunities; iii) Student sense of identity. While there have been significant departmental improvements, there are some cultural, policy, and structural issues to be addressed in order to foster a sense of belonging and success for all students.

CCS CONCEPTS

• **Social and professional topics → Computer science education**;

KEYWORDS

Diversity, case study, mentorship, professional teaching track

ACM Reference format:
Heather E. Metcalf, Tanya L. Crenshaw, Erin Wolf Chambers, and Cinda Heeren. 2018. Diversity Across a Decade: A Case Study on Undergraduate Computing Culture at the University of Illinois. In *Proceedings of The 49th ACM Technical Symposium on Computer Science Education, Baltimore, Maryland USA, February 21–24, 2018 (SIGCSE'18)*, 6 pages.
https://doi.org/10.1145/3159450.3159497

SIGCSE'18, February 21–24, 2018, Baltimore, Maryland USA

ACM ISBN 978-1-4503-5103-4/18/02...$15.00
https://doi.org/10.1145/3159450.3159497

1 INTRODUCTION

Ten years ago, we conducted a culture study of the Computer Science Department at the University of Illinois at Urbana-Champaign, a large research institution ranked among the top in the country. At the time, we found that the emphasis placed on research was at the cost of students' sense of belonging. Students did not perceive that the department valued teaching excellence. Undergraduate mentorship and research opportunities were limited, and students felt isolated from the department faculty and from each other [5].

In 2008, authors Crenshaw, Chambers, and Metcalf provided four recommendations to the Computer Science Department with respect to fostering undergraduate sense of belonging [7]:

(1) Facilitate more interaction between students and faculty.
(2) Improve quality of teaching.
(3) Increase early research opportunities.
(4) Create multiple and diverse mentoring opportunities.

Quoting a letter of support from the 2016 Computer Science Department Head [23], the specific changes informed by our original study included:

(1) A formal teaching requirement for all Ph.D. students.
(2) Significant improvements in undergraduate advising policies, including an assigned Faculty Mentor to every undergraduate as well as two full time student-facing academic professionals.
(3) Professionalization of our instructional faculty, including well-defined promotions paths, persistent course assignments – All introductory undergraduate courses are now assigned to faculty whose primary focus is teaching.

It is worth noting that other significant changes have occurred. In particular, enrollments have almost tripled, from 650 in 2005 to 1686 in 2016. At the same time the proportion of women enrolled in the program has increased from 9% to 24%. This is due, in part, to the recent dramatic increases of women's enrollment into computer science programs, reported at multiple institutions [11, 22, 24]. The racial demographics have also changed. The department has larger populations of Asian and International students. That said, other racial categories have not changed much, with African American and Hispanic student populations hovering at 1-4%.

In this paper, we report on a follow-up study to our original work. We investigate how these changes have affected the attitudes and perceptions of undergraduates now enrolled in the CS department. Our larger study investigates undergraduate, graduate, and faculty experiences in the department via surveys and one-on-one interviews. For the purposes of this paper, we focus primarily on our survey findings from the undergraduate student data. In particular, we explore undergraduate students' sense of identity, mentorship and mentoring opportunities, and teaching. After sharing our findings and relating them to those uncovered in 2006, we discuss lessons learned over the past ten years and offer future directions for improvement. It is our hope that other computing departments can learn from our findings, apply our recommendations within the context of their own organizations, and gain valuable insights about the role of such data collection efforts in informing programmatic, practical, and policy changes that benefit their entire community and bolster their recruitment and retention efforts.

2 RELATED WORK

Computer Science undergraduate enrollment and degree attainment have been of interest for many decades. Foremost, women and people of color are miserably underrepresented among bachelor's degree earners in Computer Science. In 2013, women earned 50.3% of science and engineering bachelor's degrees but only 18% of bachelor's in Computer Science [3].

Much research has explored why these differences exist. Underrepresented groups are particularly likely to feel a lack of fit or expertise compared to their peers [4, 18]. Exacerbating this is extensive evidence of cultural barriers and biases experienced by members of these groups that not only influence sense of fit, self-efficacy, and scientific identity, but also influence every core aspect of their scientific career pathway including classroom experiences, internship opportunities, mentoring experiences, hiring, evaluation, access to funding, promotion, salary, and more [10, 13, 17, 18].

While many efforts have attempted to address this problem through interventions to provide tools, support, and resources to women and people of color in scientific fields, research illustrates that these efforts are limited in their ability to effect the kinds of long-term, sustainable change needed to truly address the root of this problem [2, 4, 17]. Instead, this body of work suggests the necessity of engaging in transformative work at a cultural level in order to impact meaningful change [8, 12, 16, 19, 21].

Universities are reporting significant growth in women's enrollment in Computer Science programs around the country [22, 24]. Among these is the University of Illinois at Urbana-Champaign where 46% of its 2016-2017 incoming freshman class was comprised of women [11]. Our hope is that, through this study's findings and recommendations, we can foster a culture in which the department's recruitment endeavors can expand into positive retention outcomes for all of its students.

One of the few of its kind, this article presents a 10-year, multi-phase case study. Except for the landmark study, "Unlocking the Clubhouse" performed at Carnegie Mellon University [15], we are unaware of other such longitudinal studies. Smaller-scale studies, however, have examined specific departmental issues, such as student retention through a curriculum [1].

	Undergraduate Population		Survey Participants	
	2005-2006	2016-2017	Spring 2017	
Total	**650**	**1686**	**339**	**222**[1]
Men	90.9%	75.6%	39.8%	60.8%
Women	9.0%	24.3%	24.8%	37.8%
Gender Minorities[2]	n/a	n/a	0.9%	1.4%
White	64.7%	27.5%	27.4%	41.9%
African American	1.3%	1.4%	0.3%	0.5%
Asian	20.9%	36.2%	32.4%	49.5%
Hispanic	4.1%	3.7%	0.6%	0.9%
Native American	0.0%	n/a[3]	0.3%	0.5%
Multiracial	n/a[4]	2.6%	4.1%	6.3%
International	6.9%	27%	17.1%	26.1%
Unknown	1.8%	1.0%	34.5%	n/a

Notes:
1. The gender and racial identity questions were not required questions in our survey. Of the 339 participants, 222 answered survey questions about gender and racial identity.
2. The Illinois Computer Science Department does not track gender minorities such as genderqueer or transgender.
3. The percentage of Native American students were too few to report by the Illinois Computer Science Department as it would allow individuals to be identified.
4. The Illinois Computer Science Department did not track "Multiracial" as a racial identity in the 2005-2006 academic year.

Figure 1: A comparison of the undergraduate demographics at the time of the original study and our 2017 study.

3 RESULTS

3.1 Methodology

We conducted this follow-up study in two-phases during Spring 2016 - Fall 2017 at the Department of Computer Science under Institutional Review Board project 16507. In the pilot phase, we updated and tested our survey instruments and interview protocols via 60 to 90 minute sessions with participants. Our preliminary findings from the pilot study are available in [6].

We then revised the instruments according to pilot feedback and launched the 63-question on-line survey, inviting the entire enrolled undergraduate student population to participate via e-mail from representatives of the department's academic office. Except for two questions necessary for consent, no question on the survey was required; participants were allowed to skip questions.

For the Spring 2017 study, survey questions covered a variety of topics about student experiences in the department, including: their pathway to the department, coursework and attendance, quality of teaching and instruction, advising needs and experiences, mentoring, sources of support, sense of fit and belonging, extracurricular activities and free time, departmental values and culture, future plans, and demographics. We expanded our demographic questions and response options to incorporate write-in answers that we received in the original study and to use more inclusive categories for social identities, such as race, ethnicity, gender, disability, and sexuality, than are typically included in such surveys. As in the original study, each topical area within the survey included open-ended response options so students could openly share their experiences with that topic. Many questions also included "other, please explain" options to provide space for students to offer up responses that best reflect their experiences, perspectives, and identities. These open-ended responses provided a rich source of qualitative data and additional context and depth to the quantitative data.

At the time of the Spring 2017 study, the department had 1686 undergraduates. As summarized in Figure 1, the department comprised 24.3% women. Among students of color, the department saw 1.4% African American students, 36.2% Asian students, and 3.7% Hispanic students. In total, 339 undergraduates participated in the survey, representing a 20.7% response rate from the 2016-2017 undergraduate population. Among these participants, 222 fully completed the demographic section of the survey. In reporting our findings in the following sections, we use this sub-sample when sharing trends disaggregated by demographic categories.

3.2 Inclusive classroom experiences

In our original 2006 survey of undergraduates, students were asked the following yes-no question about teaching, "Do you think that the computer science department values excellent teaching?" Of the 61 participants, 21 answered "No". We asked a similar question in our Spring 2017, this time allowing students to answer "somewhat". Only 10 out of 334 undergraduates answered "no" to the same question. Figure 2 compares these results.

Figure 2 compares the results. We acknowledge that the questions differ in response options. That said, the large number of "somewhat" responses and the qualitative responses then and now indicate a shift in undergraduates' perception of how teaching is valued by the department. In our original study, comments and suggestions on improving the teaching quality in the department were one of the most heavily discussed topics both in interviews and the survey [7].

Looking at students' qualitative comments in the Spring 2017 survey, we see this shift in perception of teaching:

"I think we have many excellent professors, especially in lower level classes/required classes. This has helped increasing students' interest in the subject tremendously."

"I've had 1 experience where I wasn't happy with my instructor. Other than that I was almost always left in awe of the dedication and love that the instructor had for the subject and for teaching."

It is likely the teaching-track faculty had significant impact on these feelings, especially given the number of undergraduates who specifically named these faculty members in their comments. In addition, as reported in our preliminary findings [6], extra training for graduate student teaching assistants has been incorporated into the program. During the pilot, many graduate students commented that such training was both useful and a strong indicator that the department valued teaching and their role as teaching assistants.

In both studies, students answered, "When you miss a class, what are the reasons motivating you to be absent? (check all that apply)" using the options in Figure 3. In 2006, 66% of students said, "I do not feel that the lectures help me learn", as opposed to only 21% in 2017. Similarly, for the statement "I do not like the teaching style of the lecturers", the original study had 49% who agreed, while the more recent survey has only 15% who agree.

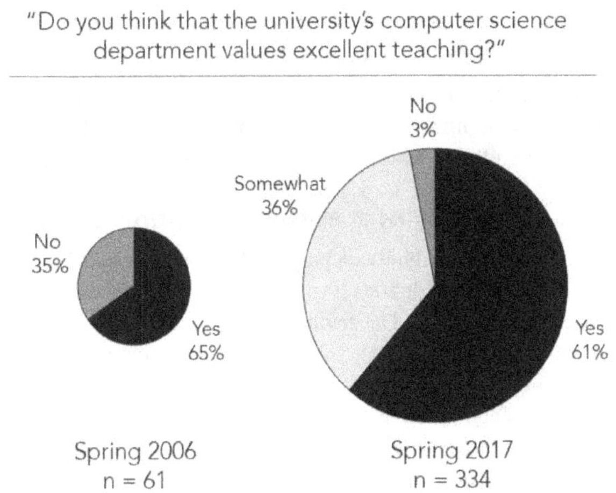

Figure 2: A comparison of the undergraduate perceptions of teaching excellence in 2006 and 2017.

However, some students do comment on issues that detract from the classroom experience, citing examples such as class sizes or professors who are more invested in research. Almost all student comments recognize the non-tenure track instructors as being gifted and innovative teachers, reinforcing our hypothesis that investing in such a track has improved student classroom experiences.

"When you miss a class, what are the reasons motivating you to be absent? (check all that apply)"

	Spring 2006	Spring 2017
I only miss a lecture if I'm unwell.	N/A	41%
I do not have time to attend all the lectures.	25%	35%
I do not feel that the lectures help me learn.	66%	41%
I do not like the teaching style of the lecturers.	49%	29%
I prefer to watch lecture videos.	8%	31%
Other. Please explain:	58%	17%

Figure 3: A comparison of undergraduate motivations to miss lectures in 2006 and 2017.

On the other side, many undergraduates made negative comments about the quality of teaching from tenure track faculty, sharing that tenure track faculty did not seem to care and behaved in ways that were detrimental to morale, even when the same students would speak highly of teaching track faculty.

"Our professors are highly qualified individuals, but they are not always the best at teaching. There are professors with highly regarded resumes, but I learn almost nothing from them in class or lecture.

"There are some professors here that are more research-oriented, and are not good at teaching. They still teach classes, to the detriment of students."

"There are many excellent teachers at Illinois but also several who rely on their status in the department or the quality of their research work to forgo their classes."

"The professors make people feel like they are worthless and can't achieve anything."

It is worth noting that almost all of these comments came from women, gender minorities, students of color, and international students, even those who reported high academic standing.

3.3 The quality of mentorship opportunities

Since the original study, the department made significant improvements in its undergraduate advising policies. For one, every undergraduate is now assigned a Faculty Mentor. Students are required to meet with their mentors once per year. This requirement is enforced using Spring registration holds. As published on the department's website, the Faculty Mentor's role for the undergraduate is to *"be a central point of contact and a liaison"* [20] between the student and faculty. Faculty mentors can offer assistance with choosing courses, identifying possible specializations within the curriculum, and provide information on career paths or graduate school.

Installing the infrastructure and processes to assign every undergraduate a Faculty Mentor is an important first step in developing student-faculty interactions and providing important educational and career support to students. To explore student experiences with these new infrastructure and processes, the survey asked:

(1) Why do you meet with your Faculty Mentor? (open-ended)

For this question, many students focused on the required aspect of this open-ended question. Of the 190 students who answered this question, 110 (or 57.8%) commented on how meetings with the Faculty Mentor are required and stated that this was the primary or only reason for meeting. Students wrote,

"Only because I have to, in order to register."

"To meet the requirement and check to make sure that I am on track and see where I want to go for my career."

"Honestly? Simply because it is required to register for classes."

Rather than experiencing mentoring meetings as a valuable component of their educational and career development, most students equated these meetings to bureaucratic hurdles to be overcome so they could register for classes. This could be, in part, because of how the mentoring relationship is framed - it is a requirement. Sixty percent of underrepresented minority women and over half of white men reported meeting with their faculty mentors because of this reason and, across demographic groups, this rationale for meeting was predominant.

3.4 Student sense of identity

A student's sense of identity and how that fits within the departmental culture and the larger computer science culture influences their experiences in belonging, membership, and inclusion. To investigate this component of belonging, we asked students two sets of questions.

3.4.1 Identity as a computer scientist. The first set of questions was on sense of self as computer scientist:

(1) Do you consider yourself a typical computer scientist? (Yes/No)
(2) Please explain. (open-ended)

In 2006, we found that nearly 60% of undergraduates felt as if they were not typical computer scientists, largely because of a sense of isolation in the department compounded with their race, gender, lifestyle and hygiene habits, social lives, and specific area of focus within the field. In the Spring 2017 study, just over 62% of students indicated that they do not consider themselves to be typical computer scientists. As summarized in Figure 4, smaller proportions of women, gender minorities, and underrepresented minority students considered themselves typical.

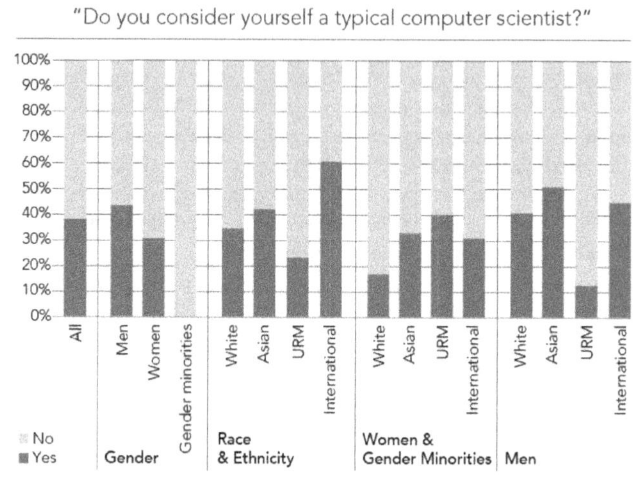

Figure 4: When asked, "Do you consider yourself a typical computer scientist", about 38% of all participants answered "Yes." Smaller proportions of women, gender minorities, and underrepresented minority students answered "Yes".

Akin to the 2006 findings, frequently cited explanations for this sense of being atypical included gender, race, personal lives/lack of constantly programming and sacrificing all else, feeling like they don't fit in, not having a lifetime of programming experience before starting college, research interests, and having to work at it:

"As a woman I feel out of place a lot."

"Haha no - / I'm a female minority, I hate video games, I don't even like CS anymore because I feel [mistreated] by my department."

"I don't think computer science comes naturally to me...for others it seems like second nature."

"I consider myself atypical because I did not have programming background prior to entering college.'"

"I am more interested in theory than engineering, while the current curriculum seems to only train engineers for Google."

International students and Asian men were more likely to report that they do feel like typical computer scientists. Common reasons included conforming to stereotypes, being male, white, fitting in with others in the department, not feeling atypical, being self-taught, and having an innate ability:

"I am a male, who enjoys video games and thinks he is smart...That's how most of us are and that's why the stereotypes have developed, such as a tendency towards introversion and coffee."

"I know a lot of other people in the department very similar to me."

"I'm a white guy, I'm pretty geeky, and I taught myself to program before I had any formal introduction to computer science."

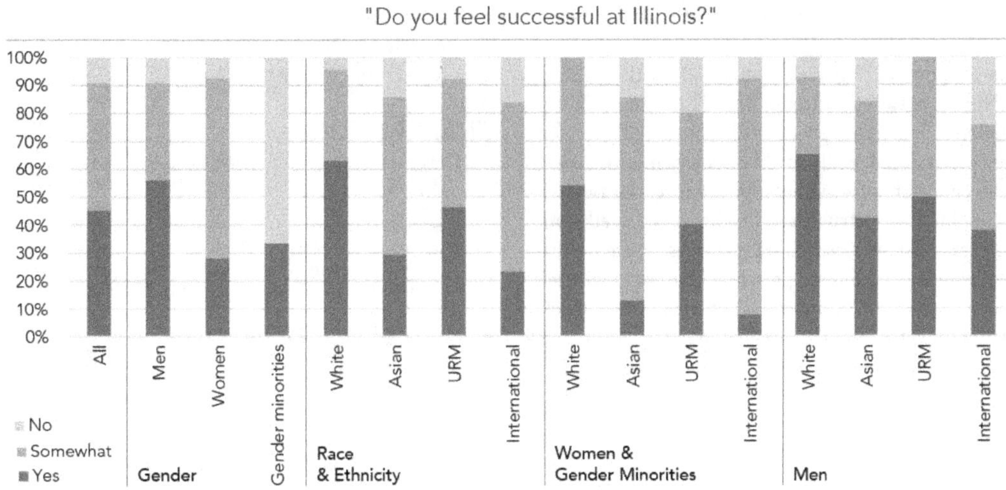

Figure 5: When asked, "Do you feel successful at Illinois?", nearly 91% of students reported feeling at least somewhat successful in 2017. Feelings of success, however, varied demographically.

3.4.2 Identity as a successful student. The second set of questions on sense of identity centered around sense and definition of success as a student:

(1) What do you consider necessary to be a successful student at the Illinois' Computer Science Department? (open-ended)
(2) Do you feel successful at Illinois? (Yes/Somewhat/No)
(3) Please explain. (open-ended)

In 2006, we found that roughly 80% of undergraduates agreed somewhat that they were as successful as their peers. In 2017, we queried them about what success means in more depth. Nearly 91% of students reported feeling at least somewhat successful. Feelings of success, however, varied demographically with white and Asian men and white women more frequently saying yes; underrepresented minority men, international and Asian women and gender minorities more likely to report somewhat; and international men and underrepresented minority women and gender minorities most likely to say no. Those who said yes were most often defining success in terms of grades, high competition internships, participation in the Registered Student Organizations (RSOs), and their own intelligence and innate ability, with the women among this group often referring to how much they've learned and what they've survived.

Among those who reported "No" and "Somewhat," they attributed this to social issues, isolation, the ease at which they see their peers doing the coursework, and expectations put forward by their peers and professors. Many women, international and underrepresented minority students called out the exclusivity of many of the RSOs and ACM in particular, referring to its culture as "toxic:"

"I don't feel like I fit in socially to the department, and constantly feel like an imposter who is just barely getting by."

"I feel incompetent seeing all my classmates land internships at high profile companies."

"I feel a surging sense of arrogance...from the community. I feel a sense of failure comparatively. Students tend to brag about how easy certain classes are despite them being difficult...Overall, it feels a little isolating."

On what it takes to succeed: "Innate ability to problem-solve, a personality conducive to competition, a high degree of focus."

"People, specially in RSOs like ACM form cliques which are not friendly/accepting to/of newcomers."

4 RECOMMENDATIONS

Overall, our follow-up study has highlighted interesting trends in the past decade. The department made progress in improving teaching through its investment in teaching-track faculty and establishing a Faculty Mentor role. However, students continue to report feelings of isolation, lack of success, abnormality, and, at times, overt hostility and ostracization in the department. Many of these problematic experiences are fueled by what appears to be a widespread belief and messages that innate talent and intelligence are required to be successful in computing. These traits create a parallel expectation that computing and the coursework should come easily, with grades and high profile internships as the primary metrics for success. Innate talent and natural ability were more often claimed by white students, largely men, while women, gender minorities, and students of color judged themselves as lacking. Much research demonstrates that the extent to which a field attributes success to innate intelligence or brilliance accurately predicts the extent to which those fields struggle with diversity and inclusion issues because women and underrepresented minority students are stereotyped as not possessing such talent [14].

Predicating success on natural brilliance not only creates dysfunctional social dynamics and potentially discriminatory evaluation processes. This is a disservice to all students. To shift this belief, departmental leadership, faculty, and staff should shift away from emphasizing talk of innate giftedness and instead focus on the importance of sustained effort, even highlighting the valuable lessons learned from "failing" or grappling with difficult problems in their own lives [14].

In addition, the proportion of students who believe the department values teaching has slightly diminished. This is largely because undergraduate student experiences with tenure-track faculty continue to be problematic, especially for historically marginalized students. Likewise, comments from students suggest that faculty mentoring in particular is not structured or supported well; this is undoubtedly exacerbated by increasing class sizes at the undergraduate level. As bridges to computing research, educational, and role-modeling experiences, student interactions with tenure-track faculty are influential in fostering a sense of belonging, success, and future career opportunities and possibilities. That these interactions are often negative, particularly for minority groups, raises concerns about departmental and field-level retention issues.

While balancing teaching, research, and service roles as a tenure-track faculty member is no easy task, our findings indicate that additional investment in quality interactions between faculty members and students in the classroom and in mentoring relationships is an important piece of improving the departmental culture. Faculty members do not automatically know how to serve as an effective mentor or teacher. Additional professional development for faculty members in these areas combined with a matching reward structure that values these aspects of faculty work would greatly improve the culture for students and faculty. Similarly, guidance for students on how to make the most of their mentoring relationships, how these relationships can contribute to their careers, and how to engage effectively as a mentee would also help shift the attitude that mentoring is a bureaucratic task. Beyond advising and informational roles, effective mentoring relationships should also offer students educational, career, and psychosocial support and access to additional professional development opportunities and should be structured in a way that the mentor experiences value from the relationship as well [9].

5 CONCLUSIONS

Fostering a sense of belonging in computing cannot occur solely through ad-hoc methods. A suite of policies and structures must be put into place to create belonging in all aspects of departmental culture. While there have been significant departmental improvements in the past decade at the University of Illinois at Urbana-Champaign, there remain cultural, policy, and structural issues to be addressed to develop belonging and success of all students.

While we have concluded survey data collection, we are still conducting follow-up interviews and analyzing graduate student and faculty data. We plan to publish a departmental whitepaper summarizing our full results and recommendations in Fall 2018. We hope our continued work will offer additional suggestions for improving the overall departmental climate and experience. Our full survey and interview instruments are available upon request for researchers to adapt them for use in other departments.

ACKNOWLEDGMENTS

The authors thank Jeff Erickson for suggesting and supporting this follow-up study. Lenny Pitt, Viveka Kudaligama, and Steve Herzog were extremely helpful with outreach efforts. We gratefully acknowledge financial support for this survey from the Illinois Computer Science Department. Erin Chambers was partially supported by NSF grants CCF 1054779 and IIS-1319573.

REFERENCES

[1] Monica Babes-Vroman, Isabel Juniewicz, Bruno Lucarelli, Nicole Fox, Thu D. Nguyen, Andrew Tjang, Georgiana Haldeman, Ashni Mehta, and Risham Chokshi. 2017. Exploring Gender Diversity in CS at a Large Public R1 Research University. In *SIGCSE*.

[2] D. Bilimoria, S. Joy, and X. Liang. 2008. Breaking barriers and creating inclusiveness: Lessons of organizational transformation to advance women faculty in academic science and engineering. *Human Resource Management* 47 (2008), 423âĂŞ441.

[3] National Science Board. 2016. *Science and engineering indicators 2016.* National Science Foundation, Arlington, VA.

[4] C. Corbett and C. Hill. 2015. Solving the equation: The variables for womenâĂŹs success in engineering and computing. *The American Association of University Women* (2015).

[5] Tanya Crenshaw, Erin Wolf Chambers, Heather Metcalf, and Umesh Thakkar. 2008. A case study of retention practices at the University of Illinois at Urbana-Champaign. In *Proceedings of the 39th SIGCSE Technical Symposium on Computer Science Education, SIGCSE 2008, Portland, OR, USA, March 12-15, 2008.* 412–416.

[6] Tanya L. Crenshaw, Erin W. Chambers, Cinda Heeren, and Heather E. Metcalf. 2017. Ten Years toward Equity: Preliminary Results from a Follow-Up Case Study of Academic Computing Culture. *Frontiers in Psychology* 8 (2017), 816. https://doi.org/10.3389/fpsyg.2017.00816

[7] Tanya L. Crenshaw, Erin W. Chambers, Heather Metcalf, and Umesh Thakkar. 2007. Recruitment, Preparation, Retention: A case study of computing culture at the University of Illinois at Urbana-Champaign. *CoRR* abs/cs/0702141 (2007).

[8] J. W. Creswell. 2008. *Research design: Qualitative, quantitative, and mixed methods approaches (3rd ed.).* Sage Publications, Inc., Thousand Oaks, CA.

[9] R. G. Hamlin and L Sage. 2011. Behavioural criteria of perceived mentoring effectiveness: An empirical study of effective and ineffective mentor and mentee behaviour within formal mentoring relationships. *Journal of European Industrial Training* 35 (2011), 7520âĂŞ778. Issue 8.

[10] Catherine Hill, Christianne Corbett, and Andresse St Rose. 2010. *Why so few? Women in Science, Technology, Engineering, and Mathematics.* ERIC.

[11] Karis Hustad. 2016. 46% of Incoming Computer Science Majors in UIUC's College of Engineering Are Women. *ChicagoInno* (25 August 2016).

[12] Lilly Irani. 2004. Understanding Gender and Confidence in CS Course Culture. *SIGCSE Bull.* 36, 1 (March 2004), 195–199. https://doi.org/10.1145/1028174.971371

[13] C. Isaac, B B. Lee, and M. Carnes. 2009. Interventions that affect gender bias in hiring: A systematic review. *Academic Medicine* 84 (2009), 1440–1446.

[14] S.J. Leslie, A. Cimpian, M. Meyer, and E. Freeland. 2015. Expectations of brilliance underlie gender distributions across academic disciplines. *Science* 347, 6219 (2015), 262–265.

[15] Jane Margolis and Allan Fisher. 2002. *Unlocking the Clubhouse: Women in Computing.* MIT Press.

[16] J. Margolis and A. Fisher. 2003. *Unlocking the clubhouse: Women in computing.* MIT press.

[17] H. E. Metcalf. 2014. Disrupting the pipeline: Critical analyses of student pathways through postsecondary STEM education. *New Directions for Institutional Research* 2013, 158 (2014), 77âĂŞ93.

[18] C. A. Moss-Racusin, J. F. Dovidio, V. L. Brescoll, M. J. Graham, and J. Handelsman. 2012. Science facultyâĂŹs subtle gender biases favor male students. In *Proceedings of the National Academy of Sciences*, Vol. 109. 16474–16479. https://doi.org/10.1073/pnas.1211286109

[19] Tia Newhall, Lisa Meeden, Andrew Danner, Ameet Soni, Frances Ruiz, and Richard Wicentowski. 2014. A Support Program for Introductory CS Courses That Improves Student Performance and Retains Students from Underrepresented Groups. In *Proceedings of the 45th ACM Technical Symposium on Computer Science Education (SIGCSE '14).* ACM, New York, NY, USA, 433–438. https://doi.org/10.1145/2538862.2538923

[20] Department of Computer Science. [n. d.]. Undergraduate Advising. ([n. d.]).

[21] Katie Redmond, Sarah Evans, and Mehran Sahami. 2013. A Large-scale Quantitative Study of Women in Computer Science at Stanford University. In *Proceeding of the 44th ACM Technical Symposium on Computer Science Education (SIGCSE '13).* ACM, New York, NY, USA, 439–444. https://doi.org/10.1145/2445196.2445326

[22] RHIT. 2016. Record-Breaking Freshman Class of Female Students Expected for 2016-17. *http://www.rose-hulman.edu/news/academics/2016/record-breaking-freshman-class-of-female-students-expected-for-2016-17.aspx* (May 2016).

[23] Rob A. Rutenbar. 2016. Letter of support for National Science Foundation Grant proposal submitted by the authors to SCIENCE, TECH & SOCIETY on 02/02/2016. (January 2016).

[24] Terri Williams. 2016. Women Total 48.5% of Carnegie MellonâĂŹs 2016 Computer Science Class. *Good Call* (26 October 2016).

Subgoal Labeled Worked Examples in K-3 Education

Johanna Joentausta
University of Helsinki
Helsinki, Finland
johanna.joentausta@helsinki.fi

Arto Hellas
University of Helsinki
Helsinki, Finland
arto.hellas@helsinki.fi

ABSTRACT

Worked examples are step-by-step instructions that are used to demonstrate and teach problem-solving processes. Subgoal labels are used to group the steps of worked examples into cohesive units that may help the learner to identify key information about the process. We conducted a study on the applicability of subgoal labeled worked examples with 9 and 10-year-old pupils (n=43) who were learning the principles of programming using LightBot. Using a between groups design, pupils in three classes were working with LightBot. One of the groups had no additional instructional materials for the LightBot environment, one of the groups had a set of worked examples without subgoal labels, and the last group had the same set of worked examples with subgoal labels. We measured pupils' success in terms of how many LightBot levels they completed during the class. In addition, pupils' beliefs and attitudes towards programming were assessed before and after the experiment. Our results indicate that in a programming environment such as LightBot, simple worked examples provide no significant benefit over no examples, but worked examples with subgoal labels can help pupils complete more levels. At the same time, the instructional materials in the study had no significant influence on the pupils' beliefs towards computer use or programming.

CCS CONCEPTS

• **Social and professional topics → K-12 education**; *Computational thinking*; • **Software and its engineering →** *Programming by example*;

ACM Reference Format:

Johanna Joentausta and Arto Hellas. 2018. Subgoal Labeled Worked Examples in K-3 Education. In *SIGCSE '18: The 49th ACM Technical Symposium on Computer Science Education, February 21–24, 2018, Baltimore, MD, USA.* ACM, New York, NY, USA, 6 pages. https://doi.org/10.1145/3159450.3159494

1 INTRODUCTION

Countries across the globe have embraced programming and included aspects of it into their school curricula [16, 21]. While the perceived difficulty of programming is rarely discussed within the context of primary schools, research into teaching programming in higher education has highlighted high drop out rates in programming courses as a problem [8, 30].

Pupils' experiences related to learning can have long-lasting effects. Success and positive feedback can lead to a reinforced self-efficacy [5], while struggling and poor feedback may lead to a complete aversion of the topic. These experiences may also influence pupils' career and study choices in the future [32]. As such, it is important for teachers to be able to support pupils in a way that the early experiences in a given subject are positive.

When teaching programming in schools, teachers often use tools such as LightBot, LOGO, and Scratch [16, 26]. These environments come in various shapes and are targeted to specific age groups [26]. Most such environments share a visual or tangible approach to learning programming; pupils control an entity or a set of entities that act in a virtual world. The environments are exploratory by nature, which also means that pupils can work in the environment either individually or in groups without explicit guidance from teachers.

When learning to use such educational programs and learning to program using them, it is possible that additional materials could be beneficial. For example, a pupil may benefit from the use of step-by-step instructions that outline the problem solving process – *worked examples* [3]. Moreover, grouping the steps into cohesive units with meaningful *subgoal labels* could help the pupil to identify key aspects of the problem solving process, and subsequently to identify reoccurring subgoals in similar problems [12]. While such studies have been conducted in higher education and teacher training [22, 23], studies on the topic in primary schools are rare.

In this article, we describe the results of a study of the benefits of using different types of instructional materials for LightBot in programming classes intended for third grade pupils who are between 9 and 10 year old. Using a between groups design with three classes, pupils used either no additional instructional materials, instructional materials with worked examples but without subgoal labels, or instructional materials with worked examples and subgoal labels. All of the three classes had two instructors present for the duration of the experiment, and pupils in all of the three classes could ask for questions and help from the instructors throughout the experiment. In addition to collecting pupils' progress, pre- and post-experiment surveys on pupils' self-beliefs and self-efficacy about computers and programming were used.

This article is organized as follows. In the next Section, we describe worked examples and subgoal labels, briefly discuss concepts related to pupils' self-beliefs, and finally outline the current state of programming education in the studied context. Then, in Section 3, we describe our research methodology, including the research questions and data. This is followed by the results and the discussion, in which we also outline the limitations of this work. Finally, Section 5 concludes this article.

SIGCSE '18, February 21–24, 2018, Baltimore, MD, USA

ACM ISBN 978-1-4503-5103-4/18/02...$15.00
https://doi.org/10.1145/3159450.3159494

2 BACKGROUND

2.1 Worked examples

Worked examples are an instructional technique in which learners are provided step-by-step guidelines for solving a problem [3, 29]. By following these guidelines, learners familiarize themselves with the problem domain and the way a particular type of a problem in that domain is solved. Worked examples have been used, for example, in mathematics, athletics and programming [3].

In general, worked examples have been shown to improve learning of novices in procedural domains. In cases where the learner is already familiar with the problem and knows how to solve it, worked examples may be detrimental and learners may consider them redundant [17]. The degree of familiarity with the problem may also influence the benefit from the worked examples; for example, some studies have suggested that learners who are given only partially worked out examples may perform as well as those with fully worked out examples [24].

Whilst the use of worked examples in the computing education domain has been suggested by various authors [1, 10, 15, 31], their use within the computing education domain has received only little empirical research [28].

The step-by-step guidelines of worked examples, while beneficial for novices who are learning a new task, may not help learners form a higher-level understanding of what they are solving or to help them to build a conceptual understanding of the problem [12]; novices may not learn to distinguish the key features from the worked examples.

2.2 Subgoal labeling

When solving problems using a set of examples, e.g. worked examples, students may memorize the steps without learning how to solve the tacit sub-problems. This may lead to a situation where students are unable to solve similar problems if the previously studied examples do not directly apply [11]. Subgoal labeling is a technique where sets of steps in a problem solving process are isolated to help students learn how specific subgoals are solved [11].

By grouping steps of worked examples together and giving the groups – that is, subgoals of the problem – meaningful names that describe the purpose of each particular group to the learner, learners may be able to focus on these higher level features of the problem while using the worked examples [2, 12]. As a consequence, students may also be able to apply the subgoals when working on new problems [11].

Studies in which subgoal labels have been used within the context of learning programming suggest that the inclusion of subgoal labels may improve learner performance over traditional worked examples [22, 23]. At the same time, it is possible that very specific goals may actually hinder the acquisition of programming comprehension skills [14].

2.3 Self-efficacy and attitudes

Self-efficacy – as defined by Albert Bandura – is the ability to see oneself as a capable individual who can succeed in a given task or in a specific situation [4]. Self-efficacy is developed through experiences and feedback, and it partially directs the actions of each individual. For example, individuals with low self-efficacy can see challenging tasks as something to avoid instead of something to master, while high self-efficacy can increase motivation and the drive to solve challenging tasks [6].

Self-efficacy is not only intertwined with school performance, but also with behavior, well-being, social relationships and performance in general [5, 6]. It can also influence career and study choices [9], leading to e.g. aversion of specific subjects. It is possible to increase self-efficacy through interventions [13, 34], however, these interventions typically take weeks. Another possibility is to use explicitly set goals, which can enhance self-efficacy as problems become easier to understand [18, 27].

2.4 Programming in Finnish schools

The Finnish national curriculum for general education (grades 1-9 $\approx$ ages 7-16) was recently revised and taken into use in fall 2016. The new curriculum places more emphasis on future competences and posits, among other things, that students are expected to learn the basics of information technology and programming.

The curriculum stipulates that pupils in grades 3-6 are expected to learn programming using visual programming tools. Programming is included to the grading of the subject mathematics – in order for a student to receive the grade 8 (out of scale 4-10, where 4 is the poorest grade and 10 is the best), the student should be able to create a working program.

The curriculum does not emphasize specific tools or programming environments. As a consequence, the teachers are free to select the tools that they feel suit their teaching the most. Commonly used tools in the grades 3-6 include LightBot[1], Scratch[2] and others. No explicit expectations are set for the third grade, in which this study took place.

3 METHODOLOGY

3.1 Research questions

Our research questions for this study are as follows:

- How do the instructional materials affect pupils' progress in LightBot?
- Does pupils' perceived self-efficacy and their attitudes towards computing change based on the instruction format?

With the first research question, *How do the instructional materials affect pupils' progress in Lightbot?*, we wish to determine the impact of different types of instructional materials (no materials, worked examples, worked examples with subgoal labels) on learning programming in a primary school setting. Our explicit focus is on LightBot, which is a commonly used novice programming environment.

With the second research question, *Does pupils' perceived self-efficacy and their attitudes towards computing change based on the instruction format?*, we wish to study whether a short intervention can influence students attitudes towards computing. Previous research suggests that explicitly set goals may influence self-efficacy, and as a consequence, it is plausible that minor effects could be observed even after a short intervention.

[1] http://lightbot.com
[2] https://scratch.mit.edu/

3.2 Context and participants

The study presented in this article was conducted in Finland. Our study focused on primary school pupils who are in the third grade (between 9 and 10 years). As the curriculum states that students in primary school should be introduced to a visual programming environment, we chose to use LightBot in our study as it is consistent with the curriculum.

A total of three classes were recruited for the study, and parental consent forms were sent to each parent of the children in the classes. In total, 47 pupils received parental consent and 4 did not. Thus, our starting population for the study was 47 pupils in three classes, labeled henceforth as groups; Group A (n = 17), Group B (n = 17) and Group C (n = 13). The gender distribution of the population was somewhat skewed; from the 47 pupils, 32 were girls.

3.3 Experimental setup

Our experiment was designed as a between groups study, where each group – class – in the experiment was given different instructional handouts, while the task and instructors were held constant.

The duration of the experiment was one class hour, which consisted of filling pre- and post-questionnaires and a 45-minute session of LightBot. The class was tutored by two experienced instructors, who had previously instructed several similar classes for 7 to 12 year old primary school pupils. One of the instructors is also the first author of this article. The main responsible teacher of each class was also present and participated in advising the pupils, but the teachers were not previously familiar with LightBot.

The pre-questionnaire included questions about gender, native language, programming experience, opinion about computing skills in general, questions related to self-efficacy, and a few questions about educational achievements and diligence. Post-questionnaire mostly focused on the programming experience, including questions such as "I could complete programming tasks" and "I was happy about the number of tasks I completed". The questionnaire was given as a Likert-like form, where the students had range of smileys that indicated their agreement. A red sad face indicated disagreement and a green happy face indicated agreement.

In the between groups design, the classes were used as a natural and convenient way to group the students, which was also requested by the schools – their preference was that students could stay with their teacher and that each student in the same class would receive the same instruction. Group A did not receive any written instructions. Group B received illustrated worked example printouts of (n = 5) levels that the instructors had previously estimated as difficult, and Group C received the same instructional materials as Group B, but with subgoal labels (Figure 1).

In each class, instructors guided any pupil who asked for help as he or she was working on levels that had not previously been estimated as difficult. However, when the pupil was working on a level that had previously been estimated as difficult by the instructors, the procedure of providing guidelines differed between the classes. In Group A with no instructional materials, the instructors provided similar guidance as before, but in Groups B and C, the instructors suggested that the pupil reads out the provided instructional materials, and if needed, also read them out themselves.

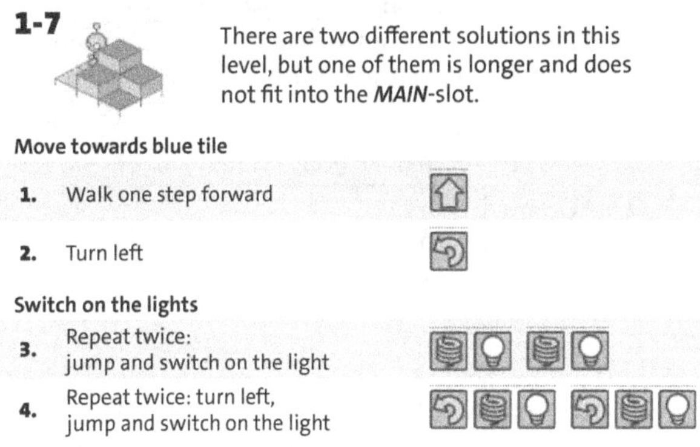

Figure 1: An example of a worked example printout with subgoal labels. The printout without subgoal labels did not have the texts "Move towards the blue tile" and "Switch on the lights".

When guidance was needed and the issue was erroneous code, the code was examined in co-operation with the pupil. If the pupil had not made any code at all, the instructor and the pupil started to think together which step would be a good one to start with. When the robot was moved, the pupil started to consider the next move, possibly with the help of the instructor. Pupils were always praised for both trying and succeeding.

3.4 Data and analysis

Pupils' progress in the game was measured as a part of the post-study questionnaire. The game consists of three different segments, where the first of them has 8 levels, the second one had 6 levels and the third one had 6 levels. During the analysis, pupils answers were numbered sequentially from 1 to 20.

The analysis of the response data was conducted using SPSS software[3].

4 RESULTS AND DISCUSSION

A total of 47 pupils had informed consent from their parents. Four of the 47 pupils did not complete the surveys, and thus, answers from 43 pupils were included into the analysis.

4.1 Materials and pupil progress

The average progress of each group is shown in Table 1. In order to determine whether the instructional format had an effect on the pupils' progress in LightBot, we used Kruskall-Wallis one-way analysis of variance [19] to assess the difference between the groups. The analysis revealed that there was no statistically significant difference between the group that had no instructional materials and the group that had the material with worked examples ($df = 2, p > 0.05$).

[3]https://www.ibm.com/analytics/us/en/technology/spss/

Table 1: Average progress in LightBot during the 45 minute class for each of the separate groups. Group A had no instructional materials, Group B had worked examples, and Group C had worked examples with subgoal labels.

Group	Average progress in LightBot
Group A	10.29
Group B	10.65
Group C	13.58

When analyzing the difference between the group that had used worked examples with subgoal labels and the other groups, a statistically significant difference between was found ($df = 2, p = 0.004$). That is, the group with worked examples with subgoal labels performed significantly better than the other groups. The difference between the groups is visualized as a Boxplot in Figure 2. We excluded one value from group B due to a very likely mistake – a pupil had indicated that he or she had completed only two levels, something that the instructors knew was false[4].

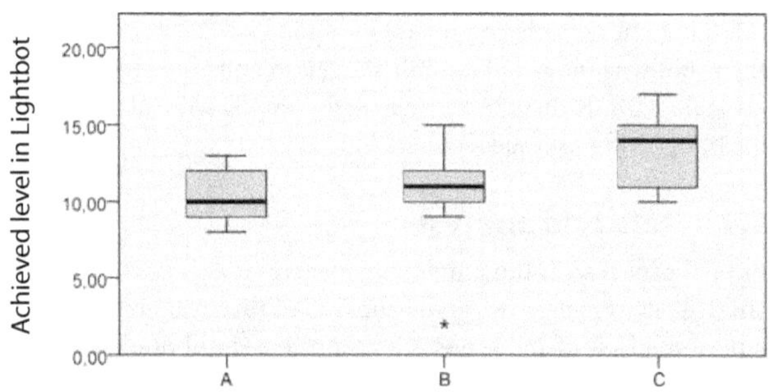

Figure 2: The difference between the average achieved LightBot level in each of the groups. Group A on the left had no instructional materials, Group B in the middle had worked examples, and Group C on the right had worked examples with subgoal labels.

To summarize, our response to the Research Question 1 *"How do the instructional materials affect pupils' progress in LightBot?"* is as follows. We did not observe a statistically significant improvement in the progress of pupils who used worked examples when compared to those who did not use any type of materials. We did, however, find that the group who used materials with subgoal labeled worked examples performed significantly better than the group with no materials and the group with worked examples but no subgoal labels.

[4]It is possible that the pupil was thinking about 2-1, that is the first level of the second segment, but wrote down 1-2, that is the second level of the first segment. As this is only speculative, the pupil was excluded from the analysis

4.2 Self-Efficacy and perceptions of programming

Students' perceived self-efficacy and perceptions of programming were assessed using a pre- and post-study survey. In this study, we limit the analysis to questions that were identical in the pre- and post-survey. These questions were as follows:

- I consider myself as a good computer user
- I believe programming is useful
- I believe programming will teach you how to use computer

In our analysis, we refer to the first question as a question that measured pupils' self-efficacy, while the two subsequent questions are related to pupils' perceptions about computing.

When analyzing the difference between pupils' answers in the pre- and post-questionnaire, no statistically significant difference was found. Moreover, the instructional format did not influence the result. We must note, however, that this result can be a side-product of a ceiling effect; vast majority of the pupils responded with very high values already during the pre-questionnaire, and there was room for only a marginal bump in the post-questionnaire.

To summarize, our response to the Research Question 2 *"Does pupils' perceived self-efficacy and their attitudes towards computing change based on the instruction format?"* is as follows. In a short, one hour computing experience, we did not observe a statistically significant change in the surveyed metrics. We note, however, that there was a ceiling effect in place, which may have influenced the outcomes.

4.3 Notes on programming experience

When asking the pupils about their background with programming, our initial goal was to exclude the few pupils with previous programming experience that we expected to find from the study. Surprisingly, nearly one half of the pupils had some previous programming experience; some had programmed using Bee-bots, some had programmed using Scratch, and some had previously used LightBot. A couple of pupils also responded that they had played Minecraft – we are unsure how they considered this as programming. The pupils with previous programming background were evenly distributed among the groups.

Given the opportunity, we also studied whether pupils' previous programming experience affected their progress in LightBot. When analyzing the pupils as two groups who had either programmed previously or had no previous programming experience, we found that there was a statistically significant difference between the groups' progress (Mann-Whitney U-Test [20], $U = 312.5, p = 0.022$). On average, the pupils with previous programming background progressed to the level 12.2, while the pupils with no previous programming background progressed to the level 10.8.

These results are in line with previous findings in higher education that indicate that previous programming experience indeed helps with programming tasks (see e.g. [33]).

4.4 Pupils' and teachers' perceptions

During the experiment, pupils' and teachers' outbursts were also monitored. Overall, in all of the classes, both pupils and teachers indicated that they had enjoyed programming a lot.

We noted an interesting observation in the groups who had the instructional materials at their disposal. When given the instructional materials, more than a single pupil (approx 2-3 in both groups B and C) stated that they did not want to cheat when studying. In other terms, some pupils saw the step-by-step instructions as cheating, and voiced out loud that they wanted to solve the problems by themselves. As we did not explicitly note down the pupils who voiced the outbursts, and our response data is anonymous, we do not know if the pupils held their mind or if they actually chose to use the provided materials in the end.

In a broader sense, this observation highlights the attitude of some of the pupils in the classroom. Having step-by-step guidelines that the pupil could use to solve a problem can be seen as cheating by some. We do not know if this is a cultural issue of if the observation holds globally.

4.5 Limitations of study

Our study has a few limitations which we address next. First, the study was conducted in a country with a rather homogeneous population; only approximately 30% of the pupils reported that their native language was not Finnish. The educational system in Finland is also such that the teachers in Kindergarten have Bachelors degrees in education, and the teachers in primary schools have Masters degrees in education. That is, it is possible that results in other contexts could be influenced by how pupils are taught to learn and act in school.

Our study was conducted as a between groups design, and as such, there may be differences between the groups. All of the groups came from similar schools and there was no significant difference in the backgrounds of the pupils. It is true that a randomized controlled trial would have possibly reduced bias, but the schools expected each pupil in the same classroom to have the same treatment.

When considering the instruction, it is possible that the instruction format influenced the way how instructors acted with the pupils. For example, the instructors may have benefited from the subgoal labels during the instruction. On the other hand, upon discussion, the instructors noted that upon problems, they attempted to teach pupils to identify key subgoals. The behavior did not change across the classes.

When measuring pupils' progress, we used self-reported metrics. In hindsight, as the levels were marked down using the notation that shows both the segment and the level, it would have been more meaningful to have the instructors mark down the highest level that each pupil achieved. In our study, at least one pupil had answered the question incorrectly, writing down that he or she had reached only the second level. The instructors knew that all of the students were able to proceed further than the second level, and as a consequence, the entry was discarded from analysis. Future studies on the topic should consider having instructors mark down the levels.

Similarly, the questionnaire used has not been validated. The questionnaire was designed by the authors based on [7, 25] and given in Finnish to the pupils. The questions were designed to be sufficiently short for the pupils, and the scale in the questionnaire was given using smiley-faces to retain attention. It is, however, possible that such design choices influenced the overall study and the results: we do not know, for example, how pupils perceive the distance between two smileys.

Finally, during the study, two additional instructors were present in the classes. We do not know whether similar results would have been achieved in a classroom with only one teacher.

5 CONCLUSIONS

In this study, we assessed the effect of different types of instructional materials in three third grade classes where 9 and 10 year old pupils were learning to program using LightBot. Each class received different instructional materials; first class received no additional instructional materials, the second class received instructional materials with worked examples, and the third class received instructional materials with worked examples and subgoal labels.

Our results show that pupils did not benefit from the worked examples when comparing to no instructional materials. There was a statistically significant improvement in the progress of the group that used worked examples with subgoal labels however. The group with worked examples and subgoal labels completed, on average, almost three more levels in LightBot than the other groups. Percentwise, this is almost a 30% improvement in the number of completed levels.

These results suggest that if the learning environment has been created to provide ample scaffolding, as LightBot does, it is possible that worked examples do not provide additional benefit. As the goals in LightBot are very specific and the LightBot environment has been constructed so that players start with small problems and eventually tackle larger ones, pupils may reach the same benefits from LightBot itself than they would gain from worked examples. Our results can also, however, be interpreted so that designers of such games as LightBot would benefit from incorporating subgoal labels into their instructional materials.

During the study, we surveyed pupils self-efficacy and attitudes towards computing, and used a pre- and post-questionnaire to study whether the attitudes were changed as a result of the experiment. We did not find any statistically significant differences between the groups nor between the pre- and post-questionnaires. We note, however, that this could be explained by a ceiling effect: majority of the pupils reported very high self-efficacy and attitudes already during the beginning of the study.

Overall, these results indicate that pupils can benefit from instructional materials with worked examples and subgoal labels when learning programming using educational environments. We did not assess long-term retention or conceptual knowledge of the students, however; in our future work, we are looking to address if this improvement in the quantity of levels that the pupils can complete has an effect on how the pupils understand programming concepts.

ACKNOWLEDGEMENTS

We would like to express our gratitude to the anonymous reviewers whose suggestions have helped us to improve the manuscript considerably. We also acknowledge and thank the teachers in the respective schools and greet Anu Riihiaho – the other instructor – thank you (again)!

REFERENCES

[1] Siti-Soraya Abdul-Rahman and Benedict Du Boulay. 2014. Learning programming via worked-examples: Relation of learning styles to cognitive load. *Computers in Human Behavior* 30 (2014), 286–298.

[2] Robert K Atkinson, Richard Catrambone, and Mary Margaret Merrill. 2003. Aiding Transfer in Statistics: Examining the Use of Conceptually Oriented Equations and Elaborations During Subgoal Learning. *Journal of Educational Psychology* 95, 4 (2003), 762.

[3] Robert K Atkinson, Sharon J Derry, Alexander Renkl, and Donald Wortham. 2000. Learning from examples: Instructional principles from the worked examples research. *Review of educational research* 70, 2 (2000), 181–214.

[4] Albert Bandura. 1977. Self-efficacy: Toward a unifying theory of behavioral change. *Psychological Review* (1977), 191–215.

[5] Albert Bandura. 1993. Perceived self-efficacy in cognitive development and functioning. *Educational psychologist* 28, 2 (1993), 117–148.

[6] Albert Bandura. 1997. *Self-efficacy: The exercise of control.* Macmillan.

[7] Albert Bandura. 2006. Guide for constructing self-efficacy scales. *Self-efficacy beliefs of adolescents* 5, 307-337 (2006).

[8] Jens Bennedsen and Michael E Caspersen. 2007. Failure rates in introductory programming. *ACM SIGCSE Bulletin* 39, 2 (2007), 32–36.

[9] Nancy E Betz and Gail Hackett. 1986. Applications of self-efficacy theory to understanding career choice behavior. *Journal of social and clinical psychology* 4, 3 (1986), 279–289.

[10] Michael E. Caspersen and Jens Bennedsen. 2007. Instructional Design of a Programming Course: A Learning Theoretic Approach. In *Proceedings of the Third International Workshop on Computing Education Research (ICER '07).* ACM, New York, NY, USA, 111–122. https://doi.org/10.1145/1288580.1288595

[11] Richard Catrambone. 1995. Aiding subgoal learning: Effects on transfer. *Journal of educational psychology* 87, 1 (1995), 5.

[12] Richard Catrambone. 1998. The subgoal learning model: Creating better examples so that students can solve novel problems. *Journal of Experimental Psychology: General* 127, 4 (1998), 355.

[13] Joanna C Dunlap. 2005. Problem-based learning and self-efficacy: How a capstone course prepares students for a profession. *Educational Technology Research and Development* 53, 1 (2005), 65–83.

[14] Chia-Yen Feng and Ming-Puu Chen. 2014. The effects of goal specificity and scaffolding on programming performance and self-regulation in game design. *British Journal of Educational Technology* 45, 2 (2014), 285–302.

[15] Simon Gray, Caroline St. Clair, Richard James, and Jerry Mead. 2007. Suggestions for Graduated Exposure to Programming Concepts Using Fading Worked Examples. In *Proceedings of the Third International Workshop on Computing Education Research (ICER '07).* ACM, New York, NY, USA, 99–110. https://doi.org/10.1145/1288580.1288594

[16] Peter Hubwieser, Michail N Giannakos, Marc Berges, Torsten Brinda, Ira Diethelm, Johannes Magenheim, Yogendra Pal, Jana Jackova, and Egle Jasute. 2015. A global snapshot of computer science education in K-12 schools. In *Proceedings of the 2015 ITiCSE on Working Group Reports.* ACM, 65–83.

[17] Slava Kalyuga, Paul Chandler, Juhani Tuovinen, and John Sweller. 2001. When problem solving is superior to studying worked examples. *Journal of educational psychology* 93, 3 (2001), 579.

[18] Steve WJ Kozlowski and Bradford S Bell. 2006. Disentangling achievement orientation and goal setting: effects on self-regulatory processes. *Journal of Applied Psychology* 91, 4 (2006), 900.

[19] William H. Kruskal and W. Allen Wallis. 1952. Use of Ranks in One-Criterion Variance Analysis. *J. Amer. Statist. Assoc.* 47, 260 (1952), 583–621. https://doi.org/10.1080/01621459.1952.10483441

[20] Henry B Mann and Donald R Whitney. 1947. On a test of whether one of two random variables is stochastically larger than the other. *The annals of mathematical statistics* (1947), 50–60.

[21] Linda Mannila, Valentina Dagiene, Barbara Demo, Natasa Grgurina, Claudio Mirolo, Lennart Rolandsson, and Amber Settle. 2014. Computational Thinking in K-9 Education. In *Proceedings of the Working Group Reports of the 2014 on Innovation & Technology in Computer Science Education Conference (ITiCSE-WGR '14).* ACM, New York, NY, USA, 1–29. https://doi.org/10.1145/2713609.2713610

[22] Lauren E. Margulieux, Mark Guzdial, and Richard Catrambone. 2012. Subgoal-labeled Instructional Material Improves Performance and Transfer in Learning to Develop Mobile Applications. In *Proceedings of the Ninth Annual International Conference on International Computing Education Research (ICER '12).* ACM, New York, NY, USA, 71–78. https://doi.org/10.1145/2361276.2361291

[23] Briana B. Morrison, Lauren E. Margulieux, and Mark Guzdial. 2015. Subgoals, Context, and Worked Examples in Learning Computing Problem Solving. In *Proceedings of the Eleventh Annual International Conference on International Computing Education Research (ICER '15).* ACM, New York, NY, USA, 21–29. https://doi.org/10.1145/2787622.2787733

[24] Fred G Paas. 1992. Training strategies for attaining transfer of problem-solving skill in statistics: A cognitive-load approach. *Journal of educational psychology* 84, 4 (1992), 429.

[25] Paul R Pintrich et al. 1991. A manual for the use of the Motivated Strategies for Learning Questionnaire (MSLQ). (1991).

[26] A Rees, Francisco J García-Peñalvo, T Toivonen, J Hughes, I Jormananinen, M Tuul, M Virnes, and D Reimann. 2016. Evaluation of existing resources (study/analysis). (2016).

[27] Dale H Schunk. 1990. Goal setting and self-efficacy during self-regulated learning. *Educational psychologist* 25, 1 (1990), 71–86.

[28] Ben Skudder and Andrew Luxton-Reilly. 2014. Worked Examples in Computer Science. In *Proceedings of the Sixteenth Australasian Computing Education Conference - Volume 148 (ACE '14).* Australian Computer Society, Inc., Darlinghurst, Australia, Australia, 59–64. http://dl.acm.org/citation.cfm?id=2667490.2667497

[29] John Sweller and Graham A Cooper. 1985. The use of worked examples as a substitute for problem solving in learning algebra. *Cognition and instruction* 2, 1 (1985), 59–89.

[30] Arto Vihavainen, Jonne Airaksinen, and Christopher Watson. 2014. A systematic review of approaches for teaching introductory programming and their influence on success. In *Proceedings of the tenth annual conference on International computing education research.* ACM, 19–26.

[31] Arto Vihavainen, Matti Paksula, and Matti Luukkainen. 2011. Extreme apprenticeship method in teaching programming for beginners. In *Proceedings of the 42nd ACM technical symposium on Computer science education.* ACM, 93–98.

[32] Xueli Wang. 2013. Why students choose STEM majors: Motivation, high school learning, and postsecondary context of support. *American Educational Research Journal* 50, 5 (2013), 1081–1121.

[33] Christopher Watson, Frederick WB Li, and Jamie L Godwin. 2014. No tests required: comparing traditional and dynamic predictors of programming success. In *Proceedings of the 45th ACM technical symposium on Computer science education.* ACM, 469–474.

[34] Amy L Zeldin and Frank Pajares. 2000. Against the odds: Self-efficacy beliefs of women in mathematical, scientific, and technological careers. *American Educational Research Journal* 37, 1 (2000), 215–246.

"I Think We Should...": Analyzing Elementary Students' Collaborative Processes for Giving and Taking Suggestions

Jennifer Tsan
North Carolina State University
Raleigh, North Carolina
jtsan@ncsu.edu

Fernando J. Rodríguez
University of Florida
Gainesville, Florida
fjrodriguez@ufl.edu

Kristy Elizabeth Boyer
University of Florida
Gainesville, Florida
keboyer@ufl.edu

Collin Lynch
North Carolina State University
Raleigh, North Carolina
cflynch@ncsu.edu

ABSTRACT

Collaboration plays an essential role in computer science. While there is growing recognition that learners of all ages can benefit from collaborative learning, little is known about how elementary-age children engage in collaborative problem solving in computer science. This paper reports on the analysis of a dataset of elementary students collaborating on a programming project. We found that children tend to make several different types of suggestions. In turn, their partners address those suggestions in different ways such as by implementing them directly in code or by replying through dialogue. We observe that students regularly accept or reject suggestions without explanation or explicit acknowledgement and that it is often unclear whether they understand the substance of the suggestion. These behaviors may inhibit the development of a shared understanding between the partners and limit the value of the collaborative process. These results can inform instructional practice and the development of new adaptive tools that facilitate productive collaborative problem solving in computer science.

CCS CONCEPTS

• **Social and professional topics → Computing education**; **Computer science education**; **K-12 education**;

KEYWORDS

Elementary school, pair programming, collaboration, dialogue.

ACM Reference format:

Jennifer Tsan, Fernando J. Rodríguez, Kristy Elizabeth Boyer, and Collin Lynch. 2018. "I Think We Should...": Analyzing Elementary Students' Collaborative Processes for Giving and Taking Suggestions. In *Proceedings of SIGCSE '18: The 49th ACM Technical Symposium on Computing Science Education, Baltimore , MD, USA, February 21–24, 2018 (SIGCSE '18)*, 6 pages. https://doi.org/10.1145/3159450.3159507

SIGCSE '18, February 21–24, 2018, Baltimore , MD, USA

ACM ISBN 978-1-4503-5103-4/18/02...$15.00
https://doi.org/10.1145/3159450.3159507

1 INTRODUCTION

Collaborative problem-solving skills play an important role in computer science education. A rich body of research has studied collaborative problem solving in CS at the undergraduate level [7, 15, 19], and we have seen the emergence of collaborative approaches such as peer instruction [4], process-oriented guided inquiry learning (POGIL) [8], and pair programming [18] that encourage students to work together on problem-solving tasks. In particular, pair programming has been shown to improve students' learning experiences [20], increase student retention in computer science courses [12], and promote good programming practices such as planning a solution before implementing it [14].

In contrast to the research on post-secondary CS learning, there has been comparably less work examining collaboration between elementary computer science students. Recent work has revealed that the equity of a relationship is dependent on how the individuals' personalities impact each other [11, 17], and in a collaborative programming context, students often discuss the problem-solving process and their achievements in that process [9].

In order to effectively support young learners in collaborative computer science learning, computer science education research needs to move toward a deeper understanding of children's collaborative practices. Our work focuses on this question in the context of elementary school pair programming. In a recent study, we found that an imbalance often exists between students not only in their prior experience, but in the extent to which they engage in talk and "driving" (controlling the keyboard and mouse). We have also discovered that suggestions to each other are the most common type of dialogue move our students made.

In this paper, we investigate the phenomenon of making and taking suggestions, addressing the following research question: *How do elementary students make and respond to suggestions during pair programming?* We examined transcripts of pair programming and the video and screen capture of collaborative work from which the transcripts originated. Our review of the dialogue contributions using a case study methodology reveals that students make suggestions through proposals, stronger commands, and suggestions about the next step to take. We also observe at least four types of responses to suggestions: implementing the suggestion (or not), combined with acknowledging the suggestion through dialogue (or not). We examine excerpts from students' interactions that illustrate these different ways of making and acting on suggestions. We hope this work can help educators promote successful collaborative dialogue among their students by identifying best practices, as well as inform instructional practice and the design and development of adaptive tools to support such collaboration.

2 RELATED WORK

This work is directly informed by a body of prior research on collaboration among young learners. This section first reviews related work on collaboration outside of the computer science domain, then focuses on the small but growing body of research on collaboration between young students learning computer science. Note that while the current paper focuses on fifth grade students (approximately ages 9-11), this discussion of related work includes young middle school students as well.

2.1 Children Collaboratively Problem-Solving in Non-CS Domains

Researchers in the learning sciences have actively studied collaborative problem solving in domains outside of computer science, chief among these mathematics. In a highly influential work, Barron studied successful and unsuccessful collaborative interactions among groups of high-achieving sixth-grade students in mathematics using both qualitative and quantitative methods [1]. One finding from that work is that groups which perform better collaboratively are more apt to accept one another's proposals and/or engage in discussion around them, while less successful groups are more prone to reject or simply ignore their partners' suggestions.

In another study of collaboration in math, Olsen and Finkelstein examined the conversations of fourth grade students collaborating on word problems within an intelligent tutoring system [13]. Students were randomly assigned to one of three conditions where they viewed problem-solving example videos: an individual student thinking aloud solving a math problem, a pair collaborating on a problem from an unrelated topic, and a pair collaborating on a math problem. Researchers annotated collaborative session segments based on the quality of the reasoning (talking about the problem) and rapport (synergy between the partners). There were significant positive correlations between the rapport and reasoning state and between the reasoning state and post test scores which indicate that pairs with better relationships may perform better when problem solving.

In a study of how roles naturally form in a collaborative group, researchers evaluated the discourse of a group of sixth grade students in a physics class [5]. Utterances were annotated as conceptual, procedural/negotiation, or social. From their analysis, the authors found that each student had a dominant discourse type, and students who contributed more conceptual utterances, or utterances about the concepts the students were learning, had the highest learning gains.

Downton studied the collaborative processes that unfold during group work on a fourth grade music production task [6], investigating how students reflected on their actions in their dialogue. The excerpt presented by the author illustrated how students reflected on aspects of the music production task and how these spoken reflections would be referenced and built upon by their partners, adding to the collective knowledge of the group.

2.2 Children Collaboratively Problem-Solving in CS Domains

Shah, Lewis, and Caires investigated the equity of elementary students pair programming in a summer CS course [11, 17]. The authors chose pairs of students where one student was in all of the pairs. For these pairs of students, the authors reviewed the distribution of talk, the content of the dialogue, and other key actions that impacted the equity of their relationships. The authors found that the student in common had inequitable relationships with two of his partners and equitable relationships with the other two. This shows that it is not necessarily an individual's characteristics that define the way an interaction plays out; instead, it is the way each individual's characteristics synergize with those of their partners.

In another study of collaborative discourse, researchers gave students the choice to work with others or work independently while solving programming problems and investigated what kinds of collaborative interactions emerged as students worked together in a computing environment. The students shifted between working independently and collaborating with a peer or teacher. The authors found that the majority of the students' interactions were about solving computational problems, off-topic discussions, or expressing excitement about their achievements during the problem solving process [9].

While research on how young students collaborate during computer science problem solving is growing, this is the first work specifically examining how elementary students give and take suggestions while pair programming. Of the papers we explored, Barron's [1] relates most closely to our current work, and we drew from its methodology. By looking into this part of the collaborative process, we can better understand how young learners solve problems together and how we may in turn support them most effectively.

3 DATA AND METHODS

3.1 Elementary CS Elective Course

Over the course of one year, we collected data from a computer science elective in an urban elementary school in the southeastern United States. The data was collected over four 30-day iterations of the class. The course did not exist prior to this research, and its curriculum was designed by the first author in collaboration with another PhD student and the elementary school teacher. In the class, the students learned about computational thinking, programming, computers in society, and other computer science topics. In the programming section, the students were taught basic concepts in Scratch including moving the visual Sprites, taking input, conditionals, and loops. In the middle of the course, students began working on their first programming project which occupied five to seven class periods. For the first programming project, the students were asked to create a program that demonstrated cause and effect using storytelling. The students were required to pair program, and the teacher assigned the students to their partners.

Pair ID	Student Pseudonyms	Gender Composition
1	Charlie and Quinn	Boy, Boy *
2	Ian and Aaron	Boy, Boy
3	Alonzo and Gigi	Boy, Girl *
4	John and Mia	Boy, Girl
5	Greg and Harry	Boy, Boy

Table 1: Identifiers, pseudonyms, and genders of the collaborating pairs. *These pairs had complete videos and screen recordings for two of their pair programming sessions, which we briefly discuss below.

Excerpt 1 (Driving: Quinn, Navigating: Charlie)

	[Quinn typed "yes" in the "«answer> = [ ]>" block.]	
154	Quinn	Until equals yes, right?
155	Charlie	I guess so.
156	Charlie	Alright.
157	Charlie	Make everything over.
	[Quinn moved a sprite.]	
158	Charlie	We did it. We did it. It actually worked. No, no go to there. Go switch the backdrop first.
	[Quinn went to the Backdrop tab and changed the backdrop.]	
159	Charlie	Now go to them, and do the (()).
	[Quinn clicked on a sprite and clicked "show".]	

3.2 Participants

Over the course of the year, 55 students signed up to take the class and 26 consented to data collection. We collected video and screen capture data from those students while they completed their projects in pairs. Before the start of the project, the teacher explained the concept of pair programming and the responsibilities of each role. Each pair programming session lasted 30-40 minutes. Due to technical problems, not every video-recorded session had screen recording data. In this work, we analyzed all of the videos and screen recordings we had of students working on their first project, a total of five pairs. Table 1 provides an overview of the five pairs on which this paper's analysis is based.

At the elementary school where we collected the data, the student body is roughly 53% African-American, 33% Caucasian, and 14% Hispanic, Latino, Native American, Asian, or mixed race. Approximately 47.4% of the students receive free or reduced cost lunch.

3.3 Methods

The present work utilizes qualitative analysis of transcribed dialogues through a case study methodology. In prior work, we transcribed the videos collected from the elective described in the previous subsection. We also previously tagged all *suggestion* dialogue moves and found that they comprised 77% of all student utterances.

We focus our case studies on the three minutes of student work that occur at the fifteen-minute mark (approximately halfway through collaboration in one class period) in each pair programming session. At this halfway mark, we are able to see students' collaboration in process because the initial setup is completed, and no pairs had finished their work.

4 CASE STUDIES

In order to answer our research questions, we examined case studies of the five pairs of students in the dataset. This led us to better understand the dynamics of the relationships and areas in which specific interactions could benefit from scaffolding.

4.1 Charlie and Quinn: "Now go to..."

We reviewed both available sessions of Charlie and Quinn pair programming. In the first session, Charlie appeared to be more open to collaborating and explained some of the code to Quinn. However, as time passed, Charlie also appeared to become frustrated with having to collaborate, and at times he did not verbally acknowledge Quinn's suggestions.

Regardless of which role he was in, Charlie spoke much more than Quinn, and gave many more suggestions than Quinn did. He also showed impatience multiple times when Quinn was driving, asking when it would be time to switch roles. We noticed that Charlie often gave specific suggestions in a series, and Quinn often followed those suggestions without verbally acknowledging them. Their behavior indicates that Charlie was the dominant member of the pair. Excerpt 1[1] further illustrates this point.

Excerpt 1 took place over approximately 30 seconds. In this time, Quinn made one specific suggestion at turn 154 while asking for confirmation from Charlie when he says, "...right?" When Charlie verbally accepted the suggestion during turn 155, Quinn continued working and implemented it. Once Quinn was done, Charlie then gave him a string of suggestions in turns 158 and 159, which Quinn followed without speaking. The suggestions that Charlie gave were very direct and confident, leaving no question of what he wanted Quinn to do. In fact, these suggestions felt more like commands.

At first blush, we might conclude that Charlie and Quinn worked relatively well together. They did not argue (a common problem for young collaborators), and they filled their respective roles roughly as expected. However, they were missing a crucial part of the collaboration process: discussion. The lack of discussion meant they simply followed one person's vision without establishing common ground [2] and may not have benefited as much from the collaboration as they could have. Throughout both sessions, Quinn implemented most solutions as a driver without questioning Charlie. He was also a quiet navigator, especially in the second session where he seemed more distracted and withdrawn. There was usually more discussion during the rare times Quinn disagreed with Charlie, but in most cases, Charlie stood firm and seemed to have the final say.

4.2 Ian and Aaron: "I know."

In this pair, Ian seemed to prefer working independently while Aaron appeared to enjoy collaborating. Aaron gave the majority of the suggestions, and Ian followed some and ignored others, often without verbally acknowledging them. Other times, when he acknowledged Aaron's suggestions, he said, "I know," before continuing to work. It is worth noting that in our previous analysis, we observed that there was one session where Aaron did not drive at

[1] (()) is used in place of inaudible speech.

all. In this session, which occurred the day after, Aaron only drove for a few minutes before Ian became frustrated and took the mouse.

In Excerpt 2, Ian made some high-level suggestions, then solicited advice by saying he did not know how to implement those solutions. Aaron then gave him some low-level suggestions, which Ian did not verbally acknowledge, but implemented. When Ian implemented the suggestions, he did not seem to find what he needed, so he went to the "Scripts" category instead while stating it out loud. While Ian soliciting advice was a positive action to take, this was another instance of how a lack of discussion is a failure to establish common ground.

Excerpt 2 (Driving: Ian, Navigating: Aaron)		
	[Ian opened their program, which he had closed when the pair went to talk to their teacher.]	
163	Ian	I think we should do this.
164	Ian	And then we have the house hide.
	[Ian moved an existing block slightly and gestured towards a sprite using his mouse.]	
165	Ian	I don't know how to.
	[Ian went to the Costumes tab.]	
166	Aaron	You gotta go to stage.
	[Ian went to the Scripts tab then went to Stage.]	
167	Aaron	Then you go to backdrops.
	[Ian went to the Backdrop tab.]	
168	Ian	(()).
169	Ian	Scripts.
	[Ian went back to the Scripts tab.]	

4.3 Alonzo and Gigi: "You're mean."

Alonzo and Gigi generally worked well together. In some ways, Gigi seemed more dominant than Alonzo, but Alonzo gave more suggestions than she did. Gigi often followed those suggestions without disagreeing with him. Alonzo's suggestions were often specific and she implemented them without problems. However, during the few times she disagreed with him, he stood his ground and they implemented his suggestions

In Excerpt 3, Alonzo gave Gigi suggestions and, similar to Charlie, Alonzo gave suggestions that were closer to commands. Then Gigi disagreed with one and said, "No," during turn 255. Alonzo responded by firmly stating that they were going to implement his idea in turn 256. Gigi protested again, but as she protested, she started to implement the change he suggested. In the end, despite the number of protests she made, they settled with his idea. This is an example of an interaction where a verbal acknowledgment and protest was not enough. The students would have benefited from self-explanation [3], where each student presents an argument for or against the idea that was presented.

Excerpt 4 illustrates Alonzo and Gigi deciding which sound to add to their program. Gigi made a suggestion in turn 440. In turn 442, Alonzo responded by telling her to wait and that he was thinking about what they needed. He did not implement her suggestion; instead, he continued searching and made his own suggestion, to which Gigi agreed. Instead of discussing Gigi's suggestion and why he did or did not agree with it, he decided not to implement it and came up with his own suggestion.

Excerpt 3 (Driving: Gigi, Navigating: Alonzo)		
	[Gigi went to the Backdrops tab.]	
253	Alonzo	Now go to mine.
	[Gigi changed the backdrop and moved a sprite.]	
254	Alonzo	My drawn one.
	[Gigi moved a different sprite.]	
255	Gigi	No.
256	Alonzo	Yes bruh, we're using that one.
257	Gigi	The ugly one?
	[Gigi goes back to Stage.]	
258	Alonzo	Yes.
	[Gigi changes the backdrop.]	
259	Gigi	You're mean.

Excerpt 4 (Driving: Alonzo, Navigating: Gigi)		
	[Alonzo is looking in the Sounds library.]	
439	Gigi	What- whatever, (()) just pick one.
	[Alonzo continues looking.]	
440	Gigi	Growl. Let's (()) growl.
441	Gigi	(())
442	Alonzo	Alright, wait. I'm tryin think of what we need bruh.
	[Alonzo goes to the animal category.]	
443	Alonzo	Alright, what do we need? An animal noise, right?
444	Gigi	Yeah.

This case study shows examples of interactions where a verbal acknowledgment and protest was not enough. In Excerpt 3, Gigi disagreed with Alonzo but conceded after he insisted multiple times. In Excerpt 4, Alonzo pushed off her suggestion to think and she did not mention it again. The students would have benefited from self-explanation, where each student presents arguments for or against the ideas that were introduced.

4.4 John and Mia: "What are you doing?"

In our previous study, we observed that John gave more suggestions than Mia did. Our current observations of their conversation and programming process revealed that Mia often did not react positively to John's suggestions or give reasons for disagreeing with him. John also did not give reasons for his suggestions.

Overall, the relationship of these two students seemed much more competitive than collaborative. Mia often attributed the problem to her partner rather than the task at hand [10]. They would sometimes even flaunt when one partner proved the other was incorrect. Additionally, neither student explained their thoughts and ideas and Mia was not open to her partner's suggestions. This undesirable behavior is illustrated in Excerpt 5.

John was making changes to the code when Mia noticed he was doing something she did not expect. Since he was working silently, she did not understand why he was making those changes and asked him what he was doing in turn 219. As John continued to work without answering her, she made a suggestion in turn 220. Once again, John did not answer and Mia repeated her question. Since John did not acknowledge her questions or suggestions and appeared not to have implemented her suggestion, Mia was obviously frustrated. It was not until the teacher asked John to explain what he was doing to Mia did John start talking to her again.

Excerpt 5 (Driving: John, Navigating: Mia)		
	[John is making changes to the code.]	
219	Mia	What are you doing?
	[John continues to work without saying anything.]	
220	Mia	We have to do the same thing that we did for the first one!
	[John goes to the Sensing category.]	
221	Mia	What are you doin'?
	[John grabs an <Ask> block.]	

4.5 Harry and Greg: "No, 'cause..."

Harry and Greg were both very engaged and excited about their project. While they did not always agree with each other's ideas, they tended to follow similar trains of thought. This pair of students had one of the most successful collaborative interactions we observed from the participants. There were times when Harry had to make the same suggestion multiple times before Greg would implement it, but they had at least one situation where they gave a reason for disagreeing with each other. This situation is shown in Excerpt 6.

While Harry was working on a task in Excerpt 6, Greg gave a general suggestion in turn 255. Harry acknowledged the suggestion but disagreed and gave a reason for it in turn 256, which Greg accepted. Even though Greg had already accepted the explanation, Harry continued to explain his thoughts in turn 257, which Greg also agreed with. This interaction is encouraging, as previous work has found that students who approve suggestions or enter into discussion have more successful collaborations [1].

Excerpt 6 (Driving: Harry, Navigating: Greg)		
255	Greg	How about when his shoes?
	[Harry modifies the x coordinate in a <Go to x:[ ] y: [ ]> block.]	
256	Harry	Touches black. No, cause then he'll be like that.
257	Greg	Yeah.
258	Harry	((He'll be like)) that looks better.
	[Harry modifies the y coordinate in a <Go to x:[ ] y: [ ]> block.]	
259	Greg	Okay.

5 DISCUSSION

Collaboration is often required in the classroom and workplace, especially in computer science. Our analysis revealed areas in which collaboration was successful and unsuccessful in an elementary computer science setting. A successful programming collaboration is one in which students are able to engage in meaningful discussion to create a program that integrates ideas from all students in a group. During the meaningful discussion, students may use various collaborative dialogue practices, including, but not limited to, self-explanation [3], question generation [16], attributing challenges to the task [10], and building on each others' ideas [2]. Students entering an elementary computer science classroom may not have had collaborative experiences or scaffolding in the past; therefore it may be beneficial to explicitly teach them collaboration and pair programming practices. Because the success of the students' collaboration process is likely to affect how much they learn, our results have implications regarding how students might better learn to collaborate and how we should design collaborative activities to foster good practices.

Type	**Example(s)**
Proposal	"So this should be no."; "How about let's test?"; "Let's try moving him up some."; "...I think we should take the ask block out."
Command	"When backdrop changes to wood, glide right here in front of her, right there. That's one thirty-four, negative one thirty-five."; "Get the apple out."; "Go to Jack."; "Now let's go to scripts."
Next Step	"We just n– need to make that turn into a horse."; "...she needs to lay down and ... she needs to wake up."; "... when backdrop changes to woods, they have to not be showing."; "And then we have the house hide."

Table 2: The list and examples of suggestion types.

A large number of the student utterances were suggestions, and previous work indicates that suggestions are vital to a collaborative interaction [6]. We identified three types of suggestions and responses from the excerpts discussed here (Table 2). A *command* is a direct instruction to the partner. A *proposal* is a suggestion that is detailed enough to inform the receiver of what exactly needs to be done next but less direct than a command. A *next step* suggestion is a more high-level suggestion, indicating a task that may need to be completed next or in the near future.

From reviewing the interactions in the excerpts we found four types of responses students had to their partners' suggestions. The response types were as follows: implement and verbally acknowledge; implement and do not verbally acknowledge; do not implement and verbally acknowledge; and do not implement and do not verbally acknowledge. Of these, perhaps the most productive response type is *implement and verbally acknowledge* because it is clear that the student understood the partner's suggestion and chose to follow it.

Implement and do not verbally acknowledge may still be a productive response because it at least implies that the partner heard and accepted the suggestion; however, without verbal acknowledgement it is unclear whether she actually heard her partner or if the action she tooks was her own idea. In addition, if she heard the suggestion and implemented it without any discussion, it is difficult to evaluate whether she understood the reason for the action.

Do not implement and acknowledge is another type of response we observed. Although choosing not to implement a suggestion is an implicit rejection of the idea, the verbal acknowledgment of the suggestion confirms that the partner actually heard it and that it may turn into a fruitful discussion about the suggestion's merit.

Do not implement and do not verbally acknowledge is when a partner does not acknowledge a suggestion, it is unclear whether she did not hear it, or the partner chose to ignore it. Such a response will likely deter the speaker from making another suggestion.

In an empirical study, Barron [1] found that students were more successful in their collaborative process if they accepted or discussed suggestions more than if they rejected or ignored them. Most commonly, the students in our dataset do not verbally acknowledge suggestions, whether they implemented them or not. Our observations and Barron's results support the notion that these actions prevent the students from having, through self-expression[3] and grounding [2], the meaningful discussion that is vital to the collaboration process. Therefore, it is important to encourage students to explain their process to their partners.

To improve students' collaborative interactions, we need to design activities that foster good collaboration practices. These activities may scaffold effective collaboration practices. While many activities require students to collaborate, they may not include the scaffolding necessary to mediate such interactions. Further research must be done in this area to find the best approach, but possible solutions could be as simple as having the students explain their thoughts to each other during specific points in the activities.

6 CONCLUSIONS AND FUTURE WORK

Collaboration and its role in learning has long been a topic of research. There have been countless studies about collaboration practices in computer science, such as pair programming, for undergraduate students. However, much is unknown about how elementary students collaborate while solving programming problems.

In our previous work, we collected a rich dataset from an elementary computer science elective and annotated students' collaborative dialogue for certain dialogue acts, including suggestions. Our current work extends this, taking a closer look at the context of the suggestions and the actions following those suggestions through a case study analysis. From this work, we identified at least three types of suggestions and four types of responses to those suggestions. In addition, we observed that more often than not, students in our dataset either accepted or rejected suggestions from their partners without verbally acknowledging them. Behaviors like this may hinder the collaboration process and the computer science education research community should continue investigating the complex phenomena associated with collaboration in elementary school. These investigations may include several open questions. For example, how soon do partners implement suggestions: do they implement them immediately after a suggestion or do they finish their current task first? How do partners solicit ideas from each other, and how often do they ask? Finally, how do students ask for help: do they ask for a high-level explanation or do they want the answer? By understanding the ways students collaborate and by scaffolding their interactions, we will help students have a better experience learning computer science and help them develop a skill they will use for life.

ACKNOWLEDGMENTS

This work is supported in part by the Wake County Public School System, Google through a CS Capacity Research Award, and the National Science Foundation through grants CNS-1453520 and DRL-1721160. Any opinions, findings, and conclusions or recommendations expressed in this material are those of the author(s) and do not necessarily reflect the views of the National Science Foundation.

REFERENCES

[1] Brigid Barron. 2003. When smart groups fail. *The Journal of the Learning Sciences* 12, 3 (2003), 307–359.
[2] Courtney B Cazden and Sarah W Beck. 2003. Classroom discourse. *Handbook of Discourse Processes* (2003), 165–197.
[3] Michelene T.H. Chi, Nicholas Leeuw, Mei-Hung Chiu, and Christian LaVancher. 1994. Eliciting self-explanations improves understanding. *Cognitive Science* 18, 3 (1994), 439–477.
[4] Catherine H. Crouch and Eric Mazur. 2001. Peer Instruction: Ten Years of Experience and Results. *American Journal of Physics* 69, 9 (2001), 970–977.
[5] Catherine Dornfeld and Sadhana Puntambekar. 2015. Emergent Roles and Collaborative Discourse Over Time. In *Proceedings of the 10th International Conference on Computer Supported Collaborative Learning (CSCL)*, Vol. 1. 380–387.
[6] Michael P. Downton. 2015. "That's What Everyone Else Is Saying...": Collaborative Reflection-in-Action during Creative Activities. In *Proceedings of the 11th International Conference on Computer-Supported Collaborative Learning (CSCL)*. International Society of the Learning Sciences, 31–38.
[7] Katrina Falkner, Nickolas J.G. Falkner, and Rebecca Vivian. 2013. Collaborative Learning and Anxiety: A Phenomenographic Study of Collaborative Learning Activities. In *Proceedings of the 44th ACM Technical Symposium on Computer Science Education (SIGCSE '13)*. 227–232.
[8] John J. Farrell, Richard S. Moog, and James N. Spencer. 1999. A Guided Inquiry General Chemistry Course. *Journal of Chemical Education* 76, 4 (1999), 570–574.
[9] Maya Israel, Quentin M. Wherfel, Saadeddin Shehab, Oliver Melvin, and Todd Lash. 2017. Describing Elementary Students' Interactions in Puzzle-based Environments using the Collaborative Computing Observation Instrument (C-COI). In *Proceedings of the Thirteenth Annual International Conference on International Computing Education Research*. ACM, 110–117.
[10] Harold H Kelley. 1967. Attribution theory in social psychology. In *Nebraska Symposium on Motivation*. University of Nebraska Press, 192–238.
[11] Colleen M Lewis and Niral Shah. 2015. How Equity and Inequity Can Emerge in Pair Programming. In *Proceedings of the Eleventh annual International Conference on International Computing Education Research*. ACM, 41–50.
[12] Clem O'Donnell, Jim Buckley, Abdulhussain E. Mahdi, John Nelson, and Michael English. 2015. Evaluating Pair-Programming for Non-Computer Science Major Students. In *Proceedings of the 46th ACM Technical Symposium on Computer Science Education (SIGCSE '15)*. 569–574.
[13] Jennifer K. Olsen and Samantha Finkelstein. 2017. Through the (Thin-Slice) Looking Glass: An Initial Look at Rapport and Co-Construction Within Peer Collaboration. In *Proceedings of the 12th International Conference on Computer-Supported Collaborative Learning (CSCL)*. International Society of the Learning Sciences., 511–518.
[14] Leo Porter and Beth Simon. 2013. Retaining Nearly One-Third More Majors with a Trio of Instructional Best Practices in CS1. In *Proceeding of the 44th ACM Technical Symposium on Computer Science Education (SIGCSE '13)*. 165–170.
[15] Fernando J. Rodríguez, Kimberly Michelle Price, and Kristy Elizabeth Boyer. 2017. Exploring the Pair Programming Process: Characteristics of Effective Collaboration. In *Proceedings of the 48th ACM Technical Symposium on Computer Science Education (SIGCSE)*. 507–512.
[16] Carolyn P Rosé, Johanna D Moore, Kurt VanLehn, and David Allbritton. 2001. A comparative evaluation of socratic versus didactic tutoring. *Proceedings of Cognitive Sciences Society* (2001), 869–874.
[17] N Shah, C Lewis, and R Caires. 2014. Analyzing equity in collaborative learning situations: A comparative case study in elementary computer science. In *Proceedings for the 11th International Conferences of the Learning Sciences (ICLS)*. 495–502.
[18] Laurie Williams. 2001. Integrating Pair Programming into a Software Development Process. In *Proceedings of the 14th Conference on Software Engineering Education and Training (CSEE&T '01)*. 27–36.
[19] Laurie Williams. 2007. Lessons Learned from Seven Years of Pair Programming at North Carolina State University. *SIGCSE Bull.* 39, 4 (Dec. 2007), 79–83.
[20] Laurie Williams, Eric Wiebe, Kai Yang, Miriam Ferzli, and Carol Miller. 2002. In support of pair programming in the introductory computer science course. *Computer Science Education* 12, 3 (2002), 197–212.

Bricklayer: Elementary Students Learn Math through Programming and Art

Michelle Friend
University of Nebraska Omaha
Omaha, Nebraska
mefriend@unomaha.edu

Michael Matthews
University of Nebraska Omaha
Omaha, NE
michaelmatthews@unomaha.edu

Victor Winter
University of Nebraska Omaha
Omaha, NE
vwinter@unomaha.edu

Betty Love
University of Nebraska Omaha
Omaha, NE
blove@unomaha.edu

Deanna Moisset
Omaha Public Schools
Omaha, NE
deanna.moisset@ops.org

Ian Goodwin
University of Nebraska Omaha
Omaha, NE
igoodwin@unomaha.edu

ABSTRACT

As computer science becomes more prevalent in the K-12 world, elementary schools are increasingly adopting computing curricula. Computer scientists have recognized the connection between math and computer science, but little work has demonstrated how and whether computer science can support improved learning in math. This paper reports on a project in which elementary students in a gifted program used Bricklayer, a functional programming environment that supports artistic and mathematical expression. A pre- and post-test design demonstrates significant learning gains in coordinate graphing and visual-spatial skills.

KEYWORDS

Elementary School, Functional Programming, Mathematics

ACM Reference Format:
Michelle Friend, Michael Matthews, Victor Winter, Betty Love, Deanna Moisset, and Ian Goodwin. 2018. Bricklayer: Elementary Students Learn Math through Programming and Art. In *Proceedings of The 49th ACM Technical Symposium on Computer Science Education (SIGCSE'18).* ACM, New York, NY, USA, 6 pages. https://doi.org/10.1145/3159450.3159515

1 INTRODUCTION

Efforts such as the CSForAll initiative [12] and Code.org have been increasingly successful at promoting the adoption of computer science across schools, particularly in elementary schools. In order to continue justifying instructional time spent on computer science, educational research must demonstrate that the time is effective - that students are indeed making sufficient progress towards instructional goals. Traditionally, language arts and math have been the two cornerstones of elementary curriculum. Computer science most closely aligns with mathematics, yet little research has demonstrated that incorporating computer science improves mathematics outcomes [10].

This paper reports on a project in which elementary school students were provided computer science lessons once per week for ten weeks in a gifted and talented education (GATE) program, and were tested for mathematics outcomes in a pre- and post-test design. The paper first explains the relationship between mathematics and computer science, particularly in elementary school. It then describes the educational intervention, using Bricklayer, a programming-based pedagogical tool that creates artistic artifacts. Finally, the research project is described, including findings related to improvements in students' coordinate graphing knowledge and visual-spatial skills following the intervention. Implications, limitations, and areas for future research are identified.

1.1 Computer science and mathematics

Computer science is in many ways an application of mathematical principles, and computer science educators have long argued the relationship between computing and math [7]. While anecdotal evidence that mathematical skill enhances students' ability to understand computing is reinforced through mathematics prerequisites for high school and college computing courses, there has been little evidence that learning programming actually leads to gains in mathematics performance [8]. This is unsurprising, as transfer between domains requires deep understanding and explicit instructions for how to take ideas from one area (such as programming) and apply them in another (such as mathematics) [1]. There is reason to believe that a strength of computing is the opportunity to apply mathematics skills and topics to a real world setting [9]; for example, programming graphics objects can motivate students' understanding of the coordinate graphing system [3]. Recently, the Bootstrap program has shown evidence that functional programming can successfully support student learning of algebraic functions [10, 11]. However, there remains a dearth of research on the explicit connections between computer science and mathematics, particularly for young children, before the introduction of algebraic reasoning.

Although it has not traditionally been a focus of mathematics curriculum and instruction, spatial reasoning has been gaining attention as an important skill underpinning mathematical and scientific learning. The National Research Council called for explicit

ACM ISBN 978-1-4503-5103-4/18/02...$15.00
https://doi.org/10.1145/3159450.3159515

attention to spatial reasoning in not just mathematics but across the entire curriculum, calling it a "major blind spot" in almost all current curricula [2]. A large longitudinal study demonstrated that spatial ability plays a critical role in the development of STEM abilities [13]. In a study of 8-year-old students, Gunderson et al. found a "strong relationship between spatial skills, number line knowledge, and math achievement" [4]. In other words, curriculum that supports student development of spatial skills is likely to support improved academic performance across the curriculum and especially in mathematics [6, 13].

A major topic in upper elementary mathematics instruction is geometry, particularly introducing students to the coordinate plane and extending their early number sense to two- and three-dimensional spaces. For example, the Common Core State Standards for Mathematics includes "Graph points on the coordinate plane to solve real-world and mathematical problems (CC.5.G.A.1 and CC.5.G.A.2)" and "Solve real-world and mathematical problems involving area, surface area, and volume (CC.6.G.A.3)." Further, elementary mathematics curricula are designed to support the underlying mathematical skills and concepts that will help students be successful in algebra, such as generating and analyzing patterns (CC.4.OA.C.5) or writing and interpreting numerical expressions (CC.5.OA.A.1, CC.5.OA.A.2).

2 BRICKLAYER

Bricklayer is an open-source, online educational ecosystem designed to teach coding to people of all ages and coding backgrounds [5, 14]. Designed with a "low-threshold, infinite-ceiling" philosophy, it provides an example-rich and problem-dense domain in which students learn to write programs in the functional programming language SML. When executed, Bricklayer programs can produce LEGO®artifacts, Minecraft artifacts, and even artifacts suitable for 3D printing.

Bricklayer is a collection of interactive web apps and downloadable software, including a Google Blockly-type coding environment called **Bricklayer-lite**, which was used by the students in this project. The pedagogical tool begins with an *unplugged* level that focuses on the exploration and understanding of various mathematical patterns such as tessellations, fractals, and elementary cellular automata - all concepts that even young students can understand through drawing exercises. Bricklayer's five coding levels provide instruction and challenges of increasing complexity, beginning with two-dimensional pixel art and progressing to the creation of three-dimensional patterns such as a Menger sponge and even more complex shapes such as those shown in Figure 1. Similar to other environments like Scratch, Bricklayer-lite has a block-based programming system and displays the output of the code, as shown in Figures 2, 3 and 4, allowing users to see their code and the output in different panes of the same window. Bricklayer itself is a text-based language with the same syntax as Bricklayer-lite, making it easy for students to transition between environments.

2.1 Bricklayer and Art

One notable element of Bricklayer is its focus on art. Although the communication with the computer takes place through coding, and the underlying concepts are mathematical such as placing objects at particular coordinate points in space, the output is artistic in nature. After introducing students to new commands and concepts, the curriculum encourages students to use creativity to design their own artifacts such as those shown in Figure 1. While early tasks are very specific, directing users to place colored bricks at particular points, users are quickly pushed to make pictures or objects based on their own artistic interests. Examples of art created by participants in this study are seen in Figures 2, 3 and 4.

Most introductory programming environments have some 'theme'; in many cases, particularly environments designed for young children, this theme is game-based. For example, both Code.org and Swift Playground lessons provide game-like challenges for users to solve. Although there are challenges built into the Bricklayer pedagogical suite, the goals are not game-like, but artistic, to create pictures and objects. In this way, Bricklayer is designed to appeal both to "STEM-y" students who are traditionally drawn to programming, and also to students with an artistic bent for whom STEM hobbies may not be intrinsically interesting.

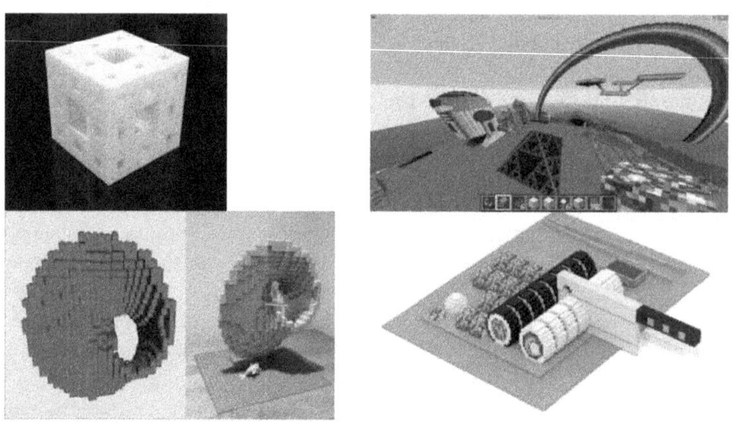

Figure 1: Artifacts created using Bricklayer.

A significant portion of the Bricklayer ecosystem has been developed specifically to help novices, especially primary school children, learn how to code. Bricklayer has been used with students from elementary school through college courses, and is currently being used in over 75 elementary, middle, and high schools. This paper reports on a project in which elementary school students used Bricklayer in a ten-week workshop one hour per week at school.

3 METHOD

This study was designed to investigate the impact of teaching Bricklayer to elementary school students. It particularly investigated whether programming in Bricklayer would promote improved mathematics skills. Thus the research question was whether students would show improvement in coordinate graphing, spatial skills, and functions following a Bricklayer unit in their GATE program.

3.1 Participants

The participants in this study represent a convenience sample. Participants were students who had been identified by the school district for GATE (gifted) services. The GATE program has considerably more leeway in implementing innovative curriculum than standard classrooms which must adhere to district-adopted curriculum. Students in the GATE program are pulled out of their regular classes for approximately one hour per week to receive instruction and resources from a trained facilitator.

Pre- and post-tests were collected from a total of 66 students in grades three through six at nine different schools in the district. Four participants were excluded for lack of consent, resulting in data from 62 participants. Data were anonymized for analysis. Tables 1 - 3 show the demographic breakdown of participants by grade level, school attended, and gender.

Table 1: Participants by grade level

Grade	3	4	5	6
Number of participants	10	14	23	15

Table 2: Number of participants at each school

School	A	B	C	D	E	F	G	H	J
Number of participants	11	8	5	1	11	6	10	3	7

Table 3: Participants by gender

Gender	Female	Male	Declined to state
Number of participants	29	29	4

3.2 Procedure

The six GATE facilitators for the nine schools were trained in Bricklayer over two evenings before teaching the students. Facilitators were trained prior to spring break and implemented the program following spring break and through mid-May; students spent no more than ten weeks using Bricklayer as a part of this program. A Piazza online community was established for the facilitators to be able to ask questions as they encountered them. The facilitators were introduced to a ten-week curriculum designed for after-school programs, and used this curriculum as a guide for their implementations.

Students took the tests on paper during their regular GATE time; the tests were administered by GATE teachers and were collected and maintained by the GATE coordinator for the district, who delivered the tests to the researchers at the conclusion of the school year.

During the Bricklayer lessons, student progressed through Bricklayer levels of increasing complexity. Examples of student work created during the project are shown in Figures 2, 3 and 4. These show a progression in conceptual complexity. Figure 2 represents level one: pixel art, created by placing each block individually. Figure 3 represents level two, and demonstrates a function which creates a simple repeating pattern. Figure 4 is a more complex function that creates a non-repeating pixelated image, from the third level of Bricklayer. Each figure shows both a Bricklayer-lite code snippet on the left, and the outcome as displayed on the screen, on the right side of the figure.

Figure 2: Early art created by a participant in Level 1

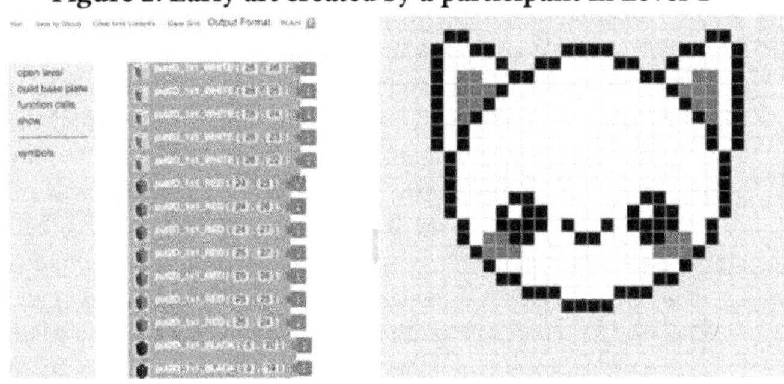

Figure 3: Intermediate art created by a participant in Level 2

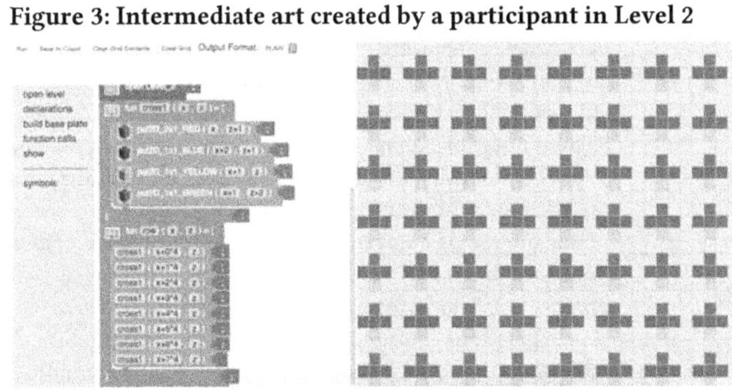

3.3 Measures

Pre- and post-test mathematics questions were isomorphic: slightly different versions of the same questions. For example, the mental

Figure 4: More complex programming by a participant in Level 3

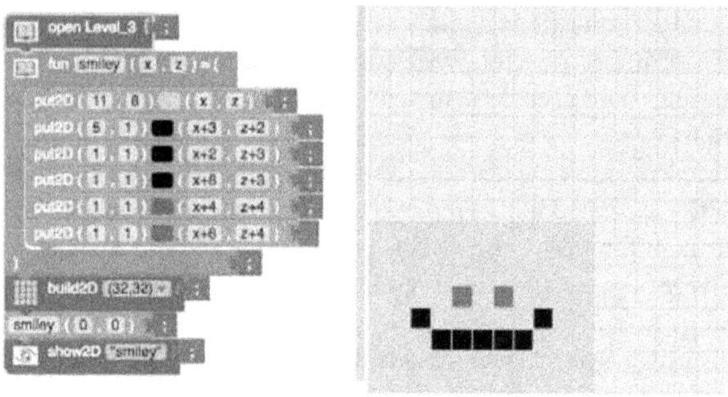

Figure 5: Sample coordinate graphing question

2. Sometimes we can't see the (0,0) spot or we don't start at the (0,0) spot. This is an example. What are the coordinates of the cell containing the ☆ ?

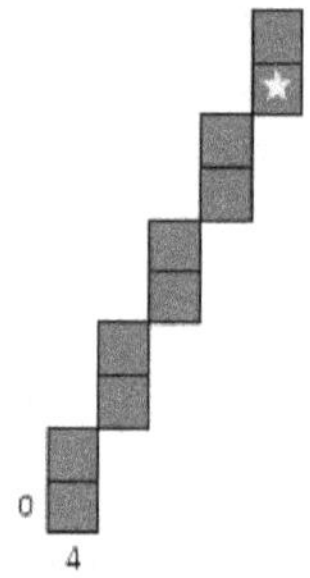

Answer_________________

Figure 6: Sample mental rotation question

7. Which of the comparison images is the same as the standard image? Circle the correct answer below.

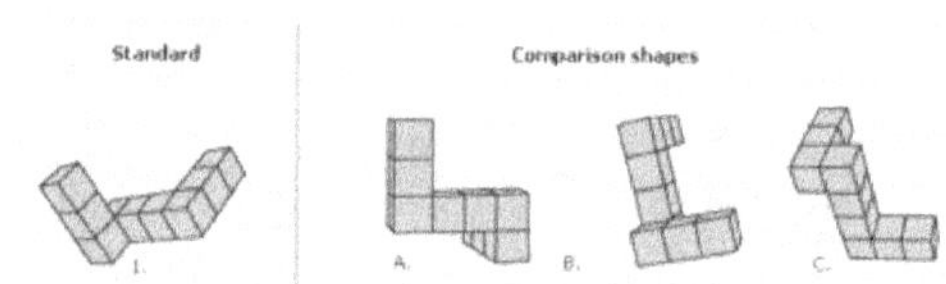

i. A only
ii. B only
iii. C only
iv. A and B
v. A and C
vi. B and C
vii. All of them
viii. None of them

Answer_________________

rotation question shown in Figure 6 had a different shape on the pre-test than the post-test. The other test questions were identical between the pre- and post-test. The following measures were analyzed:

- **Demographics** Participants were asked their *grade*, *age*, *gender identification*, and *ethnicity*. The first two pieces of demographic information were at the beginning of the test, and the last two at the end of the test in order to decrease the likelihood of stereotype threat. The grade level reported on the post-test was used for analysis because not all students answered the question on the pre-test. Four students did not report their gender. The GATE coordinator identified the school associated with each set of tests.
- **Attitudes about math & computers** Participants were asked to respond to ten statements using a five-point Likert scale. The statements broke into three constructs: *Computer Interest* such as "Computers are interesting to me", *Computer Confidence* such as "I am good with computers", and *Math Confidence* such as "I feel confident about my ability to do math problems." For each construct, responses were averaged and normed to result in a single score between 1 and 5.
- **Mathematics** A mathematics score represented how many questions were answered correctly out of twelve; unanswered questions were marked wrong. These were further divided into three subsections:
  - Three questions about *coordinate graphing* prompted students to identify the coordinates of a cell containing a particular symbol such as that shown in Figure 5
  - Four questions allowed students to demonstrate *visual-spatial ability* such as the task shown in Figure 6 that requires mentally rotating an image.
  - Five questions inquired into students' understanding of mathematical *functions*. For example, "A mathematical function can sometimes be written in words like this. Let's say I have a function called 'Almost double'. Here is what almost double does. Take any number, double it, then take away 1. What would you get if you used 7 with the 'almost double' function?"

3.4 Data Analysis

At the end of the school year, the tests were returned to the researchers. One author entered the responses into a spreadsheet. The data was analyzed using R. Because the data was non-normal, Yuen's test for trimmed means was used to compare means.

The analysis addressed the following hypotheses:

(1) Average score on the test of mathematics would increase between pre-test and post-test.
(2) Average score on the coordinate graphing mathematics sub-section would increase between pre-test and post-test.
(3) Average score on the visual-spatial mathematics sub-section would increase between pre-test and post-test.
(4) Average score on the functions mathematics sub-section would increase between pre-test and post-test.
(5) There would be no significant difference between boys and girls in terms of improvement on the tests
(6) There would be no significant difference between schools in terms of improvement on the tests
(7) Average score increase on the test of mathematics would be different for different grades. Either a ceiling effect would occur where older students (e.g. grade 6) would already have

mastered the skills and so a smaller change would occur, or the intervention would be less effective with younger students (e.g. grade 3) who had not yet learned coordinate graphing and functions, or both.

(8) Students would increase their computing interest and confidence and their mathematics confidence

4 FINDINGS

4.1 Overall Score

There was a significant increase in average test scores between the pre- and post-test across all questions from 36% correct (*se* = 2.6) on the pre-test to 47% correct (*se* = 2.6) on the post-test on average ($t(37) = 5.51$, $p<.0001$), representing a large effect ($r = .67$). This confirmed the first hypothesis.

4.2 Coordinate Graphing

There was a significant increase in scores on the coordinate graphing section of the test. On average, scores went from 26% correct (*se* = 4.2) on the pre-test to 42% correct (*se* = 4.0) on the post-test ($t(37) = 3.84$, $p = 0.0005$) with a moderate effect size ($r = .53$). The smaller significance and effect size despite a larger change in percentage correct is due to the much smaller number of questions: only three rather than 12 on the composite score. This confirmed the second hypothesis.

4.3 Visual-Spatial Skill

There was a similarly large increase in scores on the visual-spatial section of the test. On average, scores went from 24% correct (*se* = 2.9) on the pre-test to 52% correct (*se* = 3.6) on the post-test ($t(37) = 4.30$, $p = 0.0001$) with a moderate effect size ($r = .53$). Like the coordinate graphing section, this represents that the visual-spatial skill section encompassed only four questions. This confirmed the third hypothesis.

4.4 Functions

On the functions section of the test, there was a small and non-significant increase in scores from 43% correct (*se* = 3.4) on the pre-test to 45% correct (*se* = 3.7) on the post-test ($t(37) = 0.82$, $p = 0.41$, $r = 0.13$). Thus, the fourth hypothesis was not confirmed, though the small improvement contributed to the improvement seen on the overall score.

4.5 Demographic differences

An Analysis of Variance (ANOVA) was conducted to compare score differences among students with various demographic differences. No significant difference was found for changes in score between pre- and post-tests for students in different grades ($F = .32$, $p = .57$) or different genders ($F = ..03$, $p = .97$). Although there was a small difference between students in different schools ($F = 2.74$, $p = .01$) the number of students at each school was small, and further research is necessary to draw any conclusions about differences between schools. Thus hypotheses five was confirmed (that there would be no difference between genders) and hypotheses six and seven were not confirmed.

4.6 Attitudes

Because Bricklayer provides an engaging, creative opportunity for students to learn programming and math, the hypothesis was that after engaging in the Bricklayer experience, students would increase their computing interest and confidence and their mathematics confidence. Although no formal qualitative data was collected, there was anecdotal evidence that students were highly engaged and enjoyed using Bricklayer. One of the teachers reported that she gave the students an opportunity to go on to another desirable curricular experience or continue using Bricklayer and that the students unanimously chose to continue using Bricklayer. However, the survey results do not demonstrate a significant increase in attitudes. Computer interest increased from 4.21 (*se* = .1) to 4.24 (*se* = .11) ($t = 0.32$, $p = .75$) on a five-point scale, computer confidence increased from 4.17 (*se* = .09) to 4.24 (*se* = .08) ($t = 0.79$, $p = .43$), and math confidence increased from 4.17 (*se* = .09) to 4.24 (*se* = .08) ($t = 0.79$, $p = .43$). Thus, hypothesis eight was not confirmed.

5 DISCUSSION

At the most basic level, this paper reports upon a successful proof of concept: that elementary students can use Bricklayer-lite to create artistic artifacts of their own design. It further suggests that Bricklayer can support students' mathematics learning.

Participants' improvement in their ability to answer questions about coordinate graphing and visual-spatial skills following the Bricklayer course is extremely promising. Although the ability to identify locations on a coordinate graph is not a traditional computer science topic, it is a fundamental skill required in elementary math standards, and is represented in graphics programming. Students' improvement in their visual-spatial ability is not currently strongly represented in math or computer science standards, but prior research has demonstrated that it is an important skill associated with strong outcomes in STEM.

Despite successfully writing functions in order to run their programs in the higher levels (2 and 3), participants did not demonstrate improvement from pre- to post-test on the functional reasoning sub-section. Further research is warranted to understand why this hypothesis was not confirmed. One possibility is that, because the functions questions were at the end of the test, students ran out of time and could not complete them. Another possibility is that in only ten sessions with Bricklayer they were not able to engage with enough of the higher levels of the curriculum that would substantially strengthen their functional reasoning. No formal record was kept of how far students progressed in the curriculum. The curriculum has 5 levels with exposure to functional reasoning increasing dramatically in levels 3, 4, and especially 5. Feedback from the teachers indicate that many of the 62 participants only made it to levels 2 or 3 material, and thus had limited exposure to functional reasoning. It may be that more exposure to Bricklayer functional reasoning would lead to more general mathematical functional reasoning. One of our in-progress initiatives involves working with Master elementary teachers with experience teaching coding to develop Bricklayer coding projects that correlate well with elementary mathematics content standards and more advanced topics like functional reasoning.

As in most educational research, causality cannot be applied to this ten-week program. It is certainly possible that other experiences, including students' regular classroom math classes and lessons were responsible for the significant increase in performance on the post-test. However, the students were distributed across nine schools and four grades as shown in Tables 1 and 2. The heterogeneity of participants' outside-workshop experience suggests that the impressive changes are likely associated with using Bricklayer, particularly since Bricklayer was explicitly designed to support the skills which were assessed. This is not itself a weakness - the hypotheses were based on prior research and understanding of the likely gains, and were objectively assessed using isomorphic questions. To confirm a causal relationship, experimental conditions must be set up in which control groups will complete a different mathematical workshop, teaching similar skills without the use of functional programming. However, we feel comfortable suggesting that this research is worthwhile, given the strength of the findings presented here.

With the increasing push to cover more and more topics in elementary grades, finding a way to address multiple content strands is one of the great potentials of Bricklayer. A significant limitation is that this work reports upon workshops run with students identified as gifted - that is, more intelligent than the average public school population. This limits the generalizability of the results, and we hope to expand the work to implement Bricklayer across math classes throughout the district rather than limiting it to pull-out classes. It would be of interest to see how exposure to learning coding with Bricklayer will lead to similar changes in a general population of elementary students. Elementary class time is increasingly constrained, particularly with the ever-present threat of standardized tests that students must pass. By demonstrating that Bricklayer has the potential to improve students' performance on these tests, we hope that teachers, principals, and district personnel would be open to incorporating Bricklayer into curricular programming more broadly.

One of the reasons touted for getting programming into mathematics classes is that it will increase student engagement - students will think it is fun and pay more attention. Anecdotal evidence does support this idea, as students indicate more interest in some ideas such as coordinate graphing when they are motivated by a "real world" context to use what is otherwise a dry practice. This was the case with Bricklayer, where teacher reports suggest that students enjoyed using it. However, the survey of student attitudes indicate that there was not a significant change in student interest or confidence about computing and math. This is likely because of a ceiling effect - the students were generally very positive on the post-test. This is not surprising from an academically-strong group, and a group who is young enough to not yet have "turned off" to mathematics or programming. Further investigation of the role of student attitudes on learning and engagement will continue to shed light into when and how such interventions may be most effective.

Recent efforts to incorporate coding and computer science across all schools have focused on the positive outcomes of computer science. This paper reports upon a successful implementation of an environment that not only teaches programming but also demonstrates mathematics learning as well. Being able to learn coding skills while at the same time improve on students' understanding of coordinates and develop students' spatial reasoning at the same time is a win-win.

REFERENCES

[1] J D Bransford and D L Schwartz. 1999. Rethinking Transfer: A Simple Proposal With Multiple Implications. *Review of Research in Education* 24, 1 (1999), 61–100. http://rre.sagepub.com/cgi/doi/10.3102/0091732X024001061

[2] Committee on Support for Thinking Spatially. 2006. *Learning to Think Spatially.* National Academies Press. DOI: https://doi.org/10.17226/11019

[3] Robert Cutler and Michelle Friend Hutton. 2010. Digitizing Data : Computational Thinking for Middle School Students through Computer Graphics. In *Proceedings of the 31st Annual Conference of the European Association for Computer Graphics (Eurographics).* 1–8.

[4] Elizabeth A. Gunderson, Gerardo Ramirez, Sian L. Beilock, and Susan C. Levine. 2012. The relation between spatial skill and early number knowledge: The role of the linear number line. *Developmental Psychology* 48, 5 (2012), 1229–1241. DOI: https://doi.org/10.1037/a0027433

[5] Betty Love. 2016. Creating an Environment in which Elementary Educators Can Teach Coding. *ACM SIGCHI Conference on Interaction Design and Children 2016* (2016), 643–648. DOI: https://doi.org/10.1145/2930674.2936008

[6] N. S. Newcombe. 2013. Seeing Relationships. Using Spatial Tinking to Teach Science, Mathematics, and Social Studies. *American Educator* (2013), 26–32.

[7] Seymour Papert. 1971. Teaching children to be mathematicians vs teaching about mathematics. *International journal of mathematical education in science and technolog* 3, 3 (1971), 249–262. DOI: https://doi.org/10.1080/0020739700030306

[8] Roy D. Pea and D. Midian Kurland. 1984. On the Cognitive Effects of Learning Computer Programming. *New Ideas in Psychology* 2, 2 (1984), 137–168.

[9] Jeremy M Roschelle, Roy D Pea, Christopher M Hoadley, Douglas N Gordin, and Barbara M Means. 2000. Changing How and What Children Learn in School with Computer-Based Technologies. *The Future of Children* 10, 2 (2000).

[10] Emmanuel Schanzer, Kathi Fisler, Shriram Krishnamurthi, and Matthias Felleisen. 2015. Transferring Skills at Solving Word Problems from Computing to Algebra Through Bootstrap. *Proceedings of the 46th ACM Technical Symposium on Computer Science Education - SIGCSE '15* (2015), 616–621. DOI: https://doi.org/10.1145/2676723.2677238

[11] Emmanuel Tanenbaum Schanzer. 2015. *Algebraic Functions, Computer Programming, and the Challenge of Transfer.* Doctoral dissertation. Harvard Graduate School of Education. DOI: https://doi.org/10.1016/S0140-6736(09)60087-8

[12] Megan Smith. 2016. CS For All. (2016). https://www.whitehouse.gov/blog/2016/01/30/computer-science-all

[13] Jonathan Wai, David Lubinski, and Camilla P. Benbow. 2009. Spatial ability for STEM domains: Aligning over 50 years of cumulative psychological knowledge solidifies its importance. *Journal of Educational Psychology* 101, 4 (2009), 817–835. DOI: https://doi.org/10.1037/a0016127

[14] Victor Winter, Betty Love, and Cindy Corritore. 2016. The Bricklayer Ecosystem - Art, Math, and Code. *Electronic Proceedings in Theoretical Computer Science* 230 (2016), 47–61. DOI: https://doi.org/10.4204/EPTCS.230.4 arXiv:1611.09472

ACKNOWLEDGMENTS

The authors would like to thank the participating GATE teachers and students.

Fix the First, Ignore the Rest: Dealing with Multiple Compiler Error Messages

Brett A. Becker
University College Dublin
Belfield, Dublin 4, Ireland
brett.becker@ucd.ie

Cormac Murray
University College Dublin
Belfield, Dublin 4, Ireland
cormac.murray@ucdconnect.ie

Tianyi Tao
Fudan University
Shanghai, China
13302010026@fudan.edu.cn

Changheng Song
Fudan University
Shanghai, China
13302010051@fudan.edu.cn

Robert McCartney
University of Connecticut
Storrs, CT, USA
robert@engr.uconn.edu

Kate Sanders
Rhode Island College
Providence, RI, USA
ksanders@ric.edu

ABSTRACT

In order to help students learning to develop computer programs, several computing education researchers have analyzed the compiler error messages generated by novices' attempts to compile their programs. The goal is to help students diagnose the errors they make through the messages generated by the compiler. This paper builds on that previous work by applying a technique based on a heuristic well-known to programmers – fix the first error and ignore the rest – to the analysis of over 21 million compiler error messages from the Blackbox dataset.

We find that the ranks and frequencies obtained by considering all error messages are generally consistent with previously published lists, but when we consider first messages only, these ranks and frequencies are different. These differences could have important implications for teaching, and can inform tool design and future research efforts.

CCS CONCEPTS

•Social and professional topics → Computer science education; CS1;

KEYWORDS

compiler error messages; cascading error messages; subsequent error messages; buried error messages; novice syntax errors; CS1; Blackbox; novice programmers; debugging

ACM Reference format:
Brett A. Becker, Cormac Murray, Tianyi Tao, Changheng Song, Robert McCartney, and Kate Sanders. 2018. Fix the First, Ignore the Rest: Dealing with Multiple Compiler Error Messages. In *Proceedings of SIGCSE'18, February 21–24, 2018, Baltimore, MD, USA*, , 6 pages.
DOI: http://dx.doi.org/10.1145/3159450.3159453

SIGCSE'18, February 21–24, 2018, Baltimore, MD, USA
 ISBN 978-1-4503-5103-4/18/02...$15.00
DOI: http://dx.doi.org/10.1145/3159450.3159453

1 INTRODUCTION

Computer programming has been shown to pose many difficulties for students, and it has been cited as contributing to low motivation, low success rates, and high dropout rates [4]. One of the challenging aspects of learning to program is debugging, and in particular, learning how to interpret compiler error messages. We are interested in how students work with the feedback they receive from the compiler: what messages they see, how they use them, and how that process can be improved.

Novices are often advised to focus on the first compiler error message only. As Ben-Ari [8, p. 6] states: "Frequently, a single small mistake will cause the compiler to issue a cascade of messages... Do not invest any effort in trying to fix multiple error messages! Concentrate on fixing the first error and then recompile." Similarly, Fincher and Barnes [17, p. 68] state: "Start with the first one, correct it in the source file, save the file and then recompile. Don't try to fix all the errors in one go. This approach is particularly important if you have cascading errors, or multiple errors that have the same cause such as misspelled identifier."

The overarching contribution of this work is a large-scale analysis of the effects of isolating first error messages from subsequent messages, using the Blackbox dataset [11, 33]. In addition, we present motivating results of a student survey, and introduce terminology that enables researchers and educators to discuss compiler error messages with more precision.

1.1 Student Perspectives

In 1984 DuBoulay and Matthew [9, p. 109] noted: "All novice programmers find that their initial programs are rejected by the compiler in a flurry of incomprehensible error messages." Our present observations indicate that this is still the case. We conducted a survey of 106 Software Engineering students in their CS1 module, of which 73 (69%) responded. These students were programming in C using Notepad++ and compiling at the command line using GCC. We sought to explore the levels of frustration, confusion and misconception surrounding compiler error messages (particularly multiple compiler error messages), and to determine whether extra help on these topics is desired. We present the results of this survey organized into the three headings of *frustration & confusion*, *misconceptions*, and *requests for help*, below.

Frustration & confusion: 85% of students reported finding compiler error messages to be a source of frustration with 92% reporting compiler error messages as being a barrier to progress. 64% reported finding multiple compiler error messages confusing.

Misconceptions: 67% of students reported that when confronted with only one compiler error message, this error *may not* represent a true error in the code. 21% believe that compiler error messages after the first *always* represent true errors in code, and 11% believe that these error messages *never* represent true errors in code. When confronted with more than one compiler error message, only 22% try to fix the first error message reported, 43% try to fix one error which may or may not be the first reported, and 34% try and fix more than one error at the same time.

Requests for help: 100% of students reported that having additional help specifically on dealing with compiler error messages would help them in learning to program. 99% of students think that having the reasons for and nature of multiple "cascading" compiler error messages explained to them would help them deal with compiler error messages more effectively.

These results suggest that deeper discussion and increased focus on error messages (including multiple error messages) are required.

1.2 A Taxonomy of Compiler Error Messages

To facilitate the discussion of compiler error messages, we introduce a taxonomy, shown in Figure 1. All messages fall into one of two types: first or subsequent. A **first** message is the first message reported by the compiler in response to a failed compile. The first message *always* corresponds to a genuine error in code. As even novices learn early, most failed compiles generate several additional error messages; we are not aware of an existing term for these not-first error messages. We use the term **subsequent** to refer to all messages reported by the compiler *after* the first message. Subsequent messages can be broken down, in turn, into two types:

cascading: Cascading error messages are spurious messages caused by an error corresponding to an earlier error message, and provide no additional (useful) information. In short these are a result of compiler confusion. This definition is consistent Schorsch's description: "multiple reported errors caused by a single mistake that can all be corrected by fixing the first reported error" [30, p. 169].

genuine subsequent: These are subsequent messages that arise due to a genuine error in code. Unlike cascading error messages these do not stem from an error for which a message has already been generated. These are the first-instance messages corresponding to genuine errors in code.

Genuine subsequent messages are then divided into two categories:

someday first: Someday first messages will eventually become a first message on a later compile.

buried: Buried messages correspond to other legitimate errors that would have become first messages but do not, because something happens before they reach the top of the list. For example, the programmer might: see and fix the underlying error without help from the compiler, stop work on the program before fixing it, or delete the whole program and start over.

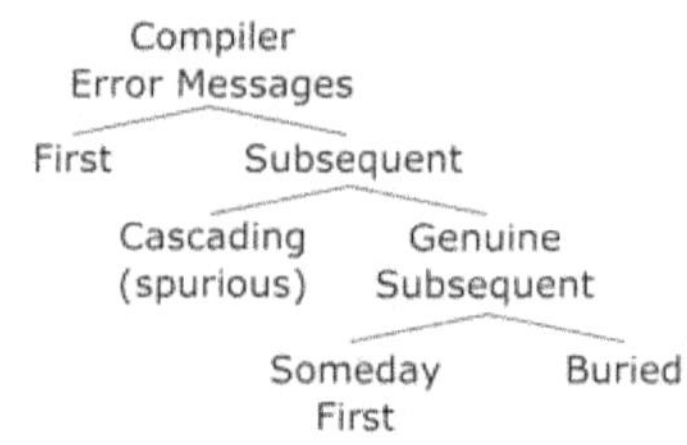

Figure 1: A Taxonomy of Compiler Error Messages.

1.3 A Motivating Example

Consider the following Java code which has an error on the third line: a regular colon (":") instead of a semicolon (";") between the initialization and the condition of the for loop.

```
public class PrintNums {
    public static void main (String[] args) {
        for(int x = 0: x < 10; x++)
            System.out.println(x);
    }
}
```

This is an easy error to make, either as a result of misreading a book or notes, or as a simple typographical error. In fact both symbols are often on the same key. When this code is compiled (using javac, Java SE JDK 1.8.0_112) the following is returned by the compiler:

```
PrintNums.java:3: error: ';' expected
        for(int x = 0: x < 10; x++)
                     ^
PrintNums.java:3: error: ';' expected
        for(int x = 0: x < 10; x++)
                        ^
PrintNums.java:3: error: illegal start of type
        for(int x = 0: x < 10; x++)
                            ^
PrintNums.java:3: error: illegal start of expression
        for(int x = 0: x < 10; x++)
                            ^
PrintNums.java:3: error: ')' expected
        for(int x = 0: x < 10; x++)
                                ^
PrintNums.java:3: error: illegal start of expression
        for(int x = 0: x < 10; x++)
                                  ^
6 errors
```

The first message accurately reflects the only genuine error in the code. The others are cascading messages resulting from the compiler being confused by the first (and only) error. Once the original error (corresponding to the first message) is rectified, all five cascading messages disappear. Time spent on the cascading messages is wasted, and confusion caused by them is unwarranted.

1.4 Research Questions

We wondered what changes if, instead of trying to help our students cope with long confusing lists of error messages, we focus on the first message generated by each compile. Specifically, our research questions are:

- RQ1: Out of all compiler error messages, what proportion are first messages?

When first error messages are considered separately:

- RQ2: How does the most-frequent list of messages change?

- RQ3: How do the frequencies of specific error messages change?

In the following sections, we discuss the related work on which this paper builds (Section 2), describe our methodology (Section 3), present our results (Section 4), discuss the results and their implications (Section 5), consider threats to validity (Section 6), and conclude with a discussion of implications for teaching, research, and future work directions (Section 7).

2 RELATED WORK

In this section, we discuss previous work related to types of compiler error messages, their frequency, and the Blackbox dataset that we have used to investigate our questions.

2.1 Errors and Error Messages

Compiler error messages have been studied for several decades [4], are essential for debugging, and can present barriers to student success [7, 13, 15]. Despite their importance they present particular difficulties for novice students [20].

Several authors have analyzed student understanding of error messages, developed tools that attempt to provide better compiler error messages, and/or supplemented standard messages with additional information [7, 13, 16, 18, 19, 24, 28, 32]. Other authors have used student error information to examine facets of student compilation or debugging behavior in general, including [1, 2, 6, 10, 12, 20]. Others, such as Ben-Ari [8], have written guides that explain what error messages mean, with examples of code that would cause them and ways to fix them.

In a recent eye-tracking study of software-engineering undergraduates, Barik et al. [3] found that participants allocated a substantial portion of their task time to reading compiler messages, and that – not surprisingly – the greater a student's difficulty with the error messages, the less likely he or she was to successfully debug the given program.

2.2 First Messages vs. Subsequent Messages

To help novices with compiler messages, Munson and Schilling [26] instructed them to focus on the first error message. Nevertheless, they found that their students did so on only 48.2% of compile attempts.

Some novice programming environments, such as CAP [30] and BlueJ [23], have forced students to focus by only displaying the first message. Consider our example in Section 1. Run on the same example, BlueJ (3.1.7) displays only the first message (`';' expected`), instead of all six messages. Kölling explains this decision in the context of Blue, a predecessor to BlueJ:

> Compilation in Blue is so fast (usually under a second for a class of 2000 lines) that the "Compile" button works as a de-facto "Next Error" button.... This has several advantages: the compiler is simpler (because no error recovery has to be attempted) and the error messages are more accurate (because incorrect messages caused by preceding errors are avoided) [22, pp. 8-9].

2.3 Determining Error Message Frequencies

Common to many studies on error messages is a presentation of the "most common" errors (in code), or error messages (resulting from errors in code), following from the reasonable assumption that helping students with the errors/messages that they most commonly deal with would be most productive. In practice however, exactly what these lists contain and particularly how they were determined vary considerably. Nonetheless these lists often inform others, and many are used as the basis for further research. Below we briefly describe some of these efforts. For a more complete summary of many of these 'common error/message lists' see [4].

An early list of Java errors was compiled by Hristova et al. [19], which began as a faculty survey on what educators believed to be the most common errors. Flowers et al. [18] chose nine common errors based on their experiences with students. Denny et al. [14] collected errors from student exercises using a custom "drill and practice" tool. Becker et al. [4, 5, 7] used an editor designed to collect and enhance error messages generated by the standard JDK compiler. Chan Mow [12] counted messages collected from three classes using JBuilder. Thompson [32] collected messages from an instrumented version of Eclipse. As an example of how such lists can have long lifetimes in informing other research, in 2017 Brown and Altadmri [10] used a set of 18 errors derived from the 20 originally presented in 2003 by Hristova et al. [19].

From these descriptions it is clear that the frequency lists reported are not always directly comparable: not all are based on compiler error messages (but errors in code); some combine certain related error messages; some use different compilers that have different messages; and others are ambiguous. By and large these studies ignore the fact that many students only ever encounter the first error message reported. One goal of this research is to develop a picture of first error messages on a large scale.

2.4 Why Blackbox?

Blackbox is a novel dataset for investigating questions about how novices learn to program. It includes student interactions with BlueJ – source code, compiler messages, etc. – collected automatically from BlueJ users around the world. Many thousands of users have opted in, agreeing to have their interactions made available (anonymously) for research. Thus, it is now possible to look at the compile information, code revisions, and error messages for student programs on a much larger scale than before [11, 33]. The dataset is fairly new, and its scale so large, that researchers are still exploring Blackbox's potential. Most papers so far have considered errors and error frequency [2, 10, 21, 29]. One paper has discussed students' use of GoTo-like control structures [31].

3 METHODOLOGY

We analyzed Blackbox error messages (excluding warnings) from United States users for the period Jan 1 - June 30, 2016 inclusive. We iterated through the data by first selecting all `bluej_start` events from which we retrieved all valid `session_id` values. For each `session_id` we retrieved all `compile_events`. From these we retrieved all error messages for each `session_id` from the `compile_outputs` table which also contains a shown flag which indicates if this message was shown to the user. This corresponds to the first error message from the JDK output as BlueJ only shows the first error to the user. All messages that are not shown are subsequent messages, which includes all cascading messages.

Many Java error messages contain tokens from source code and may be unique. For instance the following error message contains a token corresponding to the package name `edu.univ.my_package`:

```
package edu.univ.my_package does not exist
```

In order to categorize error messages such as this we processed all messages using regular expressions stored in JSON files. This allowed us to categorize all such messages into the general category `package ... does not exist`. We did similar for all other messages that contained unique tokens. This resulted in a set of 202 error message categories. Other than those containing potentially unique tokens, we did not combine any similar error messages. The source code used for our research is available at https://github.com/TTY112358/JavaErrorCollector.

4 RESULTS

We analyzed 21,511,098 error messages from 135,629 users initiating 1,444,260 BlueJ sessions and calculated frequencies for the following message categories: *first* (*F*); *subsequent* (*S*); and *all* messages (*A*).

4.1 RQ1: Proportion of First Error Messages

Out of the 21,511,098 error messages in our dataset, 28.5% (6,139,013) were first messages. The average failed compile generated 3.50 error messages, 2.50 of which were subsequent error messages. When we focus on the first error messages only, a different picture of error message distribution begins to emerge.

4.2 RQ2: Changes in the Most-Frequent Lists

There is a gap between what instructors advise and what researchers examine: although educators have recommended focusing on the first message for some time, most of the literature analyzing compiler error messages only considers the overall frequency of error messages. In this section we explore how the picture changes when taking a first-error-message-only view.

The top 85% of all first messages are shown in Table 1, sorted by increasing frequency rank (R_F), along with their corresponding percent frequencies ($\%_F$). We refer to this set of error messages as F_{85}. We choose 85% as this incorporates all individual errors with percent frequencies $\geq 1\%$. The size of F_{85} compared to A_{85} (the top 85% of all error messages) and S_{85} (the top 85% of subsequent messages) provides initial insight into the shifts that occur when isolating first and subsequent error messages. F_{85} contains 23 error messages, A_{85} contains 17, and S_{85} contains only 14.

A_{85} consists of the 14 unshaded messages in column R_A in Table 1 (that also appear in F_{85}) plus three messages not in F_{85} (and therefore also not in Table 1). S_{85} consists of the 11 unshaded messages in column R_S in Table 1 (that also appear in F_{85}) plus the same three messages not in F_{85} (and therefore also not in Table 1). These three messages are shown below with their corresponding ranks as overall (R_A) and subsequent (R_S) messages.

(1) illegal start of type ($R_A = 10, R_S = 10$)
(2) illegal character ($R_A = 13, R_S = 11$)
(3) non-static variable cannot be referenced from a static context ($R_A = 17, R_S = 14$)

Compared to A_{85} and S_{85}, a very different picture emerges for the most-frequent first error messages; scanning the ranks of each message in Table 1 reveals that the ranks R_A and R_S are more similar than either is to R_F. Only in the case of rank 1 does the same message appear at the same rank for all three lists. Further, when investigating first error messages only, more error messages are brought into play. F_{85} is larger than A_{85} and S_{85}; There are 9 messages in F_{85} that are not in A_{85} (R_A shaded in Table 1, where $R_A > 17$), and there are 12 messages in F_{85} that are not in S_{85} (R_S shaded in Table 1, where $R_A > 14$).

4.3 RQ3: Changes in Message Frequencies

The frequencies of individual error messages change notably when looking at first messages only. In Table 1, $\%_F$ and $\%_S$ are calculated by dividing the number of occurrences of the message at rank i by the total number of first and subsequent messages respectively. These values indicate the likelihood that a given message will appear as a first or as a subsequent message. For instance, Table 1 shows that `missing return statement` is 5.6 times more likely to appear as a first message (3.20%) than as a subsequent message (0.57%).

In order to facilitate this type of comparison we calculated the $\log_2$ fold-change between $\%_S$ and $\%_F$ [$\log_2(\%_S/\%_F)$]. When this value is 1, $\%_S$ is twice $\%_F$; 2 indicates that $\%_S$ is four times $\%_F$; and 3 indicates that $\%_S$ is eight times $\%_F$. Unlike the simple calculation $\%_S/\%_F$, the $\log_2$ fold-change has two advantages: First, it is centered on 0 – if $\%_S$ and $\%_F$ are equivalent, $\log_2(\%_S/\%_F)$ is 0). Second, it is symmetric – positive values mean $\%_S$ is greater than $\%_F$, and negative values mean the opposite. In order to similarly compare F with A, we also calculated $\log_2(\%_A/\%_F)$.

Figure 2 shows $\log_2(\%_S/\%_F)$ and $\log_2(\%_A/\%_F)$ for the top 23 first error messages (F_{85}), making up 85% of F. It can be seen that the differences between first and subsequent, and first and all, follow a similar trend. There are six messages lying between 0 and 1 indicating that these messages are less than two times as likely to occur as a subsequent error message, or at an unspecified location in the error output, than as a first message. For one error message (first rank 12) this likelihood is between two and four times greater. The remaining 16 error messages are negative indicating that these error messages are more likely to occur as first messages than as subsequent messages, or at an unspecified location in the output. For some messages the likelihood of occurring as a first message are nearly eight times greater than as a subsequent message.

An example of an error message that is much more frequent as a first message is `missing return statement` (~5.5 times more likely than subsequent and ~2.5 times more likely than overall). An example of an error message that is much less frequent as a first message is `class, interface, or enum expected` (~3.75 times less likely than subsequent and ~3 times less likely than overall).

5 DISCUSSION

The percentage of first error messages we found (28.5%), average number of messages per failed compile (3.50), and average number of subsequent messages (2.50) were comparable to those found by others. Murray [27] investigated Irish Blackbox users from July 1, 2015 to June 30, 2016 inclusive, including 3,708 users and 22,440 sessions. He found 23.1% first messages, with an average of 4.34

Table 1: The top 85% of first messages (set F_{85}) and their ranks and percent frequency as first (R_F, $\%_F$), subsequent (R_S, $\%_S$), and overall messages (R_A, $\%_A$). Shaded cells correspond to messages that do not appear in the top 85% of subsequent messages (column R_S) or all messages (column R_A).

Error Message Description	R_F	R_S	R_A	$\%_F$	$\%_S$	$\%_A$
cannot find symbol - variable	1	1	1	19.12	23.88	22.52
cannot find symbol - method	2	3	3	8.94	7.49	7.90
';' expected	3	2	2	8.20	13.33	11.86
incompatible types	4	9	7	6.96	3.57	4.54
cannot find symbol - class	5	5	4	6.56	6.84	6.76
')' expected	6	12	11	4.39	1.74	2.49
illegal start of expression	7	6	6	4.01	5.29	4.93
missing return statement	8	22	14	3.20	0.57	1.32
<identifier> expected	9	7	8	2.74	4.09	3.70
not a statement	10	8	9	2.59	3.77	3.43
reached end of file while parsing	11	13	12	2.31	1.70	1.88
class, interface, or enum expected	12	4	5	1.98	7.38	5.84
constructor in class cannot be applied to ...	13	19	18	1.81	0.73	1.04
method in class cannot be applied to ...	14	16	15	1.79	0.87	1.13
invalid method declaration; return type required	15	23	20	1.71	0.47	0.83
variable is already defined in method	16	20	19	1.50	0.67	0.91
variable ... might not have been initialized	17	27	24	1.37	0.38	0.66
package ... does not exist	18	15	16	1.19	1.00	1.06
no suitable method found for ...	19	24	25	1.10	0.43	0.62
... is not abstract and does not override abstract method ... in ...	20	39	30	1.06	0.15	0.41
operator ... cannot be applied to ...	21	21	22	1.04	0.60	0.72
'.class' expected	22	28	26	1.02	0.37	0.56
'(' expected	23	32	28	1.00	0.27	0.48

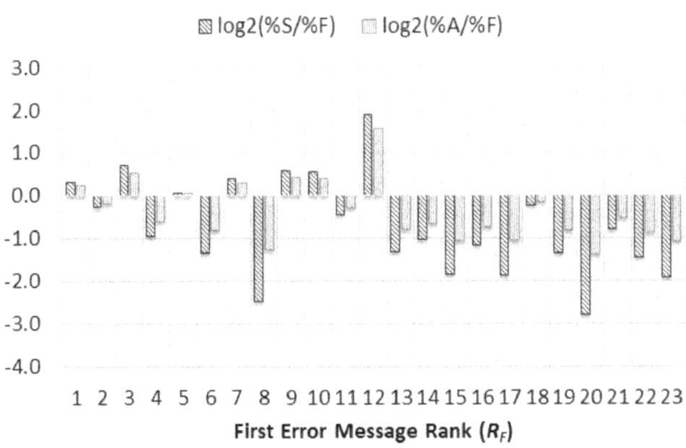

Figure 2: $\log_2(\%_S/\%_F)$ and $\log_2(\%_A/\%_F)$ for the error messages in Table 1 making up 85% of all first error messages.

per failed compile (3.34 subsequent). In a 1997 study of 42 novice Ada programmers, Moore et al. [25] reported 4.06 average error messages (3.06 subsequent) per failed compile.

The list of most-frequent first messages is notably different from the corresponding list for all messages, and from similar lists that have been reported before [11, 16, 20]. There are 23 distinct messages in the list of first messages, as opposed to 17 overall. The first-messages list includes nine messages that are not on the overall list, and omits three that are (as discussed in Section 4.2). Of those appearing on both lists, only one has the same rank, and all have differences in frequencies. For example, `missing return statement` and `')' expected` are much more common as first messages, and `class, interface, or enum expected` is much less common as a first message.

Our most-frequent first messages include all messages with at least 1% frequency. Students using editors that only show first error messages, or students following advice to only focus on first messages would (statistically) see each of these error messages from 1 to 19 times each in an average session, given 100 failed compiles in a programming session, which is quite realistic based on our data. These students would therefore see nine different messages per session not in the overall lists of frequent error messages reported by the literature (that are based on overall frequencies). Further, these students would not see three common error messages that do feature in the literature. This not only affects the students, but CS1 lecturers and lab instructors in particular, as a significant portion of their time is devoted to helping students rectify error messages. As the authors of [14] note, as educators the more we understand about the nature of compiler errors and how students respond to them, the more effective our teaching can be.

6 THREATS TO VALIDITY

The limitations of the Blackbox dataset have been characterized by Brown et al. [11]. Notably, Blackbox only includes BlueJ users and they are predominantly novices; but we are primarily interested in novices. Also, BlueJ users don't see the subsequent messages; but we are looking at compiler messages, not user responses to those messages, and the underlying messages for a given compile are essentially the same for BlueJ and other IDEs that use the standard JDK. BlueJ users *might* generate a different sequence of program versions, and therefore a different overall message frequency compared to users of other IDEs. We believe these effects are negligible, however, since our overall list of errors is similar to lists found by other researchers.

Our results may also be affected by the fact that BlueJ is an opt-in dataset. Thus, the results of this study may be subject to volunteer bias. This is an issue we share with all studies based on Blackbox, and indeed, most computing education studies based on human-subjects data. Finally, our sample, while large, is still only a subset of the Blackbox data. It is possible that non-United-States users or different time periods would show different characteristics.

7 CONCLUSIONS AND IMPLICATIONS

When teaching students, it is desirable to focus only on the first messages as often advised by educators and enforced by some novice programming environments. Our contributions are a taxonomy for discussing compiler error messages more precisely and data on how the error message landscape changes when focusing on first messages only. When we consider first messages only, message ranks and frequencies are different. We analyzed over 21 million compiler error messages from the Blackbox dataset and found that only ~28.5% of all error messages are first messages, and that the list of the most frequent *first* messages is markedly different from the corresponding list based on all compiler error messages.

We introduced a new taxonomy to make it possible for researchers and instructors to talk about errors with more precision. The Blackbox dataset includes all compiler error messages, with the first from each failed compile tagged as a "first message." In theory, the subsequent messages can be broken down into three groups: the "cascading messages" (spurious messages, which disappear when some real error is fixed); the "someday first messages" (corresponding to a distinct error and become a first message on a later compile); and the "buried messages" (corresponding to a distinct error but never become first messages). Future work will look at categorizing errors according to this taxonomy.

Our results also have implications for research. While the first messages are most relevant to investigations of student interactions with the compiler, studies that use compiler messages as a proxy for (or stepping stone towards identifying) student errors might choose to look at first messages plus buried messages. Designing and implementing an algorithm to extract the buried messages from Blackbox would be an interesting challenge in itself.

8 ACKNOWLEDGMENTS

The authors would like to acknowledge the BlueJ team at King's College London and the University of Kent for providing the Blackbox dataset that made this research possible.

REFERENCES

[1] Marzieh Ahmadzadeh, Dave Elliman, and Colin Higgins. 2005. An Analysis of Patterns of Debugging Among Novice Computer Science Students. In *ITiCSE '05*. ACM, 84–88.

[2] Amjad Altadmri and Neil C.C. Brown. 2015. 37 Million Compilations: Investigating Novice Programming Mistakes in Large-Scale Student Data. In *SIGCSE '15*. ACM, 522–527.

[3] Titus Barik, Justin Smith, Kevin Lubick, Elisabeth Holmes, Jing Feng, Emerson Murphy-Hill, and Chris Parnin. 2017. Do Developers Read Compiler Error Messages? *(ICSE '17)*. 575–585. DOI: http://dx.doi.org/10.1109/ICSE.2017.59

[4] Brett A. Becker. 2015. *An Exploration of the Effects of Enhanced Compiler Error Messages for Computer Programming Novices*. Master's thesis. Dublin Institute of Technology.

[5] Brett A. Becker. 2016. An Effective Approach to Enhancing Compiler Error Messages. In *SIGCSE '16*. ACM, 126–131.

[6] Brett A. Becker. 2016. A new metric to quantify repeated compiler errors for novice programmers. In *ITiCSE '16*. ACM, 296–301.

[7] Brett A. Becker, Graham Glanville, Ricardo Iwashima, Claire McDonnell, Kyle Goslin, and Catherine Mooney. 2016. Effective compiler error message enhancement for novice programming students. *Computer Science Education* 26, 2-3 (2016), 148–175.

[8] Mordechai Ben-Ari. 2007. Compile and Runtime Errors in Java. http://www.weizmann.ac.il/sci-tea/benari/software-and-learning-materials/errors.pdf. (2007). Accessed 12 Jan 2017.

[9] Benedict du Boulay and Ian Matthew. 1984. Fatal error in pass zero: How not to confuse novices. *Behaviour & Information Technology* 3, 2 (1984), 109–118.

[10] Neil CC Brown and Amjad Altadmri. 2017. Novice Java programming mistakes: large-scale data vs. educator beliefs. *ACM Transactions on Computing Education (TOCE)* 17, 2 (2017), 7.

[11] Neil Christopher Charles Brown, Michael Kölling, Davin McCall, and Ian Utting. 2014. Blackbox: A large scale repository of novice programmers' activity. In *SIGCSE '14*. ACM, 223–228.

[12] Ioana Tungalei Chan Mow. 2012. Analyses of student programming errors in Java programming courses. *J. Emerging Trends in Computing and Information Sciences* 3, 5 (2012), 739–749.

[13] Paul Denny, Andrew Luxton-Reilly, and Dave Carpenter. 2014. Enhancing syntax error messages appears ineffectual. In *ITiCSE '14*. ACM, 273–278.

[14] Paul Denny, Andrew Luxton-Reilly, and Ewan Tempero. 2012. All syntax errors are not equal. In *ITiCSE '12*. ACM, 75–80.

[15] Paul Denny, Andrew Luxton-Reilly, Ewan Tempero, and Jacob Hendrickx. 2011. CodeWrite: Supporting student-driven practice of Java. In *SIGCSE '11*. ACM, 471–476.

[16] Thomas Dy and Ma. Mercedes Rodrigo. 2010. A Detector for Non-literal Java Errors. In *Koli Calling '10*. ACM, 118–122.

[17] Sally Fincher and David Barnes. 2006. *Studying Programming*. Palgrave Macmillan.

[18] T. Flowers, C.A. Carver, and J. Jackson. 2004. Empowering students and building confidence in novice programmers through Gauntlet. In *FIE '04*. IEEE, T3H–10.

[19] Maria Hristova, Ananya Misra, Megan Rutter, and Rebecca Mercuri. 2003. Identifying and Correcting Java Programming Errors for Introductory Computer Science Students. In *SIGCSE '03*. ACM, 153–156.

[20] Matthew C Jadud. 2006. *An exploration of novice compilation behaviour in BlueJ*. Ph.D. Dissertation. Univ. of Kent.

[21] Matthew C. Jadud and Brian Dorn. 2015. Aggregate Compilation Behavior: Findings and Implications from 27,698 Users. In *ICER '15*. ACM, 131–139.

[22] Michael Kölling. 1999. Teaching object orientation with the Blue environment. *J. Object Oriented Programming* 12 (1999), 14–23.

[23] Michael Kölling, Bruce Quig, Andrew Patterson, and John Rosenberg. 2003. The BlueJ system and its pedagogy. *Computer Science Education* 13, 4 (2003), 249–268.

[24] Guillaume Marceau, Kathi Fisler, and Shriram Krishnamurthi. 2011. Measuring the Effectiveness of Error Messages Designed for Novice Programmers. In *SIGCSE '11*. 499–504.

[25] Deanne Moore, Allen Parrish, and David Cordes. 1997. Analyzing syntax error patterns among novice programmers. In *ACM-SE '97*. ACM, 188–190.

[26] Jonathan P. Munson and Elizabeth A. Schilling. 2016. Analyzing Novice Programmers' Response to Compiler Error Messages. *J. Comput. Sci. Coll.* 31, 3 (2016), 53–61.

[27] Cormac Murray. 2016. *A Comparative Study of Java Compiler Error Profiles Using the Blackbox Dataset*. Master's thesis. University College Dublin.

[28] James Prather, Raymond Pettit, Kayla Holcomb McMurry, Alani Peters, John Homer, Nevan Simone, and Maxine Cohen. 2017. On Novices' Interaction with Compiler Error Messages: A Human Factors Approach. In *ICER '17*. 74–82.

[29] David Pritchard. 2015. Frequency Distribution of Error Messages. In *PLATEAU 2015*. ACM, 1–8.

[30] Tom Schorsch. 1995. CAP: An automated self-assessment tool to check Pascal programs for syntax, logic and style errors. In *SIGCSE '95*. ACM, 168–172.

[31] Stewart D. Smith, Nicholas Zemljic, and Andrew Petersen. 2015. Modern Goto: Novice Programmer Usage of Non-standard Control Flow. In *Koli Calling '15*. ACM, 171–172.

[32] Suzanne Marie Thompson. 2004. *An Exploratory Study of Novice Programming Experiences and Errors*. Master's thesis. Univ. of Victoria.

[33] Ian Utting, Neil Brown, Michael Kölling, Davin McCall, and Philip Stevens. 2012. Web-scale Data Gathering with BlueJ. In *ICER '12*. ACM, 1–4.

The Effects of Enhanced Compiler Error Messages on a Syntax Error Debugging Test

Brett A. Becker
University College Dublin
Belfield, Dublin 4, Ireland
brett.becker@ucd.ie

Kyle Goslin
CCT College Dublin
Dublin 2, Ireland
kyle.goslin@cct.ie

Graham Glanville
CCT College Dublin
Dublin 2, Ireland
graham.glanville@cct.ie

ABSTRACT

There is an active strand of research in the literature exploring the effects of Enhanced Compiler Error Messages on student programming behavior, however many results seem conflicting. This is compounded by the fact that directly comparing these results is difficult as these studies utilize different metrics, and what metrics are best suited to measure the effects of enhanced compiler error messages is not known. Common to most studies to-date is that the metrics employed measure how many errors students produce, and/or rectify while writing programs.

This study takes a different approach by measuring how many *pre-existing* syntax errors are rectified by students while debugging programs. Specifically, we measured the effect of enhanced compiler error messages in an empirical control/intervention experiment where students were given the task of removing syntax errors from non-compiling source code they did not write. We find a significant positive effect on the overall number of errors rectified, as well as the number of certain specific error types, but no significant effect on the number of non-compiling submissions or student scores. These results (in different ways) support the findings of several recent studies and suggest that their results may not be as conflicting as they seem. This is evidence that enhanced error messages may be effective, but also that the signal of these effects are relatively weak, indicating that how and what is measured when attempting to observe these effects is important.

CCS CONCEPTS

•Social and professional topics → Computer science education; CS1;

KEYWORDS

compiler error messages; enhanced compiler error messages; syntax error messages; CS1; Java; novice programmers; debugging

ACM Reference format:
Brett A. Becker, Kyle Goslin, and Graham Glanville. 2018. The Effects of Enhanced Compiler Error Messages on a Syntax Error Debugging Test. In *Proceedings of SIGCSE'18, February 21–24, 2018, Baltimore, MD, USA*, , 6 pages.
DOI: http://dx.doi.org/10.1145/3159450.3159461

SIGCSE'18, February 21–24, 2018, Baltimore, MD, USA
© 2018 ACM. ISBN 978-1-4503-5103-4/18/02...$15.00
DOI: http://dx.doi.org/10.1145/3159450.3159461

1 INTRODUCTION

The difficulty that compiler error messages present to students have been pervasive themes in teaching beginners computer programming since at least the 1970s, and in many ways the situation is very little improved [2]. In 1984 it was noted that "Many students are quite unable to relate the messages from the compiler to the mistakes which they have made" [7, p. 110]. Thirty years later Ko wrote a blog post titled "Programming languages are the least usable, but most powerful human-computer interfaces ever invented", calling a particular PHP compiler error message "inscrutable" [12]. Mark Guzdial followed up with a post on the Communications of the ACM blog two days later, augmenting Ko's title to include "and learnable" after "least usable" [10].

Enhanced compiler error messages (ECEMs) have been explored in an attempt to alleviate the struggles that programming students continue to face. A currently evolving thread of research in the literature involving several groups has been attempting to measure the effects of ECEMs with varied approaches and increasing empiricism. So far the results are 'inconclusive' to borrow a word from the title of [17]; some authors have reported positive results [3, 5, 18] while others have not [8, 17]. It is important to note that for the most part, these authors have been utilizing different metrics, making direct and useful comparisons of their results difficult.

Despite their differences, these studies do share similarities in their methodologies – typically they directly or indirectly measure the number or frequency of errors *produced* by students writing programs, and sometimes the number of *self-produced* errors that are rectified. This study takes a different approach by measuring the number of *common, pre-existing errors* rectified by two groups of students – an intervention group whose code editor provides enhanced error messages, and a control group who are provided with the default Java compiler error messages. In addition we explore if the following are affected by ECEMs: number of non-compiling submissions, number of programming tasks correctly completed, number of errors rectified, and student scores.

Besides being motivated by the current debate on the effectiveness of enhanced compiler error messages, we are motivated by very recent results that show that students do read compiler error messages, that reading them takes a substantial portion of their time, and that reading compiler error messages presents a difficulty comparable to reading source code itself. We review the details of this and related studies in section 3. We are also motivated by the utility of error messages in other metrics – for instance the Error Quotient [11], Repeated Error Density [4], and Watwin [20] all incorporate student interaction with error messages.

Our research questions (see Section 4.1) are formulated to help answer the overarching questions: *Do enhanced compiler error messages have an effect on the results of a syntax error debugging test?* and if so, *What should be measured to observe these effects?*

We attempted to answer these questions by conducting an empirical control/intervention experiment where students complete a debugging test using an editor that enhances compiler error messages. We find a statistically significant effect on the number of rectified syntax errors, and we identify several specific syntax errors which the intervention group rectified more successfully. We also find that there is not a significant effect on the number of compiling submissions, the number of correct tasks, and student scores. These results (positive and negative) corroborate several previous studies.

The main contributions of this paper are:

(1) Our results (both positive and negative) support a total of four different recent studies.
(2) We offer evidence that the effects of enhanced compiler error messages may be too weak to measure with high-level metrics such as number of non-compiling submissions, and therefore the metrics used to measure these effects (at least initially) should be low-level, such as error frequency.

These contributions have important implications for the active strand of research on the effects of enhanced compiler error messages, which to-date has shown apparently conflicting results.

This paper is organized as follows. Section 2 presents our motivations and Section 3 reviews recent results on the effects of compiler error message enhancement. Section 4 presents our methodology and research questions. Section 5 presents our results. In Section 6 we discuss these results, and in Section 7 we discuss threats to validity, before concluding in Section 8.

For consistency and to avoid repeating specific long phrases, at times we use the terminology in Table 1 that was introduced by [2] and has been used by others [3, 5, 18] recently.

Table 1: Compiler error message terminology from [2].

Term	Meaning
CEM	Compiler Error Message
ECEM	Enhanced Compiler Error Message
Error	An error in code that generates a CEM

2 MOTIVATIONS

Recently, Denny et al. noted: "As educators, we have a limited amount of time to spend with each student so providing students with automated and useful feedback about why they are getting syntax errors is very important" [9, p. 278]. Besides many other altruistic motivations, we are specifically motivated by these factors:

(1) Recent studies with seemingly conflicting results on the effectiveness of ECEMs, specifically [3, 5, 8, 17, 18]. We explore these results in Section 3.
(2) A recent survey showing that students struggle with, and want help with CEMs (discussed in this section).
(3) Recent results showing that students do read CEMs, specifically [1, 18].

In tandem with another experiment, we conducted a survey of 106 Software Engineering students in their CS1 module, of which 73 (69%) responded. These students were programming in C using Notepad++ and compiling at the command line using GCC. We sought to explore the levels of frustration, confusion and misconception they have surrounding compiler error messages.

The survey revealed that students find compiler error messages to be a source of frustration (85%), a barrier to progress (92%), and confusing (64%). Interestingly, 100% of students reported that having additional help specifically on dealing with compiler errors would help them in learning to program.

A recent study by Barik et al. [1] provides substantial motivation. In their eye-tracking study they found:

(1) Students read compiler error messages and the difficulty of reading them is comparable to the difficulty of reading source code.
(2) Difficulty reading error messages significantly predicts participants' task performance.
(3) Difficulty reading error messages contributes to the overall difficulty of resolving a compiler error message.
(4) Students allocate 12-25% of their total task time to reading error messages, which is substantial, considering the brevity of most compiler error messages compared to source code.

These results "offer empirical justification for the need to improve compiler error messages" [1, p. 575]. Prather et al. [18] also provide evidence that students do read compiler error messages. We discuss their findings in more detail in the following section.

3 RELATED WORK

Several authors have explored the effect of enhanced compiler error messages on students learning to program. Becker [2] presented a fairly comprehensive historical view dating back to the 1970s. Much of the work through the early 2000s either presented anecdotal results or were based on small student numbers.

In 2014, Denny et al. [8] conducted a control/intervention study using an enhanced feedback system within CodeWrite, a web-based tool in which students complete a series of exercises that require them to write the body of a method in Java [9]. Their analysis found no effect of ECEMs on the following metrics: number of consecutive non-compiling submissions, the total number of non-compiling submissions, and the number of attempts needed to resolve the three most common student-committed syntax errors.

In 2017, Pettit et al. [17] also measured the effects of enhanced compiler error messages using a different language (C++), different assessment tool (Athene), and a different number of assignments. They found no evidence of effect on their metrics, which included the likelihood of successive compilation errors, which is important as repeated compiler errors strongly affect other metrics such as the EQ [11] and RED [4]. Despite the lack of effect that Denny et al. and Pettit et al. observed, Becker [3] and Becker et al. [5] reported positive results. In these 2015 and 2016 control/intervention studies, enhanced error messages were found to have a significant reduction in several metrics including the number of overall errors, number of errors per student, and number of repeated (consecutive) errors.

Becker [3] also identified eight specific Java compiler error messages that have a significantly reduced frequency when enhanced compiler error messages were provided.

Very recently, Prather et al. [18] applied a human-factors approach to investigating the effects of ECEMs. That study looked into the above mentioned studies (Denny et al. [8], Becker [3], and Pettit et al. [17]) and offered five potential reasons for the inconsistent conclusions concerning ECEMs: (1) students do not read them, (2) researchers are measuring the wrong thing, (3) the effects are hard to measure, (4) the messages are not properly designed, and (5) the messages are properly designed, but students do not understand them in context due to increased cognitive load.

They conducted mixed-methods experiments designed to address reasons 1 and 5 using the same tool that reported inconclusive results in Pettit et al. [17]. They sought specifically to determine if students read ECEMs, and if they are helpful in settings with high and low cognitive loads. Their results corroborate the evidence provided by Barick et al. [1] regarding whether novices read ECEMs, stating that "Observational and ethnographic data seem to indicate that novices in CS1 do, in fact, read ECEMs" [18, p. 81]. In low cognitive load settings results showed a statistically significant decrease in incorrect understanding of ECEMs compared to standard CEMs. In high cognitive load settings, quantitative data seemed inconclusive, but qualitative data indicated that ECEMs were helpful, noting that students that struggled to complete a quiz successfully used the ECEMs to arrive at a correct solution.

Quantitative results from think-aloud sessions did not show a substantial increase in student learning outcomes over the control group. However, qualitative results from these sessions indicated that most students were reading the ECEMs and generally made effective changes after encountering them.

It will be important to note that Becker [3], Becker et al. [5], Denny et al. [8], Pettit et al. [17], and Prather et al. [18], utilized a number of different metrics. Some of these can be considered fairly low-level, such as the counts of specific error messages, while others can be considered more high-level, such as the number of non-compiling student submissions. In this study we measure both of these. Finally it should be noted that although this study and those reviewed in this section focus on novice programmers (with the exception of [1] who studied undergraduate and graduate students), there is evidence that compiler error messages also pose difficulty for experienced developers [14, 19].

4 METHODOLOGY AND RESEARCH QUESTIONS

We constructed a test containing 24 syntax errors generating 11 syntax error message types, as detailed in Table 2. Like similar studies, we are primarily interested in the errors that students encounter most frequently, and we wanted our test to be representative of the errors that students normally encounter. Correspondingly, the eight error messages with frequencies of 3% or greater account for 88% of the errors on the test. It should be noted that these eight error messages are included in the 15 most frequent error messages accounting for 86% of all errors as measured in the control group of [3]. Thus, although our test contains only a subset of all possible error messages, it is in this way representative of the proportions of error messages students would normally encounter.

Table 2: Compiler errors included in test. Quantity is the number of errors in each test generating the corresponding compiler error message type. Rank is the overall frequency rank (1 is most frequent) from [3]. Frequency is the frequency, measured in a control group, from [3].

Compiler error message type	Quantity	Rank	Frequency
cannot find symbol	4	1	19%
';' expected	4	3	12%
not a statement	4	4	9%
illegal start of expression	3	5	7%
bad operand types for binary operator *op*	1	8	5%
incompatible types	2	9	4%
<identifier> expected	1	10	4%
variable *v_name* is already defined in method *m_name*	2	13	3%
']' expected	1	16	<2%
missing return statement	1	*17*	<2%
package *p_name* does not exist	1	25	<1 %

The test contained 107 lines of code (including 40 blank or comment lines) and was logically divided into five tasks, each producing its own pre-specified output, provided all errors were rectified properly. No additional effort was required of the students to arrive at a working program. The test was designed to have a specified output to keep students from rectifying errors in valid yet unconventional (and undesired) manners, such as simply deleting the line of code containing the error. Certain lines of code were marked with comments instructing students that they must not be modified. For instance, one of the `cannot find symbol` error messages was generated by a misspelled variable name. The variable was declared and used several times before being misspelled, and therefore the natural method of rectifying this error would be to correct the single instance where it is misspelled. Of course, it would be effective to change all of the properly spelled instances to match the misspelled one causing the error. However this could have the effect of *introducing* more errors in the code, which is not desirable.

The test was devised by writing a working program that completed all five tasks, then intentionally introducing the 24 syntax errors. The required program output was given to the students before the test, so they were aware what the output of the correctly fixed program should be. Students were given two hours to rectify as many of the 24 errors as possible with the goal of rectifying them all, and having a finished program that matched the provided output. The test code can be accessed at: www.brettbecker.com/sigcse18/.

The test was taken by two groups of students from the same first year cohort in their CS1 'Introduction to Programming' course at the middle and last authors' institution. Fortuitously these two groups were split (in terms of teaching) due to logistical reasons. The only difference between the groups was the time of day that their lectures were scheduled. They were taught by the same staff with the same notes, at the same pace, etc. Across both groups the gender balance was 32% female, 68% male. Both groups were learning with the editor described in [2, 3, 5]. The intervention group were experiencing the ECEMs provided by the editor and the control group were experiencing standard Java CEMs.

The test was administered in week 10 of semester 1. There were 109 control group and 43 intervention group submissions. In order to compare an equal-sized sample from each group we analyzed all 43 intervention submissions, and a random sample of 43 control. In analyzing the source code, we tabulated the following:

(1) whether the submission compiled
(2) if the program compiled, whether the output of each of the five tasks was correct
(3) whether each of the 24 errors were rectified in a manner consistent with the specified output
(4) a student score based on number of errors rectified

As discussed, it is possible for a given syntax error to be rectified in several ways. Some of these, for instance simply deleting a given line of code, or removing all instances of a given variable name, may not be considered legitimate. Fortunately, designing the test to require certain outputs kept this to a minimum, but some cases necessarily involved human judgment. For this reason two raters separately analyzed all submissions and compared their results on the rectification of individual error types. We then calculated Cohen's Kappa (κ) for each of the 11 error message types. Three error message types had $\kappa > 0.80$, eight types had $0.60 < \kappa \leq 0.80$, and one had $0.40 < \kappa \leq 0.60$. [15] describes these bands as 'almost perfect', 'substantial', and 'moderate' agreement, respectively. The category with the lowest κ was one of the error message types with a very low frequency (< 2%). Differences were resolved by both raters re-inspecting the errors in question and agreeing on a common result.

4.1 Research Questions

Our research questions were formulated to help answer the overarching questions: *Do enhanced compiler error messages have an effect on the results of a syntax error debugging test?* If so, *What should be measured to observe these effects?*

RQ1: Do enhanced compiler error messages have an effect on the number of successfully compiling submissions?
RQ2: Do enhanced compiler error messages have an effect on the number of tasks completed correctly?
RQ3: Do enhanced compiler error messages have an effect on the number of rectified syntax errors?
RQ4: Do enhanced compiler error messages have an effect on student scores?

5 RESULTS

5.1 RQ1: Successfully Compiling Submissions

The intervention group submitted 20 compiling submissions and the control group submitted 17. A chi-squared test indicated that the difference between groups is not significant, $\chi^2 = 0.43, p = 0.513$ ($\alpha = 0.05$).

5.2 RQ2: Tasks Completed Correctly

Table 3 shows the number of compiling submissions from each group correctly completing each of the 5 tasks (A-E). A chi-squared test indicated that none of the results are significant ($\alpha = 0.05$).

Table 3: Number of correctly completed tasks per group (control and intervention). χ^2 and p are results of a chi-squared test.

Task	Control	Intervention	χ^2	p
A	10	10	-	-
B	12	13	0.06	0.813
C	13	12	0.06	0.813
D	13	13	-	-
E	10	12	0.24	0.621

5.3 RQ3: Syntax Errors Rectified

There were 43 students in each group and each test had 24 compiler errors for a total of 1,032 errors per group (2,064 errors overall). The control group rectified 665 (64.4%) of their errors while the intervention group rectified 790 (76.6%). A chi-squared test indicated that this is statistically significant, $\chi^2 = 36.40$, $p < 0.001$ ($\alpha = 0.05$).

We next sought to determine which compiler error message types contributed to this result. Table 4 shows the number of rectified compiler errors for each group by type, χ^2 and p-values of a chi-squared test, and whether the result is significant ($\alpha = 0.05$) using the Benjamini-Hochberg procedure to account for multiple tests. By raw numbers, the intervention group rectified more errors than the control group for every error message type, and this difference is significant for six of these error types accounting for more than 2/3 of the total number of errors on the test.

5.4 RQ4: Student Scores

We calculated a score per student based on the number of errors corrected (perfect score = 24). The average/median scores were 15.16/16.5 (control) and 17.95/21 (intervention). A Shapiro-Wilk test revealed neither distribution was normal. A Mann-Whitney U test (two-tail, independent samples) showed no statistically significant difference between groups, $U = 805.5, p = 0.172$ ($\alpha = 0.05$).

6 DISCUSSION

Our first research question was *Do enhanced compiler error messages have an effect on the number of successfully compiling submissions?* The intervention group submitted three more compiling submissions (20) than the control group (17) and a chi-squared test showed that this difference is not statistically significant.

Our second research question was *Do enhanced compiler error messages have an effect on the number of tasks completed correctly?* For tasks A and D, the control and intervention groups had an equal number of students completing the task correctly. For tasks B and C the difference was one and for Task E the difference was two. For the tasks where there is a difference, a chi-squared test revealed no statistically significant difference.

Our third research question was *Do enhanced compiler error messages have an effect on the number of rectified syntax errors?* We found that the intervention group rectified a greater number of syntax errors than the control group (790 vs. 665) and a chi-squared test showed that this difference is statistically significant. Further, six of the eleven error message types (accounting for more than 2/3 of the total number of errors) had a statistically significant increase in the number of errors rectified by the intervention group.

Table 4: Compiler error message groups for research question 3. Total Errors is the number of errors per group (errors/test × 43 tests/group). Rectified (Control) and (Intervention) are the number of errors rectified by the Control and Intervention groups respectively. χ^2 and p are results of a chi-squared test. Sig(B-H)? indicates if the result is significant ($\alpha = 0.05$), corrected with Benjamini-Hochberg procedure (false discovery rate $Q = 0.1$). Sig[3]? indicates if there was a significant reduction in the number of errors in each error message group reported in [3], discussed in Section 6.

Compiler Error Message Type	Total Errors	Rectified (Control)	Rectified (Intervention)	χ^2	p	**Sig(B-H)?**	Sig[3]?
cannot find symbol	172	121	145	9.55	0.003	**Y**	Y
';' expected	172	111	131	5.57	0.018	**Y**	N
not a statement	172	116	135	5.32	0.021	**Y**	Y
illegal start of expression	129	87	95	1.19	0.275	**N**	Y
bad operand types for binary operator *op*	43	23	28	1.20	0.272	**N**	N
incompatible types	86	57	70	5.09	0.024	**Y**	Y
<identifier> expected	43	23	30	2.41	0.121	**N**	Y
variable *v_name* is already defined in method *m_name*	86	49	57	1.57	0.210	**N**	Y
']' expected	43	35	37	0.34	0.559	**N**	N/A
missing return statement	43	13	23	4.78	0.029	**Y**	N/A
package *p_name* does not exist	43	30	39	5.94	0.015	**Y**	N/A

Becker [3] measured if an intervention group experiencing enhanced compiler error messages experienced a statistically significant decrease in the number of errors committed compared to a control group experiencing the standard Java error messages. The column labeled sig[3]? in Table 4 indicates if [3] found a statistically significant reduction in the number of syntax errors generating the given error message type. That study only reported details for the 15 most frequent error message types, and as three of the messages in Table 4 were less frequent, sig[3]? is N/A for those messages. The present study agrees with [3] for four of the remaining eight error message types, and disagrees for the other four.

In investigating these discrepancies we noticed that half of the 10 errors in the test code that result in the four error message types where this study and [3] disagree, occur in the final third of the test program. In fact three of the `';' expected` errors are among the six errors making up the final quarter of the test. When this became apparent we reflected on our analysis of the submitted source code and recalled several submissions where it seemed that the student had completely given up somewhere around the halfway point, not even attempting to rectify the final errors on the test. We wondered if this behavior was more indicative of one group or the other.

We revisited the source code and categorized submissions into two types, those that had attempted to rectify at least one of the final eight errors (representing the final third of the test), and those that had not. The control group had 17 of the latter, and the intervention group had 8. A chi-squared test indicated that this difference is statistically significant, $\chi^2 = 4.57$, $p < 0.033$ ($\alpha = 0.05$). For some reason fewer control students attempted the final third of the test. It is possible that ECEMs are a contributing factor in explaining this. Further, as error types are not evenly distributed in the code, this effect could possibly explain some of the discrepancies between these results and those of [3].

These observations are similar to effects observed by Prather et al. [18] whose qualitative data seems to indicate that ECEMs are also effective in an environment with a higher cognitive load. In that study, students that struggled to complete their quiz successfully were observed using the ECEMs to arrive at a correct solution. As our students were working against the clock, in an 'exam' environment, it is safe to assume that their cognitive load was relatively high, and it is not unreasonable to expect some of the observations made by [18] to also be observed in our study.

7 THREATS TO VALIDITY

As discussed in Section 4, it is possible for a given syntax error to be rectified in several ways. This did lead to some student fixes of questionable merit, such as deleting the offending line of code altogether, which if there are no dependencies, can successfully resolve an error. We attempted to mitigate some of this threat by requiring the test program to have a specified output. In addition, we had two raters analyze all submissions and work out any discrepancies. In all cases, prior to working out discrepancies, Cohen's Kappa indicated 'substantial' or 'nearly perfect' agreement (as defined by [15]) in all cases other than one 'moderate' case, which was one of the error types with a frequency of less than 2% in Table 2.

It should also be considered that providing students with non-compiling source code that produces a specified output when the errors are rectified, imposes a fairly well-defined context. Other studies such as [8] involved an arguably less-defined context (providing method declarations), while [3] imposed a very minimal context as students were programming from scratch – completing assignments, working on lab exercises, or often just practicing. We include this as a consideration as [16] showed that context can have an effect on Jadud's EQ [11], which is a measure of how students deal with syntax errors, and is therefore much related to this work. In fact we would expect the students that did well on our test to have a lower (better) EQ than those that struggled, and if context can affect the EQ, it is possible that the context enforced by our test affected our students' ability. Another way of stating this is: It is most probable that a different test, but with the same number of the same syntax error message types, would generate different results. It should be noted that the different contexts explored by

[16] were diverse, up to and including different programming languages. Therefore we may be over-considering the possible effect of the context of the test used in this study.

There is also a threat to the validity of the argument presented in the end of Section 6, where we hypothesize that a lack of ECEMs prevented a large number of the control group students from even attempting to rectify some of the errors that appeared later in the test. The threat is in assuming that most students set out rectifying errors in a top-down manner, which may or may not be true. Complicating this scenario is the fact that the intervention group were only presented with the first compiler error message at each compilation (we used the same editor as [2, 3, 5]), which forces a rigid and largely top-down progression through a source file. The control group students were experiencing all error messages at each compile and their paths of progression through the source code (and the order in which they rectify errors) may have been quite different to each other, and to the intervention group. Further, it has been shown that the frequency of error messages changes when only the first error from each compilation is considered [6].

8 CONCLUSIONS AND IMPLICATIONS

This study presents results on the effects of enhanced compiler error messages (ECEMs) on a debugging test in an empirical control/intervention manner. To our knowledge this is the first time that the effects of ECEMs have been measured in this way. This study offers two lines of evidence that both support previous results. The first is that we observe statistically significant effects of ECEMs on the number of overall errors and the number of several specific types of errors committed by students, supporting the results of Becker et al. [3, 5]. We also observe effects that may corroborate observations made by Prather et al. [18]. The second line of evidence is that we do not observe statistically significant effects of ECEMs on the number of compiling submissions, supporting the results of Denny et al. [8] and Pettit et al. [17]. Additionally, we do not observe a difference in student scores.

A potential implication of these results is that the results of Becker et al. and Denny et al. may not be as conflicting as they appear. It is possible that the present results, taken together with those of Becker et al., Denny et al., Pettit et al., and Prather et al., demonstrate that ECEMs do have measurable effects, but the signals are weak. This would explain why these results are observed at the level of error frequencies (as found by this study and Becker et al.), but not at higher levels such as student scores (as found by this study), and the number of compiling submissions (as found by this study, Denny et al. and Pettit et al.). This is evidence that Prather et al. may have been correct when they postulated that researchers may be measuring the wrong thing [18].

If this is the case, it is possible that the effects of ECEMs (and therefore the benefit to students) could be strengthened by going back to the drawing board and working to ensure that the error messages themselves are well-designed and as effective as possible. In short, it is possible that studies on ECEMs need more qualitative rigor before applying statistical measures. Additionally, working towards a mechanism for the universal application of rubrics such as [13] would serve to allow the comparison of the results of separate research studies in more straight-forward and robust manners.

REFERENCES

[1] Titus Barik, Justin Smith, Kevin Lubick, Elisabeth Holmes, Jing Feng, Emerson Murphy-Hill, and Chris Parnin. 2017. Do developers read compiler error messages? *(ICSE '17)*. 575–585. DOI: http://dx.doi.org/10.1109/ICSE.2017.59

[2] Brett A. Becker. 2015. *An exploration of the effects of enhanced compiler error messages for computer programming novices.* Master's thesis. Dublin Institute of Technology.

[3] Brett A. Becker. 2016. An Effective Approach to Enhancing Compiler Error Messages. In *Proceedings of the 47th ACM Technical Symposium on Computing Science Education (SIGCSE '16)*. ACM, 126–131. DOI: http://dx.doi.org/10.1145/2839509.2844584

[4] Brett A. Becker. 2016. A new metric to quantify repeated compiler errors for novice programmers. In *Proceedings of the 2016 ACM Conference on Innovation and Technology in Computer Science Education (ITiCSE '16)*. ACM, 296–301. DOI: http://dx.doi.org/10.1145/2899415.2899463

[5] Brett A. Becker, Graham Glanville, Ricardo Iwashima, Claire McDonnell, Kyle Goslin, and Catherine Mooney. 2016. Effective compiler error message enhancement for novice programming students. *Computer Science Education* 26, 2-3 (2016), 148–175. DOI: http://dx.doi.org/10.1080/08993408.2016.1225464

[6] Brett A. Becker, Cormac Murray, Tianyi Tao, Changheng Song, Robert McCartney, and Kate Sanders. 2018. Fix the first, ignore the rest: Dealing with multiple compiler error messages. In *Proceedings of the 49th ACM Technical Symposium on Computing Science Education (SIGCSE '18)*. ACM. DOI: http://dx.doi.org/10.1145/3159450.3159453 to appear.

[7] Benedict du Boulay and Ian Matthew. 1984. Fatal error in pass zero: How not to confuse novices. *Behaviour & Information Technology* 3, 2 (1984), 109–118.

[8] Paul Denny, Andrew Luxton-Reilly, and Dave Carpenter. 2014. Enhancing syntax error messages appears ineffectual. In *Proceedings of the 2014 Conference on Innovation & Technology in Computer Science Education (ITiCSE '14)*. ACM, New York, NY, USA, 273–278. DOI: http://dx.doi.org/10.1145/2591708.2591748

[9] Paul Denny, Andrew Luxton-Reilly, Ewan Tempero, and Jacob Hendrickx. 2011. CodeWrite: Supporting student-driven practice of Java. In *Proceedings of the 42nd ACM Technical Symposium on Computer Science Education (SIGCSE '11)*. ACM, 471–476. DOI: http://dx.doi.org/10.1145/1953163.1953299

[10] Mark Guzdial. March 27, 2014 (accessed August 6, 2017). *Programming languages are the most powerful, and least usable and learnable user interfaces.* https://cacm.acm.org/blogs/blog-cacm/173328-programming-languages-are-the-most-powerful-and-least-usable-and-learnable-user-interfaces/fulltext

[11] Matthew C Jadud. 2006. *An exploration of novice compilation behaviour in BlueJ.* Ph.D. Dissertation. University of Kent.

[12] Andy Ko. March 25, 2014 (accessed August 6, 2017). *Programming languages are the least usable, but most powerful human-computer interfaces ever invented.* http://blogs.uw.edu/ajko/2014/03/25/programming-languages-are-the-least-usable-but-most-powerful-human-computer-interfaces-ever-invented/

[13] Guillaume Marceau, Kathi Fisler, and Shriram Krishnamurthi. 2011. Measuring the effectiveness of error messages designed for novice programmers. In *Proceedings of the 42Nd ACM Technical Symposium on Computer Science Education (SIGCSE '11)*. ACM, 499–504. DOI: http://dx.doi.org/10.1145/1953163.1953308

[14] Guillaume Marceau, Kathi Fisler, and Shriram Krishnamurthi. 2011. Mind your language: On novices' interactions with error messages. In *Proceedings of the 10th SIGPLAN Symposium on New Ideas, New Paradigms, and Reflections on Programming and Software (Onward! 2011)*. ACM, 3–18. DOI: http://dx.doi.org/10.1145/2048237.2048241

[15] Mary L McHugh. 2012. Interrater reliability: the kappa statistic. *Biochemia medica* 22, 3 (2012), 276–282. DOI: http://dx.doi.org/10.11613/BM.2012.031

[16] Andrew Petersen, Jaime Spacco, and Arto Vihavainen. 2015. An exploration of error quotient in multiple contexts. In *Proceedings of the 15th Koli Calling Conference on Computing Education Research (Koli Calling '15)*. ACM, New York, NY, USA, 77–86. DOI: http://dx.doi.org/10.1145/2828959.2828966

[17] Raymond S. Pettit, John Homer, and Roger Gee. 2017. Do enhanced compiler error messages help students?: results inconclusive.. In *Proceedings of the 2017 ACM SIGCSE Technical Symposium on Computer Science Education (SIGCSE '17)*. ACM, New York, NY, USA, 465–470. DOI: http://dx.doi.org/10.1145/3017680.3017768

[18] James Prather, Raymond Pettit, Kayla Holcomb McMurry, Alani Peters, John Homer, Nevan Simone, and Maxine Cohen. 2017. On novices' interaction with compiler error messages: A human factors approach. In *Proceedings of the 2017 ACM Conference on International Computing Education Research (ICER '17)*. ACM, 74–82. DOI: http://dx.doi.org/10.1145/3105726.3106169

[19] V. Javier Traver. 2010. On compiler error messages: What they say and what they mean. *Advances in Human-Computer Interaction* 2010 (2010), 3:1–3:26. http://dx.doi.org/10.1155/2010/602570

[20] Christopher Watson, Frederick WB Li, and Jamie L Godwin. 2013. Predicting performance in an introductory programming course by logging and analyzing student programming behavior. In *Proceedings of the 2013 IEEE 13th international conference on Advanced learning Technologies (ICALT)*. IEEE, 319–323. DOI: http://dx.doi.org/10.1109/ICALT.2013.99

Novice Programmers' Reasoning about Reversing Conditional Statements

Cruz Izu
The University of Adelaide
Adelaide, Australia
cruz.izu@adelaide.edu.au

Claudio Mirolo
University of Udine
Udine, Italy
claudio.mirolo@uniud.it

Amali Weerasinghe
The University of Adelaide
Adelaide, Australia
amali.weerasinghe@gmail.com

ABSTRACT

We want undergraduate students to develop higher-order thinking skills that enable them to master program behaviour. Nonetheless, many students of both introductory and advanced programming courses appear to struggle with the abstraction required for this purpose. In particular, a recent think-aloud study showed a group of students were able to reason about and reverse the effect of assignments and vector updates, but most of them failed when asked to reverse a seemingly simple conditional statement.

We have extended that study by assigning a similar task to two cohorts of novice programmers as part of their final exam paper. Students' answers, including code and short explanations, have been analysed through the lens of the SOLO taxonomy: 28% of the solutions were correct (classified as relational); an additional 23% were partially correct but failed to identify the overlap between the two paths of the conditional statement (classified as multistructural). Furthermore, the concept of reversibility and related "low-ceiling" tasks, such as the one discussed in this study, could be useful resources for educators to assess and develop students' understanding of program behaviour.

KEYWORDS

novice programmers; program comprehension; reversibility; program state; SOLO taxonomy

ACM Reference Format:

Cruz Izu, Claudio Mirolo, and Amali Weerasinghe. 2018. Novice Programmers' Reasoning about Reversing Conditional Statements. In *SIGCSE '18: SIGCSE '18: The 49th ACM Technical Symposium on Computing Science Education, February 21–24, 2018, Baltimore , MD, USA.* ACM, New York, NY, USA, 6 pages. https://doi.org/10.1145/3159450.3159499

1 INTRODUCTION

The ability to reason about program behaviour is considered to be an advanced skill that CS2 students should develop [12]. The standard implementations of CS1/CS2, however, are usually focused on practical abilities such as tracing and testing, whereas little guidance is given as to how to approach the program behaviour in a systematic way, i.e. by considering *every* possible state or data flow caused by program execution. Recent work has investigated the level of program comprehension of CS2/CS3 students by exploring an abstract related concept: *reversibility* [5]. Tasks requiring the reversal of a piece of code were first proposed by Lister [7] as a device to test an "archetypal manifestation of concrete thinking" of novice programmers. Then, Teague and Lister [16] evaluated the **coding** ability of a large group (n=603) of CS1/CS2 students to reverse a short program. Later on, Izu et al. [5] asked students to ascertain if small code fragments were reversible, in order to assess students' ability to systematically **reason** about state transformation. However, to test their full understanding we should combine both **reasoning** and **coding** in one task.

SIGCSE '18, February 21–24, 2018, Baltimore , MD, USA

ACM ISBN 978-1-4503-5103-4/18/02...$15.00
https://doi.org/10.1145/3159450.3159499

The present study involves a task on reversibility of *conditional* statements, where students are required to reason as well as to code. To complete it successfully, they need a well-formed mental model of the program state. We are interested in a task of this type in that (i) it relates to the core concept of state that students are usually exposed to, (ii) it forces them to analyse the "overlaps" of alternate data flows, and (iii) it appeared to be a stumbling block in [5].

The assignment was part of the final examination for two cohorts of first year students in different countries, hence it had to be simple and clear. In the same task we covered both the accuracy of students' analysis of potential changes to the program state and their mastery of the implications of the code they are able to write. More specifically, this was accomplished as follows: firstly we asked them to decide if a given conditional statement is reversible or not; secondly they had to justify their decision by providing the code that would undo the state if their answer was *Yes*, or an example of a state (in fact, the value of a variable) that cannot be reversed if their answer was *No*. By this instrument we intended to address the following research questions:

- Can novice programmers[1] reverse a conditional statement?
- How comprehensively can novice programmers envisage the impact of conditionals in state variables?

The main contribution of this study is to evaluate for the first time novices' understanding of the overall effect that *the alternate paths* of a conditional statement can have on program state. In addition, from a pedagogical perspective, targeted tasks exploiting the reversibility concept can also serve as helpful tools to explore students' mental models of program behaviour and to provide them with more effective feedback to overcome latent misconceptions.

The rest of the paper is organised as follows: after setting in Section 2 some background for this study, Section 3 describes how the empirical data were collected and analysed; Section 4 summarizes the quantitative and qualitative results, which are then discussed

[1]Here by novice programmers we mean undergraduate students that have completed up to one year's programming instruction at tertiary level.

in Section 5 both in terms of the research questions and from a pedagogical viewpoint.

2 RELATED WORK

Reversibility is the mental process of determining if a set of events can be undone to return to the original state. In Piaget's theory of cognitive development, reversibility is a key step toward more advanced thinking: it represents the change from using and manipulating symbols to extending their meaning and making an increased use of logical thinking. Moreover, according to a neo-Piagetian perspective, corresponding learning stages are relevant independently of the age when approaching new knowledge domains [15].

In order to cope with reversibility of programming constructs, program behaviour has to be understood as a whole. Pennington [11] investigated the role in program comprehension of different types of "abstractions" relating to code components, namely: *function* (goals to achieve), *data flow* (dependencies between values), *control flow* (action sequence), *operations* (individual actions), and *state* (preconditions for actions). These concepts are inter-related; for example, data flow is about "transformations that data objects undergo" during execution, which result from the combination of control flow and operations that change the object state. From this perspective, our reversibility task relates to both data flow and state, which, according to Pennington's empirical studies, turned out to be more difficult to master than operations and control flow.

A number of CS education papers discuss program behaviour from a variety of perspectives, such as code comprehension [3], code-reading abilities [9] and mental models [2]. However, most often the emphasis is not on reasoning about program behaviour comprehensively, but on supporting students to learn specific concepts or to improve their programming skills. Ragonis et al. [12], for instance, examined students' difficulties with the object-oriented program flow, and suggested appropriate support, in particular visualisation, to improve their understanding. Lister et al. [8], on the other hand, explored the ability to summarise a program's goal in one sentence, i.e. to do "chunking".

With regard to studies that explore the behaviour of conditional statements, it is worth mentioning what Cherenkova et al. report while discussing the most frequent sources of students' problems with conditionals [4, p. 698]:

> A significant fraction of the students do have trouble with basic structural issues of syntax and indentation. [...] However, a significant number [...] exhibit the common errors of failing to check the border condition [26.7%] or reversing the conditional [28.5%].

3 METHODOLOGY

This section describes the exam's task and the rationale for using it as an instrument to investigate program comprehension. Next, it outlines the data collection process. Finally, it presents the criteria underlying our analysis and, in particular, the application of the SOLO taxonomy.

3.1 Task

Valid assessment of higher order thinking skills requires students to be unfamiliar with the given task. Accordingly, on their tutorial or class exercises students were not exposed to reversibility. Nevertheless, they were expected to have sufficient prior knowledge to complete the proposed task, since at several points of the course they were asked to determine the outcome of small pieces of code. For the sake of our investigation, we selected a mixed method that combines the three item formats useful in measuring higher order skills: *selection*, *explanation*, and *creation* [6]. Firstly, students had to identify whether a code segment is reversible or not (selection); then they were required either to provide an example of a state not being reversible (explanation), or to write a piece of code to undo the reversible command (creation). The exam question is shown in Figure 1. Note in the exam paper the question was preceded by a basic introduction on reversibility with examples, not shown here due to space limitations.[2]

Analyse the following code fragments and determine if they are reversible:

- if your answer is *Yes, reversible* (i.e. the command is reversible), write a piece of code which restores the original state of the program variables.
- If your answer is *No* (i.e. it is not always possible to undo the effect), provide an example where it is not possible to infer the original state from the outcome.

(i)

```
// int x;
if ( x > 10 ) {
  x = x - 1;
}
```

(ii)

```
// int x;
if ( x > 10 ) {
  x = x + 1;
}
```

Figure 1: Exam question on reversibility.

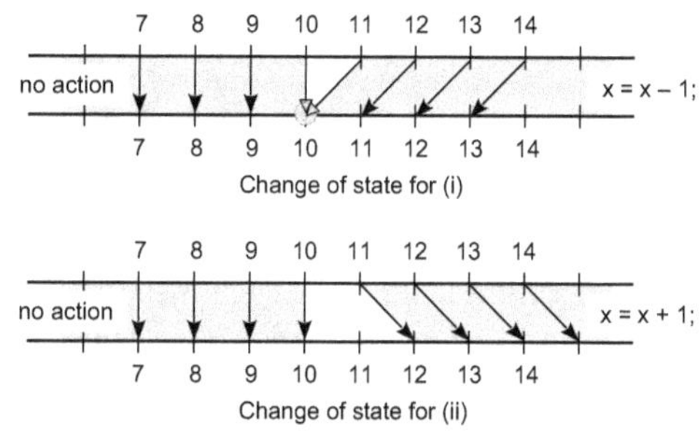

Figure 2: Depiction of the general effect of the two code fragments on the value of state variable x.

The code block inside each conditional statement is simple and clearly reversible. Adding or subtracting a constant value is easily reversed, as explained in the introduction to the task. The key insight required to analyse the reversibility of the given statements is that there are two flows of control whose outcomes may overlap: the *if* path, when the condition is true and the *else* or empty path when the condition is false.

Figure 2 illustrates how these two paths "merge" or "separate". When there is no overlap, as in conditional statement (ii), the code is reversible. To reverse the code we may need to adjust the condition so that it reflects the change of state of its variables. When the two paths overlap, as in conditional statement (i), the code is not reversible for that set of values, for example for the value 10 which may result from two original states of x: 10 and 11. Thus, the statement is not reversible as a whole.

[2]both versions available at https://goo.gl/YRXzqk

Note it may be possible to reverse the effect of the conditional statement for the range of values that do not overlap. For example, if x's current value is 15 we could deduce or calculate its original value to be 16. Similarly, if x's current value is 8 we could deduce its original value was still 8. Thus, to recognise reversibility we need to focus on the borderline cases.

3.2 Data collection

We collected the exam answers from two first year CS undergraduate cohorts at an Italian and an Australian university. Each exam paper was anonymised and digitized prior to analysis.

Cohort UN1, comprising 73 students from the University of Udine in Italy, had attended a full year programming course (24 weeks: overall about 80 hours of lessons + 60 hours of Lab and classroom exercises) following a functional-first approach with Scheme (functional programming) and then Java (imperative programming and basic notions of object-orientation). The reversibility task included 6 questions—only the first two of which are anlysed here—and was the first one of four exercises, worth 25% of the marks.

Cohort UN2 consisted of 155 students from the University of Adelaide, Australia, who had taken a 12-week course focused on object-oriented programming in C++. The task was part of the fourth exam question, worth 5% of the marks.

The Australian cohort was mixed in terms of tertiary instruction: 71% have already completed a 12-week introductory programming course, thus having a full year of instruction (but only 56% took the courses in consecutive semesters). For the rest of the cohort, this was their first programming course (and semester) of undergraduate study, having acquired basic programming skills prior to starting their degree. It may also be noticed that 17% of students were repeating this course as it is core to their degrees.

Incidentally, both cohorts did not present remarkable demographic differences, and the percentage of female students—about 6% overall—was too low in order for an analysis from the gender perspective to have any statistical significance.

3.3 Analysis

As a first step, after classifying students' selected options (reversible or not) and their code or explanations as correct/incorrect, we carried out a straightforward quantitative analysis to measure the percentages of students who had mastered the task.

However, from a pedagogical perspective it is important to dig a little deeper into the reasons that caused students to fail. Thus, in order to gain insight into latent misconceptions, we also conducted a qualitative analysis addressing their two answers in combination.

To this aim, we identified the SOLO taxonomy [1] as an appropriate instrument, since it has been widely used to classify the answers to code reading and writing questions [9, 14, 17]. Shuhidan et al., for instance, recommend "the SOLO Taxonomy, to measure the novices' understanding of the particular concepts tested. The SOLO Taxonomy provides a means of evaluating cognitive or mental models, to see if the novices are able to make connections between what they have learnt" [14, p. 152]. In other words, besides classifying a task at a given level, it helps to observe the progress made by each student towards that target level.

We considered the proposed task to be at the topmost *Relational* level for novice programmers, and we mapped each student's pair of answers into SOLO categories in accordance with the criteria described in Table 1. Two of the researchers assessed all students' answers and performed a deductive content analysis [10] based on the four SOLO categories. Overall, the rate of agreement was about 93%. By considering each category separately, the percentage of agreement varied from about 95% (*Multistructural* level) to almost 99% (*Prestructural* level). Cohen's Kappa measure of the intercoder reliability was in the range 0.83–0.96. Eventually, further discussion led to the final classification summarized in Table 2, which shall be discussed in the next section.

Table 1: SOLO Classification guidelines.

SOLO Level	Conditional statement and state
Prestructural (P)	poor answer that shows lack of understanding of the task, poor programing skills or misinterpretation of what reversiblity means.
Unistructural (U)	partial understanding of reversibility; student makes a simplistic attempt to reverse the code inside the if.
Multistructural (M)	clear understanding of the reversibility task, but one of the two exercises fail in some way, such as being able to correctly reverse the second conditional statement, but failing to identify or explain the overlap between the two paths.
Relational (R)	concept well understood and applied correctly to both questions: they explain the overlap for (i) and provide code to reverse (ii).

Table 2: Distribution of students' answers in SOLO levels.

SOLO Level	Udine (UN1)	Adelaide (UN2)
(4) Relational	38.4%	23.2%
(3) Multistructural	43.8%	34.8%
(2) Unistructural	12.3%	15.5%
(1) Prestructural	5.5%	16.8%
(0) *Empty*	0.0%	9.7%
SOLO mean	3.15	2.45

4 RESULTS

4.1 Quantitative analysis

Table 3 shows the rate of successful answers for the task presented in Figure 1. As we can see, a similar percentage of students in the two cohorts, close to 50%, selected the correct option relative to code fragment (i), although the Italian cohort (UN1) provided more accurate justifications. Note that in the think-aloud investigation [5], based on a small sample, only 20% of the subjects were able to recognise part (i) as not reversible. Thus, contrary to the outcome of that previous study, it seems that reasoning about reversibility is within the reach of novice programmers after 12/24 weeks of instruction.

Table 3: Percentages of correct answers to the question "is this code reversible?" and of accurate justifications.

	(i) not reversible	explains overlap	(ii) reversible	correct code
UN1	49.3%	39.7%	97.3%	89.0%
UN2	49.0%	27.7%	83.2%	51.0%

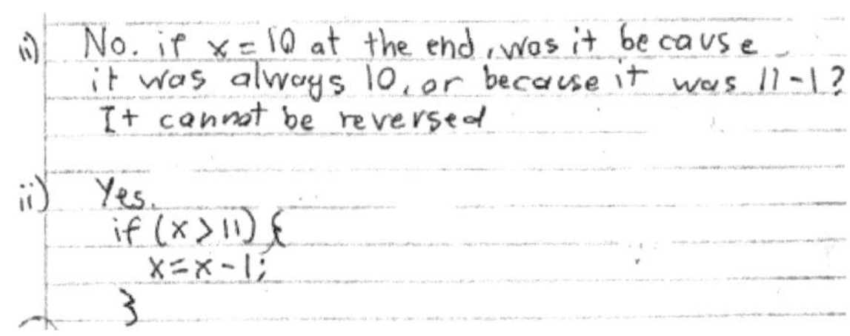

Figure 3: Answer pertaining to the Relational level.

4.2 Qualitative analysis

We next move to the SOLO analysis. Table 2 summarizes the results of classifying the answers according to the criteria outlined in Table 1. The means reported in the bottom row are obtained by assigning values in the range 1–4 to SOLO levels as shown in Table 2, and then averaging over these values. Relational answers, which are correct and accurate on both questions as in the example shown in Figure 3, amount to 28.1% of all the rated sheets. As educators, however, we are particularly interested in identifying common patterns which could reveal misconceptions that prevent students from reaching the Relational level. Thus, in the rest of this section we characterize the range of non-Relational answers, from the lowest level up.

Prestructural answers. Prestructural answers (13.2% overall) have poor code or vague explanations and mostly indicate insufficient preparation for a programming exam. However, a few of them illustrate some lack of understanding of the reversibility concept. The leftmost example of Figure 4 shows how a student approached the task by flipping the condition "x > 10" to "x < 10", which indicates a very superficial grasp of reversibility. Other students attempted to reverse the action inside the original code as shown in the middle excerpt of Figure 4. A couple of students tried to prove it can be reversed for all values by including a for loop in their code as shown in the last example of Figure 4. These three samples are representative of the answers of students who master the C++ syntax, but do not yet have a clear idea of the corresponding semantics.

Unistructural answers. Answers at this SOLO level (14.5%) suggest that students' focus was limited to the block inside the conditional statement, but they ignored the control flow. Figure 5 shows a few variations of this theme. Students just reported the command they modified, or copied the rest of the "if" conditional as provided. Most of them answered "Yes" to both question as in three of the four samples in Figure 5. In the case where the answer to question (i) is "No", however, the logic is flawed as there is no risk of underflow; moreover, the second part fits the pattern described above.

Multistructural answers. Answers at this level (37.7%) are less naive, but still unsatisfactory in some way. Most of them fell into two patterns. In the first case (23.2% of the sheets) the students deemed both conditionals to be reversible, as in the example on the left in Figure 6. They changed the assignment, as seen in the Unistructural level, but they also adjusted the condition accordingly. As a result, the answer for (ii) is correct, whereas that for (i) misses the data flow overlap.

In the answers matching the second pattern (11.0%) the students realised that the typical naive solution classified at the Unistructural level would not work with code (i) when the initial value of x is 11. Nevertheless, they failed to identify the overlap as the key reason for code (i) not to be reversible. One such example can be seen in the middle of Figure 6, and a more explicit illustration of this way of reasoning about item (i) appears in the last excerpt. Moreover, this group of students did not adjust the condition of code (ii). Note that the code they wrote is not incorrect—as if x's original value was 11, it would be changed to 12, which is still greater than 10—but it is unclear if they were actually aware of this or not.

There remain about 3.5% of the answers which do not conform to the two patterns outlined above. In a couple of them, for example, we can also find non-legitimate pieces of code introducing a new variable to save the initial value of x in order to restore it directly, after the execution of the given conditional statement.

5 DISCUSSION

We now revisit the research questions in light of the results presented in the previous section.

To answer our first question—Can novice programmers reverse a conditional statement?—we need to look at how many students succeeded in reversing part (ii). According to the data presented in Section 4.1, 63% of students were able to reverse the code correctly. However, this figure includes all variants of code that return to the original state, including those using the condition "x > 10" without modifications. On the other hand, if we only take into account the Multistructural answers where the condition is adjusted to reflect the change of state, plus those at the Relational level then only 51.3% were able to reverse the code.

As to the second question—How comprehensively can novice programmers envisage the impact of conditionals in state variables?—we have addressed this issue through the lens of the SOLO taxonomy. Since both the code and the answers implied by the assigned task are brief, our focus has been on students' awareness of the two alternate execution paths, and in the quality of their explanations.

It is worth observing that a SOLO mean of 2.67, across the two cohorts, is similar to or above those resulting from other studies which apply this taxonomy to assess first year undergraduate performance. Sheard et al. [13], in particular, classified students' reading skills relative to short code fragments to swap the values of two variables (*swap*) and to check if an array is sorted (*loop*). They report mean scores of 2.39 for the *swap* question and 2.15 for the *loop* one. As a further example, Shuhidan et al. [14] investigated on students' ability to write a piece of code to compute the min/max integers stored in an array, and their findings correspond to a SOLO mean of 2.52. Note that in our study both the reversibility concept and the task were completely unfamiliar to the students. Hence,

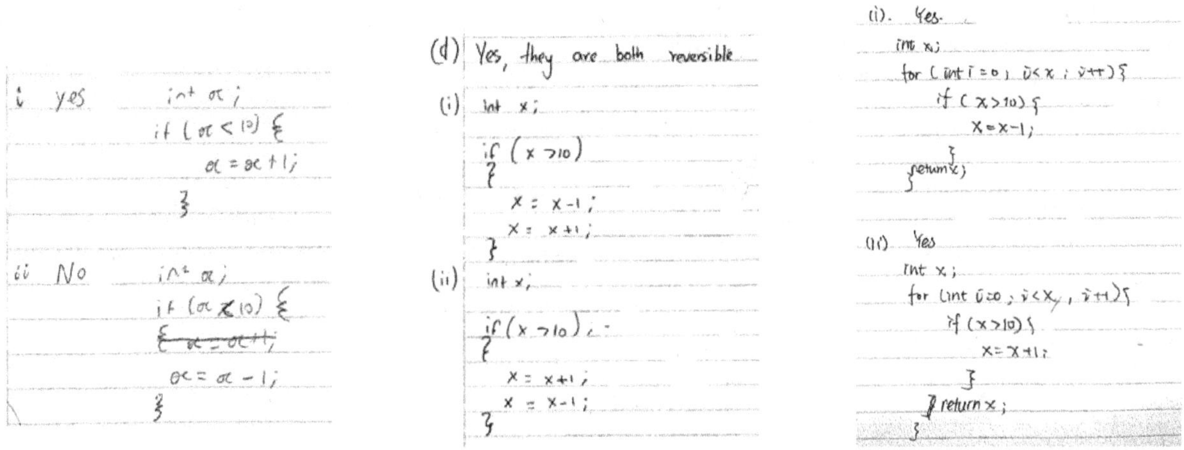

Figure 4: Examples of Prestructural answers, denoting serious misconceptions of either reversibility or program behaviour.

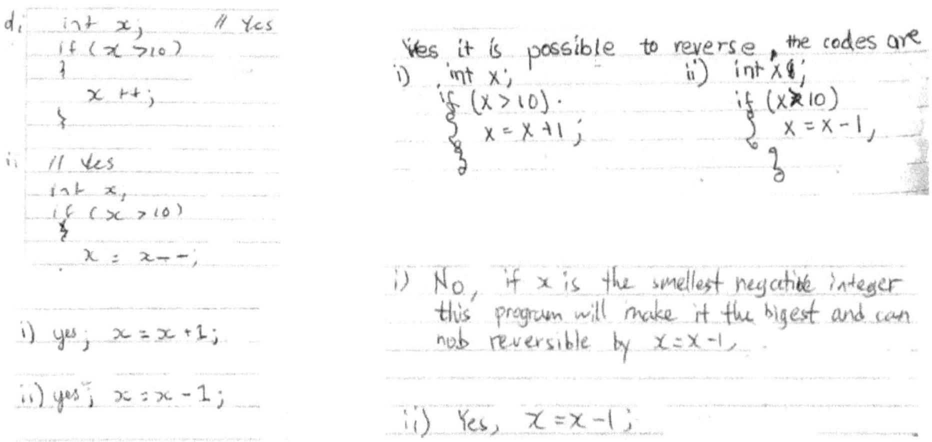

Figure 5: Examples of Unistructural answers, usually being concerned only with the assignment inside the *if* branch.

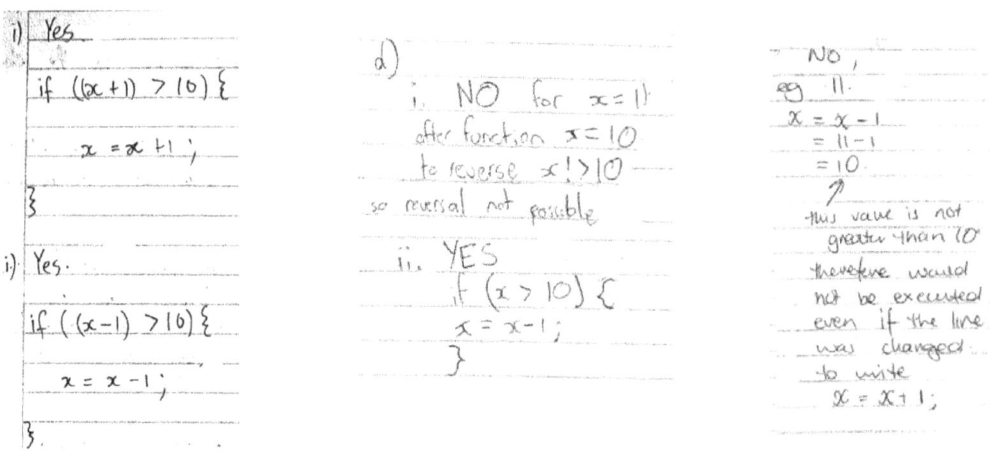

Figure 6: Examples of Multistructural answers, failing to analyse all the implications of part (i) convincingly.

relative to other more common tasks, which students have been exposed to and received feedback during instruction, our findings have exceeded the expectations, especially for the Italian cohort, who scored a SOLO mean of 3.15.

Also in terms of understanding reversibility, both student cohorts performed better than those in the range investigated by Teague and Lister [16]. After 12/24 weeks of class instruction, indeed, only 32% of their best class—and 25% on average—were successful in reversing a loop which rotates the values in an array.

Limitations. When students decided the code is reversible, they had just to provide the 'undoing' code, from which we cannot infer their reasoning. Thus, even if the code for part (ii) is correct, some may still have had a shallow understanding of reversibility.

Two possible sources of bias for the Australian cohort are the time constraints and the low percentage of marks assigned to the task (5% of exam score). Both may have led some students to skip over it, as suggested by the number of empty answers, and others to rush their answers in order to complete more familiar questions.

Implications for educators. This work demonstrates that the concept of reversibility and low-ceiling tasks such as those proposed here can serve as instruments to explore program comprehension at a fine-grained level, and then can be exploited as opportunities for students to improve their higher-order thinking skills.

When providing feedback on students' code, it is not sufficient to point out how it can be adjusted to meet the intended purpose, but we should also focus on their reasoning. For example, in class activities we could ask them to explain how their programs behave so that we can observe/revise their mental models and support abstraction. This would be especially helpful to those students who are close to developing a correct solution. In these respects, it is also important to understand what type of instruction may be appropriate in order to make students aware of the potential 'confluences' between the alternate data flows arising from a conditional statement.

As a final remark, a possible way to help students explore their reasoning is to propose peer review activities about reversing or debugging code, again with a focus on explaining the work done.

6 CONCLUSIONS

Although most novice programmers are able to explain the operational semantics of a conditional statement, recent work indicated that many students may fail to consider comprehensively the impact of this program construct on the state of the affected variables.

To contribute additional insights into this issue, we have investigated in depth the students' ability to reverse short code fragments. In particular, two first year undergraduate cohorts from different countries were asked to complete a reasoning and coding task on reversibility of simple "if" statements as part of their final exam paper. The concept, unfamiliar to the students, was introduced through examples presented in the exam paper itself.

In spite of the minimal data flow overlap, 28% of the students did realize that different flows (decrementing a variable versus doing nothing) can result in the same final state. In addition, more than half appeared to be definitely able to devise correct code for undoing a *reversible* conditional statement. Besides, it is encouraging that only 13% of the students exhibited a serious lack of understanding of the reversibility concept and/or the *if* semantics.

We are currently extending our investigation on reversibility to cover different code fragments, namely conditionals with both branches made explicit ("if-else" statements) and simple loops, while also looking for opportunities to include other student cohorts. This work has addressed one specific aspect of program comprehension—program state in connection with reversibility—and, as a future perspective, it may be interesting to design and evaluate tasks that help students to explore other aspects related to efficiency, testing and maintenance, code complexity and code security.

REFERENCES

[1] J. B. Biggs and K. F Collis. 1982. *Evaluating the quality of learning: The SOLO taxonomy.* Academic Press, New York, NY, USA.
[2] R. Bornat, S. Dehnadi, and D. Barton. 2012. Observing Mental Models in Novice Programmers. In *Proc. 24th Annual Workshop of the Psychology of Programming Interest Group.* Article 6, 7 pages.
[3] Ibrahim Cetin. 2015. Student's Understanding of Loops and Nested Loops in Computer Programming: An APOS Theory Perspective. *Canadian Journal of Science, Mathematics and Technology Education* 15, 2 (Feb. 2015), 155–170. https://doi.org/10.1080/14926156.2015.1014075
[4] Yuliya Cherenkova, Daniel Zingaro, and Andrew Petersen. 2014. Identifying Challenging CS1 Concepts in a Large Problem Dataset. In *Proceedings of the 45th ACM Technical Symposium on Computer Science Education (SIGCSE '14).* ACM, New York, NY, USA, 695–700. https://doi.org/10.1145/2538862.2538966
[5] Cruz Izu, Cheryl Pope, and Amali Weerasinghe. 2017. On the Ability to Reason About Program Behaviour: A Think-Aloud Study. In *Proceedings of the 2017 ACM Conference on Innovation and Technology in Computer Science Education (ITiCSE '17).* ACM, New York, NY, USA, 305–310. https://doi.org/10.1145/3059009.3059036
[6] F.J. King, L. Goodson, and F. Rohani. 1998. Higher order thinking skills: Definitions, strategies, assessment. Florida State University - Center for Advancement of Learning and Assessment. (1998). http://www.cala.fsu.edu/files/higher_order_thinking_skills.pdf (accessed Nov. 2017).
[7] Raymond Lister. 2011. Concrete and other neo-piagetian forms of reasoning in the novice programmer. *Conf. Res. Pract. Inf. Technol. Ser.* 114 (2011), 9–18.
[8] Raymond Lister, Beth Simon, Errol Thompson, Jacqueline L. Whalley, and Christine Prasad. 2006. Not Seeing the Forest for the Trees: Novice Programmers and the SOLO Taxonomy. In *Proceedings of the 11th Annual SIGCSE Conference on Innovation and Technology in Computer Science Education (ITICSE '06).* ACM, New York, NY, USA, 118–122. https://doi.org/10.1145/1140124.1140157
[9] Mike Lopez, Jacqueline Whalley, Phil Robbins, and Raymond Lister. 2008. Relationships Between Reading, Tracing and Writing Skills in Introductory Programming. In *Proc. 4th Int. Workshop on Computing Education Research (ICER '08).* ACM, New York, NY, USA, 101–112. https://doi.org/10.1145/1404520.1404531
[10] Philipp Mayring. 2014. *Qualitative content analysis: theoretical foundation, basic procedures and software solution.* Klagenfurt, Austria.
[11] Nancy Pennington. 1987. Comprehension Strategies in Programming. In *Empirical Studies of Programmers: Second Workshop,* Gary M. Olson, Sylvia Sheppard, and Elliot Soloway (Eds.). Ablex Publishing Corp., Norwood, NJ, USA, 100–113.
[12] Noa Ragonis and Mordechai Ben-Ari. 2005. On Understanding the Statics and Dynamics of Object-oriented Programs. In *Proceedings of the 36th SIGCSE Technical Symposium on Computer Science Education (SIGCSE '05).* ACM, New York, NY, USA, 226–230. https://doi.org/10.1145/1047344.1047425
[13] Judy Sheard, Angela Carbone, Raymond Lister, Beth Simon, Errol Thompson, and Jacqueline L. Whalley. 2008. Going SOLO to Assess Novice Programmers. In *Proceedings of the 13th Annual Conference on Innovation and Technology in Computer Science Education (ITiCSE '08).* ACM, New York, NY, USA, 209–213. https://doi.org/10.1145/1384271.1384328
[14] Shuhaida Shuhidan, Margaret Hamilton, and Daryl D'Souza. 2009. A Taxonomic Study of Novice Programming Summative Assessment. In *Proc. 11th Australasian Conf. on Computing Education - Volume 95 (ACE '09).* Australian Computer Society, Inc., Darlinghurst, Australia, Australia, 147–156.
[15] Peter Sutherland. 1999. The application of Piagetian and Neo-Piagetian ideas to further and higher education. *International Journal of Lifelong Education* 18, 4 (1999), 286–294. https://doi.org/10.1080/026013799293702
[16] Donna Teague and Raymond Lister. 2014. Programming: Reading, Writing and Reversing. In *Proceedings of the 2014 Conference on Innovation and Technology in Computer Science Education (ITiCSE '14).* ACM, New York, NY, USA, 285–290. https://doi.org/10.1145/2591708.2591712
[17] Jacqueline Whalley, Tony Clear, Phil Robbins, and Errol Thompson. 2011. Salient elements in novice solutions to code writing problems. *Conferences in Research and Practice in Information Technology Series* 114 (2011), 37–45.

Game Development with a Serious Focus

Devorah Kletenik*
Brooklyn College, City University of New York
kletenik@sci.brooklyn.cuny.edu

Deborah Sturm*
College of Staten Island, City University of New York
Deborah.Sturm@csi.cuny.edu

ABSTRACT

We report our experience teaching elective game development courses at two colleges at a public university. Over the past nine years these courses have been taught in a variety of languages on several platforms. As the courses evolved we introduced serious games with game-based-learning as a focus for the projects and ultimately offered a special topics elective in serious game development. In this paper, we discuss the merits of using serious games as a focus in game programming, including the benefits for students without a strong interest in gaming. We also describe the novel restructuring of one college's Computer Science elective sequence in response to recommendations from students, alumni, and an advisory board of computing professionals. By introducing 200-level electives, students are able to sample advanced topics including game development early in their academic sequence. This has led to involving more students in game-based undergraduate research which can result in increased interest and retention in Computer Science. We discuss our curriculum design and lessons learned including challenges and successes, and data from student surveys indicating student motivation and engagement.

CCS CONCEPTS

• **Social and professional topics → Model curricula; Computer science education;** • **Applied computing → Computer games;**

KEYWORDS

game development, serious games, game-based learning, curriculum design

ACM Reference Format:

Devorah Kletenik and Deborah Sturm. 2018. Game Development with a Serious Focus. In *SIGCSE '18: The 49th ACM Technical Symposium on Computer Science Education, February 21–24, 2018, Baltimore , MD, USA.* ACM, New York, NY, USA, 6 pages. https://doi.org/10.1145/3159450.3159588

1 INTRODUCTION

Many Computer Science curricula now include a course in game development; such courses have been shown to motivate and engage a wide range of students. [3, 5, 26]. Game development has also been incorporated into other courses and has been used to teach the introductory programming course [1, 4, 9, 23], Software Engineering [7, 25], Artificial Intelligence [2, 34]), Computer Graphics [33] and other topics (e.g. [22]). Game development courses typically cover at minimum, game genres, sprites, movement, assets, animation, collisions, and user interaction. Additional topics include AI, effects, shaders, physics, and 3D development. They also usually include a major project that, because of its size, is often designed and coded as a team. In our experience in teaching game development we found that it is useful to have a common project theme. We proposed that the students create serious games with a purpose, specifically those that employ game-based learning techniques [16] to teach a college-level topic. Part of the project included playtesting and assessing whether the game met learning outcomes.

In this paper, we discuss the game development courses at two senior colleges of City University of New York (CUNY). CUNY is the public university system of New York City and the largest urban university system in the United States; we focus on two senior colleges of CUNY, The College of Staten Island (henceforth, "Institution 1") and Brooklyn College ("Institution 2").

We first review other attempts to teach game development courses both with and without a serious game focus. We discuss platforms and languages that we tried in our courses, along with our final recommendation for the use of Unity. We describe the curriculum of the courses and list the required deliverables. Finally we present data from student surveys.

2 BACKGROUND

Game development courses are popular at many colleges because they engage students by allowing them to use their programming skills in real-world applications that interest them. The use of games motivates students across a range of courses, from introductory programming through research capstones [26] and many college now include courses in game programming [4, 15, 27, 29]. The field is so large that at this point, it is now a concentration within the CS major [10].

Game programming courses have been taught using a variety of different languages. Doss et al. [14] present a number of them, including XNA, Game Maker, and Scratch. More recently, Dickson [13] and Ivanov [19] reported on the use of Unity in game design courses.

Serious games is the term for games that accomplish a goal in addition to entertainment. Examples of serious games include games used for crowd-sourcing problem solving (e.g. Foldit[1]), recruitment (e.g. America's Army[2]), simulations (e.g. Zero Hour: America's Medic[3]), or to encourage exercising (e.g. Wii-Fit[4]). Probably the

*Both authors contributed equally to the paper

SIGCSE '18, February 21–24, 2018, Baltimore , MD, USA

ACM ISBN 978-1-4503-5103-4/18/02...$15.00
https://doi.org/10.1145/3159450.3159588

[1] https://fold.it/portal
[2] https://www.americasarmy.com/
[3] http://www.virtualheroes.biz/zerohour
[4] http://wiifit.com

most popular subset of serious games is games used for education, or Game Based Learning (GBL). Computer games for education (Digital GBL, or DGBL) have been popular since the dawn of personal computers and are used in a variety of fields and levels of education. We describe our experiences in using serious games, specifically DGBL, as the focus of a game development course.

Involving students as creators of educational games has a long history. As early as 1992, Ritchie and Dodge report on their creation of an adventure game authoring template that allowed middle-school students to design educational games in a variety of disciplines [28].

More recently, Chaffin and Barnes [8] presented a detailed informative paper about their creation of a serious games course, including a report on successes and failures in their pilot version. Kapralos wrote a comprehensive paper about a serious game course that was offered as part of a Game Development and Entrepreneurship undergraduate degree program [20] and followed up in 2015 in [21]. A difference in our approach is that students who took the serious games courses described in the aforementioned work already had a solid background in creating games. We, on the other hand, recommend offering a serious games course at an early stage of the major, or *as a replacement for* the game development course. In a degree program that offers only one game development course, we have found that a project-based learning approach to the course centered around serious games has been successful.

Brown et al. [6] describe a capstone project in creating educational video games. This project was offered to Computer Science, Education, and Digital Media students in the hopes of creating multidisciplinary teams. The games were created using Scratch, and the emphasis was on non-technical "soft skills," such as teamwork and presenting. This differs from our approach, which is to use serious games to teach a complete course in game programming.

3 WHY SERIOUS GAMES?

We identify the following benefits to focusing on serious games in a game development course rather than focusing on recreational games:

(1) It offers students a meaningful goal for their project. It is our belief that students engaged in learning that has a socially-minded component are more engaged and more motivated, and develop the perspective to think in bigger pictures. As one student commented, *"Before this class, I honestly thought games were a waste of time. I had no idea that you could use games for good. [I learned] that you could accomplish a lot with games."*
(2) It offers students a clear focus for their work, giving students a clear place to begin and a means to structure their game.
(3) It encourages creativity and discourages recycling code from online tutorials, articles, assets and scripts.
(4) We hypothesize that this focus appeals to non-gamers, including some women. Non-gamers who take game design/ programming courses are often at a disadvantage due to their limited exposure to the medium. It has been observed that there are fundamental differences in the ways that male and female players play computer games: for example, males tend to play games more frequently and for longer durations than do their female peers [11]. In our experience, our gamer students tend to be predominantly male. As a result, female students can feel marginalized from the beginning. We suggest that the use of serious games levels the playing field.
(5) It can serve as a hook to engage undergraduate students in research. Involving undergraduates in research contributes to student retention, interest in careers in STEM, and graduate school enrollment [24, 30]. However, it can be challenging to attract students to research. We find that game development is a major draw for student research: it's engaging, fun, and appeals to what they already know. In our approach, we recommend introducing research-based games early in the curriculum and to encourage students to design games that could be used as part of a research project.

4 EARLY ELECTIVES

The NSF's Integrative Computing Education and Research (ICER) Initiative recommends five strategic initiatives; the third Strategic Initiative includes: "Improve retention by recasting introductory courses as pumps, not filters" [12]. These recommendations motivated restructuring the elective sequence at Institution 1 [31].

These changes were further informed by several issues reported by the Departmental Outcomes Assessment Committee during a periodic review of assessment data. Several constituencies, including graduating seniors, alumni, and computing professionals, recommended introducing new courses to keep pace with the rapidly changing computing field. They specifically mentioned Game Development as an example of a course that would be helpful to graduates.

As a result of this recommendation, in 2007, Institution 1 introduced several new electives at the 200-level that only required CS1 as a prerequisite. By positioning them early in the major sequence, advanced and applied topics were introduced earlier in the major in line with the ICER recommendation to create "pump" rather than "filter" courses. The early electives include Hacking Revealed, Robotics, Web Database Applications, Introductory Game Development and Introduction to High Performance Computing. In order to make the coursework more practically oriented and lower the barrier to entry, courses such as Game Development make use of pre-built scripts and prefabs.

The restructuring of the elective sequence resulted in three positive outcomes: (1) potential Computer Science majors can sample advanced and/or applied topics early in their academic career; (2) students from other disciplines can take interesting and popular courses without completing several prerequisites; (3) Computer Science students are able to take electives (two early electives = one full elective) earlier and not overload themselves with several courses in their last semester. Additionally, moving the game electives earlier in the pipeline allows students to be hooked and begin working on research immediately, rather than waiting until they complete a 400-level course, when they are already poised to graduate. We discuss some of our student research projects in Section 7.2.

Game development was a perfect way to engage students in programming. As one student commented, *" This course had me more motivated to program without really realizing that I was programming. Meaning, that I got so immersed in the creation process that I stopped thinking about programming as this formal entity that is presented in other classes. It almost felt like I was taking an art class and I was looking for new techniques to create something in front of me, when in fact later I realized I had written hundreds of lines of code. . . . It was one of the few classes where you literally saw your code come to life."*

5 CURRICULUM AND DELIVERABLES

Our game programming with a serious games focus at both colleges have a similar curriculum and for ease of presentation, we discuss both curricula as one. We begin with an overview of known games with a purpose. We discuss and play several serious games including Foldit and Eyewire[5]. We then showcase game-based learning games such as Oregon Trail, Zoombinis[6] and Spent[7]. We concluded the semester with TED talks by game designer Jane McGonigal[8,9], which demonstrate the power of serious games.

We used James Paul Gee's Principles of Learning as a framework for how to design the learning components of the games [16]. Dr. Gee proposes designing games to produce "Empowered Learners." We emphasized his principles including co-design, customizing, identity and presenting well-ordered problems. We emphasized that the games should be pleasantly frustrating so that the player wants to play (i.e. learn) and persist. The game shouldn't be too easy so that the player is bored and stops playing, nor should it be too difficult to avoid quitting because of frustration. Instead the game should get more difficult at a pleasant pace to increase learning and persistence. The feedback to the player should be positive when learning is occurring and not overly negative when the player doesn't succeed. We also suggested his "on demand" information and "just-in-time" instructions. Our rubrics for peer-evaluation asked about whether the game incorporated these principles and whether it was working for the player.

The student group assignments were organized around designing, creating, and evaluating a serious game. The first group assignment was to research a game-based learning game, test it and report on its objectives and learning outcomes by completing a provided rubric. Each group then chose a college-level topic to teach and a genre. The next deliverable was a pitch to their peers where they also presented how each learning objective would be assessed. They then prepared a game design document (based on a template) with most of the chosen assets, including graphics, music, sound effects. Students demoed the project to their peers again after completing a teaching and assessment level. We didn't dictate content or genres but we encouraged students to design games to teach material at the introductory to advanced college level. We specified that each game have both teaching and assessment components. We also encouraged including high scores (using PlayerPrefs in Unity) to show the player their progress. The penultimate week of the semester was reserved to give each group a chance to evaluate the games of all other groups, using the same game evaluation rubric that they used in the first assignment. The students then had the chance to incorporate the feedback that they received into their final game submissions.

Each group prepared pre-surveys to assess the prior knowledge of their players and post-surveys to test whether their game met their learning outcomes. For example the pre- and post- surveys for the Linear Algebra game had dot-product problems to fill in. The final project included the completed surveys with a report summarizing the results.

Our students produced an array of impressive serious games for education with educational content that spanned the fields of biology, chemistry, physics, health, English, foreign languages, music, computer science, math, and history. We present a list of our student projects (from students at both colleges) in Table 2.

6 DEVELOPMENT TOOLS - WHY UNITY?

There are many excellent free game development tools available and our introductory and advanced courses have been taught using a variety of environments. As organized by user interface, Scratch and Appinventor are both visual. XNA and Xcode/objective C are primarily code-based. The Unity game engine is the most integrated in that the visual environment can be manipulated using drag-and-drop (including code) yet the more advanced developer can code their own scripts.

For the 200-level course we initially used Scratch and Appinventor. These are both excellent at conveying gaming principles without getting sidetracked by syntax and deployment issues. We later added XNA and Xcode using Objective C. In both cases we gave the student templates to get their projects started in this introductory course. In the 400-level electives we used XNA and Xcode/Objective C. Student feedback at both levels was overwhelmingly in favor of XNA and this enthusiasm was matched by stellar projects. However, when Microsoft stopped supporting XNA we researched other options. Unity was an appealing choice since it is used to produce professional games and can still be programmed by relative beginners. It uses a combination of a drag-and-drop user interface and C# scripting, which enables students of all levels to develop games; it supports both 2D and 3D game creation; and it can create games for multiple platforms, including Web players and mobile apps. Students are very aware of the commercial success of Unity and were excited and motivated to learn the interface. The Mac and Windows versions are very similar and there were few deployment issues. In our post-course survey, students unanimously reported that they enjoyed Unity. In their list of reasons, they included that they found it easy to learn and that they liked coding with the C# scripts.

At Institution 2, a game design course has also taught using Processing. Processing is based on Java, and was therefore easy for our students (all of whom had taken a course in Java) to learn. It easily supports graphics and is useful for highly visual programs. It also supports many external libraries (such as the `minim` audio library that one group of students used for a music-based game). However, it is not built for game development and many students found it clunky and difficult to use for that purpose. Due to student demand, we switched to Unity for the game programming course.

[5]http://eyewire.org/explore
[6]https://itunes.apple.com/us/app/zoombinis/id961739806?mt=8
[7]http://playspent.org/
[8]https://www.ted.com/talks/jane_mcgonigal_gaming_can_make_a_better_world
[9]https://www.ted.com/talks/jane_mcgonigal_the_game_that_can_give_you_10_extra_years_of_life

Week #	Topics covered	Student assignment/deliverables
1	Intro to game development, serious games, principles of GBL	game evaluation
2	Intro to Unity (assets, sprites, prefabs, scenes, gravity, tags)	
3	movement, user controls, transformation & rotations, velocity	game concept document "pitch" (and peer evaluation)
4	collision detection, audio effects & volume control, spawning	
5	sprite sheets & animations	
6	text, scenes	midterm
7	buttons and time	first submission of game (and peer evaluation)
8	data persistence: static classes	
9-10	data persistence, particle systems, Google Analytics	
11	2.5D games, models & textures, camera projections	final games due
12	peer evaluation of final games	submission of pre-/post-tests for review, lab assignments due
13	final review, summary of serious games	evaluations (peer) and pre- and post-test evaluations
14	final	final projects due with user data (scores on pre- and post- tests)

Table 1: Curriculum and Student Deliverables

Game name	Topic	Genre
American Revolution	History	Turn-based Strat.
Balance	physics	Physics puzzle
Binary Battleship	binary numbers	Turn-based Tact.
Egg Bash!	decimal ↔ binary	Drag/Drop
The GREat Escape	GRE vocabulary	Platform
HangukeoBaeUgi	Korean characters	FPS
The Happiness Crusade	drugs & alcohol	RPG
Khemicalz	chemistry	Puzzle-platform
Loop()	programming	Puzzle
Lunario	chemistry	Platform
Math Tac Toe	vector operations	Strategy
Miss Match	pattern matching	Platform
Night Of The Cancer	cancer facts	Action-adventure
Orchestroids	pitch	3D FPS
Recycle Hero	recycling	Platform
Siege of Bastogne	WWII history	Tower Defense
Spell Invaders	homonyms	FPS

Table 2: Student Game Projects

Inst.	Course Title	Level	Environment / Lang.
2	Game Development	400	Processing
2	Game Programming (Serious games)	400	Unity
1	Intro Game Devel.	200	XNA (C#) XCode (Objective C)
1	Serious Game Devel.	200	Unity
1	Advanced Game Devel.	400	Unity

Table 3: Languages used in game courses at both colleges

7 STUDENT OUTCOMES

At the end of the most recent semester that this course was taught, students were given a survey measuring their attitude towards the course and its aims. Twelve out of the twenty-one students in Institution 1 and all thirty-six out of thirty-six in Institution 2 completed the survey. The results of the survey were anonymous. About half of the students in both courses preferred to create a serious game over one purely for entertainment. Three-quarters of the students in Institution 2 and over 90% in Institution 1 would be interested in creating a serious game for research. In both schools, almost all the students replied that they would recommend the course to a friend and that they enjoyed the use of Unity. In Table 4, we present all the questions responses.

We also gave an open-ended question as a follow-up for question #1: *Why did you enjoy creating a serious game or why would you have preferred to create one purely for entertainment?* Here is one representative response:

"A serious game is meaningful. When we were creating the game, we were thinking. We were thinking how to make people learn from our game and enjoy our game. Making a serious game is beneficial for the creator and players. Players learn stuff creators want to teach them. Creators learn those stuff while they create their games."

7.1 Non-gamer students

Most but not all of the students took the games courses because they already had an interest in games. Some of the non-gamers reported that developing a game with a purpose leveled the playing field for them. We hope that this serious focus will encourage more non-gamers to take the game development courses, especially women. The following are quote from female students who took the course: *"I preferred that the class focused on serious games. I'm not a game player at all. I never played video games or computer games as a child. I barely ever play games on my iPhone. Even if someone has not played many games, almost everyone has played an educational game at some point in their life (whether in school or at home). Therefore, being assigned a serious game made the task more relatable and less daunting. If we had to create an adventure game I would find it difficult to figure out all the concepts involved because I don't have extensive experience playing video games."*

"I rarely play computer games. . . . I liked having the serious requirement for our group project. Giving the requirement of an educational game helped to focus the group and narrow down ideas. I think that in terms of gender parity, this is the way to go. In my experience, most

General questions about the course

	Institution 1, $n = 12$			Institution 2, $n = 36$		
Question	**yes**	**no**	**no opinion**	**yes**	**no**	**no opinion**
Did you prefer to have a serious focus instead one purely for fun?	41.7%	33.3%	25%	48.5%	27.3%	24.2%
Did you enjoy using Unity?	100%	0%	0%	93.9%	3.0%	3.0%
Would you be interested in creating a serious game for research?	91.7%	0%	8.3%	78.5%	3.0%	21.2%
Would you recommend this course to a friend?	100%	0%	0%	97.0%	0%	3%

Specific questions about Unity and the format of the course. Multiple choices allowed.

I liked Unity because	Inst. 1	Inst. 2
It's easy to learn	91.7%	57.58%
It's used in commercial games	41.7%	63.64%
It has the capability to do lots of cool things.	66.7%	78.788%
Other	8.3%	3.0%

What did you like about the format of the course?	Inst. 1	Inst. 2
Peer feedback	91.7%	36.7%
Working in groups	66.7%	51.5%
Using Unity	75%	93.9%
Testing the educational objective through pre- and post- tests	33.3%	21.2%
Having a Web player version	41.7%	54.5%

Table 4: Student responses to survey

educational games are fairly gender neutral, whereas many entertainment games are marketed towards men (e.g. first person shooter games that sell so well, but very rarely feature female protagonists)."

We suggest that using a serious games focus to the course will ultimately encourage more female students to be interested in the course and will offer a way to recruit more female students into a very heavily male-dominated course.

7.2 Student Research

As we pointed out in Sections 3 and 4, one major goal of both focusing on serious games and positioning this course as an early elective is to use the course as a hook to involve students in research. We have successfully recruited students who enjoyed the course to engage in research in serious games, including in the creation of two games for players on the autism spectrum. One game for the iPad assesses emotion recognition [32]; the second is a Kinect game that assesses and encourages collaborative learning [17]. For each we are working with domain experts from our Psychology department. One novel aspect of this project is that during the design phase, we are getting feedback from college students on the autism spectrum. Another area of undergraduate research in serious games was in gamifying the statistics lab for the Psychology department. The students collaborated with the instructors to design and develop a game-based set of labs that are currently in use in the course [18]. Yet another team is working on measuring the impact of game design elements such as storyline, sound effects, and power-ups in serious games for CS education. Students have presented their research at three game-based-learning conferences, one game expo, and at nine college undergraduate research conferences. One student was hired as as a Unity Developer for an educational gaming company based directly on his course and research experience.

8 LESSONS LEARNED

Our combined 9 years of teaching game development to over 200 students has led to several take-away lessons. In this discussion we include our experience in having students work on game-related undergraduate research projects during and following the courses.

8.1 Challenges

It is challenging to cover all the material and have the students produce a project they are proud of in a one semester course. We have had several students interested in continuing to work on independent study projects in order to deepen their knowledge of gaming and to get research experience. However if the game development course is an advanced elective, students will typically take the course in their last or penultimate semester. They graduate just as they are prepared for a substantive research project. As in other team-based projects, another issue that we deal with is managing team dynamics. In the institution where we have early electives, the intro to game development has two challenges that we needed to address. One is that some students only have the minimal prerequisite of introductory programming whereas others have completed data structures and object oriented development. We dealt with this disparity by making sure the teams were balanced so that no group had only beginners.

Finally we had to address assessment issues since the typical student did not have any background in this area. We provided examples of pre- and post-tests that meaningfully assess student learning, taught students how to create customized tests to assess the impact of their games, and had students submit their tests separately for our critique before using them for evaluation.

8.2 Successes

Although having students on varying technical levels was a challenge, having diverse teams was very beneficial. Students learned from each other especially when one team member was an expert in the subject being taught. For example in the group that produced the game to teach elements of Korean, the student who did not know Korean made sure that players learned the basics. Having students taking an early elective in game development allowing for early training in this area. Students were then more prepared to work on research projects spanning more than one semester. By choosing college level topics to teach, the students were able to easily find friends and relatives who did not know the topic and to then assess if their game taught the material. For example one group wrote a game to teach elements of Linear Algebra such as the dot product.

When a group demoed their game to the class, we assigned a different member of the class to play the game. In this way the group could see whether the game-play was intuitive. Also, towards the end of the semester, we told the students that we were asking our faculty colleagues to play the games to get their feedback. This motivated them to add polish to their games. Additionally, the level of the games produced rose significantly when we moved the web versions of the games onto the college server.

Another suggestion that we felt worked well was to allow our students to create an educational game on any topic of their choice. Our students enjoyed applying their unique backgrounds and interests to their projects, and created games on a broad array of topics.

We had excellent attendance (even when one section ran from 8 to 10:00 pm) and responsible team-work. Student satisfaction was high and most significantly, several students continued working on projects after the semester ended and presented their work at game-based learning conferences. We think that our experiences can offer guidance to other instructors who teach game development courses.

9 CONCLUSIONS

We found teaching game development with a serious focus to be a successful strategy in teaching gaming concepts, motivating high-level projects and generating interest in game-based research for both gamer and non-gamer students. The use of Unity in the course motivates students and provides a widely-used and flexible platform for game development. We successfully implemented the course in two colleges, and as a 200-level course in one institution. Having a 200-level game development course introduced students to this topic earlier in their academic careers and prepared interested students to work on game-based research projects. In the future, we would like to introduce the course at the 200-level at Institution 2 as well, and we recommend this to others who would like to try this course. Offering the course as an early elective helps flatten the curriculum, thereby making computer science more available for all.

REFERENCES

[1] Jessica D Bayliss. 2007. The effects of games in CS1-3. In *Microsoft Academic Days Conference on Game Development in Computer Science Education.* 59–63.

[2] Jessica D. Bayliss. 2012. Teaching game AI through Minecraft mods. In *Games Innovation Conference (IGIC), 2012 IEEE International.* IEEE, 1–4.

[3] Jessica D. Bayliss and Sean Strout. 2006. *Games as a Flavor of CS1.* Vol. 38. ACM.

[4] Katrin Becker and JR Parker. 2007. Serious games+ computer science= serious CS. *Journal of Computing Sciences in Colleges* 23, 2 (2007), 40–46.

[5] Kevin Bierre, Phil Ventura, Andrew Phelps, and Chris Egert. 2006. Motivating OOP by blowing things up: an exercise in cooperation and competition in an intro. Java programming course. In *SIGCSE Bulletin*, Vol. 38. ACM, 354–358.

[6] Quincy Brown, Frank Lee, and Suzanne Alejandre. 2009. Emphasizing soft skills and team development in an educational digital game design course. In *Proceedings of the 4th international Conference on Foundations of Digital Games.* ACM, 240–247.

[7] Nergiz Ercil Cagiltay. 2007. Teaching software engineering by means of computer-game development: Challenges and opportunities. *British Journal of Educational Technology* 38, 3 (2007), 405–415.

[8] Amanda Chaffin and Tiffany Barnes. 2010. Lessons from a course on serious games research and prototyping. In *Proceedings of the Fifth International Conference on the Foundations of Digital Games.* ACM, 32–39.

[9] Daniel C. Cliburn and Susan Miller. 2008. Games, stories, or something more traditional: the types of assignments college students prefer. *ACM SIGCSE Bulletin* 40, 1 (2008), 138–142.

[10] Ron Coleman, Mary Krembs, Alan Labouseur, and Jim Weir. 2005. Game design & programming concentration within the computer science curriculum. In *ACM SIGCSE Bulletin*, Vol. 37. ACM, 545–550.

[11] T.M. Connolly, E.A. Boyle, M.H. Stansfield, and T. Hainey. 2007. The potential of online games as a collaborative learning environment. *Journal of Advanced Technology for Learning* (2007).

[12] Judy Cushing, Rob Bryant, Genevieve Orr, Sylvia Spengler, Sharon Tuttle, and Ken Yasuhara. 2006. NSF'S Integrative Computing Education and Research initiative: whither the northwest. *J. of Computing Sciences in Colleges* 22, 2 (2006), 49–51.

[13] Paul E. Dickson. 2015. Using Unity to Teach Game Development: When You've Never Written a Game. In *Proceedings of the 2015 ACM Conference on Innovation and Technology in Computer Science Education.* ACM, 75–80.

[14] Kathlyn Doss, Valerie Juarez, Daniel Vincent, Peggy Doerschuk, and Jiangjiang Liu. 2011. Work in progress – A survey of popular game creation platforms used for computing education. In *Frontiers in Education Conference (FIE).* IEEE, F1H–1.

[15] Shannon Duvall. 2009. Creating a games class: a walkthrough. In *Proceedings of the 4th International Conference on Foundations of Digital Games.* ACM, 279–284.

[16] James Paul Gee. 2003. What video games have to teach us about learning and literacy. *Computers in Entertainment (CIE)* 1, 1 (2003), 20–20.

[17] Kristen Gillespie, Gabriel Goldstein, David Shane Smith, Ariana Riccio, Michael Kholodovsky, Cali Merendino, Stanislav Leskov, Rayan Arab, Hassan Elsherbini, Pavel Asanov, and Deborah Sturm. 2017. Connecting Through Kinect: Designing and Evaluating a Collaborative Game with and for Autistic Individuals. In *International Conference of Design, User Experience, and Usability.* Springer, 398–413.

[18] Evan Grandoit, Rose Bergdoll, Jenny Chan, Laura Rabin, Devorah Kletenik, Chelsea Chung, Wei Zhang, Ecem Olcum, Christopher Menedes, Ali Rishty, and Beliz Hazan. 2017. Comparison of learning efficiency with and without relevant extrinsic rewards in gamified psychological statistics classrooms. Northeast Conference for Teachers of Psychology (NECTOP) Poster Session.

[19] Lubomir Ivanov. 2015. 3D game development with unity in the computer science curriculum. *Journal of Computing Sciences in Colleges* 31, 1 (2015), 167–173.

[20] Bill Kapralos. 2012. A course on the design and development of serious games and virtual simulations. In *Games Innovation Conference (IGIC), IEEE Intl.* 1–4.

[21] Bill Kapralos, Stephanie Fisher, Jessica Clarkson, and Roland van Oostveen. 2015. A course on serious game design and development using an online problem-based learning approach. *Interactive Tech and Smart Education* 12, 2 (2015), 116–136.

[22] Stan Kurkovsky. 2009. Engaging students through mobile game development. *ACM SIGCSE Bulletin* 41, 1 (2009), 44–48.

[23] Scott Leutenegger and Jeffrey Edgington. 2007. A games first approach to teaching introductory programming. *ACM SIGCSE Bulletin* 39, 1 (2007), 115–118.

[24] David Lopatto. 2007. Undergraduate research experiences support science career decisions and active learning. *CBE-Life Sciences Education* 6, 4 (2007), 297–306.

[25] Manuel Palomo-Duarte, Juan Manuel Dodero, José Tomás Tocino, Antonio García-Domínguez, and Antonio Balderas. 2012. Competitive evaluation in a video game development course. In *Proceedings of the 17th ACM annual conference on Innovation and technology in computer science education.* ACM, 321–326.

[26] Ian Parberry, Timothy Roden, and Max B Kazemzadeh. 2005. Experience with an industry-driven capstone course on game programming. In *ACM SIGCSE Bulletin*, Vol. 37. ACM, 91–95.

[27] Yolanda Rankin, Amy Gooch, and Bruce Gooch. 2008. The impact of game design on students' interest in CS. In *Proceedings of the 3rd international conference on Game development in computer science education.* ACM, 31–35.

[28] Donn Ritchie and Bernard Dodge. 1992. Integrating Technology Usage across the Curriculum through Educational Adventure Games. (1992).

[29] Timothy E Roden. 2014. Benefits of an introductory course in computer game development. In *Computer Science & Education (ICCSE), 2014 9th International Conference on.* IEEE, 316–321.

[30] Susan Russell, Mary Hancock, and James McCullough. 2007. Benefits of undergraduate research experiences. *Science(Washington)* 316, 5824 (2007), 548–549.

[31] Deborah Sturm and Roberta Klibaner. 2012. Early introduction of advanced CS topics to increase student satisfaction. *Journal of Computing Sciences in Colleges* 27, 6 (2012), 26–33.

[32] Deborah Sturm, Ed Peppe, and Bertram Ploog. 2016. eMot-iCan: Design of an assessment game for emotion recognition in players with Autism. In *Serious Games and Applications for Health (SeGAH), 2016 IEEE Intl Conference.* IEEE, 1–7.

[33] Kelvin Sung, Peter Shirley, and Becky Reed Rosenberg. 2007. Experiencing aspects of games programming in an introductory computer graphics class. In *ACM SIGCSE Bulletin*, Vol. 39. ACM, 249–253.

[34] Scott A Wallace, Robert McCartney, and Ingrid Russell. 2010. Games and machine learning: a powerful combination in an artificial intelligence course. *Computer Science Education* 20, 1 (2010), 17–36.

Catch 'em Early: Internship and Assistantship CS Mentoring Programs for Underclassmen

Meg Fryling, MaryAnne Egan, Robin Y. Flatland, Scott Vandenberg, Sharon Small
Computer Science Department, Siena College
mfryling, maegan, flatland, vandenberg, ssmall@siena.edu

ABSTRACT

Recruiting and retaining STEM majors has been an ongoing challenge for colleges and universities. This research paper describes two initiatives to recruit and retain Computer Science (CS) majors that were implemented at Siena College starting in the fall of 2014. Both initiatives are directed at rising sophomores who have completed the first year CS sequence as an early strategy to encourage them to declare and complete the CS major. The first initiative is an early internship program directed at providing students an opportunity to apply those technical skills, extend their skill set, and introduce them to meaningful real-world projects between their freshman and sophomore years. The second initiative is a lab/classroom assistant program where sophomore or older students provide mentoring during lecture and lab sessions for the introductory CS courses. The paper provides preliminary findings, lessons learned, and directions for the future.

KEYWORDS

Internships, Undergraduate Teaching Assistants, Recruitment, Outreach, Mentoring

ACM Reference format:
Meg Fryling, MaryAnne Egan, Robin Y. Flatland, Scott Vandenberg, Sharon Small. 2018. Catch 'em Early: Internship and Assistantship CS Mentoring Programs for Underclassmen. In *Proceedings of The 49th ACM Technical Symposium on Computer Science Education, Baltimore, MD, USA, Feb. 21–24, 2018 (SIGCSE '18),* 6 pages.
https://doi.org/10.1145/3159450.3159556

1 INTRODUCTION

Recruiting and retaining STEM majors has been an ongoing challenge for colleges and universities. Only about 28 percent of bachelor's degree candidates and 20 percent of associate degree candidates declare a STEM major [18]. Of those students, approximately half do not complete a STEM degree and the bachelor degree attrition rate is highest for computer/information sciences majors [18]. It has been projected that in order for the United States to remain competitive in science and technology, it will need to increase STEM undergraduate degrees by approximately 34% annually over current rates [8]. The perception of an unfriendly environment and the lack of sufficient mentoring are cited as some of the reasons why the attrition rate for STEM majors is so high [8, 14], despite the high demand for these skills. An additional challenge for Computer Science (CS) is that not all students are exposed to the discipline in high school.

Fewer than ten states require a computing course for high school graduation and that course may be a computer applications or literacy course, which is not a true CS course [12]. In addition, fewer than half of U.S. states offer a CS K-12 teacher certification so there are insufficient resources to offer adequate CS education in secondary schools [12]. Given there is so little exposure to CS education in U.S. high schools, it is not surprising that few students pursue a CS major in higher education. However, research has found that undergraduate engagement outreach programs in STEM education have had a positive impact on recruiting and retaining STEM students, particularly underrepresented groups [6, 7, 9–11, 15].

In the remainder of this paper we present details of both the early internship and assistantship programs. Section 2 examines related work while Section 3 presents the program structure, student selection process, logistics, and specifically for the internship program, examples of participating sites and projects. Section 4 includes outcomes and data about the program from our initial evaluations. Section 5 presents lessons learned and plans for future implementations of the program, and we summarize the paper in Section 6.

2 RELATED WORK

2.1 Early Internships

Programs have been developed that focus on early inclusion in research projects, for example, the NSF STEP program at Appalachian State University [19] which used a multi-pronged approach that included early participation in a research project. The project was based entirely on campus with various faculty members working with different groups of students. However, to our knowledge, there are no programs that focus on early inclusion in internships as these opportunities are typically reserved for upperclassmen. In 2002, Cohoon presented 19 recommendations for recruiting and retaining women in undergraduate computing majors [2]. One of the recommendations was to "use the local job market to provide students with work experience". She went on to state that

> "employers can foster students' persistence in computing programs by their employment experiences. Employment offers students the chance to produce something of value and to see it used. Employment also offers expanded access to role

SIGCSE '18, Feb. 21–24, 2018, Baltimore, MD, USA

ACM ISBN 978-1-4503-5103-4/18/02...$15.00
https://doi.org/10.1145/3159450.3159556

> models, mentors, and professional peers. Likewise, internships with competent supervisors can have a positive influence on student persistence (as cited in Cohoon, 2002) [1]. For these reasons, departments should work with local employers to facilitate an appropriate degree of student work experience (i.e., not so much that it interferes with students' academic responsibilities.)"

Our program is an implementation of this concept of involving local employers to give students real world experience.

2.2 Early Assistantships

As enrollments have increased in CS, several colleges and universities (e.g. Stanford, Harvard, Duke, Mount Holyoke, University of Washington) have started employing undergraduate teaching assistants (UTAs) to improve the student experience and their academic outcomes [16]. Stanford has used UTAs, who they refer to as "section leaders", for over 20 years [5, 17]. Texas A&M University has an undergraduate leadership teaching assistant (ULTA) program, which focuses specifically on developing the leadership skills of its participants [13]. These institutions have reported many positive results from these programs, including benefits for both the students attending these classes and the assistants. Our program is similar, but focuses on recruiting from the rising sophomores instead of upper-level students.

3 OUR PROGRAMS

3.1 Early Internship Program

Our institution already has a strong undergraduate internship program in place, with most CS majors participating in an internship during their junior or senior year. While these internships provide outstanding opportunities and insight into CS careers, they only benefit students that have already committed to the CS major. Students just starting the major, or considering the major, have little opportunity to develop an awareness of how the concepts presented in class translate into real-world applications. We hypothesized that student involvement in early internships would yield similar benefits as student participation in early research. These benefits include sense of belonging and greater confidence, positive relationships with peers and faculty mentors, higher retention rate, and improved problem solving [19].

Beginning with summer 2015, we developed an early career internship experience that offers rising sophomores an opportunity to apply and improve their technical skills. Offering an internship earlier in a student's undergraduate career not only allows participants to gain confidence in their ability to apply their skills to real world problems, but is particularly helpful in the recruitment and retention of women in CS [2].

Our program is unique in that we do not restrict our applicants to CS majors. In fact, we encourage all freshman who have completed the first two courses in our CS majors sequence to apply for this program. When reviewing applications we make every effort to include non-CS majors and members of underrepresented groups.

3.1.1 Program Structure. As part of this program, students work with an internship site for six weeks during the summer between their freshman and sophomore year. The students receive a stipend, and there are some funds available for room and board for non-local students. The faculty supervisors identify sites that are willing to foster a beginning student's interest and skills in CS.

The students are selected in pairs for each site - some work on-site at the company/agency offering the internship, some at our institution in a lab near the faculty, and some split their time between the two. The students are placed in pairs so that they do not feel isolated by working alone on the assigned project. The faculty supervisors act as a technological resource and facilitate communication between students and site supervisors throughout the course of the six week internship.

3.1.2 Selection. Students (CS majors and non-CS majors) apply to a small committee of faculty internship supervisors during their second semester freshman year and must have taken, or be enrolled in, the first two CS courses to be considered. The first course is a breadth-first introduction to computer science with a programming component in Python or Perl. The second course is an introduction to Java programming, which is the prerequisite to our data structures course. Students learn about the internship opportunity through public postings, email, and encouragement from the instructors of the first two courses. The students provide a reference, but the committee supplements this information by soliciting additional input from the faculty of these first two courses.

The committee meets to evaluate the applicants on several criteria, listed here in order of priority:

- faculty input as to independence, reliability, maturity
- best fit for the available sites
- need for housing (as we have limited funds)
- member of underrepresented group
- GPA
- major

We try to identify candidates that are likely to be successful, with preference given to non-majors and students of underrepresented groups.

Once students are selected for the program, the faculty supervisors work with them to create a resume to submit to sites for approval. Some sites choose to interview interns before accepting them, other sites trust the decision of the committee.

3.1.3 Participating Sites. Each summer, we work with three sites and send two students to each site. We try to find both on-campus and off-campus placements. Having the School of Science internship coordinator on the committee has helped in identifying sites. One placement every year has been with Siena's Information Technology Services (ITS) and another placement every year has been with NY State ITS. Third placement sites have varied between other departments of NY State or non-ITS groups on campus. Most sites have provided a place for the students to work at their site, but there is also space available on campus for the interns.

Faculty supervisors and interns meet with internship site supervisors to ensure the scope of the project is appropriate for students

[1]ITWF: Departmental Factors in Gendered Attrition from Undergraduate Computing Majors. Grant #EIA-0089959

with limited experience. Sites are aware that there are faculty supervisors available if the students should need guidance or technical help.

3.1.4 Types of Projects. The projects have had varying technical requirements, with several of the projects requiring students to learn basic web programming (HTML, CSS, Javascript) and other projects required students to learn a software product that is used by the site (GIS, Splunk, Processmaker). Faculty supervisors have helped to identify good resources to learn these skills and have been available for help. Some of the projects the internship students have worked on include:

- Create online form that students can use to change their major
- Make iPad game for a state agency to be used at the state fair
- Requirements gathering
- Augment an expense report submission form
- Using GIS, create a tool to allow others to identify "food deserts" in urban areas
- Create a dashboard application to monitor web logs
- Evaluate and explore the capabilities of a web publishing software system

This is a nice variety of projects that students can do with just a year of CS and some training during the first weeks of the internship.

3.1.5 Logistics. As stated earlier, students work in pairs at a site for a six week period. They work in pairs for companionship to help dispel the myth that CS is a solitary profession and to compensate for their limited experience. Students and faculty supervisors meet at least once or twice with the site supervisors to discuss the project, determine scope, identify suitable software, and determine if it would be best for the students to work on-site, on campus, or a combination of both. Because students have limited experience, students may use a portion of their internship time reviewing books and tutorials to learn specialized software tools and applications needed for their internship projects.

The students maintain a log of hours and a summary of each day's work. These logs are shared with the faculty supervisors so problems may be identified early. The faculty supervisors also reach out at least once a week if they haven't heard from interns at a particular site. At least one lunch is scheduled during the internship providing an informal atmosphere for students to discuss their work, meet other interns, and find out what other groups are doing.

3.1.6 Faculty Supervisors. Those familiar with coordinating internships for undergraduates will understand the time commitment involved in cultivating internship sites, recruiting and selecting students, and determining placements. Since this internship program involves students with very limited CS experience, the faculty mentoring is much more extensive and hands-on. As such, this program has some added commitments in terms of time and responsibilities which vary by project, site, and student team. Examples of some of the time commitments or responsibilities of the two faculty supervisors, beyond those normally expected for coordinating internships, are listed below:

- Meetings with each site supervisor with students in attendance
- Lunch meetings to check in with the internship groups (two such meetings this past summer)
- Mid-internship meeting with site supervisors and students
- Training in necessary software which amounts to at least four days per faculty supervisor each summer. The first summer was significantly more due to project requirements, student knowledge, and faculty expertise (or lack thereof)
- At least one faculty member should be available every day during the course of the internship. Having two faculty members ensures that this is always true.

Because the students need more faculty supervision than a typical internship, the number of students that can participate in the program is limited. This is certainly a limitation and could make it difficult to scale up the program, but the students' positive experiences make it worthwhile.

3.2 Early Assistantship Program

As part of an initiative to recruit and retain CS students, an early classroom/lab assistantship experience was implemented in the fall of 2014 to give participants an opportunity to build mentoring skills and sharpen their CS abilities. High-impact programs such as undergraduate teaching assistants and undergraduate research experiences have been found to improve STEM major retention [1, 3]. As such, we theorized that engaging students as classroom/lab assistants would yield similar results.

3.2.1 Student Selection. Students who have completed the first year CS sequence are invited to apply for our early assistantship program. Classroom/lab assistants are recruited at the beginning of each semester, giving preference to sophomores and non-CS majors. Faculty then make recommendations on which students from this pool they believe will make good classroom assistants (e.g. technical skills, communication skills, mentoring skills). We also take into consideration if the applications would benefit from seeing the material again.

As with our internship program, we make every effort to recruit non-CS majors and students from underrepresented groups. Each year we give preference to sophomores so that we can better recruit and retain this critical and vulnerable population. As such, students may only end up working as a classroom/lab assistant for one year. The assistantship program has become competitive so we usually can fill most sections with sophomores. However, if we are unable to cover a section, and funds are available, we solicit assistants that have participated in previous years (i.e. upperclassmen). This population is also targeted to work as CS student tutors, which is a separately funded program at our institution.

3.2.2 Program Structure. As classroom/lab assistants, the students either assist CS faculty and students in the freshman-level Introduction to CS or Java Programming courses. They are supervised by the faculty member and provide student assistance with hands-on lecture and laboratory activities. In addition to benefiting the lab/classroom assistant, the initiative gives students enrolled in the course the benefit of more personal attention, which can also support their recruitment and retention in CS by providing a better introductory course experience [4]. While we initially called these positions Teaching Assistants, we eventually changed the name to Classroom/Lab Assistants because our assistants do not prepare course material, conduct lectures, grade assignments, or hold office hours. The assistant's responsibilities are limited to helping students during lecture/lab only, which differs from many of the UTA programs at other colleges and universities.

Although the assistants have already taken the courses for which they are assisting, they are required to work through all the lab/class exercises to ensure they are able to assist the students in class. By reviewing the material in-depth an additional time, we expect to see improved confidence and academic performance from the assistants. Assistants are paid for their time in the classroom as well as preparation time so they may work through all the exercises ahead of time.

4 OUTCOMES

4.1 Internships

This program has not only recruited CS majors, but also retained them. In its first two years, five of the 12 students who have completed the internship were not CS majors when they participated in the program. Four of these five students became CS majors afterwards. Looking at the one year retention rate of students in the program, we find that 83.3% of the students who were interns were retained in the major (this includes students who were already CS majors at the start of the internship as well as those who declared CS after the internship) versus 78.8% of their cohorts (same academic years) who did not participate.

While women make up only 20% (30 of 148) of our CS majors, 39% of the interns were female. Only 11% of our interns have come from other underrepresented groups (American Indian, Alaskan Native, African American, Hispanic, Native Hawaiian or other Pacific Islander) which is similar to the national average of bachelor degrees awarded to underrepresented groups (11.1%) [2] and the percentage of underrepresented groups at our institution (11.8%). We accepted 28.6% of the non-international minority students who applied, and we intend to better target these groups in future calls for applications. As for female applicants, 63.4% of those that applied were hired and 38.9% of the interns have been female.

As part of our grant, an outside evaluator met with the interns to discuss the outcomes of the internship. It was noted that students' confidence increased when they completed a project and received positive feedback. Student feedback from the external evaluator's assessment:

> "Some of the internships required students to program in languages in which they had no experience. They stated that this made their experience challenging, but that they appreciated the opportunity to build on their existing knowledge of programming languages. Students also appreciated the fact that they got to experience what it feels like to have a job in the computer science field."

[2]http://cra.org/crn/wp-content/uploads/sites/7/2017/05/2016-Taulbee-Survey.pdf

Finally, the internship program develops community not only among interns, but also between our institution and the placement sites. Several sites have hosted interns every year demonstrating that this is not overly burdensome on the site. Feedback from placement sites has been unsolicited, but positive, as in this example from an internship supervisor this year:

> "[The students'] high quality products are already being used by four different organizations; and will produce the data necessary to communicate to a host of stakeholders interested in improving food security in our four-county area. I can honestly tell you that your [students'] professionalism, work ethic and attention to detail have surpassed all experiences I've had with undergraduate students..."

4.2 Assistantships

Since the classroom/lab assistant program began in Fall 2014 we have employed 28 unique students as assistants. Eight of the 28 classroom assistants are non-international minority students. This percentage (28.6%) is encouraging compared to our institution's non-international minority student population, which is 11.6%. In addition, 35.7% of the assistants have been female students. Of the 22 assistants that started as CS majors, 21 are still in (or have completed) the major. In addition, two of the six students who were not CS majors at the start of their assistantship added the major after their experience.

As part of our program assessment, an external evaluator conducted focus groups with the lab/classroom assistants. The evaluator provided us with the following general category feedback from the assistants:

- Improved their CS/Programming knowledge and confidence
- Increased interest in education careers
- Provided opportunity to get to know other students within the department
- Increased their appreciation of the CS field
- Helped them with their current courses

The focus group data shows that our objective to improve the skills and confidence of the students participating in the assistantship program is being achieved. The assistants also reported that they felt some students in the class were more comfortable asking questions of them versus the professor, thus increasing class participation. Assistants provided additional suggestions on how to improve the experience, such as providing clearer expectations and regular feedback on their performance.

Students in the Introduction to Computer Science course reported that classroom assistants encouraged student learning and participation, provided quality feedback, and were knowledgeable (see Figure 1). However, students in the Java Programming course did not report these qualities as strongly (see Figure 2). [3]

[3]Figures based on a 1-5 scale where 1=Strongly Disagree, 2=Disagree, 3=Neither Agree nor Disagree, 4=Agree, 5=Strongly Agree

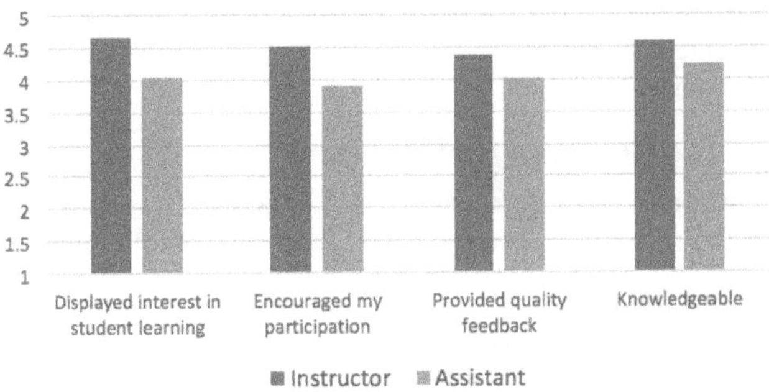

Figure 1: Fall 2014 - Spring 2017 Introduction to CS Course Evaluation Data (177 Respondents)

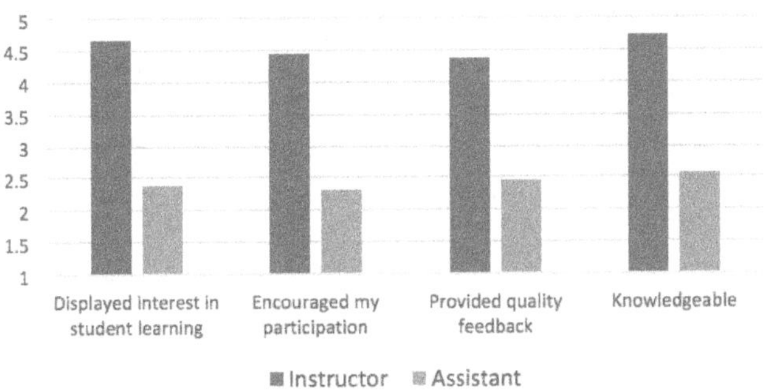

Figure 2: Fall 2014 - Spring 2017 Java Programming Course Evaluation Data (94 Respondents)

It is not known why the student feedback was more positive for the Introduction to CS assistants than the Java Programing assistants. This discrepancy is definitely something that will be investigated moving forward. It could be that the material is just more difficult in the Java Programming course and/or the course structure/delivery had an impact (e.g. some Java sections were delivered in the flipped classroom model).

5 CONCLUSIONS, LESSONS LEARNED, AND NEXT STEPS

These recruitment and retention initiatives are unique in that they are programs that would normally be offered to upper-level undergraduate or graduate students and only those that have already committed to the major. Our programs specifically target the sophomore population, which is a critical year in which many students make decisions regarding adding or dropping a major. In addition, both CS and non-CS majors participate in these programs, and we have successfully recruited some of the non-majors into the CS major.

At the beginning of these programs we predicted that the early internship and assistantship activities would strengthen recruitment and retention of students completing the first-year CS sequence. Prior to the start of these initiatives, each year on average two freshmen and two sophomore CS majors switched to a different major. Between fall 2014 and spring 2017, thirty-six unique students participated in one of these programs as an intern or assistant, with four students participating in both. For the students participating in one or both these two programs, we had a net increase in CS majors of four students. In addition, 24 out of the 26 students that were a CS major prior to the program have remained in the major.

We have some general comparison data showing that more students taking the courses with classroom/lab assistants stayed in the CS major or added the CS major. While we can't entirely attribute this to the positive influence of the classroom assistants, the numbers are compelling. Between Fall 2011 and Spring 2014, 4.9% of the undecided majors that took one or both of the two first year CS courses subsequently added the CS major. After the start of the assistantship program, between Fall 2014 and Spring 2017, with no other major changes in content or delivery style, 16.9% of the undecided majors that took one or both of the two first year CS courses subsequently added the CS major (see Table 1).

Table 1: Number of Undecided Majors Taking First Year CS Courses and Adding a CS Major

Time Period	Took Intro CS Course	Added CS Major
F 2011- S 2014	123	6 (4.9%)
F 2014- S 2017	142	24 (16.9%)

5.1 Internship Program Lessons Learned

Major lessons learned from the internship program include:

- Have interns work the same 6-week period. It makes faculty mentoring easier but it also allows students to use each other as resources.
- Provide a workplace for students on campus that is close to faculty mentor offices. This will also provide an environment where the interns can help each other.
- Maintain frequent communication with students and site to ensure scope remains appropriate. It is important that the students not be overwhelmed to the point that they give up, but you also want to challenge them and provide valuable service to the placement sites.
- Have more than one faculty mentor to cover knowledge of various software, act as a resource, and maintain communication.
- Set supervisor and student expectations. They are rising sophomores so they have little programming experience (and typically no web and no database).

5.2 Assistantship Program Lessons Learned

Major lessons learned from the assistantship program include:

- Provide clear expectations and regular feedback to assistants
- Assistants need guidance on how to properly help (e.g. get students unstuck vs. give them the answer).
- Ask faculty for feedback so best assistants are kept. These are also great candidates to become CS tutors.

It is unclear why there is such a distinct difference between the student feedback regarding classroom assistants in the Introduction to CS and the Java Programming courses. Often the same students assisted in both classes so one might speculate the cause may be related to the differences in course material and/or structure of the course. These theories will be further investigated.

5.3 Next Steps

Our next steps include completing the last two years of the grant period, through Spring 2019. During that time we intend to further improve and mature both the internship and assistantship initiatives. We will be seeking institutional support to maintain both programs after the grant period.

The current cost of the internship program is $25,550 per year. This includes $17,550 in stipends/room/board for six students and $8,100 in summer stipends for two faculty members (see Table 2).

Table 2: Yearly Internship Program Costs

Description	Cost/Intern	Number Interns	Cost
Student Stipend	$2,205	6	$13,230
Room/Board	$1,440	3	$4,320
Faculty Stipend	$1,350	6	$8,100
Total Cost			**$25,550**

The assistantship program is fairly inexpensive, on average only costing approximately $5,600 per year for student assistant salary. There are no other direct administrative costs or release time needed to manage the program. This minimal cost allowed us to have undergraduate assistants in nearly all of our Introduction to CS and Java Programming sections for the last three years (see Table 3 for a breakdown of the number of lectures and labs with assistants each year of the grant period). This program had a high value for cost since it reached not only the 28 students working as assistants but the students in the courses that have assistants.

Table 3: Classes with Assistants by Academic Year (AY)

AY	Intro CS Labs	Java Labs	Java Lectures	Total
2014-15	8	7	5	20
2015-16	13	7	6	26
2016-17	15	5	5	25

6 SUMMARY

The program has been a great success, based on our increase in new majors and retention of existing majors. The program is valuable for the students who participate as interns or assistants, but also for students who may be in an introductory course that has a student assistant to help with questions. The internship program offers students a chance to produce something of value and to experience CS in the workplace during a critical time when many students are still deciding on a major. The assistantship program gives the assistants a boost in their confidence in their programming ability and better appreciation of the CS field. Additionally, assistants in the classroom give students taking the course increased opportunities to ask questions and better understand the material, thus lowering frustration levels commonly associated with beginning programming courses.

We have presented two initiatives directed at sophomores to recruit and retain CS majors. Both the early internship program and lab/classroom assistant program have shown promising results in increasing the numbers of new majors and retaining existing majors. We hope to continue the program beyond the duration of the grant and encourage other institutions to implement similar programs.

7 ACKNOWLEDGMENTS

This work was supported by NSF grant 1432198. Thank you to our external evaluator, Joseph King, for his support and guidance.

REFERENCES

[1] Bethany Bowling, Heather Bullen, Maureen Doyle, and John Filaseta. 2013. Retention of STEM Majors Using Early Undergraduate Researchexperiences. In *Proceeding of the 44th ACM Technical Symposium on Computer Science Education (SIGCSE '13)*. ACM, New York, NY, USA, 171–176. DOI: http://dx.doi.org/10.1145/2445196.2445249

[2] J. McGrath Cohoon. 2002. Recruiting and retaining women in undergraduate computing majors. *SIGCSE Bulletin* 34, 2 (June 2002), 48–52.

[3] Teresa Dahlberg, Tiffany Barnes, Audrey Rorrer, Eve Powell, and Lauren Cairco. 2008. Improving Retention and Graduate Recruitment Through Immersive Research Experiences for Undergraduates. *SIGCSE Bull.* 40, 1 (March 2008), 466–470. DOI: http://dx.doi.org/10.1145/1352322.1352293

[4] P.E. Dickson. 2011. Using undergraduate teaching assistants in a small college environment. In *In Proceedings of the 42nd ACM technical symposium on Computer science education SIGCSE '11*. ACM.

[5] Jeffrey Forbes, David J. Malan, Heather Pon-Barry, Stuart Reges, and Mehran Sahami. 2017. Scaling Introductory Courses Using Undergraduate Teaching Assistants. In *Proceedings of the 2017 ACM SIGCSE Technical Symposium on Computer Science Education (SIGCSE '17)*. ACM, New York, NY, USA, 657–658. DOI: http://dx.doi.org/10.1145/3017680.3017694

[6] D. Hodge, K. Pasquesi, and M. Hirsh. 2007. From convocation to capstone: Developing the student as scholar. In *Keynote address at the Association of American Colleges and Universities Network for Academic Renewal Conference.*

[7] Nancy Hoffman. 2005. *Add and Subtract Dual Enrollment as a State Strategy to Increase Postsecondary Success for Underrepresented Students.* Double the Numbers: A Jobs for the Future Initiative.

[8] J.P. Holdren and E. Lander. 2012. *Engage to Excel: Producing One Million Additional College Graduates with Degrees in Science, Technology, Engineering, and Mathematics, in Report to the President by the President's Council of Advisors on Science and Technology.*

[9] IHEP. 2007. *Model Institutions for Excellence: 2007 national report. A model of success: The Model Institutions for Excellence program's successful leadership in STEM education 1995-2007.* Institute for Higher Education Policy.

[10] M.M. Karp and D.W. Jeong. 2008. *Conducting Research to Answer Your Questions About Dual Enrollment.* U.S. Department of Education.

[11] C.C. Landry. 2002/2003. Retention of Women and People of Color: Unique Challenges and Institutional Responses. *Journal of College Student Retention* 4, 1 (2002/2003), 1–13.

[12] K. Lang, Ria Galanos, Joanna Goode, Deborah Seehorn, and Fran Trees. 2013. *Bugs in the System: Computer Science Teacher Certification in the U.S., A report by The Computer Science Teachers Association and The Association for Computing Machinery.*

[13] S. F. Odom, S. P. Ho, and L. L. Moore. 2014. The undergraduate leadership teaching assistant (ULTA): A high-impact practice for undergraduates studying leadership. *Journal of Leadership Education* 13, 2 (2014), 152–161.

[14] National Academy of Sciences, National Academy of Engineering, and Institute of Medicine. 2007. *Rising Above the Gathering Storm: Energizing and Employing America for a Brighter Economic Future.* The National Academies Press, Washington, DC. DOI: http://dx.doi.org/10.17226/11463

[15] A. Olowoyeye, K.J. Stewart, and G.C. Townsen. 2010. A dozen ideas for engaging CS1 students. *J.Comput. Small Coll.* 26, 1 (2010), 93–102.

[16] E. Roberts and E. Lazowska. 2014. Tsunami or Sea Change? Responding to the Explosion of Student Interest in Computer Science. In *In Proceedings of the 2014 NCWIT Summit on Women and IT.*

[17] Eric Roberts, John Lilly, and Bryan Rollins. 1995. Using undergraduates as teaching assistants in introductory programming courses: an update on the Stanford experience. In *In Proceedings of the twenty-sixth SIGCSE technical symposium on Computer science education (SIGCSE '95), Curt M. White, James E. Miller, and Judy Gersting (Eds.).* ACM, 48–52.

[18] Megan Rogers. 2013. STEM-ming the Tide. *Inside Higher Ed* (November 2013).

[19] Rahman Tashakkori, Barry L. Kurtz, Dolores A. Parks, Jr. James B. Fenwick, and Alice A. McRae. 2011. Early participation of CS students in research. In *In Proceedings of the 42nd ACM technical symposium on Computer science education (SIGCSE '11)*. ACM, 63–68.

How Near Peer Mentoring Affects Middle School Mentees

Jody Clarke-Midura
Instructional Technology
and Learning Sciences
Utah State University
USA
jody.clarke@usu.edu

Frederick Poole
Instructional Technology
and Learning Sciences
Utah State University
USA
frederick.poole@usu.edu

Katarina Pantic
Instructional Technology
and Learning Sciences
Utah State University
USA
katarina.pantic@aggiemail.usu.edu

Megan Hamilton
Instructional Technology
and Learning Sciences
Utah State University
USA
megan.hamilton@usu.edu

Chongning Sun
Instructional Technology
and Learning Sciences
Utah State University
USA
vincent.sun@aggiemail.usu.edu

Vicki Allan
Computer Science
Utah State University
USA
vicki.allan@usu.edu

ABSTRACT

In response to the national demand to increase participation in CS, we argue that youth's interest in computer science (CS) can be sparked by providing them with role models who are relatable and who resonate with their identities. To that end, we developed a mentoring model in which we train high schoolers to be near-peer mentors for middle schoolers learning to program in summer camps. In this paper, we present results from a mixed-methods study where we examined the relationship between mentor relatability and middle school campers' self-efficacy and interest in CS. Pre- and post-surveys were used to measure campers' affective outcomes around computing and mentor relatability. In addition, interviews and observations were used to illustrate the mechanisms that led to change in affect. Our findings suggest that mentor relatability is a significant predictor of campers' self-efficacy and interest in CS. Results from the qualitative data further exemplify how mentor relatability was perceived and manifested in the camps.

ACM Reference format:

J. Clarke-Midura, F. Poole, K. Pantic, M. Hamilton, C. Sun, V. Allan. 2018. How Near Peer Mentoring Affects Middle School Mentees. In *Proceedings of ACM SIGCSE conference, Baltimore, MD USA, February 2018 (SIGCSE'18)*, 6 pages.
DOI: http://dx.doi.org/10.1145/3159450.3159525

1 INTRODUCTION

With the Bureau of Labor Statistics [7] projecting an increase in computer related jobs and US graduates being able to fill up only about 30% of those openings [1], finding ways to get youth interested in CS has become a national priority [3]. While we acknowledge the effectiveness of a variety of strategies already identified in literature, in this paper, we argue that one way to increase youth's interest in CS is to provide them with role models who are relatable and who resonate with their identities. Such connections may help them envision their future selves and CS as a possible path. Bandura [3] wrote that "seeing or visualizing people similar to oneself perform successfully, typically raises self-efficacy beliefs in observers that they themselves possess the capabilities to master comparable activities" (p.87). However, if the model does not seem similar or the youth perceives the model to have disparities in experience they "are likely to view skills exemplified by an experienced model as beyond their reach and are thus declined to invest the effort needed to master them fully" (p. 234) [2]. Youth are thus more likely to imitate those who they perceive as similar to themselves [3]. We argue that near-peer mentors, who resemble their protégés in age, status, skills, and/or interest, will make more credible role models in comparison to non-peer mentors, such as university professors or undergraduates, who are not considered "near peers."

For the past three years, we have been offering summer camp programming experiences for middle and high school youth using App Inventor. We have been using a near-peer mentoring model through which we train high school students to be near-peer mentors for middle school aged campers. We have written about the success of this model for the mentors themselves in increasing their self-efficacy and interest in computing [10, 11]. In this paper, we explore how working with near-peer mentors affects campers' self-efficacy and interest in computing. In the following sections, we review previous work around near-peer mentoring. We then describe our camps, research, and findings.

SIGCSE'18, February 21-24, 2018, Baltimore, MD, USA.

ACM ISBN 978-1-4503-5103-4/18/02...$15.00.
DOI: http://dx.doi.org/10.1145/3159450.3159525

2 RELATED WORK

The cognitive processes explaining the relationship and methods for learning in a mentor/mentee model are difficult to define because mentors operate in a social space between formal teacher, friend, role model, and coach [15]. In this research, we use the lens of social competency modeling, based on Bandura's social cognitive theory [3]. According to Bandura [4-5], a mentee's self-efficacy is directly impacted by (1) the social relationships with those who act as models (e.g. mentors, etc.), (2) the similarity they perceive between themselves and their models, and (3) watching a credible model effectively perform a task. As such, we expect that mentors who share common traits or backgrounds salient to participants' concept of self will be more credible models and, will therefore, stimulate greater enthusiasm and improve self-efficacy in CS. However, it is critical to identify the contexts in which positive attitudes are fostered as well as the mechanisms that support or hinder attitudes. Role models must also resonate with campers' identities and help them envision their future selves and CS as a possible pathway.

2.1 Defining Near-Peers

We found inconsistencies in how the term near-peer was used and defined (e.g. [6], [17], [27]). In the context of our study, we define near-peers as mentors who are proximal in age but slightly more skilled in programming. If we consider programing skills and expertise on a spectrum, the mentor's expertise would fall somewhere between the skill level of mentees and experts. This distance from mentees grants near-peer mentors with an ample knowledge base to provide the appropriate guidance and aid to a mentee. At the same time, the proximity in skill level allows the near-peer mentors to be more relatable and approachable.

2.2 Effectiveness of Near-Peer Role Models

Research on near-peer role models has lent support to our claim that near-peers are credible role models [18-22, 27]. However, the majority of studies on near-peer mentoring were conducted in the sciences and/or medical settings (e.g., [22-26, 30], with only a few studies in CS (e.g., [8, 10, 14, 17-18]). In addition, most research focused on older populations such as high school students, undergraduates and graduate students. Only a few studies (e.g., [27]) have looked at the impact of near-peers on middle school mentees. To the best of our knowledge, no study has focused primarily on the relationship between high school mentors and middle school mentees in CS. In addition, many studies tend to focus on highly skilled mentors with in-depth experience who are usually treated as experts, rather than mentors with comparatively higher expertise than the mentees. Thus, in our study, we expand on the near-peer mentoring research by exploring the effect of high school aged near-peer mentors on middle school youth in the context of CS.

3 METHODS

The purpose of this study was to explore the effect of near-peer mentoring on the mentees' self-efficacy and interest in CS. The research questions that guided our study were: *(1) Is there a relationship between the campers' connection with near-peer mentors and their intrinsic interest in computing? (2) In their self-efficacy? (3) How do campers describe their relationship with their near-peer mentors?*

We used a mixed-methods approach to answer our research questions. Mixed-methods approaches are often used in educational settings in which relationships between constructs can be very complex [12]. Given the complex nature of the relationship between mentor and mentee, we first used survey data to determine if there was a relationship between camper perceptions of their mentors and their change in affect. The interview data was analyzed to provide further insight into how campers perceived their relationship with their near-peer mentors.

3.1 App Camps

During the summer of 2017, we ran five camps on learning how to program using App Inventor. In the first camp, we trained high school students to use App Inventor and how to be a mentor. Then, mentors helped us run four additional camps for middle school youth.

3.1.1 Mentor Training. The mentors received a five-day training on programming in App Inventor and mentoring (6 ½ hours per day). During training, the mentors learned to program 11 apps that built on several key concepts. As the training progressed, the apps progressed in complexity and difficulty. By the end of the week, mentors were expected to create their own apps without instructions. They also completed debugging activities in which they learned to troubleshoot erroneous scripts which simulated problems that mentees may encounter in practice. For a full description of the apps, as well as which skills and concepts each of them targeted, see our website [http://appcamp.usu.edu/]. In addition, we had lead mentors help with mentor training. Lead mentors were youth who participated as mentors the previous summer and returned only for the week of mentor training. Each lead mentor worked with five mentors during the training. During mentor training, the mentors were exposed to three types of activities: social activities with their lead mentors, modeled behavior from their lead mentors, and mentor training activities. Each day started with social activities (e.g. Scavenger hunt, etc.) with the lead mentors. The goal of the social activities was to emphasize the importance of putting in the effort to get to know your mentees and help them feel more comfortable around you. Lead mentors also modeled desired behavior for the mentors in training, such as asking constructive questions, and being available, helpful and encouraging. Finally, each day of the camp, mentors would engage in a mentor training activity: *How to help someone debug, Role Play: good mentor/bad mentor scenarios, Questioning strategies, Mentoring practice,* and *Constructive feedback.* For instance, on Day 3, in the Questioning strategies activity, they were trained to recast questions as learning opportunities and guide their mentees through the problem-solving process rather than simply providing a direct solution. Similarly, on Day 5, in the Constructive feedback activity, we asked them to reflect on different types of feedback. Relying on those examples, we came up with several strategies for providing constructive feedback.

3.1.2 AppCamp. Middle school aged youth attended a five-day camp on programming in App Inventor (3 hours per day). The campers were provided with a similar curriculum as the mentors in which they programmed the same 11 apps. They did not engage in as many open-ended projects as the mentors; however, they did engage in some debugging activities.

3.2 Sample

All the participants in this sample came from a rural area in the Intermountain West of the United States.

3.2.1 Mentors. We selected twenty-five students to be mentors (6 males and 19 females, average age = 16). They were selected based on availability and their response to why they wanted to be mentors. Mentor ethnicities included Asian/Pacific Islander (16%), Native American (4%), Latino/a (4%) and Caucasian (76%). Thirty-two percent of our mentors reported being on free or reduced lunch.

3.2.2 Campers. We recruited 112 campers to attend our camps. One camper was excluded from the research due to lack of parental consent. The sample used for this research was 111 campers (40 males and 71 females) ranging in age from 10 to 14 years (average age = 11.98). Camper ethnicities included Asian/Pacific Islander (1%), Native American (4%), Latino/a (5%), Other (2%) and Caucasian (88%). Seventeen percent of our campers reported being on free and reduced lunch.

3.2.3 Camp Assignments. We ran four camps: two mixed gender and two single gender (girls only) camps. Each camp either had all female or mixed gender (males and females) mentors. The breakdown of each camp can be found in Table 1.

Table 1: Camp Description (N_{mentor} = 25, N_{camper} = 111).

Camp	Mentor	N_{mentor}	Camper	N_{camper}
1	Female	(9F)	Mixed	(19M, 15F)
2	Mixed	(2M, 3F)	Female	(21 F)
3	Female	(4F)	Female	(20 F)
4	Mixed	(4M, 5F)	Mixed	(21M, 16F)

3.3 Data Collection Procedures

3.3.1 Surveys. Students took an affective survey prior to the camp on day 1 (pre) and then again on the last day of camp (post). Surveys were administered via the online survey software Qualtrics. Please see measures for more details.

3.3.2 Interviews. Forty-two campers across the four camps were randomly selected to be interviewed on the first day of camp and then again on the last day. Interview protocols focused on interest, self-efficacy, perceived support and camp experience. All interviews were audio recorded and transcribed verbatim.

3.4 Measures

The affective survey contained 32 items and asked students to rate the items on a scale of 1 to 8 from strongly disagree to strongly agree. The items were modified from existing surveys [9, 13, 16] and focused on campers' self-efficacy, interest, utility value, technical curiosity, and perceived support in CS. The post survey contained 7 additional questions developed by the research team that focused on the campers' experience with the mentors.

Composite scores were derived by averaging responses for each construct (three to six items). We ran analyses to confirm unidimensionality of the constructs and conducted Cronbach's alpha, a measure of internal consistency. For the purpose of this paper, we focus only on interest and self-efficacy. Descriptive statistics and pre-post differences are presented in Table 2.

Table 2: Descriptive Statistics of Results from All Camps

	N	M	SD	Alpha
Self-Efficacy (Pre)	109	5.00	1.70	0.87
Self-Efficacy (Post)*	107	6.29	1.45	0.90
Interest (Pre)	109	6.76	1.09	0.78
Interest (Post)*	107	7.09	1.07	0.85
Mentor Relatability (Post)	107	6.11	1.48	0.81

Note. M=Mean. SD= Standard Deviation. Alpha = Cronbach's alpha. *Indicates a significant difference between pre-and post- scores.

4 RESULTS

In order to answer our first two research questions, we conducted two multiple linear regression analyses in R [23]. To ensure there were no violations of assumptions of normality, linearity, multicollinearity, and homoscedasticity, preliminary analysis were first conducted. In both models, post-test scores were used as the dependent variables. Then pretest scores were entered into the model to control for pre-camp differences in self-efficacy and interest in CS. Gender of the participant and camp type (e.g. mixed vs. single-gender camps) were also added to the null model to account for differences in context. Mentor relatability was then added to the model, and an ANOVA was run to determine if the added variable significantly increased the amount of variance explained by the model.

Intrinsic Interest

	Dependent variable:	
	Intrinsic Interest (Post)	
	Null Model	Full Model
Intrinsic Interest (Pre)	0.441^{***}	0.323^{***}
	(0.266, 0.617)	(0.168, 0.477)
Gender (Male)	-0.190	0.070
	(-0.668, 0.287)	(-0.347, 0.487)
Camp (Same-Gender)	0.131	0.186
	(-0.338, 0.601)	(-0.216, 0.587)
Mentor Relatability		0.327^{***}
		(0.223, 0.431)
Constant	4.121^{***}	2.825^{***}
	(2.907, 5.335)	(1.708, 3.942)
Model Fit (ChiSq)		.000***
Observations	105	105
R^2	0.202	0.423
Residual Std. Error	0.976 (df = 101)	0.834 (df = 100)
F Statistic	8.545^{***} (df = 3; 101)	18.296^{***} (df = 4; 100)
Note:		*p<0.05; **p<0.01; ***p<0.001

Figure 1 Intrinsic Interest Model

4.1 Mentor Relatability and Interest

Our first research question asked about the relationship between campers' connection with near-peer mentors and their intrinsic interest in computing. Figure 1 shows the results of the analyses.

The full model with the addition of mentor relatability explains significantly more variance in intrinsic interest than the null model ($\chi^2(1)= 40.37$, $p < .001$) and is significant ($F(4, 100) = 18.29$, $p < .001$), with an R^2 of .423. The addition of mentor relatability accounted for approximately 22.1% more variance than the null model. In this model, a one-unit increase in mentor relatability on an 8-point scale is associated with a .327 increase in intrinsic interest. In other words, in our sample, as campers' perceptions of mentor relatability increased, their intrinsic interest in CS increased. In the full model, gender of the participant and type of camp were not significant predictors. However, mentor relatability was a significant predictor of change in intrinsic interest.

4.2 Mentor Relatability and Self-Efficacy

Our second question asked about the relationship between campers' connection with near-peer mentors and their self-efficacy in computing. For the self-efficacy model, similar dependence on mentor relatability was discovered. The full regression model for self-efficacy with the addition of mentor relatability explains significantly more variance in self-efficacy than the null model ($\chi^2(1)= 38.12$, $p <.001$) and is significant ($F(4, 100) = 33.52$, $p < .001$), with an R^2 of .573. The full model accounted for approximately 17.3% more variance than the null model which included the pretest, gender and camp type. In this model, for a one-unit increase in mentor relatability on an 8-point scale, self-efficacy increases by .396. In other words, in our sample, as campers' perceptions of mentor relatability increased, their self-efficacy increased. In this final model, gender and camp type were not significant. However, mentor relatability was a significant predictor of self-efficacy. Figure 2 shows the results of the analyses.

Self-Efficacy

	Dependent variable:	
	Self-Efficacy (Post)	
	Null Model	Full Model
Self-Efficacy (Pre)	0.556***	0.454***
	(0.423, 0.689)	(0.336, 0.571)
Gender (Male)	-0.389	-0.062
	(-0.952, 0.174)	(-0.550, 0.427)
Camp (Same-Gender)	-0.210	-0.125
	(-0.764, 0.345)	(-0.595, 0.346)
Mentor Relatability		0.396***
		(0.274, 0.518)
Constant	3.702***	1.663***
	(2.951, 4.452)	(0.769, 2.558)
Model Fit (ChiSq)		.000***
Observations	105	105
R^2	0.400	0.573
Residual Std. Error	1.148 (df = 101)	0.974 (df = 100)
F Statistic	22.468*** (df = 3; 101)	33.516*** (df = 4; 100)
Note:		*p<0.05; **p<0.01; ***p<0.001

Figure 2 Self-efficacy Model

4.3 Relationship with Near-Peer Mentors

Our third research question focused on how campers describe their relationship with their near-peer mentors. In order to answer this question, we analyzed interview and observation data. We conducted a thematic analysis of 42 post-interviews with campers and observation notes collected from the four middle school camps, which resulted in 105 units of analysis. Four themes emerged from the data: positive relationships mentors built with their mentees (Approachability) (*n*=43), the similarities campers perceived between themselves and their mentors (Similarities) (*n*=24), performance effectiveness that mentees perceived (In the Trenches: Credible Models) (*n*=19) and seeing the mentors as role models (Role Models) (*n*=19). In the following sections, we illustrate these themes through examples from camper interviews.

4.3.1 Approachability. The most prominent theme in campers' interviews was approachability of the mentors. The fact that mentees established a good relationship with their mentors was evident from the data as they were described as "*easy to talk to*", "*nice*", "*fun*", "*friendly*", "*kind*", "*approachable*", or a combination of a few of those adjectives. More importantly, no one labeled their mentor as annoying, rude or unapproachable. The campers seemed to have appreciated the fact that the mentors made an effort to get to know them on a more personal level. This effort made the campers comfortable to address the mentors or ask them questions. As an example, one camper said that her mentor made an effort to talk to her about their mutual interest, such as books, in addition to programming. This was important to her as she felt a mentor who knew her better could help her better. In other words, this camper felt connected to her mentor, because her mentor took the time to get to know her. This is important as it testifies that social relationships were established between campers and mentors, which is important to Bandura's social competency modeling framework [4-5].

4.3.2 Similarities. The second theme that emerged in our analysis were the similarities the mentees perceived between themselves and their mentors. In other words, many campers felt that they had a lot in common with their mentors. These similarities ranged from simple to more complex, such as age, personality traits (e.g. "*laid back*", "*shy*", "*likes helping people*" or "*cheerful*"), likes/dislikes, background (e.g. they went to the same school or came from a small town), and/or programming experience and skill level.

As an example, one camper expressed excitement that one of the reasons she really liked her mentor was because she felt they had similar personalities and they were very much alike. She saw her mentor as someone who was "*not that much older than her*" and who "*always knows that there is a way past something. Like if the computer isn't working and it's hard to fix, you know? Like it has a bug or something. She'll call [someone] over. They'll work together. They'll get it working again.*" As a result of all the perceived similarities she enjoyed working with her mentor. Even though we do not know if these similarities were realistically present or just perceived, the fact that they were perceived stands as a testament that the campers related to their mentors. This is important as it has been shown to contribute to an increase in self-efficacy [5].

4.3.3 In the Trenches: Credible Role Models. Next, we learned that the level of expertise of the mentors, or their level of effectiveness in completing programming and mentoring tasks made learning enjoyable for the mentees, which consequently, allowed them to relate to their mentors. For some, the fact that mentors were good programmers, knew what they were doing and were able to provide help was comforting, inspiring and more importantly, they felt like it boosted their self-confidence, or got them more interested in programming. As an example, one camper explained how seeing her mentor's projects made her more interested in what she herself could do with programming:

> *"Faith was showing us an app that she had made. It was a game where there was like cats coming down from the sky, and you had to catch them in a little basket. I thought that was way cool. I have no idea how you could do that. I wanna figure it out."*

Faith was one of the most advanced mentor programmers that we had in the camp. As seen from the excerpt above, seeing her game provided some campers with a better understanding of what can be done with programming. As we mentioned, the level of experience mentors possess is on a spectrum. While Faith was possibly closer to expert on the spectrum than other mentors, the mentees were still able to relate to her.

About a third of the campers we interviewed felt encouraged by the fact that the mentors did not know everything, were not yet the best programmers or were not afraid to ask for help themselves. This encouraged the campers to keep mastering the skill and made them feel better about their own confusions or "*failures*". As an example, one camper described his mentor in the following manner:

> *"The [mentor] that I was working with was nice. She showed me what she did and helped me out when I was really stuck. She got confused, too, so I wasn't the only one being confused."*

Being confused or having a buggy program can be embarrassing. However, debugging and problem solving are an important part of programming. To that end, we emphasized the importance of modeling problem solving, which the mentors did through their own problem-solving techniques. This approach created an environment in which asking questions was okay, not knowing everything was okay and collaboration was welcome.

In addition, the campers liked that the mentors went through the same experience not that long ago, they still remembered what it was like to learn App Inventor, and they faced similar programing problems. For Becca, for instance, the crucial moment in developing a relationship with her mentor, Summer, was when Summer shared the "*problems she had had when she was coding things and how she had fixed them*". Summer talked openly about her own programming struggles, which helped her mentees relate to her. Other campers mentioned that working closely with someone closer to their age, as their mentor, who experienced similar struggles and is still cognizant of them, made them feel more confident about overcoming their own problems. They also believed younger mentors were more likely to sympathize with their programming "*troubles*". This finding came as the biggest surprise to us. Though we hoped that having mentors closer to their age would help the middle schoolers relate better and build their self-confidence, we did not expect that a somewhat modest programming experience of the mentors would serve as a bonding experience for the campers. And yet, the campers not only liked it, but found it comforting and encouraging.

4.3.4 Role Models. The forth theme that we found confirms that some campers did develop a sense of future self throughout the camp. Approximately half of the campers interviewed perceived their mentors as role models. This happened for a variety of reasons. Campers mentioned looking up to their mentors, or wanting to program or mentor like them. Some of the reasons for those aspirations were mentors' subject matter expertise (e.g. "*she is a good programmer*"), ease of programming or an assumption that they started programming in a camp similar to the one they were attending.

Observing the work of mentors, "*what they do and how they know all this stuff*", as well as the amount of help they provided, encouraged one camper to put more effort into her programming, because she wanted to be a mentor one day.

Another camper was also interested in the prospects of being a mentor herself. To her, however, the mentor served as a teaching role model, because she felt that if she wanted to teach people about programming one day, she could "*learn from [her mentor] about it.*"

During mentor training we emphasized the importance of being good role models for the campers, which included both being knowledgeable and being good teachers by modeling certain types of behavior. Campers did identify with their mentors and saw them as models of their future self, which provides another possible reason as to how mentor relatability affected campers' interest and self-efficacy.

5 DISCUSSION AND CONCLUSION

In this study, we set out to explore the effect of near-peer mentors on their mentees' affect gains during a one-week app camp. We found that middle school campers' perceptions of mentor relatability were shown to significantly predict both self-efficacy and interest gains. In other words, campers who perceived their mentor as more relatable were associated with higher gains in self-efficacy and intrinsic interest in computing when accounting for pre-camp affect differences, gender, and camp type (mixed-gender vs same-gender camps). Four themes were identified from the qualitative data that potentially explain why and how mentor relatability influenced self-efficacy and intrinsic interest gains. In line with Bandura's [3-4] argument for mentors as agents for self-efficacy and interest growth, we found that mentees perceived their mentors as both approachable and similar to themselves. Such perceptions were viewed as positive for the campers as they provided motivation to learn and a supportive learning environment. In addition, mentees noted the benefits of having a mentor who was both more knowledgeable than themselves, but not too much of an expert that they had disparate experiences [3-4]. Viewing the mentors as more capable versions of themselves provided the mentees with a credible but attainable model that helped them increase their interest and self-efficacy in CS.

These findings suggest that when designing CS experiences, one must not only take into account factors that promote learning, but must also attend to social aspects that lead to identity formation and a sense of community and belonging. This can be done through near-peer mentors who are approachable, similar and credible. However, it also important to note that expertise should not be the only qualification for hiring mentors because mentors with less experience may have a lot to offer.

ACKNOWLEDGMENTS

This work was supported by a grant (#1614849) from the National Science Foundation. Any opinions, findings, and conclusions or recommendations expressed in this paper are those of the authors and do not necessarily reflect the views of the National Science Foundation, or Utah State University.

REFERENCES

[1] Catherine Ashcraft, Elizabeth Eger, and Michelle Friend. 2012. Girls in IT: The Facts, Boulder, CO: National Center for Women & IT. Retrieved from: http://austinwomenintechnology.wildapricot.org/Resources/Documents/Girls%20in%20IT.%20The%20Facts.pdf

[2] Albert Bandura. 1977. Self-efficacy: Toward a unifying theory of behavioral change. *Phycological Review, Vol. 84*(2), 191.

[3] Albert Bandura. 1977. *Social learning theory.* Englewood Cliffs, N.J.: Prentice-Hall.

[4] Albert Bandura. 1981. Self-referent thought: A developmental analysis of self-efficacy. In J. H. Flavell & L. Ross (Eds.), *Social Cognitive Development: Frontiers and Possible Futures,* 200-239. Cambridge: Cambridge University Press.

[5] Albert Bandura. 1997. *Self-efficacy: The exercise of control.* New York: Freeman.

[6] Carolein Bulte, Aaron Betts, Kathryn Garner, and Steven Durning. 2007. Student teaching: Views of student near-peer teachers and learners. Medical Teacher, Vol. 29, 583-590. doi:10.1080/01421590701583824

[7] Bureau of Labor Statistics, Projections of occupational employment, 2014–24, https://www.bls.gov/careeroutlook/2015/article/projections-occupation.htm, Washington, DC: U.S. Department of Labor, 2014.

[8] Jennifer Burg, Paúl V. Pauca, William Turkett, Errin Fulp, Samuel S. Cho, Peter Santago, Daniel Cañas, and H. Donald Gage. 2015. Engaging Non-Traditional Students in Computer Science through Socially-Inspired Learning and Sustained Mentoring. In Proceedings of the *46th ACM Technical Symposium on Computer Science Education,* 639-644. ACM.

[9] Cheryl Carrico, and Chosang Tendhar. 2012. The use of the social cognitive career theory to predict engineering students' motivation in the PRODUCED program, In *the Am. Society for Eng. Education.*

[10] Jody Clarke-Midura, Vicki Allan, and Kevin Close. 2016. Investigating the role of being a mentor as a way of increasing interest in CS. In *Proceedings of the 47th ACM Technical Symposium on Computing Science Education,* 297-302. ACM. doi:10.1145/2839509.2844581

[11] Jody Clarke-Midura, Frederick Poole, Katarina Pantic, and Vicki Allan. In press. Playing mentor: A new strategy for recruiting young women into computer science. Journal of Women and Minorities in Science and Engineering. doi:10.1615/JWomenMinorScienEng.2017019307

[12] John W. Creswell, and Vicki L. Plano. 2011. Designing and Conducting Mixed Methods Research (2nd ed.). Thousand Oaks, CA: Sage Publication.

[13] Jill Denner, 2011. What Predicts Middle School Girls' Interest in Computing? *Int. Journal of Gender, Science and Technology 3,* Vol. 1. Available at: http://genderandset.open.ac.uk/index.php/genderandset/article/view/106

[14] Daryl D'Souza, Margaret Hamilton, James Harland, Peter Muir, Charles Thevathayan, and Cecily Walker. 2008.. Transforming learning of programming: a mentoring project. In *Proc. of the tenth Conf. on Australasian Comp. Edu.,* Vol. 78, 75-84. Australian Computing Society, Inc.

[15] David F. Feldon, Michelle A. Maher, Melissa Hurst, and Briana Timmerman. 2015. Faculty mentors', graduate students', and performance-based assessments of students' research skill development. *American educational research journal, 52*(2), 334-370.

[16] Elizabeth Fennema, and Julia A. Sherman. 1976. Fennema-Sherman mathematics attitudes scales: Instruments designed to measure attitudes toward the learning of mathematics by females and males. Journal for Research in Mathematics Education, Vol. 5, 324-326. doi:10.2307/748467

[17] Yasmin B. Kafai, Shiv Desai, Kylie Peppler, Grace Chiu, and Jesse Moya. 2008. Mentoring partnerships in a community technology centre: A constructionist approach for fostering equitable service learning. *Mentoring & Tutoring: Partnership in Learning,* Vol. *16,* 191-205. doi:10.1080/13611260801916614

[18] Yasmin B. Kafai, Jean Griffin, Quinn Burke, Michelle Slattery, Deborah Fields, Rita Powell, Michele Grab, Susan Davidson, and Joseph Sun. 2013. A cascading mentoring pedagogy in a CS service learning course to broaden participation and perceptions. In *Proc. for SIGCSE'13.* Denver, Colorado. doi: 10.1145/2445196.2445228

[19] Michael J. Karcher, Alice J. Davidson, Jean E. Rhodes, and Carla Herrera. 2010. Pygmalion in the program: The role of teenage peer mentors' attitudes in shaping their mentees' outcomes. *Applied Developmental Science,* vol. *14*(4), 212-227. doi:10.1080/10888691.2010.516188

[20] Tim Murphey, and Hiriko Arao. 2001. Reported belief changes through near peer role modeling. *The Electronic Journal for English as a Second Language,* Vol. *5*(3). Retrieved from http://tesl-ej.org/ej19/a1.html

[21] Tim Murphey, and K. Murakami. 1998. Near peer role models and changing beliefs. *Academia, 65,* 1-29.

[22] Michael D. Pluth, Shannon W. Boettcher, George V. Nazin, Ann L. Greenaway, and Matthew D. Hartle. 2015. Collaboration and near-peer mentoring as a platform for sustainable science education outreach. *Journal of Chemical Education, 92*(4), 625-630. doi:10.1021/ed500377m

[23] R Core Team (2017). R: A language and environment for statistical computing. R Foundation for Statistical Computing, Vienna, Austria. URL http://www.R-project.org/.

[24] Mustafa S. Rashid, Oluwaseun Sobowale, and David Gore. 2011. A near-peer teaching program developed and delivered exclusively by recent medical graduates for final year medical students sitting the final objective structured clinical examination (OSCE). *BMC Medical Education, 11,* 11.

[25] Nicholas Tayler, Samuel Hall, Norman J. Carr, Jonny R. Stephens, and Scott Border. 2015. Near peer teaching in medical curricula: Integrating student teachers in pathology tutorials. *Medical Education Online,* Vol. *20*(1). Retrieved from http://dx.doi.org/10.3402/meo.v20.27921

[26] Olle Ten Cate, O., Irene van de Vorst, and Sjoukje van den Broek, S. 2012. Academic achievement of students tutored by near-peers. *International Journal of Medical Education, 3,* 6-13.

[27] Laura S. Tenenbaum, Margery K. Anderson, Marti Jett, and Debra L. Yourick. 2014. An innovative near-peer mentoring model for undergraduate and secondary students: STEM focus. *Innovative Higher Education,* Vol. *39*(5), 375-385.

[28] Wang, J., Hong, H., Ravitz, J., and Ivory, M., Gender differences in factors influencing pursuit of computer science and related fields, Proc. ACM Tech. Symp. CS Educ., pp. 117-122, 2015.

[29] Brett Williams, and James Fowler. 2014. Can near-peer teaching improve academic performance? *International Journal of Higher Education,* Vol. *3*(4), 142-149.

[30] Williams, B. & Fowler, J. (2014). Can near-peer teaching improve academic performance? *International Journal of Higher Education, 3*(4), 142-149.

Alternative Paths to Computing Careers and Their Role in Broadening Participation

Kathleen J. Lehman
(moderator)
University of California, Los Angeles
Los Angeles, CA 90095
kate.j.lehman@gmail.com

Maureen Doyle
Northern Kentucky University
GH 400D
Highland Heights, KY 41099
doylem3@nku.edu

Louise Ann Lyon
ETR
100 Enterprise Way
Ste G300
Scotts Valley, CA 95066
louann.lyon@etr.org

Kyle Thayer
University of Washington
Box 352350
185 E Stevens Way NE
Seattle, WA 98195
kthayer@cs.washington.edu

ACM Reference format:
Kathleen J. Lehman, Maureen Doyle, Louise Ann Lyon, and Kyle Thaer. 2018. Alternative Paths to Computing Careers and Their Role in Broadening Participation. In *SIGCSE '18: 49th ACM Technical Symposium on Computer Science Education, Feb. 21–24, 2018, Baltimore, MD, USA.* ACM, NY, NY, USA, 2 pages. https://doi.org/10.1145/3159450.3159624

1. SUMMARY

Declaring a computer science (CS) major at the outset of college and going on to earn a computing degree may be the most direct route to a career in computing, but it is certainly not the only pathway. However, much of the work on pathways to computing careers focuses on those who have taken this traditional route, while less attention has been paid to those who pursue alternative pathways into computing. Understanding alternative pathways into computing may be particularly important to discussions about diversity in the field, as some research has shown that women and underrepresented minority (URM) students who enroll in CS courses are more likely than men and other majority students to be non-computing majors and to take computing courses later in their academic careers. This panel will provide perspectives from individuals with expertise in several alternative pathways into computing, such as through coding boot camps, undecided students, community colleges, and retrained end-user programmers.

2. ALTERNATIVE PATHS

2.1 Coding Boot Camps

A new breed of intensive training ground for software development dubbed "coding boot camps" has blossomed. These camps teaching coding to novices over 8 to 104 weeks at a price tag of $11,400 on average [4]. With female enrollments at 35%, compared to 15.7% in university CS programs [4], and a heavily post-traditional, career changers student population [6], boot camps are situated to help diversify the computing workforce.

2.2 Undecided Students

As computing departments seek to broaden access to computing fields, CS department chairs often cite a lack of control over the admissions process as a key obstacle to their success [8]. That is, at many institutions, students are admitted into the university and their majors through a central process, and department chairs have limited ability to influence the types of students who matriculate as computing majors. In response to this challenge, prominent scholars and non-profit organizations have encouraged computing departments to recruit undecided students into computing [2]. Undecided students include students who do not have a major as well as those who have a "declared" major but feel a significant amount of indecision about that choice, and nearly 10% of students enter college with an undecided/undeclared major [3]. Undecided students represent an important opportunity for CS departments, as they may serve as a pool of students who could be recruited to the CS major. Little research exists on pathways for undecided students to choose a STEM or CS major or how their experiences in the field might encourage or dissuade them to pursue computing.

2.3 Community Colleges

Community colleges in the United States are public institutions that offer postsecondary, technical, and continuing education to regional populations. These colleges are open access – open to anyone, no application necessary – and they serve large numbers of students that are traditionally underrepresented in computing fields. In the U.S., 43% of community college students are non-white [1], and over half of women who earn a STEM (Science, Technology, Engineering, and Math) degree started out at a community college [7]. Community colleges also serve a post-traditional (older or working) population of students. Encouraging more students at community colleges to consider computing certificates, degrees, and transfer preparation could serve to diversify computing.

2.4 From End User to End User Programmer

The number of people who say they write computer code at work vastly outnumber professional programmers [9]. Adoption of the Salesforce Customer Relationship Management (CRM) cloud-based software platform has created a demand for knowledgeable technicians who can administer software for the many businesses that have converted to the Salesforce platform. Among these "Salesforce admins" (system administrators who are configuring the software) are women who are finding that they have strong reasons to want to learn to code in Salesforce's Java-based language, Apex, to customize applications of Salesforce in ways that are not possible through the administrator interface. Salesforce provides a variety of open resources for individuals to learn to code, but some women are finding that a more structured format of coaching and learning in all-female groups is preferable. A current, NSF-funded qualitative study (#1612527) investigates the backgrounds and

ACM ISBN 978-1-4503-5103-4/18/02.
DOI: https://doi.org/10.1145/3159450.3159624

learning experiences of the participants in this group to suggest ways that women could be supported in their entry into programming while in the workforce.

3. PANELISTS

3.1 Kathleen J. Lehman

Dr. Lehman serves as the Associate Director for BRAID Research, a nationwide mixed-method study focused on recruiting women and URM students to computing. Prior to her work with BRAID, she was project manager for an NSF-funded study on the gender gap across STEM fields. Dr. Lehman completed a mixed-methods dissertation on undecided students who enroll in introductory CS courses. She found that while undecided students are a small group (approximately 7-10% of introductory CS students), they represent an important opportunity to recruit more women into the major. Her findings suggest that undecided students enrolled in intro CS courses are significantly more likely to be women as compared to CS majors taking intro courses. Further, approximately 40% of undecided students go on to choose a computing major by the end of their introductory course. Her research suggests that social interactions with computing peers is the most important factor in undecided students' decision to pursue a computing degree.

3.2 Louise Ann Lyon

Louise Ann ("Lou Ann") Lyon, PhD, Senior Research Associate at ETR, brings industry experience as well as research knowledge from Learning Sciences and Feminist Studies. Dr. Lyon is currently PI on two NSF funded projects. The first is a project to study pathways to CS for women who are teaching themselves to code motivated by current job needs or improved employment opportunities. The second is a collaborative project with Dr. Quinn Burke at the College of Charleston that looks at the alignment with workforce needs of training provided at coding boot camps versus university computing majors. Dr. Lyon also completed a study funded by Google on perspectives of students from underrepresented groups as they move through community colleges in California to transfer and completion of a bachelor's degree in CS [5].

3.3 Maureen Doyle

Maureen Doyle has worked on a number of 2+2 pathways with community colleges in Kentucky, Ohio and Indiana in roles as Associate Dean of Informatics and Chair of CS at Northern Kentucky University (NKU). NKU is a regional university located in greater Cincinnati. There are multiple successful collaborations between NKU and area community colleges, but Maureen has worked most closely with Bluegrass Community and Technical College (BCTC) in Lexington, KY. The collaboration has proved a success, with more students transferring from BCTC to NKU in the past 2 years than in the previous 10. The numbers are low (7 students in 2015 and 2016, but only 5 total students in the previous 10 years), but considerable since BCTC is 90 miles away from NKU. BCTC teaches NKU courses for an Associate in Informatics degree and they have established pathways in CS and IT.

3.4 Kyle Thayer

Kyle's researching coding boot camps are part of his PhD work in the Paul G. Allen School of CS & Engineering at the University of Washington. As part of his PhD work, he also studies how culture influences the use of programming tools and API documentation as a barrier to programming. Kyle received a MS in CS at Emory University and a BS in CS and Math at Colorado State University.

Kyle interviewed twenty-six current and former students in coding bootcamps [10]. He found some attended boot camps as an alternative to getting an undergraduate degree and that boot camps provided a second chance for those who missed earlier computing education opportunities, particularly for women. Students in boot camps faced great personal costs and risks and their paths in the software industry were often long and complicated. These long paths often including significant time, money and effort spent on activities such as online courses, in-person courses, portfolio building, attending hackathons, getting short-term contracts, and even attending sections of multiple boot camps. Some boot camp students already had CS degrees before attending while others had never tried programming before. Though the coursework of bootcamps only ranged from three to six months, career change could take students a year or more,

4. REFERENCES

[1] American Association of Community Colleges. 2016. Fact Sheet. Retrieved from http://www.aacc.nche.edu/AboutCC/Documents/AACCFactSheetsR2.pdf.

[2] Cohoon, J. M. (2002). Recruiting and retaining women in undergraduate computing majors. ACM SIGCSE Bulletin, 34(2), 48-52.

[3] Eagan, K., Stolzenberg, E. B., Ramirez, J. J., Aragon, M. C., Suchard, M. R., & Hurtado, S. (2014). The American freshman: National norms fall 2014. Los Angeles: Higher Education Research Institute, UCLA.

[4] Eggleston, L. (2017, July 19). 2017 Coding Bootcamp Market Size Study. Retrieved from: www.coursereport.com/reports/2017-coding-bootcamp-market-size-research

[5] Lyon, L. A. and Denner, J. 2016. Student Perspectives of Community College Pathways to Computer Science Bachelor's Degrees. Mountain View, CA: Google Inc. Retrieved from https://goo.gl/Q0wJJv.

[6] Lyon, L.A., Burke, Q., Denner, J., & Bowring, J. 2017. Should Your College Computer Science Program Partner with a Coding Boot Camp? Poster presented at the 48th technical symposium on computer science education (SIGCSE '17) (Seattle, WA, March 8-11, 2017).

[7] Moughari, L., Gunn-Wright, R., & Gault, B. (2012, April). Gender Segregation in Fields of Study at Community Colleges and Implications for Future Earnings. Retrieved from https://iwpr.org/wp-content/uploads/wpallimport/files/iwpr-export/publications/C395.pdf

[8] Sax, L. J., Zimmerman, H. B., Blaney, J. M., Toven-Lindsey, B., & Lehman, K. J. (2017). Diversifying Undergraduate Computer Science: The Role of Department Chairs in Promoting Gender and Racial Diversity. *Journal of Women and Minorities in Science and Engineering, 23*(2).

[9] Scaffidi, C., Shaw, M., and Myers, B. 2005. Estimating the numbers of end users and end user programmers. Paper presented at the IEEE Symposium on Visual Languages and Human-Centric Computing (VL/HCC).

[10] Thayer, K. & Ko, A. J. (2017). Barriers Faced by Coding Bootcamp Students. Proceedings of the International Computer Science Education Research Workshop. 245-253.

Best Practices in Academia to Remedy Gender Bias in Tech

Ursula Wolz (moderator)
Bennington College
1 College Dr,
North Bennington, VT 05257
ursulawolz@bennington.edu

Lina Battestilli
Department of Computer Science
North Carolina State University
Raleigh, NC 27695
lbattestilli@ncsu.edu

Bruce Maxwell
Department of Computer Science
Colby College
Waterville, ME 04901
bmaxwell@colby.edu

Susan Rodger
Department of Computer Science
Duke University
Durham, NC 27708
rodger@cs.duke.edu

Michelle Trim
College of Information and
Computer Sciences
University of Massachusetts, Amherst
Amherst, MA 01003
mtrim@cs.umass.edu

ACM Reference format:
Ursula Wolz, Lina Battestilli, Bruce Maxwell, Susan Rodger, and Michelle Trim. 2018. Best Practices in Academia to Remedy Gender Bias in Tech. In *SIGCSE '18: 49th ACM Technical Symposium on Computer Science Education, Feb. 21–24, 2018, Baltimore, MD, USA*. ACM, NY, NY, USA, 2 pages. https://doi.org/10.1145/3159450.3159618

1. SUMMARY

The New York Times published an op-ed by Anita Hill [3] suggesting that women in tech consider class action to remedy the gender bias that is increasingly being reported in the mass-media. This panel raises the question "what are we doing in undergraduate programs to reduce the 'Mad Men', "Brogrammer" culture she describes that is increasingly being reported in the popular press. Part of our mission as educators is to develop professional behavior so that our students entering the workforce not only understand what it means to act professionally, but understand that it is their responsibility to actively push back on the existing bias within the tech culture. As moderator Ursula Wolz brings a depth of insight from 40 years of industrial and academic experience, including a National Science Foundation project to broaden participation in computing [5]. She does not believe this problem can be solved through quantitative data collection on who does well in computer science, but that SIGCSE needs to begin to collect good stories (ala Sally Fincher [2]) on what constitute best practices to support diversity. The panelists present a range of perspectives that have the potential to establish new cultural norms in the single most influential industry in our economy.

2. LINA BATTESTILLI

I teach two different CS1-type courses (JAVA for majors and MATLAB for engineering students). I am also part of the Senior Design center so I also work with students right before they graduate. I observe some students earn their degree right from the beginning, all the way until then graduate! Here a few things that we can do to retain and encourage women (and minorities!) to earn a CS degree:

SIGCSE '18, February 21–24, 2018, Baltimore , MD, USA

ACM ISBN 978-1-4503-5103-4/18/02.
https://doi.org/10.1145/3159450.3159618

(1) At NCSU, we make sure that our **Women In Computer Science (WiCS) Student organization** is active and supported financially. We have lots of events where women in the department can meet each other and thus not feel isolated because they are a minority. We also create connections to industry and promote job opportunities. We also sponsor 8-12 students each year to attend the Grace Hopper Conference.

(2) Students are taught to adopt **Growth Mindset** rather than Fixed Mindset [1]. It is not that you are NOT good at something but rather you have not spent the time to get better at it. Intelligence can be developed! At NCSU, we have produced a series of 5 videos that teach Growth Mindset and all students watch them during their CS1 course. In the videos, we have students and faculty from our department and industry representatives discuss their experience with CS. Topics include Balancing Talent vs Effort, Failure is Part of Success, Characteristic of a successful computer scientists, etc. After watching these videos, the CS1 students reflect and discuss on what they have learned.

(3) Careful **team formation and managing of relationships** in the classroom. This is hard in a large class but at least during lab(discussion) can be tackled. If possible at least two women should be grouped in each team so they don't feel as a minority and thus can feel comfortable in speaking up.

(4) Include and encourage **peer instruction, collaboration and pair programming** to courses. These are successful teaching techniques, widely supported by research evidence.

(5) Getting **Unconscious Bias Training** both for faculty, TAs and students. There are two types of discrimination -- conscious vs. unconscious. Most of us will not allow conscious, obvious discrimination. However, we might have unconscious bias that we are not even aware of. It is necessary to think carefully through the examples/problems given in the class. One famous example is *Lenna* a photo often used to teach image processing [4].

(6) Selection of **Relevant Topics for Course Assignments**. There is so much work out there in this topic and yet so many really boring CS1 assignments. Female students get discouraged pursing a CS degree if they don't see how it can be connected in solving/helping our societal problems.

3. SUSAN RODGER

I have been teaching CS1 for over 25 years. Our enrollments have grown to around 300 per semester and around 50% of them are women. Here are some of the things I do to remedy gender bias.

1) In 2010 we changed to Python and began to put in a diverse set of examples and assignment to appeal to a broad set of students.

2) I send a survey to the students right before the first day of class. The survey includes questions about their programming experience. I show the survey results on the first day of class to make it clear that 80 percent of them are beginners.

3) From time to time in lecture I remind them that most of them are beginners. We do a lot of work during lecture with Google Forms and whenever a question indicates a lot of them missed it, I re-emphasize that most of them are beginners.

4) In each lecture, I have one or two slides that highlight either someone who previously took this course and what they are doing now, or someone prominent in the computer field. I select a diverse set of people to highlight among women and underrepresented groups. Not all the alums are in Computer Science, but I want to those who take the course for the problem solving skills.

5) I talk about the Grace Hopper conference and encourage students to apply for scholarships. Our program takes students every year.

6) I reach out to women and underrepresented groups who did well in the course and encourage them to be an undergraduate teaching assistant (UTA) for the course. I found they will not apply unless they get encouragement. For example, out of 31 UTAs last semester for this course 5 were African American, 9 were Asian, 15 were women, at least 2 were Hispanic. These UTAs run our labs.

7) Finally, we do training with the UTAs and meet with them once a week and include talking about how to deal with issues with students and to be aware of bias. For example, "Are you helping only a particular type of student?" For our consulting hours, in order to make sure students are helped in a fair manner, they sign up and we process them in that order.

4. BRUCE MAXWELL

Over the past five years our department has grown from 11 students pursuing CS-related degrees in the class of 2013 to 45 in the class of 2018. For the past ten years we have emphasized a CS community based on cooperation and respect. We have also followed a number of best practices, including giving women and under-represented groups summer research opportunities, funding our women to attend Grace Hopper Conference, ensuring we hire at least as many women as men for lab and evening TAs, and restructuring all of our core courses to focus around some context for the application of computer science.

The growth of our department to 80+ upper-class students, and some changes in demographics has allowed separate cliques to form, where before that was difficult. When there were fewer than 20 juniors and seniors, all taking the same courses, they all knew one another and spent time together. To address some of this loss of community, we held a meeting with of our upper-class students as well as all of our TAs. Before the meeting we had them read an article on Google's findings on what makes effective teams. One of their primary findings was that in the most effective teams, members felt that team was a safe place and that their opinions were valued. It was an effective article, because it tied team success to the kind of culture that we want to encourage. That it came out of Google also gave it some validity in the minds of those we most wanted to reach.

One of the lessons from this experience was to highlight the importance of individuals in creating or destroying the culture of the CS space. We have one big lab that is used mainly by upper-class students. Before the growth in majors, there was a senior who spent a lot of time in the lab and was also socially adept and strongly encouraged people to be civil. She graduated, and no one stepped up to take her place. We then had one or two of our alpha students become juniors or seniors, and just that flip of 2-3 people changed the character of the lab. The discussion session and the Google article helped us to reach those individuals, without directly targeting them, and collectively we developed a set of ground rules for the lab. Because we were able to reach them and get the students actively thinking about the lab culture, it engendered a change in the atmosphere of the lab that persisted for the rest of the year.

5. MICHELLE TRIM

UMass Amherst requires all students to complete an advanced writing course in their major in either their junior or senior year. The computer science version of this course is titled "Social Issues in Computing." As the coordinator for this course, I've designed it to engage students on issues related to gender and race, among others, through specific readings, discussions, and writing assignments. Since each section of this course is typically populated with only a couple of female-identified students (out of 25), discussions of gender in computer science take on an increased level of urgency. The course culminates in a reflective writing assignment that reinforces the teaching and learning about gender (and identity) that takes place in our class. This assignment serves two key purposes in combating gender bias. First, it provides students with an opportunity to write about their own learning experiences. Although gender is not a prescribed topic, many male-identified students identify changed understandings of or awakened perceptions of gender bias as powerful course outcomes. The very low-stakes nature of this assignment speaks to the validity of students' claims. This assignment also combats gender bias is through the stories it unexpectedly elicits from students regarding their experiences in the field – including those involving peers, professors, and internship co-workers/supervisors. Those stories, de-identified and compiled together provide a clear window to this student population's perceptions of gender bias in our field.

6. REFERENCES

[1] Dweck, Carol S.. *Mindset: The New Psychology Of Success.* New York : Ballantine Books, 2008.

[2] Fincher, S, et. al.. *Change Stories.* Technical Report 12-1, Computing Laboratory, University of Kent, Canterbury, Kent, UK, February 2012.

[3] Hill, A. https://www.nytimes.com/2017/08/08/opinion/anita-hill-women-in-tech-should-take-sexism-to-court.html?mcubz=3&_r=0

[4] Medel, P & V. Pournaghshband. 2017. Eliminating Gender Bias in Computer Science Education Materials. In Proceedings of the 2017 ACM SIGCSE Technical Symposium on Computer Science Education).

[5] Wolz, U., et. al. "Computational Thinking and Expository Writing in the Middle School: A novel approach to broadening participation in computing", *Transactions on Computing Education,* July 2011, Volume 2, article 9

The Role of Researcher-Practitioner Partnerships in CS4All: Lessons from the Field

Lucia Dettori (moderator)
DePaul University
lucia@cdm.depaul.edu

Don Yanek
Chicago Public Schools
dgyanek@cps.edu

Helen Hu
Westminster College
hhu@westminstercollege.edu

Dennis Brylow
Marquette University
brylow@mscs.mu.edu

CCS CONCEPTS

• **Social and professional topics → K-12 education**; *Computational thinking*; *Accreditation*; *Model curricula*; *Student assessment*;

KEYWORDS

researcher-practitioner partnerships; equity; high school; coaching; Exploring Computer Science; teacher professional development

ACM Reference Format:
Lucia Dettori (moderator), Don Yanek, Helen Hu, and Dennis Brylow. 2018. The Role of Researcher-Practitioner Partnerships in CS4All: Lessons from the Field. In *SIGCSE '18: The 49th ACM Technical Symposium on Computer Science Education, February 21–24, 2018, Baltimore , MD, USA.* ACM, New York, NY, USA, 2 pages. https://doi.org/10.1145/3159450.3159626

1 SUMMARY

Researcher Practitioner Partnerships (RPP) are "long-term, mutualistic collaborations between practitioners and researchers that are intentionally organized to investigate problems of practice and solutions for improving district [and school] outcomes." [1] As highlighted in NSF solicitation NSF 17-525, RPPs are critical for the success of CS For All initiatives aimed at providing all K–12 students access to CS education.

The panelists represent three examples of mature RPPs that have successfully implemented CS4All programs in three states working with school districts with different characteristics and at different scales. The projects share similar approaches to the goal of increasing equity in CS education by providing all high school students access to a rigorous and relevant CS course. All projects chose to focus on the Exploring Computer Science (ECS) Curriculum and Professional Development. While the specifics of the implementation vary, the projects encountered similar challenges especially when transitioning from a pilot stage to igniting systemic change across the region. Challenges vary in importance and scale across a wide range of issues including: teacher capacity building, fidelity of implementation, leadership structure and buy-in, personnel turnover and continuity of funding. The open ended commitment of RPPs to work together on the specific problems that the educational partners face and grounding solutions on rigorous research has allowed these projects to flourish.

The discussion will focus on how the programs were able to organically build an RPP and leverage it to deploy, scale and sustain their initiatives. The panel will share obstacles, successes and lessons learned from each implementation. Nascent and more established partnerships will benefit from learning how these three RPPs overcame challenges so that they can leverage those lessons to accelerate their own implementation.

2 DON YANEK – CAFÉCS

The Chicago Alliance For Equity in Computer Science (CAFÉCS) RPP started 8 years ago as an informal alliance between a Chicago Public School (CPS) high school CS teacher (Yanek), a CPS administrator (Wilkerson), and three university computer scientists (Dettori, Greenberg, and Reed). As the group sought to become better grounded in educational research practice, they added an educational researcher (McGee). The goal was to provide quality access to ECS to all high school students in CPS. With its 167 high schools, CPS is the third largest urban school district in the country. CPS 110,000 students includes: 47% Hispanic, 38% African American, and 80% economically disadvantaged students.

CAFÉCS has grown significantly since starting with a pilot cohort of 11 teachers. With the support of multiple public and private grants (NSF: CNS-1138417, 1543217, 1542971, 1738691, 1738776, DRL-1640215), the alliance has developed 15 ECS facilitators who have provided ECS PD to over 250 CPS teachers. In the alliance's first 5 years, ECS has been taught in 40 CPS high schools to over 13,000 students reflecting the diversity of CPS student body. In addition, 44% of the students are female. Currently, ECS is being taught in 63 schools to over 11,000 students by over 150 teachers. A Principals PD program and a peer coaching program have also been established. The alliance has contributed to the literature on the impact of the ECS course on students' attitudes towards CS [2], students' choices about future CS coursework [5], and students' development of computational thinking practices [6]. A proud moment for this alliance came when Mayor Emanuel felt confident enough in the direction of the alliance to launch the K–12 CS for All initiative (CS4All) in 2013. Two years later, the members of the alliance stood together in support as the Chicago School Board approved the institution of CS as a graduation requirement for all CPS high school students starting with the 2020 graduating class. It would have been easy to declare victory and disband the alliance,

ACM ISBN 978-1-4503-5103-4/18/02.
https://doi.org/10.1145/3159450.3159626

but it soon became clear that as much work as went into laying the groundwork for enacting the graduation policy, even more work would go into ensuring high quality implementation of the policy.

The need to reach every high school within the four year timeline dictated by the graduation requirement highlighted existing hurdles and uncovered new ones. Challenges revolve around teacher capacity building, improving and diversifying the support for novice teachers, ensuring fidelity of implementation, measuring impact on student learning, cultivating buy-in from school leadership and facilitating institutional changes within CPS to progressively transition ownership of logistics.

3 HELEN HU – UTAH ECS INITIATIVE

The Utah Exploring Computer Science Initiative grew out of discussions of the Utah Computer Science Teachers Association (CSTA) chapter on how to respond when 9th and 10th graders were not being allowed to take CS classes. The Utah State Specialist for Computer Science (Lyman), three university computer scientists (Hu, McCarthy and Heiner), and high school computer science teacher-leaders (Reitz-Larsen) collaborated to introduce a one-semester version of ECS to fulfill an existing Utah high school graduation requirement. NSF award CNS-1240977 supported four years of ECS summer workshops for over 200 Utah teachers [3, 4]. ECS workshops are now supported by a combination of funding from the Utah State Board of Education (USBE), the Utah STEM Action Center, and a Code.org state partnership.

The partnership between the USBE and university CS researchers has been key to the explosive adoption of ECS in the state. ECS has served as one of two options for the statewide high school Computer Technology graduation requirement set by the USBE. Similarly, Utah teachers were quick to sign up for ECS workshops because the summer workshops and the follow-up PD were requirements for earning an ECS endorsement as well as a more advanced CS endorsement for in-service teachers.

One of the challenge of the partnership has been reaching all students in Utah. ECS students were only 37% female in 2015–16. The lack of gender equity reflects a preconception by guidance counselors, parents, teachers and even students that female students may not benefit from ECS as much as male students. The partnership also struggled to break into the most rural school districts, where administrators were less enthusiastic about teaching students programming skills that would cause students to leave the community. Many rural teachers were already teaching seven or more different courses each semester and were not eager to add a new course to their teaching load. We are slowly making progress in both these areas by leveraging other STEM projects and state legislative funding in support of CS education through the USBE and the STEM Action Center.

4 DENNIS BRYLOW – PUMP-CS

The PUMP-CS project (Preparing the Upper Midwest / Urban Milwaukee for Principles of Computer Science) grew out of an effort in 2010 to bring together stakeholders from Wisconsin's Department of Public Instruction, high school CS teachers, and several universities, with Brylow representing Marquette's CS faculty. With the shared goal of promoting CS education across the state, the steering group planned the first CS-specific professional development workshops and worked to secure funding from local sponsors, Google CS4HS, and ultimately NSF. With support through NSF awards CNS-1339392 (Marquette University) and CNS-1339179 (University of Wisconsin - La Crosse) beginning in 2013, the PUMP team began rolling out ECS courses in high schools all over the state, including urban, suburban, small town and rural districts. Over three academic years, 62 teachers and over 1,800 students have participated in the project.

The greatest challenge in partnering with school districts has been getting good information into the right hands in each school. Although many affluent suburban districts quickly signed on, reaching socioeconomically disadvantaged students in very urban and very rural schools has proven persistently difficult. Many administrators still do not know what CS is, or assume that they must be teaching it because there are devices or digital literacy courses in the school. At the next tier of familiarity, district decision-makers may realize there is a need for CS, but fear that special equipment costs or the difficulty of hiring and retaining qualified CS teachers will be a prohibitive strain on limited resources. For schools that are ready to staff and run CS courses, the most daunting challenge is choosing a safe pathway through the ever-expanding universe of CS curriculum resources.

The greatest success of the PUMP-CS partnership has been to leverage university and state resources to help curate coherent curriculum choices, to promulgate sensible content standards, and to support our K–12 colleagues in developing reflective communities of professional development at various levels.

With new CS courses planted in seven of the largest Milwaukee Public School (MPS) system high schools by 2016, the PUMP team extended its focus to promoting CS education in every school of our state's largest and most diverse public school district. Continuing NSF support through 2019 is under award CNS-1640217 for Marquette, in collaboration with University of Wisconsin - Milwaukee and MPS. As is the case in many large districts, the central administration often has limited power to directly affect change in individual clusters and schools, and the case for CS education must frequently be made building by building.

REFERENCES

[1] Cynthia E. Coburn, William R. Penuel, and Kimberly E. Geil. 2013. Research-Practice Partnerships: A Strategy for Leveraging Research for Educational Improvement in School Districts. A white paper prepared for the William T. Grant Foundation. (Jan. 2013). http://rpp.wtgrantfoundation.org/library/uploads/2016/01/R-P-Partnerships-White-Paper-Jan-2013-Coburn-Penuel-Geil.pdf

[2] Lucia Dettori, Ronald I. Greenberg, Steven McGee, and Dale Reed. 2016. The Impact of The Exploring Computer Science Instructional Model in Chicago Public Schools. *Computing in Science & Engineering (Special Issue: Best of RESPECT 2015)* 18, 2 (March/April 2016), 10–17. http://doi.org/10.1109/MCSE.2016.39

[3] Helen H. Hu, Cecily Heiner, , Thomas Gagne, and Carl Lyman. 2017. Building a Statewide Computer Science Teacher Pipeline. In *SIGCSE '17*. 291–296.

[4] Helen H. Hu, Cecily Heiner, and Jay McCarthy. 2016. Deploying Exploring Computer Science Statewide. In *SIGCSE '16*. 72–77.

[5] Steven McGee, Randi McGee-Tekula, Jennifer Duck, Ronald I. Greenberg, Lucia Dettori, Dale F. Reed, Brenda Wilkerson, Don Yanek, Andrew M. Rasmussen, and Gail Chapman. 2017. Does a Taste of Computing Increase Computer Science Enrollment? *Computing in Science & Engineering (Special Issue: Best of RESPECT 2016)* 19, 3 (April 2017), 8–18. http://doi.org/10.1109/MCSE.2017.50

[6] Steven McGee, Randi McGee-Tekula, Jennifer Duck, Catherine McGee, Lucia Dettori, Ronald I. Greenberg, Eric Snow, Daisy Rutstein, Dale Reed, Brenda Wilkerson, Don Yanek, Andrew Rasmussen, and Dennis Brylow. 2018. Equal Outcomes 4 All: A Study of Student Learning in ECS. In *SIGCSE '18*.

Preparing, Visualizing, and Using Real-world Data in Introductory Courses

Austin Cory Bart
Virginia Tech
Blacksburg, Virginia
acbart@vt.edu

Kalpathi Subramanian
The University of North Carolina at Charlotte
Charlotte, North Carolina
krs@uncc.edu

Ruth E. Anderson
University of Washington
Seattle, Washington
rea@cs.washington.edu

Nadeem Abdul Hamid
Berry College
Mount Berry, Georgia
nadeem@acm.org

CCS CONCEPTS

• **Information systems → Information integration**; Data management systems; • **Social and professional topics** → *Model curricula*; Computing literacy;

KEYWORDS

Real world data, data science, visualization

ACM Reference format:
Austin Cory Bart, Kalpathi Subramanian, Ruth E. Anderson, and Nadeem Abdul Hamid. 2018. Preparing, Visualizing, and Using Real-world Data in Introductory Courses. In *Proceedings of SIGCSE '18: The 49th ACM Technical Symposium on Computer Science Education, Baltimore , MD, USA, February 21–24, 2018 (SIGCSE '18),* 2 pages.
https://doi.org/10.1145/3159450.3159616

1 SUMMARY

Working with real-world data has increasingly become a popular context for introductory computing courses [1, 5, 7, 9, 10]. As a valuable 21st century skill, preparing students to be able to divine meaning from data can be useful to their long-term careers [4]. Because Data Science aligns so closely with computing, many of the topics and problems it affords as a context can support the core learning objectives in introductory computing classes. In many instances, incorporating a real-world dataset to provide concrete context for an activity or assignment can improve student engagement and understanding of the abstract educational content being presented.

However, there are many problems inherent to bringing real-world data into introductory courses. How do instructors, with finite amounts of time and energy, find and prepare suitable datasets for their pedagogical needs? Once the datasets are ready, how can students conveniently interact with and draw meaning from the datasets, especially when they are used in complex projects that are typical of later introductory courses? On the other hand, how does an instructor balance the complexities of using real-world datasets in the classroom, making sure that students appreciate the meaningfulness of course activities and their connection to learning objectives?

This panel brings together experts with experience in using real-world data in introductory computing courses. Each panelist provides unique perspectives and skills to the problem of preparing, interacting, visualizing, and using pedagogical datasets. This panel should be of particular interest to instructors who are considering integrating current and real-world data into their assignments and projects, and to educational developers who want to create and manage datasets for pedagogical purposes. The panel will follow a conventional format: 5 minutes of introduction, 10 minutes for each panelist to present, and then 30 minutes for audience Q&A.

SIGCSE '18, February 21–24, 2018, Baltimore , MD, USA

ACM ISBN 978-1-4503-5103-4/18/02.
https://doi.org/10.1145/3159450.3159616

2 AUSTIN CORY BART(MODERATOR)

Austin Cory Bart is the lead developer for the CORGIS project (https://think.cs.vt.edu/corgis), which seeks to make a **C**ollection of **R**eally **G**reat and **I**nteresting data**S**ets available to computing educators [2]. The CORGIS site has over 40 datasets in a range of topics including health, literature, geological sciences, history, and much more. Each dataset is available in various data formats, through convenient language bindings, and in a powerful exploratory web interface. In addition to the datasets, the CORGIS project has infrastructure for managing its complex collection and myriad formats. The development of this infrastructure and these datasets have led to the authoring of an on-line text targeted at educational developers on the subject of preparing pedagogical datasets (https://think.cs.vt.edu/pragmatics).

Pedagogical Datasets are distinctive from regular datasets in that they are meant to be embedded in assignments and projects, and therefore can be tied to learning objectives and a learner context. After collection, their structure and information must be suitably scaffolded to ensure that the learners are capable of processing the data. Usability and navigability are crucial in their design, but there are many other design choices to consider. This presentation will briefly highlight the problems, strategies, and experiences that Bart has encountered while designing datasets for the CORGIS project.

3 KALPATHI SUBRAMANIAN

Kalpathi Subramanian is an associate professor of computer science at the University of North Carolina at Charlotte. For the past few years, he has led a team of investigators and developers as part of the BRIDGES project[3]. BRIDGES (**B**ridging **R**eal-world **I**nfrastructure **D**esigned to **G**oal-align, **E**ngage, and **S**timulate) provides a software infrastructure designed to enable the creation of more engaging assignments in data structures and algorithms courses by providing students with a simplified API (Java, C++ supported, with Python API in progress), allowing them to populate their own data structure implementations with live, real-world, and interesting data sets, such as those from social networks, entertainment, scientific, social or cultural data. In addition, the BRIDGES system provides the capability to visualize and share the constructed data structures via a web link, which can be highly engaging to freshmen/sophomore students.

In this talk, Dr. Subramanian will present recent work using BRIDGES, new datasets that have been integrated into BRIDGES, its impact on students over the past few years, and experiences of external users of BRIDGES. A key and current goal of BRIDGES is to continue interfacing with new datasets, creation of highly engaging assignments, and mechanisms for dissemination to the larger CS education community. In this regard, work is underway on building interfaces to CORGIS datasets, led by Bart et al. [2].

4 RUTH ANDERSON

Ruth Anderson is a Senior Lecturer in computer science at the University of Washington. For the past four years she has taught CSE 160 Data Programming [1], which aims to equip students with the skills necessary to use programming to answer questions about data sets. The course is an introduction to programming that teaches the basics of Python with a focus on language constructs needed to process data files. Assignments are drawn from science, engineering, business, and the humanities and expose students to a variety of data types (output from a DNA sequencer, images, text, election results, social networks). For early assignments students are given starter code that handles much of the file reading. Later assignments introduce students to the concept of data cleaning and give them experience doing so. The course culminates in an individual or partner project of students' own design. Students are required to propose a data set they will use and an analysis they will complete. They independently design and implement a program to answer a question about a data set and present their results in written and oral formats. The goal is that by the end of the course students can use programming to pose and answer interesting questions about data sets they care about from a variety of domains.

5 NADEEM ABDUL HAMID

Nadeem Abdul Hamid is an associate professor of computer science at Berry College. For the past several years, he has been developing a software framework [8] to facilitate the use of online data sources in introductory computer science courses. The Sinbad (**S**tructure **IN**ference and **B**inding **A**utomatically to **D**ata) library enables students to easily access online data sources in standard formats (CSV, JSON, XML) with minimal syntactic overhead and no need to deal with low-level issues related to parsing and extracting data. Given a data source URL, the library (currently implemented in Java with a Python version in active development) infers the structure of available data, downloads, caches, parses, and binds the data to programmer-defined data structures and representations. Nadeem has used this library for three years in an introductory programming course for non-majors, using Processing [6]. Students are provided a set of labs to practice accessing data at increasing levels of complexity - from primitive data and simple objects to lists of objects (where the class definitions can be provided by students themselves rather than by the instructor or the Sinbad library). For the final project in the course, students are then asked to find a data source on their own and develop an interactive GUI visualization of the data using Processing. This presentation will highlight the goals and rationale behind the design of the Sinbad project, technical and pedagogical challenges and opportunities, and reflect on the complementary nature of this project to the approaches adopted by the other panel participants.

ACKNOWLEDGMENTS

The work for BRIDGES is supported by the National Science Foundation under Grant No. DUE-1245841, DUE-1726809. The work for CORGIS is supported in part by National Science Foundation grants DUE 1624320, DUE 1444094, and DGE 0822220.

REFERENCES

[1] Ruth E. Anderson, Michael D. Ernst, Robert Ordóñez, Paul Pham, and Ben Tribelhorn. 2015. A Data Programming CS1 Course. In *Proceedings of the 46th ACM Technical Symposium on Computer Science Education (SIGCSE '15)*. ACM, New York, NY, USA, 150–155. https://doi.org/10.1145/2676723.2677309

[2] Austin Cory Bart, Ryan Whitcomb, Dennis Kafura, Clifford A Shaffer, and Eli Tilevich. 2017. Computing with corgis: Diverse, real-world datasets for introductory computing. In *Proceedings of the 2017 ACM SIGCSE Technical Symposium on Computer Science Education*. 57–62.

[3] David Burlinson, Mihai Mehedint, Chris Grafer, Kalpathi Subramanian, Jamie Payton, Paula Goolkasian, Michael Youngblood, and Robert Kosara. 2016. BRIDGES: A System to Enable Creation of Engaging Data Structures Assignments with Real-World Data and Visualizations. In *Proceedings of the 47th ACM Technical Symposium on Computing Science Education (SIGCSE '16)*. ACM, New York, NY, USA, 18–23. https://doi.org/10.1145/2839509.2844635

[4] Thomas H Davenport and DJ Patil. 2012. Data Scientist: The Sexiest Job of the 21st Century-A new breed of professional holds the key to capitalizing on big data opportunities. But these specialists aren't easy to findâĂŤAnd the competition for them is fierce. *Harvard Business Review* (2012), 70.

[5] Peter DePasquale. [n. d.]. Exploiting On-line Data Sources As the Basis of Programming Projects. In *Proceedings of the 37th SIGCSE Technical Symposium on Computer Science Education (SIGCSE '06)*. 283–287.

[6] Processing Foundation. 2017. Processing. http://processing.org/overview/. (August 2017).

[7] Olaf A. Hall-Holt and Kevin R. Sanft. [n. d.]. Statistics-infused Introduction to Computer Science. In *Proceedings of the 46th ACM Technical Symposium on Computer Science Education (SIGCSE '15)*. 138–143.

[8] Nadeem Abdul Hamid. 2016. A Generic Framework for Engaging Online Data Sources in Introductory Programming Courses. In *Proceedings of the 2016 ACM Conference on Innovation and Technology in Computer Science Education (ITiCSE '16)*. ACM, New York, NY, USA, 136–141. https://doi.org/10.1145/2899415.2899437

[9] Daniel E. Stevenson and Paul J. Wagner. [n. d.]. Developing Real-world Programming Assignments for CS1. In *Proceedings of the 11th Annual SIGCSE Conference on Innovation and Technology in Computer Science Education (ITICSE '06)*. 158–162.

[10] David G. Sullivan. [n. d.]. A Data-centric Introduction to Computer Science for Non-majors. In *Proceeding of the 44th ACM Technical Symposium on Computer Science Education (SIGCSE '13)*. 71–76.

Asking "CS4What?" as a Basis for CS4All

Workshop Tools to Support Sustainable K-12 CS Implementations

Rafi Santo
New York University
New York, NY
rafi.santo@nyu.edu

Sara Vogel
The Graduate Center of the
City University of New York
New York, NY
svogel@gradcenter.cuny.edu

Leigh Ann DeLyser
CSNYC
New York, NY
leighann@csnyc.org

June Ahn
New York University
New York, NY
june.ahn@nyu.edu

CCS CONCEPTS

• **Applied computing → Education**

KEYWORDS

CS for All, computing education purposes, K-12, professional development, policy implementation, coherent instructional systems

ACM Reference format:
Rafi Santo, Sara Vogel, Leigh Ann DeLyser and June Ahn. 2018. Asking "CS4What?" as a Basis for CS4All: Workshop Tools to Support Sustainable K-12 CS Implementations. In *SIGCSE '18: 49th ACM Technical Symposium on Computer Science Education, Feb. 21–24, 2018, Baltimore, MD, USA. ACM, NY, NY, USA,* 2 pages.
https://doi.org/10.475/3159450.3159644

SUMMARY

The rapid expansion of the Computer Science for All (CSforAll) movement in the United States has catalyzed promising policies, tools, and pedagogies for K-12 universal CS education. It has also created significant challenges for schools and districts, namely, decision-making around the programs, curricula, and professional development that will best align to their communities' broader visions and goals around equitable computing education for all.

In this session, participants will be introduced to a set of research- based workshop tools designed to support schools and districts to surface their visions for CS education and make implementation decisions aligned with those visions. The tools do not presume the use of specific curricula or languages, rather our activities support stakeholders to first articulate what their visions are for CS education implementations - the projected individual and societal impacts - that can then inform choices around CS curriculum, pedagogies, assessments and the broader instructional infrastructures they sit within.

Participants from a range of settings will be able to take these activities back to their own institutions for local use. The target audience includes stakeholders working in K-12 CSforAll implementation at all levels, including district and school leaders and educators, as well as researchers and CS education faculty who are studying and supporting CS for All efforts in local schools and districts. In addition, given that the workshop will provide practical tools for supporting vision-setting and decision-making around CS curriculum and pedagogy, this session will also benefit course designers and professors at postsecondary institutions who may be redesigning CS coursework or adding new programs to expand the kinds of purposes that CS courses might meet (for example, data science, cyber-security, or ethics in computing).

ACM ISBN 978-1-4503-5103-4/18/02.
https://doi.org/10.475/ 3159450.3159644

OVERALL OBJECTIVES

In this special session, participants will engage in a series of hands- on activities that first have them consider their rationales for bringing CS education to students using the "CSed Visions" framework, ([6]). They will consider the extent to which their priorities tend towards various projected impacts, including: (1) economic and workforce development, (2) equity and social justice, (3) competencies and literacies, (4) citizenship and civic engagement, (5) technological, social and scientific innovation, (6) school reform and improvement and (7) personal agency, joy, and fulfillment.

Participants will then evaluate professional development and curricular resources, considering how those materials may or may not be aligned with their particular visions. The session will be interactive and discussion-based, with time built in for participants to ask questions and provide feedback to the presenters.

BACKGROUND

The Computer Science for All (CSforAll) movement in the United States is in a pivotal moment. While there are many promising policies, curricula, and practices for K-12 universal CS education, there are daunting challenges for school districts, especially those without CS education specialists. The curricular options available to schools and teachers have outpaced the supports necessary for districts to thoughtfully develop their local visions for CS4All implementations, and select CS education partners aligned with those visions to facilitate teacher professional development and curricular implementation. Selection of CS education partners requires an understanding of how to coordinate vision, implementation, and curriculum to plan an approach that is sustainable, adaptive to the unique needs of each local setting and provides all students with a sequence of learning opportunities through their school years. Education policy implementation research asserts that visioning and implementing are non-trivial processes that will be the key to successful and sustainable adoption of CSforAll programs (see [2]; [3]; [4]).

To address this problem of practice regarding how schools and districts set, implement, and sustain visions for CS for All in their localities, the researchers who will be presenting this session developed a series of activities they call the CS Visions, Implementation, and Enactment Workshops (CS VIEWs). They worked alongside practitioners within the context of research practice partnerships (RPPs) and participatory knowledge building activities [5] to create them. In an initial pilot project, they engaged 53 New York City-based formal and informal CS educators, school leaders, and tool designers in a participatory knowledge building process with the goal of surfacing diverse rationales for CS education. The process resulted in the creation of the "CSed Visions" framework for understanding a range of arguments for and projected impacts of computer science education [6].

This framework was then drawn upon during a more extensive research-practice partnership, between researchers at New York University and the CSforAll Consortium - a body which connects content providers, researchers, and funders of CS education with education associations such as school districts, regional education agencies, and state departments of education [1]. The CS VIEWs emerged from the joint work of the Consortium and university researchers during the process of supporting school districts. Specifically, the CS-VIEWs were implemented in partnership with one small town and 7 rural school districts in New York State together with the Education Service Cooperative (BOCES) that works with those districts. The workshops were developed to support district leaders, school principals, educators, library media specialists and technologists in bringing CSforAll to their localities through rooting implementation plans in a set of core visions for CS education that can form the basis of coherent instructional plans ([4]). Feedback from those sessions has helped the RPP refine the workshops' goals and activities.

OUTLINE OF THE SESSION

This session is structured as a condensed version of the CS VIEWs facilitated workshops:

Introduction (10 mins): Participants will hear from researchers involved with the development of the CS Ed visions framework and the research practice partnerships that led to the development of the CS VIEWs (workshops).

Part 1 - Surfacing Visions (20 min): Participants will have the opportunity to test out a card game-style activity which helps stakeholders in CS education at schools and districts gain exposure to a range of arguments for computer science education – including some they may not yet be familiar with. They will come away having prioritized some of their commitments around the impacts they project for CS for All in their localities in the form of a "heat map." They will compare and contrast their visions to those of other participants in the room, and discuss their rationale for selecting particular vision statements.

Part 2 - Visions in Action (20 min): Participants will engage with a series of curricular examples and CS pedagogical approaches using a rubric to assess the ways in which their own visions are or are not aligned with those pedagogies. Through this process, they will be able to experience how vision-setting can inform the process of making pedagogical choices within CS education implementations.

Part 3 - Discussion and Feedback (10 min): Participants and facilitators will engage in discussions about how such activities might be used in their relevant contexts, where they might require adaptation, and how they might be improved.

Part 4 - Q and A (15 minutes)

SUITABILITY FOR SPECIAL SESSION

This presentation is most suitable for a special session format because the activities we will present are designed to spark reflection through interaction, hands-on activities and conversation. By making connections between CS education visions and practice, stakeholders will promote more coherent and ultimately, more equitable instructional systems.

FACILITATORS

The four authors listed will be co-facilitating the session. Each of them have facilitated many versions of these activities with CS educational stakeholders.

ACKNOWLEDGMENTS

The activities in this special session were developed with the support of the National Science Foundation through award #DRL-#1738675. Any opinions, findings, conclusions or recommendations expressed in this material are those of the author(s) and do not necessarily reflect those of the National Science Foundation. Additional thanks go to educators and leaders within the Mozilla Hive NYC Learning Network, the NYC Department of the Education's CS4All team and the Thompkins- Seneca-Tioga BOCES for their contributions to the development of these activities.

REFERENCES

[1] Rick Adrion, Renee Fall, Barbara Ericson, and Mark Guzdial. 2016. Broadening access to computing education state by state. *Commun. ACM* 59, 2 (2016). https: //par-nsf-gov.ezproxy.gc.cuny.edu/servlets/purl/10028006

[2] Anthony S. Bryk, Valerie E. Lee, and Peter B. Holland. 1993. *Catholic Schools and the Common Good* (revised ed. edition ed.). Harvard University Press, Cambridge.

[3] Paul Cobb, Kara Jackson, Thomas Smith, and Erin Henrick. 2017. Supporting Improvements in the Quality of Mathematics Teaching on a Large Scale. In *Making Change Happen*. Springer, 203–221. http://link.springer.com.ezproxy.gc.cuny.edu/chapter/10.1007/978-3-658-14979-6_17

[4] Fred M. Newmann, BetsAnn Smith, Elaine Allensworth, and Anthony S. Bryk. 2001. Instructional program coherence: What it is and why it should guide school improvement policy. *Educational evaluation and policy analysis* 23, 4 (2001), 297–321. http://journals.sagepub.com.ezproxy.gc.cuny.edu/doi/abs/10.3102/01623737023004297

[5] Rafi Santo, Dixie Ching, Kylie Peppler, and Chris Hoadley. 2017. Participatory knowledge building within research-practice partnerships in education. In *SAGE Research Methods Cases*. SAGE, London, UnitedKingdom.

[6] Sara Vogel, Rafi Santo, and Dixie Ching. 2017. Visions of Computer Science Education: Unpacking Arguments for and Projected Impacts of CS4All Initiatives. In *Proceedings of the 47th ACM Technical Symposium on Computing Science Education (SIGCSE '17)*. ACM, Seattle, WA. https://doi.org/10.1145/3017680.3017755

Author Index

www.ingramcontent.com/pod-product-compliance
Lightning Source LLC
LaVergne TN
LVHW080109011026
849160LV00013B/1059